Constitutional La

Constitutional Law

Geoffrey R. Stone
Harry Kalven, Jr. Professor of Law
University of Chicago Law School

Louis M. Seidman
Professor of Law
Georgetown University Law Center

Cass R. Sunstein
Professor of Law
University of Chicago Law School

Mark V. Tushnet
Professor of Law
Georgetown University Law Center

Little, Brown and Company
Boston   Toronto

Library of Congress Catalog Card No. 85-81679
ISBN 0-316-81759-7

First Edition

Fourth Printing

MV NY

Published simultaneously in Canada
by Little, Brown & Company (Canada) Limited

Printed in the United States of America

For our families

Summary of Contents

Contents   xi
Preface   xxix
Acknowledgments   xxxiii
Editorial Notice   xxxvii
U.S. Constitution   xxxix
Biographical Notes on Selected U.S. Supreme Court Justices   lv
The Supreme Court since 1789   lxxiii

I

The Role of the Supreme Court in the Constitutional

Scheme   1

A. Introduction: Some Notes on the History and Theory of the
   Constitution   1
B. The Basic Framework   18
C. The Sources of Judicial Decisions: Text,
   "Representation-Reinforcement," and Natural Law   47
D. The Power of Reprisal: Political Control of the Supreme
   Court   65
E. "Case or Controversy" Requirements and the Passive Virtues   76
F. The Jurisdiction of the Supreme Court   111

II

The Powers of Congress   115

A. Introduction   115
B. The Classical View   127
C. Formalism and Realism in Interpreting the Commerce
    Clause to Limit and Authorize Congressional Action   138
D. The New Deal Crisis and the Rise of the Welfare State   155
E. The Purported Demise of Judicially Enforced Federalism
    Limits on Congressional Power   181
F. Other Powers of Congress: Are They More (or Less) Plenary
    Than the Commerce Power?   212

III

Judicial Efforts to Protect the Expansion of the Market

against Assertions of Local Power   249

A. The Fundamental Framework   249
B. Protection against Discrimination   258
C. Facially Neutral Statutes with Significant Effects on
    Interstate Commerce   290
D. Preemption   313
E. Other Doctrines Protecting the National Market   321

IV

The Distribution of National Powers   339

A. Introduction   339
B. The Basic Allocation   346
C. The Distribution of National Powers in an Administrative
    State   365
D. Legislative and Executive Immunities: Impeachment   395
E. Foreign Affairs   413

V

Equality and the Constitution   435

A. Race and the Constitution   435
B. Equal Protection Methodology: Rational Basis Review   495

C. Equal Protection Methodology: Heightened Scrutiny and the
    Problem of Race   528
D. Equal Protection Methodology: Heightened Scrutiny and the
    Problem of Gender   610
E. Equal Protection Methodology: Other Candidates for
    Heightened Scrutiny   652

VI

Implied Fundamental Rights

691

A. Introduction   691
B. The Privileges or Immunities Clause   698
C. The Incorporation Controversy   707
D. Substantive Due Process: The Protection of Economic
    Interests   724
E. "Fundamental Interests" and the Equal Protection Clause   751
F. "Modern" Substantive Due Process: Privacy, Personhood,
    and Family   840
G. Procedural Due Process   900

VII

Freedom of Expression

925

A. Introduction   925
B. Content-Based Restrictions: Dangerous Ideas and
    Information   938
C. Overbreadth, Vagueness, and Prior Restraint   1036
D. Content-Based Restrictions: "Low" Value Speech   1058
E. Content-Neutral Restrictions: Limitations on the Means of
    Communication   1169
F. Additional Problems   1244

VIII

The Constitution and Religion

1361

A. Introduction: Historical and Analytical Overview   1361
B. The Establishment Clause   1373
C. The Free Exercise Clause   1410

IX

Economic Liberties and the Constitution: The Contracts and Takings Clauses 1427

A. The Contracts Clause 1428
B. The Eminent Domain Clause 1445

X

The Constitution and the Problem of Private Power 1467

A. State Action, Federalism, and Individual Autonomy 1468
B. Pure Inaction and the Theory of Governmental Neutrality 1478
C. Constitutionally Impermissible Departures from Neutrality: State Subsidization, Approval, and Encouragement 1499
D. Constitutionally Required Departures from Neutrality: The Public Function Doctrine 1521
E. The Constitution and Private Power: Some Final Thoughts 1534

Table of Cases 1537
Table of Authorities 1549
Index 1569

Contents

Preface   xxix
Acknowledgments   xxxiii
Editorial Notice   xxxvii
U.S. Constitution   xxxix
Biographical Notes on Selected U.S. Supreme Court Justices   lv
The Supreme Court since 1789   lxxiii

I

The Role of the Supreme Court in the Constitutional

Scheme   1

A. Introduction: Some Notes on the History and Theory of the
    Constitution   1
    1. The Antifederalist Case   5
    2. The Federalist Response   6
            The Federalist No. 10 (Madison)   7
            Note: Madisonian Republicanism   11
            The Federalist No. 51 (Hamilton or Madison)   13
            Note: Madisonian Republicanism, Checks and
                Balances, and Private Property   16
B. The Basic Framework   18
            Marbury v. Madison   18
            Note: Marbury v. Madison   25
            Note: Judicial Review, Democracy, and Some
                Notes on Interpretation   31
            Martin v. Hunter's Lessee   38
            Note: Supreme Court Review of State Courts and
                State Laws   42

         Note: Judicial Exclusivity in Constitutional
            Interpretation?   44
C.   The Sources of Judicial Decisions: Text,
     "Representation-Reinforcement," and Natural Law   47
         McCulloch v. Maryland   48
         Note: Constitutional Methodology and
            Constitutional Interpretation in *McCulloch*   57
         Calder v. Bull   61
         Note: Natural Law and the Supreme Court   62
D.   The Power of Reprisal: Political Control of the Supreme
     Court   65
         Note: Amendment, Appointment, Impeachment,
            and the Election Returns   65
         Ex Parte McCardle   69
         Note: Political Control over Jurisdiction of Article
            III Courts   70
         Note: The Power of Reprisal — General Thoughts   75
E.   "Case or Controversy" Requirements and the Passive Virtues   76
     1. Advisory Opinions   77
     2. Standing   78
         Allen v. Wright   78
         Note: The "Law" of Standing   85
     3. Political Questions   95
         Baker v. Carr   95
         Note: Political Questions   101
         Note: Questions of Timing — Ripeness and
            Mootness   109
F.   The Jurisdiction of the Supreme Court   111

II

The Powers of Congress   **115**

A.   Introduction   115
         Note: A Government of Enumerated Powers   115
         The Federalist Nos. 45 and 46 (Madison)   117
         Note: Enforcing Enumeration as a Limitation on
            Power   120
         Note: The Values and Forms of Federalism   122
B.   The Classical View   127
         Gibbons v. Ogden   127
         Note: *Gibbons v. Ogden*   136
C.   Formalism and Realism in Interpreting the Commerce
     Clause to Limit and Authorize Congressional Action   138

United States v. E. C. Knight Co.   139
Houston, East & West Texas Railway v.
  United States (The Shreveport Rate Cases)   141
Stafford v. Wallace   142
Note: Direct, Indirect, and Stream of Commerce
  Tests   142
Champion v. Ames (The Lottery Case)   145
Note: Prohibiting Interstate Transportation —
  Proper Regulation or Improper Pretext?   149
Hammer v. Dagenhart (The Child Labor Case)   150
Note: Formalism, Realism, and Prohibiting
  Interstate Shipment   154

D. The New Deal Crisis and the Rise of the Welfare State   155
A. L. A. *Schechter Poultry Corp. v. United States*   156
Carter v. Carter Coal Co.   160
Note: New Deal Legislation and Commerce
  Clause Tests in the 1930s   166
NLRB v. Jones & Laughlin Steel Corp.   169
Wickard v. Filburn   174
Note: The Adoption of the "Realist" Approach   176
United States v. Darby   177
Note: The Adoption of the "Formalist"
  Approach   181

E. The Purported Demise of Judicially Enforced Federalism
Limits on Congressional Power   181
Perez v. United States   182
Note: Congressional Processes and Federalism   184
Heart of Atlanta Motel v. United States   187
Katzenbach v. McClung   191
Note: Federalism and Congressional Motivation   195
*Garcia v. San Antonio Metropolitan Transit
  Authority*   196
Note: From *National League of Cities* to *Garcia*
  and Beyond   208
Note: Intergovernmental Tax Immunities   210

F. Other Powers of Congress: Are They More (or Less) Plenary
Than the Commerce Power?   212
1. The War Power   212
2. The Treaty Power   213
   Missouri v. Holland   213
   Note: Federalism and the Treaty Power   215
3. The Taxing Power   216
4. The Spending Power   219
   United States v. Butler   219
   Note: The Spending Power and Dual Federalism   225
   Steward Machine Co. v. Davis   226
   Note: Conditional Spending, Coercion, and the
     Political Process   228

5. The Power to Enforce the Reconstruction Amendments   233
    Katzenbach v. Morgan   233
    Note: Congressional Power to Enforce or
      Interpret(?) the Constitution   238
    Note: Congressional Power to Regulate "Private"
      Action for Civil Rights Purposes   245
    Note: Concluding Observations on Congress's
      Powers   247

III

Judicial Efforts to Protect the Expansion of the Market

against Assertions of Local Power

against Assertions of Local Power   249

A. The Fundamental Framework   249
    Note: The Classical View   249
    Note: The Modern View — Allocating the Burden
      of Inertia via Preemption and Consent   253
B. Protection against Discrimination   258
    Note: General Considerations   259
    City of Philadelphia v. New Jersey   263
    Note: Facial/Intentional Discrimination   268
    *Hunt v. Washington State Apple Advertising
      Commission*   271
    Note: Facially Neutral Statutes with
      Discriminatory Effects — Gerrymandering?   275
    Exxon Corp. v. Governor of Maryland   276
    Note: Facially Neutral Statutes with (Merely?)
      Disproportionate Effects   284
    Note: Inferring Intent   285
    Note: Taxation of Interstate Commerce   287
C. Facially Neutral Statutes with Significant Effects on
    Interstate Commerce   290
    Note: For Commercial Purposes   290
    Note: For Police Power Purposes   293
    South Carolina Highway Department v.
      Barnwell Brothers   293
    Southern Pacific Co. v. Arizona   294
    Kassel v. Consolidated Freightways Corp.   298
    Note: Are Burdens (Inevitably) Discriminatory?   312
D. Preemption   313
    *Pacific Gas & Electric v. State Energy Resources
      Conservation Commission*   313
    Note: Preemption   318
E. Other Doctrines Protecting the National Market   321
    South-Central Timber Development v. Wunnicke   321
    Note: The Market Participant Doctrine   326

United Building & Construction Trades Council
    v. Camden   328
Note: The Privileges and Immunities Clause of
    Article IV   334
Note: The Equal Protection Clause   336

IV

The Distribution of National Powers   339

A. Introduction   339
    The Federalist No. 47 (Madison)   339
    The Federalist No. 48 (Madison)   340
    Note: The Theory of Separation and Checks and
        Balances   342
B. The Basic Allocation   346
    Youngstown Sheet & Tube Co. v. Sawyer (The
        Steel Seizure Case)   346
    Note: *Youngstown* and the Power of the President   359
    Note: Impoundment, Law Enforcement, and the
        "Take Care" Clause   362
C. The Distribution of National Powers in an Administrative
    State   365
    Note: The Nondelegation Doctrine   365
    INS v. Chadha   371
    Note: The Separation of Powers and *Chadha*   381
    Note: Where Do Administrative Agencies "Fit" in
        the Separation of Powers Scheme?   385
    Buckley v. Valeo   389
    Note: The Appointments Clause   392
D. Legislative and Executive Immunities: Impeachment   395
    Note: The Speech or Debate Clause   395
    United States v. Nixon   398
    Nixon v. Administrator of General Services   403
    Note: Executive Privilege   406
    Note: Impeachment   412
E. Foreign Affairs   413
    United States v. Curtiss-Wright Corp.   414
    Note: The President and Foreign Affairs   416
    Dames & Moore v. Regan   418
    Note: Iranian Claims and Executive Power   422
    Note: The Allocation of Warmaking Authority   424
    The Prize Cases   425
    Note: The Prize Cases and the Constitutional
        Allocation of Warmaking Power   426
    The War Powers Resolution   428
    Note: The War Powers Resolution   431

Note: Distribution of National Powers — Final
    Thoughts   433

V

Equality and the Constitution   435

A. Race and the Constitution   435
    1. Slavery and the Constitution   436
            State v. Post   437
            Note: Constitutional Attacks on Slavery   439
            Dred Scott v. Sandford   440
            Note: Dred Scott and the Power of Judicial Review   443
    2. Reconstruction and Retreat   444
            Note: The Work of the Reconstruction Congress   445
            Note: The Judicial Reaction   447
            Plessy v. Ferguson   451
            Note: Separate but Equal   454
    3. The Attack on Jim Crow   456
            Note: The NAACP's Legal Strategy   456
                Missouri ex rel. Gaines v. Canada   457
            Note: Separate but Equal between Gaines and
                Brown   458
            Brown v. Board of Education of Topeka (Brown I)   461
            Note: Justifications and Explanations for Brown   463
            Brown v. Board of Education of Topeka (Brown II)   467
            Note: "All Deliberate Speed"   468
    4. Southern Desegregation   470
            Note: The Response to Brown   470
            Swann v. Charlotte-Mecklenburg Board of
                Education   475
            Note: Swann and the Collapse of Southern
                Resistance   479
    5. Northern Desegregation   482
            Keyes v. School District No. 1, Denver, Colo.   482
            Note: Northern Desegregation   486
    6. Desegregation and the Limits of Judicial Power   488
            Note: Potential Limits on the Duty to Desegregate   488
            Note: Final Thoughts on School Desegregation
                and the Efficacy of Judicial Review   493
B. Equal Protection Methodology: Rational Basis Review   495
            New York City Transit Authority v. Beazer   496
            Note: The Structure of Equal Protection Review   499
            Note: The Means/Ends Nexus   501
            Note: The Problem of Judicial Review   504
            Railway Express Agency v. New York   504
            Williamson v. Lee Optical   506
            Minnesota v. Clover Leaf Creamery Co.   506

Note: Deferential Review — Abdication or
  Self-Restraint?   507
City of Cleburne v. Cleburne Living Center   510
U.S. Railroad Retirement Board v. Fritz   513
Note: Equal Protection as a Tautology   518
  U.S. Department of Agriculture v. Moreno   519
Note: Equality as a Limitation on Permissible
  Government Purposes   520
Schweiker v. Wilson   524
Note: "Actual Purpose" Review   526

C. Equal Protection Methodology: Heightened Scrutiny and the
  Problem of Race   528
  1. Race-Specific Classifications That Expressly Disadvantage
    Racial Minorities   528
    Strauder v. West Virginia   528
    Korematsu v. United States   530
    Note: Justifications for Special Scrutiny of Racial
      Classifications   535
    Note: The Nature of Special Scrutiny   541
  2. Non-Race-Specific Classifications That Disadvantage
    Racial Minorities   543
    Washington v. Davis   543
    Note: Rational Basis Review of Non-Race-Specific
      Classifications   546
    Note: Heightened Scrutiny for Improperly
      Motivated Classifications   549
    Village of Arlington Heights v. Metropolitan
      Housing Development Corp.   553
    Personnel Administrator v. Feeney   554
    Note: The Definition of Discriminatory Purpose   556
    Note: The Problem of Proof   557
    Note: Strict Scrutiny of Facially Neutral Statutes
      — Beyond Purpose   562
  3. Race-Specific Classifications That Are Facially Neutral   565
    Loving v. Virginia   565
    Washington v. Seattle School District No. 1   567
    Crawford v. Board of Education   573
    Note: Strict Scrutiny for "Neutral" Race-Specific
      Classifications   575
  4. Race-Specific Classifications That Benefit Racial
    Minorities   578
    Note: The Pre-*Bakke* Cases   578
    Regents of the University of California v. Bakke   582
    Fullilove v. Klutznick   596
    Note: What Did *Bakke* Hold?   601
    Note: The Constitutionality of "Benign" Racial
      Classifications   602

D. Equal Protection Methodology: Heightened Scrutiny and the
  Problem of Gender   610

	1.	The Early Cases	611
	2.	The Road to Intermediate Scrutiny	612
		Reed v. Reed	612
		Frontiero v. Richardson	613
		Note: From *Reed* to *Craig* — Evolution and Doctrinal Confusion	614
		Craig v. Boren	616
		Note: Heightened Scrutiny for Gender Classifications?	622
	3.	Archaic and Overbroad Generalizations versus Real Differences	627
		Michael M. v. Sonoma County Superior Court	627
		Rostker v. Goldberg	631
		Note: Identifying and Defining "Real Differences"	634
	4.	Benign Gender Classifications and Discrimination against Men	640
		Califano v. Goldfarb	640
		Califano v. Webster	645
		Note: The Problem of "Benign" Gender Classifications	646
	5.	The Equal Rights Amendment	651
E.	Equal Protection Methodology: Other Candidates for Heightened Scrutiny		652
	1.	Alienage	652
		Sugarman v. Dougall	653
		In re Griffiths	658
		Note: Strict Scrutiny for Aliens — Defining the Political Community	659
		Note: Alienage and Federal Preemption	663
	2.	Nonmarital Children	667
		Note: Working with the *Levy/Glona* Test	668
	3.	Wealth Classifications	675
		Note: Wealth Discrimination and the Problem of Affirmative Rights	679
	4.	Other Disadvantaged Groups	685
		City of Cleburne v. Cleburne Living Center	685
		Note: Evaluating the Claims of Other Disadvantaged Groups	687

VI

Implied Fundamental Rights   691

A.	Introduction	691
	Note: Theories of Constitutional Construction — "Interpretivism" and "Noninterpretivism"	691
B.	The Privileges or Immunities Clause	698
	Slaughter-House Cases	698

		Note: The Demise of the Privileges or Immunities	
		Clause	704
C.	The Incorporation Controversy		707
		Barron v. Mayor & City Council of Baltimore	708
		Murray v. Hoboken Land & Improvement	
		Co.	709
		Twining v. New Jersey	710
		Palko v. Connecticut	711
		Adamson v. California	713
		Note: The Black/Frankfurter Debate	715
		Duncan v. Louisiana	717
		Note: Incorporation since *Duncan*	721
D.	Substantive Due Process: The Protection of Economic		
	Interests		724
		Note: The Road to *Lochner*	725
		Lochner v. New York	728
		Note: The "Vices" of *Lochner*	734
		Note: The *Lochner* Era — 1905-1934	739
		Nebbia v. New York	741
		West Coast Hotel Co. v. Parrish	743
		Note: The End of an Era	744
		United States v. Carolene Products Co.	745
		Williamson v. Lee Optical of Oklahoma	746
		Ferguson v. Skrupa	747
		Note: Restraint or Abdication?	748
E.	"Fundamental Interests" and the Equal Protection Clause		751
		Skinner v. Oklahoma	751
		Note: The Fundamental "Right to Have	
		Offspring"	754
	1.	Voting	756
	a.	Denial of the "Right to Vote"	756
		Harper v. Virginia State Board of Elections	757
		Note: Is the Right to Vote "Fundamental"?	759
		Kramer v. Union Free School District	761
		Note: *Kramer* and Its Progeny	763
	b.	Dilution of the "Right to Vote"	767
		Reynolds v. Sims	768
		Note: *Reynolds* and Its Progeny	772
		City of Mobile v. Bolden	777
		Note: Vote Dilution and the Interests of Groups	783
	c.	Denial of "Access to the Ballot"	786
		Williams v. Rhodes	786
		Note: *Williams* and Its Progeny	787
	2.	Access to the Judicial Process	791
		Griffin v. Illinois	792
		Douglas v. California	792
		Note: "Fundamental" Interests and the Criminal	
		Justice System	794
		Boddie v. Connecticut	798
		Note: Access to the Judicial Process in Civil Cases	799

3. Travel   802
    Shapiro v. Thompson   802
    Note: The Right to Travel as a "Fundamental
      Interest"   807
    Note: "Penalizing" the Right to Travel   808
4. Welfare   815
    Dandridge v. Williams   818
    Note: *Dandridge* — Principled Limitation or
      Retreat?   819
5. Education and the Continuing Effort to Define
   "Fundamental" Interests   821
    San Antonio Independent School District v.
      Rodriguez   *821*
    Note: The *Rodriguez* Reformulation   830
    Plyler v. Doe   *831*
    Note: "Fundamental Interests" and the Equal
      Protection Clause — A New Direction?   839
F. "Modern" Substantive Due Process: Privacy, Personhood,
  and Family   840
  1. The Right of Privacy   841
      Griswold v. Connecticut   *841*
      Note: *Griswold* and the Right of Privacy   850
  2. Abortion   854
      Roe v. Wade   854
      Note: The Abortion Decision   861
      Maher v. Roe   869
      Harris v. McRae   872
      Note: The Abortion-Funding Cases   873
      City of Akron v. Akron Center for
        Reproduction Health, Inc.   874
      Note: Regulating Abortion   880
  3. Family and Other "Privacy" Interests   886
      Moore v. City of East Cleveland   886
      Zablocki v. Redhail   890
      Stanley v. Illinois   893
      Note: The Limits of Privacy   895
G. Procedural Due Process   900
  1. Liberty and Property Interests   900
      Board of Regents of State Colleges v. Roth   901
      Perry v. Sindermann   903
      Cleveland Board of Education v. Loudermill   904
      Note: Defining "Liberty" and "Property"   907
      Note: Developments since *Roth* — Statutory
        Entitlements and Natural Liberty   910
  2. What Process Is Due   913
      Mathews v. Eldridge   *913*
      Note: Balancing Tests and the Due Process Clause   917
      Note: The Irrebuttable Presumption Doctrine   921
      Note: Procedural Due Process and "Legislative"
        Determinations   923

VII

Freedom of Expression   925

A. Introduction   925
          Note: The History of Free Expression   925
          Note: The Philosophy of Free Expression   931
          Note: Organization   938
B. Content-Based Restrictions: Dangerous Ideas and
     Information   938
     1. Expression That Induces Unlawful Conduct   939
              Shaffer v. United States   940
              Masses Publishing Co. v. Patten   *941*
              Schenck v. United States   943
              Note: *Shaffer, Masses,* and *Schenck*   944
              Frohwerk v. United States   947
              Debs v. United States   948
              Abrams v. United States   *949*
              Note: *Abrams* and the Emergence of the
                  Holmes/Brandeis Tradition   952
              Gitlow v. New York   *954*
              Note: *Gitlow* and the Question of Deference   958
              Whitney v. California   *960*
              Note: The Brandeis Concurrence and the Right of
                  Association   965
              Note: The Road to *Dennis*   966
              Dennis v. United States   *969*
              Note: *Dennis*, the Communist "Conspiracy," and
                  Some Approaches to First Amendment
                  Methodology   977
              Note: Revising the *Dennis* Approach   980
              Note: The Smith Act in Context — Other Federal
                  Anticommunist Legislation   983
              Note: The Road to *Brandenburg*   985
              Brandenburg v. Ohio   987
              Note: The *Brandenburg* Formulation   989
     2. Criticism of the Judicial Process   991
              Bridges v. California   *992*
              Note: *Bridges*, Contempt by Publication, and the
                  Subversive Advocacy Analogy   994
     3. Expression That Provokes a Hostile Audience Reaction   997
              Terminiello v. Chicago   997
              Cantwell v. Connecticut   *998*
              Note: *Cantwell*, the Hostile Audience, and the
                  Subversive Advocacy Analogy   999
              Feiner v. New York   *1001*
              Note: *Feiner, Kunz,* and the Search for
                  Mechanisms of Control   1003
              Edwards v. South Carolina   1005

Cox v. Louisiana   1006
Gregory v. City of Chicago   1007
Note: Mass Demonstrations and the Hostile
    Audience   1008
Chaplinsky v. New Hampshire   *1009*
Note: Fighting Words   1011
Note: The Skokie Controversy   1015
4. Expression That Discloses Confidential Information   1017
Landmark Communications, Inc. v. Virginia   1017
Note: *Landmark* and the Problem of
    Confidentiality   1018
Nebraska Press Association v. Stuart   *1019*
New York Times Co. v. United States; United
    States v. Washington Post Co.   *1023*
Note: *Nebraska Press* and the Pentagon Papers   1030
Note: *The Progressive* Controversy   1033
Note: Dangerous Ideas and Information — Final
    Thoughts   1035
C. Overbreadth, Vagueness, and Prior Restraint   1036
1. Overbreadth and Vagueness   1036
Gooding v. Wilson   *1036*
Note: Overbreadth   1039
Note: Vagueness   1043
2. Prior Restraint   1046
Lovell v. Griffin   *1047*
Note: Licensing as Prior Restraint   1048
Near v. Minnesota   *1052*
Note: Injunction as Prior Restraint   1054
D. Content-Based Restrictions: "Low" Value Speech   1058
1. False Statements of Fact   1059
New York Times Co. v. Sullivan   *1059*
Note: "The Central Meaning" of *New York Times*
    v. Sullivan   1064
Curtis Publishing Co. v. Butts; Associated
    Press v. Walker   1068
Gertz v. Robert Welch, Inc.   *1069*
Note: Public and Private Figures, Public and
    Private Speech   1076
Dun & Bradstreet v. Greenmoss Builders   1078
Note: Other False Statements of Fact   1080
2. Group Defamation   1082
Beauharnais v. Illinois   *1082*
Note: Group Defamation   1085
3. "Non-Newsworthy" Disclosures of "Private" Information   1086
Cox Broadcasting Corp. v. Cohn   *1086*
Note: Invasion of Privacy and the First
    Amendment   1089
4. Commercial Speech   1091
Virginia State Board of Pharmacy v. Virginia
    Citizens Consumer Council   1092

Note: *Virginia Pharmacy* and "the Free Flow of
Commercial Information" 1098
Bates v. State Bar of Arizona 1101
Linmark Associates v. Township of
Willingboro 1102
Note: Limitations on the Protection of
Commercial Speech 1103
Ohralik v. Ohio State Bar 1106
Central Hudson Gas v. Public Service
Commission of New York 1107
Metromedia, Inc. v. San Diego 1109
Note: *Ohralik, Central Hudson,* and *Metromedia*
— Retreat on Commercial Speech? 1111
Note: Labor Disputes and the First Amendment 1111
5. Obscenity 1114
Roth v. United States; Alberts v. California 1115
Note: Obscenity and Free Expression 1117
Note: Developments in the Law "Obscenity" —
1957-1973 1120
Miller v. California 1124
Paris Adult Theatre I v. Slaton 1127
Note: The 1973 Reformulation and Its Aftermath 1132
Note: Pornography and Feminism 1136
New York v. Ferber 1139
Note: The Regulation of Obscenity — A
Procedural Perspective 1141
6. Offensive Speech 1146
Cohen v. California 1146
Note: Offensive Language, *Cohen,* and the
Captive Audience 1150
Ernoznik v. Jacksonville 1153
FCC v. Pacifica Foundation 1154
Young v. American Mini-Theatres 1161
Note: *Young* and *Pacifica* 1161
Note: "Low" Value Speech — Final Thoughts 1169
E. Content-Neutral Restrictions: Limitations on the Means of
Communication 1169
1. General Principles 1170
Schneider v. State 1170
Martin v. City of Struthers 1171
Kovacs v. Cooper 1172
Metromedia, Inc. v. San Diego 1173
Note: The Search for Principles 1175
2. Speech on Public Property: The Public Forum 1177
a. The Public Forum: Streets and Parks 1177
Commonwealth v. Davis 1177
Hague v. CIO 1178
Schneider v. State 1179
Note: Regulating the Public Forum 1180
Note: Devices for Regulating the Public Forum 1183

	b.	The Public Forum: Other Publicly Owned Property	1186
		Brown v. Louisiana	1186
		Adderley v. Florida	*1187*
		Note: "No Less Than a Private Owner of Property"?	1189
		Greer v. Spock	1190
		Heffron v. International Society for Krishna Consciousness	1191
		U.S. Postal Service v. Council of Greenburgh Civic Associations	1193
		Members of the City Council of Los Angeles v. Taxpayers for Vincent	1195
		Note: Modern Public Forum Doctrine	1197
		Note: The Right to a "Private" Forum	1198
	3.	Symbolic Conduct	1201
		United States v. O'Brien	*1202*
		Note: Draft Card Burning and the First Amendment	1207
		Note: Flag Desecration and Misuse	1211
		Note: Political Boycotts	1215
	4.	Money and Free Expression: Regulation of Solicitation, Contribution, and Expenditure	1218
		Village of Schaumburg v. Citizens for a Better Environment	1218
		Buckley v. Valeo	*1220*
		Note: *Buckley* and *Bellotti* — Abridging Speech to "Enhance" the Electoral Process	1228
		Note: Additional Regulation of the Electoral Process	1234
	5.	Other Means of Expression: Litigation and Association	1236
		NAACP v. Button	1236
		Note: Litigation and the First Amendment	1239
		Roberts v. U.S. Jaycees	1241
F.		Additional Problems	1244
	1.	Equality and Free Expression	1244
		Police Department of Chicago v. Mosley	*1244*
		Note: *Mosley* and the "Equality" of Ideas	1246
		Lehman v. City of Shaker Heights	*1250*
		Note: *Lehman* and the Limits of *Mosley*	1254
		Southeastern Promotions v. Conrad	1260
		Board of Education, Island Trees Union Free School District v. Pico	1262
		Regan v. Taxation with Representation of Washington	1266
	2.	Restricted Environments: The Military, Schools, and Prisons	1267
		Parker v. Levy	1267
		Tinker v. Des Moines School District	1269
		Jones v. North Carolina Prisoners' Union	1272

3. Public Employment   1273
    a. Partisan Political Activity   1275
        *U.S. Civil Service Commission v. National
            Association of Letter Carriers*   1275
        Note: *Mitchell, Letter Carriers,* and *Broadrick*   1277
    b. Criticizing Government Policy   1278
        Pickering v. Board of Education   1278
        Note: *Pickering* and Its Implications   1280
    c. Patronage   1283
        Elrod v. Burns   1283
        Branti v. Finkel   1286
    d. Subversive Advocacy and Associations   1287
        Adler v. Board of Education   1288
        Elfbrandt v. Russell   1288
        Note: Loyalty Programs and the First
            Amendment   1290
    e. Confidential Information   1295
        Snepp v. United States   1295
        Note: *Snepp,* Public Employment, and the
            Disclosure of Confidential Information   1298
4. Compelled Affirmation, Expression, and Association: The
    Right *Not* to Speak   1300
        West Virginia State Board of Education v.
            Barnette   1300
        Wooley v. Maynard   1301
        PruneYard Shopping Center v. Robins   1301
        Elrod v. Burns   1302
        Abood v. Detroit Board of Education   1302
        Note: The Right *Not* to Speak — Variations   1304
5. Compelled Disclosure of Expression, Belief, and
    Association   1306
    a. General Principles   1307
        NAACP v. Alabama   1307
        Talley v. California   1308
        Buckley v. Valeo   1309
    b. Public Employees and Licensees   1310
        Shelton v. Tucker   1310
        Konigsberg v. State Bar   1312
        Note: *Baird, Stolar,* and *Wadmond*   1313
    c. Legislative Investigations   1316
        Barenblatt v. United States   1316
        Gibson v. Florida Legislative Investigating
            Committee   1319
        Note: Intelligence Activities   1321
6. Freedom of the Press   1322
    a. A "Preferred" Status for the Press?   1322
    b. Differential Treatment of the Press   1323
        Minneapolis Star & Tribune Co. v.
            Minnesota Commissioner of Revenue   1323

    c. Regulating the Press to "Improve" the Marketplace
       of Ideas   1326
       Miami Herald Publishing Co. v. Tornillo   1326
       Red Lion Broadcasting Co. v. FCC   1327
       Note: Regulating the Airwaves   1330
       Columbia Broadcasting System v. Democratic
         National Committee   1333
    d. A Right to "Gather" News?   1336
       Branzburg v. Hayes   1336
       Note: A Right to Gather News?   1340
       Pell v. Procunier   1343
       Houchins v. KQED   1345
       Note: A Press Right of Access to Government
         Information?   1347
       Richmond Newspapers v. Virginia   1350
       Globe Newspaper Co. v. Superior Court   1355
       Note: A Public Right of Access to Government
         Information?   1357
       Note: Conditioned Access to Information   1359
       Note: Free Expression — Final Thoughts   1360

VIII

The Constitution and Religion   1361

A. Introduction: Historical and Analytical Overview   1361
      Everson v. Board of Education   1361
      Note: The History of the Religion Clauses   1364
      Note: General Approaches to the Religion Clauses   1367
      Note: Defining Religion   1369
B. The Establishment Clause   1373
    1. Impermissible Purposes: The School Prayer Cases   1374
    2. Permissible Purposes: De Facto Establishments?   1377
       Lynch v. Donnelly   1377
       Note: How Are Purpose and Effect Relevant? —
         De Facto Establishments   1391
    3. Facially Neutral Statutes That (Incidentally?) Aid
      Religion   1396
       Note: The Problem and Its Background   1396
       Mueller v. Allen   1399
       Aguilar v. Felton   1404
       Note: Purpose and Effect in Aid to Nonpublic
         Education — Benevolent Neutrality?   1405
       Note: Additional Problems   1408
       Note: Concluding Observations   1410
C. The Free Exercise Clause   1410
      Braunfeld v. Brown   1410

Sherbert v. Verner	1411
Wisconsin v. Yoder	1416
United States v. Lee	1417
Note: Accommodation — Required and Permissible	1418
Note: Religion as a Form of Belief	1423
Note: Concluding Observations	1425

IX

Economic Liberties and the Constitution: The Contracts and Takings Clauses   1427

A. The Contracts Clause	1427
Note: Early Interpretive Problems	1428
Home Building & Loan Association v. Blaisdell	1430
Note: Market Ordering and Constitutional Interpretation	1435
United States Trust Co. v. New Jersey	1437
Allied Structural Steel Co. v. Spannaus	1439
Note: *United States Trust, Spannaus,* and the Possible Revival of the Contracts Clause	1442
B. The Eminent Domain Clause	1445
Hawaii Housing Authority v. Midkiff	1445
Note: The Public Use Requirement and the Takings Clause	1447
Pennsylvania Coal Co. v. Mahon	1448
Miller v. Schoene	1451
Penn Central Transportation Co. v. New York City	1452
Note: "Takings" and the Police Power	1459
Note: *Penn Central,* Takings, and Related Problems	1462

X

The Constitution and the Problem of Private Power   1467

A. State Action, Federalism, and Individual Autonomy	1468
1. State Action and Federalism	1468
The Civil Rights Cases	1469
Note: Federalism and the Substantive Content of the State Action Doctrine	1474
2. State Action and Individual Autonomy	1476

B.   Pure Inaction and the Theory of Governmental Neutrality   1478
     1.   Pure Inaction   1479
               Flagg Brothers v. Brooks   1479
               Lugar v. Edmondson Oil Co.   1484
               Note: *Flagg Brothers* and the Problem of the
                 Passive State   1485
     2.   Judicial Action and the Theory of Government
          Neutrality   1488
               Shelley v. Kraemer   1488
               Note: *Shelley v. Kraemer*, State Inaction, and the
                 Theory of Government Neutrality   1491
C.   Constitutionally Impermissible Departures from Neutrality:
     State Subsidization, Approval, and Encouragement   1499
     1.   State Subsidization of Private Conduct   1500
               Burton v. Wilmington Parking Authority   1500
               Note: Subsidies, Penalties, and the Search for a
                 Baseline   1503
               Blum v. Yaretsky   1507
               Rendell-Baker v. Kohn   1511
               Note: State Action as Coercion or Significant
                 Encouragement   1511
     2.   State Licensing and Authorization   1513
               Public Utility Commission v. Pollack   1513
               Moose Lodge No. 107 v. Irvis   1513
               Jackson v. Metropolitan Edison Co.   1517
               Note: Licensing and Authorization as State Action   1520
D.   Constitutionally Required Departures from Neutrality: The
     Public Function Doctrine   1521
               Marsh v. Alabama   1521
               Note: The "Public Function" Theory and the
                 Passive State   1523
               Jackson v. Metropolitan Edison Co.   1529
               Note: Public Functions as "Exclusive Prerogatives"
                 of the State   1530
E.   The Constitution and Private Power: Some Final Thoughts   1534

Table of Cases   1537
Table of Authorities   1549
Index   1569

Preface

American constitutional law has undergone significant changes over the past decade. The Supreme Court has revised its understanding of broad areas of constitutional doctrine, and scholarly commentary has flourished on the proper role of the Court, the scope of individual rights, and methods of constitutional interpretation. This casebook takes account of these developments by presenting and organizing its materials according to the categories suggested by contemporary constitutional doctrine and by drawing throughout on a wide range of theoretical materials that illuminate the Court's work and may influence it in the future.

Three aspects of our approach deserve special attention. (1) We stress the conceptions of politics and government that underlie constitutional doctrine, by directing attention to the premises of the constitutional order as understood both by the generation of the Framers and by our own generation. (2) Because it is impossible to have a full understanding of constitutional doctrine without having a grasp on the setting out of which doctrines arise, we stress issues of social and historical context. (3) Throughout the casebook, we recur to general problems of constitutional interpretation, such as the possibility of objective interpretation, sources of interpretation, and constraints on the interpretive process.

In approaching these issues, the casebook draws on a variety of disciplines: political theory, history, economics, public choice theory, ethics, and critical theory. We believe that students cannot have a full appreciation of constitutional law without having some acquaintance with these materials. Yet we have been sensitive to the need for the casebook to be useful in the classroom; the views of the authors span a considerable range, both methodologically and substantively, and we have been careful to ensure that the casebook can be used by teachers with widely varying approaches. Some cases are presented in a way that is generous enough to enable students to study the Court's use of precedent and to engage in close textual analysis. Others are presented in a more abbreviated fashion to inform students of the current state of the doctrine and to raise questions about the direction in which the Court is heading. Some material is presented historically to allow students to see how the Court interacts with other political and economic forces in the society; other problems are presented in a manner designed to enable students to study the development of doctrine over time; and still other materials are organized around recurring philosophical issues in constitutional adjudication.

The casebook's organization is designed to direct attention to substantive and institutional issues: the values promoted by various constitutional provisions; the extent to which constitutional law, operating largely but not exclusively through the courts, has promoted or might promote these values; the institutional arrangements that allow both courts and legislatures to determine how and to what extent the values should be promoted.

The first part of the casebook, which deals largely with issues of constitutional structure, also introduces the general themes pursued throughout. Chapter 1 deals with the role of the Supreme Court, by setting it in the context of the theory of the Constitution held by the framers' generation. It introduces students to the institutional elements that promote the values embedded in the Constitution and to the role of the courts as one of those elements. It also provides an introductory examination of various theories of judicial review. Chapters 2 and 3 deal with federalism. Chapter 2, on the powers of Congress, provides a historical overview of constitutional doctrine, examines the usefulness of judicial review of statutes challenged on grounds of federalism, and explores the theoretical bases for federalism and judicial review of federalism questions. Chapter 3, on the role of Congress and the courts in assuring that state legislatures not impair the operation of the national economy, is organized on the basis of contemporary doctrine. Again, the economics of federalism and theories of judicial review are explored in this context. Further, the chapter provides an introduction to the Court's use of principles of discrimination, a topic further examined in Chapters 5, 7, and 8. Chapter 4 completes the study of the basic structures of government, emphasizing the role that political accommodations play in the development of the effective distribution of powers among the branches of the national government. The first chapters thus deal, broadly speaking, with the ways in which the structures of government are designed to promote effective government while protecting individual liberty.

The remaining chapters deal with the protections the Constitution directly provides for individual rights. Chapter 5 examines the Court's treatment of questions of equality and inequality. Its first section provides a historical examination of the constitutional treatment of race. The remaining sections explore in detail the structure of the contemporary equal protection doctrine, raising questions about the suitability of that doctrine and about its theoretical premises. Chapter 6, on implied fundamental rights, offers a detailed study of contemporary controversies over methods of constitutional interpretation. Its presentation of constitutional doctrine is informed by discussions of "interpretivism" and "noninterpretivism," and of moral philosophy, to which it introduces students. Chapter 7 presents the modern law of free expression by showing how it has developed and the ways in which contemporary doctrine differs from that regarded as settled in the recent past. Questions about neutrality and discrimination provide one of the major organizing themes of this chapter, as they do in Chapter 8, on the Constitution and religion. Chapter 9 deals with economic liberties and asks students to consider the extent to which contemporary doctrine does and should distinguish between economic and other liberties. Finally, Chapter 10 examines the role of constitutional law in constraining "private" power.

We believe that this book will assist readers in confronting the fundamental questions of the constitutional order: whether it is possible to create a government energetic enough to promote the common good while at the same time secure enough to protect individual liberty. These questions have been with us since the beginning, but perhaps never as urgently.

G.R.S.
L.M.S.
C.R.S.
M.V.T.

June 1986

Acknowledgments

We gratefully acknowledge Susan Donner, Daniel Ernst, Jeremy Friedman, Robert Friedman, John Gomperts, Katherine Goodman, Kathleen Griesser, Mary Morton, Robert Rasmussen, Rebecca Smith, Barbara St. Clair, Kathleen Tenoever, Enid Van Hoven, and Philip Weber for their diligent research and editorial assistance; Charles Abernathy, David Currie, E. Donald Elliott, Barry Friedman, John Kramer, Thomas Krattenmaker, William Marshall, Elizabeth Natter, Girardeau Spann, and Richard Posner for their helpful comments on various sections of earlier drafts of this book; Sandra Leone, Robin Tavakoli, Susan Carol Weiss, and the members of the Georgetown University Law Center Faculty Support Service for their invaluable secretarial assistance; and a host of former students who have struggled through prior versions of this material and whose criticisms and suggestions have helped shape the final product.

Excerpts from the following books and articles appear with the kind permission of the copyright holders:

Bickel, Alexander, The Least Dangerous Branch. Copyright © 1965 by MacMillan Publishing Co. Reprinted by permission.

Blasi, Vincent A., Toward a Theory of Prior Restraint: The Central Linkage, 66 Minnesota Law Review 87-91 (1981). Copyright © 1981 by the Minnesota Law Review Association. Reprinted by permission.

Bollinger, Lee, The *Skokie* Legacy: Reflections on an "Easy Case" and Free Speech Theory, 80 Michigan Law Review 617, 629-631 (1972). Copyright © 1972 by Michigan Law Review. Reprinted by permission.

Bork, Robert H., Neutral Principles and Some First Amendment Problems, 47 Indiana Law Journal 1, 2-3, 8, 26-28 (1971). Copyright © 1971 by Indiana Law Journal and Fred B. Rothman & Company. Reprinted by permission.

Chaffee, Zechariah, Jr., Free Speech in the United States, pp. 18-20. Copyright © 1941 by Harvard University Press. Reprinted by permission.

Choper, Jesse, Congressional Power to Expand Judicial Definitions of the Substantive Terms of the Civil War Amendments, 67 Minnesota Law Review

308-309 (1982). Copyright © 1982 by the Minnesota Law Review Association. Reprinted by permission.

Clark, Loren, Liberalism and Pornography, in Pornography and Censorship, pp. 52-57. Copyright © 1983 by Prometheus Books. Reprinted by permission.

Clark, J. Morris, Guidelines for the Free Exercise Clause, 83 Harvard Law Review 345 (1969). Copyright © 1969 by the Harvard Law Review Association. Reprinted by permission.

Currie, David, The Constitution in the Supreme Court: The Process of the Federal Courts, 49 University of Chicago Law Review 646, 655-657, 660, 685-686 (1982). Copyright © 1982 by University of Chicago Law Review. Reprinted by permission.

Ely, John, Democracy and Distrust, pp. 1, 7-8, 48-50, 56-58, 60, 62, 87-88, 130-131, 135-136, 153, 159, 162. Copyright © 1981 by Harvard University Press. Reprinted by permission.

———, Flag Desecration: A Case Study in the Roles of Categorization and Balancing in First Amendment Analysis, 88 Harvard Law Review 1482, 1503-1504, 1506-1508 (1975). Copyright © 1975 by the Harvard Law Review Association. Reprinted by permission.

Emerson, Thomas, The Doctrine of Prior Restraint, 20 Law & Contemporary Problems 648, 656-660 (1955). Copyright © 1955 by Duke University School of Law. Reprinted by permission.

Fairman, Charles, Does the Fourteenth Amendment Incorporate the Bill of Rights? The Original Understanding, 2 Stanford Law Review 5, 132, 137-139 (1949). Copyright © 1949 by Stanford Law Review. Reprinted by permission.

Grey, Thomas C., Eros, Civilization, and the Burger Court, 43 Law & Contemporary Problems 83, 86-97 (1980). Copyright © 1980 by Duke University School of Law. Reprinted by permission.

Hafen, Bruce, The Constitutional Status of Marriage, Kinship and Sexual Privacy — Balancing the Individual and Social Interests, 81 Michigan Law Review 403, 559, 487, 494-497 (1980). Copyright © by Michigan Law Review. Reprinted by permission.

Henkin, Louis, Privacy and Autonomy, 74 Columbia Law Review 1410 (1974). Copyright © by the Directors of the Columbia Law Review Association. Reprinted by permission.

Howe, Mark De Wolfe, The Garden and the Wilderness, pp. 11-12. Copyright © 1965 by The Frank L. Weil Institute. Reprinted by permission.

Hutchinson, Dennis, More Substantive Equal Protection? A Note on *Plyler v. Doe*, 1982 Supreme Court Review 167, 168-169, 191-192. Copyright © by University of Chicago Press. Reprinted by permission.

Kadish, Sanford, Methodology and Criteria in Due Process Adjudication — A Survey and Criticism, 66 Yale Law Journal 319, 327-328, 337-338 (1957). Copyright © 1957 by the Yale Law Journal Company and Fred B. Rothman & Company. Reprinted by permission.

Kauper, Paul, Penumbras, Peripheries, Emanations, Things Fundamental and Things Forgotten: The *Griswold* Case, 64 Michigan Law Review 235, 252-253 (1965). Copyright © by Michigan Law Review. Reprinted by permission.

Kluger, Richard, Simple Justice: The History of *Brown v. Board of Education* and Black America's Struggle for Equality, pp. 132-133. Copyright © 1976 by Alfred A. Knopf, Inc. Reprinted by permission.

Kurland, Philip, The Religion Clauses and the Burger Court, 34 Catholic University Law Review 13-14 (1984). Copyright © 1984 Catholic University Law Review. Reprinted by permission.

Mashaw, Jerry L., The Supreme Court's Due Process Calculus for Administrative Adjudication in *Mathews v. Eldridge:* Three Factors in Search of a Theory of Value, 44 University of Chicago Law Review 28, 29-51 (1976). Copyright © 1976 by University of Chicago Law Review. Reprinted by permission.

Mayton, William T., Seditious Libel and the Lost Guarantee of Expression, 84 Columbia Law Review 91, 95, 97, 117-120 (1984). Copyright © 1984 by the Directors of the Columbia Law Review Association. Reprinted by permission.

McCloskey, Robert, Economic Due Process and the Supreme Court: An Exhumation and Reburial, pp. 34, 38. Copyright © 1962 by University of Chicago Press. Reprinted by permission.

McLaughlin, Andrew, A Constitutional History of the United States, pp. 118-136. Copyright © 1935 by Irvington Publishing Company. Reprinted by permission.

Meiklejohn, Alexander, Free Speech and Its Relation to Self-Government, pp. 15-16, 24-27, 39. Copyright © 1948 by Harper & Row, Publishers. Reprinted by permission.

Michelman, Frank I., Property, Utility, and Fairness: Comments on the Ethical Foundations of Just Compensation Law, 80 Harvard Law Review 1165, 1225 (1967). Copyright © 1967 by the Harvard Law Review Association. Reprinted by permission.

———, Welfare Rights in a Constitutional Democracy, Washington University Law Quarterly 659, 677 (1979). Copyright © 1979 by Washington University Law Quarterly. Reprinted by permission.

Mill, John Stuart, On Liberty, pp. 490-494. Copyright © 1859 by Oxford University Press. Reprinted by permission.

Note, Anti-Pornography Laws and First Amendment Values, 98 Harvard Law Review 460, 470, 473-475 (1984). Copyright © 1984 by the Harvard Law Review Association. Reprinted by permission.

———, Congress, The President, and the Power to Commit Forces to Combat, 81 Harvard Law Review 1771 (1968). Copyright © 1968 by the Harvard Law Review Association. Reprinted by permission.

———, Developments in the Law — The Constitution and the Family, 93 Harvard Law Review 1156, 1177, 1186-1187 (1980). Copyright © 1980 by the Harvard Law Review Association. Reprinted by permission.

Perry, Michael, The Authority of Text, Tradition, and Reason: A Theory of Constitutional "Interpretation," 58 Southern California Law Review 565-566 (1985). Copyright © 1985 by the Southern California Law Review. Reprinted by permission.

Prichard, Robert, Securing the Canadian Economic Union, in M. J. Treblicock, ed., Federalism and the Canadian Economic Union, pp. 3, 6, 17-18. Copyright © 1983 by University of Toronto Press. Reprinted by permission.

Robinson, Donald L., Slavery and the Structure of American Politics, pp. 209-210, 244-246. Copyright © 1971 by Donald L. Robinson. Reprinted by permission.

Sager, Lawrence, Fair Measure: The Status of Underenforced Constitutional

Norms, 91 Harvard Law Review 1220-1221, 1227 (1978). Copyright © 1978 by the Harvard Law Review Association. Reprinted by permission.

Scanlon, Thomas, A Theory of Freedom of Expression, 1 Philosophy & Public Affairs, 204, 213-218 (1972). Copyright © 1972 by Princeton University Press. Reprinted by permission.

Siegan, Bernard, Economic Liberties and the Constitution, pp. 23, 30-31, 83, 260, 262, 284, 302-303. Copyright © 1978 by University of Chicago Press. Reprinted by permission.

Stone, Geoffrey R., Content Regulation and the First Amendment, 25 William & Mary Law Review 189, 244-251 (1983). Copyright © 1983 by the College of William and Mary. Reprinted by permission.

———, Restrictions of Speech Because of Its Content: The Peculiar Case of Subject-Matter Restrictions, 46 University of Chicago Law Review 81, 83, 108 (1978). Copyright © 1978 by University of Chicago Law Review. Reprinted by permission.

Teibout, Charles, A Pure Theory of Local Expenditures, 64 Journal of Political Economy 418 (1956). Copyright © 1956 by University of Chicago Press. Reprinted by permission.

Thayer, James Bradley, John Marshall, pp. 103-107. Copyright © 1901 by Houghton Mifflin Company. Reprinted by permission.

Tribe, Laurence, American Constitutional Law, pp. 436, 439, 564, 816-819, 826-828. Copyright © 1978 by Foundation Press. Reprinted by permission.

———, American Constitutional Law Supplement, p. 25. Copyright © 1979 by Foundation Press. Reprinted by permission.

———, Constitutional Choices, pp. 243-244. Copyright © 1985 by Harvard University Press. Reprinted by permission.

Tushnet, Mark, Following the Rules Laid Down: A Critique of Interpretivism and Neutral Principles, 96 Harvard Law Review 781, 800-804 (1983). Copyright © 1983 by the Harvard Law Review Association. Reprinted by permission.

Van Alstyne, William W., A Critical Guide to *Marbury v. Madison*, 1969 Duke Law Journal 17, 22. Copyright © 1969 by Duke University School of Law. Reprinted by permission.

Wechsler, Herbert, The Political Safeguards of Federalism, in Principles, Politics, and Fundamental Law, pp. 49-82. Copyright © 1961 by Harvard University Press. Reprinted by permission.

Williamson, A., The Crucible of Race, pp. 109-111, 116-117, 224-225. Copyright © 1984 by Oxford University Press. Reprinted by permission.

Wilson, James Q., The Politics of Regulation, pp. 366-370. Copyright © 1980 by Basic Books. Reprinted by permission.

Wright, J. Skelly, Politics and the Constitution: Is Money Speech?, 85 Yale Law Journal 1001, 1005, 1015-1019 (1976). Copyright © 1976 by the Yale Law Journal Company and Fred B. Rothman & Company. Reprinted by permission.

Editorial Notice

Throughout this book additions to quoted material are indicated by brackets, and deletions are indicated either by brackets or ellipses. Citations and footnotes are sometimes omitted without notice.

The Constitution of
the United States

We the People of the United States, in Order to form a more perfect Union, establish Justice, insure domestic Tranquility, provide for the common defence, promote the general Welfare, and secure the Blessings of Liberty to ourselves and our Posterity, do ordain and establish this Constitution for the United States of America.

ARTICLE I

Section 1. All legislative Powers herein granted shall be vested in a Congress of the United States, which shall consist of a Senate and House of Representatives.

   Section 2. [1] The House of Representatives shall be composed of Members chosen every second Year by the People of the several States, and the Electors in each State shall have the Qualifications requisite for Electors of the most numerous Branch of the State Legislature.

   [2] No Person shall be a Representative who shall not have attained to the Age of twenty five Years, and been seven Years a Citizen of the United States, and who shall not, when elected, be an Inhabitant of that State in which he shall be chosen.

   [3] Representatives and direct Taxes shall be apportioned among the several States which may be included within this Union, according to their respective Numbers, which shall be determined by adding to the whole Number of free Persons, including those bound to Service for a Term of Years, and excluding Indians not taxed, three fifths of all other Persons. The actual Enumeration shall be made within three Years after the first Meeting of the Congress of the United States, and within every subsequent Term of ten Years, in such Manner as they shall by Law direct. The Number of Representatives shall not exceed one for every thirty Thousand, but each State shall have at Least one Representative; and until such enumeration shall be made, the State of New Hampshire shall be entitled to chuse three, Massachusetts eight, Rhode Island and Providence Plan-

tations one, Connecticut five, New York six, New Jersey four, Pennsylvania eight, Delaware one, Maryland six, Virginia ten, North Carolina five, South Carolina five, and Georgia three.

[4] When vacancies happen in the Representation from any State, the Executive Authority thereof shall issue Writs of Election to fill such Vacancies.

[5] The House of Representatives shall chuse their Speaker and other Officers; and shall have the sole Power of Impeachment.

Section 3. [1] The Senate of the United States shall be composed of two Senators from each State, chosen by the Legislature thereof, for six Years; and each Senator shall have one Vote.

[2] Immediately after they shall be assembled in Consequence of the first Election, they shall be divided as equally as may be into three Classes. The Seats of the Senators of the first Class shall be vacated at the Expiration of the second Year, of the second Class at the Expiration of the fourth Year, and of the third Class at the Expiration of the sixth Year, so that one third may be chosen every second Year; and if Vacancies happen by Resignation, or otherwise, during the Recess of the Legislature of any State, the Executive thereof may make temporary Appointments until the next Meeting of the Legislature, which shall then fill such Vacancies.

[3] No Person shall be a Senator who shall not have attained to the Age of thirty Years, and been nine Years a Citizen of the United States, and who shall not, when elected, be an Inhabitant of that State for which he shall be chosen.

[4] The Vice President of the United States shall be President of the Senate, but shall have no Vote, unless they be equally divided.

[5] The Senate shall chuse their other Officers, and also a President pro tempore, in the absence of the Vice President, or when he shall exercise the Office of President of the United States.

[6] The Senate shall have the sole Power to try all Impeachments. When sitting for that Purpose, they shall be on Oath or Affirmation. When the President of the United States is tried, the Chief Justice shall preside: And no Person shall be convicted without the Concurrence of two thirds of the Members present.

[7] Judgment in Cases of Impeachment shall not extend further than to removal from Office, and disqualification to hold and enjoy any Office of honor, Trust or Profit under the United States: but the Party convicted shall nevertheless be liable and subject to Indictment, Trial, Judgment and Punishment, according to Law.

Section 4. [1] The Times, Places and Manner of holding Elections for Senators and Representatives, shall be prescribed in each State by the Legislature thereof; but the Congress may at any time by Law make or alter such Regulations, except as to the Places of chusing Senators.

[2] The Congress shall assemble at least once in every Year, and such Meeting shall be on the first Monday in December, unless they shall by Law appoint a different Day.

Section 5. [1] Each House shall be the Judge of the Elections, Returns and Qualifications of its own Members, and a Majority of each shall constitute a Quorum to do Business; but a smaller Number may adjourn from day to day, and may be authorized to compel the Attendance of absent Members, in such Manner, and under such Penalties as each House may provide.

[2] Each House may determine the Rules of its Proceedings, punish its Mem-

bers for disorderly Behavior, and, with the Concurrence of two thirds, expel a Member.

[3] Each House shall keep a Journal of its Proceedings, and from time to time publish the same, excepting such Parts as may in their Judgment require Secrecy; and the Yeas and Nays of the Members of either House on any question shall, at the Desire of one fifth of those Present, be entered on the Journal.

[4] Neither House, during the Session of Congress, shall, without the Consent of the other, adjourn for more than three days, nor to any other Place than that in which the two Houses shall be sitting.

Section 6. [1] The Senators and Representatives shall receive a Compensation for their Services, to be ascertained by Law, and paid out of the Treasury of the United States. They shall in all Cases, except Treason, Felony and Breach of the Peace, be privileged from Arrest during their Attendance at the Session of their respective Houses, and in going to and returning from the same; and for any Speech or Debate in either House, they shall not be questioned in any other Place.

[2] No Senator or Representative shall, during the Time for which he was elected, be appointed to any civil Office under the Authority of the United States, which shall have been created, or the Emoluments whereof shall have been encreased during such time; and no Person holding any Office under the United States, shall be a Member of either House during his Continuance in Office.

Section 7. [1] All Bills for raising Revenue shall originate in the House of Representatives; but the Senate may propose or concur with Amendments as on other Bills.

[2] Every Bill which shall have passed the House of Representatives and the Senate, shall, before it become a Law, be presented to the President of the United States; If he approve he shall sign it, but if not he shall return it, with his Objections to the House in which it shall have originated, who shall enter the Objections at large on their Journal, and proceed to reconsider it. If after such Reconsideration two thirds of that House shall agree to pass the Bill, it shall be sent, together with the Objections, to the other House, by which it shall likewise be reconsidered, and if approved by two thirds of that House, it shall become a Law. But in all such Cases the Votes of both Houses shall be determined by yeas and Nays, and the Names of the Persons voting for and against the Bill shall be entered on the Journal of each House respectively. If any Bill shall not be re-turned by the President within ten Days (Sundays excepted) after it shall have been presented to him, the Same shall be a Law, in like Manner as if he had signed it, unless the Congress by their Adjournment prevents its Return, in which Case it shall not be a Law.

[3] Every Order, Resolution, or Vote to Which the Concurrence of the Senate and House of Representatives may be necessary (except on a question of Adjourn-ment) shall be presented to the President of the United States; and before the Same shall take Effect, shall be approved by him, or being disapproved by him, shall be repassed by two thirds of the Senate and House of Represenatatives, according to the Rules and Limitations prescribed in the Case of a Bill.

Section 8. [1] The Congress shall have Power To lay and collect Taxes, Duties, Imposts and Excises, to pay the Debts and provide for the common Defence and general Welfare of the United States; but all Duties, Imposts and Excises shall be uniform throughout the United States;

[2] To borrow money on the credit of the United States;

[3] To regulate Commerce with foreign Nations, and among the several States, and with the Indian Tribes;

[4] To establish an uniform Rule of Naturalization, and uniform Laws on the subject of Bankruptcies throughout the United States;

[5] To coin Money, regulate the Value thereof, and of foreign Coin, and fix the Standard of Weights and Measures;

[6] To provide the Punishment of counterfeiting the Securities and current Coin of the United States;

[7] To establish Post Offices and post Roads;

[8] To promote the Progress of Science and useful Arts, by securing for limited Times to Authors and Inventors the exclusive Right to their respective Writings and Discoveries;

[9] To constitute Tribunals inferior to the supreme Court;

[10] To define and punish Piracies and Felonies committed on the high Seas, and Offenses against the Law of Nations:

[11] To declare War, grant Letters of Marque and Reprisal, and make Rules concerning Captures on Land and Water;

[12] To raise and support Armies, but no Appropriation of Money to that Use shall be for a longer Term than two Years;

[13] To provide and maintain a Navy;

[14] To make Rules for the Government and Regulation of the land and naval Forces;

[15] To provide for calling forth the Militia to execute the Laws of the Union, suppress Insurrections and repel Invasions;

[16] To provide for organizing, arming, and disciplining, the Militia, and for governing such Part of them as may be employed in the Service of the United States, reserving to the States respectively, the Appointment of the Officers, and the Authority of training the Militia according to the discipline prescribed by Congress;

[17] To exercise exclusive Legislation in all Cases whatsoever, over such District (not exceeding ten Miles square) as may, by Cession of particular States, and the Acceptance of Congress, become the Seat of the Government of the United States, and to exercise like Authority over all Places purchased by the Consent of the Legislature of the State in which the Same shall be, for the Erection of Forts, Magazines, Arsenals, dock-Yards, and other needful Buildings; — And

[18] To make all Laws which shall be necessary and proper for carrying into Execution the foregoing Powers, and all other Powers vested by this Constitution in the Government of the United States, or in any Department or Officer thereof.

Section 9. [1] The Migration or Importation of such Persons as any of the States now existing shall think proper to admit, shall not be prohibited by the Congress prior to the Year one thousand eight hundred and eight, but a Tax or duty may be imposed on such Importation, not exceeding ten dollars for each Person.

[2] The privilege of the Writ of Habeas Corpus shall not be suspended, unless when in Cases of Rebellion or Invasion the public Safety may require it.

[3] No Bill of Attainder or ex post facto Law shall be passed.

[4] No Capitation, or other direct, Tax shall be laid, unless in Proportion to the Census or Enumeration herein before directed to be taken.

[5] No Tax or Duty shall be laid on Articles exported from any State.

[6] No Preference shall be given by any Regulation of Commerce or Revenue to the Ports of one State over those of another: nor shall Vessels bound to, or from, one State, be obliged to enter, clear, or pay Duties in another.

[7] No Money shall be drawn from the Treasury, but in Consequence of Appropriations made by Law; and a regular Statement and Account of the Receipts and Expenditures of all public Money shall be published from time to time.

[8] No Title of Nobility shall be granted by the United States: And no Person holding any Office of Profit or Trust under them, shall, without the Consent of the Congress, accept of any present, Emolument, Office, or Title, of any kind whatever, from any King, Prince, or foreign State.

Section 10. [1] No State shall enter into any Treaty, Alliance, or Confederation; grant Letters of Marque and Reprisal; coin Money; emit Bills of Credit; make any Thing but gold and silver Coin a Tender in Payment of Debts; pass any Bill of Attainder, ex post facto Law, or Law impairing the Obligation of Contracts, or grant any Title of Nobility.

[2] No State shall, without the Consent of the Congress, lay any Imposts or Duties on Imports or Exports, except what may be absolutely necessary for executing its inspection Laws: and the net Produce of all Duties and Imposts, laid by any State on Imports or Exports, shall be for the Use of the Treasury of the United States; and all such Laws shall be subject to the Revision and Controul of the Congress.

[3] No State shall, without the Consent of Congress, lay any Duty of Tonnage, keep Troops, or Ships of War in time of Peace, enter into any Agreement or Compact with another State, or with a foreign Power, or engage in War, unless actually invaded, or in such imminent Danger as will not admit of delay.

ARTICLE II

Section 1. [1] The executive Power shall be vested in a President of the United States of America. He shall hold his Office during the Term of four Years, and, together with the Vice President, chosen for the same Term, be elected, as follows:

[2] Each State shall appoint, in such Manner as the Legislature thereof may direct, a Number of Electors, equal to the whole Number of Senators and Representatives to which the State may be entitled in the Congress: but no Senator or Representative, or Person holding an Office of Trust or Profit under the United States, shall be appointed an Elector.

[3] The Electors shall meet in their respective States, and vote by Ballot for two Persons, of whom one at least shall not be an Inhabitant of the same State with themselves. And they shall make a List of all the Persons voted for, and of the Number of Votes for each; which List they shall sign and certify, and transmit sealed to the Seat of the Government of the United States, directed to the President of the Senate. The President of the Senate shall, in the Presence of the Senate and House of Representatives, open all the Certificates, and the Votes shall then be counted. The Person having the greatest Number of Votes shall be the President, if such Number be a Majority of the whole Number of Electors

appointed; and if there be more than one who have such Majority, and have an equal Number of Votes, then the House of Representatives shall immediately chuse by Ballot one of them for President; and if no Person have a Majority, then from the five highest on the List the said House shall in like Manner chuse the President. But in chusing the President, the Votes shall be taken by States, the Representation from each State having one Vote; a quorum for this Purpose shall consist of a Member or Members from two thirds of the States, and a Majority of all the States shall be necessary to a Choice. In every Case, after the Choice of the President, the Person having the greatest Number of Votes of the Electors shall be the Vice President. But if there should remain two or more who have equal Votes, the Senate shall chuse from them by Ballot the Vice President.

[4] The Congress may determine the Time of chusing the Electors, and the Day on which they shall give their Votes; which Day shall be the same throughout the United States.

[5] No person except a natural born Citizen, or a Citizen of the United States, at the time of the Adoption of this Constitution, shall be eligible to the Office of President; neither shall any Person be eligible to that Office who shall not have attained to the Age of thirty five Years, and been fourteen Years a Resident within the United States.

[6] In case of the removal of the President from Office, or of his Death, Resignation or Inability to discharge the Powers and Duties of the said Office, the Same shall devolve on the Vice President, and the Congress may by Law provide for the Case of Removal, Death, Resignation or Inability, both of the President and Vice President, declaring what Officer shall then act as President, and such Officer shall act accordingly, until the Disability be removed, or a President shall be elected.

[7] The President shall, at stated Times, receive for his Services, a Compensation, which shall neither be increased nor diminished during the Period for which he shall have been elected, and he shall not receive within that Period any other Emolument from the United States, or any of them.

[8] Before he enter on the Execution of his Office, he shall take the following Oath or Affirmation: "I do solemnly swear (or affirm) that I will faithfully execute the Office of President of the United States, and will to the best of my Ability, preserve, protect and defend the Constitution of the United States."

Section 2. [1] The President shall be Commander in Chief of the Army and Navy of the United States, and of the Militia of the several States, when called into the actual Service of the United States; he may require the Opinion, in writing, of the principal Officer in each of the executive Departments, upon any subject relating to the Duties of their respective Offices, and he shall have Power to grant Reprieves and Pardons for Offenses against the United States, except in Cases of Impeachment.

[2] He shall have Power, by and with the Advice and Consent of the Senate, to make Treaties, provided two thirds of the Senators present concur; and he shall nominate, and by and with the Advice and Consent of the Senate, shall appoint Ambassadors, other public Ministers and Consuls, Judges of the supreme Court, and all other Officers of the United States, whose Appointments are not herein otherwise provided for, and which shall be established by Law: but the Congress may by Law vest the Appointment of such inferior Officers, as they think proper, in the President alone, in the Courts of Law, or in the Heads of Departments.

[3] The President shall have Power to fill up all Vacancies that may happen during the Recess of the Senate, by granting Commissions which shall expire at the End of their next Session.

Section 3. He shall from time to time give to the Congress Information of the State of the Union, and recommend to their Consideration such Measures as he shall judge necessary and expedient; he may, on extraordinary Occasions, convene both Houses, or either of them, and in Case of Disagreement between them, with Respect to the Time of Adjournment, he may adjourn them to such Time as he shall think proper; he shall receive Ambassadors and other public Ministers; he shall take Care that the Laws be faithfully executed, and shall Commission all the Officers of the United States.

Section 4. The President and all civil Officers of the United States, shall be removed from Office on Impeachment for, and Conviction of, Treason, Bribery, or other high Crimes and Misdemeanors.

ARTICLE III

Section 1. The judicial Power of the United States, shall be vested in one supreme Court, and in such inferior Courts as the Congress may from time to time ordain and establish. The Judges, both of the supreme and inferior Courts, shall hold their Offices during good Behaviour, and shall, at stated Times, receive for their Services, a Compensation, which shall not be diminished during their Continuance in Office.

Section 2. [1] The Judicial Power shall extend to all Cases, in Law and Equity, arising under this Constitution, the Laws of the United States, and Treaties made, or which shall be made, under their Authority; — to all Cases affecting Ambassadors, other public Ministers and Consuls; — to all Cases of admiralty and maritime Jurisdiction; — to Controversies to which the United States shall be a Party; — to Controversies between two or more States; — between a State and Citizens of another State; — between Citizens of different States; — between Citizens of the same State claiming Lands under Grants of different States, and between a State, or the Citizens thereof, and foreign States, Citizens or Subjects.

[2] In all Cases affecting Ambassadors, other public Ministers and Consuls, and those in which a State shall be a Party, the supreme Court shall have original Jurisdiction. In all the other Cases before mentioned, the supreme Court shall have appellate Jurisdiction, both as to Law and Fact, with such Exceptions, and under such Regulations as the Congress shall make.

[3] The trial of all Crimes, except in Cases of Impeachment, shall be by Jury; and such Trial shall be held in the State where the said Crimes shall have been committed; but when not committed within any State, the Trial shall be at such Place or Places as the Congress may by Law have directed.

Section 3. [1] Treason against the United States, shall consist only in levying War against them, or in adhering to their Enemies, giving them Aid and Comfort. No person shall be convicted of Treason unless on the Testimony of two Witnesses to the same overt Act, or on Confession in open Court.

[2] The Congress shall have Power to declare the Punishment of Treason, but no Attainder of Treason shall work Corruption of Blood, or Forfeiture except during the Life of the Person attainted.

ARTICLE **IV**

Section 1. Full Faith and Credit shall be given in each State to the public Acts, Records, and judicial Proceedings of every other State. And the Congress may by general Laws prescribe the Manner in which such Acts, Records and Proceedings shall be proved, and the Effect thereof.

Section 2. [1] The Citizens of each State shall be entitled to all Privileges and Immunities of Citizens in the several States.

[2] A Person charged in any State with Treason, Felony, or other Crime, who shall flee from Justice, and be found in another State, shall on demand of the executive Authority of the State from which he fled, be delivered up, to be removed to the State having Jurisdiction of the Crime.

[3] No Person held to Service or Labour in one State, under the Laws thereof, escaping into another, shall, in Consequence of any Law or Regulation therein, be discharged from such Service or Labour, but shall be delivered up on Claim of the Party to whom such Service or Labour may be due.

Section 3. [1] New States may be admitted by the Congress into this Union; but no new State shall be formed or erected within the Jurisdiction of any other State; nor any State be formed by the Junction of two or more States, or Parts of States, without the Consent of the Legislatures of the States concerned as well as of the Congress.

[2] The Congress shall have Power to dispose of and make all needful Rules and Regulations respecting the Territory or other Property belonging to the United States; and nothing in this Constitution shall be so construed as to Prejudice any Claims of the United States, or of any particular State.

Section 4. The United States shall guarantee to every State in this Union a Republican Form of Government, and shall protect each of them against Invasion; and on Application of the Legislature, or of the Executive (when the Legislature cannot be convened) against domestic Violence.

ARTICLE **V**

The Congress, whenever two thirds of both Houses shall deem it necessary, shall propose Amendments to this Constitution, or, on the Application of the Legislatures of two thirds of the several States, shall call a Convention for proposing Amendments, which, in either Case, shall be valid to all Intents and Purposes, as part of this Constitution, when ratified by the Legislatures of three fourths of the several States, or by Conventions in three fourths thereof, as the one or the other Mode of Ratification may be proposed by the Congress; Provided that no Amendment which may be made prior to the Year One thousand eight hundred and eight shall in any Manner affect the first and fourth Clauses in the Ninth Section of the first Article; and that no State, without its Consent, shall be deprived of its equal Suffrage in the Senate.

ARTICLE **VI**

[1] All Debts contracted and Engagements entered into, before the Adoption of this Constitution, shall be as valid against the United States under this Constitution, as under the Confederation.

[2] This Constitution, and the Laws of the United States which shall be made in Pursuance thereof; and all Treaties made, or which shall be made, under the Authority of the United States, shall be the supreme Law of the Land; and the Judges in every State shall be bound thereby, any Thing in the Constitution or Laws of any State to the Contrary notwithstanding.

[3] The Senators and Representatives before mentioned, and the Members of the several State Legislatures, and all executive and judicial Officers, both of the United States and of the several States, shall be bound by Oath or Affirmation, to support this Constitution; but no religious Test shall ever be required as a Qualification to any Office or public Trust under the United States.

ARTICLE VII

The Ratification of the Conventions of nine States shall be sufficient for the Establishment of this Constitution between the States so ratifying the Same.

Done in Convention by the Unanimous Consent of the States present the Seventeenth Day of September in the Year of our Lord one thousand seven hundred and Eighty seven and of the Independence of the United States of America the Twelfth.

ARTICLES IN ADDITION TO, AND AMENDMENT OF, THE CONSTITUTION OF THE UNITED STATES OF AMERICA, PROPOSED BY CONGRESS, AND RATIFIED BY THE LEGISLATURES OF THE SEVERAL STATES, PURSUANT TO THE FIFTH ARTICLE OF THE ORIGINAL CONSTITUTION

AMENDMENT I [1791]

Congress shall make no law respecting an establishment of religion, or prohibiting the free exercise thereof; or abridging the freedom of speech, or of the press; or the right of the people peaceably to assemble, and to petition the Government for a redress of grievances.

AMENDMENT II [1791]

A well regulated Militia, being necessary to the security of a free State, the right of the people to keep and bear Arms, shall not be infringed.

AMENDMENT III [1791]

No Soldier shall, in time of peace be quartered in any house, without the consent of the Owner, nor in time of war, but in a manner to be prescribed by law.

AMENDMENT IV [1791]

The right of the people to be secure in their persons, houses, papers, and effects, against unreasonable searches and seizures, shall not be violated, and no Warrants shall issue, but upon probable cause, supported by Oath or affirmation, and particularly describing the place to be searched, and the persons or things to be seized.

AMENDMENT V [1791]

No person shall be held to answer for a capital, or otherwise infamous crime, unless on a presentment or indictment of a Grand Jury, except in cases arising in the land or naval forces, or in the Militia, when in actual service in time of War or public danger; nor shall any person be subject for the same offence to be twice put in jeopardy of life or limb; nor shall be compelled in any criminal case to be a witness against himself, nor be deprived of life, liberty, or property, without due process of law; nor shall private property be taken for public use, without just compensation.

AMENDMENT VI [1791]

In all criminal prosecutions, the accused shall enjoy the right to a speedy and public trial, by an impartial jury of the State and district wherein the crime shall have been committed, which district shall have been previously ascertained by law, and to be informed of the nature and cause of the accusation; to be confronted with the witnesses against him; to have compulsory process for obtaining witnesses in his favor, and to have the Assistance of Counsel for his defence.

AMENDMENT VII [1791]

In Suits at common law, where the value in controversy shall exceed twenty dollars, the right of trial by jury shall be preserved, and no fact tried by a jury, shall be otherwise re-examined in any Court of the United States, than according to the rules of the common law.

AMENDMENT VIII [1791]

Excessive bail shall not be required, nor excessive fines imposed, nor cruel and unusual punishments inflicted.

AMENDMENT IX [1791]

The enumeration in the Constitution, of certain rights, shall not be construed to deny or disparage others retained by the people.

AMENDMENT X [1791]

The powers not delegated to the United States by the Constitution, nor prohibited by it to the States, are reserved to the States respectively, or to the people.

Amendment XI [1798]

The Judicial power of the United States shall not be construed to extend to any suit in law or equity, commenced or prosecuted against one of the United States by Citizens of another State, or by Citizens or Subjects of any Foreign State.

Amendment XII [1804]

The Electors shall meet in their respective states and vote by ballot for President and Vice-President, one of whom, at least, shall not be an inhabitant of the same state with themselves; they shall name in their ballots the person voted for as President, and in distinct ballots the person voted for as Vice-President, and they shall make distinct lists of all persons voted for as President, and of all persons voted for as Vice-President, and of the number of votes for each, which lists they shall sign and certify, and transmit sealed to the seat of the government of the United States, directed to the President of the Senate; — The President of the Senate shall, in the presence of the Senate and House of Representatives, open all the certificates and the votes shall then be counted; — The person having the greatest number of votes for President, shall be the President, if such number be a majority of the whole number of Electors appointed; and if no person have such majority, then from the persons having the highest numbers not exceeding three on the list of those voted for as President, the House of Representatives shall choose immediately, by ballot, the President. But in choosing the President, the votes shall be taken by states, the representation from each state having one vote; a quorum for this purpose shall consist of a member or members from two-thirds of the states, and a majority of all the states shall be necessary to a choice. And if the House of Representatives shall not choose a President whenever the right of choice shall devolve upon them, before the fourth day of March next following, then the Vice-President shall act as President, as in the case of the death or other constitutional disability of the President. — The person having the greatest number of votes as Vice-President, shall be the Vice-President, if such number be a majority of the whole number of Electors appointed, and if no person have a majority, then from the two highest numbers on the list, the Senate shall choose the Vice-President; a quorum for the purpose shall consist of two-thirds of the whole number of Senators, and a majority of the whole number shall be necessary to a choice. But no person constitutionally ineligible to the office of President shall be eligible to that of Vice-President of the United States.

Amendment XIII [1865]

Section 1. Neither slavery nor involuntary servitude, except as a punishment for crime whereof the party shall have been duly convicted, shall exist within the United States, or any place subject to their jurisdiction.

    Section 2. Congress shall have power to enforce this article by appropriate legislation.

Amendment XIV [1868]

Section 1. All persons born or naturalized in the United States, and subject to the jurisdiction thereof, are citizens of the United States and of the State wherein they reside. No State shall make or enforce any law which shall abridge the privileges or immunities of citizens of the United States; nor shall any State deprive any person of life, liberty, or property, without due process of law; nor deny to any person within its jurisdiction the equal protection of the laws.

Section 2. Representatives shall be apportioned among the several States according to their respective numbers, counting the whole number of persons in each State, excluding Indians not taxed. But when the right to vote at any election for the choice of electors for President and Vice President of the United States, Representatives in Congress, the Executive and Judicial officers of a State, or the members of the Legislature thereof, is denied to any of the male inhabitants of such State, being twenty-one years of age, and citizens of the United States, or in any way abridged, except for participation in rebellion, or other crime, the basis of representation therein shall be reduced in the proportion which the number of such male citizens shall bear to the whole number of male citizens twenty-one years of age in such State.

Section 3. No person shall be a Senator or Representative in Congress, or elector of President and Vice President, or hold any office, civil or military, under the United States, or under any State, who, having previously taken an oath, as a member of Congress, or as an officer of the United States, or as a member of any State legislature, or as an executive or judicial officer of any State, to support the Constitution of the United States, shall have engaged in insurrection or rebellion against the same, or given aid or comfort to the enemies thereof. But Congress may by a vote of two-thirds of each House, remove such disability.

Section 4. The validity of the public debt of the United States, authorized by law, including debts incurred for payment of pensions and bounties for services in suppressing insurrection or rebellion, shall not be questioned. But neither the United States nor any State shall assume or pay any debt or obligation incurred in aid of insurrection or rebellion against the United States, or any claim for the loss of emancipation of any slave; but all such debts, obligations and claims shall be held illegal and void.

Section 5. The Congress shall have power to enforce, by appropriate legislation, the provisions of this article.

AMENDMENT XV [1870]

Section 1. The right of citizens of the United States to vote shall not be denied or abridged by the United States or by any State on account of race, color, or previous condition of servitude.

Section 2. The Congress shall have power to enforce this article by appropriate legislation.

AMENDMENT XVI [1913]

The Congress shall have power to lay and collect taxes on incomes, from whatever source derived, without apportionment among the several States, and without regard to any census or enumeration.

Amendment XVII [1913]

[1] The Senate of the United States shall be composed of two Senators from each State, elected by the people thereof, for six years; and each Senator shall have one vote. The electors in each State shall have the qualifications requisite for electors of the most numerous branch of the State legislatures.

[2] When vacancies happen in the representation of any State in the Senate, the executive authority of such State shall issue writs of election to fill such vacancies: *Provided,* That the legislature of any State may empower the executive thereof to make temporary appointments until the people fill the vacancies by election as the legislature may direct.

[3] This amendment shall not be so construed as to affect the election or term of any Senator chosen before it becomes valid as part of the Constitution.

Amendment XVIII [1919]

Section 1. After one year from the ratification of this article the manufacture, sale, or transportation of intoxicating liquors within, the importation thereof into, or the exportation thereof from the United States and all territory subject to the jurisdiction thereof for beverage purposes is hereby prohibited.

Section 2. The Congress and the several States shall have concurrent power to enforce this article by appropriate legislation.

Section 3. This article shall be inoperative unless it shall have been ratified as an amendment to the Constitution by the legislatures of the several States, as provided in the Constitution, within seven years from the date of the submission hereof to the States by the Congress.

Amendment XIX [1920]

[1] The right of citizens of the United States to vote shall not be denied or abridged by the United States or by any State on account of sex.

[2] Congress shall have power to enforce this article by appropriate legislation.

Amendment XX [1933]

Section 1. The terms of the President and Vice President shall end at noon on the 20th day of January, and the terms of Senators and Representatives at noon on the 3d day of January, of the years in which such terms would have ended if this article had not been ratified; and the terms of their successors shall then begin.

Section 2. The Congress shall assemble at least once in every year, and such meeting shall begin at noon on the 3d day of January, unless they shall by law appoint a different day.

Section 3. If, at the time fixed for the beginning of the term of the President, the President elect shall have died, the Vice President elect shall become President. If a President shall not have been chosen before the time fixed for the beginning of his term, or if the President elect shall have failed to qualify, then the Vice President elect shall act as President until a President shall have qualified; and the

Congress may by law provide for the case wherein neither a President elect nor a Vice President elect shall have qualified, declaring who shall then act as President, or the manner in which one who is to act shall be selected, and such person shall act accordingly until a President or Vice President shall have qualified.

Section 4. The Congress may by law provide for the case of the death of any of the persons from whom the House of Representatives may choose a President whenever the right of choice shall have devolved upon them, and for the case of the death of any of the persons from whom the Senate may choose a Vice President whenever the right of choice shall have devolved upon them.

Section 5. Sections 1 and 2 shall take effect on the 15th day of October following the ratification of this article.

Section 6. This article shall be inoperative unless it shall have been ratified as an amendment to the Constitution by the legislatures of three-fourths of the several States within seven years from the date of its submission.

AMENDMENT **XXI** [1933]

Section 1. The eighteenth article of amendment to the Constitution of the United States is hereby repealed.

Section 2. The transportation or importation into any State, Territory, or possession of the United States for delivery or use therein of intoxicating liquors, in violation of the laws thereof, is hereby prohibited.

Section 3. This article shall be inoperative unless it shall have been ratified as an amendment to the Constitution by conventions in the several States, as provided in the Constitution, within seven years from the date of the submission hereof to the States by the Congress.

AMENDMENT **XXII** [1951]

Section 1. No person shall be elected to the office of the President more than twice, and no person who has held the office of President, or acted as President, for more than two years of a term to which some other person was elected President shall be elected to the office of the President more than once. But this Article shall not apply to any person holding the office of President when this Article was proposed by the Congress, and shall not prevent any person who may be holding the office of President, or acting as President, during the term within which the Article becomes operative from holding the office of President or acting as President during the remainder of such term.

Section 2. This article shall be inoperative unless it shall have been ratified as an amendment to the Constitution by the legislatures of three-fourths of the several States within seven years from the date of its submission to the States by the Congress.

AMENDMENT **XXIII** [1961]

Section 1. The District constituting the seat of Government of the United States shall appoint in such manner as the Congress may direct:

A number of electors of President and Vice President equal to the whole number of Senators and Representatives in Congress to which the District would be entitled if it were a State, but in no event more than the least populous State; they shall be in addition to those appointed by the States, but they shall be considered, for the purposes of the election of President and Vice President, to be electors appointed by a State; and they shall meet in the District and perform such duties as provided by the twelfth article of amendment.

Section 2. The Congress shall have power to enforce this article by appropriate legislation.

Amendment XXIV [1964]

Section 1. The right of citizens of the United States to vote in any primary or other election for President or Vice President, for electors for President or Vice President, or for Senator or Representative in Congress, shall not be denied or abridged by the United States or any State by reason of failure to pay any poll tax or other tax.

Section 2. The Congress shall have power to enforce this article by appropriate legislation.

Amendment XXV [1967]

Section 1. In case of the removal of the President from office or of his death or resignation, the Vice President shall become President.

Section 2. Whenever there is a vacancy in the office of the Vice President, the President shall nominate a Vice President who shall take office upon confirmation by a majority vote of both Houses of Congress.

Section 3. Whenever the President transmits to the President pro tempore of the Senate and the Speaker of the House of Representatives his written declaration that he is unable to discharge the powers and duties of his office, and until he transmits to them a written declaration to the contrary, such powers and duties shall be discharged by the Vice President as Acting President.

Section 4. Whenever the Vice President and a majority of either the principal officers of the executive departments or of such other body as Congress may by law provide, transmit to the President pro tempore of the Senate and the Speaker of the House of Representatives their written declaration that the President is unable to discharge the powers and duties of his office, the Vice President shall immediately assume the powers and duties of the office as Acting President.

Thereafter, when the President transmits to the President pro tempore of the Senate and the Speaker of the House of Representatives his written declaration that no inability exists, he shall resume the powers and duties of his office unless the Vice President and a majority of either the principal officers of the executive department or of such other body as Congress may by law provide, transmit within four days to the President pro tempore of the Senate and the Speaker of the House of Representatives their written declaration that the President is unable to discharge the powers and duties of his office. Thereupon Congress shall decide the issue, assembling within forty-eight hours for that purpose if not in session. If the Congress, within twenty-one days after receipt of the latter written declaration, or, if Congress is not in session, within twenty-one days after Congress is required to assemble, determines by two-thirds vote of both Houses that the President is unable to discharge the powers and duties of his office, the Vice President shall continue to discharge the same as Acting President; otherwise, the President shall resume the powers and duties of his office.

AMENDMENT XXVI [1971]

Section 1. The right of citizens of the United States, who are eighteen years of age or older, to vote shall not be denied or abridged by the United States or by any State on account of age.

Section 2. The Congress shall have power to enforce this article by appropriate legislation.

Biographical Notes on Selected U.S. Supreme Court Justices

The brief sketches that follow are designed to offer at least some sense of the background, personality, and intellectual style of the justices who have had the greatest impact on modern constitutional law. They are no substitute for serious biography. Thus, we have frequently suggested additional sources for further investigation. On less significant justices, see Currie, The Most Insignificant Justice: A Preliminary Inquiry, 50 U. Chi. L. Rev. 466 (1983); Easterbrook, The Most Insignificant Justice: Further Evidence, 50 U. Chi. L. Rev. 481 (1983).

HUGO L. BLACK (1886-1971): In 1937 President Roosevelt chose Hugo Black to fill the first available vacancy on the Court. A southern progressive who had defended the rights of labor organizers and investigated police brutality before coming to Washington, Black served in the United States Senate for ten years prior to his appointment. As a senator he strongly defended New Deal programs, including Roosevelt's "Court-packing" plan. Shortly after his confirmation, he became the subject of controversy when it was revealed that he had belonged to the Ku Klux Klan for two years in the 1920s. The controversy subsided after Black, in a dramatic radio address, admitted his prior membership, but added that he had resigned many years before and would comment no further. As a justice Black was known for his insistence that the Court should literally enforce constitutional guarantees, especially the first amendment guarantee of free speech. Although frequently characterized as an "activist" because of his willingness to subject to intensive review legislation that arguably violated express constitutional provisions, Black himself thought that literalism was necessary to confine judicial power. Thus, his insistence that the fourteenth amendment incorporated and made applicable to the states the guarantees of the first eight amendments was premised in part on his belief that any other approach would leave justices free to read their own values into the Constitution. See Adamson v. California, 332 U.S. 46 (1947). Consistent with this view, in cases such as Griswold v. Connecticut, 381 U.S. 479 (1965), Black rejected the notion that the Constitution contained general guarantees of "privacy" or "natural rights" beyond those expressly articulated in the text. See G. Dunne, Hugo Black and the Judicial Revolution (1977).

HARRY A. BLACKMUN (1908-　　): Harry Blackmun was President Nixon's third choice to fill the seat vacated by Abe Fortas's resignation in 1970. After failing to secure confirmation of Clement Haynsworth of South Carolina and G. Harrold Carswell of Florida, Nixon announced that the Senate "as it is presently constituted" would not confirm a Southerner and turned to Blackmun, a judge on the Eighth Circuit Court of Appeals. A boyhood friend of Chief Justice Burger, Blackmun was quickly dubbed "the Minnesota Twin" by the press. During his early years on the Court, he regularly voted with the chief justice. Later, he distanced himself from the Court's conservative bloc and increasingly joined Justices Marshall and Brennan in dissent. Blackmun is best known for his majority opinion in Roe v. Wade, 410 U.S. 113 (1973), upholding the constitutional right of women to decide for themselves whether to have an abortion. It has been suggested that the opinion was influenced by Blackmun's pre-judicial experience as house counsel for the Mayo Clinic, where he frequently advised doctors and defended their right to make medical judgments.

JOSEPH P. BRADLEY (1813-1892): The oldest of eleven children, Bradley was raised in poverty on a small farm. As a lawyer, he specialized in corporate and commercial law and represented several railroads. A Whig before the Civil War, Bradley was an avid supporter of the Union cause and became identified with the radical wing of the Republican Party in the postwar period. His appointment to the Court by President Grant in 1870 was later the subject of controversy because it made possible the reversal of the Court's earlier decision involving the validity of the Civil War legal tender acts. Compare Hepburn v. Griswold, 75 U.S. (8 Wall.) 603 (1870), with The Legal Tender Cases, 79 U.S. (12 Wall.) 457 (1871). As a justice Bradley supported the power of Congress to regulate the interstate movement of goods even if the regulation limited state authority. His dissent in the Slaughter-House Cases, 83 U.S. (16 Wall.) 36 (1873), also showed a willingness to read the newly enacted fourteenth amendment as an important expansion of federal authority. In 1877 Bradley was a last-minute substitute on the electoral commission established to resolve the disputed presidential election of 1876. With the commission deadlocked 7 to 7, Bradley cast the deciding vote to make Rutherford B. Hayes president. See G. White, The American Judicial Tradition, ch. 4 (1976); Fairman, Mr. Justice Bradley, in A. Dunham & P. Kurland, Mr. Justice 65-93 (1956).

LOUIS D. BRANDEIS (1856-1941): The son of Jewish immigrants from Bohemia, Brandeis successfully practiced law in Boston for forty years before his nomination to the Court. Although he became wealthy from his practice, Brandeis preferred to live simply and set a ceiling on personal expenditures of one-fifth of his income. Even after his appointment to the Court, he provided financial support for the work of his protégés, one of whom was Felix Frankfurter. He devoted himself to a host of public causes. He defended municipal control of Boston's subway system, opposed monopolistic practices of the New Haven Railroad, arbitrated labor disputes in New York's garment industry, and argued in support of the constitutionality of state maximum hour and minimum wage statutes. His nomination to the Court by President Wilson in 1916 sparked heated opposition, including protests from seven ex-presidents of the American Bar Association. During his long tenure on the Court, Brandeis insisted on respect for jurisdictional and procedural limitations on the Court's power. His distrust of large and powerful institutions, and of dogmatic adherence to the received wisdom, led him to support the constitutional authority of the states to experiment with unconventional social and economic theories. He also frequently dissented from the Court's conservative majority when it blocked efforts of the federal government to intervene in the economy. Some of his most eloquent opinions, however, were written in defense of limits on governmental power when civil liberties were at issue. His famous concurring opinion in Whitney v. California, 274 U.S. 357 (1927), argued for freedom of expression on the ground that "it is hazardous to discourage thought, hope and imagination; that fear breeds repression; that repression breeds hate; that hate menaces stable government; that the path of safety lies in the opportunity to discuss freely supposed grievances and proposed remedies; and that the fitting remedy for evil counsels is good ones." And in Olmstead v. United States, 277 U.S. 438 (1928), Brandeis dissented from the Court's refusal to condemn wiretapping, noting that "Our Government is the potent, the omnipresent teacher. For good or for ill, it teaches the whole people by its example." See L. Paper, Brandeis (1983); M. Urofsky, A Mind of One Piece: Brandeis and American Reform (1971).

WILLIAM J. BRENNAN, JR. (1906-   ): After graduating near the top of his Harvard Law School class, William Brennan returned to his native Newark where he joined a prominent law firm and specialized in labor law. As his practice grew, Brennan, a devoted family man, resented the demands it made on his time and accepted an appointment on the New Jersey Superior Court in order to lessen his work load. Brennan attracted attention as an efficient and fairminded judge and was elevated to the New Jersey Supreme Court in 1952. President Eisenhower appointed him to the Supreme Court in 1956. The appointment was criticized at the time as "political" on the ground that the nomination of a Catholic Democrat on the eve of the 1956 presidential election was intended to win votes. Once on the Court, Justice Brennan firmly established himself as a leader of the "liberal" wing. He authored important opinions in the areas of free expression, criminal procedure, and reapportionment. Often credited with providing critical behind-the-scenes leadership during the Warren Court years, Brennan continued to play a significant role — although more often as a dissenter lamenting what he believed to be the evisceration of Warren Court precedents — as the ideological complexion of the Court shifted in the 1970s and 1980s. Brennan's own spirit is perhaps best captured in his celebration in New York Times v. Sullivan, 376 U.S. 255 (1964), of "our profound national commitment to the principle that debate on public issues should be uninhibited, robust, and wide-open."

WARREN E. BURGER (1907-   ): The son of financially hard-pressed parents, Warren Burger attended college and law school at night while selling life insurance during the day. After graduation, he entered private practice and assisted Harold Stassen in his unsuccessful bid for the Republican presidential nomination in 1948. In 1953 he came to Washington to serve as assistant attorney general for the Civil Division. While in that post, he attracted public attention for defending the government's dismissal of John F. Peters for disloyalty after Solicitor General Sobeloff refused to argue the case on grounds of conscience. Shortly thereafter, President Eisenhower appointed him to the United States Court of Appeals for the District of Columbia Circuit. His tenure on that Court was marked by sharp clashes with the Court's liberal majority, especially over criminal justice issues. In 1969 President Nixon named Burger chief justice to replace Earl Warren. A strong advocate of "strict construction" and a "plain meaning" approach to statutory and constitutional interpretation, Burger firmly identified himself with the Court's conservative wing and often voted to limit Warren Court decisions. But he also authored important opinions upholding the right of trial judges to order busing as a remedy for school segregation, interpreting federal civil rights statutes as imposing an "effects" test for employment discrimination, and upholding the right of the press to remain free of prior restraints in covering criminal trials. Burger wrote for a unanimous Court in United States v. Nixon, 418 U.S. 683 (1974), upholding the subpoena for the Watergate tapes which, a few days later, resulted in President Nixon's resignation.

BENJAMIN N. CARDOZO (1870-1938): The son of a Tammany Hall judge who was implicated in the Boss Tweed scandal and resigned rather than face impeachment, Benjamin Cardozo began his judicial career by narrowly defeating a Tammany candidate for a position on the New York Supreme Court. Shortly thereafter, he was appointed to the New York Court of Appeals, where he served for eighteen years, during the last six of which he was chief judge. Cardozo is probably best remembered for his skills as a state common law judge. He was responsible for making the New York Court of Appeals the most respected state court in the country, and his judicial writings and lectures were immensely influential. On Justice Holmes's retirement, President Hoover was inundated with requests that Cardozo be elevated to the Supreme Court. But there were already two New Yorkers and one Jew serving on the Court, and Hoover resisted. Only when Justice Stone offered to resign to make way for Cardozo did the President relent. Cardozo was a bachelor who had very few friends and lived for most of his life with his unmarried sister. Called "the hermit philosopher" by some, Cardozo was remembered by others for "the strangely compelling power of [his] reticient, sensitive almost mystical personality." See G. Hellman, Benjamin N. Cardozo (1940).

TOM C. CLARK (1899-1977): Long active in Texas Democratic politics, Tom Clark came to Washington in 1937 as a special assistant in the Justice Department, where he worked on antitrust matters and served as civilian coordinator of the forced evacuation of Japanese-American citizens from the West Coast. His prosecution of fraudulent war claims brought him into contact with Senator Truman, whose Senate War Investigating Committee was holding well-publicized hearings concerning war profiteering. Clark and Truman became good friends, and when Truman assumed the presidency, he named Clark attorney general. While in that post, Clark actively participated in the prosecution of top Communist Party leaders and ordered the creation of the first Attorney General's list of dangerous political organizations. Appointed to the Court in 1949, Clark served until 1967 when he resigned to avoid any appearance of conflict of interest after President Johnson appointed his son, Ramsey Clark, to serve as attorney general. Clark remained active for years after his resignation. Long interested in judicial administration, he founded the Federal Judicial Center, a part of the judicial branch that studies the operation of federal courts, and served as its first director. Until his death in 1977, he frequently accepted assignments to serve on panels of United States Courts of Appeals in various circuits to help relieve case load pressures.

WILLIAM O. DOUGLAS (1898-1980):   Widely regarded as one of the most brilliant, eccentric, and independent persons to serve on the Court, William Douglas sat as an associate justice for thirty-six years, seven months — longer than any other justice. Born in poverty in Minnesota, he spent his early years in Yakima, Washington. Although financially hard pressed, he managed to go east to study law at Columbia Law School, where he taught before joining the Yale faculty in 1929. President Roosevelt named him to the newly created Securities and Exchange Commission in 1934, and he became its chairman in 1937. Roosevelt nominated him to be an associate justice in 1939. Douglas's early opinions gave little hint of the controversy that would surround him in later years. Indeed, Roosevelt came close to choosing him as his running mate in 1944 — a decision that would have made him President on Roosevelt's death a year later. In subsequent years, however, Douglas's controversial statements both on and off the bench, his strong support for unpopular political causes, and his unconventional lifestyle (he was married four times) stirred up a whirlwind of political opposition. Congress twice began impeachment proceedings against him, although neither effort came close to success. A prodigiously rapid worker, Douglas often ridiculed his colleagues for complaining about the Court's work load. By his own account, he once assisted a colleague, who had fallen behind in his work, by ghostwriting a majority opinion that responded to his own dissent. He often finished his work for the term early and retreated to his nearly inaccessible summer home in Yakima, to which lawyers were forced to trek when emergency matters arose. Critics claimed that his opinions showed the signs of haste; admirers emphasized the forceful, blunt manner in which he cut through legal doctrine to reach the core issue in a case. His opinions were marked by a fierce commitment to individual rights and distrust of government power. See V. Countryman, Douglas of the Supreme Court (1959); W. Douglas, The Court Years 1939-1975 (1980); W. Douglas, Go East Young Man (1974).

STEPHEN J. FIELD (1816-1899):   In 1863 Congress authorized an additional seat on the Court, in part to assure a majority sympathetic to the Union cause in the Civil War. President Lincoln named Stephen Field, a Democrat who had nonetheless staunchly opposed secession, to fill the seat. Field was part of an illustrious family: His brothers included a well-known politician and lawyer, a widely read author, and a famous entrepreneur; he served for the last seven years of his tenure on the Court with his nephew, Justice Brewer; his niece was Anita Whitney, the left-wing activist who gained notoriety in Whitney v. California, 274 U.S. 357 (1927). Justice Field himself was personally involved in a landmark Supreme Court case. When his personal bodyguard killed former Chief Justice Terry of the California Supreme Court, allegedly while defending Justice Field's life, the ensuing litigation ended in In re Neagle, 135 U.S. 1 (1890). In light of the circumstances surrounding his appointment, it was ironic that, once on the

Court, Field tended to defend the South in particular and state sovereignty in general against extension of federal power during the Reconstruction period. In the period before substantive due process secured majority support on the Court, Field sought to provide constitutional protection for business enterprises. His dissenting opinion in the Slaughter-House Cases, 83 U.S. (16 Wall.) 36 (1873), for example, read the fourteenth amendment as providing significant protection to property rights and was an important precursor of Lochner v. New York, 198 U.S. 45 (1905). By the time of his retirement in 1897, Field had surpassed John Marshall's record for length of service. See C. Swisher, Stephen J. Field: Craftsman of the Law (1930).

ABE FORTAS (1910-1984): Founder of the Washington law firm Arnold, Fortas, and Porter, Abe Fortas provided behind-the-scenes advice to Democratic politicians for years before his appointment to the Court in 1965. As a young man, Fortas held a series of jobs in the Roosevelt administration, including Under-Secretary of the Interior under Harold Ickes. After entering private practice, Fortas found time to defend victims of McCarthyism and to litigate several important civil rights cases, including Gideon v. Wainwright, 372 U.S. 335 (1963). In 1948 Fortas successfully represented Congressman Lyndon Johnson when his forty-eight-vote victory in the Democratic senatorial primary was challenged. (The election earned Johnson the nickname "Landslide Lyndon.") Fortas became one of Johnson's close friends, and when Justice Goldberg resigned to become United Nations Ambassador, Johnson appointed him to the Court. In 1968, when Chief Justice Warren indicated that he intended to retire, Johnson chose Fortas as Warren's succesor. The nomination had long-term consequences that neither man could have foreseen. Republicans and conservative Democrats charged Johnson with "cronyism" and ultimately forced him to withdraw the nomination, but not before it was revealed that Fortas had received $15,000 to teach a course at a local university while on the bench. The next year, Life magazine revealed that Fortas had accepted and then returned $20,000 from a charitable foundation controlled by the family of an indicted stock manipulator. Although denying any wrongdoing, Fortas resigned from the Court. As a consequence, President Nixon was able to fill two vacancies early in his term, thereby helping to fulfill his campaign promise to "roll back" the Warren Court revolution.

FELIX FRANKFURTER (1882-1965): An immigrant from Austria, Felix Frankfurter grew up in poverty on New York's lower east side. Before his appointment to the Court by President Roosevelt in 1939, he taught at the Harvard Law School, helped found the New Republic, served in a variety of public positions, and provided important, informal advice to Roosevelt in formulating the New Deal. Frankfurter's scholarly writings contributed significantly to understanding of administrative law, labor law, and the relationship between federal and state courts. As a justice, Frankfurter's career was marked by a preoccupation with problems of judicial legitimacy and self-restraint. He frequently clashed with Justices Douglas and Black, also Roosevelt appointees, over the "preferred position" of the first amendment and the incorporation doctrine. His concern over the countermajoritarian aspect of judicial review led him to argue for deference to legislative judgment in such landmark cases as Dennis v. United States, 341 U.S. 494 (1951), and Baker v. Carr, 369 U.S. 186 (1962). See P. Kurland, Felix Frankfurter on the Supreme Court (1970); J. Lash, From the Diaries of Felix Frankfurter (1974).

JOHN MARSHALL HARLAN (1833-1911): Although a slave holder and a member of the southern aristocracy, John Harlan remained loyal to the Union during the Civil War and commanded a regiment of Kentucky volunteers in the Union forces. At a critical moment in the deadlocked Republican convention of 1876, Harlan threw the support of the Kentucky delegation behind Rutherford B. Hayes, who rewarded him a year later with an appointment to the Court. Before his appointment, Harlan opposed the postwar amendments ending slavery and guaranteeing equal rights for blacks. (He opposed Lincoln and supported Democrat John MacClellan in the 1864 presidential election.) Once on the Court, however, he advocated a broad reading of these amendments. His famous dissenting opinions in The Civil Rights Cases, 109 U.S. 3 (1883), and Plessy v. Ferguson, 163 U.S. 537 (1896), argued for Congress's power to defend the newly freed slaves from "private" discrimination and against the constitutionality of state mandated separation of the races. It was in *Plessy* that Harlan declared that "Our Constitution is color blind," and rightly predicted that "the judgment this day rendered will, in time, prove to be quite as pernicious as the decision . . . in the *Dred Scott* case." Well known for his distinctive personal style, Harlan often delivered his opinions extemporaneously in the fashion of an old-time Kentucky stump speech. Justice Holmes described him as "the last of the tobacco-spitting judges." See F. Latham, The Great Dissenter: John Marshall Harlan (1970).

  JOHN MARSHALL HARLAN (1899-1971): The grandson of the first Justice Harlan, John Harlan was appointed to the Court by President Eisenhower in 1955. Before his appointment, Harlan spent a quarter of a century in practice with a prominent Wall Street law firm, served as chief counsel to the New York State Crime Commission, and sat briefly on the Court of Appeals for the Second Circuit. On the Court, Justice Harlan became the intellectual leader of the "conservative" wing, often dissenting from "activist" decisions during the stewardship of Chief Justice Warren. He defended the values of federalism and never accepted the incorporation of the bill of rights against the states. Nor was he ever reconciled to the Court's broad reading of the equal protection clause, especially when strict scrutiny was utilized to defend "fundamental" values. There was also a strong libertarian strain in Justice Harlan's opinions, however. His belief in federalism and rejection of "judicial activism" did not prevent him from finding, for example, that the due process clause precluded the states from restricting the use of contraceptives by married couples. He also wrote for the Court in a series of important first amendment decisions, narrowly construing federal statutes prohibiting subversive advocacy, and defending the right of a Vietnam War protestor to wear a jacket inscribed with the message "Fuck the Draft." It was in the latter case that Harlan proclaimed that "one man's vulgarity is another's lyric." During his tenure, Harlan was widely respected, even by opponents of his philosophy, for his thoroughness, candor, and civility. Although he often disagreed publicly with Justice Black, they were close friends in private. They were hospitalized together during their final illnesses and died within a short period of each other. See D. Shapiro, The Evolution of a Judicial Philosophy: Selected Opinions and Papers of Justice John M. Harlan (1969).

OLIVER WENDELL HOLMES, JR. (1841-1935): Justice Holmes, the son of a famous poet and essayist, survived three wounds in the Civil War. He had already enjoyed a distinguished career as a practitioner, author, professor, and justice on the Supreme Judicial Court of Massachusetts before his appointment to the Supreme Court by President Roosevelt in 1902. Holmes, then sixty-two years old, seemed to be at the close of his career. A life-long Republican, he was expected to be a loyal supporter of the President on the bench. Few could have anticipated that he would serve on the Court for twenty-nine years, that his tenure would be marked by a fierce independence, and that he would exercise virtually unparalleled influence over modern constitutional theory. Holmes is perhaps best remembered for his formulation of the "clear and present danger test" for subversive advocacy and his rejection of substantive due process as a limitation on state social and economic legislation. His judicial philosophy was marked by skepticism, particularism, and pragmatism. He doubted that general abstract propositions were useful in deciding particular cases or that broad value judgments could be objectively defended. He thought that the law was necessarily unconcerned with the thought processes of those it regulated and that it had no independent existence apart from what people did in response to what judges said. For twenty-five years, he walked daily the two and one-half miles from his home to the Court, never missing a session. He finally retired at ninety years of age and died two days before his ninety-fourth birthday. See F. Biddle, Mr. Justice Holmes (1943); M. Howe, Justice Oliver Wendell Holmes: The Proving Years (1963); M. Howe, Justice Oliver Wendell Holmes: The Shaping Years (1957).

CHARLES EVANS HUGHES (1862-1948): After defeating William Randolph Hearst for the governorship of New York, Charles Evans Hughes served as governor for one term and part of another until 1910, when President Taft appointed him to the Court. In 1916 he resigned to run for the presidency on the Republican and Progressive tickets against Woodrow Wilson. On election eve, he went to bed thinking that he was President, but when the final returns were counted, he had lost by a scant twenty-three electoral votes. Hughes returned to New York law practice until President Harding appointed him Secretary of State. In 1930 President Hoover returned Hughes to the Court, this time as chief justice. Hughes served as chief justice during the tumultuous eleven-year period when the Court blocked much of President Roosevelt's New Deal, then survived a direct attack on its independence, and finally reconciled itself to the fundamental changes wrought by Roosevelt's program. Throughout this period, Hughes occupied a centrist position. Although closely identified with the conservative New York bar, he often joined the liberals on the Court who dissented from invalidation of social and economic legislation. But he also defended the institutional independence of the Court when it was attacked by President Roosevelt. At a crucial point in the "Court-packing" controversy, Hughes sent a letter to Senator Wheeler arguing that the Court was current in its work and that the addition of new justices would create serious inefficiencies. On his retirement in 1941 Justice Frankfurter likened his leadership ability to that of "Toscanini lead[ing] an orchestra." See M. Pusey, Charles Evans Hughes (1951).

ROBERT H. JACKSON (1892-1954): A skillful advocate and brilliant legal stylist, Robert Jackson rose quickly in the early Roosevelt administration, eventually becoming one of President Roosevelt's closest advisors. After serving as counsel to the Internal Revenue Bureau, where he won a $750,000 judgment against former Treasury Secretary Andrew W. Mellon, Jackson served successively as assistant attorney general, solicitor general, and attorney general. President Roosevelt named him to the Supreme Court in 1941 to fill the seat vacated by Justice Stone when Stone was appointed chief justice. Jackson is perhaps best remembered for his graceful prose and his subtle and original efforts to articulate a coherent theory of separation of powers in his opinions in such cases as Youngstown Sheet & Tube Co. v. Sawyer, 342 U.S. 579 (1952), and Korematsu v. United States, 323 U.S. 214 (1944). In 1945, while still on the Court, Jackson served as the chief United States prosecutor at the Nuremburg war crimes trial. This exposure to German fascism may have influenced Jackson's subsequent approach to constitutional interpretation. Many of his later first amendment opinions, for example, were preoccupied with the attempt to draw a bright line between protected freedom of conscience and unprotected speech that threatened the public peace and order. Jackson's willingness to permit government regulation of subversive or abusive advocacy in cases such as Dennis v. United States, 341 U.S. 494 (1951), and Terminiello v. Chicago, 337 U.S. 1 (1949), brought him into sharp conflict with Justices Black and Douglas — conflict that was exacerbated by deteriorating personal relationships. When Chief Justice Stone died, it was reported that several justices threatened to resign if Jackson was elevated to the chief justiceship. Jackson never became chief justice, but remained on the Court until his death in 1954. See E. Gerhart, America's Advocate: Robert A. Jackson (1958); G. White, The American Judicial Tradition, ch. 11 (1976).

WILLIAM JOHNSON (1771-1834): In 1804 President Jefferson had his first opportunity to make a Republican appointment to the Federalist-dominated Supreme Court. His choice was William Johnson, who had served on the South Carolina Court of Common Pleas immediately before his appointment. The son of a blacksmith and Revolutionary War patriot, Johnson graduated first in his class at Princeton and studied law under Charles Cotesworth Pinckney, one of President Washington's leading advisers. In 1794 Johnson was elected to the South Carolina House of Representatives as a member of Jefferson's new Republican Party and served as speaker before beginning his judicial career. Jefferson hoped that Johnson would temper the nationalist bias of a Court heavily influenced by Chief Justice Marshall's dominant personality. Johnson did quickly gain a reputation for independence. Indeed, he was largely responsible for establishing the legitimacy of dissenting opinions, and he has been called "the first great Court dissenter." But the very independence that Jefferson valued meant that Johnson could not be relied on to reflexively support the Republican position. Thus, his doubts about judicial supremacy led him to validate congressional powers that significantly trenched on local interests, and his concurrence in Gibbons v. Ogden, 22 U.S. (9 Wheat.) 1 (1824), would in some respects have carried the Court further toward the nationalist camp than even Justice Marshall felt called on to go. Although Johnson was often unhappy on the Court (he wrote Jefferson that the job was no "bed of roses" and attempted unsuccessfully to obtain another appointment), he served for thirty years until his death in 1834. See Morgan, Mr. Justice William Johnson and the Constitution, 57 Harv. L. Rev. 328 (1944).

JOHN MARSHALL (1755-1835): A century and a half after his death, John Marshall remains perhaps the most important single figure in American constitutional history. Born in a log cabin on the Virginia frontier, he served in the Continental Army during the Revolutionary War. After only the briefest formal instruction, he began the practice of law, specializing in the defense of Virginians against British creditors. Before entering public life, Marshall himself was constantly hounded by creditors. He wrote his five-volume biography of George Washington in an unsuccessful effort to raise money to pay off his debts. In 1799, Marshall entered the House of Representatives, and the following year, he became Secretary of State in the Adams administration. During his brief tenure, he signed and sealed, but failed to deliver, the famous commission naming William Marbury Justice of the Peace for the District of Columbia. In 1800, Adams appointed Marshall chief justice after John Jay, the Court's first chief justice, declined reappointment to the position. Marshall served for thirty-four years, participated in more than one thousand decisions, and wrote over five hundred opinions. He is best remembered for establishing the Court's power to declare congressional statutes unconstitutional in Marbury v. Madison, 5 U.S. (1 Cranch) 137 (1803), although his contemporaries found the portion of *Marbury* asserting judicial control over presidential appointees much more controversial. But in some ways his *refusal* to invalidate a statute enacted pursuant to Congress's implied powers in McCulloch v. Maryland, 17 U.S. (4 Wheat) 316 (1819), and his willingness to strike down *state* statutes interfering with federal powers or individual rights in such cases as *McCulloch*, Gibbons v. Ogden, 22 U.S. (9 Wheat) 1 (1824), and Fletcher v. Peck 10 U.S. (6 Cranch.) 87 (1810), were even more influential on modern constitutional theory. In 1807 Marshall presided over the the treason trial of former Vice President Aaron Burr. In the course of that trial he signed the famous subpoena directing President Jefferson to produce various documents relevant to the trial — a precedent much cited over a century and a half later when another president asserted "executive privilege" to resist a judicial subpoena. When Marshall died at age seventy-nine, the liberty bell cracked when it tolled in mourning. See L. Baker, John Marshall: A Life in the Law (1974); A. Beveridge, The Life of John Marshall (1916).

THURGOOD MARSHALL (1908-   ): The son of a primary school teacher and a club steward, Thurgood Marshall became the first black to serve on the Court when he was appointed by President Johnson in 1967. But Marshall had already made an enduring mark on American legal history decades before his judicial career began. After graduating first in his class from Howard Law School, Marshall began his long involvement with the National Association for the Advancement of Colored People. For two decades, he traveled across the country coordinating the NAACP's attack on segregation in housing, employment, voting, public accommodations, and, especially, education. His most famous victory during this period came in Brown v. Board of Education, 347 U.S. 483 (1954), where he successfully argued that segregated public education violated the equal protection clause. In 1961 President Kennedy nominated him to serve on the United States Court of Appeals for the Second Circuit. Although southern senators blocked his confirmation for a year, he finally assumed his seat, where he served until 1965 when President Johnson appointed him solicitor general. As a justice, Marshall is known primarily for his unstinting defense of racial and other minorities, his liberal interpretation of free speech and press guarantees, his "multi-tiered" theory of equal protection analysis, and his fervent opposition to capital punishment.

JAMES C. McREYNOLDS (1862-1946):   Although remembered today primarily as one of the "four horsemen of reaction" who helped block Franklin Roosevelt's New Deal, Justice McReynolds first came to public attention as a vigorous "trust buster" in the Theodore Roosevelt and Wilson administrations. In the year that he served as Wilson's attorney general, he angered many members of Congress and of the administration with his arrogance and ill-temper. President Wilson named him to the Court in 1914 largely to quiet this controversy. His judicial career was marked by an unyielding commitment to strict constructionism and conservative principles. His personal manner continued to alienate many of his colleagues. After the Gold Clause Cases were decided in 1935, he proclaimed, "Shame and humiliation are on us now. Moral and financial chaos may confidently be expected." Chief Justice Taft remarked that McReynolds "has a continual grouch" and "seems to delight in making others uncomfortable." Widely accused of antisemitism, McReynolds conspicuously failed to sign the letter of affection and regret drafted by his brethren on Justice Brandeis's retirement from the Court.

FRANCIS W. MURPHY (1890-1949):   Justice Murphy came to the Court in 1940 after a long and distinguished career in local, state, and national politics. Elected mayor of Detroit in 1930, Murphy was a strong supporter of the New Deal, and President Roosevelt rewarded him with an appointment as governor general of the Philippine Islands. In 1937 he was elected governor of Michigan, but his refusal to call out state troopers to break up a sit-down strike by automotive workers cost him re-election in 1938. Although Murphy would have preferred to serve as secretary of war, President Roosevelt named him attorney general in 1939. During the brief period he held that post, he secured the indictment of a number of corrupt Democratic politicians, most notably Tom Pendergast, the Kansas City political boss who was an early sponsor of Harry Truman. On the death of Justice Butler in 1940 Roosevelt nominated Murphy to the Court. One of the most committed liberals ever to serve on the Court, Justice Murphy voted consistently in favor of civil rights, freedom of speech, and religious liberty during his tenure. Contemporaries doubted that he had the intellectual capacity of some of his colleagues (one wag remarked that his persistent moralizing on the bench led to "justice tempered with Murphy"), but many of his opinions have stood the test of time. He agreed with Justice Black that the fourteenth amendment made the first eight amendments applicable to the states, but he also shared Justice Frankfurter's view that the due process clause required invalidation of some state laws not prohibited by those amendments. Although a practicing Catholic, he strongly supported the rights of Jehovah's Witnesses, an anti-Catholic sect. He was sufficiently committed to the war effort to spend his time during court recesses as an infantry officer in Fort Benning, Georgia. Yet he was one of only three justices to dissent when the Supreme Court upheld the wartime exclusion of Japanese-American citizens from the west coast. See S. Fine, Frank Murphy: The Court Years (1985), The New Deal Years (1979), The Detroit Years (1975).

SANDRA DAY O'CONNOR (1930-   ):   The first woman ever to serve on the Court, Sandra Day O'Connor was appointed by President Reagan in 1981. O'Connor was a classmate of Justice Rehnquist at the Stanford Law School, where she was an editor of the Stanford Law Review. Despite her outstanding academic achievements, O'Connor found it difficult to locate a job on graduation. When she applied to the firm in which future Attorney General William French Smith was a partner, she was offered the position of secretary. After briefly serving as deputy county attorney for San Mateo County in California, she worked as a civilian attorney for the army while her husband served his tour of duty. She then spent eight years as a mother, homemaker, and volunteer while her three children grew up. When she resumed her legal career, she became an assistant attorney general in Arizona. In 1970 she was elected to the Arizona senate and eventually became majority leader. She then served on the Superior Court for Maricopa County and the Arizona Court of Appeals. Although her nomination to the Supreme Court was opposed by some conservatives, Justice O'Connor generally aligned herself with the conservative wing of the Court. When the Court strongly reaffirmed the constitutional right of women to secure abortions in Akron v. Akron Center for Reproductive Health, 462 U.S. 416 (1983), Justice O'Connor dissented, arguing that the Court should reconsider its analysis of abortion. She stopped short of urging that Roe v. Wade be overruled, however, and she wrote for a 5-to-4 majority in Mississippi University for Women v. Hogan, 458 U.S. 718 (1982), to invalidate a state nursing school's single-sex admissions policy. Widely respected for her incisive and informed questioning at oral argument, O'Connor is known for her deference to the political branches of government and her concern that courts not obstruct their power to govern. See Comment, The Emerging Jurisprudence of Justice O'Connor, 52 U. Chi. L. Rev. 389 (1985).

LEWIS F. POWELL, JR. (1907-   ):   Following his graduation from Harvard Law School, Lewis Powell returned to his native Virginia, where he joined one of Richmond's most prestigious law firms. As president of the Richmond school board during a period of intense controversy concerning school desegregation, Powell gained a reputation as a racial moderate. Despite intense pressure from those advocating "massive resistance," he insisted on keeping the schools open. Powell was elected president of the American Bar Association in 1964. In that capacity, he worked to establish a legal services program within the Office of Economic Opportunity and spoke out against civil disobedience and "parental permissiveness." In 1971 President Nixon fulfilled his promise to name a southerner to the Court by selecting Powell to fill the vacancy created by the resignation of Justice Black. A few years after his appointment, Powell seemed to speak for the south in his concurring opinion in Keyes v. School District, 413 U.S. 189 (1973), in which he argued that there was no significant legal distinction between northern and southern school segregation. Over time, Powell gained the reputation as an ad hoc "balancer," often casting the critical "swing vote" in important decisions. In Regents of University of California v. Bakke, 438 U.S. 265 (1978), Trimble v. Gordon, 430 U.S. 762 (1977), and Branzburg v. Hayes, 408 U.S. 665 (1972), for example, he controlled the disposition even though he was the only justice adopting his particular view of affirmative action, the rights of nonmarital children, and press rights, respectively.

WILLIAM H. REHNQUIST (1924-   ): After graduation from Stanford Law School, William Rehnquist came to Washington in 1952 to clerk for Associate Justice Robert Jackson. During his clerkship, he wrote a controversial memorandum for Justice Jackson supporting the constitutionality of "separate but equal" education for blacks. When the memorandum surfaced years later during Rehnquist's confirmation hearings, he explained that it represented Jackson's views and not his own. Following his clerkship, Rehnquist moved to Phoenix, Arizona, where he became involved in Republican politics. A strong supporter of Barry Goldwater, Rehnquist headed the Justice Department's office of legal counsel in the Nixon administration. President Nixon named him to the Court in 1971. Justice Rehnquist is known for his commitment to judicial restraint and majoritarianism. His opinions in the areas of equal protection, due process, and free speech consistently reflect a narrow construction of constitutional rights. For example, he would limit strict scrutiny under the equal protection clause to cases involving racial discrimination. Unlike conservative justices of an earlier era, however, Rehnquist would maintain the same deferential stance when reviewing state legislation arguably interfering with private markets and the free flow of commerce. (See, for example, his dissenting opinions in Virginia Pharmacy Board v. Virginia Consumer Council, 425 U.S. 748 (1976), and Kassel v. Consolidated Freightways Corp., 450 U.S. 662 (1981).) Nonetheless, Rehnquist has supported judicial intervention to protect the prerogatives of the states from federal interference and to place constitutional limits on affirmative action programs arguably discriminating in favor of racial minorities. See Shapiro, Mr. Justice Rehnquist: A Preliminary View, 90 Harv. L. Rev. 293 (1976).

JOHN PAUL STEVENS (1920-   ): A graduate of Northwestern Law School, John Paul Stevens clerked for Justice Wiley B. Rutledge before joining a Chicago law firm specializing in antitrust work. He taught part time at the University of Chicago and Northwestern Law Schools until his appointment to the Seventh Circuit Court of Appeals in 1970. Although a registered Republican, Justice Stevens was never active in partisan politics. President Ford elevated him to the Supreme Court in 1975. Stevens is known for his independence and an unwillingness to be bound by rigid formulas. He rejected the position that equal protection analysis can be reduced to various "tiers" of review, for example, arguing that various factors must be weighed under the same standard in every case to ensure that the state has met its obligation to govern impartially. And in free speech cases, Stevens staked out his own theory that fits comfortably within neither the traditional "liberal" nor "conservative" ideology. See, e.g., Smith v. United States, 431 U.S. 291 (1977); Young v. American Mini Theatres, 427 U.S. 50 (1976).

POTTER STEWART (1915-1985): Son of the Republican mayor of Cincinnati, Potter Stewart became active in Ohio Republican politics at an early age. He was twice elected to the city council and served one term as vice mayor before President Eisenhower appointed him to the Sixth Circuit Court of Appeals in 1954. In 1958 Eisenhower elevated him to the Supreme Court, where he served until his retirement in 1981. Although his political background was conservative, Stewart occupied a centrist position on the Court. He frequently voted with the liberal justices on first amendment issues (an orientation perhaps influenced by his experience as editor of a student newspaper while at Yale) but with conservative justices on equal protection issues. On many questions, his position simply could not be predicted in advance, and he had little difficulty in changing his mind about views he had expressed in earlier opinions. Perhaps his most famous opinion was a concurrence in Jacobellis v. Ohio, 378 U.S. 184 (1964), in which he said of "hard core" pornography, "I shall not today attempt further to define the kinds of material I understand to be embraced within that shorthand description; and perhaps I could never succeed in intelligibly doing so. But I know it when I see it, and the motion picture involved in this case is not that." Although sometimes ridiculed, this statement in some ways summarized Stewart's judicial philosophy, which tended to be particularistic, intuitive, and pragmatic.

HARLAN FISKE STONE (1872-1946):   For twenty-five years, Harlan Fiske Stone practiced law with a Wall Street law firm and served as a professor and the dean of the Columbia Law School. In 1924 President Coolidge appointed Stone, his old friend and classmate, to head a Department of Justice demoralized by the Teapot Dome scandal. A year later, Coolidge appointed Stone to the Court. Although a Republican and moderate conservative, Stone sided with the wing of the Court willing to uphold New Deal programs during the great controversy that engulfed the Court in the early 1930s. In 1941 President Roosevelt elevated Stone to chief justice, an appointment that Archibald MacLeish called "the perfect word spoken at the perfect moment." Justice Stone's footnote 4 in United States v. Carolene Products, 304 U.S. 144 (1938), is doubtless the most famous footnote in constitutional law and has formed the basis of much of modern constitutional theory. During his twenty-one years on the bench, Stone occupied every seat from junior associate justice, to senior associate justice, to chief justice — a feat accomplished by no other justice. He died "with his boots on" — stricken while reading a dissenting opinion from the bench in 1946. See A. Mason, Harlan Fiske Stone: A Pillar of the Law (1956); G. White, The American Judicial Tradition, ch. 10 (1976); Dunham, Mr. Chief Justice Stone, in A. Dunham and P. Kurland, Mr. Justice 229-251 (1956).

JOSEPH STORY (1779-1845):   Joseph Story was only thirty-two years old and had had no judicial experience when James Madison appointed him to the Court in 1811. Although a Republican, Story had strong nationalist sympathies and sided with John Marshall throughout much of his judicial career. His opinion in Martin v. Hunter's Lessee, 14 U.S. (1 Wheat.) 304 (1816), established the finality of the Court's constitutional authority against the states. His nationalist inclinations were also reflected in Swift v. Tyson, 41 U.S. (16 Pet.) 1 (1842), which upheld the power of federal courts to create a national commercial law. As a circuit justice, Story was said to absorb "jurisdiction as a sponge took up water," and some claimed that "if a bucket of water were brought into his court with a corn cob floating in it, he would at once extend the admiralty jurisdiction of the United States over it." A serious scholar, Story was elected to the Harvard Board of Overseers and played a key role in the founding of the Harvard Law School. His Commentaries on the Constitution, published in 1833, was a classic of its time. On Marshall's death in 1835, Story hoped to be nominated chief justice, but Andrew Jackson, who had called him "the most dangerous man in America," named Roger Taney instead. Story was frequently in dissent during the nine years he sat on the Taney Court. See, e.g., Charles River Bridge v. Warren Bridge, 36 U.S. (11 Pet.) 420 (1837). Frustrated by the direction of the Court, which he saw as undermining the Marshall Court's conception of the Constitution, he planned to resign in 1845 but fell ill and died before he could complete his unfinished business. See G. Dunne, Justice Joseph Story and the Rise of the Supreme Court (1970); K. Neumyer, Supreme Court Justice Joseph Story (1984).

GEORGE SUTHERLAND (1862-1942): A friend and close adviser to President Harding, George Sutherland was appointed to the Court in 1922. Before his appointment, he served in the United States Senate for twelve years, where he developed a reputation as an authority on constitutional questions and a conservative who nonetheless occasionally supported progressive causes. While on the Court, he was the intellectual leader of the conservative wing. He strongly objected to what he considered the evisceration of the contract clause and vigorously opposed the constitutionality of minimum wage laws. See Home Building & Loan Association v. Blaisdell, 290 U.S. 398 (1934); Adkins v. Children's Hospital, 261 U.S. 525 (1923). But his concern for the rights of the individual and broad reading of the due process clause also led him to write for the majority in Powell v. Alabama, 287 U.S. 45 (1932), which reversed the conviction of the "Scottsboro Boys" and began the process of applying constitutionally based rules of criminal procedure to the states. See J. Paschal, Mr. Justice Sutherland: A Man against the State (1951).

WILLIAM HOWARD TAFT (1857-1930): The only person to serve as both President and chief justice, William Howard Taft's career was marked by genial conservatism and a commitment to the institutional independence of each branch of the federal government. Taft served as Secretary of War in Theodore Roosevelt's administration and became one of Roosevelt's closest advisers. With support from Roosevelt, he was elected President in 1908. Soon after his inauguration, however, he and Roosevelt split, and he lost his bid for reelection in 1912 when Roosevelt splintered the Republican vote by running as an independent. After leaving the presidency, Taft taught constitutional law at Yale University and served for a year as president of the American Bar Association. Along with several other former ABA presidents, Taft fought to block Louis Brandeis's nomination to the Court in 1916. President Harding named Taft chief justice in 1921. Taft was responsible for passage of the Judiciary Act of 1925, which gave the Supreme Court effective control over its own appellate jurisdiction and for the appropriation of funds for construction of the present Supreme Court building. See A. Mason, William Howard Taft: Chief Justice (1964).

ROGER B. TANEY (1777-1864): Prior to his appointment as chief justice by President Jackson in 1835, Roger Taney served as Jackson's attorney general and Secretary of the Treasury. While serving in Jackson's cabinet, he became enmeshed in the controversy surrounding the second Bank of the United States. As attorney general Taney drafted Jackson's message vetoing the Bank's recharter, and when the Secretary of the Treasury refused to withdraw federal funds from the Bank, Jackson named Taney to the post so that he could do so. But when Jackson submitted Taney's name to the Senate for confirmation, he was defeated and forced to resign. Senate Whigs, who feared that Taney was too radical, again blocked his nomination as associate justice in 1835. Shortly thereafter, however, he was successfully nominated to replace John Marshall as chief justice. Taney's career on the Court is overshadowed by his opinion in Scott v. Sandford, 60 U.S. (19 How.) 393 (1857), widely viewed as one of the great legal and moral blunders in the Court's history. The rest of his tenure, however, was marked by the cautious and careful use of judicial power. Contrary to the expectations of his contemporaries, he did not support the wholesale abandonment of the Marshall legacy. Instead, he steered a middle course between the extreme nationalism and extreme localism of his colleagues. But as the nation approached Civil War, the ground in the middle became increasingly unstable, and Taney's one spasmodic effort to end the nation's agony over slavery by imposing a constitutional solution in *Dred Scott* ended in a tragedy that permanently marred his reputation. See C. Swisher, Roger B. Taney (1935); G. White, The American Judicial Tradition, ch. 3 (1976).

WILLIS VAN DEVANTER (1859-1941):   A lawyer's lawyer, Justice Van Devanter invariably sided with the conservative wing of the Court but, unlike some of his colleagues, never resorted to divisive ideological rhetoric. Instead, he relied on his mastery of technical doctrine to become a "master of formulas that decided cases without creating precedents." Van Devanter, who was active in Republican politics in Wyoming, came to Washington during the McKinley administration and was named to the Eighth Circuit Court of Appeals by Theodore Roosevelt. When President Taft nominated him to serve as an associate justice, William Jennings Bryan complained that he was "the judge that held that two railroads running parallel to each other for two thousand miles were not competing lines, one of the roads being that of Union Pacific," one of Van Devanter's former clients. It has been said that Van Devanter came to the Court "fully equipped with a lawyer's understanding of federal jurisdiction, a frontiersman's knowledge of Indian affairs, and a native hostility to governmental regulation." His years on the Court were marked by a concern for technical jurisdictional questions and opposition to government intervention in all forms. His retirement in June of 1937 gave Franklin Roosevelt his first appointment and helped defuse the crisis created by the Court's opposition to the New Deal.

EARL WARREN (1891-1974):   Both vilified and canonized during his tenure, Earl Warren presided as chief justice over one of the most tumultuous and portentous periods in the Court's history. The emotions that he aroused are hard to reconcile with his political stance, which was, essentially, centrist and pragmatic. As Republican governor of California, he denounced "communistic radicals" and supported the wartime order to forcibly evacuate Japanese-Americans. (The Court subsequently upheld the constitutionality of the evacuation in Korematsu v. United States, 323 U.S. 214 (1944).) In his later years as governor, however, he developed the reputation as a progressive and proposed state programs for prepaid medical insurance and liberal welfare benefits. In 1948 he ran for Vice President on the ticket headed by Thomas Dewey. In 1952 he mounted his own presidential effort. At the Republican convention, however, he threw his support behind Dwight Eisenhower. President Eisenhower repaid Warren by nominating him as chief justice in 1953 — a nomination Eisenhower later called "the biggest damn-fool mistake I ever made." Perhaps his greatest accomplishment on the Court was his painstaking and successful effort to maintain a united front as the Court overturned the separate but equal doctrine in Brown v. Board of Education, 347 U.S. 873 (1954), and then confronted southern violence and intransigence. Warren himself believed that his opinion in Reynolds v. Sims, 377 U.S. 533 (1964), establishing the one-person/one-vote formula, was of greater significance. In the end, however, it may have been his opinions in the field of criminal procedure — especially Miranda v. Arizona, 384 U.S. 436 (1966) — that attracted the most controversy. This controversy tended to obscure the fact that there was a strong conservative and moralistic tone to many of Warren's opinions. He opposed constitutional protection for "pornographic" literature, for example, and dissented in Shapiro v. Thompson, 394 U.S. 618 (1969), in which the Court invalidated durational residency requirements for welfare recipients. Warren was distrustful of complex doctrinal argument. His opinions were thus marked by a confident, intuitively grounded insistence on fair play and fundamental justice. See B. Schwartz, Superchief (1983); E. Warren, The Memoirs of Earl Warren (1977); G. White, Earl Warren (1982).

BYRON R. WHITE (1917-   ): An outstanding scholar-athlete, "Whizzer" White was first in his class at the University of Colorado, a Rhodes scholar, and a professional football player with the Detroit Lions before beginning his legal career. White served in the navy during World War II and graduated from Yale Law School magna cum laude. After serving as law clerk to Chief Justice Fred Vinson, he returned to his native Colorado where he practiced with a prominent Denver law firm for fourteen years. A long-time friend of John Kennedy, White headed Kennedy's preconvention presidential campaign in Colorado in 1960 and became chairman of National Citizens for Kennedy after Kennedy secured the nomination. After the election, Kennedy named him deputy attorney general. Kennedy named White an associate justice in 1962. As a justice, White is known as a strong advocate of school desegregation and a defender of the rights of minorities. Although more ready than his colleagues to find legislation lacking in a "rational basis" when challenged under "low-level" equal protection review, he also criticized his colleagues for too aggressive use of substantive due process analysis. For example, joined only by Justice Rehnquist, White dissented in Roe v. Wade, 410 U.S. 113 (1973), which held that women have a constitutionally protected liberty interest in securing abortions. White opposed many of the Warren Court decisions extending new protections to criminal defendants and in later years often voted to limit the scope of those holdings.

The Supreme Court since 1789

The Supreme Court since 1789

Year	Administration	Chief Justice	2	3	4	5	6	7	8	9	Major Cases
1789	Washington	John Jay	John Rutledge	William Cushing	James Wilson	John Blair	James Iredell				
1790			Thomas Johnson								
			William Paterson								
1795	J. Adams	John Rutledge			Bushrod Washington	Samuel Chase					
		Oliver Ellsworth									
1800	Jefferson	John Marshall (Adams)					Alfred Moore				
			H. Brockholst Livingston				William Johnson				Marbury v. Madison (1803)
1805								Thomas Todd			
1810	Madison			Joseph Story		Gabriel Duvall					

McCulloch v. Maryland (1819)

Gibbons v. Ogden (1824)

Barron v. Baltimore (1833)

John McKinley

John Catron

Robert Trimble

John McLean

James M. Wayne

Philip P. Barbour

Peter V. Daniel (Van Buren)

Henry Baldwin

Smith Thompson

Roger B. Taney

Monroe

J. Q. Adams

Jackson

Van Buren

W. Harrison Tyler

1815　1820　1825　1830　1835　1840

Year	Administration	Chief Justice	2	3	4	5	6	7	8	9	Major Cases
1845	Polk		Samuel Nelson (Tyler)	Levi Woodbury	Robert C. Grier						
1850	Taylor / Fillmore			Benjamin R. Curtis							
1855	Pierce			Nathan Clifford							
	Buchanan									John A. Campbell	Dred Scott v. Sandford (1857)
1860	Lincoln					Samuel F. Miller		Noah H. Swayne	10 Stephen J. Field	David Davis	
1865**	A. Johnson	Salmon P. Chase									
1870	Grant		Ward Hunt		William Strong		Joseph P. Bradley				Slaughter-House Cases (1873)

Civil Rights Cases (1883)

John M. Harlan

Joseph McKenna

Stanley Matthews (Garfield)

David J. Brewer

George Shiras

Henry B. Brown

William B. Woods

Lucius Q. C. Lamar

Howell E. Jackson (Harrison)

Rufus W. Peckham

Horace Gray (Arthur)

Samuel Blatchford

Edward D. White

Morrison R. Waite

Melville W. Fuller

Plessy v. Ferguson (1896)

Hayes

Garfield
Arthur

Cleveland

B. Harrison

Cleveland

McKinley

T. Roosevelt

1875 — 1880 — 1885 — 1890 — 1895 — 1900

Administration	Chief Justice	2	3	4	5	6	7	8	9	Major Cases
			Oliver W. Holmes			William R. Day				
										Lochner v. N.Y. (1905)
					William H. Moody					
Taft	Edward D. White	Willis Van Devanter		Horace H. Lurton	Joseph R. Lamar		Charles E. Hughes		Mahlon Pitney	
Wilson				James C. McReynolds	Louis D. Brandeis		John H. Clarke			
										Schenk v. U.S. (1919)
Harding	William H. Taft					Pierce Butler	George Sutherland			
Coolidge								Harlan F. Stone	Edward T. Sanford (Harding)	

lxxviii

Hoover

F. D. Roosevelt

Truman

Charles E. Hughes

Harlan F. Stone

Fred M. Vinson

Benjamin N. Cardozo

Hugo L. Black

Felix Frankfurter

Owen J. Roberts

Stanley F. Reed

Frank Murphy

William O. Douglas

James F. Byrnes

Wiley B. Rutledge

Robert H. Jackson

Harold H. Burton

Tom C. Clark

Sherman Minton

Schechter Poultry v. U.S. (1935)

West Coast Hotel v. Parrish (1937)

U.S. v. Carolene Prods. (1938)

Dennis v. U.S. (1951)

Youngstown Sheet v. Sawyer (1952)

1930   1935   1940   1945   1950

Administration	Chief Justice	2	3	4	5	6	7	8	9	Major Cases
Eisenhower	Earl Warren							John M. Harlan		Brown v. Bd. of Ed. (1954)
									Potter Stewart	
				William J. Brennan			Charles E. Whittaker			
Kennedy			Arthur J. Goldberg							
L. B. Johnson							Byron R. White			N.Y. Times v. Sullivan (1964)
			Abe Fortas			Thurgood Marshall				
Nixon	Warren E. Burger		Harry A. Blackmun					William H. Rehnquist		Brandenburg v. Ohio (1969)
										N.Y. Times v. U.S. (1971)

1955 1960 1965 1970

Roe v. Wade
(1973)

U.S. v. Nixon
(1974)

Washington v.
Davis (1976)

U. Cal. v. Bakke
(1978)

Sandra
Day
O'Connor

John Paul
Stevens

Lewis F.
Powell

Ford

Carter

Reagan

1975

1980

1985

* In 1863 Congress established a tenth seat, to which Stephen J. Field was appointed.
** In 1866 Congress reduced the size of the Court to six justices. Consequently, the seats of Justices Catron and Wayne remained unfilled after their deaths in 1865 and 1867. Congress restored the Court to nine seats in 1869.

Constitutional Law

I

The Role of
the Supreme Court in
the Constitutional Scheme

This chapter deals with the role of the Supreme Court in the constitutional scheme. What is the nature of the authority of the Supreme Court over Congress, the President, and the states? What are the sources and limits of that authority? And what devices are available to Congress and the President if they disagree with the Court?

It is important to understand, however, that constitutional law is not concerned solely with judicial review and the role of the Supreme Court in American government. The Constitution binds members of Congress, of the executive branch, and of state government as well as Supreme Court justices. It therefore imposes on them the responsibility of obeying constitutional requirements regardless of whether a litigated case deals with the question. Moreover, much of constitutional "law" consists of informal accommodations and historical practices among the various parts of the national government and between the federal government and the states. Consider, for example, the extent to which power over foreign affairs is shared not because of constitutional text, but because of traditions that have grown up between Congress and the executive branch. Those accommodations and practices in turn play an important role in Supreme Court decisions when and if the issues are litigated.

Notwithstanding these disclaimers, the Supreme Court has now been established as an important and perhaps as the preeminent interpreter of the Constitution. This section explores the nature and limits of that role.

A. INTRODUCTION: SOME NOTES ON THE HISTORY AND THEORY OF THE CONSTITUTION

The Declaration of Independence was signed in 1776. Hostilities with England substantially ceased in 1781 after the Yorktown campaign; the American Revolution was formally completed in 1783 with the signing of a final peace treaty with England. In February of 1781 the thirteen colonies ratified the Articles of Confederation, under which they lived for seven years. The Constitution was written in 1787 and ratified in 1788. Two years later, the bill of rights was added.

Why did the states find it necessary to adopt a new Constitution in 1787? What were the problems for which the Constitution was supposed a remedy? Views about the Constitution and its framers span a wide range. To some, the framers were intellectual giants, equipped with extraordinary foresight, vision, and faith in democracy and self-rule, who were able to rise above the squabbles of the day in order to institute into law principles that are timeless or at least enduring. See J. Fiske, The Critical Period of American History (1888). To others, the Constitution is best understood as a series of ad hoc compromises, designed to resolve very specific issues over which the young country was divided. See M. Farrand, The Framing of the Constitution of the United States (1913). A third strand in American historical thought treats the Constitution as a product of aristocratic conservatives who, far from trusting the people and believing in self-rule, intended to protect private property, and the position of the well-to-do, from the workings of democratic politics. See C. Beard, An Economic Interpretation of the Constitution of the United States (1913). There are of course numerous variations on these general approaches. For discussion, see G. Wood, Creation of the American Republic, 1776-1787 (1969); R. Horowitz, ed., The Moral Foundations of the American Republic (2d ed. 1979); G. Wood, ed., The Confederation and the Constitution (1978).

To understand the Constitution, and the surrounding debates on its purposes and effects, it is useful to have some understanding of the Articles of Confederation, which the Constitution replaced. The articles were adopted shortly after the Revolution in order to ensure some unification of the states for common foreign and domestic problems; but the overriding understanding was that the states would remain sovereign. The first substantive provision of the articles announced that "each state retains its sovereignty, freedom, and independence, and every Power, Jurisdiction, and right, which is not by this confederation expressly delegated to the United States, in Congress assembled." A number of powers were, however, conferred on "the united states in Congress assembled." These powers included "the sole and exclusive right and power of determining on peace and war," the authority to resolve disputes between the states, the power to regulate "the alloy and value of coin struck by their own authority, or by that of the respective states," the authority to control dealings with Indian tribes, to establish or regulate post offices, and to appoint naval and other offices in federal service.

But at least by modern standards, there were conspicuous gaps. Two of the most important powers of the modern national government were missing altogether — the power to tax and the power to regulate commerce. Moreover, two of the three branches of the national government were absent. There was no executive authority. There was no general national judicial authority; the only relevant provision authorized Congress to establish a national appellate tribunal to decide maritime cases.

There is considerable dispute about the nature and extent of the problems encountered by the states under the Articles. The conventional wisdom refers to Congress's inability to raise revenue to perform necessary functions; to the perceived need for executive authority in domestic and foreign affairs; and to interstate jealousies, which produced retaliatory trade measures and inhibited the flow of interstate commerce. For a suggestion that national power in fact expanded under the articles, see Note, The United States and the Articles of Confederation: Drifting toward Anarchy or Inching toward Commonwealth, 88 Yale L.J. 142 (1978). Consider the following account of the situation:

Almost everything points in only one direction — toward the need of a competent central government and the necessity of finding a system of union which could maintain itself. [The] whole story is one of gradually increasing ineptitude; of a central government which could less and less function as it was supposed to function; of a general system which was creaking in every joint and beginning to hobble at every step. . . .

Interstate jealousy [added] to the complexities of the situation. The contest for local rights under the old imperial system had strengthened the sense of state reality; men were conscious of their states; the states were in a sense their own creation. It was difficult, after the strain of war had gone, to feel acutely the reality of America and the dependence of its members one upon another; and as the days went by disorganization rather than integration seemed to be gathering headway, until the more serious patriots and watchers of the night feared for the safety of their country. States with commodious harbors had an advantage over their neighbors, and they did not shrink from using it. [The] experience of those years brought clearly home to thinking men the need of some general regulation of commerce.

The industrial and commercial conditions after the war were in considerable confusion. [Commercial] treaties were desirable, and some steps were taken in that direction; but it was hard to do anything effectively as long as the individual states could not be relied on to fulfill their obligations. Foreign nations naturally queried whether America was one or many, or, perhaps, one to-day and thirteen to-morrow. . . .

The pivotal problem, the immediate and unrelenting problem, was how to get revenue for the pressing needs of the Confederation. Financial affairs were in a pitiful shape and conditions daily grew worse. [The] sums due for interest on the domestic and foreign debts were piling up to staggering heights and even the principal of the debts — for, strange as it may seem, Congress had succeeded in borrowing — was increasing ominously.

[Within] the individual states, paper money added to the confusion and made recovery of economic stability difficult. Some of the states refused to be drawn down into the whirlpool; but seven of the thirteen had entered upon the scheme. . . .

Social unrest passed beyond the grumbling stage in Massachusetts where Shay's rebellion broke out and aroused the anxieties of the conservatives from one end of the continent to the other. [It] unquestionably had the effect of prompting men of mind as well as men of property to strengthen the union and to create self-respecting government. "There are combustibles in every State," Washington wrote in 1786, "which a spark might set fire to." . . .

Men interested in public affairs were actively discussing the nature and the defects of the union. [Hamilton] in 1783 drafted resolutions "Intended to be submitted to Congress, but abandoned for want of support." He enumerated at length the defects of the Confederation, and made a severe arraignment of the system. The first defect consisted in "confining the power of the Federal Government within too narrow limits." [He] plainly objected not only to the inconsistencies of the Articles, but to the impracticability of their effective operation. In 1785, Noah Webster [announced]: ". . . in all the affairs that respect the whole, Congress must have the same power to enact laws and compel obedience throughout the continent, as the legislatures of the several states have in their respective jurisdictions."

Of most significance, however, is the report (August, 1786) of a grand committee of Congress. [The] report proposed that Congress [should] be given the power to regulate interstate and foreign trade, with the consent of nine states, and the power of levying additional requisitions in the way of punishment upon any state not promptly complying with requisitions for men or money. If the delinquent and disobedient state should persist in its conduct, while the majority had lived up to their obligations, then Congress should have power to levy and collect taxes and in the last extremity compel the local officers in the delinquent state to do their duty; should such a step prove ineffective, then Congress might itself appoint assessors and collectors.

Nothing could more amply demonstrate the feebleness and distraction of Congress and the necessity for energetic reform, if the union was to last many days. The cumbersome methods proposed for getting money, the practical admission of a continuing and probably inescapable refusal of the states to comply with reasonable requests to defray the absolutely necessary common expenses, and above all, the more pitiful suggestion of measures which might induce members from the states to come to Congress and attend to business, were a confession of masterly incapacity.

Another source of anxiety was the light-hearted way in which treaties were regarded by the states. . . .

[In] March, 1787, resolutions were passed by Congress declaring treaties constitutionally made were "part of the law of the land"; the states were called upon to repeal acts violating the treaty with Britain and to direct the state courts to adjudge cases in accord with the treaty, "any thing in [other] . . . acts to the contrary . . . notwithstanding."

But what was the very center of the difficulty? What was the chief problem of the time? The trouble and confusion were manifestly caused by the failure of the states to abide by their obligations. The problem was to find a method, if union was to subsist at all, for overcoming the difficulty, to find therefore some arrangement, some scheme or plan of organization wherein there would be reasonable assurance that the states would fulfill their obligations and play their part under established articles of union and not make mockery of union by willing disregard or negligent delay. That was the chief problem of the day.

A. McLaughlin, A Constitutional History of the United States 137-147 (1936).

A revisionist view has it that the Articles of Confederation did not generate severe general problems. In this view, the problems were faced principally by commercial and mercantile interests who were adversely affected by the various states and who needed national authority for protection against states that had not fully respected rights of private property and private contract. See, e.g., M. Jensen, Articles of Confederation (1940); M. Jensen, The New Nation (1950).

However those questions may be resolved, there was by 1786 agreement on the part of many that amendments to the articles were required. In that year, state representatives met in Annapolis to discuss problems that had arisen under the articles; they adopted a resolution to hold a convention in Philadelphia to remedy those problems. But the nation's charge to the framers was much more narrow than the ultimate product would suggest. The framers, chosen by state legislatures, were instructed "to meet at Philadelphia [to] take into consideration the situation of the United States, to devise such further provisions as shall appear to them necessary to render the constitution of the federal government adequate to the exigencies of the Union." The limited character of this charge proved an embarrassment to the framers, whose product reflected their view that it was necessary to provide, not "further provisions," but an entirely new governing document whose character was not clearly proportionate to the weaknesses of the articles. There is therefore a sense in which the Constitution was itself an unlawful act. In addition, the Convention disregarded the amending procedure set out in the Articles, which required approval by all thirteen state legislatures. The Constitution was instead sent to Congress, with a request that it be sent in turn to state legislatures. The state legislatures would then send it to popularly elected state ratifying conventions.

The Constitution changed the framework set up by the Articles of Confederation in a number of ways. Among the most important changes were the creation of an executive branch; the grant to Congress of the powers to tax and to regulate commerce; and the creation of a federal judiciary, including the Supreme Court and, if Congress chose, lower federal courts. The tenth amendment, added two years later, was a pale echo of the first provisions of the Articles of Confederation, deleting the word "expressly," and it was countered by the clause granting Congress the authority to make "all laws necessary and proper" to effectuate its enumerated powers.

What was the underlying theory to which the Constitution responded? In this section we discuss some of the issues and problems with which the framers attempted to deal. We explore some of the general theoretical issues here; discussion of more particular issues and provisions is deferred until later chapters.

1. The Antifederalist Case

One of the best ways of approaching the thought of the framers is with the views of their adversaries — the so-called antifederalists, opponents of the Constitution who contended that the document amounted to a betrayal of the principles underlying the Revolution. See H. Storing, What the Antifederalists Were For (1981). Antifederalist thought derived in large measure from classical republicanism, a theory of government that influenced, among others, Montesquieu and Rousseau. The animating principle of the republican and antifederalist case was that of civic virtue — the willingness of citizens to subordinate their private interests to the general good. Politics thus consisted of self-rule; but it was self-rule of a particular sort. Self-rule was not a matter of pursuing self-interest but instead of selecting the values that ought to control public and private life. Dialogue and discussion among the citizenry were critical features in the governmental process. Political participation should be active and frequent and not limited to voting or other similar statements of preference. The model for government was the town meeting, a metaphor that played an explicit role in the antifederalist conception of politics. Consider in this regard Thomas Jefferson's suggestion that the Constitution should be amended in every generation, partly in order to promote general attention to public affairs. See Letter to Samuel Kercheval, July 12, 1816, in The Portable Thomas Jefferson 557-558 (M. Peterson ed. 1975).

In the view of the antifederalists, government's first task was to ensure the flourishing of the necessary public-spiritedness. The antifederalists thus believed in decentralization, for only in small communities would it be possible to find and develop the unselfishness and devotion to the public good on which genuine freedom depends. In these respects, the antifederalists echoed traditional republican theory.

The antifederalists were therefore hostile to a dramatic expansion in the powers of the national government. In a decentralized society, it would be possible to achieve the sort of homogeneity, and dedication to the public good, that would prevent the government from degenerating into a clash of private interests. A powerful national government would be inconsistent with the spirit of civic virtue, creating heterogeneity and distance from the sphere of power, both of which would undermine the citizens' willingness to subordinate their private interests to the public good. Civil society was to operate as a sort of teacher, inculcating virtue, and not merely as a regulator of private conduct. Closely connected to this view was the antifederalists' desire to avoid extreme disparities in wealth, education, and power.

It should not be difficult to see why the antifederalists would have had at best an ambivalent attitude toward a system in which decisions were made by representatives of the people rather than by the people themselves. In their ideal world, all decisions would be made during a face-to-face process of deliberation and debate. Such a process would inculcate civic virtue in the public at large, virtue from which the process itself would simultaneously benefit.

The antifederalists acknowledged, however, that representation was necessary at both the state and national levels. The size of both governments made it impossible to conduct political affairs on the model of the town meeting. But representation was hardly to be welcomed and was understood as an evil made necessary only because of the impracticability of governance by the people themselves.

From this perspective, the proposed Constitution would undermine the system of decentralization on which true liberty depended. It would prevent citizens from having effective control over their representatives and deprive them of an opportunity to participate in public affairs. It would thus pose a severe threat to the underlying principle of civic virtue. Rule by remote national leaders would attenuate the scheme of representation, rupturing the alliance of interests between the rulers and the ruled. The antifederalists foresaw a system in which the people would be effectively excluded from the world of public affairs and in which national leaders, only weakly accountable, would have enormous discretion to make law and policy.

The antifederalists were also skeptical of the emerging interest in commercial development that played a prominent role in the decision to abandon the Articles of Confederation. In the antifederalists' view, commerce was a threat to the principles underlying the Revolution, for it gave rise to ambition and avarice and thus to the dissolution of communal bonds. Insofar as the proposed Constitution was designed to promote commerce and commercial mores, it would undermine the Revolution itself.

In sum, the antifederalists attacked the proposed Constitution on the ground that it was inconsistent with the underlying principles of republicanism. The removal of the people from the political process, the creation of a powerful and remote national government, and the new emphasis on commerce — all of these threatened to undermine the purposes for which the Revolution had been fought.

2.   The Federalist Response

The antifederalist objections to the proposed Constitution provoked a theoretical justification that amounted in many respects to a new conception of politics — in

Gordon Wood's words, a "political theory worthy of a prominent place in the history of Western thought." G. Wood, The Creation of the American Republic 1787-1789, at 615 (1969). That conception consisted of a reformulation of the principles of republicanism — a reformulation that attempted to synthesize elements of traditional republicanism with an emerging theory that understood self-interest as the motivating force for political actors.

Part of that reformulation can be found in The Federalist Papers — essays attempting to defend the proposed Constitution to the country against antifederalist attack. The Federalist Papers were published under the name "Publius," but were in fact written by James Madison, Alexander Hamilton, and John Jay. Although the papers are often consulted as a means of understanding the theory underlying the Constitution, and the "intentions" of its drafters, it is important to keep in mind that the essays were in many respects propaganda pieces, designed to persuade the ambivalent.

The Federalist No. 10 (Madison)

(1787)

To the People of the State of New York:

Among the numerous advantages promised by a well-constructed Union, none deserves to be more accurately developed than its tendency to break and control the violence of faction. The friend of popular governments never finds himself so much alarmed for their character and fate, as when he contemplates their propensity to this dangerous vice. [The] instability, injustice, and confusion introduced into the public councils, have, in truth, been the mortal diseases under which popular governments have everywhere perished; as they continue to be the favorite and fruitful topics from which the adversaries to liberty derive their most specious declamations. [Complaints] are everywhere heard from our most considerate and virtuous citizens, equally the friends of public and private faith, and of public and personal liberty, that our governments are too unstable, that the public good is disregarded in the conflicts of rival parties, and that measures are too often decided, not according to the rules of justice and the rights of the minor party, but by the superior force of an interested and overbearing majority. However anxiously we may wish that these complaints had no foundation, the evidence of known facts will not permit us to deny that they are in some degree true. [The] distresses under which we labor [must] be chiefly, if not wholly, effects of the unsteadiness and injustice with which a factious spirit has tainted our public administrations.

By a faction, I understand a number of citizens, whether amounting to a majority or minority of the whole, who are united and actuated by some common impulse of passion, or of interest, adverse to the rights of other citizens, or to the permanent and aggregate interests of the community.

There are two methods of curing the mischiefs of faction: the one, by removing its causes; the other, by controlling its effects.

There are again two methods of removing the causes of faction: the one, by destroying the liberty which is essential to its existence; the other, by giving to every citizen the same opinions, the same passions, and the same interests.

It could never be more truly said than of the first remedy, that it was worse than the disease. Liberty is to faction what air is to fire, an aliment without which it instantly expires. But it could not be less folly to abolish liberty, which is essential to political life, because it nourishes faction, than it would be to wish the annihilation of air, which is essential to animal life, because it imparts to fire its destructive agency.

The second expedient is as impracticable as the first would be unwise. As long as the reason of man continues fallible, and he is at liberty to exercise it, different opinions will be formed. As long as the connection subsists between his reason and his self-love, his opinions and his passions will have a reciprocal influence on each other; and the former will be objects to which the latter will attach themselves. The diversity in the faculties of men, from which the rights of property originate, is not less an insuperable obstacle to a uniformity of interests. The protection of these faculties is the first object of government. From the protection of different and unequal faculties of acquiring property, the possession of different degrees and kinds of property immediately results; and from the influence of these on the sentiments and views of the respective proprietors, ensues a division of the society into different interests and parties.

The latent causes of faction are thus sown in the nature of man; and we see them everywhere brought into different degrees of activity, according to the different circumstances of civil society. A zeal for different opinions, concerning religion, concerning government, and many other points, as well of speculation as of practice; an attachment to different leaders ambitiously contending for pre-eminence and power; or to persons of other descriptions whose fortunes have been interesting to the human passions, have, in turn, divided mankind into parties, inflamed them with mutual animosity, and rendered them much more disposed to vex and oppress each other than to co-operate for their common good. So strong is this propensity of mankind to fall into mutual animosities, that where no substantial occasion presents itself, the most frivolous and fanciful distinctions have been sufficient to kindle their unfriendly passions and excite their most violent conflicts. But the most common and durable source of factions has been the various and unequal distribution of property. Those who hold and those who are without property have ever formed distinct interests in society. Those who are creditors, and those who are debtors, fall under a like discrimination. A landed interest, a manufacturing interest, a mercantile interest, a moneyed interest, with many lesser interests, grow up of necessity in civilized nations, and divide them into different classes, actuated by different sentiments and views. The regulation of these various and interfering interests forms the principal task of modern legislation, and involves the spirit of party and faction in the necessary and ordinary operations of the government.

No man is allowed to be a judge in his own cause, because his interest would certainly bias his judgment, and, not improbably, corrupt his integrity. With equal, nay with greater reason, a body of men are unfit to be both judges and parties at the same time; yet what are many of the most important acts of legislation, but so many judicial determinations, not indeed concerning the rights, of single persons, but concerning the rights of large bodies of citizens? And what are the different classes of legislators but advocates and parties to the causes which they determine? Is a law proposed concerning private debts? It is a question to which the creditors are parties on one side and the debtors on the other. Justice ought to hold the balance between them. Yet the parties are, and must be, themselves, the judges; and the most numerous party, or, in other words, the most powerful faction must be expected to prevail. Shall domestic manufacturers be encouraged, and in what degree, by restrictions on foreign manufactures? are questions which would be differently decided by the landed and the manufacturing classes, and probably by neither with a sole regard to justice and the public good.

It is in vain to say that enlightened statesmen will be able to adjust these clashing interests, and render them all subservient to the public good. Enlightened statesmen will not always be at the helm. . . .

The inference to which we are brought is, that the *causes* of faction cannot be removed, and that relief is only to be sought in the means of controlling its *effects*.

If a faction consists of less than a majority, relief is supplied by the republican principle, which enables the majority to defeat its sinister views by regular vote. It may clog the administration, it may convulse the society; but it will be unable to execute and mask its violence under the forms of the Constitution. When a majority is included in a faction, the form of popular government, on the other hand, enables it to sacrifice to its ruling passion or interest both the public good and the rights of other citizens. To secure the public good and private rights against the danger of such a faction, and at the same time to preserve the spirit and the form of popular government, is then the great object to which our inquiries are directed. Let me add that it is the great desideratum by which this form of government can be rescued from the opprobrium under which it has so long labored, and be recommended to the esteem and adoption of mankind.

By what means is this object attainable? Evidently by one of two only. Either the existence of the same passion or interest in a majority at the same time must be prevented, or the majority, having such coexistent passion or interest, must be rendered, by their number and local situation, unable to concert and carry into effect schemes of oppression. If the impulse and the opportunity be suffered to coincide, we well know that neither moral nor religious motives can be relied on as an adequate control. They are not found to be such on the injustice and violence of individuals, and lose their efficacy in proportion to the number combined together, that is, in proportion as their efficacy becomes needful.

From this view of the subject it may be concluded that a pure democracy, by which I mean a society consisting of a small number of citizens, who assemble and administer the government in person, can admit of no cure for the mischiefs of faction. A common passion or interest will, in almost every case, be felt by a majority of the whole; a communication and concert result from the form of government itself; and there is nothing to check the inducements to sacrifice the weaker party or an obnoxious individual. Hence it is that such democracies have ever been spectacles of turbulence and contention; have ever been found incompatible with personal security or the rights of property; and have in general been as short in their lives as they have been violent in their deaths. Theoretic politicians, who have patronized this species of government, have erroneously supposed that by reducing mankind to a perfect equality in their political rights, they would, at the same time, be perfectly equalized and assimilated in their possessions, their opinions, and their passions.

A republic, by which I mean a government in which the scheme of representation takes place, opens a different prospect, and promises the cure for which we are seeking. . . .

The two great points of difference between a democracy and a republic are: first, the delegation of the government, in the latter, to a small number of citizens elected by the rest; secondly, the greater number of citizens, and greater sphere of country, over which the latter may be extended.

The effect of the first difference is, on the one hand, to refine and enlarge the public views, by passing them through the medium of a chosen body of citizens, whose wisdom may best discern the true interest of their country, and whose patriotism and love of justice will be least likely to sacrifice it to temporary or partial considerations. Under such a regulation, it may well happen that the public voice, pronounced by the representatives of the people, will be more consonant to the public good than if pronounced by the people themselves, convened for the purpose. On the other hand, the effect may be inverted. Men of factious tempers, of local prejudices, or of sinister designs, may, by intrigue, by corruption, or by other means, first obtain the suffrages, and then betray the interests, of the people. The question resulting is, whether small or extensive republics are more favorable to the election of proper guardians of the public weal; and it is clearly decided in favor of the latter by two obvious considerations:

In the first place, it is to be remarked that, however small the republic may be, the representatives must be raised to a certain number, in order to guard against the cabals of a few; and that, however large it may be, they must be limited to a certain number, in order to guard against the confusion of a multitude. Hence, the number of representatives in the two cases not being in proportion to that of the two constituents, and being proportionally greater in the small republic, it follows that, if the proportion of fit characters be not less in the large than in the small republic, the former will present a greater option, and consequently a greater probability of a fit choice.

In the next place, as each representative will be chosen by a greater number of citizens in the large than in the small republic, it will be more difficult for unworthy candidates to practise with success the vicious arts by which elections are too often carried; and the suffrages of the people being more free, will be more likely to centre in men who possess the most attractive merit and the most diffusive and established characters.

It must be confessed that in this, as in most other cases, there is a mean, on both sides of which inconveniences will be found to lie. By enlarging too much the number of electors, you render the representative too little acquainted with all their local circumstances and lesser interests as by reducing it too much, you render him unduly attached to these, and too little fit to comprehend and pursue great and national objects. The federal Constitution forms a happy combination in this respect; the great and aggregate interests being referred to the national, the local and particular to the State legislatures.

The other point of difference is, the greater number of citizens and extent of territory which may be brought within the compass of republican than of democratic government; and it is this circumstance principally which renders factious combinations less to be dreaded in the former than in the latter. The smaller the society, the fewer probably will be the distinct parties and interests composing it; the fewer the distinct parties and interests, the more frequently will a majority be found of the same party; and the smaller the number of individuals composing a majority, and the smaller the compass within which they are placed, the more easily will they concert and execute their plans of oppression. Extend the sphere, and you take in a greater variety of parties and interests; you make it less probable that a majority of the whole will have a common motive to invade the rights of other citizens; or if such a common motive exists, it will be more difficult for all who feel it to discover their own strength, and to act in unison with each other. Besides other impediments, it may be remarked that, where there is a consciousness of unjust or dishonorable purposes, communication is always checked by distrust in proportion to the number whose concurrence is necessary.

Hence, it clearly appears, that the same advantage which a republic has over a democracy, in controlling the effects of faction, is enjoyed by a large over a small republic, — is enjoyed by the Union over the States composing it. Does the advantage consist in the substitution of representatives whose enlightened views and virtuous sentiments render them superior to local prejudices and to schemes of injustice? It will not be denied that the representation of the Union will be most likely to possess these requisite endowments. Does it consist in the greater security afforded by a greater variety of parties, against the event of any one party being able to outnumber and oppress the rest? In an equal degree does the increased variety of parties comprised within the Union, increase this security. Does it, in fine, consist in the greater obstacles opposed to the concert and accomplishment of the secret wishes of an unjust and interested majority? Here, again, the extent of the Union gives it the most palpable advantage.

The influence of factious leaders may kindle a flame within their particular States, but will be unable to spread a general conflagration through the other States. A religious sect may degenerate into a political faction in a part of the Confederacy; but the variety of sects dispersed over the entire face of it must secure the national councils against any danger from that source. A rage for paper money, for an abolition of debts, for an equal division of property, or for any other improper or wicked project, will be less apt to pervade the whole body of the Union than a particular member of it; in the same proportion as such a malady is more likely to taint a particular county or district, than an entire State.

In the extent and proper structure of the Union, therefore, we behold a republican remedy for the diseases most incident to republican government. And according to the degree of pleasure and pride we feel in being republicans, ought to be our zeal in cherishing the spirit and supporting the character of Federalists.

Publius

Note: Madisonian Republicanism

The Federalist No. 10 reveals that for Madison the primary problem of governance consists in control of faction. The antifederalists rooted the problem of faction in that of corruption; their solution rested in the effort to control the factional spirit and the power of representatives. In their view, the civic virtue of the citizenry and of its representatives would work as a safeguard against factional tyranny.

The Federalist No. 10 turned the antifederalist understanding on its head. For

Madison, and for the other federalists, the question of corruption was transformed into that of faction, which was itself a natural product of liberty and its consequence — inequality in the ownership of property. This redefinition meant that the basic problem could not be solved by the traditional republican means of education and inculcation of virtue. Moreover, the problem of faction was likely to be most, not least, severe in a small republic. It was in a small republic that a self-interested private group would be most likely to be able to seize political power in order to distribute wealth or opportunities in its favor. Indeed, in the view of the federalists, this was precisely what had happened in the years since the Revolution. In that period, factions had usurped the processes of state government, putting both liberty and property at risk. Consider in this regard Madison's rejection of Jefferson's proposal of frequent constitutional amendment on the ground that such a proposal would produce "the most violent struggle between the parties interested in reviving and those interested in reforming the antecedent state of property." M. Meyers, ed., The Mind of the Founder 232 (1969). For Jefferson, by contrast, turbulence is "productive of good. It prevents the degeneracy of government, and nourishes a general attention to the public affairs. I hold that a little rebellion now and then is a good thing." Letter to Madison, Jan. 30, 1787, in The Portable Thomas Jefferson 416-417 (M. Peterson ed. 1975).

To Madison, the recent history furnished sufficient evidence that traditional conceptions of civic virtue, or public education, could not guard against factional tyranny. Such devices would be unable to overcome the natural self-interest of men and women, even in their capacity as political actors. To this point Madison added the familiar idea that "education" of that sort would carry a risk of tyranny of its own; for him, inculcating virtue in the citizenry was not a proper task of government.

All this was sufficient to justify rejection of the antifederalist understanding that, in a small republic, the problem of faction could be overcome. But it supplied no positive solution to that problem. It was in developing a solution that Madison was particularly original. The solution began with the insight that in a direct democracy, the problem posed by factions is especially acute, for a "common passion or interest will, in almost every case, be felt by a majority of the whole," and there will be no protection for the minority. But safeguards would be found in a large republic. There, the diversity of interests would ensure against the possibility that a common desire would be felt by sufficient numbers of people to oppress minorities. In this respect, the likelihood of factional tyranny contained a built-in check in a large republic.

Nor was this the only virtue of size. The other feature of the large republic was that the principle of representation would serve in that setting as a substantial solution to the problem of faction. The central phrase here is Madison's suggestion that that principle would "refine and enlarge the public views by passing them through the medium of a chosen body of citizens, whose wisdom may best discern the true interest of their country and whose patriotism and love of justice will be least likely to sacrifice it to temporary or partial considerations." This is so in part because in a large republic, the dangers produced by undue attachment to local interests would be reduced.

This conception of representation appears throughout The Federalist and indeed throughout Madison's work. In No. 57, Madison urges that "the aim of every political constitution is, or ought to be, first to obtain for rulers men who possess most wisdom to discern, and most virtue to pursue, the common good of society; and in the next place, to take the most effectual precautions for keeping them virtuous while they continue to hold the public trust." Elsewhere he suggests that "wisdom" and "virtue" will characterize national representatives. Where the antifederalists accepted representation as a necessary evil, Madison regarded it as an opportunity for achieving governance by officials devoted to a public good distinct from the struggle of private interests. Representatives were to have the time and temperament to engage in a form of collective reasoning. The hope, in short, was for a genuinely national politics. The representatives of the people — not the people themselves — would be free to engage in the process of discussion and debate from which the common good would emerge.

This was not, however, the entire story. The structural provisions of the Constitution attempt to bring about public-spirited representation, to provide safeguards in the event that it is absent, and to ensure an important measure of popular control. Bicameralism — the division of Congress into the House and the Senate, with two-year and six-year terms respectively — was thus intended to ensure that some representatives would be relatively isolated from the people and that others would be relatively close to them. Indirect election of representatives played a far more important role at the time of ratification than it does today. Only the house of representatives was to be directly elected, thus providing additional insulation from political pressure and factional tyranny. The electoral college is an important example; it was to be a deliberative body standing to some degree apart from constituent pressures.

Perhaps most important, the separation of powers scheme was designed with the recognition that even national representatives may be prone to the influence of "interests" that are inconsistent with the public welfare. In The Federalist No. 10 itself, Madison recognizes that "enlightened statesmen will not always be at the helm." The Federalist No. 51 is the most celebrated elaboration of this point.

The Federalist No. 51 (Hamilton or Madison)

(1788)

In order to lay a due foundation for that separate and distinct exercise of the different powers of government, which to a certain extent is admitted on all hands to be essential to the preservation of liberty, it is evident that each department should have a will of its own; and consequently should be so constituted that the members of each should have as little agency as possible in the appointment of the members of the others. Were this principle rigorously adhered to, it would require that all the appointments for the supreme executive, legislative, and judiciary magistracies should be drawn from the same fountain of authority, the people, through channels having no communication whatever with one another. [Some] difficulties, and some additional expense would attend the execution of it. Some deviations, therefore, from the principle must be admitted. In the constitution of the judiciary department in particular, it might be inexpedient to insist rigorously on the principle: first, because peculiar qualifications being essential in the members, the primary consideration ought to be to select that mode of choice which best secures these qualifications; secondly, because the permanent tenure by which the appointments are held in that department, must soon destroy all sense of dependence on the authority conferring them.

It is equally evident, that the members of each department should be as little dependent as possible on those of the others, for the emoluments annexed to their offices. Were the executive magistrate, or the judges, not independent of the legislature in this particular, their independence in every other would be merely nominal.

But the great security against a gradual concentration of the several powers in the same department, consists in giving to those who administer each department the necessary constitutional means and personal motives to resist encroachments of the others. The provision for defence must in this, as in all other cases, be made commensurate to the danger of attack. Ambition must be made to counteract ambition. The interest of the man must be connected with the constitutional rights of the place. It may be a reflection on human nature, that such devices should be necessary to control the abuses of government. But what is government itself, but the greatest of all reflections on human nature? If men were angels, no government would be necessary. If angels were to govern men, neither external nor internal controls on government would be necessary. In framing a government which is to be administered by men over men, the great difficulty lies in this: you must first enable the government to control the governed; and in the next place oblige it to control itself. A dependence on the people is, no doubt, the primary control on the government; but experience has taught mankind the necessity of auxiliary precautions.

This policy of supplying, by opposite and rival interests, the defect of better motives, might be traced through the whole system of human affairs, private as well as public. We see it particularly displayed in all the subordinate distributions of power, where the constant aim is to divide and arrange the several offices in such a manner as that each may be a check on the other — that the private interest of every individual may be a sentinel over the public rights. These inventions of prudence cannot be less requisite in the distribution of the supreme powers of the State.

But it is not possible to give to each department an equal power of self-defence. In republican government, the legislative authority necessarily predominates. The remedy for this inconveniency is to divide the legislature into different branches; and to render them, by different modes of election and different principles of action, as little connected with each other as the nature of their common functions and their common dependence on the society will admit. It may even be necessary to guard against dangerous encroachments by still further precautions. As the weight of the legislative authority requires that it should be thus divided, the weakness of the executive may require, on the other hand, that it should be fortified. An absolute negative on the legislature appears, at first view, to be the natural defence with which the executive magistrate should be armed. But perhaps it would be neither altogether safe nor alone sufficient. On ordinary occasions it might not be exerted with the requisite firmness, and on extraordinary occasions it might be perfidiously abused. May not this defect of an absolute negative be supplied by some qualified connection between this weaker department and the weaker branch of the stronger department, by which the latter may be led to support the constitutional rights of the former, without being too much detached from the rights of its own department?

There are, moreover, two considerations particularly applicable to the federal system of America, which place that system in a very interesting point of view.

First. In a single republic, all the power surrendered by the people is submitted to the administration of a single government; and the usurpations are guarded against by a division of the government into distinct and separate departments. In the compound republic of America, the power surrendered by the people is first divided between two distinct governments, and then the portion allotted to each subdivided among distinct and separate departments. Hence a double security arises to the rights of the people. The different governments will control each other, at the same time that each will be controlled by itself.

Second. It is of great importance in a republic not only to guard the society against the oppression of its rulers, but to guard one part of the society against the injustice of the other part. Different interests necessarily exist in different classes of citizens. If a majority be united by a common interest, the rights of the minority will be insecure. There are but two methods of providing against this evil: the one by creating a will in the community independent of the majority — that is, of the society itself; the other, by comprehending in the society so many separate descriptions of citizens as will render an unjust combination of a majority of the whole very improbable, if not impracticable. The first method [is] but a precarious security; because a power independent of the society may as well espouse the unjust views of the major, as the rightful interests of the minor party, and may possibly be turned against both parties. The second method will be exemplified in the federal republic of the United States. Whilst all authority in it will be derived from and dependent on the society, the society itself will be broken into so many parts, interests and classes of citizens, that the rights of individuals, or of the minority, will be in little danger from interested combinations of the majority. In a free government the security for civil rights must be the same as that for religious rights. It consists in the one case in the multiplicity of interests, and in the other in the multiplicity of sects. The degree of security in both cases will depend on the number of interests and sects; and this may be presumed to depend on the extent of country and number of people comprehended under the same government. This view of the subject must particularly recommend a proper federal system to all the sincere and considerate friends of republican government, since it shows that in exact proportion as the territory of the Union may be formed into more circumscribed Confederacies, or States, oppressive combinations of a majority will be facilitated; the best security, under the republican forms, for the rights of every class of citizens, will be diminished; and consequently the stability and independence of some member of the government, the only other security, must be proportionally increased.

[In] a society under the forms of which the stronger faction can readily unite and oppress the weaker, anarchy may as truly be said to reign as in a state of nature, where the weaker individual is not secured against the violence of the stronger; and as, in the latter state, even the stronger individuals are prompted, by the uncertainty of their condition, to submit to a government which may protect the weak as well as themselves; so, in the former state, will the more powerful factions or parties be gradually induced, by a like motive, to wish for a government which will protect all parties, the weaker as well as the more powerful. It can be little doubted that if the State of Rhode Island was separated from the Confederacy and left to itself, the insecurity of rights under the popular form of government, within such narrow limits would be displayed by such reiterated oppressions of factious majorities that some power altogether independent of the people would soon be called for by the voice of the very factions whose misrule had proved the necessity of it. In the extended republic of the United States, and among the great variety of interests, parties, and sects which it embraces, a coalition of a majority of the whole society could seldom take place on any other principles than those of justice and the general good; whilst there being thus less danger to a minor from the will of a major party, there must be less pretext, also, to provide for the security of the former, by introducing into the government a will not dependent on the latter, or, in other words, a will independent of the society itself. It is no less certain than it is important, notwithstanding the contrary opinions which have been entertained, that the larger the society, provided it lie within a practical sphere, the more duly capable it will be of self-government. And happily for the *republican cause*, the practicable sphere may be carried to a very great extent, by a judicious modification and mixture of the *federal principle*.

Publius

Note: *Madisonian Republicanism, Checks and Balances, and Private Property*

The system of checks and balances within the federal structure was thus intended to operate as a check against self-interested representation. If a segment of rulers obtained interests that diverged from those of the people, other national officials would have both the incentive and the means to resist. The result is an additional protection against tyranny. (For more detailed discussion, see Chapter 4 infra.)

The federal system, too, would act as an important safeguard. The "different governments will control each other" and ensure stalemate rather than action at the behest of particular private interests. The jealousy of state governments, and the attachment of the citizenry to local interests, would provide additional protection against the aggrandizement of power in national institutions.

The result is a complex system of checks: national representation, bicameralism, indirect election, distribution of powers, and the federal/state relationship would operate in concert to counteract the effects of faction in spite of the inevitability of the factional spirit. And the Constitution itself, enforced by disinterested judges and adopted in a moment in which that spirit had been perhaps temporarily extinguished, would prevent majorities or minorities from usurping government power to distribute wealth or opportunities in their favor.

There has been no discussion thus far of the problem of private property, whose protection was a principal interest of the framers. But there is a close practical relationship between the desire to protect private property from governmental intrusion and the devices set up by the framers to guard against the dangers posed by faction. For the framers, the problem of faction lay partly in the danger that a self-interested group would obtain governmental power in order to put rights of property at risk. The experience under the Articles of Confederation, in which popular majorities had operated as factions in state legislatures, confirmed the existence of this danger. The various safeguards, including that of representation by officials who would be able to take a broader view of the relevant issues, may be understood as having the protection of property rights from majoritarian incursion as one of its principal purposes. In this respect as well, the federalists may be contrasted with their antifederalist opponents, whose relatively weaker concern for private property coexisted easily with their preference for decentralized democracy. Moreover, the federalists' hospitable view toward lengthy deliberation and government inaction may be associated with a desire to protect private property. Inaction of course preserves the existing distribution of wealth.

The picture that emerges is in a sense one of a government that was intended to engage in deliberation. But politics was to be deliberative in a special sense. Representatives were to be accountable to the public; their deliberative task was not disembodied. The framers were thus careful to create political checks designed to ensure that representatives would not stray too far from the desires of their constituents. The result was a kind of hybrid conception of representation, in which legislators were neither to respond blindly to constituent pressures nor to undertake their deliberations in a vacuum.

In these respects, the federalists managed a kind of synthesis of the republican conception and the emerging principles of pluralism, in accordance with which politics should be seen as an inevitably self-interested struggle among competing social groups. See, e.g., A. Bentley, The Process of Government (1908); R. Dahl, A Preface to Democratic Theory (1956); D. Truman, the Governmental Process (1962). For the federalists, politics rightly consisted of deliberation and discussion about the public good. But that process could not be brought about in the traditional republican fashion; such an effort, in light of human nature, would deteriorate into a struggle among warring factions. A partial solution lay in principles of representation. At the same time, the representatives would be kept accountable to the public. The mechanisms of accountability would prevent representatives from acquiring interests distinct from those of their constituents. The separation of powers would ensure that if representatives became self-interested, or if a particular group acquired too much power over one set of representatives, there would be safeguards to prevent either representatives or private groups from obtaining authority over the national government in general.

Where does judicial review fit into this framework? To a large degree, the Court was intended to enforce the lines of division set down in the Constitution, in order to ensure that the areas marked off from politics would not be subject to political revision. The boundaries set in the Constitution were thus to be unrevisable by electoral majorities — a safeguard that would buttress the other institutional checks. This role responded to the distinction drawn by the framers between "law" — the realm of judgment — and "politics" — the realm of will, or personal preference. See The Federalist No. 78, infra. The existence of a realm of "law" immune from "politics" fit securely within a system intended to protect both the public good and private rights from perceived majoritarian excesses.

Consider to what extent the Constitution has achieved its intended purposes and, in particular, the contribution (if any) made by judicial review to that achievement. Consider also whether and to what degree constitutional law reflects or should reflect elements of the antifederalist position on the one hand and modern pluralism on the other.

B. THE BASIC FRAMEWORK

Marbury v. Madison

5 U.S. (1 Cranch) 137 (1803)

[William Marbury had been appointed a justice of the peace by the defeated incumbent Federalist President, John Adams, in the closing stages of the Adams administration. The Federalist-controlled Senate confirmed the appointments of Adams's last-minute appointees, including Marbury, on March 3, 1801. The formal commissions had not been delivered when Thomas Jefferson, the Republican President, assumed office several days later. Jefferson refused to deliver the commissions of the justices appointed by Adams. Marbury and others sought a writ of mandamus to compel Madison, Jefferson's Secretary of State (replacing John Marshall, Adams's Secretary of State), to deliver the commissions. (The underlying controversy is set out in more detail in a historical note that follows the opinion.)]

Opinion of the Court [by MARSHALL, CHIEF JUSTICE].

At the last term on the affidavits then read and filed with the clerk, a rule was granted in this case, requiring the secretary of state to show cause why a mandamus should not issue, directing him to deliver to William Marbury his commission as a justice of the peace for the county of Washington, in the district of Columbia.

No cause has been shown, and the present motion is for a mandamus. The peculiar delicacy of this case, the novelty of some of its circumstances, and the real difficulty attending the points which occur in it, require a complete exposition of the principles on which the opinion to be given by the court is founded.

In the order in which the court has viewed this subject, the following questions have been considered and decided.

   1st.   Has the applicant a right to the commission he demands?

   2dly.   If he has a right, and that right has been violated, do the laws of his country afford him a remedy?

   3dly.   If they do afford him a remedy, is it a mandamus issuing from this court?

The first object of inquiry is,

1st. Has the applicant a right to the commission he demands?

His right originates in an act of congress passed in February, 1801, concerning the district of Columbia. . . .

In order to determine whether he is entitled to this commission, it becomes necessary to inquire whether he has been appointed to the office. For if he has been appointed, the law continues him in office for five years, and he is entitled to the possession of those evidences of office, which, being completed, became his property.

The last act to be done by the president is the signature of the commission: he has then acted on the advice and consent of the senate to his own nomination. The time for deliberation has then passed. . . .

It is, [decidedly] the opinion of the court, that when a commission has been signed by the president, the appointment is made; and that the commission is complete, when the seal of the United States has been affixed to it by the secretary of state.

Where an officer is removable at the will of the executive, the circumstance which completes his appointment is of no concern; because the act is at any time revocable; and the commission may be arrested, if still in the office. But when the officer is not removable at the will of the executive, the appointment is not revocable, and cannot be annulled: it has conferred legal rights which cannot be resumed. [To] withhold his commission, therefore, is an act deemed by the court not warranted by law, but violative of a vested legal right.

2. This brings us to the second inquiry; which is: If he has a right, and that right has been violated, do the laws of his country afford him a remedy? The very essence of civil liberty certainly consists in the right of every individual to claim the protection of the laws, whenever he receives an injury. One of the first duties of government is to afford that protection. In Great Britain, the king himself is sued in the respectful form of a petition, and he never fails to comply with the judgment of his court.

The government of the United States has been emphatically termed a government of laws, and not of men. It will certainly cease to deserve this high appellation, if the laws furnish no remedy for the violation of a vested legal right. If this obloquy is to be cast on the jurisprudence of our country, it must arise from the peculiar character of the case.

It behooves us, then, to inquire whether there be in its composition any ingredient which shall exempt it from legal investigation, or exclude the injured party from legal redress. . . .

Is it in the nature of the transaction? Is the act of delivering or withholding a commission to be considered as a mere political act, belonging to the executive department alone, for the performance of which entire confidence is placed by our constitution in the supreme executive; and for any misconduct respecting which, the injured individual has no remedy? That there may be such cases is not to be questioned; but that every act of duty, to be performed in any of the great departments of government, constitutes such a case, is not to be admitted.

It follows, then, that the question, whether the legality of an act of the head of a department be examinable in a court of justice or not, must always depend on the nature of that act. If some acts be examinable, and others not, there must be some rule of law to guide the court in the exercise of its jurisdiction. In some instances, there may be difficulty in applying the rule to particular cases; but there cannot, it is believed, be much difficulty in laying down the rule.

By the constitution of the United States, the president is invested with certain important political powers, in the exercise of which he is to use his own discretion, and is accountable only to his country in his political character, and to his own conscience. To aid him in the performance of these duties, he is authorized to appoint certain officers, who act by his authority, and in conformity with his orders. In such cases, their acts are his acts; and whatever opinion may be entertained of the manner in which executive discretion may be used, still there exists, and can exist, no power to control that discretion. The subjects are political: they respect the nation, not individual rights, and being entrusted to the executive, the decision of the executive is conclusive. The application of this remark will be perceived, by adverting to the act of congress for establishing the department of foreign affairs. This officer, as his duties were prescribed by that act, is to conform precisely to the will of the president: he is the mere organ by whom that will is communicated. The acts of such an officer, as an officer, can never be examinable by the courts. But when the legislature proceeds to impose on that officer other duties; when he is directed peremptorily to perform certain acts; when the rights of individuals are dependent on the performance of those acts; he is so far the officer of the law; is amenable to the laws for his conduct; and cannot, at his discretion, sport away the vested rights of others.

The conclusion from this reasoning is, that where the heads of departments are the political or confidential agents of the executive, merely to execute the will of the president, or rather to act in cases in which the executive possesses a constitutional or legal discretion, nothing can be more perfectly clear, than that their acts are only politically examinable. But where a specific duty is assigned by law, and individual rights depend upon the performance of that duty, it seems equally clear, that the individual who considers himself injured, has a right to resort to the laws of his country for a remedy.

The question whether a right has vested or not, is, in its nature, judicial, and must be tried by the judicial authority. If, for example, Mr. Marbury had taken the oaths of a magistrate, and proceeded to act as one; in consequence of which, a suit has been instituted against him, in which his defence had depended on his being a magistrate, the validity of his appointment must have been determined by judicial authority. So, if he conceives that, by virtue of his appointment, he has a legal right either to the commission which has been made out for him, or to a copy of that commission, it is equally a question examinable in a court, and the decision of the court upon it must depend on the opinion entertained of his appointment. That question has been discussed, and the opinion is, that the latest point of time which can be taken as that at which the appointment was complete, and evidenced, was when, after the signature of the president, the seal of the United States was affixed to the commission.

It is, then, the opinion of the Court: 1st. That by signing the commission of Mr. Marbury, the President of the United States appointed him a justice of peace [and] that the appointment conferred on him a legal right to the office for the space of five years. 2d. That, having this legal title to the office, he has a consequent right to the commission; a refusal to deliver which is a plain violation of that right, for which the laws of his country afford him a remedy.

3. It remains to be inquired whether he is entitled to the remedy for which he applies? This depends on — 1st. The nature of the writ applied for; and 2d. The power of this court.

1st. The nature of the writ. . . . .

[To] render the mandamus a proper remedy, the officer to whom it is to be directed, must be one to whom, on legal principles, such writ may be directed; and the person applying for it must be without any other specific and legal remedy.

1. With respect to the officer to whom it would be directed. The intimate political relation subsisting between the president of the United States and the heads of departments, necessarily renders any legal investigation of the acts of one of those high officers peculiarly irksome, as well as delicate; and excites some hesitation with respect to the propriety of entering into such investigation. Impressions are often received, without much reflection or examination, and it is not wonderful, that in such a case as this, the assertion, by an individual, of his

legal claims in a court of justice, to which claims it is the duty of that court to attend, should at first view be considered by some, as an attempt to intrude into the cabinet, and to intermeddle with the prerogatives of the executive.

It is scarcely necessary for the court to disclaim all pretensions to such a jurisdiction. An extravagance, so absurd and excessive, could not have been entertained for a moment. The province of the court is, solely, to decide on the rights of individuals, not to inquire how the executive, or executive officers, perform duties in which they have a discretion. Questions in their nature political, or which are, by the constitution and laws, submitted to the executive, can never be made in this court.

But, if this be not such a question; if, so far from being an intrusion into the secrets of the cabinet, it respects a paper which, according to law, is upon record, and to a copy of which the law gives a right, on the payment of ten cents; if it be no intermeddling with a subject over which the executive can be considered as having exercised any control; what is there, in the exalted station of the officer, which shall bar a citizen from asserting, in a court of justice, his legal rights, or shall forbid a court to listen to the claim, or to issue a mandamus, directing the performance of a duty, not depending on executive discretion, but on particular acts of congress, and the general principles of law?

[Where the head of a department] is directed by law to do a certain act affecting the absolute rights of individuals, [it] is not perceived on what grounds the courts of the country are [excused] from the duty of giving judgment. . . .

[This,] then, is a plain case for a mandamus, either to deliver the commission, or a copy of it from the record; and it only remains to be inquired,

Whether it can issue from this court.

The act to establish the judicial courts of the United States authorizes the supreme court "to issue writs of mandamus, in cases warranted by the principles and usages of law, to any courts appointed, or persons holding, office, under the authority of the United States."*

The secretary of state, being a person holding an office under the authority of the United States, is precisely within the letter of the description; and if this court is not authorized to issue a writ of mandamus to such an officer, it must be because the law is unconstitutional, and therefore absolutely incapable of conferring the authority, and assigning the duties which its words purport to confer and assign.

The constitution vests the whole judicial power of the United States in one

---

* The full text of Section 13 of the Judiciary Act of 1789, 1 Stat. 73, reads:

And be it further enacted, That the Supreme Court shall have exclusive jurisdiction of all controversies of a civil nature, where a state is a party, except between a state and its citizens; and except also between a state and citizens of other states, or aliens, in which latter case it shall have original but not exclusive jurisdiction. And shall have exclusively all such jurisdiction of suits or proceedings against ambassadors, or other public ministers, or their domestics, or domestic servants, as a court of law can have or exercise consistently with the law of nations; and original, but not exclusive jurisdiction of all suits brought by ambassadors, or other public ministers, or in which a consul, or vice consul, shall be a party. And the trial of issues of fact in the Supreme Court, in all actions at law against citizens of the United States, shall be by jury. The Supreme Court shall also have appellate jurisdiction from the circuit courts and courts of the several states, in the cases herein after specially provided for; and shall have power to issue writs of prohibition to the district courts, when proceeding as courts of admiralty and maritime jurisdiction, and writs of mandamus, in cases warranted by the principles and usages of law, to any courts appointed, or persons holding office, under the authority of the United States.

supreme court, and such inferior courts as congress shall, from time to time, ordain and establish. This power is expressly extended to all cases arising under the laws of the United States; and, consequently, in some form, may be exercised over the present case; because the right claimed is given by a law of the United States.

In the distribution of this power it is declared that "the supreme court shall have original jurisdiction in all cases affecting ambassadors, other public ministers and consuls, and those in which a state shall be a party. In all other cases, the supreme court shall have appellate jurisdiction."

It has been insisted, at the bar, that as the original grant of jurisdiction, to the supreme and inferior courts, is general, and the clause, assigning original jurisdiction to the supreme court, contains no negative or restrictive words, the power remains to the legislature, to assign original jurisdiction to that court in other cases than those specified in the article which has been recited; provided those cases belong to the judicial power of the United States.

If it had been intended to leave it in the discretion of the legislature to apportion the judicial power between the supreme and inferior courts according to the will of that body, it would certainly have been useless to have proceeded further than to have defined the judicial power, and the tribunals in which it should be vested. The subsequent part of the section is mere surplusage, is entirely without meaning, if such is to be the construction. If congress remains at liberty to give this court appellate jurisdiction, where the constitution has declared their jurisdiction shall be original; and original jurisdiction where the constitution has declared it shall be appellate; the distribution of jurisdiction, made in the constitution, is form without substance.

Affirmative words are often, in their operation, negative of other objects than those affirmed; and in this case, a negative or exclusive sense must be given to them, or they have no operation at all.

It cannot be presumed that any clause in the constitution is intended to be without effect; and, therefore, such a construction is inadmissible, unless the words require it. . . .

When an instrument organizing fundamentally a judicial system, divides it into one supreme, and so many inferior courts as the legislature may ordain and establish; then enumerates its powers, and proceeds so far to distribute them, as to define the jurisdiction of the supreme court by declaring the cases in which it shall take original jurisdiction, and that in others it shall take appellate jurisdiction; the plain import of the words seems to be, that in one class of cases its jurisdiction is original, and not appellate; in the other it is appellate, and not original. If any other construction would render the clause inoperative, that is an additional reason for rejecting such other construction, and for adhering to their obvious meaning.

To enable this court, then, to issue a mandamus, it must be shown to be an exercise of appellate jurisdiction, or to be necessary to enable them to exercise appellate jurisdiction.

It has been stated at the bar that the appellate jurisdiction may be exercised in a variety of forms, and that if it be the will of the legislature that a mandamus should be used for that purpose, that will must be obeyed. This is true, yet the jurisdiction must be appellate, not original.

It is the essential criterion of appellate jurisdiction, that it revises and corrects the proceedings in a cause already instituted, and does not create that cause. Although, therefore, a mandamus may be directed to courts, yet to issue such a writ to an officer for the delivery of a paper, is in effect the same as to sustain an original action for that paper, and, therefore, seems not to belong to appellate, but to original jurisdiction. Neither is it necessary in such a case as this, to enable the court to exercise its appellate jurisdiction.

The authority, therefore, given to the supreme court, by the act establishing the judicial courts of the United States, to issue writs of mandamus to public officers, appears not to be warranted by the constitution; and it becomes necessary to inquire whether a jurisdiction so conferred can be exercised.

The question, whether an act, repugnant to the constitution, can become the law of the land, is a question deeply interesting to the United States; but, happily, not of an intricacy proportioned to its interest. It seems only necessary to recognise certain principles, supposed to have been long and well established, to decide it.

That the people have an original right to establish, for their future government, such principles as, in their opinion, shall most conduce to their own happiness is the basis on which the whole American fabric has been erected. The exercise of this original right is a very great exertion; nor can it, nor ought it, to be frequently repeated. The principles, therefore, so established, are deemed fundamental. And as the authority from which they proceed is supreme, and can seldom act, they are designed to be permanent.

This original and supreme will organizes the government, and assigns to different departments their respective powers. It may either stop here, or establish certain limits not to be transcended by those departments.

The government of the United States is of the latter description. The powers of the legislature are defined and limited; and that those limits may not be mistaken, or forgotten, the constitution is written. To what purpose are powers limited, and to what purpose is that limitation committed to writing, if these limits may, at any time, be passed by those intended to be restrained? The distinction between a government with limited and unlimited powers is abolished, if those limits do not confine the persons on whom they are imposed, and if acts prohibited and acts allowed, are of equal obligation. It is a proposition too plain to be contested, that the constitution controls any legislative act repugnant to it; or, that the legislature may alter the constitution by an ordinary act.

Between these alternatives there is no middle ground. The constitution is either a superior paramount law, unchangeable by ordinary means, or it is on a level with ordinary legislative acts, and, like other acts, is alterable when the legislature shall please to alter it.

If the former part of the alternative be true, then a legislative act contrary to the constitution is not law: if the latter part be true, then written constitutions are absurd attempts, on the part of the people, to limit a power in its own nature illimitable.

Certainly all those who have framed written constitutions contemplate them as forming the fundamental and paramount law of the nation, and, consequently, the theory of every such government must be, that an act of the legislature, repugnant to the constitution, is void.

This theory is essentially attached to a written constitution, and, is consequently, to be considered, by this court, as one of the fundamental principles of our society. It is not therefore to be lost sight of in the further consideration of this subject.

If an act of the legislature, repugnant to the constitution, is void, does it, notwithstanding its invalidity, bind the courts, and oblige them to give it effect? Or, in other words, though it be not law, does it constitute a rule as operative as if it was a law? This would be to overthrow in fact what was established in theory; and would seem, at first view, an absurdity too gross to be insisted on. It shall, however, receive a more attentive consideration.

It is emphatically the province and duty of the judicial department to say what the law is. Those who apply the rule to particular cases, must of necessity expound and interpret that rule. If two laws conflict with each other, the courts must decide on the operation of each.

Judicial Duty

So if a law be in opposition to the constitution; if both the law and the constitution apply to a particular case, so that the court must either decide that case conformably to the law, disregarding the constitution; or conformably to the constitution, disregarding the law; the court must determine which of these conflicting rules governs the case. This is of the very essence of judicial duty.

If, then, the courts are to regard the constitution, and the constitution is superior to any ordinary act of the legislature, the constitution, and not such ordinary act, must govern the case to which they both apply.

Those, then, who controvert the principle that the constitution is to be considered, in court, as a paramount law, are reduced to the necessity of maintaining that courts must close their eyes on the constitution, and see only the law.

This doctrine would subvert the very foundation of all written constitutions. It would declare that an act which, according to the principles and theory of our government, is entirely void, is yet, in practice, completely obligatory. It would declare that if the legislature shall do what is expressly forbidden, such act, notwithstanding the express prohibition, is in reality effectual. It would be giving to the legislature a practical and real omnipotence, with the same breath which professes to restrict their powers within narrow limits. It is prescribing limits, and declaring that those limits may be passed at pleasure.

That it thus reduces to nothing what we have deemed the greatest improvement on political institutions, a written constitution, would of itself be sufficient, in America, where written constitutions have been viewed with so much reverence, for rejecting the construction. But the peculiar expressions of the constitution of the United States furnish additional arguments in favour of its rejection.

The judicial power of the United States is extended to all cases arising under the constitution.

Could it be the intention of those who gave this power, to say that in using it the constitution should not be looked into? That a case arising under the constitution should be decided without examining the instrument under which it arises?

This is too extravagant to be maintained.

In some cases, then, the constitution must be looked into by the judges. And if they can open it at all, what part of it are they forbidden to read or to obey?

There are many other parts of the constitution which serve to illustrate this subject.

It is declared that "no tax or duty shall be laid on articles exported from any state." Suppose a duty on the export of cotton, of tobacco, or of flour; and a suit instituted to recover it. Ought judgment to be rendered in such a case? ought the judges to close their eyes on the constitution, and only see the law.

The constitution declares "that no bill of attainder or ex post facto law shall be passed."

If, however, such a bill should be passed, and a person should be prosecuted under it; must the court condemn to death those victims whom the constitution endeavours to preserve?

"No person," says the constitution, "shall be convicted of treason unless on the testimony of two witnesses to the same overt act, or on confession in open court."

Here the language of the constitution is addressed especially to the courts. It prescribes, directly for them, a rule of evidence not to be departed from. If the legislature should change that rule, and declare *one* witness, or a confession *out* of court, sufficient for conviction, must the constitutional principle yield to the legislative act?

From these, and many other selections which might be made, it is apparent, that the framers of the constitution contemplated that instrument as a rule for the government of *courts*, as well as of the legislature.

Why otherwise does it direct the judges to take an oath to support it? This oath certainly applies in an especial manner, to their conduct in their official character. How immoral to impose it on them, if they were to be used as the instruments, and the knowing instruments, for violating what they swear to support!

The oath of office, too, imposed by the legislature, is completely demonstrative of the legislative opinion on this subject. It is in these words: "I do solemnly swear that I will administer justice without respect to persons, and do equal right to the poor and to the rich; and that I will faithfully and impartially discharge all the duties incumbent on me as, according to the best of my abilities and understanding, agreeably to *the constitution* and laws of the United States."

Why does a judge swear to discharge his duties agreeably to the constitution of the United States, if that constitution forms no rule for his government? if it is closed upon him, and cannot be inspected by him? If such be the real state of things, this is worse than solemn mockery. To prescribe, or to take this oath, becomes equally a crime.

It is also not entirely unworthy of observation, that in declaring what shall be the *supreme* law of the land, the *constitution* itself is first mentioned; and not the laws of the United States generally, but those only which shall be made in *pursuance* of the constitution, have that rank.

Thus, the particular phraseology of the constitution of the United States confirms and strengthens the principle, supposed to be essential to all written constitutions, that a law repugnant to the constitution is void; and that courts, as well as other departments, are bound by that instrument.

The rule must be discharged.

Note: *Marbury v. Madison*

1. *Historical background.* The *Marbury* case was decided against a complex background and was in some respects the culmination of a lengthy political battle. The Federalist President, John Adams, had been defeated by the Republican

candidate, Thomas Jefferson, who was to take office on March 4, 1801. The Federalist Congress responded by, among other things, attempting to obtain control of the federal judiciary. On February 16, 1801, that Congress enacted the Circuit Court Act, creating sixteen new circuit judges and eliminating the circuit-riding duties of the Supreme Court. Congress also decreased the size of the Supreme Court in order to deny the incoming President Jefferson the power to appoint a successor to Justice Cushing. Two weeks later Congress enacted another statute creating forty-two positions for justices of the peace in the District of Columbia. President Adams nominated the authorized judges, who were confirmed on March 2 and 3, just one day before President Jefferson was to assume office.

At this point John Marshall, then Secretary of State under President Adams — who had appointed Marbury and the other petitioners in the *Marbury* case — became involved in the circumstances that gave rise to the case. Although Marshall took his oath of office as Chief Justice on February 4, 1801, he continued to serve as Secretary of State at least until March 3 of that year. President Adams and Acting Secretary of State Marshall had signed the commissions of the petitioners in the *Marbury* case by March 3, but the commissions had not been delivered by the time Adams and Marshall left the executive branch. Adams's successor, Thomas Jefferson, thereafter refused to deliver the commissions, claiming that they were nullities. (Should Marshall have disqualified himself from *Marbury?*)

In the next year — before *Marbury* was decided — the Circuit Court Act was repealed by the Republican Congress; the statute creating justices of the peace was left intact. But Congress also abolished the June and December terms of the Court, leaving the Court adjourned from December 1801 until February 1803 — and thus abolishing the 1802 term. The reason for Congress's actions was to avoid a constitutional challenge to the repeal of the Circuit Court Act.

A footnote: Six days after *Marbury* was decided, the Court upheld the repeal. Stuart v. Laird, 5 U.S. (1 Cranch 299) (1803).

2. *Method, antecedents*. What does the opinion in Marbury v. Madison indicate about opinion-writing method? What are the sources of the decision?

a. Note that Marshall does not begin the opinion in *Marbury* with the question of jurisdiction, although a court's jurisdiction is usually the first problem to be examined. Why did Marshall fail to deal first with the jurisdictional issue?

b. The actual holding of *Marbury* is that the Supreme Court is without power to direct the President to deliver Marbury's commission. This conclusion allowed the Court to avoid the problem of ordering President Jefferson to deliver commissions to President Adams's appointees. There was of course no assurance that President Jefferson would have complied with such a decree. The existence of judicial review was therefore established in a case in which the Court concluded that it had no power to do anything to remedy official illegality. Consider in this regard the suggestion that the "decision is a masterwork of indirection, a brilliant example of Marshall's capacity to sidestep danger while seeming to court it, to advance in one direction while his opponents are looking in another." R. Mc-Closkey, The American Supreme Court 40 (1960).

What is the basis for Marshall's conclusion that the Court lacked jurisdiction? Consider the following rejoinders to Marshall's reasoning: (1) The categories of original and appellate jurisdiction are not mutually exclusive. The Constitution sets up a provisional allocation, which Congress can alter if it wishes. The power to alter is recognized in the "exceptions" clause. It is therefore constitutional for Congress to grant to the Court original jurisdiction over cases over which it had appellate jurisdiction under the Constitution's provisional allocation. (2) The Constitution defines an irreducible minimum of original jurisdiction, but permits Congress to expand original jurisdiction if it chooses to do so. Is either of these views less persuasive, as a textual matter, than Marshall's?

Note in this regard that the reasoning of *Marbury* has been rejected insofar as it suggests that Congress may not give the lower courts jurisdiction over cases falling within the original jurisdiction of the Supreme Court. See, e.g., Illinois v. Milwaukee, 406 U.S. 91 (1972).

c. Marshall acknowledges that "where the heads of departments are the political or confidential agents of the executive, merely to execute the will of the President, or rather to act in cases in which the executive professes a constitutional or legal discretion, nothing can be more clear than that their acts are only politically examinable." This acknowledgment created the category of cases involving "political questions," which are not subject to judicial review. See Chapter 1, section E, infra. What falls in this category? In Marshall's view, is there any case of official illegality that is not judicially cognizable? Note also the contrast drawn by Marshall between cases involving "individual rights" and cases involving "discretion." What is the relationship between those two categories of cases?

d. *Judicial review.* The most important holding in the case is that the Supreme Court has the power to declare acts of Congress unconstitutional. It is striking to many modern readers that Chief Justice Marshall's principal arguments rely not on the text of the Constitution but instead on its structure and on the consequences of a conclusion that judicial review was unavailable.

Consider the view that the

issue of judicial review was by no means new. The Privy Council had occasionally applied the ultra vires principle to set aside legislative acts contravening municipal or colonial charters. State courts had set aside state statutes under constitutions no more explicit about judicial review than the federal. The Supreme Court itself had measured a state law against a state constitution in Cooper v. Telfair, 4 U.S. (4 Dall.) 14 (1800), and had struck down another under the supremacy clause in Ware v. Hylton, 3 U.S. (3 Dall.) 199 (1796); in both cases the power of judicial review was expressly affirmed. Even Acts of Congress had been struck down by federal circuit courts, and the Supreme Court, while purporting to reserve the question of its power to do so, had reviewed the constitutionality of a federal statute in Hylton v. United States, 3 U.S. (3 Dall.) 171 (1796). Justice James Iredell had explicitly asserted this power both in Chisholm v. Georgia and in Calder v. Bull, and Chase had acknowledged it in *Cooper*. In the Convention, moreover, both proponents and opponents of the proposed Council of Revision had recognized that the courts would review the validity of congressional legislation, and Alexander Hamilton had proclaimed the same doctrine in The Federalist. Yet though Marshall's principal arguments echoed those of Hamilton, he made no mention of any of this material, writing as if the question had never arisen before.

Currie, The Constitution in the Supreme Court: The Powers of the Federal Courts, 1801-1835, 49 U. Chi. L. Rev. 646, 655-656 (1982). In what ways was the issue in *Ware* and *Cooper* different from that in *Marbury*?

3. *The justifications for judicial review.* Consider the various bases for the power of judicial review.

a. *Written Constitution.* Marshall's first argument is that judicial review is a necessary inference from the fact of a written Constitution. "The distinction between a government with limited and unlimited power is abolished, if those limits do not confine the persons on whom they are imposed, and if acts prohibited and acts allowed, are of equal obligation."

Does this argument confound two different issues? (1) Is the Constitution binding on the national government? (2) Are the courts authorized to enforce their interpretation of the Constitution against that of other branches of the national government? Everyone agreed on the first question. The dispute centered on the second. Consider Van Alstyne, A Critical Guide to *Marbury v. Madison*, 1969 Duke L.J. 1, 17:

> That the Constitution is a "written" one yields little or nothing as to whether acts of Congress may be given the force of positive law notwithstanding the opinion of judges, the executive, a minority or majority of the population, or even of Congress itself [that] such Acts are repugnant to the Constitution. That this is so is clear enough simply from the fact that even in Marshall's time (and to a great extent today), a number of nations maintained written constitutions and yet gave national legislative acts the full force of positive law without providing any constitutional check to guarantee the compatibility of those acts with their constitution.

Would it be plausible to respond that the Constitution would be ineffective or merely hortatory if it were not subject to judicial enforcement? Consider in this regard The Federalist No. 78, infra. Consider also Currie, supra, at 657: "Surely the Framers were reasonable people, and surely they could not have meant to appoint the fox as guardian of the henhouse." But on the facts of *Marbury*, who was the fox?

b. *Notions of judicial role.* Marshall claims that the ordinary role of the courts is to interpret the law. That role, Marshall claims, requires judges to construe the Constitution in the ordinary course of conducting judicial business. But might it be responded that constitutional interpretation — when it takes the form of invalidation of the outcomes reached by the more political branches — is special, because of its highly intrusive and largely final character? Should this difference mean that the ordinary interpretive task is no longer appropriate?

c. *Supremacy clause.* The supremacy clause provides that the "Constitution, and the Laws of the United States which shall be made in Pursuance thereof . . . shall be the supreme Law of the Land." Does this establish the existence of judicial review?

> Assuming that an act repugnant to the Constitution is not a law "in pursuance thereof" and thus must not be given effect as the supreme law of the land, who according to the Constitution, is to make the determination as to whether any given law is in fact repugnant to the Constitution itself? [Marshall] never confronts this question. His substitute question, whether a law repugnant to the Constitution still binds the courts, assumes that such repugnance has appropriately been determined by those granted such power under the Constitution. It is clear, however, that the supremacy clause itself cannot be the clear textual basis for a claim by the judiciary that this prerogative to determine repugnancy belongs to it.

Van Alstyne, supra, at 22.

Note also that Marshall gains rhetorical force for his position by referring to clauses that, in his view, have a "plain meaning" opposed to acts of Congress. Do those clauses have such plain meanings? Are constitutional provisions likely to have such a meaning in many cases on which Congress and Court will differ? In any event, consider the possibility that the use of these hypothetical cases is misleading in light of the more open-ended character of most constitutional interpretation — of which *Marbury* itself is an example.

d. *Grant of jurisdiction.* The Constitution extends the judicial power of the United States to all cases arising under the Constitution. Marshall argues that the grant of jurisdiction would be meaningless if the courts did not have authority to examine the constitutionality of acts of Congress. Consider A. Bickel, The Least Dangerous Branch 6 (1965):

> If it were impossible to conceive a case "arising under the Constitution" which would not require the Court to pass on the constitutionality of congressional legislation, then [Marshall might be correct, for without judicial review] this clause [would be] quite senseless. But there are such cases which may call into question the constitutional validity of judicial, administrative, or military actions without attacking legislative or even presidential acts as well, or which call upon the Court, under appropriate statutory authorization, to apply the Constitution to acts of the states. Any reading but his own was for Marshall "too extravagant to be maintained." His own, although out of line with the general scheme of Article III, may be possible; but it is optional. This is the strongest bit of textual evidence in support of Marshall's view, but it is merely a hint.

Consider also Currie, The Constitution in the Supreme Court, 1801-1835, 49 U. Chi. L. Rev. 646, 660 (1982): "On its face [the] arising under clause appears to be merely a jurisdictional provision; it need not be taken to dictate when the Constitution must be given precedence over other laws."

e. *Judges' oath.* Marshall relies on the fact that judges take an oath to uphold the Constitution. But consider the fact that the

> oath to support the Constitution is not peculiar to the judges, but is taken indiscriminately by every officer of the government, and is designed rather as a test of the political principles of the man, than to bind the officer in the discharge of his duty. [But] granting it to relate to the official conduct of the judge, as well as every other officer, and not to his political principles, still it must be understood in reference to supporting the constitution, *only as far as that may be involved in his official duty*; and consequently, if his official duty does not comprehend an inquiry into the authority of the legislature, neither does his oath.

Eakin v. Raub, 12 S. & R. 330, 353 (Pa. 1825). In short, the oath requires judges to support the Constitution; but if the Constitution assigns ultimate interpretive power to the legislature, or to the President, then judicial review is not contemplated by the Constitution but is in violation of it. Does this suggest that the "oath" argument is a makeweight?

Do these various arguments in combination appear more forceful than they appear when separated? One might claim that while none is independently decisive, the various arguments together suggest that judicial review is a part of the constitutional structure.

5. *The view of the framers.* The relevant documents at the time of the framing indicate that judicial review was generally contemplated. See P. Bator, P. Mishkin, D. Shapiro & H. Wechsler, Hart & Wechsler's The Federal Courts and the Federal System 9n. (2d ed. 1977). See also A. Bickel, The Least Dangerous Branch 15-16 (1965):

> [It] is as clear as such matters can be that the Framers of the Constitution specifically, if tacitly, expected that the federal courts would assume a power — of whatever exact dimensions — to pass on the constitutionality of actions of the Congress and the President, as well as of the several states. Moreover, not even a colorable showing of decisive historical evidence to the contrary can be made. Nor can it be maintained that the language of the Constitution is compellingly the other way. At worst it may be said that the intentions of the Framers cannot be ascertained with finality.

Consider The Federalist No. 78:

> Some perplexity respecting the rights of the courts to pronounce legislative acts void, because contrary to the constitution, has arisen from an imagination that the doctrine would imply a superiority of the judiciary to the legislative power. It is urged that the authority which can declare the acts of another void, must necessarily be superior to the one whose acts may be declared void. . . .
>
> There is no position which depends on clearer principles, than that every act of a delegated authority, contrary to the tenor of the commission under which it is exercised, is void. No legislative act, therefore, contrary to the Constitution, can be valid. To deny this, would be to affirm, that the deputy is greater than his principal; that the servant is above his master; that the representatives of the people are superior to the people themselves; that men acting by virtue of powers, may do not only what their powers do not authorize, but what they forbid.
>
> If it be said that the legislative body are themselves the constitutional judges of their own powers, and that the construction they put upon them is conclusive upon the other departments, it may be answered, that this cannot be the natural presumption, where it is not to be collected from any particular provisions in the Constitution. It is not otherwise to be supposed, that the Constitution could intend to enable the representatives of the people to substitute their *will* to that of their constituents. It is far more rational to suppose, that the courts were designed to be an intermediate body between the people and the legislature, in order, among other things, to keep the latter within the limits assigned to their authority. The interpretation of the laws is the proper and peculiar province of the courts. A constitution is, in fact, and must be regarded by the judges, as a fundamental law. It therefore belongs to them to ascertain its meaning, as well as the meaning of any particular act proceeding from the legislative body. If there should happen to be an irreconcilable variance between the two, that which has the superior obligation and validity ought, of course, to be preferred; or, in other words, the Constitution ought to be preferred to the statute, the intention of the people to the intention of their agents.
>
> Nor does this conclusion by any means suppose a superiority of the judicial to the legislative power. It only supposes that the power of the people is superior to both; and that where the will of the legislature, declared in its statutes, stands in opposition to that of the people, declared in the Constitution, the judges ought to be governed by the latter rather than the former. They ought to regulate their decisions by the fundamental laws, rather than by those which are not fundamental. . . .
>
> [In] regard to the interfering acts of a superior and subordinate authority, of an original and derivative power, the nature and reason of the thing indicate the con-

verse of that rule as proper to be followed. They teach us that the prior act of a
superior ought to be preferred to the subsequent act of an inferior and subordinate
authority; and that accordingly, whenever a particular statute contravenes the Constitution, it will be the duty of the judicial tribunals to adhere to the latter and
disregard the former.

It can be of no weight to say that the courts, on the pretence of a repugnancy, may
substitute their own pleasure to the constitutional intentions of the legislature. This
might as well happen in the case of two contradictory statutes; or it might as well
happen in every adjudication upon any single statute. The courts must declare the
sense of the law; and if they should be disposed to exercise WILL instead of JUDG-
MENT, the consequence would equally be the substitution of their pleasure to that
of the legislative body. The observation, if it prove any thing, would prove that there
ought to be no judges distinct from that body.

How, if at all, do Hamilton's justifications for judicial review differ from Marshall's? Is the distinction between "will" and "judgment" a plausible one? On what
premises might it rest?

Note: *Judicial Review, Democracy, and Some Notes on Interpretation*

One of the most important dilemmas in American constitutional law arises
from the tension between the basic principle that the Constitution reposes sovereign authority in the people, who elect their representatives, and the (perhaps)
competing principle that, in interpreting the Constitution under the doctrine of
judicial review, the courts have final say over the political process. Judicial review
is a mechanism by which the courts may invalidate decisions of Congress and the
President, subject only to the burdensome process of constitutional amendment.
Because they are subject to electoral control, Congress and the President are
generally regarded as more accountable to the citizenry than federal judges, who
have life tenure. In these circumstances the existence of judicial review gives rise
to a "countermajoritarian difficulty." See A. Bickel, The Least Dangerous Branch
16 (1962). Under what premises can the allocation of power in *Marbury* be justified? At least some answers tend to turn on particular conceptions about the
process of constitutional "interpretation."

1. *Democracy, judicial review, and "mechanical" interpretation.* It is often suggested that the tension between judicial review and democracy would be eliminated, or at least sharply reduced, if judicial review were simply a mechanical
process of deciding whether an act of Congress violated some decision made by
the drafters of the Constitution. If the act of interpretation were essentially mechanical, and involved no exercise of discretion or will on the part of the judges,
the problems of democracy would be minimized. In such circumstances, the
judges would not be imposing their own value choices, but would instead be
forcing current legislatures to conform to earlier choices made by the people.
This understanding reflects Hamilton's distinction between "will" — the province
of politics — and "judgment" — the province of the courts. Is this a coherent
distinction in all or many constitutional cases? Consider also the possibility that
Hamilton, like Marshall, was relying on a "plain meaning" approach to constitutional provisions.

The understanding of judicial review as essentially mechanical is captured in United States v. Butler, 297 U.S. 1 (1936), where the Court wrote,

> It is sometimes said that the court assumes a power to overrule or control the action of the people's representatives. This is a misconception. [When] an act of Congress is appropriately challenged in the courts as not conforming to the constitutional mandate the judicial branch of the Government has only one duty, — to lay the article of the Constitution which is invoked beside the statute which is challenged and to decide whether the latter squares with the former.

Consider whether this understanding of constitutional interpretation is (a) similar to the Court's understanding of the interpretive process in *Marbury* and to Hamilton's understanding in The Federalist No. 78 and (b) an accurate description of how the various constitutional questions in *Marbury* were in fact resolved.

If *Butler* does capture the nature of constitutional interpretation, is it a good thing to have such interpretation carried out by judges rather than elected officials? One view is that judges are better at interpretation precisely because of their insulation from political pressures. That insulation permits them to follow "the ways of the scholar," A. Bickel, The Least Dangerous Branch 26 (1962), in finding the meaning of the text. Those who are subject to political pressures, by contrast, are likely to have the process of interpretation infected or distorted by prevailing political sentiments. Consider, for example, the difference between a judge and a legislator in deciding the meaning of freedom of speech in a climate of popular hostility to a particular point of view. Accountability might in such circumstances be a vice rather than a virtue. Note, on the other hand, the fact that judges have sometimes been less than hospitable to first amendment claims in times of such hostility. See Chapter 7 infra.

Is it clear that such a judicial role would eliminate the tension between judicial review and democracy? Even if the judicial role were or could be purely mechanical in the sense suggested in Butler, there would remain the problem of deciding why current legislators should be forced to conform to the will of the people, all of them dead, expressed many years ago. There is also the problem of explaining why the comparative accountability of the legislative and executive branches should not be regarded as a virtue in giving meaning to constitutional provisions.

See, in this regard, Ackerman, Discovering the Constitution, 93 Yale L.J. 1013, 1023, 1049 (1984):

> We must reconsider the levelling opinion that indicts the Supreme Court as a "deviant institution of American democracy," doomed forever to bear the stigma of the "countermajoritarian difficulty." [Consider] the obvious sense in which it is false. When the Court invokes the Constitution, it appeals to legal enactments that *were* approved by a whole series of majorities — namely the majorities of those representative bodies that proposed and ratified the original Constitution and its subsequent amendments. Rather than a countermajoritarian difficulty, the familiar platitude identifies an intertemporal difficulty.

Ackerman adds that constitutional provisions are adopted in a time of "appeals to the common good, ratified by a mobilized mass of American citizens expressing their assent through extraordinary institutional forms." He contrasts this form of politics, termed "constitutional politics," which is "the highest kind," with "a second form of activity" in which "factions try to manipulate the constitutional forms of political life to pursue their own narrow interests." In this framework, judicial review, by preventing normal politics from overcoming constitutional politics, is a means of ensuring that "the ignorance, apathy and selfishness of normal politics" is not permitted to overcome decisions made by "the public during a period of heightened mobilization and public-spiritness." In what respects does this position differ from Hamilton's in The Federalist No. 78? Compare the conceptions of politics set out in The Federalist No. 10, discussed supra. Consider also the possibility that in Madison's view, at least, the system was to be structured so as to ensure that factional manipulation would not occur even in periods without "heightened mobilization."

Does this view undervalue the consequences of judicial review for "normal politics"? Consider J. Thayer, John Marshall 103-107 (1901), suggesting that in light of the existence of judicial review, legislatures

> more and more readily incline [to] shed the consideration of constitutional restraints, [turning] that subject over to the courts; and, what is worse, they insensibly fall into a habit of assuming that whatever they can constitutionally do they may do, — as if honor and fair dealing and common honesty were not relevant to their inquiries. [It] should be remembered that the exercise of judicial review, even when unavoidable, is always attended with a serious evil, namely, that the correction of legislative mistakes comes from the outside, and the people thus lose the political experience, and the moral education and stimulus that come from fighting the question out in the ordinary way, and correcting their own errors. [The] tendency of a common and easy resort to this great function [is] to dwarf the political capacity of the people, and to deaden its sense of moral responsibility. It is no light thing to do that.

See also Brest, The Conscientious Legislator's Guide to Constitutional Interpretation, 27 Stan. L. Rev. 585 (1975).

The claim here is that the institution of judicial review tends to remove questions of principle from the political process. How realistic is the idea that such review has a significant adverse impact on the public's "sense of moral responsibility"?

Concerns about the perceived tension between judicial review and democracy have led to suggestions that courts should strike down statutes only

> when those who have the right to make laws have not merely made a mistake, but have made a very clear one, — so clear that it is not open to rational question. [This] rule recognizes that, having regard to the great, complex, ever-unfolding exigencies of government, much which will seem unconstitutional to one man, or body of men, may reasonably not seem so to another[,] that there is often a range of choice and judgment[,] and that whatever choice is rational is constitutional.

Thayer, The Origin and Scope of the American Doctrine of Constitutional Law, 7 Harv. L. Rev. 129, 144 (1893). Might this approach undo the advantages supposed to derive from judicial independence and insulation?

2. Marbury *and the discretionary character of interpretation.* Most of the doubts raised about judicial review rest on a concern that in interpreting the Constitution, the judges will not be enforcing the judgments of its drafters, but will instead be influenced by their own views about how society should be ordered.

(Consider whether that is a sensible or coherent dichotomy.) Many of the Constitution's provisions are vague and ambiguous. Their interpretation calls for the exercise of discretion. Interpretation of such provisions, in the view of some, inevitably involves the exercise of a "political" judgment by the judges. (We put to one side the question of what "political" means in this context.) It is in these circumstances that the tension between judicial review and democracy becomes most acute. Consider, for example, judicial efforts to decide whether capital punishment is "cruel and unusual" under the eighth amendment, whether school segregation denies blacks "equal protection of the laws," whether a law providing for prayer in the public schools is a "law respecting an establishment of religion," and whether a prohibition of second-trimester abortions is a deprivation of "life, liberty, or property, without due process of law."

Acknowledging the existence of discretion, the Court has said that

> It is no answer [to] insist that what the provision of the Constitution meant to the vision of [the framers'] day it must mean to the vision of our time. If by the statement that what the Constitution meant at the time of its adoption it means today, it is intended to say that the great clauses of the Constitution must be confined to the interpretation which the framers, with the conditions and outlook of their time, would have placed upon them, the statement carries its own refutation.

Home Building & Loan Association v. Blaisdell, 290 U.S. 398, 442-443 (1934).

There have been numerous efforts to respond to or to escape the countermajoritarian difficulties produced by the discretionary character of interpretation. Most of them are rooted in the notion that it is critically important to ensure that constitutional decisions rest on something other than the value judgments, or policy preferences, of the judges. Numerous disputes in constitutional law are in fact about the adequacy of these various efforts to control judicial discretion. We deal with those efforts in more detail below. Consider at the outset the appeal and limitations of the following. Which, if any, of the following is a useful or appropriate *source* of constitutional outcomes? Which, if any, limits judicial discretion? What is the proper conception of constitutional interpretation? It may be useful to keep the death penalty, school segregation, and abortion examples in mind.

a. *The intent of the framers.* It is sometimes suggested that the meaning of a constitutional provision should be ascertained by reference to the intent of its framers. But note the following difficulties.

(1) *Whose intent?* The relevant intent might be that of the drafters of the Constitution or the people in the various states who ratified it. But the problem of ascertaining the "intention" of a collective decisionmaking body is enormous. Usually there are disagreements among the various decisionmakers. Often they will have no "intent" with respect to a particular question that arises in the future. How serious are these obstacles to a finding of framers' intent?

(2) *Intent at what level of generality; the problem of interpretive intent.* As noted above, many constitutional provisions are vague and ambiguous. Consider, for example, the commerce clause, the equal protection clause, the cruel and unusual punishments clause, and the freedom of speech clause. Those provisions might be read to enact either a particular "conception" or a general "concept" to be filled in over time. The choice between the two will have enormous

consequences for constitutional interpretation. For example, the question might be whether the equal protection clause applies only to discrimination against blacks — the principal historical concern — or whether it sets forth a more general prohibition of unjustifiable distinctions between classes of people. How does one decide whether a provision establishes specific conceptions or general concepts?

(a) From the text of the Constitution, it is often plausible to suggest that the framers intended to delegate, to people in the future, the power to make decisions about what the provision means in the particular circumstances. Some framers, in short, may have intended the provision to set forth a general concept and to delegate to others the decision about the meaning of the provision in new settings. "If the abstract statement is chosen as the appropriate mode or level of investigation into the original intention, then judges must make substantive decisions of political morality not in place of judgments made by the 'Framers' but rather in service of those judgments." Dworkin, The Forum of Principle, 56 N.Y.U. L. Rev. 469, 490 (1981). This is the problem of interpretive intent.

How does one decide whether, with respect to a particular provision, the framers intended to enact a general concept or a particular conception? Consider the following possibilities. (i) The language of the Constitution is the best evidence, and most of the important provisions read as general concepts. (ii) It is implausible to attribute to the framers a desire to set out general concepts because interpretive freedom would then be unlimited. If courts were empowered to wield general concepts against the political branches, there would be a significant risk of judicial tyranny — and it is hardly plausible to impute that to the framers. (iii) It is highly unlikely that one will be able to identify a coherent interpretive intention on the part of the framers. With respect to most provisions, there was a mixture of general concepts and particular conceptions. Very few, if any, of the framers made a decision between the two. The notion that "they" had any particular position on the question is fanciful. On the framers' own view of intent, see Powell, The Original Understanding of Original Intent, 99 Harv. L. Rev. 885 (1985).

(b) Suppose that the framers did in fact intend to set forth conceptions, not concepts. It would still remain to show that their intention *on that matter* is controlling. One might believe that the constitutional text binds future decisionmakers — that that conclusion is rightly taken as axiomatic — but that it is up to future decisionmakers, not to the framers, to decide how the document should be interpreted. "Some part of any constitutional theory must be independent of the intentions or beliefs or indeed acts of the people the theory designates as Framers. Some part must stand on its own in political or moral theory; otherwise the theory would be wholly circular." Dworkin, supra, at 496. In this view, a decision to rely on the interpretive intent of the framers must be independently justified. Can it be? How?

(c) Suppose that circumstances have changed dramatically since the framers wrote. How does one understand the framers' "intent" with respect to (i) a new problem or (ii) an old problem in dramatically changed circumstances? See Tushnet, Following the Rules Laid Down: A Critique of Interpretivism and Neutral Principles, 96 Harv. L. Rev. 781 (1983). Consider, for example, the vastly changed role of both public education and the status of blacks in the period between the framing of the fourteenth amendment and the time of the desegregation decision, Brown v. Board of Education, in 1954. How does one apply their "intent" in light of such changes? Consider the view that courts must uphold all measures that the framers did not mean to invalidate, since without a decision by the framers, the judges will be unable to trace judicial outcomes to decisions made by others. Easterbrook, Legal Interpretation and the Power of the Judiciary, 7 Harv. J.L. & Pub. Policy 87, 94-99 (1984).

While it is important at the outset to have some understanding of the role of the framers' intent in constitutional interpretation, one should be able to recognize as well other possible sources of constitutional rulings. Each of these sources is discussed in more detail in subsequent chapters; we outline some of the principal sources here, as an aid to understanding the implications of *Marbury* and for future reference.

What constraints do the following impose on interpretation? How helpful were they in *Marbury* itself? How helpful might they be in a case posing the constitutionality of capital punishment, school prayer, abortion, or school segregation? What, in short, does or should the process of constitutional interpretation consist of?

b. *The text of the Constitution.* There is general agreement that the text of the Constitution is binding on courts. But what constraints does it impose? See Schauer, Easy Cases, 58 S. Cal. L. Rev. 399, 414 (1985):

> Once we expand our notion of a case to include all legal events, it becomes clear that there *are* easy cases in constitutional law — lots of them. The parties concerned know, for example, that Ronald Reagan cannot run for a third term; [that] bills receiving less than a majority of votes in either the House or the Senate are not laws of the United States; [and] that a twenty-nine-year-old is not going to be President of the United States. [The] foregoing is only a small sample of the legal events that are "easy" constitutional cases.

But consider Perry, The Authority of Text, Tradition, and Reason: A Theory of Constitutional "Interpretation," 58 S. Cal. L. Rev. 551, 566 (1985): "[Just] about any choice a majority of the Supreme Court is likely to make would probably fall within [the] boundary [set by] accepted canons of judicial behavior, even in conjunction with the constitutional text."

c. *Tradition; precedent.* Sometimes the scope of a provision is determined in part by reference to tradition and the Court's own precedents. Under this approach, constitutional law operates as a form of common law, developing over time but constrained by the past. See Wellington, Common Law Rules and Constitutional Double Standards: Some Notes on Adjudication, 83 Yale L.J. 221 (1973). See also Perry, supra, at 565:

> As I conceive it, the constitutional text is a symbol of the aspirations of the political tradition and, as such, constrains in the way and to the extent that aspirations of a tradition constrain. There is no question that the aspirations of a tradition constrain. [But], depending on the particular resources they bear, language, culture, and traditions can liberate. [In] the American political tradition, one of the most important resources of which is its self-critical aspect, we use our tradition to revise, to reform and re-present, our tradition.

Is the countermajoritarian character of judicial review a reason to reject a common law or tradition-based model of constitutional adjudication?

d. *Prevailing morality, or social consensus.* An open-ended constitutional provision might be given content by referring to prevailing morality or to some form of consensus. But this possibility raises two questions. First, Why should judges be supposed to be better than legislators as registers of social consensus? Second, in light of the fact that the Constitution, or at least the bill of rights, is often regarded as a shield against social consensus, is it not odd to suggest that its content derives from that consensus?

e. *Conceptions of justice; principle.* See A. Bickel, The Least Dangerous Branch 23-28 (1962):

> Courts have certain capacities for dealing with matters of principle that legislatures and executives do not possess. Judges have, or should have, the leisure, the training, and the insulation to follow the ways of the scholar in pursuing the ends of government. This is crucial in sorting out the enduring values of a society. [Their] insulation and the marvelous mystery of time give courts the capacity to appeal to men's better natures, to call forth their aspirations, which may have been forgotten in the moment's hue and cry.

Compare with this justification Madison's conception of the role of national representatives in The Federalist No. 10, supra, who were to "refine" rather than reflect the public view. Note also the view that the distinctive role of courts is to set out "principles," a role that is distinct from the legislative task of making "policy." See R. Dworkin, A Matter of Principle (1985); R. Dworkin, Taking Rights Seriously (1977).

How does this justification differ from that offered by Hamilton and Marshall? Does the distinction between principle and policy seem to have sufficient crispness to justify the allocation of one to the courts and the other to the legislature? Note the position of Thayer, supra, that the legislature should be and often is concerned with issues of principle. And consider Brest, Who Decides?, 58 S. Cal. L. Rev. 661, 664, 670 (1985):

> The mere demography of the judiciary suggests that judges, especially federal judges, are far from a representative cross section of American society. They are overwhelmingly Anglo, male, well educated, and upper or upper middle class. They are also members of the legal profession — an affiliation that by definition sets them apart from other members of society. [The] net effect [of judicial review] is to systematically exclude citizens and their representatives from the most fundamental decisions of the polity. This is completely at odds with the classical conception of citizenship held by political theorists such as Aristotle, J. S. Mill, Rousseau, and Jefferson, for whom the very concept of citizenship involved participation in those decisions.

3. *The countermajoritarian difficulty: escape routes.* A separate effort to respond to the countermajoritarian difficulty suggests that, in reality, there is no such difficulty, since the role of the court is to promote rather than to undermine democracy, properly understood. This effort in turn takes several forms.

Under one view, the judicial effort to impose constitutional constraints on the political process promotes democracy, since those constraints were adopted by the people in a time of heightened democratic awareness and therefore occupy a superior status to the decisions of temporary majorities. This is the position taken in Ackerman, supra, and might be said to have roots in Hamilton's position in The Federalist No. 78 and in *Marbury* itself.

Under another view, the role of the courts is to protect certain groups that are for one reason or another excluded from or unable fully to participate in politics. The relative inability of such groups to participate in or to be represented by the political process is said to justify a judicial role designed to bring about better democracy. See McCulloch v. Maryland, infra, and, generally, J. Ely, Democracy and Distrust (1980), which is an extended elaboration of this theme.

A third position would suggest that the role of the Court is indeed to improve democracy, but not only by protecting the opportunity of traditionally disadvantaged groups to participate or to be represented. In this view, the Court might attempt to ensure that, for example, legislation is not merely a response to the factional pressures described in The Federalist No. 10, or that it does not reflect existing relations of power as between whites and blacks or men and women.

These various positions attempt to defuse the countermajoritarian difficulty by suggesting that in reality there is no such difficulty at all. See M. Shapiro, Freedom of Speech: The Supreme Court and Judicial Review 32 (1966):

> [The] lawmaker to whom the nasty old undemocratic Supreme Court is supposed to yield so reverently because of his greater democratic virtues is the entire mass of majoritarian-antimajoritarian, elected-appointed, special interest-general interest, responsible-irresponsible elements that make up American national politics. If we are off on a democratic quest, the dragon begins to look better and better and St. George worse and worse.

But this position of course depends on a controversial portrait of national lawmaking institutions, and an equally controversial understanding that the remedy for defects in those institutions might be found in judicial review instead of — for example — institutional reform through the political process itself. We return to these themes at numerous points below.

The following case raises issues similar to but distinct from that in *Marbury*: the authority of the Supreme Court over decisions by state courts. That question is closely related to the question of Supreme Court review of state as distinct from federal laws.

Martin v. Hunter's Lessee

14 U.S. (1 Wheat.) 304 (1816)

[This case arose out of a dispute over the ownership of land in Virginia. Hunter claimed the land pursuant to a grant from the state of Virginia in 1789, which confiscated lands owned by British subjects. Martin, a British subject, claimed that the attempted confiscation was ineffective under anticonfiscation clauses of treaties between the United States and England.

The Virginia trial court held in favor of Martin; the Virginia Court of Appeals reversed, concluding that the state's title to the land had vested before the relevant treaties and, alternatively, that Martin's claim was defeated by a 1796 Act of Compromise between the state and Martin's uncle, from whom Martin's claim derived. The Supreme Court of the United States reversed the Virginia Court of Appeals, neglecting to mention the Act of Compromise but claiming that Virginia had not perfected its title before the relevant treaties. Fairfax's Devisee v. Hunter's Lessee, 7 Cranch 603 (1813). The Supreme Court remanded the case to the Virginia Court of Appeals with instructions to enter judgment for the appellant. But on remand, the Virginia court declined. The court said that section 25 of the Judiciary Act was unconstitutional insofar as it extended the appellate jurisdiction of the Supreme Court to the Virginia court.

In its opinion, the court emphasized that the act placed the courts of one sovereign — Virginia — under the direct control of another, an arrangement incompatible with the notion of sovereignty. "It must have been foreseen that controversies would sometimes arise as to the boundaries of the two jurisdictions. Yet the constitution has provided no umpire, has erected no tribunal by which they shall be settled. The omission proceeded, probably, from the belief, that such a tribunal would produce evils greater than those of the occasional collisions which it would be designed to remedy."

The excerpts here deal only with the question of whether the Supreme Court has appellate jurisdiction over constitutional decisions by state courts.]

MR. JUSTICE STORY delivered the opinion of the Court. . . .

[The] appellate power is not limited by the terms of the third article to any particular courts. The words are, "the judicial power (which includes appellate power) shall extend *to all cases,*" &c., and "in all other cases before mentioned the supreme court shall have appellate jurisdiction." It is the *case,* then, and not *the court,* that gives the jurisdiction. If the judicial power extends to the case, it will be in vain to search in the letter of the constitution for any qualification as to the tribunal where it depends. [If] the text be clear and distinct, no restriction upon its plain and obvious import ought to be admitted, unless the inference be irresistible.

If the constitution meant to limit the appellate jurisdiction to cases pending in the courts of the United States, it would necessarily follow that the jurisdiction of these courts would, in all the cases enumerated in the constitution, be exclusive of state tribunals. How otherwise could the jurisdiction extend to *all* cases arising under the constitution, laws, and treaties of the United States, or *to all cases* of admiralty and maritime jurisdiction? If some of these cases might be entertained by state tribunals, and no appellate jurisdiction as to them should exist, then the appellate power would not extend to *all,* but to *some,* cases. If state tribunals might exercise concurrent jurisdiction over all or some of the other classes of cases in the constitution without control, then the appellate jurisdiction of the United States might, as to such cases, have no real existence, contrary to the manifest intent of the constitution. [This] construction would abridge the jurisdiction of such court far more than has been ever contemplated in any act of congress. . . .

[It] is plain that the framers of the constitution did contemplate that cases within the judicial cognizance of the United States not only might but would arise in the state courts, in the exercise of their ordinary jurisdiction. With this view the sixth article declares, that "this constitution, and the laws of the United States, which shall be made in pursuance thereof, and all treaties made, or which shall be made, under the authority of the United States, shall be the supreme law of the land, and the judges in every state shall be bound thereby, any thing in the constitution or laws of any state to the contrary notwithstanding." It is obvious that this obligation is imperative upon the state judges in their official, and not merely in their private, capacities. From the very nature of their judicial duties they would be called upon to pronounce the law applicable to the case in judgment. They were not to decide merely according to the laws or constitution of the state, but according to the constitution, laws and treaties of the United States — "the supreme law of the land."

A moment's consideration will show us the necessity and propriety of this provision in cases where the jurisdiction of the state courts is unquestionable.

Suppose a contract for the payment of money is made between citizens of the same state, and performance thereof is sought in the courts of that state; no person can doubt that the jurisdiction completely and exclusively attaches, in the first instance, to such courts. Suppose at the trial the defendant sets up in his defence a tender under a state law, making paper money a good tender, or a state law, impairing the obligation of such contract, which law, if binding, would defeat the suit. The constitution of the United States has declared that no state shall make any thing but gold or silver coin a tender in payment of debts, or pass a law impairing the obligation of contracts. If congress shall not have passed a law providing for the removal of such a suit to the courts of the United States, must not the state court proceed to hear and determine it? [Suppose] an indictment for a crime in a state court, and the defendant should allege in his defence that the crime was created by an ex post facto act of the state, must not the state court, in the exercise of a jurisdiction which has already rightfully attached, have a right to pronounce on the validity and sufficiency of the defence? It would be extremely difficult, upon any legal principles, to give a negative answer to these inquiries. Innumerable instances of the same sort might be stated, in illustration of the position; and unless the state courts could sustain jurisdiction in such cases, this clause of the sixth article would be without meaning or effect, and public mischiefs, of a most enormous magnitude, would inevitably ensue.

It must, therefore, be conceded that the constitution not only contemplated, but meant to provide for cases within the scope of the judicial power of the United States, which might yet depend before state tribunals. It was foreseen that in the exercise of their ordinary jurisdiction, state courts would incidentally take cognizance of cases arising under the constitution, the laws, and treaties of the United States. Yet to all these cases the judicial power, by the very terms of the constitution, is to extend. It cannot extend by original jurisdiction if that was already rightfully and exclusively attached in the state courts, which (as has been already shown) may occur; it must, therefore, extend by appellate jurisdiction, or not at all. It would seem to follow that the appellate power of the United States must, in such cases, extend to state tribunals; and if in such cases, there is no reason why it should not equally attach upon all others within the purview of the constitution.

It has been argued that such an appellate jurisdiction over state courts is inconsistent with the genius of our governments, and the spirit of the constitution. That the latter was never designed to act upon state sovereignties, but only upon the people, and that if the power exists, it will materially impair the sovereignty-of the states, and the independence of their courts. . . .

It is a mistake that the constitution was not designed to operate upon states, in their corporate capacities. It is crowded with provisions which restrain or annul the sovereignty of the states in some of the highest branches of their prerogatives. The tenth section of the first article contains a long list of disabilities and prohibitions imposed upon the states. Surely, when such essential portions of state sovereignty are taken away, or prohibited to be exercised, it cannot be correctly asserted that the constitution does not act upon the states. The language of the constitution is also imperative upon the states as to the performance of many duties. It is imperative upon the state legislatures to make laws prescribing the time, places, and manner of holding elections for senators and representatives, and for electors of president and vice-president. And in these, as well as some other cases, congress have a right to revise, amend, or supercede the laws which may be passed by state legislatures. When, therefore, the states are stripped of some of the highest attributes of sovereignty, and the same are given to the United States; when the legislatures of the states are, in some respects, under the control of congress, and in every case are, under the constitution, bound by the paramount authority of the United States; it is certainly difficult to support the argument that the appellate power over the decisions of state courts is contrary to the genius of our institutions. The courts of the United States can, without question, revise the proceedings of the executive and legislative authorities of the states, and if they are found to be contrary to the constitution, may declare them to be of no legal validity. Surely the exercise of the same right over judicial tribunals is not a higher or more dangerous act of sovereign power.

Nor can such a right be deemed to impair the independence of state judges. It is assuming the very ground in controversy to assert that they possess an absolute independence of the United States. In respect to the powers granted to the United States, they are not independent; they are expressly bound to obedience by the letter of the constitution; and if they should unintentionally transcend their authority, or misconstrue the constitution, there is no more reason for giving their judgments an absolute and irresistible force, than for giving it to the acts of the other co-ordinate departments of state sovereignty.

The argument urged from the possibility of the abuse of the revising power, is equally unsatisfactory. It is always a doubtful course, to argue against the use or existence of a power, from the possibility of its abuse. It is still more difficult, by such an argument, to ingraft upon a general power a restriction which is not to be found in the terms in which it is given. From the very nature of things, the absolute right of decision, in the last resort, must rest somewhere — wherever it may be vested it is susceptible of abuse. In all questions of jurisdiction the inferior, or appellate court, must pronounce the final judgment; and common sense, as well as legal reasoning, has conferred it upon the latter.

It is further argued, that no great public mischief can result from a construction which shall limit the appellate power of the United States to cases in their own courts: first, because state judges are bound by an oath to support the constitution of the United States, and must be presumed to be men of learning and integrity; and, secondly, because congress must have an unquestionable right to remove all cases within the scope of the judicial power from the state courts to the courts of the United States, at any time before final judgment, though not after final judgment. As to the first reason — admitting that the judges of the state courts are, and always will be, of as much learning, integrity, and wisdom, as those of the courts of the United States, (which we very cheerfully admit,) it does not aid the argument. It is manifest that the constitution has proceeded upon a theory of its own, and given or withheld powers according to the judgment of the American people, by whom it was adopted. [The] constitution has presumed (whether rightly or wrongly we do not inquire) that state attachments, state prejudices, state jealousies, and state interests, might sometimes obstruct, or control, or be supposed to obstruct or control, the regular administration of justice. Hence, in controversies between states; between citizens of different states; between citizens claiming grants under different states; between a state and its citizens, or foreigners, and between citizens and foreigners, it enables the parties, under the authority of congress, to have the controversies heard, tried, and determined before the national tribunals. No other reason than that which has been stated can be assigned, why some, at least, of those cases should not have been left to the cognizance of the state courts. In respect to the other enumerated cases — the cases arising under the constitution, laws, and treaties of the United States, cases affecting ambassadors and other public ministers, and cases of admiralty and maritime jurisdiction — reasons of a higher and more extensive nature, touching the safety, peace, and sovereignty of the nation, might well justify a grant of exclusive jurisdiction.

This is not all. A motive of another kind, perfectly compatible with the most sincere respect for state tribunals, might induce the grant of appellate power over their decisions. That motive is the importance, and even necessity of *uniformity* of decisions throughout the whole United States, upon all subjects within the purview of the constitution. Judges of equal learning and integrity, in different states, might differently interpret a statute, or a treaty of the United States, or even the constitution itself: If there were no revising authority to control these jarring and discordant judgments, and harmonize them into uniformity, the laws, the treaties, and the constitution of the United States would be different in different states, and might, perhaps, never have precisely the same construction, obligation, or efficacy, in any two states. The public mischiefs that would attend such a state of things would be truly deplorable; and it cannot be believed that they could have escaped the enlightened convention which formed the constitution. What, indeed, might then have been only prophecy, has now become fact; and the appellate jurisdiction must continue to be the only adequate remedy for such evils.

There is an additional consideration, which is entitled to great weight. The constitution of the United States was designed for the common and equal benefit of all the people of the United States. The judicial power was granted for the same benign and salutary purposes. It was not to be exercised exclusively for the benefit of parties who might be plaintiffs, and would elect the national forum, but also for the protection of defendants who might be entitled to try their rights, or assert their privileges, before the same forum. Yet, if the construction contended for be correct, it will follow, that as the plaintiff may always elect the state court, the defendant may be deprived of all the security which the constitution intended in aid of his rights. Such a state of things can, in no respect, be considered as giving equal rights. . . .

On the whole, the court are of opinion, that the appellate power of the United States does extend to cases pending in the state courts; and that the 25th section of the judiciary act, which authorizes the exercise of this jurisdiction in the specified cases, by a writ of error, is supported by the letter and spirit of the constitution. We find no clause in that instrument which limits this power; and we dare not interpose a limitation where the people have not been disposed to create one. . . .

[Reversed.]

Note: Supreme Court Review of State Courts and State Laws

1. *Supreme Court review of state court decisions — underlying concerns.* In what ways does the issue in *Martin* differ from that in *Marbury*? Why is it impor-

tant to have Supreme Court jurisdiction over the state courts? Justice Story's opinion stresses that if there were "no revising authority," the federal system would make possible "jarring and discordant judgment." The appellate jurisdiction of the Supreme Court is, in this view, necessary to assure the uniformity of federal law. But that raises the question why federal law must be uniform. As a general rule, legal requirements may vary from one state to another. What would be the evil in having disparate interpretations of the federal Constitution?

The Virginia judges in *Martin* made two arguments for their conclusion. First, they claimed not that the Constitution did not bind state judges, but that one sovereign could not control another; the risk of centralization thus outweighed the risk of disharmony. Second, they contended that other devices were available to minimize that latter risk and in order to bring about uniformity. Congress could, for example, allow removal of all cases involving a federal question. The position of the Virginia judges was that Congress had to take action to eliminate the risk of lack of uniformity through creating lower federal courts and expanding removal jurisdiction. The Court's view, by contrast, is that the more direct mechanism of control — appellate jurisdiction — is constitutionally permissible.

In addition to the uniformity point, note the possibility that Supreme Court review is necessary because of state hostility, or lack of sympathy, to federal rights. The argument here is that state judges will be less likely to react sympathetically to federal claims — either because they lack the tenure and salary protections of Article III, and are thus more susceptible to political influence, or because they have a natural alliance with the legislative and executive parts of the government. Neuborne, The Myth of Parity, 90 Harv. L. Rev. 1105, 1127-1128 (1977), speaks of the difference between federal district judges and state trial judges, but the arguments are applicable to appellate judges as well:

> Federal district judges [are] as insulated from majoritarian pressures as is functionally possible, precisely to insure their ability to enforce the Constitution without fear of reprisal. State trial judges, on the other hand, generally are elected for a fixed term, rendering them vulnerable to majoritarian pressure when deciding constitutional cases. [This] insulation factor, I suggest, explains the historical preference for federal enforcement of controversial constitutional norms.

This view has often played an important role in constitutional history.

Another justification for Supreme Court review of state court decisions stresses the comparative expertise of the federal courts in dealing with federal constitutional questions. Neuborne, supra at 1120, suggests that "federal trial courts tend to be better equipped to analyze complex, often conflicting lines of authority and more likely to produce competently written, persuasive opinions than are state trial courts." Why should this be the case?

2. *Supreme Court review of state laws — constitutional basis.* Martin involved Supreme Court review of state court decisions, not of state laws; but elements of the Court's reasoning are applicable to that latter problem. Do the textual arguments for the power of judicial review of state laws carry more force than those for judicial review of federal laws? The arguments from the structure of the Constitution or its underlying purposes? Consider Holmes's view: "I do not think the United States would come to an end if we lost our power to declare an Act of Congress void. I do think the Union would be imperiled if we could not make that

declaration as to the laws of the several States." O. W. Holmes, Collected Legal
Papers 295-296 (1920). Does this conclusion depend on a justifiable belief in the
existence of institutional safeguards at the federal level?

3. *Justice Story and article III.* In *Martin*, Justice Story interpreted article III to
require that "the whole judicial power of the United States should be, at all times,
vested, either in an original or appellate form, in some courts created under its
authority." If it were accepted, this conclusion would have dramatic practical
consequences. It means that at any time, some federal court must have the power
to decide any case to which the federal judicial power extends. On what does
Story base his conclusion?

Consider Currie, The Constitution in the Supreme Court, 1801-1835, 49 U.
Chi. L. Rev. 646, 685-686 (1982), suggesting that Story's conclusion

> was contrary to Supreme Court precedent [as] well as to consistent congressional
> practice. [The] strongest argument against giving a natural reading to the ostensibly
> unlimited discretion of Congress to limit federal jurisdiction is *Marbury*'s principle
> that the courts were intended to enforce constitutional limits on legislative power.
> Story's interpretation poorly comports with that principle, for it outlaws such minor
> caseload adjustments as the jurisdictional amount while allowing Congress to evade
> any substantial check by vesting sole power over important constitutional questions
> in a single lower court selected for the complaisance of its judges.

4. *Cohens v. Virginia.* In Cohens v. Virginia, 19 U.S. (6 Wheat.) 264 (1821), the
Court reaffirmed *Martin* in the context of review of state criminal proceedings.
The case involved defendants who had been convicted of the unlawful sale of
lottery tickets in Virginia. They defended on the ground that an act of Congress
authorized the local government of the District of Columbia to establish a lottery.
The Court, per Chief Justice Marshall, affirmed, concluding that the congressional statute did not authorize the sale outside the territorial boundaries of
the District of Columbia. But the importance of the case lies in the holding that
the Supreme Court could exercise jurisdiction over decisions of the state courts
in criminal cases and in cases in which the state was a party. As to the fact that
the state was a party, Marshall noted that "the judicial power, as originally
given, extends to all cases arising under the constitution or a law of the United
States, whoever may be the party." The language of article III, Marshall
claimed, referred to "all" federal question cases. The same reasoning applied to
the claim that the fact that a criminal case was involved made *Cohens* different
from *Martin*.

Note: *Judicial Exclusivity in Constitutional*
Interpretation?

In Cooper v. Aaron, 358 U.S. 1 (1958), Arkansas had failed to comply with a
district court order requiring desegregation. Its brief stated that the "legislative,
executive, and judicial departments of the state government opposed the desegregation of Little Rock schools by enacting laws, calling out troops, making statements villifying federal law and federal courts, and failing to utilize state law
enforcement agencies and judicial processes to maintain public peace."

The state argued that desegregation would lead to undue violence and disorder
and that those consequences justified disobedience of the decree. The Court

rejected that argument on the ground that "law and order are not here to be preserved by depriving the Negro children of their constitutional rights." But the Court went on to meet the view that "the Governor and Legislature [are] not bound by our holding in the *Brown* case":

> Article VI of the Constitution makes the Constitution the "supreme Law of the Land." In 1803, Chief Justice Marshall, speaking for a unanimous Court, referring to the Constitution as "the fundamental and paramount law of the nation," declared in the notable case of Marbury v. Madison [that] "It is emphatically the province and duty of the judicial department to say what the law is." This decision declared the basic principle that the federal judiciary is supreme in the exposition of the law of the Constitution, and that principle has ever since been respected by this Court and the Country as a permanent and indispensible feature of our constitutional system. It follows that the interpretation of the Fourteenth Amendment enunciated by this Court in the *Brown* case is the supreme law of the land, and Art. VI of the Constitution makes it of binding effect on the States "any Thing in the Constitution or Laws of any State to the Contrary notwithstanding." Every state legislator and executive and judicial officer is solemnly committed by oath taken pursuant to Art. VI, cl. 3, "to support this Constitution."

Does *Cooper* go beyond *Marbury*? *Marbury* established that in the course of deciding cases, courts must look to the Constitution as an enforceable source of law. When there is a conflict between the Constitution and a statute, and when the conflict is relevant to the resolution of a justiciable controversy, the courts must allow the Constitution to prevail. Does that principle establish any *special* judicial authority to interpret the Constitution? On one view, *Marbury* means only that every branch of government, acting within its sphere, is authorized to interpret the Constitution.

Cooper v. Aaron suggests that the courts have been entrusted with a special role as guardians of the meaning of the Constitution and that other government officials must not interpret the Constitution for themselves but instead look to the courts' interpretation and take it as authoritative. The result would be that judicial rulings are authoritative even if there is no decree against the relevant officials in a litigated case.

If the passage from *Cooper* should be so understood, does it go too far in establishing "judicial supremacy"? And what are the practical differences between *Cooper* and the narrower interpretation of *Marbury*?

1. *The view from the presidency.* Consider in this regard the responsibility of political actors, including most prominently the President, in circumstances in which (1) they believe that a statute is unconstitutional in the face of a court's conclusion that it is, or in the expectation that the court will uphold it and (2) they believe that the statute or measure is constitutional in the face of a judicial conclusion that is unconstitutional, or in the expectation that the court would invalidate it. Are there differences between the two situations?

Consider the following view with respect to the first situation. The Constitution imposes on all branches of government a duty to comply with the Constitution. A necessary inference is that the President and members of Congress must make their own judgments on constitutional issues. This responsibility is especially insistent in light of the fact that moral issues frequently become constitutional issues. If the courts' duty is exclusive, politics become drained of morality, and political actors will be making decisions on the basis of expediency alone. See

Brest, A Conscientious Legislators' Guide to Constitutional Interpretation, 27 Stan. L. Rev. 585 (1975). Thus, for example, if the President or a member of Congress believes that a restriction of abortion is unconstitutional, he or she must invalidate the restriction even if the Court would uphold it. See veto message of Andrew Jackson, 1832, on act to recharter bank of the United States, 2 Messages and Papers of the Presidents 576, 581-582 (J. Richardson ed. 1900) (vetoing on constitutional grounds a measure that had been upheld by the Court; "[the] opinion of the judges has no more authority over Congress than the opinion of Congress has over the judges, and on that point the President is independent of both").

But how likely is it — now or at the time of the framing — that a legislator or President who believed a statute to be sound as a matter of public policy would sincerely believe it to be unconstitutional?

Consider the views expressed by Jefferson, Letter to Abigail Adams, Sept. 11, 1804, in 8 The Writings of Thomas Jefferson 310 (Ford ed. 1897):

> You seem to think it devolved on the judges to decide on the validity of the sedition law. But nothing in the Constitution has given them a right to decide for the Executive, any more than to the Executive to decide for them. Both magistracies are equally independent in the sphere of action assigned to them. The judges, believing the law constitutional, had a right to pass a sentence of fine and imprisonment, because that power was placed in their hands by the Constitution. But the Executive, believing the law to be unconstitutional, was bound to remit the execution of it; because that power has been confided to him by the Constitution. That instrument meant that its coordinate branches should be checks on each other. But the opinion which gives to the judges the right to decide what laws are constitutional, and what not, not only for themselves in their sphere of action, but for the Legislature and Executive also, would make the judiciary a despotic branch.

With respect to the second situation, suppose the President, or some other public official, believes that the Supreme Court has wrongly invalidated a statute. Recent examples include decisions invalidating laws calling for segregation, laws restricting abortions, and laws requiring school prayer. What is the President's duty in the face of such laws? May he sign or request legislation that would run afoul of the Court's decision? May he attempt to get the Court to overrule its decision? May he campaign against the Court? See Lincoln's First Inaugural Address, March 4, 1861, in 6 Messages and Papers of the Presidents 5 (J. Richardson ed. 1900):

> I do not forget the position assumed by some that constitutional questions are to be decided by the Supreme Court; nor do I deny that such decisions must be binding, in any case, upon the parties to a suit, as to the object of that suit, while they are also entitled to a very high respect and consideration in all parallel cases by all other departments of the government. And, while it is obviously possible that such decision may be erroneous in any given case, still the evil effect following it, being limited to that particular case, with the chance that it may be overruled and never become a precedent for other cases, can better be borne than could the evils of a different practice. At the same time, the candid citizen must confess that if the policy of the government, upon vital questions affecting the whole people, is to be irrevocably fixed by decisions of the Supreme Court, the instant they are made, in ordinary litigation between parties in personal actions, the people will have ceased to be their own rulers, having to that extent practically resigned the government into

the hands of that eminent tribunal. Nor is there in this view any assault upon the court or the judges. It is a duty from which they may not shrink to decide cases properly brought before them, and it is no fault of theirs if others seek to turn their decisions to political purposes.

Other Presidents, including Roosevelt and Nixon, have expressed similar views. Can this position be distinguished from the refusal of Governor Faubus to comply with the decision in Brown v. Board of Education?

3. *"Underenforced" constitutional norms.* Might it be argued that the Constitution sometimes invalidates official action, even if the Supreme Court declines so to hold? There is, in this view, a difference between what the Constitution requires and what the Court says it requires. The Court might decide, because of the need to defer to other branches of government or because of other limitations on its own competence, that some measure does not violate the Constitution; but such a holding might not bind other officials in the process of deciding whether a proposed course of action is constitutional, since those officials are not constrained by principles of deference.

See Sager, Fair Measure: The Status of Underenforced Constitutional Norms, 91 Harv. L. Rev. 1212, 1220-1221, 1227 (1978):

> Conventional analysis does not distinguish between fully enforced and underenforced constitutional norms; as a general matter, the scope of a constitutional norm is considered to be coterminous with the scope of its judicial enforcement. [Where] a federal judicial construct is found not to extend to certain official behavior because of institutional concerns rather than analytical perceptions, it seems strange to regard the resulting decision as a statement about the meaning of the constitutional norm in question. After all, what the members of the federal tribunal have actually determined is that there are good reasons for stopping short of exhausting the content of the constitutional concept with which they are dealing; the limited judicial construct which they have fashioned or accepted is occasioned by this determination and does not derive from a judgment about the scope of the constitutional concept itself.
>
> [The] most direct consequence of adopting this revised view is the perception that government officials have a legal obligation to obey an underenforced constitutional norm which extends beyond its interpretation by the federal judiciary to the full dimensions of the concept which the norm embodies. This obligation to obey constitutional norms at their underenforced margins requires governmental officials to fashion their own conceptions of these norms and measure their conduct by reference to these conceptions. Public officials cannot consider themselves free to act at what they perceive or ought to perceive to be peril to constitutional norms merely because the federal judiciary is unable to enforce these norms at their margins.

C. THE SOURCES OF JUDICIAL DECISIONS: TEXT, "REPRESENTATION-REINFORCEMENT," AND NATURAL LAW

Much of constitutional law is concerned with the question, What are the appropriate sources of constitutional doctrine? This section explores three possible sources that have played an important role in constitutional adjudication: the text, natural law and natural rights, and "reinforcement," or improvement, of democratic processes. For example, the abortion decision — Roe v. Wade, Chapter 6, section F, infra — has been justified on grounds of "natural law" and "representation-reinforcement"; so too the desegregation decision — Brown v. Board of Education — where the text itself has also been invoked. The roots of the resulting debates can be found in early decisions by the Supreme Court.

McCulloch v. Maryland

17 U.S. (4 Wheat.) 316 (1819)

[This was an action brought by John James, for himself and the state of Maryland, against James McCulloch, cashier of a branch of the Bank of the United States. James alleged that McCulloch had failed to pay a state tax assessed against the bank. The court below held for the plaintiff. For background, see the notes following the opinion.]

MR. CHIEF JUSTICE MARSHALL delivered the opinion of the Court.

In the case now to be determined, the defendant, a sovereign State, denies the obligation of a law enacted by the legislature of the Union, and the plaintiff, on his part, contests the validity of an act which has been passed by the legislature of that State. The constitution of our country, in its most interesting and vital parts, is to be considered; the conflicting powers of the government of the Union and of its members, as marked in that constitution, are to be discussed; and an opinion given, which may essentially influence the great operations of the government. No tribunal can approach such a question without a deep sense of its importance, and of the awful responsibility involved in its decision. But it must be decided peacefully, or remain a source of hostile legislation, perhaps of hostility of a still more serious nature; and if it is to be so decided, by this tribunal alone can the decision be made. On the Supreme Court of the United States has the constitution of our country devolved this important duty.

The first question made in the cause is, has Congress power to incorporate a bank?

It has been truly said, that this can scarcely be considered as an open question, entirely unprejudiced by the former proceedings of the nation respecting it. The principle now contested was introduced at a very early period of our history, has been recognized by many successive legislatures, and has been acted upon by the judicial department, in cases of peculiar delicacy, as a law of undoubted obligation.

It will not be denied, that a bold and daring usurpation might be resisted, after an acquiescence still longer and more complete than this. But it is conceived that a doubtful question [ought] to receive a considerable impression from that practice. An exposition of the constitution, deliberately established by legislative acts, on the faith of which an immense property has been advanced, ought not to be lightly disregarded.

The power now contested was exercised by the first Congress elected under the present constitution. The bill for incorporating the bank of the United States did not steal upon an unsuspecting legislature, and pass unobserved. Its principle was completely understood, and was opposed with equal zeal and ability. After being resisted, first in the fair and open field of debate, and afterwards in the executive cabinet, with as much persevering talent as any measure has ever experienced, and being supported by arguments which convinced minds as pure and as intelligent as this country can boast, it became a law. The original act was permitted to expire; but a short experience of the embarrassments to which the refusal to revive it exposed the government, convinced those who were most prejudiced against the measure of its necessity, and induced the passage of the present law. It would require no ordinary share of intrepidity to assert that a measure adopted under these circumstances was a bold and plain usurpation, to which the constitution gave no countenance.

These observations belong to the cause; but they are not made under the impression that, were the question entirely new, the law would be found irreconcilable with the constitution.

In discussing this question, the counsel for the State of Maryland have deemed it of some importance, in the construction of the constitution, to consider that instrument not as emanating from the people, but as the act of sovereign and independent States. The powers of the general government, it has been said, are delegated by the States, who alone are truly sovereign; and must be exercised in subordination to the States, who alone possess supreme dominion.

It would be difficult to sustain this proposition. The Convention which framed the constitution was indeed elected by the State legislatures. But the instrument, when it came from their hands, was a mere proposal, without obligation, or pretensions to it. It was reported to the then existing Congress of the United States, with a request that it might "be submitted to a Convention of Delegates, chosen in each State by the people thereof, under the recommendation of its Legislature, for their assent and ratification." This mode of proceeding was adopted; and by the Convention, by Congress, and by the State Legislatures, the instrument was submitted to the people. They acted upon it in the only manner in which they can act safely, effectively, and wisely, on such a subject, by assembling in Convention. It is true, they assembled in their several States — and where else should they have assembled? No political dreamer was ever wild enough to think of breaking down the lines which separate the States, and of compounding the American people into one common mass. Of consequence, when they act, they act in their States. But the measures they adopt do not, on that account, cease to be the measures of the people themselves, or become the measures of the State governments.

From these Conventions the constitution derives its whole authority. The government proceeds directly from the people; is "ordained and established" in the name of the people; and is declared to be ordained, "in order to form a more perfect union, establish justice, ensure domestic tranquillity, and secure the blessings of liberty to themselves and to their posterity." The assent of the States, in their sovereign capacity, is implied in calling a Convention, and thus submitting that instrument to the people. But the people were at perfect liberty to accept or reject it; and their act was final. It required not the affirmance, and could not be negatived, by the State governments. The constitution, when thus adopted, was of complete obligation, and bound the State sovereignties. . . .

The government of the Union, then, (whatever may be the influence of this fact on the case,) is emphatically, and truly, a government of the people. In form and in substance it emanates from them. Its powers are granted by them, and are to be exercised directly on them, and for their benefit.

This government is acknowledged by all to be one of enumerated powers. The principle that it can exercise only the powers granted to it [is] now universally admitted. But the question respecting the extent of the powers actually granted, is perpetually arising, and will probably continue to arise, as long as our system shall exist.

In discussing these questions, the conflicting powers of the general and State governments must be brought into view, and the supremacy of their respective laws, when they are in opposition, must be settled.

If any one proposition could command the universal assent of mankind, we might expect it would be this — that the government of the Union, though limited in its powers, is supreme within its sphere of action. This would seem to result necessarily from its nature. It is the government of all; its powers are delegated by all; it represents all, and acts for all. Though any one State may be willing to control its operations, no State is willing to allow others to control them. The nation, on those subjects on which it can act, must necessarily bind its component parts. But this question is not left to mere reason: the people have, in express terms, decided it, by saying, "this constitution, and the laws of the United States, which shall be made in pursuance thereof," "shall be the supreme law of the land," and by requiring that the members of the State legislatures, and the officers of the executive and judicial departments of the States, shall take the oath of fidelity to it. . . .

Among the enumerated powers, we do not find that of establishing a bank or creating a corporation. But there is no phrase in the instrument which, like the articles of confederation, excludes incidental or implied powers; and which requires that every thing granted shall be expressly and minutely described. Even the 10th amendment, which was framed for the purpose of quieting the excessive jealousies which had been excited, omits the word "expressly," and declares only that the powers "not delegated to the United States, nor prohibited to the States, are reserved to the States or to the people" thus leaving the question, whether the particular power which may become the subject of contest has been delegated to the one government, or prohibited to the other, to depend on a fair construction of the whole instrument. The men who drew and adopted this amendment had experienced the embarrassments resulting from the insertion of this word in the articles of confederation, and probably omitted it to avoid those embarrassments. A constitution, to contain an accurate detail of all the subdivisions of which its great powers will admit, and of all the means by which they may be carried into execution, would partake of the prolixity of a legal code, and could scarcely be embraced by the human mind. It would probably never be understood by the public. Its nature, therefore, requires, that only its great outlines should be marked, its important objects designated, and the minor ingredients which compose those objects be deduced from the nature of the objects themselves. That this idea was entertained by the framers of the American constitution, is not only to be inferred from the nature of the instrument, but from the language. Why else were some of the limitations, found in the ninth section of the 1st article, introduced? It is also, in some degree, warranted by their having omitted to use any restrictive term which might prevent its receiving a fair and just interpretation. In considering this question, then, we must never forget, that it is *a constitution* we are expounding.

Although, among the enumerated powers of government, we do not find the word "bank" or "incorporation," we find the great powers to lay and collect taxes;

to borrow money; to regulate commerce; to declare and conduct a war; and to raise and support armies and navies. The sword and the purse, all the external relations, and no inconsiderable portion of the industry of the nation, are entrusted to its government. It can never be pretended that these vast powers draw after them others of inferior importance, merely because they are inferior. Such an idea can never be advanced. But it may with great reason be contended, that a government, entrusted with such ample powers, on the due execution of which the happiness and prosperity of the nation so vitally depends, must also be entrusted with ample means for their execution. The power being given, it is the interest of the nation to facilitate its execution. It can never be their interest, and cannot be presumed to have been their intention, to clog and embarrass its execution by withholding the most appropriate means. Throughout this vast republic, from the St. Croix to the Gulph of Mexico, from the Atlantic to the Pacific, revenue is to be collected and expended, armies are to be marched and supported. The exigencies of the nation may require that the treasure raised in the north should be transported to the south, that raised in the east conveyed to the west, or that this order should be reversed. Is that construction of the constitution to be preferred which would render these operations difficult, hazardous, and expensive? Can we adopt that construction, (unless the words imperiously require it,) which would impute to the framers of that instrument, when granting these powers for the public good, the intention of impeding their exercise by withholding a choice of means? . . .

It is not denied, that the powers given to the government imply the ordinary means of execution. That, for example, of raising revenue, and applying it to national purposes, is admitted to imply the power of conveying money from place to place, as the exigencies of the nation may require, and of employing the usual means of conveyance. . . .

But the constitution of the United States has not left the right of Congress to employ the necessary means, for the execution of the powers conferred on the government, to general reasoning. To its enumeration of powers is added that of making "all laws which shall be necessary and proper, for carrying into execution the foregoing powers, and all other powers vested by this constitution, in the government of the United States, or in any department thereof."

The counsel for the State of Maryland have urged various arguments, to prove that this clause, though in terms a grant of power, is not so in effect; but is really restrictive of the general right, which might otherwise be implied, of selecting means for executing the enumerated powers. . . .

[The] argument on which most reliance is placed, is drawn from the peculiar language of this clause. Congress is not empowered by it to make all laws, which may have relation to the powers conferred on the government, but such only as may be "necessary and proper" for carrying them into execution. The word "necessary," is considered as controlling the whole sentence, and as limiting the right to pass laws for the execution of the granted powers, to such as are indispensable, and without which the power would be nugatory. That it excludes the choice of means, and leaves to Congress, in each case, that only which is most direct and simple.

Is it true, that this is the sense in which the word "necessary" is always used? Does it always import an absolute physical necessity, so strong, that one thing, to which another may be termed necessary, cannot exist without that other? We think it does not. If reference be had to its use, in the common affairs of the world, or in approved authors, we find that it frequently imports no more than that one thing is convenient, or useful, or essential to another. To employ the means necessary to an end, is generally understood as employing any means calculated to produce the end, and not as being confined to those single means, without which the end would be entirely unattainable. Such is the character of human language, that no word conveys to the mind, in all situations, one single definite idea; and nothing is more common than to use words in a figurative sense. Almost all compositions contain words, which, taken in their rigorous sense, would convey a meaning different from that which is obviously intended. It is essential to just construction, that many words which import something excessive, should be understood in a more mitigated sense — in that sense which common usage justifies. The word "necessary" is of this description. It has not a fixed character peculiar to itself. It admits of all degrees of comparison; and is often connected with other words, which increase or diminish the impression the mind receives of the urgency it imports. A thing may be necessary, very necessary, absolutely or indispensably necessary. To no mind would the same idea be conveyed, by these several phrases. This comment on the word is well illustrated, by the passage cited at the bar, from the 10th section of the 1st article of the constitution. It is, we think, impossible to compare the sentence which prohibits a State from laying "imposts, or duties on imports or exports, except what may be *absolutely* necessary for executing its inspection laws," with that which authorizes Congress "to make all laws which shall be necessary and proper for carrying into execution" the powers of the general government, without feeling a conviction that the convention understood itself to change materially the meaning of the word "necessary," by prefixing the word "absolutely." This word, then, like others, is used in various senses; and, in its construction, the subject, the context, the intention of the person using them, are all to be taken into view.

Let this be done in the case under consideration. The subject is the execution of those great powers on which the welfare of a nation essentially depends. It must have been the intention of those who gave these powers, to insure, as far as human prudence could insure, their beneficial execution. This could not be done by confiding the choice of means to such narrow limits as not to leave it in the power of Congress to adopt any which might be appropriate, and which were conducive to the end. This provision is made in a constitution intended to endure for ages to come, and, consequently, to be adapted to the various *crises* of human affairs. To have prescribed the means by which government should, in all future time, execute its powers, would have been to change, entirely, the character of the instrument, and give it the properties of a legal code. It would have been an unwise attempt to provide, by immutable rules, for exigencies which, if foreseen at all, must have been seen dimly, and which can be best provided for as they occur. To have declared that the best means shall not be used, but those alone without which the power given would be nugatory, would have been to deprive the legislature of the capacity to avail itself of experience, to exercise its reason, and to accommodate its legislation to circumstances. If we apply this principle of construction to any of the powers of the government, we shall find it so pernicious in its operation that we shall be compelled to discard it. . . .

So, with respect to the whole penal code of the United States: whence arises the power to punish in cases not prescribed by the constitution? All admit that the government may, legitimately, punish any violation of its laws; and yet, this is not among the enumerated powers of Congress. The right to enforce the observance of law, by punishing its infraction, might be denied with the more plausibility, because it is expressly given in some cases. Congress is empowered "to provide for the punishment of counterfeiting the securities and current coin of the United States," and "to define and punish piracies and felonies committed on the high seas, and offences against the law of nations." The several powers of Congress may exist, in a very imperfect state to be sure, but they may exist and be carried into execution, although no punishment should be inflicted in cases where the right to punish is not expressly given.

Take, for example, the power "to establish post offices and post roads." This power is executed by the single act of making the establishment. But, from this has been inferred the power and duty of carrying the mail along the post road, from one post office to another. And, from this implied power, has again been inferred the right to punish those who steal letters from the post office, or rob the mail. It may be said, with some plausibility, that the right to carry the mail, and to punish those who rob it, is not indispensably necessary to the establishment of a post office and post road. This right is indeed essential to the beneficial exercise of the power, but not indispensably necessary to its existence. So, of the punishment of the crimes of stealing or falsifying a record or process of a Court of the United States, or of perjury in such Court. To punish these offences is certainly conducive to the due administration of justice. But courts may exist, and may decide the causes brought before them, though such crimes escape punishment.

The baneful influence of this narrow construction in all the operations of the government, and the absolute impracticability of maintaining it without rendering the government incompetent to its great objects, might be illustrated by numerous examples drawn from the constitution, and from our laws. . . .

In ascertaining the sense in which the word "necessary" is used in this clause of the constitution, we may derive some aid from that with which it is associated. Congress shall have power "to make all laws which shall be necessary and *proper* to carry into execution" the powers of the government. If the word "necessary" was used in that strict and rigorous sense for which the counsel for the State of Maryland contend, it would be an extraordinary departure from the usual course of the human mind, as exhibited in composition, to add a word, the only possible effect of which is to qualify that strict and rigorous meaning; to present to the mind the idea of some choice of means of legislation not straitened and compressed within the narrow limits for which gentlemen contend.

But the argument which most conclusively demonstrates the error of the construction contended for by the counsel for the State of Maryland, is founded on the intention of the Convention, as manifested in the whole clause. To waste time and argument in proving that, without it, Congress might carry its powers into execution, would be not much less idle than to hold a lighted taper to the sun. As little can it be required to prove, that in the absence of this clause, Congress would have some choice of means. That it might employ those which, in its judgment, would most advantageously effect the object to be accomplished. That any means adapted to the end, any means which tended directly to the execution of the constitutional powers of the government, were in themselves constitutional. This clause, as construed by the State of Maryland, would abridge, and almost annihilate this useful and necessary right of the legislature to select its means. That this could not be intended, is, we should think, had it not

been already controverted, too apparent for controversy. We think so for the
following reasons:

    1st. The clause is placed among the powers of Congress, not among the limita-
tions on those powers.

    2nd. Its terms purport to enlarge, not to diminish the powers vested in the
government. It purports to be an additional power, not a restriction on those
already granted. No reason has been, or can be assigned for thus concealing an
intention to narrow the discretion of the national legislature under words which
purport to enlarge it. . . .

    The result of the most careful and attentive consideration bestowed upon this
clause is, that if it does not enlarge, it cannot be construed to restrain the powers
of Congress, or to impair the right of the legislature to exercise its best judgment
in the selection of measures to carry into execution the constitutional powers of
the government. If no other motive for its insertion can be suggested, a sufficient
one is found in the desire to remove all doubts respecting the right to legislate on
that vast mass of incidental powers which must be involved in the constitution, if
that instrument be not a splendid bauble.

    We admit, as all must admit, that the powers of the government are limited,
and that its limits are not to be transcended. But we think the sound construction
of the constitution must allow to the national legislature that discretion, with
respect to the means by which the powers it confers are to be carried into execution, which will enable that body to perform the high duties assigned to it, in the
manner most beneficial to the people. Let the end be legitimate, let it be within
the scope of the constitution, and all means which are appropriate, which are
plainly adapted to that end, which are not prohibited, but consist with the letter
and spirit of the constitution, are constitutional. . . .

    If a corporation may be employed indiscriminately with other means to carry
into execution the powers of the government, no particular reason can be assigned for excluding the use of a bank, if required for its fiscal operations. To use
one, must be within the discretion of Congress, if it be an appropriate mode of
executing the powers of government. That it is a convenient, a useful, and
essential instrument in the prosecution of its fiscal operations, is not now a
subject of controversy. All those who have been concerned in the administration
of our finances, have concurred in representing its importance and necessity; and
so strongly have they been felt, that statesmen of the first class, whose previous
opinions against it had been confirmed by every circumstance which can fix the
human judgment, have yielded those opinions to the exigencies of the nation.
Under the confederation, Congress, justifying the measure by its necessity, transcended perhaps its powers to obtain the advantage of a bank; and our own
legislation attests the universal conviction of the utility of this measure. The time
has passed away when it can be necessary to enter into any discussion in order to
prove the importance of this instrument, as a means to effect the legitimate
objects of the government.

    But, were its necessity less apparent, none can deny its being an appropriate
measure; and if it is, the degree of its necessity, as has been very justly observed, is
to be discussed in another place. Should Congress, in the execution of its powers,
adopt measures which are prohibited by the constitution; or should Congress,
under the pretext of executing its powers, pass laws for the accomplishment of
objects not entrusted to the government; it would become the painful duty of this

tribunal, should a case requiring such a decision come before it, to say that such an act was not the law of the land. But where the law is not prohibited, and is really calculated to effect any of the objects entrusted to the government, to undertake here to inquire into the degree of its necessity, would be to pass the line which circumscribes the judicial department, and to tread on legislative ground. This court disclaims all pretensions to such a power. . . .

It being the opinion of the Court, that the act incorporating the bank is constitutional; and that the power of establishing a branch in the State of Maryland might be properly exercised by the bank itself, we proceed to inquire —

2. Whether the State of Maryland may, without violating the constitution, tax that branch?

That the power of taxation is one of vital importance; that it is retained by the States; that it is not abridged by the grant of a similar power to the government of the Union; that it is to be concurrently exercised by the two governments: are truths which have never been denied. But, such is the paramount character of the constitution, that its capacity to withdraw any subject from the action of even this power, is admitted. The States are expressly forbidden to lay any duties on imports or exports, except what may be absolutely necessary for executing their inspection laws. If the obligation of this prohibition must be conceded — if it may restrain a State from the exercise of its taxing power on imports and exports; the same paramount character would seem, to restrain, as it certainly may restrain, a State from such other exercise of this power, as is in its nature incompatible with, and repugnant to, the constitutional laws of the Union. A law, absolutely repugnant to another, as entirely repeals that other as if express terms of repeal were used.

On this ground the counsel for the bank place its claim to be exempted from the power of a State to tax its operations. There is no express provision for the case, but the claim has been sustained on a principle which so entirely pervades the constitution, is so intermixed with the materials which compose it, so interwoven with its web, so blended with its texture, as to be incapable of being separated from it, without rendering it into shreds.

This great principle is, that the constitution and the laws made in pursuance thereof are supreme; that they control the constitution and laws of the respective States, and cannot be controlled by them. From this, which may be almost termed an axiom, other propositions are deduced as corollaries, on the truth or error of which, and on their application to this case, the cause has been supposed to depend. These are, 1st. that a power to create implies a power to preserve. 2nd. That a power to destroy, if wielded by a different hand, is hostile to, and incompatible with these powers to create and to preserve. 3d. That where this repugnancy exists, that authority which is supreme must control, not yield to that over which it is supreme. . . .

That the power of taxing it by the States may be exercised so as to destroy it, is too obvious to be denied. But taxation is said to be an absolute power, which acknowledges no other limits than those expressly prescribed in the constitution, and like sovereign power of every other description, is trusted to the discretion of those who use it. But the very terms of this argument admit that the sovereignty of the State, in the article of taxation itself, is subordinate to, and may be controlled by the constitution of the United States. How far it has been controlled by that instrument must be a question of construction. In making this construction, no principle not declared, can be admissible, which would defeat the legitimate operations of a supreme government. It is of the very essence of supremacy to remove all obstacles to its action within its own sphere, and so to modify every power vested in subordinate governments, as to exempt its own operations from their own influence. This effect need not be stated in terms. It is so involved in the declaration of supremacy, so necessarily implied in it, that the expression of it could not make it more certain. We must, therefore, keep it in view while construing the constitution.

The argument on the part of the State of Maryland, is, not that the States may directly resist a law of Congress, but that they may exercise their acknowledged powers upon it, and that the constitution leaves them this right in the confidence that they will not abuse it.

Before we proceed to examine this argument, and to subject it to the test of the constitution, we must be permitted to bestow a few considerations on the nature and extent of this original right of taxation, which is acknowledged to remain with the States. It is admitted that the power of taxing the people and their property is essential to the very existence of government, and may be legitimately exercised on the objects to which it is applicable, to the utmost extent to which the government may chuse to carry it. The only security against the abuse of this power, is found in the structure of the government itself. In imposing a tax the legislature acts upon its constituents. This is in general a sufficient security against erroneous and oppressive taxation.

The people of a State, therefore, give to their government a right of taxing themselves and their property, and as the exigencies of government cannot be limited, they prescribe no limits to the exercise of this right, resting confidently on the interest of the legislator, and on the influence of the constituents over their representative, to guard them against its abuse. But the means employed by the government of the Union have no such security, nor is the right of a State to tax them sustained by the same theory. Those means are not given by the people of a particular State, not given by the constituents of the legislature, which claim the right to tax them, but by the people of all the States. They are given by all for the benefit of all — and upon theory, should be subjected to that government only which belongs to all. . . .

We find, then, on just theory, a total failure of this original right to tax the means employed by the government of the Union, for the execution of its powers. The right never existed, and the question whether it has been surrendered, cannot arise.

But, waiving this theory for the present, let us resume the inquiry, whether this power can be exercised by the respective States, consistently with a fair construction of the constitution?

That the power to tax involves the power to destroy; that the power to destroy may defeat and render useless the power to create; that there is a plain repugnance, in conferring on one government a power to control the constitutional measures of another, which other, with respect to those very measures, is declared to be supreme over that which exerts the control, are propositions not to be denied. But all inconsistencies are to be reconciled by the magic of the word CONFIDENCE. Taxation, it is said, does not necessarily and unavoidably destroy. To carry it to the excess of destruction would be an abuse, to presume which, would banish that confidence which is essential to all government.

But is this a case of confidence? Would the people of any one State trust those of another with a power to control the most insignificant operations of their State government? We know they would not. Why, then, should we suppose that the people of any one State should be willing to trust those of another with a power to control the operations of a government to which they have confided their most important and most valuable interests? In the legislature of the Union alone, are all represented. The legislature of the Union alone, therefore, can be trusted by the people with the power of controlling measures which concern all, in the confidence that it will not be abused. This, then, is not a case of confidence, and we must consider it as it really is. . . .

If we apply the principle for which the State of Maryland contends, to the constitution generally, we shall find it capable of changing totally the character of that instrument. We shall find it capable of arresting all the measures of the government, and of prostrating it at the foot of the States. [If] the states may tax one instrument, [they] may tax any and every other instrument. [The] American people [did] not design to make their government dependent on the states. . . .

It has also been insisted, that, as the power of taxation in the general and State governments is acknowledged to be concurrent, every argument which would sustain the right of the general government to tax banks chartered by the States, will equally sustain the right of the States to tax banks chartered by the general government.

But the two cases are not on the same reason. The people of all the States have created the general government, and have conferred upon it the general power of taxation. The people of all the States, and the States themselves, are represented in Congress, and, by their representatives, exercise this power. When they tax the chartered institutions of the States, they tax their constituents; and these taxes must be uniform. But, when a State taxes the operations of the government of the United States, it acts upon institutions created, not by their own constituents, but by people over whom they claim no control. It acts upon the measures of a government created by others as well as themselves, for the benefit of others in common with themselves. The difference is that which always exists, and always must exist, between the action of the whole on a part, and the action of a part on the whole — between the laws of a government declared to be supreme, and those of a government which, when in opposition to those laws, is not supreme.

But if the full application of this argument could be admitted, it might bring into question the right of Congress to tax the State banks, and could not prove the right of the States to tax the Bank of the United States. . . .

[We] conclude that the states have no power, by taxation or otherwise, to retard, impede, burden, or in any manner control, the operations of the constitutional laws enacted by Congress. . . .

[Reversed.]

Note: Constitutional Methodology and Constitutional Interpretation in McCulloch

McCulloch resolves a number of important questions, relating both to the judicial role and to the allocation of powers as between the federal government and the states. Those issues are explored in more detail throughout this book. We outline some of the key points here.

1. *Background.* The first bank of the United States was created in 1790, shortly after ratification of the Constitution, in order to furnish loans to the federal government and to help collect taxes. The constitutional issue was sharply debated. Madison, a member of the House of Representatives, spoke against the bank, claiming that Congress had no constitutional authority to create it. Hamilton, Secretary of the Treasury, was one of its staunchest supporters and indeed drafted the plan for the bank. Jefferson also opposed the first bank on constitutional grounds, invoking the tenth amendment and venturing as well that "the Constitution allows only the means which are *necessary,* not merely 'convenient,' for effecting the enumerated powers. If such a latitude of construction be allowed to this phrase as to give any non-enumerated power [to Congress,] it would swallow up all the delegated powers, and reduce the whole to one power." Opinion on the Constitutionality of the Bill for Establishing a National Bank, in 19 Papers of Thomas Jefferson 275, 279-280 (1974). Hamilton in turn offered a defense of the constitutionality of the bank that was quite close to Chief Justice Marshall's. See A. Hamilton, Opinion on the Constitutionality of an Act to Establish a Bank, 8 Papers of Alexander Hamilton 97 (1965):

> It is essential to the being of the National government, that so erroneous a conception of the meaning of the word *necessary,* should be exploded.
>   It is certain, that neither the grammatical, nor popular sense of the term requires that construction. According to both, *necessary* often means no more than *needful, requisite, incidental, useful,* or *conducive to.* . . .
>   [This] is the true [meaning] in which it is to be understood as used in the constitution. The whole turn of the clause containing it indicates that it was the intent of the convention, by that clause to give a liberal latitude to the existence of the specified powers. . . .
>   [Any other] interpretation would beget endless uncertainty & embarrassment. The cases must be palpable and extreme in which it could be pronounced with certainty, that a measure was absolutely necessary, or one without which the exercise of a given power would be nugatory. . . .

Hamilton went on to explain that the creation of a national bank had "a relation more or less direct to the power of collecting taxes; to that of borrowing money; to that of regulating trade between the states; and to those of raising, supporting & maintaining fleets and armies."

In 1811 the bank's charter lapsed, and Congress did not renew it. The private business and banking communities vigorously opposed renewal. In 1815, however, Congress created a second Bank of the United States, responding to a period of considerable economic turmoil following the War of 1812. At this stage there was little discussion of the constitutional question. Jefferson himself supported the Bank, partly in response to political pressures and perceived practical necessities, and Madison wrote that the issue had been settled in favor of its constitutionality. But many states objected to the creation of a second bank and imposed taxes of the sort at issue in *McCulloch.* To what extent, if any, do you think the decision in *McCulloch* was or should have been different in 1819 from what it would have been if the issue had arisen in 1791?

2. *Methods of constitutional interpretation.* Note Chief Justice Marshall's remarks on the distinctive character of constitutions and of constitutional interpretation.

Marshall's suggestion that "it is a *constitution* we are expounding" has been called, by no less an authority than Justice Frankfurter, "the single most important utterance in the literature of constitutional law — most important because most comprehensive and most comprehending." Frankfurter, John Marshall and the Judicial Function, 69 Harv. L. Rev. 217, 219 (1955). But the statement and the interpretive strategies to which it has led are not universally admired. Compare, for example, Justice Frankfurter's suggestion that "precisely *because* 'it is a *constitution* we are expounding,' we ought not to take liberties with it." National Mutual Insurance Co. v. Tidewater Transfer Co., 337 U.S. 581, 647 (1949) (Frankfurter, J., dissenting). See also Kurland, Curia Regis: Some Comments on the Divine Right of Kings and Courts to Say What the Law Is, 23 Ariz. L. Rev. 582, 591 (1981), suggesting that whenever a judge quotes this passage "you can be sure that the court will be throwing the constitutional text, its history, and its structure to the winds in reaching its conclusion."

What is distinctive about the process of constitutional interpretation, as compared with that of statutory interpretation? Under Marshall's view of interpretation, how much latitude does a judge have in the process of construing the Constitution?

Consider the following possible interpretations of Marshall's position. (1) The power-granting provisions of the Constitution should be broadly construed. Those provisions are meant to endure over time; they should be interpreted flexibly as new and unforeseen problems arise. (2) All provisions of the Constitution, including those granting powers and those creating rights, should be broadly construed. (3) The meaning of the Constitution changes over time with changing circumstances, in accordance with changing social needs; judges need not adhere to the specific "intent" of the framers, but must interpret the legal text flexibly in light of contemporary necessities. See the discussion of framers' intent, supra.

In contrasting Marshall's approach to interpretation in *McCulloch* to his approach in *Marbury*, consider the following view: *Marbury* rested on a perception that the process of interpretation was essentially mechanical. That understanding was the ground on which the institution of judicial review was founded. In *McCulloch*, the understanding of interpretation is different, for it recognizes that judges and other interpreters will have considerable discretion. What consequences does this difference have for constitutional law? And what light did the framers' "intent" cast on the various questions in *McCulloch*? What are the implications of the fact that Hamilton and Madison were in disagreement?

3. *Structural approaches to constitutional interpretation.* In the view of some, the approach in *McCulloch* is distinctive in large part because of Marshall's willingness to rely on the "structures and relationships" set up by the Constitution, and not only the text, in resolving constitutional questions.

> I am inclined to think well of the method of reasoning from structure and relation. I think well of it, above all, because to succeed it has to make sense — current, practical sense. The textual-explication method, operating on general language, [contains] within itself no guarantee that it will make sense, for a court may always present itself or even see itself as being bound by the stated intent, however nonsensical, of somebody else. [With structural approaches] we can and must begin to argue at once about the practicalities and proprieties of the thing, without getting out dictionaries whose entries will not really respond to the question we are putting. [We] will have to deal with policy and not with grammar.

C. Black, Structure and Relationship in Constitutional Law 22-23 (1969). Does Black's position mean that the Constitution should be interpreted to mean whatever the judges think it *should* mean? Does it leave more or less interpretive freedom than a "textual-explication" approach? Does it point to the right or the wrong questions?

3. *The necessary and proper clause; implied powers.* a. What, if anything, does the necessary and proper clause add, in the Court's view, to the constitutional powers granted to the Congress? Note that the Court's analysis of the problem of "implied" powers depends in the first instance not on the language or history of the Constitution, but on the perceived adverse consequences that would arise from a contrary construction. What role should such perceptions of consequences play in constitutional interpretation?

Did the *McCulloch* decision recognize implied powers at all? Or did it merely recognize that a power includes appropriate means for achieving the intended end? What is the difference between these formulations?

b. The Court's construction of the necessary and proper clause resolved an extraordinarily important interpretive question that had divided, among others, Thomas Jefferson and Alexander Hamilton. On what does Marshall base his acceptance of the Hamilton position? Note the pertinence of the suggestion that that "provision is made in a constitution intended to endure for ages to come, and, consequently, to be adapted to the various crises of human affairs."

c. Even with the Court's interpretation of the necessary and proper clause, it is necessary to explain how the creation of a national bank is "necessary and proper" to the exercise of one of Congress's enumerated powers. What enumerated powers are helpful here? Consider Currie, The Constitution in the Supreme Court: State and National Powers, 1801-1835, 49 U. Chi. L. Rev. 887, 932-933, noting that Marshall "mentioned in passing various enumerated powers to which the creation of a bank might be incidental. [What] is striking is that he made no serious effort to demonstrate how the bank was necessary and proper, or even conducive, to any one of them." But consider the implications of Marshall's reference to the extended territory of the United States. Is Hamilton's explanation persuasive in this regard?

d. What limitations does Marshall recognize on congressional power? The key sentence here, frequently quoted by the Supreme Court throughout its history, is: "Let the end be legitimate, let it be within the scope of the Constitution, and all means which are appropriate, which are plainly adapted to that end, which are not prohibited, but consist with the letter and spirit of the Constitution, are constitutional." The Court adds that if Congress enacts a law "for the accomplishment of objects not entrusted to the national government," and if Congress has acted under the "pretext" of using its enumerated powers, the law will be invalidated. Does this mean that the Court will scrutinize the motivations of legislators? (The benefits and disadvantages of motivation-centered inquiries are explored infra at Chapter 3.) What else might it mean?

4. *The tenth amendment.* The second principal provision interpreted in *McCulloch* is the tenth amendment. How does Marshall construe this provision? Does the tenth amendment add anything of substance to the Constitution, in Marshall's view? Note that in the Articles of Confederation, the word "expressly" preceded the limitation analogous to the tenth amendment. How much support does the deletion of that word add to Marshall's construction?

5. *Representation-reinforcement.* Marshall finds an implicit prohibition on state taxation of the national bank. What constitutional provision does the tax violate?

Marshall's analysis of the problem is largely an inquiry, not into the constitutional text and history, but into the operation of representative government. "In imposing a tax the legislature acts upon its constituents. This is in general a sufficient security against erroneous and oppressive taxation." And in "the legislature of the Union alone, are all represented." The claim here is that the power to elect representatives will act as a safeguard against the abuse of political power by elected officials. The judicial role is defined by reference to the understanding that the political process itself will ensure against improper conduct. Does Marshall overlook the possibility that constituents, or subgroups thereof, might not have sufficient political power to prevent oppression?

Marshall also indicates that the ordinary presumption — that the processes of representation are an effective safeguard against abuse — disappears when a state imposes taxes on a national instrumentality because in so doing, the state is harming people who are not represented in the state legislature. Judicial intervention is justified in order to make up for the absence of political remedies for those burdened by legislative action. But if citizens generally are oppressed by state taxation of national banks, doesn't Congress have the power to enact a law to outlaw state taxation? Why is judicial intervention necessary or appropriate? Consider the possibility that the immunity is conferred by the statute creating the Bank, interpreted in light of the concerns about representation.

Note, by contrast, Marshall's suggestion that while the federal government has an (implicit) immunity from state taxation, states may not be immune from federal taxation. How does Marshall's theory of representation operate differently here? For further discussion of intergovernmental immunity, see Chapter 3 infra.

McCulloch might be understood as the foundation for the notion of "representation-reinforcement" as a justification of and guide for judicial action — a prominent theme in constitutional law. The central idea is that the judicial role is to make up for defects in the ordinary operation of representative government; the source of judicial decision is a breakdown in political processes. See generally J. Ely, Democracy and Distrust (1980). How does this approach differ from that in *Marbury*? The problem of representation-reinforcement is taken up below in Chapters 3 and 5.

CALDER v. BULL, 3 U.S. (3 Dall.) 386 (1798): The Connecticut legislature ordered a new trial in a will contest, setting aside a judicial decree. The Court unanimously held that the legislature's action was not an "ex post facto Law" forbidden the states by article I, section 10. Although Justices Chase and Iredell agreed on the "ex post facto" issue, they disagreed over the appropriate role of "natural law" in constitutional interpretation. Justice Chase wrote:

"I cannot subscribe to the omnipotence of a state legislature, or that it is absolute and without control; although its authority should not be expressly restrained by the constitution, or fundamental law of the state. The people of the United States erected their constitutions or forms of government, to establish justice, to promote the general welfare, to secure the blessings of liberty, and to protect their persons and property from violence. The purposes for which men enter into society will determine the nature and terms of the social compact; and as they are the foundation of the legislative power, they will decide what are the proper objects of it. The nature, and ends of legislative power will limit the exercise of it. This fundamental principle flows from the very nature of our free republican governments. [There] are acts which the federal, or state legislature cannot do, without exceeding their authority. There are certain vital principles in our free republican governments, which will determine and overrule an apparent and flagrant abuse of legislative power. [An] act of the legislature (for I cannot call it a law), contrary to the great first principles in the social compact, cannot be considered a rightful exercise of legislative authority. [A] law that punishes a citizen for an innocent [action;] a law that destroys or impairs the lawful private contracts of citizens; a law that makes a man a judge in his own cause; or a law that takes property from A. and gives it to B.: it is against all reason and justice, for a people to entrust a legislature with such powers; and therefore, it cannot be presumed that they have done it. The genius, the nature and the spirit of our state governments, amount to a prohibition of such acts of legislation; and the general principles of law and reason forbid them. [To] maintain that our federal, or state legislature possesses such powers, if they had not been expressly restrained, would, in my opinion, be a political heresy, altogether inadmissible in our free republican governments." (Chase upheld the legislature's action, however, for "it impaired no vested right and therefore was consistent with natural justice." Currie, The Constitution in the Supreme Court: 1789-1801, 48 U. Chi. L. Rev. 819, 872 (1981).)

Justice Iredell replied: "[Some] speculative jurists have held, that a legislative act against natural justice must, in itself, be void; but I cannot think that, under such a government any court of justice would possess a power to declare it so. [It] has been the policy of all the American states, [and] of the people of the United States, [to] define with precision the objects of the legislative power, and to restrain its exercise within marked and settled boundaries. If any act of congress, or of the legislature of a state, violates those constitutional provisions, it is unquestionably void. [If,] on the other hand, the legislature of the Union, or the legislature of any member of the Union, shall pass a law, within the general scope of their constitutional power, the court cannot pronounce it to be void, merely because it is, in their judgment, contrary to the principles of natural justice. The ideas of natural justice are regulated by no fixed standard: the ablest and the purest men have differed upon the subject; and all that the court could properly say, in such an event, would be, that the legislature (possessed of an equal right of opinion) had passed an act which, in the opinion of the judges, was inconsistent with the abstract principles of natural justice. [If] the legislature pursue the authority delegated to them, their acts are valid. [In such circumstances,] they exercise the discretion vested in them by the people, to whom alone they are responsible for the faithful discharge of their trust."

Note: Natural Law and the Supreme Court

The dispute between Justice Chase and Justice Iredell has proved fundamental to constitutional law. It has two basic elements. First, did the framers intend to confer on the Supreme Court the authority to invalidate statutes that do not transgress any judgment specifically attributable to the framers of the Constitution? Does the Constitution — either in general or in some of its provisions — authorize judges to invalidate laws on normative grounds that are independent of the specific value judgments of the framers? Such questions raise an objection to a "natural law court" that might be called the argument from contract.

Second, and quite apart from the framers' "intent" or constitutional authorization, is it desirable to authorize judges to invalidate laws on such grounds? Some argue that recognition of such authority is indispensable as a protection against the potential injustice of majoritarian government. Others contend that a judicial role of that sort would be intolerable in light of the basic constitutional commitment to electoral control of public officials. This position raises an objection to a natural law court that might be called the argument from democracy.

1. *The framers' "intent."* Marbury v. Madison rested in part on the understanding that a written Constitution necessarily contemplated judicial enforcement of its terms. Otherwise, the restrictions imposed by the Constitution would be meaningless. We have seen that the argument is in some respects vulnerable. But Justice Chase goes further. His position is that there is an "unwritten" Constitution, consisting of principles of natural law, which is enforceable as against the states even though it cannot be found in the Constitution.

Justice Iredell's response is that the very fact of a written Constitution is authority against the position that courts may call on principles of natural justice. But does Justice Chase's position itself show that at least some of the framers believed in the existence of a natural law supplement to the Constitution's explicit prohibitions? See in this regard Grey, Do We Have an Unwritten Constitution?, 27 Stan. L. Rev. 703 (1975); Grey, Origins of the Unwritten Constitution, 30 Stan. L. Rev. 843 (1978), suggesting that the framers believed that judges would enforce a category of natural law constraints on state and federal legislation. But see J. Ely, Democracy and Distrust (1980), for a skeptical view. On the ninth amendment, see Chapter 6 infra.

2. *A natural law Court.* What would be the advantages and disadvantages of recognizing judicial authority of the sort claimed by Justice Chase? Consider M. Perry, The Courts, the Constitution, and Human Rights 100-101 (1982):

> In any recent generation, certain political issues have been widely perceived to be fundamental moral issues as well — issues that challenge and unsettle conventional ways of understanding the moral universe and that serve as occasions for forging alternative ways of understanding. In twentieth-century America, there have been several such issues: for example, distributive justice and the role of government, freedom of political dissent, racism and sexism, the death penalty, human sexuality. Our electorally accountable policymaking institutions are not well suited to deal with such issues in a way that is faithful to the notion of moral evolution. [Those] institutions, when finally they confront such issues at all, tend simply to rely on established moral conventions and to refuse to see in such issues occasions for moral revaluation and possible moral growth. [Executive] and especially legislative officials tend to deal with fundamental political-moral problems, at least highly controversial ones, by reflexive reference to the established moral conventions of the greater part of their particular constituencies.

See also A. Bickel, The Least Dangerous Branch (1962); Dworkin, The Forum of Principle, 56 N.Y.U. L. Rev. 469 (1981); Wellington, Common Law Rules and Constitutional Double Standards: Some Notes on Adjudication, 83 Yale L.J. 221 (1973).

This view seems to depend on a skeptical view of the political process as consisting of a more or less mechanical reflection of constituent pressures. In its most extreme form, this view treats politics as an unprincipled power struggle among self-interested groups, or factions. This view has played a prominent role in modern political and economic theory. See Stigler, A Theory of Economic Regulation, 2 Bell. J.L. & Mgmt. Sci. 3 (1971); R. Dahl, A Preface to Democratic Theory (1956). In this view, Justice Chase's classic violation of natural law — taking from A to give to B — is a frequent occurrence. If the skeptical view is accepted, an active judicial role in deciding moral issues might seem attractive.

But does this view depend on an unduly pessimistic view of politics, an unwarranted belief in the possibility of "right answers" to political questions, an unduly optimistic view of judicial decisionmaking, or all three? Whether representatives in fact respond mechanically to political pressures is a sharply disputed question. A. Maass, Congress and the Common Good (1983), suggests that members of Congress often engage in some form of deliberation about what the public good requires. Note also that Perry's view — like Chase's acceptance of natural law — depends on the existence of "right answers" to moral questions; it thus rests on a rejection of ethical or moral skepticism — the view that issues of politics or morality present problems of taste or aesthetics and are not susceptible to answer. Consider, for example, the issues of abortion, segregation, and discrimination on the basis of gender. Are there right answers to the dilemmas those issues pose? If not, might interest-group politics be the best available alternative? On natural law and moral skepticism, see Chapter 6 infra.

Even if one accepts the skeptical view of politics, and believes that ethical and political questions have right answers, one might respond as did Judge Learned Hand: "For myself it would be most irksome to be ruled by a bevy of nine Platonic Guardians, even if I knew how to choose them, which I assuredly do not." L. Hand, The Bill of Rights 73 (1958). One might be mistrustful of courts even if one is not skeptical about the existence of at least some form of natural law. Consider also Hand's claim that "A society so riven that the spirit of moderation is gone, no court can save; a society where that spirit flourishes, no court need save; and in a society which evades its responsibilities by thrusting upon the courts the nurture of that spirit, that spirit in the end will perish." L. Hand, The Contribution of an Independent Judiciary to Civilization (1944), in I. Dilliard, ed., The Spirit of Liberty 155, 164 (1960). Underlying this view is a perception, first, that an active judicial role like that set out by Justice Chase is an impermissible intrusion on the workings of electoral democracy and, second, that there is no assurance against usurpation by the judges. This latter claim forces one to return to the various possible bases for preventing judicial outcomes from amounting to the imposition of personal preferences. See Chapter 7 infra.

See also A. Cox, The Role of the Supreme Court in American Government 116 (1976): "I should be no less irked than Judge Hand if the Supreme Court were to void an ordinance adopted in the open Town Meeting in the New England town in which I live — a meeting in which all citizens can participate — but I should have little such feeling about a statute enacted by the Massachusetts legislature in the normal political pattern, and none about a law made in that pattern by the Congress of the United States." Does this view undervalue the fact that state and federal laws are at least in some sense the product of representative processes?

D. THE POWER OF REPRISAL: POLITICAL CONTROL OF THE SUPREME COURT

However the power of judicial review may be limited by constraints that are internal to the interpretive process, that power grants to the Supreme Court considerable authority over the structure and substance of U.S. government. This section examines ways in which the Court's authority is subject to *external political control*. A principal issue here is whether and to what extent those mechanisms of control affect the perceived tension between the power of judicial review and conventional notions of representative democracy.

Note: Amendment, Appointment, Impeachment, and the Election Returns

1. *Constitutional amendment.* The most straightforward way for the people to respond to a Supreme Court decision with which they disagree is to amend the Constitution. But an amendment is difficult to obtain. Under article V, the amending process may begin only if two-thirds of both Houses propose an amendment or if the legislatures of two-thirds of the states call for a constitutional convention. No amendment may be adopted until it is ratified by three-fourths of the states. These requirements were a deliberate effort to make it difficult to amend the Constitution. Why were constitutional amendments to be discouraged? Why should judges be the principal constitutional decisionmakers?

Consider in this regard Jefferson's view that the Constitution should be rewritten by the people every generation, on the theory that without frequent constitution-making, there would be too little participation in and concern for the affairs of government. See Letter to Samuel Kercheval, July 12, 1816, in The Portable Thomas Jefferson 552, 558-561 (1975). Note in particular the view that.

> Some men look at constitutions with sanctimonious reverence, and deem them like the ark of the covenant, too sacred to be touched. They ascribe to the men of the preceding age a wisdom more than human, and suppose what they did to be beyond amendment. I knew that age well. [It] was very like the present, but without the experience of the present. [Let] us [not] weakly believe that one generation is not as capable as another of taking care of itself, and of ordering its own affairs.

Id. at 558-559. See generally H. Arendt, On Revolution (1965), for discussion of Jefferson's preference for citizen participation in affairs of government.

Madison rejected such proposals on the ground that they would produce "the most violent struggle between the parties interested in reviving and those interested in reforming the antecedent state of property." Letter to Thomas Jefferson, February 4, 1790, in M. Meyers, ed., The Mind of the Founder 232 (1969). Compare The Federalist Nos. 10 and 51, section A supra. Jefferson's contrary view was that even turbulence "is productive of good. It prevents the degeneracy of government, and nourishes a general attention to the public affairs. I hold that a little rebellion now and then is a good thing." Letter to Madison, Jan. 30, 1787, in

The Portable Thomas Jefferson, supra, at 416-417. Under this view, frequent revision of basic institutional arrangements might be welcomed. But as Madison's view suggests, the stability of the Constitution is often taken to be one of its great virtues. Consider in this regard the discussion of the separation of the realm of law and the realm of politics in The Federalist No. 78 and in *Marbury* itself. If frequent constitutional amendments were permitted, that distinction would be much less crisp; the effect of insulating certain decisions from politics would be undermined. Would that be a good or a bad thing?

Note also that many states make it possible to amend the Constitution through simple referendum. As a result, state constitutions are frequently altered. Under such regimes, the public is frequently involved in the process of constitutional decisionmaking. Consider the views expressed by Thayer, supra. What are the advantages and disadvantages of such systems? Might they operate as a salutary check on judicial review? Or do they erase the advantages of ensuring that an insulated body will decide constitutional issues?

There are now twenty-six amendments to the federal Constitution. Four of them represent successful efforts to overturn decisions by the Supreme Court. See U.S. Const. amends. XI (limiting jurisdiction of federal courts to hear suits brought against states); XIV (deeming Americans of African descent citizens of the United States); XVI (expanding power of Congress to tax); XXVI (setting voting age). Numerous other amendments have been offered, but without success. They have dealt with, for example, child labor, abortion, school desegregation, school prayer, and a balanced budget. Consider also the lengthy history of the proposed Equal Rights Amendment, discussed in Chapter 5 infra, which would have provided that equality under the law may not be denied on the basis of sex. See J. Mansbridge, Why We Lost the ERA (forthcoming 1986). For what issues is constitutional amendment desirable?

Consider the following views. (a) For reasons hinted at by Madison, there should be a strong presumption against any constitutional amendment. The Constitution is a broad charter of government with sufficient flexibility to accommodate changes in circumstances. It is a mistake to "constitutionalize" any particular set of norms in the absence of exceptional circumstances. (b) For reasons set out by Jefferson, proposed amendments should be welcomed. There is no reason to give special deference to past decisions. The amendment process involves the democratic process in constitutional law; and that is a good thing. (c) Constitutional amendments should be adopted only if they are structural. The Constitution is concerned by and large with institutional design; structural provisions allow flexibility for current majorities. Under this view, a balanced budget amendment, for example, should be disfavored; it "would impose a controversial economic doctrine on the Constitution." Note, The Balanced Budget Amendment: An Inquiry into Appropriateness, 96 Harv. L. Rev. 1600, 1619 (1983). Where does an individual rights provision fit in this framework?

Might it be argued that even if efforts at amendment are unsuccessful, they should be welcomed because of the effect that they have on the public and the Court itself? Consider the possibility that amendment efforts, like political pressure generally, exercise some influence over Supreme Court decisions.

If a constitutional convention is called, would its authority be limited to particular issues, or would it have general authority to amend the constitution as it chooses? See Special Constitutional Convention Study Committee, American Bar Association, Amendment of the Constitution by the Convention Method under Article V (1974). Should a court decide the issue? See the materials on the political question doctrine, section E infra.

On the amending process generally, see C. Vose, Constitutional Change: Amendment Politics and Supreme Court Litigation since 1900 (1972); Corwin & Ramsey, The Constitutional Law of Constitutional Amendment, 26 Notre Dame Law. 165 (1951); Dellinger, The Legitimacy of Constitutional Change: Rethinking the Amendment Process, 87 Harv. L. Rev. 386 (1983); Symposium on the Article V Convention Process, 66 Mich. L. Rev. 837 (1968).

2. *The power to appoint.* Members of the Supreme Court are appointed by the President, subject to the advice and consent of the Senate. As a result, the President has an opportunity to put justices on the Court who share his views. The appointing power has been important in controlling the direction of the Supreme Court. President Roosevelt responded to the efforts of the Court to invalidate aspects of the New Deal by appointing, among others, Justices Black, Douglas, Frankfurter, Stone, and Jackson. All of them turned out to be generally sympathetic to government regulation of the economy, although there developed sharp disputes among them over the scope of judicial protection of individual rights. After election campaigns marked by an emphasis on obtaining "strict constructionists" on the Court, President Nixon appointed Chief Justice Burger and Justices Blackmun, Powell, and Rehnquist. Those appointments led to a more conservative Court and brought about some changes of direction, albeit of disputed scope, see V. Blasi, ed., The Burger Court: The Counterrevolution That Wasn't (1983).

But Presidents have sometimes been surprised to find that their appointees' performance on the bench was more "liberal" or more "conservative" than expected. President Eisenhower, for example, appointed Earl Warren as Chief Justice, relying in part on Warren's conservative, law-and-order reputation as governor of California. Eisenhower later claimed that the appointment was one of the worst mistakes he had ever made. Eisenhower also appointed Justice Brennan, whose record turned out to be quite different from what had been expected.

Events of this sort indicate that the appointments process is not a guarantee of political control. But the record suggests that the appointments process makes it unlikely that Supreme Court justices will diverge too sharply or for too long from the desires of those with political power. See generally H. Abraham, Justices and Presidents (1985); J. Schmidhauser, Judges and Justices (1979). Note, however, that ideology is far from the only consideration in the appointments process. Region, race, gender, and religion of the appointee will often play a role in the President's decision. For general discussion, see id. at 41-82.

The appointment decision is not the President's alone. Consider the view that "the role of the Senate as well as interest groups cannot be overlooked. Particularly in periods in which a president lacked party or ideological support in the Senate, the influence of senatorial confirmation assumed far-reaching importance. Approximately one-fifth of the presidential nominations for Supreme Court appointments have been dealt with negatively by the Senate." Id. at 91. The Senate's power to advise and consent may affect the composition of the Court in two ways. First, it may lead the President to avoid highly controversial appointees. Second, the Senate may refuse to confirm presidential appointees — for reasons of incompetence, venality, or ideology. In this century, however, Supreme Court nominees have been rejected on only three occasions — President Nixon's appointments of Judges Haynesworth and Carswell and President Hoover's appointment of Judge John Parker. Earlier Senates exercised a more active role. See generally L. Tribe, God Save This Honorable Court (1985).

Would a resumption of that earlier role be desirable? Should the Senate disapprove Supreme Court nominees who are perceived to be too "conservative" or too "liberal"?

3. *Impeachment.* Justices of the Supreme Court "hold their Offices during good Behavior." U.S. Const. art. III, §1. They may "be removed from Office on Impeachment for, and Conviction of, Treason, Bribery, or other high Crimes and Misdemeanors." Under what circumstances may federal judges be impeached? See, for general discussion, Chapter 4 infra; R. Berger, Impeachment (1970).

No Supreme Court justice has been impeached in the nation's history. But there have been a number of efforts to impeach federal judges, including members of the lower federal courts. See K. Hall, The Politics of Justice (1979). The most celebrated recent example involved Justice Douglas. A resolution calling for an investigation referred, among other things, to Justice Douglas's having married four times; to the fact that one of his former wives was "a cocktail waitress"; to his votes in favor of defendants in cases involving "subversive questions"; to his traveling to Peking; and to various "left-wing" statements in his book, Points of Rebellion. See 116 Cong. Rec. H12,111-12,114 (daily ed. April 16, 1970). An impeachment resolution was introduced against him in part on the basis of articles published in Playboy magazine, in which Justice Douglas, among other things, expressed some sympathy for rebellious groups in the 1960s. In the course of the proceedings, then-Representative Ford argued that the grounds for impeachment were "whatever a majority of the House of Representatives considers them to be at a given moment in history." 116 Cong. Rec. H3113-3114 (daily ed. April 15, 1970).

Notwithstanding the latter suggestion, the device of impeachment has not been used as a means of obtaining political control over the Supreme Court. This phenomenon may be attributable in part to the prestige of an independent judiciary, in part to general acceptance of Marbury v. Madison, and in part to legal doubts about the wisdom and legality of the impeachment mechanisms for such purposes. On the latter question, see Chapter 4 infra.

4. *Controlling sitting judges; informal mechanisms and self-imposed limits.* To what extent is the Supreme Court subject to informal mechanisms of control? Mr. Dooley — the pen name and principal character of Finley Peter Dunne, who wrote around the turn of the century — explained in a now-celebrated statement that "No matter whether th' constitution follows th' flag or not, th' supreme coort follows th' ilection returns." P. Dunne, The Supreme Court's Decisions, in Mr. Dooley's Opinions 26 (1900). This statement is not literally true, but there can be little doubt that the Court is reluctant to make decisions that depart too sharply from what it perceives as a political consensus. As some have suggested, the Court has, or perceives itself as having, a limited amount of "political capital," and it tends to budget its expenditure of that capital in the number and kinds of controversial decisions it renders. See J. Choper, Judicial Review and the National Political Process (1981); A. Bickel, The Least Dangerous Branch (1962).

The Court's perception of its limited political capital may sometimes manifest itself in sensitivity to the views of elected officials and private citizens. Thus, for example, the fall of the *Lochner* period — in which the Court struggled against government regulation of the economy, see Chapter 7 infra — may be under-stood in part as a response to popular pressures, though the problem of identify-ing "cause and effect" is formidable. See C. Vose, Constitutional Change, supra. There are few occasions in the nation's history in which the Court has persisted in a course to which the country is sharply opposed. See A. Bickel, supra. On the other hand, the Court's decisions may themselves help to shape a national con-sensus (is that a good or a bad thing?), and it is undoubtedly true that on occasion the Court has been willing to insist on a course of action notwithstanding consid-erable public disagreement. Consider in this regard the school prayer contro-versy, Chapter 8 infra, the problem of school desegregation, Chapter 5 infra, and the abortion controversy, Chapter 6 infra. There is little empirical work on the effect of popular opinion on Supreme Court decisions, perhaps because of the difficulties in tracing causation. Perhaps the most that can be said is that the Court is sometimes sensitive to the perceived mood of the country and that it is generally unwilling to continue for long periods on courses that face intense popular disagreement.

Ex Parte McCardle

74 U.S. (7 Wall.) 506 (1869)

[McCardle published articles in a newspaper in Mississippi, which was then under the control of the national army pursuant to the Reconstruction plan adopted by Congress after the Civil War. He was arrested under charges of libel, disturbing the peace, inciting insurrection, disorder, and violence, and impeding recon-struction. McCardle sought habeas corpus from a federal court in Mississippi, claiming that Congress lacked constitutional authority to establish a system of military government in the states. The case was in this sense a fundamental challenge to Congress's reconstruction power. After losing in the trial court, McCardle appealed, invoking a habeas corpus act enacted in 1867. Congress feared that the case would be a vehicle for invalidating the reconstruction plan. Congress therefore enacted — while the case was pending, and over presidential veto on constitutional grounds — a statute that repealed the provision of the 1867 habeas corpus act that McCardle had invoked.]

THE CHIEF JUSTICE delivered the opinion of the court.

The first question necessarily is that of jurisdiction; for, if the act of March, 1868, takes away the jurisdiction defined by the act of February, 1867, it is useless, if not improper, to enter into any discussion of other questions.

It is quite true, as was argued by the counsel for the petitioner, that the appel-late jurisdiction of this court is not derived from acts of Congress. It is, strictly speaking, conferred by the Constitution. But it is conferred "with such exceptions and under such regulations as Congress shall make."

It is unnecessary to consider whether, if Congress had made no exceptions and no regulations, this court might not have exercised general appellate jurisdiction under rules prescribed by itself. For among the earliest acts of the first Congress, at its first session, was the act of September 24th, 1789, to establish the judicial courts of the United States. That act provided for the organization of this court, and prescribed regulations for the exercise of its jurisdiction. . . .

The principle that the affirmation of appellate jurisdiction implies the negation of all such jurisdiction not affirmed having been thus established, it was an almost necessary consequence that acts of Congress, providing for the exercise of jurisdiction, should come to be spoken of as acts granting jurisdiction, and not as acts making exceptions to the constitutional grant of it.

The exception to appellate jurisdiction in the case before us, however, is not an inference from the affirmation of other appellate jurisdiction. It is made in terms. The provision of the act of 1867, affirming the appellate jurisdiction of this court in cases of habeas corpus is expressly repealed. It is hardly possible to imagine a plainer instance of positive exception.

We are not at liberty to inquire into the motives of the legislature. We can only examine into its power under the Constitution; and the power to make exceptions to the appellate jurisdiction of this court is given by express words.

What, then, is the effect of the repealing act upon the case before us? We cannot doubt as to this. Without jurisdiction the court cannot proceed at all in any cause. Jurisdiction is power to declare the law, and when it ceases to exist, the only function remaining to the court is that of announcing the fact and dismissing the cause. And this is not less clear upon authority than upon principle.

Counsel seem to have supposed, if effect be given to the repealing act in question, that the whole appellate power of the court, in cases of habeas corpus, is denied. But this is an error. The act of 1868 does not except from that jurisdiction any cases but appeals from Circuit Courts under the act of 1867. It does not affect the jurisdiction which was previously exercised.

The appeal of the petitioner in this case must be dismissed for want of jurisdiction.

Note: Political Control over Jurisdiction of Article III Courts

Does Ex parte McCardle stand for the proposition that Congress has plenary power over the appellate jurisdiction of the Supreme Court? In Ex parte Yerger, 75 U.S. (8 Wall.) 85 (1869), the Court converted into a holding the last paragraph of the McCardle opinion. In Yerger, the Court asserted appellate jurisdiction over a habeas corpus proceeding brought by a petitioner in military detention. The source of jurisdiction was certiorari based on pre-1867 legislation. The language of Ex parte McCardle suggests that there are no constitutional constraints on Congress's power over the appellate jurisdiction of the Supreme Court; but its holding might be read more narrowly in light of the conclusion, noted in McCardle itself and made clear in Yerger, that there was an alternative means of obtaining Supreme Court review.

The question of congressional power over the appellate jurisdiction of the Supreme Court has assumed considerable importance in light of recent proposals to prevent the Supreme Court from hearing cases involving (among other things) school prayer, reapportionment, school desegregation, and abortion. No such proposal has yet passed Congress. But there has been substantial debate about the constitutionality of the proposals, versions of which have been introduced at numerous stages in the history of the nation. Consider the following:

Notwithstanding the provision of sections 1253, 1254, 1257 of this chapter the Supreme Court shall not have jurisdiction to review, by appeal, writ of certiorari, or otherwise, any case arising out of any State statute, ordinance, rule, regulation, or any part thereof, or arising out of any act interpreting, applying, or enforcing a State statute, ordinance, rule, or regulation, which relates to voluntary prayers in public schools and public buildings.

1. *Restricting jurisdiction and the separation of powers.* If plenary power to restrict jurisdiction existed, Congress could immunize state and federal laws from Supreme Court review. Congress could, for example, enact a law and provide that the Supreme Court could not assess its constitutionality. Indeed, Congress could for all practical purposes cut the Supreme Court out of the constitutional scheme — for example, by depriving the Court of jurisdiction in all federal question cases. At first glance, such a power might seem to be a striking intrusion on the separation of powers scheme.

Would it be possible to argue that the power to restrict jurisdiction is not such an intrusion at all but is instead a means of making it tolerable to have judicial review in a system of representative government? See P. Bator, P. Mishkin, D. Shapiro & H. Wechsler, Hart & Wechsler's The Federal Courts and the Federal System 363 (1973); C. Black, Decision According to Law (1981). Under this view, the availability of the power to limit jurisdiction is an important check on the Supreme Court, discouraging it from straying too far from "popular will," as expressed in legislative and executive enactments, and allowing the legislature to retain ultimate control over the Court. At the same time, the existence of an unexercised but broad exceptions power gives reason to find public acquiescence in or ratification of Supreme Court decisions. Do such arguments attribute too much to legislative inaction?

In any event, the nature and limits of the exceptions power remain shrouded in uncertainty. The remainder of this Note outlines some of the competing views.

2. *The plenary power argument.* To some, the exceptions clause grants Congress plenary power over the appellate jurisdiction of the Supreme Court. Congress may make exceptions whenever and for whatever reasons it chooses. This view draws support from the literal language of the Constitution. The text itself contains no limits on congressional power to make "exceptions" to the appellate jurisdiction of the Supreme Court. The only limits, in this view, are those that derive from the political process. The plenary power argument obtains support from McCardle and from numerous dicta in early cases. See Van Alstyne, A Critical Guide to *Ex Parte McCardle*, 15 Ariz. L. Rev. 229 (1973).

3. *Separation of powers constraints: the "essential functions" hypothesis.* One argument against recognition of a plenary power under the exceptions clause is based on the proposition that Congress cannot "destroy the essential role of the Supreme Court in the constitutional plan." Hart, The Power of Congress to Limit the Jurisdiction of Federal Courts: An Exercise in Dialectic, 66 Harv. L. Rev. 1362, 1365 (1953). The argument is largely a structural one. The framers, it is claimed, intended the Court to perform an important function in the separation of powers scheme: to ensure that Congress and the states are kept within constitutional limits. (Consider The Federalist No. 78 and Martin v. Hunter's Lessee.) If Congress had power to remove the Court's jurisdiction, it could insulate its own

laws, or those of the states, from constitutional attack, effectively writing the Court out of the constitutional system. Such a power, it is sometimes claimed, is not consistent with the intended function of courts in the separation of powers scheme. See Ratner, Congressional Power over the Appellate Jurisdiction of the Supreme Court, 109 U. Pa. L. Rev. 157 (1960); Letter from Attorney General Smith to Senator Strom Thurmond, May 6, 1982, in 128 Cong. Rec. S4727-4730 (daily ed. May 12, 1982).

Can this view be reconciled with the language of the exceptions clause? Proponents suggest that the use of the term "exceptions" itself contemplates a narrow power, one that is consistent with the general view that the Court would exercise jurisdiction in all or most federal question cases. See Ratner, supra; Sager, Foreword: Constitutional Limitations on Congress' Authority to Regulate the Jurisdiction of the Federal Courts, 95 Harv. L. Rev. 17 (1981). In this view, the extent of Congress's power may not be subject to precise limits, but it is clear that Congress cannot deprive the Court of jurisdiction in (all or some?) constitutional cases. See also R. Berger, Congress vs. the Supreme Court (1969) (suggesting that the exceptions power is limited to issues of fact).

Is this position supported or undermined by Marbury v. Madison? Consider Wechsler, The Courts and the Constitution, 65 Colum. L. Rev. 1001, 1005-1006 (1965):

> The plan of the Constitution for the courts [was] quite simply that the Congress would decide from time to time how far the federal judicial institution should be used within the limits of the federal judicial power. [Federal] courts, including the Supreme Court, do not pass on constitutional questions because there is a special function vested in them to enforce the Constitution or police the other agencies of government. They do so rather for the reason that they must decide a litigated case that is otherwise within their jurisdiction and in doing so must give effect to the supreme law of the land. That is, at least, what Marbury v. Madison was all about.

Is this a proper reading of Marbury? Consider the following view: Marbury and The Federalist No. 78 rest on the broader ground that the Supreme Court was accorded a distinctive role as the guarantor of the supremacy of the federal constitution as against the states and the federal legislature. Recognition of an unlimited power to make exceptions would be inconsistent with the intended role of the Supreme Court in the separation of powers scheme, generating precisely the evils that led Hamilton to support the existence of judicial review. Cf. Cooper v. Aaron, supra.

Does it matter whether the exceptions power is used to insulate federal or state laws from judicial review? Would the dangers be different in the two different cases? See Sager, Foreword: Constitutional Limitations on Congress' Authority to Regulate the Jurisdiction of the Federal Courts, 95 Harv. L. Rev. 17, 55 (1981):

> To remove or permit the removal from the entire federal judiciary, including the Supreme Court, of the constitutional review of state conduct would be to alter the balance of federal authority fundamentally and dangerously. In an observation intended to defuse rather than ignite the sense of crisis that surrounded the Court in 1913, Justice Holmes uttered his famous words on the matter of Supreme Court jurisdiction: "I do not think the United States would come to an end if we lost our

power to declare an Act of Congress void. I do think the Union would be imperiled if we could not make that declaration as to the laws of the several States." [The] case for regarding federal judicial supervision of the states as essential to the scheme of the Constitution is a strong one.

Even if it is accepted that there is an "essential functions" limitation on jurisdictional restrictions, the question remains whether particular provisions are inconsistent with the Court's "essential function." Would the bill reprinted above, eliminating federal court jurisdiction in school prayer cases, destroy the Supreme Court's "essential role"? Consider the fact that the Court would retain jurisdiction in all other cases raising constitutional questions. For the view that *any* restriction of the jurisdiction of the Supreme Court runs afoul of the "essential functions" test, see Ratner, supra. Compare Redish, Constitutional Limitations on Congressional Power to Control Federal Jurisdiction, 77 N.W.L. Rev. 143 (1982).

3. *Independent constitutional barriers.* There is little doubt that other constitutional provisions, like the equal protection clause, limit Congress's power under the exceptions clause. For example, Congress could not constitutionally provide that Republicans, but no one else, may have access to the Supreme Court. Such a provision would violate the first amendment and thus would be independently unconstitutional.

How far does this rationale extend? Does it justify a conclusion that selective withdrawals of jurisdiction — for example, busing, abortion, or school prayer — are unconstitutional? See Tribe, Jurisdictional Gerrymandering: Zoning Disfavored Rights out of the Federal Courts, 16 Harv. C.R.-C.L. L. Rev. 129 (1981). In the view of some, the answer might depend on the purpose of the withdrawal of jurisdiction. Suppose jurisdiction is withdrawn in school prayer cases in order to make it harder for litigants to vindicate their federal constitutional rights. Congress may think that state courts will be subject to popular control and thus be less willing to enforce the Constitution. (Recall Martin v. Hunter's Lessee.) If so, the argument goes, the withdrawal of jurisdiction in school prayer cases would be analytically equivalent to a denial of jurisdiction in cases involving Democrats as plaintiffs; in both cases, the motivation — to undo a constitutional decision or to interfere with a constitutional right — would be impermissible. Do you agree? Is the school prayer bill above unconstitutionally motivated? Does it violate the establishment clause? (For discussion of the relationship between school prayer and the clause, see Chapter 8 infra.) What constitutional provision would be violated by a statute denying jurisdiction in desegregation actions? Suppose that a jurisdictional limitation did not in fact make it harder to vindicate constitutional rights, because the state courts were available and willing to do so. Would the intent of Congress matter?

Consider Bator, Congressional Power over the Jurisdiction of the Federal Courts, 27 Villanova L. Rev. 1030, 1036-1037 (1982):

Neither the equal protection clause nor any other clause of the Constitution requires equal jurisdiction treatment for different subject-matters of litigation. [A] somewhat narrower argument is that if it is shown that Congress' motive in requiring a certain category of case to be brought in the exclusive original jurisdiction of the state courts is "hostility" to the substantive constitutional right in question, it can be struck down. I do not understand how such a rule could be administered. What would be an adequate indication of hostility? [The] state courts, equally with the federal, are charged with the task of enforcing and protecting federal constitutional rights.

4. *The relevance of United States v. Klein.* Consider in this regard United States v. Klein, 80 U.S. (13 Wall.) 128 (1872). Klein had sued for indemnification of property taken during the Civil War. It was a necessary predicate for relief that the claimant show that he was not a supporter of the rebellion against the national government; and the courts had held that a presidential pardon was evidence that the claimant had not in fact participated.

A statute, enacted while the United States' appeal was pending from a decision awarding indemnification to Klein, provided that a presidential pardon was to be used as evidence that the person pardoned had participated in a rebellion. The statute added that courts should dismiss suits involving such claimants for want of jurisdiction. The Court invalidated the statute on the ground that dismissal would allow Congress to "prescribe rules of decision to the Judicial Department of the government in cases pending before it." According to the Court, this was inconsistent with the separation of powers. The Court added that the statute would be permissible under the exceptions clause if it were a denial of "the right to appeal in a particular class of cases." The problem here was that it was "a means to an end," that is, denial "to pardons granted by the President of the effect which this court had adjudged them to have."

How might *Klein* be distinguished from *McCardle?* Did *Klein* involve not merely a withdrawal of jurisdiction, but an effort "to bind the Court to decide [the] case in accordance with a rule of law [that is] independently unconstitutional"? See P. Bator, P. Mishkin, D. Shapiro & H. Wechsler, Hart & Wechsler's The Federal Courts and the Federal System 316 (1973). Might *Klein* be distinguished from other selective withdrawals of jurisdiction?

Note also Justice Douglas's contention that "There is a serious question whether the *McCardle* case could command a majority view today." Glidden Co. v. Zdanok, 370 U.S. 530, 605 (1962) (dissenting opinion).

5. *The lower federal courts.* The power of Congress over the jurisdiction of the lower federal courts raises somewhat different issues. It is generally agreed that article III imposes on Congress no obligation to create lower federal courts at all. See Sheldon v. Sill, 49 U.S. (8 How.) 441 (1850). If Congress need not create lower federal courts, a natural inference might be that Congress has plenary power over the sorts of issues that lower courts might hear. This is a classic "lesser included" argument: The authority to create the lower courts necessarily includes the power to restrict the lower courts to certain specified issues.

The argument is also, however,

> based on the fact that this reading is the only one consistent with the understanding which animated the compromise adopted by the Framers. The essence of that compromise was an agreement that the question whether access to the lower courts was necessary to assure the effectiveness of federal law [should] be left a matter of political and legislative judgment, to be made from time to time in the light of particular circumstances. It would make nonsense of that notion to hold that the only power to be exercised is the all-or-nothing power to decide whether *none* or *all* of the cases to which the federal judicial power extends need the haven of a lower court.

Bator, Congressional Power over the Jurisdiction of the Federal Courts, 27 Villanova L. Rev. 1030, 1031 (1982).

Are there any limits on Congress's power over the lower federal courts? Suppose, for example, that Congress bars the lower federal courts from hearing cases involving abortion, school prayer, or desegregation — as numerous bills introduced in the late 1970s and 1980s threatened to do. Consider the following possibilities.

a. Eisenberg, in Congressional Authority to Restrict Lower Federal Court Jurisdiction, 83 Yale L.J. 498, 532-533 (1974), relies on the expansion of the caseload of the lower federal courts and their important role in protecting federal rights, to argue:

> The inability of the Supreme Court to do justice in every case within the Article III grant of jurisdiction has broad implications. It means that Congress cannot deny lower federal courts jurisdiction on the ground that Supreme Court review of state court judgments provides an adequate vindication for federal rights. [The] lower federal courts are thus indispensable if the judiciary is to be a co-equal branch and if the "judicial Power of the United States" is to remain the power to protect rights guaranteed by the Constitution and its amendments. Abolition of the lower federal courts is no longer constitutionally permissible.

b. The "independent constitutional constraints" on congressional limits on the jurisdiction of the Supreme Court apply as well to limits on the jurisdiction of the lower courts. Here the same considerations apply as discussed above. See supra.

c. Note also the position of Justice Story in Martin v. Hunter's Lessee, supra, to the effect that at any time, *some* federal court must have jurisdiction over any case to which the article III power extends. This view, however, has been rejected. Note that the diversity jurisdiction extends only to cases in which the amount in controversy is over $10,000.

Note: The Power of Reprisal — General Thoughts

What conclusions do these various mechanisms of control — constitutional amendment, appointment, impeachment, popular opinion, and jurisdictional limits — suggest? Do Congress and the President have enough, or too much, authority over the Court? Consider the following views. (1) In light of the various mechanisms of control, the countermajoritarian difficulty said to be produced by the existence of judicial review is much less severe than it appears at first glance. The various safeguards make it much less troublesome that interpretation is often or inevitably discretionary. (2) The mechanisms of control make the courts so dependent on the political branches that justifications for *Marbury* that rely on the political insulation of the judges tend to break down. It turns out that the judges are not insulated at all. (3) The various mechanisms are insufficient to allay the countermajoritarian difficulty. It remains the case that the power of judicial review permits unelected judges to have what is in effect the final say on issues of public importance. The fact that the judges are subject to some control through other means does not respond to the basic problem.

E. "CASE OR CONTROVERSY" REQUIREMENTS AND THE PASSIVE VIRTUES

A number of devices require or permit federal courts not to hear certain issues. Most of these devices are, in whole or in part, an inference from article III, section 2, providing that the "Judicial Power shall extend" to enumerated "cases" and "controversies." This provision, it is often said, forbids the courts from invalidating legislative or executive action "merely" because it is unconstitutional. The courts may rule only in the context of a constitutional case.

This principle has a number of concrete implications. In general, it means that courts may not issue "advisory opinions"; may not decide "political questions"; must have before them someone with "standing," or some kind of personal stake in the controversy; and may not decide issues that are either "premature" or "moot." What purposes are served by the "case or controversy" requirement? There are several candidates.

First, the requirement might serve the end of judicial restraint. By limiting the occasions for judicial intervention into legislative or executive processes, the case or controversy requirement reduces the friction between the branches produced by judicial review. This rationale is often tied to a concern with the countermajoritarian difficulty. The questions raised by this rationale are whether judicial restraint, thus understood, is desirable and, if so, whether the case and controversy requirement is a sensible way to promote such restraint. Note in particular that judicial restraint is promoted, not with a deferential approach to the merits, but by preventing the courts from reaching the merits at all.

Second, the case or controversy requirement might ensure that constitutional issues will be resolved only in the context of concrete disputes, rather than in response to problems that may be hypothetical, abstract, or speculative. This consequence, it is sometimes said, distinguishes legislative and judicial decision-making and promotes sound constitutional conclusions.

Third, the case or controversy requirement is said to promote the ends of self-determination by ensuring that constitutional decisions are rendered at the behest of those actually injured, rather than at the behest of bystanders attempting to disrupt mutually advantageous accommodations or to impose their own views of public policy on government. Consider, for example, the fact that the rights of those subject to racial discrimination, or environmental harm, can be raised only by those subject to those harms. Outsiders with an ideological interest are barred. This rationale is sometimes accompanied by a suggestion that case or controversy limitations ensure real adversity between the parties and thus ensure against collusive litigation. But note that sometimes, the fact that a lawsuit has not resulted stems from ignorance, poverty, or alienation rather than from satisfaction with the status quo.

Consider also A. Bickel, The Least Dangerous Branch 115-116 (1965):

> One of the chief faculties of the judiciary, which is lacking in the legislature and which fits the courts for the function of evolving and applying constitutional principles, is that the judgment of courts can come later, after the hopes and prophecies expressed in legislation have been tested in the actual workings of our society; the judgment of courts may be had in concrete cases that exemplify the actual conse-

quences of legislative or executive actions. [It] may be added that the opportunity to relate a legislative policy to the flesh-and-blood facts of an actual case [to] observe and describe in being what the legislature may or may not have foreseen as probable — this opportunity as much as, or more than, anything else enables the Court to appeal to the nation's second thought. Moreover, [these requirements] create a time lag between legislation and adjudication. [Hence] it cushions the clash between the Court and any given legislative majority.

Consider the further view that

At the root is the question — in the large — of the role of principle in democratic government. [The] Court is able to play its full role [because] it has available the many devices of mediating between the ultimates of legitimation and invalidation. [It] follows that the techniques and allied devices for staying the Court's hand [cannot] themselves be principled in the sense in which we have a right to expect adjudications on the merits to be principled.

Id. at 132-133. In Bickel's view, the "passive virtues" of inaction operate as a necessary means of mediating between the two (competing) ideas at work in U.S. government: electoral accountability and governance according to principle. The "passive virtues" operate to ensure that the latter idea does not swallow up the former, by permitting the court to defer to the political process without resolving the issue either way. But see Gunther, The Subtle Vices of the Passive Virtues, 64 Colum. L. Rev. 1 (1964), objecting that an "unprincipled" approach to justiciability issues is unacceptable and will ultimately undermine the Court's role.

1. Advisory Opinions

Early on the Supreme Court said that it was constitutionally forbidden to issue "advisory opinions" — opinions on the constitutionality of legislative or executive actions that did not grow out of a case or controversy. President Washington, through Secretary of State Thomas Jefferson, asked the justices whether he might request their views about legal questions growing out of a war, in which the United States was neutral, between England and France. The justices responded:

The three departments of the government [being] in certain respects checks upon each other, and our being judges of a court in the last resort, are considerations which accord strong arguments against the propriety of our extrajudicially deciding the questions alluded to, especially as the power given by the Constitution to the President, of calling on the heads of departments for opinions, seems to have been purposely as well as expressly united to the executive departments. We exceedingly regret every event that may cause embarrassment to your administration, but we derive consolation from the reflection that your judgment will discern what is right.

Quoted in P. Bator, P. Mishkin, D. Shapiro & H. Wechsler, Hart & Wechsler's The Federal Courts and the Federal System 65-66 (2d ed. 1973).

What might be the advantages and disadvantages of permitting courts to issue advisory opinions? Is the Court's conclusion a natural or inevitable interpretation of article III? Note that such a power would enable executive and legislative officials to obtain authoritative judgments on constitutional issues before relevant actions are taken — something that would have significant advantages. Some state supreme courts are authorized to issue advisory opinions. Note also that the Office of Legal Counsel of the Department of Justice has, at least for the executive branch, assumed an advice-giving role, informing the President and other members of the executive branch of its views about the constitutionality of proposed courses of action. Does the text of article III, or the understanding set out by Professor Bickel, support a judicial refusal to fulfill that role?

Some of the gains provided by advisory opinions are furnished by the declaratory judgment procedure. Why is that procedure constitutional? See Nashville, Cincinnati & St. Louis Railway v. Wallace, 288 U.S. 249 (1933).

2. Standing

Allen v. Wright

468 U.S. — , 104 S. Ct. 3315 (1984)

[This was a nationwide class action brought by parents of black school children against the Internal Revenue Service (IRS), contending that the IRS had not carried out its obligation to deny tax-exempt status to private schools that discriminated on the basis of race. The IRS generally does require, as a condition for tax-exempt status (and eligibility to receive deductible charitable contributions), that schools not discriminate on that basis. In Bob Jones University v. United States, 461 U.S. 574 (1983), the Court held that the governing statute disqualified such schools from receiving tax-exempt status as "charities."

According to the parents — respondents in this case representing several million people — the IRS's regulations, procedures, and policies resulted in a failure to enforce the statutory mandate: The IRS had not denied tax-exempt status to many schools that in fact discriminate on the basis of race. Some schools, for example, receive the exemption as a result of the tax-exempt status of "umbrella" organizations that support or operate such schools. According to the parents, the failure to carry out the statutory mandate (1) amounted to federal support for segregated schools and (2) fostered the organization and expansion of such schools, thus interfering with the efforts of federal agencies and courts to bring about desegregation in public school districts that had been segregated in the past. Respondents did not allege that they had applied to the private schools in question but claimed instead that the IRS's unlawful activities had harmed their children attending schools that are undergoing or might undergo desegregation. They claimed that by failing to deny the exemption, the IRS subsidized discriminatory public schools and thus decreased the likelihood that desegregation plans would be effective. Respondents sought declaratory and injunctive relief requiring the IRS to issue guidelines so as to deny tax exemptions to all private schools that discriminated on the basis of race. The court of appeals held in their favor.]

JUSTICE O'CONNOR delivered the opinion of the Court.

Article III of the Constitution confines the federal courts to adjudicating actual "cases" and "controversies." As the Court explained in Valley Forge Christian College v. Americans United for Separation of Church and State, Inc., 454 U.S. 464, 471-476 (1982), the "case or controversy" requirement defines with respect to the Judicial Branch the idea of separation of powers on which the Federal Government is founded. The several doctrines that have grown up to elaborate that requirement are "founded in concern about the proper — and properly limited — role of the courts in a democratic society."

> All of the doctrines that cluster about Article III — not only standing but mootness, ripeness, political question, and the like — relate in part, and in different though overlapping ways, to an idea, which is more than an intuition but less than a rigorous and explicit theory, about the constitutional and prudential limits to the powers of an unelected, unrepresentative judiciary in our kind of government.

Vander Jagt v. O'Neill, 699 F.2d 1166, 1178-1179 (1983) (Bork, J., concurring). The case-or-controversy doctrines state fundamental limits on federal judicial power in our system of government.

The Art. III doctrine that requires a litigant to have "standing" to invoke the power of a federal court is perhaps the most important of these doctrines. "In essence the question of standing is whether the litigant is entitled to have the court decide the merits of the dispute or of particular issues." Standing doctrine embraces several judicially self-imposed limits on the exercise of federal jurisdiction, such as the general prohibition on a litigant's raising another person's legal rights, the rule barring adjudication of generalized grievances more appropriately addressed in the representative branches, and the requirement that a plaintiff's complaint fall within the zone of interests protected by the law invoked. [The] requirement of standing, however, has a core component derived directly from the Constitution. A plaintiff must allege personal injury fairly traceable to the defendant's allegedly unlawful conduct and likely to be redressed by the requested relief.

Like the prudential component, the constitutional component of standing doctrine incorporates concepts concededly not susceptible of precise definition. The injury alleged must be, for example, " 'distinct and palpable,' " [and] not "abstract" or "conjectural" or "hypothetical." [The] injury must be "fairly" traceable to the challenged action, and relief from the injury must be "likely" to follow from a favorable decision. [These] terms cannot be defined so as to make application of the constitutional standing requirement a mechanical exercise.

In many cases the standing question can be answered chiefly by comparing the allegations of the particular complaint to those made in prior standing cases. [More] important, the law of Art. III standing is built on a single basic idea — the idea of separation of powers. Determining standing in a particular case may be facilitated by clarifying principles or even clean rules developed in prior cases. Typically, however, the standing inquiry requires careful judicial examination of a complaint's allegations to ascertain whether the particular plaintiff is entitled to an adjudication of the particular claims asserted. Is the injury too abstract, or otherwise not appropriate, to be considered judicially cognizable? Is the line of causation between the illegal conduct and injury too attenuated? Is the prospect of obtaining relief from the injury as a result of a favorable ruling too speculative? These questions and any others relevant to the standing inquiry must be answered by reference to the Art. III notion that federal courts may exercise power only "in the last resort, and as a necessity," and only when adjudication is "consistent with a system of separated powers and [the dispute is one] traditionally thought to be capable of resolution through the judicial process."

Respondents allege two injuries in their complaint to support their standing to bring this lawsuit. First, they say that they are harmed directly by the mere fact of Government financial aid to discriminatory private schools. Second, they say that the federal tax exemptions to racially discriminatory private schools in their communities impair their ability to have their public schools desegregated.[19] [Respondents'] first claim of injury [might] be a claim simply to have the Government avoid the violation of law alleged in respondents' complaint. Alternatively, it might be a claim of stigmatic injury, or denigration, suffered by all members of a racial group when the Government discriminates on the basis of race. Under neither interpretation is this claim of injury judicially cognizable.

This Court has repeatedly held that an asserted right to have the Government act in accordance with law is not sufficient, standing alone, to confer jurisdiction on a federal court. [Recently,] in [*Valley Forge*, infra] we rejected a claim of standing to challenge a Government conveyance of property to a religious institution. Insofar as the plaintiffs relied simply on " 'their shared individuated right' " to a Government that made no law respecting an establishment of religion [we] held that plaintiffs had not alleged a judicially cognizable injury. . . .

Neither do they have standing to litigate their claims based on the stigmatizing injury often caused by racial discrimination. There can be no doubt that this sort of noneconomic injury is one of the most serious consequences of discriminatory government action and is sufficient in some circumstances to support standing.

[Our] cases make clear, however, that such injury accords a basis for standing only to "those persons who are personally denied equal treatment" by the challenged discriminatory conduct. . . . [If] the abstract stigmatic injury were cognizable, standing would extend nationwide to all members of the particular racial groups against which the Government was alleged to be discriminating by its grant of a tax exemption to a racially discriminatory school, regardless of the location of that school. All such persons could claim the same sort of abstract stigmatic injury respondents assert in their first claim of injury. A black person in Hawaii could challenge the grant of a tax exemption to a racially discriminatory school in Maine. Recognition of standing in such circumstances would transform the federal courts into "no more than a vehicle for the vindication of the value interests of concerned bystanders." It is in their complaint's second claim of injury that respondents allege harm to a concrete, personal interest that can support standing in some circumstances. The injury they identify — their children's diminished ability to receive an education in a racially integrated school — is, beyond any doubt, not only judicially cognizable but, as shown by cases from Brown v. Board of Education, 347 U.S. 483 (1954), to Bob Jones University v. United States, 461 U.S. — (1983), one of the most serious injuries recognized in

---

19. The "fairly traceable" and "redressability" components of the constitutional standing inquiry were initially articulated by this Court as "two facets of a single causation requirement." C. Wright, Law of Federal Courts §13, p.68, n.43 (4th ed. 1983). To the extent there is a difference, it is that the former examines the causal connection between the assertedly unlawful conduct and the alleged injury, whereas the latter examines the causal connection between the alleged injury and the judicial relief requested. Cases such as this, in which the relief requested goes well beyond the violation of law alleged, illustrate why it is important to keep the inquiries separate if the "redressability" component is to focus on the requested relief. Even if the relief respondents request might have a substantial effect on the desegregation of public schools, whatever deficiencies exist in the opportunities for desegregated education for respondents' children might not be traceable to IRS violations of law — grants of tax exemptions to racially discriminatory schools in respondents' communities.

our legal system. Despite the constitutional importance of curing the injury alleged by respondents, however, the federal judiciary may not redress it unless standing requirements are met. In this case, respondents' second claim of injury cannot support standing because the injury alleged is not fairly traceable to the Government conduct respondents challenge as unlawful.

The illegal conduct challenged by respondents is the IRS's grant of tax exemptions to some racially discriminatory schools. The line of causation between that conduct and desegregation of respondents' schools is attenuated at best. From the perspective of the IRS, the injury to respondents is highly indirect and "results from the independent action of some third party not before the court."

The diminished ability of respondents' children to receive a desegregated education would be fairly traceable to unlawful IRS grants of tax exemptions only if there were enough racially discriminatory private schools receiving tax exemptions in respondents' communities for withdrawal of those exemptions to make an appreciable difference in public-school integration. Respondents have made no such allegation. It is, first, uncertain how many racially discriminatory private schools are in fact receiving tax exemptions. Moreover, it is entirely speculative [whether] withdrawal of a tax exemption from any particular school would lead the school to change its policies. [It] is just as speculative whether any given parent of a child attending such a private school would decide to transfer the child to public school as a result of any changes in educational or financial policy made by the private school once it was threatened with loss of tax-exempt status. It is also pure speculation whether, in a particular community, a large enough number of the numerous relevant school officials and parents would reach decisions that collectively would have a significant impact on the racial composition of the public schools.

The links in the chain of causation between the challenged Government conduct and the asserted injury are far too weak for the chain as a whole to sustain respondents' standing. In [*Eastern Kentucky Welfare Rights Org.*, infra] (EKWRO) supra, the Court held that standing to challenge a Government grant of a tax exemption to hospitals could not be founded on the asserted connection between the grant of tax-exempt status and the hospitals' policy concerning the provision of medical services to indigents. The causal connection depended on the decisions hospitals would make in response to withdrawal of tax-exempt status, and those decisions were sufficiently uncertain to break the chain of causation between the plaintiff's injury and the challenged Government action. [The] chain of causation is even weaker in this case. It involves numerous third parties (officials of racially discriminatory schools receiving tax exemptions and the parents of children attending such schools) who may not even exist in respondents' communities and whose independent decisions may not collectively have a significant effect on the ability of public-school students to receive a desegregated education.

The idea of separation of powers that underlies standing doctrine explains why our cases preclude the conclusion that respondents' alleged injury "fairly can be traced to the challenged action" of the IRS. That conclusion would pave the way generally for suits challenging, not specifically identifiable Government violations of law, but the particular programs agencies establish to carry out their legal obligations. Such suits, even when premised on allegations of several instances of violations of law, are rarely if ever appropriate for federal-court adjudication.

Carried to its logical end, [respondents'] approach would have the federal courts as virtually continuing monitors of the wisdom and soundness of Executive action; such a role is appropriate for the Congress acting through its committees and the 'power of the purse'; it is not the role of the judiciary, absent actual present or immediately threatened injury resulting from unlawful governmental action.

The same concern for the proper role of the federal courts is reflected in cases like O'Shea v. Littleton, 414 U.S. 488 (1974), Rizzo v. Goode, 423 U.S. 362 (1976), and City of Los Angeles v. Lyons, 461 U.S. — (1983). In all three cases plaintiffs sought injunctive relief directed at certain systemwide law enforcement practices. The Court held in each case that, absent an allegation of a specific threat of being subject to the challenged practices, plaintiffs had no standing to ask for an injunction. Animating this Court's holdings was the principle that "[a] federal court . . . is not the proper forum to press" general complaints about the way in which government goes about its business. . . .

Case-or-controversy considerations, the Court observed in O'Shea v. Littleton, supra, 414 U.S., at 499, "obviously shade into those determining whether the complaint states a sound basis for equitable relief." The latter set of considerations should therefore inform our judgment about whether respondents have standing. Most relevant to this case is the principle articulated in [Rizzo]: "When a plaintiff seeks to enjoin the activity of a government agency, even within a unitary court system, his case must contend with 'the well-established rule that the Government has traditionally been granted the widest latitude in the "dispatch of its own internal affairs." When transported into the Art. III context, that principle, grounded as it is in the idea of separation of powers, counsels against recognizing standing in a case brought, not to enforce specific legal obligations whose violation works a direct harm, but to seek a restructuring of the apparatus established by the Executive Branch to fulfill its legal duties. The Constitution, after all, assigns to the Executive Branch, and not to the Judicial Branch, the duty to "take Care that the Laws be faithfully executed." U.S. Const., Art. II, §3. We could not recognize respondents' standing in this case without running afoul of that structural principle. . . .

"The necessity that the plaintiff who seeks to invoke judicial power stand to profit in some personal interest remains an Art. III requirement." Respondents have not met this fundamental requirement. The judgment of the Court of Appeals is accordingly reversed, and the injunction issued by that court is vacated.

It is so ordered.

Justice Marshall took no part in the decision of the case.

Justice Brennan, dissenting.

[By] relying on generalities concerning our tripartite system of government, the Court is able to conclude that the respondents lack standing to maintain this action without acknowledging the precise nature of the injuries they have alleged. In so doing, the Court displays a startling insensitivity to the historical role played by the federal courts in eradicating race discrimination from our nation's schools — a role that has played a prominent part in this Court's decisions from [Brown]. . . .

In these cases, the respondents have alleged at least one type of injury that satisfies the constitutional requirement of "distinct and palpable injury."[3] In particular, they claim that the IRS' grant of tax-exempt status to racially discriminatory private schools directly injures their children's opportunity and ability to receive a desegregated education. . . .

Viewed in light of the injuries they claim, the respondents have alleged a direct causal relationship between the government action they challenge and the injury they suffer: their inability to receive an education in a racially integrated school is directly and adversely affected by the tax-exempt status granted by the IRS to racially discriminatory schools in their respective school districts. [The] elimination of tax-exempt status for racially discriminatory private schools would serve to lessen the impact that those institutions have in defeating efforts to desegregate the public schools. . . .

[The] respondents specifically refer by name to at least 32 private schools that discriminate on the basis of race and yet continue to benefit illegally from tax-exempt status. Eighteen of those schools — including at least 14 elementary schools, two junior high schools, and one high school — are located in the city of Memphis, Tennessee, which has been the subject of several court orders to desegregate. . . .

[At] least with respect to these school districts, as well as the others specifically mentioned in the complaint, there can be little doubt that the respondents have identified communities containing "enough racially discriminatory private schools receiving tax exemptions . . . to make an appreciable difference in public-school integration." . . .

[EKWRO] is plainly distinguishable from the case at hand. The respondents in this case do not challenge the denial of any service by a tax-exempt institution; admittedly, they do not seek access to racially discriminatory private schools. Rather, the injury they allege, and the injury that clearly satisfies constitutional requirements, is the deprivation of their children's opportunity and ability to receive an education in a racially integrated school district. This injury [is] of a kind that is directly traceable to the governmental action being challenged. . . .

More than one commentator has noted that the causation component of the Court's standing inquiry is no more than a poor disguise for the Court's view of the merits of the underlying claims. The Court today does nothing to avoid that criticism.

JUSTICE STEVENS, with whom JUSTICE BLACKMUN joins, dissenting.

In final analysis, the wrong the respondents allege that the Government has committed is to subsidize the exodus of white children from schools that would otherwise be racially integrated. The critical question in this case, therefore, is

---

3. Because I conclude that the second injury alleged by the respondents is sufficient to satisfy constitutional requirements, I do not need to reach what the Court labels the "stigmatic injury." I note, however, that the Court has mischaracterized this claim of injury by misreading the complaint filed by the respondents. In particular, the respondents have not simply alleged that, as blacks, they have suffered the denigration injury "suffered by all members of a racial group when the Government discriminates on the basis of race." Rather, the complaint, fairly read, limits the claim of stigmatic injury from illegal governmental action to black children attending public schools in districts that are currently desegregating yet contain discriminatory private schools benefitting from illegal tax exemptions. . . .

whether respondents have alleged that the Government has created that kind of subsidy. If the granting of preferential tax treatment would "encourage" private segregated schools to conduct their "charitable" activities, it must follow that the withdrawal of the treatment would "discourage" them, and hence promote the process of desegregation. [When] a subsidy makes a given activity more or less expensive, injury can be fairly traced to the subsidy for purposes of standing analysis because of the resulting increase or decrease in the ability to engage in the activity.

This causation analysis is nothing more than a restatement of elementary economics: when something becomes more expensive, less of it will be purchased. [The] process of desegregation will be advanced [since the] withdrawal of the subsidy for segregated schools means the incentive structure facing white parents who seek such schools for their children will be altered.

Considerations of tax policy, economics, and pure logic all confirm the conclusion that respondents' injury in fact is fairly traceable to the Government's allegedly wrongful conduct. The Court therefore is forced to introduce the concept of "separation of powers" into its analysis.

[The] Court could be saying that it will require a more direct causal connection when it is troubled by the separation of powers implications of the case before it. That approach confuses the standing doctrine with the justiciability of the issues that respondents seek to raise. The purpose of the standing inquiry is to measure the plaintiff's stake in the outcome, not whether a court has the authority to provide it with the outcome it seeks. . . . [The] strength of the plaintiff's interest in the outcome has nothing to do with whether the relief it seeks would intrude upon the prerogatives of other branches of government; the possibility that the relief might be inappropriate does not lessen the plaintiff's stake in obtaining that relief. If a plaintiff presents a nonjusticiable issue, or seeks relief that a court may not award, then its complaint should be dismissed for those reasons, and not because the plaintiff lacks a stake in obtaining that relief and hence has no standing. Imposing an undefined but clearly more rigorous standard for redressability for reasons unrelated to the causal nexus between the injury and the challenged conduct can only encourage undisciplined, ad hoc litigation, a result that would be avoided if the Court straightforwardly considered the justiciability of the issues respondents seek to raise, rather than using those issues to obfuscate standing analysis.[10]

[The] Court could be saying that it will not treat as legally cognizable injuries that stem from an administrative decision concerning how enforcement resources will be allocated. [Respondents] do seek to restructure the IRS' mechanisms for enforcing the legal requirement that discriminatory institutions not receive tax-exempt status. Such restructuring would dramatically affect the way in which the IRS exercises its prosecutorial discretion. The Executive requires latitude to decide how best to enforce the law, and in general the Court may well be correct that the exercise of that discretion, especially in the tax context, is unchallengeable.

10. . . . [We] have made it clear that the courts have authority to restructure both school attendance patterns and curriculum when necessary to eliminate the effects of a dual school system. [Standing] doctrine has never stood as a barrier to such "restructuring." In the seminal case of Baker v. Carr, 369 U.S. 186 (1962), the Court accorded voters standing to challenge population variations between electoral districts despite the fact that the legislative reapportionment sought would and eventually did have dramatic "restructuring" effects.

However, this principle does not apply when suit is brought "to enforce specific legal obligations whose violation works a direct harm." For example, despite the fact that they were challenging the methods used by the Executive to enforce the law, citizens were accorded standing to challenge a pattern of police misconduct that violated the constitutional constraints on law enforcement activities in Allee v. Medrano, 416 U.S. 802 (1974). Here, respondents contend that the IRS is violating a specific constitutional limitation on its enforcement discretion. . . .

Respondents contend that [the] IRS cannot provide "cash grants" to discriminatory schools through preferential tax treatment without running afoul of a constitutional duty to refrain from "giving significant aid" to these institutions. Similarly, respondents claim that the Internal Revenue Code itself [constrains] enforcement discretion. It has been clear since [Marbury v. Madison,] that "[i]t is emphatically the province and duty of the judicial department to say what the law is." Deciding whether the Treasury has violated a specific legal limitation on its enforcement discretion does not intrude upon the prerogatives of the Executive, for in so deciding we are merely saying "what the law is."

In short, I would deal with the question of the legal limitations on the IRS' enforcement discretion on its merits, rather than by making the untenable assumption that the granting of preferential tax treatment to segregated schools does not make those schools more attractive to white students and hence does not inhibit the process of desegregation.

Note: The "Law" of Standing

1. *Constitutional and prudential limits.* The Court has recently broken down standing limitations into "constitutional" and "prudential" categories. In Valley Forge Christian College v. Americans United, 454 U.S. 464 (1982), the Court said:

> [At] an irreducible minimum, Art. III requires the party who invokes the court's authority to "show that he personally has suffered some actual or threatened injury as a result of the putatively illegal conduct of the defendant," [and] that the injury "fairly can be traced to the challenged action" and "is likely to be redressed by a favorable decision." [In] this manner does Art. III limit the federal judicial power "to those disputes which confine federal courts to a role consistent with a system of separated powers and which are traditionally thought to be capable of resolution through the judicial process."
>
> The requirement of "actual injury redressable by the court," [serves] several of the "implicit policies embodied in Article III." [It] tends to assure that the legal questions presented to the court will be resolved, not in the rarified atmosphere of a debating society, but in a concrete factual context conducive to a realistic appreciation of the consequences of judicial action. The "standing" requirement serves other purposes. Because it assures an actual factual setting in which the litigant asserts a claim of injury in fact, a court may decide the case with some confidence that its decision will not pave the way for lawsuits which have some, but not all, of the facts of the case actually decided by the court.
>
> The Art. III aspect of standing also reflects a due regard for the autonomy of those persons likely to be most directly affected by a judicial order. The federal courts have abjured appeals to their authority which would convert the judicial process into no more than a vehicle for the vindication of the value interests of concerned by-

standers. Were the federal courts merely publicly funded forums for the ventilation of public grievances or the refinement of jurisprudential understanding, the concept of "standing" would be quite unnecessary. But the "cases and controversies" language of Art. III forecloses the conversion of courts of the United States into judicial versions of college debating forums. [The] exercise of judicial power, which can so profoundly affect the lives, liberty, and property of those to whom it extends, is therefore restricted to litigants who can show "injury in fact" resulting from the action which they seek to have the court adjudicate.

The exercise of the judicial power also affects relationships between the coequal arms of the National Government. The effect is, of course, most vivid when a federal court declares unconstitutional an act of the Legislative or Executive Branch. While the exercise of that "ultimate and supreme function," is a formidable means of vindicating individual rights, when employed unwisely or unnecessarily it is also the ultimate threat to the continued effectiveness of the federal courts in performing that role. While the propriety of such action by a federal court has been recognized since [*Marbury*] it has been recognized as a tool of last resort on the part of the federal judiciary throughout its nearly 200 years of existence.

[Proper] regard for the complex nature of our constitutional structure requires neither that the Judicial Branch shrink from a confrontation with the other two coequal branches of the Federal Government, nor that it hospitably accept for adjudication claims of constitutional violation by other branches of government where the claimant has not suffered cognizable injury. Thus, this Court has "refrain[ed] from passing upon the constitutionality of an act [of the representative branches] unless obliged to do so in the proper performance of our judicial function, when the question is raised by a party whose interests entitle him to raise it." The importance of this precondition should not be underestimated as a means of "defin[ing] the role assigned to the judiciary in a tripartite allocation of power."

Beyond the constitutional requirements, the federal judiciary has also adhered to a set of prudential principles that bear on the question of standing. Thus, this Court has held that "the plaintiff generally must assert his own legal rights and interests, and cannot rest his claim to relief on the legal rights or interests of third parties." In addition, even when the plaintiff has alleged redressable injury sufficient to meet the requirements of Art. III, the Court has refrained from adjudicating "abstract questions of wide public significance" which amount to "generalized grievances," pervasively shared and most appropriately addressed in the representative branches. [Finally,] the Court has required that the plaintiff's complaint fall within the zone of interests to be protected or regulated by the statute or constitutional guarantee in question.

2. *Underlying concerns.* What functions are served by standing limitations? Consider the following possibilities. (a) They ensure that the courts will decide cases that are concrete rather than abstract or hypothetical. To what extent is this so? Was the dispute in *Allen* abstract or hypothetical? (b) They promote judicial restraint by limiting the occasions for judicial intervention into the political process. But are standing limitations any better than other possible ways of limiting such intrusions? Does the fact that injuries to citizens at large are not cognizable judicially, but only politically, help to answer that question? (c) They ensure that decisions will be made at the behest of those directly affected, rather than on behalf of outsiders with a purely ideological interest in the controversy. This factor will simultaneously promote vigorous advocacy. Was there a danger of insufficiently vigorous advocacy in *Allen*? Note that sometimes those directly affected will fail to sue for reasons other than contentment with the status quo.

3. *Doctrinal components.* a. *Injury in fact.* The injury in fact requirement evolved from the earlier requirement of a "legal injury." A legal injury was a far more limited category than that of "injury in fact." To show a legal injury, one had to show an injury to an interest

> entitled to the protection of the common law. [This] limitation on standing was consistent with the two central tenets of the then prevailing theory of individual rights against the government: first, that the only valid basis for government intrusion into private autonomy was the consent of the governed (as expressed through valid legislation); and second, that the common law of property and contract defined the sphere of private autonomy protected against both individuals and the state.

Stewart, The Reformation of American Administrative Law, 88 Harv. L. Rev. 1667, 1723-1724 (1975). The consequence was that at its inception, the law of standing was highly libertarian in character: One had to show a common law interest to obtain standing; potential beneficiaries of government action — consumers, public interests groups, victims of discrimination — were denied standing. As a result, courts could be invoked by those trying to fend off government activity, but not by those trying to obtain government protection. Private property was thus the usual basis for obtaining review. See generally J. Vining, Legal Identity (1978).

The key case was Association of Data Processing Services Organizations v. Camp, 397 U.S. 150 (1970), which abandoned the legal interest test in favor of an injury in fact requirement. The Court emphasized that this requirement is relatively lenient; it may include a wide variety of economic, aesthetic, environmental, and other harms. The consequence is that beneficiaries of government regulation, not merely those trying to fend off government action, could have standing to sue. But even under *Data Processing*, a merely ideological interest — or an interest in bringing about compliance with the law — is insufficient. What is the line between an "injury in fact" and a "mere" ideological injury?

Standing was denied on "injury in fact" grounds in Sierra Club v. Morton, 405 U.S. 727 (1972). The case involved an effort by an organization with "a special interest in the conservation and sound maintenance of the national parks" to challenge construction of a recreation area in a national forest. In the plaintiffs' view, the construction would have violated federal law. The Court denied standing, saying that the fact that an aesthetic, conservational, or recreational harm would be sufficient did not mean that it would abandon "the requirement that the party seeking review must have himself suffered an injury." In this case the "Sierra Club failed to allege that it or its members" used the site in question.

What is the purpose of denying standing in *Sierra Club*? Would the Sierra Club have been an ineffective or half-hearted advocate? Was there no case or controversy? Consider the view that the Sierra Club was litigating the rights of others who had a more direct stake in the controversy, and the idea that those others, and not an intermeddling bystander, should have an exclusive right to raise the underlying legal issues.

Insofar as it involved a "stigmatic" injury, the Court treated Allen v. Wright as a variation on the *Sierra Club* case. But *Allen* was somewhat different because (1) there was no problem of litigating the rights of others and (2) a "stigmatic" injury might be different from a generalized interest in law enforcement. Compare

Allen v. Wright with Heckler v. Mathews, — U.S. — , 104 S. Ct. 1387 (1984) (holding that stigmatic injury incurred as a result of gender discrimination in pension plans was sufficient to confer standing).

Sierra Club might be contrasted with United States v. SCRAP, 412 U.S. 669 (1973), in which the Court held that environmental groups could challenge the ICC's failure to suspend a surcharge on railroad freight rates as unlawful under the Interstate Commerce Commission Act. The plaintiffs claimed that their members "used the forests, streams, mountains, and other resources in the Washington metropolitan area for camping, hiking, fishing, and sightseeing." According to the Court, the Constitution was satisfied by the

> attenuated line of causation to the eventual injury of which the [plaintiffs] complained — a general rate increase would allegedly cause increased use of nonrecyclable commodities as compared to recyclable goods, thus resulting in the need to use more natural resources to produce such goods, some of which resources might be taken from the Washington area, and resulting in more refuse that might be discarded in national parks in the Washington area.

b. *Widely diffused harms.* Should the Court refuse to decide cases in which the harm caused by government action is widely diffused — in the sense that many or all citizens feel it equally? Consider in this regard Schlesinger v. Reservists to Stop the War, 418 U.S. 208 (1974), which involved a claim, made by an association of present and former members of the Reserves, that the Reserve membership of certain members of Congress violated the incompatibility clause. That clause provides that "no Person holding any Office under the United States, shall be a member of either House during his Continuance in Office." The Court said:

> The only interest [is one] shared by all citizens. [The] claimed nonobservance [of that Clause], standing alone, would adversely affect only the generalized interest of all citizens in constitutional governance, and that is an abstract injury. . . .
> To permit a complainant who has no concrete injury to require a court to rule on important constitutional issues in the abstract would create the potential for abuse of the judicial process, distort the role of the Judiciary in its relationship to the Executive and the Legislature and open the Judiciary to an arguable charge of "government by injunction."

The Court added that the plaintiffs did not meet the requirements of *Flast,* infra. Justices Douglas, Brennan, and Marshall dissented.

Consider also United States v. Richardson, 418 U.S. 166 (1974), an effort by a taxpayer to challenge the Central Intelligence Agency Act of 1949, which provides that CIA expenditures may not be made public. According to the plaintiff, the act violated article I, section 9, clause 7, of the Constitution, which provides that "a regular statement of Account of the Receipts and Expenditures of all public Money shall be published from time to time." The Court responded that the plaintiff's claim was only "a generalized grievance" that was "common to all members of the public. While we can hardly dispute that this respondent has a genuine interest in the use of funds and that his interest may be prompted by his status as a taxpayer, he has not alleged that, as a taxpayer, he is in danger of suffering any particular concrete injury as a result of the operation of this statute." The Court added:

It can be argued that if respondent is not permitted to litigate this issue, no one can do so. In a very real sense, the absence of any particular individual or class to litigate these claims gives support to the argument that the subject matter is committed to the surveillance of Congress, and ultimately to the political process. Any other conclusion would mean that the Founding Fathers intended to set up something in the nature of an Athenian democracy or a New England town meeting to oversee the conduct of the National Government by means of lawsuits in federal courts. The Constitution created a *representative* Government with the representatives directly responsible to their constituents at stated periods of two, four, and six years; that the Constitution does not afford a judicial remedy does not, of course, completely disable the citizen who is not satisfied with the "ground rules" established by the Congress for reporting expenditures of the Executive Branch. Lack of standing within the narrow confines of Art. III jurisdiction does not impair the right to assert his views in the political forum or at the polls. Slow, cumbersome, and unresponsive though the traditional electoral process may be thought at times, our system provides for changing members of the political branches when dissatisfied citizens convince a sufficient number of their fellow electors that elected representatives are delinquent in performing duties committed to them.

In an influential concurring opinion, Justice Powell added:

The power recognized in [*Marbury*] is a potent one. Its prudent use seems to me incompatible with unlimited notions of taxpayer and citizen standing. [Due] to what many have regarded as the unresponsiveness of the Federal Government to recognized needs or serious inequities in our society, recourse to the federal courts has attained an unprecedented popularity in recent decades. Those courts have often acted as a major instrument of social reform. But this has not always been the case, as experiences under the New Deal illustrate. The public reaction to the substantive due process holdings of the federal courts during that period requires no elaboration, and it is not unusual for history to repeat itself.

Quite apart from this possibility, we risk a progressive impairment of the effectiveness of the federal courts if their limited resources are diverted increasingly from their historic role to the resolution of public-interest suits brought by litigants who cannot distinguish themselves from all taxpayers or all citizens. The irreplaceable value of the power articulated by Mr. Chief Justice Marshall lies in the protection it has afforded the constitutional rights and liberties of individual citizens and minority groups against oppressive or discriminatory government action. It is this role, not some amorphous general supervision of the operations of government, that has maintained public esteem for the federal courts and has permitted the peaceful coexistence of the countermajoritarian implications of judicial review and the democratic principles upon which our Federal Government in the final analysis rests.

The considerations outlined above underlie, I believe, the traditional hostility of the Court to federal taxpayer or citizen standing where the plaintiff has nothing at stake other than his interest as a taxpayer or citizen. It merits noting how often and how unequivocally the Court has expressed its antipathy to efforts to convert the Judiciary into an open forum for the resolution of political or ideological disputes about the performance of government.

The problem of widely diffused injuries is associated with that of taxpayer standing. The Court has rarely recognized such standing, but did so in Flast v. Cohen, 392 U.S. 83 (1968), which involved a taxpayer challenge to aid to religious schools. The Court said that taxpayer standing would be permitted in *Flast* because there was "a logical nexus between the status asserted and the claim thought to be adjudicated." According to the Court,

> the nexus demanded of federal taxpayers has two aspects to it. First, the taxpayer must establish a logical link between that status and the type of legislative enactment attacked. [It] will not be sufficient to allege an incidental expenditure of tax funds in the administration of an essentially regulatory measure. Secondly, the taxpayer must establish a nexus between that status and the precise nature of the constitutional infringement alleged. Under this requirement, the taxpayer must show that the challenged enactment exceeds specific constitutional limitations imposed upon the exercise of the congressional taxing and spending powers.

The Court held that the requirement was satisfied in the case of a taxpayer challenging an expenditure of public funds as violative of the establishment clause.

In two other cases, the Court has denied taxpayer standing. See Frothingham v. Mellon, 262 U.S. 447 (1923) (refusing to allow taxpayer to enjoin, under the tenth amendment, expenditures made to reduce maternal and infant mortality under federal statute), and Valley Forge Christian College v. Americans United, supra, in which the Court refused to permit a taxpayer to challenge, under the establishment clause, a conveyance of property formerly used as a military hospital to the Valley Forge Christian College. In *Valley Forge*, the Court emphasized that the plaintiffs challenged a property transfer, not an expenditure of funds. Justices Brennan, Marshall, Blackmun, and Stevens dissented. Justice Brennan stressed that the "taxpayer was the direct and intended beneficiary of the prohibition on financial aid to religion."

Why should a widely diffused injury be an insufficient basis for judicial relief? Consider the following views. (1) *Richardson, Schlesinger,* and *Valley Forge* were rightly decided, and *Flast* wrongly. If a harm is shared by the plaintiff in common with all other citizens or taxpayers, the appropriate forum is the legislature, not the court. The mechanisms of political accountability are a sufficient guaranty. And if those mechanisms fail, the problem must not be severe in any event. The Constitution requires more than able litigants and a legal question. (2) Constitutional requirements are not meant to vary with popular opinion; they operate largely as constraints on outcomes even if they accurately reflect popular opinion. *Richardson, Schlesinger,* and *Valley Forge* are incorrectly decided because they render constitutional constraints unenforceable. If the plaintiffs in those cases do not have standing, no one ever will.

Why is the "generalized injury" requirement prudential rather than constitutional in nature?

c. *Nexus.* Allen v. Wright was decided in part on "nexus" grounds. As suggested by *Allen* and by *Valley Forge*, the nexus requirement has two prongs: The plaintiff must show that (1) the allegedly unlawful conduct has caused his or her "injury in fact" and (2) the injury is likely to be redressed by a favorable decision. In practice, these two prongs almost always amount to the same thing.

The nexus requirement has been an important limitation in recent standing cases. One of the key cases was Linda R. S. v. Richard D., 410 U.S. 614 (1972), which involved an action by an unwed mother of an illegitimate child to enjoin discriminatory application of a Texas criminal statute that penalized any parent who failed to support his children. Plaintiffs contended that judicial interpretation had excluded illegitimate fathers from prosecution and sought to require a prosecutor to initiate criminal proceedings for failure to provide child support. The Court denied standing, claiming that because prosecution might lead only to the father's incarceration, the "prospect that prosecution will [result] in payment of support can, at best, be termed only speculative." *Linda R. S.* took place in an unusual setting, for criminal prosecutors have usually been held to have unreviewable discretion whether to bring enforcement actions. Should the decision have been based on standing grounds? Consider Easterbrook, Foreword: The Court and the Economic System, 98 Harv. L. Rev. 4, 40 (1984): "[It] is hard to take seriously the claim that enforcement of legal rules does not affect bystanders. [I] suffer an injury if the police announce that they will no longer enforce [the rule against murder] in my neighborhood. [A] plaintiff need not show a sure gain from winning in order to prove that some probability of gain is better than none, and thus he suffers injury in fact."

Another case in the same vein as *Linda R. S.* is Simon v. Eastern Kentucky Welfare Rights Organization, 426 U.S. 26 (1976). The action was brought by several indigents and organizations challenging an Internal Revenue Service Revenue Ruling that granted favorable tax treatment to certain nonprofit hospitals that limited aid to indigents to emergency room services. According to the plaintiffs, the ruling was unlawful because it reduced the amount of services necessary to qualify as charitable corporations. The consequence, plaintiffs claimed, was that the indigents would have less in the way of medical services available to them.

The Court, in an opinion by Justice Powell, held that there was no standing. In the Court's view, the plaintiffs' contention that the new ruling "encouraged" denial of services to indigents was inadequate.

> It is purely speculative whether the denials of service specified in the complaint fairly can be traced to the Service's "encouragement" or instead result from decisions made by hospitals without regard to their tax implications. [It] is equally speculative whether the desired exercise of the court's remedial powers in this suit would result in the availability [of] such services. So far as the complaint sheds light, it is just as plausible that the hospitals to which plaintiffs may apply for service would elect to forego favorable tax treatment to avoid the undetermined financial drain of an increase in the level of uncompensated services.

Justice Brennan, joined by Justice Marshall, dissented. Justice Brennan claimed that the relevant injury was to the "opportunity and ability" to receive free medical services, that that interest was not too diffuse to support standing, and that the further requirement imposed by the Court served no purpose. Under what circumstances should a plaintiff have standing to bring suit against the government for "encouraging" harmful activity? Should the intervening conduct of third parties — hospitals in Eastern Kentucky Welfare Right Organization v. Simon and schools in Allen v. Wright — play a role in the standing inquiry?

Compare Warth v. Seldin, 422 U.S. 490 (1975), where various organizations and individuals in Rochester, New York, brought suit against the town of Penfield to enjoin application of its exclusionary zoning ordinance. The Court denied the assertion of standing by people of low or moderate income and as members of minority groups. The Court said that it was necessary to resolve the question

> whether petitioners' inability to locate suitable housing in Penfield reasonably can be said to have resulted, in any concretely demonstrable way, from respondents' alleged constitutional and statuatory infractions. Petitioners must allege facts from which it reasonably could be inferred that, absent the respondents' restrictive zone practices, there is a substantial probability that they would have been able to purchase or lease in Penfield and that, if the court affords the relief requested, the asserted inability of petitioners will be removed.
>
> We find the record devoid of the necessary allegations. None of these petitioners has a present interest in any Penfield property; none is himself subject to the ordinance's strictures; and none has ever been denied a variance or permit by respondent officials. [Here,] by their own admission, realization of petitioners' desire to live in Penfield always has depended on the efforts and willingness of third parties to build low and moderate-cost housing. [But] the record is devoid of any indication that [were] the court to remove the obstacles attributable to respondents, such relief would benefit petitioners. Indeed, petitioners' descriptions of their individual financial situations and housing needs suggest precisely the contrary — that their inability to reside in Penfield is the consequence of the economics of the area housing market, rather than of respondents' assertedly illegal acts.

Justice Brennan's dissenting opinion replied, among other things, that petitioners

> cannot be expected, prior to discovery and trial, to know the future plans of building companies, the precise details of the housing market in Penfield, or everything which has transpired in 15 years of application of the Penfield zoning ordinance, including every housing plan suggested and refused. To require them to allege such facts is to require them to prove their case on paper in order to get into court at all, reverting to a form of fact-pleading long abjured in the federal courts.

Compare Duke Power Co. v. Carolina Environmental Study Group, 438 U.S. 59 (1978). In that case, the plaintiffs — consisting of forty people who lived near planned power plants, an environmental group, and a labor organization — sought a declaration to challenge the Price-Anderson Act. The act limited aggregate liability for a single nuclear power plant accident to $560 million. Plaintiffs claimed that the plant would produce environmental and aesthetic injuries. The Court found a sufficiently concrete injury: "It is enough that several of the 'immediate' impacts were found to harm appellees. Certainly the environmental and aesthetic consequences of the thermal pollution of the two lakes in the vicinity of the disputed power plants is the type of harmful effect which has been deemed adequate in prior cases to satisfy the 'injury in fact' standard."

Are EKWRO and Warth consistent with Duke Power and United States v. SCRAP, supra? Note also University of California Regents v. Bakke, 438 U.S. 265 (1978), where plaintiff challenged an affirmative action program established by the University of California at Davis without alleging that, if the program were not in place, he would have been admitted to the medical school. The Court responded:

> The constitutional element of standing is plaintiff's demonstration of any injury to himself that is likely to be redressed by favorable decision of his claim. The trial

court found such an injury, apart from failure to be admitted, in the University's decision not to permit Bakke to compete for all 100 places in the class, simply because of his race. Hence the constitutional requirements of Art. III were met. The question of Bakke's admission vel non is merely one of relief.

If the Court is correct on this point, are *EKWRO* and *Warth* wrongly decided? For discussion, see Tushnet, The New Law of Standing: A Plea for Abandonment, 62 Cornell L. Rev. 663 (1977); Fallon, Of Justiciability, Remedies, and Public Law Litigations: Notes on the Jurisprudence of *Lyons*, 59 N.Y.U. L. Rev. 1 (1984); Nichol, Causation as a Standing Requirement: The Unprincipled Use of Judicial Restraint, 69 Ky. L. Rev. 185 (1980-1981).

What is the purpose of the "nexus" or "causation" requirement? Is that requirement merely one of pleading — or does it establish a threshold requirement of proof on the plaintiff's part? One possibility is that the requirement operates as a safeguard against advisory opinions. If the plaintiff is unable to show that the requested relief would remedy his injury, it becomes necessary to ask why the court should become involved at all. Is this a persuasive justification for the results in *Linda R. S.*, *Warth*, and *EKWRO*? What level of certainty should be necessary in order to justify judicial relief?

Consider Chayes, Public Law Litigation and the Burger Court, 96 Harv. L. Rev. 4, 18-19 (1982), suggesting that in *Warth*,

> The Court stacked the deck [by] its characterization of the injury in fact that plaintiffs asserted. [If] the plaintiffs [were] asserting injury to their interest in participating in a housing market not fundamentally warped by unconstitutional zoning practices, then obviously the injury was caused by those practices and would be cured by their prohibition. [In *EKWRO*], it is easy to conceive of a different characterization of the interest assertedly harmed. It is not the interest in obtaining free medical services at a particular hospital but in having hospitals' decisions reflect accurately the incentive structure that Congress established. [Any] first-year law student, at least after he has read the *Palsgraf* case, could predict what would happen when the metaphysically undisciplined concept of causation is introduced into this kind of doctrinal formula. [There] are no "direct" and "indirect" injuries. There are only causal chains of different lengths. The question is, "how long is too long?" The answer can readily be made to vary, if not with the length of the Chancellor's foot, then with the interests and sympathies of shifting configurations of five Justices.

Does this analysis suggest that the causation requirement should be abandoned or recast? If so, how?

d. *Injuries to third parties and "the zone of interests."* In *Valley Forge*, the Court referred to two other prudential limitations. The "zone of interests" test derives from *Data Processing*, supra, which, in the course of discussing standing requirements under the Administrative Procedure Act, said that a plaintiff must show that he or she is "arguably within the zone of interests" protected or regulated by the statutory scheme. As applied in the constitutional context, the notion is that the plaintiff must be an intended beneficiary of the constitutional provision at issue. This requirement has never been the basis for denying standing in a constitutional case.

The notion that a plaintiff may not litigate the rights of third parties is closely related to the "injury in fact" requirement. The plaintiff must litigate on the basis of an injury to him or her; it is up to third parties to litigate their own rights. See, e.g., Tileston v. Ullman, 318 U.S. 44 (1943) (doctor may not challenge statute on ground that it would deprive patients of their lives without due process). See generally Monaghan, Third Party Standing, 84 Colum. L. Rev. 567 (1984); Brilmayer, The Jurisprudence of Article III: Perspectives on the "Case or Controversy" Requirement, 93 Harv. L. Rev. 297 (1979).

3. *Threatened injury.* The "injury in fact" requirement is usually met by those who can show a sufficient threat of future injury, as *Duke Power* and *SCRAP* make clear. This threat must, however, be real and immediate rather than "merely" speculative or hypothetical. The refusal to recognize speculative or hypothetical harms plays an important role in suits seeking injunctive relief. Consider City of Los Angeles v. Lyons, 461 U.S. 95 (1983), an action brought against the Los Angeles police department and city officials, seeking injunctive relief to prevent the use of "chokeholds" in arrest. Lyons, the plaintiff, had in fact been the victim of a chokehold; he also brought an action for damages. But the Court said that the fact that he was also seeking damages did not mean he could obtain an injunction when he was not "likely to suffer future injury from the use of chokeholds by police officers." In order to show such a likelihood, he would have "to make the incredible assertion either, (1) that *all* police officers in Los Angeles *always* choke any citizen with whom they happen to have an encounter whether for the purpose of arrest, issuing a citation or for questioning or, (2) that the City ordered or authorized police officers to act in such a manner." Assume that the practice at issue in *Lyons* is unconstitutional. Would anyone have standing to enjoin it?

For other cases along the same lines, see Rizzo v. Goode, 423 U.S. 362 (1976); O'Shea v. Littleton, 414 U.S. 488 (1974).

4. *Standing and separation of powers.* One of the distinctive features of Allen v. Wright is the use of "separation of powers" considerations to illuminate the standing inquiry. Why are separation of powers questions raised by an effort to "restructure" executive branch operations — if the restructuring is required by law? In such circumstances, can one argue that separation of powers considerations point in favor of recognizing standing? Consider Nichol, Abusing Standing: A Comment on *Allen v. Wright*, 133 U. Pa. L. Rev. 635, 642, 648 (1984):

> [The] infusion of separation of powers analysis [departs] sharply from standing law as we have come to know it. [Not] surprisingly, federal constitutional claims often call into question the validity of actions of another organ of government. By definition, therefore, they raise the specter of judicial intrusion. Most often, however, such cases cannot in good faith be deemed political. If the standing determination may appropriately be "skewed" by separation of powers concerns in such cases, courts will be increasingly tempted simply to deny standing on undisclosed grounds.

On the other hand, might *Allen* be a reasonable response to the spectre of judicial management of executive branch operations?

5. *Final thoughts.* Modern standing doctrine is often criticized as highly manipulable and ad hoc — and further, as a means of disguising judgments on the merits. Are such criticisms justified in light of the preceding materials? How might standing doctrine be reformulated? Which of the current requirements should be retained, restricted, or broadened? Should other requirements be added?

3. Political Questions

Baker v. Carr

369 U.S. 186 (1962)

[Voters in Tennessee brought suit challenging a state statute, passed in 1901, that apportioned the members of the state General Assembly among the state's ninety-five counties. Under the 1901 standard, representation was allocated among those counties in accordance with the number of qualified voters in those counties. But substantial growth in Tennessee and redistribution of the population between 1901 and 1961 led, in the plaintiffs' view, to a system in which apportionment was made "arbitrarily and capriciously" and "without reference to any logical or reasonable formula whatever." Claiming that their votes were diluted under the 1901 system, the plaintiffs sought an injunction prohibiting elections under that system and requiring either a reapportionment in accordance with the number of voters under federal census figures or "at-large" elections.]

MR. JUSTICE BRENNAN delivered the opinion of the Court.

[We] hold that this challenge to an apportionment presents no nonjusticiable "political question." . . .

Of course the mere fact that the suit seeks protection of a political right does not mean it presents a political question. Such an objection "is little more than a play upon words." Rather, it is argued that apportionment cases, whatever the actual wording of the complaint, can involve no federal constitutional right except one resting on the guaranty of a republican form of government, and that complaints based on that clause have been held to present political questions which are nonjusticiable.

We hold that the claim pleaded here neither rests upon nor implicates the Guaranty Clause. [To] show why we reject the argument based on the Guaranty Clause, we must examine the authorities under it. But because there appears to be some uncertainty as to why those cases did present political questions, and specifically as to whether this apportionment case is like those cases, we deem it necessary first to consider the contours of the "political question" doctrine.

Our discussion [requires] review of a number of political question cases, in order to expose the attributes of the doctrine — attributes which, in various settings, diverge, combine, appear, and disappear in seeming disorderliness.

We have said that "In determining whether a question falls within [the political question] category, the appropriateness under our system of government of attributing finality to the action of the political departments and also the lack of satisfactory criteria for a judicial determination are dominant considerations." The nonjusticiability of a political question is primarily a function of the separation of powers. Much confusion results from the capacity of the "political question" label to obscure the need for case-by-case inquiry. Deciding whether a matter has in any measure been committed by the Constitution to another branch of government, or whether the action of that branch exceeds whatever authority has been committed, is itself a delicate exercise in constitutional interpretation, and is a responsibility of this Court as ultimate interpreter of the Constitution.

Foreign relations: There are sweeping statements to the effect that all questions touching foreign relations are political questions. Not only does resolution of such issues frequently turn on standards that defy judicial application, or involve the exercise of a discretion demonstrably committed to the executive or legislature; but many such questions uniquely demand single-voiced statement of the Government's views. Yet it is error to suppose that every case or controversy which touches foreign relations lies beyond judicial cognizance. Our cases in this field seem invariably to show a discriminating analysis of the particular question posed, in terms of the history of its management by the political branches, of its susceptibility to judicial handling in the light of its nature and posture in the specific case, and of the possible consequences of judicial action.

Dates of duration of hostilities: Though it has been stated broadly that "the power which declared the necessity is the power to declare its cessation, and what the cessation requires," here too analysis reveals isolable reasons for the presence of political questions, underlying this Court's refusal to review the political departments' determination of when or whether a war has ended. Dominant is the need for finality in the political determination, for emergency's nature demands "A prompt and unhesitating obedience." . . . . Further, clearly definable criteria for decision may be available. In such cases the political question barrier falls away. . . .

Validity of enactments: In Coleman v. Miller, [307 U.S. 433 (1939)], this Court held that the questions of how long a proposed amendment to the Federal Constitution remained open to ratification, and what effect a prior rejection had on a subsequent ratification, were committed to congressional resolution and involved criteria of decision that necessarily escaped the judicial grasp. Similar considerations apply to the enacting process: "The respect due to coequal and independent departments," and the need for finality and certainty about the status of a statute contribute to judicial reluctance to inquire whether, as passed, it complied with all requisite formalities. . . .

It is apparent that several formulations which vary slightly according to the settings in which the questions arise may describe a political question, although each has one or more elements which identify it as essentially a function of the separation of powers. Prominent on the surface of any case held to involve a political question is found a textually demonstrable constitutional commitment of the issue to a coordinate political department; or a lack of judicially discoverable and manageable standards for resolving it; or the impossibility of deciding without an initial policy determination of a kind clearly for nonjudicial discretion; or the impossibility of a court's undertaking independent resolution without expressing lack of the respect due coordinate branches of government; or an unusual need for unquestioning adherence to a political decision already made; or the potentiality of embarrassment from multifarious pronouncements by various departments on one question.

Unless one of these formulations is inextricable from the case at bar, there should be no dismissal for nonjusticiability on the ground of a political question's presence. The doctrine of which we treat is one of "political questions," not one of "political cases." . . .

But it is argued that this case shares the characteristics of decisions that constitute a category not yet considered, cases concerning the Constitution's guaranty [of] a republican form of government. [Guaranty] Clause claims involve those elements which define a "political question," and for that reason and no other, they are nonjusticiable. In particular, [the] nonjusticiability of such claims has nothing to do with their touching upon matters of state governmental organization.

Luther v. Borden, [7 How. 1 (1849)], though in form simply an action for damages for trespass was, as Daniel Webster said in opening the argument for the defense, "an unusual case." The defendants, admitting an otherwise tortious breaking and entering, sought to justify their action on the ground that they were agents of the established lawful government of Rhode Island, which State was then under martial law to defend itself from active insurrection; that the plaintiff was engaged in that insurrection; and that they entered under orders to arrest the plaintiff. The case arose "out of the unfortunate political differences which agitated the people of Rhode Island in 1841 and 1842," [and] which had resulted in a situation wherein two groups laid competing claims to recognition as the lawful government. The plaintiff's right to recover depended upon which of the two groups was entitled to such recognition; but the lower court's refusal to receive evidence or hear argument on that issue, its charge to the jury that the earlier established or "charter" government was lawful, and the verdict for the defendants, were affirmed upon appeal to this Court.

Chief Justice Taney's opinion for the Court reasoned as follows: (1) If a court were to hold the defendants' acts unjustified because the charter government had no legal existence during the period in question, it would follow that all of that government's actions — laws enacted, taxes collected, salaries paid, accounts settled, sentences passed — were of no effect; and that "the officers who carried their decisions into operation [were] answerable as trespassers, if not in some cases as criminals." [A] decision for the plaintiff would inevitably have produced some significant measure of chaos. . . .

(2) No state court had recognized as a judicial responsibility settlement of the issue of the locus of state governmental authority. Indeed, the courts of Rhode Island had in several cases held that "it rested with the political power to decide whether the charter government had been displaced or not," and that that department had acknowledged no change.

(3) Since "[t]he question relates, altogether, to the constitution and laws of [the] . . . State," the courts of the United States had to follow the state courts' decisions unless there was a federal constitutional ground for overturning them.

(4) No provision of the Constitution could be or had been invoked for this purpose except Art. IV, §4, the Guaranty Clause. Having already noted the absence of standards whereby the choice between governments could be made by a court acting independently, Chief Justice Taney now found further textual and practical reasons for concluding that, if any department of the United States was empowered by the Guaranty Clause to resolve the issue, it was not the judiciary:

> Under this article of the Constitution it rests with Congress to decide what government is the established one in a State. . . .
> [After] the President has acted and called out the militia, is a Circuit Court of the United States authorized to inquire whether his decision was right? . . . If the judicial power extends so far, the guarantee contained in the Constitution of the United States is a guarantee of anarchy, and not of order. . . .

Clearly, several factors were thought by the Court in *Luther* to make the question there "political": the commitment to the other branches of the decision as to which is the lawful state government; the unambiguous action by the President, in recognizing the charter government as the lawful authority; the need for finality in the executive's decision; and the lack of criteria by which a court could determine which form of government was republican.

But the only significance that *Luther* could have for our immediate purposes is in its holding that the Guaranty Clause is not a repository of judicially manageable standards which a court could utilize independently in order to identify a State's lawful government. . . .

We come, finally, to the ultimate inquiry whether our precedents as to what constitutes a nonjusticiable "political question" bring the case before us under the umbrella of that doctrine. A natural beginning is to note whether any of the common characteristics which we have been able to identify and label descriptively are present. We find none: The question here is the consistency of state action with the Federal Constitution. We have no question decided, or to be decided, by a political branch of government coequal with this Court. Nor do we risk embarrassment of our government abroad, or grave disturbance at home if we take issue with Tennessee as to the constitutionality of her action here challenged. Nor need the appellants, in order to succeed in this action, ask the Court to enter upon policy determinations for which judicially manageable standards are lacking. Judicial standards under the Equal Protection Clause are well developed and familiar, and it has been open to courts since the enactment of the Fourteenth Amendment to determine, if on the particular facts they must, that a discrimination reflects *no* policy, but simply arbitrary and capricious action.

This case does, in one sense, involve the allocation of political power within a State, and the appellants might conceivably have added a claim under the Guaranty Clause. Of course, as we have seen, any reliance on that clause would be futile. But because any reliance on the Guaranty Clause could not have succeeded it does not follow that appellants may not be heard on the equal protection claim which in fact they tender. True, it must be clear that the Fourteenth Amendment claim is not so enmeshed with those political question elements which render Guaranty Clause claims nonjusticiable as actually to present a political question itself. But we have found that not to be the case here.

[Reversed and remanded.]

MR. JUSTICE FRANKFURTER, whom MR. JUSTICE HARLAN joins, dissenting.

The Court today reverses a uniform course of decision established by a dozen cases, including one by which the very claim now sustained was unanimously rejected only five years ago. The impressive body of rulings thus cast aside reflected the equally uniform course of our political history regarding the relationship between population and legislative representation — a wholly different matter from denial of the franchise to individuals because of race, color, religion or sex. [Disregard] of inherent limits in the effective exercise of the Court's "judicial Power" not only presages the futility of judicial intervention in the essentially political conflict of forces by which the relation between population and representation has time out of mind been and now is determined. It may well impair the Court's position as the ultimate organ of "the supreme Law of the Land" in that vast range of legal problems, often strongly entangled in popular feeling, on which this Court must pronounce. The Court's authority — possessed of neither the purse nor the sword — ultimately rests on sustained public confidence in its moral sanction. Such feeling must be nourished by the Court's complete detachment, in fact and in appearance, from political entanglements and by abstention from injecting itself into the clash of political forces in political settlements.

A hypothetical claim resting on abstract assumptions is now for the first time made the basis for affording illusory relief for a particular evil even though it foreshadows deeper and more pervasive difficulties in consequence. The claim is hypothetical and the assumptions are abstract because the Court does not vouchsafe the lower courts — state and federal — guidelines for formulating specific, definite, wholly unprecedented remedies for the inevitable litigations that today's umbrageous disposition is bound to stimulate in connection with politically motivated reapportionments in so many States. In such a setting, to promulgate jurisdiction in the abstract is meaningless. It is as devoid of reality as "a brooding omnipresence in the sky," for it conveys no intimation what relief, if any, a District Court is capable of affording that would not invite legislatures to play ducks and drakes with the judiciary. [To] charge courts with the task of accommodating the incommensurable factors of policy that underlie these mathematical puzzles is to attribute, however flatteringly, omnicompetence to judges. . . .

We were soothingly told at the bar of this Court that we need not worry about the kind of remedy a court could effectively fashion once that abstract constitutional right to have courts pass on a state-wide system of electoral districting is recognized as a matter of judicial rhetoric, because legislatures would heed the Court's admonition. This is not only a euphoric hope. It implies a sorry confession of judicial impotence in place of a frank acknowledgment that there is not under our Constitution a judicial remedy for every political mischief, for every undesirable exercise of legislative power. [Appeal] must be to an informed, civically militant electorate. In a democratic society like ours, relief must come through an aroused popular conscience that sears the conscience of the people's representatives. In any event there is nothing judicially more unseemly nor more self-defeating than for this Court to make in terrorem pronouncements, to indulge in merely empty rhetoric, sounding a word of promise to the ear, sure to be disappointing to the hope.

[From] its earliest opinions this Court has consistently recognized a class of controversies which do not lend themselves to judicial standards and judicial remedies. . . .

1. The cases concerning war or foreign affairs, for example, are usually explained by the necessity of the country's speaking with one voice in such matters. While this concern alone undoubtedly accounts for many of the decisions, others do not fit the pattern. It would hardly embarrass the conduct of war were this Court to determine, in connection with private transactions between litigants, the date upon which war is to be deemed terminated. But the Court has refused to do so. [A] controlling factor in such cases is that [there] exists no standard ascertainable [by] reference to which a political decision affecting the question at issue between the parties can be judged. . . .

2. The Court has been particularly unwilling to intervene in matters concerning the structure and organization of the political institutions of the States. The abstention from judicial entry into such areas has been greater even than that which marks the Court's ordinary approach to issues of state power challenged under broad federal guarantees. . . .

Where, however, state law has made particular federal questions determinative of relations within the structure of state government, not in challenge of it, the

Court has resolved such narrow, legally defined questions in proper proceedings. In such instances there is no conflict between state policy and the exercise of federal judicial [power.] . . .

3. The cases involving Negro disfranchisement are no exception to the principle of avoiding federal judicial intervention into matters of state government in the absence of an explicit and clear constitutional imperative. For here the controlling command of Supreme Law is plain and unequivocal. An end of discrimination against the Negro was the compelling motive of the Civil War Amendments. . . .

4. The Court has refused to exercise its jurisdiction to pass on "abstract questions of political power, of sovereignty, of government." [The] "political question" doctrine, in this aspect, reflects the policies underlying the requirement of "standing": that the litigant who would challenge official action must claim infringement of an interest particular and personal to himself, as distinguished from a cause of dissatisfaction with the general frame and functioning of government — a complaint that the political institutions are awry. [What] renders cases of this kind non-justiciable is not necessarily the nature of the parties to them, for the Court has resolved other issues between similar parties; nor is it the nature of the legal question involved, for the same type of question has been adjudicated when presented in other forms of controversy. The crux of the matter is that courts are not fit instruments of decision where what is essentially at stake is the composition of those large contests of policy traditionally fought out in non-judicial forums, by which governments and the actions of governments are made and unmade. . . .

5. The influence of these converging considerations — the caution not to undertake decision where standards meet for judicial judgment are lacking, the reluctance to interfere with matters of state government in the absence of an unquestionable and effectively enforceable mandate, the unwillingness to make courts arbiters of the broad issues of political organization historically committed to other institutions and for whose adjustment the judicial process is ill-adapted — has been decisive of the settled line of cases, reaching back more than a century, which holds that Art. IV, §4, of the Constitution, guaranteeing to the States "a Republican Form of Government," is not enforceable through the courts. . . .

The present case involves all of the elements that have made the Guarantee Clause cases non-justiciable. It is, in effect, a Guarantee Clause claim masquerading under a different label. But it cannot make the case more fit for judicial action that appellants invoke the Fourteenth Amendment rather than Art. IV, §4, where, in fact, the gist of their complaint is the same — unless it can be found that the Fourteenth Amendment speaks with greater particularity to their situation. We have been admonished to avoid "the tyranny of labels." Art. IV, §4, is not committed by express constitutional terms to Congress. It is the nature of the controversies arising under it, nothing else, which has made it judicially unenforceable. But where judicial competence is wanting, it cannot be created by invoking one clause of the Constitution rather than another.

[Appellants] invoke the right to vote[, but] they are permitted to vote and their votes are counted. [Their] complaint is simply that the representatives are not sufficiently numerous or powerful. [It] will add a virulent source of friction and tension in Federal-state relations to embroil the Federal judiciary in [apportionment battles]. . . .

[Concurring opinions by Justices Douglas, Clark, and Stewart are omitted here. Justice Clark stressed that Tennessee's apportionment scheme was "a crazy quilt." A dissenting opinion by Justice Harlan, arguing that no federal constitutional right was at stake, is also omitted.]

Note: Political Questions

1. *In general.* Alexis deToqueville observed that "There is hardly a political question in the United States that does not sooner or later turn into a judicial one." Democracy in America 270 (J. P. Mayer ed. 1969). After Baker v. Carr, the narrowness of the political question doctrine might be thought to support the point. At least if there are constitutional constraints on the executive or legislative conduct at issue, the political question doctrine is unlikely to come into play. Note that this conclusion was presaged by Marbury v. Madison, in which Chief Justice Marshall said questions would be deemed "political" if there was "legal discretion" in the circumstances.

Has standing doctrine been altered to diminish the "friction" between the branches after (what some consider) the narrow interpretation of the political question doctrine in Baker v. Carr? Consider the possibility that Allen v. Wright, *Richardson*, and *Schlesinger* reflect lurking "political question" concerns.

2. *Justiciable standards.* The primary ground on which to find a political question is that there are no "judicially cognizable standards" by which to assess the claim of unconstitutionality. This understanding means that, in order to say whether there is a political question, the court has to examine both the relevant constitutional provision and the plaintiff's legal claim: Does the former set out criteria by which a court can assess the latter? If it does not, the question is labeled "political."

If this is the correct approach, is there any difference between saying that a suit presents a political question and saying that there is no constitutional violation on the merits? If there is no difference, one might conclude that there is no "political question doctrine" at all; cases are deemed "political" only when there is no constitutional violation. See Henkin, Is There a Political Question Doctrine?, 85 Yale L.J. 597 (1976).

Note also that in cases in which there are no legal standards for assessing a claim of unconstitutionality, there is no tension between the political question doctrine and Marbury v. Madison. The Court retains the authority to "say what the law is." The reason the case is nonjusticiable is that the law does not say anything that is relevant to the dispute.

3. *Prudential concerns and* Marbury. Should the Court find nonjusticiable, on political question grounds, any cases or issues that do not fall within the category of "no judicially cognizable standards"? Would such a conclusion be inconsistent with *Marbury?* On what premises might one conclude that even if there is a constitutional violation, courts ought not to have the authority to intervene? Consider cases in which recognition of the constitutional claim might require a change in relations with a foreign government, a substantial expenditure of federal funds, or, in the words of the Court in Allen v. Wright, a restructuring of the operations of a coordinate branch of government. If political safeguards are

available to redress the challenged action, should a court be less willing to hear the case? Note the discussion of *Richardson* and *Schlesinger*, supra.

Some of the "political question" cases have been connected in some way to foreign affairs; and even when the Court does review a claim of unconstitutionality in that context, it is often quite deferential to the President and Congress. How might this phenomenon be justified? Is it because the costs of error, on the part of the Court, are unusually high?

Consider the following cases.

a. *Congressional power: excluding representatives, foreign affairs, and impeachment.* Powell v. McCormack, 395 U.S. 486 (1969), involved a House resolution that forbade Adam Clayton Powell from taking his seat in the House because of a finding that Powell had, among other things, "wrongfully diverted House funds for the use of others and himself" and had "made false reports on expenditures of foreign currency to the Committee on House Administration." Noting that he satisfied the age, citizenship, and residence requirements of article I, section 2, clause 2, Powell sought a declaration that his exclusion was unconstitutional.

The defendant invoked article 1, section 5, clause 1, which states that "each House shall be the Judge of the . . . Qualification of its own Members," contending that this clause revealed a textually demonstrable commitment to the House of power to set qualifications for membership and to judge whether those qualifications had been met. The Court said:

> In order to determine whether there has been a textual commitment to a co-ordinate department of the Government, we must interpret the Constitution. In other words, we must first determine what power the Constitution confers upon the House through Art. I, §5, before we can determine to what extent, if any, the exercise of that power is subject to judicial review. Respondents maintain that the House has broad power under §5, and, they argue, the House may determine which are the qualifications necessary for membership. . . .
>
> If examination of §5 disclosed that the Constitution gives the House judicially unreviewable power to set qualifications for membership and to judge whether prospective members meet those qualifications, further review of the House determination might well be barred by the political question doctrine. On the other hand, if the Constitution gives the House power to judge only whether elected members possess the three standing qualifications set forth in the Constitution, further consideration would be necessary to determine whether any of the other formulations of the political question doctrine are inextricable from the case at bar.
>
> In other words, whether there is a "textually demonstrable constitutional commitment of the issue to a coordinate political department" of government and what is the scope of such commitment are questions we must resolve for the first time in this case.
>
> In order to determine the scope of any "textual commitment" under Art. I, §5, we necessarily must determine the meaning of the phrase to "be the Judge of the Qualifications of its own Members." Petitioners argue that the records of the debates during the Constitutional Convention; available commentary from the post-Convention, pre-ratification period; and early congressional applications of Art. I, §5, support their construction of the section. Respondents insist, however, that a careful examination of the pre-Convention practices of the English Parliament and American colonial assemblies demonstrates that by 1787, a legislature's power to judge the qualifications of its members was generally understood to encompass exclusion or expulsion on the ground that an individual's character or past conduct rendered him unfit to serve. When the Constitution and the debates over its adop-

tion are thus viewed in historical perspective, argue respondents, it becomes clear that the "qualifications" expressly set forth in the Constitution were not meant to limit the long-recognized legislative power to exclude or expel at will, but merely to establish "standing incapacities," which could be altered only by a constitutional amendment. Our examination of the relevant historical materials leads us to the conclusion that petitioners are correct and that the Constitution leaves the House without authority to *exclude* any person, duly elected by his constituents, who meets all the requirements for membership expressly prescribed in the Constitution.

[Respondents'] alternate contention is that the case presents a political question because judicial resolution of petitioners' claim would produce a "potentially embarrassing confrontation between coordinate branches" of the Federal Government. But, as our interpretation of Art. I, §5, discloses, a determination of petitioner Powell's right to sit would require no more than an interpretation of the Constitution. Such a determination falls within the traditional role accorded courts to interpret the law, and does not involve a "lack of the respect due [a] coordinate [branch] of government," nor does it involve an "initial policy determination of a kind clearly for nonjudicial discretion." [Baker v. Carr.] Our system of government requires that federal courts on occasion interpret the Constitution in a manner at variance with the construction given the document by another branch. The alleged conflict that such an adjudication may cause cannot justify the courts' avoiding their constitutional responsibility.

Nor are any of the other formulations of a political question "inextricable from the case at bar." [Baker v. Carr.] Petitioners seek a determination that the House was without power to exclude Powell from the 90th Congress, which, we have seen, requires an interpretation of the Constitution — a determination for which clearly there are "judicially . . . manageable standards." Finally, a judicial resolution of petitioners' claim will not result in "multifarious pronouncements by various departments on one question." For [it] is the responsibility of this Court to act as the ultimate interpreter of the Constitution. [*Marbury.*] Thus, we conclude that petitioners' claim is not barred by the political question doctrine, and, having determined that the claim is otherwise generally justiciable, we hold that the case is justiciable.

Compare with *Powell* the decision in Goldwater v. Carter, 444 U.S. 996 (1979), summarily reversing a court of appeals decision that the President has authority to terminate a treaty with Taiwan without congressional approval. Justice Rehnquist, in an opinion joined by The Chief Justice and Justices Stewart and Stevens, wrote an opinion concurring in the judgment:

I am of the view that the basic question presented by the petitioners in this case is "political" and therefore nonjusticiable because it involves the authority of the President in the conduct of our country's foreign relations and the extent to which the Senate or the Congress is authorized to negate the action of the President. In Coleman v. Miller, 307 U.S. 433 (1939), a case in which members of the Kansas Legislature brought an action attacking a vote of the State Senate in favor of the ratification of the Child Labor Amendment, Mr. Chief Justice Hughes wrote in what is referred to as the "Opinion of the Court":

We think that . . . the question of the efficacy of ratifications by state legislatures, in the light of previous rejection or attempted withdrawal, should be regarded as a political question pertaining to the political departments, with the ultimate authority in the Congress in the exercise of its control over the promulgation of the adoption of the Amendment. . . .

Thus, Mr. Chief Justice Hughes' opinion concluded that "Congress in controlling the promulgation of the adoption of a constitutional amendment has the final determination of the question whether by lapse of time its proposal of the amendment had lost its vitality prior to the required ratifications."

I believe it follows a fortiori from *Coleman* that the controversy in the instant case is a nonjusticiable political dispute that should be left for resolution by the Executive and Legislative Branches of the Government. Here, while the Constitution is express as to the manner in which the Senate shall participate in the ratification of a treaty, it is silent as to that body's participation in the abrogation of a treaty. [In] light of the absence of any constitutional provision governing the termination of a treaty, and the fact that different termination procedures may be appropriate for different treaties the instant case in my view also "must surely be controlled by political standards."

I think that the justifications for concluding that the question here is political in nature are even more compelling than in *Coleman* because it involves foreign relations — specifically a treaty commitment to use military force in the defense of a foreign government if attacked.

The present case differs in several important respects from [*Youngstown*, infra, Chapter 4]. [Here we] are asked to settle a dispute between coequal branches of our Government, each of which has resources available to protect and assert its interests, resources not available to private litigants outside the judicial forum. Moreover, [the] effect of this action, as far as we can tell, is "entirely external to the United States, and [falls] within the category of foreign affairs." Finally, as already noted, the situation presented here is closely akin to that presented in *Coleman*, where the Constitution spoke only to the procedure for ratification of an amendment, not to its rejection.

Justice Powell wrote a separate concurring opinion:

Although I agree with the result reached by the Court, I would dismiss the complaint as not ripe for judicial review.

[No] constitutional provision explicitly confers upon the President the power to terminate treaties. Further, Art. II, §2, of the Constitution authorizes the President to make treaties with the advice and consent of the Senate. Article VI provides that treaties shall be a part of the supreme law of the land. These provisions add support to the view that the text of the Constitution does not unquestionably commit the power to terminate treaties to the President alone.

[There] is no "lack of judicially discoverable and manageable standards for resolving" this case; nor is a decision impossible "without an initial policy determination of a kind clearly for nonjudicial discretion." We are asked to decide whether the President may terminate a treaty under the Constitution without congressional approval. Resolution of the question may not be easy, but it only requires us to apply normal principles of interpretation to the constitutional provisions at issue. The present case involves neither review of the President's activities as Commander in Chief nor impermissible interference in the field of foreign affairs. [This] case "touches" foreign relations, but the question presented to us concerns only the constitutional division of power between Congress and the President.

[Interpretation] of the Constitution does not imply lack of respect for a coordinate branch. If the President and the Congress had reached irreconcilable positions, final disposition of the question presented by this case would eliminate, rather than create, multiple constitutional interpretations. The specter of the Federal Government brought to a halt because of the mutual intransigence of the President and the Congress would require this Court to provide a resolution pursuant to our duty " 'to say what the law is.' "

Justice Brennan dissented:

> In stating that this case presents a nonjusticiable "political question," Mr. Justice Rehnquist, in my view, profoundly misapprehends the political-question principle as it applies to matters of foreign relations. Properly understood, the political-question doctrine restrains courts from reviewing an exercise of foreign policy judgment by the coordinate political branch to which authority to make that judgment has been "constitutional[ly] commit[ted]." But the doctrine does not pertain when a court is faced with the *antecedent* question whether a particular branch has been constitutionally designated as the repository of political decisionmaking power. The issue of decisionmaking authority must be resolved as a matter of constitutional law, not political discretion; accordingly, it falls within the competence of the courts.
>
> The constitutional question raised here is prudently answered in narrow terms. Abrogation of the defense treaty with Taiwan was a necessary incident to Executive recognition of the Peking Government, because the defense treaty was predicated upon the now-abandoned view that the Taiwan Government was the only legitimate political authority in China. Our cases firmly establish that the Constitution commits to the President alone the power to recognize, and withdraw recognition from, foreign regimes. That mandate being clear, our judicial inquiry into the treaty rupture can go no further.

Consider the following case after Powell v. McCormack and Goldwater v. Carter. The Senate impeaches the President for a "high crime and misdemeanor." The Senate's view that the presidential misconduct is a "high crime and misdemeanor" would be rejected by the Court if it were to reach the question. But the Constitution grants to the Senate the "sole power to try all impeachments." Is judicial review of impeachment foreclosed because of a textual commitment to the Senate? Because of some other concern? Cf. Roudebush v. Hartke, 405 U.S. 15 (1972) (decision as to which candidate has received more lawful votes in an election is constitutionally committed to Senate).

b. *The peculiar case of the "republican form of government" clause.* Section 4 of article IV of the Constitution provides that "The United States shall guarantee to every State in this Union a Republican Form of Government." Several times this provision has been invoked by private litigants; but as Baker v. Carr suggests, the Supreme Court appears to have rendered it a dead letter with the political question doctrine.

The key case is Luther v. Borden, 7 How. 1 (1849), an action for trespass. *Luther* grew out of the Door Rebellion in Rhode Island and a conflict between various people claiming authority to act for the government of Rhode Island. The defendants claimed that the acts charged as a trespass were done under the authority of the charter government during a period of martial law in order to aid in the suppression of a revolt by supporters of an insurrectionary government. The defendants thus admitted that they had trespassed but claimed that they were agents of the lawful government of Rhode Island and that their acts were authorized as part of an order to arrest the plaintiff. The plaintiffs claimed that the charter government was unlawful. They invoked the republican form of government clause, claiming that the people have the ultimate power of sovereignty and that if the government was to be free, they must have a right to change their constitution. The case thus turned on which of the two groups was entitled to recognition as the lawful government.

The Court responded:

> [It] rests with congress to decide what government is the established one in a State. For, as the United States guarantee to each State a republican government, congress must necessarily decide what government is established in the State before it can determine whether it is republican or not. And when the senators and representatives of a State are admitted into the councils of the Union, the authority of the government under which they are appointed, as well as its republican character, is recognized by the proper constitutional authority. And its decision is binding on every other department of the government, and could not be questioned in a judicial tribunal. It is true that the contest in this case did not last long enough to bring the matter to this issue; and as no senators or representatives were elected under the authority of the government of which Mr. Dorr was the head, Congress was not called upon to decide the controversy. Yet the right to decide is placed there, and not in the courts.

Recall the Court's explanation of *Luther* in Baker v. Carr. Is the explanation faithful to the opinion in *Luther?*

In Pacific Telephone Co. v. Oregon, 223 U.S. 118 (1912), plaintiffs challenged a citizen initiatives provision in the Oregon constitution, which allowed a stated number of voters to secure, at any time, a submission to popular vote for approval of any matter which it wished to have enacted into law. Any proposal approved in that way would become law. The law at issue in *Pacific Telephone* taxed certain telephone and telegraph companies at a certain rate. According to those companies, the initiative procedure violated the "republican form of government" clause.

The Court responded by referring to "the inconceivable expansion of the judicial power" that would result from an adjudication:

> [However] perfect and absolute may be the establishment and dominion in fact of a state government, however complete may be its participation in and enjoyment of all its powers and rights as a member of national Government, [nevertheless] every citizen of such State [may] be heard, for the purpose of defeating the payment of such taxes or avoiding the discharge of such duty, to assail in a court of justice the rightful existence of the State.

Is *Pacific Telephone* consistent with Baker v. Carr? Note that the republican form of government clause is addressed to the "United States," not only to Congress. Did that clause fail to provide justiciable standards in *Luther* and *Pacific Telephone?* For discussion, see W. Wiecek, The Guarantee Clause of the United States Constitution (1947); Bonfield, The Guarantee Clause of Article IV, Section 4: A Study in Constitutional Desuetude, 46 Minn. L. Rev. 513 (1962); Note, A Niche for the Guarantee Clause, 94 Harv. L. Rev. (1981).

    c. *Constitutional amendments.* Assume that there is some irregularity in the process by which a constitutional amendment is ratified. Should a court declare the amendment ineffective? The principal case here is Coleman v. Miller, 307 U.S. 433 (1939), which involved a proposed child labor amendment to the Constitution. Of the forty senators in Kansas, twenty had voted in favor and twenty against; the lieutenant governor cast his vote in favor, and the amendment was eventually considered to have been adopted by the Kansas legislature. The twenty senators who had voted against ratification brought suit, contending that the lieutenant governor had no right to cast the tiebreaking vote and that the proposed amendment lost its vitality because of its rejection by Kansas and other states within what they claimed to be the requisite reasonable time. The remedy sought was a writ of mandamus to compel the Kansas secretary of the state to endorse on the relevant documents that the amendment had not been passed and to restrain state officials from signing the resolution and delivering it to the governor.

On the question whether the lieutenant governor was part of the legislature for article V purposes, the Court was evenly divided on the "political question" issue and therefore expressed no view. But on the "reasonable time" question, the Court concluded that the case was not justiciable:

> Where are to be found the criteria for such a judicial determination? None are to be found in the Constitution itself. In their endeavor to answer this question petitioners' counsel have suggested that at least two years should be allowed; that six years would not seem to be unreasonably long. [To] this list of variables, counsel add that "the nature and extent of publicity and the activity of the public and of legislatures of the several States in relation to any particular proposal should be taken into consideration." This statement is pertinent, but there are additional matters to be examined and weighed. [In] short, the question of a reasonable time in many cases would involve, as this case does involve, an appraisal of a great variety of relevant conditions, political, social and economic, which can hardly be said to be within the appropriate range of evidence receivable in a court of justice. [These] conditions are appropriate for the consideration of the political departments of the Government.

Several separate opinions were filed. Justice Black, joined by Justices Roberts, Frankfurter, and Douglas, expressed a somewhat broader view. He wrote that the

> Constitution grants Congress exclusive power to control submission of constitutional amendments. [In] the exercise of that power, Congress, of course, is governed by the Constitution. However, whether submission, intervening procedure, or Congressional determination of ratification conforms to the commands of the Constitution, calls for decisions by a "political department" of questions of a type which this Court has frequently designated "political."

Justice Frankfurter expressed the view that the state senators had no standing to bring suit. Justice Butler dissented. In his view, "Article V impliedly requires amendments submitted to be ratified within a reasonable time after proposal," and "more than a reasonable time had elapsed" in this case.

To what extent should *Coleman* be read to immunize the amendment process from judicial supervision? This issue arose most recently over the equal rights amendment, in the context both of efforts by some states to rescind earlier ratifications — efforts that, in the view of some, were not legally effective — and of an attempted extension by Congress of the period for ratification. Should the Court decide either or both of these questions?

Consider Dellinger, The Legitimacy of Constitutional Change: Rethinking the Amendment Process, 97 Harv. L. Rev. 386, 397-398, 411 (1983), which labels *Coleman* an "aberration" and contends that

> The assumption that judicial review is precluded by the existence of the exclusive power of the promulgating Congress to determine the validity of ratifications is, in

my view, wholly unwarranted. Neither the text of the Constitution nor prior congressional practice nor judicial precedent supports this bestowal of exclusive power on Congress. [Whether] or not judicial review of Article V issues would materially advance larger goals of the amendment process, such review is justified as an initial matter by the same considerations that have made judicial review an accepted part of the Constitution since Marbury v. Madison.

Professor Dellinger stresses the increased certainty that would result from some judicial supervision of the amendment process.

Compare Tribe, A Constitution We Are Amending: In Defense of a Restrained Judicial Role, 97 Harv. L. Rev. 433, 435-446 (1983), rejecting the view that

> added certainty in the application of article V is enough of a virtue to warrant the enormous vices that exclusive judicial review [would] entail. Among those vices is the danger [of] having the Supreme Court closely "oversee the very constitutional process used to reverse its decision." [The] resort to amendment — to constitutional politics as opposed to constitutional law — should be taken as a sign that the legal system has come to a point of discontinuity, a point at which something less radical than revolution but distinctly more radical than ordinary legal evolution is called for. To say that at such a moment in history we should necessarily conduct our legal business as usual, seeking certainty and harmony rather than tolerating discord, is to miss the very essence of the event at hand.

d. *Foreign affairs.* Some of the political question cases have arisen in the field of foreign affairs. Consider Goldwater v. Carter, supra, and the discussion in Baker v. Carr. What considerations support a deferential judicial posture? The high costs of error? The need for the nation to speak with one voice?

Consider the following case. The President initiates a war in circumstances in which he is not constitutionally authorized to do so. (On the question of presidential warmaking authority, see Chapter 4, infra.) If a declaration or injunction is sought, is judicial review available? Some of these issues arose in the context of the Vietnam War. See Mora v. McNamara, 389 U.S. 934 (1967) (Stewart, J., dissenting from denial of certiorari in case involving legality of Vietnam War); Orlando v. Laird, 443 F.2d 1039 (2d Cir. 1971) (finding some issues raised by Vietnam War to be justiciable). See generally Tigar, The "Political Question" Doctrine and Foreign Relations, 17 U.C.L.A. L. Rev. 1135 (1970); Velvel, The War in Viet Nam: Unconstitutional, Justiciable, and Jurisdictionally Attackable, 16 Kan. L. Rev. 449 (1968). Are political safeguards sufficient in this context?

e. *Miscellaneous cases.* In many cases, of course, the Court has reached the merits of a constitutional controversy notwithstanding the implications for foreign affairs, the high stakes, or the fact of interbranch disagreement. In INS v. Chadha, 462 U.S. 919 (1983), the Court rejected a political question challenge to its power to consider the legality of the "legislative veto" — a device, opposed by every President from Wilson to Reagan, by which one House of Congress might "veto" executive action by a majority vote. The Court observed that the controversy "may, in a sense, be termed 'political.' But the presence of constitutional issues with significant political overtones does not automatically invoke the political question doctrine. Resolution of litigation challenging the constitutional authority of one of the three branches cannot be evaded by courts because the issues have political implications in the sense urged by Congress."

See also Dames & Moore v. Regan, 453 U.S. 654 (1981) (reaching merits of dispute over legality of President Carter's executive agreement for the release of U.S. hostages in Iran); United States v. Nixon, 418 U.S. 683 (1974) (ordering President Nixon to turn over Watergate tapes); Youngstown Sheet & Tube Co. v. Sawyer, 343 U.S. 579 (1952) (invalidating President Truman's seizure of the steel mills despite President's claim that national emergency required seizure); United States v. Curtiss-Wright Export Corp., 299 U.S. 304 (1936) (reaching merits of congressional delegation of power to President to prohibit sale of arms to countries engaged in armed conflict).

6. *Concluding thoughts.* Consider Henkin, supra, at 622-624:

> The "political question doctrine," I conclude, is an unnecessary, deceptive packaging of several established doctrines that has misled lawyers and courts to find in it things that were never put there. [I] see its proper content as consisting of the following propositions: 1. The courts are bound to accept decisions by the political branches within their constitutional authority. 2. The courts will not find limitations or prohibitions on the powers of the political branches where the Constitution does not prescribe any. 3. Not all constitutional limitations or prohibitions imply rights and standing to object in favor of private parties. 4. The courts may refuse some (or all) remedies for want of equity. 5. In principle, finally, there might be constitutional provisions which can properly be interpreted as wholly or in part "self-monitoring" and not the subject of judicial review. (But the only one courts have found is the "guarantee clause" as applied to challenges to state action, and even that interpretation was not inevitable.) [These] propositions do not include any basis for refusing to consider, in a category of cases uncertain in rationale and definition, an allegation that the political branches have acted unconstitutionally.

Note that this approach would permit courts to reach issues, in both domestic and foreign realms, no matter how great the level of friction thereby created between courts and other branches of the government. And consider the fact that on perhaps rare occasions, the Court seems to have found a "political question" because of the high stakes involved and the consequences of judicial intrusion. Does Henkin's approach unduly limit the political question doctrine, for these reasons or for any other?

Note: Questions of Timing — Ripeness and Mootness

1. *In general.* Additional justiciability barriers relate to the timing of judicial review. The doctrine of ripeness bars courts from deciding cases that are premature — too speculative or remote to warrant judicial intervention. A classic example would be a case brought to challenge a criminal statute before a prosecution is initiated, in circumstances in which the mere existence of the statute is not alleged to produce actual harm. The doctrine of mootness prevents courts from hearing cases when events subsequent to the institution of the lawsuit have deprived the plaintiff of a stake in the action. A classic example would be a case

brought by a plaintiff challenging a statute prohibiting her from obtaining employment where the plaintiff has been given the job before the appeal. A case is not ripe when it is brought too soon; it is moot when it is brought too late.

2. *Ripeness.* Laird v. Tatum, 408 U.S. 1 (1972), involved a class action brought for injunctive relief against alleged "surveillance of lawful citizen political activity" by the U.S. Army. According to the plaintiffs, the army had collected information about political activities that had some potential for civil disorder; plaintiffs also claimed that they were targets of the surveillance and that, as a result, they were "chilled" from engaging in constitutionally protected activity. The Court held that the plaintiffs did not present "a case for resolution by the courts."

According to the Court, a "chilling effect" was insufficient if it arose "merely from the individual's knowledge that a government agency was engaged in certain activities or from the individual's concomitant fear that, armed with the fruits of those activities, the agency might in the future take some *other* and additional action detrimental to that individual." The Court said that the plaintiff's "approach would have the federal courts as virtually continuing monitors of the wisdom and soundness of Executive action; such a role is appropriate for the Congress rather than the judiciary, absent actual present or immediately threatened injury resulting from unlawful governmental action." Justice Douglas, joined by Justice Marshall, dissented. What was the timing problem in *Tatum?* When might these litigants be able to challenge the surveillance?

Compare with *Tatum* the decision in Adler v. Board of Education, 342 U.S. 485 (1952), which involved a challenge to a state law disqualifying from employment in public school anyone who was a member of assorted "subversive organizations." The plaintiffs, seeking a declaratory judgment, included parents and teachers of school children. The Court reached the merits without discussion, notwithstanding a dissent on ripeness grounds by Justice Frankfurter, who invoked United Public Workers v. Mitchell, 330 U.S. 75 (1947). In *Mitchell* federal civil service employees sought a declaratory judgment against the Hatch Act, which prohibits federal employees from participating in the management of political campaigns. The Court said that the plaintiffs' affidavits

> declare a desire to act contrary to the rule against political activity but not that the rule has been violated. [Appellants] seem clearly to seek advisory opinions upon broad claims. [Appellants] want to engage in "political management and political campaigns," [but] such generality of objection is really an attack on the political expediency of the Hatch Act, not a presentation of legal issues. It is beyond the competence of courts to render such a decision.

Did *Mitchell* in fact involve a legal question? Why was the threat of prosecution in *Mitchell* (or *Tatum*) insufficient to justify judicial relief? Was the abstract character of the dispute a real problem?

See also Socialist Labor Party v. Gilligan, 406 U.S. 583 (1972) (refusing to hear challenge to a statute requiring party members to pledge that they were not engaged in "an attempt to overthrow the government by force"; Court notes that the pleadings did not allege that party members have ever refused in the past or will now refuse to sign the oath, which has been in existence since 1941); Poe v. Ullman, 367 U.S. 497 (1961) (refusing to hear challenge to Connecticut prohibition on use of contraceptive devices on ground that there was no allegation that state threatened prosecution).

3. *Mootness*. DeFunis v. Odegaard, 416 U.S. 312 (1974), involved a challenge to a preferential admissions program adopted by the University of Washington Law School. By the time the case reached the Court, DeFunis was in his third year of law school as a result of a decision below ordering his admission. According to the law school, his registration would not be cancelled regardless of the Supreme Court's decision. The Court noted that voluntary cessation of allegedly unlawful conduct does not make the case moot; if it did, the defendant would be "free to return to his old ways." Here, however, mootness "depends not at all upon a 'voluntary cessation' of the admissions practices that were the subject of this litigation. It depends, instead, upon the simple fact that DeFunis is now in the final quarter of the final year of his course of study, and the settled and unchallenged policy of the Law School to permit him to complete the term for which he is now enrolled." The lower court found the case moot.

Compare Roe v. Wade, 410 U.S. 113 (1973), involving a challenge to abortion statutes. Roe herself was no longer pregnant by the time the case came to the Supreme Court. The Court nonetheless held that it was not moot, relying on the exception for cases that are "capable of repetition, yet evading review." If the termination of a pregnancy, the Court said, "makes a case moot, pregnancy litigation seldom will survive much beyond the trial stage, and appellate review will be effectively denied."

For general discussion, see Monaghan, Constitutional Adjudication: The Who and the When, 82 Yale L.J. 1381 (1974); Note, The Mootness Doctrine in the Supreme Court, 88 Harv. L. Rev. 373 (1974).

F. THE JURISDICTION OF THE SUPREME COURT

1. *In general.* For constitutional purposes, the jurisdiction of the Supreme Court is set out in article III. But Congress has never granted litigants access to the Court in all cases for which article III provides authorization. The governing provisions are set out in 28 U.S.C. §§1251-1257.

These provisions furnish two principal routes to the Supreme Court. The first is through an appeal; the second is through certiorari. It is generally said that the appellate jurisdiction is "mandatory." If a party who has lost below seeks review, the Court must hear any case that falls within its appellate jurisdiction. Certiorari jurisdiction, by contrast, is discretionary. The Court may deny certiorari for some reason other than its agreement with the decision below — the unimportance of the issue, the unusual character of the particular facts, the desire to see the issue "percolate" in the lower courts, the controversial character of the problem, or the wish to allow the political process time to consider the problem before an authoritative resolution is obtained. (Consider the views expressed by Bickel, supra.)

The most important provisions of the governing statutes grant the Supreme Court jurisdiction by way of an "appeal": (1) from a United States court of appeals when the decision below invalidates a state statute; (2) from a state court when the decision below invalidates a federal treaty or statute; and (3) from a state court when the decision below upholds a state statute against a claim that the statute violates federal constitutional or statutory law. The provisions grant the Supreme Court jurisdiction by way of "certiorari" (1) from a United States court of appeals in any civil or criminal case and (2) from a state court whenever (a) a challenge to a state or federal law is based on a federal issue or (b) a federal right, privilege, or immunity is set up or claimed. There is also a direct appeal from U.S. district courts in cases invalidating acts of Congress. Note that the availability of an appeal will sometimes turn on the skill of counsel: For an appeal from state court, for example, it is necessary to plead that a state statute is constitutionally invalid, not simply that a constitutional issue is at stake.

Litigants seeking certiorari must file a "petition for certiorari" setting out the reasons the case deserves plenary consideration. Rule 17 of the Supreme Court rules "while neither controlling nor fully measuring the Court's discretion, [indicates] the character of the reasons that will be considered":

> (a) When a federal court of appeals has rendered a decision in conflict with the decision of another federal court of appeals on the same matter; or has decided a federal question in a way in conflict with a state court of last resort; or has so far departed from the accepted and usual course of judicial proceedings [as] to call for an exercise of this Court's power of supervision.
>
> (b) When a state court of last resort has decided a federal question in a way in conflict with the decision of another state court of last resort or of a federal court of appeals.
>
> (c) When a state court or a federal court of appeals has decided an important question of federal law which has not been, but should be, settled by this Court, or has decided a federal question in way in conflict with apoplicable decisions of this Court.

Rules of the Supreme Court, 445 U.S. 983, 1003 (1980).

The manner of screening cases varies among the justices. Some members of the Court rely on law clerks to write brief memoranda about cases presented for certiorari; some justices read all or some of the petitions themselves; many of them participate in a "cert pool," in which one law clerk is assigned responsibility for writing a memorandum circulated to many of the chambers. Cases perceived to be of importance are placed on the "Discuss List" — the list of cases to be discussed by the justices in conference. From that list, the Court decides which cases to hear. See generally Alsup, A Policy Assessment of the National Court of Appeals, 25 Hast. L.J. 1313 (1974).

The general rule is that a denial of certiorari does not have any precedential value. Why might the Court be careful to ensure the perpetuation of that rule?

2. *The distinction between appeal and certiorari.* What explains the distinction between the cases subject to appeal and those subject to certiorari? The traditional rationale is that in some cases, there is a special need for Supreme Court review. The arguments offered in both *Marbury* and Martin v. Hunter's Lessee play an important role here. Is the current standard justifiable in light of those arguments?

Even if some classes of cases present a more compelling argument for Supreme Court review than others, one might conclude that such arguments should be taken into account by the Court itself in deciding whether to grant certiorari, and that there should be no mandatory appellate jurisdiction. Note that there is also some question about the practical importance of the appeal/certiorari distinction. Before an appeal is heard on the merits, the appellant must file a jurisdictional statement that is in many respects the same as a petition for certiorari. Frequently an appeal is disposed of "summarily," without full briefing and argument; the Court may dismiss for want of a substantial question, affirm, or dismiss for want of jurisdiction on the basis of the jurisdictional statement. The Court thus has considerable power to "screen" appeals. That power is limited by the fact that summary dispositions — unlike denials of certiorari — have some precedential value. But there is controversy over the extent of that value. See Hicks v. Miranda, 422 U.S. 332 (1975) (lower courts bound by such dispositions); Illinois State Board of Elections v. Socialist Workers Party, 440 U.S. 173 (1979) (such decisions "have considerably less precedential value than an opinion on the merits"). Some justices have suggested that the Court in fact treats jurisdictional statements in much the same way it treats certiorari petitions and that the distinction between mandatory and discretionary jurisdiction has become quite thin in practice.

In recent years, there have been many recommendations for abolition of the appeal/certiorari distinction. Many of these cases coming to the Court by way of appeal do not, it is said, have sufficient importance to merit plenary consideration, even if they fit within the current categories for mandatory jurisdiction. A state court may, for example, uphold a state statute against federal constitutional attack, but the ground for the attack may be frivolous. Should the Court be required to hear such a case? Should the mandatory jurisdiction be abolished?

3. *Independent and adequate state grounds.* Note also that the Court does not have jurisdiction under the relevant statutes to hear a case when the decision below rests on "adequate and independent state ground" — that is, when an issue of state law was actually decided that is sufficient to support the outcome. See Herb v. Pitcarin, 324 U.S. 117, 125 (1945); Michigan v. Long, 463 U.S. 1032 (1983). What is the reason for this rule? Can it be related to the ban on advisory opinions?

4. *The workload problem.* Considerable concern is sometimes expressed about the Supreme Court's workload, which had grown rapidly until the last few years. In recent years the Court has faced over 4,000 annual filings; in the 1940s, the Court faced fewer than 1,500. The number of full opinions, however, has not changed dramatically. For general discussion of the caseload problem of the federal courts, see R. Posner, Federal Courts: Crisis and Reform (1985); for the caseload in the Supreme Court, see G. Casper & R. Posner, The Workload of the Supreme Court (1976), and the annual Supreme Court issue of the Harvard Law Review.

II

The Powers of Congress

A. INTRODUCTION

Note: A Government of Enumerated Powers

1. *The origins of enumeration.* After the Revolution, the American colonists faced the task of creating one or more governments. Their first efforts, in which self-governing states joined a loose confederation, proved unsatisfactory. The government established under the Articles of Confederation was unable to guarantee that international commitments would be honored, to assure that sufficient force could be amassed to combat threats to security originating both within and without the states, or to establish a framework within which stable economic growth might proceed unhampered by localist jealousies.

Provoked by these difficulties, a number of leading political figures gathered in a convention designed nominally to amend but actually to replace the Articles of Confederation. Their goals were stated in the Preamble to the Constitution they drafted:

> We the People of the United States, in Order to form a more perfect Union, establish Justice, insure domestic Tranquility, provide for the common defence, promote the general Welfare, and secure the Blessings of Liberty to ourselves and our Posterity, do ordain and establish this Constitution for the United States of America.

(The framers regarded it as significant that, while the prior government was a federation created by the States, the new one was created by "the People." Before the Civil War and after Brown v. Board of Education, some Southerners argued that states could nullify the effect of national legislation. Does the language of the Preamble shed light on the cogency of such arguments?)

The background of the Constitution made it clear to the framers that the primary defect in the Articles of Confederation was its failure to give sufficient power to the national government. The framers therefore wanted to increase the power of the new government as compared to the old. But this raised two problems: (1) The framers believed that states ought to remain as significant units of government. The national government ought to exercise its power only on distinctively national subjects, while states would exercise control over most matters of general government. (2) Power granted to the national government might be improvidently used, so as to suppress liberty and choke economic development.

The framers sought to respond to those concerns by enumerating the powers granted to the national government.

2. *How enumeration limits powers: explicit limitations as an alternative.* In The Federalist No. 84, Hamilton argued that the enumeration made unnecessary a bill of rights, which would explicitly limit Congress's powers:

> It has been several times truly remarked that bills of rights are, in their origin, stipulations between kings and their subjects, abridgments of prerogative in favor of privilege, reservations of rights not surrendered to the prince. [Here,] in strictness, the people surrender nothing; and as they retain everything they have no need of particular reservations. . . .
>
> But a minute detail of particular rights is certainly far less applicable to a Constitution like that under consideration, which is merely intended to regulate the general political interests of the nation, than to a constitution which has the regulation of every species of personal and private concerns. . . .
>
> I go further and affirm that bills of rights [are] not only unnecessary in the proposed Constitution but would even be dangerous. They would contain various exceptions to powers not granted; and, on this very account, would afford a colorable pretext to claim more than were granted. For why declare that things shall not be done which there is no power to do? Why, for instance, should it be said that the liberty of the press shall not be restrained, when no power is given by which restrictions may be imposed? I will not contend that such a provision would confer a regulating power; but it is evident that it would furnish, to men disposed to usurp, a plausible pretense for claiming that power. They might urge with a semblance of reason that the Constitution ought not to be charged with the absurdity of providing against the abuse of an authority which was not given, and that the provision against restraining the liberty of the press afforded a clear implication that a power to prescribe proper regulations concerning it was intended to be vested in the national government. This may serve as a specimen of the numerous handles which would be given to the doctrine of constructive powers, by the indulgence of an injudicious zeal for bills of rights.
>
> On the subject of the liberty of the press, as much as has been said, I cannot forbear adding a remark or two. [What] is the liberty of the press? Who can give it any definition which would not leave the utmost latitude for evasion? I hold it to be impracticable; and from this I infer that its security, whatever fine declarations may be inserted in any constitution respecting it, must altogether depend on public opinion, and on the general spirit of the people and of the government.* And here, after all, [must] we seek for the only solid basis of all our rights.

As you study the materials that follow, consider whether Hamilton was right.

---

* To show that there is a power in the Constitution by which the liberty of the press may be affected, recourse has been had to the power of taxation. It is said that duties may be laid upon the publications so high as to amount to a prohibition. I know not by what logic it could be maintained that the declarations in the State constitutions, in favor of the freedom of the press, would be a constitutional impediment to the imposition of duties upon publications by the State legislatures. It cannot certainly be pretended that any degree of duties, however low, would be an abridgment of the liberty of the press. We know that newspapers are taxed in Great Britain, and yet it is notorious that

The Federalist Nos. 45 and 46 (Madison)

(1788)

The State governments will have the advantage of the federal government, whether we compare them in respect to the immediate dependence of the one on the other; to the weight of personal influence which each side will possess; to the powers respectively vested in them; to the predilection and probable support of the people; to the disposition and faculty of resisting and frustrating the measures of each other.

The State governments may be regarded as constituent and essential parts of the federal government; whilst the latter is nowise essential to the operation or organization of the former. Without the intervention of the State legislatures, the President of the United States cannot be elected at all. They must in all cases have a great share in his appointment, and will, perhaps, in most cases, of themselves determine it. The Senate will be elected absolutely and exclusively by the State legislatures. Even the House of Representatives, though drawn immediately from the people, will be chosen very much under the influence of that class of men whose influence over the people obtains for themselves an election into the State legislatures. Thus, each of the principal branches of the federal government will owe its existence more or less to the favor of the State governments, and must consequently feel a dependence, which is much more likely to beget a disposition too obsequious than too overbearing towards them. On the other side, the component parts of the State governments will in no instance be indebted for their appointment to the direct agency of the federal government, and very little, if at all, to the local influence of its members.

The number of individuals employed under the Constitution of the United States will be much smaller than the number employed under the particular States. There will consequently be less of personal influence on the side of the former than of the latter. The members of the legislative, executive, and judiciary departments of thirteen and more States, the justices of peace, officers of militia, ministerial officers of justice, with all the county, corporation, and town officers, for three millions and more of people, intermixed and having particular acquaintance with every class and circle of people must exceed, beyond all proportion, both in number and influence, those of every description who will be employed in the administration of the federal system. Compare the members of the three great departments of the thirteen States, excluding from the judiciary department the justices of peace, with the members of the corresponding departments of the single government of the Union; compare the militia officers of three millions of people with the military and marine officers of any establishment which is within the compass of probability, or, I may add, of possibility, and in this view alone, we may pronounce the advantage of the States to be decisive. . . .

---

the press nowhere enjoys greater liberty than in that country. And if duties of any kind may be laid without a violation of that liberty, it is evident that the extent must depend on legislative discretion, regulated by public opinion; so that, after all, general declarations respecting the liberty of the press will give it no greater security than it will have without them. The same invasions of it may be effected under the State constitutions which contain those declarations through the means of taxation, as under the proposed Constitution, which has nothing of the kind. It would be quite as significant to declare that government ought to be free, that taxes ought not to be excessive, etc., as that the liberty of the press ought not to be restrained.

The powers delegated by the proposed Constitution to the federal government are few and defined. Those which are to remain in the State governments are numerous and indefinite. The former will be exercised principally on external objects, as war, peace, negotiation, and foreign commerce; with which last the power of taxation will, for the most part, be connected. The powers reserved to the several States will extend to all the objects which, in the ordinary course of affairs, concern the lives, liberties, and properties of the people, and the internal order, improvement, and prosperity of the State.

The operations of the federal government will be most extensive and important in times of war and danger; those of the State governments in times of peace and security. As the former periods will probably bear a small proportion to the latter, the State governments will here enjoy another advantage over the federal government. The more adequate, indeed, the federal powers may be rendered to the national defense, the less frequent will be those scenes of danger which might favor their ascendancy over the governments of the particular States. . . .

[The] federal and State governments are in fact but different agents and trustees of the people, constituted with different powers and designed for different purposes. The adversaries of the Constitution seem to have lost sight of the people altogether in their reasonings on this subject; and to have viewed these different establishments not only as mutual rivals and enemies, but as uncontrolled by any common superior in their efforts to usurp the authorities of each other. These gentlemen must here be reminded of their error. They must be told that the ultimate authority, wherever the derivative may be found, resides in the people alone, and that it will not depend merely on the comparative ambition or address of the different governments whether either, or which of them, will be able to enlarge its sphere of jurisdiction at the expense of the other. . . .

Many considerations [seem] to place it beyond doubt that the first and most natural attachment of the people will be to the governments of their respective States. Into the administration of these a greater number of individuals will expect to rise. From the gift of these a greater number of offices and emoluments will flow. By the superintending care of these, all the more domestic and personal interests of the people will be regulated and provided for. With the affairs of these, the people will be more familiarly and minutely conversant. And with the members of these will a greater proportion of the people have the ties of personal acquaintance and friendship, and of family and party attachments; on the side of these, therefore, the popular bias may well be expected most strongly to incline. . . .

If, therefore, [the] people should in future become more partial to the federal than to the State governments, the change can only result from such manifest and irresistible proofs of a better administration as will overcome all their antecedent propensities. And in that case, the people ought not surely to be precluded from giving most of their confidence where they may discover it to be most due; but even in that case the State governments could have little to apprehend, because it is only within a certain sphere that the federal power can, in the nature of things, be advantageously administered. . . .

[The] prepossessions, which the members themselves will carry into the federal government, will generally be favorable to the States; whilst it will rarely happen that the members of the State governments will carry into the public councils a bias in favor of the general government. A local spirit will infallibly prevail much more in the members of Congress than a national spirit will prevail in the legislatures of the particular States. Everyone knows that a great proportion of the errors committed by the State legislatures proceeds from the disposition of the members to sacrifice the comprehensive and permanent interest of the State to the particular and separate views of the counties or districts in which they reside. And if they do not sufficiently enlarge their policy to embrace the collective welfare of their particular State, how can it be imagined that they will make the aggregate prosperity of the Union, and the dignity and respectability of its government, the objects of their affections and consultations? For the same reason that the members of the State legislatures will be unlikely to attach themselves sufficiently to national objects, the members of the federal legislature will be likely to attach themselves too much to local objects. The States will be to the latter what counties and towns are to the former. Measures will too often be decided according to their probable effect, not on the national prosperity and happiness, but on the prejudices, interests, and pursuits of the governments and people of the individual States. What is the spirit that has in general characterized the proceedings of Congress? A perusal of their journals, as well as the candid acknowledgments of such as have had a seat in that assembly, will inform us that the members have but too frequently displayed the character rather of partisans of their respective States than of impartial guardians of a common interest; that where on one occasion improper sacrifices have been made of local considerations to the aggrandizement of the federal government, the great interests of the nation have suffered on a hundred from an undue attention to the local prejudices, interests, and views of the particular States. [The] new federal government [will] partake sufficiently of the spirit of both to be disinclined to invade the rights of the individual States, or the prerogatives of their governments. The motives on the part of the State governments to augment their prerogatives by defalcations from the federal government will be overruled by no reciprocal predispositions in the members.

Were it admitted, however, that the federal government may feel an equal disposition with the State governments to extend its power beyond the due limits, the latter would still have the advantage in the means of defeating such encroachments. If an act of a particular State, though unfriendly to the national government, be generally popular in that State, and should not too grossly violate the oaths of the State officers, it is executed immediately and, of course, by means on the spot and depending on the State alone. The opposition of the federal government, or the interposition of federal officers, would but inflame the zeal of all parties on the side of the State, and the evil could not be prevented or repaired, if at all, without the employment of means which must always be resorted to with reluctance and difficulty. On the other hand, should an unwarrantable measure of the federal government be unpopular in particular States, which would seldom fail to be the case, or even a warrantable measure be so, which may sometimes be the case, the means of opposition to it are powerful and at hand. The disquietude of the people; their repugnance and, perhaps, refusal to co-operate with the officers of the Union; the frowns of the executive magistracy of the State; the embarrassments created by legislative devices, which would often be added on such occasions, would oppose, in any State, difficulties not to be despised; would form, in a large State, very serious impediments; and where the sentiments of several adjoining States happened to be in unison, would present obstructions which the federal government would hardly be willing to encounter.

But ambitious encroachments of the federal government on the authority of the State governments would not excite the opposition of a single State, or of a few States only. They would be signals of general alarm. Every government would espouse the common cause. A correspondence would be opened. Plans of resistance would be concerted. One spirit would animate and conduct the whole. . . .

The only refuge left for those who prophesy the downfall of the State governments is the visionary supposition that the federal government may previously accumulate a military force for the projects of ambition. [That] the people and the States should, for a sufficient period of time, elect an uninterrupted succession of men ready to betray both; that the traitors should, throughout this period, uniformly and systematically pursue some fixed plan for the extension of the military establishment; that the governments and the people of the States should silently and patiently behold the gathering storm and continue to supply the materials until it should be prepared to burst on their own heads must appear to everyone more like the incoherent dreams of a delirious jealousy, or the misjudged exaggerations of a counterfeit zeal, than like the sober apprehensions of genuine patriotism. . . .

The argument under the present head may be put into a very concise form, which appears altogether conclusive. Either the mode in which the federal government is to be constructed will render it sufficiently dependent on the people, or it will not. On the first supposition, it will be restrained by that dependence from forming schemes obnoxious to their constituents. On the other supposition, it will not possess the confidence of the people, and its schemes of usurpation will be easily defeated by the State governments, who will be supported by the people.

Note: *Enforcing Enumeration as a Limitation on Power*

1. *Enforcing enumeration as a limitation on power.* How was the national government to be confined to exercising only enumerated powers? By judicial enforcement of the express terms of the document? Consider here Hamilton's arguments in favor of judicial review in The Federalist No. 78, discussed in Chapter 1 supra. Are the grants of power susceptible of narrow interpretation? Do the terms in which they are stated compel such interpretations? We will explore these questions, and other related ones, in the material on the commerce power.

Hamilton suggests another method of "enforcement": Members of Congress will be so imbued with respect for local governments that they will rarely exercise even broad grants of power improvidently.

According to Madison, why is it unlikely that Congress will exercise its powers improvidently? Do his reasons seem persuasive under modern conditions?

a. A generation ago Herbert Wechsler updated Madison's argument in The Political Safeguards of Federalism, in H. Wechsler, Principles, Politics, and Fundamental Law 49-82 (1961; first published in 1954). Wechsler began by noting that "national action has [always] been regarded as exceptional in our polity. [Those] who would advocate [the] exercise [of national power] must [answer] the preliminary question why the matter should not be left to the states." He argued that variations among the states in the problems they face justify imposing this "burden of persuasion on those favoring national intervention." To Wechsler, "Madison's analysis has never lost its thrust" despite "the rise of national parties [and] the shift to popular election of the Senate."

> To the extent that federalist values have real significance they must give rise to local sensitivity to central intervention; to the extent that such a local sensitivity exists, it cannot fail to find reflection in the Congress. Indeed, the problem of the Congress is and always has been to attune itself to national opinion and produce majorities for action called for by the voice of the entire nation. It is remarkable that it should function thus as well as it does, given its intrinsic sensitivity to any insular opinion that is dominant in a substantial number of the states.

Wechsler augmented Madison's argument by invoking more modern political devices that led the Senate "to function as the guardian of state interest as such," including seniority and the filibuster. As to the House, he relied on "the states' control of voters' qualifications [and] of districting." Even though the President must "balance the localism and the separatism of the Congress by presenting programs that reflect the needs of the entire nation," that office is influenced by localism as well. The allocation of votes in the electoral college affects the allocation of time in presidential campaigns; party rules allocate convention votes based on some localist considerations. To build a winning coalition, a presidential candidate must appeal to groups that "approach balance-of-power status in important states"; some of these groups may promote "local values."

Wechsler concluded that "the national political process [is] intrinsically well adapted to retarding or restraining new intrusions by the center on the domain of the states." National authority is not "expansionist by nature." The size of the present national government is attributable "mainly to the magnitude of unavoidable responsibility under the circumstances of our time."

Wechsler drew the conclusion that judicial review was intended to maintain

> national supremacy against nullification or usurpation by the individual states. [The] Court is on weakest ground when it opposes its interpretation of the Constitution to that of Congress in the interest of the states, whose representatives control the legislative process and, by hypothesis, have broadly acquiesced in sanctioning the challenged Act of Congress. Federal intervention as against the states is thus primarily a matter for congressional determination in our system as it now stands.

b. J. Choper, Judicial Review and the National Political Process 171-259 (1980), offers a modern version of Madison's argument. Under his "Federalism Proposal," "[The] federal judiciary should not decide constitutional questions respecting the ultimate power of the national government vis-à-vis the states" because "structural aspects of the national political system serve to assure that states' rights will not be trampled, and the lesson of practice is that they have not been." In addition to the factors discussed by Madison and Wechsler, Choper mentions bloc voting by bipartisan state delegations in the House and patterns of committee assignments responsive to local interests. Also, "from the 1790s, usually more than three-fourths of the members of Congress have graduated from state and municipal offices. In the [1977-78] Senate [fifteen] of the Senators had been state governors, thirty-three others had occupied various state government positions, and fourteen more had served in local government. [Congressmen] have characteristically had very long, resolute, and intimate ties to their districts."

Do these considerations continue to have force? Consider the impact of increasing mobility among the population (and among people with political ambitions). Note that in the past service in state and local government may have been the best method to gain exposure to congressional-district and statewide constituencies, and consider the extent to which candidates may today gain similar exposure by other methods. Is the party system so strong as to overcome localist biases? The power of special interest groups? Of single-issue lobbies? What is the impact of decisions requiring that states district strictly according to population? Did Madison have something else — or in addition — in mind, other than these political considerations?

c. Does the Madisonian argument, as modernized by Wechsler and Choper to take account of present political practices, meet the objection that judicial review may sometimes eliminate legislation enacted by Congress that serves the interest of several regions at the expense of the interests of another region? Consider the implications of the Civil War and its outcome. What is "the lesson of practice" to which Choper refers? After studying the materials in this chapter, consider whether judicial review of issues regarding Congress's power vis-à-vis the states has on balance promoted the goals of the Constitution.

d. Is Madison's argument in The Federalist No. 10, Chapter 1 supra, consistent with that in The Federalist Nos. 45 and 46? For contrasting views, compare R. Dahl, A Preface to Democratic Theory (1963) (maintaining that the arguments are inconsistent and that The Federalist No. 10 states the better view), with G. Wills, Explaining America: The Federalist (1981) (maintaining that the arguments are consistent).

Suppose Congress arguably exceeds its proper role. Should the courts enforce the limited grants of power? Should the frequency with which Congress does so affect the analysis? Note that if the courts are available, they will entertain arguments about Congress's power even in cases where Congress has not acted improvidently and may themselves invalidate legislation that (in what sense?) ought to be upheld. As you study the history of congressional and judicial action under the commerce clause, consider whether that history shows the need for judicial enforcement of limits on Congress's power, or the unwisdom of the exercise of judicial review.

Note: The Values and Forms of Federalism

1. *The values of federalism.* What values are served by a system that distributes governmental authority between state and nation, that is, by federalism?

a. *Encouraging experimentation.* Justice Brandeis, dissenting in New State Ice Co. v. Liebman, 285 U.S. 262 (1932), wrote:

> To stay experimentation in things social and economic is a grave responsibility. Denial of the right to experiment may be fraught with serious consequences to the Nation. It is one of the happy incidents of the federal system that a single courageous State may, if its citizens choose, serve as a laboratory; and try novel social and economic experiments without risk to the rest of the country. This Court has the

power to prevent an experiment. [But] in the exercise of this high power, we must ever be on our guard, lest we erect our prejudices into legal principles. If we would guide by the light of reason, we must let our minds be bold.

The majority in *New State Ice* held that a *state* law unconstitutionally limited the operation of the national market; the case does not (directly) involve questions about national power.

One list of recent innovations begun at the state or local level includes "sunset legislation, zero based budgeting, equal housing, no fault insurance and the senior executive service," as well as "pioneering actions in gun control, pregnancy benefits for working women, limited access highways, education for handicapped children, auto pollution standards and energy assistance for the poor." Advisory Commission on Intergovernmental Relations, The Question of State Government Capability 23-24 (1985).

Rose-Ackerman, Risk Taking and Reelection: Does Federalism Promote Innovation?, 9 J. Legal Stud. 593 (1980), develops a formal model that suggests that Brandeis overstated his case. She assumes that politicians seek only to be reelected, that voters "have a wide range of risk preferences," and that risk preferrers "are unlikely to concentrate in a single jurisdiction" because of moving costs. She argues that innovations in one jurisdiction that turn out to be successful can be copied in other jurisdictions, which will not have to bear the costs associated with undertaking risky projects. In a federal system, "the hope of running for higher office may give low-level politicians an incentive to search for new ways of doing things," but "the reelection motive, the lack of sorting by risk preferences, external effects, and the impact of migration combine to prevent many searches [for innovation] from being carried out. [If] state and local governments are supposed to be 'laboratories,' then my model predicts that few useful experiments will be carried out in them." Rose-Ackerman explains that her assumptions about politicians' motivations and about the passive role of bureaucracies in the development of policy impose limits on the realism of her model.

b. *Efficiency.* Given wide variations in the circumstances obtaining in different areas of the country, it is likely that different solutions to specific problems will be appropriate in different areas. Prichard, Securing the Canadian Economic Union: Federalism and Internal Barriers to Trade, in Federalism and the Canadian Economic Union 6 (M. Trebilcock et al. eds. 1983), argues that "economic integration" allows gains to all participants by "spreading the risk of economic instability" and by allowing "cooperation in the provision of joint services (e.g., defence, transport, communications) characterized by economies of scale." Do state borders correspond to the boundaries of areas in which circumstances are roughly similar?

c. *Promoting individual choice.* By disabling the national government from acting on some subjects while allowing states to act in varying ways, federalism allows people to move from one area to another in order to select the kind of government policies they prefer.

The consumer-voter may be viewed as picking that community which best satisfies his preference pattern for public goods. This is a major difference between central and local provision of public goods. At the central level the preferences of the consumer-voter are given, and the government tries to adjust to the pattern of these preferences, whereas at the local level various governments have their revenue and expenditure patterns more or less set. Given these revenue and expenditure patterns, the consumer-voter moves to that community whose local government best satisfies his set of preferences. The greater the number of communities and the greater the variance among them, the closer the consumer will come to fully realizing his preference position.

Tiebout, A Pure Theory of Local Expenditures, 64 J. Pol. Econ. 416, 418 (1956). Prichard, supra, at 17-18:

> Public choice theory suggests [a] bias in favour of decentralization. First, interest groups that may be minorities nationally are more likely to be majorities locally. Second, [the] greater the homogeneity of interests on a geographical basis, the more often minorities become majorities as decentralization increases. Third, decentralization of functions in a hierarchical way disaggregates policy packages and allows a citizen to cast different votes on different components of policy because they are vested in different levels of government in the jurisdictional hierarchy. Fourth, decentralization, by creating a diversity of jurisdictions, allows a better matching of preferences and policies because voters can choose that jurisdiction which offers the most preferred policy package. That is, citizens may "vote with their feet," searching out the jurisdiction offering the most attractive set of policies. Simultaneously, the threat of exit by voters from a jurisdiction forces the decentralized governments to reflect the policy preferences of their existing or potential constituents as the jurisdictions compete for voters. Fifth, given the greater homogeneity of tastes as boundaries contract, decentralization reduces the likelihood of policy compromises being adopted that create minimum winning coalitions but do not accurately reflect the interests of any particular interest group. . . .
>
>   A sixth advantage of decentralization is the reduction of "signalling" and other "transactions costs" for expressing citizen preferences [such as] participation in efforts to influence the actions of lobbies and large pressure groups [and] voting or the act of giving one's support to or withholding it from a candidate of a political party or, in very special cases, a policy.

Decentralization may also impede the realization of economies of scale. Note that this view of federalism may overestimate the ease with which voters may relocate. For elaboration and critique, see A. Hirschman, Exit, Voice, and Loyalty (1970); D. Mueller, Public Choice 125-147 (1979).

d. *Promoting democracy.* Madison argued in The Federalist Nos. 45 and 46 that state and local governments provided the opportunity for people to participate directly in the activities of a government that had significant effects on their lives. This participation would make them the active citizens valued in one version of democratic theory, rather than the passive subjects of a remote national government. Does federalism serve this value today?

Consider these observations by the Advisory Commission on Intergovernmental Relations, supra, at 364:

> States' competence to handle their own [affairs] has been questioned continuously. Critics have pointed to out-moded constitutions, jerry-built governmental structures, and unrepresentative and poorly run legislatures. They have deplored the inadequate tools and cumbersome procedures employed by state governments. They have charged state governments with lack of openness, with inaction in meeting public needs, and with incompetence and corruption.

Much of this criticism was deserved. States in the middle of the 20th century had failed to modernize their governments and to change with the times. Their legislatures were malapportioned, their constitutions archaic, and their governmental structures and processes in need of remodeling. They often neglected to deal with the pressing public problems facing them, especially as these related to urban areas. In many instances, particularly in the south, they were more concerned with promoting states' rights than with protecting the rights of citizens and assuring them equal access to governmental institutions and services.

Since the mid-1950s, states across the country have been reexamining and remodeling their institutions and processes. One by one, and little by little, particularly in the decades of the 1960s and 1970s, they changed them to conform more closely to the models reformers had advocated for years. Sometimes this reformation was accomplished at the behest of national actions but more frequently it was the result of indigenous initiatives. The changes were so piecemeal and intermittent, so disconnected in geography and so largely unrelated in media notice, however, that few people realized the profound restructuring of the state governmental landscape. Today, states, in formal representational, policymaking and implementation terms at least, are more representative, more responsive, more activist and more professional in their operations than they ever have been.

The developments the Commission studied included improved pay for legislators and their staffs, greater openness in legislative processes, and the increasing professionalism of state agency managers and staffs. Consider whether some of these developments might be inconsistent with other conceptions of democratic self-governance.

A national government with plenary power might choose to exercise that power in ways that encouraged experimentation, efficiency, and choice. It could divide the nation into administrative regions, and give revocable grants of autonomy to the regions with respect to certain subjects. What values of federalism would be impaired by such a system? Do national lawmakers have incentives to set up such a system?

2. *The forms of federalism.* In considering the material in this chapter, you should keep in mind that there are a number of ways to distribute power in a federal system.

a. *Neither* state nor nation may have power to act. The first amendment, applicable to the states through the fourteenth amendment, exemplifies this situation: If some regulation violates the first amendment, neither state governments nor Congress may adopt it (although sometimes the substantive standards applicable to analyze the constitutional question will vary depending on whether the enacting body is a state government or Congress).

b. The *national* government may be given *exclusive* power to regulate in some area. Article I, section 10, itemizes a number of activities in which states may not engage even though Congress is given power in article I, section 8, to do so: States may not, but Congress may, "coin Money," for example.

c. *State* governments may have *exclusive* power to regulate some area. The central controversies in this chapter involve two related questions about this category: Are there *any* subjects in the category, and if so, *what* subjects may the states but not Congress regulate?

d. State and national governments may have *concurrent* power to regulate some area. The supremacy clause, article VI, paragraph 2, establishes that, where the nation and the states have concurrent power that Congress chooses to exercise, the national legislation prevails over conflicting state legislation. Chapter 3 examines such questions as: Has Congress chosen to exercise its concurrent power? Does state legislation conflict with national statutes? Does Congress's failure to exercise its power authorize — or prohibit — state legislation in the area?

3. *Methods of using enumeration as a limit on power.* Consider the commerce clause, article I, section 8, clause 3, as an example of an enumerated power. It states, "The Congress shall have Power [To] regulate Commerce with foreign Nations, and among the several states, and with the Indian Tribes." This power could be limited in two ways: (a) *"Internal" limits:* The clause might define a specific subject matter, ". . . such that Congress would lack power (1) to do anything other than regulate (2) anything other than interstate and foreign commerce." These limits are imposed, as Hamilton and Madison argued, to protect the values of federalism. (b) *"External" limits:* The clause might grant plenary power to Congress, by allowing it to do anything reasonably regarded as regulation of anything reasonably regarded as interstate or foreign commerce, but other provisions of the Constitution, such as the first amendment, might bar the exercise of a power concededly granted. Recall here Marshall's statement in *McCulloch*:

> Let the end be legitimate, let it be within the scope of the constitution, and all means which are appropriate, which are plainly adapted to that end, which are not prohibited, but consist with the letter and spirit of the constitution, are constitutional. [Should] Congress, in the execution of its powers, adopt measures which are prohibited by the constitution; or should Congress, under the pretext of executing its powers, pass laws for the accomplishment of objects not entrusted to the government; it would become the painful duty of this tribunal, should a case requiring such a decision come before it, to say that such an act was not the law of the land. But where the law is not prohibited, and is really calculated to effect any of the objects entrusted to the government, to undertake here to inquire into the degree of its necessity, would be to pass the line which circumscribes the judicial department, and to tread on legislative ground.

Does this imply that the courts will enforce both internal and external limits?

The distinction between internal and external limits, though not always stated in those terms, pervades discussions of Congress's powers. The distinction is closely tied to resolution of questions about judicial enforcement of limits on Congress's powers: It is usually conceded that the courts can enforce such external limits such as the first amendment. But judicial enforcement of federalism-based limits is more controversial, in part because they seem to be internal limits. Much of the discussion consists of efforts to transform federalism-based internal limits into external limits or to resist that transformation. As you study the following material, consider the implications of the claim that although limits such as the first amendment are relatively clear, there are no equivalently clear provisions available for the courts to rely on in enforcing federalism-based limits on Congress's power.

4. *Why study federalism?* As you will learn, contemporary constitutional law places few judicially enforced federalism-based limits — if it places any at all — on Congress's powers. Those limits have only a minor impact on Congress's ability to establish an essentially unitary national system of government. Why then study this area in detail?

a. *Historical reasons.* Controversies over the proper relation between state and nation have been at the heart of political contention for nearly the entire course of the nation's history. These controversies persist. By examining their constitutional versions, you will be able to understand some of the policy reasons for the positions people take on these matters.

b. *Analytical reasons.* The Supreme Court's cases develop a set of analytical devices — such as the distinction between "direct" and "indirect" regulation — that are used in other areas of constitutional law. By examining these devices here, you will be able to understand how the devices can be deployed, modified, argued against each other, and so on.

c. *Theoretical reasons.* The propriety and form of judicial review is a central theme in the study of constitutional law. Cases involving Congress's power provide an opportunity to examine the operation of judicial review over a long period and to see how its operation was related to general developments in politics, economics, and culture. In addition, the cases provide an opportunity to consider the merits and defects of two general theories of judicial review: originalism or interpretivism, and representation-reinforcing review, both introduced in Chapter 1 supra.

As you read the material in this chapter, note the theoretical justifications offered for the positions taken, and consider whether those justifications are sound and properly invoked in the circumstances.

B. THE CLASSICAL VIEW

Gibbons v. Ogden

22 U.S. (9 Wheat.) 1 (1824)

[The New York legislature enacted a statute granting Robert Fulton and Robert Livingston the exclusive right to operate steamboats in New York waters. The statute was designed to encourage investment in the development of the then-novel technology of steamboats. Fulton and Livingston licensed Ogden to operate a ferry between New York City and Elizabethtown Point in New Jersey. Gibbons began operating a competing ferry service that, because it necessarily entered New York waters, violated the grant to Fulton and Livingston, and the license to Ogden. Gibbons's ferries were, however, licensed as "vessels [in] the coasting trade" under a statute enacted by Congress in 1793. Ogden obtained an injunction against Gibbons from the New York courts.]

Mr. Chief Justice Marshall delivered the opinion of the Court. . . .

The appellant contends that this decree is erroneous, because the laws which purport to give the exclusive privilege it sustains, are repugnant to [that] clause in the constitution which authorizes Congress to regulate commerce. . . .

The State of New-York maintains the constitutionality of these laws; and their Legislature, their Council of Revision, and their Judges, have repeatedly concurred in this opinion. It is supported by great names — by names which have all the titles to consideration that virtue, intelligence, and office, can bestow. No tribunal can approach the decision of this question, without feeling a just and real respect for that opinion which is sustained by such authority; but it is the province of this Court, while it respects, not to bow to it implicitly; and the Judges must exercise, in the examination of the subject, that understanding which Providence has bestowed upon them, with that independence which the people of the United States expect from this department of the government.

The words are, "Congress shall have power to regulate commerce with foreign nations, and among the several States, and with the Indian tribes."

The subject to be regulated is commerce; and our constitution being, as was aptly said at the bar, one of enumeration, and not of definition, to ascertain the extent of the power, it becomes necessary to settle the meaning of the word. The counsel for the appellee would limit it to traffic, to buying and selling, or the interchange of commodities, and do not admit that it comprehends navigation. This would restrict a general term, applicable to many objects, to one of its significations. Commerce, undoubtedly, is traffic, but it is something more: it is intercourse. It describes the commercial intercourse between nations, and parts of nations, in all its branches, and is regulated by prescribing rules for carrying on that intercourse. The mind can scarcely conceive a system for regulating commerce between nations, which shall exclude all laws concerning navigation, which shall be silent on the admission of the vessels of the one nation into the ports of the other, and be confined to prescribing rules for the conduct of individuals, in the actual employment of buying and selling, or of barter. . . .

[All] America understands, and has uniformly understood, the word "commerce," to comprehend navigation. It was so understood, and must have been so understood, when the constitution was framed. The power over commerce, including navigation, was one of the primary objects for which the people of America adopted their government, and must have been contemplated in forming it. The convention must have used the word in that sense, because all have understood it in that sense; and the attempt to restrict it comes too late. . . .

The word used in the constitution, then, comprehends, and has been always understood to comprehend, navigation within its meaning; and a power to regulate navigation, is as expressly granted, as if that term had been added to the word "commerce."

To what commerce does this power extend? The constitution informs us, to commerce "with foreign nations, and among the several States, and with the Indian tribes."

It has, we believe, been universally admitted, that these words comprehend every species of commercial intercourse between the United States and foreign nations. No sort of trade can be carried on between this country and any other, to which this power does not extend. It has been truly said, that commerce, as the word is used in the constitution, is a unit, every part of which is indicated by the term.

If this be the admitted meaning of the word, in its application to foreign nations, it must carry the same meaning throughout the sentence, and remain a unit, unless there be some plain intelligible cause which alters it.

The subject to which the power is next applied, is to commerce "among the several States." The word "among" means intermingled with. A thing which is among others, is intermingled with them. Commerce among the States, cannot stop at the external boundary line of each State, but may be introduced into the interior.

It is not intended to say that these words comprehend that commerce, which is completely internal, which is carried on between man and man in a State, or between different parts of the same State, and which does not extend to or affect other States. Such a power would be inconvenient, and is certainly unnecessary.

Comprehensive as the word "among" is, it may very properly be restricted to that commerce which concerns more States than one. The phrase is not one which would probably have been selected to indicate the completely interior traffic of a State, because it is not an apt phrase for that purpose; and the enumeration of the particular classes of commerce to which the power was to be extended, would not have been made, had the intention been to extend the power to every description. The enumeration presupposes something not enumerated; and that something, if we regard the language or the subject of the sentence, must be the exclusively internal commerce of a State. The genius and character of the whole government seem to be, that its action is to be applied to all the external concerns of the nation, and to those internal concerns which affect the States generally; but not to those which are completely within a particular State, which do not affect other States, and with which it is not necessary to interfere, for the purpose of executing some of the general powers of the government. The completely internal commerce of a State, then, may be considered as reserved for the State itself.

But, in regulating commerce with foreign nations, the power of Congress does not stop at the jurisdictional lines of the several States. It would be a very useless power, if it could not pass those lines. The commerce of the United States with foreign nations, is that of the whole United States. Every district has a right to participate in it. The deep streams which penetrate our country in every direction, pass through the interior of almost every State in the Union, and furnish the means of exercising this right. If Congress has the power to regulate it, that power must be exercised whenever the subject exists. If it exists within the States, if a foreign voyage may commence or terminate at a port within a State, then the power of Congress may be exercised within a State.

This principle is, if possible, still more clear, when applied to commerce "among the several States." They either join each other, in which case they are separated by a mathematical line, or they are remote from each other, in which case other States lie between them. What is commerce "among" them; and how is it to be conducted? Can a trading expedition between two adjoining States, commence and terminate outside of each? And if the trading intercourse be between two States remote from each other, must it not commence in one, terminate in the other, and probably pass through a third? Commerce among the States must, of necessity, be commerce with the States. [The] power of Congress, then, whatever it may be, must be exercised within the territorial jurisdiction of the several States. The sense of the nation on this subject, is unequivocally manifested by the provisions made in the laws for transporting goods, by land, between Baltimore and Providence, between New-York and Philadelphia, and between Philadelphia and Baltimore.

We are now arrived at the inquiry — What is this power?

It is the power to regulate; that is, to prescribe the rule by which commerce is to be governed. This power, like all others vested in Congress, is complete in itself, may be exercised to its utmost extent, and acknowledges no limitations, other than are prescribed in the constitution. [If,] as has always been understood, the sovereignty of Congress, though limited to specified objects, is plenary as to those objects, the power over commerce with foreign nations, and among the several States, is vested in Congress as absolutely as it would be in a single government, having in its constitution the same restrictions on the exercise of the power as are found in the constitution of the United States. The wisdom and the discretion of Congress, their identity with the people, and the influence which their constituents possess at elections, are, in this, as in many other instances, as that, for example, of declaring war, the sole restraints on which they have relied, to secure them from its abuse. They are the restraints on which the people must often rely solely, in all representative governments.

The power of Congress, then, comprehends navigation, within the limits of every State in the Union; so far as that navigation may be, in any manner, connected with "commerce with foreign nations, or among the several States, or with the Indian tribes." It may, of consequence, pass the jurisdictional line of New-York, and act upon the very waters to which the prohibition now under consideration applies.

But it has been urged with great earnestness, that, although the power of Congress to regulate commerce with foreign nations, and among the several States, be co-extensive with the subject itself, and have no other limits than are prescribed in the constitution, yet the States may severally exercise the same power, within their respective jurisdictions. In support of this argument, it is said, that they possessed it as an inseparable attribute of sovereignty, before the formation of the constitution, and still retain it, except so far as they have surrendered it by that instrument; that this principle results from the nature of the government, and is secured by the tenth amendment; that an affirmative grant of power is not exclusive, unless in its own nature it be such that the continued exercise of it by the former possessor is inconsistent with the grant, and that this is not of that description.

The appellant, conceding these postulates, except the last, contends, that full power to regulate a particular subject, implies the whole power, and leaves no residuum; that a grant of the whole is incompatible with the existence of a right in another to any part of it. . . .

In discussing the question, whether this power is still in the States, in the case under consideration, we may dismiss from it the inquiry, whether it is surrendered by the mere grant to Congress, or is retained until Congress shall exercise the power. We may dismiss that inquiry, because it has been exercised, and the regulations which Congress deemed it proper to make, are now in full operation. The sole question is, can a State regulate commerce with foreign nations and among the States, while Congress is regulating it? . . .

[Ogden argued that state laws requiring inspections of cargo demonstrated that the power to regulate commerce was not exclusively in Congress.]

That inspection laws may have a remote and considerable influence on commerce, will not be denied; but that a power to regulate commerce is the source from which the right to pass them is derived, cannot be admitted. The object of inspection laws, is to improve the quality of articles produced by the labour of a country; to fit them for exportation; or, it may be, for domestic use. They act upon the subject before it becomes an article of foreign commerce, or of commerce among the States, and prepare it for that purpose. They form a portion of that immense mass of legislation, which embraces everything within the territory of a State, not surrendered to the general government: all which can be most advantageously exercised by the States themselves. Inspection laws, quarantine laws, health laws of every description, as well as laws for regulating the internal commerce of a State, and those which respect turnpike roads, ferries, &c., are component parts of this mass.

No direct general power over these objects is granted to Congress; and, consequently, they remain subject to State legislation. If the legislative power of the Union can reach them, it must be for national purposes; it must be where the power is expressly given for a special purpose, or is clearly incidental to some power which is expressly given. It is obvious, that the government of the Union, in the exercise of its express powers, that, for example, of regulating commerce with foreign nations and among the States, may use means that may also be employed by a State, in the exercise of its acknowledged powers; that, for example, of regulating commerce within the State. If Congress license vessels to sail from one port to another, in the same State, the act is supposed to be, necessarily, incidental to the power expressly granted to Congress, and implies no claim of a direct power to regulate the purely internal commerce of a State, or to act directly on its system of police. So, if a State, in passing laws on subjects acknowledged to be within its control, and with a view to those subjects, shall adopt a measure of the same character with one which Congress may adopt, it does not derive its authority from the particular power which has been granted, but from some other, which remains with the State, and may be executed by the same means. All experience shows, that the same measures, or measures scarcely distinguishable from each other, may flow from distinct powers; but this does not prove that the powers themselves are identical. Although the means used in their execution may sometimes approach each other so nearly as to be confounded, there are other situations in which they are sufficiently distinct to establish their individuality.

In our complex system, presenting the rare and difficult scheme of one general government, whose action extends over the whole, but which possesses only certain enumerated powers; and of numerous State governments, which retain and exercise all powers not delegated to the Union, contests respecting power must arise. Were it even otherwise, the measures taken by the respective governments to execute their acknowledged powers, would often be of the same description, and might, sometimes, interfere. This, however, does not prove that the one is exercising, or has a right to exercise, the powers of the other. . . .

It has been contended by the counsel for the appellant, that, as the word "to regulate" implies in its nature, full power over the thing to be regulated, it excludes, necessarily, the action of all others that would perform the same operation on the same thing. That regulation is designed for the entire result, applying to those parts which remain as they were, as well as to those which are altered. It produces a uniform whole, which is as much disturbed and deranged by changing what the regulating power designs to leave untouched, as that on which it has operated.

There is great force in this argument, and the Court is not satisfied that it has been refuted.

Since, however, in exercising the power of regulating their own purely internal affairs, whether of trading or police, the States may sometimes enact laws, the validity of which depends on their interfering with, and being contrary to, an act of Congress passed in pursuance of the constitution, the Court will enter upon the inquiry, whether the laws of New-York, as expounded by the highest tribunal of that State, have, in their application to this case, come into collision with an act of Congress, and deprived a citizen of a right to which that act entitles him. Should this collision exist, it will be immaterial whether those laws were passed in virtue of a concurrent power "to regulate commerce with foreign nations and among the several States," or, in virtue of a power to regulate their domestic trade and police. In one case and the other, the acts of New-York must yield to the law of Congress; and the decision sustaining the privilege they confer, against a right given by a law of the Union, must be erroneous.

This opinion has been frequently expressed in this Court, and is founded, as well on the nature of the government as on the words of the constitution. In argument, however, it has been contended, that if a law passed by a State, in the exercise of its acknowledged sovereignty, comes into conflict with a law passed by Congress in pursuance of the constitution, they affect the subject, and each other, like equal opposing powers.

But the framers of our constitution foresaw this state of things, and provided for it, by declaring the supremacy not only of itself, but of the laws made in pursuance of it. The nullity of any act, inconsistent with the constitution, is produced by the declaration, that the constitution is the supreme law. The appropriate application of that part of the clause which confers the same supremacy on laws and treaties, is to such acts of the State Legislatures as do not transcend their powers, but, though enacted in the execution of acknowledged State powers, interfere with, or are contrary to the laws of Congress, made in pursuance of the constitution, or some treaty made under the authority of the United States. In every such case, the act of Congress, or the treaty, is supreme; and the law of the State, though enacted in the exercise of powers not controverted, must yield to it. . . .

[Chief Justice Marshall then interpreted the 1793 statute as authorizing Gibbons's ferries to enter New York waters. The New York monopoly was therefore invalid under the supremacy clause, and the injunction was accordingly dissolved. The opinion concluded:]

Powerful and ingenious minds, taking, as postulates, that the powers expressly granted to the government of the Union, are to be contracted by construction, into the narrowest possible compass, and that the original powers of the States are retained, if any possible construction will retain them, may, by a course of well digested, but refined and metaphysical reasoning, founded on these premises, explain away the constitution of our country, and leave it, a magnificent structure, indeed, to look at, but totally unfit for use. They may so entangle and perplex the understanding, as to obscure principles, which were before thought quite plain, and induce doubts where, if the mind were to pursue its own course, none would be perceived. In such a case, it is peculiarly necessary to recur to safe and fundamental principles to sustain those principles, and when sustained, to make them the tests of the arguments to be examined.

MR. JUSTICE JOHNSON. . . .

In attempts to construe the constitution, I have never found much benefit resulting from the inquiry, whether the whole, or any part of it, is to be construed strictly, or literally. The simple, classical, precise, yet comprehensive language, in which it is couched, leaves, at most, but very little latitude for construction; and when its intent and meaning is discovered, nothing remains but to execute the will of those who made it, in the best manner to effect the purposes intended. The great and paramount purpose, was to unite this mass of wealth and power, for the protection of the humblest individual; his rights, civil and political, his interests and prosperity, are the sole *end*; the rest are nothing but the *means*. But the principal of those means, one so essential as to approach nearer the characteristics of an end, was the independence and harmony of the States, that they may the better subserve the purposes of cherishing and protecting the respective families of this great republic.

The strong sympathies, rather than the feeble government, which bound the States together during a common war, dissolved on the return of peace; and the very principles which gave rise to the war of the revolution, began to threaten the confederacy with anarchy and ruin. The States had resisted a tax imposed by the parent State, and now reluctantly submitted to, or altogether rejected, the moderate demands of the confederation. Every one recollects the painful and threatening discussions, which arose on the subject of the five per cent duty. Some States rejected it altogether; others insisted on collecting it themselves; scarcely any acquiesced without reservations, which deprived it altogether of the character of a national measure; and at length, some repealed the laws by which they had signified their acquiescence.

For a century the States had submitted, with murmurs, to the commercial restrictions imposed by the parent State; and now, finding themselves in the unlimited possession of those powers over their own commerce, which they had so long been deprived of, and so earnestly coveted, that selfish principle which, well controlled, is so salutary, and which, unrestricted, is so unjust and tyrannical, guided by inexperience and jealousy, began to show itself in iniquitous laws and impolitic measures, from which grew up a conflict of commercial regulations, destructive to the harmony of the States, and fatal to their commercial interests abroad.

This was the immediate cause, that led to the forming of a convention. . . .

The history of the times will, therefore, sustain the opinion, that the grant of power over commerce, if intended to be commensurate with the evils existing, and the purpose of remedying those evils, could be only commensurate with the power of the States over the subject. And this opinion is supported by a very remarkable evidence of the general understanding of the whole American people, when the grant was made.

There was not a State in the Union, in which there did not, at that time, exist a variety of commercial regulations; concerning which it is too much to suppose, that the whole ground covered by those regulations was immediately assumed by actual legislation, under the authority of the Union. But where was the existing statute on this subject, that a State attempted to execute? or by what State was it ever thought necessary to repeal those statutes? By common consent, those laws dropped lifeless from their statute books, for want of the sustaining power, that had been relinquished to Congress. . . .

The "power to regulate commerce," here meant to be granted, was that power to regulate commerce which previously existed in the States. But what was that power? The States were, unquestionably, supreme; and each possessed that power over commerce, which is acknowledged to reside in every sovereign State.

[The] power of a sovereign state over commerce, therefore, amounts to nothing more than a power to limit and restrain it at pleasure. And since the power to prescribe the limits to its freedom, necessarily implies the power to determine what shall remain unrestrained, it follows, that the power must be exclusive; it can reside but in one potentate; and hence, the grant of this power carries with it the whole subject, leaving nothing for the State to act upon. . . .

It is impossible, with the views which I entertain of the principle on which the commercial privileges of the people of the United States, among themselves, rests, to concur in the view which this Court takes of the effect of the coasting licence in this cause. I do not regard it as the foundation of the right set up in behalf of the appellant. If there was any one object riding over every other in the adoption of the constitution, it was to keep the commercial intercourse among the States free from all invidious and partial restraints. And I cannot overcome the conviction, that if the licensing act was repealed to-morrow, the rights of the appellant to a reversal of the decision complained of, would be as strong as it is under this license. One half the doubts in life arise from the defects of language, and if this instrument had been called an *exemption* instead of a license, it would have given a better idea of its character. Licensing acts, in fact, in legislation, are universally restraining acts; as, for example, acts licensing gaming houses, retailers of spiritous liquors, &c. . . .

Yet there is one view, in which the license may be allowed considerable influence in sustaining the decision of this Court.

It has been contended, that the grants of power to the United States over any subject, do not, necessarily, paralyze the arm of the States, or deprive them of the capacity to act on the same subject. That this can be the effect only of prohibitory provisions in their own constitutions, or in that of the general government. The vis vitæ of power is still existing in the States, if not extinguished by the constitution of the United States. That, although as to all those grants of power which may be called aboriginal, with relation to the government, brought into existence by the constitution, they, of course, are out of the reach of State power; yet, as to all concessions of powers which previously existed in the States, it was otherwise. The practice of our government certainly has been, on many subjects, to occupy so much only of the field opened to them, as they think the public interests require. [But] the license furnishes a full answer to this objection; for, although one grant of power over commerce, should not be deemed a total relinquishment of power over the subject, but amounting only to a power to assume, still the power of the States must be at an end, so far as the United States have, by their legislative act, taken the subject under their immediate superintendence. So far as relates to the commerce coastwise, the act under which this license is granted, contains a full expression of Congress on this subject. . . .

But the principal objections to these opinions arise, 1st. From the unavoidable action of some of the municipal powers of the States, upon commercial subjects.

2d. From passages in the constitution, which are supposed to imply a *concurrent* power in the States in regulating commerce.

It is no objection to the existence of distinct, substantive powers, that, in their application, they bear upon the same subject. The same bale of goods, the same cask of provisions, or the same ship, that may be the subject of commercial regulation, may also be the vehicle of disease. And the health laws that require them to be stopped and ventilated, are no more intended as regulations on commerce, than the laws which permit their importation, are intended to innoculate the community with disease. Their different purposes mark the distinction between the powers brought into action; and while frankly exercised, they can produce no serious collision. As to laws affecting ferries, turnpike roads, and other subjects of the same class, so far from meriting the epithet of commercial regulations, they are, in fact, commercial facilities, for which, by the consent of mankind, a compensation is paid, upon the same principle that the whole commercial world submit to pay light money to the Danes. Inspection laws are of a more equivocal nature, and it is obvious that the constitution has viewed that subject with much solicitude. But so far from sustaining an inference in favour of the power of the States over commerce, I cannot but think that the guarded provisions of the 10th section, on this subject, furnish a strong argument against that inference. It was obvious, that inspection laws must combine municipal with commercial regulations; and, while the power over the subject is yielded to the States, for obvious reasons, an absolute control is given over State legislation on the subject, as far as that legislation may be exercised, so as to affect the commerce of the country. The inferences, to be correctly drawn, from this whole article, appear to me to be altogether in favour of the exclusive grants to Congress of power over commerce, and the reverse of that which the appellee contends for.

This section contains the positive restrictions imposed by the constitution upon State power. The first clause of it, specifies those powers which the States are precluded from exercising, even though the Congress were to permit them. The second, those which the States may exercise with the consent of Congress. And here the sedulous attention to the subject of State exclusion from commercial power, is strongly marked. Not satisfied with the express grant to the United States of the power over commerce, this clause negatives the exercise of that power to the States, as to the only two objects which could ever tempt them to assume the exercise of that power, to wit, the collection of a revenue from imposts and duties on imports and exports; or from a tonnage duty. As to imposts on imports or exports, such a revenue might have been aimed at *directly*, by express legislation, or *indirectly*, in the form of inspection laws; and it became necessary to guard against both. Hence, first, the consent of Congress to such imposts or duties, is made necessary; and as to inspection laws, it is limited to the minimum of expenses. Then, the money so raised shall be paid into the treasury of the United States, or may be sued for since it is declared to be for their use. And lastly, all such laws may be modified, or repealed, by an act of Congress. It is impossible for a right to be more guarded. . . . .

It would be in vain to deny the possibility of a clashing and collision between the measures of the two governments. The line cannot be drawn with sufficient distinctness between the municipal powers of the one, and the commercial powers of the other. In some points they meet and blend so as scarcely to admit of separation. Hitherto the only remedy has been applied which the case admits of; that of a frank and candid co-operation for the general good. Witness the laws of Congress requiring its officers to respect the inspection laws of the States, and to aid in enforcing their health laws; that which surrenders to the States the superintendence of pilotage, and the many laws passed to permit a tonnage duty to be levied for the use of their ports. Other instances could be cited, abundantly to prove that collision must be sought to be produced; and when it does arise, the question must be decided how far the powers of Congress are adequate to put it down. Whenever the powers of the respective governments are frankly exercised, with a distinct view to the ends of such powers, they may act upon the same object, or use the same means, and yet the powers be kept perfectly distinct. A resort to the same means, therefore, is no argument to prove the identity of their respective powers. . . .

Note: Gibbons v. Ogden

1. *The purposes of the commerce clause.* What were the purposes for which Congress was given the power to regulate interstate commerce? Consider Justice Johnson's description of the problems under the Articles of Confederation. Does the history he recounts justify interpreting the commerce clause to do more than authorize Congress to override state laws that obstruct the free flow of trade across state and national borders? Note that Johnson regards this as a major enhancement of national power. On this view, does the commerce clause authorize Congress to enact regulations that it regards as appropriate to the development of the national economy? Note, however, (a) that obstructing the free flow of commerce is an evil only because it interferes with efficient economic development, so that the rationale Johnson must rely on would justify direct congressional action to promote economic development, and (b) that subsequent cases demonstrated that any state law — or any failure on the part of a state to enact a law — could readily be construed as an "obstruction" of the sort with which Johnson was concerned. Consider here the implications of Marshall's concluding paragraph.

2. *Internal limits.* What "internal" limits might be found in the commerce clause? Marshall considers three:

a. *"Commerce."* How does Marshall define "commerce"? Is there a plausible theory under which the operation of a ferry, or navigation, is not commerce? Because the ferry adds no value to the products it carries? Note that, when discussing state inspection laws, Marshall suggests that they act on the subject "before it becomes an article of" interstate commerce. Does this indicate a retreat from the broad definition he offered earlier in the opinion? This phrase occurs in a different context, where Marshall is considering whether the national power is exclusive. Does the difference in context explain or justify a difference in definition?

b. *"Among the several States."* Marshall says that the clause does not extend to "that commerce which is completely internal [and] which does not [affect] other states." Later Marshall adds that Congress may lack power only if, in addition to these conditions being satisfied, it was "not necessary" to regulate commerce. Note the conjunctive form of the statements. Was there such commerce in 1824? Can any commercial activity today satisfy all three requirements? Are the courts in a good position to determine whether congressional regulation of some (arguably or clearly) intrastate commerce is necessary? Whether that intrastate commerce affects other states? Why would giving power to Congress to regulate "completely internal" commerce be "inconvenient"?

c. *"Regulate."* How does Marshall define "regulation"? According to his definition, must a statute, in order to qualify as a "regulation," be directed at commercial goals? Note that Marshall struggles with the implications of his broad definition in dealing with inspection laws. Why do such laws pose a problem for him? Does Johnson offer an alternative definition of "regulation"?

3. *Enforcement of limits.* How are limits on Congress's power to be enforced? In discussing the definition of "regulation," Marshall emphasizes the political constraints on Congress. Does he intend to rely on enforcement through the political process for *all* limits? Should he? Does Johnson have — implicitly — a different theory of enforcement?

4. *Exclusive and concurrent power.* Much in both opinions is devoted to the argument, which Marshall says has "great force," that Congress's power here is exclusive rather than concurrent. That argument, part of which was foreshadowed in the discussion of the power to tax in McCulloch v. Maryland, Chapter 1 supra, was typical of nineteenth-century legal thought, which strove to divide the legal universe into sharply demarcated spheres of activity. Within its sphere, some decisionmaker — the individual, a state, the nation — was sovereign and had unlimited authority. Outside its sphere, that decisionmaker had no authority at all. In a federal system, these spheres of authority could not readily be defined by territorial boundaries, as Marshall argues in his discussion of the definition of "commerce."

How could they be defined? Marshall and Johnson are both attracted to "subject-matter" or "purpose" definitions. Inspection laws are within the states' exclusive sphere, and outside of Congress's, because they are not designed to promote or hinder interstate commerce. Are these definitions satisfactory? Note the difficulties that Marshall would face if he adopted the position that Congress's power is exclusive, and simultaneously defined Congress's power broadly. Many subjects would go unregulated entirely because the states would lack the power, and Congress would lack the time, to regulate.

The "concurrent power" position creates its own difficulties, discussed in Chapter 3 below.

5. *Commerce, national power, and slavery.* Controversies over the scope of the commerce clause, and over the breadth of Congress's powers generally, were inextricable from the issue of slavery in the antebellum period. Southerners feared that broad affirmations of congressional power would license Congress to regulate slavery as a form of commerce. Note the first proviso in article V, with its reference to article I, section 9, clause 1. (The Passenger Cases, 48 U.S. (7 How.) 283 (1849), eliminated the possibility that transportation of persons would be excluded from the definition of "commerce.") Even where the Constitution uncontroversially granted Congress power, its exercise was frequently controversial because it was thought that Congress might both become accustomed to exercising its power and do so in ways that would weaken the political constraints to which Madison and Marshall alluded. Further, as midcentury approached, Southerners became increasingly concerned that westward expansion of the country would eventually disrupt the rough balance of power that had been maintained in Congress between the free and slave states.

Consider in this connection the position on "exclusive v. concurrent" powers taken in Prigg v. Pennsylvania, 41 U.S. (16 Pet.) 539 (1842): Article IV, section 2, clause 3, of the Constitution provides that fugitive slaves "shall be delivered up on Claim" of their owners. To implement this provision Congress enacted the Fugitive Slave Act of 1793. The act authorized the owner to seize the fugitive slave and bring him or her before a federal or state judge, who would then issue a certificate of ownership once persuaded that the person seized was the claimant's slave. Pennsylvania enacted a statute in 1826 that made it a crime to remove a fugitive without a certificate. Prigg applied to a state judge for a certificate of removal; when it was refused, Prigg seized the slave. The Supreme Court reversed his conviction for violating the 1826 statute. Justice Story's opinion for the Court held that Congress had power to enact the Fugitive Slave Act, and that Pennsylvania could not interfere with the rendition of a fugitive (because either the Fugitive Slave Act or article IV, section 2, was supreme). He indicated in dicta that Pennsylvania could deny the aid of its officials to a rendition, relying on the theory that Pennsylvania had exclusive authority to regulate the activities of its officials. Justice Story regarded the dictum as a strong defense of the interests of blacks. Was he right? In the context of the holding of the case? Note the role that notions of exclusive power play here.

C.   FORMALISM AND REALISM IN INTERPRETING THE COMMERCE CLAUSE TO LIMIT AND AUTHORIZE CONGRESSIONAL ACTION

Until the late nineteenth century Congress rarely exercised its power to regulate interstate commerce. It acted to promote economic growth by establishing, for part of the era, the Bank of the United States, by transferring public lands to private owners, and by securing the nation's borders and its trade against foreign attack. The slavery controversy limited the opportunities for a consensus to form in favor of extensive exercise of the commerce power.

The Civil War and its aftermath inaugurated an era in which Congress began to act more vigorously. The very success of the national economy created problems. The economy became obviously interconnected; problems were no longer localized, so that it became difficult to imagine a purely internal commerce that affected no other states. During the Reconstruction era, supporters of the Union saw that the rights of freed slaves and their friends in the South were not adequately protected by state governments. They concluded that national intervention was appropriate and developed theories of federalism that justified broad exercises of national power. Finally, the mobilization of the Northern economy to fight the Civil War showed that national power could be used efficiently rather than wastefully, and the experience of the Civil War demonstrated that national power could indeed be used to promote liberty. Useful historical introductions to alterations in conceptions of the relative roles of state and nation are G. Fredrickson, The Inner Civil War (1968); H. Hyman, A More Perfect Union (1973); R. Harrison, The "Weakened Spring of Government" Revisited: The Growth of Federal Power in the Late Nineteenth Century, in The Growth of Federal Power in American History (R. Jeffreys-Jones & B. Collins eds. 1983).

These factors combined to make Congress more willing to exercise its power to regulate interstate commerce. The Interstate Commerce Act of 1887 and the Sherman Antitrust Act of 1890 illustrate the opening of the new era. Congress's earlier interventions in the economy, such as its disposal of public lands, had not created a constituency that strongly objected to the interventions. But the new regulatory mode of action automatically generated such a constituency, in the groups newly burdened by regulation. When these groups objected to national legislation on the ground that only the states could regulate their activities, they could provide relatively concrete examples of how in their view the national legislation threatened liberty and impaired the incentives needed to promote economic growth.

This section examines a number of doctrinal devices that the Supreme Court developed to deal with federalism-based objections to national legislation. As you read the materials, note that congressional legislation took two forms. Sometimes Congress imposed regulation on the industry, and sometimes it prohibited the shipment across state lines of goods that failed to meet specified conditions. Do the doctrinal tests differ depending on the form of the legislation? Should they?

Note also that congressional legislation only sometimes was designed to promote commercial goals directly. (Were those goals always the promotion of the free flow of goods?) At other times Congress acted to promote social goals, which were viewed as valuable wholly apart form their relation to economic development. Are such uses of the power to regulate interstate commerce appropriate? Are they constitutional? Do the doctrinal tests differ depending on the goal of the legislation? Should they? Observe in this connection the Court's use of the "pretext" test derived from McCulloch v. Maryland. Is it possible to sustain the distinction between commercial and social goals?

The cases invoke two general approaches. Under the *formal* approach, the Court examines the statute and the regulated activity to determine whether certain objective criteria are satisfied. For example, upholding regulation triggered by the fact that goods cross state lines is a formal approach that ignores actual economic effects and actual legislative motivation. In contrast, the *realist* approach attempts to determine the actual economic impact of the regulation or the actual motivation of Congress. Both formalism and realism were used to invalidate legislation and to uphold it. Can you discern any pattern to the results? Do the availability and use of competing approaches to yield varying results illuminate the question of whether courts should enforce limits on Congress's power in the name of federalism?

UNITED STATES v. E. C. KNIGHT CO., 156 U.S. 1 (1895): The United States invoked the Sherman Act to set aside the acquisition by the American Sugar Refining Company of four competing refineries. The acquisition left only one independent refinery in operation, which produced 2 percent of the sugar refined in the country. The Supreme Court, through Chief Justice Fuller, held that the Sherman Act did not reach this monopoly because the Constitution did not allow Congress to regulate "manufacturing." The government argued "that the power to control the manufacture of refined sugar is a monopoly over a necessary of life, to the enjoyment of which by a large part of the population of the United States interstate commerce is indispensable, and that, therefore, the general government may repress such monopoly directly and set aside the instruments which have created it. But this argument cannot be confined to necessaries of life merely, and must include all articles of general consumption. Doubtless the power to control the manufacture of a given thing involves in a certain sense the control of its disposition, but this is a secondary and not the primary sense;

and although the exercise of that power may result in bringing the operation of commerce into play, it does not control it, and affects it only incidentally and indirectly. Commerce succeeds to manufacture, and is not a part of it."

The distinction between the national commerce power and the local police power had to be maintained, "for while the one furnishes the strongest bond of union, the other is essential to the preservation of the autonomy of the States as required by our dual form of government; and acknowledged evils, however grave and urgent they may appear to be, had better be borne, than the risk be run, in the effort to suppress them, of more serious consequences by resort to expedients of even doubtful constitutionality."

It would be "far-reaching" to allow Congress to act "whenever interstate or international commerce may be ultimately affected. [The] fact that an article is manufactured for export to another State does not of itself make it an article of interstate commerce, and the intent of the manufacturer does not determine the time when the article or product passes from the control of the State and belongs to commerce." A monopoly in "manufacture, agriculture, [or] mining" might restrain interstate commerce, but that "would be an indirect result, however inevitable and whatever its extent, and such result would not necessarily determine the object" of the monopoly. American Sugar's action "bore no direct relation" to interstate commerce. "The object was manifestly private gain in the manufacture of the commodity, but not through control of interstate or foreign commerce." Rather, "trade and commerce [only] served manufacture to fulfill its function." Chief Justice Fuller agreed that some refined sugar was "forwarded" out of state. But the acquisition was not an attempt to monopolize interstate commerce, "even though, in order to dispose of the product, the instrumentality of commerce was necessarily invoked."

Justice Harlan wrote a typically long and impassioned dissent. Agreeing that it was important to preserve "the just authority of the States," he insisted that it was equally important to preserve national authority, whose "destruction [would] be fatal to the peace and well-being of the American people." To him, a monopoly that "obstructs freedom in buying and selling articles" to be sold out of state "affects, not incidentally, but directly, the people of all the States. [When] manufacture ends, that which has been manufactured becomes a subject of commerce; [buying] and selling succeed manufacture, come into existence after the process of manufacture is completed, precede transportation, and are as much commercial intercourse, where articles are bought *to be* carried from one State to another, as is the manual transportation of such articles after they have been so purchased." "[Whatever] improperly obstructs the free course of interstate intercourse and trade, as involved in the buying and selling of articles to be carried from one State to another, may be reached by Congress."

He suggested that Congress could prohibit the transportation across state lines of articles manufactured by monopolies, and that "it is not within the functions of the judiciary to adjudge that Congress shall employ particular means in execution of a given power." Rather, Congress had "discretion as to choice of means" and had chosen to regulate "in advance of transportation." "Congress sought to prevent the coming into existence of combinations, the purpose or tendency of which was to impose unlawful restraints upon interstate commerce."

"[In] my judgment, the general government is not placed by the Constitution in such a condition of helplessness that it must fold its arms and remain inactive while capital combines, under the name of a corporation, to destroy competition, not in one State only, but throughout the entire country, in the buying and selling of articles — especially the necessaries of life — that go into commerce among the States. The doctrine of the autonomy of the States cannot properly be invoked to justify a denial of power in the national government to meet such an emergency. . . .

"[To] the general government has been committed the control of commercial intercourse among the States, to the end that it may be free at all times from any restraints except such as Congress may impose or permit for the benefit of the whole country. The common government of all the people is the only one that can adequately deal with a matter which directly and injuriously affects the entire commerce of the country, which concerns equally all the people of the Union, and which, it must be confessed, cannot be adequately controlled by any one State. Its authority should not be so weakened by construction that it cannot reach and eradicate evils that, beyond all question, tend to defeat an object which that government is entitled, by the Constitution, to accomplish."

HOUSTON, EAST & WEST TEXAS RAILWAY v. UNITED STATES (The Shreveport Rate Cases), 234 U.S. 342 (1914): The Railway operated lines between Texas and Louisiana. Shipments from Dallas to Marshall, Texas, a distance of 150 miles, cost 37 cents; shipments from Shreveport, Louisiana, to Marshall (42 miles), cost 56 cents. The Interstate Commerce Commission set a maximum rate for shipments from Shreveport to Texas and ordered the railway to charge no higher rates per mile for shipments to Marshall from Shreveport or Dallas, to eliminate the "discrimination" against Shreveport. The Supreme Court, in an opinion by Justice Hughes, held that the Commission could set rates for the intrastate Dallas-to-Marshall route.

Congress's "authority, extending to these interstate carriers as instruments of interstate commerce, necessarily embraces the right to control their operations in all matters having such a close and substantial relation to interstate traffic that the control is essential or appropriate to the security of that traffic, to the efficiency of the interstate service, and to the maintenance of conditions under which interstate commerce may be conducted upon fair terms and without molestation or hindrance. As it is competent for Congress to legislate to these ends, unquestionably it may seek their attainment by requiring that the agencies of interstate commerce shall not be used in such manner as to cripple, retard or destroy it. The fact that carriers are instruments of intrastate commerce, as well as of interstate commerce, does not derogate from the complete and paramount authority of Congress over the latter or preclude the Federal power from being exerted to prevent the intrastate operations of such carriers from being made a means of injury to that which has been confided to Federal care. Wherever the interstate and intrastate transactions of carriers are so related that the government of the one involves the control of the other, it is Congress, and not the State, that is entitled to prescribe the final and dominant rule, for otherwise Congress would be denied the exercise of its constitutional authority and the State, and not the Nation, would be supreme within the national field. . . .

"Congress in the exercise of its paramount power may prevent the common instrumentalities of interstate and intrastate commercial intercourse from being used in their intrastate operations to the injury of interstate commerce. This is not to say that Congress possesses the authority to regulate the internal commerce of a State, as such, but that it does possess the power to foster and protect interstate commerce, and to take all measures necessary or appropriate to that end, although intrastate transactions of interstate carriers may thereby be controlled.

"This principle is applicable here. We find no reason to doubt that Congress is entitled to keep the highways of interstate communication open to interstate traffic upon fair and equal terms. That an unjust discrimination in the rates of a common carrier, by which one person or locality is unduly favored as against another under substantially similar conditions of traffic, constitutes an evil is undeniable; and where this evil consists in the action of an interstate carrier in unreasonably discriminating against interstate traffic over its line, the authority of Congress to prevent it is equally clear. It is immaterial, so far as the protecting power of Congress is concerned, that the discrimination arises from intrastate rates as compared with interstate rates. The use of the instrument of interstate commerce in a discriminatory manner so as to inflict injury upon that commerce, or some part thereof, furnishes abundant ground for Federal intervention."

Justices Lurton and Pitney dissented.

STAFFORD v. WALLACE, 258 U.S. 495 (1922): The Packers and Stockyards Act of 1921 authorized the Secretary of Commerce to regulate rates and prescribe standards for the operation of stockyards where livestock was kept for sale or shipment in interstate commerce. It was designed to reduce the power of packers over prices they paid for cattle and to eliminate collusion between the stockyard managers and the packers. Collusive practices raised prices to consumers. Chief Justice Taft's opinion for the Court upholding the act said that the "only question [is] whether the business done in the stockyards between the receipt of the live stock in the yards and the shipment of them therefrom is a part of interstate commerce. [The] stockyards are but a throat through which the current flows, and the transactions which occur therein are only incident to this current from the West to the East, and from one State to another. Such transactions can not be separated from the movement to which they contribute and necessarily take on its character. [The] sales are not in this aspect merely local transactions. They create a local change of title, it is true, but they do not stop the flow; they merely change the private interests in the subject of the current, not interfering with, but, on the contrary, being indispensable to its continuity. The origin of the live stock is in the West, its ultimate destination known to, and intended by, all engaged in the business is in the Middle West and East either as meat products or stock for feeding and fattening." Chief Justice Taft wrote that the Court would not "defeat [the] purpose" of the commerce clause as to "such streams of commerce [by] a nice and technical inquiry into the non-interstate character of some of its necessary incidents and facilities when considered alone and without reference to their association with the movement of which they were an essential but subordinate part." Justice McReynolds dissented.

Note: Direct, Indirect, and Stream of Commerce Tests

1. *Intent and Congress's power.* Suppose the government proved that American Sugar intended by its near-monopoly to restrict production. (Isn't that the whole point of acquiring a monopoly: to charge a monopoly price higher than the

competitive price, with the effect of restricting production?) On Chief Justice Fuller's analysis, would Congress then have power to regulate? Would he require an even more specific intent, not just to restrict production but to restrict interstate commerce? Why should the company's intent be so important?

Coronado Coal Co. v. United Mine Workers, 268 U.S. 295 (1925), applied the Sherman Act to a strike against mine operators. Carter v. Carter Coal Co., section D infra, distinguished *Coronado* from *E. C. Knight*: "The acts of the persons involved were local in character, but the intent was to restrain interstate commerce, and the means employed were calculated to carry that intent into effect. Interstate commerce was the direct object of attack; and the restraint of such commerce was the necessary consequence of the acts and the immediate end in view." Reducing the supply of a good is "ordinarily an indirect and remote obstruction" of interstate commerce, but "when the intent [is] to restrain or control the supply" in interstate commerce, the Sherman Act is violated. Is the distinction between *E. C. Knight* and *Coronado* persuasive? Intelligible?

2. *Formalist and realist approaches.* Chief Justice Fuller and Justice Harlan take different approaches to determining what federalism-based limits on national power might be. The former argues that "commerce succeeds to manufacture." He could not mean that manufacturing does not affect commerce. Rather, he defines limits by identifying certain categories of activities that he defines as "not commerce." Recall Chief Justice Marshall's discussion of navigation in *Gibbons*. On what basis can we use this "categorical" approach to *exclude* matters from interstate commerce? Note that Chief Justice Fuller appears to have some temporal sequence in mind as the basis for his exclusion: Certain activities, which are not commerce, precede it (manufacturing), and presumably other activities, which are also not commerce, succeed it (retail sales?). Does Chief Justice Fuller explain why the relevant temporal line is drawn to exclude manufacturing, rather than at an earlier point, such as acquisition of raw materials?

Justices Harlan and Hughes offer a "practical" approach to determining federalism-based limits on congressional power. Justice Harlan emphasizes the actual economic consequences of the American Sugar Company's near-monopoly. If you find his approach more congenial or realistic than Chief Justice Fuller's, consider whether that is because you find it difficult to imagine an economy divided into distinct spheres of activity or because you approve of Justice Harlan's result in the case.

3. *National power where state cannot effectively act.* American Sugar conceded that New Jersey could prohibit locally chartered corporations from acquiring monopolies. Note that so long as a single state is willing to allow its competitors to acquire monopolies — for example, in exchange for an annual tax that is less than the monopolistic profits — the practical consequence of American Sugar's position is to make it impossible to have effective antimonopoly legislation anywhere. For further discussion, see Hammer v. Dagenhart, section C infra. See also McCurdy, The *Knight* Sugar Decision of 1895 and the Modernization of American Corporation Law, 1869-1903, 53 Bus. Hist. Rev. 304 (1979). Does the inability of any single state or group of states to control monopolies justify finding power in Congress to do so? Compare the last paragraph of Justice Harlan's dissent with McCulloch v. Maryland.

4. *Regulation versus prohibition of shipment across state lines.* Is Justice Harlan correct in suggesting that Congress would not violate the Constitution if it prohib-

ited the shipment in interstate commerce of sugar manufactured by a monopoly? If that statute is constitutional, why is it unconstitutional to regulate manufacturing by directly prohibiting monopolies?

5. *Consistent precedents?* Outline an opinion relying on *E. C. Knight* to find the regulation in the Shreveport Rate cases unconstitutional. Note that Justice Hughes develops a practical, economically oriented test. Would Chief Justice Fuller have agreed with the result in the Shreveport Rate cases? If not, what accounts for the change in the position of the Court? Consider whether, in light of *Coronado Coal*, the Court over the period from 1890 to 1930 had and used a coherent notion of "good" versus "bad" regulation. What might that notion have been? In this connection, you might find it interesting to look ahead to Lochner v. New York, Chapter 6 infra, and Muller v. Oregon, Chapter 5 infra. Consider also whether the apparent change resulted from an increasing sense that it was no longer possible to think of the economy as divided into self-contained spheres of activity.

6. Gibbons *revisited.* Is the result in the Shreveport Rate cases consistent with Chief Justice Marshall's definition of "interstate" in Gibbons v. Ogden?

7. *"Stream of commerce."* In *Stafford*, Chief Justice Taft relies on a practical, economically oriented test: Congress may regulate an activity if it affects interstate commerce. Does such a test exclude anything? In addition, he relies on the metaphor of a "stream of commerce." Is that metaphor helpful? How do you know when a stream begins and ends? Why doesn't *Stafford* involve two streams of commerce, one ending with the arrival of the cattle at the stockyards and the other beginning with their departure? Consider this argument as you read the *Schechter* case, section D infra.

8. *Formalist and realist approaches — a preliminary summary.* As Congress began to regulate the national economy more extensively, the Supreme Court generally focused on practical reality and found that Congress had exercised its power in accordance with the Constitution. In addition to the principal cases, see Southern Railway v. United States, 222 U.S. 20 (1911) (upholding Federal Safety Appliance Act as applied to railroad cars with defective couplers, because although the cars were used in intrastate traffic, the act applied to cars "used on any railroad engaged in interstate commerce"). Even *E. C. Knight* had limited effects. Swift & Co. v. United States, 196 U.S. 375 (1905), sustained the application of the Sherman Act to meat dealers, invoking the "current of commerce" metaphor and calling interstate commerce "not a technical legal conception, but a practical one."

Why did the Court retain the formalist approach? Consider the following arguments:

a. As the national economy became more interconnected, both Congress and the Court recognized that national regulation was appropriate. This made the "realist" approach attractive. But the Court remained affected by the view that Congress's power to regulate interstate commerce was exclusive. On that view, recognizing a broad power in Congress to regulate, based on a practical analysis of the economy, entailed the elimination of state power to regulate. For example, Wabash, St. Louis & Pacific Railway v. Illinois, 118 U.S. 557 (1886), decided before the enactment of the Interstate Commerce Act, held unconstitutional a state's effort to regulate rates on shipments to and from the state. The powerful centralizing impetus of this combination of doctrines would have substantially reduced state authority. Some method to reduce its force seemed necessary, and the formalism of *E. C. Knight* was the Court's response. Formalism too must be contained, and intent, as invoked in *Coronado Coal*, was its doctrinal form.

b. Having available both the formalist and the realist approaches maximized the Court's power to assure that only legislation that it thought wise would be effective.

In the next principal cases, a version of formalism leads to upholding statutes and a version of realism leads to invalidating them. Are these versions sufficiently similar to the ones you have already examined to justify treating "formalism" and "realism" as unifying themes?

Champion v. Ames (The Lottery Case)

188 U.S. 321 (1903)

[The Federal Lottery Act of 1895 prohibited the interstate transportation of foreign lottery tickets. Champion was indicted for shipping a box of Paraguayan lottery tickets from Texas to California. The circuit court rejected his challenge to the constitutionality of the act.]

MR. JUSTICE HARLAN delivered the opinion of the Court.

The appellant insists that the carrying of lottery tickets from one State to another State [does] not constitute [*commerce*] among the States. . . .

[Undoubtedly,] the carrying from one State to another by independent carriers of things or commodities that are ordinary subjects of traffic, and which have in themselves a recognized value in money, constitutes interstate commerce. But does not commerce among the several States include something more? Does not the carrying from one State to another, by independent carriers, of lottery tickets that entitle the holder to the payment of a certain amount of money therein specified also constitute commerce among the States? . . .

But it is said that the statute in question does not regulate the carrying of lottery tickets from State to State, but by punishing those who cause them to be so carried Congress in effect prohibits such carrying; that in respect of the carrying from one State to another of articles or things that are, in fact, or according to usage in business, the subjects of commerce, the authority given Congress was not to *prohibit*, but only to *regulate*. . . .

It is to be remarked that the Constitution does not decline what is to be deemed a legitimate regulation of interstate commerce. In Gibbons v. Ogden it was said that the power to regulate such commerce is the power to prescribe the rule by which it is to be governed. But this general observation leaves it to be determined, when the question comes before the court, whether Congress in prescribing a particular rule has exceeded its power under the Constitution. While our Government must be acknowledged by all to be one of enumerated powers, McCulloch v. Maryland, 4 Wheat. 316, 405, 407, the Constitution does not attempt to set forth all the means by which such powers may be carried into execution. It leaves to Congress a large discretion as to the means that may be employed in executing a given power. . . .

We have said that the carrying from State to State of lottery tickets constitutes interstate commerce, and that the regulation of such commerce is within the power of Congress under the Constitution. Are we prepared to say that a provision which is, in effect, a *prohibition* of the carriage of such articles from State to State is not a fit or appropriate mode for the *regulation* of that particular kind of commerce? If lottery traffic, *carried on through interstate commerce,* is a matter of which Congress may take cognizance and over which its power may be exerted, can it be possible that it must tolerate the traffic, and simply regulate the manner in which it may be carried on? Or may not Congress, for the protection of the people of all the States, and under the power to regulate interstate commerce, devise such means, within the scope of the Constitution, and not prohibited by it, as will drive that traffic out of commerce among the States?

In determining whether regulation may not under some circumstances properly take the form or have the effect of prohibition, the nature of the interstate traffic which it was sought by the act of May 2, 1895, to suppress cannot be overlooked. When enacting that statute Congress no doubt shared the views upon the subject of lotteries heretofore expressed by this court. In Phalen v. Virginia, 8 How. 163, 168, after observing that the suppression of nuisances injurious to public health or morality is among the most important duties of Government, this court said:

> Experience has shown that the common forms of gambling are comparatively innocuous when placed in contrast with the widespread pestilence of lotteries. The former are confined to a few persons and places, but the latter infests the whole community; it enters every dwelling; it reaches every class; it preys upon the hard earnings of the poor; it plunders the ignorant and simple. . . .

If a State, when considering legislation for the suppression of lotteries within its own limits, may properly take into view the evils that inhere in the raising of money, in that mode, why may not Congress, invested with the power to regulate commerce among the several States, provide that such commerce shall not be polluted by the carrying of lottery tickets from one State to another? In this connection it must not be forgotten that the power of Congress to regulate commerce among the States is plenary, is complete in itself, and is subject to no limitations except such as may be found in the Constitution. What provision in that instrument can be regarded as limiting the exercise of the power granted? What clause can be cited which, in any degree, countenances the suggestion that one may, of right, carry or cause to be carried from one State to another that which will harm the public morals? [We] have said that the liberty protected by the Constitution embraces the right to be free in the enjoyment of one's faculties; "to be free to use them in all lawful ways; to live and work where he will; to earn his livelihood by any lawful calling; to pursue any livelihood or avocation, and for that purpose to enter into all contracts that may be proper." Allgeyer v. Louisiana, 165 U.S. 578, 589. But surely it will not be said to be a part of any one's liberty, as recognized by the supreme law of the land, that he shall be allowed to introduce into commerce among the States an element that will be confessedly injurious to the public morals.

If it be said that the act of 1895 is inconsistent with the Tenth Amendment, reserving to the States respectively or to the people the powers not delegated to the United States, the answer is that the power to regulate commerce among the States has been expressly delegated to Congress.

Besides, Congress, by that act, does not assume to interfere with traffic or commerce in lottery tickets carried on exclusively within the limits of any State, but has in view only commerce of that kind among the several States. It has not assumed to interfere with the completely internal affairs of any State, and has only legislated in respect of a matter which concerns the people of the United States. As a State may, for the purpose of guarding the morals of its own people, forbid all sales of lottery tickets within its limits, so Congress, for the purpose of guarding the people of the United States against the "widespread pestilence of lotteries" and to protect the commerce which concerns all the States, may prohibit the carrying of lottery tickets from one State to another. In legislating upon the subject of the traffic in lottery tickets, as carried on through interstate commerce, Congress only supplemented the action of those States — perhaps all of them — which, for the protection of the public morals, prohibit the drawing of lotteries, as well as the sale or circulation of lottery tickets, within their respective limits. It said, in effect, that it would not permit the declared policy of the States, which sought to protect their people against the mischiefs of the lottery business, to be overthrown or disregarded by the agency of interstate commerce. We should hesitate long before adjudging that an evil of such appalling character, carried on through interstate commerce, cannot be met and crushed by the only power competent to that end. We say competent to that end, because Congress alone has the power to occupy, by legislation, the whole field of interstate commerce. [If] the carrying of lottery tickets from one State to another be interstate commerce, and if Congress is of opinion that an effective regulation for the suppression of lotteries, carried on through such commerce, is to make it a criminal offense to cause lottery tickets to be carried from one State to another, we know of no authority in the courts to hold that the means thus devised are not appropriate and necessary to protect the country at large against a species of interstate commerce which, although in general use and somewhat favored in both national and state legislation in the early history of the country, has grown into disrepute and has become offensive to the entire people of the Nation. It is a kind of traffic which no one can be entitled to pursue as of right.

That regulation may sometimes appropriately assume the form of prohibition is also illustrated by the case of diseased cattle, transported from one State to another. . . .

It is said, however, that if, in order to suppress lotteries carried on through interstate commerce, Congress may exclude lottery tickets from such commerce, that principle leads necessarily to the conclusion that Congress may arbitrarily exclude from commerce among the States any article, commodity or thing, of whatever kind or nature, or however useful or valuable, which it may choose, no matter with what motive, to declare shall not be carried from one State to another. It will be time enough to consider the constitutionality of such legislation when we must do so. The present case does not require the court to declare the full extent of the power that Congress may exercise in the regulation of commerce among the States. We may, however, repeat, in this connection, what the court has heretofore said, that the power of Congress to regulate commerce among the States, although plenary, cannot be deemed arbitrary, since it is subject to such limitations or restrictions as are prescribed by the Constitution. This power, therefore, may not be exercised so as to infringe rights secured or protected by that instrument. It would not be difficult to imagine legislation that would be justly liable to such an objection as that stated, and be hostile to the objects for the accomplishment of which Congress was invested with the general power to regulate commerce among the several States. But, as often said, the possible abuse of a power is not an argument against its existence. There is probably no governmental power that may not be exerted to the injury of the public. If what is done by Congress is manifestly in excess of the powers granted to it, then upon the courts will rest the duty of adjudging that its action is neither legal nor binding upon the people. But if what Congress does is within the limits of its power, and is simply unwise or injurious, the remedy is that suggested by Chief Justice Marshall in Gibbons v. Ogden, when he said:

> The wisdom and the discretion of Congress, their identity with the people, and the influence which their constituents possess at elections, are, in this, as in many other instances, as that, for example, of declaring war, the sole restraints on which they have relied, to secure them from its abuse. They are the restraints on which the people must often rely solely, in all representative governments.

[Affirmed.]

MR. CHIEF JUSTICE FULLER, with whom concur MR. JUSTICE BREWER, MR. JUSTICE SHIRAS and MR. JUSTICE PECKHAM, dissenting. . . .

The naked question is whether the prohibition by Congress of the carriage of lottery tickets from one State to another by means other than the mails is within the powers vested in that body by the Constitution of the United States. That the purpose of Congress in this enactment was the suppression of lotteries cannot reasonably be denied. . . .

The power of the State to impose restraints and burdens on persons and property in conservation and promotion of the public health, good order and prosperity is a power originally and always belonging to the States, not surrendered by them to the General Government nor directly restrained by the Constitution of the United States, and essentially exclusive, and the suppression of lotteries as a harmful business falls within this power, commonly called of police.

It is urged, however, that because Congress is empowered to regulate commerce between the several States, it, therefore, may suppress lotteries by prohibiting the carriage of lottery matter. Congress may indeed make all laws necessary and proper for carrying the powers granted to it into execution, and doubtless an act prohibiting the carriage of lottery matter would be necessary and proper to the execution of a power to suppress lotteries; but that power belongs to the State and not to Congress. To hold that Congress has general police power would be to hold that it may accomplish objects not entrusted to the General Government, and to defeat the operation of the Tenth Amendment. . . .

Is the carriage of lottery tickets from one State to another commercial intercourse?

The lottery ticket purports to create contractual relations and to furnish the means of enforcing a contract right.

This is true of insurance policies, and both are contingent in their nature. Yet this court has held that the issuing of fire, marine, and life insurance policies, in one State, and sending them to another, to be there delivered to the insured on payment of premium, is not interstate commerce. . . .

[To] say that the mere carrying of an article which is not an article of commerce in and of itself nevertheless becomes such the moment it is to be transported from one State to another, is to transform a non-commercial article into a commercial one simply because it is transported. I cannot conceive that any such result can properly follow.

It would be to say that everything is an article of commerce the moment it is taken to be transported from place to place, and of interstate commerce if from State to State.

An invitation to dine, or to take a drive, or a note of introduction, all become articles of commerce under the ruling in this case, by being deposited with an express company for transportation. This in effect breaks down all the differences between that which is, and that which is not, an article of commerce, and the necessary consequence is to take from the States all jurisdiction over the subject so far as interstate communication is concerned. It is a long step in the direction of wiping out all traces of state lines, and the creation of a centralized Government.

Does the grant to Congress of the power to regulate interstate commerce impart the absolute power to prohibit it? . . .

It will not do to say — a suggestion which has heretofore been made in this case — that state laws have been found to be ineffective for the suppression of lotteries, and therefore Congress should interfere. The scope of the commerce clause of the Constitution cannot be enlarged because of present views of public interest. . . .

"Should Congress," said [Marshall] in McCulloch v. Maryland, 4 Wheat. 316, 423, "under the pretext of executing its powers, pass laws for the accomplishment of objects not entrusted to the Government; it would become the painful duty of this tribunal, should a case requiring such a decision come before it, to say that such an act was not the law of the land." . . .

The power to prohibit the transportation of diseased animals and infected goods over railroads or on steamboats is an entirely different thing, for they would be in themselves injurious to the transaction of interstate commerce, and, moreover, are essentially commercial in their nature. And the exclusion of diseased persons rests on different ground, for nobody would pretend that persons could be kept off the trains because they were going from one State to another to engage in the lottery business. However enticing that business may be, we do not understand these pieces of paper themselves can communicate bad principles by contact. . . .

Note: Prohibiting Interstate Transportation — Proper Regulation or Improper Pretext?

1. *Defining commerce — Gibbons revisited.* What arguments did *Champion* make against the act? Given *Gibbons*, what is the argument that lottery tickets are not items of commerce? That they do not have "a recognized value"? That they simply provide evidence of an underlying local contractual agreement? Why do lottery operators issue tickets? Given *Gibbons*, what is the argument that prohibition is not regulation? Would *Champion's* argument be avoided by a statute that prohibited the interstate transportation of tickets in lotteries that paid off less than

98 percent of the amount collected? Of all tickets except those of the Ecuadoran national lottery?

2. *Enforcement of limits again.* Does Justice Harlan define any judicially enforceable limits on Congress's power to regulate by means of prohibiting interstate shipment? Note the concluding quotation from Gibbons v. Ogden. What reasons does he suggest for Congress's action? Can its reason for prohibiting the shipment of lottery tickets be distinguished from the usual reasons for exercising a general police power? Note Justice Harlan's treatment of the claim that the due process clause limits Congress's power.

3. *Regulation or pretext?* Under the majority's holding, is there anything left to the "pretext" limitation stated by Chief Justice Marshall in *McCulloch* and quoted by the dissent? *Champion* involves a regulation whose apparent purpose is less "commercial" than those we have examined so far. Should that make a difference? Develop a "commercial" argument for the statute in *Champion*.

If the statute's purpose were to promote moral or social goals, would the use of the commerce power be a pretext of the sort Chief Justice Marshall disapproved in *McCulloch*? Consider that applying a "pretext" test requires a definition of the proper purposes for which a power may be exercised. Did Chief Justice Marshall in *Gibbons* say or assume that the commerce power was limited to commercial purposes? Did Justice Johnson? If it is not limited to commercial purposes, how might a "pretext" test be applied?

4. *Later developments.* In Hipolite Egg Co. v. United States, 220 U.S. 45 (1911), the government seized a shipment of preserved eggs because their labels failed to comply with the requirements of the Pure Food and Drugs Act of 1906. The act prohibited interstate shipment of noncomplying foods. The mislabeling would mislead consumers, but the eggs were not unhealthful. The eggs had reached their destination when they were seized. The Court upheld the seizure, calling the goods "outlaws of commerce [which] may be seized wherever found." They could not "escape the consequences of their illegal transportation by being mingled at the place of destination with other property." The power to seize after arrival was an "appropriate means" to preventing interstate shipment.

Hoke v. United States, 227 U.S. 308 (1913), upheld the Mann Act's prohibition of transportation of women in interstate commerce for immoral purposes. "Congress has power over transportation, [and] may adopt [means] that have the quality of police regulation."

Hammer v. Dagenhart (The Child Labor Case)

247 U.S. 251 (1918)

[In 1916 Congress responded to a decade-long lobbying effort by enacting the Child Labor Act. The act prohibited the transportation in interstate commerce of goods produced in factories employing children under age fourteen, or employing fourteen- to sixteen-year-olds for more than eight hours a day, or six days a week, or at night. Two children, one under age fourteen and the other under age sixteen, were employed in a cotton mill in North Carolina. Their father secured an injunction against the enforcement of the act on grounds of its unconstitutionality. For a comprehensive study of the origins of the Child Labor Act and the test-case litigation that culminated in Hammer v. Dagenhart and Bailey v. Drexel Furniture Co., section G infra, see S. Wood, Constitutional Politics in the Progressive Era (1968).]

MR. JUSTICE DAY delivered the opinion of the Court. . . .

[The] power [to regulate interstate commerce] is one to control the means by which commerce is carried on, which is directly the contrary of the assumed right to forbid commerce from moving and thus destroy it as to particular commodities. But it is insisted that adjudged cases in this court establish the doctrine that the power to regulate given to Congress incidentally includes the authority to prohibit the movement of ordinary commodities and therefore that the subject is not open for discussion. The cases demonstrate the contrary. They rest upon the character of the particular subjects dealt with and the fact that the scope of governmental authority, state or national, possessed over them is such that the authority to prohibit is as to them but the exertion of the power to regulate. . . .

In [*Champion, Hipolite Egg,* and *Hoke*] the use of interstate transportation was necessary to the accomplishment of harmful results. In other words, although the power over interstate transportation was to regulate, that could only be accomplished by prohibiting the use of the facilities of interstate commerce to effect the evil intended.

This element is wanting in the present case. The thing intended to be accomplished by this statute is the denial of the facilities of interstate commerce to those manufacturers in the States who employ children within the prohibited ages. The act in its effect does not regulate transportation among the States, but aims to standardize the ages at which children may be employed in mining and manufacturing within the States. The goods shipped are of themselves harmless. [When] offered for shipment, and before transportation begins, the labor of their production is over, and the mere fact that they were intended for interstate commerce transportation does not make their production subject to federal control under the commerce power. . . .

[The] making of goods and the mining of coal are not commerce, nor does the fact that these things are to be afterwards shipped or used in interstate commerce, make their production a part thereof.

Over interstate transportation, or its incidents, the regulatory power of Congress is ample, but the production of articles, intended for interstate commerce, is a matter of local regulation. . . .

[If] it were otherwise, all manufacture intended for interstate shipment would be brought under federal control to the practical exclusion of the authority of the States, a result certainly not contemplated by the framers of the Constitution when they vested in Congress the authority to regulate commerce among the States.

It is further contended that the authority of Congress may be exerted to control interstate commerce in the shipment of child-made goods because of the effect of the circulation of such goods in other States where the evil of this class of labor has been recognized by local legislation, and the right to thus employ child labor has been more rigorously restrained than in the State of production. In other words, that the unfair competition, thus engendered, may be controlled by closing the channels of interstate commerce to manufacturers in those States where the local laws do not meet what Congress deems to be the more just standard of other States.

There is no power vested in Congress to require the States to exercise their police power so as to prevent possible unfair competition. Many causes may cooperate to give one State, by reason of local laws or conditions, an economic advantage over others. The Commerce Clause was not intended to give to Congress a general authority to equalize such conditions. In some of the States laws have been passed fixing minimum wages for women, in others the local law regulates the hours of labor of women in various employments. Business done in such states may be at an economic disadvantage when compared with States which have no such regulations; surely, this fact does not give Congress the power to deny transportation in interstate commerce to those who carry on business where the hours of labor and the rate of compensation for women have not been fixed by a standard in use in other States and approved by Congress.

The grant of power to Congress over the subject of interstate commerce was to enable it to regulate such commerce, and not to give it authority to control the States in their exercise of the police power over local trade and manufacture.

The grant of authority over a purely federal matter was not intended to destroy the local power always existing and carefully reserved to the States in the Tenth Amendment to the Constitution.

In interpreting the Constitution it must never be forgotten that the Nation is made up of States to which are entrusted the powers of local government. And to them and to the people the powers not expressly delegated to the National Government are reserved. Lane County v. Oregon, 7 Wall. 71, 76. The power of the States to regulate their purely internal affairs by such laws as seem wise to the local authority is inherent and has never been surrendered to the general government. To sustain this statute would not be in our judgment a recognition of the lawful exertion of congressional authority over interstate commerce, but would sanction an invasion by the federal power of the control of a matter purely local in its character, and over which no authority has been delegated to Congress in conferring the power to regulate commerce among the States.

We have neither authority nor disposition to question the motives of Congress in enacting this legislation. The purposes intended must be attained consistently with constitutional limitations and not by an invasion of the powers of the States. This court has no more important function than that which devolves upon it the obligation to preserve inviolate the constitutional limitations upon the exercise of authority, federal and state, to the end that each may continue to discharge, harmoniously with the other, the duties entrusted to it by the Constitution.

In our view the necessary effect of this act is, by means of a prohibition against the movement in interstate commerce of ordinary commercial commodities, to regulate the hours of labor of children in factories and mines within the States, a purely state authority. Thus the act in a twofold sense is repugnant to the Constitution. It not only transcends the authority delegated to Congress over commerce but also exerts a power as to a purely local matter to which the federal authority does not extend. The far reaching result of upholding the act cannot be more plainly indicated than by pointing out that if Congress can thus regulate matters entrusted to local authority by prohibition of the movement of commodities in interstate commerce, all freedom of commerce will be at an end, and the power of the States over local matters may be eliminated, and thus our system of government be practically destroyed.

[Affirmed.]

MR. JUSTICE HOLMES, dissenting. . . .

[If] an act is within the powers specifically conferred upon Congress, it seems to me that it is not made any less constitutional because of the indirect effects that it may have, however obvious it may be that it will have those effects, and that we are not at liberty upon such grounds to hold it void.

The first step in my argument is to make plain what no one is likely to dispute — that the statute in question is within the power expressly given to Congress if considered only as to its immediate effects and that if invalid it is so only upon some collateral ground. The statute confines itself to prohibiting the carriage of certain goods in interstate or foreign commerce. Congress is given power to regulate such commerce in unqualified terms. It would not be argued today that the power to regulate does not include the power to prohibit. Regulation means the prohibition of something, and when interstate commerce is the matter to be regulated I cannot doubt that the regulation may prohibit any part of such commerce that Congress sees fit to forbid. [Champion v. Ames.] . . .

The question then is narrowed to whether the exercise of its otherwise constitutional power by Congress can be pronounced unconstitutional because of its possible reaction upon the conduct of the States in a matter upon which I have admitted that they are free from direct control. I should have thought that that matter had been disposed of so fully as to leave no room for doubt. I should have thought that the most conspicuous decisions of this Court had made it clear that the power to regulate commerce and other constitutional powers could not be cut down or qualified by the fact that it might interfere with the carrying out of the domestic policy of any State.

The manufacture of oleomargarine is as much a matter of state regulation as the manufacture of cotton cloth. Congress levied a tax upon the compound when colored so as to resemble butter that was so great as obviously to prohibit the manufacture and sale. In a very elaborate discussion the present Chief Justice excluded any inquiry into the purpose of an act which apart from that purpose was within the power of Congress. McCray v. United States, 195 U.S. 27. Fifty years ago a tax on state banks, the obvious purpose and actual effect of which was to drive them, or at least their circulation, out of existence, was sustained, although the result was one that Congress had no constitutional power to require. The Court made short work of the argument as to the purpose of the act. "The judicial cannot prescribe to the legislative department of the government limitations upon the exercise of its acknowledged powers." Veazie Bank v. Fenno, 8 Wall. 533. . . .

The notion that prohibition is any less prohibition when applied to things now thought evil I do not understand. But if there is any matter upon which civilized countries have agreed — far more unanimously than they have with regard to intoxicants and some other matters over which this country is now emotionally aroused — it is the evil of premature and excessive child labor. I should have thought that if we were to introduce our own moral conceptions where in my opinion they do not belong, this was preeminently a case for upholding the exercise of all its powers by the United States.

But I had thought that the propriety of the exercise of a power admitted to exist in some cases was for the consideration of Congress alone and that this Court always had disavowed the right to intrude its judgment upon questions of policy or morals. It is not for this Court to pronounce when prohibition is necessary to regulation if it ever may be necessary — to say that it is permissible as against strong drink but not as against the product of ruined lives.

The act does not meddle with anything belonging to the States. They may regulate their internal affairs and their domestic commerce as they like. But when they seek to send their products across the state line they are no longer within their rights. If there were no Constitution and no Congress their power to cross the line would depend upon their neighbors. Under the Constitution such commerce belongs not to the States but to Congress to regulate. It may carry out its views of public policy whatever indirect effect they may have upon the activities of the States. Instead of being encountered by a prohibitive tariff at her boundaries the State encounters the public policy of the United States which it is for Congress to express. The public policy of the United States is shaped with a view to the benefit of the nation as a whole. If, as has been the case within the memory of men still living, a State should take a different view of the propriety of sustaining a lottery from that which generally prevails, I cannot believe that the fact would require a different decision from that reached in Champion v. Ames. Yet in that case it would be said with quite as much force as in this that Congress was attempting to intermeddle with the State's domestic affairs. The national welfare as understood by Congress may require a different attitude within its sphere from that of some self-seeking State. It seems to me entirely constitutional for Congress to enforce its understanding by all the means at its command.

MR. JUSTICE MCKENNA, MR. JUSTICE BRANDEIS and MR. JUSTICE CLARKE concur in this opinion.

Note: Formalism, Realism, and Prohibiting Interstate Shipment

1. *Handling precedents.* How does Justice Day distinguish *Champion* and *Hipolite Egg*? In what sense was interstate transportation necessary in those cases to accomplish the evil, but unnecessary here? In what sense are lottery tickets "of themselves" harmful?

The dissent cites cases involving the power to tax in which the Court disclaimed the effort to inquire into purpose. For a discussion of whether the power to tax differs from the power to regulate commerce, see section F3 infra. How can a "pretext" test be applied without inquiring into purpose?

2. *Dual federalism.* Justice Day says that the act violates the Constitution "in a twofold sense." One is that Congress has only its enumerated powers; the other is that states have authority over local matters "to which the federal authority does not extend." Does the second sense mean that Congress cannot regulate a local matter even in the course of an unquestioned exercise of an enumerated power? Is that consistent with the theory of enumeration? With the Shreveport Rate cases, decided four years earlier? With Stafford v. Wallace, decided four years later?

3. *Enforcement of limits again.* Justice Day's strongest argument seems to be that if this statute is upheld, there will be no (judicially enforceable) limits on Congress' power. Does the opinion recognize the relevance of the parenthetical qualification? Does the dissent suggest judicially enforceable limits? Should it have? Develop an "affecting commerce" and "stream of commerce" defense of

the statute. Does child labor really "affect commerce" in any way other than by creating the "unfair competition" that Justice Day argues Congress has no power to prevent?

4. *Concluding remarks.* Does the Court's record from the 1880s to the 1920s on the issues considered here reflect (a) a principled effort to develop a coherent body of law in an area where determining appropriate doctrine is difficult; (b) an unprincipled effort to uphold laws that enough justices thought wise and to strike down those they thought unwise; (c) an effort to ensure that Congress attend to considerations of federalism by developing a doctrinal repertoire that allowed the Court occasionally to hold a statute unconstitutional? Can you draw a "lesson of history" from these materials?

Whatever the Court's intentions, by 1930 it had at hand a group of precedents that gave it substantial flexibility in assessing the constitutionality of Congress's efforts to regulate the economy. Over the following decade those precedents were applied and then abandoned.

D. THE NEW DEAL CRISIS AND THE RISE OF THE WELFARE STATE

As soon as Franklin D. Roosevelt took office in 1933, he proposed — and Congress quickly enacted — a series of statutes designed to ameliorate the consequences of the ongoing economic crisis and to stabilize the economy so that such a severe crisis could not recur. It was possible to find analogues in the past for each specific item of legislation, yet their sheer numbers, the swiftness with which they were enacted, and the sense of national crisis joined to make the New Deal legislation unprecedented in an important sense.

Much of the legislation interfered with what many had come to regard as the prerogatives of private property and, incidentally, the proper domain of the states. The New Deal statutes were sure to generate challenges to their constitutionality. As we have seen, supporters of the statutes, and those who attacked them, could draw on a complex, well-developed, and not entirely coherent body of law regarding the extent of Congress's power to regulate interstate commerce. (In addition, a similarly complex and not entirely coherent body of law existed regarding external limits — notably the due process clause — on Congress's power.)

In 1934 and 1935 the first challenges reached the Supreme Court. A useful discussion of the overall litigation is P. Irons, The New Deal Lawyers (1982). The Court's first signals were mixed. By 5-to-4 votes the Court rejected challenges to state legislation designed to alleviate the effects of the Depression in Home Building & Loan Assn. v. Blaisdell, Chapter 9 infra (obligation of contracts clause), and Nebbia v. New York, 291 U.S. 502 (1934) (due process clause). It also upheld the Roosevelt administration's repudiation of contractual duties to repay debts in gold, Norman v. Baltimore & Ohio Railroad, 294 U.S. 240 (1935). But the Court invalidated a portion of the National Industrial Recovery Act of 1933, holding that the act excessively delegated power to the President, Panama Refining Co. v. Ryan, 293 U.S. 388 (1935).

Railroad Retirement Board v. Alton Railroad, 295 U.S. 330 (1935), foreshadowed what was to come. There the Court invalidated the Railroad Retirement Act of 1934. Justice Roberts's opinion for a five-person majority held that, though Congress had power to regulate the safety of railroad operation, it lacked power to establish a compulsory retirement and pension plan. Such a plan was not "related to efficiency of transportation" and was too "remote from any regulation of commerce as such." Three weeks later the Court decided the *Schechter* case, invalidating the National Industrial Recovery Act of 1933, in many ways the conceptual centerpiece of the New Deal recovery program.

A. L. A. Schechter Poultry Corp. v. United States

295 U.S. 495 (1935)

[The National Industrial Recovery Act authorized the President to approve "codes of fair competition" developed by boards from various industries. President Roosevelt approved a Live Poultry Code applicable in metropolitan New York, the largest live poultry market in the country. The code established a forty-hour work week and a minimum wage of 50 cents per hour; it prohibited child labor and established the right of employees to organize and bargain collectively. The code also regulated a variety of trade practices.

Virtually all of the live poultry sold in New York was shipped by railroad from other states. After arrival, the poultry was assigned to commission sales agents, who sold the poultry to slaughterhouse operators such as the Schechters. They bought poultry for slaughter and resale. The poultry was shipped by truck from the rail terminals to the Schechters' slaughterhouse in Brooklyn, and from there, within twenty-four hours, to butchers who sold directly to consumers. The Schechters were convicted of violating the wage and hour provisions of the code, as well as a trade practice requirement that purchasers buy an entire "run" of a coop, including sick poultry. The Court of Appeals affirmed their convictions.]

MR. CHIEF JUSTICE HUGHES delivered the opinion of the Court. . . .

Two preliminary points are stressed by the Government with respect to the appropriate approach to the important questions presented. We are told that the provision of the statute authorizing the adoption of codes must be viewed in light of the grave national crisis with which Congress was confronted. Undoubtedly, the conditions to which power is addressed are always to be considered when the exercise of power is challenged. Extraordinary conditions may call for extraordinary remedies. But the argument necessarily stops short of an attempt to justify action which lies outside the sphere of constitutional authority. Extraordinary conditions do not create or enlarge constitutional power. The Constitution established a national government with powers deemed to be adequate, as they have proved to be both in war and peace, but these powers of the national government are limited by the constitutional grants. Those who act under these grants are not at liberty to transcend the imposed limits because they believe that more or different power is necessary. Such assertions of extra-constitutional authority were anticipated and precluded by the explicit terms of the Tenth Amendment. . . .

The further point is urged that the national crisis demanded a broad and intensive coöperative effort by those engaged in trade and industry, and that this necessary coöperation was sought to be fostered by permitting them to initiate the adoption of codes. But the statutory plan is not simply one for voluntary effort. [It] involves the coercive exercise of the law-making power. . . .

THIRD.   THE QUESTION OF THE APPLICATION OF THE PROVISIONS
         OF THE LIVE POULTRY CODE TO INTRASTATE
         TRANSACTIONS

[This] aspect of the case presents the question whether the particular provisions of the Live Poultry Code, which the defendants were convicted for violating and for having conspired to violate, were within the regulating power of Congress. . . .

(1) Were these transactions "*in*" interstate commerce? Much is made of the fact that almost all the poultry coming to New York is sent there from other States. But the code provisions, as here applied, do not concern the transportation of the poultry from other States to New York, or the transactions of the commission men or others to whom it is consigned, or the sales made by such consignees to defendants. When defendants had made their purchases, whether at the West Washington Market in New York City or at the railroad terminals serving the City, or elsewhere, the poultry was trucked to their slaughterhouses in Brooklyn for local disposition. The interstate transactions in relation to that poultry then ended. Defendants held the poultry at their slaughterhouse markets for slaughter and local sale to retail dealers and butchers who in turn sold directly to consumers. Neither the slaughtering nor the sales by defendants were transactions in interstate commerce.

The undisputed facts thus afford no warrant for the argument that the poultry handled by defendants at their slaughterhouse markets was in a "*current*" or "*flow*" of interstate commerce and was thus subject to congressional regulation. The mere fact that there may be a constant flow of commodities into a State does not mean that the flow continues after the property has arrived and has become commingled with the mass of property within the State and is there held solely for local disposition and use. So far as the poultry here in question is concerned, the flow in interstate commerce had ceased. The poultry had come to a permanent rest within the State. It was not held, used, or sold by defendants in relation to any further transactions in interstate commerce and was not destined for transportation to other States. Hence, decisions which deal with a stream of interstate commerce — where goods come to rest within a State temporarily and are later to go forward in interstate commerce — and with the regulations of transactions involved in that practical continuity of movement, are not applicable here. See [Swift & Co.; Stafford v. Wallace].

(2) Did the defendants' transactions directly "*affect*" interstate commerce so as to be subject to federal regulation? The power of Congress extends not only to the regulation of transactions which are part of interstate commerce, but to the protection of that commerce from injury. It matters not that the injury may be due to the conduct of those engaged in intrastate operations. . . .

In determining how far the federal government may go in controlling intrastate transactions upon the ground that they "affect" interstate commerce, there is a necessary and well-established distinction between direct and indirect effects. The precise line can be drawn only as individual cases arise, but the distinction is clear in principle. Direct effects are illustrated by [the] effect of failure to use prescribed safety appliances on railroads which are the highways of both interstate and intrastate commerce, injury to an employee engaged in interstate transportation by the negligence of an employee engaged in an intrastate movement, the fixing of rates for intrastate transportation which unjustly discriminate against interstate commerce. But where the effect of intrastate transactions upon interstate commerce is merely indirect, such transactions remain within the domain of state power. If the commerce clause were construed to reach all enterprises and transactions which could be said to have an indirect effect upon interstate commerce, the federal authority would embrace practically all the activities of the people and the authority of the State over its domestic concerns would exist only by sufferance of the federal government. Indeed, on such a theory, even the development of the State's commercial facilities would be subject to federal control. . . .

The distinction between direct and indirect effects has been clearly recognized in the application of the Anti-Trust Act. Where a combination or conspiracy is formed, with the intent to restrain interstate commerce or to monopolize any part of it, the violation of the statute is clear. Coronado Coal Co. v. United Mine Workers, 268 U.S. 295, 310. But where that intent is absent, and the objectives are limited to intrastate activities, the fact that there may be an indirect effect upon interstate commerce does not subject the parties to the federal statute, notwithstanding its broad provisions. This principle has frequently been applied in litigation growing out of labor disputes. . . .

The question of chief importance relates to the provisions of the Code as to the hours and wages of those employed in defendants' slaughterhouse markets. It is plain that these requirements are imposed in order to govern the details of defendants' management of their local business. The persons employed in slaughtering and selling in local trade are not employed in interstate commerce. Their hours and wages have no direct relation to interstate commerce. The question of how many hours these employees should work and what they should be paid differs in no essential respect from similar questions in other local businesses which handle commodities brought into a State and there dealt in as a part of its internal commerce. This appears from an examination of the considerations urged by the Government with respect to conditions in the poultry trade. Thus, the Government argues that hours and wages affect prices; that slaughterhouse men sell at a small margin above operating costs; that labor represents 50 to 60 per cent. of these costs; that a slaughterhouse operator paying lower wages or reducing his cost by exacting long hours of work, translates his saving into lower prices; that this results in demands for a cheaper grade of goods; and that the cutting of prices brings about a demoralization of the price structure. Similar conditions may be adduced in relation to other businesses. The argument of the Government proves too much. If the federal government may determine the wages and hours of employees in the internal commerce of a State, because of their relation to cost and prices and their indirect effect upon interstate commerce, it would seem that a similar control might be exerted over other elements of cost, also affecting prices, such as the number of employees, rents, advertising, methods of doing business, etc. All the processes of production and distribution that enter into cost could likewise be controlled. If the cost of doing an intrastate business is in itself the permitted object of federal control, the extent of the regulation of cost would be a question of discretion and not of power.

The Government also makes the point that efforts to enact state legislation establishing high labor standards have been impeded by the belief that unless similar action is taken generally, commerce will be diverted from the States adopting such standards, and that this fear of diversion has led to demands for federal legislation on the subject of wages and hours. The apparent implication is that the federal authority under the commerce clause should be deemed to extend to the establishment of rules to govern wages and hours in intrastate trade and industry generally throughout the country, thus overriding the authority of the States to deal with domestic problems arising from labor conditions in their internal commerce.

It is not the province of the Court to consider the economic advantages or disadvantages of such a centralized system. It is sufficient to say that the Federal Constitution does not provide for it. Our growth and development have called for wide use of the commerce power of the federal government in its control over the expanded activities of interstate commerce, and in protecting that commerce from burdens, interferences, and conspiracies to restrain and monopolize it. But the authority of the federal government may not be pushed to such an extreme as to destroy the distinction, which the commerce clause itself establishes, between commerce "among the several States" and the internal concerns of a State. The same answer must be made to the contention that is based upon the serious economic situation which led to the passage of the Recovery Act, — the fall in prices, the decline in wages and employment, and the curtailment of the market for commodities. Stress is laid upon the great importance of maintaining wage distributions which would provide the necessary stimulus in starting "the cumulative forces making for expanding commercial activity." Without in any way disparaging this motive, it is enough to say that the recuperative efforts of the federal government must be made in a manner consistent with the authority granted by the Constitution.

We are of the opinion that the attempt through the provisions of the Code to fix the hours and wages of employees of defendants in their intrastate business was not a valid exercise of federal power.

[Reversed.]

MR. JUSTICE CARDOZO, concurring. . . .

I find no authority [for] the regulation of wages and hours of labor in the intrastate transactions that make up the defendants' business. [There] is a view of causation that would obliterate the distinction between what is national and what is local in the activities of commerce. Motion at the outer rim is communicated perceptibly, though minutely, to recording instruments at the center. A society such as ours "is an elastic medium which transmits all tremors throughout its territory; the only question is of their size." Per Learned Hand, J., in the court below. The law is not indifferent to considerations of degree. Activities local in their immediacy do not become interstate and national because of distant repercussions. What is near and what is distant may at times be uncertain. There is no penumbra of uncertainty obscuring judgment here. To find immediacy or directness here is to find it almost everywhere. If centripetal forces are to be isolated to the exclusion of the forces that oppose and counteract them, there will be an end to our federal system. . . .

I am authorized to state that MR. JUSTICE STONE joins in this opinion.

Carter v. Carter Coal Co.

298 U.S. 238 (1936)

[The Bituminous Coal Conservation Act of 1935 was intended to stabilize the industry during a period of sustained industrial crisis. The first section of the act contained a long recitation of the importance of coal to the national economy, the need for "just and rational relations" between labor and management, and the existence of inefficient practices that "directly affect[ed]" interstate commerce." The act established a system of local coal boards to set minimum prices, with variations for particular mines as each board thought appropriate. The boards were to administer a code that allowed employees to bargain collectively. Once a sufficient number of collective bargaining agreements had been negotiated, their wage and hour terms would bind all mine operators in the area. A stockholder in Carter Coal sued to enjoin the company from complying with the code. The lower courts sustained the act.]

MR. JUSTICE SUTHERLAND delivered the opinion of the Court. . . .

[The] recitals contained in [the first section of] the act plainly suggest that its makers were of opinion that its constitutionality could be sustained under some general federal power, thought to exist, apart from the specific grants of the Constitution. [These] affirmations [do] not constitute an exertion of the *will* of Congress which is legislation, but a recital of considerations which in the *opinion* of that body existed and justified the expression of its will in the present act. Nevertheless, this preamble may not be disregarded. On the contrary it is important, because it makes clear, except for the pure assumption that the conditions described "directly" affect interstate commerce, that the powers which Congress undertook to exercise are not specific but of the most general character — namely, to protect the general public interest and the health and comfort of the people, to conserve privately-owned coal, maintain just relations between producers and employees and others, and promote the general welfare, by controlling nation-wide production and distribution of coal. These, it may be conceded, are objects of great worth; but are they ends, the attainment of which has been committed by the Constitution to the federal government? This is a vital question; for nothing is more certain than that beneficent aims, however great or well directed, can never serve in lieu of constitutional power.

The ruling and firmly established principle is that the powers which the general government may exercise are only those specifically enumerated in the Constitution, and such implied powers as are necessary and proper to carry into effect the enumerated powers. Whether the end sought to be attained by an act of Congress is legitimate is wholly a matter of constitutional power and not at all of legislative discretion. Legislative congressional discretion begins with the choice of means and ends with the adoption of methods and details to carry the delegated powers into effect. The distinction between these two things — power and discretion — is not only very plain but very important. For while the powers are rigidly limited to the enumerations of the Constitution, the means which may be employed to carry the powers into effect are not restricted, save that they must be appropriate, plainly adapted to the end, and not prohibited by, but consistent with, the letter and spirit of the Constitution. [McCulloch v. Maryland.] Thus, it may be said that to a constitutional end many ways are open; but to an end not within the terms of the Constitution, all ways are closed.

The proposition, often advanced and as often discredited, that the power of the federal government inherently extends to purposes affecting the nation as a whole with which the states severally cannot deal or cannot adequately deal, and the related notion that Congress, entirely apart from those powers delegated by the Constitution, may enact laws to promote the general welfare, have never been accepted but always definitely rejected by this court. . . .

There are many subjects in respect of which the several states have not legislated in harmony with one another, and in which their varying laws and the failure of some of them to act at all have resulted in injurious confusion and embarrassment. The state laws with respect to marriage and divorce present a case in point; and the great necessity of national legislation on that subject has been from time to time vigorously urged. Other pertinent examples are laws with respect to negotiable instruments, desertion and non-support, certain phases of state taxation, and others which we do not pause to mention. In many of these fields of legislation, the necessity of bringing the applicable rules of law into general harmonious relation has been so great that a Commission on Uniform State Laws, composed of commissioners from every state in the Union, has for many years been industriously and successfully working to that end by preparing and securing the passage by the several states of uniform laws. If there be an easier and constitutional way to these desirable results through congressional action, it thus far has escaped discovery.

The general rule with regard to the respective powers of the national and the state governments under the Constitution, is not in doubt. The states were before the Constitution; and, consequently, their legislative powers antedated the Constitution. Those who framed and those who adopted that instrument meant to carve from the general mass of legislative powers, then possessed by the states, only such portions as it was thought wise to confer upon the federal government; and in order that there should be no uncertainty in respect of what was taken and what was left, the national powers of legislation were not aggregated but enumerated — with the result that what was not embraced by the enumeration remained vested in the states without change or impairment. . . .

[And] since every addition to the national legislative power to some extent detracts from or invades the power of the states, it is of vital moment that, in order to preserve the fixed balance intended by the Constitution, the powers of the general government be not so extended as to embrace any not within the express terms of the several grants or the implications necessarily to be drawn therefrom. It is no longer open to question that the general government, unlike the states, possesses no *inherent* power in respect of the internal affairs of the states; and emphatically not with regard to legislation. The question in respect of the inherent power of that government as to the external affairs of the nation and in the field of international law is a wholly different matter which it is not necessary now to consider. . . .

[Every] journey to a forbidden end begins with the first step; and the danger of such a step by the federal government in the direction of taking over the powers of the states is that the end of the journey may find the states so despoiled of their powers, or — what may amount to the same thing — so relieved of the responsibilities which possession of the powers necessarily enjoins, as to reduce them to little more than geographical subdivisions of the national domain. It is safe to say that if, when the Constitution was under consideration, it had been thought that any such danger lurked behind its plain words, it would never have been ratified. . . .

[Since] the validity of the act depends upon whether it is a regulation of interstate commerce, the nature and extent of the power conferred upon Congress by the commerce clause becomes the determinative question in this branch of the case. . . .

[The] word "commerce" is the equivalent of the phrase "intercourse for the purposes of trade." Plainly, the incidents leading up to and culminating in the mining of coal do not constitute such intercourse. The employment of men, the fixing of their wages, hours of labor and working conditions, the bargaining in respect of these things — whether carried on separately or collectively — each and all constitute intercourse for the purposes of production, not of trade. The latter is a thing apart from the relation of employer and employee, which in all producing occupations is purely local in character. Extraction of coal from the mine is the aim and the completed result of local activities. Commerce in the coal mined is not brought into being by force of these activities, but by negotiations, agreements, and circumstances entirely apart from production. Mining brings the subject matter of commerce into existence. Commerce disposes of it. . . .

[The effect of the labor] provisions of the act [primarily] falls upon production and not upon commerce; and confirms the further resulting conclusion that production is a purely local activity. It follows that none of these essential antecedents of production constitutes a transaction in or forms any part of interstate commerce. [Schechter Corp. v. United States.] Everything which moves in interstate commerce has had a local origin. Without local production somewhere, interstate commerce, as now carried on, would practically disappear. Nevertheless, the local character of mining, of manufacturing and of crop growing is a fact, and remains a fact, whatever may be done with the products.

Certain decisions of this court, superficially considered, seem to lend support to the defense of the act now under review. But upon examination, they will be seen to be inapposite. Thus, Coronado Coal Co. v. United Mine Workers, and kindred cases, involved conspiracies to restrain interstate commerce in violation of the Anti-trust laws. The acts of the persons involved were local in character, but the intent was to restrain interstate commerce, and the means employed were calculated to carry that intent into effect. Interstate commerce was the direct object of attack; and the restraint of such commerce was the necessary consequence of the acts and the immediate end in view. . . .

But §1 (the preamble) of the act now under review declares that all production and distribution of bituminous coal "bear upon and directly affect its interstate commerce"; and that regulation thereof is imperative for the protection of such commerce. The contention of the government is that the labor provisions of the act may be sustained. . . .

Whether the effect of a given activity or condition is direct or indirect is not always easy to determine. The word "direct" implies that the activity or condition invoked or blamed shall operate proximately — not mediately, remotely, or collaterally — to produce the effect. It connotes the absence of an efficient intervening agency or condition. And the extent of the effect bears no logical relation to its character. The distinction between a direct and an indirect effect turns, not upon the magnitude of either the cause or the effect, but entirely upon the manner in which the effect has been brought about. If the production by one man of a single ton of coal intended for interstate sale and shipment, and actually so sold and shipped, affects interstate commerce indirectly, the effect does not become direct by multiplying the tonnage, or increasing the number of men employed, or adding to the expense or complexities of the business, or by all combined. It is quite true that rules of law are sometimes qualified by considerations of degree, as the government argues. But the matter of degree has no bearing upon the question here, since that question is not — What is the *extent* of the local activity or condition, or the *extent* of the effect produced upon interstate commerce? but — What is the *relation* between the activity or condition and the effect?

Much stress is put upon the evils which come from the struggle between employers and employees over the matter of wages, working conditions, the right of collective bargaining, etc., and the resulting strikes, curtailment and irregularity of production and effect on prices; and it is insisted that interstate commerce is *greatly* affected thereby. But, in addition to what has just been said, the conclusive answer is that the evils are all local evils over which the federal government has no legislative control. The relation of employer and employee is a local relation. At common law, it is one of the domestic relations. The wages are paid for the doing of local work. Working conditions are obviously local conditions. The employees are not engaged in or about commerce, but exclusively in producing a commodity. And the controversies and evils, which it is the object of the act to regulate and minimize, are local controversies and evils affecting local work undertaken to accomplish that local result. Such effect as they may have upon commerce, however extensive it may be, is secondary and indirect. An increase in the greatness of the effect adds to its importance. It does not alter its character.

The government's contentions in defense of the labor provisions are really disposed of adversely by our decision in the *Schechter* case. The only perceptible difference between that case and this is that in the *Schechter* case the federal power was asserted with respect to commodities which had come to rest after their interstate transportation; while here, the case deals with commodities at rest before interstate commerce has begun. That difference is without significance. The federal regulatory power ceases when interstate commercial intercourse ends; and, correlatively, the power does not attach until interstate commercial intercourse begins.

[Reversed.]

Separate opinion of MR. CHIEF JUSTICE HUGHES. . . .

The power to regulate interstate commerce embraces the power to protect that commerce from injury, whatever may be the source of the dangers which threaten it, and to adopt any appropriate means to that end. Congress thus has adequate authority to maintain the orderly conduct of interstate commerce and to provide for the peaceful settlement of disputes which threaten it. But Congress may not use this protective authority as a pretext for the exertion of power to regulate activities and relations within the States which affect interstate commerce only indirectly. Otherwise, in view of the multitude of indirect effects, Congress in its discretion could assume control of virtually all the activities of the people to the subversion of the fundamental principle of the Constitution. If the people desire to give Congress the power to regulate industries within the State, and the relations of employers and employees in those industries, they are at liberty to declare their will in the appropriate manner, but it is not for the Court to amend the Constitution by judicial decision. . . .

But that is not the whole case. The Act also provides for the regulation of the prices of bituminous coal sold in interstate commerce and prohibits unfair methods of competition in interstate commerce.

Whether the policy of fixing prices of commodities sold in interstate commerce is a sound policy is not for our consideration. The question of that policy, and of its particular applications, is for Congress. The exercise of the power of regulation is subject to the constitutional restriction of the due process clause, and if in fixing rates, prices or conditions of competition, that requirement is transgressed, the judicial power may be invoked to the end that the constitutional limitation may be maintained. . . .

In this view, the Act, and the Code for which it provides, may be sustained in relation to the provisions for marketing in interstate commerce, and the decisions of the courts below, so far as they accomplish that result, should be affirmed.

MR. JUSTICE CARDOZO, dissenting. . . .

Regulation of prices being an exercise of the commerce power in respect of interstate transactions, the question remains whether it comes within that power as applied to intrastate sales where interstate prices are directly or intimately affected. Mining and agriculture and manufacture are not interstate commerce considered by themselves, yet their relation to that commerce may be such that for the protection of the one there is need to regulate the other. [Schechter Poultry Corp. v. United States]. Sometimes it is said that the relation must be "direct" to bring that power into play. In many circumstances such a description will be sufficiently precise to meet the needs of the occasion. But a great principle of constitutional law is not susceptible of comprehensive statement in an adjective. The underlying thought is merely this, that "the law is not indifferent to considerations of degree." [Schechter, concurring opinion] It cannot be indifferent to them without an expansion of the commerce clause that would absorb or imperil the reserved powers of the states. At times, as in the case cited, the waves of causation will have radiated so far that their undulatory motion, if discernible at all, will be too faint or obscure, too broken by crosscurrents, to be heeded by the law. In such circumstances the holding is not directed at prices or wages considered in the abstract, but at prices or wages in particular conditions. The relation may be tenuous or the opposite according to the facts. Always the setting of the facts is to be viewed if one would know the closeness of the tie. Perhaps, if one group of adjectives is to be chosen in preference to another, "intimate" and "remote" will be found to be as good as any. At all events, "direct" and "indirect," even if accepted as sufficient, must not be read too narrowly. A survey of the cases shows that the words have been interpreted with suppleness of adaptation and flexibility of meaning. The power is as broad as the need that evokes it.

One of the most common and typical instances of a relation characterized as direct has been that between interstate and intrastate rates for carriers by rail where the local rates are so low as to divert business unreasonably from interstate competitors. In such circumstances Congress has the power to protect the business of its carriers against disintegrating encroachments. [*Shreveport Case.*] To be sure, the relation even then may be characterized as indirect if one is nice or over-literal in the choice of words. Strictly speaking, the intrastate rates have a primary effect upon the intrastate traffic and not upon any other, though the repercussions of the competitive system may lead to secondary consequences affecting interstate traffic also. What the cases really mean is that the causal relation in such circumstances is so close and intimate and obvious as to permit it to be called direct without subjecting the word to an unfair or excessive strain. There is a like immediacy here. Within rulings the most orthodox, the prices for intrastate sales of coal have so inescapable a relation to those for interstate sales that a system of regulation for transactions of the one class is necessary to give adequate protection to the system of regulation adopted for the other. . . .

The commerce clause being accepted as a sufficient source of power, the next inquiry must be whether the power has been exercised consistently with the Fifth Amendment. In the pursuit of that inquiry, Nebbia v. New York, 291 U.S. 502, lays down the applicable principle. There a statute of New York prescribing a minimum price for milk was upheld against the objection that price-fixing was forbidden by the Fourteenth Amendment. We found it a sufficient reason to uphold the challenged system that "the conditions or practices in an industry make unrestricted competition an inadequate safeguard of the consumer's interest, produce waste harmful to the public, threaten ultimately to cut off the supply of a commodity needed by the public, or portend the destruction of the industry itself." 291 U.S. at p. 538.

All this may be said, and with equal, if not greater force, of the conditions and practices in the bituminous coal industry, not only at the enactment of this statute in August, 1935, but for many years before. Overproduction was at a point where free competition had been degraded into anarchy. Prices had been cut so low that profit had become impossible for all except the lucky handful. Wages came down along with prices and with profits. There were strikes, at times nationwide in extent, at other times spreading over broad areas and many mines, with the accompaniment of violence and bloodshed and misery and bitter feeling. The sordid tale is unfolded in many a document and treatise. During the twenty-three years between 1913 and 1935, there were nineteen investigations or hearings by Congress or by specially created commissions with reference to conditions in the coal mines. The hope of betterment was faint unless the industry could be subjected to the compulsion of a code. In the weeks immediately preceding the passage of this Act the country was threatened once more with a strike of ominous proportions. The plight of the industry was not merely a menace to owners and to mine workers; it was and had long been a menace to the public, deeply concerned in a steady and uniform supply of a fuel so vital to the national economy.

Congress was not condemned to inaction in the face of price wars and wage wars so pregnant with disaster. Commerce had been choked and burdened; its normal flow had been diverted from one state to another; there had been bankruptcy and waste and ruin alike for capital and for labor. The liberty protected by the Fifth Amendment does not include the right to persist in this anarchic riot. [There] is testimony in these records, testimony even by the assailants of the statute, that only through a system of regulated prices can the industry be stabilized and set upon the road of orderly and peaceful progress. If further facts are looked for, they are narrated in the findings as well as in congressional reports and a mass of public records. After making every allowance for difference of opinion as to the most efficient cure, the student of the subject is confronted with the indisputable truth that there were ills to be corrected, and ills that had a direct relation to the maintenance of commerce among the states without friction or diversion. An evil existing, and also the power to correct it, the lawmakers were at liberty to use their own discretion in the selection of the means. . . .

My vote is for affirmance.

I am authorized to state that Mr. JUSTICE BRANDEIS and Mr. JUSTICE STONE join in this opinion.

Note: New Deal Legislation and Commerce Clause Tests in the 1930s

1. Schechter's *significance*. At the start of the New Deal the NIRA was a popular and apparently successful program, less because the codes of fair competition established a sensible regime for developing macroeconomic policy than because the evidence of concerted national action gave the public confidence that something was being done. Over the next two years, however, the regulatory apparatus became much less popular. The codes had done little to stabilize, much less restore, production, and opponents fearing congressional control of the economy obtained injunctions against some codes that further weakened the program. The act was due to expire a few weeks after *Schechter* was decided, and there had been no effort to extend its life even before the decision. The decision in *Schechter* was thus less important for its precise holding than for the approaches it articulated toward Congress's powers.

What values of federalism are served by limiting Congress's power in *Schechter*?

2. *New Deal economics.* What were the National Industrial Recovery Act and the Bituminous Coal Conservation Act designed to do? Were their provisions well adapted to their goals? Economists usually argue that minimum price statutes promote inefficient uses of resources: The guaranteed minimums induce capital investment (for example, in mining) when more efficient production would result from investment elsewhere. Is Justice Cardozo's response in *Carter* to these and similar arguments persuasive? Note also the manner in which areawide minimum wages were set. Again, economists usually argue that such methods enhance the economic position of unions that negotiate the initial agreements, at the expense of nonunionized workers (in other areas or industries) and of the consuming public. Should these arguments, if correct, affect the analysis of the statute's constitutionality?

3. *"Stream of commerce."* Why were the chickens not still part of a flow of interstate commerce? Does the Court explain why the flow ended at the slaughterhouses and not, for example, at the butcher's final sale? Or even further at the disposition of the chickens' bones at the garbage dump? What case would you cite to counter the Court's analysis?

4. *"Direct effects."* Chief Justice Hughes, Justice Sutherland, and Justice Cardozo distinguish between direct and indirect effects on interstate commerce.

Justice Sutherland invokes the *E. C. Knight* approach, treating directness as a logical category defined in terms of a beginning and an end to interstate commerce. Within the terms of that approach, does he effectively distinguish *Cor-*

onado Coal, which allowed Congress to prohibit strikes in mining and manufacturing? Does he effectively distinguish the earlier "stream of commerce" cases?

Justice Cardozo argues that the directness of an effect on interstate commerce is a matter of degree. Why should the Court's judgment of degree prevail over Congress's? Because, unless the Court were in a position to displace Congress's judgment, the issue would be reduced to one of "discretion and not of power," as Chief Justice Hughes puts it? He argues that the "affecting commerce" theory urged by the government would allow Congress completely to displace state authority in many areas. So what?

Justice Cardozo treats directness as he would the tort law concept of proximate cause, in which directness is determined with reference to the purposes sought to be achieved by the test. According to Justice Cardozo, what are those purposes? Could Justice Sutherland have used Justice Cardozo's test to hold the Bituminous Coal Act unconstitutional? Is Cardozo's effort to distinguish *Schechter* and *Carter* persuasive?

To which of the various approaches were the congressional declarations responsive?

5. *Enforcement again.* Using Justice Cardozo's approach, develop an argument supporting the constitutionality of a statute enacted by Congress creating a system of no-fault divorce nationwide. Does this suggest difficulties with that approach? Note that Congress has not attempted to enact such a statute and has instead tended to act only when faced with arguably national problems. Why? What bearing, if any, does this have on the question of judicial enforcement of federalism-based limits on congressional power?

Why does Justice Sutherland mention the Commission on Uniform State Laws? Consider this argument: No system of government is perfect. One imperfection in the federal system of the United States is that it is sometimes difficult to solve national problems. Coordinated action by the states is possible but costly. Coordinated action by the national government is less costly, but it may threaten important values of a federal system. To Sutherland the costs of obtaining coordinated action by the states were worth bearing in order to avoid threats to the values promoted by federalism. How persuasive is that argument in general? In the circumstances of *Carter*? If its persuasiveness varies with the context, what are the implications for judicial enforcement of federalism-based limits on congressional power?

Article I, section 10, prohibits states from entering into agreements with each other, unless Congress consents. The section contains a number of provisions designed to ensure national unity by prohibiting states from taking actions that might destroy the unitary nature of the national government or draw the nation into foreign difficulties. Interstate compacts can be used to alleviate regional difficulties. The affected states can negotiate acceptable agreements among themselves and present them to Congress for approval. Members of Congress representing other states are less likely to tinker with such agreements than they would with a statute originating in Congress. Compacts typically involve distribution of interstate resources such as water and sewage. They have also been used to regulate the penal treatment of prisoners who have violated or are charged with violating the laws of a number of states. To what extent are compacts a satisfactory substitute for direct congressional action?

6. *The New Deal response to the Court.* Because *Schechter* dealt with an activity near the retailing end of the spectrum of economic activity, supporters of the New Deal thought that their program could survive in areas closer to the center of the economy. The Bituminous Coal Conservation Act of 1935 was enacted after *Schechter*. It was invalidated in Carter v. Carter Coal Co. The National Labor Relations Act became effective after *Schechter*, and supporters of the New Deal believed that the Court might hold it unconstitutional. See also United States v. Butler, 297 U.S. 1 (1936), section F4 infra (holding Agricultural Adjustment Act of 1933 unconstitutional as beyond the scope of the spending power); Morehead v. New York ex rel. Tipaldo, 298 U.S. 587 (1936) (invalidating state minimum wage law for women as violating due process).

These decisions, coupled with his massive victory in the elections of 1936, led Roosevelt to propose changes in the structure of the Supreme Court. Seizing on the fact that six justices were over seventy years old in 1937, Roosevelt proposed that one additional justice, up to a total of fifteen, be appointed for each justice over seventy who did not resign or retire. His message to Congress argued that older justices were unable to fulfill their responsibilities, thus increasing the workload of the younger justices. Yet it was widely understood that the real point of the proposal was to increase the numbers of justices who would find New Deal legislation constitutional and that the workload argument was essentially a makeweight.

The proposal encountered substantial opposition: It was attacked as disingenuous and contrary to the spirit of the Constitution. (Was it the latter? See Chapter 1 supra.) During the debate over the proposal, Justice Van Devanter retired. In addition, the Court upheld a state minimum wage statute in West Coast Hotel Co. v. Parrish, 300 U.S. 379 (1937). Justice Roberts, who had voted with the five-person majority in *Morehead*, now voted to uphold a similar statute. The Court had taken a preliminary vote in *West Coast Hotel* before Roosevelt submitted his "Court-packing" plan. A later memorandum by Justice Roberts explained that he had joined the majority in *Morehead* only because those seeking to uphold the minimum wage statute sought to distinguish prior cases, instead of urging that they be overruled. When in *West Coast Hotel* the argument for overruling was made, Justice Roberts agreed with it. Note his position in National Labor Relations Board v. Jones & Laughlin Steel Co., Section D infra, decided while the Senate was debating the Court-packing plan. Whether or not his behavior made sense to him, his position was widely characterized as "the switch in time that saved Nine." The Senate Judiciary Committee on June 14, after *Jones & Laughlin* and *West Coast Hotel*, emphatically rejected Roosevelt's proposal. The majority leader of the Senate, Joseph Robinson, exerted a great deal of personal pressure on other senators and appeared to have accumulated enough votes to secure passage of a slightly modified Court-packing bill by early July. However, Robinson died of a heart attack before the vote was taken, and the plan was rejected in the Senate in mid-July. See Leuchtenberg, The Origins of Franklin D. Roosevelt's Court-Packing Plan, 1966 Sup. Ct. Rev. 347.

As you read the material that follows, note that the New Deal position on national powers was completely vindicated. Why did that occur? Should *Schechter* and *Carter* be understood as aberrational deviations from well-established prior law? Should the more recent cases be so understood? If choices of doctrine were available in the 1930s, why did the justices choose one rather than another doctrine?

NLRB v. Jones & Laughlin Steel Corp.

301 U.S. 1 (1937)

[The National Labor Relations Act established a comprehensive system for regulating labor/management relations. It established the right of employees to organize and bargain collectively, and created a board to supervise elections and to enforce the act's prohibition of such unfair labor practices as discrimination against union members. The act contained the following "findings":

> The denial by employers of the right of employees to organize and the refusal by employers to accept the procedure of collective bargaining lead to strikes and other forms of industrial strife or unrest, which have the intent or the necessary effect of burdening or obstructing commerce by (a) impairing the efficiency, safety, or operation of the instrumentalities of commerce; (b) occurring in the current of commerce; (c) materially affecting, restraining, or controlling the flow of raw materials or manufactured or processed goods from or into the channels of commerce, or the prices of such materials or goods in commerce; or (d) causing diminution of employment and wages in such volume as substantially to impair or disrupt the market for goods flowing from or into the channels of commerce.
>
> The inequality of bargaining power between employees who do not possess full freedom of association or actual liberty of contract, and employers who are organized in the corporate or other forms of ownership association substantially burdens and affects the flow of commerce, and tends to aggravate recurrent business depressions, by depressing wage rates and the purchasing power of wage earners in industry and by preventing the stabilization of competitive wage rates and working conditions within and between industries.
>
> Experience has proved that protection by law of the right of employees to organize and bargain collectively safeguards commerce from injury, impairment, or interruption, and promotes the flow of commerce by removing certain recognized sources of industrial strife and unrest, by encouraging practices fundamental to the friendly adjustment of industrial disputes arising out of differences as to wages, hours, or other working conditions, and by restoring equality of bargaining power between employers and employees.
>
> It is hereby declared to be the policy of the United States to eliminate the causes of certain substantial obstructions to the free flow of commerce and to mitigate and eliminate these obstructions when they have occurred by encouraging the practice and procedure of collective bargaining and by protecting the exercise by workers of full freedom of association, self-organization, and designation of representatives of their own choosing, for the purpose of negotiating the terms and conditions of their employment or other mutual aid or protection.

The Board charged Jones & Laughlin with the unfair labor practice of firing employees because they sought to organize a union. The Court of Appeals held the act unconstitutional.]

MR. CHIEF JUSTICE HUGHES delivered the opinion of the Court. . . .

[Jones & Laughlin] is engaged in the business of manufacturing iron and steel in plants situated in Pittsburgh and nearby Aliquippa, Pennsylvania. It manufactures and distributes a widely diversified line of steel and pig iron, being the fourth largest producer of steel in the United States. With its subsidiaries — nineteen in number — it is a completely integrated enterprise, owning and operating ore, coal and limestone properties, lake and river transportation facilities and terminal railroads located at its manufacturing plants. It owns or controls mines in Michigan and Minnesota. It operates four ore steamships on the Great Lakes, used in the transportation of ore to its factories. It owns coal mines in Pennsylvania. It operates towboats and steam barges used in carrying coal to its factories. It owns limestone properties in various places in Pennsylvania and West Virginia. It owns the Monongahela connecting railroad which connects the plants of the Pittsburgh works and forms an interconnection with the Pennsylvania, New York Central and Baltimore and Ohio Railroad systems. It owns the Aliquippa and Southern Railroad Company which connects the Aliquippa works with the Pittsburgh and Lake Erie part of the New York Central system. Much of its product is shipped to its warehouses in Chicago, Detroit, Cincinnati and Memphis, — to the last two places by means of its own barges and transportation equipment. In Long Island City, New York, and in New Orleans it operates structural steel fabricating shops in connection with the warehousing of semi-finished materials sent from its works. Through one of its wholly-owned subsidiaries it owns, leases and operates stores, warehouses and yards for the distribution of equipment and supplies for drilling and operating oil and gas wells and for pipe lines, refineries and pumping stations. It has sales offices in twenty cities in the United States and a wholly-owned subsidiary which is devoted exclusively to distributing its product in Canada. Approximately 75 percent. of its product is shipped out of Pennsylvania.

Summarizing these operations, the Labor Board concluded that the works in Pittsburgh and Aliquippa "might be likened to the heart of a self-contained, highly integrated body. They draw in the raw materials from Michigan, Minnesota, West Virginia, Pennsylvania in part through arteries and by means controlled by the respondent; they transform the materials and then pump them out to all parts of the nation through the vast mechanism which the respondent has elaborated."

To carry on the activities of the entire steel industry, 33,000 men mine ore, 44,000 men mine coal, 4,000 men quarry limestone, 16,000 men manufacture coke, 343,000 men manufacture steel, and 83,000 men transport its product. Respondent has about 10,000 employees in its Aliquippa plant, which is located in a community of about 30,000 persons.

Respondent points to evidence that the Aliquippa plant, in which the discharged men were employed, contains complete facilities for the production of finished and semi-finished iron and steel products from raw materials. [The] iron ore which is procured from mines in Minnesota and Michigan and transported to respondent's plant is stored in stock piles for future use, the amount of ore in storage varying with the season but usually being enough to maintain operations from nine to ten months. . . .

First. The Scope of the Act

The Act is challenged in its entirety as an attempt to regulate all industry, thus invading the reserved powers of the States over their local concerns. It is asserted that the references in the Act to interstate and foreign commerce are colorable at best; that the Act is not a true regulation of such commerce or of matters which directly affect it but on the contrary has the fundamental object of placing under the compulsory supervision of the federal government all industrial labor relations within the nation. . . .

[The] Act [defines] the term "affecting commerce" (§2(7)):

> The term "affecting commerce" means in commerce, or burdening or obstructing
> commerce or the free flow of commerce, or having led or tending to lead to a labor
> dispute burdening or obstructing commerce or the free flow of commerce.

This definition is one of exclusion as well as inclusion. The grant of authority to the Board does not purport to extend to the relationship between all industrial employees and employers. Its terms do not impose collective bargaining upon all industry regardless of effects upon interstate or foreign commerce. It purports to reach only what may be deemed to burden or obstruct that commerce and, thus qualified, it must be construed as contemplating the exercise of control within constitutional bounds. It is a familiar principle that acts which directly burden or obstruct interstate or foreign commerce, or its free flow, are within the reach of the congressional power. Acts having that effect are not rendered immune because they grow out of labor disputes. It is the effect upon commerce, not the source of the injury, which is the criterion. Whether or not particular action does affect commerce in such a close and intimate fashion as to be subject to federal control, and hence to lie within the authority conferred upon the Board, is left by the statute to be determined as individual cases arise. We are thus to inquire whether in the instant case the constitutional boundary has been passed.

SECOND. THE UNFAIR LABOR PRACTICES IN QUESTION . . .

[In] its present application, the statute goes no further than to safeguard the right of employees to self-organization and to select representatives of their own choosing for collective bargaining or other mutual protection without restraint or coercion by their employer.

That is a fundamental right. Employees have as clear a right to organize and select their representatives for lawful purposes as the respondent has to organize its business and select its own officers and agents. Discrimination and coercion to prevent the free exercise of the right of employees to self-organization and representation is a proper subject for condemnation by competent legislative authority. Long ago we stated the reason for labor organizations. We said that they were organized out of the necessities of the situation; that a single employee was helpless in dealing with an employer; that he was dependent ordinarily on his daily wage for the maintenance of himself and family; that if the employer refused to pay him the wages that he thought fair, he was nevertheless unable to leave the employ and resist arbitrary and unfair treatment; that union was essential to give laborers opportunity to deal on an equality with their employer. . . .

THIRD. THE APPLICATION OF THE ACT TO EMPLOYEES ENGAGED
         IN PRODUCTION. THE PRINCIPLE INVOLVED

Respondent says that whatever may be said of employees engaged in interstate commerce, the industrial relations and activities in the manufacturing department of respondent's enterprise are not subject to federal regulation. The argument rests upon the proposition that manufacturing in itself is not commerce.

[*Coronado Coal Co.*; Schechter Corp. v. United States; Carter v. Carter Coal Co.]

The Government distinguishes these cases. The various parts of respondent's enterprise are described as interdependent and as thus involving "a great movement of iron ore, coal and limestone along well-defined paths to the steel mills, thence through them, and thence in the form of steel products into the consuming centers of the country — a definite and well-understood course of business." It is urged that these activities constitute a "stream" or "flow" of commerce, of which the Aliquippa manufacturing plant is the focal point, and that industrial strife at that point would cripple the entire movement. Reference is made to [Stafford v. Wallace]. . . .

Respondent contends that the instant case presents material distinctions. Respondent says that the Aliquippa plant is extensive in size and represents a large investment in buildings, machinery and equipment. The raw materials which are brought to the plant are delayed for long periods and, after being subjected to manufacturing processes, "are changed substantially as to character, utility and value." The finished products which emerge "are to a large extent manufactured without reference to pre-existing orders and contracts and are entirely different from the raw materials which enter at the other end." Hence respondent argues that "If importation and exportation in interstate commerce do not singly transfer purely local activities into the field of congressional regulation, it should follow that their combination would not alter the local situation."

We do not find it necessary to determine whether these features of defendant's business dispose of the asserted analogy to the "stream of commerce" cases. The instances in which that metaphor has been used are but particular, and not exclusive, illustrations of the protective power which the Government invokes in support of the present Act. The congressional authority to protect interstate commerce from burdens and obstructions is not limited to transactions which can be deemed to be an essential part of a "flow" of interstate or foreign commerce. Burdens and obstructions may be due to injurious action springing from other sources. The fundamental principle is that the power to regulate commerce is the power to enact "all appropriate legislation" for "its protection and advancement" (The Daniel Ball, 10 Wall. 557, 564); to adopt measures "to promote its growth and insure its safety" (Mobile County v. Kimball, 102 U.S. 691, 696, 697); "to foster, protect, control and restrain." Second Employers' Liability Cases, p.47. That power is plenary and may be exerted to protect interstate commerce "no matter what the source of the dangers which threaten it." Second Employers' Liability Cases, Schechter Corp. v. United States. Although activities may be intrastate in character when separately considered, if they have such a close and substantial relation to interstate commerce that their control is essential or appropriate to protect that commerce from burdens and obstructions, Congress cannot be denied the power to exercise that control. Schechter Corp. v. United States. Undoubtedly the scope of this power must be considered in the light of our dual system of government and may not be extended so as to embrace effects upon interstate commerce so indirect and remote that to embrace them, in view of our complex society, would effectually obliterate the distinction between what is national and what is local and create a completely centralized government. The question is necessarily one of degree. . . .

[The] Anti-Trust Act has been applied to the conduct of employees engaged in production. [*Coronado Coal.*]

It is thus apparent that the fact that the employees here concerned were engaged in production is not determinative. The question remains as to the effect upon interstate commerce of the labor practice involved. In the *Schechter* case, we found that the effect there was so remote as to be beyond the federal power. To find "immediacy or directness" there was to find it "almost everywhere," a result inconsistent with the maintenance of our federal system. In the *Carter* case, the Court was of the opinion that the provisions of the statute relating to production were invalid upon several grounds, — that there was improper delegation of legislative power, and that the requirements not only went beyond any sustainable measure of protection of interstate commerce but were also inconsistent with due process. These cases are not controlling here.

FOURTH. EFFECTS OF THE UNFAIR LABOR PRACTICE IN
         RESPONDENT'S ENTERPRISE

Giving full weight to respondent's contention with respect to a break in the complete continuity of the "stream of commerce" by reason of respondent's manufacturing operations, the fact remains that the stoppage of those operations by industrial strife would have a most serious effect upon interstate commerce. In view of respondent's far-flung activities, it is idle to say that the effect would be indirect or remote. It is obvious that it would be immediate and might be catastrophic. We are asked to shut our eyes to the plainest facts of our national life and to deal with the question of direct and indirect effects in an intellectual vacuum. Because there may be but indirect and remote effects upon interstate commerce in connection with a host of local enterprises throughout the country, it does not follow that other industrial activities do not have such a close and intimate relation to interstate commerce as to make the presence of industrial strife a matter of the most urgent national concern. When industries organize themselves on a national scale, making their relation to interstate commerce the dominant factor in their activities, how can it be maintained that their industrial labor relations constitute a forbidden field into which Congress may not enter when it is necessary to protect interstate commerce from the paralyzing consequences of industrial war? We have often said that interstate commerce itself is a practical conception. It is equally true that interferences with that commerce must be appraised by a judgment that does not ignore actual experience.

Experience has abundantly demonstrated that the recognition of the right of employees to self-organization and to have representatives of their own choosing for the purpose of collective bargaining is often an essential condition of industrial peace. Refusal to confer and negotiate has been one of the most prolific causes of strife. . . .

These questions have frequently engaged the attention of Congress and have been the subject of many inquiries. The steel industry is one of the great basic industries of the United States, with ramifying activities affecting interstate commerce at every point. The Government aptly refers to the steel strike of 1919-1920 with its far-reaching consequences. The fact that there appears to have been no major disturbance in that industry in the more recent period did not dispose of the possibilities of future and like dangers to interstate commerce which Congress was entitled to foresee and to exercise its protective power to forestall. It is not necessary again to detail the facts as to respondent's enterprise. Instead of being beyond the pale, we think that it presents in a most striking way the close and intimate relation which a manufacturing industry may have to interstate commerce and we have no doubt that Congress had constitutional authority to safeguard the right of respondent's employees to self-organization and freedom in the choice of representatives for collective bargaining. . . .

[Reversed.]

[JUSTICES MCREYNOLDS, VAN DEVANTER, SUTHERLAND, and BUTLER dissented.]

Wickard v. Filburn

317 U.S. 111 (1942)

[Under the Agricultural Adjustment Act, the Secretary of Agriculture set a quota for wheat production, after finding that the total supply of wheat would substantially exceed a normal year's domestic consumption and export needs. The 1941 quota was approved in a referendum of wheat growers, required by the act, by 81 to 19 percent. Under the quota, each wheat grower was given an allotment. Filburn had a dairy farm in Montgomery County, Ohio, on which he also raised small amounts of wheat for his livestock, for making flour at home, for seed purposes, and for sale. His 1941 allotment was 222 bushels, but he harvested 461 bushels. Under the act he was penalized $117. Filburn sued the Secretary of Agriculture to enjoin enforcement of the penalty. The lower court issued the injunction.]

MR. JUSTICE JACKSON delivered the opinion of the Court. . . .

It is urged that under the Commerce Clause, [Congress] does not possess the power it has in this instance sought to exercise. The question would merit little consideration [except] for that fact that this Act extends federal regulation to production not intended in any part for commerce but wholly for consumption on the farm. [Marketing] quotas not only embrace all that may be sold without penalty but also what may be consumed on the premises. . . .

Appellee says that this is a regulation of production and consumption of wheat. Such activities are, he urges, beyond the reach of Congressional power under the Commerce Clause, since they are local in character, and their effects upon interstate commerce are at most "indirect." In answer the Government argues that the statute regulates neither production nor consumption, but only marketing; and, in the alternative, that if the Act does go beyond the regulation of marketing it is sustainable as a "necessary and proper" implementation of the power of Congress over interstate commerce.

The Government's concern lest the Act be held to be a regulation of production or consumption, rather than of marketing, is attributable to a few dicta and decisions of this Court which might be understood to lay it down that activities such as "production," "manufacturing," and "mining" are strictly "local" and, except in special circumstances which are not present here, cannot be regulated under the commerce power because their effects upon interstate commerce are, as matter of law, only "indirect." Even today, when this power has been held to have great latitude, there is no decision of this Court that such activities may be regulated where no part of the product is intended for interstate commerce or intermingled with the subjects thereof. We believe that a review of the course of decision under the Commerce Clause will make plain, however, that questions of the power of Congress are not to be decided by reference to any formula which would give controlling force to nomenclature such as "production" and "indirect" and foreclose consideration of the actual effects of the activity in question upon interstate commerce.

At the beginning Chief Justice Marshall described the federal commerce power with a breadth never yet exceeded. [Gibbons v. Ogden.] He made emphatic the embracing and penetrating nature of this power by warning that effective restraints on its exercise must proceed from political rather than from judicial processes.

[Justice Jackson then reviewed the decisions from E. C. Knight through the Shreveport Rate cases.]

The Court's recognition of the relevance of the economic effects in the application of the Commerce Clause [has] made the mechanical application of legal formulas no longer feasible. Once an economic measure of the reach of the power granted to Congress in the Commerce Clause is accepted, questions of federal power cannot be decided simply by finding the activity in question to be "production," nor can consideration of its economic effects be foreclosed by calling them "indirect." . . .

Whether the subject of the regulation in question was "production," "consumption," or "marketing" is, therefore, not material for purposes of deciding the question of federal power before us. That an activity is of local character may help in a doubtful case to determine whether Congress intended to reach it. [But] even if appellee's activity be local and though it may not be regarded as commerce, it may still, whatever its nature, be reached by Congress if it exerts a substantial economic effect on interstate commerce, and this irrespective of whether such effect is what might at some earlier time have been defined as "direct" or "indirect."

The parties have stipulated a summary of the economics of the wheat industry. Commerce among the states in wheat is large and important. Although wheat is raised in every state but one, production in most states is not equal to consumption. Sixteen states on average have had a surplus of wheat above their own requirements for feed, seed, and food. Thirty-two states and the District of Columbia, where production has been below consumption, have looked to these surplus-producing states for their supply as well as for wheat for export and carryover.

The wheat industry has been a problem industry for some years. Largely as a result of increased foreign production and import restrictions, annual exports of wheat and flour from the United States during the ten-year period ending in 1940 averaged less than 10 per cent of total production, while during the 1920's they averaged more than 25 per cent. The decline in the export trade has left a large surplus in production which, in connection with an abnormally large supply of wheat and other grains in recent years, caused congestion in a number of markets; tied up railroad cars; and caused elevators in some instances to turn away grains, and railroads to institute embargoes to prevent further congestion. . . .

In the absence of regulation, the price of wheat in the United States would be much affected by world conditions. During 1941, producers who cooperated with the Agricultural Adjustment program received an average price on the farm of about $1.16 a bushel, as compared with the world market price of 40 cents a bushel. . . .

The effect of consumption of home-grown wheat on interstate commerce is due to the fact that it constitutes the most variable factor in the disappearance of the wheat crop. Consumption on the farm where grown appears to vary in an amount greater than 20 per cent of average production. The total amount of wheat consumed as food varies but relatively little, and use as seed is relatively constant.

The maintenance by government regulation of a price for wheat undoubtedly can be accomplished as effectively by sustaining or increasing the demand as by limiting the supply. The effect of the statute before us is to restrict the amount which may be produced for market and the extent as well to which one may forestall resort to the market by producing to meet his own needs. That appellee's own contribution to the demand for wheat may be trivial by itself is not enough to remove him from the scope of federal regulation where, as here, his contribution, taken together with that of many other similarly situated, is far from trivial.

It is well established by decisions of this Court that the power to regulate commerce includes the power to regulate the prices at which commodities in that commerce are dealt in and practices affecting such prices. One of the primary purposes of the Act in question was to increase the market price of wheat, and to that end to limit the volume thereof that could affect the market. It can hardly be denied that a factor of such volume and variability as home-consumed wheat would have a substantial influence on price and market conditions. This may arise because being in marketable condition such wheat overhangs the market and, if induced by rising prices, tends to flow into the market and check price increases. But if we assume that it is never marketed, it supplies a need of the man who grew it which would otherwise be reflected by purchases in the open market. Home-grown wheat in this sense competes with wheat in commerce. The stimulation of commerce is a use of the regulatory function quite as definitely as prohibitions or restrictions thereon. This record leaves us in no doubt that Congress may properly have considered that wheat consumed on the farm where grown, if wholly outside the scheme of regulation, would have a substantial effect in defeating and obstructing its purpose to stimulate trade therein at increased prices.

It is said, however, that this Act, forcing some farmers into the market to buy what they could provide for themselves, is an unfair promotion of the markets and prices of specializing wheat growers. It is of the essence of regulation that it lays a restraining hand on the self-interest of the regulated and that advantages from the regulation commonly fall to others. The conflicts of economic interest between the regulated and those who advantage by it are wisely left under our system to resolution by the Congress under its more flexible and responsible legislative process. Such conflicts rarely lend themselves to judicial determination. And with the wisdom, workability, or fairness, of the plan of regulation we have nothing to do.

[Reversed.]

Note: The Adoption of the "Realist" Approach

1. *The "realist" approach.* In these cases the Court chose the "economic" or "pragmatic" approach to determining whether an activity affects interstate commerce. Note that in *Wickard*, the Court focused on the national market in wheat, while in *Jones & Laughlin* it focused on Jones & Laughlin's own steel plants.

Compare the facts in *Schechter*. Are the factual differences relevant to the doctrinal distinctions between *Schechter* and *Jones & Laughlin*? Consider whether the factual differences may have affected the majority's view of the constitutional issue. Both *Wickard* and *Jones & Laughlin* say that Congress's power turns on whether the activity it regulates has a "substantial economic effect on interstate commerce." Are the tests of "substantiality" the same?

2. *Precedents*. Does the Court in *Jones & Laughlin* fairly distinguish *E. C. Knight*, *Schechter*, and *Carter*? Does it fairly rely on *Schechter*? How did all this come about?

3. *Aggregation and economic reality*. *Wickard* makes substantiality turn on the aggregate effect of the regulated activity, "taken together with that of many others similarly situated." How do you determine what activities are sufficiently similar so as to be aggregated for these purposes? Here are some candidates: wheat growing in Montgomery County, wheat growing, food production, production for national and international markets. The outcome of the aggregation will obviously depend on the choice of the activities regarded as similar enough to justify aggregation. What guides that choice? Note that neither of the principal cases discusses the values of federalism as the basis for the choices they make.

4. *The scope of the doctrine*. Consider whether, by joining the "economic" approach in *Jones & Laughlin* to the "aggregation" approach in *Wickard*, the Court could in practice eliminate all judicial enforcement of federalism-based limits on congressional power. Is that a troubling result? If so, how can it be avoided without repudiating these cases?

United States v. Darby

312 U.S. 100 (1941)

[Darby was charged with violating the Fair Labor Standards Act of 1938. The act prohibited the shipment in interstate commerce of goods manufactured by employees who were paid less than a prescribed minimum wage or who worked more than a prescribed maximum hours, and prohibited the employment of workers in production "for interstate commerce" at other than the prescribed wages and hours. The District Court sustained Darby's objections to the constitutionality of the act.]

MR. JUSTICE STONE delivered the opinion of the Court. . . .

[The purpose of the act] is to exclude from interstate commerce goods produced for the commerce and to prevent their production for interstate commerce, under conditions detrimental to the maintenance of the minimum standards of living necessary for health and general well-being; and to prevent the use of interstate commerce as the means of competition in the distribution of goods so produced, and as the means of spreading and perpetuating such substandard labor conditions among the workers of the several states. . . .

THE PROHIBITION OF SHIPMENT OF THE PROSCRIBED GOODS IN INTERSTATE COMMERCE . . .

While manufacture is not of itself interstate commerce, the shipment of manufactured goods interstate is such commerce and the prohibition of such shipment by Congress is indubitably a regulation of the commerce. The power to regulate commerce is the power "to prescribe the rule by which commerce is governed." Gibbons v. Ogden. It extends not only to those regulations which aid, foster and protect the commerce, but embraces those which prohibit it. [*Lottery Case*.] It is conceded that the power of Congress to prohibit transportation in interstate commerce includes noxious articles, [*Lottery Case; Hipolite Egg Co.*], stolen articles, kidnapped persons, and articles such as intoxicating liquor or convict made goods, traffic in which is forbidden or restricted by the laws of the state of destination. Kentucky Whip & Collar Co. v Illinois Central R. Co., 299 U.S. 334.

But it is said that the present prohibition falls within the scope of none of these categories; that while the prohibition is nominally a regulation of the commerce its motive or purpose is regulation of wages and hours of persons engaged in manufacture, the control of which has been reserved to the states and upon which Georgia and some of the states of destination have placed no restriction; that the effect of the present statute is not to exclude the proscribed articles from interstate commerce in aid of state regulation [but] instead, under the guise of a regulation of interstate commerce, it undertakes to regulate wages and hours within the state contrary to the policy of the state which has elected to leave them unregulated.

The power of Congress over interstate commerce "is complete in itself, may be exercised to its utmost extent, and acknowledges no limitations other than are prescribed in the Constitution." Gibbons v. Ogden. [Congress,] following its own conception of public policy concerning the restrictions which may appropriately be imposed on interstate commerce, is free to exclude from the commerce articles whose use in the states for which they are destined it may conceive to be injurious to the public health, morals, or welfare, even though the state has not sought to regulate their use. [*Lottery Case.*]

Such regulation is not a forbidden invasion of state power merely because either its motive or its consequence is to restrict the use of articles of commerce within the states of destination; and is not prohibited unless by other Constitutional provisions. It is no objection to the assertion of the power to regulate interstate commerce that its exercise is attended by the same incidents which attend the exercise of the police power of the states.

The motive and purpose of the present regulation are plainly to make effective the Congressional conception of public policy that interstate commerce should not be made the instrument of competition in the distribution of goods produced under substandard labor conditions, which competition is injurious to the commerce and to the states from and to which the commerce flows. The motive and purpose of a regulation of interstate commerce are matters for the legislative judgment upon the exercise of which the Constitution places no restriction and over which the courts are given no control. "The judicial cannot prescribe to the legislative department of the government limitations upon the exercise of its acknowledged power." Veazie Bank v. Fenno, 8 Wall. 533. Whatever their motive and purpose, regulations of commerce which do not infringe some constitutional prohibition are within the plenary power conferred on Congress by the Commerce Clause. Subject only to that limitation, presently to be considered, we conclude that the prohibition of the shipment interstate of goods produced under the forbidden substandard labor conditions is within the constitutional authority of Congress.

In the more than a century which has elapsed since the decision of Gibbons v. Ogden, these principles of constitutional interpretation have been so long and repeatedly recognized by this Court as applicable to the Commerce Clause, that there would be little occasion for repeating them now were it not for the decision of this Court twenty-two years ago in Hammer v. Dagenhart, 247 U.S. 251. . . .

Hammer v. Dagenhart has not been followed. The distinction on which the decision was rested that Congressional power to prohibit interstate commerce is limited to articles which in themselves have some harmful or deleterious property — a distinction which was novel when made and unsupported by any provision of the Constitution — has long since been abandoned. The thesis of the opinion that the motive of the prohibition or its effect to control in some measure the use or production within the states of the article thus excluded from the commerce can operate to deprive the regulation of its constitutional authority has long since ceased to have force. . . .

The conclusion is inescapable that Hammer v. Dagenhart, was a departure from the principles which have prevailed in the interpretation of the Commerce Clause both before and since the decision and that such vitality, as a precedent, as it then had has long since been exhausted. It should be and now is overruled.

VALIDITY OF THE WAGE AND HOUR REQUIREMENTS

Section 15(a)(2) and §§6 and 7 require employers to conform to the wage and hour provisions with respect to all employees engaged in the production of goods for interstate commerce. As appellee's employees are not alleged to be "engaged in interstate commerce" the validity of the prohibition turns on the question whether the employment, under other than the prescribed labor standards, of employees engaged in the production of goods for interstate commerce is so related to the commerce and so affects it as to be within the reach of the power of Congress to regulate it. . . .

[The] phrase "produced for interstate commerce" [embraces] at least the case where an employer [manufactures] his product with the intent or expectation that according to the normal course of his business all or some part of it will be selected for shipment to those customers.

[The] obvious purpose of the Act was not only to prevent the interstate transportation of the proscribed product, but to stop the initial step toward transportation, production with the purpose of so transporting it. Congress was not unaware that most manufacturing businesses shipping their product in interstate commerce make it in their shops without reference to its ultimate destination and then after manufacture select some of it for shipment interstate and some intrastate according to the daily demands of their business, and that it would be practically impossible, without disrupting manufacturing businesses, to restrict the prohibited kind of production to the particular pieces of lumber, cloth, furniture or the like which later move in interstate rather than intrastate commerce. . . .

There remains the question whether such restriction on the production of goods for commerce is a permissible exercise of the commerce power. The power of Congress over interstate commerce is not confined to the regulation of commerce among the states. It extends to those activities intrastate which so affect interstate commerce or the exercise of the power of Congress over it as to make regulation of them appropriate means to the attainment of a legitimate end, the exercise of the granted power of Congress to regulate interstate commerce. . . .

Congress, having by the present Act adopted the policy of excluding from interstate commerce all goods produced for the commerce which do not conform to the specified labor standards, it may choose the means reasonably adapted to the attainment of the permitted end, even though they involve control of intrastate activities. Such legislation has often been sustained with respect to powers, other than the commerce power granted to the national government, when the means chosen, although not themselves within the granted power, were nevertheless deemed appropriate aids to the accomplishment of some purpose within an admitted power of the national government. A familiar like exercise of power is the regulation of intrastate transactions which are so commingled with or related to interstate commerce that all must be regulated if the interstate commerce is to be effectively controlled. [*Shreveport Case.*] . . .

We think also that §15(a)(2), now under consideration, is sustainable independently of §15(a)(1), which prohibits shipment or transportation of the proscribed goods. As we have said the evils aimed at by the Act are the spread of substandard labor conditions through the use of the facilities of interstate commerce for competition by the goods so produced with those produced under the prescribed or better labor conditions; and the consequent dislocation of the commerce itself caused by the impairment or destruction of local businesses by competition made effective through interstate commerce. The Act is thus directed at the suppression of a method or kind of competition in interstate commerce which it has in effect condemned as "unfair," as the Clayton Act has condemned other "unfair methods of competition" made effective through interstate commerce. . . .

The means adopted by §15(a)(2) for the protection of interstate commerce by the suppression of the production of the condemned goods for interstate commerce is so related to the commerce and so affects it as to be within the reach of the commerce power. Congress, to attain its objective in the suppression of nationwide competition in interstate commerce by goods produced under substandard labor conditions, has made no distinction as to the volume or amount of shipments in the commerce or of production for commerce by any particular shipper or producer. It recognized that in present day industry, competition by a small part may affect the whole and that the total effect of the competition of many small producers may be great. The legislation aimed at a whole embraces all its parts. . . .

Our conclusion is unaffected by the Tenth Amendment which provides: "The powers not delegated to the United States by the Constitution, nor prohibited by it to the States, are reserved to the States respectively, or to the people." The amendment states but a truism that all is retained which has not been surrendered. There is nothing in the history of its adoption to suggest that it was more than declaratory of the relationship between the national and state governments as it had been established by the Constitution before the amendment or that its purpose was other than to allay fears that the new national government might seek to exercise powers not granted, and that the states might not be able to exercise fully their reserved powers.

[Reversed.]

Note: The Adoption of the "Formalist" Approach

Darby is divided into two parts. Are the analyses the same in both?

1. *Prohibiting interstate shipment.* Congress prohibited the shipment in interstate commerce of certain goods. Does this intrude on state policies in a way distinguishable from the statutes in the *Lottery Case* or *Hipolite Egg Co.?* Note that the Court refuses to use Congress's "motive and purpose" as a basis for its constitutional analysis. Can that be reconciled with the "pretext" language of *McCulloch?* Can a "pretext" test ever be applied without the courts' exercising "control" over motive and purpose? But is a "pretext" test necessary? Recall Madison's and Wechsler's arguments as you read the following comments.

2. *Regulating directly.* Congress directly regulated the wages and hours of employees producing goods for interstate commerce.

a. In light of *Wickard*, was the "interstate commerce" restriction constitutionally compelled? The statute was amended in 1961 and 1966 to cover the wages and hours of every employee of "an enterprise engaged in commerce." The constitutionality of the amendment was upheld in Maryland v. Wirtz, 392 U.S. 183 (1968). Justice Harlan for the Court stated: "Neither here nor in *Wickard* has the Court declared that Congress may use a relatively trivial impact on commerce as an excuse for broad general regulation of [private] activities. The Court has said only that where a general regulatory statute bears a substantial relation to commerce, the de minimis character of individual instances arising under that statute is of no consequence." Is that a fair characterization of *Wickard?* If it is, does it state a federalism-based limitation that courts can enforce?

b. The Court in *Darby* justifies the direct regulation as a necessary and proper means of enforcing the ban on interstate shipment. Are there any limitations to the use of this technique that are independent of whatever limitations there are on the commerce-prohibiting technique? Does this approach eliminate all distinctions between direct regulation and a prohibition on interstate shipment, on the theory that direct regulation will always be a necessary and proper method of ensuring that the prohibition will not be violated? Would *Darby* require the courts to find constitutional a national no-fault divorce law? Design a national no-fault divorce statute and describe the findings you think Congress might make in its support. Would such a statute be constitutional under *Darby?* Under what circumstances would Congress be likely to enact such a statute? What is the relation between the two preceding questions?

c. The Court justifies the direct regulation on an "independent" ground, that of eliminating unfair competition. In what sense is the competition "unfair"? Note that, absent the federal statute, paying sub-"minimum" wages was lawful in some states. Paying such wages is "unfair" only in that some states chose to require employers located there to pay higher wages. Consider the effects on state minimum wage laws of the mobility of capital in determining where to locate.

E.   THE PURPORTED DEMISE OF JUDICIALLY ENFORCED FEDERALISM LIMITS ON CONGRESSIONAL POWER

By 1945 the Supreme Court has come to the position that the primary and perhaps exclusive federalism-based constraints on Congress were imposed by the political process. Although Congress's regulation of the national economy has continued to grow, nearly all of its work falls well within the boundaries set by cases such as *Wickard* and *Darby*.

How substantially have the courts reduced their role? The diminution of judicial oversight of Congress's output might have been accompanied by an increased concern for congressional process. This section explores the Court's position on three aspects of congressional process: the importance of congressional investigation into the facts that it concludes justify regulation under the commerce clause, the use of the commerce power to accomplish goals that perhaps should be advanced by using some other power, and the adequacy of the contemporary political process to protect federalism-based interests.

Perez v. United States

402 U.S. 146 (1971)

[The Consumer Credit Protection Act of 1968 prohibits "extortionate credit transactions" — loan-sharking enforced by threats of violence — in an effort to control organized crime. Perez was convicted of loan-sharking; his threats had led the borrower to sell his store. The court of appeals rejected Perez's constitutional attack on the act.]

MR. JUSTICE DOUGLAS delivered the opinion of the Court. . . .

Petitioner is one of the species commonly known as "loan sharks" which Congress found are in large part under the control of "organized crime."[1] . . .

Two "loan shark" amendments to the bill that became this Act were proposed in the House. . . .

The House debates include a long article from the New York Times Magazine for January 28, 1968, on the connection between the "loan shark" and organized crime. The gruesome and stirring episodes related have the following as a prelude:

> The loan shark, then, is the indispensable "money-mover" of the underworld. He takes "black" money tainted by its derivation from the gambling or narcotics rackets and turns it "white" by funneling it into channels of legitimate trade. In so doing, he exacts usurious interest that doubles the black-white money in no time; and, by his special decrees, by his imposition of impossible penalties, he greases the way for the underworld takeover of entire businesses.

---

1. Section 201(a) of Title II contains the following findings by Congress:

(1) Organized crime is interstate and international in character. Its activities involve many billions of dollars each year. It is directly responsible for murders, willful injuries to person and property, corruption of officials, and terrorization of countless citizens. A substantial part of the income of organized crime is generated by extortionate credit transactions.

(2) Extortionate credit transactions are characterized by the use, or the express or implicit threat of the use, of violence or other criminal means to cause harm to person, reputation, or property as a means of enforcing repayment. Among the factors which have rendered past efforts at prosecution almost wholly ineffective has been the existence of exclusionary rules of evidence stricter than necessary for the protection of constitutional rights.

(3) Extortionate credit transactions are carried on to a substantial extent in interstate and foreign commerce and through the means and instrumentalities of such commerce. Even where extortionate credit transactions are purely intrastate in character, they nevertheless directly affect interstate and foreign commerce.

There were objections on constitutional grounds. Congressman Eckhardt of Texas said:

> Should it become law, the amendment would take a long stride by the Federal Government toward occupying the field of general criminal law and toward exercising a general Federal police power; and it would permit prosecution in Federal as well as State courts of a typically State offense. . . .

In [*Darby*] *a class of activities* was held properly regulated by Congress without proof that the particular intrastate activity against which a sanction was laid had an effect on commerce. . . .

[Petitioner] is clearly *a member of the class* which engages in "extortionate credit transactions" as defined by Congress and the description of that class has the required definiteness. . . .

Where the *class of activities* is regulated and that *class* is within the reach of federal power, the courts have no power "to excise, as trivial, individual instances" of the class. Maryland v. Wirtz, 392 U.S. 183, 193.

Extortionate credit transactions, though purely intrastate, may in the judgment of Congress affect interstate commerce. . . .

The findings by Congress are quite adequate on that ground. The McDade Amendment in the House [was] the one ultimately adopted. As stated by Congressman McDade it grew out of a "profound study of organized crime, its ramifications and its implications" undertaken by some 22 Congressmen in 1966–1967. The results of that study were included in a report, The Urban Poor and Organized Crime, submitted to the House on August 29, 1967, which revealed that "organized crime takes over $350 million a year from America's poor through loan-sharking alone." Congressman McDade also relied on The Challenge of Crime in a Free Society, A Report by the President's Commission on Law Enforcement and Administration of Justice (February 1967) which stated that loan sharking was "the second largest source of revenue for organized crime," and is one way by which the underworld obtains control of legitimate businesses.

The Congress also knew about New York's Report, An Investigation of the Loan Shark Racket (1965). That report shows the loan shark racket is controlled by organized criminal syndicates, either directly or in partnership with independent operators; that in most instances the racket is organized into three echelons, with the top underworld "bosses" providing the money to their principal "lieutenants," who in turn distribute the money to the "operators" who make the actual individual loans; that loan sharks serve as a source of funds to bookmakers, narcotics dealers, and other racketeers; that victims of the racket include all classes, rich and poor, businessmen and laborers; that the victims are often coerced into the commission of criminal acts in order to repay their loans; that through loan sharking the organized underworld has obtained control of legitimate businesses, including securities brokerages and banks which are then exploited; and that "[e]ven where extortionate credit transactions are purely intrastate in character, they nevertheless directly affect interstate and foreign commerce."

Shortly before the Conference bill was adopted by Congress a Senate Committee had held hearings on loan sharking and that testimony was made available to members of the House.

The essence of all these reports and hearings was summarized and embodied in formal congressional findings. They supplied Congress with the knowledge that the loan shark racket provides organized crime with its second most lucrative source of revenue, exacts millions from the pockets of people, coerces its victims into the commission of crimes against property, and causes the takeover by racketeers of legitimate businesses.

We have mentioned in detail the economic, financial, and social setting of the problem as revealed to Congress. We do so not to infer that Congress need make particularized findings in order to legislate. We relate the history of the Act in detail to answer the impassioned plea of petitioner that all that is involved in loan sharking is a traditionally local activity. It appears, instead, that loan sharking in its national setting is one way organized interstate crime holds its guns to the heads of the poor and the rich alike and syphons funds from numerous localities to finance its national operations.

Affirmed.

Mr. Justice Stewart, dissenting. . . .

[Under] the statute before us a man can be convicted without any proof of interstate movement, of the use of the facilities of interstate commerce, or of facts showing that his conduct affected interstate commerce. I think the Framers of the Constitution never intended that the National Government might define as a crime and prosecute such wholly local activity through the enactment of federal criminal laws.

In order to sustain this law we would, in my view, have to be able at least to say that Congress could rationally have concluded that loan sharking is an activity with interstate attributes that distinguish it in some substantial respect from other local crime. But it is not enough to say that loan sharking is a national problem, for all crime is a national problem. It is not enough to say that some loan sharking has interstate characteristics, for any crime may have an interstate setting. And the circumstance that loan sharking has an adverse impact on interstate business is not a distinguishing attribute, for interstate business suffers from almost all criminal activity, be it shoplifting or violence in the streets.

Because I am unable to discern any rational distinction between loan sharking and other local crime, I cannot escape the conclusion that this statute was beyond the power of Congress to enact. The definition and prosecution of local, intrastate crime are reserved to the States under the Ninth and Tenth Amendments.

Note: *Congressional Processes and Federalism*

1. *Congressional fact-finding processes.* In light of *Perez*, could Congress make shoplifting a crime? On what theory? (Spouse-beating? See Katzenbach v. Morgan, section F5 infra.) Would the Court require that appropriate findings be made? Findings serve to alert Congress to the necessity for its action. How likely is it that Congress would act unnecessarily even if it made no findings? What was the congressional inquiry into the facts that preceded the enactment of the statute in *Perez*? Consider that most, though not all, legislation is adopted after committee hearings and reports, sometimes extending through several sessions and Congresses.

2. *Regulation of local activities.* Is regulation of loan sharking inherently more or less local than regulation of wages and hours? Why? What about regulation of violent street crime? Note the relation between these questions and the theory of Wickard v. Filburn.

Hodel v. Virginia Surface Mining Association, 452 U.S. 264 (1981), upheld provisions of a federal statute regulating the operation of strip mines. On the commerce clause issue, the Court said that "when Congress has determined that an activity affects interstate commerce, the courts need inquire only whether the finding is rational." The statute contained a finding that strip-mining affected commerce "by destroying [the] utility of land, [by] causing erosion, [by] polluting the water, by destroying fish and wildlife habitats, [and] by impairing natural beauty." The Court said that these findings were amply supported in the hearings on the act. It quoted the House Committee's Report: "The most widespread damages [are] environmental. [Reduced] recreational values, fishkills, reductions in normal waste assimilation capacity, impaired water supplies, metals and masonry corrosion and deterioration, increased flood frequencies and flood damages, [and] higher operating costs for commercial waterway users are some of the most obvious effects that stem from mining-related pollution and sedimentation." In light of this evidence, the Court "[could not] say that Congress did not have a rational basis for concluding that surface coal mining has substantial effects on interstate commerce."

Do the quoted legislative materials establish that there was a problem with interstate dimensions? Consider the final paragraph of the Court's discussion of the commerce clause issue:

> [The] Act responds to a congressional finding that nationwide "surface mining and reclamation standards are essential in order to insure that competition in interstate commerce among sellers of coal produced in different States will not be used to undermine the ability of the several States to improve and maintain adequate standards on coal mining operations within their borders." The prevention of this sort of destructive interstate competition is a traditional role for congressional action under the Commerce Clause [*Darby*].

Would that have been sufficient to support the statute?

Justice Rehnquist, concurring in the judgment, argued that there are internal limits on the commerce power:

> It would be a mistake to conclude that Congress' power to regulate [is] unlimited. Some activities may be so private or local in nature that they simply may not be *in* commerce. Nor is it sufficient that the person or activity reached have *some* nexus with interstate commerce. Our cases have consistently held that the regulated activity must have a *substantial* effect on interstate commerce. E.g., [*Jones & Laughlin*]. Moreover, simply because Congress may conclude that a particular activity substantially affects interstate commerce does not necessarily make it so. Congress' findings must be supported by a "rational basis" and are reviewable by the courts. Cf. [*Perez*] (Stewart, J., dissenting). . . .
>
> [The] Court asserts that regulation will be upheld if Congress had a rational basis for finding that the regulated activity affects interstate commerce. [But] it has long been established that the commerce power does not reach activity which merely "affects" interstate commerce. There must instead be a showing that regulated

activity has a *substantial effect* on that commerce. As recently as Maryland v. Wirtz, 392 U.S. 183, 197, n.27 (1968), Justice Harlan stressed that: "[neither] here nor in *Wickard* has the Court declared that Congress may use a relatively trivial impact on commerce as an excuse for broad general regulation of state or private activities.". . .

[The] Court often seems to forget that legislation enacted by Congress is subject to two different kinds of challenge, while that enacted by the States is subject to only one kind of challenge. Neither Congress nor the States may act in a manner prohibited by any provision of the Constitution. Congress must show that the activity it seeks to regulate has a substantial effect on interstate commerce.

Does Justice Rehnquist fairly describe the law?

3. *Federalism in statutory interpretation.* Recall that in *Wickard* Justice Jackson said that considerations of federalism might affect the courts' construction of a statute: "That an activity is of local character may help in a doubtful case to determine whether Congress intended to reach it." Why? What is a "doubtful case"? In United States v. Bass, 404 U.S. 336 (1971), the Court held that a defendant could not be convicted for possessing a gun under the following statute without proof that the gun had been possessed "in commerce or affecting commerce": "Any person who — (1) has been convicted [of] a felony [and] who receives, possesses, or transports in commerce or affecting commerce [any] firearm shall be fined not more than $10,000 or imprisoned for not more than two years, or both." It found the statute ambiguous on the question of whether the "in or affecting commerce" phrase modified "transports" only, or "receives [or] possesses" as well. If it modified "transports" only, the Court said, the statute would have the "curious" effect of criminalizing all possessions and receipts while not criminalizing some (purely intrastate) transportations that result in the criminalized possessions and receipts. (The provision was a floor amendment to a broader statute; it "was hastily passed, with little discussion, no hearings and no report.")

Justice Blackmun's dissent argued that there was no ambiguity:

The statute[, although] arguably ambiguous and, as the Government concedes, "not a model of logic or clarity," is clear enough. The structure of the vital language and its punctuation make it refer to one who receives, to one who possesses, and to one who transports in commerce. If one wished to say that he would welcome a cat, would welcome a dog, or would welcome a cow that jumps over the moon, he would likely say "I would like to have a cat, a dog, or a cow that jumps over the moon." So it is here.

Given the ambiguity it found, the majority invoked two canons of statutory construction:

First, ["ambiguity] concerning the ambit of criminal statutes should be resolved in favor of lenity." . . .

[Second,] unless Congress conveys its purpose clearly, it will not be deemed to have significantly changed the federal-state balance. Congress has traditionally been reluctant to define as a federal crime conduct readily denounced as criminal by the States. [In] traditionally sensitive areas, such as legislation affecting the federal balance, the requirement of clear statement assures that the legislature has in fact faced, and intended to bring into issue, the critical matters involved in the judicial decision. [The] broad construction urged by the Government renders traditionally local criminal conduct a matter for federal enforcement and would also involve a substantial extension of federal police resources. Absent proof of some interstate commerce nexus in each case, [the statute] dramatically intrudes upon traditional state criminal jurisdiction. [The] legislative history provides scanty basis for concluding that Congress faced these serious questions and meant to affect the federal-state balance in the way now claimed by the Government. Absent a clearer statement of intention than is present here, we do not interpret [the statute] to reach the "mere possession" of firearms.

The Court noted that it did "not reach the question whether, upon appropriate findings, Congress can constitutionally punish the 'mere possession' of firearms." In Scarborough v. United States, 431 U.S. 563 (1977), the Court held that the "commerce" element of the possession offense in *Bass* could be established by proof that "the firearm had been, at some time, in interstate commerce." Does that in itself resolve the question reserved in *Bass*? When coupled with Wickard v. Filburn?

Heart of Atlanta Motel v. United States

379 U.S. 241 (1964)

[The motel sought a declaratory judgment that Title II of the 1964 Civil Rights act was unconstitutional. The motel, located in downtown Atlanta, had 216 rooms. It advertised in national magazines and on billboards. About 75 percent of its registered guests were from out-of-state. It refused to rent its rooms to blacks. The lower court upheld the act.]
    MR. JUSTICE CLARK delivered the opinion of the Court. . . .

2.   THE HISTORY OF THE ACT . . .

[On] June 19, 1963, the late President Kennedy called for civil rights legislation in a message to Congress to which he attached a proposed bill. Its stated purpose was

> to promote the general welfare by eliminating discrimination based on race, color, religion, or national origin in . . . public accommodations through the exercise by Congress of the powers conferred upon it . . . to enforce the provisions of the fourteenth and fifteenth amendments, to regulate commerce among the several States, and to make laws necessary and proper to execute the powers conferred upon it by the Constitution.

Bills were introduced in each House of the Congress. . . .
    After extended hearings each of these bills was favorably reported to its respective house. Although each bill originally incorporated extensive findings of fact these were eliminated from the bills as they were reported. The House passed its bill in January 1964 and sent it to the Senate. Through a bipartisan coalition of Senators Humphrey and Dirksen, together with other Senators, a substitute was worked out in informal conferences. This substitute was adopted by the Senate and sent to the House where it was adopted without change. This expedited

procedure prevented the usual report on the substitute bill in the Senate as well as a Conference Committee report ordinarily filed in such matters. Our only frame of reference as to the legislative history of the Act is, therefore, the hearings, reports and debates on the respective bills in each house.

The Act as finally adopted was most comprehensive, undertaking to prevent through peaceful and voluntary settlement discrimination in voting, as well as in places of accommodation and public facilities, federally secured programs and in employment. Since Title II is the only portion under attack here, we confine our consideration to those public accommodation provisions.

3. Title II of the Act

This Title is divided into seven sections beginning with §201(a) which provides that:

> All persons shall be entitled to the full and equal enjoyment of the goods, services, facilities, privileges, advantages, and accommodations of any place of public accommodation, as defined in this section, without discrimination or segregation on the ground of race, color, religion, or national origin.

There are listed in §201(b) four classes of business establishments, each of which "serves the public" and "is a place of public accommodation" within the meaning of §201(a) "if its operations affect commerce, or if discrimination or segregation by it is supported by State action." The covered establishments [include]:

> any inn, hotel, motel, or other establishment which provides lodging to transient guests, other than an establishment located within a building which contains not more than five rooms for rent or hire and which is actually occupied by the proprietor of such establishment as his residence. . . .

Section 201(c) defines the phrase "affect commerce" as applied to the above establishments. It first declares that "any inn, hotel, motel, or other establishment which provides lodging to transient guests" affects commerce per se. . . .

5. The Civil Rights Cases, 109 U.S. 3 (1883), and Their Application

In light of our ground for decision, it might be well at the outset to discuss the Civil Rights Cases, which declared provisions of the Civil Rights Act of 1875 unconstitutional. We think that decision inapposite, and without precedential value in determining the constitutionality of the present Act. Unlike Title II of the present legislation, the 1875 Act broadly proscribed discrimination in "inns, public conveyances on land or water, theaters, and other places of public amusement," without limiting the categories of affected businesses to those impinging upon interstate commerce. In contrast, the applicability of Title II is carefully limited to enterprises having a direct and substantial relation to the interstate flow of goods and people, except where state action is involved. Further, the fact that certain kinds of businesses may not in 1875 have been sufficiently involved in interstate commerce to warrant bringing them within the ambit of the commerce power is not necessarily dispositive of the same question today. Our populace had not reached its present mobility, nor were facilities, goods and services circulating as readily in interstate commerce as they are today. Although the principles which we apply today are those first formulated by Chief Justice Marshall in Gibbons v. Ogden, 9 Wheat. 1 (1824), the conditions of transportation and commerce have changed dramatically, and we must apply those principles to the present state of commerce. The sheer increase in volume of interstate traffic alone would give discriminatory practices which inhibit travel a far larger impact upon the Nation's commerce than such practices had on the economy of another day. . . .

6. The Basis of Congressional Action

While the Act as adopted carried no congressional findings the record of its passage through each house is replete with evidence of the burdens that discrimination by race or color places upon interstate commerce. This testimony included the fact that our people have become increasingly mobile with millions of people of all races traveling from State to State; that Negroes in particular have been the subject of discrimination in transient accommodations, having to travel great distances to secure the same; that often they have been unable to obtain accommodations and have had to call upon friends to put them up overnight; and that these conditions had become so acute as to require the listing of available lodging for Negroes in a special guidebook which was itself "dramatic testimony to the difficulties" Negroes encounter in travel. These exclusionary practices were found to be nationwide, the Under Secretary of Commerce testifying that there is "no question that this discrimination in the North still exists to a large degree" and in the West and Midwest as well. This testimony indicated a qualitative as well as quantitative effect on interstate travel by Negroes. The former was the obvious impairment of the Negro traveler's pleasure and convenience that resulted when he continually was uncertain of finding lodging. As for the latter, there was evidence that this uncertainty stemming from racial discrimination had the effect of discouraging travel on the part of a substantial portion of the Negro community. This was the conclusion not only of the Under Secretary of Commerce but also of the Administrator of the Federal Aviation Agency who wrote the Chairman of the Senate Commerce Committee that it was his "belief that air commerce is adversely affected by the denial to a substantial segment of the traveling public of adequate and desegregated public accommodations." We shall not burden this opinion with further details since the voluminous testimony presents overwhelming evidence that discrimination by hotels and motels impedes interstate travel.

7. The Power of Congress over Interstate Travel . . .

The same interest in protecting interstate commerce which led Congress to deal with segregation in interstate carriers and the white-slave traffic has prompted it to extend the exercise of its power to gambling, [Lottery Case]; to criminal enter-prises, Brooks v. United States, 267 U.S. 432 (1925); to deceptive practices in the sale of products, Federal Trade Comm'n v. Mandel Bros., Inc., 359 U.S. 385 (1959); to fraudulent security transactions, Securities & Exchange Comm'n v. Ralston Purina Co., 346 U.S. 119 (1953); to misbranding of drugs, Weeks v. United States, 245 U.S. 618 (1918); to wages and hours, United States v. Darby; to members of labor unions, Labor Board v. Jones & Laughlin; to crop control, Wickard v. Filburn; to discrimination against shippers, United States v. Baltimore & Ohio R. Co., 333 U.S. 169 (1948); to the protection of small business from injurious price cutting, Moore v. Mead's Fine Bread Co., 348 U.S. 115 (1954); to resale price maintenance, Hudson Distributors, Inc. v. Eli Lilly & Co., 377 U.S. 386 (1964), Schwegmann v. Calvert Distillers Corp., 341 U.S. 384 (1951); to pro-fessional football, Radovich v. National Football League, 352 U.S. 445 (1957); and to racial discrimination by owners and managers of terminal restaurants, Boynton v. Virginia, 364 U.S. 454 (1960).

That Congress was legislating against moral wrongs in many of these areas rendered its enactments no less valid. In framing Title II of this Act Congress was also dealing with what it considered a moral problem. But that fact does not detract from the overwhelming evidence of the disruptive effect that racial dis-crimination has had on commercial intercourse. It was this burden which em-powered Congress to enact appropriate legislation, and, given this basis for the exercise of its power, Congress was not restricted by the fact that the particular obstruction to interstate commerce with which it was dealing was also deemed a moral and social wrong.

It is said that the operation of the motel here is of a purely local character. But, assuming this to be true, "[i]f it is interstate commerce that feels the pinch, it does not matter how local the operation which applies the squeeze." United States v. Women's Sportswear Mfrs. Assn., 336 U.S. 460, 464 (1949). [Thus] the power of Congress to promote interstate commerce also includes the power to regulate the local incidents thereof, including local activities in both the States of origin and destination, which might have a substantial and harmful effect upon that com-merce. One need only examine the evidence which we have discussed above to see that Congress may — as it has — prohibit racial discrimination by motels serving travelers, however "local" their operations may appear.

Nor does the Act deprive appellant of liberty or property under the Fifth Amendment. The commerce power invoked here by the Congress is a specific and plenary one authorized by the Constitution itself. The only questions are: (1) whether Congress had a rational basis for finding that racial discrimination by motels affected commerce, and (2) if it had such a basis, whether the means it selected to eliminate that evil are reasonable and appropriate. If they are, appel-lant has no "right" to select its guests as it sees fit, free from governmental regulation. . . .

It is doubtful if in the long run appellant will suffer economic loss as a result of the Act. Experience is to the contrary where discrimination is completely obliter-ated as to all public accomodations. But whether this be true or not is of no consequence since this Court has specifically held that the fact that a "member of the class which is regulated may suffer economic losses not shared by others . . . has never been a barrier" to such legislation. Bowles v. Willingham, at 518. . . .

We, therefore, conclude that the action of the Congress in the adoption of the

Act as applied here to a motel which concededly serves interstate travelers is within the power granted it by the Commerce Clause of the Constitution, as interpreted by this Court for 140 years. It may be argued that Congress could have pursued other methods to eliminate the obstructions it found in interstate commerce caused by racial discrimination. But this is a matter of policy that rests entirely with the Congress not with the courts. How obstructions in commerce may be removed — what means are to be employed — is within the sound and exclusive discretion of the Congress. It is subject only to one caveat — that the means chosen by it must be reasonably adapted to the end permitted by the Constitution. We cannot say that its choice here was not so adapted. The Constitution requires no more.

Affirmed.

[For concurring opinions, see Katzenbach v. McClung, infra.]

Katzenbach v. McClung

379 U.S. 294 (1964)

[The lower court sustained a challenge to the constitutionality of the application of Title II of the 1964 Civil Rights Act to a restaurant.]

Mr. Justice Clark delivered the opinion of the Court. . . .

2. The Facts

Ollie's Barbecue is a family-owned restaurant in Birmingham, Alabama, specializing in barbecued meats and homemade pies, with a seating capacity of 220 customers. It is located on a state highway 11 blocks from an interstate one and a somewhat greater distance from railroad and bus stations. The restaurant caters to a family and white-collar trade with a take-out service for Negroes. It employs 36 persons, two-thirds of whom are Negroes.

In the 12 months preceding the passage of the Act, the restaurant purchased locally approximately $150,000 worth of food, $69,683 or 46% of which was meat that it bought from a local supplier who had procured it from outside the State. The District Court expressly found that a substantial portion of the food served in the restaurant had moved in interstate commerce. The restaurant has refused to serve Negroes in its dining accommodations since its original opening in 1927, and since July 2, 1964, it has been operating in violation of the Act. The court below concluded that if it were required to serve Negroes it would lose a substantial amount of business. . . .

3. The Act as Applied. . . .

[Sections] 201(b)(2) and (c) place any "restaurant . . . principally engaged in selling food for consumption on the premises" under the Act "if . . . it serves or offers to serve interstate travelers or a substantial portion of the food which it serves . . . has moved in commerce."

Ollie's Barbecue admits that it is covered by these provisions of the Act. [The] sole question, therefore, narrows down to whether Title II, as applied to a restaurant annually receiving about $70,000 worth of food which has moved in commerce, is a valid exercise of the power of Congress. The Government has contended that Congress had ample basis upon which to find that racial discrimination at restaurants which receive from out of state a substantial portion of the food served does, in fact, impose commercial burdens of national magnitude upon interstate commerce. . . .

4. THE CONGRESSIONAL HEARINGS

As we noted in *Heart of Atlanta Motel* both Houses of Congress conducted prolonged hearings on the Act. And, as we said there, while no formal findings were made, which of course are not necessary, it is well that we make mention of the testimony at these hearings the better to understand the problem before Congress and determine whether the Act is a reasonable and appropriate means toward its solution. The record is replete with testimony of the burdens placed on interstate commerce by racial discrimination in restaurants. A comparison of per capita spending by Negroes in restaurants, theaters, and like establishments indicated less spending, after discounting income differences, in areas where discrimination is widely practiced. This condition, which was especially aggravated in the South, was attributed in the testimony of the Under Secretary of Commerce to racial segregation. This diminutive spending springing from a refusal to serve Negroes and their total loss as customers has, regardless of the absence of direct evidence, a close connection to interstate commerce. The fewer customers a restaurant enjoys the less food it sells and consequently the less it buys. In addition, the Attorney General testified that this type of discrimination imposed "an artificial restriction on the market" and interfered with the flow of merchandise. In addition, there were many references to discriminatory situations causing wide unrest and having a depressant effect on general business conditions in the respective communities.

Moreover there was an impressive array of testimony that discrimination in restaurants had a direct and highly restrictive effect upon interstate travel by Negroes. This resulted, it was said, because discriminatory practices prevent Negroes from buying prepared food served on the premises while on a trip, except in isolated and unkempt restaurants and under most unsatisfactory and often unpleasant conditions. This obviously discourages travel and obstructs interstate commerce for one can hardly travel without eating. Likewise, it was said, that discrimination deterred professional, as well as skilled, people from moving into areas where such practices occurred and thereby caused industry to be reluctant to establish there.

We believe that this testimony afforded ample basis for the conclusion that established restaurants in such areas sold less interstate goods because of the discrimination, that interstate travel was obstructed directly by it, that business in general suffered and that many new businesses refrained from establishing there as a result of it. Hence the District Court was in error in concluding that there was no connection between discrimination and the movement of interstate commerce. The court's conclusion that such a connection is outside "common experience" flies in the face of stubborn fact.

It goes without saying that, viewed in isolation, the volume of food purchased by Ollie's Barbecue from sources supplied from out of state was insignificant when compared with the total foodstuffs moving in commerce. . . .

[While] the focus of the legislation was on the individual restaurant's relation to interstate commerce, Congress appropriately considered the importance of that connection with the knowledge that the discrimination was but "representative of many others throughout the country, the total incidence of which if left unchecked may well become far-reaching in its harm to commerce." Polish Alliance v. Labor Board, 322 U.S. 643, 648 (1944). . . .

5.   THE POWER OF CONGRESS TO REGULATE LOCAL ACTIVITIES . . .

The appellees contend that Congress has arbitrarily created a conclusive presumption that all restaurants meeting the criteria set out in the Act "affect commerce." Stated another way, they object to the omission of a provision for a case-by-case determination — judicial or administrative — that racial discrimination in a particular restaurant affects commerce. . . .

Here, as [in *Darby*], Congress has determined for itself that refusals of service to Negroes have imposed burdens both upon the interstate flow of food and upon the movement of products generally. Of course, the mere fact that Congress has said when particular activity shall be deemed to affect commerce does not preclude further examination by this Court. But where we find that the legislators, in light of the facts and testimony before them, have a rational basis for finding a chosen regulatory scheme necessary to the protection of commerce, our investigation is at an end. The only remaining question — one answered in the affirmative by the court below — is whether the particular restaurant either serves or offers to serve interstate travelers or serves food a substantial portion of which has moved in interstate commerce.

The appellees urge that Congress, in passing the Fair Labor Standards Act and the National Labor Relations Act, made specific findings which were embodied in those statutes. Here, of course, Congress has included no formal findings. But their absence is not fatal to the validity of the statute, see United States v. Carolene Products Co., 304 U.S. 144, 152 (1938), for the evidence presented at the hearing fully indicated the nature and effect of the burdens on commerce which Congress meant to alleviate.

Confronted as we are with the facts laid before Congress, we must conclude that it had a rational basis for finding that racial discrimination in restaurants had a direct and adverse effect on the free flow of interstate commerce. Insofar as the sections of the Act here relevant are concerned, §§201(b)(2) and (c), Congress prohibited discrimination only in those establishments having a close tie to interstate commerce, i.e., those, like the McClungs', serving food that has come from out of the State. We think in so doing that Congress acted well within its power to protect and foster commerce in extending the coverage of Title II only to those restaurants offering to serve interstate travelers or serving food, a substantial portion of which has moved in interstate commerce.

The absence of direct evidence connecting discriminatory restaurant service with the flow of interstate food, a factor on which the appellees place much reliance, is not, given the evidence as to the effect of such practices on other aspects of commerce, a crucial matter.

The power of Congress in this field is broad and sweeping; where it keeps within its sphere and violates no express constitutional limitation it has been the rule of this Court, going back almost to the founding days of the Republic, not to interfere. The Civil Rights Act of 1964, as here applied, we find to be plainly appropriate in the resolution of what the Congress found to be a national commercial problem of the first magnitude. We find it in no violation of any express limitations of the Constitution and we therefore declare it valid.

The judgment is therefore reversed.

MR. JUSTICE BLACK, concurring. . . .

It requires no novel or strained interpretation of the Commerce Clause to sustain Title II as applied in either of these cases. . . .

[There] can be no doubt that the operations of both the motel and the restaurant here fall squarely within the measure Congress chose to adopt in the Act and deemed adequate to show a constitutionally prohibitable adverse effect on commerce. The choice of policy is of course within the exclusive power of Congress; but whether particular operations affect interstate commerce sufficiently to come under the constitutional power of Congress to regulate them is ultimately a judicial rather than a legislative question, and can be settled finally only by this Court. I agree that as applied to this motel and this restaurant the Act is a valid exercise of congressional power, in the case of the motel because the record amply demonstrates that its practice of discrimination tended directly to interfere with interstate travel, and in the case of the restaurant because Congress had ample basis for concluding that a widespread practice of racial discrimination by restaurants buying as substantial a quantity of goods shipped from other States as this restaurant buys could distort or impede interstate trade. . . .

[Ollie's Barbeque] bought $69,683 worth [of meat] (representing 46% of its total expenditures for supplies), which had been shipped into Alabama from outside the State. Plainly, 46% of the goods it sells is a "substantial" portion and amount. Congress concluded that restaurants which purchase a substantial quantity of goods from other States might well burden and disrupt the flow of interstate commerce if allowed to practice racial discrimination, because of the stifling and distorting effect that such discrimination on a wide scale might well have on the sale of goods shipped across state lines. Certainly this belief would not be irrational even had there not been a large body of evidence before the Congress to show the probability of this adverse effect. . . .

[I] recognize that every remote, possible, speculative effect on commerce should not be accepted as an adequate constitutional ground to uproot and throw into the discard all our traditional distinctions between what is purely local, and therefore controlled by state laws, and what affects the national interest and is therefore subject to control by federal laws. I recognize too that some isolated and remote lunchroom which sells only to local people and buys almost all its supplies in the locality may possibly be beyond the reach of the power of Congress to regulate commerce, just as such an establishment is not covered by the present Act. But in deciding the constitutional power of Congress in cases like the two before us we do not consider the effect on interstate commerce of only one isolated, individual, local event, without regard to the fact that this single local event when added to many others of a similar nature may impose a burden on interstate commerce by reducing its volume or distorting its flow. There are approximately 20,000,000 Negroes in our country. Many of them are able to, and do, travel among the States in automobiles. Certainly it would seriously discourage such travel by them if, as evidence before the Congress indicated has been true in the past, they should in the future continue to be unable to find a decent place along their way in which to lodge or eat. And the flow of interstate commerce may be impeded or distorted substantially if local sellers of interstate food are permitted to exclude all Negro consumers. Measuring, as this Court has so often held is required, by the aggregate effect of a great number of such acts of discrimination, I am of the opinion that Congress has constitutional power under the Commerce and Necessary and Proper Clauses to protect interstate commerce from the injuries bound to befall it from these discriminatory practices. . . .

MR. JUSTICE DOUGLAS, concurring.

Though I join in the Court's opinions, I am somewhat reluctant [to] rest solely on the Commerce Clause. My reluctance is not due to any conviction that Congress lacks power to regulate commerce in the interests of human rights. It is rather my belief that the right of people to be free of state action that discriminates against them because of race, like the "right of persons to move freely from State to State" "occupies a more protected position in our constitutional system than does the movement of cattle, fruit, steel and coal across state lines." . . .

Hence I would prefer to rest on the assertion of legislative power contained in §5 of the Fourteenth Amendment. . . .

A decision based on the Fourteenth Amendment would have a more settling effect, making unnecessary litigation over whether a particular restaurant or inn is within the commerce definitions of the Act or whether a particular customer is an interstate traveler. Under my construction, the Act would apply to all customers in all the enumerated places of public accommodation. And that construction would put an end to all obstructionist strategies and finally close one door on a bitter chapter in American history.

The Senate Committee laid emphasis on the Commerce Clause. [But] it is clear that the objectives of the Fourteenth Amendment were by no means ignored. . . .

Thus while I agree with the Court that Congress in fashioning the present Act used the Commerce Clause to regulate racial segregation, it also used (and properly so) some of its power under §5 of the Fourteenth Amendment. . . .

MR. JUSTICE GOLDBERG, concurring. . . .

The primary purpose of the Civil Rights Act of 1964, however, as the Court recognizes, and as I would underscore, is the vindication of human dignity and not mere economics. . . .

Moreover, that this is the primary purpose of the Act is emphasized by the fact that while §201(c) speaks only in terms of establishments which "affect commerce," it is clear that Congress based this selection not only on its power under the Commerce Clause but also on §5 of the Fourteenth Amendment. . . .

Note: Federalism and Congressional Motivation

1. *Commerce clause versus (?) fourteenth amendment motivations.* The central issues arising from these cases involve the tension between the evident motivation

behind the enactment of the statute — an antidiscrimination, moral motivation — and the use of the commerce power. Consider the following argument: The Court in *Heart of Atlanta* and *McClung* improperly refused to examine the motivation of Congress. *Darby* disclaimed inquiry into motive, but there Congress had prohibited the movement in interstate commerce of certain goods. Where Congress uses the "affecting commerce" rationale of Wickard v. Filburn, the Court must examine Congress's motive.

Should Congress have relied on the fourteenth amendment instead of the commerce clause? Brest, The Conscientious Legislator's Guide to Constitutional Interpretation, 27 Stan. L. Rev. 585 (1975), argues that in deciding whether to support a proposed statute, members of Congress ought to consider whether in their judgment the statute is consistent with constitutional norms. Reconsider here the discussion of Cooper v. Aaron, Chapter 1 supra. Members of Congress will have views on the wisdom of the proposal as a matter of public policy and will estimate the political consequences of supporting or opposing it. Given the Madison/Wechsler argument concerning the relation between federalism and congressional power, what more is there that the "conscientious legislator" should consider in this context?

Suppose a member of Congress believed that the Civil Rights Act actually served the equality goals of the fourteenth amendment and (a) that the Civil Rights Cases had been wrongly decided, or (b) that the Supreme Court in 1964 would have overruled the Civil Rights Cases, or (c) was uncertain about the Court's position in 1964. How, if at all, would these views affect the design of the statute? Should they affect the member's vote on the statute in the form actually presented? That is, what are the consequences of a conscientious legislator's coming to an independent judgment on the statute's constitutionality? Is the legislator who thinks the Civil Rights Cases were correctly decided likely to believe that the proposed act is sound policy?

2. *The scope of the rationale.* Must there be a connection between the activities found to "affect" commerce and the regulations Congress imposes? Consider in this connection the role played in the analysis by the food Ollie's Barbeque purchased. Do the food purchases demonstrate that the restaurant's actions "affect" interstate commerce? Could Congress require that the restaurant comply with regulations for the disposal by its carry-out customers of their trash? Regulations regarding the maintenance of its lawn and parking lot?

Alternatively, is the activity that affects commerce the discrimination? If so, do the questions in the preceding paragraph arise? What is the function in the Court's analysis of the purchases of food Ollie's makes?

Garcia v. San Antonio Metropolitan Transit Authority

— U.S. — , 105 S. Ct. 1005 (1985)

JUSTICE BLACKMUN delivered the opinion of the Court.

We revisit in [this case] an issue raised in National League of Cities v. Usery, 426 U.S. 833 (1976). In that litigation, this Court, by a sharply divided vote, ruled that the Commerce Clause does not empower Congress to enforce the minimum-wage and overtime provisions of the Fair Labor Standards Act (FLSA) against the States "in areas of traditional governmental functions." . . .

[Garcia sought overtime pay from the Transit Authority under FLSA. The trial court, applying the "traditional governmental functions" test, held that application of the act to the Authority would violate the Constitution.]

II

Appellees have not argued that SAMTA is immune from regulation under the FLSA on the ground that it is a local transit system engaged in intrastate commercial activity. In a practical sense, SAMTA's operations might well be characterized as "local." Nonetheless, it long has been settled that Congress' authority under the Commerce Clause extends to intrastate economic activities that affect interstate commerce. See, e.g., [Heart of Atlanta, Wickard, Darby.] Were SAMTA a privately owned and operated enterprise, it could not credibly argue that Congress exceeded the bounds of its Commerce Clause powers in prescribing minimum wages and overtime rates for SAMTA's employees. Any constitutional exemption from the requirements of the FLSA therefore must rest on SAMTA's status as a governmental entity rather than on the "local" nature of its operations.

The prerequisites for governmental immunity under National League of Cities were summarized by this Court in Hodel [v. Virginia Surface Mining Assn., 452 U.S. 264 (1981)]. Under that summary, four conditions must be satisfied before a state activity may be deemed immune from a particular federal regulation under the Commerce Clause. First, it is said that the federal statute at issue must regulate "the 'States as States.' " Second, the statute must "address matters that are indisputably 'attribute[s] of state sovereignty.' " Third, state compliance with the federal obligation must "directly impair [the States'] ability 'to structure integral operations in areas of traditional governmental functions.' " Finally, the relation of state and federal interests must not be such that "the nature of the federal interest . . . justifies state submission."

[After reviewing lower court cases, and a related line of tax immunity cases, the Court concluded that the "traditional governmental functions" test was "unworkable."]

[The] most obvious defect of a historical approach to state immunity is that it prevents a court from accommodating changes in the historical functions of States, changes that have resulted in a number of once-private functions like education being assumed by the States and their subdivisions. At the same time, the only apparent virtue of a rigorous historical standard, namely, its promise of a reasonably objective measure for state immunity, is illusory. Reliance on history as an organizing principle results in linedrawing of the most arbitrary sort; the genesis of state governmental functions stretches over a historical continuum from before the Revolution to the present, and courts would have to decide by fiat precisely how longstanding a pattern of state involvement had to be for federal regulatory authority to be defeated.

A nonhistorical standard for selecting immune governmental functions is likely to be just as unworkable as is a historical standard. . . .

We believe, however, that there is a more fundamental problem at work here. [The] problem is that [no] distinction [that] purports to separate out important governmental functions can be faithful to the role of federalism in a democratic society. The essence of our federal system is that within the realm of authority left open to them under the Constitution, the States must be equally free to engage in any activity that their citizens choose for the common weal, no matter how unorthodox or unnecessary anyone else — including the judiciary — deems state involvement to be. Any rule of state immunity that looks to the "traditional," "integral," or "necessary" nature of governmental functions inevitably invites an unelected federal judiciary to make decisions about which state policies it favors and which ones it dislikes. . . .

We therefore now reject, as unsound in principle and unworkable in practice, a rule of state immunity from federal regulation that turns on a judicial appraisal of whether a particular governmental function is "integral" or "traditional." Any such rule leads to inconsistent results at the same time that it disserves principles of democratic self-governance, and it breeds inconsistency precisely because it is divorced from those principles. If there are to be limits on the Federal Government's power to interfere with state functions — as undoubtedly there are — we must look elsewhere to find them. We accordingly return to the underlying issue that confronted this Court in *National League of Cities* — the manner in which the Constitution insulates States from the reach of Congress' power under the Commerce Clause.

III

The central theme of *National League of Cities* was that the States occupy a special position in our constitutional system and that the scope of Congress' authority under the Commerce Clause must reflect that position. Of course, the Commerce Clause by its specific language does not provide any special limitation on Congress' actions with respect to the States. See EEOC v. Wyoming, 460 U.S. 226, 248 (1983) (concurring opinion). It is equally true, however, that the text of the Constitution provides the beginning rather than the final answer to every inquiry into questions of federalism, for "[b]ehind the words of the constitutional provisions are postulates which limit and control." Monaco v. Mississippi, 292 U.S. 313, 322 (1934). *National League of Cities* reflected the general conviction that the Constitution precludes "the National Government [from] devour[ing] the essentials of state sovereignty." Maryland v. Wirtz, 392 U.S., at 205 (dissenting opinion). In order to be faithful to the underlying federal premises of the Constitution, courts must look for the "postulates which limit and control."

What has proved problematic is not the perception that the Constitution's federal structure imposes limitations on the Commerce Clause, but rather the nature and content of those limitations. . . .

We doubt that courts ultimately can identify principled constitutional limitations on the scope of Congress' Commerce Clause powers over the States merely by relying on *a priori* definitions of state sovereignty. . . .

The States unquestionably do "retai[n] a significant measure of sovereign authority." EEOC v. Wyoming, 460 U.S., at 269 (Powell, J., dissenting). They do so, however, only to the extent that the Constitution has not divested them of their original powers and transferred those powers to the Federal Government. In the words of James Madison to the Members of the First Congress: "Interference with the power of the States was no constitutional criterion of the power of Congress. If the power was not given, Congress could not exercise it; if given, they might exercise it, although it should interfere with the laws, or even the Constitution of the States." 2 Annals of Cong. 1897 (1791). . . .

[With] rare exceptions, like the guarantee, in Article IV, §3, of state territorial integrity, the Constitution does not carve out express elements of state sovereignty that Congress may not employ its delegated powers to displace. [The] fact that the States remain sovereign as to all powers not vested in Congress or denied them by the Constitution offers no guidance about where the frontier between state and federal power lies. In short, we have no license to employ freestanding conceptions of state sovereignty when measuring congressional authority under the Commerce Clause.

When we look for the States' "residuary and inviolable sovereignty," The Federalist No. 39 (J. Madison), in the shape of the constitutional scheme rather than in predetermined notions of sovereign power, a different measure of state sovereignty emerges. Apart from the limitation on federal authority inherent in the delegated nature of Congress' Article I powers, the principal means chosen by the Framers to ensure the role of the States in the federal system lies in the structure of the Federal Government itself. It is no novelty to observe that the composition of the Federal Government was designed in large part to protect the States from overreaching by Congress.[11] . . .

The extent to which the structure of the Federal Government itself was relied on to insulate the interests of the States is evident in the views of the Framers. James Madison explained that the Federal Government "will partake sufficiently of the spirit [of the States], to be disinclined to invade the rights of the individual States, or the prerogatives of their governments." The Federalist No. 46. [In] short, the Framers chose to rely on a federal system in which special restraints on federal power over the States inhered principally in the workings of the National Government itself, rather than in discrete limitations on the objects of federal authority. State sovereign interests, then, are more properly protected by procedural safeguards inherent in the structure of the federal system than by judicially created limitations on federal power.

The effectiveness of the federal political process in preserving the States' interests is apparent even today in the course of federal legislation. On the one hand, the States have been able to direct a substantial proportion of federal revenues into their own treasuries in the form of general and program-specific grant in aid.

[Moreover,] at the same time that the States have exercised their influence to obtain federal support, they have been able to exempt themselves from a wide variety of obligations imposed by Congress under the Commerce Clause. For example, the Federal Power Act, the National Labor Relations Act, the Labor-Management Reporting and Disclosure Act, the Occupational Safety and Health Act, the Employee Retirement Insurance Security Act, and the Sherman Act all contain express or implied exemptions for States and their subdivisions. The fact that some federal statutes such as the FLSA extend general obligations to the States cannot obscure the extent to which the political position of the States in the federal system has served to minimize the burdens that the States bear under the Commerce Clause.

We realize that changes in the structure of the Federal Government have taken place since 1789, not the least of which has been the substitution of popular

_____

11. See, e.g., [Choper; Wechsler].

election of Senators by the adoption of the Seventeenth Amendment in 1913, and that these changes may work to alter the influence of the States in the federal political process. Nonetheless, against this background, we are convinced that the fundamental limitation that the constitutional scheme imposes on the Commerce Clause to protect the "States as States" is one of process rather than one of result. Any substantive restraint on the exercise of Commerce Clause powers must find its justification in the procedural nature of this basic limitation, and it must be tailored to compensate for possible failings in the national political process rather than to dictate a "sacred province of state autonomy." EEOC v. Wyoming, 460 U.S., at 236.

Insofar as the present cases are concerned, then, we need go no further than to state that we perceive nothing in the overtime and minimum-wage requirements of the FLSA, as applied to SAMTA, that is destructive of state sovereignty or violative of any constitutional provision. . . .

IV

This analysis makes clear the Congress' action in affording SAMTA employees the protections of the wage and hour provisions of the FLSA contravened no affirmative limit on Congress' power under the Commerce Clause. The judgment of the District Court therefore must be reversed.

Of course, we continue to recognize that the States occupy a special and specific position in our constitutional system and that the scope of Congress' authority under the Commerce Clause must reflect that position. But the principal and basic limit on the federal commerce power is that inherent in all congressional action — the built-in restraints that our system provides through state participation in federal governmental action. The political process ensures that the laws that unduly burden the States will not be promulgated. In the factual setting of these cases the internal safeguards of the political process have performed as intended.

These cases do not require us to identify or define what affirmative limits the constitutional structure might impose on federal action affecting the States under the Commerce Clause. See Coyle v. Oklahoma, 221 U.S. 559 (1911). We note and accept Justice Frankfurter's observation in New York v. United States, 326 U.S. 572, 583 (1946):

> The process of Constitutional adjudication does not thrive on conjuring up horrible possibilities that never happen in the real world and devising doctrines sufficiently comprehensive in detail to cover the remotest contingency. Nor need we go beyond what is required for a reasoned disposition of the kind of controversy now before the Court. . . .

[Reversed.]

JUSTICE POWELL, with whom THE CHIEF JUSTICE, JUSTICE REHNQUIST, and JUSTICE O'CONNOR join, dissenting.

The Court today, in its 5–4 decision, overrules National League of Cities v. Usery, 426 U.S. 833 (1976), a case in which we held that Congress lacked authority to impose the requirements of the Fair Labor Standards Act on state and local governments. Because I believe this decision substantially alters the federal system embodied in the Constitution, I dissent.

I . . .

[The] extent to which the States may exercise their authority, when Congress purports to act under the Commerce Clause, henceforth is to be determined from time to time by political decisions made by members of the federal government, decisions the Court says will not be subject to judicial review. I note that it does not seem to have occurred to the Court that *it* — an unelected majority of five Justices — today rejects almost 200 years of the understanding of the constitutional status of federalism. . . .

II . . .

B

Today's opinion does not explain how the State's role in the electoral process guarantees that particular exercises of the Commerce Clause power will not infringe on residual State sovereignty.[7] Members of Congress are elected from the various States, but once in office they are members of the federal government.[8] Although the States participate in the Electoral College, this is hardly a reason to view the President as a representative of the States' interest against federal encroachment. We noted recently "the hydraulic pressure inherent within each of the separate Branches to exceed the outer limits of its power. . . ." *Immigration and Naturalization Service v. Chadha,* 462 U.S. 919, 951 (1983). The Court offers no reason to think that this pressure will not operate when Congress seeks to invoke its powers under the Commerce Clause, notwithstanding the electoral role of the States.[9]

---

7. Late in its opinion, the Court suggests that after all there may be some "affirmative limits the constitutional structure might impose on federal action affecting the States under the Commerce Clause." The Court asserts that "[i]n the factual setting of these cases the internal safeguards of the political process have performed as intended." The Court does not explain the basis for this judgment. Nor does it identify the circumstances in which the "political process" may fail and "affirmative limits" are to be imposed. Presumably, such limits are to be determined by the Judicial Branch even though it is "unelected." Today's opinion, however, has rejected the balancing standard and suggests no other standard that would enable a court to determine when there has been a malfunction of the "political process." The Court's failure to specify the "affirmative limits" on federal power, or when and how these limits are to be determined, may well be explained by the transparent fact that any such attempt would be subject to precisely the same objections on which it relies to overrule *National League of Cities.*

8. One can hardly imagine this Court saying that because Congress is composed of individuals, individual rights guaranteed by the Bill of Rights are amply protected by the political process. Yet, the position adopted today is indistinguishable in principle. The Tenth Amendment also is an essential part of the Bill of Rights.

9. At one time in our history, the view that the structure of the federal government sufficed to protect the States might have had a somewhat more practical, although not a more logical, basis. Professor Wechsler, whose seminal article in 1954 proposed the view adopted by the Court today, predicated his argument on assumptions that simply do not accord with current reality. Professor Wechsler wrote: "National action has . . . always been regarded as exceptional in our polity, an

The Court apparently thinks that the States' success at obtaining federal funds for various projects and exemptions from the obligations of some federal statutes is indicative of the "effectiveness of the federal political process in preserving the States' interests. . . ." But such political success is not relevant to the question whether the political *processes* are the proper means of enforcing constitutional limitations.[11] The fact that Congress generally does not transgress constitutional limits on its power to reach State activities does not make judicial review any less necessary to rectify the cases in which it does do so.[12] The States' role in our system of government is a matter of constitutional law, not of legislative grace. "The powers not delegated to the United States by the Constitution, nor prohibited by it to the States, are reserved to the States, respectively, or to the people." U.S. Const., Amend. 10.

More troubling than the logical infirmities in the Court's reasoning is the result of its holding, i.e., that federal political officials, invoking the Commerce Clause, are the sole judges of the limits of their own power. This result is inconsistent with the fundamental principles of our constitutional system. See, e.g., The Federalist No. 78 (Hamilton). At least since Marbury v. Madison it has been the settled province of the federal judiciary "to say what the law is" with respect to the constitutionality of acts of Congress. 1 Cranch 137, 177 (1803). In rejecting the role of the judiciary in protecting the States from federal overreaching, the Court's opinion offers no explanation for ignoring the teaching of the most famous case in our history.[13]

---

intrusion to be justified by some necessity, the special rather than the ordinary case." [Wechsler.] Not only is the premise of this view clearly at odds with the proliferation of national legislation over the past 30 years, but "a variety of structural and political changes in this century have combined to make Congress particularly *insensitive* to state and local values." Advisory Comm'n on Intergovernmental Relations [ACIR], Regulatory Federalism: Policy, Process, Impact and Reform 50 (1984). The adoption of the Seventeenth Amendment (providing for direct election of senators), the weakening of political parties on the local level, and the rise of national media, among other things, have made Congress increasingly less representative of State and local interests, and more likely to be responsive to the demands of various national constituencies. As one observer explained, "As Senators and members of the House develop independent constituencies among groups such as farmers, businessmen, laborers, environmentalists, and the poor, each of which generally supports certain national initiatives, their tendency to identify with state interests and the positions of state officials is reduced." Kaden, "Federalism in the Courts: Agenda for the 1980s," in ACIR, The Future of Federalism in the '80s, at 97 (1981). [Thus,] even if one were to ignore the numerous problems with the Court's position in terms of constitutional theory, there would remain serious questions as to its factual premises.

11. Apparently in an effort to reassure the States, the Court identifies several major statutes that thus far have not been made applicable to State governments. [The] Court does not suggest that this restraint will continue after its decision here. Indeed, it is unlikely that special interest groups will fail to accept the Court's open invitation to urge Congress to extend these and other statutes to apply to the States and their local subdivisions.

12. This Court has never before abdicated responsibility for assessing the constitutionality of challenged action on the ground that affected parties theoretically are able to look out for their own interests through the electoral process. As the Court noted in *National League of Cities*, a much stronger argument as to inherent structural protections could have been made in either Buckley v. Valeo, 424 U.S. 1 (1976) or Myers v. United States, 272 U.S. 52 (1926), than can be made here. In these cases, the President signed legislation that limited his authority with respect to certain appointments and thus arguably "it was no concern of this Court that the law violated the Constitution." 426 U.S., at 841-842 n.12. The Court nevertheless held the laws unconstitutional because they infringed on presidential authority, the President's consent notwithstanding. The Court does not address this point; nor does it cite any authority for its contrary view.

13. [The] Court does not explain how leaving the States virtually at the mercy of the federal government, without recourse to judicial review, will enhance their opportunities to experiment and serve as "laboratories."

III

A

In our federal system, the States have a major role that cannot be preempted by the national government. As contemporaneous writings and the debates at the ratifying conventions make clear, the States' ratification of the Constitution was predicated on this understanding of federalism. Indeed, the Tenth Amendment was adopted specifically to ensure that the important role promised the States by the proponents of the Constitution was realized.

Much of the initial opposition to the Constitution was rooted in the fear that the national government would be too powerful and eventually would eliminate the States as viable political entities. This concern was voiced repeatedly until proponents of the Constitution made assurances that a bill of rights, including a provision explicitly reserving powers in the States, would be among the first business of the new Congress. . . .

This history, which the Court simply ignores, documents the integral role of the Tenth Amendment in our constitutional theory. It exposes as well, I believe, the fundamental character of the Court's error today. Far from being "unsound in principle," judicial enforcement of the Tenth Amendment is essential to maintaining the federal system so carefully designed by the Framers and adopted in the Constitution.

B

The Framers had definite ideas about the nature of the Constitution's division of authority between the federal and state governments. . . .

The Framers believed that the separate sphere of sovereignty reserved to the States would ensure that the States would serve as an effective "counterpoise" to the power of the federal government. The States would serve this essential role because they would attract and retain the loyalty of their citizens. The roots of such loyalty, the Founders thought, were found in the objects peculiar to state government. For example, Hamilton argued that the States "regulat[e] all those personal interests and familiar concerns to which the sensibility of individuals is more immediately awake. . . ." The Federalist No. 17. Thus, he maintained that the people would perceive the States as "the immediate and most visible guardian of life and property," a fact which "contributes more than any other circumstance to impressing upon the minds of the people affection, esteem and reverence towards the government." [Like] Hamilton, Madison saw the States' involvement in the everyday concerns of the people as the source of their citizens' loyalty. See also Nagel, Federalism as a Fundamental Value: *National League of Cities* in Perspective, 1981 Sup. Ct. Rev. 81 (1981).

Thus, the harm to the States that results from federal overreaching under the Commerce Clause is not simply a matter of dollars and cents. Nor is it a matter of the wisdom or folly of certain policy choices. Rather, by usurping functions traditionally performed by the States, federal overreaching under the Commerce Clause undermines the constitutionally mandated balance of power between the

States and the federal government, a balance designed to protect our fundamental liberties.

C

The emasculation of the powers of the States that can result from the Court's decision is predicated on the Commerce Clause as a power "delegated to the United States" by the Constitution. . . .

To be sure, this Court has construed the Commerce Clause to accommodate unanticipated changes over the past two centuries. As these changes have occurred, the Court has had to decide whether the federal government has exceeded its authority by regulating activities beyond the capability of a single state to regulate or beyond legitimate federal interests that outweighed the authority and interests of the States. In so doing, however, the Court properly has been mindful of the essential role of the States in our federal system. . . .

D

In contrast, the Court today propounds a view of federalism that pays only lip service to the role of the States. Although it says that the States "unquestionably do retai[n] a significant measure of sovereign authority,' " (quoting EEOC v. Wyoming, 460 U.S. 226, 269 (Powell, J., dissenting)), it fails to recognize the broad yet specific areas of sovereignty that the Framers intended the States to retain. [The] Court's view of federalism appears to relegate the States to precisely the trivial role that opponents of the Constitution feared they would occupy.

In *National League of Cities*, we spoke of the fire prevention, police protection, sanitation, and public health as "typical of [the services] performed by state and local governments in discharging their dual functions of administering the public law and furnishing public services." Not only are these activities remote from any normal concept of interstate commerce, they are also activities that epitomize the concerns of local, democratic self-government. In emphasizing the need to protect traditional governmental functions, we identified the kinds of activities engaged in by state and local governments that affect the everyday lives of citizens. These are services that people are in a position to understand and evaluate, and in a democracy, have the right to oversee.[18] We recognized that "it is functions such as these which governments are created to provide. . . ." and that the states

18. The Framers recognized that the most effective democracy occurs at local levels of government, where people with first hand knowledge of local problems have more ready access to public officials responsible for dealing with them. E.g., The Federalist No. 17; No. 45. This is as true today as it was when the Constitution was adopted. "Participation is likely to be more frequent, and exercised at more different stages of a governmental activity at the local level, or in regional organizations, than at the state and federal levels. [Additionally,] the proportion of people actually involved from the total population tends to be greater, the lower the level of government, and this, of course, better approximates the citizen participation ideal." ACIR, Citizen Participation in the American Federal System 95 (1979).

Moreover, we have witnessed in recent years the rise of numerous special interest groups that engage in sophisticated lobbying, and make substantial campaign contributions to some members of Congress. These groups are thought to have significant influence in the shaping and enactment of certain types of legislation. Contrary to the Court's view, a "political process" that functions in this way is unlikely to safeguard the sovereign rights of States and localities.

and local governments are better able than the national government to perform them.

The Court maintains that the standard approved in *National League of Cities* "disserves principles of democratic self government." In reaching this conclusion, the Court looks myopically only to persons elected to positions in the federal government. It disregards entirely the far more effective role of democratic self-government at the state and local levels. One must compare realistically the operation of the state and local governments with that of the federal government. Federal legislation is drafted primarily by the staffs of the congressional committees. In view of the hundreds of bills introduced at each session of Congress and the complexity of many of them, it is virtually impossible for even the most conscientious legislators to be truly familiar with many of the statutes enacted. Federal departments and agencies customarily are authorized to write regulations. Often these are more important than the text of the statutes. As is true of the original legislation, these are drafted largely by staff personnel. The administration and enforcement of federal laws and regulations necessarily are largely in the hands of staff and civil service employees. These employees may have little or no knowledge of the States and localities that will be affected by the statutes and regulations for which they are responsible. In any case, they hardly are as accessible and responsive as those who occupy analogous positions in State and local governments.

In drawing this contrast, I imply no criticism of these federal employees or the officials who are ultimately in charge. The great majority are conscientious and faithful to their duties. My point is simply that members of the immense federal bureaucracy are not elected, know less about the services traditionally rendered by States and localities, and are inevitably less responsive to recipients of such services, than are state legislatures, city councils, boards of supervisors, and state and local commissions, boards, and agencies. It is at these state and local levels — not in Washington as the Court so mistakenly thinks — that "democratic self-government" is best exemplified.

IV

The question presented in this case is whether the extension of the FLSA to the wages and hours of employees of a city-owned transit system unconstitutionally impinges on fundamental state sovereignty. . . .

I return now to the balancing test approved in *National League of Cities*. [The] state interest is compelling. The financial impact on States and localities of displacing their control over wages, hours, overtime regulations, pensions, and labor relations with their employees could have serious, as well as unanticipated, effects on state and local planning, budgeting, and the levying of taxes. . . .

The Court emphasizes that municipal operation of an intracity mass transit system is relatively new in the life of our country. It nevertheless is a classic example of the type of service traditionally provided by local government. It is *local* by definition. It is indistinguishable in principle from the traditional services of providing and maintaining streets, public lighting, traffic control, water, and sewerage systems. Services of this kind are precisely those "with which citizens are more 'familiarly and minutely conversant.' " The Federalist, No. 46. State and local officials of course must be intimately familiar with these services and sensitive to their quality as well as cost. Such officials also know that their constituents and the press respond to the adequacy, fair distribution, and cost of these services. It is this kind of state and local control and accountability that the Framers understood would insure the vitality and preservation of the federal system that the Constitution explicitly requires. . . .

JUSTICE REHNQUIST, dissenting. . . .

Justice Powell's reference to the "balancing test" approved in *National League of Cities* is not identical with the language in that case, which recognized that Congress could not act under its commerce power to infringe on certain fundamental aspects of state sovereignty that are essential to "the States' separate and independent existence." Nor is either test, or Justice O'Connor's suggested approach, precisely congruent with Justice Blackmun's views in 1976, when he spoke of a balancing approach which did not outlaw federal power in areas "where the federal interest is demonstrably greater." But under any one of these approaches the judgment in this case should be affirmed, and I do not think it incumbent on those of us in dissent to spell out further the fine points of a principle that will, I am confident, in time again command the support of a majority of this Court.

JUSTICE O'CONNOR, with whom JUSTICE POWELL and JUSTICE REHNQUIST join, dissenting. . . .

In my view, federalism cannot be reduced to the weak "essence" distilled by the majority today. There is more to federalism than the nature of the constraints that can be imposed on the States in "the realm of authority left open to them by the Constitution." The central issue of federalism, of course, is whether any realm *is* left open to the States by the Constitution — whether any area remains in which a State may act free of federal interference. "The issue . . . is whether the federal system has any *legal* substance, any core of constitutional right that courts will enforce." C. Black, Perspectives in Constitutional Law 30 (1963). The true "essence" of federalism is that the States *as States* have legitimate interests which the National Government is bound to respect even though its laws are supreme. If federalism so conceived and so carefully cultivated by the Framers of our Constitution is to remain meaningful, this Court cannot abdicate its constitutional responsibility to oversee the Federal Government's compliance with its duty to respect the legitimate interests of the States.

Due to the emergence of an integrated and industrialized national economy, this Court has been required to examine and review a breathtaking expansion of the powers of Congress. In doing so the Court correctly perceived that the Framers of our Constitution intended Congress to have sufficient power to address national problems. But the Framers were not single-minded. The Constitution is animated by an array of intentions. Just as surely as the Framers envisioned a National Government capable of solving national problems, they also envisioned a republic whose vitality was assured by the diffusion of power not only among the branches of the Federal Government, but also between the Federal Government and the States. In the 18th century these intentions did not conflict because technology had not yet converted every local problem into a national one. A conflict has now emerged, and the Court today retreats rather than reconcile the Constitution's dual concerns for federalism and an effective commerce power. . . .

[The] Framers perceived the interstate commerce power to be important but limited, and expected that it would be used primarily if not exclusively to remove interstate tariffs and to regulate maritime affairs and large-scale mercantile enterprise. This perception of a narrow commerce power is important not because it suggests that the commerce power should be as narrowly construed today. Rather, it explains why the Framers could believe the Constitution assured significant state authority even as it bestowed a range of powers, including the commerce power, on the Congress. In an era when interstate commerce represented a tiny fraction of economic activity and most goods and services were produced and consumed close to home, the interstate commerce power left a broad range of activities beyond the reach of Congress.

In the decades since ratification of the Constitution, interstate economic activity has steadily expanded. . . .

Incidental to this expansion of the commerce power, Congress has been given an ability it lacked prior to the emergence of an integrated national economy. Because virtually every *state* activity, like virtually every activity of a private individual, arguably "affects" interstate commerce, Congress can now supplant the States from the significant sphere of activities envisioned for them by the Framers. It is in this context that recent changes in the workings of Congress, such as the direct election of Senators and the expanded influence of national interest groups, become relevant. These changes may well have lessened the weight Congress gives to the legitimate interests of States as States. As a result, there is now a real risk that Congress will gradually erase the diffusion of power between state and nation on which the Framers based their faith in the efficiency and vitality of our Republic. . . .

It is not enough that the "end be legitimate"; the means to that end chosen by Congress must not contravene the spirit of the Constitution. Thus many of this Court's decisions acknowledge that the means by which national power is exercised must take into account concerns for state autonomy. [The] operative language of these cases varies, but the underlying principle is consistent: state autonomy is a relevant factor in assessing the means by which Congress exercises its powers.

This principle requires the Court to enforce affirmative limits on federal regulation of the States to complement the judicially crafted expansion of the interstate commerce power. National League of Cities v. Usery represented an attempt to define such limits. . . .

[With] the abandonment of *National League of Cities*, all that stands between the remaining essentials of state sovereignty and Congress is the latter's underdeveloped capacity for self-restraint.

The problems of federalism in an integrated national economy are capable of more responsible resolution than holding that the States as States retain no status apart from that which Congress chooses to let them retain. The proper resolution, I suggest, lies in weighing state autonomy as a factor in the balance when interpreting the means by which Congress can exercise its authority on the States as States. It is insufficient, in assessing the validity of congressional regulation of a State pursuant to the commerce power, to ask only whether the same regulation would be valid if enforced against a private party. That reasoning, embodied in the majority opinion, is inconsistent with the spirit of our Constitution. It remains relevant that a *State* is being regulated, as *National League of Cities* and every recent case have recognized. As far as the Constitution is concerned, a State should not be equated with any private litigant. Instead, the autonomy of a State is an essential component of federalism. If state autonomy is ignored in assessing the means by which Congress regulates matters affecting commerce, then federalism becomes irrelevant simply because the set of activities remaining beyond the reach of such a commerce power "may well be negligible."

It has been difficult for this Court to craft bright lines defining the scope of the state autonomy protected by *National League of Cities*. Such difficulty is to be expected whenever constitutional concerns as important as federalism and the effectiveness of the commerce power come into conflict. Regardless of the difficulty, it is and will remain the duty of this Court to reconcile these concerns in the final instance. That the Court shuns the task today by appealing to the "essence of federalism" can provide scant comfort to those who believe our federal system requires something more than a unitary, centralized government. I would not shirk the duty acknowledged by *National League of Cities* and its progeny, and I share JUSTICE REHNQUIST's belief that this Court will in time again assume its constitutional responsibility.

Note: *From* National League of Cities *to* Garcia *and Beyond*

1. *The background. Garcia* states the holding and the test in *National League of Cities*, and recites the test used in *Hodel*, which upheld the constitutionality of a federal statute regulating the operation of strip mines. The statute required strip-mine operators to return the area to its "approximate original contour," which substantially increased the cost of operating certain strip mines. The Court held that this did not affect "State as States." The lower court had held that the federal statute interfered with the "traditional governmental function" of land use regulation. From the states' point of view, why should it matter that a federal regulation affects them directly, rather than by increasing the operating costs of locally important industries? Consider that some private activities, because they are taxable by the States, may be more important to the states than is the power to set the wages and hours of state employees.

United Transportation Union v. Long Island Railroad, 455 U.S. 678 (1982), upheld the constitutionality of applying the Railway Labor Act's collective bargaining provisions to the state-owned Long Island Rail Road. The state had operated the line for thirteen years before challenging the act's applicability. The Court said that the *League of Cities* test "was not meant to impose a static historical view of state functions." Consider the proposition that maintaining the railroad was as essential to the infrastructure of economic and social activities in New York as is setting wages and hours of state employees.

Federal Energy Regulatory Commission v. Mississippi, 456 U.S. 742 (1982), upheld by votes of 5 to 4 and 6 to 3 certain provisions of the Public Utilities Regulatory Policies Act (PURPA) of 1978. PURPA requires state utilities commissions to consider a specified list of approaches to structuring rates and to consider adopting standards regarding rate disclosure and the recovery of advertising costs in rates. It requires the commissions to consider these standards at public hearings and to issue written statements if the standards are not adopted. PURPA also authorizes the Federal Energy Regulatory Commission to adopt rules encouraging small power production facilities. These rules would be enforced by the state commissions. The Court held that the state commissions could be required to enforce federal standards, relying on Testa v. Katt, 330 U.S. 386 (1947). It upheld the mandatory consideration requirement on the ground that Congress, having the power to preempt state regulation entirely, could adopt the less instrusive scheme of PURPA. Justice O'Connor's dissent argued that the mandatory consideration provisions displaced the essential attribute that sovereign governments have of setting their own agendas for public policy.

EEOC v. Wyoming, 460 U.S. 226 (1983), upheld by a 5 to 4 vote the application of the Age Discrimination in Employment Act to state employees. The Court found that the act did not impair states' abilities to structure their integral operations to a degree making the act unconstitutional. The act allows employees to be discharged for cause and authorizes mandatory retirement policies that are shown to be bona fide occupational qualifications. The costs of eliminating mandatory retirement policies were said to be neither "direct" nor "obvious."

Between *National League of Cities* and *Garcia*, the Court had not found a federal statute unconstitutional under the *League of Cities/Hodel* test. Does this show the adequacy of that test, or its failure?

2. *The issue(s) in* Garcia. Justice Powell devotes a section of his dissent to the argument that federalism serves important values. Does the majority necessarily disagree? Isn't the real dispute over how the values of federalism are to be protected? (a) Is Justice Powell's quotation from *Marbury* apposite? Could the Court reply that it has performed its "duty" by determining that the Constitution requires federalism issues to be decided by Congress alone? Is that compatible with the premises of the constitutional scheme? See also United States v. Nixon, Chapter 4, section D, infra. (b) Does Justice Powell describe the national political process more accurately than the Court does? The state and local political process?

3. *The implications of* Garcia. The Court argues that the *League of Cities/Hodel* test turned out to be a failure. Note that Justice Rehnquist, the author of *League of Cities,* appears not to accept the test(s) offered by Justices Powell and O'Connor. What then is the "principle" that he believes will again gain the Court's endorsement? Are the tests offered by the other dissenters likely to be satisfactory?

a. Justice Powell advocates the use of a balancing test. Did Congress balance national interests against state ones in 1974 when it extended the Fair Labor Standards Act to state and local governments? In 1978 when it enacted PURPA? Can the Court more effectively balance the interests?

b. Justice O'Connor says that the impact on states is a "relevant consideration" in assessing a statute's constitutionality. How is that test to be applied?

c. The dissenters suggest that the Court will eventually return to the effort to develop judicially enforced federalist limitations on Congress's power. What doctrinal forms might such a return take? Consider the proposition that the doctrine should focus not on protecting attributes of sovereignty but on insulating private activities from federal regulation, on the ground that the most important functions of states involve sheltering private actors from uniform national regulation. What does the period from *National League of Cities* to *Garcia* suggest about the viability of a return to the effort abandoned in *Garcia?*

4. *Did* League of Cities *make sense?* Most of the commentary on the *League of Cities* line of cases was highly critical. See, e.g., Barber, *National League of Cities v. Usery:* New Meaning for the Tenth Amendment, 1976 Sup. Ct. Rev. 161; Alfange, Congressional Regulation of the "States Qua States": From *National League of Cities* to *EEOC v. Wyoming,* 1983 Sup. Ct. Rev. 215. Some authors suggested that, notwithstanding difficulties with the Court's doctrinal formulations, it was engaged in a valuable enterprise.

a. P. Bobbitt, Constitutional Fate 191–195 (1982), describes *National League of Cities* as a "cue" to Congress that its members must "[judge] their own actions to see if they conform to the limits and restraints placed on them by the Constitution." Did Congress need such a reminder in 1974 or 1976? In 1985? Consider whether Congress today is likely to enact legislation without seriously considering whether its impact on state and local governments is justified by overriding national interests. Note that under Bobbitt's theory, *National League of Cities* will have served its function so long as Congress remembers what its duties are.

b. Nagel, Federalism as a Fundamental Value: *National League of Cities* in Perspective, 1981 Sup. Ct. Rev. 81, argues that the courts should enforce federalism-based limits on Congress's power to assure that the value inherent in federalism of promoting self-government will not be undermined. Which, if any, of the statutes at issue in the cases from *National League of Cities* to *Garcia* threatened the values of self-government? Were the threats, if any, justified by other values?

5. *Concluding observations.* Over its history the Court has sporadically attempted to enforce federalism-based limitations on Congress's power. It has repeatedly abandoned those efforts after a time, only to revive them a while later. What accounts for this pattern? Consider the proposition that the Court has from time to time forgotten what the Constitution means. But did it forget during the periods of enforcement or of nonenforcement of such limits?

Note: Intergovernmental Tax Immunities

Garcia establishes that states cannot claim that the Constitution protects them from congressional exercises of the power to regulate interstate commerce. McCulloch v. Maryland, Chapter 1 supra, stated that "the power to tax is the power to destroy" and held unconstitutional a state tax imposed on a federal instrumentality. Dobbins v. Erie County, 41 U.S. (16 Pet.) 435 (1842), held unconstitutional a local tax on the income of a federal employee. Collector v. Day, 78 U.S. (11 Wall.) 113 (1871), held that Congress could not impose a tax on the income of a state judge. These decisions created a system of reciprocal intergovernmental tax immunities designed to assure that each government would be able to exercise its proper powers through its own employees. Helvering v. Gerhardt, 304 U.S. 405 (1938), and Graves v. O'Keefe, 306 U.S. 466 (1939), overruled these cases and held that employees of one government were not immune from taxes imposed by the other.

Are the governments themselves immune from taxation? A divided Court upheld the imposition of a federal tax on mineral waters bottled and sold by the state of New York, but there was no majority opinion. New York v. United States, 326 U.S. 572 (1946). May taxes be distinguished from regulation in a way that leaves this issue open after *Garcia?*

May states tax the activities of the federal government? The Court summarized a complex body of law in United States v. New Mexico, 455 U.S. 720 (1982). A state may not "directly" tax the United States. But it does not necessarily do so "simply because the tax has an effect on the United States, or even because the Federal Government shoulders the entire economic burden of the levy." Nor does the immunity arise "simply because the state tax falls on the earnings of a contractor providing services to the Government [or] simply because the State is levying [a] tax on the use of federal property in private hands, even if the private entity is using the Government property to provide the United States with goods or services." Immunity "is appropriate [only when] the levy falls on the United States itself, or an agency or instrumentality so closely connected to the Government that the two cannot realistically be viewed as separate entities." What result in *McCulloch* under this test?

The Court regarded this narrow immunity as based on the Constitution. It stated that Congress could "expand" the immunity "beyond its narrow constitutional limits" by enacting appropriate statutes exempting various activities from state taxes. In the Court's view, the political process is "uniquely adapted to accommodating the competing demands" for revenue on the one hand and for effective governmental operations on the other. Could Congress waive the immunity from direct taxation? If so, why should there be a constitutional doctrine of immunity? Is the doctrine asymmetrical? Is it correct to say that Congress may protect the federal government from the states, while no single state may protect itself from the national government? Consider the implications of *Garcia*.

Congress's power to "expand" the immunity converts previously constitutional questions about nondirect taxation into statutory ones. Instead of asking whether the Constitution creates an immunity for the activity or actor involved, courts must ask whether Congress intended to confer an immunity on the activity or actor. Should the courts require an express statement conferring immunity? May they infer that Congress intended to confer an immunity from the importance of the claimant's activities or the economic incidence of the tax? Note that United States v. New Mexico rejected such considerations in the constitutional context. Should they be reinstated in a statutory one?

States may not impose taxes that "discriminate against" the federal government. Memphis Bank & Trust Co. v. Garner, 459 U.S. 392 (1983): A federal statute exempts federal obligations from state taxes other than nondiscriminatory franchise taxes. Tennessee's bank franchise tax was based on a bank's net earnings, defined to include interest on obligations of the federal government and of the other states but not to include interest on Tennessee obligations. The Court held that the tax was discriminatory. It stated that the statute was "principally a restatement of the constitutional rule." What result in *McCulloch* under this branch of the doctrine?

Washington has a sales and use tax. For construction projects the tax is imposed on the landowner, not the contractor, and so is based on labor costs and contractor's markups as well as the cost of materials. The tax cannot be imposed in this form on federal construction projects. (Why not?) Washington therefore enacted a tax on the contractors for materials used in federal construction projects. Even though this tax was applicable only to federal projects, the Court held that it was nondiscriminatory. Because the tax did not include labor costs and markups, it was lower than the tax imposed on equivalent projects done for private parties. Four dissenters argued that the Court's approach would require an analysis of the entire set of state taxes to see if a tax imposed solely on a federal activity was offset by exemptions from other taxes. Washington v. United States, 460 U.S. 536 (1983).

Should different principles be applied where states attempt to regulate rather tax federal activities?

F. OTHER POWERS OF CONGRESS: ARE THEY MORE (OR LESS) PLENARY THAN THE COMMERCE POWER?

The preceding examination of the history of constitutional doctrine regarding the commerce clause explored the scope of Congress's power under that clause, the dimensions of judicially enforceable limits on that power in the name of federalism, and the justifications for those limits. Many other clauses of the Constitution confer power on Congress. This section examines a number of those other powers. With respect to each of them, consider the following questions, versions of which will be raised throughout: Is the scope of this power broader or narrower than, or the same as, the scope of the commerce power? Do the words of the Constitution provide sufficient guidance to answer that question? Are the political constraints on Congress different with respect to this power, such that the courts should be more (or less) willing to enforce federalism-based limitations on congressional power?

1. The War Power

In Woods v. Cloyd W. Miller Co., 333 U.S. 138 (1948), the Supreme Court upheld the constitutionality of the Housing and Rent Act of 1947. It concluded that "the war power sustains this legislation." Even though the President had declared hostilities terminated on December 31, 1946, before the statute was enacted, "the war power does not necessarily end with the cessation of hostilities." When Congress acted, there was a

deficit in housing which in considerable measure was caused by the heavy demobilization of veterans and by the cessation or reduction in residential construction during the period of hostilities due to the allocation of building materials to military projects. Since the war effort contributed heavily to that deficit, Congress has the power even after the cessation of hostilities to act to control the forces that a short supply of the needed article created. . . .

We recognize the force of the argument that the effects of war under modern conditions may be felt in the economy for years and years, and that if the war power can be used in days of peace to treat all the wounds which war inflicts on our society, it may not only swallow up all other powers of Congress but largely obliterate the Ninth and Tenth Amendments as well. There are no such implications in today's decision. We deal here with the consequences of a housing deficit greatly intensified during the period of hostilities by the war effort. Any power, of course, can be abused. But we cannot assume that Congress is not alert to its constitutional responsibilities. And the question whether the war power has been properly employed in cases such as this is open to judicial inquiry.

The question of the constitutionality of action taken by Congress does not depend on recitals of the power which it undertakes to exercise. Here it is plain from the legislative history that Congress was invoking its war power to cope with a current condition of which the war was a direct and immediate cause. Its judgment on that score is entitled to the respect granted like legislation enacted pursuant to the police power.

Justice Jackson's concurring opinion expressed "misgivings" about "this vague, undefined and indefinable 'war power.'"

No one will question that this power is the most dangerous one to free government in the whole catalogue of powers. It is usually invoked in haste and excitement when calm legislative consideration of constitutional limitation is difficult. It is executed in a time of patriotic fervor that makes moderation unpopular. And, worst of all, it is interpreted by judges under the influence of the same passions and pressures. Always, as in this case, the Government urges hasty decision to forestall some emergency or serve some purposes and pleads that paralysis will result if its claims to power are denied or their confirmation delayed.

Particularly when the war power is invoked to do things to the liberties of people, or to their property or economy that only indirectly affect conduct of the war and do not relate to the management of the war itself, the constitutional basis should be scrutinized with care.

He concluded that "the present state of war [was not] merely technical" and that the statute was constitutional.

What is "the war power" on which the Court relies? There are particular powers related to the waging of war and the management of foreign affairs. Would the analysis or result in *Woods* differ if the Court had asked whether the statute fell within one of those enumerated powers as the grants of power were interpreted in McCulloch v. Maryland?

Congress's exercise of the "war powers" may raise separation of powers issues and individual rights issues. Are the textual sources of separation of powers or individual rights limitations clearer than those of federalism limitations? Justice Jackson suggests that the political constraints on congressional action are loosened in all areas when the war powers are invoked. Is he correct?

2. The Treaty Power

Missouri v. Holland

252 U.S. 416 (1920)

Mr. Justice Holmes delivered the opinion of the court.

This is a bill in equity brought by the State of Missouri to prevent a game warden of the United States from attempting to enforce the Migratory Bird Treaty Act of 1918 and the regulations made by the Secretary of Agriculture in pursuance of the same. The ground of the bill is that the statute is an unconstitutional interference with the rights reserved to the States by the Tenth Amendment, and that the acts of the defendant done and threatened under that authority invade the sovereign right of the State and contravene its will manifested in statutes. . . .

On December 8, 1916, a treaty between the United States and Great Britain was proclaimed by the President. It recited that many species of birds in their annual migrations traversed certain parts of the United States and of Canada, that they were of great value as a source of food and in destroying insects injurious to vegetation, but were in danger of extermination through lack of adequate protection. It therefore provided for specified close seasons and protection in other forms, and agreed that the two powers would take or propose to their law-making bodies the necessary measures for carrying the treaty out. [The act] prohibited the killing, capturing or selling any of the migratory birds included in the terms of the treaty except as permitted by regulations compatible with those terms, to be made by the Secretary of Agriculture. . . .

[It] is not enough to refer to the Tenth Amendment, reserving the powers not delegated to the United States, because by Article II, §2, the power to make treaties is delegated expressly, and by Article VI treaties made under the authority of the United States, along with the Constitution and laws of the United States made in pursuance thereof, are declared the supreme law of the land. If the treaty is valid there can be no dispute about the validity of the statute under Article I, §8, as a necessary and proper means to execute the powers of the Government. . . .

It is said that a treaty cannot be valid if it infringes the Constitution, that there are limits, therefore, to the treaty-making power, and that one such limit is that what an act of Congress could not do unaided, in derogation of the powers reserved to the States, a treaty cannot do. An earlier act of Congress that attempted by itself and not in pursuance of a treaty to regulate the killing of migratory birds within the States had been held bad in the District Court. United States v. Shauver, 214 Fed. Rep. 154. United States v. McCullagh, 221 Fed. Rep. 288. . . .

Whether the two cases cited were decided rightly or not they cannot be accepted as a test of the treaty power. Acts of Congress are the supreme law of the land only when made in pursuance of the Constitution, while treaties are declared to be so when made under the authority of the United States. It is open to question whether the authority of the United States means more than the formal acts prescribed to make the convention. We do not mean to imply that there are no qualifications to the treaty-making power; but they must be ascertained in a different way. It is obvious that there may be matters of the sharpest exigency for the national well being that an act of Congress could not deal with but that a treaty followed by such an act could, and it is not lightly to be assumed that, in matters requiring national action, "a power which must belong to and somewhere reside in every civilized government" is not to be found. [When] we are dealing with words that also are a constituent act, like the Constitution of the United States, we must realize that they have called into life a being the development of which could not have been foreseen completely by the most gifted of its begetters. It was enough for them to realize or to hope that they had created an organism; it has taken a century and has cost their successors much sweat and blood to prove that they created a nation. The case before us must be considered in the light of our whole experience and not merely in that of what was said a hundred years ago. The treaty in question does not contravene any prohibitory words to be found in the Constitution. The only question is whether it is forbidden by some invisible radiation from the general terms of the Tenth Amendment. We must consider what this country has become in deciding what that Amendment has reserved. . . .

Here a national interest of very nearly the first magnitude is involved. It can be protected only by national action in concert with that of another power. The subject matter is only transitorily within the State and has no permanent habitat therein. But for the treaty and the statute there soon might be no birds for any powers to deal with. We see nothing in the Constitution that compels the Government to sit by while a food supply is cut off and the protectors of our forests and our crops are destroyed. It is not sufficient to rely upon the States. The reliance is vain, and were it otherwise, the question is whether the United States is forbidden to act. We are of opinion that the treaty and statute must be upheld.

Decree affirmed.

MR. JUSTICE VAN DEVANTER and MR. JUSTICE PITNEY dissent.

Note: Federalism and the Treaty Power

1. *The scope of* Missouri v. Holland *as applied to federalism.* What is the "different way" that federalism-based limits on the treaty power are to be ascertained? Is it "different" in light of commerce clause doctrine in 1920? Note the reference to the prior statute and its invalidation by the lower courts. "Different" in light of today's commerce clause doctrine?

Can courts determine what are "matters requiring national action" by treaty followed by legislation rather than by legislation alone? How likely is the President to negotiate and the Senate to ratify a treaty on a matter not requiring national action in Holmes's sense?

2. *Self-executing treaties.* What different issues would arise had the treaty been "self-executing," that is, had the treaty as a matter of U.S. law not required implementing legislation in order to impose legally enforceable obligations on Americans? How would the political process differ?

3. *The scope of* Missouri v. Holland *as applied to separation of powers and individual rights.* Does Missouri v. Holland deal only with federalism-based limitations on national power?

a. In the early 1950s a coalition of conservative Republicans and Southern Democrats sponsored the Bricker Amendment, which would have added to the Constitution provisions that stated (1) "a provision of a treaty which conflicts with this Constitution shall not be of any force or effect" and (2) "a treaty shall become effective as internal law [only] through legislation which would be valid in the absence of treaty." Was the first provision necessary in light of Missouri v. Holland? What effects would the second provision have had? The Southern Democrats who supported the Bricker Amendment did so out of concern that provisions of the United Nations Charter and associated treaties would make unlawful aspects of the existing system of race discrimination. In light of *Heart of Atlanta* and *McClung*, supra, would the Bricker Amendment have had any effects in this area? The Bricker Amendment fell short of adoption by the Senate in 1954 by a vote of 60 in favor, 31 opposed.

b. Consider Reid v. Covert, 354 U.S. 1 (1957): Mrs. Covert, a civilian residing with her serviceman husband on a military base in England, was convicted by a military tribunal of killing him. The Supreme Court held that a civilian in her position could not be tried in the military courts. The plurality emphasized that all of Congress's powers, including its power to regulate the armed forces, were limited by the bill of rights, including its requirement of trial by jury. The plurality also discussed the effects of treaties and executive agreements on congressional power:

> [No] agreement with a foreign nation can confer power on the Congress, or on any other branch of Government, which is free from the restraints of the Constitution. . . .
>
> [There] is nothing in [the supremacy clause] which intimates that treaties and laws enacted pursuant to them do not have to comply with the provisions of the Constitution. Nor is there anything in the debates which accompanied the drafting and ratification of the Constitution which even suggests such a result. These debates as well as the history that surrounds the adoption of the treaty provision in Article VI make it clear that the reason treaties were not limited to those made in "pursuance" of the Constitution was so that agreements made by the United States under the Articles of Confederation, including the important peace treaties which concluded the Revolutionary War, would remain in effect. It would be manifestly contrary to the objectives of those who created the Constitution, as well as those who were responsible for the Bill of Rights — let alone alien to our entire constitutional history and tradition — to construe Article VI as permitting the United States to exercise power under an international agreement without observing constitutional prohibitions. In effect, such construction would permit amendment of that document in a manner not sanctioned by Article V. The prohibitions of the Constitution were designed to apply to all branches of the National Government and they cannot be nullified by the Executive or by the Executive and the Senate combined. . . .
>
> There is nothing in Missouri v. Holland, 252 U.S. 416, which is contrary to the position taken here. There the Court carefully noted that the treaty involved was not inconsistent with any specific provision of the Constitution. The Court was concerned with the Tenth Amendment which reserves to the States or the people all power not delegated to the National Government. To the extent that the United States can validly make treaties, the people and the States have delegated their power to the National Government and the Tenth Amendment is no barrier.

Does this fairly distinguish Missouri v. Holland? Should such a distinction be made? What implications, if any, does Justice Jackson's analysis in Woods v. Miller have for these questions?

3. The Taxing Power

After Hammer v. Dagenhart, section B supra, Congress enacted the Child Labor Tax Act. The statute required that anyone who employed child labor, defined as it had been in the statute invalidated in *Hammer*, pay an excise tax equivalent to 10 per cent of the entire net profits of the mine or factory. In Bailey v. Drexel Furniture Co., 259 U.S. 20 (1922), the Supreme Court held the act unconstitutional. It posed the issue in this way: "Does this law impose a tax with only that incidental restraint and regulation which a tax must inevitably involve? Or does it regulate by the use of the so-called tax as a penalty?" The "detailed and specified course of conduct in business" set out in the act demonstrated its purpose, as did provisions authorizing inspection of factories and mines by the Department of Labor, "whose normal function is the advancement and protection of the welfare of workers." In the light of these features of the act, a court must be blind not to see that the so-called tax is imposed to stop the employment of children within the age limits prescribed. Its prohibitory and regulatory effect and purpose are palpable. All others can see and understand this. How can we properly shut our minds to it?"

The Court continued:

> [The] good sought in unconstitutional legislation is an insidious feature because it leads citizens and legislators of good purpose to promote it without thought of the serious breach it will make in the ark of our covenant or the harm which will come from breaking down recognized standards. In the maintenance of local self government, on the one hand, and the national power, on the other, our country has been able to endure and prosper for near a century and a half.
>
> Out of a proper respect for the acts of a coordinate branch of the Government, this court has gone far to sustain taxing acts as such, even though there has been ground for suspecting from the weight of the tax it was intended to destroy its subject. But, in the act before us, the presumption of validity cannot prevail, because the proof of the contrary is found on the very face of its provisions. Grant the validity of this law, and all that Congress would need to do, hereafter, in seeking to take over to its control any one of the great number of subjects of public interest, jurisdiction of which the States have never parted with, and which are reserved to them by the Tenth Amendment, would be to enact a detailed measure of complete regulation of the subject and enforce it by a so-called tax upon departures from it. To give such magic to the word "tax" would be to break down all constitutional limitation of the powers of Congress and completely wipe out the sovereignty of the States.
>
> The difference between a tax and a penalty is sometimes difficult to define and yet the consequences of the distinction in the required method of their collection often are important. Where the sovereign enacting the law has power to impose both tax and penalty the difference between revenue production and mere regulation may be immaterial, but not so when one sovereign can impose a tax only, and the power of regulation rests in another. Taxes are occasionally imposed in the discretion of the legislature on proper subjects with the primary motive of obtaining revenue from them and with the incidental motive of discouraging them by making their continuance onerous. They do not lose their character as taxes because of the incidental motive. But there comes a time in the extension of the penalizing features of the so-called tax when it loses its character as such and becomes a mere penalty with the characteristics of regulation and punishment. Such is the case in the law before us. Although Congress does not invalidate the contract of employment or expressly declare that the employment within the mentioned ages is illegal, it does exhibit its intent practically to achieve the latter result by adopting the criteria of wrongdoing and imposing its principal consequence on those who transgress its standard.

Is the distinction between a penalty and a tax cogent? Does it turn on Congress's motive? Recall the discussion of motive in *Darby* and *Heart of Atlanta*, and consider whether distinctions between the commerce power and the taxing power make it easier to determine motive with respect to the use of the taxing power. Is there any other difference between the tax and commerce powers that makes the "pretext" analysis more cogent? Recall that a "pretext" analysis requires a prior determination of the proper purposes for which a power may be exercised. Are the purposes of the power to tax more clearly defined than those of the power to regulate interstate commerce? Note that many taxes serve both revenue-raising and regulatory purposes. Is it helpful to say that taxes must raise nontrivial amounts of revenue even if they have a substantial regulatory effect? Rejecting a challenge to the federal occupational tax levied on people in the business of accepting bets, in United States v. Kahriger, 345 U.S. 22 (1953), the Court listed cases in which it had upheld taxes on colored oleomargarine, McCray v. United States, 195 U.S. 27 (1904), on narcotics, United States v. Doremus, discussed below, and on firearms, Sonzinsky v. United States, 300 U.S. 506 (1937). A footnote added:

> One of the indicia which appellee offers to support his contention that the wagering tax is not a proper revenue measure is that the tax amount collected under it was $4,371,869, as compared with an expected amount of $400,000,000 a year. The figure of $4,371,869, however, is relatively large when it is compared with the $3,501 collected under the tax on adulterated and process or renovated butter and filled cheese, the $914,910 collected under the tax on narcotics, including marihuana and special taxes, and the $28,911 collected under the tax on firearms, transfer and occupational taxes.

(The Court later held that the occupational tax violated the self-incrimination clause of the fifth amendment. Marchetti v. United States, 390 U.S. 39 (1968).)

Does the distinction between a penalty and a tax turn on "detail[ing a] specified course of conduct"? Why isn't that just a description of the activity subject to tax? Does the distinction turn on the presence of a complex enforcement scheme? In *Kahriger* the statute required the tax collector to furnish copies of a list of those who paid the wagering tax to state law enforcement officials.

Consider the discussion in Bailey v. Drexel of United States v. Doremus, 249 U.S. 86 (1919):

> [*Doremus*] involved the validity of the Narcotic Drug Act, which imposed a special tax on the manufacture, importation and sale or gift of opium or coca leaves or their compounds or derivatives. It required every person subject to the special tax to register with the Collector of Internal Revenue his name and place of business and forbade him to sell except upon the written order of the person to whom the sale was made on a form prescribed by the Commissioner of Internal Revenue. The vendor was required to keep the order for two years, and the purchaser to keep a duplicate for the same time and both were to be subject to official inspection. Similar requirements were made as to sales upon prescriptions of a physician and as to the dispensing of such drugs directly to a patient by a physician. The validity of a special tax in the nature of an excise tax on the manufacture, importation and sale of such drugs was, of course, unquestioned. The provisions for subjecting the sale and distribution of the drugs to official supervision and inspection were held to have a reasonable relation to the enforcement of the tax and were therefore held valid.
>
> The court [in *Doremus*] said that the act could not be declared invalid just because another motive than taxation, not shown on the face of the act, might have contributed to its passage. This case does not militate against the conclusion we have reached in respect of the law now before us. The court, there, made manifest its view that the provisions of the so-called taxing act must be naturally and reasonably

adapted to the collection of the tax and not solely to the achievement of some other purpose plainly within state power.

Are you persuaded that *Doremus* is distinguishable from Bailey v. Drexel?

In light of these materials, can you conclude that federalism-based limitations on the use of the taxing power are more substantial than those on the use of the commerce power?

4. *The Spending Power*

United States v. Butler

297 U.S. 1 (1936)

[The Agricultural Adjustment Act of 1933 was designed to stabilize production in agriculture by assuring farmers that their products would be sold at a fair price. The act imposed a tax on processors of agricultural commodities such as cotton. The proceeds of the tax were to be used to subsidize farmers who agreed to restrict their production. The Court, in an opinion by Justice Roberts, held that the act was beyond Congress's powers. The tax was an integral part of the acreage reduction system and, the Court held, that system was not a valid exercise of Congress's power to spend for the general welfare.]

There should be no misunderstanding as to the function of this court in such a case. It is sometimes said that the court assumes a power to overrule or control the action of the people's representatives. This is a misconception. The Constitution is the supreme law of the land ordained and established by the people. All legislation must conform to the principles it lays down. When an act of Congress is appropriately challenged in the courts as not conforming to the constitutional mandate the judicial branch of the Government has only one duty, — to lay the article of the Constitution which is invoked beside the statute which is challenged and to decide whether the latter squares with the former. All the court does, or can do, is to announce its considered judgment upon the question. The only power it has, if such it may be called, is the power of judgment. This court neither approves nor condemns any legislative policy. Its delicate and difficult office is to ascertain and declare whether the legislation is in accordance with, or in contravention of, the provisions of the Constitution; and, having done that, its duty ends.

The question is not what power the Federal Government ought to have but what powers in fact have been given by the people. It hardly seems necessary to reiterate that ours is a dual form of government; that in every state there are two governments, — the state and the United States. Each State has all governmental powers save such as the people, by their Constitution, have conferred upon the United States, denied to the States, or reserved to themselves. The federal union is a government of delegated powers. It has only such as are expressly conferred upon it and such as are reasonably to be implied from those granted. . . .

The clause thought to authorize the legislation [confers] upon the Congress power "to lay and collect Taxes, Duties, Imposts and Excises, to pay the Debts and provide for the common Defence and general Welfare of the United

States. . . ." It is not contended that this provision grants power to regulate agricultural production upon the theory that such legislation would promote the general welfare. The Government concedes that the phrase "to provide for the general welfare" qualifies the power "to lay and collect taxes." The view that the clause grants power to provide for the general welfare, independently of the taxing power, has never been authoritatively accepted. Mr. Justice Story points out that if it were adopted "it is obvious that under color of the generality of the words, to 'provide for the common defence and general welfare,' the government of the United States is, in reality, a government of general and unlimited powers, notwithstanding the subsequent enumeration of specific powers." The true construction undoubtedly is that the only thing granted is the power to tax for the purpose of providing funds for payment of the nation's debts and making provision for the general welfare.

Nevertheless the Government asserts that warrant is found in this clause for the adoption of the Agricultural Adjustment Act. The argument is that Congress may appropriate and authorize the spending of moneys for the "general welfare"; that the phrase should be liberally construed to cover anything conducive to national welfare; that decision as to what will promote such welfare rests with Congress alone, and the courts may not review its determination; and finally that the appropriation under attack was in fact for the general welfare of the United States. . . .

Since the foundation of the Nation sharp differences of opinion have persisted as to the true interpretation of the phrase. Madison asserted it amounted to no more than a reference to the other powers enumerated in the subsequent clauses of the same section; that, as the United States is a government of limited and enumerated powers, the grant of power to tax and spend for the general national welfare must be confined to the enumerated legislative fields committed to the Congress. In this view the phrase is mere tautology, for taxation and appropriation are or may be necessary incidents of the exercise of any of the enumerated legislative powers. Hamilton, on the other hand, maintained the clause confers a power separate and distinct from those later enumerated, is not restricted in meaning by the grant of them, and Congress consequently has a substantive power to tax and to appropriate, limited only by the requirement that it shall be exercised to provide for the general welfare of the United States. [We] conclude that the reading advocated by [Hamilton] is the correct one. While, therefore, the power to tax is not unlimited, its confines are set in the clause which confers it, and not in those of §8 which bestow and define the legislative powers of the Congress. It results that the power of Congress to authorize expenditure of public moneys for public purposes is not limited by the direct grants of legislative power found in the Constitution.

But the adoption of the broader construction leaves the power to spend subject to limitations. . . .

We are not now required to ascertain the scope of the phrase "general welfare of the United States" or to determine whether an appropriation in aid of agriculture falls within it. Wholly apart from that question, another principle embedded in our Constitution prohibits the enforcement of the Agricultural Adjustment Act. The act invades the reserved rights of the states. It is a statutory plan to regulate and control agricultural production, a matter beyond the powers delegated to the federal government. The tax, the appropriation of the funds raised, and the direction for their disbursement, are but parts of the plan. They are but means to an unconstitutional end. . . .

[If] the taxing power may not be used as the instrument to enforce a regulation of matters of state concern with respect to which the Congress has no authority to interfere, may it, as in the present case, be employed to raise the money necessary to purchase a compliance which the Congress is powerless to command? The Government asserts that whatever might be said against the validity of the plan if compulsory, it is constitutionally sound because the end is accomplished by voluntary co-operation. There are two sufficient answers to the contention. The regulation is not in fact voluntary. The farmer, of course, may refuse to comply, but the price of such refusal is the loss of benefits. The amount offered is intended to be sufficient to exert pressure on him to agree to the proposed regulation. The power to confer or withhold unlimited benefits is the power to coerce or destroy. If the cotton grower elects not to accept the benefits, he will receive less for his crops; those who receive payments will be able to undersell him. The result may well be financial ruin. . . .

But if the plan were one for purely voluntary co-operation it would stand no better so far as the federal power is concerned. At best it is a scheme for purchasing with federal funds submission to federal regulation of a subject reserved to the states.

It is said that Congress has the undoubted right to appropriate money to executive officers for expenditure under contracts between the government and individuals; that much of the total expenditures is so made. But appropriations and expenditures under contracts for proper governmental purposes cannot justify contracts which are not within federal power. And contracts for the reduction of acreage and the control of production are outside the range of that power. An appropriation to be expended by the United States under contracts calling for violation of a state law clearly would offend the Constitution. Is a statute less objectionable which authorizes expenditure of federal moneys to induce action in a field in which the United States has no power to intermeddle? The Congress cannot invade state jurisdiction to compel individual action; no more can it purchase such action. . . .

We are not here concerned with a conditional appropriation of money, nor with a provision that if certain conditions are not complied with the appropriation shall no longer be available. By the Agricultural Adjustment Act the amount of the tax is appropriated to be expended only in payment under contracts whereby the parties bind themselves to regulation by the Federal Government. There is an obvious difference between a statute stating the conditions upon which moneys shall be expended and one effective only upon assumption of a contractual obligation to submit to a regulation which otherwise could not be enforced. Many examples pointing the distinction might be cited. We are referred to appropriations in aid of education, and it is said that no one has doubted the power of Congress to stipulate the sort of education for which money shall be expended. But an appropriation to an educational institution which by its terms is to become available only if the beneficiary enters into a contract to teach doctrines subversive of the Constitution is clearly bad. An affirmance of the authority of Congress so to condition the expenditure of an appropriation would tend to nullify all constitutional limitations upon legislative power.

But it is said that there is a wide difference in another respect, between compulsory regulation of the local affairs of a state's citizens and the mere making of a contract relating to their conduct; that, if any state objects, it may declare the contract void and thus prevent those under the state's jurisdiction from complying with its terms. The argument is plainly fallacious. The United States can make the contract only if the federal power to tax and to appropriate reaches the subject matter of the contract. If this does reach the subject matter, its exertion cannot be displaced by state action. To say otherwise is to deny the supremacy of the laws of the United States; to make them subordinate to those of a State. This would reverse the cardinal principle embodied in the Constitution and substitute one which declares that Congress may only effectively legislate as to matters within federal competence when the States do not dissent.

Congress has no power to enforce its commands on the farmer to the ends sought by the Agricultural Adjustment Act. It must follow that it may not indirectly accomplish those ends by taxing and spending to purchase compliance. The Constitution and the entire plan of our government negative any such use of the power to tax and to spend as the act undertakes to authorize. It does not help to declare that local conditions throughout the nation have created a situation of national concern; for this is but to say that whenever there is a widespread similarity of local conditions, Congress may ignore constitutional limitations upon its own powers and usurp those reserved to the states. If, in lieu of compulsory regulation of subjects within the states' reserved jurisdiction, which is prohibited, the Congress could invoke the taxing and spending power as a means to accomplish the same end, clause 1 of §8 of Article I would become the instrument for total subversion of the governmental powers reserved to the individual states.

If the act before us is a proper exercise of the federal taxing power, evidently the regulation of all industry throughout the United States may be accomplished by similar exercises of the same power. It would be possible to exact money from one branch on an industry and pay it to another branch in every field of activity which lies within the province of the states. The mere threat of such a procedure might well induce the surrender of rights and the compliance with federal regulation as the price of continuance in business. A few instances will illustrate the thought.

Let us suppose Congress should determine that the farmer, the miner or some other producer of raw materials is receiving too much for his products, with consequent depression of the processing industry and idleness of its employes. Though, by confession, there is no power vested in Congress to compel by statute a lowering of the prices of the raw material, the same result might be accomplished, if the questioned act be valid, by taxing the producer upon his output and appropriating the proceeds to the processors, either with or without conditions imposed as the consideration for payment of the subsidy.

We have held in [Schechter], that Congress has no power to regulate wages and hours of labor in a local business. If the petitioner is right, this very end may be accomplished by appropriating money to be paid to employers from the federal treasury under contracts whereby they agree to comply with certain standards fixed by federal law or by contract. . . .

Suppose that there are too many garment workers in the large cities; that this results in dislocation of the economic balance. Upon the principle contended for an excise might be laid on the manufacture of all garments manufactured and the proceeds paid to those manufacturers who agree to remove their plants to cities having not more than a hundred thousand population. Thus, through the asserted power of taxation, the federal government, against the will of individual states, might completely redistribute the industrial population.

A possible result of sustaining the claimed federal power would be that every business group which thought itself under-privileged might demand that a tax be laid on its vendors or vendees, the proceeds to be appropriated to the redress of its deficiency of income.

These illustrations are given, not to suggest that any of the purposes mentioned are unworthy, but to demonstrate the scope of the principle for which the Government contends; to test the principle by its applications; to point out that, by the exercise of the asserted power, Congress would, in effect, under the pretext of exercising the taxing power, in reality accomplish prohibited ends. It cannot be said that they envisage improbable legislation. The supposed cases are no more improbable than would the present act have been deemed a few years ago. . . .

[Affirmed.]

MR. JUSTICE STONE, dissenting. . . .

The power of courts to declare a statute unconstitutional is subject to two guiding principles of decision which ought never to be absent from judicial consciousness. One is that courts are concerned only with the power to enact statutes, not with their wisdom. The other is that while unconstitutional exercise of power by the executive and legislative branches of the government is subject to judicial restraint, the only check upon our own exercise of power is our own sense of self-restraint. For the removal of unwise laws from the statute books appeal lies not to the courts but to the ballot and to the processes of democratic government. . . .

As the present depressed state of agriculture is nation wide in its extent and effects, there is no basis for saying that the expenditure of public money in aid of farmers is not within the specifically granted power of Congress to levy taxes to "provide for the . . . general welfare." The opinion of the Court does not declare otherwise. . . .

[In] saying that this method of spending public moneys is an invasion of the reserved powers of the states, the Court does not assert that the expenditure of public funds to promote the general welfare is not a substantive power specifically delegated to the national government, as Hamilton [pronounced] it to be. It does not deny that the expenditure of funds for the benefit of farmers and in aid of a program of curtailment of production of agricultural products, and thus of a supposedly better ordered national economy, is within the specifically granted power. But it is declared that state power is nevertheless infringed by the expenditure of the proceeds of the tax to compensate farmers for the curtailment of their cotton acreage. Although the farmer is placed under no legal compulsion to reduce acreage, it is said that the mere offer of compensation for so doing is a species of economic coercion which operates with the same legal force and effect as though the curtailment were made mandatory by Act of Congress. In any event it is insisted that even though not coercive the expenditure of public funds to induce the recipients to curtail production is itself an infringement of state power, since the federal government cannot invade the domain of the states by the "purchase" of performance of acts which it has no power to compel.

Of the assertion that the payments to farmers are coercive, it is enough to say that no such contention is pressed by the taxpayer, and no such consequences were to be anticipated or appear to have resulted from the administration of the Act. The suggestion of coercion finds no support in the record or in any data showing the actual operation of the Act. Threat of loss, not hope of gain, is the essence of economic coercion. Members of a long depressed industry have undoubtedly been tempted to curtail acreage by the hope of resulting better prices and by the proffered opportunity to obtain needed ready money. . . . .

It is upon the contention that state power is infringed by purchased regulation of agricultural production that chief reliance is placed. It is insisted that, while the Constitution gives to Congress, in specific and unambiguous terms, the power to tax and spend, the power is subject to limitations which do not find their origin in any express provision of the Constitution and to which other expressly delegated powers are not subject.

The Constitution requires that public funds shall be spent for a defined purpose, the promotion of the general welfare. Their expenditure usually involves payment on terms which will insure use by the selected recipients within the limits of the constitutional purpose. Expenditures would fail of their purpose and thus lose their constitutional sanction if the terms of payment were not such that by their influence on the action of the recipients the permitted end would be attained. The power of Congress to spend is inseparable from persuasion to action over which Congress has no legislative control. Congress may not command that the science of agriculture be taught in state universities. But if it would aid the teaching of that science by grants to state institutions, it is appropriate, if not necessary, that the grant be on the condition, incorporated in the Morrill Act, that it be used for the intended purpose. Similarly it would seem to be compliance with the Constitution, not violation of it, for the government to take and the university to give a contract that the grant would be so used. It makes no difference that there is a promise to do an act which the condition is calculated to induce. Condition and promise are alike valid since both are in furtherance of the national purpose for which the money is appropriated. . . . .

The limitation now sanctioned must lead to absurd consequences. The government may give seeds to farmers, but may not condition the gift upon their being planted in places where they are most needed or even planted at all. The government may give money to the unemployed, but may not ask that those who get it shall give labor in return, or even use it to support their families. It may give money to sufferers from earthquake, fire, tornado, pestilence or flood, but may not impose conditions — health precautions designed to prevent the spread of disease, or induce the movement of population to safer or more sanitary areas. All that, because it is purchased regulation infringing state powers, must be left for the states, who are unable or unwilling to supply the necessary relief. [If] the expenditure is for a national public purpose, that purpose will not be thwarted because payment is on condition which will advance that purpose. The action which Congress induces by payments of money to promote the general welfare, but which it does not command or coerce, is but an incident to a specifically granted power, but a permissible means to a legitimate end. If appropriation in aid of a program of curtailment of agricultural production is constitutional, and it is not denied that it is, payment to farmers on condition that they reduce their crop acreage is constitutional. It is not any the less so because the farmer at his own option promises to fulfill the condition.

That the governmental power of the purse is a great one is not now for the first time announced. . . .

The suggestion that it must now be curtailed by judicial fiat because it may be abused by unwise use hardly rises to the dignity of argument. [The] power to tax and spend is not without constitutional restraints. One restriction is that the purpose must be truly national. Another is that it may not be used to coerce action left to state control. Another is the conscience and patriotism of Congress and the Executive. "It must be remembered that legislators are the ultimate guardians of the liberties and welfare of the people in quite as great a degree as the courts." Justice Holmes, in Missouri, Kansas & Texas Ry. Co. v. May, 194 U.S. 267, 270.

A tortured construction of the Constitution is not to be justified by recourse to extreme examples of reckless congressional spending which might occur if courts could not prevent — expenditures which, even if they could be thought to effect any national purpose, would be possible only by action of a legislature lost to all sense of public responsibility. Such suppositions are addressed to the mind accustomed to believe that it is the business of courts to sit in judgment on the wisdom of legislative action. Courts are not the only agency of government that must be assumed to have capacity to govern. Congress and the courts both unhappily may falter or be mistaken in the performance of their constitutional duty. But interpretation of our great charter of government which proceeds on any assumption that the responsibility for the preservation of our institutions is the exclusive concern of any one of the three branches of government, or that it alone can save them from destruction is far more likely, in the long run, "to obliterate the constituent members" of "an indestructible union of indestructible states" than the frank recognition that language, even of a constitution, may mean what it says: that the power to tax and spend includes the power to relieve a nationwide economic maladjustment by conditional gifts of money.

Mr. Justice Brandeis and Mr. Justice Cardozo join in this opinion.

Note: The Spending Power and Dual Federalism

1. *Dual federalism.* Having adopted the Hamiltonian position on the scope of the spending power, is the Court consistent in finding the act unconstitutional? Does Justice Roberts take the position that there are no judicially enforceable *internal* limitations on the spending power — the courts will not determine whether an expenditure promotes the "general welfare" — but that there are judicially enforceable federalism-based *external* limitations on that power? Consider his discussion of the "reserved rights of the states." (Note however Roberts's discussion of the state's power to invalidate the contracts.) If this analytic structure is coherent in the abstract, is it coherently used in *Butler?*

2. Butler's *doctrine.* What if anything is the limitation the Court enforces? That Congress may not use the spending power to do what it may not do under other grants of power? That appears to contradict the adoption of the Hamiltonian position. That Congress may not "coerce" those it wishes to regulate into accepting the regulation, if Congress could not impose the regulation directly? In what sense is there coercion in *Butler?* (This issue is explored in more detail after Steward Machine Co. v. Davis, below.) Notice Roberts's discussion of the plan considered as "one for purely voluntary co-operation."

3. *Political restraints.* What answers does Justice Stone offer to the Court's parade of horribles? He says that "the purpose must be truly national." Could the courts enforce such a restriction in the face of action by the national legislature, by saying that although action was taken, it was not for a truly national purpose? Note Stone's invocation of the legislature's "sense of public responsibility." Does this provide a better answer than Roberts does to the problem posed by the Morrill Act, granting federal aid to state universities on the condition that they teach agriculture? (Does Roberts have any answer to that problem?)

Steward Machine Co. v. Davis

301 U.S. 548 (1937)

[The Supreme Court, in an opinion by Justice Cardozo, upheld the constitutionality of the federal unemployment compensation system. Under that system, an employer paid a tax to the United States Treasury. If the employer also made contributions to a state unemployment fund that had been certified by the Secretary of the Treasury as meeting certain "minimum criteria" designed to assure financial stability and accountability, the employer received a credit of up to 90 per cent against the federal tax. This system, the Court said, did not "[involve] the coercion of the States in contravention of the Tenth Amendment or of restrictions implicit in our federal form of government."]

MR. JUSTICE CARDOZO delivered the opinion of the Court. . . .

[Before] the statute succumbs to an assault[, there] must be a showing [that] the tax and credit in combination are weapons of coercion, destroying or impairing the autonomy of the states. . . .

To draw the line intelligently between duress and inducement there is need to remind ourselves of facts as to the problem of unemployment that are now matters of common knowledge. [Justice Cardozo then recited facts drawn from the government's brief describing the national problem of unemployment. "The fact developed quickly that the states were unable to give the requisite relief."]

In the presence of this urgent need for some remedial expedient, the question is to be answered whether the expedient adopted has overlept the bounds of power. The assailants of the statute say that its dominant end and aim is to drive the state legislatures under the whip of economic pressure into the enactment of unemployment compensation laws at the bidding of the central government. Supporters of the statute say that its operation is not constraint, but the creation of a larger freedom, the states and the nation joining in a coöperative endeavor to avert a common evil. Before Congress acted, unemployment compensation insurance was still, for the most part, a project and no more. Wisconsin was the pioneer. Her statute was adopted in 1931. At times bills for such insurance were introduced elsewhere, but they did not reach the stage of law. In 1935, four states (California, Massachusetts, New Hampshire and New York) passed unemployment laws on the eve of the adoption of the Social Security Act, and two others did likewise after the federal act and later in the year. The statutes differed to some extent in type, but were directed to a common end. In 1936, twenty-eight other states fell in line, and eight more the present year. But if states had been holding back before the passage of the federal law, inaction was not owing, for the most part, to the lack of sympathetic interest. Many held back through alarm lest, in laying such a toll upon their industries, they would place themselves in a position of economic disadvantage as compared with neighbors or competitors. Two consequences ensued. One was that the freedom of a state to contribute its fair share to the solution of a national problem was paralyzed by fear. The other was that in so far as there was failure by the states to contribute relief according to the measure of their capacity, a disproportionate burden, and a mountainous one, was laid upon the resources of the Government of the nation.

The Social Security Act is an attempt to find a method by which all these public agencies may work together to a common end. Every dollar of the new taxes will continue in all likelihood to be used and needed by the nation as long as states are unwilling, whether through timidity or for other motives, to do what can be done at home. At least the inference is permissible that Congress so believed, though retaining undiminished freedom to spend the money as it pleased. On the other hand fulfilment of the home duty will be lightened and encouraged by crediting the taxpayer upon his account with the Treasury of the nation to the extent that his contributions under the laws of the locality have simplified or diminished the problem of relief and the probable demand upon the resources of the fisc. . . .

Who then is coerced through the operation of this statute? Not the taxpayer. He pays in fulfilment of the mandate of the local legislature. Not the state. Even now she does not offer a suggestion that in passing the unemployment law she was affected by duress. For all that appears she is satisfied with her choice, and would be sorely disappointed if it were now to be annulled. The difficulty with the petitioner's contention is that it confuses motive with coercion. "Every tax is in some measure regulatory. To some extent it interposes an economic impediment to the activity taxed as compared with others not taxed." Sonzinsky v. United States. In like manner every rebate from a tax when conditioned upon conduct is in some measure a temptation. But to hold that motive or temptation is equivalent to coercion is to plunge the law in endless difficulties. The outcome of such a doctrine is the acceptance of a philosophical determinism by which choice becomes impossible. Till now the law has been guided by a robust common sense which assumes the freedom of the will as a working hypothesis in the solution of its problems. The wisdom of the hypothesis has illustration in this case. Nothing in the case suggests the exertion of a power akin to undue influence, if we assume that such a concept can ever be applied with fitness to the relations between state and nation. Even on that assumption the location of the point at which pressure turns into compulsion, and ceases to be inducement, would be a question of degree, — at times, perhaps, of fact. The point had not been reached when Alabama made her choice. We cannot say that she was acting not of her unfettered will, but under the strain of a persuasion equivalent to undue influence, when she chose to have relief administered under laws of her own making, by agents of her own selection, instead of our federal laws, administered by federal officers, with all the ensuing evils, at least to many minds, of federal patronage and power. . . .

In ruling as we do, we leave many questions open. We do not say that a tax is valid, when imposed by act of Congress, if it is laid upon the condition that a state may escape its operation through the adoption of a statute unrelated in subject matter to activities fairly within the scope of national policy and power. No such question is before us. In the tender of this credit Congress does not intrude upon fields foreign to its function. The purpose of its intervention, as we have shown, is to safeguard its own treasury and as an incident to that protection to place the states upon a footing of equal opportunity. Drains upon its own resources are to be checked; obstructions to the freedom of the states are to be leveled. It is one thing to impose a tax dependent upon the conduct of the taxpayers, or of the state in which they live, where the conduct to be stimulated or discouraged is unrelated to the fiscal need subserved by the tax in its normal operation, or to any other end legitimately national. [It] is quite another thing to say that a tax will be abated upon the doing of an act that will satisfy the fiscal need, the tax and the alternative being approximate equivalents. In such circumstances, if in no others, inducement or persuasion does not go beyond the bounds of power. We do not fix the outermost line. Enough for present purposes that wherever the line may be, this statute is within it. Definition more precise must abide the wisdom of the future. . . .

[The] statute does not call for a surrender by the states of powers essential to their quasi-sovereign existence.

Argument to the contrary has its source in two sections of the act [defining] the minimum criteria to which a state compensation system is required to conform if it is to be accepted by the Board as the basis for a credit. . . .

A credit to taxpayers for payments made to a State under a state unemployment law will be manifestly futile in the absence of some assurance that the law leading to the credit is in truth what it professes to be. [What] is basic and essential may be assured by suitable conditions. The terms embodied in these sections are directed to that end. A wide range of judgment is given to the several states as to the particular type of statute to be spread upon their books. [What] they may not do, if they would earn the credit, is to depart from those standards which in the judgment of Congress are to be ranked as fundamental. Even if opinion may differ as to the fundamental quality of one or more of the conditions, the difference will not avail to vitiate the statute. In determining essentials Congress must have the benefit of a fair margin of discretion. One cannot say with reason that this margin has been exceeded, or that the basic standards have been determined in any arbitrary fashion. . . .

[Affirmed.]

[JUSTICES McREYNOLDS, SUTHERLAND, VAN DEVANTER, and BUTLER dissented.]

Note: Conditional Spending, Coercion, and the Political Process

1. *Distinguishing* Butler. Is *Steward Machine Co.* consistent with *Butler?* The Court distinguished *Butler* on four grounds: The proceeds of the tax were not "earmarked for a special group"; the system operated in a state only if the state gave its approval; the state could repeal its law "at its pleasure"; and the end, unemployment relief, was one on which "nation and state may lawfully cooperate."

a. Note that the first ground may assert that in *Butler* the Court had found the Agricultural Adjustment Act unconstitutional because it did not promote the "general" welfare. Is that a tenable reading of *Butler?* The best reading?

b. Consider the proposition that the unemployment system is more objectionable than the Agricultural Adjustment Act because the former "coerces" the states directly while the latter does so only indirectly, by allowing contracts between the United States and private parties that have the effect of undermining local policy. Recall however the suggestion in *Butler* that states could invalidate those contracts by enacting appropriate legislation. If that suggestion is correct, can the distinction between direct and indirect coercion of the states be sustained? Note that the states are "coerced" into participating by a provision that affects the taxes paid by private parties, who thus have an incentive to locate in participating states.

c. As the Court adopted broader views of the power granted Congress elsewhere in article I, the differences between the Hamiltonian and the Madisonian views on the scope of the spending power diminished substantially. Does Justice Roberts disagree with the proposition that if Congress can regulate directly under the commerce clause, it can regulate indirectly by granting tax exemptions or subsidies to people who meet specified conditions, under the taxing and spending clause?

2. *Coercion and states' rights.* Why is the state *not* coerced into participating in the unemployment system, by fear of the flight of business to states that have qualifying unemployment systems? In *Butler* Justice Stone said, "Threat of loss, not hope of gain, is the essence of economic coercion." Which one is operating in *Steward Machine Co.?* Suppose someone is entitled to A, happens to have B, and would like to have C as well. That person can be coerced by the threat of loss: "Unless you relinquish A, we will take B away from you." Suppose the offer is, "We'll give you C if you relinquish A, but it's up to you; you decide whether C is more important to you than A." Would Stone have considered that coercion? Is it? Suppose an outside observer would consider both A and C to be quite important. These questions raise deep conceptual issues. For an introduction, see Nozick, Coercion, in Philosophy, Science and Method (S. Morgenbesser ed. 1969); Zimmerman, Coercive Wage Offers, 10 Phil. & Pub. Affairs 121 (1981).

The difficulty of the questions turns on the assumption that the person is entitled to A. Otherwise we can call A "money" and C "goods available for purchase," and the questions reduce to ones about the propriety of a market system for distributing goods. In the present context, the baseline set of "entitlements" held by states would be the set of activities in which the states and not the national government can engage. Note that Justice Cardozo argues that "the statute does not call for a surrender [of] powers essential to their quasi-sovereign existence."

Test your understanding of the foregoing by considering whether Congress could grant financial aid to students on the condition that they not oppose the draft (or — see note 3(b) below — on condition that they not oppose the conduct of military research on their campuses). A full analysis would require a discussion of the free speech dimensions of the problem. See Kreimer, Allocational Sanctions: The Problem of Negative Rights in a Positive State, 132 U. Pa. L. Rev. 1293 (1984).

3. *States' rights limitations on conditional spending.* What limitations does the Court suggest? Is it helpful to say that the issues are ones of degree and fact? What sort of facts?

a. In analyzing the "surrender of essential powers" issue, Justice Cardozo finds that the conditions imposed were within the "margin of discretion" Congress has in determining what standards are "fundamental." What criteria might there be for a judicial determination that the margin had been exceeded, that is, that Congress had adopted arbitrary conditions? How likely is it that Congress would do so? Does it make sense to hold in reserve a doctrine authorizing judicial review for arbitrariness, to remind Congress of its obligations? Recall the discussion of the "cueing" theory after *Garcia*.

b. Does the Court suggest that the conditions imposed be related to the activity receiving the federal subsidy? Note that the Court's precise formulation is "unrelated to the fiscal need [or] to any other end legitimately national." Is the latter anything more than the Madisonian position on the scope of the spending power? Could Congress require that state universities whose students receive federally guaranteed loans (a) not discriminate on the basis of race and gender in their admissions policies; (b) not discriminate on the basis of race and gender in faculty employment; (c) conduct research for federal agencies on the development of nuclear power? Could Congress require that states whose universities have students who receive federally guaranteed loans pay the maintenance personnel at the universities the federal minimum wage? Pay their police and fire officers the federal minimum wage? What would Justice Stone have said about these questions?

4. *Avoiding the race to the bottom.* Note Justice Cardozo's discussion of the impediments to adoption by the states of local unemployment systems. Consider the following argument in support of the national legislation: Every state desires to alleviate the burdens of unemployment by adopting some sort of unemployment system. But any state that does so runs the risk that a neighboring state will not, or will adopt a somewhat different system. If the neighboring state has no unemployment system, or has one financed more favorably to employers, the state that adopts the less favorable system runs the risk that employers will relocate. In order to assure that no risk of "unfair competition" of this sort — sometimes called a "race to the bottom" — can occur, coordinated action on the national level is necessary.

Note the following points about this argument: (a) Mechanisms of voluntary coordination exist, as the Court discussed in Carter v. Carter Coal Co. Recall the discussion of the relative costs and benefits of using those mechanisms rather than using congressional legislation. (b) Can we distinguish between failure of a state legislature to act because it fears unfair competition from a neighboring state and failure to act because it believes that unemployment compensation systems are unsound as a matter of policy? Is it sufficient to answer that that is the kind of judgment we leave to Congress? Suppose both senators and the majority of the representatives from some state voted against the national legislation. How confident can we be that national action was needed to avoid a universally undesired race to the bottom? And if the race is not universally undesired, does the preceding argument retain its force? Even if the senators and representatives from a state favored the legislation, might there be differences between their constituencies and the constituencies of local legislators such that we still could not be confident that the state legislature that failed to enact an unemployment compensation system did so from fear of unfair competition? (c) Note that five states, including New York and California, had adopted unemployment compensation systems before Congress acted. Does that cast doubt on the argument that states failed to act out of fear of unfair competition? Why should those states fear such competition any less than other states did?

In order to control health care costs, the National Health Planning and Resources Development Act of 1974 required each state to enact legislation, conforming to federal standards, requiring the state's health planning agency to approve all major capital development projects by hospitals. If it did not enact such legislation, the state would lose not only the planning funds made available by the act but also federal funds for a variety of public health, mental health, and alcohol abuse services as well. Two years after *National League of Cities*, the Supreme Court summarily affirmed a judgment that the act was constitutional. North Carolina v. Califano, 435 U.S. 962 (1978). Is the act a program of cooperation or coercion?

5. *Statutory interpretation as a limiting technique.* The questions raised above can be avoided by construing ambiguous statutes so as not impose the problematic obligations on the states. Consider in this connection Pennhurst State School & Hospital v. Halderman, 451 U.S. 1 (1981): The court of appeals, after holding that the Developmentally Disabled Assistance and Bill of Rights Act of 1975 "created substantive rights in favor of the mentally retarded," affirmed a decree that required a substantial alteration in, and federal judicial supervision of, the operation of Pennsylvania's major institution for the mentally retarded. The Supreme Court reversed, holding that the act did not create substantive rights. The act "is a federal-state grant program whereby the federal government provides financial assistance to participating states to aid them in creating programs to care for and treat the developmentally disabled. Like other federal-state cooperative programs, the Act is voluntary and the states are given the choice of complying with the conditions set forth in the act or forgoing the benefits of federal funding." Its statement of purposes declares that the act is designed "to assist" the states in treating persons with developmental disabilities. The act imposes

> a variety of conditions for the receipt of federal funds [including that] "as a condition of providing assistance [each] recipient of such assistance take affirmative action" to hire qualified handicapped individuals, [that each state] submit [a] plan to evaluate the services provided under the act [and] "provide [satisfactory] assurances that each program [which] receives funds from the state's allotment [has] in effect for each developmentally disabled person who receives services from or under the program a habilitation plan."

The act also includes a "bill of rights":

> Congress makes the following findings respecting the rights of persons with developmental disabilities:
>
> (1) Persons with developmental disabilities have a right to appropriate treatment, services, and habilitation for such disabilities.
>
> (2) The treatment, services, and habilitation for a person with developmental disabilities should be designed to maximize the developmental potential of the person and should be provided in the setting that is least restrictive of the person's personal liberty.
>
> (3) The Federal Government and the States both have an obligation to assure that public funds are not provided to any institutio[n] . . . that — (A) does not provide treatment, services, and habilitation which is appropriate to the needs of such person; or (B) does not meet the following minimum standards. . . .

Noticeably absent from §6010 is any language suggesting that §6010 is a condition for the receipt of federal funding under the Act.

The Court examined the spending clause as a source of legislative authority and its relation to the question of statutory interpretation:

> [Legislation] enacted pursuant to the spending power is much in the nature of a contract: in return for federal funds, the States agree to comply with federally imposed conditions. The legitimacy of Congress' power to legislate under the spend-

ing power thus rests on whether the State voluntarily and knowingly accepts the terms of the contract. See [*Steward Machine Co*]. There can, of course, be no knowing acceptance if a State is unaware of the conditions or is unable to ascertain what is expected of it. Accordingly, if Congress intends to impose a condition on the grant of federal moneys, it must do so unambiguously. [By] insisting that Congress speak with a clear voice, we enable the States to exercise their choice knowingly, cognizant of the consequences of their participation. . . .

Applying those principles to these cases, we find nothing in the Act or its legislative history to suggest that Congress intended to require the States to assume the high cost of providing "appropriate treatment" in the "least restrictive environment" to their mentally retarded citizens. . . .

[We] are persuaded that §6010 when read in the context of other more specific provisions of the Act, does no more than express a congressional preference for certain kinds of treatment. It is simply a general statement of findings and, as such, is too thin a reed to support the rights and obligations read into it by the court below. The closest one can come in giving §6010 meaning is that it justifies and supports Congress' appropriation of money under the Act and guides the Secretary in his review of state applications for federal funds. . . .

The legislative history buttresses our conclusion that Congress intended to encourage rather than mandate the provisions of better services to the developmentally disabled. . . .

The fact that Congress granted to Pennsylvania only $1.6 million in 1976, a sum woefully inadequate to meet the enormous financial burden of providing appropriate treatment in the "least restrictive" setting, confirms that Congress must have had a limited purpose in enacting §6010. When Congress does impose affirmative obligations on the States, it usually makes a far more substantial contribution to defray costs. It defies common sense, in short, to suppose that Congress implicitly imposed this massive obligation on participating States.

Our conclusion is also buttressed by the rule of statutory construction established above that Congress must express clearly its intent to impose conditions on the grant of federal funds so that the States can knowingly decide whether or not to accept those funds. That canon applies with greatest force where, as here, a State's potential obligations under the Act are largely indeterminate. It is difficult to know what is meant by providing "appropriate treatment" in the "least restrictive" setting, and it is unlikely that a State would have accepted federal funds had it known it would be bound to provide such treatment. The crucial inquiry, however, is not whether a State would knowingly undertake that obligation, but whether Congress spoke so clearly that we can fairly say that the State could make an informed choice. In this case, Congress fell well short of providing clear notice to the States that they, by accepting funds under the Act, would indeed be obligated to comply with §6010. [Though] Congress' power to legislate under the spending power is broad, it does not include surprising participating States with postacceptance or "retroactive" conditions.

A footnote stated, "There are limits on the power of Congress to impose conditions on the States pursuant to its spending power. [*Steward Machine Co.*]; see [*National League of Cities*]."

Justice White, joined by Justices Brennan and Marshall, agreed that the remedial order was inappropriate, but dissented on the question of statutory interpretation:

The language and scheme of the Act make it plain enough to me that Congress intended §6010, although couched in terms of rights, to serve as requirements that the participating States must observe in receiving federal funds under the provisions of the Act. That Congress was deadly serious in stating that the developmentally disabled had entitlements which a State must respect if it were to participate in a program can hardly be doubted. . . .

It is true that the terms [are] not self-defining. But it does not follow that the participating States are free to ignore them. . . .

Why the language of an express "condition" which §6010 lacks, should be the only touchstone for identifying a State's obligation is difficult to fathom. Indeed, identifying "rights" and requiring the participating State to observe them seems a far stronger indicia of congressional intent than a mere statement of "conditions."

To argue that Congress could not have intended to obligate the States under §6010 because those obligations would be large and for the most part unknown is also unpersuasive. [The] content and reach of the federal requirements will, as a practical matter, emerge from the process of preparing a state plan and securing its approval by the Secretary. [There] is no indication in the record before us that the cost of compliance with §6010 would be "massive."

Did constitutional concerns influence the Court's construction of the statute? Should they have? What does the Bill of Rights section of the act accomplish? Does the Court construe it in light of ordinary assumptions about the political process? With respect to Congress's desire to accomplish something by legislating? With respect to federalism?

5. The Power to Enforce the Reconstruction Amendments

Katzenbach v. Morgan

384 U.S. 641 (1966)

[Section 4(e) of the Voting Rights Act of 1965 provides that no person who has completed sixth grade in a Puerto Rican school, where instruction was in Spanish, shall be denied the right to vote because of his or her inability to read or write English. The legislative history made it clear that this provision, sponsored in the Senate by both senators from New York and in the House by a representative from New York, was designed to enfranchise several hundred thousand people who had migrated to New York from Puerto Rico, by overriding a New York statute requiring that voters be literate in English. Section 4(e) was challenged on constitutional grounds. Previously, in Lassiter v. Northampton Election Board, 360 U.S. 45 (1959), the Court had held that an English-language literacy requirement did not violate the substantive guarantees of the fourteenth and fifteenth amendments.]

MR. JUSTICE BRENNAN delivered the opinion of the Court. . . .

[We] hold that, in the application challenged in these cases, §4(e) is a proper exercise of the powers granted to Congress by §5 of the Fourteenth Amendment[5]

---

5. "The Congress shall have power to enforce, by appropriate legislation, the provisions of this article."

It is therefore unnecessary for us to consider whether §4(e) could be sustained as an exercise of power under the Territorial Clause, Art. IV, §3; or as a measure to discharge certain treaty obligations of the United States. Nor need we consider whether §4(e) could be sustained insofar as it relates to the and that by force of the Supremacy Clause, Article VI, the New York English literacy requirement cannot be enforced to the extent that it is inconsistent with §4(e).

Under the distribution of powers effected by the Constitution, the States establish qualifications for voting. [But] of course, the States have no power to grant or withhold the franchise on conditions that are forbidden by the Fourteenth Amendment, or any other provision of the Constitution. Such exercises of state power are no more immune to the limitations of the Fourteenth Amendment than any other state action. The Equal Protection Clause itself has been held to forbid some state laws that restrict the right to vote.

The Attorney General of the State of New York argues that an exercise of congressional power under §5 of the Fourteenth Amendment that prohibits the enforcement of a state law can only be sustained if the judicial branch determines that the state law is prohibited by the provisions of the Amendment that Congress sought to enforce. More specifically, he urges that §4(e) cannot be sustained as appropriate legislation to enforce the Equal Protection Clause unless the judiciary decides — even with the guidance of a congressional judgment — that the application of the English literacy requirement prohibited by §4(e) is forbidden by the Equal Protection Clause itself. We disagree. Neither the language nor history of §5 supports such a construction. As was said with regard to §5 in Ex parte Virginia, 100 U.S. 339, 345, "It is the power of Congress which has been enlarged. Congress is authorized to *enforce* the prohibitions by appropriate legislation. Some legislation is contemplated to make the amendments fully effective." A construction of §5 that would require a judicial determination that the enforcement of the state law precluded by Congress violated the Amendment, as a condition of sustaining the congressional enactment, would depreciate both congressional resourcefulness and congressional responsibility for implementing the Amendment. It would confine the legislative power in this context to the insignificant role of abrogating only those state laws that the judicial branch was prepared to adjudge unconstitutional, or of merely informing the judgment of the judiciary by particularizing the "majestic generalities" of §1 of the Amendment.

Thus our task in this case is not to determine whether the New York English literacy requirement as applied to deny the right to vote to a person who successfully completed the sixth grade in a Puerto Rican school violates the Equal Protection Clause. Accordingly, our decision in *Lassiter* [is] inapposite. *Lassiter* did not present the question before us here: Without regard to whether the judiciary would find that the Equal Protection Clause itself nullifies New York's English literacy requirement as so applied, could Congress prohibit the enforcement of the state law by legislating under §5 of the Fourteenth Amendment? In answering this question, our task is limited to determining whether such legislation is, as required by §5, appropriate legislation to enforce the Equal Protection Clause.

By including §5 the draftsmen sought to grant to Congress, by a specific provision applicable to the Fourteenth Amendment, the same broad powers expressed in the Necessary and Proper Clause Art. I, §8, cl. 18. The classic formulation of

election of federal officers as an exercise of congressional power under Art. I, §4, nor whether §4(e) could be sustained, insofar as it relates to the election of state officers, as an exercise of congressional power to enforce the clause guaranteeing to each State a republican form of government, Art. IV, §4; Art. I, §8, cl. 18.

Court interpreting 14TH AMEND.

the reach of those powers was established by Chief Justice Marshall in McCulloch v. Maryland. . . .

We therefore proceed to the consideration whether §4(e) is "appropriate legislation" to enforce the Equal Protection Clause, that is, under the McCulloch v. Maryland standard, whether §4(e) may be regarded as an enactment to enforce the Equal Protection Clause, whether it is "plainly adapted to that end" and whether it is not prohibited by but is consistent with "the letter and spirit of the constitution."[10]

There can be no doubt that §4(e) may be regarded as an enactment to enforce the Equal Protection Clause. Congress explicitly declared that it enacted §4(e) "to secure the rights under the fourteenth amendment of persons educated in American-flag schools in which the predominant classroom language was other than English." [Section] 4(e) may be viewed as a measure to secure for the Puerto Rican community residing in New York nondiscriminatory treatment by government — both in the imposition of voting qualifications and the provision or administration of governmental services, such as public schools, public housing and law enforcement.

Section 4(e) may be readily seen as "plainly adapted" to furthering these aims of the Equal Protection Clause. The practical effect of §4(e) is to prohibit New York from denying the right to vote to large segments of its Puerto Rican community. Congress has thus prohibited the State from denying to that community the right that is "preservative of all rights." Yick Wo v. Hopkins, 118 U.S. 356, 370. This enhanced political power will be helpful in gaining nondiscriminatory treatment in public services for the entire Puerto Rican community.[11] Section 4(e) thereby enables the Puerto Rican minority better to obtain "perfect equality of civil rights and the equal protection of the laws." It was well within congressional authority to say that this need of the Puerto Rican minority for the vote warranted federal intrusion upon any state interests served by the English literacy requirement. It was for Congress, as the branch that made this judgment, to assess and weigh the various conflicting considerations — the risk or pervasiveness of the discrimination in governmental services, the effectiveness of eliminating the state restriction on the right to vote as a means of dealing with the evil, the adequacy or availability of alternative remedies, and the nature and significance of the state interests that would be affected by the nullification of the English literacy requirement as applied to residents who have successfully completed the sixth grade in a Puerto Rican school. It is not for us to review the congressional resolution of these factors. It is enough that we be able to perceive a basis upon which the Congress might resolve the conflict as it did. There plainly was such a basis to support §4(e) in the application in question in this case. Any contrary conclusion would require us to be blind to the realities familiar to the legislators.

10. Contrary to the suggestion of the dissent, §5 does not grant Congress power to exercise discretion in the other direction and to enact "statutes so as in effect to dilute equal protection and due process decisions of this Court." We emphasize that Congress' power under §5 is limited to adopting measures to enforce the guarantees of the Amendment; §5 grants Congress no power to restrict, abrogate, or dilute these guarantees. Thus, for example, an enactment authorizing the States to establish racially segregated systems of education would not be — as required by §5 — a measure "to enforce" the Equal Protection Clause since that clause of its own force prohibits such state laws.

11. Cf. [the] settled principle applied in the *Shreveport Case* and expressed in [*Darby*], that the power of Congress to regulate interstate commerce "extends to those activities intrastate which so affect interstate commerce or the exercise of the power of Congress over it as to make regulation of then appropriate means to the attainment of a legitimate end. . . ."

The result is no different if we confine our inquiry to the question whether §4(e) was merely legislation aimed at the elimination of an invidious discrimination in establishing voter qualifications. We are told that New York's English literacy requirement originated in the desire to provide an incentive for non-English speaking immigrants to learn the English language and in order to assure the intelligent exercise of the franchise. Yet Congress might well have questioned, in light of the many exemptions provided and some evidence suggesting that prejudice played a prominent role in the enactment of the requirement whether these were actually the interests being served. Congress might have also questioned whether denial of a right deemed so precious and fundamental in our society was a necessary or appropriate means of encouraging persons to learn English, or of furthering the goal of an intelligent exercise of the franchise. Finally, Congress might well have concluded that as a means of furthering the intelligent exercise of the franchise, an ability to read or understand Spanish is as effective as ability to read English for those to whom Spanish-language newspapers and Spanish-language radio and television programs are available to inform them of election issues and governmental affairs. Since Congress undertook to legislate so as to preclude the enforcement of the state law, and did so in the context of a general appraisal of literacy requirements for voting, to which it brought a specially informed legislative competence,[17] it was Congress' prerogative to weigh these competing considerations. Here again, it is enough that we perceive a basis upon which Congress might predicate a judgment that the application of New York's English literacy requirement to deny the right to vote to a person with a sixth grade education in Puerto Rican schools in which the language of instruction was other than English constituted an invidious discrimination in violation of the Equal Protection Clause.

There remains the question whether the congressional remedies adopted in §4(e) constitute means which are not prohibited by, but are consistent "with the letter and spirit of the constitution." The only respect in which appellees contend that §4(e) fails in this regard is that the section itself works an invidious discrimination in violation of the Fifth Amendment by prohibiting the enforcement of the English literacy requirement only for those educated in American-flag schools (schools located within the United States jurisdiction) in which the language of instruction was other than English, and not for those educated in schools beyond the territorial limits of the United States in which the language of instruction was also other than English. [The] argument, in our view, falls on the merits. . . .

We therefore conclude that §4(e), in the application challenged in this case, is appropriate legislation to enforce the Equal Protection Clause and that the judgment of the District Court must be and hereby is reversed.

Mr. Justice Douglas joins the Court's opinion except for the discussion of the question whether the congressional remedies adopted in §4(e) constitute means which are not prohibited by, but are consistent with "the letter and spirit of the constitution." On that question, he reserves judgment until such time as it is

17. See, e.g., 111 Cong. Rec. 11061 (Senator Long of Louisiana and Senator Young), 11064 (Senator Holland), drawing on their experience with voters literate in a language other than English. See also an affidavit from Representative Willis of Louisiana expressing the view that on the basis of his thirty years' personal experience in politics he has "formed a definite opinion that French-speaking voters who are illiterate in English generally have as clear a grasp of the issues and an understanding of the candidates, as do people who read and write the English language."

presented by a member of the class against which that particular discrimination is directed.

MR. JUSTICE HARLAN, whom MR. JUSTICE STEWART joins, dissenting.

Worthy as its purposes may be thought by many, I do not see how §4(e) [can] be sustained except at the sacrifice of fundamentals in the American constitutional system — the separation between the legislative and judicial function and the boundaries between federal and state political authority. . . .

The pivotal question in this instance is what effect the added factor of a congressional enactment has on the straight equal protection argument. [The] Court declares that since §5 of the Fourteenth Amendment gives to the Congress power to "enforce" the prohibitions of the Amendment by "appropriate" legislation, the test for judicial review of any congressional determination in this area is simply one of rationality; that is, in effect, was Congress acting rationally in declaring that the New York statute is irrational? Although §5 most certainly does give to the Congress wide powers in the field of devising remedial legislation to effectuate the Amendment's prohibition on arbitrary state action, Ex parte Virginia, 100 U.S. 339, I believe the Court has confused the issue of how much enforcement power Congress possesses under §5 with the distinct issues of what questions are appropriate for congressional determination and what questions are essentially judicial in nature.

When recognized state violations of federal constitutional standards have occurred, Congress is of course empowered by §5 to take appropriate remedial measures to redress and prevent the wrongs. See Strauder v. West Virginia, 100 U.S. 303, 310. But it is a judicial question whether the condition with which Congress has thus sought to deal is in truth an infringement of the Constitution, something that is the necessary prerequisite to bringing the §5 power into play at all. . . .

Section 4(e), however, presents a significantly different type of congressional enactment. The question here is not whether the statute is appropriate remedial legislation to cure an established violation of a constitutional command, but whether there has in fact been an infringement of that constitutional command, that is whether a particular state practice or, as here, a statute is so arbitrary or irrational as to offend the command of the Equal Protection Clause of the Fourteenth Amendment. That question is one for the judicial branch ultimately to determine. Were the rule otherwise, Congress would be able to qualify this Court's constitutional decisions under the Fourteenth and Fifteenth Amendments, let alone those under other provisions of the Constitution, by resorting to congressional power under the Necessary and Proper Clause. In view of this Court's holding in Lassiter, that an English literacy test is a permissible exercise of state supervision over its franchise, I do not think it is open to Congress to limit the effect of that decision as it has undertaken to do by §4(e). In effect the Court reads §5 of the Fourteenth Amendment as giving Congress the power to define the *substantive* scope of the Amendment. If that indeed be the true reach of §5, then I do not see why Congress should not be able as well to exercise its §5 "discretion" by enacting statutes so as in effect to dilute equal protection and due process decisions of this Court. In all such cases there is room for reasonable men to differ as to whether or not a denial of equal protection or due process has occurred, and the final decision is one of judgment. Until today this judgment has always been one for the judiciary to resolve.

I do not mean to suggest in what has been said that a legislative judgment of the type incorporated in §4(e) is without any force whatsoever. Decisions on questions of equal protection and due process are based not on abstract logic, but on empirical foundations. To the extent "legislative facts" are relevant to a judicial determination, Congress is well equipped to investigate them, and such determinations are of course entitled to due respect. . . .

But no such factual data provide a legislative record supporting §4(e)[9] by way of showing that Spanish-speaking citizens are fully as capable of making informed decisions in a New York election as are English-speaking citizens. Nor was there any showing whatever to support the Court's alternative argument that §4(e) should be viewed as but a remedial measure designed to cure or assure against unconstitutional discrimination of other varieties, e.g., in "public schools, public housing and law enforcement," to which Puerto Rican minorities might be subject in such communities as New York. There is simply no legislative record supporting such hypothesized discrimination of the sort we have hitherto insisted upon when congressional power is brought to bear on constitutionally reserved state concerns.

Thus, we have here not a matter of giving deference to a congressional estimate, based on its determination of legislative facts, bearing upon the validity vel non of a statute, but rather what can at most be called a legislative announcement that Congress believes a state law to entail an unconstitutional deprivation of equal protection. . . .

[Federal] authority, legislative no less than judicial, does not intrude unless there has been a denial by state action of Fourteenth Amendment limitations, in this instance a denial of equal protection. At least in the area of primary state concern a state statute that passes constitutional muster under the judicial standard of rationality should not be permitted to be set at naught by a mere contrary congressional pronouncement unsupported by a legislative record justifying that conclusion.

To deny the effectiveness of this congressional enactment is not of course to disparage Congress' exertion of authority in the field of civil rights; it is simply to recognize that the Legislative Branch like the other branches of federal authority is subject to the governmental boundaries set by the Constitution. To hold, on this record, that §4(e) overrides the New York literacy requirement seems to me tantamount to allowing the Fourteenth Amendment to swallow the State's constitutionally ordained primary authority in this field. For if Congress by what, as here, amounts to mere *ipse dixit* can set that otherwise permissible requirement partially at naught I see no reason why it could not also substitute its judgment for that of the States in other fields of their exclusive primary competence as well.

I would affirm the judgment. . . .

Note: Congressional Power to Enforce or Interpret (?) the Constitution

This Note examines some interpretations of the holding in Katzenbach v. Morgan. To what extent is each supported by language in the opinion? Which, if

---

9. There were no committee hearings or reports referring to this section, which was introduced from the floor during debate on the full Voting Rights Act.

any, is more strongly supported by that language? On what basis should we choose among permissible interpretations of the case?

1. *Remedial interpretations.* a. Congress may provide remedies for violations of rights that the courts have found or would themselves find protected by the Constitution. On this interpretation, what does section 5 of the fourteenth amendment add to the substantive provisions of section 1? (1) It might authorize Congress to confer jurisdiction on the federal courts to enforce section 1's guarantees. Would Congress have had that authority without section 5? (2) It might authorize Congress to create remedies that courts would have difficulty in developing on their own in the ordinary course of case-by-case adjudication.

Consider in this connection South Carolina v. Katzenbach, 383 U.S. 301 (1966): After an extensive investigation into racial discrimination in voting practices, Congress enacted the Voting Rights Act of 1965, a peripheral provision of which was at issue in Katzenbach v. Morgan. The central provisions established the following mechanism to "remedy" racial discrimination in voting. The attorney general and the director of the Census were given unreviewable authority, the first to determine that a literacy test or other device had been used in a state or political subdivision, the second to determine that less than 50 percent of its voting residents were registered to vote or had voted. Once those findings were made, the use of "tests or devices" was suspended. In addition, the state or subdivision could not adopt any new standards or procedures with respect to voting, without prior submission of the standards to federal authorities, who would determine whether their use would violate the fifteenth amendment. If this "preclearance" resulted in a conclusion by the federal agency that the changes were motivated by or would have the effect of discriminating on the basis of race, the changes could not be implemented until the state or subdivision secured an appropriate ruling from a federal court. The Court upheld these provisions as permissible exercises of Congress' power under section 2 of the fifteenth amendment "to enforce . . . by appropriate legislation" the right guaranteed by section 1 of that amendment. (The cases have not distinguished between the enforcement powers granted Congress by the fourteenth amendment and those granted by the fifteenth. Is there any ground for such a distinction?) The coverage formula was "rational in both practice and theory." Congress had acted on the basis of a factual record that showed that "the Fifteenth Amendment has clearly been violated." Note the role that the factual determinations play in this analysis.

Is it possible to sustain the distinction between substantive rights and remedies? There is a sense in which the remedies available to rectify violations define the scope of the rights themselves. This question is explored in more detail in Chapter 5, section A, infra.

b. Congress has the power to forestall the occurrence of acts that would violate rights that the courts have found or would find protected by the Constitution. Note that the "remedy" here occurs before the "violation" does. See City of Rome v. United States, 446 U.S. 156 (1980): The city challenged the application of the preclearance provisions of the Voting Rights Act on various grounds. One was that the fifteenth amendment prohibited only purposeful discrimination, an issue canvassed in City of Mobile v. Bolden, 446 U.S. 55 (1980), decided on the same day. The Voting Rights Act required preclearance of changes that had discriminatory effects even if they had no discriminatory purposes. The attorney general had found that the city's changes had the impermissible effects but not the impermissible purposes. Under those circumstances, the city argued, Congress's power to enforce the fifteenth amendment did not extend to its proposed changes. The Court, through Justice Marshall, rejected the city's argument. It assumed that the fifteenth amendment prohibited only intentional discrimination. But "Congress could rationally have concluded that, because electoral changes by jurisdictions with a demonstrable history of intentional racial discrimination in voting create the risk of purposeful discrimination, it was proper to prohibit changes that have a discriminatory impact." Is the "risk" that at some time in the future the city will adopt purposefully discriminatory changes? If so, why won't preclearance then, and judicial scrutiny directly under the fifteenth amendment, be enough to preclude the adoption of those — but only those — changes? Or is the "risk" that neither the attorney general nor the courts will be able accurately to determine in every instance whether a change had a discriminatory purpose? How substantial must either of these risks be? Is it enough that Congress found them substantial, or must the Court agree, based on its independent analysis of the situation? Justice Marshall said that accepting the city's arguments would mean "overruling" South Carolina v. Katzenbach. Is that true? Justice Rehnquist's dissent, joined by Justice Stewart, argued that, having established that it had no discriminatory purpose, the city would not violate the Constitution in adopting its new rules, and that Congress therefore lacked power to "remedy" a nonexistent violation by requiring preclearance of the changes. It also argued that a preventive "remedy" was constitutional only if the Court agreed that the risk of a substantive violation was substantial.

In EEOC v. Wyoming, section E supra, the Court held that Congress had power under the commerce clause to require that states follow federal standards prohibiting age discrimination in employment. It did not decide whether the prohibition "could also be upheld under §5." A footnote stated that "Congress need [not] recite the words 'section 5' or 'Fourteenth Amendment' or 'equal protection' [citing Woods v. Miller]," so long as the Court could "discern some legislative purpose or factual predicate that supports the exercise of that power." Chief Justice Burger's dissent, joined by three others, addressed the question of Congress's power under section 5 to prohibit age discrimination in state employment.

> Congress may act only where a violation lurks. [In] this instance, no one — not the Court, not the Congress — has determined that mandatory retirement plans violate any rights protected by these amendments. We cannot say that the Judiciary made this determination, for we have considered the constitutionality of mandatory retirement schemes twice [in Murgia and Vance v. Bradley, Chapter 5, section E, infra]; we rejected both equal protection challenges. . . .
>
> Nor can appellant claim that Congress has used the powers we recognized in [Katzenbach v. Morgan], to enact legislation that prohibits conduct not in itself unconstitutional because it considered the prohibition necessary to guard against encroachment of guaranteed rights or to rectify past discrimination. There has been no finding [that] the abrogated state law infringed on rights identified by this Court. Nor did Congress use [its] "specifically informed legislative competence" to decide that the state law it invalidated was too intrusive on federal rights to be an appropriate means to achieve the ends sought by the state.

Is this a fair reading of the precedents?

c. Congress may provide remedies for violations of rights that *arguably* are protected by the Constitution, that is, where there are good grounds for thinking that, given what the courts have said about a problem, the courts *might* find a constitutional violation.

> Congress may scrutinize any state regime which the Court has found to be constitutionally questionable because it involves a suspect classification or a fundamental right. [Congress may] investigate the facts surrounding state action of this type and then prohibit the practice if, in Congress' judgment, it lacks the compelling basis which the Court demands to uphold it. [Under] this reading [Congress] is free to invalidate government actions that the Court has already upheld or might otherwise uphold in the future. But this would only permit Congress to "expand" on judicial conceptions [in] those very limited situations where Congress, with its special competence in the circumstances, has appraised the relevant factors and concluded that the law (already declared vulnerable by the judiciary) is not justified by the required state interest — a decision which differs from that which the Court, with its more limited capabilities, either has already reached or would otherwise make when the issue was presented to it. Thus, in enacting section 4(e) of the Voting Rights Act, Congress might be said to have concluded that, in its judgment, contrary to the Court's holding in [*Lassiter*], there was no compelling basis for states' denying the franchise to persons not literate in English.

Choper, Congressional Power to Expand Judicial Definitions of the Substantive Terms of the Civil War Amendments, 67 Minn. L. Rev. 299, 308-309 (1982). Suppose, on examining the record compiled by Congress, the Court concludes that the state law does indeed have a compelling basis. What result under Choper's analysis? Can his analysis be extended to other cases, in which the courts require that the state law satisfy a "mere rationality" standard, and yet Congress has acted? What result in EEOC v. Wyoming under Choper's analysis? The first two "remedial" interpretations of Katzenbach v. Morgan rest on the proposition that somewhere in the situation lurks a constitutional violation that the courts would themselves declare to be a violation. Does Choper's analysis rest on that proposition or a similar one? If not, what reason is there for adopting it?

2. *Substantive interpretations.* "Congress, in the field of state activities and except as confined by the Bill of Rights, has the power to enact any law which may be viewed as a measure for correction of any condition which Congress might believe involves a denial of equality or other fourteenth amendment rights." Cox, Constitutional Adjudication and the Promotion of Human Rights, 80 Harv. L. Rev. 91, 107 (1966). On what bases might we rest this independent power in Congress to interpret the Constitution in ways that the Court would (might?) not?

a. *Fact-finding ability.* Cox argues that "the Court has long been committed both to the presumption that facts exist which sustain congressional legislation and also to deference to congressional judgment about questions of degree and proportion." The due process and equal protection requirements depend "to a large extent upon finding and appraisal of the practical importance of relevant facts," and "there is often room for differences of opinion in interpreting the available data." Note that the provision upheld in Katzenbach v. Morgan was a floor amendment, and examine carefully the evidence the Court cites in support of the proposition that Congress has a "specially informed legislative competence."

b. *The "footnote 10" ratchet.* Why does Congress have power to "enforce" (i.e., under a substantive theory "expand") but not to "dilute" constitutional guarantees? Consider the possibility that (1) with respect to some constitutional guarantees there is a (broad or narrow) range of permissible interpretations, and (2) the courts are sometimes constrained by their institutional characteristics, for example by limits on their ability to define rules with sufficient clarity, to adopt only one interpretation within that range. Congress, lacking the same kinds of institutional characteristics, might adopt another interpretation yet still remain within the range of permissible interpretations. In the context of remedies, Congress might replace a judicially developed remedy with an equally efficacious one. In those circumstances, is it appropriate to speak of "dilution"?

Consider the following variation on this analysis: The courts enforce a substantive right whose content is developed by applying a balancing test. Enforcement occurs through the use of a remedy developed by the courts. Congress replaces the judicially developed remedy with another one. The statutory remedy is slightly less efficacious than the judicial one, because Congress thought it wise to promote somewhat more effectively one of the values the courts took into account in formulating the substantive right. Is the statute constitutional? Note the possibility suggested by this variation that Congress's power may vary depending on whether the substantive right is formulated in balancing terms or as a more rigid rule. For further discussion of the issue of balancing versus rules, see Chapter 7, section B, infra.

The preceding analysis, particularly where the statutory remedy is as effective as the judicial one, is relatively easy to understand in the area of remedies. Can it be extended to issues of substantive constitutional law without threatening the theory of Marbury v. Madison? For a full discussion, see Monaghan, Constitutional Common Law, 89 Harv. L. Rev. 1 (1975); Burt, *Miranda* and Title II: A Morganatic Marriage, 1969 Sup. Ct. Rev. 81.

In what sense do constitutional guarantees "of their own force" prohibit anything? If the sense of that phrase is that the courts will strike down some statutes as unconstitutional, does footnote 10 mean only that Congress may do what the courts think wise?

c. *Federalism.* Note that the challengers in Katzenbach v. Morgan made two kinds of attack on the statute. One, discussed at the end of the Court's opinion, was that the statute violated rights of equal treatment. (Note that the final paragraphs of the Court's opinion reject this attack on the merits, applying directly a judicially developed standard incorporating deference to legislative judgments.) The other, more important one, was that the statute was beyond Congress's powers. The second challenge was based on a theory of federalism. Cohen, Congressional Power to Interpret Due Process and Equal Protection, 27 Stan. L. Rev. 603 (1975), argues that Katzenbach v. Morgan is defensible as an ordinary application of the general proposition, derived from Madison and Wechsler, that the courts will not enforce federalism-based limitations on congressional power because the political constraints on Congress are sufficient to protect against improvident national action. Is this different from the footnote 10 ratchet? Considering the political constraints on Congress, can you identify differences between Congress's article I powers on the one hand and its powers to enforce the fourteenth and fifteenth amendments on the other? If you can, do the differences argue in favor of or against more expansive interpretations of the latter than the former? Note that essentially all of the problems raised in the preceding notes become relatively simple under this interpretation.

3. *The application of* Katzenbach. Consider the proposed "human life statute": In Roe v. Wade, Chapter 6, section F, infra, the Court held unconstitutional state laws restricting the availability of abortions. The states defended their laws in part on the ground that "life begins at conception." The Court responded, "We need not resolve the difficult question of when life begins. When those trained in the respective disciplines of medicine, philosophy, and theology are unable to arrive at any consensus, the judiciary [is] not in a position to speculate as to the answer." Taking this as an assertion of a distinctive judicial incapacity (is it?), and relying on Katzenbach v. Morgan, Senator Helms and Representative Hyde in 1981 proposed the following statute:

> The Congress finds that present-day scientific evidence indicates a significant likelihood that actual human life exists from conception.
>
> The Congress further finds that the fourteenth amendment to the Constitution of the United States was intended to protect all human beings.
>
> Upon the basis of these findings, and in the exercise of the powers of the Congress, including its power under section 5 of the fourteenth amendment to the Constitution of the United States, the Congress hereby declares that for the purpose of enforcing the obligation of the States under the fourteenth amendment not to deprive persons of life without due process of law, human life shall be deemed to exist from conception, without regard to race, sex, age, health, defect, or condition of dependency; and for this purpose "person" shall include all human life as defined herein.

Construct a remedial theory in support of the statute, then construct a "fact-finding" one. Try to articulate the differences between the kind of "fact" involved here and in Katzenbach v. Morgan. One candidate is that Katzenbach v. Morgan involved facts about social reality that were causally related to effects on ultimate moral values, while the facts here describe a moral conclusion directly. But note that this distinction rests on a (controversial) theory about the nature of morality.

What are the arguments based on Katzenbach v. Morgan supporting and opposing the constitutionality of statutes: (a) prohibiting state governments from adopting affirmative action programs; (b) requiring state governments to adopt affirmative action programs; (c) prohibiting states from regulating the distribution of sexually explicit materials; (d) requiring the states to regulate the distribution of sexually explicit materials; (e) prohibiting the imposition of capital punishment? Does the explicitness of the constitutional guarantee involved affect the persuasiveness of the arguments?

Could Congress rely on Katzenbach v. Morgan to require that states pay out of their own resources a minimum annual income to their residents? Construct the appropriate remedial and substantive theories.

Note that a full understanding of the arguments based on Katzenbach v. Morgan may (unless Cohen's federalism argument is correct) depend on an understanding of the substantive constitutional provisions "expanded" or "diluted."

4. *The Court's position.* In recent years no member of the Court has rejected the first remedial interpretation of Katzenbach v. Morgan. The other remedial interpretations, and the substantive ones, remain controversial. Consider the

bearing of Oregon v. Mitchell, 400 U.S. 112 (1970), on the present state of the law: In 1970 Congress amended the Voting Rights Act to prohibit literacy tests nationwide and to prohibit denying the vote to eighteen-year-olds. The nationwide ban on literacy tests was upheld unanimously, on a remedial theory. (The Court and Justice Rehnquist in City of Rome v. United States disagreed over which remedial theory was involved in Oregon v. Mitchell.) By a 5 to 4 vote the Court upheld the eighteen-year-old vote provision as it applied to federal elections. Four justices who accepted a Katzenbach v. Morgan rationale were joined by Justice Black, who regarded the statute as an appropriate exercise of Congress's power under article I, section 4, to "make Regulations" regarding voter qualifications for federal elections, a matter on which article I, section 2 gave the states initial responsibility. (To see how idiosyncratic that view is, examine the text of article I, section 4.)

By a 5 to 4 vote, Justice Black again in the majority, the Court found the eighteen-year-old vote provision unconstitutional as it applied to state elections. Justice Black emphasized the centrality of the power to determine voter qualifications to "the separate and independent existence of the States." Katzenbach v. Morgan, he argued, should be confined to the area of racial discrimination. Otherwise, he argued, Congress's power to enforce the equal protection clause would "blot out all state power, leaving the 50 States as little more than impotent figureheads." Chief Justice Burger and Justices Stewart, Blackmun, and Harlan rejected both the broad remedial and the substantive interpretations of Katzenbach v. Morgan, and would have held the statute unconstitutional as to both state and federal elections. They adopted the first remedial interpretation and concluded that there was no antecedent constitutional violation to remedy or threatened one to be forestalled. Justice Harlan wrote:

> Although Congress' expression of the view that it does have power to alter state suffrage requirements is entitled to the most respectful consideration by the judiciary, coming as it does from a coordinate branch of government, this cannot displace the duty of this Court to make an independent determination whether Congress has exceeded its powers [Marbury]. [Congress] is subject to none of the institutional restraints imposed on judicial decisionmaking; it is controlled only by the political process. [To] allow a simple majority of Congress to have final say on matters of constitutional interpretation is [fundamentally] out of keeping with the constitutional structure. . . .
>
> Judicial deference is based, not on relative factfinding competence, but on due regard for the decision of the body constitutionally appointed to decide. Establishment of voting qualifications is a matter for state legislatures. Assuming any authority at all, only when the Court can say with some confidence that the legislature has demonstrably erred in adjusting the competing interests is it justified in striking down the legislative judgment. . . .
>
> The same considerations apply, and with almost equal force, to Congress' displacement of state decisions with its own ideas of wise policy. The sole distinction between Congress and the Court in this regard is that Congress, being an elective body, presumptively has popular authority for the value judgment it makes. But since the state legislature has a like authority, this distinction between Congress and the judiciary falls short of justifying a congressional veto on the state judgment. The perspectives and values of national legislators on the issue of voting qualifications are likely to differ from those of state legislators, but I see no reason a priori to prefer those of the national figures, whose collective decision, applying nationwide, is

necessarily less able to take account of peculiar local conditions. Whether one agrees with this judgment or not, it is the one expressed by the Framers in leaving voting qualifications to the States.

Does Justice Harlan's analysis completely dispose of all but the narrowest interpretations of *Katzenbach?* Consider whether it adequately deals with the federalism interpretation.

Justices Brennan, White, and Marshall dissented. They expressed doubt about the constitutionality of state statutes denying the vote to eighteen-year-olds and found reasonable Congress's determination that such denials failed to promote a compelling state interest. Their opinion emphasized Congress's superior fact-finding ability. Justice Douglas also dissented.

Three months after the decision, Congress submitted the twenty-sixth amendment to the states for ratification, which was completed after another three months. (Is there a lesson in that?)

Note: Congressional Power to Regulate "Private" Action for Civil Rights Purposes

1. *The thirteenth amendment.* Jones v. Alfred H. Mayer Co., 392 U.S. 409 (1968): Plaintiffs alleged that Mayer, the developer of a large suburban housing complex, had refused to sell them a home solely because one of them was black. They claimed that this violated 42 U.S.C. §1982, which provides: "All citizens [shall] have the same right, in every State and Territory, as is enjoyed by white citizens thereof, to inherit, purchase, lease, sell, hold, and convey real and personal property." The Court, through Justice Stewart, held that the statute barred private racial discrimination in the sale of property, and that, "thus construed, [it] is a valid exercise of the power of Congress to enforce the Thirteenth Amendment." Citing the Civil Rights Cases, Chapter 10, section A, infra, the Court said that the Amendment is " 'an absolute declaration that slavery or involuntary servitude shall not exist in any part of the United States.' " Its second section "clothed 'Congress with power to pass *all laws necessary and proper for abolishing all badges and incidents of slavery in the United States*' (emphasis added). [Surely] Congress has the power [rationally] to determine what are the badges and the incidents of slavery." It was not "irrational" for Congress to conclude that private restraints on the ability of blacks to engage in otherwise normal market transactions were such badges and incidents.

[When] racial discrimination herds men into ghettos and makes their ability to buy property turn on the color of their skin, then it too is a relic of slavery. [The Amendment would be pointless] if Congress were powerless to assure that a dollar in the hands of a Negro will purchase the same thing as a dollar in the hands of a white man. At the very least, the freedom that Congress is empowered to secure [includes] the freedom to buy whatever a white man can buy, the right to live wherever a white man can live. . . .

Justice Harlan, joined by Justice White, would have dismissed the writ of certiorari as improvidently granted because the Civil Rights Act of 1968 covered essentially the same ground as that raised by Jones's complaint. He argued that the Court's construction of the statute was subject to serious question.

2. *The fourteenth amendment.* The fourteenth amendment provides that "no state shall [deny] to any person [the] equal protection of the laws." The reference to "states" has generated a large body of doctrine regarding the so-called state action doctrine, discussed in detail in Chapter 10 infra. For present purposes, the doctrine means that, for the fourteenth amendment to be implicated (and therefore for Congress to have power to enforce its protections), there must be either a sufficient degree of state involvement with the action, or a failure by the state to act in circumstances where the Constitution affirmatively requires action. (Justice Douglas, concurring in Jones v. Mayer, argued that the developer's actions amounted to "zoning" and so satisfied the state action requirements.)

In United States v. Guest, 383 U.S. 745 (1966), the Court sustained an indictment for a criminal conspiracy to violate 18 U.S.C. §241, which prohibits conspiracies to deprive citizens of rights protected by the Constitution. The defendants were charged with violating the rights of civil rights workers; two of the defendants had been acquitted in state court in a trial for murdering Lemuel Penn, one such worker. The court found that an allegation that the defendants had caused the arrests of blacks by making false reports of criminal activity to police officers established sufficient state involvement.

Congress has provided a civil remedy for conspiracies to deny "the equal protection of the laws." May the statute constitutionally reach purely private conspiracies? Assume that state officials may not beat blacks for distributing leaflets on a public street or refuse to hire members of the Socialist Party as janitors. Could members of the Ku Klux Klan be made liable under this statute for doing so? The problem is puzzling because it is not immediately obvious how a private person can deny another the protection of laws enforced by public officials. A full answer can be given only after you study the state action doctrine.

The Court has avoided some of the more difficult questions raised by these statutes by finding that the rights alleged to have been violated were defined by the Constitution as rights protected against private invasions. See *Guest* (right to travel); Griffin v. Breckinridge, 403 U.S. 88 (1971) (thirteenth amendment, right to travel).

3. *Problems of statutory interpretation.* a. The statutes discussed in this Note are the legacy of Reconstruction, a period when concepts of civil rights and federalism were different from our own. The Court has been criticized and praised for infusing these old statutes with contemporary content. See, e.g., Casper, *Jones v. Mayer:* Clio, Bemused and Confused Muse, 1968 Sup. Ct. Rev. 89; Kohl, The Civil Rights Act of 1866, Its Hour Come Round at Last, 55 Va. L. Rev. 272 (1969). If the language of the statutes is fairly susceptible to the Court's interpretations, should it matter that its adopters had a narrower understanding of civil rights? What if their understanding was confused (on our terms or theirs)? These questions raise broader issues of interpretation, discussed in more detail in Chapter 6, section A, infra.

b. Modern civil rights statutes cover many of the acts also covered by the Reconstruction statutes under the Court's interpretations. The Civil Rights Act of 1968, for example, makes unlawful the activity at issue in Jones v. Mayer. The act is broader than the 1866 act in some ways, by covering other forms of discrimination and providing additional forms of remedial assistance to a complainant, and is narrower in others, by containing some exemptions. Is it appropriate to revive old statutes when Congress has recently addressed the general problem in a different way?

c. The statutes refer broadly to rights secured by the Constitution. What those rights are may not be immediately clear to a nonlawyer. Is it proper to use such general terms as the basis for criminal or civil liability? Screws v. United States, 325 U.S. 91 (1945), held that a conviction under the criminal statute required that the defendant had "a purpose to deprive a person of a specific constitutional right." Harlow v. Fitzgerald, 457 U.S. 800 (1982), held that officials could be held liable under the civil statute only if they violated clearly established rights of which a reasonable person should have known.

d. Could all of the activities discussed in this Note be reached by a statute enacted pursuant to the power to regulate interstate commerce? Does it matter that the Reconstruction Congress did not focus on that power as a source of its authority? That it may have had a different conception of the scope of that power than does the Court today?

Note: Concluding Observations on Congress's Powers

Consider this statement from the Advisory Commission on Intergovernmental Relations, Regulatory Federalism: Policy, Process, Impact and Reform 93 (1984), based on a study of the impact of federal regulations of the states:

[1] Most of the regulations [used] federal grants to state and local governments, or they affected functions and activities traditionally within the orbit of state responsibilities. In many cases, related regulations had been initiated at the state level prior to the federal legislation. [2] The initial enactments [tended] to encounter serious and prolonged opposition in the legislative process. [3] These early regulations often were developed in response to perceived failures of less intrusive federal measures to achieve their goals. [4] Once a regulatory instrument has been successfully established in a given field of policy, there has been a tendency for other programs in that field to duplicate its use. [5] The most openly coercive forms of intergovernmental regulation [have] been adopted much less frequently than seemingly more cooperative regulatory instruments. [6] Finally, state and local officials generally have been ineffective in opposing new intergovernmental regulations. Often they have supported the goals of regulations. In other cases, they have focused their attention on grant benefits provided by many regulatory programs, overlooking the adverse consequences of the program as a whole.

Assume that this is an accurate summary of what Congress has done and of the political processes behind its actions. Does it indicate that Madison, Wechsler, and Choper are correct in believing that there is no need for judicial supervision of the exercise of Congress's powers in order to assure that the goals of federalism are advanced? Or does it indicate that in this area the political process is an inadequate safeguard of important interests? Even if the political process is inadequate in that sense, is judicial review likely to improve matters? What, in the end, is the lesson of experience?

III

Judicial Efforts to Protect the Expansion of the Market against Assertions of Local Power

Since the early years of constitutional adjudication, the Supreme Court has asserted the authority to invalidate state and local laws that the Court finds to interfere improperly with interstate and foreign commerce. A recent example is Hunt v. Washington State Apple Advertising Commission, 432 U.S. 333 (1977), where the Court held unconstitutional a North Carolina regulation that prohibited the sale of apples from cartons that were labeled "Washington State Grade A." (The case is considered in more detail below.) The provision of the Constitution said to be violated was the commerce clause. This chapter deals with two major problems: (a) What is the *source* of the Court's authority in this area (the primary subject of section A), and (b) what are the *criteria* for determining when a state or local law improperly interferes with interstate commerce (the primary subject of the remainder of the chapter). A comprehensive survey, using a framework similar to that adopted here, is Eule, Laying the Dormant Commerce Clause to Rest, 91 Yale L.J. 425 (1982).

A. THE FUNDAMENTAL FRAMEWORK

Note: The Classical View

1. *The vices of "protectionism."* As *Gibbons* showed, the framers were concerned that states would erect barriers to trade in order to protect the economic activities of local residents. Protectionism impedes economic development by making it more difficult for goods and capital to move to places where they are more valued. It also impairs the development of a sense of national unity. These two vices of protectionism may have different implications for the constitutional scheme. Regardless of the reasons for their creation, barriers to trade impede economic development. But they need not impair national unity, if out-of-state residents understand that the barriers were created to further important local goals unrelated to the suppression of free trade.

The materials that follow address several aspects of the vices of protectionism. (a) Whatever free trade norms the Constitution embodies, which branch — Congress or the courts — should enforce them? (b) How may protectionist legislation be identified? Some statutes apply one rule to economic activity originating locally and another to activity originating elsewhere. Must such statutes be protectionist? Other statutes have a disparate impact on local and out-of-state trade. When should they be characterized as protectionist? Will the degree of the disparate impact matter? Still other statutes erect barriers to trade without regard to its origin locally or elsewhere. Should such statutes ever be considered protectionist or otherwise constitutionally suspect?

2. *A congressional veto of state laws?* At the constitutional convention, Madison proposed that Congress have the power to veto state laws contravening the Constitution and that a Council of Revision composed of the President and Supreme Court justices have authority to review such vetoes. Apparently because the Council of Revision would also have had authority to review all federal legislation as well, and believing that the ordinary processes of judicial review would be sufficient as to federal legislation, the convention rejected the entire proposal. J. Goebel, 1 History of the Supreme Court: Antecedents and Beginnings to 1801, 208-210 (1971). Does the rejection shed any light on whether the Court may invalidate state laws in the absence of congressional action?

3. *Preemption and judicial authority.* Article I, section 8, gives Congress the power to regulate interstate commerce. It may exercise that power to displace ("preempt") state laws, whenever interstate commerce is involved. Recall that Justice Johnson's opinion in Gibbons v. Ogden emphasized the importance the framers placed on that grant of power to Congress as a way of assuring that no unnecessary impediments be placed in the way of interstate commerce. Where Congress has failed to exercise its affirmative power to preempt state law, why may the Court invalidate state laws that impede interstate commerce?

4. *Exclusive congressional power?* In *Gibbons* Chief Justice Marshall found "great force" in the argument, made in more detail by Justice Johnson, that Congress's power to regulate interstate commerce was exclusive — that is, that the Constitution necessarily withdrew that power from the states. Under this view the states lacked power to enact laws that regulated interstate commerce, and the courts could invalidate any such laws on the ground that they exceeded the states' authority in our federal system.

This view derived from a more general political theory in which sovereign powers were indivisible. See *Cooley,* infra this note. If a power was lodged in one sovereign such as the national government, it could not simultaneously be lodged in another such as the states. Is that the theory of the Constitution? Note that article I, section 10, expressly disables states from certain activities that are elsewhere committed to Congress (e.g., the power to coin money and to grant letters of marque and reprisal). Why should the commerce power standing alone be exclusive when these other powers require a specific provision denying state power, for them to be exclusive? Consider whether the modern theory of the Court's authority, infra, provides a satisfactory resolution of the textual difficulty.

Whatever its analytic merits or defects, the exclusive power argument was troublesome for political reasons, discussed in note 4 infra, and for practical ones as well. The latter stem from the fact that, where Congress's power is exclusive, the states may not act even if Congress too has failed to act. (Note that the acceptability of the "exclusive power" argument may turn on the scope one gives to the affirmative grant of power to Congress.) If *some* regulation is thought appropriate, the "exclusive power" argument may go too far in insisting that the regulation always derive from Congress.

Difficulties with the breadth of the "exclusive power" argument led the Court to develop a number of doctrines designed to limit it.

a. *Purpose*. Recall that in *Gibbons* Justice Johnson coupled his "exclusive power" argument with the contention that Congress was granted the power to regulate interstate commerce only to achieve commercial ends. It followed that the states lacked power only insofar as they sought to achieve similar ends, such as the protection of local enterprises from out-of-state competition, but not insofar as they exercised their general "police" powers, those designed to promote the health and safety of their citizens. Note that this limitation requires the Court to distinguish between statutes designed to serve commercial goals and those designed to serve police power ones, and that examination of the legislature's purpose in light of the impact of its actions may be quite difficult.

In Willson v. Black Bird Creek Marsh Co., 27 U.S. (2 Pet.) 245 (1829), a Delaware statute authorized the company to erect a dam on a stream deep enough to be used by boats in interstate commerce. The dam helped dry up a marsh in the area. Chief Justice Marshall's brief opinion for the Court held that the statute did not violate the commerce clause. "The value of the property on [the] banks [of the creek] must be enhanced [by the dam], and the health of the inhabitants probably improved. Measures calculated to produce these objects, provided they do not come into collision with the powers of the general government, are undoubtedly within those reserved to the states." Does this adopt a "purpose" limitation? Why did Marshall speak of the "powers" of the national government rather than, for example, its "statutes"?

b. *Direct/indirect*. DiSanto v. Pennsylvania, 273 U.S. 34 (1927), invalidated a licensing statute for those wishing to sell tickets for transportation to or from foreign countries. The state argued that the statute was designed to prevent exploitation of recent immigrants who wished to purchase tickets for relatives still in Europe; before the licensing scheme was adopted, some ticket agents had required the immigrants to make payments into an account with the agents, who would not purchase the tickets until full payment had been made. The majority, noting that "Congress has complete and paramount authority to regulate foreign commerce and [to] protect the public against [frauds,]" stated that a "statute which by its necessary operation directly interferes with or burdens foreign commerce is a prohibited regulation and invalid, regardless of the purpose with which it was passed. Such legislation cannot be sustained as an exertion of the police power of the State to prevent possible fraud." Justice Stone's dissent called the "direct/indirect" test "too mechanical, too uncertain in its application, and too remote from actualities to be of value." He called the terms "labels to describe a result rather than any trustworthy formula by which it is reached." Recall the use of the "direct/indirect" test with respect to Congress's power.

c. *Inherently local/national*. Cooley v. Board of Port Wardens, 53 U.S. (12 How.) 299 (1851), involved a Pennsylvania law, adopted in 1803, requiring all ships entering or leaving the port of Philadelphia to use a local pilot or pay a fine into a fund to support retired pilots and their dependents. The Court agreed that the regulation of pilots was a regulation of interstate commerce even though pilots stayed with the ships for only brief periods. It upheld the statute:

[The] power to regulate commerce, embraces a vast field, containing not only many, but exceedingly various subjects, quite unlike in their nature; some imperatively demanding a single uniform rule, operating equally on the commerce of the United States in every port; and some, like the subject now in question, as imperatively demanding that diversity, which alone can meet the local necessities of navigation.

Either absolutely to affirm, or to deny that the nature of this power requires exclusive legislation by Congress, is to lose sight of the nature of the subjects of this power, and to assert concerning all of them, what is really applicable but to a part. Whatever subjects of this power are in their nature national, or admit only of one uniform system [may] justly be said to be of such a nature as to require exclusive legislation by Congress. That this cannot be affirmed of laws for the regulation of [pilotage] is clear.

The Court supported this conclusion by referring to a federal statute, adopted in 1789, providing that "all pilots [shall be] regulated in conformity with [such] laws as the States may respectively hereafter enact for the purpose, until further legislative provision shall be made by Congress." This statute did not dispose of the case for the Court, because if the subject-matter was local Congress lacked power to act, and if it was national it was questionable whether Congress could "regrant" the power to regulate back to the states. But the statute "[manifested] the understanding of Congress [that] the nature of this subject is not such as to require its exclusive legislation."

Cooley requires that the Court determine whether a "subject" is of "a nature" requiring uniform national regulation or diverse local regulation. (1) What are the criteria for determining what is the national or local nature of the "subject" of the legislation? The Court treats *Cooley* as involving the subject of pilotage; would the analysis or result differ if the subject were "retirement systems"? (2) Why does the Court refuse to recognize the possibility of diverse national regulation? On the Court's assumptions, Congress cannot achieve diversity by piggybacking on state legislation, but it clearly could do so by directly adopting regulations specific to each named port (or by creating an administrative agency charged with developing appropriate regulations for each port). Yet if uniformity does not necessarily follow from the exercise of national power, how can we decide whether a subject ought to be local or national?

As you study the modern cases, note the extent to which intuitions or express judgments about (1) the "national versus local" nature of the problem, (2) the "commercial versus police powers" purposes of the regulation, and (3) the directness of the effect on interstate commerce appear to influence outcomes and doctrinal formulations.

5. *"Exclusive power" and the slavery issue.* Before the Civil War, discussions of the exclusivity as well as those of the scope of Congress's power were deeply influenced by the issue of slavery. Supporters of slavery were concerned that, if slavery were treated as involving interstate commerce in human beings, they would lose the power to regulate slavery. Mayor of New York v. Miln, 36 U.S. (11 Pet.) 102 (1837), invoked the "police powers" test to uphold a statute requiring shipmasters to report the names and residences of passengers. Justice Story's dissent noted that Marshall, who had heard the case argued before he died, would have held the statute unconstitutional. In the Passenger Cases, 48 U.S. (7 How.) 283 (1849), the Court, dividing 5 to 4 with each justice writing an opinion, held unconstitutional one statute imposing a tax on each incoming passenger, to be

used to defray the costs of health inspections and treatment, and another requiring a bond to be posted for each immigrant likely to become a public charge. (Similar doctrinal divisions appeared in the License Cases, 46 U.S. (5 How.) 504 (1847).)

The issue of slavery affected these discussions directly and indirectly. The Passenger Cases held that people could be objects of commerce. That raised questions about Congress's power to regulate the interstate trade in slaves. If Congress's power were exclusive, not only could it regulate the trade, but the states could not. Southern interests were opposed to treating people as objects of commerce because that would affirm national power. But once they were so treated, the same interests opposed the "exclusive power" position because it would bar southern states from regulating the interstate slave trade, yet the slave-exporting states of the upper South and the slave-importing states of the lower South both wanted to regulate that trade.

More generally, lodging "exclusive power" in the national government meant that if people wanted action on some matter within the exclusive national power, they had to direct their attention to the national government. If states had concurrent power, people could look to their states first. After the early years of the nineteenth century, Southern interests were less confident that they could retain permanent control of the national government and more devoted to enhancing local authority. Yet they were simultaneously attracted to the view that all governing authority was absolute within its sphere because that view captured their sense of the proper relation between master and slave. But if governments were absolute within their spheres, then the "exclusive power" position was correct. The confusions in the antebellum law regarding state authority to regulate commerce derive in large measure from the tension between the immediate interest Southerners had in restricting national authority and their interest in developing a comprehensive view of governing authority that explained why they had absolute power over slaves. See generally M. Tushnet, The American Law of Slavery, 1810-1860 (1981).

6. *The demise of the classical framework.* After the Civil War the doctrinal tensions became less important. The slavery issue of course disappeared. Further, as *DiSanto* suggests, for a while it did not trouble a majority of the Court that the "exclusive power" position led to a regime in which economic activity was unregulated: The states could not act because they lacked power, and Congress did not act because it had other things to do that it regarded as more pressing. The various limitations on the "exclusive power" argument could be deployed to allow deviations from a regime of laissez faire in practice, where a majority of the Court believed that deviations were appropriate. (Consider here the extent to which the statute in *DiSanto* rested on an expansive definition of fraud.) Eventually the classical framework was abandoned.

Note: *The Modern View — Allocating the Burden of Inertia via Preemption and Consent*

In Exxon Corp. v. Governor of Maryland, 437 U.S. 117 (1978), the Court rejected a commerce clause challenge to a statute that prohibited gasoline producers and refiners from operating retail gas stations in the state. (The case is considered in more detail below.) Suppose the major gasoline producers such as Exxon continue to object to the burdens the statute places on them. What avenues do they have available to alleviate those burdens? The precise holding in *Gibbons* was that the federal licensing law preempted New York's grant of a monopoly. Thus, the major producers might seek congressional action to preempt Maryland's law. Once Congress acts, its statutes prevail over conflicting state laws, by reason of the Supremacy Clause. (Standards for determining when a state law conflicts with a federal one are discussed in section D below.)

Suppose the Court had held that the Maryland statute violated the commerce clause. Could the local retailers who supported the statute have it reinstated by persuading Congress to act on their behalf?

1. *Early formulations of congressional power to consent or preempt.* In 1827 the Supreme Court held that states could not exercise their power to tax items of interstate commerce so long as the items remained in their original packages. Brown v. Maryland, 25 U.S. (12 Wheat.) 419 (1827), limited in Michelin Tire Co. v. Wages, 423 U.S. 276 (1976). In 1873 Iowa passed a statute prohibiting the sale of beer. In Leisy v. Hardin, 135 U.S. 100 (1890), the Leisys brewed beer in Illinois and shipped it to Iowa, where they sought to sell it in the original kegs. When Hardin, the town marshal, seized the kegs, the Leisys sued for their return. They argued that although Iowa had the power to regulate liquor consumption, the original package doctrine barred it from regulating the sale of beer in its original kegs. A divided Supreme Court agreed. Chief Justice Fuller's majority opinion emphasized that Congress's power to regulate interstate commerce was plenary and exclusive:

> [While a] State may provide for the security of the lives, limbs, health, and comfort of persons and [property,] yet a subject matter which has been confided exclusively to Congress [is] not within the [police] power of the State, unless placed there by congressional action. The power to regulate commerce among the States is a unit, but if particular subjects within its operation do not require the application of a general or uniform system, the States may legislate in regard to them with a view to local needs and circumstances, until Congress otherwise directs; but the power thus exercised by the States is not identical in its extent with the power to regulate commerce among the States. The power to pass laws in respect to internal commerce [belongs] to the class of powers pertaining to the locality [and] to the [welfare] of society, originally necessarily belonging to, and upon the adoption of the Constitution reserved by, the States, except so far as falling within the scope of a power confided to the general government.

After restating the *Cooley* test, Chief Justice Fuller continued:

> Whenever [a] particular power of the general government is one which must necessarily be exercised by it, and Congress remains silent, [the] only legitimate conclusion is that the general government intended that power should not be affirmatively exercised, and the action of the States cannot be permitted to effect that which would be incompatible with such intention. Hence, inasmuch as [the] transportation [of] commodities, is national in its character, and must be governed by a uniform system, so long as Congress does not pass any law to regulate it, or allowing the states to do so, it thereby indicates its will that such commerce shall be free and untrammelled. . . .

[As] the grant of the power to regulate commerce among the states, so far as one system is required, is exclusive, the States cannot exercise that power without the assent of Congress, and, in the absence of legislation, it is left for the courts to determine when state action does or does not amount to such exercise, or, in other words, what is or is not a regulation of such commerce.

Chief Justice Fuller concluded that Iowa's prohibition statute "[inhibited], directly or indirectly, the receipt of an imported commodity" and was therefore unconstitutional. His opinion stated that "the responsibility is upon Congress [to] remove the restriction upon the State [if] in its judgment the end to be secured justifies and requires such action." If Congress has the power to displace the Court's judgment, in what sense was Iowa's statute "unconstitutional"?

Supporters of prohibition accepted the Court's suggestion that they seek congressional permission for state prohibition laws. In August 1890, a few months after *Leisy*, Congress enacted the Wilson Act, which stated that liquor imported into a state "shall upon arrival [be] subject to" local laws as if it had been locally produced, "and shall not be exempt therefrom by reason of being [in] original packages." In re Rahrer, 140 U.S. 545 (1891), held that the Wilson Act was a constitutional exercise of Congress's exclusive power to regulate interstate commerce and that Rahrer's conviction for selling liquor in its original package, contrary to Kansas law, did not violate the Constitution. Chief Justice Fuller again wrote the Court's opinion. Rahrer argued that, as *Cooley* showed, Congress could not "delegate its own powers [or] enlarge those of a State," and Chief Justice Fuller agreed. But, he argued, the Constitution transferred authority to regulate from the states to Congress; it did not give an "affirmative guaranty" that any activity would remain unregulated:

> Congress could [in] the exercise of the discretion reposed in it, concluding that the common interests did not require entire freedom in the traffic in ardent spirits, enact the law in question. In so doing Congress has not attempted to delegate the power to regulate commerce [or] to grant a power not possessed by the States, or to adopt state laws. It has taken its own course and made its own regulation, applying to these subjects of interstate commerce one common rule, whose uniformity is not affected by variations in state laws in dealing with such property. . . .
>
> [If] Congress chooses to provide that certain designated subjects of interstate commerce shall be governed by a rule which divests them of that character, [it may] do so. . . .
>
> [The] framers of the Constitution never intended that the legislative power of the nation should find itself incapable of disposing of a subject matter specifically committed to its charge. The manner of that disposition [in the Wilson Act] involves no ground for adjudging the act of Congress inoperative and void.

Does the Court adequately explain why the Wilson Act differs from the federal pilotage law involved in *Cooley*?

2. *Congressional silence and inertia.* The contortions in Chief Justice Fuller's logic notwithstanding, the rule became settled that Congress could consent to state regulations that the courts, in the absence of congressional action, would have found to violate the commerce clause. The logical difficulties disappeared once the theory of exclusive powers was abandoned: Congress may exercise its plenary power to regulate commerce by transferring regulatory authority to states, just as it could by transferring regulatory authority to an administrative

agency. See Cohen, Congressional Power to Validate Unconstitutional State Laws, 35 Stan. L. Rev. 387 (1983).

Taken together, the doctrines of preemption and consent mean that a judicial decision on a commerce clause challenge need not be final. If the challenge is rejected, those who oppose state regulation may secure federal legislation pre-empting it. If the challenge is sustained, those who support state regulation may secure federal legislation permitting it. Under these circumstances, why should the courts intervene rather than let the burdens of regulation lay where they fall and allow the political process to adjust the balance between burdens and benefits?

Concurring in Duckworth v. Arkansas, 314 U.S. 390 (1941), Justice Robert Jackson said that:

> [These] restraints are individually too petty, too diversified, and too local to get the attention of a Congress hard pressed with more urgent matters. [The] sluggishness of government, the multitude of matters that clamor for attention, and the relative ease with which men are persuaded to postpone troublesome decisions, all make inertia one of the most decisive powers in determining the course of our affairs and frequently gives [sic] to the established order of things a longevity and vitality much beyond its merits.

Thus, he concluded, the courts should intervene because of congressional iner-tia. If the restraints are indeed petty, in what sense could they unduly burden interstate commerce? Should the assumption rather be that restraints serious enough to violate the Constitution ought to be of such economic significance as to attract congressional attention? How can we distinguish congressional inaction due to inertia from inaction due to a considered judgment that on balance the state regulation does not unduly burden interstate commerce? For discussions of congressional silence, see Bikle, The Silence of Congress, 41 Harv. L. Rev. 200 (1927); Tribe, Toward a Syntax of the Unsaid: Construing the Sounds of Congres-sional and Constitutional Silence, 57 Indiana L.J. 515 (1982).

Note however that securing congressional action is costly. If the costs of mobi-lizing Congress to act exceed the burdens a regulation places on interstate com-merce, Congress's failure to act reflects not inertia but a rational calculation of the costs and benefits of political action. Judicial intervention might be justified if it is less expensive than the burdens on interstate commerce and the cost of mobilizing Congress. Should Congress create an administrative agency to review state regulations? Note (a) that such an agency might be seen as a modern version of Madison's proposed Council of Revision; (b) that it would plainly be a body exercising the power Congress has to regulate commerce; (c) that an agency is an attractive substitute for direct congressional action because it is relatively easier to bring a problem to its attention than to Congress's; and finally (d) that the courts could be seen as the proposed agency. Is there anything wrong in taking this last step? As you study the materials in section B of this chapter, consider whether review of state regulations is a sound use of the courts' time, compared to other possible uses of that time.

3. *Allocating the burden of inertia.* Under the modern view, the fundamental issue in this area is who should bear the burden of overcoming congressional inertia. Note that Justice Jackson's justification for judicial intervention con-cludes with a reference to the "merits" of the status quo. What are the criteria for determining the "merits" in this setting?

a. *Substantive preference for free trade.* H. P. Hood & Sons v. DuMond, 336 U.S. 525 (1949) (by Jackson, J.):

The Commerce Clause is one of the most prolific sources of national power and an equally prolific source of conflict with legislation of the state. While the Constitution vests in Congress the power to regulate commerce among the states, it does not say what the states may or may not do in the absence of congressional action. [This] Court has advanced the solidarity and prosperity of this Nation by the meaning it has given to these great silences of the Constitution. . . .

[The] principle that our economic unit is the Nation, which alone has the gamut of powers necessary to control the economy, including the vital power of erecting customs barriers against foreign competition, has as its corollary that the states are not separable economic units. . . .

The material success that has come to inhabitants of the states which make up this federal free trade unit has been the most impressive in the history of commerce, but the established interdependence of the states only emphasizes the necessity of protecting interstate movement of goods against local burdens and repressions. We need only consider the consequences if each of the few states that produce copper, lead, [cotton,] oil or gas should decree that industries located in that state shall have priority. What fantastic rivalries and dislocations and reprisals would ensue if such practices were begun! [May] Michigan provide that automobiles cannot be taken out of the State until local dealers' demands are fully met? [Could] Ohio then pounce upon the rubber-tire industry, on which she has a substantial grip, to retaliate for Michigan's auto monopoly?

Our system, fostered by the Commerce Clause, is that every farmer and every craftsmen shall be encouraged to produce by the certainty that he will have free access to every market in the Nation, that no home embargoes will withhold his exports, and no foreign state will by customs duties or regulations exclude them. Likewise, every consumer may look to the free competition from every producing area in the Nation to protect him from exploitation by any. Such was the vision of the Founders; such has been the doctrine of this Court which has given it reality.

Justice Jackson's description of the political and economic benefits of free trade reflects (a) the preconstitutional history of interstate commercial rivalries, discussed by Justice Johnson in *Gibbons,* and (b) the modern economic theory of free trade. On the latter, consider Prichard, Securing the Canadian Economic Union: Federalism and Internal Barriers to Trade, in Federalism and the Canadian Economic Union 1, 6 (M. Trebilcock et al. eds. 1983):

[The] tension between political autonomy and economic integration is inescapable in any non-unitary political system. Only by the mutual sacrifice of independence of action can states reap the full advantages of integration, because [they] flow from the adoption of common [rather] than competing policies. [Through] integration the participants may reap the benefits of the theory of comparative advantage through specialization and exchange. These gains are maximized when the factors of production and the resulting goods and services are allowed to move freely among participants to locations where the highest value is put on them. Thus gains from trade should increase the gross national product [as] long as the free movement of factors is maintained. . . .

[In] the absence of affirmative consent a Congressional negative will be presumed in the courts against state action which in its effect upon interstate commerce constitutes an unreasonable interference with national interests, the presumption being rebuttable at the pleasure of Congress.

Dowling, Interstate Commerce and State Power, 27 Va. L. Rev. 1, 20 (1940). (This article and its successor, Interstate Commerce and State Power — Revised Version, 47 Colum. L. Rev. 547 (1947), remain the most useful overviews of the problems addressed in this section.)

b. *Minimizing costs.* Obtaining congressional preemption or consent requires interest groups to invest time and effort in the political process. If the burden of overcoming inertia is placed on the group *less* likely to succeed in that effort, it may be discouraged from the investment. If that occurs, the courts will have arrived at the outcome that Congress would have, and at a lower cost. How accurately can the courts determine who is less likely to succeed? What if the loser in the courts is not discouraged?

Consider the extent to which the distinction in *Cooley* between national and local subject matters, and that in *Gibbons* between commercial and police power regulations, assist in determining who should bear the burden of overcoming congressional inertia. Finally, note Powell, The Still Small Voice of the Commerce Clause, in 3 Selected Essays on Constitutional Law 932 (1938): "If congress keeps silent about the interstate commerce that is not national in character, [then] congress is silently silent, and the states may regulate. But if congress keeps silent about the kind of commerce that is national in character, [then] congress is silently vocal and says that the commerce must be free from state regulation."

4. *The availability of nonconstitutional grounds for decision.* Note in the following materials the cases in which federal statutes might have been used as the basis for decisions on preemption or consent grounds. Consider what reasons the Court might have for relying on "constitutional" rather than statutory grounds.

B. PROTECTION AGAINST DISCRIMINATION

In Lewis v. BT Investment Managers, 447 U.S. 27 (1980), the Court held unconstitutional a Florida statute barring out-of-state banks from owning Florida investment advisory businesses. Other out-of-state businesses could own Florida investment advisors, and out-of-state banks were not barred by Florida law from owning other kinds of businesses. Why was the statute passed? Who benefits from it? Who bears the costs? Consider this observation by Justice Stone in South Carolina State Highway Department v. Barnwell Bros., 303 U.S. 177 (1938):

> State regulations affecting interstate commerce, whose purpose or effect is to gain for those within the state an advantage at the expense of those without, or to burden those out of the state without any corresponding advantage to those within, have been thought to impinge upon the constitutional prohibition even though Congress has not acted.
>
> Underlying the stated rule has been the thought, often expressed in judicial opinion, that when the regulation is of such a character that its burden falls principally upon those without the state, legislative action is not likely to be subjected to those political restraints which are normally exerted on legislation where it affects adversely some interests within the state. See [*Cooley*].

Does this "thought" explain the outcome in *Lewis?* The implications of Stone's observations provide the structure for this section.

Note: General Considerations

1. *The politics of regulation.* State (and federal) regulations of economic activities impose costs and provide benefits. There are a number of ways in which costs and benefits can be spread among various segments of the population. Consider the following classification, offered by J. Q. Wilson, in The Politics of Regulation 366-370 (1980):

[Policy] proposals, especially those involving economic stakes, can be classified in terms of the perceived distribution of their costs and benefits. These costs and benefits may be monetary or nonmonetary, and the value assigned to them, as well as beliefs about the likelihood of their materializing, can change. . . .

The political significance of costs and benefits arises out of their distribution as well as their magnitude. To simplify the analysis, I will emphasize the distributional effect. Magnitudes are certainly important (politics is replete with discussions of "windfall profits," "tax burdens," and "unmet needs"), but the incidence of these magnitudes is especially relevant to political action. As we shall see, the distribution of consequences affects the incentive to form political organizations and to engage in collective action. Moreover, perceptions of the fairness and unfairness of a policy profoundly affect the extent to which it is regarded as legitimate and thus the difficulty (or cost) of finding persuasive justifications for that policy. . . .

Costs and benefits may be widely distributed or narrowly concentrated. Income and social security taxes are widely distributed; subsidies to a particular industry or regulations imposing costs on an industry that cannot be fully passed through to consumers are narrowly concentrated. Though there are many intermediate cases, four political situations can be distinguished by considering all combinations of the dichotomous cases.

When both costs and benefits are widely distributed, we expect to find *majoritarian* politics. All or most of society expects to gain; all or most of society expects to pay. Interest groups have little incentive to form around such issues because no small, definable segment of society (an industry, an occupation, a locality) can expect to capture a disproportionate share of the benefits or avoid a disproportionate share of the burdens. Not all measures that seem to offer a net gain to popular majorities are passed: proposals must first get onto the political agenda, people must agree that it is legitimate for the government to take action, and ideological objections to the propriety or feasibility of the measures must be overcome. All these issues had to be dealt with in the case of such conspicuously majoritarian policies as the Social Security Act of 1935 and the proposal to maintain a large standing army just before and just after World War II.

The passage of the Sherman Antitrust Act, and perhaps also of the Federal Trade Commission Act, arose out of circumstances that approximate those of majoritarian politics. No single industry was to be regulated; the nature and scope of the proposed regulations were left quite vague; any given firm could imagine ways in which these laws might help them (in dealing with an "unscrupulous" competitor, for example). But though there was no determined industry opposition, neither was there strong business support. The measures could not be passed until popular sentiment supported them (Grangers and muckrakers had first to persuade people that a problem existed and that there was a gain to be had) and elite opinion was convinced that it was legitimate for the federal government to pass such laws. . . .

When both costs and benefits are narrowly concentrated, conditions are ripe for *interest-group politics.* A subsidy or regulation will often benefit a relatively small group at the expense of another comparable small group. Each side has a strong incentive to organize and exercise political influence. The public does not believe it will be much affected one way or another; though it may sympathize more with one side than the other, its voice is likely to be heard in only weak or general terms. The passage of the Commerce Act in 1886 resulted from interest-group politics as each affected party — long-haul and short-haul railroads, farm groups, oil companies, and businessmen representing various port cities — contended over how, if at all, railroad rates should be regulated. Much labor legislation — the Wagner Act, the Taft-Hartley Act, the Landrum-Griffin Act, the proposed labor law reform act of 1978 — is also a product of interest-group politics. . . .

When the benefits of a prospective policy are concentrated but the costs widely distributed, *client politics* is likely to result. Some small, easily organized group will benefit and thus has a powerful incentive to organize and lobby; the costs of the benefit are distributed at a low per capita rate over a large number of people, and hence they have little incentive to organize in opposition — if, indeed, they even hear of the policy. [An] important organizational change has occurred that has altered the normal advantage enjoyed by the client group in these circumstances — the emergence of "watchdog" or "public interest" associations that have devised ways of maintaining themselves without having to recruit and organize the people who will be affected by a policy. Absent such watchdog organizations, however, client politics produces regulatory legislation that most nearly approximates the producer-dominance model. Countless industries and occupations have come to enjoy subsidies and regulations that, in effect, spare them the full rigors of economic competition.

The Civil Aeronautics Board arose from circumstances conducive to client politics and, after its formation, the CAB operated in a manner most solicitous of the health of the domestic aviation industry. Public utility commissions were created in part at the urging of electric utility executives; though one cannot be certain, the desires of these industry spokesmen may well have been the most important source of the PUC movement. But [neither] the CAB nor the PUCs conform exactly to the model of client politics. There was much public discussion of the matter, nonbusiness groups were important parts of the supportive coalition, and public-serving arguments were made and taken seriously. These circumstances are somewhat different from those normally associated with client politics: backstairs intrigue, quiet lobbying, and quick passage with a minimum of public discussion. . . .

Finally, a policy may be proposed that will confer general (though perhaps small) benefits at a cost to be borne chiefly by a small segment of society. When this is attempted, we are witnessing *entrepreneurial politics*. Antipollution and auto-safety bills were proposed to make air cleaner or cars safer for everyone at an expense that was imposed, at least initially, on particular segments of industry. Since the incentive to organize is strong for opponents of the policy but weak for the beneficiaries, and since the political system provides many points at which opposition can be registered, it may seem astonishing that regulatory legislation of this sort is ever passed. It is, and with growing frequency in recent years — but it requires the efforts of a skilled entrepreneur who can mobilize latent public sentiment (by revealing a scandal or capitalizing on a crisis), put the opponents of the plan publicly on the defensive (by accusing them of deforming babies or killing motorists), and associate the legislation with widely shared values (clean air, pure water, health, and safety). The entrepreneur serves as the vicarious representative of groups not directly part of the legislative process.

Into which categories do the statutes in *Hunt* and *Lewis* fall? A statute limiting the weights of trucks on local highways? In reading the materials that follow, consider whether Wilson's classification assists your understanding of the legal issues discussed.

2. *Cost-benefit analysis generally.* If an individual decided to alter his or her economic activity, we could be confident that the benefits to the individual of the

change exceeded its costs. But as Stone and Wilson make clear, the costs of economic regulation are not always paid by those who receive its benefits. The distribution of costs and benefits across different groups means that the mere adoption of a regulation need not establish that its benefits to the entire society exceed its costs. Further, the distribution of costs and benefits across different groups affects the political forces supporting and opposing adoption or repeal of regulations. Under what conditions might regulations be adopted when their total social costs exceed their total social benefits?

Wilson's discussion of client politics indicates one set of conditions. If benefits will be conferred on a relatively small group, each member can agree to finance lobbying efforts to secure the legislation (on the condition that every other member also contribute). (Why is the condition important?) Each will expect to recover its investment in political activity from the benefits to be gained by the legislation. If the regulation also imposes costs on a broad group, those who bear the costs will find it difficult to organize in opposition. The costs imposed on each member of the group are likely to be smaller than the amount each would have to invest in an effective lobbying effort. Further, there is a free-rider problem: Each member of the group may hang back, expecting that others will engage in lobbying which, if successful, would benefit the free rider at no cost to him or herself. This theory is developed in detail in M. Olson, The Logic of Collective Action (1965). To what extent is it weakened by the development of "watchdog" organizations? (How and why are they funded?)

Consider the extent to which a theory like Olson's may underlie (1) the "undue burden" cases in section C below; (2) the discrimination cases that follow; (3) cases such as Lochner v. New York, Chapter 6, section D, infra.

3. *"Exporting" costs.* Regulations may be adopted when the beneficiaries within the jurisdiction adopting it outweigh in political power those within the jurisdiction who will bear (some of) its costs. They may do so because of numbers or because of the organizational factors discussed by Wilson and Olson. Total social costs may still exceed total social benefits, but if the local beneficiaries can export enough costs so that the local benefits exceed the local costs, the regulation may be adopted. Is this the "thought" Stone described? Consider whether the statutes in *Hunt* and *Lewis* involve this kind of cost-exporting.

Note that in every case some local residents — those who prefer doing business with out-of-staters — will be worse off. In the simplest case the benefits to local residents exceed the costs to local residents. Even though some local residents (and therefore voters) will bear some costs, the "gross state product" will be greater after the regulation is adopted than before. The local beneficiaries may then use some of their new profits to subsidize the local cost-bearers, reducing the political opposition to the adoption of the regulation. Consider in this connection Dean Milk Co. v. Madison, below.

Although Congress may not "export" costs of national regulations in the same way, note that it may distribute costs and benefits among various geographical areas. Two constitutional provisions have been interpreted to require geographical uniformity in regulation: Article I, section 8, clause 4 (power "to establish [uniform] Laws [on] Bankruptcies"), and article I, section 8, clause 1 (power to tax requires that "all Duties, Imposts, and Excises [be] uniform throughout the United States"). The latter clause was applied in United States v. Ptasynski, 462 U.S. 74 (1983), which found constitutional a provision of the Windfall Profit Tax of 1980 that excluded "exempt Alaskan oil" from its coverage. The Court noted that the exempt oil could have been described in nongeographical terms and, after "closely" examining the statute, concluded that the exemption was based on "neutral factors" such as climate and difficulty of extraction. Would a tax imposed only on Alaskan oil violate the Uniformity Clause? For a discussion of the clause's background, see Knowlton v. Moore, 178 U.S. 41 (1900). Consider Comment, The Uniformity Clause, 51 U. Chi. L. Rev. 1193, 1194: "[The] uniformity clause should be read in light of the Constitution's general preference for free markets and unrestrained economic competition." Is there such a general preference?

4. *Incidence analysis.* Under what circumstances can a state export the costs of regulation? This is the subject of a branch of economics called incidence analysis. McLure, Incidence Analysis and the Supreme Court: An Examination of Four Cases from the 1980 Term, 1 Sup. Ct. Econ. Rev. 69 (1982), provides a useful introduction to this complex subject, with illustrations taken from the matters covered in this section.

McLure identifies the following as among the "pervasive determinants of incidence": (a) "Short-term versus long-term" perspectives: In the short run a state may be able to export the costs of regulation by imposing the regulation on an activity where fixed capital investments (in plants and equipment, for example) out-of-state are proportionally more significant than fixed capital in-state. But over time investors will adjust their activities to take account of the regulation. Consider in this connection Justice Jackson's reference to the monopolies in automobile and tire manufacture held by Michigan and Ohio. (b) "Market dominance": If the state has a monopoly or near-monopoly on the regulated activity, the costs of regulation can be shifted to consumers. If the consumers are largely out-of-state, the costs will be exported even if the regulated activity takes place entirely within the state. For an example (a tax placed on the extraction of coal), see Commonwealth Edison Co. v. Montana, below. For a detailed examination of this aspect of the problem, see Levmore, Interstate Exploitation and Judicial Intervention, 69 Va. L. Rev. 563 (1983). (c) "Substitution": Costs can be exported if there are no or few substitutes for the regulated activity at almost equal prices and (again) if consumers are largely out-of-state. For example, if a commodity like coal must be shipped out of state on railroads, the costs of railroad regulation can be exported. If shippers can switch to trucks, the costs of railroad regulation cannot be exported. McLure notes that careful definition of the relevant market is essential when considering the latter two determinants.

Try to apply this analysis to the *Lewis* case that introduced this section. Which of the cases that follow involve regulations that have the characteristic of allowing enough costs to be exported so that local benefits will exceed local costs?

5. *Possible burdens on the local economy.* In *Lewis,* out-of-state banks were deprived of some opportunities to make profits on their Florida operations. Could they raise the prices they charge to Floridians to make up for the lost profits? The regulation also diminished the competition faced by in-state investment advisors. Could they raise the prices they charged? If prices rise in this manner, costs are not exported. Note however that Olson's free-rider analysis might still explain why the regulation was adopted. Should the courts be concerned about that problem?

6. *An alternative framework.* The materials in this chapter are organized around the theme of cost-exporting. After working through the materials, consider whether that organization is more helpful than one focused on the subject

matter of the regulation (e.g., transportation, natural resources, end products of complex manufacturing processes). (One reason for adopting this organization is that its basic structure duplicates that of the material on the equal protection clause, Chapter 5 infra. Consider whether this indicates something about the premises of the Constitution as a whole.) Be careful to note as well the varying doctrinal formulations the Court offers. Are the variations associated with relevant differences (a) in the likelihood of cost-exporting, or (b) in the subject matter, or (c) anything?

City of Philadelphia v. New Jersey
437 U.S. 617 (1978)

MR. JUSTICE STEWART delivered the opinion of the Court.

A New Jersey law prohibits the importation of most "solid or liquid waste which originated or was collected outside the territorial limits of the State." In this case we are required to decide whether this statutory prohibition violates the Commerce Clause of the United States Constitution. . . .

[Private landfill operators challenged the statute on preemption and constitutional grounds. The state Supreme Court found that the statute "advanced vital health and environmental objectives with no economic discrimination against, and with little burden upon, interstate commerce." It also found no preemption.]

We agree with the New Jersey court that the state law has not been pre-empted by federal legislation.[4] The dispositive question, therefore, is whether the law is constitutionally permissible in light of the Commerce Clause of the Constitution.

II

Before it addressed the merits of the appellants' claim, the New Jersey Supreme Court questioned whether the interstate movement of those wastes banned by ch. 363 is "commerce" at all within the meaning of the Commerce Clause. Any doubts on that score should be laid to rest at the outset. . . .

[All] objects of interstate trade merit Commerce Clause protection; none is excluded by definition at the outset. Hence, we reject the state court's suggestion that the banning of "valueless" out-of-state wastes by [the statute] implicates no constitutional protection. Just as Congress has power to regulate the interstate movement of these wastes, States are not free from constitutional scrutiny when they restrict that movement.

---

4. [From] our review of this federal legislation, we find no "clear and manifest purpose of Congress," Rice v. Santa Fe Elevator Corp., 331 U.S. 218, 230, to pre-empt the entire field of interstate waste management or transportation, either by express statutory command, or by implicit legislative design. To the contrary, Congress expressly has provided that "the collection and disposal of solid wastes should continue to be primarily the function of State, regional, and local agencies. . . ." 42 U.S.C. §6901 (a)(4)(1976 ed.). Similarly, [the statute] is not pre-empted because of a square conflict with particular provisions of federal law or because of general incompatibility with basic federal objectives. In short, [the statute] can be enforced consistently with the program goals and the respective federal-state roles intended by Congress when it enacted the federal legislation.

III

A

Although the Constitution gives Congress the power to regulate commerce among the States, many subjects of potential federal regulation under that power inevitably escape congressional attention "because of their local character and their number and diversity." South Carolina State Highway Dept. v. Barnwell Bros., Inc., 303 U.S. 177, 185. In the absence of federal legislation, these subjects are open to control by the States so long as they act within the restraints imposed by the Commerce Clause itself. The bounds of these restraints appear nowhere in the words of the Commerce Clause, but have emerged gradually in the decisions of this Court giving effect to its basic purpose. That broad purpose was well expressed by Mr. Justice Jackson in his opinion for the Court in H. P. Hood & Sons, Inc. v. Du Mond, [quoted above]. . . .

The opinions of the Court through the years have reflected an alertness to the evils of "economic isolation" and protectionism, while at the same time recognizing that incidental burdens on interstate commerce may be unavoidable when a State legislates to safeguard the health and safety of its people. Thus, where simple economic protectionism is effected by state legislation, a virtually per se rule of invalidity has been erected. See, e.g., H. P. Hood & Sons, Inc., v. Du Mond. The clearest example of such legislation is a law that overtly blocks the flow of interstate commerce at a State's borders. But where other legislative objectives are credibly advanced and there is no patent discrimination against interstate trade, the Court has adopted a much more flexible approach, the general contours of which were outlined in Pike v. Bruce Church, Inc., 397 U.S. 137, 142:

> Where the statute regulates evenhandedly to effectuate a legitimate local public interest, and its effects on interstate commerce are only incidental, it will be upheld unless the burden imposed on such commerce is clearly excessive in relation to the putative local benefits. . . . If a legitimate local purpose is found, then the question becomes one of degree. And the extent of the burden that will be tolerated will of course depend on the nature of the local interest involved, and on whether it could be promoted as well with a lesser impact on interstate activities.

The crucial inquiry, therefore, must be directed to determining whether [the statute] is basically a protectionist measure, or whether it can fairly be viewed as a law directed to legitimate local concerns, with effects upon interstate commerce that are only incidental.

B

The purpose of [the statute] is set out [as] follows:

> The Legislature finds and determines that . . . the volume of solid and liquid waste continues to rapidly increase, that the treatment and disposal of these wastes continues to pose an even greater threat to the quality of the environment of New Jersey, that the available and appropriate land fill sites within the State are being diminished, that the environment continues to be threatened by the treatment and

disposal of waste which originated or was collected outside the State, and that the
public health, safety and welfare require that the treatment and disposal within this
State of all wastes generated outside of the State be prohibited.

The New Jersey Supreme Court accepted this statement of the state legislature's purpose. The state court additionally found that New Jersey's existing
landfill sites will be exhausted within a few years; that to go on using these sites or
to develop new ones will take a heavy environmental toll, both from pollution and
from loss of scarce open lands; that new techniques to divert waste from landfills
to other methods of disposal and resource recovery processes are under development, but that these changes will require time; and finally, that "the extension of
the lifespan of existing landfills, resulting from the exclusion of out-of-state waste,
may be of crucial importance in preventing further virgin wetlands or other
undeveloped lands from being devoted to landfill purposes." Based on these findings, the court concluded that [the statute] was designed to protect, not the
State's economy, but its environment, and that its substantial benefits outweigh
its "slight" burden on interstate commerce.

The appellants strenuously contend that [the statute], "while outwardly cloaked
'in the currently fashionable garb of environment protection,' . . . is actually no
more than a legislative effort to suppress competition and stabilize the cost of
solid waste disposal for New Jersey residents. . . ." They cite passages of legislative history suggesting that the problem [is] primarily financial: Stemming the flow
of out-of-state waste into certain landfill sites will extend their lives, thus delaying
the day when New Jersey cities must transport their waste to more distant and
expensive sites.

The appellees, on the other hand, deny that [the statute] was motivated by
financial concerns or economic protectionism. In the words of their brief, "[n]o
New Jersey commercial interests stand to gain advantage over competitors from
outside the state as a result of the ban on dumping out-of-state waste." Noting
that New Jersey landfill operators are among the plaintiffs, the appellee's brief
argues that "[t]he complaint is not that New Jersey has forged an economic
preference for its own commercial interests, but rather that it has denied a small
group of its entrepreneurs an economic opportunity to traffic in waste in order to
protect the health, safety and welfare of the citizenry at large."

This dispute about ultimate legislative purpose need not be resolved, because
its resolution would not be relevant to the constitutional issue to be decided in
this case. Contrary to the evident assumption of the state court and the parties,
the evil of protectionism can reside in legislative means as well as legislative ends.
Thus, it does not matter whether the ultimate aim of [the statute] is to reduce the
waste disposal costs of New Jersey residents or to save remaining open lands from
pollution, for we assume New Jersey has every right to protect its residents'
pocketbooks as well as their environment. And it may be assumed as well that
New Jersey may pursue those ends by slowing the flow of *all* waste into the State's
remaining landfills, even though interstate commerce may incidentally be affected. But whatever New Jersey's ultimate purpose, it may not be accomplished
by discriminating against articles of commerce from outside the State unless there
is some reason, apart from their origin, to treat them differently. Both on its face
and in its plain effect, [the statute] violates this principle of nondiscrimination.

The Court has consistently found parochial legislation of this kind to be consti-

tutionally invalid, whether the ultimate aim of the legislation was to assure a
steady supply of milk by erecting barriers to allegedly ruinous outside competition, Baldwin v. G. A. F. Seelig, Inc., [infra]; or to create jobs by keeping industry
within the State, or to preserve the State's financial resources from depletion by
fencing out indigent immigrants. In each of these cases, a presumably legitimate
goal was sought to be achieved by the illegitimate means of isolating the State
from the national economy.

Also relevant here are the Court's decisions holding that a State may not accord
its own inhabitants a preferred right of access over consumers in other States to
natural resources located within its borders. These cases stand for the basic
principle that a "State is without power to prevent privately owned articles of
trade from being shipped and sold in interstate commerce on the ground that they
are required to satisfy local demands or because they are needed by the people of
the State." Foster-Fountain Packaging Co. v. Haydel, [278 U.S. 1], at 10.

The New Jersey law at issue in this case falls squarely within the area that the
Commerce Clause puts off limits to state regulation. On its face, it imposes on
out-of-state commercial interests the full burden of conserving the state's remaining landfill space. It is true that in our previous cases the scarce natural resource
was itself the article of commerce, whereas here the scarce resource and the
article of commerce are distinct. But that difference is without consequence. In
both instances, the State has overtly moved to slow or freeze the flow of commerce for protectionist reasons. It does not matter that the State has shut the
article of commerce inside the State in one case and outside the State in the
other. What is crucial is the attempt by one State to isolate itself from a problem
common to many by erecting a barrier against the movement of interstate trade.

The appellees argue that not all laws which facially discriminate against out-of-
state commerce are forbidden protectionist regulations. In particular, they point
to quarantine laws, which this Court has repeatedly upheld even though they
appear to single out interstate commerce for special treatment. See Baldwin v.
G. A. F. Seelig, Inc., at 525. In the appellees' view, [the statute] is analogous to
such health-protective measures, since it reduces the exposure of New Jersey
residents to the allegedly harmful effects of landfill sites.

It is true that certain quarantine laws have not been considered forbidden
protectionist measures, even though they were directed against out-of-state commerce. But those quarantine laws banned the importation of articles such as
diseased livestock that required destruction as soon as possible because their very
movement risked contagion and other evils. Those laws thus did not discriminate
against interstate commerce as such, but simply prevented traffic in noxious
articles, whatever their origin.

The New Jersey statute is not such a quarantine law. There has been no claim
here that the very movement of waste into or through New Jersey endangers
health, or that waste must be disposed of as soon and as close to its point of
generation as possible. The harms caused by waste are said to arise after its
disposal in landfill sites, and at that point, as New Jersey concedes, there is no
basis to distinguish out-of-state waste from domestic waste. If one is inherently
harmful, so is the other. Yet New Jersey has banned the former while leaving its
landfill sites open to the latter. The New Jersey law blocks the importation of
waste in an obvious effort to saddle those outside the State with the entire burden
of slowing the flow of refuse into New Jersey's remaining landfill sites. That

legislative effort is clearly impermissible under the Commerce Clause of the Constitution.

Today, cities in Pennsylvania and New York find it expedient or necessary to send their waste into New Jersey for disposal, and New Jersey claims the right to close its borders to such traffic. Tomorrow, cities in New Jersey may find it expedient or necessary to send their waste into Pennsylvania or New York for disposal, and those States might then claim the right to close their borders. The Commerce Clause will protect New Jersey in the future, just as it protects her neighbors now, from efforts by one State to isolate itself in the stream of interstate commerce from a problem shared by all. The judgment is reversed.

MR. JUSTICE REHNQUIST, with whom THE CHIEF JUSTICE joins, dissenting.

A growing problem in our Nation is the sanitary treatment and disposal of solid waste. For many years, solid waste was incinerated. Because of the significant environmental problems attendant on incineration, however, this method of solid waste disposal has declined in use in many localities, including New Jersey. "Sanitary" landfills have replaced incineration as the principal method of disposing of solid waste. [But] landfills also present extemely serious health and safety problems. First, in New Jersey, "virtually all sanitary landfills can be expected to produce leachate, a noxious and highly polluted liquid which is seldom visible and frequently pollutes . . . ground and surface waters." The natural decomposition process which occurs in landfills also produces large quantities of methane and thereby presents a significant explosion hazard. Landfills can also generate "health hazards caused by rodents, fires and scavenger birds" and, "needless to say, do not help New Jersey's aesthetic appearance nor New Jersey's noise or water or air pollution problems."

The health and safety hazards associated with landfills present appellees with a currently unsolvable dilemma. Other, hopefully safer, methods of disposing of solid wastes are still in the development stage and cannot presently be used. But appellees obviously cannot completely stop the tide of solid waste that its citizens will produce in the interim. For the moment, therefore, appellees must continue to use sanitary landfills to dispose of New Jersey's own solid waste despite the critical environmental problems thereby created.

The question presented in this case is whether New Jersey must also continue to receive and dispose of solid waste from neighboring States, even though these will inexorably increase the health problems discussed above. The Court answers this question in the affirmative. New Jersey must either prohibit *all* landfill operations, leaving itself to cast about for a presently nonexistent solution to the serious problem of disposing of the waste generated within its own borders, or it must accept waste from every portion of the United States, thereby multiplying the health and safety problems which would result if it dealt only with such wastes generated within the State. Because past precedents establish that the Commerce Clause does not present appellees with such a Hobson's choice, I dissent. . . .

[New] Jersey may require germ-infected rags or diseased meat to be disposed of as best as possible within the State, but at the same time prohibit the *importation* of such items for disposal at the facilities that are set up within New Jersey for disposal of such material generated *within* the State. The physical fact of life that New Jersey must somehow dispose of its own noxious items does not mean that it must serve as a depository for those of every other State. Similarly, New Jersey should be free under our past precedents to prohibit the importation of solid waste because of the health and safety problems that such waste poses to its citizens. The fact that New Jersey continues to, and indeed must continue to, dispose of its own solid waste does not mean that New Jersey may not prohibit the importation of even more solid waste into the State. I simply see no way to distinguish solid waste, on the record of this case, from germ-infected rags, diseased meat, and other noxious items.

The Court's effort to distinguish these prior cases is unconvincing. . . .

[I] do not see why a State may ban the importation of items whose movement risks contagion, but cannot ban the importation of items which, although they may be transported into the State without undue hazard, will then simply pile up in an ever increasing danger to the public's health and safety. The Commerce Clause was not drawn with a view to having the validity of state laws turn on such pointless distinctions.

Second, the Court implies that the challenged laws must be invalidated because New Jersey has left its landfills open to domestic waste. But, as the Court notes, this Court has repeatedly upheld quarantine laws "even though they appear to single out interstate commerce for special treatment." The fact that New Jersey has left its landfill sites open for domestic waste does not, of course, mean that solid waste is not innately harmful. Nor does it mean that New Jersey prohibits importation of solid waste for reasons other than the health and safety of its population. New Jersey must out of sheer necessity treat and dispose of its solid waste in some fashion, just as it must treat New Jersey cattle suffering from hoof-and-mouth disease. It does not follow that New Jersey must, under the Commerce Clause, accept solid waste or diseased cattle from outside its borders and thereby exacerbate its problems.

Note: Facial/Intentional Discrimination

1. *Cost-benefit analysis.* Who gains the benefits and who bears the costs of New Jersey's statute? There are four groups to consider: Out-of-state waste producers, out-of-state landfill operators, in-state waste producers, and in-state landfill operators. (a) Costs: The statute reduces the supply of landfill available to out-of-state waste producers and may therefore increase the price they must pay for disposal. It reduces the demand for New Jersey landfills and may therefore decrease the profits of in-state landfill operators. (b) Benefits: The statute benefits in-state waste producers by reducing demand and decreasing prices and by improving their environment, and out-of-state landfill operators by increasing demand and raising profits. Note that from the point of view of cost-exporting, New Jersey does not care whether the benefits to out-of-state landfill operators exceed the costs to out-of-state waste producers. Its sole concern is that the decreased prices paid by New Jersey waste producers exceed the profits New Jersey operators lose by being unable to accept out-of-state waste. Is it likely that the local benefits exceed the local costs? (What is the relevance, if any, of the fact that New Jersey landfill operators are among the plaintiffs in the case?)

2. *Local versus overall benefits.* Suppose that local benefits exceed local costs. It may nonetheless be true that the total social benefits of the regulation exceed the total social costs. Why should New Jersey be barred from enforcing its statute without the opponents showing that total costs also exceed total benefits? Reduc-

ing the supply of landfills in the Northeast may encourage the development of alternative means of waste disposal (a "long-run" consideration in McLure's terms). Or waste producers in the Northeast may have refrained from making economically sound investments in local waste disposal plants because they relied on the availability of New Jersey's landfills. There may also be issues of distribution: The welfare of the Northeast might be increased by making New Jersey a little less polluted and Pennsylvania a little more. (It is sometimes argued that distributional goals can be reached more effectively by direct transfers of wealth than by regulation. For a presentation and critique of this contention, see Kronman, Contract Law and Distributive Justice, 89 Yale L.J. 472 (1980).)

Recall that the fundamental issue in this section is determining who should bear the burden of overcoming congressional inertia. Is the possibility that exporting costs will produce a situation in which total costs exceed total benefits enough to justify placing that burden on a state that manages to export enough of the costs of regulation? ("Enough" means sufficient to make local benefits exceed local costs.) Consider in this connection the interpretation of the federal statutes in footnote 4 of *City of Philadelphia*. Should the Court have considered whether the statute gave New Jersey permission to do what it did?

3. *Intent.* Is it fair to say that the Court infers from the use of the statute's distinction between in-state and out-of-state waste producers, an intent to benefit local interests and harm out-of-state ones? Suppose the statute fails to export enough costs. Should the intent to export costs matter then? Suppose the statute does export enough costs. Should a noncommercial intent matter then? Does the use of a local/out-of-state distinction justify a presumption of intent to export costs? If so, should the effect of the presumption be to invalidate the statute unless the state persuades the court that it had a noncommercial intent, or to invalidate the statute until the state persuades Congress to permit the state to regulate for either anticommercial or noncommercial purposes?

Consider in this connection the following facts about the regulation at issue in the *Lewis* case, above: On October 3, 1972, Bankers Trust, a New York corporation, filed a proposal with federal regulatory officials to operate an investment management subsidiary in Florida. As of that date, Florida prohibited out-of-state bank holding companies such as Bankers Trust from owning a local bank and from offering investment advisory services to local banks. It did not prohibit them from offering investment advisory services directly to the public. Florida banking interests responded by filing objections with the federal regulators to Bankers Trust's proposal. In addition, on November 30, the Florida legislature adopted the statute challenged in *Lewis*. According to the Supreme Court, "there [was] evidence that the [statute] was a direct response to Bankers Trust's pending application, and that it had the strong backing of the local financial community."

How typical are these facts? Recall Wilson's comments on client politics, and see the facts relied on by some justices in Kassel v. Consolidated Freightways, below. (Note, as always, the presence of a federal regulatory scheme that opens the way for preemption/consent arguments.)

4. *"Quarantining" pollution.* The primary precedents supporting New Jersey are the quarantine cases. Does the majority or the dissent better characterize those cases and their relation to the principal case?

5. *Variations.* Are the following statutes constitutional? In analyzing this question, consider (a) who bears the costs and gains the benefits, to see if it is likely that enough costs are exported; (b) the possible protectionist, police power, or

other purposes of the statutes; and (c) the importance, local and regional, of the subject matter the statutes regulate.

a. An Oklahoma statute provides that "no person may [ship] minnows for sale outside the state which were seined [within] the waters of the state." The statute bars local residents who catch minnows from exporting them, and allows out-of-state buyers to purchase minnows raised in nurseries. Hughes v. Oklahoma, 441 U.S. 322 (1979) (statute held unconstitutional).

b. A New Hampshire statute prohibits companies whose plants generate electricity from conveying the electricity out of state without the permission of the state's public utilities commission. The Commission prohibited exportation on the ground that the electricity was "reasonably required" for local use. New England Power Company had 10 percent of its generating capacity in New Hampshire; it serviced 6 percent of New Hampshire's population. The state's largest utility had costs about 25 percent higher than those of New England Power, largely because New England Power used hydroelectric generation, a cheaper method than the one used by the other utility. Hydroelectric generation produces electricity by using the force of water flowing downstream. See New England Power Co. v. New Hampshire, 455 U.S. 331 (1982) (statute held unconstitutional). Reconsider this case after reading South-Central Timber Development v. Wunnicke, below.

How confident are you that the courts can reliably determine whether enough costs can be exported in these cases? Should the courts use the appearance of discrimination on the face of the statute, or anticommercial intent, as a rough approximation of the incidence analysis? As the basis for allocating the burden of overcoming congressional inertia?

6. *The relevance of retaliation.* The principal case concludes by invoking fears of retaliatory responses by other states. Why should that be a matter of concern? Retaliation would increase the costs borne by local residents, thus eliminating the export of costs and reducing the incentive to adopt the regulation. Note however that retaliation may not be completely effective, so that it inflicts some pure economic losses on the states involved with neither an economic nor a distributive justification, and that retaliation, at least until the trade barriers are lowered, is likely to alter the patterns of investment, as resources shift to take account of the costs imposed by retaliatory regulations in one sector of the economy but not in another.

Sporhase v. Nebraska, 458 U.S. 941 (1982): A Nebraska statute prohibited the withdrawal of ground water from any well within Nebraska intended for use in another state that fails to grant reciprocal rights to withdraw and transport ground water to Nebraska. Colorado does not grant reciprocal rights. Owners of contiguous land on the Nebraska/Colorado border claimed that the statute unconstitutionally barred them from transferring ground water from a Nebraska well to the Colorado land. The Supreme Court agreed. After holding that ground water was an article of commerce (see note 7 infra), the Court considered Nebraska's "legitimate and highly important" interest in conserving ground water, a scarce and valuable resource in the region. Water conservation was important for health as well as economic reasons. The Court upheld portions of Nebraska's statutes restricting exportation of ground water unless exportation was "reasonable [and] not contrary to [conservation,]" in part because Nebraska heavily regulated transfer of ground water from one part of Nebraska to another. It found the reciprocity requirement not "narrowly tailored" to serve conservation goals. Citing A&P Tea

Co. v. Cottrell, 424 U.S. 366 (1976), it noted that the reciprocity requirement could not be justified "as a response to another State's unreasonable burden on commerce." Why not?

Cottrell defended its position that retaliation was not permitted even if it was intended to provide an incentive to eliminate trade barriers, on the ground that the state's proper remedy for trade barriers was a challenge in court, not retaliation. Retaliation is common in the international sphere. It is dealt with by the negotiation of bilateral and multilateral trade agreements. Have the states already negotiated such an agreement, calling it the commerce clause rather than a trade treaty? As is always true in this area, the problem is again reduced to one regarding allocating the burden of overcoming congressional inertia.

7. *What is commerce?* *Hughes* and *Sporhase* are two in a series of recent cases overruling older ones exempting certain items from the commerce clause. See, e.g., Geer v. Connecticut, 161 U.S. 519 (1896) (game birds not articles of commerce because state "owns" them); Hudson County Water Co. v. McCarter, 209 U.S. 349 (1908) (relying on *Geer* to find water not an article of commerce). See also Commonwealth Edison Co. v. Montana, infra (rejecting argument based on Heisler v. Thomas Colliery, 260 U.S. 245 (1922), that extraction of coal occurs prior to commerce). The older cases rested on aspects of the "exclusive power" view, and as that view has been rejected so have been what were thought of as its consequences.

Hunt v. Washington State Apple Advertising Commission

432 U.S. 333 (1977)

MR. CHIEF JUSTICE BURGER delivered the opinion of the Court.

In 1973, North Carolina enacted a statute which required [all] closed containers of apples sold [or] shipped into the State to bear "no grade other than the applicable U.S. grade or standard." [A federal court invalidated the statute "on the ground that it unconstitutionally discriminated against interstate commerce."]

Washington State is the Nation's largest producer of apples. [It requires that apples be tested and graded under a system of grades superior to the standards adopted by the United States Department of Agriculture.] . . .

In 1972, the North Carolina Board of Agriculture adopted an administrative regulation, unique in the 50 States, which in effect required all closed containers of apples shipped into or sold in the State to display either the applicable USDA grade or a notice indicating no classification. State grades were expressly prohibited. In addition to its obvious consequence — prohibiting the display of Washington State apple grades on containers of apples shipped into North Carolina, the regulation presented the Washington apple industry with a marketing problem of potentially nationwide significance. Washington apple growers annually ship in commerce approximately 40 million closed containers of apples, nearly 500,000 of which eventually find their way into North Carolina, stamped with the applicable Washington State variety and grade. It is the industry's practice to purchase these containers preprinted with the various apple varieties and grades, prior to harvest. [Since] the ultimate destination of these apples is unknown at the time they are placed in storage, compliance with North Carolina's unique regulation would have required Washington growers to obliterate the printed labels on containers shipped to North Carolina, thus giving their product a damaged appearance. Alternatively, they could have changed their marketing practices to accommodate the needs of the North Carolina market, i.e., repack apples to be shipped to North Carolina in containers bearing only the USDA grade, and/or store the estimated portion of the harvest destined for that market in such special containers. As a last resort, they could discontinue the use of the preprinted containers entirely. None of these costly and less efficient options was very attractive to the industry. Moreover, in the event a number of other States followed North Carolina's lead, the resultant inability to display the Washington grades could force the Washington growers to abandon the State's expensive inspection and grading system which their customers had come to know and rely on over the 60-odd years of its existence. . . .

[Appellants] do not really contest the District Court's determination that the challenged statute burdened the Washington apple industry by increasing its costs of doing business in the North Carolina market and causing it to lose accounts there. Rather, they maintain that any such burdens on the interstate sale of Washington apples were far outweighed by the local benefits flowing from what they contend was valid exercise of North Carolina's inherent police powers designed to protect its citizenry from fraud and deception in the marketing of apples.

Prior to the statute's enactment, appellants point out, apples from 13 different States were shipped into North Carolina for sale. Seven of those States, including the State of Washington, had their own grading systems which, while differing in their standards, used similar descriptive labels (e.g., fancy, extra fancy, etc.). This multiplicity of inconsistent state grades [posed] dangers of deception and confusion not only in the North Carolina market, but in the Nation as a whole. The North Carolina statute, appellants claim, was enacted to eliminate this source of deception and confusion by replacing the numerous state grades with a single uniform standard. Moreover, it is contended that North Carolina sought to accomplish this goal of uniformity in an evenhanded manner as evidenced by the fact that its statute applies to all apples sold in closed containers in the State without regard to their point of origin. Nonetheless, appellants argue that the District Court gave "scant attention" to the obvious benefits flowing from the challenged legislation and to the long line of decisions from this Court holding that the States possess "broad powers" to protect local purchasers from fraud and deception in the marketing of foodstuffs.

[Not] every exercise of state authority imposing some burden on the free flow of commerce is invalid. [Our] opinions have long recognized that, "in the absence of conflicting legislation by Congress, there is a residuum of power in the state to make laws governing matters of local concern which nevertheless in some measure affect interstate commerce or even, to some extent, regulate it." Southern Pacific Co. v. Arizona ex rel. Sullivan, 325 U.S. 761, 767 (1945). Moreover, [that] "residuum" is particularly strong when the State acts to protect its citizenry in matters pertaining to the sale of foodstuffs. By the same token, however, a finding that state legislation furthers matters of legitimate local concern, even in the health and consumer protection areas, does not end the inquiry. Such a view, we have noted, "would mean that the Commerce Clause of itself imposes no limitations on state action . . . save for the rare instance where a state artlessly discloses an avowed purpose to discriminate against interstate goods." [*Dean Milk Co.*, infra.] Rather, when such state legislation comes into conflict with the Commerce Clause's overriding requirement of a national "common market," we are confronted with the task of effecting an accommodation of the competing national and local interests. We turn to that task.

As the District Court correctly found, the challenged statute has the practical effect of not only burdening interstate sales of Washington apples, but also discriminating against them. This discrimination takes various forms. The first, and most obvious, is the statute's consequence of raising the costs of doing business in the North Carolina market for Washington apple growers and dealers, while leaving those of their North Carolina counterparts unaffected. [This] disparate effect results from the fact that North Carolina apple producers, unlike their Washington competitors, were not forced to alter their marketing practices in order to comply with the statute. They were still free to market their wares under the USDA grade or none at all as they had done prior to the statute's enactment. Obviously, the increased costs imposed by the statute would tend to shield the local apple industry from the competition of Washington apple growers and dealers who are already at a competitive disadvantage because of their great distance from the North Carolina market.

Second, the statute has the effect of stripping away from the Washington apple industry the competitive and economic advantages it has earned for itself through its expensive inspection and grading system. [The] Washington apple-grading system has gained nationwide acceptance in the apple trade. [Apple] brokers and dealers located both inside and outside of North Carolina [state] their preference [for] apples graded under the Washington, as opposed to the USDA, system because of the former's greater consistency, its emphasis on color, and its supporting mandatory inspections. Once again, the statute had no similar impact on the North Carolina apple industry and thus operated to its benefit.

Third, by prohibiting Washington growers and dealers from marketing apples under their State's grades, the statute has a leveling effect which insidiously operates to the advantage of local apple producers. [The] Washington State grades are equal or superior to the USDA grades in all corresponding categories. Hence, with free market forces at work, Washington sellers would normally enjoy a distinct market advantage vis-à-vis local producers in those categories where the Washington grade is superior. However, because of the statute's operation, Washington apples which would otherwise qualify for and be sold under the superior Washington grades will now have to be marketed under their inferior USDA counterparts. Such "downgrading" offers the North Carolina apple industry the very sort of protection against competing out-of-state products that the Commerce Clause was designed to prohibit. At worst, it will have the effect of an embargo against those Washington apples in the superior grades as Washington dealers withhold them from the North Carolina market. At best, it will deprive Washington sellers of the market premium that such apples would otherwise command.

Despite the statute's facial neutrality, the Commission suggests that its discriminatory impact on interstate commerce was not an unintended byproduct and there are some indications in the record to that effect. The most glaring is the response of the North Carolina Agriculture Commissioner to the Commission's request for an exemption following the statute's passage in which he indicated that before he could support such an exemption, he would "want to have the sentiment from our apple producers *since they were mainly responsible for this legislation being passed. . . .*" Moreover, we find it somewhat suspect that North Carolina singled out only closed containers of apples, the very means by which apples are transported in commerce, to effectuate the statute's ostensible consumer protection purpose when apples are not generally sold at retail in their shipping containers. However, we need not ascribe an economic protection motive to the North Carolina Legislature to resolve this case; we conclude that the challenged statute cannot stand insofar as it prohibits the display of Washington State grades even if enacted for the declared purpose of protecting consumers from deception and fraud in the marketplace.

When discrimination against commerce of the type we have found is demonstrated, the burden falls on the State to justify it both in terms of the local benefits flowing from the statute and the unavailability of nondiscriminatory alternatives adequate to preserve the local interests at stake. [*Dean Milk Co.*; *Pike v. Bruce Church, Inc.*] North Carolina has failed to sustain that burden on both scores.

The several States unquestionably possess a substantial interest in protecting their citizens from confusion and deception in the marketing of foodstuffs, but the challenged statute does remarkably little to further that laudable goal at least with respect to Washington apples and grades. The statute, as already noted, permits the marketing of closed containers of apples under *no* grades at all. Such a result can hardly be thought to eliminate the problems of deception and confusion created by the multiplicity of differing state grades; indeed, it magnifies them by depriving purchasers of all information concerning the quality of the contents of closed apple containers. Moreover, although the statute is ostensibly a consumer protection measure, it directs its primary efforts, not at the consuming public at large, but at apple wholesalers and brokers who are the principal purchasers of closed containers of apples. And those individuals are presumably the most knowledgeable individuals in this area. Since the statute does nothing at all to purify the flow of information at the retail level, it does little to protect consumers against the problems it was designed to eliminate. Finally, we note that any potential for confusion and deception created by the Washington grades was not of the type that led to the statute's enactment. Since Washington grades are in all cases equal or superior to their USDA counterparts, they could only "deceive" or "confuse" a consumer to his benefit, hardly a harmful result.

In addition, it appears that nondiscriminatory alternatives to the outright ban of Washington State grades are readily available. For example, North Carolina could effectuate its goal by permitting out-of-state growers to utilize state grades only if they also marked their shipments with the applicable USDA label. In that case, the USDA grade would serve as a benchmark against which the consumer could evaluate the quality of the various state grades. If this alternative was for some reason inadequate to eradicate problems caused by state grades inferior to those adopted by the USDA, North Carolina might consider banning those state grades which, unlike Washington's, could not be demonstrated to be equal or superior to the corresponding USDA categories. Concededly, even in this latter instance, some potential for "confusion" might persist. However, it is the type of "confusion" that the national interest in the free flow of goods between the States demands be tolerated.

The judgment of the District Court is affirmed.

MR. JUSTICE REHNQUIST took no part in the consideration or decision of the case.

Note: Facially Neutral Statutes with Discriminatory Effects — Gerrymandering?

1. *Cost-benefit analysis.* Who bears the costs and gains the benefits of North Carolina's statute? How does it differ from that in Philadelphia v. New Jersey? Is the difference relevant to the incidence analysis?

2. *Inferring intent from effect.* The criteria triggering the regulation in *Hunt* do not identify in terms in-state and out-of-state sources of the problem it purports to address. Its effect is to treat Washington producers differently from North Carolina ones. Should the courts infer a discriminatory or anticommercial purpose from neutral criteria that have the effect of distinguishing in-state and out-of-state producers? How precisely must the neutral criteria target out-of-state producers to justify that inference? How important should be the presence or absence of evidence like that taken from the state's Agriculture Commissioner?

3. *Doctrinal formulations.* Is the Court's stated test in *Hunt* different from the stated test in Philadelphia v. New Jersey? Should it be? Note that the statute in *Hunt* did not in terms apply one rule to local apples and another to out-of-state apples. Consider the proposition that varying doctrinal formulations are appropriate methods of screening out protectionist motivations in varying circumstances.

4. *Reasonable alternatives and facial neutrality.* Dean Milk Co. v. Madison, 340 U.S. 349 (1951), invalidated an ordinance adopted by the Madison City Council that prohibited the sale of milk in the city unless it had been bottled at an approved plant within five miles of the city. The "avowed purpose," ensuring by inspection of bottling plants that milk was bottled under sanitary conditions, was acceptable. But the "practical effect" was to prevent the sale in Madison of wholesome milk produced in Illinois and in parts of Wisconsin. "In thus erecting an economic barrier protecting a major local industry against competition from without the State, Madison plainly discriminates against interstate commerce. This it cannot do, even in the exercise of its unquestioned power to protect the health and safety of its people, if reasonable nondiscriminatory alternatives, adequate to serve legitimate local interests, are available." The Court concluded that two alternatives existed: Madison could send its inspectors to Illinois and charge the reasonable costs of inspection to the importing producers, or it could rely on inspections by federal authorities complying with the regulatory standards in the Madison ordinance, which itself adopted the provisions of a model ordinance recommended by a federal agency. "To permit Madison to adopt a regulation not essential for the protection of local health interests and placing a discriminatory burden on interstate commerce would invite a multiplication of preferential trade areas destructive of the very purpose of the Commerce Clause."

Justice Black dissented. He believed that the courts should not engage in the essentially legislative task of determining whether some suggested method of inspection was a reasonable alternative to the one Madison's elected legislators had chosen. He noted for example that charging the processors for the inspections had in other jurisdictions led to "prolonged litigation over the calculation and collection of the charges," and that federal inspections were far less frequent than those of local plants by Madison officials.

The majority opinion stated in a footnote, "It is immaterial that Wisconsin milk from outside the Madison area is subjected to the same proscription as that moving in interstate commerce." Why? Doesn't that show that Madison is not exporting as much of the costs of regulation outside the state as would a statewide requirement? Think about why legislators from other parts of Wisconsin might have allowed Madison to adopt its ordinance.

5. *Regulation v. subsidy.* Bacchus Imports v. Dias, 468 U.S. — , 104 S. Ct. 3049 (1984), invalidated an exemption from Hawaii's liquor tax given to "ti root okolehao," a brandy distilled from a shrub indigenous to Hawaii, and "fruit wine manufactured in the State from products grown in the State." The purpose of the exemption was to stimulate the local wine industry. Should it matter that indigenous shrubs can, once discovered, be grown elsewhere? Is the remedy for the discrimination a refund of the taxes paid by the out-of-state liquor producers (approximately $45 million) or the collection of the taxes from the local ones (a much smaller amount)? (The Court did not address this issue.) Suppose the taxes foregone amounted to $1 million. Would it violate the Constitution for Hawaii's legislature to impose the general tax in year 1, and then to appropriate $1 million in year 2 as a subsidy to the local liquor industry? Note that the visibility in the political process of an annual direct appropriation may be greater than that of a one-time "permanent" exemption and that the annual appropriations are unlikely to be exact in compensating for the increased prices consumers pay due to the tax.

Exxon Corp. v. Governor of Maryland
437 U.S. 117 (1978)

MR. JUSTICE STEVENS delivered the opinion of the Court.

A Maryland statute provides that a producer or refiner of petroleum products [may] not operate any retail service station within the State.

The Maryland statute is an outgrowth of the 1973 shortage of petroleum. In response to complaints about inequitable distribution of gasoline among retail stations, the Governor of Maryland directed the State Comptroller to conduct a market survey. The results of that survey indicated that gasoline stations operated by producers or refiners had received preferential treatment during the period of short supply. The Comptroller therefore proposed legislation which, according to the Court of Appeals, was "designed to correct the inequities in the distribution and pricing of gasoline reflected by the survey." After legislative hearings and a "special veto hearing" before the Governor, the bill was enacted and signed into law. . . .

[All] of the gasoline sold by Exxon in Maryland is transported into the State from refineries located elsewhere. Although Exxon sells the bulk of this gas to wholesalers and independent retailers, it also sells directly to the consuming public through 36 company-operated stations. Exxon uses these stations to test innovative marketing concepts or products. . . .

[Other plaintiffs], or their subsidiaries, sell their gasoline in Maryland exclusively through company-operated stations. These refiners, using trade names such as "Red Head" and "Scot," concentrate largely on high-volume sales with prices consistently lower than those offered by independent dealer-operated major brand stations. Testimony presented by these refiners indicated that company ownership is essential to their method of private brand, low-priced competition. . . .

[Approximately] 3,800 retail service stations in Maryland sell over 20 different brands of gasoline. However, no petroleum products are produced or refined in Maryland, and the number of stations actually operated by a refiner or an affiliate is relatively small, representing about 5% of the total number of Maryland retailers.

The refiners introduced evidence indicating that their ownership of retail service stations has produced significant benefits for the consuming public. Moreover, the three refiners that now market solely through company-operated stations may elect to withdraw from the Maryland market altogether if the statute is enforced. There was, however, no evidence that the total quantity of petroleum products shipped into Maryland would be affected by the statute. . . .

Plainly, the Maryland statute does not discriminate against interstate goods, nor does it favor local producers and refiners. Since Maryland's entire gasoline supply flows in interstate commerce and since there are no local producers or refiners, such claims of disparate treatment between interstate and local commerce would be meritless. Appellants, however, focus on the retail market, arguing that the effect of the statute is to protect in-state independent dealers from out-of-state competition. They contend that the divestiture provisions "create a protected enclave for Maryland independent dealers. . . ." As support for this proposition, they rely on the fact that the burden of the divestiture requirements falls solely on interstate companies. But this fact does not lead, either logically or as a practical matter, to a conclusion that the State is discriminating against interstate commerce at the retail level.

As the record shows, there are several major interstate marketers of petroleum that own and operate their own retail gasoline stations.[15] These interstate dealers, who compete directly with the Maryland independent dealers, are not affected by the Act because they do not refine or produce gasoline. In fact, the Act creates no barriers whatsoever against interstate independent dealers; it does not prohibit the flow of interstate goods, place added costs upon them, or distinguish between instate and out-of-state companies in the retail market. The absence of any of these factors fully distinguishes this case from those in which a State has been found to have discriminated against interstate commerce. See, e.g. [Dean Milk Co.] For instance, the Court in Hunt noted that the challenged state statute raised the cost of doing business for out-of-state dealers, and, in various other ways, favored the in-state dealer in the local market. No comparable claim can be made here. While the refiners will no longer enjoy their same status in the Maryland market, in-state

---

15. For instance, as of July 1, 1974, such interstate, nonrefining or nonproducing, companies as Sears, Roebuck & Co., Hudson Oil Co., and Pantry Pride operated retail gas stations in Maryland.

independent dealers will have no competitive advantage over out-of-state dealers. The fact that the burden of a state regulation falls on some interstate companies does not, by itself, establish a claim of discrimination against interstate commerce.[16]

Appellants argue, however, that this fact does show that the Maryland statute impermissibly *burdens* interstate commerce. They point to evidence in the record which indicates that, because of the divestiture requirements, at least three refiners will stop selling in Maryland, and which also supports their claim that the elimination of company-operated stations will deprive the consumer of certain special services. Even if we assume the truth of both assertions, neither warrants a finding that the statute impermissibly burdens interstate commerce.

Some refiners may choose to withdraw entirely from the Maryland market, but there is no reason to assume that their share of the entire supply will not be promptly replaced by other interstate refiners. The source of the consumers' supply may switch from company-operated stations to independent dealers, but interstate commerce is not subjected to an impermissible burden simply because an otherwise valid regulation causes some business to shift from one interstate supplier to another.

The crux of appellants' claim is that, regardless of whether the State has interfered with the movement of goods in interstate commerce, it has interfered "with the natural functioning of the interstate market either through prohibition or through burdensome regulation." Hughes v. Alexandria Scrap Corp., 426 U.S. 794, 806. Appellants then claim that the statute "will surely change the market structure by weakening the independent refiners. . . ." We cannot, however, accept appellants' underlying notion that the Commerce Clause protects the particular structure or methods of operation in a retail market. As indicated by the Court in *Hughes*, the Clause protects the interstate market, not particular interstate firms, from prohibitive or burdensome regulations. It may be true that the consuming public will be injured by the loss of the high-volume, low-priced stations operated by the independent refiners, but again that argument relates to the wisdom of the statute, not to its burden on commerce.

Finally, we cannot adopt appellants' novel suggestion that because the economic market for petroleum products is nationwide, no State has the power to regulate the retail marketing of gas. Appellants point out that many state legislatures have either enacted or considered proposals similar to Maryland's,[18] and that the cumulative effect of this sort of legislation may have serious implications for their national marketing operations. While this concern is a significant one, we do not find that the Commerce Clause, by its own force, pre-empts the field of retail gas marketing. [This] Court has only rarely held that the Commerce Clause

16. If the effect of a state regulation is to cause local goods to constitute a larger share, and goods with an out-of-state source to constitute a smaller share, of the total sales in the market — as in *Hunt* and *Dean Milk* — the regulation may have a discriminatory effect on interstate commerce. But the Maryland statute has no impact on the relative proportions of local and out-of-state goods sold in Maryland and, indeed, no demonstrable effect whatsoever on the interstate flow of goods. The sales by independent retailers are just as much a part of the flow of interstate commerce as the sales made by the refiner-operated stations.

18. California, Delaware, the District of Columbia, and Florida have adopted laws restricting refiner's operation of service stations. Similar proposals have been before the legislatures of 32 other jurisdictions.

itself pre-empts an entire field from state regulation, and then only when a lack of national uniformity would impede the flow of interstate goods. [*Cooley.*] The evil that appellants perceive in this litigation is not that the several States will enact differing regulations, but rather that they will all conclude that divestiture provisions are warranted. The problem thus is not one of national uniformity. In the absence of a relevant congressional declaration of policy, or a showing of a specific discrimination against, or burdening of, interstate commerce, we cannot conclude that the States are without power to regulate in this area.

[The Court also rejected a preemption argument made by Exxon.]

The judgment is affirmed.

So ordered.

MR. JUSTICE POWELL took no part in the consideration or decision of these cases.

MR. JUSTICE BLACKMUN, [dissenting] [as to the commerce clause issue].

[The] divestiture provisions preclude out-of-state competitors from retailing gasoline within Maryland. The effect is to protect in-state retail service station dealers from the competition of the out-of-state businesses. This protectionist discrimination is not justified by any legitimate state interest that cannot be vindicated by more evenhanded regulation. . . .

I

In Maryland the retail marketing of gasoline is interstate commerce, for all petroleum products come from outside the State. Retailers serve interstate travelers. To the extent that particular retailers succeed or fail in their businesses, the interstate wholesale market for petroleum products is affected. Cf. [*Dean Milk Co.*] The regulation of retail gasoline sales is therefore within the scope of the Commerce Clause.

A

The Commerce Clause forbids discrimination against interstate commerce, which repeatedly has been held to mean that States and localities may not discriminate against the transactions of out-of-state actors in interstate markets. E.g., [*Hunt; Dean Milk Co.*] The discrimination need not appear on the face of the state or local regulation. "The commerce clause forbids discrimination, whether forthright or ingenious. In each case it is our duty to determine whether the statute under attack, whatever its name may be, will in its practical operation work discrimination against interstate commerce." The state or local authority need not intend to discriminate in order to offend the policy of maintaining a free-flowing national economy. As demonstrated in *Hunt*, a statute that on its face restricts both intrastate and interstate transactions may violate the Clause by having the "practical effect" of discriminating in its operation.

If discrimination results from a statute, the burden falls upon the state or local government to demonstrate legitimate local benefits justifying the inequality and to show that less discriminatory alternatives cannot protect the local interests. [*Dean Milk Co.*] This Court does not merely accept without analysis purported local interests. Instead, it independently identifies the character of the interests and judges for itself whether alternatives will be adequate. . . .

B

With this background, the unconstitutional discrimination in the Maryland statute becomes apparent. No facial inequality exists. [But] given the structure of the retail gasoline market in Maryland, the effect [is] to exclude a class of predominantly out-of-state gasoline retailers while providing protection from competition to a class of nonintegrated retailers that is overwhelmingly composed of local businessmen. [Of] the class of stations statutorily insulated from the competition of the out-of-state integrated firms [more] than 99% were operated by local business interests. Of the class of enterprises excluded entirely from participation in the retail gasoline market, 95% were out-of-state firms, operating 98% of the stations in the class.

The discrimination suffered by the out-of-state integrated producers and refiners is significant. Five of the excluded enterprises, Ashland Oil, Inc., BP Oil, Inc., Kayo Oil Co., Petroleum Marketing Corp., and Southern States Cooperative, Inc., market nonbranded gasoline through price competition rather than through brand recognition. Of the 98 stations marketing gasoline in this manner, all but 6 are company operated. The company operations result from the dominant fact of price competition marketing. [Such] nonbranded stations can compete successfully only if they have day-to-day control of the retail price of their products, the hours of operation of their stations, and related business details. Only with such control can sufficient sales volume be achieved to produce satisfactory profits at prices two to three cents a gallon below those of the major branded stations. [For] the same reason 32 other out-of-state national nonbranded integrated marketers, who operate their own stations without dealers, will be precluded from entering the Maryland retail gasoline market.

The record also contains testimony that the discrimination will burden the operations of major branded companies, such as appellants Exxon, Phillips, Shell, and Gulf, all of which are out-of-state firms. Most importantly, [the statute] will preclude these companies [from] competing directly for the profits of retail marketing. [In] addition, the ban of the sections will preclude the majors from enhancing brand recognition and consumer acceptance through retail outlets with company-controlled standards. Their ability directly to monitor consumer preferences and reactions will be diminished. And their opportunity for experimentation with retail marketing techniques will be curtailed. In short, the divestiture provisions, which will require the appellant majors to cease operation of property valued at more than $10 million, will inflict significant economic hardship on Maryland's major brand companies, all of which are out-of-state firms.

Similar hardship is not imposed upon the local service station dealers by the divestiture provisions. Indeed, rather than restricting their ability to compete, the Maryland Act effectively and perhaps intentionally improves their competitive position by insulating them from competition by out-of-state integrated producers and refiners. In its answers to the various complaints in this case, the State repeatedly conceded that the Act was intended to protect "the retail dealer as an independent businessman [by] reducing the control and dominance of the vertically integrated petroleum producer and refiner in the retail market." At trial the

State's expert said that the legislation would have the effect of protecting the local dealers against the out-of-state competition. In short, the foundation of the discrimination in this case is that the local dealers may continue to enter retail transactions and to compete for retail profits while the statute will deny similar opportunities to the class composed almost entirely of out-of-state businesses.

With discrimination proved against interstate commerce, the burden falls upon the State to justify the distinction with legitimate state interests that cannot be vindicated with more evenhanded regulation. On the record before the Court, the State fails to carry its burden. It asserts only in general terms a desire to maintain competition in gasoline retailing. Although this is a laudable goal, it cannot be accepted without further analysis, just as the Court could not accept the mere assertion of a public health justification in *Dean Milk*. Here, the State ignores the second half of its responsibility; it does not even attempt to demonstrate why competition cannot be preserved without banning the out-of-state interests from the retail market.

The State's showing may be so meager because any legitimate interest in competition can be vindicated with more evenhanded regulation. First, to the extent that the State's interest in competition is nothing more than a desire to protect particular competitors — less efficient local businessmen — from the legal competition of more efficient out-of-state firms, the interest is illegitimate under the Commerce Clause. A national economy would hardly flourish if each State could effectively insist that local nonintegrated dealers handle product retailing to the exclusion of out-of-state integrated firms that would not have sufficient local political clout to challenge the influence of local businessmen with their local government leaders.[8] Each State would be encouraged to "legislate according to its estimate of its own interests, the importance of its own products, and the local advantages or disadvantages of its position in a political or commercial view." J. Story, Commentaries on the Constitution of the United States §259 (4th ed. 1873), quoted in [H. P. Hood & Sons v. Du Mond]. The Commerce Clause simply does not countenance such parochialism.

Second, a legitimate concern of the State could be to limit the economic power

---

8. There is support in the record for the inference that the Maryland Legislature passed the divestiture provisions in response to the pleas of local gasoline dealers for protection against the competition of both the price marketers and the major oil companies. For example, the executive director of the Greater Washington/Maryland Service Station Association, which represents almost 700 local Maryland dealers, testified before the Economic Matters Committee of the Maryland Senate:

> I would like to begin by telling you gentlemen that these are desperate days for service station dealers. . . .
> Now beset by the critical gasoline supply situation, the squeeze by his landlord-supplier and the shrinking service and tire, battery and accessory market, the dealer is now faced with an even more serious problem.
> That is the sinister threat of the major oil companies to complete their takeover of the retail-marketing of gasoline, not just to be in competition with their own branded dealers, but to squeeze them out and convert their stations to company operation. . . .
> Our oil industry has grown beyond the borders of our country to where its American character has been replaced by a multinational one.
> Are the legislators of Maryland now about to let this octopus loose and unrestricted in the state of Maryland, among our small businessmen to devour them? We sincerely hope not.
> The men that you see here today are the back-bone of American small business. . . .
> We are here today asking you, our own legislators to protect us from an economic giant who would take away our very livelihood and our children's future in its greed for greater profits. Please give us the protection we need to save our stations.

of vertical integration. But nothing in the record suggests that the vertical integration that has already occurred in the Maryland petroleum market has inhibited competition. . . .

Third, the State appears to be concerned about unfair competitive behavior such as predatory pricing or inequitable allocation of petroleum products by the integrated firms. These are the only examples of specific misconduct asserted in the State's answers. But none of the concerns support the discrimination. [There] is no proof in the record that any significant portion of the class of out-of-state firms burdened by the divestiture sections has engaged in such misconduct. Furthermore, predatory pricing and unfair allocation already have been prohibited by both state and federal law. Less discriminatory legislation, which would regulate the leasing of all service stations, not just those owned by the out-of-state integrated producers and refiners, could prevent whatever evils arise from short-term leases. . . .

II . . .

[The] Court says that the discrimination against the class of out-of-state producers and refiners does not violate the Commerce Clause because the State has not imposed similar discrimination against other out-of-state retailers.[13] This is said to distinguish the present case from [Hunt]. In fact, however, the unconstitutional discrimination in *Hunt* was not against all out-of-state interests. [The] provision imposed no discrimination on growers from States that employed only the United States Department of Agriculture grading system. Despite this lack of universal discrimination, the Court declared the provision unconstitutional because it discriminated against a single segment of out-of-state marketers of apples, namely, the Washington State growers who employed the superior grading system. In this regard, the Maryland divestiture provisions are identical to, not distinguishable from, the North Carolina statute in *Hunt*. Here, the discrimination has been imposed against a segment of the out-of-state retailers of gasoline, namely, those who also refine or produce petroleum.

To accept the argument of the Court, that is, that discrimination must be universal to offend the Commerce Clause, naively will foster protectionist discrimination against interstate commerce. In the future, States will be able to

---

13. The Court also notes that [the statute does] not discriminate against interstate goods and [does] not favor local producers and refiners. While true, the observation is irrelevant because it does not address the discrimination inflicted upon retail marketing in the State.

Footnote 16 of the Court's opinion suggests that unconstitutional discrimination does not exist unless there is an effect on the quantity of out-of-state goods entering a State. This is too narrow a view of the Commerce Clause. First, interstate commerce consists of far more than mere production of goods. It also consists of transactions — of repeated buying and selling of both goods and services. By focusing exclusively on the quantity of goods, the Court limits the protection of the Clause to producers and handlers of goods before they enter a discriminating State. In our complex national economy, commercial transactions continue after the goods enter a State. The Court today permits a State to impose protectionist discrimination upon these latter transactions to the detriment of out-of-state participants. Second, the Court cites no case in which this Court has held that a burden on the flow of goods is a prerequisite to establishing a case of unconstitutional discrimination against interstate commerce. Neither *Hunt* nor *Dean Milk* contains such a holding. In both of those cases the Court upheld the claims of discrimination; in neither did it say that a burden on the wholesale flow of goods was a necessary part of its holding. [This] case presents a threat to the flow of gasoline in Maryland identical to the threat to the flow of milk in *Dean Milk*. [Relocated footnote.]

insulate in-state interests from competition by identifying the most potent segments of out-of-state business, banning them, and permitting less effective out-of-state actors to remain. The record shows that the Court permits Maryland to effect just such discrimination in this case. The State bans the most powerful out-of-state firms from retailing gasoline within its boundaries. It then insulates the forced divestiture of 199 service stations from constitutional attack by permitting out-of-state firms [to] continue to operate 34 gasoline stations. Effective out-of-state competition is thereby emasculated — no doubt, an ingenious discrimination. But as stated at the outset, "the commerce clause forbids discrimination, whether forthright or ingenious."

[Merely] demonstrating a burden on some out-of-state actors does not prove unconstitutional discrimination. But when the burden is significant, when it falls on the most numerous and effective group of out-of-state competitors, when a similar burden does not fall on the class of protected in-state businessmen, and when the State cannot justify the resulting disparity by showing that its legislative interests cannot be vindicated by more evenhanded regulation, unconstitutional discrimination exists. The facts of this litigation demonstrate such discrimination, and the Court does not argue persuasively to the contrary. . . .

[The state] Court of Appeals reasoned that [the statute] did not discriminate against the class of out-of-state refiners and producers because the wholesale flow of petroleum products into the State was not restricted. [The] Maryland statute has not effected discrimination with regard to the wholesaling or interstate transport of petroleum. The discrimination exists with regard to retailing. The fact that gasoline will continue to flow into the State does not permit the State to deny out-of-state firms the opportunity to retail it once it arrives.

[*Dean Milk*] cannot be distinguished on the ground asserted by the Court of Appeals. . . .

In *Dean Milk* out-of-state producers could bring their milk to Madison, have it pasteurized in Madison, and sell it in Madison. [If] the flow of milk were at all restricted, it was merely because the out-of-state producers chose not to deal with the Madison pasteurizers. Similarly, the flow of gasoline into Maryland may be restricted if the out-of-state producers and refiners choose not to supply the dealers who replace the company-owned operations. . . .

[The] State argues that discrimination against interstate commerce has not occurred because "[n]o nexus between interstate as opposed to local interests inheres in the production or refining of petroleum." Although this statement might be correct in the abstract, it is incorrect in reality, given the structure of the Maryland petroleum market. Due to geological formation as so far known, no petroleum is produced in Maryland; due to the economics of production and refining, as well as to the geology, no petroleum is refined in Maryland. As a matter of actual fact, then, an inherent nexus does exist between the out-of-state status of producers and refiners and the distribution and retailing of gasoline in Maryland. The Commerce Clause does not forbid only legislation that discriminates under all factual circumstances. It forbids discrimination in effect against interstate commerce on the specific facts of each case. If production or refining of gasoline occurred in Maryland, [the statute] might not be unconstitutional. Under those different circumstances, however, the producers and refiners would have a fair opportunity to influence their local legislators and thereby to prevent the enactment of economically disruptive legislation. Under those circumstances, the economic disruption would be felt directly in Maryland, which would tend to make the local political processes responsive to the problems thereby created. Under those circumstances, [the statute] might never have been passed. In this case, however, the economic disruption of the sections is visited upon out-of-state economic interests and not upon in-state businesses. One of the basic assumptions of the Commerce Clause is that local political systems will tend to be unresponsive to problems not felt by local constituents; instead, local political units are expected to act in their constituents' interests. One of the basic purposes of the Clause, therefore, is to prevent the vindication of such self-interest from unfairly burdening out-of-state concerns and thereby disrupting the national economy. . . .

III

The Court's decision brings to mind the well-known words of Mr. Justice Cardozo:

> To give entrance to [protectionism] would be to invite a speedy end of our national solidarity. The Constitution was framed under the dominion of a political philosophy less parochial in range. It was framed upon the theory that the peoples of the several states must sink or swim together, and that in the long run prosperity and salvation are in union and not division.

Baldwin v. G. A. F. Seelig, Inc., 294 U.S. 511, 523 (1935). Today, the Court fails to heed the Justice's admonition. The parochial political philosophy of the Maryland Legislature thereby prevails. I would reverse the judgment of the Maryland Court of Appeals.

Note: Facially Neutral Statutes with (Merely?) Disproportionate Effects

1. *Cost-benefit analysis.* Who bears the costs and gains the benefits of Maryland's statutes? How substantial are the higher prices that Maryland consumers are likely to face? Consider L. Tribe, American Constitutional Law 25 (Supp. 1979):

> Behind Justice Stevens' analysis stands an important doctrinal theme: the negative implications of the Commerce Clause derive centrally from a political theory of union, not primarily from an economic theory of free trade. The function of the clause is to insure national solidarity, not national efficiency. Although the Court's Commerce Clause opinions have often employed the language of economics, the decisions have not interposed the Constitution to the end of merely facilitating the natural functioning of the market-place. More particularly, the constitutional vice of "economic protectionism" is not implicated by a regulation which makes impossible the economies of scale that a fully open market permits.

How is national solidarity promoted other than by economic integration? By prohibiting states from enacting statutes designed to hurt other states' interests? Why did Maryland not impair national solidarity?

2. *Commerce — gasoline or retailing?* The Court argues that interstate commerce in gasoline will be unaffected by the statute because all it can do is force Maryland consumers to switch from cheaper brands of gasoline originating out-of-state to more expensive brands also originating out-of-state. (Apply this argument by recharacterizing the subjects regulated in *Lewis* and *Hunt*.) Justice Blackmun argues that in determining discriminatory effects/gerrymandering, the courts should confine their attention to the subject regulated — here, retailing. Why? Consider the implications of the following argument: In a strongly interconnected economy, local regulations can do no more than alter the patterns of interstate trade; they cannot reduce it. In *Hunt*, some prospective apple purchasers, seeing higher prices for Washington State apples, will purchase Florida oranges instead. Even if some other producers substitute local apples, the North Carolina apple growers will eventually spend their money on goods originating out of state. (Isn't this the lesson of Wickard v. Filburn and Katzenbach v. McClung?) States may succeed in protecting particular local industries, but they cannot protect their entire economies. Thus, local regulations serve only distributional goals, altering the relative wealth of in-state and out-of-state producers (e.g., of apples and oranges) and of consumers. What if anything is there in the materials presented here that suggests that the Constitution is concerned with these goals? See Chapter 6, section D, infra.

3. *Preemption.* Are you satisfied with the Court's response to the argument that the commerce clause "by its own force pre-empts the field of retail gas marketing"? Why should the precedents be read in the Court's way?

4. *Gerrymandering?* Is the inference of anticommercial intent weaker here than in *Hunt*? Note footnote 8 in Justice Blackmun's opinion. Does *Exxon* involve anticommercial intent but no significant anticommercial impact? Is it harder to perform the incidence analysis in *Exxon* than it was in *Hunt*? Consider whether the cases make a statute's use of express or strongly implied discrimination conclusive. Is such formalism justified on the ground that form is strongly though not perfectly correlated with cost-exporting, and that the gains from allowing courts to look beyond form are outweighed by its costs in encouraging complex litigation? Can that be reconciled with the concern for representation expressed by Justice Stone in *Barnwell* and reiterated by Justice Blackmun's dissent in *Exxon*?

Note: Inferring Intent

Consider Minnesota v. Clover Leaf Creamery Co., 449 U.S. 456 (1981). Minnesota prohibited the sale of milk in plastic disposable containers but allowed its sale in paper nonreturnable cartons. The Supreme Court accepted the argument that the statute served its stated purposes of promoting conservation, easing waste disposal problems, and conserving energy. The state's trial court had found that the "actual basis" of the statute "was to promote the economic interests of certain segments of the local dairy and pulpwood industries at the expense of the economic interests of other segments of the dairy industry and the plastics industry." It also had found that banning the use of plastic bottles would not in fact promote conservation or save energy because paper containers are "a more environmentally harmful product." The Supreme Court responded:

"Minnesota's statute does not effect 'simple protectionism,' but 'regulates even-handedly' by prohibiting all milk retailers from selling their products in plastic, nonreturnable milk containers, without regard to whether the milk, the containers, or the sellers are from outside the State. This statute is therefore unlike statutes discriminating against interstate commerce, which we have consistently struck down. E.g., [Lewis; Hughes; Philadelphia v. New Jersey; Hunt].

"Since the statute does not discriminate between interstate and intrastate commerce, the controlling question is whether the incidental burden imposed on interstate commerce by the Minnesota Act is 'clearly excessive in relation to the putative local benefits' [Pike v. Bruce Church.] We conclude that it is not.

"The burden imposed on interstate commerce by the statute is relatively minor. Milk products may continue to move freely across the Minnesota border, and since most dairies package their products in more than one type of containers, the inconvenience of having to conform to different packaging requirements in Minnesota and the surrounding States should be slight. Within Minnesota, business will presumably shift from manufacturers of plastic nonreturnable containers to producers of paperboard cartons, refillable bottles, and plastic pouches, but there is no reason to suspect that the gainers will be Minnesota firms, or the losers out-of-state firms. Indeed, two of the three dairies, the sole milk retailer, and the sole milk container producer challenging the statute in this litigation are Minnesota firms.[17]

"Pulpwood producers are the only Minnesota industry likely to benefit significantly from the Act at the expense of out-of-state firms. Respondents point out that plastic resin, the raw material used for making plastic nonreturnable milk jugs, is produced entirely by non-Minnesota firms, while pulpwood, used for making paperboard, is a major Minnesota product. Nevertheless, it is clear that respondents exaggerate the degree of burden on out-of-state interests, both because plastics will continue to be used in the production of plastic pouches, plastic returnable bottles, and paperboard itself, and because out-of-state pulpwood producers will presumably absorb some of the business generated by the Act.

"Even granting that the out-of-state plastics industry is burdened relatively more heavily than the Minnesota pulpwood industry, we find that this burden is not 'clearly excessive' in light of the substantial state interest in promoting conservation of energy and other natural resources and easing solid waste disposal problems. [We] find these local benefits ample to support Minnesota's decision under the Commerce Clause. Moreover, we find that no approach with a lesser impact on interstate activities, [Pike v. Bruce Church, Inc.] is available. Respondents have suggested several alternative statutory schemes, but these alternatives are either more burdensome on commerce than the Act (as, for example, banning all nonreturnables) or less likely to be effective (as, for example, providing incentives for recycling).

"In [Exxon we] stressed that the Commerce Clause 'protects the interstate market, not particular interstate firms, from prohibitive or burdensome regula-

___

17. The existence of major in-state interests adversely affected by the Act is a powerful safeguard against legislative abuse. [Barnwell Bros.]

tions.' A nondiscriminatory regulation serving substantial state purposes is not invalid simply because it causes some business to shift from a predominantly out-of-state industry to a predominantly in-state industry. Only if the burden on interstate commerce clearly outweighs the State's legitimate purposes does such a regulation violate the Commerce Clause."

Is this analysis of the issue of intent persuasive? Is the problem addressed here different from that in *Hunt?* In Philadelphia v. New Jersey?

Note: Taxation of Interstate Commerce

Consider Commonwealth Edison Co. v. Montana, 453 U.S. 609 (1981). In 1975 Montana imposed a tax on the severance of coal. The rate of 30 percent of the contract sales price was substantially higher than the rate in similar severance taxes in most other states. The proceeds of the tax were to be put into a permanent trust fund from which appropriations of principal could be made only by a three-fourths vote of both houses of the state legislature. The tax produced almost 20 percent of the state's revenue. Montana has 25 percent of the nation's coal reserves and over 50 percent of its low-sulfur coal reserves. Low sulfur coal can be burned to produce electricity while complying with environmental regulations in plants that do not require extensive modification. Approximately 90 percent of the coal is shipped out-of-state.

The Court rejected a commerce clause challenge to the tax. It applied a four-part test as stated in Complete Auto Transit v. Brady, 430 U.S. 274 (1977): The tax must be "applied to an activity with a substantial nexus with the taxing State, [must be] fairly apportioned, [must] not discriminate against interstate commerce, and [must be] fairly related to services provided by the State." On the discrimination issue, the Court said:

"[The] Montana tax is computed at the same rate regardless of the final destination of the coal, and there is no suggestion here that tax is administered in a manner that departs from this evenhanded formula. We are not, therefore, confronted here with the type of differential tax treatment of interstate and intrastate commerce that the Court has found in other 'discrimination' cases. [Philadelphia v. New Jersey.]

"Instead, the gravamen of appellants' claim is that a state tax must be considered discriminatory for purposes of the Commerce Clause if the tax burden is borne primarily by out-of-state consumers. . . .

"[Appellants'] assertion that Montana may not 'exploit' its 'monopoly' position by exporting tax burdens to other States, cannot rest on a claim that there is need to protect the out-of-state consumers of Montana coal from discriminatory tax treatment. [There] is no real discrimination in this case; the tax burden is borne according to the amount of coal consumed and not according to any distinction between in-state and out-of-state consumers. Rather, appellants assume that the Commerce Clause gives residents of one State a right of access at reasonable prices to resources located in another State that is richly endowed with such resources, without regard to whether and on what terms residents of the resource-rich State have access to resources. We are not convinced that the Commerce Clause, of its own force, gives the residents of one State the right to control in this fashion the terms of resource development and depletion in a sister State. Cf. Philadelphia v. New Jersey.][8]

"In any event, appellants' discrimination theory ultimately collapses into their claim that the Montana tax is invalid under the fourth prong of the *Complete Auto Transit* test: that the tax is not 'fairly related to the services provided by the State.' Because appellants concede that Montana may impose *some* severance tax on coal mined in the State, the only remaining foundation for their discrimination theory is a claim that the tax burden borne by the out-of-state consumers of Montana coal is excessive. This is, of course, merely a variant of appellants' assertion that the Montana tax does not satisfy the 'fairly related' prong of the *Complete Auto Transit* test, and it is to this contention that we now turn. . . .

"The Montana Supreme Court held that the coal severance tax is 'imposed for the general support of the government' and we have no reason to question this characterization of the Montana tax as a general revenue tax.[11] . . .

[There] is no requirement under the Due Process Clause that the amount of general revenue taxes collected from a particular activity must be reasonably related to the value of the services provided to the activity.

"There is no reason to suppose that this latitude afforded the States under the Due Process Clause is somehow divested by the Commerce Clause merely because the taxed activity has some connection to interstate commerce; particularly when the tax is levied on an activity conducted within the State. . . .

"Against this background, we have little difficulty concluding that the Montana tax satisfies the fourth prong of the *Complete Auto Transit* test. The 'operating incidence' of the tax is on the mining of coal within Montana. Because it is measured as a percentage of the value of the coal taken, the Montana tax is in 'proper proportion' to appellants' activities within the State and, therefore, to their 'consequent enjoyment of the opportunities and protections which the State has afforded' in connection with those activities. When a tax is assessed in proportion to a taxpayer's activities or presence in a State, the taxpayer is shouldering its fair share of supporting the State's provision of 'police and fire protection, the benefit of a trained work force, and the advantages of a civilized society.'

"[In] essence, appellants ask this Court to prescribe a test for the validity of state taxes that would require state and federal courts, as a matter of federal constitutional law, to calculate acceptable rates or levels of taxation of activities that are conceded to be legitimate subjects of taxation. This we decline to do.

"In the first place, it is doubtful whether any legal test could adequately reflect the numerous and competing economic, geographic, demographic, social, and political considerations that must inform a decision about an acceptable rate or

---

8. Nor do we share appellants' apparent view that the Commerce Clause injects principles of antitrust law into the relations between the States by reference to such imprecise standards as whether one State is "exploiting" its "monopoly" position with respect to a natural resource when the flow of commerce among them is not otherwise impeded. The threshold questions whether a State enjoys a "monopoly" position and whether the tax burden is shifted out of state, rather than borne by in-state producers and consumers, would require complex factual inquiries about such issues as elasticity of demand for the product and alternative sources of supply. Moreover, under this approach, the constitutionality of a state tax could well turn on whether the in-state producer is able, through sales contracts or otherwise, to shift the burden of the tax forward to its out-of-state customers. . . .

11. Contrary to appellants' suggestion, the fact that 50% of the proceeds of the severance tax is paid into a trust fund does not undermine the Montana court's conclusion that the tax is a general revenue tax. Nothing in the Constitution prohibits the people of Montana from choosing to allocate a portion of current tax revenues for use by future generations.

level of state taxation, and yet be reasonably capable of application in a wide variety of individual cases. But even apart from the difficulty of the judicial undertaking, the nature of the factfinding and judgment that would be required of the courts merely reinforces the conclusion that questions about the appropriate level of state taxes must be resolved through the political process. Under our federal system, the determination is to be made by state legislatures in the first instance and, if necessary, by Congress, when particular state taxes are thought to be contrary to federal interests.[18]

"Furthermore, the reference in the cases to police and fire protection and other advantages of civilized society is not, as appellants suggest, a disingenuous incantation designed to avoid a more searching inquiry into the relationship between the *value* of the benefits conferred on the taxpayer and the *amount* of taxes it pays. Rather, when the measure of a tax is reasonably related to the taxpayer's activities or presence in the State — from which it derives some benefit such as the substantial privilege of mining coal — the taxpayer will realize, in proper proportion to the taxes it pays, '[t]he only benefit to which the taxpayer is constitutionally entitled . . .[:] that derived from his enjoyment of the privileges of living in an organized society, established and safeguarded by the devotion of taxes to public purposes.' Carmichael v. Southern Coal & Coke Co., 301 U.S. at 522. Correspondingly, when the measure of a tax bears no relationship to the taxpayers' presence or activities in a State, a court may properly conclude under the fourth prong of the *Complete Auto Transit* test that the State is imposing an undue burden on interstate commerce. We are satisfied that the Montana tax, assessed under a formula that relates the tax liability to the value of appellant coal producers' activities within the State, comports with the requirements of the *Complete Auto Transit* test."

The Court also rejected a preemption argument. Justice White began his concurring opinion by calling the case "very troublesome," but concluded: "Congress has the power to protect interstate commerce from intolerable or even undesirable burdens. It is also very much aware of the Nation's energy needs, of the Montana tax, and of the trend in the energy-rich States to aggrandize their position and perhaps lessen the tax burdens on their own citizens by imposing unusually high taxes on mineral extraction. But Congress is so far content to let the matter rest. [The] constitutional authority and the machinery to thwart efforts such as those of Montana, if thought unacceptable, are available to Congress, and surely Montana and other similarly situated States do not have the political power to impose their will on the rest of the country. As I presently see it, therefore, the better part of both wisdom and valor is to respect the judgment of the other branches of the Government."

Justice Blackmun, joined by Justices Powell and Stevens, dissented, saying that the case should be remanded for a full trial to determine the actual incidence of the tax.

As the discussion of *Complete Auto Transit* indicates, the stated tests in cases challenging taxes as undue burdens on interstate commerce differ from the stated

---

18. The controversy over the Montana tax has not escaped the attention of the Congress. Several bills were introduced during the 96th Congress to limit the rate of state severance taxes. Similar bills have been introduced in the 97th Congress.

tests in cases challenging regulations. Should they? Recall the discussion of the comparative scope of the tax and commerce powers of Congress, Chapter 2 supra. The doctrines applying the commerce clause to state taxes are extremely complex, but *Complete Auto Transit* and *Commonwealth Edison* suggest that doctrines regarding taxes and regulations are in the process of converging. Did Justice White properly allocate the burden of securing congressional action?

C.   FACIALLY NEUTRAL STATUTES WITH SIGNIFICANT EFFECTS ON INTERSTATE COMMERCE

Note: For Commercial Purposes

1. *"Obstructing" commerce.* In Buck v. Kuykendall, 267 U.S. 307 (1925), Buck, a citizen of Washington, wished to operate an "auto stage" line between Portland, Oregon, and Seattle, Washington. After obtaining a license from Oregon, he applied to the Washington authorities for a certificate that would allow him to begin operations. The certificate was denied on the ground that the route was already adequately served by railroads and four other auto stage lines. The Court held that the denial violated the commerce clause. The purpose was "the prohibition of competition." Its effect was "not merely to burden [interstate commerce], but to obstruct it." The Court also noted that the prohibition "[defeated] the purpose of Congress" in legislation providing federal aid for highway construction.

Aside from preemption, why should Washington be barred from limiting competition in transportation? Who bears the burdens and gains the benefits of Washington's statute? Assuming that the statute protects existing carriers from competition, is it protectionist in the sense of promoting local carriers at the expense of out-of-state ones? (All four of the competing auto stage lines operated in interstate commerce and were not shown to be Washington-based.) Is it possible to develop a *Barnwell*-type explanation of the result? If not, does the case rest on the proposition that the Constitution embodies a substantive preference for free trade sufficient to place the burden of overcoming congressional inertia on those who support regulations that have significant though nondiscriminatory effects on interstate commerce?

2. *Subsidizing local industry.* Suppose a state finds that an important local industry is undergoing a decline. Its legislators believe that the industry provides important benefits to the state. These benefits are not merely economic. In addition, the industry engages people in a form of production that encourages the development of character traits, such as emotional stability and cooperation, that have important political consequences. The legislators therefore develop a program to stabilize the industry. They conclude that a direct subsidy would undermine the development of the desired character traits, but that an indirect subsidy, accomplished by imposing regulations that have the effect of raising prices and therefore profits, would not. However, they wish to assure that the regulatory subsidy be given only to the local industry and not to its out-of-state competitors. Does the Constitution allow them to develop a regulatory system to do this? If

not, is it because subsidies to local industries are impermissible, because regulatory subsidies are particularly undesirable, or for some other reason?

This issue is explored in the following cases. Nebbia v. New York, 291 U.S. 502 (1934), upheld a New York law setting minimum prices paid to milk producers, as applied to purchases by New York retailers from New York producers. One year later the Court in Baldwin v. G. A. F. Seelig, Inc., 294 U.S. 511 (1935), considered the constitutionality of a provision designed "to keep the system unimpaired by competition from afar." The provision required that milk purchased from out-of-state (in this case, Vermont) producers could not be sold in New York unless the out-of-state producers had received the New York minimum price. Justice Cardozo's opinion for the Court treated this as a "customs [duty] equal to the price differential" and found it unconstitutional because its "purpose [as] well as its necessary tendency, is to suppress or mitigate the consequences of competition between the states." This opened up the possibility of destructive "rivalries and reprisals." The opinion rejected two noncommercial justifications for the statute. New York could not claim that it promoted "a regular and adequate supply of pure and wholesome milk" by guaranteeing that farmers "earn a living income." "This would be to eat up the rule under the guise of an exception. Economic welfare is always related to health, for there can be no health if men are starving. [To] give entrance to that excuse would be to invite a speedy end of our national solidarity. The Constitution [was] framed upon the theory that the peoples of the several states must sink or swim together, and that in the long run prosperity and salvation are in union and not division." Nor could the statute be defended on the theory that Vermont's producers might have gained their cost advantages by cutting corners on sanitary precautions. There was no evidence of that, and "apart from such defects of proof, [one] state may not put pressure of that sort upon others to reform their economic standards. [If a problem exists,] the legislature of Vermont and not that of New York must supply the fitting remedy." The Court concluded that New York's statute was "designed to neutralize advantages belonging to the place of origin. [It is] thus hostile in conception as well as burdensome in result."

Does Justice Cardozo's opinion fairly characterize the purposes of New York's statute? In what sense did the lower prices charged by Vermont producers "belong to the place of origin"? Suppose Vermont had provided a direct subsidy to its milk producers. Suppose instead that its legislature had rejected proposals to adopt a program like New York's, either deeming it unsound as a matter of policy or desiring to capitalize on the opportunities New York's system opened up for Vermont producers. (These latter questions are related to those discussed under "state action" in Chapter 10 infra.)

In Milk Control Board v. Eisenberg Farm Products, 306 U.S. 346 (1936), the Court upheld Pennsylvania's price control statute as applied to purchasers of milk in Pennsylvania by a dealer who intended to ship all the milk out of state. The Court said that the purpose was "to reach a domestic situation" and that the activity regulated was "essentially local." If purchasers for out-of-state sale could escape the minimum price requirements, "the uniform operation of the statute locally would be crippled." Baldwin was distinguished on the ground that the statute there was "aimed solely at interstate commerce attempting to affect and regulate the price to be paid for milk in a sister state." Is that a satisfactory distinction as to the provision at issue in Baldwin? As to New York's overall regulatory scheme? Suppose New York's system allowed purchases out-of-state at any price, but sales in-state only at the required minimum plus a markup for transportation costs. Is that different from the scheme in *Baldwin?* In *Eisenberg?*

At issue in H. P. Hood & Sons v. DuMond, 336 U.S. 525 (1949), was a New York statute requiring that milk distributors obtain licenses, which could be denied if the authorities determined that the licensed facility would "tend to a destructive competition in a market already adequately served." Hood was denied a license. The authorities found that existing plants were adequate for milk produced in the area and that some plants had excess capacity. The new plant would probably reduce the amounts purchased by Hood's competitors, who served primarily New York cities. For example, the new plant was likely to divert milk from a plant shipping primarily to Troy, New York, to Boston, Hood's primary outlet. Justice Jackson's opinion for the Court contained the discussion of free trade excerpted above. It described the denial as "for the avowed purpose and with the practical effect of curtailing the volume of interstate commerce to aid local economic interests" and held the denial unconstitutional. Justice Black's dissent observed that under New York law it was irrelevant that Hood served Boston consumers. If a dealer supplying New York customers had applied for a license, the authorities would have had to protect Hood's plant supplying Boston consumers. If that characterization of New York law is correct, did Justice Jackson properly describe the purpose and effect of the New York law? Of its application in this case? Justice Frankfurter, in dissent, would have remanded the case for a trial to explore such issues as the following:

> [It] is impossible to say whether or not the restriction of competition among dealers in milk does in fact contribute to their economic well-being and, through them, to that of the entire industry. And if we assume that some contribution is made, we cannot guess how much. Why, when the State has fixed a minimum price for producers, does it take steps to keep competing dealers from increasing the price by bidding against each other for the existing supply? Is it concerned with protecting consumers from excessive prices? Or is it concerned with seeing that marginal dealers, forced by competition to pay more and charge less, are not driven either to cut corners in the maintenance of their plants or to close them down entirely? Might these consequences follow from operation at less than capacity? What proportion of capacity is necessary to enable the marginal dealer to stay in business? Could Hood's potential competitors in the Greenwich area maintain efficient and sanitary standards of operation on a lower margin of profit? How would their closing down affect producers? Would the competition of Hood affect dealers other than those in that area? How many of those dealers are also engaged in interstate commerce? How much of a strain would be put on the price structure maintained by the State by a holding that it cannot regulate the competition of dealer buying for an out-of-state market? Is this a situation in which State regulation, by supplementing federal regulation, is of benefit to interstate as well as to intrastate commerce?

For a discussion of the issues this approach raises, see Southern Pacific Co. v. Arizona, infra.

Finally, consider Henneford v. Silas Mason Co., 300 U.S. 577 (1937). Washington adopted a 2 percent tax. To avoid losing business to retailers in other states, it also adopted a 2 percent "compensating use tax," levied on the price of goods purchased elsewhere for the "privilege of using" them in Washington. Justice

Cardozo's opinion for the Court, upholding the compensating use tax, described it as designed to promote equality. *Baldwin* was distinguished in this way: New York

> was attempting to project its legislation within the borders of another state by regulating the price to be paid in that state for milk acquired there. She said in effect to farmers in Vermont: your milk cannot be sold by dealers to whom you ship it in New York unless you sell it to them in Vermont at a price determined here. What Washington is saying to sellers beyond her borders is something very different. In substance what she says is this: You may ship your goods in such amounts and at such prices as you please, but the goods when used in Washington after the transit is completed, will share an equal burden with goods that have been purchased here.

Does that make economic sense? Is the underlying distinction one between taxes and regulations? Between price competition due to "natural" advantages and that due to "state-created" ones? Is either distinction coherent?

Do the cases establish any coherent approach to the problem of neutral regulations? Consider the following possibilities: (a) *Regulations intended to restrict commerce are invalid.* Nebbia rejects that position. (b) *Regulations intended to restrict interstate commerce are invalid.* That is the rationale of *Hood.* Is the regulation in *Hood* actually so intended? (c) A *territorial theory:* A state may regulate transactions that occur within its borders (*Eisenberg*) but not those that occur elsewhere (*Baldwin*). How would that theory be applied to the statute proposed after the discussion of *Eisenberg*, requiring in-state sales of out-of-state milk to be at a stated minimum price? Note that in *Hood* the transactions occur within the regulating state. What is the transaction in *Silas Mason* — the purchase or the use? Note that the territorial formalism has nothing to do with economic realities. Is it fair to say in addition that none of the cases discussed in this note implicates issues of disparities in representation? If so, consider whether these cases are confused because the *Barnwell* approach to the problems had not completely crystallized when the cases were decided. Do the following materials undermine that suggestion?

Note: For Police Power Purposes

SOUTH CAROLINA HIGHWAY DEPARTMENT v. BARNWELL BROTHERS, 303 U.S. 177 (1938): The Court upheld the constitutionality of a South Carolina statute prohibiting the use on state highways of trucks that were over ninety inches wide or over 20,000 pounds in gross weight. Approximately 85 to 90 percent of the nation's trucks exceeded these limits. The trial court found that gross weight was not an accurate measure of a truck's potential to cause damage to highways, whereas axle weight was, and that trucks weighing over 20,000 pounds in gross weight could be used without damaging the highways. Justice Stone's opinion for the Court cited *Cooley* to show that "there are matters of local concern, the regulation of which unavoidably involves some regulation of interstate commerce but which, because of their local character and their number and diversity, may never be fully dealt with by Congress. Notwithstanding the commerce clause, such regulation in the absence of Congressional action has for the most part been left to the states. . . .

"The commerce clause, by its own force, prohibits discrimination [even] when state legislation nominally of local concern is in point of fact aimed at interstate commerce, or by its necessary operation is a means of gaining a local benefit by throwing the attendant burdens on those without the state. [However,] few subjects of state regulation are so peculiarly of local concern as is the use of state highways." Sometimes such regulations burdened interstate commerce, but "so long as the state action does not discriminate, the burden is one which the Constitution permits because it is an inseparable incident of the exercise of a legislative authority, which, under the Constitution, has been left to the states."

In the absence of congressional action, the test was "whether the state legislature in adopting regulations such as the present has acted within its province, and whether the means of regulation chosen are reasonably adapted to the end sought." In "resolving the second [inquiry], the courts do not sit as Legislatures [to weigh] all the conflicting interests. [Fairly] debatable questions as to [a regulation's] reasonableness, wisdom and propriety are not for the determination of courts, but for the legislative body." The court must decide "upon the whole record whether it is possible to say that the legislative choice is without rational basis." Here the state reasonably chose to use gross weight for "convenience of application and consequent lack of need for rigid supervisory enforcement." Further, many of the state's roads were old and liable to crack more frequently than newer roads. As to width limitation, 100 miles of the state's roads were sixteen feet wide, which left no margin for passing a ninety-six-inch-wide truck.

SOUTHERN PACIFIC CO. v. ARIZONA, 325 U.S. 761 (1945): The Court, again through Chief Justice Stone, found unconstitutional a 1912 statute limiting train lengths to fourteen passenger or seventy freight cars. After rejecting the railroad's argument that the Interstate Commerce Act, even "in the absence of administrative implementation by the [Interstate Commerce] Commission," itself "[curtailed] state power to regulate train lengths," the Court turned to the commerce clause issue. Citing *Gibbons*, it said that states may not regulate subjects "which, because of the need for national uniformity, demand that their regulation, if any, be prescribed by a single authority." At this point a footnote said, "In applying this rule the Court has often recognized that to the extent that the burden of state regulation falls on interests outside the state, it is unlikely to be alleviated by the operation of those political restraints normally exerted when interests within the state are affected." Reviewing the Court's prior decisions, it concluded that "the states [have] wide scope for the regulation of matters of local state concern, even though it in some measure affects the commerce, provided it does not materially restrict the free flow of commerce across state lines, or interfere with it in matters with respect to which uniformity of regulation is of predominant national concern."

Chief Justice Stone then stated "the matters for ultimate determination": "the nature and extent of the burden which the state regulation, [adopted] as a safety measure, imposes on interstate commerce, and whether the relative weights of the state and national interests are such as to make inapplicable the rule [that] the free flow of interstate commerce [in] matters requiring uniformity of regulation" is protected by the commerce clause. The Court reviewed "detailed findings of fact" made in a long trial below. The operation of trains longer than those allowed in Arizona was "standard practice." Over 90 percent of the rail traffic in Arizona was interstate. Railroads had to operate 30 percent more trains in Arizona than they otherwise would, at a cost of over $1 million a year. Breaking up and remaking long trains at the state's borders delayed traffic. "Enforcement of the law in Arizona [must] inevitably result in an impairment of efficient railroad operation because the railroads are subjected to regulation which is not uniform in its application. [Either trains are broken up and reconstituted or] the carrier [must] conform to the lowest train limit restriction of any of the states through which its trains pass, whose laws thus control the carriers' operations both within and without the regulating state."

The Court then turned to the safety benefits of the law: "The decisive question is whether in the circumstances the total effect of the law as a safety measure in reducing accidents and casualties is so slight or problematical as not to outweigh the national interest in keeping interstate commerce free from interferences which seriously impede it and subject it to local regulation which does not have a uniform effect on the interstate train journey which it interrupts." Longer trains cause accidents by "slack action," the movement of one car before it transmits its momentum to the next one to which it is loosely coupled. The more slack action, the more likely are injuries to workers, especially on freight trains. But the evidence showed that, in states leaving train lengths unregulated, the accident rate on long trains was the same as that on Arizona's shorter trains. Further, because the regulation meant that more trains had to be used, there were more grade-crossing collisions and collisions between trains in the course of switching tracks. The Court found that the regulation, "viewed as a safety measure, affords at most slight and dubious advantage, if any, over unregulated train lengths, because it results in an increase in the number of trains and train operations and the consequent increases in train accidents of a character generally more severe than those due to slack action."

The Court distinguished *Barnwell* by stressing its point about the peculiarly local nature of highway control. "The fact that [regulations of highways] affect alike shippers in interstate and intrastate commerce in great numbers, within as well as without the state, is a safeguard against regulatory abuses." It concluded, "Here examination of all the relevant factors makes it plain that the state interest is outweighed by the interest of the nation in an adequate, economical and efficient railway transportation service, which must prevail."

Justice Black's long dissenting opinion described the Arizona statute as the product of a long-standing political struggle between railroads and railroad workers, conducted in state legislatures and in Congress. He called the trial in *Southern Pacific* "extraordinary" in that the issue was "whether the law was unconstitutional [because] the legislature had been guilty of misjudging the facts concerning the degree of the danger of long trains. [This] new pattern of trial procedure makes it necessary for a judge to hear all the evidence offered as to why a legislature passed a law and to make findings of fact as to the validity of those reasons. [In] this respect, [this] Court today is acting as a 'super-legislature.' "

Justice Black's examination of the record convinced him that there was evidence to justify the conclusion that the statute promoted safety to some extent. "Under those circumstances, the determination of whether it is in the interest of society for the length of trains to be governmentally regulated is a matter of public policy. Someone must fix that policy — either the Congress, or the state, or the courts. A century and a half of constitutional history and government admonishes this Court to leave that choice to the elected legislative representatives [where] it properly belongs both on democratic principles and the requirements of efficient government."

Stating that "Congress knew about the Arizona law" and that the appropriate congressional committees "keep in close and intimate touch with the affairs of railroads," he concluded that Congress has made "a deliberate choice" to "leave the state free in this field." "We are not left in doubt as to why, as against the potential peril of injuries to employees, the Court tips the scales on the side of 'uniformity.' For the evil it finds in a lack of uniformity is that it (1) delays interstate commerce, (2) increases its cost and (3) impairs its efficiency. All three of these boil down to the same thing, and that is that running shorter trains would increase the cost of railroad operations. The 'burden' on interstate commerce reduces itself to mere cost because there was no [evidence] to support a finding that by the expenditure of sufficient sums of money, the railroads could not enable themselves to carry goods and passengers just as quickly and efficiently with short trains as with long trains. Thus the conclusion that a requirement for long trains will 'burden interstate commerce' is a mere euphemism for the statement that a requirement for long trains will increase the cost of railroad operations. He criticized the Court for "requiring that money costs outweigh human values" in the name of "an 'economical national railroad system.' I cannot believe that if Congress had defined what it meant by 'economical,' it would have required money to be saved at the expense of the personal safety of railway employees."

Justice Douglas also dissented, saying that "the courts should intervene only where the state legislation discriminated against interstate commerce or was out of harmony with laws which Congress had enacted." It was "particularly appropriate" for the courts to abstain, given the ability of the "expert" Interstate Commerce Commission "to police the field." He also suggested that a state law "requiring all railroads within its borders to operate on [non-standard] tracks" would be unconstitutional. "The question is one of degree and calls for a close appraisal of the facts." He was unpersuaded that the railroads' evidence overcame the "presumption of validity to which this train-limit law is entitled."

---

1. *Cost-benefit analysis — the benefits.* Who gains the benefits of Arizona's statute? Consider these two lines of analysis.

a. The net safety benefits are positive: The reduction in slack-action accidents (slightly) offsets the increase in grade crossing and other accidents. Should this alone establish that the balance between benefits and burdens on interstate commerce favors the statute no matter what the burdens are? Consider in this connection Justice Black's observations in his opinion for the Court in Brotherhood of Locomotive Firemen & Engineers v. Chicago, Rock Island & Pacific Railroad, 393 U.S. 129 (1968). The lower court had found that requiring trains to carry a stipulated number of crew members imposed "substantial financial burdens" on railroads in light of technological changes that reduced the need for crews as large as had been needed in the past, and had "no substantial effect on safety." Applying the *Southern Pacific* balancing test, it found the statute unconstitutional. The Supreme Court reversed. Justice Black wrote:

[The District Court should not have placed] a value on the additional safety in terms of dollars and cents, in order to see whether this value, as calculated by the court, exceeded the financial cost to the railroads. [It] is difficult at best to say that financial losses should be balanced against the loss of lives and limbs of workers and people using the highways.

On the assumption that the net safety benefits in *Southern Pacific* are positive, are the cases distinguishable? Doesn't the tort system regularly place a value on life and limb, and why shouldn't its processes be adequate in constitutional adjudication? (Why do states replace compensation via the tort system with direct regulation to accomplish their safety goals?) How can burdens on interstate commerce be balanced against the accomplishment of police power goals unless some sort of monetary value can be placed on both?

b. The net safety benefits are negative: The increase in grade crossing accidents exceeds the reduction in slack-action accidents. Railroad employees gain at the expense of road users and others injured in grade crossing accidents. If both groups are largely composed of Arizonans, the statute redistributes wealth from one group of Arizonans to another. Should the courts be concerned about that? See Lochner v. New York, Chapter 6, section D, infra. How can the distributive impact be balanced against the cost imposed on interstate commerce?

Which of these lines of analysis did the Court pursue?

2. *Cost-benefit analysis — the costs.* Does the statute discriminate against interstate commerce, either in terms or in effect? If not, why should the Court intervene? Who bears the costs of Arizona's statute? Recall the analysis in *Exxon*, above. Does the cost of complying with the regulation measure the burden on interstate commerce? Suppose railroads have a slight cost advantage over trucks in transporting goods through Arizona to California. By complying with the statute, the railroads face cost increases which they either must absorb or pass on to their customers. If they pass the costs on, they lose business to trucks. In either event, how exactly is interstate commerce burdened? To what extent?

Ultimately someone has to pay for Arizona's regulation, either in increased prices for goods shipped to California on railroads, or in increased prices for goods shipped on the more expensive trucks. Is this what the Court meant by the footnote reiterating the "thought" from *Barnwell Brothers* that opened this section? Does *Southern Pacific* persuasively distinguish *Barnwell*? What prevents the railroads from raising the prices they charge for delivering goods to Arizona?

3. *Balancing and judicial capacity.* During the late 1940s, Justice Black was concerned about the propriety of balancing as a technique of adjudication in other areas as well. See Dennis v. United States, Chapter 7, section B, infra. Are Black's criticisms of the nature of the trial in *Southern Pacific* well taken? Why are legislators better, in Justice Black's view, than courts in balancing the probabilities that increased safety to workers will be offset by greater danger of grade-crossing accidents? Is this a factual or a normative issue? Are the considerations the same when the statute is discriminatory? Reconsider these questions after reading the next principal case.

4. *The scope of the balancing inquiry.* In balancing costs and benefits, should (can) the courts take into account broader social effects, such as the strengthening of the union movement by its ability to show potential members that it is a

powerful force in politics? If they cannot, is the balance they strike an accurate one? (Justice Black began his legal career representing injured railroad workers.)

5. *Conflicting regulations.* Does *Southern Pacific* turn on an implicit decision that, under *Cooley,* the regulation of train lengths is an inherently national subject? Then the burden would be on the railroad workers to secure congressional permission for state regulation of train lengths. Is Justice Black persuasive in finding such permission in congressional knowledge of the existence of train limit laws and its failure to act?

In Bibb v. Navajo Freight Lines, 359 U.S. 520 (1959), Justice Douglas wrote the Court's opinion invalidating an Illinois law requiring that trucks in the state use curved mudguards to prevent spatter and promote safety. Straight mudflaps were legal in forty-five other states, curved mudflaps were illegal in Arkansas and were required in no other state. The trial court found that curved mudflaps have "no" safety advantages over straight ones, and introduce "hazards previously unknown to those using the highways," by increasing the heat around the tires and thereby reducing the effectiveness of the trucks' brakes. However, the Court said, "If we had here only a question whether the cost of adjusting an interstate operation to these new local safety regulations [unduly] burdened interstate commerce, we would have to sustain the law. [The] same result would obtain if we had to resolve the much discussed issues of safety." The case was different, though, because of the impossibility of using a single truck whose mudflaps complied with both Illinois and Arkansas law. Further, the Illinois law "seriously [interfered] with" interlining, the practice of having one carrier bring a trailer to a depot and another take it to its destination without unloading and reloading. The case was "one of those cases — few in number — where local safety measures that are nondiscriminatory place an unconstitutional burden on interstate commerce." Is Justice Douglas consistent in *Bibb* and *Southern Pacific?* In what sense do the Arkansas and Illinois regulations conflict other than that complying with both would increase costs enormously by requiring unloading and reloading? Why is it a problem for Illinois rather than for Arkansas that a shipper could not use a single trailer that complied with both states' regulations?

Kassel v. Consolidated Freightways Corp.
450 U.S. 662 (1981)

JUSTICE POWELL announced the judgment of the Court and delivered an opinion, in which JUSTICE WHITE, JUSTICE BLACKMUN, and JUSTICE STEVENS joined.

The question is whether an Iowa statute that prohibits the use of certain large trucks within the State unconstitutionally burdens interstate commerce.

I

Appellee Consolidated Freightways Corporation of Delaware (Consolidated) is one of the largest common carriers in the country. It offers service in 48 States under a certificate of public convenience and necessity issued by the Interstate Commerce Commission. Among other routes, Consolidated carries commodities through Iowa on Interstate 80, the principal east-west route linking New York, Chicago, and the west coast, and on Interstate 35, a major north-south route.

Consolidated mainly uses two kinds of trucks. One consists of a three-axle tractor pulling a 40-foot two-axle trailer. This unit, commonly called a single, or "semi," is 55 feet in length overall. Such trucks have long been used on the Nation's highways. Consolidated also uses a two-axle tractor pulling a single-axle trailer which, in turn, pulls a single-axle dolly and a second single-axle trailer. This combination, known as a double, or twin, is 65 feet long overall. Many trucking companies, including Consolidated, increasingly prefer to use doubles to ship certain kinds of commodities. Doubles have larger capacities, and the trailers can be detached and routed separately if necessary. Consolidated would like to use 65-foot doubles on many of its trips through Iowa.

The State of Iowa, however, by statute restricts the length of vehicles that may use its highways. Unlike all other States in the West and Midwest, Iowa generally prohibits the use of 65-foot doubles within its borders. Instead, most truck combinations are restricted to 55 feet in length. Doubles, mobile homes, trucks carrying vehicles such as tractors and other farm equipment, and singles hauling livestock, are permitted to be as long as 60 feet. Notwithstanding these restrictions, Iowa's statute permits cities abutting the state line by local ordinance to adopt the length limitations of the adjoining State. Where a city has exercised this option, otherwise oversized trucks are permitted within the city limits and in nearby commercial zones.[6]

Iowa also provides for two other relevant exemptions. An Iowa truck manufacturer may obtain a permit to ship trucks that are as large as 70 feet. Permits also are available to move oversized mobile homes, provided that the unit is to be moved from a point within Iowa or delivered for an Iowa resident.[7]

Because of Iowa's statutory scheme, Consolidated cannot use its 65-foot doubles to move commodities through the State. Instead, the company must do one of four things: (i) use 55-foot singles; (ii) use 60-foot doubles; (iii) detach the trailers of a 65-foot double and shuttle each through the State separately; or (iv) divert 65-foot doubles around Iowa.

Dissatisfied with these options, Consolidated filed this suit in the District Court averring that Iowa's statutory scheme unconstitutionally burdens interstate commerce. Iowa defended the law as a reasonable safety measure enacted pursuant to its police power. The State asserted that 65-foot doubles are more dangerous than 55-foot singles and, in any event, that the law promotes safety and reduces road wear within the State by diverting much truck traffic to other States.

In a 14-day trial, both sides adduced evidence on safety, and on the burden on interstate commerce imposed by Iowa's law. On the question of safety, the Dis-

---

6. The Iowa Legislature in 1974 passed House Bill 671, which would have permitted 65-foot doubles. But Iowa Governor Ray vetoed the bill, noting that it "would benefit only a few Iowa-based companies while providing a great advantage for out-of-state trucking firms and competitors at the expense of our Iowa citizens." The "border-cities exemption" was passed by the General Assembly and signed by the Governor shortly thereafter. . . .

7. The parochial restrictions in the mobile home provision were enacted after Governor Ray vetoed a bill that would have permitted the interstate shipment of all mobile homes through Iowa. Governor Ray commented, in his veto message: "This bill . . . would make Iowa a bridge state as these oversized units are moved into Iowa after being manufactured in another state and sold in a third. None of this activity would be of particular economic benefit to Iowa."

trict Court found that the "evidence clearly establishes that the twin is as safe as the semi." For that reason,

> there is no valid safety reason for barring twins from Iowa's highways because of their configuration.
>
> The evidence convincingly, if not overwhelmingly, establishes that the 65 foot twin is as safe as, if not safer than, the 60 foot twin and the 55 foot semi. . . .
>
> Twins and semis have different characteristics. Twins are more maneuverable, are less sensitive to wind, and create less splash and spray. However, they are more likely than semis to jackknife or upset. They can be backed only for a short distance. The negative characteristics are not such that they render the twin less safe than semis overall. Semis are more stable but are more likely to 'rear end' another vehicle.

In light of these findings, the District Court applied the standard we enunciated in Raymond Motor Transportation, Inc. v. Rice, 434 U.S. 429 (1978), and concluded that the state law impermissibly burdened interstate commerce:

> [T]he balance here must be struck in favor of the federal interests. The *total effect* of the law as a safety measure in reducing accidents and casualties is so slight and problematical that it does not outweigh the national interest in keeping interstate commerce free from interferences that seriously impede it.

The Court of Appeals for the Eighth Circuit affirmed. . . .

II . . .

[A] State's power to regulate commerce is never greater than in matters traditionally of local concern. For example, regulations that touch upon safety — especially highway safety — are those that "the Court has been most reluctant to invalidate." Indeed, "if safety justifications are not illusory, the Court will not second-guess legislative judgment about their importance in comparison with related burdens on interstate commerce." *Raymond*, at 449 (Blackmun, J., concurring). Those who would challenge such bona fide safety regulations must overcome a "strong presumption of validity." [*Bibb.*]

But the incantation of a purpose to promote the public health or safety does not insulate a state law from Commerce Clause attack. Regulations designed for that salutary purpose nevertheless may further the purpose so marginally, and interfere with commerce so substantially, as to be invalid under the Commerce Clause. In the Court's recent unanimous decision in *Raymond*, we declined to "accept the State's contention that the inquiry under the Commerce Clause is ended without a weighing of the asserted safety purpose against the degree of interference with interstate commerce." This "weighing" by a court requires — and indeed the constitutionality of the state regulation depends on — "a sensitive consideration of the weight and nature of the state regulatory concern in light of the extent of the burden imposed on the course of interstate commerce."

III

Applying these general principles, we conclude that the Iowa truck-length limitations unconstitutionally burden interstate commerce. [The] State failed to present any persuasive evidence that 65-foot doubles are less safe than 55-foot singles. Moreover, Iowa's law is now out of step with the laws of all other Midwestern and Western States. Iowa thus substantially burdens the interstate flow of goods by truck. In the absence of congressional action to set uniform standards, some burdens associated with state safety regulations must be tolerated. But where, as here, the State's safety interest has been found to be illusory, and its regulations impair significantly the federal interest in efficient and safe interstate transportation, the state law cannot be harmonized with the Commerce Clause.[12]

A . . .

[The] District Court found that the "evidence clearly establishes that the twin is as safe as the semi." The record supports this finding.

The trial focused on a comparison of the performance of the two kinds of trucks in various safety categories. The evidence showed, and the District Court found, that the 65-foot double was at least the equal of the 55-foot single in the ability to brake, turn, and maneuver. The double, because of its axle placement, produces less splash and spray in wet weather. And, because of its articulation in the middle, the double is less susceptible to dangerous "off-tracking," and to wind.

None of these findings is seriously disputed by Iowa. Indeed, the State points to only three ways in which the 55-foot single is even arguably superior: singles take less time to be passed and to clear intersections; they may back up for longer distances; and they are somewhat less likely to jackknife.

The first two of these characteristics are of limited relevance on modern interstate highways. As the District Court found, the negligible difference in the time required to pass, and to cross intersections, is insignificant on 4-lane divided highways because passing does not require crossing into oncoming traffic lanes, and interstates have few, if any, intersections. The concern over backing capability also is insignificant because it seldom is necessary to back up on an interstate.[15] In any event, no evidence suggested any difference in backing capability between the 60-foot doubles that Iowa permits and the 65-foot doubles that it bans. Similarly, although doubles tend to jackknife somewhat more than singles, 65-foot doubles actually are less likely to jackknife than 60-foot doubles.

Statistical studies supported the view that 65-foot doubles are at least as safe overall as 55-foot singles and 60-foot doubles.[16] . . .

B

Consolidated, meanwhile, demonstrated that Iowa's law substantially burdens interstate commerce. Trucking companies that wish to continue to use 65-foot

---

12. It is highly relevant that here, as in *Raymond*, the state statute contains exemptions that weaken the deference traditionally accorded to a state safety regulation.

15. Evidence at trial did show that doubles could back up far enough to move around an accident.

16. In suggesting that Iowa's law actually promotes safety, the dissenting opinion ignores the findings of the courts below and relies on largely discredited statistical evidence. The dissent implies that a statistical study identified doubles as more dangerous than singles. At trial, however, the author of that study — Iowa's own statistician — conceded that his calculations were statistically biased, and therefore "not very meaningful."

The dissenting opinion also suggests that its conclusions are bolstered by the fact that the American Association of State Highway and Transportation Officials (AASHTO) recommends that States limit truck lengths. The dissent fails to point out, however, that AASHTO specifically recommends that States permit 65-foot doubles. [Relocated footnote.]

doubles must route them around Iowa or detach the trailers of the doubles and ship them through separately. Alternatively, trucking companies must use the smaller 55-foot singles or 60-foot doubles permitted under Iowa law. Each of these options engenders inefficiency and added expense. The record shows that Iowa's law added about $12.6 million each year to the costs of trucking companies. Consolidated alone incurred about $2 million per year in increased costs.

In addition to increasing the costs of the trucking companies (and, indirectly, of the service to consumers), Iowa's law may aggravate, rather than ameliorate, the problem of highway accidents. Fifty-five foot singles carry less freight than 65-foot doubles. Either more small trucks must be used to carry the same quantity of goods through Iowa, or the same number of larger trucks must drive longer distances to bypass Iowa. In either case, as the District Court noted, the restriction requires more highway miles to be driven to transport the same quantity of goods. Other things being equal, accidents are proportional to distance traveled. Thus, if 65-foot doubles are as safe as 55-foot singles, Iowa's law tends to *increase* the number of accidents, and to shift the incidence of them from Iowa to other States.[18]

IV

Perhaps recognizing the weakness of the evidence supporting its safety argument, and the substantial burden on commerce that its regulations create, Iowa urges the Court simply to "defer" to the safety judgment of the State. It argues that the length of trucks is generally, although perhaps imprecisely, related to safety. The task of drawing a line is one that Iowa contends should be left to its legislature.

The Court normally does accord "special deference" to state highway safety regulations. [*Raymond*.] This traditional deference "derives in part from the assumption that where such regulations do not discriminate on their face against interstate commerce, their burden usually falls on local economic interests as well as other States' economic interests, thus insuring that a State's own political processes will serve as a check against unduly burdensome regulations." Less deference to the legislative judgment is due, however, where the local regulation bears disproportionately on out-of-state residents and businesses. Such a disproportionate burden is apparent here. Iowa's scheme, although generally banning large doubles from the State, nevertheless has several exemptions that secure to Iowans many of the benefits of large trucks while shunting to neighboring States many of the costs associated with their use.

At the time of trial there were two particularly significant exemptions. First, singles hauling livestock or farm vehicles were permitted to be as long as 60 feet. As the Court of Appeals noted, this provision undoubtedly was helpful to local interests. Cf. *Raymond* (exemption in Wisconsin for milk shippers). Second, cities abutting other States were permitted to enact local ordinances adopting the larger length limitation of the neighboring State. This exemption offered the

---

18. The District Court, in denying a stay pending appeal, noted that Iowa's law causes "more accidents, more injuries, more fatalities and more fuel consumption." Appellant Kassel conceded as much at trial. Kassel explained, however, that most of these additional accidents occur in States other than Iowa because truck traffic is deflected around the State. He noted: "Our primary concern is the citizens of Iowa and our own highway system we operate in this state."

benefits of longer trucks to individuals and businesses in important border cities without burdening Iowa's highways with interstate through traffic. Cf. *Raymond* (exemption in Wisconsin for shipments from local plants).

The origin of the "border cities exemption" also suggests that Iowa's statute may not have been designed to ban dangerous trucks, but rather to discourage interstate truck traffic. In 1974, the legislature passed a bill that would have permitted 65-foot doubles in the State. Governor Ray vetoed the bill. He said:

> I find sympathy with those who are doing business in our state and whose enterprises could gain from increased cargo carrying ability by trucks. However, with this bill, the Legislature has pursued a course that would benefit only a few Iowa-based companies while providing a great advantage for out-of-state trucking firms and competitors at the expense of our Iowa citizens.

After the veto, the "border cities exemption" was immediately enacted and signed by the Governor.

It is thus far from clear that Iowa was motivated primarily by a judgment that 65-foot doubles are less safe than 55-foot singles. Rather, Iowa seems to have hoped to limit the use of its highways by deflecting some through traffic. In the District Court and Court of Appeals, the State explicitly attempted to justify the law by its claimed interest in keeping trucks out of Iowa. [A] State cannot constitutionally promote its own parochial interests by requiring safe vehicles to detour around it.

V

In sum, the statutory exemptions, their history, and the arguments Iowa has advanced in support of its law in this litigation, all suggest that the deference traditionally accorded a State's safety judgment is not warranted. The controlling factors thus are the findings of the District Court, accepted by the Court of Appeals, with respect to the relative safety of the types of trucks at issue, and the substantiality of the burden on interstate commerce.

Because Iowa has imposed this burden without any significant countervailing safety interest, its statute violates the Commerce Clause. The judgment of the Court of Appeals is affirmed.

It is so ordered.

JUSTICE BRENNAN, with whom JUSTICE MARSHALL, joins, concurring in the judgment.

Iowa's truck-length regulation challenged in this case is nearly identical to the Wisconsin regulation struck down in [*Raymond*] as in violation of the Commerce Clause. In my view the same Commerce Clause restrictions that dictated that holding also require invalidation of Iowa's regulation insofar as it prohibits 65-foot doubles.

The reasoning bringing me to that conclusion does not require, however, that I engage in the debate between my Brothers Powell and Rehnquist over what the District Court record shows on the question whether 65-foot doubles are more dangerous than shorter trucks. With all respect, my Brothers ask and answer the wrong question.

For me, analysis of Commerce Clause challenges to state regulations must take into account three principles: (1) The courts are not empowered to second-guess the empirical judgments of lawmakers concerning the utility of legislation. (2) The burdens imposed on commerce must be balanced against the local benefits actually sought to be achieved by the State's lawmakers, and not against those suggested after the fact by counsel. (3) Protectionist legislation is unconstitutional under the Commerce Clause, even if the burdens and benefits are related to safety rather than economics.

I

Both the opinion of my Brother Powell and the opinion of my Brother Rehnquist are predicated upon the supposition that the constitutionality of a state regulation is determined by the factual record created by the State's lawyers in trial court. But that supposition cannot be correct, for it would make the constitutionality of state laws and regulations depend on the vagaries of litigation rather than on the judgments made by the State's lawmakers.

In considering a Commerce Clause challenge to a state regulation, the judicial task is to balance the burden imposed on commerce against the local benefits sought to be achieved by the State's *lawmakers*. In determining those benefits, a court should focus ultimately on the regulatory purposes identified by the lawmakers and on the evidence before or available to them that might have supported their judgment. See generally [*Clover Leaf*]. Since the court must confine its analysis to the purposes the lawmakers had for maintaining the regulation, the only relevant evidence concerns whether the lawmakers could rationally have believed that the challenged regulation would foster those purposes. See Locomotive Firemen v. Chicago, R.I. & P.R. Co., 393 U.S. 129, 138-139 (1968). It is not the function of the court to decide whether *in fact* the regulation promotes its intended purpose, so long as an examination of the evidence before or available to the lawmaker indicates that the regulation is not wholly irrational in light of its purposes. See [*Clover Leaf*].[1]

II

My Brothers Powell and Rehnquist make the mistake of disregarding the intention of Iowa's lawmakers and assuming that resolution of the case must hinge upon the argument offered by Iowa's attorneys: that 65-foot doubles are more danger-

---

1. Moreover, I would emphasize that in the field of safety — and perhaps in other fields where the decisions of state lawmakers are deserving of a heightened degree of deference — the role of the courts is not to balance asserted burdens against intended benefits as it is in other fields. Compare [*Raymond*] (Blackmun, J., concurring) (safety regulation), with Pike v. Bruce Church, Inc., 397 U.S. 137, 143 (1970) (regulation intended "to protect and enhance the reputation of growers within the State"). In the field of safety, once the court has established that the intended safety benefit is not illusory, insubstantial, or nonexistent, it must defer to the State's lawmakers on the appropriate balance to be struck against other interests. I therefore disagree with my Brother Powell when he asserts that the degree of interference with interstate commerce may in the first instance be "weighed" against the State's safety interests. . . .

ous than shorter trucks. They then canvass the factual record and findings of the courts below and reach opposite conclusions as to whether the evidence adequately supports that empirical judgment. I repeat: my Brothers Powell and Rehnquist have asked and answered the wrong question. For although Iowa's lawyers in this litigation have defended the truck-length regulation on the basis of the safety advantages of 55-foot singles and 60-foot doubles over 65-foot doubles, Iowa's actual rationale for maintaining the regulation had nothing to do with these purported differences. Rather, Iowa sought to discourage interstate truck traffic on Iowa's highways. Thus, the safety advantages and disadvantages of the types and lengths of trucks involved in this case are irrelevant to the decision.[3] . . .

III

Though my Brother Powell recognizes that the State's actual purposes in maintaining the truck-length regulation was "to limit the use of its highways by deflecting some through traffic," he fails to recognize that this purpose, being *protectionist* in nature, is *impermissible* under the Commerce Clause. The Governor admitted that he blocked legislative efforts to raise the length of trucks because the change "would benefit only a few Iowa-based companies while providing a great advantage for out-of-state trucking firms and competitors at the expense of our Iowa citizens." Appellant Raymond Kassel, Director of the Iowa Department of Transportation, while admitting that the greater 65-foot length

3. My Brother Rehnquist claims that the "argument" that a court should defer to the actual purposes of the lawmakers rather than to the *post hoc* justifications of counsel "has been consistently rejected by the Court in other contexts." Apparently he has overlooked such cases. Weinberger v. Wiesenfeld, 420 U.S. 636, 648, n.16 (1975), [where] we said: "This Court need not . . . accept at face value assertions of legislative purposes, when an examination of the legislative scheme and its history demonstrates that the asserted purpose could not have been a goal of the legislation." And in Massachusetts Board of Retirement v. Murgia, 427 U.S. 307, 314 (1976), we stated that a classification challenged as being discriminatory will be upheld only if it "rationally furthers the purpose identified by the State." See also [*Clover Leaf*; Califano v. Goldfarb, infra].

The extent to which we may rely upon post hoc justifications of counsel depends on the circumstances surrounding passage of the legislation. Where there is no evidence bearing on the actual purpose for a legislative classification, our analysis necessarily focuses on the suggestions of counsel. Even then, "marginally more demanding scrutiny" is appropriate to "test the plausibility of the tendered purpose." But where the lawmakers' purposes in enacting a statute are explicitly set forth, e.g., [*Clover Leaf*] or are clearly discernible from the legislative history, this Court should not take — and, with the possible exception of United States Railroad Retirement Board v. Fritz [infra] has not taken — the extraordinary step of disregarding the *actual* purpose in favor of some "imaginary basis or purpose." The principle of separation of powers requires, after all, that we defer to the elected lawmakers' judgment as to the appropriate means to accomplish an end, not that we defer to the arguments of lawyers.

If, as here, the only purpose ever articulated by the State's lawmakers for maintaining a regulation is illegitimate, I consider it contrary to precedent as well as to sound principles of constitutional adjudication for the courts to base their analysis on purposes never conceived by the lawmakers. This is especially true where, as the dissent's strained analysis of the relative safety of 65-foot doubles to shorter trucks amply demonstrates, the post hoc justifications are implausible as well as imaginary. I would emphasize that, although my Brother Powell's plurality opinion does not give as much weight to the illegitimacy of Iowa's actual purpose as I do, both that opinion and this concurrence have found the actual motivation of the Iowa lawmakers in maintaining the truck-length regulation highly relevant to, if not dispositive of, the case.

standard would be *safer* overall, defended the more restrictive regulations because of their benefits *within Iowa:*

> Q: Overall, there would be fewer miles of operation, fewer accidents and fewer fatalities?
> A: Yes, on the national scene.
> Q: Does it not concern the Iowa Department of Transportation that banning 65-foot twins causes more accidents, more injuries and more fatalities?
> A: Do you mean outside of our state border?
> Q: Overall.
> A: Our primary concern is the citizens of Iowa and our own highway system we operate in this state.

The regulation has had its predicted effect. As the District Court found:

> Iowa's length restriction causes the trucks affected by the ban to travel more miles over more dangerous roads in other states which means a greater overall exposure to accidents and fatalities. More miles of highway are subjected to wear. More fuel is consumed and greater transportation costs are incurred.

Iowa may not shunt off its fair share of the burden of maintaining interstate truck routes, nor may it create increased hazards on the highways of neighboring States in order to decrease the hazards on Iowa highways. Such an attempt has all the hallmarks of the "simple . . . protectionism" this Court has condemned in the economic area. [Philadelphia v. New Jersey.] Just as a State's attempt to avoid interstate competition in economic goods may damage the prosperity of the Nation as a whole, so Iowa's attempt to deflect interstate truck traffic has been found to make the Nation's highways as a whole more hazardous. That attempt should therefore be subject to "a virtually per se rule of invalidity."

This Court's heightened deference to the judgments of state lawmakers in the field of safety, is largely attributable to a judicial disinclination to weigh the interests of safety against other societal interests, such as the economic interest in the free flow of commerce. Thus, "if safety justifications are not illusory, the Court will not second-guess legislative judgment about their importance *in comparison with related burdens on interstate commerce.*" [*Raymond*] (Blackmun, J., concurring). Here, the decision of Iowa's lawmakers to promote *Iowa's* safety and other interests at the direct expense of the safety and other interests of neighboring States merits no such deference. No special judicial acuity is demanded to perceive that this sort of parochial legislation violates the Commerce Clause. As Justice Cardozo has written, the Commerce Clause "was framed upon the theory that the peoples of the several states must sink or swim together, and that in the long run prosperity and salvation are in union and not division." [Baldwin v. G.A.F. Seelig.]

I therefore concur in the judgment.

JUSTICE REHNQUIST, with whom THE CHIEF JUSTICE and JUSTICE STEWART join, dissenting.

The result in this case suggests, to paraphrase Justice Jackson, that the only state truck-length limit "that is valid is one which this Court has not been able to get its hands on." Jungersen v. Ostby & Barton Co., 335 U.S. 560, 572 (1949) (dissenting opinion). . . .

I

It is necessary to elaborate somewhat on the facts as presented in the plurality opinion to appreciate fully what the Court does today. Iowa's action in limiting the length of trucks which may travel on its highway is in no sense unusual. Every State in the Union regulates the length of vehicles permitted to use the public roads. Nor is Iowa a renegade in having the length limits which operate to exclude the 65-foot doubles favored by Consolidated. These trucks are prohibited in other areas of the country as well, some 17 States and the District of Columbia, including all of New England and most of the Southeast.[1] While pointing out that Consolidated carries commodities through Iowa on Interstate 80, "the principal east-west route linking New York, Chicago, and the west coast," the plurality neglects to note that both Pennsylvania and New Jersey, through which Interstate 80 runs before reaching New York, also ban 65-foot doubles. In short, the persistent effort in the plurality opinion to paint Iowa as an oddity standing alone to block commerce carried in 65-foot doubles is simply not supported by the facts.

Nor does the plurality adequately convey the extent to which the lower courts permitted the 65-foot doubles to operate in Iowa. Consolidated sought to have the 60-foot length limit declared an unconstitutional burden on commerce when applied to the seven Interstate Highways in Iowa and "access routes to and from Plaintiff's terminals, and reasonable access from said Interstate Highways to facilities for food, fuel, repairs, or rest." The lower courts granted this relief, permitting the 65-foot doubles to travel *off the Interstates* as far as five miles for access to terminal and other facilities, or less if closer facilities were available. To the extent the plurality relies on characteristics of the Interstate Highways in rejecting Iowa's asserted safety justifications, it fails to recognize the scope of the District Court order it upholds.

With these additions to the relevant facts, we can now examine the appropriate analysis to be applied.

II . . .

A determination that a state law is a rational safety measure does not end the Commerce Clause inquiry. A "sensitive consideration" of the safety purpose in relation to the burden on commerce is required. *Raymond* at 441. When engaging in such a consideration the Court does not directly compare safety benefits to commerce costs and strike down the legislation if the latter can be said in some vague sense to "outweigh" the former. Such an approach would make an empty gesture of the strong presumption of validity accorded state safety measures, particularly those governing highways. It would also arrogate to this Court functions of forming public policy, functions which, in the absence of congressional

1. Doubles are prohibited in Maine, New Hampshire, Vermont, Massachusetts (except turnpike), Rhode Island, Connecticut, Pennsylvania, West Virginia, Virginia, Tennessee, North Carolina, South Carolina, Alabama, and the District of Columbia. Doubles are permitted to a maximum length of 55 feet in New York (on designated highways only, longer permitted on turnpike), New Jersey, Mississippi, and Georgia. Sixty-five foot doubles are restricted to designated highways in Oregon, North Dakota, Minnesota, Wisconsin, Michigan, Illinois, Missouri, Louisiana, Kentucky, Maryland, and Florida.

action, were left by the Framers of the Constitution to state legislatures. "[I]n reviewing a state highway regulation where Congress has not acted, a court is not called upon, as are state legislatures, to determine what, in its judgment, is the most suitable restriction to be applied of those that are possible, or to choose that one which in its opinion is best adapted to all the diverse interests affected." [*Barnwell Brothers.*] See [*Locomotive Firemen*] ("[T]he question of safety in the circumstances of this case is essentially a matter of public policy, and public policy can, under our constitutional system, be fixed only by the people acting through their elected representatives"); [*Bibb*] ("If there are alternative ways of solving a problem, we do not sit to determine which of them is best suited to achieve a valid state objective. Policy decisions are for the state legislature"). These admonitions are peculiarly apt when, as here, the question involves the difficult comparison of financial losses and "the loss of lives and limbs of workers and people using the highways." [*Locomotive Firemen.*][4]

The purpose of the "sensitive consideration" referred to above is rather to determine if the asserted safety justification, although rational, is merely a pretext for discrimination against interstate commerce. We will conclude that it is if the safety benefits from the regulation are demonstrably trivial while the burden on commerce is great. . . .

III

Iowa defends its statute as a highway safety regulation. There can be no doubt that the challenged statute is a valid highway safety regulation and thus entitled to the strongest presumption of validity against Commerce Clause challenges. As noted, all 50 States regulate the length of trucks which may use their highways. The American Association of State Highway and Transportation Officials (AASHTO) has consistently recommended length as well as other limits on vehicles. [There] can also be no question that the particular limit chosen by Iowa — 60 feet — is rationally related to Iowa's safety objective. Most truck limits are between 55 and 65 feet, and Iowa's choice is thus well within the widely accepted range.

Iowa adduced evidence supporting the relation between vehicle length and highway safety. The evidence indicated that longer vehicles take greater time to pass, thereby increasing the risks of accidents, particularly during the inclement weather not uncommon in Iowa. The 65-foot vehicle exposes a passing driver to visibility-impairing splash and spray during bad weather for a longer period than do the shorter trucks permitted in Iowa. Longer trucks are more likely to clog intersections, and although there are no intersections on the Interstate Highways, the order below went beyond the highways themselves and the concerns about greater length at intersections would arise "[a]t every trip origin, every trip destination, every intermediate stop for picking up trailers, reconfiguring loads,

---

4. It should not escape notice that a majority of the Court goes on record today as agreeing that courts in Commerce Clause cases do not sit to weigh safety benefits against burdens on commerce when the safety benefits are not illusory. Even the plurality gives lip service to this principle. I do not agree with my Brother Brennan, however, that only those safety benefits somehow articulated by the legislature as *the* motivation for the challenged statute can be considered in supporting the state law.

change of drivers, eating, refueling — every intermediate stop would generate this type of situation." The Chief of the Division of Patrol in the Iowa Department of Public Safety testified that longer vehicles pose greater problems at the scene of an accident. For example, trucks involved in accidents often must be unloaded at the scene, which would take longer the bigger the load.

In rebuttal of Consolidated's evidence of the relative safety of 65-foot doubles to trucks permitted on Iowa's highways, Iowa introduced evidence that doubles are more likely than singles to jackknife or upset. The District Court concluded that this was so and that singles are more stable than doubles. Iowa also introduced evidence from Consolidated's own records showing that Consolidated's overall accident rate for doubles exceeded that of semis for three of the last four years, and that some of Consolidated's own drivers expressed a preference for the handling characteristics of singles over doubles.

In addition Iowa elicited evidence undermining the probative value of Consolidated's evidence. For example, Iowa established that the more experienced drivers tended to drive doubles, because they have seniority and driving doubles is a higher paying job than driving singles. Since the leading cause of accidents was driver error, Consolidated's evidence of the relative safety record of doubles may have been based in large part not on the relative safety of the vehicles themselves but on the experience of the drivers. Although the District Court, the Court of Appeals, and the plurality all fail to recognize the fact, Iowa also negated much of Consolidated's evidence by establishing that it considered the relative safety of doubles to singles, and not the question of length alone. Consolidated introduced much evidence that its doubles were as safe as singles. Such evidence is beside the point. The trucks which Consolidated wants to run in Iowa are prohibited because of their length, not their configuration. Doubles are allowed in Iowa, up to a length of 60 feet, and Consolidated in fact operates 60-foot doubles in Iowa. Consolidated's experts were often forced to admit that they could draw no conclusions about the relative safety of 65-foot doubles and 60-foot doubles, as opposed to doubles and singles. Conclusions that the double configuration is as safe as the single do not at all mean the 65-foot double is as safe as the 60-foot double, or that length is not relevant to vehicle safety. For example, one of Consolidated's experts testified that doubles "off track" better than singles, because of their axle placement, but conceded on cross-examination that a 60-foot double would off-track better than a 65-foot double. In sum, there was sufficient evidence presented at trial to support the legislative determination that length is related to safety, and nothing in Consolidated's evidence undermines this conclusion.

The District Court approached the case as if the question were whether Consolidated's 65-foot trucks were as safe as others permitted on Iowa highways, and the Court of Appeals as if its task were to determine if the District Court's factual findings in this regard were "clearly erroneous." The question, however, is whether the Iowa Legislature has acted rationally in regulating vehicle lengths and whether the safety benefits from this regulation are more than slight or problematical. "The classification of the traffic for the purposes of regulation . . . is a legislative, not a judicial, function. Its merits are not to be weighed in the judicial balance and the classification rejected merely because the weight of the evidence in court appears to favor a different standard." Clark v. Paul Gray, Inc., 306 U.S. 583, 594 (1939). "Since the adoption of one weight or width regulation, rather than another, is a legislative and not a judicial choice, its constitutionality is not to be determined by weighing in the judicial scales the merits of the legislative choice and rejecting it if the weight of evidence presented in court appears to favor a different standard." [*Barnwell Brothers.*][8]

The answering of the relevant question is not appreciably advanced by comparing trucks slightly over the length limit with those at the length limit. It is emphatically not our task to balance any incremental safety benefits from prohibiting 65-foot doubles as opposed to 60-foot doubles against the burden on interstate commerce. Lines drawn for safety purposes will rarely pass muster if the question is whether a slight increment can be permitted without sacrificing safety. [The] question is rather whether it can be said that the benefits flowing to Iowa from a rational truck-length limitation are "slight or problematical." See [*Bibb.*] The particular line chosen by Iowa — 60 feet — is relevant only to the question whether the limit is a rational one. Once a court determines that it is, it considers the overall safety benefits *from the regulation* against burdens on interstate commerce, and not any marginal benefits from the scheme the State established as opposed to that the plaintiffs desire.

The difficulties with the contrary approach are patent. While it may be clear that there are substantial safety benefits from a 55-foot truck as compared to a 105-foot truck, these benefits may not be discernible in 5-foot jumps. Appellee's approach would permit what could not be accomplished in one lawsuit to be done in 10 separate suits, each challenging an additional five feet. . . .

[Striking] down Iowa's law because Consolidated has made a voluntary business decision to employ 65-foot doubles, a decision based on the actions of other state legislatures, would essentially be compelling Iowa to yield to the policy choices of neighboring States. Under our constitutional scheme, however, there is only one legislative body which can pre-empt the rational policy determination of the Iowa Legislature and that is Congress. Forcing Iowa to yield to the policy choices of neighboring States perverts the primary purpose of the Commerce Clause, that of vesting power to regulate interstate commerce in Congress, where all the States are represented. In *Barnwell Brothers*, the Court upheld a South Carolina width limit of 90 inches even though "all other states permit a width of 96 inches, which is the standard width of trucks engaged in interstate commerce." Then Justice Stone, writing for the Court, stressed:

> The fact that many states have adopted a different standard is not persuasive. . . .
> The legislature, being free to exercise its own judgment, is not bound by that of
> other legislatures. It would hardly be contended that if all the states had adopted a

___

8. The opinion of my Brother Brennan concurring in the judgment mischaracterizes this dissent when it states that I assume "resolution of the case must hinge upon the argument offered by Iowa's attorneys: that 65-foot doubles are more dangerous than shorter trucks." I assume nothing of the sort. As noted in the immediately preceding paragraph, the point of this dissent is that the District Court and the Court of Appeals erred when they undertook to determine if the prohibited trucks were as safe as the permitted ones on the basis of evidence presented at trial. As I read this Court's opinions, the State must simply prove, aided by a "strong presumption of validity," that the safety benefits of its law are not illusory. I review the evidence presented at trial simply to demonstrate that Iowa made such a showing in this case, not because the validity of Iowa's law depends on its proving by a preponderance of the evidence that the excluded trucks are unsafe. As I thought was made clear, it is my view that Iowa must simply show a relation between vehicle length limits and safety, and that the benefits from its length limit are not illusory. Iowa's arguments on passing time, intersection obstruction, and problems at the scene of accidents have validity beyond a comparison of the 65- and 60-foot trucks. In sum, I fully agree with Justice Brennan that the validity of Iowa's length limit does not turn on whether 65-foot trucks are less safe than 60-foot trucks.

single standard none, in the light of its own experience and in the exercise of its judgment upon all the complex elements which enter into the problem, could change it.

Nor is Iowa's policy preempted by Consolidated's decision to invest in 65-foot trucks, particularly since this was done when Iowa's 60-foot limit was on the books. . . .

[The] exception to the Wisconsin prohibition which the Court specifically noted in *Raymond* finds no parallel in this case. The exception in *Raymond* permitted oversized vehicles to travel from plant to plant in Wisconsin or between a Wisconsin plant and the border. As the Court noted, this discriminated on its face between Wisconsin industries and the industries of other States. The border-cities exception to the Iowa length limit does not. Iowa shippers in cities with border-city ordinances may use longer vehicles in interstate commerce, but interstate shippers coming into such cities may do so as well. Cities without border-city ordinances may neither export nor import on oversized vehicles. Nor can the border-cities exception be "[v]iewed realistically," as was the Wisconsin exception, to "be the product of compromise between forces within the State that seek to retain the State's general truck-length limit, and industries within the State that complain that the general limit is unduly burdensome." [*Raymond*], 434 U.S. at 447. The Wisconsin exception was available to all Wisconsin industries wanting to ship out of State from Wisconsin plants. The border-cities exception is of much narrower applicability: only 5 of Iowa's 16 largest cities and only 8 cities in all permit oversized trucks under the border-cities exception. The population of the eight cities with border-city ordinances is only 13 percent of the population of the State.

My Brother Brennan argues that the Court should consider only *the* purpose the Iowa legislators *actually* sought to achieve by the length limit, and not the purposes advanced by Iowa's lawyers in defense of the statute. This argument calls to mind what was said of the Roman Legions: that they may have lost battles but they never lost a war, since they never let a war end until they had won it. The argument has been consistently rejected by the Court in other contexts, compare, e.g., United States Railroad Retirement Board v. Fritz [infra], and Michael M. v. Superior Court of Sonoma County [infra]. Justice Brennan can cite no authority for the proposition that possible legislative purposes suggested by a State's lawyers should not be considered in Commerce Clause cases. The problems with a view such as that advanced in the opinion concurring in the judgment are apparent. To name just a few, it assumes that individual legislators are motivated by one discernible "actual" purpose, and ignores the fact that different legislators may vote for a single piece of legislation for widely different reasons. How, for example, would a court adhering to the views expressed in the opinion concurring in the judgment approach a statute, the legislative history of which indicated that 10 votes were based on safety considerations, 10 votes were based on protectionism, and the statute passed by a vote of 40–20? What would the *actual* purpose of the *legislature* have been in that case? This Court has wisely "never insisted that a legislative body articulate its reasons for enacting a statute." *Fritz*, at 461.

Both the plurality and concurring opinions attach great significance to the Governor's veto of a bill passed by the Iowa Legislature permitting 65-foot doubles. Whatever views one may have about the significance of legislative motives, it must be emphasized that the law which the Court strikes down today was not passed to achieve the protectionist goals the plurality and the concurrence ascribe to the Governor. Iowa's 60-foot length limit was established in 1963, at a time when very few States permitted 65-foot doubles. Striking down legislation on the basis of asserted legislative motives is dubious enough, but the plurality and concurrence strike down the legislation involved in this case because of asserted impermissible motives for *not* enacting *other* legislation, motives which could not possibly have been present when the legislation under challenge here was considered and passed. Such action is, so far as I am aware, unprecedented in this Court's history.

Furthermore, the effort in both the plurality and concurring opinions to portray the legislation involved here as protectionist is in error. Whenever a State enacts more stringent safety measures than its neighbors, in an area which affects commerce, the safety law will have the incidental effect of deflecting interstate commerce to the neighboring States. Indeed, the safety and protectionist motives cannot be separated: The whole purpose of safety regulation of vehicles is to *protect* the State from unsafe vehicles. If a neighboring State chooses *not* to protect its citizens from the danger discerned by the enacting State, that is its business, but the enacting State should not be penalized when the vehicles it considers unsafe travel through the neighboring State.

The other States with truck-length limits that exclude Consolidated's 65-foot doubles would not at all be paranoid in assuming that they might be next on Consolidated's "hit list." The true problem with today's decision is that it gives no guidance whatsoever to these States as to whether their laws are valid or how to defend them. For that matter, the decision gives no guidance to Consolidated or other trucking firms either. Perhaps, after all is said and done, the Court today neither says nor does very much at all. We know only that Iowa's law is invalid and that the jurisprudence of the "negative side" of the Commerce Clause remains hopelessly confused.

Note: Are Burdens (Inevitably) Discriminatory?

1. *Discrimination*. Did Iowa discriminate against interstate commerce? Are any of the in-staters who benefit from the statute competitors of out-of-staters who bear its costs? Are there nondiscriminatory explanations for the exceptions in the statute? (Is the "farm vehicles" exemption relevant at all?)

Justice Rehnquist argues that the existence of an undue burden triggers inquiry into whether the regulation is a pretext for discrimination but does not in itself establish a commerce clause violation. Is that an accurate characterization of *Southern Pacific* and *Bibb*?

2. *Economic isolationism?* If Iowa's statute is treated as nondiscriminatory, what benefits does it provide? Does it enhance safety in Iowa? In the region? Justice Brennan says that Iowa must bear its "fair share" of safety problems in the region. Why? Suppose Iowa provides so little maintenance on its highways that shippers choose to send their trucks on routes through Missouri. Would Iowa's policy violate the commerce clause? If not, how might Justice Brennan distinguish that policy from the prohibition on sixty-five foot trucks?

3. *Judicial capacity*. *Kassel* has been edited to present substantial information about the factual matters said to bear on the constitutional analysis. How apt were

Justice Black's concerns in his *Southern Pacific* dissent over the capacity of trial and appellate courts to base their decisions on the results of such factual inquiries? In *Raymond*, Chief Justice Burger, and Justices Blackmun, Brennan, and Rehnquist joined in a concurring opinion that stated, "If safety justifications are not illusory, the Court will not second guess legislative judgment about their importance in comparison with related burdens on interstate commerce. [Here] the Court does not engage in a balance of policies; it does not make a legislative choice. Instead, after searching the factual record, [it] concludes that the safety interests have not been shown to exist as a matter of law." The concurrence mentioned "the overwhelming empirical data" supporting the safety of doubles. Did Justice Rehnquist and Chief Justice Burger (and Justice Stewart) change their minds, or did they find Iowa's factual presentation more adequate than Wisconsin's? If the latter, should a sound body of constitutional law include a rule that allows one state to maintain a policy that another may not, simply because the lawyers for the former were better than those for the latter?

4. *Congress intervenes.* What is the relevance of the following? In 1981 Congress enacted the Economic Recovery Tax Act, which substantially reduced individual income tax rates. In 1982 it enacted the Surface Transportation Act. One provision of the act recaptured some of the lost revenue by increasing the excise tax on trucks and the tax on gasoline and diesel fuel. Trucking interests opposed these increased taxes, but withdrew their opposition in exchange for another provision in the act eliminating the restrictions states placed on the use of doubles on interstate highways, to take effect in 1984. Although the increased tax on gasoline went into effect relatively quickly, collection of the excise tax on trucks was deferred until 1985 because of technical difficulties in defining truck weights. A 1984 amendment to the act allows the Secretary of Transportation, rather than the states, to invoke safety reasons for excluding doubles from some portions of the interstate system. Governors may petition the Secretary for such an exclusion and must demonstrate that the safety reasons are genuine. In addition, the Secretary may, with the permission of a state's governor, open primary noninterstate highways to doubles.

D. PREEMPTION

Pacific Gas & Electric v. State Energy Resources Conservation Commission

461 U.S. 190 (1983)

JUSTICE WHITE delivered the opinion of the Court.

The turning of swords into plowshares has symbolized the transformation of atomic power into a source of energy in American society. To facilitate this development the federal government relaxed its monopoly over fissionable materials and nuclear technology, and in its place, erected a complex scheme to promote the civilian development of nuclear energy, while seeking to safeguard the public and the environment from the unpredictable risks of a new technology. Early on, it was decided that the states would continue their traditional role in the regulation of electricity production. The interrelationship of federal and state authority in the nuclear energy field has not been simple; the federal regulatory structure has been frequently amended to optimize the partnership.

This case emerges from the intersection of the federal government's efforts to ensure that nuclear power is safe with the exercise of the historic state authority over the generation and sale of electricity. At issue is whether provisions in the 1976 amendments to California's Warren-Alquist Act, which condition the construction of nuclear plants on findings by the State Energy Resources Conservation and Development Commission that adequate storage facilities and means of disposal are available for nuclear waste, are preempted by the Atomic Energy Act of 1954.

I

A nuclear reactor must be periodically refueled and the "spent fuel" removed. This spent fuel is intensely radioactive and must be carefully stored. The general practice is to store the fuel in a water-filled pool at the reactor site. For many years, it was assumed that this fuel would be reprocessed; accordingly, the storage pools were designed as short-term holding facilities with limited storage capacities. As expectations for reprocessing remained unfulfilled, the spent fuel accumulated in the storage pools, creating the risk that nuclear reactors would have to be shutdown. This could occur if there were insufficient room in the pool to store spent fuel and also if there were not enough space to hold the entire fuel core when certain inspections or emergencies required unloading of the reactor. In recent years, the problem has taken on special urgency. Some 8,000 metric tons of spent nuclear fuel have already accumulated, and it is projected that by the year 2000 there will be some 72,000 metric tons of spent fuel. . . .

There is a second dimension to the problem. Even with water-pools adequate to store safely all the spent fuel produced during the working lifetime of the reactor, permanent disposal is needed because the wastes will remain radioactive for thousands of years. A number of long-term nuclear waste management strategies have been extensively examined. These range from sinking the wastes in stable deep seabeds, to placing the wastes beneath ice sheets in Greenland and Antarctica, to ejecting the wastes into space by rocket. The greatest attention has been focused on disposing of the wastes in subsurface geologic repositories such as salt deposits. Problems of how and where to store nuclear wastes has engendered considerable scientific, political, and public debate. There are both safety and economic aspects to the nuclear waste issue: first, if not properly stored, nuclear wastes might leak and endanger both the environment and human health; second, the lack of a long-term disposal option increases the risk that the insufficiency of interim storage space for spent fuel will lead to reactor-shutdowns, rendering nuclear energy an unpredictable and uneconomical adventure.

The California laws at issue here are responses to these concerns. In 1974, California adopted the Warren-Alquist State Energy Resources Conservation and Development Act. The Act requires that a utility seeking to build in California any electric power generating plant, including a nuclear power plant, must apply for certification to the State Energy Resources and Conservation Commission (Energy Commission).

Section 25524.2 deals with the long-term solution to nuclear wastes. This section imposes a moratorium on the certification of new nuclear plants until the

Energy Commission "finds that there has been developed and that the United States through its authorized agency has approved and there exists a demonstrated technology or means for the disposal of high-level nuclear waste." "Disposal" is defined as a "method for the permanent and terminal disposition of high-level nuclear waste. . . ." Such a finding must be reported to the state legislature, which may nullify it.

In 1978, petitioners Pacific Gas and Electric Company and Southern California Edison Company filed this action in the United States District Court, requesting a declaration that numerous provisions of the Warren-Alquist Act, including the [section] challenged here, are invalid under the Supremacy Clause because [it is] preempted by the Atomic Energy Act. . . .

III

It is well-established that within Constitutional limits Congress may preempt state authority by so stating in express terms. Jones v. Rath Packing Co., 430 U.S. 519, 525 (1977). Absent explicit preemptive language, Congress' intent to supersede state law altogether may be found from a "scheme of federal regulation so pervasive as to make reasonable the inference that Congress left no room to supplement it," "because the Act of Congress may touch a field in which the federal interest is so dominant that the federal system will be assumed to preclude enforcement of state laws on the same subject," or because "the object sought to be obtained by the federal law and the character of obligations imposed by it may reveal the same purpose." Fidelity Federal Savings & Loan Ass'n v. de la Cuesta, 458 U.S. 141, 153 (1982); Rice v. Santa Fe Elevator Corp., 331 U.S. 218, 230 (1947). Even where Congress has not entirely displaced state regulation in a specific area, state law is preempted to the extent that it actually conflicts with federal law. Such a conflict arises when "compliance with both federal and state regulations is a physical impossibility." Florida Lime & Avocado Growers, Inc. v. Paul, 373 U.S. 132, 142-143 (1963), or where state law "stands as an obstacle to the accomplishment and execution of the full purposes and objectives of Congress." Hines v. Davidowitz, 312 U.S. 52, 67 (1941).

Petitioners, the United States, and supporting amici, present three major lines of argument as to why §25524.2 is preempted. First, they submit that the statute — because it regulates construction of nuclear plants and because it is allegedly predicated on safety concerns — ignores the division between federal and state authority created by the Atomic Energy Act, and falls within the field that the federal government has preserved for its own exclusive control. Second, the statute, and the judgments that underlie it, conflict with decisions concerning the nuclear waste disposal issue made by Congress and the Nuclear Regulatory Commission. Third, the California statute frustrates the federal goal of developing nuclear technology as a source of energy. We consider each of these contentions in turn.

A

Even a brief perusal of the Atomic Energy Act reveals that, despite its comprehensiveness, it does not at any point expressly require that States construct or authorize nuclear power plants or prohibit the States from deciding, as an absolute or conditional matter, not to permit the construction of any further reactors. Instead, petitioners argue that the Act is intended to preserve the federal government as the sole regulator of all matters nuclear, and that §25524.2 falls within the scope of this impliedly preempted field. But as we view the issue, Congress, in passing the 1954 Act and in subsequently amending it, intended that the federal government should regulate the radiological safety aspects involved in the construction and operation of a nuclear plant, but that the States retain their traditional responsibility in the field of regulating electrical utilities for determining questions of need, reliability, cost and other related state concerns.

Need for new power facilities, their economic feasibility, and rates and services, are areas that have been characteristically governed by the States. . . .

[From] the passage of the Atomic Energy Act in 1954, through several revisions, and to the present day, Congress has preserved the dual regulation of nuclear-powered electricity generation: the federal government maintains complete control of the safety and "nuclear" aspects of energy generation; the states exercise their traditional authority over the need for additional generating capacity, the type of generating facilities to be licensed, land use, ratemaking, and the like.

The above is not particularly controversial. But deciding how §25524.2 is to be construed and classified is a more difficult proposition. At the outset, we emphasize that the statute does not seek to regulate the construction or operation of a nuclear powerplant. It would clearly be impermissible for California to attempt to do so, for such regulation, even if enacted out of non-safety concerns, would nevertheless directly conflict with the NRC's exclusive authority over plant construction and operation. . . .

That being the case, it is necessary to determine whether there is a non-safety rationale for §25524.2. California has maintained, and the Court of Appeals agreed, that §25524.2 was aimed at economic problems, not radiation hazards. The California Assembly Committee On Resources [reported] that the waste disposal problem was "largely economic or the result of poor planning, *not* safety related." The Committee explained that the lack of a federally approved method of waste disposal created a "clog" in the nuclear fuel cycle. Storage space was limited while more nuclear wastes were continuously produced. Without a permanent means of disposal, the nuclear waste problem could become critical leading to unpredictably high costs to contain the problem or, worse, shutdowns in reactors. "Waste disposal *safety*," the Reassessment Report notes, "is not directly addressed by the bills, which ask only that a method [of waste disposal] be chosen and accepted by the federal government." . . .

[Petitioners] and amici nevertheless attempt to upset this interpretation in a number of ways. First, they maintain that §25524.2 evinces no concern with the economics of nuclear power. The statute states that the "development" and "existence" of a permanent disposal technology approved by federal authorities will lift the moratorium; the statute does not provide for considering the economic costs of the technology selected. This view of the statute is overly myopic. Once a technology is selected and demonstrated, the utilities and the California Public Utilities Commission would be able to estimate costs; such cost estimates cannot be made until the federal government has settled upon the method of long-term waste disposal. Moreover, once a satisfactory disposal technology is found and demonstrated, fears of having to close down operating reactors should largely evaporate.

Second, it is suggested that California, if concerned with economics, would have banned California utilities from building plants outside the state. This objection carries little force. There is no indication that California utilities are contemplating such construction; the state legislature is not obligated to address purely hypothetical facets of a problem.

Third, petitioners note that there already is a body, the California Public Utilities Commission, which is authorized to determine on economic grounds whether a nuclear power plant should be constructed. While California is certainly free to make these decisions on a case-by-case basis, a state is not foreclosed from reaching the same decision through a legislative judgment, applicable to all cases. The economic uncertainties engendered by the nuclear waste disposal problems are not factors that vary from facility to facility; the issue readily lends itself to more generalized decisionmaking and California cannot be faulted for pursuing that course. . . .

Although these specific indicia of California's intent in enacting §25524.2 are subject to varying interpretation, there are two further reasons why we should not become embroiled in attempting to ascertain California's true motive. First, inquiry into legislative motive is often an unsatisfactory venture. [United States v. O'Brien, infra.] What motivates one legislator to vote for a statute is not necessarily what motivates scores of others to enact it. Second, it would be particularly pointless for us to engage in such inquiry here when it is clear that the states have been allowed to retain authority over the need for electrical generating facilities easily sufficient to permit a state so inclined to halt the construction of new nuclear plants by refusing on economic grounds to issue certificates of public convenience in individual proceedings. In these circumstances, it should be up to Congress to determine whether a state has misused the authority left in its hands.

Therefore, we accept California's avowed economic purpose as the rationale for enacting §25524.2. Accordingly, the statute lies outside the occupied field of nuclear safety regulation.[28]

B

Petitioners' second major argument concerns federal regulation aimed at the nuclear waste disposal problem itself. It is contended that §25524.2 conflicts with federal regulation of nuclear waste disposal, with the NRC's decision that it is permissible to continue to license reactors, notwithstanding uncertainty surrounding the waste disposal problem, and with Congress' recent passage of legislation directed at that problem. . . .

The NRC's imprimatur, however, indicates only that it is safe to proceed with such plants, not that it is economically wise to do so. Because the NRC order does

28. Petitioners correctly cite Perez v. Campbell, 402 U.S. 637, 651 (1971) for the proposition that state law may not frustrate the operation of federal law simply because the state legislature in passing its law had some purpose in mind other than one of frustration. In Perez, however, unlike this case, there was an actual conflict between state and federal law. Perez involved an Arizona law that required uninsured motorists who had not satisfied judgments against them or had failed to pay settlements after accidents to prove their financial responsibility before the state would license them to drive again. The Arizona law, contrary to the Federal Bankruptcy Act, specified that this obligation would not be discharged in bankruptcy. We held the state law preempted, despite the fact that its purpose was to deter irresponsible driving rather than to aid in the collection of debts. Only if there were an actual conflict between §25524.2 and the Atomic Energy Act, such that adherence to both were impossible or the operation of state law frustrated accomplishment of the federal objective, would Perez be apposite.

not and could not compel a utility to develop a nuclear plant, compliance with both it and §25524.2 are possible. Moreover, because the NRC's regulations are aimed at insuring that plants are safe, not necessarily that they are economical, §25524.2 does not interfere with the objective of the federal regulation.

Nor has California sought through §25524.2 to impose its own standards on nuclear waste disposal. The statute accepts that it is the federal responsibility to develop and license such technology. As there is no attempt on California's part to enter this field, one which is occupied by the federal government, we do not find §25524.2 preempted any more by the NRC's obligations in the waste disposal field than by its licensing power over the plants themselves. . . .

C

Finally, it is strongly contended that §25524.2 frustrates the Atomic Energy Act's purpose to develop the commercial use of nuclear power. It is well established that state law is preempted if it "stands as an obstacle to the accomplishment of the full purposes and objectives of Congress."

There is little doubt that a primary purpose of the Atomic Energy Act was, and continues to be, the promotion of nuclear power. . . .

The Court of Appeals is right [that] the promotion of nuclear power is not to be accomplished "at all costs." The elaborate licensing and safety provisions and the continued preservation of state regulation in traditional areas belie that. Moreover, Congress has allowed the States to determine — as a matter of economics — whether a nuclear plant vis-à-vis a fossil fuel plant should be built. The decision of California to exercise that authority does not, in itself, constitute a basis for preemption. Therefore, while the argument of petitioners and the United States has considerable force, the legal reality remains that Congress has left sufficient authority in the states to allow the development of nuclear power to be slowed or even stopped for economic reasons. Given this statutory scheme, it is for Congress to rethink the division of regulatory authority in light of its possible exercise by the states to undercut a federal objective. The courts should not assume the role which our system assigns to Congress.

IV

The judgment of the Court of Appeals is affirmed.

[JUSTICE BLACKMUN, joined by JUSTICE STEVENS, concurred except insofar as the Court "suggest[ed] that a State may not prohibit the construction of nuclear power plants if the State is motivated by concerns about the safety of such plants."]

Note: Preemption

PG & E states that there are three ways in which Congress may preempt state regulation: expressly, or by enacting a regulation with which the state regulation in fact conflicts, or by enacting a system of regulations so comprehensive as to displace all state regulations even if they do not conflict with any specific federal one (by "occupying the field").

1. *Express preemption*. A federal statute may state that it preempts state law, but the extent of the "express" preemption may be questioned to determine whether the state law at issue falls within the category of laws that are preempted. See Shaw v. Delta Air Lines, 463, U.S. 85 (1983): The federal Employment Retirement Income Security Act preempts "all State laws insofar as they [relate] to any employee benefit plan" covered by ERISA, but also provides that the preemption provision shall not impair any other federal law. New York's Human Rights Law prohibits sex-based discrimination. Employers whose employee benefit plans treat pregnancy differently from other non-occupational disabilities violate the Human Rights Law. (For federal law on this issue, see Chapter 5 infra.) Delta had a disability plan that did not provide benefits to employees disabled by pregnancy. It claimed that the Human Rights Law was preempted by ERISA. The Court held that the state law "related to" employee benefit plans. It was saved by the exception because preempting it would impair the enforcement of federal antidiscrimination laws that rely on state agencies for enforcement. Thus, state law was preempted only with respect to practices it prohibited but were permitted by federal law. (How close is this to saying that state laws conflicting with federal law were preempted?)

2. *Conflicting regulations*. Conflicts may occur when it is impossible to comply with both state and federal law, or when the state law "stands as an obstacle to the accomplishment of the full purposes and objectives of Congress." Hines v. Davidowitz, 312 U.S. 52 (1941). In addition to *PG & E*, consider Perez v. Campbell, 402 U.S. 637 (1971): Arizona suspends the driver's license of people who have not satisfied judgments against them in accident cases. A discharge in a federal bankruptcy proceeding, which relieves the debtor of the duty to satisfy the judgment, does not lift the suspension, which thus remains as an inducement to satisfy the judgment. Adolfo Perez was in an accident in 1965. Judgment was entered against him on November 8, 1967. Two days earlier he had filed a petition in bankruptcy, and he received a discharge from all debts, including the accident judgment, on July 8, 1968. The Court held that Arizona's use of license suspension as a means of inducing financial responsibility conflicted with and so was preempted by the federal bankruptcy law. Four justices dissented, arguing that Arizona's purpose was to "assure driving competence" and therefore its statute did not conflict with federal law. Note the discussion of *Perez* in *PG & E*.

3. *Occupying the field*. Traditionally the Court has required a strong showing that Congress intended to preempt by occupying the field. The usual test is taken from Rice v. Santa Fe Elevator Co., cited in *PG & E*. Note the consequences of finding this sort of preemption: There is no federal regulation with which the state law conflicts (otherwise preemption by conflict would occur); finding preemption therefore means that the matter is left unregulated by both federal and state law. Does that justify a strong presumption against preemption of this sort? What if a system of nonregulation makes social or economic sense? See Farmers Educational & Cooperative Union v. WDAY, Inc., 360 U.S. 525 (1959), holding that the Federal Communications Act, which required broadcasters to carry some political speeches without censoring them, occupied the field and therefore immunized broadcasters from liability under state libel laws.

4. *Unifying Themes?* *PG & E*, which has been heavily edited to eliminate extensive discussion of the relevant federal statutes, makes it appear that preemption decisions are so closely tied to particular statutes that no unifying themes can

be articulated. Consider here the Court's decision in Silkwood v. Kerr-McGee Corp., 464 U.S. 283 (1984): *PG & E* holds that federal statutes regulating the safety aspects of nuclear energy preempt state regulations. (Is the distinction between safety and economic regulations coherent? Sensibly applied in *PG & E*?) In *Silkwood*, a divided Court held that state laws awarding punitive damages for injuries resulting from the escape of plutonium, presumably a safety hazard, were not preempted. The Court examined a number of aspects of the federal regulatory scheme, and concluded that Congress's desire to preempt state substantive standards did not extend to include preemption of state remedies. Is that a coherent distinction where the state remedies are designed, as punitive damages are, to deter undesired conduct? The four dissenters thought not. There may however be some unifying themes:

a. The Court's view on the relative wisdom of the state and federal laws may influence its decision. In addition to *Perez*, consider Pennsylvania v. Nelson, 350 U.S. 497 (1956), which held that the federal Smith Act, prohibiting the knowing advocacy of the overthrow of the national government by force and violence, preempted the Pennsylvania Sedition Act. Nelson, a leader in the Communist Party, had been sentenced to twenty years in prison for violating the Pennsylvania Act. In contemporaneous decisions discussed in Chapter 7, section B, infra, the Court was influenced by first amendment concerns to construe the Smith Act fairly narrowly.

b. Individual justices' general attitudes about federalism may influence its decision. Note that *PG & E* and *Silkwood* both arise in an era in which the doctrine of *National League of Cities* attracted some members of the Court. See Note, The Preemption Doctrine: Shifting Perspectives on Federalism and the Burger Court, 75 Colum. L. Rev. 623 (1975), which ably surveys the changing doctrinal presumptions favoring and, more recently, disfavoring findings of preemption. (That views on federalism and the wisdom of the state and federal laws at issue may conflict is suggested by the fact that three of the dissenters in *Silkwood* were Chief Justice Burger and Justices Powell and Blackmun. That such views are not dispositive is suggested that the fourth dissenter was Justice Marshall.)

c. Preemption may be used to avoid other constitutional issues. In addition to *Nelson*, consider that the Court's decision in *Perez* also involved Mrs. Perez, against whom the liability judgment had been entered because Arizona was a community property state. The Court unanimously found Arizona's statute preempted as to her. Might there be due process or equal protection problems in depriving her of her license "solely because she is the impecunious wife of an impecunious, negligent driver in a community property state," as Justice Blackmun put it? See also Note, Pre-emption as a Preferential Ground: A New Canon of Construction, 12 Stan. L. Rev. 208 (1959).

d. Preemption decisions may be influenced by the same considerations that enter into dormant commerce clause decisions. For example, finding that federal statutes "occupy the field" in some area may not be significantly different from finding that the area is inherently national under *Cooley*. Consider in this connection the history of Florida Lime & Avocado Growers v. Paul, 373 U.S. 132 (1963). The Court decided by a 5-to-4 vote that federal marketing regulations did not preempt California's statute prohibiting the sale in California of avocados containing less than 8 percent of oil. The oil content is one measure of an avocado's maturity, and its maturity when picked affects its appearance and taste.

Immature avocados may be indistinguishable in appearance on the grocer's shelf from mature ones, but they may become unpalatable after purchase. The federal marketing regulations for Florida avocados, developed by a committee of Florida growers, determined maturity based on a schedule of picking dates, sizes, and weights. As a result, some mature Florida avocados do not satisfy California's oil-content test. The majority held that California's statute did not conflict with the federal marketing system. Florida avocados could be left on their trees until they met the 8 percent oil requirement. "The maturity of avocados seems to be an inherently unlikely candidate for exclusive federal regulation. [The] supervision of the readying of foodstuffs for market has always been deemed a matter of peculiarly local concern."

Finding the record inadequate to determine whether California's statute unduly burdened or discriminated against interstate commerce, the Court remanded for a trial. It noted that "the Florida industry was well-developed when the California industry was in its infancy," that "the passage of the California statute was immediately and vigorously protested by Florida producers," and that there was "contemporaneous recognition that [the] statute severely restricted the access of Florida growers to [some California] markets." However, California growers have had "difficulty meeting the oil content requirement, and sizable shipments must be destroyed." Ten years later a federal district court in California held the California statute unconstitutional on commerce clause grounds. (Consider how arguments might be drawn from *Hunt, Dean Milk*, and *Kassel* to support that result.)

The cases are discussed in Deutsch, Precedent and Adjudication, 83 Yale L.J. 1553 (1974), a profound and difficult work that ranges deeply into important matters of constitutional theory in general.

What result in *PG & E* under the commerce clause?

E.   OTHER DOCTRINES PROTECTING THE NATIONAL MARKET

South-Central Timber Development v. Wunnicke
467 U.S. 82 (1984)

[Alaska proposed to sell 49 million board feet of timber it owned. Its proposed contract required that the successful bidder process the timber before it was shipped out of Alaska. The stated purpose of this requirement was to protect existing timber-processing industries, promote new industries, and derive revenue from all timber resources. South-Central is an Alaska corporation that purchases and logs timber, then ships it elsewhere, primarily to Japan, where it is processed. It sought an injunction against the local processing requirement as a violation of the commerce clause. The court of appeals denied the injunction, finding implicit congressional authorization for the requirement.

Justice White, in a portion of his opinion joined by six members of the Court, found no authorization, after examining federal policies regarding Alaska timber, including a regulation that prohibited the export of unprocessed federally-owned timber from Alaska to other states. Congressional consent "must be unmistakably clear," in order to avoid economic balkanization.

> Unrepresented interests will often bear the brunt of regulations imposed by one State having a significant effect on persons or operations in other States [*Barnwell Brothers, Southern Pacific*]. On the other hand, when Congress acts, all segments of the country are represented and there is significantly less danger that one State will be in a position to exploit others. Furthermore, if a State is in such a position, the decision to allow it is a collective one. A rule requiring a clear expression of approval by Congress ensures that there is, in fact, such a collective decision and reduces significantly the risk that unrepresented interests will be adversely affected by restraints on commerce.

Justice White addressed the commerce clause issue in a plurality opinion joined by Justices Brennan, Blackmun, and Stevens.]

Our cases make clear that if a State is acting as a market participant, rather than as a market regulator, the dormant Commerce Clause places no limitation on its activities. See White v. Massachusetts Council of Construction Employers, Inc., 460 U.S. 204 (1983); Reeves, Inc. v. Stake, 447 U.S. 429, 436-437 (1980); Hughes v. Alexandria Scrap Corp., 426 U.S. 794, 810 (1976). The precise contours of the market-participant doctrine have yet to be established, however, the doctrine having been applied in only three cases of this Court to date.

The first of the cases, Hughes v. Alexandria Scrap Corp., involved a Maryland program designed to reduce the number of junked automobiles in the State. A "bounty" was established on Maryland-licensed junk cars, and the State imposed more stringent documentation requirements on out-of-state scrap processors than on in-state ones. The Court rejected a Commerce Clause attack on the program, although it noted that under traditional Commerce Clause analysis the program might well be invalid because it had the effect of reducing the flow of goods in interstate commerce. The Court concluded that Maryland's action was not "the kind of action with which the Commerce Clause is concerned," because "[n]othing in the purposes animating the Commerce Clause prohibits a State, in the absence of congressional action, from participating in the market and exercising the right to favor its own citizens over others."

In Reeves, Inc. v. Stake, the Court upheld a South Dakota policy of restricting the sale of cement from a state-owned plant to state residents, declaring that "[t]he basic distinction drawn in *Alexandria Scrap* between States as market participants and States as market regulators makes good sense and sound law." The Court relied upon "the long recognized right of trader or manufacturer, engaged in an entirely private business freely to exercise his own independent discretion as to parties with whom he will deal." In essence, the Court recognized the principle that the Commerce Clause places no limitations on a State's refusal to deal with particular parties when it is participating in the interstate market in goods.

The most recent of this Court's cases developing the market-participant doctrine is White v. Massachusetts Council of Construction Employers, Inc., in which the Court sustained against a Commerce Clause challenge an executive order of the Mayor of Boston that required all construction projects funded in whole or in part by city funds or city administered funds to be performed by a work force of at least 50% city residents. The Court rejected the argument that the city was not entitled to the protection of the doctrine because the order had the effect of regulating employment contracts between public contractors and their employees. Recognizing that "there are some limits on a state or local government's ability to impose restrictions that reach beyond the immediate parties with which the government transacts business," the Court found it unnecessary to define those limits because "[e]veryone affected by the order [was], in a substantial if informal sense, 'working for the city.' " The fact that the employees were "working for the city" was "crucial" to the market-participant analysis in *White*.

The State of Alaska contends that its primary-manufacture requirement fits squarely within the market-participant doctrine, arguing that "Alaska's entry into the market may be viewed as precisely the same type of subsidy to local interests that the Court found unobjectionable in *Alexandria Scrap*." However, when Maryland became involved in the scrap market it was as a purchaser of scrap; Alaska, on the other hand, participates in the timber market, but imposes conditions downstream in the timber-processing market. Alaska is not merely subsidizing local timber processing in an amount "roughly equal to the difference between the price the timber would fetch in the absence of such a requirement and the amount the state actually receives." If the State directly subsidized the timber-processing industry by such an amount, the purchaser would retain the option of taking advantage of the subsidy by processing timber in the State or forgoing the benefits of the subsidy and exporting unprocessed timber. Under the Alaska requirement, however, the choice is made for him: if he buys timber from the State he is not free to take the timber out of state prior to processing.

The State also would have us find *Reeves* controlling. It states that "*Reeves* made it clear that the Commerce Clause imposes no limitation on Alaska's power to choose the terms on which it will sell its timber." Such an unrestrained reading of *Reeves* is unwarranted. Although the Court in *Reeves* did strongly endorse the right of a State to deal with whomever it chooses when it participates in the market, it did not — and did not purport to — sanction the imposition of any terms that the State might desire. For example, the Court expressly noted in *Reeves* that "Commerce Clause scrutiny may well be more rigorous when a restraint on foreign commerce is alleged," that a natural resource "like coal, timber, wild game, or minerals," was not involved, but instead the cement was "the end product of a complex process whereby a costly physical plant and human labor act on raw materials," and that South Dakota did not bar resale of South Dakota cement to out-of-state purchasers. In this case, all three of the elements that were not present in *Reeves* — foreign commerce, a natural resource, and restrictions on resale — are present.

Finally, Alaska argues that since the Court in *White* upheld a requirement that reached beyond "the boundary of formal privity of contract," then, a fortiori, the primary-manufacture requirement is permissible, because the State is not regulating contracts for resale of timber or regulating the buying and selling of timber, but is instead "a seller of timber, pure and simple." Yet it is clear that the State is more than merely a seller of timber. In the commercial context, the seller usually has no say over, and no interest in, how the product is to be used after sale; in this case, however, payment for the timber does not end the obligations of the purchaser, for, despite the fact that the purchaser has taken delivery of the timber and has paid for it, he cannot do with it as he pleases. Instead, he is obligated to deal with a stranger to the contract after completion of the sale.[9]

That privity of contract is not always the outer boundary of permissible state activity does not necessarily mean that the Commerce Clause has no application within the boundary of formal privity. The market-participant doctrine permits a State to influence "a discrete, identifiable class of economic activity in which [it] is a major participant." [*White.*] Contrary to the State's contention, the doctrine is not carte blanche to impose any conditions that the State has the economic power to dictate, and does not validate any requirement merely because the State imposes it upon someone with whom it is in contractual privity.

The limit of the market-participant doctrine must be that it allows a State to impose burdens on commerce within the market in which it is a participant, but allows it to go no further. The State may not impose conditions, whether by statute, regulation, or contract, that have a substantial regulatory effect outside of that particular market.[10] Unless the "market" is relatively narrowly defined, the doctrine has the potential of swallowing up the rule that States may not impose substantial burdens on interstate commerce even if they act with the permissible state purpose of fostering local industry.

At the heart of the dispute in this case is disagreement over the definition of the market. Alaska contends that it is participating in the processed timber market, although it acknowledges that it participates in no way in the actual processing. South-Central argues, on the other hand, that although the State may be a participant in the timber market, it is using its leverage in that market to exert a regulatory effect in the processing market, in which it is not a participant. We agree with the latter position.

There are sound reasons for distinguishing between a State's preferring its own residents in the initial disposition of goods when it is a market participant and a State's attachment of restrictions on dispositions subsequent to the goods coming to rest in private hands. First, simply as a matter of intuition a State market participant has a greater interest as a "private trader" in the immediate transaction than it has in what its purchaser does with the goods after the State no longer has an interest in them. The common law recognized such a notion in the doctrine of restraints on alienation. Similarly, the antitrust laws place limits on vertical restraints. It is no defense in an action charging vertical trade restraints that the

9. The facts of the present case resemble closely the facts of Foster-Fountain Packing Co. v. Haydel, 278 U.S. 1 (1928), in which the Court struck down a Louisiana law prohibiting export from the State of any shrimp from which the heads and hulls had not been removed. The Court rejected the claim that the fact that the shrimp were owned by the State authorized the State to impose such limitations. Although not directly controlling here, because of the Court's recognition that "the State owns, or has power to control, the game and fish within its borders not absolutely or as proprietor or for its own use or benefit but in its sovereign capacity as representative of the people," the Court's reasoning is relevant. The Court noted that the State might have retained the shrimp for consumption and use within its borders, but "by permitting its shrimp to be taken and all the products thereof to be shipped and sold in interstate commerce, the State necessarily releases its hold and, as to the shrimp so taken, definitely terminates its control."

10. The view of the market-participant doctrine expressed by Justice Rehnquist would validate under the Commerce Clause any contractual condition that the State had the economic power to impose, without regard to the relationship of the subject matter of the contract and the condition imposed. If that were the law, it would have been irrelevant that the employees in [*White*] were in effect "working for the city." If the only question were whether the condition is imposed by contract, a residency requirement could have been imposed with respect to the work force on all projects of any employer doing business with the city.

same end could be achieved through vertical integration; if it were, there would be virtually no antitrust scrutiny of vertical arrangements. We reject the contention that a State's action as a market regulator may be upheld against Commerce Clause challenge on the ground that the State could achieve the same end as a market participant. We therefore find it unimportant for present purposes that the State could support its processing industry by selling only to Alaska processors, by vertical integration, or by direct subsidy.

Second, downstream restrictions have a greater regulatory effect than do limitations on the immediate transaction. Instead of merely choosing its own trading partners, the State is attempting to govern the private, separate economic relationships of its trading partners; that is, it restricts the post-purchase activity of the purchaser, rather than merely the purchasing activity. In contrast to the situation in *White*, this restriction on private economic activity takes place after the completion of the parties' direct commercial obligations, rather than during the course of an ongoing commercial relationship in which the city retained a continuing proprietary interest in the subject of the contract.[11] In sum, the State may not avail itself of the market-participant doctrine to immunize its downstream regulation of the timber-processing market in which it is not a participant.

Finally, the State argues that even if we find that Congress did not authorize the processing restriction, and even if we conclude that its actions do not qualify for the market-participant exception, the restriction does not substantially burden interstate or foreign commerce under ordinary Commerce Clause principles. We need not labor long over that contention.

Viewed as a naked restraint on export of unprocessed logs, there is little question that the processing requirement cannot survive scrutiny under the precedents of the Court. [Because] of the protectionist nature of Alaska's local-processing requirement and the burden on commerce resulting therefrom, we conclude that it falls within the rule of virtual *per se* invalidity of laws that "bloc[k] the flow of interstate commerce at a State's borders." [Philadelphia v. New Jersey.]

We are buttressed in our conclusion that the restriction is invalid by the fact that foreign commerce is burdened by the restriction. It is a well-accepted rule that state restrictions burdening foreign commerce are subjected to a more rigorous and searching scrutiny. It is crucial to the efficient execution of the Nation's foreign policy that "the Federal Government . . . speak with one voice when regulating commercial relations with foreign governments." Michelin Tire Corp. v. Wages, 423 U.S. 276, 285 (1976). In light of the substantial attention given by Congress to the subject of export restrictions on unprocessed timber, it would be peculiarly inappropriate to permit state regulation of the subject.

The judgment of the Court of Appeals is reversed and the case is remanded for proceedings consistent with the opinion of this Court.

It is so ordered.

[JUSTICE POWELL and CHIEF JUSTICE BURGER would have remanded the case for consideration of the commerce clause issue.]

JUSTICE MARSHALL took no part in the decision of this case.

---

11. This is not to say that the State could evade the reasoning of this opinion by merely including a provision in its contract that title does not pass until the processing is complete. It is the substance of the transaction, rather than the label attached to it, that governs Commerce Clause analysis.

JUSTICE BRENNAN, concurring.

I join Justice White's opinion in full because I believe Alaska's in-state process-ing requirement constitutes market regulation that is not authorized by Congress. In my view, Justice White's treatment of the market-participant doctrine and the response of Justice Rehnquist point up the inherent weakness of the doctrine.

JUSTICE REHNQUIST, with whom JUSTICE O'CONNOR joins, dissenting.

In my view, the line of distinction drawn in the plurality opinion between the State as market participant and the State as market regulator is both artificial and unconvincing. The plurality draws this line "simply as a matter of intuition," but then seeks to bolster its intuition through a series of remarks more appropriate to antitrust law than to the Commerce Clause.* . . .

The contractual term at issue here no more transforms Alaska's sale of timber into "regulation" of the processing industry than the resident-hiring preference imposed by the city of Boston in [White] constituted regulation of the construc-tion industry. Alaska is merely paying the buyer of the timber indirectly, by means of a reduced price, to hire Alaska residents to process the timber. Under existing precedent, the State could accomplish that same result in any number of ways. For example, the State could choose to sell its timber only to those companies that maintain active primary-processing plants in Alaska. [Reeves, Inc. v. Stake.] Or the State could directly subsidize the primary-processing industry within the State. [Hughes v. Alexandria Scrap Corp.] The State could even pay to have the logs processed and then enter the market only to sell processed logs. It seems to me unduly formalistic to conclude that the one path chosen by the State as best suited to promote its concerns is the path forbidden it by the Commerce Clause.

For these reasons, I would affirm the judgment of the Court of Appeals.

Note: The Market Participant Doctrine

1. *States as economic actors*. Justice Blackmun's opinion for the Court in Reeves v. Stake called the "basic distinction [between] States as market partici-pants and States as market regulators [good] sense and sound law." When states act in the marketplace, he wrote, they resemble private businesses and should be free to exercise a similar discretion to choose the parties with whom they deal. Note that, in the absence of statutory restrictions, private businesses may pur-chase from or sell to whites or Democrats only. Are states similarly free of such restrictions? See Elrod v. Burns, Chapter 7, section F, infra. Note also that private businesses are constrained to some extent by competition and the profit motive to purchase from the cheapest seller and sell to the buyer willing to pay most. States in contrast may buy and sell without that constraint, using their

---

* The plurality does offer one other reason for its demarcation of the boundary between these two concepts. "[D]ownstream restrictions have a greater regulatory effect than do limitations on the immediate transaction. Instead of merely choosing its own trading partners, the State is attempting to govern the private, separate economic relationships of its trading partners; that is, it restricts the post-purchase activity of the purchaser, rather than merely the purchasing activity." But, of course, this is not a "reason" at all, but merely a restatement of the conclusion. The line between participation and regulation is what we are trying to determine. To invoke that very distinction in support of the line drawn is merely to fall back on intuition.

power to tax as the mechanism to force some taxpayers to subsidize "uneconomic" transactions. See generally Wells & Hellerstein, The Governmental-Proprietary Distinction in Constitutional Law, 66 Va. L. Rev. 1073 (1980).

2. *The scope of the doctrine.* The plurality in *Wunnicke* says that the "market participant" doctrine must be narrowly confined. Consider the following argument: In *New England Power Co.* and Hughes v. Oklahoma, above, the state owned the water used to generate hydroelectric power and the minnows, respectively. Why should the "regulations" invalidated in those cases not be treated as contractual conditions imposed by the states as sellers of resources they owned? Chief Justice Burger's opinion in *New England Power* stated, "New Hampshire has done more than regulate the use of a resource it assertedly owns; it has restricted the sale of electric energy, a product entirely distinct from the river waters used to produce it." Using that criterion, was *White* correctly decided? Note that *White* involves a "downstream" transaction between the contractor and the employee, not a transaction between the state and the contractor. Reeves v. Stake distinguished *Hughes* on the ground that cement "is the end product of a complex process whereby a costly physical plant and human labor act on raw materials." Justice Powell's dissent, joined by Justices Brennan, White, and Stevens, noted that this "describes all sophisticated economic activity, including the exploitation of natural resources." What is the relevant "complex process" in *Hughes*? In Philadelphia v. New Jersey? Is the state's participation in that process less significant than its participation in the market for cement?

3. *States as market subsidizers.* Can the "market participant" doctrine be defended as allowing states to capture the benefits of their tax expenditures? Consider L. Tribe, Constitutional Choices 145 (1985): The doctrine is justified by "the sense of fairness in allowing a community to retain the public benefits created by its own public investment. [The] broader theme that underlies each case seems to be *creation* of commerce: whatever the state's ultimate goal, the state is approaching that goal by channeling its resources into commerce rather than by placing restrictions on commerce already in existence."

In *White* the public expenditure is the outlay for construction contracts. How does that differ from the state's expenditures for the general provision of social order in Hughes v. Oklahoma and Philadelphia v. New Jersey? The expenditures differ in the specificity with which they affect particular transactions, but is that relevant to any constitutionally significant matters?

Do the relevant expenditures differ in amount? The budget for the cement plant in *Reeves* may be larger than that portion of the general state budget properly allocated to support for the minnow market in Hughes v. Oklahoma. But the relevant figure is not the total budget of the cement plant; it is that portion of its budget that constitutes a subsidy to South Dakota purchasers because that is the state's net outflow of taxes. Consider finally that we have now seen three types of subsidy: via regulation, via participation in the market, and via direct appropriations (recall the note on Bacchus v. Dias, above). Only the former is subject to commerce clause scrutiny, even though all three types are economically identical. Recall the suggestion that direct appropriations have more political visibility than do regulatory subsidies. Which does a market-participation subsidy more closely resemble?

4. *States as monopolists or competitors.* Can market participation be distinguished from regulation on the ground that the latter affects all actors in the

market, while the former affects only those whom the state chooses as its buyers or sellers? South Central can buy timber from other sellers; a regulation requiring local processing would affect it no matter from whom it bought. Consider however that this ignores the actual economic effect on South Central of Alaska's participation in the market. Given its opportunities, South Central preferred to buy Alaska's timber without local processing over purchasing someone else's; a competitor willing to comply with the local processing requirement can displace South Central to the same extent that a uniform regulation would. Doesn't the same argument establish that *White* was wrongly decided?

Can the argument be strengthened by considering the market power of the state as a market participant? The greater its market power, the more coercive its contractual conditions are and so the more they resemble regulations. Does this in fact distinguish the cases? Note that the state has "monopoly power" over the transaction in which South Central wishes to participate. (So do ordinary businesses, but they face market pressures to act efficiently.) If the state has little market power, how can its decisions as market participant burden interstate commerce? On this view, the "market participant" doctrine is a convenient shorthand for the application of ordinary dormant commerce clause tests to a set of activities that do not burden interstate commerce. Note however that this version requires reconsideration of the almost automatic invalidation of facially discriminatory regulations.

5. *State sovereignty. Reeves* stated that "restraint [by the courts] in [the] area [of market participation] is also counseled by considerations of state sovereignty." Hughes v. Alexandria Scrap was decided on the same day as *National League of Cities*, supra, and three of the *League of Cities* dissenters also dissented there. Justices White and Brennan have never supported the market participant doctrine; Justices Rehnquist and O'Connor (and Chief Justice Burger, his position in *Wunnicke* aside) have never dissented from its application. What is the relation between the doctrine and state sovereignty? Could Congress prohibit Alaska's local processing requirement? If states may be regulated as market participants, the market participant doctrine does not completely exempt state activities from compliance with the norms of the commerce clause. Instead, it exempts them in the absence of a congressional prohibition. This reverses the "presumption" Dowling's analysis would have established against burdensome regulations. Is it plausible to think that Congress will be more alert to burdens imposed on commerce by states as market participants than to those imposed by states as regulators?

United Building & Construction Trades Council v. Camden

465 U.S. 208 (1984)

[Acting under a state statute authorizing cities to adopt affirmative action plans, Camden passed an ordinance requiring that at least 40 percent of the employees of contractors and subcontractors on city projects be Camden residents. The council challenged the ordinance as a violation of the privileges and immunities clause, article IV, clause 2: "The citizens of each State shall be entitled to all the Privileges and Immunities of Citizens in the several States." The New Jersey Supreme Court upheld the ordinance. After the state court's decision the Supreme Court decided White v. Massachusetts Council, described in *South-Central Timber*, supra, upholding a similar ordinance against a commerce clause challenge.]

JUSTICE REHNQUIST delivered the opinion of the Court. . . .

[We] first address the argument, accepted by the Supreme Court of New Jersey, that the Clause does not even apply to a *municipal* ordinance such as this. Two separate contentions are advanced in support of this position: first, that the Clause only applies to laws passed by a *State* and, second, that the Clause only applies to laws that discriminate on the basis of state citizenship.

The first argument can be quickly rejected. The fact that the ordinance in question is a municipal, rather than a state, law does not somehow place it outside the scope of the Privileges and Immunities Clause. . . .

[A] municipality is merely a political subdivision of the State from which its authority derives. It is as true of the Privileges and Immunities Clause as of the Equal Protection Clause that what would be unconstitutional if done directly by the State can no more readily be accomplished by a city deriving its authority from the State. Thus, even if the ordinance had been adopted solely by Camden, and not pursuant to a state program or with state approval, the hiring preference would still have to comport with the Privileges and Immunities Clause.

The second argument merits more consideration. The New Jersey Supreme Court concluded that the Privileges and Immunities Clause does not apply to an ordinance that discriminates solely on the basis of *municipal* residency. The Clause is phrased in terms of *state* citizenship and was designed "to place the citizens of each State upon the same footing with citizens of other States, so far as the advantages resulting from citizenship in those States are concerned." Paul v. Virginia, 8 Wall. 168, 180 (1869).

> The primary purpose of this clause, like the clauses between which it is located — those relating to full faith and credit and to interstate extradition of fugitives from justice — was to help fuse into one Nation a collection of independent, sovereign States. It was designed to insure to a citizen of State A who ventures into State B the same privileges which the citizens of State B enjoy. For protection of such equality the citizen of State A was not to be restricted to the uncertain remedies afforded by diplomatic processes and official retaliation.

Toomer v. Witsell, 334 U.S. 385, 395 (1948). Municipal residency classifications, it is argued, simply do not give rise to the same concerns.

We cannot accept this argument. . . .

Given the Camden ordinance, an out-of-state citizen who ventures into New Jersey will not enjoy the same privileges as the New Jersey citizen residing in Camden. It is true that New Jersey citizens not residing in Camden will be affected by the ordinance as well as out-of-state citizens. And it is true that the disadvantaged New Jersey residents have no claim under the Privileges and Immunities Clause. But New Jersey residents at least have a chance to remedy at the polls any discrimination against them. Out-of-state citizens have no similar opportunity, and they must "not be restricted to the uncertain remedies afforded by diplomatic processes and official retaliation." [Toomer v. Witsell.][9]

Application of the Privileges and Immunities Clause to a particular instance of discrimination against out-of-state residents entails a two-step inquiry. As an initial matter, the court must decide whether the ordinance burdens one of those privileges and immunities protected by the Clause. Baldwin v. Montana Fish and Game Comm'n, 436 U.S. 371 (1978). [As] a threshold matter, [we] must determine whether an out-of-state resident's interest in employment on public works contracts in another State is sufficiently "fundamental" to the promotion of interstate harmony so as to "fall within the purview of the Privileges and Immunities Clause."

Certainly, the pursuit of a common calling is one of the most fundamental of those privileges protected by the Clause. [Public] employment, however, is qualitatively different from employment in the private sector; it is a subspecies of the broader opportunity to pursue a common calling. We have held that there is no fundamental right to government employment for purposes of the Equal Protection Clause. Massachusetts v. Murgia, 427 U.S. 307, 313 (1976) (per curiam). And in *White*, we held that for purposes of the Commerce Clause everyone employed on a city public works project is, "in a substantial if informal sense, 'working for the city.' "

It can certainly be argued that for purposes of the Privileges and Immunities Clause everyone affected by the Camden ordinance is also "working for the city" and, therefore, has no grounds for complaint when the city favors its own residents. But we decline to transfer mechanically into this context an analysis fashioned to fit the Commerce Clause. Our decision in *White* turned on a distinction between the city acting as a market participant and the city acting as a market regulator. The question whether employees of contractors and subcontractors on public works projects were or were not, in some sense, working for the city was crucial to that analysis. The question had to be answered in order to chart the boundaries of the distinction. But the distinction between market participant and market regulator relied upon in *White* to dispose of the Commerce Clause challenge is not dispositive in this context. The two Clauses have different aims and set different standards for state conduct.

---

9. The dissent suggests that New Jersey citizens not residing in Camden will adequately protect the interests of out-of-state residents and that the scope of the Privileges and Immunities Clause should be measured in light of this political reality. [But] the Camden ordinance at issue in this case was adopted pursuant to a comprehensive, state-wide program applicable in all New Jersey cities. The Camden resident-preference ordinance has already received state sanction and approval, and every New Jersey city is free to adopt a similar protectionist measure. Some have already done so. Thus, it is hard to see how New Jersey residents living outside Camden will protect the interests of out-of-state citizens.

More fundamentally, the dissent's proposed blanket exemption for all classifications that are less than state-wide would provide States with a simple means for evading the strictures of the Privileges and Immunities Clause. Suppose, for example, that California wanted to guarantee that all employees of contractors and subcontractors working on construction projects funded in whole or in part by state funds are state residents. Under the dissent's analysis, the California legislature need merely divide the State in half, providing one resident-hiring preference for Northern Californians on all such projects taking place in Northern California, and one for Southern California on all projects taking place in Southern California. State residents generally would benefit from the law at the expense of out-of-state residents; yet, the law would be immune from scrutiny under the Clause simply because it was not phrased in terms of *state* citizenship or residency. Such a formalistic construction would effectively write the Clause out of the Constitution.

The Commerce Clause acts as an implied restraint upon state regulatory powers. Such powers must give way before the superior authority of Congress to legislate on (or leave unregulated) matters involving interstate commerce. When the State acts solely as a market participant, no conflict between state *regulation* and federal regulatory authority can arise. The Privileges and Immunities Clause, on the other hand, imposes a direct restraint on state action in the interests of interstate harmony. This concern with comity cuts across the market regulator-market participant distinction that is crucial under the Commerce Clause. It is discrimination against out-of-state residents on matters of fundamental concern which triggers the Clause, not regulation affecting interstate commerce. Thus, the fact that Camden is merely setting conditions on its expenditures for goods and services in the marketplace does not preclude the possibility that those conditions violate the Privileges and Immunities Clause.

In Hicklin v. Orbeck, 437 U.S. 518 (1978), we struck down as a violation of the Privileges and Immunities Clause an "Alaska Hire" statute containing a resident hiring preference for all employment related to the development of the State's oil and gas resources. Alaska argued in that case "that because the oil and gas that are the subject of Alaska Hire are *owned* by the State, this ownership, of itself, is sufficient justification for the Act's discrimination against nonresidents, and takes the Act totally without the scope of the Privileges and Immunities Clause." We concluded, however, that the State's interest in controlling those things it claims to own is not absolute. "Rather than placing a statute completely beyond the Clause, a State's ownership of the property with which the statute is concerned is a factor — although often the crucial factor — to be considered in evaluating whether the statute's discrimination against noncitizens violates the Clause." Much the same analysis, we think, is appropriate to a city's efforts to bias private employment decisions in favor of its residents on construction projects funded with public monies. The fact that Camden is expending its own funds or funds it administers in accordance with the terms of a grant is certainly a factor — perhaps the crucial factor — to be considered in evaluating whether the statute's discrimination violates the Privileges and Immunities Clause. But it does not remove the Camden ordinance completely from the purview of the Clause.

In sum, Camden may, without fear of violating the Commerce Clause, pressure private employers engaged in public works projects funded in whole or in part by the city to hire city residents. But that same exercise of power to bias the employment decisions of private contractors and subcontractors against out-of-state residents may be called to account under the Privileges and Immunities Clause. A determination of whether a privilege is "fundamental" for purposes of that Clause does not depend on whether the employees of private contractors and subcontractors engaged in public works projects can or cannot be said to be "working for the city." The opportunity to seek employment with such private employers is "sufficiently basic to the livelihood of the Nation," [*Baldwin*], as to fall within the purview of the Privileges and Immunities Clause even though the contractors and subcontractors are themselves engaged in projects funded in whole or part by the city.

The conclusion that Camden's ordinance discriminates against a protected privilege does not, of course, end the inquiry. We have stressed in prior cases that "[l]ike many other constitutional provisions, the privileges and immunities clause is not an absolute." [*Toomer.*] It does not preclude discrimination against citizens of other States where there is a "substantial reason" for the difference in treatment. "[T]he inquiry in each case must be concerned with whether such reasons do exist and whether the degree of discrimination bears a close relation to them." As part of any justification offered for the discriminatory law, nonresidents must somehow be shown to "constitute a peculiar source of the evil at which the statute is aimed."

The city of Camden contends that its ordinance is necessary to counteract grave economic and social ills. Spiralling unemployment, a sharp decline in population, and a dramatic reduction in the number of businesses located in the city have eroded property values and depleted the city's tax base. The resident hiring preference is designed, the city contends, to increase the number of employed persons living in Camden and to arrest the "middle class flight" currently plaguing the city. The city also argues that all nonCamden residents employed on city public works projects, whether they reside in New Jersey or Pennsylvania, constitute a "source of the evil at which the statute is aimed." That is, they "live off" Camden without "living in" Camden. Camden contends that the scope of the discrimination practiced in the ordinance, with its municipal residency requirement, is carefully tailored to alleviate this evil without unreasonably harming nonresidents, who still have access to 60% of the available positions.

Every inquiry under the Privileges and Immunities Clause "must . . . be conducted with due regard for the principle that the states should have considerable leeway in analyzing local evils and in prescribing appropriate cures." [*Toomer.*] This caution is particularly appropriate when a government body is merely setting conditions on the expenditure of funds it controls. The Alaska Hire statute at issue in [*Hicklin*] swept within its strictures not only contractors and subcontractors dealing directly with the State's oil and gas; it also covered suppliers who provided goods and services to those contractors and subcontractors. We invalidated the Act as "an attempt to force virtually all businesses that benefit in some way from the economic ripple effect of Alaska's decision to develop its oil and gas resources to bias their employment practices in favor of the State's residents." No similar "ripple effect" appears to infect the Camden ordinance. It is limited in scope to employees working directly on city public works projects.

Nonetheless, we find it impossible to evaluate Camden's justification on the record as it now stands. No trial has ever been held in the case. No findings of fact have been made. [We,] therefore, deem it wise to remand the case to the New Jersey Supreme Court. That court may decide, consistent with state procedures, on the best method for making the necessary findings. . . .

Reversed and remanded.

JUSTICE BLACKMUN, dissenting.

For over a century the underlying meaning of the Privileges and Immunities Clause of the Constitution's Article IV has been regarded as settled: at least absent some substantial, noninvidious justification, a State may not discriminate between its own residents and residents of other States on the basis of state citizenship. . . .

[Because] I believe that the Privileges and Immunities Clause was not intended to apply to the kind of municipal discrimination presented by this case, I would affirm the judgment of the Supreme Court of New Jersey.

I

The historical underpinnings of the Privileges and Immunities Clause are not in serious dispute. The Clause was derived from the fourth Article of Confederation and was designed to carry forward that provision's prescription of interstate comity. . . .

While the Framers thus conceived of the Privileges and Immunities Clause as an instrument for frustrating discrimination based on state citizenship, there is no evidence of any sort that they were concerned by intrastate discrimination based on municipal residence. The most obvious reason for this is also the most simple one: by the time the Constitution was enacted, such discrimination was rarely practiced and even more rarely successful. Even had attempts to practice the kind of economic localism at issue here been more widespread, moreover, there is little reason to believe that the Framers would have devoted their limited institutional resources to bringing such conduct within the ambit of the Privileges and Immunities Clause. Whatever the weaknesses of the new state governments in suppressing section conflicts that gave rise to outright physical violence, like Shays' Rebellion in 1786-1787, the States had more than adequate powers to prevent localities from disrupting the States' internal economic affairs through discriminatory ordinances and regulations. . . .

[In] Zobel v. Williams, 457 U.S. 55 (1982), the Court held that an Alaska statute which allocated state treasury refunds to state residents on the basis of the length of their residence violated the Equal Protection Clause. The Court declined, however, to hold that the statute violated the Privileges and Immunities Clause. It observed that the statute "does not simply make distinctions between native-born Alaskans and those who migrate to Alaska from other States;" instead, it "also discriminates among long-time residents and even native-born residents." As a result: "The statute does not involve the kind of discrimination which the Privileges and Immunities Clause of Art. IV was designed to prevent. That Clause 'was designed to insure to a citizen of State A who ventures into State B the same privileges which the citizens of State B enjoy.' [Toomer.] The Clause is thus not applicable to this case."

I am somewhat at a loss to understand how the Court's decision today can be reconciled with its reasoning in Zobel. The Alaska statute at issue in Zobel fell outside the scope of the Privileges and Immunities Clause for the elementary reason that it did not discriminate between state residents and nonresidents on the basis of state residence; rather, it discriminated among state residents in a way that disadvantaged nonresidents as well but did not thereby implicate the underlying concerns of the Privileges and Immunities Clause. The Camden ordinance presently before the Court occupies precisely the same position. . . .

Finally, the Court fails to attend to the functional considerations that underlie the Privileges and Immunities Clause. The Clause has been a necessary limitation on state autonomy not simply because of the self-interest of individual States, but because state parochialism is likely to go unchecked by state political processes when those who are disadvantaged are by definition disenfranchised as well. The Clause remedies this breakdown in the representative process by requiring state residents to bear the same burdens that they choose to place on nonresidents; "by constitutionally tying the fate of outsiders to the fate of those possessing political power, the framers insured that their interests would be well looked after." J. Ely,

Democracy and Distrust 83 (1980). As a practical matter, therefore, the scope of the Clause may be measured by asking whether failure to link the interests of those who are disadvantaged with the interests of those who are preferred will consign the former group to "the uncertain remedies afforded by diplomatic processes and official retaliation." [*Toomer.*]

   Contrary to the Court's tacit assumption, discrimination on the basis of munic-' ipal residence is substantially different in this regard from discrimination on the basis of state citizenship. The distinction is simple but fundamental: discrimination on the basis of municipal residence penalizes persons within the State's political community as well as those without. The Court itself points out that while New Jersey citizens who reside outside Camden are not protected by the Privileges and Immunities Clause, they may resort to the State's political processes to protect themselves. What the Court fails to appreciate is that this avenue of relief for New Jersey residents works to protect residents of other States as well; disadvantaged state residents who turn to the state legislature to displace ordinances like Camden's further the interests of nonresidents as well as their own.[14]

Note: *The Privileges and Immunities Clause of Article IV*

1. *History and scope.* In Corfield v. Coryell, Fed. Cas. No. 3,230 (Cir. Ct. E.D. Pa. 1823), Justice Bushrod Washington stated that the clause protected interests "which are fundamental; which belong, of right, to the citizens of all free governments. [These] may [all be] comprehended under the following general heads: Protection by the government, the enjoyment of life and liberty, with the right to acquire and possess property of every kind, and to pursue and obtain happiness and safety; subject nevertheless to such restraints as the government may prescribe for the general good of the whole." *Corfield* held that a New Jersey statute forbidding nonresidents from gathering clams from state waters did not violate the clause because the clams were the property of the state. (What result under modern commerce clause doctrine?) See generally Varat, State "Citizenship" and Interstate Equality, 48 U. Chi. L. Rev. 487 (1981).

   The fourteenth amendment also contains a privileges and immunities clause, which has been held to prohibit state infringements of the privileges of national citizenship. Those privileges might also be identified as fundamental rights.

---

14. [The] Court raises the [prospect] that a State might evade the Privileges and Immunities Clause by dividing itself in half and granting the residents in each half of the State employment preferences over residents in the other half of the State. The Clause exists to protect against those classifications that a State's political process cannot be relied on to prevent, however, not those that it can, and there is no reason to believe that state residents will be willing to forgo access to employment in one half of a State merely to obtain privileged access to jobs in the other half. The fact that no State has attempted anything resembling the Court's proposed maneuver in the two centuries since the adoption of the Clause, despite the fact that none of this Court's precedents has foreclosed the option, strongly suggests that state political processes can be trusted to prevent this kind of Balkanization. The Court cannot justify deforming the Constitution's response to real problems by invoking imaginary and unrealistic ones. [Relocated footnote.]

See Chapter 6, section E, infra. What is the difference between a fundamental right as defined in *Corfield* and a fundamental right under the fourteenth amendment?

2. *The commerce clause.* What does article IV, section 2, add to the commerce clause? Toomer v. Witsell invoked article IV to hold unconstitutional a South Carolina statute imposing a $2,500 license fee on nonresident commercial shrimp fishermen, in contrast to the $25 fee for residents. What result under recent commerce clause cases? Suppose Camden had imposed the residency requirement on all businesses located in Camden or supplying goods to the city. What result under the commerce clause? In many ways, the modern function of article IV, section 2, appears to be that of carving out an exception to the "market participant" exception to the commerce clause. Note, however, that corporations are not "citizens" within the meaning of the privileges and immunities clause. Paul v. Virginia, 75 U.S. (8 Wall.) 168 (1868). See also Doe v. Bolton, 410 U.S. 179 (1973) (statute permitting only residents to obtain abortions violates privileges and immunities clause; what result under equal protection clause?). Is the test formulated by the Court in *Camden* different from the "undue burden" test under the commerce clause? Note however that Camden's ordinance is discriminatory. What commerce clause test would apply to it?

Supreme Court of New Hampshire v. Piper, 470 U.S. —, 105 S. Ct. 1272 (1985), held that a rule limiting bar admission to local residents violated the privileges and immunities clause. Justice Powell's opinion for the Court stated that the clause "was intended to create a national economic union." The practice of law was a "privilege" because of "the lawyer's role in the national economy" and the profession's "noncommercial role [in representing] persons who raise unpopular federal claims." Applying the twofold standard discussed in *Camden*, the Court found none of the asserted justifications for the discrimination substantial: There was no evidence that nonresident lawyers would fail to keep up with developments in local law or behave unethically. Nonresidents, especially those living far from the state, might be less available for hearings and for local pro bono work, but the state could "protect its interests through less restrictive means" such as requiring that a nonresident lawyer "who resides at a great distance [retain] a local attorney." The "professional interests" of nonresident lawyers would be served by keeping current with local law and doing pro bono work. Justice White concurred in the result. Justice Rehnquist's dissent argued that the practice of law is "fundamentally different" from other occupations because of the role lawyers play in a state's "self-governance": "[Law] is one occupation that does not readily translate across state lines." He found "less restrictive means analysis [out] of place" here; the courts should not "independently [scrutinize] each asserted state interest to see if it could devise a better way than the State to accomplish that goal." On "less restrictive means" analysis in first amendment cases, see Chapter 7, section C, infra.

What result in *Piper* under the commerce clause tests (a) for facial discrimination, (b) for other forms of discrimination, and (c) for undue burdens? Is New Hampshire a market regulator or a market participant in *Piper*?

3. *Political constraints.* Why does the Court reject Justice Blackmun's argument that New Jersey residents adversely affected by Camden's ordinance will protect the interests of out-of-state residents? Is this problem different from that in *Dean Milk*?

Note: The Equal Protection Clause

Consider Metropolitan Life Insurance Co. v. Ward, 470 — U.S. — , 105 S. Ct. 1676, (1985). Paul v. Virginia, 75 U.S. (8 Wall.) 168 (1868), held that insurance contracts were not in interstate commerce. As a result, states developed extensive systems for regulating insurance. In 1944 the Court rejected that analysis in United States v. South-Eastern Underwriters Assn., 322 U.S. 533 (1944). Congress responded by passing the McCarran-Ferguson Act, which declared it to be national policy that "the continued regulation and taxation by the several States of the business of insurance is in the public interest, and that silence on the part of Congress shall not be construed to impose any barrier to the regulation or taxation of such business by the several States." Alabama placed a 1 percent tax on the gross receipts of local insurance companies, while requiring that out-of-state companies pay a tax of 3 to 4 percent, which could be lowered by 1 percent if the companies invested substantially in Alabama. The equal protection clause allows such discrimination if it is a rational means to accomplish a "legitimate state purpose." The Court, dividing 5 to 4, held that the state's purpose of "encouraging the formation of new insurance companies in Alabama" was an impermissible one. It was "purely and completely discriminatory" for Alabama "to [erect] barriers to foreign companies [in] order to improve its domestic insurers' ability to compete at home." This is "the very sort of parochial discrimination that the Equal Protection Clause was intended to prevent." The state may encourage the growth of new business by granting out-of-state companies exemptions from regulations but not by imposing burdens on them that are not placed on local ones. Further, the McCarran-Ferguson Act was irrelevant because it lifted commerce clause restrictions but not equal protection ones. "Under Commerce Clause analysis, the State's interest, if legitimate, is weighed against the burden the state law would impose on interstate commerce. In the equal protection context, however, if the State's purpose is found to be legitimate, the state law stands as long as the burden it imposes is found to be rationally related to that purpose, a relationship that is not difficult to establish. The two [provisions] perform different functions — [one] protects interstate commerce, and the other protects persons from unconstitutional discrimination." The Court conceded that "the *effect* of the discrimination in this case is similar to the type of burden with which the Commerce Clause would also be concerned," but said that "acceptance of [the] contention that promotion of domestic industry is always a legitimate state purpose under equal protection analysis would eviscerate the Equal Protection Clause in this context." It said that it had rejected that position "in an analogous context arising under the Commerce Clause," citing *Bacchus*, supra.

Justice O'Connor's long dissent was joined by Justices Brennan, Marshall, and Rehnquist. She said that "it is obviously legitimate for a State to seek to promote local business," and described the different markets served by domestic and out-of-state insurers to point up Alabama's goals: the former served rural and less affluent purchasers, the latter urban, high volume, and more affluent ones. Justice O'Connor criticized the Court for "collapsing the two prongs of the rational relationship test into one" by its declaration that "the ends of promoting a domestic insurance industry and attracting investments to the State *when accomplished through the means of discriminatory taxation* are not legitimate state purposes."

To the extent that the equal protection clause served a nationalizing goal, "any federalism component of equal protection is fully vindicated where Congress has explicitly validated a parochial focus," as in the McCarran-Ferguson Act. Western & Southern Life Insurance Co. v. State Board of Equalization, 451 U.S. 648 (1981), had upheld a California statute imposing a higher tax on out-of-state insurance companies whose home states imposed a similar tax on California companies because the retaliatory tax promoted the interstate business of domestic insurers. To Justice O'Connor, the Court's decision in *Metropolitan Life* said, "We will excuse an unequal burden on foreign investors if the State's purpose is to foster its domestic insurers' activities in *other* States, but the same unequal burden will be unconstitutional when employed to further a policy that places a higher social value on the domestic insurer's *home-state* than interstate activities. [This] "engrafts [the Court's] own economic values on the Equal Protection Clause."

Why is encouraging entry by exempting out-of-state companies from regulation different from doing so by differential taxation? Note that in *Metropolitan Life*, if the state's policy succeeds, local insurers will face greater competition. What result in *Metropolitan Life* under the commerce clause? Is the Court's distinction between the purposes of the two clauses persuasive where, as in *Metropolitan Life*, the commerce clause challenge rests on facial discrimination? Would the Court "weigh" the competing interests in a commerce clause challenge to Alabama's statute? What is the effect of the McCarran-Ferguson Act after *Metropolitan Life?*

IV

The Distribution of National

Powers

A. INTRODUCTION

The Constitution distributes power horizontally as well as vertically. Dispersion of authority is a product not only of the separation between the national government and the states, but also of the allocation of power among the legislative, executive, and judicial branches. This chapter explores the purposes and effects of that allocation.

The Federalist No. 47 (Madison)
(1787)

One of the principal objections inculcated by the more respectable adversaries to the Constitution is its supposed violation of the political maxim that the legislative, executive, and judiciary departments ought to be separate and distinct. . . .

No political truth is certainly of greater intrinsic value, or is stamped with the authority of more enlightened patrons of liberty than that on which the objection is founded. The accumulation of all powers, legislative, executive, and judiciary, in the same hands, whether of one, a few, or many, and whether hereditary, self-appointed, or elective, may justly be pronounced the very definition of tyranny. . . .

The oracle who is always consulted and cited on this subject, is the celebrated Montesquieu.

The British constitution was to Montesquieu, [the] standard, or to use his own expression, [the] mirror of political liberty.

On the slightest view of the British Constitution, we must perceive that the legislative, executive, and judiciary departments are by no means totally separate and distinct from each other. The executive magistrate forms an integral part of the legislative authority. He alone has the prerogative of making treaties with foreign sovereigns which, when made, have, under certain limitations, the force of legislative acts. All the members of the judiciary department are appointed by him, can be removed by him on the address of the two Houses of Parliament, and form, when he pleases to consult them, one of his constitutional councils. One branch of the legislative department forms also a great constitutional council to the executive chief, as, on another hand, it is the sole depositary of judicial power in cases of impeachment, and is invested with the supreme appellate jurisdiction in all other cases. The judges, again, are so far connected with the legislative department as often to attend and participate in its deliberations, though not admitted to a legislative vote.

[Thus Montesquieu] did not mean that these departments ought to have no *partial agency* in, or no *control* over, the acts of each other. His meaning, [can] amount to no more than this, that where the *whole* power of one department is exercised by the same hands which possess the *whole* power of another department, the fundamental principles of a free constitution are subverted. . . .

The reasons on which Montesquieu grounds his maxim are a further demonstration of his meaning. "When the legislative and executive powers are united in the same person or body," says he, "there can be no liberty, because apprehensions may arise lest *the same* monarch or senate should *enact* tyrannical laws to *execute* them in a tyrannical manner." Again: "Were the power of judging joined with the legislative, the life and liberty of the subject would be exposed to arbitrary control, for *the judge* would then be *the legislator*. Were it joined to the executive power, *the judge* might behave with all the violence of *an oppressor*." . . .

If we look into the constitutions of the several States we find that, notwithstanding the emphatical and, in some instances, the unqualified terms in which this axiom has been laid down, there is not a single instance in which the several departments of power have been kept absolutely separate and distinct. . . .

[The] charge brought against the proposed Constitution of violating the sacred maxim of free government is warranted neither by the real meaning annexed to that maxim by its author, nor by the sense in which it has hitherto been understood in America.

The Federalist No. 48 (Madison)
(1787)

It was shown in the last paper that the political apothegm there examined does not require that the legislative, executive, and judiciary departments should be wholly unconnected with each other. I shall undertake, in the next place, to show that unless these departments be so far connected and blended as to give to each a constitutional control over the others, the degree of separation which the maxim requires, as essential to a free government, can never in practice be duly maintained.

It is agreed on all sides that the powers properly belonging to one of the departments ought not to be directly and completely administered by either of the other departments. It is equally evident that none of them ought to possess, directly or indirectly, an overruling influence over the others in the administration of their respective powers. It will not be denied that power is of an encroaching nature and that it ought to be effectually restrained from passing the limits assigned to it. After discriminating, therefore, in theory, the several classes of power, as they may in their nature be legislative, executive or judiciary, the next and most difficult task is to provide some practical security for each, against the invasion of the others. What this security ought to be is the great problem to be solved.

Will it be sufficient to mark, with precision, the boundaries of these departments in the constitution of the government, and to trust to these parchment barriers against the encroaching spirit of power? This is the security which appears to have been principally relied on by the compilers of most of the American constitutions. But experience assures us that the efficacy of the provision has been greatly overrated; and that some more adequate defense is indispensably necessary for the more feeble against the more powerful members of the government. The legislative department is everywhere extending the sphere of its activity and drawing all power into its impetuous vortex.

The founders of our republics [seem] never for a moment to have turned their eyes from the danger, to liberty, from the overgrown and all-grasping prerogative of an hereditary magistrate, supported and fortified by an hereditary branch of the legislative authority. They seem never to have recollected the danger from legislative usurpations, which, by assembling all power in the same hands, must lead to the same tyranny as is threatened by executive usurpations.

In a government where numerous and extensive prerogatives are placed in the hands of an hereditary monarch, the executive department is very justly regarded as the source of danger, and watched with all the jealousy which a zeal for liberty ought to inspire. In a democracy, where a multitude of people exercise in person the legislative functions and are continually exposed, by their incapacity for regular deliberation and concerted measures, to the ambitious intrigues of their executive magistrates, tyranny may well be apprehended, on some favorable emergency, to start up in the same quarter. But in a representative republic where the executive magistracy is carefully limited, both in the extent and the duration of its power; and where the legislative power is exercised by an assembly, which is inspired by a supposed influence over the people with an intrepid confidence in its own strength; which is sufficiently numerous to feel all the passions which actuate a multitude, yet not so numerous as to be incapable of pursuing the objects of its passions by means which reason prescribes; it is against the enterprising ambition of this department that the people ought to indulge all their jealousy and exhaust all their precautions.

The legislative department derives a superiority in our governments from other circumstances. Its constitutional powers being at once more extensive, and less susceptible of precise limits, it can, with the greater facility, mask, under complicated and indirect measures, the encroachments which it makes on the co-ordinate departments. It is not unfrequently a question of real nicety in legislative bodies whether the operation of a particular measure will, or will not, extend beyond the legislative sphere. On the other side, the executive power being restrained within a narrower compass and being more simple in its nature, and the judiciary being described by landmarks still less uncertain, projects of usurpation by either of these departments would immediately betray and defeat themselves. Nor is this all: as the legislative department alone has access to the pockets of the people, and has in some constitutions full discretion, and in all a prevailing influence, over the pecuniary rewards of those who fill the other departments, a dependence is thus created in the latter, which gives still greater facility to encroachments of the former. . . .

Note: The Theory of Separation and Checks and Balances

1. *In general.* The Constitution distributes national power among the legislative, executive, and judicial branches of the national government. The resulting scheme is usually described as one of either "separation of powers" or "checks and balances." The former description captures the constitutional effort to allocate different sorts of power among three governmental entities that are constituted in different ways. The latter description, in some ways more accurate, focuses on the constitutional effort to ensure that the system will be able to guard against usurpation of authority by any one branch.

The two descriptions emphasize different aspects of the distribution of national powers. Indeed, to some extent the two work against each other. The principle of separation suggests three autonomous entities, working independently. The principle of checks and balances suggests overlapping functions in which each branch is able to intrude on and thereby to check the power of the others. The constitutional framework is best understood as a scheme that embodies a partial, rather than complete, separation of powers, and that supplements the separation by creating devices by which one branch can monitor and check the others. In order to provide the important checking function, the Constitution had to allow some of the branches to play a role in functions assigned to the others.

The Constitution does not separate rigidly the powers of the three branches. The President is expressly given a role in legislation; no law may be enacted without allowing him an opportunity to veto. On the other hand, the Senate is required to consent to presidential appointments, and the power to withhold consent has sometimes been important in permitting Congress to impose its views on the executive branch.

The roles of the respective branches are especially blurred in the area of foreign affairs. Congress is authorized to declare war, but the President is made commander-in-chief of the armed services. "The foreign relations powers appear not so much 'separated' as fissured, along jagged lines indifferent to classical categories of governmental power. [Irregular], uncertain division renders claims of usurpation more difficult to establish." L. Henkin, Foreign Affairs and the Constitution 32 (1965).

Although the separation of powers was not complete, the basic principle of separation was to many of the framers the most fundamental element in the Constitution — in Madison's view, "the basis of all free governments." Political theorists have attempted to show the relationship between the separation of powers and the preservation of liberty. Aristotle, Montesquieu, and Locke were among its many defenders. See W. B. Gwyn, The Meaning of the Separation of Powers (1965); M. Vile, Constitutionalism and the Separation of Powers (1967). The principle has also been the occasion for some of the most dramatic cases in all of constitutional law. Three questions are of special importance: Precisely what functions is the constitutional distribution of powers intended to serve? How does the Constitution distribute powers? Is judicial review a useful device for ensuring the preservation of the constitutional boundary lines?

2. *The purposes of separation.* Throughout American history, the separation of powers has been said to serve two distinct purposes. The first is efficiency. In this view, a division of labor among the various branches makes government more efficient, especially because of the concentration of executive power in the President, who can act with dispatch. The second purpose is the prevention of tyranny. The separation of powers diffuses governmental power, diminishing the likelihood that any one branch will be able to use its power against the citizenry.

a. *Efficiency.* One of the principal concerns of the framers was to bring about a strong executive. A central defect of the Articles of Confederation was the failure to provide for such an executive. See Chapter 1, supra. In these circumstances, the distribution of powers in the Constitution was intended to promote efficiency by ensuring a sensible division of labor with an energetic executive.

Consider Miller, An Inquiry into the Relevance of the Intentions of the Founding Fathers, with Special Emphasis upon the Doctrine of Separation of Powers, 27 Ark. L. Rev. 583, 588-589 (1973):

> Efficiency was stressed as a principal reason for establishing an executive independent from the legislature by, among others, John Adams, Thomas Jefferson, John Jay, and James Wilson. [Wilson's] views are particularly apposite:
>
>> In the active scenes of government, there are emergencies, in which the man [who] deliberates, is lost. But, can either secrecy or dispatch be expected, when, to every enterprise, mutual communication, mutual consultation, and mutual agreement among men, perhaps of discordant views, are indispensably necessary? [If,] on the other hand, the executive power of government is placed in the hands of one person, is there not reason to expect, in his plans and conduct, promptitude, activity, firmness, consistency, and energy?
>
> Despite the assertions to the contrary, the efficiency version has been dominant throughout American constitutional history. Separation of powers has never been a barrier to a high level of cooperation between the political branches of government — a situation that, speaking generally, has found judicial acceptance.

Consider also The Federalist No. 70, defending the Constitution's expansion of the power of the executive on the ground that such power "is essential to the protection of the community against foreign attacks; it is not less essential to the steady administration of the laws; to the protection of property against those irregular and highhanded combinations which sometimes interrupt the ordinary course of justice; to the security of liberty against the enterprises and assaults of ambition, of faction, and of anarchy."

b. *Preventing tyranny.* The Federalist No. 47 stresses a different justification for separating government powers: "The accumulation of all powers, legislative, executive, and judiciary, in the same hands, whether of one, a few, or many, and whether hereditary, self-appointed, or elective, may justly be pronounced the very definition of tyranny."

The same theme can be found in Justice Brandeis's celebrated suggestion that the "doctrine of the separation of powers was adopted by the Convention of 1787, not to promote efficiency but to preclude the exercise of arbitrary power. The purpose was, not to avoid friction, but, by means of the inevitable friction incident to the distribution of the governmental powers among three departments, to save the people from autocracy." Myers v. United States, 272 U.S. 52, 293 (1926) (Brandeis, J., dissenting).

(1) *The rule of law.* The separation of powers ensures that the power to make the law is not in the hands of those who execute it. Lawmakers cannot enact oppressive laws knowing that they will be exempt from their operation. Under this view, the central safeguard of the separation of powers is that it

> makes the laws apply to the lawmakers. This is probably the meaning of Montesquieu's statement concerning tyrannical laws tyrannically applied; if the legislators cannot ensure a tyrannical execution, i.e., one which favors themselves, they will be less likely to make tyrannical laws for fear that they themselves will be tyrannically ruled by them. [If] a separate executive will enforce the law even against the lawmakers, the lawmakers will not have a "distinct interest from the rest of the Community."

D. Epstein, The Political Theory of the Federalist 129-130 (1984).

(2) *Rulers versus ruled.* One of the principal concerns of the framers involved the need to ensure that government officials would act not in their own interests but in the interest of the public. If power were concentrated in one branch, there would be an increased risk that that branch would act to increase its own power — the power of government — at the expense of the governed. The separation of powers was intended to act as a partial remedy, thus safeguarding both liberty and private property against governmental action. If one branch tried to use its power in an oppressive manner, "ambition would counteract ambition," The Federalist No. 51, and another branch would provide resistance. In this respect, the separation of powers "was based upon the skeptical idea that only the division of power among three governmental institutions — executive, legislative, and judicial — could counteract the inevitable tendency of concentrated power to overreach and threaten liberty." Levi, Some Aspects of the Separation of Powers, 76 Colum. L. Rev. 371, 374 (1976).

The power of the legislature posed the primary danger. The period immediately before the Constitutional Convention of 1787 was characterized, in the view of many of the framers, by dangerous intrusions by the legislature into the sphere of liberty and private property. The separation of powers was therefore intended to ensure "the protection of individual rights against all governmental encroachments, particularly by the legislature, the body which the Whigs has traditionally cherished as the people's exclusive repository of their public liberty." G. Wood, The Creation of the American Republic 609 (1969). Consider in this regard Madison's concerns about legislative power in The Federalist No. 48.

Note that this justification depends on a sharp distinction between the interests of the rulers and the interests of the ruled. If the citizenry was thought to control its representatives, or if the interests of the two were allied, the separation of powers and system of checks and balances might seem antidemocratic: They make it harder for the public to bring about change.

(3) *Limited government.* A different rationale for the constitutional distribution of powers stresses the goal, important to some of the framers, of limited government. Under that distribution, no law can be brought to bear against the citizenry without a broad consensus. The executive and judiciary must concur with the legislature in order for a law to be enforced. This system tends to make it difficult

for government to act unless there is something like a consensus that it ought to do so. In this respect, there is an intimate connection between the separation of powers and the protection of private ordering. Note also the connection between the distribution of national powers and the desire to limit the power of democratic politics to alter the status quo. In particular, the system of checks and balances ensures that it will be difficult to obtain substantial reforms. Compare in this regard the respective views of Madison and Jefferson about stability and turbulence, Chapter 1, section A, supra.

(4) *The problem of factions.* The separation of powers was also a partial solution to the problem posed by factions — the risk that governmental power will be usurped by private groups seeking to obtain distribution of wealth or opportunities in their favor. Such private groups, whether minorities or (as was more likely) majorities, might use the authority of government to oppress others. See The Federalist No. 10, Chapter 1 supra. The distribution of national powers was intended to reduce that risk. A faction may be able to acquire power over one of the branches; but it was unlikely that it could do so over all three. (Has this proved to be true?) In this respect, a goal of the separation of powers was to protect minorities against tyranny.

3. *The constitutional distribution of powers: contemporary criticism.* The constitutional distribution of national powers has come under sharp attack in recent years. See, e.g., T. Lowi, The End of Liberalism (2d ed. 1980); Cutler & Johnson, Regulation and the Political Process, 84 Yale L.J. 1395 (1975). Part of the attack is based on the perceived inefficiency of the system. The concern is that in light of the existence of powerful checks, it is difficult for the federal government to accomplish anything. Instead it is reduced to a series of stalemates. Sometimes this critique is attached to a belief that the separation of powers interferes with democratic processes by preventing popular majorities from bringing about change. This belief in turns raises the question whether insulation from dramatic change is a good or a bad thing.

A related attack is that the separation of powers scheme, instead of solving the problem of factions, aggravates it by allowing well-organized private groups to block necessary regulation. In these circumstances, it is sometimes urged that constitutional doctrine should be altered to recognize a greater role for the President.

A different attack is that power is now concentrated in the executive branch and it is thus necessary to restore Congress to its original status of preeminence. Finally, it is sometimes suggested that the growth of an enormous national bureaucracy, operating for the most part within the executive branch, has fundamentally altered the original constitutional framework, and requires some sort of response if the original constitutional concerns are to be satisfied. We return to these issues below.

4. *The judicial role.* What role should the courts play in preserving the barriers against combination of powers and the maintenance of checks and balances? Should the judicial role differ from that in cases involving (1) civil rights and liberties or (2) federalism disputes?

Consider J. Choper, Judicial Review and the National Political Process 263, 269, 275 (1982):

> The federal judiciary should not decide constitutional questions concerning the respective powers of Congress and the President vis-à-vis one another; rather, the

ultimate constitutional issues [should] be held nonjusticiable, their final resolution to be remitted to the interplay of the national political process. [The] important message [to] be gleaned from [the] founders' thinking is that the checks on legislative autocracy that they contemplated exist independently of judicial supervision of the constitutionally mandated separation of powers between the President and Congress. . . .

[The] participation of the Supreme Court is unnecessary to police constitutional violations by one political department against the other. Each branch — legislative and executive — has tremendous incentives jealously to guard its constitutional boundaries and assigned prerogatives against invasion by the other. [In] Hamilton's simple but telling statement, each has the "necessary constitutional means and personal motives to resist encroachments of the other." Without judicial review, neither Congress nor the executive will act as the final judge of its own power vis-à-vis the other. Rather both will effectively participate in defining the reach of their respective authorities — a process that promises trustworthy resolution without the expenditure of precious judicial capital.

Does this argument disregard the possibility that a judicial role is necessary to prevent a stalemate between the branches and potential constitutional crises? Does it overemphasize the usefulness of nonjudicial techniques in reaching accommodation? Consider the perhaps more conventional view that the Supreme Court has performed an important function in resolving separation of powers problems that could not be solved through other means, thus averting potential constitutional crises.

Although the Court has not considered separation of powers cases to be nonjusticiable, it has had relatively few occasions in which to set out the governing constitutional principles. It is for this reason that there is perhaps less guidance here than in other areas of constitutional law. What principles there are derive from a relatively few "great cases" involving conflicts between two branches of the federal government. Much of the "law" in the area therefore amounts to historical practices, informal and formal, of the various branches, and to understandings that take the Constitution as their starting point but that derive in large part from perceived practical necessities.

B. THE BASIC ALLOCATION

Youngstown Sheet & Tube Co. v. Sawyer (The Steel Seizure Case)

343 U.S. 579 (1952)

Mr. Justice Black delivered the opinion of the Court.

We are asked to decide whether President Truman was acting within his constitutional power when he issued an order directing the Secretary of Commerce to take possession of and operate most of the Nation's steel mills. The mill owners argue that the President's order amounts to lawmaking, a legislative function which the Constitution has expressly confided to the Congress and not to the President. The Government's position is that the order was made on findings of the President that his action was necessary to avert a national catastrophe which would inevitably result from a stoppage of steel production, and that in meeting this grave emergency the President was acting within the aggregate of his constitutional powers as the Nation's Chief Executive and the Commander in Chief of the Armed Forces of the United States. The issue emerges here from the following series of events:

In the latter part of 1951, a dispute arose between the steel companies and their employees over terms and conditions that should be included in new collective bargaining agreements. Long-continued conferences failed to resolve the dispute. On December 18, 1951, the employees' representative, United Steelworkers of America, C.I.O., gave notice of an intention to strike when the existing bargaining agreements expired on December 31. The Federal Mediation and Conciliation Service then intervened in an effort to get labor and management to agree. This failing, the President on December 22, 1951, referred the dispute to the Federal Wage Stabilization Board to investigate and make recommendations for fair and equitable terms of settlement. This Board's report resulted in no settlement. On April 4, 1952, the Union gave notice of a nation-wide strike called to begin at 12:01 A.M. April 9. The indispensability of steel as a component of substantially all weapons and other war materials led the President to believe that the proposed work stoppage would immediately jeopardize our national defense and that governmental seizure of the steel mills was necessary in order to assure the continued availability of steel. Reciting these considerations for his action, the President, a few hours before the strike was to begin, issued Executive Order 10340. [The] order directed the Secretary of Commerce to take possession of most of the steel mills and keep them running. The Secretary immediately issued his own possessory orders, calling upon the presidents of the various seized companies to serve as operating managers for the United States. They were directed to carry on their activities in accordance with regulations and directions of the Secretary. The next morning the President sent a message to Congress reporting his action.

[Twelve] days later he sent a second message. [Congress] has taken no action. . . .

[The Court noted that the companies had obeyed the Secretary's order under protest and brought suit against him in district court. On April 30, that court issued a temporary restraining order prohibiting the Secretary from continuing the seizure and possession of the plants. On the same day, the district court's order was stayed by the court of appeals. The Supreme Court granted certiorari on May 3 and heard argument on May 12; the decision was announced on June 2.]

The President's power, if any, to issue the order must stem either from an act of Congress or from the Constitution itself. There is no statute that expressly authorizes the President to take possession of property as he did here. Nor is there any act of Congress to which our attention has been directed from which such a power can fairly be implied. [There] are two statutes which do authorize the President to take both personal and real property under certain conditions. However, the Government admits that these conditions were not met and that the President's order was not rooted in either of the statutes. The Government refers to the seizure provisions of one of these statutes as "much too cumbersome, involved, and time-consuming for the crisis which was at hand."

Moreover, the use of the seizure technique to solve labor disputes in order to prevent work stoppages was not only unauthorized by any congressional enactment; prior to this controversy, Congress had refused to adopt that method of settling labor disputes. When the Taft-Hartley Act was under consideration in 1947, Congress rejected an amendment which would have authorized such governmental seizures in cases of emergency. Apparently it was thought that the technique of seizure, like that of compulsory arbitration, would interfere with the process of collective bargaining. [Instead,] the plan sought to bring about settlements by use of the customary devices of mediation, conciliation, investigation by boards of inquiry, and public reports. In some instances temporary injunctions were authorized to provide cooling-off periods. All this failing, unions were left free to strike. . . .

It is clear that if the President had authority to issue the order he did, it must be found in some provision of the Constitution. And it is not claimed that express constitutional language grants this power to the President. The contention is that presidential power should be implied from the aggregate of his powers under the Constitution. Particular reliance is placed on provisions in Article II which say that "The executive Power shall be vested in a President . . ."; that "he shall take Care that the Laws be faithfully executed"; and that he "shall be Commander in Chief of the Army and Navy of the United States."

The order cannot properly be sustained as an exercise of the President's military power as Commander in Chief of the Armed Forces. The Government attempts to do so by citing a number of cases upholding broad powers in military commanders engaged in day-to-day fighting in a theater of war. Such cases need not concern us here. Even though "theater of war" be an expanding concept, we cannot with faithfulness to our constitutional system hold that the Commander in Chief of the Armed Forces has the ultimate power as such to take possession of private property in order to keep labor disputes from stopping production. This is a job for the Nation's lawmakers, not for its military authorities.

Nor can the seizure order be sustained because of the several constitutional provisions that grant executive power to the President. In the framework of our Constitution, the President's power to see that the laws are faithfully executed refutes the idea that he is to be a lawmaker. The Constitution limits his functions in the lawmaking process to the recommending of laws he thinks wise and the vetoing of laws he thinks bad. And the Constitution is neither silent nor equivocal about who shall make laws which the President is to execute. The first section of the first article says that "All legislative Powers herein granted shall be vested in a Congress of the United States. . . ." After granting many powers to the Congress, Article I goes on to provide that Congress may "make all Laws which shall be necessary and proper for carrying into Execution the foregoing Powers, and all other Powers vested by this Constitution in the Government of the United States, or in any Department or Officer thereof."

The President's order does not direct that a congressional policy be executed in a manner prescribed by Congress — it directs that a presidential policy be executed in a manner prescribed by the President. The preamble of the order itself, like that of many statutes, sets out reasons why the President believes certain policies should be adopted, proclaims these policies as rules of conduct to be followed, and again, like a statute, authorizes a government official to promulgate additional rules and regulations consistent with the policy proclaimed and needed to carry that policy into execution. The power of Congress to adopt such public policies as those proclaimed by the order is beyond question. It can authorize the taking of private property for public use. It can make laws regulating the relationships between employers and employees, prescribing rules designed to settle labor disputes, and fixing wages and working conditions in certain fields of our economy. The Constitution does not subject this lawmaking power of Congress to presidential or military supervision or control.

It is said that other Presidents without congressional authority have taken possession of private business enterprises in order to settle labor disputes. But even if this be true, Congress has not thereby lost its exclusive constitutional authority to make laws necessary and proper to carry out the powers vested by the Constitution "in the Government of the United States, or any Department or Officer thereof."

The Founders of this Nation entrusted the lawmaking power to the Congress alone in both good and bad times. It would do no good to recall the historical events, the fears of power and the hopes for freedom that lay behind their choice. Such a review would but confirm our holding that this seizure order cannot stand.

The judgment of the District Court is affirmed.

Mr. Justice Frankfurter, concurring.

[Not] so long ago it was fashionable to find our system of checks and balances obstructive to effective government. It was easy to ridicule that system as outmoded — too easy. The experience through which the world has passed in our own day has made vivid the realization that the Framers of our Constitution were not inexperienced doctrinaires. These long-headed statesmen had no illusion that our people enjoyed biological or psychological or sociological immunities from the hazards of concentrated power. It is absurd to see a dictator in a representative product of the sturdy democratic traditions of the Mississippi Valley. The accretion of dangerous power does not come in a day. It does come, however slowly, from the generative force of unchecked disregard of the restrictions that fence in even the most disinterested assertion of authority. . . .

The pole-star for constitutional adjudications is John Marshall's greatest judicial utterance that "it is a *constitution* we are expounding." [*McCulloch*.] That requires both a spacious view in applying an instrument of government "made for an undefined and expanding future," and as narrow a delimitation of the constitutional issues as the circumstances permit. Not the least characteristic of great statesmanship which the Framers manifested was the extent to which they did not attempt to bind the future. . . .

Marshall's admonition that "it is a *constitution* we are expounding" is especially relevant when the Court is required to give legal sanctions to an underlying principle of the Constitution — that of separation of powers. "The great ordinances of the Constitution do not establish and divide fields of black and white." . . .

[We] must therefore put to one side consideration of what powers the President would have had if there had been no legislation whatever bearing on the authority asserted by the seizure, or if the seizure had been only for a short, explicitly temporary period, to be terminated automatically unless Congressional approval were given. . . .

The question before the Court comes in this setting. Congress has frequently — at least 16 times since 1916 — specifically provided for executive seizure of production, transportation, communications, or storage facilities. In every case it has qualified this grant of power with limitations and safeguards. This body of enactments demonstrates that Congress deemed seizure so drastic a power as to require that it be carefully circumscribed whenever the President was vested with this extraordinary authority. . . .

In any event, nothing can be plainer than that Congress made a conscious choice of policy in a field full of perplexity and peculiarly within legislative responsibility for choice. In formulating legislation for dealing with industrial conflicts, Congress could not more clearly and emphatically have withheld authority than it did in 1947. . . .

It cannot be contended that the President would have had power to issue this order had Congress explicitly negated such authority in formal legislation. Congress has expressed its will to withhold this power from the President as though it had said so in so many words. . . .

Apart from his vast share of responsibility for the conduct of our foreign relations, the embracing function of the President is that "he shall take Care that the Laws be faithfully executed. . . . ." Art. II, §3. The nature of that authority has for me been comprehensively indicated by Mr. Justice Holmes. "The duty of the President to see that the laws be executed is a duty that does not go beyond the laws or require him to achieve more than Congress sees fit to leave within his power." Myers v. United States, 272 U.S. 52, 177. The powers of the President are not as particularized as are those of Congress. But unenumerated powers do not mean undefined powers. . . .

To be sure, the content of the three authorities of government is not to be derived from an abstract analysis. The areas are partly interacting, not wholly disjointed. The Constitution is a framework for government. Therefore the way the framework has consistently operated fairly establishes that it has operated according to its true nature. Deeply embedded traditional ways of conducting government cannot supplant the Constitution or legislation, but they give meaning to the words of a text or supply them. It is an inadmissibly narrow conception of American constitutional law to confine it to the words of the Constitution and to disregard the gloss which life has written upon them. In short, a systematic, unbroken, executive practice, long pursued to the knowledge of the Congress and never before questioned, engaged in by Presidents who have also sworn to uphold the Constitution, making as it were such exercise of power part of the structure of our government, may be treated as a gloss on "executive Power" vested in the President by §1 of Art. II. . . .

Down to the World War II period, [the] record is barren of instances comparable to the one before us. Of twelve seizures by President Roosevelt prior to the enactment of the War Labor Disputes Act in June, 1943, three were sanctioned by existing law, and six others were effected after Congress, on December 8, 1941, had declared the existence of a state of war. In this case, reliance on the powers that flow from declared war has been commendably disclaimed by the Solicitor General. Thus the list of executive assertions of the power of seizure in circumstances comparable to the present reduces to three in the six-month period from June to December of 1941. [Without] passing on their validity, as we are not called upon to do, it suffices to say that these three isolated instances do not add

up, either in number, scope, duration or contemporaneous legal justification, to
the necessary kind of executive construction of the Constitution. [Nor] do they
come to us sanctioned by long-continued acquiescence of Congress giving decisive weight to a construction by the Executive of its powers. [No] doubt a government with distributed authority, subject to be challenged in the courts of law, at
least long enough to consider and adjudicate the challenge, labors under restrictions from which other governments are free. It has not been our tradition to
envy such governments. In any event our government was designed to have such
restrictions. The price was deemed not too high in view of the safeguards which
these restrictions afford. . . .

[A lengthy historical appendix was added to this opinion.]

Mr. Justice Jackson, concurring in the judgment and opinion of the Court.

[A] judge, like an executive adviser, may be surprised at the poverty of really
useful and unambiguous authority applicable to concrete problems of executive
power as they actually present themselves. Just what our forefathers did envision,
or would have envisioned had they foreseen modern conditions, must be divined
from materials almost as enigmatic as the dreams Joseph was called upon to
interpret for Pharaoh. A century and a half of partisan debate and scholarly
speculation yields no net result but only supplies more or less apt quotations from
respected sources on each side of any question. They largely cancel each other.
And court decisions are indecisive because of the judicial practice of dealing with
the largest questions in the most narrow way.

The actual art of governing under our Constitution does not and cannot conform to judicial definitions of the power of any of its branches based on isolated
clauses or even single Articles torn from context. While the Constitution diffuses
power the better to secure liberty, it also contemplates that practice will integrate
the dispersed powers into a workable government. It enjoins upon its branches
separateness but interdependence, autonomy but reciprocity. Presidential powers
are not fixed but fluctuate, depending upon their disjunction or conjunction with
those of Congress. We may well begin by a somewhat over-simplified grouping of
practical situations in which a President may doubt, or others may challenge, his
powers, and by distinguishing roughly the legal consequences of this factor of
relativity.

1. When the President acts pursuant to an express or implied authorization of
Congress, his authority is at its maximum, for it includes all that he possesses in
his own right plus all that Congress can delegate. In these circumstances, and in
these only, may he be said (for what it may be worth) to personify the federal
sovereignty. If his act is held unconstitutional under these circumstances, it
usually means that the Federal Government as an undivided whole lacks power.
A seizure executed by the President pursuant to an Act of Congress would be
supported by the strongest of presumptions and the widest latitude of judicial
interpretation, and the burden of persuasion would rest heavily upon any who
might attack it.

2. When the President acts in absence of either a congressional grant or denial
of authority, he can only rely upon his own independent powers, but there is a
zone of twilight in which he and Congress may have concurrent authority, or in
which its distribution is uncertain. Therefore, congressional inertia, indifference
or quiescence may sometimes, at least as a practical matter, enable, if not invite,

measures on independent presidential responsibility. In this area, any actual test of power is likely to depend on the imperatives of events and contemporary imponderables rather than on abstract theories of law.

3. When the President takes measures incompatible with the expressed or implied will of Congress, his power is at its lowest ebb, for then he can rely only upon his own constitutional powers minus any constitutional powers of Congress over the matter. Courts can sustain exclusive presidential control in such a case only by disabling the Congress from acting upon the subject. Presidential claim to a power at once so conclusive and preclusive must be scrutinized with caution, for what is at stake is the equilibrium established by our constitutional system.

Into which of these classifications does this executive seizure of the steel industry fit? It is eliminated from the first by admission, for it is conceded that no congressional authorization exists for this seizure. . . .

Can it then be defended under flexible tests available to the second category? It seems clearly eliminated from that class because Congress has not left seizure of private property an open field but has covered it by three statutory policies inconsistent with this seizure. . . .

This leaves the current seizure to be justified only by the severe tests under the third grouping, where it can be supported only by any remainder of executive power after subtraction of such powers as Congress may have over the subject. In short, we can sustain the President only by holding that seizure of such strikebound industries is within his domain and beyond control by Congress. . . .

The Solicitor General seeks the power of seizure in three clauses of the Executive Article, the first reading, "The executive Power shall be vested in a President of the United States of America." [I] quote the interpretation which his brief puts upon it: "In our view, this clause constitutes a grant of all the executive powers of which the Government is capable." If that be true, it is difficult to see why the forefathers bothered to add several specific items, including some trifling ones.

The example of such unlimited executive power that must have most impressed the forefathers was the prerogative exercised by George III, and the description of its evils in the Declaration of Independence leads me to doubt that they were creating their new Executive in his image. [And] if we seek instruction from our own times, we can match it only from the executive powers in those governments we disparagingly describe as totalitarian. I cannot accept the view that this clause is a grant in bulk of all conceivable executive power but regard it as an allocation to the presidential office of the generic powers thereafter stated.

The clause on which the Government next relies is that "The President shall be Commander in Chief of the Army and Navy of the United States. . . ." These cryptic words [imply] something more than an empty title. But just what authority goes with the name has plagued presidential advisers who would not waive or narrow it by nonassertion yet cannot say where it begins or ends. It undoubtedly puts the Nation's armed forces under presidential command. Hence, this loose appellation is sometimes advanced as support for any presidential action, internal or external, involving use of force, the idea being that it vests power to do anything, anywhere, that can be done with an army or navy.

That seems to be the logic of an argument tendered at our bar — that the President having, on his own responsibility, sent American troops abroad derives from that act "affirmative power" to seize the means of producing a supply of steel for them. . . .

I cannot foresee all that it might entail if the Court should indorse this argument. Nothing in our Constitution is plainer than that declaration of a war is entrusted only to Congress. Of course, a state of war may in fact exist without a formal declaration. But no doctrine that the Court could promulgate would seem to me more sinister and alarming than that a President whose conduct of foreign affairs is so largely uncontrolled, and often even is unknown, can vastly enlarge his mastery over the internal affairs of the country by his own commitment of the Nation's armed forces to some foreign venture. I do not, however, find it necessary or appropriate to consider the legal status of the Korean enterprise to discountenance argument based on it.

Assuming that we are in a war *de facto*, whether it is or is not a war *de jure*, does that empower the Commander in Chief to seize industries he thinks necessary to supply our army? The Constitution expressly places in Congress power "to raise and *support* Armies" and "to *provide* and *maintain* a Navy." (Emphasis supplied.) This certainly lays upon Congress primary responsibility for supplying the armed forces. Congress alone controls the raising of revenues and their appropriation and may determine in what manner and by what means they shall be spent for military and naval procurement. . . .

There are indications that the Constitution did not contemplate that the title Commander in Chief *of the Army and Navy* will constitute him also Commander in Chief of the country, its industries and its inhabitants. He has no monopoly of "war powers," whatever they are. . . .

The third clause in which the Solicitor General finds seizure powers is that "he shall take Care that the Laws be faithfully executed. . . ." That authority must be matched against words of the Fifth Amendment that "No person shall be . . . deprived of life, liberty or property, without due process of law. . . ." One gives a governmental authority that reaches so far as there is law, the other gives a private right that authority shall go no farther. These signify about all there is of the principle that ours is a government of laws, not of men, and that we submit ourselves to rulers only if under rules.

The Solicitor General lastly grounds support of the seizure upon nebulous, inherent powers never expressly granted but said to have accrued to the office from the customs and claims of preceding administrations. The plea is for a resulting power to deal with a crisis or an emergency according to the necessities of the case, the unarticulated assumption being that necessity knows no law.

Loose and irresponsible use of adjectives colors all nonlegal and much legal discussion of presidential powers. "Inherent" powers, "implied" powers, "incidental" powers, "plenary" powers, "war" powers and "emergency" powers are used, often interchangeably and without fixed or ascertainable meanings.

The vagueness and generality of the clauses that set forth presidential powers afford a plausible basis for pressures within and without an administration for presidential action beyond that supported by those whose responsibility it is to defend his actions in court. The claim of inherent and unrestricted presidential powers has long been a persuasive dialectical weapon in political controversy. While it is not surprising that counsel should grasp support from such unadjudicated claims of power, a judge cannot accept self-serving press statements of the attorney for one of the interested parties as authority in answering a constitutional question, even if the advocate was himself. But prudence has counseled that actual reliance on such nebulous claims stop short of provoking a judicial test. . . .

The appeal, however, that we declare the existence of inherent powers ex necessitate to meet an emergency asks us to do what many think would be wise, although it is something the forefathers omitted. They knew what emergencies were, knew the pressures they engender for authoritative action, knew, too, how they afford a ready pretext for usurpation. We may also suspect that they suspected that emergency powers would tend to kindle emergencies. Aside from suspension of the privilege of the writ of habeas corpus in time of rebellion or invasion, when the public safety may require it, they made no express provision for exercise of extraordinary authority because of a crisis. I do not think we rightfully may so amend their work. . . .

In view of the ease, expedition and safety with which Congress can grant and has granted large emergency powers, certainly ample to embrace this crisis, I am quite unimpressed with the argument that we should affirm possession of them without statute. Such power either has no beginning or it has no end. If it exists, it need submit to no legal restraint. I am not alarmed that it would plunge us straightway into dictatorship, but it is at least a step in that wrong direction.

As to whether there is imperative necessity for such powers, it is relevant to note the gap that exists between the President's paper powers and his real powers. The Constitution does not disclose the measure of the actual controls wielded by the modern presidential office. That instrument must be understood as an Eighteenth-Century sketch of a government hoped for, not as a blueprint of the Government that is. Vast accretions of federal power, eroded from that reserved by the States, have magnified the scope of presidential activity. Subtle shifts take place in the centers of real power that do not show in the face of the Constitution.

Executive power has the advantage of concentration in a single head in whose choice the whole Nation has a part, making him the focus of public hopes and expectations. In drama, magnitude and finality his decisions so far overshadow any others that almost alone he fills the public eye and ear. No other personality in public life can begin to compete with him in access to the public mind through modern methods of communications. By his prestige as head of state and his influence upon public opinion he exerts a leverage upon those who are supposed to check and balance his power which often cancels their effectiveness.

Moreover, rise of the party system has made a significant extraconstitutional supplement to real executive power. No appraisal of his necessities is realistic which overlooks that he heads a political system as well as a legal system. Party loyalties and interests, sometimes more binding than law, extend his effective control into branches of government other than his own and he often may win, as a political leader, what he cannot command under the Constitution. . . .

But I have no illusion that any decision by this Court can keep power in the hands of Congress if it is not wise and timely in meeting its problems. A crisis that challenges the President equally, or perhaps primarily, challenges Congress. If not good law, there was worldly wisdom in the maxim attributed to Napoleon that "The tools belong to the man who can use them." We may say that power to legislate for emergencies belongs in the hands of Congress, but only Congress itself can prevent power from slipping through its fingers.

The essence of our free Government is "leave to live by no man's leave, underneath the law" — to be governed by those impersonal forces which we call law.

Our Government is fashioned to fulfill this concept so far as humanly possible. [The] executive action we have here originates in the individual will of the President and represents an exercise of authority without law. No one, perhaps not even the President, knows the limits of the power he may seek to exert in this instance and the parties affected cannot learn the limit of their rights. We do not know today what powers over labor or property would be claimed to flow from Government possession if we should legalize it, what rights to compensation would be claimed or recognized, or on what contingency it would end. With all its defects, delays and inconveniences, men have discovered no technique for long preserving free government except that the Executive be under the law, and that the law be made by parliamentary deliberations.

Such institutions may be destined to pass away. But it is the duty of the Court to be last, not first, to give them up.

MR. JUSTICE BURTON, concurring.

[Does] the President [have] inherent constitutional power to seize private property which makes congressional action in relation thereto unnecessary? We find no such power available to him under the present circumstances. The present situation is not comparable to that of an imminent invasion or threatened attack. We do not face the issue of what might be the President's constitutional power to meet such catastrophic situations. Nor is it claimed that the current seizure is in the nature of a military command addressed by the President, as Commander-in-Chief, to a mobilized nation waging, or imminently threatened with, total war.

MR. JUSTICE CLARK, concurring.

[The] Constitution does grant to the President extensive authority in times of grave and imperative national emergency. In fact, to my thinking, such a grant may well be necessary to the very existence of the Constitution itself. As Lincoln aptly said, "[is] it possible to lose the nation and yet preserve the Constitution?" In describing this authority I care not whether one calls it "residual," "inherent," "moral," "implied," "aggregate," "emergency," or otherwise. . . .

[Three] statutes furnish the guideposts for decision in this case. [The fact] remains that neither the Defense Production Act nor Taft-Hartley authorized the seizure challenged here, and the Government made no effort to comply with the procedures established by the Selective Service Act of 1948, a statute which expressly authorizes seizures when producers fail to supply necessary defense matériel.

For these reasons I concur in the judgment of the Court.

MR. JUSTICE DOUGLAS, concurring. . . .

The legislative nature of the action taken by the President seems to me to be clear. . . .

[The] President might seize and the Congress by subsequent action might ratify the seizure. But until and unless Congress acted, no condemnation would be lawful. The branch of government that has the power to pay compensation for a seizure is the only one able to authorize a seizure or make lawful one that the President has effected. That seems to me to be the necessary result of the condemnation provision in the Fifth Amendment. It squares with the theory of checks and balances expounded by Mr. Justice Black in the opinion of the Court in which I join.

If we sanctioned the present exercise of power by the President, we would be expanding Article II of the Constitution and rewriting it to suit the political conveniences of the present emergency. . . .

We pay a price for our system of checks and balances, for the distribution of power among the three branches of government. It is a price that today may seem exorbitant to many. Today a kindly President uses the seizure power to effect a wage increase and to keep the steel furnaces in production. Yet tomorrow another President might use the same power to prevent a wage increase, to curb trade-unionists, to regiment labor as oppressively as industry thinks it has been regimented by this seizure.

MR. CHIEF JUSTICE VINSON, with whom MR. JUSTICE REED and MR. JUSTICE MINTON join, dissenting.

The President of the United States directed the Secretary of Commerce to take temporary possession of the Nation's steel mills during the existing emergency because "a work stoppage would immediately jeopardize and imperil our national defense and the defense of those joined with us in resisting aggression, and would add to the continuing danger of our soldiers, sailors, and airmen engaged in combat in the field." . . .

In passing upon the question of Presidential powers in this case, we must first consider the context in which those powers were exercised. . . .

The President has the duty to execute [legislative programs.] Their successful execution depends upon continued production of steel and stabilized prices for steel. Accordingly, when the collective bargaining agreements between the Nation's steel producers and their employees, represented by the United Steel Workers, were due to expire on December 31, 1951, and a strike shutting down the entire basic steel industry was threatened, the President acted to avert a complete shutdown of steel production. . . .

One is not here called upon even to consider the possibility of executive seizure of a farm, a corner grocery store or even a single industrial plant. Such considerations arise only when one ignores the central fact of this case — that the Nation's entire basic steel production would have shut down completely if there had been no Government seizure. Even ignoring for the moment whatever confidential information the President may possess as "the Nation's organ for foreign affairs," the uncontroverted affidavits in this record amply support the finding that "a work stoppage would immediately jeopardize and imperil our national defense."

Plaintiffs do not remotely suggest any basis for rejecting the President's finding that *any* stoppage of steel production would immediately place the Nation in peril. [Under the plaintiffs'] view, the President is left powerless at the very moment when the need for action may be most pressing and when no one, other than he, is immediately capable of action. Under this view, he is left powerless because a power not expressly given to Congress is nevertheless found to rest exclusively with Congress. [But the] whole of the "executive Power" is vested in the President. . . .

This comprehensive grant of the executive power to a single person was bestowed soon after the country had thrown the yoke of monarchy. Only by instilling initiative and vigor in all of the three departments of Government, declared Madison, could tyranny in any form be avoided. [It] is thus apparent that the Presidency was deliberately fashioned as an office of power and independence. Of course, the Framers created no autocrat capable of arrogating any power unto himself at any time. But neither did they create an automaton impotent to exercise the powers of Government at a time when the survival of the Republic itself may be at stake.

In passing upon the grave constitutional question presented in this case, we must never forget, as Chief Justice Marshall admonished, that the Constitution is "intended to endure for ages to come, and, consequently, to be adapted to the various *crises* of human affairs," and that "[i]ts means are adequate to its ends." Cases do arise presenting questions which could not have been foreseen by the Framers. In such cases, the Constitution has been treated as a living document adaptable to new situations. But we are not called upon today to expand the Constitution to meet a new situation. For, in this case, we need only look to history and time-honored principles of constitutional law. . . . .

A review of executive action demonstrates that our Presidents have on many occasions exhibited the leadership contemplated by the Framers when they made the President Commander in Chief, and imposed upon him the trust to "take Care that the Laws be faithfully executed." With or without explicit statutory authorization, Presidents have at such times dealt with national emergencies by acting promptly and resolutely to enforce legislative programs, at least to save those programs until Congress could act. Congress and the courts have responded to such executive initiative with consistent approval. . . .

[Chief Justice Vinson discussed historical practices, including:]

Our first President displayed at once the leadership contemplated by the Framers. When the national revenue laws were openly flouted in some sections of Pennsylvania, President Washington, without waiting for a call from the state government, summoned the militia and took decisive steps to secure the faithful execution of the laws. [Hamilton,] whose defense of the Proclamation [of Neutrality issued during the French Revolution] has endured the test of time, invoked the argument that the Executive has the duty to do that which will preserve peace until Congress acts and, in addition, pointed to the need for keeping the Nation informed of the requirements of existing laws and treaties as part of the faithful execution of the laws. . . .

In an action furnishing a most apt precedent for this case, President Lincoln without statutory authority directed the seizure of rail and telegraph lines leading to Washington. [In] his autobiography, President Roosevelt expounded the "Stewardship Theory" of Presidential power, stating that "the executive is subject only to the people, and, under the Constitution, bound to serve the people affirmatively in cases where the Constitution does not explicitly forbid him to render the service." . . .

[During] World War I, President Wilson established a War Labor Board without awaiting specific direction by Congress. [Twenty years later] the President directed seizure of the Nation's coal mines to remove an obstruction to the effective prosecution of the war.

The procedures adopted by President Roosevelt closely resembled the methods employed by President Wilson. A National War Labor Board, like its predecessor of World War I, was created by Executive Order to deal effectively and fairly with disputes affecting defense production. Seizures were considered necessary, upon disobedience of War Labor Board orders, to assure that the mobilization effort remained a "going concern," and to enforce the economic stabilization program. . . .

[This] is but a cursory summary of executive leadership. But it amply demonstrates that Presidents have taken prompt action to enforce the laws and protect the country whether or not Congress happened to provide in advance for the particular method of execution. [The] fact that Congress and the courts have consistently recognized and given their support to such executive action indicates that such a power of seizure has been accepted throughout our history.

History bears out the genius of the Founding Fathers, who created a Government subject to law but not left subject to inertia when vigor and initiative are required. . . .

Much of the argument in this case has been directed at straw men. We do not now have before us the case of a President acting solely on the basis of his own notions of the public welfare. Nor is there any question of unlimited executive power in this case. The President himself closed the door to any such claim when he sent his Message to Congress stating his purpose to abide by any action of Congress, whether approving or disapproving his seizure action. Here, the President immediately made sure that Congress was fully informed of the temporary action he had taken only to preserve the legislative programs from destruction until Congress could act.

The absence of a specific statute authorizing seizure of the steel mills as a mode of executing the laws — both the military procurement program and the anti-inflation program — has not until today been thought to prevent the President from executing the laws. Unlike an administrative commission confined to the enforcement of the statute under which it was created, or the head of a department when administering a particular statute, the President is a constitutional officer charged with taking care that a "mass of legislation" be executed. Flexibility as to mode of execution to meet critical situations is a matter of practical necessity. . . .

The diversity of views expressed in the six opinions of the majority, the lack of reference to authoritative precedent, the repeated reliance upon prior dissenting opinions, the complete disregard of the uncontroverted facts showing the gravity of the emergency and the temporary nature of the taking all serve to demonstrate how far afield one must go to affirm the order of the District Court.

The broad executive power granted by Article II to an officer on duty 365 days a year cannot, it is said, be invoked to avert disaster. Instead, the President must confine himself to sending a message to Congress recommending action. Under this messenger-boy concept of the Office, the President cannot even act to preserve legislative programs from destruction so that Congress will have something left to act upon. There is no judicial finding that the executive action was unwarranted because there was in fact no basis for the President's finding of the existence of an emergency for, under this view, the gravity of the emergency and the immediacy of the threatened disaster are considered irrelevant as a matter of law. . . .

[There] is no question that the possession was other than temporary in character and subject to congressional direction — either approving, disapproving or regulating the manner in which the mills were to be administered and returned to the owners. The President immediately informed Congress of his action and clearly stated his intention to abide by the legislative will. No basis for claims or arbitrary action, unlimited powers or dictatorial usurpation of congressional power appears from the facts of this case. On the contrary, judicial, legislative and executive precedents throughout our history demonstrate that in this case the President acted in full conformity with his duties under the Constitution. . . .

Note: Youngstown *and the Power of the President*

1. *Background.* The Steel Seizure Case was decided against a complex background. At the end of 1950, U.S. steel producers and the steelworkers union had agreed on a wage increase. Shortly thereafter, however, the Economic Stabilization Agency effectively froze all price and wage increases, thus preventing implementation of the agreement. In these circumstances, the labor force threatened a strike in December 1951. Because the President feared that a strike would endanger the Korean effort, he postponed the strike while his Wage Stabilization Board — made up of representatives of steel producers, workers, and the general public — could study the problem. The board recommended certain staggered wage increases and union benefits, but the proposals were rejected by the industry. The steelworkers union set a strike date for April 9, 1952.

At this time, President Truman's popularity, which had soared during the start of the Korean War, had fallen drastically. Disillusionment over the war effort, fear of economic deterioration, charges that the administration was riddled with Communism and corruption, and numerous political defeats in Congress had contributed to Truman's announcement that he would not run for reelection that year. Despite the decline in his popularity, Truman refused to waver on his plans in Korea or — more particularly — to impose any labor injunctions that might be available to him through the Taft-Hartley Act. Truman had had a long and close political alliance with organized labor. In order to preserve steel production, Truman set out an executive order transferring control over the industries to the government. Instead of defending his decision as a national defense measure to secure steel for the undeclared and unofficial war in Korea, President Truman invoked a general constitutional privilege of his office.

The *Youngstown* decision was reached only two months after Truman seized the industries — a rapid timetable for which the Court has been criticized, especially in light of the importance of the issues. Notably, the legal and political consequences of the President's actions appear much more significant than the economic and military harms that had motivated the seizure. After the Court's ruling on June 2, the union struck for fifty-three days. No steel shortage materialized, and industry owners finally negotiated an agreement similar to the Wage Stabilization Board's recommendations. For discussion, see S. Marcus, Truman and the Steel Seizure Case: The Limits of Presidential Power (1977); A. Westin, The Anatomy of a Constitutional Case (1958).

2. *The text.* The President asserted three textual bases for his action in seizing the steel mills: the vesting of executive power in the President, the "take Care" clause, and the commander-in-chief provision. What power does each of these

provisions confer on the President? What are the conflicting views of the justices on this question? If the text turned out to be unhelpful to the President, is there any other basis for upholding the President's action?

3. *The view from the White House.* Consider 2 Harry S Truman, Memoirs: Years of Trial and Hope 478 (1956):

> Whatever the six justices of the Supreme Court meant by their differing opinions about the constitutional powers of the President, he must always act in a national emergency. We live in an age when hostilities begin without polite exchanges of diplomatic notes. There are no longer sharp distinctions between combatants and noncombatants, between military targets and the sanctuary of civilian areas. Nor can we separate the economic facts from the problems of defense and security. [The] President, who is Commander in Chief and who represents the interests of all the people, must be able to act at all times to meet any sudden threat to the nation's security.

The Court appears to reject this position in *Youngstown*. Should it have?

4. *The problem of methodology.* There are significant differences between the views expressed in the majority opinion by Justice Black and those expressed by other members of the Court both in dissent and in concurrence. Justice Black's approach is largely one of classification: Does the asserted power fall within the category of "legislation" or that of "execution," as those terms are conventionally understood? By contrast, Justice Jackson (and to some extent Justice Frankfurter) examine (1) whether Congress has granted or refused to grant the relevant power, (2) whether historical practices support the assertion of power, and (3) whether "contemporary imponderables," or "the imperatives of events," argue in favor of or against the asserted power. Note also Justice Jackson's "tripartite" approach.

Does Justice Black oversimplify a complicated problem? Consider the view that separation of powers questions cannot be resolved through a mechanical process of classification. The terms "legislation" and "execution" are too loaded with ambiguity to support the Court's rationale; it was by no means clear that the seizure of the steel mills was a "legislative" act. Does Justice Douglas's approach meet these criticisms?

On the other hand, does Justice Jackson's alternative position involve an unduly open-ended, discretionary inquiry — and allow irrelevant factors to influence the analysis? Precisely how does one resolve cases within Justice Jackson's "twilight zone"? What is the role of "history" and "contemporary imponderables"?

Note that the Court (or at least the group of the justices who comprise the majority position) assumes (a) that Congress had at least implicitly disapproved of the asserted presidential power and (b) that Congress's view is important to the outcome. Did Congress in fact disapprove? Imagine that Congress had expressed no view on the question of presidential authority in Youngstown. Same result? Compare the Court's treatment of a similar problem in Dames & Moore v. Regan, section E infra.

5. *The role of history.* Note that Justices Frankfurter and Jackson agree that the text of the Constitution is not conclusive. Both believe not only that Congress's view is important to resolution of the constitutional question but also that "history" is relevant as a "gloss" on the text. Does this view permit the Constitution to be amended through historical practices, amounting to a kind of adverse possession rule for constitutional interpretation? Would such a mechanism of "amend-

ment" be legitimate? Exactly why and to what extent are historical considerations relevant?

6. *Implied and emergency powers.* What would be the dangers of recognizing a presidential power of the sort asserted in the *Youngstown* case? Would recognition of such a power pose any of the dangers that the framers sought to prevent through the constitutional distribution of national powers? Does the President have any implied or emergency powers after *Youngstown?*

The existence of implied or emergency presidential powers has been sharply disputed throughout the nation's history. Note that article I refers to "legislative powers herein granted," while article II refers to "executive power" without a "herein granted" qualification. In Alexander Hamilton's view, the "different modes of expression in regard to the two powers confirm the inference that the authority vested in the President is not limited to the specific cases of executive power delineated in Article II." 7 Works of Alexander Hamilton 80 (1851).

This line of reasoning led to the conclusion, reached by Theodore Roosevelt and adhered to by many subsequent Presidents, that the President "was a steward of the people bound actively and affirmatively to do all he could for the people [unless] such action was forbidden by the Constitution or by the law." T. Roosevelt, Autobiography 372 (1914). Contrast with this the view, of President Taft and others, that the President may exercise only those powers traceable to a constitutional grant of authority. Does *Youngstown* resolve the problem?

Consider In re Debs, 158 U.S. 564 (1894). President Cleveland requested a U.S. attorney in Chicago to seek an injunction designed (1) to continue the operation of the train system during the Pullman strike and (2) to prevent the strike because of unlawful interference with interstate commerce and the flow of mail. There was no statutory authorization for the injunction. The Court upheld the injunction. It pointed to the breadth of federal power over interstate commerce and the postal system and to the existence of numerous statutes regulating railroads and the postal system. In these circumstances, it was unnecessary to have a precise statute "[prescribing] by legislation that any interference with these matters shall be offenses against the United States, and prosecuted and punished by indictment in the proper courts." The Court said that "here is no such impotency in the national government. The entire strength of the nation may be used to enforce in any part of the land the full and free exercise of all national powers and the security of all rights entrusted by the Constitution to its care. The strong arm of the national government may be put forth to brush away all obstructions to the freedom of interstate commerce or the transportation of the mails." With respect to the question whether the government had the power to obtain an injunction, the Court added that "the right to use force does not exclude the right to appeal to the courts for a judicial determination and for the exercise of all their powers of prevention." Is *Debs* distinguishable from *Youngstown?*

See also In re Neagle, 135 U.S. 1 (1890), upholding an order by the Attorney General to a U.S. marshal to protect a Supreme Court justice whose life had been threatened by a litigant, notwithstanding the absence of express statutory authorization. Compare United States v. City of Philadelphia, 644 F.2d 187 (3d Cir. 1980) (no implied power to bring suit to challenge unconstitutional practices of Philadelphia police department).

For general discussion of *Youngstown*, see Marcus, Truman and the Steel Seizure Case: The Limits of Presidential Power (1977); Kauper, The Steel Seizure

Case: Congress, the President, and the Supreme Court, 51 Mich. L. Rev. 141 (1952); Corwin, The Steel Seizure Case: A Judicial Brick without Straw, 53 Colum. L. Rev. 53 (1953).

7. *The reach of* Youngstown. Consider the following cases after *Youngstown*. Under the approaches of the Court, Justice Douglas, Justice Jackson, or Justice Frankfurter, what results? (a) The Attorney General, acting at the behest of the President, brings suit to challenge unconstitutional racial discrimination by the Philadelphia police department. Congress has provided no authority to bring the suit. See United States v. City of Philadelphia, supra. (b) The President orders federal troops into a city experiencing urban riots. Congress has enacted no legislation expressly granting or denying such authority. (c) A potentially catastrophic accident has occurred at a privately owned but federally regulated nuclear power plant. The federal regulations impose a series of safety requirements with which the power plant owner has failed to comply. The President seizes control of the plant in order to confine the harm from the accident, concluding that the private owner will be unable to control the damage. (d) U.S. hostages have been taken by a foreign government. The President retaliates with military action, consisting of a naval blockade of that country. The President also takes the families of the hostages into federal custody in order to limit the publicity growing out of the crisis. On the release of the hostages, he orders the Central Intelligence Agency to identify, capture, and bring to trial in the United States the people who took the U.S. citizens hostage.

Note: *Impoundment, Law Enforcement, and the "Take Care" Clause*

1. *The impoundment controversy.* The meanings of the clause vesting executive power in the President and of the "take Care" clause have received attention in connection with presidential refusal to appropriate funds or otherwise to carry out laws enacted by Congress. Several Presidents have argued that they have "inherent" authority to refuse to spend funds. President Nixon claimed that it was essential to recognize this power to enable the President to combat inflation.

Such authority would go far beyond the power to veto legislation. The veto power applies only to legislation across-the-board. If the President successfully vetoes legislation, none of it becomes law. If there is an impoundment power, by contrast, the President could sign a bill, thus permitting it to be enacted as law, but decline to carry out particular provisions. For example, he might sign a bill providing for various sorts of social spending but refuse to expend funds for a particular area of spending.

The argument on behalf of President Nixon's assertion of impoundment power included an assertion that "authority for the President to establish reserves is derived basically from the constitutional provisions which vest the executive power in the President. [Returning] now to the provisions of Article II, we believe the power to withhold appropriated funds is implicit in them." Hearings on Executive Impoundment of Appropriated Funds before the Subcommittee on Separation of Powers of the Senate Committee on the Judiciary, 92d Cong., 1st Sess. 95 (1971) (statement of OMB deputy director Casper Weinberger). This position led to a claim by President Nixon that if spending would result in "increasing prices or increasing taxes," there was constitutional authorization to impound. The claim was buttressed by reference to occasional assertions of impoundment power by previous presidents and considerations of policy.

But such statements were generally rejected by courts and commentators. See, e.g., Mikva & Hertz, Impoundment of Funds — the Courts, the Congress and the President: A Constitutional Triangle, 69 Nw. L. Rev. 335, 376-381 (1974):

> Although the Constitution does not expressly condemn impoundment, it contains no support for the practice and many provisions cast serious doubt on the legality of the practice. [The] power to repeal or nullify a law is a legislative power. Since impoundment in effect repeals a law, the President violates this provision when he withholds funds. [The] Constitution provides that the President "shall take Care that the Laws be faithfully executed." An appropriations act constitutes a law which the President must faithfully execute. [The] Constitution does not require the President to be a mere clerk, and his power to execute the laws must necessarily involve some discretion. However, to imply from this discretion a power so great as impoundment is to have the exception swallow the rule and to ignore the basic tenor of the Constitution. [*Youngstown*] repudiates the concept of inherent Executive powers. Although some of the opinions in the *Youngstown* case suggest that the President has inherent powers to cope with an emergency, it seems clear that an inflationary economy does not meet the requisite standard of crisis.

Do you agree with the President's claim that, at the level of policy, impoundment authority would be highly desirable? Would it promote or undermine the separation of powers? Consider in this regard the view of former Deputy Attorney General Sneed:

> Despite the statutory policy and fiscal necessity to protect purchasing power by avoiding intolerable inflation, the structure of Congress does not enable it to assume the executive responsibility for achieving this end. The harsh reality is that time and time again Congress has passed swollen appropriation acts and failed to levy the taxes necessary to avoid inflation. [Presidents] have been forced to resort to their veto power and, ultimately, to impounding of appropriations.

Statement before the Ad Hoc Subcommittee on Impoundment of Funds of the Senate Committee on Government Operations and the Subcommittee on Separation of Powers of the Senate Committee on the Judiciary, 93d Cong., 1st Sess. 364, 268 (1973). See generally Abascal & Kramer, Presidential Impoundment, 62 Geo. L.J. 1549 (1974); Note, Presidential Impoundment: Constitutional Theories and Political Realities, 61 Geo. L.J. 1295 (1973).

The Supreme Court has not resolved the legal issue. In Train v. New York, 420 U.S. 35 (1975), the Court rejected, as a matter of statutory construction, the President's claim that the Federal Water Pollution Control Act left the executive discretion to withhold funds. The Court concluded that Congress intended "to provide a firm commitment of substantial sums within a relatively limited period of time" and that it did not intend to undermine "the entire effort by providing the Executive with the seemingly limitless power to withhold funds from allotment and obligation." But the President did not assert his constitutional claim in the Supreme Court.

2. *Statutory resolution? A "framework statute."* Congress attempted to solve the impoundment controversy in the Congressional Budget and Impoundment

Control Act of 1974, 31 U.S.C. §§1400-1407. That statute contains provisions governing two kinds of impoundment. The first is deferral of budget authority, defined as delaying or withholding an expenditure for a period not to exceed one fiscal year. If the President proposes to undertake such a deferral, he is required to notify Congress. The proposal will take effect unless either house of Congress passes a resolution disapproving the proposal. (Consider the implications of INS v. Chadha, section C supra). The second kind of impoundment is a rescission of budget authority, defined as a decision that "all or part of any budget authority will not be required to carry out the full objectives or scope of programs." A proposal to rescind will not take effect unless, within forty-five days after notification, Congress has enacted "a rescission bill rescinding all or part of the amount proposed to be rescinded."

In practice, the act has largely resolved the impoundment controversy, at least thus far. There has been little litigation and the process seems to have worked through mutual accommodation between the President and Congress. For this reason, the act may be regarded as a "framework statute," Casper, Constitutional Constraints on the Conduct of Foreign and Defense Policy: A Nonjudicial Model, 43 U. Chi. L. Rev. 463, 482 (1976), designed by Congress and the President to operate as a foundation on which future decisions may be based. See also Dam, The American Fiscal Constitution, 44 U. Chi. L. Rev. 271 (1977), discussing various other "framework statutes" and describing them as "quasi-constitutional" rather than as ordinary legislation. See also the discussion of the War Powers Resolution, section E infra.

Construct an argument that the Impoundment Control Act is unconstitutional. Does the *Youngstown* decision strengthen or weaken that argument?

3. *Failure to enforce the law.* What if the President or a subordinate official in the executive branch refuses to enforce a particular law? Suppose the executive branch concludes that enforcement of an environmental statute would be detrimental to the nation and therefore enforces the statute very little or not at all. Traditional principles of prosecutorial discretion have allowed executive officials some leniency in deciding when and how to enforce the law. Courts have thus concluded that the exercise of prosecutorial discretion is sometimes unreviewable, occasionally referring to the "take Care" clause for support. See Heckler v. Chaney, — U.S. — , 105 S. Ct. 1649 (1985) (failure of Food and Drug Administration to regulate drugs used in human executions is not subject to judicial review under the Administrative Procedure Act). In this view, the separation of powers prohibits courts from ordering the executive to execute the laws. That power is vested in the President, not the federal courts. Would this position accord too much power to the presidency? Note that it would permit the President effectively to nullify, through nonenforcement, laws enacted by Congress — including those enacted over his veto. Are political checks a sufficient safeguard against this possibility?

In more recent years, courts have concluded that the executive branch is not authorized to refuse to enforce statutes and that such a refusal may in practice amount to an impermissible act of lawmaking subject to judicial correction. See, e.g., Adams v. Richardson, 480 F.2d 1159 (D.C. Cir. 1973); Nader v. Saxbe, 497 F.2d 676, 679 & n.18 (D.C. Cir. 1974). In this view, the "take Care" clause argues in precisely the opposite direction: it imposes on the President a duty to enforce the law and does not grant him discretion to enforce only those laws with which he agrees.

The Supreme Court has not had an opportunity to resolve the question. What light does *Youngstown*, or the impoundment controversy, cast on the problem? In Allen v. Wright, Chapter 1 supra, the Court said that more stringent standing requirements would be applied to those seeking to "restructure" executive branch operations by requiring law enforcement because "separation of powers" considerations argued against judicial requirements of law enforcement. Does this suggestion mean that even if the *Allen* plaintiffs had standing, the Court would have assumed a deferential posture, or stayed out altogether, on separation of powers grounds?

Note that no separation of powers problems are raised if a court orders the executive branch *not* to take action, so long as the order is based on a statutory or constitutional violation. If a statute or the Constitution requires the executive to act, why are separation of powers concerns any more powerful? Perhaps the answer lies in a libertarian conception of the role of courts, whose traditional role has been to fend off rather than to help bring about government intervention. To what extent can that conception be sustained in an era in which Congress often imposes affirmative obligations on the executive branch? Consider the implications of the rise and fall of *Lochner*, Chapter 6 infra.

4. *The separation of powers and the budget; alternatives.* Even if the President lacks impoundment authority, there can be little doubt that the case for structural provisions bringing about control of the budget is a serious one. Consider in this regard two possibilities. (a) A balanced budget amendment would require Congress to ensure that total outlays do not exceed total receipts. Would such a provision be desirable? How, if at all, would it differ from other structural provisions that can be found in the Constitution? Under what premises might such an amendment be defended? See Note, The Balanced Budget Amendment: An Inquiry into Appropriateness, 96 Harv. L. Rev. 1600 (1983). Consider the criticism that such a provision would import a controversial economic theory into the Constitution. (b) A statutory or constitutional provision would permit the President to veto any particular item in a proposed law or appropriation. Under the current scheme, the President is often confronted with the choice of approving of proposed laws as a whole or not at all. The "line-item" veto would permit him to veto particular appropriations or provisions. Would such a veto enhance or undermine the separation of powers? How would you compare such a presidential power with the authority (1) not to enforce laws or (2) to impound funds?

C. THE DISTRIBUTION OF NATIONAL POWERS IN AN ADMINISTRATIVE STATE

Note: The Nondelegation Doctrine

1. *Introduction.* Both *Youngstown* and the impoundment controversy reflect the conventional understanding that in the separation of powers scheme, the legislature, rather than the executive, makes the laws. The reason for this alloca-

tion of power is that the legislature is supposed to be peculiarly accountable to the public as a whole. Its distinctive sort of accountability, it is hoped, will operate as a guarantee against the effects of faction. (To what extent is that a realistic hope?)

But the conventional understanding — that the legislature is the exclusive lawmaker — no longer reflects reality. In every industrialized nation, administrative agencies, which are generally part of the executive branch, have been granted considerable lawmaking power. Congress has given such agencies regulatory authority, but often it offers them little guidance for the task. It has, for example, told agencies to regulate "unreasonable risks" to consumers and to promote "the public interest" in broadcasting regulation. The process of giving content to these vague standards — a process undertaken by the executive — can be understood only as one of lawmaking.

Why does Congress delegate broad discretionary power to administrative agencies? Consider the following possibilities: (1) Congress may know that there is a general problem but may be unaware of how to solve it. Administrators will have the necessary expertise. (2) The area may be one that changes rapidly. Congress may not want to freeze into law a solution that will become outmoded. (3) There are severe political costs to precise solutions of problems; no such costs attach if Congress merely identifies a problem and asks administrators to solve it. If the administrators fail, members of Congress may blame them. A broad delegation of authority thus allows Congress to claim the credit for identification of a problem while insulating it from attack if particular solutions exacerbate that problem. In particular, Congress may delegate lawmaking authority if the benefits extend to a broad and diffuse class. (Can you see why? Consider the discussion in Chapter 2 supra.) See, for general discussion, Stewart, The Reformation of American Administrative Law, 88 Harv. L. Rev. 1667 (1975); T. Lowi, The End of Liberalism (2d ed. 1977); Fiorina, Legislative Choice of Regulatory Forms: Legal Process or Administrative Process, 39 Pub. Choice 33 (1982).

What constraints does the Constitution impose on the delegation of congressional power to the executive branch? The current answer is: Very few. But it was not always so. Early on the Court made clear that article I, by vesting legislative power in Congress, imposed constraints on the national legislature's authority to delegate that power to others. Thus, for example, the Court stated that the applicable test was whether Congress has laid "down by legislative act an intelligible principle to which the person or body authorized to take action is directed to conform." J. W. Hampton, Jr. & Co. v. United States, 276 U.S. 394, 409 (1928).

This principle, sometimes known as the nondelegation doctrine, is intended to serve several functions. First, and foremost, it is supposed to ensure that the fundamental policy choices will be made by the legislature, and not by officials within the executive branch (who are thought to be less, or differently, accountable). Second, it promotes predictability for those benefited or burdened by regulation. Third, it tends to work against arbitrariness or caprice on the part of administrators because it cabins their discretion in the enforcement process. In the latter two respects, the nondelegation doctrine is intended to promote the rule of law.

2. *Panama Refining and* Schechter. The issues raised by the nondelegation doctrine came to a head in two cases involving legislation designed to ease the Depression during President Roosevelt's famous first "100 days." The National Industrial Recovery Act of 1933 (NIRA) attempted to permit representatives of

labor and management in each industry to meet and to design codes of "fair competition." The goal was to help stabilize wages and prices in order to stop the precipitous decline of both, thus restoring the confidence of industry and stabilizing the economy.

The act's declaration of policy referred to Congress's desire to promote cooperative action among trade groups, to maintain united action on the part of management and labor, to eliminate unfair competitive practices, to increase purchasing power and thus consumption of industrial and agricultural products, and to avoid undue restriction of production (except as may be temporarily required). The President was supposed to approve such codes if he made several findings, including (1) that there were "no inequitable restrictions on admission to membership" and (2) that the codes were not designed to promote monopoly or to oppress small enterprises.

In the first case decided under the NIRA, Panama Refining Co. v. Ryan, 293 U.S. 388 (1935), the Court invalidated a provision of the NIRA authorizing the President to prohibit, as part of a petroleum code, the transportation in interstate commerce of oil produced in violation of state-imposed production quotas. The Court emphasized that the statute did not supply standards that would tell the President when to exercise that power. In the Court's view, the NIRA authorized the President to prohibit transportation of "hot oil" whenever he chose.

The second case, Schechter Poultry Corp. v. United States, 295 U.S. 495 (1935), involved the "live poultry code," which contained maximum hour and minimum wage provisions and prohibited various practices said to be "unfair methods of competition." The code identified such practices in provisions that, among other things, (1) barred the sale of unfit chickens and (2) stated that buyers could not be allowed to select particular chickens but instead must "accept the run of any half coop, coop, or coops." Schechter Poultry was prosecuted for violating both of these provisions. It sought to invalidate the statute authorizing creation of the code on the ground that it was an impermissible delegation of legislative authority. The Court, unanimous on the point, said:

> The Congress is not permitted to abdicate or to transfer to others the essential legislative function with which it is thus vested. We have repeatedly recognized the necessity of adapting legislation to complex conditions involving a host of details with which the national legislature cannot deal directly. [The] Constitution has never been regarded as denying to Congress the necessary resources of flexibility and practicality, which will enable it to perform its function in laying down policies and establishing standards, while leaving to selected instrumentalities the making of subordinate rules within prescribed limits and the determination of facts to which the policy as declared by the legislature is to apply. But we said that the constant recognition of the necessity and validity of such provisions, and the wide range of administrative authority which has been developed by means of them cannot be allowed to obscure the limitations of the authority to delegate, if our constitutional system is to be maintained. . . .
>
> What is meant by "fair competition" as the term is used in the Act? Does it refer to a category established in the law, and is the authority to make codes limited accordingly? Or is it used as a convenient designation for whatever set of laws the formulators of a code for a particular trade or industry may propose and the President may approve [as] being wise and beneficient provisions for the government of the trade industry in order to accomplish the broad purposes of rehabilitation, correction and expansion which are stated in the first section of Title I? . . .

For a statement of the authorized objectives and content of the "codes of fair competition" we are referred repeatedly to the "Declaration of Policy" in Section 1 of Title 1 of the Recovery Act. [That] declaration embraces a broad range of objectives. . . .

Under Section 3, whatever "may tend to effectuate" these general purposes may be included in the codes of fair competition. [The] purpose is clearly disclosed to authorize new and controlling prohibitions through codes of laws which would embrace what the formulators would propose and what the President would approve, or prescribe, as wise and beneficent measures for the government of trade and industries in order to bring about their rehabilitation, correction and development, according to the general declaration of policy in section one. . . .

The Government urges that the codes will "consist of rules of competition deemed fair for each industry by representative members of that industry — by the persons most vitally concerned and most familiar with its problems." Instances are cited in which Congress has availed itself of such assistance; as, e.g., in the exercise of its authority over the public domain, with respect to the recognition of local customers or rules of miners as to mining claims, or, in matters of a more or less technical nature, as in designating the standard height of drawbars. But would it be seriously contended that Congress could delegate its legislative authority to trade or industrial associations or groups so as to empower them to enact the laws they deem to be wise and beneficent for the rehabilitation and expansion of their trade or industries? Could trade or industrial associations or groups be constituted legislative bodies for that purpose because such associations or groups are familiar with the problem of their enterprises? [Such] a delegation of legislative power is known to our law and is utterly inconsistent with the constitutional prerogatives and duties of Congress.

The President is required to find that the code is not "designed to promote monopolies or to eliminate or oppress small enterprises and will not operate to discriminate against them." [But] these restrictions leave virtually untouched the field of policy envisaged by Section 1. . . .

Section 3 of the Recovery Act is without precedent. It supplies no standards for any trade, industry or activity. [We] think that the code-making authority thus conferred is an unconstitutional delegation of legislative power.

To what extent did each of the following factors contribute to the result in *Schechter?* (1) The absence of a historical tradition by which to give content to the notion of "fair competition." (2) The fact that the delegation was made expressly to private groups, thus increasing the danger of capture of governmental power by faction. (3) The existence of open-ended and self-contradictory instructions in the statute. (4) The broad coverage of the statute, encompassing virtually all industries.

3. *The demise of the nondelegation doctrine.* The nondelegation doctrine has all but disappeared as a constraint on the delegation of authority to administrative agencies. Indeed, *Panama Refining* and *Schechter* are the only two decisions that have invalidated federal statutes on nondelegation grounds in the nation's history. Statutes authorizing regulation of "unreasonable risks" or of administrative action "in the public interest" appear immune from attack. See, for an example of the modern approach, Amalgamated Meat Cutters v. Connally, 337 F. Supp. 737 (D.D.C. 1971). In that case, the court upheld a statute authorizing the President to impose wage and price controls on the ground that implicit standards of "broad fairness and avoidance of gross inequity" were sufficient. The court referred in particular to the temporary character of the delegation, to the fact that the President could not discriminate unreasonably among industries, and to an im-

plicit requirement that the President come up with standards to limit his own discretion.

In general, the nondelegation doctrine is of little or no practical importance today. On rare occasions, the doctrine has been invoked as an aid to statutory construction: the fear of a broad delegation is a reason to construe administrative authority narrowly. See Industrial Union Department v. American Petroleum Institute, 448 U.S. 607 (1980) (plurality opinion) (narrowing authority of OSHA to regulate toxic substances in the workplace); National Cable Television Assn. v. United States, 415 U.S. 336 (1974) (narrowly construing fee-setting authority of federal agencies). Moreover, *Schechter* itself has not been overruled, and a massive delegation of authority of the sort involved in that case might be struck down today. But the doctrine has not been invoked in modern cases, notwithstanding the breadth of delegations to administrative agencies.

Should the nondelegation doctrine be revived? Some have recently suggested that it should be. Consider the following.

a. Justice Rehnquist attempted to use the doctrine in Industrial Union v. American Petroleum Institute, 448 U.S. 607 (1980), which involved the interpretation of the Occupational Safety and Health Act. Two provisions were relevant. The first defined occupational safety and health standards as those "reasonably necessary or appropriate to provide safe or healthful employment." The second required the Secretary of Labor to "set the standard which most adequately assures, to the extent feasible, on the basis of the best available evidence, that no employee will suffer material impairment of health." The plurality concluded that the "reasonably necessary or appropriate" language required the Secretary to show a "significant risk" before undertaking to regulate. But Justice Rehnquist would have decided the case on nondelegation grounds:

> We ought not to shy away from our judicial duty to invalidate unconstitutional delegations of legislative authority solely out of concern that we should thereby reinvigorate discredited constitutional doctrines of the pre-New Deal era. [If] we are ever to reshoulder the burden of ensuring that Congress itself make the critical policy decisions, these are surely the cases in which to do it. It is difficult to imagine a more obvious example of Congress simply avoiding a choice which was both fundamental for purposes of the statute and yet so politically divisive that the necessary decision or compromise was difficult, if not impossible, to hammer out in the legislative forge. [If] Congress wishes to legislate in an area which it has not previously sought to enter, it will in today's political world undoubtedly run into opposition no matter how the legislation is formulated. But that is the very essence of legislative authority under our system. It is the hard choices, and not the filling in of the blanks, which must be made by the elected representatives of the people. When fundamental policy decisions underlying important legislation about to be enacted are to be made, the buck stops with Congress and the President insofar as he exercises his constitutional role in the legislative process.

See also American Textile Manufacturers Institute v. Donovan, 452 U.S. 490, 543-548 (1981) (Rehnquist, J., joined by Burger, C.J., dissenting).

b. J. Ely, Democracy and Distrust 131-134 (1980):

> In theory it is the legislature that makes the laws and the administrators who apply them. Anyone who has seen Congress in action, however, [will] know that the actual situation is very nearly upside down. [There] can be little point in worrying about the

distribution of the franchise and other personal political rights unless the important policy choices are being made by elected officials. Courts thus should ensure not only that administrators follow those legislative policy directions that do exist [but] also that such directions are given. The reason this isn't a popular idea probably has mainly to do with its history, but sometimes reasons are given. One is that the world is a complicated and volatile place and therefore detailed legislative instructions would simply prove unworkable. To this two different answers seem appropriate. The first is that most legislatures, certainly the Congress, can call on staffs as expert as those the administrators have available, and that at least in the federal government they are also entitled to the assistance of the executive departments' technical staffs. The second and more fundamental answer is that the nondelegation doctrine, even at its high point, never insisted either on more detail than was feasible or that matters be settled with more permanence than the subject matter would allow. Policy direction is all that was ever required, and policy direction is what is lacking in much contemporary legislation.

c. Stewart, The Reformation of American Administrative Law, 88 Harv. L. Rev. 1667, 1695-1697 (1975):

In many government endeavors it may be impossible in the nature of the subject matter to specify with particularity the course to be followed. This is most obvious when a new field of regulation is undertaken. Administration is an exercise in experiment. [Constant] changes in the basic parameters of the problem may preclude the development of a detailed policy that can consistently be pursued for any length of time.

In addition, there appear to be serious institutional constraints on Congress' ability to specify regulatory policy in meaningful detail. Legislative majorities typically represent coalitions of interests that must not only compromise among themselves but also with opponents. Individual politicians often find far more to be lost than gained in taking a readily identifiable stand on a controversial issue of social or economic policy. Detailed legislative specification of policy would require intensive and continuous investigation, decision, and revision of specialized and complex issues. [Moreover,] quite apart from these factors, one may question whether a legislature is likely in many instances to generate more responsible decisions on questions of policy than agencies.

Finally, there are serious problems in relying upon the judiciary to enforce the nondelegation doctrine. [How] is the judge to decide the degree of policy specification that is possible, for example, in wage and price regulation when it is initially undertaken? [What] if the political situation is such that the legislative process cannot be made to yield any more detailed policy resolution? [Such] judgments are necessarily quite subjective, and a doctrine that made them determinative of an administrative program's legitimacy could cripple the program by exposing it to continuing threats of invalidation and encouraging the utmost recalcitrance by those opposed to its effectuation. Given such subjective standards, and the controversial character of decisions on whether to invalidate legislative delegations, such decisions will almost inevitably appear partisan, and might often be so.

d. Consider the following assessment of the "new" Constitution:

Article II. The separation of powers notwithstanding, the center of the national government is the presidency. Said office is authorized to use any powers, real or imagined, to set our nation to rights by making any rules or regulations the president deems appropriate; the president may subdelegate this authority to any other official or agency. . . .

Article III. Congress exists, but only as a consensual body. Congress possesses all legislative authority but should limit itself to the broad grants of unstructured authority to the President. . . .

Article IV. There exists a separate administrative branch composed of persons whose right to govern is based upon two principles: (1) the delegations of power flowing from Congress; and (2) the authority inherent in professional training and promotion through an administrative hierarchy. . . .

Article VII. [Actual] policymaking will not come from voter preferences or congressional enactments but from a process of tripartite bargaining between the specialized administrators, relevant members of Congress, and the representatives of self-interested organized interests.

T. Lowi, The End of Liberalism xi-xii (2d ed. 1979).

If the nondelegation doctrine is not revived, and if it proves impossible for Congress to set forth clear standards to govern decisions by administrative agencies, is there an alternative means by which Congress might reassert its original position as lawmaker? The following case deals with one possible method.

INS v. Chadha

462 U.S. 919 (1983)

CHIEF JUSTICE BURGER delivered the opinion of the Court.

Chadha is an East Indian who was born in Kenya and holds a British passport. He was lawfully admitted to the United States in 1966 on a nonimmigrant student visa. His visa expired on June 30, 1972. On October 11, 1973, the District Director of the Immigration and Naturalization Service ordered Chadha to show cause why he should not be deported for having "remained in the United States for a longer time than permitted." [After a hearing, an immigration judge ordered] that Chadha's deportation be suspended. The immigration judge found that Chadha met the requirements of [the statute]: he had resided continuously in the United States for over seven years, was of good moral character, and would suffer "extreme hardship" if deported.

Pursuant to [statute the] immigration judge suspended Chadha's deportation and a report of the suspension was transmitted to Congress.

Once the Attorney General's recommendation for suspension of Chadha's deportation was conveyed to Congress, Congress had the power under [statute to] veto the Attorney General's determination that Chadha should not be deported. . . .

On December 12, 1975, Representative Eilberg, Chairman of the Judiciary Subcommittee on Immigration, Citizenship, and International Law, introduced a resolution opposing "the granting of permanent residence in the United States to [six] aliens," including Chadha. [So] far as the record before us shows, the House consideration of the resolution was based on Representative Eilberg's statement from the floor that

> [i]t was the feeling of the committee, after reviewing 340 cases, that the aliens contained in the resolution [Chadha and five others] did not meet these statutory

requirements, particularly as it relates to hardship; and it is the opinion of the committee that their deportation should not be suspended.

The resolution was passed without debate or recorded vote.[3] Since the House action was pursuant to [the statute] the resolution was not treated as an Article I legislative act; it was not submitted to the Senate or presented to the President for his action.

After the House veto of the Attorney General's decision to allow Chadha to remain in the United States, the immigration judge reopened the deportation proceedings and [Chadha] was ordered deported pursuant to the House action. [Chadha] filed a petition for review of the deportation order in the United States Court of Appeals for the Ninth Circuit. The Immigration and Naturalization Service agreed with Chadha's position before the Court of Appeals and joined him in arguing that §244(c)(2) is unconstitutional. In light of the importance of the question, the Court of Appeals invited both the Senate and the House of Representatives to file briefs amici curiae.

After full briefing and oral argument, the Court of Appeals held that the House was without constitutional authority to order Chadha's deportation. [The] essence of its holding was that §244(c)(2) violates the constitutional doctrine of separation of powers. . . .

[The Court held that the case was justiciable.[13]]

3. It is not at all clear whether the House generally, or Subcommittee Chairman Eilberg in particular, correctly understood the relationship between H.R. Res. 926 and the Attorney General's decision to suspend Chadha's deportation. Exactly one year previous to the House veto of the Attorney General's decision in this case, Representative Eilberg introduced a similar resolution disapproving the Attorney General's suspension of deportation in the case of six other aliens. H.R. Res. 1518, 93d Cong., 2d Sess. The following colloquy occurred on the floor of the House:

> Mr. Wylie.   Mr. Speaker, further reserving the right to object, is this procedure to expedite the ongoing operations of the Department of Justice, as far as these people are concerned. Is it in any way contrary to whatever action the Attorney General has taken on the question of deportation; does the gentleman know?
>
> Mr. Eilberg.   Mr. Speaker, the answer is no to the gentleman's final question. These aliens have been found to be deportable and the Special Inquiry Officer's decision denying suspension of deportation has been reversed by the Board of Immigration Appeals. We are complying with the law since all of these decisions have been referred to us for approval or disapproval, and there are hundreds of cases in this category. In these six cases however, we believe it would be grossly improper to allow these people to acquire the status of permanent resident aliens.
>
> Mr. Wylie.   In other words, the gentleman has been working with the Attorney General's office?
>
> Mr. Eilberg.   Yes.
>
> Mr. Wylie.   This bill then is in fact a confirmation of what the Attorney General intends to do?
>
> Mr. Eilberg.   The gentleman is correct insofar as it relates to the determination of deportability which has been made by the Department of Justice in these cases.
>
> Mr. Wylie.   Mr. Speaker, I withdraw my reservation of objection.

120 Cong. Rec. 41412 (1974). Clearly, this was an obfuscation of the effect of a veto under §244(c)(2). Such a veto in no way constitutes "a confirmation of what the Attorney General intends to do." To the contrary, such a resolution was meant to overrule and set aside, or "veto," the Attorney General's determination that, in a particular case, cancellation of deportation would be appropriate under the standards set forth in §244(a)(1).

13. The suggestion is made that §244(c)(2) is somehow immunized from constitutional scrutiny because the Act containing §244(c)(2) was passed by Congress and approved by the President. [Marbury] resolved that question. The assent of the Executive to a bill which contains a provision contrary to the Constitution does not shield it from judicial review. In any event, eleven Presidents, from Mr. Wilson through Mr. Reagan, who have been presented with this issue have gone on record at some point to challenge Congressional vetoes as unconstitutional. . . .

We turn now to the question whether action of one House of Congress under §244(c)(2) violates strictures of the Constitution. [The] fact that a given law or procedure is efficient, convenient, and useful in facilitating functions of the government, standing alone, will not save it if it is contrary to the Constitution. Convenience and efficiency are not the primary objectives — or the hallmarks — of democratic government and our inquiry is sharpened rather than blunted by the fact that Congressional veto provisions are appearing with increasing frequency in statutes which delegate authority to executive and independent agencies:

> Since 1932, when the first veto provision was enacted into law, 295 congressional veto-type procedures have been inserted in 196 different statutes as follows: from 1932 to 1939, five statutes were affected; from 1940-49, nineteen statutes; between 1950-59, thirty-four statutes; and from 1960-69, forty-nine. From the year 1970 through 1975, at least one hundred sixty-three such provisions were included in eighty-nine laws.

Justice White undertakes to make a case for the proposition that the one-House veto is a useful "political invention." [But] policy arguments supporting even useful "political inventions" are subject to the demands of the Constitution which defines powers and, with respect to this subject, sets out just how those powers are to be exercised.

Explicit and unambiguous provisions of the Constitution prescribe and define the respective functions of the Congress and of the Executive in the legislative process. [Art.] I provides:

> All legislative Powers herein granted shall be vested in a Congress of the United States, which shall consist of a Senate *and* a House of Representatives.

Art. I, §1. (Emphasis added).

> Every Bill which shall have passed the House of Representatives and the Senate, *shall*, before it becomes a Law, be presented to the President of the United States; . . .

Art. I, §7, cl. 2. (Emphasis added).

> Every Order, Resolution, or Vote to which the Concurrence of the Senate and House of Representatives may be necessary (except on a question of Adjournment) *shall be* presented to the President of the United States; and before the Same shall take Effect, *shall be* approved by him, or being disapproved by him, *shall be* repassed by two thirds of the Senate and House of Representatives, according to the Rules and Limitations prescribed in the Case of a Bill.

Art. I, §7, cl. 3. (Emphasis added).

These provisions of Art. I are integral parts of the constitutional design for the separation of powers. . . .

The records of the Constitutional Convention reveal that the requirement that all legislation be presented to the President before becoming law was uniformly accepted by the Framers. . . .

The decision to provide the President with a limited and qualified power to nullify proposed legislation by veto was based on the profound conviction of the

Framers that the powers conferred on Congress were the powers to be most carefully circumscribed. [In] The Federalist No. 73 Hamilton focused on the President's role in making laws:

> If even no propensity had ever discovered itself in the legislative body to invade the rights of the Executive, the rules of just reasoning and theoretic propriety would of themselves teach us that the one ought not to be left to the mercy of the other, but ought to possess a constitutional and effectual power of self-defense.

The President's role in the lawmaking process also reflects the Framers' careful efforts to check whatever propensity a particular Congress might have to enact oppressive, improvident, or ill-considered measures. The President's veto role in the legislative process was described later during public debate on ratification:

> It establishes a salutary check upon the legislative body, calculated to guard the community against the effects of faction, precipitancy, or of any impulse unfriendly to the public good which may happen to influence a majority of that body. . . . The primary inducement to conferring the power in question upon the Executive is to enable him to defend himself; the secondary one is to increase the chances in favor of the community against the passing of bad laws through haste, inadvertence, or design.

The Federalist No. 73. [The] Court also has observed that the Presentment Clauses serve the important purpose of assuring that a "national" perspective is grafted on the legislative process:

> The President is a representative of the people just as the members of the Senate and of the House are, and it may be, at some times, on some subjects, that the President elected by all the people is rather more representative of them all than are the members of either body of the Legislature whose constituencies are local and not countrywide. . . .

The bicameral requirement of Art. I, §§1, 7 was of scarcely less concern to the Framers than was the Presidential veto and indeed the two concepts are interdependent. By providing that no law could take effect without the concurrence of the prescribed majority of the Members of both Houses, the Framers reemphasized their belief [that] legislation should not be enacted unless it has been carefully and fully considered by the Nation's elected officials. . . .

Hamilton argued that a Congress comprised of a single House was antithetical to the very purposes of the Constitution. Were the Nation to adopt a Constitution providing for only one legislative organ, he warned:

> we shall finally accumulate in a single body, all the most important prerogatives of sovereignty, and thus entail upon our posterity one of the most execrable forms of government that human infatuation ever contrived. Thus we should create in reality that very tyranny which the adversaries of the new Constitution either are, or affect to be, solicitous to avert.

The Federalist No. 22.

This view was rooted in a general skepticism regarding the fallibility of human nature. . . .

However familiar, it is useful to recall that apart from their fear that special interests could be favored at the expense of public needs, the Framers were also concerned, although not of one mind, over the apprehensions of the smaller states. Those states feared a commonality of interest among the larger states would work to their disadvantage; representatives of the larger states on the other hand were skeptical of a legislature that could pass laws favoring a minority of the people. [It] need hardly be repeated here that the Great Compromise, under which one House was viewed as representing the people and the other the states, allayed the fears of both the large and small states.

We see therefore that the Framers were acutely conscious that the bicameral requirement and the Presentment Clauses would serve essential constitutional functions. The President's participation in the legislative process was to protect the Executive Branch from Congress and to protect the whole people from improvident laws. The division of the Congress into two distinctive bodies assures that the legislative power would be exercised only after opportunity for full study and debate in separate settings. The President's unilateral veto power, in turn, was limited by the power of two thirds of both Houses of Congress to overrule a veto thereby precluding final arbitrary action of one person. [It] emerges clearly that the prescription for legislative action in Art. I, §§1, 7 represents the Framers' decision that the legislative power of the Federal government be exercised in accord with a single, finely wrought and exhaustively considered, procedure.

[When] the Executive acts, it presumptively acts in an executive or administrative capacity as defined in Art. II. And when, as here, one House of Congress purports to act, it is presumptively acting within its assigned sphere. Beginning with this presumption, we must nevertheless establish that the challenged action under §244(c)(2) is of the kind to which the procedural requirements of Art. I, §7 apply. Not every action taken by either House is subject to the bicameralism and presentment requirements of Art. I. [Whether] actions taken by either House are, in law and fact, an exercise of legislative power depends not on their form but upon "whether they contain matter which is properly to be regarded as legislative in its character and effect." . . .

Examination of the action taken here by one House [reveals] that it was essentially legislative in purpose and effect. In purporting to exercise power defined in Art. I, §8, cl. 4 to "establish an uniform Rule of Naturalization," the House took action that had the purpose and effect of altering the legal rights, duties and relations of persons, including the Attorney General, Executive Branch officials and Chadha, all outside the legislative branch. [The] one-House veto operated in this case to overrule the Attorney General and mandate Chadha's deportation; absent the House action, Chadha would remain in the United States. Congress has *acted* and its action has altered Chadha's status.

The legislative character of the one-House veto in this case is confirmed by the character of the Congressional action it supplants. Neither the House of Representatives nor the Senate contends that, absent the veto provision, [either] of them, or both of them acting together, could effectively require the Attorney General to deport an alien once the Attorney General, in the exercise of legislatively delegated authority,[16] had determined the alien should remain in the

16. Congress protests that affirming the Court of Appeals in this case will sanction "lawmaking by the Attorney General. . . ." [To] be sure, some administrative agency action — rule making, for example — may resemble "lawmaking." [This] Court has referred to agency activity as being "quasi-

United States. Without the challenged provision, [this] could have been achieved, if at all, only by legislation requiring deportation. . . .

The nature of the decision implemented by the one-House veto in this case further manifests its legislative character. After long experience with the clumsy, time consuming private bill procedure, Congress made a deliberate choice to delegate to the Executive Branch, [the] authority to allow deportable aliens to remain in this country in certain specified circumstances. It is not disputed that this choice to delegate authority is precisely the kind of decision that can be implemented only in accordance with the procedures set out in Art. I. Disagreement with the Attorney General's decision on Chadha's deportation — that is, Congress' decision to deport Chadha — no less than Congress' original choice to delegate to the Attorney General the authority to make that decision, involves determinations of policy that Congress can implement in only one way, bicameral passage followed by presentment to the President. Congress must abide by its delegation of authority until that delegation is legislatively altered or revoked.

Finally, we see that when the Framers intended to authorize either House of Congress to act alone and outside of its prescribed bicameral legislative role, they narrowly and precisely defined the procedure for such action. There are but four provisions in the Constitution, explicit and unambiguous, by which one House may act alone with the unreviewable force of law, not subject to the President's veto.

[The Court referred to the House's power to initiate impeachments, the Senate's power to impeach, the Senate's power over presidential appointments, and the Senate's power to ratify treaties.[21]]

---

legislative" in character. [Clearly,] however, "[i]n the framework of our Constitution, the President's power to see that the laws are faithfully executed refutes the idea that he is to be a lawmaker." [*Youngstown.*] When the Attorney General performs his duties pursuant to §244, he does not exercise "legislative" power. The bicameral process is not necessary as a check on the Executive's administration of the laws because his administrative activity cannot reach beyond the limits of the statute that created it — a statute duly enacted pursuant to Art. I, §§1, 7. The constitutionality of the Attorney General's execution of the authority delegated to him by §244 involves only a question of delegation doctrine. The courts, when a case or controversy arises, can always "ascertain whether the will of Congress has been obeyed," Yakus v. United States, 321 U.S. 414, 425, and can enforce adherence to statutory standards. See [*Youngstown.*] It is clear, therefore, that the Attorney General acts in his presumptively Art. II capacity when he administers the Immigration and Nationality Act. Executive action under legislatively delegated authority that might resemble "legislative" action in some respects is not subject to the approval of both Houses of Congress and the President for the reason that the Constitution does not so require. That kind of Executive action is always subject to check by the terms of the legislation that authorized it, and if that authority is exceeded it is open to judicial review as well as the power of Congress to modify or revoke the authority entirely. A one-House veto is clearly legislative in both character and effect and is not so checked; the need for the check provided by Art. I, §§1, 7 is therefore clear. Congress' authority to delegate portions of its power to administrative agencies provides no support for the argument that Congress can constitutionally control administration of the laws by way of a Congressional veto.

21. Justice Powell's position is that the one-House veto in this case is a *judicial* act, and therefore unconstitutional as beyond the authority vested in Congress by the Constitution. We agree that there is a sense in which one-House action pursuant to §244(c)(2) has a judicial cast, since it purports to "review" Executive action. [But] the attempted analogy between judicial action and the one-House veto is less than perfect. Federal courts do not enjoy a roving mandate to correct alleged excesses of administrative agencies; we are limited by Art. III to hearing cases and controversies and no justiciable case or controversy was presented by the Attorney General's decision to allow Chadha to remain in this country. We are aware of no decision [where] a federal court has reviewed a decision of the Attorney General suspending deportation of an alien pursuant to the standards set out in §244(a)(1). This is not surprising, given that no party to such action has either the motivation or the right to appeal from it. As Justice White correctly notes, "the courts have not been given the authority to

[These provisions give] further support for the conclusion that Congressional authority is not to be implied. . . .[22]

The choices we discern as having been made in the Constitutional Convention impose burdens on governmental processes that often seem clumsy, inefficient, even unworkable, but those hard choices were consciously made by men who had lived under a form of government that permitted arbitrary governmental acts to go unchecked. There is no support in the Constitution or decisions of this Court for the proposition that the cumbersomeness and delays often encountered in complying with explicit Constitutional standards may be avoided, either by the Congress or by the President. See [*Youngstown.*] With all the obvious flaws of delay, untidiness, and potential for abuse, we have not yet found a better way to preserve freedom than by making the exercise of power subject to the carefully crafted restraints spelled out in the Constitution.

We hold that the Congressional veto provision [is unconstitutional.] Accordingly, the judgment of the Court of Appeals is affirmed.

JUSTICE POWELL, concurring in the judgment.

On its face, the House's action appears clearly adjudicatory. The House did not enact a general rule; rather it made its own determination that six specific persons did not comply with certain statutory criteria. It thus undertook the type of decision that traditionally has been left to other branches.

The impropriety of the House's assumption of this function is confirmed by the fact that its action raises the very danger the Framers sought to avoid — the exercise of unchecked power. In deciding whether Chadha deserves to be deported, Congress is not subject to any internal constraints that prevent it from arbitrarily depriving him of the right to remain in this country. Unlike the judiciary or an administrative agency, Congress is not bound by established substantive rules. Nor is it subject to the procedural safeguards, such as the right to counsel and a hearing before an impartial tribunal, that are present when a court or an agency adjudicates individual rights. The only effective constraint on Congress' power is political, but Congress is most accountable politically when it prescribes rules of general applicability. When it decides rights of specific persons, those rights are subject to "the tyranny of a shifting majority."

[In] my view, when Congress undertook to apply its rules to Chadha, it exceeded the scope of its constitutionally prescribed authority. I would not reach the broader question whether legislative vetoes are invalid under the Presentment Clauses.

---

review whether an alien should be given permanent status; review is limited to whether the Attorney General has properly applied the statutory standards for" *denying* a request for suspension of deportation. [Thus,] Justice Powell's statement that the one-House veto in this case is "clearly adjudicatory," simply is not supported by his accompanying assertion that the House has "assumed a function ordinarily entrusted to the federal courts." We are satisfied that the one-House veto is legislative in purpose and effect and subject to the procedures set out in Art. I.

22. [Justice] White suggests that the Attorney General's action suspending deportation is equivalent to a *proposal* for legislation and that because Congressional approval is indicated "by failure to veto, the one-House veto satisfies the requirement of bicameral approval." [However,] as the Court of Appeals noted, that approach "would analogize the effect of the one house disapproval to the failure of one house to vote affirmatively on a private bill." Even if it were clear that Congress entertained such an arcane theory when it enacted §244(c)(2), which Justice White does not suggest, this would amount to nothing less than an amending of Art. I. The legislative steps outlined in Art. I are not empty formalities; they were designed to assure that both Houses of Congress and the President participate in the exercise of lawmaking authority.

JUSTICE WHITE, dissenting.

Today the Court not only invalidates §244(c)(2) of the Immigration and Nationality Act, but also sounds the death knoll for nearly 200 other statutory provisions in which Congress has reserved a "legislative veto." For this reason, the Court's decision is of surpassing importance. And it is for this reason that the Court would have been well-advised to decide the case, if possible, on the narrower grounds of separation of powers, leaving for full consideration the constitutionality of other congressional review statutes operating on such varied matters as war powers and agency rulemaking, some of which concern the independent regulatory agencies.

The prominence of the legislative veto mechanism in our contemporary political system and its importance to Congress can hardly be overstated. It has become a central means by which Congress secures the accountability of executive and independent agencies. Without the legislative veto, Congress is faced with a Hobson's choice: either to refrain from delegating the necessary authority, leaving itself with a hopeless task of writing laws with the requisite specificity to cover endless special circumstances across the entire policy landscape, or in the alternative, to abdicate its lawmaking function to the executive branch and independent agencies. To choose the former leaves major national problems unresolved; to opt for the latter risks unaccountable policymaking by those not elected to fill that role. Accordingly, over the past five decades, the legislative veto has been placed in nearly 200 statutes. The device is known in every field of governmental concern: reorganization, budgets, foreign affairs, war powers, and regulation of trade, safety, energy, the environment and the economy.

[Justice White summarized the history of the legislative veto, noting that it was a response to "the sprawling government structure" created after the depression; that it "balanced delegations of statutory authority in new areas," and that it played an important role in disputes in the 1970s over impoundment, war, and national emergency powers.]

Even this brief review suffices to demonstrate that the legislative veto [is an] important if not indispensable political invention that allows the President and Congress to resolve major constitutional and policy differences, assures the accountability of independent regulatory agencies, and preserves Congress' control over lawmaking. . . .

The history of the legislative veto also makes clear that it has not been a sword with which Congress has struck out to aggrandize itself at the expense of the other branches — the concerns of Madison and Hamilton. Rather, the veto has been a means of defense, a reservation of ultimate authority necessary if Congress is to fulfill its designated role under Article I as the nation's lawmaker. While the President has often objected to particular legislative vetoes, generally those left in the hands of congressional committees, the Executive has more often agreed to legislative review as the price for a broad delegation of authority. To be sure, the President may have preferred unrestricted power, but that could be precisely why Congress thought it essential to retain a check on the exercise of delegated authority. . . .

[The] Constitution does not directly authorize or prohibit the legislative veto. Thus, our task should be to determine whether the legislative veto is consistent with the purposes of Art. I and the principles of Separation of Powers. [We] should not find the lack of a specific constitutional authorization for the legislative veto surprising, and I would not infer disapproval of the mechanism from its absence. From the summer of 1787 to the present the government of the United States has become an endeavor far beyond the contemplation of the Framers. Only within the last half century has the complexity and size of the Federal Government's responsibilities grown so greatly that the Congress must rely on the legislative veto as the most effective if not the only means to insure their role as the nation's lawmakers. But the wisdom of the Framers was to anticipate that the nation would grow and new problems of governance would require different solutions. Accordingly, our Federal Government was intentionally chartered with the flexibility to respond to contemporary needs without losing sight of fundamental democratic principles. . . .

[The presentation and bicameralism requirements do] not [answer] the constitutional question before us. The power to exercise a legislative veto is not the power to write new law without bicameral approval or presidential consideration. The veto must be authorized by statute and may only negative what an Executive department or independent agency has proposed. On its face, the legislative veto no more allows one House of Congress to make law than does the presidential veto confer such power upon the President. Accordingly, the Court properly recognizes that it "must establish that the challenged action [is] of the kind to which the procedural requirements of Art. I, §7 apply". . . .

The terms of the Presentment Clauses suggest only that bills and their equivalent are subject to the requirements of bicameral passage and presentment to the President.

Although the Clause does not specify the actions for which the concurrence of both Houses is "necessary," the proceedings at the Philadelphia Convention suggest its purpose was to prevent Congress from circumventing the presentation requirement in the making of new legislation. . . .

When the Convention did turn its attention to the scope of Congress' lawmaking power, the Framers were expansive. The Necessary and Proper Clause, Art. I, §8, cl. 18, vests Congress with the power "to make all laws which shall be necessary and proper for carrying into Execution the foregoing Powers [the enumerated powers of §8], and all other Powers vested by this Constitution in the government of the United States, or in any Department or Officer thereof." It is long-settled that Congress may "exercise its best judgment in the selection of measures, to carry into execution the constitutional powers of the government," and "avail itself of experience, to exercise its reason, and to accommodate its legislation to circumstances." [*McCulloch.*]

The Court heeded this counsel in approving the modern administrative state. The Court's holding today that all legislative type action must be enacted through the lawmaking process ignores that legislative authority is routinely delegated to the Executive branch, to the independent regulatory agencies, and to private individuals and groups. "The rise of administrative bodies probably has been the most significant legal trend of the last century. . . . They have become a veritable fourth branch of the Government, which has deranged our three-branch legal theories. . . ."

This Court's decisions sanctioning such delegations make clear that Article I does not require all action with the effect of legislation to be passed as a law.

Theoretically, agencies and officials were asked only to "fill up the details," and the rule was that "Congress cannot delegate any part of its legislative power except under a limitation of a prescribed standard." In practice, however, restrictions on the scope of the power that could be delegated diminished and all but disappeared. . . .

The wisdom and the constitutionality of these broad delegations are matters that still have not been put to rest. But for present purposes, these cases establish that by virtue of congressional delegation, legislative power can be exercised by independent agencies and Executive departments without the passage of new legislation. For some time, the sheer amount of law — the substantive rules that regulate private conduct and direct the operation of government — made by the agencies has far outnumbered the lawmaking engaged in by Congress through the traditional process. There is no question but that agency rulemaking is law-making in any functional or realistic sense of the term.

If Congress may delegate lawmaking power to independent and executive agencies, it is most difficult to understand Article I as forbidding Congress from also reserving a check on Legislative power for itself. Absent the veto, the agencies receiving delegations of legislative or quasi-legislative power may issue regulations having the force of law without bicameral approval and without the President's signature. It is thus not apparent why the reservation of a veto over the exercise of that legislative power must be subject to a more exacting test. In both cases, it is enough that the initial statutory authorizations comply with the Article I requirements. . . .

Nor are there strict limits on the agents that may receive such delegations of legislative authority so that it might be said that the legislature can delegate authority to others but not to itself. While most authority to issue rules and regulations is given to the executive branch and the independent regulatory agencies, statutory delegations to private persons have also passed this Court's scrutiny. [More] fundamentally, even if the Court correctly characterizes the Attorney General's authority under §244 as an Article II Executive power, the Court concedes that certain administrative agency action, such as rulemaking, "may resemble lawmaking" and recognizes that "[t]his Court has referred to agency activity as being 'quasi-legislative' in character." [Such] rules and adjudications by the agencies meet the Court's own definition of legislative action for they "alter[] the legal rights, duties, and relations of persons . . . outside the legislative branch," and involve "determinations of policy." Under the Court's analysis, the Executive Branch and the independent agencies may make rules with the effect of law while Congress, in whom the Framers confided the legislative power, Art. I, §1, may not exercise a veto which precludes such rules from having operative force. If the effective functioning of a complex modern government requires the delegation of vast authority which, by virtue of its breadth, is legislative or "quasi-legislative" in character, I cannot accept that Article I — which is, after all, the source of the non-delegation doctrine — should forbid Congress from qualifying that grant with a legislative veto.

The Court also takes no account of perhaps the most relevant consideration: However resolutions of disapproval under §244(c)(2) are formally characterized, in reality, a departure from the status quo occurs only upon the concurrence of opinion among the House, Senate, and President. Reservations of legislative authority to be exercised by Congress should be upheld if the exercise of such reserved authority is consistent with the distribution of and limits upon legislative power that Article I provides. . . .

[JUSTICE WHITE argued that the veto "did not alter the division of actual authority between Congress and the executive," since a change in the alien's legal status could occur only with the concurrence of the President and both Houses. Thus the purposes of the presentation and bicameralism requirements were satisfied.]

[The] history of the separation of powers doctrine is also a history of accommodation and practicality. Apprehensions of an overly powerful branch have not led to undue prophylactic measures that handicap the effective working of the national government as a whole. The Constitution does not contemplate total separation of the three branches of Government.

[The] legislative veto provision does not "prevent the Executive Branch from accomplishing its constitutionally assigned functions." First, it is clear that the Executive Branch has no "constitutionally assigned" function of suspending the deportation of aliens. " 'Over no conceivable subject is the legislative power of Congress more complete than it is over' the admission of aliens." . . .

Moreover, the Court believes that the legislative veto [is] best characterized as an exercise of legislative or quasi-legislative authority. Under this characterization, the practice does not, even on the surface, constitute an infringement of executive or judicial prerogative. The Attorney General's suspension of deportation is equivalent to a proposal for legislation. . . .

Nor does §244 infringe on the judicial power, as Justice Powell would hold. Section 244 makes clear that Congress has reserved its own judgment as part of the statutory process. Congressional action does not substitute for judicial review of the Attorney General's decisions. . . .

I do not suggest that all legislative vetoes are necessarily consistent with separation of powers principles. A legislative check on an inherently executive function, for example that of initiating prosecutions, poses an entirely different question. But the legislative veto device here — and in many other settings — is far from an instance of legislative tyranny over the Executive. It is a necessary check on the unavoidably expanding power of the agencies, both executive and independent, as they engage in exercising authority delegated by Congress.

[The court's decision] reflects a profoundly different conception of the Constitution than that held by the Courts which sanctioned the modern administrative state. Today's decision strikes down in one fell swoop provisions in more laws enacted by Congress than the Court has cumulatively invalidated in its history. I fear it will now be more difficult "to insure that the fundamental policy decisions in our society will be made not by an appointed official but by the body immediately responsible to the people," Arizona v. California, 373 U.S. 546, 625 (1963)(Harlan, J., dissenting). I must dissent.

[JUSTICE REHNQUIST dissented on the ground that the legislative veto provision was not severable.]

Note: *The Separation of Powers and* Chadha

1. *Background.* The *Chadha* decision resolved a fifty-year dispute between Congress and the President. And it is important to understand that the legislative veto

has been used in many contexts. It was invoked during efforts to sell arms to Saudi Arabia, and a two-house veto was used to override an FTC rule requiring automobile dealers to disclose known defects in used cars to potential customers. The peculiar facts of *Chadha* — in which the veto was used in a relatively unattractive setting — should not obscure the possibility that the veto might serve important ends. Indeed, members of Congress urged that the legislative veto device was an indispensable means for the national legislature to reassert its proper role in the lawmaking process. Members of the executive branch responded that the legislative veto was an impermissible effort to bypass the requirements of article I. How does one explain the frequent insertion of the legislative veto in modern statutes, notwithstanding the constitutional controversy?

In the twentieth century, the delegation of power to administrative agencies has resulted in a dramatic increase in the power of the executive branch. In addition, many believe that the delegation of lawmaking power to the executive branch itself amounts to a circumvention of the article I safeguards for lawmaking, thus creating an increased risk of the usurpation of government power to distribute wealth or opportunities in favor of particular groups. In these circumstances, the legislative veto was in part an effort to respond to the danger of factionalism, and the increased power of the executive branch, by allowing Congress to exercise a supervisory role over regulatory decisions. At the same time, it was extremely attractive to members of Congress, who were often unwilling or unable to set out clear guidelines in statute but who were allowed, with the veto device, to exercise a powerful supervisory role without requiring the initial statement of standards to govern the exercise of discretion by administrators.

To some, however, the legislative veto did not reduce the dangers caused by the delegation of power to the executive branch, but instead increased them. Consider in this regard Bruff & Gellhorn, Congressional Control of Administrative Regulation: A Study of Legislative Vetoes, 90 Harv. L. Rev. 1369, 1417-1418 (1977):

> A primary purpose of the legislative veto is to increase the political accountability of administrative regulation. In theory, the veto power insures that agency rulemaking is consistent with the intent of Congress. Experience under existing vetoes, however, reveals that political accountability is likely to be attenuated in practice. [Much] settlement of policy occurred in behind-the-scenes negotiations between the staffs of the committees and the agencies. [The] "stacking" of oversight committees with members favorable to an agency or to the group it regulates is not unknown; this practice can forge agency-committee alliances which reinforce the capture of agencies by the interest groups they purport to regulate. Whenever it does not report a veto resolution to the floor of a house, the committee, with its narrow constituency, wields all of Congress' review power. In such a case, the ideal of The Federalist — national responsibility to a national constituency — is not achieved.

2. *Chadha in context: legislative control of the bureaucracy.* The legislative veto is one of a number of means by which Congress has attempted to control administrative agencies to which Congress has delegated substantial discretionary authority. For example, congressional committees or subcommittees might hold "oversight hearings," in which they call executive officials before them and question the officials about past and future conduct. Such hearings may produce considerable publicity and lead to pressure for changes in executive policy; on the

other hand, those pressures are entirely informal. A more formal mechanism is the appropriations rider — an attachment to an authorization of expenditure of federal funds that prohibits the agency from engaging in certain courses of conduct. Similarly, Congress may decrease or increase an agency's budget, in the annual appropriations process, in order to express its views on the mission of the agency and on whether more or less enforcement is desirable. Alternatively, Congress might enact "sunset" legislation, providing that agency authority will terminate after a certain period unless Congress reenacts the substantive statute. The most formal device is a repeal of agency authority, through ordinary legislation, to engage in a particular course of conduct. Even more extreme, Congress might rewrite the statute itself to limit agency authority. Congress has invoked all of these methods on various occasions.

How do these devices compare with the legislative veto? Do they suggest that the veto is in fact dispensable? For discussion, see Elliott, *INS v. Chadha:* The Constitution, The Administrative Constitution, and the Legislative Veto, 1983 Sup. Ct. Rev. 125, 156-160.

3. *The reach of* Chadha. Should the *Chadha* decision apply to *all* legislative vetoes? The case itself involved, as Justice Powell emphasized, an "adjudicatory" proceeding involving a single person. But in Process Gas Consumers Group v. Consumers Energy Council of America, 459 U.S. — , 103 S. Ct. 3556 (1983), the Court summarily affirmed, on the authority of *Chadha,* a decision invalidating a legislative veto as applied to certain Federal Energy Regulatory Commission regulations of natural gas pricing. See also U.S. Senate v. FTC, 459 U.S. — , 103 S. Ct. 3556 (1983) (summarily affirming decision invalidating legislative veto as applied to rulemaking by FTC). Both of these summary affirmances also involved independent agencies; the FTC case involved a "two-house veto," in which both houses of Congress must agree before the veto may become effective. The summary affirmances thus confirm Justice White's suggestion that the reach of the decision is quite broad.

Should the decision have been drawn more narrowly? In addition to Justice Powell's views, consider that the bill of attainder clause, article I, section 10, forbids laws that combine rulemaking and rule-applying functions by specifically tailoring sanctions to particular persons. The bill of attainder clause may thus be regarded as a separation of powers provision, ensuring a certain measure of generality in legislation. See United States v. Lovett, 328 U.S. 303 (1946). Was the bill of attainder clause applicable to *Chadha?* Some doubt is created by the fact that the relevant "sanction" was deportation, which may not amount to a declaration of guilt or a punishment that would trigger the clause.

4. *The veto and the separation of powers: general considerations.* What are the purposes of the presentation and bicameralism provisions? What is the relationship between those provisions and the general constitutional concern about the effects of faction? Consider how those provisions might be related to the other purposes of the distribution of national powers.

5. *The Court's approach.* Many commentators have been critical of the reasoning in *Chadha.* See, e.g., Elliott, *INS v. Chadha:* The Administrative Constitution, the Constitution, and the Legislative Veto, 1983 Sup. Ct. Rev. 125; Strauss, Was There a Baby in the Bathwater? A Comment on the Supreme Court's Legislative Veto Decision, 1983 Duke L.J. 789; Tribe, The Legislative Veto Decision: A Law by Any Other Name?, 21 Harv. J. Legis. 1 (1984). In their view, there is no

doubt that the bicameralism and presentation requirements are applicable to the enactment of a law. But the question in *Chadha* was whether the legislative veto was the sort of action to which those requirements were applicable. Congress does many things without being bound by the formal requirements for legislation: It holds hearings, engages in investigations, confirms presidential appointments, and so forth. Consider Strauss, supra, at 794: "The Chief Justice essentially overcomes this problem by assertion." Does anything in the Court's opinion help to solve the problem?

a. The Court refers to a "presumption" that action taken by the legislature is "legislative." See Elliott, supra, at 133:

> The Court's presumption sweeps in too much and proves too little. [The] Constitution does not require presentment to the President of all congressional actions within Article I legislative power. On the contrary, the text restricts presentment to "Bills" and to "Every Order, Resolution, or Vote to which the Concurrence of the Senate and House of Representatives may be necessary. . . ." The most that can be said about the drafting history is that the Constitutional Convention wanted the presentment requirement to apply to bills and to functional equivalents of bills. Not every exercise of Article I legislative power comes within these categories, as the Court concedes.

b. The Court argues that the veto "alters legal rights." Consider these responses. (1) Before Congress acted, Chadha had no "right" that could be altered. The only right at issue must be defined by reference to positive law — which included the legislative veto. Cf. the discussion of procedural due process, Chapter 6, infra. (2) Strauss, supra, argues that that fact "is no measure of legislative activity in the functional sense. Judicial activity also 'alter(s) [legal] rights.' [Executive] activity also has this effect. . . ."

c. The Court observes that "when the Framers intended to authorize either House of Congress to act alone and outside of its prescribed bicameral role, they narrowly and precisely defined the procedure for such action." Elliott, supra, argues that the use of this canon of construction — expressio unius est exclusio alterius — is an improper basis for constitutional interpretation. At most, he argues, it creates a weak inference "negated entirely if other circumstances show that the list of specifics was not intended to be exhaustive"; and conventional principles of constitutional interpretation counsel against attributing such an intent to the framers.

Would it be plausible to respond that the expressio unius argument is supported by structural arguments having to do with the framers' fear of factional tyranny? The bicameralism and presentation requirements, everyone agrees, were part of a general effort to ensure against the possibility that private groups would be able to use government power to distribute wealth or opportunities in their favor. The legislative veto might be regarded as a process by which that possibility was in fact increased. Consider in this regard the views of Bruff & Gellhorn, supra. How would an opinion emphasizing this rationale be written? Would it be preferable to the opinion the Court wrote?

d. Note that the Court has recognized that Congress may subpoena witnesses and indeed punish noncomplying witnesses for contempt. See McGrain v. Doherty, 273 U.S. 135 (1927). Do these holdings suggest that Congress may "affect legal rights" and yet not "legislate"? If so, are they inconsistent with *Chadha*?

6. *The necessary and proper clause.* Why does the Court reject the view that the necessary and proper clause justifies the legislative veto? Is it persuasive to suggest that just as the clause does not permit an infringement on a provision of the bill of rights, so it does not permit an infringement on the lawmaking provisions of article I?

7. *A return to the text?* *Chadha* might be understood as an effort to reassert an understanding of the text of the Constitution as more or less self-contained, with clear answers to at least some problems. The Court's opinion seems to assume that the text is itself dispositive of the constitutional question. Thus understood, the decision might fit within the category of "interpretivist" or "originalist" approaches to the Constitution, discussed above in Chapter 1. Consider in this regard Justice White's complaint that the Court's approach is inconsistent with its previous flexible attitude toward separation of powers disputes. If so, is the Court's analysis naive and mechanical? Or is it a salutary return to the text and underlying intent? In *Chadha*, what sort of guidance did text and intent in fact provide? Consider the view that in light of the enormous expansion of the bureaucracy, application of the framers' views on the distribution of national powers counseled in favor of, rather than against, the legislative veto arrangement.

8. *Future directions.* Whatever one thinks of *Chadha*, it seems clear that the rise of the administrative state is an important feature of the modern separation of powers scheme and that it has dramatic consequences for current thinking. The executive does not merely enforce the law but also makes it. What consequences should this have for the separation of powers?

What solutions are available for this problem? Consider, in addition to the options suggested supra pp. 382-383, the following possibilities. (a) "Report and wait" provisions. Congress might provide that before rules may become effective, they must be submitted to Congress to allow it an opportunity to legislate on the subject. The Federal Rules of Civil Procedure are already controlled by such provisions. Would they be constitutional after *Chadha*? (b) A statute might provide that no agency rule may become effective unless enacted by Congress with the participation of the President. Such a statute would convert administrative agencies largely into advisory bodies. What problems might arise with such a system? (c) Congress might provide that agency authority would "lapse" after a certain number of years, requiring a new statute to permit the agency to continue to exist. (d) Congress might provide that action pursuant to a certain statute be taken only if it is approved by both houses of Congress; such approval could consist of a joint resolution. Would such a measure be constitutional?

Note: Where Do Administrative Agencies "Fit" in the Separation of Powers Scheme?

1. *Introduction.* Article II vests the executive power in the President, not in subordinate officials. The decision to vest that power exclusively in the President was based on a rejection of the notion of a "plural executive." See The Federalist No. 70; E. Corwin, The President — Office and Powers 3-30 (1957). The decision

to create a unitary executive branch, headed by one person, can be thus understood in terms of the "efficiency" justification for the separation of powers scheme — that is, a justification that stresses the need to ensure expeditious, centralized, and coordinated authority in law enforcement.

But the Constitution does not explicitly resolve the question whether Congress may immunize subordinate officials from presidential control. Suppose, for example, that Congress provides that the Environmental Protection Agency, or the Civil Rights Commission, should do its work free from interference by the President. Would such a statute be constitutional under the necessary and proper clause? Would such a statute be inconsistent with the framers' decision to create a unitary executive and to vest all of the executive power in one person — the President? See Strauss, The Place of Agencies in Government: Separation of Powers and the Fourth Branch, 84 Colum. L. Rev. 452 (1984). The question is important, especially in an era in which lawmaking authority has been concentrated in executive officials.

There are very few cases on the problem. What guidance there is comes from three cases decided early in the days of the creation of administrative agencies.

2. Myers *and Presidential Supremacy.* Myers v. United States, 272 U.S. 52 (1926), involved a statute that provided that postmasters "shall be appointed and may be removed by the President and with the advice and consent of the Senate." President Wilson attempted to remove Myers, a postmaster appointed for a four-year term in Portland, Oregon, before the expiration of his term. The Court, in an opinion by Chief Justice (and former President) Taft, held that the removal was lawful because the attempted limitation on the President's removal power was unconstitutional under article II. The Court relied on several conclusions: (1) the act of removal is itself executive in nature and must therefore be performed by the President; (2) under the "take Care" clause, it is the President, not his subordinates, who must take care that the laws be faithfully executed; and (3) article II vests executive power in the President, not subordinate officials. The Court explained:

> Made responsible under the Constitution for the effective enforcement of the law, the President needs as an indispensable aid to meet it the disciplinary influence upon those who act under him of a reserve power of removal. [The] highest and most important duties which his subordinates perform are those in which they act for him. In such cases they are exercising not their own but his discretion. . . .
>
> In all such cases, the discretion to be exercised is that of the President in determining the national public interest and in directing the action to be taken by his executive subordinates to protect it. [To] require him to file charges and submit them to the consideration of the Senate might make impossible that unity and co-ordination in executive administration essential to effective action. . . .
>
> The ordinary duties of officers prescribed by statute come under the general administrative control of the President by virtue of the general grant to him of the executive power, and he may properly supervise and guide their construction of the statutes under which they act in order to secure that unitary and uniform execution of the laws which Article II of the Constitution evidently contemplated in vesting general executive power in the President alone.

Justices Holmes, Brandeis, and McReynolds dissented. Justice Holmes wrote: "We have to deal with an office that owes its existence to Congress and that

Congress may abolish tomorrow. [With] such power over its own creation, I have no more trouble in believing that Congress has power to prescribe a term of life for it free from any interference than I have in accepting the undoubted power of Congress to decree its end."

Under *Myers*, are the civil services statutes — immunizing lower-level federal officials from power to discharge "at will" — constitutionally acceptable? If so, is it because such officials are not "officers of the United States"; see Buckley v. Valeo, infra? Consider the view that *Myers* is satisfied so long as the official who is in charge of the basic chain of command is subject to presidential control.

3. Humphrey's Executor, Wiener, *and the rise of "independent" agencies.* Humphrey's Executor v. United States, 295 U.S. 602 (1935), involved a statute providing that members of the Federal Trade Commission could be "removed by the President for inefficiency, neglect of duty, or malfeasance in office." The history of the statute indicated that the legislative goal was to entrust regulatory decisions to a body of nonpartisan "experts," insulated from political pressures. President Roosevelt removed Humphrey from office, contending not that removal was justified by one of the statutory conditions but that the limitation of the removal power was unconstitutional under *Myers*. In short, President Roosevelt urged that any subordinate official served, by virtue of article II as interpreted in *Myers*, at the pleasure of the President. A unanimous Court disagreed, distinguishing and confining the reach of *Myers*:

> The office of a postmaster is so essentially unlike the office now involved that the decision in the *Myers* case cannot be accepted as controlling our decision here. A postmaster is an executive officer restricted to the performance of executive functions. He is charged with no duty at all related to either the legislative or judicial power. The actual decision in the *Myers* case finds support in the theory that such an officer is merely one of the units in the executive department and, hence, inherently subject to the exclusive and illimitable power of removal by the Chief Executive, whose subordinate and aid he is. [The] necessary reach of the decision goes far enough to include all purely executive officers. It goes no farther; much less does it include an officer who occupies no place in the executive department and who exercises no part of the executive power vested by the Constitution in the President.
>
> The Federal Trade Commission is an administrative body created by Congress to carry into effect legislative policies embodied in the statute in accordance with the legislative standard therein prescribed, and to perform other specified duties as a legislative or as a judicial aid. Such a body cannot in any proper sense be characterized as an arm or an eye of the executive. Its duties are performed without executive leave and, in the contemplation of the statute, must be free from executive control. [The] Commission acts in part quasi-legislatively and in part quasi-judicially. . . .
>
> The *Myers* decision, affirming the power of the President alone to make the removal, is confined to purely executive officers; and as to officers of the kind here under consideration, we hold that no removal can be made during the prescribed term for which the officer is appointed, except for one or more of the causes named in the applicable statute.

Wiener v. United States, 357 U.S. 349 (1958), involved the War Claims Commission, an adjudicatory body created by Congress to resolve disputed claims arising out of World War II. The statute was silent on the question of presidential removal power. The Court concluded that because of the adjudicatory nature of the Commission's decisions, there was an implicit limitation on the President's power to remove. Plenary removal authority would, in the Court's view, be inconsistent with the statutory purpose.

Humphrey's Executor and *Wiener* recognize a congressional power to create "independent" agencies — governmental entities that are free from presidential removal power and, to some uncertain degree, presidential power to supervise and control the decisions of their officers. The Federal Trade Commission, the Federal Energy Regulatory Commission, and the Federal Communications Commission are examples of independent agencies.

4. *Answered and unanswered questions: the continuing debate.* Myers, *Humphrey's Executor*, and *Wiener* leave many questions open, but this much is clear. The critical line is between executive agencies, which are subject to full presidential removal power and to considerable presidential control, and "independent" agencies, which can be insulated from full presidential removal power and from full presidential control. In order to qualify as an "independent" agency, the agency in question must (a) perform "quasi-legislative" or "quasi-judicial" functions and (b) be protected by a statutory provision (or an implicit decision by Congress) that insulates the agency from removal at the pleasure of the president. "Quasi-judicial" functions are those that are adjudicative in nature; many administrative agencies perform such functions. "Quasi-legislative" functions apparently include investigating duties to aid lawmaking and perhaps administrative rulemaking — the process by which administrative agencies make general rules to govern diverse factual situations and many persons.

Myers and *Humphrey's Executor* are concerned with the removal power. They do not speak directly to the question of presidential control of administrative agencies. But the decisions do have implications for the question of presidential control. The power to remove may well imply the power to control. Thus it is generally agreed that the executive agencies are subject to considerable presidential supervisory power. The independent agencies are more insulated and sometimes feel free to ignore the will of the President. For general discussion, see Bruff, Presidential Power and Administrative Rulemaking, 88 Yale L.J. 451 (1978); Strauss, supra.

Consider the following assessments of *Myers* and *Humphrey's Executor*:

a. *Humphrey's Executor* creates a "headless fourth branch" of government subject to the control of none of the three constitutionally recognized branches. There is no constitutional basis for administrative agencies exercising power without presidential supervision. That was the lesson of *Myers*, which was a correct reading of article II. The references in *Humphrey's Executor* to quasi-legislative and quasi-judicial functions are confused and confusing. Ever since the Constitution was enacted, agencies have engaged in rulemaking; and rulemaking, within the bounds set up by statute, is execution of the law, not "quasi-legislation." If it is not execution — if it is really lawmaking — it cannot constitutionally be done by administrative agencies. The same goes for quasi-judicial functions. *Humphrey's Executor* should be overruled.

b. *Humphrey's Executor* was a necessary response to the growth of administrative agencies and the grant of legislative and judicial functions to those agencies. If the delegation of those powers were permitted, and if those powers were to be exercised by the President, the system of separation of powers would be skewed in favor of the executive branch. *Humphrey's Executor*, in short, was a necessary quid pro quo for the downfall of the nondelegation doctrine. Moreover, the growth of administrative agencies was at least in part a response to a belief that it was important to vest regulatory power in nonpartisan experts. That goal would be defeated if the President has plenary power of removal and control. Finally, it is impossible merely to "apply" the framers' decision to create a unitary executive in an administrative era, in which extraordinary lawmaking power is conferred on regulatory agencies. To conclude that such agencies must be subject to executive control would create a further imbalance in the constitutional scheme. *Humphrey's Executor* implements that scheme more faithfully than does *Myers*.

c. The *Myers* decision is a conceptual anachronism. It is based on an outmoded understanding of the separation of powers scheme. The grant of "executive power" to the President, and the rejection of a plural executive, will not bear the weight that the Court put on them. When Congress creates a subordinate body, it is under no obligation to make its members subject to presidential control. Such a result would produce an unduly powerful executive branch.

Buckley v. Valeo

424 U.S. 1 (1976)

[A suit was brought challenging the Federal Election Campaign Act of 1971, as amended in 1974. The plaintiffs' attack raised numerous constitutional issues. The act created an eight-member Federal Election Commission to oversee federal elections. The Commission was authorized to investigate, to maintain records, to make rules governing federal elections, and to impose sanctions on those who violated the act and its own regulations.

The Commission was constituted as follows. The Secretary of the Senate and the Clerk of the House of Representatives were ex officio members, not having the right to vote. Two members were appointed by the President pro tempore of the Senate "upon the recommendation of the majority leader of the Senate and the minority leader of the Senate." Two were appointed by the Speaker of the House, also on recommendation of the majority and minority leaders. The remaining two members were appointed by the President. Each of the six voting members had to be confirmed by a majority of the House and Senate. Each of the three appointing authorities was barred from choosing both appointees from the same political party. The following excerpts deal with separation of powers attacks on the Commission, which the lower Court rejected.]

Appellants urge that since Congress has given the Commission wide-ranging rulemaking and enforcement powers with respect to the substantive provisions of the Act, Congress is precluded under the principle of separation of powers from vesting in itself the authority to appoint those who will exercise such authority. Their argument is based on the language of Art. II, §2, cl. 2, of the Constitution, which provides in pertinent part as follows:

[The President] shall nominate, and by and with the Advice and Consent of the Senate, shall appoint . . . all other Officers of the United States, whose Appointments are not herein otherwise provided for, and which shall be established by Law: but the Congress may by Law vest the Appointment of such inferior Officers, as they think proper, in the President alone, in the Courts of Law, or in the Heads of Departments.

[The] further concern of the Framers of the Constitution with maintenance of the separation of powers is found in the so-called "Ineligibility" and "Incompatibility" Clauses contained in Art. I, §6:

> No Senator or Representative shall, during the Time for which he was elected, be appointed to any civil Office under the Authority of the United States, which shall have been created, or the Emoluments whereof shall have been encreased during such time; and no Person holding any Office under the United States, shall be a Member of either House during his Continuance in Office.

[The] Appointments Clause could, of course, be read as merely dealing with etiquette or protocol in describing "Officers of the United States," but the drafters had a less frivolous purpose in mind. [We] think that the term "Officers of the United States" as used in Art. II, [is] a term intended to have substantive meaning. We think its fair import is that any appointee exercising significant authority pursuant to the laws of the United States is an "Officer of the United States," and must, therefore, be appointed in the manner prescribed by §2, cl. 2, of that Article. . . .

Although two members of the Commission are initially selected by the President, his nominations are subject to confirmation not merely by the Senate, but by the House of Representatives as well. The remaining four voting members of the Commission are appointed by the President pro tempore of the Senate and by the Speaker of the House. While the second part of the Clause authorizes Congress to vest the appointment of the officers described in that part in "the Courts of Law, or in the Heads of Departments," neither the Speaker of the House nor the President pro tempore of the Senate comes within this language.

The phrase "Heads of Departments," used as it is in conjunction with the phrase "Courts of Law," suggests that the Departments referred to are themselves in the Executive Branch or at least have some connection with that branch. While the Clause expressly authorizes Congress to vest the appointment of certain officers in the "Courts of Law," the absence of similar language to include Congress must mean that neither Congress nor its officers were included within the language "Heads of Departments" in this part of cl. 2.

Thus with respect to four of the six voting members of the Commission, neither the President, the head of any department, nor the Judiciary has any voice in their selection.

The Appointments Clause specifies the method of appointment only for "Officers of the United States" whose appointment is not "otherwise provided for" in the Constitution. But there is no provision of the Constitution remotely providing any alternative means for the selection of the members of the Commission or for anybody like them. . . .

The position that because Congress has been given explicit and plenary authority to regulate a field of activity, it must therefore have the power to appoint those who are to administer the regulatory statute is both novel and contrary to the language of the Appointments Clause. . . .

Appellee Commission [contends] that whatever shortcomings the provisions for the appointment of members of the Commission might have under Art. II, Congress had ample authority under the Necessary and Proper Clause of Art. I to effectuate this result. We do not agree. The proper inquiry when considering the Necessary and Proper Clause is not the authority of Congress to create an office or a commission, which is broad indeed, but rather its authority to provide that its own officers may make appointments to such office or commission.

So framed, the claim that Congress may provide for this manner of appointment under the Necessary and Proper Clause of Art. I stands on no better footing than the claim that it may provide for such manner of appointment because of its substantive authority to regulate federal elections. Congress could not, merely because it concluded that such a measure was "necessary and proper" to the discharge of its substantive legislative authority, pass a bill of attainder or ex post facto law contrary to the prohibitions contained in §9 of Art. I. No more may it vest in itself, or in its officers, the authority to appoint officers of the United States when the Appointments Clause by clear implication prohibits it from doing so. . . .

Thus, on the assumption that all of the powers granted in the statute may be exercised by an agency whose members *have been* appointed in accordance with the Appointments Clause, the ultimate question is which, if any, of those powers may be exercised by the present voting Commissioners, none of whom *was* appointed as provided by that Clause. . . .

[The] Commission's powers fall generally into three categories: functions relating to the flow of necessary information — receipt, dissemination, and investigation; functions with respect to the Commission's task of fleshing out the statute — rulemaking and advisory opinions; and functions necessary to ensure compliance with the statute and rules — informal procedures, administrative determinations and hearings, and civil suits.

Insofar as the powers confided in the Commission are essentially of an investigative and informative nature, falling in the same general category as those powers which Congress might delegate to one of its own committees, there can be no question that the Commission as presently constituted may exercise them. . . .

But when we go beyond this type of authority to the more substantial powers exercised by the Commission, we reach a different result. The Commission's enforcement power, exemplified by its discretionary power to seek judicial relief, is authority that cannot possibly be regarded as merely in aid of the legislative function of Congress. A lawsuit is the ultimate remedy for a breach of the law, and it is to the President, and not to the Congress, that the Constitution entrusts the responsibility to "take Care that the Laws be faithfully executed." Art. II, §3.

Congress may undoubtedly under the Necessary and Proper Clause create "offices" in the generic sense and provide such method of appointment to those "offices" as it chooses. But Congress' power under that Clause is inevitably bounded by the express language of Art. II, §2, cl. 2, and unless the method it provides comports with the latter, the holders of those offices will not be "Officers of the United States." They may, therefore, properly perform duties only in aid of those functions that Congress may carry out by itself, or in an area sufficiently removed from the administration and enforcement of the public law as to permit their being performed by persons not "Officers of the United States."

We hold that these provisions of the Act, vesting in the Commission primary responsibility for conducting civil litigation in the courts of the United States for vindicating public rights, violate Art. II, §2, cl. 2, of the Constitution. Such functions may be discharged only by persons who are "Officers of the United States" within the language of that section.

All aspects of the Act are brought within the Commission's broad administrative powers: rulemaking, advisory opinions, and determinations of eligibility for funds and even for federal elective office itself. These functions, exercised free from day-to-day supervision of either Congress or the Executive Branch, are more legislative and judicial in nature than are the Commission's enforcement powers, and are of kinds usually performed by independent regulatory agencies or by some department in the Executive Branch under the direction of an Act of Congress. Congress viewed these broad powers as essential to effective and impartial administration of the entire substantive framework of the Act. Yet each of these functions also represents the performance of a significant governmental duty exercised pursuant to a public law. While the President may not insist that such functions be delegated to an appointee of his removable at will, [*Humphrey's Executor*], none of them operates merely in aid of congressional authority to legislate or is sufficiently removed from the administration and enforcement of public law to allow it to be performed by the present Commission. These administrative functions may therefore be exercised only by persons who are "Officers of the United States."

[Reversed.]

Note: The Appointments Clause

1. *In general.* The appointments and incompatibility clauses should be understood in relation to the general purposes of the distribution of national powers. Note that both clauses tend to promote the goal of a unitary executive and at the same time to guard against concentration of the executive and legislative powers in the same hands.

2. Buckley's *holding.* The Court defines "officers of the United States" — who must be appointed by the President — to include all those performing "a significant governmental duty exercised pursuant to a public law." This holding is an extremely important one, for it prevents Congress from vesting in itself the power to appoint subordinate officials. Frequently members of Congress introduce legislation designed to create administrative agencies whose membership would be determined, in whole or in part, by Congress or some subgroup thereof. Congress might, for example, seek some authority to appoint members of a commission that would oversee presidential behavior. *Buckley* appears to forbid such arrangements. What separation of powers goals are promoted by this conclusion?

3. *Appointments by those outside the executive branch?* Despite the foregoing, under the Constitution Congress is still permitted, in at least some circumstances, to vest the appointment power in "the courts of law." What is the meaning of this provision? There are two leading cases. Ex parte Hennen, 38 U.S. 230 (1839), involved a congressional decision to assign to the federal courts the power to appoint judicial clerks. The court stated that the "appointing power here designated, in the latter part of the section was no doubt intended to be exercised by

the department of the government to which the officer to be appointed most appropriately belonged. The appointment of clerks of Courts properly belongs to the Courts of law. . . ." This language appears to suggest that the appointment power can be vested in the courts only with respect to judicial duties.

Ex parte Siebold, 100 U.S. 371 (1879), involved a statute calling for the creation of a board of election commissioners to oversee certain elections. The commissioners were appointed by federal judges. The Court rejected the argument that "no power can be conferred upon the courts of the United States to appoint officers whose duties are not connected with the judicial department of the government":

> It is no doubt usual and proper to vest the appointment of inferior officers in that department of the government (to) which the duties of such officers appertain. But there is no absolute requirement to that effect in the Constitution; and if there were, it would be difficult in many cases to determine to which department an office properly belonged. . . .
>
> As the Constitution stands, the selection of the appointing power, as between the functionaries named, is a matter resting in the discretion of Congress. [The] observation in the case of Hennen [was] not intended to define the constitutional power of Congress in this regard, but rather to express the law or rule by which it should be governed. [It] cannot be affirmed that the appointment of the officers in question could, with any greater impropriety, and certainly not with equal regard to convenience, have been assigned to any other depository of official power capable of exercising it.

What limitations, if any, on the appointment power does this suggest?

4. *The Special Prosecutor Act.* Consider the constitutionality of the Special Prosecutor Act, 28 U.S.C. §§591 et seq. The act, passed in the aftermath of the Watergate scandal, is designed to allow for prosecution, by an "independent counsel," of certain high-level government officials. The act is triggered "whenever the Attorney General receives information sufficient to constitute grounds to investigate that any of [the enumerated officials] has committed a violation of any Federal law [subject to various exceptions]." The enumerated officials include the President, the Vice President, assistant attorneys general in the Department of Justice, various people working in the Executive Office of the President, the director and deputy director of Central Intelligence, and the Commissioner of Internal Revenue.

If the Attorney General finds "no reasonable grounds to believe that further investigation or prosecution is warranted," the matter is terminated. If the Attorney General conducts such an investigation and finds "reasonable grounds to believe that further investigation or prosecution is warranted," then the Attorney General must apply to a district court for appointment, by the court, of a special prosecutor. The court is also authorized to define the prosecutorial jurisdiction of the special prosecutor. The special prosecutor in turn has "with respect to all matters" in the counsel's "prosecutorial jurisdiction, full power and independent authority to exercise all investigative functions and powers of the Department of Justice [and] the Attorney General." The independent counsel may be removed by impeachment and by the Attorney General "only for good cause, physical disability, mental incapacity, or any other condition that substantially impairs the performance of such independent counsel's duties."

The purpose of the act is to ensure that someone largely independent of the executive branch — appointed by the court and removable only in limited circumstances — will be entrusted with the duty of prosecuting high-level executive branch officials. Independence, it is thought, will avoid the appearance and the reality of a conflict of interest. But is the act constitutional? In the Carter administration, the Justice Department concluded that it was; in the Reagan administration during the early 1980s, Attorney General William French Smith expressed doubts.

Defenders of the statute contend that it is authorized by the provision allowing vesting of the appointment power in the "courts of law." The *Siebold* case is said to be especially relevant here. Those who attack the statute claim that special prosecutors exercise "significant governmental duties pursuant to a public law," that their functions are quintessentially executive, and that they must therefore be appointed (and subject to removal) by the President. Who is right? Consider also the constitutionality of proposals, set forth during the Watergate era, to create a Department of Justice that would be independent of the President.

5. *The Civil Rights Commission controversy.* Issues involved in both *Buckley* and *Myers* were raised when President Reagan announced on May 26, 1983, that he planned to replace three commissioners on the Civil Rights Commission with nominees reflecting the President's opposition to school busing and racial quotas. The Commission was established in 1957 as an investigatory and reportorial entity, examining private and government policies on civil rights. The agency, which has no formal enforcement powers, evaluates civil rights measures and reports recommendations to Congress and the public. (Were the commissioners "officers of the United States" under *Buckley*?) The original legislation located the Commission "in the executive branch." The Commission was to expire in September 1983, unless Congress extended its life with new legislation, as it had done several times in the past.

President Reagan's attempt to discharge the commissioners in favor of his own appointees came in the aftermath of criticism by the Commission of President Reagan's policies; the President claimed that such criticism amounted to an unjustified vendetta. Congress delayed the President's replacement effort, contending that it undermined the independence of the agency. Could one argue, on the basis of *Wiener*, that the effort to discharge the commissioners was unlawful?

After President Reagan's announcement, the Commission became the focus of a heated political battle. On August 4, the House passed a bill designed to expand the Commission and to insulate it from political control by the President. Hours before the Senate was to consider the bill on October 25, President Reagan formally fired the three commissioners. Two commissioners appointed by President Carter filed suit in a district court to restrain the President's order, citing *Humphrey's Executor* and *Wierner*. Experts had testified before Congress that the case was controlled by *Myers*; but a district court held for the plaintiffs, concluding that the commissioners could not be removed at the pleasure of the President. On November 30, while the expired Commission was in its sixty-day "winding down" period awaiting new legislation, Congress ratified Public Law 98-183 in a compromise to revitalize the Commission. New provisions in the act, 42 U.S.C. §1975, took the Commission out of the executive branch, allowing four appointments from the President and two each from the House and Senate. (Is this arrangement permissible under *Buckley*?) In addition, commissioners could only be removed from their staggered six-year terms for neglect of duty or malfeasance in office. The compromise also reinstated the three discharged commissioners.

A footnote: In December of 1983, the administration refused to adhere to an unofficial agreement to appoint an agreed-on person as a commissioner. This unofficial understanding had been an important feature of the November 30th compromise. The result was that President Reagan obtained a five-member majority on the Commission.

Does this incident support or undermine the proposition that institutional safeguards are sufficient to resolve separation of powers controversies?

D. LEGISLATIVE AND EXECUTIVE IMMUNITIES: IMPEACHMENT

Note: The Speech or Debate Clause

1. *In general*. The speech or debate clause provides that senators and representatives "shall not be questioned in any other place" for "any speech or debate in either house." It is the only explicit immunity provision in the Constitution.

Why would the framers grant immunity to members of Congress for any "speech or debate in either house"? Two general purposes can be identified. First, the clause ensures legislators that they will not be called into court in order to defend acts undertaken in their legislative capacities. This protection might be thought necessary to protect legislators against a possibly hostile judiciary that might be influenced in its deliberations by its views about the representatives in question. More generally, the immunity ensures against distraction of legislators or an undue "chilling effect" on candid debate in the performance of legislative functions. The immunity guarantees legislators that they may say whatever they want, free from legal scrutiny. The remedies are political rather than legal.

Second, the clause blocks efforts by the executive to use grand jury investigations and criminal prosecutions in order to call into question legislative acts. In this respect, the clause serves an important separation of powers function by protecting legislators from politically motivated prosecutions. The prosecutorial power of the executive is, by virtue of the clause, rendered unavailable as a weapon in the separation of powers scheme. Recall The Federalist No. 51.

2. *Scope of the immunity*. The speech or debate clause does, however, contain a number of ambiguities. Those ambiguities primarily have to do with the scope of the immunity: What sorts of legislative acts are covered? And who is protected by the privilege? Consider the following cases:

a. *Work of legislative aides; private publication; hearings*. At issue in Gravel v. United States, 408 U.S. 606 (1972), were certain actions taken by Senator Gravel and his aide, Dr. Rodberg. Gravel had read from the Pentagon Papers and placed the forty-seven volumes in the public record of subcommittee hearings. He also was alleged to have arranged for private publication of the papers. The United States initiated an investigation. A federal grand jury examined the matter, calling Rodberg as a witness. Senator Gravel intervened in the proceedings and moved to quash the subpoenas, invoking the speech or debate clause. There were three principal issues: Could Gravel be held liable for reading the papers into the hearing records? Did the clause protect Rodberg as well as Gravel? Did it extend to protect private publication of the papers?

The Court concluded, first, that the clause applied to the events at the subcommittee hearing; it "protects Members against prosecutions that directly impinge upon or threaten the legislative process." Second, the Court ruled that the clause covered legislative aides as well as members of Congress. "[The] day-to-day work of such aides is so critical to the Members' performance that they must be treated as the latter's alter ego" in order to "prevent intimidation of legislators by the Executive and accountability before a possibly hostile judiciary." The Court acknowledged that this conclusion went beyond the constitutional text, but "sought to implement its fundamental purpose of freeing the legislator from executive and judicial oversight." To say this did not mean that all acts by such employees would be protected; the question was whether the acts were "essential to legislating." Cf. Dombrowski v. Eastland, 387 U.S. 486 (1969) (privilege unavailable to Senate subcommittee counsel conspiring to seize records unlawfully). How does one answer that question? Is the nature of the conduct in question relevant? If it is, does the issue of immunity become intertwined with the merits — something that immunity is supposed to avoid?

At the same time, the Court concluded that the private publication would be unprotected. "The heart of the Clause is speech or debate in either House." Other matters could be immunized if they were "an integral part of the deliberative and communicative processes by which Members participate in committee and House proceedings with respect to the consideration and passage or rejection of proposed legislation or with respect to other matters which the Constitution places within the jurisdiction of either House." But private publication was "in no way essential to the deliberations of the Senate; nor does questioning as to private publication threaten the integrity or independence of the Senate by impermissibly exposing its deliberations to executive influence. The Senator had conducted his hearings. [We] cannot but conclude that the Senator's arrangements with Beacon Press were not part and parcel of the legislative process." In the Court's view, the focus of the clause was on "the legislative sphere. That Senators generally perform certain acts in their official capacity as Senators does not necessarily make all such acts legislative in nature."

Justice Brennan, joined by Justices Douglas and Marshall, disagreed. He concluded that the "legislator's duty to inform the public about matters affecting the administration of government" was part of "the class of things 'generally done in a session of the House by one of its members in relation to the business before it.' " Justice Douglas added that "publication was but another way of informing the public as to what had gone on in the privacy of the Executive Branch concerning the conception and pursuit of the so-called 'war' in Vietnam." How does one resolve this disagreement?

b. *Bribes.* In United States v. Brewster, 408 U.S. 501 (1972), the Court held by a 6-to-3 margin that the clause permits a prosecution of a former legislator for acceptance of a bribe if — but only if — "the Government's case does not rely on legislative acts or the motivation for legislative acts." The Court reasoned that the clause does not protect "all conduct relating to the legislative process." In its view, the immunity is "limited to an act which was clearly a part of the legislative process — the *due* functioning of the process." Does this position also entangle immunity with the merits? The Court added that it would be unsound "to extend the privilege beyond its intended scope, its literal language, and its history, to include all things in any way related to the legislative process." In this case, "examination of the indictment [reveals] that no inquiry into legislative acts or motivation is necessary for the Government to make out a prima facie case."

Justice Brennan, in dissent, urged that the crime of bribery was one "whose proof calls into question the very motive behind his legislative acts." In a separate dissent, Justice White attacked the Court's distinction between a promise made in the course of bribery and the performance of a legislative act. In his view, the clause was intended to ensure that "the power to discipline" members of Congress for legislative acts remains in Congress. "I would insist that those Houses develop their own institutional procedures for dealing with those in their midst who would prostitute the legislative process."

See also United States v. Helstoski, 442 U.S. 477 (1979), holding that references to past legislative acts were inadmissible in a bribery prosecution.

c. *Enjoining subcommittee activity.* Eastland v. United States Servicemen's Fund, 421 U.S. 491 (1975), dealt with a legislative subpoena directed by Senator Eastland to a bank where the Servicemen's Fund had an account. The subpoena was issued in connection with the Senate's investigation into the allegedly subversive activities of the fund.

The fund brought suit in federal court to enjoin implementation of the subpoena. The Supreme Court concluded that the actions of the subcommittee, Senator Eastland, and the subcommittee's chief counsel were immunized from judicial interference under the speech or debate clause. The Court reasoned that "a private civil action, whether for an injunction or damages, creates a distraction and forces Members to divert their time, energy, and attention from their legislative tasks to defend the litigation. [Judicial] power is still brought to bear on Members of Congress and legislative independence is imperiled." Acknowledging that there was no "literal speech or debate" in the case, the Court found immunity because the "power to investigate and to do so through compulsory process" falls within the sphere of "deliberative and communicative processes" central to the legislative function. Justice Douglas dissented.

d. *Dissemination of congressional reports.* Doe v. McMillan, 412 U.S. 306 (1973), involved a subcommittee report that contained a "somewhat derogatory" view of the school system of the District of Columbia. The report identified students by name in connection with disciplinary problems, with alleged sexual perversion, and with criminal violations. The report was distributed publicly by private persons with the authorization of Congress. Suit was brought on behalf of the children, alleging invasion of privacy and injury to reputation.

The Court held that the action was barred "insofar as it sought relief from the Congressmen-Committee members, from the Committee staff, from the consultant, or from the investigator, for introducing material at Committee hearings that identified particular individuals, for referring the report that included the material to the Speaker of the House, and for voting for publication of the report." Such acts were "legislative" and therefore protected.

On the other hand, the Court concluded that the clause did not protect private persons who brought about the public distribution of the report — even though such distribution was with the authorization of Congress. Public dissemination by private persons was not, in the Court's view, within the realm of protected "legislative activities." To hold otherwise would be "to invite gratuitous injury to citizens for little if any public purpose."

e. *Press releases and newsletters.* In Hutchinson v. Proxmire, 443 U.S. 111 (1979), the Court held that the immunity did not extend to press releases and newsletters. The case involved Senator Proxmire's annual "Golden Fleece" award for wasteful government spending. Proxmire had given the award to federal agencies that had funded Hutchinson's studies of aggressive behavior in animals and humans. In a speech on the Senate floor, Senator Proxmire referred to the "worthlessness" of the project. He also distributed a press release incorporating the text of the speech, and he referred to the "award," and the reasons for it, in various other places. Hutchinson brought a defamation action.

The Court stated that the immunity applied to statements on the Senate floor but did not attach to the newsletters or the press release. The latter were neither "essential to the deliberations of the Senate" nor "part of the deliberative process." Nothing "in history or in the explicit language of the Clause suggests any intention to create an absolute privilege for defamatory statements made outside the Chamber." It may be "the duty of Members to tell the public about their activities," but "the transmittal of [information] by individuals in order to inform the public [is] not a part of the legislative function." Justice Brennan dissented, claiming that "public criticism by legislators of unnecessary governmental expenditures, whatever its form, is a legislative act shielded by" the clause.

United States v. Nixon
418 U.S. 683 (1974)

Mr. Chief Justice Burger delivered the opinion of the Court.

This litigation presents for review the denial of a motion, filed in the District Court on behalf of [President Nixon] in the case of United States v. Mitchell, to quash a third-party subpoena *duces tecum* issued by the [District Court] pursuant to Fed. Rule Crim. Proc. 17 (c). The subpoena directed the President to produce certain tape recordings and documents relating to his conversations with aides and advisers.

On March 1, 1974, a grand jury of the United States District Court for the District of Columbia returned an indictment charging seven named individuals with various offenses, including conspiracy to defraud the United States and to obstruct justice. Although he was not designated as such in the indictment, the grand jury named the President, among others, as an unindicted coconspirator. On April 18, 1974, upon motion of the Special Prosecutor, [a] subpoena duces tecum was issued [to] the President by the United States District Court [requiring] the production, in advance of the September 9 trial date, of certain tapes, memoranda, papers, transcripts, or other writings relating to certain precisely identified meetings between the President and others. [On] April 30, the President publicly released edited transcripts of 43 conversations; portions of 20 conversations subject to subpoena in the present case were included. On May 1, 1974, the President's counsel filed a "special appearance" and a motion to quash the subpoena [on grounds] of privilege.

On May 20, 1974, the District Court denied the motion to quash and [ordered the] "President or any subordinate officer, official, or employee with custody or control of the documents or objects subpoenaed," [to] deliver to the District Court, on or before May 31, 1974, the originals of all subpoenaed items. [The President sought review in the court of appeals, but the Supreme Court granted review before judgment. The Court held that the subpoena met the requirements of Fed. R. Crim. Proc. 17c. The various prerequisites, including relevance, specificity, and admissibility were satisfied. The Court also held that the case was justiciable.]

[W]e turn to the claim that the subpoena should be quashed because it demands "confidential conversations between a President and his close advisors that it would be inconsistent with the public interest to produce." [The] first contention is a broad claim that the separation of powers doctrine precludes judicial review of a President's claim of privilege. The second contention is that if he does not prevail on the claim of absolute privilege, the court should hold as a matter of constitutional law that the privilege prevails over the subpoena duces tecum.

In the performance of assigned constitutional duties each branch of the Government must initially interpret the Constitution, and the interpretation of its powers by any branch is due great respect from the others. The President's counsel [reads] the Constitution as providing an absolute privilege of confidentiality for all Presidential communications. Many decisions of this Court, however, have unequivocally reaffirmed the holding of [Marbury, that] "[i]t is emphatically the province and duty of the judicial department to say what the law is." . . .

No holding of the Court has defined the scope of judicial power specifically relating to the enforcement of a subpoena for confidential Presidential communications for use in a criminal prosecution, but other exercises of power by the Executive Branch and the Legislative Branch have been found invalid as in conflict with the Constitution. Powell v. McCormack, 395 U.S. 486 (1969); [Youngstown]. [In] a series of cases, the Court interpreted the explicit immunity conferred by express provisions of the Constitution on Members of the House and Senate by the Speech or Debate Clause. Since this Court has consistently exercised the power to construe and delineate claims arising under express powers, it must follow that the Court has authority to interpret claims with respect to powers alleged to derive from enumerated powers.

Our system of government "requires that federal courts on occasion interpret the Constitution in a manner at variance with the construction given the document by another branch." [Notwithstanding] the deference each branch must accord the others, the "judicial Power of the United States" vested in the federal courts [can] no more be shared with the Executive Branch than the Chief Executive, for example, can share with the Judiciary the veto power. [Any] other conclusion would be contrary to the basic concept of separation of powers and the checks and balances that flow from the scheme of a tripartite government. [We] therefore reaffirm that it is the province and duty of this Court "to say what the law is" with respect to the claim of privilege presented in this case.

In support of his claim of absolute privilege, the President's counsel urges two grounds, one of which is common to all governments and one of which is peculiar to our system of separation of powers. The first ground is the valid need for protection of communications between high Government officials and those who advise and assist them in the performance of their manifold duties; the importance of this confidentiality is too plain to require further discussion. Human experience teaches that those who expect public dissemination of their remarks may well temper candor with a concern for appearances and for their own inter-ests to the detriment of the decisionmaking process. Whatever the nature of the privilege of confidentiality of Presidential communications in the exercise of Art. II powers, the privilege can be said to derive from the supremacy of each branch within its own assigned area of constitutional duties. Certain powers and privileges flow from the nature of enumerated powers;[16] the protection of the confidentiality of Presidential communications has similar constitutional underpinnings.

The second ground asserted by the President's counsel in support of the claim of absolute privilege rests on the doctrine of separation of powers. Here it is argued that the independence of the Executive Branch within its own sphere [insulates] a President from a judicial subpoena in an ongoing criminal prosecu-tion, and thereby protects confidential Presidential communications.

However, neither the doctrine of separation of powers, nor the need for confi-dentiality of high-level communications, without more, can sustain an absolute, unqualified Presidential privilege of immunity from judicial process under all circumstances. The President's need for complete candor and objectivity from advisers calls for great deference from the courts. However, when the privilege depends solely on the broad, undifferentiated claim of public interest in the confidentiality of such conversations, a confrontation with other values arises. Absent a claim of need to protect military, diplomatic, or sensitive national secu-rity secrets, we find it difficult to accept the argument that even the very impor-tant interest in confidentiality of Presidential communications is significantly diminished by production of such material for *in camera* inspection with all the protection that a district court will be obliged to provide.

The impediment that an absolute, unqualified privilege would place in the way of the primary constitutional duty of the Judicial Branch to do justice in criminal prosecutions would plainly conflict with the function of the courts under Art. III. In designing the structure of our Government and dividing and allocating the sovereign power among three co-equal branches, the Framers of the Constitution sought to provide a comprehensive system, but the separate powers were not intended to operate with absolute independence.

[To] read the Art. II powers of the President as providing an absolute privilege as against a subpoena essential to enforcement of criminal statutes on no more than a generalized claim of the public interest in confidentiality of nonmilitary and nondiplomatic discussions would upset the constitutional balance of "a work-able government" and gravely impair the role of the courts under Art. III.

Since we conclude that the legitimate needs of the judicial process may out-weigh Presidential privilege, it is necessary to resolve those competing interests in a manner that preserves the essential functions of each branch. The right and indeed the duty to resolve that question does not free the Judiciary from accord-ing high respect to the representations made on behalf of the President.

---

16. The Special Prosecutor argues that there is no provision in the Constitution for a Presidential privilege as to the President's communications corresponding to the privilege of Members of Congress under the Speech or Debate Clause. But the silence of the Constitution on this score is not dispositive. "The rule of constitutional interpretation announced in McCulloch v. Maryland, 4 Wheat. 316, that that which was reasonably appropriate and relevant to the exercise of a granted power was to be considered as accompanying the grant, has been so universally applied that it suffices merely to state it."

The expectation of a President to the confidentiality of his conversations and correspondence, like the claim of confidentiality of judicial deliberations, for example, has all the values to which we accord deference for the privacy of all citizens and, added to those values, is the necessity for protection of the public interest in candid, objective, and even blunt or harsh opinions in Presidential decisionmaking. A President and those who assist him must be free to explore alternatives in the process of shaping policies and making decisions and to do so in a way many would be unwilling to express except privately. These are the considerations justifying a presumptive privilege for Presidential communications. The privilege is fundamental to the operation of Government and inextricably rooted in the separation of powers under the Constitution. . . .

But this presumptive privilege must be considered in light of our historic commitment to the rule of law. This is nowhere more profoundly manifest than in our view that "the twofold aim [of criminal justice] is that guilt shall not escape or innocence suffer." We have elected to employ an adversary system of criminal justice in which the parties contest all issues before a court of law. The need to develop all relevant facts in the adversary system is both fundamental and comprehensive. The ends of criminal justice would be defeated if judgments were to be founded on a partial or speculative presentation of the facts. The very integrity of the judicial system and public confidence in the system depend on full disclosure of all the facts, within the framework of the rules of evidence. To ensure that justice is done, it is imperative to the function of courts that compulsory process be available for the production of evidence needed either by the prosecution or by the defense. . . .

[But evidentiary privileges] are designed to protect weighty and legitimate competing interests. Thus, the Fifth Amendment to the Constitution provides that no man "shall be compelled in any criminal case to be a witness against himself." And, generally, an attorney or a priest may not be required to disclose what has been revealed in professional confidence. These and other interests are recognized in law by privileges against forced disclosure. [Whatever] their origins, these exceptions to the demand for every man's evidence are not lightly created nor expansively construed, for they are in derogation of the search for truth.

In this case the President challenges a subpoena served on him as a third party requiring the production of materials for use in a criminal prosecution; he does so on the claim that he has a privilege against disclosure of confidential communications. He does not place his claim of privilege on the ground they are military or diplomatic secrets. As to these areas of Art. II duties the courts have traditionally shown the utmost deference to Presidential responsibilities.

[No] case of the Court, however, has extended this high degree of deference to a President's generalized interest in confidentiality. Nowhere in the Constitution [is] there any explicit reference to a privilege of confidentiality, yet to the extent this interest relates to the effective discharge of a President's powers, it is constitutionally based.

The right to the production of all evidence at a criminal trial similarly has constitutional dimensions. The Sixth Amendment explicitly confers upon every defendant in a criminal trial the right "to be confronted with the witnesses against him" and "to have compulsory process for obtaining witnesses in his favor." Moreover, the Fifth Amendment also guarantees that no person shall be deprived of liberty without due process of law. . . .

In this case we must weigh the importance of the general privilege of confidentiality of Presidential communications in performance of the President's responsibilities against the inroads of such a privilege on the fair administration of criminal justice.[19] The interest in preserving confidentiality is weighty indeed and entitled to great respect. However, we cannot conclude that advisers will be moved to temper the candor of their remarks by the infrequent occasions of disclosure because of the possibility that such conversations will be called for in the context of a criminal prosecution.

On the other hand, the allowance of the privilege to withhold evidence that is demonstrably relevant in a criminal trial would cut deeply into the guarantee of due process of law and gravely impair the basic function of the courts. A President's acknowledged need for confidentiality in the communications of his office is general in nature, whereas the constitutional need for production of relevant evidence in a criminal proceeding is specific and central to the fair adjudication of a particular criminal case in the administration of justice. Without access to specific facts a criminal prosecution may be totally frustrated. The President's broad interest in confidentiality of communications will not be vitiated by disclosure of a limited number of conversations preliminarily shown to have some bearing on the pending criminal cases.

 We conclude that when the ground for asserting privilege as to subpoenaed materials sought for use in a criminal trial is based only on the generalized interest in confidentiality, it cannot prevail over the fundamental demands of due process of law in the fair administration of criminal justice. The generalized assertion of privilege must yield to the demonstrated, specific need for evidence in a pending criminal trial.

[If] a President concludes that compliance with a subpoena would be injurious to the public interest he may properly, as was done here, invoke a claim of privilege on the return of the subpoena. Upon receiving a claim of privilege from the Chief Executive, it became the further duty of the District Court to treat the subpoenaed material as presumptively privileged and to require the Special Prosecutor to demonstrate that the Presidential material was "essential to the justice of the [pending criminal] case." [We] are unable to conclude that the District Court erred in ordering the inspection. Accordingly we affirm the order of the District Court that subpoenaed materials be transmitted to that court. We now turn to the important question of the District Court's responsibilities in conducting the in camera examination of Presidential materials or communications delivered under the compulsion of the subpoena duces tecum. . . .

[Statements] that meet the test of admissibility and relevance must be isolated; all other material must be excised. At this stage the District Court is not limited to representations of the Special Prosecutor as to the evidence sought by the subpoena; the material will be available to the District Court. It is elementary that in camera inspection of evidence is always a procedure calling for scrupulous protection against any release or publication of material not found by the court, at that stage, probably admissible in evidence and relevant to the issues of the trial

---

19. We are not here concerned with the balance between the President's generalized interest in confidentiality and the need for relevant evidence in civil litigation, nor with that between the confidentiality interest and congressional demands for information, nor with the President's interest in preserving state secrets. We address only the conflict between the President's assertion of a generalized privilege of confidentiality and the constitutional need for relevant evidence in criminal trials.

for which it is sought. That being true of an ordinary situation, it is obvious that the District Court has a very heavy responsibility to see to it that Presidential conversations, which are either not relevant or not admissible, are accorded that high degree of respect due the President of the United States. Mr. Chief Justice Marshall, sitting as a trial judge in the [trial of Aaron Burr for treason] was extraordinarily careful to point out that "[i]n no case of this kind would a court be required to proceed against the president as against an ordinary individual." Marshall's statement cannot be read to mean in any sense that a President is above the law, but relates to the singularly unique role under Art. II of a President's communications and activities, related to the performance of duties under that Article. Moreover, a President's communications and activities encompass a vastly wider range of sensitive material than would be true of any "ordinary individual." It is therefore necessary in the public interest to afford Presidential confidentiality the greatest protection consistent with the fair administration of justice. The need for confidentiality even as to idle conversations with associates in which casual reference might be made concerning political leaders within the country or foreign statesmen is too obvious to call for further treatment. We have no doubt that the District Judge will at all times accord to Presidential records [a] high degree of deference and will discharge his responsibility to see to it that until released to the Special Prosecutor no in camera material is revealed to anyone. . . .

Affirmed.

Mr. Justice Rehnquist took no part in the consideration or decision of these cases.

Nixon v. Administrator of General Services

433 U.S. 425 (1977)

Mr. Justice Brennan delivered the opinion of the Court.

[The] Presidential Recordings and Materials Preservation Act [directs] the Administrator of General Services, an official of the Executive Branch, to take custody of the Presidential papers and tape recordings of former President [Nixon] and promulgate regulations that (1) provide for the orderly processing and screening by Executive Branch archivists of such materials for the purpose of returning to [him] those that are personal and private in nature, and (2) determine the terms and conditions upon which public access may eventually be had to those materials that are retained. The question for decision is whether [the act] is unconstitutional on its face as a violation of (1) the separation of powers; (2) Presidential privilege doctrines. . . .

[The lower court upheld the statute.]

We reject at the outset appellant's argument that the Act's regulation of the disposition of Presidential materials within the Executive Branch constitutes, without more, a violation of the principle of separation of powers. Neither President Ford nor President Carter supports this claim. The Executive Branch became a party to the Act's regulation when President Ford signed the Act into law, and the administration of President Carter, acting through the Solicitor General, vigorously supports [its] constitutionality. Moreover, the control over the materials remains in the Executive Branch. The Administrator of General Services, who must promulgate and administer the regulations that are the keystone of the statutory scheme, is himself an official of the Executive Branch, appointed by the President. . . .

Appellant's argument is in any event based on an interpretation of the separation-of-powers doctrine inconsistent with the origins of that doctrine, recent decisions of the Court, and the contemporary realities of our political system. True, it has been said that "each of the three general departments of government [must remain] entirely free from the control or influence, direct or indirect, of either of the others. . . ."

But the more pragmatic, flexible approach [was] expressly affirmed by this Court only three years ago in [Nixon.]

[The] unanimous Court essentially embraced Mr. Justice Jackson's view [in] his concurrence in [Youngstown.] [Thus,] in determining whether the Act disrupts the proper balance between the coordinate branches, the proper inquiry focuses on the extent to which it prevents the Executive Branch from accomplishing its constitutionally assigned functions. [Only] where the potential for disruption is present must we then determine whether that impact is justified by an overriding need to promote objectives within the constitutional authority of Congress.

It is therefore highly relevant that the Act provides for custody of the materials in officials of the Executive Branch and that employees of that branch have access to the materials, [for] it is clearly less intrusive to place custody and screening of the materials within the Executive Branch itself than to have Congress or some outside agency perform the screening function. [Nothing in] the Act renders it unduly disruptive of the Executive Branch and, therefore, unconstitutional on its face. . . .

The appellant bases his claim of Presidential privilege [on] the assertion that the potential disclosure of communications given to the appellant in confidence would adversely affect the ability of future Presidents to obtain the candid advice necessary for effective decisionmaking. [But there] is no reason to believe that the restriction on public access ultimately established by regulation will not be adequate to preserve executive confidentiality. An absolute barrier to all outside disclosure is not practically or constitutionally necessary. [There] has never been an expectation that the confidences of the Executive Office are absolute and unyielding. All former Presidents from President Hoover to President Johnson have deposited their papers in Presidential libraries [for] governmental preservation and eventual disclosure.

[We] are thus left with the bare claim that the mere screening of the materials by the archivists will impermissibly interfere with candid communication of views by Presidential advisers. [Thus] framed, the question is readily resolved. The screening constitutes a very limited intrusion by personnel in the Executive Branch sensitive to executive concerns. These very personnel have performed the identical task in each of the Presidential libraries without any suggestion that such activity has in any way interfered with executive confidentiality. . . .

Other substantial public interests that led Congress to seek to preserve [these] materials were the desire to restore public confidence in our political processes by preserving the materials as a source for facilitating a full airing of the events leading to appellant's resignation, and Congress' need to understand how those political processes had in fact operated in order to gauge the necessity for remedial legislation. Thus by preserving these materials, the Act may be thought to aid the legislative process and thus to be within the scope of Congress' broad investigative power. [And,] of course, the Congress repeatedly referred to the importance of the materials to the Judiciary in the event that they shed light upon issues in civil or criminal litigation, a social interest that cannot be doubted.

In light of these objectives, the scheme adopted by Congress for preservation of the appellant's Presidential materials cannot be said to be overbroad. . . .

In short, we conclude that the screening process contemplated by the Act will not constitute a more severe intrusion into Presidential confidentiality than the in camera inspection by the District Court approved in United States v. Nixon.

[Affirmed.]

Mr. Justice Rehnquist, dissenting.

My conclusion that the Act violates the principle of separation of powers is based upon three fundamental propositions. First, candid and open discourse among the President, his advisers, foreign heads of state and ambassadors, Members of Congress, and the others who deal with the White House on a sensitive basis is an absolute prerequisite to the effective discharge of the duties of that high office. Second, [the] Act [will] undoubtedly restrain the necessary free flow of information to and from the [President. Third,] any substantial intrusion upon the effective discharge of the duties of the President is sufficient to violate the principle of separation of powers, and our prior cases do not permit the sustaining of an Act such as this by "balancing" an intrusion of substantial magnitude against the interests assertedly fostered by the Act.

With respect to the second point, it is of course true that the Act is directed solely at the papers of former President Nixon. Although the terms of the Act, therefore, have no direct application to the present occupant or future occupants of the Office, the effect upon candid communication to and from these future Presidents depends, in the long run, not upon the limited nature of the present Act, but upon the precedential effect of today's decision. Unless the authority of Congress to seize the papers of this appellant is limited only to him in some principled way, future Presidents and their advisers will be wary of a similar Act directed at their papers out of pure political hostility. [But] the Court's opinion [is] obscure, to say the least, as to the circumstances that will justify Congress in seizing the papers of an ex-President. A potpourri of reasons is advanced as to why the Act is not an unconstitutional infringement upon the principle of separation of powers, but the weight to be attached to any of the factors is left wholly unclear. . . .

It thus appears to me indisputable that this Act is a significant intrusion into the operations of the Presidency. I do not think that this severe dampening of free communication to and from the President may be discounted by the Court's adoption of a novel "balancing" test for determining whether it is constitutional. I agree with the Court that the three branches of Government need not be airtight, and that the separate branches are not intended to operate with absolute independence. [But] I find no support [for] the Court's pronouncement that the operations of the Office of the President may be severely impeded by Congress simply because Congress had a good reason for doing so.

Surely if ever there were a case for "balancing," and giving weight to the asserted "national interest" to sustain governmental action, it was in [Youngstown]. There the challenged Presidential Executive Order recited, without contradiction by its challengers, that "American fighting men [are] now engaged in deadly combat with the forces of aggression in Korea" [and] that a work stoppage in the steel industry "would immediately jeopardize and imperil our national defense [and] would add to the continuing danger of our soldiers, sailors, and airmen engaged in combat in the field." [Although] the "legislative" actions by the President could have been quickly overridden by an Act of Congress, [this] Court struck down the Executive Order as violative of the separation-of-powers principle with nary a mention of the national interest to be fostered by what could have been characterized as a relatively minimal and temporary intrusion upon the role of Congress. The analysis was simple and straightforward: Congress had exclusive authority to legislate; the President's Executive Order was an exercise of legislative power that impinged upon that authority of Congress, and was therefore unconstitutional.

I think that not only the Executive Branch of the Federal Government, but the Legislative and Judicial Branches as well, will come to regret this day when the Court has upheld an Act of Congress that trenches so significantly on the functioning of the Office of the President.

[CHIEF JUSTICE BURGER also dissented.]

Note: Executive Privilege

1. *The historical setting: the Watergate affair.* The United States v. Nixon case was decided in the midst of a constitutional crisis. Employees of the reelection committee for President Nixon broke into the Democratic National Headquarters at the Watergate Hotel on June 17, 1972. In February of the next year, a Senate Select Committee on the Watergate affair was set up by a unanimous vote of the Senate. The committee was charged with investigating the alleged illegal break-in and the question of White House involvement. In late May, under considerable public pressure, President Nixon appointed Archibald Cox as special prosecutor to investigate, among other things, any participation by the White House in the Watergate affair. The President was himself implicated by former White House Counsel John Dean in testimony before the House in June, and in July, one member of the House introduced an impeachment resolution.

On February 6, 1974, the House formally authorized the Judiciary Committee to begin impeachment hearings. On July 25 the Supreme Court handed down the decision in *Nixon*. On July 27 the Judiciary Committee adopted the first article of impeachment, charging the President with obstruction of justice with respect to the Watergate break-in and other activities. On July 29 it adopted the second article of impeachment, involving abuse of power by misusing executive agencies and violating constitutional rights of the citizenry. On July 30 the Committee adopted the third article, charging the President with willful disobedience of subpoenas issued by the Judiciary Committee. (The articles are reproduced infra.) On August 6, twelve days after the Supreme Court decision, President Nixon decided to make the transcript of the tapes available to the public. Three days thereafter, on August 9, he resigned. On August 20 the Judiciary Committee filed its impeachment report with the House, which took no further action.

In these circumstances, was the Court's intervention undesirable? Consider

Gunther, Judicial Hegemony and Legislative Autonomy: the *Nixon* Case and the Impeachment Process, 22 U.C.L.A. L. Rev. 30, 31 (1974):

> the most admirable feature of our recent constitutional history lies in the demonstration that the House of Representatives is capable of taking its impeachment responsibilities seriously. [To] a regrettable extent, the triumph of the legislative branch was diminished by the Supreme Court's performance. For most of the first half of 1974, the Judiciary Committee proceedings were at center stage. That is where they belonged. The impeachment route is the most appropriate one in our Constitution for the pursuit of problems such as those raised by Watergate.

Consider too the discussion at Chapter 1, section B, supra of the adverse effects of judicial review on the exercise of political responsibility by representatives and the public as a whole. But why did the Judiciary Committee proceedings belong at center stage? Did the Court do the nation a disservice by requiring disclosure of the tapes, or did it bring about a more orderly conclusion to the whole affair?

2. *Reviewability of the presidential determination.* In the *Nixon* case, the President's counsel made three separate arguments. The first was that while in office, the President was immune to judicial process and could be subject only to the specified constitutional sanction of impeachment; the second, that the President had absolute discretion to determine the scope of executive privilege; the third, that even if the President's determination was subject to judicial review, it was correct in this case. Consider how, if at all, the Court responded to these separate contentions.

In Mississippi v. Johnson, 71 U.S. (4 Wall.) 475 (1867), the Court refused to hear a suit attempting to enjoin the President's enforcement of the reconstruction laws. The Court concluded that courts did not have power to issue an injunction against the President. The Court referred in particular to the difficulties of enforcement and to the alternative route of impeachment. Moreover, it has often been argued that impeachment is the exclusive sanction for improper conduct by a sitting President. (Can you generate a structural argument for this view, relying on the constitutional text?) Note, however, that the Constitution does not create any express presidential immunity from judicial process. Would such an immunity be a proper inference from the impeachment provision? Is impeachment too blunt and crude an instrument for handling what might be isolated instances of presidential illegality? To what extent does *Nixon* reject an inference that impeachment is an exclusive route? Note finally that while President Truman was not the named defendant in *Youngstown*, his order was in fact the subject of the Court's injunction.

With respect to the President's first two claims, the following exchange occurred during oral argument in the Supreme Court. The exchange dealt with the President's claim that executive privilege is absolute as against both the special prosecutor and the impeachment discovery power of Congress:

> *Question:* How are you going to impeach him if you don't know about it?
> Mr. *St. Clair* [the President's lawyer]: Well, if you know about it, then you can state the case. If you don't know about it, you don't have it.
> *Question:* So there you are. You're on the prongs of a dilemma; hunh?
> Mr. *St. Clair:* No, I don't think so.

> *Question:* If you know the President is doing something wrong, you can im-
>   peach him; but the only way you can find out is this way; you can't impeach
>   him, so you don't impeach him. You lose me some place along there.
> (Laughter)

Record of Oral Argument of United States v. Nixon (1974), at 108.

Why did the Court reject the President's second claim — that his decision about the scope of executive privilege was unreviewable? Consider the following:

> Central to Chief Justice Burger's reasoning, and used for more than it is worth, is
> Chief Justice Marshall's famous Marbury v. Madison statement that "[i]t is emphati-
> cally the province and duty of the judicial department to say what the law is." [I] do
> not disagree with the appropriateness of that statement in the [*Marbury*] context. I
> do question the use made of it in United States v. Nixon. There it seems to me to
> convey a misleadingly broad view of judicial competence, exclusivity and suprem-
> acy. [Chief] Justice Burger's handling of the issue suggests that recognizing absolute
> executive privilege as a matter of constitutional interpretation would somehow be
> contrary to Marbury v. Madison's view of the proper judicial role. But there is
> nothing in Marbury v. Madison that precludes a constitutional interpretation which
> gives final authority to another branch.

Gunther, Judicial Hegemony and Legislative Autonomy: The *Nixon* Case and the Impeachment Process, 22 U.C.L.A. L. Rev. 30, 33-34 (1974). What would be the consequences of a judicial ruling accepting the President's claim in the *Nixon* case? Does Cooper v. Aaron, see Chapter 1, section B, supra, support the Court? Consider too the views of Jefferson, Lincoln, and others about the presidential power to interpret the Constitution independently of the courts. Was Nixon's position different from theirs?

3. *Executive privilege.* a. *The existence of the privilege.* Though the President lost the *Nixon* case, the presidency may have won a great victory. For the first time, the decision established the existence of executive privilege. The question whether the Constitution implicitly creates such a privilege had for a long period been the subject of heated debate among Congress, the President, and academic commentators. Indeed, the privilege had been asserted by many Presidents, in-cluding President Washington, who claimed that such a privilege was necessary for the execution of the laws. Frequently, Congress denied the existence of the privilege, claiming that it was without constitutional foundation. See generally R. Berger, Executive Privilege: A Constitutional Myth (1974), arguing that the his-tory of the Constitution demonstrates that there was no intention to create any such privilege.

Why did the Court recognize the privilege when it is not expressly provided for in the Constitution? Does the necessary and proper clause help? Note also the fact that in light of the existence of an explicit legislative privilege, it might be argued that an executive privilege should not be understood to have been "im-plied." This argument, based on the canon of construction "expressio unius est exclusio alterius," was adopted by the Court in the *Chadha* case. Is it weaker in *Nixon* than it was in *Chadha?* Outline an opinion in favor of the *Nixon* Court's view, using structural arguments akin to that in *McCulloch.*

b. *The search for limits.* What are the limits of the privilege recognized in *Nixon?* In the case itself, the Court concluded that the privilege was "presumptive," not absolute, and that it could be overcome by the interests of the criminal justice system. This is of course a balancing test. In *Nixon* itself, the President's own interest was said to be relatively weak because "generalized." The countervailing interest, the Court said, was strong because of the need for the materials sought in the pending criminal proceeding. Do you agree with the Court's assessment of the relevant interests?

Consider Cox, Executive Privilege, 122 U. Pa. L. Rev. 1383, 1414-1415 (1974):

[The] crucial test is probably relevance and admissibility [which] may seem at first blush to indicate that despite the talk about a defeasible privilege the duty to produce evidence of confidential communications between a President and his aides actually depends upon the same rules of competency, relevancy and materiality that govern the testimony of any private person when proper objection is made. Two important additional requirements are implicit in the case, however. First, the case involved serious criminal charges against high government officials. The public interest in having all competent, relevant and material evidence available in such a case is higher than in any other kind. Second, because the subpoena sought evidence for use upon trial of an indictment, there was already an implicit determination of probable cause to believe that the officials named as defendants had committed serious crimes.

Consider how the decision would apply in the following contexts.

(1) *National security interests.* Suppose President Nixon had asserted a national security need for secrecy with respect to some of the tapes. Consider in this regard United States v. American Telephone & Telegraph, 567 F.2d 121 (D.C. Cir. 1977), which involved an effort by Congress to obtain information from the defendant concerning wiretaps ordered by the executive branch. Rejecting the executive's claim that national security barred the subpoena, the court wrote: "The executive would have it that the Constitution confers on the executive absolute discretion in the area of national security. This does not stand up. [The] Constitution [confers] upon Congress [powers] equally inseparable from the national security." The court called for a compromise solution and set forth a procedure involving limited committee access and in camera resolution of disputes.

(2) *Legislative investigations, executive investigations, and civil proceedings.* Suppose a committee of the House or Senate seeks material in connection with an investigation into certain conduct by the President and his subordinates. In what circumstances may the President successfully interpose a claim of executive privilege? Suppose the committee makes a showing of need. Does a civil proceeding differ in this respect from a criminal case? See Senate Select Committee on Presidential Campaign Committees v. Nixon, 370 F. Supp. 521 (D.D.C. 1974), where a senate committee sought access to the tapes in connection with an investigation. The court held that the Committee's need to know was insufficient to outweigh the privilege. See also Dellums v. Powell, 561 F.2d 242 (D.C. Cir. 1977), holding that the presidential privilege was outweighed in a civil action brought by people who alleged that they had been unconstitutionally arrested during a demonstration on Capitol Hill.

(3) *Lower-level officials.* Suppose the claim is asserted by lower-level officials in the executive branch. Do they have the same privilege as the President? In 1983,

for example, Administrator Anne Gorsuch Buford of the Environmental Protection Agency asserted executive privilege as a basis for resisting disclosure, to the U.S. Senate, of law enforcement files. The files contained discussions of possible criminal investigations. The executive branch argued that *Nixon*, read in light of *Myers*, controlled the constitutional issue. In their view, *Myers* established the existence of a unitary executive branch. When subordinate officials in the executive branch take action, they do so as the President's representative. Thus, if an EPA administrator is involved in prosecutorial duties, she is only a surrogate for the President, and she acts with his powers and his responsibilities. If he could claim executive privilege if he himself were involved in the conversation, she could as well, at least if he directs that she do so. Do you agree?

(4) *Law enforcement activities.* The Gorsuch incident also raised the question whether and how executive privilege applies in the context of congressional investigations into law enforcement activities by the executive branch. The executive's claim was that disclosure of law enforcement files would inevitably compromise ongoing investigations, thus interfering with the executive's power to "take Care that the Laws be faithfully executed." If an executive investigation is in fact in process, is the claim for secrecy substantially greater than in *Nixon* itself? What must Congress show in order to overcome such a claim? Can one foresee difficulties in deciding whether an investigation is "ongoing"?

4. *Bills of attainder.* Note that in Nixon v. General Services, it was also argued that the statute amounted to an impermissible "bill of attainder" against Nixon. See art. I, §9. As the Court put it, a bill of attainder is "a law that legislatively determines guilt and inflicts punishment upon an identifiable individual without provision of the protections of a judicial trial." Consider the bill of attainder clause as a separation of powers provision, in connection with both *General Services* and *Chadha*, supra, Chapter 4, section B. Which of the purposes of the separation of powers are served by the separation of the power of lawmaking on the one hand and conviction on the other? Note in particular the possibility that the clause is designed as a part of the constitutional effort to bring about "generality" in lawmaking and law-application, on the theory that such generality is a safeguard against factional tyranny.

In *General Services*, the Court found no bill of attainder because *Nixon* "constituted a legitimate class of one," because the punishment at issue did not fall within the basic prohibition, and because the statute was not punitive in nature.

5. *Damage actions.* Nixon v. Fitzgerald, 457 U.S. 731 (1982), was an action for damages brought against President Nixon for an unconstitutional discharge from federal employment. The allegation was that the President had fired Fitzgerald because he had exercised his right to freedom of speech. The Court held, by a 5-to-4 vote, that the President was immune from an action for damages. The opinion was written by Justice Powell. According to the Court, "the President occupies a unique position in the constitutional scheme. [Because] of the singular importance of the President's duties, diversion of his energies by concern with private lawsuits would raise unique risks to the effective functioning of government." The Court referred to "the sheer prominence of the President's office," which would make him "an easily identifiable target for suits for civil damages. Cognizance of this personal vulnerability frequently could distract a President from his public duties, to the detriment not only of the President and his office but also the Nation that the Presidency was designed to serve."

The Court also responded to the suggestion that absolute immunity would "leave the Nation without sufficient protection against misconduct on the part of the Chief Executive." A number of safeguards were already in place: the remedy of impeachment; "constant scrutiny by the press"; "vigilant oversight by Congress"; "a desire to earn re-election, the need to maintain prestige as an element of Presidential influence, and a President's traditional concern for his historical stature" would all play a role. The Court left open, however, the question whether Congress might constitutionally subject the President to liability for damages.

In his dissenting opinion, joined by Justices Brennan, Marshall, and Blackmun, Justice White noted that with respect to presidential immunity, there was no provision akin to the speech or debate clause. In this light, it was necessary to find such immunity in "the constitutional principle of separation of powers and ['public] policy.'" Justice White noted that the Court had previously held that the President was not immune from suits for injunctive relief or other sorts of judicial process.

> These two lines of cases establish, then, that neither subjecting Presidential actions to a judicial determination of their constitutionality, nor subjecting the President to judicial process violates the separation-of-powers doctrine. [With] respect to intrusion by the judicial process itself on executive functions, subjecting the President to private claims for money damages involves no more than this.

And with respect to the distinctive nature of the remedy, Justice White argued that "the question that must be answered is who should bear the cost of the resulting injury — the wrongdoer or the victim." In his view, "the President should have the same remedial obligations toward those whom he injures as any other federal officer." The result of such a rule "should be to deter unconstitutional, or otherwise illegal, behavior."

Justice White concluded with a response to the Court's reasoning:

> It cannot be seriously argued that the President must be placed beyond the law and beyond judicial enforcement of constitutional restraints upon executive officers in order to implement the principle of separation of powers. [There] is no reason to think that, in the future, the protection afforded by summary judgment procedures would not be adequate to protect the President, as they currently protect other executive officers from unfounded litigation. [Furthermore,] in no instance have we previously held legal accountability in itself to be an unjustifiable cost. The availability of the courts to vindicate constitutional and statutory wrongs has been perceived and protected as one of the virtues of our system of delegated and limited powers. [Except] for the empty generality that the President should have "'the maximum ability to deal fearlessly and impartially with' the duties of his office," the majority nowhere suggests a particular, disadvantageous effect on a specific Presidential function. The caution that comes from requiring reasonable choices in areas that may intrude on individuals' legally protected rights has never before been counted as a cost.

Should the *Fitzgerald* ruling be extended to presidential aides? The Court held that it should not be in Harlow v. Fitzgerald, 457 U.S. 800 (1982). Is it persuasive to argue that the distinctive position of the presidency affords nonjudicial safeguards against unlawful conduct? Consider (1) the view that those safeguards are too blunt to ensure against more or less isolated activities rather than a general pattern of misconduct and (2) the response that sometimes the public may react with indifference or even approval to such misconduct. For general discussion, see Carter, The Political Aspects of Judicial Power: Some Notes on the Presidential Immunity Decision, 131 U. Pa. L. Rev. 1341 (1984).

Note: Impeachment

The Constitution provides the ultimate weapon against presidential misconduct in the form of the impeachment remedy. The House of Representatives may impeach the President, and remove him from office, for "Treason, Bribery, or other high Crimes and Misdemeanors." U.S. Const. art. II, §4.

The impeachment mechanism has been invoked quite rarely in the nation's history. Andrew Johnson is alone among presidents in having been impeached; he escaped conviction by a single vote. The House has voted to impeach a number of federal judges; the Senate voted to convict in four cases. Most recently, issues associated with the impeachment mechanism arose during the Watergate affair. The Articles of Impeachment adopted by the House Judiciary Committee, which never reached the full House because of President Nixon's resignation, are outlined below.

In part because of the sparse history, there is no clear answer to the central question: What is the meaning of the phrase "high crimes and misdemeanors"? May the President be impeached for activities that are not criminal offenses? Consider the following views.

1. *Legislative discretion:*

> What, then, is an impeachable offense? The only honest answer is that an impeachable offense is whatever a majority of the House of Representatives considers it to be at a given moment in history; conviction results from whatever offense or offenses two-thirds of the other body considers to be sufficiently serious to require removal of the accused from office.

Remarks of Congressman Gerald Ford, proposing the impeachment of Justice William O. Douglas, 116 Cong. Rec. H3113-3114 (daily ed. April 15, 1970).

2. *Crimes:*

> The decided weight of authority is, that no impeachment will lie except for a true crime [or] a breach of the common or statute law, which [would] be the subject of indictment.

Theodore Dwight, Trial by Impeachment, 6 Am. L. Reg. (N.S.) 257, 264 (1867).

3. *Words of art:*

> "High crimes and misdemeanors" appear to be words of art confined to impeachments, without roots in the ordinary criminal law and which, so far as I could discover, had no relation to whether an indictment would lie in the particular circumstances. [Charges] drawn from impeachment cases disclose that impeachable conduct was patently not "criminal" in the ordinary sense. [But the framers' intention was] to preclude resort to impeachment of the President for petty misconduct.

R. Berger, Impeachment 62-63, 67, 90 (1973).

Which interpretation best accords with the text of the clause? With a sensible allocation of power as between the Congress and the President? Consider the view that the position set out by then-Representative Ford should be accepted because, as history shows, there are powerful political and institutional checks on improperly motivated impeachment proceedings. For such proceedings to go forward, there must be a substantial consensus that the President's conduct warrants sanction. Does this view undervalue the damaging effects of politically inspired impeachment proceedings? Would it accord an undue weapon to Congress?

Should judicial review be available of decisions to impeach that, according to the President, do not involve "high crimes and misdemeanors"? Consider the materials on the political question doctrine, Chapter 1, section E, supra, and the position set out by Choper, Chapter 4, section A, supra.

Consider, finally, the three articles of impeachment voted against President Nixon. Which theory does each of them adopt?

Article I of the Articles of Impeachment asserted that President Nixon had obstructed the administration of justice by delaying and impeding the investigation into the unlawful entry into the headquarters of the Democratic National Committee. Among other things, the article said that Nixon had made false statements to investigative officers; withheld relevant evidence; approved of false and misleading testimony by government employees; interfered with investigations by the Federal Bureau of Investigation and the Department of Justice; and made false statements to the American public in order to deceive it into believing that a thorough investigation had been conducted.

Article II claimed that President Nixon had engaged in conduct violating the constitutional rights of citizens and impairing the administration of justice. Among other things, the article referred to use of the Internal Revenue Service to produce tax audits in a discriminatory manner; the effort to obtain tax information for unauthorized purposes; the misuse of the FBI through authorization of unlawful electronic surveillance; and creation of a secret investigative unit that used the Central Intelligence Agency for unlawful activities.

Article III contended that President Nixon failed without lawful cause to produce papers and things as directed by subpoenas issued by the House Committee on the Judiciary. The article stated that the relevant documents were deemed necessary by the committee to resolve questions relevant to the impeachment process.

E.   FOREIGN AFFAIRS

In the domestic sphere, analysis of separation of powers questions can be guided by the division of authority among the executive, legislative, and judicial branches. That division is ambiguous, with hard intermediate cases; but as the *Youngstown* case suggests, it provides a fruitful starting point for analysis.

The foreign sphere is different. There the allocation of authority

is not determined by any "natural" division. As they have evolved, the foreign relations powers appear [fissured]: [some] powers and functions belong to the President, some to Congress, some to the President-and-Senate; some can be exercised by either the President or the Congress, some require the joint authority of both. Irregular, uncertain division renders claims of usurpation more difficult to establish and the courts have not been available to adjudicate them.

L. Henkin, Foreign Affairs and the Constitution 32 (1972).

In these circumstances, much of the "law" is the product of historical practice and practical accommodations, formal and informal, between the executive and legislative branches. The relevant practices and accommodations take their starting point in the Constitution. But the text of the Constitution can hardly be said to compel the particular outcomes that have been reached. And because of the frequent unavailability of judicial review (why is judicial review so frequently unavailable?), history, perceived practical necessities, and "contemporary imponderables" have operated, even more here than elsewhere, as a "gloss" on the provisions of articles I and II. Consider in this regard the views of Justices Frankfurter and Jackson in the Steel Seizure case, which are frequently used as the basis for assessment of separation of powers issues in the foreign realm.

Consider, too, the cautionary suggestion that

> where foreign relations are concerned the Constitution seems a strange, laconic document: although it explicitly lodges important foreign affairs powers in one branch or another of the federal government, and denies important powers to the States, many others are not mentioned. [Traditional] interpreters have attempted to find the missing powers by traditional doctrines of constitutional construction. [But] the attempt to build all the foreign affairs powers of the federal government with the few bricks provided by the Constitution has not been accepted as successful. It requires considerable stretching of language, much reading between lines, and bold extrapolation from "the Constitution as a whole," and that still does not plausibly add up to all the power which the federal government in fact exercises.

Henkin, supra, at 16-17.

United States v. Curtiss-Wright Corp.
299 U.S. 304 (1936)

MR. JUSTICE SUTHERLAND delivered the opinion of the Court.

[An] indictment was returned in the court below, the first count of which charges that appellees [conspired] to sell in the United States certain arms of war, namely fifteen machine guns, to Bolivia, a country then engaged in armed conflict in the Chaco, in violation of the Joint Resolution of Congress approved May 28, 1934, and the provisions of a proclamation issued on the same day by the President [pursuant] to authority conferred by §1 of the resolution. [The] Joint Resolution [provided that:]

[If] the President finds that the prohibition of the sale of arms and munitions of war in the United States to those countries now engaged in armed conflict in the Chaco may contribute to the reëstablishment of peace between those countries, and if [he] makes proclamation to that effect, it shall be unlawful to sell [any] arms or munitions of war in any place in the United States to the countries now engaged in that armed conflict, [until] otherwise ordered by the President or by Congress. . . .

[The lower court held that the Joint Resolution was an unconstitutional delegation of legislative power to the President.]

Whether, if the Joint Resolution had related solely to internal affairs it would be open to the challenge that it constituted an unlawful delegation of legislative power to the Executive, we find it unnecessary to determine. The whole aim of the resolution is to affect a situation entirely external to the United States, and falling within the category of foreign affairs. [Assuming] (but not deciding) that the challenged delegation, if it were confined to internal affairs, would be invalid, may it nevertheless be sustained on the ground that its exclusive aim is to afford a remedy for a hurtful condition within foreign territory?

It will contribute to the elucidation of the question if we first consider the differences between the powers of the federal government in respect of foreign or external affairs and those in respect of domestic or internal affairs. . . .

The two classes of powers are different, both in respect of their origin and their nature. The broad statement that the federal government can exercise no powers except those specifically enumerated in the Constitution, and such implied powers as are necessary and proper to carry into effect the enumerated powers, is categorically true only in respect of our internal affairs. In that field, the primary purpose of the Constitution was to carve from the general mass of legislative powers *then possessed by the states* such portions as it was thought desirable to vest in the federal government, leaving those not included in the enumeration still in the states. [That] this doctrine applies only to powers which the states had, is self evident. And since the states severally never possessed international powers, such powers could not have been carved from the mass of state powers but obviously were transmitted to the United States from some other source. . . .

As a result of the separation from Great Britain by the colonies acting as a unit, the powers of external sovereignty passed from the Crown not to the colonies severally, but to the colonies in their collective and corporate capacity as the United States of America. [Rulers] come and go; governments end and forms of government change; but sovereignty survives. A political society cannot endure without a supreme will somewhere. Sovereignty is never held in suspense. When, therefore, the external sovereignty of Great Britain in respect of the colonies ceased, it immediately passed to the Union. . . .

It results that the investment of the federal government with the powers of external sovereignty did not depend upon the affirmative grants of the Constitution. The powers to declare and wage war, to conclude peace, to make treaties, to maintain diplomatic relations with other sovereignties, if they had never been mentioned in the Constitution, would have vested in the federal government as necessary concomitants of nationality. . . .

Not only, as we have shown, is the federal power over external affairs in origin and essential character different from that over internal affairs, but participation in the exercise of the power is significantly limited. In this vast external realm, with its important, complicated, delicate and manifold problems, the President alone has the power to speak or listen as a representative of the nation. He *makes* treaties with the advice and consent of the Senate; but he alone negotiates. Into the field of negotiation the Senate cannot intrude; and Congress itself is powerless to invade it. As Marshall said [in] the House of Representatives, "The President is the sole organ of the nation in its external relations, and its sole representative with foreign nations." . . .

It is important to bear in mind that we are here dealing not alone with an authority vested in the President by an exertion of legislative power, but with such an authority plus the very delicate, plenary and exclusive power of the President as the sole organ of the federal government in the field of international relations — a power which does not require as a basis for its exercise an act of Congress. [It] is quite apparent that if, in the maintenance of our international relations, embarrassment — perhaps serious embarrassment — is to be avoided and success for our aims achieved, congressional legislation [must] often accord to the President a degree of discretion and freedom from statutory restriction which would not be admissible were domestic affairs alone involved. Moreover, he, not Congress, has the better opportunity of knowing the conditions which prevail in foreign countries, and especially is this true in time of war. He has his confidential sources of information. He has his agents in the form of diplomatic, consular and other officials. Secrecy in respect of information gathered by them may be highly necessary, and the premature disclosure of it productive of harmful results. . . .

In the light of the foregoing observations, it is evident that this court should not be in haste to apply a general rule which will have the effect of condemning legislation like that under review as constituting an unlawful delegation of legislative power. The principles which justify such legislation find overwhelming support in the unbroken legislative practice which has prevailed almost from the inception of the national government to the present day. . . .

[Reversed.]

MR. JUSTICE McREYNOLDS dissented without opinion.

Note: The President and Foreign Affairs

Two aspects of *Curtiss-Wright* are of special importance. The first, involving the distribution of power between the states and the federal government, is the conclusion that the national government has exclusive authority in the realm of foreign affairs. The second, involving the distribution of power between the legislature and the executive, is the expansive view of presidential authority in that realm.

1. *Federal authority*. The Court concludes that national power over foreign affairs is exclusive; the states are thus disabled from acting in the arena of foreign relations. Cf. Cooley v. Board of Wardens, Chapter 2 supra (dormant commerce clause creates exclusive sphere of federal authority). This was a highly controversial judgment, not clearly supported by the relevant history. What is the basis for the Court's position?

Consider the following view:

Surely [the evidence] is not manifestly all [the Court's] way: there is disagreement whether the Declaration of Independence declared a single sovereign entity or thirteen independent nation-states; there is evidence that, after independence, at least some of the erstwhile colonies, at least for some time and for some purposes, considered themselves sovereign, independent states; even under the Articles of Confederation it is not wholly clear that "the United States" was a sovereign entity rather than a band of sovereigns acting together through the agency of the Congress. But Sutherland's view of the locus of sovereignty between 1776 and 1789 has strong support; and — what Sutherland's critics have largely overlooked — challenging his history does not necessarily destroy his constitutional doctrine. . . .

The Constitution, Sutherland might point out, does not explicitly terminate the sovereignty of the States or declare or recognize the United States a nation, does not confer upon the federal government the powers of national sovereignty generally, or specify many of the powers implied in sovereignty. It is reasonable to conclude, he might say, that the Framers intended to deal in full only with the governance of domestic affairs where the distribution between nation and States was new and critical, where the States retained most of the powers and the new central government was to have only what was given it; but, with a few explicable exceptions, they did not deal with, enumerate, allocate powers in foreign affairs where the federal government was to have all.

Henkin, supra, at 23-24. But if this view is correct, why did the framers believe it necessary to confer foreign affairs powers at all?

2. *Presidential power. Curtiss-Wright* itself involved a delegation from Congress to the President. The Court's broad pronouncements about presidential power were therefore unnecessary to the decision. Be that as it may, why does the Court believe that the President is "the sole organ of the federal government in the field of international relations"? Three candidates suggest themselves: the constitutional text; historical practices; and contemporary policy, or the need to avoid "serious embarrassment." But the text does not make the President the sole organ of the federal government. Indeed, it vests in Congress a number of foreign affairs powers, including the power to declare war, the power to regulate commerce with foreign nations, the power to raise and support armies, the power to provide and maintain a navy, the power to provide for organizing, arming, and disciplining the militia, and the power to make rules for calling forth the militia to repel invasions. The President, to be sure, is Commander-in-Chief of the armed forces and the militia; and he is given other authority as well. But the text hardly provides unambiguous support for the Court's broad statements.

The history is also uncertain. From the first it was clear that the President would have to assume a special role of leadership and initiative in the realm of foreign policy. Many Presidents assumed such a role, concluding that the necessities of international relations prevented Congress, with its many members, from acting expeditiously. Consider in this regard the framers' desire to ensure an energetic executive. But that raises two questions. First, does the somewhat ambiguous history in fact support the Court's conclusion? Second, what role should historical practices have in interpreting the relevant constitutional provisions? Why should those practices not be considered a usurpation of the original allocation of constitutional authority?

The final justification for the Court's view involves considerations of policy. Several considerations may support broad presidential authority. He may act more expeditiously than Congress, which after all consists of many people with diverse viewpoints. The President may have more expertise. He may be better at keeping secrets. And he may have better access to the necessary information. If you were arguing on behalf of a strong congressional role, could you meet these arguments? What part, if any, should these considerations play in constitutional interpretation? Consider in this regard the opinions in the Steel Seizure case.

3. *The implications of* Curtis-Wright. How much "inherent" authority does *Curtis-Wright* recognize on the part of the President in the field of foreign relations? How far does that authority extend if (a) Congress has been silent or has attempted to deny the President the authority in question or (b) the attempted assertion of presidential authority is not directly traceable to the particular enumerated powers in article II? Cf. Goldwater v. Carter, Chapter 1, section E, supra, where Justice Brennan found presidential authority to terminate a treaty without congressional consent. See also United States v. Belmont, 301 U.S. 324 (1937) (sustaining executive agreement growing out of U.S. recognition of Soviet Union, notwithstanding contrary public policy of state of New York). Note that the President often sets out "executive orders," purporting to have binding effect, and traces his authority to constitutional or statutory provisions. To what extent is Justice Jackson's framework in *Youngstown* useful here?

Dames & Moore v. Regan

453 U.S. 654 (1981)

JUSTICE REHNQUIST delivered the opinion of the Court.

The questions presented by this case touch fundamentally upon the manner in which our Republic is to be governed. Throughout the nearly two centuries of our Nation's existence under the Constitution, this subject has generated considerable debate. We have had the benefit of commentators such as John Jay, Alexander Hamilton, and James Madison writing in The Federalist Papers at the Nation's very inception, the benefit of astute foreign observers of our system such as Alexis de Tocqueville and James Bryce writing during the first century of the Nation's existence, and the benefit of many other treatises as well as more than 400 volumes of reports of decisions of this Court. As these writings reveal it is doubtless both futile and perhaps dangerous to find any epigrammatical explanation of how this country has been governed. . . .

Our decision today will not dramatically alter this situation, for the Framers "did not make the judiciary the overseer of our government." [*Youngstown*] (Frankfurter, J., concurring). We are confined to a resolution of the dispute presented to us. That dispute involves various Executive Orders and regulations by which the President nullified attachments and liens on Iranian assets in the United States, directed that these assets be transferred to Iran, and suspended claims against Iran that may be presented to an International Claims Tribunal. This action was taken in an effort to comply with an Executive Agreement between the United States and Iran.

[The] decisions of the Court in this area have been rare, episodic, and afford little precedential value for subsequent cases. The tensions present in any exercise of executive power under the tripartite system of Federal Government established by the Constitution have been reflected in opinions by Members of this Court more than once.

[Justice] Jackson in his concurring opinion in *Youngstown*, [which] both parties agree brings together as much combination of analysis and common sense as there is in this area, focused not on the "plenary and exclusive power of the President" but rather responded to a claim of virtually unlimited powers for the Executive by noting:

> The example of such unlimited executive power that must have most impressed the forefathers was the prerogative exercised by George III, and the description of its evils in the Declaration of Independence leads me to doubt that they were creating their new Executive in his image.

343 U.S., at 641.

As we now turn to the factual and legal issues in this case, we freely confess that we are obviously deciding only one more episode in the never-ending tension between the President [and] the Constitution. . . .

On November 4, 1979, the American Embassy in Tehran was seized and our diplomatic personnel were captured and held hostage. In response to that crisis, President Carter, acting pursuant to the International Emergency Economic Powers Act, declared a national emergency on November 14, 1979, and blocked the removal or transfer of "all property and interests in property of the Government of Iran, its instrumentalities and controlled entities and the Central Bank of Iran which are or become subject to the jurisdiction of the United States. . . ." [On] November 14, 1979, the Treasury Department's Office of Foreign Assets Control issued a regulation providing that "[u]nless licensed or authorized . . . any attachment, judgment, decree, lien, execution, garnishment, or other judicial process is null and void with respect to any property in which on or since [November 14, 1979] there existed an interest of Iran." . . .

On December 19, 1979, petitioner Dames & Moore filed suit in the United States District Court [against] the Government of Iran, the Atomic Energy Organization of Iran, and a number of Iranian banks. [Petitioner] alleged that its wholly owned subsidiary, Dames & Moore International, S.R.L., was a party to a written contract with the Atomic Energy Organization, and that the subsidiary's entire interest in the contract had been assigned to petitioner. [Petitioner] contended [that] it was owed $3,436,694.30 plus interest for services performed under the contract prior to the date of termination. The District Court issued orders of attachment directed against property of the defendants, and the property of certain Iranian banks was then attached to secure any judgment that might be entered against them.

On January 20, 1981, the Americans held hostage were released by Iran pursuant to an Agreement entered into the day [before. The] Agreement stated that "[i]t is the purpose of [the United States and Iran] . . . to terminate all litigation as between the Government of each party and the nationals of the other, and to bring about the settlement and termination of all such claims through binding arbitration." In furtherance of this goal, the Agreement called for the establishment of an Iran-United States Claims Tribunal which would arbitrate any claims not settled within six months. Awards of the Claims Tribunal are to be "final and binding" and "enforceable . . . in the courts of any nation in accordance with its laws." Under the Agreement, the United States is obligated

> to terminate all legal proceedings in United States courts involving claims of United States persons and institutions against Iran and its state enterprises, to nullify all attachments and judgments obtained therein, to prohibit all further litigation based on such claims, and to bring about the termination of such claims through binding arbitration.

In addition, the United States must "act to bring about the transfer" by July 19, 1981, of all Iranian assets held in this country by American banks. One billion dollars of these assets will be deposited in a security account in the Bank of England, to the account of the Algerian Central Bank, and used to satisfy awards rendered against Iran by the Claims Tribunal.

On January 19, 1981, President Carter issued a series of Executive Orders implementing the terms of the agreement. . . .

On February 24, 1981, President Reagan issued an Executive Order in which he "ratified" the January 19th Executive Orders. Moreover, he "suspended" all "claims which may be presented to the . . . Tribunal" and provided that such claims "shall have no legal effect in any action now pending in any court of the United States." The suspension of any particular claim terminates if the Claims Tribunal determines that it has no jurisdiction over that claim; claims are discharged for all purposes when the Claims Tribunal either awards some recovery and that amount is paid, or determines that no recovery is due. . . .

[The lower court upheld the executive actions at issue.]

The parties and the lower courts [have] all agreed that much relevant analysis is contained in [*Youngstown*]. Justice Black's opinion for the Court in that case [recognized] that "[t]he President's power, if any, to issue the order must stem either from an act of Congress or from the Constitution itself." Justice Jackson's concurring opinion elaborated in a general way the consequences of different types of interaction between the two democratic branches in assessing Presidential authority to act in any given case.

Although we have in the past found and do today find Justice Jackson's classification of executive actions into three general categories analytically useful, [Justice] Jackson himself recognized that his three categories represented "a somewhat over-simplified grouping," and it is doubtless the case that executive action in any particular instance falls, not neatly in one of three pigeonholes, but rather at some point along a spectrum running from explicit congressional authorization to explicit congressional prohibition. This is particularly true as respects cases such as the one before us, involving responses to international crises the nature of which Congress can hardly have been expected to anticipate in any detail.

[The] Government has principally relied on §203 of the [International Emergency Economic Powers Act, or IEEPA] [as] authorization for these actions. [That section] provides in part:

> [The] President may [nullify,] void, prevent or prohibit, any acquisition, holding, withholding, use, transfer, withdrawal, transportation, importation or exportation of, or dealing in, or exercising any right, power, or privilege with respect to, or transactions involving, any property in which any foreign country or a national thereof has any interest; by any person, or with respect to any property, subject to the jurisdiction of the United States.

The Government contends that the acts of "nullifying" the attachments and ordering the "transfer" of the frozen assets are specifically authorized by the plain language of the above statute. . . .

Petitioner contends that we should ignore the plain language of this statute because an examination of its legislative history as well as the history of §5(b) of the Trading with the Enemy Act (hereinafter TWEA), from which the pertinent language of §1702 is directly drawn, reveals that the statute was not intended to give the President such extensive power over the assets of a foreign state during times of national emergency. . . . .

We do not [agree. Nothing] in the legislative history of [§5(b)] of the TWEA requires such a result. To the contrary, we think both the legislative history and cases interpreting the TWEA fully sustain the broad authority of the Executive when acting under this congressional grant of power. . . .

Because the President's action in nullifying the attachments and ordering the transfer of the assets was taken pursuant to specific congressional authorization, it is "supported by the strongest of presumptions and the widest latitude of judicial interpretation, and the burden of persuasion would rest heavily upon any who might attack it." *Youngstown*, 343 U.S., at 637 (Jackson, J., concurring). Under the circumstances of this case, we cannot say that petitioner has sustained that heavy burden. A contrary ruling would mean that the Federal Government as a whole lacked the power exercised by the President, and that we are not prepared to say.

Although we have concluded that the IEEPA constitutes specific congressional authorization to the President to nullify the attachments and order the transfer of Iranian assets, there remains the question of the President's authority to suspend claims pending in American courts. Such claims have, of course, an existence apart from the attachments which accompanied them. In terminating these claims [the] President purported to act under authority of both the IEEPA and [the] so-called "Hostage Act." We conclude that neither the IEEPA nor the Hostage Act constitutes specific authorization of the President's action suspending claims. This is not to say[, however,] that these statutory provisions are entirely irrelevant to the question of the validity of the President's action. We think both statutes highly relevant in the looser sense of indicating congressional acceptance of a broad scope for executive action in circumstances such as those presented in this case. [The] IEEPA delegates broad authority to the President to act in times of national emergency with respect to property of a foreign country. The Hostage Act similarly indicates congressional willingness that the President have broad discretion when responding to the hostile acts of foreign sovereigns. . . .

[We] cannot ignore the general tenor of Congress' legislation in this area in trying to determine whether the President is acting alone or at least with the acceptance of Congress. [Congress] cannot anticipate and legislate with regard to every possible action the President may find it necessary to take or every possible situation in which he might act. Such failure of Congress specifically to delegate authority does not, "especially . . . in the areas of foreign policy and national security," imply "congressional disapproval" of action taken by the Executive. On the contrary, the enactment of legislation closely related to the question of the President's authority in a particular case which evinces legislative intent to accord the President broad discretion may be considered to "invite" "measures on independent presidential responsibility." *Youngstown* (Jackson, J., concurring). At least this is so where there is no contrary indication of legislative intent and when, as here, there is a history of congressional acquiescence in conduct of the sort engaged in by the President. It is to that history which we now turn.

Not infrequently in affairs between nations, outstanding claims by nations of one country against the government of another country are "sources of friction" between the two sovereigns. To resolve these difficulties, nations have often entered into agreements settling the claims of their respective nations. [Under] such agreements, the President has agreed to renounce or extinguish claims of United States nationals against foreign governments in return for lump-sum payments or the establishment of arbitration procedures. . . .

Crucial to our decision today is the conclusion that Congress has implicitly approved the practice of claim settlement by executive agreement. This is best demonstrated by Congress' enactment of the International Claims Settlement Act of 1949. . . .

Over the years Congress has frequently amended the International Claims Settlement Act to provide for particular problems arising out of settlement agreements, thus demonstrating Congress' continuing acceptance of the President's claim settlement authority. . . .

In light of all of the foregoing — the inferences to be drawn from the character of the legislation Congress has enacted in the area such as the IEEPA and the Hostage Act, and from the history of acquiescence in executive claims settlement — we conclude that the President was authorized to suspend pending claims. [As] Justice Frankfurter pointed out in *Youngstown*, "a systematic, unbroken, executive practice, long pursued to the knowledge of the Congress and never before questioned . . . may be treated as a gloss on 'Executive Power' vested in the President by §1 of Art. II." Past practice does not, by itself, create power, but "long-continued practice, known to and acquiesced in by Congress, would raise a presumption that the [action] had been [taken] in pursuance of its consent. . . ." United States v. Midwest Oil Co., 236 U.S. 459, 474 (1915). . . .

Our conclusion is buttressed by the fact that the means chosen by the President to settle the claims of American nationals provided an alternative forum, the Claims Tribunal, which is capable of providing meaningful relief. . . .

Just as importantly, Congress has not disapproved of the action taken here. Though Congress has held hearings on the Iranian Agreement itself, Congress has not enacted legislation, or even passed a resolution, indicating its displeasure with the Agreement. Quite the contrary, the relevant Senate Committee has stated that the establishment of the Tribunal is "of vital importance to the United States." We are thus clearly not confronted with a situation in which Congress has in some way resisted the exercise of Presidential authority.

Finally, we re-emphasize the narrowness of our decision. We do not decide that the President possesses plenary power to settle claims, even as against foreign governmental entities. [But] where, as here, the settlement of claims has been determined to be a necessary incident to the resolution of a major foreign policy dispute between our country and another, and where, as here, we can conclude that Congress acquiesced in the President's action, we are not prepared to say that the President lacks the power to settle such claims.

[Affirmed.]

[A concurring opinion by JUSTICE POWELL is omitted.]

Note: *Iranian Claims and Executive Power*

1. *The setting. Dames & Moore* must be understood as a late stage of the crisis growing out of the holding of U.S. citizens as hostages by Iranian terrorists. President Carter was able to secure the release of the hostages in return for the

various agreements at issue in the Court's opinion. In these circumstances, there was considerable pressure for the Court to decide the case as it did.

See in this regard Miller, *Dames & Moore v. Regan*: A Political Decision by a Political Court, 29 U.C.L.A. L. Rev. 1104, 1105, 1127 (1982):

> Although crafted in familiar lawyers' language, Justice Rehnquist's opinion for the Court reeks with the odor of compromise forced by necessity. Principle, as usual, gave way to *realpolitik*. The Justices had, in the last analysis, no choice save to sustain the validity of President Carter's hurried deal for the release of the hostages. Invalidation of the executive agreement would have placed the prospective conduct of American policy in an intolerable position. [I] do not suggest that the Constitution, as written, is irrelevant in such cases as *Dames & Moore*. Of course it has pertinence, but only as a point of departure for political decisions politically made.

Do you agree? Or does the text of the relevant constitutional provisions, read in the light of their purposes and the precedents, justify a different conclusion?

2. Dames & Moore *versus* Youngstown. Does the Court's opinion resolve the question of methodology raised by *Youngstown*? Consider the possibility that it represents a rejection of the approach taken by Justice Black, at least in cases involving foreign affairs, in favor of an approach that borrows from Justices Frankfurter and Jackson.

Questions of methodology to one side, can the result in *Dames & Moore* be reconciled with that in *Youngstown*? The Court appears to assume that the President's acts belong in Justice Jackson's category one, that is, acts with implied congressional consent — unlike in *Youngstown*, which involved an implied negation of authority. But did the Court properly read congressional silence? Where did the implied authorization derive from? One might have argued that Congress had carefully considered the question whether to grant the relevant presidential power and expressly refused to do so — just as in *Youngstown*. The failure to grant the precise power in question might be understood as a refusal to do this; where Congress stopped is surely as important as the general direction in which it was headed. On this score, *Dames & Moore* can be understood as indistinguishable from *Youngstown*. Do you agree? What result in *Chadha* if Congress had expressed no view one way or the other?

Note also that in *Chadha* the Court held that Congress may make law only through the mechanisms specified in article I. Does the Court's reliance on congressional silence and inaction as a form of lawmaking run afoul of the understanding in *Chadha*?

Compare *Youngstown* and *Dames & Moore* in terms of historical considerations and "contemporary imponderables." How would Justices Frankfurter and Jackson have resolved *Dames & Moore*? Note also the differences between the classification analysis of the Court in *Youngstown* and the more open-ended inquiry of *Dames & Moore*. Might one suggest that the Court adopted Chief Justice Vinson's position in *Youngstown*?

3. *The emergency powers of the President.* To what extent does *Dames & Moore*, explicitly or implicitly, recognize an emergency power on the part of the President? With respect to that question, should foreign affairs be treated differently from domestic matters? Reconsider the situations set out at page 362 supra.

Note: The Allocation of Warmaking
Authority

The Constitution is notoriously ambiguous on the allocation of warmaking power as between the President and the Congress. The President is made commander-in-chief of the armed forces, and there is no doubt that the framers intended the President to play the principal role as the representative of the United States in relations with other nations. On the other hand, Congress is expressly empowered to "declare war." How should these provisions be reconciled? Some guidance was provided during the constitutional convention:

"To make war."

Mr. Pinkney opposed the vesting this power in the Legislature. Its proceedings were too slow. It wd. meet but once a year. The Hs. of Reps. would be too numerous for such deliberations. The Senate would be the best depositary, being more acquainted with foreign affairs, and most capable of proper resolutions. If the States are equally represented in Senate, so as to give no advantage to large States, the power will notwithstanding be safe, as the small have their all at stake in such cases as well as the large States. It would be singular for one authority to make war, and another peace.

Mr. Butler. The Objections agst the Legislature lie in a great degree agst the Senate. He was for vesting the power in the President, who will have all the requisite qualities, and will not make war but when the Nation will support it.

Mr. M⟨adison⟩ and Mr. Gerry moved to insert "*declare*," striking out "*make*" war; leaving to the Executive the power to repel sudden attacks.

Mr. Sharman thought it stood very well. The Executive shd. be able to repel and not to commence war. "Make" better than "declare" the latter narrowing the power too much.

Mr. Gerry never expected to hear in a republic a motion to empower the Executive alone to declare war.

Mr. Elseworth. There is a material difference between the cases of making *war*, and making *peace*. It shd. be more easy to get out of war, than into it. War also is a simple and overt declaration, peace attended with intricate & secret negociations.

Mr. Mason was agst giving the power of war to the Executive, because not ⟨safely⟩ to be trusted with it; or to the Senate, because not so constructed as to be entitled to it. He was for clogging rather than facilitating war; but for facilitating peace. He preferred "*declare*" to "*make*".

On the Motion to insert *declare* — in place of *Make*, ⟨it was agreed to.⟩

This colloquy seems to indicate a constitutional judgment that the President should be able to act to "repel sudden attacks." But in other contexts, he could not initiate "war" without a congressional declaration. How much weight should such a colloquy have? Note that even if it is accorded considerable authority, the colloquy leaves open a number of questions: (1) Is the power to "repel sudden attacks" a part of the Constitution as well as its drafting history? (2) Exactly what does that power include? Does it extend beyond purely defensive measures? (3) May the President do anything other than repel sudden attacks without a congressional declaration? (4) What is a "war" within the meaning of the Constitution?

You should keep these questions in mind while reading the materials that follow.

The Prize Cases
67 U.S. [2 Black] 635 (1863)

MR. JUSTICE GRIER delivered the opinion of the Court

[After the purported secession of a number of Southern states, President Lincoln proclaimed a blockade of Southern ports. A series of cases were brought challenging the proclamation; the lower courts upheld the President's action.]

[Had] the President a right to institute a blockade of ports in possession of persons in armed rebellion against the Government, on the principles of international law, as known and acknowledged among civilized States?

Let us enquire whether, at the time this blockade was instituted, a state of war existed which would justify a resort to these means of subduing the hostile force. [It] is not necessary to constitute war, that both parties should be acknowledged as independent nations or sovereign States. A war may exist where one of the belligerents, claims sovereign rights as against the other. [A] civil war is never solemnly declared. [When] the party in rebellion occupy and hold in a hostile manner a certain portion of territory; have declared their independence; have cast off their allegiance; have organized armies; have commenced hostilities against their former sovereign, the world acknowledges them as belligerents, and the contest a *war. They* claim to be in arms to establish their liberty and independence, in order to become a sovereign State, while the sovereign party treats them as insurgents and rebels who owe allegiance, and who should be punished with death for their treason. . . .

As a civil war is never publicly proclaimed, [its] actual existence is a fact in our domestic history which the Court is bound to notice and to know. . . .

By the Constitution, Congress alone has the power to declare a national or foreign war. It cannot declare war against a State, or any number of States, by virtue of any clause in the Constitution. The Constitution confers on the President the whole Executive power. He is bound to take care that the laws be faithfully executed. He is Commander-in-chief of the Army and Navy of the United States, and of the militia of the several States when called into the actual service of the United States. He has no power to initiate or declare a war either against a foreign nation or a domestic State. But by [Acts] of Congress, [he] is authorized to [call] out the militia and use the military and naval forces of the United States in case of invasion by foreign nations, and to suppress insurrection against the government of a State or of the United States.

If a war be made by invasion of a foreign nation, the President is not only authorized but bound to resist force by force. He does not initiate the war, but is bound to accept the challenge without waiting for any special legislative authority. And whether the hostile party be a foreign invader, or States organized in rebellion, it is none the less a war, although the declaration of it be *"unilateral."* . . .

Whether the President in fulfilling his duties, as Commander in-chief, in suppressing an insurrection, has met with such armed hostile resistance, and a civil war of such alarming proportions as will compel him to accord to them the character of belligerents, is a question to be decided *by him*, and this Court must be governed by the decisions and acts of the political department of the Government to which this power was entrusted. "He must determine what degree of force the crisis demands." The proclamation of blockade is itself official and conclusive evidence to the Court that a state of war existed which demanded and authorized a recourse to such a measure, under the circumstances peculiar to the case.

[We] are of the opinion that the President had a right, jure belli, to institute a blockade of ports in possession of the States in rebellion, which neutrals are bound to regard. [Affirmed.]

MR. JUSTICE NELSON, dissenting.

By our Constitution [the] war power is lodged in Congress. Congress shall have power "to declose war, grant letters [of] reprisal, and make rules concerning captures on land and water." [We] are asked, what would become of the peace and integrity of the Union in case of an insurrection at home or invasion from abroad if this power could not be exercised by the President in the recess of Congress, and until that body could be assembled?

The framers of the Constitution fully comprehended this question, and provided for the contingency. [The] Constitution declares that Congress shall have power "to provide for calling forth the militia to execute the laws of the Union, suppress insurrections, and repel invasions." Another clause, "that the President shall be Commander-in-chief of the Army and Navy of the United States, and of the militia of the several States when called into the actual service of the United States"; and, again, "He shall take care that the laws shall be faithfully executed." Congress passed laws on this subject in 1792 and 1795.

The last Act provided that whenever the United States shall be invaded or be in imminent danger of invasion from a foreign nation, it shall be lawful for the President to call forth such number of the militia most convenient to the place of danger, and in case of insurrection in any State against the Government thereof, it shall be lawful for the President, on the application of the Legislature of such State, [to] call forth such number of militia of any other State or States as he may judge sufficient to suppress such insurrection. . . .

It will be seen [that] ample provision has been made under the Constitution and laws against any sudden and unexpected disturbance of the public peace from insurrection at home or invasion from abroad. The whole military and naval power of the country is put under the control of the President to meet the emergency.

[It] has also been argued that this power of the President from necessity should be construed as vesting him with the war power, or the Republic might greatly suffer or be in danger from the attacks of the hostile party before the assembling of Congress. But we have seen that the whole military and naval force are in his hands under the municipal laws of the country. He can meet the adversary upon land and water with all the forces of the Government. The truth is, this idea of the existence of any necessity for clothing the President with the war power, under the Act of 1795, is simply a monstrous exaggeration; for, besides having the command of the whole of the army and navy, Congress can be assembled within any thirty days, if the safety of the country requires that the war power shall be brought into operation.

[CHIEF JUSTICE TANEY and JUSTICES CASTROM and CLIFFORD joined in this dissent.]

Note: The Prize Cases *and the Constitutional* *Allocation of Warmaking Power*

1. *Breadth and implications.* Whatever one thinks of the decision, it is clear that The Prize Cases covered a relatively narrow problem. What implications

does the decision have for the more general issue of presidential authority? Consider Mora v. McNamara, 389 U.S. 934 (1967) (Douglas, J., dissenting), stressing that the conflicts between Justice Grier and Justice Nelson "have continued to be voiced" during "all subsequent periods in our history — through the Spanish-American War, the Boxer Rebellion, two World Wars, Korea, and [Vietnam]."

2. *The Vietnam War.* There were numerous efforts to obtain some answers to the constitutional questions during the Vietnam War. Most courts held the issue to present a nonjusticiable political question. See Chapter 1, section E, infra. In Orlando v. Laird, 443 F.2d 1039 (2d Cir. 1971), cert. denied, 404 U.S. 869 (1971), the court held that the Constitution required participation on the part of Congress for the Vietnam War but that Congress had provided sufficient authorization to the President.

Note also that the question of U.S. involvement in international hostilities raises issues of treaty interpretation and of international law as well as of constitutional interpretation. See, for general discussion, Department of State, Office of Legal Advisor, The Legality of United States Participation in the Defense of Vietnam, 75 Yale L.J. 1085 (1966); Monaghan, Presidential Warmaking, 50 B.U. L. Rev. 19 (1970).

3. *Some ambiguities: "war" and "repelling sudden attack."* If it is assumed that the Constitution authorizes the President to act unilaterally to "repel a sudden attack" but that he must obtain a declaration of war in order to commence hostilities, how much authority does he have? Note also the changes in the nature of the international context since the Constitution was drafted. Might "repel sudden attack" and "war" mean something different today from what they meant in that era? Consider the following views.

a. Ratner, The Coordinated Warmaking Power — Legislative, Executive, and Judicial Roles, 44 S. Cal. L. Rev. 461, 466-469 (1971):

> In 1787, "repel sudden attack" probably meant "resist invasion or rebellion." But the constitutional policy [is] not congealed in the mold of 1787 referents. [Aggression] beyond the seas could not threaten Americans in the eighteenth century as it can in the twentieth. Underlying the constitutional language is a long-range purpose that authorizes the President to protect Americans from external force in an emergency.
>
> The amorphous distinction between offense and defense does not effectively delineate the scope of the President's emergency war power. In a world where increasingly mobile weapons enhance the advantage of military initiative, the distinction turns, for the most part, on an appraisal of motives and intentions. With his heavy load of responsibility, the President may sometimes conclude that offense is the best defense. And, though his characterization may be debatable, the President must necessarily be accorded a broad discretion.

b. Note, Congress, the President, and the Power to Commit Forces to Combat, 81 Harv. L. Rev. 1771 (1968):

> The historical development of the self-defense rationale would limit independent presidential power to engage in war to certain cases involving direct attacks against the United States. [There] are a number of difficulties with the theory that [an] attack on another country is equivalent to an attack on the United States. [The] fact that "security" interests are involved does not in itself alter the normal processes for deciding whether such interests are worth defending at the price of war. That decision [will] depend on a variety of factors. [Where], on the other hand, the attack is against the United States itself, there can be no question [that] the "security

interest" involved warrants defending at the cost of war if necessary. [Still,] there may be *some* cases where [an] eruption of violence abroad poses a threat so inimical to our own security that the defense of the United States itself is immediately involved.

How does one decide what cases fall in that category? Is there a role for the courts here?

    c. Id.:

> From the beginning it has been recognized that not every involvement of the armed forces can be a "war" requiring congressional action. In the modern context where international conflict has so many forms, the problem is even more difficult. [The] meaning of war [must] be determined with reference to the purpose of the war-declaring clause: to safeguard the United States against unchecked executive decisions to commit the country to a trial of force.
>
>   There are two possible reasons for requiring such a safeguard from the body most directly representative of popular sentiment. The first is that such a decision involves risk of great economic and physical sacrifice. [The] second is that [the] very act of using force [entails] moral and legal consequences sufficiently significant to require an expression of popular approval. [The] first argues for a definition phrased in quantitative terms, which would require congressional action prior to engaging in "major" hostilities. [The] second would result in a more comprehensive, qualitative definition which would forbid any use of force against a foreign sovereign without prior congressional approval.

How helpful are such guidelines?

    4. *Some examples.* In the absence of a congressional declaration of war, and putting to one side any obligations imposed by treaty, may the President do the following? (a) Use military force to protect a U.S. military base in West Germany from an attack that has already begun; (b) send troops to West Germany to protect it from an anticipated attack; (c) send troops to (1) Canada or (2) France to protect it from an attack that has already begun; (d) send troops on a mission to rescue U.S. hostages held abroad. Consider also the bearing of the War Powers Resolution on these questions and note the examples described below.

The War Powers Resolution

50 U.S.C. §§1545-1548 (1973)

Purpose and Policy

Sec. 2. (a) It is the purpose of this joint resolution to fulfill the intent of the framers of the Constitution of the United States and insure that the collective judgment of both the Congress and the President will apply to the introduction of United States Armed Forces into hostilities, or into situations where imminent involvement in hostilities is clearly indicated by the circumstances, and to the continued use of such forces in hostilities or in such situations.

    (b) Under article I, section 8, of the Constitution, it is specifically provided that the Congress shall have the power to make all laws necessary and proper for carrying into execution, not only its own powers but also all other powers vested by the Constitution in the Government of the United States, or in any department or officer thereof.

→(c) The constitutional powers of the President as Commander-in-Chief to introduce United States Armed Forces into hostilities, or into situations where imminent involvement in hostilities is clearly indicated by the circumstances, are exercised only pursuant to (1) a declaration of war, (2) specific statutory authorization, or (3) a national emergency created by attack upon the United States, its territories or possessions, or its armed forces.

CONSULTATION

Sec. 3. The President in every possible instance shall consult with Congress before introducing United States Armed Forces into hostilities or into situations where imminent involvement in hostilities is clearly indicated by the circumstances, and after every such introduction shall consult regularly with the Congress until United States Armed Forces are no longer engaged in hostilities or have been removed from such situations.

REPORTING

Sec. 4. (a) In the absence of a declaration of war, in any case in which United States Armed Forces are introduced —

(1) into hostilities or into situations where imminent involvement in hostilities is clearly indicated by the circumstances;

(2) into the territory, airspace or waters of a foreign nation, while equipped for combat, except for deployments which relate solely to supply, replacement, repair, or training of such forces; or

(3) in numbers which substantially enlarge United States Armed Forces equipped for combat already located in a foreign nation;

the President shall submit within 48 hours to the Speaker of the House of Representatives and to the President pro tempore of the Senate a report, in writing [setting forth "the circumstances necessitating the introduction of armed forces," "the constitutional and legislative authority" under which it occurred, "the estimated scope and duration of the hostilities," and "such other information as the Congress may request."]

CONGRESSIONAL ACTION . . .

Sec. 5. . . . . (b) Within sixty calendar days after a report is submitted or is required to be submitted pursuant to section 4(a)(1), whichever is earlier, the President shall terminate any use of United States Armed Forces with respect to which such report was submitted (or required to be submitted), unless the Congress (1) has declared war or has enacted a specific authorization for such use of United States Armed Forces, (2) has extended by law such sixty-day period, or (3) is physically unable to meet as a result of an armed attack upon the United States. Such sixty-day period shall be extended for not more than an additional thirty days if the

President determines and certifies to the Congress in writing that unavoidable military necessity respecting the safety of United States Armed Forces requires the continued use of such armed forces in the course of bringing about a prompt removal of such forces.

(c) Notwithstanding subsection (b), at any time that United States Armed Forces are engaged in hostilities outside the territory of the United States, its possessions and territories without a declaration of war or specific statutory authorization, such forces shall be removed by the President if the Congress so directs by concurrent resolution. . . .

INTERPRETATION OF JOINT RESOLUTION

Sec. 8. (a) Authority to introduce United States Armed Forces into hostilities or into situations wherein involvement in hostilities is clearly indicated by the circumstances shall not be inferred —

(1) from any provision of law (whether or not in effect before the date of the enactment of this joint resolution), including any provision contained in any appropriation Act, unless such provision specifically authorizes the introduction of United States Armed Forces into hostilities or into such situations and states that it is intended to constitute specific statutory authorization within the meaning of this joint resolution; or

(2) from any treaty heretofore or hereafter ratified unless such treaty is implemented by legislation specifically authorizing the introduction of United States Armed Forces into hostilities or into such situations and stating that it is intended to constitute specific statutory authorization within the meaning of this joint resolution.

(b) Nothing in this joint resolution shall be construed to require any further specific statutory authorization to permit members of United States Armed Forces to participate jointly with members of the armed forces of one or more foreign countries in the headquarters operations of high-level military commands which were established prior to the date of enactment of this joint resolution and pursuant to the United Nations Charter or any treaty ratified by the United States prior to such date.

(c) For purposes of this joint resolution, the term "introduction of United States Armed Forces" includes the assignment of members of such armed forces to command, coordinate, participate in the movement of, or accompany the regular or irregular military forces of any foreign country or government when such military forces are engaged, or there exists an imminent threat that such forces will become engaged, in hostilities.

(d) Nothing in this joint resolution —

(1) is intended to alter the constitutional authority of the Congress or of the President, or the provisions of existing treaties; or

(2) shall be construed as granting any authority to the President with respect to the introduction of United States Armed Forces into hostilities or into situations wherein involvement in hostilities is clearly indicated by the circumstances which authority he would not have had in the absence of this joint resolution. . . .

Note: *The War Powers Resolution*

1. *Background.* Before the enactment of the War Powers Resolution in 1973, the President enjoyed considerable discretion in the use of military force to accomplish foreign policy objectives. After the Vietnam controversy, and the popular distrust of the presidency of Richard Nixon after Watergate, Congress enacted the War Powers Resolution in an attempt to define and enlarge the congressional role in the use of military power. The resolution was enacted in spite of a veto by President Nixon, who invoked grounds of policy and constitutionality. President Nixon contended that the act attempted to intrude on "authorities which the President has properly exercised under the Constitution for almost 200 years."

Congressional use of its newly defined role in military activities did not materialize until resistance emerged over the presence of U.S. Marines in Lebanon in 1983. But some Presidents had followed the act's procedures under §4(a)(1) in informing Congress of military involvement in foreign hostilities within forty-eight hours. On May 14, 1975, President Ford informed Congress of his rescue mission of the U.S. merchant ship *Mayaguez* and its thirty-nine member crew from Cambodian Communist troops. In that mission, forty-one U.S. servicemen died. In the month before that action, President Ford invoked military help on two occasions to evacuate U.S. and Cambodian citizens from Saigon and Phnom Penh. While taking note of the War Powers Resolution in these actions, President Ford did not rely on its provisions for authority but instead invoked his constitutional prerogative as head executive and the chief of the armed forces. Although recognizing the existence of the resolution, President Ford insisted that the President always retains authority to use force in protecting the lives of U.S. citizens. Some members of Congress complained that the President did not consult with them in advance, as stipulated in the resolution, but Congress took no formal action. Similarly, President Carter did not consult Congress on the attempted rescue mission of the Iranian hostages on April 24, 1980. (Was he required to do so under the terms of the resolution?) When the mission was aborted, and eight Americans died in a helicopter crash, Carter formally informed Congress of his actions. Again, the President did not rely on the War Powers Resolution for his authority, but gave notice pursuant to §4(a)(1) of the act.

Congress has never formally enacted any resolution pursuant to the War Powers Resolution; discussions in Congress have focused on its ability to make effective use of the resolution while keeping within constitutional boundaries. Congressional action under the act was most vigorous in 1983 after military hostilities in Lebanon involving U.S. Marines. Initially, President Reagan ignored the provisions of the War Powers Resolution in involving U.S. troops, as he had in October of 1983 when troops invaded the island of Grenada. But while popular support for the Grenada affair prohibited Congress from carrying on any formal protest to the President's military programs, the situation in Lebanon furnished fertile grounds for political confrontation.

When U.S. troops initially landed in Lebanon in September 1982, President Reagan declared that they were not to be involved in "hostilities" — which would have required congressional approval under the War Powers Resolution — but were there as a peacekeeping measure. In August of 1983, two marines were killed and fourteen injured. On September 5 two more were killed. Three days later, a

U.S. warship retaliated by shelling targets in Lebanon. These events led Congress to insist that U.S. involvement be recognized as participation in "hostile" activities and that President Reagan seek Congress's approval. A resulting compromise between Congress and Reagan in October produced a joint resolution invoking the War Powers Resolution and requiring the marines to remain only for eighteen months. Neither Congress nor the President was willing to provoke a large-scale political crisis over the affair.

For general discussion, see Note, The Future of the War Powers Resolution, 36 Stan. L. Rev. 1407 (1984); Glennon, War Powers Resolution: Sad Record, Dismal Promise, 17 Loyola L. Rev. 657 (1984).

2. *Some questions of interpretation.* What does the act mean by "introduction" of U.S. Armed Forces "into hostilities"? When is "imminent involvement in hostilities" clearly indicated by the circumstances? Suppose the President (a) attempts a military action to rescue U.S. citizens held hostage overseas or (b) orders the marines into a foreign country, as a show of force, in order to prevent revolutionary acts. Must he inform Congress? If it is assumed that he need not do so, should he? Should the President construe the resolution broadly or narrowly? Consider also the possible need for secrecy in such operations.

Note that the War Powers Resolution contains a legislative veto. Is the veto constitutional after *Chadha*? See Comment, Congressional Control of Presidential War-Making under the War Powers Act: The Status of a Legislative Veto after *Chadha*, 132 U. Pa. L. Rev. 1217 (1984).

3. *The constitutional issue.* Consider, in the light of the preceding materials, the constitutionality of the War Powers Resolution. Which provisions are most troublesome? Consider also the following views:

a. *The War Powers Resolution is an unconstitutional infringement on the powers of the President.* The Constitution gives the President the authority to introduce armed forces into hostilities without a congressional declaration of war. Moreover, at least in cases of an effort to "repel sudden attacks" on the United States and its allies, the resolution is far too broad. It allows a congressional role in areas in which such a role is constitutionally proscribed.

Consider Rostow, Great Cases Make Bad Law: The War Powers Act, 50 Tex. L. Rev. 833, 855-856, 900 (1972):

> The pattern against which the [Resolution] protests is old, familiar, and rooted in the nature of things. There is nothing constitutionally illegitimate or even dubious about "undeclared" wars. We and other nations fought them frequently in the eighteenth and nineteenth centuries, as well as in the twentieth. [The Resolution] would turn the clock back to the Articles of Confederation, and destroy the Presidency which it was one of the chief aims of the men of Annapolis and Philadelphia to create.

See also Emerson, The War Powers Resolution Tested: The President's Independent Defense Power, 51 Notre Dame Law. 187 (1975).

b. *The War Powers Resolution is constitutional.* It merely restores the constitutional balance that had been upset by a long period of congressional inactivity before its passage. In essence, the resolution allows Congress to ensure that there is no undeclared war. Indeed, to the extent that it suffers from any constitutional defect, it is in yielding undue power to the President — for the resolution seems to allow the President to wage war without a declaration in far too many circumstances.

Consider Carter, The Constitutionality of the War Powers Resolution, 70 Va. L. Rev. 101, 125 (1984):

> The "inherent" powers to which opponents of the War Powers Resolution make reference are really [powers] thought to be inherent because the President has historically exercised them. But they are powers the President has exercised in the absence of any congressional objection. [Mere] historical acquiescence by Congress in the President's exercise of a particular power does not by itself prove that Congress lacks the authority to limit the exercise of that power when it gathers the wisdom and courage to do so.

c. *Provision (d)(1) makes the preceding provisions of the resolution effectively meaningless.* It restores the constitutional status quo and remits those deciding on the distribution of the war powers — in the executive, legislative, and judicial branches — to the Constitution itself. Why was provision (d)(1) included?

For general discussion, see, in addition to the sources cited above, Javits, Who Makes War? (1973); Van Alstyne, Congress, the President, and the Power to Declare War, 121 U. Pa. L. Rev. 1 (1972).

Note: *Distribution of National Powers — Final Thoughts*

Do the preceding materials suggest that the distribution of national powers has served its intended function? Has it limited factional control over governmental processes? Has it served as an important safeguard of liberty? Or has it created so many "checks" that (1) democratic processes are unable to bring about substantial reform or (2) the government is prevented from taking necessary action? Recall the debate between Jefferson and Madison about the value of stability in government. What consequences does the growth of administrative agencies have for these issues? Consider the possibility that in light of that development, original understandings of the distribution of national powers must be radically changed.

The preceding materials raise institutional issues as well. To what extent has judicial review contributed to the development of the present distribution of national powers? What has been the effect of "framework" legislation like the Impoundment Control Act and the War Powers Resolution? Consider the possibility that the written Constitution has played a surprisingly small role. Do the materials support the suggestion that the process of bargaining between Congress and the executive branch is a sufficient safeguard against abuse? What *is* abuse in this context?

V

Equality and the Constitution

This chapter explores the Court's struggle to define and apply the Constitution's requirement of equal treatment. Section A is devoted to an historical case study. It examines the ways in which the Court has interacted with other social forces in dealing with the race problem. The remaining sections focus on constitutional doctrine. Section B explores the meaning of "equality" in the context of "rational basis" review of "ordinary" social or economic classifications. Section C then returns to racial classifications as the prime example of "suspect" classifications subject to "heightened scrutiny." Section D discusses the problem of classifications based on gender. Finally, Section E explores the claims of other "disadvantaged" groups, such as aliens, nonmarital children, and the poor, to special scrutiny of laws arguably discriminating against them.

A. RACE AND THE CONSTITUTION

This section traces the evolution of constitutional doctrine concerning discrimination against blacks. There are several reasons for beginning the study of constitutionally protected individual rights with this issue.

First, in one form or another, the controversy about the legal status of blacks has been central to U.S. politics since the founding of the republic. As you read through this material, consider the extent to which judicial decisions have shaped that controversy and the extent to which they have been shaped by it. At each stage, could the Court have acted differently? Was its power meaningfully restrained by the language and history of the Constitution? By the constellation of social and political forces at the time? By widely held ethical norms?

Second, the Court's analysis of discrimination against blacks has served as a prototype for the development of other constitutional doctrines. In the nineteenth century, the argument over slavery provoked a fundamental realignment of federal and state power and gave birth to a new strategy for the protection of individual rights. In our own time, controversies over school segregation, racial discrimination in access to political power, and "affirmative action" have shaped attitudes toward the proper scope of constitutional protection for minorities generally. To what extent is our experience with discrimination against blacks generalizable? Have the special problems faced by black Americans distorted constitutional law?

Finally, a chronological examination of this issue provides insight into the influence of history on constitutional adjudication. What factors are most important in determining the course of judicial decisions? The strategy of individual litigants? The Court's formulation of the issues? The reactions of the other branches of government? Does the Supreme Court ultimately have the power to impose its own solution to the race problem? Or are its decisions merely the product of broad historical forces over which it exercises little control?

1. Slavery and the Constitution

Three provisions in the original Constitution recognize and arguably legitimate slavery. Article I, section 9, prohibits Congress from outlawing the slave trade until 1808. Article I, section 2, requires apportionment of legislators on the basis of the "whole number of free persons" in each state and "three fifths of all other persons." Article IV, section 2, clause 3, requires states to "[deliver] up" escaped slaves and prohibits states from discharging them.

Do these provisions make the Constitution a proslavery document? Consider Robinson, Slavery in the Structure of American Politics 1765–1820, at 209, 210, 244–246 (1971):

> In the drama that produced the Constitution, Southern delegates were unmistakably prominent players. James Madison, the man whose leadership during the Convention earned him the title "Father of the Constitution," was a Southerner, a slave-owning Virginian. [John] Rutledge, certainly a leading nationalist and chairman of the important Committee of Detail, which provided the first definition of legislative powers under the Constitution, was one of the wealthiest and best-established planters at the Convention, and deliberately represented the most candid slave owners. [George] Washington [was] an exceedingly rich man, whose fortune arose largely from the labor of slaves in and around Mount Vernon, Virginia. In fact, of the fifteen delegates whom Clinton Rossiter has termed either "principals" or "influentials," seven were planters. . . .
>
> The South's enthusiastic participation in the nationalizing thrust of 1787 carried one portentous qualification: the national government could be as powerful as the vision of a great national empire demanded, *provided that it keep its hands off slavery.* . . .
>
> The framers [dealt] with slavery by seeking, so far as possible, to take it out of the national political arena. They were unable in 1787 to settle the issue, one way or the other. They could not establish straightforward Constitutional guarantees against emancipation, as the South Carolinians desired, because many Northerners, and perhaps some Southerners, would not permit it. Nor could they give Congress power to regulate slavery in any way, much less abolish it, because Southerners refused to yield control over the institution. Realizing that is was utterly beyond their power to fashion a national consensus on slavery, or to "govern" the issue in the absence of one, they had contented themselves with measures aimed at prevent-

ing friction over slavery between the states and sections. Thus, when it was decided to tie representation to population, it became necessary to set a date when the slave trade could be terminated, because of the relationship it now bore to the balance of political forces in the union. And when Pierce Butler raised the question of escaped slaves, the Convention was willing to oblige, because most Northerners were as reluctant for blacks to flee north as Southern slave owners were to lose their property. The fugitive-slave clause, like the slave-trade clause, was intended to remove a potential sore point between the states. . . .

There is no evidence that any framer thought the Constitution contained power to abolish slavery. They all knew how the Deep Southerners felt, and however much some of them may have regretted the hold that slavery had on the South, they were all fully sympathetic with the determination of the Deep Southerners to resist abolition in the present circumstances. . . .

But there was no guarantee that powers of emancipation were forever denied to the federal government.

The evidence there is permits the conclusion that the future, with respect to possible public action against slavery, was left open on purpose. [The] framers, as of 1787, agreed unanimously to place the institution of slavery, as it existed within the South, not "in the course of ultimate extinction," as Lincoln argued, but beyond national regulation.

State v. Post

20 N.J.L. 368 (1845)

NEVIUS, J.

This proceeding is designed to present for our adjudication the question, whether slavery can exist within the limits of this state under its present constitution and laws; and it derives signal and solemn importance from its bearing upon a class of human beings, still claimed to be lawfully held in slavery, and upon the interest of those communities where most of that class are still found. I have listened with great pleasure and deep interest to the arguments and remarks and the pathetic appeals, which have been urged before us, in support of this demurrer, and in behalf of the colored race; and whilst I most sincerely respect the zeal and humane spirit by which they were dictated, and the ingenuity, talents and research of the counsel, I am nevertheless constrained to say, that much of the argument seemed rather addressed to the feelings than to the legal intelligence of the court. . . .

[Abolitionists argued that slavery was made illegal in New Jersey by a State constitutional provision declaring that "all men are by nature free and independent, and have certain natural and unalienable rights, among which are those of enjoying and defending life and liberty, acquiring, possessing and protecting property, and of pursuing and obtaining safety and happiness."]

If the [New Jersey constitutional] convention intended to say that all men, in a state of civil or political society, were free and independent and entitled to the exercise and enjoyment of the rights mentioned, the expression must be understood in a modified sense according to the nature, the condition and laws of the society to which they belong. For man, under no form of government, can be said

to be absolutely free and independent, and have the absolute and uncontrollable
right over his own actions, according to his own free will, unrestrained by the
rights of others and the laws of the government, under which he lives. Authority
and subordination are essential under every form of civil society, and one of its
leading principles is that the citizen yields to it a portion of his natural rights, for
the better protection of the remainder. In such a state, man's right to freedom
and independence, to enjoy and defend life and liberty, to acquire, possess and
protect property, and to pursue and obtain safety and happiness, are ever subject
to, and regulated by, laws fundamental or otherwise, which the majority of the
people in a republic, have established for their government. . . . .

[Had] the convention intended to abolish slavery and domestic relations, well
known to exist in this state and to be established by law, and to divest the master
of his right of property in his slave and the slave of his right to protection and
support from the master, no one can doubt but that it would have adopted some
clear and definite provision to effect it, and not have left so important and grave a
question, involving such extensive consequences, to depend upon the doubtful
construction of an indefinite abstract political proposition. . . . .

The declaration of independence, the basis of our free government, declares
that all men are created free and equal, and the constitution of the United States
proclaims that the people have formed it to secure the blessings of liberty to
themselves and their posterity; yet by the express language of the latter instrument, the relation of master and slave is recognized; showing that the framers of
that constitution did not deem their general declaration in favor of liberty, incompatible with its other provisions; and it has never been judicially determined that
slavery, in the United States, was thereby abrogated. On the contrary it has been
often adjudged, both by the State and Federal courts, that slavery still exists; that
the master's right of property in the slave has not been affected either by the
declaration of independence, or the constitution of the United States. [It] was
argued before us, that, under the declaration of rights in the constitution of
Massachusetts, which contains the same language, it has been judicially held,
that slavery was no more. And we are referred to Commonwealth v. Ives, 18 Pick.
R. 193. [In *Ives*.] Chief Justice Shaw declares "that slavery is contrary to natural
right, to the principles of justice and humanity, and repugnant to the constitution." I am unwilling to yield to any one, in high respect for the supreme judicial
tribunal of that enlightened state; but [I] do not find the reason or argument,
which satisfies my mind of the soundness of its conclusion. [How] far the humane
spirit of abolitionism, which prevailed in that state, the fewness or worthlessness
of that species of property, the feebleness of the defence made by masters, or the
collateral mode in which the question was presented, or the fact that slavery had
only been tolerated, but never actually established by law, may have influenced
the opinion of the court, [I] will not undertake to determine. By this remark I
mean to cast no imputation upon the judicial intelligence or integrity of that
court; but judges must be more than men, if they can always escape the influence
of a strong popular opinion of society upon great questions of state policy and
human benevolence, which have been long agitated and much discussed; and it is
no matter of surprise that Chief Justice Shaw, entertaining the opinions he did
upon this question of slavery, should have found it repugnant to the spirit of their
constitution. . . . .

Note: Constitutional Attacks on Slavery

1. Post *and the problem of judicial power.* For 150 years, U.S. courts have vacillated between attempts to impose a judicial solution to the race problem and attempts to leave the matter to the political process. In *Post* the Court chose the latter course. Is the decision an example of moral cowardice or of fidelity to law?

Was the Court bound to reach the result it did by the words of the provision in question? By the intent of the framers? Where else might it have looked for guidance? See Chapter 1 section C, supra.

Do you agree with Justice Nevius that judges should attempt to "escape the influence of strong popular opinion of society upon great questions of state policy and human benevolence"? That appeals to "feelings" rather than the "legal intelligence of the court" are inappropriate? What exactly does the Court mean by "legal intelligence" in this context?

Justice Nevius says judges must be "more than men" to ignore "strong popular opinion." Does this susceptibility to public pressure suggest that he should have used his power more confidently? How likely is it that a court would construe the Constitution in a manner most people violently opposed? That it would succeed in enforcing such a construction in the long run? Consider R. Cover, Justice Accused 54–55 (1975):

> In mid-century New Jersey, slavery was not an important economic fact of life. In 1804 the state had adopted a scheme for gradual emancipation. By 1845 there were only an estimated seven hundred slaves left. Perhaps as many as 50 percent of these seven hundred Negroes were over fifty-five. For these older slaves it is at least conceivable that the security supposedly guaranteed by the Act was as valuable as a few years of freedom. The abolition of slavery in New Jersey in 1845 would only have accelerated, by a few years, the end of the process started forty years earlier.

Do these additional facts make the result in *Post* more defensible on the ground that judicial abolition of slavery would have made little practical difference? Do they make the result less defensible on the ground that judicial abolition could have been accomplished relatively easily?

Of course, in a southern state in 1845, a judicial decision abolishing slavery would have been revolutionary. If a southern judge had written such a decision, what do you suppose the result would have been? Would such a decision have been wise?

2. *Constitutional attacks on slavery.* Post typifies judicial analysis of slavery prior to the Civil War. Although abolitionist lawyers won isolated victories, even judges strongly opposed to slavery usually ruled against them. See generally Cover, supra; L. Levy, the Law of the Commonwealth and Chief Justice Shaw (1957).

Although *Post* dealt exclusively with *state* constitutional issues, Alvan Stewart, the abolitionist lawyer who argued *Post*, relied on the federal constitution as well. See J. TenBroek, The Antislavery Origins of the Fourteenth Amendment 43–45 (1951). See also E. Foner, Free Soil, Free Labor, Free Men: The Ideology of the Republican Party before the Civil War 76–77 (1970). The Court apparently thought these arguments too flimsy to merit a response. Are the arguments tenable?

3. *Judicial support for slavery*. From the perspective of the present, it may seem that courts should have done more to combat the evils of slavery. In fact, however, when the courts did intervene in the pre-Civil War period, it was more often to invalidate political arrangements that tended to *limit* slavery.

Most of the federal litigation centered on the Fugitive Slave Clause, Article IV, section 2, which required the return of escaped slaves. In Prigg v. Pennsylvania, 41 U.S. (16 Pet.) 539 (1842), the Court held unconstitutional a Pennsylvania statute prohibiting any person from removing blacks from the state by force or violence with the intention of detaining them as slaves. The Court explained that article IV, section 2, "contemplates the existence of a positive, unqualified right on the part of the owner of the slave, which no state law or regulation can in any way qualify, regulate, control, or restrain." The Court therefore held the statute invalid as applied to an escaped slave because "any state law or state regulation, which interrupts, limits, delays, or postpones the right of the owner to the immediate possession of the slave, and the immediate command of his service and labor, operates, pro tanto, a discharge of the slave therefrom." The Court further held that article IV, section 2, implicitly vested Congress with the power to assist owners in securing the return of escaped slaves, that Congress had exercised that power by enacting the Fugitive Slave Act of 1793, that this national power was exclusive, and that any state laws regulating the means by which slaves were to be delivered up were unconstitutional.

Superficially, *Prigg* seemed a proslavery decision. But its legacy was not unambiguous. The decision left intact the power of both free states and the national government to limit the growth of slavery by freeing slaves brought into free areas. Moreover, by nationalizing the rendition question, the Court relieved free states of this distasteful obligation and intensified the political struggle over the future of slavery on a national level. See 5 C. Swisher, History of the Supreme Court of the United States: The Taney Period 1836–64, at 546 (1974). Fifteen years after *Prigg*, the Court attempted to cut off the political struggle in an opinion which presaged the Civil War.

4. *The road to* Dred Scott. Consider D. Fehrenbacher, The *Dred Scott* Case: Its Significance in American Law and Politics 192–194, 206–208 (1978):

> [The] pressures for judicial intervention in the mounting sectional conflict over slavery [were very] strong. [The] tendency to constitutionalize the territorial issue dated back many years. It was reinforced in 1856 by the peculiar needs of the Democratic party and especially by the strategy of unity through evasion, [with] a consequent increase in talk about "leaving it to the Supreme Court." The Court, furthermore, was the one major agency of government that had not yet tried its hand at resolving the conflict. More than a few Americans apparently believed that at its command, agitation of the slavery question would subside and the years of crisis would come to an end. Indeed, some members of the Court itself seem to have harbored the belief that it possessed some such extraordinary power.

Dred Scott v. Sandford

60 U.S. (19 How.) 393 (1857)

MR. CHIEF JUSTICE TANEY delivered the opinion of the Court. . . .

[Dred Scott, admittedly once a slave but claiming now to be a citizen of Missouri, brought an action for trespass in the Circuit Court of the United States for the District of Missouri against John F. A. Sandford, a citizen of New York. Federal jurisdiction was premised on diversity of citizenship. In 1834 Scott's former owner had taken him from Missouri to Illinois, where they resided for two years before moving to Minnesota, then part of the Louisiana Territory. In 1838 they returned to Missouri, and Scott was sold as a slave to Sandford. Although slavery was legal in Missouri, it was prohibited in Illinois by the state constitution and in the Louisiana Territory by the federal statute embodying the Missouri Compromise — the Act of March 6, 1820, 3 Stat. 545. Scott argued that these provisions made him a free man. In response, Sandford contended that even if Scott were free, he was not a citizen of Missouri and that the court therefore lacked jurisdiction under the diversity of citizenship provisions of article III. Moreover, Scott was not free, since his presence in Illinois and the Territory could not deprive his former owner of his property interest in Scott when he returned to Missouri.]

I

[The Court first addressed the question whether Scott was a citizen of Missouri for diversity purposes.]

The words "people of the United States" and "citizens" are synonymous terms, and mean the same thing. They both describe the political body who, according to our republican institutions, form the sovereignty, and who hold the power and conduct the Government through their representatives. They are what we familiarly call the "sovereign people," and every citizen is one of this people, and a constituent member of this sovereignty. The question before us is, whether the class of persons described in the plea in abatement compose a portion of this people, and are constituent members of this sovereignty? We think they are not, and that they are not included, and were not intended to be included, under the word "citizens" in the Constitution, and can therefore claim none of the rights and privileges which that instrument provides for and secures to citizens of the United States. On the contrary, they were at that time considered as a subordinate and inferior class of beings, who had been subjugated by the dominant race, and, whether emancipated or not, yet remained subject to their authority, and had no rights or privileges but such as those who held the power and the Government might choose to grant them.

It is not the province of the court to decide upon the justice or injustice, the policy or impolicy, of these laws. The decision of that question belonged to the political or law-making power; to those who formed the sovereignty and framed the Constitution. The duty of the court is, to interpret the instrument they have framed, with the best lights we can obtain on the subject, and to administer it as we find it, according to its true intent and meaning when it was adopted.

In discussing this question, we must not confound the rights of citizenship which a State may confer within its own limits, and the rights of citizenship as a member of the Union. [The] Constitution has conferred on Congress the right to establish an uniform rule of naturalization, and this right is evidently exclusive, and has always been held by this court to be so. Consequently, no State, since the adoption of the Constitution, can by naturalizing an alien invest him with the

rights and privileges secured to a citizen of a State under the Federal Government, although, so far as the State alone was concerned, he would undoubtedly
be entitled to the rights of a citizen, and clothed with all the rights and immunities
which the Constitution and laws of the State attached to that character. . . .

In the opinion of the court, the legislation and histories of the times, and
the language used in the Declaration of Independence, show, that neither
the class of persons who had been imported as slaves, nor their descendants,
whether they had become free or not, were then acknowledged as a part of the
people, nor intended to be included in the general words used in that memorable
instrument.

It is difficult at this day to realize the state of public opinion in relation to that
unfortunate race, which prevailed in the civilized and enlightened portions of the
world at the time of the Declaration of Independence, and when the Constitution
of the United States was framed and adopted. But the public history of every
European nation displays it in a manner too plain to be mistaken.

They had for more than a century before been regarded as beings of an inferior
order, and altogether unfit to associate with the white race, either in social or
political relations; and so far inferior, that they had no rights which the white man
was bound to respect; and that the negro might justly and lawfully be reduced to
slavery for his benefit. He was bought and sold, and treated as an ordinary article
of merchandise and traffic, whenever a profit could be made by it. This opinion
was at that time fixed and universal in the civilized portion of the white race. It
was regarded as an axiom in morals as well as in politics, which no one thought of
disputing, or supposed to be open to dispute; and men in every grade and position
in society daily and habitually acted upon it in their private pursuits, as well as in
matters of public concern, without doubting for a moment the correctness of this
opinion. . . .

[Upon] a full and careful consideration of the subject, the court is of opinion,
that, upon the facts stated in the plea in abatement, Dred Scott was not a citizen
of Missouri within the meaning of the Constitution of the United States, and not
entitled as such to sue in its courts; and, consequently, that the Circuit Court had
no jurisdiction of the case, and that the judgment on the plea in abatement is
erroneous. . . .

II . . .

[The Court then discussed whether Scott remained a slave after his sojourn in the
Louisiana Territory and Illinois.]

The act of Congress, upon which the plaintiff relies, declares that slavery and
involuntary servitude, except as a punishment for crime, shall be forever prohibited in all that part of the territory ceded by France, under the name of Louisiana,
which lies north of thirty-six degrees thirty minutes north latitude, and not
included within the limits of Missouri. And the difficulty which meets us at the
threshold of this part of the inquiry is, whether Congress was authorized to pass
this law under any of the powers granted to it by the Constitution; for if the
authority is not given by that instrument, it is the duty of this court to declare it
void and inoperative, and incapable of conferring freedom upon any one who is
held as a slave under the laws of any one of the States. . . .

[The] power of Congress over the person or property of a citizen can never be a mere discretionary power under our Constitution and form of Government. The powers of the Government and the rights and privileges of the citizen are regulated and plainly defined by the Constitution itself. [An] act of Congress which deprives a citizen of the United States of his liberty or property, merely because he came himself or brought his property into a particular Territory of the United States, and who had committed no offence against the laws, could hardly be dignified with the name of due process of law. . . .

[The] right of property in a slave is distinctly and expressly affirmed in the Constitution. The right to traffic in it, like an ordinary article of merchandise and property, was guaranteed to the citizens of the United States, in every State that might desire it, for twenty years. And the Government in express terms is pledged to protect it in all future time, if the slave escapes from his owner. This is done in plain words — too plain to be misunderstood. And no word can be found in the Constitution which gives Congress a greater power over slave property, or which entitles property of that kind to less protection than property of any other description. The only power conferred is the power coupled with the duty of guarding and protecting the owner in his rights.

Upon these considerations, it is the opinion of the court that the act of Congress which prohibited a citizen from holding and owning property of this kind in the territory of the United States north of the line therein mentioned, is not warranted by the Constitution, and is therefore void; and that neither Dred Scott himself, nor any of his family, were made free by being carried into this territory; even if they had been carried there by the owner, with the intention of becoming a permanent resident.

[Finally, the Court addressed Scott's contention that he had been made free by his visit to Illinois, a free state. The Court held that his status on his return to Missouri was to be determined by Missouri law rather than Illinois law and that under that law, he remained a slave.

Justices Wayne, Daniel, Campbell, Grier, Nelson, and Catron each wrote separate concurring opinions. Justices McLean and Curtis dissented].

Note: Dred Scott *and the Power of Judicial Review*

1. *The meaning of* Dred Scott. After *Dred Scott*, were free blacks in northern states citizens of those states for federal constitutional purposes? Short of amending the Constitution, was there anything that either those states or the federal government could do to make them citizens? If Scott and his owner had remained in the Louisiana Territory, could Congress have prohibited the owner from holding Scott as a slave?

2. *Chief Justice Taney's opinion and the problem of judicial review.* It is frequently noted that the Supreme Court first asserted the power to invalidate acts of Congress in Marbury v. Madison. Less often mentioned is the fact that the Court's second assertion of this power came fifty-four years later in Scott v. Sandford. What lessons does *Dred Scott* teach about power of judicial review?

It is generally acknowledged that *Dred Scott* is one of the great disasters in the history of the Supreme Court. But what, precisely, is wrong with Justice Taney's opinion? Consider the following possibilities:

a. *The Court's decision is racist in its premises and morally obtuse in its result.*
Is this fair? Notice that Justice Taney does not claim that blacks *are* "a subordinate
and inferior class of beings" but only that they were so viewed by the authors of
the Constitution. See 2 C. Warren, The Supreme Court in United States History
303 (1922). If that assertion is correct, does it establish that the framers wished to
exclude the free blacks from ever becoming citizens? Even if the framers' attitude
toward free blacks was ambiguous, can it be doubted that they viewed slaves as a
form of property? Is the problem with *Dred Scott* that the Court was too "passive"
in rigidly saddling the country with outdated moral attitudes or that it was too
"active" in reading the contemporary moral attitudes of the Justices into the
constitutional text?

b. *The Court unnecessarily and unwisely reached out to decide an issue not
properly presented.* The first part of Justice Taney's opinion held that Scott was
not a citizen of Missouri and that the court below therefore lacked jurisdiction.
Was it proper for the Court to decide the questions addressed in the second part
of the opinion? Why was it necessary to determine Scott's status outside Missouri?
Even if Scott was free when he lived outside Missouri, did the Constitution
preclude Missouri from enslaving him when he returned?

Did Justice Taney have to read the diversity clause as establishing federal
standards for state citizenship? Why wasn't it sufficient to hold that Scott, even if
free, was not a citizen under Missouri law?

c. *The Court unwisely assumed that it could finally resolve a divisive political
issue by taking it "out of politics."* Modern constitutional doctrines are sometimes
justified on the ground that they remove highly divisive questions from the political process. For example, the abortion decisions and expansive readings of the
first amendment religion clauses are sometimes defended on the ground that the
underlying questions are inappropriate for political resolution. What are the characteristics of such questions? Was the future and spread of slavery such a question?

d. *The problem was not that the Court attempted to impose a solution to the
slavery problem but that it attempted to impose the wrong solution.* The decision
failed to solve the problem, exacerbated sectional tensions, and, ultimately,
helped cause the Civil War. Should Supreme Court decisions be judged by
whether they "work" in this sense? Should justices consider whether their decisions will be "accepted"? Whether they will produce "wise" social policy? Judged
by this standard, is it clear that *Dred Scott* did not "work"? In the long run, the
decision contributed to a war that brought about a fundamental realignment of
political power and initiated a new stage in the struggle over racial equality.

2. Reconstruction and Retreat

A central paradox in constitutional law is that in order to enforce limitations on
governmental power, it is necessary to create governmental power. A constitutional provision may, by its terms, prohibit certain forms of governmental action.
That limitation might be obeyed simply because actors in the system recognize a
moral obligation not to transgress it. But if the prohibition is to be legally enforceable, then some other branch of government must be invested with the power to
enforce it. The risk, of course, is that this power will be misused and will serve to
undermine the very rights it was created to protect. Does it follow that the real

choice for the framers of a constitution is not between individual rights and government power, but between different distributions of government power providing more or less effective enforcement of individual rights with more or less risk of abuse?

Before the Civil War, there were few constitutional constraints on the power of state governments. Although the first eight amendments to the Constitution protected individual rights against federal intrusion, the Supreme Court held in 1833 that they did not limit state power. See Barron v. Mayor of Baltimore, 32 U.S. (7 Pet.) 243 (1833), infra Chapter 6, section C. The failure of the framers to protect individual rights from state governments was a product of neither indifference nor oversight. It stemmed instead from the view that the most serious threat to individual liberty came from the federal government and that the states could be relied on to "afford complete security against invasions of the public liberty by the national authorities." The Federalist No. 28 (Hamilton). A federal bill of rights applicable to the states would have enhanced federal power at the expense of the states and thus increased the risk of federal domination.

By the close of the Civil War, it was clear that this strategy required some modification. The southern states could not be depended on to protect the rights of the newly freed slaves, and it could hardly be maintained that the main threat to those rights came from the federal government. Under the pressure of this reality, a shift occurred: Instead of viewing the Constitution as a protection from federal power and the states as a bulwark against federal interference, at least some people came to see constitutional rights as a basis for the *assertion* of federal power to protect individuals against *state* interference.

Note: The Work of the Reconstruction Congress

The Reconstruction Congress laid the groundwork for the expansion of federal authority by enacting three constitutional amendments, each of which conferred additional substantive power on Congress. On December 31, 1865, the thirteenth amendment became part of the Constitution. The amendment ratified and extended President Lincoln's Emancipation Proclamation by prohibiting slavery and involuntary servitude throughout the United States. In addition, section 2 of the amendment granted Congress the power "to enforce this article by appropriate legislation."

But the formal eradication of slavery was insufficient to change the real status of southern blacks. The bonds of slavery were quickly replaced by "Black Codes" in many southern states. The Supreme Court subsequently described the effect of these provisions as follows:

> [Blacks] were [forbidden] to appear in the towns in any other character than menial servants. They were required to reside on and cultivate the soil without the right to purchase or own it. They were excluded from many occupations of gain, and were not permitted to give testimony in the courts of any case where a white man was a party. It was said that their lives were at the mercy of bad men, either because the laws for their protection were insufficient or were not enforced.

The Slaughter-House Cases, 83 U.S. (16 Wall.) 36 (1873).

Congress attempted to make the thirteenth amendment effective against the challenge posed by the Black Codes through enactment of the Civil Rights Act of 1866. Passed over President Johnson's veto, the act declared that "all persons born in the United States and not subject to any foreign power, excluding Indians not taxed," were citizens of the United States. Such citizens were granted the same right to make and enforce contracts, sue, give evidence, acquire property, and "to full and equal benefit of all laws and proceedings for the security of person and property as is enjoyed by white citizens." Moreover, all citizens were to be "subject to like punishment, pains, and penalties, and to none other, any law, statute, ordinance, regulation or custom to the contrary notwithstanding."

Even before the Civil Rights Bill was enacted, doubt arouse about Congress's power to enact such a law. Thus, on February 13 and 26, 1866, Congressman Bingham introduced the first version of what was to become the fourteenth amendment. It stated that "The Congress shall have the power to make all laws which shall be necessary and proper to secure the citizens of each State all privileges and immunities of citizens in the several States, and to all persons in the several States equal protection in the rights of life, liberty, and property." Cong. Globe, 39th Cong., 1st Sess. 813, 1034 (1866).

On April 30, 1866, after extensive debate, the Joint Committee on Reconstruction reported a new proposal that provided that "No state shall make or enforce any law which shall abridge the privileges or immunities of citizens of the United States, nor shall any State deprive any person of life, liberty, or property without due process of law; nor deny any person within its jurisdiction the equal protection of the laws." These substantive prohibitions were coupled with another grant of power to Congress to enforce them "by appropriate legislation." The amendment was adopted by the House in this form. When the amendment reached the Senate, the first sentence of section 1 — making all persons born or naturalized in the United States and subject to the jurisdiction thereof citizens of the United States and of the state wherein they reside — was added. The amendment was ratified on July 28, 1868.

Two years later, on March 30, 1879, Congress added the last of the Reconstruction amendments, which prohibited both the United States and any state from denying or abridging the right to vote on account of race, color, or previous condition of servitude. The amendment granted Congress the power to enforce this provision by appropriate legislation.

Invoking this new constitutional authority, the Reconstruction Congress enacted an extensive legislative program. In 1870 Congress reenacted the 1866 Civil Rights Act and added criminal penalties for deprivation of rights under the law. In the same year, Congress passed the "Enforcement Act," which attached criminal penalties to interference with the right to vote and made it a felony to conspire to injure, oppress, threaten, or intimidate any citizen with the intent to prevent or hinder the free exercise of any right granted by the Constitution or laws of the United States. One year later, Congress enacted the Ku Klux Klan Act, which criminally punished conspiracies to deprive a class of persons of equal protection of the laws and created civil liability for state officials who deprived persons of federal rights under the color of state laws. Finally, in 1875 Congress enacted a sweeping public accommodations law requiring all inns, public conveyances, theaters, and other places of public amusement to admit all persons regardless of race, color, or previous condition of servitude.

Did this flurry of legislative activity fundamentally alter the constitutional structure that existed before the Civil War? This question has two dimensions. First, how did the Reconstruction Congress alter the power balance between the federal and state governments? No doubt, the Reconstruction amendments were intended to provide a new source of federal power to protect the newly freed slaves. But were they also a more general rejection of the traditional theory that state governments would serve to protect individual liberties? Or was the federal government to intervene only interstitially when the states were unwilling or unable to provide protection? Second, how did the amendments alter the balance of power between the judiciary and the political branches? As noted above, the primary impetus for passage of the fourteenth amendment was the need to provide a basis for federal *legislative* action against the states. But was it intended as well as a basis for federal *judicial* power?

Note: The Judicial Reaction

1. *The Slaughter-House cases and the reassertion of federalism constraints.* The Supreme Court's first opportunity to assess the impact of the Reconstruction amendments came in The Slaughter-House Cases, 83 U.S. (16 Wall.) 36 (1873), in which the Court rejected a thirteenth and fourteenth amendment attack on a Louisiana statute granting to a single company the right to engage in the slaughterhouse business within an area including the City of New Orleans. (These cases are dealt with at greater length at page 698, infra.) Justice Miller's analysis in his opinion for the Court begins with a ringing declaration that "the one pervading purpose" of the amendments was "The freedom of the slave race, the security and firm establishment of that freedom, and the protection of the newly-made freeman and citizen from the oppressions of those who had formerly exercised unlimited dominion over him." The Court emphasized that it did not follow from this purpose that the framers of the amendments intended to transfer general responsibility for protection of civil rights from the states to the federal government. Such a broad reading of the amendments would "degrade the State governments by subjecting them to the control of Congress, in the exercise of powers heretofore universally conceded to them of the most ordinary and fundamental character" and "radically [change] the whole theory of the relations of the State and Federal governments to each other and both of these governments to the people." Thus, the privileges and immunities clause of the fourteenth amendment did not provide general federal protection for citizens. Rather, it protected only a few rights "which owe their existence to the Federal government, its National character, its Constitution, or its laws." Nor was the due process clause implicated by the Louisiana statute. As for petitioners' equal protection clause arguments, the Court "[doubted] very much whether any action of a State not directed by way of discrimination against the negroes as a class, or on account of their race, will ever be held to come within the purview of this provision."

2. *Federalism and protection of the newly freed slaves.* The Slaughter-House Cases suggest a two-tier approach to the fourteenth amendment: When the rights of newly freed slaves are at stake, the amendment must be read expansively to provide comprehensive federal protection. But when racial discrimination is not at issue, the protections of federal citizenship are narrower, and a state resident's primary recourse for protection of his rights remains to his own state government. This approach is consistent with the history of the fourteenth amendment, which was unquestionably written primarily to protect the newly freed slaves.

Note, however, that the language of the amendment provides no support for the distinction. Was the Court correct in emphasizing the history rather than the language?

In some measure, the Court's treatment of the fourteenth amendment in the wake of *Slaughter-House* conformed to the two-tier approach and, indeed, remnants of it remain today. Thus, on the one hand, the fourteenth amendment privileges and immunities clause has never recovered from the narrow reading it received in *Slaughter-House* and remains virtually a dead letter, although the modern Court's expansive reading of the equal protection and due process clauses has largely mooted the issue. See Chapter 6, infra. On the other hand, the Court quickly established that federal protection was available when the states singled out blacks for discriminatory treatment. In Strauder v. West Virginia, 100 U.S. 303 (1879), for example, the Court relied on the fourteenth amendment to reverse the murder conviction of a black tried before a jury from which members of his race were excluded by law. The Court was careful to note that the fourteenth amendment erected no general barrier against discrimination in jury selection. The state could "confine the selection to males, to freeholders, to citizens, to persons within certain ages, or to persons having educational qualifications." But the history of the Reconstruction amendments made clear that racial discrimination was on a different footing. The fourteenth amendment contained

> A necessary implication of a positive immunity, or right, most valuable to the colored race, — the right to exemption from unfriendly legislation against them distinctly as colored, — exemption from legal discriminations, implying inferiority in civil society, lessening the security of their enjoyment of the rights which others enjoy, and discriminations which are steps towards reducing them to the condition of a subject race.

See also Ex parte Virginia, 100 U.S. 339 (1880).

3. *Judicial invalidation of civil rights legislation.* The result in *Strauder* seems to follow logically from the Court's opinion in *Slaughter-House*. What was less predictable, however, was that the Court's narrow interpretation of the Reconstruction amendments would eventually obstruct federal efforts to protect newly freed slaves.

The first intimations of difficulty came in United States v. Reese, 92 U.S. 214 (1875), which involved a federal criminal prosecution against two Kentucky municipal elections inspectors who were charged with refusing to permit a black to vote. The defendants were charged with violating two of the voting rights sections of the 1870 Enforcement Act. Because the relevant sections of the act were not expressly limited to actions that were racially motivated, the Court held that they exceeded Congress's power under the fifteenth amendment and that the prosecution therefore could not proceed. See also Virginia v. Rives, 100 U.S. 313 (1879).

In United States v. Cruikshank, 92 U.S. 542 (1875), the Court held that the criminal conspiracy section of the 1870 act could not be applied to three persons convicted of lynching two blacks and thereby interfering with their right of peaceable assembly. Since there was no claim that the blacks had assembled to petition the federal government, the prosecution had not alleged that the rights of national citizenship were violated, and punishment of the killings therefore exceeded Congress's power under the fourteenth amendment. Nor could the prosecution proceed on the theory that the due process rights of blacks were violated, since "the fourteenth amendment prohibits a State from depriving any person of life, liberty, or property, without due process of law; but this adds nothing to the rights of one citizen as against another."

In United States v. Harris, 106 U.S. 629 (1882), the Court reached a similar result with respect to the criminal conspiracy sections of the Ku Klux Klan Act of 1871. The Court held that because the fourteenth amendment did not reach purely private conduct, Congress lacked the power to punish members of a lynch mob who had seized prisoners held by a state deputy sheriff.

But the most damaging judicial attack on Reconstruction legislation came in The Civil Rights Cases, 109 U.S. 3 (1883), where the Court invalidated the public accommodation sections of the 1875 Civil Rights Act. (The Civil Rights Cases are excerpted more fully in Chapter 10, section A1, infra.) The Court, in an opinion by Justice Bradley, denied that either the thirteenth or fourteenth amendments conferred on Congress the power to prohibit private discrimination in public accommodations. The Court's discussion of the fourteenth amendment is usually treated as establishing the requirement of "state action" for a fourteenth amendment violation — a requirement examined in greater detail in Chapter 10. The Court held that "The first section of the Fourteenth Amendment [is] prohibitory in its character, and prohibitory upon the States. [It] is State action of a particular character that is prohibited. Individual invasion of individual rights is not the subject matter of the amendment."

Note, however, that this reading of the fourteenth amendment grew out of the same view of the states as the primary protector of individual rights that the Court expressed in Slaughter-House. The Court in The Civil Rights Cases found the statute constitutionally offensive, in part, because "It applies equally to cases arising in States which have the justest laws respecting the personal rights of citizens, and whose authorities are ever ready to enforce such laws, as to those which arise in States that may have violated the prohibition of the amendment." In the Court's view, "An individual cannot deprive a man of his [rights]; he may, by force or fraud, interfere with the enjoyment of the right in a particular case; [but] unless protected in these wrongful acts by some shield of State law or State authority, he cannot destroy or injure the right; he will only render himself amenable to satisfaction or punishment." It followed that "in all those cases where the Constitution seeks to protect the rights of the citizen against discriminative and unjust laws of the State, [it] is not individual offences, but abrogation and denial of rights which it denounces, and for which it clothes the Congress with power to provide a remedy."

Would the result in The Civil Rights Cases have been different if the prosecution had alleged that state law permitted owners of public accommodations to discriminate? If the Civil Rights Act of 1875 applied only in states that provided no remedy for such discrimination?

Turning to the thirteenth amendment, the Court agreed that laws enacted under this head of authority "may be primary and direct in [character]; for the thirteenth amendment is not a mere prohibition of State laws establishing or upholding slavery, but an absolute declaration that slavery or involuntary servitude shall not exist in any part of the United States." The Court also agreed that Congress was empowered under the amendment "to pass all laws necessary and proper for abolishing all badges and incidents of slavery in the United States." But the crucial question was whether the discriminatory refusal to serve a black in a public accommodation was such a badge or incident. The Court thought that accepting this position "would be running the slavery argument into the ground." A refusal of service "has nothing to do with slavery or involuntary servitude. [If] it is violative of any right of the party, his redress is to be sought under the laws of the State; or if those laws are adverse to his rights and do not protect him, his remedy will be found in the corrective legislation which Congress has adopted, or may adopt, for counteracting the effect of State laws, or State action, prohibited by the Fourteenth Amendment."

Was the Reconstruction Court concerned primarily with what the rights of blacks should be, with the source of interference with those rights, or with which organ of government should have the power to vindicate them? In cases where racial discrimination affected federal rights, the Court upheld Reconstruction legislation. Thus, in Ex parte Yarbrough, 110 U.S. 651 (1884), the Court sustained a conviction of a private individual under the Ku Klux Klan Act of 1871 for using violence against blacks voting in a *congressional* election. See also Ex parte Siebold, 100 U.S. 371 (1879). Similarly, in Logan v. United States, 144 U.S. 263 (1892), the Court held that Congress had the power to punish conspiracies to injure persons in custody of a U.S. marshal. It is at least possible to argue from these cases that the justices were authentically concerned about the expansion of federal power. But what about the expansion of federal *judicial* power that The Civil Rights Cases represented? Was that expansion consistent with the approach of The Slaughter-House Cases? With the intent of the framers of the Reconstruction amendments? In the context of the 1880s, was it meaningful to speak of the rights of blacks without an expansion of federal power?

At the same time that the Court was dismantling much of the Reconstruction legislation, the political coalition behind Reconstruction was also collapsing. The turning point is usually said to have come with the disputed election of 1876. In return for accepting Hayes's election, Democratic leaders were promised the withdrawal of federal troops from the South and the inclusion of southern Democrats in the cabinet. The post-Reconstruction status of blacks was not, however, a foregone conclusion. As C. Vann Woodward writes in his classic study, "Southern white people themselves [were not] so united on that subject at first as has been generally assumed. The determination of the Negro's 'place' took shape gradually under the influence of economic and political conflicts among divided white people — conflicts that were eventually resolved in part at the expense of the Negro." The Strange Career of Jim Crow 6-7 (1957).

Consider also J. Williamson, The Crucible of Race 109-111, 116-117, 224-225 (1984):

> [Southern] Racial Conservatives, ruling again in the 1880s, built their power, in part, upon the assumption that the Negro would remain in the South and that he would be willingly and harmoniously subordinate. They resisted strenuously both attempts in the 1880s to raise blacks substantially higher in the scale of white civilization and efforts in the 1890s to exclude them altogether. [In] the late 1880s and on through the 1890s, caught in a depression in which opportunities for everyone diminished with sickening rapidity, racial Conservatives found themselves losing power and fighting for survival. . . .
>
> Racialism appeared in strength in 1889 and spread rapidly through the South. The core of the Radical mentality was the concept that Negroes, freed from the restrain-

ing influences of slavery, were rapidly "retrogressing" toward their natural state of bestiality. [Ultimately], Radicals believed, there would be no place for blacks in the South or in America. . . .

The assault upon idealized Southern womanhood by the "nigger beast" was the keen cutting edge of Radicalism. Let Benjamin Ryan Tillman of South Carolina catch the scene for us, as he did for his colleagues on the floor of the United States Senate in 1907. As he drew the picture, white women in the rural South were virtually besieged by Negro brutes who roamed almost without restraint, their "breasts pulsating with the desire to sate their passions upon white maidens and wives." . . .

Rapes and the lynchings that followed became the special studies of the Radicals, and provided the most vital of their statistics. It is vastly significant that the lynching of black men for the rape of white women was not the subject of intense observation and comment in the South before 1889. [In] and after 1889, however, that crime and its punishment commanded a new and tremendously magnified attention. . . .

Violence and the great threat of violence was one way in which Radicals sought to lower the self-esteem of blacks and thus render them more controllable on the way to their demise. But there were other, more subtle means to effect that end. . . .

Two of the tools used to reduce and, hence, to manage blacks were disfranchisement and segregation. . . .

Radicalism had a special motive in its effort to pass laws to disfranchise black men and to separate the races in public places, one that was distinctly different from the special motive of Conservatism in the same process. The Radical motive was to depress the expectations of blacks, especially black men, to make them less secure and ultimately less aggressive, to lead them to follow with minimal resistance the inevitable path to racial extinction. Radicals readily recognized [that] blacks were already practically disfranchised and segregated, but to Radicals the laws were useful in showing explicitly and blatantly the power of whites. They were tokens of hard and present truths and signs of things to come — of the surety of white supremacy and the futility of black resistance.

Plessy v. Ferguson
163 U.S. 537 (1896)

MR. JUSTICE BROWN delivered the opinion of the court.

[A Louisiana statute enacted in 1890 required railroad companies to provide "equal but separate accommodations for the white and colored races," with the provision that "nothing in this act shall be construed as applying to nurses attending children of the other race." A passenger using facilities intended for the other race was made criminally liable. Plessy, who claimed to be seven-eighths Caucasian, was prosecuted under the statute when he failed to leave the coach reserved for whites. The state supreme court upheld the constitutionality of the statute].

The object of the [fourteenth] amendment was undoubtedly to enforce the absolute equality of the two races before the law, but, in the nature of things, it could not have been intended to abolish distinctions based upon color, or to enforce social, as distinguished from political, equality, or a commingling of the two races upon terms unsatisfactory to either. Laws permitting, and even requiring, their separation, in places where they are liable to be brought into contact, do not necessarily imply the inferiority of either race to the other, and have been generally, if not universally, recognized as within the competency of the state legislatures in the exercise of their police power. The most common instance of this is connected with the establishment of separate schools for white and colored children, which have been held to be a valid exercise of the legislative power even by courts of states where the political rights of the colored race have been longest and most earnestly enforced. . . .

[Counsel for Plessy suggests] that the same argument that will justify the state legislature in requiring railways to provide separate accommodations for the two races will also authorize them to require separate cars to be provided for people whose hair is of a certain color, or who are aliens, or who belong to certain nationalities, or to enact laws requiring colored people to walk upon one side of the street, and white people upon the other, or requiring white men's houses to be painted white, and colored men's black, or their vehicles or business signs to be of different colors, upon the theory that one side of the street is as good as the other, or that a house or vehicle of one color is as good as one of another color. The reply to all this is that every exercise of the police power must be reasonable, and extend only to such laws as are enacted in good faith for the promotion of the public good, and not for the annoyance or oppression of a particular class. . . .

So far, then, as a conflict with the fourteenth amendment is concerned, the case reduces itself to the question whether the statute of Louisiana is a reasonable regulation, and with respect to this there must necessarily be a large discretion on the part of the legislature. In determining the question of reasonableness, it is at liberty to act with reference to the established usages, customs, and traditions of the people, and with a view to the promotion of their comfort, and the preservation of the public peace and good order. Gauged by this standard, we cannot say that a law which authorizes or even requires the separation of the two races in public conveyances is unreasonable, or more obnoxious to the fourteenth amendment than the acts of congress requiring separate schools for colored children in the District of Columbia, the constitutionality of which does not seem to have been questioned, or the corresponding acts of state legislatures.

We consider the underlying fallacy of the plaintiff's argument to consist in the assumption that the enforced separation of the two races stamps the colored race with a badge of inferiority. If this be so, it is not by reason of anything found in the act, but solely because the colored race chooses to put that construction upon it. The argument necessarily assumes that if, as has been more than once the case, and is not unlikely to be so again, the colored race should become the dominant power in the state legislature, and should enact a law in precisely similar terms, it would thereby relegate the white race to an inferior position. We imagine that the white race, at least, would not acquiesce in this assumption. The argument also assumes that social prejudices may be overcome by legislation, and that equal rights cannot be secured to the negro except by an enforced commingling of the two races. We cannot accept this proposition. If the two races are to meet upon terms of social equality, it must be the result of natural affinities, a mutual appreciation of each other's merits, and a voluntary consent of individuals. [Legislation] is powerless to eradicate racial instincts, or to abolish distinctions based upon physical differences, and the attempt to do so can only result in accentuating the difficulties of the present situation. If the civil and political rights of both races be equal, one cannot be inferior to the other civilly or politically. If one race be inferior to the other socially, the constitution of the United States cannot put them upon the same plane. . . .

MR. JUSTICE HARLAN, dissenting. . . .

In respect of civil rights, common to all citizens, the constitution of the United States does not, I think, permit any public authority to know the race of those entitled to be protected in the enjoyment of such rights. Every true man has pride of race, and under appropriate circumstances, when the rights of others, his equals before the law, are not to be affected, it is his privilege to express such pride and to take such action based upon it as to him seems proper. But I deny that any legislative body or judicial tribunal may have regard to the race of citizens when the civil rights of those citizens are involved. Indeed, such legislation as that here in question is inconsistent not only with that equality of rights which pertains to citizenship, national and state, but with the personal liberty enjoyed by every one within the United States. . . .

It was said in argument that the statute of Louisiana does not discriminate against either race, but prescribes a rule applicable alike to white and colored citizens. But this argument does not meet the difficulty. Every one knows that the statute in question had its origin in the purpose, not so much to exclude white persons from railroad cars occupied by blacks, as to exclude colored people from coaches occupied by or assigned to white persons. . . .

[If] a state can prescribe, as a rule of civil conduct, that whites and blacks shall not travel as passengers in the same railroad coach, why may it not so regulate the use of the streets of its cities and towns as to compel white citizens to keep on one side of a street and black citizens to keep on the other? Why may it not, upon like grounds, punish whites and blacks who ride together in street cars or in open vehicles on a public road or street? . . .

The answer given at the argument to these questions was that regulations of the kind they suggest would be unreasonable, and could not, therefore, stand before the law. Is it meant that the determination of questions of legislative power depends upon the inquiry whether the statute whose validity is questioned is, in the judgment of the courts, a reasonable one, taking all the circumstances into consideration? A statute may be unreasonable merely because a sound public policy forbade its enactment. But I do not understand that the courts have anything to do with the policy or expediency of legislation. . . .

The white race deems itself to be the dominant race in this country. And so it is, in prestige, in achievements, in education, in wealth, and in power. So, I doubt not, it will continue to be for all time, if it remains true to its great heritage, and holds fast to the principles of constitutional liberty. But in view of the constitution, in the eye of the law, there is in this country no superior, dominant, ruling class of citizens. There is no caste here. Our constitution is color-blind, and neither knows nor tolerates classes among citizens. In respect of civil rights, all citizens are equal before the law. The humblest is the peer of the most powerful. The law regards man as man, and takes no account of his surroundings or of his color when his civil rights as guaranteed by the supreme law of the land are involved. It is therefore to be regretted that this high tribunal, the final expositor of the fundamental law of the land, has reached the conclusion that it is competent for a state to regulate the enjoyment by citizens of their civil rights solely upon the basis of race.

In my opinion, the judgment this day rendered will, in time, prove to be quite as pernicious as the decision made by this tribunal in the *Dred Scott Case*. [The] present decision, it may well be apprehended, will not only stimulate aggressions, more or less brutal and irritating, upon the admitted rights of colored citizens, but will encourage the belief that it is possible, by means of state enactments, to defeat the beneficent purposes which the people of the United States had in view when they adopted the recent amendments of the constitution. [Sixty] millions of whites are in no danger from the presence here of eight millions of blacks. The destinies of the two races, in this country, are indissolubly linked together, and the interests of both require that the common government of all shall not permit the seeds of race hate to be planted under the sanction of law. What can more certainly arouse race hate, what more certainly create and perpetuate a feeling of distrust between these races, than state enactments which, in fact, proceed on the ground that colored citizens are so inferior and degraded that they cannot be allowed to sit in public coaches occupied by white citizens? That, as all will admit, is the real meaning of such legislation as was enacted in Louisiana.

Note: Separate but Equal

1. *Equality of separate facilities.* Plessy v. Ferguson is often said to have inaugurated the "separate but equal" doctrine. But note that *Plessy* says not one word about the equality of separate facilities. Why not? If one reads *Plessy* together with The Civil Rights Cases, was the railroad constitutionally obligated to provide equal facilities? Was a state that required private entities to maintain separate facilities constitutionally obligated to enforce an equality requirement as well?

Three years after *Plessy* the Court squarely addressed the equality problem for the first time in Cumming v. Board of Education, 175 U.S. 528 (1899). Petitioners, black taxpayers and parents, challenged their tax assessment on the ground that the money was utilized to support a high school open only to white students. The school board had initially operated a separate black high school, but the facility had been closed to free funds for the education of black primary school students. In an opinion by Justice Harlan, who had dissented in *Plessy* and The Civil Rights Cases, the Court rejected the challenge. The basis for and scope of the Court's holding is not altogether clear. The Court thought it significant that

> the substantial relief asked is an injunction that would either impair the efficiency of the high school provided for white children or compel the Board to close it. But if that were done, the result would only be to take from white children educational privileges enjoyed by them, without giving to colored children additional opportunities for the education furnished in high schools. [If,] in some appropriate proceeding instituted directly for that purpose, the plaintiffs had sought to compel the Board of Education, out of funds in its hands or under its control, to establish and maintain a high school for colored children, and if it appeared that the Board's refusal to maintain such a school was in fact an abuse of its discretion and in hostility to the colored population because of their race, different questions might have arisen in the state court.

The Court made clear, however, that local authorities were to be accorded substantial discretion in allocating funds between white and black facilities, and that "any interference on the part of Federal authority with the management of such schools cannot be justified except in the case of a clear and unmistakable disregard of rights secured by the supreme law of the land."

Compare *Plessy* and *Cumming* with McCabe v. Atchison, Topeka & Santa Fe Railway, 235 U.S. 151 (1914). An Oklahoma statute required railroads to provide separate but equal coach facilities. The statute also authorized railroads to haul sleeping cars, dining cars, and chair cars to be used exclusively by one race but not the other. The state justified this latter provision on the ground that the minimal black demand for sleeping and dining facilities made it impractical to haul separate cars for this purpose. The Court found this argument "without merit" because

> [it] makes the constitutional right depend upon the number of persons who may be discriminated against, whereas the essence of the constitutional right is that it is a personal one. Whether or not particular facilities shall be provided may doubtless be conditioned upon there being a reasonable demand therefor, but if facilities are provided, substantial equality of treatment of persons traveling under like conditions cannot be refused. It is the individual who is entitled to the equal protection of the laws, and if he is denied by a common carrier, acting in the matter under the authority of a state law, a facility of convenience in the course of his journey which under substantially the same circumstances is furnished to another traveler, he may properly complain that his constitutional privilege has been invaded.

Can *McCabe* be reconciled with *Cumming?* With *Plessy?* After *McCabe*, suppose a black student sought admission to a white public school on the ground that it was closer to his home than the nearest black school? Cf. Gong Lum v. Rice, 275 U.S. 78 (1927).

2. *The state interest in separate facilities.* Note that *Plessy* does not approve all statutes mandating separate treatment. Only those which are "reasonable" are permissible. What state interest made racial separation "reasonable" in *Plessy?* Consider the following hypothetical cases:

a. A white person sits in his assigned seat on a railway coach. When a black person sits next to him, the white asks the conductor if he can change his seat because he does not wish to sit next to a black. No sooner has the white assumed his new seat than the black follows him and sits next to him again. The black is prosecuted under a breach of the peace statute.

b. During rush hour, commuter railways are extremely crowded with standing passengers packed tightly in the aisles. Female passengers complain that their privacy is invaded by these arrangements and prevail on the legislature to require separate cars for men and women during busy periods.

c. After repeated episodes of racial violence, state officials provide separate prison cells for whites and blacks. Cf. Lee v. Washington, 390 U.S. 333 (1968).

Compare *Plessy* with Berea College v. Kentucky, 211 U.S. 45 (1908). The college, a private institution, was convicted under a statute making it a crime to operate a school "where persons of the white and negro races are both received as pupils for instruction." The Court affirmed the conviction, but on the ground that the college was a corporation that did not have all the rights of individuals. In light of *Plessy*, why did the Court think it necessary to qualify its holding in this way? If an individual had been prosecuted under the same statute, what result?

In Buchanan v. Warley, 245 U.S. 60 (1917), the Court held that a statute prohibiting whites from occupying a residence in a block where the majority of houses were occupied by blacks, and vice versa, violated the fourteenth amendment. The challenge to the statute arose in the context of a suit by a white seller to enforce specifically a contract with a black purchaser, who claimed that the law barred him from occupying the residence. The Court acknowledged that "there exists a serious and difficult problem arising from a feeling of race hostility which the law is powerless to control, and to which it must give a measure of consideration." But the Court believed that "such legislation must have its limitations" and that these legitimate objectives could not "be accomplished by laws or ordinances which deny rights created or protected by the Federal Constitution." The Court distinguished *Plessy* and *Berea College*: "In each instance the complaining person was afforded the opportunity to ride, or to attend institutions of learning, or afforded the thing of whatever nature to which in the particular case he was entitled. The most that was done was to require him as a member of a class to conform with reasonable rules in regard to separation of races. In none of them was he denied the right to use, control, or dispose of his property, as in this case."

Does this distinction make sense? Can you formulate a general principle that explains the results in *Plessy, Cumming, McCabe, Berea College,* and *Buchanan?*

3.   The Attack of Jim Crow

As the previous section indicates, the framers of the Reconstruction amendments almost certainly intended that the rights of newly freed slaves would be protected by federal *legislative* action authorized by the new sources of congressional power contained in those amendments. This intent was frustrated by the Court's adherence to an older version of federalism and by the collapse of the political consensus supporting civil rights legislation.

One ironic consequence of the Court's invalidation of such Reconstruction legislation was that when meaningful reform finally came, it was the courts, rather than Congress, that provided the impetus for change. From 1938, when the NAACP won its first Supreme Court victory in a school desegregation case, until the 1960s, when a political consensus favoring civil rights again emerged, the courts stood virtually alone in articulating and enforcing the law of race discrimination. What difference might it make that the protection of blacks was left to judicial interpretations of the Constitution rather than to legislative action? Are we in the long run better off because prohibitions on racial discrimination were given firm constitutional roots? Or did the short-circuiting of the arduous task of building a political consensus for civil rights ultimately weaken those prohibitions?

Note: The NAACP's Legal Strategy

1. *The Garland Fund.* Consider R. Kluger, Simple Justice 132-133 (1976):

> In 1922, a twenty-one-year-old Harvard undergraduate named Charles Garland had chosen not to accept his share of the estate left by his father, a Boston millionaire. Believing that it was wrong for anyone to be handed a fortune he had done nothing to create, young Garland announced, "I am placing my life on a Christian basis," and gave some $800,000 to establish a foundation for the support of liberal and radical causes. He tarried long enough to see it christened the American Fund for Public Service before he himself took up a farmer's life.

[A committee formed to administer the Garland Fund] recommended that [it] finance a large-scale, widespread dramatic campaign to give the Southern Negro his constitutional rights, his political and civil equality, and therewith a self-conscious-ness and self-respect which would inevitably tend to effect a revolution in the eco-nomic life of the country. [A] grant of $100,000 to the NAACP to carry out such a legal campaign was suggested, along with a memorandum of proposed legal strategy, especially in the education area. Taxpayers' suits were urged, to assure equal as well as separate public schools in the seven states that most flagrantly discriminated against Negroes in their school allocations. . . .

Not everyone at the Garland Fund was enthusiastic about the idea. Indeed, the man who had most experience in such undertakings — Roger Baldwin of the ACLU — was the most skeptical. He was convinced that the legal approach would misfire "because the forces that keep the Negro under subjection will find some way of accomplishing their purposes, law or no law." [Baldwin] favored "the union of white and black workers against their common exploiters." But the committee report carried anyway, the $100,000 was earmarked for the effort, and the first $8,000 transferred to the NAACP for drawing up a detailed blueprint of the legal campaign.

2. *Strategy*. Suppose you were a member of the NAACP's governing board. What use of the Garland Fund money would you favor? Consider the following possibilities?

a. Contributions to scholarship funds for needy black students;
b. Contributions to the political campaigns of candidates sympathetic to the plight of black Americans;
c. Financing litigation demanding the equalization of separate black facilities;
d. Financing litigation demanding the admission of blacks to white facilities on the ground that parallel black facilities were unequal;
e. Financing litigation that frontally attacked *Plessy* and demand integrated facilities.

In fact, the NAACP did not unwaveringly pursue any single strategy to end discrimination. Rather, it "attacked what might be called targets of opportunity. [If] the military metaphor referring to a litigation campaign is helpful, the cam-paign was conducted on a terrain that repeatedly required changes in maneu-vers." M. Tushnet, Segregated Schools and Legal Strategy: The NAACP's Campaign against Segregated Education, 1925-1950, at 8-13 (unpub. ms. 1985).

Although the NAACP's campaign was neither systematic nor invariably suc-cessful, it did succeed in slowly remaking the law.

MISSOURI EX REL. GAINES v. CANADA, 305 U.S. 337 (1938): Mis-souri law required separate education for whites and blacks. Although the Univer-sity of Missouri operated a law school, the parallel black institution, Lincoln University, did not. A Missouri statute, however, authorized the board of cura-tors to arrange for attendance of black residents at institutions in neighboring states and to pay reasonable tuition rates for such attendance when no black instate facility was available. Lloyd Gaines, a black denied admission at the Uni-versity of Missouri law school, brought this action to compel the curators to admit him. The state court denied relief, holding that he should have applied for aid to attend an out-of-state institution. The Supreme Court reversed. Chief Justice Hughes delivered the Court's opinion:

"The state court stresses the advantages that are afforded by the law schools of the adjacent States [which] admit non-resident negroes. The court considered that these were schools of high standing where one desiring to practice law in Missouri can get 'as sound, comprehensive, valuable legal education' as in the University of Missouri. [Petitioner] insists that for one intending to practice in Missouri there are special advantages in attending a law school there. [Proceeding] with its examination of relative advantages, the state court found that the difference in distances to be traveled afforded no substantial ground of complaint and that there was an adequate appropriation to meet the full tuition fees which petitioner would have to pay.

"We think that these matters are beside the point. The basic consideration is not as to what sort of opportunities other States provide, or whether they are as good as those in Missouri, but as to what opportunities Missouri itself furnishes to white students and denies to negroes solely upon the ground of color. [By] the operation of the laws of Missouri a privilege has been created for white law students which is denied to negroes by reason of their race. The white resident is afforded legal education within the State; the negro resident having the same qualifications is refused it there and must go outside the State to obtain it. That is a denial of the equality of legal right to the enjoyment of the privilege which the State has set up, and the provision for the payment of tuition fees in another State does not remove the discrimination.

"Nor can we regard the fact that there is but a limited demand in Missouri for the legal education of negroes as excusing the discrimination in favor of whites. [See *McCabe*]. . . .

"Here, petitioner's right was a personal one. It was as an individual that he was entitled to the equal protection of the laws, and the State was bound to furnish him within its borders facilities for legal education substantially equal to those which the State there afforded for persons of the white race, whether or not other negroes sought the same opportunity."

Justice McReynolds, joined by Justice Butler, dissented: "The State has offered to provide the negro petitioner opportunity for study of the law — if perchance that is the thing really desired — by paying his tuition at some nearby school of good standing. This is far from unmistakable disregard of his rights and in the circumstances is enough to satisfy any reasonable demand for specialized training. It appears that never before has a negro applied for admission to the Law School and none has ever asked that Lincoln University provide legal instruction.

"The problem presented obviously is a difficult and highly practical one. A fair effort to solve it has been made by offering adequate opportunity for study when sought in good faith. The State should not be unduly hampered through theorization inadequately restrained by experience."

Note: *Separate but Equal between* Gaines *and* Brown

1. *The aftermath of* Gaines. Some of the frustrations inherent in attempting to achieve social change through litigation are illustrated by the aftermath of

Gaines. Shortly after the decision, the Missouri legislature appropriated some money to establish a black law school at Lincoln University. The NAACP thought the facility was blatantly unequal, but the client — Mr. Gaines — had disappeared without a trace. A frantic search failed to locate him, and eventually, the NAACP was forced to accept dismissal of the suit. See Bluford, The Lloyd Gaines Story, 1958 J. Educ. Soc. 242, 245-246 (1959). Should the resolution of a great public issue turn on the wishes or whereabouts of a single client? Was the real point of the *Gaines* litigation to assure an adequate legal education for Mr. Gaines? Should it have been?

2. Gaines *and the meaning of equal treatment.* Can you state precisely why the *Gaines* court thought that the out-of-state education provided to blacks was not equal to the in-state education provided to whites? If Missouri had established a special in-state law school for blacks attended by one student (Gaines), would such a facility have satisfied the Constitution?

Note that there are two questions at issue in cases like *Gaines:* which institution of government should determine whether the facilities are equal and how that determination should be made. Cumming v. Board of Education was preoccupied with the first question. The Court argued that state officials should be left free to make their own determinations of equality as long as they acted in good faith and their determinations were reasonable. In *Gaines,* however, the Court assumed without discussion that it must make a de novo determination of equality. What is the justification for this change? Would the *Cumming* approach necessarily have made the equality requirement meaningless?

Because of the way it answered the first question, the Court in *Gaines* was forced to confront the second. This is a problem of dizzying complexity. Presumably, the equality requirement does not mean that parallel facilities must be identical. If classrooms in the University of Missouri are painted green and those in Lincoln University yellow, this fact alone would not violate the equal protection clause. How is the Court to evaluate which differences in facilities are relevant for equality purposes? Suppose, for example, that Missouri has an outstanding mathematics department but a weak history department, while Lincoln excels in history but does poorly in mathematics. Can a court evaluate the equality of the two institutions without deciding a priori on the relative worth of education in mathematics and history? How is a court to do that?

The *McCabe* principle complicates matters further. For under *McCabe,* which held that the constitutional right is an individual one, the state could not defend Lincoln's weak mathematics department on the ground that the vast majority of its students valued history more highly. How can one determine the worth of an entity apart from the value that most people place on it? Suppose a single student at Lincoln attached extraordinary value to attending an institution with green walls. Might yellow walls violate the equality principle after all?

3. *From* Gaines *to* Brown. The analysis above suggests that the way the Court answered the first question in *Gaines* led, inevitably, to the ultimate abandonment of the effort to answer the second. This was true not only because there were difficulties in finding a principled way for courts to evaluate the equality of different facilities, but also because the task of performing the evaluation, in the context of thousands of separate facilities each of which had countless different variables to compare, was unmanageable. In fact, it is possible to draw a fairly

straight line from *Gaines* to the ultimate abandonment of the separate but equal formula sixteen years later. The Court decided three school segregation cases between *Gaines* and *Brown*:

a. In Sipuel v. Board of Regents, 332 U.S. 631 (1948), petitioner applied to the only state law school and was denied admission because of her race. In a unanimous, four-paragraph per curiam opinion issued only four days after oral argument, the Court reaffirmed *Gaines* and held that the state was constitutionally obligated to provide her with an equal legal education. On remand, the trial court gave the state the option of either admitting Sipuel or immediately establishing a separate black law school. Sipuel thereupon sought mandamus in the Supreme Court, claiming that this disposition was inconsistent with the Court's mandate, since the hastily established black school could not possibly provide an equal education. In Fisher v. Hurst, 333 U.S. 147 (1948), the Court, over two dissents, denied relief. The Court noted that "the petition for certiorari in [*Sipuel*] did not present the issue whether a state might not satisfy the equal protection clause of the Fourteenth Amendment by establishing a separate school for Negroes." For an account of the Court's deliberations over *Sipuel* and *Fisher*, see Hutchinson, Unanimity and Desegregation: Decisionmaking in the Supreme Court, 1948-1958, 68 Geo. L.J. 1, 6-9 (1979).

b. In Sweatt v. Painter, 339 U.S. 629 (1950), the Court did what it had declined to do in *Fisher* — order the admission of a black student to a white school. Sweatt was denied admission to the University of Texas Law School on the ground that a parallel black school, opened after the litigation commenced, was a substantially equal facility. The Court held that the facility was not in fact equal and that Sweatt therefore could not be denied admission to the white school. In reaching this conclusion, the Court was aided by the obvious inequality between the two schools in objectively measurable factors like size of library and number of full-time faculty. But the Court did not limit its examination to these factors:

> What is more important, the University of Texas Law School possesses to a far greater degree those qualities which are incapable of objective measurement but which make for greatness in a law school. Such qualities, to name but a few, include reputation of the faculty, experience of the administration, position and influence of the alumni, standing in the community, traditions and prestige. It is difficult to believe that one who had a free choice between these law schools would consider the question close.
>
> Moreover, although the law is a highly learned profession, we are well aware that it is an intensely practical one. The law school, the proving ground for legal learning and practice, cannot be effective in isolation from the individuals and institutions with which the law interacts. Few students and no one who has practiced law would choose to study in an academic vacuum, removed from the interplay of ideas and the exchange of views with which the law is concerned. The law school to which Texas is willing to admit petitioner excludes from its student body members of the racial groups which number 85% of the population of the State and include most of the lawyers, witnesses, jurors, judges and other officials with whom petitioner will inevitably be dealing when he becomes a member of the Texas Bar. With such a substantial and significant segment of society excluded, we cannot conclude that the education offered petitioner is substantially equal to that which he would receive if admitted to the University of Texas Law School.

[handwritten margin note: Gave historical precedent to Brown v. Board]

✴ c. The Court further elaborated on this theme in McLaurin v. Oklahoma State Regents, 339 U.S. 637 (1950), decided the same day as *Sweatt*. In *McLaurin* the state, under the pressure of litigation, admitted petitioner to the previously all-white University of Oklahoma Department of Education. However, McLaurin was made to sit in a special seat in the classroom reserved for blacks, could not eat with other students in the cafeteria, and was given a special table in the library. Although McLaurin could not claim that the physical facilities provided him were unequal, the Court held the restrictions unconstitutional because they "[impaired] and [inhibited] his ability to study, to engage in discussions and exchange views with other students, and, in general, to learn his profession."

After *Sweatt* and *McLaurin*, was there anything left for the Court to decide in *Brown?*

Brown v. Board of Education of Topeka (*Brown I*)
347 U.S. 483 (1954)

MR. CHIEF JUSTICE WARREN delivered the opinion of the Court. . . .

In each of [these] cases, minors of the Negro race, through their legal representatives, seek the aid of the courts in obtaining admission to the public schools of their community on a nonsegregated basis. In each instance, they had been denied admission to schools attended by white children under laws requiring or permitting segregation according to race. This segregation was alleged to deprive the plaintiffs of the equal protection of the laws under the Fourteenth Amendment. . . .

Reargument was largely devoted to the circumstances surrounding the adoption of the Fourteenth Amendment in 1868. It covered exhaustively consideration of the Amendment in Congress, ratification by the states, then existing practices in racial segregation, and the views of proponents and opponents of the Amendment. This discussion and our own investigation convince us that, although these sources cast some light, it is not enough to resolve the problem with which we are faced. At best, they are inconclusive. The most avid proponents of the post-War Amendments undoubtedly intended them to remove all legal distinctions among "all persons born or naturalized in the United States." Their opponents, just as certainly, were antagonistic to both the letter and the spirit of the Amendments and wished them to have the most limited effect. What others in Congress and the state legislatures had in mind cannot be determined with any degree of certainty.

An additional reason for the inconclusive nature of the Amendment's history, with respect to segregated schools, is the status of public education at that time. In the South, the movement toward free common schools, supported by general taxation, had not yet taken hold. Education of white children was largely in the hands of private groups. Education of Negroes was almost nonexistent, and practically all of the race were illiterate. In fact, any education of Negroes was forbidden by law in some states. Today, in contrast, many Negroes have achieved outstanding success in the arts and sciences as well as in the business and professional world. It is true that public school education at the time of the Amendment had advanced further in the North, but the effect of the Amendment on North-

History as precedent (handwritten marginalia)

ern States was generally ignored in the congressional debates. Even in the North, the conditions of public education did not approximate those existing today. The curriculum was usually rudimentary; ungraded schools were common in rural areas; the school term was but three months a year in many states; and compulsory school attendance was virtually unknown. As a consequence, it is not surprising that there should be so little in the history of the Fourteenth Amendment relating to its intended effect on public education. . . .

In approaching this problem, we cannot turn the clock back to 1868 when the Amendment was adopted, or even to 1896 when [*Plessy*] was written. We must consider public education in the light of its full development and its present place in American life throughout the Nation. Only in this way can it be determined if segregation in public schools deprives these plaintiffs of the equal protection of the laws.

Today, education is perhaps the most important function of state and local governments. Compulsory school attendance laws and the great expenditures for education both demonstrate our recognition of the importance of education to our democratic society. It is required in the performance of our most basic public responsibilities, even service in the armed forces. It is the very foundation of good citizenship. Today it is a principal instrument in awakening the child to cultural values, in preparing him for later professional training, and in helping him to adjust normally to his environment. In these days, it is doubtful that any child may reasonably be expected to succeed in life if he is denied the opportunity of an education. Such an opportunity, where the state has undertaken to provide it, is a right which must be made available to all on equal terms.

We come then to the question presented: Does segregation of children in public schools solely on the basis of race, even though the physical facilities and other "tangible" factors may be equal, deprive the children of the minority group of equal educational opportunities? We believe that it does.

In [*Sweatt*], in finding that a segregated law school for Negroes could not provide them equal educational opportunities, this Court relied in large part on "those qualities which are incapable of objective measurement but which make for greatness in a law school." In [*McLaurin*], the Court, in requiring that a Negro admitted to a white graduate school be treated like all other students, again resorted to intangible considerations: " . . . his ability to study, to engage in discussions and exchange views with other students, and, in general, to learn his profession." Such considerations apply with added force to children in grade and high schools. To separate them from others of similar age and qualifications solely because of their race generates a feeling of inferiority as to their status in the community that may affect their hearts and minds in a way unlikely ever to be undone. The effect of this separation on their educational opportunities was well stated by a finding in the Kansas case by a court which nevertheless felt compelled to rule against the Negro plaintiffs:

> Segregation of white and colored children in public schools has a detrimental effect upon the colored children. The impact is greater when it has the sanction of the law; for the policy of separating the races is usually interpreted as denoting the inferiority of the negro group. A sense of inferiority affects the motivation of a child to learn. Segregation with the sanction of law, therefore, has a tendency to [retard] the educational and mental development of negro children and to deprive them of some of the benefits they would receive in a racial[ly] integrated school system.

Whatever may have been the extent of psychological knowledge at the time of [*Plessy*], this finding is amply supported by modern authority.[11] Any language in [*Plessy*] contrary to this finding is rejected.

We conclude that in the field of public education the doctrine of "separate but equal" has no place. Separate educational facilities are inherently unequal. Therefore, we hold that the plaintiffs and others similarly situated for whom the actions have been brought are, by reason of the segregation complained of, deprived of the equal protection of the laws guaranteed by the Fourteenth Amendment.

Note: Justifications and Explanations for Brown

1. *The Court's justifications*. Did *Brown* adequately explain why segregation denied minority students equal educational opportunity even when "tangible" factors were equalized? Consider the following arguments:

a. *The legislative history of the equal protection clause is consistent with the position that segregated education is unconstitutional*. Note that the Court does not assert that the framers of the fourteenth amendment specifically intended to outlaw segregated education. Is such an assertion plausible? In 1868 eight northern states permitted segregated schools and five additional northern states excluded black children entirely from public education. See R. Kluger, Simple Justice 633-634 (1976). The Reconstruction Congress itself permitted the District of Columbia schools to remain segregated, see Frank & Munro, The Original Understanding of "Equal Protection of the Laws," 1972 Wash. U. L.Q. 421, 460-462, and even the spectators in the gallery listening to the Senators debate the fourteenth amendment were segregated by race. See R. Berger, Government by Judiciary: The Transformation of the Fourteenth Amendment 123-125 (1977). Moreover, the sponsors of the Civil Rights Act of 1866, which the fourteenth amendment was intended to constitutionalize, specifically disclaimed any intent to interfere with segregated education. See, e.g., Statement of James Wilson, Cong. Globe, 39th Cong. 1st Sess. 1117-1118 (1866). See generally Bickel, The Original Understanding and the Segregation Decision, 69 Harv. L. Rev. 1, 11-40 (1955).

Might it nonetheless be argued that the equal protection clause represented "a compromise permitting [Moderates and Radicals] to go to the country with language which they could, where necessary, defend against damaging alarms raised by the opposition, but which at the same time was sufficiently elastic to permit reasonable future advances"? Id. at 61. But even if the legislative history "left the way open to, in fact invited, a decision based on the moral and material state of the nation in 1954, not 1866," id. at 65, does not the burden remain on the defenders of *Brown* to explain why segregation in 1954 denied equality?

11. K. B. Clark, Effect of Prejudice and Discrimination on Personality Development (Midcentury White House Conference on Children and Youth, 1950); Witmer and Kotinsky, Personality in the Making (1952), c. VI; Deutscher and Chein, The Psychological Effects of Enforced Segregation: A Survey of Social Science Opinion, 26 J. Psychol. 259 (1948); Chein, What are the Psychological Effects of Segregation under Conditions of Equal Facilities?, 3 Int. J. Opinion and Attitude Res. 229 (1949); Brameld, Educational Costs, in Discrimination and National Welfare (MacIver, ed., 1949), 44-48; Frazier, The Negro in the United States (1949), 674-681. And see generally Myrdal, An American Dilemma (1944).

In Bolling v. Sharpe, 347 U.S. 497 (1954), decided on the same day as *Brown*, the Court unanimously held school segregation in the District of Columbia unconstitutional. Since the fourteenth amendment applies only to the states, the Court could not rely on the equal protection clause. But although equal protection and due process are not "interchangeable phrases," the Court held that "discrimination may be so unjustifiable as to be violative of [the due process clause of the Fifth Amendment]." Moreover, "In view of our decision that the Constitution prohibits the States from maintaining racially segregated public schools, it would be unthinkable that the same Constitution would impose a lesser duty on the Federal Government."

Does the legislative history of the fifth and fourteenth amendments really make this result "unthinkable"? When the fifth amendment was adopted, most blacks in the United States were slaves and the Constitution itself implicitly acknowledged that fact. Does *Bolling* suggest that the fourteenth amendment somehow modified the fifth amendment? The framers of the fourteenth amendment chose to make the equal protection guarantee applicable solely to the states. This decision presumably reflected the view that institutional safeguards on the federal level made a constitutional guarantee of equality unnecessary. Does the Court care what those who wrote the fifth and fourteenth amendments meant by them? Should it?

Consider Tushnet, Following the Rules Laid Down: A Critique of Interpretivism and Neutral Principles, 96 Harv. L. Rev. 781, 800-801 (1983):

> Suppose that we [turned] back the clock so that we could talk to the framers of the fourteenth amendment. If we asked them whether the amendment outlawed segregation in public schools, they would answer "No." [But the framers] had in mind a relatively new and peripheral social institution. [In] contrast they thought that freedom of contract was extremely important because it was the foundation of individual achievement, and they certainly wanted to outlaw racial discrimination with respect to this freedom. Returning to 1954 and the question for the Court in *Brown*, we might, in an antic moment, challenge the interpretivists with their own weapons. [Public] education as it exists today — a central institution for the achievement of individual goals — is in fact the functional equivalent not of public education in 1868, but of freedom of contract in 1868. . . .
>
> The problem raised by this interpretation of *Brown* is that the need to identify functional equivalents over time necessarily imports significant indeterminacy — and therefore discretion — into the interpretivist account.

See also the discussion of original intent in constitutional interpretation in Chapter 1, supra, and Chapter 6, infra.

b. *"Today, education is perhaps the most important function of state and local governments."* Does this observation, even if correct, in any way advance the argument that segregated education is per se discriminatory? Is *Brown* supported by the deep-seated view of U.S. public schools as a "secular, nationalizing, assimilationist agent [charged] with the task of Americanization, of melding backgrounds, and creating one nation"? A. Bickel, The Supreme Court and the Idea of Progress 121-122 (1970). Does the Constitution require this view of education, or does it permit (compel?) recognition of competing values such as cultural diversity, parental control, and freedom of association? See Board of Education v. Pico, Chapter 7, section F1, infra.

In a series of terse per curiam opinions handed down in the years immediately after *Brown*, the Court held unconstitutional segregation in a wide variety of other public facilities. See, e.g., Gayle v. Browder, 352 U.S. 903 (1956) (buses); Holmes v. City of Atlanta, 350 U.S. 879 (1955) (municipal golf courses); Mayor of Baltimore v. Dawson, 350 U.S. 877 (1955) (public beaches and bathhouses). In light of these decisions, is it possible to maintain that *Brown* rested on the special status of public education?

c. *"To separate [minority] children from others of similar age and qualifications solely because of their race generates a feeling of inferiority as to their status in the community that may affect their hearts and minds in a way unlikely ever to be undone."* Is stigma alone a sufficient injury to constitute a denial of equal protection? Is the perception of stigma sufficient to invalidate a law that is supported by a valid, neutral purpose? In *Bolling* the Court observed that "Segregation in public education is not reasonably related to any proper governmental objective, and thus it imposes on Negro children [a] burden that constitutes an arbitrary deprivation of their liberty."

Consider Black, The Lawfulness of the Segregation Decisions, 69 Yale L.J. 421, 424-426 (1960): "[Segregation was] set up and continued for the very purpose of keeping [blacks] in an inferior station. [This purpose was a] matter of common notoriety [not] so much for judicial notice as for background knowledge of educated men who live in the world." Would segregated education have achieved this purpose if all tangible facilities were really equalized in black and white schools? Suppose that segregation was imposed for the purpose of disadvantaging blacks but that overwhelmingly persuasive data demonstrated that blacks in fact benefited from a segregated but truly equal environment?

d. *"Segregation with the sanction of law [has] a tendency to [retard] the educational and mental development of Negro children."* *Brown*'s reliance on empirical, social science data to support this conclusion has been the subject of continuing controversy. See, e.g., Cahn, Jurisprudence, 30 N.Y.U. L. Rev. 150 (1955); Van den Haag, Social Science Testimony in the Desegregation Cases — A Reply to Professor Kenneth Clark, 6 Vill. L. Rev. 69 (1960). See generally Symposium, The Courts, Social Science and School Desegregation, 39 Law & Contemp. Probs. (Winter/Spring 1975). Indeed, it appears that "Virtually everyone who has examined the question now agrees that the Court erred [in relying upon the social science data]. The proffered evidence was methodologically unsound." Yudof, School Desegregation: Legal Realism, Reasoned Elaboration, and Social Science Research in the Supreme Court, 42 Law & Contemp. Probs. 57, 70 (1978).

The conflict over the reliability of the data has tended to obscure more fundamental questions. Even if it could be demonstrated unambiguously that blacks perform better in an integrated than a segregated environment, why should that fact be constitutionally determinative? Does the Constitution require the arrangement that maximizes the achievement of black students?

If whites in an integrated classroom receive better test scores than blacks, does *Brown* suggest that the class must be *segregated* so that blacks can be given a different curriculum that will produce equal test scores? Is the *Brown* Court's reliance on social science data consistent with *McCabe*'s holding that the fourteenth amendment protects *individual* rights? Suppose a minority of black students, or their parents, would prefer a segregated education? Does *Brown* hold that the equal protection clause protects group rights, even at the expense of individuals?

2. *Alternative rationales and explanations.* If the Court's reasoning in *Brown* is less than satisfactory, are there better justifications for the result? Even if it can't be justified legally, are there plausible explanations for the Court's decision? Consider the following possibilities:

a. Wechsler, Toward Neutral Principles of Constitutional Law, 73 Harv. L. Rev. 1, 34 (1959):

> Assuming equal facilities, the question posed by state-enforced segregation is not one of discrimination at all. Its human and its constitutional dimensions lie entirely elsewhere, in the denial by the state of freedom to associate, a denial that impinges in the same way on any groups or races that may be involved.

Wechsler goes on to ask whether in

> a situation where the state must practically choose between denying the association to those individuals who wish it or imposing it on those who would avoid it, [there is] a basis in neutral principles for holding that the Constitution demands that the claims for association should prevail.

Is *Brown* premised on the assumption that in a white-dominated society, segregation harms blacks more severely than whites? That blacks are harmed more severely by forced separation than whites are harmed by forced association? Does it matter to the freedom of association argument that in the school context, it is generally parents who have the freedom, but children who do the associating?

b. Bell, *Brown v. Board of Education* and the Interest-Convergence Dilemma, 93 Harv. L. Rev. 518, 524-525 (1980):

> [The] decision in *Brown* to break with the Court's long-held position on these issues cannot be understood without some consideration of the decision's value to whites [able] to see the economic and political advantages at home and abroad that would follow the abandonment of segregation. [*Brown* provided] immediate credibility to America's struggle with Communist countries to win the hearts and minds of emerging third world people [and] offered much needed reassurance to American blacks. [Moreover,] there were whites who realized that the South could make the transition from a rural, plantation society to the sunbelt with all its potential and profit only when it ended its struggle to remain divided by state-sponsored segregation.

If desegregation was really in the interest of the white majority, why did it have to be judicially imposed? Was the campaign to overrule *Plessy* ultimately successful because "the dominant elites in the South, even if they controlled public opinion there, [were] only a fragment of the national ruling class, and [the] interests of the ruling class as a whole [differed] from those of its southern fragment"? M. Tushnet, Segregated Schools and Legal Strategy: The NAACP's Campaign against Segregated Education, 1925-1950, at 1-19 (unpub. ms. 1985). If the result in *Brown* was in the interest of the white majority, does that support the decision by answering those who claimed that the Court had unjustifiably imposed its own social views on the country?

c. Consider the following argument: Most critics of *Brown* have treated the decision as an unjustified assertion of judicial power. But *Brown* can be viewed instead as a product of the institutional *weakness* of the judiciary. Prior to *Brown*, the Court had committed itself to the position that separate educational facilities had to be equalized and that the courts were duty bound to decide de novo whether such equality actually existed. Might such a doctrine, by requiring the courts to evaluate the level of "equality" in thousands of segregated school systems throughout the country, have produced an even more serious judicial intrusion on the political branches than *Brown*? Note that even if you believe that segregated schools as they existed in the southern states in 1954 violated the equal protection clause, it does not follow that *Brown* was correctly decided. The hard question is why desegregation was the constitutionally required alternative to a judicially mandated regime of real equality. Did the *Brown* Court abandon a truly serious effort to achieve racial justice for a slogan? Could it have done otherwise?

3. *The meaning of* Brown. What, precisely, did *Brown* require southern school systems to do? Could that question be answered before the ambiguity as to *Brown*'s reasoning was resolved? For example, if *Brown* was premised on the stigma associated with state-enforced segregation, then presumably a simple declaration that race would no longer be considered in school assignments would be sufficient. But if *Brown* meant that educational equality could be achieved only if blacks and whites attended school together, something more might be required.

The initial *Brown* opinion did not answer the remedy question. Instead, the Court restored the case to the docket for reargument. As you read the opinion that follows, think about whether the Court answered or avoided the substantive questions that remained after *Brown I*.

Brown v. Board of Education of Topeka (*Brown II*)
349 U.S. 294 (1955)

Mr. Chief Justice Warren delivered the opinion of the Court.

These cases were decided on May 17, 1954. The opinions of that date, declaring the fundamental principle that racial discrimination in public education is unconstitutional, are incorporated herein by reference. All provisions of federal, state, or local law requiring or permitting such discrimination must yield to this principle. There remains for consideration the manner in which relief is to be accorded.

Because these cases arose under different local conditions and their disposition will involve a variety of local problems, we requested further argument on the question of relief. In view of the nationwide importance of the decision, we invited the Attorney General of the United States, and the Attorneys General of all states requiring or permitting racial discrimination in public education to present their views on that question. The parties, the United States, and the States of Florida, North Carolina, Arkansas, Oklahoma, Maryland, and Texas filed briefs and participated in the oral argument. . . .

Full implementation of these constitutional principles may require solution of varied local school problems. School authorities have the primary responsibility for elucidating, assessing, and solving these problems; courts will have to consider whether the action of school authorities constitutes good faith implementation of the governing constitutional principles. Because of their proximity to local conditions and the possible need for further hearings, the courts which originally heard these cases can best perform this judicial appraisal. Accordingly, we believe it appropriate to remand the cases to those courts.

In fashioning and effectuating the decrees, the courts will be guided by equitable principles. Traditionally equity has been characterized by a practical flexibility in shaping its remedies and by a facility for adjusting and reconciling public and private needs. These cases call for the exercise of these traditional attributes of equity power. At stake is the personal interest of the plaintiffs in admission to public schools as soon as practicable on a nondiscriminatory basis. To effectuate this interest may call for elimination of a variety of obstacles in making the transition to school systems operated in accordance with the constitutional principles set forth in our May 17, 1954, decision. Courts of equity may properly take into account the public interest in the elimination of such obstacles in a systematic and effective manner. But it should go without saying that the vitality of these constitutional principles cannot be allowed to yield simply because of disagreement with them.

While giving weight to these public and private considerations, the courts will require that the defendants make a prompt and reasonable start toward full compliance with our May 17, 1954, ruling. Once such a start has been made, the courts may find that additional time is necessary to carry out the ruling in an effective manner. The burden rests upon the defendants to establish that such time is necessary in the public interest and is consistent with good faith compliance at the earliest practicable date. To that end, the courts may consider problems related to administration, arising from the physical condition of the school plant, the school transportation system, personnel, revision of school districts and attendance areas into compact units to achieve a system of determining admission to the public schools on a nonracial basis, and revision of local laws and regulations which may be necessary in solving the foregoing problems. They will also consider the adequacy of any plans the defendants may propose to meet these problems and to effectuate a transition to a racially nondiscriminatory school system. During this period of transition, the courts will retain jurisdiction of these cases.

The judgments below, except that in the Delaware case, are accordingly reversed and the cases are remanded to the District Courts to take such proceedings and enter such orders and decrees consistent with this opinion as are necessary and proper to admit to public schools on a racially nondiscriminatory basis with all deliberate speed the parties to these cases. The judgment in the Delaware case — ordering the immediate admission of the plaintiffs to schools previously attended only by white children — is affirmed on the basis of the principles stated in our May 17, 1954, opinion, but the case is remanded to the Supreme Court of Delaware for such further proceedings as that Court may deem necessary in light of this opinion.

Note: "All Deliberate Speed"

Brown II's "all deliberate speed" formulation has been widely criticized. See, e.g., Carter, The Warren Court and Desegregation, 67 Mich. L. Rev. 237, 243 (1968); Lusky, Racial Discrimination and the Federal Law: A Problem in Nullification, 63 Colum. L. Rev. 1163 (1963). What are the weaknesses of the approach?

Do you agree that "the harsh truth is that the first *Brown* decision was a great decision; and the second *Brown* decision was a great mistake"? L. Miller, The Petitioners: The Story of the Supreme Court of the United States and the Negro 351 (1966). Or do the problems in *Brown II* (if there are any) grow logically from the weaknesses in *Brown I?* Consider the following arguments:

1. *If segregation is unconstitutional, the Court cannot legitimately tolerate continued segregation while jurisdictions make "a prompt and reasonable start toward" desegregation.* Was *Brown II* premised on the notion that "Negroes (unlike whites) possess rights as a race rather than as individuals, so that a particular Negro can rightly be delayed in the enjoyment of his established rights if progress is being made in improving the legal status of Negroes generally"? Lusky, The Stereotype: Hard Core of Racism, 13 Buffalo L. Rev. 450, 457 (1963). See also Carter, The Warren Court and Desegregation, 67 Mich. L. Rev. 237, 243-244 (1968). Did *Brown I* involve the rights of individual black students? For example, after *Brown I*, could a school board argue that a particular black child in a particular district would receive a better education in a segregated rather than an integrated school? If *Brown I* was designed to protect the rights of blacks *as a group,* is it fair to attack *Brown II* for providing group-oriented remedies?

2. Brown II *needlessly encouraged white resistance to desegregation by failing to demand an immediate remedy.* See, e.g., Black, The Unfinished Business of the Warren Court, 46 Wash. L. Rev. 3, 22 (1970). *Brown II* was followed by an extended period of "massive resistance" during which there was virtually no actual desegregation in the South. See infra pages 470–475. But the causal link between *Brown II* and the slow pace of desegregation is uncertain, and some have defended the decision on the ground that "any head-on challenge to the segregated South in 1955 would have produced civil strife sufficient to make Little Rock and Birmingham seem gatherings of good will." J. Wilkinson, From *Brown* to *Bakke* 68 (1979). See also Bickel, The Decade of School Desegregation: Progress and Prospects, 64 Colum. L. Rev. 193, 201-202 (1964). What could the Court have done if an order for immediate desegregation had simply been defied? Note that in 1955 it was uncertain whether either the President or the Congress would support the Court if such an order were disobeyed. Where did that leave the Court? Consider A. Bickel, The Least Dangerous Branch 252 (1962):

> [Congress and the President] are uncomfortable in the presence of hard and fast principles calling for universal and sudden execution. [They] can most readily be expected to exert themselves when some leeway to expediency has been left open. Therefore, time and an opportunity for accommodation were required [to] form part of the invitation that the Court might be extending to the political institutions to join with it in what amounted to a major enterprise of social reform.

Does *Brown II* prove that the Court "was a white court which would protect the interests of White America in the maintenance of stable institutions"? Steel, Nine Men in Black Who Think White, New York Times Magazine, Oct. 13, 1968, at 112, col. 4. Or does the decision merely reflect the inherent limits of judicial power — limits that arguably influenced the formulation of the *Brown I* standard in the first place?

3. Brown II *overstated the administrative difficulties of desegregation.* What, precisely, were the "varied local school problems" that might justify delay? Does

the answer to that question depend, in part, on what *Brown I* required? If *Brown I* required no more than the repeal of laws prohibiting blacks from attending white schools, it is hard to see why this could not be accomplished instantly. But if *Brown I* required school boards to take affirmative steps to dismantle dual school systems and produce actual integration, the process might be more complex. Did the Court act responsibly in authorizing a period of delay without specifying what was to be accomplished during that period?

4. *The Court acted unwisely in remitting the task of enforcement and elucidation of* Brown I *to the lower federal courts.* To the extent that the remaining difficulties were solely remedial and technical, it was perhaps appropriate to remand the cases to local federal judges familiar with local conditions. But could these courts be expected to devise appropriate remedies when the content of the right to be vindicated remained so vague? As the next Note indicates, *Brown II* was followed by an extended period during which the lower courts wrestled with the question of remedy in the face of intransigence and subterfuge. When, some fifteen years after *Brown II*, the Court finally returned to the question of rights, its views were crucially influenced by this remedial struggle.

4. *Southern Desegregation*

Note: *The Response to* Brown

1. *Tokenism and massive resistance.* Suppose you were a southern governor in 1955 determined to minimize the impact of *Brown*. What policies would you pursue? In retrospect, it seems at least possible that the immediate, good-faith dismantling of the formal structure of segregation might have satisfied the courts while producing only modest integration. Instead, *Brown* was greeted throughout the South with defiance and evasion. In the short term, this approach stymied judicial enforcement efforts. But in the longer term, the strategy had two unanticipated consequences. First, it helped mobilize political support for desegregation. Second, the long struggle to impose meaningful remedies in the face of "massive resistance" subtly influenced the way in which the fourteenth amendment was interpreted.

Southern resistance took several different forms. In part, it was rhetorical. For example, most southern members of Congress signed the "Southern Manifesto" asserting the illegitimacy of *Brown* and the right of the states to ignore the decision. See 102 Cong. Rec. H3948, 4004 (daily ed. March 12, 1956). Other southern politicians advanced their careers by vowing never to permit integration. In some communities, this verbal resistance was supplemented by intimidation and violence. And throughout the South, school districts devised a bewildering variety of legal strategies designed to slow or stop desegregation. A few communities took the extreme measure of closing their public schools altogether to avoid desegregation. Others adopted complex pupil placement laws giving local officials discretion to place students in different schools on the basis of supposedly nonracial criteria. Still others utilized "freedom-of-choice" plans whereby students were assigned to their old schools unless they applied for transfer. The common feature of all these plans was that they produced virtually no actual integration. For accounts of early efforts to circumvent *Brown*, see McKay, "With All Deliberate

Speed," 31 N.Y.U. L. Rev. 991 (1956); Powe, The Road to *Swann:* Mobile County Crawls to the Bus, 51 Tex. L. Rev. 505 (1973). Some of the rhetoric from the period is collected in J. Wilkinson, From *Brown* to *Bakke* 69–74 (1979).

2. *The early judicial response.* The judicial response to these strategems varied. Pupil placement, freedom of choice, and grade-per-year plans were all both invalidated and upheld by various lower courts. In the face of massive community opposition, a few district court judges insisted on far-reaching and effective desegregation plans. See generally J. Peltason, Fifty-Eight Lonely Men (1971). But the more common judicial attitude toward *Brown* ranged from caution to outright hostility. In one widely quoted opinion written shortly after *Brown,* a district court held that *Brown* did not require "the states [to] mix persons of different races in the schools. [What] it has decided [is] that a state may not deny any person on account of race the right to attend any school that it maintains. [The] Constitution, in other words, does not require integration. [It] merely forbids the use of governmental power to enforce segregation." Briggs v. Elliott, 132 F. Supp. 776, 777 (E.D.S.C. 1955). Other judges read *Brown* even more narrowly. For example, one judge announced at the conclusion of a suit to desegregate the Dallas schools that "the white man has a right to maintain his racial integrity and it can't be done so easily in integrated schools. [We] will not name any date or issue any order. [The] School Board should further study this question and perhaps take further action, maybe an election." Peltason, supra, at 118–119. Overall, the pace of desegregation was painfully slow. By 1964, ten years after *Brown I,* only 2.3 percent of the black children in the South were attending desegregated schools. See Dunn, Title VI, the Guidelines, and School Desegregation in the South, 53 Va. L. Rev. 42, 44 n.9 (1967).

Despite the lack of uniformity and absence of progress, the Supreme Court remained almost entirely silent during this early period. It intervened only once — and then only in the face of outright defiance. Cooper v. Aaron, 358 U.S. 1 (1958), grew out of efforts to desegregate the Little Rock public school system. Pursuant to a plan developed by the Little Rock School Board, nine black children were scheduled to enroll in all-white Central High School at the start of the 1957 term. These plans were stymied by Arkansas Governor Orville Faubus, who ordered the Arkansas National Guard to block the entry of the children. The students were admitted only after President Eisenhower dispatched troops to enforce federal law. Under the protection of these troops and the federalized National Guard, the black students remained in Central High School through February 1958. The School Board then sought permission from the federal district court to terminate the desegregation program because of the extreme public hostility. The district court granted the board's request, but the court of appeals reversed. In an extraordinary opinion, signed by all nine justices, the Supreme Court affirmed the court of appeals and ordered desegregation to proceed. The Court held that "the constitutional rights of respondents are not to be sacrificed or yielded to the violence and disorder which have followed upon the actions of the Governor and Legislature. [Law] and order are not here to be preserved by depriving the Negro children of their constitutional rights." In response to the governor's assertion that he was not bound by *Brown,* the Court declared that "the federal judiciary is supreme in the exposition of the law of the Constitution" and that "the interpretation of the Fourteenth Amendment enunciated by this Court in the *Brown* case is the supreme law of the land."

3. *The end of deliberate speed.* Cooper v. Aaron was a powerful statement of judicial supremacy and an attack on outright defiance of *Brown*. It did little, however, to clarify the confusion concerning what *Brown* required. It was not until the early 1960s that the Court began to intervene more effectively and systematically to oversee the desegregation process. Even then, it purported to address only the nature and speed of the remedy *Brown* required.

The first signs of judicial restiveness came in Watson v. Memphis, 373 U.S. 526 (1963), a case involving segregated municipal recreation facilities. The Court held the *Brown II* "all deliberate speed" formulation inapplicable to such facilities and ordered immediate desegregation. Moreover, the Court hinted that its tolerance for "deliberate speed" in the school context might be coming to an end:

> Given the extended time which has elapsed, it is far from clear that the mandate of the second *Brown* decision requiring that desegregation proceed with "all deliberate speed" would today be fully satisfied by types of plans or programs for desegregation of public educational facilities which eight years ago might have been deemed sufficient. *Brown* never contemplated that the concept of "deliberate speed" would countenance indefinite delay in elimination of racial barriers in schools.

One week later, in Goss v. Board of Education, 373 U.S. 683 (1963), the Court repeated this warning in a school case, noting that "eight years after [*Brown II*] and over nine years after the first *Brown* decision, the context in which we must interpret and apply [the 'all deliberate speed'] language [has] significantly altered." In *Goss* the Court invalidated a school desegregation plan under which students were permitted the option of "one-way transfers" from schools where they were in a racial minority to those where they enjoyed majority status. The Court held that such a one-way plan "lends itself to perpetuation of segregation" and was therefore invalid. But it stopped short of questioning "freedom-of-choice" plans permitting transfers without regard to race, noting that they posed "an entirely different case" because students "could then at their option [choose], entirely free of any imposed racial considerations, to remain in the school of their zone or to transfer to another."

A year after *Goss*, in Griffin v. County School Board, 377 U.S. 218 (1964), the Court considered another technique for avoiding the requirements of *Brown* — the school closing. Faced with a court order requiring immediate steps toward desegregation, the supervisors of Prince Edward County, Virginia, refused to levy school taxes and closed the public schools. For four years, blacks in the county went without formal education, while whites attended private schools supported in part by state tuition grants and property tax credits. The black children argued that the closing of the Prince Edward schools to avoid integration while public schools in the rest of the state remained open violated the equal protection clause. Rejecting the county's suggestion that it delay reaching this issue until state law questions could be resolved, the Court again expressed its dissatisfaction with the pace of desegregation:

> [The] issues here imperatively call for decision now. The case has been delayed since 1951 by resistance at the state and county level, by legislation, and by lawsuits. The original plaintiffs have doubtless all passed high school age. There has been entirely too much deliberation and not enough speed in enforcing the constitutional rights which we held in Brown v. Board of Education [had] been denied Prince Edward County Negro children.

Turning to the merits, the Court conceded that a state is not always constitutionally required to provide the same services to citizens in different communities. Nonetheless, the closing of Prince Edward schools while other state schools remained open violated the equal protection clause because

> the record in the present case could not be clearer that [the] schools were closed and private schools operated in their place with state and county assistance, for one reason, and one reason only: to ensure, through measures taken by the county and the State, that white and colored children in Prince Edward County would not, under any circumstances, go to the same school. Whatever nonracial grounds might support a State's allowing a county to abandon public schools, the object must be a constitutional one, and grounds of race and opposition to desegregation do not qualify as constitutional.

What group was unequally treated by the Prince Edward school closing? Would the result in *Griffin* have been different if all the public schools in Virginia had been closed to avoid desegregation? Was it the availability of tuition benefits — to blacks and whites alike — that made the school closing unconstitutional? Cf. Norwood v. Harrison, 413 U.S. 455 (1973) (Mississippi practice of lending textbooks to students attending both public and private schools without reference to whether the private schools were racially segregated unconstitutional). The *Griffin* district court had merely enjoined the provision of such benefits. But the Supreme Court, over the dissent of Justices Harlan and Clark, held that the Court also had the power to order the reopening of the schools even if no tuition benefits were provided.

Compare *Griffin* with Palmer v. Thompson, 403 U.S. 217 (1971), where the Court upheld the decision of the Jackson, Mississippi, City Council to close its municipal swimming pools after they were ordered desegregated. Justice Black, the author of the *Griffin* opinion, also wrote for the Court in *Palmer*. In *Palmer* the Court characterized *Griffin* as turning on the state involvement in financing the private schools. *Griffin*, the Court said, "simply treated the school program for what it was — an operation of Prince Edward County schools under a thinly disguised 'private' school system actually planned and carried out by the State and the county to maintain segregated education with public funds." Does this characterization of *Griffin* explain why the Court ordered the reopening of the public schools rather than the termination of tuition benefits?

In a footnote in *Palmer*, the Court distinguished Bush v. Orleans Parish School Board, 187 F. Supp. 42 (E.D. La. 1960), affd., 365 U.S. 569 (1961), in which the Supreme Court summarily affirmed the invalidation of a Louisiana statute authorizing the governor to close any school ordered to integrate. The Court explained: "That case did not involve swimming pools but rather public schools, an enterprise we have described as 'perhaps the most important function of state and local governments.' [Quoting Brown I.] More important, the laws struck down in *Bush* were part of an elaborate package of legislation through which Louisiana sought to maintain public education on a segregated basis, not to end public education."

Is *Griffin* merely about remedy, or does it implicitly define the substantive rights protected by *Brown*? Is *Griffin* consistent with the view that "the Constitution [does] not require integration. [It] merely forbids the use of governmental power to enforce segregation"? Briggs v. Elliott, supra. With the view that freedom-of-choice plans producing little actual integration are permissible because they leave students able to "choose, entirely free of any racial considerations, to remain in the school of their zone or to transfer to another"? Goss v. Board of Education, supra.

The Court's renewed interest in the pace of school desegregation coincided with the reemergence of an effective political coalition supporting black equality for the first time since Reconstruction. The changed political atmosphere finally provided the Court with needed support — support that translated into real progress toward southern desegregation.

An important turning point was passage of the Civil Rights Act of 1964, 42 U.S.C. §§2000a et seq. Although the most widely debated sections of the act prohibited racial discrimination in places of public accommodation, the act also had important provisions dealing with school desegregation. Title IV authorized the Attorney General to institute desegregation suits in the name of the United States, thereby ending the need to rely on individual lawsuits by private plaintiffs. More significantly, Title VI established a parallel desegregation mechanism that avoided the necessity of lawsuits altogether. Racial discrimination was prohibited in any program receiving federal assistance, and federal agencies were authorized to issue regulations enforcing this prohibition and to terminate funding upon noncompliance. Pursuant to this authority, the Department of Health, Education, and Welfare promulgated desegregation guidelines in 1965. The first guidelines did not require substantially more than was already mandated by contemporary case law, but revised guidelines, issued in March 1966, were considerably stiffer. They provided, inter alia, that attendance zones could not be drawn to "maintain what is essentially a dual school structure" and that freedom of choice plans would be "[scrutinized] with special care" and judged by whether "minority group students have in fact transferred from segregated schools."

The guidelines were important not only because the threatened fund cutoff provided an impetus for desegregation, but also because they provided the courts with an escape from the morass of case-by-case litigation over individual desegregation plans. In a series of landmark decisions, the Fifth Circuit Court of Appeals used the guidelines to formulate model decrees, applicable throughout the Circuit, which regulated every detail of the desegregation process. See, e.g., United States v. Jefferson County Board of Education, 380 F.2d 385 (5th Cir.), cert. denied, 389 U.S. 840 (1967). The effect was dramatic. The percentage of southern black children attending desegregated schools jumped from 2.3 percent in 1964, to 7.5 percent in 1965, to 12.5 percent in 1966. See Dunn, Title VI, the Guidelines, and School Desegregation in the South, 53 Va. L. Rev. 42, 43 n.8 (1967). For a discussion of the effect of the guidelines, see Note, The Courts, HEW, and Southern School Desegregation, 77 Yale L.J. 321 (1967).

What explains the sudden success of southern desegregation efforts after ten years of stagnation? Why was it an administrative agency, rather than the courts, that formulated the standards that produced actual integration?

Four years after passage of the 1964 Civil Rights Act, the Court began dismantling the last barriers to desegregation in the rural south by questioning the "freedom of choice" plans widely used throughout the region. In Green v. County School Board, 391 U.S. 430 (1968), the Court invalidated a "freedom of choice" plan that the district had adopted to avoid loss of federal funds. The district had only two schools, one of which had been all black and the other all white prior to Brown. Since there was little residential segregation, a plan utilizing geographical districts would have created integrated schools. Instead, each pupil was required to choose between the two schools on entering first and eighth grades. Children in other grades were permitted to choose but were assigned to the school last attended if they made no choice. After the plan had been in effect for three years, 85 percent of the black children and none of the white children were attending the black school.

A unanimous Court held that this freedom of choice plan could not "be accepted as a sufficient step to 'effectuate a transition' to a unitary school system." Justice Brennan's opinion emphasized the Court's impatience at the pace of desegregation: "In determining whether [the Board satisfied *Brown*] by adopting its 'freedom-of-choice' plan, it is relevant that this first step did not come until some 11 years after *Brown I* was decided and 10 years after *Brown II* directed the making of a 'prompt and reasonable start.' [The] burden on a school board today is to come forward with a plan that promises realistically to work, and promises realistically to work *now*."

Moreover, the Court rejected the argument that the institution of "freedom of choice" itself satisfied the Board's constitutional obligation. Rather, freedom of choice had to be judged by its effectiveness as a means to achieve a unitary school system. The ultimate test was whether the plan [promises] realistically to convert promptly to a system without a 'white' school and a 'Negro' school, but just schools."

Like most of the Court's pronouncements on school desegregation since *Brown II*, *Green* focused on the adequacy of remedy. Did the Court explain what *substantive* deprivation the Board had failed to remedy? What made the *Green* school system nonunitary? As a practical matter, a network of formal and informal sanctions made black freedom wholly illusory under many "freedom of choice" plans. But *Green* did not rely on the illusory nature of the choice in invalidating the plan. Rather, the Court suggested that a system is not unitary even if truly free choice fails to produce integration. In a system where each child freely chooses his school, how has the *state* erected racial barriers violative of equal protection? Does the state violate the Constitution when it fails affirmatively to encourage racial mixing in the schools? If so, can *Green* be confined to districts with a prior history of legally imposed segregation?

The *Green* Court hinted that, on the facts of the case, a plan for neighborhood schools would have made the system "unitary." In *Green*, and in much of the rural South, neighborhood schools would have produced substantial integration. Would a neighborhood school system be "unitary" in urban areas, where residential segregation patterns would be mirrored in school populations? If free choice failing to produce integration is unconstitutional, does it now follow a fortiori that *Brown* is not satisfied when children are compelled to attend one-race schools in their neighborhoods?

Swann v. Charlotte-Mecklenburg Board of Education

402 U.S. 1 (1971)

MR. CHIEF JUSTICE BURGER delivered the opinion of the Court. . . .

This case and those argued with it arose in States having a long history of maintaining two sets of schools in a single school system deliberately operated to carry out a governmental policy to separate pupils in schools solely on the basis of race. That was what Brown v. Board of Education was all about. These cases present us with the problem of defining in more precise terms than heretofore the scope of the duty of school authorities and district courts in implementing *Brown I* and the mandate to eliminate dual systems and establish unitary systems at once.

[The Charlotte-Mecklenburg school system was segregated by law prior to 1954. In 1965 the system adopted a court-approved desegregation plan involving geographic zoning and free transfers. The plan left over half of the black students attending schools at least 99 percent black. In 1968 petitioners sought further relief, claiming that the plan failed to satisfy the standards enunciated in *Green*. The District Court adopted a new plan involving gerrymandering of school districts and busing of students between inner-city and outlying schools. On appeal, the Court of Appeals vacated that portion of the District Court's plan pairing and grouping elementary schools on the ground that it unreasonably burdened the school board and the system's pupils.]

The objective today remains to eliminate from the public schools all vestiges of state-imposed segregation. . . .

If school authorities fail in their affirmative obligations [judicial] authority may be invoked. Once a right and a violation have been shown, the scope of a district court's equitable powers to remedy past wrongs is broad, for breadth and flexibility are inherent in equitable remedies. . . .

In seeking to define even in broad and general terms how far this remedial power extends it is important to remember that judicial powers may be exercised only on the basis of a constitutional violation. Remedial judicial authority does not put judges automatically in the shoes of school authorities whose powers are plenary. Judicial authority enters only when local authority defaults.

School authorities are traditionally charged with broad power to formulate and implement educational policy and might well conclude, for example, that in order to prepare students to live in a pluralistic society each school should have a prescribed ratio of Negro to white students reflecting the proportion for the district as a whole. To do this as an educational policy is within the broad discretionary powers of school authorities; absent a finding of a constitutional violation, however, that would not be within the authority of a federal court. As with any equity case, the nature of the violation determines the scope of the remedy. In default by the school authorities of their obligation to proffer acceptable remedies, a district court has broad power to fashion a remedy that will assure a unitary school system. . . .

The central issue in this case is that of student assignment, and there are essentially four problem areas. . . .

(1) RACIAL BALANCES OR RACIAL QUOTAS

[The] target of the cases from *Brown I* to the present was the dual school system. The elimination of racial discrimination in public schools is a large task and one that should not be retarded by efforts to achieve broader purposes lying beyond the jurisdiction of school authorities. One vehicle can carry only a limited amount of baggage. [We] do not reach in this case the question whether a show-ing that school segregation is a consequence of other types of state action, with-out any discriminatory action by the school authorities, is a constitutional violation requiring remedial action by a school desegregation decree. This case does not present that question and we therefore do not decide it. . . .

If we were to read the holding of the District Court to require, as a matter of substantive constitutional right, any particular degree of racial balance or mixing, that approach would be disapproved and we would be obliged to reverse. The constitutional command to desegregate schools does not mean that every school in every community must always reflect the racial composition of the school system as a whole [But here] the use made of mathematical ratios was no more than a starting point in the process of shaping a remedy, rather than an inflexible requirement. [As] we said in *Green*, a school authority's remedial plan or a district court's remedial decree is to be judged by its effectiveness. Awareness of the racial composition of the whole school system is likely to be a useful starting point in shaping a remedy to correct past constitutional violations. [The] very limited use made of mathematical ratios was within the equitable remedial discretion of the District Court.

(2) ONE-RACE SCHOOLS

[The] existence of some small number of one-race, or virtually one-race, schools within a district is not in and of itself the mark of a system that still practices segregation by law. [But] in a system with a history of segregation the need for remedial criteria of sufficient specificity to assure a school authority's compliance with its constitutional duty warrants a presumption against schools that are sub-stantially disproportionate in their racial composition. Where the school author-ity's proposed plan for conversion from a dual to a unitary system contemplates the continued existence of some schools that are all or predominately of one race, they have the burden of showing that [their] racial composition is not the result of present or past discriminatory action on their part. . . .

(3) REMEDIAL ALTERING OF ATTENDANCE ZONES

[One] of the principal tools employed by school planners and by courts to break up the dual school system has been a frank — and sometimes drastic — gerry-mandering of school districts and attendance zones. An additional step was pair-ing, "clustering," or "grouping" of schools with attendance assignments made deliberately to accomplish the transfer of Negro students out of formerly segre-gated Negro schools and transfer of white students to formerly all-Negro schools. More often than not, these zones are neither compact nor contiguous; indeed they may be on opposite ends of the city. As an interim corrective measure, this cannot be said to be beyond the broad remedial powers of a court.

Absent a constitutional violation there would be no basis for judicially ordering assignment of students on a racial basis. All things being equal, with no history of discrimination, it might well be desirable to assign pupils to schools nearest their homes. But all things are not equal in a system that has been deliberately con-structed and maintained to enforce racial segregation. The remedy for such segregation may be administratively awkward, inconvenient, and even bizarre in some situations and may impose burdens on some; but all awkwardness and inconvenience cannot be avoided in the interim period when remedial adjustments are being made to eliminate the dual school systems.

No fixed or even substantially fixed guidelines can be established as to how far a court can go, but it must be recognized that there are limits. The objective is to dismantle the dual school system. "Racially neutral" assignment plans proposed by school authorities to a district court may be inadequate; such plans may fail to counteract the continuing effects of past school segregation resulting from discriminatory location of school sites or distortion of school size in order to achieve or maintain an artificial racial separation. When school authorities present a district court with a "loaded game board," affirmative action in the form of remedial altering of attendance zones is proper to achieve truly nondiscriminatory assignments. In short, an assignment plan is not acceptable simply because it appears to be neutral.

In this area, we must of necessity rely to a large extent, as this Court has for more than 16 years, on the informed judgment of the district courts in the first instance and on courts of appeals.

We hold that the pairing and grouping of noncontiguous school zones is a permissible tool and such action is to be considered in light of the objectives sought. . . .

(4) TRANSPORTATION OF STUDENTS

The scope of permissible transportation of students as an implement of a remedial decree has never been defined by this Court and by the very nature of the problem it cannot be defined with precision. No rigid guidelines as to student transportation can be given for application to the infinite variety of problems presented in thousands of situations. Bus transportation has been an integral part of the public education system for years, and was perhaps the single most important factor in the transition from the one-room schoolhouse to the consolidated school. Eighteen million of the Nation's public school children, approximately 39%, were transported to their schools by bus in 1969-1970 in all parts of the country. . . .

[We] find no basis for holding that the local school authorities may not be required to employ bus transportation as one tool of school desegregation. Desegregation plans cannot be limited to the walk-in school.

An objection to transportation of students may have validity when the time or distance of travel is so great as to either risk the health of the children or significantly impinge on the educational process. District courts must weigh the soundness of any transportation plan in light of what is said in subdivisions (1), (2), and (3) above. It hardly needs stating that the limits on time of travel will vary with many factors, but probably with none more than the age of the students. The reconciliation of competing values in a desegregation case is, of course, a difficult task with many sensitive facets but fundamentally no more so than remedial measures courts of equity have traditionally employed. . . .

[On] the facts of this case, we are unable to conclude that the order of the District Court is not reasonable, feasible and workable. However, in seeking to define the scope of remedial power or the limits on remedial power of courts in an area as sensitive as we deal with here, words are poor instruments to convey the sense of basic fairness inherent in equity. Substance, not semantics, must govern, and we have sought to suggest the nature of limitations without frustrating the appropriate scope of equity.

At some point, these school authorities and others like them should have achieved full compliance with this Court's decision in *Brown I*. The systems will then be "unitary" in the sense required by our decisions. . . .

It does not follow that the communities served by such systems will remain demographically stable, for in a growing, mobile society, few will do so. Neither school authorities nor district courts are constitutionally required to make year-by-year adjustments of the racial composition of student bodies once the affirmative duty to desegregate has been accomplished and racial discrimination through official action is eliminated from the system. This does not mean that federal courts are without power to deal with future problems; but in the absence of a showing that either the school authorities or some other agency of the State has deliberately attempted to fix or alter demographic patterns to affect the racial composition of the schools, further intervention by a district court should not be necessary.

For the reasons herein set forth, the judgment of the Court of Appeals is affirmed as to those parts in which it affirmed the judgment of the District Court. The order of the District Court [directing that its plan remain in effect] is also affirmed.

Note: Swann *and the Collapse of Southern Resistance*

1. Swann *and the role of the lower courts.* Chief Justice Burger's opinion asserts that "the nature of the violation determines the scope of the remedy" and that judicial intervention is permissible only so long as the system is not "unitary." The opinion also emphasizes the broad discretion of district courts in selecting particular remedies to achieve unitary schools. Does *Swann* thus implicitly grant district courts discretion to determine what *is* a unitary school? Suppose, for example, that in District A, a judge orders extensive busing creating a high degree of integration but in identical District B, a different judge declines to enter such an order, thereby leaving the schools less integrated. Under *Swann*, both decisions may be lawful. Moreover, since both courts are constitutionally obligated to create unitary schools, it would also seem to follow that both systems would be unitary after complying with the courts' remedial orders. Does this mean that what is "unitary" in District B is "nonunitary" in District A? Does this suggest that it is folly to think about remedies before defining the scope of the constitutional right at stake?

2. Swann *and the definition of substantive rights.* Does *Swann* help to define the substantive right initially articulated in *Brown*? Consider the distinction between a "process-oriented" and "result-oriented" view of *Brown*. A process-oriented view insists merely that school boards make assignments on a basis other than race. A result-oriented view insists that school boards make assignments on a basis that in fact produces integration. See Fiss, The Fate of an Idea Whose Time Has Come: Antidiscrimination Law in the Second Decade after *Brown v. Board of*

Education, 41 U. Chi. L. Rev. 742 (1974). Which of these views does *Swann* embrace? The Court states rather clearly that the Constitution prohibits only "[deliberate attempts] to fix or alter demographic patterns to affect the racial composition of the schools." But are the remedial measures authorized in *Swann* consistent with this view? If, as the Court says, the Constitution does not require "any particular degree of racial balance or mixing," what is the source of the district court's power to use "mathematical ratios [as] a starting point in the process of shaping a remedy"? And why is the district court under a duty to "make every effort to achieve the greatest possible degree of actual desegregation"? In Davis v. School Commissioners of Mobile County, 402 U.S. 33 (1971), decided the same day as *Swann*, the Court was even more emphatic in endorsing result-oriented remedies: "[Neighborhood schools are not] per se adequate to meet the remedial responsibilities of local boards. [A] district court may and should consider the use of all available techniques including restructuring of attendance zones and both contiguous and noncontiguous attendance zones. The measure of any desegregation plan is its effectiveness."

Note that the emphasis on result-oriented remedies may render efforts to *remove* race from the decisionmaking process unconstitutional. In North Carolina State Board of Education v. Swann, 402 U.S. 43 (1971), another companion case to the main *Swann* decision, the Court struck down a North Carolina statute providing that no student shall be assigned or compelled to attend any school on account of race or for the purpose of creating a balance or ratio of race. The Court held that this requirement "against the background of segregation, would render illusory the promise of [*Brown*]. [To] forbid, at this stage, all assignments made on the basis of race would deprive school authorities of the one tool absolutely essential to fulfillment of their constitutional obligation to eliminate existing dual school systems." See also McDaniel v. Barresi, 402 U.S. 39 (1971) (assignment of students on the basis of race to achieve greater racial balance does not violate equal protection). Do these decisions turn *Brown* on its head?

3. Swann *and the definition of appropriate remedies.* Whether or not *Swann* endorsed a result-oriented view of the substantive right, it clearly permitted — perhaps even required — result-oriented remedies. But what results does the decision mandate? If "mathematical ratios" are only a "starting point" in shaping a remedy, what is the end point? Does *Swann* offer district judges any meaningful guidance as to how to balance a marginal increase in integration against a marginal increase in cost or inconvenience necessary to achieve that integration? See, e.g., Kaplan, Segregation Litigation and the Schools — Part II: The General Northern Problem, 58 Nw. U. L. Rev. 157, 183 (1963) ("How can the courts weigh the value of a 30 percent increase in integration against a requirement that students cross a dangerous traffic artery or walk five extra blocks?"). Does the difficulty in answering these questions help explain why the Court left the scope of the remedy to district judges? Does leaving the problem to the district courts make it go away?

Notice the connection between the way one characterizes the *Brown* right and the nature of the remedial dilemma. If *Brown* requires a school system unpolluted by racially motivated decisions, then the court must refashion the system to make it function the way it would have functioned had the decisions been made on a neutral basis. This requires the court to determine what motivated decisions, often made years ago by collective bodies, and to trace through the consequences of those decisions. To avoid these problems, the court might adopt a result-oriented approach — either defining the right in terms of result, or presuming that racially segregated schools result from racially motivated decisions. The question then becomes not what the system would have looked like had nonracist decisions been made, but what the system should look like to achieve the requisite degree of racial mixing. Answering that question requires the court to formulate a rule for trading off integration against the costs of producing it.

Which approach puts less pressure on the institutional weaknesses of courts? Which does *Swann* adopt?

4. Swann *as the end of an era.* *Swann* was the last major desegregation decision that was entirely "southern" in its orientation. It thus ended an era begun with *Brown II*. In one sense, the Court's efforts to desegregate the South were stunningly successful. The Court's studied ambiguity concerning the scope of *Brown I* provided it with the flexibility to respond to each of the subterfuges advanced to defeat desegregation. Moreover, the "all deliberate speed" formulation allowed the Court to avoid defeat when significant progress was not politically feasible and then to push forward when a coalition for change finally emerged. The results of this strategy speak for themselves: By 1971, 44 percent of the black students in the South attended majority white schools, compared to only 28 percent in the North and West. See 18 Cong. Rec. §564 (daily ed, Jan. 20, 1972) (remarks of Sen. Stennis).

Yet in another sense, the strategy carried with it serious weaknesses. Southern intransigence forced the Court to adopt broader and broader statements of what *Brown* required. But the gradual expansion of *Brown*, in the long term, helped to undermine the political support that made progress possible. To avoid endless litigation with school boards operating in bad faith, the Court moved toward result-oriented, bright-line remedies. This made the promise of *Brown* a reality in hundreds of school districts. But the Court paid for these advances by sacrificing the claim that it was merely announcing principles of "simple justice" directly commanded by the Constitution. And by conceding that judges had discretion in the remedy they imposed, the Court lost the political insulation that came with the argument that the constitutional text left the judiciary with no choice. Moreover, the Court's preoccupation with empirical results made it vulnerable to empirical attack. So long as *Brown* prohibited only decisions made on racist grounds, the decision could be defended as a matter of principle. But if the constitutionality of a particular plan turned on the results it produced, then it became relevant to ask what tangible results in terms of educational quality integration actually achieved.

Finally, the expansion of *Brown* — and, indeed, the Court's very success in enforcing the decision — helped erode the distinction between North and South. To be sure, *Swann* clung to the position that judicial intervention was permissible only to correct deliberate segregative acts. But the result-oriented remedies *Swann* approved, and the fact that the South had become the most integrated area of the country, made it increasingly difficult to defend the proposition that judicial intervention was permissible only below the Mason-Dixon line. The Court was therefore faced with a dilemma. If *Brown* remained applicable only to the South, southerners could, with some justice, complain of hypocrisy and a double standard. Yet if the fight for integrated education was pressed in the North and West, the collapse of political support was inevitable.

5. *Northern Desegregation*

Keyes v. School District No. 1, Denver, Colo.
413 U.S. 189 (1973)

MR. JUSTICE BRENNAN delivered the opinion of the Court.

[This was the first case in which the Supreme Court considered the lawfulness of school segregation in a northern city that had never mandated segregated education by statute. The District Court found that the Denver School Board had, for a period of ten years, maintained deliberately segregated schools in the Park Hill section of the city through use of gerrymandered attendance zones and similar devices. Although the District Court ordered desegregation of the Park Hill schools, it held that the finding of purposeful segregation in this area did not require the Board to remedy racial imbalance in other areas of the city. The Court of Appeals affirmed this portion of the District Court's order, and the Supreme Court granted certiorari to consider petitioners' claim that they were entitled to systemwide relief.]

Petitioners apparently concede for the purposes of this case that in the case of a school system like Denver's, where no statutory dual system has ever existed, plaintiffs must prove not only that segregated schooling exists but also that it was brought about or maintained by intentional state action. [Respondent] argues, however, that a finding of state-imposed segregation as to a substantial portion of the school system can be viewed in isolation from the rest of the district, and that even if state-imposed segregation does exist in a substantial part of the Denver school system, it does not follow that the District Court could predicate on that fact a finding that the entire school system is a dual system. We do not agree. We have never suggested that plaintiffs in school desegregation cases must bear the burden of proving the elements of *de jure* segregation as to each and every school or each and every student within the school system. . . .

[Common] sense dictates the conclusion that racially inspired school board actions have an impact beyond the particular schools that are the subjects of those actions. This is not to say, of course, that there can never be a case in which the geographical structure of, or the natural boundaries within a school district may have the effect of dividing the district into separate, identifiable and unrelated units. Such a determination is essentially a question of fact to be resolved by the trial court in the first instance, but such cases must be rare. In the absence of such a determination, proof of state-imposed segregation in a substantial portion of the district will suffice to support a finding by the trial court of the existence of a dual system. . . .

[Moreover,] inquiry whether the District Court and the Court of Appeals applied the correct legal standards in addressing petitioners' contention of deliberate segregation in the core city schools is not at an end even if it be true that Park Hill may be separated from the rest of the Denver school district as a separate, identifiable, and unrelated unit. [Plainly], a finding of intentional segregation as to a portion of a school system is not devoid of probative value in assessing the school authorities' intent with respect to other parts of the same school system. . . .

[We] hold that a finding of intentionally segregative school board actions in a meaningful portion of a school system, as in this case, creates a presumption that other segregated schooling within the system is not adventitious. It establishes, in other words, a prima facie case of unlawful segregative design on the part of school authorities, and shifts to those authorities the burden of proving that other segregated schools within the system are not also the result of intentionally segregative actions. This is true even if it is determined that different areas of the school district should be viewed independently of each other because, even in that situation, there is high probability that where school authorities have effectuated an intentionally segregative policy in a meaningful portion of the school system, similar impermissible considerations have motivated their actions in other areas of the system. . . .

In discharging [their] burden, it is not enough, of course, that the school authorities rely upon some allegedly logical, racially neutral explanation for their actions. Their burden is to adduce proof sufficient to support a finding that segregative intent was not among the factors that motivated their actions. The courts below attributed much significance to the fact that many of the Board's actions in the core city area antedated our decision in *Brown*. We reject any suggestion that remoteness in time has any relevance to the issue of intent. . . .

This is not to say, however, that the prima facie case may not be met by evidence supporting a finding that a lesser degree of segregated schooling in the core city area would not have resulted even if the Board had not acted as it did. [Thus,] if respondent School Board cannot disprove segregative intent, it can rebut the prima facie case only by showing that its past segregative acts did not create or contribute to the current segregated condition of the core city schools. . . .

[The] case is remanded to the District Court for further proceedings consistent with this opinion.

Mr. Justice Douglas.

While I join the opinion of the Court, I agree with my Brother Powell that there is, for the purposes of the Equal Protection Clause of the Fourteenth Amendment as applied to the school cases, no difference between de facto and de jure segregation. The school board is a state agency and the lines that it draws, the locations it selects for school sites, the allocation it makes of students, the budgets it prepares are state action for Fourteenth Amendment purposes. . . .

Mr. Justice Powell concurring in part and dissenting in part. . . .

The situation in Denver is generally comparable to that in other large cities across the country in which there is a substantial minority population and where desegregation has not been ordered by the federal courts. There is segregation in the schools of many of these cities fully as pervasive as that in southern cities prior to the desegregation decrees of the past decade and a half. The focus of the school desegregation problem has now shifted from the South to the country as a whole. Unwilling and footdragging as the process was in most places, substantial progress toward achieving integration has been made in Southern States. No comparable progress has been made in many nonsouthern cities with large minority populations primarily because of the de facto/de jure distinction nurtured by the courts and accepted complacently by many of the same voices which denounced the evils of segregated schools in the South. But if our national concern is for those who attend such schools, rather than for perpetuating a legalism rooted in history rather than present reality, we must recognize that the evil of operating separate schools is no less in Denver than in Atlanta. . . .

In my view we should abandon a distinction which long since has outlived its time, and formulate constitutional principles of national rather than merely regional application. . . .

Whereas *Brown I* rightly decreed the elimination of state-imposed segregation in that particular section of the country where it did exist, *Swann* imposed obligations on southern school districts to eliminate conditions which are not regionally unique but are similar both in origin and effect to conditions in the rest of the country. As the remedial obligations of *Swann* extend far beyond the elimination of the outgrowths of the state-imposed segregation outlawed in *Brown*, the rationale of *Swann* points inevitably toward a uniform, constitutional approach to our national problem of school segregation. [I] would hold, quite simply, that where segregated public schools exist within a school district to a substantial degree, there is a prima facie case that the duly constituted public authorities [are] sufficiently responsible to warrant imposing upon them a nationally applicable burden to demonstrate they nevertheless are operating a genuinely integrated school system. [This] means that school authorities, consistent with the generally accepted educational goal of attaining quality education for all pupils, must make and implement their customary decisions with a view toward enhancing integrated school opportunities. . . .

An integrated school system does not mean — and indeed could not mean in view of the residential patterns of most of our major metropolitan areas — that *every school* must in fact be an integrated unit. A school which happens to be all or predominantly white or all or predominantly black is not a "segregated" school in an unconstitutional sense if the system itself is a genuinely integrated one.

Having school boards operate an integrated school system provides the best assurance of meeting the constitutional requirement that racial discrimination, subtle or otherwise, will find no place in the decisions of public school officials. . . .

Public schools are creatures of the State, and whether the segregation is state-created or state-assisted or merely state-perpetuated should be irrelevant to constitutional principle. The school board exercises pervasive and continuing responsibility over the long-range planning as well as the daily operations of the public school system. [School] board decisions obviously are not the sole cause of segregated school conditions. But if, after such detailed and complete public supervision, substantial school segregation still persists, the presumption is strong that the school board, by its acts or omissions, is in some part responsible. . . .

Where school authorities have defaulted in their duty to operate an integrated school system, district courts must insure that affirmative desegregative steps ensue. Many of these can be taken effectively without damaging state and parental interests in having children attend schools within a reasonable vicinity of home. Where desegregative steps are possible within the framework of a system of "neighborhood education," school authorities must pursue them. . . .

A *constitutional requirement* of extensive student transportation solely to achieve integration presents a vastly more complex problem. It promises, on the one hand, a greater degree of actual desegregation, while it infringes on what may fairly be regarded as other important community aspirations and personal rights.

Such a requirement is also likely to divert attention and resources from the foremost goal of any school system: the best quality education for all pupils. The Equal Protection Clause does, indeed, command that racial discrimination not be tolerated in the decisions of public school authorities. But it does not require that school authorities undertake widespread student transportation solely for the sake of maximizing integration.

This obviously does not mean that bus transportation has no place in public school systems or is not a permissible means in the desegregative process. [The] crucial issue is when, under what circumstances, and to what extent such transportation may appropriately be ordered. The answer to this turns — as it does so often in the law — upon a sound exercise of discretion under the circumstances. . . .

[This] would [require] that the legitimate community interests in neighborhood school systems be accorded far greater respect. [As] a minimum, this Court should not require school boards to engage in the unnecessary transportation away from their neighborhoods of elementary-age children. . . .

MR. JUSTICE REHNQUIST, dissenting. . . .

It is conceded that the State of Colorado and the city of Denver have never had a statute or ordinance [mandating racially segregated schools]. The claim made by these plaintiffs, as described in the Court's opinion, is that the School Board by "use of various techniques such as the manipulation of student attendance zones, schoolsite selection and a neighborhood school policy" took race into account in making school assignments in such a way as to lessen that mixing of races which would have resulted from a racially neutral policy of school assignment. If such claims are proved, those minority students who as a result of such manipulative techniques are forced to attend schools other than those that they would have attended had attendance zones been neutrally drawn are undoubtedly deprived of their constitutional right to equal protection of the laws just as surely as were the plaintiffs in Brown v. Board of Education by the statutorily required segregation in that case. But the fact that invidious racial discrimination is prohibited by the Constitution in the North as well as the South must not be allowed to obscure the equally important fact that the consequences of manipulative drawing of attendance zones in a school district the size of Denver does not necessarily result in denial of equal protection to all minority students within that district. There are significant differences between the proof which would support a claim such as that alleged by plaintiffs in this case, and the total segregation required by statute which existed in Brown. . . .

Underlying the Court's entire opinion is its apparent thesis that a district judge is at least permitted to find that if a single attendance zone between two individual schools in the large metropolitan district is found by him to have been "gerrymandered," the school district is guilty of operating a "dual" school system, and is apparently a candidate for what is in practice a federal receivership. [It] would therefore presumably be open to the District Court to require, inter alia, that pupils be transported great distances throughout the district to and from schools whose attendance zones have not been gerrymandered. Yet, unless the Equal Protection Clause of the Fourteenth Amendment now be held to embody a principle of "taint," found in some primitive legal systems but discarded centuries ago in ours, such a result can only be described as the product of judicial fiat. . . .

The Court has taken a long leap in this area of constitutional law in equating the district-wide consequences of gerrymandering individual attendance zones in a district where separation of the races was never required by law with statutes or ordinances in other jurisdictions which did so require. It then adds to this potpourri a confusing enunciation of evidentiary rules in order to make it more likely that the trial court will on remand reach the result which the Court apparently wants it to reach. Since I believe neither of these steps is justified by prior decisions of this Court, I dissent.

Note: Northern Desegregation

1. *Post-*Keyes *developments.* The Court placed an important gloss on *Keyes* in cases arising out of efforts to desegregate the Dayton and Columbus school systems.

a. Dayton I. In 1973 the district court held that the Dayton School Board's failure to correct a substantial racial imbalance, its use of optional attendance zones with demonstrable racial effects in some high schools, and its decision to rescind an earlier resolution assuming responsibility for racial imbalance constituted a cumulative violation of the equal protection clause. Based on these findings, the district court ordered a limited remedy not requiring large-scale transportation of students. The court of appeals held that the trial court's finding of constitutional violations was supported by the record but that the court below had erred in not imposing a systemwide remedy.

In Dayton Board of Education v. Brinkman, 433 U.S. 406 (1977) (*Dayton I*), the Court vacated the judgment of the court of appeals and remanded for further proceedings. Justice Rehnquist's opinion for the Court cast doubt on some of the inferences the district court drew from its findings. Specifically, "The finding that the pupil population in the various Dayton schools is not homogeneous, standing by itself, is not a violation of the Fourteenth Amendment in the absence of a showing that this condition resulted from intentionally segregative action on the part of the Board."

Moreover, the Court held that even assuming the existence of constitutional violations, the court of appeals had erred in requiring a systemwide remedy — a remedy "entirely out of proportion to the constitutional violations found by the District Court." On finding violations, the court should have determined "how much incremental segregative effect [they] had on the racial distribution of the Dayton school population as presently constituted, when that distribution is compared to what it would have been in the absence of such constitutional violations. The remedy must be designed to redress that difference, and only if there has been a systemwide impact may there be a systemwide remedy."

b. Dayton II. On remand after *Dayton I*, the district court held an additional evidentiary hearing and dismissed the complaint. Although finding numerous additional constitutional violations, the district court held that plaintiffs had failed to prove any current incremental segregative effects stemming from them. The court of appeals again reversed and again ordered a systemwide remedy. It viewed the evidence as establishing the existence of a dual school system prior to 1954. Since the school board had failed to meet its affirmative obligation to dismantle the system, judicial intervention was required.

In Dayton Board of Education v. Brinkman, 443 U.S. 526 (1979) (*Dayton II*), the Court by a 5-to-4 vote affirmed the court of appeals. On the supplemented record, the Court, in an opinion by Justice White, saw no reason to challenge the court of appeals' conclusion that the board had purposefully operated segregated schools in a substantial part of the district. Given the finding of substantial violations, the district court's reliance on *Dayton I* was misplaced, and it was unnecessary for plaintiffs "to prove with respect to each individual act of discrimination precisely what effect it has had on current patterns of segregation." Rather, the finding of purposeful segregation in a substantial part of the district "furnished prima facie proof that current segregation in Dayton schools was caused at least in part by prior intentional segregative official acts." Moreover, the district court also erred in ignoring postviolation actions of the school board perpetuating or aggravating segregation on the ground that no segregative purpose had been shown: "[The] measure of the post-*Brown I* conduct of a school board under an unsatisfied duty to liquidate a dual system is the effectiveness, not the purpose of the actions in decreasing or increasing the segregation caused by the dual system."

c. Columbus. In Columbus Board of Education v. Penick, 443 U.S. 449 (1979), decided the same day as *Dayton II*, the Court again affirmed an order requiring systemwide desegregation. The Court found "no reason [to] disturb the judgment of the Court of Appeals, based on the findings and conclusions of the District Court, that the Board's conduct at the time of trial and before not only was animated by an unconstitutional segregative purpose, but also had current, segregative impact that was sufficiently systemwide to warrant the remedy ordered by the District Court." These findings served to distinguish *Dayton I*, which the Court characterized as involving "only a few apparently isolated discriminatory practices." The Court adhered to the view that the Constitution required the remedying of only that school segregation caused by purposeful state action but emphasized that "actions having foreseeable and anticipated disparate impact are relevant evidence to prove the ultimate fact, forbidden purpose. [Adherence] to a particular policy or practice, with full knowledge of the predictable effects of such adherence upon racial imbalance in a school system is one factor among many others which may be considered by a court in determining whether an inference of segregative intent should be drawn."

2. *A hypothetical problem.* In light of *Swann, Keyes, Dayton I* and *II*, and *Columbus*, consider the following problem:

A school district has two junior high schools located in the eastern and western parts of the city, respectively. A busy highway, running north/south, bisects the city. The eastern half of the city is substantially white and the western half substantially black. Thus, if the school board divides the city into a northern and southern zone, the schools will be integrated, but many students will be forced to cross the highway at some risk to their safety. If it instead chooses eastern and western zones, the schools will be segregated, but no student need cross the highway. Cf. Davis v. Board of School Commissioners, 402 U.S. 33 (1971).

a. Suppose the district is in a northern state and has no prior history of intentional segregation. Does the board violate the Constitution if it chooses eastern and western zones?

b. Suppose the board chooses these zones because, although it favors integration, it thinks that the safety costs would be too high.

c. Should the result be different if the board is hostile to integration and, therefore, is especially unwilling to incur safety costs to achieve it?

d. Suppose the board creates north/south zones, but subsequent population shifts make the two schools substantially segregated. Black parents petition the board to shift to east/west zones, which will now create more integration. The board refuses to do so because it opposes integration. Is there a constitutional violation?

e. Should it change any of these results if, fifteen years earlier, a school board with different membership had deliberately gerrymandered a substantial number of elementary school districts to maintain segregated schools?

f. What if the district were located in a southern state and had practiced de jure segregation prior to 1954?

g. Suppose that in 1970, before the highway was built, a federal judge ordered north/south zones to remedy prior deliberate segregation and create unitary schools. The highway is then constructed in 1982, and the board moves to amend the order to allow east/west zones. What result?

6. Desegregation and the Limits of Judicial Power

As the preceding material demonstrates, modern cases make the constitutional obligation to operate unitary schools a matter of degree, and the degree of integration required turns on some sort of assessment of costs and benefits. What kinds of costs and benefits should a court consider in deciding how much integration is constitutionally mandated? Is it appropriate for a court to consider the actual educational impact of a particular plan before approving it? Is it relevant that widespread community opposition to a plan may exacerbate the costs or dissipate the benefits? That a too-aggressive desegregation effort might spark a political counterattack likely to destroy the court's effectiveness?

Note: Potential Limits on the Duty to Desegregate

1. *Interdistrict relief.* In Milliken v. Bradley, 418 U.S. 717 (1974) (*Milliken I*), the Court held that federal courts lack the power to impose interdistrict remedies for school segregation absent an interdistrict violation or interdistrict effects. After a lengthy trial, the district court found that the Detroit schools had been deliberately segregated and that any Detroit-only remedy "would make the Detroit school system more identifiably black [thereby] increasing the flight of whites from the city and the system." Consequently, the court ordered a desegregation plan encompassing fifty-three suburban school districts surrounding Detroit. The court of appeals affirmed after noting that "any less comprehensive [solution would] result in an all black school system immediately surrounded by practically all white suburban school systems, with an overwhelmingly white majority population in the local metropolitan area."

The Court, in an opinion by Chief Justice Burger, reversed. The Court rejected the "notion that school district lines may be casually ignored or treated as a mere administrative convenience. [No] single tradition in public education is more deeply rooted than local control over the operation of schools." To be sure, in cases where school district lines violate constitutional rights, a federal court can order an appropriate remedy. But no such violation occurs simply because the racial composition of schools within a district fails to reflect the racial composition of the metropolitan area as a whole. To justify interdistrict relief

> it must be shown that racially discriminatory acts of the state or local school districts, or of a single school district have been a substantial cause of interdistrict segregation. Thus, an interdistrict remedy might be in order where the racially discriminatory acts of one or more school districts caused racial segregation in an adjacent district, or where district lines have been deliberately drawn on the basis of race. [But] without an interdistrict violation and interdistrict effect, there is no constitutional wrong calling for an interdistrict remedy.

These conclusions were unaffected by the fact that the state of Michigan had exercised substantial control over the activity of local school districts and that state agencies had participated in the deliberate segregation of the Detroit schools. Despite this state activity, "Disparate treatment of white and Negro students occurred within the Detroit school system, and not elsewhere, and on this record the remedy must be limited to that system."

In a dissenting opinion that was joined by Justices Douglas, Brennan, and White, Justice Marshall complained that the Court had rendered the district judge

> powerless to require the State to remedy its constitutional violation in any meaningful fashion. Ironically purporting to base its result on the principle that the scope of the remedy in a desegregation case should be determined by the nature and extent of the constitutional violation, the Court's answer is to provide no remedy at all for the violation proved in this case, thereby guaranteeing that Negro children in Detroit will receive the same separate and inherently unequal education in the future as they have been unconstitutionally afforded in the past.

Justices Douglas and White also filed separate dissenting opinions. Is *Milliken's* limitation on interdistrict remedies consistent with *Keyes*? If it is appropriate to infer districtwide effect from segregative acts in a portion of a district, why is it inappropriate to infer interdistrict effects from segregative acts within a district? If proof of deliberate segregative acts in part of a school district creates a presumption that other school board conduct creating segregation is deliberate, why doesn't Michigan's participation in maintenance of a dual school system in Detroit shift the burden of proving that it was not manipulating district lines?

Are there special costs associated with interdistrict relief that justify limitations on this remedy? Compare *Milliken I* with Hills v. Gautreaux, 425 U.S. 284 (1976), in which a unanimous Court affirmed the power of a district judge to order the U.S. Department of Housing and Urban Development to take action outside the Chicago city limits to remedy discriminatory site selection for public housing that had occurred only within Chicago. The Court in *Hills* rejected the notion that *Milliken I* established "a per se rule [prohibiting] remedial efforts beyond the municipal boundaries of the city where the violation occurred." The district court's decree in *Milliken I* was impermissible "not because it envisioned relief against a wrongdoer extending beyond the city in which the violation occurred but because it contemplated a judicial decree restructuring the operation of local governmental entities that were not implicated in any constitutional violation." In light of *Milliken I* and *Hills*, would the result in *Keyes* have differed if Denver had accorded substantial local control to individual schools within the Denver school district?

What impact does *Milliken I* have on the prospects for achieving meaningful school desegregation? About half of all nonwhite school children reside in twenty to thirty of the nation's large school districts, with minority enrollment averaging about 60 percent in these districts. Only a handful of these districts have a majority of white students. See Ravitch, The "White Flight" Controversy, 51 Pub. Interest 135, 145-147 (1978). Does *Milliken I* mean, in effect, that only those whites too poor to escape to the suburbs or private schools must bear the cost of desegregation?

After remand in *Milliken I*, the district court confronted the task of attempting to desegregate a school system that was approximately 70 percent black. The court rejected a plan establishing schools reflecting Detroit's racial balance — a plan that, inter alia, would have required the busing of large numbers of minority students from one majority-black school to another. Instead, the court ordered a plan requiring extensive educational reform, including remedial education, counseling, and career guidance. In Milliken v. Bradley, 433 U.S. 267 (1977) (*Milliken II*), the Supreme Court affirmed. The Court rejected the notion that desegregation remedies were limited to pupil assignment and held that a district judge could order the expenditure of state funds for remedial education as part of an effort to return victims of unconstitutional conduct to the position they would have enjoyed but for the violation. Taken together, do *Milliken I* and *II* represent a turning away from *Brown* and a return to the "separate but equal" philosophy? Has the Court resolved the difficulties with that philosophy that caused its abandonment in the first place?

2. *Resegregation.* In Pasadena Board of Education v. Spangler, 427 U.S. 424 (1976), the Court in an opinion by Justice Rehnquist disapproved a lower court order requiring annual readjustments of school boundary lines to ensure that no school had a majority of minority pupils. The Court conceded that the Pasadena school system might not yet have achieved unitary status. Nonetheless, once the district implemented a racially neutral student assignment plan, the district court's remedial powers were exhausted. Specifically,

> the District Court was not entitled to require [the Board] to rearrange its attendance zones each year so as to ensure that the racial mix desired by the court was maintained in perpetuity. For having once implemented a racially neutral attendance pattern in order to remedy the perceived constitutional violations on the part of the defendants, the District Court had fully performed its function of providing the appropriate remedy for previous racially discriminatory attendance patterns.

Is *Spangler* consistent with the notion that illegally segregated systems have an affirmative duty to attain unitary status? The Court carefully noted in *Spangler* that there was no proof that changes in the racial mix of the schools were caused by segregative acts of the board or by "white flight" attributable to the initial decree. But there was no proof that failure of the *Green* freedom of choice plan was attributable to the school board either. Does *Spangler* mean that if a freedom of choice plan produces integration for a single year, the board is thereafter insulated from constitutional attack?

Spangler limited the power of federal courts to require continual *readjustments* of district lines. What implications does it have for a court's ability to *freeze* the lines it initially imposes? Since district courts are obligated to create unitary schools, a board that complies with a district court decree is, presumably, operating a unitary system. Does this mean that all desegregation decrees promptly self-destruct? If not, when should offending school boards be freed of federal control?

3. *"White flight."* Should a district court considering a desegregation plan take into account the risk that if the plan is too rigorous, whites will flee the public schools, thereby creating more, rather than less, segregation? See, e.g., Brunson v. Clarendon School District, 429 F.2d 820 (4th Cir. 1970). Might it even be argued that a school board under a duty to dismantle dual schools is constitutionally *obligated* to take "white flight" into account as part of its duty under *Green* to fashion a plan that "works"? Consider Schools Try to Attract Whites by Easing Integration Efforts, New York Times, June 21, 1982, at 1, col. 1: "in a risky bid to salvage some of the desegregation that is left and to regain broad-based support for the public schools, some local school boards in the South and West are trying to lure whites by reducing busing and re-establishing neighborhood schools. They are acting, sometimes with the endorsement of blacks, even if the result is further racial segregation of some schools."

In Monroe v. Board of Commissioners, 391 U.S. 450 (1968), a companion case to *Green*, the school board defended its "free transfer" plan on the ground that it was necessary to prevent whites from leaving the system altogether. A unanimous Court rejected the argument, citing *Brown II* for the proposition that "The vitality of these constitutional principles cannot be allowed to yield simply because of disagreement with them." See also United States v. Scotland Neck City Board of Education, 407 U.S. 484, 490-491 (1972). Was this reliance on *Brown II* justified? Consider L. Graglia, Disaster by Decree 82 (1976): "Insistence on principle and legality in the face of threatened lawlessness can be justified even where great immediate costs are involved, but to ignore the existence of perfectly legal means of avoiding a requirement is to bury one's head in the sand." But is there not a risk that recognizing the reality of white flight might encourage more of it? Consider J. Wilkinson, From *Brown* to *Bakke* 182 (1979): "Certainly the Supreme Court could not openly announce that busing was appropriate only where whites were least likely to flee. That would impose, on nothing more than demographic proclivities, gross disparities in the burdens different communities would undergo."

The extent to which court-ordered desegregation in fact causes whites to abandon urban public schools has been hotly debated in the social science literature. Compare, e.g., J. Coleman, S. Kelly & J. Moore, Trends in School Segregation 1968-73 (1975), with Pettigrew and Green, School Desegregation in Large Cities: A Critique of the Coleman "White Flight" Thesis, 46 Harv. Educ. Rev. 1, (1976). See also Rossell, School Desegregation and White Flight, 90 Pol. Sci. Q. 675 (1975-76). It is beyond dispute, however, that for whatever reason, the percentage of whites in many urban public schools has declined. Do you agree that "Whether busing is the foremost factor in causing whites to flee urban schools [may] be beside the point" because "It certainly does not encourage them to stay, or to come back once the system is installed" and that "The issue is no longer what causes whites to flee the city but what now can be done to induce them to return"? Wilkinson, supra, at 183.

Compare Gewirtz, Remedies and Resistance, 92 Yale L.J. 585, 661 (1983):

> Whether using racial ceilings will actually produce the greatest desegregation depends upon the extent to which white flight and integration really will occur under alternative remedial schemes. This empirical question highlights a serious problem with ceilings: Unlike other strategies to avoid tipping, ceilings assure remedial imperfection on the face of the decree. [While] the premise of ceilings is that white flight must be addressed, realism can be a dangerous aspiration for people, such as judges or law professors, who are often accused of not being realistic enough. Newly initiated into the jurisprudence of limitation, judges may become too "realistic," taking reality to be more resistant than it is.

May a district that has never had a dual school system bus black children past predominantly white schools so as to avoid "white flight" and thereby reduce de facto segregation? See, e.g., Johnson v. Board of Education, 604 F.2d 504 (7th Cir. 1979), cert. granted, 448 U.S. 910 (1980), vacated and remanded, 449 U.S. 915 (1980). In a sense, the case for such busing is weaker in the de facto situation, since it cannot be justified as necessary to remedy a prior constitutional violation. But is it sensible to permit only jurisdictions that have operated dual systems in the past to deny blacks admission to white schools?

4. *Political constraints.* Polls show that about three-fourths of Americans believe that it would be "too hard" on their children to be bused to another part of town to go to school with children of all races. In contrast, of the white families who have actually experienced busing to go to school with children of other races, 88 percent report the experience was very satisfactory or partially satisfactory, and only 11 percent unsatisfactory.

What relevance do these figures have on the possibility — or desirability — of the Court's continued insistence on busing to remedy segregation?

Recall the manner in which progress toward southern desegregation coincided with the emergence of the political branches as effective allies of the courts. As the desegregation effort spread north, and as the southern problem began to look like the northern one, some of this support dissipated. In 1968 Richard Nixon, while seeking the presidential nomination, told southern Republican leaders that he thought "all deliberate speed" required reinterpretation and that he opposed compulsory busing of students. See T. White, The Making of the President: 1968, 137-138 (1969). When President Nixon assumed office, the Justice Department for the first time since 1954 intervened on behalf of a southern school board to seek additional time for desegregation. Although the Supreme Court emphatically rejected the request, see Alexander v. Holmes County Board of Education, 396 U.S. 19 (1969), the episode nonetheless marked a significant turning point away from the alliance that produced change in the 1960s.

After *Swann* Congress enacted legislation purporting to limit the use of busing as a remedy for desegregation. The Education Amendments of 1972, 20 U.S.C. §§1651-1656, prohibit the appropriation of federal funds for transportation of students to achieve racial balance. Moreover, federal agencies are prohibited from requiring states to use funds for this purpose unless constitutionally required. See 20 U.S.C. §1652. In 1974 Congress went further and prohibited any "court, department, or agency of the United States [from ordering] transportation of any student to a school other than the school closest or next closest to his place of residence which provides the appropriate grade level, and type of education for such student." Equal Education Opportunities Act of 1974, 20 U.S.C. §1714. This legislation has had little effect on judicial conduct. Relying on another provision of the 1972 act stating that it is "not intended to modify or diminish the authority of the courts of the United States to enforce fully the fifth and four-teenth amendments to the Constitution of the United States," courts have inter-preted the 1972 legislation as applicable only to efforts to remedy de facto segregation. See, e.g., Drummond v. Acree, 409 U.S. 1228 (1972) (Powell, C.J.); United States v. Texas Education Agency, 532 F.2d 380, 394 n.18 (5th Cir.), vacated on other grounds sub nom. Austin Independent School District v. United States, 429 U.S. 990 (1976).

Far more sweeping measures have been proposed in Congress, however, in-cluding constitutional amendments prohibiting any court from requiring the as-signment or exclusion of any person from any school on the basis of race (see H.R.J. Res. 56, 97th Cong., 2d Sess. (1982)), and statutes purporting to deprive the Supreme Court and lower courts of jurisdiction in cases where transportation orders are requested or to otherwise limit the remedies available to lower courts in desegregation cases. See S. 37, 99th Cong, 1st Sess. (1985); H.R. 81, 99th Cong. 1st Sess (1985); H.R. 1211, 99th Cong., 1st Sess. (1985); H.R. 527, 99th Cong. 1st Sess. (1985). Are statutory efforts to control judicial desegregation orders consti-tutional? For a discussion of the constitutionality of jurisdiction limiting mea-sures, see chapter 1, section D, supra.

The Reagan administration also opposed transportation remedies and promised not to seek them. See Testimony of William Bradford Reynolds before the Sub-committee on Civil and Constitutional Rights of the House Judiciary Committee, 97th Cong., 1st Sess. 614 (1982). Indeed, administration officials indicated that "In deciding to initiate litigation, we will not rely on the Keyes presumption, but will define the violation precisely and seek to limit the remedy only to those schools in which racial imbalance is the product of intentional segregative acts of State officials." Id. at 618.

What conclusion follows from the opposition of the public and the political branches to judicial desegregation remedies? Does such opposition legitimate the Court's decisions by showing that they were necessary to counteract majoritarian pressures? Does it, alternatively, dissipate fear of judicial dictatorship by demon-strating that the Court's powers are not completely unchecked? Does the public opposition suggest that the Court has overstepped the bounds appropriate for it in a democratic society?

Note: Final Thoughts on School Desegregation and the Efficacy of Judicial Review

What does the Court's long struggle to define and implement the principle of racial equality reveal about the efficacy of judicial review? Has the Court been able to achieve the objectives it established in Brown?

How one answers this question turns in part on how one defines the objectives. Consider, first, the Court's performance from a purely doctrinal perspective. Has the Court succeeded in enunciating a legal principle that is reasoned and internally consistent? That adequately reflects the wording of the equal protection clause and the intent of its framers? That is consistent with the ideals of a free society? Has the Court performed these tasks more effectively than the political branches would have if left to themselves?

Presumably, the *Brown* Court was not engaged in a purely aesthetic or symbolic exercise. It is therefore relevant to ask not only whether the justices adequately articulated and defended their vision but also whether they succeeded in imposing it on the real world. The Court has been overwhelmingly successful in removing legally mandated segregation. The results in terms of actual integration are more mixed, however. Data collected by the federal government indicate that in 1980 about a third of black students nationwide attended schools with virtually all-black enrollments and almost 63 percent attended schools that were at least 50 percent black. Progress has been substantial in the South, where less than a quarter of blacks are in nearly all-black schools — down from 77.8 percent in 1968. In the Northeast, however, almost half of the black children did not attend school with a substantial number of whites, and the percentage is growing. See G. Orfield, Public School Desegregation in the United States, 1968-1980 (1983). Finally, even in schools that are formally integrated, the interracial contact envisioned by *Brown* has frequently not materialized. Thus, a significant percentage of blacks attending integrated schools are assigned to segregated, or substantially segregated, classrooms. See Fulfilling the Letter and Spirit of the Law: Desegregation of the Nation's Public Schools 233-234 (U.S. Commission on Civil Rights 1976). Indeed, "tracking" schemes and assignment of black children to special education programs in disproportionate numbers may have aggravated the sense of inferiority *Brown* was designed to combat. See G. Orfield, How to Make Desegregation Work: The Adaptation of Schools to Their Newly Integrated Bodies 327-328 (1976). See generally D. Bell, Race, Racism and American Law 424-428 (2d ed. 1980).

If one asks whether integration, where it has occurred, has produced equal educational opportunity, the evidence is even more mixed. While there is no proof that integration has reduced white achievement levels, neither is there proof that it has aided blacks in any demonstrable fashion. See, e.g., St. John, The Effects of Desegregation on Children, in Yarmolinsky, Liebman & Schelling, Race and Schooling in the City 85-102 (1981); Armor, The Evidence on Busing, Pub. Interest 90 (Summer 1972).

What if one asks, more broadly still, whether the Court has succeeded in implementing the great aims of the Reconstruction amendments — eliminating the wounds of slavery and integrating blacks into the mainstream of U.S. life?

Consider the following argument: *Brown* was a great success. Before *Brown* it was constitutionally legitimate in our society for government to legislate the separation of the races. *Brown* put an end to the most degrading and most humiliating form of discrimination — state-mandated, legally enforced racial separation. Moreover, *Brown* opened the door to the civil rights movement. In so doing, the Court took a critical first step toward forming the political coalition that produced the civil rights legislation of the 1960s.

Is this optimistic view consistent with the position that blacks presently occupy in U.S. society? Blacks have made great strides in educational achievement since Brown. See H. Levin, Education and Earnings of Blacks and the *"Brown"* Decision 12 (1981). In 1975, 58 percent more of the black population ages 25 to 34 had completed high school than in 1940, and 9 percent more had graduated from college. See U.S. Department of Commerce, Bureau of the Census, The Social and Economic Status of the Black Population in the United States: An Historical View, 1790-1978, at 94, table 71 (1979). But educational gains have not been uniformly translated into economic progress. A 1984 study showed that black high school graduates are more than twice as likely to be unemployed as white high school graduates. Black male college graduates have an unemployment rate three times the rate of white male college graduates. Indeed, young black college graduates have an unemployment rate almost as high as that of white high school dropouts. See Children's Defense Fund, Black and White Children in America: Key Facts 61, 65 (1985).

Moreover, although black median income has more than doubled in constant dollars since 1947, there has been no narrowing of the substantial black/white median income gap for families. See R. Hill, The Economic Status of Black Americans 57, table 5 (1981). Indeed, the gap is growing. Whereas black family income was 61.3 percent of white family income in 1970, it had declined to 56.3 percent in 1983. See U.S. Department of Commerce, Current Population Reports, Series P-60, No. 145 (1984). In 1984 black families were about twice as likely as white families to live in poverty, and almost half of all black children were poor. See Children's Defense Fund, supra, at 50-51.

Do such statistics provide appropriate criteria by which to judge the Court's work? If not, what criteria would you suggest? In reviewing the Court's performance from before the Civil War through the modern desegregation controversies, think about the extent to which the Court has been able to function as an effective alternative power center for dealing with the race question. Has the Court's effectiveness been hampered (augmented?) by the necessity of formulating public policy through the litigation process? By the obligation to write opinions tying its conclusions to the constitutional text?

When the Court has opposed the political branches, has it done so effectively? Has it been right?

B. EQUAL PROTECTION METHODOLOGY: RATIONAL BASIS REVIEW

The preceding section examined the development of equal protection principles in the context of race. Standing alone, however, this material provides an incomplete picture of the equal protection clause in two respects: First, although the impetus for passage of the equal protection clause was the problem of the newly freed slaves, its language is more general. It is therefore not surprising that the Court has applied the clause to controversies unrelated to race. Second, while historical circumstances undoubtedly influenced the development of equal protection doctrine, it is also true that the doctrine has taken on a life of its own and that it shapes the way lawyers think about equal protection problems. One therefore cannot understand the equal protection clause without first understanding the general methodology courts use to resolve equal protection disputes.

This section and those following it examine that methodology in both racial and nonracial contexts. In recent years, the Court's approach has involved creation of various "tiers" of review. Classifications based on race and a few other suspect characteristics are subject to varying degrees of heightened review and are frequently invalidated. In contrast, classifications not drawn on a "suspect basis" are subject to "low level" or "rational basis" review and are usually upheld. The remainder of this chapter examines the characteristics of each form of review and the bases on which the Court has placed various types of classifications in each tier.

New York City Transit Authority v. Beazer
440 U.S. 568 (1979)

MR. JUSTICE STEVENS delivered the opinion of the Court.

The New York City Transit Authority refuses to employ persons who use methadone. The District Court found that this policy violates the Equal Protection Clause of the Fourteenth Amendment. [The] Court of Appeals affirmed. [We] now reverse.

[A New York City Transit Authority (TA) rule prohibits employment of persons who use narcotic drugs. TA applied the rule to persons receiving methadone — a synthetic narcotic that, when taken orally, blocks the effect of heroin. The drug is widely used in the treatment of heroin addiction.]

This litigation was brought by the four respondents as a class action on behalf of all persons who have been, or would in the future be, subject to discharge or rejection as employees of TA by reason of participation in a methadone maintenance program. . . .

The trial record contains extensive evidence concerning the success of methadone maintenance programs, the employability of persons taking methadone, and the ability of prospective employers to detect drug abuse or other undesirable characteristics of methadone users. In general, the District Court concluded that there are substantial numbers of methadone users who are just as employable as other members of the general population and that normal personnel-screening procedures — at least if augmented by some method of obtaining information from the staffs of methadone programs — would enable TA to identify the unqualified applicants on an individual basis. On the other hand, the District Court recognized that at least one-third of the persons receiving methadone treatment — and probably a good many more — would unquestionably be classified as unemployable.

After extensively reviewing the evidence, the District Court briefly stated its conclusion that TA's methadone policy is unconstitutional. The conclusion rested on the legal proposition that a public entity "cannot bar persons from employment on the basis of criteria which have no rational relation to the demands of the jobs to be performed." [Because] it is clear that substantial numbers of methadone users are capable of performing many of the jobs at TA, the court held that the Constitution will not tolerate a blanket exclusion of all users from all jobs.

The District Court enjoined TA from denying employment to any person solely because of participation in a methadone maintenance program. Recognizing, however, the special responsibility for public safety borne by certain TA employees and the correlation between longevity in a methadone maintenance program and performance capability, the injunction authorized TA to exclude methadone users from specific categories of safety-sensitive positions and also to condition eligibility on satisfactory performance in a methadone program for at least a year. In other words, the court held that TA could lawfully adopt general rules excluding all methadone users from some jobs and a large number of methadone users from all jobs. . . .

At its simplest, the District Court's conclusion was that TA's rule is broader than necessary to exclude those methadone users who are not actually qualified to work for TA. We may assume not only that this conclusion is correct but also that it is probably unwise for a large employer like TA to rely on a general rule instead of individualized consideration of every job applicant. But these assumptions concern matters of personnel policy that do not implicate the principle safeguarded by the Equal Protection Clause. As the District Court recognized, the special classification created by TA's rule serves the general objectives of safety and efficiency.[39] Moreover, the exclusionary line challenged by respondents "is not one which is directed 'against' any individual or category of persons, but rather it represents a policy choice . . . made by that branch of Government vested with the power to make such choices." Marshall v. United States, 414 U.S. 417, 428. Because it does not circumscribe a class of persons characterized by some unpopular trait or affiliation, it does not create or reflect any special likelihood of bias on the part of the ruling majority. Under these circumstances, it is of no constitutional significance that the degree of rationality is not as great with respect to certain ill-defined subparts of the classification as it is with respect to the classification as a whole.

No matter how unwise it may be for TA to refuse employment to individual car cleaners, track repairmen, or busdrivers simply because they are receiving methadone treatment, the Constitution does not authorize a federal court to interfere in that policy decision. The judgment of the Court of Appeals is reversed.

[JUSTICE POWELL's opinion, concurring in part and dissenting in part, and JUSTICE BRENNAN's dissenting statement are omitted.]

Mr. Justice White, with whom Mr. Justice Marshall joins, dissenting. . . .

The question before us is the rationality of placing successfully maintained or recently cured persons in the same category as those just attempting to escape heroin addiction or who have failed to escape it, rather than in with the general population. The asserted justification for the challenged classification is the objective of a capable and reliable work force, and thus the characteristic in question is employability. "Employability," in this regard, does not mean that any particular applicant, much less every member of a given group of applicants, will turn out to be a model worker. Nor does it mean that no such applicant will ever become or be discovered to be a malingerer, thief, alcoholic, or even heroin addict. All employers take such risks. Employability, as the District Court used it in reference to successfully maintained methadone users, means only that the

---

39. "[L]egislative classifications are valid unless they bear no rational relationship to the State's objectives. Massachusetts Bd. of Retirement v. Murgia, [427 U.S. 307, 314]. State legislation 'does not violate the Equal Protection Clause merely because the classifications [it makes] are imperfect.' Dandridge v. Williams, 397 U.S. 471, 485." Washington v. Yakima Indian Nation, 439 U.S. 463, 501–502. . . .

employer is no more likely to find a member of that group to be an unsatisfactory employee than he would an employee chosen from the general population.

Petitioners had every opportunity, but presented nothing to negative the employability of successfully maintained methadone users as distinguished from those who were unsuccessful. [That] 20% to 30% are unsuccessful after one year in a methadone program tells us nothing about the employability of the successful group, and it is the latter category of applicants that the District Court and the Court of Appeals held to be unconstitutionally burdened by the blanket rule disqualifying them from employment. . . .

Of course, the District Court's order permitting total exclusion of all methadone users maintained for less than one year, whether successfully or not, would still exclude some employables and would to this extent be overinclusive. "Overinclusiveness" as to the primary objective of employability is accepted for less successful methadone users because it fulfills a secondary purpose and thus is not "overinclusive" at all. Although many of those who have not been successfully maintained for a year are employable, as a class they, unlike the protected group, are not as employable as the general population. Thus, even assuming the bad risks could be identified, serving the end of employability would require unusual efforts to determine those more likely to revert. But that legitimate secondary goal is not fulfilled by excluding the protected class: The District Court found that the fact of successful participation for one year could be discovered through petitioners' normal screening process without additional effort and, I repeat, that those who meet that criterion are no more likely than the average applicant to turn out to be poor employees. Accordingly, the rule's classification of successfully maintained persons as dispositively different from the general population is left without any justification and, with its irrationality and invidiousness thus uncovered, must fall before the Equal Protection Clause.[15]

Finally, even were the District Court wrong, and even were successfully maintained persons marginally less employable than the average applicant, the blanket exclusion of only these people, when but a few are actually unemployable and when many other groups have varying numbers of unemployable members, is arbitrary and unconstitutional. Many persons now suffer from or may again suffer from some handicap related to employability. But petitioners have singled

---

15. [Heroin] addiction is a special problem of the poor, and the addict population is composed largely of racial minorities that the Court has previously recognized as politically powerless and historical subjects of majoritarian neglect. Persons on methadone maintenance have few interests in common with members of the majority, and thus are unlikely to have their interests protected, or even considered, in governmental decisionmaking. Indeed, petitioners stipulated that "[o]ne of the reasons for the . . . drug policy is the fact that [petitioners] fee[l] an adverse public reaction would result if it were generally known that [petitioners] employed persons with a prior history of drug abuse, including persons participating in methadone maintenance programs." It is hard for me to reconcile that stipulation of animus against former addicts with our past holdings that "a bare . . . desire to harm a politically unpopular group cannot constitute a *legitimate* governmental interest." United States Dept. of Agriculture v. Moreno, 413 U.S. 528, 534 (1973). On the other hand, the afflictions to which petitioners are more sympathetic, such as alcoholism and mental illness, are shared by both white and black, rich and poor.

Some weight should also be given to the history of the rule. Petitioners admit that it was not the result of a reasoned policy decision and stipulated that they had never studied the ability of those on methadone maintenance to perform petitioners' jobs. Petitioners are not directly accountable to the public, are not the type of official body that normally makes legislative judgments of fact such as those relied upon by the majority today, and are by nature more concerned with business efficiency than with other public policies for which they have no direct responsibility. . . .

out respondents — unlike ex-offenders, former alcoholics and mental patients, diabetics, epileptics, and those currently using tranquilizers, for example — for sacrifice to this at best ethereal and likely nonexistent risk of increased unemployability. Such an arbitrary assignment of burdens among classes that are similarly situated with respect to the proffered objectives is the type of invidious choice forbidden by the Equal Protection Clause.

Note: The Structure of Equal Protection Review

1. *The nature of equality.* What does it mean to treat two people, or two groups of people, "equally" for purposes of the equal protection clause? Consider, for example, whether any of the following hypothetical employment rules for the New York City Transit Authority provide for equal treatment:

a. No position shall be filled by a woman.
b. No position shall be filled by a person weighing less than 175 pounds.
c. No position shall be filled by a person without a high school diploma.
d. All positions shall be filled by lot.
e. All persons applying for any position shall be hired.

In a trivial sense, of course, each of these rules provides for equal treatment. Under each of them, every applicant is equally subject to the same criteria. Thus, under rule *c*, all applicants are equally subject to the requirement of a high school diploma, and under rule *a*, all applicants are equally subject to the requirement that they be male. Indeed, it is impossible to imagine a rule that does not provide for equality in this sense.

In a similarly trivial sense, each of the hypothetical employment rules denies equal treatment. Under each of them, some people are denied a benefit that is granted to others. Inequality in this sense is also inescapable. Even rule *e*, which requires hiring all people who apply for the position, discriminates against the class of people who have not applied. In theory at least, one could provide that every person, whether they applied or not, would be employed by the Transit Authority. But even this (clearly absurd) rule would not provide equal treatment, for the class of persons wishing to work for the Transit Authority would be guaranteed the job of their choice, whereas the class of persons wishing to work for the police department, for example, would not.

This illustrates another difficulty with the concept of equality: Providing similar treatment to two groups will not result in equal treatment if the groups are not similarly situated. Rule *b*, for example, provides similar treatment to all applicants: They cannot weigh less than 175 pounds. But in one obvious sense the rule does not provide equal treatment because applicants are not similarly situated with respect to the rule. Similarly, rule *d* gives everyone an equal chance to win a job in a lottery. But even if the lottery is "fairly" conducted, the rule denies equal treatment, for the winner may be less qualified for the job or less in need of it or less "deserving" of it than the loser.

2. *The "relevant difference" requirement.* One might therefore say that the principle of equal treatment requires that all individuals be treated similarly to the

extent that they are the same and treated differently to the extent that they are different. But individuals are both the same and different in an infinite variety of respects. For example, although competing applicants under rule *a* are different in that some are men and some are women, they are all persons wishing to work for the Transit Authority.

Thus, the equality principle must be modified to provide that differences in treatment can be justified only by *relevant* differences between individuals. A difference is relevant if, but only if, it bears an empirical relationship to the purpose of the rule. This is, presumably, what the Court means in *Beazer* when it says that "legislative classifications are valid unless they bear no rational relationship to the State's objectives." Even though the Transit Authority's no methadone rule treated methadone users and nonusers differently, the Court thought that the rule did not violate the equality principle because there was a difference between the two classes relevant to the state's objective of a safe and efficient transit system. Had the Transit Authority required the employment of males only, the Court might have thought that gender bears no empirical relationship to these objectives and, so, invalidated the rule. Had the Authority limited employment to persons weighing more than 175 pounds or persons with high school diplomas, the result presumably would have turned on the extent to which possession of these qualities was useful in doing the work performed by Authority employees.

3. *Efficiency and relevant differences.* Is there a sound reason why we should insist that legislative classifications be based on relevant distinctions in this sense? This seems to turn the equality requirement into no more than a mandate for economic efficiency. Note, for example, that the requirement of a relevant distinction provides no guidance as to how the social costs of achieving the state's objective are to be distributed when different distributions are equally efficacious in achieving the state's goal. Nor does it provide any protection against the concentration of extreme costs on a small group when a "fairer" distribution of the costs over a larger group would be equally efficient.

Another problem with this version of the "relevant difference" requirement is that it becomes meaningless unless some restriction is placed upon the kinds of purposes the legislature may pursue. For example, if one supposes a Transit Authority uninterested in operating a safe subway, but determined to provide enhanced employment opportunities for men, then rule *a* satisfies the equality principle. Indeed, without a limit on the kinds of purposes that may be pursued, one can formulate a purpose for every possible rule, for every rule may be said to have the purpose of doing what it does.

Do these difficulties make the equality principle "empty?" Consider Westen, The Empty Idea of Equality, 95 Harv. L. Rev. 537, 548, 551 (1982):

> To say that two persons are the same in a certain respect is to presuppose a rule — a prescribed standard for treating them — that both fully satisfy. Before such a rule is established, no standard of comparison exists. After such a rule is established, equality between them is a "logical consequence" of the established rule. [It] is true that rules should be applied equally [if] by "equally," [one] means the tautological proposition that the rule should be applied in all cases to which the terms of the rule dictate that it be applied. [To] say that a rule should be applied "equally" [means] simply that the rule should be applied to the cases to which it applies.

4. *Relevant differences and the public interest.* Can these problems be avoided if rationality review is understood not as a requirement of efficiency, but rather as a guarantor of a political process that is public-regarding and not merely the product of self-serving activity? On this view, differential treatment violates the equality principle when its purpose is to advance the interests of politically powerful individuals but is permissible when it serves the public welfare. The requirement that the government show a connection between the means chosen and a public end might then be understood as a method of seeing whether the public end in fact accounts for the classification. If there is a close connection between the classification and a public end, the court may be persuaded that the legitimate end is in fact at work. If there is no such connection, there is reason to suspect that the legitimate end is a fraud. See J. Ely, Democracy and Distrust 145–48 (1980); Sunstein, Naked Preferences and the Constitution, 84 Colum. L. Rev. 1689, 1713 (1984).

Does this "public interest" requirement adequately capture the equality principle? Does it provide adequate protection against the infliction of very severe deprivations on small groups when those deprivations serve the public interest? As the material below illustrates, the judicial application of the rationality test has generally (although not always) led to validation of statutory classifications. Is this because of the difficulty in defining a "public interest" that is different from the fair aggregation of private preferences? Is it because the Court believes that there is really nothing wrong with interest-group politics? Is it because the Court has an unduly optimistic view of representative government?

5. *A note on organization.* The material below discusses these issues in greater detail. The material immediately following discusses the relationship between means and ends necessary to satisfy the equality requirement.

Presumably, a legislator determined to fulfill his or her constitutional obligations would undertake this means/ends analysis before voting for legislation. Material at pages 504-518 discusses whether the analysis is changed when a judge is reviewing the constitutional adequacy of the legislature's work.

Finally, as noted above, the meaningfulness of judicial review of the means/ends nexus ultimately rests on the court's ability to limit the universe of purposes that can be advanced to justify the classification. Material at pages 518-528 discusses whether the equal protection clause makes certain legislative purposes illegitimate. Should the range of justifying purposes be limited to those that actually motivated the legislature, or should the court entertain hypothetical purposes advanced post hoc by advocates defending the classification?

Note: The Means/Ends Nexus

To survive equal protection attack, the different treatment of two classes of persons must be justified by a relevant difference between them. But when is a difference relevant, and what constitutes an adequate justification? Suppose, first, that every member of the disadvantaged class has a trait that every member of the advantaged class lacks and that the trait is related in some way to achievement of the state's goal. Suppose, for example, that it could be shown that every methadone user is an unsafe worker, while every nonuser is a safe worker. The difference between users and nonusers would then justify the difference in treatment if, but only if, the benefit derived from a safer transit system outweighs the cost imposed on users denied employment. How does one measure "cost" and "benefit" in this context? Note that the "benefit" calculation requires an assessment of both the importance of the state's goal and the degree to which the classification advances it. Suppose, for example, that every methadone user poses a 1 percent greater risk of causing accidents than every nonuser. The issue would then be whether a 1 percent improvement in the safety of the transit system outweighs the cost imposed on methadone users in order to achieve it.

As complex as this analysis is, it vastly oversimplifies the problems encountered in the real world. For in almost all cases, the classification will not be perfectly efficient, but will be either "overinclusive" or "underinclusive" or both. A classification is "overinclusive" if it disadvantages some people who do not in fact threaten the state's interest. It is "underinclusive" if some people are not disadvantaged even though they threaten the state's interest.

1. *Overinclusion.* Consider first the problem of overinclusion in *Beazer.* If every methadone user were a safe and efficient worker, the exclusion of the class would not advance the state's purpose at all and, hence, would be unconstitutional. Both the majority and the dissent seem to agree, however, that at least *some* methadone users were unsuited for transit work. Is it sufficient to uphold the classification to show that it advances the state's purpose to some extent — if, for example, the transit system would be somewhat safer without methadone users than with them? Such a test would permit the state to impose severe deprivations in exchange for trivial benefits.

A rule requiring the state to demonstrate that every member of the disadvantaged class possesses the trait relevant to the state's objective is no more satisfactory. This test would make legislation virtually impossible, for almost all laws clump people together based on generalizations that do not universally hold. It may be that there is somewhere a ten-year-old who would make a perfectly safe transit worker. Yet the Transit Authority is surely justified in imposing a minimum age requirement on the individuals it employs.

It seems clear, therefore, that the permissibility of a legislative generalization must turn on the cost of the generalization as compared to the cost of a more individualized judgment. Making this comparison involves a complex process. In *Beazer,* for example, a no-methadone rule eliminates some unsafe workers but at the cost of denying jobs to some safe ones. A more individualized judgment would permit more safe workers to be employed but arguably at the cost of employing more unsafe workers who might go undetected. To strike the balance, one must first weigh the importance of safety against the importance of employment and then discount each side of the equation by the risk of error. Moreover, even if one concludes that the cost imposed on safe methadone users wrongly denied employment under the no-methadone rule outweighs the cost imposed by unsafe methadone users wrongly employed under a more individualized approach, it does not follow that the no methadone rule is invalid. The administrative costs associated with a more individualized assessment might still justify use of a prophylactic rule. For example, if the Transit Authority must conduct lengthy interviews with each methadone user to assure his or her safety, it might reasonably conclude that the cost of such interviews outweighs the cost of denying employment to those users who would be safe workers.

2. *Underinclusion.* A similarly complex weighing process is required when it is alleged that a classification is underinclusive. Is the Transit Authority's rule unconstitutional because it applies only to methadone users, and not to ex-offenders, former alcoholics and mental patients, diabetics, epileptics, and others who arguably pose an equal or greater safety risk? The Court has sometimes said that the equal protection clause permits the legislature to deal with one problem at a time, or to proceed step by step. See, e.g., Williamson v. Lee Optical Co., 348 U.S. 483, 489 (1955). One cannot, however, take these statements literally. If the legislature were completely free to select which part of a problem to attack, the equal protection clause would be meaningless. For example, such a rule would permit the state to deny driver's licenses to all people with green eyes on the theory that such people cause traffic accidents (albeit not a disproportionate number) and that their exclusion therefore advances the state's goal of traffic safety. If the legislature may disqualify a group posing a lesser risk while leaving untouched another group posing an equal or greater risk, then it could arbitrarily disadvantage virtually any group.

One might therefore conclude that the equal protection clause prohibits any law that denies a benefit to a group but grants the benefit to other groups imposing equal or greater costs. Such a rule once again oversimplifies the analysis, however. Suppose, for example, that 25 percent of persons suffering from epilepsy would make unsafe transit workers, while only 10 percent of methadone users pose an unacceptable risk. But suppose further that only a small number of epileptics apply for employment, while large numbers of methadone users seek transit jobs. May the Transit Authority disqualify methadone users but not epileptics on the theory that by doing so, it is dealing with a larger share of the total problem? May it disqualify epileptics but not methadone users on the theory that a given epileptic is more likely to cause safety problems than a given methadone user?

Closely associated with this problem is the difficulty of relative administrative costs. It may be, for example, that methadone users are easier to identify than epileptics or that unsafe epileptics are easier to identify than unsafe methadone users. In either event, the state might be justified in excluding users of methadone, even though they cause less of the problem, because the cost of exclusion is less.

Moreover, the cost calculation must also include the cost of not achieving ancillary goals that may qualify the purpose of achieving a safe transit system. Suppose, for example, that persons suffering from epilepsy impose greater safety costs than methadone users. The transit authority might nonetheless employ epileptics but not methadone users, if it believes that drug addicts but not victims of epilepsy are responsible for their plight.

Finally, the underinclusion analysis is affected by the manner in which the advantaged class is characterized. In *Beazer*, for example, it may seem quite sensible to disadvantage methadone users but not epileptics if methadone users pose more of a problem. There is no reason in principle, however, to compare methadone users to the class of epileptics as opposed to, for example, the class of epileptics, ex-offenders, and ex-mental patients, who, taken together, may pose more of a problem than methadone users alone. Indeed, one could characterize the advantaged class still more broadly. The methadone users might ask why the state is worried about the social cost of their unsafe conduct, when it does nothing to control the arguably greater social cost imposed by automobile drivers who do not wear seat belts or cigarette smokers who pollute the air around them or parents who abuse their children.

Note: The Problem of Judicial Review

The preceding material demonstrates that a serious effort to evaluate the nexus between means and ends is extraordinarily complex. In fact, however, courts rarely rigorously pursue such analysis when assessing the validity of statutes subject to equal protection attack.

The Supreme Court has not been altogether consistent in formulating a standard against which to measure statutes subject to "low level" scrutiny. In F. S. Royster Guano Co. v. Virginia, 253 U.S. 412 (1920), the Court said that "the classification must be reasonable, not arbitrary, and must rest upon some ground of difference having a fair and substantial relation to the object of the legislation, so that all persons similarly circumstanced shall be treated alike." Other cases suggest a more lenient standard of review. In New Orleans v. Dukes, 427 U.S. 297 (1976), for example, the Court held that the equal protection clause is satisfied so long as the classification is "rationally related to a legitimate state interest." Other cases purport to follow an even more deferential standard. In McGowan v. Maryland, 366 U.S. 420 (1961), for example, the Court said that "The constitutional safeguard is offended only if the classification rests on grounds wholly irrelevant to the achievement of the State's objective. State legislatures are presumed to have acted within their constitutional power despite the fact that, in practice, their laws result in some inequality. A statutory discrimination will not be set aside if any state of facts reasonably may be conceived to justify it."

Compare these formulations with the methods of analyzing the means/ends nexus outlined above. Can you state precisely what relationship between the classification and the legislative purpose must be shown to satisfy the Court? Must proponents of the law demonstrate that the classification advances the legislative purpose to some extent? That a rational person would so believe? That a rational person would so believe if the facts were as the legislature supposed them to be? Or must the proponents demonstrate that the various trade-offs outlined above between the costs of narrower and broader classifications are "rational?"

Regardless of the verbal distinctions, in practice the applications of any of the standards has usually led to validation of the legislative scheme. Three examples illustrate the Court's approach:

RAILWAY EXPRESS AGENCY v. NEW YORK, 336 U.S. 106 (1949): A New York traffic regulation prohibited the operation of "advertising vehicles" but permitted placing "business notices upon business delivery vehicles, so long as such vehicles are engaged in the usual business or regular work of the owner and not used merely or mainly for advertising." Justice Douglas delivered the Court's opinion:

"[The] regulation draws the line between advertisements of products sold by the owner of the truck and general advertisements. It is argued that unequal treatment on the basis of such a distinction is not justified by the aim and purpose of the regulation. It is said, for example, that one of appellant's trucks carrying the advertisement of a commercial house would not cause any greater distraction of pedestrians and vehicle drivers than if the commercial house carried the same advertisement on its own truck. . . .

"That, however, is a superficial way of analyzing the problem. [The] local authorities may well have concluded that those who advertise their own wares on their trucks do not present the same traffic problem in view of the nature or extent of the advertising which they use. [And] the fact that New York City sees fit to eliminate from traffic this kind of distraction but does not touch what may be even greater ones in a different category, such as the vivid displays on Times Square, is immaterial. It is no requirement of equal protection that all evils of the same genus be eradicated or none at all."

Justice Jackson wrote a concurring opinion: "There are two clauses of the Fourteenth Amendment which this Court may invoke to invalidate ordinances by which municipal governments seek to solve their local problems [— the due process clause and the equal protection clause.]. . .

"The burden should rest heavily upon one who would persuade us to use the due process clause to strike down a substantive law or ordinance. [Invalidation] of a statute [on] due process grounds leaves ungoverned and ungovernable conduct which many people find objectionable.

"Invocation of the equal protection clause, on the other hand, does not disable any governmental body from dealing with the subject at hand. It merely means that the prohibition or regulation must have a broader impact. I regard it as a salutary doctrine that [governments] must exercise their powers so as not to discriminate between their inhabitants except upon some reasonable differentiation fairly related to the object of regulation. [There] is no more effective practical guaranty against arbitrary and unreasonable government than to require that the principles of law which officials would impose upon a minority must be imposed generally. Conversely, nothing opens the door to arbitrary action so effectively as to allow those officials to pick and choose only a few to whom they will apply legislation and thus to escape the political retribution that might be visited upon them if larger numbers were affected. . . .

"This case affords an illustration. Even casual observations from the sidewalks of New York will show that an ordinance which would forbid all advertising on vehicles would run into conflict with many interests, including some, if not all, of the great metropolitan newspapers, which use that advertising extensively. [But] any regulation applicable to all such advertising would require much clearer justification in local conditions to enable its enactment than does some regulation applicable to a few. . . .

"There is not even a pretense here that the traffic hazard created by the advertising which is forbidden is in any manner or degree more hazardous than that which is permitted. It is urged with considerable force that this local regulation does not comply with the equal protection clause because it applies unequally upon classes whose differentiation is in no way relevant to the objects of the regulation. . . .

"The question in my mind comes to this. Where individuals contribute to an evil or danger in the same way and to the same degree, may those who do so for hire be prohibited, while those who do so for their own commercial ends but not for hire be allowed to continue? I think the answer has to be that the hireling may be put in a class by himself and may be dealt with differently than those who act on their own. But this is not merely because such a discrimination will enable the lawmaker to diminish the evil. That might be done by many classifications, which I should think wholly unsustainable. It is rather because there is a real difference between doing in self-interest and doing for hire, so that it is one thing to tolerate action from those who act on their own and it is another thing to permit the same action to be promoted for a price."

WILLIAMSON v. LEE OPTICAL, 348 U.S. 483 (1955): An Oklahoma statute made it unlawful for any person not a licensed optometrist or ophthamologist to fit lenses to a face or to duplicate or replace into frames lenses except on a written prescription of a ophthamologist or optometrist. In practical effect, the statute prevented opticians from fitting old glasses into new frames or supplying new or duplicate lenses without a prescription. However, the statute specifically exempted sellers of ready-to-wear glasses. The district court held that this discrimination against opticians violated the equal protection clause. In a unanimous opinion written by Justice Douglas, the Supreme Court reversed:

"The problem of legislative classification is a perennial one, admitting of no doctrinaire definition. Evils in the same field may be of different dimensions and proportions, requiring different remedies. Or so the legislature may think. Or the reform may take one step at a time, addressing itself to the phase of the problem which seems most acute to the legislative mind. The legislature may select one phase of one field and apply a remedy there, neglecting the others. The prohibition of the Equal Protection Clause goes no further than the invidious discrimination. We cannot say that the point has been reached here. For all this record shows, the ready-to-wear branch of this business may not loom large in Oklahoma or may present problems of regulation distinct from the other branch."

MINNESOTA v. CLOVER LEAF CREAMERY CO., 449 U.S. 456 (1981): This case concerned the constitutionality of a Minnesota law that banned the retail sale of milk in plastic nonreturnable, nonrefillable containers, but permitted such sale in nonreturnable paperboard milk cartons. A state trial court held the law violative of the equal protection clause in part because the "actual basis" for the law was to promote the economic interests of local dairy and pulpwood industries rather than to serve the environmental objectives that supporters of the law advanced for it. On appeal, the Minnesota Supreme Court concluded that the law was indeed designed to serve environmental purposes. Nonetheless, it affirmed the trial court on the ground that the ban on plastic containers was not rationally related to these purposes. The Supreme Court reversed. Justice Brennan wrote the Court's opinion:

"The parties agree that the standard of review applicable to this case under the Equal Protection Clause is the familiar 'rational basis' test.[6] Moreover, they agree that the purposes of the Act cited by the legislature — promoting resource

---

6. Justice Stevens' dissenting opinion argues that the Minnesota Supreme Court when reviewing a challange to a Minnesota statute on equal protection grounds is not bound by the limits applicable to federal courts, but may independently reach conclusions contrary to those of the legislature concerning legislation. This argument, though novel, is without merit. [When] a state court reviews state legislation challenged as violative of the Fourteenth Amendment, it is not free to impose greater restrictions as a matter of federal constitutional law than this Court has imposed.

conservation, easing solid waste disposal problems, and conserving energy — are legitimate state purposes.[7] [Respondents] apparently have not challenged the *theoretical* connection between a ban on plastic nonreturnables and the purposes articulated by the legislature; instead, they have argued that there is no *empirical* connection between the two. They produced impressive supporting evidence at trial to prove that the probable consequences of the ban on plastic nonreturnable milk containers will be to deplete natural resources, exacerbate solid waste disposal problems, and waste energy, because consumers unable to purchase milk in plastic containers will turn to paperboard milk cartons, allegedly a more environmentally harmful product.

"But States are not required to convince the courts of the correctness of their legislative judgments. . . .

"Although parties challenging legislation under the Equal Protection Clause may introduce evidence supporting their claim that it is irrational, they cannot prevail so long as "it is evident from all the considerations presented to [the legislature], and those of which we may take judicial notice, that the question is at least debatable." [United States v. Carolene Products Co., 304 U.S. 144, 154 (1938)]. Where there was evidence before the legislature reasonably supporting the classification, litigants may not procure invalidation of the legislation merely by tendering evidence in court that the legislature was mistaken."

Justice Stevens wrote a dissenting opinion: "The State of Minnesota has told us in unambiguous language that this statute is not rationally related to any environmental objective; it seems to me to be a matter of indifference, for purposes of applying the federal Equal Protection Clause, whether that message to us from the State of Minnesota is conveyed by the State Supreme Court, or by the state legislature itself.

"I find it extraordinary that this federal tribunal feels free to conduct its own de novo review of a state legislative record in search of a rational basis that the highest court of the State has expressly rejected. [It] is not our business to disagree with the state tribunal's evaluation of the State's own lawmaking process."

[Justice Powell's opinion concurred in part and dissented in part. Justice Rehnquist did not participate in the case.]

Note: *Deferential Review — Abdication or Self-Restraint?*

1. *Evaluating the means/ends nexus: the problem of fact.* Whether a particular means is "rationally related" to the legislature's ends frequently turns on the answers to antecedent questions of fact — e.g., will the prohibition of plastic milk containers in fact make for a cleaner environment, how much expertise is neces-

---

7. [In] equal protection analysis, this Court will assume that the objectives articulated by the legislature are actual purposes of the statute, unless an examination of the circumstances forces us to conclude that they "could not have been a goal of the legislation." [Weinberger v. Wiesenfeld, 420 U.S. 636, 648 n.16 (1975)]. Here, a review of the legislative history supports the Minnesota Supreme Court's conclusion that the principal purposes of the Act were [environmental]. The contrary evidence cited by respondents [is] easily understood, in context, as economic defense of an Act genuinely proposed for environmental reasons. We will not invalidate a state statute under the Equal Protection Clause merely because some legislators sought to obtain votes for the measure on the basis of its beneficial side effects on state industry.

sary to fit lenses into an eyeglass frame. How should these answers be ascertained? Has the Court gone too far in curtailing the right of litigants to prove that the facts are not as the legislature supposed them to be? A Court faced with a factual dispute generally resolves it pursuant to detailed procedural rules designed to give both parties a fair opportunity to bring to the factfinder's attention all relevant evidence. Although legislatures frequently hold hearings before enacting statutes, their procedures tend to be far less careful and structured. Indeed, there is no requirement that a legislator hear any of the evidence or know anything about the subject before voting on a bill. See Chapter 6 section G, infra. If the court, after a full trial, determines that the legislature is factually mistaken, why should the statute nonetheless be upheld?

Do the inherent problems with litigation suggest that the Court has been wise in restricting the ability of litigants to mount factual attacks on the means/ends nexus? Note, for example, that at least in traditional litigation, individuals who are not parties are unrepresented and that different courts may make different factual findings depending on the particular evidence presented and the skill of the advocates. The same statute might therefore be both constitutional and unconstitutional depending on the parties to the lawsuit and the evidence they happened to introduce. See Chapter 3, section C, supra. Note also that the adequacy of the factual predicate for statutes may vary depending on the time and place where the question is asked. Suppose, for example, that the legislature correctly perceives a nexus between the means and ends at the time it enacts the law, but that a few years later, the facts change so that the statute is no longer effectual. Does a constitutional statute then become unconstitutional? Does it become constitutional again if the facts change once again? If the means are effectual in achieving the ends in one part of the state but not in another part, is the statute constitutional only in certain places?

Does the Court's insistence that the challenger of a statute demonstrate that the legislature was irrational solve these problems?

2. *Evaluating the means/ends nexus: the problem of value.* If we assume agreement about the underlying facts, should the Court be more aggressive in evaluating legislative means? Or are there sound institutional reasons for deference to the legislative judgment? Consider Gunther, Foreword: In Search of Evolving Doctrine on a Changing Court: A Model for a Newer Equal Protection, 86 Harv. L. Rev. 1, 21 (1972):

> invigorated [equal] protection scrutiny would not involve adjudication on the basis of fundamental interests with shaky constitutional roots. Nor would it require a critical evaluation of the relative weights of asserted state purposes. Rather, it would permit the state to achieve a wide range of objectives. The yard-stick for the acceptability of the means would be the purpose chosen by the legislatures, not "constitutional" interests drawn from the value perception of the Justices.

But is it really possible to balance the environmental benefits associated with the prohibition of plastic milk containers against the burden imposed on consumers without "[evaluating] the relative weights of asserted state purposes"? Could the Court decide whether persons hired to advertise should be distinguished from those advertising their own products without reference to the "value perceptions of the Justices"? Consider Bennett, "Mere" Rationality in Constitutional Law: Judicial Review and Democratic Theory, 67 Calif. L. Rev. 1049, 1065 (1979): "Usually there will be no way to quantify or otherwise objectify [the] cost-benefit balancing. [To] recognize that rationality is a function of costs, benefits, and alternatives is to recognize that judicial value judgments at some level are unavoidable even when applying [the] most minimal of constitutional standards."

Does the unavoidability of such value judgments necessarily make even a highly deferential rationality test meaningless? For a negative answer, consider id. at 1067:

> Of course, the external spectator will have no ready way of comparing the value of the burdens to the minority with the value of the benefits to the majority. This means no more than that ascribing irrationality to legislative actions must be a matter of judgment, not science. [This fact] may counsel caution [but] it does not make the conclusion meaningless. On occasion we may call an individual's cost-benefit balance "irrational" even though he has decided that it is satisfactory to him.

Even if there is no problem with the judicial value judgments arguably inherent in rationality review, might there not still be a risk that the sporadic nature of judicial review will cause the Court to overlook the overall political context that makes a legislative judgment rational? For example, one might believe that requiring prescriptions from optometrists before opticians can replace lenses imposes costs that cannot be justified in terms of the marginal improvement in public safety. But suppose consumer groups agreed not to oppose the law in exchange for passage of measures that regulated the price that optometrists could charge their customers? Can a state defend an otherwise irrational classification on the ground that it is the product of compromise? Is a court competent to make judgments concerning the kinds of trade-offs between groups that are permissible? Consider Posner, The DeFunis Case and the Constitutionality of Preferential Treatment of Racial Minorities, 1974 Sup. Ct. Rev. 1, 27-29:

> The Court's expressed view, perhaps dictated by its dependence on the good will of the legislative branch, is that the political process is one of honestly attempting to promote efficiency or justice, or some other equally general conception of the public good. [But many] public policies are better explained as the outcome of a pure power struggle — clothed in a rhetoric of public interest that is a mere figleaf — among narrow interest or pressure groups. [If] it is true that we have a government of powers and interests rather than of general-welfare maximization, and if this pattern is an inevitable, and perhaps ultimately a desirable, feature of our society (the impartial pursuit of the public interest might incite a revolution by those disadvantaged in the pursuit) then it would be a mistake to require that legislation, to withstand a challenge based on alleged arbitrariness or discrimination, be reasonably related to some general social goal. The real "justification" for most legislation is simply that it is the product of the constitutionally created political process of our society.

Does this beg the question of what political process the Constitution creates? Consider Michelman, Politics and Values or What's Really Wrong with Rationality Review?, 13 Creighton L. Rev. 487, 509 (1979): "[Majoritarian] politics cannot be only the individualistically self-serving activity 'realistically' portrayed by economics-minded political scientists and theorists. Politics must also be a joint and mutual search for good or right answers to the question of directions for our evolving selves." Does this conception of the political process support rationality review under the equal protection clause? Michelman argues that it makes rationality review impossible because the standard against which statutes are measured should emerge from the very political process under review. "If [the] values that justify [statutes] are just the ones that they themselves shape and express for us, then inviting courts to judge their legitimacy by the test of whether they are aptly designed to promote the satisfaction of *preexisting* values — which is just the question posed by the test of minimum economic rationality — must cause either stifling judicial intervention or unprincipled judicial abstention." Id. at 510. Compare Sunstein, Naked Preferences and the Constitution, 84 Colum. L. Rev. 1689, 1713 (1984):

> Although the rationality test is highly deferential, its function is to ensure that classifications rest on something other than a naked preference for one person or group over another. Thus, [in] *Williamson*, [the] Court upheld differential treatment of optometrists and opticians on the ground not that the equal protection clause tolerated an unprincipled distribution of wealth to one rather than to the other — though there is a plausible argument that such a naked preference was indeed taking place — but that the differential treatment was a means of protecting consumers. The Court has made clear in rationality cases that the government must be able to invoke some public value that the classification at issue can be said to serve.

Is it plausible to find a public value truly at work in *Williamson*?

3. *The underenforcement thesis*. Even if problems inherent in judicial review preclude vigorous judicial enforcement of the rationality requirement, might not that requirement still retain significance for other actors in the system? Consider the following view: Pure interest group deals, justified by nothing other than the political strength of the beneficiaries, are prohibited by the equal protection clause. This prohibition is not subject to principled judicial enforcement because inquiries into the legislative process would prove unmanageable and strain judicial competence and authority. But although this prohibition is "underenforced," it nonetheless remains binding on legislators and administrators who have an obligation to obey the Constitution. See generally Sager, Fair Measure: The Status of Underenforced Constitutional Norms, 91 Harv. L. Rev. 122 (1978).

4. *The controversy over nondeferential low-level review*. The Court has generally been extremely deferential to legislative judgments when utilizing "low-level" scrutiny. It would be a mistake, however, to assume that such scrutiny inevitably leads to validation of the legislative scheme. Consider the following decisions:

City of Cleburne v. Cleburne Living Center
— U.S. — , 105 S. Ct. 3249 (1985)

JUSTICE WHITE delivered the opinion of the Court.

A Texas city denied a special use permit for the operation of a group home for the mentally retarded, acting pursuant to a municipal zoning ordinance requiring permits for such homes. The Court of Appeals [held that] the ordinance violated the Equal Protection Clause. [We affirm].

[Respondent purchased a building with the intention of converting it into a group home for thirteen mentally retarded men and women who would reside there under the constant supervision of staff members. A city zoning ordinance permitted a wide variety of structures on the proposed site, including "Hospitals, sanitariums, nursing homes or homes for convalescents or aged." However, the ordinance specifically excepted "homes for [the] insane or feeble-minded or alcoholics or drug addicts." Another section of the ordinance required "special use permits," renewable annually, for "Hospitals for the insane or feeble-minded, or alcoholic or drug addicts, or penal or correctional institutions." The City determined that the proposed home should be classified as a "hospital for the feeble-minded." After holding a public hearing, the city council voted to deny respondent a special use permit.

[In the first part of the opinion, the Court held that the lower court erred in treating the mentally retarded as a "quasi-suspect classification" and subjecting the law to "middle-level scrutiny." This portion of the opinion is discussed at Chapter 5, section E4, infra.]

Our refusal to recognize the retarded as a quasi-suspect class does not leave them entirely unprotected from invidious discrimination. To withstand equal protection review, legislation that distinguishes between the mentally retarded and others must be rationally related to a legitimate governmental purpose. . . .

The constitutional issue is clearly posed. [May] the city require the permit for this facility when other care and multiple dwelling facilities are freely permitted?

[The] mentally retarded as a group are indeed different from others not sharing their misfortune, and in this respect they may be different from those who would occupy other facilities that would be permitted [without] a special permit. But this difference is largely irrelevant unless the [home] and those who would occupy it would threaten legitimate interests of the city in a way that other permitted uses such as boarding houses and hospitals would not. . . .

The District Court found that the City Council's insistence on the permit rested on several factors. [The] Council was concerned with the negative attitude of the majority of property owners located within 200 feet of the [facility], as well as with the fears of elderly residents of the neighborhood. But mere negative attitudes, or fear, unsubstantiated by factors which are properly cognizable in a zoning proceeding, are not permissible bases for treating a home for the mentally retarded differently from apartment houses, multiple dwellings, and the like. It is plain that the electorate as a whole [could] not order city action violative of the Equal Protection Clause, and the City may not avoid the strictures of that Clause by deferring to the wishes or objections of some fraction of the body politic. . . .

[The] Council had two objections to the location of the facility. It was concerned that the facility was across the street from a junior high school, and it feared that the students might harass the occupants of the [home.] But the school itself is attended by about 30 mentally retarded students, and denying a permit based on such vague, undifferentiated fears is again permitting some portion of the community to validate what would otherwise be an equal protection violation. The other objection to the home's location was that it was located on "a five hundred year flood plain." This concern with the possibility of a flood, however, can hardly be based on a distinction between the [home] and, for example, nursing homes, homes for convalescents or the aged, or sanitariums or hospitals, any of which could be located on the [site] without obtaining a special use permit.

[Handwritten margin note: Mentally retarded are subject to higher level of scrutiny.]

The same may be said of another concern of the Council — doubts about the legal responsibility for actions which the mentally retarded might take. If there is no concern about legal responsibility with respect to other uses that would be permitted in the area, such as boarding and fraternity houses, it is difficult to believe that the groups of mildly or moderately mentally retarded individuals who would live at [the home] would present any different or special hazard.

[The] Council was concerned with the size of the home and the number of people that would occupy it. [But], there would be no restrictions on the number of people who could occupy this home as a boarding house, nursing home, family dwelling, fraternity house, or dormitory. The question is whether it is rational to treat the mentally retarded differently. It is true that they suffer disability, not shared by others; but why this difference warrants a density regulation that others need not observe is not at all apparent. . . .

The short of it is that requiring the permit in this case appears to us to rest on an irrational prejudice against the mentally retarded, including those who would occupy the [facility] and who would live under the closely supervised and highly regulated conditions expressly provided for by state and federal law. . . .

JUSTICE STEVENS, with whom [CHIEF JUSTICE BURGER] joins, concurring.

[Our] cases reflect an continuum of judgmental responses to differing classifications which have been explained in opinions by terms ranging from "strict scrutiny" at one extreme to "rational basis" at the other. I have never been persuaded that these so called "standards" adequately explain the decisional process. [In] my own approach to these cases, I have always asked myself whether I could find a "rational basis" for the classification at issue. The term "rational," of course, includes a requirement that an impartial lawmaker could logically believe that the classification would serve a legitimate public purpose that transcends the harm to the members of the disadvantaged class. Thus, the word "rational" — for me at least — includes elements of legitimacy and neutrality that must always characterize the performance of the sovereign's duty to govern impartially. . . .

In every equal protection case, we have to ask certain basic questions. What class is harmed by the legislation, and has it been subjected to a "tradition of disfavor" by our laws? What is the public purpose that is being served by the law? What is the characteristic of the disadvantaged class that justifies the disparate treatment? In most cases the answer to these questions will tell us whether the statute has a "traditional basis." . . .

Every law that places the mentally retarded in a special class is not presumptively irrational. The differences between mentally retarded persons and those with greater mental capacity are obviously relevant to certain legislative decisions. . . .

Even so, the Court of Appeals correctly observed that through ignorance and prejudice the mentally retarded "have been subjected to a history of unfair and often grotesque mistreatment." The discrimination against the mentally retarded that is at issue in this case is the city's decision to require an annual special use permit before property in an apartment house district may be used as a group home for persons who are mildly retarded. The record convinces me that this permit was required because of the irrational fears of neighboring property owners, rather than for the protection of the mentally retarded persons who would reside in [the] home.

JUSTICE MARSHALL, with whom JUSTICE BRENNAN and JUSTICE BLACKMUN join, concurring in the judgment in part and dissenting in part. . . .

[The] Court holds the ordinance invalid on rational basis grounds and disclaims that anything special, in the form of heightened scrutiny, is taking place. Yet Cleburne's ordinance surely would be valid under the traditional rational basis test applicable to economic and commercial regulation. . . .

The Court, for example, concludes that legitimate concerns for fire hazards or the serenity of the neighborhood do not justify singling out respondents to bear the burdens of these concerns, for analogous permitted uses appear to pose similar threats. Yet under the traditional and most minimal version of the rational basis test, "reform may take one step at a time, addressing itself to the phase of the problem which seems most acute to the legislative mind." [*Williamson*]. The "record" is said not to support the ordinance's classifications, but under the traditional standard we do not sift through the record to determine whether policy decisions are squarely supported by a firm factual foundation. Finally, the Court further finds it "difficult to believe" that the retarded present different or special hazards than other groups. In normal circumstances, the burden is not on the legislature to convince the Court that the lines it has drawn are sensible; legislation is presumptively constitutional, and a State "is not required to resort to close distinctions or to maintain a precise, scientific uniformity with reference" to its goals. Allied Stores of Ohio, Inc. v. Bowers, 358 U.S. 522, 527 (1959).

I share the Court's criticisms of the overly broad lines that Cleburne's zoning ordinance has drawn. But if the ordinance is to be invalidated for its imprecise classifications, it must be pursuant to more powerful scrutiny than the minimal rational-basis test used to review classifications affecting only economic and commercial matters. The same imprecision in a similar ordinance that required opticians but not optometrists to be licensed to practice, see [*Williamson*], [would] hardly be fatal to the statutory scheme.

The refusal to acknowledge that something more than minimum rationality review is at work here is, in my view, unfortunate in at least two respects. The suggestion that the traditional rational basis test allows this sort of searching inquiry creates precedent for this Court and lower courts to subject economic and commercial classifications to similar and searching "ordinary" rational basis review. [Moreover,] by failing to articulate the factors that justify today's "second order" rational basis review, the Court provides no principled foundation for determining when more searching inquiry is to be invoked. Lower courts are thus left in the dark on this important question, and this Court remains unaccountable for its decisions employing, or refusing to employ, particularly searching scrutiny. . . .

U.S. Railroad Retirement Board v. Fritz

449 U.S. 166 (1980)

JUSTICE REHNQUIST delivered the opinion of the Court.

[Before 1974 federal law permitted retired persons who worked in both railroad and nonrailroad jobs to receive dual benefits under social security and the railroad retirement systems. In 1974 Congress restructured the railroad retirement system in order to place it on a sound financial basis by eliminating future accrual of dual benefits. Congress chose not to make these changes fully retroactive, however, and this case concerned the constitutionality of the distinction Congress drew between those workers continuing to receive dual benefits and those workers denied them.

The 1974 act provided that workers who, as of January 1, 1975, lacked the ten years railroad employment necessary to qualify for a railroad pension would not receive dual benefits. In contrast, workers who had already retired and were presently receiving dual benefits would continue to receive them. Workers who had not yet retired but had already qualified for railroad and social security benefits could receive them only if they (1) had performed some railroad work in 1974; or (2) had a "current connection" with the railroad industry as of December 31, 1974; or (3) had completed 25 years of railroad service as of December 31, 1974.

Appellees represented the class of active railroad workers who had qualified for dual benefits under the old scheme but would be denied them under the new law because they did not satisfy any of these three criteria. They claimed that depriving them of dual benefits while continuing them for active workers who satisfied the criteria violated the equal protection component of the fifth amendment's due process clause.]

The District Court agreed with appellee that a differentiation based solely on whether an employee was "active" in the railroad business as of 1974 was not "rationally related" to the congressional purposes of insuring the solvency of the railroad retirement system and protecting vested benefits. We disagree and reverse.

The initial issue presented by this case is the appropriate standard of judicial review to be applied when social and economic legislation enacted by Congress is challenged as being violative of the Fifth Amendment to the United States Constitution. . . .

Despite the narrowness of the issue, this Court in earlier cases has not been altogether consistent in its pronouncements in this area. . . .

In more recent years, however, the Court in cases involving social and economic benefits has consistently refused to invalidate on equal protection grounds legislation which it simply deemed unwise or unartfully drawn. [Applying this principle] to this case, the plain language of [the statute] marks the beginning and end of our inquiry. There Congress determined that some of those who in the past received full windfall benefits would not continue to do so. Because Congress could have eliminated windfall benefits for all classes of employees, it is not constitutionally impermissible for Congress to have drawn lines between groups of employees for the purpose of phasing out those benefits.

The only remaining question is whether Congress achieved its purpose in a patently arbitrary or irrational way. The classification here is not arbitrary, says appellant, because it is an attempt to protect the relative equities of employees and to provide benefits to career railroad employees. . . .

Congress could properly conclude that persons who had actually acquired statutory entitlement to windfall benefits while still employed in the railroad industry had a greater equitable claim to those benefits than the members of appellees' class who were no longer in railroad employment when they became eligible for dual benefits. [Congress] could assume that those who had a current connection with the railroad industry when the Act was passed in 1974, or who returned to the industry before their retirement, were more likely than those who had left the industry prior to 1974 and who never returned, to be among the class of persons who pursue careers in the railroad industry, the class for whom the Railroad Retirement Act was designed.

Where, as here, there are plausible reasons for Congress' action, our inquiry is at an end. It is, of course, "constitutionally irrelevant whether this reasoning in fact underlay the legislative decision," [quoting Flemming v. Nestor, 363 U.S. 603, 612 (1960)] because this Court has never insisted that a legislative body articulate its reasons for enacting a statute. This is particularly true where the legislature must necessarily engage in a process of line drawing. . . .

Finally, we disagree with the District Court's conclusion that Congress was unaware of what it accomplished or that it was misled by the groups that appeared before it. If this test were applied literally to every member of any legislature that ever voted on a law, there would be very few laws which would survive it. The language of the statute is clear, and we have historically assumed that Congress intended what it enacted. To be sure, appellees lost a political battle in which they had a strong interest, but this is neither the first nor the last time that such a result will occur in the legislative forum. What we have said is enough to dispose of the claims that Congress not only failed to accept appellees' argument as to restructuring in toto, but that such failure denied them equal protection of the laws guaranteed by the Fifth Amendment.

For the foregoing reasons, the judgment of the District Court is reversed.

JUSTICE STEVENS, concurring in the judgment. . . .

[Justice] Brennan correctly points out that if the analysis of legislative purpose requires only a reading of the statutory language in a disputed provision, and if any "conceivable basis" for a discriminatory classification will repel a constitutional attack on the statute, judicial review will constitute a mere tautological recognition of the fact that Congress did what it intended to do. . . .

I do not, however, share Justice Brennan's conclusion that every statutory classification must further an objective that can be confidently identified as the "actual purpose" of the legislature. Actual purpose is sometimes unknown. Moreover, undue emphasis on actual motivation may result in identically worded statutes being held valid in one State and invalid in a neighboring State. I therefore believe that we must discover a correlation between the classification and either the actual purpose of the statute or a legitimate purpose that we may reasonably presume to have motivated an impartial legislature. If the adverse impact on the disfavored class is an apparent aim of the legislature, its impartiality would be suspect. If, however, the adverse impact may reasonably be viewed as an acceptable cost of achieving a larger goal, an impartial lawmaker could rationally decide that that cost should be incurred.

In this case, however, we need not look beyond the actual purpose of the legislature. [The] congressional purpose to eliminate dual benefits is unquestionably legitimate. [Some] hardship — in the form of frustrated long-term expectations — must inevitably result from any reduction in vested benefits. Arguably, therefore, Congress had a duty — and surely it had the right to decide — to eliminate no more vested benefits than necessary to achieve its fiscal purpose. Having made that decision, any distinction it chose within the class of vested beneficiaries would involve a difference of degree rather than a difference in entitlement. I am satisfied that a distinction based upon currency of railroad employment represents an impartial method of identifying that sort of difference. Because retirement plans frequently provide greater benefits for recent retirees than for those who retired years ago — and thus give a greater reward for recent service than for past service of equal duration — the basis for the statutory discrimination is supported by relevant precedent. . . .

JUSTICE BRENNAN, with whom JUSTICE MARSHALL joins, dissenting. . . .

[When] faced with a challenge to a legislative classification under the rational basis test, the court should ask, first, what the purposes of the statute are, and second, whether the classification is rationally related to achievement of those purposes. . . .

[A] "principal purpose" of the Railroad Retirement Act of 1974, as explicitly stated by Congress, was to preserve the vested earned benefits of retirees who had already qualified for them. The classification at issue here, which deprives some retirees of vested dual benefits that they had earned prior to 1974, directly conflicts with Congress' stated purpose. As such, the classification is not only rationally unrelated to the congressional purpose; it is inimical to it.

The Court today avoids the conclusion that [the statute] must be invalidated by deviating in three ways from traditional rational basis analysis. First, the Court adopts a tautological approach to statutory purpose, thereby avoiding the necessity for evaluating the relationship between the challenged classification and the legislative purpose. Second, it disregards the actual stated purpose of Congress in favor of a justification which was never suggested by any Representative or Senator, and which in fact conflicts with the stated congressional purpose. Third, it upholds the classification without any analysis of its rational relationship to the identified purpose.

The Court states that "the plain language of [the statute] marks the beginning and end of our inquiry." This statement is strange indeed, for the "plain language" of the statute can tell us only what the classification is; it can tell us nothing about the purpose of the classification, let alone the relationship between the classification and that purpose. Since [the] Act deprives the members of appellee class of their vested earned dual benefits, the Court apparently assumes that Congress must have *intended* that result. But by presuming purpose from result, the Court reduces analysis to tautology. It may always be said that Congress intended to do what it in fact did. If that were the extent of our analysis, we would find every statute, no matter how arbitrary or irrational, perfectly tailored to achieve its purpose. But equal protection scrutiny under the rational basis test requires the courts first to deduce the independent objectives of the statute, usually from statements of purpose and other evidence in the statute and legislative history, and second to analyze whether the challenged classification rationally furthers achievement of those objectives. The Court's tautological approach will not suffice.

The Court analyzes the rationality of [the statute] in terms of a justification suggested by Government attorneys, but never adopted by Congress. The Court states that it is "constitutionally irrelevant whether this reasoning in fact underlay the legislative decision." [Over] the past 10 years, this Court has frequently recognized that the actual purposes of Congress, rather than the post hoc justifications offered by Government attorneys, must be the primary basis for analysis under the rational basis test. . . .

[The] standard we have applied is properly deferential to the Legislative Branch: where Congress has articulated a legitimate governmental objective, and the challenged classification rationally furthers that objective, we must sustain the provision. In other cases, however, the courts must probe more deeply. Where Congress has expressly stated the purpose of a piece of legislation, but where the challenged classification is either irrelevant to or counter to that purpose, we must view any post hoc justifications proffered by Government attorneys with skepticism. A challenged classification may be sustained only if it is rationally related to achievement of an *actual* legitimate governmental purpose.

The Court argues that Congress chose to discriminate against appellees for reasons of equity. [But] Congress expressed the view that it would be inequitable to deprive any retirees of any portion of the benefits they had been promised and that they had earned under prior law. The Court is unable to cite even one statement in the legislative history by a Representative or Senator that makes the equitable judgment it imputes to Congress. . . .

[In] 1970, Congress established a Commission to investigate the actuarial soundness of the Railroad Retirement system and to make recommendations for its reform. . . .

After receiving the Commission report, Congress asked railroad management and labor representatives to negotiate and submit a bill to restructure the Railroad Retirement system, which should "take into account the specific recommendations of the Commission on Railroad Retirement." The members of this Joint Labor-Management Negotiating Committee were not appointed by public officials, nor did they represent the interests of the appellee class, who were no longer active railroaders or union members.

In an initial proposed restructuring of the system, the Joint Committee devised a means whereby the system's deficit could be completely eliminated without depriving retirees of vested earned benefits. However, labor representatives demanded that benefits be increased for their current members, the cost to be offset by divesting the appellee class of a portion of the benefits they had earned under prior law. . . .

Congress conducted hearings to consider the Joint Committee's recommendations, but never directed its attention to their effect on persons in appellee class' situation. In fact, the Joint Committee negotiators and Railroad Retirement Board members who testified at congressional hearings perpetuated the inaccurate impression that all retirees with earned vested dual benefits under prior law would retain their benefits unchanged. . . .

Of course, a misstatement or several misstatements by witnesses before Congress would not ordinarily lead us to conclude that Congress misapprehended what it was doing. In this instance, however, where complex legislation was drafted by outside parties and Congress relied on them to explain it, where the misstatements are frequent and unrebutted, and where no Member of Congress can be found to have stated the effect of the classification correctly, we are entitled to suspect that Congress may have been misled. . . .

Therefore, I do not think that this classification was rationally related to an *actual* governmental purpose.

The third way in which the Court has deviated from the principles of rational basis scrutiny is its failure to analyze whether the challenged classification is genuinely related to the purpose identified by the Court. . . .

An unadorned claim of "equitable" considerations is, of course, difficult to assess. It seems to me that before a court may accept a litigant's assertion of "equity," it must inquire what principles of equity or fairness might genuinely support such a judgment. But apparently the Court does not demand such inquiry, for it has failed to address any equitable considerations that might be relevant to the challenged classification.

In my view, the following considerations are of greatest relevance to the equities of this case: (1) contribution to the system; (2) reasonable expectation and reliance; (3) need; and (4) character of service to the railroad industry. With respect to each of these considerations, I would conclude that appellees have as great an equitable claim to their earned dual benefits as do their more favored coworkers, who remain entitled to their earned dual benefits under [the statute].

Note: Equal Protection as a Tautology

1. City of Cleburne *and the rational basis test.* Did the Court in *Cleburne* in fact apply the rational basis test? If you agree with Justice Marshall that the Court was actually using some form of heightened scrutiny, what was it about the case that triggered this more careful review?

2. City of Cleburne, Fritz, *and the "rationality" of aesthetic and value preferences.* Are *Cleburne* and *Fritz* consistent? If the legislature can benefit a certain class of railroad workers simply because it feels that they have a greater "equitable claim," why can't it take into account the aesthetic or attitudinal preferences of the surrounding property owners in *Cleburne?* The Court is surely correct when it argues that it would render the equal protection clause meaningless if the legislature could "avoid the strictures of that Clause by deferring to the wishes or objections of some fraction of the body politic." But how can a court evaluate the "rationality" of these wishes and objections when they are premised on ultimate value judgments rather than on instrumental considerations? Is it "irrational," for example, for the legislature to conclude that factories or buildings over a certain height are inappropriate in residential neighborhoods? Would "mere negative attitudes" be an insufficient basis for a zoning ordinance excluding such structures?

3. Fritz *and the effort to escape the tautology.* Is Justice Brennan correct when he asserts that "by presuming purpose from result, the Court [in *Fritz*] reduces analysis to tautology"? Consider Note, Legislative Purpose, Rationality, and Equal Protection, 82 Yale L.J. 123, 128 (1972):

> It is always possible to define the legislative purpose of a statute in such a way that the statutory classification is rationally related to it. When a statute names a class, that class must share some common characteristic for that is the definitional attribute of a "class." The nature of the burdens or benefits created by a statute and the nature of the chosen class's commonality will always suggest a statutory purpose — to so burden or benefit the common trait shared by members of the identified class. A statute's classification will be rationally related to such a purpose because the reach of the purpose has been derived from the classifications themselves.

Is there an escape from this tautology? Two possibilities suggest themselves. First, some statutes might be invalidated on the theory that even though they promote the purpose the legislature actually had, that purpose is illegitimate. In *Cleburne*, for example, the Court assumes arguendo that the ordinance was based in part on the desire to vindicate the preferences of surrounding property owners. While there is no doubt that the ordinance was "rationally related" to this purpose, this relationship does not save the statute because "mere negative attitudes [are] not permissible bases" for differential treatment of a home for the mentally retarded.

Second, even if the legislature's purpose is legitimate, statutes might nonetheless be invalidated if they are judged on the basis of that actual purpose, rather than on the basis of post hoc justifications. One might then say that the law fails because there is no reasonable nexus between the classification and what the legislature *actually* wished to achieve, even though one might hypothesize a *possible* purpose advanced by the statute. For example, in *Fritz*, Justice Brennan's dissent argues that even if equity considerations are a legitimate hypothetical basis for the statute, they cannot be advanced to support it because they are merely "post hoc justifications proffered by Government attorneys," which did not actually motivate Congress to enact the law.

On occasion, the Court has relied on both of these techniques to invalidate statutes as "irrational," although both remain controversial. The controversy is explored below.

U.S. DEPARTMENT OF AGRICULTURE v. MORENO, 413 U.S. 528 (1973): Section 3(e) of the Food Stamp Act of 1964 (as amended in 1971) excluded from participation in the food stamp program any household containing an individual who is unrelated to any other member of the household. Appellees in this case consisted of several groups of individuals who alleged that, although they satisfied the income eligibility requirements for the program, they were excluded solely because persons in each group were not related to each other. For example, one appellee had a daughter with an acute hearing deficiency who required special instruction in a school for the deaf. Because the school was located in an area in which appellee could not afford to live, she agreed to share an apartment near the school with another woman on public assistance. Since she was not related to the woman, she was threatened with termination of food stamp assistance. Appellees claimed that the "unrelated persons" provision created an irrational classification in violation of the equal protection component of the due process clause of the Fifth Amendment. Justice Brennan delivered the Court's opinion:

"Under traditional equal protection analysis, a legislative classification must be sustained if the classification itself is rationally related to a legitimate governmental interest. [The act stated that it was the policy of Congress to 'raise levels of nutrition among low-income households' and increase utilization of food so as to 'strengthen our agricultural economy.'] The challenged statutory classification [is] clearly irrelevant to [these purposes]. . . .

"Thus, if it is to be sustained, the challenged classification must rationally further some legitimate governmental interest other than those specifically stated in [the act]. Regrettably, there is little legislative history to illuminate the purposes of the [act]. The legislative history that does exist, however, indicates that that amendment was intended to prevent so-called 'hippies' and 'hippie communes' from participating in the food stamp program. The challenged classification clearly cannot be sustained by reference to this congressional purpose. For if the constitutional conception of 'equal protection of the laws' means anything, it must at the very least mean that a bare congressional desire to harm a politically unpopular group cannot constitute a *legitimate* governmental interest. . . .

"Although apparently conceding this point, the Government maintains that the challenged classification should nevertheless be upheld as rationally related to the clearly legitimate governmental interest in minimizing [fraud]. In essence, the Government contends that, in adopting the [act], Congress might rationally have thought (1) that households with one or more unrelated members are more likely than 'fully related' households to contain individuals who abuse the program by fraudulently failing to report sources of income or by voluntarily remaining poor; and (2) that such households are 'relatively unstable,' thereby increasing the difficulty of detecting such abuses. But even if we were to accept as rational the Government's wholly unsubstantiated assumptions concerning the differences between 'related' and 'unrelated' households, we still could not agree with the Government's conclusion that the denial of essential federal food assistance to *all* otherwise eligible households containing unrelated members constitutes a rational effort to deal with these concerns.

"At the outset, it is important to note that the [act] itself contains provisions, wholly independent of §3(e), aimed specifically at the problems of fraud and of the voluntary poor. . . .

"Moreover, in practical effect, the challenged classification simply does not operate so as rationally to further the prevention of fraud. . . .

"[The act] excludes from participation [*not*] those persons who are 'likely to abuse the program' but, rather, *only* those persons who are so desperately in need of aid that they cannot even afford to alter their living arrangements so as to retain their eligibility.

Justice Douglas wrote a separate concurring opinion. Justice Rehnquist, with whom Chief Justice Burger joined, dissented: "I do not think it is unreasonable for Congress to conclude that the basic unit which it was willing to support with federal funding [is] some variation on the family as we know it — a household consisting of related individuals. This unit provides a guarantee which is not provided by households containing unrelated individuals that the household exists for some purpose other than to collect federal food stamps."

Note: Equality as a Limitation on Permissible Governmental Purposes

1. *Other examples of impermissible purpose review.* a. Zobel. An Alaska statute distributed income derived from the state's oil resources based on length of residence in the state. Under the statute, Alaska residents were granted one "dividend unit" for each year they had resided within the state since 1959. Appellants, who had moved to Alaska two years before passage of the law, argued that it was unconstitutional to distinguish between them and persons who had arrived earlier. In Zobel v. Alaska, 457 U.S. 55 (1982), Chief Justice Burger, writing for seven

members of the Court (Justice O'Connor concurred in the judgment only; Justice Rehnquist dissented) agreed. Assuming arguendo that the statute had to satisfy only a minimum rationality standard, the Court nonetheless found it defective. The law could not be justified as an effort to encourage people to establish and maintain Alaskan residences, since this end was "not in any way served by granting greater dividends to persons for their residency during the 21 years prior to [its] enactment." Nor could the state justify the scheme as an effort to manage its oil resources prudently and avoid rapacious development. "Even if we assume that [this interest] is served by increasing the dividend for each year of residency beginning with the date of enactment, [it is not] rationally served by granting greater dividends in varying amounts to those who resided in Alaska during the 21 years prior to enactment." Finally, the Court rejected the argument that the classification was justified by the policy of rewarding long-time residents for "past contributions" to the state. This objective was simply "not a legitimate state purpose," since such reasoning "could open the door to state apportionment of other rights, benefits and services according to length of residency" and "Such a result would be clearly impermissible."

b. Hooper. The Court elaborated in slightly more detail on the length of residence problem in Hooper v. Bernalillo County Assessor, — U.S. — , 105 S. Ct. 2862 (1985). Under New Mexico law, a Vietnam veteran currently residing in New Mexico was entitled to a $2,000 annual property tax exemption if the veteran had established New Mexican residence before May 8, 1976. A veteran who had established residence after this date argued that the limitation violated equal protection, and the Court agreed. Again writing for the majority, Chief Justice Burger held that

> The New Mexico statute, by singling out previous residents for tax exemption, rewards only those citizens for their "past contributions" toward our nation's military effort in Vietnam. *Zobel* teaches that such an objective is "not a legitimate state purpose." The State may not favor established residents over new residents based on the view that the State may take care of "its own," if such is defined by prior residence. Newcomers, by establishing bona fide residence in the State, become the State's "own."

Justice Brennan filed a brief concurring opinion. Justice Stevens filed a dissenting opinion in which Justices Rehnquist and O'Connor joined.

c. Ward. In Metropolitan Life Insurance Co. v. Ward, — U.S. — (1985), the Court made clear that at least in some contexts, a desire to favor current residents over nonresidents is also an impermissible basis for legislative classifications. The Alabama statute in question imposed a substantially lower gross premiums tax on domestic insurance companies than on out-of-state companies doing business in Alabama. Since federal legislation specifically exempted state regulation of insurance companies from commerce clause limitations, the foreign companies could not argue that discrimination against them violated the dormant commerce clause. See Chapter 3, section A, supra. Instead, they argued that the discrimination violated equal protection principles. In a 5-to-4 decision, the Supreme Court agreed. In an opinion by Justice Powell, the Court rejected the state's argument that the classification advanced the legitimate purpose of encouraging the formation of new domestic companies in Alabama. "Alabama's aim to promote domestic industry is purely and completely discriminatory, designed only to favor domestic industry within the State, no matter what the cost to foreign corporations also seeking to do business there. [This] constitutes the very sort of parochial discrimination that the Equal Protection Clause was intended to prevent." Justice O'Connor wrote a dissenting opinion, which was joined by Justices Brennan, Marshall, and Rehnquist. See also Williams v. Vermont, — U.S. — , 105 S. Ct. 2465 (1985) (state statute granting credit for sales tax paid in other states on cars purchased by present state residents, but denying credit for sales tax paid by those purchasing cars before becoming state residents, violates equal protection; state "may not treat those within its borders unequally solely on the basis of their different residences.")

2. *Defining "impermissible purposes" under the equal protection clause.* What makes the legislative purposes in these cases constitutionally impermissible? Of course, if the legislature is pursuing a goal that is independently unconstitutional, a classification designed to accomplish that goal is presumably unconstitutional as well. But one could then rely on the substantive constitutional provision to invalidate the law, and reference to the equal protection clause would be superfluous. In *Ward*, for example, the desire of a state to discourage foreign competition is normally considered impermissible under the dormant commerce clause. But once Congress removed this objection through reverse preemption, see Chapter 3, section A, supra, why should the state be precluded from pursuing this objective? Does the equal protection clause of its own force prohibit the government from pursuing certain ends that are otherwise constitutionally permissible? If so, what ends does it prohibit? Consider the following suggestions:

a. Do you agree that the "desire to harm a politically unpopular group cannot constitute a *legitimate* governmental interest"? If the unadorned desire to harm a group disadvantaged by a statute could shield the statute from equal protection attack, wouldn't the clause be a nullity? On the other hand, the disadvantaged group is always defined in the statute by some trait shared by its members. Why, then, can't such statutes be justified by the legislature's desire to discourage that trait? For example, even if the *Moreno* statute was aimed at disadvantaging hippies, persons harmed by it could nonetheless escape its force if they adopted a more conventional lifestyle. Is it really unconstitutional for the legislature to determine that one lifestyle is preferable to another and therefore more worthy of support? Would it be unconstitutional, for example, for the legislature to subsidize small family farms, but not large-scale industry, on the theory that farm life is "wholesome"?

Does this suggest that laws should be subject to special scrutiny when they disadvantage groups based on immutable traits, since the immutability eliminates the possibility that the legislature is attempting to change behavior? See Chapter 5, section C, infra. For example, although the *Moreno* statute could be justified as an attempt to discourage certain lifestyles, the zoning ordinance in *Cleburne* could not sensibly be defended as a measure designed to deter mental retardation.

On the other hand, the "immutability" of the classifying trait might be viewed as a kind of protection because it ensures that the legislature is not attempting to change behavior in an impermissible way. In *Ward*, for example, the very fact that foreign insurance companies could change their behavior by establishing an Alabama domicile might suggest that the legislature is pursuing an impermissible purpose. Moreover, aren't some traits relevant to legitimate governmental objectives even if a person is powerless to change them?

b. Is the equal protection clause violated when the legislature pursues a purpose that is not derived from the aggregation of the personal preferences of its constituents? Consider R. Dworkin, Taking Rights Seriously 275 (1978):

> Utilitarian arguments fix on the fact that a particular constraint on liberty will make more people happier, or satisfy more of their preference. [But] people's overall preference for one policy rather than another may be seen to include, on further analysis, both preferences that are *personal*, because they state a preference for the assignment of one set of goods or opportunities to him and preferences that are *external*, because they state a preference for one assignment of goods or opportunities to others. But a utilitarian argument that assigns critical weight to the external preferences of members of the community will not be egalitarian. [It] will not respect the right of everyone to be treated with equal concern and respect.
>
> Suppose, for example, that a number of individuals in the community hold racist rather than utilitarian political theories. They believe, not that each man is to count for one and no more than one in the distribution of goods, but rather that a black man is to count for less and a white man therefore to count for more than one. [If] this preference or pleasure is given the normal weight in a utilitarian calculation and blacks suffer accordingly, then their own assignment of goods and opportunities will depend, not simply on the competition among personal preferences that abstract statements of utilitarianism suggest, but precisely on the fact that they are thought less worthy of concern and respect than others are.

Does the equal protection clause prohibit a classification designed to vindicate "external preferences"? Consider Hart, Between Utility and Rights, 79 Colum. L. Rev. 828, 843 (1979):

> What is fundamentally wrong [with Dworkin's argument] is the suggested interpretation of denials of freedom as denials of equal concern or respect. This surely is mistaken. It is indeed least credible where the denial of a liberty is the upshot of a utilitarian decision procedure or majority vote in which the defeated minority's preferences or votes for the liberty were weighed equally with others and outweighed by numbers. Then the message need not be, as Dworkin interprets it, "You and your views are inferior, not entitled to equal consideration concern or respect," but "You and your supporters are too few. You, like everyone else, are counted as one but no more than one. Increase your numbers and then your views may win out."

c. Might it be argued that Dworkin's theory is precisely backwards — that the equal protection clause prohibits vindication of *personal* preferences and requires that the state purpose be based on *external* preferences? Consider Sunstein, Public Values, Private Interests, and the Equal Protection Clause, 1982 Sup. Ct. Rev. 127, 134:

> When the government operates to benefit A and burden B, it can do so only if it is prepared to justify its decision by reference to a public value. [Legislation] may not be merely the adjustment of private interests, or the transfer of wealth or opportunity from one person to another; it must be in some sense public-serving. [Nor] is political strength a legitimate justification. [The] institution that made the discrimination must be attempting to remedy a perceived public evil, and must not be responding only to the interests or preferences of some of its constituents.

Can the distinction between public and private interests, on which this theory rests, be maintained? What is the public interest if not the aggregation of the private preferences of individual participants in the political process? Consider Michelman, Political Markets and Community Self-Determination: Competing Judicial Models of Local Government Legitimacy, 53 Ind. L.J. 145, 148-150 (1977-1978):

> In the economic or public choice model, all substantive values or ends are regarded as strictly private and subjective. [Legislative] intercourse is not public spirited but self-interested. Legislators do not deliberate toward goals, they bicker towards terms. . . .
>
> The opposed, public-interest model depends at bottom on a belief in the reality — or at least the possibility — of public or objective values and ends for human action. In this public-interest model the legislature is regarded as a forum for identifying or defining, and acting towards those ends. The process is one of mutual search through joint deliberation, relying on the use of reason supposed to have persuasive force. [This] model, no doubt, is as sentimental as the public-choice model is un-lovely; but though public interest may in that sense be a less "realistic" way of looking at the world than public choice, I doubt that it is less real as a description of our actual way of experiencing and interpreting our political life; nor is it less real [as] a description of the way judges perceive that life.

3. *Low-level review based on "actual" purposes.* Even if one does not believe that the equal protection clause places substantive limits on the purposes that the state may pursue, rationality review might still be possible if defenders of a statute are permitted to justify it only in terms of the legislature's actual purpose, rather than in terms of any conceivable purpose. Is this limitation appropriate? Consider the following:

SCHWEIKER v. WILSON, 450 U.S. 221 (1981): Under the federal Supplemental Security Income (SSI) program, a subsistence allowance is provided to the needy aged, blind, and disabled. Although the Act excludes from coverage "[inmates] of a public institution," such inmates are provided a small amount of money (not exceeding $300 per year) for their personal needs if they are confined in a facility receiving payments under the federal Medicaid program. Appellees represented the class of individuals between ages 21 and 64 who resided in public mental institutions. Persons within this age range residing in such institutions are not eligible for Medicaid. Consequently, they do not receive the personal expense money. They claimed that Congress had inadvertently excluded them from coverage because of their political powerlessness and that the exclusion violated the equal protection component of the due process clause. The lower court agreed and granted appellees' motion for summary judgment. Justice Blackmun delivered the opinion of the Court:

"[The] pertinent inquiry is whether the classification employed in [the statute] advances legitimate legislative goals in a rational fashion. . . .

"We believe that the decision to incorporate the Medicaid eligibility standards into the SSI scheme must be considered Congress' deliberate, considered choice. . . .

"The legislative history shows that Congress was aware [of] the limitations in the Medicaid program that would restrict eligibility for the reduced SSI benefits; we decline to regard such deliberate action as the result of inadvertence or ignorance.

"Having found the adoption of the Medicaid standards intentional, we deem it logical to infer from Congress' deliberate action an intent to further the same subsidiary purpose that lies behind the Medicaid exclusion, which, as no party denies, was adopted because Congress believed the States to have a 'traditional' responsibility to care for those institutionalized in public mental institutions. The Secretary, emphasizing the then existing congressional desire to economize in the disbursement of federal funds, argues that the decision to limit distribution of the monthly stipend to inmates of public institutions who are receiving Medicaid funds 'is rationally related to the legitimate legislative desire to avoid spending federal resources on behalf of individuals whose care and treatment are being fully provided for by state and local government units' and 'may be said to implement a congressional policy choice to provide supplemental financial assistance for only those residents of public institutions who already receive significant federal support in the form of Medicaid coverage.' We cannot say that the belief that the States should continue to have the primary responsibility for making this small 'comfort money' allowance available to those residing in state-run institutions is an irrational basis for withholding from them federal general welfare funds. . . .

"We conclude that Congress did not violate appellees' rights to equal protection by denying them the supplementary benefit. The judgment of the District Court is reversed."

Justice Powell, with whom Justices Brennan, Marshall, and Stevens joined, dissented: "In my view, Congress thoughtlessly has applied a statutory classification developed to further legitimate goals of one welfare program to another welfare program serving entirely different needs. The result is an exclusion of wholly dependent people from minimal benefits, serving no government interest. This irrational classification violates the equal protection component of the Due Process Clause of the Fifth Amendment. . . .

"The legislative history of [the challenged statute] sheds no light on why Congress made the exclusion from reduced SSI benefits coextensive with the exclusion from Medicaid payments. The Secretary argues that Congress might rationally have concluded that the States have the primary responsibility for making payments of comfort allowances to appellees, because they already bear the responsibility for paying for their treatment. . . .

"The deference to which legislative accommodations of conflicting interests is entitled rests in part upon the principle that the political process of our majoritarian democracy responds to the wishes of the people. Accordingly, an important touchstone for equal protection review of statutes is how readily a policy can be discerned which the legislature intended to serve. When a legitimate purpose for a statute appears in the legislative history or is implicit in the statutory scheme itself, a court has some assurance that the legislature has made a conscious policy choice. Our democratic system requires that legislation intended to serve a discernible purpose receive the most respectful deference. Yet, the question of whether a statutory classification discriminates arbitrarily cannot be divorced from whether it was enacted to serve an identifiable purpose. When a legislative purpose can be suggested only by the ingenuity of a government lawyer litigating the constitutionality of a statute, a reviewing court may be presented not so much with a legislative policy choice as its absence.

"In my view, the Court should receive with some skepticism post hoc hypotheses about legislative purpose, unsupported by the legislative history. When no indication of legislative purpose appears other than the current position of the Secretary, the Court should require that the classification bear a 'fair and substantial relation' to the asserted purpose. See F. S. Royster Guano Co. v. Virginia, 253 U.S. 412, 415 (1920). This marginally more demanding scrutiny indirectly would test the plausibility of the tendered purpose, and preserve equal protection review as something more than 'a mere tautological recognition of the fact that Congress did what it intended to do.' [*Fritz* (Stevens, J., concurring in the judgment.)]

"Neither the structure of [the statute] nor its legislative history identifies or even suggests any policy plausibly intended to be served by denying appellees the small SSI allowance. . . .

"I conclude that Congress had no rational reason for refusing to pay a comfort allowance to appellees while paying it to numerous otherwise identically situated disabled indigents. This unexplained difference in treatment must have been a legislative oversight. I therefore dissent."

Note: "Actual Purpose" Review

1. *Some preliminary questions.* Does it make sense to invalidate a law that advances a legitimate state purpose simply because the legislators were not think-ing of that purpose when they enacted it? Once such a law is struck down, could the legislature reenact it if it thinks of that purpose while doing so? What if the legislature enacted the law for irrational reasons but fails to repeal it because it turns out to advance important goals? On the other hand, why should deference to the legislature require upholding a statute that advances a policy that the legislature had no interest in pursuing? Even if a law turns out to advance legiti-mate purposes, we do not know that it would have been enacted if the legislature had not believed that it advanced other goals that, in fact, it does not achieve.

2. *The state of the law.* Neither the Court nor individual justices have been altogether consistent on the issue of review based on actual purpose. Justice Rehnquist's opinion for the Court in *Fritz* flatly rejects the notion that the Court should investigate the actual purpose motivating the legislature. Yet Justice Rehnquist has also insisted that the Court should not strictly scrutinize a facially neutral statute that has the effect of disadvantaging a racial minority unless the challenger can prove that the legislature intended to produce this effect. See, e.g., Jefferson v. Hackney, 406 U.S. 535 (1972) (Rehnquist, J.). See generally Chapter 5, section C2, infra. Can these positions be reconciled?

Recall Minnesota v. Clover Leaf Creamery Co., supra page 506, decided the same term as *Fritz*. In his opinion for the Court, Justice Brennan (the author of the *Fritz* dissent) makes the following observations regarding review based on actual purpose:

> In equal protection analysis, the Court will assume that the objectives articulated by the legislature are actual purposes of the statute, unless an examination of the circumstances forces us to conclude that they "could not have been the goal of the legislation." [Weinberger v. Wiesenfeld, 420 U.S. 636, 648 n.16 (1975)]. Here, review of the legislative history supports the Minnesota Supreme Court's conclusion that the principal purposes of the Act were to promote conservation and ease solid waste disposal problems.

Does this formulation treat as "constitutionally irrelevant" the reasons that "in fact underlay the legislative decision" as *Fritz* requires? (Note that Justice Rehnquist, the author of *Fritz*, did not participate in *Clover Leaf Creamery*.)

For an extended debate on the present state of the law concerning actual purpose review, compare the concurring and dissenting opinions of Justices Brennan and Rehnquist in Kassel v. Consolidated Freightways Corp., Chapter 3, section C, supra.

3. *The epistemological problem.* Does the difficulty in discovering the legislature's "actual purpose" counsel against utilizing this standard of review? Consider Kassel v. Consolidated Freightways Corp., supra (Rehnquist, J., dissenting):

> [Actual purpose review] assumes that individual legislators are motivated by one discernible "actual" purpose, and ignores the fact that different legislators may vote for a single piece of legislation for widely different reasons. [How], for example, would a court adhering to [actual purpose review] approach a statute, the legislative history of which indicated that 10 votes were based on [permissible considerations], 10 votes were based on [impermissible considerations] and the statute passed by a vote of 40-20?

Justice Rehnquist has also pointed out that under actual purpose review, "litigants who wish to succeed in invalidating a law [must] have a certain schizophrenia if they are to be successful in their advocacy: They must first convince this Court that the legislature had a particular purpose in mind in enacting the law, and then convince it that the law was not at all suited to the accomplishment of that purpose." Trimble v. Gordon, 430 U.S. 762, 783 (1977) (dissenting opinion).

Are these problems insurmountable? Need an advocate be "schizophrenic" in a case where the statute itself or its legislative history makes plain that the legislature intended to accomplish results that fail to validate the statute? Is that the point of Justice Brennan's observation in *Clover Leaf Creamery* that a court should not entertain a hypothetical purpose when "an examination of the circumstances forces us to conclude that [it] 'could not have been the goal of the legislation' "? Note, however, that in *Clover Leaf Creamery* itself, the state trial court, which invalidated the law, relied upon legislative history indicating that its "actual basis" was to promote the economic interests of the local dairy and pulpwood industries, rather than to serve the environmental interests the state's lawyers advanced when the law was challenged. Justice Brennan disposed of this legislative history by observing that "The [evidence] is easily understood, in context, as an economic defense of an Act genuinely proposed for environmental reasons. We will not invalidate a state statute under the Equal Protection Clause merely because some legislators sought to obtain votes for the measure on the basis of its beneficial side effects on state industry."

Is this formulation consistent with the kind of actual purpose review the Court in *Clover Leaf Creamery* purported to apply? If a court cannot deduce the statute's purpose from what it does, and it is also precluded from deducing its purpose from what its supporters say it does, how *is* purpose to be discovered?

4. *Requirement of statement of purpose.* Do these epistemological difficulties suggest that the Court should require or encourage the legislature to state explicitly the purposes it wishes a statute to achieve? Lawyers for the state would then be limited to these purposes in defending the constitutionality of the statute. Is this the point of Justice Powell's dissent in *Schweiker*? Justice Powell would require "marginally more demanding scrutiny" of a statute when the only indication of purpose is "the current position of [an executive officer]." Presumably this heightened scrutiny is designed to provide incentives for the legislature to state its

purpose explicitly. Might not the result of this requirement be no more than "boilerplate" statements of worthwhile purposes that failed to state the legislature's true objectives? Doesn't Justice Powell's position turn actual purpose review on its head by according "the most respectful deference" in precisely those cases where the legislative purpose is clear, and rigorous judicial review is therefore possible?

Compare Justice Powell's views in *Schweiker* with Justice Brennan's *Fritz* dissent. Justice Brennan argued that "Where Congress has expressly stated the purpose of a piece of legislation, but where the challenged classification is either irrelevant to or counter to that purpose, we must view any post hoc justifications proffered by Government attorneys with skepticism." Doesn't this suggest that legislative classifications may be subject to *more* rigorous review when the legislature articulates its purpose? Wouldn't such enhanced review discourage the legislators from candidly stating why they enacted the statute?

In any event, is there a legitimate constitutional basis for the Court skewing review in an effort to force legislative articulation of purpose? Consider J. Ely, Democracy and Distrust 130-131 (1980):

> the common case of nonaccountability involves not a situation where the legislature has drawn a distinction whose range of informing purposes won't be readily apparent, but rather a situation where the legislature (in large measure precisely in order to escape accountability) has refused to draw the legally operative distinctions, leaving that chore to others who are not politically accountable. Perhaps, therefore, the most effective way to get our representatives to be clearer about what they are up to in their legislation is to get them to legislate.

C. EQUAL PROTECTION METHODOLOGY: HEIGHTENED SCRUTINY AND THE PROBLEM OF RACE

This section, and those that follow it, explore the circumstances under which the Court has subjected classifications to some form of review more rigorous than the "rational relationship" test. When is such review appropriate? What must be shown to satisfy the more demanding standard?

The best established case for heightened review is for classifications based on race. This section explores four different varieties of classifications arguably discriminating on the basis of race and the Court's response to each.

1. Race-Specific Classifications That Expressly Disadvantage Racial Minorities

Strauder v. West Virginia
100 U.S. (10 Otto) 303 (1879)

MR. JUSTICE STRONG delivered the opinion of the court.

[Strauder, a black man, was convicted of murder before an all-white jury in a West Virginia trial court. A West Virginia statute limited jury service to "white male persons who are twenty-one years of age and who are citizens of this State."

Strauder claimed that his conviction by a jury chosen pursuant to this provision violated the fourteenth amendment.]

[The] controlling [question is] whether by the Constitution and laws of the United States, every citizen of the United States has a right to a trial of an indictment against him by a jury selected and impanelled without discrimination against his race or color, because of race or color. . . .

It is to be observed that the [question] is not whether a colored man, when an indictment has been preferred against him, has a right to a grand or a petit jury composed in whole or in part of persons of his own race or color, but it is whether, in the composition or selection of jurors by whom he is to be indicted or tried, all persons of his race or color may be excluded by law, solely because of their race or color, so that by no possibility can any colored man sit upon the jury. . . .

[The fourteenth amendment] is one of a series of constitutional provisions having a common purpose; namely, securing to a race recently emancipated, a race that through many generations had been held in slavery, all the civil rights that the superior race enjoy. The true spirit and meaning of the amendments, as we said in the Slaughter-House Cases, cannot be understood without keeping in view the history of the times when they were adopted, and the general objects they plainly sought to accomplish. At the time when they were incorporated into the Constitution, it required little knowledge of human nature to anticipate that those who had long been regarded as an inferior and subject race would, when suddenly raised to the rank of citizenship, be looked upon with jealousy and positive dislike, and that State laws might be enacted or enforced to perpetuate the distinctions that had before existed. Discriminations against them had been habitual. It was well known that in some States laws making such discriminations then existed, and others might well be expected. The colored race, as a race, was abject and ignorant, and in that condition was unfitted to command the respect of those who had superior intelligence. Their training had left them mere children, and as such they needed the protection which a wise government extends to those who are unable to protect themselves. They especially needed protection against unfriendly action in the States where they were resident. It was in view of these considerations the Fourteenth Amendment was framed and adopted. It was designed to assure to the colored race the enjoyment of all the civil rights that under the law are enjoyed by white persons, and to give to that race the protection of the general government, in that enjoyment, whenever it should be denied by the States. It not only gave citizenship and the privileges of citizenship to persons of color, but it denied to any State the power to withhold from them the equal protection of the laws, and authorized Congress to enforce its provisions by appropriate legislation. . . .

[What] is this but declaring that the law in the States shall be the same for the black as for the white; that all persons, whether colored or white, shall stand equal before the laws of the States, and, in regard to the colored race, for whose protection the amendment was primarily designed, that no discrimination shall be made against them by law because of their color? The words of the amendment, it is true, are prohibitory, but they contain a necessary implication of a positive immunity, or right, most valuable to the colored race, — the right to exemption from unfriendly legislation against them distinctively as colored, — exemption from legal discriminations, implying inferiority in civil society, lessening the security of their enjoyment of the rights which others enjoy, and discriminations which are steps towards reducing them to the condition of a subject race.

That the West Virginia statute respecting juries — the statute that controlled the selection of the grand and petit jury in the case of the plaintiff in error — is such a discrimination ought not to be doubted. [The] very fact that colored people are singled out and expressly denied by a statute all right to participate in the administration of the law, as jurors, because of their color, though they are citizens, and may be in other respects fully qualified, is practically a brand upon them, affixed by the law, an assertion of their inferiority, and a stimulant to that race prejudice which is an impediment to securing to individuals of the race that equal justice which the law aims to secure to all others.

The right to a trial by jury is guaranteed to every citizen of West Virginia by the Constitution of that State, and the constitution of juries is a very essential part of the protection such a mode of trial is intended to secure. The very idea of a jury is a body of men composed of the peers or equals of the person whose rights it is selected or summoned to determine; that is, of his neighbors, fellows, associates, persons having the same legal status in society as that which he holds. . . .

[It] is well known that prejudices often exist against particular classes in the community, which sway the judgment of jurors, and which, therefore, operate in some cases to deny to persons of those classes the full enjoyment of that protection which others enjoy. . . .

In view of these considerations, it is hard to see why the statute of West Virginia should not be regarded as discriminating against a colored man when he is put upon trial for an alleged criminal offence against the State. It is not easy to comprehend how it can be said that while every white man is entitled to a trial by a jury selected from persons of his own race or color, or, rather, selected without discrimination against his color, and a negro is not, the latter is equally protected by the law with the former. Is not protection of life and liberty against race or color prejudice, a right, a legal right, under the constitutional amendment? And how can it be maintained that compelling a colored man to submit to a trial for his life by a jury drawn from a panel from which the State has expressly excluded every man of his race, because of color alone, however well qualified in other respects, is not a denial to him of equal legal protection?

We do not say that within the limits from which it is not excluded by the amendment a State may not prescribe the qualifications of its jurors, and in so doing make discriminations. It may confine the selection to males, to freeholders, to citizens, to persons within certain ages, or to persons having educational qualifications. We do not believe the Fourteenth Amendment was ever intended to prohibit this. Looking at its history, it is clear it had no such purpose. Its aim was against discrimination because of race or color. . . .

The judgment of the Supreme Court of West Virginia will be reversed, and the case remitted with instructions to reverse the judgment of the Circuit Court of Ohio county; and it is so ordered.

[JUSTICE FIELD and JUSTICE CLIFFORD dissented.]

Korematsu v. United States

323 U.S. 214 (1944)

MR. JUSTICE BLACK delivered the opinion of the Court.

[On February 19, 1942, some two months after the United States declared war against Japan, the President issued Executive Order 9066, which authorized military commanders to "prescribe military areas [from] which any or all persons may be excluded, and with respect to which, the right of any person to enter, remain in, or leave shall be subject to whatever restrictions [the Military] Commander may impose in his discretion." On March 21, 1942, Congress enacted legislation making it a crime to violate an order issued by a military commander pursuant to this authority. Three days later, the military commander of the western defense command ordered imposition of a curfew on all persons of Japanese ancestry living on the West Coast. The Supreme Court upheld the constitutionality of this order in Hirabayashi v. United States, 320 U.S. 81 (1943).

On May 3, 1942, the same military commander issued one of a series of exclusion orders, requiring persons of Japanese descent, whether or not they were United States citizens, to leave their homes on the West Coast. Persons so ordered were required to report to "Assembly Centers." While some detainees were released from these centers on condition that they remain outside the prohibited zone, others were shipped to "Relocation Centers," which they were prohibited from leaving without permission of the military commander.

Korematsu, a U.S. citizen of unchallenged loyalty but of Japanese descent, was tried and convicted for remaining in his home contrary to the exclusion order.]

It should be noted, to begin with, that all legal restrictions which curtail the civil rights of a single racial group are immediately suspect. That is not to say that all such restrictions are unconstitutional. It is to say that courts must subject them to the most rigid scrutiny. Pressing public necessity may sometimes justify the existence of such restrictions; racial antagonism never can. . . .

In the light of the principles we announced in the *Hirabayashi* case, we are unable to conclude that it was beyond the war power of Congress and the Executive to exclude those of Japanese ancestry from the West Coast war area at the time they did. True, exclusion from the area in which one's home is located is a far greater deprivation than constant confinement to the home from 8 P.M. to 6 A.M. Nothing short of apprehension by the proper military authorities of the gravest imminent danger to the public safety can constitutionally justify either. But exclusion from a threatened area, no less than curfew, has a definite and close relationship to the prevention of espionage and sabotage. The military authorities, charged with the primary responsibility of defending our shores, concluded that curfew provided inadequate protection and ordered exclusion. . . .

Here, as in the *Hirabayashi* case,

> . . . we cannot reject as unfounded the judgment of the military authorities and of Congress that there were disloyal members of that population, whose number and strength could not be precisely and quickly ascertained. We cannot say that the war-making branches of the Government did not have ground for believing that in a critical hour such persons could not readily be isolated and separately dealt with, and constituted a menace to the national defense and safety, which demanded that prompt and adequate measures be taken to guard against it.

Like curfew, exclusion of those of Japanese origin was deemed necessary because of the presence of an unascertained number of disloyal members of the group, most of whom we have no doubt were loyal to this country. It was because we could not reject the finding of the military authorities that it was impossible to bring about an immediate segregation of the disloyal from the loyal that we sustained the validity of the curfew order as applying to the whole group. In the instant case, temporary exclusion of the entire group was rested by the military on the same ground. The judgment that exclusion of the whole group was for the same reason a military imperative answers the contention that the exclusion was in the nature of group punishment based on antagonism to those of Japanese origin. That there were members of the group who retained loyalties to Japan has been confirmed by investigations made subsequent to the exclusion. Approximately five thousand American citizens of Japanese ancestry refused to swear unqualified allegiance to the United States and to renounce allegiance to the Japanese Emperor, and several thousand evacuees requested repatriation to Japan.

We uphold the exclusion order as of the time it was made and when the petitioner violated it. [In] doing so, we are not unmindful of the hardships imposed by it upon a large group of American citizens. But hardships are part of war, and war is an aggregation of hardships. All citizens alike, both in and out of uniform, feel the impact of war in greater or lesser measure. Citizenship has its responsibilities as well as its privileges, and in time of war the burden is always heavier. Compulsory exclusion of large groups of citizens from their homes, except under circumstances of direst emergency and peril, is inconsistent with our basic governmental institutions. But when under conditions of modern warfare our shores are threatened by hostile forces, the power to protect must be commensurate with the threatened danger. . . .

It is said that we are dealing here with the case of imprisonment of a citizen in a concentration camp solely because of his ancestry, without evidence or inquiry concerning his loyalty and good disposition towards the United States. Our task would be simple, our duty clear, were this a case involving the imprisonment of a loyal citizen in a concentration camp because of racial prejudice. Regardless of the true nature of the assembly and relocation centers — and we deem it unjustifiable to call them concentration camps with all the ugly connotations that term implies — we are dealing specifically with nothing but an exclusion order. To cast this case into outlines of racial prejudice, without reference to the real military dangers which were presented, merely confuses the issue. Korematsu was not excluded from the Military Area because of hostility to him or his race. He *was* excluded because we are at war with the Japanese Empire, because the properly constituted military authorities feared an invasion of our West Coast and felt constrained to take proper security measures, because they decided that the military urgency of the situation demanded that all citizens of Japanese ancestry be segregated from the West Coast temporarily, and finally, because Congress, reposing its confidence in this time of war in our military leaders — as inevitably it must — determined that they should have the power to do just this. There was evidence of disloyalty on the part of some, the military authorities considered that the need for action was great, and time was short. We cannot — by availing ourselves of the calm perspective of hindsight — now say that at that time these actions were unjustified.

Affirmed.

[A concurring opinion by Justice Frankfurter and a dissenting opinion by Justice Roberts have been omitted.]

MR. JUSTICE MURPHY, dissenting.

This exclusion of "all persons of Japanese ancestry, both alien and non-alien," from the Pacific Coast area on a plea of military necessity in the absence of martial law ought not to be approved. Such exclusion goes over "the very brink of constitutional power" and falls into the ugly abyss of racism.

In dealing with matters relating to the prosecution and progress of a war, we must accord great respect and consideration to the judgments of the military authorities who are on the scene and who have full knowledge of the military facts. The scope of their discretion must, as a matter of necessity and common sense, be wide. And their judgments ought not to be overruled lightly by those whose training and duties ill-equip them to deal intelligently with matters so vital to the physical security of the nation.

At the same time, however, it is essential that there be definite limits to military discretion, especially where martial law has not been declared. Individuals must not be left impoverished of their constitutional rights on a plea of military necessity that has neither substance nor support. Thus, like other claims conflicting with the asserted constitutional rights of the individual, the military claim must subject itself to the judicial process of having its reasonableness determined and its conflicts with other interests reconciled. . . .

It must be conceded that the military and naval situation in the spring of 1942 was such as to generate a very real fear of invasion of the Pacific Coast, accompanied by fears of sabotage and espionage in that area. The military command was therefore justified in adopting all reasonable means necessary to combat these dangers. In adjudging the military action taken in light of the then apparent dangers, we must not erect too high or too meticulous standards; it is necessary only that the action have some reasonable relation to the removal of the dangers of invasion, sabotage and espionage. But the exclusion, either temporarily or permanently, of all persons with Japanese blood in their veins has no such reasonable relation. And that relation is lacking because the exclusion order necessarily must rely for its reasonableness upon the assumption that *all* persons of Japanese ancestry may have a dangerous tendency to commit sabotage and espionage and to aid our Japanese enemy in other ways. It is difficult to believe that reason, logic or experience could be marshalled in support of such an assumption. . . .

The main reasons relied upon by those responsible for the forced evacuation, therefore, do not prove a reasonable relation between the group characteristics of Japanese Americans and the dangers of invasion, sabotage and espionage. The reasons appear, instead, to be largely an accumulation of much of the misinformation, half-truths and insinuations that for years have been directed against Japanese Americans by people with racial and economic prejudices — the same people who have been among the foremost advocates of the evacuation. A military judgment based upon such racial and sociological considerations is not entitled to the great weight ordinarily given the judgments based upon strictly military considerations. Especially is this so when every charge relative to race, religion, culture, geographical location, and legal and economic status has been substantially discredited by independent studies made by experts in these matters. . . .

[No] one denies, of course, that there were some disloyal persons of Japanese descent on the Pacific Coast who did all in their power to aid their ancestral land. Similar disloyal activities have been engaged in by many persons of German, Italian and even more pioneer stock in our country. But to infer that examples of individual disloyalty prove group disloyalty and justify discriminatory action against the entire group is to deny that under our system of law individual guilt is the sole basis for deprivation of rights. . . .

MR. JUSTICE JACKSON, dissenting. . . .

It would be impracticable and dangerous idealism to expect or insist that each specific military command in an area of probable operations will conform to conventional tests of constitutionality. When an area is so beset that it must be put under military control at all, the paramount consideration is that its measures be successful, rather than legal. . . .

But if we cannot confine military expedients by the Constitution, neither would I distort the Constitution to approve all that the military may deem expedient. That is what the Court appears to be doing, whether consciously or not. . . .

The limitation[s] under which courts always will labor in examining the necessity for a military order are illustrated by this case. How does the Court know that these orders have a reasonable basis in necessity? No evidence whatever on that subject has been taken by this or any other court. . . .

Much is said of the danger to liberty from the Army program for deporting and detaining these citizens of Japanese extraction. But a judicial construction of the due process clause that will sustain this order is a far more subtle blow to liberty than the promulgation of the order itself. A military order, however unconstitutional, is not apt to last longer than the military emergency. Even during that period a succeeding commander may revoke it all. But once a judicial opinion rationalizes such an order to show that it conforms to the Constitution, or rather rationalizes the Constitution to show that the Constitution sanctions such an order, the Court for all time has validated the principle of racial discrimination in criminal procedure and of transplanting American citizens. The principle then lies about like a loaded weapon ready for the hand of any authority that can bring forward a plausible claim of an urgent need. Every repetition imbeds that principle more deeply in our law and thinking and expands it to new purposes. . . .

I should hold that a civil court cannot be made to enforce an order which violates constitutional limitations even if it is a reasonable exercise of military authority. The courts can exercise only the judicial power, can apply only law, and must abide by the Constitution, or they cease to be civil courts and become instruments of military policy.

Of course the existence of a military power resting on force, so vagrant, so centralized, so necessarily heedless of the individual, is an inherent threat to liberty. But I would not lead people to rely on this Court for a review that seems to me wholly delusive. The military reasonableness of these orders can only be determined by military superiors. If the people ever let command of the war power fall into irresponsible and unscrupulous hands, the courts wield no power equal to its restraint. The chief restraint upon those who command the physical forces of the country, in the future as in the past, must be their responsibility to the political judgments of their contemporaries and to the moral judgments of history.

My duties as a justice as I see them do not require me to make a military judgment as to whether General DeWitt's evacuation and detention program was a reasonable military necessity. I do not suggest that the courts should have attempted to interfere with the Army in carrying out its task. But I do not think they may be asked to execute a military expedient that has no place in law under the Constitution. I would reverse the judgment and discharge the prisoner.

Note: Justifications for Special Scrutiny of Racial Classifications

Korematsu is frequently said to mark the last occasion on which the Supreme Court has upheld a race-specific statute disadvantaging a racial minority. But cf. Swain v. Alabama, 380 U.S. 202 (1965) (refusal to invalidate prosecutorial use of peremptory challenges to remove blacks from juries); Morton v. Mancari, 417 U.S. 535, 555 (1974) (special treatment of Indians will be upheld where rationally tied to Congress's unique obligation toward Indians). Moreover, even though its decision came in the midst of a military emergency, the Court's willingness to uphold the classification in *Korematsu* has been widely and severely criticized. See, e.g., R. Daniels, Concentration Camps: North America, Japanese in the United States and Canada during World War II (rev. ed. 1981); J. ten Broek, E. Barnhart & F. Matson, Prejudice, War and the Constitution (1954). What explains this special aversion to statutes that distinguish on the basis of race? Consider the following arguments:

1. *Intent of the framers.* The Court in *Strauder* argues that the framers of the equal protection clause meant to provide special protection for blacks against "unfriendly action in the States where they were resident." Even if this is a correct account of the framers' intent, does it explain the special scrutiny accorded statutes directed against Japanese or other racial or ethnic minorities? Note that the words of the fourteenth amendment provide no support for special treatment of race cases. Moreover, it is far from clear that the Reconstruction Congress meant to invalidate all statutory classifications based on race. Consider, R. Berger, Government by Judiciary 10, 15 (1977):

> The key to an understanding of the Fourteenth Amendment is that the North was shot through with Negrophobia, that the Republicans, except for a minority of extremists, were swayed by the racism that gripped their constituents rather than by abolitionist ideology. [While] most men were united in a desire to protect the freedmen from outrage and oppression in the South by prohibiting discrimination with respect to "fundamental rights," without which freedom was illusory, to go beyond this with a campaign for political and social equality was, as Senator James R. Doolittle of Wisconsin confessed, "frightening" to the Republicans who "represented States containing the despised and feared negroes."

See also Perry, Modern Equal Protection: A Conceptualization and Appraisal, 79 Colum. L. Rev. 1023, 1027-1028 (1979) (framers meant to outlaw racial discrimination only with respect to physical security, freedom of movement, and capacity to contract and own property). Cf. Frank & Munro, The Original Understanding of "Equal Protection of the Laws," 1972 Wash. U. L.Q. 421, 442-443, 450 ("insiders" who drafted amendment split on whether all distinctions based on race banned; many supporters of amendment thought it established "civil equality" but not "social equality.")

2. *The antidiscrimination principle.* Might it be argued that a principle disfavoring racial classifications is warranted under the fourteenth amendment, even

if not required by the specific intent of the framers? Consider, e.g., Brest, Foreword: In Defense of the Antidiscrimination Principle, 90 Harv. L. Rev. 1, 5-6 (1976):

> The antidiscrimination principle rests on fundamental moral values that are widely shared in our society. [The] text and history of the [equal protection] clause are vague and ambiguous and cannot, in any event, infuse the antidiscrimination principle with moral force or justify its extension to novel circumstances and new beneficiaries. Therefore, the argument [against racial classifications] does not ultimately turn on authority, but on whether it comports with the reader's reflective understanding of the antidiscrimination principle.

But if the antidiscrimination principle really "rests on fundamental moral values widely shared in our society," why is special judicial scrutiny required when it is violated? Doesn't the very fact that the principle is widely shared and deeply engrained provide a built-in guarantee that when it is overridden, there is a very good reason for doing so? On the other hand, if the principle is not widely shared, and if it is not required by the text or history of the Constitution, what justification is there for judicial enforcement of it?

Even if we ignore the problem of linking it to the Constitution, does the antidiscrimination principle state a sound rule of decision? To be sure, racial criteria may often be irrational. But the fact that such criteria would often be invalidated under traditional low-level review hardly explains why enhanced scrutiny is required in cases where use of race would pass a rational basis test. If one individual is denied a benefit on racial grounds, and another denied precisely the same benefit on some other grounds, are the costs incurred by one different from those incurred by the other? In *Strauder*, for example, the Court makes clear that if the defendant had been convicted by an all-white jury chosen by lot from a fair cross-section of the community, his conviction would have been affirmed. But if the actual composition of the jury is the same, why should it matter whether this result is achieved by luck or by design?

3. *Stigma.* The Court in *Strauder* thought the exclusion of blacks from juries was "practically a brand upon them" and "an assertion of inferiority." Does infliction of this additional injury justify enhanced review? Consider Brest, supra, at 10:

> Generalizations based on immutable personal traits such as race [are] especially frustrating because we can do nothing to escape their operation. These generalizations are still more pernicious, for they are often premised on the supposed correlation between the inherited characteristic and the undesirable voluntary behavior of those who possess the characteristic. [Because] the behavior is voluntary, and hence the proper object of moral condemnation, individuals as to whom the generalization is inaccurate may justifiably feel that the decisionmaker has passed moral judgment on them.

If this psychic injury is caused by the mere knowledge of the victim that the legislature is making an adverse moral judgment on him, how is that injury remedied by invalidating the law? Why, in any event, should we be more concerned with this sort of psychic injury than with the very real, material injuries the law regularly inflicts on the few for the benefit of the many?

4. *Representation reinforcement theories.* Can special review of racial classifications be justified on the ground that defects in the political process make it

especially likely that such classifications will be based on "hostility" or inaccurate stereotypes?

In United States v. Carolene Products, 304 U.S. 144 (1938), Chapter 6, section D, infra, the Court upheld under rational basis review a federal statute prohibiting interstate shipment of filled milk. Today, the case is less significant for its holding than for its famous footnote 4, in which Justice Stone, writing for the Court, intimated that a more stringent standard of review might apply to statutes "directed at particular religious or national or racial minorities." Justice Stone argued that stricter review might be appropriate in such cases because "prejudice against discrete and insular minorities may be a special condition, which tends seriously to curtail the operation of those political processes ordinarily to be relied upon to protect minorities." It followed that "correspondingly more searching judicial inquiry" was appropriate.

The *Carolene Products* footnote has been called "the most celebrated footnote in constitutional law." Powell, *Carolene Products* Revisited, 82 Colum. L. Rev. 1087, 1087 (1982). See also Fiss, The Supreme Court, 1978 Term — Foreword: The Forms of Justice, 93 Harv. L. Rev. 1, 6 (1979) (*Carolene Products* footnote "[the] great and modern charter for ordering the relations between judges and other agencies of government.") It has been the subject of extensive scholarly commentary. See, e.g., Ackerman, Beyond *Carolene Products*, 98 Harv. L. Rev. 713 (1985); Ball, Judicial Protection of Powerless Minorities, 59 Iowa L. Rev. 1059 (1974); Cover, The Origins of Judicial Activism in the Protection of Minorities, 91 Yale L.J. 1287 (1982). For an interesting exposition of the history of the footnote, see Lusky, Footnote Redux: A *Carolene Products* Reminiscence, 82 Colum. L. Rev. 1093 (1982).

Does the *Carolene Products* footnote provide a principled basis for judicial intervention to protect minorities? Why does the "discreteness" and "insularity" of these minorities interfere with their ability to protect themselves in the political process? Consider Ackerman, supra, at 728:

> In fact, for all our *Carolene* talk about the powerlessness of insular groups, we are perfectly aware of the enormous power such voting blocs have in American politics. The story of the protective tarriff is [the] classic illustration of insularity's power in American history. Over the past half-century, we have been treated to an enormous number of welfare-state variations on the theme of insularity by the farm bloc, the steel lobby, the auto lobby, and others too numerous to mention. In this standard scenario of pluralistic politics, it is precisely the diffuse character of the majority forced to pay the bill for tariffs, agricultural subsidies, and the like, that allows strategically located Congressmen to deliver the goods to their well-organized constituents. Given these familiar stories, it is really quite remarkable to hear lawyers profess concern that insular interests have too little influence in Congress.

Is it the "prejudice" directed against discrete and insular minorities that justifies judicial intervention? The concept of prejudice lies at the heart of the most comprehensive and careful modern elaboration of the theory behind footnote 4 — J. Ely, Democracy and Distrust (1980). Ely begins with the premise that "the Constitution [cannot] coherently be interpreted as outlining some 'appropriate' distributional pattern against which actual allocations of hurts and benefits can be traced to see if they are constitutional. The constitutionality of most distributions thus cannot be determined simply by looking to see who ended up with what, but rather can be approached intelligibly only by attending to the process that brought about the distribution in question." Generally, the Constitution prescribes a process of representative democracy to allocate costs and benefits. This process includes "the sort of pluralist wheeling and dealing by which the various minorities that make up our society typically interact to protect their interests."

This process sometimes breaks down. Prejudice directed at certain minorities may obstruct their ability to form coalitions, so that "a system of 'mutual defense pacts' will prove recurrently unavailing." Prejudice is relevant in two respects. First, "it is a lens that distorts reality. We are a nation of minorities and our system thus depends on the ability and willingness of various groups to apprehend those overlapping interests that can bind them into a majority on a given issue; prejudice blinds us to overlapping interests that in fact exist." Second,

> If the doctrine of suspect classifications is a roundabout way of uncovering official attempts to inflict inequality for its own sake — to treat a group worse not in the service of some overriding social goal but largely for the sake of disadvantaging its members — it would seem to follow that one set of classifications we should treat as suspicious are those that disadvantage groups we know to be objects of widespread villification, groups we know others (specifically those who control the legislative process) might wish to injure.

In order to identify those generalizations that are the product of prejudice, Ely would investigate "where [they] come from — who came up with [them] and whether [they serve] their interests."

> Thus, generalizations to the effect, say, that whites in general are smarter or more industrious than blacks, men more stable emotionally than women, or native-born Americans more patriotic than Americans born elsewhere, are likely to go down pretty easily — and in fact we know they have — with groups whose demography is that of the typical American legislature. Few will suppose there aren't counterexamples, but the overall validity of such a generalization is likely to be quite readily accepted. By seizing upon the positive myths about the groups to which they belong and the negative myths about those to which they don't, or for that matter the realities respecting some or most members of the two classes, legislators, like the rest of us, are likely to assume too readily that not many of "them" will be unfairly deprived, nor many of "us" unfairly benefited by a classification of this type. Generalizations of the opposite sort, which attribute superiority to a group to which most legislators do not belong — say, that blacks are better basketball players or that Jews are better students — are a different matter.

Is this an adequate defense of enhanced judicial review of racial classifications? Do you agree that the equal protection clause speaks only to the process by which decisions are made, and not to the results of those decisions? Consider Fiss, Groups and the Equal Protection Clause, 5 J. Phil. & Pub. Affairs 107, 133 (1976):

> [Imagine] it is the 1940s, the state electorate is predominantly white and the state legislature directs the law school to adopt a preferential admission policy in favor of whites. Assume also that this policy is justified on the ground that whites are better prepared academically (given the dual school system) and that the state wishes to have the most brilliant persons as members of the bar. Color is used because of

administrative convenience. Under the [Ely] analysis, there is reason to be suspicious about this explanation of this use of race. [But] it would seem to me that even if that suspicion were refuted, even if it were (somehow) demonstrated that the argument about administrative convenience were sincere and well-founded and in some sense accurate, the result would still be unacceptable under the Equal Protection Clause.

Does Ely's analysis adequately distinguish between groups that are unfairly treated in the political process and groups that are simply outvoted? Consider Powell, *Carolene Products* Revisited, supra, at 1090:

> [In] one sense, any group that loses a legislative battle can be regarded as both "discrete" and "insular." It is discrete because it supported or opposed legislation not supported or opposed by the majority. It is insular because it was unable to form coalitions with other groups that would have enabled it to achieve its desired ends through the political process. On this view the drug cult — or for that matter public utilities — could be considered discrete and insular.

Ely would limit judicial intervention to cases where a group consistently loses because of inaccurate generalizations about its members. But the very question at issue is when courts should substitute their judgment for that of legislatures. Can that question be answered by assuming ab initio the right of the courts to determine that a legislative generalization is inaccurate? Consider Ackerman, supra, at 739:

> It is simply self-congratulatory to suppose that members of our own persuasion have reached their convictions in a deeply reflective way, whereas those espousing opinions we hate are superficial. [Given] the complexity of the human comedy, a judge is bound on a fool's errand if he imagines that the good guys and bad guys of American politics can be neatly classified according to the seriousness with which they have considered opposing points of view. Processual prejudice is a pervasive problem in the American political system.

Even if a defect in the political process does lead to unfair treatment of some groups, does it follow that substituting a judicial for a legislative judgment would improve matters? Is there good reason to believe that excluded groups are better represented in the judiciary, or that judges are less susceptible to prejudiced, inaccurate generalizations about such groups?

5. *Group rights.* The arguments discussed above are premised on the assumption that the equal protection clause protects individuals from being unfairly pigeonholed in disfavored groups. Might special review of racial classifications be defended on the alternative theory that the equal protection clause protects the rights of particular social groups as such? Consider Fiss, supra, at 150-151:

> We must [realize that blacks] are a very special type of social group. [They] are very badly off, probably our worst-off class (in terms of material well-being second only to the American Indians), and in addition they have occupied the lowest rung for several centuries. In a sense, they are America's perpetual underclass. It is both of these characteristics — the relative position of the group and the duration of the position — that makes efforts to improve the status of the group defensible. This

redistribution may be rooted in a theory of compensation — blacks as a group were *put* in that position by others and the redistributive means are *owed* to the group as a form of compensation. . . .

[But] a redistributive strategy need not rest on this idea of compensation. [The] redistributive strategy could give expression to an ethical view against caste, one that would make it undesirable for any social group to occupy a position of subordination for any extended period of time.

Is Fiss's view of the equal protection clause too narrow because "it is unjust for society to attach negative significance to a morally irrelevant factor even when doing so does not eventuate in a specially disadvantaged group, but only in harm to, and suffering on the part of, the particular individual affected"? Perry, The Principle of Equal Protection, 32 Hastings L. Rev. 1133, 1146 (1981). Is Fiss's view too broad because it confers special rights on members of a subjugated group even if an individual member enjoying these rights is not himself subjugated? Consider also Brest, supra, at 49-50:

If a society can be said to have an underlying political theory, ours has not been a theory of organic groups but of liberalism, focusing on the rights of individuals including rights of distributive justice. . . .

[Although] the practices of nations — including our own — often fall short of their aspirations, most societies in which power is formally allocated among racial and national groups are strikingly oppressive, unequal and unstable. In view of all this, it seems reasonable to place the burden on proponents of a theory of group racial justice to show that it is morally tenable and consistent with other values we cherish.

Even if the equal protection clause does protect the rights of blacks as a group, does it follow that racial classifications should be strictly scrutinized? On the one hand, a law restricting blacks in a trivial fashion might not meaningfully contribute to their subjugation. On the other, a facially neutral law might well have a devastating impact on blacks. Why, then, should anything turn on whether the law uses race as a classifying principle?

6. *Nonpluralist theories.* Is it possible to formulate a theory of heightened scrutiny not dependent on the notion of groups selfishly utilizing the political process to advance their self-interest? Consider Ackerman, supra, at 743:

We must repudiate [the] reduction of the American Constitution to a simple system of pluralist bargaining if we are to reassert the legitimacy of the courts' critical function. Although the bargaining model captures an important aspect of American politics, it does not do justice to the most fundamental episodes of our constitutional history. We make a mistake, for example, to view the enactment of the Bill of Rights and the Civil War Amendments as if they were outcomes of ordinary pluralist bargaining. Instead, these constitutional achievements represent the highest legal expression of a different kind of politics — one characterized by mass mobilization and struggle that [yielded] fundamental principles transcending the normal processes of interest group accommodation.

Can strict scrutiny of racial classifications be understood as an effort to ensure that public deliberation involves something more than a power struggle between competing interest groups? Consider Sunstein, Interest Groups in American Public Law, 38 Stan. L. Rev. 1 — (1985):

> Underlying the Court's approach is a perception that classifications in [certain contexts] are likely to reflect private power, even if it is possible to come up with a public value that the relevant classification can be said to serve. . . .
>
> This understanding is in important respects classically republican. The role of the representative is to deliberate on the public good, not to respond mechanically to existing social conceptions. Under the Court's framework, such conceptions must themselves be subjected to critical review. They cannot be automatically translated into law. The result is to apply the deliberative task to social practices that had previously been accepted as natural and inviolate.

Note that this view, unlike Ely's, does not take individual private preferences as the starting point for analysis. Instead, it assumes that "politics properly has, as one of its central functions, the selection, evaluation, and shaping of preferences. [There] is, in short, something like a 'common good' or 'public interest' that in some contexts amounts to something other than the aggregation of private preferences or utilities." Id. at — .

How can one know that racial classifications merely reflect "existing social conceptions" and are not, in fact, in the "public interest"? How likely is it that courts will be able to stand above existing power relationships and determine what is truly in the "common good"? If the "public interest" is in fact different from the aggregation of our private preferences, why does it follow that our private desires should be subordinated to those that emerge from public processes?

Note: The Nature of Special Scrutiny

Korematsu held that racial classifications should be subject to "rigid scrutiny." If some sort of enhanced review is in fact appropriate, what should it consist of? Can the scrutiny be structured to avoid the problem of judicial value judgments encountered in connection with rational relationship review? Consider the following possibilities:

1. *Ends scrutiny. Korematsu* held that a racial classification must be supported by a "pressing public necessity." Presumably, this language means that the end purportedly advanced by the classification must be unusually important. But how should a court rank the importance of various constitutionally permissible ends?

In any event, if the evil to be avoided is race prejudice and stereotyping, why should the importance of the end matter? Ends scrutiny is sometimes defended as a mechanism for filtering out statutes motivated by prejudice. On this theory, if the legitimate ends advanced to justify the statute are relatively unimportant, the claim that the statute was motivated by these ends becomes correspondingly less plausible. A court is therefore more justified in concluding that the real purpose of the law is to harm an unpopular group.

Are you persuaded? One can hardly doubt that winning World War II counts as a "pressing public necessity." Does it follow that the decision to advance that goal by interning Japanese-Americans was not infected by race prejudice? Conversely, a publicly financed production of *Othello* presumably ranks as something less than a necessity. Yet a race-based classification in casting the lead might well be uninfluenced by race-prejudice. If, alternatively, the reason for ends scrutiny is to avoid making powerless minorities bear disproportionate social costs, should not the test require consideration of not only the importance of the state's end but also the gravity of the injury inflicted to achieve it? Suppose, for example, the state's goal is legitimate albeit relatively unimportant but the deprivation required to achieve it is more trivial still?

2. *Means scrutiny.* It is possible to read the *Korematsu* test as focusing not only on ends but also on means. Thus, even if winning World War II was a "pressing public necessity," it is hard to see how that necessity justified a racial classification that only marginally contributed to achieving the end. In other cases, the Court has been more explicit in requiring a tight fit between means and ends when reviewing racial classifications. In McLaughlin v. Florida, 379 U.S. 184, 196 (1964), for example, the Court said that racial classifications "[bear] a heavy burden of justification [and] will be upheld only if [necessary] and not merely rationally related, to the accomplishment of a permissible state policy." See also In re Griffiths, 413 U.S. 717, 721-722 (1973).

Does means-oriented strict scrutiny escape the problem of judicial value judgments? If the scrutiny is so strict that the existence of *any* alternative means, regardless of cost, is sufficient to invalidate a racial classification, then, presumably, the Court would be freed from the necessity of balancing. But could any racial classification survive this test? If, alternatively, a balance must be struck between the cost of the classification and the cost of foregoing it, must not the Court somehow attach values to these factors so that they can be weighed against each other?

Note how fact dependent means-oriented scrutiny is. In *Korematsu*, for example, the necessity of a racial classification turned on questions such as how serious the threat of sabotage was, how many Japanese-Americans were disloyal, how hard it would have been to separate the loyal from the disloyal. A modern student of the *Korematsu* case has concluded that the military's fear of subversion by Japanese-Americans was greatly overstated, that Justice Department lawyers who prepared the *Korematsu* brief knew that the evidence of such subversion was extremely weak, but that they failed to alert the Supreme Court to the defects in the evidence. See P. Irons, Justice at War 278-310 (1983). Did the *Korematsu* court "rigidly scrutinize" the military commander's judgment? Would it be tolerable for nine justices in Washington to substitute their judgment for that of the military on questions such as these? Does "rigid scrutiny" amount to anything more than a rubber stamp if the Court is unwilling to look behind the factual judgments made by other branches?

3. *Absolute prohibition.* In light of the difficulties posed by both means and ends scrutiny, would it be preferable for the Court to adopt a bright-line rule prohibiting all racial classifications that burden racial minorities? See, e.g., A. Bickel, The Morality of Consent 133 (1975) ("discrimination on the basis of race is illegal, immoral, unconstitutional, inherently wrong, and destructive of democratic society"). But see Greenawalt, Judicial Scrutiny of "Benign" Racial Preference in Law School Admissions, 75 Colum. L. Rev. 559, 568 (1975) (nighttime curfew on all Japanese-Americans might have been reasonable if hard evidence that a substantial percentage of them were training to commit sabotage in aid of much more probable and imminent invasion).

Consider Palmore v. Sidoti, 466 U.S. — , 104 S. Ct. 1879 (1984). The case arose from a custody battle between Palmore and Sidoti (who were both white) following their divorce. Originally the trial court awarded custody of the couple's three-year-old daughter to the mother. When the mother remarried a black man, however, the court determined that the best interests of the child required that the father be awarded custody. The trial court ruled that "despite the strides that have been made in bettering relations between the races in this country, it is inevitable that [the child] will, if allowed to remain in her present situation [suffer] from the social stigmatization that is sure to come."

A unanimous Supreme Court reversed. Chief Justice Burger's opinion for the Court acknowledged that the state had "a duty of the highest order to protect the interests of minor children" and that "There is a risk that a child living with a step-parent of a different race may be subject to a variety of pressures and stresses not present if the child were living with parents of the same racial or ethnic origin." But the Court nonetheless held that the "reality of private biases and the possible injury they might inflict" were not "permissible considerations. [Private] biases may be outside the reach of the law, but the law cannot, directly or indirectly, give them effect."

The law cannot perpetuate these private biases.

Would the result in *Sidoti* have been the same if detailed empirical study demonstrated that children in mixed-race homes suffered psychological damage? Would a statute giving preference to prospective adoptive parents who are the same race as the child to be adopted be constitutional? See, e.g., In the Matter of the Petition of RMG and EMG, No. 79-747 (D.C.C.A. 1982) (preference for same-race adoptions survives strict scrutiny, but absolute prohibition of cross-racial adoptions unconstitutional).

Would you be satisfied with a rule that automatically invalidated a statute requiring blacks but not whites contemplating marriage to be tested for sickle-cell anemia and to undergo genetic counseling if they have it? See J. Ely, Democracy and Distrust 247-248 n.46 (1980). A statute requiring persons whose skin pigmentation is darker than a certain shade to wear light clothing at night? See Kaplan, Equal Justice in an Unequal World: Equality for the Negro — the Problem of Special Treatment, 61 Nw. U. L. Rev. 363, 383 (1966).

2. Non-Race-Specific Classifications That Disadvantage Racial Minorities

Court is allowing defacto effects of education.

Washington v. Davis

426 U.S. 229 (1976)

Mr. Justice White delivered the opinion of the Court.

This case involves the validity of a qualifying test administered to applicants for positions as police officers in the District of Columbia Metropolitan Police Department. The test was sustained by the District Court but invalidated by the Court of Appeals. We are in agreement with the District Court and hence reverse the judgment of the Court of Appeals. . . .

[Respondents, unsuccessful black applicants for positions on the police force, claimed that a test measuring verbal ability, vocabulary, and reading comprehension unconstitutionally discriminated against them. According to the District

Test 21 for civil servants

Court, respondents' evidence supported the conclusion that a higher percentage of blacks than whites failed the test and that the test had not been validated to establish its reliability for measuring subsequent job performance. Respondents made no claim that administration of the test constituted an "intentional" or "purposeful" act of discrimination.]

The central purpose of the Equal Protection Clause of the Fourteenth Amendment is the prevention of official conduct discriminating on the basis of race. [But] our cases have not embraced the proposition that a law or other official act, without regard to whether it reflects a racially discriminatory purpose, is unconstitutional *solely* because it has a racially disproportionate impact.

Almost 100 years ago, Strauder v. West Virginia established that the exclusion of Negroes from grand and petit juries in criminal proceedings violated the Equal Protection Clause, but the fact that a particular jury or a series of juries does not statistically reflect the racial composition of the community does not in itself make out an invidious discrimination forbidden by the Clause. . . .

The rule is the same in other contexts. Wright v. Rockefeller, 376 U.S. 52 (1964), upheld a New York congressional apportionment statute against claims that district lines had been racially gerrymandered. The challenged districts were made up predominantly of whites or of minority races, and their boundaries were irregularly drawn. The challengers did not prevail because they failed to prove that [the] statute "was the product of a state contrivance to segregate on the basis of race or place of origin." . . .

The school desegregation cases have also adhered to the basic equal protection principle that the invidious quality of a law claimed to be racially discriminatory must ultimately be traced to a racially discriminatory purpose. That there are both predominantly black and predominantly white schools in a community is not alone violative of the Equal Protection Clause. The essential element of de jure segregation is "a current condition of segregation resulting from intentional state action." Keyes v. School Dist. No. 1.

[The] Court has also recently rejected allegations of racial discrimination based solely on the statistically disproportionate racial impact of various provisions of the Social Security Act because "[t]he acceptance of appellants' constitutional theory would render suspect each difference in treatment among the grant classes, however lacking in racial motivation and however otherwise rational the treatment might be." Jefferson v. Hackney, 406 U.S. 535, 548 (1972).

This is not to say that the necessary discriminatory racial purpose must be express or appear on the face of the statute, or that a law's disproportionate impact is irrelevant in cases involving Constitution-based claims of racial discrimination. A statute, otherwise neutral on its face, must not be applied so as invidiously to discriminate on the basis of race. . . .

Necessarily, an invidious discriminatory purpose may often be inferred from the totality of the relevant facts, including the fact, if it is true, that the law bears more heavily on one race than another. It is also not infrequently true that the discriminatory impact — in the jury cases for example, the total or seriously disproportionate exclusion of Negroes from jury venires — may for all practical purposes demonstrate unconstitutionality because in various circumstances the discrimination is very difficult to explain on nonracial grounds. Nevertheless, we have not held that a law, neutral on its face and serving ends otherwise within the power of government to pursue, is invalid under the Equal Protection Clause simply because it may affect a greater proportion of one race than of another. Disproportionate impact is not irrelevant, but it is not the sole touchstone of an invidious racial discrimination forbidden by the Constitution. Standing alone, it does not trigger the rule, that racial classifications are to be subjected to the strictest scrutiny and are justifiable only by the weightiest of considerations. . . .

[We] have difficulty understanding how a law establishing a racially neutral qualification for employment is nevertheless racially discriminatory and denies "any person . . . equal protection of the laws" simply because a greater proportion of Negroes fail to qualify than members of other racial or ethnic groups. Had respondents, along with all others who had failed [the test], whether white or black, brought an action claiming that [it] denied each of them equal protection of the laws as compared with those who had passed with high enough scores to qualify them as police recruits, it is most unlikely that their challenge would have been sustained. [The test], which is administered generally to prospective Government employees, concededly seeks to ascertain whether those who take it have acquired a particular level of verbal skill; and it is untenable that the Constitution prevents the Government from seeking modestly to upgrade the communicative abilities of its employees rather than to be satisfied with some lower level of competence, particularly where the job requires special ability to communicate orally and in writing. Respondents, as Negroes, could no more successfully claim that the test denied them equal protection than could white applicants who also failed. The conclusion would not be different in the face of proof that more Negroes than whites had been disqualified by [the test]. That other Negroes also failed to score well would, alone, not demonstrate that respondents individually were being denied equal protection of the laws by the application of an otherwise valid qualifying test being administered to prospective police recruits.

Nor on the facts of the case before us would the disproportionate impact of [the test] warrant the conclusion that it is a purposeful device to discriminate against Negroes and hence an infringement of the constitutional rights of respondents as well as other black applicants. As we have said, the test is neutral on its face and rationally may be said to serve a purpose the Government is constitutionally empowered to pursue. Even agreeing with the District Court that the differential racial effect of [the test] called for further inquiry, we think the District Court correctly held that the affirmative efforts of the Metropolitan Police Department to recruit black officers, the changing racial composition of the recruit classes and of the force in general, and the relationship of the test to the training program negated any inference that the Department discriminated on the basis of race or that "a police officer qualifies on the color of his skin rather than ability." . . . .

A rule that a statute designed to serve neutral ends is nevertheless invalid, absent compelling justification, if in practice it benefits or burdens one race more than another would be far reaching and would raise serious questions about, and perhaps invalidate, a whole range of tax, welfare, public service, regulatory, and licensing statutes that may be more burdensome to the poor and to the average black than to the more affluent white. . . . .

MR. JUSTICE STEVENS, concurring. . . .

The requirement of purposeful discrimination is a common thread running through the cases summarized in [the majority's opinion]. These cases include criminal convictions which were set aside because blacks were excluded from the grand jury, a reapportionment case in which political boundaries were obviously influenced to some extent by racial considerations, a school desegregation case, and a case involving the unequal administration of an ordinance purporting to prohibit the operation of laundries in frame buildings. Although it may be proper to use the same language to describe the constitutional claim in each of these contexts, the burden of proving a prima facie case may well involve differing evidentiary considerations. The extent of deference that one pays to the trial court's determination of the factual issue, and indeed, the extent to which one characterizes the intent issue as a question of fact or a question of law, will vary in different contexts.

Frequently the most probative evidence of intent will be objective evidence of what actually happened rather than evidence describing the subjective state of mind of the actor. For normally the actor is presumed to have intended the natural consequences of his deeds. This is particularly true in the case of governmental action which is frequently the product of compromise, of collective decisionmaking, and of mixed motivation. It is unrealistic, on the one hand, to require the victim of alleged discrimination to uncover the actual subjective intent of the decisionmaker or, conversely, to invalidate otherwise legitimate action simply because an improper motive affected the deliberation of a participant in the decisional process. A law conscripting clerics should not be invalidated because an atheist voted for it.

My point in making this observation is to suggest that the line between discriminatory purpose and discriminatory impact is not nearly as bright, and perhaps not quite as critical, as the reader of the Court's opinion might assume. I agree, of course, that a constitutional issue does not arise every time some disproprotionate impact is shown. On the other hand, when the disproportion is dramatic, ... [it] really does not matter whether the standard is phrased in terms of purpose or effect. Therefore, although I accept the statement of the general rule in the Court's opinion, I am not yet prepared to indicate how that standard should be applied in the many cases which have formulated the governing standard in different language. . . .

[A dissenting opinion by JUSTICE BRENNAN is omitted].

Note: Rational Basis Review of Non-Race-Specific Classifications

1. *Some preliminary questions.* After Washington v. Davis, a court confronted with a classification that disadvantages a racial minority must first determine whether it is race specific. If it is, either because it explicitly draws racial lines or because it is motivated by a racial purpose, the court will use strict scrutiny and, probably, invalidate it. If the classification is non-race specific, the court will use rational basis review despite its disproportionate impact on the minority group. Has the Supreme Court given an adequate account of why non-race-specific classifications that harm racial minorities should not be strictly scrutinized in the absence of a discriminatory purpose? Is it because such classifications are less likely to stigmatize? Because they are less likely to perpetuate stereotypes? Because it would be impractical to invalidate all the "tax, welfare, public service, regulatory, and licensing statutes that may be more burdensome to [the] average

black than to the [average] white"? Even if strict scrutiny and virtual per se invalidation is inappropriate for non-race-specific classifications, why shouldn't the fact that they disproportionately impact on racial minorities trigger some form of intermediate review more rigorous than the rational relationship test?

2. *Effects tests and the problem of preferential treatment.* In what sense are racial minorities denied equal treatment if the disproportionate impact of a non-race-specific classification is merely the adventitious byproduct of a "neutral" government policy? So long as racial effects are unintended, isn't it likely that, over the range of policies, those that harm blacks will be counterbalanced by those that help them? Consider Bennett, "Mere" Rationality in Constitutional Law: Judicial Review and Democratic Theory, 67 Calif. L. Rev. 1049, 1076 (1977): "If members of racial minorities stochastically obtain benefits and suffer detriments as one or another piece of legislation is passed without attention to its racial impact, they are obtaining, not being deprived of, equal protection of the laws. To forbid all legislation that disadvantages them would give them the gains from political bargaining without the losses."

Would heightened review of non-race-specific classifications that disadvantage racial minorities turn the equal protection clause on its head by constitutionally requiring legislatures to be race conscious as to outcomes, rather than race neutral as to the legal rules producing those outcomes? Consider Ely, Legislative and Administrative Motivation in Constitutional Law, 79 Yale L. J. 1205, 1255, 1260 (1970):

> A number of commentators have asserted that government officials may, if they wish, go out of their way to favor the members of minority races without violating the Constitution. But none of whom I am aware, and certainly not the Court, has argued that such favoritism is constitutionally required. . . .
>
> [So] long as the Court remains unwilling to order states to take race into account [judicial] review must await proof of racial motivation and cannot be triggered by disproportion per se. To undertake automatically to invalidate [state actions] because of racial disproportion would obviously be to order that balance be intentionally achieved.

3. *The problem of remedy.* These arguments against an effects test assume that so long as a disproportionate impact is unintended, it is merely a matter of chance. Is this assumption warranted? Would an effects test require preferential treatment for blacks if blacks and whites are differently situated with respect to the law because of *prior* unequal treatment by government? Consider Perry, The Disproportionate Impact Theory of Racial Discrimination, 125 U. Pa. L. Rev. 540, 558 (1977):

> Laws having a disproportionate racial impact burden blacks *because* of their especially disadvantaged position in American society. A failure to require government to take account of that especially disadvantaged social position by selecting and fine-tuning laws to avoid the unnecessary or thoughtless aggravation of the situation would effectively ignore American society's responsibility for that social position. Furthermore, the failure would compound the responsibility.

The Court has recognized that its proscription of an effects test is inapplicable to situations where the state has an affirmative duty to remedy a previously established constitutional violation. See section A4 supra. Can you state precisely why this should be so? If two individuals are equally deprived, one because of an unconstitutional act that has already occurred, and the other because of bad luck, why does the first, but not the second, have a constitutional entitlement to affirmative measures designed to remedy his situation?

Once such an entitlement is acknowledged, difficult problems concerning its scope must be resolved. It might be argued that virtually all statutes that have a disproportionate impact on blacks have this effect because of our long history of slavery and government-sanctioned racial discrimination. Moreover, even statutes that do not have the effect of making things worse for blacks might be subject to attack on the theory that they fail to meet the government's affirmative constitutional obligation to make things better. Ought a court to undertake responsibility for weighing that obligation against the government's competing responsibility to pursue policies benefiting the majority?

4. *Disproportionate impact and the theory of passive government.* Even if the government is not responsible for the fact that blacks are differently situated with respect to a non-race-specific classification, why should that fact matter? Doesn't treating people the same when they are relevantly different deny equality just as effectively as treating them differently when they are relevantly the same? Compare, for example, the following two hypothetical admissions policies followed by a state university:

a.   No blind applicants will be admitted.
b.   All applicants, whether sighted or blind, must take a written examination, and those receiving the highest score will be admitted.

The first treats blind and sighted applicants differently although they are (arguably) relevantly the same. The second treats blind and sighted applicants the same, although they are (arguably) relevantly different. Does either satisfy the equality principle?

Recall the suggestion that race-specific classifications are strictly scrutinized in order to deal with problems of legislative purpose. When the classification is race specific, the purpose question is not whether the legislature intended to treat blacks and whites differently. The classification itself establishes that purpose. Rather, the question is whether the legislature intended to disadvantage a racial minority simply for the sake of harming it, rather than for the sake of achieving some permissible goal. The strict scrutiny doctrine holds that only a showing of a close fit and an overriding governmental interest can overcome the inference that the classification was motivated by a desire to harm the minority. See section C1 supra. See also Personnel Administrator v. Feeney, 442 U.S. 256, 272 (1979); Bennett, supra, at 1077. But why shouldn't the same inference be drawn, and the same strict scrutiny required, when a non-race-specific classification disproportionately disadvantages a racial minority? Isn't treating blacks and whites the same despite the fact that they are differently situated just as effective a strategy for disadvantaging blacks as treating them differently despite the fact that they are similarly situated?

Consider the following argument: The Washington v. Davis test ultimately rests on a theory of constitutional law that associates individual rights with limits on government power. The implicit premise of the opinion is that the alignment of groups in the private sphere is "equal" for constitutional purposes so long as the government does not intervene to make it unequal. This theory, in turn, rests on two problematic assumptions. First, it assumes that discriminatory effects are just "there" and are not the product of present and previous governmental choices. Second, it assumes that the interaction of private forces will automatically yield just outcomes so long as governmental coercion is avoided. During the "*Lochner* era," when the Court invalidated social legislation on the theory that it violated "freedom of contract," these assumptions were seen as the basis for limitations on legislative power. See Chapter 6, section D, infra. Today, *Lochner* is widely viewed as discredited. Yet Washington v. Davis demonstrates that the *Lochner* approach survives as a constraint on judicial power. The burden is on defenders of Washington v. Davis to explain why the assumptions are more plausible in the judicial than in the legislative sphere.

Note: *Heightened Scrutiny for Improperly Motivated Classifications*

Washington v. Davis makes clear that a facially neutral classification is not race specific and, hence, not subject to strict scrutiny merely because of its disproportionate racial impact. Does such a classification become race specific if the disproportionate racial impact was intentional?

1. *Discriminatory administration.* In Yick Wo v. Hopkins, 118 U.S. 351 (1886), petitioner was convicted of violating a local ordinance prohibiting operation of a laundry not located in a brick or stone building without the consent of the board of supervisors. He alleged that he and more than 200 other Chinese nationals had petitioned the board of supervisors for consent but that all of the petitions were denied, whereas all but one of the petitions filed by non-Chinese were granted. The Court unanimously reversed Yick Wo's conviction. The Court held that "the facts shown establish an administration directed so exclusively against a particular class of persons as to warrant and require the conclusion, that, whatever may have been the intent of the ordinances as adopted, they are applied by the public authorities charged with their administration, and thus representing State itself, with a mind so unequal and oppressive as to amount to a practical denial by the State of [equal] protection of the laws."

Is there any functional difference between the discriminatory administration shown in *Yick Wo* and a statute that facially applied only to Chinese nationals? Should the result in *Yick Wo* have been the same if the state specifically prohibited discrimination in the granting of licenses and administrative officials were subject to sanctions for violating the prohibition? If the ordinance is facially constitutional, why should the legislature's constitutionally permissible purpose be frustrated by reversal of Yick Wo's conviction? Does *Yick Wo* have any ground for complaint if the state can show that he would have been denied a permit even if non-Chinese had been denied permits as well? See People v. Walker, 14 N.Y.2d 901, 200 N.E.2d 779, 252 N.Y.S.2d 96 (1964). Cf. Arlington Heights v. Metropolitan Housing Corp., infra this section, at 270-271 n.21 (proof of unconstitutional purpose not dispositive where defendant can show that same decision would have resulted without impermissible purpose).

There is a well-developed line of authority reversing convictions where it is shown that facially neutral jury selection statutes are administered in discriminatory fashion. See, e.g., Castaneda v. Partida, 430 U.S. 482 (1977); Carter v. Jury Commission, 396 U.S. 320 (1970); Avery v. Georgia, 345 U.S. 559 (1953). Moreover, in the jury context, reversal is required even in the absence of a showing that any prejudice resulted from the discriminatory policy. See Rose v. Mitchell, 443 U.S. 545 (1979).

2. *Statutes enacted for discriminatory purposes.* Is discriminatory purpose review less problematical when a statute contains a classification that is deliberately "gerrymandered" to produce a disproportionate impact on racial minorities? Compare *Yick Wo* with Gomillion v. Lightfoot, 364 U.S. 339 (1960). An Alabama statute altered the shape of the City of Tuskegee from a square to an "uncouth twenty-eight sided figure." Petitioners alleged that the new boundary lines removed from the city all but four or five of the 400 black voters, while not removing a single white voter. The Court held that if these allegations were proved, the statute infringed on the right of blacks to vote in violation of the fifteenth amendment.

> If these allegations upon a trial remained uncontradicted or unqualified, the conclusion would be irresistible, tantamount for all practical purposes to a mathematical demonstration, that the legislation is solely concerned with segregating white and colored voters by fencing Negro citizens out of town so as to deprive them of their pre-existing municipal vote. It is difficult to appreciate what stands in the way of adjudging a statute having this inevitable effect invalid.

Is there a meaningful difference between the *Gomillion* statute and a law that expressly directed administrative officials to draw the boundary line so as to exclude all blacks? Would there be such a difference in the improbable event that these lines had in fact been drawn to serve nonracial ends? If they in fact served nonracial ends but were drawn for the purpose of serving racial ends?

3. *Racially motivated classifications that are not strictly scrutinized.* Does it follow from *Yick Wo* and *Gomillion* that racially motivated classifications should always be subject to strict scrutiny? The Court has demonstrated some reluctance to strictly scrutinize such classifications in three situations:

a. Palmer v. Thompson *and the problem of racially motivated classifications with neutral effects.* Compare *Gomillion* with Palmer v. Thompson, 403 U.S. 217 (1971), in which a city council closed municipal swimming pools following court-ordered integration. In a 5-to-4 decision, the Court held that the closing did not violate the equal protection clause. After observing that "no case in this Court has held that a legislative act may violate equal protection solely because of the motivations of the men who voted for it," the Court advanced several reasons why investigation of purpose was improper:

> First, it is extremely difficult for a court to ascertain the motivation, or collection of different motivations, that lie behind a legislative enactment. [Furthermore], there is an element of futility in a judicial attempt to invalidate a law because of the bad motives of its supporters. If the law is struck down for this reason, rather than because of its facial content or effect, it would presumably be valid as soon as the legislature or relevant governing body repassed it for different reasons.

The Court distinguished *Gomillion* as a case resting "on the actual effect of the [enactment], not upon the motivation which led the [State] to behave as [it] did."

Are *Gomillion* and *Palmer* distinguishable on this ground? Was it the "effect" of the *Gomillion* ordinance that made it unconstitutional, or was the effect relevant only because it amounted to a "mathematical demonstration" that a discriminatory purpose was at work? Are the cases distinguishable on the ground that the overwhelmingly discriminatory effect of the *Gomillion* statute greatly reduced the difficulties of ascertaining purpose that worried the Court in *Palmer*?

Does Palmer v. Thompson survive Washington v. Davis? In *Washington*, the Court attempted to reconcile *Palmer* on the ground that the pool closing extended "identical treatment to both whites and Negores." Taken together, do *Palmer* and *Washington* mean that a facially neutral statute is subject to enhanced review only when it has *both* a discriminatory purpose *and* a disproportionate impact? Is a holding that the closing of integrated pools does not produce a disproportionate racial impact consistent with Brown v. Board of Education? See Brest, *Palmer v. Thompson:* An Approach to the Problem of Unconstitutional Legislative Motive, 1971 Sup. Ct. Rev. 95, 132. Is it conceivable that the Court would uphold a statute that, by its terms, required the closing of any municipal facility ordered desegregated? Cf. Bush v. Orleans Parish School Board, 187 F. Supp. 42 (E.D. La. 1960), aff'd, 365 U.S. 569 (1961) (statute providing for closing of all integrated schools unconstitutional).

b. *"Discretionary" decisions.* Compare *Yick Wo* and the jury cases cited above with Swain v. Alabama, 380 U.S. 202 (1965). Swain claimed that he was denied equal protection when the prosecutor used his peremptory challenges to remove all blacks from the jury pool. The Court held that even if the prosecutor removed the jurors because of their race, an equal protection claim had not been made out. "The essential nature of the peremptory challenge is that it is one exercised without a reason stated, without inquiry and without being subject to the court's control. [To] subject the prosecutor's challenge in any particular case to the demands and traditional standards of the Equal Protection Clause would entail a radical change in the nature and operation of the challenge." The Court went on to note, however, that if the prosecutor used his peremptory challenges to remove blacks "in case after case, whatever the circumstances, whatever the crime and whoever the defendant or the victim may be" an equal protection claim would be stronger. "Such proof might support a reasonable inference that Negroes are excluded from juries for reasons wholly unrelated to the outcome of the particular case on trial and that the peremptory system is being used to deny the Negro the same right and opportunity to participate in the administration of justice enjoyed by the white population."

In light of *Yick Wo* and *Swain*, how should a court treat the decision of a high public official to use racial criteria in the hiring of a close aide? Consider Mayor of Philadelphia v. Educational Equality League, 415 U.S. 605 (1974). Respondents alleged that the mayor had violated the equal protection clause by discriminating against blacks in appointments to the nine-member Educational Nominating Panel, a body with statutory responsibility for submitting nominees for the School Board to the mayor. The Court, in an opinion by Justice Powell, labeled the mayor's appointment power as "discretionary" and expressed concern that "judicial oversight of discretionary appointments may interfere with the ability of an elected official to respond to the mandate of his constituency." The Court found it unnecessary to decide what the equal protection clause required in this context, however, since it held that, on the facts, racial discrimination had not been established.

Compare *Mayor of Philadelphia* with Davis v. Passman, 442 U.S. 228 (1979). Davis, a deputy administrative assistant to Congressman Passman, brought a constitutionally based action against the congressman after he fired her because she was a woman. The Court held that Davis had asserted a constitutionally protected right that could be judicially enforced if Passman's conduct was not protected by the speech and debate clause of article I, section 6 (a question that the Court did not reach). Writing in dissent, Chief Justice Burger objected that

> A Member of Congress has a right to expect that every person on his or her staff will give total loyalty to the political positions of the Member, total confidentiality, and total support. This may, on occasion, lead a Member to employ a particular person on a racial, ethnic, religious, or gender basis thought to be acceptable to the constituency represented. [Presidents] consciously select — and dispense with — their appointees on this basis and have done so since the beginning of the Republic.

Do cases such as *Swain* and *Mayor of Philadelphia* suggest that there is an area in which even government officials should be permitted to engage in racial discrimination? If so, is this because the ends served by such discrimination are sufficiently weighty to survive strict scrutiny? Because the institutional costs of judicial enforcement are too high?

c. *The causation requirement.* Should an improperly motivated classification be subject to strict scrutiny if the state is able to show that the same classification would have been utilized even in the absence of the improper motive? Consider Mt. Healthy City School District Board of Education v. Doyle, 429 U.S. 274 (1979). The District Court found that Doyle was not rehired as a teacher because he had engaged in conduct protected by the first amendment. Although accepting these findings of fact, the Supreme Court held that it did not necessarily follow that he was entitled to reinstatement and back pay. Writing for a unanimous court, Justice Rehnquist observed that

> A rule of causations which focuses solely on whether protected conduct played a [substantial] part in a decision not to rehire could place an employee in a better position as a result of the exercise of constitutionally protected conduct than he would have occupied had he done nothing. . . .
>
> Initially, in this case, the burden was properly placed upon [Doyle] to show that his conduct was constitutionally protected, and that this conduct was a "substantial factor" [in] the Board's decision not to rehire him. [Doyle] having carried that burden, however, the District Court should have gone on to determine whether the Board had shown by a preponderance of the evidence that it would have reached the same decision as to [Doyle's] reemployment even in the absence of the protected conduct.

Compare *Mt. Healthy* to Village of Arlington Heights v. Metropolitan Housing Development Corp., 429 U.S. 252 (1977), a case decided on the same day. (*Arlington Heights* is considered in greater detail infra this section.) Writing for the Court, Justice Powell said that

> [Washington v. Davis] does not require a plaintiff to prove that challenged action rested solely on racially discriminatory purposes. Rarely can it be said that a legisla-

ture or administrative body operating under a broad mandate made a decision motivated solely by a single concern, or even that a particular purpose was the "dominant" or "primary" one. [When] there is a proof that a discriminatory purpose has been a motivating factor in the decision, [judicial] deference is no longer justified.

Is this language consistent with *Mt. Healthy?* In a footnote later in the same opinion, the Court declared that "Proof that [a] decision [was] motivated in part by a racially discriminatory purpose [does] not necessarily [require] invalidation of the challenged decision. Such proof would, however, [shift] to the [defendant] the burden of establishing that the same decision would have resulted even had the impermissible purpose not been considered. [See *Mt. Healthy.*]" Does this mean that the Court will require proof of "but-for" causation? Is such a requirement consistent with the Court's recognition that the illicit purpose need not be "dominant" or "primary" to invalidate the classification?

Consider Hunter v. Underwood, — U.S. — , — S. Ct. — (1985). A provision in the Alabama Constitution, adopted in 1901, disfranchised all persons convicted of crimes of moral turpitude. Appellees attacked the provision on the ground that it was motivated by the desire to disfranchise blacks. Although conceding this was one of the provision's purposes, the state maintained that the framers had also been motivated by the desire to deprive poor whites of the vote. A unanimous Court, in an opinion by Justice Rehnquist, rejected this argument and held the provision unconstitutional.

> Whether or not intentional disenfranchisements of poor whites would qualify as a "permissible motive," [it] is clear that where both impermissible racial motivation and racially discriminatory impact are demonstrated, *Arlington Heights* and *Mt. Healthy* supply the proper analysis. [An] additional purpose to discriminate against poor whites would not render nugatory the purpose to discriminate against all blacks, and it is beyond peradventure that the latter was a "but-for" motivation for the enactment of [the provision].

Is the Court's approach in *Mt. Healthy, Arlington Heights,* and *Underwood* consistent with its treatment of statutes that facially discriminate against racial minorities? The Court has never suggested that such statutes can be saved from strict scrutiny by a showing that the same classification would have been utilized in the absence of racial animus. Indeed, on one view, the reason why the Court requires a compelling government interest and a tight fit between means and ends is to ascertain whether the same law would have been adopted if the legislature were not "prejudiced." Does it follow that strict scrutiny is also the appropriate technique for investigating the causation question when facially neutral statutes are infected by a discriminatory purpose?

VILLAGE OF ARLINGTON HEIGHTS v. METROPOLITAN HOUSING DEVELOPMENT CORP., 429 U.S. 252 (1977): Respondent applied to the Village of Arlington Heights for rezoning of a fifteen-acre parcel so as to permit construction of low- and moderate-income housing. When the request was denied, respondent brought this suit claiming that the denial was racially discriminatory and violated the equal protection clause. Justice Powell wrote the Court's opinion:

"Determining whether invidious discriminatory purpose was a motivating factor demands a sensitive inquiry into such circumstantial and direct evidence of intent as may be available. The impact of the official action [may] provide an important starting point. Sometimes a clear pattern, unexplainable on grounds other than race, emerges from the effect of the state action even when the governing legislation appears neutral on its face. The evidentiary inquiry is then relatively easy. But such cases are rare. Absent a pattern as stark as that in *Gomillion* or *Yick Wo*, impact alone is not determinative, and the Court must look to other evidence.

"The historical background of the decision is one evidentiary source, particularly if it reveals a series of official actions taken for invidious purposes. The specific sequence of events leading up to the challenged decision also may shed some light on the decisionmaker's purposes. [Departures] from the normal procedural sequence also might afford evidence that improper purposes are playing a role. Substantive departures too may be relevant, particularly if the factors usually considered important by the decisionmaker strongly favor a decision contrary to the one reached.

"The legislative or administrative history may be highly relevant, especially where there are contemporary statements by members of the decisionmaking body, minutes of its meetings, or reports. In some extraordinary instances the members might be called to the stand at trial to testify concerning the purpose of the official action, although even then such testimony frequently will be barred by privilege. . . .

"[Here, respondents] simply failed to carry their burden of proving that discriminatory purpose was a motivating factor in the Village's decision."

PERSONNEL ADMINISTRATOR v. FEENEY, 442 U.S. 256 (1979): Justice Stewart delivered the Court's opinion: "This case presents a challenge to the constitutionality of the Massachusetts veterans' preference statute on the ground that it discriminates against women in violation of the Equal Protection Clause of the Fourteenth Amendment. Under [the statute], all veterans who qualify for state civil service positions must be considered for appointment ahead of any qualifying nonveterans. The preference operates overwhelmingly to the advantage of males. . . .

"[The] District Court [concluded] that a veterans' hiring preference is inherently nonneutral because it favors a class from which women had traditionally been excluded, and that the consequences of the Massachusetts absolute-preference formula for the employment opportunities of women were too inevitable to have been 'unintended.' . . .

"If the impact of this statute could not be plausibly explained on a neutral ground, impact itself would signal that the real classification made by the law was in fact not neutral. See [*Washington; Arlington Heights*]. But there can be but one answer to the question whether this veteran preference excludes significant numbers of women from preferred state jobs because they are women or because they are nonveterans. Apart from the facts that the definition of 'veterans' in the statute has always been neutral as to gender and that Massachusetts has consistently defined veteran status in a way that has been inclusive of women who have served in the military, this is not a law that can plausibly be explained only as a gender-based classification. Indeed, it is not a law that can rationally be explained

on that ground. Veteran status is not uniquely male. Although few women benefit from the preference, the nonveteran class is not substantially all female. . . .

Moreover, [the] purposes of the statute provide the surest explanation for its
impact. Just as there are cases in which impact alone can unmask an invidious
classification, cf. [*Yick Wo*], there are others, in which — notwithstanding impact — the legitimate noninvidious purposes of the law cannot be missed. This is
one. The distinction made by [the statute] is, as it seems to be, quite simply
between veterans and nonveterans, not between men and women.

"The appellee's ultimate argument rests upon the presumption, common to the
criminal and civil law, that a person intends the natural and foreseeable consequences of his voluntary actions. . . .

"[It] cannot seriously be argued that the Legislature of Massachusetts could
have been unaware that most veterans are men. It would thus be disingenuous to
say that the adverse consequences of this legislation for women were unintended,
in the sense that they were not volitional or in the sense that they were not
foreseeable.

"'Discriminatory purpose,' however, implies more than intent as volition or
intent as awareness of consequences. It implies that the decisionmaker [selected]
or reaffirmed a particular course of action at least in part 'because of,' not merely
'in spite of,' its adverse effects upon an identifiable group. Yet nothing in the
record demonstrates that this preference for veterans was originally devised or
subsequently re-enacted because it would accomplish the collateral goal of keeping women in a stereotypic and predefined place in the Massachusetts Civil
Service.

"Veterans' hiring preferences represent an awkward — and, many argue, unfair — exception to the widely shared view that merit and merit alone should
prevail in the employment policies of government. [The substantial] edge granted
to veterans by [the Massachusetts statute] may reflect unwise policy. The appellee, however, has simply failed to demonstrate that the law in any way reflects a
purpose to discriminate on the basis of sex."

Justice Marshall wrote a dissenting opinion, which Justice Brennan joined:
"That a legislature seeks to advantage one group does not [exclude] the possibility that it also intends to disadvantage another. Individuals in general and lawmakers in particular frequently act for a variety of reasons. [Thus], the critical
constitutional inquiry is not whether an illicit consideration was the primary or
but-for cause of a decision, but rather whether it had an appreciable role in
shaping a given legislative enactment. . . .

"To discern the purposes underlying facially neutral policies, this Court has
[considered] the degree, inevitability, and foreseeability of any disproportionate
impact as well as the alternatives reasonably available.

"In the instant case, the impact of the Massachusetts statute on women is
undisputed. [Because] less than 2% of the women in Massachusetts are veterans,
the absolute preference formula has rendered desirable state civil service employment an almost exclusively male prerogative. . . .

"Where the foreseeable impact of a facially neutral policy is so disproportionate, the burden should rest on the State to establish that sex-based considerations
played no part in the choice of the particular legislative scheme.

"Clearly, that burden was not sustained here. The legislative history of the
statute reflects the Commonwealth's patent appreciation of the impact the prefer-

ence system would have on women, and an equally evident desire to mitigate that impact only with respect to certain traditionally female occupations. Until 1971, the statute and implementing civil service regulations exempted from operation of the preference any job requisitions 'especially calling for women.' In practice, this exemption, coupled with the absolute preference for veterans, has created a gender-based civil service hierarchy, with women occupying the low-grade clerical and secretarial jobs and men holding more responsible and remunerative positions."

Note: The Definition of Discriminatory Purpose

1. A *hypothetical problem*. What, precisely, is the mental state a legislator must have when voting for a non-race-specific statute for a court to subject it to heightened review? Consider the following hypothetical:

A playground located in a predominately white neighborhood attracts a large number of black youths. There have been a number of racial incidents involving fights between the blacks and a smaller number of white youths who also use the playground. White homeowners adjoining the playground complain, and the City Council votes to close it.

a. Councilmember A votes to close the playground because she dislikes blacks and blacks are getting most of the benefit from it;

b. Councilmember B has nothing against blacks personally, but his constituents wish the playground closed because they dislike blacks. B votes to close the playground because he wishes to be reelected;

c. Councilmember C has nothing against blacks personally but wishes to preserve racial peace. She votes to close the playground because she believes that keeping blacks out of white neighborhoods is a necessary, although unfortunate, means to this end;

d. Councilmember D believes that if the playground is not closed, it will have to be policed more closely. She votes to close it because she thinks that the money used for that purpose could better be used for other purposes;

e. Councilmember E shares D's concern about the expense of more police and therefore votes to close the playground. However, if the playground had been used primarily by whites, he would have found the money somewhere to keep it open.

Which (if any) of these legislative purposes would make the Council's decision unconstitutional? Suppose the motion to close the playground carries by a vote of 5 to 3, with the three dissenters voting to keep it open because it primarily benefits blacks. If the closure is challenged in court, what result?

2. *The problem of selective insensitivity*. Does the Court's formulation of the intent requirement in *Feeney* adequately heed the risk that legislatures will be selectively indifferent to the welfare of politically powerless groups? Consider the following argument: Of course, the equal protection clause prohibits governmental action deliberately undertaken to harm racial and other minorities. But few laws are passed because legislators have a sadistic desire to inflict disabilities on such groups. The more common problem arises when the legislature is pursuing a neutral aim but, in doing so, is selectively indifferent to the welfare of certain groups. Thus the question the *Feeney* Court should have asked is not whether the

veteran's preference was designed to harm women, but rather whether the legislature would have been willing to impose the same burdens on men that it imposed on women in order to have the preference. Cf. Brest, Foreword: In Defense of the Antidiscrimination Principle, 90 Harv. L. Rev. 1, 6-8 (1976).

Does the Constitution require legislatures to be equally sensitive to the psychological as well as material impact of facially neutral statutes? Consider Memphis v. Greene, 451 U.S. 100 (1981). At the request of homeowners of Hein Park, an historically all-white section of Memphis, the city closed a street passing through the community. The street was utilized primarily by blacks, and the barrier erected by the city demarcated the boundary between the all-white enclave and the black section of the city. Although the closing had a disproportionate racial impact, the trial court found that it was not motivated by a racially discriminatory intent. In light of this finding, the Supreme Court held, inter alia, that an equal protection attack on the city's action was foreclosed and that the burden imposed on blacks inconvenienced by the road closing was not a badge of slavery prohibited by the Thirteenth Amendment. Writing in dissent, Justice Marshall quarreled with

> the majority's suggestion that "[t]he injury to respondents established by the record is the requirement that one public street rather than another must be used for certain trips within the city" and that this requirement amounts to no more than "some slight inconvenience." [I] can only agree with the Court of Appeals, which viewed the city's action as nothing more than "one more of the many humiliations which society has historically visited" on Negro citizens. [Respondents] are being sent a clear, though sophisticated, message that because of their race, they are to stay out of the all-white enclave of Hein Park and should instead take the long way around in reaching their destinations to the south.

If the trial court's findings regarding purpose are correct, is it consistent with the principle of equality for the city negligently to inflict the psychological harm on a racial minority that Justice Marshall describes? Is it unrealistic to expect a court to administer an "equal sensitivity" test fairly and uniformly?

Note: The Problem of Proof

Stated abstractly, there appears to be a sharp distinction between a "purpose" and an "effects" test for the constitutionality of facially neutral statutes that disproportionately disadvantage racial minorities. In practical effect, however, the importance of the distinction turns on the willingness of courts to infer discriminatory purpose from either discriminatory effect or the absence of other plausible purposes. The more willing the courts are to infer purpose from effect or to insist on proof of important nondiscriminatory purposes, the less important the distinction. In *Arlington Heights* and *Feeney*, the Court maintained a fairly sharp distinction between the treatment of race-specific classifications on the one hand and facially neutral classifications with a disproportionate racial impact on the other. In other contexts, however, the Court has been more willing to infer purpose from effect and to evaluate the strength of a putative permissible purpose in deciding whether the actual purpose of a facially neutral statute is discriminatory:

1. *The jury cases.* When jury selection procedures are challenged as racially discriminatory, the Court has been receptive to arguments based on effect alone, at least as a device for shifting the burden of proof to the state. Castaneda v. Partida, 430 U.S. 482 (1977) sets out the standard method of proof:

> [In] order to show that an equal protection violation has occurred [the] defendant must show that the procedure employed resulted in substantial underrepresentation of his race or of the identifiable groups to which he belongs. The first step is to establish that the group is one that is a recognizable, distinct class, singled out for different treatment under the laws, as written or as applied. [Next], the degree of underrepresentation must be proved, by comparing the proportion of the group in the total population to the proportion called to serve as [jurors], over a significant period of time. [Finally, a] selection procedure that is susceptible of abuse or is not racially neutral supports the presumption of discrimination raised by the statistical showing. [Once] the defendant has shown substantial underrepresentation of his group, he has made out a prima facie case of discriminatory purpose, and the burden then shifts to the State to rebut that case.

What explains the Court's greater willingness to infer purpose from effect in the jury context? Does the reiterative nature of the decision make statistical analysis more relevant than it would be for "one shot" decisions like whether to grant a zoning variance or institute a veteran's preference? Cf. Mayor of Philadelphia v. Educational Equality League, 415 U.S. 605, 621 (1974) (percentage comparison between racial composition of thirteen-member panel and city population irrelevant because sample too small). Does the independent constitutional requirement that juries represent a fair cross-section of the community make the Court less tolerant in the jury context of possible nondiscriminatory purposes that might explain the disproportionate impact?

2. *The school desegregation cases.* Review pages 475-488 supra. Swann v. Charlotte-Mecklenburg Board of Education, section A supra, establishes that important inferences about the constitutional adequacy of a school desegregation plan can be drawn from its effect. Thus, there is a presumption against plans providing for one-race schools, and mathematical ratios can serve as "a starting point in the process of shaping a remedy." Moreover, the state interests in avoiding student transportation and maintaining compact attendance zones, although rational, are not sufficiently weighty to establish the constitutionality of neighborhood schools. Can *Swann* be distinguished from *Arlington Heights* and *Feeney* on the ground that it speaks to the remedies for constitutional violations, rather than to the proof necessary to establish the violation? Is this distinction consistent with the assertion in *Swann* that "judicial powers may be exercised only on the basis of a constitutional violation" and that "the nature of the violation determines the scope of the remedy"? Why couldn't an effects test be justified in cases like Washington v. Davis and Personnel Administrator v. Feeney on a remedial theory? Even when determining the existence of a violation, the Court has been more ready to infer purpose from effect in the school desegregation context than one might expect from reading *Arlington Heights*. In Keyes v. School District No. 1, page 482 supra, for example, a pre-*Arlington Heights* decision, the Court held that once intentional segregative acts were proven with regard to one portion of a school system, the burden shifted to the school board to prove that other acts having a segregative effect were not intentional. In Columbus Board of Educa-

tion v. Penick and Dayton Board of Education v. Brinkman (*Dayton II*), section A5 supra, decided after *Arlington Heights*, the Court strongly reaffirmed *Keyes*. Moreover, in the *Columbus* case, the Court rejected the school board's argument that the district court had acted contrary to *Arlington Heights* by inferring a segregative purpose solely from the segregative effect of the board's actions. The Court noted that while "disparate impact and foreseeable consequences, without more, do not establish a constitutional violation," adherence to a policy "with full knowledge of the predictable effects of such adherence upon racial imbalance in a school system is one factor among many others which may be considered by a court in determining whether an inference of segregative intent should be drawn."

What explains the greater emphasis on effects in the school desegregation context? Does the emphasis grow out of the nature of the *Brown* right itself, which the Court derived from the effect of segregated education on black students? Does the Court believe that the state interests competing with integrated education are less important than those at stake in cases like *Arlington Heights* and *Feeney*? Or does the emphasis on effect result from the historical fact that school desegregation law was formulated in a context of massive evasion and subterfuge by resisting school districts?

3. *The vote-dilution cases.* What sort of proof of discriminatory purpose suffices when a particular electoral system is challenged on the ground that it results in inadequate representation of minority groups? This issue divided the Court in Mobile v. Bolden, 446 U.S. 55 (1980), which concerned the constitutionality of at-large elections for the City Commission of Mobile, Alabama. Plaintiffs argued that the at-large, winner-take-all system unconstitutionally discriminated against black voters, who were consistently outvoted by the white majority. The district court agreed and ordered imposition of a mayor-city council form of government with councilmembers elected from single-member districts. The Supreme Court reversed, but no opinion attracted a majority of the justices. Writing for himself and three others, Justice Stewart began by noting that the test for the constitutionality of multimember districts was whether the purpose of such a system was to minimize the voting potential of racial minorities. Thus, the district court had erred in premising its finding of unconstitutionality solely on objective factors demonstrating that the at-large system had a discriminatory effect. Although acknowledging that effect "may provide an important starting point," Justice Stewart emphasized that "where the character of a law is readily explainable on grounds apart from race, as would nearly always be true where, as here, an entire system of local governance is brought into question, disproportionate impact alone cannot be decisive."

Here, the objective factors relied on by the court below "were most assuredly insufficient to prove an unconstitutionally discriminatory purpose." Specifically, the district court had placed undue weight on the fact that no black had ever been elected to the Mobile City Commission. "It may be that Negro candidates have been defeated, but that fact alone does not work a constitutional deprivation." Nor was it sufficient that persons elected to the commission discriminated against blacks in municipal employment and dispensing of public services, since "evidence of discrimination by white officials in Mobile is relevant only as the most tenuous and circumstantial evidence of the constitutional invalidity of the electoral system under which they attained their offices." Finally, the substantial history of prior racial discrimination in Alabama did not demonstrate that this electoral system had a discriminatory purpose. "[Past] discrimination cannot, in the manner of original sin, condemn government action that is not itself unlawful."

Justices Blackmun and Stevens also voted to reverse the district court, but neither joined the plurality opinion. Justices White, Brennan, and Marshall each filed dissenting opinions.

Two years after the *Mobile* decision, a majority of the Court was able to agree on a test for vote-dilution cases that, although relying on purpose analysis, seemingly placed far greater emphasis on inference of purpose from effect. *Rogers v. Lodge*, 458 U.S. 613 (1982), once again concerned an equal protection attack on an at-large voting system that effectively submerged the black minority of voters. Although blacks composed 53.6 percent of the population and 38 percent of the registered voters in Burke County, Georgia, no black had ever been elected to the county Board of Commissioners. The district court struck down the system of at-large elections, holding that the system had a racially neutral purpose when adopted but was maintained for the purpose of diluting black voting strength. This time, the Court affirmed in an opinion written by Justice White, one of the *Mobile* dissenters. The Court emphasized that it was not abandoning the *Mobile* requirement of proof of discriminatory purpose in vote dilution cases. It distinguished *Mobile* on the ground that here, the trial judge had relied on the impact of the system to infer discriminatory purpose rather than concluding that the impact alone made the system unconstitutional. In analyzing the district court's opinion, however, the Court seemed to place great weight on some of the same factors that *Mobile* had held were insufficient to establish discriminatory purpose. Thus, the fact that no black had ever been elected to the board was "important evidence of purposeful exclusion." While this evidence alone was insufficient to establish discriminatory purpose, the district court's conclusion was also supported by findings of past discrimination in voting and schooling that limited black participation in the political process, unresponsiveness of elected officials to black concerns, and the depressed socioeconomic status of blacks. Moreover, the size of the district made it difficult for blacks to get to polling places, and the absence of residency requirements meant that all candidates could reside in "lily-white" neighborhoods.

In a long dissenting opinion, Justice Stevens argued that the Court erred in judging the constitutionality of local electoral systems based on the subjective intent of the legislature rather than on the objective effect of the rules in question. Although certain features of Burke County's at-large voting system were questionable under this test because of their effect on minority representation, the plaintiffs had not argued that the system was objectively deficient, and the record was therefore inadequate to support such a finding. In a shorter dissent, Justice Powell, joined by Justice Rehnquist, complained that the majority had based its decision on the very factors that *Mobile* had held were insufficient to establish discriminatory purpose. Although agreeing with the majority that a purpose test should be utilized, Justice Powell noted that he also shared Justice Stevens's concern that the majority was inviting federal courts to engage in "deeply subjective inquiries into the motivations of local officials" which were "unseemly" and "[intruded] federal courts — with only the vaguest constitutional direction — into an area of intensely local and political concern." In order to avoid these problems, Justice Powell argued that federal courts should be limited to consideration of objective factors tending to prove discriminatory intent.

Although disagreeing as to the ultimate outcome, all nine Justices in *Rogers* placed heavy emphasis on the impact of Burke County's voting system. What explains the reliance on effect in this context? Recall that in *Feeney* the Court was able to discount a claim of discriminatory purpose even though the adverse effect on women was foreseeable on the ground that this effect was simply a byproduct of the state's legitimate policy of aiding veterans. Could a similar analysis have been utilized in *Rogers*? Are there legitimate policies, analogous to aiding veterans, that the state may pursue in the voting context? Whatever voting system Burke County adopted, the system would have some effect on the distribution of political power between various groups within the county. Would it be constitutional for the county to pursue *any* policy designed to affect that distribution? If you think that the pursuit of any such policy is impermissible, how could the county avoid acting pursuant to an impermissible purpose?

Is emphasis on effect particularly appropriate in the voting context because the voting system utilized will affect the composition of the very body that determines the system to be utilized in the future? Should the judiciary accord deference to a legislative voting scheme disadvantaging blacks when the scheme is formulated by a legislative body elected by a method that, itself, disadvantages blacks? Is it a sufficient response that blacks are, presumably, fairly represented in the state legislature, which could, if it wished, alter Burke County's electoral system? That they are fairly represented in Congress, which could presumably utilize its power under the fourteenth and fifteenth amendments to prohibit at-large voting in this context? See Chapter 2, section F5, supra.

If the Court's emphasis on effect is justified in cases like Rogers v. Lodge, precisely what effect is it that the Constitution prohibits? Does the equal protection clause guarantee blacks the right to elect representatives in rough proportion to their numbers? To a fair chance to elect representatives in rough proportion to their numbers insofar as black candidates reflect the majority's concerns on the issues? To a fair chance to elect candidates — black or white — responsive to black concerns on the issues? Consider Whitcomb v. Chavis, 403 U.S. 124 (1971):

> [It] seems reasonable to infer that had the Democrats won all of the elections or even most of them, the ghetto would have had no justifiable complaints about representation. The fact is, however, that four of the five elections were won by Republicans, which was not the party of the ghetto and which would not always slate ghetto candidates. [If] this is the proper view of this case, the failure of the ghetto to have legislative seats in proportion to its population emerges more as a function of losing elections than of built-in bias against poor Negroes. The voting power of ghetto residents may have been "cancelled out" as the District Court held, but this seems a mere euphemism for political defeat at the polls.

How should an effects-based test be administered in light of the fact that a system having the effect of enhancing the voting power of one minority group will often have the effect of diluting the power of another such group? Consider, e.g., United Jewish Organizations v. Carey, 430 U.S. 144 (1977). Petitioners challenged the constitutionality of New York's deliberate use of racial criteria in drawing district lines for the state legislature. New York deliberately attempted to enhance black voting strength in order to satisfy the U.S. Attorney General, whose approval was required under the 1965 Voting Rights Act, that the redistricting did not dilute the black vote. One effect of the redistricting was to divide the 30,000 member Hasidic Jewish community, which had previously been located in one district, into two districts, each of which had a substantial nonwhite majority. The Supreme Court refused to invalidate this deliberate use of racial criteria. In the course of so holding, Justice White, writing for a plurality, noted that the plan "represented no racial slur or stigma with respect to whites or any other race" and that "there was no fencing out of the white population from participation in the political processes of the county." In a concurring opinion, Justice Stewart emphasized that "Under the Fourteenth Amendment the question is whether the reapportionment plan represents purposeful discrimination against white voters." While disproportionate impact had some bearing on this question, "The clear purpose with which the New York legislature acted — in response to the position of the United States Department of Justice under the Voting Rights Act — forecloses any finding that it acted with the invidious purpose of discriminating against white voters." Under a test emphasizing the effect of an electoral scheme on minority voting power, how should the claim of the Hasidic Jews have been resolved? For further discussion of the right to vote, see Chapter 6, section, infra.

Note: Strict Scrutiny of Facially Neutral Statutes — Beyond Purpose

Washington v. Davis makes clear that a facially neutral statute will not be treated as race specific merely because of its disproportionate impact on a racial minority. On the other hand, if the classification was formulated for a discriminatory purpose, the Court generally (although not always) has strictly scrutinized it. In the absence of a discriminatory purpose, is strict scrutiny ever appropriate for facially neutral statutes? The Court has sometimes treated such statutes as race specific in two situations: when they permit or facilitate discrimination and when they effectively describe a racial minority.

1. *Facially neutral statutes permitting or facilitating discrimination.* Are statutes that invite racially discriminatory administration, or are readily susceptible to such administration, facially invalid even in the absence of proof of actual discrimination? Consider Louisiana v. United States, 380 U.S. 145 (1965), where the Court invalidated under the fifteenth amendment a state law requiring all voters to be able to understand and give a reasonable interpretation of any section of the state or federal constitution when read to them by the registrar. There was ample evidence to show that the provision had been administered in discriminatory fashion to keep blacks from voting. However, the Court did not stop with a holding that application of the law was unconstitutional. It went on to find the statute facially invalid on the ground that it gave officials "uncontrolled power to determine whether the applicant's understanding of the Federal or State Constitution is satisfactory. [The] cherished right of people in a country like ours to vote cannot be obliterated by the use of laws like this, which leave the voting fate of a citizen to the passing whim of impulse of an individual registrar."

Does United States v. Louisiana remain good law after Washington v. Davis? Compare United States v. Louisiana with Swain v. Alabama, supra this section.

In addition to his challenge to the prosecutor's use of peremptory challenges discussed above, Swain attacked the overall composition of the jury pool from which his jury was drawn. Under Alabama law, a three-person jury commission was directed to place on the jury rolls all "honest, intelligent men [esteemed] for their integrity, good character and sound judgment." In practice, the commissioners exercised considerable discretion in deciding who to place on the rolls, and blacks were substantially underrepresented in the pool chosen. Nonetheless, the Court rejected Swain's challenge, holding that "purposeful discrimination based on race alone [was not] satisfactorily proved. [Undoubtedly] the selection of prospective jurors was somewhat haphazard and little effort was made to ensure that all groups in the community were fully represented. But an imperfect system is not equivalent to purposeful discrimination based on race." But cf. Castaneda v. Partida, 430 U.S. 482 (1977) (jury selection procedure "susceptible of abuse" supports presumption that statistical disparity results from deliberate discrimination).

After *Swain* and *Davis*, should the result in cases like United States v. Louisiana turn on whether those drafting the statute granted administrative discretion *for the purpose of* having that discretion exercised in a racially discriminatory fashion? The Court's opinion in United States v. Louisiana in fact relies heavily on the state's long history of legislative efforts to subvert black voting rights. But if the legislature has a choice between outlawing discriminatory enforcement and remaining silent, what legitimate purpose could it ever have for failing to outlaw it?

Suppose a statute not only permits but also in some way facilitates or encourages administrative discrimination? Should such a statute be treated as if it discriminated on its face even in the absence of discriminatory enforcement? Or should the opportunity for discriminatory enforcement be treated simply as some evidence that there was in fact discrimination? Compare Anderson v. Martin, 375 U.S. 399 (1964) (state law requiring designation of race of candidates on ballot facially unconstitutional because it places "the power of the State behind a racial classification that induces racial prejudice at the polls"), with Alexander v. Louisiana, 405 U.S. 625 (1972) (racial designation of forms used by jury commissioners, taken together with statistical disparity, make out prima facie case of purposeful administrative discrimination in jury selection).

2. *Statutes that describe racial minorities.* Should a statute be subject to strict scrutiny even if it does not use race per se as a classifying principle, if it disadvantages individuals based on characteristics that effectively describe members of a minority race?

Suppose, for example, that it could be shown that, as a statistical matter, blacks default on loans more frequently than whites. Obviously, a law requiring a state lender to charge higher interest rates to blacks than to whites would be subject to strict scrutiny. But suppose further that there is a high degree of residential segregation in the state. It is therefore also possible to show a correlation between default rates and the zip code of the borrower — a correlation that is entirely the product of the fact that blacks live in the neighborhoods with high default rates. How should a court treat a statute requiring higher interest rates for borrowers with certain zip codes? Is such a statute subject only to low-level review because the purpose of its drafters was to avoid defaults rather than to harm blacks? Or is it subject to strict scrutiny because, whatever their purpose, the drafters of the statute are using zip codes as a proxy for race? Would the case be different if there was a high correlation between zip code and race, but the correlation between zip code and default rates was unrelated to race?

Consider Guinn v. United States, 238 U.S. 347 (1915). Shortly after its admission to the Union, Oklahoma amended its constitution to require prospective voters to pass a literacy test, except that all persons entitled to vote on January 1, 1866, and all lineal descendants of such persons were not required to pass the test. Although disclaiming any "right to question the motive of the State in establishing [this] standard," the United States claimed that it violated the fifteenth amendment. In response, the state contended that the standard did not constitute impermissible race discrimination because it did "not in terms make any discrimination on account of race, color, or previous condition of servitude." A unanimous Court rejected the state's argument and invalidated the provision. "It is true [the law] contains no express words of an exclusion from the standard which it establishes of any person on account of race, color or previous condition of servitude prohibited by the Fifteenth Amendment, but the standard itself inherently brings that result into existence since it is based purely upon a period of time before the enactment of the Fifteenth Amendment and makes that period the controlling and dominant test of the right of suffrage." (As an apparently alternative ground for decision, the opinion also noted that "the same result [is] demonstrated by considering whether it is possible to discover any basis of reason for the standard [other] than the purpose above stated.")

Does Guinn depend on the sort of effects analysis prohibited by Washington v. Davis, or is the case distinguishable because the Oklahoma law was "really" a racial classification subject to strict scrutiny regardless of its purpose? In modern cases, arising under the fourteenth amendment, the Court has struggled to distinguish between classifications that are subject to strict scrutiny because they describe a suspect class and classifications subject only to rational relationship review because they merely create a disproportionate impact on such a class. Although the modern cases concern statutes that allegedly discriminate along arguably suspect lines that are not racial, they are discussed here because of the analogy between defining racial and other suspect classifications.

Consider first Geduldig v. Aiello, 417 U.S. 484 (1974). A state-administered disability insurance system excluded from coverage certain disabilities relating to pregnancy. The Court, in an opinion by Justice Stewart, upheld the exclusion after finding that it was rationally related to legitimate state objectives. The Court rejected the argument that the exclusion constituted gender discrimination subject to heightened scrutiny:

> The California insurance program does not exclude anyone from benefit eligibility because of gender but merely removes one physical condition — pregnancy — from the list of compensable disabilities. While it is true that only women can become pregnant, it does not follow that every legislative classification concerning pregnancy is a sex-based classification. [The] lack of identity between the excluded disability and gender as such under this insurance program becomes clear under the most cursory analysis. The program divides potential recipients into two groups — pregnant women and nonpregnant persons. While the first group is exclusively female, the second includes members of both sexes.

Compare Aiello with Personnel Administrator v. Feeney, supra this section. Appellee claimed that a Massachusetts statute granting preference to veterans in state employment decisions amounted to unconstitutional gender discrimination. Despite the overwhelming advantage the preference gave to males, the Court, again in an opinion by Justice Stewart, rejected the claim and, utilizing a rational basis test, upheld the statute. On this occasion, however, the Court suggested that in some cases, describing a trait of a suspect class might subject the classification to strict scrutiny even in the absence of discriminatory purpose:

> When a statute gender-neutral on its face is challenged on the ground that its effects upon women are disproportionably adverse, a two-fold inquiry is appropriate. The first question is whether the statutory classification is indeed neutral in the sense that it is not gender based. If the classification itself, *covert or overt*, is not based upon gender, the second question is whether the adverse effect reflects invidious gender-based discrimination.

(Emphasis added.) On the facts before it, the Court found that the veteran's preference was not a "covert" gender classification because "significant numbers of nonveterans are men, and all nonveterans — male as well as female — are placed at a disadvantage. Too many men are affected by [the statute] to permit the inference that [it] is but a pretext for preferring men over women." Having found the classification gender-neutral, the Court then proceeded to hold that it was not infected by a gender-based discriminatory purpose. (This portion of the opinion is summarized supra this section, pages 554-556.) In a brief concurring opinion, Justice Stevens noted that he was "not at all sure that there is any difference between the two questions posed [by the Court]. If a classification is not overtly based on gender, I am inclined to believe the question whether it is covertly gender based is the same as the question whether its adverse effects reflect invidious gender-based discrimination."

Do you agree? Suppose a law grants a hiring preference only to persons who are not capable of becoming pregnant. Would such a law be subject to heightened review only if its opponents could prove a discriminatory purpose? Is the Massachusetts statute meaningfully different from this hypothetical because of the large number of men who are ineligible for the veterans' preference? Should a law granting a preference exclusively to male veterans be subject to heightened review?

3.   Race-Specific Classifications That Are Facially Neutral

Loving v. Virginia

388 U.S. 1 (1967)

Mr. Chief Justice Warren delivered the opinion of the Court.

This case presents a constitutional question never addressed by this Court: whether a statutory scheme adopted by the State of Virginia to prevent marriages between persons solely on the basis of racial classifications violates the Equal Protection and Due Process Clauses of the Fourteenth Amendment. For reasons which seem to us to reflect the central meaning of those constitutional commands, we conclude that these statutes cannot stand consistently with the Fourteenth Amendment. . . .

[The Lovings challenged their conviction under a Virginia statute making it a felony for "any white person [to] intermarry with a colored person, or any colored person [to] intermarry with a white person." The Supreme Court of Appeals of Virginia upheld the statute's constitutionality. The state court relied on its own earlier decision holding that the statute served the legitimate state purposes of preserving the "racial integrity" of its citizens and preventing "corruption of blood," the creation of "a mongrel breed of citizens," and "the obliteration of racial pride."]

[The] State argues that the meaning of the Equal Protection Clause, as illuminated by the statements of the Framers, is only that state penal laws containing an interracial element as part of the definition of the offense must apply equally to whites and Negroes in the sense that members of each race are punished to the same degree. Thus, the State contends that, because its miscegenation statutes punish equally both the white and the Negro participants in an interracial marriage, these statutes, despite their reliance on racial classifications, do not constitute an invidious discrimination based upon race. . . .

Because we reject the notion that the mere "equal application" of a statute containing racial classifications is enough to remove the classifications from the Fourteenth Amendment's proscription of all invidious racial discriminations, we do not accept the State's contention that these statutes should be upheld if there is any possible basis for concluding that they serve a rational purpose. The mere fact of equal application does not mean that our analysis of these statutes should follow the approach we have taken in cases involving no racial discrimination. . . .

The State finds support for its "equal application" theory in the decision of the Court in Pace v. Alabama, 106 U.S. 583 (1883). In that case, the Court upheld a conviction under an Alabama statute forbidding adultery or fornication between a white person and a Negro which imposed a greater penalty than that of a statute proscribing similar conduct by members of the same race. The Court reasoned that the statute could not be said to discriminate against Negroes because the punishment for each participant in the offense was the same. However, as recently as the 1964 Term, in rejecting the reasoning of that case, we stated "Pace represents a limited view of the Equal Protection Clause which has not withstood analysis in the subsequent decisions of this Court." McLaughlin v. Florida, [379 U.S. 184, 188 (1964)]. As we there demonstrated, the Equal Protection Clause requires the consideration of whether the classifications drawn by any statute constitute an arbitrary and invidious discrimination. The clear and central purpose of the Fourteenth Amendment was to eliminate all official state sources of invidious racial discrimination in the States.

There can be no question but that Virginia's miscegenation statutes rest solely upon distinctions drawn according to race. The statutes proscribe generally accepted conduct if engaged in by members of different races. [At] the very least, the Equal Protection Clause demands that racial classifications, especially suspect in criminal statutes, be subjected to the "most rigid scrutiny," Korematsu v. United States, 323 U.S. 214, 216 (1944), and, if they are ever to be upheld, they must be shown to be necessary to the accomplishment of some permissible state objective, independent of the racial discrimination which it was the object of the Fourteenth Amendment to eliminate. . . .

There is patently no legitimate overriding purpose independent of invidious racial discrimination which justifies this classification. The fact that Virginia prohibits only interracial marriages involving white persons demonstrates that the racial classifications must stand on their own justification, as measures designed to maintain White Supremacy.[11] We have consistently denied the constitutionality of measures which restrict the rights of citizens on account of race. There can be no doubt that restricting the freedom to marry solely because of racial classifications violates the central meaning of the Equal Protection Clause. . . .

These convictions must be reversed.

It is so ordered.

MR. JUSTICE STEWART, concurring.

I have previously expressed the belief that "it is simply not possible for a state law to be valid under our Constitution which makes the criminality of an act depend upon the race of the actor." McLaughlin v. Florida, 379 U.S. 184, 198 (concurring opinion). Because I adhere to that belief, I concur in the judgment of the Court.

Washington v. Seattle School District No. 1

458 U.S. 457 (1982)

JUSTICE BLACKMUN delivered the opinion of the Court.

We are presented here with an extraordinary question: whether an elected local school board may use the Fourteenth Amendment to *defend* its program of busing for integration from attack by the State.

[In 1978 the Seattle School Board voluntarily adopted a plan to alleviate racial isolation in the schools. The plan made extensive use of busing and mandatory reassignment. Opponents of the plan responded by drafting a statewide initiative designed to terminate use of mandatory busing for purposes of racial integration. The proposal, known as Initiative 350, prohibited school boards from requiring students to attend schools not nearest or next nearest to the student's place of residence. The initiative included a series of exceptions, however, which permitted such assignments for a variety of nonracial reasons, such as overcrowding or special education needs. It also permitted racial reassignments when a court found that they were constitutionally required.

The initiative was adopted by a substantial statewide majority, including a majority of Seattle voters. The Seattle School Board thereupon initiated this litigation, challenging the constitutionality of the initiative under the equal protection clause of the fourteenth amendment. The district court held that the initiative was unconstitutional, and the court of appeals affirmed.]

II

The Equal Protection Clause of the Fourteenth Amendment guarantees racial minorities the right to full participation in the political life of the community. It is

---

11. Appellants point out that the State's concern in these statutes, as expressed in the words of the 1924 Act's title, "An Act to Preserve Racial Integrity," extends only to the integrity of the white race. While Virginia prohibits whites from marrying any nonwhite. . . . Negroes, Orientals, and any other racial class may intermarry without statutory interference. Appellants contend that this distinction renders Virginia's miscegenation statutes arbitrary and unreasonable even assuming the constitutional validity of an official purpose to preserve "racial integrity." We need not reach this contention because we find the racial classifications in these statutes repugnant to the Fourteenth Amendment, even assuming an even-handed state purpose to protect the "integrity" of all races.

beyond dispute, of course, that given racial or ethnic groups may not be denied the franchise, or precluded from entering into the political process in a reliable and meaningful manner. But the Fourteenth Amendment also reaches "a political structure that treats all individuals as equals," Mobile v. Bolden, 446 U.S. 55, 84 (1980) (Stevens, J., concurring in the judgment), yet more subtly distorts governmental processes in such a way as to place special burdens on the ability of minority groups to achieve beneficial legislation.

This principle received its clearest expression in Hunter v. Erickson, [393 U.S. 385 (1969)], a case that involved attempts to overturn antidiscrimination legislation in Akron, Ohio. The Akron city council, pursuant to its ordinary legislative processes, had enacted a fair housing ordinance. In response, the local citizenry, using an established referendum procedure, amended the city charter to provide that ordinances regulating real estate transactions "'on the basis of race, color, religion, national origin or ancestry must first be approved by a majority of the electors voting on the question at a regular or general election before said ordinance shall be effective.'" This action "not only suspended the operation of the existing ordinance forbidding housing discrimination, but also required the approval of the electors before any future [fair housing] ordinance could take effect." In essence, the amendment changed the requirements for the adoption of one type of local legislation: to enact an ordinance barring housing discrimination on the basis of race or religion, proponents had to obtain the approval of the city council *and* of a majority of the voters citywide. To enact an ordinance preventing housing discrimination on other grounds, or to enact any other type of housing ordinance, proponents needed the support of only the city council.

In striking down the charter amendment, the *Hunter* Court recognized that, on its face, the provision "draws no distinctions among racial and religious groups." But it did differentiate "between those groups who sought the law's protection against racial . . . discriminations in the sale and rental of real estate and those who sought to regulate real property transactions in the pursuit of other ends," thus "disadvantag[ing] those who would benefit from laws barring racial . . . discriminations as against those who would bar other discriminations or who would otherwise regulate the real estate market in their favor." In "reality," the burden imposed by such an arrangement necessarily "falls on the minority. The majority needs no protection against discrimination and if it did, a referendum might be bothersome but no more than that." In effect, then, the charter amendment served as an "explicitly racial classification treating racial housing matters differently from other racial and housing matters." Id., at 339. This made the amendment constitutionally suspect: "the State may no more disavantage any *particular* group by making it more difficult to enact legislation in its behalf than it may dilute any person's vote or give any group a smaller representation than another of comparable size. . . .

[This case yields] a simple but central principle. [The] political majority may generally restructure the political process to place obstacles in the path of everyone seeking to secure the benefits of governmental action. But a different analysis is required when the State allocates governmental power non-neutrally, by explicitly using the *racial* nature of a decision to determine the decisionmaking process. State action of this kind, the Court said, "places *special* burdens on racial minorities within the governmental process. . . ."

III

In our view, Initiative 350 must fall because it does "not attemp[t] to allocate governmental power on the basis of any general principle." Hunter v. Erickson. Instead, it uses the racial nature of an issue to define the governmental decision-making structure, and thus imposes substantial and unique burdens on racial minorities.

A

Noting that Initiative 350 nowhere mentions "race" or "integration," appellants suggest that the legislation has no racial overtones; they maintain that *Hunter* is inapposite because the initiative simply permits busing for certain enumerated purposes while neutrally forbidding it for all other reasons. We find it difficult to believe that appellants' analysis is seriously advanced, however, for despite its facial neutrality there is little doubt that the initiative was effectively drawn for racial purposes. [It] is beyond reasonable dispute, then, that the initiative was enacted " 'because of,' not merely 'in spite of,' its adverse effects upon" busing for integration. Personnel Administrator of Massachusetts v. Feeney. . . .

[It] undoubtedly is true, as the United States suggests, that the proponents of mandatory integration cannot be classified by race: Negroes and whites may be counted among both the supporters and the opponents of Initiative 350. And it should be equally clear that white as well as Negro children benefit from exposure to "ethnic and racial diversity in the classroom." Columbus Board of Education v. Penick, 443 U.S. 449 (1979) (Powell, J., dissenting). But neither of these factors serves to distinguish *Hunter*, for we may fairly assume that members of the racial majority both favored and benefited from Akron's fair housing ordinance.

In any event, our cases suggest that desegregation of the public schools, like the Akron open housing ordinance, at bottom inures primarily to the benefit of the minority, and is designed for that purpose. . . .

B

We are also satisfied that the practical effect of Initiative 350 is to work a reallocation of power of the kind condemned in *Hunter*. The initiative removes the authority to address a racial problem — and only a racial problem — from the existing decisionmaking body, in such a way as to burden minority interests. . . .

The state appellants and the United States, in response to this line of analysis, argue that Initiative 350 has not worked *any* reallocation of power. They note that the State necessarily retains plenary authority over Washington's system of education, and therefore they suggest that the initiative amounts to nothing more than an unexceptional example of a State's intervention in its own school system. . . .

But "insisting that a State may distribute legislative power as it desires . . . furnish[es] no justification for a legislative structure which otherwise would violate the Fourteenth Amendment. [It] is irrelevant that the State might have vested all decisionmaking authority in itself, so long as the political structure it in fact erected imposes comparative burdens on minority interests; that much is settled by *Hunter*. And until the passage of Initiative 350, Washington law in fact had established the local school board, rather than the State, as the entity charged with making decisions of the type at issue here. . . .

[Before] adoption of the initiative, the power to determine what programs would most appropriately fill a school district's educational needs — including programs involving student assignment and desegregation — was firmly committed to the local board's discretion. The question whether to provide an integrated learning environment rather than a system of neighborhood schools surely involved a decision of that sort. After passage of Initiative 350, authority over all but one of those areas remained in the hands of the local board. By placing power over desegregative busing at the state level, then, Initiative 350 plainly "differentiates between the treatment of problems involving racial matters and that afforded other problems in the same area."[23] . . .

C

To be sure, "the simple repeal or modification of desegregation or anti-discrimination laws, without more, never has been viewed as embodying a presumptively invalid racial classification."

Initiative 350, however, works something more than the "mere repeal" of a desegregation law by the political entity that created it. It burdens all future attempts to integrate Washington schools in districts throughout the State, by lodging decisionmaking authority over the question at a new and remote level of government. Indeed, the initiative, like the charter amendment at issue in *Hunter*, has its most pernicious effect on integration programs that do "*not* arouse extraordinary controversy." In such situations the initiative makes the enactment of racially beneficial legislation difficult, though the particular program involved might not have inspired opposition had it been promulgated through the usual legislative processes used for comparable legislation. . . .

IV

In the end, appellants are reduced to suggesting that *Hunter* has been effectively overruled by more recent decisions of this Court. As they read it, *Hunter* applied a simple "disparate impact" analysis: it invalidated a facially neutral ordinance because of the law's adverse effects upon racial minorities. Appellants therefore contend that *Hunter* was swept away, along with the disparate impact approach to

---

23. Throughout his dissent, Justice Powell insists that the Court has created a "vested constitutional right to local decisionmaking," that under our holding "the people of the State of Washington apparently are forever barred from developing a different policy on mandatory busing where a School District previously has adopted one of its own," and that today's decision somehow raises doubts about "the authority of a State to abolish school boards altogether." These statements evidence a basic misunderstanding of our decision. Our analysis vests no rights, and has nothing to do with whether school board action predates that taken by the State. Instead, what we find objectionable about Initiative 350 is the comparative burden it imposes on minority participation in the political process — that is, the racial nature of the way in which it structures the *process* of decisionmaking. It is evident, then, that the horribles paraded by the dissent — which have nothing to do with the ability of minorities to participate in the process of self-government — are entirely unrelated to this case. It is equally clear, as we have noted at several points in our opinion, that the State remains free to vest all decisionmaking power in state officials, or to remove authority from local school boards in a race-neutral manner.

equal protection, in Washington v. Davis, 426 U.S. 229 (1976), and Arlington Heights v. Metropolitan Housing Dev. Corp., 429 U.S. 252 (1977).

Appellants unquestionably are correct when they suggest that "purposeful discrimination is 'the condition that offends the Constitution.'" [Thus,] when facially neutral legislation is subjected to equal protection attack, an inquiry into intent is necessary, to determine whether the legislation in some sense was designed to accord disparate treatment on the basis of racial considerations. Appellants' suggestion that this analysis somehow conflicts with *Hunter*, however, misapprehends the basis of the *Hunter* doctrine. . . .

There is one immediate and crucial difference between *Hunter* and the cases cited by appellants. While decisions such as Washington v. Davis and *Arlington Heights* considered classifications facially unrelated to race, the charter amendment at issue in *Hunter* dealt in explicitly racial terms with legislation designed to benefit minorities "as minorities," not legislation intended to benefit some larger group of underprivileged citizens among whom minorities were disproportionately represented. This does not mean, of course, that every attempt to address a racial issue gives rise to an impermissible racial classification. But when the political process or the decisionmaking mechanism used to *address* racially conscious legislation — and only such legislation — is singled out for peculiar and disadvantageous treatment, the governmental action plainly "rests on 'distinctions based on race.'"[29] And when the State's allocation of power places unusual burdens on the ability of racial groups to enact legislation specifically designed to overcome the "special condition" of prejudice, the governmental action seriously "curtail[s] the operation of those political processes ordinarily to be relied upon to protect minorities." United States v. Carolene Products Co., 304 U.S. 144, 152-153, n.4 (1938). In a most direct sense, this implicates the judiciary's special role in safeguarding the interests of those groups that are "relegated to such a position of political powerlessness as to command extraordinary protection from the majoritarian political process." . . .

V

In reaching this conclusion, we do not undervalue the magnitude of the State's interest in its system of education. Washington could have reserved to state officials the right to make all decisions in the areas of education and student assignment. It has chosen, however, to use a more elaborate system; having done so, the State is obligated to operate that system within the confines of the Fourteenth Amendment. That, we believe, it has failed to do.

Accordingly, the judgment of the Court of Appeals is affirmed.

JUSTICE POWELL, with whom [CHIEF JUSTICE BURGER], JUSTICE REHNQUIST, and JUSTICE O'CONNOR join, dissenting. . . .

[In] the absence of a prior constitutional violation, the States are under no constitutional duty to adopt integration programs in their schools, and certainly

---

29. Thus we do not hold, as the dissent implies, that the State's attempt to repeal a desegregation program creates a racial classification, while "identical action" by the Seattle School Board does not. It is the State's race-conscious restructuring of its decisionmaking process that is impermissible, not the simple repeal of the Seattle Plan.

they are under no duty to establish a regime of mandatory busing. Nor does the Federal Constitution require that particular decisions concerning the schools or any other matter be made on the local as opposed to the State level. It does not require the States to establish local governmental bodies or to delegate unreviewable authority to them. . . .

Application of these settled principles demonstrates the serious error of today's decision — an error that cuts deeply into the heretofore unquestioned right of a State to structure the decisionmaking authority of its government. In this case, by Initiative 350, the State has adopted a policy of racial neutrality in student assignments. The policy in no way interferes with the power of State or Federal Courts to remedy constitutional violations. And if such a policy had been adopted by any of the school districts in this litigation there could have been no question that the policy was constitutional.

The issue here arises only because the Seattle School District — in the absence of a then established State policy — chose to adopt race specific school assignments with extensive busing. It is not questioned that the District itself, at any time thereafter, could have changed its mind and cancelled its integration program without violating the Federal Constitution. Yet this Court holds that neither the legislature nor the people of the State of Washington could alter what the District had decided.

The Court argues that the people of Washington by Initiative 350 created a racial classification, and yet must agree that identical action by the Seattle School District itself would have created no such classification. This is not an easy argument to answer because it seems to make no sense. School boards are the creation of supreme State authority, whether in a State Constitution or by legislative enactment. Until today's decision no one would have questioned the authority of a State to abolish school boards altogether, or to require that they conform to any lawful State policy. And in the State of Washington, a neighborhood school policy would have been lawful.

Under today's decision this heretofore undoubted supreme authority of a State's electorate is to be curtailed whenever a school board — or indeed any other state board or local instrumentality — adopts a race specific program that arguably benefits racial minorities. Once such a program is adopted, *only* the local or subordinate entity that approved it will have authority to change it. The Court offers no authority or relevant explanation for this extraordinary subordination of the ultimate sovereign power of a State to act with respect to racial matters by subordinate bodies. It is a strange notion — alien to our system — that local governmental bodies can forever preempt the ability of a State — the sovereign power — to address a matter of compelling concern to the State. The Constitution of the United States does not require such a bizarre result. . . .

[Initiative] 350 places no "special burdens on racial minorities within the governmental process," [*Hunter*], such that interference with the State's distribution of authority is justified. Initiative 350 is simply a reflection of the State's political process at work. It does not alter that process in any respect. It does not require, for example, that all matters dealing with race — or with integration in the schools — must henceforth be submitted to a referendum of the people. Cf. Hunter v. Erickson, supra. The State has done no more than precisely what the Court has said that it should do: It has "resolved through the political process" the "desirability and efficacy of [mandatory] school desegregation" where there has been no unlawful segregation.

The political process in Washington, as in other States, permits persons who are dissatisfied at a local level to appeal to the State legislature or the people of the State for redress. It permits the people of a State to preempt local policies, and to formulate new programs and regulations. Such a process is inherent in the continued sovereignty of the States. This is our system. Any time a State chooses to address a major issue some persons or groups may be disadvantaged. In a democratic system there are winners and losers. But there is no inherent unfairness in this and certainly no Constitutional violation. . . .

Nothing in *Hunter* supports the Courts extraordinary invasion into the State's distribution of authority. Even could it be assumed that Initiative 350 imposed a burden on racial minorities, it simply does not place unique political obstacles in the way of racial minorities. In this case, unlike in *Hunter*, the political system has *not* been redrawn or altered. The authority of the State over the public school system, acting through Initiative or the legislature, is plenary. Thus, the State's political system is not altered when it adopts for the first time a policy, concededly within the area of its authority, for the regulation of local school districts. And certainly racial minorities are not uniquely or comparatively burdened by the State's adoption of a policy that would be lawful if adopted by any School District in the State.

Hunter, therefore, is simply irrelevant. It is the *Court* that by its decision today disrupts the normal course of State government. Under its unprecedented theory of a vested constitutional right to local decisionmaking, the State apparently is now forever barred from addressing the perplexing problems of how best to educate fairly *all* children in a multi-racial society where, as in this case, the local school board has acted first.[16] . . .

CRAWFORD v. BOARD OF EDUCATION, 458 U.S. 527 (1982): In this case, decided on the same day as *Seattle*, petitioners challenged the constitutionality of an amendment to the California constitution prohibiting state courts from ordering mandatory pupil assignment or transportation unless a federal court would do so to remedy a violation of the federal equal protection clause. The amendment followed a decision by the California Supreme Court interpreting the state constitution as prohibiting de facto segregation and ordering "reasonable

---

16. Responding to this dissent, the Court denies that its opinion limits the authority of the people of the State of Washington and the Legislature to control or regulate school boards. It further states that "the State remains free to vest all decisionmaking power in state officials, or to remove authority from local school boards in a race-neutral manner." These are puzzling statements that seem entirely at odds with much of the text of the Court's opinion. It will be surprising if officials of the State of Washington — with the one exception mentioned below — will have any clear idea as to what the State now lawfully may do.

The Court does say that "[i]t is the State's race-conscious restructuring of its decisionmaking process that is impermissible, not the simple repeal of the Seattle plan." Apparently the Court is saying that, despite what else may be said in its opinion, the people of the State — or the State legislature — may repeal the *Seattle plan*, even though neither the people nor the legislature validly may prescribe statewide standards. I perceive no logic in — and certainly no constitutional basis for — a distinction between repealing the Seattle plan of mandatory busing and establishing a statewide policy to the same effect. The people of a State have far greater interest in the general problems associated with compelled busing for purpose of integration than in the plan of a single school board.

[handwritten margin note: — No structural change — No effects argument]

steps" to alleviate it. Opponents of this decision succeeded in placing Proposition I, which embodied the amendment, on the ballot, and the Proposition was approved in a statewide referendum. Justice Powell delivered the Court's opinion:

"We agree with the California Court of Appeal in rejecting the contention that once a State chooses to do "more" than the Fourteenth Amendment requires, it may never recede. We reject an interpretation of the Fourteenth Amendment so destructive of a State's democratic processes and of its ability to experiment. . . .

"Proposition I does not inhibit enforcement of any federal law or constitutional requirement. Quite the contrary, by its plain language the Proposition seeks only to embrace the requirements of the Federal Constitution with respect to mandatory school assignments and transportation. It would be paradoxical to conclude that by adopting the Equal Protection Clause of the Fourteenth Amendment, the voters of the State thereby had violated it. . . .

"We would agree that if Proposition I employed a racial classification it would be unconstitutional unless necessary to further a compelling state interest. [But] Proposition I does not embody a racial classification. It neither says nor implies that persons are to be treated differently on account of their race. It simply forbids state courts to order pupil school assignment or transportation in the absence of a Fourteenth Amendment violation. The benefit it seeks to confer — neighborhood schooling — is made available regardless of race in the discretion of school boards. [In] addition, this Court previously has held that even when a neutral law has a disproportionately adverse effect on a racial minority, the Fourteenth Amendment is violated only if a discriminatory purpose can be shown.

"Similarly, the Court has recognized that a distinction may exist between state action that discriminates on the basis of race and state action that addresses, in neutral fashion, race related matters. This distinction is implicit in the Court's repeated statement that the Equal Protection Clause is not violated by the mere repeal of race related legislation or policies that were not required by the Federal Constitution in the first place. . . .

"Relying primarily on the decision in Hunter v. Erickson, [petitioners] contend that Proposition I does not simply repeal a state created right but fundamentally alters the judicial system so that 'those seeking redress from racial isolation in violation of state law must be satisfied with less than full relief from a state court.' We do not view *Hunter* as controlling here, nor are we persuaded by petitioners' characterization of Proposition I as something more than a mere repeal. . . .

"[It cannot be said] that Proposition I distorts the political process for racial reasons or that it allocates governmental or judicial power on the basis of a discriminatory principle. . . .

"[Having] gone beyond the requirements of the Federal Constitution, the State was free to return in part to the standard prevailing generally throughout the United States."

Justice Blackmun, joined by Justice Brennan, concurred: "While I join the opinion of the Court, I write separately to address what I believe are the critical distinctions between this case and Washington v. Seattle School District No. 1 . . . .

"State courts do not create the rights they enforce; those rights originate elsewhere — in the state legislature, in the State's political subdivisions, or in the state constitution itself. When one of those rights is repealed, and therefore is rendered unenforceable in the courts, that action hardly can be said to restructure the State's decisionmaking mechanism. While the California electorate may have made it more difficult to achieve desegregation when it enacted Proposition I, to my mind it did so not by working a structural change in the political *process* so much as by simply repealing the right to invoke a judicial busing remedy. Indeed, ruling for petitioners on a *Hunter* theory seemingly would mean that statutory affirmative action or antidiscrimination programs never could be repealed, for a repeal of the enactment would mean that enforcement authority previously lodged in the state courts was being removed by another political entity."

Justice Marshall wrote a dissenting opinion: "In my view [the principles announced in *Seattle*] lead to the conclusion that California's Proposition I works an unconstitutional reallocation of state power by depriving California courts of the ability to grant meaningful relief to those seeking to vindicate the State's guarantee against de facto segregation in the public schools. . . .

"Prior to the enactment of Proposition I, those seeking to vindicate the rights enumerated by the California Supreme Court just as those interested in attaining any other educational objective, followed a two-stage procedure. First, California's minority community could attempt to convince the local school board voluntarily to comply with its constitutional obligation to take reasonably feasible steps to eliminate racial isolation in the public schools. If the board was either unwilling or unable to carry out its constitutional duty, those seeking redress could petition the California state courts to require school officials to live up to their obligations. Busing could be required as part of a judicial remedial order. . . .

"Whereas Initiative 350 attempted to deny minority children the first step of this procedure, Proposition I eliminates by fiat the second stage: the ability of California courts to order meaningful compliance with the requirements of the State Constitution. After the adoption of Proposition I, the only method of enforcing against a recalcitrant school board the state constitutional duty to eliminate racial isolation is to petition either the state legislature or the electorate as a whole. Clearly, the rules of the game have been significantly changed for those attempting to vindicate this state constitutional right."

Note: Strict Scrutiny for "Neutral" Race-Specific Classifications

1. *Why strict scrutiny?* Compare Justice Warren's opinion in *Loving* with his opinion in Brown v. Board of Education (*Brown I*), section A3 supra. Does *Loving* provide a more satisfactory account of why neutral race-specific laws are strictly scrutinized?

What class of people was disadvantaged by the statute invalidated in *Loving*? Since the class necessarily includes an equal number of blacks and whites (for every black/white marriage, there must be one black and one white who wish to marry each other) how can the Court say that the statute constitutes "invidious racial discrimination"? Is the point that in a culture dominated by whites, blacks are harmed more than whites by laws separating the races or suggesting that race is a relevant factor in decisionmaking? That because there are fewer blacks than whites, a higher percentage of the total black community will be prospective partners in mixed-race marriages? Why should these disproportionate impact arguments trigger strict scrutiny when the disproportionate impact shown in Washington v. Davis did not? Is the point, then, that race-specific classifications, even when facially neutral, are particularly likely to be motivated by race prejudice? See Palmore v. Sidoti, section C1 supra: "Classifying persons according to their race is more likely to reflect racial prejudice than legitimate public concerns; the race, not the person, dictates the category." But why should one suspect that such laws reflect racial prejudice apart from the fact that they have a disproportionate racial impact?

2. *What makes a neutral statute race specific?* The antimiscegenation statute invalidated in *Loving* was race specific in the sense that the legal consequence of a marriage turned on the races of the married couple. But the statute invalidated in *Seattle* nowhere mentioned race. What made it race specific and therefore subject to strict scrutiny?

Consider Sunstein, Public Values, Private Interests and the Equal Protection Clause, 1982 Sup. Ct. Rev. 127, 158:

> Noninvidious justifications are more plausibly made in opposition to busing than in support of statutes that distinguish on their face between blacks and whites. . . .
> [It] would be unrealistic to suggest, [however], that invidious motives may not play a part in how best, and how enthusiastically, to desegregate the public schools. [A] selective effort to prevent enactment of measures designed to desegregate [may] well not be an effort to promote a public value, but [simply] unprincipled redistribution of wealth or opportunity. [Even] if the Court were incorrect to characterize Initiative 350 as a conventional racial classification, then, it was right in approaching the initiative with more than usual suspicion.

Does this argument explain why statutes dealing with "racial subjects" should be viewed with suspicion, while those having severely disproportionate racial impacts should not be? Compare *Seattle* with James v. Valtierra, 402 U.S. 137 (1971), where the Court upheld a provision of the California constitution prohibiting state entities from constructing low rent housing projects unless approved by a majority of those voting in a community election. The Court held that the provision was not a racial classification, since it "[required] referendum approval for any low-rent public housing project, not only for projects which will be occupied by a racial minority. And the record here would not support any claim that a law seemingly neutral on its face is in fact aimed at a racial minority." Can this language be reconciled with the *Seattle* Court's holding that Initiative 350 was race specific because school desegregation "inures primarily to the benefit of the minority" and because "In reality, the burden imposed by [the Initiative] necessarily 'falls on the minority' " (quoting from Hunter v. Erickson). Is *Seattle* consistent with Washington v. Davis and *Arlington Heights*, where the Court treated state actions disproportionately burdening blacks as facially neutral? Note that the Court in *Seattle* distinguishes *Davis* and *Arlington Heights* on the ground that those cases "considered classifications facially unrelated to race." Does this distinction beg the very question the Court is attempting to answer?

3. *Mere repeals and restructuring the political process.* The Court was careful in *Seattle* to note that "every attempt to address a racial issue [does not give] rise to an impermissible racial classification." Thus, the Court made clear that the mere

repeal of previously enacted legislation benefiting blacks need not survive strict scrutiny. Why not? Surely, such legislation is race specific and impacts adversely on blacks. Moreover, the risk that repeal is motivated by racial animus will often be substantial. If the Court had held that a mere repeal must be strictly scrutinized, wouldn't it logically follow that failure to enact the law in the first place must be strictly scrutinized as well? Could the Court have reached that result without overruling Washington v. Davis?

The majority in Seattle thought that Initiative 350 was more than a mere repeal because it also restructured the political process in a manner that made it more difficult for communities to promulgate future voluntary desegregation plans. Even if the Court is correct that Initiative 350 involved such a restructuring (see below), why should that matter? There is no suggestion in Loving that the Virginia antimiscegenation statute involved a restructuring of the political process. Why was restructuring crucial to the result in Seattle but irrelevant in Loving?

In what sense did Initiative 350 restructure the political process? Both before and after adoption of the initiative, the state's political process permitted opponents of local school board policies to reverse them by securing the votes of a majority of the participants in a statewide referendum. True, opponents of busing used this political process to make it more difficult for local governments to promulgate busing plans in the future. But the process itself was race neutral. Proponents of voluntary integration plans were not excluded from it and, indeed, could have used the same process to repeal Initiative 350 or, for that matter, to require localities to eliminate de facto segregation. It might be supposed that there was a substantial risk that persons voting for Initiative 350 were motivated by racial prejudice. But surely this risk is no greater than it would have been if the Washington voters had defeated an initiative requiring local integration — a result that clearly would have been constitutional.

After Seattle is there anything a majority of Washington's citizens can do to stop busing in local communities? Would a statewide initiative restricted to invalidation of the Seattle plan be constitutional? Would it be constitutional for the state to enact separate initiatives banning specific voluntary desegregation plans whenever local governments promulgated them? Does it make any sense to distinguish between individual, post hoc invalidations of desegregation plans on the one hand and a prophylactic invalidation of all future plans on the other?

4. Seattle and Crawford. Can the results in Seattle and Crawford be reconciled? (Note that five of the nine justices thought that the cases were indistinguishable; the Court reached different results only because this majority was divided between four justices who thought that both measures were constitutional and one justice who thought that both were unconstitutional.) In Seattle the political process was "restructured" in the sense that after the referendum local governments were unable to promulgate transportation plans to remedy de facto segregation. In Crawford the political process was "restructured" in the sense that after the referendum, state courts were unable to promulgate transportation plans to remedy de facto segregation. Is it relevant that in Seattle a local program was repealed by statewide action, while in Crawford both the program and repeal were statewide? Note that in Hunter v. Erickson, the Court invalidated the result of a referendum even though both it and the fair housing legislation it repealed were local. Justice Blackmun argued in his Crawford concurrence that Proposition I was a mere repeal because the state did no more than withdraw from the courts

power that it had initially vested in the judicial system. But did not the Seattle school board's power to order desegregation ultimately stem from the state as well?

5. *The source of the difficulty.* What explains the Court's problem in formulating consistent results and persuasive opinions in cases like *Seattle* and *Crawford*? Consider the following argument: The Court's difficulty in *Seattle* and *Crawford* stems from its effort to reconcile two lines of authority that are ultimately inconsistent. On the one hand, Washington v. Davis and its progeny suggest an approach to the race problem that eschews an effort to guarantee any substantive position for blacks in U.S. society. Rather than focusing on the substantive content of statutes affecting blacks, it directs attention to the process by which the statutes are enacted. Thus, facially neutral statutes that have an adverse impact on blacks are subject only to rational basis review so long as the process by which they are enacted is not infected by an illegitimate purpose. These precedents inevitably channeled the Court's *Seattle* and *Crawford* opinions into an irrelevant and fruitless discussion of whether the political process had been unfairly restructured. On the other hand, *Loving* as well as its lineal antecedent, Brown v. Board of Education, are fundamentally inconsistent with this process approach. These cases can be read as outlawing certain outcomes of even a "fair" process when those outcomes disadvantage blacks in certain ways. They suggest that race-specific classifications are evil because their effect, at least in our culture, is to leave blacks in a permanently subservient position. In *Seattle* and *Crawford* the analogy to *Brown* and *Loving* was too close for the Court to ignore. Yet it is hardly surprising that the Court failed to pursue the logic of these precedents. To do so would require the justices to articulate and justify a substantive theory about the distribution of resources among groups in our society, and the Court is simply not prepared to undertake that task. But trying to think about *Seattle* and *Crawford* without a theory of distribution is like trying to think about the race problem without a theory of justice.

4. Race-Specific Classifications That Benefit Racial Minorities

What standard of review should a court use to evaluate so-called benign racial classifications that purportedly benefit a racial minority? What kinds of justifications are constitutionally adequate to support such classifications? If "benign" classifications should be judged by some test less rigorous than strict scrutiny, how should a court determine whether a classification is in fact benign? Although the Court has wrestled with these questions in recent years, much of the law of "affirmative action" remains confused.

Note: The Pre-Bakke Cases

1. *Remedies for school segregation.* The Court's first exposure to these problems came almost by accident when it became clear that "benign" racial classifications were a necessary consequence of constitutionally required remedies for school

segregation. Implicit in the Court's insistence on desegregation plans that "worked," see Green v. County School Board, 391 U.S. 430 (1968), was an emphasis on the actual effect of school board policy in producing "unitary schools." See section A4 supra. Thus, a school board under an affirmative obligation to desegregate its schools was necessarily required to employ assignment policies that were race conscious. See United States v. Montgomery County Board of Education, 395 U.S. 225, 235 (1969).

This requirement, implicit in *Green*, was made explicit in Swann v. Charlotte-Mecklenburg Board of Education, section A4 supra, in which the Court held that a district judge could consider the racial composition of individual schools in formulating a desegregation remedy. In two companion cases decided on the same day, the Court not only rejected the argument that the equal protection clause *prohibited* racial classifications in this context; it also held that the *refusal* to permit use of such classifications was unconstitutional. See McDaniel v. Barresi, 402 U.S. 39 (1971) (the remedying of prior unconstitutional segregation "will almost invariably require that students be assigned 'differently because of their race.' Any other approach would freeze the status quo that is the very target of all desegregation processes"); North Carolina State Board of Education v. Swann, 402 U.S. 43 (1971) (invalidating a state statute, enacted in the midst of desegregation litigation, providing that "No student shall be assigned or compelled to attend any school on account of race, creed, color, or national origin, or for the purpose of creating a balance or ratio of race, religion, or national origin").

These early cases approving the use of racial criteria generated little controversy on the Court, since the Court's premise made the argument for the use of such criteria in the school desegregation context extremely strong. If, as the Court assumed, racial classifications were absolutely essential to remedy prior unconstitutional conduct, then it could hardly be maintained that the classifications were themselves unconstitutional. Note, however, that dicta in Swann v. Charlotte-Mecklenberg Board of Education suggested that benign classifications might be constitutionally permissible even when not constitutionally compelled. "School authorities [might] well conclude [that] in order to prepare students to live in a pluralistic society each school should have a prescribed ratio of Negro to white students reflecting the proportion for the district as a whole. To do this as an educational policy is within the broad discretionary powers of school authorities."

2. *Employment discrimination.* In cases dealing with private employment discrimination, the Court went beyond mere dicta and apparently approved race-conscious remedies even though the underlying violations were statutory rather than constitutional. In Franks v. Bowman Transportation Co., 424 U.S. 747 (1976), and International Brotherhood of Teamsters v. United States, 431 U.S. 324 (1977), the Court upheld the power of district courts to order the hiring of blacks who had been subject to employment discrimination in violation of Title VII of the 1964 Civil Rights Act. The Court also held that a victim of such discrimination might be accorded retroactive seniority, even though this remedy might disadvantage white co-workers who were not themselves responsible for the discrimination. Since job discrimination by private employers does not violate the Constitution, it could not be argued that these remedies were constitutionally compelled. But the employment cases were careful to limit the remedy to making whole the particular individual illegally deprived of a job because of his race.

They therefore left unsettled whether the government could require a preference for blacks as a class in order to remedy broader, societywide discrimination. The kind of voluntary school integration approved in the *Swann* dicta is class-based in character. Such programs do involve racial classifications, but no child is entirely deprived of an education, and, typically, both black and white children bear part of the burden of attending distant schools in order to achieve integration. Thus, neither *Swann* nor the employment cases need be read as approving the provision of special benefits to blacks alone or a preference for blacks in situations where a race classification was not necessary to remedy a specific constitutional violation.

3. *Voting discrimination.* These issues were arguably presented in United Jewish Organizations v. Carey, 430 U.S. 144 (1977), a case concerning the constitutionality of race-conscious remedies adopted to comply with the Voting Rights Act of 1965. Section 5 of the act prohibits covered jurisdictions from implementing legislative reapportionment plans without first obtaining either a declaratory judgment from the District Court for the District of Columbia or a ruling from the Attorney General that the change does not have the purpose or effect of abridging the right to vote on racial grounds. Although there was no showing that New York had unconstitutionally infringed the right of any group to vote, section 4 of the act made certain New York counties subject to this preclearance requirement because they had utilized a literacy test in 1968 and fewer than 50 percent of the voting-age residents had voted in the presidential election of that year. In order to secure the Attorney General's approval for its new apportionment, New York devised a redistricting plan that deliberately concentrated black voters in certain districts, thereby enhancing their opportunity to elect black candidates. The plan also had the effect of splitting into two adjoining districts the Hasidic Jewish community, which had previously been in one district. Plaintiffs, representing this community, challenged the constitutionality of the reapportionment, arguing that the deliberate use of racial criteria to enhance black voting strength violated the fourteenth and fifteenth amendments.

The Supreme Court rejected this challenge, but no opinion attracted a majority of the Justices. Justice White, joined by Justices Stevens, Brennan, and Blackmun, wrote that the Constitution did not prohibit the deliberate creation of black majorities in particular districts in order to ensure that reapportionment plans complied with section 5. Nor was the use of such racial criteria limited to situations where necessary to eliminate the effects of past unconstitutional discrimination. New York's conduct was constitutionally permissible because it amounted to no more than satisfying the requirement imposed by the 1965 act that redistricting not have the effect of diminishing black voting strength. Moreover, in a separate section of his opinion, joined only by Justices Stevens and Rehnquist, Justice White argued that the use of racial criteria and the deliberate creation of black majorities in some districts were permissible, even if not required by the 1965 act, so long as whites were not "fenced out" of participation in the political process and the plan did not unfairly cancel white voting strength on a statewide basis.

In a lengthy concurring opinion, Justice Brennan emphasized that even supposedly benign racial criteria might stigmatize minority groups, disguise a policy that actually disadvantages the minority, or require "discrete and insular" white groups to bear a disproportionate share of the cost of benign discrimination. In this context, however, Brennan concluded that the procedural protections of the

1965 act and the congressional judgment that it embodied were sufficient to protect against misuse of racial criteria. Since New York had done no more than comply with the act's requirements, the redistricting survived constitutional attack.

In a separate concurrence, Justice Stewart, joined by Justice Powell, argued that under Washington v. Davis the issue was whether the reapportionment plan represented purposeful discrimination against white voters. Mere awareness of race when the lines were drawn was insufficient to establish discriminatory intent, since the clear purpose for which the legislature acted — to satisfy the Attorney General under the 1965 act — foreclosed any finding that it acted in order to discriminate against white voters.

Chief Justice Burger was the sole dissenter. He objected to "mechanical racial gerrymandering," arguing that manipulating the racial composition of electoral districts did not promote the goal of a racially neutral legislature. Instead, it put the imprimatur of the state on the concept that race is a proper consideration in the electoral process, thereby "[moving] us one step farther away from a truly homogeneous society." Justice Marshall did not participate.

4. *Preferential admissions.* *United Jewish Organizations* seemed to endorse the use of racial criteria despite the absence of a proven constitutional violation. But it did so in a context where it was difficult for individual whites to demonstrate cognizable injury, since the challenged redistricting did not lead to underrepresentation of white voters generally. Moreover, the use of racial criteria was mandated by a federal statute and supported by elaborate congressional findings, to which the Court accorded considerable deference. When state-supported graduate schools adopt admissions programs favoring minority applicants, however, unsuccessful white applicants can sometimes demonstrate that they have been denied admission because "less qualified" blacks have been admitted in their place, and such programs are often promulgated by relatively low-level administrative officials whose actions are not supported by legislative findings.

The Court first considered the preferential admissions problem in DeFunis v. Odegaard, 416 U.S. 312 (1974), a case decided several years before *United Jewish Organizations.* Petitioner, who was denied admission to the University of Washington Law School, claimed that his fourteenth amendment rights were violated because less qualified blacks were admitted under the university's affirmative action program. Although the constitutional issue was elaborately briefed and argued, the Court failed to reach the merits. Instead, it held that the case was moot because petitioner, who had been ordered admitted by a lower court, was nearing graduation. Four justices dissented from the mootness determination, but only Justice Douglas spoke to the merits. He would have utilized the "strictest scrutiny" to evaluate even "benign" racial classifications. He argued that such classifications lead to racial polarization and unintentionally stigmatize blacks by suggesting that they cannot succeed on the basis of individual merit. So long as candidates are evaluated in an individual, racially neutral fashion, however, Douglas was prepared to allow schools to consider the fact that an applicant had overcome economic or cultural barriers to attain a given achievement level. He was also willing to permit schools to utilize a separate selection process for racial minorities to the extent that this was necessary to compensate for the cultural bias of standardized admissions tests.

Regents of the University of California v. Bakke

438 U.S. 265 (1978)

MR. JUSTICE POWELL announced the judgment of the Court.

This case presents a challenge to the special admissions program of the petitioner, the Medical School of the University of California at Davis, which is designed to assure the admission of a specified number of students from certain minority groups. [The] Supreme Court of California affirmed those portions of the trial court's judgment declaring the special admissions program unlawful and enjoining petitioner from considering the race of any applicant. . . .

For the reasons stated in the following opinion, I believe that so much of the judgment of the California court as holds petitioner's special admissions program unlawful and directs that respondent be admitted to the Medical School must be affirmed. For the reasons expressed in a separate opinion, my Brothers [CHIEF JUSTICE BURGER], MR. JUSTICE STEWART, MR. JUSTICE REHNQUIST, and MR. JUSTICE STEVENS concur in this judgment.

I also conclude for the reasons stated in the following opinion that the portion of the court's judgment enjoining petitioner from according any consideration to race in its admissions process must be reversed. For reasons expressed in separate opinions, my Brothers MR. JUSTICE BRENNAN, MR. JUSTICE WHITE, MR. JUSTICE MARSHALL, and MR. JUSTICE BLACKMUN concur in this judgment.

Affirmed in part and reversed in part.

I‡

[In order to increase minority enrollment in its medical school, the University of California at Davis created a special admissions program operating in coordination with the regular admissions process. Candidates for admission were asked to indicate on their admissions form whether they wished to be considered as members of a "minority group," a category that the medical school apparently viewed as limited to "Blacks," "Chicanos," "Asians," and "American Indians." If the applicant responded affirmatively, the application was forwarded to a special admissions committee, a majority of whom were members of minority groups. The chairman of the committee screened these applications to determine whether the applicant suffered from economic or educational deprivation. Applicants who met this requirement were then considered by the special committee, which recommended its top choices to the general admissions committee. The special committee continued to recommend candidates until sixteen of the 100 seats in the entering class had been filled. Thus, persons admitted through the special admissions program did not have their credentials rated against students competing for the other eighty-four seats. Minorities were not precluded from competing for the regular seats, however, so that it remained possible for more than sixteen minority students to be admitted in a particular year.

[Petitioner was a white, male applicant whose application for admission was rejected in two successive years although on each occasion students who ranked significantly lower according to the criteria used to evaluate candidates were

‡ Mr. Justice Brennan, Mr. Justice White, Mr. Justice Marshall, and Mr. Justice Blackmun join Parts I and V-C of this opinion. Mr. Justice White also joins Part III-A of this opinion.

admitted through the special admissions program. After his second rejection, he sued respondent in state court, alleging that the special admissions program violated his rights under the equal protection clause of the fourteenth amendment, the California Constitution, and section 601 of Title VI of the 1964 Civil Rights Act. The trial court held that the special admissions program was unlawful, and the California Supreme Court affirmed.]

II

[In this section of his opinion, Justice Powell addresses respondent's claim that the special admissions program violated Title VI of the 1964 Civil Rights Act, 42 U.S.C. §2000d. The act provides that "No person in the United States shall, on the ground of race, color, or national origin, be excluded from participation in, be denied the benefits of, or be subjected to discrimination under any program or activity receiving Federal financial assistance." Justice Powell concludes that he need not decide whether a right of action for private parties exists under Title VI, since, in any event, the statute does no more than to prohibit racial discrimination similar to that also prohibited by the Constitution. It was therefore necessary to address respondent's underlying constitutional claim.]

III

A . . .

It is settled beyond question that the "rights created by the first section of the Fourteenth Amendment are, by its terms, guaranteed to the individual. The rights established are personal rights," Shelley v. Kraemer, [334 U.S. 1, 22 (1948)]. . . .

[The] guarantee of equal protection cannot mean one thing when applied to one individual and something else when applied to a person of another color. If both are not accorded the same protection, then it is not equal.

Nevertheless, petitioner argues that the court below erred in applying strict scrutiny to the special admissions program because white males, such as respondent, are not a "discrete and insular minority" requiring extraordinary protection from the majoritarian political process. [United States v. Carolene Products Co., 304 U.S. 144, 152-153 n.4]. This rationale, however, has never been invoked in our decisions as a prerequisite to subjecting racial or ethnic distinctions to strict scrutiny. Nor has this Court held that discreteness and insularity constitute necessary preconditions to a holding that a particular classification is invidious. . . .

[These] characteristics may be relevant in deciding whether or not to add new types of classifications to the list of "suspect" categories or whether a particular classification survives close examination. . . .

[Racial] and ethnic classifications, however, are subject to stringent examination without regard to these additional characteristics. . . .

B . . .

Petitioner urges us to adopt for the first time a more restrictive view of the Equal Protection Clause and hold that discrimination against members of the white "majority" cannot be suspect if its purpose can be characterized as "benign."[34] The clock of our liberties, however, cannot be turned back to 1868. . . .

[It] is far too late to argue that the guarantee of equal protection to *all* persons permits the recognition of special wards entitled to a degree of protection greater than that accorded others. "The Fourteenth Amendment is not directed solely against discrimination due to a 'two-class theory' — that is, based upon differences between 'white' and Negro." [Hernandez v. Texas, 347 U.S. 475, 478 (1954).]

Once the artificial line of a "two-class theory" of the Fourteenth Amendment is put aside, the difficulties entailed in varying the level of judicial review according to a perceived "preferred" status of a particular racial or ethnic minority are intractable. The concepts of "majority" and "minority" necessarily reflect temporary arrangements and political judgments. [The] white "majority" itself is composed of various minority groups, most of which can lay claim to a history of prior discrimination at the hands of the State and private individuals. Not all of these groups can receive preferential treatment and corresponding judicial tolerance of distinctions drawn in terms of race and nationality, for then the only "majority" left would be a new minority of white Anglo-Saxon Protestants. There is no principled basis for deciding which groups would merit "heightened judicial solicitude" and which would not. . . .

Moreover, there are serious problems of justice connected with the idea of preference itself. First, it may not always be clear that a so-called preference is in fact benign. Courts may be asked to validate burdens imposed upon individual members of a particular group in order to advance the group's general interest. See United Jewish Organizations v. Carey, 430 U.S., at 172-173 (Brennan, J., concurring in part). Nothing in the Constitution supports the notion that individuals may be asked to suffer otherwise impermissible burdens in order to enhance the societal standing of their ethnic groups. Second, preferential programs may only reinforce common stereotypes holding that certain groups are unable to achieve success without special protection based on a factor having no relationship to individual worth.

[Third,] there is a measure of inequity in forcing innocent persons in respondent's position to bear the burdens of redressing grievances not of their making. . . .

Also, the mutability of a constitutional principle, based upon shifting political and social judgments, undermines the chances for consistent application of the Constitution from one generation to the next, a critical feature of its coherent interpretation. . . .

If it is the individual who is entitled to judicial protection against classifications based upon his racial or ethnic background because such distinctions impinge

34. In the view of Mr. Justice Brennan, Mr. Justice White, Mr. Justice Marshall, and Mr. Justice Blackmun, the pliable notion of "stigma" is the crucial element in analyzing racial classifications. The Equal Protection Clause is not framed in terms of "stigma." Certainly the word has no clearly defined constitutional meaning. It reflects a subjective judgment that is standardless. *All* state-imposed classifications that rearrange burdens and benefits on the basis of race are likely to be viewed with deep resentment by the individuals burdened. [Moreover,] Mr. Justice Brennan, Mr. Justice White, Mr. Justice Marshall, and Mr. Justice Blackmun offer no principle for deciding whether preferential classifications reflect a benign remedial purpose or a malevolent stigmatic classification, since they are willing in this case to accept mere post hoc declarations by an isolated state entity — a medical school faculty — unadorned by particularized findings of past discrimination, to establish such a remedial purpose.

upon personal rights, rather than the individual only because of his membership in a particular group, then constitutional standards may be applied consistently. Political judgments regarding the necessity for the particular classification may be weighed in the constitutional balance, Korematsu v. United States, 323 U.S. 214 (1944), but the standard of justification will remain constant. This is as it should be, since those political judgments are the product of rough compromise struck by contending groups within the democratic process. When they touch upon an individual's race or ethnic background, he is entitled to a judicial determination that the burden he is asked to bear on that basis is precisely tailored to serve a compelling governmental interest. . . .

IV

We have held that in "order to justify the use of a suspect classification, a State must show that its purpose or interest is both constitutionally permissible and substantial, and that its use of the classification is 'necessary . . . to the accomplishment' of its purpose or the safeguarding of its interest." In re Griffiths, 413 U.S. 717, 721-722 (1973) (footnotes omitted). The special admissions program purports to serve the purposes of: (i) "reducing the historic deficit of traditionally disfavored minorities in medical schools and in the medical profession." (ii) countering the effects of societal discrimination;[43] (iii) increasing the number of physicians who will practice in communities currently underserved; and (iv) obtaining the educational benefits that flow from an ethnically diverse student body. It is necessary to decide which, if any, of these purposes is substantial enough to support the use of a suspect classification.

A

If petitioner's purpose is to assure within its student body some specified percentage of a particular group merely because of its race or ethnic origin, such a preferential purpose must be rejected not as insubstantial but as facially invalid. Preferring members of any one group for no reason other than race or ethnic origin is discrimination for its own sake. This the Constitution forbids.

B

The State certainly has a legitimate and substantial interest in ameliorating, or eliminating where feasible, the disabling effects of identified discrimination. The line of school desegregation cases, commencing with Brown, attests to the importance of this state goal and the commitment of the judiciary to affirm all lawful

---

43. [Racial] classifications in admissions conceivably could serve a fifth purpose, one which petitioner does not articulate: fair appraisal of each individual's academic promise in the light of some cultural bias in grading or testing procedures. To the extent that race and ethnic background were considered only to the extent of curing established inaccuracies in predicting academic performance, it might be argued that there is no "preference" at all. Nothing in this record, however, suggests either that any of the quantitative factors considered by the Medical School were culturally biased or that petitioner's special admissions program was formulated to correct for any such biases. Furthermore, if race or ethnic background were used solely to arrive at an unbiased prediction of academic success, the reservation of fixed numbers of seats would be inexplicable.

means toward its attainment. In the school cases, the States were required by court order to redress the wrongs worked by specific instances of racial discrimination. That goal was far more focused than the remedying of the effects of "societal discrimination," an amorphous concept of injury that may be ageless in its reach into the past.

We have never approved a classification that aids persons perceived as members of relatively victimized groups at the expense of other innocent individuals in the absence of judicial, legislative, or administrative findings of constitutional or statutory violations. After such findings have been made, the governmental interest in preferring members of the injured groups at the expense of others is substantial, since the legal rights of the victims must be vindicated. In such a case, the extent of the injury and the consequent remedy will have been judicially, legislatively, or administratively defined. Also, the remedial action usually remains subject to continuing oversight to assure that it will work the least harm possible to other innocent persons competing for the benefit. Without such findings of constitutional or statutory violations, it cannot be said that the government has any greater interest in helping one individual than in refraining from harming another. Thus, the government has no compelling justification for inflicting such harm.

Petitioner does not purport to have made, and is in no position to make, such findings. Its broad mission is education, not the formulation of any legislative policy or the adjudication of particular claims of illegality. [Isolated] segments of our vast governmental structures are not competent to make those decisions, at least in the absence of legislative mandates and legislatively determined criteria. . . .

Hence, the purpose of helping certain groups whom the faculty of the Davis Medical School perceived as victims of "societal discrimination" does not justify a classification that imposes disadvantages upon persons like respondent, who bear no responsibility for whatever harm the beneficiaries of the special admissions program are thought to have suffered. To hold otherwise would be to convert a remedy heretofore reserved for violations of legal rights into a privilege that all institutions throughout the Nation could grant at their pleasure to whatever groups are perceived as victims of societal discrimination. That is a step we have never approved.

C

Petitioner identifies, as another purpose of its program, improving the delivery of health-care services to communities currently underserved. . . .

[But] Petitioner simply has not carried its burden of demonstrating that it must prefer members of particular ethnic groups over all other individuals in order to promote better health-care delivery to deprived citizens. Indeed, petitioner has not shown that its preferential classification is likely to have any significant effect on the problem.

D

The fourth goal asserted by petitioner is the attainment of a diverse student body. This clearly is a constitutionally permissible goal for an institution of higher education. Academic freedom, though not a specifically enumerated constitutional right, long has been viewed as a special concern of the First Amendment. The freedom of a university to make its own judgments as to education includes the selection of its student body. . . .

[The] atmosphere of "speculation, experiment and creation" — so essential to the quality of higher education — is widely believed to be promoted by a diverse student body. . . .

Thus, in arguing that its universities must be accorded the right to select those students who will contribute the most to the "robust exchange of ideas," petitioner invokes a countervailing constitutional interest, that of the First Amendment. In this light, petitioner must be viewed as seeking to achieve a goal that is of paramount importance in the fulfillment of its mission. . . .

As the interest of diversity is compelling in the context of a university's admissions program, the question remains whether the program's racial classification is necessary to promote this interest.

V

A

It may be assumed that the reservation of a specified number of seats in each class for individuals from the preferred ethnic groups would contribute to the attainment of considerable ethnic diversity in the student body. But petitioner's argument that this is the only effective means of serving the interest of diversity is seriously flawed.

[The] diversity that furthers a compelling state interest encompasses a far broader array of qualifications and characteristics of which racial or ethnic origin is but a single though important element. Petitioner's special admissions program, focused *solely* on ethnic diversity, would hinder rather than further attainment of genuine diversity.

Nor would the state interest in genuine diversity be served by expanding petitioner's two-track system into a multitrack program with a prescribed number of seats set aside for each identifiable category of applicants. Indeed, it is inconceivable that a university would thus pursue the logic of petitioner's two-track program to the illogical end of insulating each category of applicants with certain desired qualifications from competition with all other applicants.

The experience of other university admissions programs, which take race into account in achieving the educational diversity valued by the First Amendment, demonstrates that the assignment of a fixed number of places to a minority group is not a necessary means toward that end. An illuminating example is found in the Harvard College program:

> In recent years Harvard College has expanded the concept of diversity to include students from disadvantaged economic, racial and ethnic groups. Harvard College now recruits not only Californians or Louisianans but also blacks and Chicanos and other minority students. . . .
>
> In practice, this new definition of diversity has meant that race has been a factor in some admission decisions. When the Committee on Admissions reviews the large middle group of applicants who are 'admissible' and deemed capable of doing good

work in their courses, the race of an applicant may tip the balance in his favor just as geographic origin or a life spent on a farm may tip the balance in other candidates' cases. A farm boy from Idaho can bring something to Harvard College that a Bostonian cannot offer. Similarly, a black student can usually bring something that a white person cannot offer. . . .

In Harvard College admissions the Committee has not set target-quotas for the number of blacks, or of musicians, football players, physicists or Californians to be admitted in a given year. . . . But that awareness [of the necessity of including more than a token number of black students] does not mean that the Committee sets a minimum number of blacks or of people from west of the Mississippi who are to be admitted. It means only that in choosing among thousands of applicants who are not only "admissible" academically but have other strong qualities, the Committee, with a number of criteria in mind, pays some attention to distribution among many types and categories of students.

In such an admissions program, race or ethnic background may be deemed a "plus" in a particular applicant's file, yet it does not insulate the individual from comparison with all other candidates for the available seats. [In] short, an admissions program operated in this way is flexible enough to consider all pertinent elements of diversity in light of the particular qualifications of each applicant, and to place them on the same footing for consideration, although not necessarily according them the same weight. . . .

It has been suggested that an admissions program which considers race only as one factor is simply a subtle and more sophisticated — but no less effective — means of according racial preference than the Davis program. A facial intent to discriminate, however, is evident in petitioner's preference program and not denied in this case. No such facial infirmity exists in an admissions program where race or ethnic background is simply one element — to be weighed fairly against other elements — in the selection process. . . .

B

In summary, it is evident that the Davis special admissions program involves the use of an explicit racial classification never before countenanced by this Court. It tells applicants who are not Negro, Asian, or Chicano that they are totally excluded from a specific percentage of the seats in an entering class. No matter how strong their qualifications, quantitative and extracurricular, including their own potential for contribution to educational diversity, they are never afforded the chance to compete with applicants from the preferred groups for the special admissions seats. At the same time, the preferred applicants have the opportunity to compete for every seat in the class.

The fatal flaw in petitioner's preferential program is its disregard of individual rights as guaranteed by the Fourteenth Amendment. Such rights are not absolute. But when a State's distribution of benefits or imposition of burdens hinges on ancestry or the color of a person's skin, that individual is entitled to a demonstration that the challenged classification is necessary to promote a substantial state interest. Petitioner has failed to carry this burden. For this reason, that portion of the California court's judgment holding petitioner's special admissions program invalid under the Fourteenth Amendment must be affirmed.

c

In enjoining petitioner from ever considering the race of any applicant, however, the courts below failed to recognize that the State has a substantial interest that legitimately may be served by a properly devised admissions program involving the competitive consideration of race and ethnic origin. For this reason, so much of the California court's judgment as enjoins petitioner from any consideration of the race of any applicant must be reversed. . . .

Opinion of MR. JUSTICE BRENNAN, MR. JUSTICE WHITE, MR. JUSTICE MARSHALL, and MR. JUSTICE BLACKMUN, concurring in the judgment in part and dissenting in part.

The Court today, in reversing in part the judgment of the Supreme Court of California, affirms the constitutional power of Federal and State Governments to act affirmatively to achieve equal opportunity for all. The difficulty of the issue presented — whether government may use race-conscious programs to redress the continuing effects of past discrimination — and the mature consideration which each of our Brethren has brought to it have resulted in many opinions, no single one speaking for the Court. But this should not and must not mask the central meaning of today's opinions: Government may take race into account when it acts not to demean or insult any racial group, but to remedy disadvantages cast on minorities by past racial prejudice, at least when appropriate findings have been made by judicial, legislative, or administrative bodies with competence to act in this area.

The Chief Justice and our Brothers Stewart, Rehnquist, and Stevens, have concluded that Title VI of the Civil Rights Act of 1964, prohibits programs such as that at the Davis Medical School. On this statutory theory alone, they would hold that respondent Allan Bakke's rights have been violated and that he must, therefore, be admitted to the Medical School. Our Brother Powell, reaching the Constitution, concludes that, although race may be taken into account in university admissions, the particular special admissions program used by petitioner, which resulted in the exclusion of respondent Bakke, was not shown to be necessary to achieve petitioner's stated goals. Accordingly, these Members of the Court form a majority of five affirming the judgment of the Supreme Court of California insofar as it holds that respondent Bakke "is entitled to an order that he be admitted to the University."

We agree with Mr. Justice Powell that, as applied to the case before us, Title VI goes no further in prohibiting the use of race than the Equal Protection Clause of the Fourteenth Amendment itself. We also agree that the effect of the California Supreme Court's affirmance of the judgment of the Superior Court of California would be to prohibit the University from establishing in the future affirmative-action programs that take race into account. Since we conclude that the affirmative admissions program at the Davis Medical School is constitutional, we would reverse the judgment below in all respects. Mr. Justice Powell agrees that some uses of race in university admissions are permissible and, therefore, he joins with us to make five votes reversing the judgment below insofar as it prohibits the University from establishing race-conscious programs in the future.

I

Our Nation was founded on the principle that "all Men are created equal." Yet candor requires acknowledgment that the Framers of our Constitution, to forge the 13 Colonies into one Nation, openly compromised this principle of equality with its antithesis: slavery. The consequences of this compromise are well known and have aptly been called our "American Dilemma." Still, it is well to recount how recent the time has been, if it has yet come, when the promise of our principles has flowered into the actuality of equal opportunity for all regardless of race or color. . . .

Against this background, claims that law must be "color-blind" or that the datum of race is no longer relevant to public policy must be seen as aspiration rather than as description of reality. This is not to denigrate aspiration; for reality rebukes us that race has too often been used by those who would stigmatize and oppress minorities. Yet we cannot — and, as we shall demonstrate, need not under our Constitution or Title VI, which merely extends the constraints of the Fourteenth Amendment to private parties who receive federal funds — let color blindness become myopia which masks the reality that many "created equal" have been treated within our lifetimes as inferior both by the law and by their fellow citizens.

II

The threshold question we must decide is whether Title VI of the Civil Rights Act of 1964 bars recipients of federal funds from giving preferential consideration to disadvantaged members of racial minorities as part of a program designed to enable such individuals to surmount the obstacles imposed by racial discrimination. We join Parts I and V-C of our Brother Powell's opinion and three of us agree with his conclusion in Part II that this case does not require us to resolve the question whether there is a private right of action under Title VI.[8] . . .

III . . .

Unquestionably we have held that a government practice or statute which [contains] "suspect classifications" is to be subjected to "strict scrutiny" and can be justified only if it furthers a compelling government purpose and, even then, only if no less restrictive alternative is available. But no fundamental right is involved here. Nor do whites as a class have any of the "traditional indicia of suspectness: the class is not saddled with such disabilities, or subjected to such a history of purposeful unequal treatment, or relegated to such a position of political powerlessness as to command extraordinary protection from the majoritarian political process." [See] United States v. Carolene Products Co., 304 U.S. 144, 152 n.4 (1938).

Moreover, if the University's representations are credited, this is not a case where racial classifications are "irrelevant and therefore prohibited." [Hirabayashi

---

8. Mr. Justice White believes we should address the private-right-of-action issue. Accordingly, he has filed a separate opinion stating his view that there is no private right of action under Title VI.

v. United States, 320 U.S. 81, 100 (1943).] Nor has anyone suggested that the University's purposes contravene the cardinal principle that racial classifications that stigmatize — because they are drawn on the presumption that one race is inferior to another or because they put the weight of government behind racial hatred and separatism — are invalid without more. . . .

On the other hand, the fact that this case does not fit neatly into our prior analytic framework for race cases does not mean that it should be analyzed by applying the very loose rational-basis standard of review that is the very least that is always applied in equal protection cases. [Instead,] a number of considerations — developed in gender-discrimination cases but which carry even more force when applied to racial classifications — lead us to conclude that racial classifications designed to further remedial purposes " 'must serve important governmental objectives and must be substantially related to achievement of those objectives.' " Califano v. Webster, [430 U.S. 313, 317 (1977)], quoting Craig v. Boren, 429 U.S. 190, 197 (1976).

First, race, like, "gender-based classifications too often [has] been inexcusably utilized to stereotype and stigmatize politically powerless segments of society." Kahn v. Shevin, 416 U.S. 351, 357 (1974) (dissenting opinion). [State] programs designed ostensibly to ameliorate the effects of past racial discrimination obviously create [a] hazard of stigma, since they may promote racial separatism and reinforce the views of those who believe that members of racial minorities are inherently incapable of succeeding on their own.

Second, race, like gender and illegitimacy, see Weber v. Aetna Casualty & Surety Co., 406 U.S. 164 (1972), is an immutable characteristic which its possessors are powerless to escape or set aside. While a classification is not per se invalid because it divides classes on the basis of an immutable characteristic, it is nevertheless true that such divisions are contrary to our deep belief that "legal burdens should bear some relationship to individual responsibility or wrongdoing," Weber, supra at 175, and that advancement sanctioned, sponsored, or approved by the State should ideally be based on individual merit or achievement, or at the least on factors within the control of an individual.

Because this principle is so deeply rooted it might be supposed that it would be considered in the legislative process and weighed against the benefits of programs preferring individuals because of their race. But this is not necessarily so: The "natural consequence of our governing processes [may well be] that the most 'discrete and insular' of whites . . . will be called upon to bear the immediate, direct costs of benign discrimination." [United Jewish Organizations v. Carey, 430 U.S. 144, 174 (1977) (opinion concurring in part)]. Moreover, it is clear from our cases that there are limits beyond which majorities may not go when they classify on the basis of immutable characteristics. See, e.g., Weber, supra. Thus, even if the concern for individualism is weighed by the political process, that weighing cannot waive the personal rights of individuals under the Fourteenth Amendment.

In sum, because of the significant risk that racial classifications established for ostensibly benign purposes can be misused, causing effects not unlike those created by invidious classifications, it is inappropriate to inquire only whether there is any conceivable basis that might sustain such a classification. Instead, to justify such a classification an important and articulated purpose for its use must be shown. In addition, any statute must be stricken that stigmatizes any group or that singles out those least well represented in the political process to bear the brunt of a benign program. . . .

IV

Davis' articulated purpose of remedying the effects of past societal discrimination is, under our cases, sufficiently important to justify the use of race-conscious admissions programs where there is a sound basis for concluding that minority underrepresentation is substantial and chronic, and that the handicap of past discrimination is impeding access of minorities to the Medical School.

A

At least since Green v. County School Board, 391 U.S. 430 (1968), it has been clear that a public body which has itself been adjudged to have engaged in racial discrimination cannot bring itself into compliance with the Equal Protection Clause simply by ending its unlawful acts and adopting a neutral stance. Three years later, Swann v. Charlotte-Mecklenburg Board of Education, 402 U.S. 1 (1971), [reiterated] that racially neutral remedies for past discrimination were inadequate where consequences of past discriminatory acts influence or control present decisions. And the Court further held both that courts could enter desegregation orders which assigned students and faculty by reference to race, and that local school boards could *voluntarily* adopt desegregation plans which made express reference to race if this was necessary to remedy the effects of past discrimination. Moreover, we stated that school boards, even in the absence of a judicial finding of past discrimination, could voluntarily adopt plans which assigned students with the end of creating racial pluralism by establishing fixed ratios of black and white students in each school. In each instance, the creation of unitary school systems, in which the effects of past discrimination had been "eliminated root and branch," was recognized as a compelling social goal justifying the overt use of race.

Finally, the conclusion that state educational institutions may constitutionally adopt admissions programs designed to avoid exclusion of historically disadvantaged minorities, even when such programs explicitly take race into account, finds direct support in our cases construing congressional legislation designed to overcome the present effects of past discrimination. Congress can and has outlawed actions which have a disproportionately adverse and unjustified impact upon members of racial minorities and has required or authorized race-conscious action to put individuals disadvantaged by such impact in the position they otherwise might have enjoyed. See Franks v. Bowman Transportation Co., 424 U.S. 747 (1976). . . .

B

Properly construed, therefore, our prior cases unequivocally show that a state government may adopt race-conscious programs if the purpose of such programs is to remove the disparate racial impact its actions might otherwise have and if there is reason to believe that the disparate impact is itself the product of past discrimination, whether its own or that of society at large. There is no question that Davis' program is valid under this test.

Certainly, on the basis of the undisputed factual submissions before this Court, Davis had a sound basis for believing that the problem of underrepresentation of minorities was substantial and chronic and that the problem was attributable to handicaps imposed on minority applicants by past and present racial discrimination. . . .

C

The second prong of our test — whether the Davis program stigmatizes any discrete group or individual and whether race is reasonably used in light of the program's objectives — is clearly satisfied by the Davis program.

It is not even claimed that Davis' program in any way operates to stigmatize or single out any discrete and insular, or even any identifiable, nonminority group. Nor will harm comparable to that imposed upon racial minorities by exclusion or separation on grounds of race be the likely result of the program. It does not, for example, establish an exclusive preserve for minority students apart from and exclusive of whites. Rather, its purpose is to overcome the effects of segregation by bringing the races together. True, whites are excluded from participation in the special admissions program, but this fact only operates to reduce the number of whites to be admitted in the regular admissions program in order to permit admission of a reasonable percentage — less than their proportion of the California population — of otherwise under-represented qualified minority applicants.[58] . . .

In addition, there is simply no evidence that the Davis program discriminates intentionally or unintentionally against any minority group which it purports to benefit. The program does not establish a quota in the invidious sense of a ceiling on the number of minority applicants to be admitted. Nor can the program reasonably be regarded as stigmatizing the program's beneficiaries or their race as inferior. The Davis program does not simply advance less qualified applicants; rather, it compensates applicants, who it is uncontested are fully qualified to study medicine, for educational disadvantages which it was reasonable to conclude were a product of state-fostered discrimination. Once admitted, these students must satisfy the same degree requirements as regularly admitted students; they are taught by the same faculty in the same classes; and their performance is evaluated by the same standards by which regularly admitted students are judged. Under these circumstances, their performance and degrees must be regarded equally with the regularly admitted students with whom they compete for standing. . . .

D

We disagree with the lower courts' conclusion that the Davis program's use of race was unreasonable in light of its objectives. First, as petitioner argues, there

58. [This] case does not raise the question whether even a remedial use of race would be unconstitutional if it admitted unqualified minority applicants in preference to qualified applicants or admitted, as a result of preferential consideration, racial minorities in numbers significantly in excess of their proportional representation in the relevant population. Such programs might well be inadequately justified by the legitimate remedial objectives. Our allusion to the proportional percentage of minorities in the population of the State administering the program is not intended to establish either that figure or that population universe as a constitutional benchmark. In this case, even respondent, as we understand him, does not argue that, if the special admissions program is otherwise constitutional, the allotment of 16 places in each entering class for special admittees is unconstitutionally high.

are no practical means by which it could achieve its ends in the foreseeable future without the use of race-conscious measures. . . .

Second, the Davis admissions program does not simply equate minority status with disadvantage. Rather, Davis considers on an individual basis each applicant's personal history to determine whether he or she has likely been disadvantaged by racial discrimination. [True], the procedure by which disadvantage is detected is informal, but we have never insisted that educators conduct their affairs through adjudicatory proceedings, and such insistence here is misplaced. A case-by-case inquiry into the extent to which each individual applicant has been affected, either directly or indirectly, by racial discrimination, would seem to be, as a practical matter, virtually impossible, despite the fact that there are excellent reasons for concluding that such effects generally exist. When individual measurement is impossible or extremely impractical, there is nothing to prevent a State from using categorical means to achieve its ends, at last where the category is closely related to the goal. . . .

E

Finally, Davis' special admissions program cannot be said to violate the Constitution simply because it has set aside a predetermined number of places for qualified minority applicants rather than using minority status as a positive factor to be considered in evaluating the applications of disadvantaged minority applicants. For purposes of constitutional adjudication, there is no difference between the two approaches. In any admissions program which accords special consideration to disadvantaged racial minorities, a determination of the degree of preference to be given is unavoidable, and any given preference that results in the exclusion of a white candidate is no more or less constitutionally acceptable than a program such as that at Davis. Furthermore, the extent of the preference inevitably depends on how many minority applicants the particular school is seeking to admit in any particular year so long as the number of qualified minority applicants exceeds that number. There is no sensible, and certainly no constitutional, distinction between, for example, adding a set number of points to the admissions rating of disadvantaged minority applicants as an expression of the preference with the expectation that this will result in the admission of an approximately determined number of qualified minority applicants and setting a fixed number of places for such applicants as was done here. . . .

V

Accordingly, we would reverse the judgment of the Supreme Court of California holding the Medical School's special admissions program unconstitutional and directing respondent's admission, as well as that portion of the judgment enjoining the Medical School from according any consideration to race in the admissions process.

[JUSTICE WHITE's separate opinion, arguing that there is no private right of action under Title VI, has been omitted.]

MR. JUSTICE MARSHALL. . . .

While I applaud the judgment of the Court that a university may consider race in its admissions process, it is more than a little ironic that, after several hundred years of class-based discrimination against Negroes, the Court is unwilling to hold that a class-based remedy for that discrimination is permissible. In declining to so hold, today's judgment ignores the fact that for several hundred years Negroes have been discriminated against, not as individuals, but rather solely because of the color of their skins. It is unnecessary in 20th-century America to have individual Negroes demonstrate that they have been victims of racial discrimination; the racism of our society has been so pervasive that none, regardless of wealth or position, has managed to escape its impact. The experience of Negroes in America has been different in kind, not just in degree, from that of other ethnic groups. It is not merely the history of slavery alone but also that a whole people were marked as inferior by the law. And that mark has endured. The dream of America as the great melting pot has not been realized for the Negro; because of his skin color he never even made it into the pot. . . .

I fear that we have come full circle. After the Civil War our Government started several "affirmative action" programs. This Court in the Civil Rights Cases and Plessy v. Ferguson destroyed the movement toward complete equality. For almost a century no action was taken, and this nonaction was with the tacit approval of the courts. Then we had Brown v. Board of Education and the Civil Rights Acts of Congress, followed by numerous affirmative-action programs. Now, we have this Court again stepping in, this time to stop affirmative-action programs of the type used by the University of California.

Mr. Justice Blackmun. . . .

I yield to no one in my earnest hope that the time will come when an "affirmative action" program is unnecessary and is, in truth, only a relic of the past. I would hope that we could reach this stage within a decade at the most. But the story of Brown v. Board of Education, 347 U.S. 483 (1954), decided almost a quarter of a century ago, suggests that that hope is a slim one. At some time, however, beyond any period of what some would claim is only transitional inequality, the United States must and will reach a stage of maturity where action along this line is no longer necessary. Then persons will be regarded as persons, and discrimination of the type we address today will be an ugly feature of history that is instructive but that is behind us. . . .

It is somewhat ironic to have us so deeply disturbed over a program where race is an element of consciousness, and yet to be aware of the fact, as we are, that institutions of higher learning, albeit more on the undergraduate than the graduate level, have given conceded preferences up to a point to those possessed of athletic skills, to the children of alumni, to the affluent who may bestow their largess on the institutions, and to those having connections with celebrities, the famous, and the powerful. . . .

I suspect that it would be impossible to arrange an affirmative-action program in a racially neutral way and have it successful. To ask that this be so is to demand the impossible. In order to get beyond racism, we must first take account of race. There is no other way. And in order to treat some persons equally, we must treat them differently. We cannot — we dare not — let the Equal Protection Clause perpetuate racial supremacy. . . .

Mr. Justice Stevens, with whom The Chief Justice, Mr. Justice Stewart, and Mr. Justice Rehnquist join, concurring in the judgment in part and dissenting in part.

It is always important at the outset to focus precisely on the controversy before the Court.[1] It is particularly important to do so in this case because correct identification of the issues will determine whether it is necessary or appropriate to express any opinion about the legal status of any admissions program other than petitioner's.

I

This is not a class action. The controversy is between two specific litigants. Allan Bakke challenged petitioner's special admissions program, claiming that it denied him a place in medical school because of his race in violation of the Federal and California Constitutions and of Title VI of the Civil Rights Act of 1964. The California Supreme Court upheld his challenge and ordered him admitted. If the state court was correct in its view that the University's special program was illegal, and that Bakke was therefore unlawfully excluded from the Medical School because of his race, we should affirm its judgment, regardless of our views about the legality of admissions programs that are not now before the Court. . . .

It is therefore perfectly clear that the question whether race can ever be used as a factor in an admissions decision is not an issue in this case, and that discussion of that issue is inappropriate.

II

Both petitioner and respondent have asked us to determine the legality of the University's special admissions program by reference to the Constitution. Our settled practice, however, is to avoid the decision of a constitutional issue if a case can be fairly decided on a statutory ground. . . .

III . . .

The University's special admissions program violated Title VI of the Civil Rights Act of 1964 by excluding Bakke from the Medical School because of his race. It is therefore our duty to affirm the judgment ordering Bakke admitted to the University.

Accordingly, I concur in the Court's judgment insofar as it affirms the judgment of the Supreme Court of California. To the extent that it purports to do anything else, I respectfully dissent.

FULLILOVE v. KLUTZNICK, 448 U.S. 448 (1980): In an effort to stimulate the national economy, Congress enacted The Public Works Employment Act of 1977, which provided financial assistance to state and local governments to

---

1. Four Members of the Court have undertaken to announce the legal and constitutional effect of this Court's judgment. See opinion of Justices Brennan, White, Marshall, and Blackmun. It is hardly necessary to state that only a majority can speak for the Court or determine what is the "central meaning" of any judgment of the Court.

build public facilities. The act required that, absent an administrative waiver, 10 percent of the funds granted for the projects had to be used to procure services or supplies from minority business enterprises (MBEs). These enterprises were defined as businesses owned or controlled by minority groups, which, in turn, were defined as "citizens of the United States who are Negroes, Spanish-speaking, Orientals, Indians, Eskimos, and Aleuts." This case concerned a facial challenge to this "set-aside" provision. Although the Court upheld its constitutionality, no opinion attracted the votes of a majority of the Justices. Chief Justice Burger announced the Court's judgment in an opinion joined by Justices White and Powell:

"A program that employs racial or ethnic criteria, even in a remedial context, calls for close examination; yet we are bound to approach our task with appropriate deference to the Congress, a co-equal [branch]. [We] stress the limited scope of our inquiry. [Petitioners] have challenged the constitutionality of the MBE provision on its face; they have not sought damages or other specific relief for injury allegedly flowing from specific applications of the program; nor have they attempted to show that as applied in identified situations the MBE provision violated the constitutional or statutory rights of any party to this case. In these circumstances, given a reasonable construction and in light of its projected administration, if we find the MBE program on its face to be free of constitutional defects, it must be upheld as within congressional power.

"Our review of the regulations and guidelines governing administration of the MBE provision reveals that Congress enacted the program as a strictly remedial measure; moreover, it is a remedy that functions prospectively, in the manner of an injunctive decree. Pursuant to the administrative program, grantees and their prime contractors are required to seek out all available, qualified, bona fide MBE's. [The] program assumes that grantees who undertake these efforts in good faith will obtain at least 10% participation by minority business enterprises. It is recognized that, to achieve this target, contracts will be awarded to available, qualified, bona fide MBE's even though they are not the lowest competitive bidders, so long as their higher bids, when challenged, are found to reflect merely attempts to cover costs inflated by the present effects of prior disadvantage and discrimination. There is available to the grantee a provision [for] administrative waiver on a case-by-case basis should there be a demonstration that, despite affirmative efforts, this level of participation cannot be achieved without departing from the objectives of the program. There is also an administrative mechanism, including a complaint procedure, to ensure that only bona fide MBE's are encompassed by the remedial program, and to prevent unjust participation in the program by those minority firms whose access to public contracting opportunities is not impaired by the effects of prior discrimination.

"As a threshold matter, we reject the contention that in the remedial context Congress must act in a wholly 'color-blind' fashion. . . .

"It is fundamental that in no organ of government [does] there repose a more comprehensive remedial power than in Congress, expressly charged by the Constitution with competence and authority to enforce equal protection guarantees. . . .

"A more specific challenge to the MBE program is the charge that it impermissibly deprives nonminority businesses of access to at least some portion of the government contracting opportunities generated by the Act. . . .

"It is not a constitutional defect in this program that it may disappoint the expectations of nonminority firms. When effectuating a limited and properly tailored remedy to cure the effects of prior discrimination, such 'a sharing of the burden' by innocent parties is not impermissible. The actual 'burden' shouldered by nonminority firms is relatively light. [Moreover], although we may assume that the complaining parties are innocent of any discriminatory conduct, it was within congressional power to act on the assumption that in the past some nonminority businesses may have reaped competitive benefit over the years from the virtual exclusion of minority firms from these contracting opportunities.

Underinclusive "Another challenge to the validity of the MBE program is the assertion that it is underinclusive — that it limits its benefit to specified minority groups rather than extending its remedial objectives to all businesses whose access to government contracting is impaired by the effects of disadvantage or discrimination. . . .

"There has been no showing in this case that Congress has inadvertently effected an invidious discrimination by excluding from coverage an identifiable minority group that has been the victim of a degree of disadvantage and discrimination equal to or greater than that suffered by the groups encompassed by the MBE program. . . .

Overinclusive "It is also contended that the MBE program is overinclusive — that it bestows a benefit on businesses identified by racial or ethnic criteria which cannot be justified on the basis of competitive criteria or as a remedy for the present effects of identified prior discrimination. It is conceivable that a particular application of the program may have this effect; however, the peculiarities of specific applications are not before us in this case. . . .

"This does not mean that the claim of overinclusiveness is entitled to no [consideration]. Even in the context of a facial challenge [the] MBE provision cannot pass muster unless, with due account for its administrative program it provides reasonable assurance that application of racial or ethnic criteria will be limited to accomplishing the remedial objectives of Congress and that misapplications of the program will be promptly and adequately remedied administratively.

"It is significant that the administrative scheme provides for waiver and exemption. . . .

"[Waiver] is available to avoid dealing with an MBE who is attempting to exploit the remedial aspects of the program by charging an unreasonable price, i.e., a price not attributable to the present effects of past discrimination. We must assume that Congress intended close scrutiny of false claims and prompt action on them. . . .

"The MBE provision may be viewed as a pilot project, appropriately limited in extent and duration, and subject to reassessment and reevaluation by the Congress prior to any extention or re-enactment. Miscarriages of administration could have only a transitory economic impact on businesses not encompassed by the program, and would not be irremediable. . . .

"That the program may press the outer limits of congressional authority affords no basis for striking it down. . . .

"This opinion does not adopt, either expressly or implicitly, the formulas of analysis articulated in such cases as [Bakke]. However, our analysis demonstrates that the MBE provision would survive judicial review under either 'test' articulated in the several Bakke opinions."

Justice Powell wrote a concurring opinion: "Although I would place greater emphasis than [Chief Justice Burger] on the need to articulate judicial standards of review in conventional terms, I view his opinion announcing the judgment as substantially in accord with my own views. . . .

"Different standards of review applied to different sorts of classifications simply illustrate the principle that some classifications are less likely to be legitimate than others. Racial classifications must be assessed under the most stringent level of review because immutable characteristics, which bear no relation to individual merit or need, are irrelevant to almost every governmental decision. In this case, however, I believe that [the statute] is justified as a remedy that serves the compelling governmental interest in eradicating the continuing effects of past discrimination identified by Congress. . . .

"Because the distinction between permissible remedial action and impermissible racial preference rests on the existence of constitutional or statutory violation, the legitimate interest in creating a race-conscious remedy is not compelling unless an appropriate governmental authority has found that such a violation has occurred. In other words, two requirements must be met. First, the governmental body that attempts to impose a race-conscious remedy must have the authority to act in response to identified discrimination. Second, the governmental body must make findings that demonstrate the existence of illegal discrimination. . . .

"The history of this Court's review of congressional action demonstrates beyond question that the National Legislature is competent to find constitutional and statutory violations. Unlike the Regents of the University of California, Congress properly may — and indeed must — address directly the problem of discrimination in our society. . . .

"The Petitioners contend that the legislative history of [the statute] reflects no congressional finding of statutory or constitutional violations. Crucial to that contention is the assertion that a reviewing court may not look beyond the legislative history of the [statute] itself for evidence that Congress believed it was combating invidious discrimination. . . .

"The petitioners' contention [is] essentially a plea that we treat Congress as if it were a lower federal court. But Congress is not expected to act as though it were duty bound to find facts and make conclusions of law. The creation of national rules for the governance of our society simply does not entail the same concept of recordmaking that is appropriate to a judicial or administrative proceeding."

Justice Marshall, joined by Justices Brennan and Blackmun, also concurred: "My resolution of the constitutional issue in this case is governed by the separate opinion I coauthored in [Bakke]. In my view the [10 percent set-aside] passes constitutional muster under the standard announced in that opinion.

"Judged under this standard, the [statute] is plainly constitutional. Indeed, the question is not even a close one. . . .

"Congress had a sound basis for concluding that minority-owned construction enterprises, though capable, qualified, and ready and willing to work, have received a disproportionately small amount of public contracting business because of the continuing effects of past discrimination. . . .

"Because the means chosen by Congress to implement the set-aside provision are substantially related to the achievement of its remedial purpose, the provision also meets the second prong of our Bakke test. Congress reasonably determined that race-conscious means were necessary to break down the barriers confronting participation by minority enterprises in federally funded public works projects. That the set-aside creates a quota in favor of qualified and available minority business enterprises does not necessarily indicate that it stigmatizes. . . .

"In sum, it is clear to me that the racial classifications employed in the set-aside provision are substantially related to the achievement of the important and congressionally articulated goal of remedying the present effects of past racial discrimination."

DISSENT

Justice Stewart, joined by Justice Rehnquist, dissented: "Under our Constitution, the government may never act to the detriment of a person solely because of that person's race. The color of a person's skin and the country of his origin are immutable facts that bear no relation to ability, disadvantage, moral culpability, or any other characteristics of constitutionally permissible interest to government. . . .

"The rule cannot be any different when the persons injured by a racially biased law are not members of a racial minority. [From] the perspective of a person detrimentally affected by a racially discriminatory law, the arbitrariness and unfairness is entirely the same, whatever his skin color and whatever the law's purpose, be it purportedly 'for the promotion of the public good' or otherwise."

Justice Stevens also dissented: "The 10% set-aside [creates] monopoly privileges in a $400 million market for a class of investors defined solely by racial characteristics. The direct beneficiaries of these monopoly privileges are the relatively small number of persons within the racial classification who represent the entrepreneurial subclass — those who have, or can borrow, working capital.

"History teaches us that the costs associated with a sovereign's grant of exclusive privileges often encompass more than the high prices and shoddy workmanship that are familiar handmaidens of monopoly; they engender animosity and discontent as well. . . .

"Our historic aversion to titles of nobility is only one aspect of our commitment to the proposition that the sovereign has a fundamental duty to govern impartially. When government accords different treatment to different persons, there must be a reason for the difference. Because racial characteristics so seldom provide a relevant basis for disparate treatment, and because classifications based on race are potentially so harmful to the entire body politic, it is especially important that the reasons for any such classification be clearly identified and unquestionably legitimate.

"The statutory definition of the preferred class includes 'citizens of the United States who are Negroes, Spanish-speaking, Orientals, Indians, Eskimos, and Aleuts.' All aliens and all nonmembers of the racial class are excluded. No economic, social geographical, or historical criteria are relevant for exclusion or inclusion. There is not one word in the remainder of the Act or in the legislative history that explains why any Congressman or Senator favored this particular definition over any other or that identifies the common characteristics that every member of the preferred class was believed to share. Nor does the Act or its history explain why 10% of the total appropriation was the proper amount to set aside. . . .

"We can never either erase or ignore the history [of discrimination]. But if that history can justify such a random distribution of benefits on racial lines as that embodied in this statutory scheme, it will serve not merely as a basis for remedial legislation, but rather as a permanent source of justification for grants of special privileges. For if there is no duty to attempt either to measure the recovery by the wrong or to distribute that recovery within the injured class in an evenhanded way, our history will adequately support a legislative preference for almost any ethnic, religious, or racial group with the political strength to negotiate 'a piece of the action' for its members. . . .

"In both its substantive and procedural aspects this Act is markedly different from the normal product of the legislative decisionmaking process. The very fact that Congress for the first time in the Nation's history has created a broad legislative classification for entitlement to benefits based solely on racial characteristics identifies a dramatic difference between this Act and the thousands of statutes that preceded it. This dramatic point of departure is not even mentioned in the statement of purpose of the Act or in the Reports of either the House or the Senate committee that processed the legislation, and was not the subject of any testimony or inquiry in any legislative hearing on the bill that was enacted. . . .

"Although it is traditional for judges to accord the same presumption of regularity to the legislative process no matter how obvious it may be that a busy Congress has acted precipitately, I see no reason why the character of their procedures may not be considered relevant to the decision whether the legislative product has caused a deprivation of liberty or property without due process of law. . . .

"[Rather] than take the substantive position expressed in Mr. Justice Stewart's dissenting opinion, I would hold this statute unconstitutional on a narrower ground. It cannot fairly be characterized as a 'narrowly tailored' racial classification because it simply raises too many serious questions that Congress failed to answer or even to address in a responsible way."

Note: What Did Bakke Hold?

After *Bakke*, what are the obligations of a conscientious lower court judge asked to rule on an admissions program identical to that employed by the Davis Medical School? Note that although Justice Powell announced the Court's judgment, he failed to attract a majority for any of the substantive portions of his opinion. Indeed, on the crucial question of the constitutionality of the Davis program, he was outvoted 4 to 1. (The four justices joining Justice Brennan's opinion would have upheld the program; the four remaining justices, who joined Justice Stevens's opinion, expressed no views on the constitutional question.) Similarly, he was the only justice who thought that the classification merited strict scrutiny and the only justice who thought that there was a relevant difference between the "Harvard" and "Davis" plans. True, Bakke himself was victorious, but he prevailed only because Justice Powell was joined by the four justices in the Stevens group who thought that his Title VI claim was meritorious. Could a lower court judge properly invalidate an identical program on Title VI grounds when a clear majority of the Supreme Court (Justices Powell and the four justices in the Brennan group) thought that Title VI went no further than the constitutional prohibition? Does it follow that a lower court judge is free to (obligated to?) adhere to the Brennan position? Assuming no change in the Court's personnel or the views of the justices, this course would result in a Supreme Court reversal. Is it senseless to argue that lower court judges, intent on following the views of a majority of the justices, are obligated to reach results that, they know, the Supreme Court will reverse?

Post-*Bakke* developments do little to clarify the law. Although the Court has granted review and heard argument in four additional cases raising aspects of the benign discrimination problem, *Fullilove* is the only other case decided on the merits, and it was also decided without a majority opinion. In each of the other cases, the Court avoided any discussion of the underlying issue. See Boston Firefighters Union v. NAACP, Boston Chapter, 461 U.S. 477 (1983) (challenge to lower court order prohibiting layoffs of municipal employees on seniority basis when such layoffs would undermine consent decree embodying color-conscious hiring requirement; case remanded for consideration of mootness after state enacted legislation requiring reemployment of all laid-off personnel); Johnson v. Board of Education, 457 U.S. 52 (1982) (challenge to voluntary desegregation plan involving racial quotas designed to arrest "white flight"; court of appeals decision vacated and remanded to allow compiling of factual record on developments occurring after initial decision); Minnick v. California Department of Corrections, 452 U.S. 105 (1981) (challenge to voluntary affirmative action plan establishing employment goals for state correctional officers; writ of certiorari dismissed on ground that ambiguities in record made it advisable to postpone consideration of constitutional issues until proceedings in lower court concluded).

When these cases are taken together with *Bakke, United Jewish Organizations,* and *DeFunis,* they total seven attempts by the Court to consider the benign discrimination problem since 1977 without a single majority opinion. Is there an explanation for this indecision? Does the court's inability to generate clear results in these cases suggest a more general inability to lead the country on divisive issues? Is studied ambiguity the essence of sound leadership in a period when a consensus on the question has not yet emerged? See generally Calabresi, *Bakke* as Pseudo-Tragedy, 28 Cath. U. L. Rev. 427 (1979).

Note: The Constitutionality of "Benign" Racial Classifications

Perhaps the only firm conclusions that can be drawn from study of the cases summarized above are that the Court is badly divided on the "affirmative action" question and that most issues concerning "benign" discrimination remain unsettled. What analytical framework should be used to resolve these issues?

1. *The level of scrutiny for classifications that benefit racial minorities.* Do the arguments supporting heightened scrutiny for racial classifications apply when the classification benefits a minority group? Consider how the following factors bear on the appropriate level of scrutiny for "affirmative action" measures:

a. *History.* Does the fact that whites as a group have not suffered from a history of discrimination justify a lower standard of review for statutes disadvantaging them? Consider Lempert, The Force of Irony: On the Morality of Affirmative Action and *United Steelworkers v. Weber,* 95 Ethics 86, 89 (1984):

> Why does racial discrimination excite us when so many other kinds of discrimination do not? It is because of the way we interpret history, associating racial discrimination

with practices that now appear self-evidently evil: forcing blacks from their home-land, enslaving blacks, lynching blacks for actions that among whites would not be criminal, intimidating blacks who sought to exercise their rights — in sum, system-atically disadvantaging a people in almost every way that mattered because of the color of their skin. [A] claim made by a white person as a member of the dominant majority draws its moral force largely from our collective horror at centuries of oppressing black people. It would be ironic indeed if evils visited on blacks had lent enough force to the moral claims of whites to prevent what appears to many at this point to be the most effective means of eliminating the legacy of those evils.

b. *Political process.* Does the fact that whites have "adequate" political power justify a lower level of scrutiny when laws disadvantage them? Consider Ely, The Constitutionality of Reverse Racial Discrimination, 41 U. Chi. L. Rev. 723, 735-36 (1974):

When the group that controls the decision making process classifies so as to advan-tage a minority and disadvantage itself, the reasons for being unusually suspicious, and, consequently, employing a stringent brand of review are lacking. A White majority is unlikely to disadvantage itself for reasons of racial prejudice; nor is it likely to be tempted either to underestimate the needs and deserts of Whites relative to those of others, or to overestimate the cost of devising an alternative classification that would extend to certain Whites the advantages generally extended to Blacks. . . .

[Whether] or not it is more blessed to give than to receive, it is surely less suspi-cious.

Is it a necessary implication of this view that a race-conscious program might be constitutional if adopted by a city council dominated by whites, but unconstitu-tional if adopted by a city council dominated by blacks? If the arguments for affirmative action are ultimately persuasive, why should it matter who is per-suaded by them?

Does this view unrealistically assume that affirmative action disadvantages a monolithic white majority capable of protecting itself politically? Doesn't the very fact that the legislature adopted an affirmative action plan demonstrate that the groups benefiting from it controlled the political process at least with regard to that issue? Consider Sandalow, Racial Preferences in Higher Education: Political Responsibility and the Judicial Role, 42 U. Chi. L. Rev. 653, 694 (1975):

Typically, political majorities are coalitions of minorities which have varying inter-ests in the issue presented for decision. The real dispute is not between a majority and a minority but between those minorities whose interests are most immediately affected.

[There] is no reason to suppose that the costs of [preferential admissions] policies are borne equally by sub-groups within the white population. To the extent that they are not, the discrimination — though nominally against a majority — is in reality against those sub-groups.

Of course, affirmative action plans do not typically discriminate on their face against these subgroups, and, in light of the Washington v. Davis principle, the impact of the program on these groups is insufficient to trigger strict scrutiny. Does an approach based on Washington v. Davis analysis make sense in this context? Consider Greenawalt, Judicial Scrutiny of "Benign" Racial Preference in Law School Admissions, 75 Colum. L. Rev. 559, 597 (1975):

> Under the rational basis standard, a law school would be left free to divide much of the "pie" of places in the student body by preferences for a multiplicity of minority groups. In many parts of the country, a number of minorities make up the majority of the population. If each minority group were assured "proportional representation," the result would be much closer to a maximum quota for presently overrepresented groups than any existing preferential policies.

c. *Public accountability*. Even if one is prepared to assume that the majority is monolithic, how realistic is the further assumption that it can make its will felt on the relatively low-level administrative officials who typically devise preferential admissions programs? Consider Greenawalt, supra, at 573-574:

> We may safely suppose that the faculty of most state law schools is almost entirely white, but we may not assume that most faculty members will identify more with marginal white applicants than with black applicants. . . .
>   [Many] intellectuals may actually find it easier to identify with the plight of the "oppressed" than the problems of the "Philistine" middle and lower middle classes, from whom many marginal white applicants may come. Furthermore, two things that are in the obvious and immediate interest of faculty members and administrators are campus peace and a minimum of administrative burdens. [Thus], it would be a mistake for judges to suppose that since most law school teachers and educational administrators are white they will not employ preferential policies ill-advisedly.

Do concerns such as these explain Justice Powell's refusal in *Bakke* to allow "isolated segments of our vast governmental structure" to formulate remedial affirmative action plans? Is Justice Powell's concern for public accountability consistent with his invocation of the first amendment and academic freedom in support of preferential admission plans designed to achieve student diversity? On its face, reliance on the first amendment seems puzzling, since the Davis Medical School is a state instrumentality and the first amendment is usually read to provide protection *from* the state, rather than protection *to* the state. Justice Powell might mean that there is a value in granting state universities relative immunity from public accountability when they decide on the composition of their student bodies. But why, then, does this immunity not extend to the university's decision to pursue a remedial policy?

Is a concern for public accountability consistent with Justice Powell's disapproval of a "Davis Plan" that makes explicit the number of seats awarded on a preferential basis and approval of a "Harvard Plan" that obscures the role played by race in any particular admissions decision? See Tribe, Perspectives on *Bakke*: Equal Protection, Procedural Fairness, or Structural Justice?, 92 Harv. L. Rev. 864, 873 (1979).

Suppose Congress, rather than a university, elects to pursue a remedial policy. Does that fact assure an adequate level of public accountability? Do any of the opinions supporting the judgment in *Fullilove* explain why Congress's decision should be treated differently from that of the California Board of Regents? Do they respond to Justice Stevens's complaint that the use of a racial criterion had not been adequately considered by a politically responsible body? Compare *Fullilove* with Hampton v. Mow Sung Wong, 426 U.S. 88 (1976), in which the Court, in an opinion by Justice Stevens, invalidated a Civil Service Commission policy excluding aliens from most civil service jobs. Although acknowledging that Congress or the President might constitutionally promulgate such a policy, the Court held that due process was violated because "the Chairman of the Civil Service Commission [was] deliberately fostering an interest so far removed from his normal responsibilities." For a further discussion of *Hampton*, see section E1 infra.

In a portion of his dissenting opinion in *Fullilove* not quoted above, Justice Stewart objected to the set-aside program precisely because it was adopted by a politically responsive institution. Although Justice Stewart would allow a court of equity to take race into account in devising a remedial decree to undo illegal racial discrimination, he thought that Congress had "neither the dispassionate objectivity nor the flexibility that are needed to mold a race-conscious remedy around the single objective of eliminating the effects of past or present discrimination."

Is the case for affirmative action ultimately strengthened or weakened when the program is promulgated by a politically accountable institution? Can the insistence on "dispassionate objectivity" be reconciled with the position that we should look to the political process to provide protection against unfair treatment of majorities?

d. *Judicial restraint.* The arguments examined above concern the assertion that affirmative action represents an abuse of legislative or executive power. Should "benign" racial classifications be strictly scrutinized on the ground that any other treatment of them would allow courts to substitute their own value judgment? How is the cause of judicial restraint advanced by empowering judges to invalidate an additional category of statutes? Consider Posner, The *DeFunis* Case and the Constitutionality of Preferential Treatment of Racial Minorities, 1974 Sup. Ct. Rev. 1, 25-26:

> [The] proper constitutional principle is not, no "invidious" racial or ethnic discrimination, but no use of racial or ethnic criteria to determine the distribution of government benefits and burdens. [To] ask whether racial exclusion may not have overriding benefits for both races in particular circumstances is to place the antidiscrimination principle at the mercy of the vagaries of empirical conjecture and thereby free the judge to enact his own personal values into constitutional doctrine.

Does this formulation avoid the problem of personal value judgments? Compare Sandalow, Racial Preferences in Higher Education: Political Responsibility and the Judicial Role, supra, at 677:

> [The equal protection] clause does not reveal the values courts are to defend against legislative incursion. [Value] choices necessarily underlie the selection of one or another principle, and [there] is no escape from the risk that the principle selected will reflect values personal to the judge. The principle Posner would have the court adopt is, thus, neither more nor less "objective" than a principle which would sanction minority preferences.

e. *"Innocent victims."* It is sometimes argued that "benign" discrimination should be strictly scrutinized because it disadvantages individuals on the basis of immutable characteristics when those individuals are not themselves responsible for the evil to be corrected. Note, however, that in a remedial context, innocent victims will be disadvantaged by their race whether or not an affirmative action program is adopted. In any event, is it tenable to insist on a general rule that the government should not disadvantage "innocent" individuals when doing so promotes the general welfare? Would a meritocratic system for dispensing scarce resources satisfy this requirement? Consider Karst & Horowitz, Affirmative Action and Equal Protection, 60 Va. L. Rev. 955, 962 (1974):

> Whether "merit" be defined in terms of demonstrated achievement or of potential achievement, it includes a large and hard-to-isolate ingredient of native talents. These talents resemble race in that they are beyond the control of the individual whose "merit" is being evaluated. If racial classifications are "suspect" partly for this reason, then it may be appropriate to insist that public rewards for native talents be justified by a showing of compelling necessity.

Note that in *Fullilove* Chief Justice Burger's plurality opinion rejects the contention that the minority set-aside program was constitutionally deficient because of its incidental effect on innocent nonminority firms deprived of government business. Should there nonetheless be some limit on the extent to which innocent third parties can be made to bear the burden of remedying conditions for which they are not responsible? Compare *Fullilove* with Firefighters Local Union No. 1784 v. Stotts, — U.S. — 104 S. Ct. 2576 (1984). In 1977 suit was filed against the Memphis Fire Department alleging that the department was engaged in a pattern or practice of employment discrimination in violation of Title VII of the 1964 Civil Rights Act. Ultimately, the parties settled the suit by entering into a consent decree requiring the department to pursue race-conscious hiring goals. The department operated under the decree for a number of years, but then was forced to embark on reductions in force required by budgetary constraints. The district court thereupon enjoined the department from laying off workers on the basis of seniority — a course that would have resulted in the discharge of some of the newly employed minority workers. Instead, the court's decision required the discharge of white officers who were, of course, in no way responsible for the prior acts of discrimination. The court of appeals affirmed, but a 6-to-3 majority of the Supreme Court reversed. Justice White's opinion for the majority held that the district court had exceeded its power under Title VII by interfering with the department's seniority system. Since the Court disposed of the issue on statutory grounds, it had no occasion to decide whether the discharges violated the equal protection clause. Had the Court reached the constitutional issue, how should it have been decided? See Spann, Simple Justice, 73 Geo. L.J. 1041, 1072-1073 n.156 (1985).

f. *Counterproductive consequences.* Should "benign" discrimination be strictly scrutinized because it demeans racial minorities? Because it encourages a racial "spoils system" under which minorities are sure to be the losers in the long run? Because it weakens the educative force of the government's position against racism? Consider Van Alstyne, Rites of Passage: Race, The Supreme Court, and the Constitution, 46 U. Chi. L. Rev. 775, 809 (1979):

> Ironically, the basic suggestion to relicense racial discrimination by government is put forward not despite its intrinsic tendency to set race against race, but as a good, benign, and thoughtful way to get beyond racism. [But] one gets beyond racism by

getting beyond it now; by a complete, resolute, and credible commitment *never* to tolerate in one's own life — or in the life or practices of one's government — the differential treatment of other human beings by race.

Do such arguments confuse the case for strict scrutiny with the result we might achieve if strict scrutiny were adopted? It may well be, for example, that *if* a court strictly scrutinized a "benign" classification, it would conclude that it promoted racial stereotyping. But it is hard to see why that fact alone advances the argument for using strict scrutiny, especially if, as is surely the case, a rational legislator could also conclude that the classification promotes racial justice.

2. *Justifications for affirmative action.* After selecting the appropriate standard of review, a court confronted with an affirmative action measure must determine what goals satisfy that standard.

a. *Diversity*. Is the desire to include racial minorities in aspects of community life where they are underrepresented a sufficient justification for affirmative action? In a portion of his dissenting opinion in *Fullilove* not quoted above, Justice Stewart argued that

> One [purpose] [of the minority set-aside] appears to have been to assure to minority contractors a certain percentage of federally funded public works contracts. But since the guarantee of equal protection immunizes from capricious governmental treatment "persons" — not "races" — it can never countenance laws that seek racial balance as a goal in and of itself. "Preferring members of any one group for no reason other than race or ethnic origin is discrimination for its own sake. This the Constitution forbids."

(Quoting from Justice Powell's *Bakke* opinion.)

Does this argument "[fail] to appreciate the social significance of race, quite apart from its statistical correlation with other attributes"? Sandalow, Racial Preferences in Higher Education: Political Responsibility and the Judicial Role, supra, at 685-686. Sandalow argues in the preferential admissions context that "Precisely because race itself is socially significant, students need knowledge of the attitudes, views, and background of racial minorities." Compare McCormack, Race and Politics in the Supreme Court: *Bakke* to Basics, 1979 Utah L. Rev. 491, 530: "Most educators would agree that some element of diversity in a student body is healthy, but few would assert that this factor is the primary motivation behind minority preferences or that it is sufficiently important to justify a practice that would otherwise be illegal or unconstitutional. Thus, one problem with this approach is that it is simply not the most honest statement of the objectives of the program."

b. *Race as a proxy.* When, if ever, can affirmative action be justified on the ground that race serves as a useful proxy for other characteristics relevant to a government program? Consider, for example, Minnick v. California Department of Corrections, 452 U.S. 105 (1981), where white, male correctional officers challenged a California Department of Corrections affirmative action plan establishing employment goals for women and minorities related in part to the percentage of minorities in the prison inmate population. There was no evidence in the record that the department had previously intentionally discriminated against these groups, so it was difficult to justify the plan on a remedial theory. Instead, the department argued that the plan was necessary to the safe and efficient operation of the prison system on the theory that minority officers could relate better to minority prisoners. After hearing oral argument, the Supreme Court dismissed the writ of certiorari on the ground that ambiguities in the record made it advisable to postpone consideration of the constitutional issue until proceedings in the courts below had been concluded. If the Court had reached the merits, how should the case have been decided?

Compare the state's justification for affirmative action in *Minnick* with the argument often advanced by state universities that a preference for black law and medical school applicants is appropriate because, as a class, they are more likely to provide assistance to segments of the population that most need it. Do you agree that "The purpose of [state law schools] cannot be to produce black lawyers for blacks, Polish lawyers for Poles, Jewish lawyers for Jews, Irish lawyers for Irish. It should be to produce good lawyers for Americans"? DeFunis v. Odegaard, 416 U.S. 312, 342 (1974) (Douglas, J., dissenting).

If black lawyers in fact will provide disproportionately greater service to the black community, and if the cost of using nonracial means to identify the group of blacks and whites that will provide such service is high, what is wrong with using race as a proxy for this characteristic? Consider Posner, The *DeFunis* Case and the Constitutionality of Preferential Treatment of Racial Minorities, supra, at 12: "use of a racial characteristic to establish a presumption that the individual also possesses other, and socially relevant, characteristics exemplifies, encourages, and legitimates the mode of thought and behavior that underlies most prejudice and bigotry in modern America." Compare Greenawalt, Discrimination and Reverse Discrimination 64 (1983): "When whites have extensive contact with black doctors, lawyers, professors, and businessmen, their stereotypes about blacks, if they have them, are likely to be affected. And blacks of all ages may take pride in the achievements of professional blacks. Thus reverse discrimination may help to shatter prejudices that have exercised a tenacious hold on American society."

c. *Remedying prior discrimination.* When, if ever, is affirmative action justified to remedy prior discrimination? Is there a constitutional duty to remedy the effects of prior constitutional violation? To remedy the lingering effects of slavery, which was constitutional at the time it was practiced? Race-conscious remedies are relatively uncontroversial when the individual benefited can demonstrate that he or she was the direct victim of unconstitutional or illegal conduct and when the remedy is directed against a person who profited from the violation. Remedial justifications are more problematical when affirmative action is designed to remedy broader, "societal" discrimination and is directed against individuals who were neither responsible for nor profited from the discriminatory conduct. Is it tenable in this context to insist on the one hand that the state has no constitutional duty to remedy prior discrimination, yet to maintain on the other that there is a compelling governmental interest in doing so?

Consider Greenawalt, Judicial Scrutiny of "Benign" Racial Preference in Law School Admissions, supra, at 582-583:

It can be debated whether the young black has a greater claim on society's resources than a young white whose predecessors were equally ill educated and destitute because they were persecuted in some other country or were lazy drunkards; but it is tenable to believe that a society has a special reason to eliminate the hardships stemming from its own injustices, and that this responsibility can survive the death of oppressors and direct victims, as long as ascertainable persons continue to suffer those hardships. This is not to say that rectifying the effects of injustice on subsequent generations is a typically desirable policy; it usually is not. It is only to say that a decision justified on that basis would not be evidently unsound.

If recognition of a remedial duty is at least permissible, how should one define its scope? Consider Fishkin, Justice, Equal Opportunity and the Family 117 (1983):

> If we were to embark upon the admittedly difficult task of imagining the alternative world (or worlds) that might have occurred had injustices to blacks not been committed, it is arguable that we might find a society in which race functioned somewhat the way eye color does now. In a racially neutral society, blacks would not constitute a social group or natural class. Their status, identity, and welfare would not be tied to their group membership. Therefore, but for the injustices for which compensation is being advocated, the group to be compensated would not exist as a social group. [The] group cannot be returned to the level of well-being it would have enjoyed, had the injustices not occurred, because had the injustices not occurred, it would not have been a group, at least in the same strict sense.

Benign discrimination

3. *Defining "benign" discrimination.* Even if one assumes that heightened scrutiny is unnecessary for "benign" discrimination and that one or more of the arguments examined above is sufficient to justify such discrimination under low-level review, a further problem remains: When is discrimination "benign"? For example, is it "benign" discrimination to bus black children past the neighborhood schools they wish to attend in order to achieve a desired racial balance? See *Johnson v. Board of Education*, 457 U.S. 52 (1982). To prevent more than a certain number of blacks from moving into public housing to avoid the racial "tipping point?" See Bittker, The Case of the Checker-Board Ordinance: An Experiment in Race Relations, 71 Yale L.J. 1387 (1962). To maintain a maximum quota on Jews admitted to a state law school in order to avoid anti-Semitic incidents? See generally Kaplan, Equal Justice in an Unequal World: Equality for the Negro — The Problem of Special Treatment, 61 Nw. L. Rev. 363 (1966).

a. *Benign purpose.* Is it satisfactory to define discrimination as "benign" whenever the legislature's purpose is to benefit a racial minority? Note that this definition would dramatically extend the Washington v. Davis principle. Under *Washington v. Davis*, "purpose" was relevant only to show that a facially neutral statute was in fact discriminatory. But a purpose-based definition of benign discrimination would mean that even facially discriminatory statutes would be constitutional so long as the legislature was properly motivated. Is this desirable? Laws discriminating against blacks have often been justified on the theory that blacks in fact benefited from them. Recall, for example, the state's assertion in *Loving* that antimiscegenation laws served the long-range interest of black people. Recall, as well, that one of the powerful arguments for strict scrutiny of racial classifications was that it avoided an individualized assessment of the good faith of claims such as these.

b. *Benign effect.* If a purpose-based definition of benign discrimination is unsatisfactory, is an effects test more useful? Should a classification be treated as benign only when both its purpose *and* effect is to benefit a racial minority?

An effects test has problems of its own. First, it is necessary to specify the effect by which the law should be judged. Should "benign" discrimination be subject to heightened review whenever opponents of the law can point to a single black person harmed by it? This standard would subject virtually every "benign" statute to heightened review. A preferential admissions plan, for example, arguably harms black applicants who would have been admitted without the preference.

Should a statute be treated as benign when the only harm it causes the minority is the imputation of inferiority created by the affirmative action measure itself? Virtually every school desegregation plan requires busing some blacks past neighborhood schools that some of them would prefer to attend. Are these plans therefore unconstitutional?

Should the test, then, be whether blacks as a group benefit from the plan in question? If so, what standard of review should a court utilize to decide whether the plan has this effect? No solution is entirely satisfactory. A rational basis standard would effectively dismantle heightened review for all racial classifications. Strict scrutiny of the effect of the plan would reintroduce heightened review of affirmative action through the back door.

Should minority groups be permitted to decide for themselves whether supposedly benign discrimination serves their interests? For example, should school segregation be constitutional in a community where a majority of blacks prefer legally separated schools? Are you troubled by the possibility that the minority's judgment on this question might be influenced by the subtle effects of the very discrimination it is approving? Consider Castaneda v. Partida, 430 U.S. 482, 503 (1977) (Marshall, J. concurring): "Social scientists agree that members of minority groups frequently respond to discrimination and prejudice by attempting to disassociate themselves from the group, even to the point of adopting the majority's negative attitudes towards the minority." Compare Ackerman, Beyond *Carolene Products*, 98 Harv. L. Rev. 713, 737 (1985):

> In branding minority politicians as victims of "false consciousness" on the pages of the United States Reports, the Supreme Court would be consigning them to a peculiarly demeaning constitutional status. Henceforth they — and they alone — would be deemed constitutionally incapable of discharging the representative functions of democratically elected legislators. [The] Court would be protecting minority rights by emphatically impugning the capacity of these very same minorities to engage in democratic politics at all.

D. EQUAL PROTECTION METHODOLOGY: HEIGHTENED SCRUTINY AND THE PROBLEM OF GENDER

Does the Constitution impose a special burden of justification when government action discriminates on the basis of gender? Does it matter whether the government action disadvantages men or women? Is it ever proper for a legislature to recognize "inherent" differences between the sexes?

1. The Early Cases

Until the 1970s, the Court applied only minimal scrutiny to gender classifications and consistently rejected constitutional attacks on statutes disadvantaging women. In Bradwell v. Illinois, 83 U.S. (16 Wall.) 130 (1873), for example, decided the day after the Slaughter-House Cases, section A2 supra, the Court rejected an attack on Illinois' refusal to license a woman to practice law. In an opinion by Justice Miller, the author of the Slaughter-House Cases, the Court held that the right to practice law was not a privilege or immunity of national citizenship and therefore was not protected by the fourteenth amendment.

Justice Bradley, who had dissented in the Slaughter-House Cases, added a much-quoted concurring opinion. In the Slaughter-House Cases, Bradley had written that "a law which prohibits a large class of citizens from adopting a lawful [employment deprives] them of liberty as well as property without due process of law." In Bradwell, however, he asserted that

> The natural and proper timidity and delicacy which belongs to the female sex evidently unfits it for many of the occupations of civil life. The constitution of the family organization, which is founded in the divine ordinance, as well as in the nature of things, indicates the domestic sphere as that which properly belongs to the domain and functions of womanhood. The harmony, not to say identity, of interests and views which belong or should belong to the family institution, is repugnant to the idea of a woman adopting a distinct and independent career from that of her husband. . . .
>
> It is true that many women are unmarried and not affected by any of the duties, complications, and incapacities arising out of the married state but these are exceptions to the general rule. The paramount destiny and mission of woman are to fulfill the noble and benign offices of wife and mother. This is the law of the Creator. And the rules of civil society must be adapted to the general constitution of things, and cannot be based upon exceptional cases.

See also In re Lockwood, 154 U.S. 116 (1894).

Two years later, in Minor v. Happersett, 88 U.S. (21 Wall.) 162 (1875), the Court acknowledged that women were "persons" and "citizens" within the meaning of the fourteenth amendment but held that the right to vote was not a privilege of United States citizenship and that women could therefore be denied the franchise.

These early cases were decided against the backdrop of the Slaughter-House Cases, which had given an extremely narrow reading to the fourteenth amendment's due process and equal protection clauses. They therefore paid little attention to claims that gender discrimination violated these provisions. But even when the Court began to invalidate other legislation on due process and equal protection grounds, it resisted application of these clauses to gender discrimination.

In Muller v. Oregon, 208 U.S. 412 (1908), for example, the Court upheld an Oregon statute prohibiting the employment of women in factories for more than ten hours per day. In doing so, it distinguished its earlier decision in Lochner v. New York, 198 U.S. 45 (1905), in which it had held that the liberty of contract implicit in the due process clause prohibited a similar restriction on the working hours of bakers. See Chapter 6, section D, infra. In *Muller* the Court maintained that "the inherent difference between the two sexes" justified limitations on a woman's right to contract. But see Adkins v. Children's Hospital, 261 U.S. 525 (1923) (invalidating minimum wage legislation for women on substantive due process grounds). *Adkins* was overruled in West Coast Hotel Co. v. Parrish, 300 U.S. 379 (1937). See generally Chapter 6, section D, infra.

The Court was similarly unsympathetic to equal protection claims. In Goesaert v. Cleary, 335 U.S. 464 (1948), for example, the Court, in an opinion by Justice Frankfurter, held that a Michigan statute prohibiting a woman from working as a bartender unless she was the wife or daughter of a male owner, did not violate the equal protection clause:

> The fact that women may now have achieved the virtues that men have long claimed as their prerogatives and now indulge in vices that men have long practiced, does not preclude the States from drawing a sharp line between the sexes, certainly in such matters as the regulation of the liquor traffic. The Constitution does not require legislatures to reflect sociological insight, or shifting social standards, any more than it requires them to keep abreast of the latest scientific standards.

See also Quong Wing v. Kirkendall, 223 U.S. 59 (1912).

As late as 1961, the Court, in Hoyt v. Florida, 368 U.S. 57 (1961), upheld as "rational" a jury selection system excluding women who did not affirmatively indicate a desire to serve. Although noting the "enlightened emancipation of women from the restrictions and protections of bygone years," Justice Harlan wrote for the Court that "woman is still regarded as the center of home and family life. We cannot say that it is constitutionally impermissible for a State, acting in pursuit of the general welfare, to conclude that a woman should be relieved from the civic duty of jury service unless she herself determines that such service is consistent with her own special responsibilities."

2. The Road to Intermediate Scrutiny

In the early 1970s the Court became more receptive to constitutional attacks on gender classifications.

REED v. REED, 404 U.S. 71 (1971): This was the first Supreme Court decision to invalidate a gender classification under the equal protection clause. An Idaho statute established a hierarchy of persons entitled to administer the estate of a decedent who died intestate (e.g., (1) parent, (2) child, (3) sibling, etc.). The statute provided further that when two or more persons were of the same entitlement class, preference should be given to the male. The state justified this preference on the ground that it eliminated an area of controversy when two or more persons, otherwise equally entitled, sought to administer an estate.

In a terse opinion, a unanimous Court held that this preference violated the equal protection clause. Chief Justice Burger, writing for the Court, characterized the issue as "whether a difference in the sex of competing applicants [bears] a rational relationship to a state objective that is sought to be advanced by the operation of [the statute]." Although recognizing that the objective of reducing the workload of probate courts by eliminating one class of contests was legitimate, the Court maintained that the means used to achieve that objective — i.e., a gender classification — was "the very kind of arbitrary legislative choice forbidden by the Equal Protection Clause."

FRONTIERO v. RICHARDSON, 411 U.S. 677 (1973): Under federal law, a male member of the uniformed services could automatically claim his spouse as a dependent thereby receiving greater quarters allowance and medical benefits. However, a woman member of the uniformed services could claim comparable benefits only if she demonstrated that her spouse was in fact dependent on her for over half his support. Although divided as to the appropriate standard of review, eight members of the Court agreed that this distinction violated the equal protection component of the fifth amendment's due process clause.

Writing for four Justices, Justice Brennan argued that classifications based on sex are inherently suspect and, like racial classifications, should be subject to close scrutiny. Brennan found "at least implicit support for such an approach" in *Reed,* since in *Reed* the Court had "implicitly rejected appellee's apparently rational explanation of the statutory scheme." Moreover, this departure from "'traditional' rational-basis analysis" was "clearly justified" in Brennan's opinion:

"There can be no doubt that our Nation has had a long and unfortunate history of sex discrimination. Traditionally, such discrimination was rationalized by an attitude of 'romantic paternalism' which, in practical effect, put women, not on a pedestal, but in a cage. . . .

"As a result of notions such as these, our statute books gradually became laden with gross, stereotyped distinctions between the sexes and, indeed, throughout much of the 19th century the position of women in our society was, in many respects, comparable to that of blacks under the pre-Civil War slave codes. Neither slaves nor women could hold office, serve on juries, or bring suit in their own names, and married women traditionally were denied the legal capacity to hold or convey property or to serve as legal guardians of their own children. And although blacks were guaranteed the right to vote in 1870, women were denied even that right [until] adoption of the Nineteenth Amendment half a century later.

"It is true, of course, that the position of women in America has improved markedly in recent decades. Nevertheless, it can hardly be doubted that, in part because of the high visibility of the sex characteristic, women still face pervasive, although at times more subtle, discrimination in our educational institutions, in the job market and, perhaps most conspicuously in the political arena.

"Moreover, since sex, like race and national origin, is an immutable characteristic determined solely by the accident of birth, the imposition of special disabilities upon the members of a particular sex because of their sex would seem to violate 'the basic concept of our system that legal burdens should bear some relationship to individual responsibility.' And what differentiates sex from such nonsuspect statutes as intelligence or physical disability, and aligns it with the recognized suspect criteria, is that the sex characteristic frequently bears no relation to ability to perform or contribute to society."

Finally, relying on Title VII of the 1964 Civil Rights Act, which prohibited employment discrimination based on gender, and congressional approval of the Equal Rights Amendment to the Constitution, Justice Brennan argued that "Congress itself has concluded that classifications based upon sex are inherently invidious, and this conclusion of a coequal branch of Government is not without significance." [At the time Justice Brennan wrote, the equal rights amendment had been submitted to the states for ratification. In 1982 the time period for ratification expired. See section D5 infra.]

Turning to the classification at issue, Justice Brennan concluded that it could not survive strict scrutiny. The Government argued that differential treatment of men and women served the purpose of administrative convenience, since, as an empirical matter, wives in our society are usually dependent upon their husbands for at least half their support, whereas husbands are rarely so dependent upon their wives. "The Government offers no concrete evidence [tending] to support its view that such differential treatment in fact saves the Government any money. [In] any case, [when] we enter the realm of 'strict judicial scrutiny,' there can be no doubt that 'administrative convenience' is not a shibboleth, the mere recitation of which dictates constitutionality. On the contrary, any statutory scheme which draws a sharp line between the sexes, *solely* for the purpose of achieving administrative convenience, necessarily commands 'dissimilar treatment for men and women who are [similarly] situated,' and, therefore, involves the 'very kind of arbitrary legislative choice forbidden by the [Constitution]' [*Reed*]."

In a separate opinion joined by Chief Justice Burger and Justice Blackmun, Justice Powell concurred in the judgment but expressly disassociated himself from Brennan's assertion that classifications based on sex are suspect. Powell thought that in light of *Reed* it was unnecessary to reach this question in order to invalidate the statute. Moreover, he noted that the equal rights amendment, which had been passed by Congress and was then pending ratification by the states would, if adopted, resolve the issue. "If this Amendment is duly adopted, it will represent the will of the people accomplished in the manner prescribed by the Constitution. By acting prematurely and unnecessarily, [the] Court has assumed a decisional responsibility at the very time when state legislatures, functioning within the traditional democratic processes, are debating the proposed Amendment."

Justice Stewart also concurred solely in the judgment with the notation that he believed "the statutes before us work an invidious discrimination in violation of the Constitution. [*Reed*]." Justice Rehnquist dissented without opinion.

Note: *From* Reed *to* Craig — *Evolution and Doctrinal Confusion*

Reed inaugurated a period of intense judicial interest in gender classifications, and the Court began to utilize a variety of techniques to invalidate laws embodying distinctions based upon sex.

1. *Due process and conclusive presumptions.* A few months after *Reed*, a divided Court in Stanley v. Illinois, 405 U.S. 645 (1972), struck down an Illinois statute that automatically made children of unwed fathers wards of the state on the death of their mothers. In contrast, unwed mothers could be deprived of their children only on a showing that they were unfit parents. The Court held that this scheme deprived fathers of due process of law by erecting a "conclusive presumption" of unfitness. In Cleveland Board of Education v. LaFleur, 414 U.S. 632 (1974), the Court used a similar technique to invalidate regulations requiring a school teacher to take maternity leave well before the expected birth date of her child.

The Court held that the due process clause did not permit a "conclusive presumption" that such women were medically unfit to teach. (In Weinberger v. Salfi, 422 U.S. 749 (1975), the Court sharply restricted use of the "conclusive presumption" technique for attacking statutory classifications. For a more detailed discussion of the problem, see Chapter 6, section G, infra.)

2. *Fair and impartial juries.* In Taylor v. Louisiana, 419 U.S. 522 (1975), the Court distinguished Hoyt v. Florida, supra this section, and held that the exclusion of women from jury service deprived the defendant of his sixth amendment right to a fair and impartial jury. The Court explained that "*Hoyt* did not involve a defendant's Sixth Amendment right to a jury drawn from a fair cross section of the community. [The] right to a proper jury cannot be overcome on merely rational grounds."

3. *Equal protection.* In Weinberger v. Wiesenfeld, 420 U.S. 636 (1975), the Court used equal protection analysis to strike down a section of the Social Security Act entitling a widowed mother, but not a widowed father, to benefits based on the earnings of the deceased spouse. The Court characterized *Frontiero* as standing for the proposition that gender classifications based on "archaic and overbroad [generalizations]" were unconstitutional. The statutory distinction between widows and widowers ran afoul of this principle by assuming "that male workers' earnings are vital to the support of their families, while the earnings of female wage earners do not significantly contribute to their families' support."

Less than a month after *Wiesenfeld*, the Court renewed its attack on "old notions" regarding sex roles as a sufficient justification for gender classifications. A Utah statute required parents to support their male children until age 21 but required support of female children only until age 18. In Stanton v. Stanton, 421 U.S. 7 (1975), the Court held that this distinction violated the equal protection clause. The state argued that it was generally the responsibility of men to provide a home and that they therefore needed a good education before undertaking this task. Women, in contrast, "tend generally to mature physically, emotionally and mentally before boys" and "tend to marry earlier." The Court categorically rejected this justification. "Notwithstanding the 'old notions' to which the [state refers], we perceive nothing rational in the distinction drawn by [the statute]. [No] longer is the female destined solely for the home and the rearing of the family, and only the male for the marketplace and the world of ideas. Women's activities and responsibilities are increasing and expanding."

4. *Unsuccessful challenges to gender classifications.* Although the post-*Reed* period was marked by dramatic advances for opponents for gender classifications, not all of their attacks were successful.

In Kahn v. Shevin, 416 U.S. 351 (1974), for example, the Court sustained a Florida statute providing a property tax exemption for widows but not widowers. The Court held that the distinction was justified by the greater financial difficulties confronting a lone woman: "Whether from overt discrimination or from the socialization process of a male-dominated culture, the job market is inhospitable to the woman seeking any but the lowest paid jobs." (The problem of affirmative action in the gender context is discussed more fully in section D3, infra.)

In Geduldig v. Aiello, 417 U.S. 484 (1974), the Court rejected an attack on California's disability insurance program that excluded pregnancy-related disabilities from coverage. The Court held that California's insurance limitation was justified by the state's "legitimate interest in maintaining the self-supporting nature of its insurance program." In a footnote, the Court added that the case was "a far cry from cases like [*Reed*] and [*Frontiero*], involving discrimination based upon gender as such. The California insurance program does not exclude anyone from benefit eligibility because of gender but merely removes one physical condition — pregnancy — from the list of compensable disabilities." (For a fuller discussion of *Geduldig* and the problem of identifying facially discriminatory classifications, see section C2 supra.)

Finally, in Schlesinger v. Ballard, 419 U.S. 498 (1975), the Court sustained a federal statute granting women in the navy a longer period in which to achieve mandatory promotion than men. The Court reasoned that this distinction, unlike those disapproved in *Frontiero* and *Reed*, was not based on "archaic and overbroad generalizations." Rather, it reflected the "demonstrable fact that male and female line officers in the Navy are *not* similarly situated with respect to opportunities for professional service." Since women were precluded from participating in combat and most sea duty, they would "not generally have compiled records of seagoing service comparable to those of male lieutenants."

5. *The legacy of* Reed. These mixed results in the period immediately following *Reed* sent confused signals. On the one hand, it was indisputable that the Court had become far more receptive to claims of sex discrimination. It seemed clear as well that, whatever it said in its opinions, the Court was subjecting gender classifications to some form of heightened scrutiny. Yet on the other hand, the justices went to extraordinary lengths to leave intact prior equal protection doctrine that had supported the old approach. Thus, in *Taylor, Stanley,* and *LaFleur,* the Court managed to overturn gender classifications without any substantial reliance on equal protection analysis. While the Court did resort to equal protection principles in *Reed, Stanley,* and *Wiesenfeld,* it purported to utilize only low-level, rational basis review to invalidate the challenged statutes. And when confronted with an express invitation to afford heightened scrutiny for gender classifications in *Frontiero,* five Justices declined to accept.

This unwillingness to dismantle the old doctrinal structure, together with the decisions in *Kahn, Geduldig,* and *Ballard,* sparked controversy over the depth and seriousness of the Court's commitment to sexual equality. See, e.g., Ginsburg, Gender in the Supreme Court: The 1973 and 1974 Terms, 1975 Sup. Ct. Rev. 1; Johnston, Sex Discrimination and the Supreme Court 1971-1974, 49 N.Y.U. L. Rev. 617 (1974). There was speculation as well concerning the actual standard of review the Court was utilizing in gender cases. See, e.g., Gunther, Foreword: In Search of Evolving Doctrine on a Changing Court: A Model for a Newer Equal Protection, 86 Harv. L. Rev. 1, 34 (1972).

When a majority of the justices finally agreed on the appropriate standard of review in gender cases, the standard was utilized to invalidate a statute that, superficially at least, favored women.

Craig v. Boren
429 U.S. 190 (1976)

MR. JUSTICE BRENNAN delivered the opinion of the Court.

The interaction of two sections of an Oklahoma statute prohibits the sale of "nonintoxicating" 3.2% beer to males under the age of 21 and to females under the age of 18. The question to be decided is whether such a gender-based differential constitutes a denial to males 18-20 years of age of the equal protection of the laws in violation of the Fourteenth Amendment. . . .

[Analysis] may appropriately begin with the reminder that *Reed* emphasized that statutory classifications that distinguish between males and females are "subject to scrutiny under the Equal Protection Clause." To withstand constitutional challenge, previous cases establish that classifications by gender must serve important governmental objectives and must be substantially related to achievement of those objectives. Thus, in *Reed*, the objectives of "reducing the workload on probate courts," and "avoiding intrafamily controversy," were deemed of insufficient importance to sustain use of an overt gender criterion in the appointment of administrators of intestate decedents' estates. Decisions following *Reed* similarly have rejected administrative ease and convenience as sufficiently important objectives to justify gender-based classifications.[6]

Reed v. Reed has also provided the underpinning for decisions that have invalidated statutes employing gender as an inaccurate proxy for other, more germane bases of classification. Hence, "archaic and overbroad" generalizations, [*Ballard*], concerning the financial position of servicewomen, [*Frontiero*], and working women, [*Wiesenfeld*], could not justify use of a gender line in determining eligibility for certain governmental entitlements. Similarly, increasingly outdated misconceptions concerning the role of females in the home rather than in the "marketplace and world of ideas" were rejected as loose-fitting characterizations incapable of supporting state statutory schemes that were premised upon their accuracy. . . .

In this case, too, "*Reed*, we feel, is controlling . . . ," [*Stanton*]. We turn then to the question whether, under *Reed*, the difference between males and females with respect to the purchase of 3.2% beer warrants the differential in age drawn by the Oklahoma statute. We conclude that it does not. . . .

We accept for purposes of discussion the District Court's identification of the objective underlying [the statute] as the enhancement of traffic safety. Clearly, the protection of public health and safety represents an important function of state and local governments. However, appellees' statistics in our view cannot support the conclusion that the gender-based distinction closely serves to achieve that objective and therefore the distinction cannot under *Reed* withstand equal protection challenge.

The appellees introduced a variety of statistical surveys. . . .

Even were this statistical evidence accepted as accurate, it nevertheless offers only a weak answer to the equal protection question presented here. The most focused and relevant of the statistical surveys, arrests of 18-20-year-olds for alcohol-related driving offenses, exemplifies the ultimate unpersuasiveness of this evidentiary record. Viewed in terms of the correlation between sex and the actual activity that Oklahoma seeks to regulate — driving while under the influence of alcohol — the statistics broadly establish that .18% of females and 2% of males in that age group were arrested for that offense. While such a disparity is not trivial

---

6. [*Kahn*] and [*Ballard*], upholding the use of gender-based classifications, rested upon the Court's perception of the laudatory purposes of those laws as remedying disadvantageous conditions suffered by women in economic and military life. Needless to say, in this case Oklahoma does not suggest that the age-sex differential was enacted to ensure the availability of 3.2% beer for women as compensation for previous deprivations.

in a statistical sense, it hardly can form the basis for employment of a gender line as a classifying device. Certainly if maleness is to serve as a proxy for drinking and driving, a correlation of 2% must be considered an unduly tenuous "fit."[12] Indeed, prior cases have consistently rejected the use of sex as a decisionmaking factor even though the statutes in question certainly rested on far more predictive empirical relationships than this.[13]

Moreover, the statistics exhibit a variety of other shortcomings that seriously impugn their value to equal protection analysis. Setting aside the obvious methodological problems,[14] the surveys do not adequately justify the salient features of Oklahoma's gender-based traffic-safety law. None purports to measure the use and dangerousness of 3.2% beer as opposed to alcohol generally, a detail that is of particular importance since, in light of its low alcohol level, Oklahoma apparently considers the 3.2% beverage to be "nonintoxicating."

There is no reason to belabor this line of analysis. It is unrealistic to expect either members of the judiciary or state officials to be well versed in the rigors of experimental or statistical technique. But this merely illustrates that proving broad sociological propositions by statistics is a dubious business, and one that inevitably is in tension with the normative philosophy that underlies the Equal Protection Clause. Suffice to say that the showing offered by the appellees does not satisfy us that sex represents a legitimate, accurate proxy for the regulation of drinking and driving. In fact, when it is further recognized that Oklahoma's statute prohibits only the selling of 3.2% beer to young males and not their drinking the beverage once acquired (even after purchase by their 18-20-year-old female companions), the relationship between gender and traffic safety becomes far too tenuous to satisfy *Reed*'s requirement that the gender-based difference be substantially related to achievement of the statutory objective.

We hold, therefore, that under *Reed*, Oklahoma's 3.2% beer statute invidiously discriminates against males 18-20 years of age. . . .

We conclude that the gender-based differential contained in [the statutes] constitutes a denial of the equal protection of the laws to males aged 18-20[23] and reverse the judgment of the District Court.

It is so ordered.

Mr. Justice Powell, concurring.

I join the opinion of the Court as I am in general agreement with it. I do have

---

12. Obviously, arrest statistics do not embrace all individuals who drink and drive. But for purposes of analysis, this "underinclusiveness" must be discounted somewhat by the shortcomings inherent in this statistical sample. In any event, we decide this case in light of the evidence offered by Oklahoma and know of no way of extrapolating these arrest statistics to take into account the driving and drinking population at large, including those who avoided arrest.

13. For example, we can conjecture that in *Reed*, Idaho's apparent premise that women lacked experience in formal business matters (particularly compared to men) would have proved to be accurate in substantially more than 2% of all cases. And in both *Frontiero* and *Wiesenfeld*, we expressly found appellees' empirical defense of mandatory dependency tests for men but not women to be unsatisfactory, even though we recognized that husbands are still far less likely to be dependent on their wives than vice versa.

14. The very social stereotypes that find reflection in age-differential laws, see [*Stanton*], are likely substantially to distort the accuracy of these comparative statistics. Hence "reckless" young men who drink and drive are transformed into arrest statistics, whereas their female counterparts are chivalrously escorted home. . . .

23. Insofar as [*Goesaert*] may be inconsistent, that decision is disapproved. . . .

reservations as to some of the discussion concerning the appropriate standard for equal protection analysis and the relevance of the statistical evidence.

Reed and subsequent cases involving gender-based classifications make clear that the Court subjects such classifications to a more critical examination than is normally applied when "fundamental" constitutional rights and "suspect classes" are not present.*

I view this as a relatively easy case. No one questions the legitimacy or importance of the asserted governmental objective: the promotion of highway safety. The decision of the case turns on whether the state legislature, by the classification it has chosen, has adopted a means that bears a "'fair and substantial relation'" to this objective.

It seems to me that the statistics offered by appellees and relied upon by the District Court do tend generally to support the view that young men drive more, possibly are inclined to drink more, and — for various reasons — are involved in more accidents than young women. Even so, I am not persuaded that these facts and the inferences fairly drawn from them justify this classification based on a three-year age differential between the sexes, and especially one that is so easily circumvented as to be virtually meaningless. Putting it differently, this gender-based classification does not bear a fair and substantial relation to the object of the legislation.

MR. JUSTICE STEVENS, concurring.

There is only one Equal Protection Clause. It requires every State to govern impartially. It does not direct the courts to apply one standard of review in some cases and a different standard in other cases. Whatever criticism may be leveled at a judicial opinion implying that there are at least three such standards applies with the same force to a double standard.

I am inclined to believe that what has become known as the two-tiered analysis of equal protection claims does not describe a completely logical method of deciding cases, but rather is a method the Court has employed to explain decisions that actually apply a single standard in a reasonably consistent fashion. I also suspect that a careful explanation of the reasons motivating particular decisions may contribute more to an identification of that standard than an attempt to articulate it in all-encompassing terms. It may therefore be appropriate for me to state the principal reasons which persuaded me to join the Court's opinion.

In this case, the classification is not as obnoxious as some the Court has condemned, nor as inoffensive as some the Court has accepted. It is objectionable because it is based on an accident of birth, because it is a mere remnant of the now almost universally rejected tradition of discriminating against males in this age bracket, and because, to the extent it reflects any physical difference between

---

* As is evident from our opinions, the Court has had difficulty in agreeing upon a standard of equal protection analysis that can be applied consistently to the wide variety of legislative classifications. There are valid reasons for dissatisfaction with the "two-tier" approach that has been prominent in the Court's decisions in the past decade. Although viewed by many as a result-oriented substitute for more critical analysis, that approach — with its narrowly limited "upper-tier" — now has substantial precedential support. As has been true of *Reed* and its progeny, our decision today will be viewed by some as a "middle-tier" approach. While I would not endorse that characterization and would not welcome a further subdividing of equal protection analysis, candor compels the recognition that the relatively deferential "rational basis" standard of review normally applied takes on a sharper focus when we address a gender-based classification. So much is clear from our recent cases. . . .

males and females, it is actually perverse.[4] The question then is whether the traffic safety justification put forward by the State is sufficient to make an otherwise offensive classification acceptable.

The classification is not totally irrational. For the evidence does indicate that there are more males than females in this age bracket who drive and also more who drink. Nevertheless, there are several reasons why I regard the justification as unacceptable. It is difficult to believe that the statute was actually intended to cope with the problem of traffic safety, since it has only a minimal effect on access to a not very intoxicating beverage and does not prohibit its consumption. Moreover, the empirical data submitted by the State accentuate the unfairness of treating all 18-20-year-old males as inferior to their female counterparts. The legislation imposes a restraint on 100% of the males in the class allegedly because about 2% of them have probably violated one or more laws relating to the consumption of alcoholic beverages. It is unlikely that this law will have a significant deterrent effect either on that 2% or on the law-abiding 98%. But even assuming some such slight benefit, it does not seem to me that an insult to all of the young men of the State can be justified by visiting the sins of the 2% on the 98%.

[Concurring opinions by Justices Stewart and Blackmun and a dissenting opinion by Chief Justice Burger are omitted.]

Mr. Justice Rehnquist, dissenting.

The Court's disposition of this case is objectionable on two grounds. First is its conclusion that *men* challenging a gender-based statute which treats them less favorably than women may invoke a more stringent standard of judicial review than pertains to most other types of classifications. Second is the Court's enunciation of this standard, without citation to any source, as being that "classifications by gender must serve *important* governmental objectives and must be *substantially* related to achievement of those objectives." The only redeeming feature of the Court's opinion, to my mind, is that it apparently signals a retreat by those who joined the plurality opinion in [*Frontiero*] from their view that sex is a "suspect" classification for purposes of equal protection analysis. I think the Oklahoma statute challenged here need pass only the "rational basis" equal protection analysis. . . .

Most obviously unavailable to support any kind of special scrutiny in this case, is a history or pattern of past discrimination, such as was relied on by the plurality in *Frontiero* to support its invocation of strict scrutiny. There is no suggestion in the Court's opinion that males in this age group are in any way peculiarly disadvantaged, subject to systematic discriminatory treatment, or otherwise in need of special solicitude from the courts. . . .

The Court's conclusion that a law which treats males less favorably than females "must serve important governmental objectives and must be substantially related to achievement of those objectives" apparently comes out of thin air. The Equal Protection Clause contains no such language, and none of our previous cases adopt that standard. I would think we have had enough difficulty with the two standards of review which our cases have recognized — the norm of "rational basis," and the "compelling state interest" required where a "suspect classifica-

---

4. Because males are generally heavier than females, they have a greater capacity to consume alcohol without impairing their driving ability than do females.

tion" is involved — so as to counsel weightily against the insertion of still another "standard" between those two. How is this Court to divine what objectives are important? How is it to determine whether a particular law is "substantially" related to the achievement of such objective, rather than related in some other way to its achievement? Both of the phrases used are so diaphanous and elastic as to invite subjective judicial preferences or prejudices relating to particular types of legislation, masquerading as judgments whether such legislation is directed at "important" objectives or, whether the relationship to those objectives is "substantial" enough. . . .

The Court "accept[s] for purposes of discussion" the District Court's finding that the purpose of the provisions in question was traffic safety, and proceeds to examine the statistical evidence in the record in order to decide if "the gender-based distinction *closely* serves to achieve that objective." [One] need not immerse oneself in the fine points of statistical analysis, however, in order to see the weaknesses in the Court's attempted denigration of the evidence at hand.

One survey of arrest statistics assembled in 1973 indicated that males in the 18-20 age group were arrested for "driving under the influence" almost 18 times as often as their female counterparts, and for "drunkenness" in a ratio of almost 10 to 1. Accepting, as the Court does, appellants' comparison of the total figures with 1973 Oklahoma census data, this survey indicates a 2% arrest rate among males in the age group, as compared to a .18% rate among females. . . .

The Court's criticism of the statistics relied on by the District Court conveys the impression that a legislature in enacting a new law is to be subjected to the judicial equivalent of a doctoral examination in statistics. Legislatures are not held to any rules of evidence such as those which may govern courts or other administrative bodies, and are entitled to draw factual conclusions on the basis of the determination of probable cause which an arrest by a police officer normally represents. In this situation, they could reasonably infer that the incidence of drunk driving is a good deal higher than the incidence of arrest.

And while, [such] statistics may be distorted as a result of stereotyping, the legislature is not required to prove before a court that its statistics are perfect. In any event, if stereotypes are as pervasive as the Court suggests, they may in turn influence the conduct of the men and women in question, and cause the young men to conform to the wild and reckless image which is their stereotype. . . .

[The] Court notes that only 2% of males (as against .18% of females) in the age group were arrested for drunk driving, and that this very low figure establishes "an unduly tenuous 'fit'" between maleness and drunk driving in the 18-20-year-old group. On this point the Court misconceives the nature of the equal protection inquiry. . . .

[The] clearest demonstration of this is the fact that the precise argument made by the Court would be equally applicable to a flat bar on such purchases by *anyone*, male or female, in the 18-20 age group; in fact it would apply *a fortiori* in that case given the even more "tenuous 'fit'" between drunk-driving arrests and femaleness. The statistics indicate that about 1% of the age group population as a whole is arrested. What the Court's argument is relevant to is not equal protection, but due process — whether there are enough persons in the category who drive while drunk to justify a bar against purchases by all members of the group. . . .

This is not a case where the classification can only be justified on grounds of administrative convenience. There being no apparent way to single out persons likely to drink and drive, it seems plain that the legislature was faced here with the not atypical legislative problem of legislating in terms of broad categories with regard to the purchase and consumption of alcohol. I trust [that] there would be no due process violation if no one in this age group were allowed to purchase 3.2% beer. Since males drink and drive at a higher rate than the age group as a whole, I fail to see how a statutory bar with regard only to them can create any due process problem.

Note: Heightened Scrutiny for Gender Classifications?

Assuming that racial classifications require heightened scrutiny, are there persuasive reasons to accord gender classifications similar treatment?

1. *History.* In the Slaughter House Cases, Justice Miller began his consideration of the fourteenth amendment by observing that its "one pervading purpose" was "the freedom of the slave race, the security and firm establishment of that freedom, and the protection of the newly-made freeman and citizen from the oppressions of those who had formerly exercised unlimited dominion over him." Is there anything in the history of the fourteenth amendment that provides analogous support for heightened scrutiny of gender classifications?

Ironically, the second section of the fourteenth amendment for the first time introduced explicit gender discrimination into the Constitution. The section, which required reduction of representation in the House of Representatives for states that "denied [the right to vote] to any of the male inhabitants of such State, being twenty-one years of age, and citizens of the United States," infuriated feminists such as Susan B. Anthony and Elizabeth Cady Stanton, who worked tirelessly, but unsuccessfully, for defeat of the amendment. See E. Flexner, Century of Struggle 146-148 (1975).

Even apart from the history surrounding section 2 of the amendment, it is hard to make the case that the framers had any intention of bringing into question laws that discriminated on the basis of gender. As a leading opponent of gender discrimination has conceded,

> Boldly dynamic interpretation, departing radically from the original understanding, is required to tie to the fourteenth amendment's equal protection clause a command that government treat men and women as individuals equal in rights, responsibilities, and opportunities. . . .
> When the post-Civil War amendments were added to the Constitution, women were not accorded the vote. [Married] women in many states could not contract, hold property, litigate on their own behalf, or even control their own earnings. The fourteenth amendment left all that untouched.

Ginsburg, Sexual Equality under the Fourteenth and Equal Rights Amendments, 1979 Wash. U. L.Q. 161, 161-163.

2. *Arguments by analogy.* Even if the framers of the equal protection clause did not specifically intend to ban gender discrimination, might the clause be read to require a special burden of justification for classifications that are relevantly similar to racial classifications? Does gender discrimination satisfy this test?

a. Should gender discrimination be treated like racial discrimination because it is based on "a trait that is immutable and highly visible" and therefore "lends itself to a system of thought dominated by stereotype, which automatically consigns an individual to a general category [often] implying the inferiority of the person so categorized"? Karst, Foreword: Equal Citizenship under the Fourteenth Amendment, 91 Harv. L. Rev. 1, 23 (1977). Compare Ackerman, Beyond *Carolene Products*, 98 Harv. L. Rev. 713, 730-731:

> the easier it is to avoid a bad situation, the less it will seem worthwhile to complain, and vice versa. [Among] efficacious forms of complaint, the possibility of organized political action will surely rank high. [Discreteness therefore frees] a minority from the organizational problem confronting an anonymous group of comparable size. [For], by definition, discrete groups do not have to convince their constituents to "come out of the closet" before they can engage in effective political activity. [A] Court concerned with pluralist bargaining power should be more, not less, attentive to the claims of anonymous minorities than to those of discrete ones.

b. Does the pervasive nature of sexual stereotypes and the historic subjugation of women make gender "like" race for purposes of the equal protection clause? Recall Justice Brennan's observation in *Frontiero* that statutory restrictions on women in the nineteenth century left them "in a position somewhat comparable to that of blacks under the pre-Civil War slave codes." Concerning the modern status of women, consider R. Wasserstrom, Philosophy and Social Issues 17 (1980):

> It is even clearer in the case of sex than in the case of race that one's sexual identity is a centrally important, crucially relevant category within the culture. [There] are substantially different [role] assignments to persons in accordance with their [gender]. We have a patriarchal society [in] which it matters enormously whether one is a male or a female. Just as with the case of race, by almost all important measures it is more advantageous to be a male rather than a female.

But does it follow from the pervasiveness of sex-role differentiation that laws reinforcing that differentiation are constitutionally suspect? Compare Rutherglen, Sexual Equality in Fringe-Benefit Plans, 65 Va. L. Rev. 199, 209 (1979):

> The more lenient constitutional treatment of sexual classifications draws support from contemporary morality. [Sexual] classifications are valued for their own sake within an important area of human life, namely sexual conduct, whereas racial classifications are neither so widely nor so openly valued in everyday life. [Disputes] over sexual discrimination do not concern the merits of a unisex society as disputes over racial discrimination concern the merits of a color-blind society.

If sex-role distinctions are in fact as deeply embedded in our culture as Wasserstrom and Rutherglen suggest, is an insistence on a state policy of gender neutrality likely to improve the situation? Consider Olsen, The Family and the Market: A Study of Ideology and Legal Reform, 96 Harv. L. Rev. 1497, 1552 (1983): "Antidiscrimination law [mainly] benefits a small percentage of women who adopt 'male' roles. Meanwhile, it legitimates the continued oppression of most women: the reforms maintain the status quo by particularizing and privatizing inequality and encouraging women to blame themselves for their failures in the market."

c. Are women, like blacks, entitled to special protection because of their exclusion from the political process? Consider J. Ely, Democracy and Distrust 164 (1980): "[Although sexual] stereotyping has been clear [so] has the noninsularity of the group affected. The degree of contact between men and women could hardly be greater. [And], lest you think I missed it, women have about half the votes, apparently more. As if it weren't enough that they're not discrete and insular, they're not even a minority!"

But might it not be argued that it is the very absence of female insularity that contributes to their powerlessness? Consider Bartky, On Psychological Oppressions, in Philosophy and Women 23, 36 (S. Bishop & M. Weinzweig eds. 1979):

> Unlike the black colonial, [women] are not now in possession of an alternate culture, a native culture which, even if regarded by everyone including ourselves as decidedly inferior to the dominant culture, we could at least recognize as our own. However degraded or distorted an image of ourselves we see reflected in the patriarchal culture, the culture of our men is still our culture. [The] subordination of women, then because it is so pervasive a feature of my culture will (if uncontested) appear to be natural — and because it is natural, unalterable.

Does it follow that "The chief obstacles to increased participation by [women] both in government and in other social arenas dominated by white men, are psychological" and that "removal of these obstacles only begins in providing access to voting and officeholding and the like. To complete the process requires the eradication of any discrimination which, without compelling justification, reinforces the substance or symbolism of female dependency." Karst, supra, at 26.

Ely responds that

> Constitutional suspiciousness should turn on evidence of blocked access, [not] on the fact that elections are coming out "wrong." There is an infinity of groups that do not act as such in the political marketplace, but we don't automatically infer that they have a "slave mentality." The cause, more often, is that (sensibly or not) the people involved are not in agreement over the significance of their shared characteristic.

Ely, supra, at 166.

d. In any event, is the premise of the political process argument — that the interests of women are politically undervalued — still plausible? In *Frontiero* Justice Brennan relied on congressional approval of the equal rights amendment and of Title VII of the 1964 Civil Rights Act barring employment discrimination on the basis of sex to support his conclusion that sexual classifications are suspect. But doesn't congressional recognition of the invidious nature of gender discrimination demonstrate that women can protect themselves in the political process and that heightened judicial scrutiny is therefore unnecessary? Justice Powell, on the other hand, thought that the Court should stay its hand because final ratification of the equal rights amendment would establish that gender classifications were suspect. See also Brown, Emerson, Falk & Freedman, The Equal Rights Amendment: A Constitutional Basis for Equal Rights for Women, 80 Yale L.J.

871 (1971). Since Justice Powell wrote, the time limit for passage of the equal rights amendment expired without the necessary three-fourths of the states endorsing it. Might it not now be argued that the *defeat* of the amendment also supports heightened scrutiny by demonstrating the continued inability of women to protect themselves in the political process? Does this paradox suggest that there is something fundamentally wrong with the basic theory underlying the political process argument?

e. Even if women currently exercise "adequate" political power, is there still an argument for heightened scrutiny when gender classifications are "archaic?" Consider Ely, supra, at 167: "most laws classifying by sex weren't passed this morning or even the day before yesterday: in fact, it is rare to see a gender-based classification enacted since the New Deal. In general, women couldn't even *vote* until the Nineteenth Amendment was ratified in 1920, and most of these laws probably predate even that: they should be invalidated." Compare Michael M. v. Superior Court, 450 U.S. 464 (1981), in which the Court upheld California's statutory rape law making men, but not women, criminally liable for acts of sexual intercourse involving a female under age 18. In a footnote to his plurality opinion, Justice Rehnquist noted that the California legislature had recently rejected a proposal to make the statute sex neutral. "That is enough to answer petitioner's contention that the statute was the 'accidental byproduct of a traditional way of thinking about females.' Certainly this decision of the California Legislature is as good a source as is this Court in deciding what is 'current' and what is 'outmoded' in the perception of women." (*Michael M.* is considered at greater length at section D3 infra.)

f. Can heightened scrutiny of even modern statutes be defended on the ground that gender classifications pose a peculiar risk of unthinking overgeneralization? Consider the suggestion in Mississippi University for Women v. Hogan, page 626 infra, that a skeptical attitude toward gender classifications is designed to ensure that government action is "determined through reasoned analysis rather than through the mechanical application of traditional, often inaccurate assertions about the proper roles of men and women." Under this view, judicial inspection of the means/ends connection and the substantiality of the state's interest is intended to ensure that such "reasoned analysis" is in fact at work.

3. *Limits to the race analogy.* As the preceding discussion suggests, gender classifications are like racial classifications in some respects but different from them in others. Does the "intermediate scrutiny" announced in *Craig* therefore represent a sensible compromise, recognizing that the analogy has force in some contexts, but not in others? In what contexts is the analogy inappropriate?

Consider gender segregation:

> [The] primary evil of [racial segregation] was that [it] designedly and effectively marked off all black persons as degraded, dirty, less than fully developed persons who were unfit for full membership in the political, social, and moral community. [It] is worth observing that the social realities of sexually segregated bathrooms appear to be different. [There] is no notion of the possibility of contamination from use; or [of] inferiority or superiority. What seems to be involved — at least in part — is the importance of inculcating and preserving a sense of secrecy concerning the genitalia of the opposite sex.

Wasserstrom, supra, at 21.

Is the analogy between gender and racial segregation more persuasive in other contexts? Recall Loving v. Virginia, in which the Court invalidated a Virginia statute prohibiting cross-racial marriages. Do laws requiring opposite-sex marriages raise nontrivial constitutional questions? Do you agree that "any prohibition against sexual classifications must be flexible enough to accommodate [the] prevailing heterosexual ethic of American society"? Rutherglen, supra, at 206.

For an example of the Court's treatment of gender segregation in a somewhat different context, consider Mississippi University for Women v. Hogan, 458 U.S. 718 (1982). Hogan, a man, claimed that his exclusion from the Mississippi University for Women school of nursing solely on the basis of gender violated the equal protection clause. In a 5-to-4 decision, the Supreme Court agreed. In an opinion by Justice O'Connor the Court recognized that Hogan could have attended classes in one of Mississippi's state-supported coeducational nursing programs. But since these programs were a considerable distance from his home, and since many students at the school of nursing were able to hold full-time jobs, "The policy of denying males the right to obtain credit toward a bacalaureate degree [imposed] upon Hogan 'a burden he would not bear were he female.' Orr v. Orr, 440 U.S. 268, 273 (1979)." This burden was unconstitutional because "excluding males from admission to the School of Nursing tends to perpetuate the stereotyped view of nursing as an exclusively woman's job. By assuring that Mississippi allots more openings in its state-supported nursing schools to women than it does to men [petitioner's] admissions policy lends credibility to the old view that women, not men, should become nurses, and makes the assumption that nursing is a field for women a self-fulfilling prophesy." The Court was careful to note, however, that it was not ruling on the constitutionality of the exclusion of males from other schools in the Mississippi University for Women or on the permissibility of a general policy of "separate but equal" education for men and women.

After Hogan must the Mississippi University for Women admit male applicants who live close to coeducational nursing programs? Could the university deny Hogan admission if it established an all-male nursing school? If the all-male program were farther from Hogan's home than the all-female program?

Are state-supported, sexually segregated athletic programs unconstitutional because they reinforce stereotypes concerning women's athletic ability? Would integrated programs be unconstitutional because they fail to take account of differences between men and women and therefore deny women an equal chance to participate?

4. The remaining questions. Craig establishes that heightened scrutiny is required for at least some forms of gender discrimination. However, the case raises two additional questions of considerable complexity. First, what sort of showing is necessary to satisfy the Court's test? Note that in Craig the state offered statistics purporting to demonstrate that ten times more men than women in the 18 to 20 age range were arrested for drunken driving. Does the Court provide an adequate explanation for why this showing was insufficient to save the law? Is it relevant to the equal protection analysis, as the Court seems to believe, that only 2 percent of the men in this age group were arrested for the offense? How does the fact that most people obey the law support the conclusion that the law is not serving an important objective? If, as the Court asserts, a statistical justification for gender classifications "is in tension with the normative philosophy that underlies the

Equal Protection Clause," what kind of justification would comport with that philosophy? The next section explores this question.

Second, as Justice Rehnquist noted in his dissent, the statute invalidated in *Craig* disadvantaged men rather than women. Does the Court explain why laws disadvantaging men should be subject to heightened scrutiny? Does it follow from *Craig* that all such laws are suspect? That such laws are suspect only when they "really" disadvantage women by reinforcing stereotypes that, in the long run, work to their disadvantage? That such laws are suspect unless they are "affirmative action" measures? Section D4 explores the problem of "benign" gender discrimination and discrimination against men. A final section briefly discusses the equal rights amendment and the effect its passage might have on current doctrine.

3. Archaic and Overbroad Generalizations versus Real Differences

Michael M. v. Sonoma County Superior Court
450 U.S. 464 (1981)

JUSTICE REHNQUIST announced the judgment of the Court and delivered an opinion, in which [CHIEF JUSTICE BURGER], JUSTICE STEWART, and JUSTICE POWELL joined.

[Petitioner, a 17½-year-old male, was convicted of "statutory rape" for having intercourse with a 16½-year-old female. California law defined this offense as "an act of sexual intercourse accomplished with a female not the wife of the perpetrator, where the female is under the age of 18 years." The statute thus made men alone criminally liable for the act of sexual intercourse. Petitioner claimed that the statute violated the equal protection clause by unlawfully discriminating on the basis of gender.]

As is evident from our opinions, the Court has had some difficulty in agreeing upon the proper approach and analysis in cases involving challenges to gender-based classifications. . . .

[We] have not held that gender-based classifications are "inherently suspect" and thus we do not apply so-called "strict scrutiny" to those classifications. See [Stanton v. Stanton]. Our cases have held, however, that the traditional minimum rationality test takes on a somewhat "sharper focus" when gender-based classifications are challenged. See [Justice Powell's concurrence in Craig v. Boren]. In Reed v. Reed, for example, the Court stated that a gender-based classification will be upheld if it bears a "fair and substantial relationship" to legitimate state ends, while in Craig v. Boren, the Court restated the test to require the classification to bear a "substantial relationship" to "important governmental objectives."

Underlying these decisions is the principle that a legislature may not "make overbroad generalizations based on sex which are entirely unrelated to any differences between men and women or which demean the ability or social status of the affected class." Parham v. Hughes, 441 U.S. 347, 354 (1979) (plurality opinion of Stewart, J.). But because the Equal Protection Clause does not "demand that a statute necessarily apply equally to all persons" or require " 'things which are

different in fact . . . to be treated in law as though they were the same,' " Rinaldi
v. Yeager, 384 U.S. 305, 309 (1966), quoting Tigner v. Texas, 310 U.S. 141, 147
(1940), this Court has consistently upheld statutes where the gender classification
is not invidious, but rather realistically reflects the fact that the sexes are not
similarly situated in certain circumstances. . . .

Applying those principles to this case, the fact that the California Legislature
criminalized the act of illicit sexual intercourse with a minor female is a sure
indication of its intent or purpose to discourage that conduct. Precisely why the
legislature desired that result is of course somewhat less clear. . . .

The justification for the statute offered by the State, and accepted by the
Supreme Court of California, is that the legislature sought to prevent illegitimate
teenage pregnancies. . . .

We are satisfied not only that the prevention of illegitimate pregnancy is at least
one of the "purposes" of the statute, but also that the State has a strong interest in
preventing such pregnancy. . . .

We need not be medical doctors to discern that young men and young women
are not similarly situated with respect to the problems and the risks of sexual
intercourse. Only women may become pregnant, and they suffer disproportionately the profound physical, emotional, and psychological consequences of sexual activity. The statute at issue here protects women from sexual intercourse at
an age when those consequences are particularly severe.[7]

The question thus boils down to whether a State may attack the problem of
sexual intercourse and teenage pregnancy directly by prohibiting a male from
having sexual intercourse with a minor female. We hold that such a statute is
sufficiently related to the State's objectives to pass constitutional muster.

Because virtually all of the significant harmful and inescapably identifiable
consequences of teenage pregnancy fall on the young female, a legislature acts
well within its authority when it elects to punish only the participant who, by
nature, suffers few of the consequences of his conduct. It is hardly unreasonable
for a legislature acting to protect minor females to exclude them from punishment. Moreover, the risk of pregnancy itself constitutes a substantial deterrence
to young females. No similar natural sanctions deter males. A criminal sanction
imposed solely on males thus serves to roughly "equalize" the deterrents on the
sexes. . . .

[We] cannot say that a gender-neutral statute would be as effective as the
statute California has chosen to enact. The State persuasively contends that a
gender-neutral statute would frustrate its interest in effective enforcement. Its
view is that a female is surely less likely to report violations of the statute if she
herself would be subject to criminal prosecution. . . .

We similarly reject petitioner's argument that [the statute] is impermissibly
overbroad because it makes unlawful sexual intercourse with prepubescent females, who are, by definition, incapable of becoming pregnant. Quite apart from

7. Although petitioner concedes that the State has a "compelling" interest in preventing teenage
pregnancy, he contends that the "true" purpose of [the statute] is to protect the virtue and chastity of
young women. As such, the statute is unjustifiable because it rests on archaic stereotypes. What we
have said above is enough to dispose of that contention. The question for us — and the only question
under the Federal Constitution — is whether the legislation violates the Equal Protection Clause of
the Fourteenth Amendment, not whether its supporters may have endorsed it for reasons no longer
generally accepted. . . .

the fact that the statute could well be justified on the grounds that very young females are particularly susceptible to physical injury from sexual intercourse, it is ludicrous to suggest that the Constitution requires the California Legislature to limit the scope of its rape statute to older teenagers and exclude young girls.

There remains only petitioner's contention that the statute is unconstitutional as it is applied to him because he, like [his partner], was under 18 at the time of sexual intercourse. Petitioner argues that the statute is flawed because it presumes that as between two persons under 18, the male is the culpable aggressor. We find petitioner's contentions unpersuasive. Contrary to his assertions, the statute does not rest on the assumption that males are generally the aggressors. It is instead an attempt by a legislature to prevent illegitimate teenage pregnancy by providing an additional deterrent for men. The age of the man is irrelevant since young men are as capable as older men of inflicting the harm sought to be prevented. . . .

Accordingly, the judgment of the California Supreme Court is affirmed.

JUSTICE STEWART, concurring. . . .

The Constitution is violated when government, state or federal, invidiously classifies similarly situated people on the basis of the immutable characteristics with which they were born. Thus, detrimental racial classifications by government always violate the Constitution, for the simple reason that, so far as the Constitution is concerned, people of different races are always similarly situated. By contrast, while detrimental gender classifications by government often violate the Constitution, they do not always do so, for the reason that there are differences between males and females that the Constitution necessarily recognizes. In this case we deal with the most basic of these differences: females can become pregnant as the result of sexual intercourse; males cannot. . . .

Experienced observation confirms the commonsense notion that adolescent males disregard the possibility of pregnancy far more than do adolescent females. And to the extent that [the statute] may punish males for intercourse with prepubescent females, that punishment is justifiable because of the substantial physical risks for prepubescent females that are not shared by their male counterparts.

[An opinion by JUSTICE BLACKMUN, concurring in the judgment, is omitted].

JUSTICE BRENNAN, with whom JUSTICE WHITE and MARSHALL join, dissenting. . . .

The State of California vigorously asserts that the "important governmental objective" to be served by [the statute] is the prevention of teenage pregnancy. It claims that its statute furthers this goal by deterring sexual activity by males — the class of persons it considers more responsible for causing those pregnancies.[4] But even assuming that prevention of teenage pregnancy is an important governmental objective and that it is in fact an objective of [the statute], California still has the burden of proving that there are fewer teenage pregnancies under its gender-based statutory rape law than there would be if the law were gender neutral. To meet this burden, the State must show that because its statutory rape

4. In a remarkable display of sexual stereotyping, the California Supreme Court stated: "The Legislature is well within its power in imposing criminal sanctions against males, alone, because they are the *only* persons who may physiologically cause the result which the law properly seeks to avoid."

law punishes only males, and not females, it more effectively deters minor females from having sexual intercourse.

The plurality assumes that a gender-neutral statute would be less effective than [this statute] in deterring sexual activity because a gender-neutral statute would create significant enforcement problems. [However,] a State's bare assertion that its gender-based statutory classification substantially furthers an important governmental interest is not enough to meet its burden of proof under Craig v. Boren. Rather, the State must produce evidence that will persuade the Court that its assertion is true. [Even] assuming that a gender-neutral statute would be more difficult to enforce, the State has still not shown that those enforcement problems would make such a statute less effective than a gender-based statute in deterring minor females from engaging in sexual intercourse. Common sense, however, suggests that a gender-neutral statutory rape law is potentially a *greater* deterrent of sexual activity than a gender-based law, for the simple reason that a gender-neutral law subjects both men and women to criminal sanctions and thus arguably has a deterrent effect on twice as many potential violators. Even if fewer persons were prosecuted under the gender-neutral law, as the State suggests, it would still be true that twice as many persons would be *subject* to arrest. . . .

Until very recently, no California court or commentator had suggested that the purpose of California's statutory rape law was to protect young women from the risk of pregnancy. Indeed, the historical development of [the statute] demonstrates that the law was initially enacted on the premise that young women, in contrast to young men, were to be deemed legally incapable of consenting to an act of sexual intercourse. Because their chastity was considered particularly precious, those young women were felt to be uniquely in need of the State's protection. In contrast, young men were assumed to be capable of making such decisions for themselves; the law therefore did not offer them any special protection. . . .

I would hold that [the statute] violates the Equal Protection Clause of the Fourteenth Amendment, and I would reverse the judgment of the California Supreme Court.

JUSTICE STEVENS, dissenting. . . .

[I] think the plurality is quite correct in making the assumption that the joint act that this law seeks to prohibit creates a greater risk of harm for the female than for the male. But the plurality surely cannot believe that the risk of pregnancy confronted by the female — any more than the risk of venereal disease confronted by males as well as females — has provided an effective deterrent to voluntary female participation in the risk-creating conduct. Yet the plurality's decision seems to rest on the assumption that the California Legislature acted on the basis of that rather fanciful notion.

In my judgment, the fact that a class of persons is especially vulnerable to a risk that a statute is designed to avoid is a reason for making the statute applicable to that class. The argument that a special need for protection provides a rational explanation for an exemption is one I simply do not comprehend.[6] . . .

---

6. A hypothetical racial classification will illustrate my point. Assume that skin pigmentation provides some measure of protection against cancer caused by exposure to certain chemicals in the atmosphere and, therefore, that white employees confront a greater risk than black employees in certain industrial settings. Would it be rational to require black employees to wear protective clothing

[If] we view the government's interest as that of a parens patriae seeking to protect its subjects from harming themselves, the discrimination is actually perverse. Would a rational parent making rules for the conduct of twin children of opposite sex simultaneously forbid the son and authorize the daughter to engage in conduct that is especially harmful to the daughter? That is the effect of this statutory classification.

In my opinion, the only acceptable justification for a general rule requiring disparate treatment of the two participants in a joint act must be a legislative judgment that one is more guilty than the other. [The] fact that the California Legislature has decided to apply its prohibition only to the male may reflect a legislative judgment that in the typical case the male is actually the more guilty party. Any such judgment must, in turn, assume that the decision to engage in the risk-creating conduct is always — or at least typically — a male decision. If that assumption is valid, the statutory classification should also be valid. But what is the support for the assumption? [The] possibility that such a habitual attitude may reflect nothing more than an irrational prejudice makes it an insufficient justification for discriminatory treatment that is otherwise blatantly unfair. . . .

Nor do I find at all persuasive the suggestion that this discrimination is adequately justified by the desire to encourage females to inform against their male partners. Even if the concept of a wholesale informant's exemption were an acceptable enforcement device, what is the justification for defining the exempt class entirely by reference to sex rather than by reference to a more neutral criterion such as relative innocence? Indeed, if the exempt class is to be composed entirely of members of one sex, what is there to support the view that the statutory purpose will be better served by granting the informing license to females rather than to males? If a discarded male partner informs on a promiscuous female, a timely threat of prosecution might well prevent the precise harm the statute is intended to minimize.

Finally, even if my logic is faulty and there actually is some speculative basis for treating equally guilty males and females differently, I still believe that any such speculative justification would be outweighed by the paramount interest in evenhanded enforcement of the law. A rule that authorizes punishment of only one of two equally guilty wrongdoers violates the essence of the constitutional requirement that the sovereign must govern impartially.

I respectfully dissent.

ROSTKER v. GOLDBERG, 453 U.S. 57 (1981): In this case, respondents challenged the constitutionality of Congress's decision to require men, but not women, to register for the draft. A federal statute authorized the President to require the registration of every male citizen and resident alien between the ages of 18 and 26 for possible conscription. In 1980 the President decided to resume registration (but not conscription) and requested funds from Congress for this purpose. At the same time, he urged Congress to amend the law to permit the registration and conscription of women. Congress agreed to provide funds for registration but after lengthy consideration declined to authorize female registra-

---

but to exempt whites from that requirement? It seems to me that the greater risk of harm to white workers would be a reason for including them in the requirement — not for granting them an exemption.

Congress taking charge of military affairs

tion. A three-judge district court held that this gender-based classification was unconstitutional.

In an opinion written by Justice Rehnquist, the Court reversed. The Court's analysis begins with a lengthy discourse on the deference owed a decision by Congress — especially when it exercises its constitutional power relating to national defense and military affairs.

"[Perhaps] in no other area has the Court accorded Congress greater deference. [Not] only is the scope of Congress' constitutional power in this area broad, but the lack of competence on the part of the courts is marked."

Turning to the specific issue raised, the Court noted that Congress had not acted "unthinkingly" or "reflexively and not for any considered reason" in rejecting female registration. "The question of registering women for the draft not only received considerable national attention and was the subject of wide-ranging public debate, but also was extensively considered by Congress in hearings, floor debate, and in committee.

"[The congressional decision to exclude women must be understood in light of the fact that registration was intended] as a prelude to a draft in a time of national emergency. [Moreover], Congress determined that any future draft, which would be facilitated by the registration scheme, would be characterized by a need for combat troops. [Women] as a group, however, unlike men as a group, are not eligible for combat [and the] President expressed his intent to continue the current military policy of precluding women from combat. . . .

"The reason women are exempt from registration is not because military needs can be met by drafting men. This is not a case of Congress arbitrarily choosing to burden one of two similarly situated groups, such as would be the case with an all-black or all-white or an all-Catholic or all-Lutheran, or an all-Republican or all-Democratic registration. Men and women, because of the combat restrictions on women, are simply not similarly situated for purposes of a draft or registration for a draft. [The] Constitution requires that Congress treat similarly situated persons similarly, not that it engage in gestures of superficial equality. . . .

"[There] was testimony that in the event of a draft of 650,000 the military could absorb some 80,000 female inductees. The 80,000 would be used to fill noncombat positions, freeing men to go to the front. In relying on this testimony in striking down the [statute], the District Court palpably exceeded its authority when it ignored Congress' response to this line of reasoning.

"In the first place, assuming that a small number of women could be drafted for noncombat roles, Congress simply did not consider it worth the added burdens of including women in the draft and registration plans. . . .

"Congress also concluded that whatever the need for women for noncombat roles during mobilization, whether 80,000 or less, it could be met by volunteers. . . .

"Most significantly, Congress determined that staffing noncombat positions with women during a mobilization would be positively detrimental to the important goal of military flexibility."

Justice White, joined by Justice Brennan, dissented: "I assume what has not been challenged in this case — that excluding women from combat positions does not offend the Constitution. Granting that, it is self-evident that if during mobilization for war, all noncombat military positions must be filled by combat-qualified personnel available to be moved into combat positions, there would be no occasion whatsoever to have any women in the Army, whether as volunteers or inductees. [I] perceive little, if any, indication that Congress itself concluded that every position in the military, no matter how far removed from combat, must be filled with combat-ready men. Common sense and experience in recent wars, where women volunteers were employed in substantial numbers, belie this view of reality. . . .

"The Court [submits] that because the primary purpose of registration and conscription is to supply combat troops and because the great majority of non-combat positions must be filled by combat-trained men ready to be rotated into combat, the absolute number of positions for which women would be eligible is so small as to be de minimis and of no moment for equal protection purposes, especially in light of the administrative burdens involved in registering all women of suitable age. There is some sense to this; but at least on the record before us, the number of women who could be used in the military without sacrificing combat-readiness is not at all small or insubstantial, and administrative convenience has not been sufficient justification for the kind of outright gender-based discrimination involved in registering and conscripting men but no women at all."

Justice Marshall filed a separate dissenting opinion, which Justice Brennan also joined: "The Government does not defend the exclusion of women from registration on the ground that preventing women from serving in the military is substantially related to the effectiveness of the Armed Forces. Indeed, the successful experience of women serving in all branches of the Armed Services would belie any such claim. . . .

[Even] assuming that precluding the use of women in combat is an important governmental interest in its own right, there can be no suggestion that the exclusion of women from registration and a draft is substantially related to the achievement of that goal. . . .

[The] majority concludes that women may be excluded from registration because they will not be needed in the event of a draft. [This] analysis, however, focuses on the wrong question. The relevant inquiry under the Craig v. Boren test is not whether a *gender-neutral* classification would substantially advance important governmental interests. Rather, the question is whether the gender-based classification is itself substantially related to the achievement of the asserted governmental interest. Thus, the Government's task in this case is to demonstrate that excluding women from registration substantially furthers the goal of preparing for a draft of combat troops. Or to put it another way, the Government must show that registering women would substantially impede its efforts to prepare for such a draft. . . .

"Nothing in the Senate Report supports the Court's intimation that women must be excluded from registration because combat eligibility is a prerequisite for *all* positions that would need to be filled in the event of a draft. [The Defense] Department indicated that conscripts would [be] needed to staff a variety of support positions having no prerequisite of combat eligibility, and which therefore could be filled by women. . . .

The Defense Department also concluded that there are no military reasons that would justify excluding women from registration. [All] four Service Chiefs agreed that there are no military reasons for refusing to register women, and uniformly advocated requiring registration of women. . . .

As such, the combat restrictions cannot by themselves supply the constitutionally required justification for the [gender-based] classification. Since the classification precludes women from being drafted to fill positions for which they would be qualified and useful, the Government must demonstrate that excluding women from those positions is substantially related to the achievement of an important governmental objective."

Note: Identifying and Defining "Real Differences"

1. *The case for selective judicial intervention.* The apparent premise behind the intermediate scrutiny mandated by *Craig* is that gender stereotypes, like race prejudice, warp legislative judgments. However, the Court has refrained from applying to gender classifications the virtual per se rule of invalidity it has applied to de jure race discrimination. This judgment presumably reflects the view that even a legislature completely free of gender prejudice would, on occasion, utilize gender classifications to achieve its goals.

Under this approach, the Court must reconstruct what the world would look like if judgments were not affected by gender prejudice. This is, presumably, the sense behind the Court's effort to distinguish between "archaic generalizations" on the one hand and "real differences" on the other. Does the Court's effort to define the "real differences" between the sexes generate confidence in its ability to perform this task? Even if judges are not immune from sexist stereotyping, might judicial intervention be defended on the ground that the Court occasionally makes things better and is unlikely to make them worse? Alternatively, might it be argued that the Court's recognition of "real differences" reenforces and legitimates gender stereotypes, thereby obstructing change?

2. Michael M. Was there any evidence before the Court in *Michael M.* demonstrating that men were more responsible for the problem of teenage pregnancy than women? In light of the fact that most forms of intercourse resulting in pregnancy involve one man and one woman, what could such evidence — even if it existed — possibly have shown? That a man is more likely to have multiple partners than a woman? That a man is more likely to be the aggressor? Is that what the Court means by avoiding overbroad, gender-based generalizations?

What, precisely, is the "real difference" between men and women justifying the disparate treatment in *Michael M.*? Is it relevant, even if true, that more women than men are deterred by the risk of pregnancy from engaging in sexual intercourse? Since the California statute prohibits *consensual* intercourse, it presently applies only in cases where the woman partner is *undeterred* by the risk of pregnancy (else the intercourse would not be consensual). What difference does it make, then, that there is another class of women, to whom the statute has no application in any event, who are deterred by this risk?

In comparing the statutes in *Craig* and *Michael M.*, which is more likely to reenforce traditional sex roles and sex stereotyping? Which is more stigmatizing?

3. Rostker. In *Rostker* the Court was unable to point to an undisputed biological fact — like the fact that only women can bear children — to support the result. Still, it rested on a premise that it seems to have viewed as almost as noncontroversial — that women are unfit to serve as combat troops or, at least, that Congress might reasonably so believe. Note that respondents chose to argue their case without challenging the combat exclusion. Is it obvious that the exclusion is constitutional? Would the result in *Rostker* have been the same if the exclusion had been challenged?

Consider Freedman, Sex Equality, Sex Differences, and the Supreme Court, 92 Yale L.J. 913, 939-940 (1983):

> The majority's acceptance [in *Rostker*] of legally created differences as a basis for other sex-based laws seems inconsistent with any serious commitment to eliminating sex discrimination. If legislatures can create "real" sex differences at will by passing sex-based laws, the equal protection clause can easily be circumvented. [It is possible] that the combat exclusion is thought to be in some way related to biological, or at least fundamental, differences between women and men, perhaps having to do with motherhood or with men's "natural" aggressiveness. Seen in this light, [the case is an example] of lax judicial review of assertions that challenged sex classifications are justified because of definitional or biological differences between women and men. It is striking, however, that the [opinion itself] [places] primary emphasis on the "real" legally-created differences between women's and men's situations and [refers] only secondarily to possible justifications for the [legislature's] creation of those differences. Thus, [the decision] significantly [dilutes] the concept of "real" differences.

Given the premise that women can be disqualified from combat service, is there any sense to a requirement that women register to facilitate a draft of people for combat positions? Might not the same objectives have been accomplished in a sex-neutral fashion by exempting all noncombat eligible persons (e.g., conscientious objectors, women, people with physical disabilities) from registration? Would grouping the class of women together with these other categories make the statute less objectionable?

Is there a constitutional problem with the military's effort to fill all noncombat positions with people who are combat qualified before resorting to others? With the decision to rely on female volunteers to fill noncombat roles before resorting to a draft? Note that even on the dissenters' view, the government could properly categorize registrants by sex and, in the event of an actual draft, choose men for all combat roles. It is at least possible, and perhaps likely, that this outcome would lead to an all-male draft. Would this result be less stigmatizing to women?

4. *Family rights*. In thinking about the Court's success in separating "real differences" from "overbroad generalizations," consider its treatment of gender classifications regarding family rights.

a. Parham. In Parham v. Hughes, 441 U.S. 347 (1979), the Court upheld the constitutionality of a Georgia statute permitting the mother, but not the father of an illegitimate child to sue for the wrongful death of the child. Although appellant was the undisputed biological father of the child, had signed the child's birth certificate, contributed to his support and visited him regularly, Georgia law prohibited him from bringing a wrongful death action because he had not formally legitimated the child. Writing for a plurality, Justice Stewart argued that the statute did not invidiously discriminate on the basis of gender because

> mothers and fathers of illegitimate children are not similarly situated. Under Georgia law, only a father can by voluntary unilateral action make an illegitimate child legitimate. Unlike the mother of an illegitimate child whose identity will rarely be in doubt, the identity of the father will frequently be unknown. By coming forward with a motion under [the applicable statute], however, a father can both establish his identity and make his illegitimate child legitimate. [Since] fathers who do legitimate their children can sue for wrongful death in precisely the same circumstances as

married fathers whose children were legitimate ab initio, the statutory classification does not discriminate against fathers as a class but instead distinguishes between fathers who have legitimated their children and those who have not.

Is the plurality correct that the ability of men to escape the classification means that the statute should not be treated under gender-discrimination principles? Writing in dissent, Justice White criticized the "startling circularity" of this argument.

> Seemingly, it is irrelevant that as a matter of state law mothers may not legitimate their children, for they are not required to do so in order to maintain a wrongful death action. That only fathers *may* resort to the legitimization process cannot dissolve the sex discrimination in *requiring* them to. Under the plurality's bootstrap rationale, a State could require that women, but not men, pass a course in order to receive a taxi license, simply by limiting admission to the course to women.

b. Kirchberg. Compare the plurality's position in *Parham* with Kirchberg v. Feenstra, 450 U.S. 455 (1981). A Louisiana statute, which had been repealed by the time the case reached the Court, gave a husband as "head and master" of property jointly owned with his wife, the unilateral right to dispose of such property without his wife's consent. Feenstra's husband utilized this power to mortgage the couple's jointly owned home, but when Kirchberg sought to foreclose on the mortgage, Feenstra resisted on the ground that the "head and master" provision was unconstitutional. The Court had little difficulty in concluding that the provision, on its face, constituted impermissible gender discrimination. Kirchberg argued, however, that Feenstra "could have taken steps to avoid the discriminatory impact of [the law by filing] a 'declaration by authentic act' prohibiting her husband from executing a mortgage on her home without her consent." By failing to do so, Kirchberg maintained, she had become the "architect of her own predicament." The Court dismissed this argument in three sentences:

> By focusing on the steps that Mrs. Feenstra could have taken to preclude her husband from mortgaging their home without her consent [appellant] overlooks the critical question: Whether [the statute] substantially furthers an important government interest. [The] "absence of an insurmountable barrier" will not redeem an otherwise unconstitutionally discriminatory law. Instead the burden remains on the party seeking to uphold a statute that expressly discriminates on the basis of sex to advance an "exceedingly persuasive justification' for the challenged classification."

Are *Parham* and *Kirchberg* consistent?

c. Caban. Apart from the ability of men to escape the statutory disability imposed by the *Parham* statute, are there other "real differences" between men and women regarding their relationship to children that justify different treatment? Compare *Parham* to Caban v. Mohammed, 441 U.S. 380 (1979), decided on the same day. In *Caban* the Court struck down a New York statute that required the consent of the mother, but not the father, for the adoption of a child born out of wedlock. The Court rejected the argument that the statute was justified by

> a fundamental difference between maternal and paternal relations. [Maternal] and paternal roles are not invariably different in importance. Even if unwed mothers as a

class were closer than unwed fathers to their newborn infants, this generalization concerning parent-child relations would become less acceptable as a basis for legislative distinctions as the age of the child increased. The present case demonstrates that an unwed father may have a relationship with his children fully comparable to that of a mother.

Appellees also argued that the statute served the end of promoting the adoption of illegitimate children, but the Court found this justification no more persuasive:

> It may be that, given the opportunity, some unwed fathers would prevent the adoption of their illegitimate children. This impediment to adoption usually is the result of a natural parental interest shared by both genders alike; it is not manifestation of any profound difference between the affection and concern of mothers and fathers for their children. [Even] if the special difficulties attendant upon locating and identifying unwed fathers at birth would justify a legislative distinction between mothers and fathers of newborns, these difficulties need not persist past infancy. [In] those cases where the father never has come forward to participate in the rearing of his child, nothing in the Equal Protection Clause precludes the State from withholding from him the privilege of vetoing the adoption of that child. [But] in cases such as this, where the father has established a substantial relationship with the child and has admitted his paternity, a State should have no difficulty in identifying the father even of children born out of wedlock.

Is *Caban* consistent with *Parham*? Dissenting in *Caban*, Justice Stevens argued that while both parents are responsible for conception of a child

> from that point on through pregnancy and infancy, the differences between the male and female have an important impact on the child's destiny. [Immediately after birth] the mother and child are together; the mother's identity is known with certainty. The father, on the other hand, may or may not be present; his identity may be unknown to the world and may even be uncertain to the mother. These natural differences between unmarried fathers and mothers make it probable that the mother, and not the father or both parents, will have custody of the newborn infant.

Stevens recognized that the particular case before the Court involved adoption of an older child against the wishes of a natural father who admitted paternity and had in fact participated in raising the child. But

> The mere fact that an otherwise valid general classification appears arbitrary in an isolated case is not sufficient reason for invalidating the entire rule. Nor, indeed, is it a sufficient reason for concluding that the application of a valid rule in a hard case constitutes a violation of equal protection principles. We cannot test the conformance of rules to the principle of equality simply by reference to exceptional cases.

Recall that *Parham*, like *Caban*, had acknowledged the paternity of his child and participated in his rearing. Why was the Court willing to invalidate the *Caban* statute because of its application to the facts actually before it, while validating the *Parham* statute without reference to the specific facts?

d. Lehr. Compare *Caban* to Lehr v. Robertson, 463 U.S. 248 (1983), where Justice Stevens, a dissenter in *Caban*, wrote the Court's opinion upholding application of a New York statute permitting adoption of appellant's child without notice to him. At the time of the adoption, New York law permitted the mother of nonmarital children to veto an adoption. A father, on the other hand, was not even entitled to notice of the proceedings unless he had registered his intent to claim paternity with a "putative father's registry" maintained by the state or met certain other statutory criteria such as living openly with the child and the child's mother. According to Justice White's dissenting opinion, appellant had made persistent efforts to see his daughter and provide financial support. These efforts were frustrated by the mother, who threatened to have appellant arrested if he did not stay away and initiated proceedings culminating in the adoption of the child by her new husband when appellant hired a lawyer to help him secure visitation rights. Emphasizing that "By mailing a postcard to the putative father registry, [appellant] could have guaranteed that he would receive notice of [the proceedings]," the Court rejected appellants constitutional challenge. The Court distinguished Caban on the ground that "appellant [has] never established a substantial relationship with his daughter. [If] one parent has an established custodial relationship with the child and the other parent has either abandoned or never established a relationship, the Equal Protection Clause does not prevent a state from according the two parents different legal rights."

Does this observation explain why the equal protection clause permits the state to allow mothers automatic veto rights over adoptions, while insisting that fathers "establish a relationship" with the child? Are there "real differences" between men and women that support this distinction? Are there sound reasons why the state might insist that men, but not women, register themselves as the parent in order to preserve their rights? Are these reasons applicable to a case where the man's paternity is not in dispute and where the mother knows that he is actively attempting to establish a relationship with the child?

When the "family rights" cases are taken together, has the Court assisted in breaking down the sex-role stereotypes that make it "suspicious" of legislative judgments in this area? Has it reinforced those stereotypes by giving them constitutional statute?

5. *The relevance of "real differences."* What, precisely, makes something a "real" difference for constitutional purposes? Must it be linked to some purely physiological distinction between the sexes? Which, if any, of the statutes considered above can be justified on this basis alone? Are demonstrated differences in behavior sufficient? It is at least conceivable that some such differences are a product of cultural expectations reinforced by the very statutes under attack. To the extent that this is true, the statutes become self-validating. Recall, for example, Justice O'Connor's concern in Mississippi University for Women v. Hogan that Mississippi's policy "makes the assumption that nursing is a field for women a self-fulfilling prophesy." Is it this phenomenon that concerned Justice Brennan in *Craig* when he wrote that statistical demonstrations are "in tension with the normative philosophy of the Equal Protection Clause"?

Does it follow that the appropriate question is what, if any, gender differences would exist in a "state of nature" before cultural forces have taken hold? Recall Justice Bradley's assertion over a century ago that a woman's duty "to fulfill the noble and benign offices of wife and mother" was "the law of the Creator." Is the current Court's search for "real differences" a modern-day analogue to this sort of reasoning? How likely is it that the justices can escape their own culture in deciding which differences are culturally determined?

Consider Wasserstrom, supra, at 34:

> It is not clear [that] this sense of "natural" is wholly intelligible; it supposes that we can meaningfully talk about how humans would behave in the absence of culture. And few if any humans have ever lived in such a state. Moreover, [the] proposal that the natural way to behave is somehow the appropriate or desirable way to behave is strikingly implausible. It is, for example, almost surely natural, in this sense of "natural" that humans would eat their food with their hands, except for the fact that they are, almost always, socialized to eat food differently.

Might it not even be argued that identification of a gender trait as "natural" makes it an especially suspect basis for classification? Recall the suggestion that there are special constitutional problems with categorizing people on the basis of "immutable characteristics" over which they have no control. Doesn't it follow from this argument that gender differences that are "real" in the sense of being inherent or unavoidable ought *not* to serve as a basis for different treatment?

6. *Real differences and substantive values.* If we cannot rely on actual differences in behavior between men and women (because they may be culturally determined) and we also cannot rely on suppositions about differences that would exist in the absence of cultural forces, what test should we utilize to identify "real" differences? Is there, in the end, any way to judge the appropriateness of gender classifications without a substantive vision of the role gender would play in a just society? Consider Freedman, Sex Equality, Sex Differences, and the Supreme Court, 92 Yale L. J. 913, 961 (1983): "The choice to pursue sex equality rather than other social goals [can] be justified only on the basis of an explicitly normative theory of sex equality that identifies with some particularity the dynamics and harmful consequences of sexism." But what is the source of this normative vision?

7. *Beyond real differences.* Do the difficulties associated with the identification of "real differences" suggest that we might be better off, after all, with a virtual per se rule prohibiting gender classifications? Consider Brown, Emerson, Falk & Freedman, The Equal Rights Amendment: A Constitutional Basis for Equal Rights for Women, 80 Yale L.J. 871, 873-874 (1971):

> Many of the efforts to create a separate legal status for women stem from a good faith attempt to advance the interests of women. Nevertheless, the preponderant effect has been to buttress the social and economic subordination of women. [Whatever] the motivation for different treatment, the result is to create a dual system of rights and responsibilities in which the rights of each group are governed by a different set of values. History and experience have taught us that in such a dual system one group is always dominant and the other subordinate. As long as woman's place is defined as separate, a male-dominated society will define her place as inferior.

But is the cause of equality advanced by insisting on gender-neutral laws that disproportionately affect women because they are differently situated with respect to the laws? Consider Law, Rethinking Sex and the Constitution, 132 U. Pa. L. Rev. 955, 1007 (1984): "[Pregnancy,] abortion, reproduction, and creation of another human being *are* special — very special. Women have these experiences. Men do not. An equality doctrine that ignores the unique quality of these experiences implicitly says that women can claim equality only insofar as they are like men. Such doctrine demands that women deny an important aspect of who they are."

4. *Benign Gender Classifications and Discrimination against Men*

[handwritten: For social security Congress don't have per se gender classifications.]

[handwritten: Intermediate Level of Scrutiny]

Califano v. Goldfarb

430 U.S. 199 (1977)

MR. JUSTICE BRENNAN announced the judgment of the Court and delivered an opinion in which MR. JUSTICE WHITE, MR. JUSTICE MARSHALL, and MR. JUSTICE POWELL joined.

Under the Federal Old-Age, Survivors, and Disability Insurance Benefits (OASDI) program, survivors' benefits based on the earnings of a deceased husband covered by the Act are payable to his widow. Such benefits on the basis of the earnings of a deceased wife covered by the Act are payable to the widower, however, only if he "was receiving at least one-half of his support" from his deceased wife. The question in this case is whether this gender-based distinction violates the Due Process Clause of the Fifth Amendment.

I

[Hannah Goldfarb worked as a secretary for the New York City public schools for almost twenty-five years until her death. Although she had paid her Social Security taxes in full during this period, her husband was denied a widower's benefit on her death because he could not show that he had been receiving one-half of his support from his wife when she died. Relying on Weinberger v. Wiesenfeld, the district court held that this requirement was unconstitutional.]

II

The gender-based distinction drawn by [the statute] — burdening a widower but not a widow with the task of proving dependency upon the deceased spouse — presents an equal protection question indistinguishable from that decided in [*Wiesenfeld*]. That decision and the decision in [*Frontiero*] plainly require affirmance of the judgment of the District Court.

[The reasoning in *Wiesenfeld*] condemns the gender-based distinction made by [the statute] in this case. For that distinction [like the distinction in *Wiesenfeld*] operates "to deprive women of protection for their families which men receive as a result of their employment": social security taxes were deducted from Hannah Goldfarb's salary during the quarter century she worked as a secretary, yet, in consequence of [the statute], she also "not only failed to receive for her [spouse] the same protection which a similarly situated male worker would have received [for his spouse] but she also was deprived of a portion of her own earnings in order to contribute to the fund out of which benefits would be paid to others." *Wiesenfeld* thus inescapably compels the conclusion reached by the District Court that the gender-based differentiation created by [the statute] — that results in the efforts of female workers required to pay social security taxes producing less protection for their spouses than is produced by the efforts of men — is forbidden by the Constitution, at least when supported by no more substantial justification than "archaic and overbroad" generalizations, [*Ballard*] or " 'old notions,' " [*Stanton*] such as "assumptions as to dependency," [*Wiesenfeld*], that are more consistent with "the role-typing society has long imposed," [*Stanton*], than with contemporary reality. . . .

III

Appellant, however, would focus equal protection analysis, not upon the discrimination against the covered wage earning female, but rather upon whether her surviving widower was unconstitutionally discriminated against by burdening him but not a surviving widow with proof of dependency. The gist of the argument is that, analyzed from the perspective of the widower, "the denial of benefits reflected the congressional judgment that aged widowers as a class were sufficiently likely not to be dependent upon their wives that it was appropriate to deny them benefits unless they were in fact dependent."

But [*Wiesenfeld*] rejected the virtually identical argument when appellant's predecessor argued that the statutory classification there attacked should be regarded from the perspective of the prospective beneficiary and not from that of the covered wage earner. . . .

From its inception, the social security system has been a program of social insurance. Covered employees and their employers pay taxes into a fund administered distinct from the general federal revenues to purchase protection against the economic consequences of old age, disability, and death. But under [this statute] female insureds received less protection for their spouses solely because of their sex. Mrs. Goldfarb worked and paid social security taxes for 25 years at the same rate as her male colleagues, but because of [the statute] the insurance protection received by the males was broader than hers. Plainly then [the statute] disadvantages women contributors to the social security system as compared to similarly situated men. . . .

[In] a sense, of course, both the female wage earner and her surviving spouse are disadvantaged by operation of the statute, but this is because "Social Security is designed . . . for the protection of the *family*," [quoting from Justice Powell's concurring opinion in *Wiesenfeld*] and the section discriminates against one particular category of family — that in which the female spouse is a wage earner covered by social security. Therefore decision of the equal protection challenge in this case cannot focus solely on the distinction drawn between widowers and widows but, as *Wiesenfeld* held, upon the gender-based discrimination against covered female wage earners as well.[8] . . .

IV . . .

B

Appellant next argues that *Frontiero* and *Wiesenfeld* should be distinguished as involving statutes with different objectives from [this one]. Rather than merely enacting presumptions designed to save the expense and trouble of determining which spouses are really dependent, providing benefits to all widows, but only to such widowers as prove dependency, [this statute], it is argued, rationally defines different standards of eligibility because of the differing social welfare needs of widowers and widows. That is, the argument runs, Congress may reasonably have presumed that nondependent widows, who receive benefits, are needier than nondependent widowers, who do not, because of job discrimination against women (particularly older women), and because they are more likely to have been more dependent on their spouses.

But "inquiry into the actual purposes" of the discrimination, [*Wiesenfeld*], proves the contrary. First, [the statute] itself is phrased in terms of *dependency*, not *need*. Congress chose to award benefits, not to widowers who could prove that they are needy, but to those who could prove that they had been dependent on their wives for more than one-half of their support. On the face of the statute, dependency, not need, is the criterion for inclusion.

Moreover, the general scheme of OASDI shows that dependence on the covered wage earner is the critical factor in determining beneficiary categories. . . .

[Nothing] whatever suggests a reasoned congressional judgment that nondependent widows should receive benefits because they are more likely to be needy than nondependent widowers. . . .

We conclude, therefore, that the differential treatment of nondependent widows and widowers results not, as appellant asserts, from a deliberate congressional intention to remedy the arguably greater needs of the former, but rather from an intention to aid the dependent spouses of deceased wage earners, coupled with a presumption that wives are usually dependent. [We] held in *Frontiero*, and again in *Wiesenfeld*, and therefore hold again here, that such assumptions do not suffice to justify a gender-based discrimination in the distribution of employment-related benefits.

Affirmed.

---

8. In any event, gender-based discriminations against men have been invalidated when they do not "serve important governmental objectives and [are not] substantially related to the achievement of those objectives." [*Craig*]. Neither [*Kahn*], nor [*Ballard*], relied on by appellant, supports a contrary conclusion. The gender-based distinctions in the statutes involved in *Kahn* and *Ballard* were justified because the only discernible purpose of each was the permissible one of redressing our society's longstanding disparate treatment of women.

But "the mere recitation of a benign, compensatory purpose is not an automatic shield which protects against any inquiry into the actual purposes underlying a statutory scheme." [*Wiesenfeld*.] That inquiry in this case demonstrates that [this statute] has no such remedial purpose. Moreover, the classifications challenged in *Wiesenfeld* and in this case rather than advantaging women to compensate for past wrongs compounds those wrongs by penalizing women "who do work and whose earnings contribute significantly to their families' support."

MR. JUSTICE STEVENS, concurring in the judgment.

Although my conclusion is the same, my appraisal of the relevant discrimination and my reasons for concluding that it is unjustified, are somewhat different from those expressed by Mr. Justice Brennan.

First, I agree with Mr. Justice Rehnquist that the constitutional question raised by this plaintiff requires us to focus on his claim for benefits rather than his deceased wife's tax obligation. She had no contractual right to receive benefits or to control their payment; moreover, the payments are not a form of compensation for her services. . . .

Second, I also agree with Mr. Justice Rehnquist that a classification which treats certain aged widows more favorably than their male counterparts is not "invidious." Such a classification does not imply that males are inferior to females; does not condemn a large class on the basis of the misconduct of an unrepresentative few; and does not add to the burdens of an already disadvantaged discrete minority.

It is also clear that the disparate treatment of widows and widowers is not the product of a conscious purpose to redress the "legacy of economic discrimination" against females. [*Kahn* (Brennan, J., dissenting)]. The widows who benefit from the disparate treatment are those who were sufficiently successful in the job market to become nondependent on their husbands. Such a widow is the least likely to need special benefits. . . .

[The] history of the statute is entirely consistent with the view that Congress simply assumed that all widows should be regarded as "dependents" in some general sense, even though they could not satisfy the statutory support test later imposed on men. It is fair to infer that habit, rather than analysis or actual reflection, made it seem acceptable to equate the terms "widow" and "dependent surviving spouse." . . .

I am therefore persuaded that this discrimination against a group of males is merely the accidental byproduct of a traditional way of thinking about females. I am also persuaded that a rule which effects an unequal distribution of economic benefits solely on the basis of sex is sufficiently questionable that "due process requires that there be a legitimate basis for presuming that the rule was actually intended to serve [the] interest" put forward by the Government as its justification. . . .

MR. JUSTICE REHNQUIST, with whom [CHIEF JUSTICE BURGER], MR. JUSTICE STEWART, and MR. JUSTICE BLACKMUN join, dissenting.

In light of this Court's recent decisions beginning with [*Reed*], one cannot say that there is no support in our cases for the result reached by the Court. One can, however, believe as I do that careful consideration of these cases affords more support for the opposite result than it does for that reached by the Court. . . .

[The] effect of the statutory scheme is to make it easier for widows to obtain benefits than it is for widowers, since the former qualify automatically while the latter must show proof of need. Such a requirement in no way perpetuates or exacerbates the economic disadvantage which has led the Court to conclude that gender-based discrimination must meet a different test from other types of classifications. . . .

Perhaps because the reasons asserted for "heightened scrutiny" of gender-based distinctions are rooted in the fact that *women* have in the past been victims of unfair treatment, see [*Frontiero*], the plurality says that the difference in treatment here is not only between a widow and a widower, but between the respective deceased spouses of the two. It concludes that wage-earning wives are deprived "'of protection for their families which men receive as a result of their employment.'"

But this is a questionable tool of analysis which can be used to prove virtually anything. It might just as well have been urged in [*Kahn*], where we upheld a Florida property tax exemption redounding to the benefit of widows but not widowers, that the real discrimination was between the deceased spouses of the respective widow and widower, who had doubtless by their contributions to the family or marital community helped make possible the acquisition of the property which was now being disparately taxed.

Since the claim to social security benefits is noncontractual in nature, the contributions of the deceased spouse cannot be regarded as creating any sort of contractual entitlement on the part of either the deceased wife or the surviving husband. Here the female wage earner has gotten the degree of protection for her family which Congress was concerned to extend to all. Neither she nor her surviving husband has any constitutional claim to more, simply because Congress has chosen, for administrative reasons, to give benefits to widows without requiring proof of dependency. . . .

[The] present statutory treatment of widows and widowers would seem to reflect a pair of legislative judgments about the needs of those two groups. The first is that the persons qualifying for spousal benefits are likely to have even more substantial needs after the passing of their spouse. . . .

The second legislative judgment implicit in the widow's and widower's provisions is that widows, as a practical matter, are much more likely to be without adequate means of support than are widowers. The plurality opinion makes much of establishing this point, that the absence of any dependency prerequisite to the award of widow's benefits reflects a judgment, resting on "administrative convenience," that dependence among aged widows is frequent enough to justify waiving the requirement entirely. I differ not with the recognition of this administrative convenience purpose but with the conclusion that such a purpose *necessarily* invalidates the resulting classification. Our decisions dealing with social welfare legislation indicate that our inquiry must go further. For rational classifications aimed at distributing funds to beneficiaries under social insurance legislation weigh a good deal more heavily on the governmental interest side of the equal protection balance than they may in other legislative contexts. The "administrative convenience" which is afforded by such classifications in choosing the administrator of a decedent's estate, see [Reed], is significantly less important to the effectiveness of the legislative scheme than is the "convenience" afforded by classifications in administering an Act designed to provide benefits to millions upon millions of beneficiaries with promptness and certainty. . . .

[Whatever] his actual needs, Goldfarb would, of course, have no complaint if Congress had chosen to require proof of dependency by widows as well as widowers, or if it had simply refrained from making any provision whatever for benefits to surviving spouses. [Any] claim which he has must therefore turn upon the alleged impropriety of giving benefits to widows without requiring them to make the same proof of dependency required of widowers. Yet, in the context of the legislative purpose, this amounts not to exclusion but to overinclusiveness for reasons of administrative convenience which, if reasonably supported by the underlying facts, is not offensive to the Equal Protection Clause in social welfare cases.[7]

This case is also distinguishable from [*Frontiero*], in the sense that social insurance differs from compensation for work done. While there is no basis for assessing the propriety of a given allocation of funds within a social insurance program apart from an identifiable legislative purpose, a compensatory scheme may be evaluated under the principle of equal pay for equal work done. This case is therefore unlike *Frontiero*, where the Court invalidated sex discrimination among military personnel in their entitlement to increased quarters allowances on account of marriage, and in the eligibility of their spouses for dental and medical care. These compensatory fringe benefits were available to male employees as a matter of course, but were unavailable to females except on proof that their husbands depended on them for over one-half of their support. . . .

[The] very most that can be squeezed out of the facts of this case in the way of cognizable "discrimination" is a classification which favors aged widows. Quite apart from any considerations of legislative purpose and "administrative convenience" which may be advanced to support the classification, this is scarcely an invidious discrimination. [The] differentiation in no way perpetuates the economic discrimination which has been the basis for heightened scrutiny of gender-based classifications, and is, in fact, explainable as a measure to ameliorate the characteristically depressed condition of aged widows. [*Kahn*] is therefore also authority for upholding it. For both of these reasons, I would reverse the judgment of the District Court.

CALIFANO v. WEBSTER, 430 U.S. 313 (1977): In this case, decided less than three weeks after *Goldfarb*, the Court unanimously sustained the constitutionality of a provision of the Social Security Act that had the effect of granting to retired female workers higher monthly old-age benefits than those received by similarly situated retired male workers. The act provided that benefits were to be computed based on the average monthly wage of the worker during certain statutorily defined "benefit computation years." Until its amendment in 1972, the statutory formula permitted women to exclude more lower earning years from this average than men could exclude. A district judge held that this gender-based distinction violated the equal protection component of the fifth amendment due process clause, but the Court, in a per curiam opinion, reversed.

The Court began its analysis by reciting the familiar *Craig* test for classifications based on gender — the classification "must serve important governmental objectives and must be substantially related to achievement of those objectives." It

---

7. There is substantial statistical evidence indicating that the differential treatment of widows and widowers is economically justifiable on the basis of administrative convenience. . . .

[The] number of married women over 55 who would satisfy the dependency test is something like 88.5% — the 77% who do not work, plus half of the remaining 23% who do. This nine-tenths correlation appears sufficiently high to justify extension of benefits to the other one-tenth for reasons of administrative convenience.

On the side of widower's benefits, the incidence of dependent husbands is certainly low enough to justify any administrative expense incurred in screening out those who are not dependent. In 1970, only 2.5% of *working* wives contributed more than 75% of the family income which renders the husband dependent. Since only 43% of all wives work, the incidence of dependent husbands among all married couples is approximately 1%. . . .

then noted that "Reduction of the disparity in economic condition between men and women caused by the long history of discrimination against women has been recognized as such as important governmental objective [*Ballard; Kahn*]." Of course, the mere recitation of a compensatory purpose did not automatically shield a statute from inquiry into its actual purpose. "Accordingly, we have rejected attempts to justify gender classifications as compensatory for past discrimination against women when the classifications in fact penalized women wage earners, or when the statutory structure and its legislative history revealed that the classification was not enacted as compensation for past discrimination [*Goldfarb; Wiesenfeld*]."

In the Court's opinion, however, this provision was more analogous to those upheld in *Kahn* and *Ballard* than to those struck down in *Wiesenfeld* and *Goldfarb*. "The more favorable treatment of the female wage earner enacted here was not a result of 'archaic and overbroad generalizations' about women [*Ballard*] or of 'the role-typing society has long imposed' upon women [*Stanton*], such as casual assumptions that women are 'the weaker sex' or are more likely to be child rearers or dependents." Rather, "The challenged statute operated directly to compensate women for past economic discrimination. Retirement benefits under the Act are based on past earnings. But as we have recognized: 'Whether from overt discrimination or from the socialization process of a male-dominated culture, the job market is inhospitable to the woman seeking any but the lowest paid jobs' [*Kahn*]. Thus, allowing women, who as such have been unfairly hindered from earning as much as men, to eliminate additional low-earning years from the calculation of their retirement benefits works directly to remedy some part of the effect of past discrimination."

Moreover, after canvassing the legislative history of the provision, the Court concluded that "the differing treatment of men and women [was] not 'the accidental byproduct of a traditional way of thinking about females,' [*Goldfarb* (Stevens, J., concurring)], but rather was deliberately enacted to compensate for particular economic disabilities suffered by women."

Chief Justice Burger, with whom Justices Stewart, Blackmun and Rehnquist joined, concurred in the judgment: "While I am happy to concur in the Court's judgment, I find it somewhat difficult to distinguish the Social Security provision upheld here from that struck down so recently in [*Goldfarb*]. Although the distinction drawn by the Court between this case and *Goldfarb* is not totally lacking in substance, I question whether certainty in the law is promoted by hinging the validity of important statutory schemes on whether five Justices view them to be more akin to the 'offensive' provisions struck down in [*Wiesenfeld*] and [*Frontiero*], or more like the 'benign' provisions upheld in [*Ballard*] and [*Kahn*]."

Note: The Problem of "Benign" Gender Classifications

1. *Discrimination against men.* In what sense did the statute invalidated in *Goldfarb* discriminate against women? Would the statute still discriminate against women if the benefits to widows and widowers were funded from general revenues?

Compare *Goldfarb* with Wengler v. Druggists Mutual Insurance Co., 446 U.S. 142 (1980), in which the Court invalidated a portion of Missouri's worker's compensation statute under which a widower of a deceased worker was entitled to death benefits only if he was mentally or physically incapacitated from wage earning or proved actual dependence on his wife's earnings. In contrast, a widow was automatically entitled to death benefits without having to demonstrate dependence. Appellees attempted to distinguish *Goldfarb* on the ground that, unlike the social security program, worker's compensation was not based on mandatory contributions from wage earnings of the employee. Therefore, women workers could not complain that they were being deprived of a portion of their earnings to contribute to a fund from which their husbands would receive no benefits. In a footnote the Court responded as follows: "We have before rejected the proposition that 'the Constitution is indifferent to a statute that conditions the availability of noncontributory welfare benefits on the basis of gender [Califano v. Westcott, 443 U.S. 76, 85 (1979)], and we refuse to part ways with our earlier decisions by applying a different standard of review in this case simply because the system is funded by employer rather than employee contributions."

In the body of the opinion, the Court argued that the challenged statute discriminated against both men and women. Women were harmed because "The benefits [that] the working woman can expect to be paid to her spouse in the case of her work-related death are less than those payable to the spouse of the deceased male wage earner." Men were also discriminated against because "the surviving male spouse must prove his incapacity or dependency [while the] widow of a deceased wage earner [is] presumed dependent and is guaranteed a weekly benefit for life or until remarriage." However the discrimination was characterized, the Court wrote, "our precedents require that gender-based discrimination must [meet the *Craig* test]." Here, the state's "claimed justification of administrative convenience fails, just as it has in our prior cases."

If, as the Court asserts, the Missouri statute discriminated against women simply because their spouses were deprived of a benefit, don't virtually all laws that discriminate against men also discriminate against women? In *Webster*, for example, might it not be argued that the wives of retired male workers were harmed by granting such workers lower old age benefits than those accorded to retired female workers?

If, as the Court asserts, the Missouri statute discriminates against both men and women, in what sense does it involve *gender* discrimination? What argument is there for heightened scrutiny of statutes that classify on the basis of gender if neither men nor women as a class are disadvantaged by them? Is the logical extension of *Wengler* that, given the close association between men and women in our society, the very concept of gender discrimination is incoherent? Is this the problem Ely had in mind when he observed that women are not an "insular" minority? See page 624 supra.

In a separate opinion concurring in the judgment, Justice Stevens renewed his attack on the notion "that this kind of gender-based classification can simultaneously disfavor the male class and the female class." Stevens argued that for purposes of this statute, there were three kinds of marriages:

> (1) those in which the husband is dependent on the wife; (2) those in which the wife is dependent on the husband; and (3) those in which neither spouse is dependent on the other.
>
> [In] either of the first two situations, if the dependent spouse survives, a death benefit will be paid regardless of whether the survivor is male or female; conversely,

if the working spouse survives, no death benefit will be paid. The only difference in the two situations is that the surviving male, unlike the surviving female, must undergo the inconvenience of proving dependency. That surely is not a discrimination against females.

In the third situation, if one spouse dies, benefits are payable to a surviving female but not to a surviving male. In my view, that is a rather blatant discrimination against males.

Nevertheless, Stevens agreed that the statute violated the equal protection clause because Missouri had failed to justify this disparate treatment of similarly situated surviving spouses.

Assuming arguendo that the Missouri statute discriminated against men, but not women, should it be subjected to heightened scrutiny? Note that in *Craig* and *Mississippi University for Women*, the Court utilized heightened scrutiny in cases where men were the disadvantaged class. But under a representation reenforcement theory, doesn't the justification for such scrutiny disappear if the discrimination operates to disadvantage a powerful group?

Consider Kanowitz, "Benign" Sex Discrimination: Its Troubles and Their Cue, 31 Hast. L.J. 1379, 1394 (1980):

> a casual glance at the treatment males have received at the hands of the law solely because they are males suggests that they have paid an awesome price for other advantages they have presumably enjoyed over females in our society. Whether one talks of the male's unique obligation of compulsory military service, his primary duty for spousal and child support, his lack of the same kinds of protective labor legislation that have traditionally been enjoyed by women, or the statutory or judicial preference in child custody disputes that has long been accorded to mothers vis-á-vis fathers of minor children, sex discrimination against males in statutes and judicial decisions has been widespread and severe.

But if it is *men* as a class who have been historically disadvantaged, why should laws discriminating against *women* be subject to heightened scrutiny? It is, of course, possible that both men and women have been harmed in different ways by sex stereotyping. But if both sexes are harmed equally, what is the basis for judicial intervention? Kanowitz argues that

> Centuries of sex-role allocations, based on "habit, rather than analysis," simply disabled Americans of either sex from restructuring the duties of military service, family support, and protections in the work place so as to permit men and women to share the burdens and benefits of social existence more equitably. Viewed in this light, the apparent power of men to change their sex-based roles in the past can be seen as being more theoretical than real. In this respect, men were as powerless as any other discrete, insular minority.

Can *both* men and women be discrete and insular minorities? Under this expansive version of the political process argument, is there any group that cannot claim judicial protection?

Is the real point of *Goldberg* and *Wengler* that even though the laws invalidated in those cases superficially benefited women, they "really" discriminated against them be reinforcing stereotypes of dependence and passivity that make women the losers in the long run? Consider MacKinnon, Sexual Harrassment of Working Women 116-117 (1979):

> sex discrimination is a system that defines women as inferior from men, that cumulatively disadvantages women for their differences from men, as well as ignores their similarities. [The] only question for litigation is whether the policy or practice in question integrally contributes to the maintenance of an underclass or a deprived position because of gender status. The disadvantage which constitutes the injury of discrimination is not the failure to be treated "without regard to" one's sex; that is the injury of arbitrary differentiation. The unfairness lies in being deprived *because of* being a woman or a man, a deprivation given meaning in the social context of the dominance or preference of one sex over the other.

Is this approach consistent with *Michael M.* and *Rostker?* Is it one that the justices who wrote those opinions could possibly administer? Compare Law, Rethinking Sex and the Constitution, 132 U. Pa. L. Rev. 955, 1005 (1984):

> Professor MacKinnon's approach is ambitious, but it adds unnecessary complexity to the application of sex equality doctrine in a large number of cases. The determination of what reinforces or undermines a sex-based underclass is exceedingly difficult. Professor MacKinnon may overestimate judges' capacities to identify and avoid socially imposed constraints on equality. She disregards our history in which laws justified as protecting women have been a central means of oppressing them. Most fundamentally, her proposed standard may incorporate and perpetuate a false belief that a judicially enforced constitutional standard can, by itself, dismantle the deep structures that "integrally contribute" to sex-based deprivation.

2. *Affirmative action for women.* The Court has adopted the view that laws disadvantaging men, like those disadvantaging women, are subject to the *Craig* test. As a result, whereas the level of review for racial classifications intended to remedy prior discrimination remains confused, see section C4 supra, it is clear that in the gender area such statutes must survive intermediate scrutiny. It seems clear as well that the remedying of disparities between men and women, at least if caused by prior discrimination, qualifies as an "important government objective" for purposes of the *Craig* test. Beyond this, however, the application of that test remains confused.

For example, what, precisely, is the distinction between the statute invalidated in *Goldfarb* and the statute upheld in *Webster?* Consider the following possibilities:

a. *Actual purpose.* Is it significant that the *Goldfarb* statute did not result "from a deliberate congressional intention to remedy the arguably greater needs of [widows]" while in Webster the statute was "deliberately enacted to compensate for particular economic disabilities suffered by women"? If the *Goldfarb* statute in fact served to remedy prior discrimination, why should it matter that this was not the original intent of its authors? Recall Justice Rehnquist's assertion in *Michael M.* that "The question for us — and the only question under the Federal Constitution — is whether the legislation violates the Equal Protection Clause of the Fourteenth Amendment, not whether its supporters may have endorsed it for reasons no longer generally accepted." Can this statement be reconciled with the Court's reliance on "actual purpose" analysis in *Goldberg* and *Webster?*

b. *Stereotyping and stigmatization*. In *Goldfarb* the Court thought that the statute was based on the "then generally accepted presumption that a man is responsible for the support of his wife and children." In contrast, the Court in *Webster* thought that the larger benefits for retired female workers "operated directly to compensate women for past economic discrimination." Is this distinction viable? Wasn't the "past economic discrimination" remedied by the *Webster* statute *based* in part on the "presumption that a man is responsible for the support of his wife and children"? Might not the *Webster* statute be viewed as reenforcing the stereotype that women should remain at home during childbearing years or work at lower-paying jobs after their children grow up? Is it ever possible to compensate women for the harm inflicted by old stereotypes without at the same time reenforcing those stereotypes?

c. *Classifications "in fact" penalizing women*. The Court in *Webster* thought it significant that the statute under consideration did not "in fact [penalize] women wage earners" by depriving them of family-protection benefits provided to men. Does this argument survive *Wengler?* If statutes discriminating against men and women are subject to the same level of scrutiny, why does it matter whether women wage earners are "in fact" penalized?

d. *The overinclusion problem*. Assuming that women are in fact benefited rather than harmed by "affirmative action" measures, what kind of showing must the state make that the benefited class has suffered from prior discrimination? Recall the Court's parallel debate over this issue in the race context in *Bakke* and *Fullilove*, section C4 supra. Neither *Goldfarb* nor *Webster* paid much attention to the problem, but the Court threw additional light on it two years later in Orr v. Orr, 440 U.S. 268 (1979). Alabama's alimony statute provided that husbands, but not wives, could be required to pay alimony on divorce. The state justified this distinction in part on the ground that it served the goal of compensating women for past discrimination during marriage that left them unprepared to fend for themselves in the working world after divorce. The Court rejected this argument and invalidated the statute. It once again acknowledged the importance of helping women in economic need and compensating them for the effects of past discrimination. But these goals did not justify the classification employed by the statute:

> Under the statute, individualized hearings at which the parties' relative financial circumstances are considered *already* occur. [Since] individualized hearings can determine which women were in fact discriminated against vis-à-vis their husbands, as well as which family units defied the stereotype and left the husband dependent on the wife, Alabama's alleged compensatory purpose may be effectuated without placing burdens solely on husbands. [Moreover], use of a gender classification actually produces perverse results in this case. As compared to a gender-neutral law placing alimony obligations on the spouse able to pay, the present Alabama statutes give an advantage only to the financially secure wife whose husband is in need. [A] gender-based classification which, as compared to a gender-neutral one, generates additional benefits only for those it has no reason to prefer cannot survive equal protection scrutiny.

Why does the Court assume that the state has "no reason to prefer" financially secure wives? Might not a woman be more secure than her husband, yet still be the victim of prior discrimination?

Why does the state's willingness to hold hearings on some issues constitutionally obligate it to hold hearings on others? Why didn't the *Webster* Court require individualized hearings to determine which retired female workers had been subject to discrimination?

3. *"Affirmative action" and the nature of equality.* In light of the difficulties posed by gender classifications allegedly designed to remedy prior discrimination, should such laws be treated as per se invalid? Consider, e.g., Olsen, The Family and the Market: A Study of Ideology and Legal Reform, 96 Harv. L. Rev. 1497, 1555 (1983):

> Although the doctrine of affirmative action presupposes prior discrimination against women, affirmative action policies pretend to have ended such discrimination. Affirmative action thus creates another reason for women to blame themselves when they fail in the marketplace. Moreover, although affirmative action may expand women's social roles, it also tends to reenforce the ideology of inequality and to reintroduce problems of paternalism.

But is the goal of equality better served by insisting on laws that are facially gender-neutral, but that, in fact, affect women unequally because they are differently situated with respect to the laws. Recall, for example, Justice Stewart's assertion in *Geduldig*, supra page 616, that the exclusion of pregnancy benefits from an insurance program was not gender discrimination because it did "not exclude anyone from benefit eligibility because of gender but merely [removed] one physical condition — pregnancy — from the list of compensable disabilities." Is that the sort of analysis that helps undercut "the ideology of inequality"?

5. The Equal Rights Amendment

In 1972, Congress approved and submitted to the states for ratification the following constitutional amendment:

> Section 1. Equality of rights under the law shall not be denied or abridged by the United States or by any State on account of sex.
> Section 2. The Congress shall have the power to enforce, by appropriate legislation, the provisions of this article.
> Section 3. This amendment shall take effect two years after the date of ratification.

Although about half of the required three-fourths of the states ratified the amendment within a few months of its submission, progress then became stalled. In 1978 Congress extended the period for ratification until June 30, 1982, but the second deadline expired with only thirty-five of the necessary thirty-eight states having approved the amendment. However, proponents of the amendment promptly introduced a new congressional resolution embodying identical language, and controversy over its adoption continues.

What advantages does a constitutional amendment have over specific statutory measures designed to correct the problems that exist? Over continued case-by-case litigation under the equal protection clause? If the Court's interpretation of the fourteenth amendment in the gender context has been less than fully satisfactory, is a constitutional amendment necessary to refocus its decisions? Does the vagueness and sweep of the proposed amendment constitute a virtual invitation to the Supreme Court to "solve" our gender problem in the manner it thinks best? Does the Court's performance to date justify confidence in the kind of solution it is likely to formulate?

E. EQUAL PROTECTION METHODOLOGY: OTHER CANDIDATES FOR HEIGHTENED SCRUTINY

What, if any, other classifications should be regarded as "suspect"? What criteria should the Court utilize in assessing the claims of other "disadvantaged" groups for heightened scrutiny? Is the analogy to race and gender useful? If so, which characteristics of blacks and women must other candidates for heightened scrutiny share? Might heightened scrutiny for some classifications be justified even though the problems of the group are entirely different from those facing blacks and women? If so, what sorts of problems should trigger judicial intervention?

1. Alienage

One way to think about heightened scrutiny for suspect classifications is that it is the appropriate judicial response to efforts by the majority to exclude certain groups from the political community. Yet many people would agree that our political institutions need not show equal concern and respect for the well being of everyone. The U.S. government does not show the same concern for people living in Mexico as it does for people living in Texas. Indeed, membership in our political community derives much of its value from the fact that it is not universal.

There is also general agreement that the government has some power to define the boundaries of the political community within our territorial limits. For example, most (although not all) people would agree that our political institutions need not show the same concern and respect for animals that it shows for people. Others would exclude fetuses from the political community.

The moral and legal legitimacy of this power to define boundaries for the political community is intensely controversial. At one time, many viewed black slaves in the way that many view animals and fetuses today. Powerful arguments have been advanced that our preference for Americans over Mexicans, for the born over fetuses, or for people over animals, represents no more than chauvinism. See, e.g., J. Noonan, The Morality of Abortion: Legal and Historical Perspectives 51-58 (1970) (moral obligation to fetuses); T. Regan & P. Singer, Animal Rights and Human Obligations (1976) (moral obligation to animals); Lopez, Mexican Migration, 28 U.C.L.A. L. Rev. 615 (1981) (moral obligation to Mexicans).

And yet at some point lines must be drawn. For example, some who claim that the U.S. government owes a duty to citizens of Mexico base the claim on physical proximity and are prepared to acknowledge that it may not owe the same duty to citizens of Pakistan. See Lopez, supra, at 698-700. And presumably even the most ardent advocates of animal rights are prepared to acknowledge the lesser status of plants.

Are these boundaries justified by the innate limits on the ability to communicate across cultural and, a fortiori, species lines? Consider J. Dunn, Western Political Theory in the Face of the Future 76-77 (1979):

> Because both what man makes himself and a large part of what he is caused to become are mediated by human speech, the potential community of those with whom men can in practice communicate, to whom they can in practice render themselves lucidly intelligible, can be a human community in an altogether deeper sense than practical aggregations of human beings of any scale who are unable to address each other or comprehend each other with such directness. [Herder], it seems, sensed this when he wrote [that] "The savage who loves himself, his wife and his child [and] works for the good of his tribe as for his own [is] in my view more genuine than that human ghost, the [citizen] of the world, who, burning with love for all his fellow ghosts, loves a chimera. The savage in his hut has room for any stranger. [The] saturated heart of the idle cosmopolitan is a home for no one."

Do these observations cast doubt as well on the characterization of the United States as a single political community? If we are willing to concede that some groups outside the political community need not receive the same attention as those within the community, what are the implications of the existence of subnational political communities? Consider whether the materials on federalism shed light on these issues.

Can the need to draw some boundaries of the political community be reconciled with heightened scrutiny for classifications disadvantaging some groups outside those boundaries? Are there principled limits on the way in which the boundaries can be defined? The Supreme Court's treatment of statutes disadvantaging aliens raises these questions.

Sugarman v. Dougall

413 U.S. 634 (1973)

Mr. Justice Blackmun delivered the opinion of the Court. . . .

[Appellees challenged the constitutionality of a New York statute that excluded aliens from all government civil service positions filled by competitive examination. Such positions included the "full range of work tasks [all] the way from the menial to the policy making." However, the exclusion did not apply to higher offices in the state executive departments and to elected officers and offices filled by the governor or by legislative appointment.]

As is so often the case, it is important at the outset to define the precise and narrow issue that is here presented. The Court is faced only with the question whether New York's flat statutory prohibition against the employment of aliens in the competitive classified civil service is constitutionally valid. The Court is not asked to decide whether a particular alien, any more than a particular citizen, may be refused employment or discharged on an individual basis for whatever legitimate reason the State might possess.

Neither is the Court reviewing a legislative scheme that bars some or all aliens from closely defined and limited classes of public employment on a uniform and consistent basis. The New York scheme, instead, is indiscriminate. . . .

It is established, of course, that an alien is entitled to the shelter of the Equal Protection Clause. [Appellants] argue, however, that [the statute] does not violate the equal protection guarantee of the Fourteenth Amendment because [it] "establishes a generic classification reflecting the special requirements of public employment in the career civil service." The distinction drawn between the citizen and the alien, it is said, "rests on the fundamental concept of identity between a government and the members, or citizens, of the state." The civil servant "participates directly in the formulation and execution of government policy," and thus must be free of competing obligations to another power. The State's interest in having an employee of undivided loyalty is substantial, for obligations attendant upon foreign citizenship "might impair the exercise of his judgment or jeopardize public confidence in his objectivity." [It] is at once apparent, however, that appellants' asserted justification proves both too much and too little. [The] State's broad prohibition of the employment of aliens applies to many positions with respect to which the State's proffered justification has little, if any, relationship. At the same time, the prohibition has no application at all to positions that would seem naturally to fall within the State's asserted purpose. Our standard of review of statutes that treat aliens differently from citizens requires a greater degree of precision.

In Graham v. Richardson, 403 U.S. 365, 372 (1971), we observed that aliens as a class "are a prime example of a 'discrete and insular' minority (see United States v. Carolene Products Co., 304 U.S. 144, 152-153, n.4 (1938))," and that classifications based on alienage are "subject to close judicial scrutiny."

[*Graham* concerned a constitutional challenge to state statutes disqualifying aliens from receipt of various forms of welfare assistance. Justice Blackmun's opinion for the Court held that "classifications based on alienage, like those based on nationality or race, are inherently suspect." Applying strict scrutiny to the challenged statutes, the Court found that the "State's desire to preserve limited welfare benefits for its own citizens is inadequate to justify [making] noncitizens ineligible for public assistance."]

Applying this standard to New York's purpose in confining civil servants in the competitive class to those persons who have no ties of citizenship elsewhere, [the statute] does not withstand the necessary close scrutiny. We recognize a State's interest in establishing its own form of government, and in limiting participation in that government to those who are within "the basic conception of a political community." Dunn v. Blumstein, 405 U.S. 330, 344 (1972). We recognize, too, the State's broad power to define its political community. But in seeking to achieve this substantial purpose, with discrimination against aliens, the means the State employs must be precisely drawn in light of the acknowledged purpose.

[The statute] is neither narrowly confined nor precise in its application. Its imposed ineligibility may apply to the "sanitation man, class B," to the typist, and to the office worker, as well as to the person who directly participates in the formulation and execution of important state policy. . . . Appellants further contend, however, that the State's legitimate interest is greater than simply limiting to citizens those high public offices that have to do with the formulation and execution of state policy. [Appellants] argue that a State constitutionally may confine public employment to citizens. Mr. Justice (the Judge) Cardozo accepted this "special public interest" argument because of the State's concern with "the restriction of the resources of the state to the advancement and profit of the members of the state." People v. Crane, 214 N.Y. 154, 161, 108 N.E. 427, 429, aff'd, 239 U.S. 195 (1915). We rejected that approach, however, in the context of public assistance in *Graham*, where it was observed that "the special public interest doctrine was heavily grounded on the notion that '[w]hatever is a privilege, rather than a right, may be made dependent upon citizenship.' People v. Crane. . . . But this Court now has rejected the concept that constitutional rights turn upon whether a governmental benefit is characterized as a 'right' or as a 'privilege.' "

We perceive no basis for holding the special-public-interest doctrine inapplicable in *Graham* and yet applicable and controlling here. A resident alien may reside lawfully in New York for a long period of time. He must pay taxes. And he is subject to service in this country's Armed Forces. The doctrine, rooted as it is in the concepts of privilege and of the desirability of confining the use of public resources, has no applicability in this case. . . .

While we rule that [the statute] is unconstitutional, we do not hold that, on the basis of an individualized determination, an alien may not be refused, or discharged from, public employment, even on the basis of noncitizenship, if the refusal to hire, or the discharge, rests on legitimate state interests that relate to qualifications for a particular position or to the characteristics of the employee. We hold only that a flat ban on the employment of aliens in positions that have little, if any, relation to a State's legitimate interest, cannot withstand scrutiny under the Fourteenth Amendment.

Neither do we hold that a State may not, in an appropriately defined class of positions, require citizenship as a qualification for office. Just as "the Framers of the Constitution intended the States to keep for themselves, as provided in the Tenth Amendment, the power to regulate elections," "[e]ach State has the power to prescribe the qualifications of its officers and the manner in which they shall be chosen." Such power inheres in the State by virtue of its obligation, already noted above, "to preserve the basic conception of a political community." And this power and responsibility of the State applies, not only to the qualifications of voters, but also to persons holding state elective or important nonelective executive, legislative, and judicial positions, for officers who participate directly in the formulation, execution, or review of broad public policy perform functions that go to the heart of representative government. . . .

We have held, of course, that such state action, particularly with respect to voter qualifications, is not wholly immune from scrutiny under the Equal Protection Clause. But our scrutiny will not be so demanding where we deal with matters resting firmly within a State's constitutional prerogatives. This is no more than a recognition of a State's historical power to exclude aliens from participation in its democratic political institutions, and a recognition of a State's constitutional responsibility for the establishment and operation of its own government, as well as the qualifications of an appropriately designated class of public office holders. This Court has never held that aliens have a constitutional right to vote or to hold high public office under the Equal Protection Clause. Indeed implicit in many of this Court's voting rights decisions is the notion that citizenship is a permissible criterion for limiting such rights. A restriction on the employment of noncitizens, narrowly confined, could have particular relevance to this important state responsibility, for alienage itself is a factor that reasonably could be employed in defining "political community."

The judgment of the District Court is affirmed.

MR. JUSTICE REHNQUIST, dissenting.

The Court [holds] that an alien is not really different from a citizen, and that any legislative classification on the basis of alienage is "inherently suspect." The Fourteenth Amendment, the Equal Protection Clause of which the Court interprets as invalidating the state legislation here involved, contains no language concerning "inherently suspect classifications," or, for that matter, merely "suspect classifications." The principal purpose of those who drafted and adopted the Amendment was to prohibit the States from invidiously discriminating by reason of race, Slaughter-House Cases, 16 Wall. 36 (1873), and, because of this plainly manifested intent, classifications based on race have rightly been held "suspect" under the Amendment. But there is no language used in the Amendment, or any historical evidence as to the intent of the Framers, which would suggest to the slightest degree that it was intended to render alienage a "suspect" classification, that it was designed in any way to protect "discrete and insular minorities" other than racial minorities, or that it would in any way justify the result reached by the Court in these two cases. . . .

[The record contains] no indication that the aliens suffered any disability that precluded them, either as a group or individually, from applying for and being granted the status of naturalized citizens. [The] "status" of these individuals was not, therefore, one with which they were forever encumbered; they could take steps to alter it when and if they chose.[1] . . .

The Court, by holding in these cases and in Graham v. Richardson that a citizen-alien classification is "suspect" in the eyes of our Constitution, fails to mention, let alone rationalize, the fact that the Constitution itself recognizes a basic difference between citizens and aliens. That distinction is constitutionally important in no less than 11 instances in a political document noted for its brevity. . . .

Not only do the numerous classifications on the basis of citizenship that are set forth in the Constitution cut against both the analysis used and the results reached by the Court in these cases; the very Amendment which the Court reads to prohibit classifications based on citizenship establishes the very distinction which the Court now condemns as "suspect." The first sentence of the Fourteenth Amendment provides:

> All persons born or naturalized in the United States and subject to the jurisdiction thereof, are citizens of the United States and of the State wherein they reside.

1. Although some of the members of the class had not been residents of the United States for five years at the time the complaint was filed, and therefore were ineligible to apply immediately for citizenship, there is no indication that these members, assuming that they are in the same "class" as the named appellees, would be prohibited from seeking citizenship status after they had resided in this country for the required period. In any event, this circumstance only underscores the fact that it is not unreasonable to assume that they have not learned about and adapted to our mores and institutions to the same extent as one who had lived here for five years would have through social contact.

In constitutionally defining who is a citizen of the United States, Congress obviously thought it was doing something, and something important. Citizenship meant something, a status in and relationship with a society which is continuing and more basic than mere presence or residence. The language of that Amendment carefully distinguishes between "persons" who, whether by birth or naturalization, had achieved a certain status, and "persons" in general. That a "citizen" was considered by Congress to be a rationally distinct subclass of all "persons" is obvious from the language of the Amendment. . . .

The [apparently] paramount "decision" upon which the Court relied in *Graham*, and which is merely quoted in the instant decisions, is a footnote from United States v. Carolene Products Co., a case involving a federal statute prohibiting the interstate shipment of filled milk. . . .

On the "authority" of this footnote, which only four Members of the Court in *Carolene Products* joined, the Court in *Graham* merely stated that "classifications based on alienage . . . are inherently suspect" because "[a]liens as a class are a prime example of a 'discrete and insular' minority . . . for whom such heightened judicial solicitude is appropriate." 403 U.S., at 372.

As Mr. Justice Frankfurter so aptly observed: "A footnote hardly seems to be an appropriate way of announcing a new constitutional doctrine, and the *Carolene* footnote did not purport to announce any new doctrine. . . ." Kovacs v. Cooper, 336 U.S. 77, 90-91 (1949) (concurring opinion). Even if that judicial approach were accepted, however, the Court is conspicuously silent as to why that "doctrine" should apply to these cases.

The footnote itself did not refer to "searching judicial inquiry" when a classification is based on alienage, perhaps because there was a long line of authority holding such classifications entirely consonant with the Fourteenth Amendment. The "national" category mentioned involved legislative attempts to prohibit education in languages other than English, which attempts were held unconstitutional as a deprivation of "liberty" within the meaning of the Fourteenth and Fifth Amendments. These cases do not mention a "citizen-alien" distinction, nor do they support a reasoning that "nationality" is the same as "alienage."

The mere recitation of the words "insular and discrete minority" is hardly a *constitutional* reason for prohibiting state legislative classifications such as are involved here, and is not necessarily consistent with the theory propounded in that footnote. The approach taken in *Graham* and these cases appears to be that whenever the Court feels that a societal group is "discrete and insular," it has the constitutional mandate to prohibit legislation that somehow treats the group differently from some other group.

Our society, consisting of over 200 million individuals of multitudinous origins, customs, tongues, beliefs, and cultures is, to say the least, diverse. It would hardly take extraordinary ingenuity for a lawyer to find "insular and discrete" minorities at every turn in the road. Yet, unless the Court can precisely define and constitutionally justify both the terms and analysis it uses, these decisions today stand for the proposition that the Court can choose a "minority" it "feels" deserves "solicitude" and thereafter prohibit the States from classifying that "minority" differently from the "majority." I cannot find, and the Court does not cite, any constitutional authority for such a "ward of the Court" approach to equal protection. . . .

[I] do not believe that it is irrational for New York to require this class of civil servants to be citizens, either natural born or naturalized. The proliferation of public administration that our society has witnessed in recent years, as a result of the regulation of conduct and the dispensation of services and funds, has vested a great deal of de facto decisionmaking or policymaking authority in the hands of employees who would not be considered the textbook equivalent of policymakers of the legislative or "top" administrative variety. . . .

It is not irrational to assume that aliens as a class are not familiar with how we as individuals treat others and how we expect "government" to treat us. An alien who grew up in a country in which political mores do not reject bribery or self-dealing to the same extent that our culture does; in which an imperious bureaucracy historically adopted a complacent or contemptuous attitude toward those it was supposed to serve; in which fewer if any checks existed on administrative abuses; in which "low-level" civil servants serve at the will of their superiors — could rationally be thought not to be able to deal with the public and with citizen civil servants with the same rapport that one familiar with our political and social mores would, or to approach his duties with the attitude that such positions exist for service, not personal sinecures of either the civil servant or his or her superior.

IN RE GRIFFITHS, 413 U.S. 717 (1973): In this case, decided on the same day as *Sugarman*, the Court held that a state could not constitutionally exclude aliens from membership in the bar. Justice Powell delivered the opinion of the Court: "Resident aliens, like citizens, pay taxes, support the economy, serve in the Armed Forces, and contribute in myriad other ways to our society. It is appropriate that a State bear a heavy burden when it deprives them of employment opportunities.

We hold that [the State] has not carried its burden. [In] order to establish a link between citizenship and the powers and responsibilities of the lawyer in Connecticut, the [State] contrasts a citizen's undivided allegiance to this country with a resident alien's possible conflict of loyalties. From this, the [State] concludes that a resident alien lawyer might in the exercise of his functions ignore his responsibilities to the courts or even his clients in favor of the interest of a foreign power.

"We find these arguments unconvincing. It in no way denigrates a lawyer's high responsibilities to observe that the powers 'to sign writs and subpoenas, take recognizances, [and] administer oaths' hardly involve matters of state policy or acts of such unique responsibility as to entrust them only to citizens. Nor do we think that the practice of law offers meaningful opportunities adversely to affect the interest of the United States. Certainly the [State] has failed to show the relevance of citizenship to any likelihood that a lawyer will fail to protect faithfully the interest of his clients. . . .

"Lawyers do indeed occupy professional positions of responsibility and influence that impose on them duties correlative with their vital right of access to the courts. Moreover, by virtue of their professional aptitudes and natural interests, lawyers have been leaders in government throughout the history of our country. Yet, they are not officials of government by virtue of being lawyers. Nor does the status of holding a license to practice law place one so close to the core of the political process as to make him a formulator of government policy."

Chief Justice Burger and Justice Rehnquist dissented.

Note: Strict Scrutiny for Aliens — Defining the Political Community

Is there an adequate justification for subjecting alienage classifications to special scrutiny? Consider the following arguments:

1. *History of discrimination.* Is strict scrutiny for alienage classifications required because aliens, like blacks and women, have suffered a history of discrimination in the United States? Historically, different states at different times have denied aliens the right to vote, prohibited them from engaging in a wide range of occupations, discriminated against them in taxation, and restricted their ownership of property. Moreover, a general sense of xenophobia has affected American attitudes and policies at various times in our history. In the Alien Act of 1798 and the "Red Scare" after World War I, for example, the federal government adopted especially severe measures to deal with suspected subversion by aliens. See generally W. Gibson, Aliens and the Law (1940); M. Konvitz, The Alien and the Asiatic in American Law (1946); J. Smith, Freedom's Fetters (1956). See also Takahashi v. Fish & Game Commission, 334 U.S. 410 (1948) (invalidating a California law restricting the right of aliens to fish); Oyama v. California, 332 U.S. 633 (1948) (invalidating a California law restricting the right of aliens to own land); Truax v. Raich, 239 U.S. 33 (1915) (invalidating an Arizona law prohibiting any business employing five or more persons to employ more than 20 percent aliens).

2. *Alienage as an immutable characteristic.* Is strict scrutiny for alienage classifications required because it is an immutable characteristic over which the disadvantaged individual can exercise no control? Consider Nyquist v. Mauclet, 432 U.S. 1 (1977). Under New York law an applicant for state higher education financial assistance must be a U.S. citizen, have made application for citizenship, or, if not qualified for citizenship, must submit a statement affirming an intent to apply for U.S. citizenship as soon as qualified to do so. The state argued that this statute need not be strictly scrutinized because it did not discriminate against aliens as such, but only against those aliens unwilling to apply for citizenship. In a 5-to-4 decision the Court rejected this argument and invalidated the law. Justice Blackmun delivered the opinion of the Court: "The important points are that [the statute] is directed at aliens and that only aliens are harmed by it. The fact that the statute is not an absolute bar does not mean that it does not discriminate against the class." Nor was it relevant that aliens could voluntarily withdraw from the disfavored status. By this logic "the suspect class for alienage would be defined to include at most only those who have resided in this country for less than five years, since after that time, if not before, resident aliens are generally eligible to become citizens. The Court has never suggested, however, that the suspect class is to be defined so narrowly."

In a dissenting opinion, Justice Rehnquist, joined by Chief Justice Burger, complained of the Court's

> somewhat mechanical application [of] equal protection jurisprudence. [Here,] unlike the other cases, the resident alien is not a member of a discrete and insular minority for purposes of the classification, even during the period that he must remain an alien, because he has at all times the means to remove himself immedi-

ately from the disfavored classification. [The] alien is not, therefore, for any period of time, forced into a position as a discrete and insular minority.

Chief Justice Burger and Justice Powell also filed separate dissenting opinions.

Does the Court adequately answer Justice Rehnquist's objection? If aliens are free to change their status at will, why aren't classifications disadvantaging this group justified as a means of encouraging naturalization? Compare Plyler v. Doe, 457 U.S. 202 (1982), where the Court invalidated a Texas policy of refusing to provide free public education to *illegally present* alien children. The court rejected the assertion that illegal aliens are a suspect class. "Unlike most of the classifications that we have recognized as suspect, entry into this class, by virtue of entry into this country, is the product of voluntary action. Indeed, entry into the class is itself a crime." But although "Persuasive arguments support the view that a State may withhold its beneficence from those whose very presence within the United States is the product of their own unlawful conduct," these arguments

> do not apply with the same force to classifications imposing disabilities on the minor *children* of such illegal entrants. [The] "parents have the ability to conform their conduct to societal norms," and presumably the ability to remove themselves from the State's jurisdiction; but the children who are plaintiffs in these cases "can affect neither their parents' conduct nor their own status" [quoting Trimble v. Gordon, 430 U.S. 762 (1977)]. Even if the State found it expedient to control the conduct of adults by acting against their children, legislation directing the onus of a parent's misconduct against his children does not comport with fundamental conceptions of justice.

Because Texas's policy "[imposed] a lifetime hardship on a discrete class of children not accountable for their disabling status," the Court concluded that the discrimination "can hardly be considered rational unless it furthers some substantial goal of the State." Chief Justice Burger filed a dissenting opinion, in which Justices White, Rehnquist, and O'Connor joined.

Illegal aliens are subject to deportation and, if deported, these aliens would be denied an education in the Texas public schools. Does it make sense, then, to say that their rights are violated when they are denied such an education while illegally residing in Texas? *Plyler* is examined more fully in Chapter 6, section E5, infra.

3. *Aliens as a "discrete" and "insular" minority.* Are aliens members of a "discrete and insular [minority]" hampered by the kind of prejudice "which tends seriously to curtail the operation of those political processes ordinarily to be relied upon to protect minorities"? United States v. Carolene Products, supra. Consider Lusky, Footnote Redux: A *Carolene Products* Reminiscence, 82 Colum. L. Rev. 1087, 1093 n.72:

> As a matter of language, "discrete" means separate or distinct and "insular" means isolated or detached. The words do not describe aliens as such; many of them, who are anglophones, pass unnoticed, and many if not most others fit into the social scene with little difficulty. Of course, there are sizeable ethnic groups, *and they include citizens as well as aliens*, who are held at arm's length — Chicanos, Orientals, and so on — but that is quite another matter.

But compare Rosberg, The Protection of Aliens from Discriminatory Treatment by the National Government, 1977 Sup. Ct. Rev. 275, 309-310:

> Given the exclusion of aliens from the political process, it is [reasonable] for the Court to demand a special showing from the state if it is to classify on the basis of alienage. The state has presumably weighed its interest in giving a preference to the members of its polity against the aliens' interest in enjoying the benefits at issue. But aliens have had no opportunity to participate in the process of measuring the relative weight of these two interests. Since the legislature has denied aliens any chance to assert their own interests in the political forum, it cannot expect the courts to maintain their usual deference to the legislature's balancing of the interests.

Does basing strict scrutiny on the political disabilities that the law itself imposes on aliens involve circular reasoning? In the second paragraph of the *Carolene Products* footnote, Justice Stone suggested that strict scrutiny might be appropriate for laws that "[restrict] those political processes which can ordinarily be expected to bring about repeal of undesirable legislation." If aliens are politically vulnerable because they lack the franchise, why isn't the appropriate solution to scrutinize strictly the laws denying them the right to vote? See generally Rosberg, Aliens and Equal Protection: Why Not the Right to Vote?, 75 Mich. L. Rev. 1092 (1977). Note that the Court in *Sugarman* affirms the states' right to restrict the franchise and policy making positions to citizens. Is there a justification for these restrictions that would survive strict scrutiny? Presumably, the justification relates to historical considerations, perceptions of the framers' "intent," and the general interest of the state in limiting political rights to members of the political community. The citizenship clause of the fourteenth amendment itself seems to recognize the legitimacy of this interest. But if fundamental political rights like the franchise may be limited to citizens, why may not the state restrict less basic benefits like public employment to members of the political community as well?

4. *Alienage and the political community.* In a series of cases since *Sugarman,* the Court has upheld a number of state restrictions on employment of aliens on the theory that the positions involve the formulation or execution of broad public policy and may therefore be limited to members of the political community. The trend begins with Foley v. Connelie, 435 U.S. 291 (1978), where the Court upheld a New York statute prohibiting aliens from serving on the state police force. Writing for five justices, Chief Justice Burger observed that it would be

> inappropriate [to] require every statutory exclusion of aliens to clear the high hurdle of "strict scrutiny." [The] act of becoming a citizen is more than a ritual with no content beyond the fanfare of ceremony. A new citizen has become a member of a Nation, part of a people distinct from others.
>
> The practical consequence of this theory is that "our scrutiny will not be so demanding where we deal with matters firmly within a State's constitutional prerogatives" [quoting *Sugarman*]. . . .
>
> [We] have recognized that citizenship may be a relevant qualification for fulfilling those "important nonelective executive, legislative, and judicial positions," held by "officers who participate directly in the formulation, execution, or review of broad public policy." [*Sugarman*]. This is not because our society seeks to reserve the better jobs to its members. Rather, it is because this country entrusts many of its most important policy responsibilities to these officers, the discretionary exercise of which can often more immediately affect the lives of citizens than even the ballot of

a voter or the choice of a legislator. In sum, then, it represents the choice, and right, of the people to be governed by their citizen peers. To effectuate this result, we must necessarily examine each position in question to determine whether it involves discretionary decisionmaking, or execution of policy, which substantially affects members of the political community.

After examining the functions of police officers, the Court concluded that they were important nonelective officials engaged in the execution of broad public policy. Because the citizenship requirement was rationally related to the demands of the position, the requirement was constitutional. One of the five votes for Chief Justice Burger's opinion was provided by Justice Stewart, who wrote separately to explain that he thought the result was "difficult if not impossible to reconcile" with prior decisions, but that he was nonetheless joining the opinion because he had "become increasingly doubtful about the validity of those decisions." Justice Blackmun concurred only in the result. Justice Marshall, joined by Justices Brennan and Stevens, dissented.

Does *Foley* adequately explain why rational relationship review is appropriate, or is its reasoning instead directed to why the classification at issue satisfies the requirements of the level of review it has chosen? Is there a coherent distinction between choosing a level of review and deciding that a classification satisfies the requirements of that level? Are any of the concerns that caused the Court to scrutinize alienage classifications strictly in the first place reduced because the classification relates to an important policy execution position? Would the *Foley* classification survive strict scrutiny?

Following *Foley* the Court upheld citizenship requirements for public school teachers (Ambach v. Norwick, 441 U.S. 68 (1979)) and probation officers (Cabell v. Chavez-Salido, 454 U.S. 432 (1982)). In Bernal v. Fainter, — U.S. —, 104 S. Ct. 2312 (1984), however, a unanimous Court invalidated a citizenship requirement for notaries public.

Can the results in these cases be reconciled? In Cabell v. Chavez-Salido, the Court acknowledged that the alienage decisions "have not formed an unwavering line over the years. [But] to say that the decisions do not fall into a neat pattern is not to say that they fall into no pattern." According to the Court,

> The cases through *Graham* dealt for the most part with attempts by the States to retain certain economic benefits exclusively for citizens. Since *Graham*, the Court has confronted claims distinguishing between the economic and sovereign functions of government. This distinction has been supported by the argument that although citizenship is not a relevant ground for the distribution of economic benefits, it is a relevant ground for determining membership in the political community.

Is this distinction sound? Note that the Court has relied on a similar distinction under the dormant commerce clause where it has been willing to uphold state actions as a "market participant" that would be invalidated if the state were acting as a "market regulator." See Chapter 3, section E, supra.

How does one separate the "economic" and "sovereign" functions of government? In *Cabell* the Court set out a two-pronged test:

> First, the specificity of the classification will be examined: a classification that is substantially overinclusive or underinclusive tends to undercut the governmental

claim that the classification serves legitimate political ends. [Second], even if the classification is sufficiently tailored, it may be applied in the particular case only to "persons holding state elective or important nonelective executive, legislative, and judicial positions," those officers who "participate directly in the formulation, execution, or review of broad public policy" and hence "perform functions that go to the heart of representative government." [*Sugarman*].

Is this test workable? How can one determine whether a classification is over- or underinclusive without first settling on the level of review under which the fit is to be measured?

The statute in *Cabell* required all "peace officers" to be citizens. This classification included over seventy positions, including toll-service employees, cemetery sextons, and inspectors. The Court held that the

District Court was wrong in striking down the statute on its face. The District Court assumed that if the statute was overinclusive at all, it could not stand. This is not the proper standard. Rather, the inquiry is whether the restriction reaches so far and is so broad and haphazard as to belie the State's claim that it is only attempting to ensure that an important function of government be in the hands of those having the "fundamental legal bond of citizenship." [*Ambach.*] Under this standard, the classifications used need not be precise; there need only be a substantial fit.

Applying this test to the case before it, the Court concluded that "the questionable classifications are comparatively few in number" and that the statutes were "sufficiently tailored in light of [the aim of limiting the exercise of coercive police power to citizens] to pass the lower level of scrutiny we articulated as the appropriate equal protection standard for such an exercise of sovereign power."

Does this formulation successfully keep the choice of the level of scrutiny separate from the scrutiny itself? Is it consistent with *Sugarman?*

What is the justification for separating the "economic" and "sovereign" functions of government? Doesn't this distinction turn the *Carolene Products* theory on its head? That theory suggests that strict scrutiny is appropriate precisely when political rather than economic, rights are at stake. If "representation reinforcement" for politically disadvantaged minorities is not the basis for the Court's intervention in this area, what is?

Consider the possibility that the decisions reflect a concern that classifications in this area are peculiarly likely to reflect hostility or prejudice and not to respond to a legitimate effort by the state to promote the public interest. Is that a plausible distinction? How does it differ from an approach based on representation reinforcement?

Note: Alienage and Federal Preemption

Can the alienage cases be explained on the ground that the states have only a narrow role to play when dealing with problems of immigration and naturalization? On this view, many state alienage classifications are invalid not simply because they discriminate against aliens, or because the policies they advance are inherently illegitimate, but rather because those policies are best pursued in a unified way on the national level. See Note, The Equal Treatment of Aliens: Preemption or Equal Protection?, 31 Stan. L. Rev. 1069 (1979).

In *Graham* itself, which first announced that alienage classifications were suspect for equal protection purposes, the Court also relied on federalism grounds as an alternative basis for invalidating the state law. State restrictions on the eligibility of aliens for welfare benefits, in the Court's view, conflicted with "overriding national policies in an area constitutionally entrusted to the Federal Government." Since *Graham* federalism and preemption concerns have become an increasingly important theme in alienage cases.

1. *The federal cases.* In Mathews v. Diaz, 426 U.S. 67 (1976), a unanimous Court upheld a federal statute limiting participation in a federal medical insurance program to citizens and aliens who had continuously resided in the United States for five years and had been admitted for permanent residence. Writing for the Court, Justice Stevens explained that

> In the exercise of its broad power over naturalization and immigration, Congress regularly makes rules that would be unacceptable if applied to citizens. [In] particular, the fact that Congress has provided some welfare benefits for citizens does not require it to provide like benefits for *all aliens*. Neither the overnight visitor, the unfriendly agent of a hostile foreign power, the resident diplomat, nor the illegal entrant, can advance even a colorable constitutional claim to a share in the bounty that a conscientious sovereign makes available to its own citizens and *some* of its guests. The decision to share that bounty with our guests may take into account the character of the relationship between the alien and this country: Congress may decide that as the alien's tie grows stronger, so does the strength of his claim to an equal share of that munificence.

Graham v. Richardson, in the Court's view, was fully consistent with this analysis. Indeed, the federalism prong of the *Graham* holding "actually supports our holding today that it is the business of the political branches of the Federal Government, rather than that of either the States or the Federal Judiciary, to regulate the conditions of entry and residence of aliens." Moreover, the equal protection analysis in *Graham* involved "significantly different considerations." Whereas the states had

> little, if any, basis for treating persons who are citizens of another State differently from persons who are citizens of another country, [a] comparable classification by the Federal Government is a routine and normally legitimate part of its business. Furthermore, whereas the Constitution inhibits every State's power to restrict travel across its own borders, Congress is explicitly empowered to exercise that type of control over travel across the borders of the United States.

After *Mathews* do any limits remain on the federal government's power to impose special rules governing the conduct of aliens? Could Congress prohibit resident aliens from having abortions? From working as lawyers? Could it insist that an alien doctor admitted to this country to practice medicine continue to do so while she or he remains here? Is the "political powerlessness" or "immutable condition" of aliens sufficient to give rise to suspicion of an impermissible motivation in these cases, or is the very concept of impermissible motivation out of place in this context?

Can federal power over aliens be justified on the ground that the federal government could exclude aliens altogether and that it therefore may condition their admission on the waiver of certain rights? Consider Rosberg, The Protection of Aliens from Discriminatory Treatment by the National Government, supra, at 334-336:

> To resolve the equal protection issue presented in [*Mathews*] the Court did not have to explore the ultimate limits of federal power to reshape the fundamental precepts of the nation's immigration policy. . . .
>
> Some conditions on admission — for example, the restrictions against foreign students' working in the United States — are open and notorious. [The] restriction is plainly an integral part of the immigration scheme, and it is debated in terms of its impact on immigration policy: How many aliens can the country reasonably admit?
>
> Unlike the rules that prevent nonimmigrants from accepting employment, the great majority of the statutory provisions discriminating against resident aliens, certainly including the provision at issue in [*Mathews*], have no explicit connection with immigration. They are not codified in the immigration laws. For the most part they did not originate in immigration legislation and were not acted upon by the congressional committees primarily concerned with immigration. [Aliens] are subject to discriminatory treatment because Congress, in the course of deciding who should receive the benefits of a particular program, decides to leave them out. [There] may, to be sure, be good reasons for excluding aliens from the program. [But the] point of treating alienage as a suspect classification is to make clear that the legislature must have more than just a good reason for treating them differently from citizens, because resident aliens cannot protect their own interests.

Compare *Mathews* with Hampton v. Mow Sun Wong, 426 U.S. 88 (1976), decided on the same day. In *Hampton* the Court invalidated a Civil Service Commission policy excluding aliens from most civil service jobs. The Court, in an opinion by Justice Stevens, acknowledged that "there may be overriding national interests which justify selective federal legislation that would be unacceptable for an individual State. [The] paramount federal power over immigration and naturalization [forecloses] a simple extension of the holding in *Sugarman*." Nonetheless, the Court held that imposition of a citizenship requirement *by the Civil Service Commission* violated due process.

> We may assume [that] if the Congress or the President had expressly imposed the citizenship requirement, it would be justified by the national interest in providing an incentive for aliens to become naturalized, or possibly even as providing the President with an expendable token for treaty negotiating purposes; but we are not willing to presume that the Chairman of the Civil Service Commission [was] deliberately fostering an interest so far removed from his normal responsibilities. [By] broadly denying this class substantial opportunities for employment, the Civil Service Commission rule deprives its members of an aspect of liberty. Since these residents were admitted as a result of decisions made by the Congress and the President, [due process] requires that the decision to impose that deprivation of an important liberty be made either at a comparable level of government or, if it is to be permitted to be made by the Civil Service Commission, that it be justified by reasons which are properly the concern of that agency.

Justice Rehnquist filed a dissenting opinion that was joined by Chief Justice Burger and Justices White and Blackmun.

If Congress could exclude aliens from civil service jobs, why is there a constitutional obstacle to congressional delegation of this power to the Civil Service Commission? Does *Hampton* suggest a revitalization of the nondelegation doctrine? See Chapter 4 section C, supra.

2. *The state cases.* Can the state cases also be read as resting on a concern that the proper unit of government make a judgment about the status of aliens, rather than on a concern about the merits of the judgment itself? On occasion, the Court has expressly relied on preemption grounds to invalidate state citizenship requirements. In Toll v. Moreno, 458 U.S. 1 (1982), for example, the Court considered a state policy denying in-state status to nonimmigrant aliens for purposes of qualifying for tuition reductions at state universities. Without reaching the equal protection question, the Court held the state policy unconstitutional under the supremacy clause. In light of the "long recognized [preeminent] role of the Federal Government with respect to the regulation of aliens within our borders," the Court held that " 'state regulation not congressionally sanctioned that discriminates against aliens lawfully admitted to the country is impermissible if it imposes additional burdens not contemplated by Congress' " [quoting De Canas v. Bica, 424 U.S. 351 (1976)].

In other cases, however, federalism concerns have played a more indirect role in the Court's reasoning. Instead of relying directly on the supremacy clause, the Court has referred to the federal government's "preeminent role" regarding aliens when it assesses the legitimacy of state concerns that might otherwise justify the classification under the equal protection clause. In Nyquist v. Mauclet, supra, for example, the state sought to justify its citizenship requirement for higher education financial assistance on the ground that it encouraged naturalization and ensured a "degree of national affinity." But the Court rejected this goal as "not a permissible one for a State. Control over immigration and naturalization is entrusted exclusively to the Federal Government, and a State has no power to interfere." Similarly, in Plyler v. Doe the Court was unimpressed by the state's claim that its refusal to enroll illegal aliens in public schools supported the federal policy against illegal immigration.

> To be sure, like all persons who have entered the United States unlawfully, these children are subject to deportation. But there is no assurance that a child subject to deportation will ever be deported. An illegal entrant might be granted federal permission to continue to reside in this country, or even to become a citizen. In light of the discretionary federal power to grant relief from deportation, a State cannot realistically determine that any particular undocumented child will in fact be deported until after deportation proceedings have been completed. It would of course be most difficult for the State to justify a denial of education to a child enjoying an inchoate federal permission to remain.

Is the Court's distinction between the "economic" and "sovereign" functions of state government explicable in terms of this desire to limit state decisionmaking to an appropriate sphere? Does the Court's decision to oversee the unit of government making these decisions rather than the substance of the decisions themselves reflect sensible judicial restraint? Or does it elevate form over substance? Note that Congress could enact preemptive laws on its own if it so desired. In these circumstances, is there a good reason why these institutional decisions should not be made by the political branches? Isn't it likely that basically the same sorts of people would be hired to make these decisions by whatever branch of government is vested with the decisionmaking authority?

2. Nonmarital Children

In a series of cases beginning in 1968, the Supreme Court has evaluated the constitutionality of a number of statutes disadvantaging nonmarital children. Although the Court has refused formally to elevate discrimination against this group to the "suspect" status, some of these statutes have been invalidated, and the Court has at least on occasion subjected them to something more than conventional rational basis review. The Court's first encounter with the problem came in Levy v. Louisiana, 391 U.S. 68 (1968), and Glona v. American Guarantee & Liability Insurance Co., 391 U.S. 73 (1968), two brief opinions written by Justice Douglas. In *Levy* the Court held that Louisiana could not constitutionally exclude nonmarital children from coverage of a wrongful death statute that generally permitted children to sue for the loss of their mother. The Court noted that the usual test for statutory classifications challenged under the equal protection clause was "whether the line drawn is a rational one" but that the Court had also "been extremely sensitive when it comes to basic civil rights," and that "The rights asserted here involve the intimate, familial relationship between a child and his own mother." Without further clarifying the applicable standard it was applying, the Court concluded that "Legitimacy or illegitimacy of birth has no relation to the nature of the wrong allegedly inflicted on the mother" and that "it is invidious to discriminate against [the children] when no action, conduct, or demeanor of theirs is possibly relevant to the harm that was done the mother."

In *Glona* the Court reached a similar conclusion in an action brought by the mother of a nonmarital child to recover for the child's wrongful death. The law could not be rationally defended, in the Court's view, as a measure to deter creation of nonmarital children. "It would, indeed, be farfetched to assume that women have illegitimate children so that they can be compensated in damages for their death." Although "Opening the courts to suits of this kind may conceivably be a temptation to some to assert motherhood fraudulently[, that] problem [concerns] burden of proof. When the claimant is plainly the mother, the State denies equal protection of the laws to withhold relief merely because the child, wrongfully killed, was born to her out of wedlock."

Justice Harlan, joined by Justices Black and Stewart, dissented in both *Levy* and *Glona*. He argued that "the interest one person has in the life of another is inherently intractable." Consequently, there was no reason for the Court's insistence that the state

> base its arbitrary definition of the plaintiff class on biological rather than legal relationships. [Neither] a biological relationship nor legal acknowledgment is indicative of the love or economic dependence that may exist between two persons. [The] rights at issue here stem from the existence of family relationship, and the State has decided only that it will not recognize the family relationship unless the formalities of marriage, or of the acknowledgment of children by the parent in question, have been complied with.

Three years after *Levy* and *Glona*, the Court appeared to limit sharply their holdings. In Labine v. Vincent, 401 U.S. 532 (1971), the three *Levy/Glona* dissenters joined with two new members of the Court to form a 5-to-4 majority upholding a Louisiana statute barring nonmarital children from sharing equally in the estate of a father who had died intestate but publicly acknowledged paternity. "Of course, it may be said that the rules adopted by the Louisiana Legislature 'discriminate' against illegitimates," Justice Black wrote for the majority.

> But the rules also discriminate against collateral relations, as opposed to ascendants, and against ascendants, as opposed to descendants. Other rules determining property rights based on family status also "discriminate" in favor of wives and against "concubines." [The] social difference between a wife and a concubine is analogous to the difference between a legitimate and an illegitimate child. One set of relationships is socially sanctioned, legally recognized, and gives rise to various rights and duties. The other set of relationships is illicit and beyond the recognition of the law.

Levy was distinguished on the ground that there, the state had created an "insurmountable barrier" to recovery by nonmarital children. Here, the deceased could have left money to his illegitimate daughter by executing a will, marrying her mother, or stating his desire to legitimate her in his acknowledgment of paternity.

One year later, in Weber v. Aetna Casualty & Surety Co., 406 U.S. 164 (1972), the Court made clear that the *Levy/Glona* doctrine survived *Labine*. With only Justice Rehnquist dissenting, the Court invalidated a statute discriminating against dependent but unacknowledged nonmarital children in the award of worker's compensation benefits on the death of their natural father. The Court reasoned that "The status of illegitimacy has expressed through the ages society's condemnation of irresponsible liaisons beyond the bonds of marriage. But visiting this condemnation on the head of an infant is illogical and unjust. Moreover, imposing disabilities on the illegitimate child is contrary to the basic concept of our system that legal burdens should bear some relationship to individual responsibility or wrongdoing." Justice Powell distinguished *Labine* as resting on "the traditional deference to a State's prerogative to regulate the disposition at death of property within its borders. [Moreover,] in *Labine* the intestate, unlike deceased in the present action, might easily have modified his daughter's disfavored position."

Note: Working with the Levy/Glona Test

In the years since *Weber* the Court has struggled to articulate a consistent position regarding the constitutional status of laws discriminating against nonmarital children. Some of its confusion almost certainly stems from underlying uncertainty about the justification for heightened scrutiny in this area.

1. *Nonmarital children as a discrete and insular minority.* Do nonmarital children suffer from the kind of prejudice that prevents their views from being fairly counted in the political process? Historically, such children have doubtless been victimized by societal disapproval that is unrelated to their own conduct. But is it likely that this kind of prejudice is still an important factor? Notice that unlike blacks, women, and aliens, nonmarital children have never been formally ex-

cluded from the political process. Moreover, although there are laws that disadvantage them, these laws relate exclusively to their status in the family. It seems doubtful that they suffer from more generalized political disabilities.

In Mathews v. Lucas, 427 U.S. 495 (1976), the Court expressly rejected the position that prejudice directed against this group justified strict scrutiny.

> [While] the law has long placed the illegitimate child in an inferior position relative to the legitimate in certain circumstances, particularly in regard to obligations of support or other aspects of family law, [perhaps] in part because the roots of the discrimination rest in the conduct of the parents rather than the child, and perhaps in part because illegitimacy does not carry an obvious badge, as race or sex do, this discrimination against illegitimates has never approached the severity or pervasiveness of the historic legal and political discrimination against women and Negroes.

2. *Nonmarital children and biological rights.* Although the Court in *Lucas* declined to apply "our most exacting scrutiny" to laws disadvantaging nonmarital children, such statutes are apparently not currently tested under ordinary rational relationship review. In Pickett v. Brown, 462 U.S. 1 (1983), for example, the Court wrote that statutory classifications based on illegitimacy were subject to a "heightened level of scrutiny. Although we have held that classifications based on illegitimacy are not 'suspect,' or subject to 'our most exacting scrutiny,' the scrutiny applied to them 'is not a toothless one.'" Similarly, in United States v. Clark, 445 U.S. 23 (1980), the Court held that classifications based on illegitimacy are "unconstitutional unless [they] bear 'an evident and substantial relation to the particular [interests the] statute is designed to serve' [quoting Lalli v. Lalli, 439 U.S. 259 (1978)]."

The Court has frequently justified this heightened scrutiny on the theory that it is particularly unjust to burden nonmarital children with disadvantages based on conduct of their parents over which they had no control. In *Lucas* itself, for example, the Court observed that

> the legal status of illegitimacy, however defined, is, like race or national origin, a characteristic determined by causes not within the control of the illegitimate individual, and it bears no relation to the individual's ability to participate in and contribute to society. [Visiting] condemnation upon the child in order to express society's disapproval of the parents' liasons "is illogical and unjust" [*Weber*]. [Where] the law is arbitrary in such a way, we have had no difficulty in finding the discrimination impermissible on less demanding standards than those advocated here.

Does the fact that the status of one's parents is "not within the control of the illegitimate individual" justify heightened scrutiny? Note that attributes not strictly within an individual's control — height, age, and intelligence, for example — are frequently used as a basis for classifications, and no constitutional question is raised as a result. If the status of one's parents should bear no relation to an individual's rights, how is it possible to justify the pervasive assumption in our legal system that parents should have control of the lives of their children and the reciprocal assumption that children have a right to expect support from their parents? For example, suppose an unmarried woman has sexual intercourse with a rich man and a poor man. Is there a good reason that the level of support to which the child is entitled should depend on the fortuity of who happens to be the father? If a child is conceived by artificial insemination, does the Constitution require states to extend a duty of support to the donor to the sperm bank? If the donor dies intestate, is it constitutionally mandatory that the child share in his estate?

Do the Court's unstated assumptions about biologically determined rights at the core of its "illegitimacy" decisions guarantee inequality of outcomes by giving children different starting points in the world? Consider J. Fishkin, Justice, Equal Opportunity and the Family 54-55 (1983):

> While empirical conditions will vary from one society to the next, the general proposition is difficult to deny: children from advantaged families in a given society will have greater opportunities to develop the skills, credentials, and motivations valued in that society. If the autonomy of the family protects the process by which parents provide those greater opportunities, and if the principle of merit sorts people accurately in terms of their skills, credentials, and motivations — as developed under those unequal conditions — then systematic inequality of life chances will result.

A program designed to reduce this inequality might substitute a system of legally for biologically determined rights. The nonmarital children cases suggest that there are limits on the state's ability to engage in such a program. The cases suggest that nonmarital children have a certain status simply because of a genetic relationship to their mother and father. Might these cases be viewed, then, as an extension of the substantive due process cases protecting traditional family groupings from government interference? See Chapter 6, section F3, infra. Is such protection consistent with a real commitment to equality?

3. *Some cases concerning nonmarital children and biological rights.* Assuming that some biologically determined rights should be recognized, how should each of the following problems be resolved?

a. Under Texas law, the natural father has a continuing and primary duty to support his legitimate children. However, fathers have no analogous duty to support nonmarital children.

In Gomez v. Perez, 409 U.S. 535 (1973), the Court held that the failure to provide support rights for nonmarital children violated the equal protection clause.

> [A] State may not invidiously discriminate against illegitimate children by denying them substantial benefits accorded children generally. We therefore hold that once a State posits a judicially enforceable right on behalf of children to needed support from their natural fathers there is no constitutionally sufficient justification for denying such an essential right to a child simply because its natural father has not married its mother.

b. In response to *Gomez* Texas amended its law to require parents to support their nonmarital children in cases where such children can establish paternity. However, the law provided that suits to establish paternity must be brought before the child reaches the age of one. The state justified this statute of limitations as necessary to prevent the prosecution of stale or fraudulent claims of paternity.

In Mills v. Habluetzel, 456 U.S. 91 (1982), the Court held that this statute of limitations violated the equal protection clause.

If *Gomez* [is] to have any meaning, it is clear that the support opportunity provided by the State to illegitimate children must be more than illusory. The period for asserting the right to support must be sufficiently long to permit those who normally have an interest in such children to bring an action on their behalf despite the difficult personal, family, and financial circumstances that often surround the birth of a child outside of wedlock. [The] fact that Texas must provide illegitimate children with a bona fide opportunity to obtain paternal support does not mean, however, that it must adopt procedures for illegitimate children that are coterminous with those accorded legitimate children. Paternal support suits on behalf of illegitimate children contain an element that such suits for legitimate children do not contain: proof of paternity. [The] equal protection analysis [therefore], focuses on two related requirements. First, the period for obtaining support [to] illegitimate children must be sufficiently long in duration to present a reasonable opportunity for those with an interest in such children to assert claims on their behalf. Second, any time limitation placed on that opportunity must be substantially related to the State's interest in avoiding the litigation of stale or fraudulent claims.

See also Pickett v. Brown, 462 U.S. 1 (1983) (two-year statute of limitations on proof of paternity for nonmarital children violates equal protection).

c. Under Georgia law, a child born in wedlock generally cannot be adopted without the consent of both parents. However, only the consent of the mother is required for adoption of nonmarital children. The father can obtain veto rights by marrying the mother and acknowledging the child as his own or by obtaining a court order declaring the child legitimate and capable of inheriting from the father. Appellant was the natural father of a child but had never married the mother or lived with the child. The mother married appellee, who sought to adopt the child. The mother gave her consent, but appellant sought to block the adoption. After a hearing at which the natural father was permitted to participate, the trial court found that the adoption was in the child's best interest and ruled for appellee.

In Quilloin v. Walcott, 434 U.S. 246 (1978), the Court unanimously upheld the adoption on these facts. The Court noted that there was "little doubt" that the Constitution would be violated

If a State were to attempt to force the breakup of a natural family, over the objections of the parents and their children, without some showing of unfitness and for the sole reason that to do so was thought to be in the children's best interest [quoting Smith v. Organization of Foster Families, 431 U.S. 816, 862-863 (1977) (Stewart, J., concurring in the judgment)]. But this is not a case in which the unwed father at any time had, or sought, actual or legal custody of his child. [Rather,] the result of the adoption in this case is to give full recognition to a family unit already in existence, a result desired by all concerned except appellant.

The Court also rejected appellant's claim that his interests were indistinguishable from those of a separated or divorced father and that equal protection principles therefore required that he be given the same veto rights.

Although appellant was subject, for the years prior to these proceedings, to essentially the same child-support obligations as a married father would have had, [he] has never exercised actual or legal custody over his child, and thus has never shouldered any significant responsibility with respect to the daily supervision, education, protection, or care of the child. [In] contrast, legal custody of children is, of course, a central aspect of the marital relationship, and even a father whose marriage has broken apart will have borne full responsibility for the rearing of his children during the period of the marriage.

See also Lehr v. Robertson, 463 U.S. 248 (1983) (upholding constitutionality of statute permitting adoption of nonmarital children without even providing notice to natural father unless he had registered intent to claim paternity with "putative father's registry" or met certain other statutory criteria such as living openly with child and child's mother). But see Caban v. Mohammed, 441 U.S. 380 (1979) (New York statute requiring consent of mother but not father for adoption of nonmarital child constitutes impermissible gender discrimination when applied to father who has established substantial relationship with child and contributed to support). See generally section D3, supra.

4. *Nonmarital children, the problem of proof, and the review of rules.* As noted above, the Court has rejected the argument that statutes disadvantaging nonmarital children can be justified as a means of deterring or punishing their parents for illicit sexual activity. It is rare, however, for modern legislatures to base such legislation explicitly on this theory. Rather, most current legislation classifying on the basis of "illegitimacy" is premised on what are perceived to be the special problems of proof of paternity posed when a child's parents are not married. When this claim has been advanced, the Court has usually not rejected it outright. Instead, the justices have asked whether the avoidance of fraud, a legitimate purpose, does in fact justify the sweeping disqualifications from benefits the legislature has sometimes imposed. These decisions may be based on an effort to ascertain whether the classification in question is rooted in hostility or prejudice, or a belief that nonmarital children are less worthy than marital children or instead rooted in an effort to respond to "real differences" between the two classes of children. Compare the Court's treatment of gender discrimination, section D3, supra.

Thus, laws that totally bar nonmarital children from benefits without giving them an opportunity to prove entitlement are frequently invalidated. But the Court has been more sympathetic to statutes that give such children some opportunity to qualify for the benefits, albeit on terms that may differ from those available to marital children. These special terms satisfy the state's need to avoid fraudulent claims of paternity. Moreover, so long as the law provides some realistic means by which nonmarital children can qualify for the benefits, perhaps they are not being penalized for a status over which they have no control if they fail to qualify. Unfortunately, however, this middle course has created problems of its own. Consider the following decisions:

a. *Jiminez.* In Jiminez v. Weinberger, 417 U.S. 628 (1974), the Court struck down a section of the Social Security Act disadvantaging certain nonmarital children of disabled workers. All marital and "legitimated" children of such workers as well as nonmarital children who could inherit under the state's intestacy laws or who could not inherit only because of a nonobvious defect in their parents' ceremonial marriage, were entitled to benefits without any showing that they were actually supported by the disabled worker. However, other nonmarital children could obtain benefits only by demonstrating that they were living with or being supported by the claimant at the time the disability began. Appellants failed to qualify for benefits because they were born after the onset of their father's disability and, therefore, were neither living with nor being supported by their father before he became disabled.

The Court, in an opinion by Chief Justice Burger, recognized the legitimacy of the government's interest in preventing spurious claims but rejected the argument that the exclusion of this subclass of illegitimates was reasonably related to this interest. "Assuming that the appellants are in fact dependent on the claimant, it would not serve the purposes of the Act to conclusively deny them an opportunity to establish their dependency and their right to insurance benefits, and it would discriminate between the two subclasses of afterborn illegitimates without any basis for the distinction since the potential for spurious claims is exactly the same as to both subclasses."

b. Mathews. In Mathews v. Lucas, supra, the Court upheld a seemingly analogous section of the Social Security Act depriving certain nonmarital children of survivors benefits. The act generally provided survivors benefits for dependent children of covered individuals. However, it conclusively presumed that all marital children were dependent on their parents. The same conclusive presumption applied to nonmarital children when the parents had gone through a marriage ceremony void because of a nonobvious legal defect, when the deceased parent had acknowledged in writing that the child was his, when a court had decreed that the deceased was the parent of the child, or when the deceased had been ordered by a court to support the child. Other nonmarital children could qualify for benefits only on a showing that the parent was living with or contributing to the child's support at the time of death.

In *Mathews* it was uncontested that appellant was the nonmarital child of a deceased covered individual. However, he was denied benefits because he failed to qualify for any of the exemptions for nonmarital children and he had not proved actual dependency by demonstrating that his father was either living with him or contributing to his support at the time of his death.

The Court observed that Congress's purpose in adopting the statutory presumption of dependence was to serve administrative convenience.

> While Congress was unwilling to assume that every child of a deceased insured was dependent at the time of death, by presuming dependency on the basis of relatively readily documented facts, such as legitimate birth, or existence of a support order or paternity decree, which could be relied upon to indicate the likelihood of continued actual dependency, Congress was able to avoid the burden and expense of specific case-by-case determination in the large number of cases where dependency is objectively probable.

These presumptions, in the Court's view, were "justified as reasonable empirical judgments that are consistent with a design to qualify entitlement to benefits upon a child's dependency at the time of the parent's death." *Jiminez* was distinguishable because there certain nonmarital children "were conclusively denied any benefits, regardless of any showing of dependency. [This] conclusiveness in denying benefits to some classes of afterborn illegitimate children, which belied the asserted legislative reliance on dependency [is] absent here, for, as we have noted, any otherwise eligible child may qualify for survivorship benefits by showing contribution to support, or cohabitation, at the time of death."

c. Trimble. In Trimble v. Gordon, 430 U.S. 762 (1977), a narrowly divided Court invalidated application of a state law excluding nonmarital children from intestate succession to the estate of their fathers. Prior to his death, a state court had found that the decedent was appellant's father and ordered him to support appellant. Decedent thereafter supported her, openly acknowledged her as his child, and lived with her until his death. An Illinois court nonetheless held that a state statute prevented appellant from sharing in the estate. This statute was unobjectionable, according to the state court, because it raised no insurmountable barrier to nonmarital children sharing in their fathers' estates. Fathers who desired this result could leave a will naming such children as heirs. In the absence of a will, the ban on intestate recovery was justified by the difficulties of proof of paternity and the risk of fraudulent claims.

The Court, in an opinion by Justice Powell, acknowledged that

> The more serious problems of proving paternity might justify a more demanding standard for illegitimate children claiming under their fathers' estates than that required [for] legitimate children. [However, the state] court failed to consider the possibility of a middle ground between the extremes of complete exclusion and case-by-case determination of paternity. For at least some significant categories of illegitimate children of intestate men, inheritance rights can be recognized without jeopardizing the orderly settlement of estates.

Nor was the statute rendered constitutionally acceptable because a nonmarital child could escape the statutory disability if the father wrote a will.

> Despite its appearance in [Labine and Weber], the focus on the presence or absence of an insurmountable barrier is somewhat of an analytical anomaly. [By] focusing on the steps that an intestate might have taken to assure some inheritance for his illegitimate children, the analysis loses sight of the essential question: the constitutionality of discrimination against illegitimates in a state intestate succession law. [Hard] questions cannot be avoided by a hypothetical reshuffling of the facts.

Four justices dissented.

d. Lalli. In Lalli v. Lalli, 439 U.S. 259 (1978), the Court distinguished Trimble and upheld a New York law providing that a nonmarital child could inherit intestate from his father only if "a court of competent jurisdiction has, during the lifetime of the father, made an order of filiation declaring paternity." Appellant, claiming to be the decedent's son, tendered a notarized document written by the decedent in which he referred to appellant as "my son" as well as several affidavits by persons who stated that decedent had acknowledged openly and often that appellant was his child. Despite this evidence, the New York court held that the statute precluded appellant from sharing in the estate.

Although no opinion attracted a majority of the justices, the Court affirmed this result. Justice Powell's plurality opinion distinguished Trimble as follows:

> The Illinois statute [was] constitutionally unacceptable because it effected a total statutory disinheritance of children born out of wedlock who were not legitimated by the subsequent marriage of their parents. The reach of the statute was far in excess of its justifiable purpose. [This statute] does not share this defect. Inheritance is barred only where there has been a failure to secure evidence of paternity during the

father's lifetime in the manner prescribed by the State. This is not a requirement that inevitably disqualifies an unnecessarily large number of children born out of wedlock.

Powell acknowledged that some nonmarital children who could easily establish their relationship to the decedent would nonetheless be disqualified by the statutory requirement. "But few statutory classifications are entirely free from the criticism that they sometimes produce inequitable results. Our inquiry under the Equal Protection Clause does not focus on the abstract 'fairness' of a state law, but on whether the statute's relation to the state interests it is intended to promote is so tenuous that it lacks the rationality contemplated by the Fourteenth Amendment." One justice, who dissented in *Trimble*, concurred in the *Lalli* judgment on the ground that *Trimble* was wrongly decided. The four justices who had joined Justice Powell to form the *Trimble* majority dissented.

5. *An evaluation.* Consider the following evaluation: The problems in the cases summarized above stem from the Court's vacillation between review based on the appropriateness of the *rule* in question and review based on the appropriateness of the *result* reached under that rule. Thus, even if the rule in question provides an escape hatch through which nonmarital children can potentially qualify for benefits, there will still be some individual cases where a child, who obviously "deserves" the benefits, will be denied them through no fault of his own. In such individual cases, it will always be possible to say that the child is being penalized because of the marital status of his parents, and that this injustice is unnecessary to advance any legitimate state objective. Yet if the Court corrects each of these individual injustices, it obstructs formulation of any rule providing differential treatment for nonmarital children, thereby preventing the state from vindicating its interest in avoiding fraudulent paternity claims.

3. Wealth Classifications

Are the poor entitled to special judicial protection under the equal protection clause? In the late 1950s and 1960s, the Court repeatedly suggested that classifications based on indigency were suspect. See, e.g., Griffin v. Illinois, 351 U.S. 12 (1956) ("In criminal trials a State can no more discriminate on account of poverty than on account of religion, race, or color"); Harper v. Virginia Board of Elections, 383 U.S. 663 (1966) ("Lines drawn on the basis of wealth or property, like those of race, are traditionally disfavored"). More recently, however, the Court has shown increasing reluctance to strictly scrutinize state practices withholding benefits because of inability to pay for them. As the Court in Maher v. Roe, 432 U.S. 464 (1977), summarized the current state of the law in the context of state refusals to fund abortions for indigents:

> An indigent woman desiring an abortion does not come within the limited category of disadvantaged classes so recognized by our cases. Nor does the fact that the impact of the regulation falls upon those who cannot pay lead to a different conclusion. In a sense, every denial of welfare to an indigent creates a wealth classification as compared to nonindigents who are able to pay for the desired goods or services. But this Court has never held that financial need alone identifies a suspect class for purposes of equal protection analysis.

a. *Facial discrimination.* As early as 1941 the Court suggested that there were serious constitutional obstacles to laws that expressly discriminated against indigents. In Edwards v. California, 314 U.S. 160 (1941), the Court invalidated a California statute barring the bringing of indigents into the state. Although the Court relied solely on the commerce clause to invalidate the statute, it suggested in passing that it would not accept stereotypical judgments about the poor as justifications for laws disadvantaging them: "Whatever may have been the [previously prevailing] notion, we do not think that it will now be seriously contended that because a person is without employment and without funds he constitutes a 'moral pestilence.' Poverty and immorality are not synonymous." Justice Jackson's concurring opinion went farther. He urged the Court to "say now, and in no uncertain terms, that a man's mere property status, without more, cannot be used by a state to test, qualify, or limit his rights as a citizen of the United States. 'Indigence' in itself is neither a source of rights nor a basis for denying them. The mere state of being without funds is a neutral fact — constitutionally an irrelevance, like race, creed or color."

b. *Heightened scrutiny for "de facto" wealth classifications.* Statutes that facially discriminate against the poor, such as the one invalidated in *Edwards*, are relatively rare. Far more common are statutes that create de facto wealth classifications either by charging money for some governmental service or benefit (e.g., a poll tax or tuition charge at a state university) or by failing to subsidize some activity that can be engaged in only if one has the money to purchase it in private markets (e.g., the exclusion of abortions from Medicaid coverage). Note that Justice Jackson's insistence that wealth be treated as a "neutral fact" does little to assist the poor when they are denied benefits on this basis.

Beginning in the late 1950s, however, a series of decisions suggested that such de facto wealth classifications were constitutionally suspect. (This line of cases is discussed more fully in conjunction with the "implied fundamental rights" strand of equal protection, Chapter 6, section E, infra.) See, e.g., Griffin v. Illinois, 351 U.S. 12 (1956) (holding that the equal protection clause requires states to provide trial transcripts or their equivalent to indigents appealing their criminal convictions); Douglas v. California, 372 U.S. 353 (1963) (holding that states must provide indigents with counsel on a first appeal of right to challenge a criminal conviction); Harper v. Virginia Board of Elections, 383 U.S. 663 (1966) (holding a state law conditioning the vote on payment of a $1.50 poll tax denied equal protection); Cipriano v. City of Houma, 395 U.S. 701 (1969) (holding invalid a state statute restricting the franchise to property owners in a state election to approve issuance of revenue bonds by a municipal utility).

During the same period, the Court also hinted that strict judicial scrutiny might be appropriate when the state failed to provide the poor with "necessities." See, e.g., Shapiro v. Thompson, 394 U.S. 618 (1969) (classification "[denies] welfare aid upon which may depend the ability of the families to obtain the very means to subsist — food, shelter, and other necessities of life"); Goldberg v. Kelly, 397 U.S. 254 (1970) ("Welfare, by meeting the basic demands of subsistence, can help bring within the reach of the poor the same opportunities that are available to others to participate meaningfully in the life of the community. [Public] assistance, then, is not mere charity, but a means to 'promote the general Welfare, and secure the Blessings of Liberty to ourselves and our Posterity' ").

But although some of the Court's rhetoric was sweeping, its actual holdings were far narrower. Those wealth classifications that were invalidated were all associated with access to "fundamental" rights such as the franchise and the ability to challenge criminal convictions. No holding during this period established that it was unconstitutional as a general matter for the state to deny services or benefits to those who could not pay for them. Moreover, even with regard to fundamental rights, the Court never suggested that absolute equality was required so long as the poor were not denied minimal benefits. (E.g., although the poor were entitled to representation on a first appeal of right, the Court never suggested that they had a constitutional right to the best lawyer that money could buy.) Finally, despite some suggestive dicta, no holding during this period established that the state had an affirmative constitutional obligation to guarantee subsistence to those in need.

c. *The Court's retreat from heightened scrutiny.* More recently, the Court has veered sharply away from its earlier suggestions that wealth classifications should be strictly scrutinized. Although none of the earlier holdings has been overturned, the Court has, in general, been unwilling to extend these holdings. See, e.g., Ross v. Moffitt, 417 U.S. 600 (1974) (refusing to extend the *Douglas* principle to require counsel in discretionary appeals beyond a first appeal of right); United States v. Kras, 409 U.S. 434 (1973) (holding that there is no general equal protection principle barring the imposition of filing fees in ordinary civil litigation, even when they prevent the indigent from securing access to the courts).

At about the same time, the Court ended speculation that it might read the equal protection clause to impose an affirmative obligation on government to provide the poor with necessities. In Dandridge v. Williams, 397 U.S. 471 (1970), for example, the Court turned aside an equal protection challenge to Maryland's practice of imposing an upper limit on the size of grants under its Aid to Families with Dependent Children Program regardless of the size of the family. Writing for the majority, Justice Stewart analogized the case to other situations where the Court had utilized low level review.

> To be sure, the cases cited [have] in the main involved state regulation of business or industry. The administration of public welfare assistance, by contrast, involves the most basic economic needs of impoverished human beings. We recognize the dramatically real factual difference between the cited cases and this one, but we can find no basis for applying a different constitutional standard. [The] intractable economic, social and even philosophical problems presented by public welfare assistance programs are not the business of this Court. The Constitution may impose certain procedural safeguards upon systems of welfare administration. But the Constitution does not empower this Court to second guess state officials charged with the difficult responsibility of allocating limited public welfare funds among the myriad of potential recipients.

Similarly, in Lindsey v. Normet, 405 U.S. 56 (1972), the Court rejected a constitutional challenge to Oregon's summary eviction procedures. Writing for the Court, Justice White rejected appellants' argument that

> the "need for decent shelter" and the "right to retain peaceful possession of one's home" are fundamental interests which are particularly important to the poor and

which may be trenched upon only after the State demonstrates some superior interest. [The] Constitution does not provide judicial remedies for every social and economic ill. We are unable to perceive in that document any constitutional guarantee
of access to dwellings of a particular quality. [Absent] constitutional mandate, the
assurance of adequate housing and the definition of landlord-tenant relationships
are legislative, not judicial, functions.

The Court's most detailed treatment of a wealth discrimination claim during
this period came in San Antonio School District v. Rodriguez, 411 U.S. 1 (1973).
The decision grew out of a constitutional challenge to the manner in which
Texas, and many other states, financed public education. Much of the revenues
needed for public schools were raised locally by an ad valorem property tax on the
property located within each district. The result of this system was that children
located in districts with more valuable property benefited from higher expenditures than children in districts with less valuable property even though both
districts made the same tax effort. Appellees claimed that this method of financing education should be strictly scrutinized under the equal protection clause
because, inter alia, it discriminated against the poor. (Appellees also argued that it
impinged on their fundamental right to education. This aspect of the case is
discussed in greater detail in Chapter 6, section E5, infra.)
In a 5 to 4 decision, the Court rejected this claim and, applying low-level
scrutiny, upheld the system. In its discussion of the wealth discrimination claim,
the Court, in an opinion by Justice Powell, said that in prior cases

> The individuals, or groups of individuals, who constituted the class discriminated
> against [shared] two distinguishing characteristics; because of their impecunity they
> were completely unable to pay for some desired benefit, and as a consequence, they
> sustained an absolute deprivation of a meaningful opportunity to enjoy that benefit.
> [Even] a cursory examination, however, demonstrates that neither of the two distin-
> guishing characteristics of wealth classifications can be found here. First, in support
> of their charge that the system discriminates against the "poor," appellees have made
> no effort to demonstrate that it operates to the peculiar disadvantage of any class
> fairly definable as indigent. [There] is no basis on the record in this case for assuming
> that the poorest people — defined by reference to any level of absolute impecunity
> — are concentrated in the poorest districts.
>   Second, [lack] of personal resources has not occasioned an absolute deprivation of
> the desired benefit. [Apart] from the unsettled and disputed question whether the
> quality of education may be determined by the amount of money expended for it, a
> sufficient answer to appellees' argument is that, at least where wealth is involved, the
> Equal Protection Clause does not require absolute equality or precisely equal advan-
> tages.

d. *Continued protection for the poor?* The Court's retreat from strict scrutiny
for wealth classifications, like its initial endorsement of the concept, has been
ambiguous, however. For example, analysis in *Rodriguez* was complicated by the
fact that the statute disadvantaged poor *districts*, but not necessarily poor *people*.
A district with valuable commercial or industrial property (and, hence, a relatively large tax base) might also contain large numbers of poor people. It was
therefore far from clear that the method of school finance at issue worked to the
disadvantage of the poor.

In a few other areas, the Court has built on some of its earlier cases strictly scrutinizing laws disadvantaging the poor. With regard to the criminal process, for example, the Court has held that a criminal defendant cannot be imprisoned for a period beyond the statutory maximum for the offense for failure to pay a fine. See Williams v. Illinois, 399 U.S. 235 (1970); Tate v. Short, 401 U.S. 395 (1971). Similarly, the Court has extended the scope of the franchise cases to invalidate filing fee requirements for candidates that effectively excluded the poor. See Bullock v. Carter, 405 U.S. 134 (1972); Lubin v. Panish, 415 U.S. 709 (1974).

Finally, although the Court has shown increasing reluctance to treat the poor as a "suspect" class for equal protection purposes, it has sometimes reached the same result through other doctrinal routes. Recall, for example, U.S. Department of Agriculture v. Moreno, section B supra, where the Court utilized rational basis review to invalidate a law disqualifying from the federal food stamp program unrelated individuals who lived together. Similarly, some cases have extended rights to the poor through due process analysis. See, e.g., Ake v. Oklahoma, — U.S. — , 105 S. Ct. 1087 (1985) (due process requires the state to pay for psychiatric assistance for indigent defendant where there is preliminary showing that sanity is likely to be significant factor at trial); Evitts v. Lucey, — U.S. — , 105 S. Ct. 830 (1985) (holding that due process requires effective assistance of counsel on first appeal of right, and suggesting that *Griffin-Douglas* line of cases rests in part on due process principles); Little v. Streater, 452 U.S. 1 (1981) (due process requires state to pay for blood test of indigent defendant in paternity action); Boddie v. Connecticut, 401 U.S. 371 (1971) (holding unconstitutional on due process grounds the imposition of court fees preventing an indigent from securing a divorce).

Do these cases suggest that the Court in fact uses heightened scrutiny for classifications that deny "necessities" to the poor? Consider Michelman, Welfare Rights in a Constitutional Democracy, 1979 Wash U. L.Q. 659, 664: "These cases could be cited in support of welfare rights should the Court eventually come to see them as a correct conclusion from accepted forms of legal argument. [The] cases alone do not establish the welfare-rights thesis, but they do go far to answer [two] objections against it — that it is purely fanciful and that it thrusts inappropriate tasks on the courts."

Note: Wealth Discrimination and the Problem of Affirmative Rights

1. *Facial discrimination.* Should laws that expressly classify on the basis of wealth be strictly scrutinized? In many respects, the poor would seem to be a prime example of a discrete and insular minority. Consider Michelman, Forward: On Protecting the Poor through the Fourteenth Amendment, 83 Harv. L. Rev. 7, 21 (1969):

> If money is power, then a class deliberately defined so as to include everyone who has less wealth or income than any person outside it may certainly be deemed, as racial minorities are by many observers deemed, to be especially susceptible to abuse by majoritarian process; and classifications of "the poor" as such may, like classifica-

tion of racial minorities as such, be popularly understood as a badge of inferiority. Especially is this so in light of the extreme difficulty of imagining proper governmental objectives which require for their achievement the explicit carving out, for relatively disadvantageous treatment, of a class defined by relative paucity of wealth or income.

But compare Bork, The Impossibility of Finding Welfare Rights in the Constitution, 1979 Wash. U. L.Q. 695, 701:

> The premise that the poor [are] underrepresented politically is quite dubious. In the past two decades we have witnessed an explosion of welfare legislation, massive income redistributions, and civil rights laws of all kinds. The poor and the minorities have had access to the political process and have done very well through it. In addition to its other defects, then, the welfare-rights theory rests less on demonstrated fact than on a liberal shibboleth.

If "the poor" are a suspect class, how should the class be defined? The concept of "poverty," unlike gender, alienage, and illegitimacy, is inherently relative and is usually associated with particular goods to which the "poor" are denied access. Cases such as *Griffin* and *Douglas* seem to define the class with reference to these goods. Does this approach make sense? Doesn't defining the class in this fashion amount to saying that there is a constitutional right to the good in question? For example, if a government hospital charges for the full cost of a kidney dialysis machine and a "middle-class" person is unable to pay the cost, does the hospital's policy discriminate against the poor? Alternatively, suppose a "poor" person were able to pay the $1.50 poll tax at issue in *Harper*. Would such a person therefore not be "poor" for equal protection purposes? (Note that in *Harper*, unlike *Griffin* and *Douglas*, the Court invalidated the tax even as applied to those who could afford to pay it. Under what theory does it violate the equality principle to require a rich person to pay $1.50 before voting?)

If the class is defined with reference to the good in question, what should be done about the individual who can barely afford the good but will be left with less money after purchasing it than the "poor" person who is not charged for it? Consider in this connection Fuller v. Oregon, 417 U.S. 40 (1974), in which the Court sustained an Oregon statute requiring convicted defendants who escaped indigency to repay the state for the cost of their defense:

> The fact that an indigent who accepts state-appointed legal representation knows that he might someday be required to repay the costs of these services in no way affects his eligibility to obtain counsel. [We] live in a society where the distribution of legal assistance, like the distribution of all goods and services, is generally regulated by the dynamics of private enterprise. A defendant in a criminal case who is just above the line separating the indigent from the nonindigent must borrow money, sell off his meager assets, or call upon his family or friends in order to hire a lawyer. We cannot say that the Constitution requires that those only slightly poorer must remain forever immune from any obligation to shoulder the expenses of their legal defense, even when they are able to pay without hardship.

But see James v. Strange, 407 U.S. 128 (1972) (recoupment provision violates equal protection when none of exemptions provided generally for other judgment debtors available to indigent defendants); Rinaldi v. Yeager, 384 U.S. 305 (1966) (recoupment provision violates equal protection when limited to defendants confined to state institutions).

2. *"De facto" wealth classifications and the* Washington v. Davis *problem.* It would be possible, of course, to define the protected class in terms of some absolute level of destitution rather than with reference to the particular good at issue. But if the class is defined in this fashion, do laws that require payment of the price for goods like counsel or a transcript in a criminal case discriminate facially against the poor? Can *Griffin* and *Douglas* be reconciled with the Court's refusal in Washington v. Davis to scrutinize statutes strictly because of the disproportionate impact they have on a suspect group? Consider J. Ely, Democracy and Distrust 162 (1980):

[Laws] that actually classify on the basis of wealth, drawing on some comparative generalization about the relative characteristics of the poor on the one hand and those who more nearly resemble the legislators on the other, are extremely rare. [What] typically disadvantage the poor are various failures on the part of the government (or anybody else) to alleviate their poverty by providing one or another good or service. [These failures], insensitive as they may often seem to some of us, do not generally result from a sadistic desire to keep the miserable in their state of misery, or a stereotypical generalization about their characteristics, but rather from a reluctance to raise the taxes needed to support such expenditures.

Does the advent of the Washington v. Davis doctrine explain the Court's recent reluctance to expand the *Griffin-Douglas* line of cases? Would the Court continue to strictly scrutinize laws that facially exclude the poor from benefits rather than merely charging a price for them? Consider James v. Valtierra, 402 U.S. 137 (1971). An amendment to the state's constitution provided that no low-rent housing project should be developed, constructed, or acquired in any manner by a state public body until the project was approved by a majority of those voting at a community election. Plaintiffs argued that this amendment violated the equal protection clause because other public programs were not subject to the mandatory referendum provision. They relied on Hunter v. Erickson, section C3 supra, where the Court invalidated a city charter provision requiring referendum approval for statutes prohibiting racial discrimination in housing. In rejecting plaintiffs' argument and upholding the statute, the Court distinguished *Hunter:*

Unlike the [*Hunter*] referendum provision, it cannot be said that California's Article XXXIV rests on "distinctions based on race." The Article requires referendum approval for any low-rent public housing project, not only for projects which will be occupied by a racial minority. [Plaintiffs] suggest that the mandatory nature of the Article XXXIV referendum constitutes unconstitutional discrimination because it hampers persons desiring public housing from achieving their objective when no such roadblock faces other groups seeking to influence other public decisions to their advantage. But of course a lawmaking procedure that "disadvantages" a particular group does not always deny equal protection. Under any such holding, presumably a State would not be able to require referendums on any subject unless referendums were required on all, because they would always disadvantage some group.

Assuming that de jure, as opposed to de facto, wealth classifications should be treated as suspect, was *James* correctly decided?

3. *"De facto" wealth discrimination and the efficient allocation of scarce resources.* Even if charging a price for a government service in some sense discriminates against the poor, might not the differential treatment be justified by the state's desire to allocate scarce resources in an efficient manner? Consider, for example, Michelman, Forward: On Protecting the Poor through the Fourteenth Amendment, supra, at 27-28:

> Unlike a de facto racial classification which usually must seek its justifications in purposes completely distinct from its race-related impacts, a de facto pecuniary classification typically carries a highly persuasive justification inseparable from the very effect which excites antipathy — i.e., the hard choices it forces upon the financially straitened. [A] de facto pecuniary classification [is] usually nothing more or less than the making of a market (e.g., in trial transcripts) or the failure to relieve someone of the vicissitudes of market pricing (e.g., for appellate legal services). But the risk of exposure to markets and their "decisions" is not normally deemed objectionable, to say the least, on our society. Not only do we not inveigh generally against unequal distribution of income or full-cost pricing for most goods. We usually regard it as both the fairest and most efficient arrangement to require each consumer to pay the full market price of what he consumes, limiting his consumption to what his income permits.

Is this argument persuasive when the government charges for "public goods" where the consumption of the goods by some does not interfere with their consumption by others? Is it constitutional, for example, for the government to charge an admission fee to cover the cost of running a municipal swimming pool when the cost remains constant regardless of the number of users?

Is the argument persuasive when the government charges for goods in circumstances where the demand declines relatively little even when the price rises? For example, could a government hospital refuse to perform life-saving surgery on a person too poor to pay the cost?

Is it constitutional for the state to substitute government regulation for the constraint normally exercised by the market when providing benefits to poor people? Would it be constitutional, for example, to provide appellate counsel for the poor only in cases where a preliminary review of the record demonstrated that there were nonfrivolous issues to be raised on appeal? Consider Draper v. Washington, 372 U.S. 487 (1963):

> The State [argues] that in practical effect there is no difference at all between the rights it affords indigents and nonindigents, because a moneyed defendant, motivated by a "sense of thrift," will choose not to appeal in exactly the same circumstances that an indigent will be denied a transcript. We reject this contention as untenable. It defies common sense to think that a moneyed defendant faced with long-term imprisonment and advised by counsel that he has substantial grounds for appeal, as petitioners were here, will choose not to appeal merely to save the cost of a transcript.

But see Anders v. California, 386 U.S. 738 (1967):

> If [appellate] counsel finds his case to be wholly frivolous, after a conscientious examination of it, he should so advise the court and request permission to withdraw. That request must, however, be accompanied by a brief referring to anything in the

record that might arguably support the appeal. A copy of counsel's brief should be furnished the indigent and time allowed him to raise any points that he chooses; the court — not counsel — then proceeds, after a full examination of all the proceedings, to decide whether the case is wholly frivolous.

Might the allocative distortions produced by government subsidization of particular goods be avoided if the Constitution were read to provide the poor with a minimum income, to be spent as they saw fit? Is the desire to maintain the incentive to work a sufficiently weighty state interest to justify the failure to enact such a program? Could the courts articulate and enforce a constitutional right to basic subsistence while staying within the bounds of their appropriate role?

Consider Bork, The Impossibility of Finding Welfare Rights in the Constitution, supra, at 699:

> The effort to apply [the representation reinforcement value to create a right to welfare] would completely transform the nature and role of courts. [Advocates of the right] apparently [conclude] that a claimant cannot go into a court and demand a welfare program as a constitutional right, but if a welfare program already exists, he can demand that it be broadened. The right to broadening rests upon the premise that there is a basic right to the program. If so, why cannot the Court order a program to start up from scratch?

But compare L. Tribe, American Constitutional Law 920-921 (1978):

> If the state and federal governments were to wash their hands altogether of the sick, hungry, and poor, none of the interstitial doctrines sketched here could provide a remedy. But that is simply a reminder of the basic point suggested as long ago as 1827 by Chief Justice Marshall [dissenting in Ogden v. Saunders] — that a government which wholly failed to discharge its duty to protect its citizens would be answerable primarily in the streets and at the polling booth, and only secondarily if at all in the courts. To say this is not to deny that government has affirmative duties to its citizens arising out of the basic necessities of bodily survival, but only to deny that all such duties are perfectly enforceable in the courts of law.

4. *The Constitution and affirmative rights.* Are the wealth cases explicable in terms of a more general principle of constitutional construction under which the Constitution is seen primarily as a limitation on governmental power and not as an affirmative guarantee against conditions for which government is not responsible? Consider, for example Justice Harlan's dissenting opinions in *Griffin* and *Douglas*, the cases establishing the equal protection right of the poor to a counsel and a trial transcript in order to pursue an appeal of right in a criminal case. In *Griffin* Harlan wrote that "All that Illinois has done is to fail to alleviate the consequences of differences in economic circumstances that exist wholly apart from any state action. [The] issue here is not the typical equal protection question of the reasonableness of a 'classification' on the basis of which the State has imposed legal disabilities, but rather the reasonableness of the State's failure to remove natural disabilities." In *Douglas*, he added that

> every financial exaction which the State imposes on a uniform basis is more easily satisfied by the well-to-do than by the indigent. Yet I take it that no one would dispute the constitutional power of the State to levy a uniform sales tax, to charge

tuition at a state university, to fix rates for the purchase of water from a municipal corporation, to impose a standard fine for criminal violations, or to establish minimum bail for various categories of offenses. Laws such as these do not deny equal protection to the less fortunate for one essential reason: the Equal Protection Clause does not impose on the States "an affirmative duty to lift the handicaps flowing from differences in economic circumstances" [quoting from his *Griffin* dissent]. To so construe it would be to read into the Constitution a philosophy of leveling that would be foreign to many of our basic concepts of the proper relations between government and society.

Note the affinity between this argument and the Washington v. Davis principle. One way to state that principle is that the equal protection clause does not impose on the states an affirmative obligation to compensate for unequal outcomes produced by a facially neutral governmental policy. The argument is also closely related to the "state action" doctrine. Under that doctrine, the Constitution in general protects individuals from state invasions of their rights and does not confer a right to affirmative governmental intervention to remedy privately imposed deprivations. (The state action doctrine is discussed in greater detail in Chapter 10, infra.) Finally, the argument is related to the more general orientation toward the equal protection clause pursuant to which different treatment of individuals similarly situated is viewed as more problematical than similar treatment of individuals differently situated.

Is Justice Harlan's argument persuasive? In what sense are the disabilities under which the poor labor "natural"? Why is the state not responsible for them? Consider Tribe, supra, at 919:

> [The] demise of the *Lochner* era [during which the Supreme Court read the due process clause to protect liberty of contract and thereby invalidated much social legislation] reflected the view that [the] system of governmental decisions — some statutory and some made by common-law judges — bore an active responsibility for the plight of those who could not earn a decent living. [It] should be stressed that this perspective does *not* entail a judicially cognizable remedy against government for every instance of substandard wages or unmet needs. [But] at least sometimes, the person who is forced to work too hard for too little, or can find no work at all, must be regarded as the victim of the system of contract and property rights rather than the author of his own plight.

Is it sensible to suppose that a court could ever ascertain the extent to which the condition of the poor is the product of government action? Even if it were possible to do so in principle, why should the answer to this question matter? Why is the equality principle satisfied by government inaction that leaves the disadvantaged at the mercy of private forces?

In connection with these issues, consider Harris v. McRae, 448 U.S. 297 (1980), wherein the Court upheld the constitutionality of the so-called Hyde Amendment prohibiting virtually all federal funding for abortions under the Medicaid program. The Court acknowledged that the Constitution protected a woman's freedom of choice regarding abortions. But in its view,

> it simply [did] not follow that a woman's freedom of choice carries with it a constitutional entitlement to financial resources to avail herself of the full range of protected

choices. [Although] government may not place obstacles in the path of a woman's exercise of her freedom of choice, it need not remove those not of its own creation. Indigency falls in the latter category. [Although] Congress has opted to subsidize medically necessary services generally, but not certain medically necessary abortions, the fact remains that the Hyde Amendment leaves an indigent woman with at least the same range of choice in deciding whether to obtain a medically necessary abortion as she would have had if Congress had chosen to subsidize no health care costs at all.

In a footnote, the Court rejected the argument that the Hyde Amendment unconstitutionally "penalized" a woman's choice to abort the fetus because funding was available for live births. It noted, however, that

A substantial constitutional question would arise if Congress had attempted to withhold all Medicaid benefits from an otherwise eligible candidate simply because that candidate had exercised her constitutionally protected freedom to terminate her pregnancy by abortion. [But] the Hyde Amendment [does] not provide for such a broad disqualification from receipt of public benefits. Rather, the Hyde Amendment [represents] simply a refusal to subsidize certain protected conduct. A refusal to fund protected activity, without more, cannot be equated with the imposition of a "penalty" on that activity.

Is the Court's distinction between penalization and refusal to subsidize convincing? If one begins with the premise that it is important for women to have the abortion option, is there a sensible theory under which it is possible to distinguish between interference with that option by state action and interference by private action which the state fails to prevent? *Harris* is examined further in Chapter 6, section F2.

4.   Other Disadvantaged Groups

Are there other "discrete and insular minorities" entitled to special judicial protection from the political process?

CITY OF CLEBURNE v. CLEBURNE LIVING CENTER, — U.S. —, 105 S. Ct. 3249 (1985): This case concerned an equal protection challenge to a zoning ordinance that prevented construction of a group home for the mentally retarded in a residential neighborhood. Although it affirmed the decision below insofar as it invalidated the ordinance as applied, the Supreme Court held that the lower court had erred in utilizing heightened scrutiny. The Court, in an opinion by Justice White, advanced several reasons for rejecting heightened scrutiny:

"First, it is undeniable [that] those who are mentally retarded have a reduced ability to cope with and function in the everyday world. [They] are thus different, immutably so, in relevant respects, and the states' interest in dealing with and providing for them is plainly a legitimate one. How this large and diversified group is to be treated under the law is a difficult and often technical matter, very much a task for legislators guided by qualified professionals and not by the perhaps ill-informed opinions of the judiciary.

"Second, the distinctive legislative response, both national and state, to the plight of those who are mentally retarded demonstrates not only that they have unique problems, but also that the lawmakers have been addressing their difficulties in a manner that belies a continuing antipathy or prejudice and a corresponding need for more intrusive oversight by the judiciary. Thus, the federal government has not only outlawed discrimination against the mentally retarded in federally funded programs, but it has also provided the retarded with the right to receive 'appropriate treatment services and habilitation' in a setting that is 'least restrictive of [their] personal liberty.' . . .

"Such legislation thus singling out the retarded for special treatment reflects the real and undeniable differences between the retarded and others. That a civilized and decent society expects and approves such legislation indicates that governmental consideration of those differences in the vast majority of situations is not only legitimate but desirable. [Even] assuming that many of these laws could be shown to be substantially related to an important governmental purpose, merely requiring the legislature to justify its efforts in these terms may lead it to refrain from acting at all. [Especially] given the wide variation in the abilities and needs of the retarded themselves, governmental bodies must have a certain amount of flexibility and freedom from judicial oversight in shaping and limiting their remedial efforts.

"Third, the legislative response, which could hardly have occurred and survived without public support, negates any claim that the mentally retarded are politically powerless in the sense that they have no ability to attract the attention of lawmakers. . . .

"Fourth, if the large and amorphous class of the mentally retarded were deemed quasi-suspect [it] would be difficult to find a principled way to distinguish a variety of other groups who have perhaps immutable disabilities setting them off from others, who cannot themselves mandate the desired legislative responses, and who can claim some degree of prejudice from at least part of the public at large. One need mention in this respect only the aging, the disabled, the mentally ill, and the infirm. We are reluctant to set out on that course, and we decline to do so.

"Doubtless, there have been and there will continue to be instances of discrimination against the retarded that are in fact [invidious]. But the appropriate method of reaching such instances is not to create a new quasi-suspect classification and subject all governmental action based on that classification to more searching evaluation."

The Court thereupon held that the refusal to permit construction of the home could not survive low-level review and was therefore unconstitutional. This portion of the Court's opinion is examined at section B supra. Justice Marshall, joined by Justices Brennan and Blackmun, wrote an opinion concurring in the judgment in part and dissenting in part:

"[The] mentally retarded have been subject to a 'lengthy and tragic history' of segregation and discrimination that can only be called grotesque. [By] the latter part of the [nineteenth] century and during the first decades of the new one, [social] views of the retarded underwent a radical transformation. Fueled by the rising tide of Social Darwinism, the 'science' of eugenics, and the extreme xenophobia of those years, leading medical authorities and others began to portray the 'feebleminded' as a 'menace to society and civilization [responsible] in a large degree for many, if not all, our social problems.' A regime of state-mandated segregation and degradation soon emerged that in its virulence and bigotry rivaled, and indeed paralleled, the worst excesses of Jim Crow. . . .

"Prejudice, once let loose, is not easily cabined. As of 1979, most states still categorically disqualified 'idiots' from voting, without regard to individual capacity and with discretion to exclude left in the hands of low-level officials. Not until Congress enacted the Education of the Handicapped Act were 'the door[s] of public education' opened wide to handicapped children. But most important, lengthy and continuing isolation of the retarded has perpetuated the ignorance, irrational fears, and stereotyping that long have plagued them.

"In light of the importance of the interest at stake and the history of discrimination the retarded have suffered, the Equal Protection Clause requires us to do more than review the distinctions drawn by Cleburne's zoning ordinance as if they appeared in a taxing statute or in economic or commercial legislation. The searching scrutiny I would give to restrictions on the ability of the retarded to establish community group homes leads me to conclude that Cleburne's vague generalizations for classifying the 'feeble minded' with drug addicts, alcoholics, and the insane, and excluding them where the elderly, the ill, the boarder, and the transient are allowed, are not substantial or important enough to overcome the suspicion that the ordinance rests on impermissible assumptions or outmoded and perhaps invidious stereotypes."

Justice Stevens, joined by Chief Justice Burger, also wrote a concurring opinion.

Note: Evaluating the Claims of Other Disadvantaged Groups

1. *The mentally retarded as a suspect class.* Does the *Cleburne* Court adequately explain why classifications disadvantaging the mentally retarded need only survive low-level review? Why is the judiciary less equipped to deal with "technical" questions concerning the mentally retarded than with the problems of gender and race? Do you think that federal judges are likely to be more poorly informed about these questions than the Cleburne City Council? Why does legislative protection for the mentally retarded, but not for blacks and women, argue against heightened review? Are the problems of affirmative action and the need for flexibility really more compelling in this context? Even if "the real and undeniable differences between the retarded and others" makes strict scrutiny inappropriate, why didn't the Court opt for intermediate review?

2. *Other potentially suspect classifications.* In light of *Cleburne*, are there any other groups that can plausibly claim suspect status? In Massachusetts Board of Retirement v. Murgia, 427 U.S. 307 (1976), the Court rejected the argument that the aged were entitled to special judicial solicitude:

> While the treatment of the aged in this Nation has not been wholly free of discrimination, such persons, unlike, say, those who have been discriminated against on the basis of race or national origin, have not experienced a "history of purposeful unequal treatment" or been subjected to unique disabilities on the basis of stereotyped characteristics not truly indicative of their abilities. [Old] age does not define a

"discrete and insular" group in need of "extraordinary protection from the majoritarian political process." Instead, it marks a stage that each of us will reach if we live out our normal span.

See also Vance v. Bradley, 440 U.S. 93 (1979) (utilizing rational basis review to uphold federal law requiring Foreign Service personnel to retire at age sixty). Cf. Schweiker v. Wilson, 450 U.S. 221 (1981) (avoiding the question whether mentally ill are a discrete and insular minority).

Are statutes disadvantaging homosexuals suspect? Consider J. Ely, Democracy and Distrust 162-163 (1980): "Homosexuals for years have been the victims of [prejudice]. Our stereotypes — whether to the effect that male homosexuals are effeminate, females "butch"; that they are untrustworthy, unusually menacing to children, or whatever — are likely to remain fixed given our obliviousness to the fact that the people around us may well be counterexamples."

But compare L. Tribe, Constitutional Choices 16-17 (1985):

Coming out of the closet could dispel ignorance, but it may not alter belief. Legislators may see homosexuals as "different" not out of ignorance, but on principle — on the basis of a morality that treats certain sexual practices as repugnant to a particular view of humanity, and, thus, regards people who engage in those practices as "other." [Process] and prejudice thus seem profoundly beside the point. Any constitutional distinction between laws burdening homosexuals and laws burdening exhibitionists [must] depend on a substantive theory of which groups are exercising fundamental rights and which are not.

Consider whether statutes disadvantaging any of the following groups should be strictly scrutinized: ethnic minorities; children; families with children; families without children; future generations; the physically disabled; the ugly or obese; residents of the District of Columbia; incarcerated individuals.

Do the Court's decisions provide reasonably clear standards under which the claims of these groups can be evaluated? Some of the Court's decisions indicate that heightened scrutiny is applied when there is a likelihood of impermissible motivation. But what is the motivation made impermissible by the equal protection clause? Can one distinguish between hostility or prejudice and good faith moral beliefs? Is the notion that legislation must be based on "reasoned analysis" and reflect something other than power subject to judicial enforcement? Do you agree with Justice Rehnquist that "It would hardly take extraordinary ingenuity for a lawyer to find 'insular and discrete' minorities at every turn of the road"? Sugarman v. Dougall, supra (dissenting opinion).

Or do you think, alternatively, that the decisions are flawed because they assume that, in general, the political system operates fairly? Has the Court not gone far enough to correct pervasive malfunctioning? Consider Parker, The Past of Constitutional Theory — and Its Future, 42 Ohio St. L.J. 223, 253 (1981):

[The] central problem is not *whether* a majority of citizens (actually) rules, but *that* a majority of citizens (supposedly) rules. Thus, the primary worry of [political process] theorists — the concern around which their theory pivots — is that "majorities" may disregard or undervalue the interests of "minorities." If they even acknowledge the opposite concern — that powerful minorities can get the state to act in ways that disregard or undervalue interests of nonmobilized majorities and that, in any event, legislative majorities often fail to champion the interests of passive popular majorities — they tend abruptly to dismiss it.

3. *The relevance of suspectness.* In *Cleburne* the Court insisted that it was not subjecting the statute to heightened scrutiny. Nonetheless, it looked closely enough at the purported justifications for the law to invalidate it. In this respect, the decision is reminiscent of the early gender discrimination cases in which the Court struck down a number of statutes disadvantaging women while insisting that it was engaged in low-level review. Only in retrospect did the Court acknowledge that these cases in fact involved heightened scrutiny. See section D2 supra.

On the other hand, the Court has upheld a number of gender-based statutes, racial affirmative action measures, and laws disadvantaging nonmarital children and aliens despite the supposedly heightened review to which these laws were subjected. These cases raise questions concerning the significance of the Court's categorization of levels of review. Is the Court really following a two-step process pursuant to which it first decides how closely to scrutinize a classification and then applies that level of scrutiny? Is it possible (desirable) to insulate the two steps of this process from each other? Might the Court's decisions more accurately be described as a series of ad hoc, intuitive judgments concerning the appropriateness of various classifications?

Is the effort to single out particular groups entitled to special judicial protection from majoritarian processes a useful way to think about constitutional law? Is there a better alternative?

VI

Implied Fundamental Rights

A. INTRODUCTION

The Constitution expressly guarantees a number of individual rights. The first amendment guarantees freedom of speech, press, and religion; the fourth amendment guarantees freedom from unreasonable searches and seizures; the fifth amendment guarantees freedom from compelled self-incrimination; the equal protection clause guarantees freedom from racial discrimination; and so on. This chapter examines whether, in reviewing laws for constitutionality, courts must confine themselves to interpreting rights that are expressly guaranteed by the Constitution or whether they may also enforce general principles of liberty and justice when the normative content of those principles is not embodied in the express provisions of the Constitution.

The debate over implied fundamental rights goes back to the very beginning of constitutional interpretation. Recall Calder v. Bull, 3 U.S. (3 Dall.) 386 (1798), supra Chapter 1, section C. Who has the better of the argument in *Calder*? What problems do you foresee in Chase's position? In Iredell's? How would you strengthen their arguments?

Note: Theories of Constitutional Construction — "Interpretivism" and "Noninterpretivism"

1. *The terms of the debate.* Interpretivism, represented by Iredell, embodies the view "that judges deciding constitutional issues should confine themselves to enforcing norms that are stated or clearly implicit in the written Constitution." Noninterpretivism, represented by Chase, reflects the view "that courts should go beyond that set of references and enforce norms that cannot be discovered within the four corners of the document." J. Ely, Democracy and Distrust 1 (1980).

Note, however, that the terms "interpretivism" and "noninterpretivism" have been quite controversial. Almost all commentators believe that the text of the

Constitution is binding. The real point of disagreement is whether the intent of the framers is binding and, if so, how that intent should be understood. "Noninterpretivists" believe that they are "interpreting" the Constitution, even if they disregard the framers' specific intent. Consider, for example, Dworkin, The Forum of Principle, 56 N.Y.U. L. Rev. 469, 472 (1981):

> Any recognizable theory of judicial review is interpretive in the sense that it aims to provide an interpretation of the Constitution as an original, foundational legal document, and also aims to integrate the Constitution into our constitutional and legal practice as a whole. No one presupposes judicial review as if on a clean slate. Each theory claims to provide the most illuminating account of what our actual constitutional tradition [really] comes to — of the "point" or "best justification" of the constitutional system that has in fact been developed in our own legal history. So the thesis that a useful distinction can be made between theories that insist on and those that reject interpretation [is] more confusing than helpful.

2. *The nature and stakes of the debate.* Whether extratextual norms are constitutionally enforceable is a question of considerable importance. There is doubt, for example, whether the "intent of the framers," at least if narrowly construed, supports the Supreme Court's decisions outlawing racial segregation, invalidating laws prohibiting abortion, recognizing a constitutional right of privacy, affording women protection against discrimination, and applying the bill of rights to the states. There are two strands in the argument against noninterpretivism. First, it is argued that noninterpretivism is objectionable because the intent of the framers controls, and the framers did not intend to permit courts to invalidate legislation for reasons other than those set out by the framers. This is the argument from contract. Second, it is argued that noninterpretivism is objectionable because it accords too much power to unelected judges. This assumes that in the U.S. system basic decisions are made by those subject to the constraints of the electoral process. If judges invalidate laws because of extratextual norms, they are acting in a way inconsistent with the basic premise of democracy. This is the argument from democracy. It is useful to keep in mind the distinction between these two arguments. In considering the various arguments below, and the possible sources of constitutional decisionmaking, it is useful also to consider whether those arguments and sources provide justifications or critiques of the Court's decisions on such issues as segregation, abortion, privacy, gender discrimination, and incorporation.

3. *An argument for interpretivism.* Consider Bork, Neutral Principles and Some First Amendment Problems, 47 Ind. L.J. 1, 2-3, 8 (1971):

> A Madisonian system is not completely democratic, if by "democratic" we mean completely majoritarian. It assumes that in wide areas of life majorities are entitled to rule for no better reason than that they are majorities. [The system] has also a countermajoritarian premise, however, for it assumes there are some areas of life that a majority should not control. There are some things a majority should not do to us no matter how democratically it decides to do them. [Some] see the model as containing an inherent, perhaps an insoluble, dilemma. [This] dilemma is resolved [by] the Supreme Court's power to define both majority and minority freedom through the interpretation of the Constitution. Society consents to be ruled un-

democratically within defined areas by certain enduring principles believed to be stated in, and placed beyond the reach of majorities by, the Constitution.

But this resolution of the dilemma imposes severe requirements upon the Court. For it follows that the Court's power is legitimate only if it has [a] valid theory, derived from the Constitution, of the respective spheres of majority and minority freedom. If it does not have such a theory but merely imposes its own value choices [the] Court violates the postulates of the Madisonian model that alone justifies its power. [On this view,] the choice of "fundamental values" by the Court cannot be justified, [for where] constitutional materials do not clearly specify the value to be preferred, there is no principled way to prefer any claimed human value to any other.

Consider the discussion of Madison in Chapter 1, supra. Does Bork accurately capture the Madisonian understanding? See also Monaghan, Our Perfect Constitution, 56 N.Y.U. L. Rev. 353 (1981); Rehnquist, The Notion of a Living Constitution, 54 Tex. L. Rev. 693 (1976).

4. *Arguments against interpretivism.* a. "[The interpretivists] suppose that the intention of the Framers [is] some complex psychological fact locked in history waiting to be winkled out from old pamphlets and letters and proceedings. But this is a serious common mistake, because there is no such thing as the intention of the Framers waiting to be [discovered]. There is only some such thing waiting to be invented." Dworkin, supra, at 477. Consider the following problems: (1) Who counts? Do we consider only the intentions of those who drafted the provision? Of those who voted for it in Congress? Those who voted against it? Those who voted in the ratification process? (2) What is the relevant psychological state? Are we interested in what a legislator expected the provision to do? What he feared it would do? What he hoped it would do? (3) What combination of individual intentions is controlling? Must we find that a majority of the relevant persons held the same "intent"? (4) Are we interested in abstract or concrete intentions? Are we interested, for example, in the framers' view of equality generally or in their view of racial segregation in the schools? Do we care how they would have liked us to resolve the conflict? See Dworkin, supra, at 476-500; Powell, The Original Understanding of Original Intent, 98 Harv. L. Rev. 885 (1985); Bennett, Objectivity in Constitutional Law, 132 U. Pa. L. Rev. 445 (1984); Brest, The Misconceived Quest for the Original Understanding, 60 B.U. L. Rev. 204 (1980).

b. Tushnet, Following the Rules Laid Down: A Critique of Interpretivism and Neutral Principles, 96 Harv. L. Rev. 781, 784-785, 800, 802 (1983):

Interpretivism [is] designed to remedy a central problem of liberal theory by constraining the judiciary sufficiently to prevent judicial tyranny. [It] attempts to implement the rule of law by assuming that the meanings of words and rules are stable over extended [periods]. But [in] imaginatively entering the world of the past, we not only reconstruct it, [we] also creatively construct it. For such creativity is the only way to bridge the gaps between that world and ours. The past, particularly the aspects that the interpretivists care about, is in its essence indeterminate; the interpretivist project cannot be carried to its conclusion. [The] hermeneutic tradition tells us that we cannot understand the acts of those in the past without entering into their mental world. [The] imagination that we have used to adjust and readjust our understandings makes it impossible to claim that any one reconstruction is uniquely correct. The past shapes the materials on which we use our imaginations; our interests, concerns, and preconceptions shape our imaginations themselves.

5. *Arguments for noninterpretivism.* Even if the attacks on interpretivism are persuasive, the arguments from contract and democracy still have to be met. To meet those arguments, one must identify and explain the appropriate sources of constitutional decisions if the intent of the framers is abandoned. Consider the following possibilities:

a. *Natural law.* Grey, Do We Have an UnWritten Constitution?, 27 Stan. L. Rev. 703, 715-716 (1975):

> For the generation that framed the Constitution, the concept of a "higher law," protecting "natural rights," and taking precedence over ordinary positive law as a matter of political obligation, was widely shared and deeply felt. An essential element of American constitutionalism was the reduction to written form — and hence to positive law — of some of the principles of natural rights. But at the same time, it was generally recognized that written constitutions could not completely codify the higher law. Thus in the framing of the original American constitutions it was widely accepted that there remained unwritten but still binding principles of higher law. [And as] it came to be accepted that the judiciary had the power to enforce the commands of the written Constitution when these conflicted with ordinary law, it was also widely assumed that judges would enforce as constitutional restraints the unwritten natural rights as well.

See also Grey, Origins of the UnWritten Constitution: Fundamental Law in American Revolutionary Thought, 30 Stan. L. Rev. 843 (1978); Corwin, The "Higher Law" Background of American Constitutional Law, 42 Harv. L. Rev. 149, 365 (1928-1929). Is this an interpretivist or noninterpretivist theory?

b. *Moral philosophy.* A. Bickel, The Least Dangerous Branch 24-26 (1962):

> [Government] should serve not only what we conceive from time to time to be our immediate material needs but also certain enduring values. [But] such values do not present themselves ready-made. They [must] be continually derived, enunciated, and seen in relevant application. [Courts] have certain capacities for dealing with matters of principle that legislatures and executives do not possess. Judges have, or should have, the leisure, the training, and the insulation to follow the ways of the scholar in pursuing the ends of government. This is crucial in sorting out the enduring values of a society.

See also M. Perry, The Constitution, the Courts, and Human Rights 101-102 (1982):

> Noninterpretative review [serves] an important, even indispensable, function. It [enables] us, as a people, to keep faith with [our commitment] to struggle incessantly to see beyond, and then to live beyond, the imperfections of [our] established moral conventions. [It] enables us to take seriously [the] possibility that there are right answers to political-moral problems.

And see Perry, The Authority of Text, Tradition, and Reason: A Theory of Constitutional "Interpretation," 58 S. Cal. L. Rev. 551, 593-594 (1985), quoting MacIntyre, Moral Arguments and Social Contexts, 80 J. Phil. 590, 591 (1983):

> Those of us who see constitutional questions [as] questions [of] political morality [must] address the problem of moral knowledge: Is there moral knowledge? Of what does it consist? How is it achieved? [It has been] suggested that moral reasoning [can]

operate only within the context [of] "a tradition-bearing community [with] shared beliefs about goods and shared dispositions educated in accordance with those [beliefs]." [To] understand precisely how *both* tradition and reason [are] authoritative for constitutional decisionmaking, and also why they should be authoritative, [we] must understand better than we do the nature [of] practical reasoning and, especially, the ways in which we use the past to transcend the past.

c. *Tradition*. Sandalow, Constitutional Interpretation, 79 Mich. L. Rev. 1033, 1036, 1068-1069, 1071 (1971):

[There is a] need to accommodate the Constitution to changing circumstances and values. [Constitutional] law thus emerges not as exegesis, but as a process by which each generation gives formal expression to the values it holds [fundamental]. Judges [who] wish to appeal to the Constitution must demonstrate that the principles upon which they propose to confer constitutional status express values that [are] rooted in history. [The] relevant past for purposes of constitutional law, thus, is to be found not only in the intentions of those who drafted and ratified the document but in the entirety of our history.

d. *Consensus*. Wellington, Common Law Rules and Constitutional Double Standards: Some Notes on Adjudication, 83 Yale L.J. 221, 244, 284 (1973):

[When] dealing with legal principles a court must take a moral point of view. Yet I doubt one would want to say that a court is entitled or required to assert *its* moral point of view. Unlike the moral philosopher, the court is required to assert *ours*. [The] Court's task is to ascertain [the] conventional morality and to convert [moral] principle[s] into [legal ones] by connecting [them] with the body of constitutional law.

See also Simon, The Authority of the Constitution and Its Meaning: A Preface to a Theory of Constitutional Interpretation, 58 S. Cal. L. Rev. 603, 613-615 (1985):

As we confront the multiple language-meanings permitted by many of the open-textured provisions of the Constitution, the only apparent standard we can bring to bear in evaluating competing arguments for one or another interpretative methodology [is] the extent to which they promote a good or just society. [That] is, each argument claims that it is authoritative because [it] is "correct" as a matter of political morality. [I] want to claim that the source or basis of our Constitution's authority is in what might be described either as a shared moral consciousness or identity, or as a deeply layered and shared consensual attitude toward certain stories about and norms of political morality that are understood by a sizable number of our people as representational of the value and importance of the Constitution. [This] consciousness consists [of] two interdependent and mutually reinforcing elements. The first consists of paradigmatic examples [of] representative or historically important episodes of our national moral [life]. The second [consists] of widespread, socialized belief in [several] very abstract values, most importantly, democracy, freedom, equality, and justice. [These] moral beliefs [that] are the basis of the Constitution's authoritativeness do and should affect its interpretation.

e. *Representation-reinforcement*. Ely, supra, at 7-8, 87-88:

[Rule] in accord with the consent of a majority [is] the core of the American governmental system. [But] that cannot be the whole story, since a majority with untrammeled power [is] in a position to deal itself benefits at the expense of the [minority]. The tricky task [is to devise] a way [of] protecting minorities from majority tyranny that is not a flagrant contradiction of the principle of majority [rule]. [To accomplish this task,] the Constitution [is] overwhelmingly concerned [with] procedural fairness [and] with ensuring broad participation in the processes [of] government. [Thus,] a representation-reinforcing approach to judicial review, [which focuses on "clearing the channels of political change" and "facilitating the representation of minorities," is] supportive of [the] underlying premises of the American system of representative democracy. [Moreover,] such an approach [involves] tasks that courts, as experts on process and [as] political outsiders, can sensibly claim to be better qualified [to] perform than political officials.

Under this view, decisions that depart from the "intent of the framers" are justifiable when they promote representation, but not if they recognize or create fundamental rights unrelated to representation. This position would support decisions protecting minorities and rights of access to the political process; it would not support decisions recognizing rights of privacy or economic liberty.

6. *Arguments against noninterpretivism.* Do the sources outlined above meet the objections from contract and democracy? Do they sufficiently constrain judicial discretion? Do they justify noninterpretivist review in a system of representative government? Consider the following objections:

a. *Natural law.* Ely, supra, at 48-50:

> At the time the original Constitution was ratified, [a] number of people espoused the existence of a system of natural law principles. [But the] historical record [is] not so uncomplicated as it is sometimes made to appear. [In any event, the] idea is a discredited one in our society, [and] for good reason. "[A]ll theories of natural law have a singular vagueness which is both an advantage and disadvantage in the application of the theories." The advantage [is] that you can invoke natural law to support anything you want. The disadvantage is that everybody understands that.

b. *Moral philosophy.* Ely, supra, at 56-58:

> [The view] that judges, in seeking constitutional value judgments, should [employ] "the method of reason familiar to the discourse of moral philosophy" [assumes] that moral philosophy is what constitutional law is properly about, that there exists a correct way of doing such philosophy, and that judges are better than others at identifying and engaging in it. [But] surely the claim here cannot be that lawyers and judges are the best imaginable people to tell good moral philosophy from bad. [Moreover, this view assumes] that something exists called "the method of moral philosophy" whose contours sensitive experts will agree on. [That] is not the way things are. [There] simply does not exist *a* method of moral philosophy.

Consider the following response: The existence of competing methods of moral philosophy no more disqualifies moral philosophy as a source of constitutional interpretation than the existence of competing methods of ascertaining the intent of the framers disqualifies original intention as a source of constitutional interpretation. The critical issue is not whether there are necessarily "right" answers to moral questions, but whether it is possible to engage in rational discourse about such questions — whether moral philosophy is ultimately about anything more than a wholly subjective and inevitably relativist choice of competing value preferences. For a defense of the proposition that it is possible to reason about ethical judgments, see R. Singer, Practical Ethics 4-13 (1979). For an illustration of moral reasoning, see Judith Jarvis Thomson's analysis of the abortion issue, excerpted at Chapter 6, section F2, infra.

c. *Tradition*. Ely, supra, at 60, 62:

> Tradition is an obvious place to seek fundamental values, but one whose problems are also obvious. [Tradition] can be invoked in support of almost any cause. [Moreover, tradition's] overtly backward-looking character highlights its undemocratic nature: it is hard to square with the theory of our government that yesterday's majority [should not] control today's. [And] "[i]f the Constitution protects only interests which comport with traditional values, the persons most likely to be penalized for their way of life will be those least likely to receive judicial protection," and that flips the point of the [Constitution] exactly upside down.

d. *Consensus*. See Ely, supra, at 63-64, 67:

> [The problem with the] idea that society's "widely shared values" should give content to the [Constitution is] that that consensus is not reliably discoverable, at least not by the courts. [In] any event the comparative judgment is devastating: as between courts and legislatures, it is clear that the latter are better suited to reflect consensus. [We] may grant until we're blue in the face that legislatures aren't wholly democratic, but that isn't going to make courts more democratic than legislatures.

e. *Representation-reinforcement*. Brest, The Substance of Process, 42 Ohio St. L.J. 131, 140, 142 (1981):

> [Most] instances of representation-reinforcing review demand value judgments not different in kind or scope from the fundamental values sort. [Indeed, the] representation-reinforcing enterprise is shot full of value choices, starting with the decision of just *how* representative our various systems of government ought to be and who ought to be included in the political community, and ending with (covert) choices about who is justifiably the object of prejudice and whether legislative goals are sufficiently important to warrant the burdens they impose on some members of society. [In his] attempt to establish a value-free mode of constitutional adjudication, [Ely] has come as close as anyone could to proving that it can't be done.

See also Tushnet, Darkness on the Edge of Town: The Contributions of John Hart Ely to Constitutional Theory, 89 Yale L.J. 1037 (1980). Consider Bork, The Impossibility of Finding Welfare Rights in the Constitution, 1979 Wash. U. L.Q. 695, 698-699:

> The idea of representation-reinforcement [is] internally contradictory. As a concept it tends to devour itself. It calls upon the judiciary to deny representation to those who have voted in a particular way to enhance the representation of others. Thus, what is reinforced is less democratic representation than judicial [power]. If I were looking at the Constitution for a suffusing principle that judges were entitled to enforce even though it was not explicitly stated, that principle would be the separation of powers or the limited political authority of courts.

5. *The literature*. The literature is extensive. In addition to sources cited in this section, see generally R. Berger, Government by Judiciary (1977); J. Choper,

Judicial Review and the National Political Process (1980); Grano, Judicial Review and a Written Constitution in a Democratic Society, 28 Wayne L. Rev. 1 (1981); Interpretation Symposium, 58 S. Cal. L. Rev. 1 (1985); Sedler, The Legitimacy Debate in Constitutional Adjudication: An Assessment and a Different Perspective, 44 Ohio St. L.J. 93 (1983); Symposium, Constitutional Adjudication and Democratic Theory, 56 N.Y.U. L. Rev. 259 (1981); Symposium, Judicial Review versus Democracy, 42 Ohio St. L.J. 1 (1981); Tribe, The Puzzling Persistence of Process-Based Constitutional Theories, 89 Yale L.J. 1063 (1980).

B. THE PRIVILEGES OR IMMUNITIES CLAUSE

Section 1 of the fourteenth amendment provides that "No State shall make or enforce any law which shall abridge the privileges or immunities of citizens of the United States." The enactment of the fourteenth amendment is examined in Chapter 5, section A, supra. Of the considerable body of literature concerning the adoption of the Civil War amendments, useful works are R. Berger, Government by Judiciary (1977); C. Fairman, Reconstruction and Reunion, 1864-1888, pt. 1, ch. 20 (1971); H. Flack, The Adoption of the Fourteenth Amendment (1908); J. James, The Framing of the Fourteenth Amendment (1956); Fairman, Does the Fourteenth Amendment Incorporate the Bill of Rights? The Original Understanding, 2 Stan. L. Rev. 5 (1949); Frank & Munro, The Original Understanding of "Equal Protection of the Laws," 1972 Wash. U. L.Q. 421.

What are the "privileges or immunities of citizens of the United States"? How would you go about answering that question? Is the interpretivist-noninterpretivist debate helpful?

Slaughter-House Cases

83 U.S. (16 Wall.) 36 (1873)

Mr. Justice Miller delivered the opinion of the Court.

[A statute passed by the Louisiana legislature granted to the Crescent City Live-Stock Landing and Slaughter-House Company the exclusive right to engage in the livestock landing and slaughterhouse business within an area including the City of New Orleans. The company was required to permit any person to slaughter animals in its slaughterhouse at charges fixed by law. Plaintiffs in error, several butchers whose businesses were restricted by the statute, sued to invalidate the monopoly.]

The plaintiffs in error [allege] that the statute is a violation of the Constitution of the United States in these several particulars:

That it creates an involuntary servitude forbidden by the thirteenth article of amendment;

That it abridges the privileges and immunities of citizens of the United States;

That it denies to the plaintiffs the equal protection of the laws; and,

That it deprives them of their property without due process of law; contrary to the provisions of the first section of the fourteenth article of amendment.

This court is thus called upon for the first time to give construction to these articles. . . .

The most cursory glance at these articles discloses a unity of purpose, when taken in connection with the history of the times, which cannot fail to have an important bearing on any question of doubt concerning their true meaning. [For] in the light of [events,] almost too recent to be called history, but which are familiar to us all; and on the most casual examination of the language of these amendments, no one can fail to be impressed with the one pervading purpose found in them all, lying at the foundation of each, and without which none of them would have been even suggested; we mean the freedom of the slave race, the security and firm establishment of that freedom, and the protection of the newly-made freeman and citizen from the oppressions of those who had formerly exercised unlimited dominion over him. . . .

We do not say that no one else but the negro can share in this protection. [But] what we do say, and what we wish to be understood is, that in any fair and just construction of any section or phrase of these amendments, it is necessary to look to the purpose which we have said was the pervading spirit of them all. . . .

The first section of the fourteenth article, to which our attention is more specially invited, opens with a definition of citizenship — not only citizenship of the United States, but citizenship of the States. . . .

"All persons born or naturalized in the United States, and subject to the jurisdiction thereof, are citizens of the United States and of the State wherein they reside."

The first observation we have to make on this clause is, that it [overturns] the *Dred Scott* decision by making *all persons* born within the United States and subject to its jurisdiction citizens of the United States. . . .

The next observation is more important in view of the arguments of counsel in the present case. It is, that the distinction between citizenship of the United States and citizenship of a State is clearly recognized and established. [There] is a citizenship of the United States, and a citizenship of a State, which are distinct from each other, and which depend upon different characteristics or circumstances in the individual.

We think this distinction and its explicit recognition in this amendment of great weight in this argument, because the next paragraph of this same section, which is the one mainly relied on by the plaintiffs in error, speaks only of privileges and immunities of citizens of the United States, and does not speak of those of citizens of the several States. . . .

The language is, "No State shall make or enforce any law which shall abridge the privileges or immunities of citizens of *the United States*." It is a little remarkable, if this clause was intended as a protection to the citizen of a State against the legislative power of his own State, that the word citizen of the State should be left out when it is so carefully used, and used in contradistinction to citizens of the United States, in the very sentence which precedes it. It is too clear for argument that the change in phraseology was adopted understandingly and with a purpose.

Of the privileges and immunities of the citizen of the United States, and of the privileges and immunities of the citizen of the State, and what they respectively are, we will presently consider; but we wish to state here that it is only the former which are placed by this clause under the protection of the Federal Constitution, and that the latter, whatever they may be, are not intended to have any additional protection by this paragraph of the amendment.

If, then, there is a difference between the privileges and immunities belonging to a citizen of the United States as such, and those belonging to the citizen of the State as such, the latter must rest for their security and protection where they have heretofore rested; for they are not embraced by this paragraph of the amendment.

The first occurrence of the words "privileges and immunities" in our [Constitution] is to be found in [article IV, section 2, which provides that] "The citizens of each State shall be entitled to all the privileges and immunities of citizens of the several States." [The] first and the leading case on [this clause] is that of Corfield v. Coryell, decided by Mr. Justice Washington in the Circuit Court for the District of Pennsylvania in 1823.

"The inquiry," he says,

> is, what are the privileges and immunities of citizens of the several States? We feel no hesitation in confining these expressions to those privileges and immunities which are *fundamental*; which belong of right to the citizens of all free governments, and which have at all times been enjoyed by citizens of the several States which compose this Union, from the time of their becoming free, independent, and sovereign. What these fundamental principles are, it would be more tedious than difficult to enumerate. They may all, however, be comprehended under the following general heads: protection by the government, with the right to acquire and possess property of every kind, and to pursue and obtain happiness and safety, subject, nevertheless, to such restraints as the government may prescribe for the general good of the whole. . . .

[Article IV, section 2] did not create those rights, which it called privileges and immunities of citizens of the States. [Its] sole purpose was to declare to the several States, that whatever those rights, as you grant or establish them to your own citizens, or as you limit or qualify, or impose restrictions on their exercise, the same, neither more nor less, shall be the measure of the rights of citizens of other States within your jurisdiction.

[Thus,] up to the adoption of the recent amendments, no claim or pretence was set up that those rights depended on the Federal government for their existence or protection. [Was] it the purpose of the fourteenth amendment, by the simple declaration that no State should make or enforce any law which shall abridge the privileges and immunities of *citizens of the United States*, to transfer the security and protection of all the civil rights which we have mentioned, from the States to the Federal government? And where it is declared that Congress shall have the power to enforce that article, was it intended to bring within the power of Congress the entire domain of civil rights heretofore belonging exclusively to the States?

All this and more must follow, if the proposition of the plaintiffs in error be sound. For not only are these rights subject to the control of Congress whenever in its discretion any of them are supposed to be abridged by State legislation, but that body may also pass laws in advance, limiting and restricting the exercise of legislative power by the States, in their most ordinary and usual functions, as in its judgment it may think proper on all such subjects. And still further, such a construction [would] constitute this court a perpetual censor upon all legislation of the States, on the civil rights of their own citizens, with authority to nullify such as it did not approve as consistent with those rights, as they existed at the time of the adoption of this amendment. The argument we admit is not always the most conclusive which is drawn from the consequences urged against the adoption of a particular construction of an instrument. But when, as in the case before us, these consequences are so serious, so far-reaching and pervading, so great a departure from the structure and spirit of our institutions; when the effect is to fetter and degrade the State governments by subjecting them to the control of Congress, in the exercise of powers heretofore universally conceded to them of the most ordinary and fundamental character; when in fact it radically changes the whole theory of the relations of the State and Federal governments to each other and of both these governments to the people; the argument has a force that is irresistible, in the absence of language which expresses such a purpose too clearly to admit of doubt.

We are convinced that no such results were intended by the Congress which proposed these amendments, nor by the legislatures of the States which ratified them.

Having shown that the privileges and immunities relied on in the argument are those which belong to citizens of the States as such, and that they are left to the State governments for security and protection, and not by this article placed under the special care of the Federal government, we may hold ourselves excused from defining the privileges and immunities of citizens of the United States which no State can abridge, until some case involving those privileges may make it necessary to do so.

But lest it should be said that no such privileges and immunities are to be found if those we have been considering are excluded, we venture to suggest some which owe their existence to the Federal government, its National character, its Constitution, or its laws.

One of these is well described in the case of Crandall v. Nevada. [73 U.S. (6 Wall.) 35 (1867)]. It is said to be the right of the citizen of this great country, protected by implied guarantees of its Constitution, "to come to the seat of government to assert any claim he may have upon that government, to transact any business he may have with it, to seek its protection, to share its offices, to engage in administering its functions. He has the right of free access to its seaports, through which all operations of foreign commerce are conducted, to the subtreasuries, land offices, and courts of justice in the several States."

Another privilege of a citizen of the United States is to demand the care and protection of the Federal government over his life, liberty, and property when on the high seas or within the jurisdiction of a foreign government. [The] right to peaceably assemble and petition for redress of grievances, the privilege of the writ of habeas corpus, are rights of the citizen guaranteed by the Federal Constitution. The right to use the navigable waters of the United States, however they may penetrate the territory of the several States, all rights secured to our citizens by treaties with foreign nations, are dependent upon citizenship of the United States, and not citizenship of a State. [To] these may be added the rights secured by the thirteenth and fifteenth articles of amendment, and by the other clause[s] of the fourteenth. . . .

But it is useless to pursue this branch of the inquiry, since we are of opinion that the rights claimed by these plaintiffs in error, if they have any existence, are not privileges and immunities of citizens of the United States within the meaning of the clause of the fourteenth amendment under consideration.

[The Court also rejected claims that the statute violated the thirteenth amendment and the equal protection and due process clauses of the fourteenth amendment.]

The judgments of the Supreme Court of Louisiana in these cases are affirmed.

MR. JUSTICE FIELD, dissenting. . . .

The act of Louisiana presents the naked case [where] a right to pursue a lawful and necessary calling, previously enjoyed by every citizen, [is] taken away and vested exclusively [in] a single corporation. . . .

The question presented is, therefore, one of the gravest importance, not merely to the parties here, but to the whole country. It is nothing less than the question whether the recent amendments to the Federal Constitution protect the citizens of the United States against the deprivation of their common rights by State legislation. In my judgment the fourteenth amendment does afford such protection, and was so intended by the Congress which framed and the States which adopted it. . . .

If [the privileges and immunities clause] only refers, as held by the majority of the court in their opinion, to such privileges and immunities as were before its adoption specially designated in the Constitution or necessarily implied as belonging to citizens of the United States, it was a vain and idle enactment, which accomplished nothing, and most unnecessarily excited Congress and the people on its passage. With privileges and immunities thus designated or implied no State could ever have interfered by its laws, and no new constitutional provision was required to inhibit such interference. The supremacy of the Constitution and the laws of the United States always controlled any State legislation of that character. But if the amendment refers to the natural and inalienable rights which belong to all citizens, the inhibition has a profound significance and consequence.

What, then, are the privileges and immunities which are secured against abridgment by State legislation?

[Mr. Justice Washington's interpretation of the "privileges and immunities" protected by article IV, section 2] appears to me to be a sound construction of the clause in question. The privileges and immunities designated are those *which of right belong to the citizens of all free governments*. Clearly among these must be placed the right to pursue a lawful employment in a lawful manner, without other restraint than such as equally affects all persons. . . .

What [article IV, section 2] did for the protection of the citizens of one State against hostile and discriminating legislation of other States, the fourteenth amendment does for the protection of every citizen of the United States against hostile and discriminating legislation against him in favor of others, whether they reside in the same or in different States. . . .

It will not be pretended that under the fourth article of the Constitution any State could create a monopoly in any known trade or manufacture in favor of her own citizens [which] would exclude an equal participation [by] citizens of other States. [And] what [article IV, section 2] does for the protection of citizens of one State against the creation of monopolies in favor of citizens of other States, the fourteenth amendment does for the protection of every citizen of the United States against the creation of any monopoly whatever. The privileges and immunities of citizens of the United States, of every one of them, is secured against abridgment in any form by any State. The fourteenth amendment places them under the guardianship of the National authority. All monopolies in any known trade or manufacture are an invasion of these privileges, for they encroach upon the liberty of citizens to acquire property and pursue happiness. . . .

This equality of right, with exemption from all disparaging and partial enactments, in the lawful pursuits of life, throughout the whole country, is the distinguishing privilege of citizens of the United States. To them, everywhere, all pursuits, all professions, all avocations are open without other restrictions than such as are imposed equally upon all others of the same age, sex, and condition. The State may prescribe such regulations for every pursuit and calling of life as will promote the public health, secure the good order and advance the general prosperity of society, but when once prescribed, the pursuit or calling must be free to be followed by every citizen who is within the conditions designated, and will conform to the regulations. This is the fundamental idea upon which our institutions rest. . . .*

I am authorized by THE CHIEF JUSTICE, MR. JUSTICE SWAYNE, and MR. JUSTICE BRADLEY, to state that they concur with me in this dissenting opinion.

MR. JUSTICE BRADLEY, also dissenting. . . .

The right of a State to regulate the conduct of its citizens is undoubtedly a very broad and extensive one, and not to be lightly restricted. But there are certain fundamental rights which this right of regulation cannot infringe. It may prescribe the manner of their exercise, but it cannot subvert the rights themselves. [In] this free country, the people of which inherited certain traditional rights and privileges from their ancestors, citizenship means something. . . .

The people of this country brought with them to its shores the rights of Englishmen; the rights which had been wrested from English sovereigns at various periods of the nation's history. [Blackstone] classifies these fundamental rights under three heads, as the absolute rights of individuals, to wit: the right of personal security, the right of personal liberty, and the right of private property. [These] are the fundamental rights which can only be [interfered with] by lawful regulations necessary or proper for the mutual good of all. . . . [And among the privileges and immunities of citizens,] none is more essential and fundamental than the right to follow such profession or employment as each one may choose, subject only to uniform regulations equally applicable to all. . . .

The keeping of a slaughter-house is part of, and incidental to, the trade of a butcher — one of the ordinary occupations of human life. To compel a butcher [to] slaughter [his] cattle in another person's slaughter-house and pay him a toll

---

* [Relocated footnote — EDS.] "The property which every man has in his own labor," says Adam Smith,

> as it is the original foundation of all other property, so it is the most sacred and inviolable. The patrimony of the poor man lies in the strength and dexterity of his own hands; and to hinder him from employing this strength and dexterity in what manner he thinks proper, without injury to his neighbor, is a plain violation of this most sacred property. It is a manifest encroachment upon the just liberty both of the workman and of those who might be disposed to employ him. As it hinders the one from working at what he thinks proper, so it hinders the others from employing whom they think proper.

(Smith's Wealth of Nations, b. 1, ch. 10, part 2.) . . .

therefor, is such a restriction upon the trade as materially to interfere with its prosecution. It is onerous, unreasonable, arbitrary, and unjust. It has none of the qualities of a police regulation. If it were really a police regulation, it would undoubtedly be within the power of the legislature. [But the] granting of monopolies, or exclusive privileges to individuals or corporations, is an invasion of the right of others to choose a lawful calling, and an infringement of personal liberty. . . .

[Great] fears are expressed that this construction of the amendment will lead to enactments by Congress interfering with the internal affairs of the States, and [that] it will lead the Federal courts to draw to their cognizance the supervision of State tribunals on every subject of judicial inquiry, on the plea of ascertaining whether the privileges and immunities of citizens have not been abridged.

In my judgment no such practical inconveniences would arise. Very little, if any, legislation on the part of Congress would be required to carry the amendment into effect. [And as] the privileges and immunities protected are only those fundamental ones which belong to every citizen, they would soon become so far defined as to cause but a slight accumulation of business in the Federal courts. [In any event, the] argument from inconvenience ought not to have a very controlling influence in questions of this sort. The National will and National interest are of far greater importance. . . .*

Note: The Demise of the Privileges or Immunities Clause

1. *The Slaughter-House Cases.* Consider the following criticisms of Justice Miller's interpretation of the privileges or immunities clause:

a. "Unique among constitutional provisions, the privileges and immunities clause of the Fourteenth Amendment enjoys the distinction of having been rendered a 'practical nullity' by a single decision of the Supreme Court within five years after its ratification." E. Corwin, The Constitution of the United States of America 965 (1953). See Currie, The Constitution in the Supreme Court: Limitations on State Power, 1865-1873, 51 U. Chi. L. Rev. 329, 348 (1983):

> [As Justice Field observed in dissent, the difficulty] was with Miller's apparent conclusion that the sole office of the clause was to protect rights already given by some other federal law. Apart from the amendment's less than conclusive reference to dual citizenship, his sole justification was that a broader holding would "radically [change] the whole theory of the relations of the State and Federal governments to each other and of both these governments to the people" — which quite arguably was precisely what the authors of the amendment had in mind.

b. Graham, Our "Declaratory" Fourteenth Amendment, 7 Stan. L. Rev. 3, 23, 25 (1954):

> A single change was made in Section One after it had been reported by the Joint Committee. This was the addition of the first sentence defining citizenship. [Significantly,] no one observed that while citizenship was made dual in this first sentence,

---

* [A dissenting opinion by Swayne, J., is omitted. — Eds.]

only the privileges or immunities of "citizens of the United States" were specifically protected in the second sentence against abridgment by the states. The reason for this apparent oversight is that [opponents] of slavery had regarded all the important "natural" and constitutional rights as being privileges or immunities of *citizens of the United States*. This had been the cardinal premise of antislavery theory. [The] real purpose of adding this citizenship definition was to [overrule *Dred Scott*]. [To] reach the conclusion of Justice Miller and the majority, one must disregard not only all antislavery from 1834 on, but one must ignore virtually every word said in the debates of 1865-66.

For a defense of Justice Miller's opinion, see Palmer, The Parameters of Constitutional Reconstruction: *Slaughter-House, Cruikshank,* and the Fourteenth Amendment, 1984 U. Ill. L. Rev. 739.

c. Kaczorowski, The Politics of Judicial Interpretation: The Federal Courts, Department of Justice and Civil Rights, 1866-1876, 154-155, 161 (1985):

Theoretical rationalizations of legal doctrine are also means to achieve political objectives. [*Slaughter-House*] may thus be explained in terms of its political goals. Miller was quite explicit about the majority's desire to resist the nationalizing impact of the Civil War by redefining American federalism as a states rights-centered dual federalism. [Although the Court may not have] shared the political objectives and values of Democratic Conservatives of the South, [it clearly was] more concerned about preserving the states' regulatory functions [than] in establishing national authority to protect the civil rights of black Americans. [Moreover, the] revitalization of states rights was crucial to the success of Northern states in their struggle to cope with the stresses of industrialization, [for] it endorsed the state police power necessary to control the growing concentrations of monopolistic power of rising business.

2. *The* Slaughter-House *dissents*. Did the dissenters offer a satisfactory basis for defining the "privileges or immunities of citizens"? The dissenters maintained that the "right to pursue a lawful employment in a lawful manner" is a "fundamental" right that belongs "to the citizens of all free governments." Is this formulation mere "question begging, because [the] question how lawfulness is to be determined is unresolved"? Kurland, The Privileges or Immunities Clause: "Its Hour Come Round at Last"?, 1972 Wash. U. L.Q. 405, 409. If the *Slaughter-House* dissenters had prevailed, what *other* rights would constitute "privileges or immunities of citizens"?

3. *Alternative interpretations*. a. "My study of the historical events that culminated in the Fourteenth Amendment [persuades] me that one of the chief objects that [the] Amendment's first section [was] intended to accomplish was to make the Bill of Rights applicable to the states." Adamson v. California, 332 U.S. 46, 71-72 (1947) (Black, J., dissenting). "[The] words 'No State shall make or enforce any law which shall abridge the privileges or immunities of citizens of the United States' seem to me an eminently reasonable way of expressing the idea that henceforth the Bill of Rights shall apply to the States. What more precious 'privilege' of American citizenship could there be than that privilege to claim the protection of our great Bill of Rights?" Duncan v. Louisiana, 391 U.S. 145, 166 (1968) (Black, J., concurring). In support of this view, note that Representative Bingham, the framer of the provision, stated that "the privileges and immunities of citizens of the United States [are] chiefly defined in the first eight amendments to the Constitution." Cong. Globe, 42d Cong., 1st Sess., app. 85 (1871).

b. Fairman, Does the Fourteenth Amendment Incorporate the Bill of Rights? The Original Understanding, 2 Stan. L. Rev. 5, 132, 137-139 (1949):

[Apart from a few isolated references, the theory that the] privileges and immunities clause incorporated Amendments I to VIII found no recognition in the practice of Congress, or the action of state legislatures, constitutional conventions, or courts. [The] freedom that the states traditionally [had] exercised to develop their own systems for administering justice repels any thought that the [Bill of Rights] provisions on grand jury, criminal jury, and civil jury were fastened upon them in 1868. Congress would not have attempted such a thing, the country would not have stood for it, the legislatures would not have ratified. . . .

If the founders of the Fourteenth Amendment did not intend the privileges and immunities clause to impose Amendments I to VIII, then what, it may be asked, did they mean? [If] one seeks some inclusive and exclusive definition, such that one could say, this is precisely what they had in mind — pretty clearly there never was any such clear conception. [The opponents of the measure magnified] the proposal to render it odious. [The advocates] offered illustrations of particular evils that would be repressed; [but] stayed away from any explanation of a fundamental principle. [Brooding] over the matter [has] slowly brought [me to] the conclusion that [the protection of those rights that are] "implicit in the concept of ordered liberty" [comes] as close as one can to catching the vague aspirations that were hung upon the privileges and immunities clause.

In support of this view, note that Senator Howard, who presented the amendment to the Senate on behalf of the Joint Committee on Reconstruction, explained that the clause protects all "fundamental rights lying at the basis of all society" and that the precise scope of the rights incorporated in the clause would be left "to be discussed and adjudicated when they should happen practically to arise." Cong. Globe, 39th Cong., 1st Sess. 2765-2766 (1866).

c. R. Berger, Government by Judiciary 18, 20 (1977):

The "privileges or immunities" clause was the central provision of the Amendment's §1, and the key to its meaning is furnished by the immediately preceding Civil Rights Act of 1866, which, all are agreed, it was the purpose of the Amendment to embody and protect. The objectives of the [Civil Rights] Act were quite limited. [The Act provided that "there shall be no discrimination in civil rights or immunities on account of race [but] the inhabitants of every race [shall] have the same right to make and enforce contracts, to sue, be parties, and give evidence; to inherit, purchase, lease, sell, hold and convey real and personal property, and to full and equal benefit of all laws and proceedings for the security of person and property, and shall be subject to like punishment [and] no other."] The three clauses of §1 [of the fourteenth amendment] were [thus] three facets of one and the same concern: to insure that there would be no discrimination against [blacks] in respect of "fundamental rights," which had clearly understood and narrow compass [as exemplified by the Civil Rights Act].

In support of this view, note Representative Garfield's comment that the proposed amendment will "lift [the Civil Rights Act] above the reach of political strife, [where] no storm of passion can shake it." Cong. Globe, 39th Cong., 1st Sess. 2462 (1866).

d. See Comment, The Privileges or Immunities Clause of the Fourteenth Amendment: The Original Intent, 79 Nw. U. L. Rev. 142, 174, 177 (1984):

[The] Republican majority in Congress was in disarray as to the proper scope of [the] privileges or immunities clause. Republicans variously thought that the clause merely constitutionalized the Civil Rights Act, incorporated also the Bill of Rights, or incorporated some conception of natural rights. [Thus,] acceptable models for constructing intent [identify] not a single, but a range of intentions, any one of which the framers are reasonably likely to have had. It follows that any choice between these possible intents cannot itself be made by reference to intentionalist theory, but must instead be guided by a non-intentionalist theory.

e. See Laycock, Taking Constitutions Seriously: A Theory of Judicial Review, 59 Tex. L. Rev. 343, 347-348, 352-353 (1981):

There is no reason not to construe section 1 of the fourteenth amendment in accord with its language. [Legislative history] can clarify ambiguities, indicate central concerns, and cast light on whether cases near the limits of the language were meant to be included. But it [cannot] limit a provision as general as the [privileges or immunities clause] to the specific terms of an earlier statute from which the Framers did not borrow as much as three consecutive words. Only the text is part of the Constitution, and in the case of conflict the text must control. [Thus,] a true interpretivism, one that gives natural scope to the language of open-ended constitutional provisions, does not narrowly constrain judicial discretion. [The privileges or immunities clause] protects a set of unenumerated substantive rights whose identification is left to the judiciary in the process of judicial review.

4. *Subsequent developments.* The Court has generally adhered to the *Slaughter-House* interpretation of the privileges or immunities clause, thus rendering the clause essentially "superfluous." L. Tribe, American Constitutional Law 423 (1978). Although the Court invoked the clause in Colgate v. Harvey, 296 U.S. 404 (1935), to invalidate a state income tax levied against in-state residents exclusively on dividends and interest earned outside the state, *Colgate* was expressly overruled only five years later in Madden v. Kentucky, 309 U.S. 83 (1940).

In several instances, a minority of the Court has relied on the clause. See, e.g., Hague v. CIO, 307 U.S. 496 (1939) (opinion of Roberts, J.) (right to assemble and discuss national issues is a privilege of national citizenship); Edwards v. California, 314 U.S. 160 (1941) (Douglas, J., concurring) (right of interstate travel is a privilege of national citizenship); Duncan v. Louisiana, 391 U.S. 145 (1968) (Black, J., concurring) (right to jury trial is a privilege of national citizenship). For suggestions that the clause may yet have importance, see Tribe, supra, at 426; Kurland, supra.

C. THE INCORPORATION CONTROVERSY

In Barron v. Baltimore, 32 U.S. (7 Pet.) 243 (1833), infra this section, the Court held that the rights guaranteed in the first eight amendments do not apply to the states. In *Slaughter-House* the Court held that the rights guaranteed in the first eight amendments are not "privileges or immunities of citizens of the United States" and thus are not applicable to the states via the privileges or immunities clause of the fourteenth amendment. The fourteenth amendment also provides, however, that "No State shall [deprive] any person of life, liberty, or property, without due process of law." To what extent, if any, does the fourteenth amendment due process clause "incorporate" the specific guarantees of the Bill of Rights? Does it, for example, incorporate such procedural rights as the fifth amendment prohibition on "double jeopardy," the sixth amendment guarantee of a "speedy and public" trial by jury in criminal cases, and the eighth amendment prohibition on "excessive" bail? If only some of these provisions are incorporated in the due process clause, how is the Court to decide which merit incorporation? What about other provisions of the bill of rights, such as the first amendment guarantee of free speech, the fourth amendment prohibition against "unreasonable searches and seizures," and the fifth amendment guarantee that "private property" shall not "be taken for public use, without just compensation"? Are these provisions excluded from incorporation because they are not sufficiently procedural in nature?

This section traces the process by which the Court, since *Slaughter-House*, has gradually held most of the rights guaranteed in the first eight amendments applicable to the states via the due process clause of the fourteenth amendment. The incorporation controversy is important, not only because of the questions it raises about the identification of fundamental values, but also because of the questions it raises about the nature and structure of the federal system.

BARRON v. MAYOR & CITY COUNCIL OF BALTIMORE, 32 U.S. (7 Pet.) 243 (1833): Barron sued the City for ruining his wharf in Baltimore harbor. Barron claimed that municipal street construction had diverted the flow of streams so that they deposited silt in front of his wharf, and that this made the water too shallow for most vessels. Barron maintained that this action violated the fifth amendment, which provides that private property shall not be "taken for public use, without just compensation." The Court rejected Barron's contention that the fifth amendment, "being in favour of the liberty of the citizens, ought to be so construed as to restrain the legislative power of a state, as well as that of the United States." Chief Justice Marshall delivered the opinion:

"The question [is] of great importance, but not of much difficulty. The constitution was ordained and established by the people of the United States for themselves, for their own government, and not for the government of the individual states. Each state established a constitution for itself, and in that constitution, provided such limitations and restrictions on the powers of its particular government, as its judgment dictated. The people of the United States framed such a government for the United States as they supposed best adapted to their situation and best calculated to promote their interests. The powers they conferred on this government were to be exercised by itself; and the limitations on power, if expressed in general terms, are naturally, and, we think, necessarily, applicable to the government created by the instrument. . . .

"[Article I., section 10, of the original constitution expressly enumerates those limitations] which were to operate on the state legislatures. [Had] the framers of [the] amendments intended them to be limitations on the powers of the state governments, they would have imitated the framers of the original constitution, and have expressed that intention. Had congress engaged in the extraordinary occupation of improving the constitutions of the several states, by affording the people additional protection from the exercise of power by their own governments, in matters which concerned themselves alone, they would have declared this purpose in plain and intelligible language.

"But it is universally understood, it is a part of the history of the day, that the great revolution which established the constitution of the United States, was not effected without immense opposition. Serious fears were extensively entertained, that those powers which the patriot statesmen, who then watched over the interests of our country, deemed essential to union, and to the attainment of those invaluable objects for which union was sought, might be exercised in a manner dangerous to liberty. In almost every convention by which the constitution was adopted, amendments to guard against the abuse of power were recommended. These amendments demanded security against the apprehended encroachments of the general government — not against those of the local governments. In compliance with a sentiment thus generally expressed, to quiet fears thus extensively entertained, amendments were proposed by the required majority in congress, and adopted by the states. These amendments contain no expression indicating an intention to apply them to the state governments. This court cannot so apply them.

"We are of opinion, that the [just compensation] provision in the fifth amendment [is] intended solely as a limitation on the exercise of power by the government of the United States, and is not applicable to legislation of the states."

"In terms of the original understanding, *Barron* was almost certainly correctly decided." J. Ely, Democracy and Distrust 196 n.58 (1980). The decision not to extend the Bill of Rights to the states reflected "a concession to state power," a "degree of ambivalence about the actual content of the personal freedoms that merited protection," and, perhaps most important, a belief that the preservation of state autonomy was itself essential to the protection of individual rights and security. L. Tribe, American Constitutional Law 3 (1978). In the framers' view, citizen control over state government would serve as an adequate safeguard of individual liberty. The enactment of the bill of rights was thus associated with special fear of the remote federal government. See Chapter 5, section A, supra. The Civil War, however, and the Civil War amendments, fundamentally realigned federal-state relations. And although the Court rejected the application of the Bill of Rights to the states through the privileges or immunities clause in the *Slaughter-House Cases*, that did not end the matter. The *Murray* case, which follows, offers a pre-fourteenth amendment perspective on "due process." The remaining cases address the issue of incorporation.

MURRAY v. HOBOKEN LAND & IMPROVEMENT CO., 59 U.S. (18 How.) 272 (1856): In *Murray*, several years before the adoption of the fourteenth amendment, Justice Curtis described the origin and scope of the due process clause of the fifth amendment: "The words, 'due process of law,' were undoubtedly intended to convey the same meaning as the words, 'by the law of the land,' in Magna Charta. [The] constitution contains no description of those processes which it was intended to allow or forbid. It does not even declare what principles are to be applied to ascertain whether it be due process. [To] what principles, then, are we to resort to ascertain whether [a particular process] is due process? [We] must look to those settled usages and modes of proceeding existing in the common and statute law of England, before the emigration of our ancestors, and which are shown not to have been unsuited to their civil and political condition by having been acted on by them after the settlement of this country."

TWINING v. NEW JERSEY, 211 U.S. 78 (1908): In a state court prosecution, the jury was instructed that it might draw an unfavorable inference against the defendants from their failure to testify. The Court rejected the defendants' contention that this instruction violated their rights under the federal Constitution: "It is not argued that the defendants are protected by that part of the Fifth Amendment which provides that 'no person . . . shall be compelled in any criminal case to be a witness against himself,' for it is recognized [that] the first ten Amendments are not operative on the States. [Citing Barron v. Baltimore.] [Moreover, there] can be no doubt, so far as [the] Slaughter-House Cases has determined the question, that the civil rights sometimes described as fundamental and inalienable, which before the war Amendments were enjoyed by state citizenship and protected by state government, were left untouched by [the privileges or immunities] clause of the Fourteenth Amendment. . . .

"The defendants, however, do not stop here. They appeal to another clause of the Fourteenth Amendment, and insist that the [jury instruction] was a denial of due process of law. This contention requires separate consideration, for it is possible that some of the personal rights safeguarded by the first eight amendments against National action may also be safeguarded against state action, because a denial of them would be a denial of due process of law. [If] this is so, it is not because those rights are enumerated in the first eight Amendments, but because they are of such a nature that they are included in the conception of due process of law. . . .

"The question under consideration may first be tested by the application of [the] settled doctrines of this court. If the statement of Mr. Justice Curtis [in *Murray*] is to be taken literally, that alone might be decisive. For nothing is more certain, in point of historical fact, than that the practice of compulsory self-incrimination [existed] for four hundred years after the granting of Magna Carta, [gained] at least some foothold among the early colonists of this country, and was not entirely omitted at trial in England until the eighteenth century. . . .

"But without repudiating or questioning the test proposed by Mr. Justice Curtis [we] prefer to rest our decision on broader grounds, and inquire whether the exemption from self-incrimination is [a] fundamental principle of liberty and justice which inheres in the very idea of free government and is the inalienable right of a citizen of such a government. [Under] the guise of interpreting the Constitution we must take care that we do not import into the discussion our own personal views of what would be wise, just and fitting rules of government [and] confound them with constitutional limitations. [One] aid to the solution of the question is to inquire how the right was rated during the time when the meaning of due process was in a formative state and before it was incorporated in American constitutional law. [None] of the great instruments in which we are accustomed to look for the declaration of the fundamental rights [such as Magna Charta and the Petition of Right] made reference to [the exemption from self-incrimination].

[Moreover, of the thirteen states which ratified the original Constitution, only four proposed amendments to incorporate] the privilege in the Constitution, [and] Congress, in submitting the amendments to [the] States, treated [due process of law and the privilege against self-incrimination] as exclusive of each other. [Thus, the] inference is irresistible that it has been the opinion of constitution makers that the privilege, if fundamental in any sense, is not fundamental in due process of law, nor an essential part of it. . . .

"Even if the historical meaning of due process of law [did] not exclude the privilege from it, it would be going far to rate it as an immutable principle of [justice]. Salutary as the principle may seem to the great majority, it cannot be ranked with the right to hearing before condemnation, the immunity from arbitrary power not acting by general laws, and the inviolability of private property. The wisdom of the exemption has never been universally assented to [and] it is best defended not as an unchangeable principle of universal justice but as a law proved by experience to be expedient. [There is no reason] for straining the meaning of due process of law to include this privilege within it."

Justice Harlan dissented.

Is *Twining's* interpretation of the due process clause consistent with the *Slaughter-House* interpretation of the privileges or immunities clause? Are they consistent because "due process of law" focuses only on "procedural" rights? Is the privilege against self-incrimination procedural or substantive?

PALKO v. CONNECTICUT, 302 U.S. 319 (1937): *Palko* concerned the constitutionality of a Connecticut statute permitting the state to appeal in criminal cases. Although the Court "assumed for the purpose of the case" that such a statute, if enacted by the United States, would violate the double jeopardy clause of the fifth amendment, it rejected appellant's contention that the challenged statute violated the due process clause of the fourteenth amendment. Justice Cardozo delivered the opinion of the Court:

"[In] appellant's view [whatever] would be a violation of the original bill of rights [if] done by the federal government is now equally unlawful by force of the Fourteenth Amendment if done by a state. There is no such general rule. [The] Fifth Amendment provides [that] no person shall be held to answer for a capital or otherwise infamous crime unless on presentment or indictment of a grand jury [but this] court has held that, in prosecutions by a state, presentment or indictment by a grand jury [is not required]. [Citing Hurtado v. California, 110 U.S. 516 (1884).] The Fifth Amendment provides also that no person shall be compelled in any criminal case to be a witness against himself [but this] court has said that, in prosecutions by a state, the exemption will fail if the state elects to end it. [Citing *Twining.*] The Sixth Amendment calls for a jury trial in criminal cases and the Seventh for a jury trial in civil cases at common law [but this] court has ruled that [trial] by jury may be modified by a state or abolished altogether. [Citing Maxwell v. Dow, 176 U.S. 581 (1900).] . . .

"On the other hand, the due process clause of the Fourteenth Amendment may make it unlawful for a state to abridge [the] freedom of speech which the First Amendment safeguards against encroachment by the Congress, [citing De Jonge v. Oregon, 299 U.S. 353 (1937)]; or the like freedom of the press, [citing

Grosjean v. American Press Co., 297 U.S. 233 (1936)]; or the free exercise of religion, [citing Hamilton v. Regents, 293 U.S. 245 (1934)]; or the right of peaceable assembly, [citing *De Jonge*]; or the right of one accused of crime to the benefit of counsel, [citing Powell v. Alabama, 287 U.S. 45 (1932)]. In these and other situations immunities that are valid as against the federal government by force of the specific pledges of particular amendments have been found to be implicit in the concept of ordered liberty, and thus, through the Fourteenth Amendment, become valid as against the states.

"The line of division may seem to be wavering and broken if there is a hasty catalogue of the cases on the one side and the other. Reflection and analysis will induce a different view. There emerges the perception of a rationalizing principle which gives to discrete instances a proper order and coherence. The right to trial by jury and the immunity from prosecution except as the result of an indictment may have value and importance. Even so, they are not of the very essence of a scheme of ordered liberty. To abolish them is not to violate a 'principle of justice so rooted in the tradition and conscience of our people as to be ranked as fundamental.' [Few] would be so narrow or provincial as to maintain that a fair and enlightened system of justice would be impossible without them. What is true of jury trials and indictments is true also [of] the immunity from compulsory self-incrimination. This too might be lost, and justice still be done. Indeed, today as in the past there are students of our penal system who look upon the immunity as a mischief rather than a benefit, and who would limit its scope, or destroy it altogether. No doubt there would remain the need to give protection against torture, physical or mental. [Citing Brown v. Mississippi, 297 U.S. 278 (1936)]. Justice, however, would not perish if the accused were subject to a duty to respond to orderly inquiry. . . .

"We reach a different plane of social and moral values when we pass to the privileges and immunities that have been taken over from the earlier articles of the federal bill of rights and brought within the Fourteenth Amendment by a process of absorption. [The] process of absorption has had its source in the belief that neither liberty nor justice would exist if they were sacrificed. [This] is true, for illustration, of freedom of thought and speech. Of that freedom one may say that it is the matrix, and indispensable condition, of nearly every other form of freedom. [Fundamental] too in the concept of due process, and so in that of liberty, is the thought that condemnation shall be rendered only after trial. [The] hearing, moreover, must be a real one, not a sham or a pretense. [For] that reason, ignorant defendants in a capital case were held to have been condemned unlawfully when in truth, though not in form, they were refused the aid of counsel. [Citing Powell v. Alabama]. The decision did not turn upon the fact that the benefit of counsel would have been guaranteed to the defendants by the provisions of the Sixth Amendment if they had been prosecuted in a federal court. The decision turned upon the fact that in the particular situation laid before us in the evidence the benefit of counsel was essential to the substance of a hearing.

"Our survey of the cases serves, we think, to justify the statement that the dividing line between them, if not unfaltering throughout its course, has been true for the most part to a unifying principle. On which side of the line the case made out by appellant has appropriate location must be the next inquiry and the final one. Is that kind of double jeopardy to which the statute has subjected him a hardship so acute and shocking that our polity will not endure it? Does it violate those 'fundamental principles of liberty and justice which lie at the base of all our civil and political institutions'? [The] answer must surely be 'no.' What the answer would have to be if the state were permitted after a trial free from error to try the accused over again or to bring another case against him, we have no occasion to consider. [Here, the state asks only] that the case against him shall go on until there shall be a trial free from [substantial] legal error. [This] is not a cruelty at all."

Justice Butler dissented.

Note that by 1937 there was no longer any doubt that "due process" could embrace not only procedural rights but also substantive rights such as freedom of speech and religion. Is this consistent with the guarantee of "due process"? Note also the Court's distinction between the privilege against compelled self-incrimination and freedom of speech. Is this a defensible distinction?

ADAMSON v. CALIFORNIA, 332 U.S. 46 (1947): In a state court prosecution, the prosecution was permitted to comment on the defendant's failure to take the stand. The Court assumed that such comment "would infringe defendant's privilege against self-incrimination [if] this were a trial in a court of the United States." Relying on *Slaughter-House*, *Twining*, and *Palko*, however, the Court, in a five-to-four decision, held that the fourteenth amendment did not incorporate the privilege and that the particular practice at issue did not deprive defendant of his due process right to a "fair trial." In a lengthy dissenting opinion, Justice Black, joined by Justice Douglas, set forth his theory of "total" incorporation:

"This decision reasserts a constitutional theory spelled out in [*Twining*], that this Court is endowed by the Constitution with boundless power under 'natural law' periodically to expand and contract constitutional standards to conform to the Court's conception of what at a particular time constitutes 'civilized decency' and 'fundamental liberty and justice.' [I] would not reaffirm the *Twining* decision. I think that decision and the 'natural law' theory of the Constitution upon which it relies degrade the constitutional safeguards of the Bill of Rights and simultaneously appropriate for this Court a broad power which we are not authorized by the Constitution to exercise. . . .

"My study of the historical events that culminated in the Fourteenth Amendment, and the expressions of those who sponsored and favored, as well as those who opposed its submission and passage, persuades me that one of the chief objects that the provisions of the Amendment's first section, separately, and as a whole, were intended to accomplish was to make the Bill of Rights applicable to the states. With full knowledge of the import of the *Barron* decision, the framers and backers of the Fourteenth Amendment proclaimed its purpose to be to overturn the constitutional rule that case had announced. . . .

"[The] 'natural law' formula which the Court uses [should] be abandoned as an incongruous excrescence on our Constitution. [I] fear to see the consequences of the Court's practice of substituting its own concepts of decency and fundamental justice for the language of the Bill of Rights as its point of departure in interpreting and enforcing that Bill of Rights. If the choice must be between the selective process of the *Palko* decision applying some of the Bill of Rights to the States, or the *Twining* rule applying none of them, I would choose the *Palko* selective process. But rather than accept either of these choices, I would follow what I believe was the original purpose of the Fourteenth Amendment — to extend to all the people of the nation the complete protection of the Bill of Rights. . . .

"Since [Marbury v. Madison] the practice has been firmly established, for better or worse, that courts can strike down legislative enactments which violate our Constitution. This process, of course, involves interpretation, and since words can have many meanings, interpretation obviously may result in contraction or extension of the original purpose of a constitutional provision, thereby affecting policy. But to pass upon the constitutionality of statutes by looking to the particular standards enumerated in the Bill of Rights and other parts of the Constitution is one thing; to invalidate statutes because of application of 'natural law' deemed to be above and undefined by the Constitution is another. 'In the one instance, courts proceeding within clearly marked constitutional boundaries seek to execute policies written into the Constitution; in the other, they roam at will in the limitless area of their own beliefs as to reasonableness and actually select policies, a responsibility which the Constitution entrusts to the legislative representatives of the people.'"

In a separate dissenting opinion, Justice Murphy, joined by Justice Rutledge, agreed with Justice Black that "the specific guarantees of the Bill of Rights should be carried over intact into the first section of the Fourteenth Amendment," but disagreed that "the latter is entirely and necessarily limited by the Bill of Rights." To the contrary, there may be occasions "where a proceeding falls so far short of conforming to fundamental standards of procedure as to warrant constitutional condemnation in terms of a lack of due process despite the absence of a specific provision in the Bill of Rights."

In a concurring opinion, Justice Frankfurter attacked Justice Black's theory of "total" incorporation: "For historical reasons a limited immunity from the common duty to testify was written into the Federal Bill of Rights, and I am prepared to agree that, as part of that immunity, comment on failure of an accused to take the witness stand is forbidden in federal prosecutions. [But] to suggest that such a limitation can be drawn out of 'due process' in its protection of ultimate decency in a civilized society is to suggest that the Due Process Clause fastened fetters of unreason upon the States. . . .

"The short answer to the suggestion that the [due process clause of the fourteenth amendment] was a way of saying that every State must thereafter initiate prosecutions through indictment by a grand jury, must have a trial by a jury of twelve in criminal cases, and must have trial by such a jury in common law suits where the amount in controversy exceeds twenty dollars, is that it is a strange way of saying it. [Those] reading the English language with the meaning which it ordinarily conveys, those conversant with the political and legal history of the concept of due process, those sensitive to the relations of the States to the central government as well as the relation of some of the provisions of the Bill of Rights to the process of justice, would hardly recognize the Fourteenth Amendment as a cover for the various explicit provisions of the first eight Amendments. Some of these are enduring reflections of experience with human nature, while some express the restricted views of Eighteenth-Century England regarding the best methods for the ascertainment of facts. The notion that the Fourteenth Amendment was a covert way of imposing upon the States all the rules which it seemed important to Eighteenth Century statesmen to write into the Federal Amendments, was rejected by judges who were themselves witnesses of the process by which the Fourteenth Amendment became part of the Constitution. . . .

"[Nor can I accept the suggestion that there is] merely a selective incorporation of the first eight Amendments into the Fourteenth Amendment. [Under that view, some] are in and some are out, but we are left in the dark as to which are in and which are out. Nor are we given the calculus for determining which go in and which stay out. If the basis of selection is merely that those provisions of the first eight Amendments are incorporated which commend themselves to individual justices as indispensable to the dignity and happiness of a free man, we are thrown back to a merely subjective test. The protection against unreasonable search and seizure might have primacy for one judge, while trial by a jury of 12 for every claim above $20 might appear to another as an ultimate need in a free society. In the history of thought 'natural law' has a much longer and much better founded meaning and justification than such subjective selection of the first eight Amendments for incorporation into the Fourteenth. If all that is meant is that due process contains within itself certain minimal standards which are 'of the very essence of a scheme of ordered liberty,' [*Palko*], putting upon this Court the duty of applying these standards from time to time, then we have merely arrived at the insight which our predecessors long ago expressed. . . .

"And so, when, as in a case like the present, a conviction in a State court is here for review under a claim that a right protected by the Due Process Clause of the Fourteenth Amendment has been denied, the issue is not whether an infraction of one of the specific provisions of the first eight Amendments is disclosed by the record. The relevant question is whether the criminal proceedings which resulted in conviction deprived the accused of the due process of law to which the [Constitution] entitled him. Judicial review of that guaranty [inescapably] imposes upon this Court an exercise of judgment upon the whole course of the proceedings in order to ascertain whether they offend those canons of decency and fairness which express the notions of justice of English-speaking peoples. [These] standards [are] not authoritatively formulated anywhere as though they were prescriptions in a pharmacopoeia. But neither does the application of the Due Process Clause imply that judges are wholly at large. The judicial judgment in applying the Due Process Clause must move within the limits of accepted notions of justice and is not to be based upon the idiosyncrasies of a merely personal judgment. [An] important safeguard against such merely individual judgment is an alert deference to the judgment of the State court under review."

Note: The Black/Frankfurter Debate

1. *"Total" incorporation.* Justice Black's "total" incorporation theory has never commanded a majority of the Court. Although he maintained in *Adamson* that "one of the chief objects" of the fourteenth amendment "was to make the Bill of Rights applicable to the states," the historical record is ambiguous, and there is no clear consensus on the actual intentions of the framers and ratifiers of the fourteenth amendment. For analysis of the historical issue, see generally R. Berger, Government by Judiciary (1977); J. Ely, Democracy and Distrust (1980); H. Flack, The Adoption of the Fourteenth Amendment (1908); W. Guthrie, The Four-

teenth Article of Amendment to the Constitution of the United States (1898); tenBroek, The Antislavery Origins of the Fourteenth Amendment (1951); Crosskey, Charles Fairman, "Legislative History," and the Constitutional Limitations on State Authority, 22 U. Chi. L. Rev. 1 (1954); Fairman, Does the Fourteenth Amendment Incorporate the Bill of Rights? The Original Understanding, 2 Stan. L. Rev. 5 (1949).

2. *"Fundamental fairness."* For about a decade-and-a-half after *Adamson*, the Court continued to employ the "fundamental fairness" approach to due process. In applying this approach, the Court struggled to avoid decisions based on what Justice Frankfurter termed "the idiosyncrasies of a merely personal judgment." Consider Kadish, Methodology and Criteria in Due Process Adjudication — A Survey and Criticism, 66 Yale L.J. 319, 327-328 (1957):

> The effort to eliminate the purely personal preference from flexible due process decision making has taken two main forms. One has been a respectful deference to the judgment of the state court or the act of the legislature under review. The other had been an attempt to rest conclusions upon external and objective evidence in such fashion that as far as possible it can be said that the Court is not so much itself creating its own policy determinations as it is interpreting and reading determinations that have already been made. [The] most significant kind of such objective data has consisted of the moral judgments already made on the point at issue, sought for in the express or implicit view of important segments of our society, past or present. [The Court has thus looked to four primary sources]: (1) the opinions of the progenitors and architects of American institutions; (2) the implicit opinions of the policy-making organs of state governments; (3) the explicit opinions of other American courts that have evaluated the fundamentality of [the asserted right]; or, (4) the opinions of other countries in the Anglo-American tradition "not less civilized than our own" as reflected in their statutes, decisions and practices.

This approach produced an "apparently chaotic array" of decisions:

> [Under the Court's analysis], a criminal conviction based on a confession obtained by physical and mental coercion violates due process regardless of its testimonial reliability, but a conviction based on incriminating evidence obtained by acts concededly violative of the due process clause is not itself violative of due process; the privilege against self-incrimination and the right to be free of convictions based upon unconstitutional searches and seizures are not protected by due process of law, but a conviction for illegally possessing narcotics based on the evidential use of narcotics unwillingly pumped out of the accused's stomach does violate due process; the use of illegally obtained evidence to procure a conviction is not violative of due process when the illegality consists of breaking into the accused's office and rifling through his papers, but does violate due process (at least in the eyes of two members of the Court) when the illegality consists of repeated and unauthorized entries for the purpose of installing a microphone[;] due process is violated by the denial of an opportunity for the accused to retain counsel, but not (necessarily) by the denial of an opportunity to have counsel appointed where a private retainer is financially impossible.

Kadish, supra, at 319.

Does the unpredictable and "apparently chaotic" quality of these decisions confirm Justice Black's contention that "fundamental fairness" should "be abandoned as an incongruous excrescence on our Constitution"? Does it argue in favor of Black's less open-ended approach?

Consider Kadish, supra, at 337-338:

> In seeking to tie due process interpretation to the specific written provisions of the Bill of Rights, Justice Black's theory of judicial review is an appealing one: it precludes unfettered judicial subjectivity by pinning down constitutional adjudication to the interpretation of specific written language, and at the same time appears to give greater assurance that [the] guarantees will be applied with the vigor he thinks appropriate. But the notion that this latter consequence follows from express directions in the written language of the Bill of Rights is hardly supported by the nature of those provisions or by the history of the interpretation by the Supreme Court. It may be conceded that some of the first eight amendments are of the specific statutory characters which admit of little play for judicial value judgment — for example, [the] guarantee of the initiation of criminal proceedings by indictment. But [most of the guarantees in the Bill of Rights are not of this nature]. The changing contours of and the vigorous divisions of the Court concerning the meaning of freedom of and from religion, double jeopardy, cruel and unusual punishments, the privilege against self-incrimination and unreasonable searches and seizures, belie the notion that the literal language of these provisions directs and confines judicial inquiry along specific lines. [The] consequence of requiring due process to be measured precisely by the provisions of the Bill of Rights is not to eliminate broad judicial inquiry, but rather to change its focus [and] to disguise its essential character.

See also Friendly, The Bill of Rights as a Code of Criminal Procedure, 53 Calif. L. Rev. 929 (1965).

For academic efforts to articulate a coherent theory of "fundamental fairness," see Kadish, supra, at 344-363; Nowak, Due Process Methodology in the Postincorporation World, 70 J. Crim. L. & Criminology 397 (1979).

3. *The "demise" of "fundamental fairness."* In the early 1960s, the Warren Court, without expressly abandoning "fundamental fairness," began to modify incorporation methodology. As the Court looked increasingly to the Bill of Rights for guidance, it "selectively" incorporated more and more of the specific guarantees of the Bill of Rights into the due process clause of the fourteenth amendment. These developments are traced in *Duncan.*

DUNCAN v. LOUISIANA, 391 U.S. 145 (1968): In *Duncan* the Court held the sixth amendment right to jury trial applicable to the states via the fourteenth amendment due process clause. Justice White delivered the opinion of the Court: "The Fourteenth Amendment denies the States the power to 'deprive any person of life, liberty, or property, without due process of law.' In resolving conflicting claims concerning the meaning of this spacious language, the Court has looked increasingly to the Bill of Rights for guidance; many of the rights guaranteed by the first eight Amendments [have] been held to be protected against state action by the Due Process Clause of the Fourteenth Amendment. That clause now protects the right to compensation for property taken by the State [Chicago, Burlington & Quincy Railroad v. Chicago, 166 U.S. 226 (1897)]; the rights of speech, press, and religion covered by the First Amendment [Fiske v. Kansas, 274 U.S. 380 (1927)]; the Fourth Amendment rights to be free from unreasonable searches and seizures and to have excluded from criminal trials any evidence illegally seized [Mapp v. Ohio, 367 U.S. 643 (1961)]; the right guaranteed by the Fifth Amendment to be free of compelled self-incrimination [Malloy v. Hogan, 378 U.S. 1 (1964), overruling *Twining* and *Adamson*]; and the Sixth Amendment rights to counsel [Gideon v. Wainwright, 372 U.S. 335 (1963)], to a speedy and public trial [Klopfer v. North Carolina, 386 U.S. 213 (1967); In re Oliver, 333 U.S. 257 (1948)], to confrontation of opposing witnesses [Pointer v. Texas, 380 U.S. 400 (1965)], and to compulsory process for obtaining witnesses [Washington v. Texas, 388 U.S. 14 (1967)].

"The test for determining whether a right extended by the Fifth and Sixth Amendments with respect to federal criminal proceedings is also protected against state action by the Fourteenth Amendment has been phrased in a variety of ways in opinions of this Court. The question has been asked whether a right is among those '"fundamental principles of liberty and justice which lie at the base of all our civil and political institutions,"' [whether] it is 'basic in our system of jurisprudence,' [and] whether it is a 'fundamental right, essential to a fair trial.' . . .

"[In] one sense recent cases applying provisions of the first eight Amendments to the States represent a new approach to the 'incorporation' debate. Earlier the Court can be seen as having asked [if] a civilized system could be imagined that would not accord the particular protection. [Citing *Palko*.] The recent cases, on the other hand, have proceeded upon the valid assumption that state criminal processes are not imaginary and theoretical schemes but actual systems bearing virtually every characteristic of the common-law system that has been developing contemporaneously in England and in this country. The question thus is whether given this kind of system a particular procedure is fundamental — whether, that is, a procedure is necessary to an Anglo-American regime of ordered liberty. . . .

"When the inquiry is approached in this way the question whether the State can impose criminal punishment without granting a jury trial appears quite different from the way it appeared in the older [cases]. A criminal process which was fair and equitable but used no juries is easy to imagine. It would make use of alternative guarantees and protections which would serve the purposes that the jury serves in the English and American systems. Yet no American State has undertaken to construct such a system. [In] every State [the] structure and style of the criminal process [are] the sort that naturally complement jury trial, and have developed in connection with and in reliance upon jury trial. . . .

"Because we believe that trial by jury in criminal cases is fundamental to the American scheme of justice, we hold that the Fourteenth Amendment guarantees a right of jury trial in all criminal cases which — were they to be tried in a federal court — would come within the Sixth Amendment's guarantee. . . .

"[By] the time our Constitution was written, jury trial in criminal cases had been in existence in England for several centuries [and its] preservation and proper operation as a protection against arbitrary rule were among the major objectives of the revolutionary settlement. [The Sixth Amendment guaranteed jury trial as did the] constitutions adopted by the original States. [This] history is impressive support for considering the right to jury trial in criminal cases to be fundamental to our system of justice. [Moreover, the] guarantees of jury trial in the Federal and State Constitutions reflect a profound judgment about the way in which law should be enforced and justice administered. A right to jury trial is granted to criminal defendants in order to prevent oppression by the Government. Those who wrote our constitution knew from history and experience that it was necessary to protect against unfounded criminal charges brought to eliminate enemies and against judges too responsive to the voice of higher authority. [Beyond] this, the jury trial provisions in the Federal and State Constitutions reflect a fundamental decision about the exercise of official power — a reluctance to entrust plenary powers over the life and liberty of the citizen to one judge or to a group of judges. [The] deep commitment of the Nation to the right of jury trial in serious criminal cases as a defense against arbitrary law enforcement qualifies for protection under the Due Process Clause of the Fourteenth Amendment, and must therefore be respected by the States."

Justice Black, joined by Justice Douglas, filed a concurring opinion: "I believe as strongly as ever that the Fourteenth Amendment was intended to make the Bill of Rights applicable to the States. I have been willing to support the selective incorporation doctrine, however, as an alternative, although perhaps less historically supportable than complete incorporation. The selective incorporation process, if used properly, does limit the Supreme Court in the Fourteenth Amendment field to the specific Bill of Rights' protections only and keeps judges from roaming at will in their own notions of what policies outside the Bill of Rights are desirable and what are not. And, most important to me, the selective incorporation process has the virtue of having already worked to make most of the Bill of Rights' protections applicable to the States."

Justice Fortas also filed a concurring opinion: "[Although] I agree with the decision of the Court, I cannot agree with the implication [that] the tail must go with the hide: that when we hold, influenced by the Sixth Amendment, that 'due process' requires that the States accord the right of jury trial for all but petty offenses, we automatically import all of the ancillary rules which have been or may hereafter be developed incidental to the right to jury trial in the federal courts. [Neither] logic nor history nor the intent of the draftsmen of the Fourteenth Amendment can possibly be said to require the Sixth Amendment or its jury trial provision be applied to the States together with the total gloss that this Court's decisions have supplied. The draftsmen of the Fourteenth Amendment intended what they said, not more or less: that no State shall deprive any person of life, liberty, or property without due process of law. It is ultimately the duty of this Court to interpret, to ascribe meaning to this phrase. There is no reason whatever for us to conclude that, in so doing, we are bound slavishly to follow not only the Sixth Amendment but all of its bag and baggage. [To] take this course, in my judgment, would be not only unnecessary but mischievous because it would inflict a serious blow upon the principle of federalism. [Our] Constitution sets up a federal union, not a monolith."

Justice Harlan, joined by Justice Stewart, dissented: "A few members of the Court have taken the position that the intention of those who drafted the first section of the Fourteenth Amendment was simply, and exclusively, to make the provisions of the first eight Amendments applicable to state action. This view has never been accepted by this Court. In my view, [the] overwhelming historical evidence [demonstrates] that [those] who wrote, debated, and ratified the Fourteenth Amendment did not think they were 'incorporating' the Bill of Rights. [Although I] fundamentally disagree with the total incorporation view of the Fourteenth Amendment, it seems to me that such a position does at least have the virtue [of] internal consistency: we look to the Bill of Rights, word for word, clause for clause, precedent for precedent because, it is said, the men who wrote the Amendment wanted it that way. . . .

"Today's Court [remains] unwilling to accept the total incorporationists' view [and] is also, apparently, unwilling to face the task of determining whether denial of trial by jury in the situation before us, or in other situations, is fundamentally unfair. Consequently, the Court has compromised on the ease of the incorporationist position, without its internal logic. It has simply assumed that the question before us is whether the Jury Trial Clause of the Sixth Amendment should be incorporated into the Fourteenth, jot-for-jot and case-for-case, or be ignored. Then the Court merely declares that the clause in question is 'in' rather than 'out.'

"The Court has justified neither its starting place nor its conclusion. If the problem is to discover and articulate the rules of fundamental fairness in criminal proceedings, there is no reason to assume that the whole body of rules developed in this Court constituting Sixth Amendment jury trial must be regarded as a unit. [Moreover, even] if I could agree that the question before us is whether Sixth Amendment jury trial is totally 'in' or totally 'out,' I can find in the Court's opinion no real reasons for concluding that it should be 'in.' [The] Court says that some clauses are more 'fundamental' than others, but [uses] this word in a sense [which] is of no help. The word does not mean 'analytically critical to procedural fairness' for no real analysis of the role of the jury in making procedures fair is even attempted. Instead, the word turns out to mean 'old,' 'much praised,' and 'found in the Bill of Rights.' The definition of 'fundamental' thus turns out to be circular. . . .

"The argument that jury trial is not a requisite of due process is quite simple. The central proposition of [*Palko*] is that 'due process of law' requires only that criminal trials be fundamentally fair. [Thus,] the inquiry in each case must be whether a state trial process was a fair one. [It] has not been demonstrated, nor, I think, can it be demonstrated, that trial by jury is the only fair means of resolving issues of fact.

"The jury is of course not without virtues. [But] the principal original virtue of the jury trial — the limitations a jury imposes on a tyrannous judiciary — has largely disappeared. We no longer live in a medieval or colonial society. Judges enforce laws enacted by democratic decision, [they] are elected by the people or appointed by the people's elected officials, and are responsible not to a distant monarch alone but to reviewing courts, including this one.

"The jury system can also be said to have some inherent defects, which are multiplied by the emergence of the criminal law from the relative simplicity that existed when the jury system was devised. It is a cumbersome process [which contributes] to delay in the machinery of justice. Untrained jurors are presumably less adept at reaching accurate conclusions of fact than judges, particularly if the issues are many or complex. [That] trial by jury is not the only fair way of adjudicating criminal guilt is well attested by the fact that it is not the prevailing way, either in England or in this country. [I] therefore see no reason why this Court should reverse the conviction of appellant, absent any suggestion that his particular trial was in fact unfair. . . .

"In sum, there is a wide range of views on the desirability of trial by jury, and on the ways to make it most effective when it is used; there is also considerable variation from State to State in local conditions such as the size of the criminal caseload, the ease or difficulty of summoning jurors, and other trial conditions bearing on fairness. We have before us, therefore, an almost perfect example of a situation in which [the states should serve as laboratories]. This Court, other courts, and the political process are available to correct any experiments in criminal procedure that prove fundamentally unfair to defendants. This is not what is being done today: instead, and quite without reason, the Court has chosen to impose upon every State one means of trying criminal cases; it is a good means, but it is not the only fair means, and it is not demonstrably better than the alternatives States might devise."

Note: Incorporation since Duncan

1. *The current scope of incorporation.* Although the Court has never embraced Justice Black's "total" incorporation theory, it has used "selective" incorporation to make almost all the specific guarantees of the bill of rights applicable to the states. To the enumeration set out in *Duncan*, the Court has added the fifth amendment prohibition on "double jeopardy," Benton v. Maryland, 395 U.S. 784 (1969), overruling *Palko*; the eighth amendment prohibition on "cruel and unusual punishment," Robinson v. California, 370 U.S. 660 (1962); and the eighth amendment prohibition on "excessive" bail, Schilb v. Kuebel, 404 U.S. 357 (1971). The only provisions of the first eight amendments that have not been incorporated are the second and third amendments, the fifth amendment's requirement of grand jury indictment, and the seventh amendment.

2. *Incorporation "jot-for-jot."* Prior to the 1960s, there were frequent suggestions that even if a specific guarantee of the bill of rights was incorporated in the due process clause of the fourteenth amendment, it did not necessarily apply to the states in the same manner as it applied to the federal government. In Wolf v. Colorado, 338 U.S. 25 (1949), for example, the Court held that the "security of one's privacy against arbitrary intrusion by the police — which is at the core of the fourth amendment — is basic to a free society" and "is therefore implicit in 'the concept of ordered liberty' and as such enforceable against the States through the Due Process Clause." Nonetheless the Court refused to apply the exclusionary rule, which was applicable to the federal government, to the states. Similarly, in Roth v. United States, 354 U.S. 476 (1957), Justice Harlan argued that the first amendment imposed fewer limits on state regulation of obscenity than it did on federal regulation. See also Beauharnais v. Illinois, 343 U.S. 250 (1952) (Jackson, J., dissenting) (different standards with respect to group libel).

As illustrated by *Duncan*, however, by the 1960s the Court had reached the conclusion that the guarantees of the bill of rights that were "selectively" incorporated in the due process clause of the fourteenth amendment should apply to the states in *precisely* the same manner as they applied to the federal government. See also Malloy v. Hogan, 378 U.S. 1 (1964) (self-incrimination); Pointer v. Texas, 380 U.S. 400 (1965) (confrontation); Benton v. Maryland, 395 U.S. 784 (1969) (double jeopardy).

Do you agree with Justice Fortas that this conclusion inflicts "a serious blow upon the principle of federalism"? Consider Pointer v. Texas, 380 U.S. 400, 413-414 (1965) (Goldberg, J., concurring):

I do not agree [that] once a provision of the Bill of Rights has been held applicable to the States [it] does not apply to the States in full strength. [While] I quite agree [that] "[i]t is one of the happy incidents of the federal system that [a State may] serve as a laboratory; and try novel social and economic experiments," [I] do not believe that this includes the power to experiment with the fundamental liberties of citizens safeguarded by the Bill of Rights. [Moreover,] I do not see that [this] view would further any legitimate interests of federalism. It would require this Court to intervene in the state judicial process with considerable lack of predictability and with a consequent likelihood of considerable friction.

Consider also *Williams* and *Apodaca:*

a. Williams. Although earlier interpretations of the sixth amendment had assumed that a twelve-person jury is constitutionally required, the Court held in Williams v. Florida, 399 U.S. 78 (1970), that "the twelve-man panel is not a necessary ingredient of 'trial by jury.'" In a concurring opinion, Justice Harlan noted that the necessary consequence of this decision is that twelve-member juries are not constitutionally required in *federal* criminal trials either and objected to the Court's "dilution" of the sixth amendment guarantee:

[The] internal logic of the selective incorporation doctrine cannot be respected if the Court is both committed to interpreting faithfully the meaning of the federal Bill of Rights and recognizing the governmental diversity that exists in this country. The "backlash" in *Williams* exposes the malaise, for [the] Court dilutes a federal guarantee in order to reconcile the logic of "incorporation" [with] the reality of federalism. [Can] we expect repeat performances when this Court is called upon to give definition and meaning to other federal guarantees that have been "incorporated"?

b. Apodaca. In Apodaca v. Oregon, 406 U.S. 404 (1972), the Court upheld the constitutionality of less-than-unanimous jury verdicts in state criminal cases. Eight justices adhered to the view that the sixth amendment right to jury trial applies to the states in the same way that it applies to the federal government. These justices divided four-to-four, however, on whether the sixth amendment requires jury unanimity. The deciding vote was cast by Justice Powell who, echoing Justice Harlan, maintained that jury unanimity is required by the sixth amendment but not by the fourteenth amendment due process clause. Justice Powell explained:

In [past] cases, the Court has presumed that unanimous verdicts are essential in federal jury trials [because] that result is mandated by [the intentions of the framers of the sixth amendment, who] desired to preserve the jury safeguard as it was known to them at common law. [But] it is the Fourteenth Amendment, rather than the Sixth, that imposes upon the States the requirement that they provide jury trials to those accused of serious crimes. [The] importance that our system attaches to trial by jury derives from the special confidence we repose in a "body of one's peers to determine guilt or innocence as a safeguard against arbitrary law enforcement." [This] is the fundamental of jury trial that brings it within the mandate of due process. It seems to me that this fundamental is adequately preserved by the [non-unanimous jury-verdict provision here at issue]. . . .

[In] holding that the Fourteenth Amendment has incorporated "jot-for-jot and case-for-case" every element of the Sixth Amendment, the Court derogates principles of federalism that are basic to our system. [It] deprives the States of freedom to experiment with adjudicatory processes different from the federal model. At the same time, the Court's understandable unwillingness to impose requirements that it finds unnecessarily rigid [citing *Williams*], has culminated in the dilution of federal rights that were, until these decisions, never seriously questioned. [Although] it is perhaps late in the day for an expression of my views, I would have been in accord with the opinions in [*Duncan* and *Williams* by Justices Harlan, Stewart, and Fortas] that, at least in defining the elements of the right to jury trial, there is no sound basis for interpreting the Fourteenth Amendment to require blind adherence by the States to all details of the federal Sixth Amendment standards.

See also Crist v. Bretz, 437 U.S. 28, 52-53 (1978) (Powell, J., joined by Burger, C.J., and Rehnquist, J., dissenting) (arguing that the fourteenth amendment does not "necessarily" impose on the states particular aspects of the fifth amendment's prohibition on "double jeopardy").

3. *Evaluation.* Consider Israel, Selective Incorporation: Revisited, 71 Mich. L. Rev. 253, 336-338 (1982):

Over the years [the Court's incorporation] opinions [have] referred largely to five concerns: (1) adhering to the language of the amendment and the intent of its framers; (2) avoiding vague standards that invite the Justices to apply their own subjective and idiosyncratic views of basic justice; (3) providing broad protection of individual liberties against state systems too often willing to sacrifice those [liberties]; (4) giving appropriate recognition to the principles of federalism; and (5) providing sufficient direction to state courts to gain consistent enforcement of federal constitutional [standards]. Perhaps no concern has been mentioned more frequently than the first, [but] neither the language nor the history has proven especially [confining]. The Court's rulings also suggest that the second concern [was] far from a dominant factor, [for the] "ordered liberty" standard remains a part of the selective incorporation doctrine. [The] third and fourth concerns have [had considerable] influence, [for the] pre-1960s Court [gave special] weight to the interests of federalism, [and] the Court of the 1960s [gave] greater weight to expanding [constitutional protections]. In the end, the fifth concern [may] have proven the most significant, [for selective incorporation's relative clarity] may do more to promote a vital federalist system than [an approach that] gives the state slightly greater leeway at the fringes.

4. *Beyond incorporation.* This section has focused on whether the specific guarantees of the bill of rights are incorporated in the due process clause of the fourteenth amendment. Is the content of "due process" *limited* to the specific guarantees of the first eight amendments? If not, how is the Court to decide on the additional content?

Consider In re Winship, 397 U.S. 358 (1970), in which the Court held that because the requirement that proof of criminal charges be beyond a reasonable doubt "plays a vital role in the American scheme of criminal procedure" and "is indispensable to command the respect and confidence of the community," the "Due Process Clause protects the accused against conviction except upon proof beyond a reasonable doubt." Justice Black dissented:

[Nowhere] in [the Constitution] is there any statement that conviction of crime requires proof beyond a reasonable doubt. The Constitution [goes] into some detail to spell out what kind of trial a defendant charged with crime should have, and I believe the Court has no power to add to or subtract from the procedures set forth by the Founders. I realize that it is far easier to substitute individual judges' ideas of "fairness" for the fairness prescribed by the Constitution, but I shall not at any time surrender my belief that that document itself should be our guide, not our own concept of what is fair, decent, and right.

Consider Justice Frankfurter's response to a similar argument in *Adamson*:

> The Due Process Clause of the Fourteenth Amendment has an independent potency, precisely as does the Due Process Clause of the Fifth Amendment in relation to the Federal Government. It ought not to require argument to reject the notion that due process of law meant one thing in the Fifth Amendment and another in the Fourteenth. [The Bill of Rights specifically guarantees certain rights that the Court has held to be incorporated within the concept of "due process," and it *also* specifically] precludes deprivation of "life, liberty, or property, without due process of law. . . ." Are Madison and his contemporaries in the framing of the Bill of Rights to be charged with writing into it a meaningless clause?

If "due process" embraces procedural rights other than those expressly enumerated in the bill of rights, does it also embrace *substantive* rights other than those enumerated in the bill of rights? That is the central inquiry of the next section.

D. SUBSTANTIVE DUE PROCESS: THE PROTECTION OF ECONOMIC INTERESTS

As we saw in section B supra, the Court held in the Slaughter-House Cases that the privileges or immunities clause of the fourteenth amendment protects only the privileges or immunities of national citizenship and thus does not protect the fundamental rights of individuals. As we saw in section C, however, the Court held in a series of decisions after *Slaughter-House* that the due process clause of the fourteenth amendment incorporates most of the express guarantees of the bill of rights and thus protects at least *those* fundamental rights. *Slaughter-House* itself, however, did not involve a right expressly guaranteed in the Bill of Rights. Rather, it involved what Justice Bradley termed the "fundamental" right of each individual "to follow such profession or employment as [he] may choose." To what extent, if any, does the Constitution protect this "right"?

The Constitution contains several provisions that expressly restrict government's power to interfere with the private economic interests of individuals. The fifth and fourteenth amendments, for example, provide that "No person shall [be] deprived of [property,] without due process of law." Article I, section 10 provides that "No State shall [pass] any [Law] impairing the Obligation of Contracts." And the fifth amendment provides that "private property" shall not "be taken for public use, without just compensation." Although these provisions reflect the importance of private property, they protect private economic interests only against certain narrowly defined forms of government interference. See Chapter 9, infra. Is there a more general constitutional limitation on the power of government to interfere with private economic decisions?

In its 1905 decision in Lochner v. New York, infra, the Court held that the due process clauses of the fifth and fourteenth amendments protect liberty of contract and private property against unwarranted government interference. This section traces the rise — and fall — of this doctrine.

Note: The Road to Lochner

1. *Early intimations.* Although the doctrine of economic substantive due process did not come into full flower until the Court's 1905 decision in *Lochner,* several pre-*Lochner* decisions flirted with analogous doctrines. In Calder v. Bull, supra Chapter 1, section C, more than a century before *Lochner,* Justice Chase's "natural law" theory clearly reflected a concern with property rights, and in Fletcher v. Peck, 10 U.S. (6 Cranch.) 87 (1810), in which the Court held that a state legislature could not constitutionally rescind land grants to individuals who had purchased the land in good faith, Chief Justice Marshall explained that the result was justified both by the contract clause and "by general principles which are common to our free institutions." Moreover, in Wynehamer v. People, 13 N.Y. 378 (1856), the New York Court of Appeals relied expressly on the state due process clause in invalidatng a liquor prohibition statute that prohibited the use or possession even of liquor owned prior to the enactment of the statute. The New York court explained that when "a law annihilates the value of property, [the] owner is deprived of it [within] the spirit of a constitutional provision intended expressly to shield private rights from the exercise of arbitrary power." A year after *Wynehamer,* in Dred Scott v. Sanford, 60 U.S. (19 How.) 393 (1857), the Court held that Congress could not prohibit slavery in the territories. The Court observed, without explanation, that an "act of Congress which deprives a citizen of the United States of his liberty or property, merely because he came himself or brought his property into a particular [Territory,] could hardly be dignified with the name of due process of law."

These intermittent intimations of economic substantive due process did not seriously challenge the prevailing view that the due process guarantee was essentially *procedural* in nature. See Den ex dem. Murray v. Hoboken Land & Improvement Co., 59 U.S. (18 How.) 272 (1856). Moreover, in the Slaughter-House Cases, the Court held not only that the Louisiana statute did not violate the privileges or immunities clause of the fourteenth amendment, but also that it did not violate the fourteenth amendment due process clause. The Court explained that "under no construction of that provision we have ever seen, or any that we deem admissible, can the restraint imposed by the State of Louisiana upon the exercise of their trade by the butchers of New Orleans be held to be a deprivation of property within the meaning of that provision."

Slaughter-House did not end the matter, however. For as Professor Corwin, the leading commentator on the era, observed: "In less than twenty years from the time of its rendition, the crucial ruling in *Wynehamer* [was] far on the way to being assimilated into the accepted constitutional law of the country. The 'due process' clause, which had been intended originally to consecrate a mode of procedure, had become a constitutional test of ever increasing reach of the substantive content of legislation." E. Corwin, Liberty against Government 114

(1948). See Corwin, The Basic Doctrine of American Constitutional Law, 12 Mich. L. Rev. 247 (1914); Corwin, The Doctrine of Due Process before the Civil War, 24 Harv. L. Rev. 366, 460 (1911); Corwin, The "Higher Law" Background of American Constitutional Law, 42 Harv. L. Rev. 149, 365 (1928-1929).

2. *The road to* Lochner. The shift identified by Professor Corwin was directed, in part, by economic and social developments. The rise of industrial organization in the late nineteenth century transformed American society. As ownership of productive property became increasingly concentrated, inequalities in private economic power grew sharper and the number of persons without significant productive property and dependent on industrial employment increased. As the twentieth century approached, state legislatures began to address working and social conditions accompanying the concentration of private power in business. Opponents of the new regulatory laws maintained that "fundamental" rights of property were not being respected by the popularly controlled state legislatures. See, e.g., C. Tiedeman, A Treatise on the Limitations of the Police Power in the United States (1886). Armed with the laissez-faire doctrines of the eighteenth-century economist Adam Smith and the nineteenth-century social Darwinist Herbert Spencer, and supported by the leading constitutional law text of the period, Thomas M. Cooley's Constitutional Limitations (1868), legal representatives of the regulated industries increasingly urged the courts to invalidate the new legislation. Gradually, the Supreme Court assumed the burden of reconciling majoritarian authority with individual property rights in the new era of large-scale private organization.

In Munn v. Illinois, 94 U.S. 113 (1877), the Court held that an Illinois law fixing the maximum charges for grain-storage warehouses did not violate the due process clause of the fourteenth amendment. The Court noted, however, that "under some circumstances" such statutes may violate due process. The critical inquiry was whether the "private property is 'affected with a public interest,' [for when] one devotes his property to a use in which the public has an interest, he, in effect, grants to the public an interest in that use, and must submit to be controlled by the public for the common good." The Court held that the businesses regulated in *Munn* were clearly "affected with a public interest," for they had a "virtual monopoly" on the storage of grain bound from the midwest to national and international markets. In such circumstances, the Court would not consider the "reasonableness" of the rates.

Consider D. Currie, The Constitution in the Supreme Court: The First Hundred Years 1789–1888 ch. 11 (1985): "By stressing the public interest in grain elevators, the Court seemed to imply that they were extraordinary, and that similar regulation of other businesses might not pass muster. By employing the rhetoric of substantive due process without ever having justified its acceptance, [Waite] made it easy for his successors to argue that the principle had already been established." For an interesting perspective on *Munn*, see Kitch & Bowler, The Facts of Munn v. Illinois, 1978 Sup. Ct. Rev. 313.

By the late 1880s, a decade after *Munn* and some fifteen years after *Slaughter-House*, the make-up of the Court had changed almost completely, and the new appointees were increasingly inclined to use the due process clause to protect substantive rights of property. Whether this shift was due to the justices' conservative economic policies, see A. Paul, Conservative Crisis and the Rule of Law (1969), their hostility to labor regulations, see L. Beth, The Development of the

American Constitution 1877–1917, at 138-168 (1971), or their acceptance of the liberty-based jurisprudence of the antislavery movement, see Nelson, The Impact of the Antislavery Movement upon Styles of Judicial Reasoning in Nineteenth Century America, 87 Harv. L. Rev. 513, 547-566 (1974), the shift in judicial attitude was evident.

In the Railroad Commission Cases, 116 U.S. 307 (1886), the Court sustained state regulation of railroad rates but emphasized that there was a limit to judicial deference: "[The] power to regulate is not a power to [destroy]. Under pretence of regulating fares and freights, the State cannot require a railroad corporation to carry persons or property without reward; neither can it do that which in law amounts to a taking of private property for public use without just compensation, or without due process of law."

Later that same year, in Santa Clara County v. Southern Pacific Railroad, 116 U.S. 394 (1886), the Court held, without argument, that corporations were "persons" within the meaning of the due process clause of the fourteenth amendment, thus opening the door for direct challenges to regulations by corporations. For the "story" behind this decision, see Graham, The "Conspiracy Theory" of the Fourteenth Amendment, 47 Yale L.J. 371 (1938). See also P. Freund, The Supreme Court of the United States 46-49 (1961); Wheeling Steel Corp. v. Glander, 337 U.S. 562, 576 (1949) (Douglas, J., dissenting) (*Santa Clara County* should be "overruled"); Connecticut General Life Insurance Co. v. Johnson, 303 U.S. 77, 85-90 (1938) (Black, J., dissenting) (same).

The following year, in Mugler v. Kansas, 123 U.S. 623 (1887), the Court upheld a state law prohibiting the sale of alcoholic beverages, but again cautioned that not every regulatory measure "is to be accepted as a legitimate exertion of the police powers of the State." The Court warned that, if "a statute purporting to have been enacted to protect the public health, the public morals, or the public safety, has no real or substantial relations to those objects, or is a palpable invasion of rights secured by the fundamental law, it is the duty of the courts to so adjudge, and thereby give effect to the Constitution." Thus, by the late 1880s "the concept of due process as a judicially enforced bar to arbitrary economic legislation was ready for action." R. McCloskey, The American Supreme Court 131 (1960).

In the Minnesota Rate Case (Chicago, Milwaukee & St. Paul Railway v. Minnesota), 134 U.S. 418 (1890), the Court held unconstitutional a state statute authorizing a commission to set final and unreviewable railroad rates, thus marking the first time that the Court relied directly on the due process clause to invalidate a state economic regulation. The Court explained:

> The question of reasonableness of a rate of charge for transportation by a railroad company [is] eminently a question for judicial investigation, requiring due process of law for its determination. If the company is deprived of the power of charging reasonable rates for the use of its property, and such deprivation takes place in the absence of investigation by judicial machinery, it is deprived of the lawful use of its property, and thus, in substance and effect, of the property itself, without due process of law.

In dissent, Justice Bradley maintained that the decision practically overruled *Munn*. Three decades later, Judge Hough, with the advantage of hindsight, said:

"It is from [the Minnesota Rate Case] that I date the flood." Hough, Due Process of Law — Today, 32 Harv. L. Rev. 218, 228 (1919). Indeed, by the end of the decade, the Court was actively in the business of reviewing the reasonableness of rates. See Smith v. Ames, 169 U.S. 466 (1898) (establishing the rule that rates must yield a fair return on a fair present value); Federal Power Commission v. Hope Natural Gas Co., 320 U.S. 591 (1944) (tracing the evolution and eventual repudiation of the rule of Smith v. Ames); Siegel, Understanding the *Lochner* Era: Lessons from the Controversy over Railroad and Utility Rate Regulation, 70 Va. L. Rev. 187 (1984).

In Allgeyer v. Louisiana, 165 U.S. 578 (1897), the Court took the final step toward *Lochner*. In *Allgeyer* the Court invalidated a state statute that prohibited any person from effecting insurance on property in the state with companies that had not been admitted to business in the state. Although Justice Peckham, writing for a unanimous Court, focused primarily on state power over foreign corporations, he also offered a comprehensive articulation of the "liberty of contract":

> The liberty mentioned in [the due process clause] means not only the right of the citizen to be free from the mere physical restraint of his person, as by incarceration, but the term is deemed to embrace the right of the citizen to be free in the enjoyment of all his faculties; to be free to use them in all lawful ways; to live and work where he will; to earn his livelihood by any lawful calling; to pursue any livelihood or avocation, and for that purpose to enter into all contracts which may be proper, necessary and essential to his carrying out to a successful conclusion the purposes mentioned above. [In] the privilege of pursuing an ordinary calling or trade and of acquiring, holding and selling property must be embraced the right to make all proper contracts in relation thereto, and although it may be conceded that this right to contract [or] to do business within the jurisdiction of the State may be regulated and sometimes prohibited when the contracts or business conflict with the policy of the State as contained in its statutes, yet the power does not and cannot extend to prohibiting a citizen from making contracts of the nature involved in this case outside of the limits and jurisdiction of the State, and which are also to be performed outside of such jurisdiction.

Lochner v. New York
198 U.S. 45 (1905)

MR. JUSTICE PECKHAM [delivered] the opinion of the Court.

[The Court held unconstitutional a New York statute providing that no employee shall "work in a biscuit, bread or cake bakery or confectionary establishment more than sixty hours in any one week, or more than ten hours in any one day."]

The statute necessarily interferes with the right of contract between the employer and employés, concerning the number of hours in which the latter may labor in the bakery of the employer. The general right to make a contract in relation to his business is part of the liberty of the individual protected by the Fourteenth Amendment of the Federal Constitution. [*Allgeyer.*] Under that provision no State can deprive any person of life, liberty or property without due process of law. The right to purchase or to sell labor is part of the liberty protected by this amendment, unless there are circumstances which exclude the right.

There are, however, certain powers, existing in the sovereignty of each State in the Union, somewhat vaguely termed police powers, the exact description and limitation of which have not been attempted by the courts. Those powers [relate] to the safety, health, morals and general welfare of the public. Both property and liberty are held on such reasonable conditions as may be imposed by the governing power of the State in the exercise of those powers, and with such conditions the Fourteenth Amendment was not designed to interfere. [*Mugler.*]

This court has recognized the existence and upheld the exercise of the police powers of the States in many cases. [Among] the [cases] where the state law has been upheld by this court is that of Holden v. Hardy, 169 U.S. 366 [1898]. A provision in the act of the legislature of Utah was there under consideration, the act limiting the employment of workmen in all underground mines or workings, to eight hours per day, "except in cases of emergency, where life or property is in imminent danger." [The] act was held to be a valid exercise of the police powers of the State. [It] was held that the kind of employment [and] the character of the employés [were] such as to make it reasonable and proper for the State to interfere to prevent the employés from being constrained by the rules laid down by the proprietors in regard to labor. [There] is nothing in Holden v. Hardy which covers the case now before us. . . .

It must, of course, be conceded that there is a limit to the valid exercise of the police power by the State. There is no dispute concerning this general proposition. Otherwise the Fourteenth Amendment would have no efficacy and the legislatures of the States would have unbounded power. [In] every case that comes before this court, therefore, where legislation of this character is concerned and where the protection of the Federal Constitution is sought, the question necessarily arises: Is this a fair, reasonable and appropriate exercise of the police power of the State, or is it an unreasonable, unnecessary and arbitrary interference with the right of the individual to his personal liberty or to enter into those contracts in relation to labor which may seem to him appropriate or necessary for the support of himself and his family? Of course the liberty of contract relating to labor includes both parties to it. The one has as much right to purchase as the other to sell labor.

This is not a question of substituting the judgment of the court for that of the legislature. If the act be within the power of the State it is valid, although the judgment of the court might be totally opposed to the enactment of such a law. But the question would still remain: Is it within the police power of the State? and that question must be answered by the court.

The question whether this act is valid as a labor law, pure and simple, may be dismissed in a few words. There is no reasonable ground for interfering with the liberty of person or the right of free contract, by determining the hours of labor, in the occupation of a baker. There is no contention that bakers as a class are not equal in intelligence and capacity to men in other trades or manual occupations, or that they are not able to assert their rights and care for themselves without the protecting arm of the State, interfering with their independence of judgment and of action. They are in no sense wards of the State. Viewed in the light of a purely labor law, with no reference whatever to the question of health, we think that a law like the one before us involves neither the safety, the morals nor the welfare of the public, and that the interest of the public is not in the slightest degree affected by such an act. The law must be upheld, if at all, as a law pertaining to the health of the individual engaged in the occupation of a baker. It does not affect any other portion of the public than those who are engaged in that occupation. Clean and wholesome bread does not depend upon whether the baker works but ten hours per day or only sixty hours a week. . . .

It is a question of which of two powers or rights shall prevail — the power of the State to legislate or the right of the individual to liberty of person and freedom of contract. The mere assertion that the subject relates though but in a remote degree to the public health does not necessarily render the enactment valid. The act must have a more direct relation, as a means to an end, and the end itself must be appropriate and legitimate, before an act can be held to be valid which interferes with the general right of an individual to be free in his person and in his power to contract in relation to his own labor. . . .

We think the limit of the police power has been reached and passed in this case. There is, in our judgment, no reasonable foundation for holding this to be necessary or appropriate as a health law to safeguard the public health or the health of the individuals who are following the trade of a baker. If this statute be valid, [there] would seem to be no length to which legislation of this nature might not go. . . .

We think that there can be no fair doubt that the trade of a baker, in and of itself, is not an unhealthy one to that degree which would authorize the legislature to interfere with the right to labor, and with the right of free contract on the part of the individual, either as employer or employé. In looking through statistics regarding all trades and occupations, it may be true that the trade of a baker does not appear to be as healthy as some other trades, and is also vastly more healthy than still others. To the common understanding the trade of a baker has never been regarded as an unhealthy one. [It] might be safely affirmed that almost all occupations more or less affect the health. There must be more than the mere fact of the possible existence of some small amount of unhealthiness to warrant legislative interference with liberty. It is unfortunately true that labor, even in any department, may possibly carry with it the seeds of unhealthiness. But are we all, on that account, at the mercy of legislative majorities? . . .

It is also urged, pursuing the same line of argument, that it is to the interest of the State that its population should be strong and robust, and therefore any legislation which may be said to tend to make people healthy must be valid as health laws, enacted under the police power. If this be a valid argument and a justification for this kind of legislation, it follows that the protection of the Federal Constitution from undue interference with liberty of person and freedom of contract is visionary, wherever the law is sought to be justified as a valid exercise of the police power. Scarcely any law but might find shelter under such assumptions. . . . Not only the hours of employés, but the hours of employers, could be regulated, and doctors, lawyers, scientists, all professional men, as well as athletes and artisans, could be forbidden to fatigue their brains and bodies by prolonged hours of exercise, lest the fighting strength of the State be impaired. We mention these extreme cases because the contention is extreme. We do not believe in the soundness of the views which uphold this law. [The] act is not, within any fair meaning of the term, a health law, but is an illegal interference with the rights of individuals, both employers and employés, to make contracts regarding labor upon such terms as they may think best, or which they may agree upon with the other parties to such contracts. Statutes of the nature of that under review, limiting the hours in which grown and intelligent men may labor to earn their living, are mere meddlesome interferences with the rights of the individual, and they are not saved from condemnation by the claim that they are passed in the exercise of the police power and upon the subject of the health of the individual whose rights are interfered with, unless there be some fair ground, reasonable in and of itself, to say that there is material danger to the public health or to the health of the employés, if the hours of labor are not curtailed. [All that the State] could properly do has been done by it with regard to the conduct of bakeries, as provided for in the other sections of the act, [which] provide for the inspection of the premises where the bakery is carried on, with regard to furnishing proper wash-rooms and water-closets, [with] regard to providing proper drainage, plumbing and painting [and] for other things of that nature. . . .

It was further urged [that] restricting the hours of labor in the case of bakers was valid because it tended to cleanliness on the part of the workers, as a man was more apt to be cleanly when not overworked, and if cleanly then his "output" was also more likely to be so. [In] our judgment it is not possible in fact to discover the connection between the number of hours a baker may work in the bakery and the healthful quality of the bread made by the workman. The connection, if any exists, is too shadowy and thin to build any argument for the interference of the legislature. [When] assertions such as we have adverted to become necessary in order to give, if possible, a plausible foundation for the contention that the law is a "health law," it gives rise to at least a suspicion that there was some other motive dominating the legislature than the purpose to subserve the public health or welfare.

This interference on the part of the legislatures of the several States with the ordinary trades and occupations of the people seems to be on the increase. . . .

It is impossible for us to shut our eyes to the fact that many of the laws of this character, while passed under what is claimed to be the police power for the purpose of protecting the public health or welfare, are, in reality, passed from other motives. We are justified in saying so when, from the character of the law and the subject upon which it legislates, it is apparent that the public health or welfare bears but the most remote relation to the law. The purpose of a statute must be determined from the natural and legal effect of the language employed; and whether it is or is not repugnant to the Constitution of the United States must be determined from the natural effect of such statutes when put into operation, and not from their proclaimed purpose. [The] court looks beyond the mere letter of the law in such cases. Yick Wo v. Hopkins, 118 U.S. 356.

It is manifest to us that the [law here] has no such direct relation to and no such substantial effect upon the health of the employé, as to justify us in regarding the section as really a health law. It seems to us that the real object and purpose were simply to regulate the hours of labor between the master and his employés (all being men, sui juris), in a private business, not dangerous in any degree to morals or in any real and substantial degree, to the health of the employés. Under such circumstances the freedom of master and employé to contract with each other in relation to their employment [cannot] be prohibited or interfered with, without violating the Federal Constitution. . . .

Reversed.

Mr. Justice Harlan, with whom Mr. Justice White and Mr. Justice Day concurred, dissenting. . . .

[The] statute must be taken as expressing the belief of the people of New York that, as a general rule, and in the case of the average man, labor in excess of sixty hours during a week in such establishments may endanger the health of those who thus labor. Whether or not this be wise legislation it is not the province of the court to inquire. Under our systems of government the courts are not concerned with the wisdom or policy of legislation. So that in determining the question of power to interfere with liberty of contract, the court may inquire whether the means devised by the State are germane to an end which may be lawfully accomplished and have a real or substantial relation to the protection of health, as involved in the daily work of the persons, male and female, engaged in bakery and confectionery establishments. But when this inquiry is entered upon I find it impossible, in view of common experience, to say that there is here no real or substantial relation between the means employed by the State and the end sought to be accomplished by its legislation. . . .

Professor Hirt in his treatise on the "Diseases of the Workers" has said:

> The labor of the bakers is among the hardest and most laborious imaginable, because it has to be performed under conditions injurious to the health of those engaged in it. It is hard, very hard work, not only because it requires a great deal of physical exertion in an overheated workshop and during unreasonably long hours, but more so because of the erratic demands of the public, compelling the baker to perform the greater part of his work at night, thus depriving him of an opportunity to enjoy the necessary rest and sleep, a fact which is highly injurious to his health.

Another writer says:

> The constant inhaling of flour dust causes inflammation of the lungs and of the bronchial tubes. The eyes also suffer through this dust. . . . The long hours of toil to which all bakers are subjected produce rheumatism, cramps and swollen legs. The intense heat in the workshops [is] another source of a number of diseases of various organs. [The] average age of a baker is below that of other workmen; they seldom live over their fiftieth year, most of them dying between the ages of forty and fifty. . . .

We judicially know that the question of the number of hours during which a workman should continuously labor has been, for a long period, and is yet, a subject of serious consideration among civilized peoples, and by those having special knowledge of the laws of health. . . .

We also judicially know that the number of hours that should constitute a day's labor in particular occupations involving the physical strength and safety of workmen has been the subject of enactments by Congress and by nearly all of the States. Many, if not most, of those enactments fix eight hours as the proper basis of a day's labor.

I do not stop to consider whether any particular view of this economic question presents the sounder theory. What the precise facts are it may be difficult to say. It is enough for the determination of this case, and it is enough for this court to know, that the question is one about which there is room for debate and for an honest difference of opinion. There are many reasons of a weighty, substantial character, based upon the experience of mankind, in support of the theory that, all things considered, more than ten hours' steady work each day, from week to week, in a bakery or confectionery establishment, may endanger the health, and shorten the lives of the workmen, thereby diminishing their physical and mental capacity to serve the State, and to provide for those dependent upon them.

If such reasons exist that ought to be the end of this case, for the State is not amenable to the judiciary, in respect of its legislative enactments, unless such enactments are plainly, palpably, beyond all question inconsistent with the Constitution of the United States. . . .

MR. JUSTICE HOLMES dissenting. . . .

This case is decided upon an economic theory which a large part of the country does not entertain. If it were a question whether I agreed with that theory, I should desire to study it further and long before making up my mind. But I do not conceive that to be my duty, because I strongly believe that my agreement or disagreement has nothing to do with the right of a majority to embody their opinions in law. It is settled by various decisions of this court that state constitutions and state laws may regulate life in many ways which we as legislators might think as injudicious or if you like as tyrannical as this, and which equally with this interfere with the liberty to contract. Sunday laws and usury laws are ancient examples. A more modern one is the prohibition of lotteries. The liberty of the citizen to do as he likes so long as he does not interfere with the liberty of others to do the same, which has been a shibboleth for some well-known writers, is interfered with by school laws, by the Post Office, by every state or municipal institution which takes his money for purposes thought desirable, whether he likes it or not. The Fourteenth Amendment does not enact Mr. Herbert Spencer's Social Statics. The other day we sustained the Massachusetts vaccination law. Jacobson v. Massachusetts, 197 U.S. 11. United States and state statutes and decisions cutting down the liberty to contract by way of combination are familiar to this court. [The] decision sustaining an eight hour law for miners is still recent. [Holden v. Hardy.] Some of these laws embody convictions or prejudices which judges are likely to share. Some may not. But a constitution is not intended to embody a particular economic theory, whether of paternalism and the organic relation of the citizen to the State or of laissez faire. It is made for people of fundamentally differing views, and the accident of our finding certain opinions natural and familiar or novel and even shocking ought not to conclude our judgment upon the question whether statutes embodying them conflict with the Constitution of the United States.

General propositions do not decide concrete cases. The decision will depend on a judgment or intuition more subtle than any articulate major premise. But I think that the proposition just stated, if it is accepted, will carry us far toward the end. Every opinion tends to become a law. I think that the word liberty in the Fourteenth Amendment is perverted when it is held to prevent the natural outcome of a dominant opinion, unless it can be said that a rational and fair man necessarily would admit that the statute proposed would infringe fundamental principles as they have been understood by the traditions of our people and our law. It does not need research to show that no such sweeping condemnation can be passed upon the statute before us. A reasonable man might think it a proper measure on the score of health. Men whom I certainly could not pronounce unreasonable would uphold it as a first instalment of a general regulation of the hours of work. . . .

Note: The "Vices" of Lochner

Lochner "is one of the most condemned cases in United States history and has been used to symbolize judicial dereliction and abuse." B. Siegan, Economic Liberties and the Constitution 23 (1980). Why? Consider the following criticisms:

1. *The "liberty of contract" protected in* Lochner *is not within the "liberty" protected by the due process clause.* In *Allgeyer* the Court announced that the "'liberty' mentioned in [the due process clause] is deemed to embrace the right [to] make all proper contracts." This view has been disputed. Consider Warren, The New "Liberty" under the Fourteenth Amendment, 39 Harv. L. Rev. 431, 440 (1926):

> The phrase, "life, liberty or property without due process of law" came to us from the English common law; and there seems to be little question that, under the common law, the word "liberty" meant simply "liberty of the person," or, in other words, "the right to have one's person free from physical restraint." [It] is unquestionable that when the First Congress adopted the Fifth Amendment and inserted the Due Process Clause, they took it with the meaning it then bore.

Suppose a law provides that no person who breaches a contract may make a binding contract for one year thereafter. May the state, in determining whether an individual has committed the initial breach, use procedures that fall short of "due process" because there is no deprivation of "liberty"? Is Warren's conception of "liberty" too narrow? Should the "liberty of contract" protected in *Lochner* be based not in the "liberty" component of the due process clause but in its "property" component? See Coppage v. Kansas, 236 U.S. 1 (1915) ("included in the right [of] personal property [is] the right to make contracts").

2. *Even if the "liberty of contract" is a "liberty" or "property" protected by the due process clause, that clause does not accord "substantive" protection to the "liberty of contract."* There are several variations on this argument. First, one might argue that the due process clause is concerned exclusively with "procedure," and thus has no relevance to the statute at issue in *Lochner*. "Substantive due process," it has been argued, "is a contradiction in terms — sort of like 'green pastel redness.'" J. Ely, Democracy and Distrust 18 (1980). Note, however, that "the words that follow 'due process' are 'of law,' and the word 'law' seems to have been the textual point of departure for substantive due process." Tribe, The Puzzling Persistence of Process-Based Constitutional Theories, 89 Yale L.J. 1063, 1066 n.9 (1980). The notion of "due process," in other words, might logically be understood as prohibiting arbitrary governance in the legislative as well as the judicial process. Note, too, that the argument limiting "due process" to the judicial sphere would require abandonment of at least some elements of the "incorporation" doctrine, which accords protection via the due process clause to such "substantive" rights as the first amendment guarantees of free speech, press, and religion, the fourth amendment guarantee of freedom from "unreasonable" searches and seizures, and the fifth amendment guarantee that "private property" will not "be taken for public use, without just compensation."

Second, one might argue, as did Justice Black in the "incorporation" context, that the due process clause accords substantive protection *only* to those rights that are expressly guaranteed in the bill of rights, thus excluding the "liberty of contract."

Third, one might argue that the due process clause accords substantive protection to all "fundamental" rights, but that the "liberty of contract" is not "fundamental." Under this view, "the error of [*Lochner*] lay not in judicial intervention to protect 'liberty' but in a misguided understanding of what liberty actually required." L. Tribe, American Constitutional Law 564 (1978).

Is the "liberty of contract" a "fundamental" right? Consider Siegan, supra, at 83:

> A free society cannot exist unless government is prohibited from confiscating private property. If government can seize something owned by a private citizen, it can exert enormous power over people. One would be reluctant to speak, write, pray, or petition in a manner displeasing to the authorities lest he lose what he has already earned and possesses. As [Alexander] Hamilton stated, a power over a man's subsistence amounts to a power over his will.

The historical commitment to the "liberty of contract" and to rights of property runs deep: "[In the view of the Framers,] a major function of government was protecting and preserving property rights. [The] Framers probably subscribed to Blackstone's definition that the right of property is 'absolute . . . [and] consists in the free use, enjoyment and disposal [by man] of all his acquisitions, without any control or diminution, save only by the laws of the land.'" Siegan, supra, at 30-31. Moreover, in Calder v. Bull, Justice Chase maintained that "natural law" prohibits "a law that destroys or impairs the lawful private contracts of citizens [or] that takes property from A. and gives it to B." In Corfield v. Coryell, 6 Fed. Cas. 546 (1823), a decision recognized by all of the justices participating in *Slaughter-House* as defining the "fundamental" rights of individuals, Justice Washington declared that the "fundamental" privileges and immunities of individuals include the "right [to] take, hold and dispose of property." And the Civil Rights Act of 1866, which provided the impetus for the fourteenth amendment, expressly protected the right of blacks "to make and enforce contracts [and to] purchase, lease, sell, hold and convey real and personal property."

In light of these considerations, on what grounds might one argue that the "liberty of contract" is not "fundamental"?

3. *The means/ends connection: Even if the "liberty of contract" is entitled to "substantive" protection under the due process clause, the statute at issue in* Lochner *was justified by the state's interest in protecting the health of bakery employees.* If it is assumed that the liberty of contract is substantively protected by the due process clause, what standard should the Court apply in deciding whether the challenged law sufficiently serves the state's interest in protecting the health of bakery employees to withstand constitutional attack? In his opinion for the Court, Justice Peckham declared that for the statute to be "saved from condemnation," there must "be some fair ground, reasonable in and of itself, to say that there is material danger to the public health or to the health of the employees, if the hours of labor are not curtailed." Is this standard too stringent? Should the Court have sustained the law because, as Justice Harlan observed, "the question

is one about which there is room for debate and for an honest difference of opinion"?

Even if one assumes that Justice Peckham stated the appropriate standard, why weren't the data offered by Justice Harlan sufficient to satisfy that standard? Do you agree with Peckham that if the Court upheld this law, "there would seem to be no length to which legislation of this nature might not go"? What *additional* evidence was needed to satisfy the Court?

The Court's careful examination of the means/ends connection might be criticized on two grounds. The first is that judges do not have the factfinding competence to engage in such inquiries; the second is that judges are unelected, and therefore lack the accountability that would support such a role. Note, however, that careful examination of the means/ends connection is a common feature of modern constitutional law. Recall, for example, the Court's analysis of "suspect" classifications under the equal protection clause. See Chapter 5, supra.

Consider Tribe, supra, at 436-437:

> [*Lochner* and similar decisions] expressed profound skepticism about academic or other experts as witnesses and especially about legislators as factfinders. Such "facts" were regarded as manipulable and thus unreliable. Instead, the Court interpreted its requirement of a substantial means-ends relationship so as to invalidate statutes which interfered with private economic transactions unless evolving common law concepts demonstrated a proper fit between the legislation and its asserted objectives. [The] result in *Holden*, [for example,] appeared to rest heavily on the characterization of mining as an activity which the courts had traditionally recognized as unusually dangerous or ultrahazardous. [The] Court was plainly more willing to trust the gradually evolving categories of the common law than the readily tailored findings of "experts," committees, or even legislative majorities.

In fact, the Court did not always follow the "common law" approach. In Muller v. Oregon, 208 U.S. 412 (1908), for example, the Court sustained against due process attack an Oregon statute forbidding the employment of women "in any mechanical establishment, or factory, or laundry" for more than ten hours in any one day because the extensive evidence marshalled by Louis D. Brandeis in his "factual" brief convinced the Court that there was ample justification for the "widespread belief that woman's physical structure, and the functions she performs in consequence thereof, justify special legislation restricting or qualifying the conditions under which she should be permitted to toil." On the "Brandeis brief," see P. Freund, On Understanding the Supreme Court 86-91 (1949); Bikle, Judicial Determination of Questions of Fact Affecting the Constitutional Validity of Legislative Action, 38 Harv. L. Rev. 6 (1924); Karst, Legislative Facts in Constitutional Litigation, 1960 Sup. Ct. Rev. 75. Is *Muller* explainable on the ground that the Court regarded women as a dependent class analogous to workers in mining camps? Recall the discussion of gender discrimination in Chapter 5, section D, supra.

4. *The problem of ends: Even if the "liberty of contract" is entitled to "substantive" protection under the due process clause, the statute at issue in* Lochner *was justified as a "labor law, pure and simple."* Why wasn't the New York statute justified as a means of compensating for the unequal bargaining position of bakery workers? On "unequal bargaining power," see Kennedy, Distributive and Paternalistic Motives in Contract and Tort Law, with Special Reference to Com-

pulsory Terms and Unequal Bargaining Power, 41 Md. L. Rev. 563 (1982). In dismissing the "health" justification, the Court conceded that "health" is a legitimate end of the police power but held that the statute did not sufficiently promote that legitimate purpose. The Court dismissed the "labor law" justification, however, as an effort to further an illegitimate end. Indeed, the Court was so concerned with the "illegitimacy" of this end that it was prepared to disregard the state's assertion that the law actually had a different, legitimate, purpose. Why? Consider the following observations:

a. Coppage v. Kansas, 236 U.S. 1, 17-18 (1915):

[It] is said [that] "employees, as a rule, are not financially able to be as independent in making contracts for the sale of their labor as are employers in making contracts of purchase thereof." No doubt, wherever the right of private property exists, there must and will be inequalities of fortune. [Thus, it is] impossible to uphold freedom of contract and the right of private property without at the same time recognizing as legitimate those inequalities of fortune that are the necessary result of the exercise of those rights. [And] since a State may not strike [those rights] down directly it is clear that it may not do so indirectly, as by declaring in effect that the public good requires the removal of those inequalities that are but the normal and inevitable result of their [exercise]. The police power is broad, [but] it cannot be given the wide scope that is here asserted for it, without in effect nullifying the constitutional guaranty.

b. Tribe, supra, at 438-439:

Perhaps more striking than [the] close scrutiny of means-ends relationships during the *Lochner* era was the strict judicial assessment of legislative ends. In this respect, judges drew heavily on earlier natural law and implied limitation notions; partly on the economic and social theories of Herbert Spencer advocating social Darwinism; and [on] the conservative legal theories of [such authors as] Thomas Cooley. [The] underlying philosophy held that the only legitimate goal of government in general, and of the police power in particular, was to protect individual rights and otherwise enhance the *total* public good; if they were to be upheld, governmental regulations thus had to promote "the general welfare" and not be "purely for the promotion of private interests." As a corollary, it followed that any statute which was [designed] to redistribute resources and thus benefit some persons at the expense of others [would] extend beyond the implicit boundaries of legislative authority. [Legislatures] could properly enact statutes which protected the interests of certain discrete groups, such as children and women, both treated by the dominant legal ideology as unable to protect themselves. [But] equalization or redistribution of economic or social power, which "takes property from A. and gives it to B.," was an impermissible end of legislation.

c. Sunstein, Naked Preferences and the Constitution, 84 Colum. L. Rev. 1689, 1697, 1718 (1984):

In the *Lochner* era, the Court attempted to create a separate category of impermissible ends, using the libertarian framework of the common law as a theoretical basis. Under that framework, the government's police power was sharply limited, and modern social legislation [appeared] not as an effort to promote a public value, but instead as a raw exercise of political power by the beneficiaries of the legislation. But the theoretical basis of the *Lochner* era [is undermined once one recognizes] that the market status quo [is] itself the product of government choices. [Once it becomes] clear that harms produced by the marketplace [are themselves] the products of public choices, efforts to alleviate those harms [must] be regarded as permissible exercises of government power.

d. Siegan, supra, at 123-124:

[Judges] who had received their education [during] the Civil War era viewed labor [in light of the antislavery tradition]. Freedom of contract for both employer and employee was strongly espoused by the antislavery movement. It was accepted that the right of the individual to bestow his labor as he pleased was among the rights for which the Civil War had been fought. [Accordingly, the Court's] contention [that] government has no legitimate interest in [protecting labor] was far less controversial than contemporary generations might suppose. The Court believed that the labor market itself would operate to support the welfare of both workers and employers.

For evaluations of this "belief," compare Kennedy, supra, with Epstein, A Common Law for Labor Relations: A Critique of the New Deal Labor Legislation, 92 Yale L.J. 1357 (1983).

5. Lochner *and the political process.* Consider the following arguments:

a. *Lochner* is defensible in terms of "representation-reinforcement." Although one can agree with Justice Holmes that a legislature's apparent lack of wisdom in passing a given statute "has nothing to do with the right of a majority to embody their opinions in law," there are circumstances in which statutes owe their existence primarily to the organized power of special interest groups and are enacted even though the majority does not approve of them and even though the majority may be harmed by their operation. Indeed, the theory of "public choice" postulates certain conditions in which even a properly functioning democratic process will frequently thwart majority values. See Stigler, The Theory of Economic Regulation, 2 Bell J. Econ. & Mgmt. Sci. 3 (1971). The theory of "public choice" is examined in more detail in the context of the dormant commerce clause. See Chapter 3, section A, supra.

In *Lochner* itself, the New York statute was arguably the product of a political process in which labor unions had an organizational advantage over consumers, who would ultimately pay for the regulation through higher prices for bread, and over nonunionized workers who were willing to accept jobs in unregulated transactions with employers. Moreover, large employers and those already engaged in collective bargaining with unions had little incentive to oppose the legislation, for it would impair the operation only of less efficient bakers and would impose on all bakers regulations that had already been extracted in collective bargaining from some. In such circumstances, the unions were able to capture the legislative process to the disadvantage of the majority, and the Court acted appropriately to rectify this defect in the operation of the representative process. For a description of the political circumstances surrounding the adoption of the New York legislation, see Siegan, supra, at 116-118; Tarrow, *Lochner versus New York:* A Political Analysis, 5 Lab. Hist. 277 (1964). For a defense of some aspects of economic substantive due process in these terms, see Wonnell, Economic Due Process and the Preservation of Competition, 11 Hast. Const. L.Q. 91 (1983).

b. *Lochner* was wrongly decided because, as Justice Holmes recognized, the political process is inevitably a process of unprincipled compromises among competing social groups. Indeed, most "public policies are better explained as the outcome of a pure power struggle — clothed in a rhetoric of public interest that is a mere figleaf — among narrow interest or pressure groups." Posner, The *DeFunis* Case and the Constitutionality of Preferential Treatment of Racial Minorities, 1974 Sup. Ct. Rev. 1, 27. Thus, the Court's search for a "public" justification for the legislation in *Lochner* was inherently incoherent. The due process clause cannot logically prohibit legislatures from passing laws merely because powerful groups want and press for them. Such an approach would ultimately prove counterproductive, for if the courts prevent powerful groups from having their way in the legislative process, the political pressures will be bottled up and eventually emerge in even more destructive forms elsewhere.

Consider the view that Holmes's position in *Lochner* was closely tied to his general acceptance of Social Darwinism: "What proximate test of excellence can be found except correspondence to the actual equilibrium of force in the community — that is, conformity to the wishes of the dominant power. Of course, such conformity may lead to destruction, and it is desirable that the dominant power be wise. But wise or not, the proximate test of a good government is that the dominant power has its way." Justice Oliver Wendell Holmes: His Book Notices and Uncollected Letters and Papers 250 (1936). See generally Rogat, Mr. Justice Holmes: Some Modern Views — The Judge as Spectator, 31 U. Chi. L. Rev. 213 (1964). Justice Holmes's related views on free expression are examined in Chapter 7, section B1, infra.

6. *Summary.* Objections to the *Lochner* decision generally fall into two camps. Some are institutional and emphasize that the Court overstepped its bounds in relation to the legislature. These objections focus on the Court's careful scrutiny of the means/ends connection and on its willingness to declare certain legislative ends impermissible. Other objections are substantive and emphasize that the Court attempted to vindicate, as a matter of constitutional law, a laissez-faire conception of the role of government that could not be sustained. Under this view, *Lochner* turned on an indefensible distinction between the "public" and "private" spheres, defined in terms of common law categories. Note that these two types of objections have very different implications. The institutional view suggests that courts should take a deferential approach to legislation — particularly in the realm of social and economic affairs. The substantive view leaves open the possibility that judicial deference might not be required if the Court acts in the service of some end other than laissez-faire.

Note: *The* Lochner *Era — 1905-1934*

From the decision in *Lochner* in 1905 to the mid-1930s, the Court invalidated approximately two hundred economic regulations, usually under the due process clause of the fourteenth amendment. These decisions centered primarily, although not exclusively, on labor legislation, the regulation of prices, and restrictions on entry into business. Although the Court employed substantive due process in an "activist" manner, it sustained as many regulations as it struck down. Moreover, as reflected in *Lochner*, the Court was often divided. Justices Holmes, Brandeis, Stone, Cardozo, and Chief Justice Hughes dissented regularly from the Court's invalidation of economic regulations. This Note describes some of the more significant decisions. For comprehensive surveys, see The Constitution of the United States 1602-1612, 1643-1709 (Government Printing Office, 1973 ed.); B. Wright, The Growth of American Constitutional Law 153-168 (1942); Jacobson, Federalism and Property Rights, 15 N.Y.U. L.Q. Rev. 319 (1938).

1. *Maximum hour legislation*. Although the Court invalidated maximum hour legislation in *Lochner*, three years later, in Muller v. Oregon, 208 U.S. 412 (1908), the Court upheld a statute prohibiting the employment of women in laundries for more than ten hours per day. The Court distinguished *Lochner* on the ground that "woman's physical structure" placed her at a disadvantage in the "struggle for subsistence" and legislation to protect women was thus "necessary to secure a real equality of right." In Bunting v. Oregon, 243 U.S. 426 (1917), the Court, in a rather cryptic opinion, upheld a statute establishing a maximum ten-hour day for factory workers of both sexes. Although *Bunting* overruled the specific holding of *Lochner* sub silentio, the constitutional theory on which *Lochner* was based continued to be enforced.

2. *"Yellow-dog" contracts*. In Adair v. United States, 208 U.S. 161 (1908), and Coppage v. Kansas, 236 U.S. 1 (1915), the Court invalidated federal and state legislation forbidding employers to require employees to agree not to join a union. The Court observed in *Adair* that "it is not within the functions of government [to] compel any person in the course of his business [to] retain the personal services of another." In *Coppage* the Court emphasized that efforts to compensate for "unequal" bargaining power were beyond the legitimate scope of the police power and maintained that although the individual has a right "to join the union, he has no inherent right to do this and still remain in the employ of one who is unwilling to employ a union man, any more than the same individual has a right to join the union without the consent of that organization."

3. *Minimum wages*. Although *Muller* upheld a law establishing maximum working hours for women, the Court invalidated a law establishing minimum wages for women in Adkins v. Children's Hospital, 261 U.S. 525 (1923). In distinguishing *Muller* the Court observed:

> But the ancient inequality of the sexes, otherwise than physical, [has] continued "with diminishing intensity." In view of the great [changes] which have taken place since [*Muller*], in the contractual, political and civil status of women, culminating in the Nineteenth Amendment, it is not unreasonable to say that these differences have now come almost, if not quite, to the vanishing point. [Thus], while the physical differences must be recognized in appropriate cases, and legislation fixing hours or conditions of work may properly take them into account, we cannot accept the doctrine that women of mature age, sui juris, require or may be subjected to restrictions upon their liberty of contract which could not lawfully be imposed in the case of men under similar circumstances.

See generally Powell, The Judiciality of Minimum Wage Legislation, 37 Harv. L. Rev. 545 (1924).

4. *Price regulation*. In a line of cases after Munn v. Illinois, the Court initially adopted a broad definition of "affected with a public interest" and thus upheld a wide range of laws regulating prices. See, e.g., German Alliance Insurance Co. v. Lewis, 233 U.S. 389 (1914) (fire insurance); Block v. Hirsh, 256 U.S. 135 (1921) (rental housing). Thereafter, the Court increasingly narrowed the *Munn* standard and thus invalidated laws regulating prices with regard to such matters as gasoline, Williams v. Standard Oil Co., 278 U.S. 235 (1929), employment agencies,

Ribnik v. McBride, 277 U.S. 350 (1928), and theater tickets, Tyson & Brother v. Banton, 273 U.S. 418 (1927). See Hamilton, Affectation with Public Interest, 39 Yale L.J. 1089 (1930).

5. *Business entry.* On several occasions, the Court invalidated laws restricting entry into particular lines of business. In New State Ice Co. v. Liebmann, 285 U.S. 262 (1932), for example, the Court invalidated a law prohibiting any person to manufacture ice without first obtaining a certificate of convenience and necessity. The Court explained that, as in the context of price regulation, the critical issue was "whether the business is [charged] with a public use," for "a regulation which has the effect of denying [the] common right to engage in a lawful private business, such as that under review, cannot be upheld." See also Louis K. Liggett Co. v. Baldridge, 278 U.S. 105 (1928) (invalidating a law limiting entry into the pharmacy business to pharmacists).

6. *The demise of* Lochner. As these decisions indicate, the Court's decisions in the *Lochner* era were often inconsistent. The unifying theme seemed to be the Court's perception of the "real" reason for the regulation. If the Court believed the regulation was truly designed to protect the health, safety, or morals of the general public, it was apt to uphold the law. But if the Court perceived the law to be an effort to readjust the market in favor of one party to the contract, it was likely to hold the regulation invalid.

By the mid-1930s, the Court was prepared to abandon *Lochner.* This was due to changes in the composition of the Court, internal tensions in the doctrine, increasing judicial and academic criticism, and, perhaps most important, the economic realities of the depression, which seemed to undermine *Lochner*'s central premises.

NEBBIA v. NEW YORK, 291 U.S. 502 (1934): During 1932, the prices received by farmers for milk fell much below the cost of production, and the situation of the families of dairy producers in New York grew "desperate." A legislative committee, established to investigate the matter, concluded that milk "is an essential item of diet" and that the failure "of producers to receive a reasonable return for their labor and investment over an extended period threatens a relaxation of vigilance against contamination." The committee further found that the "production and distribution of milk is a paramount industry of the state" and that the "milk industry is affected by factors of [price] instability [which] call for special methods of control." The legislature thus established the Milk Control Board, which was authorized to fix minimum and maximum retail prices for milk. Nebbia, the owner of a grocery store in Rochester, was convicted of selling milk below the minimum price fixed by the Board. The Court, in a five-to-four decision, upheld the law. Justice Roberts delivered the opinion of the Court:

"The legislature adopted [the law] as a method of correcting the evils, which the report of the committee showed could not be expected to right themselves through the ordinary play of the forces of supply and demand, owing to the peculiar and uncontrollable factors affecting the industry. [Under] our form of government the use of property and the making of contracts are normally matters of private and not of public concern. The general rule is that both shall be free of governmental interference. But neither property rights nor contract rights are absolute; for government cannot exist if the citizen may at will use his property to the detriment of his fellows, or exercise his freedom of contract to work them harm. [Thus] has this court from the early days affirmed that the power to promote the general welfare is inherent in government. [These] correlative rights, that of the citizen to exercise exclusive dominion over property and freely to contract about his affairs, and that of the state to regulate the use of property and the conduct of business, are always in collision. [But] subject only to constitutional restraint the private right must yield to the public need.

"The Fifth Amendment, in the field of federal activity, and the Fourteenth, as respects state action, do not prohibit governmental regulation for the public welfare. They merely condition the exertion of the admitted power, by securing that the end shall be accomplished by methods consistent with due process. And the guaranty of due process, as has often been held, demands only that the law shall not be unreasonable, arbitrary or capricious, and that the means selected shall have a real and substantial relation to the object sought to be attained. [The] Constitution does not guarantee the unrestricted privilege to engage in a business or to conduct it as one pleases. . . .

"But we are told that because the law essays to control prices it denies due process. Notwithstanding the admitted power to correct existing economic ills by appropriate regulation of business, [the] appellant urges that direct fixation of prices [is] per se unreasonable and unconstitutional, save as applied to businesses affected with a public interest; [and that no] business is so affected [unless it is in the nature of a public utility or a monopoly]. But this is a misconception. [There] is no closed class or category of businesses affected with a public interest, and the function of courts in the application of the Fifth and Fourteenth Amendments is to determine in each case whether circumstances vindicate the challenged regulation as a reasonable exertion of governmental authority or condemn it as arbitrary or discriminatory. [The] phrase 'affected with a public interest' can, in the nature of things, mean no more than that an industry, for adequate reason, is subject to control for the public good. . . .

"So far as the requirement of due process is concerned, [a] state is free to adopt whatever economic policy may reasonably be deemed to promote public welfare, and to enforce that policy by legislation adapted to its purpose. The courts are without authority either to declare such policy, or, when it is declared by the legislature, to override it. [If] the legislative policy be to curb unrestrained and harmful competition [it] does not lie with the courts to determine that the rule is unwise. [Times] without number we have said that the legislature is primarily the judge of the necessity of such an enactment, that every possible presumption is in favor of its validity, and that though the court may hold views inconsistent with the wisdom of the law, it may not be annulled unless palpably in excess of legislative power. [Price] control, like any other form of regulation, is unconstitutional only if arbitrary, discriminatory, or demonstrably irrelevant to the policy the legislature is free to adopt, and hence an unnecessary and unwarranted interference with individual liberty."

Justice McReynolds, joined by Justices Van Devanter, Sutherland, and Butler, dissented: "This is not regulation, but management, control, dictation — it amounts to the deprivation of the fundamental right which one has to conduct his own affairs honestly and along customary lines. [It is the duty of this Court to inquire] whether the means proposed have reasonable relation to something within legislative power. [Here,] we find direct interference with guaranteed rights defended upon the ground that the purpose was to promote the public welfare by increasing milk prices at the farm. [But it is unclear] how higher charges at stores to impoverished customers when the output is excessive [can] possibly increase receipts at the farm. [I]t appears to me wholly unreasonable to expect this legislation to accomplish the proposed end."

WEST COAST HOTEL CO. v. PARRISH, 300 U.S. 379 (1937): In a five-to-four decision, the Court explicitly overruled Adkins v. Children's Hospital and upheld a state law establishing a minimum wage for women. Chief Justice Hughes delivered the opinion of the Court:

"[The] violation alleged by those attacking minimum wage regulation for women is deprivation of freedom of contract. What is this freedom of contract? The Constitution does not speak of freedom of contract. It speaks of liberty and prohibits the deprivation of liberty without due process of law. [Regulation] which is reasonable in relation to its subject and is adopted in the interests of the community is due process. . . .

"What can be closer to the public interest than the health of women and their protection from unscrupulous and overreaching employers? And if the protection of women is a legitimate end of the exercise of state power, how can it be said that the requirement of the payment of a minimum wage fairly fixed in order to meet the very necessities of existence is not an admissible means to that end? The legislature of the State was clearly entitled to consider the situation of women in employment, the fact that they are in the class receiving the least pay, that their bargaining power is relatively weak, and that they are the ready victims of those who would take advantage of their necessitous circumstances. The legislature was entitled to adopt measures to reduce the evils of the 'sweating system,' the exploiting of workers at wages so low as to be insufficient to meet the bare cost of living, thus making their very helplessness the occasion of a most injurious competition. The legislature had the right to consider that its minimum wage requirements would be an important aid in carrying out its policy of protection. The adoption of similar requirements by many States evidences a deep-seated conviction both as to the presence of the evil and as to the means adapted to check it. Legislative response to that conviction cannot be regarded as arbitrary or capricious, and that is all we have to decide. Even if the wisdom of the policy be regarded as debatable and its effects uncertain, still the legislature is entitled to its judgment. . . .

"There is an additional and compelling consideration which recent economic experience has brought into a strong light. The exploitation of a class of workers who are in an unequal position with respect to bargaining power and are thus relatively defenseless against the denial of a living wage is not only detrimental to their health and well being but casts a direct burden for their support upon the community. What these workers lose in wages the taxpayers are called upon to pay. The bare cost of living must be met. We may take judicial notice of the unparalleled demands for relief which arose during the recent period of depression. [The] community is not bound to provide what is in effect a subsidy for unconscionable employers. The community may direct its law-making power to correct the abuse which springs from their selfish disregard of the public interest. [Adkins] should be, and it is, overruled."

Justice Sutherland, joined by Justices Van Devanter, McReynolds, and Butler, dissented.

For discussion of the "political" context of *West Coast Hotel*, and the possible significance of President Roosevelt's "Court-packing plan," see Chapter 2, section D, supra.

Note the suggestion in *West Coast Hotel* that the "community is not bound to provide what is in effect a subsidy for unconscionable employers." Consider the possibility that in *West Coast Hotel* the Court largely abandoned the *Lochner*-era understanding that private ordering, within the common law framework, was natural and not the result of governmental choice. On this view, *West Coast Hotel* suggests that governmental "inaction" is itself a constitutionally significant decision. Consider Sunstein, Naked Preferences and the Constitution, 84 Colum. L. Rev. 1689, 1726 (1984):

> [The] new conception of the market status quo as neither natural nor inviolate led the way after the *Lochner* era toward a dramatically expanded understanding of the police power. [If] government inaction can be understood as government action — if a decision not to act is understood as an intrusion in the same way as "affirmative" regulation — then the traditional notion of private property as natural and prepolitical loses much of its coherence.

This theme is echoed in other decisions of the era. See, e.g., Miller v. Schoene, infra Chapter 9, section B. The issue of governmental inaction as governmental action is explored more fully in Chapter 10, infra.

Note: The End of an Era

Since 1937 the Court's abandonment of *Lochner*-style substantive due process review of economic regulation has been unequivocal. In the years after *West Coast Hotel* the Court overruled prior decisions and consistently rejected challenges to legislation based on assertions of a constitutional preference for laissez-faire economics.

In United States v. Darby, 312 U.S. 100 (1941), for example, the Court unanimously rejected a substantive due process challenge to the provisions of the Fair Labor Standards Act establishing maximum hours and minimum wages for all covered employees. Later that term, in Phelps Dodge Corp. v. National Labor Relations Board, 313 U.S. 177 (1941), the Court upheld a provision of the NLRA declaring it an unfair labor practice for an employer to encourage or discourage union membership. The Court noted that "decisions in this Court since [*Adair*] and [*Coppage*] have completely sapped those cases of their authority." That same day, in Olsen v. Nebraska, 313 U.S. 236 (1941), the Court unanimously upheld a state statute fixing the maximum fee that an employment agency could collect from employees, thus overruling Ribnik v. McBride, 277 U.S. 350 (1928). The Court observed that "the only constitutional prohibitions or restraints which respondents have suggested for invalidation of this legislation are those notions of public policy embodied in earlier decisions of this Court but which, as Mr. Justice Holmes long admonished, should not be read into the Constitution." In Lincoln

Federal Union v. Northwestern Iron & Metal Co., 335 U.S. 525 (1949), the Court upheld a state right-to-work law that prohibited closed shops. The Court explained that it had abandoned "the *Allgeyer-Lochner-Adair-Coppage* constitutional doctrine" and returned "to the earlier constitutional principle that states have power to legislate against what are found to be injurious practices in their internal commercial and business affairs, so long as their laws do not run afoul of some specific federal constitutional prohibition." And in Day-Brite Lighting, Inc. v. Missouri, 342 U.S. 421 (1952), the Court upheld a law authorizing employees to take four hours' leave with full pay on election day, noting that, "if our recent cases mean anything, they leave debatable issues as respects business, economic, and social affairs to legislative decision."

Although these and similar decisions unambiguously repudiated *Lochner*-style substantive due process, the question remains — what review of economic regulation is appropriate? Should the Court employ the standard suggested in Justice Harlan's dissent in *Lochner?* Should it abandon substantive due process review entirely? Consider the following three decisions:

UNITED STATES v. CAROLENE PRODUCTS CO., 304 U.S. 144 (1938): After extensive hearings, two congressional committees made the following findings:

> There is an extensive commerce in milk compounds made of condensed milk from which the butter fat has been extracted and an equivalent amount of vegetable oil [has been] substituted. [By] reason of the extraction of the natural milk fat the compounded product [known as "filled milk"] can be manufactured and sold at a lower cost than pure milk. Butter fat [is] rich in vitamins [that] are wanting in vegetable oils. The use of filled milk as a dietary substitute for pure milk results [in] undernourishment. [Despite] compliance with the branding and labeling requirements of the Pure Food and Drugs Act, there is widespread use of filled milk as a substitute for pure milk. This is aided by their identical taste and appearance, by the similarity of the containers in which they are sold, by the practice of dealers in offering the inferior product to customers as being as good as or better than pure condensed milk sold at a higher price, by customers' ignorance of the respective food values of the two products, and in many sections of the country by their inability to read the labels.

Based on these findings, Congress enacted the Filled Milk Act of 1923, which declared that "filled milk" is an "adulterated article of food, injurious to the public health" and that "its sale constitutes a fraud upon the public." The act therefore prohibited any person to ship filled milk in interstate commerce. In *Carolene Products* the Court upheld the act. Justice Stone delivered the opinion of the Court:

"We may assume for present purposes that no pronouncement of a legislature can forestall attack upon the constitutionality of [a prohibition] by applying opprobrious epithets to the prohibited act, and that a statute would deny due process which precluded the disproof in judicial proceedings of all facts which would show or tend to show that a statute depriving the suitor of life, liberty or property had a rational basis.

"But such we think is not the purpose [of] the statutory characterization of filled milk as injurious to health and as a fraud upon the public. There is no need to consider it here as more than a declaration of the legislative findings deemed to support and justify the action taken, [aiding] informed judicial review, as do the reports of legislative committees, by revealing the rationale of the legislation. Even in the absence of such aids the existence of facts supporting the legislative judgment is to be presumed, for regulatory legislation affecting ordinary commercial transactions is not to be pronounced unconstitutional unless in the light of the facts made known or generally assumed it is of such a character as to preclude the assumption that it rests upon some rational basis. . . .

"Where the existence of a rational basis for legislation [depends] upon facts beyond the sphere of judicial notice, such facts may properly be made the subject of judicial inquiry, [and] the constitutionality of a statute predicated upon the existence of a particular state of facts may be challenged by showing to the court that those facts have ceased to exist. [Similarly] we recognize that the constitutionality of a statute, valid on its face, may be assailed by proof of facts tending to show that the statute as applied to a particular article is without support in reason because the article, although within the prohibited class, is so different from others of the class as to be without the reason for the prohibition, [though] the effect of such proof depends on the relevant circumstances of each case, as for example the administrative difficulty of excluding the article from the regulated class. [But] by their very nature such inquiries, where the legislative judgment is drawn in question, must be restricted to the issue whether any state of facts either known or which could reasonably be assumed affords support for it. Here the [appellee] challenges the validity of the statute on its face and it is evident from all the considerations presented to Congress, and those of which we may take judicial notice, that the question is at least debatable whether commerce in filled milk should be left unregulated, or in some measure restricted, or wholly prohibited. As that decision was for Congress, neither the finding of a court arrived at by weighing the evidence, nor the verdict of a jury can be substituted for it. [The Act is] constitutional."

Does *Carolene Products* accord too much deference to legislative judgment? Consider the following variations:

1. At trial, appellee presents expert witnesses who testify that filled milk is just as nourishing as pure milk.

2. At trial, appellee presents expert witnesses who testify that *his* filled milk is just as nourishing as pure milk.

3. At trial, appellee demonstrates that his product is packaged in a container that expressly and conspicuously states: "Filled Milk. Not as Nourishing as Pure Milk. But Cheaper."

4. Suppose Congress had enacted the act without the express legislative findings and that at trial appellee presents expert witnesses who testify that filled milk is just as nourishing as pure milk.

WILLIAMSON v. LEE OPTICAL OF OKLAHOMA, 348 U.S. 483 (1955): An ophthalmologist is a licensed physician who specializes in the care of the eyes. An optometrist examines for refractive error, recognizes diseases of the eye, and fills prescriptions for eyeglasses. An optician is an artisan qualified to grind lenses, fill prescriptions, and fit frames. In *Lee Optical* the Court considered the constitutionality of an Oklahoma statute that made it unlawful for an optician to fit or duplicate lenses without a prescription from an ophthalmologist or optometrist. The district court held that through "ordinary skills the optician could take a broken lens or a fragment thereof, measure its power, and reduce it to prescriptive terms," that the requirement of a prescription from an ophthalmologist or optometrist was thus not "reasonably and rationally related to the health and welfare of the people," and that the law therefore "violated the Due Process Clause by arbitrarily interfering with the optician's right to do business." The Supreme Court reversed. Justice Douglas delivered the opinion of the Court:

"The Oklahoma law may exact a needless, wasteful requirement in many cases. But it is for the legislature, not the courts, to balance the advantages and disadvantages of the new requirement. It appears that in many cases the optician can easily supply the new frames or new lenses without reference to the old written prescription. [But] in some cases the directions contained in the prescription are essential. [The] legislature might have concluded that the frequency of occasions when a prescription is necessary was sufficient to justify this regulation of the fitting of eyeglasses. [Or] the legislature may have concluded that eye examinations were so critical, not only for correction of vision but also for detection of latent ailments or diseases, that every change in frames and every duplication of a lens should be accompanied by a prescription from a medical expert. To be sure, the present law does not require a new examination of the eyes every time the frames are changed or the lenses duplicated. [But] the law need not be in every respect logically consistent with its aims to be constitutional. It is enough that there is an evil at hand for correction, and that it might be thought that the particular legislative measure was a rational way to correct it. [The] day is gone when this Court uses the Due Process Clause [to] strike down state laws, regulatory of business and industrial conditions, because they may be unwise, improvident, or out of harmony with a particular school of thought."

FERGUSON v. SKRUPA, 372 U.S. 726 (1963): A Kansas statute declared it unlawful for any person to engage in the business of debt adjusting except as incident to "the lawful practice of law." The statute defined "debt adjusting" as the making of a contract with a debtor whereby the debtor pays money periodically to the adjuster who then distributes it to the debtor's creditors in accordance with an agreed-on plan. Skrupa, a debt adjustor who was put out of business by the statute, filed this action. The district court held that the statute was an unreasonable regulation of a "lawful business" and thus violative of due process. The Supreme Court reversed. Justice Black delivered the opinion of the Court:

"Under the system of government created by our Constitution, it is up to legislatures, not courts, to decide on the wisdom and utility of legislation. There was a time when the Due Process Clause was used by this Court to strike down laws which were thought unreasonable, that is, unwise or incompatible with some particular economic or social philosophy. [That doctrine] has long since been discarded. [It] is now settled that States 'have power to legislate against what are found to be injurious practices in their internal commercial and business affairs, so long as their laws do not run afoul of some specific federal constitutional prohibition. . . .' [The] Kansas legislature was free to decide for itself that legislation was needed to deal with the business of debt adjusting. Unquestionably, there are arguments showing that the business of debt adjusting has social utility, but such arguments are properly addressed to the legislature, not to us. [The] Kansas debt adjusting statute may be wise or unwise. But relief, if any be needed, lies not with us but with the body constituted to pass laws for the State of Kansas."

Justice Harlan concurred in the judgment "on the ground that this state measure bears a rational relation to a constitutionally permissible objective. See [*Lee Optical*]."

Note: Restraint or Abdication?

1. *Economic substantive due process today.* In *Carolene Products* the Court indicated that it would uphold economic legislation if any state of facts either known or reasonably inferable could support the legislative judgment. In *Lee Optical*, however, the Court went even further and resorted to wholly hypothetical facts and reasons to sustain the legislation. And in *Ferguson* the Court appeared to uphold the legislation without any inquiry into the rationality of the means/ends connection.

It has been argued that economic substantive due process review has become so deferential in the post-*Lochner* era in part because "a wide range of justifications count as exercises of the police power and are not treated as naked wealth transfers." Sunstein, Naked Preferences and the Constitution, 84 Colum. L. Rev. 1689, 1718 (1984). In the post-*Lochner* era what, if anything, constitutes an "impermissible" end? Are governmental actions based only on raw power and unsupported by *any* public value "impermissible?" Would *Carolene Products*, *Williamson*, and *Ferguson* pass muster under such a standard? Consider Komesar, Taking Institutions Seriously: Introduction to a Strategy for Constitutional Analysis, 51 U. Chi. L. Rev. 366, 416 (1984):

> It does not take much scrutiny to see the dairy lobby at work behind the passage [of] the "filled milk" act. Indeed, [it] is not too uncharitable, perhaps, to suggest that concern for the dairies' pocketbooks rather than for the consumer's health best explains the dairy lobby's efforts. In fact, though [the] legislation seemed to be aimed at helping consumers, it may have harmed them. They were "saved" from "adulterated" products, but only at the cost of higher prices, while the dairy industry benefited from reduced competition.

In any event, after decisions like *Carolene Products*, *Williamson*, and *Ferguson*, "there could be little doubt as to the practical result: no claim of substantive economic rights would now be sustained by the Supreme Court. The judiciary had abdicated the field." McCloskey, Economic Due Process and the Supreme Court: An Exhumation and Reburial, 1962 Sup. Ct. Rev. 34, 38. Indeed, the Court has not invalidated an economic regulation on substantive due process grounds since 1937. For recent decisions rejecting substantive due process challenges to economic regulation, see, e.g., Texaco v. Short, 454 U.S. 516 (1982); Pruneyard Shopping Center v. Robins, 447 U.S. 74 (1980); Duke Power Co. v. Carolina Environmental Study Group, Inc., 438 U.S. 59 (1978); Exxon Corp. v. Governor of Maryland, 437 U.S. 117 (1978). Due process review has persisted with some vitality in state adjudication, however. See Hetherington, State Economic Regulation and Substantive Due Process of Law, 53 Nw. U.L. Rev. 13, 226 (1958); Note, State Economic Substantive Due Process: A Proposed Approach, 88 Yale L.J. 1487 (1979); Paulsen, The Persistence of Substantive Due Process in the States, 34 Minn. L. Rev. 91 (1950). Cf. Struve, The Less-Restrictive-Alternative Principle and Economic Due Process, 80 Harv. L. Rev. 1463 (1967).

2. *Alternatives to abdication?* Has the Court gone too far in its withdrawal from the substantive review of economic legislation? Should it have adhered to the *Nebbia* standard — "that the means selected shall have a real and substantial relation to the object sought to be attained"? Is it possible to apply such a standard without reinviting the "vices" of the *Lochner* era? How would you apply such a standard in *Carolene Products? Lee Optical? Ferguson?*

Consider McCloskey, supra, at 40-44:

> Why did the Court move all the way from the inflexible negativism of the old majority to the all-out tolerance of the new? Why did it not establish a halfway house between the extremes, retaining a measure of control over economic legislation but exercising that control with discrimination and self-restraint? [Assuming] that this standard [was] consciously and purposefully rejected, what explains the rejection? [One possibility] is that extremism had bred extremism in thinking about the role of the Supreme Court.
>
> [During the *Lochner* era], a conservative majority had, from time to time, embraced a policy of adamant resistance to economic experiment, and this obstructionist spirit [tended] to discredit the whole concept of judicial supervision in the minds of those who felt that government must have reasonable leeway to experiment with the economic order. [The] extreme of the past had generated the extreme of the present. . . .
>
> Factors like [this] may help to explain the impulse to discard the old due process doctrine, bag and baggage. Yet one would like to think [that] the policy of virtual abdication was not merely a reflex against the excesses of the past but a considered and justified decision about the proper scope of judicial review. The written record to support such a supposition is not, alas, very convincing. Scattered remarks [assailed] the dead horse of "the *Allgeyer-Lochner-Adair-Coppage*" doctrine, [but] they did not explain why the abuses of power in those earlier decisions justified abandonment of the power itself, nor why the deference to the legislature should be carried to the point of complete submission.

3. *The "costs" of abdication.* Consider B. Siegan, Economic Liberties and the Constitution 260, 262, 284, 302-303 (1980):

> Society condemns censorship [of expression] for two reasons: first, because it would operate tyrannically and oppressively, and second, because the censors would perform their task incompetently, and even counterproductively. [Reprehensible] practices are not exclusive to the regulators of expression. Neither are the unfortunate consequences of decisions. Government is no more wise, compassionate, or understanding when it regulates the economic marketplace than when it censors expression. . . .
>
> The low esteem in which economic due process is held suggests to many that judicial review of economic matters is undesirable and harmful and that the judiciary should accept without reservation almost all legislative and administrative solutions to social and economic problems. Society was worse off, the proponents of this

approach contend, as a result of the interventions of the "laissez-faire" Court. [But] studies effectively disclose the error in [the] New Deal emphasis on government intervention to solve existing economic problems. The studies demonstrate that the very people who [most] require the regulators' assistance — those at the lower end of the economic spectrum — actually suffer greatly from regulation. [The studies] are proving the wisdom of the Old Court's guiding principle, that freedom of contract is the rule and restraint the exception. [The] conclusion is warranted that the Old Court's policy of review is [preferable] to the contemporary Supreme Court's abdication.

4. *The implications of abdication: the decline of* Lochner *and the doctrine of governmental action.* Consider the following view: The position suggested in *West Coast Hotel* and other decisions marking the decline of *Lochner* — that government's failure to act may in some circumstances amount to governmental action — does not justify judicial abdication as a general rule. To the contrary, the understanding that the "private" sphere is itself a governmental creation suggests that a wide range of subjects might be vulnerable to constitutional attack. Perhaps most dramatically, the unequal distribution of resources and the existence of poverty itself may be understood as in part the product of governmental "inaction." See Chapter 10, infra.

5. *The implications of abdication: the decline of* Lochner *and the rise of the "double standard."* Why is there a "presumption of constitutionality" when the Court reviews economic legislation? Does this presumption govern all constitutional review? All substantive due process review? All substantive due process review except where the right at issue is expressly guaranteed in the bill of rights? All substantive due process review except where the right at issue is "fundamental?"

Consider Justice Stone's famous footnote 4 in *Carolene Products:*

There may be narrower scope for operation of the presumption of constitutionality when legislation appears on its face to be within a specific prohibition of the Constitution, such as those of the first ten amendments, which are deemed equally specific when held to be embraced within the Fourteenth. . . .

It is unnecessary to consider now whether legislation which restricts those political processes [such as voting, expression, and political association] which can ordinarily be expected to bring about repeal of undesirable legislation, is to be subjected to more exacting judicial scrutiny under the general prohibitions of the Fourteenth Amendment than are most other types of legislation. . . .

Nor need we enquire whether similar considerations enter into the review of statutes directed at particular religious, [or] national, [or] racial minorities[;] whether prejudice against discrete and insular minorities may be a special condition, which tends seriously to curtail the operation of those political processes ordinarily to be relied upon to protect minorities, and which may call for a correspondingly more searching judicial inquiry.

Does the "double standard" suggested by footnote 4 — active review in some contexts, deferential review in others — reflect a coherent, defensible constitutional theory? Does it leave room for the recognition of "implied fundamental rights"? Does it suggest what those rights might be? For an interesting account of the origins of footnote 4, see Lusky, Footnote Redux: A *Carolene Products* Reminiscence, 82 Colum. L. Rev. 1093 (1982).

E. "FUNDAMENTAL INTERESTS" AND THE EQUAL PROTECTION CLAUSE

This section explores the intersection of equal protection and implied fundamental rights jurisprudence. Chapter 5, supra, examined two basic models of equal protection analysis. The first model focuses on classifications based on race or other "suspect" criteria. As we saw, the Court tests such classifications by varying forms of "strict" scrutiny. The second model focuses on classifications in the economic and social realm that do not involve "suspect" criteria. As we saw, the Court tests such classifications by a highly deferential form of "rational basis" review, similar to the standard that the Court currently employs in considering substantive due process challenges to economic regulation.

This section asks whether there is a third model of equal protection analysis. That is, should the degree of scrutiny vary, not only with the "suspectness" of the criterion on which the classification is based, but also with the "importance" or "fundamentality" of the interest that is distributed or affected "unequally"? Should inequalities involving "fundamental" interests be analyzed differently than inequalities involving "nonfundamental" interests?

The Court first invoked fundamental interest analysis in the equal protection context in Skinner v. Oklahoma, 316 U.S. 535 (1942), in which the Court considered the constitutionality of an Oklahoma statute that authorized the sterilization of some criminals, but not others. Interestingly, *Skinner* was decided only five years after *West Coast Hotel* and at the height of the Court's repudiation of economic substantive due process. This section begins with *Skinner,* and then examines several arguably "fundamental" interests, including voting, access to the judicial process, travel, welfare, and education.

Several years before *Skinner,* in Buck v. Bell, 274 U.S. 200 (1927), the Court upheld a Virginia statute authorizing the sterilization of inmates of state institutions who were found, after a hearing, to be afflicted with an hereditary form of insanity or imbecility. Justice Holmes, writing for the Court, observed: "It is better for all the world, if instead of waiting to execute degenerate offspring for crime, or to let them starve for their imbecility, society can prevent those who are manifestly unfit from continuing their kind. [Three] generations of imbeciles are enough."

Skinner v. Oklahoma
316 U.S. 535 (1942)

MR. JUSTICE DOUGLAS delivered the opinion of the Court.

This case touches a sensitive and important area of human rights. Oklahoma deprives certain individuals of a right which is basic to the perpetuation of a race — the right to have offspring. . . .

The statute involved is Oklahoma's Habitual Criminal Sterilization Act. That Act defines an "habitual criminal" as a person who [has been convicted three] or more times for crimes "amounting to felonies involving moral turpitude." [Machinery] is provided for the institution by the Attorney General of a proceeding against such a person in the Oklahoma courts for a judgment that such person shall be rendered sexually sterile. [If] the court or jury finds that the defendant is an "habitual criminal" and that he "may be rendered sexually sterile without deteriment to his or her general health," then the court "shall render judgment to the effect that said defendant be rendered sexually sterile" by the operation of vasectomy in case of a male, and of salpingectomy in case of a female. Only one other provision of the Act is material here, and that provides that "offenses arising out of the violation of the prohibitory laws, revenue acts, embezzlement, or political offenses, shall not come or be considered within the terms of this Act."

Petitioner was convicted in 1926 of the crime of stealing chickens, [and in 1929 and 1934] he was convicted of robbery with firearms. . . . In 1936 the Attorney General instituted proceedings against him. [A] judgment directing that the operation of vasectomy be performed on petitioner was affirmed by the Supreme Court of Oklahoma. . . .

Several objections to the constitutionality of the Act have been pressed upon us. It is urged that the Act cannot be sustained as an exercise of the police power, in view of the state of scientific authorities respecting inheritability of criminal traits. It is argued that due process is lacking because, under this Act, unlike the Act upheld in Buck v. Bell, 274 U.S. 200, the defendant is given no opportunity to be heard on the issue as to whether he is the probable potential parent of socially undesirable offspring. [It] is also suggested that the Act is penal in character and that the sterilization provided for is cruel and unusual punishment and violative of the Fourteenth Amendment. [We] pass those points without intimating an opinion on them, for there is a feature of the Act which clearly condemns it. That is, its failure to meet the requirements of the equal protection clause of the Fourteenth Amendment.

We do not stop to point out all of the inequalities in this Act. A few examples will suffice. In Oklahoma, grand larceny is a felony. Larceny is grand larceny when the property taken exceeds $20 in value. Embezzlement is punishable "in the manner prescribed for feloniously stealing property of the value of that embezzled." Hence, he who embezzles property worth more than $20 is guilty of a felony. A clerk who appropriates over $20 from his employer's till and a stranger who steals the same amount are thus both guilty of felonies. If the latter repeats his act and is convicted three times, he may be sterilized. But the clerk is not subject to the pains and penalties of the Act no matter how large his embezzlements nor how frequent his convictions. A person who enters a chicken coop and steals chickens commits a felony and he may be sterilized if he is thrice convicted. If, however, he is a bailee of the property and fraudulently appropriates it, he is an embezzler. Hence, no matter how habitual his proclivities for embezzlement are and no matter how often his conviction, he may not be sterilized. Thus, the nature of the two crimes is intrinsically the same and they are punishable in the same manner. . . .

It was stated in [Buck v. Bell] that the claim that state legislation violates the equal protection clause of the Fourteenth Amendment is "the usual last resort of constitutional arguments." Under our constitutional system the States in determining the reach and scope of particular legislation need not provide "abstract symmetry." They may mark and set apart the classes and types of problems according to the needs and as dictated or suggested by experience. [Thus,] if we had here only a question as to a State's classification of crimes, such as embezzlement or larceny, no substantial federal question would be raised. [For] a State is not constrained in the exercise of its police power to ignore experience which marks a class of offenders or a family of offenses for special treatment. Nor is it prevented by the equal protection clause from confining "its restrictions to those classes of cases where the need is deemed to be clearest." . . .

But the instant legislation runs afoul of the equal protection clause, though we give Oklahoma that large deference which the rule of the foregoing cases requires. We are dealing here with legislation which involves one of the basic civil rights of man. Marriage and procreation are fundamental to the very existence and survival of the race. The power to sterilize, if exercised, may have subtle, far-reaching and devastating effects. In evil or reckless hands it can cause races or types which are inimical to the dominant group to wither and disappear. There is no redemption for the individual whom the law touches. Any experiment which the State conducts is to his irreparable injury. He is forever deprived of a basic liberty. We mention these matters not to reexamine the scope of the police power of the States. We advert to them merely in emphasis of our view that strict scrutiny of the classification which a State makes in a sterilization law is essential, lest unwittingly, or otherwise, invidious discriminations are made against groups or types of individuals in violation of the constitutional guaranty of just and equal laws. The guaranty of "equal protection of the laws is a pledge of the protection of equal laws." When the law lays an unequal hand on those who have committed intrinsically the same quality of offense and sterilizes one and not the other, it has made as invidious a discrimination as if it had selected a particular race or nationality for oppressive treatment. Sterilization of those who have thrice committed grand larceny, with immunity for those who are embezzlers, is a clear, pointed, unmistakable discrimination. Oklahoma makes no attempt to say that he who commits larceny by trespass or trick or fraud has biologically inheritable traits which he who commits embezzlement lacks. [We] have not the slightest basis for inferring that that line has any significance in eugenics, nor that the inheritability of criminal traits follows the neat legal distinctions which the law has marked between those two offenses. In terms of fines and imprisonment, the crimes of larceny and embezzlement rate the same under the Oklahoma code. Only when it comes to sterilization are the pains and penalties of the law different. The equal protection clause would indeed be a formula of empty words if such conspicuously artificial lines could be drawn. . . .

Reversed.

MR. CHIEF JUSTICE STONE, concurring.

I concur in the result, but I am not persuaded that we are aided in reaching it by recourse to the equal protection clause.

If Oklahoma may resort generally to the sterilization of criminals on the assumption that their propensities are transmissible to future generations by inheritance, I seriously doubt that the equal protection clause requires it to apply the measure to all criminals in the first instance, or to none.

Moreover, if we must presume that the legislature knows — what science has been unable to ascertain — that the criminal tendencies of any class of habitual offenders are transmissible regardless of the varying mental characteristics of its individuals, I should suppose that we must likewise presume that the legislature, in its wisdom, knows that the criminal tendencies of some classes of offenders are more likely to be transmitted than those of others. And so I think the real question we have to consider is not one of equal protection, but whether the wholesale condemnation of a class to such an invasion of personal liberty, without opportunity to any individual to show that his is not the type of case which would justify resort to it, satisfies the demands of due process.

There are limits to the extent to which the presumption of constitutionality can be pressed, especially where the liberty of the person is concerned (see United States v. Carolene Products Co., 304 U.S. 144, 152, n.4) and where the presumption is resorted to only to dispense with a procedure which the ordinary dictates of prudence would seem to demand for the protection of the individual from arbitrary action. Although petitioner here was given a hearing to ascertain whether sterilization would be detrimental to his health, he was given none to discover whether his criminal tendencies are of an inheritable type. . . .

Science has found and the law has recognized that there are certain types of mental deficiency associated with delinquency which are inheritable. But the State does not contend — nor can there be any pretense — that either common knowledge or experience, or scientific investigation, has given assurance that the criminal tendencies of any class of habitual offenders are universally or even generally inheritable. In such circumstances, inquiry whether such is the fact in the case of any particular individual cannot rightly be dispensed with. [A] law which condemns, without hearing, all the individuals of a class to so harsh a measure as the present because some or even many merit condemnation, is lacking in the first principles of due process. [And] so, while the state may protect itself from the demonstrably inheritable tendencies of the individual which are injurious to society, the most elementary notions of due process would seem to require it to take appropriate steps to safeguard the liberty of the individual by affording him, before he is condemned to an irreparable injury in his person, some opportunity to show that he is without such inheritable tendencies. The state is called on to sacrifice no permissible end when it is required to reach its objective by a reasonable and just procedure adequate to safeguard rights of the individual which concededly the Constitution protects.*

Note: The Fundamental "Right to Have Offspring"

1. *Alternative bases of resolution.* The Court in *Skinner* found it unnecessary to address three "objections to the constitutionality of the Act" that did not involve the equal protection clause. First, it was argued that "the Act cannot be sustained as an exercise of the police power, in view of the state of scientific authorities respecting inheritability of criminal traits." This argument sounds in substantive due process. Could the Court have invalidated the act because criminality is not inheritable? At the time of *Skinner* the scientific evidence was inconclusive. See, e.g., W. Healy, The Individual Delinquent 188-189 (1915) ("Inheritance of certain types of feeblemindedness, epilepsy and insanity is [a] well-established fact, and [there is a] close relationship of these abnormalities to criminalism. [But] we would warn [against] the danger of drawing easy conclusions about heredity being the main factor back of misdeeds simply because some progenitors [were] guilty of delinquency."); D. Sutherland, Principles of Criminality 90 (1947) (4th ed.) ("there is no evidence that there can be such a thing as a born criminal. No one has such an heredity that he must inevitably be a criminal regardless of [environ-

---

* [A concurring opinion of Mr. Justice Jackson is omitted. — Eds.]

ment]. Both the individual trait and the situation must be included in the statement of the causation; neither one works alone to produce crime."); Landman, The History of Human Sterilization in the United States — Theory, Statute, and Adjudication, 23 Ill. L. Rev. 463, 471 (1929) ("the inheritance of mental disorders has not been fully worked out; the results obtained by different observers are not altogether concordant").

Second, it was argued "that due process is lacking because, under this Act, unlike the Act upheld in Buck v. Bell, the defendant is given no opportunity to be heard on the issue as to whether he is the probable potential parent of socially undesirable offspring." This, of course, is the argument relied on by Chief Justice Stone. This argument sounds in procedural due process. Or does it? Suppose, for example, a state prohibits any person under age seventeen from driving. Does this violate due process unless everyone under age seventeen is granted a hearing on actual ability to drive? Is Stone confusing a conventional problem of equal protection "overinclusion" with an issue of procedural due process? The problem of "conclusive" presumptions is considered more fully in section G, infra.

Third, it was argued that "the Act is penal in character and that the sterilization provided for is cruel and unusual punishment." The Oklahoma Supreme Court disposed of this argument as follows: "[The prohibition on cruel and unusual punishment is] not applicable where the operation of vasectomy is required as a eugenic measure, and not as a punishment. In such case it is said to be analogous to compulsory vaccination and is non-punitive. [We] think it was the intention of the legislature that this act should be a eugenic measure to improve the safety and general welfare of the race by preventing from being born persons who will probably become criminals." Skinner v. State, 115 P.2d 123, 126 (Okla. 1941). For a more recent manifestation of a similar analysis, see Bell v. Wolfish, 441 U.S. 520 (1979) ("double-bunking" of pretrial detainees does not constitute cruel and unusual punishment because it is not intended as punishment).

2. *Equal protection: rational basis review.* Could the Court have invalidated the act on the ground that the distinction between embezzlers and larceners was "irrational"? Note Justice Douglas's observation that "a classification of crimes, such as embezzlement or larceny," would "raise no substantial federal question." If the classification is rational for those purposes, is it any less rational when it is drawn for purposes of sterilization? Could the legislature believe that larceners are more likely than embezzlers to have inheritable criminal tendencies? Could it believe that larceny is a more serious crime, and that sterilization should be used only on individuals who commit crimes more serious than embezzlement?

3. *"Fundamental" interests and the equal protection clause.* Is Skinner consistent with the Court's essentially contemporaneous renunciation of economic substantive due process? Because the right to have offspring, unlike the liberty of contract, is a true "fundamental" right? Because "fundamental" interest analysis is more appropriate in equal protection jurisprudence than in due process jurisprudence?

Does *Skinner* recognize an independent constitutional right to have offspring, or does it merely elevate the standard of equal protection review because the interest affected is "fundamental"? Consider the following arguments: (a) An inequality with respect to a trivial interest is not as significant as an inequality with respect to an important interest. (b) Inequality with respect to a "fundamental" interest is inherently irrational unless there are very good reasons for the inequality. (c) Inequality with respect to a "fundamental" interest suggests a possible improper motivation, for it is unlikely that those who framed the classification would have deprived themselves of the fundamental interest in the absence of extraordinary necessity. (d) The 1866 Civil Rights Act, on which the fourteenth amendment was based, protected blacks against inequality only with respect to certain specified interests, thus suggesting that the importance of the interest affected is central to the constitutionality of a classification.

4. *Is the "right to have offspring" a "fundamental" interest?* Is the right to have offspring more "fundamental" than the "liberty of contract"? Is this difference reflected in the considerations identified by Chief Justice Stone in his *Carolene Products* footnote 4? Consider the following views:

a. "[The] Court in *Skinner* was moved to recognize the fundamental personal character of a right to reproductive autonomy in part because of fear about the invidious and potentially genocidal way in which governmental control over reproductive matters might be exercised if the choice of whether or when to beget a child were to be transferred from the individual to the state." L. Tribe, American Constitutional Law 923 (1978). Note in this regard that the statutory distinction in *Skinner* was itself at least arguably class-based.

b. "[The] right of procreation [rests] most securely on the interest in status and dignity. [The] choice to be [a] parent is, among other things, a choice of social role and of self-concept. For the state to deny such a choice is for the organized society to deny the individual [the] presumptive right to be treated as a person, one of equal worth among citizens." Karst, Foreword: Equal Citizenship under the Fourteenth Amendment, 91 Harv. L. Rev. 1, 32 (1977).

5. *A right not to have offspring?* In *Skinner* the Court held that the right to have offspring is "fundamental." Is there also a fundamental right *not* to have offspring? See section F, infra.

1. Voting

In footnote 4 of *Carolene Products* Chief Justice Stone suggested that there "may be a narrower scope for operation of the presumption of constitutionality when [legislation] restricts those political processes which can ordinarily be expected to bring about repeal of undesirable legislation." He then offered "restrictions upon the right to vote" as a specific example. This section examines three aspects of the right to vote: denial of the right to vote, dilution of the right to vote, and denial of access to the ballot.

a. Denial of the "Right to Vote"

The original Constitution left it entirely to the states to determine the qualifications of voters for both national and state elections. See U.S. Const. art. I, §2, cl. 1; art. II, §1. The fourteenth amendment, enacted in 1868, did not directly prohibit discrimination in voting. Section 2 of the amendment, however, provided for a reduction in representation in the House of Representatives in proportion to the number of "male inhabitants of [the] State, being twenty-one years of age, and citizens of the United States," who were not permitted to vote. The fifteenth amendment, adopted in 1870, provided that the right of citizens to vote "shall not be denied or abridged [on] account of race, color or previous condition of servitude." The nineteenth amendment, enacted in 1920, provided that the right of citizens to vote "shall not be denied or abridged [on] account of sex." The twenty-fourth amendment, adopted in 1964, provided that the right of any citizen to vote in any election for president, vice-president, or members of Congress "shall not be denied or abridged [by] reason of failure to pay any poll tax or other tax." And the twenty-sixth amendment, enacted in 1971, provided that the right of any citizen eighteen years or older to vote "shall not be denied or abridged [on] account of age."

Except where a particular qualification was expressly prohibited by a specific amendment, the Court, until the 1960s, generally deferred to the states in determining the qualifications to vote. In Breedlove v. Suttles, 302 U.S. 277 (1937), for example, the Court unanimously upheld a Georgia statute requiring the payment of a $1 poll tax as a precondition for voting. Similarly, in Lassiter v. Northampton County Board of Elections, 360 U.S. 45 (1959), the Court unanimously upheld a North Carolina statute providing that to be eligible to vote an individual must "be able to read and write any section of the [state constitution] in the English language." The Court explained:

> The States have long been held to have broad powers to determine the conditions under which the right of suffrage may be [exercised]. Residence requirements, age, previous criminal record [are] obvious examples indicating factors which a State may take into consideration in determining the qualifications of voters. The ability to read and write likewise has some relation to standards designed to promote intelligent use of the ballot. [Literacy] and intelligence are obviously not synonymous. Illiterate people may be intelligent voters. Yet in our society where newspapers, periodicals, books, and other printed matter canvass and debate campaign issues, a State might conclude that only those who are literate should exercise the franchise.

In 1964, however, in Reynolds v. Sims, infra section E1b, a decision involving dilution of the right to vote, the Court observed: "[The] right of suffrage is a fundamental matter in a free and democratic society. Especially since the right to exercise the franchise in a free and unimpaired manner is preservative of other basic civil and political rights, any alleged infringement of the right of citizens to vote must be carefully and meticulously scrutinized." Reynolds opened the door to a more active judicial scrutiny of voter qualifications.

Harper v. Virginia State Board of Elections
383 U.S. 663 (1966)

[The Court, overruling Breedlove v. Suttles, invalidated a Virginia law requiring the payment of a poll tax not to exceed $1.50 as a precondition for voting. The Court held that "a State violates the Equal Protection Clause [whenever] it makes the affluence of the voter or payment of any fee an electoral standard."]

MR. JUSTICE DOUGLAS delivered the opinion of the Court. . . .

[The] right to vote in state elections is nowhere expressly mentioned [in the Constitution]. It is argued that the right to vote in state elections is implicit, particularly by reason of the First Amendment. [We] do not stop to canvass the relation between voting and political expression. For it is enough to say that once the franchise is granted to the electorate, lines may not be drawn which are inconsistent with the Equal Protection Clause of the Fourteenth Amendment. . . .

[The] *Lassiter* case does not govern the result here, because, unlike a poll tax, the "ability to read and write . . . has some relation to standards designed to promote intelligent use of the ballot." [Voter] qualifications have no relation to wealth nor to paying or not paying this or any other tax. . . .

Long ago in [*Yick Wo*] the Court referred to "the political franchise of voting" as a "fundamental political right, because preservative of all rights." Recently in Reynolds v. Sims, we said, "[Any] alleged infringement of the right of citizens to vote must be carefully and meticulously scrutinized." . . .

It is argued that a State may exact fees from citizens for many different kinds of licenses; that if it can demand from all an equal fee for a driver's license, it can demand from all an equal poll tax for voting. But we must remember that the interest of the State, when it comes to voting, is limited to the power to fix qualifications. Wealth, like race, creed, or color, is not germane to one's ability to participate intelligently in the electoral process. Lines drawn on the basis of wealth or property, like those of race [are] traditionally disfavored. See [Griffin v. Illinois and Douglas v. California, infra section E2]. To introduce wealth or payment of a fee as a measure of a voter's qualifications is to introduce a capricious or irrelevant factor. . . .

We agree, of course, with Mr. Justice Holmes that the Due Process Clause of the Fourteenth Amendment "does not enact Mr. Herbert Spencer's Social Statics." [*Lochner.*] Likewise, the Equal Protection Clause is not shackled to the political theory of a particular era. In determining what lines are unconstitutionally discriminatory, we have never been confined to historic notions of [equality]. Notions of what constitutes equal treatment for purposes of the Equal Protection Clause *do* change. [Comparing Plessy v. Ferguson with Brown v. Board of Education.] Our conclusion [is] founded not on what we think governmental policy should be, but on what the Equal Protection Clause requires.

We have long been mindful that where fundamental rights and liberties are asserted under the Equal Protection Clause, classifications which might invade or restrain them must be closely scrutinized and carefully confined. See, e.g., [*Skinner*].

Those principles apply here. For to repeat, wealth or fee paying has, in our view, no relation to voting qualifications; the right to vote is too precious, too fundamental to be so burdened or conditioned.

Reversed.

MR. JUSTICE BLACK, dissenting. . . .

[Under] a proper interpretation of the Equal Protection Clause States are to have the broadest kind of leeway in areas where they have a general constitutional competence to act. [State] poll tax legislation can "reasonably," "rationally" and without an "invidious" or evil purpose to injure anyone be found to rest on a number of state policies including (1) the State's desire to collect its revenue, and (2) its belief that voters who pay a poll tax will be interested in furthering the State's welfare when they vote. [And] history is on the side of "rationality" of the State's poll tax policy. Property qualifications existed in the Colonies and were continued by many States after the Constitution was adopted. . . .

Another reason for my dissent [is that the Court] seems to be using the old "natural-law-due-process formula" to justify striking down state laws as violations of the Equal Protection Clause. I have heretofore had many occasions to express my strong belief that there is no constitutional support whatever for this Court to use the Due Process Clause as though it provided a blank check to alter the meaning of the Constitution as written so as to add to it substantive constitutional changes which a majority of the Court at any given time believes are needed to meet present-day problems. [Recall Justice Black's dissenting opinion in Adamson v. California, supra section C.] Nor is there in my opinion any more constitutional support for this Court to use the Equal Protection Clause, as it has today, to write into the Constitution its notions of what it thinks is good governmental policy. . . .

Mr. Justice Harlan, whom Mr. Justice Stewart joins, dissenting. . . .
[The Court uses] captivating phrases, but they are wholly inadequate to satisfy the standard governing adjudication of the equal protection issue: Is there a rational basis for Virginia's poll tax as a voting qualification? I think the answer to that question is undoubtedly "yes."
Property qualifications and poll taxes have been a traditional part of our political structure. In the Colonies the franchise was generally a restricted one. [It] is certainly a rational argument that payment of some minimal poll tax promotes civic responsibility, weeding out those who do not care enough about public affairs to pay $1.50 or thereabouts a year for the exercise of the franchise. It is also · arguable, indeed it was probably accepted as sound political theory by a large percentage of Americans through most of our history, that people with some property have a deeper stake in community affairs, and are consequently more responsible, more educated, more knowledgeable, more worthy of confidence, than those without means, and that the community and Nation would be better managed if the franchise were restricted to such citizens. . . .
These viewpoints, to be sure, ring hollow on most contemporary ears. Their lack of acceptance today is evidenced by the fact that nearly all of the States, left to their own devices, have eliminated property or poll tax qualifications. [Such] qualifications, very simply, are not in accord with current egalitarian notions of how a modern democracy should be organized. It is of course entirely fitting that legislatures should modify the law to reflect such changes in popular attitudes. However, it is all wrong, in my view, for the Court to adopt the political doctrines popularly accepted at a particular moment of our history and to declare all others to be irrational and invidious, barring them from the range of choice by reasonably minded people acting through the political process. It was not too long ago that Mr. Justice Holmes felt impelled to remind the Court that the Due Process Clause of the Fourteenth Amendment does not enact the laissez-faire theory of society, [Lochner]. The times have changed, and perhaps it is appropriate to observe that neither does the Equal Protection Clause of that Amendment rigidly impose upon America an ideology of unrestrained egalitarianism. . . .

Note: Is the Right to Vote "Fundamental"?

1. *The equal protection clause, voting, and the intent of the framers.* In his dissenting opinion in Reynolds v. Sims, 377 U.S. 533 (1964), infra section E1b,

Justice Harlan argued that the equal protection clause was "never intended" to inhibit the states in setting the qualifications for voting. Justice Harlan emphasized several factors: (a) Section 2 of the fourteenth amendment "expressly recognizes" the power of the states to deny the right to vote and expressly provides a remedy for such denial — a proportionate reduction in their representation in Congress. (b) The debates on the amendment reflected "the understanding of those who proposed and ratified it" that it would not affect the "power of a State to withhold the right to vote." (c) The adoption of the fifteenth amendment, which guaranteed the right to vote to blacks, only two years after the adoption of the fourteenth amendment, demonstrates that the framers of the fourteenth amendment did not intend it to guarantee the right to vote. For further elaboration of this view, see Oregon v. Mitchell, 400 U.S. 112, 152 (1970) (Harlan, J.); R. Berger, Government by Judiciary ch. 4 (1977). For a contrary view, see Oregon v. Mitchell, 400 U.S. 112, 229 (1970) (Brennan, J.); Van Alstyne, The Fourteenth Amendment, the "Right" to Vote, and the Understanding of the Thirty-Ninth Congress, 1965 Sup. Ct. Rev. 33.

2. *The basis of* Harper: *wealth as a "suspect classification."* The Court relied in *Harper* on both the "suspect classification" and "fundamental interest" aspects of equal protection analysis. To what extent, if any, can *Harper* be explained on the ground that "lines drawn on the basis of wealth [are] traditionally disfavored"? Consider that (a) the poll tax does not expressly classify on the basis of wealth; (b) like ordinary license fees, it has a differential effect on the poor; and (c) the Court invalidated the poll tax in its entirety, not only as applied to the poor.

3. *The basis of* Harper: *voting as a "fundamental" interest.* The Court conceded in *Harper* that there is no constitutional right to vote in state elections. How, then, does it justify its conclusion that the right to vote is "fundamental"? Note the Court's assertion that "[notions] of what constitutes equal treatment for purposes of the Equal Protection Clause *do* change," but that its conclusion in *Harper* is founded not on what it thinks "governmental policy should be, but on what the Equal Protection Clause requires." Is this coherent? Is *Harper* founded "on what the Equal Protection Clause requires" or on the currently prevailing "ideology of unrestrained egalitarianism"?

Consider J. Ely, Democracy and Distrust 77, 101-103 (1980):

> *Carolene Products* [focused, in part,] on whether the opportunity to participate [in] the political [process] has been unduly constricted. [The framers of the Constitution created a representative democracy in which] the people in their self-interest would choose representatives whose interests intertwined with [theirs]. The Constitution has [proceeded] from the quite sensible assumption that an effective majority will not inordinately threaten its own rights, and has sought to assure that such a majority will not systematically treat others less well than it treats [itself]. Malfunction occurs when [the] ins are choking off the channels of political change to ensure that they will stay in and the outs will stay out. [Unblocking] stoppages in the democratic process is what judicial review ought preeminently to be about, and denial of the vote seems the quintessential stoppage. [We] cannot trust the ins to decide who stays out, and it is therefore incumbent on the courts to ensure not only that no one is denied the vote for no reason, but also that where there is a reason [it] had better be a very convincing one.

But consider Bork, Neutral Principles and Some First Amendment Problems, 47 Ind. L. J. 1, 19 (1971), arguing that to approach cases like *Harper* "as involving rights derived from the requirements of our form of government is [to] say that they involve the guarantee clause," and that "Madison's writing [on] the guarantee clause suggests that representative democracy may properly take many forms, so long as the forms do not become 'aristocratic or monarchical.'" Thus, even if constitutional interpretation appropriately considers "considerations of constitutional structure and political practice," restrictions on the franchise should be upheld so long as they do not "'permit the systematic frustration of the will of a majority of the electorate of the State.'"

Kramer v. Union Free School District
395 U.S. 621 (1969)

Mr. Chief Justice Warren delivered the opinion of the Court.

[Section 2012] of the New York Education Law [provides] that in certain New York school districts residents [may] vote in the school district election only if they (1) own (or lease) taxable real property within the district, or (2) are parents (or have custody of) children enrolled in the local public schools. Appellant, a bachelor who neither owns nor leases taxable real property, [claims] that §2012 denied him equal protection of the laws. . . .

At the outset, it is important to note what is *not* at issue in this case. [Appellant] agrees that the States have the power to impose reasonable citizenship, age, and residency requirements on the availability of the ballot. The sole issue in this case is whether the *additional* requirements of §2012 [are constitutional].

In determining whether or not [this] law violates the Equal Protection Clause, [we] must give the statute a close and exacting examination. [This] careful examination is necessary because statutes distributing the franchise constitute the foundation of our representative society. Any unjustified discrimination in determining who may participate in political affairs or in the selection of public officials undermines the legitimacy of representative government.

Statutes granting the franchise to residents on a selective basis always pose the danger of denying some citizens any effective voice in the governmental affairs which substantially affect their lives. Therefore, if a challenged state statute grants the right to vote to some bona fide residents of requisite age and citizenship and denies the franchise to others, the Court must determine whether the exclusions are necessary to promote a compelling state interest.

And, for these reasons, [when] we are reviewing statutes which deny some residents the right to vote, the general presumption of constitutionality afforded state statutes and the traditional approval given state classifications if the Court can conceive of a "rational basis" for the distinctions made are not applicable. See [*Harper*]. The presumption of constitutionality and the approval given "rational" classifications in other types of enactments are based on an assumption that the institutions of state government are structured so as to represent fairly all the people. However, when the challenge to the statute is in effect a challenge of this basic assumption, the assumption can no longer serve as the basis for presuming constitutionality. And, the assumption is no less under attack because the legislature which decides who may participate at the various levels of political choice is fairly elected. Legislation which delegates decision making to bodies elected by only a portion of those eligible to vote for the legislature can cause unfair representation. . . .

The need for exacting judicial scrutiny of statutes distributing the franchise is undiminished simply because, under a different statutory scheme, the offices subject to election might have been filled through appointment. [For] "once the franchise is granted to the electorate, lines may not be drawn which are inconsistent with the Equal Protection Clause of the Fourteenth Amendment." [*Harper.*]*

We turn therefore to question whether the exclusion is necessary to promote a compelling state interest. [Appellees] argue that the State has a legitimate interest in limiting the franchise in school district elections [to] those "primarily interested in such elections" [and] that the State may reasonably and permissibly conclude that "property taxpayers" (including lessees of taxable property who share the tax burden through rent payments) and parents of the children enrolled in the district's schools are those "primarily interested" in school affairs. . . .

We need express no opinion as to whether the State in some circumstances might limit the exercise of the franchise to those "primarily interested" or "primarily affected." [For,] assuming, arguendo, that New York legitimately might limit the franchise in these school district elections to those "primarily interested in school affairs," close scrutiny of the §2012 classifications demonstrates that they do not accomplish this purpose with sufficient precision to justify denying appellant the franchise.

Whether classifications allegedly limiting the franchise to those resident citizens "primarily interested" deny those excluded equal protection of the laws depends, inter alia, on whether all those excluded are in fact substantially less interested or affected than those the statute includes. In other words, the classifications must be tailored so that the exclusion of appellant and members of his class is necessary to achieve the articulated state goal.[14] Section 2012 does not meet the exacting standard of precision we require of statutes which selectively distribute the franchise. The classifications in §2012 permit inclusion of many persons who have, at best, a remote and indirect interest in school affairs and, on the other hand, exclude others who have a distinct and direct interest in the school meeting decisions.[15] [The] requirements of §2012 are not sufficiently tailored to limiting the franchise to those "primarily interested" in school affairs to justify the denial of the franchise to appellant and members of his class. . . .

Mr. Justice Stewart, with whom Mr. Justice Black and Mr. Justice Harlan join, dissenting. . . .

[Appellant concedes] the validity of voting requirements relating to residence,

---

* [The Court noted: "Besides appellant and others who similarly live in their parents' homes, the statute also disenfranchises the following persons (unless they are parents or guardians of children enrolled in the district public school): senior citizens and others living with children or relatives; clergy, military personnel, and others who live on tax-exempt property; boarders and lodgers; parents who neither own nor lease qualifying property and whose children are too young to attend school [or] attend private schools." — Eds.]

14. Of course, if the exclusions are necessary to promote the articulated state interest, we must then determine whether the interest promoted by limiting the franchise constitutes a compelling state interest. We do not reach that issue in this case.

15. For example, appellant resides with his parents in the school district, pays state and federal taxes and is interested in and affected by school board decisions; however, he has no vote. On the other hand, an uninterested unemployed young man who pays no state or federal taxes, but who rents an apartment in the district, can participate in the election.

literacy, and age. Yet he argues — and the Court accepts the argument — that the voting qualifications involved here somehow have a different constitutional status. I am unable to see the distinction.

Clearly a State may reasonably assume that its residents have a greater stake in the outcome of elections held within its boundaries than do other persons. Likewise, it is entirely rational for a state legislature to suppose that residents, being generally better informed regarding state affairs than are nonresidents, will be more likely than nonresidents to vote responsibly. And the same may be said of legislative assumptions regarding the electoral competence of adults and literate persons on the one hand, and of minors and illiterates on the other. It is clear, of course, that lines thus drawn cannot infallibly perform their intended legislative function. Just as "[i]lliterate people may be intelligent voters," nonresidents or minors might also in some instances be interested, informed, and intelligent participants in the electoral process. Persons who commute across a state line to work may well have a great stake in the affairs of the State in which they are employed; some college students under 21 may be both better informed and more passionately interested in political affairs than many adults. But such discrepancies are the inevitable concomitant of the line drawing that is essential to law making. So long as the classification is rationally related to a permissible legislative end, therefore — as are residence, literacy, and age requirements imposed with respect to voting — there is no denial of equal protection.

Thus judged, the statutory classification involved here seems to me clearly to be valid. [The] Court does not really argue the contrary. Instead, it strikes down New York's statute by asserting that the traditional equal protection standard is inapt in this case. . . . But the asserted justification for applying [its stricter] standard cannot withstand analysis. The voting qualifications at issue have been promulgated, not by [the School District], but by the New York State Legislature, and the appellant is of course fully able to participate in the election of representatives in that body. There is simply no claim whatever here that the state government is not "structured so as to represent fairly all the people," including the appellant.

Nor is there any other justification for imposing the Court's "exacting" equal protection test. This case does not involve racial classifications [and] this statute is not one that impinges upon a constitutionally protected right, [for] "the Constitution of the United States does not confer the right of suffrage upon any one." . . .

Today's decision can only be viewed as irreconcilable with the established principle that "[t]he States have . . . broad powers to determine the conditions under which the right of suffrage may be exercised. . . ." Since I think that principle is entirely sound, I respectfully dissent. . . .

Note: Kramer *and Its Progeny*

Does *Kramer* satisfactorily explain why the right to vote is a "fundamental interest" for equal protection purposes even though there is no constitutional right to vote? Can you answer Justice Stewart's argument that the Court's theory is inapplicable in *Kramer*, for the "voting qualifications at issue" were promulgated by the New York Legislature, and appellant participated fully "in the election of representatives in that body"? So long as appellant was represented in the legislature, is that body's "unequal" distribution of the franchise any more problematic than its "unequal" distribution of economic benefits?

Consider Tushnet, Darkness on the Edge of Town: The Contributions of John Hart Ely to Constitutional Theory, 89 Yale L. J. 1037, 1049 (1980):

> [It] is significant that the statute that *Kramer* challenged was not of statewide uniformity. According to the market theory of local government, [each] local government provides a distinctive bundle of services; individuals "vote with their feet," by moving to the locality that gives them their preferred combination of services at a cost that they are willing to pay. From this perspective, New York offered Kramer a choice: live with your parents and have no vote in school district elections, or live in [a different district] and have a vote. [Why] should the Court refuse to hold him to [his] choice [and] override the preferences of those who live in [his] district?

In examining the Court's decisions since *Kramer*, consider what the Court means in this context by "strict scrutiny."

1. *Property requirements: special purpose elections.* In Cipriano v. City of Houma, 395 U.S. 701 (1969), decided on the same day as *Kramer*, the Court invalidated a Louisiana law permitting only property-owning taxpayers to vote whether to issue municipal utility bonds. The Court emphasized that the revenue bonds were to be paid entirely from the operation of the utilities, and that they therefore did not especially burden the owners of real property.

The following year, in Phoenix v. Kolodziejski, 399 U.S. 204 (1970), the Court invalidated an Arizona law permitting only property-owning taxpayers to vote whether to issue general obligation bonds. Although the bonds in *Kolodziejski*, unlike those in *Cipriano*, were to be paid substantially from property taxes, the Court observed that nonproperty owners had a substantial interest in the services and facilities financed by the bonds and that the differences between the interests of property owners and nonproperty owners were therefore "not sufficiently substantial to justify excluding the latter from the franchise." Justice Stewart, joined by Chief Justice Burger and Justice Harlan, dissented. Stewart maintained that the state could reasonably conclude that bonds should not be issued "without the approval of a majority of those upon whom the weight of repaying those bonds will legally fall."

2. *Property requirements: limited purpose government units.* In Salyer Land Co. v. Tulare Lake Basin Water Storage District, 410 U.S. 719 (1973), the Court upheld a California statute permitting only landowners to vote in water storage district elections and allocating votes in proportion to the assessed valuation of the land. The main purpose of the districts was to provide water for farming. The districts' project costs were assessed against the land in proportion to the benefits received. Emphasizing that the district does "not exercise what might be thought of as 'normal governmental' authority," the Court held that the "strict scrutiny" demanded by *Kramer*, *Cipriano*, and *Kolodziejski* was inapplicable to the district "by reason of its special limited purpose and of the disproportionate effect of its activities on landowners as a group." It then concluded that the franchise restriction was constitutional because it was not "'wholly irrelevant to achievement'" of a legitimate objective. Justice Douglas, joined by Justices Brennan and Marshall, dissented.

In Ball v. James, 451 U.S. 355 (1981), the Court extended *Salyer* and upheld a "one acre-one vote" scheme for voting for directors of a large water reclamation district in Arizona. Unlike the water district in *Salyer*, which covered only a sparsely populated agricultural area, the water reclamation district in *Ball* financed most of its water operations by selling electricity to several hundred thousand residents. Nonetheless, the Court found *Salyer*, rather than *Kramer*, controlling. The Court explained that the district "cannot enact any laws governing the conduct of citizens, nor does it administer such normal functions of government as the maintenance of streets, the operation of schools, or sanitation, health, and welfare services." Moreover, the Court rejected the argument that "the sheer size of the power operations and the great number of people they affect serve to transform the [district] into an entity of general governmental power." Rather, the relationship between nonvoting residents and the district was "essentially that between consumers and a business enterprise from which they buy."

Justice White, joined by Justices Brennan, Marshall, and Blackmun, dissented. The dissenters objected to the Court's assertion that "the provision of electricity and water is essentially private enterprise and not sufficiently governmental" and maintained that the district "is an integral governmental actor providing important governmental services to residents" who are being denied the opportunity "to participate in any meaningful way in the conduct of the [district's] operations."

Is the *Salyer/Ball* "limited purpose" doctrine a sensible exception to *Kramer?* Concurring in *Ball*, Justice Powell observed that "it must be evident that some of the reasoning in [*Kramer*] has been questioned." What factors should the Court consider in deciding whether a governmental authority falls within the "limited purpose" doctrine?

3. *Durational residency requirements.* In Dunn v. Blumstein, 405 U.S. 330 (1972), the Court expressly reaffirmed the states' power to limit the franchise to bona fide residents, but invalidated a Tennessee statute conditioning eligibility to vote on one year's residence in the state and three months' residence in the county. The Court explained that because durational residence requirements curtail the "fundamental interest" in voting, they are unconstitutional "unless the State can demonstrate that [they] 'are *necessary* to promote a *compelling* governmental interest.'" The Court added: "Thus phrased, the constitutional question may sound like a mathematical formula. But legal 'tests' do not have the precision of mathematical formulas. The key words emphasize a matter of degree: that a heavy burden of justification is on the State, and that the statute will be closely scrutinized in light of its asserted purposes."

Tennessee offered two such purposes: to "insure purity of the ballot box" by protecting against fraud and to assure a "knowledgeable voter." The Court conceded that prevention of fraud was a legitimate interest, but concluded that "30 days appears to be an ample period of time [to] complete whatever administrative tasks are necessary to prevent fraud." And although also conceding the legitimacy of the state's interest in having "knowledgeable" voters, the Court concluded that "the conclusive presumptions of durational residence requirements are much too crude."

Chief Justice Burger dissented: "Some lines must be drawn. To challenge such lines by the 'compelling state interest' standard is to condemn them all. So far as I am aware, no state law has ever satisfied this seemingly insurmountable standard, and I doubt one ever will."

In Marston v. Lewis, 410 U.S. 679 (1973), and Burns v. Fortson, 410 U.S. 686 (1973), the Court upheld fifty-day durational residence requirements, noting that the fifty-day period was "necessary" to serve the states' "important interest in accurate voter lists." Justice Marshall, joined by Justices Douglas and Brennan, dissented on the ground that thirty days was sufficient.

4. *Absentee ballots.* In McDonald v. Board of Election Commissioners, 394 U.S. 802 (1969), decided after *Harper* but shortly before *Kramer,* the Court upheld an Illinois statute that granted absentee ballots to some classes of persons but not to "unsentenced inmates awaiting trial." The Court noted that "there is nothing in the record to indicate [that] Illinois has in fact precluded appellants from voting," for "the record is barren of any indication that the State might not [furnish] the jails with special polling booths [or] provide guarded transportation to the polls." It thus concluded that it "is [not] the right to vote that is at stake here but a claimed right to receive absentee ballots." It therefore applied the "traditional standards" of equal protection review and sustained the statute.

In O'Brien v. Skinner, 414 U.S. 524 (1974), the Court invalidated a New York statute that did not provide absentee ballots to persons in jail awaiting trial. The Court explained that since the statute provided absentee ballots to persons absent from their home county, those held in jail in a county other than their residence could vote, but "persons confined for the same reason in the county of their residence are completely denied the ballot." The Court concluded that this distinction was "wholly arbitrary." Justice Blackmun, joined by Justice Rehnquist, dissented.

After *Kramer* and *O'Brien,* is the state prohibited from denying absentee ballots to persons who are otherwise unable to vote? Is it prohibited from providing absentee ballots to some persons who are otherwise unable to vote but not to others? What constitutes "inability" to vote?

5. *Disenfranchising felons.* In Richardson v. Ramirez, 418 U.S. 24 (1974), the Court upheld a California law that denied the vote to convicted felons, even if they had completed their sentences and paroles. The Court, in an opinion by Justice Rehnquist, adopted an "intent of the framers" approach. The Court observed that many state constitutions in effect when the fourteenth amendment was adopted denied the vote to convicted felons and that section 2 of the amendment expressly reduced the representation in the House to the extent a state denied the vote to adult male citizens, "except for participation in rebellion, or other crime." It then concluded that "the exclusion of felons from the vote has an affirmative sanction [which] was not present in the case of the other restrictions on the franchise" invalidated in the *Harper/Kramer* line of cases.

Justice Marshall, joined by Justice Brennan, dissented on the ground that "§2 was not intended and should not be construed to be a limitation on the other sections of the Fourteenth Amendment," and that, under "strict scrutiny," "the blanket disenfranchisement of ex-felons cannot stand." Justice Douglas dissented on other grounds.

Consider Note, The Supreme Court — 1973 Term, 88 Harv. L. Rev. 41, 108 (1974):

[The] Court rejected [the] view expressed in prior cases that "the Equal Protection Clause is not shackled to the political theory of a particular era," and that "[notions] of what constitutes equal [treatment] *do* change." Although the Court's exploration of the legislative history of section 2 demonstrates convincingly that the framers of the fourteenth amendment did not object to disenfranchisement following criminal conviction, it does not establish that section 2 restricts the expansive potential of section 1.

6. *Enrollment requirements for voting in primaries.* In Rosario v. Rockefeller, 410 U.S. 752 (1973), the Court upheld a New York statute requiring voters to register their party affiliation at least thirty days before a general election in order to be eligible to vote in the next party primary, which might be as many as eleven months later. The Court distinguished Dunn v. Blumstein and held that the law did not violate the right of petitioners to vote in the primary "of their choice" because the law "did not absolutely disenfranchise" petitioners but "merely imposed a time deadline" and that petitioners' inability to vote in the primary of their choice was caused "by their own failure to take timely steps to effect their enrollment." The Court maintained that the law furthered the "important state goal" of inhibiting party raiding, "whereby voters in sympathy with one party designate themselves as voters of another party [to] influence [the] results of the other party's primary."

Justice Powell, joined by Justices Douglas, Brennan, and Marshall, dissented. Powell complained that the majority had failed to "identify the standard of scrutiny" it applied. He argued that the challenged law imposed a "substantial" burden on voting rights, that strict scrutiny was the appropriate standard, and that even if the state's interest in deterring "raiding" was "compelling," the law was invalid because the state's interest "may be protected adequately by lesser measures."

Several months later, in Kusper v. Pontikes, 414 U.S. 51 (1973), the Court distinguished *Rosario* and invalidated an Illinois statute that prohibited any person "from voting in the primary election of a political party if he has voted in the primary of any other party within the preceding 23 months." The Court explained that "The Illinois law, unlike [the law in *Rosario*,] 'locks' voters into a pre-existing party affiliation from one primary to the next, and the only way to break the 'lock' is to forgo voting in *any* primary for a period of almost two years." It concluded that such a scheme "substantially restricts an Illinois voter's freedom to change his political party affiliation" and is not the least drastic means of attaining the state's objectives. Justices Blackmun and Rehnquist dissented.

b. Dilution of the "Right to Vote"

Until 1962 the Court held that legislative districting controversies were nonjusticiable. In Colgrove v. Green, 328 U.S. 549 (1946), for example, the Court declined to consider a claim that an Illinois law unconstitutionally prescribed congressional districts that were not approximately equal in population. Justice Frankfurter, writing for a plurality, explained that "this controversy concerns matters that bring courts into immediate and active relations with party contests. [It] is hostile to a democratic system to involve the judiciary in the politics of the people. [Courts] ought not to enter this political thicket."

In Baker v. Carr, 369 U.S. 186 (1962), however, which involved a claim that the apportionment of the Tennessee General Assembly violated the appellants' rights under the equal protection clause "by virtue of the debasement of their votes," the Court held "that a justiciable cause of action is stated upon which appellants would be entitled to appropriate relief." Justice Brennan explained:

> The question here is the consistency of state action with the Federal Constitution. We have no [need] to enter upon policy determinations for which judicially manageable standards are lacking. Judicial standards under the Equal Protection Clause are well developed and [familiar]. [Moreover, claims such as these] are not [nonjusticiable merely] because they touch matters of state governmental [organization]. We conclude that the complaint's allegations of a denial of equal protection present a justiciable constitutional cause of [action].

Baker is examined more fully in Chapter 1, section E3, supra.

Reynolds v. Sims
377 U.S. 533 (1964)

[In *Reynolds* and five companion cases, the Court held that in six states the system of apportionment of one or both houses of the legislature was unconstitutional. *Reynolds* involved Alabama; the others involved Colorado, Delaware, Maryland, New York, and Virginia. The Court observed: "Legislative apportionment in Alabama is signally illustrative and symptomatic of the seriousness of this problem in a number of States. [There has] been no reapportionment of seats in the Alabama Legislature for over 60 years. [This has resulted] in the perpetuated scheme becoming little more than an irrational anachronism [enabling] a minority stranglehold on the State Legislature."]

MR. CHIEF JUSTICE WARREN delivered the opinion of the Court. . . .

A predominant consideration in determining whether a State's legislative apportionment scheme constitutes an invidious discrimination violative of rights asserted under the Equal Protection Clause is that the rights allegedly impaired are individual and personal in nature. [Since] the right of suffrage is a fundamental matter in a free and democratic society [and] is preservative of other basic civil and political rights, any alleged infringement of the right of citizens to vote must be carefully and meticulously scrutinized. . . .

Legislators represent people, not trees or acres. Legislators are elected by voters, not farms or cities or economic interests. As long as ours is a representative form of government, [the] right to elect legislators in a free and unimpaired fashion is a bedrock of our political system. It could hardly be gainsaid that a constitutional claim had been asserted by an allegation that certain otherwise qualified voters had been entirely prohibited from voting for members of their state legislature. And, if a State should provide that the votes of citizens in one part of the State should be given two times, or five times, or 10 times the weight of votes of citizens in another part of the State, it could hardly be contended that the right to vote of those residing in the disfavored areas had not been effectively diluted. [Of] course, the effect of state legislative districting schemes which give the same number of representatives to unequal numbers of constituents is identical. . . .

Logically, in a society ostensibly grounded on representative government, it would seem reasonable that a majority of the people of a State could elect a majority of that State's legislators. [To] sanction minority control of state legislative bodies, would appear to deny majority rights in a way that far surpasses any possible denial of minority rights that might otherwise be thought to result. [The] concept of equal protection has been traditionally viewed as requiring the uniform treatment of persons standing in the same relation to the governmental action questioned or challenged. With respect to the allocation of legislative representation, all voters, as citizens of a State, stand in the same relation regardless of where they live. Any suggested criteria for the differentiation of citizens are insufficient to justify any discrimination, as to the weight of their votes, unless relevant to the permissible purposes of legislative apportionment. Since the achieving of fair and effective representation for all citizens is concededly the basic aim of legislative apportionment, we conclude that the Equal Protection Clause guarantees the opportunity for equal participation by all voters in the election of state legislators. Diluting the weight of votes because of place of residence impairs basic constitutional rights under the Fourteenth Amendment. [Our] constitutional system amply provides for the protection of minorities by means other than giving them majority control of state legislatures. . . .

We are told that the matter of apportioning representation in a state legislature is a complex and many-faceted one. We are advised that States can rationally consider factors other than population in apportioning legislative representation. We are admonished not to restrict the power of the States to impose differing views as to political philosophy on their citizens. We are cautioned about the dangers of entering into political thickets and mathematical quagmires. Our answer is this: a denial of constitutionally protected rights demands judicial protection; our oath and our office require no less of us. [To] the extent that a citizen's right to vote is debased, he is that much less a citizen. [The] weight of a citizen's vote cannot be made to depend on where he lives. Population is, of necessity, the starting point for consideration and the controlling criterion for judgment in legislative apportionment controversies. A citizen, a qualified voter, is no more nor no less so because he lives in the city or on the farm. This is the clear and strong command of our Constitution's Equal Protection Clause. . . .

We hold that, as a basic constitutional standard, the Equal Protection Clause requires that the seats in both houses of a bicameral state legislature must be apportioned on a population basis. Simply stated, an individual's right to vote for state legislators is unconstitutionally impaired when its weight is in a substantial fashion diluted when compared with votes of citizens living in other parts of the State. . . .

Much has been written since our decision in Baker v. Carr about the applicability of the so-called federal analogy to state legislative apportionment arrangements. [We] find the federal analogy inapposite and irrelevant to state legislative districting schemes. . . .

The system of representation in the two Houses of the Federal Congress is one ingrained in our Constitution [and] is based on the consideration that in establishing our type of federalism a group of formerly independent States bound themselves together under one national government. [A] compromise between the larger and smaller States on this matter averted a deadlock in the Constitutional Convention which had threatened to abort the birth of our Nation. . . .

Political subdivisions of States — counties, cities, or whatever — never were and never have been considered as sovereign entities. Rather, they have been traditionally regarded as subordinate governmental instrumentalities created by the State to assist in the carrying out of state governmental functions. [The] relationship of the States to the Federal Government could hardly be less analogous. . . .

By holding that as a federal constitutional requisite both houses of a state legislature must be apportioned on a population basis, we mean that the Equal Protection Clause requires that a State make an honest and good faith effort to construct districts, in both houses of its legislature, as nearly of equal population as is practicable. We realize that it is a practical impossibility to arrange legislative districts so that each one has an identical number of residents, or citizens, or voters. Mathematical exactness or precision is hardly a workable constitutional requirement. [So] long as the divergences from a strict population standard are based on legitimate considerations incident to the effectuation of a rational state policy, some deviations from the equal-population principle are constitutionally permissible [but] neither history alone, nor economic or other sorts of group interests, are permissible factors in attempting to justify disparities from population-based representation. Citizens, not history or economic interests, cast votes. Considerations of area alone provide an insufficient justification for deviations from the equal-population principle. Again, people, not land or trees or pastures, vote. Modern developments and improvements in transportation and communications make rather hollow, in the mid-1960's, most claims [for] allowing such deviations in order to insure effective representation for sparsely settled areas and to prevent legislative districts from becoming so large that the availability of access of citizens to their representatives is impaired. . . .

A consideration that appears to be of more substance in justifying some deviations from population-based representation in state legislatures is that of insuring some voice to political subdivisions, as political subdivisions. [In] many States much of the legislature's activity involves the enactment of so-called local legislation, directed only to the concerns of particular political subdivisions. And a State may legitimately desire to construct districts along political subdivision lines to deter the possibilities of gerrymandering. [But] if, even as a result of a clearly rational state policy of according some legislative representation to political subdivisions, population is submerged as the controlling consideration in the apportionment of seats in the particular legislative body, then the right of all of the State's citizens to cast an effective and adequately weighted vote would be unconstitutionally impaired. . . .

[Affirmed and remanded.]

Mr. Justice Harlan, dissenting [in all six cases]. . . .

The Court's constitutional discussion [is remarkable] for its failure to address itself at all to the Fourteenth Amendment as a whole or to the legislative history of the Amendment pertinent to the matter at hand. [The] history of the adoption of the Fourteenth Amendment provides conclusive evidence that neither those who proposed nor those who ratified the Amendment believed that the Equal Protection Clause limited the power of the States to apportion their legislatures as they saw fit. Moreover, the history demonstrates that the intention to leave this power undisturbed was deliberate and was widely believed to be essential to the adoption of the Amendment. [Justice Harlan's extensive historical analysis is omitted.]

The Court's elaboration of its new "constitutional" doctrine indicates how far — and how unwisely — it has strayed from the appropriate bounds of its authority. The consequence of today's decision is that in all but the handful of States which may already satisfy the new requirements the [courts] are given blanket authority and the constitutional duty to supervise apportionment of the State Legislatures. It is difficult to imagine a more intolerable and inappropriate interference by the judiciary with the independent legislatures of the States. . . .

Although the Court — necessarily, as I believe — provides only generalities in elaboration of its main thesis, its opinion nevertheless fully demonstrates how far removed these problems are from fields of judicial competence. [In] one or another of today's opinions, the Court declares it unconstitutional for a State to give effective consideration to any of the following in establishing legislative districts:

  (1)   history;
  (2)   "economic or other sorts of group interests";
  (3)   area;
  (4)   geographical considerations;
  (5)   a desire "to insure effective representation for sparsely settled areas";
  (6)   "availability of access of citizens to their representatives";
  (7)   theories of bicameralism (except those approved by the Court);
  (8)   occupation;
  (9)   "an attempt to balance urban and rural power";
 (10)   the preference of a majority of voters in the State.

So far as presently appears, the *only* factor which a State may consider, apart from numbers, is political subdivisions. But even "a clearly rational state policy" recognizing this factor is unconstitutional if "population is submerged as the controlling consideration. . . ."

I know of no principle of logic or practical or theoretical politics, still less any constitutional principle, which establishes all or any of these exclusions. [The] Court says [only] that "legislators represent people, not trees or acres." [This] may be conceded. But it is surely equally obvious, and, in the context of elections, more meaningful to note that people are not ciphers and that legislators can represent their electors only by speaking for their interests — economic, social, political — many of which do reflect the place where the electors live. The Court does not establish, or indeed even attempt to make a case for the proposition that conflicting interests within a State can only be adjusted by disregarding them when voters are grouped for purposes of representation. . . .

MR. JUSTICE STEWART, whom MR. JUSTICE CLARK joins, dissenting [in the Colorado and New York cases]. . . .

[My] own understanding of the various theories of representative government is that no one theory has ever commanded unanimous assent. [But] even if it were thought that the rule announced today by the Court is, as a matter of political theory, the most desirable general rule which can be devised, [I] could not join in the fabrication of a constitutional mandate which imports and forever freezes one theory of political thought into our Constitution. . . .

Representative government is a process of accommodating group interests through democratic institutional arrangements. [Appropriate] legislative apportionment, therefore, should ideally be designed to insure effective representation in the State's legislature, in cooperation with other organs of political power, of the various groups and interests making up the electorate. [Population] factors must often to some degree be subordinated in devising a legislative apportionment plan which is to achieve the important goal of ensuring a fair, effective, and balanced representation of the regional, social, and economic interests within a State. [What] constitutes a rational plan reasonably designed to achieve this objective will vary from State to State, since each State is unique, in terms of topography, geography, demography, history, heterogeneity and concentration of population, variety of social and economic interests, and in the operation and interrelation of its political institutions. But so long as a State's apportionment plan reasonably achieves, in the light of the State's own characteristics, effective and balanced representation of all substantial interests, without sacrificing the principle of effective majority rule, that plan cannot be considered irrational.

[I] think the cases should be decided by application of accepted principles of constitutional adjudication under the Equal Protection Clause. [The] Equal Protection Clause demands but two basic attributes of any plan of state legislative apportionment. First, it demands that, in the light of the State's own characteristics and needs, the plan must be a rational one. Secondly, it demands that the plan must be such as not to permit the systematic frustration of the will of a majority of the electorate of the State. [But,] beyond this, I think there is nothing in the Federal Constitution to prevent a State from choosing any electoral legislative structure it thinks best suited to the interests, temper, and customs of its people.

[Applying these standards, Justice Stewart voted to uphold the Colorado and New York plans of legislative apportionment. The Colorado House was apportioned on a population basis, but rural areas were significantly "overrepresented" in the Senate. Stewart maintained that this departure from a population-based apportionment was permissible because it had been adopted in a statewide referendum and because it accommodated the distinct interests and characteristics of the state's various regions. Stewart thought that smaller population districts were reasonable in sparsely populated areas, for example, to enable senators "to maintain close contact with [constituents]," and he thought they were reasonable in certain agricultural areas to prevent the grouping of this portion of the electorate "in districts with larger numbers of voters with wholly different interests." Moreover, Stewart noted, because of the strength of the urban areas, "no possible combination of Colorado senators from rural districts [could] control the Senate." Stewart thus concluded that the Colorado scheme represented a reasonable "choice to protect the minority's interests." The New York plan assured smaller counties greater representation in the Assembly than would be warranted under a population-based apportionment and limited representation of the largest counties. Justice Stewart argued that this was justified as a counterweight to New York City's "concentration of population, homogeneity of interest, and political cohesiveness."]

Note: Reynolds *and Its Progeny*

1. *"One person, one vote."* Note that *Kramer* was denied the right to vote, whereas no one in *Reynolds* was denied that right. Does "one person, one

vote" follow logically from the equality principle? Does it follow from the conclusion that the "right to vote" is "fundamental"? Does Justice Stewart's emphasis on "systematic frustration of the majority" provide a preferable focus for judicial inquiry? Consider the following views.

a. Auerbach, The Reapportionment Cases: One Person, One Vote — One Vote, One Value, 1964 Sup. Ct. Rev. 1, 2:

It is paradoxical for the judicial activists, who extol the Court as the protector of minorities, to praise it for helping to erase the power of minorities to curb majority rule in our state legislatures. But it is also paradoxical for the advocates of judicial self-limitation to criticize the Court for helping to make majority rule effective, because the case for self-restraint rests on the assumption that the Court is reviewing the legislative acts of representatives who are put in office [by] a majority of the people. Since malapportionment destroys this assumption, judicial intervention to remove this obstacle to majority rule may be less intolerable than the self-perpetuation of minority rule.

b. Neal, *Baker v. Carr:* Politics in Search of Law, 1962 Sup. Ct. Rev. 252, 275-278, 284:

[The] principle that representation must be based primarily on equality of voting strength [is] too gross an oversimplification [to] serve as the controlling constitutional rule, [for fair] representation depends on more than the weight of individual votes in voting for legislative representatives. [The] principle of equal weight for each vote would be fully satisfied, [for example,] by a system under which all representatives were elected at large, [but such a system] could leave the Negro largely without effective political participation unless Negro voters become a majority. [Moreover, districting, which gives] representation to interests which would [otherwise] be submerged by majorities, [suggests how] the problem of apportionment cannot be divorced from the problem of gerrymander. [If] the test of equality goes so short a distance in guiding judicial judgment, it remains uncertain not only what the other determinants are but whether any exist which will enable a court to claim more for its conclusion than that it is a political judgment.

c. M. Shapiro, Law and Politics in the Supreme Court 230, 249 (1964):

[The] electoral process is not the only political process. Indeed, a major share of our politics consists of negotiations [among] various interest groups and segments of government. [By] adopting the most simplistic view of the political process, and particularly of the process of representation, the Court equates the electoral and the political processes. [Such a] vision of the political process [cannot] serve even the most populist philosophy. For in the complex politics of group bargaining and shifting temporary majorities that we actually have in the United States, inequalities in voting strength may contribute [to] the over-all equality of all participants in the political process as a whole. Blanket and blind enforcement of electoral equality will [thus have effects that are] largely random.

d. Deutsch, Neutrality, Legitimacy, and the Supreme Court: Some Intersections between Law and Political Science, 20 Stan. L. Rev. 169, 246-247 (1968):

What [Justice Stewart] would require the Court to do in apportionment cases is to examine the realities of the distribution of political power within the State — the existence of voting blocs, the degree of party control over voters and officials, the position of the mass media, and the extent of financial backing available to the various factions, to mention only a few of the crucial inquiries. [Given] the Court's institutional arrangements, however, it could investigate these matters only by requiring lower courts to build records on these issues. Is this a demand we can reasonably make of our courts?

e. J. Ely, Democracy and Distrust 124 (1980):

[There] were two ways to avoid the unadministrability thicket. One was to stay out of the area altogether. That would have meant, however, that the ins would simply have gone on maintaining their positions by valuing one person's vote at a sixth of another's. Everyone [agreed] that that was no more compatible with the underlying theory of our Constitution than taking away some people's votes altogether. So the Court entered, and *precisely because of considerations of administrability*, soon found itself with no perceived alternative but to move to a one person, one vote standard.

2. *Reapportionment: a "success story"?* Consider McKay, Reapportionment: Success Story of the Warren Court, 67 Mich. L. Rev. 223, 226-229 (1968):

By 1960 malapportionment in the United States had attained such proportions that the integrity of representative government was in many instances endangered. [*Reynolds*, however, was viewed by some] as an abuse of judicial power. [Opponents] of reapportionment swiftly mounted an attack [that included] efforts to limit the jurisdiction of the federal courts [and to amend the Constitution. These] efforts were unsuccessful [for] the simple reason that the public did not oppose the decisions. [Moreover, while] there was some footdragging, and judicial proceedings were often necessary, [within four years of *Reynolds* congressional and state legislative district lines had been redrawn in almost every state].

For a more skeptical view, see A. Bickel, The Supreme Court and the Idea of Progress (1970).

3. *Popularly mandated malapportionment. Reynolds* was designed, in part, to protect majoritarianism and to prevent "minority control of state legislative bodies." Is malapportionment unconstitutional even if it is approved by a majority of the state's voters? In Lucas v. Forty-Fourth General Assembly, 377 U.S. 713 (1964), a companion case to *Reynolds*, the Colorado scheme, which apportioned only one of the two houses on the basis of population, had been approved in 1962 by a statewide referendum in which the voters specifically rejected a plan to apportion both houses on the basis of population. Nonetheless, the Court held the scheme invalid: "An individual's constitutionally protected right to cast an equally weighted vote cannot be denied even by a vote of a majority of a State's electorate, if the apportionment scheme [fails] to measure up to the requirements of the Equal Protection Clause. [A] citizen's constitutional rights can hardly be infringed simply because a majority of the people choose that it be."

4. *Supermajorities.* If *Reynolds* was designed, in part, to protect majoritarianism and to prevent minority control of government, may a state constitutionally require the assent of a "supermajority" to enact legislation or take other action? Is such a practice invalid because it accords a "veto" to the minority? In Gordon v. Lance, 403 U.S. 1 (1971), the Court upheld a West Virginia law prohibiting

political subdivisions from incurring bonded indebtedness without the approval of 60 percent of the voters in a referendum election. The Court explained:

> [Any] departure from strict majority rule gives disproportionate power to the minority. But there is nothing in the language of the Constitution, our history or our cases that requires that a majority always prevail on every issue. [The] Constitution itself provides that a simple majority vote is insufficient on some issues. [We] conclude that so long as such provisions do not discriminate against or authorize discrimination against any identifiable class they do not violate the Equal Protection Clause.

The Court added in a footnote: "We intimate no view on the constitutionality of a provision requiring unanimity or giving a veto power to a very small group. Nor do we decide whether a State may [require] extraordinary majorities for the election of public officers."

Consider Wilkinson, The Supreme Court, The Equal Protection Clause, and the Three Faces of Constitutional Equality, 61 Va. L. Rev. 943, 945 (1975): "The supermajority requirement in [Lance] predictably and repeatedly benefits one side of a political issue. It invariably dilutes the votes of those supporting capital improvements in public services [and] invariably magnifies the votes of those opposing [them]."

After Lance, may a state require a 60 percent majority in the legislature to increase taxes? May it require a 60 percent majority to unseat an incumbent? May it prohibit a new county charter from being adopted unless it is approved by "majorities of the voters who live in the cities within the county, and of those who live outside the cities"? See Lockport v. Citizens for Community Action, 430 U.S. 259 (1977), in which the Court upheld such a scheme. The Court reasoned that "The equal protection principles applicable in gauging the fairness of an election involving the choice of legislative representatives are of limited relevance [in] analyzing the propriety of recognizing distinctive voter interests in a 'single-shot' referendum." The Court concluded that the "differing interests of city and non-city voters in the adoption of a new county charter" were sufficient to justify the scheme.

5. *Local government units.* In Avery v. Midland County, 390 U.S. 474 (1968), the Court extended *Reynolds* to subunits of state government. The Midland County Commissioners Court, which had "general responsibility and power for local affairs," consisted of five commissioners, one elected at large, and one elected from each of four districts. One of these districts had 67,000 residents, the other three had less than 1,000 each. Noting that the commissioners had jurisdiction over tax rates and adoption of the county budget, the Court rejected an argument that the commissioners' responsibilities were "insufficiently legislative" to require their election to conform to the principle of one person, one vote. It concluded "that the Constitution permits no substantial variation from equal population in drawing districts for units of local government having general governmental powers over the entire geographic area served by the body." Justices Harlan, Fortas, and Stewart dissented.

In Hadley v. Junior College District, 397 U.S. 50 (1970), the Court extended *Avery* to a junior college district consisting of eight districts, where one district with 60 percent of the population was authorized to elect only 50 percent of the junior college district's trustees. The Court explained that the district's powers to run the schools, levy taxes, and issue bonds were "general enough and [had] sufficient impact throughout the district" to require equal apportionment. It noted, however, "that there might be some cases in which a State elects certain functionaries whose duties are so far removed from normal governmental activities and so disproportionately affect different groups that a popular election in compliance with *Reynolds* [might] not be required." Chief Justice Burger and Justices Harlan and Stewart dissented.

6. *Permissible deviations from "one person, one vote."* The courts have developed a number of statistical indices to measure malapportionment. The most prominent index is the "maximum percentage deviation." For example, if a state with a population of 10 million is allotted ten congressmen, the ideal district will have a population of 1 million. If the largest district has a population of 1.1 million (10 percent above the ideal) and the smallest has 0.9 million (10 percent below the ideal), the maximum percentage deviation is 20 percent. What is the maximum percentage deviation that should satisfy *Reynolds?* How should one measure "population" — eligible voters, registered voters, total population?

a. *Congressional districting.* In Wesberry v. Sanders, 376 U.S. 1 (1964), the Court held that the provision of article I, section 2, that United States representatives "be chosen 'by the People of the several States' means that as nearly as is practicable one man's vote in a congressional election is to be worth as much as another's." The Court thus invalidated a Georgia congressional districting scheme with a maximum percentage deviation of more than 140 percent. The Court has relied on *Wesberry* to invalidate congressional districting plans with much smaller deviations. See Kirkpatrick v. Preisler, 394 U.S. 526 (1969) (5.97 percent); Wells v. Rockefeller, 394 U.S. 542 (1969) (13.1 percent); White v. Weiser, 412 U.S. 783 (1973) (4.13 percent); Karcher v. Daggett, 462 U.S. 725 (1983) (0.7 percent).

In *Kirkpatrick* the Court held that no variance from absolute equality could be justified as de minimis. The Court emphasized that the states must make "a good-faith effort to achieve precise mathematical equality," that they must justify every deviation from the ideal, and that deviations cannot be justified by a desire to avoid the fragmentation of political subdivisions. In *Karcher* the Court reaffirmed *Kirkpatrick*. It again explained that states must "come as nearly as practicable to population equality." Although the Court indicated that certain "consistently applied legislative policies might justify some variance, including, for instance, making districts compact, respecting municipal boundaries, preserving the cores of prior districts, and avoiding contests between incumbent Representatives," it stressed that the state must "show with some specificity that a particular objective required the specific deviations in its plan, rather than simply relying on general assertions." Justice White, joined by Chief Justice Burger and Justices Powell and Rehnquist, dissented, concluding that if *Kirkpatrick* required the invalidation of a districting plan with a maximum percentage deviation of only 0.7 percent, then it was time to reconsider *Kirkpatrick*.

b. *State districting.* Under the equal protection clause, the Court has tolerated significant deviations from the mathematical ideal in its review of state and local districting plans. In Mahan v. Howell, 410 U.S. 315 (1973), the Court upheld a Virginia legislative districting plan with a maximum percentage deviation of 16.4 percent. The Court distinguished *Kirkpatrick* and explained that "more flexibility was constitutionally permissible with respect to state legislative reapportionment" because of the interest in "the normal functioning of state and local governments." It held that the deviations in the Virginia plan satisfied *Reynolds's* goal of "substantial equality of population" and were justified by "the State's policy of maintaining the integrity of political subdivision lines." The Court cautioned, however, that even rational state interests could not "be permitted to emasculate the goal of substantial equality." The deviation in *Mahan*, it noted, "may well approach tolerable limits." Justice Brennan, joined by Justices Douglas and Marshall, dissented. Brennan conceded that a state might have a broader range of *justifications* for deviations in the state legislative context, but objected to the idea of "different constitutional *standards*" for state and congressional districting.

Later that term, in Gaffney v. Cummings, 412 U.S. 735 (1973), and White v. Regester, 412 U.S. 755 (1973), the Court recognized a category of "minor" deviations that require no justification at all. In opinions by Justice White, the Court upheld state legislative districting plans with maximum percentage deviations of 9.9 and 7.8 percent. The Court observed that these "relatively minor" deviations were insufficient to meet the "threshold requirement of proving a prima facie case of invidious discrimination" and thus required no justification. It distinguished these cases from cases like *Reynolds*, which involved "enormous" and unjustifiable deviations, and cases like *Mahan*, which involved deviations "sufficiently large to require justification" but which were justifiable. It concluded that *Reynolds's* goal of "substantial equality" did "not in any commonsense way depend upon eliminating the insignificant population variation [in these cases]." Again, Justices Douglas, Brennan, and Marshall dissented. In subsequent decisions, the Court has "established that, as a general matter, an apportionment plan with a maximum population deviation of under 10 percent falls within [the] category of minor deviations." Brown v. Thompson, 462 U.S. 835 (1983).

7. *Political gerrymandering.* In Gaffney v. Cummings, 412 U.S. 735 (1973), the challengers of the districting plan maintained that even if the plan satisfied the one person, one vote requirement of *Reynolds*, it was nonetheless "invidiously discriminatory" because it was admittedly drawn to "achieve a rough approximation of statewide political strengths of the Democratic and Republican Parties." The Court held that the "political fairness principle" was not unconstitutional:

> Politics and political considerations are inseparable from districting and apportionment. [It] may be suggested that those who redistrict and reapportion should work with census, not political, data and achieve population equality without regard for political impact. But this politically mindless approach may produce, whether intended or not, the most grossly gerrymandered results. [Districting schemes may be invalid] if racial or political groups [are] fenced out of the political process and their voting strength invidiously minimized, [but there is no] constitutional warrant to invalidate a state plan, otherwise within tolerable population limits, because it undertakes, not to minimize or eliminate the political strength of any group or party, but to recognize it and, through districting, provide a rough sort of proportional representation in the legislative halls of the State.

Suppose a districting scheme adversely affects the relative political power of an identifiable political or racial group? Consider City of Mobile v. Bolden.

City of Mobile v. Bolden
446 U.S. 55 (1980)

[Since 1911 the city of Mobile, Alabama, has been governed by a City Commission consisting of three commissioners who jointly exercise all legislative, executive, and administrative power. The commissioners are elected, not by the residents of three distinct districts but by the residents of the city at large. This electoral system "is followed by literally thousands of municipalities." Although Mobile has a substantial black population, no black has ever been elected to the commission. In *Bolden* the Court rejected a claim that the retention of the at-large electoral system in such circumstances unconstitutionally diluted the voting strength of blacks.]

MR. JUSTICE STEWART announced the judgment of the Court and delivered an opinion, in which THE CHIEF JUSTICE, MR. JUSTICE POWELL, and MR. JUSTICE REHNQUIST joined.

[At the outset, Justice Stewart observed that the "claim that at-large electoral schemes" violate the equal protection clause "'is rooted in their winner-take-all aspects, their tendency to submerge minorities.'" Stewart noted that, despite this feature, multimember legislative districts "are not unconstitutional per se." Rather, he maintained, they are invalid only if their purpose is "invidiously to minimize or cancel out the voting potential of racial or ethnic minorities." "A plaintiff," in other words, "must prove that the disputed plan was 'conceived or operated' as [a] purposeful devic[e] to further [racial] discrimination." Stewart explained that this "burden of proof is simply one aspect of the basic principle that only if there is purposeful discrimination can there be a violation of the Equal Protection Clause." To illustrate, Stewart pointed to Gomillion v. Lightfoot, 364 U.S. 339 (1960), in which the Court had invalidated a "racially motivated gerry-mander of municipal boundaries"; White v. Register, 412 U.S. 755 (1973), in which the Court had invalidated a multimember district plan which minimized the voting strength of blacks and Mexican-Americans where it was proved that "the political processes [were] not equally open to participation by the group[s] in question"; and Wright v. Rockefeller, 376 U.S. 52 (1964), in which the Court had sustained a state congressional reapportionment statute against claims that the district lines had been racially gerrymandered, because the plaintiffs had failed to prove that the legislature had been "motivated by racial considerations." Applying the intent standard, Stewart concluded that "the evidence [falls] far short of showing that the appellants 'conceived or operated [a] purposeful devic[e] to further racial [discrimination].'" (This aspect of *Bolden* is addressed in Chapter 5, section C2, supra.)]

We turn finally to the arguments advanced in [Mr.] Justice Marshall's dissenting opinion. The theory [appears] to be that every "political group," or at least every such group that is in the minority, has a federal constitutional right to elect candidates in proportion to its numbers.[22] Moreover, a political group's "right" to have its candidates elected is said to be a "fundamental interest," the infringement of which may be established without proof that a State has acted with the purpose of impairing anybody's access to the political process. This dissenting

---

22. The dissenting opinion seeks to disclaim this description of its theory by suggesting that a claim of vote dilution may require, in addition to proof of electoral defeat, some evidence of "historical and social factors" indicating that the group in question is without political influence. [Putting] to the side the evident fact that these gauzy sociological considerations have no constitutional basis, it remains far from certain that they could, in any principled manner, exclude the claims of any discrete political group that happens, for whatever reason, to elect fewer of its candidates than arithmetic indicates it might. Indeed, the putative limits are bound to prove illusory if the express purpose informing their application would be, as the dissent assumes, to redress the "inequitable distribution of political influence."

opinion finds the "right" infringed in the present case because no Negro has been elected to the Mobile City Commission.

Whatever appeal the dissenting opinion's view may have as a matter of political theory, it is not the law. The Equal Protection Clause [does] not require proportional representation as an imperative of political organization. The entitlement that the dissenting opinion assumes to exist simply is not to be found in the Constitution of the United States.

It is of course true that a law that impinges upon a fundamental right [is] presumptively unconstitutional. [And it is true] that the Equal Protection Clause confers a substantive right to participate in elections on an equal basis with other qualified voters. See [Dunn v. Blumstein; Reynolds v. Sims]. But this right to equal participation in the electoral process does not protect any "political group," however defined, from electoral defeat.

The dissenting opinion erroneously discovers the asserted entitlement to group representation within the "one person, one vote" principle of Reynolds v. Sims, supra, and its progeny. [The] Court [there] recognized that a voter's right to "have an equally effective voice" in the election of representatives is impaired where representation is not apportioned substantially on a population basis. [There] can be, of course, no claim that the "one person, one vote" principle has been violated in this case, because the city of Mobile is a unitary electoral district and the Commission elections are conducted at large. It is therefore obvious that nobody's vote has been "diluted" in the sense in which that word was used in the *Reynolds* case. [It] is, of course, true that the right of a person to vote on an equal basis with other voters draws much of its significance from the political associations that its exercise reflects, but it is an altogether different matter to conclude that political groups themselves have an independent constitutional claim to representation.[26]. . .

[Reversed and remanded.]

Mr. Justice Blackmun, concurring in the result.

Assuming that proof of intent is a prerequisite to appellees' prevailing on their constitutional claim of vote dilution, I am inclined to agree with Mr. Justice White that, in this case, "the findings of the District Court amply support an inference of purposeful discrimination." I concur in the Court's judgment of reversal, however, because I believe that the relief afforded appellees by the District Court, [changing the form of the city's government to a mayor-council system], was not commensurate with the sound exercise of judicial discretion.

---

26. It is difficult to perceive how the implications of the dissenting opinion's theory of group representation could rationally be cabined. Indeed, certain preliminary practical questions immediately come to mind: Can only members of a minority of the voting population in a particular municipality be members of a "political group"? How large must a "group" be to be a "political group"? Can any "group" call itself a "political group"? If not, who is to say which "groups" are "political groups"? Can a qualified voter belong to more than one "political group"? Can there be more than one "political group" among white voters (e.g., Irish-American, Italian-American, Polish-American, Jews, Catholics, Protestants)? Can there be more than one "political group" among nonwhite voters? Do the answers to any of these questions depend upon the particular demographic composition of a given city? Upon the total size of its voting population? Upon the size of its governing body? Upon its form of government? Upon its history? Its geographic location? The fact that even these preliminary questions may be largely unanswerable suggests some of the conceptual and practical fallacies in the constitutional theory espoused by the dissenting opinion, putting to one side the total absence of support for that theory in the Constitution itself.

[In] my view, the District Court at least should have considered alternative remedial orders that would have maintained some of the basic elements of the commission system, [such as] joint exercise of legislative and executive power. . . .

MR. JUSTICE STEVENS, concurring in the judgment. . . .

In my view, there is a fundamental distinction between state action that inhibits an individual's right to vote and state action that affects the political strength of various groups that compete for leadership in a democratically governed community. That distinction divides so-called vote dilution practices into two different categories "governed by entirely different constitutional considerations."

In the first category are practices such as poll taxes or literacy tests that deny individuals access to the ballot. Districting practices that make an individual's vote in a heavily populated district less significant than an individual's vote in a smaller district also belong in that category. [Such] practices must be tested by the strictest of constitutional standards. . . .

This case does not fit within the first category. [Rather,] this case draws into question a political structure that treats all individuals as equals but adversely affects the political strength of a racially identifiable group. . . .

Whatever the proper standard for identifying an unconstitutional gerrymander may be, [it] must apply equally to all forms of political gerrymandering — not just to racial gerrymandering. [This follows] from the very nature of a gerrymander. By definition, gerrymandering involves drawing district boundaries (or using multimember districts or at-large elections) in order to maximize the voting strength of those loyal to the dominant political faction and to minimize the strength of those opposed to it. In seeking the desired result, legislators necessarily make judgments about the probability that the members of certain identifiable groups, whether racial, ethnic, economic, or religious, will vote in the same way. The success of the gerrymander from the legislators' point of view, as well as its impact on the disadvantaged group, depends on the accuracy of those predictions.

A prediction based on a racial characteristic is not necessarily more reliable than a prediction based on some other group characteristic. Nor, since a legislator's ultimate purpose in making the prediction is political in character, is it necessarily more invidious or benign than a prediction based on other group characteristics.[9] In the line-drawing process, racial, religious, ethnic, and economic gerrymanders are all species of political gerrymanders. . . .

My conclusion that the same standard should be applied to racial groups as is applied to other groups leads me also to conclude that the standard cannot condemn every adverse impact on one or more political groups without spawning more dilution litigation than the judiciary can manage. [Nothing] comparable to the mathematical yardstick used in apportionment cases is available to identify the difference between permissible and impermissible adverse impacts on the voting strength of political groups.

[Today], the plurality [holds] that the primary, if not the sole, focus of the inquiry must be on the intent of the political body responsible for making the districting decision. [I] do not believe that it is appropriate to focus on the subjective intent of the decisionmakers.

_____

9. Thus, for example, there is little qualitative difference between the motivation behind a religious gerrymander designed to gain votes on the abortion issue and a racial gerrymander designed to gain votes on an economic issue.

In my view [a challenged scheme should be invalidated if three objective factors are present]: (1) [it] was manifestly not the product of a routine or a traditional political decision; (2) it [has] a significant adverse impact on a minority group; and (3) it [is] unsupported by any neutral justification and thus [is] either totally irrational or entirely motivated by a desire to curtail the political strength of the minority. . . .

[In] this case, if the commission form of government in Mobile were extraordinary, or if it were nothing more than a vestige of history, with no [rational] justification, it would surely violate the Constitution [because of] its adverse impact on black voters plus the absence of any legitimate justification for the system. [And this would be so] without reference to the subjective intent of the political body that has refused to alter it.

Conversely, I [am] persuaded that a political decision that affects group voting rights may be valid even if it can be proved that irrational or invidious factors have played some part in its enactment or retention. The [process of] drawing political boundaries [inevitably] involves a series of compromises among different group interests. If the process is to work, it must reflect an awareness of group interests and it must tolerate some attempts to advantage or to disadvantage particular segments of the voting populace. [The] standard cannot, therefore, be so strict that any evidence of a purpose to disadvantage a bloc of voters will justify a finding of "invidious discrimination"; otherwise, the facts of political life would deny legislatures the right to perform the districting function. Accordingly, a political decision that is supported by valid and articulable justifications cannot be invalid simply because some participants in the decisionmaking process were motivated by a purpose to disadvantage a minority group.

The decision to retain the commission form of government in Mobile, Ala., is such a decision. [The] fact that these at-large systems characteristically place one or more minority groups at a significant disadvantage in the struggle for political power cannot invalidate all such systems. Nor can it be the law that such systems are valid when there is no evidence that they were instituted or maintained for discriminatory reasons, but that they may be selectively condemned on the basis of the subjective motivation of some of their supporters. A contrary view "would spawn endless litigation" [and] would entangle the judiciary in a voracious political thicket.

In sum, I believe we must accept the choice to retain Mobile's commission form of government as constitutionally permissible even though that choice may well be the product of mixed motivation, some of which is invidious. . . .

MR. JUSTICE BRENNAN, dissenting.

I dissent because I agree with Mr. Justice Marshall that proof of discriminatory impact is sufficient in these cases. I also dissent because, even accepting the plurality's premise that discriminatory purpose must be shown, I agree with Mr. Justice Marshall and Mr. Justice White that the appellees have clearly met that burden.

MR. JUSTICE WHITE, dissenting.

[In a lengthy opinion, Justice White maintained] that the findings of the District Court amply support an inference of purposeful discrimination. . . .

MR. JUSTICE MARSHALL, dissenting. . . .

"[O]nly if there is purposeful discrimination," announces the plurality, "can there be a violation of the Equal Protection Clause of the Fourteenth Amendment." That proposition is plainly overbroad. It fails to distinguish between two distinct lines of equal protection decisions: those involving suspect classifications, and those involving fundamental rights. . . .

Under the Equal Protection Clause, if a classification "impinges upon a fundamental right [strict] judicial scrutiny" is required, regardless of whether the infringement was intentional. [There is] a fundamental right to equal electoral participation that encompasses protection against vote dilution. Proof of discriminatory purpose is, therefore, not required to support a claim of vote dilution. . . .

[The] equal protection problem attacked by the "one person, one vote" principle is [one] of vote dilution: under *Reynolds*, each citizen must have an "equally effective voice" in the election of representatives. In the present cases, the alleged vote dilution, though caused by the combined effects of the electoral structure and social and historical factors rather than by unequal population distribution, is analytically the same concept: the unjustified abridgment of a fundamental right. . . .

The plurality's response is that my approach amounts to nothing less than a constitutional requirement of proportional representation for groups. [I] explicitly reject the notion that the Constitution contains any such requirement. The constitutional protection against vote dilution [does] not extend to those situations in which a group has merely failed to elect representatives in proportion to its share of the population. To prove unconstitutional vote dilution, the group is also required to carry the far more onerous burden of demonstrating that it has been effectively fenced out of the political process. Typical of the plurality's mischaracterization of my position is its assertion that I would provide protection against vote dilution for "every 'political group,' or at least every such group that is in the minority." The vote-dilution doctrine can logically apply only to groups whose electoral discreteness and insularity allow dominant political factions to ignore them. In short, the distinction between a requirement of proportional representation and the discriminatory-effect test I espouse is by no means a difficult one, and it is hard for me to understand why the plurality insists on ignoring it.

The plaintiffs [proved] that no Negro had ever been elected to the Mobile City Commission, despite the fact that Negroes constitute about one-third of the electorate, and that the persistence of severe racial bloc voting made it highly unlikely that any Negro could be elected at large in the foreseeable future. [The] plaintiffs convinced the District Court that Mobile Negroes were unable to use alternative avenues of political influence. They showed that Mobile Negroes still suffered pervasive present effects of massive historical official and private discrimination, and that the City Commission had been quite unresponsive to the needs of the minority community. [Negroes] are grossly underrepresented on city boards and committees. [The] city's distribution of public services is racially discriminatory. . . .

[The] protection against vote dilution [serves] as a minimally intrusive guarantee of political survival for a discrete political minority that is effectively locked out of governmental decisionmaking processes.[22] [The] doctrine is a simple reflection of the basic principle that the Equal Protection Clause protects "[t]he right of a citizen to equal representation and to have his vote weighted equally with those of all other citizens." [*Reynolds.*] . . .

[Even if] it is assumed that proof of discriminatory intent is necessary to support the vote-dilution claims in these cases, the question becomes what evidence will satisfy this requirement.

The plurality assumes, without any analysis, that these cases are appropriate for the application of the rigid test developed in [such cases as Washington v. Davis and Personnel Administrator v. Feeney, see Chapter 5, section C2, supra]. In my view, [that] standard creates a burden of proof far too extreme to apply in vote-dilution cases.

I would apply the common-law foreseeability presumption to the present cases. [Because] the foreseeable disproportionate impact was so severe, the burden of proof should have shifted to the defendants, and they should have been required to show that they refused to modify the districting schemes in spite of, not because of, their severe discriminatory effect. Reallocation of the burden of proof is especially appropriate in these cases, where the challenged state action infringes the exercise of a fundamental right. The defendants would carry their burden of proof only if they showed that they considered submergence of the Negro vote a detriment, not a benefit, of the multimember systems, that they accorded minority citizens the same respect given to whites, and that they nevertheless decided to maintain the systems for legitimate reasons. . . .

The plurality [fails] to recognize that the maintenance of multimember districts in the face of foreseeable discriminatory consequences strongly suggests that officials are blinded by "racially selective sympathy and indifference." Like outright racial hostility, selective racial indifference reflects a belief that the concerns of the minority are not worthy of the same degree of attention paid to problems perceived by whites. When an interest as fundamental as voting is diminished along racial lines, a requirement that discriminatory purpose must be proved should be satisfied by a showing that official action was produced by this type of pervasive bias. . . .

Note: *Vote Dilution and the Interests of Groups*

1. A *"fundamental interest"* in *"proportional"* representation? Do you agree with Justice Stewart that there is no constitutional right to proportional representation? How would you distinguish between "one person, one vote" and "one

---

22. It is at this point that my view most diverges from the position expressed by my Brother Stevens. He would strictly scrutinize state action having an adverse impact on an individual's right to vote. In contrast, he would apply a less stringent standard to state action diluting the political influence of a group. The facts of the present cases, however, demonstrate that severe and persistent racial bloc voting, when coupled with the inability of the minority effectively to participate in the political arena by alternative means, can effectively disable the individual Negro as well as the minority community as a whole. In these circumstances, Mr. Justice Stevens' distinction between the rights of individuals and the political strength of groups becomes illusory.

group, one representative"? Consider Note, The Constitutional Imperative of Proportional Representation, 94 Yale L. J. 163, 172-173, 175-176, 182 (1984):

> Two fundamental values underlie the Supreme Court's debate about constitutional rights in voting: majority rule and minority representation. The debate has taken the traditional system of winner-take-all single-member districts as a given. [But this] system contains a strong majoritarian bias. If the supporters of two parties were distributed uniformly throughout the area of the elections, the party winning the most votes would win every seat in the legislature. The votes for the minority candidate would in effect be wasted. [Under the Court's analysis, majority] rule is conceptualized [as] an individual right deserving the strongest protection, whereas minority representation is conceptualized [as] a group right that will not be vindicated without proof of invidious discrimination. But the opposition of individual and group rights is logically [untenable]: The rights labeled as group rights are also individual rights and vice versa. [The] real distinction [is] not between individual and group rights but between the right to an equally weighted vote and the right to an equally powerful or equally meaningful vote. [The relevant] constitutional values [can] be fully guaranteed only by [proportional representation, for] proportional representation [is the only system that both achieves] majority rule [and] simultaneously guarantee[s] the individual and group right to both an equally weighted vote and an equally meaningful vote.

2. A *"fundamental" interest in "fair" representation?* Consider Justice Marshall's argument that there is a "fundamental interest" in "political survival for a discrete political minority that is effectively locked out of governmental decision-making processes" and that this "doctrine is a simple reflection of the basic principle that the Equal Protection Clause protects 'The right of a citizen to equal representation and to have his vote weighted equally with those of all other citizens.'" How does this differ from a right to proportional representation?

Consider Note, The Supreme Court — 1979 Term, 94 Harv. L. Rev. 75, 143-145 (1980):

> Voting has been recognized as a fundamental interest [because] it is "preservative of all rights." [*Reynolds*] emphasized the functional importance of voting by recognizing every citizen's "inalienable right to full and effective participation in the political [process]." [T]he "one man, one vote" rule established by *Reynolds* [was] designed to give voters an equal chance to be heard by their elected representatives. [This] requires that an electoral system be structured so as to allow all voters a "fair chance" to influence the choice of representatives. [When] a districting or electoral scheme operates systematically to deny to a distinct group of voters [a] "fair chance" of playing a role in determining who will represent them, voting itself becomes a futile and meaningless gesture.

See also Casper, Apportionment and the Right to Vote: Standards of Judicial Scrutiny, 1973 Sup. Ct. Rev. 1; Carpeneti, Legislative Apportionment: Multimember Districts and Fair Representation, 120 U. Pa. L. Rev. 666 (1972); Sickels, Dragons, Bacon Strips and Dumbbells — Who's Afraid of Reapportionment?, 75 Yale L. J. 1300 (1966).

3. *Discriminatory purpose.* As is evident in *Bolden*, the Court will invalidate a gerrymander or multimember district plan if it is adopted or retained for the

purpose of minimizing the relative voting strength of blacks. See Rogers v. Lodge, 458 U.S. 613 (1982) (invalidating an at-large system because it was maintained for a racially discriminatory purpose); Gomillion v. Lightfoot, 364 U.S. 339 (1960) (invalidating a districting plan because the lines were drawn with a racially discriminatory purpose). The issue of discriminatory purpose is examined more fully in Chapter 5, section C2, supra. Should the standard for proving discriminatory purpose be relaxed when the challenged law involves a "fundamental interest"? Should it be relaxed when, as in *Bolden*, it involves the structure of political representation? Consider, on the other hand, Justice Stevens's argument that the Court should not invalidate a gerrymander or multimember district plan because "irrational or invidious factors [played] a part in its enactment or retention" because the process of drawing "political boundaries [must] reflect an awareness of group interests and [must] tolerate some attempts to advantage or to disadvantage particular segments of the voting populace." Justice Stevens paints a picture of politics as consisting of inevitably self-interested efforts by representatives to get reelected and interest groups to maximize their power — efforts that will include self-interested gerrymanders. Stevens seems to think that in this context, perhaps uniquely, such motivations are not unconstitutional. Is he right?

If racially motivated gerrymanders are impermissible, what about gerrymanders designed to minimize the relative voting strength of particular political parties, ethnic groups, or economic factions? Suppose, for example, a state draws district lines in order to minimize the relative voting strength of farmers. Should protection against gerrymandering be available only to "suspect" classes? Should it extend to "any discernible group having coherent and identifiable legislative goals"? Clinton, Further Explorations in the Political Thicket: The Gerrymander and the Constitution, 59 Iowa L. Rev. 1, 35 (1973).

May a state draw district lines in order to assure at least proportional representation for particular groups? In *Gaffney* the Court upheld the "fairness principle" as applied to political parties. Is that principle acceptable as applied to racial groups?

Consider United Jewish Organizations v. Carey, 430 U.S. 144 (1977), in which New York redrew district lines in Brooklyn in order to maintain black representation in the state legislature. To achieve this result, the redistrict divided the local Hasidic community into several districts, thus assuring that each district had a substantial nonwhite majority. The Court upheld the plan. Justice White, joined by Justices Brennan, Blackmun, and Stevens, concluded that the Constitution did not prohibit the use of race in this manner where the redistricting was authorized by the Voting Rights Act and the percentage of districts in the county with substantial nonwhite majorities did not exceed the percentage of the population of the county that was nonwhite. In a separate part of his opinion, Justice White, joined by Justices Stevens and Rehnquist, concluded that, wholly apart from the Voting Rights Act, this use of race was permissible because it "represented no racial slur or stigma with respect to whites or any other race" and did not "minimize or unfairly cancel out white voting strength." White observed that racial voting is a common, if "unfortunate," practice and stated that it is "permissible for a State, employing sound districting principles [to] attempt to prevent racial minorities from being repeatedly outvoted." Justice Stewart, joined by Justice Powell, concluded that there had been no showing of racial discrimination and that racial awareness in legislative reapportionment is not per se unconstitutional.

Chief Justice Berger dissented on the ground that the Constitution mandates reapportionment along racially neutral lines.

May a state, as a form of "affirmative action," draw district lines in order to give blacks *greater* than proportional representation? The issue of "affirmative action" is examined more fully in Chapter 5, section C4, supra.

4. *Beyond discriminatory purpose: Justice Stevens's view.* Do you agree with Justice Stevens that the "appropriate" test should focus on "objective" factors rather than "on the subjective intent of the decisionmakers"? Is Stevens's approach an effort to balance the interest in fair representation against competing state interests, or is it merely an objective means of ascertaining intent?

Justice Stevens elaborated on his *Bolden* dissent in Karcher v. Daggett, 462 U.S. 725 (1983) (Stevens, J., concurring):

> [Judicial] preoccupation with the goal of perfect population equality is an inadequate method of judging the constitutionality of an apportionment plan. [Although numerical equality] directly protects individuals, it protects groups only indirectly at best, [for] a standard "of absolute equality is perfectly compatible with 'gerrymandering' of the worst sort." [In] evaluating equal protection challenges to districting plans, [I] would consider whether the plan has a significant adverse impact on an identifiable political group, whether the plan has objective indicia of irregularity, and then, whether the State is able to produce convincing evidence that the plan nevertheless serves neutral, legitimate interests of the community as a whole. [To demonstrate that there are "objective indicia of irregularity," the plaintiffs might prove that the districts have "dramatically irregular shapes," or that they deviate extensively "from established political boundaries," or that "the process for formulating and adopting a plan excluded divergent viewpoints, openly reflected the use of partisan criteria, and provided no explanation of the reasons for selecting one plan over another."] Although a scheme in fact worsens the voting position of a particular group, and though its geographic configuration or genesis is sufficiently irregular to violate one or more of the criteria just [mentioned], it will nevertheless be constitutionally valid if the State can demonstrate that the plan as a whole [advances] "legitimate considerations incident to the effectuation of a rational state policy." [But] if a State is unable to respond to a plaintiff's prima facie case by showing that its plan is supported by adequate neutral criteria, I believe a court could properly conclude that the challenged scheme is either totally irrational or entirely motivated by a desire to curtail the political strength of the affected group.

See also Rogers v. Lodge, 458 U.S. 613 (1982) (Stevens, J., dissenting). What, exactly, is the difference between Justice Stevens's approach and that of the plurality?

c. Denial of "Access to the Ballot"

WILLIAMS v. RHODES, 393 U.S. 23 (1968): Under Ohio law, political parties that had received 10 percent of the vote in the prior gubernatorial election automatically qualified for the next presidential election ballot. Other political parties, however, could earn a place on the ballot only if they had an elaborate party structure, held "a primary election conforming to detailed and rigorous standards," and filed a petition nine months before the election signed "by qualified electors totaling 15 percent of the number of ballots cast in the last preceding gubernatorial election." Noting that the law had "made it virtually impossible for a new political party [to] be placed on [the] ballot," the Court invalidated the Ohio scheme. Justice Black delivered the opinion of the Court:

"In determining whether or not a state law violates the Equal Protection Clause, we must consider the facts and circumstances behind the law, the interests which the State claims to be protecting, and the interests of those who are disadvantaged by the classification. [Here] the state laws [burden] two different, although overlapping, kinds of rights — the right of individuals to associate for the advancement of political beliefs, and the right of qualified voters [to] cast their votes effectively. [The challenged laws] give the two old, established parties a decided advantage [and] thus place substantially unequal burdens on both the right to vote and the right to associate. [In] determining whether the State has power to place such unequal burdens on minority groups where rights of this kind are at stake, [we] have consistently held that 'only a compelling interest [can] justify limiting [such] freedoms.' . . .

"The State asserts that [it] may validly promote a two-party system in order to encourage compromise and political stability. [But] the Ohio system does not merely favor a 'two-party system'; it favors two particular parties — the Republicans and the Democrats — and in effect [gives] them a complete monopoly. [Ohio argues further] that its highly restrictive provisions are justified because without them a large number of parties might qualify for the ballot, and the voters would then be confronted with a choice so confusing that the popular will could be frustrated. But [experience] demonstrates that no more than a handful of parties attempts to qualify for ballot positions even when a very low number of signatures, such as 1% of the electorate, is required. [Thus,] at the present time this danger [is] no more than 'theoretically imaginable.' No such remote danger can justify the immediate and crippling impact on the basic constitutional rights involved in this case."

Justice Harlan concurred in the result on the ground "that Ohio's statutory scheme violates the basic right of political association assured by the First Amendment." Chief Justice Warren and Justices Stewart and White dissented.

Note: Williams and Its Progeny

1. *Access to the ballot.* If there is a fundamental interest in gaining access to the franchise, is there necessarily also a fundamental interest in gaining access to the ballot? Whose right is the Court protecting: The candidate's? The party member's? The potential voter's? Should the Court have analyzed the Ohio statute in first amendment rather than equal protection terms? Consider Casper, *Williams v. Rhodes* and Public Financing of Political Parties under the American and German Constitutions, 1969 Sup. Ct. Rev. 271, 282-283: "I find it very difficult to see how the right 'to vote effectively' [or] the right 'to associate effectively' [can] be the heart of the matter. [To] be sure, the right freely to form political parties [derives] from a systematic interpretation of the various political rights guaranteed in the Constitution, [but] once this has been established, the [question] of which requirements may be imposed on political parties [is] essentially a problem of equal political opportunities." Suppose the Ohio statute was amended to apply equally to *all* political parties. How would that affect the analysis? For

further analysis of *Williams*, see Barton, The General-Election Ballot: More Nominees or More Representative Nominees?, 22 Stan. L. Rev. 165 (1970).

2. *Petition requirements.* In *Williams* the Court invalidated the requirement that, to gain access to the presidential election ballot, a new or minor party must file a petition nine months before the election "signed by qualified electors totaling 15% of the number of ballots cast in the last preceding gubernatorial election." In Jenness v. Forston, 403 U.S. 431 (1971), the Court unanimously upheld a Georgia law providing that any political organization whose candidate received 20 percent of the vote at the most recent gubernatorial or presidential election automatically qualified for the ballot, but that a nominee of any other political organization must file a petition five months before the election signed by at least 5 percent of those eligible to vote at the last election for the office he is seeking. The Court explained:

> [*Williams*] presented a statutory scheme vastly different from the one before us here. Unlike Ohio, Georgia freely provides for write-in votes, [it] does not require every candidate to be the nominee of a political party, [it] does not fix an unreasonably early filing deadline, [and it] does not impose upon a small party or a new party [the] requirement of establishing elaborate primary election [machinery]. In a word, Georgia in no way freezes the status [quo]. [It] is true that a [major political party] in Georgia is assured of having the name of its nominee [printed] on the ballot, whereas the name of the nominee of a [minor political party] will be printed only if nominating petitions have been [filed]. [But a major political party, unlike a minor party, is required to conduct elaborate primary elections.] The fact is that there are obvious differences [between] the needs [of] a political party with historically established broad support [and] a new or small political [organization]. Georgia has not been guilty of invidious discrimination in recognizing these differences and providing different routes to the printed ballot. [There] is surely an important state interest in requiring some preliminary showing of a significant modicum of support before printing the name of a political organization's candidate on the ballot — the interest [in] avoiding confusion, deception, and even frustration of the democratic [process]. [And although the] 5% figure [is] apparently somewhat higher than the percentage [required] in many States, [this] is balanced by the fact that Georgia [permits a registered voter] to sign as many nominating petitions as he wishes.

Similarly, in American Party of Texas v. White, 415 U.S. 767 (1974), the Court upheld a Texas law providing that candidates of "major" parties could gain access to the ballot by being nominated in a primary election but that "minor" parties could obtain ballot access only by holding nominating conventions and obtaining signatures totaling at least 1 percent of the persons voting in the last preceding gubernatorial election. As in *Jenness* the Court emphasized that this scheme "in no way freezes the status quo." The Court explained that the equal protection clause did not forbid the requirement that small parties proceed by convention rather than primary election, for "the convention process [had not been shown to be] invidiously more burdensome than the primary election." Moreover, the Court held that "So long as the larger parties must demonstrate major support among the electorate at the last election, [the] smaller parties [may] be required to establish their position in some other [reasonable] manner." The Court thus upheld the 1 percent requirement, a provision stating that a voter could not sign a nominating petition if he had voted in a major party's primary or signed another nominating petition, a fifty-five-day time limit on the circulation of petitions, and a requirement that the signatures be notarized, as not "so excessive or impractical as to be in reality [devices to] exclude parties with significant support from the ballot." See also Illinois State Board of Elections v. Socialist Workers Party, 440 U.S. 173 (1979) (invalidating a state statute that had the effect of requiring more signatures to qualify for access to the ballot in Chicago elections than in statewide elections).

3. *Filing fees.* In Lubin v. Panish, 415 U.S. 709 (1974), the Court invalidated, as applied to indigents, a California law requiring payment of a filing fee of 2 percent of the annual salary for the office sought. The Court explained:

> [The] State's interest in keeping its ballots within manageable, understandable limits is of the highest order [but it] must be achieved by a means that does not unfairly or unnecessarily burden either a minority party's or an individual candidate's equally important interest in the continued availability of political opportunity. [The] process of qualifying candidates [may] not constitutionally be measured solely in dollars. [A] wealthy candidate with not the remotest chance of election may secure a place on the ballot by writing a check [while] impecunious but serious candidates may be prevented from running. [A] State may [not] require from an indigent candidate filing fees he cannot pay.

See also Bullock v. Carter, 405 U.S. 134 (1972) (invalidating a filing fee designed to shift to candidates the cost of primary elections).

The Court suggested in *Lubin* that, as an alternative to a filing fee, the State may require minor parties or impecunious candidates "to demonstrate the 'seriousness' of [their candidacies] by persuading a substantial number of voters to sign [petitions in their] behalf." May a state require that *only* those who cannot pay the filing fee demonstrate the "seriousness of [their] candidac[ies]" by such other means?

4. *Party loyalty requirements.* In Storer v. Brown, 415 U.S. 724 (1974), the Court upheld a California statute forbidding ballot position to an independent candidate who "had a registered affiliation with [a] political party at any time within one year prior to the immediately preceding primary election." The Court explained:

> [The challenged provision] involves no discrimination against independents. [Just as] the independent candidate must be clear of political party affiliations for a year before the primary, the party candidate must not have been registered with another party for a year before he files his [declaration]. [The challenged provision] protects the direct primary process by refusing to recognize independent candidates who do not make early plans to leave a [party]. It works against independent candidacies prompted by short-range political goals, pique, or personal quarrel. [It thus] furthers the State's [compelling] interest in the stability of its political system.

Justices Douglas, Brennan, and Marshall dissented.

5. *Disqualification of public officials.* In Clements v. Fashing, 457 U.S. 957 (1982), the Court upheld two provisions of the Texas Constitution. Section 19 provides that certain public officials shall not "be eligible to the Legislature" until the expiration of their current term of office. Section 65 provides that certain public officials who run for any other state or federal office must automatically resign their current position.

In a plurality opinion, Justice Rehnquist, joined by Chief Justice Burger and Justices Powell and O'Connor, reasoned:

[We have never held that] candidacy [is] a "fundamental right." [Rather, our] ballot access cases [focus] on the degree to which the challenged restrictions operate as a mechanism to exclude certain classes of candidates from the electoral process. The inquiry is whether the challenged restriction unfairly or unnecessarily burdens the "availability of political opportunity." [The] Court has departed from traditional equal protection analysis [in] two [lines] of ballot access cases. One line [involves] classifications based on wealth. [E.g., *Lubin; Bullock.*] The second [involves] classification schemes that impose burdens on new or small political parties or independent candidates. [E.g., *Williams; White; Storer.*] The provisions [challenged] in this case do not [fall within either of these lines]. [It is thus] necessary to examine the provisions in question in terms of the extent of the burdens that they place on the candidacy of current holders of public office. [Section 19] merely prohibits office-holders from cutting short their current term of office in order to serve in the Legislature. [As applied to appellee, a Justice of the Peace, section 19 establishes] a maximum "waiting period" of two [years]. A "waiting period" is hardly a significant barrier to candidacy. [Citing *Storer.*] We conclude that this sort of insignificant interference with access to the ballot need only rest on a rational predicate in order to [survive]. Section 19 clearly rests on a rational predicate [for] Texas has a legitimate interest in discouraging its Justices of the Peace from vacating their current terms of office. [The] burdens that §65 imposes on candidacy are even less substantial than those imposed by §19 [and the] two provisions [serve] essentially the same state interests.

Justice Stevens concurred in the judgment:

[The] burdens imposed [by these provisions are not] inconsistent with the First Amendment. [The] State's interest in having its officeholders faithfully perform the public responsibilities they have voluntarily undertaken is adequate to justify the restrictions placed on their ability to run for other offices. [The] only complaint [under the Equal Protection Clause] is that certain officeholders are treated differently from other officeholders. [There is no] claim that the classes are treated differently because of any characteristic of the persons who happen to occupy the various [offices]. [Rather,] the disparate treatment of different officeholders is entirely a function of the different offices that they occupy. The question presented then is whether there is any federal interest in requiring a State to define the benefits and burdens of different elective state offices in any particular manner. In my opinion there is not. [Thus,] there need be no justification at all for treating [these] classes differently.

Justice Brennan, joined by Justices Marshall, Blackmun, and White, dissented:

Although we have never defined candidacy as a fundamental right, we have clearly recognized that restrictions on candidacy impinge on First Amendment rights of candidates and voters. [With] this consideration in mind, we have applied strict scrutiny in reviewing most restrictions on ballot [access]. The plurality dismisses our prior cases as dealing with only two kinds of ballot access restrictions — classifications based on wealth and classifications imposing burdens on new or small political parties or independent candidates. But strict scrutiny was required in those cases because of their impact on the First Amendment *rights* of candidates and voters, [not] because the *class* of candidates or voters that was burdened was somehow suspect. [The] plurality offers no explanation as to why the restrictions at issue here, which completely bar some candidates from running and require other candidates to give up their present employment, are less "substantial" in their impact on candidates and their supporters than, for example, [the] filing fee at issue in *Lubin*.

Finally, Justice Brennan put "to one side the question of the proper level of equal protection scrutiny" and concluded that the classification among officeholders was irrational and could not "survive even minimal equal protection scrutiny."

6. *A new approach?* In Anderson v. Celebrezze, 460 U.S. 780 (1983), the Court invalidated an Ohio law requiring independent candidates to file their nominating petitions in mid-March in order to qualify for the ballot in the November election. Interestingly, Justice Stevens's majority opinion relied on the first amendment rather than the equal protection clause:

> [We] base our conclusions directly on the First [Amendment] and do not engage in a separate Equal Protection Clause analysis. We rely, however, on the analysis in a number of our prior election cases resting on the Equal Protection Clause. [These] cases, applying the "fundamental rights" strand of equal protection analysis, have identified the First [Amendment] rights implicated by restrictions on the eligibility of voters and [candidates]. Constitutional challenges to specific provisions of a State's election laws [cannot] be resolved by any "litmus-paper test" that will separate valid from invalid restrictions. Instead, a court [must] first consider the character and magnitude of the asserted injury to [First Amendment rights]. It then must identify and evaluate the precise interests put forward by the State as justifications for the burden imposed. [The] Court must not only determine the legitimacy and strength of each of those interests; it also must consider the extent to which those interests make it necessary to burden [First Amendment] rights. Only after weighing all these factors is the reviewing court in a position to decide whether the challenged provision is unconstitutional.

The Court concluded that Ohio's interests in "voter education, equal treatment for partisan and independent candidates, and political stability" were either illegitimate or too remotely related to the early filing deadline to justify such a substantial barrier to independent candidates. Justice Rehnquist, joined by Justices White, Powell, and O'Connor, dissented.

Is *Anderson* a step in the right direction? Consider Note, The Supreme Court — 1982 Term, 97 Harv. L. Rev. 1, 163 (1983): "The case-by-case multifactor balancing test employed in *Anderson* is unpredictable in application. [One] is left with the impression that evaluating each filing deadline requires weighing anew the interests in associational freedom with those in [political] stability."

2. Access to the Judicial Process

If there is a "fundamental" interest in equal access to the franchise, is there also a "fundamental" interest in equal access to the judicial process? Consider Michelman, The Supreme Court and Litigation Access Fees: The Right to Protect One's Rights — Part II, 1974 Duke L.J. 527, 534-540:

> There are a number of striking resemblances between the interests in voting and in litigating. [Both] the voting and litigating interests base a claim to "fundamentality"

on the idea that they are "preservative of all rights"; of both it can be said that "in social compact terms, in exchange for this legal and orderly method of resolving disputes, one restricts his power to satisfy his claims by force"; [and that] "ability to litigate just claims, like availability of the franchise, gives legitimacy to the state's coercive power." [Indeed,] litigation and legislation [are] bound up with one another in an entire, political-legal order in which the court's part is no less critical than the [legislature's]. Access to courts and access to legislatures are [thus] claims that merge into one another, [and you] cannot, without confusion, call a person a citizen and at the same time sanction [his] exclusion [from] that process.

GRIFFIN v. ILLINOIS, 351 U.S. 12 (1956): The Court held in *Griffin* that a state must furnish an indigent criminal defendant with a free trial transcript if such a transcript is necessary for "adequate and effective appellate review" of his conviction. In a plurality opinion, Justice Black, joined by Chief Justice Warren and Justices Douglas and Clark, explained: "[Our] constitutional guaranties of due process and equal protection both call for procedures in criminal trials which allow no invidious discriminations between persons and different groups of persons. [In] criminal trials a State can no more discriminate on account of poverty than on account of religion, race, or color. Plainly the ability to pay costs in advance bears no rational relationship to a defendant's guilt or innocence and could not be used as an excuse to deprive a defendant of a fair trial. [It] is true that a State is not required by the Federal Constitution to provide appellate courts or a right to appellate review at all. See, e.g., McKane v. Durston, 153 U.S. 684 [1894]. But that is not to say that a State that does grant appellate review can do so in a way that discriminates against some convicted defendants on account of their poverty. . . .

"All of the States now provide some method of appeal from criminal convictions, recognizing the importance of appellate review to a correct adjudication of guilt or innocence. Statistics show that a substantial proportion of criminal convictions are reversed by state appellate courts. Thus to deny adequate appellate review to the poor means that many of them may lose their life, liberty or property because of unjust convictions which appellate courts would set aside. Many States have recognized this and provided aid for convicted defendants who have a right to appeal and need a transcript but are unable to pay for it. A few have not. Such a denial is a misfit in a country dedicated to affording equal justice to all and special privileges to none in the administration of its criminal law. There can be no equal justice where the kind of trial a man gets depends on the amount of money he has. Destitute defendants must be afforded as adequate appellate review as defendants who have money enough to buy transcripts."

Justice Frankfurter concurred in the judgment. Justices Burton, Minton, Reed, and Harlan dissented.

DOUGLAS v. CALIFORNIA, 372 U.S. 353 (1963): In a six-to-three decision, the Court held unconstitutional a California rule requiring state appellate courts, on the request of an indigent criminal defendant for counsel on appeal, to make "an independent investigation of the record" and to "appoint counsel [only] if in their opinion it would be helpful to the defendant or the court." Justice Douglas delivered the opinion of the Court:

"[The denial] 'of counsel on appeal [to an indigent] would seem to be at least as invidious [a discrimination] as that condemned in [*Griffin*].' [Under the California rule,] the type of an appeal a person is afforded [hinges] upon whether or not he can pay for the assistance of counsel. . . .

"We are not here concerned with problems that might arise from the denial of counsel for the preparation of a petition for discretionary or mandatory review beyond the stage in the appellate process at which the claims have once been presented by a lawyer and passed upon by an appellate court. We are dealing only with the *first appeal*, granted as a matter of right to rich and poor [alike,] from a criminal conviction. . . .

"When an indigent is forced to run this gauntlet of a preliminary showing of merit, the right to appeal does not comport with fair procedure. [The] discrimination is not between 'possibly good and obviously bad cases,' but between cases where the rich man can require the court to listen to argument of counsel before deciding on the merits, but a poor man cannot. There is lacking that equality demanded by the Fourteenth Amendment where the rich man, who appeals as of right, enjoys the benefit of counsel's examination into the record, research of the law, and marshalling of arguments on his behalf, while the indigent, already burdened by a preliminary determination that his case is without merit, is forced to shift for himself. The indigent, where the record is unclear or the errors are hidden, has only the right to a meaningless ritual, while the rich man has a meaningful appeal."

Justice Harlan, joined by Justice Stewart, dissented: "[To] approach the present problem in terms of the Equal Protection Clause is, I submit, but to substitute resounding phrases for analysis. [The] States, of course, are prohibited by the Equal Protection Clause from discriminating between 'rich' and 'poor' *as such* in the formulation and application of their laws. But it is a far different thing to suggest that this provision prevents the State from adopting a law of general applicability that may affect the poor more harshly than it does the [rich]. Every financial exaction which the State imposes on a uniform basis is more easily satisfied by the well-to-do than by the indigent. Yet I take it that no one would dispute the constitutional power of the State to levy a uniform sales tax, to charge tuition at a state university, to fix rates for the purchase of water from a municipal corporation, [or] to establish minimum bail for various categories of offenses. [Laws] such as these do not deny equal protection to the less fortunate for one essential reason: the Equal Protection Clause does not impose on the States 'an affirmative duty to lift the handicaps flowing from differences in economic circumstances.' [The] State may have a moral obligation to eliminate the evils of poverty, but it is not required by the Equal Protection Clause to give to some whatever others can afford. . . .

"The real question in this case [and] the only one that permits of satisfactory analysis, is whether or not the state rule [is] consistent with the requirements of fair procedure guaranteed by the Due Process Clause. [It] bears reiteration that California's procedure [denies] to no one the right to appeal. This is not a case [in] which a court rule or statute bars all consideration of the merits of an [appeal, and there] is nothing in the present case [to] indicate that the [California] system has resulted in injustice. . . .

"We have today held that in [criminal prosecutions] there is an absolute right to the services of counsel at trial. Gideon v. Wainwright, [372 U.S. 335 (1963)]. But the appellate procedures involved here stand on an entirely different constitutional footing. First, appellate review is in itself not required by the Fourteenth

Amendment. [Second], the kinds of questions that may arise on appeal are circumscribed by the record of the proceedings that led to the conviction. [Third], as California applies its rule, the indigent appellant receives the benefit of expert and conscientious legal appraisal of the merits of his case on the basis of the trial record, and whether or not he is assigned counsel, is guaranteed full consideration of his appeal. It would be painting with too broad a brush to conclude that under these circumstances an appeal is just like a trial. . . .

"I cannot agree that the Constitution prohibits a State, in seeking to redress economic imbalances at its bar of justice and to provide indigents with full review, from taking reasonable steps to guard against needless expense."

Justice Clark also dissented.

Note: "Fundamental" Interests and the Criminal Justice System

1. *The basis of* Griffin *and* Douglas: *wealth as a "suspect" classification.* As in *Harper,* supra section E1a, the Court in *Griffin* and *Douglas* relied on both the "suspect" classification and the "fundamental" interest aspects of equal protection analysis. To what extent, if any, can *Griffin* and *Douglas* be explained on the ground that "a State can no more discriminate on account of poverty than on account of religion, race, or color"? Consider that the rules invalidated in *Douglas* and *Griffin* (a) do not expressly classify on the basis on wealth; (b) like ordinary license fees, have a differential effect on the poor; and (c) unlike the poll tax, were invalidated not in their entirety, but only as applied to the poor.

2. *The basis of* Griffin *and* Douglas: *equal access to appeal as a "fundamental" interest.* Justice Black conceded in *Griffin* that there is no constitutional right "to appellate review." How, then, does he justify his implicit conclusion that the right "to appellate review" is fundamental? In *Harper* the Court suggested that the right to vote is fundamental because it is "preservative of all rights." Is the "right to sue and defend in the courts" similarly fundamental because "it is the right conservative of all other rights, and lies at the foundation of orderly government"? Chambers v. Baltimore & Ohio Railroad, 207 U.S. 142, 148 (1907). Consider Note, The Supreme Court — 1972 Term, 87 Harv. L. Rev. 57, 66 (1973): "The right to vote and the right to hold office are means of participation in the democratic process which are fundamental to the protection of other interests. A function of similar importance is performed by the judiciary. If the election of the public officials who make and administer the laws is so fundamental as to require access, it would make little sense to deny indigents access to the only forum in which rights arising under those laws may be enforced."

3. *Equal protection or due process?* What is the "real" concern in *Griffin* and *Douglas* — the inequality or the lack of an effective opportunity to appeal? Consider Clune, The Supreme Court's Treatment of Wealth Discriminations under the Fourteenth Amendment, 1975 Sup. Ct. Rev. 289, 298: "Harlan thought the equal protection model was quite wrong. [The defendants] were asking to be treated differently rather than similarly, asking in fact, for a specific entitlement. Because they could not be entitled constitutionally to every resource needed or wanted for an appeal, Harlan argued that the particular necessity of this resource was the true issue, a traditional due process inquiry."

If the due process clause guarantees a right to appeal, *Griffin* and *Douglas* would pose a coherent due process issue. But everyone seems to agree that the due process clause does not require the states to create an appeals system and that there is thus no due process right to appeal. That being so, can one sensibly argue that the restrictions at issue in *Griffin* and *Douglas* violate due process because they limit the opportunity to appeal? Consider the following argument: Even if the due process clause does not require a state to create an appeals system, it does require a state that decides voluntarily to create such a system to permit access to the system unless its restrictions are justified by important government interests.

If there is no due process right to appeal, can one nonetheless argue that the interest in equal access to appeal is "fundamental" for purposes of the equal protection clause?

4. *The limits of* Griffin *and* Douglas: Ross v. Moffitt. In Ross v. Moffitt, 417 U.S. 600 (1974), the Court held that the Constitution does not require states to provide counsel for indigent defendants petitioning for discretionary state appellate review or for review in the United States Supreme Court. Justice Rehnquist delivered the opinion of the Court:

> The precise rationale for the *Griffin* and *Douglas* lines of cases has never been explicitly stated, some support being derived from the Equal Protection Clause [and] some from the Due Process [Clause]. Neither clause by itself provides an entirely satisfactory basis for the result reached, each depending on a different inquiry which emphasizes different factors. . . .
>
> We do not believe that the Due Process Clause requires North Carolina to provide [counsel in this situation]. [T]he State need not provide any appeal at all. [The] fact that an appeal *has* been provided does not automatically mean that a State then acts unfairly by refusing to provide counsel to indigent defendants at every stage of the way. [Unfairness] results only if indigents are singled out by the State and denied meaningful access to the appellate system because of their poverty. That question is more profitably considered under an equal protection analysis. . . .
>
> The [equal protection clause] "does not require absolute equality or precisely equal advantages," nor does it require the State to "equalize economic conditions." It does require that the state appellate system be "free of unreasoned distinctions," and that indigents have an adequate opportunity to present their claims fairly within the adversary system. The State cannot adopt procedures which leave an indigent defendant "entirely cut off from any appeal at all," by virtue of his indigency, or extend to such indigent defendants merely a "meaningless ritual" while others in better economic circumstances have a "meaningful appeal." That question is not one of absolutes, but one of degrees. . . .
>
> North Carolina has followed the mandate of Douglas v. California [and] authorized appointment of counsel for a convicted defendant appealing to the intermediate Court of Appeals, but has not gone beyond *Douglas* to provide for appointment of counsel for a defendant who seeks [review] in the Supreme Court of North Carolina or a writ of certiorari here. We do not believe that [a] defendant in respondent's circumstances is denied meaningful access to the [state] Supreme Court [or to this Court] simply because the State does not appoint counsel to aid him in seeking [review]. At that stage he will have, at the very least, a transcript or other record of trial proceedings, a brief on his behalf in the Court of Appeals setting forth his claims of error, and in many cases an opinion by the Court of Appeals disposing of his case. These materials [would] appear to provide [an] adequate basis for [the] decision to grant or deny review. [This] is not to say, of course, that a skilled lawyer [would] not prove helpful to any litigant able to employ him. [But] the fact that a particular

service might be of benefit to an indigent defendant does not mean that the service is constitutionally required. The duty of the State [is] not to duplicate the legal arsenal that may be privately [retained,] but only to assure the indigent defendant an adequate opportunity to present his claims fairly in the context of the State's appellate process. We think respondent was given that opportunity under the existing North Carolina system.

Justice Douglas, joined by Justices Brennan and Marshall, dissented: "The right to seek discretionary review is a substantial one, and one where a lawyer can be of significant assistance to an indigent defendant. [The] 'same concepts of fairness and equality, which require counsel in a first appeal of right, require counsel in other and subsequent discretionary appeals.'"

Consider Kamisar, Poverty, Equality, and Criminal Procedure, in National College of District Attorneys, Constitutional Law Deskbook (1977): "Perhaps the most potentially significant feature of [the *Ross* opinion] is that its 'equal protection analysis' closely resembles a 'due process analysis.' [*Ross* suggests that so] long as the indigent defendant's 'brand of justice' satisfies certain minimal standards [it] need not be the same brand of justice [as] the wealthy man's."

See also United States v. MacCollom, 426 U.S. 317 (1976), in which the Court, relying on *Ross*, held in a five-to-four decision that an indigent criminal defendant does not have a constitutional right to a free trial transcript for use in a collateral attack on a federal conviction if a federal judge finds that the claim is "frivolous" and that the transcript is not "needed to decide the issue."

5. *The limits of* Griffin *and* Douglas: Fuller v. Oregon. When a state assists an indigent in the criminal process, may it claim reimbursement for its expenditures on his behalf? In Fuller v. Oregon, 417 U.S. 40 (1974), the Court held that a state may recoup legal expenses paid on behalf of a convicted defendant to the extent that he later becomes able to pay. The Court rejected the argument that "a defendant's knowledge that he may remain under an obligation to repay the expenses incurred in providing him legal representation might impel him to decline the services of an appointed attorney and thus 'chill' his constitutional right to counsel." The Court explained:

> We live in a society where the distribution of legal assistance, like the distribution of all goods and services, is generally regulated by the dynamics of private enterprise. A defendant in a criminal case who is just above the line separating the indigent from the nonindigent must borrow money, sell off his meager assets, or call upon his family or friends in order to hire a lawyer. We cannot say that the Constitution requires that those only slightly poorer must remain forever immune from any obligation to shoulder the expenses of their legal defense.

See also James v. Strange, 407 U.S. 128 (1972) (invalidating a statute providing for the recoupment of all state expenditures for indigent defendants because the statute deprived such defendants of all the exemptions and restrictions ordinarily afforded civil judgment debtors and thus failed to accord "even treatment of indigent criminal defendants with other classes of debtors"); Rinaldi v. Yeager, 384 U.S. 305 (1966) (invalidating on similar grounds a statute requiring unsuccessful appellants confined to prison, but not those receiving suspended sentences, placed on probation, or penalized only by a fine, to repay the state for the cost of transcripts).

6. *The reach of* Griffin *and* Douglas: Williams v. Illinois. In Williams v. Illinois, 399 U.S. 235 (1970), appellant, who had been convicted of petty theft, received the maximum authorized sentence of one year in prison and a $500 fine. A state statute provided that defendants in default of payment of a fine must remain in jail to "work off" their obligations at a rate of $5 per day. "Applying the teaching [of] *Griffin*," the Court held the statute unconstitutional as applied to an indigent defendant insofar as it authorized imprisonment beyond the maximum statutory term. The Court reasoned that "when the aggregate imprisonment exceeds the maximum period fixed by the statute and results directly from an involuntary nonpayment of a fine or court costs we are confronted with an impermissible discrimination that rests on ability to pay." The Court concluded that no substantial state interest justified the discriminatory impact, for the state had "numerous alternatives," including the use of installment plans, for recouping the monetary penalties from indigents.

Consider Justice Harlan's objection to the equal protection rationale, expressed in his concurring opinion in *Williams*: "If equal protection implications of the Court's opinion were to be fully realized, it would require that the consequence of punishment be comparable for all individuals; the State would be forced to embark on the impossible task of developing a system of individualized fines, so that the total disutility of the entire fine, or the marginal disutility of the last dollar taken, would be the same for all individuals." Consider also Clune, supra, at 306: "One possibility would be a fine of an equal percentage of [earnings]. Such a system would go most of the way toward curing the wrong but would not represent a great interference with the states' systems of criminal justice."

See also Tate v. Short, 401 U.S. 395 (1971), in which the Court held that a state could not constitutionally imprison an indigent defendant for failure to pay traffic fines not otherwise punishable by imprisonment, but added that *Williams* did not necessarily preclude imprisonment "as an enforcement method when alternative means are unsuccessful despite the defendant's reasonable efforts to satisfy the fines by those means"; Bearden v. Georgia, 461 U.S. 660 (1983), in which the Court, relying on *Williams* and *Tate*, held that probation may be revoked for nonpayment of a fine only if the probationer made no bona fide effort to pay or there are no "adequate alternative forms of punishment."

7. *The reach of* Griffin *and* Douglas: *noneconomic classifications.* In the voting context, the Court in *Harper* invalidated the poll tax, which involved both the "fundamental" interest in voting and a disproportionate impact on the poor, but then extended the doctrine to all restrictions on voting, whether or not they implicated the poor. Do *Griffin* and *Douglas* invite a similar extension? Suppose, for example, a state authorizes appeal only by those convicted of capital offenses. Suppose it permits appeal by embezzlers but not other larceners? Should a court subject such classifications to heightened scrutiny because they implicate the "fundamental" interest in equal access to appeal?

The Court has generally required only a rational basis for non-wealth-related classifications in the criminal justice context. In McGinnis v. Royster, 410 U.S. 263 (1973), for example, the Court upheld a New York law granting "good time" credit toward parole eligibility for time spent in a state prison after sentencing, but not for time spent in a county jail before sentencing. The Court, applying a rational basis standard, rejected a claim that the law discriminated against defendants who did not make bail before trial. It explained that "good time" was designed to reflect a prisoner's rehabilitation, and that the state reasonably offered rehabilitative programs only in its prisons.

Similarly, in Marshall v. United States, 414 U.S. 417 (1974), the Court, applying a rational basis standard, upheld a provision of the Narcotic Addict Rehabilitation Act excluding convicted addicts with two or more prior felony convictions from participation in a drug rehabilitation program in lieu of penal incarceration. The Court explained that Congress "could rationally have assumed that a person who has committed two or more prior felonies [is] less likely to be susceptible of rehabilitation [and would pose] a greater threat to society upon release."

BODDIE v. CONNECTICUT, 401 U.S. 371 (1971): In *Boddie* the Court held unconstitutional, as applied to indigents, a state requirement that individuals pay court fees and costs of about $60 in order to sue for divorce. Justice Harlan delivered the opinion of the Court: "American society [bottoms] its systematic definition of individual rights and duties [on] the common-law model. It is to courts [that] we ultimately look for the implementation of a regularized, orderly process of dispute settlement. [It] is upon this premise that this Court has [put] flesh upon the due process principle. [Past] litigation has, however, typically involved rights of defendants — not, as here, persons seeking access to the judicial process in the first instance. This is because our society has been so structured that resort to the courts is not usually the only available, legitimate means of resolving private disputes. Indeed, private structuring of individual relationships [is] largely encouraged in American life, [and] this Court has [thus] seldom been asked to view access to the courts as an element of due process. . . .

"As this Court [has] recognized, marriage involves interests of basic importance in our society. See, e.g., Loving v. Virginia [supra Chapter 5, section C3]; Skinner v. Oklahoma [supra section E]; Meyer v. Nebraska [infra section F]. It is not surprising, then, that the States have seen fit to oversee many aspects of that institution. Without a prior judicial imprimatur, individuals may freely enter into and rescind commercial contracts, for example, but we are unaware of any jurisdiction where private citizens may covenant for or dissolve marriages without state approval. [The] State's refusal to admit these appellants to its courts, the sole means in Connecticut for obtaining a divorce, must be regarded as the equivalent of denying them an opportunity to be heard upon their claimed right to a dissolution of their marriages, and, in the absence of a sufficient countervailing [justification,] a denial of due process."

The Court emphasized that "We do not decide that access for all individuals to the courts is a right that is, in all circumstances, guaranteed by the Due Process Clause," but only that, "given the basic position of the marriage relationship in this society's hierarchy of values and the concomitant state monopolization of the means for legally dissolving this relationship, due process does prohibit a State from denying, solely because of inability to pay, access to its courts to individuals who seek judicial dissolution of their marriages."

Justice Douglas filed a concurring opinion: "[This] case should be decided upon the principles developed in the line of cases marked by [*Griffin*]. The Due Process Clause on which the Court relies has proven very elastic in the hands of judges. [The] Court today puts 'flesh' upon the Due Process Clause by concluding that marriage and its dissolution are so important that an unhappy couple who are indigent should have access to the divorce courts free of charge. [I] do not see the length of the road we must follow if we accept my Brother Harlan's invitation. [Although the] reach of the Equal Protection Clause is not definable with mathematical [precision,] rather definite guidelines have been [developed]. Here the invidious discrimination is based on [poverty]. Just as denying [appellate] counsel in *Douglas*, and a transcript in *Griffin* created an invidious distinction based on wealth, so, too, does [affluence] not pass muster under the Equal Protection Clause for determining who must remain married and who shall be allowed to separate."

Justice Brennan also concurred: "[I] cannot join the Court's opinion insofar as [it] is made to depend upon the factor that only the State can grant a divorce and that an indigent would be locked into a marriage if unable to pay the fees required to obtain a divorce. A State has an ultimate monopoly of all judicial process and attendant enforcement machinery. [The] right to be heard [extends] to all proceedings entertained by courts. The possible distinctions suggested by the Court [will] not withstand analysis."

Justice Black dissented: "[*Griffin* is distinguishable]. Civil lawsuits [are] not like government prosecutions for crime. [In] such cases the government is not usually involved as a party, and there is no deprivation of life, liberty, or property as punishment for crime. [There] is consequently no necessity [why] government should in civil trials be hampered [by the strict] due process rules the Constitution has provided to protect people charged with crime. [The] Court's opinion appears to rest solely on a philosophy that any law violates due process if it is unreasonable, arbitrary, indecent, deviates from the fundamental, is shocking to the conscience, or fails to meet other tests [equally] lacking in any possible constitutional precision. [The] Due Process and Equal Protection Clauses [do not justify] judges in trying [to] hold laws constitutional or not on the basis of a judge's sense of fairness."

Note: Access to the Judicial Process in Civil Cases

1. *The rationale of* Boddie. Note the three distinct positions on the constitutionality of filing fees that preclude indigents from initiating civil litigation: (a) constitutional (Black); (b) unconstitutional (Brennan); (c) unconstitutional only if the litigation involves "interests of basic importance in our society" and there is "state monopolization of the means" for protecting such interests (Harlan). Which position is most consistent with the *Griffin/Douglas* principle? Does *Boddie* implicitly reject the voting analogy and the proposition that there is a "fundamental" interest in equal access to the judicial process?

2. *Monopolization.* Why the "monopolization" requirement? Consider Michelman, The Supreme Court and Litigation Access Fees: The Right to Protect One's Rights — Part I, 1973 Duke L.J. 1153, 1178-1180:

> The monopoly notion is disarmingly simple. Divorce [is] different from most other kinds of affirmative relief [in] that it is absolutely unavailable except in the form of a judicial decree. It takes judicial action to dissolve a marriage, but not to release a creditor's claim. [In practical effect, however, the court] has a monopoly on lawful deployment of remedial force; and this monopoly applies to plaintiffs across the board. [Consider] the case of an impoverished person who objects to emission of poisonous gases near his residence. [Although] out-of-court settlement [is theoreti-

cally available, it is in fact unlikely if] the complaining party lacks [the money even to file a] lawsuit. [Moreover, the monopolization notion] is unpersuasive [for another reason as well]. The notion appears to have been conceived by Justice Harlan [to assimilate] the predicament of the *Boddie* petitioners to the plight common to civil defendants. [Just as a person once married cannot become unmarried without gaining access to a court, so a person once haled into court cannot avoid an adverse judgment without making an appearance. But is the latter proposition true? Quite plainly it is not, [for it assumes] that the defendant will fail in any attempt to gain [a settlement]. [Thus, monopoly] fails to distinguish [civil plaintiffs] from civil defendants.

On the other hand, consider Lupu, Untangling the Strands of the Fourteenth Amendment, 77 Mich. L. Rev. 981, 1007-1008 (1979):

[Abandonment] of the monopoly concept [would] leave the Court with two unpalatable choices. [First, the Court might] require that the state provide or fully subsidize all services necessary to the exercise of preferred rights. In the first amendment context, [for example], such a doctrine would produce [an] allocation of state resources toward a socialized system of access to expressive media. [This would be wholly "unmanageable."] [Second, the Court might in each instance] explore the *adequacy* of the marketplace to provide the [benefit. This] alternative would lead the Court to demand state satisfaction of a claim if the private sector were [unlikely] to relieve the financial obstacles to access to a constitutional opportunity. [But this] might work as a significant disincentive to private charity [and, more] fundamentally, the question of the sufficiency of the private services to the poor is not amenable to principled resolution.

3. *Due process or equal protection?* Note Justice Harlan's reliance on due process rather than equal protection. Is this a preferable basis for decision? Does Harlan's analysis invalidate *every* limitation on the filing of divorce actions, or only those that exclude the poor? Consider Clune, The Supreme Court's Treatment of Wealth Discriminations under the Fourteenth Amendment, 1975 Sup. Ct. Rev. 289, 309-310: "Harlan's effort to forge due process into a tool that bridges the civil and criminal processes and also operates solely for the benefit of the poor is impressive. [T]o limit the holding to the poor, [Harlan recognized] that poor people have a unique claim [because they] have an acceptable excuse for not paying; poverty is important [because] it removes the ordinary interpretation put on nonpayment, that is, waiver or default."

Is *Boddie* a case of procedural or substantive due process? Note that the Court grants procedural rights, but only if the litigation involves "interests of basic importance in our society." What, then, is *Boddie* really about — the constitutionality of restrictions on access to the judicial process or the constitutionality of restrictions on the formation and dissolution of marriage? On marriage, privacy, and modern substantive due process, see Chapter 6, section F3, infra.

4. *The limits of* Boddie: Kras. In United States v. Kras, 409 U.S. 434 (1973), the Court upheld a provision of the Bankruptcy Act requiring individuals seeking voluntary discharge to pay costs and fees of about $50. Justice Blackmun delivered the opinion of the Court:

The denial of access to the judicial forum in *Boddie* touched directly [on] the marital relationship and on the associational interests that surround the establishment and dissolution of that relationship. On many occasions we have recognized the fundamental importance of these interests under our Constitution. [Kras's] alleged interest in the elimination of his debt burden [does] not rise to the same constitutional level. If Kras is not discharged in bankruptcy, his position will not be materially altered in any constitutional sense. . . .

Nor is the government's control over the establishment, enforcement, or dissolution of debts nearly so exclusive as [its] control over the marriage relationship. [In] contrast with divorce, bankruptcy is not the only method available to a debtor for the adjustment of his legal relationship with his creditors. . . .

We are also of the opinion that the filing fee requirement does not deny Kras the equal protection of the laws. Bankruptcy is hardly akin to free speech or marriage or to those other rights [that] the Court has come to regard as fundamental and that demand the lofty requirement of a compelling governmental interest before they may be significantly regulated.

Justice Stewart, joined by Justices Douglas, Brennan, and Marshall, dissented:

The violation of due process seems to me [as] clear in the present case [as in *Boddie*]. [The] bankrupt is bankrupt precisely for the reason that the State stands ready to exact all of his debts through [the] panoply of [creditor] remedies. [In] the unique situation of the indigent bankrupt, the Government provides the only effective means of his ever being free of these Government-imposed obligations. [Unless] the Government provides him access to the bankruptcy court, Kras will remain in the totally hopeless situation he now finds himself. [The] Court today holds that Congress may say that some of the poor are too poor even to go bankrupt. I cannot agree.

Justice Marshall filed a separate dissent: "The majority says that '[t]he denial of access to the judicial forum in *Boddie* touched directly . . . on the marital relationship.' It sees 'no fundamental interest that is gained or lost depending on the availability of a discharge in bankruptcy.' [But] I view the case as involving the right of access to the courts, the opportunity to be heard when one claims a legal right."

5. *The limits of* Boddie: Ortwein. In Ortwein v. Schwab, 410 U.S. 656 (1973), the Court, in a per curiam opinion, upheld a $25 appellate court filing fee as applied to indigents who sought to appeal administrative decisions reducing their welfare benefits:

[The] interest [in increased welfare payments], like [the interest at issue in] *Kras*, has far less constitutional significance than the interest of the *Boddie* appellants. [Moreover, each] of the present appellants has received an agency [hearing, and this] Court has long recognized that, even in criminal cases, due process does not require a State to provide an appellate system. [Under] the facts of this case, appellants were not denied due process. [Nor does the filing fee violate equal protection on the ground that it discriminates] against the poor. As in *Kras*, this [litigation] "is in the area of economics and social welfare" [and the] applicable standard is [thus] that of rational justification.

Justices Douglas, Stewart, Brennan, and Marshall dissented. On welfare as a "fundamental" interest, see Chapter 6, section E4, infra.

6. *Variations.* Consider the following: (a) A state law authorizes state courts to grant a divorce only if both parties reside in the state. Cf. Sosna v. Iowa, 419 U.S.

393 (1975) (upholding a requirement that an individual reside in the state for one year before suing a nonresident for divorce, and distinguishing *Boddie* on the ground that the one-year residency requirement involves "not total deprivation, as in *Boddie*, but only delay"). (b) A state law imposes a filing fee for all civil actions, as applied to an indigent seeking to sue for a claimed violation of first amendment rights. (c) A state law requires the party moving for blood grouping tests in a paternity action to pay for the tests, as applied to an indigent party. Cf. Little v. Streater, 452 U.S. 1 (1981) (invalidating such a statute). (d) A state law requires all civil parties to pay an appearance fee, as applied to an indigent who is sued for repossession of his furniture.

3. Travel

Shapiro v. Thompson
394 U.S. 618 (1969)

MR. JUSTICE BRENNAN delivered the opinion of the Court.

[Each of these three appeals is] from a decision [holding] unconstitutional a State or District of Columbia statutory provision which denies welfare assistance to residents [who] have not resided within their jurisdictions for at least one year immediately preceding their applications for such assistance. We affirm. . . .

There is no dispute that the effect of the waiting-period requirement [is] to create two classes of needy resident families indistinguishable from each other except that one is composed of residents who have resided a year or more, and the second of residents who have resided less than a year, in the jurisdiction. [The] second class is denied welfare aid upon which may depend the ability of the families to obtain the very means to subsist — food, shelter, and other necessities of life. [This scheme] constitutes an invidious discrimination [denying] equal protection of the laws. [The] interests which appellants assert are promoted by the classification either may not constitutionally be promoted by government or are not compelling governmental interests.

Primarily, appellants justify the waiting-period requirement as a protective device to preserve the fiscal integrity of state public assistance programs. It is asserted that people who require welfare assistance during their first year of residence in a State are likely to become continuing burdens on state welfare programs. Therefore, the argument runs, if such people can be deterred from entering the jurisdiction by denying them welfare benefits during the first year, state programs to assist long-time residents will not be impaired by a substantial influx of indigent newcomers. . . .

We do not doubt that the one-year waiting-period device is well suited to discourage the influx of poor families in need of assistance. An indigent who desires to migrate, resettle, find a new job, and start a new life will doubtless hesitate if he knows that he must risk making the move without the possibility of falling back on state welfare assistance during his first year of residence, when his need may be most acute. But the purpose of inhibiting migration by needy persons into the State is constitutionally impermissible.

This Court long ago recognized that the nature of our Federal Union and our constitutional concepts of personal liberty unite to require that all citizens be free to travel throughout the length and breadth of our land uninhibited by statutes, rules, or regulations which unreasonably burden or restrict this movement. . . .

We have no occasion to ascribe the source of this right to travel interstate to a particular constitutional provision.[3] It suffices that, as Mr. Justice Stewart said for the Court in United States v. Guest, 383 U.S. 745, 757-758 (1966): "The constitutional right to travel from one State to another . . . occupies a position fundamental to the concept of our Federal Union. It is a right that has been firmly established and repeatedly recognized. . . ."

Thus, the purpose of deterring the in-migration of indigents cannot serve as justification for the classification created by the one-year waiting period, since that purpose is constitutionally impermissible. If a law has "no other purpose . . . than to chill the assertion of constitutional rights by penalizing those who choose to exercise them, then it [is] patently unconstitutional."

Alternatively, appellants argue that even if it is impermissible for a State to attempt to deter the entry of all indigents, the challenged classification may be justified as a permissible state attempt to discourage those indigents who would enter the State solely to obtain larger benefits. [But] a State may no more try to fence out those indigents who seek higher welfare benefits than it may try to fence out indigents generally. [We] do not perceive why a mother who is seeking to make a new life for herself and her children should be regarded as less deserving because she considers, among other factors, the level of a State's public assistance. Surely such a mother is no less deserving than a mother who moves into a particular State in order to take advantage of its better educational facilities.

Appellants argue further that the challenged classification may be sustained as an attempt to distinguish between new and old residents on the basis of the contribution they have made to the community through the payment of taxes. [But this] would logically permit the State to bar new residents from schools, parks, and libraries or deprive them of police and fire protection. Indeed it would permit the State to apportion all benefits and services according to the past tax contributions of its citizens. The Equal Protection Clause prohibits such an apportionment of state services.[10]

We recognize that a State [may] legitimately attempt to limit its expenditures, whether for public assistance, public education, or any other program. But a State may not accomplish such a purpose by invidious distinctions between classes of its citizens. It could not, for example, reduce expenditures for education by barring indigent children from its schools. Similarly, [appellants] must do more than show that denying welfare benefits to new residents saves money. The saving of welfare costs cannot justify an otherwise invidious classification. . . .

---

3. In Corfield v. Coryell, 6 F. Cas. 546, 552 (No. 3230) (C.C.E.D. Pa. 1825), Paul v. Virginia, 8 Wall. 168, 180 (1869), and Ward v. Maryland, 12 Wall. 418, 430 (1871), the right to travel interstate was grounded upon the Privileges and Immunities Clause of Art. IV, §2. See also Slaughter-House Cases, 16 Wall. 36, 79 (1873); Twining v. New Jersey, 211 U.S. 78, 97 (1908). In Edwards v. California, 314 U.S. 160, 181, 183-185 (1941) (Douglas and Jackson, JJ., concurring), and Twining v. New Jersey, supra, reliance was placed on the Privileges and Immunities Clause of the Fourteenth Amendment. See also Crandall v. Nevada, 6 Wall. 35 (1868). In Edwards v. California, supra, and the Passenger Cases, 7 How. 283 (1849), a Commerce Clause approach was employed.

See also Kent v. Dulles, 357 U.S. 116, 125 (1958); Aptheker v. Secretary of State, 378 U.S. 500, 505-506 (1964); Zemel v. Rusk, 381 U.S. 1, 14 (1965), where the freedom of Americans to travel outside the country was grounded upon the Due Process Clause of the Fifth Amendment.

10. We are not dealing here with state insurance programs which may legitimately tie the amount of benefits to the individual's contributions.

Appellants next advance as justification certain administrative and related governmental objectives allegedly served by the waiting-period requirement. They argue that the requirement (1) facilitates the planning of the welfare budget; (2) provides an objective test of residency; (3) minimizes the opportunity for recipients fraudulently to receive payments from more than one jurisdiction; and (4) encourages early entry of new residents into the labor force.

At the outset, we reject appellants' argument that a mere showing of a rational relationship between the waiting period and these four admittedly permissible state objectives will suffice to justify the classification, [for] in moving from State to State or to the District of Columbia appellees were exercising a constitutional right, and any classification which serves to penalize the exercise of that right, unless shown to be necessary to promote a *compelling* governmental interest, is unconstitutional. Cf. [*Skinner*].

The argument that the waiting-period requirement facilitates budget predictability is wholly unfounded. The records [are] utterly devoid of evidence that either State or the District of Columbia in fact uses the one-year requirement as a means to predict the number of people who will require assistance in the budget year. . . .

The argument that the waiting period serves as an administratively efficient rule of thumb for determining residency similarly will not withstand scrutiny. [Before] granting an application, the welfare authorities investigate the applicant [and] in the course of the inquiry necessarily learn the facts upon which to determine whether the applicant is a resident.

Similarly, there is no need for a State to use the one-year waiting period as a safeguard against fraudulent receipt of benefits; for less drastic means are available, and are employed, to minimize that hazard. . . .

[Finally, a] state purpose to encourage employment provides no rational basis for imposing a one-year waiting-period restriction on new residents only, [for there is no reason not to require a similar waiting period for this reason for long-term residents].

We conclude therefore that appellants [have] no need to use the one-year requirement for the governmental purposes suggested. Thus, even under traditional equal protection tests a classification of welfare applicants according to whether they have lived in the State for one year would seem irrational and unconstitutional. But, of course, the traditional criteria do not apply in these cases. Since the classification here touches on the fundamental right of interstate movement, its constitutionality must be judged by the stricter standard of whether it promotes a *compelling* state interest. Under this standard, the waiting-period requirement clearly violates the Equal Protection Clause.[21]

[The Court also rejected the states' argument that Congress had expressly authorized the one-year waiting period and added that "even if . . . Congress did approve the imposition of a . . . waiting period," such an approval "would be unconstitutional," for "Congress may not authorize the States to violate the Equal Protection Clause."]

---

21. We imply no view of the validity of waiting-period *or* residence requirements determining eligibility to vote, eligibility for tuition-free education, to obtain a license to practice a profession, to hunt or fish, and so forth. Such requirements may promote compelling state interests on the one hand, or, on the other, may not be penalties upon the exercise of the constitutional right of interstate travel.

MR. JUSTICE STEWART, concurring.

In joining the opinion of the Court, I add a word in response to the dissent of my Brother Harlan, who, I think, has quite misapprehended what the Court's opinion says.

The Court today does *not* "pick out particular human activities, characterize them as 'fundamental,' and give them added protection. . . ." To the contrary, the Court simply recognizes, as it must, an established constitutional right, and gives to that right no less protection than the Constitution itself demands. [As] Mr. Justice Harlan wrote for the Court more than a decade ago, "[T]o justify the deterrent effect . . . on the free exercise . . . of their constitutionally protected right . . . a '. . . subordinating interest of the State must be compelling.'" [NAACP v. Alabama.] . . .

MR. CHIEF JUSTICE WARREN, with whom MR. JUSTICE BLACK joins, dissenting. . . .

Congress has imposed a residence requirement in the District of Columbia and authorized the States to impose similar requirements. The issue before us must therefore be framed in terms of whether Congress may create minimal residence requirements, not whether the States, acting alone, may do so. . . .

Congress, pursuant to its commerce power, has enacted a variety of restrictions upon interstate travel. It has taxed air and rail fares and the gasoline needed to power cars and trucks which move interstate. Many of the federal safety regulations of common carriers which cross state lines burden the right to travel. And Congress has prohibited by criminal statute interstate travel for certain purposes. Although these restrictions operate as a limitation upon free interstate movement of persons, their constitutionality appears well settled. . . .

The Court's right-to-travel cases lend little support to the view that congressional action is invalid merely because it burdens the right to travel. Most of our cases fall into two categories: those in which *state*-imposed restrictions were involved, see, e.g., Edwards v. California, 314 U.S. 160 (1941); Crandall v. Nevada, 6 Wall. 35 (1868), and those concerning congressional decisions to remove impediments to interstate movement, see e.g., United States v. Guest, 383 U.S. 745 (1966). Since the focus of our inquiry must be whether Congress would exceed permissible bounds by imposing residence requirements, neither group of cases offers controlling principles. [Here,] travel itself is not prohibited. Any burden inheres solely in the fact that a potential welfare recipient might take into consideration the loss of welfare benefits for a limited period of time if he changes his residence. Not only is this burden of uncertain degree, but appellees themselves assert there is evidence that few welfare recipients have in fact been deterred by residence requirements. . . .

The insubstantiality of the restriction imposed by residence requirements must then be evaluated in light of the possible congressional reasons for such requirements. [Our] cases require only that Congress have a rational basis for finding that a chosen regulatory scheme is necessary to the furtherance of interstate commerce. Certainly, a congressional finding that residence requirements allowed each State to concentrate its resources upon new and increased programs of rehabilitation ultimately resulting in an enhanced flow of commerce as the economic condition of welfare recipients progressively improved is rational and would justify imposition of residence requirements under the Commerce Clause.

[Since] the congressional decision is rational and the restriction on travel insubstantial, I conclude that residence requirements can be imposed by Congress as an exercise of its power to control interstate commerce consistent with the constitutionally guaranteed right to travel.

Mr. Justice Harlan, dissenting.

In upholding the equal protection argument, the Court has applied an equal protection doctrine of relatively recent vintage: the rule that statutory classifications which [affect] "fundamental rights" will be held to deny equal protection unless justified by a "compelling" governmental interest.

[This] rule was foreshadowed in [*Skinner*]. After a long hiatus, [it] reemerged in Reynolds v. Sims [and] Harper v. Virginia Bd. of Elections. It has reappeared today in the Court's cryptic suggestion that the "compelling interest" test is applicable merely because the result of the classification may be to deny the appellees "food, shelter, and other necessities of life," as well as in the Court's statement that "[s]ince the classification here touches on the fundamental right of interstate movement, its constitutionality must be judged by the stricter standard of whether it promotes a *compelling* state interest."

I think this [doctrine] particularly unfortunate [because] it creates an exception which threatens to swallow the standard equal protection rule. Virtually every state statute affects important rights. This Court has repeatedly held, for example, that the traditional equal protection standard is applicable to statutory classifications affecting such fundamental matters as the right to pursue a particular occupation, the right to receive greater or smaller wages or to work more or less hours, and the right to inherit property. Rights such as these are in principle indistinguishable from those involved here, and to extend the "compelling interest" rule to all cases in which such rights are affected would go far toward making this Court a "super-legislature." [The] doctrine is also unnecessary. When the right affected is one assured by the Federal Constitution, any infringement can be dealt with under the Due Process Clause. But when a statute affects only matters not mentioned in the Federal Constitution and is not arbitrary or irrational, I must reiterate that I know of nothing which entitles this Court to pick out particular human activities, characterize them as "fundamental," and give them added protection under an unusually stringent equal protection test. . . .

[If] the issue is regarded purely as one of equal protection, [this] classification should be judged by ordinary equal protection standards. [And in] light of [the] undeniable relation of residence requirements to valid legislative aims, [I] can find no objection to these residence requirements under the Equal Protection Clause. . . .

The next issue [is] whether a one-year welfare residence requirement amounts to an undue burden upon the right of interstate travel [which I conclude] is a "fundamental" right [which] should be regarded as having its source in the Due Process Clause of the Fifth Amendment. . . .

[The decisive question is] whether the governmental interests served by residence requirements outweigh the burden imposed upon the right to travel. [Taking] all of [the] competing considerations into account, I believe that the balance definitely favors constitutionality. In reaching that conclusion, I do not minimize the importance of the right to travel interstate. However, the impact of residence conditions upon that right is indirect and apparently quite insubstantial. On the other hand, the governmental purposes served by the requirements are legitimate and real, and the residence requirements are clearly suited to their accomplishment. To abolish residence requirements might well discourage highly worthwhile experimentation in the welfare field. The statutes come to us clothed with the authority of Congress and attended by a correspondingly heavy presumption of constitutionality. Moreover, although [it is argued] that the same objectives could have been achieved by less restrictive means, this is an area in which the judiciary should be especially slow to fetter [legislative] judgment. . . . Residence requirements have advantages, such as administrative simplicity and relative certainty, which are not shared by the alternative solutions. . . . In these circumstances, I cannot find that the burden imposed by residence requirements upon ability to travel outweighs the governmental interests in their continued employment. . . .

Note: The Right to Travel as a "Fundamental Interest"

1. *The right to travel.* As noted in *Shapiro* the Court has long recognized a constitutional right to travel, even though the precise source of the right remains somewhat obscure. In Crandall v. Nevada, 73 U.S. (6 Wall.) 35 (1868), for example, the Court invalidated a state law imposing a capitation tax of one dollar on "every person leaving the State by any [vehicle engaged] in the business of transporting passengers for hire." The Court explained that "For all the great purposes for which the Federal Government was formed we are one people, with one common country [and] as members of the same community must have the right to pass and repass through every part of it without interruption." Similarly, in Edwards v. California, 314 U.S. 160 (1941), the Court, relying on the commerce clause, invalidated a state statute prohibiting any person from "bringing into the State any indigent person who is not a resident of the State." Four justices concurred on the ground that the statute violated the privileges or immunities clause of the fourteenth amendment. Recall the Slaughter-House Cases, supra section B.

2. *The right to travel versus equal protection.* Given the Court's view that there is an independent constitutional right to travel, why did the Court rely in *Shapiro* on the equal protection clause? Do the durational residence requirements at issue in *Shapiro* violate the right to travel? Consider the following views.

a. Perry, Modern Equal Protection: A Conceptualization and Appraisal, 79 Colum. L. Rev. 1023, 1075 (1979):

It made little sense [for] the Court in *Shapiro* to treat the question [as] an equal protection problem. The state had drawn a line on the basis of the exercise of a constitutional right and had disadvantaged those on one side of the line — those who had exercised the right — relative to those on the other side. Because such a scheme strongly suggests that government is seeking to discourage exercise of the constitutional right in question, obviously not a legitimate governmental interest, the [Court should have held the scheme violative of] the constitutional right of interstate migration.

b. McCoy, Recent Equal Protection Decisions — Fundamental Right to Travel or "Newcomers" as a Suspect Class?, 28 Vand. L. Rev. 987, 996-999 (1975):

[*Shapiro*] did not involve the infringement of [the right to travel]. No criminal prohibition against travelling into the state [was] enforced, nor was [there] even the minimal restriction of [a] tax on entry [or] departure. [Of] course, the state may infringe upon an individual right through means other than direct regulation. [But with] respect to the defendant states [in *Shapiro*] the plaintiffs [were] no worse off [after] than before their moves. To be sure, the defendant states were not as attractive a destination as they would have been had welfare benefits been made available to new residents, [but] failing to offer benefits that would make the state a more attractive place does not in any ordinary sense constitute penalizing those who travel [or] inhibiting [those who do not. Indeed,] if the defendant states had provided no welfare system at all, the unavailability of welfare benefits to the plaintiffs would have constituted exactly the same burden on plaintiffs' right to travel. [And] the fact that [the defendant] states chose to pay welfare to [long-term] residents in no way increased the burden on the plaintiffs' right to travel.

c. Reinstein, The Welfare Cases: Fundamental Rights, the Poor, and the Burden of Proof in Constitutional Litigation, 44 Temp. L.Q. 1, 39 (1970):

The maximum impact on the right to travel would have been caused [if] a state abolished its welfare program. But the state's justification for doing [this] would be overriding, and a court would probably not view a case challenging this action as a right to travel case at all. Even though the residence test affected the exercise of the right to travel to a lesser extent, the discriminatory features enhanced the constitutional challenge, [for the] four objectives asserted by the state [were belied] by the state's failure to seek to obtain them in the much larger class of welfare recipients.

3. *The right to travel as a "fundamental" interest.* In *Shapiro* the Court held that "Since the classification here touches on the fundamental right of interstate movement, its constitutionality must be judged [by] whether it promotes a compelling state interest" and that "Under this standard, the waiting-period requirement clearly violates the Equal Protection Clause." Is it superfluous to call an independent constitutional right a "fundamental" interest for equal protection purposes? If durational residence requirements do not violate the right to travel, does it make sense to call the right to travel a "fundamental" interest and then to invalidate the requirements under the equal protection clause?

Are *all* independent constitutional rights "fundamental" interests? If not, how do we decide? Recall the incorporation doctrine. In at least one other context — freedom of expression — the Court has held an independent constitutional right to be a "fundamental" interest under the equal protection clause. See Chapter 7, section F1, infra. For analysis of the intersection of the right to abortion and equal protection analysis, see section F2, infra.

4. *The right to travel and the "necessities of life."* Note the Court's reference in *Shapiro* to the "necessities of life." To what extent does *Shapiro* turn on this aspect of the case? Do laws that unequally distribute the "necessities of life" infringe a "fundamental" interest? This issue is examined in section E4, infra.

Note: "Penalizing" the Right to Travel

1. *Impermissible purposes.* The Court in *Shapiro* distinguished between two types of state purposes — those that are "constitutionally impermissible" and those that are permissible but insufficient to satisfy the "compelling" interest

standard. Do you agree that it is "constitutionally impermissible" for a state (a) to attempt to deter "the in-migration of indigents"; (b) to "attempt to discourage those indigents who would enter the State solely to obtain larger benefits"; and (c) to "attempt to distinguish between new and old residents on the basis of the contribution they have made to the community through the payment of taxes"?

In Zobel v. Williams, 457 U.S. 55 (1982), the Court held that an Alaska statute distributing the income derived from its natural resources to adult citizens in varying amounts depending on length of residence in the state violated the equal protection clause. Citing *Shapiro* the Court dismissed the state's objective of rewarding "citizens for past contributions" as "not a legitimate state purpose."

Consider Justice O'Connor's observations in a concurring opinion:

> [The] Court misdirects its criticism when it labels Alaska's objective illegitimate. A desire to compensate citizens for their prior contributions is neither inherently invidious nor irrational. [The] difficulty is that plans enacted to further this objective necessarily treat new residents of a State less favorably than the longer-term residents who have past contributions to "reward." This inequality [conflicts] with the constitutional purpose of maintaining a Union rather than a mere "league of States." [The] Court's task, therefore, should be (1) to articulate this constitutional principle, explaining its textual sources, and (2) to test the strength of Alaska's objective against the constitutional imperative. [The] Privileges and Immunities Clause of Article IV [addresses] just this type of discrimination. [In this case, the statute is invalid, not because the objective is illegitimate, but because] Alaska has not shown that its new residents are the "peculiar source" of any evil [or that there is] a "substantial relationship" between the evil and the discrimination practiced against the noncitizens.

Consider also the views expressed by Justice Brennan in a separate concurring opinion, joined by Justices Marshall, Blackmun, and Powell:

> [The] illegitimacy of [the] state purpose [reflects] not the structure of the Federal Union but the idea of constitutionally protected equality. [Even if] the Alaska plan [did not] apply to migrants from sister States [the discrimination would] be constitutionally suspect. [Length] of residence has only the most tenuous relation to the actual service of individuals to the State. Thus, the past contribution rationale proves much too little to provide a rational predicate for discrimination on the basis of length of residence. But it also proves far too much, for "it would permit the State to apportion all benefits and services according to the [past] contributions of its citizens." [*Shapiro*.] In my view, it is difficult to escape from the recognition that underlying any scheme of classification on the basis of duration of residence, we shall almost invariably find the unstated premise that "some citizens are more equal than others." We rejected that premise [when] we adopted the Equal Protection Clause.

In Hooper v. Bernalillo County Assessor, 105 S. Ct. 2862 (1985), the Court held that a New Mexico statute granting a special tax exemption to Vietnam veterans who were New Mexico residents before May 8, 1976, violated the equal protection clause. The Court distinguished *Shapiro*, *Sosna*, *Dunn*, and *Maricopa County* on the ground that they involved waiting periods, whereas the New Mexico statute, like the Alaska law invalidated in *Zobel*, "creates 'fixed, permanent distinctions between . . . classes of concededly bona fide residents' based on when they arrived in the State." The Court held that, "stripped of its asserted justifications, the New Mexico statute suffers from the same constitutional flaw as the Alaska statute in *Zobel*." The Court explained:

> The New Mexico statute, by singling out previous residents for the tax exemption, rewards only those citizens for their "past contributions" toward our nation's military effort in Vietnam. *Zobel* teaches that such an objective is "not a legitimate state purpose." The State may not favor established residents over new residents based on the view that the State may take care of "its own," if such is defined by prior residence. Newcomers, by establishing bona fide residence in the State, become the State's "own" and may not be discriminated against solely on the basis of their arrival in the State after May 8, 1976. [The] Constitution will not tolerate a state benefit program that creates "fixed, permanent distinctions . . . between . . . classes of concededly bona fide residents," based on how long they have been in the State.

Justice Stevens, joined by Justices Rehnquist and O'Connor, dissented.

2. *"Penalizing" the right to travel.* In what circumstances may a state burden the right to travel in order to further a constitutionally *permissible* objective? In *Shapiro* the Court invoked strict scrutiny because the durational residence requirements "penalized" the right to travel. Do you accept the "penalty" characterization? Consider the following arguments:

a. In the usual "penalty" case, the existence of a condition on eligibility for a state's program makes a person worse off with respect to the constitutional right in question than if there were no program at all. For example, if a state grants welfare benefits only to persons who agree not to vote, the right to vote is pressured in a way it would not be if there were no welfare program at all. The situation is different, however, in *Shapiro*. If state X has a durational residence requirement for the receipt of welfare benefits, a person contemplating a move to state X is no worse off with respect to the right to travel than if state X had no welfare system at all.

b. In the usual "penalty" case, a state withholds an otherwise available benefit from an individual unless she forgoes a constitutional right. For example, if a state grants welfare benefits only to persons who agree not to vote, an individual who exercises her constitutional right to vote will lose a benefit she would otherwise receive. The benefit program thus "penalizes" the exercise of her right. The situation is different, however, in *Shapiro*. If state X has a durational residence requirement for the receipt of welfare benefits, a person contemplating a move to state X will not receive benefits from state X even if she decides not to travel. If she exercises her right to travel, she does not lose a benefit she would otherwise have received from state X. Thus, insofar as state X is concerned, the individual is no worse off if she moves than if she stays put. State X's residence requirement therefore does not "penalize" her right to travel.

Consider the following answers to these arguments: (a) The individual might have been eligible for benefits in her prior state of residence. (b) State X has singled out those who have exercised a constitutional right for special disability.

3. *Other penalties on the right to travel.* Are all durational residence requirements unconstitutional "penalties" on the right to travel? Note footnote 21 in *Shapiro*, and consider the following cases:

a. *Voting.* In Dunn v. Blumstein, 405 U.S. 330 (1972), the Court, in a six-to-one decision, held that Tennessee's one-year residence requirement for voting violated the equal protection clause. The Court employed strict equal protection scrutiny both because the requirement interfered with the "fundamental" right to vote, see supra section E1, and because it "penalized" the "fundamental" right to travel. On the latter issue, the Court explained:

> Tennessee seeks to avoid the clear command of *Shapiro* by arguing that durational residence requirements for voting neither seek to nor actually do deter [travel]. This view represents a fundamental misunderstanding of the law. It is irrelevant whether disenfranchisement or denial of welfare is the more potent deterrent to travel. *Shapiro* did not rest upon a finding that denial of welfare actually deterred travel. [In] *Shapiro* we explicitly stated that the compelling-state-interest test would be triggered by "any classification which serves to *penalize* the exercise of that right. . . ." [Durational] residence laws impermissibly condition and penalize the right to travel by imposing their prohibitions on only those persons who have recently exercised that right. In the present case, such laws force a person [to] choose between travel and the basic right to vote. [Absent] a compelling state interest, a State may not burden the right to travel in this way.

Chief Justice Burger dissented.

b. *Nonemergency medical care.* In Memorial Hospital v. Maricopa County, 415 U.S. 250 (1974), the Court held that an Arizona statute requiring a year's residence in a county as a condition to receiving nonemergency medical care at county expense violated the equal protection clause. The Court explained:

> Although any durational residence requirement imposes a potential cost on migration, [*Shapiro*] cautioned that some "waiting-period[s] . . . may not be penalties." [In *Dunn*], the Court found that the denial of the franchise, "a fundamental political right," [was] a penalty requiring application of the compelling-state-interest test. In *Shapiro*, the Court found denial of the basic "necessities of life" to be a penalty. [Whatever] the ultimate parameters of the *Shapiro* penalty analysis, it is at least clear that medical care is as much "a basic necessity of life" to an indigent as welfare assistance. [It] would be odd, indeed, to find that [Arizona] was required to afford [appellant] welfare assistance to keep him from the discomfort of inadequate housing or the pangs of hunger but could deny him the medical care necessary to relieve him from the wheezing and gasping for breath that attend his illness. [Thus, the challenged requirement] penalizes indigents for exercising their right to migrate [and], "unless shown to be necessary to promote a compelling governmental interest, is unconstitutional."

The Court held that the state's justifications for the requirement were not "compelling." Chief Justice Burger and Justice Blackmun concurred in the result. Justice Douglas concurred in a separate opinion. Justice Rehnquist was the lone dissenter:

> Since the Court concedes that "some 'waiting period[s] . . . may not be penalties,'" one would expect to learn [how] to distinguish a waiting period which is a penalty from one which is not. Any expense imposed on citizens crossing state lines but not imposed on those staying put could theoretically be deemed a penalty on travel; the toll exacted from persons crossing from Delaware to New Jersey by the Delaware Memorial Bridge is a "penalty" on interstate travel in the most literal sense of all. But such charges [have] been upheld by this [Court]. [See Evansville-Vanderburgh Airport v. Delta Airlines, 405 U.S. 707 (1972) (upholding a $1 municipal charge for

each commercial airline passenger).] It seems to me that the line to be derived from our prior cases is that some financial impositions [have] such indirect or inconsequential impact on travel that they simply do not constitute the type of direct purposeful barriers struck down in [cases like *Shapiro*. The] solicitude which the Court has shown in cases involving the right to vote, and the virtual denial of entry inherent in denial of welfare benefits [ought] not be so casually extended to the alleged deprivation here. [The] barrier here is hardly a counterpart to the barriers condemned in earlier cases. That being so, the Court should observe its traditional respect for the State's allocation of its limited financial resources rather than unjustifiably imposing its own preferences.

Consider the following views: (1) "The degree of penalization requisite for strict scrutiny [is] never made clear. [Indeed,] courts have no judicially manageable standards [for] drawing essentially legislative-like distinctions concerning the practical significance of the benefits and rights denied to migrants. [Thus,] severity-of-the-penalty analysis offers nothing more than the illusion of a principled judicial framework." Note, Durational Residence Requirements from *Shapiro* through *Sosna*: The Right to Travel Takes a New Turn, 50 N.Y.U. L. Rev. 622, 669 (1975).

(2) "[The] Court should consider the deterrent effect that various durational residence requirements have on travel, rather than attempt as does Justice Marshall's 'penalty' analysis, to assess the importance of various state benefits to immigrants. Insofar as the validity of a given requirement depends upon the latter, what is being protected is not the right to travel, but the right to the withheld benefit." Note, The Supreme Court — 1973 Term, 88 Harv. L. Rev. 41, 117–118 (1974).

c. *Divorce.* In Sosna v. Iowa, 419 U.S. 393 (1975), the Court upheld a one-year residence requirement for bringing a divorce action against a nonresident. The Court, in an opinion by Justice Rehnquist, explained:

> Appellant was not irretrievably foreclosed from obtaining some part of what she sought, as was the case with the welfare recipients in *Shapiro*, the voters in *Dunn*, or the indigent patient in *Maricopa County*. [Iowa's] requirement delayed her access to the courts, but, by fulfilling it, she could ultimately have obtained the same opportunity for adjudication which she asserts ought to have been hers at an earlier point in time. [Moreover, unlike the residency requirements invalidated in *Shapiro*, *Dunn*, and *Maricopa County*,] Iowa's residency requirement may reasonably be justified on grounds other than purely budgetary considerations or administrative convenience. [A] decree of divorce [may affect the parties' marital status, their property rights, and their children]. With consequences of such moment riding on a divorce decree [Iowa] may insist that one seeking to initiate such a proceeding have the modicum of attachment to the State required here. Such a requirement additionally furthers the State's parallel interests both in avoiding officious intermeddling in matters in which another State has a paramount interest, and in minimizing the susceptibility of its own divorce decrees to collateral attack. [Iowa] may quite reasonably decide that it does not wish to become a divorce mill.

Justice Marshall, joined by Justice Brennan, dissented:

> The Court today departs sharply from the course we have followed in analyzing durational residency requirements since [*Shapiro*]. In its stead, the Court has em-

ployed what appears to be an ad hoc balancing [test]. The Court omits altogether what should be the first inquiry: whether the right to obtain a divorce is of sufficient importance that its denial to recent immigrants constitutes a penalty on interstate travel. [The] previous decisions of this Court make it plain that the right of marital association is one of the most basic rights conferred on the individual by the State. [E.g., *Boddie*.] [It] is clear beyond cavil [that] denial of this right to the class of recent interstate travelers penalizes interstate travel within the meaning of *Shapiro*, *Dunn*, and *Maricopa County*. [The] Court, however, has not only declined to apply the "compelling interest" test to this case, it has conjured up possible justifications for the State's restriction in a manner much more akin to the lenient standard we have in the past applied in analyzing equal protection challenges to business regulations. [The] Court proposes three defenses for the Iowa statute: first, the residency requirement merely delays receipt of the benefit in question; [second,] significant social consequences may follow from the conferral of a divorce; [and] third, the State has interests both in protecting itself from use as a "divorce mill" and in protecting its judgments from possible collateral attack in other States. [The] first justification [seems] to me specious. [It] ignores the severity of the deprivation suffered by the divorce petitioner who is forced to wait a year for relief. [The] second argument [is] no more persuasive. [Although] the stakes in a divorce are weighty [I] fail to see how any legitimate objective of Iowa's divorce regulations would be frustrated by granting equal access to new state residents. [The] third justification [is] the only one that warrants close consideration. [But Iowa's interests in this regard] would adequately be protected by a simple requirement of domicile [which would permit] the State to restrict the availability of its divorce process to citizens who are genuinely its own.

Justice White dissented on other grounds.

Consider the following views: (1) "What is disturbing about Justice Rehnquist's opinion in *Sosna* is his abandonment of penalty analysis, which could have produced the same result. [Divorce] is neither a necessity of life nor a fundamental right, and its denial for a year is not a penalty. Even if one assumes that the fundamental importance of divorce triggers strict scrutiny, the state's interest in avoiding collateral challenges of its decrees may be compelling." Comment, A Strict Scrutiny of the Right to Travel, 22 U.C.L.A. L. Rev. 1129, 1158 (1975).

(2) See Clark, Legislative Motivation and Fundamental Rights in Constitutional Law, 15 San Diego L. Rev. 953, 986–987 (1978):

Sosna makes some sense with respect to the underlying concerns of the constitutional right-to-travel provisions and to the danger against which they are designed to guard. [The] interstate commerce clause, the interstate privileges and immunities clause, the equal protection clause, and the penumbral right to travel [all] are centrally concerned with the prevention of repeated attempts by state legislatures to exclude undesirable persons, such as paupers or foreign business competitors, from their borders. [Unlike] indigents seeking welfare benefits, divorce plaintiffs hardly constitute a class of persons the state has any invidious reason for excluding. In the absence of any reason to suspect the state legislature of invidious motives, strict judicial scrutiny [does] not seem warranted.

d. *Variations*. In the light of *Shapiro*, *Dunn*, *Maricopa County*, and *Sosna*, consider the following: (a) a one-year residency requirement for admittance to the bar, cf. Supreme Court of New Hampshire v. Piper, 105 S. Ct. 1272 (1985) (holding that a bona fide residency requirement for admission to the bar violates the privileges and immunities clause of article IV, section 2); (b) a one-year residency requirement for reduced tuition at a state university, cf. Vlandis v. Kline, 412 U.S. 441 (1973) (invalidating such a requirement under the due process clause as an unconstitutional "irrebuttable presumption"); (c) a state statute making it a misdemeanor for a parent to abandon a dependent child and a felony for the parent to leave the state after the abandonment, see Jones v. Helms, 452 U.S. 412 (1981) (upholding such a statute).

4. *Alternative rationales for the invalidation of durational residency requirements.* Consider the following arguments. Are they preferable to the Court's "penalty on the exercise of a fundamental right" analysis?

a. Cohen, Equal Treatment for Newcomers: The Core Meaning of National and State Citizenship, 1 Const. Comm. 9, 17-18 (1984):

> The only hope for analysis is a new beginning, abandoning the doctrinal false leads of burdens or penalties on the right to travel or migrate, equal protection, and strict scrutiny. The new citizen's right to equality depends on none of those things. [Under] the fourteenth amendment, any United States citizen becomes a full-fledged member of the state community immediately upon establishing residence there. [A] state's decision that old-timers deserve a greater share of state-owned resources cannot be squared with a constitutional structure that demands that newcomers be treated as full members of the state community.

See also Varat, State "Citizenship" and Interstate Equality, 48 U. Chi. L. Rev. 487 (1981).

b. McCoy, Recent Equal Protection Decisions — Fundamental Right to Travel or "Newcomers" as a Suspect Class?, 28 Vand. L. Rev. 987, 1016-1022 (1975):

> None of the reasoning in the classic cases applying strict equal protection to unequal regulation of fundamental rights provides a firm theoretical basis for the *Shapiro-Dunn* [rationale]. On the other hand, reading *Shapiro, Dunn,* and *Maricopa* to establish "newcomers" as a suspect class is perfectly consistent with the reasoning of the Court in the classic cases creating the suspect class rationale for strict equal protection. ["Newcomers"] as a class are almost always a minority in the governmental unit, unable to protect their interests through the political process. [As] with blacks and aliens, the members of the class of "newcomers" are viewed as sufficiently different by oldtimers in the political majority [that] the class is easily stereotyped as ignorant, unreliable, or in some other way inadequate and unworthy. [And] as is the case with blacks and aliens, the social tendency to exclude newcomers has regularly been embodied in state law. [Indeed, one may fairly presume] that most instances of such discriminatory treatment are explained by the social tendency to discriminate against newcomers as newcomers, [and that] presumption [is] tantamount to the establishment of "newcomers" as a suspect class.

See also Loewy, A Different and More Viable Theory of Equal Protection, 57 N.C. L. Rev. 1, 35-39 (1978).

5. *Bona fide residency requirements. Shapiro* dealt with the right to travel in the sense of changing one's residence from one state to another. After *Shapiro* could a state constitutionally deny welfare benefits to nonresidents who are in the state temporarily? Is such a law permissible because it does not implicate the right to travel?

Shapiro dealt with a classification between two groups of residents. After *Shapiro* could a state constitutionally deny welfare benefits to former residents who had moved to another state? Consider McCarthy v. Philadelphia Civil Service Commission, 424 U.S. 645 (1976), in which the Court upheld the dismissal of an employee of the fire department who was terminated because he moved to New Jersey in violation of a requirement that city employees be residents of Philadelphia. In a summary per curiam disposition, the Court explained that *Shapiro* dealt only with durational residence requirements, and "did not question 'the validity [of] bona fide residence requirements.'" Consider also Martinez v. Bynum, 461 U.S. 321 (1983), in which the Court upheld a bona fide residence requirement for attending a state's public schools. The Court explained: "A bona fide residence requirement [furthers] the substantial state interest in assuring that services provided for its residents are enjoyed only by residents. Such a requirement with respect to attendance in public free schools does not violate the Equal Protection Clause. [It] does not burden or penalize the constitutional right of interstate travel, for any person is free to move to a State and to establish residence there."

Is the distinction between bona fide and durational residence requirements tenable? Consider Cohen, supra, at 17: "The reality of the existence of states qua states, rather than as departments of a national government, requires a conception that the state's citizens own state-owned resources, and that a state is not required to share its treasury with the nation at large."

Is the issue in *McCarthy* and *Martinez* more sensibly analyzed under the privileges and immunities clause of article IV, section 2? See Supreme Court of New Hampshire v. Piper, 105 S. Ct. 1272 (1985) (bona fide residence requirement for admission to the bar violates article IV, section 2); United Building & Construction Trades Council v. Mayor of Camden, 104 S. Ct. 1020 (1984) (ordinance requiring at least 40 percent of employees of contractors working on city projects to be city residents may violate article IV, section 2); Hicklin v. Orbeck, 437 U.S. 518 (1978) (Alaska statute requiring private employers to grant hiring preferences to Alaska residents violates article IV, section 2); Baldwin v. Fish & Game Commission, 436 U.S. 371 (1978) (upholding against article IV, section 2 and equal protection attack a requirement that nonresidents pay higher fees than residents for hunting licenses). The privileges and immunities clause of article IV, section 2 is examined more fully in Chapter 3, section E, supra.

4. Welfare

In *Harper, Griffin,* and *Douglas,* the Court emphasized the impact of certain forms of inequality on the poor. In *Shapiro* the Court observed that durational residence requirements for welfare affect "the ability [of] families to obtain the very means to subsist — food, shelter, and other necessities of life." After *Shapiro* a number of courts and commentators maintained that welfare constituted a "fundamental" interest for purposes of equal protection review.

Is welfare, like voting and access to the judicial process, a "fundamental" interest because it is "preservative of all rights"? Consider Michelman, Welfare Rights in a Constitutional Democracy, 1979 Wash. U. L.Q. 659, 677:

> [What] hope is there of effective participation in [the] political system [without] health and vigor, presentable attire, and shelter not only from the elements but from

the physical and psychological onslaughts of social debilitation? Are not these interests the universal, rock-bottom prerequisites of effective participation in democratic representation — even paramount in importance to [the] niceties of apportionment, districting, and ballot access on which so much judicial and scholarly labor has been lavished? How can there be those sophisticated rights to a formally unbiased majoritarian system, but no rights to the indispensable means of effective participation in that system?

In an earlier article, Professor Michelman offered a broader argument for the recognition of welfare as a "fundamental" interest:

[The] judicial "equality" explosion of recent times has largely been ignited by reawakened sensitivity, not to equality, but to a quite different sort of value or claim which might better be called "minimum welfare." In [cases like *Harper*, *Griffin*, *Douglas*, and *Shapiro*,] the Court has directly shielded poor persons from the most elemental consequence of poverty: lack of funds to exchange for needed goods, services, or privileges of access. . . .

The argument for minimum [welfare is] that justice requires *more* than a fair opportunity to realize an income which can cover [basic] needs. [Rather, it requires] absolute assurance that [these needs] will be met when and as felt, free of any remote contingencies pertaining to effort, thrift, or foresight.

We might take our cue from Professor Rawls' idea of "justice as fairness." Rawls grants that social institutions and practices may be just, even though they produce unequal incomes and accumulations. Yet for an unequal system to be just, it must be the case that a rational person, hypothetically ignorant of what particular place in society awaits him, would find the inequalities acceptable. . . .

The identity of "just wants" would then be determined according to a judgment arrived at through the following process of reasoning. Assume that a man has no idea what his social and economic station in a predominantly competitive society is to [be]. Will he nevertheless wish to have each person insured against the risk that certain needs will remain unfulfilled as and when they accrue — and what specific risks of that sort, if any, will he say should be insured against? Might he, for example, say that insofar as the society provides for "democratic" political participation, [access to such participation] should never be blocked by economic vicissitude? Or that persons must at all times be assured of effective access to some impartial [forum] for the peaceful settlement [of] disputes? Or that everyone at all times must be assured of facilities for a modicum of privacy, intimacy, confidentiality, self-expression? Or that each child must be guaranteed the means of developing his competence, self-knowledge, and tastes for living? . . .

It is not difficult to imagine reasons why a court, even if we supposed that it was inspired [by] notions of minimum protection and just wants, might [clothe] its decisions in the verbiage of inequality and discrimination. [Because] of unhappy connotations associated with "substantive due process," [the] Court seems [more] comfortable in staking out and valuing "fundamental" interests under the aegis of equal protection. [Moreover], there is an independent problem of standards which would be likely to induce reliance [on] equality. [How else] could the Court say when "enough" protection had been furnished? [Further,] while the idea of "just wants" or "severe deprivations" expresses an ethical precept distinct from that of "equality," detecting a failure to provide the required minimum may nonetheless depend in part upon the detection of inequalities. [Widening] inequalities become increasingly suggestive of failure to furnish the just minimum. [Finally, what] others have [may be particularly relevant] when the want in question is deemed [special because] of its importance for success in competitive activities.

Michelman, Foreword: On Protecting the Poor through the Fourteenth Amendment, 83 Harv. L. Rev. 7, 9, 14-19 (1969).

Consider, on the other hand, Bork, The Impossibility of Finding Welfare Rights in the Constitution, 1979 Wash. U. L.Q. 695, 695-696, 699-700:

> The effect of Professor Michelman's style of argument [is] to create rights by arguments from moral philosophy rather than from constitutional text, history, and structure. The end result would be to convert our government from one by representative assembly to one by judiciary. That result seems to me unfortunate for a variety of reasons.
>
> [There] is a certain seductiveness to the notion of judges gathered in conference and engaged in the sort of subtle philosophical analysis advanced by Professor Michelman. But the hard truth is that this kind of reasoning is impossible for committees. The violent disagreements among the legal philosophers alone demonstrate that there is no single path down which philosophical reasoning must lead. On arguments of this type, one can demonstrate that the obligation to pay for welfare is a violation of a right as easily as that there is a constitutional right to receive welfare. [For such an argument, see Epstein, Takings: Private Property and the Power of Eminent Domain, ch. 19 (1985).] Under these impossible circumstances, courts — perhaps philosophers, also — will reason toward conclusions that appeal to them for reasons other than those expressed. [The] consequence of this philosophical approach to constitutional law almost certainly would be the destruction of the idea of law. . . .
>
> [Professor] Michelman's basic argument [is] that people will have better access to the political process if their basic needs are met. [But suppose a state that has repealed its welfare laws argues that it did so] precisely for the purpose of reinforcing representation. The legislature had at last become convinced that welfare payments tend to relegate entire groups to a condition of permanent dependency so that they are not the active and independent political agents that they ought to be; moreover, these groups had lost political influence because they had been stigmatized as people on welfare. Experience had convinced the legislature that it would be better for people of that class, and for their participation in the political process, to struggle without state support as other poor groups have done successfully in our history. [What] is the Court to do when faced [with] arguments of this [sort]? Is [it] to make a sociological estimate of which actions will, in fact, reinforce representation in society? [Courts] simply are not equipped, much less authorized, to make such decisions.

Consider also Winter, Poverty, Economic Equality, and the Equal Protection Clause, 1972 Sup. Ct. Rev. 41, 100-102:

> The reduction of economic inequality [seems] a classic issue calling for the resolution of the claims of competing [groups. It] is precisely that judgment [which] ought to be the routine grist of the political mill. [Indeed, it] is for these reasons [that] most students of constitutional law believe the Court's vigorous use [of] substantive due process to upset economic regulation earlier in the century [was] a misuse of the power of judicial review. [All] economic regulation involves the allocation of scarce resources and the distribution of income. One may prefer one kind of regulation [and] distribution over another kind, but the judgment must be based on personal value preferences [and on] one's view of the social and economic impact of particular policies. [Such judgments cannot support] a legitimate exercise of judicial review.

DANDRIDGE v. WILLIAMS, 397 U.S. 471 (1970): The Court upheld a
provision of Maryland's Aid to Families with Dependent Children program that
granted most eligible families their computed "standard of need," but imposed a
maximum monthly grant of $250 per family, regardless of family size or computed
need. Justice Stewart delivered the opinion of the Court: "[Here] we deal with
state regulation in the social and economic field, not affecting freedoms guaranteed by the Bill of Rights, and claimed to violate the Fourteenth Amendment only
because the regulation results in some disparity in grants of welfare payments to
the largest AFDC families. For this Court to approve the invalidation of state
economic or social regulation [here] would be far too reminiscent of an era when
the Court thought the Fourteenth Amendment gave it power to strike down state
laws 'because they may be unwise, improvident, or out of harmony with a particular school of thought,' [Williamson v. Lee Optical Co.].

"In the area of economics and social welfare, a State does not violate the Equal
Protection Clause merely because the classifications made by its laws are imperfect. If the classification has some 'reasonable basis,' it does not offend the [Con-
stitution]. To be sure, the cases [enunciating] this [standard] have in the main
involved state regulation of business or industry. The administration of public
welfare assistance, by contrast, involves the most basic economic needs of impoverished human beings. We recognize the dramatically real factual difference
between the [business] cases and this one, but we can find no basis for applying a
different constitutional standard. . . .

"[The] maximum grant regulation is constitutionally valid. [By] keying the
maximum family AFDC grants to the minimum wage a steadily employed head of
a household receives, [the regulation encourages employment and avoids discrimination between welfare families and the families of the working poor]. [Al-
though the regulation may be both over- and under-inclusive,] the Equal
Protection Clause does not require that a State must choose between attacking
every aspect of a problem or not attacking the problem at all. [It] is enough that
the State's action be rationally based and free from invidious discrimination. The
regulation before us meets that test."

Justice Marshall, joined by Justice Brennan, dissented: "[The] maximum grant
regulation [creates] two classes of eligible families: those small families [who]
receive payments to cover their subsistence needs and those large families who do
not. This classification [produces] a basic denial of equal treatment. [The] Court
[focuses] upon the abstract dichotomy between two different approaches to equal
protection [problems]. Under the so-called 'traditional test,' a classification [is]
permissible [unless] it is 'without any reasonable basis.' [On] the other hand, if the
classification affects a 'fundamental right,' then the state interest [must] be 'compelling.' . . .

"This case simply defies easy characterization in terms of one or the other of
these 'tests.' The cases [that used] a 'mere rationality' test [involved] the regulation of business interests. [But this] case, involving the literally vital interests of a
powerless minority — poor families without breadwinners — is far removed from
the area of business regulation. [On the other hand, in] my view, equal protection
analysis of this case is not appreciably advanced by the a priori definition of a
'right,' fundamental or otherwise. Rather, concentration must be placed upon the
character of the classification in question, the relative importance to individuals

in the class discriminated against of the governmental benefits that they do not receive, and the asserted state interests in support of the classification. . . .

"It is the individual interests here at stake [that] most clearly distinguish this case from the 'business regulation' equal protection cases. AFDC support to needy dependent children provides the stuff that sustains those children's lives: food, clothing, shelter. And this Court has already recognized [that] when a benefit [is] necessary to sustain life, stricter constitutional standards, both procedural and substantive, are applied to the deprivation of that benefit. [Citing, e.g., Shapiro v. Thompson; Goldberg v. Kelly, infra section G.] . . .

"Appellees are not a gas company or an optical dispenser, they are needy dependent children and families who are discriminated against by the State. The basis of that discrimination [is] too arbitrary, [the] impact on those discriminated against [too] great, and the supposed interests served [too] attenuated to meet the requirements of the Constitution."

Justice Douglas dissented on the ground that the challenged regulation was inconsistent with the Social Security Act.

Note: Dandridge — *Principled Limitation or Retreat?*

1. Dandridge. Note that the Court in *Dandridge* did not directly address the claim that welfare is a "fundamental" interest. Rather, it simply asserted that rational basis review governs because the case involved "state regulation in the social and economic field, not affecting freedoms guaranteed by the Bill of Rights." Why isn't welfare a fundamental interest? In what way is it different from voting, access to the courts, and travel?

Consider Note, The Supreme Court — 1969 Term, 84 Harv. L. Rev. 1, 69-70 (1970): "The Court's decision to restrict active review [must] have been grounded in two related fears. The first was its apprehension that once strict scrutiny was extended to welfare there would be no way to limit its further extension [to] other important interests. [The] second fear was that since there are no easy standards for defining equality for purposes of welfare, strict scrutiny might require declaring all inequalities in its distribution invalid."

Note that in the welfare context, the claimant is not asking the government to leave him alone, but is asking it to *give* him something. The Constitution is ordinarily thought of, however, as creating limitations on government, rather than as establishing affirmative rights. In this sense, constitutional doctrine has a powerful libertarian dimension. Recall the discussion of *Lochner* in section D, supra. Does this fact distinguish welfare from other interests that have been declared "fundamental"? Does the fact that the issue is *equality*, rather than a right to welfare as such, eliminate the problem?

Note also that spending decisions have a "polycentric" character. If the Court expands the class of beneficiaries, the state may simply reduce the benefits for all recipients. Thus, the effect of declaring welfare to be a fundamental interest may not be to benefit the poor as a class but to benefit some poor persons at the expense of others. To what extent might this explain *Dandridge?* For discussion of "polycentricity," see Fuller, The Forms and Limits of Adjudication, 92 Harv. L. Rev. 353, 394-404 (1978).

2. *The Marshall dissent.* Note that Justice Marshall also did not directly address the claim that welfare is a "fundamental" interest. Rather, he simply asserted that "analysis of this case is not appreciably advanced by the a priori definition of a 'right,' fundamental or otherwise," and offered a more open-ended approach. Is Marshall's "sliding-scale" analysis an effective response to the Court's "fears"?

3. *Procreation.* Should the Court have subjected the regulation at issue in *Dandridge* to strict scrutiny because it imposed a penalty on the "fundamental" interest in procreation? Consider Justice Marshall's view, expressed in his dissenting opinion in *Dandridge,* that "the effect of the maximum grant regulation upon the right of procreation is marginal and indirect at best, totally unlike the compulsory sterilization law that was at issue in *Skinner.*"

4. *The reach of* Dandridge: *welfare.* Since *Dandridge* the Court has generally adhered to the view that rational basis review is the appropriate standard for the evaluation of welfare classifications. See, e.g., Califano v. Boles, 443 U.S. 282 (1979) (upholding a provision of the Social Security Act restricting "mothers' insurance benefits" to widows and divorced wives of wage earners); Jefferson v. Hackney, 406 U.S. 535 (1972) (upholding a provision of a state welfare program authorizing payment of a lower percentage of need to recipients of AFDC than to recipients of other forms of categorical welfare assistance); Richardson v. Belcher, 404 U.S. 78 (1971) (upholding a provision of the Social Security Act reducing disability benefits for amounts received from worker's compensation but not for amounts received from private insurance).

5. *The reach of* Dandridge: *housing.* In Lindsey v. Normet, 405 U.S. 56 (1972), the Court upheld a state's summary "forcible entry and wrongful detainer" procedures for the eviction of tenants after alleged nonpayment of rent. The Court rejected a claim that "the 'need for decent shelter' and the 'right to retain peaceful possession of one's home' are fundamental interests which are particularly important to the poor and which may be trenched upon only after the State demonstrates some superior interest." The Court explained:

> We do not denigrate the importance of decent, safe, and sanitary housing. But the Constitution does not provide judicial remedies for every social and economic ill. We are unable to perceive in that document any constitutional guarantee of access to dwellings of a particular quality, or any recognition of the right of a tenant to occupy the real property of his landlord beyond the term of his [lease]. Absent constitutional mandate, the assurance of adequate housing and the definition of landlord-tenant relationships are legislative, not judicial, functions.

Applying rational basis review, the Court found no constitutional defect in the fact that eviction actions are more summary than "other litigation," for the "unique factual and legal characteristics of the landlord-tenant relationship [justify] special statutory treatment." Justices Douglas and Brennan dissented.

6. *The limits of* Dandridge: *Moreno.* In U.S. Department of Agriculture v. Moreno, 413 U.S. 528 (1973), supra Chapter 5, section B, the Court, in a seven-to-two decision, invalidated a provision of the Food Stamp Act excluding from participation in the program any household containing an individual who is unrelated to any other household member. The government argued that the challenged classification was rationally related to the legitimate government interest in minimizing fraud, because "Congress might rationally have thought [that]

households with one or more unrelated members are more likely than 'fully related' households to contain individuals who abuse the program by fraudulently failing to report sources of income." In rejecting this argument, the Court maintained that "the challenged classification [does] not operate so as rationally to further the prevention of fraud," for "even if we were to accept as rational the Government's [assumptions] concerning the differences between 'related' and 'unrelated' households, we still could not agree" that the challenged provision "constitutes a rational effort to deal with" this concern, for "in practical operation," it "excludes from participation in [the] program, *not* those persons who are 'likely to abuse the program' but, rather, *only* those persons who are so desperately in need of aid that they cannot even afford to alter their living arrangements so as to retain their eligibility."

Does *Moreno* suggest that, despite *Dandridge*, the Court may apply a more stringent standard where a law involves not a mere *relative* deprivation of welfare benefits, as in *Dandridge*, but an *absolute* deprivation, as in *Moreno?*

7. *The implications of* Dandridge. Consider Gunther, Foreword: In Search of Evolving Doctrine on a Changing Court: A Model for a Newer Equal Protection, 86 Harv. L. Rev. 1, 12-18 (1972):

> The anticipations spurred by the Warren Court have not fared well. The new Justices are disinclined to add to the list of fundamental interests unearthed by their predecessors. [Even] Justice Marshall's effort in [*Dandridge* reflects the] growing malaise about the [dichotomy between strict and minimal scrutiny]. [The] attempted reformulations in [these opinions] are less important for their content than for the mood they reflect. None of these gropings has produced a fully developed alternative, but all signify a widespread inclination to reexamine old rationales.

5. Education and the Continuing Effort to Define "Fundamental" Interests

As *Dandridge* suggests, by the early 1970s there was growing dissatisfaction with the Court's "fundamental" interest equal protection jurisprudence. This dissatisfaction derived from two quite distinct sources: First, there were those who thought that the entire enterprise was nothing more than a return to substantive due process, for it involved the Court in the highly subjective selection of so-called fundamental interests. Second, there were those who thought that the enterprise was legitimate, but that the Court's two-tier analysis was too rigid, and called for a more flexible approach. Matters came to a head in *Rodriguez*.

San Antonio Independent School District v. Rodriguez

411 U.S. 1 (1973)

[Public school education has long been financed largely by means of property taxes imposed by local school districts. This suit challenged the constitutionality of Texas's use of this financing system on the ground that it produced substantial interdistrict disparities in per-pupil expenditures. For example, the Edgewood

Independent School District, the least affluent of the seven school districts in metropolitan San Antonio, had an assessed property value of $5,960 per student. By imposing a property tax of $1.05 per $100 of assessed property value — the highest rate in the metropolitan area — the district raised $26 per student in local funds. In contrast, the Alamo Heights Independent School District, the most affluent in the area, had an assessed property value per student of more than $49,000 and with a tax rate of only $.85 per $100 was able to raise $333 per student. Although contributions from a state-funded "foundation program" tended to reduce interdistrict disparities, the inclusion of such funds still left a substantial difference — $248 per pupil in Edgewood as compared to $558 in Alamo Heights. A federal district court, applying strict scrutiny, held that the Texas scheme violated the equal protection clause. The Supreme Court reversed.]

MR. JUSTICE POWELL delivered the opinion of the Court. . . .

I

[We] must decide, first, whether the Texas system of financing public education operates to the disadvantage of some suspect class or impinges upon a fundamental right explicitly or implicitly protected by the Constitution, thereby requiring strict judicial scrutiny. If so, the judgment of the District Court should be affirmed. If not, the Texas scheme must still be examined to determine whether it rationally furthers some legitimate, articulated state purpose and therefore does not constitute an invidious discrimination in violation of the Equal Protection Clause of the Fourteenth Amendment.

II

[We] find neither the suspect-classification nor the fundamental-interest analysis persuasive.

A

[The Court rejected the claim that strict scrutiny was appropriate because the Texas system discriminated against the "poor." The Court explained that, in prior cases, like Griffin, Douglas, and Bullock v. Carter, the "individuals, or groups of individuals, who constituted the class discriminated against [shared] two distinguishing characteristics: because of their impecunity they were completely unable to pay for some desired benefit, and as a consequence, they sustained an absolute deprivation of a meaningful opportunity to enjoy that benefit." The Court maintained here that "neither of the two distinguishing characteristics of wealth classifications" is present. First, "appellees have made no effort to demonstrate that [the Texas system] operates to the peculiar disadvantage" of the poor. To the contrary, "there is reason to believe that the poorest families are not necessarily clustered in the poorest property districts," for the poor are often "clustered around commercial and industrial areas," which produce a relatively high property tax income. Second, the Texas system "has not occasioned an absolute deprivation of the desired benefit." Rather, the sole claim is that appellees "are receiving a poorer quality education [than] children" in other districts,[56] and "at least where wealth is involved, the Equal Protection Clause does not [require] precisely equal advantages." The Court thus concluded that the "disadvantaged class is not susceptible of identification in traditional terms."[60] The issue of wealth discrimination in *Rodriguez* is addressed more fully in Chapter 5, supra.]

B

In Brown v. Board of Education, a unanimous Court recognized that "education is perhaps the most important function of state and local governments." . . .

Nothing this Court holds today in any way detracts from our historic dedication to public education. [But] the importance of a service performed by the State does not determine whether it must be regarded as fundamental for purposes of examination under the Equal Protection Clause.

The lesson of [Dandridge v. Williams and Lindsey v. Normet] is plain. It is not the province of this Court to create substantive constitutional rights in the name of guaranteeing equal protection of the laws. Thus, the key to discovering whether education is "fundamental" is not to be found in comparisons of the relative societal significance of education as opposed to subsistence or housing. Nor is it to be found by weighing whether education is as important as the right to travel. Rather, the answer lies in assessing whether there is a right to education explicitly or implicitly guaranteed by the Constitution. Dunn v. Blumstein, 405 U.S. 330 (1972);[74] Police Dept. of Chicago v. Mosley, 408 U.S. 92 (1972);[75] Skinner v. Oklahoma, 316 U.S. 535 (1942).[76]

56. Each of appellees' possible theories of wealth discrimination is founded on the assumption that the quality of education varies directly with the amount of funds expended on it and that, therefore, the difference in quality between two schools can be determined simplistically by looking at the difference in per-pupil expenditures. This is a matter of considerable dispute among educators and commentators.

60. An educational financing system might be hypothesized, however, in which the analogy to the wealth discrimination cases would be considerably closer. If elementary and secondary education were made available by the State only to those able to pay a tuition assessed against each pupil, there would be a clearly defined class of "poor" people — definable in terms of their inability to pay the prescribed sum — who would be absolutely precluded from receiving an education. That case would present a far more compelling set of circumstances for judicial assistance than the case before us today. After all, Texas has undertaken to do a good deal more than provide an education to those who can afford it. It has provided what it considers to be an adequate base education for all children and has attempted, though imperfectly, to ameliorate by state funding and by the local assessment program the disparities in local tax resources.

74. *Dunn* fully canvasses this Court's voting rights cases and explains that "this Court has made clear that a citizen has a *constitutionally protected right* to participate in elections on an equal basis with other citizens in the jurisdiction. The constitutional underpinnings of the right to equal treatment in the voting process can no longer be doubted even though, as the Court noted in Harper v. Virginia Bd. of Elections, 383 U.S., at 665, "the right to vote in state elections is nowhere expressly mentioned." . . .

75. In *Mosley*, the Court struck down a Chicago antipicketing ordinance that exempted labor picketing from its prohibitions. The ordinance was held invalid under the Equal Protection Clause after subjecting it to careful scrutiny and finding that the ordinance was not narrowly drawn. The stricter standard of review was appropriately applied since the ordinance was one "affecting First Amendment interests."

76. *Skinner* applied the standard of close scrutiny to a state law permitting forced sterilization of "habitual criminals." Implicit in the Court's opinion is the recognition that the right of procreation is among the rights of personal privacy protected under the Constitution. See Roe v. Wade, 410 U.S. 113, 152 (1973).

Education, of course, is not among the rights afforded explicit protection under our Federal Constitution. Nor do we find any basis for saying it is implicitly so protected. As we have said, the undisputed importance of education will not alone cause this Court to depart from the usual standard for reviewing a State's social and economic legislation. It is appellees' contention, however, that education is distinguishable from other services and benefits provided by the State because it bears a peculiarly close relationship to other rights and liberties accorded protection under the Constitution. Specifically, they insist that education is itself a fundamental personal right because it is essential to the effective exercise of First Amendment freedoms and to intelligent utilization of the right to vote. In asserting a nexus between speech and education, appellees urge that the right to speak is meaningless unless the speaker is capable of articulating his thoughts intelligently and persuasively. . . .

A similar line of reasoning is pursued with respect to the right to vote.[78] Exercise of the franchise, it is contended, cannot be divorced from the educational foundation of the voter. . . .

We need not dispute any of these propositions. The Court has long afforded zealous protection against unjustifiable governmental interference with the individual's rights to speak and to vote. Yet we have never presumed to possess either the ability or the authority to guarantee to the citizenry the most *effective* speech or the most *informed* electoral choice. That these may be desirable goals [is] not to be doubted. [But] they are not values to be implemented by judicial intrusion into otherwise legitimate state activities.

[Whatever] merit appellees' argument might have if a State's financing system occasioned an absolute denial of educational opportunities to any of its children, that argument provides no basis for finding an interference with fundamental rights where only relative differences in spending levels are involved and where — as is true in the present case — no charge fairly could be made that the system fails to provide each child with an opportunity to acquire the basic minimal skills necessary for the enjoyment of the rights of speech and of full participation in the political process.

Furthermore, the logical limitations on appellees' nexus theory are difficult to perceive. How, for instance, is education to be distinguished from the significant personal interests in the basics of decent food and shelter? Empirical examination might well buttress an assumption that the ill-fed, ill-clothed, and ill-housed are among the most ineffective participants in the political process, and that they derive the least enjoyment from the benefits of the First Amendment. If so, appellees' thesis would cast serious doubt on the authority of Dandridge v. Williams and Lindsey v. Normet. . . .

C

[We] need not rest our decision, however, solely on the inappropriateness of the strict-scrutiny test. A century of Supreme Court adjudication under the Equal

---

78. Since the right to vote, per se, is not a constitutionally protected right, we assume that appellees' references to that right are simply shorthand references to the protected right, implicit in our constitutional system, to participate in state elections on an equal basis with other qualified voters whenever the State has adopted an elective process for determining who will represent any segment of the State's population.

Protection Clause affirmatively supports the application of the traditional standard of review, which requires only that the State's system be shown to bear some rational relationship to legitimate state purposes.

[We] have here nothing less than a direct attack on the way in which Texas has chosen to raise and disburse state and local tax revenues. [A]ppellees would have the Court intrude in an area in which it has traditionally deferred to state legislatures. [No] scheme of taxation, whether the tax is imposed on property, income, or purchases of goods and services, has yet been devised which is free of all discriminatory impact. In such a complex arena in which no perfect alternatives exist, the Court does well not to impose too rigorous a standard of scrutiny lest all local fiscal schemes become subjects of criticism under the Equal Protection Clause.

[Moreover], this case also involves the most persistent and difficult questions of educational policy, another area in which this Court's lack of specialized knowledge and experience counsels against premature interference with the informed judgments made at the state and local levels. Education, perhaps even more than welfare assistance, presents a myriad of "intractable economic, social, and even philosophical problems." [In] such circumstances, the judiciary is well advised to refrain from imposing on the States inflexible constitutional restraints that could circumscribe [continued] research and experimentation. . . .

III

[While] assuring a basic education for every child in the State, [the Texas system of school financing] permits and encourages a large measure of participation in and control of each district's schools at the local level. In an era that has witnessed a consistent trend toward centralization of the functions of government, local sharing of responsibility for public education has survived. [In] part, local control means [the] freedom to devote more money to the education of one's children. Equally important, however, is the opportunity it offers for participation in the decisionmaking process that determines how those local tax dollars will be spent. Each locality is free to tailor local programs to local needs. Pluralism also affords some opportunity for experimentation, innovation, and a healthy competition for educational [excellence]. Appellees suggest that local control could be preserved and promoted under other financing systems that resulted in more equality in educational expenditures. While it is no doubt true that reliance on local property taxation for school revenues provides less freedom of choice with respect to expenditures for some districts than for others, the existence of "some inequality" in the manner in which the State's rationale is achieved is not alone a sufficient basis for striking down the entire system. [Nor] must the financing system fail because, as appellees suggest, other methods of satisfying the State's interest, which occasion "less drastic" disparities in expenditures, might be conceived. Only where state action impinges on the exercise of fundamental constitutional rights or liberties must it be found to have chosen the least restrictive alternative. [It] is also well to remember that even those districts that have reduced ability to make free decisions with respect to how much they spend on education still retain under the present system a large measure of authority as to how available funds will be allocated. They further enjoy the power to make numerous other decisions with respect to the operation of the schools. The people of Texas may be justified in believing that other systems of school financing, which place more of the financial responsibility in the hands of the State, will result in a comparable lessening of desired local autonomy. . . .

Appellees further urge that the Texas system is unconstitutionally arbitrary because it allows the [quality] of education to fluctuate on the basis of the fortuitous positioning of the boundary lines of political subdivisions. [But] any scheme of local taxation — indeed the very existence of identifiable local governmental units — requires the establishment of jurisdictional boundaries that are inevitably arbitrary. [And] if local taxation for local expenditures were an unconstitutional method of providing for education then it might be an equally impermissible means of providing other necessary services customarily financed largely from local property taxes, including local police and fire protection, public health and hospitals, and public utility facilities of various kinds. We perceive no justification for such a severe denigration of local property taxation and control. . . .

In sum, to the extent that the Texas system of school financing results in unequal expenditures between children who happen to reside in different districts, we cannot say that such disparities are the product of a system that is so irrational as to be invidiously discriminatory. [The] constitutional standard under the Equal Protection Clause is whether the challenged state action rationally furthers a legitimate state purpose or interest. We hold that the Texas plan abundantly satisfies this standard. . . .

Reversed.*

MR. JUSTICE WHITE, with whom MR. JUSTICE DOUGLAS and MR. JUSTICE BRENNAN join, dissenting.

[This] case would be quite different if it were true that the Texas system, while insuring minimum educational expenditures in every district through state funding, extended a meaningful option to all local districts to increase their per-pupil [expenditures. But for] districts with a low per-pupil real estate tax base [the] Texas system utterly fails to extend a realistic choice to parents because the property tax, which is the only revenue-raising mechanism extended to school districts, is practically and legally unavailable. . . .

In order to equal the highest yield in any other Bexar County district, [Edgewood] would be required to tax at the prohibitive rate of $5.76 per $100. But state law places a $1.50 per $100 ceiling on the maintenance tax rate. [Edgewood] is thus precluded in law, as well as in fact, from achieving a yield even close to that of some other districts. [Requiring] the State to establish only that unequal treatment is in furtherance of a permissible goal, without also requiring the State to show that the means chosen to effectuate that goal are rationally related to its achievement, makes equal protection analysis no more than an empty gesture. . . .

MR. JUSTICE MARSHALL, with whom MR. JUSTICE DOUGLAS concurs, dissenting.

[The] Court apparently seeks to establish today that equal protection cases fall into one of two neat categories which dictate the appropriate standard of review

---

* [The concurring opinion of Justice Stewart and the dissenting opinion of Justice Brennan are omitted. — EDS.]

— strict scrutiny or mere rationality. But this Court's decisions in the field of equal protection defy such easy categorization. A principled reading of what this Court has done reveals that it has applied a spectrum of standards in reviewing discrimination allegedly violative of the Equal Protection Clause. This spectrum clearly comprehends variations in the degree of care with which the Court will scrutinize particular classifications, depending, I believe, on the constitutional and societal importance of the interest adversely affected and the recognized invidiousness of the basis upon which the particular classification is drawn. . . .

I therefore cannot accept the majority's labored efforts to demonstrate that fundamental interests, which call for strict scrutiny of the challenged classification, encompass only established rights which we are somehow bound to recognize from the text of the Constitution itself. To be sure, some interests which the Court has deemed to be fundamental for purposes of equal protection analysis are themselves constitutionally protected rights. [Citing Police Department of Chicago v. Mosley (free speech); Shapiro v. Thompson (right to travel).] But it will not do to suggest that the "answer" to whether an interest is fundamental for purposes of equal protection analysis is *always* determined by whether that interest "is a right . . . explicitly or implicitly guaranteed by the Constitution."[59]

I would like to know where the Constitution guarantees the right to procreate, [Skinner v. Oklahoma], or the right to vote in state elections, [Reynolds v. Sims],[60] or the right to an appeal from a criminal conviction, [*Griffin*].[61] These are instances in which, due to the importance of the interests at stake, the Court has displayed a strong concern with the existence of discriminatory state treatment. But the Court has never said or indicated that these are interests which independently enjoy full-blown constitutional protection. . . .

The majority is, of course, correct when it suggests that the process of determining which interests are fundamental is a difficult one. But I do not think the problem is insurmountable. [The] determination of which interests are fundamental should be firmly rooted in the text of the Constitution. The task in every case should be to determine the extent to which constitutionally guaranteed rights are dependent on interests not mentioned in the Constitution. As the nexus between the specific constitutional guarantee and the nonconstitutional interest draws closer, the nonconstitutional interest becomes more fundamental and the degree of judicial scrutiny applied when the interest is infringed on a discriminatory basis must be adjusted accordingly. Thus, it cannot be denied that interests such as procreation, the exercise of the state franchise, and access to criminal

59. Indeed, the Court's theory would render the established concept of fundamental interests in the context of equal protection analysis superfluous, for the substantive constitutional right itself requires that this Court strictly scrutinize any asserted state interest for restricting or denying access to any particular guaranteed right.

60. It is interesting that in its effort to reconcile the state voting rights cases with its theory of fundamentality the majority can muster nothing more than the contention that "[t]he constitutional underpinnings of the *right to equal treatment in the voting process* can no longer be doubted. . . ." If, by this, the Court intends to recognize a substantive constitutional "right to equal teatment in the voting process" independent of the Equal Protection Clause, the source of such a right is certainly a mystery to me.

61. It is true that *Griffin* [also] involved discrimination against indigents, that is, wealth discrimination. But, as the majority points out, the Court has never deemed wealth discrimination alone to be sufficient to require strict judicial scrutiny; rather, such review of wealth classifications has been applied only where the discrimination affects an important individual interest, see, e.g., [*Harper*]. Thus, I believe *Griffin* [can] only be understood as premised on a recognition of the fundamental importance of the criminal appellate process.

appellate processes are not fully guaranteed to the citizen by our Constitution. But these interests have nonetheless been afforded special judicial consideration in the face of discrimination because they are, to some extent, interrelated with constitutional guarantees. Procreation is now understood to be important because of its interaction with the established constitutional right of privacy. The exercise of the state franchise is closely tied to basic civil and political rights inherent in the First Amendment. And access to criminal appellate processes enhances the integrity of the range of rights implicit in the [guarantee] of due process of law. Only if we closely protect the related interests from state discrimination do we ultimately ensure the integrity of the constitutional guarantee itself. This is the real lesson that must be taken from our previous decisions involving interests deemed to be fundamental. . . .

[It] is true that this Court has never deemed the provision of free public education to be required by the Constitution. [Nevertheless] the fundamental importance of education is amply indicated by the prior decisions of this Court, by the unique status accorded public education by our society, and by the close relationship between education and some of our most basic constitutional values. . . .

Education directly affects the ability of a child to exercise his First Amendment rights, both as a source and as a receiver of information and ideas. [Of] particular importance is the relationship between education and the political process [and] the demonstrated effect of education on the exercise of the franchise by the electorate. [It] is this very sort of intimate relationship between a particular personal interest and specific constitutional guarantees that has heretofore caused the Court to attach special significance, for purposes of equal protection analysis, to individual interests such as procreation and the exercise of the state franchise.[74] [These factors] compel us to recognize the fundamentality of education and to scrutinize with appropriate care the bases for state discrimination affecting equality of educational opportunity in Texas' school districts — a conclusion which is only strengthened when we consider the character of the classification in this case.

[On the "wealth" issue, Justice Marshall maintained that *Harper*, *Griffin*, and *Douglas* refuted the Court's contention "that we have in the past required an absolute deprivation before subjecting wealth classifications to strict scrutiny." Marshall conceded, however, that "the form of wealth classification in this case" differs "from those recognized [in] previous decisions," for "the children of the disadvantaged Texas school districts are being discriminated against not necessar-

---

74. I believe that the close nexus between education and our established constitutional values with respect to freedom of speech and participation in the political process makes this a different case from our prior decisions concerning discrimination affecting public welfare, see, e.g., [*Dandridge*] or housing, see, e.g., [Lindsey v. Normet]. There can be no question that, as the majority suggests, constitutional rights may be less meaningful for someone without enough to eat or without decent housing. But the crucial difference lies in the closeness of the relationship. Whatever the severity of the impact of insufficient food or inadequate housing on a person's life, they have never been considered to bear the same direct and immediate relationship to constitutional concerns for free speech and for our political processes as education has long been recognized to bear. Perhaps, the best evidence of this fact is the unique status which has been accorded public education as the single public service nearly unanimously guaranteed in the constitutions of our States. Education, in terms of constitutional values, is much more analogous, in my judgment, to the right to vote in state elections than to public welfare or public housing. Indeed, it is not without significance that we have long recognized education as an essential step in providing the disadvantaged with the tools necessary to achieve economic self-sufficiency.

ily because of their personal wealth, [but] because of the taxable property wealth of the residents of the district in which they happen to live." Nonetheless, Marshall concluded that "discrimination on the basis of group wealth in this case likewise calls for careful judicial scrutiny," for "it bears no relationship whatsoever to the interest of Texas schoolchildren in the educational opportunity afforded them," it "involves wealth over which the disadvantaged individual has no significant control," and it was the State, not the operation of the market, "that has [tied] educational funding [to] local district wealth."]

The nature of our inquiry into the justifications for state discrimination is essentially the same in all equal protection cases: We must consider the substantiality of the state interests sought to be served, and we must scrutinize the reasonableness of the means by which the State has sought to advance its interests. Differences in the application of this test are, in my view, a function of the constitutional importance of the interests at stake and the invidiousness of the particular classification. Here, both the nature of the interest and the classification dictate close judicial scrutiny of the purposes which Texas seeks to serve with its present educational financing scheme and of the means it has selected to serve that purpose.

The only justification offered [to] sustain the discrimination in educational opportunity caused by the Texas financing scheme is local educational control. [But] on this record, it is apparent that the State's purported concern with local control is offered primarily as an excuse rather than as a justification for interdistrict inequality.

In Texas, statewide laws regulate [the] most minute details of local public education. [But] even if we accept Texas' general dedication to local control in educational matters, it is difficult to find any evidence of such dedication with respect to fiscal matters. [If] Texas had a system truly dedicated to local fiscal control, one would expect the quality of the educational opportunity provided in each district to vary with the decision of the voters in that district as to the level of sacrifice they wish to make for public education. In fact, the Texas scheme produces precisely the opposite result. Local school districts cannot choose to have the best education in the State by imposing the highest tax rate. Instead, the quality of the educational opportunity offered by any particular district is largely determined by the amount of taxable property located in the district — a factor over which local voters can exercise no control. . . .

In my judgment, any substantial degree of scrutiny of the operation of the Texas financing scheme reveals that the State has selected means wholly inappropriate to secure its purported interest in assuring its school districts local fiscal control.[96] At the same time, appellees have pointed out a variety of alternative financing schemes which may serve the State's purported interest in local control as well as, if not better than, the present scheme without the current impairment

96. My Brother White, in concluding that the Texas financing scheme runs afoul of the Equal Protection Clause, likewise finds on analysis that the means chosen by Texas — local property taxation dependent upon local taxable wealth — is completely unsuited in its present form to the achievement of the asserted goal of providing local fiscal control. Although my Brother White purports to reach this result by application of that lenient standard of mere rationality traditionally applied in the context of commercial interests, it seems to me that the care with which he scrutinizes the practical effectiveness of the present local property tax as a device for affording local fiscal control reflects the application of a more stringent standard of review, a standard which at the least is influenced by the constitutional significance of the process of public education.

of the educational opportunity of vast numbers of Texas schoolchildren.[98] I see no need, however, to explore the practical or constitutional merits of those suggested alternatives at this time for, whatever their positive or negative features, experience with the present financing scheme impugns any suggestion that it constitutes a serious effort to provide local fiscal control. . . .

Note: The Rodriguez Reformulation

1. *The competing views.* There are two critical points of disagreement in *Rodriguez*: (1) The Court confined "fundamental" interests to only those rights that are "explicitly or implicitly guaranteed by the Constitution," whereas Justice Marshall offered a "nexus" approach, focusing on the "extent to which constitutionally protected rights are dependent on interests not mentioned in the Constitution." (2) The Court adhered to the "two-tier" theory of equal protection review, whereas Justice Marshall, as in *Dandridge*, offered his "sliding-scale" approach.

How would you argue in favor of the competing views? As a matter of precedent? As a matter of first principle?

2. *The court and "middle-class" values.* Consider Bennett, The Burger Court and the Poor, in The Burger Court: The Counter-Revolution That Wasn't 46, 53-55 (Blasi ed. 1983):

> [Commentators] have chided the Court for pursuing middle-class values in the name of fundamental rights, while ignoring the pressing problems of those, including the poor, with fewer resources to bring to bear on legislative decision-making. Perhaps the most dramatic evidence for the validity of such a charge is [*Rodriguez*]. [The] arguments for implicit protection of [travel, for example,] seem no stronger than those for education. Against this background the charge becomes plausible that the Court in *Rodriguez* used the distinction between implicit constitutional interests and those outside the document's protection as a shield to stave off an assault by the poor on the middle-class prerogative of well-financed public schools. [But the decision is also] understandable in terms other than those of class conflict. An important prudential constraint in constitutional decision-making is the extent to which a court can provide an adequate remedy once it has defined a wrong. [In] *Rodriguez*, the Court may well have thought that attacking the school financing problem would have required [a] willingness to devote extraordinary judicial resources to a continu-

---

98. [Even] centralized financing would not deprive local school districts of what has been considered to be the essence of local educational control. Central financing would leave in local hands the entire gamut of local educational policymaking — teachers, curriculum, school sites, the whole process of allocating resources among alternative educational objectives.

A second possibility is the much-discussed theory of district power equalization put forth by Professors Coons, Clune, and Sugarman in their seminal work, Private Wealth and Public Education 201-242 (1970). Such a scheme would truly reflect a dedication to local fiscal control. Under their system, each school district would receive a fixed amount of revenue per pupil for any particular level of tax effort regardless of the level of local property tax base. . . .

District wealth reapportionment is yet another alternative. . . .

A fourth possibility would be to remove commercial, industrial, and mineral property from local tax rolls, to tax this property on a statewide basis, and to return the resulting revenues to the local districts in a fashion that would compensate for remaining variations in the local tax bases.

None of these particular alternatives are necessarily constitutionally compelled; rather, they indicate the breadth of choice which would remain to the State if the present interdistrict disparities were eliminated.

ing process of overseeing the responsive actions of other branches of government. [That] prospect could have chilled the enthusiasm even of a Court quite appalled by unequal education financing.

3. *Education as a "fundamental" interest.* To what extent, if any, does footnote 60 impeach the Court's conclusion that education is not a "fundamental" interest? To what extent does the Court's reiteration that the Texas system did not involve an "absolute deprivation" of education impeach this conclusion?

What is an "absolute deprivation" of education? After *Rodriguez*, is a state constitutionally obligated to provide bilingual education for language minorities or special educational facilities for the physically and mentally handicapped? See generally Levin, The Courts, The Congress, and Educational Adequacy: The Equal Protection Predicament, 39 Md. L. Rev. 187 (1979).

If education *were* a "fundamental" interest, how would the Court decide what kind of education, and how much education, a person is entitled to receive? Would public schools be required to adopt standardized curricula? Would state universities be required to pay the tuition costs of indigents?

4. *The impact of* Rodriguez. The Court attempted in *Rodriguez* to add a measure of certainty to equal protection jurisprudence and to withdraw from the arguably "subjective" enterprise of selecting "fundamental" interests. Since 1973 the Court has generally adhered to the *Rodriguez* reformulation. That is, although the Court has continued to enforce "fundamental" interest analysis in the areas of procreation, voting, access to the courts, and travel, it has essentially frozen the list of "fundamental" interests and maintained its "two-tier" approach. But not entirely. Consider Plyler v. Doe.

Plyler v. Doe

457 U.S. 202 (1982)

JUSTICE BRENNAN delivered the opinion of the Court. . . .

[The Court held unconstitutional a Texas statute that authorized local school districts to deny free public education to children who had not been "legally admitted" into the United States. Pursuant to this statute, the Tyler Independent School District required "undocumented" children to pay a "tuition fee" in order to enroll.]

[In] applying the Equal Protection Clause to most forms of state action, we [seek] only the assurance that the classification at issue bears some fair relationship to a legitimate public purpose.

But we would not be faithful to our obligations under the Fourteenth Amendment if we applied so deferential a standard to every classification. The Equal Protection Clause was intended as a restriction on state legislative action inconsistent with elemental constitutional premises. Thus we have treated as presumptively invidious those classifications that disadvantage a "suspect class,"[14] or that

14. Several formulations might explain our treatment of certain classifications as "suspect." Some classifications are more likely than others to reflect deep-seated prejudice rather than legislative rationality in pursuit of some legitimate objective. Legislation predicated on such prejudice is easily recognized as incompatible with the constitutional understanding that each person is to be judged individually and is entitled to equal justice under the law. Classifications treated as suspect tend to be

impinge upon the exercise of a "fundamental right."[15] With respect to such classifications, it is appropriate to enforce the mandate of equal protection by requiring the State to demonstrate that its classification has been precisely tailored to serve a compelling governmental interest. In addition, we have recognized that certain forms of legislative classification, while not facially invidious, nonetheless give rise to recurring constitutional difficulties; in these limited circumstances we have sought the assurance that the classification reflects a reasoned judgment consistent with the ideal of equal protection by inquiring whether it may fairly be viewed as furthering a substantial interest of the State.[16] We turn to a consideration of the standard appropriate for the evaluation of [the challenged law].

Sheer incapability or lax enforcement of the laws barring entry into this country, [has] resulted in the creation of a substantial "shadow population" of illegal migrants — numbering in the millions — within our borders. This situation raises the specter of a permanent caste of undocumented resident aliens, encouraged by some to remain here as a source of cheap labor, but nevertheless denied the benefits that our society makes available to citizens and lawful residents. The existence of such an underclass presents most difficult problems for a Nation that prides itself on adherence to principles of equality under law.[19]

The children who are plaintiffs in these cases are special members of this underclass. [Adults] who elect to enter our territory by stealth and in violation of our law should be prepared to bear the consequences, including, but not limited to, deportation. But the children [of] illegal entrants are not comparably situated. [They] "can affect neither their parents' conduct nor their own status." [Trimble v. Gordon.] Even if the State found it expedient to control the conduct of adults by acting against their children, legislation directing the onus of a parent's misconduct against his children does not comport with fundamental conceptions of justice. [Citing Weber v. Aetna Casualty.]

Of course, undocumented status is not irrelevant to any proper legislative goal. Nor is undocumented status an absolutely immutable characteristic since it is the product of conscious, indeed unlawful, action. But [the challenged law] is di-

---

irrelevant to any proper legislative goal. Finally, certain groups, indeed largely the same groups, have historically been "relegated to such a position of political powerlessness as to command extraordinary protection from the majoritarian political process." [Carolene Products.] [Legislation] imposing special disabilities upon groups disfavored by virtue of circumstances beyond their control suggests the kind of "class or caste" treatment that the Fourteenth Amendment was designed to abolish.

15. In determining whether a class-based denial of a particular right is deserving of strict scrutiny under the Equal Protection Clause, we look to the Constitution to see if the right infringed has its source, explicitly or implicitly, therein. But we have also recognized the fundamentality of participation in state "elections on an equal basis with other citizens in the jurisdiction," even though "the right to vote, per se, is not a constitutionally protected right." With respect to suffrage, we have explained the need for strict scrutiny as arising from the significance of the franchise as the guardian of all other rights. See [Harper].

16. See [Craig v. Boren and Lalli v. Lalli in Chapter 5, section D2, supra]. This technique of "intermediate" scrutiny permits us to evaluate the rationality of the legislative judgment with reference to well-settled constitutional principles. [Only] when concerns sufficiently absolute and enduring can be clearly ascertained from the Constitution and our cases do we employ this standard to aid us in determining the rationality of the legislative choice.

19. We reject the claim that "illegal aliens" are a "suspect class." No case in which we have attempted to define a suspect class [has] addressed the status of persons unlawfully in our country. Unlike most of the classifications that we have recognized as suspect, entry into this class, by virtue of entry into this country, is the product of voluntary action. Indeed, entry into the class is itself a crime. In addition, it could hardly be suggested that undocumented status is a "constitutional irrelevancy." . . .

rected against children, and imposes its discriminatory burden on the basis of a legal characteristic over which children can have little control. It is thus difficult to conceive of a rational justification for penalizing these children for their presence within the United States. Yet that appears to be precisely the effect of [the law].

Public education is not a "right" granted to individuals by the Constitution. [*Rodriguez.*] But neither is it merely some governmental "benefit" indistinguishable from other forms of social welfare legislation. Both the importance of education in maintaining our basic institutions, and the lasting impact of its deprivation on the life of the child, mark the distinction. ["Some] degree of education is necessary to prepare citizens to participate effectively and intelligently in our open political system if we are to preserve freedom and independence." [In] addition, education provides the basic tools by which individuals might lead economically productive lives to the benefit of us all. In sum, education has a fundamental role in maintaining the fabric of our society. We cannot ignore the significant social costs borne by our Nation when select groups are denied the means to absorb the values and skills upon which our social order rests.

In addition to the pivotal role of education in sustaining our political and cultural heritage, denial of education to some isolated group of children poses an affront to one of the goals of the Equal Protection Clause: the abolition of governmental barriers presenting unreasonable obstacles to advancement on the basis of individual merit. [Illiteracy] is an enduring disability. The inability to read and write will handicap the individual deprived of a basic education each and every day of his life. The inestimable toll of that deprivation on the social, economic, intellectual, and psychological well-being of the individual, and the obstacle it poses to individual achievement, make it most difficult to reconcile [a] status-based denial of basic education with the framework of equality embodied in the Equal Protection Clause.[20] . . .

These well-settled principles allow us to determine the proper level of deference to be afforded [the Texas statute]. Undocumented aliens [are not] a suspect class [and] education [is not] a fundamental [right]. But more is involved in [this case] than the abstract question whether [the Texas statute] discriminates against a suspect class, or whether education is a fundamental right. [The statute] imposes a lifetime hardship on a discrete class of children not accountable for their disabling status. [In] determining the rationality of [the challenged statute], we may appropriately take into account its costs to the Nation and to the innocent children who are its victims. In light of these countervailing costs, the discrimination contained in [the statute] can hardly be considered rational unless it furthers some substantial goal of the State.

---

20. Because the State does not afford noncitizens the right to vote, and may bar noncitizens from participating in activities at the heart of its political community, appellants argue that denial of a basic education to these children is of less significance than the denial to some other group. Whatever the current status of these children, the courts below concluded that many will remain here permanently and that some indeterminate number will eventually become citizens. The fact that many will not is not decisive, even with respect to the importance of education to participation in core political institutions. [In] addition, although a noncitizen "may be barred from full involvement in the political arena, he may play a role — perhaps even a leadership role — in other areas of import to the community." Moreover, the significance of education to our society is not limited to its political and cultural fruits. The public schools are an important socializing institution, imparting those shared values through which social order and stability are maintained.

It is the State's principal argument [that] the undocumented status of these children vel non establishes a sufficient rational basis for denying them benefits that a State might choose to afford other residents. The State notes that while other aliens are admitted "on an equality of legal privileges with all citizens under non-discriminatory laws," the asserted right of these children to an education can claim no implicit congressional imprimatur.[21] Indeed, in the State's view, Congress' apparent disapproval of the presence of these children within the United States [provides] authority for its decision to impose upon them special disabilities. Faced with an equal protection challenge respecting the treatment of aliens, we agree that the courts must be attentive to congressional policy; [but] we are unable to find in the congressional immigration scheme any statement of policy that might weigh significantly in arriving at an equal protection balance concerning the State's authority to deprive these children of an education.

Congress has developed a complex scheme governing admission to our Nation and status within our borders. The obvious need for delicate policy judgments has counseled the Judicial Branch to avoid intrusion into this field. But this traditional caution does not persuade us that unusual deference must be shown the [challenged classification]. The States enjoy no power with respect to the classification of aliens. This power is "committed to the political branches of the Federal Government." [And although] the States do have some authority to act with respect to illegal aliens, at least where such action mirrors federal objectives and furthers a legitimate state [goal], there is no indication that the disability imposed by [the challenged law] corresponds to any identifiable congressional policy. . . .

To be sure, like all persons who have entered the United States unlawfully, these children are subject to deportation. But there is no assurance that a child subject to deportation will ever be deported. [We] are reluctant to impute to Congress the intention to withhold from these children, for so long as they are present in this country through no fault of their own, access to a basic education. In other contexts, undocumented status, coupled with some articulable federal policy, might enhance state authority with respect to the treatment of undocumented aliens. But in the area of special constitutional sensitivity presented by these cases, and in the absence of any contrary indication fairly discernible in the present legislative record, we perceive no national policy that supports the State in denying these children an elementary education. . . .

[The State argues further] that the classification at issue furthers an interest in the "preservation of the state's limited resources for the education of its lawful residents." [But the] State must do more than justify its classification with a concise expression of an intention to discriminate. [We] discern three colorable state interests that might support [the classification].

First, [the State suggests that it may] protect itself from an influx of illegal immigrants. [But there] is no evidence in the record suggesting that illegal entrants impose any significant burden on the State's economy. To the contrary, the

21. If the constitutional guarantee of equal protection was available only to those upon whom Congress affirmatively granted its benefit, the State's argument would be virtually unanswerable. But the Equal Protection Clause operates of its own force to protect anyone "within [the State's] jurisdiction" from the State's arbitrary action. The question we examine in text is whether the federal *disapproval* of the presence of these children assists the State in overcoming the presumption that denial of education to innocent children is not a rational response to legitimate state concerns.

available evidence suggests that illegal aliens underutilize public services, while contributing their labor to the local economy and tax money to the state fisc. The dominant incentive for illegal entry into the State of Texas is the availability of employment; few if any illegal immigrants come [in] order to avail themselves of a free education. Thus, even making the doubtful assumption that the net impact of illegal aliens on the economy of the State is negative, we think it clear that "[c]harging tuition to undocumented children constitutes a ludicrously ineffectual attempt to stem the tide of illegal immigration," at least when compared with the alternative of prohibiting the employment of illegal aliens.

Second, [the State suggests] that undocumented children are appropriately singled out for exclusion because of the special burdens they impose on the State's ability to provide high-quality public education. But the record in no way supports the claim that exclusion of undocumented children is likely to improve the overall quality of education in the State. [Moreover], even if improvement in the quality of education were a likely result of barring some *number* of children from the schools of the State, the State must support its selection of *this* group as the appropriate target for exclusion. In terms of educational cost and need, however, undocumented children are "basically indistinguishable" from legally resident alien children.

Finally, [the State suggests] that undocumented children are appropriately singled out because their unlawful presence within the United States renders them less likely than other children to remain within the [State], and to put their education to productive social or political use within the State. Even assuming that such an interest is legitimate, it is an interest that is most difficult to quantify. The State has no assurance that any child, citizen or not, will employ the education provided by the State within the confines of the State's borders. In any event, the record is clear that many of the undocumented children disabled by this classification will remain in this country indefinitely, and that some will become lawful residents or citizens of the United States. It is difficult to understand precisely what the State hopes to achieve by promoting the creation and perpetuation of a subclass of illiterates within our boundaries, surely adding to the problems and costs of unemployment, welfare, and crime. It is thus clear that whatever savings might be achieved by denying these children an education, they are wholly insubstantial in light of the costs involved to these children, the State, and the Nation.

If the State is to deny a discrete group of innocent children the free public education that it offers to other children residing within its borders, that denial must be justified by a showing that it furthers some substantial state interest. No such showing was made here. . . .

Affirmed.

JUSTICE MARSHALL, concurring.

While I join the Court opinion, I do so without in any way retreating from my opinion in [*Rodriguez*]. I continue to believe that an individual's interest in education is fundamental. [Furthermore], I believe that the facts of [this case] demonstrate the wisdom of rejecting a rigidified approach to equal protection analysis, and of employing an approach that allows for varying levels of scrutiny depending upon "the constitutional and societal importance of the interest adversely affected and the recognized invidiousness of the [classification]."

JUSTICE BLACKMUN, concurring.

I join the opinion and judgment of the Court.

Like Justice Powell, I believe that the children involved in this litigation "should not be left on the streets uneducated." I write separately, however, because in my view the nature of the interest at stake is crucial to the proper resolution of these cases.

[The] Court in *Rodriguez* [articulated] a firm rule: fundamental rights are those that "explicitly or implicitly [are] guaranteed by the Constitution." It therefore squarely rejected the notion that "an ad hoc determination as to the social or economic importance" of a given interest is relevant to the level of scrutiny accorded classifications involving that interest, and made clear that "[i]t is not the province of this Court to create substantive constitutional rights in the name of guaranteeing equal protection of the laws."

[I] continue to believe that [*Rodriguez*] provides the appropriate model for resolving most equal protection disputes. [But] experience has demonstrated that the [*Rodriguez*] formulation does not settle every issue of "fundamental rights" arising under the Equal Protection Clause. Only a pedant would insist that there are *no* meaningful distinctions among the multitude of social and political interests regulated by the States, and *Rodriguez* does not stand for quite so absolute a proposition. To the contrary, *Rodriguez* implicitly acknowledged that certain interests [like the right to vote], though not constitutionally guaranteed, must be accorded a special place in equal protection analysis. [It] is arguable, of course, that the Court never should have [gone that far, but] it is too late to debate that point. . . .

In my view, when the State provides an education to some and denies it to others, it immediately and inevitably creates class distinctions of a type fundamentally inconsistent with [the purposes] of the Equal Protection Clause. Children denied an education are placed at a permanent and insurmountable competitive disadvantage, for an uneducated child is denied even the opportunity to achieve. And when those children are members of an identifiable group, that group — through the State's action — will have been converted into a discrete underclass. Other benefits provided by the State, such as housing and public assistance, are of course important; to an individual in immediate need, they may be more desirable than the right to be educated. But classifications involving the complete denial of education are in a sense unique, for they strike at the heart of equal protection values by involving the State in the creation of permanent class distinctions. In a sense, then, denial of an education is the analogue of denial of the right to vote: the former relegates the individual to second-class social status; the latter places him at a permanent political disadvantage.

This conclusion is fully consistent with *Rodriguez*, [for the] Court there reserved judgment on the constitutionality of a state system that "occasioned an absolute denial of educational opportunities to any of its children." . . .

JUSTICE POWELL, concurring.

I join the opinion of the Court, and write separately to emphasize the unique character of the [case] before us. . . .

Although the analogy is not perfect, our holding today does find support in decisions of this Court with respect to the status of illegitimates. [In this case],

Texas effectively denies to the school-age children of illegal aliens the opportunity to attend the free public schools that the State makes available to all residents. They are excluded only because of a status resulting from the violation by parents or guardians of our immigration laws and the fact that they remain in our country unlawfully. The appellee children are innocent in this respect. They can "affect neither their parents' conduct nor their own status." [Trimble v. Gordon.]

Our review in a case such as [this] is properly heightened.[2] Cf. [Craig v. Boren]. The classification at issue deprives a group of children of the opportunity for education afforded all other children simply because they have been assigned a legal status due to a violation of law by their parents. These children thus have been singled out for a lifelong penalty and stigma. A legislative classification that threatens the creation of an underclass of future citizens and residents cannot be reconciled with one of the fundamental purposes of the Fourteenth Amendment. In these unique circumstances, the Court properly may require that the State's interests be substantial and that the means bear a "fair and substantial relation" to these interests.[3] . . .

CHIEF JUSTICE BURGER, with whom JUSTICE WHITE, JUSTICE REHNQUIST, and JUSTICE O'CONNOR join, dissenting.

Were it our business to set the Nation's social policy, I would agree without hesitation that it is senseless for an enlightened society to deprive any children — including illegal aliens — of an elementary education. I fully agree that it would be folly — and wrong — to tolerate creation of a segment of society made up of illiterate persons, many having a limited or no command of our language. However, the Constitution does not constitute us as "Platonic Guardians" nor does it vest in this Court the authority to strike down laws because they do not meet our standards of desirable social policy, "wisdom," or "common sense." . . .

[The] Court expressly — and correctly — rejects any suggestion that illegal aliens are a suspect class, or that education is a fundamental right. Yet by patching together bits and pieces of what might be termed quasi-suspect-class and quasi-fundamental-rights analysis, the Court spins out a theory custom-tailored to the facts of [this case]. If ever a court was guilty of an unabashedly result-oriented approach, this case is a prime example.

The Court first suggests that these illegal alien children, although not a suspect class, are entitled to special solicitude under the Equal Protection Clause because they lack "control" over or "responsibility" for their unlawful entry into this country. Similarly, the Court appears to take the position that [the law] is presumptively "irrational" because it has the effect of imposing "penalties" on "inno-

2. I emphasize the Court's conclusion that strict scrutiny is not appropriately applied to this classification. This exacting standard of review has been reserved for instances in which a "fundamental" constitutional right or a "suspect" classification is present. Neither is present in these cases, as the Court holds.

3. The Chief Justice argues [that] this heightened standard of review is inconsistent with [Rodriguez]. But in Rodriguez no group of children was singled out by the State and then penalized because of their parents' status. Rather, funding for education varied across the State because of the tradition of local control. Nor, in that case, was any group of children totally deprived of all education as in these cases. If the resident children of illegal aliens were denied welfare assistance, made available by government to all other children who qualify, this also — in my opinion — would be an impermissible penalizing of children because of their parents' status.

cent" children. However, the Equal Protection Clause does not preclude legislators from classifying among persons on the basis of factors and characteristics over which individuals may be said to lack "control." [A] state legislature is not barred from considering, for example, relevant differences between the mentally healthy and the mentally ill, or between the residents of different counties,[5] simply because these may be factors unrelated to individual choice or to any "wrongdoing." The Equal Protection Clause protects against arbitrary and irrational classifications, and against invidious discrimination stemming from prejudice and hostility; it is not an all-encompassing "equalizer" designed to eradicate every distinction for which persons are not "responsible."

The Court does not presume to suggest that appellees' purported lack of culpability for their illegal status prevents them being deported or otherwise "penalized" under federal law. Yet would deportation be any less a "penalty" than denial of privileges provided to legal residents? [The] Court's analogy to cases involving discrimination against illegitimate children is grossly misleading. The State has not thrust any disabilities upon appellees due to their "status of birth." Rather, appellees' status is predicated upon the circumstances of their concededly illegal presence in this country. . . .

The second strand of the Court's analysis rests on the premise that, although public education is not a constitutionally guaranteed right, "neither is it merely some governmental 'benefit' indistinguishable from other forms of social welfare legislation." [This] opaque observation [has] no bearing on the issues at hand. [The] importance of education is beyond dispute. Yet we have held repeatedly that the importance of a governmental service does not elevate it to the status of a "fundamental right" for purposes of equal protection analysis. Moreover, the Court points to no meaningful way to distinguish between education and other governmental benefits in this context. Is the Court suggesting that education is more "fundamental" than food, shelter, or medical care? [The] Equal Protection Clause [does] not mandate a constitutional hierarchy of governmental services. . . .

Once it is conceded [that] illegal aliens are not a suspect class, and that education is not a fundamental right, our inquiry should focus on and be limited to whether the legislative classification at issue bears a rational relationship to a legitimate state purpose. [*Dandridge.*] [It] simply is not "irrational" for a state to conclude that it does not have the same responsibility to provide benefits for persons whose very presence in the state and this country is illegal as it does to provide for persons lawfully present. [The] Federal Government has seen fit to exclude illegal aliens from numerous social welfare programs, such as the food stamp program, the old-age assistance, aid to families with dependent children, aid to the blind, aid to the permanently and totally disabled, and supplemental security income [programs]. [These] exclusions [support] the rationality of [the challenged statute]. . . .

---

5. Appellees "lack control" over their illegal residence in this country in the same sense as lawfully resident children lack control over the school district in which their parents reside. Yet in [*Rodriguez*] we declined to review under "heightened scrutiny" a claim that a State discriminated against residents of less wealthy school districts in its provision of educational benefits. There was no suggestion in that case that a child's "lack of responsibility" for his residence in a particular school district had any relevance to the proper standard of review of his claims. The result was that children lawfully here but residing in different counties received different treatment.

Note: "Fundamental Interests" and the Equal Protection Clause — A New Direction?

1. Plyler: *a "landmark" or a "sport"?* Consider the following views:

a. Hutchinson, More Substantive Equal Protection? A Note on *Plyler v. Doe*, 1982 Sup. Ct. Rev. 167, 168-169, 191-192:

Justice Brennan's opinion [carries] no hint that the opinion is either a landmark or a sport. [Justice] Marshall's point, lightly made, was that [the] Court had finally adopted [his] "sliding-scale" test. [It] would have been easy enough for Justice Marshall to detail his case, [for no] better summary of the new content of heightened scrutiny could have been found than that in Marshall's dissent in *Dandridge*. [The] importance of *Rodriguez* [was] that it preserved the two-tier model of [equal protection review]. Three years later, however, Craig v. Boren added an intermediate tier — then apparently limited to gender-based [classifications.] Taken together, [*Craig* and *Plyler*] demonstrate that *Rodriguez* is now a constitutional relic whose only significance is its holding; as doctrine, it is irrelevant. [Whatever] the deficiencies of the old two-tier model, it at least provided some predictability and a common ground of discourse. The new three-tier model promises to be nowhere near as predictable, either as to content or result.

b. Tushnet, The Optimist's Tale, 132 U. Pa. L. Rev. 1257, 1263-1264 (1984):

Justice Brennan's opinion [is] analytically indefensible. It jams together doctrines that other cases carefully held [apart]. But its very awkwardness reveals much about what Justice Brennan was really doing: not writing a carefully crafted opinion, [but] building a coalition. [According to this view, Justices Brennan and Marshall were prepared to invalidate the statute because it] embodies a dreadfully unwise social policy. [The problem was how] to get three more votes. [Justice Brennan knew that Justice Blackmun] thinks that it's not a nice thing to penalize kids for their parents' actions, [so he stressed the] analogy to illegitimacy. [He knew that] Justice Powell knows, from Virginia's experience during the period of massive resistance to desegregation, the severity of the social costs of wholesale denials of education, [so he stressed that the case] involves absolute deprivations of education. [And because] Justice Stevens has this bizarre attraction to the idea that equal protection cases involving state regulation affecting aliens are rather like preemption cases, [he stressed] the primary responsibility of the national government for regulating aliens.

2. *The limits of* Plyler. In Martinez v. Bynum, 461 U.S. 321 (1983), the Court upheld a Texas statute that authorized local school districts to deny tuition-free admission to public schools to minors who live apart from their parents or guardians and whose presence in the district is "for the primary purpose of attending the public free schools." Justice Powell wrote the opinion of the Court:

[The challenged bona fide residence] requirement implicates no "suspect" classification; [it] does not burden or penalize the constitutional right of interstate travel, for any person is free to move to [the] State and to establish residence there; [and] the "service" [denied] to nonresidents is not a fundamental right protected by the Constitution. [Citing *Plyler*.] [Moreover, as a bona fide residence requirement, the challenged statute furthers] the substantial state interest in assuring that [educational] services provided for its residents are enjoyed only by residents. [The requirement thus] satisfies constitutional standards.

Justice Marshall dissented. Is *Martinez* consistent with *Plyler?*

3. *"Fundamental" interests and the equal protection clause: concluding thoughts.* How would you characterize "fundamental" interest equal protection: As a necessary and proper interpretation of the fourteenth amendment? As an illegitimate exercise of raw judicial power? As the effort of conscientious Justices to interpret an ambiguous constitutional provision while maintaining at least minimal standards of decency and common sense?

Consider Justice Rehnquist's evaluation:

> The relationship of [the] "fundamental personal right" analysis to the constitutional guarantee of equal protection of the law is approximately the same as that of "freedom of contract" to the constitutional guarantee that no person shall be deprived of life, liberty, or property without due process of law. It is an invitation for judicial exegesis over and above the commands of the Constitution, in which values that cannot possibly have their source in that instrument are invoked to either validate or condemn the countless laws enacted by the various States.

Weber v. Aetna Casualty & Surety Co., 406 U.S. 164, 182 (1972) (Rehnquist, J., dissenting).

F. "MODERN" SUBSTANTIVE DUE PROCESS: PRIVACY, PERSONHOOD, AND FAMILY

Although the Court employed substantive due process in the *Lochner* era primarily in the realm of economic regulation and the liberty of contract, not all of its decisions were so limited. In Meyer v. Nebraska, 262 U.S. 390 (1923), for example, the Court invalidated a state law prohibiting the teaching of any modern language other than English in any public or private grammar school. The Court explained:

> [The "liberty" guaranteed by the due process clause of the fourteenth amendment] denotes not merely freedom from bodily restraint but also the right of the individual to contract, to engage in any of the common occupations of life, to acquire useful knowledge, to marry, establish a home and bring up children, to worship God according to the dictates of his own conscience, and generally to enjoy those privileges long recognized at common law as essential to the orderly pursuit of happiness by free men. [This] liberty may not be interfered with [by] legislative action which is arbitrary or without reasonable relation to some purpose within the competency of the state to effect. [That] the State may do much [to] improve the quality of its citizens [is] clear; but the individual has certain fundamental rights which must be respected. [Here, no] emergency has arisen which renders knowledge of a child of some language other than English so clearly harmful as to justify [its] infringement of the right long freely enjoyed.

Justice Holmes, joined by Justice Sutherland, dissented. Similarly, in Pierce v. Society of Sisters, 268 U.S. 510 (1925), the Court invalidated a state statute requiring students to attend public rather than private schools. The Court held that the statute "unreasonably [interfered] with the liberty of parents and guardians to direct the upbringing and education of children under their control."

Did the demise of *Lochner* implicitly mark the end of the *Meyers/Pierce* line of authority? Or is the real "objection to [*Lochner*] that it generally selected the 'wrong' values for protection"? Lupu, Untangling the Strands of the Fourteenth Amendment, 77 Mich. L. Rev. 981, 989 (1979). Consider the gradual reemergence of the *Meyers/Pierce* branch of substantive due process.

1. The Right of Privacy

Griswold v. Connecticut

381 U.S. 479 (1965)

MR. JUSTICE DOUGLAS delivered the opinion of the Court.

Appellant Griswold is Executive Director of the Planned Parenthood League of Connecticut. Appellant Buxton is a licensed physician and a professor at the Yale Medical School who served as Medical Director for the League. . . .

They gave information, instruction, and medical advice to *married persons* as to the means of preventing conception. [Fees] were usually charged, although some couples were serviced free.

[A Connecticut statute prohibits any person to use "any drug, medicinal article or instrument for the purpose of preventing conception."]

The appellants were found guilty as accessories and fined $100 each, against the claim that the accessory statute as so applied violated the Fourteenth Amendment. . . .

We think that appellants have standing to raise the constitutional rights of the married people with whom they had a professional relationship. [Certainly] the accessory should have standing to assert that the offense which he is charged with assisting is not, or cannot constitutionally be, a crime. . . .

Coming to the merits, we are met with a wide range of questions that implicate the Due Process Clause of the Fourteenth Amendment. Overtones of some arguments suggest that [*Lochner*] should be our guide. But we decline that invitation as we did in [West Coast Hotel Co. v. Parrish, and Williamson v. Lee Optical Co., supra section D]. We do not sit as a super-legislature to determine the wisdom, need, and propriety of laws that touch economic problems, business affairs, or social conditions. This law, however, operates directly on an intimate relation of husband and wife and their physician's role in one aspect of that relation.

The association of people is not mentioned in the Constitution nor in the Bill of Rights. The right to educate a child in a school of the parents' choice — whether public or private or parochial — is also not mentioned. Nor is the right to study any particular subject or any foreign language. Yet the First Amendment has been construed to include certain of those rights. [As Pierce v. Society of Sisters, Meyer v. Nebraska, and other decisions suggest, the] right of freedom of speech and press includes not only the right to utter or to print, but the right to distribute, the right to receive, the right to read and freedom of inquiry, freedom of thought, and freedom to teach — indeed the freedom of the entire university community. Without those peripheral rights the specific rights would be less secure. And so we reaffirm the principle of the *Pierce* and the *Meyer* cases.

In NAACP v. Alabama, [infra Chapter 7, section F5], we protected the "freedom to associate and privacy in one's associations," noting that freedom of association was a peripheral First Amendment right. Disclosure of membership lists of a constitutionally valid association, we held, was invalid. [In] other words, the First Amendment has a penumbra where privacy is protected from governmental intrusion. In like context, we have protected forms of "association" that are not political in the customary sense but pertain to the social, legal, and economic benefit of the members. NAACP v. Button, [infra Chapter 7, section E5]. [While association] is not expressly included in the First Amendment its existence is necessary in making the express guarantees fully meaningful.

The foregoing cases suggest that specific guarantees in the Bill of Rights have penumbras, formed by emanations from those guarantees that help give them life and substance. See Poe v. Ullman, 367 U.S. 497, 516-522 [Douglas, J., dissenting]. Various guarantees create zones of privacy. The right of association contained in the penumbra of the First Amendment is one, as we have seen. The Third Amendment in its prohibition against the quartering of soldiers "in any house" in time of peace without the consent of the owner is another facet of that privacy. The Fourth Amendment explicitly affirms the "right of the people to be secure in their persons, houses, papers, and effects, against unreasonable searches and seizures." The Fifth Amendment in its Self-Incrimination Clause enables the citizen to create a zone of privacy which government may not force him to surrender to his detriment. The Ninth Amendment provides: "The enumeration in the Constitution, of certain rights, shall not be construed to deny or disparage others retained by the people."

The Fourth and Fifth Amendments were described in Boyd v. United States, 116 U.S. 616, 630, as protection against all governmental invasions "of the sanctity of a man's home and the privacies of life." We recently referred in Mapp v. Ohio, 367 U.S. 643, 656, to the Fourth Amendment as creating a "right to privacy, no less important than any other right carefully and particularly reserved to the people."

We have had many controversies over these penumbral rights of "privacy and repose." [Skinner v. Oklahoma and other] cases bear witness that the right of privacy which presses for recognition here is a legitimate one.

The present case, then, concerns a relationship lying within the zone of privacy created by several fundamental constitutional guarantees. And it concerns a law which, in forbidding the *use* of contraceptives rather than regulating their manufacture or sale, seeks to achieve its goals by means having a maximum destructive impact upon that relationship. Such a law cannot stand in light of the familiar principle, so often applied by this Court, that a "governmental purpose to control or prevent activities constitutionally subject to state regulation may not be achieved by means which sweep unnecessarily broadly and thereby invade the area of protected freedoms." [NAACP v. Alabama.] Would we allow the police to search the sacred precincts of marital bedrooms for telltale signs of the use of contraceptives? The very idea is repulsive to the notions of privacy surrounding the marriage relationship.

We deal with a right of privacy older than the Bill of Rights. [Marriage] is a coming together for better or for worse, hopefully enduring, and intimate to the degree of being sacred. It is an association that promotes a way of life, not causes; a harmony in living, not political faiths; a bilateral loyalty, not commercial or social projects. Yet it is an association for as noble a purpose as any involved in our prior decisions.

Reversed.

MR. JUSTICE GOLDBERG, whom THE CHIEF JUSTICE and MR. JUSTICE BRENNAN join, concurring.

I [join the Court's opinion]. Although I have not accepted the view that "due process" as used in the Fourteenth Amendment incorporates all of the first eight Amendments, [I] do agree that the concept of liberty protects those personal rights that are fundamental, and is not confined to the specific terms of the Bill of Rights. My conclusion that the concept of liberty [embraces] the right of marital privacy though that right is not mentioned explicitly in the Constitution is supported both by numerous decisions of this Court, referred to in the Court's opinion, and by the language and history of the Ninth Amendment [which] reveal that the Framers of the Constitution believed that there are additional fundamental rights, protected from governmental infringement. . . .

The Ninth Amendment [was] proffered to quiet expressed fears that a bill of specifically enumerated rights could not be sufficiently broad to cover all essential rights and that the specific mention of certain rights would be interpreted as a denial that others were protected. . . .

While this Court has had little occasion to interpret the Ninth Amendment,[6] "[i]t cannot be presumed that any clause in the constitution is intended to be without effect." [To] hold that a right so basic and fundamental and so deep-rooted in our society as the right of privacy in marriage may be infringed because that right is not guaranteed in so many words by the first eight amendments to the Constitution is to ignore the Ninth Amendment and to give it no effect whatsoever. . . .

I do not mean to imply that the Ninth Amendment is applied against the States by the Fourteenth. [Rather,] the Ninth Amendment [simply] lends strong support to the view that the "liberty" protected by the Fifth and Fourteenth Amendments from infringement by the Federal Government or the States is not restricted to rights specifically mentioned in the first eight amendments. . . .

In determining which rights are fundamental, judges are not left at large to decide cases in light of their personal and private notions. Rather, they must look to the "traditions and [collective] conscience of our people" to determine whether a principle is "so rooted [there] . . . as to be ranked as fundamental." The inquiry is whether a right involved "is of such a character that it cannot be denied without violating those 'fundamental principles of liberty and justice which lie at the base of all our civil and political institutions.' . . ."

The entire fabric of the Constitution and the purposes that clearly underlie its specific guarantees demonstrate that the rights to marital privacy and to marry and raise a family are of similar order and magnitude as the fundamental rights specifically protected.

6. This Amendment has been referred to as "The Forgotten Ninth Amendment," in a book with that title by Bennett B. Patterson (1955). . . .

Although the Constitution does not speak in so many words of the right of privacy in marriage, I cannot believe that it offers these fundamental rights no protection. The fact that no particular provision of the Constitution explicitly forbids the State from disrupting the traditional relation of the family — a relation as old and as fundamental as our entire civilization — surely does not show that the Government was meant to have the power to do so. . . .

The logic of the dissents would sanction federal or state legislation that seems to me even more plainly unconstitutional than the statute before us. Surely the Government, absent a showing of a compelling subordinating state interest, could not decree that all husbands and wives must be sterilized after two children have been born to them. Yet by their reasoning such an invasion of marital privacy would not be subject to constitutional challenge because, while it might be "silly," no provision of the Constitution specifically prevents the Government from curtailing the marital right to bear children and raise a family. . . .

In a long series of cases this Court has held that where fundamental personal liberties are involved, they may not be abridged by the States simply on a showing that a regulatory statute has some rational relationship to the effectuation of a proper state purpose. "Where there is a significant encroachment upon personal liberty, the State may prevail only upon showing a subordinating interest which is compelling." The law must be shown "necessary, and not merely rationally related, to the accomplishment of a permissible state policy."

[The] State, at most, argues that there is some rational relation between this statute and what is admittedly a legitimate subject of state concern — the discouraging of extra-marital relations. It says that preventing the use of birth-control devices by married persons helps prevent the indulgence by some in such extra-marital relations. The rationality of this justification is dubious, particularly in light of the admitted widespread availability to all persons [in] Connecticut, unmarried as well as married, of birth-control devices for the prevention of disease, as distinguished from the prevention of conception. But, in any event, it is clear that the state interest in safeguarding marital fidelity can be served by a more discriminately tailored statute, which does not, like the present one, sweep unnecessarily broadly, reaching far beyond the evil sought to be dealt with and intruding upon the privacy of all married couples. [Connecticut] does have statutes, the constitutionality of which is beyond doubt, which prohibit adultery and fornication. These statutes demonstrate that means for achieving the same basic purpose of protecting marital fidelity are available to Connecticut without the need to "invade the area of protected freedoms." . . .

In sum, I believe that the right of privacy in the marital relation is fundamental and basic — a personal right "retained by the people" within the meaning of the Ninth Amendment. Connecticut cannot constitutionally abridge this fundamental right, which is protected by the Fourteenth Amendment from infringement by the States. . . .

Mr. Justice Harlan, concurring in the judgment.

[I] fully agree with the judgment of reversal, but [cannot] join the Court's opinion [because it evinces the view that] the Due Process Clause of the Fourteenth Amendment does not touch this Connecticut statute unless the enactment is found to violate some right assured by the letter or penumbra of the Bill of Rights. . . .

In my view, the proper constitutional inquiry in this case is whether this Connecticut statute infringes the Due Process Clause of the Fourteenth Amendment because the enactment violates basic values "implicit in the concept of ordered liberty," [Palko v. Connecticut]. For reasons stated at length in my dissenting opinion in Poe v. Ullman, [367 U.S. 497 (1961)], I believe that it does. While the relevant inquiry may be aided by resort to one or more of the provisions of the Bill of Rights, it is not dependent on them or any of their radiations. The Due Process Clause of the Fourteenth Amendment stands, in my opinion, on its own bottom. . . .

While I could not more heartily agree that judicial "self restraint" is an indispensable ingredient of sound constitutional adjudication, I do submit that the formula suggested [by the dissenters] for achieving it is more hollow than real. "Specific" provisions of the Constitution, no less than "due process," lend themselves as readily to "personal" interpretations by judges whose constitutional outlook is simply to keep the Constitution in supposed "tune with the times." . . .

Judicial self-restraint will not, I suggest, be brought about in the "due process" area by the historically unfounded incorporation formula long advanced by my Brother Black. It will be achieved in this area, as in other constitutional areas, only by continual insistence upon respect for the teachings of history, solid recognition of the basic values that underlie our society, and wise appreciation of the great roles that the doctrines of federalism and separation of powers have played in establishing and preserving American freedoms. . . .

[Justice Harlan dissented in Poe v. Ullman, in which the Court dismissed on justiciability grounds a challenge to the Connecticut statute invalidated in *Griswold*. Harlan argued:]

[I] believe that a statute making it a criminal offense for *married couples* to use contraceptives is an intolerable and unjustifiable invasion of privacy in the conduct of the most intimate concerns of an individual's personal life. [Since this contention draws its] basis from no explicit language of the Constitution, [I] feel it desirable [to] state the framework of Constitutional principles in which I think the issue must be judged.

[Because] it is the Constitution alone which warrants judicial interference in sovereign operations of the State, the basis of judgment as to the Constitutionality of state action must be a rational one, approaching the text [not] in a literalistic way, as if we had a tax statute before us, but as the basic charter of our society, setting out in spare but meaningful terms the principles of government. . . .

It is but a truism to say that [the Due Process Clause] is not self-explanatory. [It] is important to note, however, that two views of the [Fourteenth] Amendment have not been accepted. . . . One view [sought] to limit the provision to a guarantee of procedural fairness. [The] other [would] have it that the Fourteenth Amendment, whether by way of the Privileges and Immunities Clause or the Due Process Clause, applied against the States only and precisely those restraints which [are embodied in the Bill of Rights]. However, "due process" in the consistent view of this Court has ever been a broader concept than the first view and more flexible than the second. . . .

[It] is not the particular enumeration of rights in the first eight Amendments which spells out the reach of Fourteenth Amendment due process, but rather, as was suggested in another context long before the adoption of that Amendment, those concepts which are considered to embrace those rights "which are . . .

fundamental; which belong . . . to the citizens of all free governments," [Corfield v. Coryell], for "the purposes [of securing] which men enter into society," [Calder v. Bull]. . . .

Due process has not been reduced to any formula; its content cannot be determined by reference to any code. The best that can be said is that through the course of this Court's decisions it has represented the balance which our Nation, built upon postulates of respect for the liberty of the individual, has struck between that liberty and the demands of organized society. If the supplying of content to this Constitutional concept has of necessity been a rational process, it certainly has not been one where judges have felt free to roam where unguided speculation might take them. The balance of which I speak is the balance struck by this country, having regard to what history teaches are the traditions from which it developed as well as the traditions from which it broke. That tradition is a living thing. . . .

[The] liberty guaranteed by the Due Process Clause [is] not a series of isolated points [represented by the Bill of Rights]. It is a rational continuum which, broadly speaking, includes a freedom from all substantial arbitrary impositions and purposeless restraints, [citing, e.g., Allgeyer v. Louisiana, Skinner v. Oklahoma], and which also recognizes, what a reasonable and sensitive judgment must, that certain interests require particularly careful scrutiny of the state needs asserted to justify their abridgment. . . .

The State [asserts] that it is acting to protect the moral welfare of its citizenry. [Society] has traditionally concerned itself with the moral soundness of its people. [Certainly,] Connecticut's judgment [here] is no more demonstrably correct or incorrect than are the varieties of judgment, expressed in law, on marriage and divorce, on adult consensual homosexuality, abortion, and sterilization, or euthanasia and suicide. If we had a case before us which required us to decide simply, and in abstraction, whether the moral judgment implicit in the [present statute] was a sound one, the very controversial nature of these questions would, I think, require us to hesitate long before concluding that the Constitution precluded Connecticut from choosing as it has. . . .

But, as might be expected, we are not presented simply with this moral judgment to be passed on as an abstract proposition. The secular state [must] operate in the realm of behavior, [and] where it does so operate, not only the underlying, moral purpose of its operations, but also the *choice of means* becomes relevant to any Constitutional judgment on what is done. . . .

Precisely what is involved here is this: the State is asserting the right to enforce its moral judgment by intruding upon the most intimate details of the marital relation with the full power of the criminal law. Potentially, this could allow the deployment of all the incidental machinery of the criminal law, arrests, searches and seizures; inevitably, it must mean at the very least the lodging of criminal charges, a public trial, and testimony as the corpus delicti. [The] statute allows the State to enquire into, prove and punish married people for the private use of their marital intimacy.

[This] enactment involves what, by common understanding throughout the English-speaking world, must be granted to be a most fundamental aspect of "liberty," the privacy of the home in its most basic sense, and it is this which requires that the statute be subjected to "strict scrutiny." [Skinner v. Oklahoma.]

That aspect of liberty which embraces the concept of the privacy of the home receives explicit Constitutional protection at two places only. These are the Third [and Fourth Amendments]. . . .

It is clear, of course, that this Connecticut statute does not invade the privacy of the home in the usual sense, since the invasion involved here may [be] accomplished without any physical intrusion [into] the home. [But it] would surely be an extreme instance of sacrificing substance to form were it to be held that the Constitutional principle of privacy against arbitrary official intrusion comprehends only physical invasions by the police. [If] the physical curtilage of the home is protected, it is surely as a result of solicitude to protect the privacies of the life within. Certainly the safeguarding of the home does not follow merely from the sanctity of property rights. The home derives its pre-eminence as the seat of family life. [Of the] whole "private realm of family life" it is difficult to imagine what is more private or more intimate than a husband and wife's marital relations. . . .

Of course, [there] are countervailing considerations. "[T]he family . . . is not beyond regulation," and it would be an absurdity to suggest either that offenses may not be committed in the bosom of the family or that the home can be made a sanctuary for crime. The right of privacy [is] not an absolute. Thus, I would not suggest that adultery, homosexuality, fornication and incest are immune from criminal enquiry, however privately practiced. [But] not to discriminate between what is involved in this case and either the traditional offenses against good morals or crimes which, though they may be committed anywhere, happen to have been committed or concealed in the home, would entirely misconceive the argument that is being made.

[The] intimacy of husband and wife is necessarily an essential and accepted feature of the institution of marriage, an institution which the State not only must allow, but which always and in every age it has fostered and protected. It is one thing when the State exerts its power either to forbid extra-marital sexuality altogether, or to say who may marry, but it is quite another when, having acknowledged a marriage and the intimacies inherent in it, it undertakes to regulate by means of the criminal law the details of that intimacy. . . .

[Since,] as it appears to me, the statute marks an abridgment of important fundamental liberties protected by the Fourteenth Amendment, it will not do to urge [that it] is rationally related to the effectuation of a proper state purpose. A closer scrutiny and stronger justification than that are required.

[Though] the State has argued the Constitutional permissibility of the moral judgment underlying this statute, [it does not] even remotely [suggest] a justification for the obnoxiously intrusive means it has chosen to effectuate that policy. To me the very circumstance that Connecticut has not chosen to press the enforcement of this statute against individual users [conduces] to the inference either that it does not consider the policy of the statute a very important one, or that it does not regard the means it has chosen for its effectuation as appropriate or necessary.

But conclusive, in my view, is the utter novelty of this enactment. Although the Federal Government and many States have at one time or other had on their books statutes forbidding or regulating the distribution of contraceptives, none, so far as I can find, has made the *use* of contraceptives a crime. . . .

MR. JUSTICE WHITE, concurring in the judgment.

[This] is not the first time this Court has had occasion to articulate that the liberty entitled to protection under the Fourteenth Amendment includes the right "to marry, establish a home and bring up children," [Meyer v. Nebraska], and "the liberty . . . to direct the upbringing and education of children," [Pierce v. Society of Sisters], and that these are among "the basic civil rights of man." [*Skinner.*] These decisions affirm that there is a "realm of family life which the state cannot enter" without substantial justification. Surely the right invoked in this case, to be free of regulation of the intimacies of the marriage relationship, "come[s] to this Court with a momentum for respect lacking when appeal is made to liberties which derive merely from shifting economic arrangements." . . .

[The] State claims [that] its anti-use statute [serves its] policy against all forms of promiscuous or illicit sexual relationships, be they premarital or extramarital, concededly a permissible and legitimate legislative goal. [But I] fail to see how the ban on the use of contraceptives by married couples in any way reinforces the State's ban on illicit sexual relationships. [Perhaps] the theory is that the flat ban on use prevents married people from possessing contraceptives and without the ready availability of such devices for use in the marital relationship, there will be no or less temptation to use them in extramarital ones. This reasoning rests on the premise that married people will comply with the ban in regard to their marital relationship, notwithstanding total nonenforcement in this context and apparent nonenforcibility, but will not comply with criminal statutes prohibiting extramarital affairs and the anti-use statute in respect to illicit sexual relationships, a premise whose validity has not been demonstrated and whose intrinsic validity is not very evident. [I] find nothing in this record justifying the sweeping scope of this statute. . . .

MR. JUSTICE BLACK, with whom MR. JUSTICE STEWART joins, dissenting. . . .

The Court talks about a constitutional "right of privacy" as though there is some constitutional [provision] forbidding any law ever to be passed which might abridge the "privacy" of individuals. But there is not. There are, of course, guarantees in certain specific constitutional provisions which are designed in part to protect privacy at certain times and places with respect to certain activities. Such, for example, is the Fourth Amendment's guarantee against "unreasonable searches and seizures." But I think it belittles that Amendment to talk about it as though it protects nothing but "privacy." [The] average man would very likely not have his feelings soothed any more by having his property seized openly than by having it seized privately and by stealth. [I] get nowhere in this case by talk about a constitutional "right of privacy" as an emanation from one or more constitutional provisions.[1] I like my privacy as well as the next one, but I am nevertheless compelled to admit that government has a right to invade it unless prohibited by some specific constitutional provision. . . .

---

1. The phrase "right to privacy" appears first to have gained currency from an article written by Messrs. Warren and (later Mr. Justice) Brandeis in 1890 which urged that States should give some form of tort relief to persons whose private affairs were exploited by others. The Right to Privacy, 4 Harv. L. Rev. 193. [Today] this Court, which I did not understand to have power to sit as a court of common law, now appears to be exalting a phrase which Warren and Brandeis used in discussing grounds for tort relief, to the level of a constitutional rule which prevents state legislatures from passing any law deemed by this Court to interfere with "privacy."

I discuss the due process and Ninth Amendment arguments together because on analysis they turn out to be the same thing — merely using different words to claim for this Court and the federal judiciary power to invalidate any legislative act which the judges find irrational, unreasonable or offensive. [If] these formulas based on "natural justice" [are] to prevail, they require judges to determine what is or is not constitutional on the basis of their own appraisal of what laws are unwise or unnecessary. The power to make such decisions is [that] of a legislative body. [No] provision of the Constitution specifically gives such blanket power to courts. . . .

Of the cases on which my Brothers White and Goldberg rely so heavily, undoubtedly the reasoning of two of them supports their result here — as would that of a number of others which they do not bother to name, e.g., [*Lochner*]. The two they do cite and quote from, [*Meyer* and *Pierce*], elaborated the same natural law due process philosophy found in [*Lochner*]. [That was a] philosophy which many later opinions repudiated, and which I cannot accept. . . .

My Brother Goldberg has adopted the recent discovery that the Ninth Amendment as well as the Due Process Clause can be used by this Court as authority to strike down all state legislation which this Court thinks violates "fundamental principles of liberty and justice," or is contrary to the "traditions and [collective] conscience of our people." He also states [that] in making decisions on this basis judges will not consider "their personal and private notions." One may ask how they can avoid considering them. Our Court certainly has no machinery with which to take a Gallup Poll. And the scientific miracles of this age have not yet produced a gadget which the Court can use to determine what traditions are rooted in the "[collective] conscience of our people." Moreover, one would certainly have to look far beyond the language of the Ninth Amendment to find that the Framers vested in this Court any such awesome veto powers over lawmaking, either by the States or by the Congress. [That] Amendment was passed [to] assure the people that the Constitution in all its provisions was intended to limit the Federal Government to the powers granted expressly or by necessary implication. [This] fact is perhaps responsible for the peculiar phenomenon that for a period of a century and a half no serious suggestion was ever made that the Ninth Amendment [could] be used as a weapon of federal power to prevent state legislatures from passing laws they consider appropriate to govern local affairs. . . .

I realize that many good and able men have eloquently spoken and written [about] the duty of this Court to keep the Constitution in tune with the times. [For] myself, I must with all deference reject that philosophy. The Constitution makers knew the need for change and provided for it. [The] Due Process Clause with an "arbitrary and capricious" or "shocking to the conscience" formula was liberally used by this Court to strike down economic legislation in the early decades of this century, threatening, many people thought, the tranquility and stability of the Nation. That formula, based on subjective considerations of "natural justice," is no less dangerous when used to enforce this Court's views about personal rights than those about economic rights. . . .

MR. JUSTICE STEWART, whom MR. JUSTICE BLACK joins, dissenting. . . .

I think this is an uncommonly silly law. [But] we are not asked in this case to say whether we think this law is unwise, or even asinine. We are asked to hold that it violates the United States Constitution. And that I cannot do.

In the course of its opinion the Court refers to no less than six Amendments to the Constitution: the First, the Third, the Fourth, the Fifth, the Ninth, and the Fourteenth. But the Court does not say which of these Amendments, if any, it thinks is infringed by this Connecticut law.

We *are* told that the Due Process Clause of the Fourteenth Amendment is not, as such, the "guide" in this case. With that much I agree.

 As to the First, Third, Fourth, and Fifth Amendments, I can find nothing in any of them to invalidate this Connecticut law. [And to] say that the Ninth Amendment has anything to do with this case is to turn somersaults with history. The Ninth Amendment, like its companion the Tenth, [was adopted] to make clear that the adoption of the Bill of Rights did not alter the plan that the *Federal* Government was to be a government of express and limited powers. . . .

What provision of the Constitution, then, does make this state law invalid? The Court says it is the right of privacy "created by several fundamental constitutional guarantees." With all deference, I can find no such general right of privacy in the Bill of Rights, in any other part of the Constitution, or in any case ever before decided by this Court. . . .

Note: Griswold and the Right of Privacy

1. Griswold. Consider the following evaluations:

a. Henkin, Privacy and Autonomy, 74 Colum. L. Rev. 1410, 1421-1422 (1974):

Justice Douglas's argument seems to go something like this: since the Constitution, in various "specifics" of the Bill of Rights and in their penumbra, protects rights which partake of privacy, it protects other aspects of privacy as well, indeed it recognizes a general, complete right of privacy. [A] legal draftsman [might] suggest the opposite: when the Constitution sought to protect private rights it specified them; that it explicitly protects some elements of privacy, but not others, suggests that it did not mean to protect those not mentioned.

b. Kauper, Penumbras, Peripheries, Emanations, Things Fundamental and Things Forgotten: The *Griswold* Case, 64 Mich. L. Rev. 235, 252-253 (1965):

I have no difficulty with [a] theory of implied rights. For example, the right to associate [seems] fairly to be implied from the first amendment. It is another thing, however, to [convert] a freedom from unreasonable police searches into a fundamental substantive right restricting legislative action in formulating social policy. [The] accordion-like qualities of the emanations-and-penumbra theory [become] evident when one considers its application to [other areas. For example], since the body of the Constitution protects against the impairment of the obligations of contracts, it does not require a far-fetched application of [the] theory to suggest that implicit in the contracts clause (or at least radiating from it) is a constitutional right to enter into contracts. [In] extending the specifics to the periphery, [the] Court is [essentially engaging in substantive due process], but dignifying it with a different name and thereby creating the illusion of greater objectivity.

Similarly, one might challenge the Court's analysis on the ground that the Court separated the values underlying the relevant clauses from the means set out in the

Constitution for promoting those values. But the values and the means cannot be separated; if the values are taken independently, and used as a basis for prohibiting additional "means," the Constitution is infinitely expandable.

c. Henkin, supra, at 1427:

> In a constitutional system in which limitations on government [are] a crucial characteristic, it is surely desirable [that] the limitations be reexamined and renovated in the light of changing philosophies of both public good and individual right. Formal amendment of our Constitution, however, [is] difficult [and] divisive. [We] have [therefore] come to [accept] constitutional modernization by the judiciary. But we try to insist that adaptations be congenial to the spirit of the Constitution, and that the Court nod more rather than less seriously to the sacred word, to its history, and to the now-traditional processes of judicial shaping of it. [Griswold] does [not] exceed the bounds of proper judicial innovation.

d. Richards, Interpretation and Historiography, 56 S. Cal. L. Rev. 490, 543-545 (1985):

> [The] maintenance of a continuous yet vital constitutional tradition [has] required the Supreme Court to interpret relevant constitutional text in terms of abstract background rights (equal liberties of religion and speech, equal treatment, cruel and unusual punishment, etc.). Continuity is insured by the common appeal to an abstract [intention]; vitality is insured by the Court's duty reasonably to articulate changes in the scope of application of the common concept in light of each generation's [experience] about what should count as basic liberties of the person, or the demands of equality, or unjustly disproportionate punishment. The constitutional right to privacy was elaborated by the Supreme Court consistent with this traditional [approach]. There is a powerful historical argument [that] the generation who drafted [the] Constitution and Bill of Rights thought of these documents as protecting not only enumerated rights, but unenumerated basic human rights as well. [There] can be little doubt that one such assumed basic human right was the natural right to marriage. Furthermore, there is quite good historical reason [to] suppose that this right was thought of as one nonexclusive example of a more abstract background right of voluntary association. [Thus], the Court has properly elaborated a right to constitutional privacy originated [in] the right to marriage, historically understood as one central example of the more abstract right to association.

Recall the general discussion of interpretivism and noninterpretivism in section A, supra.

2. *The ninth amendment.* Consider the following views:

a. J. Ely, Democracy and Distrust 34-38 (1980):

> The received account of the Ninth Amendment, [offered by Justice Black in *Griswold*, goes] like this. There was fear that the inclusion of a bill of rights [would] be taken to imply that federal power was [not] limited to the authorities enumerated in Article I, Section 8, [but] extended all the way up to the edge of the rights stated in the first eight amendments. [The] Ninth Amendment, the received version goes, was attached to the Bill of Rights [to] negate that inference. [But the] Tenth Amendment, submitted and ratified at the same time, completely fulfills [that] function. [Moreover, the legislative history of the Ninth Amendment is consistent with Justice Goldberg's view, and] the conclusion that the Ninth Amendment was intended to signal the existence of federal constitutional rights beyond those specifically enu-

merated in the Constitution is the only conclusion its language seems comfortably able to support.

b. Berger, The Ninth Amendment, 66 Cornell L. Rev. 1, 2-3, 20, 14 (1980):

[The ninth and tenth amendments] are complementary: the ninth deals with *rights* "retained by the people," the tenth with *powers* "reserved" to the states or the people. [Madison] made clear that the retained rights [constitute] an area in which the "Government ought not to act." This means, in my judgment, that the courts have not been empowered to enforce the retained rights. [Rather, in] "retaining" the unenumerated rights, the people reserved to themselves power to add to or subtract from the rights enumerated in the Constitution by the process of amendment. [If] this be deemed supererogatory, be it remembered that according to Madison the ninth amendment itself was "inserted merely for greater caution."

c. Caplan, The History and Meaning of the Ninth Amendment, 69 Va. L. Rev. 223, 264-265, 227-228 (1983):

[The] ninth amendment was drafted in order to allay concern that the Constitution might abolish rights traditionally guaranteed by state law. [These] "other" rights were understood to refer to the common law, along with the state constitutions and statutes engrafted onto it. [But the] ninth amendment [did] not transform these unenumerated rights into constitutional [rights]. Instead, it simply provides that the individual rights contained in state law are to continue in force under the Constitution until modified or eliminated by state enactment, by federal preemption, or by a judicial determination of unconstitutionality.

Since *Griswold* various justices have alluded to the ninth amendment but without offering a comprehensive theory of precisely what unenumerated rights it protects. See, e.g., Richmond Newspapers v. Virginia, 448 U.S. 555, 579 n.15 (1980) (opinion of Burger, C.J.) (concerning the right of the people to attend criminal trials); Lubin v. Panish, 415 U.S. 709, 721 n.* (1974) (Douglas, J., concurring) (concerning right to vote in state elections).

3. *The right of "privacy."* What is the nature of the right of "privacy" protected in *Griswold?* Is *Griswold* about the privacy of the home? The privacy of information concerning intimate matters? The integrity of the marriage relationship? Sexual freedom? Autonomy over decisions relating to childbearing? Autonomy generally?

After *Griswold,* consider the following: (a) a law prohibiting the use of marijuana, as applied to married persons who use marijuana in their home as a sexual stimulant; (b) a law prohibiting the sale or distribution of contraceptives, as applied to prohibit the sale or distribution of contraceptives to married persons; (c) a law prohibiting the use of contraceptives by unmarried persons.

4. *The reach of* Griswold: *the unmarried.* In Eisenstadt v. Baird, 405 U.S. 438 (1972), the Court, in a six-to-one decision, held that a Massachusetts statute prohibiting the distribution of any drug or device to unmarried persons for the prevention of conception violated the equal protection clause because it provided dissimilar treatment for married and unmarried persons.

Purporting to apply traditional rational basis review, the Court, in an opinion by Justice Brennan, held that none of the interests asserted in defense of the statute was sufficient to justify the challenged classification. First, the Court concluded that the deterrence of premarital sex could not reasonably be regarded as the purpose of the law. This was so because (a) the statute did not prohibit the distribution of contraceptives to prevent the "spread of disease," and thus was "so riddled with exceptions" that its effect "has at best a marginal relation to the proffered objective," and (b) in any event, it "would be plainly unreasonable to assume that Massachusetts has prescribed pregnancy and the birth of an unwanted child as punishment for fornication, which is a misdemeanor under Massachusetts [law]."

Second, the Court rejected the contention that the classification was designed to "serve the health needs of the community by regulating the distribution of potentially harmful articles." This was so because (a) "not all contraceptives are potentially dangerous" and (b) this rationale does not serve to distinguish between married and unmarried persons.

Finally, the Court rejected the argument that the statute could be sustained on moral grounds "as a prohibition on contraception." The Court explained:

> [Whatever] the rights of the individual to access to contraceptives may be, the rights must be the same for the unmarried and the married alike. If under *Griswold* the distribution of contraceptives to married persons cannot be prohibited, a ban on distribution to unmarried persons would be equally impermissible. It is true that in *Griswold* the right of privacy in question inhered in the marital relationship. Yet the marital couple is not an independent entity with a mind and heart of its own, but an association of two individuals each with a separate intellectual and emotional makeup. If the right of privacy means anything, it is the right of the *individual*, married or single, to be free from unwarranted governmental intrusion into matters so fundamentally affecting a person as the decision whether to bear or beget a child. [On] the other hand, if *Griswold* is no bar to a prohibition on the distribution of contraceptives, the State could not, consistently with the Equal Protection Clause, outlaw distribution to unmarried but not to married persons. In each case the evil, as perceived by the State, would be identical, and the underinclusion would be invidious.

Chief Justice Burger dissented.

Note that the Connecticut statute would easily satisfy the traditional rational basis review. Does *Eisenstadt* shed any light on the meaning of *Griswold*? Consider the following: (a) "[Whether] the 'different classes' (married, not married) are 'wholly unrelated to the objective of the statute,' depends on whether, as *Griswold* insists, the marriage relationship is important to that aspect of liberty that the Court calls privacy. [*Eisenstadt* thus implies] a new rationale for *Griswold*." Wellington, Common Law Rules and Constitutional Double Standards: Some Notes on Adjudication, 83 Yale L.J. 221, 296 (1973). (b) "*Griswold* had at least attempted to relate the right to use contraceptives to familiar notions of privacy by speculating on the intrusive methods by which a statute banning the use of contraceptives might be enforced. This ground was unavailable in [*Eisenstadt*] because the [Massachusetts statute] forbade not the use, but only the distribution, of contraceptives. [*Eisenstadt* thus] unmasks *Griswold* as based on the idea of sexual liberty rather than privacy." Posner, The Uncertain Protection of Privacy by the Supreme Court, 1979 Sup. Ct. Rev. 173, 198.

5. *The reach of* Griswold: *access to contraceptives.* In Carey v. Population Services International, 431 U.S. 678 (1977), the Court, in a seven-to-two decision,

invalidated a New York law prohibiting any person other than a licensed pharmacist to distribute contraceptives. The Court, in an opinion by Justice Brennan, explained:

> *Griswold* may no longer be read as holding only that a State may not prohibit a married couple's use of contraceptives. Read in light of its progeny, the teaching of *Griswold* is that the Constitution protects individual decisions in matters of childbearing from unjustified intrusion by the State. Restrictions on the distribution of contraceptives clearly burden the freedom to make such decisions. [Limiting] the distribution of nonprescription contraceptives to licensed pharmacists clearly imposes a significant burden on the right of individuals to use contraceptives if they choose to do so. [Accordingly, the challenged law] "may be justified only by a 'compelling state interest' [and] must be narrowly drawn to express only the legitimate state interests at stake." [None of the interests asserted in defense of this statute is] compelling.

Chief Justice Burger and Justice Rehnquist dissented.

2. Abortion

Roe v. Wade
410 U.S. 113 (1973)

MR. JUSTICE BLACKMUN delivered the opinion of the Court.

This [appeal presents] constitutional challenges to state criminal abortion legislation. The Texas statutes under attack here [make procuring an abortion a crime except "by medical advice for the purpose of saving the life of the mother." These statutes] are typical of those that have been in effect in many States for approximately a century. . . .

We forthwith acknowledge our awareness of the sensitive and emotional nature of the abortion controversy, of the vigorous opposing views, even among physicians, and of the deep and seemingly absolute convictions that the subject inspires. . . .

Our task, of course, is to resolve the issue by constitutional measurement, free of emotion and of predilection. We seek earnestly to do this, and, because we do, we have inquired into, and in this opinion place some emphasis upon, medical and medical-legal history and what that history reveals about man's attitudes toward the abortion procedure over the centuries. . . .

[The] restrictive criminal abortion laws in effect in a majority of States today are of relatively recent vintage. [They] derive from statutory changes effected, for the most part, in the latter half of the 19th century.

[Abortion] was practiced in Greek times as well as in the Roman Era. [Most] Greek thinkers [commended] abortion, at least prior to viability. [At] common law, abortion performed *before* "quickening" — the first recognizable movement of the fetus in utero, appearing usually from the 16th to the 18th week of pregnancy — was not an indictable offense. [It] was not until [the] middle and late 19th century [that] the quickening distinction [was abandoned] and the degree of the offense [increased]. [Thus,] at common law, at the time of the adoption of our

Constitution, and throughout the major portion of the 19th century, [a] woman enjoyed a substantially broader right to terminate a pregnancy than she does in most States today. . . .

Three reasons have been advanced to explain historically the enactment of criminal abortion laws in the 19th century and to justify their continued existence.

It has been argued occasionally that these laws were [designed] to discourage illicit sexual conduct. Texas, however, does not advance this justification in the present case. . . .

A second reason is concerned with abortion as a medical procedure. When most criminal abortion laws were first enacted, the procedure was [hazardous]. [Thus,] it has been argued that a State's real concern in enacting a criminal abortion law was to protect the pregnant woman. [Modern] medical techniques have altered this situation. [Mortality] rates for women undergoing early abortions [appear] to be as low as or lower than the rates for normal childbirth. [Of] course, important state interests in the areas of health and medical standards do remain. The State has a legitimate interest in seeing to it that abortion, like any other medical procedure, is performed under circumstances that insure maximum safety for the patient [and] the State retains a definite interest in protecting the woman's own health and safety when an abortion is proposed at a late stage of pregnancy.

The third reason is the State's interest [in] protecting prenatal life. Some of the argument for this justification rests on the theory that a new human life is present from the moment of conception. [But in] assessing the State's interest, recognition may [also] be given to the less rigid claim that [at] least *potential* life is involved. . . .

The Constitution does not explicitly mention any right of privacy. [But] the Court has recognized that a right of personal privacy, or a guarantee of certain areas or zones of privacy, does exist under the Constitution. In varying contexts, the Court or individual Justices have, indeed, found at least the roots of that right in the First Amendment, Stanley v. Georgia, [infra Chapter 7, section D5]; in the Fourth and Fifth Amendments; in the penumbras of the Bill of Rights, [*Griswold*]; in the Ninth Amendment, id., (Goldberg, J., concurring); or in the concept of liberty guaranteed by the first section of the Fourteenth Amendment, see Meyer v. Nebraska. These decisions make it clear that only personal rights that can be deemed "fundamental" or "implicit in the concept of ordered liberty," are included in this guarantee of personal privacy. They also make it clear that the right has some extension to activities relating to marriage, Loving v. Virginia, [supra Chapter 5, section C3]; procreation, [*Skinner*]; contraception, [*Eisenstadt*]; family relationships, Prince v. Massachusetts, 321 U.S. 158 (1944); and child rearing and education, [*Pierce; Meyer*].

This right of privacy, whether it be founded in the Fourteenth Amendment's concept of personal liberty [as] we feel it is, or [in] the Ninth [Amendment], is broad enough to encompass a woman's decision whether or not to terminate her pregnancy. The detriment that the State would impose upon the pregnant woman by denying this choice altogether is apparent. Specific and direct harm medically diagnosable even in early pregnancy may be involved. Maternity, or additional offspring, may force upon the woman a distressful life and future. Psychological harm may be imminent. Mental and physical health may be taxed by child care. There is also the distress, for all concerned, associated with the unwanted child, and there is the problem of bringing a child into a family already unable, psychologically and otherwise, to care for it. In other cases, [the] additional difficulties and continuing stigma of unwed motherhood may be involved. All these are factors the woman and her responsible physician necessarily will consider in consultation.

On the basis of elements such as these, appellant [argues] that the woman's right is absolute and that she is entitled to terminate her pregnancy at whatever time, in whatever way, and for whatever reason she alone chooses. With this we do not agree. [The] Court's decisions recognizing a right of privacy also acknowledge that some state regulation in areas protected by that right is appropriate. . . .

Where certain "fundamental rights" are involved, the Court has held that regulation limiting these rights may be justified only by a "compelling state interest," and that legislative enactments must be narrowly drawn to express only the legitimate state interests at stake. . . .

The appellee [argues] that the fetus is a "person" within the language and meaning of the Fourteenth Amendment. [If] this suggestion of personhood is established, the appellant's case, of course, collapses, for the fetus' right to life would then be guaranteed specifically by the Amendment. . . .

The Constitution does not define "person" in so many words. Section 1 of the Fourteenth Amendment contains three references to "person." ["Person"] is used in other places in the Constitution: in the listing of qualifications for Representatives and Senators, Art. I, §2, cl. 2, and §3, cl. 3; in the Apportionment Clause, Art. I, §2, cl. 3;[53] in the Migration and Importation provision, Art. I, §9, cl. 1; in the Emolument Clause, Art. I, §9, cl. 8; in the Electors provisions, Art. II, §1, cl. 2, and the superseded cl. 3; in the provision outlining qualifications for the office of President, Art. II, §1, cl. 5; in the Extradition provisions, Art. IV, §2, cl. 2, and the superseded Fugitive Slave Clause 3; and in the Fifth, Twelfth, and Twenty-second Amendments, as well as in §§2 and 3 of the Fourteenth Amendment. But in nearly all these instances, the use of the word is such that it has application only postnatally. None indicates, with any assurance, that it has any possible prenatal application.[54]

All this, together with our observation that throughout the major portion of the 19th century prevailing legal abortion practices were far freer than they are today, persuades us that the word "person," as used in the Fourteenth Amendment, does not include the unborn. [Thus,] we pass on to other considerations. The pregnant woman cannot be isolated in her privacy. She carries an embryo and, later, a fetus. [The] situation therefore is inherently different from marital intimacy, or bedroom possession of obscene material, or marriage, or procreation, or education, with which *Eisenstadt* and *Griswold, Stanley, Loving, Skinner,* and

53. We are not aware that in the taking of any census under this clause, a fetus has ever been counted.

54. When Texas urges that a fetus is entitled to Fourteenth Amendment protection as a person, it faces a dilemma. Neither in Texas nor in any other State are all abortions prohibited. Despite broad proscription, an exception always exists. The exception [in the Texas law] for an abortion procured or attempted by medical advice for the purpose of saving the life of the mother, is typical. But if the fetus is a person who is not to be deprived of life without due process of law, and if the mother's condition is the sole determinant, does not the Texas exception appear to be out of line with the Amendment's command? . . .

Pierce and *Meyer* were respectively concerned. [It] is reasonable and appropriate for a State to decide that at some point in time another interest, that of health of the mother or that of potential human life, becomes significantly involved. . . .

Texas urges that, apart from the Fourteenth Amendment, life begins at conception and is present throughout pregnancy, and that, therefore, the State has a compelling interest in protecting that life from and after conception. We need not resolve the difficult question of when life begins. When those trained [in] medicine, philosophy, and theology are unable to arrive at any consensus, the judiciary, at this point in the development of man's knowledge, is not in a position to speculate as to the answer.

It should be sufficient to note briefly the wide divergence of thinking on [this] question. There has always been strong support for the view that life does not begin until live birth. This was the belief of the Stoics. It appears to be the predominant, though not the unanimous, attitude of the Jewish faith. It may be taken to represent also the position of a large segment of the Protestant community. [The] common law found greater significance in quickening. Physicians and their scientific colleagues have [tended] to focus either upon conception, upon live birth, or upon the interim point at which the fetus becomes "viable," that is, potentially able to live outside the mother's womb, albeit with artificial aid. Viability is usually placed at about seven months (28 weeks) but may occur earlier, even at 24 weeks. [The Catholic church recognizes] the existence of life from the moment of conception. . . .

In areas other than criminal abortion [such as torts and inheritance], the law has been reluctant to endorse any theory that life, as we recognize it, begins before live birth or to accord legal rights to the unborn except in narrowly defined situations and except when the rights are contingent upon live birth. . . .

In view of all this, we do not agree that, by adopting one theory of life, Texas may override the rights of the pregnant woman that are at stake. We repeat, however, that the State does have an important and legitimate interest in preserving and protecting the health of the pregnant woman [and] that it has still *another* important and legitimate interest in protecting the potentiality of human life. These interests are separate and distinct. Each grows in substantiality as the woman approaches term and, at a point during pregnancy, each becomes "compelling."

With respect to [the] interest in the health of the mother, the "compelling" point, in the light of present medical knowledge, is at approximately the end of the first trimester. This is so because of the now-established medical fact [that] until the end of the first trimester mortality in abortion may be less than mortality in normal childbirth. It follows that, from and after this point, a State may regulate the abortion procedure to the extent that the regulation reasonably relates to the preservation and protection of maternal health. Examples of permissible state regulation in this area are requirements as to the qualifications of the person who is to perform the abortion; [as] to the facility in which the procedure is to be performed; [and] the like.

This means, on the other hand, that, for the period of pregnancy prior to this "compelling" point, the attending physician, in consultation with his patient, is free to determine, without regulation by the State, that, in his medical judgment, the patient's pregnancy should be terminated. If that decision is reached, the judgment may be effectuated by an abortion free of interference by the State.

With respect to [the] interest in potential life, the "compelling" point is at viability. This is so because the fetus then presumably has the capability of meaningful life outside the mother's womb. State regulation protective of fetal life after viability thus has both logical and biological justifications. If the State is interested in protecting fetal life during that period, it may go so far as to proscribe abortion during that period, except when it is necessary to preserve the life or health of the mother.

Measured against these standards, [the Texas statute] sweeps too broadly [and] therefore, cannot survive the constitutional attack made upon it here. . . .

To summarize and to repeat: . . .

(a) For the stage prior to approximately the end of the first trimester, the abortion decision and its effectuation must be left to the medical judgment of the pregnant woman's attending physician.

(b) For the stage subsequent to approximately the end of the first trimester, the State, in promoting its interest in the health of the mother, may, if it chooses, regulate the abortion procedure in ways that are reasonably related to maternal health.

(c) For the stage subsequent to viability, the State in promoting its interest in the potentiality of human life may, if it chooses, regulate, and even proscribe, abortion except where it is necessary, in appropriate medical judgment, for the preservation of the life or health of the mother. . . .

This holding, we feel, is consistent with the relative weights of the respective interests involved, with the lessons and examples of medical and legal history, with the lenity of the common law, and with the demands of the profound problems of the present day. . . .

MR. JUSTICE STEWART, concurring.

In 1963, this Court, in Ferguson v. Skrupa, purported to sound the death knell for the doctrine of substantive due process. [Barely] two years later, in [Griswold], the Court held a Connecticut birth control law unconstitutional. In view of what had been so recently said in Skrupa, the Court's opinion in Griswold understandably did its best to avoid reliance on the Due Process Clause of the Fourteenth Amendment as the ground for decision. [But] it was clear to me then, and it is equally clear to me now, that the Griswold decision can be rationally understood only as a holding that the Connecticut statute substantively invaded the "liberty" that is protected by the Due Process Clause of the Fourteenth Amendment. As so understood, Griswold stands as one in a long line of pre-Skrupa cases decided under the doctrine of substantive due process, and I now accept it as such.

[The] Constitution nowhere mentions a specific right of personal choice in matters of marriage and family life, but the "liberty" protected by the Due Process Clause of the Fourteenth Amendment covers more than those freedoms explicitly named in the Bill of Rights. [In Eisenstadt], we recognized "the right of the individual, married or single, to be free from unwarranted governmental intrusion into matters so fundamentally affecting a person as the decision whether to bear or beget a child." That right necessarily includes the right of a woman to decide whether or not to terminate her pregnancy. . . .

It is evident that the Texas abortion statute infringes that right directly. [The] question then becomes whether the state interests advanced to justify this abridgment can survive the "particularly careful scrutiny" that the Fourteenth Amendment here requires.

The asserted state interests are protection of the health and safety of the pregnant woman, and protection of the potential future human life within her. These are legitimate objectives, [but as] the Court today has thoroughly demonstrated, [these] state interests cannot constitutionally support the broad abridgment of personal liberty worked by the existing Texas law. . . .

MR. JUSTICE DOUGLAS, concurring.

While I join the opinion of the Court, I add a few words. . . .

The Ninth Amendment [does] not create federally enforceable rights. [But] a catalogue of [the rights "retained by the people"] includes customary, traditional, and time-honored rights, amenities, privileges, and immunities that come within the sweep of "the Blessings of Liberty" mentioned in the preamble to the Constitution. Many of them, in my view, come within the meaning of the term "liberty" as used in the Fourteenth Amendment.

First is the autonomous control over the development and expression of one's intellect, interests, tastes, and personality.

These are rights protected by the First Amendment and, in my view, they are absolute. . . .

Second is freedom of choice in the basic decisions of one's life respecting marriage, divorce, procreation, contraception, and the education and upbringing of children.

These rights, unlike those protected by the First Amendment, are subject to some control by the police power. [These] rights are "fundamental," and we have held that in order to support legislative action the statute must be narrowly and precisely drawn and that a "compelling state interest" must be shown in support of the limitation.[4] . . .

Third is the freedom to care for one's health and person, freedom from bodily restraint or compulsion, freedom to walk, stroll, or loaf.

These rights, though fundamental, are likewise subject to regulation on a showing of "compelling state interest." . . .

[A] woman is free to make the basic decision whether to bear an unwanted child. [Childbirth] may deprive a woman of her preferred lifestyle and force upon her a radically different and undesired future. [But the] State [too] has interests to protect. [While] childbirth endangers the lives of some women, voluntary abortion at any time and place regardless of medical standards would impinge on a rightful concern of society. The woman's health is part of that concern; as is the life of the fetus after quickening. These concerns justify the State in treating the procedure as a medical one. . . .[*]

MR. JUSTICE WHITE, with whom MR. JUSTICE REHNQUIST joins, dissenting.

At the heart of the controversy in these cases are those recurring pregnancies that pose no danger whatsoever to the life or health of the mother but are, nevertheless, unwanted for any one or more of a variety of reasons — conven-

---

4. My Brother Stewart [says] that our decision in *Griswold* reintroduced substantive due process that had been rejected in [*Ferguson v. Skrupa*]. [I do not agree. *Griswold* had] nothing to do with substantive due process. [The right recognized in *Griswold* was protected because it is] peripheral to other rights that are expressed in the Bill of Rights. . . .

[*] [A concurring opinion of Chief Justice Burger, noting that "the Court today rejects any claim that the Constitution requires abortion on demand," is omitted. — EDS.]

ience, family planning, economics, dislike of children, the embarrassment of illegitimacy, etc. The common claim before us is that for any one of such reasons, or for no reason at all, and without asserting or claiming any threat to life or health, any woman is entitled to an abortion at her request if she is able to find a medical advisor willing to undertake the procedure.

The Court for the most part sustains this position: During the period prior to the time the fetus becomes viable, the Constitution of the United States values the convenience, whim, or caprice of the putative mother more than the life or potential life of the fetus; the Constitution, therefore, guarantees the right to an abortion as against any state law or policy seeking to protect the fetus from an abortion not prompted by more compelling reasons of the mother.

With all due respect, I dissent. I find nothing in the language or history of the Constitution to support the Court's judgment. The Court simply fashions and announces a new constitutional right for pregnant mothers and, with scarcely any reason or authority for its action, invests that right with sufficient substance to override most existing state abortion statutes. The upshot is that the people and the legislatures of the 50 States are constitutionally disentitled to weigh the relative importance of the continued existence and development of the fetus, on the one hand, against a spectrum of possible impacts on the mother, on the other hand. As an exercise of raw judicial power, the Court perhaps has authority to do what it does today; but in my view its judgment is an improvident and extravagant exercise of the power of judicial review that the Constitution extends to this Court. . . .

MR. JUSTICE REHNQUIST, dissenting. . . .

I have difficulty in concluding [that] the right of "privacy" is involved in this case. Texas [bars] the performance of a medical abortion by a licensed physician on a plaintiff such as Roe. A transaction resulting in an operation such as this is not "private" in the ordinary usage of that word. Nor is the "privacy" that the Court finds here even a distant relative of the freedom from searches and seizures protected by the Fourth Amendment. . . .

If the Court means by the term "privacy" no more than that the claim of a person to be free from unwanted state regulation of consensual transactions may be a form of "liberty" protected by the Fourteenth Amendment, there is no doubt that similar claims have been upheld in our earlier decisions on the basis of that liberty. I agree [that] the "liberty," against deprivation of which without due process the Fourteenth Amendment protects, embraces more than the rights found in the Bill of Rights. But that liberty is not guaranteed absolutely against deprivation, only against deprivation without due process of law. The test traditionally applied in the area of social and economic legislation is whether or not a law such as that challenged has a rational relation to a valid state objective. [Williamson v. Lee Optical.] The Due Process Clause of the Fourteenth Amendment undoubtedly does place a limit, albeit a broad one, on legislative power to enact laws such as this. If the Texas statute were to prohibit an abortion even where the mother's life is in jeopardy, I have little doubt that such a statute would lack a rational relation to a valid state objective under the test stated in [Williamson]. But the Court's sweeping invalidation of any restrictions on abortion during the first trimester is impossible to justify under that standard, and the conscious weighing of competing factors that the Court's opinion apparently substitutes for the established test is far more appropriate to a legislative judgment than to a judicial one. While the Court's opinion quotes from the dissent of Mr. Justice Holmes in [*Lochner*], the result it reaches is more closely attuned to the majority opinion of Mr. Justice Peckham in that case. . . .

The fact that a majority of the States reflecting, after all, the majority sentiment in those States, have had restrictions on abortions for at least a century is a strong indication, it seems to me, that the asserted right to an abortion is not "so rooted in the traditions and conscience of our people as to be ranked as fundamental." Even today, when society's views on abortion are changing, the very existence of the debate is evidence that the "right" to an abortion is not so universally accepted as the appellant would have us believe.

To reach its result, the Court necessarily has had to find within the scope of the Fourteenth Amendment a right that was apparently completely unknown to the drafters of the Amendment. [By] the time of the adoption of the Fourteenth Amendment in 1868, there were at least 36 laws enacted by state or territorial legislatures limiting abortion. [The] only conclusion possible from this history is that the drafters did not intend to have the Fourteenth Amendment withdraw from the States the power to legislate with respect to this matter. . . .

Note: The Abortion Decision

1. Griswold *to* Eisenstadt *to* Roe. A central issue in *Roe* was whether there was a constitutional basis for the woman's right of "privacy." The Court relied heavily on precedent to establish this right, but critics argue that the precedents did not establish a general right of privacy, let alone a right broad enough to reach abortion. Consider, for example, Ely, The Wages of Crying Wolf: A Comment on *Roe v. Wade*, 82 Yale L. J. 920, 930 (1973):

[The] Court in *Griswold* stressed that it was invalidating only that portion of the Connecticut law that proscribed the *use*, as opposed to the manufacture, sale, or other distribution of contraceptives. That distinction [makes] sense [only] if the case is rationalized on the ground that [enforcement of the challenged provision] *would have been virtually impossible without* the most outrageous sort of governmental prying into the privacy of the home. [No] such rationalization is [possible in *Roe*], for whatever else may be involved, it is not a case about governmental snooping.

Defenders of *Roe*, on the other hand, argue that, taken together, the *Meyer/Pierce/Griswold/Eisenstadt* line of cases delineates a sphere of interests — which the Court now groups and denominates "privacy" — implicit in the "liberty" protected by the fourteenth amendment:

At the core of this sphere is the right of the individual to make for himself [the] fundamental decisions that shape family life: whom to marry; whether and when to have children; and with what values to rear those children. [Plainly] the right [to an abortion] falls within [this] class of [interests]. The question of constitutionality [in *Roe*] is a more difficult one than that involved in *Griswold* and *Eisenstadt* only because the asserted state interest is more important, not because of any difference in the individual interests involved.

Heymann & Barzelay, The Forest and the Trees: *Roe v. Wade* and Its Critics, 53 B.U. L. Rev. 765, 772, 75 (1973).

2. *The right of privacy.* The Court concluded in *Roe* that there is a constitutional right of privacy, that the right is based in the due process clause, and that it is "broad enough to encompass a woman's decision whether or not to terminate her pregnancy." Is the right of privacy enforced in *Roe* any more legitimate than the "liberty of contract" enforced in *Lochner*? Consider Ely, supra, at 935-936, 947:

> What is frightening about *Roe* is that [its] super-protected right is not inferable from the language of the Constitution, the framers' thinking respecting the specific problem in issue, any general value derivable from the provisions they included, or the nation's governmental structure. Nor is it explainable in terms of the unusual political impotence of the group judicially protected vis-à-vis the interest that legislatively prevailed over it. [*Roe*] is bad because it is bad constitutional law, or rather because it is *not* constitutional law and gives almost no sense of an obligation to try to be.

Does Ely's list exhaust the legitimate bases for the recognition of constitutional rights? Recall the interpretivism/noninterpretivism debate, in section A, supra.

3. *In defense of* Roe. Defenders of *Roe* have drawn on tradition, consensus, political theory, and moral philosophy to support the decision. Consider the following arguments:

a. L. Tribe, American Constitutional Law 893, 923 (1978):

> The Constitution was consecrated to the blessings of liberty for ourselves and our posterity — yet it contains no discussion of the right to be a *human* being; no definition of a person; and, indeed, no express provisions guaranteeing to persons the right to carry on their lives protected from the "vicissitudes of the political process" by a zone of privacy or a right of personhood. Nor, apart from the obviously incomplete listing in the Bill of Rights, does the document enumerate those aspects of self which must be preserved and allowed to flourish if we are to promote the fullest development of human faculties and ensure the greatest breadth to personal liberty and community life. But the Constitution is not a totalitarian design, depending for its success upon the homogenization or depersonalization of humanity. The judiciary has thus reached into the Constitution's spirit and structure, and has elaborated from the spare text an idea of "human" and a conception of "being" not merely contemplated but required. [This conception recognizes] the fundamental personal character of a right to reproductive autonomy.

b. Heymann & Barzelay, supra, at 772-773:

[The] family unit [is] an integral part of [our constitutional system]. In democratic theory as well as in practice, it is in the family that children are expected to learn the values and beliefs that democratic institutions later draw on. [The] immensely important power of deciding about matters of early socialization has been allocated to the family, not to the government. [If] a state government decided that all children would be reared [from] birth under [complete] control of a state [official], the effect on our present notions of democratic government would be immense. [The] long line of precedent in this area [is] entirely principled. For the Court to have declined strict review of state legislation that limits the private right to choose whom to marry and whether to raise a family, or to decide within wide bounds how to rear one's children, would have been to leave the most basic substructure of our society and government [to] political whim.

c. Before offering the view set out in *a* above, Professor Tribe offered an alternative defense of *Roe.* See Tribe, Foreword: Toward a Model of Roles in the Due Process of Life and Law, 87 Harv. L. Rev. 1, 11, 15, 22 (1973):

> [The Court in *Roe* was choosing, not] between the alternatives of abortion and continued pregnancy, [but] among alternative allocations of decisionmaking authority. [The] Court [transferred] the role of decisionmaker from the government to the woman herself. [In] the role-allocation model, the due process clause is violated whenever the state [assumes] a role the Constitution entrusts to another. [The] highly charged and distinctly sectarian religious controversy [at the center of the abortion issue] strongly supports the basic allocation of roles mandated by *Roe.* For [the] "first and most immediate purpose" of the establishment clause was to prevent "a union of government and religion."

Several years later, Tribe changed his view: "[On] reflection, [my former] view appears to give too little weight to the value of allowing religious groups freely to express their convictions in the political process, underestimates the power of moral convictions unattached to religious beliefs on this issue, and makes the unrealistic assumption that a constitutional ruling could somehow disentangle religion from future public debate on the question." L. Tribe, American Constitutional Law 928 (1978).

d. Perry, Substantive Due Process Revisited: Reflections On (And Beyond) Recent Cases, 71 Nw. U. L. Rev. 417, 419-421 (1976); Perry, Abortion, the Public Morals, and the Police Power: The Ethical Function of Substantive Due Process, 23 U.C.L.A. L. Rev. 689, 733 (1976):

> [Substantive] due process refers to the principle that a law adversely affecting an individual's life, liberty or property is invalid, even though offending no specific constitutional prohibition, unless the law serves a legitimate governmental objective. [Conventional] morality is the touchstone of the legitimacy of governmental objectives. [Consequently], to say that the right of privacy protects a woman's decision to have an abortion is necessarily to say that the objective of prohibiting such decisions lacks support in conventional morality. [The] Court's implicit evaluation of conventional moral culture [in *Roe* was] essentially accurate.

This argument turns on the notion that *Roe* rests on moral notions widely shared among the American people. It asserts, in effect, that Americans generally believe that government may not coerce intimate acts and that given such a principle, restrictions on abortions are inherently suspect. Note, however, that this defense is effective only if the principle of conventional morality is stated at a relatively high level of generality. If we look at enacted statutes as evidence of what Americans conventionally believe is correct, we may acquire a more precise — and quite different — understanding of what conventional morality requires. Which focus, if either, is appropriate?

Several years later, Perry changed his mind: "[I am now convinced that] there are no consensual values sufficiently determinate to be of help to the Court, and [that] the values that do enjoy significant support are, in our pluralist culture, fragmented and point in many different directions." M. Perry, The Constitution, the Courts, and Human Rights 94 (1982).

e. Only women become pregnant, and only women need abortions. Thus, laws prohibiting abortion might be understood as embodying a severe form of gender discrimination. On this view, the Court's decisions in *Griswold, Eisenstadt,* and *Roe,* and its decisions granting special protection to women under the equal protection clause (see Chapter 5, section B3b), "present various faces of a single issue: the roles women are to play in our society." It "is simply inconceivable that the majority Justices in *Roe* were indifferent to this question." Karst, Book Review, 89 Harv. L. Rev. 1028, 1036-1037 (1976).

Consider L. Tribe, Constitutional Choices 243 (1985):

> [Although] current law nowhere forces *men* to sacrifice their bodies and restructure their lives even in those tragic situations (of needed organ transplants, for example) where nothing less will permit their children to survive, those who would outlaw abortion [would] rely [on] physiological circumstances — the supposed dictates of the natural — to conscript women [as] involuntary incubators and thus to usurp a control over sexual activity and its consequences that men [take] for granted. To one who regards this outcome as unjust, a right to end pregnancy might be seen more plausibly as a matter of resisting sexual [domination] than as a matter of shielding from public control "private" transactions.

See also Regan, Rewriting *Roe v. Wade,* 77 Mich. L. Rev. 1569 (1979).

For a feminist analysis of *Roe,* see MacKinnon, *Roe v. Wade:* A Study in Male Ideology in Abortion: Moral and Legal Perspectives 45, 49, 51 (J. Garfield ed. 1985):

> In feminist terms, [*Roe*] translates the ideology of the private sphere into the individual woman's legal right to privacy as a means of subordinating women's collective needs to the imperatives of male supremacy. [Under] conditions of gender inequality, [*Roe*] does not free women, it frees male sexual aggression. The availability of abortion [removes] the one remaining legitimized reason that women have had for refusing sex besides the headache.

Do laws that discriminate against persons who are pregnant discriminate against women? See Geduldig v. Aiello, supra Chapter 5, section D. Consider also Ely, supra, at 933-935:

> In his famous *Carolene Products* footnote, Justice Stone suggested that the interests to which the Court can responsibly give extraordinary constitutional protection include not only those expressed in the Constitution but also those that are unlikely to receive adequate consideration in the political process, specifically the interests of "discrete and insular minorities" unable to form effective political alliances. [But] *Roe* is not an appropriate case for [the] invocation [of this theory]. Compared with men, very few women sit in our legislatures. [But] *no* fetuses sit [there]. [Footnote 4] should be reserved for those interests which, *as compared with the interests to which they have been subordinated,* constitute minorities unusually incapable of protecting themselves. Compared with men, women may constitute such a "minority"; compared with the unborn, they do not.

4. "*Compelling state interests.*" Even if there is a constitutional "right of privacy," and even if that right is "broad enough to encompass a woman's decision

whether or not to terminate her pregnancy," the question remains whether the prohibition of abortion serves a "compelling state interest." The Court in *Roe* identified two such interests — protecting the health of the pregnant woman and protecting the "potentiality of human life" of the fetus. The Court held that, at various points, these interests become "compelling." How did the Court make these determinations?

Consider A. Cox, The Role of the Supreme Court in American Government 113-114 (1976):

> My criticism of *Roe* [is] that the Court failed [to] lift the ruling above the level of a political judgment based upon the evidence currently available from the medical, physical and social sciences. [The opinion reads] like a set of hospital rules and regulations, whose validity [will] be destroyed with new statistics upon the medical risks of childbirth and abortion or new advances in providing for the separate existence of a foetus. Neither historian, layman, nor lawyer will be persuaded that all the details prescribed in *Roe* [are] part [of] the Constitution.

Can the decision whether a state interest outweighs an individual's interest ever rise above a "political judgment"?

5. *The fetus as "person."* Does the state have a "compelling" interest in preserving the life of the fetus? Do you agree with the Court that, to decide *Roe*, it need not "resolve the difficult question of when life begins"? Given the inability of those trained in "medicine, philosophy, and theology [to] arrive at [a] consensus," should the Court simply have deferred to the legislative judgment? Consider the following views:

a. Dellapenna, Nor Piety Nor Wit: The Supreme Court on Abortion, 6 Colum. Human Rights L. Rev. 379, 399, 409 (1974-1975):

> Who is a "person" [is not] the sort of question which can be left to [individual] decision. Too many basic rights hinge upon the answer. Are [blacks] "persons"? [By] concluding [that] the foetus could be no more than potential life, the Court [as in Plessy v. Ferguson, supra Chapter 5, section A2] has gained support by sacrificing invisible people. [Will] future generations ponder these abortion decisions with the same incredulity with which many have come to view the segregation decisions?

b. Epstein, Substantive Due Process by any Other Name: The Abortion Cases, 1973 Sup. Ct. Rev. 159, 172, 176, 182:

> [We must] face the definitional question: who is a person? [We should] reject the suggestion, however tempting, that the problem should be left to individual choice. [The] preference for individual choice is quite proper when we ask whether a person should take advantage of a liberty that is his, but it cannot be accepted where the very question raised concerns the appropriate social limits to be placed upon individual choice. [It] makes no sense to hold in conclusionary terms that "by adopting one theory of life, Texas may [not] override the rights of the pregnant [woman]." [We] could as well claim that the Court, by adopting another theory of life, has decided to override the rights of the unborn child.

c. To decide "when life begins" inevitably involves a "moral" judgment. Although "moral" judgments may satisfy the rational basis standard (recall Justice Harlan's discussion of this issue in Poe v. Ullman, set out in his concurring opinion in *Griswold*), such judgments can never, standing alone, constitute *compelling* state interests. See Henkin, Privacy and Autonomy, 74 Colum. L. Rev. 1410, 1431-1432 (1974). But consider L. Tribe, American Constitutional Law 928 (1978): "[*All*] normative judgments are rooted in moral premises; surely the judgment that it is wrong to kill a two-week old infant is no less 'moral' in inspiration than the judgment [that] it is wrong to kill a two-day old fetus. [*Roe*] must [thus] be wrong if it rests on the premise that a state can never interfere with individual decisions relating to sex or procreation 'with only moral justification.' "

d. The real issue in *Roe* concerns the allocation of uncertainty. There is no way to determine with certainty when life begins. Ordinarily, government may act on the basis of uncertain but rational legislative judgments. When fundamental constitutional rights such as free speech, freedom from racial discrimination, and privacy are at stake, however, government must demonstrate that it has a compelling interest. An uncertain interest is by definition not compelling. Thus, just as free speech may not be restrained to prevent a possibly harmful consequence, privacy may not be invaded to prevent a possibly compelling interest. Under this view, the Court in *Roe* decided not that life begins at viability but only that the government had not sufficiently proved that life begins at conception.

6. *The fetus as "person": a "dispositive" issue?* It is often assumed that if the fetus is a "person," *Roe* is necessarily wrong. But consider the following views.

a. L. Tribe, American Constitutional Law 931 (1978):

> [Prior to *Roe*, antiabortion laws] were not consistently enforced [either] against the affluent, who could evade them by obtaining lawful abortions outside their own restrictive jurisdictions, or against the poor, untold numbers of whom would unavoidably "subject themselves to the notorious backstreet abortion . . . fraught with the myriad possibilities of mutilation, infection, sterility and death." Thus, [in] view of the realities too commonplace to be ignored, the Court might understandably have viewed restrictive abortion laws less as meaningful protections for unborn life than as relatively pointless and economically skewed expressions of outdated worry about the health of the women involved coupled with disapproval of their moral choices.

b. Thomson, A Defense of Abortion, 1 Phil. & Pub. Affairs 47, 48-49, 55-59 (1971):

> I propose [that] we grant [for the sake of argument] that the fetus is a person from the moment of conception. How does the [antiabortion] argument go from here? Something like this, I take it. Every person has a right to life. So the fetus has a right to life. No doubt the mother has a right to decide what shall happen in and to her body; [but] surely a person's right to life is stronger [than] the mother's right to decide what happens in and to her body, and so outweighs it. So the fetus may not be killed; an abortion may not be performed.
>
> It sounds plausible. But now let me ask you to imagine this. You wake up in the morning and find yourself back to back in bed with an unconscious violinist. [He] has been found to have a fatal kidney ailment, and the Society of Music Lovers has canvassed all the available medical records and found that you alone have the right blood type to help. They have therefore kidnapped you [and] plugged [the violinist's circulatory system] into yours. [To] unplug you would be to kill him. But never mind, it's only for nine months. By then he will have recovered [and] can safely be unplugged. [Is] it morally incumbent on you to accede to this situation? . . .

The emendation which may be made at this point is this: the right to life consists not in the right not to be killed, but rather in the right not to be killed unjustly. [This enables] us to square the fact that the violinist has a right to life with the fact that you do not act unjustly toward him in unplugging yourself, thereby killing him. For if you do not kill him unjustly, you do not violate his right to life. [But] if this emendation is accepted, the gap in the argument against abortion stares us plainly in the face: it is by no means enough to show that the fetus is a person, and to remind us that all persons have a right to life — we need to be shown also that killing the fetus violates its right to life, i.e., that abortion is unjust killing. And is it?

I suppose we may take it as a datum that in the case of pregnancy due to rape the mother has not given the unborn person a right to the use of her body for food and shelter. [But suppose] a woman voluntarily indulges in intercourse, knowing of the chance it will issue in pregnancy, and then she does become pregnant; is she not in part responsible for the presence, in fact the very existence, of the unborn person inside her? No doubt she did not invite it in. But doesn't her partial responsibility for its being there itself give it a right to the use of her body? If so, then her aborting it [would] be depriving it of what it does have a right to, and thus would be doing it an injustice. . . .

[But] it is not at all plain that this argument really [goes as] far as it purports to. [Suppose] it were like this: people-seeds drift about in the air like pollen, and if you open your windows, one may drift in and take root in your carpets or upholstery. You don't want children, so you fix up your windows with fine mesh screens, the very best you can buy. As can happen, however, [one] of the screens is defective; and a seed drifts in and takes root. Does the person-plant who now develops have a right to the use of your house? Surely [not]. Someone may argue that you are responsible for its rooting, that it does have a right to your house, because after all you *could* have lived out your life with bare floors and furniture, or with sealed windows and doors. But this won't do — for by the same token anyone can avoid a pregnancy due to rape by having a hysterectomy, or anyway by never leaving home without a (reliable!) army.

For further elaboration of this view, see Regan, supra.

For criticism of this view, consider M. Tooley, Abortion and Infanticide 45-49 (1983):

[There] is a possibly crucial difference between the situation of the violinist and that of the foetus. Both need the use of a certain person's body if they are to survive. But in the case of the violinist, the relevant person is in no way responsible for the violinist's being in need of assistance, whereas in the case of the foetus it can be said that the woman is among those who are at least partially responsible [for] the foetus's being in need of a life-support system — assuming that the pregnancy did not result from rape. . . .

Thomson raises this objection herself [but concludes] it is not convincing. [But] consider the structure of [her] argument. First, she has offered an argument that lends support to the view that abortion is justified at least in the case of rape. Second, she has pointed out that one cannot drive a wedge between rape and other cases simply by appealing to the fact that in other cases the woman is responsible for there being a foetus that needs assistance, since the woman is also to some extent responsible in cases of rape. [She therefore concludes] that abortion is morally permissible in at least some cases where intercourse is voluntary. . . .

[But there is] the following disanalogy between the people-seed case and that of pregnancy resulting from voluntary intercourse. In the people-seed case, there are only two sorts of alternatives. Either one exposes oneself to the danger of people-seeds taking root in one's house, or one reconciles oneself to a somewhat dreary existence in rooms that are stuffy and uncarpeted. In contrast, it does not seem that one is thus limited in the real life case; the choice is not confined to chastity on the one hand, and the risk of pregnancy on the other. [There] are delightfully unchaste alternatives to normal intercourse.

7. *Viability.* The court held that, with "respect to [the] interest in potential life, the 'compelling' point is at viability [because] the fetus then presumably has the capability of meaningful life outside the mother's womb." Does this conclusion "mistake a definition for a syllogism"? Ely, supra, at 924. Consider Tribe, Foreword: Toward a Model of Roles in the Due Process of Life and Law, 87 Harv. L. Rev. 1, 27-28 (1973): "Once the fetus can be severed from the woman by a process which enables it to survive, leaving the abortion decision to private choice would confer not only a right to remove an unwanted fetus from one's body, but also an entirely separate right to ensure its death. [Viability] thus marks a point after which [the] state could properly conclude that permitting abortion would be tantamount to permitting murder."

The viability principle poses several potential problems.

a. *Shifting viability.* Viability is not biologically fixed. It will arrive earlier in gestation as better techniques are developed for sustaining existence outside the womb. At some point, viability may be pushed so far back into the gestation process as to eliminate the right to abortion. Is this a problem? One might see this as a built-in social safety valve. If society really cares about fetal life, it can do something about it by advancing technology. See Tribe, Structural Due Process, 10 Harv. C.R.-C.L. L. Rev. 269 (1975). Is the right of privacy recognized in *Roe* about the right not to continue an unwanted pregnancy or is it about the right not to have unwanted children? If *Roe* is about the right not to be a mother, shifting viability should not matter. But the viability line itself suggests that *Roe* is about the right not to be pregnant, not the right not to be a mother.

b. *Uncertain viability.* The point of viability varies from fetus to fetus, and it is extremely difficult to determine the precise point of viability for any particular fetus. How, then, should viability be defined? On a case-by-case basis? At the point at which the average fetus is viable? At the earliest point at which a fetus has been found viable? The Court has held that "it is not the proper function of the legislature or the courts to place viability [at] a specific point in the gestation period," but that "the determination of whether a particular fetus is viable [must be] a matter for the judgment of the responsible attending physician." Planned Parenthood of Missouri v. Danforth, 428 U.S. 52, 64 (1976). Consider King, The Juridical Status of the Fetus: A Proposal for Legal Protection of the Unborn, 77 Mich. L. Rev. 1647, 1679-1681 (1976):

[States] should be permitted to assert a compelling interest in potential life at the earliest point at which there has been verified fetal survival. [This] would be consistent with the reasons for giving fetuses legal protection in the first place. If we want to ensure that no human being is denied fair consideration [we] should err on the safe side by protecting all who might have such an entitlement. [The] Court's extraordinary deference to the medical profession [seems] unwarranted. Physicians [have no] peculiar competence to decree that a specific probability of survival is the critical one for determining when a state's interest in potential life becomes compelling. [Moreover,] the Court's apparent refusal to permit states to assert a compelling interest at the earliest moment of known fetal survival sacrifices the objectivity and ease of administration which that system offers.

c. *Post-viability abortion.* The Court stated in *Roe* that "If the State is interested in protecting fetal life after viability, it may go so far as to proscribe abortion during that period, except when it is necessary to preserve the life or health of the mother." Do you agree that the "health" of the mother outweighs the "life" of the viable fetus?

8. *Regulating abortion.* Although the Court held in *Roe* that a state may not prohibit abortion entirely, it left many subsidiary questions unanswered: May the government provide funds to pay for childbirth but not abortion? May it prohibit abortion except in a hospital? May it require spousal consent? Parental consent? Parental notification? The following cases and Note deal with these and related issues.

MAHER v. ROE, 432 U.S. 464 (1977): In a six-to-three decision, the Court upheld a state regulation granting Medicaid benefits for childbirth, but denying such benefits for nontherapeutic abortions (i.e., abortions that are not "medically necessary"). Justice Powell delivered the opinion of the Court:

"The Constitution imposes no obligation on the States to pay the pregnancy-related medical expenses of indigent women, or indeed to pay any of the medical expenses of indigents. But when a State decides to alleviate some of the hardships of poverty by providing medical care, the manner in which it dispenses benefits is subject to constitutional limitations. Appellees' claim is that [the State] must accord equal treatment to both abortion and childbirth, and may not evidence a policy preference by funding only the medical expenses incident to childbirth. This [presents] a question [under] the Equal Protection Clause. . . .

"This case involves no discrimination against a suspect class. An indigent woman desiring an abortion does not come within the limited category of [suspect classes]. Nor does the fact that the impact of the regulation falls upon those who cannot pay lead to a different conclusion. In a sense, every denial of welfare to an indigent creates a wealth classification as compared to nonindigents who are able to pay for the desired goods or services. But this Court has never held that financial need alone identifies a suspect [class]. [Cases such as *Griffin* and *Douglas* are distinguishable. Such cases] are grounded in the criminal justice system, a governmental monopoly in which participation is compelled. Our subsequent decisions have made it clear that the principles underlying *Griffin* and *Douglas* do not extend to legislative classifications generally.

"[Accordingly], the central question in this case is whether a regulation 'impinges upon a fundamental right explicitly or implicitly protected by the Constitution.' [Quoting San Antonio Independent School District v. Rodriguez.] The District Court read [*Roe*] as establishing a fundamental right to abortion and therefore concluded that nothing less than a compelling state interest would justify [the] different treatment of abortion and childbirth. [This misconceives] the nature and scope of the fundamental right recognized in *Roe*.

"[*Roe* involved] a Texas law [prohibiting] abortion, except [to save] the life of the mother. [We] held that only a compelling state interest would justify such a sweeping restriction on a constitutionally protected [interest]. [Although] a state-created obstacle [to abortion] need not be absolute to be impermissible, see Doe

v. Bolton, 410 U.S. 179 (1973) [invalidating a law requiring that all first-trimester abortions be performed in a hospital], [*Roe*] did not declare an unqualified 'constitutional right to an abortion.' [Rather], the right protects the woman [only] from unduly burdensome interference with her freedom to decide whether to terminate her pregnancy. It implies no limitation on the authority of a State to make a value judgment favoring childbirth over abortion, and to implement that judgment by the allocation of public funds.

"The [regulation] before us is different in kind from the laws invalidated in our previous [decisions. It] places no obstacles — absolute or otherwise — in the pregnant woman's path to an abortion. An indigent woman who desires an abortion suffers no disadvantage as a consequence of [the State's] decision to fund childbirth; she continues as before to be dependent on private sources for the service she desires. The State may have made childbirth a more attractive alternative, thereby influencing the woman's decision, but it has imposed no restriction on access to abortions that was not already there. The indigency that may make it difficult — and in some cases, perhaps, impossible — for some women to have abortions is neither created nor in any way affected by [the] regulation. [The challenged] regulation does not impinge upon the fundamental right recognized in *Roe*.

"[Appellees] rely on [Shapiro v. Thompson and *Maricopa County*]. Appellees' reliance on the penalty analysis of [those decisions] is misplaced. [*Shapiro*] and *Maricopa County* recognized that denial of welfare to one who had recently exercised the right to travel [was] sufficiently analogous to a criminal fine to justify strict judicial scrutiny. If [the State] denied general welfare benefits to all women who had obtained abortions and who were otherwise entitled to the benefits, we would have a close analogy [to] *Shapiro*, and strict scrutiny might be [appropriate]. But the claim here is that the State 'penalizes' the woman's decision to have an abortion by refusing to pay for it. *Shapiro* and *Maricopa County* did not hold that States would penalize the right to travel [by] refusing to pay the bus fares of the indigent [travelers]. Sherbert v. Verner [see Justice Brennan's dissenting opinion], similarly is inapplicable here. . . .

"Our conclusion signals no retreat from [*Roe*]. There is a basic difference between direct state interference with a protected activity and state encouragement of an alternative [activity]. Constitutional concerns are greatest when the State attempts to impose its will by force of law; the State's power to encourage actions deemed to be in the public interest is necessarily far broader. . . .

"The question remains whether [the challenged] regulation can be sustained under the less demanding test of [rationality]. [*Roe*] itself explicitly acknowledged the State's strong interest in protecting the potential life of the fetus. [The] State unquestionably has a 'strong and legitimate interest in encouraging normal childbirth.' [There can be no] question that the [regulation] rationally furthers that interest. . . . [We] certainly are not unsympathetic to the plight of an indigent woman who desires an abortion, but 'the Constitution does not provide judicial remedies for every social and economic ill.' . . ."

Justice Brennan, joined by Justices Marshall and Blackmun, dissented: "[A] distressing insensitivity to the plight of impoverished pregnant women is inherent in the Court's analysis. The stark reality for too many, not just 'some,' indigent pregnant women is that indigency makes access to competent licensed physicians not merely 'difficult' but 'impossible.' As a practical matter, many indigent women will feel they have no choice but to carry their pregnancies to term because the State will pay for the associated medical services, even though they would have chosen to have abortions if the State had also provided funds for that procedure, or indeed if the State had provided funds for neither procedure. This disparity in funding [clearly] operates to coerce indigent pregnant women to bear children they would not otherwise choose to have. . . .

"None can take seriously the Court's assurance that its 'conclusion signals no retreat from [Roe].' [Indeed, today's] decision seriously erodes [Roe]. The Court's premise is that only an equal protection claim is presented here. [The] Court plainly errs in ignoring [the] unanswerable argument [that] the regulation unconstitutionally impinges upon [the right] of privacy by bringing financial pressures on indigent women that force them to bear children they would not otherwise have. [The] fact that the [challenged] scheme may not operate as an absolute bar preventing all indigent women from having abortions is not critical. What is critical is that the State has inhibited their fundamental right to make that choice free from state interference. [Citing, e.g., Doe v. Bolton; Carey v. Population Services International.] [Indeed], cases involving other fundamental rights [make] clear that [the] compelling-state-interest test is applicable not only to outright denials but also to restraints that make exercise of those rights more difficult. [Citing, e.g., Reynolds v. Sims; Shapiro v. Thompson; Griffin v. Illinois.]

"Nor does the manner in which [the State] has burdened the right [save its] program. The [challenged] scheme cannot be distinguished from other grants and withholdings of financial benefits that we have held unconstitutionally burdened a fundamental right. Sherbert v. Verner, [374 U.S. 398 (1963),] struck down [a] statute that denied unemployment compensation to a woman who for religious reasons could not work on Saturday. [Sherbert] held that 'the pressure upon her to forgo [her religious] practice [was] unmistakable,' [and that] the effect was the same as a fine imposed for Saturday worship. Here, though the burden is upon the right to privacy [and] not upon freedom of religion, [the] governing principle is the same. . . .

"[The] Court [says] that a state requirement is unconstitutional [only] if it 'unduly burdens the right to seek an abortion.' [The challenged regulation] has 'unduly' burdened the fundamental right of pregnant women to be free to choose to have an abortion because the State has advanced no compelling state interest to justify its interference in that choice. . . ."

Justice Marshall also filed a dissenting opinion: "It is all too obvious that the [challenged regulation], ostensibly [adopted] to 'encourage' women to carry pregnancies to term, [is] in reality intended to impose a moral viewpoint that no State may constitutionally enforce. Since efforts to overturn [Roe] have been unsuccessful, the opponents of abortion have attempted every imaginable means to circumvent the commands of the Constitution and impose their moral choices upon the rest of society. [The] present [case involves] the most vicious [attack] yet devised. [I] am appalled at the ethical bankruptcy of those who preach a 'right to life' that means, under present social policies, a bare existence in utter misery for so many poor women and their children. [Today's decision] will be an invitation to public officials [to] approve more such restrictions. [When] elected leaders cower before public pressure, this Court, more than ever, must not shirk its duty to enforce the Constitution for the benefit of the poor and powerless."

Policy malfunction

HARRIS v. McRAE, 448 U.S. 297 (1980): In a five-to-four decision, the Court upheld the "Hyde Amendment," which prohibited the use of federal Medicaid funds "to perform abortions except where the life of the mother would be endangered if the fetus were carried to term; or except for such medical procedures necessary for the victims of rape or incest." Justice Stewart delivered the opinion of the Court:

"The present case [differs] factually from *Maher* insofar as that case involved a failure to fund nontherapeutic abortions, whereas the Hyde Amendment withholds funding of certain medically necessary abortions. [Appellees] argue that because the Hyde Amendment affects a significant interest not present [in] *Maher* — the interest of a woman in protecting her health during pregnancy — and because that interest lies at the core of the personal constitutional freedom recognized in [*Roe*], the present case is constitutionally different from *Maher*. [It] is evident that a woman's interest in protecting her health was an important theme in [*Roe*]. [But], regardless of whether the freedom of a woman to choose to terminate her pregnancy for health reasons lies at the core or the periphery of the due process liberty recognized in [*Roe*], it simply does not follow that a woman's freedom of choice carries with it a constitutional entitlement to the financial resources to avail herself of the full range of protected choices. The reason why was explained in *Maher*: although government may not place obstacles in the path of a woman's exercise of her freedom of choice, it need not remove those not of its own creation. Indigency falls in the latter category. [The] Hyde Amendment leaves an indigent woman with at least the same range of choice in deciding whether to obtain a medically necessary abortion as she would have had if Congress had chosen to subsidize no health care costs at all. [To invalidate the Hyde Amendment] would mark a drastic change in our understanding of the Constitution. It cannot be that because government may not prohibit the use of contraceptives, [*Griswold*], or prevent parents from sending their child to a private school, [*Pierce*], government, therefore, has an affirmative constitutional obligation to ensure that all persons have the financial resources to obtain contraceptives or send their children to private schools. [Nothing] in the Due Process Clause supports such an extraordinary result."

Justice Stewart rejected the equal protection challenge for reasons similar to those stated in *Maher*: "[Because Congress] has neither invaded a substantive constitutional right [nor] enacted legislation [that] operates to the detriment of a suspect class, [strict scrutiny is inappropriate. And it is not] irrational that Congress has authorized federal reimbursement for medically necessary services generally, but not [for] medically necessary abortions, [for] no other [medical] procedure involves the purposeful termination of a potential life."

Justice Brennan, joined by Justices Marshall and Blackmun, dissented for essentially the reasons stated in his *Maher* dissent: "The proposition for which [*Roe* stands] is not that the State is under an affirmative obligation to ensure access to abortions for all who may desire them; it is that the State must refrain from wielding its enormous power and influence in a manner that might burden the pregnant woman's freedom to choose whether to have an abortion. [What] the Court fails to appreciate is that it is not simply the woman's indigency that interferes with her freedom of choice, but the combination of her own poverty and the Government's unequal subsidization of abortion and childbirth."

Justice Stevens was the only member of the *Maher* majority to dissent in *Harris:* "[This case involves women] who, by definition, are confronted with a choice [between] serious health damage to themselves [and abortion]. [In *Roe*, the Court held that, even after viability, a State cannot constitutionally prohibit an abortion that is necessary to preserve the "health of the mother." Thus, *Roe*] squarely held that state interference is unreasonable if it attaches a greater importance to the interest in potential life than to the interest in protecting the mother's health. [Having] decided to alleviate some of the hardships of poverty by providing necessary medical care, the government must use neutral criteria in distributing benefits. [It] may not create exceptions for the sole purpose of furthering a governmental interest that is constitutionally subordinate to the individual interest that the entire program was designed to protect."

Note: The Abortion-Funding Cases

Consider the following views:

1. Perry, Why the Supreme Court Was Plainly Wrong in the Hyde Amendment Case: A Brief Comment on *Harris v. McRae*, 32 Stan. L. Rev. 1113, 1115-1116, 1125 (1980):

> In *Roe* the Court held [that] in the previability period a woman's interest in terminating her pregnancy [is] weightier, as a constitutional matter, than government's interest in preventing the taking of fetal life, *where preventing the taking of fetal life is government's ultimate interest.* [This reasoning] necessarily entails the proposition that *no* governmental action can be predicated on the view that in the previability period abortion is per se morally objectionable. [This is so] because if some governmental action could be predicated on the view that abortion is per se morally objectionable, it would follow that the government's interest in preventing abortion would be weightier than a woman's interest in terminating her pregnancy. [McRae was thus "plainly wrong," for the] view, constitutionally illicit under *Roe*, that in and of itself abortion is morally objectionable indisputably played a determinative role in the passage of the Hyde Amendment.

For a contrary view, consider Westen, Correspondence, 33 Stan. L. Rev. 1187 (1981): "No one can deny that Professor Perry's conclusion follows from his premises. As with most syllogisms, however, the real issue is the validity of the major premise — that *Roe* necessarily prohibited the state from taking *any* action premised on moral objections to abortion."

2. Simson, Abortion, Poverty and the Equal Protection of the Laws, 13 Ga. L. Rev. 505, 507-508, 511-512 (1979):

> [By] offering to pay indigent women's childbirth expenses but not the costs of their having abortions, [the regulations challenged in *Maher* and *Harris*] substantially [interfered] with needy women's decisions as to whether or not to have an abortion. [According to the Court, however, the challenged regulations did] not disadvantage indigent women with regard to the interest declared fundamental in *Roe*. [This conclusion] ought to be perceived as a strategic device for avoiding the constraints of [two-tier analysis]. [If] the Court [had] conceded that the law before it impinged on

the interest discussed in *Roe*, it would have been obliged under two-tier review to demand the same high level of justification as it demanded for the prohibition invalidated in *Roe*. [But] the Court may well have felt that [government] reasonably should not be expected to present as strong a justification for a law that inhibits a woman's abortion decision as for one, like the criminal statute in *Roe*, that deprives her of the decision entirely.

Should the Court deal with this problem by (a) testing *all* laws that inhibit the exercise of a fundamental right by the compelling interest standard; (b) testing laws that do not *substantially* inhibit the exercise of a fundamental right by only the rationality standard; or (c) using a "sliding-scale" analysis? If *Maher* and *Harris* were rightly decided, could a state pay a fee to every woman who has a child in order to discourage abortion? Could it impose a special tax on every woman who has an abortion? On the other hand, if *Maher* and *Harris* were wrongly decided, could a state engage in an "educational" campaign to discourage abortion? To encourage women to have more children?

3. The Court reasoned in *Maher* and *Harris* that "burdens," in the relevant sense, do not arise when the government leaves the allocation of a good or service to the ordinary operation of the market. But this assumes that the basic rule is that goods are allocated by market processes. If the government allocates most goods, relegating some particular good to the market isolates that good from the rest, presumably because the government wishes to see less consumption of the good than would occur if it were subsidized. And actions designed to discourage consumption place burdens on the decision to consume in any reasonable sense. In our society, the government allocates most of the goods that poor people consume. Their shelter is subsidized in public housing, their consumption of food is subsidized by food stamps, their use of most medical services is subsidized by Medicaid, and they have few remaining resources to devote to purchases of unsubsidized goods. Thus, they are in precisely the situation described, where a decision not to subsidize constitutes a burden. See Tushnet, The Supreme Court on Abortion, in Abortion, Medicine and the Law (ed. J. D. Butler & D. Walbert).

4. L. Tribe, Constitutional Choices 243-244 (1985):

> The Court's willingness to uphold laws whose apparent injustice is thought simply to reflect the world's own cruelty [seems] most vivid in a case like [*Harris*]. [In *Roe*], abortion was not perceived as involving the intensely [public] question of the subordination of the poor to the rich through the instrument of coerced childbirth for those unable to afford medical procedures placed by the state on an ability-to-pay basis. [If the issue had been seen in this light], then even the state's use of selective funding to encourage the birth of unwanted children might resemble a program to foster involuntary servitude more closely than an exercise of government's prerogative to set its own priorities.

CITY OF AKRON v. AKRON CENTER FOR REPRODUCTIVE HEALTH, INC., 462 U.S. 416 (1983): In *City of Akron*, the Court considered the constitutionality of "several provisions of an ordinance" designed "to regulate the performance of abortions." In an amicus brief in defense of the challenged provisions, the Solicitor General argued that "Because the legislature has superior fact-finding capabilities, is directly responsible to the public for its resolution of the policy issues it treats, and has greater flexibility than the courts to fine-tune and redirect its efforts if a particular solution is ill-founded or unwise, the courts should test the constitutionality of legislation impacting upon the abortion choice by an appropriately deferential standard." Justice Powell delivered the opinion of the Court:

"[This case comes] to us a decade after we held in [Roe] that the right of privacy [encompasses] a woman's right to decide whether to terminate her pregnancy. [Arguments] continue to be made [that] we erred in interpreting the Constitution. Nonetheless, the doctrine of stare decisis, while perhaps never entirely persuasive on a constitutional question, is a doctrine that demands respect in a society governed by the rule of law. We respect it today, and reaffirm [Roe]. [There] are especially compelling reasons for adhering to stare decisis in applying the principles of [Roe]. That case was considered with special care. It was first argued during the 1971 Term, and reargued — with extensive briefing — the following Term. The decision was joined by [seven] Justices. Since [Roe], the Court repeatedly and consistently has [applied] the basic principle that a woman has a fundamental right to make the highly personal choice whether or not to terminate her pregnancy.

"[The] Court in Roe acknowledged that the woman's fundamental right 'is not unqualified and must be considered against important state interests in abortion.' [But] restrictive state regulation of the right to choose abortion, as with other fundamental rights subject to searching judicial examination, must be supported by a compelling state interest.

"[Roe held that, until the end of the first trimester], a pregnant woman must be permitted, in consultation with her physician, to decide to have an abortion and to effectuate that decision 'free of interference by the State.' [This] does not mean that a State never may enact a regulation touching on the woman's abortion right during the first weeks of pregnancy. Certain regulations that have no significant impact on the woman's exercise of her right may be permissible where justified by important state health objectives. In [Planned Parenthood of Central Missouri v. Danforth, 428 U.S. 52 (1976), for example], we [upheld] provisions, applicable to the first trimester, requiring the woman to provide her informed written consent to the abortion and [requiring] the physician to keep certain records. [The] decisive factor was that [these] regulations furthered important health-related State concerns. But even these minor regulations [during] the first trimester may not interfere with the physician-patient consultation or with the woman's choice between abortion and childbirth.

"[From] approximately the end of the first trimester of pregnancy, the State 'may regulate the abortion procedure to the extent that the regulation reasonably relates to the preservation and protection of maternal health.' [The] State's discretion to regulate on this basis does not, however, permit it to adopt abortion regulations that depart from accepted medical practice. [In Danforth, supra, for example, we] rejected a State's attempt to ban [the saline amniocentesis method of abortion in the second trimester], where the ban would have increased the costs and limited the availability of abortions without promoting important health benefits. . . .

"Section 1870.03 of the Akron ordinance requires that any [second-trimester abortion] must be 'performed in a hospital.' [The] ordinance thus prevents the performance of abortions in outpatient facilities that are not part of an acute-care, full-service hospital. [In Doe v. Bolton, 410 U.S. 179 (1973), we held that a

State could not constitutionally require all first-trimester abortions to be performed in a hospital, because the State had failed to show] ' "that only the full resources of a licensed hospital, rather than those of some other appropriately licensed institution," ' [such as an outpatient clinic,] could satisfy 'its acknowledged interest in insuring [the] full protection of the patient.' Here, however, we deal with second-trimester abortions.

"We reaffirm [that] a State's interest in health regulation becomes compelling at approximately the end of the first trimester. The existence of a compelling state interest in health, however, is only the beginning of the inquiry. The State's regulation may be upheld only if it is reasonably designed to further that state interest. [And if a] regulation 'depart[s] from accepted medical practice' [during] a substantial portion of the second trimester, [it] may not be upheld simply because it may be reasonable for the remaining portion of the trimester. Rather, the State is obligated to make a reasonable effort to limit the effect of its regulations to the period in the trimester during which its health interest will be furthered.

"There can be no doubt that [the] second-trimester hospitalization requirement places a significant obstacle in the path of women seeking an abortion. A primary burden created by the requirement is additional cost to the woman. [Moreover, experience since *Roe*] indicates that [at least during the early weeks of the second trimester, certain types of abortion procedures] may be performed safely on an outpatient basis in appropriate nonhospital facilities. [Indeed, this experience has] convinced the American Public Health Association to abandon its prior recommendation of hospitalization for all second-trimester abortions. [We] conclude, therefore, that 'present medical knowledge' [convincingly] undercuts Akron's justification for requiring that *all* second-trimester abortions be performed in a hospital. [The challenged provision is unconstitutional, for it] unreasonably infringes upon a woman's constitutional right to obtain an abortion. . . .*

"[Section 1870.06(A) of the Akron ordinance] provides that no abortion shall be performed except 'with the informed written consent of the pregnant woman [given] freely and without coercion.' [Section 1870.06(B) provides that], 'in order to insure that the consent for an abortion is truly informed consent,' the woman must be 'orally informed by her attending physician' of the status of her pregnancy, the development of her fetus, the date of possible viability, the physical and emotional complications that may result from an abortion, and the availability of agencies to provide her with assistance and information with respect to birth control, adoption, and childbirth. [In] *Danforth,* supra, we upheld a Missouri law requiring a pregnant woman to 'certif[y] in writing her consent to the [abortion].' We explained: 'The decision to abort [is] an important, and often a stressful one, and it is [imperative] that it be made with full knowledge of its nature and consequences. The [woman's] awareness of the decision and its significance may be assured, constitutionally, by the State to the extent of requiring her prior written consent.' . . .

---

* [In Simopoulos v. Virginia, 462 U.S. 506 (1983), decided on the same day as *City of Akron*, the Court upheld a requirement that second-trimester abortions be performed in either licensed hospitals or licensed outpatient clinics. The Court explained that "Unlike the provisions at issue in *City of Akron*," the challenged requirement "appears to comport with accepted medical practice," it "is not an unreasonable means of furthering the State's compelling interest in 'protecting the woman's own health and safety,' " and it "leaves the method and timing of the abortion precisely where they belong — with the physician and the patient." — Eds.]

"[The] State legitimately may seek to ensure that [the] decision to have an abortion [has] been made 'in the light of all attendant [circumstances,' but it may not use the informing function as a means] to influence the woman's informed choice between abortion or childbirth. [We] believe that §1870.06(B) attempts to extend the State's interest in ensuring 'informed consent' beyond permissible limits. [Much] of the information required is designed not to inform the woman's consent but rather to persuade her to withhold it altogether. Subsection (3) requires the physician to inform his patient that 'the unborn child is a human life from the moment of conception,' a requirement inconsistent with the Court's holding in [Roe] that a State may not adopt one theory of when life begins to justify its regulation of abortions. [And] subsection (5) [begins] with the dubious statement that 'abortion is a major surgical procedure' and proceeds to describe numerous [possible] complications [in] a 'parade of horribles' intended to suggest that abortion [is] particularly dangerous. . . .

"Section 1870.06(C) [provides that] the 'attending physician' must inform the woman 'of the particular risks associated with her own pregnancy [and provide] her with at least a general description of the medical instructions to be followed subsequent to the [abortion].' The information required clearly is related to maternal health and to the State's legitimate purpose in requiring informed consent. [But requiring] physicians personally to discuss the abortion decision [with] each patient may in some cases add to the [cost]. [Although] we have left no doubt that, to ensure the safety of the abortion procedure, the States may mandate that only physicians perform abortions, [we] are not convinced [that] there is as vital a state need for insisting that [a physician] counsel the patient. [The] critical factor is whether [the woman] obtains the necessary information and counseling from a qualified person, not the identity of the person from whom she obtains it. [Section 1870.06(C) is thus unreasonable and] invalid. . . .

"[Section 1870.07] prohibits a physician from performing an abortion until 24 hours after the pregnant woman signs a consent form. [This] increases the cost of obtaining an abortion by requiring the woman to make two separate trips to the abortion facility. [Akron] has failed to demonstrate that any legitimate state interest is furthered by an arbitrary and inflexible waiting period. [In] accordance with the ethical standards of the profession, a physician will advise the patient to defer the abortion when he thinks this will be beneficial to her. But if a woman, after appropriate counseling, is prepared to give her written informed consent and proceed with the abortion, a State may not demand that she delay the effectuation of that decision. . . ."

Justice O'Connor, joined by Justices White and Rehnquist, dissented: "[Neither] sound constitutional theory nor our need to decide cases based on the application of neutral principles can accommodate an analytical framework that varies according to the 'stages' of pregnancy, where those stages, and their concomitant standards of review, differ according to the level of medical technology available when a particular challenge to state regulation occurs. [Our] recent cases indicate that a regulation imposed on 'a lawful abortion "is not unconstitutional unless it unduly burdens the right to seek an abortion."' [Maher.] In my view, this 'unduly burdensome' standard should be applied [throughout] the entire pregnancy without reference to the particular 'stage' of pregnancy involved. If the particular regulation does not 'unduly burden[]' the fundamental right, [then] our evaluation of that regulation is limited to our determination that the regulation rationally relates to a legitimate state purpose. . . .

"The trimester [approach adopted in *Roe*] cannot be supported as a legitimate or useful framework for accommodating the woman's right and the State's interests. [As] the Court indicates today, the State's compelling interest in maternal health changes as medical technology changes, and any health regulation must not 'depart from accepted medical practice.' [Thus,] despite the Court's purported adherence to the trimester [approach], the lines drawn in [*Roe*] have now been 'blurred' [and] the State must continuously [study] contemporary medical and scientific literature in order to determine whether the effect of a particular regulation is to 'depart from accepted medical practice.' [It] is difficult to believe that our Constitution *requires* [legislative bodies to do this, and it] is even more difficult to believe that this Court [believes] itself competent to make these inquiries and to revise these standards every time the American College of Obstetricians and Gynecologists [revises] its views. . . .

"The Court adheres to the *Roe* framework because the doctrine of stare decisis 'demands respect in a society governed by the rule of law.' [Although] respect for stare decisis cannot be challenged, 'this Court's considered practice [is] not to apply stare decisis as rigidly in constitutional as in nonconstitutional cases.' [Although] we must be mindful of the 'desirability of continuity of decision in constitutional questions, [when] convinced of former error, this Court has never felt constrained to follow precedent. In constitutional questions, when correction depends on amendment and not upon legislative action this Court throughout its history has freely exercised its power to reexamine the basis of its constitutional decisions.' [In my view, even] assuming that there is a fundamental right to terminate pregnancy in some situations, there is no justification in law or logic for [adhering to] the trimester framework. . . .

"The Court in *Roe* correctly realized that the State has important interests 'in the areas of health and medical standards' [and] 'in protecting the potentiality of human life.' [In] my view, the point at which these interests become compelling does not depend on the trimester of pregnancy. Rather, these interests are present *throughout* pregnancy. . . .

"Under the *Roe* framework, [the] state interest in maternal health cannot become compelling until the onset of the second trimester of pregnancy because 'until [that time] mortality in abortion may be less than mortality in normal childbirth.' [The] fallacy inherent in [this] framework is apparent: just because the State has a compelling interest in ensuring maternal safety once an abortion may be more dangerous [than] childbirth, it simply does not follow that the State has *no* interest before that point that justifies state regulation to ensure that first-trimester abortions are performed as safely as possible.

"The state interest in potential human life is likewise extant throughout pregnancy. In *Roe*, the Court held that although the State had an important and legitimate interest in protecting potential life, that interest could not become compelling until the point at which the fetus was viable. The difficulty with this analysis is clear: *potential* life is no less potential in the first weeks of pregnancy than it is at viability or afterward. [The] choice of viability as the point at which the state interest in *potential* life becomes compelling is no less arbitrary than choosing any point before viability or any point afterward.

"[Although] the State possesses compelling interests in the protection of potential human life and in maternal health throughout pregnancy, not every regulation [must] be measured against the State's compelling interests and examined with strict scrutiny. '[*Roe*] did not declare an unqualified "right to an abortion." [Rather], the right protects the woman [only] from unduly burdensome interference with her freedom to decide whether to terminate her pregnancy.' [*Maher.*]

"The requirement that state interference 'infringe substantially' or 'heavily burden' a right before heightened scrutiny is applied is not novel in our fundamental-rights jurisprudence, or restricted to the abortion context. In [San Antonio Independent School Dist. v. Rodriguez], we observed that we apply 'strict judicial scrutiny' only when legislation may be said to have ' "deprived," "infringed," or "interfered" with the free exercise of [some] fundamental personal right or liberty.' [Even] in the First Amendment context, we have required in some circumstances that state laws 'infringe substantially' on protected [conduct]. [Citing Gibson v. Florida Legislative Investigating Committee, 372 U.S. 539 (1963); Bates v. Little Rock, 361 U.S. 516 (1960). . . .

"The 'undue burden' required in the abortion cases represents the required threshold inquiry that must be conducted before this Court can require a State to justify its legislative actions under the exacting 'compelling state interest' standard. [An] 'undue burden' [should be] found [only] in situations involving absolute obstacles or severe limitations on the abortion decision. [In] determining whether the State imposes an 'undue burden,' we must keep in mind that when we are concerned with extremely sensitive issues, such as the one involved here, 'the appropriate forum' for their resolution in a democracy is the legislature. [This] does not mean that in determining whether a regulation imposes an 'undue burden' [we must] defer to the judgments made by state legislatures. 'The point is, rather, that [we] do well to pay careful attention to how the other branches of Government have addressed the same problem.' [And we] must always be mindful that '[t]he Constitution does not compel a state [to] encourage or facilitate abortions.' To the contrary, state action 'encouraging childbirth except in the most urgent circumstances' is 'rationally related to the legitimate government objective of protecting potential life.' [*Harris.*]

"Section 1870.03 of the Akron ordinance requires that second-trimester abortions be performed in hospitals. [I would uphold this provision because] the hospitalization requirement does not impose an undue burden on [the abortion] decision. The Court's reliance on increased abortion costs and decreased availability is misplaced. [There] is no evidence [that hospitals in the Akron area do] not provide second-trimester abortions. Further, almost *any* state regulation, including [licensing] requirements that the Court *would* allow, inevitably [entails] increased costs. [Because the] hospitalization requirement does not impose an undue burden, [it] is not necessary to apply an exacting standard of review. Further, the regulation has a 'rational relation' to a valid state objective of ensuring the health and welfare of its citizens. See [Williamson v. Lee Optical Co.]. . . .

"The Court invalidates the informed consent provisions of §1870.06(B) and §1870.06(C). [The] validity of subsections (3) [and] (5) [of §1870.06(B), which are emphasized by the Court,] are not before the Court because it appears that the [City] conceded their unconstitutionality before the court below. [In] my view, the remaining [provisions of §§1870.06(B) & (C)] are separable from the subsections conceded to be unconstitutional [and they] impose no undue burden or drastic limitation on the abortion decision. [Thus, they] do not impermissibly affect any privacy right under the Fourteenth Amendment.

"Section 1870.07 [requires] a 24-hour waiting [period]. [It is] interesting to note that the American College of Obstetricians and Gynecologists recommends that '[p]rior to abortion, the woman should [have] sufficient time for reflection [to make] an informed decision.' [Although] the waiting period may impose an additional cost on the abortion decision, this increased cost does not unduly burden the availability of abortions or impose an absolute obstacle to access to abortions. [And assuming] arguendo that any additional costs are such as to impose an undue [burden], the State's compelling interests in [maternal] health and protection of fetal life clearly justify the waiting period. [The] waiting period is surely a small cost to impose to ensure that the woman's decision is well-considered in light of its certain and irreparable consequences on fetal life, and the possible effects on her own."

Note: Regulating Abortion

1. City of Akron. Consider the following:

a. Do the hospitalization, informed consent, and waiting-period requirements invalidated in *City of Akron* more substantially impair the right recognized in *Roe* than the funding regulations upheld in *Maher* and *Harris*?

b. Is the disagreement between Justices Powell and O'Connor about the "regulation" of abortion, or is it more basic? Note Justice O'Connor's claim that "The state interest in potential human life is [extant] throughout pregnancy." Does this suggest that the state can prohibit *all* abortions (except, perhaps, those necessary to protect the life or health of the mother) in order to protect this interest?

c. Do you agree with Justice O'Connor's attack on the trimester approach of *Roe?* Is O'Connor's "undue burden" approach more sensible? Is it more consistent with the Court's general fundamental rights jurisprudence?

d. Consider Justice Powell's response to Justice O'Connor, set forth in a footnote to his opinion for the Court:

[The] dissenting opinion rejects the basic premise of *Roe* and its progeny. The dissent stops short of arguing flatly that *Roe* should be overruled. Rather, it adopts reasoning that, for all practical purposes, would accomplish precisely that result. [The] dissent does not think that even one of the numerous abortion regulations at issue [in this case] imposes a sufficient burden on the "limited" fundamental right [to] require heightened scrutiny. [Indeed, the] dissent [would] hold that a requirement that all abortions be performed in an acute-care, general hospital does not impose an unacceptable burden on the abortion decision. It requires no great familiarity with the cost and limited availability of such hospitals to appreciate that the effect of the dissent's views would be to drive the performance of many abortions back underground free of effective regulation and often without the attendance of a physician. In sum, it appears that the dissent would uphold virtually any abortion regulation under a rational-basis test. It also appears that even where heightened scrutiny is deemed appropriate, the dissent would uphold virtually any abortion-inhibiting regulation because of the State's interest in preserving potential human life. [Citing Justice O'Connor's analysis of the waiting period requirement.] This analysis is wholly incompatible with the existence of the fundamental right recognized in [*Roe*].

2. *Spousal consent.* In Planned Parenthood of Central Missouri v. Danforth, 428 U.S. 52 (1976), the Court invalidated a Missouri statute requiring the prior written consent of the spouse of the woman seeking an abortion, unless "the abortion is certified by a licensed physician to be necessary in order to preserve the life of the mother." The Court explained:

[We] recognize that the decision whether to undergo or to forgo an abortion may have profound effects on the future of any marriage, effects that are both physical and mental, and possibly deleterious. [Ideally], the decision to terminate a pregnancy should be one concurred in by both the wife and her husband. [But] it is difficult to believe that the goal of fostering mutuality and trust in a marriage [will] be achieved by giving the husband a veto [power]. We recognize, of course, that when a woman, [without] the approval of her husband, decides to terminate her pregnancy, it could be said that she is acting unilaterally. The obvious fact is that when the wife and the husband disagree on this decision, the view of only [one] can prevail. Inasmuch as it is the woman who physically bears the child and who is the more directly and immediately affected by the pregnancy, as between the two, the balance weighs in her favor.

Justice White, joined by Chief Justice Burger and Justice Rehnquist, dissented:

A father's interest in having a child — perhaps his only child — may be unmatched by any other interest in his life. [It] is truly surprising that the majority finds in the [Constitution] a rule that the State must assign a greater value to a mother's decision to cut off a potential human life by abortion than to a father's decision to let it mature into a live child. [These] are matters which a State should be able to decide free from the suffocating power of the federal judge.

Suppose the father favors an abortion but the mother refuses. Can the State compel the abortion? Can it eliminate any responsibility the father might otherwise have to support the child?

Consider the following views: (a) "The Court's apparent position that the mother always has the superior claim and interest, no matter how much the father might show that her burden in childbearing would be less than his burden in losing his child, appears to me an invidious sex discrimination." Burt, The Constitution of the Family, 1979 Sup. Ct. Rev. 329, 394. (b) "[If] the whole issue is one of balancing, might it not be that the state's interest [and the husband's interest *added together* outweigh] the interests of the [woman]?" Regan, Rewriting *Roe v. Wade*, 77 Mich. L. Rev. 1569, 1644 (1979).

3. *Parental consent.* In *Danforth,* supra, the Court, in a five-to-four decision, invalidated a Missouri statute prohibiting an unmarried woman under age eighteen from obtaining an abortion without the written consent of a parent or person in loco parentis, unless "the abortion is certified by a licensed physician as necessary in order to preserve the life of the mother." The Court explained:

Just as with the requirement of consent from the spouse, so here, the State does not have the constitutional authority to give a third party an absolute, and possibly arbitrary, veto over the decision [to] terminate [a pregnancy]. Constitutional rights do not mature and come into being magically only when one attains the state-defined age of majority. Minors, as well as adults, are protected by the Constitution and possess constitutional rights. [Citing, e.g., Tinker v. Des Moines School District, 393 U.S. 503 (1969); In re Gault, 387 U.S. 1 (1967).] [And although the Court has long] recognized that the State has somewhat broader authority to regulate the activities of children than of adults, [it] is difficult [to] conclude [in this context] that providing a parent with absolute power [to prohibit an abortion] will serve to strengthen the family unit.

Justice White, joined by the Chief Justice and Justice Rehnquist, dissented:

Missouri is entitled to protect the minor unmarried woman from making the decision [whether to have an abortion] in a way which is not in her own best interests, and it seeks to achieve this goal by requiring parental consultation and consent. This is the traditional way by which States have sought to protect children from their own immature and improvident decisions; and there is absolutely no reason [why] the State may not utilize that method here.

Justice Stevens also dissented.

In Bellotti v. Baird, 443 U.S. 622 (1979) (*Bellotti II*), the Court invalidated a Massachusetts statute prohibiting an unmarried woman under age eighteen from obtaining an abortion unless both of her parents consent or a court orders the abortion "for good cause shown." In a plurality opinion, Justice Powell, joined by Chief Justice Burger and Justices Stewart and Rehnquist, explained:

We have recognized three reasons justifying the conclusion that the constitutional rights of children cannot be equated with those of adults: the peculiar vulnerability of children; their inability to make critical decisions in an informed, mature manner; and the importance of the parental role in child rearing. [For these reasons,] a State reasonably may determine that parental consultation [is desirable] with respect to the abortion decision — [a decision] that for some people raises profound moral and religious concerns. [At the same time, however,] we are concerned here with a constitutional [right]. The abortion decision differs in important ways from other decisions that may be made during minority. [The] potentially severe detriment facing a pregnant woman [is] not mitigated by her minority. Indeed, [unwanted] motherhood may be exceptionally burdensome for a minor. [We] therefore conclude that if the State decides to require a pregnant minor to obtain [parental] consent to an abortion, it also must provide an alternative procedure whereby authorization for the abortion can be obtained. A pregnant minor is entitled in such a proceeding to show either: (1) that she is mature enough and well enough informed to make her abortion decision [independently] of her parents' wishes; or (2) that even if she is not able to make this decision independently, the desired abortion would be in her best interests. [This] proceeding [must] assure that a resolution [will] be completed with anonymity and [expedition].

Justice Powell concluded that the challenged statute was unconstitutional because it failed to provide such an "alternative" procedure.

Justice Stevens, joined by Justices Brennan, Marshall, and Blackmun, concurred on the ground that the Massachusetts statute was unconstitutional under *Danforth*. Justice White dissented.

In Planned Parenthood Association of Kansas City v. Ashcroft, 462 U.S. 476 (1983), the Court upheld a parental consent requirement that contained an "alternative procedure" sufficient to meet the standards established in Justice Powell's plurality opinion in *Bellotti II*. Justice Powell, joined by Chief Justice Burger, sustained the statute on the basis of his opinion in *Bellotti II*. Justice O'Connor, joined by Justices White and Rehnquist, sustained the statute on the ground that "it imposes no undue burden on any right that a minor may have to undergo an abortion." Justice Blackmun, joined by Justices Brennan, Marshall, and Stevens, dissented on the ground that "any judicial-consent statute [suffers] from the same flaw the Court identified in *Danforth*: it [gives] a third party [i.e., the court] an absolute veto over the decision of the physician and his patient."

4. *Parental notification.* In his plurality opinion in *Bellotti II*, supra, Justice Powell discussed the extent to which a minor employing the "alternative procedure" has a constitutional right "to obtain judicial consent to an abortion" without parental consultation:

> [Many] parents hold strong views on the subject of abortion, and young pregnant minors, especially those living at home, are particularly vulnerable to their parents' efforts to obstruct both an abortion and their access to court. [We] conclude, therefore, that [every] minor must have the opportunity [to] go directly to a court without first consulting or notifying her parents. If she satisfies the court that she is mature and well enough informed to make intelligently the abortion decision on her own, the court must authorize her to act without parental consultation or consent. If she fails to satisfy the court that she is competent to make this decision independently, she must be permitted to show that an abortion nevertheless would be in her best interests. [In making this determination, the court may consider whether] her best interests would be served [by parental consultation]. But this is the full extent to which parental involvement may be required.

Justice White stated in dissent that "I would have thought inconceivable a holding that the [Constitution] forbids even notice to parents when their minor child who seeks surgery objects to such notice and is able to convince a judge that the parents should be denied participation in the decision." Justices Brennan, Marshall, Blackmun, and Stevens did not address the issue.

H. L. v. Matheson, 450 U.S. 398 (1981), concerned a Utah statute requiring a physician to notify, if possible, the parents or guardian of any minor woman on whom an abortion is to be performed. The Court held that the plaintiff lacked standing to challenge the statute "on its face." In a narrow decision, the Court upheld the statute as applied to minor women who are "living with and dependent upon [their] parents," who are "not emancipated by marriage or otherwise," and who have "made no claim or showing as to [their] maturity." The Court explained that, as "applied to immature and dependent minors, the statute plainly serves the important considerations of family integrity and protecting adolescents" and provides "an opportunity for parents to supply essential medical and other information to a physician." Although conceding that "the requirement of notice to parents may inhibit some minors from seeking abortions," the Court maintained that this is "not a valid basis to void the statute as applied [to] the class [before] us." The Court thus concluded that although "a state may not constitutionally legislate a blanket, unreviewable power of parents to veto their daughter's abortion, a statute setting out a 'mere requirement of parental notice' does not violate the constitutional rights of an immature, dependent minor."

In a concurring opinion, Justice Powell, joined by Justice Stewart, reaffirmed the view he stated in *Bellotti II* and emphasized that "a State may not validly require notice to parents in all cases, without providing an independent decision-maker to whom a pregnant minor can have recourse if she believes that she is mature enough to make the abortion decision independently or that notification otherwise would not be in her best interests."

In a dissenting opinion, Justice Marshall, joined by Justices Brennan and Blackmun, maintained that the plaintiff had standing to challenge the statute "on its face." Marshall concluded that, because the statute required parental notification in all cases, it was "plainly overbroad."

5. *Minors and contraceptives.* If minors have a right to an abortion, do they also have a right to contraceptives? In what circumstances, and to what extent, may a state regulate a minor's access to contraceptives? In Carey v. Population Services International, 431 U.S. 678 (1977), the Court invalidated a New York statute prohibiting the distribution of contraceptives to persons under age sixteen. In a plurality opinion, Justice Brennan, joined by Justices Stewart, Marshall, and Blackmun, reasoned:

> [The] right to privacy in connection with decisions affecting procreation extends to minors as well as adults. [Citing *Danforth.*] [The State argues], however, that significant state interests are served by restricting minors' access to contraceptives, because free availability to minors of contraceptives would lead to increased sexual activity among the [young]. The same argument, however, would support a ban on abortions for [minors]. [As we said in *Eisenstadt*]: "It would be plainly unreasonable to assume that [the State] has prescribed pregnancy [as] punishment for fornication." [Moreover], there is substantial reason for doubt whether limiting access to contraceptives will in fact substantially discourage early sexual behavior. [When] a State, as here, burdens the exercise of a fundamental right, its attempt to justify that burden as a rational means for the accomplishment of some significant state policy requires more than a bare assertion [that] the burden is connected to such a policy.

Justice White concurred in the result. White emphasized that "the legality of state laws forbidding premarital intercourse is not at issue here." White concurred because "the State has not demonstrated that the prohibition against distribution of contraceptives to minors measurably contributes to the deterrent purposes which the State advances."

Justice Powell also concurred in the result. In Powell's view, the challenged statute was "defective" because it "prohibits parents from distributing contraceptives to their children, a restriction that unjustifiably interferes with parental interests in rearing their children. [Citing, e.g., *Pierce* and *Meyer.*]" Powell added that, in his view, a State could constitutionally require "prior parental consultation" as a condition of minors obtaining contraceptives.

Justice Stevens also concurred in the result. Stevens emphasized that the holding in *Danforth* "that a minor's decision to abort her pregnancy may not be conditioned on parental consent, is not dispositive here," for the Constitution does not provide "the same measure of protection to the minor's right to use contraceptives as to the pregnant female's right to abort." This is so, Stevens explained, because the "already pregnant minor [must] bear a child unless she aborts," whereas "nonpregnant minors [can] and generally will avoid childbearing by abstention." Nonetheless, Stevens maintained that the challenged statute was analogous to a state effort "to dramatize its disapproval of motorcycles by forbidding the use of safety helmets" and that such an effort is "irrational and perverse" and, hence, a violation of due process. Chief Justice Burger and Justice Rehnquist dissented.

6. *Protecting the viable fetus.* In *Danforth*, supra, the Court upheld a statute that defined "viability" as "that stage of fetal development when the life of the unborn child may be continued indefinitely outside the womb by natural or artificial life-supportive systems." The Court rejected the contention "that a specified number of weeks in pregnancy must be fixed by statute as the point of viability": "it is not the proper function of the legislature or the courts to place viability, which essentially is a medical concept, at a specific point in the gestation period. The time when viability is achieved may vary with each pregnancy, and the determination of whether a particular fetus is viable is, and must be, a matter for the judgment of the responsible attending physician."

At the same time, however, the Court in *Danforth* invalidated another section of the statute providing that "No person who performs [an] abortion shall fail to exercise that degree of professional skill, care and diligence to preserve the life and health of the fetus which such person would be required to exercise in order to preserve the life and health of any fetus intended to be [born]." Noting that the provision "does not specify that such care need be taken only after [viability]," the Court concluded that the provision "impermissibly requires the physician to preserve the life and health of the fetus, whatever the stage of pregnancy," and thus "effectively precludes abortion."

In Colautti v. Franklin, 439 U.S. 379 (1979), the Court invalidated a Pennsylvania statute that requires every person who performs an abortion first to determine, "based on his experience, judgment or professional competence," that the fetus is not viable. If the person performing the abortion determines that the fetus "is viable," or "if there is sufficient reason to believe that the fetus may be viable," the statute requires the person performing the abortion to exercise the same care to preserve the life and health of the fetus as would be required if the fetus were intended to be born alive, and to use the abortion technique providing the best opportunity for the fetus to be born alive, so long as a different technique is not necessary to preserve the life or health of the mother. The Court held the provision "void-for-vagueness" because (a) the "distinction between the phrases 'is viable' and 'may be viable' [is] elusive," (b) the standard-of-care provision is "uncertain" as to whether the physician may "consider his duty to the patient to be paramount [or] whether it requires the physician to make a 'trade-off' between the woman's health and additional percentage points of fetal survival," and (c) the provision "subjects the physician to potential criminal liability without regard to fault," thus compounding the problem of vagueness. Justice White, joined by Chief Justice Burger and Justice Rehnquist, dissented.

In Planned Parenthood Association of Kansas City v. Ashcroft, 462 U.S. 476 (1983), the Court upheld a Missouri statute requiring the attendance of a second physician at all postviability abortions. Missouri permits postviability abortions only when necessary to preserve the life or health of the mother. The statute requires the second physician to "provide immediate medical care" to the "child." Although conceding that the second-physician requirement is "costly," that "Missouri does not require two physicians in attendance for any other medical or surgical procedure," and that only a small percentage of aborted fetuses can be saved, Justice Powell, joined by Chief Justice Burger, nonetheless concluded that "the second-physician requirement reasonably furthers the State's compelling interest in protecting the lives of viable fetuses" because "the second physician," by "giving immediate medical attention to a fetus that is delivered alive, [will] assure that the State's interests are protected more fully than the first physician alone would be able to do." Justice O'Connor, joined by Justices White and Rehnquist, concurred on the ground that "the State possesses a compelling interest in protecting and preserving fetal life." Justice Blackmun, joined by Justices Brennan, Marshall, and Stevens, dissented on the ground that the statute is "overbroad" because it requires a second physician even when the necessary method of abortion renders the "chance of a live birth . . . nonexistent." For discussion of related issues, see Rhoden, The Neonatal Dilemma: Live Births from Late Abortions, 72 Geo. L.J. 1451 (1984).

7. *Miscellaneous regulations.* For the Court's analysis of other regulations of abortion, see *Danforth,* supra (upholding a recordkeeping requirement even as applied to first-trimester abortions); *Ashcroft,* supra (upholding a requirement that when an abortion is performed, a tissue sample be submitted to a certified pathologist for a report); *Danforth,* supra (invalidating a prohibition on the use of saline amniocentesis abortions); *City of Akron,* supra (invalidating on vagueness grounds a requirement that physicians dispose of "the remains of the unborn child [in] a humane and sanitary manner").

3. Family and Other "Privacy" Interests

The modern substantive due process decisions we have examined thus far — *Griswold, Eisenstadt, Roe,* and so on — have all involved the freedom to decide "whether to bear or beget a child." Is modern substantive due process so limited? *Meyer* and *Pierce,* of course, dealt with matters beyond procreation. The three primary cases in this section examine the relationship between the right of privacy and the integrity of the "family." The Note that follows those cases examines other possible extensions of the right.

MOORE v. CITY OF EAST CLEVELAND, 431 U.S. 494 (1977): In *Moore* the Court invalidated a city ordinance limiting occupancy of any dwelling unit to members of the same "family," where the ordinance narrowly defined "family" as including only "a few categories of related individuals." Appellant lived with her son, Dale, and her two grandsons, Dale, Jr., and John. Under the ordinance, John could not live in the home because he was not "sufficiently related" to his uncle, Dale, and his cousin, Dale, Jr., to constitute a "family" within the meaning of the ordinance. In a plurality opinion, Justice Powell, joined by Justices Brennan, Marshall, and Blackmun, concluded that the ordinance violated the due process clause of the fourteenth amendment:

  "The city argues that our decision in Village of Belle Terre v. Boraas, 416 U.S. 1 (1974), requires us to sustain the ordinance attacked here. Belle Terre, like East Cleveland, imposed limits on the types of groups that could occupy a single dwelling unit. [We] sustained the Belle Terre ordinance on the ground that it bore a rational relationship to permissible state objectives. But one overriding factor sets this case apart from *Belle Terre.* The ordinance there affected only *unrelated* individuals. It expressly allowed all who were related by 'blood, adoption, or marriage' to live [together]. East Cleveland, in contrast, has chosen to regulate the occupancy of its housing by slicing deeply into the family itself. [The ordinance] selects certain categories of relatives who may live together and declares that others may not. In particular, it makes a crime of a grandmother's choice to live with her grandson in circumstances like those presented here.

"When a city undertakes such intrusive regulation of the family, [*Belle Terre* does not govern, and] the usual judicial deference to the legislature is inappropriate. 'This Court has long recognized that freedom of personal choice in matters of marriage and family life is one of the liberties protected by the Due Process Clause of the Fourteenth Amendment.' [Citing, e.g., *Meyer*; *Pierce*; *Roe*; *Griswold*; *Skinner*.] [When] government intrudes on choices concerning family living arrangements, this Court must examine carefully the importance of the governmental interests advanced and the extent to which they are served by the challenged regulation. When thus examined, this ordinance cannot survive. The city seeks to justify it as a means of preventing overcrowding, minimizing traffic and parking congestion, and avoiding an undue financial burden on [the] school system. Although these are legitimate goals, the ordinance [serves] them marginally, at best. . . .

"Substantive due process has at times been a treacherous field for this Court. There *are* risks when the judicial branch gives enhanced protection to certain substantive liberties without the guidance of the more specific provisions of the Bill of Rights. As the history of the *Lochner* era demonstrates, there is reason for concern lest the only limits to such judicial intervention become the predilections of those who happen at the time to be Members of this Court. That history counsels caution and restraint. But it does not counsel abandonment. . . .

"Appropriate limits on substantive due process come [from] careful 'respect for the teachings of history [and] solid recognition of the basic values that underlie our society.' [*Griswold* (Harlan, J., concurring).] Our decisions establish that the Constitution protects the sanctity of the family precisely because the institution of the family is deeply rooted in this Nation's history and tradition. It is through the family that we inculcate and pass down many of our most cherished values, moral and cultural. [And ours] is by no means a tradition limited to respect for [the] nuclear family. The tradition of uncles, aunts, cousins, and especially grandparents sharing a household along with parents has roots equally venerable and equally deserving of constitutional recognition. [Out] of choice, necessity, or a sense of family responsibility, it has been common for close relatives to draw [together]. Especially in times of adversity [the] broader family has tended to come together for mutual [sustenance]. [The] choice of relatives in this degree of kinship to live together may not lightly be denied by the State. [The] Constitution prevents East Cleveland from standardizing its children — and its adults — by forcing all to live in certain narrowly defined family patterns."

Justice Stevens concurred in the result on the ground that the challenged ordinance "constitutes a taking of property without due process and without just compensation." Justice Stewart, joined by Justice Rehnquist, dissented:

"[Appellant's] claim that the ordinance [invades the] constitutionally protected [right] of association [is] in large part answered by [*Belle Terre*]. To suggest [that] related persons [have] constitutional rights of association superior to those of unrelated persons is to misunderstand the nature of the associational freedoms that the Constitution has been understood to protect. Freedom of association has been constitutionally recognized because it is often indispensable to effectuation of explicit First Amendment guarantees. [Citing, e.g., NAACP v. Alabama, 357 U.S. 449 (1958).] [The] 'association' in this case is not for any purpose relating to the promotion of speech, assembly, the press, or religion. And wherever the outer boundaries of constitutional protection of freedom of association may eventually turn out to be, they surely do not extend to those who assert no interest other than the gratification, convenience, and economy of sharing the same residence.

"[Appellant] is considerably closer to the constitutional mark in asserting that [the] ordinance intrudes upon 'the private realm of family life which the state cannot enter.' [But] appellant's desire to share a single-dwelling unit [can] hardly be equated with any of the interests protected in [our prior decisions]. The ordinance [did] not impede her choice to have or not to have children, and it did not dictate to her how her own children were to be nurtured and reared. The ordinance [does] not prevent parents from living together or living with their unemancipated offspring. [When] the Court has found that the Fourteenth Amendment placed a substantive limitation on a State's power to regulate, it has been in those rare cases in which the personal interests at issue have been deemed 'implicit in the concept of ordered liberty.' The interest [that] appellant may have in permanently sharing a single kitchen and a suite of contiguous rooms with some of her relatives simply does not rise to that level. To equate this interest with the fundamental decisions to marry and to bear and raise children is to extend the limited substantive contours of the Due Process Clause beyond recognition."

Justice White also dissented: "[Although] the Due Process Clause extends substantial protection to various phases of family life, [the challenged] ordinance [merely] denies appellant the opportunity to live with all her grandchildren in this particular [suburb]. [Her] claim is hardly one of which it could be said that 'neither liberty nor justice would exist if [it] were sacrificed.' [Justice] Powell would apparently construe the Due Process Clause to protect from all but quite important state regulatory interests any right or privilege that in his estimation is deeply rooted in the country's traditions. For me, this suggests a far too expansive charter for this [Court]. What the deeply rooted traditions of the country are is arguable; which of them deserve the protection of the Due Process Clause is even more debatable. The suggested view would broaden enormously the horizons of the Clause; and, if the interest involved here is any measure of what the States would be forbidden to regulate, the courts would be substantively weighing and very likely invalidating a wide range of measures that Congress and state legislatures think appropriate to respond to a changing economic and social order."

Chief Justice Burger dissented on procedural grounds.

---

1. Do you agree with the plurality that the Court should employ strict scrutiny when government "intrudes on choices concerning family living arrangements"?

2. Is *Belle Terre* distinguishable from *Moore* because the ordinance upheld in *Belle Terre* "allowed all who were related by 'blood, adoption, or marriage' to live [together]"? Is that the constitutionally mandated definition of "family" because of tradition? If so, is tradition an appropriate basis for the definition and limitation of constitutional rights? Is there any other basis for a constitutional definition of family?

Consider Note, Developments in the Law — The Constitution and the Family, 93 Harv. L. Rev. 1156, 1177, 1186-1187, 1180-1182 (1980):

In the family cases, the Court has consistently turned to tradition as a source of previously unrecognized aspects of the liberty protected by the due process clauses. [Recourse] to traditional values enables the Court to afford constitutional protection to rights Americans traditionally have assumed to be part of our nation's scheme of liberty. [The] use of tradition [appeals] to the Court's need for a sense of impartiality in the application of substantive due process. [Reference] to tradition does not involve the Court in the ambitious task of developing its own unified theory of political liberty; rather, the initial appeal is to a relatively objective history.

[Once] a traditional value has been accepted as an aspect of constitutional liberty, the Court must give that value a consistent and principled interpretation. Otherwise, the actual contours tradition supplies may reflect the same prejudice and insensitivity that necessitate judicial protection of unenumerated rights in the first place. [Justice] Powell stated this clearly in *Moore*, refusing to confine constitutional protection to the nuclear [family]. Because a functional approach extends the scope of a traditional right beyond its historical contours, it may be criticized as manipulation of the level of generality of the relevant tradition so that rights not historically regarded as important liberties are brought within the scope of protection. This criticism misses the point. A court which extends the right of procreative autonomy from a marital to a nonmarital context is not contending that the procreative rights of the unmarried are traditional. It is merely claiming that, given a longstanding cultural consensus that procreative activities [are special], there must be some principled basis for treating the unmarried and married differently.

3. Did the Court in *Moore* fail to see the real nature of the dispute? Consider Burt, The Constitution of the Family, 1979 Sup. Ct. Rev. 329, 391:

[Victory] for Mrs. Moore was total defeat for the other residents of East Cleveland, while victory for them was not total defeat for her, except insofar as she wished to remain in their community while transforming [it] to her taste. If Mrs. Moore were shut out from many different [communities] — if, that is, the city ordinance was not [unusual] — then the Court might properly have seen some role for itself in protecting her interests. [But] the very oddity of [the] ordinance suggests [that] the city residents are more the vulnerable, isolated dissenters than [she]. The Court in *Moore* myopically saw the case as a dispute between "a family" and "the state" rather than as a dispute among citizens about the meaning of "family."

4. After *Belle Terre* and *Moore*, could a city constitutionally prohibit "significant others" from living together? Consider the following views:

a. Karst, The Freedom of Intimate Association, 89 Yale L.J. 624, 686-689 (1980):

When the freedom of intimate association is seen in the perspective of our recent appreciation of cultural [diversity], the principle extends without difficulty to family living arrangements that are alternatives to those of [even] the extended family given a blessing-by-plurality in [*Moore*]. Families of choice, from lesbian mothers and their children to communes of the young and the old are responses to what their members often see as the failings of other familial arrangements. [A] legislature that prohibits unmarried cohabitation, or homosexual relations, or other disapproved forms of intimate association does so primarily to promote a certain view of morality, and to protect the sensibilities of those who share that view. Although the freedom of intimate association does not wholly disable government from seeking to promote majoritarian morals, just as surely the state cannot defeat every claim to the freedom of intimate association by invoking conventional moral values. [The] power to reinforce one type of relationship must not extend to an authority to stamp out another.

   b. Hafen, The Constitutional Status of Marriage, Kinship, and Sexual Privacy — Balancing the Individual and Social Interests, 81 Mich. L. Rev. 463, 559, 487 (1983):

When the legal system [protects] such relationships as kinship and formal marriage, it advances not only the immediate individual interests involved, but society's interest in social and political structures that sustain long-term individual liberty. [The] structure of marriage and kinship responds to that social interest by maximizing the interest of children and society in a stable family environment; by ensuring a socialization process and an attitude toward personal obligation that maximizes democracy's interest in the voluntary "public virtue" of its citizens; by maintaining marriage and kinship as legally recognizable structures that mediate between the individual and the State, thereby limiting governmental power; and by maintaining sources of objective jurisprudence that will ensure stable personal expectations, [thereby] minimizing the arbitrary power of the State. In these ways, the structure of formal family life emphasizes that sense of "*ordered* liberty" necessary to achieve individual liberty as a *long-range* objective. [Moreover, the] natural boundary created by the objective nature of legal marriage [and kinship] is [significant]. Once these limits are breached, there is no realistic boundary [that] will confine [the right] according to any meaningful standards. A boundary based on the degree of commitment to a relationship [would] require intolerable inquiries into the most private realm [of] individuals' lives. [And if the right were so expanded, the] power of family life [to] promote the ends of a democratic society would [be] seriously impaired.

   5. If, as *Moore* suggests, the traditional concept of "family" is fundamental, in what circumstances, if any, may the State interfere with the individual's ability to enter into a traditional "family" relationship? Consider *Zablocki*.

   ZABLOCKI v. REDHAIL, 434 U.S. 374 (1978): In *Zablocki* the Court invalidated a Wisconsin statute providing that any resident "having minor issue not in his custody and which he is under an obligation to support by court order" may not marry without a prior judicial determination that the support obligation has been met and that the children "are not then and are not likely thereafter to become public charges." The Court, in an opinion by Justice Marshall, held that the statute violated the equal protection clause:
   "[The] decisions of this Court confirm that the right to marry is of fundamental importance for all individuals. [Citing, e.g., Loving v. Virginia, 388 U.S. 1 (1967) (invalidating state miscegenation laws); *Griswold*; *Skinner*; *Meyer*.] It is not surprising that the decision to marry has been placed on the same level of importance as decisions relating to procreation, childbirth, child rearing, and family relationships. [It] would make little sense to recognize a right of privacy with respect to other matters of family life and not with respect to the decision to enter the relationship that is the foundation of the family in our society. [If the] right to procreate means anything at all, it must imply some right to enter the only relationship in which the [State] allows sexual relations legally to take place. [We]

do not mean to suggest that every state regulation which relates in any way to the incidents of or prerequisites for marriage must be subjected to rigorous scrutiny. To the contrary, reasonable regulations that do not significantly interfere with decisions to enter into the marital relationship may legitimately be imposed. [Citing, e.g., Califano v. Jobst, infra.]

"The statutory classification at issue here, however, [interferes] directly and substantially with the right to marry. Under the challenged statute, [some persons] will never be able to obtain the necessary court order, because they either lack the financial means to meet their support obligations or cannot prove that their children will not become public charges. These persons are absolutely prevented from getting married. Many others, able in theory to satisfy the statute's requirements, will be sufficiently burdened by having to do so that they will [forgo] their right to marry. And even those who can [meet] the statute's requirements suffer a serious intrusion into their freedom of choice in an area in which we have held such freedom to be fundamental.

"When a statutory classification significantly interferes with the exercise of a fundamental right, it cannot be upheld unless it is supported by sufficiently important state interests and is closely tailored to effectuate only those interests. [The State argues that the statute protects the welfare of the out-of-custody children, but this] 'collection device' rationale cannot justify the statute's broad infringement on the right to marry. First, with respect to individuals who are unable to [pay], the statute merely prevents the applicant from getting married, without delivering any money at all into the hands of [the] children. More importantly, [the] State already has numerous other means for exacting compliance with support obligations [that] do not impinge upon the right to marry."

Justice Stewart concurred in the judgment: "To hold [that] the Wisconsin statute violates the Equal Protection Clause [misconceives] the meaning of that constitutional guarantee. [The] problem in this case is not one of discriminatory classifications, but of unwarranted encroachment upon a constitutionally protected freedom. [The] statute is unconstitutional because it exceeds the bounds of permissible state regulation of marriage, and invades the sphere of liberty protected by the Due Process Clause of the Fourteenth Amendment. [On] several occasions this Court has held that a person's inability to pay [does] not justify the total deprivation of a constitutionally protected liberty. [Citing Boddie.] The principle of [Boddie] applies [here]. We [may] assume that [the law is permissible] as applied to those who can afford to [pay] but choose not to do [so]. [But] some people simply cannot afford to [pay]. To deny these people permission to marry penalizes them for failing to do that which they cannot do. Insofar as it applies to indigents, the [law] is [irrational]."

Justice Powell also concurred in the judgment: "The Court apparently would subject all state regulation which 'directly and substantially' interferes with the decision to marry in a traditional family setting [to] 'compelling state interest' analysis. [We must recognize, however, that] domestic relations [is] 'an area that has long been regarded as a virtually exclusive province of the States.' [The] State, representing the collective expression of moral aspirations, has an undeniable interest in ensuring that its rules of domestic relations reflect the widely held values of its people. [State] regulation has included bans on incest, bigamy, and homosexuality, as well as various preconditions to marriage, such as blood tests. Likewise, a showing of fault [traditionally] has been a prerequisite to [divorce]. A 'compelling state purpose' inquiry would cast doubt on [such restrictions]." Justice Powell then argued for a more flexible approach: "The Due Process Clause requires a showing of justification 'when the government intrudes on choices concerning family living arrangements' in a manner which is contrary to deeply rooted traditions. [Quoting his plurality opinion in *Moore*.] Furthermore, under the Equal Protection Clause the means chosen by the State in this case must bear 'a fair and substantial relation' to the object of the legislation. [Quoting Reed v. Reed, 404 U.S. 71 (1971).] The [challenged statute] does not pass muster under either due process or equal protection standards. [I] do not agree with the [Court] that a State may never condition the right to marry on satisfaction of existing support obligations [where] the [person is] able to make the required support payments but simply wish[es] to shirk [his] moral and legal [obligation]. The vice inheres, not in the collection concept, but in the failure to [exempt] those without the means to [pay]. [Citing *Boddie*.]"

Justice Stevens also concurred in the judgment: "The individual's interest in making the marriage decision independently is sufficiently important to merit special constitutional protection. It is not, however, an interest which is constitutionally immune from evenhanded regulation. Thus, laws prohibiting marriage to a child, a close relative, or a person afflicted with venereal disease, are unchallenged even though they 'interfere directly and substantially with the right to marry.' [The challenged] statute has a different character. Under this statute, a person's economic status may determine his eligibility to [marry]. This type of statutory discrimination [is] inconsistent with our tradition of administering justice equally to the rich and to the poor. [Neither] the fact that the appellee's interest is constitutionally protected, nor the fact that the classification is based on economic status is sufficient to justify a 'level of scrutiny' so strict that a holding of unconstitutionality is virtually foreordained. [But] the presence of these factors precludes a holding that [rational explanation] is [sufficient]. [Here, the] discrimination between the rich and the poor is irrational in so many ways that it cannot withstand scrutiny under the Equal Protection Clause."

Justice Rehnquist was the lone dissenter: "I [agree with Justice Powell] that marriage is [not] the sort of 'fundamental right' which must invariably trigger the strictest judicial scrutiny. I disagree with his imposition of an 'intermediate' standard of [review]. I would view this [statute] in the light of the traditional presumption of validity. [The] statute so viewed is a permissible exercise of the State's power to regulate family life and to assure the support of minor children."

---

1. Why did the Court rely on due process in *Moore* but on equal protection in *Zablocki*? Does it matter whether the Court emphasizes liberty or equality? Consider Lupu, Untangling the Strands of the Fourteenth Amendment, 77 Mich. L. Rev. 981, 982-985 (1979):

[The] fourteenth amendment companionship of liberty and equality [has] created opportunities for misunderstanding as well as for creative linkage. In particular, the judicial selection of values for special protection against the majoritarian processes has wavered [between] a liberty base and an equality base. [This] has led the Court into a tangle. [The] tangling is [most] serious when viewed in its relationship to the so-called "fundamental rights" developments in both equal protection and due process clause interpretation. [This] doctrinal imprecision has bred unpredictability, disrespect, and charges of outcome-orientation. [The] equal protection clause and the due process clause are complementary — not interchangeable — [safeguards]. Whether the fourteenth amendment remains a credible source of protection for the individual depends upon the process of untangling. [Judicial] discovery of fundamental [values] outside the constitutional text [should be grounded in the due process clause. The] equality strand [should] not bear a substantive content — [equal] protection [should] remain substantially rooted in the pure anti-discrimination concerns that sparked the [clause].

2. In Califano v. Jobst, 434 U.S. 47 (1977), the Court unanimously upheld a section of the Social Security Act providing that benefits received by a disabled dependent child of a covered wage earner shall terminate when the child marries an individual who is not independently entitled to benefits under the act, even though that individual is also disabled. The Court applied the rational basis standard:

> Both tradition and common experience support the conclusion that marriage is an event which normally marks an important change in economic status. [Frequently], of course, financial independence and marriage do not go hand in hand. [But] there can be no question about the validity of the assumption that a married person is less likely to be dependent on his parents for support than one who is unmarried. [The challenged provision thus satisfies] the constitutional test normally applied in cases like this. That general rule is not rendered invalid simply because some persons who might otherwise have married were deterred by the rule or because some who did marry were burdened thereby. For the [challenged] rule cannot be criticized as merely [an] attempt to interfere with the individual's freedom to make a decision as important as marriage [or] to foist orthodoxy on the unwilling by banning, or criminally prosecuting, nonconforming marriages.

Is *Jobst* consistent with *Zablocki?* In *Zablocki* the Court maintained that "The directness and substantiality of the interference with the freedom to marry distinguish the instant case from [*Jobst*]. [The provision challenged in *Jobst*] placed no direct legal obstacle in the path of persons desiring to get married, [and] there was no evidence that the [law] significantly discouraged [or] made 'practically impossible' any marriages." Is *Jobst* consistent with *Zablocki* because the provisions challenged in *Jobst* did not disadvantage the poor? Because, as Justice Stevens argued in *Zablocki*, "A classification based on marital status [e.g., *Jobst*] is fundamentally different from a classification which determines who may lawfully enter into the marriage relationship [e.g., *Zablocki*]"?

3. After *Zablocki* are marriage license fees constitutional? Recall *Harper, Griffin, Douglas,* and *Boddie.*

4. If there is a constitutional right to marry, is there a correlative right to divorce? Recall Boddie v. Connecticut, supra section E2. Consider Karst, supra, at 671: "To condition divorce on a showing of fault is to place an insuperable burden on some spouses [and] to interfere very significantly with such a spouse's decision to associate with another person in marriage. [Thus,] no-fault divorce seems implied [unless] the state can demonstrate some very strong interest in the fault requirement."

STANLEY v. ILLINOIS, 405 U.S. 645 (1972): "Joan Stanley lived with Peter Stanley intermittently for 18 years, during which time they had three children. [Then Joan Stanley died.] Under Illinois law, the children of unwed fathers [automatically] become wards of the State upon the death of the mother. [Stanley maintained] that he had never been shown to be an unfit parent and that since married fathers [could] not be deprived of their children without such a showing, he had been deprived of the equal protection of the laws." The Supreme Court agreed. Justice White delivered the opinion:

"[The] interest of a parent in the companionship, care, custody, and management of his or her children 'come[s] to this Court with a momentum for respect lacking when appeal is made to liberties which derive merely from shifting economic arrangements.' The Court has frequently emphasized the importance of the family. [Nor] has the law refused to recognize those family relationships unlegitimized by a marriage ceremony. ['To] say that the test of equal protection should be the "legal" rather than the biological relationship is to avoid the issue. For the Equal Protection Clause necessarily limits the authority of a State to draw such "legal" lines as it chooses.' . . .

"It may be [that] most unmarried fathers are unsuitable and neglectful parents. [But] all unmarried fathers are not in this category. [Given] the opportunity to make his case, Stanley may have been seen to be deserving of custody of his offspring. [Procedure] by presumption is always cheaper and easier than individualized determination. But when, as here, the procedure [needlessly] risks running roughshod over the important interests of both parent and child [it] cannot stand."

Justices Powell and Rehnquist did not participate.

Chief Justice Burger, joined by Justice Blackmun, dissented: "[The] Equal Protection Clause is not violated when Illinois gives full recognition only to those father-child relationships that arise in the context of family units bound together by legal [obligations]. Quite apart from the religious or quasi-religious connotations that marriage has [historically enjoyed], it is in law an essentially contractual relationship, the parties to which have legally enforceable rights and duties, with respect both to each other and to any children born to them. Stanley and the mother of these children never entered such a relationship. [Stanley] did not seek the burdens when he could have freely assumed them."

---

1. Do these decisions — *Moore*, *Zablocki*, and *Stanley* — present a coherent vision of the "family"? Is *Stanley* consistent with *Moore*'s emphasis on "traditional" family values? By legitimating relationships that do not fit within the "traditional" family structure, it can be argued that *Stanley* undermines the very values that *Moore* sought to protect. Consider also in this regard Eisenstadt v. Baird, supra (unmarried persons have a constitutional right to use contraceptives); Planned Parenthood v. Danforth, supra (minors in some circumstances have a constitutional right to an abortion without parental consent); Mathews v. Lucas, 427 U.S. 495 (1976) (laws disadvantaging illegitimate children must be tested by intermediate scrutiny); Parham v. J. R., 442 U.S. 584 (1979) (due process requires at least an inquiry before a "neutral factfinder," although not a full-scale adversary hearing, before a parent may commit a minor child to a state mental hospital). See generally Burt, The Constitution of the Family, 1979 Sup. Ct. Rev. 329.

2. If an unwed father may have a constitutional right to custody of his illegitimate children when the mother dies, does he also have a constitutional right to veto the adoption of his illegitimate children by the mother's husband? In Quil-

loin v. Walcott, 434 U.S. 246 (1978), the Court unanimously held that a state could constitutionally deny such a veto to an unwed father, even though granting it to married and divorced fathers, where the unwed father had "never exercised actual or legal custody" over the child and there had been a determination that the adoption was in the "best interests of the child."

Consider Hafen, supra, at 497-499:

> [Despite *Stanley*, *Quilloin* makes] clear that [only] when [an unwed] father has admitted his paternity, "established a substantial relationship with the child," and "shouldered significant responsibility" for his child, will his parental interests receive constitutional protection. [The] difference between the law's treatment of a married man and an unmarried man was justified [in *Quilloin*] because of what [the Court] called a "difference in the extent of the commitment to the welfare of the child." In other words, a man's unwillingness to marry [raises a] presumption that he is unwilling to make long-term commitments to his children. [Those] concerned about the welfare of an illegitimate [child] cannot keep the child [waiting] to see what "functional equivalents" of marriage the father will [demonstrate]. The marriage commitment enables the courts [to] make certain assumptions [about] what to expect.

3. May a state take a child from his legitimate parents in order to serve the "best interests of the child"? In *Quilloin* the Court observed: "We have little doubt that the Due Process Clause would be offended '[i]f a State were to attempt to force the breakup of a natural family, over the objections of the parents and their children, without some showing of unfitness and for the sole reason that to do so was thought to be in the children's best interest.'" When *may* a state "break up" a "natural family"? May a state remove a child from his parents because they engage in criminal, adulterous, or otherwise immoral activity?

To date, the Court has focused more on the procedures than on the substantive limits of parental termination actions. See, e.g., Santosky v. Kramer, 455 U.S. 745 (1982) (holding that "Before a State may sever completely and irrevocably the rights of parents in their natural child [on the ground that the child was 'permanently neglected'], due process requires that the State support its allegations by at least clear and convincing evidence"); Lassiter v. Department of Social Services, 452 U.S. 18 (1981) (holding that due process does not require the appointment of counsel for an indigent parent in a parental termination proceeding where the petition to terminate contained no allegations on which criminal charges could be based, the case presented no especially troublesome points of law, the presence of counsel could not have made a determinative difference, and the parent had failed without cause to attend a prior custody hearing).

For analysis of the constitutional status of parental rights in divorce proceedings, see Strickman, Marriage, Divorce and the Constitution, 22 B.C. L. Rev. 935 (1981). See also Palmore v. Sidoti, 104 S. Ct. 1879 (1984) (the equal protection clause prohibits a state from divesting a divorced mother of custody of her child, on petition of the child's natural father, because of the mother's remarriage to a man of a different race).

Note: *The Limits of Privacy*

1. *Freedom of intimate association.* In Roberts v. United States Jaycees, 104 S. Ct. 3244 (1984), the Court upheld as applied to the Jaycees a Minnesota statute

prohibiting discrimination on the basis of sex in "places of public accommodation." In the course of its opinion the Court explained that there are two facets to the constitutionally protected freedom of association — one concerned with the exercise of first amendment rights, see Chapter 7, section E5, infra, and the other concerned with "intimate human relationships." The Court offered the following view on the freedom of "intimate" association:

> The Court has long recognized that, because the Bill of Rights is designed to secure individual liberty, it must afford the formation and preservation of certain kinds of highly personal relationships a substantial measure of sanctuary from unjustified interference by the State. [We] have noted that certain kinds of personal bonds have played a critical role in the culture and traditions of the Nation by cultivating and transmitting shared ideals and beliefs; they thereby foster diversity and act as critical buffers between the individual and the power of the State. Moreover, the constitutional shelter afforded such relationships reflects the realization that individuals draw much of their emotional enrichment from close ties with others. Protecting these relationships from unwarranted state interference therefore safeguards the ability independently to define one's identity that is central to any concept of liberty.
>
>   The personal affiliations that exemplify these considerations, and that therefore suggest some relevant limitations on the relationships that might be entitled to this sort of constitutional protection, are those that attend the creations and sustenance of a family — marriage; childbirth; the raising and education of children; and cohabitation with one's relatives. Family relationships, by their nature, involve deep attachments and commitments to the necessarily few other individuals with whom one shares not only a special community of thoughts, experiences, and beliefs but also distinctively personal aspects of one's life. Among other things, therefore, they are distinguished by such attributes as relative smallness, a high degree of selectivity in decisions to begin and maintain the affiliation, and seclusion from others in critical aspects of the relationship. As a general matter, only relationships with these sorts of qualities are likely to reflect the considerations that have led to an understanding of freedom of association as an intrinsic element of personal liberty. Conversely, an association lacking these qualities — such as a large business enterprise — seems remote from the concerns giving rise to this constitutional protection. [Between] these poles, of course, lies a broad range of human relationships that may make greater or lesser claims to constitutional protection.

The Court held that because "the local chapters of the Jaycees are large and basically unselective groups," they are "clearly [outside] the category of relationships worthy of this kind of constitutional protection." The first amendment aspects of *Roberts* are explored in Chapter 7, section E5, infra.

2. *Sexual autonomy: homosexuality, adultery, and fornication.* Does the right of privacy have sexual as well as procreative and family components? Consider Doe v. Commonwealth's Attorney for Richmond, 403 F. Supp. 1199 (E.D. Va. 1975), in which a divided three-judge district court upheld a Virginia antisodomy statute as applied to the private, consensual homosexual acts of two adult males. The majority reasoned:

> [The Supreme Court's decisions condemn] State legislation that trespasses upon the privacy of the incidents of marriage, upon the sanctity of the home, or upon the nurture of family life. [Homosexuality] is obviously no portion of marriage, home or family life. [If] a State determines that punishment therefor, even when committed

in the home, is appropriate in the promotion of morality and decency, it is not for the courts to say that the State is not free to do so.

Judge Merhige dissented:

> To say [that] the right of privacy [is] limited to matters of marital, home or family life is unwarranted. [*Eisenstadt* seriously impaired the] marital-nonmarital distinction [and] to a great extent vitiated any implication that the state [can] forbid extra-marital sexuality. [*Eisenstadt* demonstrates] that intimate personal decisions on private matters of substantial importance to the well-being of the individuals involved are protected by the Due Process Clause. The right to select consenting adult sexual partners must be considered within this category. The exercise of that right, whether heterosexual or homosexual, should not be proscribed [absent] compelling justification.

The Supreme Court summarily affirmed the district court's judgment, 425 U.S. 901 (1976). Justices Brennan, Marshall, and Stevens dissented from the summary disposition. They would have noted probable jurisdiction and set the case for argument. Consider the following views:

a. Richards, Sexual Autonomy and the Constitutional Right to Privacy: A Case Study in Human Rights and the Unwritten Constitution, 30 Hastings L.J. 957, 975, 978, 981 (1979):

> [The] constitutional right to privacy is, in part, to be understood in terms of a transvaluation of values: certain areas of conduct, traditionally conceived as morally wrong, [are] now perceived as affirmative goods [and] no longer a proper object of public critical concern. [This] understanding of *Griswold* and its progeny [turns on its] repudiation of the procreational model of sexual [love]. [Under that model], certain rigidly defined kinds of intercourse [are] alone moral; contraception, [extra-marital] and, of course, homosexual intercourse are forbidden since these do not involve intent to procreate. [The] constitutional right to privacy [developed] because the procreational model of sexuality could no longer be sustained by sound empirical or conceptual argument. Lacking such support, the procreational model could no longer be legally enforced on the grounds of the "public morality." [And if] the right to privacy extends to sex among unmarried couples [citing *Eisenstadt* and *Roe*], it is difficult to understand how in a principled way the Court could decline to [extend] this right to private, consensual, deviant sex acts.

b. Wilkinson & White, Constitutional Protection for Personal Lifestyles, 62 Corn. L. Rev. 563, 588, 591, 593, 595 (1977):

> [The] issue is whether the state has an interest in confining intimate sexual conduct to "acceptable" [contexts.] Essential to a blanket prohibition of "unnatural" sexual conduct on moral grounds is a firm and generally shared belief that the prohibited conduct is in fact immoral. [Arguably, such a consensus] does not exist to justify the prohibition of "unnatural" sexual conduct. [Nonetheless], state interests of significant strength support a prohibition of homosexuality. [The] most threatening aspect of homosexuality is its potential to become a viable alternative to heterosexual intimacy. [This state concern] should not be minimized. The nuclear, heterosexual family is charged with several of society's most essential functions. [If] allegiance to traditional family arrangements declines, society as a whole [may] suffer.

c. Grey, Eros, Civilization, and the Burger Court, 43 L. & Contemp. Probs. 83, 86-97 (Summer 1980):

[The] Court has given no support to the notion that the right of privacy protects sexual freedom. [Rather,] the Court has consistently protected traditional familial institutions, [and where] less traditional values have been directly protected, [as] in the cases involving contraception and abortion, the decisions reflect not any Millian glorification of diverse individuality, but the stability-centered concerns of moderate conservative family and population policy.

What would be the features of a contrary attitude, one that would be conducive to the development of a constitutional right of sexual freedom? Such a point of view would have two aspects: First, it would ascribe to sexuality a considerable importance in the lives of individuals; and second, it would hold that the way sexual relations are carried on, at least among consenting adults, has no great effect on the welfare of society outside the sexual sphere, so that it is reasonable to regard adults' sex lives as their own business. [But the second of these elements is false. The] repression of sex is of [great] importance to the general welfare of society. . . .

[Modern] civilization is built upon [the] repression of sexual drives. [One] of Freud's central themes was that communal life, whether in the family or the larger society, depends directly on sexual repression. [Western civilization has exacted such repression because] "a large amount of the physical energy [it needs] for its own purposes [must] be drawn from sexuality." [But as] capitalism churned forth material wealth [it] undermined [the] asceticism on which its structures were based and substituted a culture characterized by relativism, materialism, and [hedonism]. [Late] capitalism requires not hardworking inner-directed Puritans, but rootless, compulsive consumers, with no emotional ties except to their own narcissistic pleasures. . . .

I expect that within a few years fornication and sodomy laws will be found unconstitutional, on something [like the] right of consenting adults to control their own sex lives that the Court has until now so rigorously avoided. But the real reasons for the decisions will have little to do with any notion [that] sexual freedom is essential to the pursuit of happiness. Rather the decisions will respond to the same demands of order and social stability that have produced the contraception and abortion decisions. Thousands of couples are living together today outside of marriage. The fornication laws [stand] in the way of providing a stable legal framework for handling child rearing and property questions within these unions. [Similarly], the homosexual community is becoming an increasingly public sector of our society. For that community to be governed effectively, it must be recognized as legitimate. [The] Supreme Court [will] step in and play its traditional role as enlightened conservator of the social interest in ordered stability, and will strike down those laws, in the glorious name of the individual.

3. *Personal appearance: hair style.* Would a state law dictating a uniform hair style for all persons infringe the "right of privacy"? In Kelley v. Johnson, 425 U.S. 238 (1976), the Court upheld a regulation limiting the length of policemen's hair. The Court explained that the "'liberty' interest" claimed in *Kelley* was "distinguishable" from those protected in *Roe, Eisenstadt, Stanley, Griswold,* and *Meyer,* for each "of those cases involved a substantial claim of infringement on the individual's freedom of choice with respect to certain basic matters of procreation, marriage, and family life." The Court thus held that the regulation was

constitutional because it was "not irrational." Justice Marshall, joined by Justice Brennan, dissented:

> I think it clear that the Fourteenth Amendment [protects] against comprehensive regulation of what citizens may or may not wear. [An] individual's personal appearance may reflect, sustain, and nourish his personality and may well be used as a means of expressing his attitude and lifestyle. In taking control over a citizen's personal appearance, the government forces him to sacrifice substantial elements of his integrity and identity as well. To say that the liberty guarantee of the Fourteenth Amendment does not encompass matters of personal appearance would be fundamentally inconsistent with the values of privacy, self-identity, autonomy, and personal integrity that [the] Constitution was designed to protect.

Justice Marshall found it unnecessary to decide whether "heightened scrutiny" is appropriate in such cases, for he concluded that the regulation failed "to pass even a minimal degree of scrutiny." On the constitutionality of regulations governing the hair styles of students in public schools, see Karr v. Schmidt, 460 F.2d 609 (5th Cir. 1972) (upholding such regulations); Wilkinson & White, supra (arguing that such regulations are unconstitutional).

4. *The reach of "privacy."* Consider the following assertions:

a. Rutherford v. United States, 438 F. Supp. 1287, 1300-1301 (W.D. Okla. 1977), rev'd on other grounds, 442 U.S. 544 (1979):

> Numerous cancer patients possess extensive first-hand experience with Laetrile which has led them to believe [that] the substance has eased their pain and prolonged their lives. [Many] perceive the drug's acquisition as a life and death [matter]. To be insensitive to the [fact] that making [this] choice [is] the sole prerogative of the person whose body is being ravaged, [in the absence of a "compelling state interest" in denying that choice,] is to display slight understanding of the essence of our free [society]. By denying the right to use a nontoxic substance in connection with one's own personal health-care, [the Food and Drug Administration] has offended the constitutional right of privacy.

b. People v. Fries, 42 Ill. 2d 446, 250 N.E.2d 149 (1969):

> The [question] presented is whether the [State may require motorcyclists to wear] protective headgear. [The] manifest function of [the] requirement [is] to safeguard the person wearing it [from] head injuries [in the event of an accident]. Such a laudable purpose, however, cannot justify the regulation of what is essentially a matter of personal safety. [The statute violates] the fourteenth amendment.

c. Whalen v. Roe, 429 U.S. 589, 606 (1977) (Brennan, J., concurring):

> The [statute] under attack requires doctors to disclose to the State information about prescriptions for certain drugs with a high potential for abuse, and provides for the storage of that information in a central computer file. [This] information [is] made available only to a small number of public health officials with a legitimate interest in the information. [Broad] dissemination by state officials of such information, however, would clearly implicate constitutionally protected privacy rights, and would presumably be justified only by compelling state interests. See [Roe].

The Court in *Whalen* found it unnecessary to decide whether the right of privacy reached this far, for in light of the safeguards of the challenged statutory scheme, "the program does [not] pose a sufficiently grievous threat to [the asserted privacy] interest to establish a constitutional violation."

G. PROCEDURAL DUE PROCESS

The text of the due process clause — "nor shall any State deprive any person of life, liberty, or property, without due process of law" — suggests that the clause is concerned above all with procedure. This section explores the question when the clause requires procedural safeguards to accompany substantive choices. That question is an important aspect of the problem of identifying "implied" fundamental rights. As the preceding materials suggest, the terms "liberty" and "property" are not self-defining. A principal issue here is how to give content to those terms when the question is, What deprivations require procedural safeguards? In exploring the materials that follow, consider how and why the procedural and substantive contexts might differ.

Note that this section does not deal with questions of procedural due process in conventional criminal and civil contexts — e.g., burden of proof rules for criminal or civil defendants and the role of the exclusionary rule. Nor are we concerned here with the problem of incorporation, dealt with in section B supra. Instead the focus is on defining and protecting "liberty" and "property" interests in cases in which the government seeks to provide less than elaborate safeguards to accompany a deprivation of some interest.

1. *Liberty and Property Interests*

Before Goldberg v. Kelly, 397 U.S. 254 (1970), the Court defined liberty and property interests by reference to the common law. If government took someone's property, or invaded his bodily integrity, the due process clause would require some kind of hearing. But the clause was inapplicable if government denied an individual some public benefit — employment, welfare, or some other advantageous opportunity. See, e.g., Bailey v. Richardson, 182 F.2d 46 (D.C. Cir. 1950), aff'd by an equally divided Court, 341 U.S. 918 (1951) (no hearing required for dismissal from government employment). This conclusion was a form of the traditional right/privilege distinction. "[Advantageous] relations with the government were mere 'privileges' or 'gratuities,' not legally protected rights. [But] with the expansion of the governmental role, it became less and less tolerable that the government should wield the degree of potentially arbitrary power over the lives of individuals implied by this doctrine." Stewart, The Reformation of American Administrative Law, 88 Harv. L. Rev. 1667, 1717-1718 (1975).

This framework was a natural outgrowth of a libertarian conception of government based on principles of laissez-faire. Reich, The New Property, 73 Yale L.J. 733 (1963), was an important critique of this framework. According to Reich, the traditional framework was anachronistic in a period in which individual security frequently depended on advantageous relationships with the government — insurance, social security benefits, employment, licenses, welfare, and so forth. In Reich's view, it was necessary to create a "new property" that would attach the traditional procedural safeguards to these benefits, in order to furnish, in the modern era, the same kind of security promoted by "old property" under a common law regime. The idea was that without such safeguards, those dependent on governmental benefits would be subject to the arbitrary will of public officials.

The Supreme Court accepted Reich's approach in Goldberg v. Kelly, 397 U.S. 254 (1970). In *Goldberg* the Court held that a welfare recipient's interest in continued receipt of welfare benefits was a "statutory entitlement" that amounted to "property" within the meaning of the due process clause. The Court referred to the "brutal need" of welfare recipients and held that a fairly elaborate hearing was required before benefits could be terminated. But what interests amount to "liberty" or "property" once it is concluded that at least some statutory benefits amount to rights?

BOARD OF REGENTS OF STATE COLLEGES v. ROTH, 408 U.S. 564 (1972): Roth was hired for a one-year term as assistant professor at Wisconsin State University. Under state law, he did not have tenure. The president of the university informed Roth that he would not be rehired; no explanation was given for the decision, and there was no opportunity to challenge it. Roth alleged that the failure to hold a hearing violated the due process clause. In an opinion by Justice Stewart, the Court rejected Roth's claim:

"The requirements of procedural due process apply only to the deprivation of interests encompassed by the Fourteenth Amendment's protection of liberty and property. [The] range of interests protected by procedural due process is not infinite.

"The District Court decided that procedural due process guarantees apply in this case by assessing and balancing the weights of the particular interests involved. [Undeniably,] the respondent's re-employment prospects were of major concern to him — concern that we surely cannot say was insignificant. And a weighing process has long been a part of any determination of the *form* of hearing required in particular situations by procedural due process. But, to determine whether due process requirements apply in the first place, we must look not to the weight, but to the *nature* of the interest at stake.

"'Liberty' and 'property' are broad and majestic terms. They are among the '[g]reat [constitutional] concepts . . . purposely left to gather meaning from experience. . . . [T]hey relate to the whole domain of social and economic fact, and the statesmen who founded this Nation knew too well that only a stagnant society remains unchanged.' For that reason, the Court has fully and finally rejected the wooden distinction between 'rights' and 'privileges' that once seemed to govern the applicability of procedural due process rights. The Court has also made clear that the property interests protected by procedural due process extend well beyond actual ownership of real estate, chattels, or money. . . .

"While this Court has not attempted to define with exactness the liberty . . . guaranteed [by the Fourteenth Amendment], the term [denotes] not merely freedom from bodily restraint but also the right of the individual to contract, to engage in any of the common occupations of life, to acquire useful knowledge, to marry, establish a home and bring up children, to worship God according to the dictates of his own conscience, and generally to enjoy those privileges long recognized . . . as essential to the orderly pursuit of happiness by free men. In a Constitution for a free people, there can be no doubt that the meaning of 'liberty' must be broad indeed.

"There might be cases in which a State refused to re-employ a person under such circumstances that interests in liberty would be implicated. But this is not such a case. [The Court noted that the statement did not make any charge against Roth damaging to his reputation and that it did not in any way foreclose his opportunity to obtain other employment opportunities.]

"The Fourteenth Amendment's procedural protection of property is a safeguard of the security of interests that a person has already acquired in specific benefits. These interests — property interests — may take many forms.

"Thus, the Court has held that a person receiving welfare benefits under statutory and administrative standards defining eligibility for them has an interest in continued receipt of those benefits that is safeguarded by procedural due process. [*Goldberg.*] [To] have a property interest in a benefit, a person clearly must have more than an abstract need or desire for it. He must have more than a unilateral expectation of it. He must, instead, have a legitimate claim of entitlement to it. It is a purpose of the ancient institution of property to protect those claims upon which people rely in their daily lives, reliance that must not be arbitrarily undermined. It is a purpose of the constitutional right to a hearing to provide an opportunity for a person to vindicate those claims.

"Property interests, of course, are not created by the Constitution. Rather, they are created and their dimensions are defined by existing rules or understandings that stem from an independent source such as state law — rules or understandings that secure certain benefits and that support claims of entitlement to those benefits.

"Just as [in *Goldberg*] the welfare recipient's 'property' interest in welfare payments was created and defined by statutory terms, so the respondent's 'property' interest in employment at Wisconsin State University-Oshkosh was created and defined by the terms of his appointment. [The] important fact in this case is that they specifically provided that the respondent's employment was to terminate on June 30. They did not provide for contract renewal absent 'sufficient cause.' Indeed, they made no provision for renewal whatsoever.

"Thus, the terms of the respondent's appointment secured absolutely no interest in re-employment for the next year. They supported absolutely no possible claim of entitlement to re-employment. Nor, significantly, was there any state statute or University rule or policy that secured his interest in re-employment or that created any legitimate claim to it. In these circumstances, the respondent surely had an abstract concern in being rehired, but he did not have a *property* interest sufficient to require the University authorities to give him a hearing when they declined to renew his contract of employment."

Justice Marshall dissented.

"[I] would go further than the Court does in defining the terms 'liberty' and 'property.'

"The prior decisions of this Court [establish] a principle that is as obvious as it is compelling — i.e., federal and state governments and governmental agencies are restrained by the Constitution from acting arbitrarily with respect to employment opportunities that they either offer or control. Hence, it is now firmly established that whether or not a private employer is free to act capriciously or unreasonably with respect to employment practices, at least absent statutory or contractual controls, a government employer is different. The government may only act fairly and reasonably. . . .

"In my view, every citizen who applies for a government job is entitled to it unless the government can establish some reason for denying the employment. This is the 'property' right that I believe is protected by the Fourteenth Amendment and that cannot be denied 'without due process of law.' And it is also liberty — liberty to work — which is the 'very essence of the personal freedom and opportunity' secured by the Fourteenth Amendment. . . .

"Employment is one of the greatest, if not the greatest, benefits that governments offer in modern-day life. When something as valuable as the opportunity to work is at stake, the government may not reward some citizens and not others without demonstrating that its actions are fair and equitable. And it is procedural due process that is our fundamental guarantee of fairness, our protection against arbitrary, capricious, and unreasonable government action. . . .

"It may be argued that to provide procedural due process to all public employees or prospective employees would place an intolerable burden on the machinery of government. The short answer to that argument is that it is not burdensome to give reasons when reasons exist. Whenever an application for employment is denied, an employee is discharged, or a decision not to rehire an employee is made, there should be some reason for the decision. It can scarcely be argued that government would be crippled by a requirement that the reason be communicated to the person most directly affected by the government's action.

"Where there are numerous applicants for jobs, it is likely that few will choose to demand reasons for not being hired. But, if the demand for reasons is exceptionally great, summary procedures can be devised that would provide fair and adequate information to all persons. As long as the government has a good reason for its actions it need not fear disclosure. It is only where the government acts improperly that procedural due process is truly burdensome. And that is precisely when it is most necessary.

"It might also be argued that to require a hearing and a statement of reasons is to require a useless act, because a government bent on denying employment to one or more persons will do so regardless of the procedural hurdles that are placed in its path. Perhaps this is so, but a requirement of procedural regularity at least renders arbitrary action more difficult. [When] the government knows it may have to justify its decisions with sound reasons, its conduct is likely to be more cautious, careful, and correct."

PERRY v. SINDERMANN, 408 U.S. 593 (1972): This was a companion case to *Roth*. Sindermann was a professor at Odessa Junior College who, like Roth, was not renewed. Sindermann claimed that Odessa had a de facto tenure program. The College had stated, in a faculty guide, that despite the absence of an actual tenure system, it "wishes each faculty member to feel that he has permanent tenure so long as his teaching services are satisfactory and as long as he displays a cooperative attitude." According to Sindermann, there was a mutual expectation that he would be renewed each year. Justice Stewart wrote the opinion of the Court:

"The respondent's lack of formal contractual or tenure security in continued employment at Odessa Junior College [may] not be entirely dispositive.

"[The] respondent's allegations [raise] a genuine issue as to his interest in continued employment at Odessa Junior College. He alleged that this interest, though not secured by a formal contractual tenure provision, was secured by a no less binding understanding fostered by the college administration. . . .

"[A] written contract with an explicit tenure provision clearly is evidence of a formal understanding that supports a teacher's claim of entitlement to continued employment unless sufficient 'cause' is shown. Yet absence of such an explicit contractual provision may not always foreclose the possibility that a teacher has a 'property' interest in re-employment. . . .

"A teacher, like the respondent, who has held his position for a number of years, might be able to show from the cirumstances of this service — and from other relevant facts — that he has a legitimate claim of entitlement to job tenure."

Cleveland Board of Education v. Loudermill
470 U.S. — , 105 S. Ct. 1487 (1985)

JUSTICE WHITE delivered the opinion of the Court.

In these cases we consider what pretermination process must be accorded a public employee who can be discharged only for cause.

In 1979 the Cleveland Board of Education [hired] respondent James Loudermill as a security guard. On his job application, Loudermill stated that he had never been convicted of a felony. Eleven months later, as part of a routine examination of his employment records, the Board discovered that in fact Loudermill had been convicted of grand larceny in 1968. By letter dated November 3, 1980, the Board's Business Manager informed Loudermill that he had been dismissed because of his dishonesty in filling out the employment application. Loudermill was not afforded an opportunity to respond to the charge of dishonesty or to challenge his dismissal. On November 13, the Board adopted a resolution officially approving the discharge.

Under Ohio law, Loudermill was a "classified civil servant." [Such] employees can be terminated only for cause, and may obtain administrative review if discharged. [Plaintiff's] federal constitutional claim depends on his having had a property right in continued employment. [If he did,] the State could not deprive [him] of this property without due process.

Property interests are not created by the Constitution, "they are created and their dimensions are defined by existing rules or understandings that stem from an independent source such as state law. . . ." [Roth.] [The] Ohio statute plainly creates such an interest. Respondents were "classified civil service employees," Ohio Rev. Code Ann. §124.11 (1984), entitled to retain their positions "during good behavior and efficient service," who could not be dismissed "except . . . for . . . misfeasance, malfeasance, or nonfeasance in office." The statute plainly supports the conclusion, reached by both lower courts, that respondents possessed property rights in continued employment. [The lower court thus required a hearing.]

The [Board] argues, however, that the property right is defined by, and conditioned on, the legislature's choice of procedures for its deprivation. [The] Board stresses that in addition to specifying the grounds for termination, the statute sets out procedures by which termination may take place. The procedures were adhered to in these cases. According to petitioner, "[t]o require additional procedures would in effect expand the scope of the property interest itself."

This argument, which was accepted by the District Court, has its genesis in the plurality opinion in Arnett v. Kennedy, 416 U.S. 134 (1974). *Arnett* involved a challenge by a former federal employee to the procedures by which he was dismissed. The plurality reasoned that where the legislation conferring the substantive right also sets out the procedural mechanism for enforcing that right, the two cannot be separated:

> The employee's statutorily defined right is not a guarantee against removal without cause in the abstract, but such a guarantee as enforced by the procedures which Congress has designated for the determination of cause.
>
> . . . [W]here the grant of a substantive right is inextricably intertwined with the limitations on the procedures which are to be employed in determining that right, a litigant in the position of appellee must take the bitter with the sweet.

This view garnered three votes in *Arnett*, but was specifically rejected by the other six Justices. See id. (Powell, J., joined by Blackmun, J.,); id. (White, J.,); id. (Marshall, J., joined by Douglas and Brennan, JJ.). Since then, this theory has at times seemed to gather some additional support. [More] recently, however, the Court has clearly rejected it. In Vitek v. Jones, 445 U.S. 480, 491 (1980), we pointed out that "minimum [procedural] requirements [are] a matter of federal law, they are not diminished by the fact that the State may have specified its own procedures that it may deem adequate for determining the preconditions to adverse official action."

In light of these holdings, it is settled that the "bitter with the sweet" approach misconceives the constitutional guarantee. If a clearer holding is needed, we provide it today. The point is straightforward: the Due Process Clause provides that certain substantive rights — life, liberty, and property — cannot be deprived except pursuant to constitutionally adequate procedures. The categories of substance and procedure are distinct. Were the rule otherwise, the Clause would be reduced to a mere tautology. "Property" cannot be defined by the procedures provided for its deprivation any more than can life or liberty. The right to due process "is conferred, not by legislative grace, but by constitutional guarantee. While the legislature may elect not to confer a property interest in [public] employment, it may not constitutionally authorize the deprivation of such an interest, once conferred, without appropriate procedural safeguards."

[Affirmed.]

[Justice Powell concurred in part and concurred in result in part.]

JUSTICE REHNQUIST, dissenting.

In [*Arnett*] six Members of this Court agreed that a public employee could be dismissed for misconduct without a full hearing prior to termination. A plurality of Justices agreed that the employee was entitled to exactly what Congress gave him, and no more. The Chief Justice, Justice Stewart, and I said:

> Here appellee did have a statutory expectancy that he not be removed other than for "such cause as will promote the efficiency of [the] service." But the very section of the statute which granted him that right, a right which had previously existed, only by virtue of administrative regulation, expressly provided also for the procedure by which "cause" was to be determined, and expressly omitted the procedural guarantees which appellee insists are mandated by the Constitution. Only by bifurcating the very sentence of the Act of Congress which conferred upon appellee the right not to be removed save for cause could it be said that he had an expectancy of that substantive right without the procedural limitations which Congress attached to it. In the area of federal regulation of government employees, where in the absence of statutory limitation the governmental employer has had virtually uncontrolled latitude in decisions as to hiring and firing, we do not believe that a statutory enactment such as the Lloyd-La Follette Act may be parsed as discretely as appellee urges. Congress was obviously intent on according a measure of statutory job security to governmental employees which they had not previously enjoyed, but was likewise intent on excluding more elaborate procedural requirements which it felt would make the operation of the new scheme unnecessarily burdensome in practice. Where the focus of legislation was thus strongly on the procedural mechanism for enforcing the substantive right which was simultaneously conferred, we decline to conclude that the substantive right may be viewed wholly apart from the procedure provided for its enforcement. The employee's statutorily defined right is not a guarantee against removal without cause in the abstract, but such a guarantee as enforced by the procedures which Congress has designated for the determination of cause.

In this case, the relevant Ohio statute provides in its first paragraph that "[t]he tenure of every officer or employee in the classified service [shall] be during good behavior and efficient service." The very next paragraph of this section [provides] that in the event of suspension of more than three days or removal the appointing authority shall furnish the employee with the stated reasons for his removal. The next paragraph provides that within ten days following the receipt of such a statement, the employee may appeal in writing to the State Personnel Board of Review or the Commission, such appeal shall be heard within 30 days from the time of its filing, and the Board may affirm, disaffirm, or modify the judgment of the appointing authority.

Thus in one legislative breath Ohio has conferred upon civil service employees such as respondents in this case a limited form of tenure during good behavior, and prescribed the procedures by which that tenure may be terminated. Here, as in *Arnett*, "[t]he employee's statutorily defined right is not a guarantee against removal without cause in the abstract, but such a guarantee as enforced by the procedures which [the Ohio legislature] has designated for the determination of cause." (Opinion of Rehnquist, J.). We ought to recognize the totality of the State's definition of the property right in question, and not merely seize upon one of several paragraphs in a unitary statute to proclaim that in that paragraph the State has inexorably conferred upon a civil service employee something which it is powerless under the United States Constitution to qualify in the next paragraph of the statute. This practice ignores our duty under *Roth* to rely on state law as the source of property interests for purposes of applying the Due Process Clause of the Fourteenth Amendment. While it does not impose a federal definition of property, the Court departs from the full breadth of the holding in *Roth* by its selective choice from among the sentences the Ohio legislature chooses to use in establishing and qualifying a right. . . .

Because I believe that the Fourteenth Amendment of the United States Constitution does not support the conclusion that Ohio's effort to confer a limited form of tenure upon respondents resulted in the creation of a "property right" in their employment, I dissent.

Note: Defining "Liberty" and "Property"

1. *The purposes of hearings.* What goals are promoted by requiring hearings before government deprives someone of a liberty or property interest?

a. *Obtaining more accurate factual determinations.* Suppose a welfare agency seeks to take away welfare benefits because the recipient's relatively high earnings disqualify her under the governing statute, but she disputes the government's claim that her earnings do in fact disqualify her. A hearing before an impartial arbiter might produce a more accurate resolution of the disputed factual issue than a unilateral decision by the administrator. (Note that the issue here is a dispute over the facts; hearings are generally not required on questions of law. Why?)

b. *Recognizing and promoting the dignity of those whose interests are at stake by allowing them to participate in the decision.* Consider Michelman, Formal and Associational Aims in Procedural Due Process, in NOMOS: Due Process 126, 127-128 (J. R. Pennock & J. Chapman eds. 1977):

> Such procedures seem responsive to demands for revelation and participation. They attach value to an individual's being told why the agent is treating him unfavorably and to his having a part in the decision. [The] information may also be wanted for introspective reasons — because, for example, it fulfills a potentially destructive gap in the individual's conception of himself. Similarly, the individual may have various reasons for wanting an opportunity to discuss the decision with the agent. Some pertain to external consequences: the individual might succeed in persuading the agent away from the harmful action. But again participatory opportunity may also be psychologically important to the individual: to have played a part in, to have made one's apt contribution to, decisions which are about oneself may be counted important even though the decision, as it turns out, is the most unfavorable one imaginable and one's efforts have not proved influential.

See also J. Mashaw, Due Process in the Administrative State (1985), which attempts to justify hearing rights in part by reference to dignitary concerns. Is this argument undermined when participation will be through a representative — the lawyer?

Hearings have costs as well. If government must spend money on procedural safeguards, it will have fewer resources at its command, and the result may be that welfare benefits or salaries are correspondingly diminished. Hearing requirements may therefore not prove beneficial for the class of intended beneficiaries as a whole. Fewer employees may be hired, fewer people may be allowed on the welfare rolls, benefit levels and salaries may be decreased. What is the relevance of these possibilities?

2. *Statutory entitlements.* Under *Roth* interests are defined by reference to positive law. The test for deciding whether a "property" interest has been created is to examine positive law to see whether the government's discretion has been confined by existing "rules or understandings." In *Perry* the tenure system, if there was one, meant that professors could be discharged only "for cause." In *Roth* there was no such "for cause" limitation of the discretion of the administrator as to renewal. We might term this approach one of "statutory entitlement," or, following Reich, supra, "new property."

But why should the due process clause be read to say that a "for clause" provision creates a property interest that is not defined by reference to the procedural provisions of the same statute? If the due process clause does not require government to create a "for cause" system at all, why does it bar the government from taking the intermediate step of providing a "for cause" system without procedural safeguards? Consider Justice Rehnquist's argument in *Arnett*:

> [The] very section of the statute which gave him that right [expressly] provided also for the procedure by which "cause" was to be determined, and expressly omitted the procedural guarantees which appellee insists are mandated by the Constitution. Only by bifurcating the very sentence of the Act of Congress which conferred upon appellee the right not to be removed for cause could it be said that he had an expectancy of that substantive right without the procedural limitations which Congress attached to it.

Note also Easterbrook, Substance and Due Process, 1982 Sup. Ct. Rev. 85, 112-113:

> Substance and process are intimately related. The procedures one uses determine how much substance is achieved, and by whom. Procedural rules are just a measure of how much the substantive entitlements are worth, of what we are willing to sacrifice to see a given goal attained. The body that creates a substantive rule is the logical judge of how much should be spent to avoid errors in the process of disposing of claims to that right. The substantive rule is itself best seen as a promised benefit coupled with a promised rate of mistake: the legislature sets up an X% probability that a person will receive a certain boon. The Court cannot logically be reticent about revising the substantive rules but unabashed about rewriting the procedures to be followed in administering those rules.

From another angle, consider Simon, The Invention and Reinvention of Welfare Rights, 44 Md. L. Rev. 1 (1985), arguing that in welfare cases, the statutory entitlement approach depends on and creates formal, adversarial relations between beneficiaries and state officials. Simon claims that the "new property" approach creates two paradoxes: First, its understanding has "curiously conservative and anti-redistributive implications," because its reliance on principles of vested rights may prevent government action intended to reallocate property rights; second, "while it was clearly designed to legitimate the expansion of the welfare state, it proceeded by portraying the state as a menace," because it rested on fear of arbitrary governance. Simon concludes that the new property approach "is incoherent as jurisprudence" and that the legal system should instead "develop an ideal and a program of public administration that recognizes the value of a responsible state as well as the dangers of an irresponsible one and that fosters conditions in which the street level public workforce can work responsibly and effectively." Consider the following attempted defenses of the statutory entitlement approach.

a. "For cause" provisions generate expectations that deserve constitutional protection. Procedural qualifications of such provisions are like fine print; they do not prevent the expectations thus generated from being reasonable. Cf. Tribe, Structural Due Process, 10 Harv. C.R.-C.L. L. Rev. 269, 280 (1975).

b. The due process clause itself distinguishes "life, liberty and property" from "due process." The legislature can decide whether there is "property." But once property has been created, the Constitution decides how much process is due. A contrary "theory could end judicial enforcement of the due process clause. Any legislature that wishes to limit procedural rights need only make the limitation part of the definition of the underlying substantive right." Laycock, Due Process and Separation of Powers: The Effort to Make the Due Process Clauses Nonjusticiable, 60 Tex. L. Rev. 875, 876 (1982). But consider Van Alstyne, Cracks in the New Property, 62 Cornell L. Rev. 445, 465 (1977), arguing that this approach "misses the point": "What 'interest' was 'conferred'? Show us a [jot] of 'interest' actually conferred by the legislature apart from the interest Kennedy held — the interest exactly bounded, as Rehnquist said, by the procedural provisions of the only source giving it any substance at all."

c. See Stewart & Sunstein, Public Programs and Private Rights, 95 Harv. L. Rev. 1193, 1261-1262 (1982):

> If Congress has chosen to mandate statutory benefits in specific terms[, hearing] rights help to ensure predictability and to combat arbitrariness in the distribution of those benefits, without endangering entire statutory programs or requiring judicial review of the legislature's decision to delegate discretion. Moreover, to some degree procedural safeguards may promote political accountability by ensuring bureaucratic conformity to legislative limitations.

d. See Van Alstyne, supra, at 497:

> Is it plausible to treat freedom from arbitrary adjudicative procedures as a substantive element of one's liberty as well — a freedom whose abridgment government must sustain the burden of justifying, even as it must do when it seeks to subordinate other freedoms, such as those of speech or privacy? I believe that it is plausible so to regard the matter, and that the ideas of liberty and of substantive due process may easily accommodate a view that government may not adjudicate the claims of individuals by unreliable means.

(This position is adopted as a construction of the state constitution in People v. Ramirez, 25 Cal. 3d 260, 599 P.2d 622, 158 Cal. Rptr. 316 (1979).) What consequences would this approach have? Consider Williams, Liberty and Property: The Problem of Government Benefits, 12 J. Legal Stud. 3, 18 (1983): "Such a view makes it pointless for the framers to have specified life, liberty, and property: there would be no need to mention any protected substantive interests if the clauses intended to establish a right to due process without regard to the substantive interest at stake."

3. *Property and liberty interests apart from positive law.* The Supreme Court has generally been reluctant to define "property" or "liberty" interests by reference to the importance of the interest at issue; even a "grievous loss" may not be enough. In some cases, however, the Court has concluded that a "liberty" interest is at issue even though there is no positive protection of the sort required in *Roth*. See Ingraham v. Wright, 430 U.S. 651 (1977) (child's interest in bodily integrity, at stake because of practice of paddling children, is a liberty interest); Vitek v. Jones, 445 U.S. 480 (1980) (inmates' interest in preventing transfer from prison to mental institution is a liberty interest); Owen v. City of Independence, 445 U.S. 662 (1980) (the right to reputation when combined with dismissal from at-will employment is a liberty interest). Note that all of these cases involve variations on "old property" — government infringements on private autonomy as understood at common law.

Why has the Court generally been unwilling to hold that all important interests are protected by the due process clause? Why has the Court been unwilling to hold that freedom from arbitrary adjudicative procedures is itself a part of the "liberty" protected by due process? Consider the following views.

a. A determination of which statutory benefits are sufficiently important to merit protection would involve an unduly open-ended and subjective inquiry. The requirement of a statutory entitlement limits the judicial inquiry without requiring comparisons among, for example, welfare benefits, employment, and parole revocation.

b. If courts were to hold that all important interests are protected by the due process clause, they would be driven to give such interests substantive as well as procedural protection. Such a revival of substantive due process is properly resisted. Consider, for example, a probationary employee fired from a government job; assume that there is no statute providing that the employee may not be discharged without "cause." If a court held that, because of the "grievous loss," there is a constitutional right to a hearing, what would the hearing be about? Unless courts implied a "for cause" provision, it is hard to see what the participants in the hearing would discuss; there would be nothing to adjudicate. Procedural safeguards make little sense without substantive rights to adjudicate; in cases with "at will" provisions, like *Roth*, there is no state-created substantive right, and there is no constitutional right to be discharged from employment without cause.

Is a partial answer that even without implying a "for cause" provision, such a hearing would serve participatory and dignitary values? For discussion, see Mashaw, Administrative Due Process: The Quest for a Dignitary Theory, 61 B.U. L. Rev. 885 (1981); Monaghan, Of "Liberty" and "Property," 62 Cornell L. Rev. 405 (1977); Tushnet, The Newer Property: Suggestions for a Revival of Substantive Due Process, 1975 Sup. Ct. Rev. 261.

Note: Developments since Roth—Statutory Entitlements and Natural Liberty

Between *Roth* and *Loudermill*, the Court decided many cases raising the question when there is a "statutory entitlement" or "grievous loss" amounting to a property or liberty interest.

1. *Property: state-created rights.* Bishop v. Wood, 426 U.S. 341 (1976), involved a dismissal of a city police officer. The officer contended that because he was classified as a "permanent employee," he had a property interest entitling him to a pretermination hearing. The Court disagreed, relying heavily on the conclusion of the federal district court that, under state law, he held his position at the will and pleasure of the city. In the Court's view, the district court interpretation indicated that notwithstanding the classification as a "permanent employee," the job of police officer was like that of the untenured professor in *Roth*.

In Goss v. Lopez, 419 U.S. 565 (1975), the plaintiffs were sixth-grade students suspended temporarily — for periods of up to ten days — from public school. The Court found a property interest because state law provided that students may be suspended only for "misconduct." In the Court's view, this provision created "legitimate claims of entitlement to a public education. [Having] chosen to extend the right to an education to people of appellees' class generally, Ohio may not withdraw that right on grounds of misconduct, absent fundamentally fair procedures to determine whether the misconduct has occurred."

Logan v. Zimmerman Brush Co., 455 U.S. 422 (1982), involved a state statute prohibiting discrimination on the basis of handicap and providing that within 120 days of the filing of a charge of unlawful discrimination, the state fair employment practices commission "shall convene a factfinding conference." In the *Logan* case the commission failed, through negligence, to hold the hearing within the requisite time, and the plaintiff's claim was extinguished by state law. The Court held that the state-created right to redress of unlawful discrimination amounted to a property interest and that, under state law, that right was to be "assessed under what is, in essence, a 'for cause' standard, based upon the substantiality of the evidence." The plaintiff was therefore entitled to a hearing.

2. *Liberty.* Paul v. Davis, 424 U.S. 693 (1976), involved a person arrested on a charge of shoplifting; Davis's name was placed on a flyer sent to 800 merchants in Louisville, designating him as an active shoplifter. The charges were dismissed and Davis brought suit, claiming that the action had deprived him of his constitutional interest in reputation. The Court concluded that reputation, standing alone, was not a constitutionally protected liberty interest. The Court acknowledged that in conjunction with some other injury — such as a failure to rehire or deprivation of a right to purchase liquor, see Wisconsin v. Constantineau, 400 U.S. 433 (1971) (injury to reputation by "posting" is a liberty interest when accompanied by ban on purchase of liquor) — an injury to reputation would trigger the due process clause. The Court expressed concern that a contrary holding would allow the Constitution to swallow up state tort law, making it enforceable in the federal courts. Is it odd that under Paul v. Davis, zero (discharge of a probationary employee) plus zero (injury to reputation) equals one? For a sharply critical view of the decision, see Monaghan, Of "Liberty" and "Property," 62 Cornell L. Rev. 405 (1977).

Compare with *Paul* the decision in Goss v. Lopez, supra, where the Court found a liberty interest, as well as a property interest, in freedom from arbitrary discharges. "School authorities here suspended appellees from school for periods of up to 10 days based on charges of misconduct. If sustained and recorded, those charges could seriously damage the students' standing with their fellow students and their teachers as well as interfere with later opportunities for higher education and employment." Does *Goss* suggest that the importance of the interest is a critical factor in deciding whether a liberty interest is at stake?

Meachum v. Fano, 427 U.S. 215 (1976), found no constitutionally protected interest in a transfer of prisoners from a medium-security prison to a maximum-security prison on the basis of the prisoners' alleged responsibility for committing arson. The Court said:

> We reject at the outset the suggestion that *any* grievous loss visited upon a person by the State is sufficient to invoke the procedural protections of the Due Process Clause. [The] determining factor is the nature of the interest involved rather than its weight. [Given] a valid conviction, the criminal defendant has been constitutionally deprived of his liberty, to the extent that the State may confine him and subject him to the rules of its prison system so long as the conditions of confinement do not otherwise violate the Constitution. [Confinement] in any of the State's institutions is within the normal limits or range of custody which the conviction has authorized the State to impose. That life in one prison is much more disagreeable than in another does not in itself signify that a Fourteenth Amendment liberty interest is implicated.

Justice Stevens, joined by Justices Brennan and Marshall, dissented on the ground that the Court's conception of liberty was

> fundamentally incorrect. [If] a man were a creature of the state, the analysis would be correct. But neither the Bill of Rights nor the laws of sovereign states create the liberty which the Due Process Clause protects. [I] had thought it self-evident that all men were endowed by their Creator with liberty, as one of the cardinal unalienable rights. It is that basic freedom which the Due Process Clause protects, rather than the particular rights or privileges conferred by specific laws or regulations.

Compare Vitek v. Jones, 445 U.S. 480 (1980), which involved a transfer of a prisoner to a state mental hospital for treatment. The Court held that the due process clause was triggered, distinguishing *Meachum* in two ways. First, the state statute at issue allowed transfer only upon a finding, by a designated physician or psychologist, that the prisoner "suffers from a mental disease or defect" and "cannot be given treatment in that facility." The prisoner therefore had a liberty interest under *Arnett*. Second, the Court held that the prisoner "retained a residuum of liberty that would be infringed by a transfer to a mental hospital." The Court pointed to the stigmatic consequences of involuntary commitment to a mental hospital; the possibility of compelled treatment in the form of mandatory behavior modification programs; and the increased limitations on freedom of action. Do these factors persuasively distinguish *Vitek* from *Meachum*? Assume that there was no statutory entitlement in *Vitek*. If there is a constitutionally protected liberty interest, does it follow that there is a substantive constitutional right not to be transferred to a mental institution without just cause?

Note finally Greenholtz v. Inmates, 442 U.S. 1 (1979), holding that without a statutory entitlement, there is no constitutionally protected interest in a denial of parole. The Court acknowledged that a revocation of parole would trigger the due process clause but found a distinction between rescinding a benefit already conferred and refusing to grant a benefit in the first instance.

3. *Concluding thoughts.* In defining liberty and property interests, the Court has had three principal options. First, it could have continued to define protected

interests by reference to the common law. Such an approach would deny procedural protection for all statutory interests by adhering to the preexisting framework; at the same time, it would have denied "new property" any constitutional protection by allowing statutes to condition the interests they grant. Second, the Court could have defined protected interests in a functional way, by looking to their importance. For example, it could have assessed whether the interests in question have as much importance in the modern era as common law rights seemed to have in a very different time. Third, it could have chosen, as it did, the current course — offering procedural protection only to statutes that create "entitlements." Which approach would be preferable? In which direction, if any, should the Court move?

2. What Process Is Due

Mathews v. Eldridge

424 U.S. 319 (1976)

[Eldridge had received disability benefits since 1968. After considering Eldridge's response to a questionnaire about his condition, reports from Eldridge's physician and a psychiatric consultant, and Eldridge's files, the relevant state agency made a tentative determination that Eldridge's disability had ceased. Eldridge was so informed, given a statement of reasons, and offered an opportunity to submit a written response. He did so, disputing the agency's decision, but benefits were nonetheless terminated. Eldridge claimed that this procedure violated the due process clause. The Court below agreed.]

MR. JUSTICE POWELL delivered the opinion of the Court.

[Procedural] due process imposes constraints on governmental decisions which deprive individuals of "liberty" or "property" interests within the meaning of the Due Process Clause of the Fifth or Fourteenth Amendment. The Secretary does not contend that procedural due process is inapplicable to terminations of Social Security disability benefits. He recognizes [that] the interest of an individual in continued receipt of these benefits is a statutorily created "property" interest protected by the Fifth Amendment. [Rather,] the Secretary contends that the existing administrative procedures [provide] all the process that is constitutionally due before a recipient can be deprived of that interest. This Court consistently has held that some form of hearing is required before an individual is finally deprived of a property interest. [The] "right to be heard before being condemned to suffer grievous loss of any kind, even though it may not involve the stigma and hardships of a criminal conviction, is a principle basic to our society." Joint Anti-Fascist Comm. v. McGrath, 341 U.S. 123, 168 (Frankfurter, J., concurring). The fundamental requirement of due process is the opportunity to be heard "at a meaningful time and in a meaningful manner." [Eldridge] agrees that the review procedures available to a claimant before the initial determination of ineligibility becomes final would be adequate if disability benefits were not terminated until after the evidentiary hearing stage of the administrative process. The dispute centers upon what process is due prior to the initial termination of benefits, pending review.

In recent years this Court increasingly has had occasion to consider the extent to which due process requires an evidentiary hearing prior to the deprivation of some type of property interest even if such a hearing is provided thereafter. In only one case, [*Goldberg*], has the Court held that a hearing closely approximating a judicial trial is necessary. In other cases requiring some type of pretermination hearing as a matter of constitutional right the Court has spoken sparingly about the requisite procedures. . . .

[Our] decisions underscore the truism that " '[d]ue process,' unlike some legal rules, is not a technical conception with a fixed content unrelated to time, place and circumstances." "[D]ue process is flexible and calls for such procedural protections as the particular situation demands." [Accordingly,] resolution of the issue whether the administrative procedures provided here are constitutionally sufficient requires analysis of the governmental and private interests that are affected. [*Arnett.*] More precisely, our prior decisions indicate that identification of the specific dictates of due process generally requires consideration of three distinct factors: First, the private interest that will be affected by the official action; second, the risk of an erroneous deprivation of such interest through the procedures used, and the probable value, if any, of additional or substitute procedural safeguards; and finally, the Government's interest, including the function involved and the fiscal and administrative burdens that the additional or substitute procedural requirement would entail.

[The Court described the relevant procedures. It noted that the worker bears a continuing burden of showing that he suffers from a medically determinable physical or mental impairment; that a state agency conducts continuing eligibility investigations, in which there is communication with the disabled worker; that when an agency's tentative assessment differs from the workers, the worker is informed that benefits may be terminated and offered an opportunity to respond in writing and to furnish new evidence; that there is review by a federal official of any state decision to terminate; that after termination, there is a right to an evidentiary hearing, in which the claimant may be represented by counsel; and that the worker may recover retroactive payments if the termination is later found erroneous.]

[Despite] the elaborate character of the administrative procedures provided by the Secretary, the courts below held them to be constitutionally inadequate, concluding that due process requires an evidentiary hearing prior to termination. In light of the private and governmental interests at stake here and the nature of the existing procedures, we think this was error.

Since a recipient whose benefits are terminated is awarded full retroactive relief if he ultimately prevails, his sole interest is in the uninterrupted receipt of this source of income pending final administrative decision on his claim.

[Only] in *Goldberg* has the Court held that due process requires an evidentiary hearing prior to a temporary deprivation. It was emphasized there that welfare assistance is given to persons on the very margin of [subsistence. Eligibility] for disability benefits, in contrast, is not based upon financial need. Indeed, it is wholly unrelated to the worker's income or support from many other sources, such as earnings of other family members, workmen's compensation awards, tort claims awards, savings, private insurance, public or private pensions, veterans' benefits, food stamps, public assistance, or the "many other important programs, both public and private, which contain provisions for disability payments affecting a substantial portion of the work force. . . ."

As *Goldberg* illustrates, the degree of potential deprivation that may be created by a particular decision is a factor to be considered in assessing the validity of any administrative decisionmaking process. The potential deprivation here is generally likely to be less than in *Goldberg*, although the degree of difference can be overstated. As the District Court emphasized, to remain eligible for benefits a recipient must be "unable to engage in substantial gainful activity." Thus, in contrast to the discharged federal employee in *Arnett*, there is little possibility that the terminated recipient will be able to find even temporary employment to ameliorate the interim loss. [Further,] "the possible length of wrongful deprivation of . . . benefits [also] is an important factor in assessing the impact of official action on the private interests." The Secretary concedes that the delay between a request for a hearing before an administrative law judge and a decision on the claim is currently between 10 and 11 months. Since a terminated recipient must first obtain a reconsideration decision as a prerequisite to invoking his right to an evidentiary hearing, the delay between the actual cutoff of benefits and final decision after a hearing exceeds one year.

In view of the torpidity of this administrative review process, and the typically modest resources of the family unit of the physically disabled worker,[26] the hardship imposed upon the erroneously terminated disability recipient may be significant. Still, the disabled worker's need is likely to be less than that of a welfare recipient. In addition to the possibility of access to private resources, other forms of government assistance will become available where the termination of disability benefits places a worker or his family below the subsistence level.[27] In view of these potential sources of temporary income, there is less reason here than in *Goldberg* to depart from the ordinary principle, [that] something less than an evidentiary hearing is sufficient prior to adverse administrative action.

An additional factor to be considered here is the fairness and reliability of the existing pretermination procedures, and the probable value, if any, of additional procedural safeguards. Central to the evaluation of any administrative process is the nature of the relevant inquiry. In order to remain eligible for benefits the disabled worker must demonstrate by means of "medically acceptable clinical and laboratory diagnostic techniques," that he is unable "to engage in any substantial gainful activity by reason of any *medically determinable* physical or mental impairment. . . ."

In short, a medical assessment of the worker's physical or mental condition is required. This is a more sharply focused and easily documented decision than the typical determination of welfare entitlement. [The] decision whether to discontinue disability benefits will turn, in most cases, upon "routine, standard, and unbiased medical reports by physician specialists," [concerning] a subject whom they have personally examined. [To] be sure, credibility and veracity may be a factor in the ultimate disability assessment in some cases. But procedural due process rules are shaped by the risk of error inherent in the truthfinding process as

26. Amici cite statistics compiled by the Secretary which indicate that in 1965 the mean income of the family unit of a disabled worker was $3,803, while the median income for the unit was $2,836. The mean liquid assets — i.e., cash, stocks, bonds — of these family units was $4,862; the median was $940. These statistics do not take into account the family unit's nonliquid assets — i.e., automobile, real estate, and the like.

27. Amici emphasize that because an identical definition of disability is employed in both the Title II Social Security Program and in the companion welfare system for the disabled, [the] terminated disability-benefits recipient will be ineligible for the SSI Program. There exist, however, state and local welfare programs which may supplement the worker's income. In addition, the worker's household unit can qualify for food stamps if it meets the financial need requirements. . . .

applied to the generality of cases, not the rare exceptions. The potential value of an evidentiary hearing, or even oral presentation to the decisionmaker, is substantially less in this context than in *Goldberg*.

The decision in *Goldberg* also was based on the Court's conclusion that written submissions were an inadequate substitute for oral presentation because they did not provide an effective means for the recipient to communicate his case to the decisionmaker. Written submissions were viewed as an unrealistic option, for most recipients lacked the "educational attainment necessary to write effectively" and could not afford professional assistance. In addition, such submissions would not provide the "flexibility of oral presentations" or "permit the recipient to mold his argument to the issues the decision maker appears to regard as important." [In] the context of the disability-benefits-entitlement assessment the administrative procedures under review here fully answer these objections.

[A] further safeguard against mistake is the policy of allowing the disability recipient's representative full access to all information relied upon by the state agency. In addition, prior to the cutoff of benefits the agency informs the recipient of its tentative assessment, the reasons therefor, and provides a summary of the evidence that it considers most relevant. Opportunity is then afforded the recipient to submit additional evidence or arguments, enabling him to challenge directly the accuracy of information in his file as well as the correctness of the agency's tentative conclusions.

Despite these carefully structured procedures, amici point to the significant reversal rate for appealed cases as clear evidence that the current process is inadequate. Depending upon the base selected and the line of analysis followed, the relevant reversal rates urged by the contending parties vary from a high of 58.6% for appealed reconsideration decisions to an overall reversal rate of only 3.3%. Bare statistics rarely provide a satisfactory measure of the fairness of a decisionmaking process. Their adequacy is especially suspect here since the administrative review system is operated on an open-file basis. A recipient may always submit new evidence, and such submissions may result in additional medical examinations. . . .

In striking the appropriate due process balance the final factor to be assessed is the public interest. This includes the administrative burden and other societal costs that would be associated with requiring, as a matter of constitutional right, an evidentiary hearing upon demand in all cases prior to the termination of disability benefits. The most visible burden would be the incremental cost resulting from the increased number of hearings and the expense of providing benefits to ineligible recipients pending decision. No one can predict the extent of the increase, but the fact that full benefits would continue until after such hearings would assure the exhaustion in most cases of this attractive option. [The] parties submit widely varying estimates of the probable additional financial cost. We only need say that experience with the constitutionalizing of government procedures suggests that the ultimate additional cost in terms of money and administrative burden would not be insubstantial.

Financial cost alone is not a controlling weight in determining whether due process requires a particular procedural safeguard prior to some administrative decision. But the Government's interest, and hence that of the public, in conserving scarce fiscal and administrative resources is a factor that must be weighed. At some point the benefit of an additional safeguard to the individual affected by the administrative action and to society in terms of increased assurance that the action is just, may be outweighed by the cost. Significantly, the cost of protecting those whom the preliminary administrative process has identified as likely to be found undeserving may in the end come out of the pockets of the deserving since resources available for any particular program of social welfare are not un-limited. . . .

[But] more is implicated in cases of this type than ad hoc weighing of fiscal and administrative burdens against the interests of a particular category of claimants. The ultimate balance involves a determination as to when, under our constitu-tional system, judicial-type procedures must be imposed upon administrative action to assure fairness. We reiterate the wise admonishment of Mr. Justice Frankfurter that differences in the origin and function of administrative agencies "preclude wholesale transplantation of the rules of procedure, trial and review which have evolved from the history and experience of courts." FCC v. Pottsville Broadcasting Co., 309 U.S. 134, 143 (1940). The judicial model of an evidentiary hearing is neither a required, nor even the most effective, method of decision-making in all circumstances. The essence of due process is the requirement that "a person in jeopardy of serious loss [be given] notice of the case against him and opportunity to meet it." Joint Anti-Fascist Comm. v. McGrath, 341 U.S., at 171-172 (Frankfurter, J., concurring). All that is necessary is that the procedures be tailored, in light of the decision to be made, to "the capacities and circumstances of those who are to be heard," [Goldberg], to insure that they are given a mean-ingful opportunity to present their case. In assessing what process is due in this case, substantial weight must be given to the good-faith judgments of the individ-uals charged by Congress with the administration of social welfare programs that the procedures they have provided assure fair consideration of the entitlement claims of individuals. . . .

We conclude that an evidentiary hearing is not required prior to the termina-tion of disability benefits and that the present administrative procedures fully comport with due process.

The judgment of the Court of Appeals is reversed.

Mr. Justice Stevens took no part in the consideration or decision of this case.

Mr. Justice Brennan, with whom Mr. Justice Marshall concurs, dissenting.

[The] Court's consideration that a discontinuance of disability benefits may cause the recipient to suffer only a limited deprivation is no argument. It is speculative. Moreover, the very legislative determination to provide disability benefits, without any prerequisite determination of need in fact, presumes a need by the recipient which is not this Court's function to denigrate. Indeed, in the present case, [because] disability benefits were terminated there was a foreclosure upon the Eldridge home and the family's furniture was repossessed, forcing Eldridge, his wife, and their children to sleep in one bed. Finally, it is also no argument that a worker, who has been placed in the untenable position of having been denied disability benefits, may still seek other forms of public assistance.

Note: Balancing Tests and the Due Process Clause

1. *The* Mathews *test in general.* In *Mathews* the Court adopted a three-part "test," sometimes called one of balancing or "cost-benefit" analysis, that has played an important role in constitutional law. In almost all cases raising ques-

tions of procedural regularity, the Court refers to the *Mathews* test. On what grounds might the test be criticized?

a. *Ignoring nonutilitarian variables.* Does the *Mathews* approach ignore participatory and dignitary concerns? Consider Mashaw, The Supreme Court's Due Process Calculus for Administrative Adjudication in *Mathews v. Eldridge:* Three Factors in Search of a Theory of Value, 44 U. Chi. L. Rev. 28, 49-51 (1976):

> The Supreme Court's analysis in *Eldridge* is not informed by systematic attention to any theory of the values underlying due process review. The approach is implicitly utilitarian but incomplete, and the Court overlooks alternative theories that might have yielded fruitful inquiry. [The] increasingly secular, scientific, and collectivist character of the modern American state reinforces our propensity to define fairness in the formal, and apparently neutral language of social utility. [Yet] the popular moral presupposition of individual dignity, and its political counterpart, self-determination, persist. State coercion must be legitimized, not only by acceptable substantive policies, but also by political processes that respond to a democratic morality's demand for participation in decisions affecting individual and group interests. [A] dignitary theory of due process might have contributed significantly to the *Eldridge* analysis. [A] disability decision is a judgment of considerable social significance, and one that the claimant should rightly perceive as having a substantive moral content.

See also J. Mashaw, Due Process in the Administrative State (1985).

b. *Vagueness.* How useful is the three-part analysis? Does it constrain judicial discretion in a helpful way? Note that in economics, cost-benefit analysis is usually based on the criterion of private willingness to pay. The benefit is measured by how much people would be willing to pay for the good in question; the cost is measured similarly. But how does one assess the benefits and costs in a case like *Mathews?*

c. *Susceptibility to misapplication.* Does a utilitarian assessment of the three factors require courts to duplicate legislative processes? That assessment, calling for ad hoc judgments of policy, may not be readily within judicial competence. What, in the text of the due process clause or in acceptable conceptions of the judicial role, authorizes such an approach?

This critique might be buttressed by reference to *Mathews* itself. Mashaw, The Supreme Court's Due Process Calculus for Administrative Adjudication, supra, argues that the Court misconceived the character of the disability determination. According to Mashaw, that determination is based much less on purely medical factors and much more on subjective impressions raising issues of credibility than the Court suggested. In these circumstances oral rather than written testimony becomes more valuable. Note also the Court's confessed inability to evaluate the costs of additional safeguards, captured in its statement that it could not say that they would be "insubstantial."

But is there an alternative to the *Mathews* approach that would avoid these various critiques and at the same time provide a sensible approach for making decisions about the extent of procedural safeguards? Would bright-line rules — requiring, for example, trial-type hearings absent a special governmental showing or deference to the legislative determination absent special individual circumstances — be preferable? See Walters v. National Association of Radiation Survivors, — U.S. — , 105 S. Ct. 3180 (1985), where the Court cited *Mathews* in upholding a statute providing that $10 is the maximum fee that may be paid to an attorney who represents a veteran seeking Veterans Administration benefits for service-related injuries. In a concurring opinion, Justice O'Connor, joined by Justice Blackmun, suggested that under the due process clause, courts should look at the individual claim to evaluate whether the statutory maximum is unconstitutional in particular applications. Justice Stevens, joined by Justices Brennan and Marshall, dissented, arguing in favor of a bright-line rule in favor of counsel. Consider also that (1) it is possible that detailed procedures may be requested only by the most educated and aggressive claimants, (2) the costs of such procedures may be taken out of the claimants' benefits elsewhere, and (3) formal procedures may increase the adversarial quality of relations that should be conducted in a more informal way.

2. *The problem of timing.* Must hearings be held before or after adverse action is taken? The traditional rule has been that a postdeprivation remedy is insufficient. In general government must afford procedural safeguards *before* it harms someone. But in North American Cold Storage Co. v. Chicago, 211 U.S. 306 (1908), the Court held that a prior hearing was not required before state officers destroyed stored food deemed by health officials to be unfit for human consumption. The Court noted that the existence of the food posed a threat to public health and that a subsequent tort action would provide sufficient protection to the owner. Would the *Mathews* approach support this outcome?

How far should the *North Carolina Cold Storage* reasoning be taken? Should it apply to cases of termination of welfare benefits? Of employment? Note that in Arnett v. Kennedy, supra, a majority of the Court held that a trial-type hearing was not required before termination of a federal employee accused of bribery. Justice Powell, undertaking a balancing approach, contended that the government "must have wide discretion and control over the management of its personnel and internal affairs. This includes the prerogative to remove employees whose conduct hinders efficient operation and to do so with dispatch. [The employee's] actual injury would consist of a temporary interruption of his income during the interim. [The] possible deprivation is considerably less severe than that involved in *Goldberg*." Note, however, that in *Arnett* there was some predeprivation procedure as well.

In *Loudermill*, supra, the Court held that the Constitution did not permit discharge of state employees without any prior procedural safeguards. The Court said: "In *Arnett* six Justices found constitutional minima satisfied where the employee had access to the material upon which the charge was based and could respond orally or in writing and present rebuttal affidavits. [The] need for some form of pretermination hearing [is] evident from a balancing of the competing interests at stake." The Court emphasized that the "private interest in retaining employment" was significant, that "some opportunity for the employee to present his side of the case is recurringly of obvious value in reaching an accurate decision," especially in light of the fact the discharge may involve a factual dispute, and that "affording the employee an opportunity to respond would impose neither a significant administrative burden nor intolerable delays."

The Court added that even when the dispute was not factual, a hearing might allow an examination of the appropriateness or necessity of discharge, and that a hearing could serve governmental interests in retaining qualified employees. The Court said, however, that the pretermination hearing need not be elaborate and could consist of "oral or written notice of the charges against him, an explanation of the employer's evidence, and an opportunity to present his side of the story."

3. *How formal?* Goldberg v. Kelly required a trial-type hearing before termination of welfare benefits, including a number of features: a right to present oral evidence, a right to confront and cross-examine witnesses, a right to counsel, a statement by the arbiter of reasons and of the evidence relied on, and a right to an impartial decisionmaker. In recent cases, however, the Court has shown some reluctance to formalize the administrative process with such requirements.

At the opposite pole from *Goldberg*, for example, is Goss v. Lopez, supra, in which the Court found that due process required only a conversation before temporary suspension of students. This included oral or written notice of the charges against them, an explanation of the evidence the authorities have, and a chance to provide the students' side of the story. The Court said:

> Even truncated trial-type procedures might well overwhelm administrative facilities in many places and, in diverting resources, cost more than it would save in educational effectiveness. Moreover, further formalizing the suspension process and escalating its formality and adversary nature may not only make it too costly as a regular disciplinary tool but also destroy its effectiveness as part of the teaching process. On the other hand, requiring effective notice and informal hearing permitting the student to give his version of the events will provide a meaningful hedge against erroneous action.

Is this a useful compromise approach, or does it deprive students, at the "what process is due" stage of the inquiry, of the benefits that should result after a conclusion that they have a property interest in continued attendance? See also Board of Curators of University of Missouri v. Horowitz, 435 U.S. 78 (1978), declining to require elaborate procedures for discharge of a woman from medical school, in part because of reluctance to "formalize the academic dismissal process." And note the various conclusions on the issue of formality in *Mathews*, *Arnett*, and *Loudermill*.

Consider, finally, Greenholtz v. Inmates, 442 U.S. 1 (1979), in which the Court held that in parole decisions, based on a subjective assessment of the whole person, an oral hearing was not required. A review of the prisoner's files, the Court said, was sufficient to satisfy due process.

4. *State remedies as due process.* In a development of potentially great importance, the Court has held that state tort remedies may provide all the process that is constitutionally "due." Ingraham v. Wright, 430 U.S. 651 (1977), involved a claim that the due process clause required some sort of procedural safeguard before teachers "paddled" students for asserted misconduct. The Court held that the interest in avoiding "paddling" was constitutionally protected liberty, but concluded that an after-the-fact state tort remedy provided sufficient procedural safeguards. "Because paddlings are usually inflicted in response to conduct directly observed by teachers in their presence, the risk that a child will be paddled without cause is typically insignificant. [In] those cases where severe punishment is contemplated, the available civil and criminal sanctions for abuse — considered in light of the openness of the school environment — afford significant protection against unjustified corporal punishment." The Court added that if a prior hearing were required, the use of corporal punishment would be signifi-

cantly burdened, and it might be eliminated or sharply curtailed. The costs of such a step, according to the Court, "cannot be dismissed as insubstantial." Justice White, in a dissent joined by Justices Brennan, Marshall, and Stevens, complained that state law was inadequate in cases of a good faith mistake in school discipline and that the "infliction of physical pain is final and irreparable."

Compare Memphis Light, Gas, & Water Division v. Craft, 436 U.S. 1 (1978), requiring a hearing in advance of termination of electricity service for nonpayment of a disputed bill. "The factors that have justified exceptions to the requirements of some prior process are not present here. Although utility service may be restored ultimately, the cessation of essential services for any appreciable time works a uniquely final deprivation. [Moreover], the probability of error in utility cut-off decisions is not so insubstantial as to warrant dispensing with all process prior to termination."

Ingraham was extended in Parratt v. Taylor, 451 U.S. 527 (1981), which involved a negligent loss of a prisoner's hobby kit. The Court held that state tort law provided a constitutionally adequate remedy. The Court noted that the case involved a "tortious loss of [property] as a result of a random and unauthorized act by a state employee [not] as a result of some established state procedure." A state tort remedy was therefore sufficient "process." Should it matter that *Parratt* involved negligence? See Hudson v. Palmer, — U.S. — ,104 S. Ct. 3194 (1984), extending *Parratt* to intentional deprivations of property, in a context of destruction of prisoners' property during search of his cell. Should it matter that property rather than liberty was at stake? That a prior hearing would seem impracticable?

In Logan v. Zimmerman Brush Co., supra, it was argued that *Parratt* was controlling and that the state tort remedy provided sufficient procedural protection for the state's failure to hold a hearing on the plaintiff's claim of discrimination. The Court rejected that argument, reasserting the general principle requiring predeprivation hearings. Unlike in *Parratt*, moreover, "it is the state system itself that destroys a complainant's property interests, by operation of law, whenever the Commission fails to convene a timely conference."

5. *Concluding note.* In exploring issues of timing, formality, and adequacy of state tort remedies, the Court has increasingly relied on the tripartite test of *Mathews*. Do the outcomes suggest that the test is vulnerable to the three criticism set out at the introduction of this note? Or taken as a whole, can one conclude that the test furnishes a sensible method of accommodating the various concerns at stake?

Note: *The Irrebuttable Presumption Doctrine*

For a period, the Court combined principles of procedural due process and equal protection in the "irrebuttable presumption doctrine," in accordance with which decisions according to rule were sometimes unconstitutional. Cleveland Board of Education v. LaFleur, 414 U.S. 632 (1974), was the leading case. At issue was a school board regulation requiring pregnant school teachers to take an unpaid maternity leave four to five months before the expected birth. The Court invalidated the regulation on the ground that it created "a conclusive presumption that every pregnant teacher who teaches the fifth or sixth month of pregnancy is physically incapable of continuing. There is no individualized determination [as] to any particular teacher's ability to continue at her job." See also Vlandis v. Kline, 412 U.S. 441 (1973), invalidating a Connecticut statute creating an irrebuttable presumption that students transferring to a state university from out of state were nonresidents and thus not entitled to reduced tuition fees.

The doctrine has been subject to sharp criticism. Decisions made in accordance with clear rules are sometimes taken to be the model of compliance with the principle of procedural regularity. Moreover, most statutes amount to conclusive presumptions; surely the Court did not mean to invalidate them all.

See Note, Irrebuttable Presumptions: An Illusory Analysis, 27 Stan. L. Rev. 449 (1975), contending that

> [Conclusive] presumption claims are correctly analyzed by determining the actual relationship between the criterion of basic fact and the consequences established by the challenged provision, the importance of the individual interest impaired by that relationship, and the extent of overlap between the relationship established and the governmental interest sought to be effected. [The] nearly automatic application of a close scrutiny test to what are essentially equal protection claims engages the Court in the type of review that it abandoned in the 1930's and from which it has assiduously sought to abstain.

To the same effect, see Note, The Irrebuttable Presumption Doctrine in the Supreme Court, 87 Harv. L. Rev. 1534 (1974).

Weinberger v. Salfi, 422 U.S. 749 (1975), seems to have marked the demise of the doctrine. The case involved a constitutional attack on a requirement of the Social Security Act that, in order to receive benefits as a spouse of a wage earner, one must have been married to the wage earner for at least nine months prior to his death. The requirement was attacked on the ground that it did not permit individualized proof on the question whether the marriage was entered into for purposes of qualifying for social security benefits. The Court distinguished La-Fleur and Vlandis on the ground that they did not involve "a noncontractual claim to receive funds from the public treasury." Extension of the doctrine here, the Court said,

> would turn the doctrine of those cases into a virtual engine of destruction for countless legislative judgments which have heretofore been thought wholly consistent with the [Constitution]. The question raised is not whether a statutory provision precisely filters out those, and only those, who are in the factual position which generated the congressional concern reflected in the statute. Such a rule would ban all prophylactic provisions.

The Court added that there were substantial benefits to an across-the-board rule, in terms of saving the costs of individuation. Applying traditional rationality review, the Court upheld the rule. Justice Brennan, joined by Justice Marshall, dissented. For a post-*Salfi* refusal either to overrule or to reaffirm Vlandis v. Kline, see Elkins v. Moreno, 435 U.S. 647 (1978). See also Usery v. Turner Elkhorne Mining Co., 428 U.S. 1 (1976) (upholding a broad "conclusive presumption").

Is any function performed by invalidation of irrebuttable presumptions that is not performed by procedural due process, as understood in *Roth* and successor cases, or by equal protection doctrine? Note that ordinary principles of procedural due process entitle a person to a hearing to determine whether the applicable rule has been violated. Such principles are, by definition, inapplicable to a conclusive presumption, where there is no doubt that the government "followed the rules." Note also that ordinary principles of equal protection require a merely rational connection between the conclusive presumption and the harm sought to be avoided. Under this framework, most conclusive presumptions — like most rules — will be upheld.

But the irrebuttable presumption doctrine has been defended on the ground that procedural due process and equal protection, ordinarily conceived, neglect the possibility that procedural irregularity may consist precisely in the failure to allow individuation. Under this view, the rule of law can sometimes produce arbitrariness and is not (always or inevitably? generally?) a guarantee against it. Consider the following view:

> There are circumstances in which individualized judgments, unbounded by rules, should not be viewed as ways of concealing arbitrary, unequal, or substantively impermissible bases for decision. The persistence of courts of equity, the emergence of concepts like "unconscionability," and, in another sphere, the vitality of successful families and other intimate communities, all belie any automatic equating of the informal with the suspect. [Is] it possible to argue that individualized and informal judgments are in some circumstances not only more "enlightened" but indeed constitutionally propelled — no less so than judgments by determinate rules are in other circumstances?

Tribe, Structural Due Process, 10 Harv. C.R.-C.L. L. Rev. 269 (1975). Tribe goes on to defend *LaFleur* on the ground that "the important interest involved in parenthood, cast in a context of social and moral flux about unmarried sex, made rulebound determination inappropriate for the issue." For an extended discussion of the premises underlying preferences for rules on the one hand and individualized decision on the other, see generally Kennedy, Form and Substance in Private Law Adjudication, 89 Harv. L. Rev. 1685, 1710-1722, 1767-1774 (1976).

Note: Procedural Due Process and "Legislative" Determinations

Congress and state legislatures may pass laws without affording procedural safeguards beyond those specifically required by the Constitution. The due process clause does not mean that, before passing laws, Congress must hear those who will be affected. Congress may, for example, reduce the welfare benefits of a class of people without offering anything in the way of procedure. Why? Does the same reasoning apply when administrative agencies make rules governing private conduct?

Some answers were spelled out in Bi-Metallic Investment Co. v. State Board of Equalization, 239 U.S. 441 (1915). *Bi-Metallic* involved an attempt to prevent the

Denver Board of Equalization and the Colorado Tax Commission from increasing the valuation of all taxable property in Denver without affording a hearing. The Court held that no hearing was required:

> Where a rule of conduct applies to more than a few people it is impracticable that every one should have a direct voice in its adoption. The Constitution does not require all public acts to be done in town meeting or an assembly of the whole. General statutes within the state power are passed that affect the person or property of individuals, sometimes to the point of ruin, without giving them a chance to be heard. Their rights are protected in the only way that they can be in a complex society, by their power, immediate or remote, over those who make the rule.

This reasoning contains two points: Processes of representation are a sufficient guarantee of legitimacy, thus serving the same ends as a hearing; and it would be impracticable to require a hearing for determinations that affect large numbers of people. Kenneth Culp Davis has added that trial-type processes are best suited for "adjudicative" facts — facts "about the parties and their activities, business, and properties. Adjudicative facts usually answer the questions of who said what, where, when, how, why, with what motive or intent." K. Davis, Administrative Law Treatise §7.02 (1958). "Legislative" facts, by contrast, raise questions of policy that are better suited to a legislative forum.

How might one challenge these claims? Skepticism has sometimes been expressed about the idea that no procedural safeguards are required in legislative-type proceedings. See, e.g., Thompson v. Washington, 497 F.2d 626 (D.C. Cir. 1973) (giving tenants a right to participate in decisions involving proposed rent increases); Marshall v. Lynn, 497 F.2d 643 (D.C. Cir. 1973) (same). Such decisions reflect skepticism about the idea that representative processes are a reliable safeguard when administrative agencies are making rules; they also reflect a view that judicially enforced procedures, giving a right to participate, are useful even when the issue at stake is one of policy rather than "adjudicative facts." How far should such rulings be taken? Consider the relevance of the discussion of the purposes of procedural safeguards, supra.

VII

Freedom of Expression

A. INTRODUCTION

The first amendment provides that "Congress shall make no law [abridging] the freedom of speech, or of the press; or the right of the people peaceably to assemble, and to petition the Government for a redress of grievances." Consider Justice Black's position: "The phrase 'Congress shall make no law' is composed of plain words, easily understood. [The] language [is] absolute. [Of] course the decision to provide a constitutional safeguard for [free speech] involves a balancing of conflicting interests. [But] the Framers themselves did this balancing when they wrote the [Constitution]. Courts have neither the right nor the power [to] make a different [evaluation]." Black, The Bill of Rights, 35 N.Y.U. L. Rev. 865, 874, 879 (1960).

The Court has never accepted Black's view. Rather, it has consistently held that "abridging" and "the freedom of speech" require interpretation and that restraints on free expression may be "permitted for appropriate reasons." Elrod v. Burns, 427 U.S. 347, 360 (1976). This section examines two sources that might aid interpretation: the history and philosophy underlying the first amendment.

clear language - Black

Note: The History of Free Expression

1. *The English background.* The notion that government "shall make no law [abridging] the freedom of speech, or of the press," received only gradual acceptance in Anglo-American law. Indeed, throughout much of English history the crown and Parliament attempted vigorously to suppress opinions deemed pernicious. Three forms of restraint were most commonly employed: licensing of the press; the doctrine of constructive treason; and the law of seditious libel.

a. *Licensing.* The invention of printing greatly magnified the danger posed by "undesirable" opinions, and shortly after the first book was printed in England in 1476 the crown claimed an authority to control printing presses as a right of prerogative. The manuscript of any work intended for publication had to be submitted to crown officials empowered to censor objectionable passages and to approve or deny a license for the printing of the work. Anything published without an imprimatur was criminal. This system of "prior restraint" remained in effect until 1694 when the authorizing legislation expired and was not renewed. The decision not to renew licensing resulted not from any commitment to free expression but rather from considerations of expediency, for licensing had proved ineffective, difficult to enforce, and conducive to bribery. See generally L. Levy, Emergence of a Free Press ch. 1 (1985); F. Siebert, Freedom of the Press in England, 1476-1776, chs. 2-3, 6-12 (1952).

b. *Constructive treason.* The law of treason in England derived from the statute 25 Edward III (1352), which defined the crime as (1) compassing or imagining the king's death, (2) levying war against the king, or (3) adhering to his enemies. During the latter part of the seventeenth century, the English judges ruled that mere written or printed matter, as well as overt acts, could constitute treason. John Twyn was the first printer to suffer under this extension of the law of treason. Government officers searched Twyn's home and seized the proofs of a book suggesting that the king was accountable to the people and that the people were entitled to self-governance. Twyn was convicted of constructive treason, hanged, drawn, and quartered.

Although constructive treason was invoked in only a few cases, the doctrine posed a serious threat to freedom of expression, for the few instances in which conviction and execution occurred served to remind potential publishers of the fate that awaited those who violated the law. The doctrine was abandoned after 1720 because juries were often reluctant to convict, the death penalty was in many cases considered too drastic, and the procedure was too detailed. See generally Siebert, supra, at 265-269.

c. *Seditious libel.* The doctrine of seditious libel first entered Anglo-American jurisprudence in a 1275 statute outlawing "any false news or tales whereby discord or occasion of discord or slander may grow between the king and his people or the great men of the realm." Violations were punished by the king's council sitting in the "starred chamber." The point of departure for the modern law of seditious libel was Sir Edward Coke's report of a Star Chamber case of 1606, which stated three central propositions: (1) A libel against a private person may be punished criminally because it may provoke revenge and thus cause a breach of the peace. (2) A libel against a government official is an even greater offense, "for it concerns not only the breach of the peace, but also the scandal of government." (3) Although the essence of the crime as fixed by the statute of 1275 was the falsity of the libel, even a true libel may be criminally punished.

The theory underlying seditious libel was explained by Chief Justice Holt in 1704: "If people should not be called to account for possessing the people with an ill opinion of the government, no government can subsist. For it is very necessary for all governments that the people should have a good opinion of it." Rex v. Tutchin, 14 Howell's State Trials 1095, 1128 (1704). Thus, a true libel is especially dangerous, for unlike a false libel, the dangers of truthful criticism cannot be defused by disproof. It was thus an oft-quoted maxim after 1606 that "the greater the truth the greater the libel."

Two procedural issues played a central role in the formulation of seditious libel in the seventeenth century. First, must the government prove that the defendant maliciously intended to cause sedition, or was it sufficient that he merely intended to publish matter having a seditious tendency? The judges in this era held that intent to publish was sufficient. Second, who would determine whether the publication had a seditious tendency — the judge or jury? The seventeenth-century judges held that the court should decide this question as a matter of law. The jury's sole function was to determine matters of fact, such as whether the defendant actually published the words. See generally Levy, supra, at 7-13.

In practice, then, seventeenth-century judges punished as seditious libel any "written censure upon any public man whatever for any conduct whatever, or upon any law or institution whatever." 2 J. Stephen, A History of the Criminal Law of England 350 (1883). As one commentator has observed, "no single method of restricting the press was as effective as the law of seditious libel as it was developed and applied by the common-law courts in the latter part of the seventeenth century." Seibert, supra, at 269. For general discussion, see Hamburger, The Development of the Law of Seditious Libel and the Control of the Press, 37 Stan. L. Rev. 661 (1985).

In 1769 Blackstone summarized the law as follows:

> The liberty of the press [consists] in laying no *previous* restraints upon publications, and not in freedom from censure for criminal matter when published. [To] subject the press to the restrictive power of a licenser [is] to subject all freedom of sentiment to the prejudices of one man, and make him the arbitrary and infallible judge of all controverted points in learning, religion, and government. But to punish (as the law does at present) any dangerous or offensive writings, which, when published, shall on a fair and impartial trial be adjudged of a pernicious tendency, is necessary for the preservation of peace and good order, of government and religion, the only solid foundations of civil liberty.

4 W. Blackstone, Commentaries on the Laws of England* 151-152.

2. *The colonial background.* The image of colonial America as a society in which freedom of expression was cherished seems largely inaccurate. Although colonial America was the scene of extraordinary diversity of opinion on religion, politics, social structure, and other subjects, each community "tended to be a tight little island clutching its own respective orthodoxy and [eager] to banish or extralegally punish unwelcome dissidents." Levy, supra, at 16.

Formal legal restraints on expression, however, were relatively rare. Licensing expired in 1725, and although there were hundreds of trials for seditious libel in England during the seventeenth and eighteenth centuries, there were not more than half a dozen such cases in colonial America. The most famous of these trials involved the prosecution of John Peter Zenger in New York in 1735. Zenger, publisher of the New York Weekly Journal, was charged with seditious libel by the Governor General of New York, whom he had criticized. Zenger was defended by Andrew Hamilton and James Alexander, who argued that the truth of the libel should be an absolute defense and that the jury, rather than the judge, should decide the questions of seditious tendency and intent. Although these propositions were rejected by the trial judge, the jury, responding to the popularity of Zenger's cause, disregarded the judge's instructions and returned a verdict of not guilty.

Although common law prosecutions for seditious libel were rare, the popularly elected colonial assemblies, imitating Parliament, assumed and vigorously exercised the power to summarily punish "seditious" expression. Any criticism of an assembly or its members was likely to be regarded as a seditious scandal against the government punishable as a "breach of privilege." Levy, supra, at 14. To cite just one example, James Franklin, the older brother of Ben, ran a brief notice in his New England Courant that the government was preparing a ship to pursue coastal pirates "sometime this month, wind and weather permitting." The insinuation that the government was not dealing effectively with the pirates angered Massachusetts's popularly elected assembly. Franklin was arrested, and after a pro forma hearing the assembly resolved that he had committed "a High affront to this Government." Franklin was imprisoned for the remainder of the session.

3. *The first amendment.* Scholars have long puzzled over the actual intentions of the framers of the first amendment. The primary dispute is over whether the framers intended to adopt the Blackstonian view — that freedom of speech consists entirely in the freedom from prior restraints — or whether they intended some broader meaning. Consider the following views.

a. Z. Chafee, Free Speech in the United States 18-20 (1941):

> If we [consider] what mischief in the existing law the [framers] wished to [remedy], we can be sure that it was not [licensing]. This had expired in England in 1695, and in the colonies by 1725. [There] was no need to go to all the trouble of pushing through a constitutional amendment just to settle an issue that had been dead for decades. What the framers did have plenty of reason to fear was an entirely different danger to political writers and speakers. For years the government here and in England had substituted for [licensing] rigorous and repeated prosecutions for seditious libel [and] for years these prosecutions were opposed by liberal opinion and popular agitation. [Two] different views of the relation of rulers and people were in conflict. According to one view, the rulers were the superiors of the people, and therefore must not be subjected to any censure that would tend to diminish their authority. [According] to the other view, the rulers were agents and servants of the people, who might therefore find fault with their servants and discuss questions of their punishment or dismissal, and of governmental policy. [In] the United States the people and not the government possess the absolute sovereignty, and [government is thus not free to punish seditious libel. Indeed, one] "of the objects of the Revolution was to get rid of the English common law on liberty of speech and of the press."

b. Mayton, Seditious Libel and the Lost Guarantee of a Freedom of Expression, 84 Colum. L. Rev. 91, 95, 97, 117-120 (1984):

> [To] understand the full constitutional protection of speech, we must look past the first amendment and consider the entire Constitution. When we do so, the plausibility of the first amendment's incorporating past practice is considerably dissipated. [For] the original Constitution, unlike the first amendment, carries with it a source of strong extrinsic evidence — the state ratification debates — concerning the extent and nature of the constitutional protection of speech. [In these] debates, the power of the national government to suppress speech was drawn into issue. [The] understanding was reached that the Constitution as [originally drafted] disarmed the national government of such power. [To] the framers the [most] important protection of speech lay in a Constitution structured to deny the national government power over speech. [By] originally enumerating and limiting government power, the whole of liberty, except for those identified areas where the government might intrude, was to be reserved to the individual. [The first] amendment was [thus]

meant to seal an understanding about speech already embodied in the text of the original Constitution [and] to continue an original understanding [that] left no room for a Blackstonian measure of the power to punish seditious libel.

The implications of the enumeration of limited powers in article I of the Constitution are explored in Chapters 2 and 3, supra.

c. Levy, supra, at xii-xv:

[The proposition has been conventionally accepted] that it was the intent of the American Revolution or the Framers of the First Amendment to abolish the common law of seditious libel. [The] evidence suggests that the proposition is supposititious and unprovable. [We] may even have to confront the possibility that the intentions of the Framers were not the most [libertarian]. But this should be expected because the Framers were nurtured on the crabbed historicism of Coke and the narrow conservatism of Blackstone, as well as Zenger's case. The ways of thought of a lifetime are not easily broken. The Declaration of Independence severed the political connection with England but the American states continued the English common-law system except as explicitly rejected by statute. If the Revolution produced any radical libertarians on the meaning of freedom of speech and press, they were not present at the Constitutional Convention or the First Congress, which drafted the Bill of Rights. Scholars and judges have betrayed a penchant for what John P. Roche called "retrospective symmetry," by giving to present convictions a patriotic lineage and tradition — in this case, the fatherhood of the "Framers."

For a critical analysis of this view, see Rabban, An Ahistorical Historian: Leonard Levy on Freedom of Expression in Early American History, 37 Stan. L. Rev. 795 (1985).

4. *The Relevance of History.* To what extent, if any, is the preceding history relevant to interpretation of the first amendment? Is the English common law important because it was what the framers rejected, or because it was what they accepted? Is it plausible that states that themselves punished seditious libel intended to prohibit Congress from punishing it? And given the enormous changes in the media and politics since the adoption of the first amendment, to what extent, if any, should the intent of the framers control the contemporary resolution of first amendment issues?

5. *The Sedition Act of 1798.* The first serious challenge to freedom of expression in the United States came with the Sedition Act of 1798. Act of July 14, 1798, 1 Stat. 596. The United States was on the verge of war with France, and many of the ideas generated by the French Revolution aroused fear and hostility in segments of the U.S. population. A bitter political and philosophical debate raged between the Federalists, then in power, and the Republicans.

Against this backdrop, the Federalists enacted the Sedition Act of 1798. The act prohibited the publication of

false, scandalous, and malicious writing or writings against the government of the United States, or either house of the Congress of the United States, or the President of the United States, with intent to defame [them]; or to bring them [into] contempt or disrepute; or to excite against them [the] hatred of the good people of the United States, or to stir up sedition within the United States, or to excite any unlawful combinations therein, for opposing or resisting any law of the United States, or any [lawful] act of the President of the United States.

The act provided further that truth would be a good defense, that malicious intent was an element of the crime, and that the jury "shall have a right to determine the law and the fact, under the direction of the court, as in other cases." Thus, as the Federalists emphasized, the act eliminated those particular aspects of the English common law that had been the focus of attack on both sides of the Atlantic during the eighteenth century. See Levy, supra, at xi.

The Sedition Act was vigorously enforced, but only against members or supporters of the Republican Party. Prosecutions were brought against the four leading Republican newspapers. The cases, often tried before openly hostile Federalist judges, resulted in ten convictions and no acquittals. Moreover, in the hands of these judges, the procedural reforms of the act proved largely illusory.

Consider, for example, the plight of Matthew Lyon, a Republican congressman from Vermont. During his reelection campaign, Lyon published an article in which he attacked the Adams administration, asserting that under President Adams "every consideration of the public welfare [was] swallowed up in a continual grasp for power, in an unbounded thirst for ridiculous pomp, foolish adulation, and selfish avarice." At Lyons's trial, the judge instructed the jury to find malicious intent unless the statement "could have been uttered with any other intent than that of making odious or contemptible the President and the government, and bringing them both into disrepute." And although Lyon was technically free to prove the "truth" of his statement in his defense, this was hardly possible given the nature of the statement. Lyon was convicted and sentenced to a fine of $1,000 and four months in prison. The Federalist press rejoiced, but Lyon became an instant martyr and was reelected while in jail. See Trial of Matthew Lyon, in F. Wharton, State Trials 333 (1849).

The Supreme Court did not rule on the constitutionality of the Sedition Act at the time. It was upheld without dissent, however, by the lower federal courts and by three Supreme Court justices sitting on circuit. The act expired of its own force on March 3, 1801. President Jefferson thereafter pardoned all those who had been convicted under the act, and Congress eventually repaid most of the fines. It is generally agreed that the act was a factor in the defeat of the Federalists in the election of 1800.

Significant cases under the Sedition Act are printed, with discerning comment, in F. Wharton, State Trials (1849). The story of the enforcement of the act is told briefly and with liveliness in J. Miller, Crisis in Freedom (1951). A more detailed account is given in James Morton Smith's Freedom's Fetters (1956). Problems of federalism, sometimes overlooked in discussions of the act, are examined in a review of Miller's book in 66 Harv. L. Rev. 189 (1952) and in Berns, Freedom of the Press and the Alien and Sedition Laws: A Reappraisal, 1970 Sup. Ct. Rev. 109.

What is the significance of the fact that the Sedition Act was approved by many of the same people who had earlier approved the first amendment?

6. *From the Sedition Act of 1798 to the Espionage Act of 1917.* The Supreme Court did not directly consider the first amendment's guarantee of free expression until Congress enacted the Espionage Act of 1917 at the outset of World War I. See section B1, infra. This is not to say, however, that controversies over free speech did not arise in the 120 years between the Sedition Act of 1798 and the Espionage Act of 1917. See generally P. Brissenden, The I.W.W.: A Study of American Syndicalism (1919) (examining government efforts to suppress radical groups in the late nineteenth century); J. Coulter, The Confederate States of

America, 1861-1865 (1950) (examining the liberties of the press in the Confederacy); R. Nye, Fettered Freedom (1949) (examining the efforts of southern states to suppress abolitionist literature during the slavery controversy); J. Randall, Constitutional Problems under Lincoln (1926) (examining the executive and military efforts to control seditious publications during the Civil War); Rabban, The First Amendment in Its Forgotten Years, 90 Yale L.J. 514 (1981) (examining academic and judicial thought about free expression prior to 1919).

Note: The Philosophy of Free Expression

"Intuition at first may suggest that an individual ought to have more freedom to speak than he has liberty in other areas. There would seem to be some truth in the adage, 'sticks and stones can break my bones, but words will never hurt me.' Yet speech often hurts. It can offend, injure reputation, fan prejudice or passion, and ignite the world. Moreover, a great deal of other conduct that the state regulates has less harmful potential." Wellington, On Freedom of Expression, 88 Yale L.J. 1105, 1106-1107 (1979). Why, then, should expression have greater immunity from government regulation than most other forms of human conduct? Why should society prohibit the making of any law "abridging the freedom of speech"?

1. *Search for truth: the "marketplace of ideas."* The "search for truth" rationale for the protection of free expression rests on the premise that "when men have realized that time has upset many fighting faiths, they may come to believe even more than they believe the very foundations of their own conduct that the ultimate good desired is better reached by free trade in ideas — that the best test of truth is the power of the thought to get itself accepted in the competition of the market, and that truth is the only ground upon which their wishes safely can be carried out." Abrams v. United States, 250 U.S. 616, 630 (1919) (Holmes, J., dissenting).

The "search for truth" rationale was first fully enunciated by John Stuart Mill in On Liberty (1859):

> [The] peculiar evil of silencing the expression of an opinion is, that it is robbing the human race; posterity as well as the existing generation; those who dissent from the opinion, still more than those who hold it. . . .
>
> First: the opinion which it is attempted to suppress [may] be true. Those who desire to suppress it [are] not infallible. They have no authority to decide the question for all mankind, and exclude every other person from the means of judging. [Of course, it is not the case] that truth always triumphs over persecution. [But the] real advantage which truth has [is] that when an opinion is true, it may be extinguished once, twice, or many times, but in the course of ages there will generally be found persons to rediscover it, until [eventually] it has made such head as to withstand all subsequent attempts to suppress it. . . .
>
> [Second: the received opinion may be true. But however true an opinion] may be, if it is not fully, frequently, and fearlessly discussed, it will be held as a dead dogma, not a living truth. [He] who knows only his own side of the case, knows little of that. [Even if] the received opinion [is] true, a conflict with the opposite error is essential to a clear apprehension and deep feeling of its truth. . . .
>
> [Finally,] the conflicting doctrines, instead of being one true and the other false, [may] share the truth between them; and the nonconforming opinion [may be] needed to supply the remainder of the truth, of which the received doctrine em-

bodies only a part. [Every] opinion which embodies somewhat of the portion of truth which the common opinion omits, ought to be considered precious.

Consider the following observations.

a. DuVal, Free Communication of Ideas and the Quest for Truth: Toward a Teleological Approach to First Amendment Adjudication, 41 Geo. Wash. L. Rev. 161, 190-191 (1972):

[One must question] the assumption [that] discussion, if it can be free, will lead to truth. The practical difficulties in [proving] such a proposition are forbidding. [It would be] necessary to show that greater progress is achieved in a society operating on a principle of free discussion than in any society in which some particular selective suppression of ideas is employed. [Apart] from [the obvious] practical difficulties, it seems questionable that [such] a determination [is] theoretically possible. To determine the relative degree of error [requires] a knowledge of what is true. [Yet] this flies in the face of the fundamental premise of the market place theory itself.

b. Baker, Scope of the First Amendment Freedom of Speech, 25 U.C.L.A. L. Rev. 964, 974-978 (1978).

[The] hope that the marketplace leads to truth, or even to the best or most desirable decision, [is] implausible. [First, experience as well as discussion contributes to understanding. Thus,] restrictions on experience-generating conduct are as likely as restrictions on [debate] to stunt the progressive development of understanding, [but the marketplace theory gives no] constitutional protection [to] experience-producing conduct. [Second, the marketplace theory assumes] that people [use] their rational capacities to eliminate distortion caused by the form and frequency of message presentation. [This] assumption cannot be accepted. Emotional or "irrational" appeals have great [impact]. [Finally, in practice, the] the marketplace of ideas appears improperly biased in favor of presently dominant groups.

c. Ingber, The Marketplace of Ideas: A Legitimizing Myth, 1984 Duke L. J. 1, 4-5:

[Courts] that invoke the marketplace model [justify] free expression because of the aggregate benefits to society, and not because an individual speaker receives a particular benefit. [Once] free expression is viewed solely as an instrumental value, [it] is easier to allow government regulation of speech if society as a whole [benefits] from a regulated system of expression. [The] imagery of the marketplace of ideas is rooted in laissez-faire economics. Although laissez-faire economic theory asserts that desirable economic conditions are best promoted by a free market system, today's economists widely admit that government regulation is needed to correct failures in the economic market caused by real world conditions. Similarly, real world conditions also interfere with the effective operation of the marketplace of [ideas]. Consequently [state] intervention [may be] necessary to correct communicative market failures.

d. Wellington, supra, at 1130-1132:

In the long run, true ideas do tend to drive out false ones. The problem is that the short run may be very long, that one short run follows hard upon another, and that we may become overwhelmed by the inexhaustible supply of freshly minted, often very seductive, false ideas. [Moreover,] most of us do believe that the book is closed on some issues. Genocide is an example. [Truth] may win, and in the long run it may almost always win, but millions of Jews were deliberately and systematically murdered in a very short period of time. [Before] those murders occurred, many individuals must have come "to have false beliefs."

2. *Self-governance*. The "self-governance" rationale is most closely identified with the work of Alexander Meiklejohn:

[The] Constitution [ordains] that all authority to exercise control, to determine common action, belongs to "We, the People." [Under this system, free men are governed] by themselves. [What,] then, does the First Amendment forbid? [The] town meeting suggests an answer. That meeting is called to discuss and, on the basis of such discussion, to decide matters of public policy. [The] voters, therefore, must be made as wise as possible. [And] this, in turn, requires that so far as time allows, all facts and interests relevant to the problem shall be fully and fairly presented to the meeting [so] that all the alternative lines of action can be wisely measured in relation to one another. . . .

The First Amendment, then, is not the guardian of unregulated talkativeness. It does not require that, on every occasion, every citizen shall take part in public debate. [Rather,] the vital point, as stated negatively, is that no suggestion of policy shall be denied a hearing because it is on one side of the issue rather than another. [Citizens] may not be barred [from speaking] because their views are thought to be false or dangerous. [The] reason for this equality of status in the field of ideas lies deep in the very foundation of the self-governing process. When men govern themselves, it is they — and no one else — who must pass judgment upon unwisdom and unfairness and danger. [Just] so far as, at any point, the citizens who are to decide an issue are denied acquaintance with information or opinion [which] is relevant to that issue, just so far the result must be ill-considered. [It] is that mutilation of the thinking process of the community against which the First Amendment [is] directed. The principle of the freedom of speech [is] not a Law of Nature or of Reason in the abstract. It is a deduction from the basic American agreement that public issues shall be decided by universal suffrage. [Thus,] the unlimited guarantee of the freedom of public discussion, which is given by the First Amendment, [protects the speech] of a citizen who is planning for the general welfare.

Meiklejohn, Free Speech and Its Relation to Self-Government 15-16, 24-27, 39 (1948).

Consider the following observations.

a. Chafee, Book Review, 62 Harv. L. Rev. 891, 899-900 (1949):

The most serious weakness in Mr. Meiklejohn's argument is that it rests on his supposed boundary between public speech and private speech. That line is extremely blurred. [The] truth is that there are public aspects to practically every subject. [Moreover, if Mr. Meiklejohn's public speech excludes scholarship,] art and literature, it is shocking to deprive these vital matters of the protection of [the] First Amendment. [Valuable] as self-government is, it is in itself only a small part of our lives. That a philosopher should subordinate all other activities to it is indeed surprising.

b. Meiklejohn's response:

The First Amendment [protects] the freedom of those activities of thought and communication by which we "govern." [But] voting is merely the external expression of a wide and diverse number of activities by means of which citizens attempt to meet the responsibilities of making judgments, which that freedom to govern lays upon them. [Self-government] can exist only insofar as the voters acquire the intelligence, integrity, sensitivity, and generous devotion to the general welfare that, in theory, casting a ballot is assumed to express. [Thus,] there are many forms of thought and expression within the range of human communications from which the voter derives the [necessary] knowledge, intelligence, [and] sensitivity to human values. [These], too, must suffer no abridgment of their freedom. [These include:] 1. Education, in all its phases. [2]. The achievements of philosophy and the sciences. [3]. Literature and the arts. [4]. Public discussions of public issues.

Meiklejohn, The First Amendment Is an Absolute, 1961 Sup. Ct. Rev. 245, 255-257.

c. Bork, Neutral Principles and Some First Amendment Problems, 47 Ind. L. J. 1, 26-28 (1971):

Professor Alexander Meiklejohn seems correct when he says: "The First Amendment [protects] the freedom of those activities of thought and communication by which we 'govern.'" [But Meiklejohn goes] further and would extend the protection of the first amendment beyond speech that is explicitly political. [I disagree.] [There is, of course,] an analogy between criticism of official behavior and the publication of a novel like Ulysses, for the latter may form attitudes that ultimately affect politics. But it is an analogy, not an identity. Other human activities and experiences also form personality, teach and create attitudes just as much as does the novel, but no one would on that account [suggest] that the first amendment strikes down regulations of economic activity, control of entry into trade, laws about sexual behavior, marriage and the like. Yet these activities, in their capacity to create attitudes that ultimately impinge upon the political process, are more like literature and science than literature and science are like political speech. If the dialectical progression is not to become an analogical stampede, the protection of the first amendment must be cut off when it reaches the outer limits of political speech. [The] notion that all valuable types of speech must be protected by the first amendment confuses the constitutionality of laws with their wisdom. Freedom of nonpolitical speech rests, as does freedom for other valuable forms of behavior, upon the enlightenment of society and its elected representatives.

d. Redish, The Value of Free Speech, 130 U. Pa. L. Rev. 591, 601, 604 (1982):

Bork and Meiklejohn [never] attempt to ascertain what basic value or values the democratic process was designed to serve. [Our nation adopted] a democratic system [because of] an implicit belief in the worth of the individual. [Political] democracy is merely a means to — or, in another sense, a logical outgrowth of — the much broader value of individual self-realization. [Bork] and Meiklejohn [have] confused one means of obtaining the ultimate value with the value itself. [The] appropriate scope of the first amendment protection is [thus] much broader than Bork or Meiklejohn would have it. Free speech aids all life-affecting decisionmaking, no matter how personally limited, in much the same manner in which it aids the political process. [There] thus is no logical basis for distinguishing the role speech plays in the political process.

e. Meiklejohn's theory is premised on a controversial conception of politics. The underlying idea is that the political process can be understood as a form of "town meeting." In that process, speech has special status as a mechanism by which citizens deliberate on the common good. This process of deliberation is, in the Meiklejohn conception, what politics is all about; and the first amendment has an indispensable role in promoting that understanding of politics. But is it sensible to conceive of the political process in these terms? According to many, the political process is more properly understood as a system in which private groups, equipped with private interests, seek to obtain gain at the expense of others. See R. Dahl, Who Governs? Democracy and Power in an American City (1961): Stigler, The Theory of Economic Regulation, 3 Bell J. Econ. & Mgmt. Sci. 3 (1971). Do you agree that, if this competing conception is all or even partly right, Meiklejohn's understanding of the first amendment must be rejected?

3. *Self-fulfillment/autonomy.* There are several versions of the "self-fulfill-ment/autonomy" rationale.

a. Richards, Free Speech and Obscenity Law: Toward a Moral Theory of the First Amendment, 123 U. Pa. L. Rev. 45, 62 (1974):

> [People] are not to be constrained to communicate or not to communicate, to believe or not to believe, to associate or not to associate. The value placed on this cluster of ideas derives from the notion of self-respect that comes from a mature person's full and untrammelled exercise of capacities central to human rationality. Thus, the significance of free expression rests on the central human capacity to create and express symbolic systems, such as speech, writing, pictures, and [music]. Freedom of expression permits and encourages the exercise of these [capacities]. In so doing, it nurtures and sustains the self-respect of the mature person. [The] value of free expression, in this view, rests on its deep relation to self-respect arising from autonomous self-determination without which the life of the spirit is meager and slavish.

b. Scanlon, A Theory of Freedom of Expression, 1 Phil. & Pub. Aff. 204, 213-218 (1972):

> There are certain harms which, although they would not occur but for certain acts of expression, nonetheless cannot be taken as part of a justification for legal restric-tions on [such expression]. These harms are: (a) harms to certain individuals which consist in their coming to have false beliefs as a result of [the] expression; [and] (b) harmful consequences of acts performed as a result of [the] expression, where the connection between [the] expression and the subsequent harmful acts consists merely in the fact that [the] expression led the [actor] to believe [the] acts to be worth performing. . . .
>
> [This principle, which I will term the Millian Principle, is "the basic principle of freedom of expression." The] Millian Principle [is] a consequence of the view that the powers of a state are limited to those that citizens could recognize while still regarding themselves as equal, autonomous, rational agents. [To] regard himself as autonomous [a] person must see himself as sovereign in deciding what to believe and in weighing competing reasons for action. [An] autonomous person cannot accept without independent consideration the judgment of others as to what he should believe or what he should do. [Thus,] autonomous citizens [could] not regard them-selves as being under an "obligation" to believe the decrees of the state to be correct, nor could they concede to the state the right to have its decrees obeyed without deliberation. The Millian Principle can be seen as a refinement of these limita-tions. . . .

The harm of coming to have false beliefs is not one that an autonomous man could allow the state to protect him against through restrictions on expression. For [if] a [person] authorized the state to protect him in this [way, he would necessarily have to bind] himself to accept the state's judgment about which views were false. [The] argument for the second half of the Millian Principle is [parallel]. Conceding to the state the right to [restrict expression] to secure compliance with its laws [is] a concession that autonomous citizens could not make, since it gives the state the right to deprive citizens of the grounds for arriving at an independent judgment as to whether the law should be obeyed.

Consider the following observations:
c. Bork, supra, at 25:

[The self-fulfillment/autonomy rationale does] not distinguish speech from any other human activity. An individual may develop his faculties or derive pleasure from trading on the stock market, [working] as a barmaid, engaging in sexual activity, [or] in any of thousands of other endeavors. Speech [can] be preferred to other activities [on the basis of this rationale] only by ranking forms of personal gratification. [One] cannot, on neutral grounds, choose to protect speech [on this basis] more than [one] protects any other claimed freedom.

d. Scanlon, Freedom of Expression and Categories of Expression, 40 U. Pitt. L. Rev. 519, 532-533 (1979):

[Is my original theory] correct? I now think that it is not. To begin with, the Millian Principle has what seem to be implausible consequences in some cases. For example, it is hard to see how laws against deceptive advertising [could] be squared with this principle. [Clause] (a) of the Millian Principle [constitutes] a rejection of paternalism that is too strong and too sweeping to be plausible. [Moreover], the problems of the Millian Principle are not limited to cases of justified paternalism. The principle is appealing because it protects important audience interests — interests in deciding for one's self what to believe and what reasons to act on. [These] interests depend not only on freedom of expression, but also on other forms of access to [information]. Why should we be willing to bear unlimited costs to allow expression to flourish [when we are unwilling to extend this immunity to other sources of information that "enhance our decision-making capacity"]?

4. *Other rationales.* Although courts and commentators have focused primarily on the "search for truth," "self-governance," and "self-fulfillment/autonomy" rationales for the protection of free expression, two further rationales merit note.
a. *The checking value.* Consider Blasi, The Checking Value in First Amendment Theory, 1977 A.B.F. Res. J. 521, 527-542:

[Another rationale for the protection of free expression] is the value that free speech [can] serve in checking the abuse of power by public officials. [The] central premise of the checking value is that the abuse of official power is an especially serious evil [because of government's unique] capacity to employ legitimized violence. [The] government's monopoly of legitimized violence means [that the] check on government must come from the power of public opinion. [Thus,] the checking value grows out of democratic theory, but it is the democratic theory of John Locke [and] not that of Alexander Meiklejohn. Under [this] view of democracy, the role of the ordinary citizen is not so much to contribute on a continuing basis to the formation of public policy as to retain a veto power to be employed when the decisions of officials pass certain bounds.

b. *The safety valve.* Consider T. Emerson, The System of Freedom of Expression 7 (1970):

[Freedom] of expression is a method of achieving a more adaptable and hence a more stable [community]. This follows because suppression of discussion makes a rational judgment impossible, substituting force for reason; because suppression promotes inflexibility and [prevents] society from adjusting to changing circumstances. [The] process of open discussion promotes greater cohesion in a society because people are more ready to accept decisions that go against them if they have a part in the decision-making process. [Freedom] of expression thus provides a framework in which the conflict necessary to the progress of a society can take place without destroying the society. It is an essential mechanism for maintaining the balance between stability and change.

Compare DuVal, supra, at 200 ("While suppression may create barriers to the achievement of consensus, even greater barriers may result from discussion, [for the] natural effect of criticism of government programs [may] be the division of society — not its unification"); Bork, supra, at 25-26 ("The safety valve function raises only issues of expediency [and such issues] are for the political branches and not for the judiciary").

5. *Philosophy and the first amendment.* To what extent, if any, are these rationales for the protection of free expression relevant to interpretation of the first amendment? Consider Bloustein, The Origin, Validity, and Interrelationships of the Political Values Served by Freedom of Expression, 33 Rutgers L. Rev. 372, 381 (1981): "[There] is no evidence [that these rationales were] discussed or debated during the period of the drafting and adoption of the [first] amendment [and we may thus conclude] that whatever validity and authority they may have do *not* derive directly from the intentions of the drafters." Whence, then, do the validity and authority of these rationales derive? Is it sufficient that they flow "readily" from "general advocacy, descriptions, and discussions of political individualism and democracy"? Bloustein, supra, at 381. Recall the interpretivism/noninterpretivism debate, examined in Chapter 6, section A, supra.

To what extent do these rationales, if relevant to interpretation of the first amendment, provide a coherent and workable basis for the decision of actual cases? Note that, in some instances, it may be necessary to choose among the competing rationales. For example, the "self-fulfillment/autonomy" rationale does not support a distinction between political and nonpolitical expression, whereas the "self-governance" theory seems to compel that distinction. Despite such potential conflicts, most commentators agree that any "adequate conception of freedom of speech must [draw] upon several strands of theory in order to protect a rich variety of expressional modes." L. Tribe, American Constitutional Law 579 (1978). As one commentator has observed, in the "democratic state," which "is founded on a tradition of free inquiry," the "attainment of knowledge," the "consensual participation in government," and the "dignity of self-expression" are "so interdependent that they really represent three aspects [of] a single value; their relationships define a kind of culture, embracing the individual, the state, and the system of knowledge, art and other such values that we call liberal." Bloustein, supra, at 395.

Note: Organization

The remaining sections in this chapter explore the Supreme Court's interpretation of the first amendment's guarantee of free speech, press, assembly, and petition. These sections are structured in accord with two distinctions that have played a central role in the Court's analysis. First, there is the distinction between "content-based" and "content-neutral" restrictions. Content-based restrictions restrict communication because of the message conveyed. Laws prohibiting the publication of "confidential" information, forbidding the hiring of teachers who advocate the violent overthrow of government, or banning the display of the swastika in certain neighborhoods illustrate this type of restriction. Content-neutral restrictions, on the other hand, restrict communication without regard to the message conveyed. Laws prohibiting noisy speeches near a hospital, banning the erection of billboards in residential communities, or requiring the disclosure of the names of all leafleteers are examples. The Court has generally employed different standards to test the constitutionality of these two types of restrictions.

Second, there is the distinction within the realm of content-based restrictions between "high" and "low" value expression. The Court has long adhered to the view that there are certain categories of expression that do not appreciably further the values underlying the first amendment. Examples are obscenity, commercial advertising, and false statements of fact. The Court has traditionally held that such categories of expression are either unprotected or only marginally protected by the first amendment.

In line with these distinctions, sections B and C focus on government efforts to suppress "high" value speech; section D explores "low" value expression; section E examines "content-neutral" restrictions; and section F explores "additional problems," such as laws that have only an "incidental" effect on free expression (e.g., compulsory disclosure of one's associations); laws that restrict the expression of persons in a "special" relation to government (e.g., students, prisoners, and public employees); and laws that restrict the "press." The point of this structure is not, of course, to insulate these distinctions from challenge. It is, rather, to illuminate the Court's jurisprudence while at the same time facilitating critical scrutiny of the Court's analysis.

B.   CONTENT-BASED RESTRICTIONS: DANGEROUS IDEAS AND INFORMATION

In what circumstances, if any, may government, consonant with the first amendment, restrict speech because the expression of particular ideas or items of information might cause some harm to government, to private individuals, or to society in general? In addressing this question, this section examines four separate but related problems: expression that induces unlawful conduct; expression that criticizes the judicial process; expression that provokes a hostile audience response; and expression that disseminates confidential information. In its effort to deal with these problems, the Court has struggled to identify the relevant considerations. The task is not easy. How serious must the harm be before speech may be suppressed? How likely must the harm be? How imminent must it be? Should it matter whether the speaker intended to cause the harm? Can these and other considerations be integrated into a single, coherent standard?

Principled standard?

1.   Expression That Induces Unlawful Conduct

The question whether government may constitutionally restrict expression because it might persuade, incite, or otherwise induce readers or listeners to engage in unlawful conduct has long absorbed the Court's attention. This was the first issue of first amendment interpretation to capture the Court's sustained interest, and the debate within the Court over this question has produced some of the most powerful and most eloquent opinions in the Court's history, engaged the energies of several of the Court's most distinguished jurists, and resulted in the articulation of a series of doctrines and precepts that have dominated first amendment jurisprudence generally. That the question has triggered such controversy and played so central a role in the evolution of first amendment theory is not surprising, for it focuses on government efforts to restrict advocacy in many respects similar to the traditional concept of seditious libel, and thus implicates values at the very core of the first amendment.

The Supreme Court first confronted this issue in a series of cases concerning agitation against the war and the draft during World War I. Such agitation was not uncommon:

> [When] the U.S. first entered the war, [many] influential groups of people were apathetic if not actually hostile to fighting. [Organizations] which identified themselves as against the war, [such as the Socialist Party of America], made strong gains during 1917 [and] over three hundred thirty thousand draft evaders or delinquents were reported during the war. [Antiwar] sentiment did not pose a threat of revolution or violence, but it did pose a threat of spreading disaffection which could paralyze the war effort. [Attorney] General Thomas Gregory, referring to war opponents in November, 1917, stated, "May God have mercy on them, for they need expect none from an outraged people and an avenging government."

R. Goldstein, Political Repression in Modern America 105-108 (1978).

Two months after our entry into the First World War, Congress enacted the Espionage Act of 1917. Although the act was directed primarily toward such matters as actual espionage and the protection of military secrets, the third section of title I of the act made it a crime when the nation is at war for any person (1) willfully to "make or convey false reports or false statements with intent to interfere" with the military success of the United States or "to promote the success of its enemies," (2) willfully to "cause or attempt to cause insubordination, disloyalty, mutiny, or refusal of duty, in the military or naval forces of the United States," or (3) willfully to "obstruct the recruiting or enlistment service of the United States." Violations were punishable by fines of up to $10,000, prison sentences of up to twenty years, or both. Act of June 15, 1917, ch. 30, tit. I, §3, 40 Stat. 219.

Eleven months later, Congress enacted the Sedition Act of 1918. The 1918 act, which was repealed in 1921, made it criminal, among other things, for any person to say anything with intent to obstruct the sale of war bonds; to utter, print, write, or publish any disloyal, profane, scurrilous, or abusive language intended to cause contempt or scorn for the form of government of the United States, the Constitution, or the flag; to urge the curtailment of production of war materials with the intent of hindering the war effort; or to utter any words supporting the cause of any country at war with the United States or opposing the cause of the United States. Act of May 16, 1918, ch. 75, §1, 40 Sta. 553.

During the war years, federal authorities initiated approximately two thousand prosecutions under these acts. Most of these prosecutions were brought under the 1917 statute. The opinions that follow represent three distinct analyses of the issue.

SHAFFER v. UNITED STATES, 255 Fed. 886 (9th Cir. 1919): Shaffer was convicted of violating the Espionage Act of 1917. The indictment alleged that Shaffer had mailed a book, The Finished Mystery, which contained several "treasonable, disloyal, and seditious utterances," specifying the following passages in particular:

> Standing opposite to these Satan has placed [a] certain delusion which is best described by the word patriotism, but which in reality is murder, the spirit of the very devil. [If] you say it is a war of defense against wanton and intolerable aggression, I must reply that [it] has yet to be proved that Germany has any intention or desire of attacking us. [The] war itself is wrong. Its prosecution will be a crime. There is not a question raised, an issued involved, a cause at stake, which is worth the life of one blue-jacket on the sea or one khaki-coat in the trenches.

The Court of Appeals affirmed the conviction:

"It is true that disapproval of war and the advocacy of peace are not crimes under the Espionage Act; but the question here [is] whether the natural and probable tendency and effect of [the publication] are such as are calculated to produce the result condemned by the statute. [It cannot] be said, as a matter of law, that the reasonable and natural effect of [the] publication was not to obstruct [the] recruiting or enlistment service, and thus to injure the service of the United States. Printed matter may tend to obstruct [the] service, even if it contains no mention of recruiting or enlistment, and no reference to the military service of the United States. [The] service may be obstructed by attacking the justice of the cause for which the war is waged, and by undermining the spirit of loyalty which inspires men to enlist or to register for conscription in the service of their country. [To] teach that patriotism is murder and the spirit of the devil, and that the war against Germany was wrong and its prosecution a crime, is to weaken patriotism and the purpose to enlist or to render military service in the war. . . .

"It is argued that the evidence fails to show that [Shaffer] committed the act willfully and intentionally. But there is enough in the evidence to show the hostile attitude of his mind against the prosecution of the war by the United States, and that the books were intentionally concealed on his premises. He must be presumed to have intended the natural and probable consequences of what he knowingly did."

Masses Publishing Co. v. Patten

244 F. 535 (S.D.N.Y. 1917)

[In July, 1917, the postmaster of New York, acting on the direction of the Postmaster General, advised the plaintiff, a publishing company engaged in the production of a monthly revolutionary journal called The Masses, that the August issue of the journal would be denied access to the mails under the Espionage Act of 1917. Plaintiff applied for a preliminary injunction to forbid the postmaster to refuse to accept the August issue for mailing. While objecting generally that the whole purport of the issue was in violation of the law, on the ground that it tended to produce a violation of the law, to encourage the enemies of the United States, and to hamper the government in the conduct of the war, the postmaster specified four cartoons and four pieces of text as especially falling within the act.]

LEARNED HAND, DISTRICT JUDGE [after stating the facts as above]. . . .

It must be remembered at the outset, and the distinction is of critical consequence throughout, that no question arises touching the war powers of Congress. It may be that Congress may forbid the mails to any matter which tends to discourage the successful prosecution of the war. It may be that the fundamental personal rights of the individual must stand in abeyance, even including the right of the freedom of the press, though that is not here in question. . . .

The next phrase [of §3 of the act] relied upon is that which forbids any one from willfully causing insubordination, disloyalty, mutiny, or refusal of duty in the military or naval forces of the United States. The defendant's position is that to arouse discontent and disaffection among the people with the prosecution of the war and with the draft tends to promote a mutinous and insubordinate temper among the troops. This [is] true; men who become satisfied that they are engaged in an enterprise dictated by the unconscionable selfishness of the rich, and effectuated by a tyrannous disregard for the will of those who must suffer and die, will be more prone to insubordination than those who have faith in the cause and acquiesce in the means. Yet to interpret the word "cause" so broadly would [involve] necessarily as a consequence the suppression of all hostile criticism, and of all opinion except what encouraged and supported the existing policies, or which fell within the range of temperate argument. It would contradict the normal assumption of democratic government that the suppression of hostile criticism does not turn upon the justice of its substance or the decency and propriety of its temper. Assuming that the power to repress such opinion may rest in Congress in the throes of a struggle for the very existence of the state, its exercise is so contrary to the use and wont of our people that only the clearest expression of such a power justifies the conclusion that it was intended.

The defendant's position, therefore, in so far as it involves the suppression of the free utterance of abuse and criticism of the existing law, or of the policies of the war, is not, in my judgment, supported by the language of the statute. Yet there has always been a recognized limit to such expressions. [One] may not counsel or advise others to violate the law as it stands. Words are not only the keys of persuasion, but the triggers of action, and those which have no purport but to counsel the violation of law cannot by any latitude of interpretation be a part of that public opinion which is the final source of government in a democratic state. The defendant asserts not only that the magazine indirectly through its propaganda leads to a disintegration of loyalty and a disobedience of law, but that in addition it counsels and advises resistance to existing law, especially to the draft. The consideration of this aspect of the case more properly arises under the third phrase of section 3, which forbids any willful obstruction of the recruiting or enlistment service of the United States, but, as the defendant urges that the magazine falls within each phrase, it is as well to take it up now. To counsel or advise a man to an act is to urge upon him either that it is his interest or his duty to do it. While, of course, this may be accomplished as well by indirection as expressly, since words carry the meaning that they impart, the definition is exhaustive, I think, and I shall use it. Political agitation, by the passions it arouses or the convictions it engenders, may in fact stimulate men to the violation of law. Detestation of existing policies is easily transformed into forcible resistance of the authority which puts them in execution, and it would be folly to disregard the causal relation between the two. Yet to assimilate agitation, legitimate as such, with direct incitement to violent resistance, is to disregard the tolerance of all methods of political agitation which in normal times is a safeguard of free government. The distinction is not a scholastic subterfuge, but a hard-bought acquisition in the fight for freedom, and the purpose to disregard it must be evident when the power exists. If one stops short of urging upon others that it is their duty or their interest to resist the law, it seems to me one should not be held to have attempted to cause its violation. If that be not the test, I can see no escape from the conclusion that under this section every political agitation which can be shown to be apt to create a seditious temper is illegal. I am confident that by such language Congress had no such revolutionary purpose in view.

It seems to me, however, quite plain that none of the language and none of the cartoons in this paper can be thought directly to counsel or advise insubordination or mutiny, without a violation of their meaning quite beyond any tolerable understanding. I come, therefore, to the third phrase of the section, which forbids any one from willfully obstructing the recruiting or enlistment service of the United States. I am not prepared to assent to the plaintiff's position that this only refers to acts other than words, nor that the act thus defined must be shown to have been successful. One may obstruct without preventing, and the mere obstruction is an injury to the service; for it throws impediments in its way. Here again, however, since the question is of the expression of opinion, I construe the sentence, so far as it restrains public utterance, as [limited] to the direct advocacy of resistance to the recruiting and enlistment service. If so, the inquiry is narrowed to the question whether any of the challenged matter may be said to advocate resistance to the draft, taking the meaning of the words with the utmost latitude which they can bear.

As to the cartoons it seems to me quite clear that they do not fall within such a test. Certainly the nearest is that entitled "Conscription," and the most that can be said of that is that it may breed such animosity to the draft as will promote resistance and strengthen the determination of those disposed to be recalcitrant. There is no intimation that, however hateful the draft may be, one is in duty bound to resist it, certainly none that such resistance is to one's interest. I cannot, therefore, even with the limitations which surround the power of the court, assent to the assertion that any of the cartoons violate the act.

The text offers more embarrassment. The poem to Emma Goldman and Alexander Berkman, at most, goes no further than to say that they are martyrs in the cause of love among nations. Such a sentiment holds them up to admiration, and hence their conduct to possible emulation. The paragraph in which the editor offers to receive funds for their appeal also expresses admiration for them, but goes no further. The paragraphs upon conscientious objectors are of the same kind. They go no further than to express high admiration for those who have held and are holding out for their convictions even to the extent of resisting the law. [That] such comments have a tendency to arouse emulation in others is clear enough, but that they counsel others to follow these examples is not so plain. Literally at least they do not, and while, as I have said, the words are to be taken, not literally, but according to their full import, the literal meaning is the starting point for interpretation. One may admire and approve the course of a hero without feeling any duty to follow him. There is not the least implied intimation in these words that others are under a duty to follow. The most that can be said is that, if others do follow, they will get the same admiration and the same approval. Now, there is surely an appreciable distance between esteem and emulation; and unless there is here some advocacy of such emulation, I cannot see how the passages can be said to fall within the law. [The] question before me is quite the same as what would arise upon a motion to dismiss an indictment at the close of the proof: Could any reasonable man say, not that the indirect result of the language might be to arouse a seditious disposition, for that would not be enough, but that the language directly advocated resistance to the draft? I cannot think that upon such language any verdict would stand. . . .

It follows that the plaintiff is entitled to the usual preliminary injunction.

Schenck v. United States

249 U.S. 47 (1919)

Mr. Justice Holmes delivered the opinion of the court. . . .

[The defendants were convicted of conspiracy to violate section 3 of the Espionage Act of 1917, by circulating "to men who had been called and accepted for military service" a document "alleged to be calculated" to obstruct the recruiting and enlistment service.]

The document in question, upon its first printed side, recited the 1st section of the Thirteenth Amendment, said that the idea embodied in it was violated by the Conscription Act, and that a conscript is little better than a convict. In impassioned language it intimated that conscription was despotism in its worst form and a monstrous wrong against humanity, in the interest of Wall Street's chosen few. It said: "Do not submit to intimidation"; but in form at least confined itself to peaceful measures, such as a petition for the repeal of the act. The other and later printed side of the sheet was headed, "Assert Your Rights." It stated reasons for alleging that anyone violated the Constitution when he refused to recognize "your right to assert your opposition to the draft," and went on: "If you do not assert and support your rights, you are helping to deny or disparage rights which it is the solemn duty of all citizens and residents of the United States to retain." It described the arguments on the other side as coming from cunning politicians and a mercenary capitalist press, and even silent consent to the Conscription Law as helping to support an infamous conspiracy. It denied the power to send our citizens away to foreign shores to shoot up the people of other lands, and added that words could not express the condemnation such cold-blooded ruthlessness deserves, etc., etc., winding up, "You must do your share to maintain, support, and uphold the rights of the people of this country." Of course the document would not have been sent unless it had been intended to have some effect, and we do not see what effect it could be expected to have upon persons subject to the draft except to influence them to obstruct the carrying of it out. The defendants do not deny that the jury might find against them on this point.

But it is said, suppose that that was the tendency of this circular, it is protected by the First Amendment to the Constitution. Two of the strongest expressions are said to be quoted respectively from well-known public men. It well may be that the prohibition of laws abridging the freedom of speech is not confined to previous restraints, although to prevent them may have been the main purpose, as intimated in Patterson v. Colorado, 205 U.S. 454, 462. We admit that in many places and in ordinary times the defendants, in saying all that was said in the circular, would have been within their constitutional rights. But the character of every act depends upon the circumstances in which it is done. The most stringent protection of free speech would not protect a man in falsely shouting fire in a theater, and causing a panic. It does not even protect a man from an injunction against uttering words that may have all the effect of force. The question in every case is whether the words used are used in such circumstances and are of such a nature as to create a clear and present danger that they will bring about the substantive evils that Congress has a right to prevent. It is a question of proximity and degree. When a nation is at war many things that might be said in time of peace are such a hindrance to its effort that their utterance will not be endured so long as men fight, and that no Court could regard them as protected by any constitutional right. It seems to be admitted that if an actual obstruction of the recruiting service were proved, liability for words that produced that effect might be enforced. The Statute of 1917, in §4, punishes conspiracies to obstruct as well as actual obstruction. If the act, (speaking, or circulating a paper,) its tendency and the intent with which it is done, are the same, we perceive no ground for saying that success alone warrants making the act a crime. Goldman v. United States, 245 U.S. 474, 477. Indeed, that case might be said to dispose of the present contention if the precedent covers all media concludendi. But as the right to free speech was not referred to specially we have thought fit to add a few words. . . .

Judgments affirmed.

Note: Shaffer, Masses, and Schenck

1. *Bad tendency. Shaffer* reflects the then prevailing view of the lower federal courts — that speech could constitutionally be punished as an attempt to cause some forbidden or otherwise undesirable conduct if the natural and reasonable tendency of the expression might be to bring about the conduct and if the speaker intended such a result. Under this view, intent could be inferred from the tendency of the speech itself, on the theory that one intends the natural and foreseeable consequences of one's acts. Through the twin doctrines of bad tendency and constructive intent, decisions like *Shaffer* routinely converted criticism of the war and the draft into criminal attempts to cause insubordination or obstruct recruiting. The relatively modest provisions of the 1917 act were thus converted into essentially open-ended restrictions on seditious expression. For detailed accounts of this era, see Z. Chafee, Free Speech in the United States 36-108 (1941); Rab-

ban, The Emergence of Modern First Amendment Theory, 50 U. Chi. L. Rev. 1205 (1983). On criminal solicitation generally, see Greenawalt, Speech and Crime, 1980 A.B.F. Res. J. 645, 653-670.

2. *Express incitement*. Although Judge Hand technically limited himself in *Masses* to a mere interpretation of the Espionage Act, the opinion has clear constitutional overtones and, as Hand himself made clear in private correspondence, *Masses* was "a distinctive, carefully considered alternative to the prevalent analyses of free speech issues." Gunther, Learned Hand and the Origins of Modern First Amendment Doctrine: Some Fragments of History, 27 Stan. L. Rev. 719, 720 (1975). In effect, Hand attempted in *Masses* to articulate a categorical, per se rule that would be "hard, conventional, difficult to evade." Id. at 749. Unlike the *Shaffer* and *Schenck* analyses, Hand focused on the content of the speech rather than on the intent of the speaker or the consequences of the communication. Under Hand's formula, the dispositive factor was whether the speaker employed express words of incitement. As Hand intimated in his opinion and made explicit in correspondence, if the effect of such speech "upon the hearers is only to counsel them to violate the law, it is unconditionally illegal." Id. at 765. But if the speaker refrains from such incitement, the speech may not be restrained. For a similar analysis, predating Hand's, see E. Freund, Police Power 509-512 (1904). Consider the following propositions:

a. *Hand's analysis of express incitement is underprotective of free speech.* Hand's analysis accords little, if any, constitutional protection to express advocacy of criminal conduct. Is this defensible on the ground, urged by Hand, that "words [which] have no purport but to counsel the violation of law cannot by any latitude of interpretation be a part of that public opinion which is the final source of government in a democratic state"? Consider Bork, Neutral Principles and Some First Amendment Problems, 47 Ind. L. Rev. 1, 31 (1971):

> Advocacy of law violation is a call to set aside the results that political speech has produced. The process of the "discovery and spread of political truth" is damaged or destroyed if the outcome is defeated by a minority that makes law enforcement, and hence the putting of political truth into practice, impossible or less effective. There should, therefore, be no constitutional protection for any speech advocating the violation of the law.

But is it so clear that counseling of law violation is not a proper part of self-governance? Might speech advocating civil disobedience be considered an aspect of public deliberation both on the law in question and on the proper response to unjust laws? See Perry, Freedom of Expression: An Essay on Theory and Doctrine, 78 Nw. U. L. Rev. 1137, 1161-1166 (1983); Scanlon, A Theory of Freedom of Expression, 1 Phil. & Pub. Aff. 204 (1972).

Even if express incitement is constitutionally "valueless," might there nonetheless be practical or institutional reasons to protect it? Consider T. Emerson, The System of Freedom of Expression 51-53 (1970): "Groups which [would] abolish democratic institutions [do] not operate in a political vacuum. They advance other ideas that may be valid [and] groups [expressing] the prohibited views usually represent real grievances, which should be heard. [Moreover, suppression] of any group in a society destroys the atmosphere of freedom essential to the life and progress of a healthy community." See also BeVier, The First Amendment and Political Speech: An Inquiry into the Substance and Limits of Principle,

30 Stan. L. Rev. 299 (1978). Should the rhetorical or hyperbolic use of express incitement ("Kill the umpire!") be constitutionally protected?

b. *The Hand formula is overprotective of the "clever" inciter.* Hand's theory distinguishes between the speaker who uses express words of incitement and the speaker who specifically intends to incite but is clever enough to avoid the use of such language. Is this sensible? Consider the following arguments:

(1) The express inciter is more dangerous because he is more likely to be effective.

(2) Case-by-case inquiries into actual subjective intent are too slippery to provide adequate protection to innocent speakers. As Chafee observed, "It is only in times of popular panic and indignation that freedom of speech becomes important as an institution, and it is precisely in those times that the protection of the jury proves [illusory]. 'Men believed during [the period of the Espionage Act prosecutions] that the only verdict in a war case, which could show loyalty, was a verdict of guilty.' " Chafee, supra, at 70. See also Monaghan, First Amendment Due Process, 83 Harv. L. Rev. 518, 526-532 (1970). Thus, to avoid the dangers of "erroneous" fact-finding, and protect the rights of innocent dissenters, it is necessary to focus on more objective considerations than intent.

(3) What really matters under the first amendment is not the intent of the speaker but the value of the expression. Since the clever inciter has not used "words [which] have no purport but to counsel the violation of the law," the value of his speech is indistinguishable from that of the speaker who utters the same words with a more honorable intent.

c. *The Hand formula is overprotective of the dangerous speaker.* Is it sensible to accord absolute protection to a speaker, without regard to the potential dangers of his speech, merely because he does not use express language of incitement? Consider the following arguments: (1) It is the actor, and not the speaker, who ultimately brings about the harm. Government should thus direct its punishment and deterrence toward actors, not speakers. (2) An essential premise of the first amendment is that, except in the most extraordinary circumstances, government may not restrict the expression of particular ideas, viewpoints, or items of information because it does not trust its citizens to make wise or desirable decisions if they are exposed to such expression. Such "paternalism" is fundamentally at odds with the very notion of free expression. (3) As Hand argued, "If that be not the test, I can see no escape from the conclusion that [every] political agitation which can be shown to be apt to create a seditious temper is illegal."

3. *The fate of* Masses. Judge Hand's opinion was reversed on appeal. Masses Publishing Co. v. Patten, 246 Fed. 24 (2d Cir. 1917). The Court of Appeals flatly rejected Hand's construction of the act: "If the natural and reasonable effect of what is said is to encourage resistance to a law, and the words are used in an endeavor to persuade to resistance, it is immaterial that the duty to resist is not mentioned, or the interest of the persons addressed in resistance is not suggested." Other reactions to Hand's formulation were equally unsupportive, and after 1921 Hand himself abandoned his advocacy of the *Masses* approach. Parts of the formula, however, have reappeared in contemporary tests of subversive advocacy. See *Yates* and *Brandenburg*, infra this section.

4. *Clear and present danger.* Whence does Justice Holmes derive the clear and present danger standard? Is Holmes's famous reference to the false shout of fire helpful? Such speech, Holmes implies, may be restricted because it creates a clear

and present danger of panic. But suppose the shout is *true*. Would that change the analysis? Perhaps the most satisfactory explanation of Holmes's use of clear and present danger in *Schenck* is that he was simply transferring his view of criminal attempts generally into the first amendment. See Rogat, Mr. Justice Holmes: Some Modern Views — The Judge as Spectator, 31 U. Chi. L. Rev. 213, 215 (1964); Rabban, supra, at 1267-1283.

Was there a clear and present danger in *Schenck* that the war effort would be jeopardized? That the recruiting and enlistment service would grind to a halt? That a single person might be influenced to refuse induction or not to enlist? How should we deal with the possibility that there may be many Schencks?

Was Holmes's clear and present danger standard designed to supplant the prevailing bad tendency/constructive intent test? Note that the jury instructions in *Schenck* could not have embodied the clear and present danger standard. Why, then, didn't the Court remand for a new trial? Was the existence of a clear and present danger so clear that no reasonable juror could have found to the contrary? Is clear and present danger a question of *law* to be decided by the court?

Consider the Court's decisions in *Frohwerk* and *Debs*, handed down on the same day, in the spring of 1919, exactly one week after *Schenck*. Consider also the Court's decision, and Justice Holmes's dissent, in *Abrams*, handed down the following fall.

FROHWERK v. UNITED STATES, 249 U.S. 204 (1919): As a result of their participation in the preparation and publication of a series of articles in the Missouri Staats Zeitung, a German language newspaper, Frohwerk and Gleeser were convicted under the Espionage Act of 1917 of conspiring to cause disloyalty, mutiny, and refusal of duty in the military and naval forces of the United States. Frohwerk was sentenced to a fine and to ten years' imprisonment. The Court, speaking through Justice Holmes, unanimously rejected Frohwerk's contention that his conviction violated the first amendment. Holmes described two of the articles as follows:

"The first begins by declaring it a monumental and inexcusable mistake to send our soldiers to France, says that it comes no doubt from the great trusts, and later that it appears to be outright murder without serving anything practical; speaks of the unconquerable spirit and undiminished strength of the German nation, and characterizes its own discourse as words of warning to the American people. [A subsequent article,] after deploring 'the draft riots in Oklahoma and elsewhere' in language that might be taken to convey an innuendo of a different sort, [says] that the previous talk about legal remedies is all very well for those who are past the draft age and have no boys to be drafted, and [then] goes on to give a picture, made as moving as the writer was able to make it, of the sufferings of a drafted man, [and of his] reaching the conviction that this is but a war to protect some rich men's money. Who then, it is asked, will pronounce a verdict of guilty upon him if he stops reasoning and follows the first impulse of nature: self-preservation; and further, whether, while technically he is wrong in his resistance, he is not more sinned against than sinning; and yet again whether the guilt of those who voted the unnatural sacrifice is not greater than the wrong of those who now seek to escape by ill-advised resistance."

Holmes began his analysis in *Frohwerk* by observing that the first amendment "cannot have been, and obviously was not, intended to give immunity for every

possible use of language. Neither Hamilton nor Madison, nor any other competent person then or later every supposed that to make criminal the counseling of
murder within the jurisdiction of Congress would be an unconstitutional interference with free speech." Moreover, Holmes argued, the Court had already
decided in *Schenck* that "a person may be convicted of a conspiracy to obstruct
recruiting by words of persuasion."

Holmes then turned to the crux of the issue: "It may be that all this may be said
or written even in time of war in circumstances that would not make it a crime.
We do not lose our right to condemn either measures or men because the Country is at war. It does not appear that there was any special effort to reach men who
were subject to the draft; and if the evidence should show that the defendant was
a poor man, turning out copy for Gleeser, his employer, at less than a day
laborer's pay, for Gleeser to use or reject as he saw fit, in a newspaper of small
circulation, there would be a natural inclination to test every question of law to be
found in the record very thoroughly before upholding the very severe penalty
imposed. But we must take the case on the record as it is, and on the record it is
impossible to say that it might not have been found that the circulation of the
paper was in quarters where a little breath would be enough to kindle a flame and
that the fact was known and relied upon by those who sent the paper out. Small
compensation would not exonerate the defendant if it were found that he expected the result, even if pay were his chief desire." Holmes therefore concluded
that "we find ourselves unable to say that the articles could not furnish a basis for
a conviction."

DEBS v. UNITED STATES, 249 U.S. 211 (1919): As a result of a speech
delivered to a public assembly in Canton, Ohio, in July of 1918, Eugene V. Debs,
national leader of the Socialist Party, was convicted under the Espionage Act of
1917 of attempting to obstruct the recruiting and enlistment service of the United
States. Debs was sentenced to a prison term of ten years. The Supreme Court,
speaking once again through Justice Holmes, unanimously rejected Debs's claim
that the conviction violated the first amendment. Holmes noted at the outset that:
"The main theme of the speech was socialism, its growth, and a prophecy of its
ultimate success. With that we have nothing to do, but if a part of the manifest
intent of the more general utterances was to encourage those present to obstruct
the recruiting service and if in passages such encouragement was directly given,
the immunity of the general theme may not be enough to protect the speech."
Indeed, if "one purpose of the speech, whether incidental or not does not matter,
was to oppose [the] war, and if, in all the circumstances, that would be its probable effect, it would not be protected."

Turning to the speech itself, Holmes observed that Debs specifically praised
several persons who had previously been convicted of aiding or encouraging
others to refuse induction. At one point, Debs stated that such persons "were
paying the penalty for standing erect and for seeking to pave the way to better
conditions for all mankind." Moreover, Debs stated "that he had to be prudent
and might not be able to say all that he thought, thus intimating to his hearers,"
Holmes reasoned, "that they might infer that he meant more." Toward the end of
his address, Debs told his audience that "you need to know that you are fit for
something better than slavery and cannon fodder."

In addition to the text of the speech, the prosecution introduced evidence at Debs's trial of an Anti-war Proclamation and Program "adopted at St. Louis in April, 1917, coupled with testimony that about an hour before his speech [Debs] had stated that he approved of that platform in spirit and in substance." The platform called for "continuous, active, and public opposition to the war, through demonstrations, mass petitions, and all other means within our power." Holmes upheld the admission of the platform on the ground that it tended to prove "that if in [Debs's] speech he used words tending to obstruct the recruiting service he meant that they should have that effect."

Debs's first amendment claim, Holmes concluded, had in practical effect been "disposed of in [Schneck]." In closing, Holmes emphasized that the jury in *Debs* had been "most carefully instructed that they could not find the defendant guilty for advocacy of any of his opinions unless the words used had as their natural tendency and reasonably probable effect to obstruct the recruiting service [and] unless the defendant had the specific intent to do so in his mind." As in *Frohwerk*, Holmes made no reference in *Debs* to clear and present danger.

In 1920, while in prison, Debs was the Socialist candidate for president. He received almost a million votes. President Harding released him from prison in 1921.

Suppose that the day after Debs's address the leading Cleveland newspaper printed the speech in full as a news item. If the paper were prosecuted and convicted under the act for attempting to obstruct the recruiting and enlistment service, and its appeal was to be heard by the Supreme Court shortly after the decision in *Debs*, how would you argue the paper's case?

Abrams v. United States

250 U.S. 616 (1919)

[Although Czarist Russia, like the United States, had declared war on Germany, the Bolsheviks, on seizing power, signed a peace treaty with Germany. In the summer of 1918, the United States sent a contingent of marines to Vladivostok and Murmansk. The defendants in *Abrams*, a group of Russian immigrants who were self-proclaimed socialists and anarchists, perceived the expedition as an attempt to "crush the Russian Revolution." In protest, they distributed several thousand copies of each of two leaflets, one of which was written in English, the other in Yiddish. The leaflets, which were thrown from a window and circulated secretly, called for a general strike. The defendants were arrested by the military police and, after a complex and controversial trial, they were convicted of conspiring to violate various provisions of the 1918 amendments to the Espionage Act of 1917. The overall flavor of the trial is captured in the trial judge's remarks just prior to sentencing:

> These defendants took the stand. They talked about capitalists and producers, and I tried to figure out what a capitalist and what a producer is as contemplated by them. After listening carefully to all they had to say, I came to the conclusion that a capitalist is a man with a decent set of clothes, a minimum of $1.25 in his pocket, and

a good character. And when I tried to find out what the prisoners had produced, I was unable to find out anything at all. So far as I can learn, not one of them ever produced so much as a single potato. The only thing they know how to raise is hell, and to direct it against the government of the United States. [But] we are not going to help carry out the plans mapped out by the Imperial German Government, and which are being carried out by Lenine and Trotsky. I have heard of the reported fate of the poor little daughters of the Czar, but I won't talk about that now. I might get mad. I will now sentence the prisoners.

The defendants were sentenced to prison terms ranging from three to twenty years. On the trial, see Z. Chafee, Free Speech in the United States 108-140 (1941): Lawrence, Eclipse of Liberty: Civil Liberties in the United States during the First World War, 21 Wayne L. Rev. 33 (1974). The Supreme Court affirmed the convictions on two counts, one charging a violation of the provision prohibiting conspiracy "to incite, provoke or encourage resistance to the United States" (count 3); the other charging a violation of the provision prohibiting conspiracy to urge curtailment of the production of war materials "with intent [to] cripple or hinder the United States in the prosecution of the war" (count 4). Speaking for the Court, Justice Clarke summarily rejected the defendants' first amendment argument, noting simply that "This contention is sufficiently discussed and is definitely negatived in [Schenck] and [Frohwerk]."]

MR. JUSTICE HOLMES dissenting. . . .

The first of these leaflets says that the President's cowardly silence about the intervention in Russia reveals the hypocrisy of the plutocratic gang in Washington. It intimates that "German militarism combined with allied capitalism to crush the Russian revolution." [It] says that there is only one enemy of the workers of the world and that is capitalism; that it is a crime for workers of America, &c., to fight the workers' republic of Russia, and ends "Awake! Awake, you Workers of the World! Revolutionists." A note adds "It is absurd to call us pro-German. We hate and despise German militarism more than do you hypocritical tyrants. We have more reasons for denouncing German militarism than has the coward of the White House."

The other leaflet, headed "Workers — Wake Up," with abusive language says that [the] hypocrites shall not fool the Russian emigrants and friends of Russia in America. It tells the Russian emigrants that they now must spit in the face of the false military propaganda by which their sympathy and help to the prosecution of the war have been called forth and says that with the money they have lent or are going to lend "they will make bullets not only for the Germans but also for the Workers Soviets of Russia," and further, "Workers in the ammunition factories, you are producing bullets, bayonets, cannon, to murder not only the Germans, but also your dearest, best, who are in Russia and are fighting for freedom." It then appeals to the same Russian emigrants at some length not to consent to the "inquisitionary expedition to Russia," and says that the destruction of the Russian revolution is "the politics of the march to Russia." The leaflet winds up by saying "Workers, our reply to this barbarous intervention has to be a general strike!," and after a few words on the spirit of revolution, exhortations not to be afraid, and some usual tall talk ends "Woe unto those who will be in the way of progress. Let solidarity live! The Rebels."

[After describing the leaflets, Holmes argued that the conviction under the fourth count was invalid because the defendants did not have the intent, required by the act, "to cripple or hinder the United States in the prosecution of the war." The defendants' specific intent, Holmes maintained, was to help Russia, with whom we were not at war. Although conceding that "the word *intent* as vaguely used in ordinary legal discussion means no more than knowledge at the time of the act that the consequences said to be intended will ensue," Holmes insisted that "this statute must be taken to use its words in a strict and accurate sense." Otherwise, Holmes reasoned, the act would "be absurd," for it would make it criminal for one who thought "we were wasting money on aeroplanes" successfully to advocate curtailment if such curtailment later turned out "to hinder the United States in the prosecution of the war." Holmes then passed to what he referred to as "a more important aspect of the case" — the first amendment.]

I never have seen any reason to doubt that the questions of law that alone were before this Court in the cases of *Schenck, Frohwerk* and *Debs* were rightly decided. I do not doubt for a moment that by the same reasoning that would justify punishing persuasion to murder, the United States constitutionally may punish speech that produces or is intended to produce a clear and imminent danger that it will bring about forthwith certain substantive evils that the United States constitutionally may seek to prevent. The power undoubtedly is greater in time of war than in time of peace because war opens dangers that do not exist at other times.

But as against dangers peculiar to war, as against others, the principle of the right to free speech is always the same. It is only the present danger of immediate evil or an intent to bring it about that warrants Congress in setting a limit to the expression of opinion where private rights are not concerned. Congress certainly cannot forbid all effort to change the mind of the country. Now nobody can suppose that the surreptitious publishing of a silly leaflet by an unknown man, without more, would present any immediate danger that its opinions would hinder the success of the government arms or have any appreciable tendency to do so. Publishing those opinions for the very purpose of obstructing, however, might indicate a greater danger and at any rate would have the quality of an attempt. So I assume that the second leaflet if published for the purposes alleged in the fourth count might be punishable. But [I] do not see how anyone can find the intent required by the statute in any of the defendants' words. The second leaflet is the only one that affords even a foundation for the charge, and there, without invoking the hatred of German militarism expressed in the former one, it is evident from the beginning to the end that the only object of the paper is to help Russia and stop American intervention there against the popular government — not to impede the United States in the war that it was carrying on. To say that two phrases taken literally might import a suggestion of conduct that would have interference with the war as an indirect and probably undesired effect seems to me by no means enough to show an attempt to produce that effect.

In this case sentences of twenty years imprisonment have been imposed for the publishing of two leaflets that I believe the defendants had as much right to publish as the Government has to publish the Constitution of the United States now vainly invoked by them. Even if I am technically wrong and enough can be squeezed from these poor and puny anonymities to turn the color of legal litmus paper; I will add, even if what I think the necessary intent were shown; the most nominal punishment seems to me all that possibly could be inflicted, unless the defendants are to be made to suffer not for what the indictment alleges but for the creed that they avow — a creed that I believe to be the creed of ignorance and immaturity when honestly held, as I see no reason to doubt that it was held here, but which, although made the subject of examination at the trial, no one has a right even to consider in dealing with the charges before the Court.

Persecution for the expression of opinions seems to me perfectly logical. If you have no doubt of your premises or your power and want a certain result with all your heart you naturally express your wishes in law and sweep away all opposition. To allow opposition by speech seems to indicate that you think the speech impotent, as when a man says that he has squared the circle, or that you do not care whole-heartedly for the result, or that you doubt either your power or your premises. But when men have realized that time has upset many fighting faiths, they may come to believe even more than they believe the very foundations of their own conduct that the ultimate good desired is better reached by free trade in ideas — that the best test of truth is the power of the thought to get itself accepted in the competition of the market, and that truth is the only ground upon which their wishes safely can be carried out. That at any rate is the theory of our Constitution. It is an experiment, as all life is an experiment. Every year if not every day we have to wager our salvation upon some prophecy based upon imperfect knowledge. While that experiment is part of our system I think that we should be eternally vigilant against attempts to check the expression of opinions that we loathe and believe to be fraught with death, unless they so imminently threaten immediate interference with the lawful and pressing purposes of the law that an immediate check is required to save the country. I wholly disagree with the argument of the Government that the First Amendment left the common law as to seditious libel in force. History seems to me against the notion. I had conceived that the United States through many years had shown its repentance for the Sedition Act of 1798, by repaying fines that it imposed. Only the emergency that makes it immediately dangerous to leave the correction of evil counsels to time warrants making any exception to the sweeping command, "Congress shall make no law . . . abridging the freedom of speech." Of course I am speaking only of expressions of opinion and exhortations, which were all that were uttered here, but I regret that I cannot put into more impressive words my belief that in their conviction upon this indictment the defendants were deprived of their rights under the Constitution of the United States.

MR. JUSTICE BRANDEIS concurs with the foregoing opinion.

Note: Abrams *and the Emergence of the*
Holmes/Brandeis Tradition

1. *The Holmes transformation.* Do you agree that the "same constitutional standard that Holmes urged in *Abrams* [was applied] in *Schenck, Frohwerk* and *Debs*"? Bogen, The Free Speech Metamorphosis of Mr. Justice Holmes, 11 Hofstra L. Rev. 97, 99 (1982). Most commentators have rejected this view and concluded that "Holmes moved from a restrictive construction of the first amendment [in] *Schenck, Frohwerk*, and *Debs* [to] a libertarian position in his dissent in *Abrams*." Rabban, The Emergence of Modern First Amendment Doctrine, 50 U. Chi. L. Rev. 1207, 1208-1209 (1983). What explains this sudden transformation in Holmes's commitment to free speech? Was Holmes simply "biding his time until the Court should have before it a conviction so clearly

wrong as to let him speak out his deepest thoughts about the First Amendment"? Z. Chafee, Free Speech in the United States 86 (1941). For a thoughtful analysis of the Holmes transformation, see Rabban, supra, at 1311-1317. For an especially critical view of Holmes in this period, see Ragan, Justice Oliver Wendell Holmes, Jr., Zechariah Chafee, Jr., and the Clear and Present Danger Test for Free Speech: The First Year, 1919, 58 J. Am. Hist. 24 (1971).

2. *Intent.* Holmes's *Abrams* dissent is traditionally identified with the emergence of clear and present danger as a highly speech protective doctrine. Note, however, that Holmes speaks of danger and intent in *Abrams* in the disjunctive. Should the fact that a speaker "intended to produce a clear and imminent danger" in itself be sufficient to justify suppression of his expression?

3. *The administrability of clear and present danger.* Is Holmes's formulation of clear and present danger in *Abrams* administratively workable? Judge Hand was largely unimpressed with Holmes's effort. As he wrote to Chafee,

> I am not wholly in love with Holmesey's test, [for once] you admit that the matter is one of degree, [you] give to Tomdickandharry, D.J., so much latitude that the jig is at once up. Besides [the] Nine Elder Statesmen have not shown themselves wholly immune from the "herd instinct" and what seems "immediate and direct" to-day may seem very remote next year even though the circumstances surrounding the utterance be unchanged. I own I should prefer a qualitative formula, hard, conventional, difficult to evade.

In short, Hand preferred "a test based upon the nature of the utterance itself." Gunther, Learned Hand and the Origins of Modern First Amendment Doctrine: Some Fragments of History, 27 Stan. L. Rev. 719, 749 (1975). For a defense of clear and present danger in this regard, see Redish, Advocacy of Unlawful Conduct and the First Amendment: In Defense of Clear and Present Danger, 70 Cal. L. Rev. 1159 (1982).

4. *Was there a clear and present danger in* Abrams? Consider Wigmore's criticism:

> [The *Abrams* dissent] is dallying with the facts and the law. [If] these five men could, without the law's restraint, urge munition workers to a general strike and armed violence, then others could lawfully do so; and a thousand disaffected undesirables, aliens and natives alike, were ready and waiting to do so. [If] such urgings were lawful, every munitions factory in the country could be stopped by them. The relevant amount of harm that one criminal act can effect is no measure of its criminality, and no measure of the danger of its criminality.

Wigmore, *Abrams v. United States:* Freedom of Speech and Freedom of Thuggery in War-Time and Peace-Time, 14 Ill. L. Rev. 539, 549-550 (1920). See also Bork, Neutral Principles and Some First Amendment Problems, 47 Ind. L.J. 1, 33 (1971).

5. *The rationale of clear and present danger.* Does the clear and present danger standard derive from Holmes's elaboration of the "marketplace of ideas" theory of the first amendment? Would the "self-fulfillment" or "self-governance" theories provide a sounder foundation for clear and present danger?

Consider the following rationales for the clear and present danger standard: (a) The test balances competing speech and societal interests — speech is important, so government can restrict it only when there is an "emergency"; an "emergency" exists only if the danger is "clear" and "present." (b) The test marks off a broad area of protected expression to avoid Hand's concern in *Masses* that government not be permitted to render unlawful "every political agitation which can be shown to be apt to create a seditious temper." (c) The test is designed to reduce the risk that government, in the guise of preventing "danger," will in fact suppress expression because it disapproves of the substantive message.

6. *Other Espionage Act decisions.* In several post-*Abrams* decisions, the Court, over the dissents of Justices Holmes and Brandeis, upheld further convictions under the Espionage Act. See Pierce v. United States, 252 U.S. 239 (1920); Schaefer v. United States, 251 U.S. 466 (1920). See also Gilbert v. Minnesota, 254 U.S. 325 (1920). Dissenting in *Schaefer*, Brandeis stated that the clear and present danger standard

> is a rule of reason. Correctly applied, it will preserve the right of free speech both from suppression by tyrannous, well-meaning majorities and from abuses by irresponsible, fanatical minorities. [The] question whether in a particular instance the words spoken or written fall within the permissible curtailment of free speech [is] one of degree. And because it is a question of degree the field in which the jury may exercise its judgment is, necessarily, a wide one. But its field is not unlimited. [If] the words were of such a nature and were used under such circumstances that men, judging in calmness, could not reasonably say that they created a clear and present danger [then] it is the duty of the trial judge to withdraw the case from the consideration of the jury.

7. *The "Red Scare."* After World War I and the Russian Revolution, the United States entered a period of intense antiradicalism. In the years 1919 and 1920, an era known as the "Red Scare," two-thirds of the states enacted laws prohibiting the advocacy of criminal syndicalism and criminal anarchy. In addition, two-thirds of the states adopted "red flag" laws, which made it a crime to display a red flag with a seditious intent. See Z. Chafee, Free Speech in the United States 141-168 (1941). It was not long before the Court had to rule on the constitutionality of such legislation.

Gitlow v. New York

268 U.S. 652 (1925)

MR. JUSTICE SANFORD delivered the opinion of the Court.

Benjamin Gitlow was indicted in the Supreme Court of New York, with three others, for the statutory crime of criminal anarchy. [He] was separately tried, convicted, and sentenced to imprisonment. . . .

The contention here is that the statute, by its terms and as applied in this case, is repugnant to the due process clause of the Fourteenth Amendment. Its material provisions are: . . .

> §161. *Advocacy of criminal anarchy.* Any person [who] advocates, advises, or teaches the duty, necessity or propriety of overthrowing [organized] government by force or violence, or by assassination of [any] of the executive officials of government, or by any unlawful means; [is] guilty of a felony. . . .

[The] defendant is a member of the Left Wing Section of the Socialist Party, a dissenting branch or faction of that party formed in opposition to its dominant policy of "moderate Socialism." [The] Left Wing Section was organized nationally at a conference in New York City in June, 1919, attended by ninety delegates from twenty different States. The conference elected a National Council, of which the defendant was a member, and left to it the adoption of a "manifesto." This was published in The Revolutionary Age, the official organ of the Left Wing. The defendant was on the board of managers of the paper and was its business manager. He arranged for the printing [and publication of the first issue of the paper, which contained the Left Wing Manifesto].

[The indictment charged that, as a result of his involvement in the publication of the Manifesto, he "had advocated, advised and taught the duty, necessity and propriety of overthrowing and overturning organized government by force, violence and unlawful means."]

There was no evidence of any effect resulting from the publication and circulation of the Manifesto. [The Manifesto] condemned the dominant "moderate Socialism" for its recognition of the necessity of the democratic parliamentary state; repudiated its policy of introducing Socialism by legislative measures; and advocated, in plain and unequivocal language, the necessity of accomplishing the "Communist Revolution" by a militant and "revolutionary Socialism," based on "the class struggle" and mobilizing the "power of the proletariat in action," through mass industrial revolts developing into mass political strikes and "revolutionary mass action," for the purpose of conquering and destroying the parliamentary state and establishing in its place, through a "revolutionary dictatorship of the proletariat," the system of Communist Socialism. . . .

The court, among other things, charged the jury, in substance, that they must determine what was the intent, purpose and fair meaning of the Manifesto; [that] a mere statement or analysis of social and economic facts and historical incidents, in the nature of an essay, accompanied by prophecy as to the future course of events, but with no teaching, advice or advocacy of action, would not constitute the advocacy, advice or teaching of a doctrine for the overthrow of government within the meaning of the statute; [and] that a mere statement that unlawful acts might accomplish such a purpose would be insufficient, unless there was a teaching, advising and advocacy of employing such unlawful acts for the purpose of overthrowing government. . . .

The defendant's counsel submitted two requests to charge [the jury] that to constitute criminal anarchy [it] was necessary that the language used or published should advocate, teach or advise the duty, necessity or propriety of doing "some definite or immediate act or acts" of force, violence or unlawfulness directed toward the overthrowing of organized government, [and] that to constitute guilt the language used or published must be "reasonably and ordinarily calculated to incite certain persons" to acts of force, violence or unlawfulness, with the object of overthrowing organized government. These were [denied]. [The] sole contention here is, essentially, that as there was no evidence of any concrete result flowing from the publication of the Manifesto or of circumstances showing the likelihood of such result, the statute as construed and applied by the trial court penalizes the mere utterance, as such, of "doctrine" having no quality of incitement, [and thus] contravenes the due process clause of the Fourteenth Amendment. . . .

The statute does not penalize the utterance or publication of abstract "doctrine" or academic discussion having no quality of incitement to any concrete action. It is not aimed against mere historical or philosophical essays. It does not restrain the advocacy of changes in the form of government by constitutional and lawful means. What it prohibits is language advocating, advising or teaching the overthrow of organized government by unlawful means. These words imply urging to action. . . .

The Manifesto, plainly, is neither the statement of abstract doctrine nor, as suggested by counsel, mere prediction that industrial disturbances and revolutionary mass strikes will result spontaneously in an inevitable process of evolution in the economic system. It advocates and urges in fervent language mass action which shall progressively foment industrial disturbances and through political mass strikes and revolutionary mass action overthrow and destroy organized parliamentary government. It concludes with a call to action in these words: "The proletariat revolution and the Communist reconstruction of society — *the struggle for these* — is now indispensable. . . . The Communist International calls the proletariat of the world to the final struggle!" This is not the expression of philosophical abstraction, the mere prediction of future events; it is the language of direct incitement. [That] the jury were warranted in finding that the Manifesto advocated not merely the abstract doctrine of overthrowing organized government by force, violence and unlawful means, but action to that end, is clear.

For present purposes we may and do assume that freedom of speech and of the press — which are protected by the First Amendment from abridgment by Congress — are among the fundamental personal rights and "liberties" protected by the due process clause of the Fourteenth Amendment from impairment by the States. . . .

It is a fundamental principle, long established, that the freedom of speech and of the press which is secured by the Constitution, does not confer an absolute right to speak or publish, without responsibility, whatever one may choose, or an unrestricted and unbridled license that gives immunity for every possible use of language and prevents the punishment of those who abuse this freedom. [A] State may punish utterances endangering the foundations of organized government and threatening its overthrow by unlawful means. These imperil its own existence as a constitutional State. Freedom of speech and press [does] not deprive a State of the primary and essential right of self preservation. . . .

By enacting the present statute the State has determined, through its legislative body, that utterances advocating the overthrow of organized government by force, violence and unlawful means, are so inimical to the general welfare and involve such danger of substantive evil that they may be penalized in the exercise of its police power. That determination must be given great weight. Every presumption is to be indulged in favor of the validity of the statute. Mulger v. Kansas, 123 U.S. 623, 661. And the case is to be considered "in the light of the principle that the State is primarily the judge of regulations required in the interest of public safety and welfare;" and that its police "statutes may only be declared unconstitutional where they are arbitrary or unreasonable attempts to exercise authority vested in the State in the public interest." Great Northern Ry. v. Clara City, 246 U.S. 434, 439. That utterances inciting to the overthrow of organized government by unlawful means, present a sufficient danger of substantive evil to bring their punishment within the range of legislative discretion, is clear. Such utterances, by their very nature, involve danger to the public peace and to the security of the State. They threaten breaches of the peace and ultimate revolution. And the immediate danger is none the less real and substantial, because the effect of a given utterance cannot be accurately foreseen. The State cannot reasonably be required to measure the danger from every such utterance in the nice balance of a jeweler's scale. A single revolutionary spark may kindle a fire that, smouldering for a time, may burst into a sweeping and destructive conflagration. It cannot be said that the State is acting arbitrarily or unreasonably when in the exercise of its judgment as to the measures necessary to protect the public peace and safety, it seeks to extinguish the spark without waiting until it has enkindled the flame or blazed into the conflagration. It cannot reasonably be required to defer the adoption of measures for its own peace and safety until the revolutionary utterances lead to actual disturbances of the public peace or imminent and immediate danger of its own destruction; but it may, in the exercise of its judgment, suppress the threatened danger in its incipiency. . . .

We cannot hold that the present statute is an arbitrary or unreasonable exercise of the police power of the State unwarrantably infringing the freedom of speech or press; and we must and do sustain its constitutionality.

This being so it may be applied to every utterance — not too trivial to be beneath the notice of the law — which is of such a character and used with such intent and purpose as to bring it within the prohibition of the statute. [In] other words, when the legislative body has determined generally, in the constitutional exercise of its discretion, that utterances of a certain kind involve such danger of substantive evil that they may be punished, the question whether any specific utterance coming within the prohibited class is likely, in and of itself, to bring about the substantive evil, is not open to consideration. It is sufficient that the statute itself be constitutional and that the use of the language comes within its prohibition.

It is clear that the question in such cases is entirely different from that involved in those cases where the statute merely prohibits certain acts involving the danger of substantive evil, without any reference to language itself, and it is sought to apply its provisions to language used by the defendant for the purpose of bringing about the prohibited results. There, if it be contended that the statute cannot be applied to the language used by the defendant because of its protection by the freedom of speech or press, it must necessarily be found, as an original question, without any previous determination by the legislative body, whether the specific language used involved such likelihood of bringing about the substantive evil as to deprive it of the constitutional protection. In such cases it has been held that the general provisions of the statute may be constitutionally applied to the specific utterance of the defendant if its natural tendency and probable effect was to bring about the substantive evil which the legislative body might prevent. [*Schenck; Debs.*] And the general statement in [*Schenck*] that the "question in every case is whether the words are used in such circumstances and are of such a nature as to create a clear and present danger that they will bring about the substantive evils," — upon which great reliance is placed in the defendant's argument — was manifestly intended, as shown by the context, to apply only in cases of this class, and has no application to those like the present, where the legislative body itself has previously determined the danger of substantive evil arising from utterances of a specified character. . . .

Affirmed.

Mr. Justice Holmes dissenting.

Mr. Justice Brandeis and I are of opinion that this judgment should be reversed. The general principle of free speech, it seems to me, must be taken to be included in the Fourteenth Amendment, in view of the scope that has been given to the word "liberty" as there used, although perhaps it may be accepted with a somewhat larger latitude of interpretation than is allowed to Congress by the sweeping language that governs, or ought to govern, the laws of the United States. If I am right, then I think that the criterion sanctioned by the full court in [Schenck] applies: "The question in every case is whether the words used are used in such circumstances and are of such a nature as to create a clear and present danger that they will bring about the substantive evils that [the state] has a right to prevent." It is true that in my opinion this criterion was departed from in [Abrams], but the convictions that I expressed in that case are too deep for it to be possible for me as yet to believe that it [has] settled the law. If what I think the correct test is applied, it is manifest that there was no present danger of an attempt to overthrow the government by force on the part of the admittedly small minority who shared the defendant's views. It is said that this Manifesto was more than a theory, that it was an incitement. Every idea is an incitement. It offers itself for belief, and, if believed, it is acted on unless some other belief outweighs it, or some failure of energy stifles the movement at its birth. The only difference between the expression of an opinion and an incitement in the narrower sense is the speaker's enthusiasm for the result. Eloquence may set fire to reason. But whatever may be thought of the redundant discourse before us, it had no chance of starting a present conflagration. If, in the long run, the beliefs expressed in proletarian dictatorship are destined to be accepted by the dominant forces of the community, the only meaning of free speech is that they should be given their chance and have their way.

If the publication of this document had been laid as an attempt to induce an uprising against government at once, and not at some indefinite time in the future, it would have presented a different question. The object would have been one with which the law might deal, subject to the doubt whether there was any danger that the publication could produce any result; or, in other words, whether it was not futile and too remote from possible consequences. But the indictment alleges the publication and nothing more.

Note: Gitlow *and the Question of Deference*

1. *Incitement.* Justice Sanford emphasized repeatedly in *Gitlow* that the New York statute was not directed against "abstract doctrine," "academic discussion," "historical or philosophical essays," the "prediction of future events," or "advocacy of changes in the form of government by constitutional and lawful means." Rather, Sanford reiterated, the statute restricted only expression "urging to action," "incitement to [concrete] action," and "the language of direct incite-

ment." Was Sanford suggesting an analysis similar to that set out by Hand? Is Holmes's assertion that "every idea is an incitement" a satisfactory response?

2. *The problem of deference.* Justice Sanford drew a sharp distinction in *Gitlow* between cases like *Schenck*, in which "the statute merely prohibits certain acts involving the danger of substantive evil, without any reference to language itself," and cases like *Gitlow*, in which the "legislative body has determined [that] utterances of a certain kind involve such danger of substantive evil that they may be punished." Is Sanford right that the problems posed by these two types of cases are "entirely different"? Did Sanford defer in *Gitlow* to the legislature's interpretation of the first amendment? To its factual assessment of the dangers of certain types of utterances?

The New York law involved in *Gitlow* was enacted in 1902 in response to the assassination of President McKinley. Although intended for use against anarchists, it was first invoked in the prosecution of Gitlow, a radical socialist. Does this pose an embarrassment for the Court? Consider Linde, "Clear and Present Danger" Reexamined: Dissonance in the Brandenburg Concerto, 22 Stan L. Rev. 1163, 1176 (1970):

> Whatever danger the new radicalism posed for New York in 1920, it was not the demonstrative assassinations that had been feared from the anarchists. Yet when Benjamin Gitlow, a former Socialist member of the New York Assembly, and his associates were prosecuted under the Criminal Anarchy Act for publishing their Left Wing Manifesto, the Supreme Court deferred to a supposed legislative judgment that their doctrines — separated from those of the anarchists by a history of bitter sectarian battles — carried with them enough substantive danger to justify their suppression.

Holmes refused in *Gitlow* to defer to the legislative judgment, insisting instead that it is for the judiciary to determine in each and every instance whether the expression creates a "clear and present danger." Was Holmes's disregard of the legislative judgment warranted? Can Holmes's persistent advocacy of judicial deference in the substantive due process context, see, e.g., Lochner v. New York (Holmes, J., dissenting), Chapter 6, section D, supra, be reconciled with his position in *Gitlow*?

3. *Underinclusion.* Note that, as drafted, the New York Criminal Anarchy Act did not prohibit the advocacy of unlawful force, violence, and assassination to *preserve* organized government. Is such underinclusion a relevant first amendment concern? The Court rejected such an argument, couched in equal protection terms, in Whitney v. California, 274 U.S. 357, 369-371 (1927).

4. *The marketplace of ideas.* In *Abrams* Holmes maintained that, as an "experiment," our Constitution embraced the "theory" that "the best test of truth is the power of the thought to get itself accepted in the competition of the market." The market, however, is not perfect, and in *Gitlow* Holmes conceded that "if, in the long run, the beliefs expressed in proletarian dictatorship are destined to be accepted by the dominant forces of the community, the only meaning of free speech is that they should be given their chance and have their way." What about ideas which, if accepted, would refuse to permit other ideas to compete in the "market"? Are some evils so grave that we cannot afford to "experiment"? Is there

a difference under the "marketplace" theory between advocacy of change through lawful processes and advocacy of change through force?

Consider Rogat & O'Fallon, Mr. Justice Holmes: A Dissenting Opinion — The Speech Cases, 36 Stan. L. Rev. 1349, 1367-1368 (1984):

> One [factor that] led Holmes to a liberal position on speech [was] his concern that judges should not impede the avenues of social change. Since Holmes was skeptical of absolute "truth," believing instead that there were only degrees of probability, he focused his attention on the clash of conflicting beliefs, and ended by accepting whatever won out and commanded the most force. He felt courts should not clog that struggle by placing impediments in the way of "the natural outcome of a dominant opinion." Ultimate strength was a curiously predestined condition for Holmes, apparently unaffected by conscious governmental attempts to impede some groups or to assist others. [The] curious fatalism he expressed in his *Gitlow* dissent reflects this outlook.

Recall Justice Holmes's dissenting opinion in Lochner v. New York, supra Chapter 6, section D.

Whitney v. California
274 U.S. 357 (1927)

MR. JUSTICE SANFORD delivered the opinion of the Court.

[In 1919 Anita Whitney attended the national convention of the Socialist Party in Chicago as a delegate of the Local Oakland branch of the party. At this convention, the party split between the "radicals" and the old-line Socialists. The "radicals," supported by the Oakland branch delegates, formed the Communist Labor Party and promulgated a platform similar in style and substance to the Left Wing Manifesto at issue in *Gitlow*. Shortly thereafter, Whitney attended a convention held in Oakland for the purpose of organizing a California branch of the Communist Labor Party. At this convention, she sponsored a moderate resolution calling for the achievement of the party's goals through the political process. This resolution was defeated, however, and the convention adopted the more militant national platform. Whitney remained at the convention until it adjourned and remained a member of the party. As a result of her activities at the Oakland convention, she was charged with violating the California Criminal Syndicalism Act, which prohibited any person to organize or knowingly become a member of any organization that advocates "the commission of crime, sabotage, or unlawful acts of force and violence or unlawful methods of terrorism as a means of accomplishing a change in industrial ownership or control, or effecting any political change."]

The first count of the information, on which the conviction was had, charged that [at the Oakland convention] the defendant, in violation of the Criminal Syndicalism Act, "did then and there [deliberately] organize and assist in organizing, and was, is, and knowingly became a member of [a group] organized [to advocate] criminal syndicalism." . . .

[At her trial, Whitney] testified that it was not her intention that the Communist Labor Party of California should be an instrument of terrorism or violence, and that it was not her purpose or that of the Convention to violate any known law. . . .

While it is not denied that the evidence warranted the jury in finding that the defendant became a member of and assisted in organizing the Communist Labor Party of California, and that this was organized to [advocate] criminal syndicalism as defined by the Act, it is urged that the Act, as here construed and applied, deprived the defendant of her liberty without due process of law in that it has made her action in attending the Oakland convention unlawful by reason of "a subsequent event brought about against her will, by the agency of others," with no showing of a specific intent on her part to join in the forbidden purpose of the association. [This] contention, while advanced in the form of a constitutional objection to the Act, is in effect nothing more than an effort to review the weight of the evidence for the purpose of showing that the defendant did not join and assist in organizing the Communist Labor Party of California with a knowledge of its unlawful character and purpose. This question [is] one of fact [which] is not open to review in this Court, involving as it does no constitutional question whatever. . . .

[That] a State in the exercise of its police power may punish those who abuse [the freedom of speech] by utterances inimical to the public welfare, tending to incite to crime, disturb the public peace, or endanger the foundations of organized government and threaten its overthrow by unlawful means, is not open to question. [*Gitlow*.]

By enacting the provisions of the Syndicalism Act the State has declared, through its legislative body, that to knowingly be or become a member of or assist in organizing an association to advocate [criminal syndicalism], involves such danger to the public peace and the security of the State, that these acts should be penalized in the exercise of its police power. That determination must be given great weight. . . .

The essence of the offense denounced by the Act is the combining with others in an association for the accomplishment of the desired ends through the advocacy and use of criminal and unlawful methods. It partakes of the nature of a criminal conspiracy. [That] such united and joint action involves even greater danger to the public peace and security than the isolated utterances and acts of individuals, is clear. We cannot hold that, as here applied, the Act is an unreasonable or arbitrary exercise of the police power of the State, unwarrantably infringing any right of free speech, assembly or association, or that those persons are protected from punishment by the due process clause who abuse such rights by joining and furthering an organization thus menacing the peace and welfare of the State. . . .

Affirmed.

Mr. Justice Brandeis, concurring. . . .

The felony which the statute created is a crime very unlike the old felony of conspiracy or the old misdemeanor of unlawful assembly. The mere act of assisting in forming a society for teaching syndicalism, of becoming a member of it, or of assembling with others for that purpose is given the dynamic quality of crime. [The] novelty in the prohibition introduced is that the statute aims, not at the practice of criminal syndicalism, nor even directly at the preaching of it, but at association with those who propose to preach it. . . .

[Although] the rights of free speech and assembly are fundamental, they are not in their nature absolute. Their exercise is subject to restriction, if the particular restriction proposed is required in order to protect the state from destruction or from serious injury, political, economic or moral. That the necessity which is essential to a valid restriction does not exist unless speech would produce, or is intended to produce, a clear and imminent danger of some substantive evil which the state constitutionally may seek to prevent has been settled. See [*Schenck*].

It is said to be the function of the legislature to determine whether at a particular time and under the particular circumstances the formation of, or assembly with, a society organized to advocate criminal syndicalism constitutes a clear and present danger of substantive evil; and that by enacting the law here in question the legislature of California determined that question in the affirmative. Compare [*Gitlow*]. The legislature must obviously decide, in the first instance, whether a danger exists which calls for a particular protective measure. But where a statute is valid only in case certain conditions exist, the enactment of the statute cannot alone establish the facts which are essential to its validity. Prohibitory legislation has repeatedly been held invalid, because unnecessary, where the denial of liberty involved was that of engaging in a particular business. The power of the courts to strike down an offending law is no less when the interests involved are not property rights, but the fundamental personal rights of free speech and assembly.

This court has not yet fixed the standard by which to determine when a danger shall be deemed clear; how remote the danger may be and yet be deemed present; and what degree of evil shall be deemed sufficiently substantial to justify resort to abridgment of free speech and assembly as the means of protection. To reach sound conclusions on these matters, we must bear in mind why a state is, ordinarily, denied the power to prohibit dissemination of social, economic and political doctrine which a vast majority of its citizens believes to be false and fraught with evil consequence.

Those who won our independence believed that the final end of the state was to make men free to develop their faculties; and that in its government the deliberative forces should prevail over the arbitrary. They valued liberty both as an end and as a means. They believed liberty to be the secret of happiness and courage to be the secret of liberty. They believed that freedom to think as you will and to speak as you think are means indispensable to the discovery and spread of political truth; that without free speech and assembly discussion would be futile; that with them, discussion affords ordinarily adequate protection against the dissemination of noxious doctrine; that the greatest menace to freedom is an inert people; that public discussion is a political duty; and that this should be a fundamental principle of the American government. They recognized the risks to which all human institutions are subject. But they knew that order cannot be secured merely through fear of punishment for its infraction; that it is hazardous to discourage thought, hope and imagination; that fear breeds repression; that repression breeds hate; that hate menaces stable government; that the path of safety lies in the opportunity to discuss freely supposed grievances and proposed remedies; and that the fitting remedy for evil counsels is good ones. Believing in the power of reason as applied through public discussion, they eschewed silence coerced by law — the argument of force in its worst form. Recognizing the occasional tyrannies of governing majorities, they amended the Constitution so that free speech and assembly should be guaranteed.

Fear of serious injury cannot alone justify suppression of free speech and assembly. Men feared witches and burned women. It is the function of speech to free men from the bondage of irrational fears. To justify suppression of free speech there must be reasonable ground to fear that serious evil will result if free speech is practiced. There must be reasonable ground to believe that the danger apprehended is imminent. There must be reasonable ground to believe that the evil to be prevented is a serious one. Every denunciation of existing law tends in some measure to increase the probability that there will be violation of it. Condonation of a breach enhances the probability. Expressions of approval add to the probability. Propagation of the criminal state of mind by teaching syndicalism increases it. Advocacy of lawbreaking heightens it still further. But even advocacy of violation, however reprehensible morally, is not a justification for denying free speech where the advocacy falls short of incitement and there is nothing to indicate that the advocacy would be immediately acted on. The wide difference between advocacy and incitement, between preparation and attempt, between assembling and conspiracy, must be borne in mind. In order to support a finding of clear and present danger it must be shown either that immediate serious violence was to be expected or was advocated, or that the past conduct furnished reason to believe that such advocacy was then contemplated.

Those who won our independence by revolution were not cowards. They did not fear political change. They did not exalt order at the cost of liberty. To courageous, self-reliant men, with confidence in the power of free and fearless reasoning applied through the processes of popular government, no danger flowing from speech can be deemed clear and present, unless the incidence of the evil apprehended is so imminent that it may befall before there is opportunity for full discussion. If there be time to expose through discussion the falsehood and fallacies, to avert the evil by the processes of education, the remedy to be applied is more speech, not enforced silence. Only an emergency can justify repression. Such must be the rule if authority is to be reconciled with freedom. Such, in my opinion, is the command of the Constitution. It is, therefore, always open to Americans to challenge a law abridging free speech and assembly by showing that there was no emergency justifying it.

Moreover, even imminent danger cannot justify resort to prohibition of these functions essential to effective democracy, unless the evil apprehended is relatively serious. Prohibition of free speech and assembly is a measure so stringent that it would be inappropriate as the means for averting a relatively trivial harm to society. A police measure may be unconstitutional merely because the remedy, although effective as means of protection, is unduly harsh or oppressive. Thus, a state might, in the exercise of its police power, make any trespass upon the land of another a crime, regardless of the results or of the intent or purpose of the trespasser. It might, also, punish an attempt, a conspiracy, or an incitement to commit the trespass. But it is hardly conceivable that this court would hold constitutional a statute which punished as a felony the mere voluntary assembly with a society formed to teach that pedestrians had the moral right to cross unenclosed, unposted, waste lands and to advocate their doing so, even if there was imminent danger that advocacy would lead to a trespass. The fact that speech is likely to result in some violence or in destruction of property is not enough to justify its suppression. There must be the probability of serious injury to the state. Among freemen, the deterrents ordinarily to be applied to prevent crime are education and punishment for violations of the law, not abridgment of the rights of free speech and assembly.

The California Syndicalism Act recites, in §4:

> [This] act concerns and is necessary to the immediate preservation of the public peace and safety, for the reason that at the present time large numbers of persons are going from place to place in this state advocating, teaching and practicing criminal syndicalism. . . .

This legislative declaration satisfies the requirement of the Constitution of the state concerning emergency legislation. [But] it does not preclude inquiry into the question whether, at the time and under the circumstances, the conditions existed which are essential to validity under the Federal Constitution. As a statute, even if not void on its face, may be challenged because invalid as applied, [the] result of such an inquiry may depend upon the specific facts of the particular case. Whenever the fundamental rights of free speech and assembly are alleged to have been invaded, it must remain open to a defendant to present the issue whether there actually did exist at the time a clear danger; whether the danger, if any, was imminent; and whether the evil apprehended was one so substantial as to justify the stringent restriction interposed by the legislature. The legislative declaration, like the fact that the statute was passed and was sustained by the highest court of the state, creates merely a rebuttable presumption that these conditions have been satisfied.

Whether, in 1919, when Miss Whitney did the things complained of, there was in California such clear and present danger of serious evil, might have been made the important issue in the case. She might have required that the issue be determined either by the court or the jury. She claimed below that the statute as applied to her violated the Federal Constitution; but she did not claim that it was void because there was no clear and present danger of serious evil, nor did she request that the existence of these conditions of a valid measure thus restricting the rights of free speech and assembly be passed upon by the court or a jury. On the other hand, there was evidence on which the court or jury might have found that such danger existed. I am unable to assent to the suggestion in the opinion of the court that assembling with a political party, formed to advocate the desirability of a proletarian revolution by mass action at some date necessarily far in the future, is not a right within the protection of the Fourteenth Amendment. In the present case, however, there was other testimony which tended to establish the existence of a conspiracy, on the part of members of the International Workers of the World, to commit present serious crimes; and likewise to show that such a conspiracy would be furthered by the activity of the society of which Miss Whitney was a member. Under these circumstances the judgment of the state court cannot be disturbed. [We] lack here the power occasionally exercised on review of judgments of lower federal courts to correct in criminal cases vital errors, although the objection was not taken in the trial court. [This] is a writ of error to a state court. Because we may not inquire into the errors now alleged, I concur in affirming the judgment of the state court.

Mr. Justice Holmes joins in this opinion.

Note: The Brandeis Concurrence and the Right of Association

1. *Clear and present danger.* Justice Brandeis attempted in *Whitney* to explicate the underlying rationale of the clear and present danger standard. Was his reliance on the intent of the framers historically sound? Do Brandeis's conceptions of clear and present danger and of the functions of the first amendment differ from Holmes's? Note that Brandeis's emphasis in not on a "marketplace of ideas," but on the "development of the faculties" and the "deliberative process."

Brandeis emphasized that if the danger is not imminent, "the remedy to be applied is more speech, not enforced silence." Is the opportunity for counter-speech an adequate explanation of the imminence requirement?

Did Brandeis clarify the role of specific intent? There can be little doubt that the Communist Labor Party specifically intended to bring about the overthrow of government by force. Should it matter that it specifically intended to accomplish this goal in the future rather than imminently?

2. *Deference and the preferred freedom.* Did Brandeis answer Sanford's contention, arguably evaded by Holmes in *Gitlow*, that the Court should defer to reasonable legislative judgments in this context? Note that, in the substantive due process decisions of the same era, Brandeis argued consistently for a deferential standard of review. See Chapter 6, section D, supra. Would Brandeis have been more convincing in *Whitney* had he argued that such deference is inappropriate "where legislation has undermined the reasons for deference by eroding the very processes of communication and opinion-formation on which one can ordinarily rely to cause the political branches to change course"? L. Tribe, American Constitutional Law 613 n.30 (1978). Under this view, a well-functioning democracy is one in which government permits free speech; when speech is suppressed, the ordinary processes of representation are no longer reliable safeguards, and the government becomes self-insulating. This view is part of the general theme of representation-reinforcement in constitutional law, a theme explored at various points in this book. See Chapter 1, section C, and Chapter 6, section A; United States v. Carolene Products Co., 304 U.S. 144, 152-153 n. 4 (1938); see generally J. Ely, Democracy and Distrust (1980). Does this argument overlook the possibility that a political community may freely decide to insulate itself from the deleterious aspects of free speech? Cf. Bork, The Impossibility of Finding Welfare Rights in the Constitution, 1979 Wash. U. L.Q. 695 (arguing that the theory of representation-reinforcement is self-contradictory).

3. *Association.* In the pre-*Whitney* cases, the various defendants were prosecuted either for engaging personally in prohibited expression or, as in *Frohwerk*, for directly and actively participating in the prohibited expression of others. The California Criminal Syndicalism Act, however, declared it unlawful for any person knowingly to be a *member* of any organization that engages in unlawful advocacy. *Whitney* thus posed, but did not necessarily answer, three new questions: First, is the act of associating with others for expression-related purposes in itself protected by the first amendment? Second, assuming that association is a protected first amendment activity, in what circumstances, if any, may the state constitutionally punish membership in an organization on the ground that the organization itself engages in unlawful advocacy? The Court in *Whitney* held

"knowing" membership unprotected. Is that the appropriate line? Third, how does the Holmes-Brandeis conception of clear and present danger apply to association? Recall the argument of Wigmore that the legislature should be permitted to consider the cumulative danger posed by many individually harmless speakers in deciding whether there is sufficient danger to warrant the suppression of speech.

Note: *The Road to* Dennis

1. *A new direction?* In the decade following *Whitney*, the Court handed down three significant decisions concerning subversive advocacy and the right of association. In each decision — *Fiske, De Jonge,* and *Herndon* — the Court held the conviction unconstitutional. Thus, after an era of nine consecutive affirmances of convictions for subversive advocacy, the Court offered three consecutive reversals. To what extent do the following three decisions reflect a shift in substantive first amendment principles?

a. In Fiske v. Kansas, 274 U.S. 380 (1927), decided on the same day as *Whitney*, the defendant was convicted under the Kansas Criminal Syndicalism Act for soliciting members for the Worker's Industrial Union, a branch of the International Workers of the World. The only evidence offered by the State at Fiske's trial of the doctrines advocated by the International Workers of the World consisted of a copy of the preamble to the organization's constitution. Although the preamble asserted that "a struggle must go on until the workers of the World [take] possession of [the] machinery of production and abolish the wage system," it did not expressly state that such goals should be attained through unlawful means. Finding that "no substantial inference" could be drawn from the preamble alone that the organization advocated criminal syndicalism within the meaning of the act, the Court unanimously held the application of the act in the context of this case to be "an arbitrary and unreasonable exercise of the police power of the State, unwarrantably infringing the liberty of the defendant in violation of the due process clause of the Fourteenth Amendment." Although *Fiske* has clear first amendment overtones, it has generally been cited as authority for the procedural due process principle that an individual may not be convicted of a crime in the absence of proof of guilt. See Jackson v. Virginia, 443 U.S. 307 (1979); Thompson v. Louisville, 362 U.S. 199 (1960).

b. In De Jonge v. Oregon, 299 U.S. 353 (1937), the defendant assisted in conducting a meeting held under the auspices of the Communist Party. The meeting was open to the public and was concerned primarily with an ongoing maritime strike, allegedly unlawful raids on workers' halls and homes, and the shooting of a striking longshoreman by local police. No one at the meeting advocated criminal syndicalism or any other unlawful conduct. As a result of his participation in this meeting, defendant was convicted under a provision of Oregon's Criminal Syndicalism Law declaring it unlawful for any person to assist "in conducting a meeting" of any organization that advocates criminal syndicalism. In sustaining De Jonge's conviction, the state courts found that the Communist Party had advocated criminal syndicalism at other times and places. The Court held the conviction invalid:

> [The first amendment] may be abused by using speech or press or assembly in order to incite to violence and crime. The people through their legislatures may protect

themselves against that abuse. But the legislative intervention can find constitutional justification only by dealing with the abuse. [It] follows [that] peaceable assembly for lawful discussion cannot be made a crime. The holding of meetings for peaceable political action cannot be proscribed. Those who assist in the conduct of such meetings cannot be branded as criminals on that score. The question, if the rights of free speech are to be preserved, is not as to the auspices under which the meeting is held but as to its purpose; not as to the relations of the speakers, but whether their utterances transcend the bounds of the freedom of speech which the Constitution protects. If the persons assembling have committed crimes elsewhere, if they have formed or are engaged in a conspiracy against the public peace and order, they may be prosecuted for their conspiracy or other violation of valid laws. But it is a different matter when the State instead of prosecuting them for such offenses, seizes upon mere participation in a peaceable assembly and a lawful public discussion as the basis for a criminal charge. [The] Oregon statute as applied to the particular charge [is] repugnant to the [Constitution].

Is *De Jonge* reconcilable with *Whitney*? If the state can constitutionally prohibit membership in the Communist Party, why can't it prohibit the party from holding meetings? Would it have made a difference in *De Jonge* if the defendant had been charged with helping to conduct the meeting with *knowledge* of the party's unlawful advocacy?

c. In Herndon v. Lowry, 301 U.S. 242 (1937), Herndon, a black, came to Atlanta as a paid organizer for the Communist Party. During his time in Atlanta, he enrolled at least five new members and held three meetings. Herndon was arrested, tried, and convicted under a never-before-used slave insurrection statute that prohibited "any attempt, by persuasion or otherwise, to induce others to join in any combined resistance to the lawful authority of the State."

At the time of his arrest, Herndon had in his possession a box containing, among other documents, membership blanks. The blanks set forth the specific aims of the party, such as unemployment insurance, emergency relief for the poor, and equal rights for blacks. Although none of these aims was expressly criminal, the state maintained that the demand for equal racial rights was rendered criminal by virtue of "extrinsic facts." The state relied principally on a booklet, found in Herndon's possession, that urged that certain southern states should be made one governmental unit, ruled by a black majority. The booklet advocated strikes, boycotts, and demonstrations, "even if the situation does not yet warrant the raising of the question of uprising."

In a five-to-four decision, the Court overturned Herndon's conviction:

[In applying the statute to this case,] the offense made criminal [is] that of soliciting members for a political party and conducting meetings of a local unit of that party when one of [its] doctrines [may] be said to be ultimate resort to violence at some indefinite future time against organized government. [Did appellant] incite to insurrection by reason of the fact that [those whom he induced to join the party] agreed to abide by [its tenets], some of them lawful, others, as may be assumed, unlawful, in absence of proof that he brought the unlawful aims to their notice, that he approved them, or that the fantastic program they envisaged was conceived of by anyone as more than an ultimate ideal? Doubtless circumstantial evidence might affect the answer to the question if appellant had been shown to have said that the Black Belt should be organized at once [and] that that objective was one of his principal aims. But here [the] only objectives appellant is proved to have urged [are] void of criminality. [In] these circumstances, to make solicitation of members [a] criminal offense [is] an unwarranted invasion of the right of freedom of speech.

What principles emerge from *Herndon*? Note that the Court placed considerable emphasis on the absence of evidence that Herndon had distributed the booklet. Why should that matter? Why wasn't it sufficient that Herndon presumably *knew* of the contents of the booklet?

Consider Z. Chafee, Free Speech in the United States 397 (1941):

> I have let my mind run over all the chief sedition defendants [to date. All] but one seem to me fairly harmless. The one exception is Herndon. Not that there was clear and present danger of the insurrection for which he was indicted. [But], given the unrest of Negroes, [his] demands for equal racial rights, lavish relief, and the virtual abolition of debts might have produced some sort of disorder in the near future. Smoking is all right, but not in a powder magazine.

2. *Clear and present danger from* Whitney *to* Dennis. Although the decisions in *Fiske, De Jonge,* and *Herndon* did more to muddle than to clarify the law governing subversive advocacy, in the quarter-century between *Whitney* and *Dennis* the Court embraced clear and present danger as the appropriate test for a wide range of first amendment issues. See, e.g., Schneider v. State, infra section E1 (leafleting); Cantwell v. Connecticut, infra section B3 (hostile audience); Bridges v. California, infra section B2 (contempt by publication); Terminiello v. Chicago, infra section B3 (breach of peace). See also Strong, Fifty Years of "Clear and Present Danger": From *Schenck* to *Brandenburg* — and Beyond, 1969 Sup. Ct. Rev. 41.

At the same time that the Court was gradually recognizing clear and present danger as the centerpiece of its first amendment jurisprudence, however, the doctrine came increasingly under attack both for its failure adequately to protect expression and for its lack of clarity. Alexander Meiklejohn, for example, in articulating his influential interpretation of the first amendment according absolute protection to all speech relating to self-governance, sharply criticized clear and present danger:

> [That standard] regards the freedom of speech as a mere device which is to be abandoned when dangers threaten the public welfare. [But] it is the very presence of those dangers which makes it imperative that, in the midst of our fears, we remember and observe a principle upon whose integrity the entire structure of government by consent of the governed rests. [By] adopting a theory which annuls the First Amendment, [the Court] has denied the belief that men can, by processes of free public discussion, govern themselves.

A. Meiklejohn, Free Speech and Its Relation to Self-Government 90 (1948). Consider also P. Freund, On Understanding the Supreme Court 27-28 (1949):

> The truth is that the clear-and-present-danger test is an oversimplified judgment unless it takes account also of a number of other factors: the relative seriousness of the danger in comparison with the value of the occasion for speech or political activity; the availability of more moderate controls than those which the state has imposed; and perhaps the specific intent with which the speech or activity is

launched. No matter how rapidly we utter the phrase "clear and present danger," or how closely we hyphenate the words, they are not a substitute for the weighing of values. They tend to convey a delusion of certitude when what is most certain is the complexity of the strands in the web of freedoms which the judge must disentangle.

See also H. Wechsler, Symposium on Civil Liberties, 9 Am. L. Sch. Rev. 881, 887 (1941), reprinted in Selected Essays on Constitutional Law 1938-1962, at 628, 634 (1963). For a contemporaneous defense of clear and present danger, see Z. Chafee, Free Speech in the United States 31-35 (1941).

3. *The war on communism.* With its 1951 decision in *Dennis*, the Court continued its quest for a satisfactory solution to the problem of subversive advocacy. During the post–World War II "cold war" era, fears over national security once again generated wide-ranging federal and state restrictions on "radical" speech. These restrictions included extensive loyalty programs, emergency detention plans, attempts to "outlaw" the Communist Party, requirements that all so-called communist-front and communist-action organizations register with the government, and extensive legislative investigations of suspected "subversives." *Dennis*, which involved the prosecution under the Smith Act of the national leaders of the Communist Party of the United States, represents but one facet of this era.

Dennis v. United States

341 U.S. 494 (1951)

MR. CHIEF JUSTICE VINSON announced the judgment of the Court and an opinion in which MR. JUSTICE REED, MR. JUSTICE BURTON and MR. JUSTICE MINTON join.

Petitioners were indicted for violation of the conspiracy provisions of the Smith Act during the period of April 1945, to July, 1948. [A] verdict of guilty as to all the petitioners was returned by the jury. [The] Court of Appeals affirmed. [We] granted certiorari limited to the following two questions: (1) Whether either §2 or §3 of the Smith Act, inherently or as construed and applied in the instant case, violates the First Amendment and other provisions of the Bill of Rights; (2) whether either §2 or §3 of the Act, inherently or as construed and applied in the instant case, violates the First and Fifth Amendments because of indefiniteness.

Sections 2 and 3 of the Smith Act, 54 Stat. 670, (see present 18 U.S.C. §2385), provide as follows:

Sec. 2.

(a) It shall be unlawful for any person —

(1) to knowingly or willfully advocate, abet, advise, or teach the duty, necessity, desirability, or propriety of overthrowing or destroying any government in the United States by force or violence, or by the assassination of any officer of such government. . . .

Sec. 3. It shall be unlawful for any person to attempt to commit, or to conspire to commit, any of the acts prohibited by the provisions of . . . this title.

The indictment charged the petitioners with willfully and knowingly conspiring (1) to organize as the Communist Party of the United States of America a society, group and assembly of persons who teach and advocate the overthrow and destruction of the Government of the United States by force and violence, and (2) knowingly and willfully to advocate and teach the duty and necessity of overthrowing and destroying the Government of the United States by force and violence. . . .

The trial of the case extended over nine months, six of which were devoted to the taking of evidence, resulting in a record of 16,000 pages. Our limited grant of the writ of certiorari has removed from our consideration any question as to the sufficiency of the [evidence]. Whether on this record petitioners did in fact advocate the overthrow of the Government by force and violence is not before us, and we must base any discussion of this point upon the conclusion [of] the Court of Appeals, which [held] that the record in this case amply supports the necessary finding of the jury that petitioners, the leaders of the Communist Party in this country, [intended] to initiate a violent revolution whenever the propitious occasion appeared. . . .

The obvious purpose of the statute is to protect existing Government, not from change by peaceable, lawful and constitutional means, but from change by violence, revolution and terrorism. That it is within the *power* of the Congress to protect the Government of the United States from armed rebellion is a proposition which requires little discussion. Whatever theoretical merit there may be to the argument that there is a "right" to rebellion against dictatorial governments is without force where the existing structure of the government provides for peaceful and orderly change. We reject any principle of governmental helplessness in the face of preparation for revolution, which principle, carried to its logical conclusion, must lead to anarchy. No one could conceive that it is not within the power of Congress to prohibit acts intended to overthrow the Government by force and violence. The question with which we are concerned here is not whether Congress has such *power*, but whether the *means* which it has employed conflict with the First and Fifth Amendments to the Constitution.

[The petitioners attack] the statute on the grounds that by its terms it prohibits academic discussion of the merits of Marxism-Leninism, that it stifles ideas and is contrary to all concepts of a free speech and a free press. [But the] very language of the Smith Act [demonstrates that it] is directed at advocacy, not discussion. Thus, the trial judge properly charged the jury that they could not convict if they found that petitioners did "no more than pursue peaceful studies and discussions or teaching and advocacy in the realm of ideas." [Congress] did not intend to eradicate the free discussion of political theories, to destroy the traditional rights of Americans to discuss and evaluate ideas without fear of governmental sanction. . . .

But although the statute is not directed at the hypothetical cases which petitioners have conjured, its application in this case has resulted in convictions for the teaching and advocacy of the overthrow of the Government by force and violence, which, even though coupled with the intent to accomplish that overthrow, contains an element of speech. For this reason, we must pay special heed to the demands of the First Amendment marking out the boundaries of speech. . . .

The rule we deduce from [the Espionage Act] cases is that where an offense is specified by a statute in nonspeech or nonpress terms, a conviction relying upon speech or press as evidence of violation may be sustained only when the speech or publication created a "clear and present danger" of attempting or accomplishing the prohibited crime. [The] dissents [in those cases] were addressed to the argument of the sufficiency of the evidence. . . .

[In *Gitlow* and *Whitney*, the] legislature had found that a certain kind of speech was, itself, harmful and unlawful. [In such circumstances, the Court held that the test was] whether the statute was "reasonable." [Although] no case subsequent to *Whitney* and *Gitlow* has expressly overruled the majority opinions in those cases, there is little doubt that subsequent opinions have inclined toward the Holmes-Brandeis rationale. . . .

In this case we are [thus] squarely presented with the application of the "clear and present danger" test, and must decide what that phrase imports. We first note that [overthrow] of the Government by force and violence is certainly a substantial enough interest for the Government to limit speech. [If], then, this interest may be protected, the literal problem which is presented is what has been meant by the use of the phrase "clear and present danger." . . .

Obviously, the words cannot mean that before the Government may act, it must wait until the putsch is about to be executed, the plans have been laid and the signal is awaited. If Government is aware that a group aiming at its overthrow is attempting to indoctrinate its members and to commit them to a course whereby they will strike when the leaders feel the circumstances permit, action by the Government is required. The argument that there is no need for Government to concern itself, for Government is strong, it possesses ample powers to put down a rebellion, it may defeat the revolution with ease needs no answer. For that is not the question. Certainly an attempt to overthrow the Government by force, even though doomed from the outset because of inadequate numbers or power of the revolutionists, is a sufficient evil for Congress to prevent. The damage which such attempts create both physically and politically to a nation makes it impossible to measure the validity in terms of the probability of success, or the immediacy of a successful attempt. In the instant case the trial judge charged the jury that they could not convict unless they found that petitioners intended to overthrow the Government "as speedily as circumstances would permit." This does not mean, and could not properly mean, that they would not strike until there was certainty of success. What was meant was that the revolutionists would strike when they thought the time was ripe. We must therefore reject the contention that success or probability of success is the criterion.

The situation with which Justices Holmes and Brandeis were concerned in *Gitlow* was a comparatively isolated event, bearing little relation in their minds to any substantial threat to the safety of the community. . . . They were not confronted with any situation comparable to the instant one — the development of an apparatus designed and dedicated to the overthrow of the Government, in the context of world crisis after crisis.

Chief Judge Learned Hand, writing for the majority below, interpreted the phrase as follows: "In each case [courts] must ask whether the gravity of the 'evil,' discounted by its improbability, justifies such invasion of free speech as is necessary to avoid the danger." [We] adopt this statement of the rule. As articulated by Chief Judge Hand, it is as succinct and inclusive as any other we might devise at this time. It takes into consideration those factors which we deem relevant, and relates their significances. More we cannot expect from words.

Likewise, we are in accord with the court below, which affirmed the trial court's finding that the requisite danger existed. The mere fact that from the period 1945 to 1948 petitioners' activities did not result in an attempt to overthrow the Government by force and violence is of course no answer to the fact that there was a group that was ready to make the attempt. The formation by petitioners of such a highly organized conspiracy, with rigidly disciplined members subject to call when the leaders, these petitioners, felt that the time had come for action, coupled with the inflammable nature of world conditions, similar uprisings in other countries, and the touch-and-go nature of our relations with countries with whom petitioners were in the very least ideologically attuned, convince us that their convictions were justified on this score. And this analysis disposes of the contention that a conspiracy to advocate, as distinguished from the advocacy itself, cannot be constitutionally restrained, because it comprises only the preparation. It is the existence of the conspiracy which creates the danger. . . .

[The defendants argue that the issue of "clear and present danger"] should have been submitted to the jury. [We] do not agree.

When facts are found that establish the violation of a statute, the protection against conviction afforded by the First Amendment is a matter of law. The doctrine that there must be a clear and present danger of a substantive evil that Congress has a right to prevent is a judicial rule to be applied as a matter of law by the courts. The guilt is established by proof of facts. Whether the First Amendment protects the activity which constitutes the violation of the statute must depend upon a judicial determination of the scope of the First Amendment applied to the circumstances of the case. [In] the very case in which the phrase was born, *Schenck*, this Court itself examined the record to find whether the requisite danger appeared, and the issue was not submitted to a jury. And in every later case in which the Court has measured the validity of a statute by the "clear and present danger" test, that determination has been by the court, the question of the danger not being submitted to the jury. . . .

[Affirmed].

Mr. Justice Clark took no part in the consideration or decision of this case.

Mr. Justice Frankfurter, concurring. . . .

The historic antecedents of the First Amendment preclude the notion that its purpose was to give unqualified immunity to every expression that touched on matters within the range of political interest. [The] demands of free speech in a democratic society as well as the interest in national security are better served by candid and informed weighing of the competing interests, within the confines of the judicial process, than by announcing dogmas too inflexible for the non-Euclidian problems to be solved.

But how are competing interests to be assessed? Since they are not subject to quantitative ascertainment, the issue necessarily resolves itself into asking, who is to make the adjustment? — who is to balance the relevant factors and ascertain which interest is in the circumstances to prevail? Full responsibility for the choice cannot be given to the courts. Courts are not representative bodies. They are not designed to be a good reflex of a democratic society. Their judgment is best informed, and therefore most dependable, within narrow limits. Their essential quality is detachment, founded on independence. History teaches that the independence of the judiciary is jeopardized when courts become embroiled in the passions of the day and assume primary responsibility in choosing between competing political, economic and social pressures.

Primary responsibility for adjusting the interests which compete in the situation before us of necessity belongs to the Congress. [We] are to set aside the judgment of those whose duty it is to legislate only if there is no reasonable basis for it. . . .

Unless we are to compromise judicial impartiality and subject these defendants to the risk of an ad hoc judgment influenced by the impregnating atmosphere of the times, the constitutionality of their conviction must be determined by principles established in cases decided in more tranquil periods. If those decisions are to be used as a guide and not as an argument, it is important to view them as a whole and to distrust the easy generalizations to which some of them lend themselves. [After canvassing the entire corpus of the Court's first amendment jurisprudence, Frankfurter set forth the following conclusions]:

First. Free-speech cases are not an exception to the principle that we are not legislators, that direct policy-making is not our province. [In] Gitlow v. New York, we put our respect for the legislative judgment in terms which, if they were accepted here, would make decision easy. [*Gitlow*] has not been expressly overruled. But it would be disingenuous to deny that the dissent in *Gitlow* has been treated with the respect usually accorded to a decision. [It] requires excessive tolerance of the legislative judgment to suppose that the *Gitlow* publication in the circumstances could justify serious concern. In contrast, there is ample justification for a legislative judgment that the conspiracy now before us is a substantial threat to national order and security. . . .

Second. A survey of the relevant decisions indicates that the results which we have reached are on the whole those that would ensue from careful weighing of conflicting interests. . . .

Third. Not every type of speech occupies the same position on the scale of values. [On] any scale of values, [speech advocating the overthrow of the Government by force and violence] ranks low. Throughout our decisions there has recurred a distinction between the statement of an idea which may prompt its hearers to take unlawful action, and advocacy that such action be taken. . . .

These general considerations underlie decision of the case before us. On the one hand is the interest in security. [In] determining whether application of the statute to the defendants is within the constitutional powers of Congress, we [must consider] whatever is relevant to a legislative judgment. [We] may take account of evidence brought forward at this trial and elsewhere, much of which has long been common knowledge, [that] would amply justify a legislature in concluding that recruitment of additional members of the Party would create a substantial danger to national security.

On the other hand is the interest in free speech. The right to exert all governmental powers in aid of maintaining our institutions and resisting their physical overthrow does not include intolerance of opinions and speech that cannot do harm although opposed and perhaps alien to dominant, traditional opinion. [Moreover, a] public interest is not wanting in granting freedom to speak their minds even to those who advocate the overthrow of the Government by force. For, as the evidence in this case abundantly illustrates, coupled with such advocacy is criticism of defects in our society. [We must also recognize that suppressing] advocates of overthrow inevitably will also silence critics who do not advocate overthrow but fear that their criticism may be so construed. [It] is self-delusion to think that we can punish [the defendants] for their advocacy without adding to the risks run by loyal citizens who honestly believe in some of the reforms these defendants advance. It is a sobering fact that in sustaining the convictions before us we can hardly escape restriction on the interchange of ideas. . . .

It is not for us to decide how we would adjust the clash of interests which this case presents were the primary responsibility for reconciling it ours. Congress has determined that the danger created by advocacy of overthrow justifies the ensuing restriction on freedom of speech. [To] make validity of legislation depend on judicial reading of events still in the womb of time [is] to charge the judiciary with duties beyond its equipment. . . .

MR. JUSTICE JACKSON, concurring. . . .

The Communist Party [does] not seek its strength primarily in numbers. Its aim is a relatively small party whose strength is in selected, dedicated, indoctrinated, and rigidly disciplined members. [Through] placements in positions of power it seeks a leverage over society that will make up in power of coercion what it lacks in power of persuasion. [Thus], either by accident or design, the Communist stratagem outwits the anti-anarchist pattern of statute aimed against "overthrow by force and violence" if qualified by the doctrine that only "clear and present danger" of accomplishing that result will sustain the prosecution. . . .

I would save [the clear and present danger standard], unmodified, for application as a "rule of reason" in the kind of case for which it was devised. When the issue is criminality of a hot-headed speech on a street corner, or circulation of a few incendiary pamphlets, or parading by some zealots behind a red flag, or refusal of a handful of school children to salute our flag, it is not beyond the capacity of the judicial process to gather, comprehend, and weigh the necessary materials for decision whether it is a clear and present danger of substantive evil or a harmless letting off of steam. It is not a prophecy, for the danger in such cases has matured by the time of trial or it was never present. The test applies and has meaning where a conviction is sought to be based on a speech or writing which does not directly or explicitly advocate a crime but to which such tendency is sought to be attributed by construction or by implication from external circumstances. The formula in such cases favors freedoms that are vital to our society, and, even if sometimes applied too generously, the consequences cannot be grave. [But] unless we are to hold our government captive in a judge-made verbal trap, we must approach the problem of a well-organized, nation-wide conspiracy, such as I have described, as realistically as our predecessors faced the trivialities that were being prosecuted until they were checked with a rule of reason.

I think reason is lacking for applying that test to this case.

If we must decide that this Act and its application are constitutional only if we are convinced that petitioner's conduct creates a "clear and present danger" of violent overthrow, we must appraise imponderables, including international and national phenomena which baffle the best informed foreign offices and our most experienced politicians. [No] doctrine can be sound whose application requires us to make a prophecy of that sort in the guise of a legal decision. The judicial process simply is not adequate to a trial of such far-flung issues. The answers given would reflect our own political predilections and nothing more.

The authors of the clear and present danger test never applied it to a case like this, nor would I. If applied as it is proposed here, it means that the Communist plotting is protected during its period of incubation; its preliminary stages of organization and preparation are immune from the law; the Government can move only after imminent action is manifest, when it would, of course, be too late.

The highest degree of constitutional protection is due to the individual acting without conspiracy. But even an individual cannot claim that the Constitution protects him in advocating or teaching overthrow of government by force or violence. I should suppose no one would doubt that Congress has power to make such attempted overthrow a crime. But the contention is that one has the constitutional right to work up a public desire and will to do what it is a crime to attempt. I think direct incitement by speech or writing can be made a crime, and I think there can be a conviction without also proving that the odds favored its success by 99 to 1, or some other extremely high ratio. . . .

Of course, it is not always easy to distinguish teaching or advocacy in the sense of incitement from teaching or advocacy in the sense of exposition or explanation. It is a question of fact in each case.

What really is under review here is a conviction of conspiracy, after a trial for conspiracy, on an indictment charging conspiracy, brought under a statute outlawing conspiracy. With due respect to my colleagues, they seem to me to discuss anything under the sun except the law of conspiracy. [The] reasons underlying the doctrine that conspiracy may be a substantive evil in itself, apart from any evil it may threaten, attempt, or accomplish, are peculiarly appropriate to conspiratorial Communism. . . .

I do not suggest that Congress could punish conspiracy to advocate something, the doing of which it may not punish. Advocacy or exposition of the doctrine of communal property ownership, or any political philosophy unassociated with advocacy of its imposition by force or seizure of government by unlawful means could not be reached through conspiracy prosecution. But it is not forbidden to put down force or violence, it is not forbidden to punish its teaching or advocacy, and the end being punishable, there is no doubt of the power to punish conspiracy for the purpose. . . .

Mr. Justice Black, dissenting. . . .

At the outset I want to emphasize what the crime involved in this case is, and what it is not. These petitioners were not charged with an attempt to overthrow the Government. They were not charged with overt acts of any kind designed to overthrow the Government. They were not even charged with saying anything or writing anything designed to overthrow the Government. The charge was that they agreed to assemble and to talk and publish certain ideas at a later date. The indictment is that they conspired to organize the Communist Party and to use speech or newspapers and other publications in the future to teach and advocate the forcible overthrow of the Government. No matter how it is worded, this is a virulent form of prior censorship of speech and press, which I believe the First Amendment forbids. . . .

[The] other opinions in this case show that the only way to affirm these convictions is to repudiate directly or indirectly the established "clear and present danger" rule. This the Court does in a way which greatly restricts the protections afforded by the First Amendment. The opinions for affirmance indicate that the chief reason for jettisoning the rule is the expressed fear that advocacy of Communist doctrine endangers the safety of the Republic. Undoubtedly, a governmental policy of unfettered communication of ideas does entail dangers. To the

Founders of this Nation, however, the benefits derived from free expression were worth the risk. They embodied this philosophy in the First Amendment's command that Congress "shall make no law abridging . . . the freedom of speech, or of the press. . . ." I have always believed that the First Amendment is the keystone of our Government, that the freedoms it guarantees provide the best insurance against destruction of all freedom. . . .

So long as this Court exercises the power of judicial review of legislation, I cannot agree that the First Amendment permits us to sustain laws suppressing freedom of speech and press on the basis of Congress' or our own notions of mere "reasonableness." Such a doctrine waters down the First Amendment so that it amounts to little more than an admonition to Congress. The Amendment as so construed is not likely to protect any but those "safe" or orthodox views which rarely need its protection. . . .

Public opinion being what it now is, few will protest the conviction of these Communist petitioners. There is hope, however, that in calmer times, when present pressures, passions and fears subside, this or some later Court will restore the First Amendment liberties to the high preferred place where they belong in a free society.

MR. JUSTICE DOUGLAS, dissenting.

If this were a case where those who claimed protection under the First Amendment were teaching the techniques of sabotage, the assassination of the President, the filching of documents from public files, the planting of bombs, the art of street warfare, and the like, I would have no doubts. The freedom to speak is not absolute; the teaching of methods of terror and other seditious conduct should be beyond the pale. [This] case was argued as if those were the facts. [But] the fact is that no such evidence was introduced at the trial. . . .

So far as the present record is concerned, what petitioners did was to organize people to teach and themselves teach the Marxist-Leninist doctrine contained chiefly in four books: Stalin, Foundations of Leninism (1924); Marx and Engels, Manifesto of the Communist Party (1848); Lenin, The State and Revolution (1917); History of the Communist Party of the Soviet Union (B.) (1939).

Those books are to Soviet Communism what Mein Kampf was to Nazism. If they are understood, the ugliness of Communism is revealed, its deceit and cunning are exposed, the nature of its activities becomes apparent, and the chances of its success less likely. That is not, of course, the reason why petitioners chose these books for their classrooms. They are fervent Communists to whom these volumes are gospel. They preached the creed with the hope that some day it would be acted upon.

The opinion of the Court does not outlaw these texts nor condemn them to the fire, as the Communists do literature offensive to their creed. But if the books themselves are not outlawed, if they can lawfully remain on library shelves, by what reasoning does their use in a classroom become a crime? It would not be a crime under the Act to introduce these books to a class, though that would be teaching what the creed of violent overthrow of the Government is. The Act, as construed, requires the element of intent — that those who teach the creed believe in it. The crime then depends not on what is taught but on who the teacher is. That is to make freedom of speech turn not on *what is said*, but on the *intent* with which it is said. Once we start down that road we enter territory dangerous to the liberties of every citizen. . . .

Intent, of course, often makes the difference in the law. An act otherwise excusable or carrying minor penalities may grow to an abhorrent thing if the evil intent is present. We deal here, however, not with ordinary acts but with speech, to which the Constitution has given a special sanction. . . .

There comes a time when even speech loses its constitutional immunity. Speech innocuous one year may at another time fan such destructive flames that it must be halted in the interests of the safety of the Republic. That is the meaning of the clear and present danger test. When conditions are so critical that there will be no time to avoid the evil that the speech threatens, it is time to call a halt. Otherwise, free speech which is the strength of the Nation will be the cause of its destruction.

Yet free speech is the rule, not the exception. The restraint to be constitutional must be based on more than fear, on more than passionate opposition against the speech, on more than a revolted dislike for its contents. There must be some immediate injury to society that is likely if speech is allowed. . . .

I had assumed that the question of the clear and present danger, being so critical an issue in the case, would be a matter for submission to the jury. [Yet], whether the question is one for the Court or the jury, there should be evidence of record on the issue. This record, however, contains no evidence whatsoever showing that the acts charged, viz., the teaching of the Soviet theory of revolution with the hope that it will be realized, have created any clear and present danger to the Nation. . . . If we are to take judicial notice of the threat of Communists within the nation, it should not be difficult to conclude that *as a political party* they are of little consequence. [Communism] in the world scene is no bogeyman; but Communism as a political faction or party in this country plainly is. Communism has been so thoroughly exposed in this country that it has been crippled as a political force. Free speech has destroyed it as an effective political party. . . .

How it can be said that there is a clear and present danger that this advocacy will succeed is, therefore, a mystery. [In] America, [the Communists] are miserable merchants of unwanted ideas; their wares remain unsold. The fact that their ideas are abhorrent does not make them powerful. [Thus], if we are to proceed on the basis of judicial notice, it is impossible for me to say that the Communists in this country are so potent or so strategically deployed that they must be suppressed for their speech. . . .

This is my view if we are to act on the basis of judicial notice. But the mere statement of the opposing views indicates how important it is that we know the facts before we act. Neither prejudice nor hate nor senseless fear should be the basis of this solemn act. Free speech — the glory of our system of government — should not be sacrificed on anything less than plain and objective proof of danger that the evil advocated is imminent.

Note: Dennis, *the Communist "Conspiracy," and Some Approaches to First Amendment Methodology*

1. *The charge in* Dennis. As suggested by Justice Black, the charge in *Dennis* was more than a little awkward, for the defendants were charged not with attempting to overthrow the government or with conspiring to overthrow the government but with conspiring to advocate the overthrow of government. Consider

M. Shapiro, Freedom of Speech: The Supreme Court and Judicial Review 63-64 (1966):

> [The charge gives rise to the suspicion that the] prosecution was instituted under the advocacy provisions because there was no sufficient evidence to meet the normal requirements of the criminal law of sedition. [Ironically, then,] the defendants were convicted in an area where they were protected by the supposedly rigorous demands of the First Amendment *precisely because* they could not be convicted in an area under the routine protections of the criminal law.

See also Nathanson, The Communist Trial and the Clear-and-Present-Danger Test, 63 Harv. L. Rev. 1167, 1172-1173 (1950).

2. *Clear and present danger: The Holmes/Brandeis formulation.* Could the Holmes/Brandeis formulation of clear and present danger sensibly be applied in *Dennis?* What "substantive evil" must be clear and present? Actual overthrow? Attempted overthrow? Conspiracy to overthrow? Conspiracy to advocate overthrow? Do you agree with Justice Jackson that the conspiracy itself can constitute the relevant "evil"?

3. *Clear and present danger: the* Dennis *formulation.* Is the *Dennis* version of clear and present danger "simply the remote bad tendency test dressed up in modern style"? Shapiro, supra, at 65. In his concurring opinion in *Whitney*, Brandeis first introduced the "seriousness" element as a means of intensifying the clear and present danger standard. The *Dennis* formulation, however, uses "gravity" to dilute the standard. Is this dilution unreasonable? If government may restrict speech that creates an immediate 70 percent chance of a relatively modest evil (such as persuading a few persons to refuse induction), shouldn't it also be permitted to restrict speech that creates a less immediate 30 percent chance of a very serious evil (such as attempted overthrow of government)? See J. Ely, Democracy and Distrust 108 (1980); Greenawalt, Speech and Crime, 1980 Am. B.F. Res. J. 645, 717.

4. *Balancing.* Is the *Dennis* version of clear and present danger really any different from Frankfurter's balancing? Is it, in effect, nothing more than a "straightforward balancing between the costs and benefits of suppressing the communication, [with] the pretense of a mathematical formula"? Ely, supra, at 108. As a matter of judicial technique, what, if anything, differentiates the Holmes/Brandeis conception of clear and present danger from balancing? Consider the following views:

a. Franz, Is the First Amendment Law?, 51 Calif. L. Rev. 729, 748-749 (1963):

> How is the judge to convert balancing into something that does not merely give him back whatever answer he feeds into it? [Even] if [the judge succeeds] in stating the [competing] interest quantitatively (or thinks he has), they are still interests of different kinds and therefore they can no more be compared quantitatively than sheep can be subtracted from goats. It is literally impossible for him to compare them unless he has some standard independent of both to which they can be referred. What is that standard to be?

b. Mendelson, On the Meaning of the First Amendment: Absolutes in the Balance, 50 Calif. L. Rev. 821, 825-826 (1962):

> We have had too many opinions that hide the inevitable weighing process by pre-

tending that decisions spring full-blown from the Constitution. [Open] balancing compels a judge to take full responsibility for his decisions, and promises a particularized, rational account of how he arrives at them — more particularized and more rational at least than the familiar parade of hallowed abstractions, elastic absolutes, and selective history. Moreover, this approach should make it more difficult for judges to rest on their predispositions without ever subjecting them to the test of [reason]. Above all, the open balancing technique is calculated to leave "the sovereign prerogative of choice" to the people — with the least interference that is compatible with our tradition of judicial review.

c. L. Tribe, American Constitutional Law 583-584 (1978):

If the judicial branch is to protect dissenters from a majority's tyranny, it cannot be satisfied with a process of review that requires a court to assess after each incident a myriad of facts, to guess at the risk created by expressive conduct, and to assign a specific value to the hard-to-measure worth of each particular instance of free expression. [Categorical] rules, by drawing clear lines, are usually less open to manipulation because they leave less room for the prejudices of the factfinder to insinuate themselves into a [decision]. The balancing approach is contrastingly a slippery slope; once an issue is seen as a matter of degree, first amendment protections become especially reliant on the sympathetic administration of the law.

5. *Deference.* One significant difference between the *Dennis* version of clear and present danger, as articulated by Vinson, and balancing, as articulated by Frankfurter, concerns the question of deference to legislative judgment. For a critical appraisal of the notion that deference was appropriate in *Dennis*, see Linde, "Clear and Present Danger" Reexamined, 22 Stan. L. Rev. 1163, 1176-1178 (1970), concluding that in light of the confused legislative history of the Smith Act, and the passage of more than a decade between the enactment of the act and the decision in *Dennis*, it was virtually impossible meaningfully to identify any particular "legislative judgment that would deserve deference for its assessment of the danger from revolutionary speech."

The Court's present position on the deference issue is set out in Landmark Communications, Inc. v. Virginia, 435 U.S. 829 (1978), which held unconstitutional a state statute barring the disclosure of information about confidential proceedings before a Judicial Inquiry and Review Commission. Chief Justice Burger, speaking for the Court, observed that:

Deference to a legislative finding cannot limit judicial inquiry when First Amendment rights are at stake. "[A legislative declaration] does not preclude enquiry into the question whether, at the time and under the circumstances, the conditions existed which are essential to validity under the Federal Constitution." [A] legislature appropriately inquires into and may declare the reasons impelling legislative action but the judicial function commands analysis of whether the specific conduct charged falls within the reach of the statute and if so whether the legislation is consonant with the Constitution. Were it otherwise, the scope of freedom of speech and of the press would be subject to legislative definition and the function of the First Amendment as a check on legislative power would be nullified.

6. *Balancing and absolutes: another look.* At the time of *Dennis*, Justice Black had not yet fully elaborated his view that first amendment rights are "absolute."

On Black's "absolutism," see Koningsberg v. State Bar of California, 366 U.S. 36 (1961); H. Black, A Constitutional Faith (1968); Black, The Bill of Rights, 35 N.Y.U. L. Rev. 865 (1960); Black & Cahn, Justice Black and First Amendment "Absolutes": A Public Interview, 37 N.Y.U. L. Rev. 549 (1962). It is noteworthy that the Black and Frankfurter views derive from a common source — their reaction to the era of economic substantive due process, see Chapter 6, section D, supra. As a consequence, they both distrusted judicial balancing tests. For Black, this led to constitutional literalism and absolutism; for Frankfurter, it led to extreme deference to legislative judgment.

For analysis of the 1960s balancing-absolutism debate, see Frantz, supra; Mendelson, supra; Bickel, The Least Dangerous Branch 93-97 (1962); Emerson, Toward a General Theory of the First Amendment, 72 Yale L.J. 877 (1963); Frantz, The First Amendment in the Balance, 71 Yale L.J. 1424 (1962). Professor Kalven concluded that the "whole balancing 'war' seems [to] have been a fruitless one, generating on the one hand an unnecessary philosophic debate and obscuring on the other, by its large rhetoric, a hard technical free speech issue." Kalven, Upon Rereading Mr. Justice Black on the First Amendment, 14 U.C.L.A. L. Rev. 428, 444 (1962). See also P. Kauper, Civil Liberties and the Constitution 167-171 (1962).

The debate seems now to have subsided, with neither side a victor. The ultimate consequence of the debate may have been acceptance of "definitional balancing" as the primary mode of first amendment jurisprudence. Definitional balancing involves the formulation, through a process of balancing, of a series of independent categorical rules to govern separate problems of first amendment analysis. See Ely, Flag Desecration: A Case Study in the Roles of Categorization and Balancing in First Amendment Analysis, 88 Harv. L. Rev. 1482 (1975); Nimmer, The Right to Speak from *Times* to *Time*: First Amendment Theory Applied to Libel and Misapplied to Privacy, 56 Calif. L. Rev. 935 (1968); Shiffrin, Defamatory Non-Media Speech and First Amendment Methodology, 25 U.C.L.A. L. Rev. 915 (1978); Van Alstyne, A Graphic Review of the Free Speech Clause, 70 Calif. L. Rev. 107 (1982).

7. *The Smith Act from* Dennis *to* Yates. Following *Dennis*, federal authorities initiated Smith Act prosecutions against more than 120 individuals constituting the secondary leadership of the Communist Party. By the time of the Court's 1957 decision in *Yates*, the government had secured convictions in almost all of these prosecutions. See T. Emerson, D. Haber & N. Dorsen, Political and Civil Rights in the United States 127-128 (1967).

Note: Revising the Dennis Approach

1. *Advocacy of doctrine versus advocacy of action.* In Yates v. United States, 354 U.S. 298 (1957), the Court, in a six-to-one decision, overturned the convictions of several members of the Communist Party for conspiracy to violate the Smith Act. Justice Harlan delivered the opinion:

> Petitioners contend that the instructions to the jury were fatally defective in that the trial court refused to charge that in order to convict the jury must find that the advocacy which the defendants conspired to promote was of a kind calculated to "incite" persons to action for the forcible overthrow of the Government. [We are

thus] faced with the question whether the Smith Act prohibits advocacy and teaching of forcible overthrow as an abstract principle, divorced from any effort to instigate action to that end, so long as such advocacy or teaching is engaged in with evil intent. We hold that it does not.

The distinction between advocacy of abstract doctrine and advocacy directed at promoting unlawful action is one that has been consistently recognized in the opinions of this Court, [and] was heavily underscored in [*Gitlow*]. [We] need not, however, decide the issue before us in terms of constitutional compulsion, for our first duty is to construe this statute. In doing so we should not assume that Congress chose to disregard a constitutional danger zone so clearly [marked. Indeed, the] legislative history of the Smith Act [shows that it] was aimed at the advocacy and teaching of concrete action for the forcible overthrow of the Government, and not of principles divorced from action.

The Government's reliance [on] *Dennis* is misplaced. [The] essence of the *Dennis* holding was that indoctrination of a group in preparation for future violent action, as well as exhortation to immediate action, by advocacy found to be directed to "action for the accomplishment" of forcible overthrow, to violence as "a rule of principle of action," and employing "language of incitement" is not constitutionally protected when the group is of sufficient size and cohesiveness, is sufficiently oriented towards action, and other circumstances are such as reasonably to justify the apprehension that action will occur. This is quite a different thing from the view [that] mere doctrinal justification of forcible overthrow, if engaged in with the intent to accomplish overthrow, is punishable per se under the Smith Act. That sort of advocacy, even though uttered with the hope that it may ultimately lead to violent revolution, is too remote from concrete action to be regarded as the kind of indoctrination preparatory to action which was condemned in *Dennis*. [The] essential distinction is that those to whom the advocacy is addressed must be urged to *do* something, now or in the future, rather than merely to *believe* in something.

Emphasizing that "vague references to 'revolutionary' or 'militant' action of an unspecified character" do not constitute advocacy of action, the Court ordered the acquittal of five of the fourteen petitioners on the ground that there was "no adequate evidence in the record" to sustain their convictions on retrial. On remand, the government requested the dismissal of the indictments against the other nine petitioners, conceding that it could not meet the evidentiary standards established in *Yates*.

Justice Black, joined by Justice Douglas, concurred in part and dissented in part. Justice Clark dissented, noting that the Court's distinctions between *Yates* and *Dennis* were too "subtle and difficult to grasp."

What is the basis of Justice Harlan's distinction between advocacy of action and advocacy of belief? Is it premised upon the relative dangerousness of the expression? The relative "value" of the speech?

In Scales v. United States, 367 U.S. 203 (1961), Justice Harlan had an opportunity to clarify the *Yates* distinction. In *Scales* the Court, in a five-to-four decision, upheld a conviction under a provision of the Smith Act prohibiting "knowing membership in any organization which advocates the overthrow of the Government of the United States by force or violence." In his majority opinion, Harlan explained that "*Yates* makes clear what type of evidence is not *in itself* sufficient to show illegal advocacy." Harlan noted that this included the teaching of Marxism-Leninism and the use of Marxist "classics" as textbooks; dissemination of the party's general literature; and statements evidencing a sympathy for the U.S.S.R.

Harlan cautioned, however, that although such evidence is not in itself sufficient to sustain a conviction, it may, in the context of other evidence, "be of value in showing illegal advocacy."

Harlan then observed that *Yates* indicated

> at least two patterns of evidence sufficient to show illegal advocacy: (a) the teaching of forceful overthrow, accompanied by directions as to the type of illegal action which must be taken when the time for revolution is reached; and (b) the teaching of forceful overthrow, accompanied by a contemporary, though legal, course of conduct clearly undertaken for the specific purpose of rendering effective the later illegal activity which is advocated.

Applying these standards, Harlan concluded that there was sufficient evidence in the record in *Scales* "to make a case for the jury on the issue of illegal Party advocacy." See also Noto v. United States, 367 U.S. 290 (1961) (reversing a conviction under the membership provision of the Smith Act because "the evidence of illegal Party advocacy was insufficient"). Scales was the last person convicted under the Smith Act.

2. *Doctrinal evolution?* Consider Gunther, Learned Hand and the Origins of Modern First Amendment Doctrine: Some Fragments of History, 27 Stan. L. Rev. 719, 753 (1975):

> Harlan found a way to curtail prosecutions under the Smith Act even though the constitutionality of the Act had been sustained in *Dennis*. He did it by [reading] the statute in terms of constitutional presuppositions; and he strove to find standards "manageable" by judges and capable of curbing jury discretion. He insisted on strict statutory standards of proof emphasizing the actual speech of the [defendants]. Harlan claimed to be interpreting *Dennis*. In fact, *Yates* and *Scales* represented doctrinal evolution in a new direction.

3. *Association. Scales* and *Noto*, like *Whitney*, posed issues concerning the right of association and the constitutional status of membership. In *Whitney* the Court concluded that mere "knowing" membership was sufficient to remove constitutional protection. In *Scales* Justice Harlan maintained that a "blanket prohibition" of knowing membership in organizations "having both legal and illegal aims" might pose "a real danger that legitimate political expression or association would be impaired." To avoid this danger, Harlan interpreted the Smith Act as making membership unlawful only if the individual was an "active" member and not merely a "nominal, passive, inactive or purely technical" member, with knowledge of the organization's illegal advocacy, and with the "specific intent" to further the organization's illegal ends. Thus, a member could be punished under the act only if he was an "active" member who specifically intended "to bring about the overthrow of government as speedily as circumstances would permit." On the other hand, Harlan concluded that he could "discern no reason why membership, when it constitutes a purposeful form of complicity in a group engaging [in] advocacy [that may constitutionally be forbidden], should receive [constitutional protection]."

Is "specific intent" required by the first amendment? "Active membership"? Assuming that the organization's advocacy could constitutionally be prohibited, is the membership provision of the Smith Act, as construed, constitutional? Consider Justice Douglas, dissenting in *Scales*:

> We legalize today guilt by association, sending a man to prison when he committed no unlawful act. [That] petitioner was an active member [is irrelevant]. None of the activity [such as actively recruiting members and directing a secret school for selected young Party members] constitutes a [crime]. Not one single illegal act is charged to petitioner. That is why the essence of the crime covered by the indictment is merely belief — belief in the proletarian revolution, belief in Communist creed.

Note: The Smith Act in Context — Other Federal Anticommunist Legislation

As noted earlier, in the post–World War II "cold war" era the federal government launched an intensive campaign against the Communist Party and its adherents. Although most facets of this campaign posed doctrinal and analytical problems somewhat distinct from those thus far examined, a brief overview of the relevant legislation and the judicial response is necessary to place the Smith Act prosecutions in proper historical perspective. Through a variety of doctrines and analytical devices, the Court eventually rendered most of the anti-Communist legislation ineffective. Many of the first amendment issues posed by these developments will be examined more fully at later points in these materials.

1. *Labor organizations.* Because of a fear that Communist officers of labor organizations might misuse their influence by calling strikes as a means of disrupting commerce and industry for purely political ends, Congress, in section 9(h) of the Labor-Management Relations Act of 1947, prohibited the National Labor Relations Board from enforcing employee representation rights of any labor union whose officers failed to execute affidavits that they were not members of the Communist Party. In American Communications Association v. Douds, 339 U.S. 382 (1950), the Court held that this provision did not violate the first amendment. See generally Meiklejohn, The First Amendment and Evils That Congress Has a Right to Prevent, 26 Ind. L.J. 477 (1951); Boudin, "Seditious Doctrines" and the "Clear and Present Danger" Rule, 38 Va. L. Rev. 143, 315, 315-324 (1952). In 1959 Congress replaced section 9(h) with section 504 of the Labor-Management Reporting and Disclosure Act, which made it a crime for any member of the Communist Party to serve as an officer or employee of a labor union except in a clerical or custodial capacity. In United States v. Brown, 381 U.S. 437 (1965), the Court held section 504 unconstitutional as a bill of attainder.

2. *The Subversive Activities Control Act: registration.* The Subversive Activities Control Act of 1950 (title I of the Internal Security Act) created a complex regulatory scheme requiring all "Communist-action organizations" to register with the Attorney General and to disclose a wide range of information, including membership lists. The act also established the Subversive Activities Control Board to administer the scheme and provided that once a board order to register became final, various sanctions would automatically be imposed on the organization and its members. The act was premised on congressional findings that the Communist movement in the United States was part of a "world Communist movement" committed to the "overthrow of the Government of the United States by force

and violence" and that the "Communist organization in the United States," combined with "the recent successes of Communist methods in other countries, and the nature and control of the world Communist movement itself, present a clear and present danger to the security of the United States."

Shortly after the act became effective, the Communist Party challenged the board's authority to order it to register. After a decade of litigation, the Court held that the order to register did not violate the party's rights under the first amendment. See Communist Party v. Subversive Activities Control Board, 367 U.S. 1 (1961). Thereafter, the Board's order that the Communist Party register became final. The party and its individual members refused to comply, however, claiming that the registration requirement violated the privilege against compelled self-incrimination, an issue left unresolved in Communist Party v. SACB for reasons of "prematurity." In Albertson v. Subversive Activities Control Board, 382 U.S. 70 (1965), the Court, noting that admission of party membership could be used in subsequent prosecutions under the membership provisions of the Smith Act, accepted the party's argument and held the registration requirement invalid. See also Communist Party v. United States, 331 F.2d 807 (D.C. Cir. 1963), cert. denied, 377 U.S. 968 (1964). As a consequence of Albertson, the registration provisions were repealed in 1968.

3. *The Subversive Activities Control Act: sanctions.* Although the Communist Party never registered under the 1950 act, a final board order to register automatically triggered various sanctions even in the absence of actual registration. Section 6, for example, prohibited any member of a "Communist-action organization" with "knowledge or notice" that a registration order had become final to use a passport. In Aptheker v. Secretary of State, 378 U.S. 500 (1964), the Court held section 6 unconstitutional as a violation of the right to travel. On the constitutional right of foreign travel, see Zemel v. Rusk, 381 U.S. 1 (1965); Haig v. Agee, 453 U.S. 280 (1981). Another provision of the act prohibited any member of a "Communist-action organization" with "knowledge or notice" that a registration order had become final to engage "in any employment in any defense facility." In United States v. Robel, 389 U.S. 258 (1967), the Court held this provision unconstitutional as a violation of the first amendment right of association. See generally, Gunther, Reflections on *Robel*, 20 Stan. L. Rev. 1140 (1968).

4. *The Communist Control Act.* The Communist Control Act of 1954, 50 U.S.C. §§841-844, purported to "outlaw" the Communist Party and declared that the party is "not entitled to any of the rights, privileges, and immunities attendant upon legal bodies created under the jurisdiction of the laws of the United States or any political subdivision thereof." The act has been only sporadically enforced, and the Supreme Court has not had occasion to rule on its constitutionality. See generally Auerbach, The Communist Control Act of 1954: A Proposed Legal-Political Theory of Free Speech, 23 U. Chi. L. Rev. 173 (1956); cf. Communist Party v. Catherwood, 367 U.S. 389 (1961) (construing the act narrowly to avoid constitutional questions).

5. *Other antisubversive programs.* Both the state and federal governments created extensive loyalty programs for government employees, and at both the state and federal levels legislative committees were used extensively to investigate Communist "infiltration." See generally E. Brown, Loyalty and Security (1958); T. Emerson, D. Haber & N. Dorsen, Political and Civil Rights in the United States 337-511 (1967). These programs generated considerable litigation. See infra

sections F3c, F5. There were also efforts to prevent the importation of Communist doctrine from abroad. See Lamont v. Postmaster General, 381 U.S. 301 (1965) (invalidating restrictions on the mailing of foreign "communist political propaganda"); Kleindienst v. Mandel, 408 U.S. 753 (1972) (upholding a provision of the Internal Security Act of 1950 declaring foreign Communists ineligible to obtain visas to visit the United States). Finally, on the FBI's anti-Communist activities and its development of a program designed extralegally to "expose, disrupt, and otherwise neutralize" the domestic Communist movement, see generally F. Donner, The Age of Surveillance (1980); A. Theoharis, Spying on Americans (1978).

Note: *The Road to* Brandenburg

A dominant theme of Justice Harlan's opinion in *Yates* was that the Court had historically recognized an "essential distinction" between express advocacy of unlawful action, on the one hand, and advocacy of abstract doctrine or general discussion of policies and ideas, on the other. If the Court tests restrictions on express advocacy of unlawful action with the *Dennis* version of clear and present danger, what standard should it use to test restrictions on advocacy of abstract doctrine or general discussion of policies and ideas? In reflecting on *Yates*, consider also the Court's post-*Yates* decisions in *Kingsley Pictures, Bond,* and *Watts.*

1. *Advocacy of immorality.* In Kingsley International Pictures Corp. v. Regents of New York, 360 U.S. 684 (1959), the Court held unconstitutional a New York statute prohibiting the issuance of a license to exhibit nonobscene motion pictures that "portray 'acts of sexual immorality [as] desirable, acceptable, or proper patterns of behavior.'" The state applied the statute to deny a license to the film Lady Chatterley's Lover because its "theme" was that adultery was "proper behavior."

Speaking for the Court, Justice Stewart observed that the state was attempting "to prevent the exhibition of a motion picture because that picture advocates an idea — that adultery under certain circumstances may be proper behavior. Yet the First Amendment's basic guarantee is of freedom to advocate ideas. The state, quite simply, has thus struck at the heart of constitutionally protected liberty." In response to the State's argument that its "action was justified because the motion picture attractively portrays a relationship which is contrary to [the] legal code of its citizenry," Stewart maintained that the state "misconceives what it is that the Constitution protects." The first amendment, he declared, "protects advocacy of the opinion that adultery may sometimes be proper, no less than advocacy of socialism or the single tax." Indeed, Stewart explained,

> advocacy of conduct proscribed by law is not, as Mr. Justice Brandeis long ago pointed out, "a justification for denying free speech where the advocacy falls short of incitement and there is nothing to indicate that the advocacy would be immediately acted on." ["Among] free men, the deterrents ordinarily to be applied to prevent crime are education and punishment for violations of the law, not abridgement of the rights of free speech. . . ." [Citing Brandeis's *Whitney* concurrence.]

2. *Support for war resisters.* In Bond v. Floyd, 385 U.S. 116 (1966), the Court held that the Georgia House of Representatives could not constitutionally refuse

to seat Julian Bond, a duly elected representative, because of his statements, and statements to which he subscribed, criticizing the policy of the federal government in Vietnam and the operation of the selective service system. Four days before Bond was scheduled to be sworn in, the Student Nonviolent Coordinating Committee, a civil rights organization of which Bond was the communications director, issued a statement declaring its "opposition to United States' involvement in Viet Nam." The statement maintained that "the United States government has been deceptive in its claims of concern for freedom of the Vietnamese people," that it "has never guaranteed the freedom of oppressed citizens, and is not yet truly determined to end the rule of terror and oppression [of blacks] within its own borders," and that its "cry of 'preserve freedom in the world' is a hypocritical mask behind which it squashes liberation movements." The statement concluded by announcing: "We are in sympathy with, and support, the men in this country who are unwilling to respond to a military draft [and] believe that work in the civil rights movement and with other human relations organizations is a valid alternative to the draft."

On the day that this statement was issued, Bond announced that although he had not participated in its drafting, he "endorsed" the statement. He said: "I'm against all war. I'm against that war in particular, and I don't think people ought to participate in it. Because I'm against war, I'm against the draft." Thereafter, at a hearing before a committee of the Georgia House of Representatives to determine whether Bond should be permitted to take the oath of office, Bond stated that he concurred in the SNCC statement "without reservation," but explained: "I have never suggested or counseled or advocated that any one other person burn their draft card. [I] do not advocate that people should break laws. What I simply try to say was that I admired the courage of someone who could act on his convictions knowing that he faces pretty stiff consequences."

During the course of his opinion for a unanimous Court, Chief Justice Warren observed that "Bond could not have been constitutionally convicted under [the federal statute] which punishes any person who 'counsels, aids, or abets another to refuse or evade registration.'" Warren explained that, although the SNCC statement expressed sympathy with, and support for, those who refused to respond to a military draft, that statement "alone cannot be interpreted as a call to unlawful refusal to be drafted." Moreover, Warren continued, Bond's statements at the hearing tended "to resolve the opaqueness in favor of legal alternatives to the draft" and did "not demonstrate any incitement to violation of law." Warren thus concluded that "Bond could not have been convicted for these statements consistently with the First Amendment. [Citing *Yates*.]"

Compare the expression in *Bond* with that in *Schenck*, *Frohwerk*, and *Debs*. Do you agree that "the distance traversed in first amendment interpretation is quite apparent"? Emerson, Freedom of Expression in Wartime, 116 U. Pa. L. Rev. 975 (1968).

3. *Hyperbole*. In Watts v. United States, 394 U.S. 705 (1969), petitioner, during a public rally at the Washington Monument, stated to a small group of persons: "I have already received my draft classification as 1-A and I have got to go for my physical this Monday coming. I am not going. If they ever make me carry a rifle the first man I want to get in my sights is L.B.J. [They] are not going to make me kill my black brothers." For this remark, petitioner was convicted of violating a 1917 federal statute prohibiting any person "knowingly and wilfully [to make] any

threat to take the life of or to inflict bodily harm upon the President of the United States." Although conceding that the statute was constitutional "on its face," the Court, in a per curiam opinion, reversed the conviction on the ground that "the kind of political hyperbole indulged in by petitioner" did not constitute a "threat" within the meaning of the statute. The statute, the Court insisted, must be interpreted "'against the background of a profound national commitment to the principle that debate on public issues should be uninhibited, robust, and wide-open, and that it may well include vehement, caustic, and sometimes unpleas-antly sharp attacks on government and public officials.'" Petitioner's "only offense," the Court concluded, "was 'a kind of very crude offensive method of stating a political opposition to the President.'"

Does *Watts* turn on petitioner's expression, his dangerousness, or his intent? How does the distinction between express advocacy of unlawful action and other forms of advocacy apply to *threats?*

Brandenburg v. Ohio

395 U.S. 444 (1969)

PER CURIAM.

The appellant, a leader of a Ku Klux Klan group, was convicted under the Ohio Criminal Syndicalism statute of "advocat[ing] . . . the duty, necessity, or propri-ety of crime, sabotage, violence, or unlawful methods of terrorism as a means of accomplishing industrial or political reform" and of "voluntarily assembl[ing] with any society, group or assemblage or persons formed to teach or advocate the doctrines of criminal syndicalism." He was fined $1,000 and sentenced to one to 10 years' imprisonment. . . .

The record shows that a man, identified at trial as the appellant, telephoned an announcer-reporter on the staff of a Cincinnati television station and invited him to come to a Ku Klux Klan "rally" to be held at a farm in Hamilton County. With the cooperation of the organizers, the reporter and a cameraman attended the meeting and filmed the events. Portions of the films were later broadcast on the local station and on a national network.

The prosecution's case rested on the films and on testimony identifying the appellant as the person who communicated with the reporter and who spoke at the rally. The State also introduced into evidence several articles appearing in the film, including a pistol, a rifle, a shotgun, ammunition, a Bible, and a red hood worn by the speaker in the films.

One film showed 12 hooded figures, some of whom carried firearms. They were gathered around a large wooden cross, which they burned. No one was present other than the participants and the newsman who made the film. Most of the words uttered during the scene were incomprehensible when the film was pro-jected, but scattered phrases could be understood that were derogatory of Ne-groes and, in one instance, of Jews. Another scene on the same film showed the appellant, in Klan regalia, making a speech. The speech, in full, was as follows:

> This is an organizers' meeting. We have had quite a few members here today which are — we have hundreds, hundreds of members throughout the State of Ohio. I can quote from a newspaper clipping from the Columbus Ohio Dispatch,

five weeks ago Sunday morning. The Klan has more members in the State of Ohio than does any other organization. We're not a revengent organization, but if our President, our Congress, our Supreme Court, continues to suppress the white, Caucasian race, it's possible that there might have to be some revengence taken.

We are marching on Congress July the Fourth, four hundred thousand strong. From there we are dividing into two groups, one group to march on St. Augustine, Florida, the other group to march into Mississippi. Thank you.

The second film showed six hooded figures one of whom, later identified as the appellant, repeated a speech very similar to that recorded on the first film. The reference to the possibility of "revengence" was omitted, and one sentence was added: "Personally, I believe the nigger should be returned to Africa, the Jew returned to Israel." Though some of the figures in the films carried weapons, the speaker did not.

The Ohio Criminal Syndicalism Statute was enacted in 1919. From 1917 to 1920, identical or quite similar laws were adopted by 20 States and two territories. . . . In 1927, this Court sustained the constitutionality of California's Criminal Syndicalism Act, [the] text of which is quite similar to that of the laws of Ohio. [Whitney.] The Court upheld the statute on the ground that, without more, "advocating violent means to effect political and economic change involves such danger to the security of the State that the State may outlaw it. [But] Whitney has been thoroughly discredited by later decisions. See [Dennis.] These later decisions have fashioned the principle that the constitutional guarantees of free speech and free press do not permit a State to forbid or proscribe advocacy of the use of force or of law violation except where such advocacy is directed to inciting or producing imminent lawless action and is likely to incite or produce such action.[1] As we said in [Noto], "the mere abstract teaching [of] the moral propriety or even moral necessity for a resort to force and violence, is not the same as preparing a group for violent action and steeling it to such action." See also [Herndon; Bond]. A statute which fails to draw this distinction impermissibly intrudes upon the freedoms guaranteed by the First and Fourteenth Amendments. It sweeps within its condemnation speech which our Constitution has immunized from governmental control. Cf. [Yates; DeJonge]. . . .

Measured by this test, Ohio's Criminal Syndicalism Act cannot be sustained. [Neither] the indictment nor the trial judge's instructions to the jury in any way refined the statue's bald definition of the crime in terms of mere advocacy not distinguished from incitement to imminent lawless action.

Accordingly, we are here confronted with a statute which, by its own words and as applied, purports to punish mere advocacy and to forbid, on pain of criminal punishment, assembly with others merely to advocate the described type of action. Such a statute falls within the condemnation of the First and Fourteenth Amendments. The contrary teaching of [Whitney] cannot be supported, and that decision is therefore overruled.

Reversed.

---

1. It was on the theory that the Smith Act [embodied] such a principle and that it had been applied only in conformity with it that this Court sustained the Act's constitutionality. [Dennis.] That this was the basis for Dennis was emphasized in [Yates], in which the Court overturned convictions for advocacy of the forcible overthrow of the Government under the Smith Act, because the trial judge's instructions had allowed convictions for mere advocacy, unrelated to its tendency to produce forcible action.

Mr. Justice Black, concurring.

I agree with the views expressed by Mr. Justice Douglas in his concurring opinion in this case that the "clear and present danger" doctrine should have no place in the interpretation of the First Amendment. I join the Court's opinion, which, as I understand it, simply cites [*Dennis*] but does not indicate any agreement on the Court's part with the "clear and present danger" doctrine on which *Dennis* purported to rely.

Mr. Justice Douglas, concurring. . . .

I see no place in the regime of the First Amendment for any "clear and present danger" test, whether strict and tight as some would make it, or free-wheeling as the Court in *Dennis* rephrased it.

When one reads the opinions closely and sees when and how the "clear and present danger" test has been applied, great misgivings are aroused. First, the threats were often loud but always puny and made serious only by judges so wedded to the status quo that critical analysis made them nervous. Second, the test was so twisted and perverted in *Dennis* as to make the trial of those teachers of Marxism an all-out political trial which was part and parcel of the cold war that has eroded substantial parts of the First Amendment. . . .

The line between what is permissible and not subject to control and what may be made impermissible and subject to regulation is the line between ideas and overt acts.

The example usually given by those who would punish speech is the case of one who falsely shouts fire in a crowded theatre.

This is, however, a classic case where speech is brigaded with action. [They] are indeed inseparable and a prosecution can be launched for the overt acts actually caused. Apart from rare instances of that kind, speech is, I think, immune from prosecution. Certainly there is no constitutional line between advocacy of abstract ideas as in *Yates* and advocacy of political action as in *Scales*. The quality of advocacy turns on the depth of the conviction; and government has no power to invade that sanctuary of belief and conscience.

Note: *The* Brandenburg *Formulation*

1. *The precedents.* Although the Court maintained that the pre-*Brandenburg* "decisions [fashioned] the principle" adopted in *Brandenburg*, *Brandenburg* seems to have gone far beyond settled law. Indeed it has been said that the *Brandenburg* formulation would "have demanded the contrary result in [both] the early Espionage Act cases and the later Communist cases," J. Ely, Democracy and Distrust 115 (1980), and that *Brandenburg* combined "the most [speech] protective ingredients of the *Masses* emphasis with the most useful elements of the clear and present danger heritage" to produce "the most speech-protective standard yet evolved by the Supreme Court." Gunther, Learned Hand and the Origins of Modern First Amendment Doctrine: Some Fragments of History, 27 Stan. L. Rev. 719, 754, 755 (1975).

2. Brandenburg *and speech that does not expressly incite.* Suppose that, during a famine, a speaker angrily asserts "to an excited mob assembled before the house of a corn-dealer" that "corn-dealers are starvers of the poor," thus inflaming the mob to burn down the corn-dealer's house. J. S. Mill, On Liberty ch. 3 (1859).

Does *Brandenburg*, interpreted in the light of *Yates* and *Bond*, accord *absolute* protection to the speaker so long as he does not use express words of incitement?

Does *Brandenburg* suggest as a general first amendment principle that expression is absolutely protected against direct criminal prohibition, regardless of dangerousness and intent, so long as the speech is not of "low" first amendment value?

3. Brandenburg *and express incitement*. Is *Brandenburg* overprotective of express incitement? Does express incitement merit such stringent protection, not because it is "valuable" in itself but because experience teaches that its *suppression* may be costly? See BeVier, The First Amendment and Political Speech: An Inquiry into the Substance and Limits of Principle, 30 Stan. L. Rev. 299 (1978).

Is *Brandenburg* underprotective of express incitement? It has been argued that *Brandenburg* permits "government interference with expression at too early a stage, allowing officials to cut speech off as soon as it shows signs of being effective." Emerson, First Amendment Doctrine and the Burger Court, 68 Calif. L. Rev. 422, 437 (1980). And, of course, Justice Douglas maintained in his *Brandenburg* concurrence that the critical line should be "the line between ideas and overt acts." See also T. Emerson, The System of Freedom of Expression (1970). Douglas has been criticized, however, on the ground that his treatment of the false shout of fire as "speech [brigaded] with action" undermines his position. Consider Ely, supra, at 109: "[Answers] like ['speech is unprotected because brigaded with action'] are simply not responsible. They refuse to display whatever reasoning in fact underlies the denial of protection, and by their transparent lack of principle substantially attenuate [whatever] value there was in the pronouncement that speech is always protected."

4. Brandenburg *and the pathological perspective*. Consider Blasi, The Pathological Perspective and the First Amendment, 85 Colum. L. Rev. 449, 449-450 (1985):

> [In] fashioning first amendment doctrines, courts ought to adopt what might be termed the pathological perspective. That is, the overriding objective at all times should be to equip the first amendment to do maximum service in those historical periods when intolerance of unorthodox ideas is most prevalent and when governments are most able and most likely to stifle dissent systematically. The first amendment, in other words, should be targeted for the worst of times.

How would you assess the Court's performance in general, and *Brandenburg* in particular, from this perspective?

5. *Subsequent decisions*. The Court has adhered to *Brandenburg* in several subsequent decisions. In Hess v. Indiana, 414 U.S. 105 (1973), for example, the Court reversed the conviction for disorderly conduct of an individual who shouted, "We'll take the fucking street later [or again]," during an antiwar demonstration. In a per curiam opinion, the Court observed that: "At best, [the] statement could be taken as counsel for present moderation; at worst, it amounted to nothing more than advocacy of illegal action at some indefinite future time." Since there was no evidence that the "words were intended to produce, and likely to produce, *imminent* disorder," they could not constitutionally be punished "on the ground that they had 'a "tendency to lead to violence." ' "

In NAACP v. Claiborne Hardware Co., 458 U.S. 886 (1982), the Court considered an NAACP-sponsored boycott of white merchants in Claiborne County, Mississippi. The boycott was designed to secure compliance by civic and business leaders with a list of demands for equality and racial justice. During the course of the boycott, Charles Evers, an NAACP official, stated in a public speech to several hundred people that "If we catch any of you going in any of them racist stores, we're gonna break your damn neck." On the basis of this and similar statements, a state court found that fear of reprisals had caused some black citizens to withhold their patronage from the boycotted businesses. Thus, in an action brought by the white merchants, the state court declared the boycott unlawful and held the organizers liable for all damages resulting therefrom. The Supreme Court reversed:

> In the passionate atmosphere in which the speeches were delivered, they might have been understood as inviting an unlawful form of discipline or, at least, as intending to create a fear of violence whether or not improper discipline was specifically intended. [This] Court has made clear, however, that mere *advocacy* of the use of force or violence does not remove speech from the protection of the First Amendment. [The] emotionally charged rhetoric of Charles Evers' speeches did not transcend the bounds of protected speech set forth in *Brandenburg*. The lengthy addresses generally contained an impassioned plea for black citizens to unify, to support and respect each other, and to realize the political and economic power available to them. In the course of those pleas, strong language was used. If that language had been followed by acts of violence, a substantial question would be presented whether Evers could be held liable for the consequences of that unlawful conduct. In this case, however, [the] acts of violence occurred weeks or months after [the] speech. Strong and effective extemporaneous rhetoric cannot be nicely channeled in purely dulcet phrases. An advocate must be free to stimulate his audience with spontaneous and emotional appeals for unity and action in a common cause. When such appeals do not incite lawless action, they must be regarded as protected speech. To rule otherwise would ignore the "profound national commitment" that "debate on public issues should be uninhibited, robust, and wide-open."

See also Carey v. Population Services International, 431 U.S. 678 (1977) (invalidating a law prohibiting the advertisement or display of contraceptives); Communist Party of Indiana v. Whitcomb, 414 U.S. 441 (1974) (invalidating a state statute that denied a place on the ballot to any new party that failed to file "an affidavit, by its officers, under oath, that it does not advocate the overthrow of local, state or national government by force or violence").

6. Brandenburg: *a test for all seasons?* To what extent is *Brandenburg* applicable to restrictions on subversive advocacy where noncriminal sanctions are imposed or where special institutional settings are involved? See generally Comment, *Brandenburg v. Ohio: A Speech Test for All Seasons?*, 43 U. Chi. L. Rev. 151 (1975). Suppose the government prohibits any person who advocates the violent overthrow of government to teach in a public high school? See infra section F3. Suppose a soldier is court-martialed for urging other soldiers not to fight when they arrive in Vietnam? See infra section F2. Suppose the government requires organizations that advocate violent overthrow to disclose their membership lists? See infra section F5.

2. Criticism of the Judicial Process

The problem of subversive advocacy, though central to the development of a jurisprudence of the first amendment, is but one example of a government effort to suppress speech because the expression of particular ideas or information may conflict with some competing social, individual, or governmental interest. To what extent should the principles that emerged in the subversive advocacy context govern other situations as well? This section explores the problem of criticism of the judicial process.

Bridges v. California
314 U.S. 252 (1941)

[*Bridges* arose out of litigation between two rival unions. While a motion for new trial was pending, Bridges, president of the union against whom the trial judge had ruled, published a copy of a telegram he had sent to the Secretary of Labor describing the judge's decision as "outrageous" and suggesting that if the decision was enforced his union would call a strike that would tie up the port of Los Angeles and involve the entire Pacific Coast. As a result of this publication, Bridges was found guilty of contempt of court. In Times-Mirror Co. v. Superior Court, a companion case, the publisher of the Los Angeles Times was found guilty of contempt for publishing a series of editorials concerning the pending sentencing of two members of a labor union who had previously been convicted of assaulting nonunion truck drivers. The key editorial, entitled Probation for Gorillas?, described the defendants as "thugs" and "gorillas," called upon the trial judge to sentence them to San Quentin, and concluded that the judge would "make a serious mistake if he grants probation to [them]." Bridges and the Times-Mirror Company maintained that the contempt convictions violated their rights of free speech and free press.]

MR. JUSTICE BLACK delivered the opinion of the Court. . . .

[The] "clear and present danger" language of the *Schenck* case has afforded practical guidance in a great variety of cases in which the scope of constitutional protections of freedom of expression was in issue. [What] finally emerges from the "clear and present danger" cases is a working principle that the substantive evil must be extremely serious and the degree of imminence extremely high before utterances can be punished.

We may appropriately begin our discussion of the judgments below by considering how much, as a practical matter, they would affect liberty of expression. [Public] interest is much more likely to be kindled by a controversial event of the day than by a generalization [of] the historian or scientist. Since [the judgments below] punish utterances made during the pendency of a case, [they] produce their restrictive results at the precise time when public interest in the matters discussed would naturally be at its height. . . .

This [threat] is, to be sure, limited in time, terminating as it does upon final disposition of the case. But this does not change its censorial quality. An endless series of moratoria on public discussion, even if each were very short, could hardly be dismissed as an insignificant abridgment of freedom of expression. [We] are [thus] convinced that the judgments below result in a curtailment of expression that cannot be dismissed as insignificant. If they can be justified at all, it must be in terms of some serious substantive evil which they are designed to avert. The substantive evil here [appears] to be double: disrespect for the judiciary; and disorderly and unfair administration of justice. The assumption that respect for the judiciary can be won by shielding judges from published criticism wrongly appraises the character of American public opinion. For [an] enforced silence, however limited, solely in the name of preserving the dignity of the bench, would probably engender resentment, suspicion, and contempt much more than it would enhance respect.

The other evil feared, disorderly and unfair administration of justice, is more plausibly associated with restricting publications which touch upon pending litigation. [Legal] trials are not like elections, to be won through the use of the meeting-hall, the radio, and the newspaper. But we cannot start with the assumption that publications of the kind here involved actually do threaten to change the nature of legal [trials]. [We] must therefore turn to the particular utterances here in question [to] determine to what extent the substantive evil of unfair administration of justice was a likely consequence, and whether the degree of likelihood was sufficient to justify summary punishment. . . .

[Turning first to the Times-Mirror Company, from] the indications in the record of the position taken by the Los Angeles Times on labor controversies in the past, there could have been little doubt of its attitude toward the probation of Shannon and Holmes. [It] is inconceivable that any judge in Los Angeles would expect anything but adverse criticism from it in the event probation were granted. [Hence], this editorial [did] no more than threaten future adverse criticism which was reasonably to be expected anyway in the event of a lenient disposition of the pending case. To regard it [as] in itself of substantial influence upon the course of justice would be to impute to judges a lack of firmness, wisdom, or honor, — which we cannot accept as a major premise.

[With respect to the Bridges situation, let] us assume that the telegram could be construed as an announcement of Bridges' intention to call a strike, something which [neither] the general law of California nor the court's decree prohibited. With an eye on the realities of the situation, we cannot assume that Judge Schmidt was unaware of the possibility of a strike as a consequence of his decision. If he was not intimidated by the facts themselves, we do not believe that the most explicit statement of them could have sidetracked the course of justice. . . .

Reversed.

MR. JUSTICE FRANKFURTER, with whom concurred the CHIEF JUSTICE, MR. JUSTICE ROBERTS and MR. JUSTICE BYRNES, dissenting. . . .

Free speech is not so absolute or irrational a conception as to imply paralysis of the means for effective protection of all the freedoms secured by the Bill of Rights. [In] the cases before us, the claims on behalf of freedom of speech and of the press encounter claims on behalf of liberties no less precious. . . .

A trial is not a "free trade in ideas," nor is the best test of truth in a courtroom "the power of the thought to get itself accepted in the competition of the market." [A] court is a forum with strictly defined limits for discussion. It is circumscribed in the range of its inquiry and in its methods by the Constitution, by laws, and by age-old traditions. . . .

Of course freedom of speech and of the press [should] be employed in comment upon the work of [courts]. But [freedom] of expression can hardly carry implications that nullify the guarantees of impartial trials. . . .

Comment however forthright is one thing. Intimidation with respect to specific matters still in judicial suspense, quite another. [To be punishable, a publication] must refer to a matter under consideration and constitute in effect a threat to its impartial disposition. It must be calculated to create an atmospheric pressure incompatible with rational, impartial adjudication. But to interfere with justice it need not succeed. As with other offenses, the state should be able to proscribe attempts that fail because of the danger that attempts may succeed. [This case thus] tenders precisely the same kind of issues as that to which the "clear and present danger" test gives rise. "It is a question of proximity and degree." [*Schenck.*] . . .

[In the Times-Mirror case], a powerful newspaper admonished a judge, who within a year would have to secure popular approval if he desired continuance in office, that failure to comply with its demands would be "a serious mistake." Clearly, the state court was justified in treating this as a threat to impartial adjudication. [California] should not be denied the right [to] assure its citizens of their constitutional right of a fair trial. Here there was a real and substantial manifestation of an endeavor to exert outside influence. A powerful newspaper brought its full coercive power to bear in demanding a particular sentence. It cannot be denied that even a judge may be affected. . . .

[With respect to Bridges, the] publication of the telegram was regarded by the state supreme court as "a threat that if an attempt was made to enforce the decision, the ports of the entire Pacific Coast would be tied up." [This] occurred immediately after counsel had moved to set aside the judgment which was criticized, so unquestionably there was a threat to litigation obviously alive. It would be inadmissible dogmatism for us to say that in the context of the immediate case [this] could not have dominated the mind of the judge before whom the matter was pending. . . .

Note: Bridges, *Contempt by Publication, and the Subversive Advocacy Analogy*

1. *The subversive advocacy analogy.* Should the principles enunciated in the subversive advocacy context govern the problem of contempt by publication? As in the subversive advocacy context, the government's claim to suppression in *Bridges* turns on the "communicative impact" of expression. That is, in both situations the government seeks to restrict speech on the ground that the *content* of the communication generates some harm that government "has a right to prevent." On the "communicative impact" concept, see Stone, Content Regulation and the First Amendment, 25 Wm. & Mary L. Rev. 189 (1983); Ely, Flag Desecration: A Case Study in the Roles of Categorization and Balancing in First Amendment Analysis, 88 Harv. L. Rev. 1482 (1975); Nimmer, The Meaning of Symbolic Speech under the First Amendment, 21 U.C.L.A. L. Rev. 29 (1973).

There are, however, differences. In the subversive advocacy context, the statutory restrictions, either explicitly, as in *Gitlow* and *Dennis*, or as interpreted and applied, as in the Espionage Act cases, constituted essentially absolute prohibitions on the expression of particular ideas or viewpoints. In practical effect, public criticism of the war or draft during World War I, and public advocacy of the violent overthrow of government from the 1920s to the 1950s, were declared unlawful. Such blanket prohibitions on the expression of particular messages may be of special first amendment concern, for they may seriously distort the thought processes of the community and thus jeopardize the effective operation of the "marketplace of ideas." The restriction at issue in *Bridges*, however, was more modest in scope, for the doctrine of contempt by publication merely "postpones" the expression until the case is no longer pending. Should this reduction in the impact on free speech lead to a less stringent standard of justification?

The subversive advocacy and contempt by publication problems differ in another way as well. As noted by Justice Frankfurter, there exists in *Bridges* a conflict between competing constitutional rights. On the one hand, there is the right of free speech and press; on the other, the "no less precious" due process right of criminal and civil litigants to the fair and impartial administration of justice. Do the policies underlying the clear and present danger standard lose force in the face of such a conflict? Is there an analogous conflict in cases like *Schenck* between the right of free speech and the war power?

2. *Clear and present danger.* Is clear and present danger a workable standard in this context? What factors are relevant? Consider the following: (a) whether the judge must seek reelection; (b) whether the newspaper or speaker is a powerful voice in the community; (c) whether the litigation is still pending; (d) the seriousness of the consequences threatened or predicted by the publication; (e) whether the judge should have anticipated these consequences even in the absence of the publication; (f) the courage and fortitude of the particular judge.

It has been said that "if Bridges' threat to cripple the economy of the entire West Coast did not present danger enough, the lesson of [*Bridges*] must be that almost nothing said outside the courtroom is punishable as contempt." L. Tribe, American Constitutional Law 624 (1978). Do you agree? In two subsequent decisions, the Court, following *Bridges*, overturned convictions for contempt by publication, rejecting arguments that the expression created a clear and present danger of actual or apparent improper influence on judicial behavior. Pennekamp v. Florida, 328 U.S. 331 (1946); Craig v. Harney, 331 U.S. 367 (1947). See also Landmark Communications, Inc. v. Virginia, 435 U.S. 829 (1978); Wood v. Georgia, 370 U.S. 375 (1962).

3. *Incitement and threats.* Did Bridges and the Times-Mirror Co. expressly "incite" the judges to act unlawfully? Did they, as suggested by Frankfurter, "threaten" the judges? If so, should they be protected? Recall Watts v. United States, supra section B1. Consider Greenawalt, Criminal Coercion and Freedom of Speech, 78 Nw. U. L. Rev. 1081, 1093-1095, 1099 (1983): "[T]hreats of action when the [person making the threat] would [not] engage in the action were it not for the threat itself [are] not the sorts of communications covered by freedom of expression. [This is so because] the major social justifications for freedom of expression [are] typically advanced with reference to assertions of fact and value [whereas] the dominant import of [such threats] lies elsewhere."

4. *Picketing near a courthouse: Cox.* In Cox v. Louisiana, 379 U.S. 559 (1965), appellant, an ordained Congregational minister and a field secretary of the Congress of Racial Equality, led a demonstration of approximately 2,000 black students to protest the arrest the previous day of twenty-three black students who had picketed stores that maintained segregated lunch counters. The demonstration took place at the local courthouse, which contained the parish jail in which the twenty-three students were confined. Appellant was convicted of violating a state statute prohibiting any person, "with the intent of interfering with, obstructing, or impeding the administration of justice, or with the intent of influencing any judge, juror, witness, or court officer, in the discharge of his duty [to picket or

parade] in or near a building housing a court of the State of Louisiana." Although overturning the conviction on technical grounds, the Court suggested in dictum that the statute was constitutional both on its face and as applied. Justice Goldberg delivered the opinion of the Court:

> There can be no question that a State has a legitimate interest in protecting its judicial system from the pressures which picketing near a courthouse might create. [Mob] law is the very antithesis of due process. [This statute does not] infringe upon the constitutionally protected rights of free speech and free assembly. [*Bridges* does] not hold to the contrary. [Here] we deal not with the contempt power — a power which is "based on a common law concept of the most general and undefined nature," [but with] a statute narrowly drawn to punish specific [conduct]. [Moreover, we] are not concerned here with such a pure form of expression as newspaper comment or a telegram by a citizen to a public official, [but] with expression mixed [with] conduct. [A] major purpose of [this] demonstration was to protest what the demonstrators considered an "illegal" arrest of 23 students the previous day. While the students had not been arraigned or their trial set for any day certain, they were charged with violation of the law, and the judges responsible for trying them and passing upon the legality of their arrest were then in the building. [The] legislature has the right to recognize the danger that some judges, jurors, and other court officials, will be consciously or unconsciously influenced by demonstrations in or near their courtrooms both prior to and at the time of the trial. A State may also properly protect the judicial process from being misjudged in the minds of the public. Suppose demonstrators paraded and picketed for weeks with signs asking that indictments be dismissed, and that a judge, completely uninfluenced by these demonstrations, dismissed the indictments. A State may protect against the possibility of a conclusion by the public under these circumstances that the judge's action was in part a product of intimidation and did not flow only from the fair and orderly working of the judicial process. . . .
>
> Appellant invokes the clear and present danger doctrine in support of his argument that the statute cannot constitutionally be applied to the conduct involved here. [We] have already pointed out the important differences between the contempt cases and the present one. [But even] assuming the applicability of a general clear and present danger test, it is one thing to conclude that the mere publication of a newspaper editorial or a telegram to a Secretary of Labor, however critical of a court, presents no clear and present danger to the administration of justice and quite another thing to conclude that crowds such as this, demonstrating before a courthouse may not be prohibited by a legislative determination based on experience that such conduct inherently threatens the judicial process.

Does Justice Goldberg satisfactorily reconcile *Cox* and *Bridges*? Note the extraordinarily limited nature of the restriction at issue in *Cox*. The challenged statute limited only a particular means of expression at only a particular location. It thus left speakers free to express the same message by other means or even by the same means at different locations. In such circumstances, is clear and present danger an appropriate standard? Consider Stone, Content Regulation and the First Amendment, 25 Wm. & Mary L. Rev. 189, 217, 225-226 (1983):

> [Some] content-based restrictions so substantially impair the communication of particular ideas, viewpoints, or items of information that, for that reason alone, they are presumptively invalid. [Other content]-based restrictions, [however,] do not *substantially* impair the communication of particular messages. Because these more

modest [restrictions] leave open alternative channels of communication, they do not as dramatically skew the thought process of the community. [There is] reason to doubt, [however], that we can confidently delineate [those] restrictions that do not significantly distort public debate. As history teaches, judicial evaluations of [content]-based restrictions are especially likely to "become involved with the ideological predispositions of those doing the evaluating." [Thus], the safest and most sensible course may be to test *all* [content]-based restrictions by the same stringent standards [of review].

3. Expression That Provokes a Hostile Audience Reaction

This section examines the circumstances, if any, in which government may restrict speech because the ideas expressed might provoke a hostile audience response. To what extent does the first amendment protect the speaker whose expression provokes a "breach of the peace"? Must society tolerate speech that leads to fistfights, riots, or even mob violence? Is there a danger that, in attempting to maintain order, we may invite a "heckler's veto"?

TERMINIELLO v. CHICAGO, 337 U.S. 1 (1949): Terminiello was convicted of disorderly conduct based on a speech he delivered under the following circumstances: "The auditorium was filled to capacity with over eight hundred persons present. [Outside] a crowd of about one thousand persons gathered to protest against the meeting. A cordon of policemen was assigned to maintain order; but they were not able to prevent several disturbances. The crowd outside was angry and turbulent." Members of the crowd threw stink bombs and broke windows. Terminiello goaded his opponents, referring to them as "slimy scum," "snakes," and "bedbugs." In his condemnation of various political and racial groups, Terminiello "followed, with fidelity that [was] more than coincidental, the pattern of European fascist leaders." The Court found it unnecessary to decide the case on its facts. At Terminiello's trial, the jury was instructed that it could convict if it found that his speech included expression that "stirs the public to anger, invites dispute, brings about a condition of unrest, or creates a disturbance." The Court held that this instruction violated the first amendment:

"A function of free speech under our system of government is to invite dispute. It may indeed best serve its high purpose when it induces a condition of unrest, creates dissatisfaction with conditions as they are, or even stirs people to anger. [That] is why freedom of speech, though not absolute, [is] nevertheless protected against censorship or punishment, unless shown likely to produce a clear and present danger of a serious substantive evil that rises far above public inconvenience, annoyance, or unrest."

Terminiello stands for the proposition that speech may not be restricted because the ideas expressed offend the audience. Is that defensible? Because there is no clear and present danger? Because the harm is too insubstantial? Because the justification for suppression is fundamentally at odds with basic first amendment principles? Are no ideas sufficiently offensive to justify suppression on this basis? On the "captive" audience, see section D6, infra.

Cantwell v. Connecticut

310 U.S. 296 (1940)

MR. JUSTICE ROBERTS delivered the opinion of the Court.

[In an effort to proselytize and solicit contributions, Jesse Cantwell, a Jehovah's Witness, played a phonograph record that sharply attacked the Roman Catholic religion to persons he encountered on the street. As a result of these activities, Cantwell was charged by information with various statutory and common law offenses. The fifth count, of concern here, charged commission of the common law offense of inciting a breach of the peace.]

Conviction on the fifth count was not pursuant to a statute evincing a legislative judgment that street discussion of religious affairs, because of its tendency to provoke disorder, should be regulated, or a judgment that the playing of a phonograph on the streets should in the interest of comfort or privacy be limited or prevented. Violation of an Act exhibiting such a legislative judgment and narrowly drawn to prevent the supposed evil, would pose a question differing from that we must here answer.[9] Such a declaration of the State's policy would weigh heavily in any challenge of the law as infringing constitutional limitations. Here, however, the judgment is based on a common law concept of the most general and undefined nature. . . .

The offense known as breach of the peace embraces a great variety of conduct destroying or menacing public order and tranquility. It includes not only violent acts but acts and words likely to produce violence in others. No one would have the hardihood to suggest that the principle of freedom of speech sanctions incitement to riot or that religious liberty connotes the privilege to exhort others to physical attack upon those belonging to another sect. When clear and present danger of riot, disorder, interference with traffic upon the public streets, or other immediate threat to public safety, peace, or order, appears, the power of the State to prevent or punish is obvious. Equally obvious is it that a State may not unduly suppress free communication of views, religious or other, under the guise of conserving desirable conditions. . . .

Having these considerations in mind, we note that Jesse Cantwell, on April 26, 1938, was upon a public street, where he had a right to be, and where he had a right peacefully to impart his views to others. There is no showing that his deportment was noisy, truculent, overbearing or offensive. He requested of two pedestrians permission to play to them a phonograph record. The permission was granted. It is not claimed that he intended to insult or affront the hearers by playing the record. It is plain that he wished only to interest them in his propaganda. The sound of the phonograph is not shown to have disturbed residents of the street, to have drawn a crowd, or to have impeded traffic. Thus far he had invaded no right or interest of the public or of the men accosted.

The record [embodies] a general attack on all organized religious systems as instruments of Satan and injurious to man; it then singles out the Roman Catholic Church for strictures couched in terms which naturally would offend not only persons of that persuasion, but all others who respect the honestly held religious faith of their fellows. The hearers were in fact highly offended. One of them said he felt like hitting Cantwell and the other that he was tempted to throw Cantwell

9. Compare [Gitlow].

off the street. The one who testified he felt like hitting Cantwell said, in answer to the question "Did you do anything else or have any other reaction?" "No, sir, because he said he would take the victrola and he went." . . .

Cantwell's conduct, in the view of the court below, considered apart from the effect of his communication upon his hearers, did not amount to a breach of the peace. One may, however, be guilty of the offense if he commit acts or make statements likely to provoke violence and disturbance of good order, even though no such eventuality be intended. Decisions to this effect are many, but examination discloses that, in practically all, the provocative language which was held to amount to a breach of the peace consisted of profane, indecent, or abusive remarks directed to the person of the hearer.

We find in the instant case no assault or threatening of bodily harm, no truculent bearing, no intentional discourtesy, no personal abuse. On the contrary, we find only an effort to persuade a willing listener to buy a book or to contribute money in the interest of what Cantwell, however misguided others may think him, conceived to be true religion.

In the realm of religious faith, and in that of political belief, sharp differences arise. In both fields the tenets of one man may seem the rankest error to his neighbor. To persuade others to his own point of view, the pleader, as we know, at times, resorts to exaggeration, to vilification of men who have been, or are, prominent in church or state, and even to false statement. But the people of this nation have ordained in the light of history, that, in spite of the probability of excesses and abuses, these liberties are, in the long view, essential to enlightened opinion and right conduct on the part of the citizens of a democracy. . . .

Although the contents of the record not unnaturally aroused animosity, we think that, in the absence of a statute narrowly drawn to define and punish specific conduct as constituting a clear and present danger to a substantial interest of the State, the petitioner's communication, considered in the light of the constitutional guarantees, raised no such clear and present menace to public peace and order as to render him liable to conviction of the common law offense in question. . . .

Reversed.

Note: Cantwell, *the Hostile Audience, and the Subversive Advocacy Analogy*

1. Cantwell. Why would the case have posed a different question had Cantwell been convicted "pursuant to a statute evincing a legislative judgment that street discussion of religious affairs, because of its tendency to provoke disorder, should be regulated"? (Note Justice Roberts's citation of *Gitlow.*) How would the Court, in 1940, have analyzed the constitutionality of Cantwell's conviction had he been convicted under a statute prohibiting the criticism of Roman Catholicism in any public place?

As Justice Roberts observed, Cantwell was not charged with violating a statute prohibiting the playing of phonographs "on the streets" or with disturbing the peace because the "sound of the phonograph [disturbed] residents of the street." Which law is "worse" from the standpoint of the first amendment — one that bans *all* use of phonographs on the streets or one that bans the use of phonographs *only* when used to criticize Roman Catholicism? Which is "worse" — a law that bans the use of phonographs when the *sound* disturbs residents of the street or one that bans phonographs when the *ideas* communicated disturb residents of the street?

Justice Roberts also observed that Cantwell did not intend "to insult or affront the hearers" and did not direct "profane, indecent, or abusive remarks" to them. Could Cantwell have been punished if he had directed "abusive remarks" to the hearers or intended "to insult" them?

Finally, Justice Roberts observed that was there no clear and present danger in *Cantwell*. But isn't it clear that Cantwell would eventually have instigated a fight? Could Cantwell have been punished if he had in fact provoked a fight?

2. *The subversive advocacy analogy.* To what extent should the principles enunciated in the subversive advocacy and criticism of the judicial process contexts govern the problem of the hostile audience? In all three situations, the government's claim to suppression turns on the "communicative impact" of expression — that is, the "harm" is caused by the content of the communication. There are, however, differences.

First, in the subversive advocacy and judicial process contexts, the speech is suppressed because it may successfully persuade the audience to act in an "undesirable" manner, whereas in the hostile audience context the speech is suppressed because the audience may react against the speaker. Which, if either, is more troublesome from the perspective of the first amendment? Is it especially inappropriate to restrict expression because its ideas are persuasive to others? See Scanlon, A Theory of Freedom of Expression, 1 Phil. & Pub. Aff. 204 (1972). Is it especially inappropriate to restrict expression because its ideas are offensive to others? See H. Kalven, The Negro and the First Amendment 140-145 (1965). See generally Stone, Content Regulation and the First Amendment, 25 Wm. & Mary L. Rev. 189, 207-217 (1983).

Second, in the subversive advocacy context, the statutory restrictions, either explicitly, as in *Gitlow* and *Dennis*, or as interpreted and applied, as in the Espionage Act cases, constituted essentially absolute prohibitions on the expression of particular ideas or viewpoints. As illustrated by *Cantwell*, however, restrictions in the hostile audience context, as in the judicial process context, tend to be more modest in scope. They are tied specifically to limited factual circumstances, and although they may in practice make the communication of some messages more difficult, they are not absolute prohibitions, for alternative means of communication are usually available.

Third, in the subversive advocacy context, the statutory restrictions were directed, either explicitly, as in *Gitlow* and *Dennis*, or implicitly, as in the Espionage Act cases, at *specific*, clearly identifiable messages. When laws are explicitly "viewpoint-based," there is a substantial possibility that lawmakers may have been influenced, not only by their concern that the speech might cause unlawful conduct, but also by their conscious or unconscious desire to suppress ideas that they themselves view as false, wrong, or otherwise undesirable. Thus, the highly speech-protective principles developed in the subversive advocacy context may reflect in part a judicial effort to minimize the potential impact of what is considered an "improper" legislative motivation. See Stone, supra, at 227-233; see also Ely, Flag Desecration: A Case Study in the Roles of Categorization and Balancing in First Amendment Analysis, 88 Harv. L. Rev. 1482 (1975); Scanlon, supra.

As illustrated by *Cantwell*, however, the restrictions in the hostile audience context generally do not single out any particular idea for suppression; rather, they prohibit *any* expression that may produce a breach of peace, without regard to the speaker's substantive message. The very breadth of such prohibitions, and their facial content-neutrality, would seem at least to reduce, if not eliminate, the possibility of "improper" motivation. There are, however, other sources of potential "improper" motivation in the hostile audience context. Consider, for example, the hostility of other citizens to the speaker's views. Is the hostility of private citizens analogous to the hostility of government? Is recognition of a "heckler's veto" incompatible with the first amendment because it is, in effect, "improper" motivation in another form? See Kalven, supra; Stone, supra, at 234-239.

Feiner v. New York
340 U.S. 315 (1951)

MR. CHIEF JUSTICE VINSON delivered the opinion of the Court.

Petitioner was convicted of the offense of disorderly conduct. . . .

On the evening of March 8, 1949, petitioner [was] addressing [a street-corner] meeting [in] the City of Syracuse. [The] police received a telephone complaint concerning the meeting, and two officers were detailed to investigate. [They] found a crowd of about seventy-five or eighty people, both Negro and white, filling the sidewalk and spreading out into the street. Petitioner, standing on a large wooden box on the sidewalk, was addressing the crowd through a loud-speaker system attached to an automobile. Although the purpose of his speech was to urge his listeners to attend a meeting to be held that night in the Syracuse Hotel, in its course he was making derogatory remarks concerning President Truman, the American Legion, the Mayor of Syracuse, and other local political officials. [Feiner referred to Truman as a "bum," to the mayor as a "champagne-sipping bum" who "does not speak for the Negro people," and to the American Legion as "a Nazi Gestapo."]

The police officers made no effort to interfere with petitioner's speech, but were first concerned with the effect of the crowd on both pedestrian and vehicular traffic. [The] crowd was restless and there was some pushing, shoving and milling around. . . .

At this time, petitioner was speaking in a "loud, high-pitched voice." He gave the impression that he was endeavoring to arouse the Negro people against the whites, urging that they rise up in arms and fight for equal rights. The statements before such a mixed audience "stirred up a little excitement." Some of the onlookers made remarks to the police about their inability to handle the crowd and at least one threatened violence if the police did not act. There were others who appeared to be favoring petitioner's arguments. Because of the feeling that existed in the crowd both for and against the speaker, the officers finally "stepped in to prevent it from resulting in a fight." One of the officers approached the petitioner, not for the purpose of arresting him, but to get him to break up the crowd. He asked petitioner to get down off the box, but the latter refused to accede to his request and continued talking. The officer waited for a minute and then demanded that he cease talking. Although the officer had thus twice requested petitioner to stop over the course of several minutes, petitioner not only ignored him but continued talking. During all this time, the crowd was pressing closer around petitioner and the officer. Finally, the officer told petitioner he was under arrest and ordered him to get down from the box, reaching up to grab him. Petitioner stepped down, announcing over the microphone that "the law has arrived, and I suppose they will take over now." In all, the officer had asked petitioner to get down off the box three times over a space of four or five minutes. Petitioner had been speaking for over a half hour.

On these facts, petitioner was specifically charged with violation of §722 of the Penal Law of New York, the pertinent part of which is set out in the margin.[1] . . .

We are not faced here with blind condonation by a state court of arbitrary police action. [The] courts below recognized petitioner's right to hold a street meeting at this locality, to make use of loud-speaking equipment in giving his speech, and to make derogatory remarks concerning public officials and the American Legion. They found that the officers in making the arrest were motivated solely by a proper concern for the preservation of order and protection of the general welfare, and that there was no evidence which could lend color to a claim that the acts of the police were a cover for suppression of petitioner's views and opinions. Petitioner was thus neither arrested nor convicted for the making or the content of his speech. Rather, it was the reaction which it actually engendered.

The language of Cantwell v. Connecticut, 310 U.S. 296 (1940), is appropriate here. ". . . When clear and present danger of riot, disorder, interference with traffic upon the public streets, or other immediate threat to public safety, peace, or order, appears, the power of the State to prevent or punish is obvious." . . .

We are well aware that the ordinary murmurings and objections of a hostile audience cannot be allowed to silence a speaker, and also mindful of the possible danger of giving overzealous police officials complete discretion to break up otherwise lawful public meetings. [But] we are not faced here with such a situation. It is one thing to say that the police cannot be used as an instrument for the suppression of unpopular views, and another to say that, when as here the speaker passes the bounds of argument or persuasion and undertakes incitement to riot, they are powerless to prevent a breach of the peace. . . .

Affirmed.*

MR. JUSTICE BLACK, dissenting.

The record before us convinces me that petitioner, a young college student, has been sentenced to the penitentiary for the unpopular views he expressed on matters of public interest while lawfully making a street-corner speech in Syracuse, New York. . . .

The Court's opinion apparently rests on this reasoning: The policeman, under

---

1. "Section 722. Any person who with intent to provoke a breach of the peace, or whereby a breach of the peace may be occasioned, commits any of the following acts shall be deemed to have committed the offense of disorderly conduct:

"1. Uses offensive, disorderly, threatening, abusive or insulting language, conduct or behavior;

"2. Acts in such a manner as to annoy, disturb, interfere with, obstruct, or be offensive to others;

"3. Congregates with others on a public street and refuses to move on when ordered by the police. . . ."

* [A concurring opinion of JUSTICE FRANKFURTER and a dissenting opinion of JUSTICE DOUGLAS, in which JUSTICE MINTON concurred, are omitted. — EDS.]

the circumstances detailed, could reasonably conclude that serious fighting or even riot was imminent; therefore he could stop petitioner's speech to prevent a breach of peace; accordingly, it was "disorderly conduct" for petitioner to continue speaking in disobedience of the officer's request. As to the existence of a dangerous situation on the street corner, it seems far-fetched to suggest that the "facts" show any imminent threat of riot or uncontrollable disorder. It is neither unusual nor unexpected that some people at public street meetings mutter, mill about, push, shove, or disagree, even violently, with the speaker. Indeed, it is rare where controversial topics are discussed that an outdoor crowd does not do some or all of these things. Nor does one isolated threat to assault the speaker forebode disorder. Especially should the danger be discounted where, as here, the person threatening was a man whose wife and two small children accompanied him and who, so far as the record shows, was never close enough to petitioner to carry out the threat.

Moreover, assuming that the "facts" did indicate a critical situation, I reject the implication of the Court's opinion that the police had no obligation to protect petitioner's constitutional right to talk. The police of course have power to prevent breaches of the peace. But if, in the name of preserving order, they ever can interfere with a lawful public speaker, they first must make all reasonable efforts to protect him. Here the policeman did not even pretend to try to protect petitioner. According to the officers' testimony, the crowd was restless but there is no showing of any attempt to quiet it; pedestrians were forced to walk into the street, but there was no effort to clear a path on the sidewalk; one person threatened to assault petitioner but the officers did nothing to discourage this when even a word might have sufficed. Their duty was to protect petitioner's right to talk, even to the extent of arresting the man who threatened to interfere. Instead, they shirked that duty and acted only to suppress the right to speak.

Finally, I cannot agree with the Court's statement that petitioner's disregard of the policeman's unexplained request amounted to such "deliberate defiance" as would justify an arrest or conviction for disorderly conduct. On the contrary, I think that the policeman's action was a "deliberate defiance" of ordinary official duty as well as of the constitutional right of free speech. For at least where time allows, courtesy and explanation of commands are basic elements of good official conduct in a democratic society. Here petitioner was "asked" then "told" then "commanded" [sic] to stop speaking, but a man making a lawful address is certainly not required to be silent merely because an officer directs it. Petitioner was entitled to know why he should cease doing a lawful act. Not once was he told. I understand that people in authoritarian countries must obey arbitrary orders. I had hoped that there was no such duty in the United States. . . .

Note: Feiner, Kunz, *and the Search for Mechanisms of* *Control*

1. Feiner. Is *Feiner* consistent with *Cantwell* because Feiner triggered a clear and present danger? Because he passed "the bounds of argument or persuasion" and undertook "incitement to riot"? In what sense did Feiner "incite to riot"? Does "incitement" mean the same thing here as in the subversive advocacy context?

2. *Police orders.* Note that Feiner, unlike Cantwell, disobeyed a specific police order to stop speaking. What is the appropriate role of the police? Consider the following propositions: (a) The first amendment requires the police to arrest the hostile members of the audience rather than stop the speaker. (b) The first amendment allows the police greater authority to disperse the audience than to order the speaker to stop speaking. (c) The first amendment allows the state greater authority to disperse the audience or order the speaker to stop speaking than to punish the speaker after-the-fact for creating an identical danger when no police were present.

May an individual who refused to obey a police order assert the unconstitutionality of the order in his defense? Consider the following argument: Whatever other remedies may be available to the victim of an unconstitutional order, such as administrative sanctions or civil remedy, an order to stop speaking *must* be obeyed. By analogy to resisting arrest, an order to stop speaking may be challenged by lawful process, but not by disobedience at the scene.

3. *Licensing and the* Kunz *case.* Kunz v. New York, 340 U.S. 290 (1951), decided on the same day as *Feiner,* concerned the constitutionality of a city ordinance declaring it unlawful to hold public worship meetings on the streets without first obtaining a permit from the police commissioner. Kunz, an ordained Baptist minister, was issued a permit in 1946, but the permit was revoked after a hearing at which it was determined that Kunz had ridiculed and denounced other religious beliefs in such a way as to cause disorder. Thereafter, the city denied Kunz's permit applications, and in 1948 he was convicted for holding a meeting without a permit in violation of the ordinance. The Court did not decide whether a permit could constitutionally be denied on the ground that the speaker had previously caused disorder, holding instead that the permit scheme was invalid on its face because it failed to provide clear standards to guide the discretion of the official charged with administering the scheme. On standardless licensing, see infra section C2.

Is a permit system preferable to the mechanism of control approved in *Feiner?* Dissenting in *Kunz,* Justice Jackson compared the two procedures: "Feiner was stopped," he noted, by "the order of patrolmen, put into immediate effect without hearing." Kunz, however, "was advised of charges, given a hearing, confronted by witnesses, and afforded a chance to deny the charges or to confess them and offer to amend his ways. The decision of revocation was made by a detached and responsible administrative official and Kunz could have had the decision reviewed in court." Jackson concluded that "this procedure better protects freedom of speech" than the procedure approved in *Feiner.*

Consider Blasi, Prior Restraints on Demonstrations, 68 Mich. L. Rev. 1481, 1514 (1970):

> [However one deals with an on-going hostile audience], the problem is not so perplexing in the permit application context. Then, the hostile audience is not an actuality but merely a threat. The threat may be largely imagined or imagined by paranoid or hostile city officials; it almost certainly will be exaggerated. Even if accurately gauged, the threat may never materialize, especially if the municipality makes it clear that it will support the demonstrators. [Moreover, the] advance notice gives the city an adequate opportunity to protect the demonstrators — if necessary by requesting the governor to call out the National Guard. [In] contrast to the on-the-spot, uncontrollable emergency, it would seem to be a greater spur to vigilantism

and a greater symbolic defeat for free speech if the legal system were to give in to a threat that *could* be contained, albeit by drastic action.

Consider also T. Emerson, The System of Freedom of Expression 342 (1970): "The ease with which the expression may be curtailed, the pressures to play safe, the speculative basis of the restriction, are all abundantly present when the standard of possible violence is used as grounds for denying a permit."

4. *Injunctions.* Are injunctions against expression a more or less desirable means of dealing with anticipated hostile audiences than permit systems, subsequent punishments, and police orders? In Carroll v. President & Commissioners of Princess Anne, 393 U.S. 175 (1968), the National States Rights Party held a meeting at which they made "aggressively and militantly racist" remarks to a crowd of both whites and blacks. Members of the party announced that the party would hold another rally the following evening. Local officials, however, obtained an ex parte temporary restraining order enjoining the party from holding meetings "which will tend to disturb and endanger the citizens of the County." The Court found it unnecessary to "decide the thorny problem of whether, on the facts of this case, an injunction against the announced rally could be justified," holding instead that the order was unconstitutional because it was unnecessarily issued "without notice to petitioners and without any effort, however informal, to invite or permit their participation in the proceedings." On injunctions against expression, infra section C2.

EDWARDS v. SOUTH CAROLINA, 372 U.S. 229 (1963): Petitioners, 187 black high school and college students, walked to the South Carolina State House grounds, an area open to the general public, to protest discrimination. About thirty law enforcement officers, who had advance knowledge of the demonstration, were present. Petitioners walked in an orderly manner through the grounds carrying placards bearing such messages as "I am proud to be a Negro" and "Down with segregation." A crowd of about 200 to 300 onlookers gathered; although some were identified as "possible trouble makers," there were no threatening remarks, hostile gestures, or offensive comments. There was no significant interference with either vehicular or pedestrian traffic.

After thirty to forty-five minutes, police authorities informed petitioners that they would be arrested if they did not disperse within fifteen minutes. One of the demonstrators then delivered a "religious harangue," inspiring petitioners to sing several patriotic songs while loudly clapping their hands and stamping their feet. After fifteen minutes, petitioners were arrested. They were convicted of the common law crime of breach of the peace.

The Court, in an opinion by Justice Stewart, held that the convictions "infringed the petitioners' constitutionally protected rights of free speech, free assembly, and freedom to petition for redress of their grievances." After making "an independent examination" of the record, the Court found that the "circumstances in this case reflect an exercise of these basic constitutional rights in their most pristine and classic form." *Edwards*, the Court explained, "was a far cry" from *Feiner*. Here, "there was no violence or threat of violence on [the part of the petitioners], or on the part of any member of the crowd watching them." Moreover, "police protection at the scene was at all times sufficient to meet any foreseeable possibility of disorder." In the Court's view, then, petitioners had been convicted because "the opinions which they were peaceably expressing were sufficiently opposed to the views of the majority of the community to attract a crowd and necessitate police protection." The Constitution, however, "does not permit a State to make criminal the peaceful expression of unpopular views." The Court thus concluded that, "as in [*Terminiello*], the Courts of South Carolina have defined a criminal offense so as to permit conviction of the petitioners if their speech 'stirred people to anger, invited public dispute, or brought about a condition of unrest. A conviction resting on any of those grounds may not stand.' "

Justice Clark, the lone dissenter, rejected the Court's distinction of *Feiner*, insisting that the demonstration in *Edwards* "created a much greater danger of riot and disorder." Indeed, in Clark's view, "anyone conversant with the almost spontaneous combustion in some Southern communities in such a situation will agree that the [town officials'] action may well have averted a major catastrophe. [To] say that the police may not intervene until the riot has occurred is like keeping out the doctor until the patient dies." Finally, Clark observed that even if the police were "honestly mistaken as to the imminence of danger, this was certainly a reasonable request [in] an effort to avoid a public brawl. But the response of petitioners and their leaders was defiance rather than cooperation."

In the subversive advocacy context, the Court is concerned, in part, that restrictions on expression may prevent speakers from persuading others to their point of view. This concern has its roots in both the "self-governance" and "search for truth" rationales. But was there really any possibility that the demonstrators in *Edwards* would "persuade" their audience? What theory of free expression supports the protection of speech when the audience is this hostile?

COX v. LOUISIANA, 379 U.S. 536 (1965): Cox, an ordained Congregational minister and a field secretary of the Congress of Racial Equality, led a demonstration of approximately 2,000 black students to protest segregation generally and, more specifically, to protest the arrest the previous day of twenty-three black students who had picketed stores that maintained segregated lunch counters. The demonstration was to take place at the local courthouse, which contained the parish jail in which the twenty-three students were confined. The demonstrators walked to the courthouse in an orderly manner, two or three abreast. As they neared the courthouse, the police chief stopped the procession and inquired as to their purpose. Cox stated that they would sing the national anthem and a freedom song and recite the Lord's Prayer and the pledge of allegiance, and that he would deliver a short speech. The police chief instructed Cox to confine the demonstration to the west side of the street, across the street from the courthouse, 101 feet from its steps. The demonstrators lined up on the west sidewalk about five deep, spread along almost the entire length of the block. A group of about 100 to 300 whites, mostly courthouse personnel, gathered across the street on the steps of the courthouse. Seventy-five to eighty policemen, several members of the fire department, and a fire truck were stationed in the street between the two groups.

The demonstration proceeded according to plan until Cox, in the course of his speech, said: "It's lunch time. Let's go eat. There are twelve stores we are protesting. [These stores won't accept your money at one of their counters.] This is an act of racial discrimination. These stores are open to the public. You are members of the public." These remarks caused some "muttering" and "grumbling" among the white onlookers. The sheriff, deeming Cox's appeal to the students to sit in at the lunch counters to be "inflammatory," ordered the demonstrators to disperse. When Cox and the students ignored the sheriff, the police fired tear gas, causing the demonstrators to flee. The following day, Cox was arrested. He was convicted of breach of the peace, obstructing public passages, and picketing before a courthouse. The conviction for breach of the peace is of primary significance here. For the Court's analyses of the picketing before a courthouse and obstructing public passages convictions, see supra section B2, and infra section E2, respectively.

In a unanimous decision, the Court overturned Cox's conviction for breach of the peace. Justice Goldberg, speaking for the Court, observed at the outset that, as in *Edwards*, the Court was required independently to examine the record. The Court explained that when constitutional rights are at stake, "'we cannot avoid our responsibilities by permitting ourselves to be "completely bound by state court determination of any [essential] issue, [else] federal law could be frustrated by distorted fact finding."'" The Court's examination of the record showed "no conduct which the State had a right to prohibit as a breach of the peace." Cox's call to the students to sit in "obviously did not deprive the demonstration of its protected character." Moreover, the Court rejected the State's contention that the conviction could be sustained because "violence was about to erupt." The demonstrators themselves "were not violent and threatened no violence." Indeed, there was "no indication that the mood of the students was ever hostile, aggressive, or unfriendly." The fear of violence was thus "based upon the reaction of the group of white citizens looking on from across the street." Although there were some "mutterings," there was no evidence "that any member of the white group threatened violence." In any event the police and other personnel present "could have handled the crowd." The Court thus concluded that the facts of *Cox* "are strikingly similar" to *Edwards* and, like *Edwards*, "a far cry" from *Feiner*.

Justices Black, Clark, and White filed separate opinions concurring in the Court's disposition of the breach of the peace conviction.

GREGORY v. CITY OF CHICAGO, 394 U.S. 111 (1969): Gregory led a march of about eighty-five protestors to the home of Chicago Mayor Richard Daley to protest segregation in the city's public schools. The protestors, accompanied by about 100 police, arrived at the mayor's home at 8:00 P.M. and began marching continuously around the block. For the first thirty minutes they sang civil rights songs and chanted slogans criticizing the mayor and referring to him as a "snake." After 8:30, the protestors marched quietly but continued to carry sharply critical placards. In the next hour, the crowd of white onlookers grew rapidly to more than 1,000 and as the evening wore on they became increasingly unruly. In several instances, spectators attempted physically to block the march. There were threatening shouts such as "Get out of here niggers — go back where you belong or we will get you out of here," and rocks and eggs were thrown at the marchers. At about 9:30, the police officer in charge informed Gregory that "the situation was dangerous and becoming riotous" and asked Gregory to lead the marchers out of the area. When Gregory refused, he and the other protestors were arrested. They were thereafter convicted under Chicago's disorderly conduct ordinance, which declared it unlawful for any person to make "any improper noise, riot, disturbance, breach of the peace, or diversion tending to a breach of the peace," or to "collect in bodies or crowds for unlawful purposes [to] the annoyance or disturbance of other persons."

The Court, in an opinion by Chief Justice Warren, unanimously overturned the convictions. The Court announced that "this is a simple case." Noting that "there is no evidence in this record that petitioners' conduct was disorderly," the Court concluded that "convictions so totally devoid of evidentiary support violate due process." (Recall *Fiske.*) Moreover, although the Illinois Supreme Court had construed the ordinance on appeal as authorizing conviction only "where there is an imminent threat of violence, the police have made all reasonable efforts to protect the demonstrators, the police have requested that the demonstration be stopped and explained the request, if there be time, and there is a refusal of the police request," the Court disregarded this narrowing construction because the petitioners had been convicted under a jury instruction that tracked the language of the ordinance itself. Because the jury instruction was cast in terms of the ordinance, it "permitted the jury to convict for acts clearly entitled to First Amendment protection."

In a concurring opinion, Justice Black characterized the ordinance as a "meat-ax" and agreed that it was too broad and too easily subject to administrative manipulation and discriminatory enforcement to withstand constitutional scrutiny. At the same time, however, Black complained that *Gregory* "is a highly important case which requires more detailed consideration than the Court's opinion gives it." *Gregory* demonstrated, Black maintained, that "when groups with diametrically opposed, deepseated views are permitted to air their emotional grievances, side by side, on city streets, tranquility and order cannot be maintained even by the joint efforts of the finest and best officers and of those who desire to be the most law-abiding protestors of their grievances." The Constitution, he argued, does not leave government powerless to deal with such situations or to "protect the public from the kind of boisterous and threatening conduct that disturbs the tranquility of spots selected by the people either for homes, wherein they can escape the hurly-burly of the outside business and political world, or for public and other buildings that require peace and quiet to carry out their functions, such as courts, libraries, schools, and hospitals." What is needed, Black concluded, are "narrowly drawn" laws "designed to regulate certain kinds of conduct such as marching or picketing or demonstrating" so as to restrict "the times or places or manner of carrying on such activities."

Note: Mass Demonstrations and the Hostile Audience

1. "A *far cry*" *from* Feiner? Why are *Edwards* and *Cox* "a far cry" from *Feiner*? Consider the following possibilities: (a) The demonstrators in *Cox* and *Edwards* did not pass "the bounds of argument or persuasion and undertake incitement to riot"; (b) there was less likelihood in *Edwards* and *Cox* of an imminent violent response; (c) the police were better able to handle the situation in *Edwards* and *Cox.*

Should mass demonstrations, which commonly pose greater potential dangers and require a greater diversion of law enforcement resources, be governed by the same standards as relatively "small-scale" confrontations like that in *Feiner?*

Are *Edwards* and *Cox* really "a far cry" from *Feiner*, or do they implicitly limit its precedential force? Do the results in *Edwards*, *Cox*, and *Gregory* suggest that the Court has implicitly embraced a set of principles for dealing with the hostile audience problem analogous to those articulated at approximately the same time for dealing with the problem of subversive advocacy?

2. *Independent examinations of the record and the "no evidence" rule.* "[In] cases raising First Amendment issues," the Court has "repeatedly held that an appellate court has an obligation to 'make an independent examination of the whole record' in order to make sure 'that the judgment does not constitute a forbidden intrusion on the field of free expression.'" Bose Corp. v. Consumers Union of the United States, — U.S. — , 104 S. Ct. 1949 (1984). On "independent examinations" of the record, see Monaghan, Constitutional Fact Review, 85 Colum. L. Rev. 229 (1985); Note, Supreme Court Review of State Findings of Fact in Fourteenth Amendment Cases, 14 Stan. L. Rev. 328 (1962). On the "no evidence" doctrine relied on by the Court in *Gregory*, see Thompson v. Louisville, 362 U.S. 199 (1960); Jackson v. Virginia, 443 U.S. 307 (1979); Blasi, Prior Restraints on Demonstrations, 68 Mich. L. Rev. 1481, 1512-1513 (1970).

3. *"Low" value speech and the hostile audience.* What is "low" value speech in this context? The difficulties of defining "incitement" in cases like *Cantwell*, *Feiner*, *Edwards*, and *Cox* have already been noted. Consider also *Chaplinsky* and the "fighting words" doctrine.

Chaplinsky v. New Hampshire

315 U.S. 568 (1942)

MR. JUSTICE MURPHY delivered the opinion of the Court.

Appellant, a member of the sect known as Jehovah's Witnesses, was convicted in the municipal court of Rochester, New Hampshire, for violation of Chapter 378, §2, of the Public Laws of New Hampshire:

> No person shall address any offensive, derisive or annoying word to any other person who is lawfully in any street or other public place, nor call him by an offensive or derisive name, nor make any noise or exclamation in his presence and hearing with intent to deride, offend or annoy him, or to prevent him from pursuing his lawful business or occupation.

The complaint charged that appellant,

> with force and arms, in a certain public place in said city of Rochester, to wit, on the public sidewalk on the easterly side of Wakefield Street, near unto the entrance of the City Hall, did unlawfully repeat, the words following, addressed to the complainant, that is to say, "You are a God damned racketeer" and "a damned Fascist and the whole government of Rochester are Fascists or agents of Fascists," the same being offensive, derisive and annoying words and names. . . .

There is no substantial dispute over the facts. Chaplinsky was distributing the literature of his sect on the streets of Rochester on a busy Saturday afternoon. Members of the local citizenry complained to the City Marshal, Bowering, that Chaplinsky was denouncing all religion as a "racket." Bowering told them that

Chaplinsky was lawfully engaged, and then warned Chaplinsky that the crowd was getting restless. Some time later, a disturbance occurred and the traffic officer on duty at the busy intersection started with Chaplinsky for the police station, but did not inform him that he was under arrest or that he was going to be arrested. On the way, they encountered Marshal Bowering, who had been advised that a riot was under way and was therefore hurrying to the scene. Bowering repeated his earlier warning to Chaplinsky, who then addressed to Bowering the words set forth in the complaint.

Chaplinsky's version of the affair was slightly different. He testified that, when he met Bowering, he asked him to arrest the ones responsible for the disturbance. In reply, Bowering cursed him and told him to come along. Appellant admitted that he said the words charged in the complaint, with the exception of the name of the Deity.

Over appellant's objection the trial court excluded, as immaterial, testimony relating to appellant's mission "to preach the true facts of the Bible," his treatment at the hands of the crowd, and the alleged neglect of duty on the part of the police. This action was approved by the court below, which held that neither provocation nor the truth of the utterance would constitute a defense to the charge. . . .

Allowing the broadest scope to the language and purpose of the Fourteenth Amendment, it is well understood that the right of free speech is not absolute at all times and under all circumstances. There are certain well-defined and narrowly limited classes of speech, the prevention and punishment of which have never been thought to raise any Constitutional problem. These include the lewd and obscene, the profane, the libelous, and the insulting or "fighting" words — those which by their very utterance inflict injury or tend to incite an immediate breach of the peace. It has been well observed that such utterances are no essential part of any exposition of ideas, and are of such slight social value as a step to truth that any benefit that may be derived from them is clearly outweighed by the social interest in order and morality. "Resort to epithets or personal abuse is not in any proper sense communication of information or opinion safeguarded by the Constitution, and its punishment as a criminal act would raise no question under that instrument." [*Cantwell.*] . . .

On the authority of its earlier decisions, the state court declared that the statute's purpose was to preserve the public peace, no words being "forbidden except such as have a direct tendency to cause acts of violence by the persons to whom, individually, the remark is addressed." It was further said:

> The word "offensive" is not to be defined in terms of what a particular addressee thinks. . . . The test is what men of common intelligence would understand would be words likely to cause an average addressee to fight. . . . The English language has a number of words and expressions which by general consent are "fighting words" when said without a disarming smile. . . . Such words, as ordinary men know, are likely to cause a fight. So are threatening, profane or obscene revilings. Derisive and annoying words can be taken as coming within the purview of the statute as heretofore interpreted only when they have this characteristic of plainly tending to excite the addressee to a breach of the peace. . . . The statute, as construed, does no more than prohibit the face-to-face words plainly likely to cause a breach of the peace by the addressee, words whose speaking constitutes a breach of the peace by the speaker — including "classical fighting words," words in current

use less "classical" but equally likely to cause violence, and other disorderly words, including profanity, obscenity and threats.

We are unable to say that the limited scope of the statute as thus construed contravenes the Constitutional right of free expression. It is a statute narrowly drawn and limited to define and punish specific conduct lying within the domain of state power, the use in a public place of words likely to cause a breach of the peace. . . .

Nor can we say that the application of the statute to the facts disclosed by the record substantially or unreasonably impinges upon the privilege of free speech. Argument is unnecessary to demonstrate that the appellations "damned racketeer" and "damned Fascist" are epithets likely to provoke the average person to retaliation, and thereby cause a breach of the peace.

The refusal of the state court to admit evidence of provocation and evidence bearing on the truth or falsity of the utterances, is open to no Constitutional objection. Whether the facts sought to be proved by such evidence constitute a defense to the charge, or may be shown in mitigation, are questions for the state court to determine. Our function is fulfilled by a determination that the challenged statute, on its face and as applied, does not contravene the Fourteenth Amendment.

Affirmed.

Note: Fighting Words

1. *The two-level theory.* Building on dictum in *Cantwell,* the Court in *Chaplinsky* first fully enunciated what Professor Kalven later termed the "two-level" theory of speech, under which speech is either "protected" or "unprotected" by the first amendment according to the court's assessment of its relative "value." Kalven, The Metaphysics of the Law of Obscenity, 1960 Sup. Ct. Rev. 1, 10. The analytical underpinnings and historical evolution of this theory, and the other varieties of "unprotected" speech mentioned in *Chaplinsky,* such as the "lewd," the "obscene," the "profane," and the "libelous," are examined more fully in section D, infra.

2. *Fighting words as "low" value speech.* Why was Chaplinsky's expression unprotected by the first amendment? Because it consisted of "epithets or personal abuse"? What distinguishes an "epithet" from bona fide criticism? The following arguments might be advanced for the proposition that fighting words are of "low" first amendment value and therefore unprotected:

a. Fighting words are unprotected because, as "epithets or personal abuse," they are intended to inflict harm rather than to communicate ideas and thus are not really "speech" at all. They are "verbal assaults," more akin to a "punch in the mouth" than to constitutionally protected expression of opinion. See Bogen, The Supreme Court's Interpretation of the Guarantee of Freedom of Speech, 35 Md. L. Rev. 555, 575-588 (1976). If Chaplinsky had actually punched Bowering, could he successfully claim that this was merely a constitutionally protected expression of his accurate evaluation of Bowering's performance of his duties? It has been argued that fighting words, even if intended to hurt, are different from actual physical assaults, and that "Chaplinsky's statement was well within the category of criticism of government policy and personnel known as seditious libel." Gard,

Fighting Words as Free Speech, 58 Wash. U. L.Q. 531, 542 (1980). Do you agree? Should Chaplinsky have been permitted to prove the "truth" of his remarks?

b. Fighting words are unprotected because they are "likely to provoke the average person to retaliation, and thereby cause a breach of the peace." The doctrine is thus merely a straightforward application of the Holmes/Brandeis version of clear and present danger. But is name-calling really likely to cause the *average* addressee to fight? Is the focus on the *average* rather than the *actual* addressee consistent with the Holmes/Brandeis formulation?

Even if the speaker creates a clear and present danger, one might argue that the state should punish the violent addressee rather than the speaker. The attractiveness of that alternative may depend on whether one thinks that the addressee's violent response is reasonable. Should that question ever be answered in the affirmative?

Should the fighting words doctrine have any application where the addressee, as in *Chaplinsky*, is an officer of the law, "trained to exercise a higher degree of restraint than the average citizen"? Lewis v. City of New Orleans, 408 U.S. 913 (1972) (Powell, J., concurring). See Gard, supra; Shea, "Don't Bother to Smile When You Call Me That" — Fighting Words and the First Amendment, 63 Ky. L.J. 1 (1975); Rutzick, Offensive Language and the Evolution of First Amendment Protection, 9 Harv. C.R.-C.L. L. Rev. 1 (1974).

c. Fighting words are unprotected because they are "no essential part of any exposition of ideas." Does the Court undervalue the use of personal insults to dramatize one's point? Is the emotive impact worth protecting? Even if fighting words are not "essential" to the exposition of ideas, is this in itself a basis for holding them unprotected? Is it, in conjunction with other factors, a relevant consideration?

3. *Fighting words?* Consider whether the following constitute "fighting words": (1) Cantwell's phonograph record, which charged that Roman Catholicism "has by means of fraud and deception brought untold sorrow and suffering upon the people" and "operates the greatest racket ever employed amongst men and robs the people of their money," when played, as it was, to Roman Catholics. (2) Terminiello's speech, in which he called his opponents, who were outside the hall, "slimy scum," "snakes," and "bedbugs." (3) Kunz's public prayer meetings, in which he labelled Catholicism "a religion of the devil," declared that the Pope is "the anti-Christ," and described Jews as "Christ-killers" and "garbage that [should] have been burnt in the incinerators [of Nazi Germany]." (4) Gregory's repeated references to Mayor Daley as a "snake." Consider also the Court's post-*Chaplinsky* decisions:

a. In Street v. New York, 394 U.S. 576 (1969), Street, a black, on learning that James Meredith, a civil rights leader, had been shot, burned an American flag in public. A small crowd gathered and Street said, "We don't need no damn flag. [If] they let that happen to Meredith we don't need an American flag." The state argued, among other things, that Street could constitutionally be convicted for this speech because of "the possible tendency of [his] words to provoke violent retaliation." The Court disagreed: "Though it is conceivable that some listeners might have been moved to retaliate upon hearing [Street's] disrespectful words, we cannot say that [his] remarks were so inherently inflammatory as to come within that small class of 'fighting words' which are 'likely to provoke the average person to retaliation, and thereby cause a breach of the peace.' [Citing *Chaplinsky.*]"

b. In Cohen v. California, 403 U.S. 15 (1971), Cohen wore a jacket bearing the words "Fuck the Draft" in a corridor of a courthouse. As a consequence, he was convicted under a California statute prohibiting any person "maliciously and willfully [to disturb] the peace or quiet of any neighborhood or person [by] offensive conduct." The state courts interpreted the phrase "offensive conduct" as "behavior which has a tendency to provoke *others* to acts of violence." In overturning the conviction, the Court rejected the state's argument that Cohen's speech constituted fighting words: "While the four-letter word displayed by Cohen in relation to the draft is not uncommonly employed in a personally provocative fashion, in this instance it was clearly not 'directed to the person of the hearer.' [Citing *Cantwell.*] No individual actually or likely to be present could reasonably have regarded the words on appellant's jacket as a direct personal insult."

c. In Gooding v. Wilson, 405 U.S. 518 (1972), Gooding said to a police officer attempting to restore access to an army induction center during an antiwar demonstration, "White son of a bitch, I'll kill you" and "You son of a bitch, I'll choke you to death." He was thereafter convicted under a Georgia statute prohibiting any person to "use to or of another, and in his [presence] opprobrious words or abusive language, tending to cause a breach of the peace." The Court found it unnecessary to decide whether Gooding's speech could constitutionally be punished under a properly drawn statute, holding instead that the Georgia law was overbroad and hence unconstitutional on its face because the state courts had repeatedly interpreted it as reaching clearly protected expression. As examples of this overbreadth, the Court noted that the state courts had failed to construe the statute as "limited in application, as in *Chaplinsky*, to words that 'have a direct tendency to cause acts of violence by the person to whom, individually, the remark is addressed,'" and, further, that the state courts had previously interpreted the statute as authorizing conviction even if, because of surrounding circumstances, the addressee might "'not be able at the time [of the remark] to assault and beat another'" so long as "'it might still tend to cause a breach of the peace at some future time.'" The Court emphasized that this went beyond the fighting words doctrine, which reached only utterances tending "to incite an immediate breach of the peace." On the overbreadth doctrine, see infra section C1.

d. Rosenfeld v. New Jersey, 408 U.S. 901 (1972), Lewis v. New Orleans, 408 U.S. 913 (1972), and Brown v. Oklahoma, 408 U.S. 914 (1972), were decided as companion cases. In *Rosenfeld*, the appellant, in the course of a public school board meeting attended by approximately 150 people, about 40 of whom were children and 25 of whom were women, used the adjective "mother-fucker" on four occasions to describe the teachers, the school board, the town, and the country. In *Lewis*, while the police were engaged in arresting appellant's son, she called them "god-damn-mother-fucker police." In *Brown*, appellant, a member of the Black Panthers, spoke by invitation to a large audience at the University of Tulsa's chapel. During the question and answer period he referred to some police officers as "mother-fucking fascist pig cops" and to one officer in particular as a "black mother-fucking pig." Each appellant was convicted under a state law prohibiting, in varying forms, the use of profanity in public. In each case, the Court summarily vacated the judgment and reversed for reconsideration in light of *Gooding.*

Chief Justice Burger and Justices Blackmun and Rehnquist dissented in all three cases. Burger observed:

> It is barely a century since men in parts of this country carried guns constantly because the law did not afford protection. In that setting, the words used in these cases, if directed toward such an armed civilian, could well have led to death or serious bodily injury. When we undermine the general belief that the law will give protection against fighting words and profane and abusive language such as the utterances involved in these cases, we take steps to return to the law of the jungle.

With respect to *Rosenfeld* in particular, Burger added that "civilized people attending such a meeting with wives and children would not likely have an instantaneous, violent response, but it does not unduly tax the imagination to think that some justifiably outraged parent whose family were exposed to the foul mouthings of the speaker would 'meet him outside' and, either alone or with others, resort to the 19th century's vigorous modes of dealing with such people."

In a series of separate opinions, dissenting in *Rosenfeld* and concurring in *Brown* and *Lewis,* Justice Powell focused primarily on the extent to which the appellants could constitutionally be convicted for "the wilfull use of scurrilous language calculated to offend the sensibilities" of the audience, an issue considered infra in section D6, infra. He did note in passing, however, that Rosenfeld's speech probably did not constitute fighting words because "the good taste and restraint of [his] audience may have made it unlikely that physical violence would result," and because "the offensive words were not directed at a specific individual." In *Lewis* he maintained that if "these words had been addressed by one citizen to another, face-to-face and in a hostile manner, I would have no doubt that they would be 'fighting words,'" but noted further that "the situation may be different where such words are addressed to a police officer trained to exercise a higher degree of restraint than the average citizen."

On remand in *Lewis* the Louisiana Supreme Court again affirmed Lewis's conviction. In so doing, the court construed the statute as prohibiting the use of "obscene or opprobrious words to a police officer while in the actual performance of his duty" because the use of such language "would be unreasonable and basically incompatible with the officer's activities." The Supreme Court reversed, holding that "it is immaterial whether the words appellant used might be punishable under a properly limited statute," for as in *Gooding* the state court failed to limit the law's scope to conform precisely to the fighting words doctrine. Lewis v. New Orleans, 415 U.S. 130 (1974). See also Norwell v. Cincinnati, 414 U.S. 14 (1973) ("fighting words" conviction held unconstitutional); Hess v. Indiana, 414 U.S. 105 (1973) (same).

4. *Fighting words reconsidered.* It has been suggested that the post-*Chaplinsky* decisions establish that the doctrine applies only to the use of insulting and provocative epithets that describe a particular individual and are addressed specifically to that individual in a face-to-face encounter. See Gard, supra. Are these limitations defensible? Should the doctrine apply when an insult descriptive of a group is directed to an individual member of that group? Are insults descriptive of

a group less likely to provoke a violent response? Are they, because of their generality, more likely to be of "high" first amendment value?

The Court has not upheld a conviction on the basis of the fighting words doctrine since *Chaplinsky*. It has been argued that the Court's post-*Chaplinsky* decisions have so narrowed the doctrine as to render it meaningless, and that the doctrine is "nothing more than a quaint remnant of an earlier morality that has no place in a democratic society dedicated to the principle of free expression." Gard, supra, at 536. Do you agree? Or is Chief Justice Burger right that "when we undermine the general belief that the law will give protection against fighting words [we] take steps to return to the law of the jungle"?

Note: *The Skokie Controversy*

In 1977, the Village of Skokie, a northern Chicago suburb, had a population of about 70,000 persons, 40,000 of whom were Jewish. Approximately 5,000 of the Jewish residents were survivors of Nazi concentration camps during World War II. In March of 1977 Frank Collin, leader of the National Socialist Party of America, informed village officials that the party intended to hold a peaceable public assembly in Skokie on May 1 to protest the village's requirement that a $350,000 insurance bond be posted before the village's parks could be used for purposes of assembly. Collin explained that the demonstration would last twenty to thirty minutes and would consist of thirty to fifty demonstrators marching in single file in front of the village hall. The marchers would wear uniforms reminiscent of those worn by members of the Nazi Party in Germany under Hitler, and they would wear swastika emblems or armbands. The marchers would carry a party banner containing a swastika emblem and signs bearing such messages as "White Free Speech" and "Free Speech for the White Man."

Village officials filed suit seeking to enjoin the marchers from wearing their uniforms, displaying the swastika, or distributing or displaying any materials "which incite or promote hatred against persons of Jewish faith or ancestry." The complaint alleged that the march, as planned, was a "deliberate and wilful attempt to exacerbate the sensitivities of the Jewish population in Skokie and to incite racial and religious hatred" and that the display of the swastika in Skokie "constitutes a symbolic assault against large numbers of the residents of the plaintiff village and an incitation to violence and retaliation."

At a hearing before the trial court, the village presented evidence that some fifteen to eighteen Jewish organizations, along with various other anti-Nazi organizations, planned to hold a counterdemonstration to protest the march. Between 12,000 and 15,000 persons were expected to participate in the counterdemonstration. The village also presented evidence that there had already been many threats of violence and that if the party was permitted to demonstrate "an uncontrollably violent situation would develop" and "bloodshed would occur." Finally, the village presented the testimony of a survivor of a Nazi concentration camp to the effect that for him and other survivors "the swastika is a symbol that his closest family was killed by the Nazis, and that the lives of him and his children are not presently safe." The village maintained that the display of the swastika in such circumstances amounted to the intentional infliction of emotional harm. The witness testified further that although he did not "intend to use violence against" the marchers, he did "not know if he [could] control himself." On April 29, the trial judge granted the injunction. The National Socialist Party appealed.

After the issuance of the injunction, the Illinois appellate courts refused to stay the injunction pending appeal, and the Illinois Supreme Court denied a petition for direct, expedited appeal. The party then sought a stay in the Supreme Court of the United States, which treated the petition as a petition for certiorari, granted the writ, and summarily reversed the state court's denial of the stay. In a five-to-four decision, the Court characterized the denial of the stay as a "final judgment for purposes of our jurisdiction" because it

> finally determined the merits of petitioners' claim that the outstanding injunction will deprive them of rights protected by the First Amendment during the period of appellate review which, in the normal course, may take a year or more to complete. If a State seeks to impose a restraint of this kind, it must provide strict procedural safeguards, [including] immediate appellate review. [Absent] such review, the State [must] allow a stay.

On remand, the Illinois appellate court, in July, modified the injunction, so as to enjoin the party only from displaying the swastika. Skokie v. Nationalist Socialist Part of America, 366 N.E.2d 347 (1977). The following January the Illinois Supreme Court held the entire injunction invalid. Skokie v. National Socialist Party of America, 373 N.E.2d 21 (1978).

During the course of the injunction litigation, Skokie enacted a series of ordinances designed to block the march. These ordinances (1) required applicants for parade permits to procure $300,000 in public liability insurance and $50,000 in property damage insurance; (2) prohibited the "dissemination of any material [including signs and clothing of symbolic significance] which promotes and incites hatred against persons by reason of their race, national origin, or religion, and is intended to do so"; and (3) prohibited anyone to demonstrate "on behalf of any political party while wearing a military-style uniform." All three ordinances were held to violate the first amendment. Collin v. Smith, 578 F.2d 1197 (7th Cir. 1978), aff'g 477 F. Supp. 676 (N.D. Ill. 1978). With the march scheduled for June 25, 1978, the village requested the Supreme Court to stay the ruling of the Court of Appeals. The Court denied the stay, Justices Blackmun and Rehnquist dissenting. Smith v. Collin, 436 U.S. 953 (1978).

On June 22 Collin cancelled the march. He explained that he had used the threat of a march in Skokie as a means to win the right to demonstrate in Chicago, a right he had won while the Skokie litigation was proceeding. On July 9, 1978, the party held an hour-long rally in Chicago at which 400 riot-helmeted policemen protected the twenty-five Nazi demonstrators. There were seventy-two arrests and some rock and bottle throwing, but no serious violence.

Consider Bollinger, The Skokie Legacy: Reflections on an "Easy Case" and Free Speech Theory, 80 Mich. L. Rev. 617, 629-631 (1982):

> [The] free speech principle is grounded as much in a desire to avoid being the slaves of our own intolerant impulses as it is in a desire to preserve an unshackled freedom to speak one's mind as one wishes. [From] this perspective upholding a right of free speech in a case like the Skokie case seems to make the most sense. [One] can

understand [the] choice to protect the free speech activities of Nazis, but not because people should value their message in the slightest or believe it should be
seriously entertained, not because a commitment to self-government or rationality
logically demands that such ideas be presented for consideration, not because a line
could not be drawn that would exclude this ideology without inevitably encroaching
on ideas that one likes — not for any of these reasons nor others related to them that
are a part of the traditional baggage of the free speech argumentation; but rather
because the danger of intolerance towards ideas is so pervasive an issue in our social
lives, the process of mastering a capacity for tolerance so difficult, that it makes
sense somewhere in the system to attempt to confront that problem and exercise
more self-restraint than may be otherwise required. [On] this basis, then, tolerance
becomes [a] symbolic act indicating an awareness of the risks and dangers of intolerance and a commitment to developing a certain attitude toward the ideas and beliefs
of others.

4. Expression That Discloses Confidential Information

This section examines government efforts to restrict the publication of factual
information it would prefer to keep secret. The interests potentially furthered by
such secrecy range from the individual's interest in privacy, to the right to a fair
trial, to the rehabilitation of juvenile offenders, to the national security. The clash
between the "right to know" and the need to "keep secret" is central to the first
amendment.

LANDMARK COMMUNICATIONS, INC. v. VIRGINIA, 435 U.S. 829
(1978): The Virginian Pilot, a Landmark newspaper, accurately reported that the
Virginia Judicial Inquiry and Review Commission was contemplating an investigation of a particular state court judge. As a result of this disclosure, Landmark
was convicted of violating a state statute prohibiting any person to divulge information regarding confidential matters pending before the commission. The
Court, in an opinion by Chief Justice Burger, held the statute invalid. The Court
found it unnecessary to decide whether "truthful reporting about public officials
in connection with their public duties is always insulated from the imposition of
criminal sanctions," holding instead that "the publication Virginia seeks to punish
under its statute lies near the core of the First Amendment, and the Commonwealth's interests advanced by the imposition of criminal sanctions are insufficient to justify the actual and potential encroachments on freedom of speech and
of the press which follow therefrom."
   The state argued that disclosure of confidential information about pending
investigations would create a clear and present danger to the effective operation
of the Commission by chilling the willingness of individuals to file complaints and
by subjecting judges and the judicial system generally to unfavorable publicity
arising out of possibly unwarranted charges. Although assuming "for purposes of
decision that confidentiality of Commission proceedings serves legitimate state
interests," the Court emphasized that the question "is whether these interests are
sufficient to justify the encroachment on First Amendment guarantees which the
imposition of criminal sanctions entails." At the outset, the Court questioned
"the relevance of [the clear and present danger] standard here." It explained,
moreover, that "Mr. Justice Holmes' test was never intended" to serve as a doc-

trine of "mechanical application." Rather, "properly applied, the test requires a court to make its own inquiry into the imminence and magnitude of the danger said to flow from the particular utterances and then to balance the character of the evil, as well as its likelihood, against the need for free and unfettered expression. The possibility that other measures will serve the State's interests should also be weighed."

Applying that standard to the facts of *Landmark*, the Court noted that "the Commission has offered little more than assertion and conjecture to support its claim that without criminal sanctions the objectives of the statutory scheme would be seriously undermined." Indeed, referring to *Bridges* and its progeny, the Court announced that "our precedents leave little doubt as to the proper outcome," for "the threat to the administration of justice posed by the speech and publications in [those cases] was, if anything, more direct and substantial than the threat posed by Landmark's article." Moreover, "much of the risk [here] can be eliminated through careful internal procedures," such as prohibiting participants in Commission proceedings from divulging confidential information. Finally, "neither the Commonwealth's interest in protecting the reputation of its judges, nor its interest in maintaining the institutional integrity of its courts is sufficient to justify the subsequent punishment of speech at issue here, even on the assumption that criminal sanctions do in fact enhance the guarantee of confidentiality."

Note: Landmark *and the Problem of Confidentiality*

Note that the Court in *Landmark* "[questioned] the relevance" of the clear and present danger standard. Should clear and present danger apply in this context? Note that Brandeis's "counter-speech" theory loses some of its force when the harm derives from the disclosure of truthful information. Does this suggest that "imminence" no longer matters? Consider also Cox, Foreword: Freedom of Expression in the Burger Court, 94 Harv. L. Rev. 1, 11 (1980): "[The Court's reliance upon the *Bridges* line of authority in *Landmark* ignores] the seemingly material difference between publishing information or commentary upon official business conducted in public and publicizing information that the state has rightfully sought to keep confidential and that has received even limited disclosure only by a criminal act."

Two other aspects of *Landmark* merit attention. First, the Court emphasized that there are other means, such as "internal procedures," to deal with the risk. Should that affect the analysis? Would such "internal procedures" eliminate *entirely* the need for restrictions on the publication of confidential information? Second, the Court focused on the seriousness of the state's interests. Compare the roles played by the gravity element in *Landmark* and *Dennis*. Which is truer to the original Holmes/Brandeis formulation? Consider also the Court's decisions in subsequent cases:

1. In Cox Broadcasting Corp. v. Cohn, 420 U.S. 469 (1975), the Georgia courts recognized a cause of action in tort for "invasion of privacy" arising out of a television station's broadcast of the name of a rape victim. A reporter employed by Cox Broadcasting had learned the victim's name by examining a copy of the indictment. The Court found it unnecessary to "address the broader question whether truthful publications may ever be subjected to civil or criminal liability,"

holding more narrowly that, "once true information is disclosed in public court documents open to public inspection, the press cannot be sanctioned for publishing it" because the publication is "offensive to the sensibilities of the supposed reasonable man." For more on "invasion of privacy," see infra section D3.

2. In Oklahoma Publishing Co. v. District Court, 430 U.S. 308 (1977), several reporters attended a hearing concerning a juvenile proceeding in which an eleven-year-old boy was charged with delinquency by second-degree murder. At this hearing, the reporters learned the boy's identity and took his photograph. Thereafter, several stories using the boy's name and picture appeared in local newspapers. The state court then entered a pretrial order prohibiting any further publication of the boy's name or photograph. The Supreme Court unanimously held the order invalid. Although recognizing that a state law required juvenile proceedings to be held in private "unless specifically ordered by the judge to be conducted in public," and that no such order had expressly been made in this case, the Court emphasized that "members of the press were in fact present at the hearing with the full knowledge of the presiding judge" and that "no objection was made" to their presence. The Court thus concluded that there was "no evidence that [the press] acquired the information unlawfully or even without the State's implicit approval." In such circumstances, "Cox [is] controlling." Whether or not the state could constitutionally have excluded the press from the hearing, "the First and Fourteenth Amendments will not permit a state court to prohibit the publication [of] information obtained at court proceedings which were in fact open to the public."

3. In Smith v. Daily Mail Publishing Co., 443 U.S. 97 (1979), a newspaper, in violation of a state law prohibiting any newspaper to publish the name of a juvenile offender "without a written order of the court," published the name and photograph of a fourteen-year-old who had been arrested for murder. Reporters for the newspaper had learned the suspect's name from several witnesses to the shooting and from police and prosecutors at the scene. The Supreme Court unanimously held the statute invalid, declaring that "if a newspaper lawfully obtains truthful information about a matter of public significance then state officials may not constitutionally punish publication of the information, absent a need to further a state interest of the highest order." Although recognizing that preservation of the anonymity of juvenile offenders may further their rehabilitation, the Court concluded that the "magnitude of [this interest] is not sufficient to justify the application of a criminal penalty to [the publication of such information]."

Note that the Court focused in these decisions on the substantiality of the state's interests rather than on clear and present danger. Does this mark a shift in doctrine? What is "a state interest of the highest order"?

Nebraska Press Association v. Stuart

427 U.S. 539 (1976)

[In anticipation of a trial for a multiple murder that had attracted widespread news coverage, respondent, a Nebraska state trial court judge, entered an order that, as modified by the Nebraska Supreme Court, restrained petitioner newspapers, broadcasters, journalists, news media associations, and national newswire services from publishing or broadcasting accounts of confessions or admissions made by the accused or any other facts "strongly implicative" of the accused. The Court, in a unanimous decision, held the order unconstitutional.]

MR. CHIEF JUSTICE BURGER delivered the opinion of the Court. . . .

The Sixth Amendment in terms guarantees "trial, by an impartial jury . . . " in federal criminal prosecutions. [The] Due Process Clause of the Fourteenth Amendment guarantees the same right in state criminal prosecutions. . . .

In the overwhelming majority of criminal trials, pretrial publicity presents few unmanageable threats to this important right. But when the case is a "sensational" one tensions develop between the right of the accused to trial by an impartial jury and the rights guaranteed others by the First Amendment. . . .

[Chief Justice Burger then examined the Court's decisions concerning the relationship between pretrial publicity and the right of the defendant in a criminal case to a fair and impartial jury. As Burger observed, in some decisions the Court had found the pretrial publicity so extensive as to render the conviction violative of due process, whereas in others the Court had reached the opposite conclusion. Compare Sheppard v. Maxwell, 384 U.S. 333 (1966), with Murphy v. Florida, 421 U.S. 794 (1975).]

Taken together, these cases demonstrate that pretrial publicity — even pervasive, adverse publicity — does not inevitably lead to an unfair trial. The capacity of the jury eventually impaneled to decide the case fairly is influenced by the tone and extent of the publicity, which is in part, and often in large part, shaped by what attorneys, police, and other officials do to precipitate news coverage. The trial judge has a major responsibility. . . .

The state trial judge in the case before us acted responsibly, out of a legitimate concern, in an effort to protect the defendant's right to a fair trial. What we must decide is not simply whether the Nebraska courts erred in seeing the possibility of real danger to the defendant's rights, but whether in the circumstances of this case the means employed were foreclosed by another provision of the Constitution. . . .

The First Amendment provides [special] protection against orders that prohibit the publication or broadcast of particular information or commentary — orders that impose a "previous" or "prior" restraint on speech. . . .

The thread running through [our] cases is that prior restraints on speech and publication are the most serious and the least tolerable infringement on First Amendment rights. A criminal penalty or a judgment in a defamation case is subject to the whole panoply of protections afforded by deferring the impact of the judgment until all avenues of appellate review have been exhausted. Only after judgment has become final, correct or otherwise, does the law's sanction become fully operative.

A prior restraint, by contrast and by definition, has an immediate and irreversible sanction. If it can be said that a threat of criminal or civil sanctions after publication "chills" speech, prior restraint "freezes" it at least for the time.

The damage can be particularly great when the prior restraint falls upon the communication of news and commentary on current events. . . .

Of course, the order at issue [does] not prohibit but only postpones publication. Some news can be delayed and most commentary can even more readily be delayed without serious injury, and there often is a self-imposed delay when responsible editors call for verification of information. But such delays are normally slight and they are self-imposed. Delays imposed by governmental authority are a different matter. [Because "the element of time is not unimportant if press coverage is to fulfill its traditional function of bringing news to the public promptly,"] the burden on the Government is not reduced by the temporary nature of a restraint. . . .

We turn now to the record in this case to determine whether, as Learned Hand put it, "the gravity of the 'evil,' discounted by its improbability, justifies such invasion of free speech as is necessary to avoid the danger." [*Dennis.*] To do so, we must examine the evidence before the trial judge when the order was entered to determine (a) the nature and extent of pretrial news coverage; (b) whether other measures would be likely to mitigate the effects of unrestrained pretrial publicity; and (c) how effectively a restraining order would operate to prevent the threatened danger. [We] must then consider whether the record supports the entry of a prior restraint on publication, one of the most extraordinary remedies known to our jurisprudence. . . .

Our review of the pretrial record persuades us that the trial judge was justified in concluding that there would be intense and pervasive pretrial publicity concerning this case. He could also reasonably conclude, based on common human experience, that publicity might impair the defendant's right to a fair trial. . . .

We find little in the record that goes to another aspect of our task, determining whether measures short of an order restraining all publication would have insured the defendant a fair trial.

[The Chief Justice then mentioned briefly several alternatives to prior restraint of publication that should have been considered by the state courts. These included "change of trial venue to a place less exposed to the intense publicity"; "postponement of the trial to allow public attention to subside"; "searching questioning of prospective jurors [to] screen out those with fixed opinions as to guilt or innocence"; the "use of emphatic and clear instructions on the sworn duty of each juror to decide the issues only on evidence presented in open court"; sequestration of jurors during trial to enhance "the likelihood of dissipating the impact of pretrial publicity"; restricting what the lawyers, the police, and the witnesses may "say to anyone"; and closure "of pretrial proceedings with the consent of the defendant."]

We have noted earlier that pretrial publicity, even if pervasive and concentrated, cannot be regarded as leading automatically and in every kind of criminal case to an unfair trial. . . .

We have therefore examined this record to determine the probable efficacy of the measures short of prior restraint on the press and speech. There is no finding that alternative measures would not have protected [the defendant's] rights, and the Nebraska Supreme Court did no more than imply that such measures might not be adequate. Moreover, the record is lacking in evidence to support such a finding.

We must also assess the probable efficacy of prior restraint on publication as a workable method of protecting [the] right to a fair trial, and we cannot ignore the reality of the problems of managing and enforcing pretrial restraining orders. The territorial jurisdiction of the issuing court is limited by concepts of sovereignty, [and the] need for in personam jurisdiction also presents an obstacle to a restraining order that applies to publication at large as distinguished from restraining publication within a given jurisdiction.

[Moreover,] the events disclosed by the record took place in a community of 850 people. It is reasonable to assume that, without any news accounts being printed or broadcast, rumors would travel swiftly by word of mouth. [Plainly] a whole community cannot be restrained from discussing a subject intimately affecting life within it.

Given these practical problems, it is far from clear that prior restraint on publication would have protected [the defendant's] rights. . . .

Of necessity our holding is confined to the record before us. But our conclusion is not simply a result of assessing the adequacy of the showing made in this case; it results in part from the problems inherent in meeting the heavy burden of demonstrating, in advance of trial, that without prior restraint a fair trial will be denied. The practical problems of managing and enforcing restrictive orders will always be present. In this sense, the record now before us is illustrative rather than exceptional. [But] we need not rule out the possibility of showing the kind of threat to fair trial rights that would possess the requisite degree of certainty to justify restraint. This Court has frequently denied that First Amendment rights are absolute and has consistently rejected the proposition that a prior restraint can never be employed. . . .*

Reversed.

Mr. Justice Brennan, with whom Mr. Justice Stewart and Mr. Justice Marshall join, concurring in the judgment.

[The] right to a fair trial by a jury of one's peers is unquestionably one of the most precious and sacred safeguards enshrined in the Bill of Rights. I would hold, however, that resort to prior restraints on the freedom of the press is a constitutionally impermissible method for enforcing that right; judges have at their disposal a broad spectrum of devices for ensuring that fundamental fairness is accorded the accused without necessitating so drastic an incursion on the equally fundamental and salutary constitutional mandate that discussion of public affairs in a free society cannot depend on the preliminary grace of judicial censors. . . .

[Commentary] and reporting on the criminal justice system is at the core of First Amendment values, for the operation and integrity of that system is of crucial import to citizens concerned with the administration of government. Secrecy of judicial action can only breed ignorance and distrust of courts and suspicion concerning the competence and impartiality of judges; free and robust reporting, criticism, and debate can contribute to public understanding of the rule of law and to comprehension of the functioning of the entire criminal justice system, as well as improve the quality of that system by subjecting it to the cleansing effects of exposure and public accountability. . . .

There is, beyond peradventure, a clear and substantial damage to freedom of the press whenever even a temporary restraint is imposed on reporting of material concerning the operations of the criminal justice system, an institution of such pervasive influence in our constitutional scheme. [The] press may be arrogant, tyrannical, abusive, and sensationalist, just as it may be incisive, probing, and

---

* [Concurring opinions of Justices White, Powell, and Stevens are omitted. — Eds.]

informative. But at least in the context of prior restraints on publication, the decision of what, when, and how to publish is for editors, not judges. . . .

New York Times Co. v. United States;
United States v. Washington Post Co.
403 U.S. 713 (1971)

[On June 12-14, 1971, the New York Times and on June 18 the Washington Post published excerpts from a top secret Defense Department study of the Vietnam War. The study, which was commissioned by Robert McNamara in 1967, filled forty-seven volumes and reviewed in great detail the formulation of United States policy towards Indochina, including military operations and secret diplomatic negotiations. The newspapers obtained the study, known popularly as the Pentagon Papers, from Daniel Ellsberg, a former Pentagon official. The government filed suit in federal district courts in New York and Washington seeking to enjoin further publication of the materials, claiming that such publication would interfere with the national security and would lead to the death of soldiers, the undermining of our alliances, the inability of our diplomats to negotiate, and the prolongation of the war. Between June 15 and June 23 the cases worked their way through the federal courts and on June 26 the Supreme Court heard argument. On June 30 the Court issued its decision. Restraining orders remained in effect throughout the Court's deliberations.]

PER CURIAM.

We granted certiorari in these cases in which the United States seeks to enjoin the New York Times and the Washington Post from publishing the contents of a classified study entitled "History of U.S. Decision-Making Process on Viet Nam Policy."

"Any system of prior restraints of expression comes to this Court bearing a heavy presumption against its constitutional validity." [The] Government "thus carries a heavy burden of showing justification for the imposition of such a restraint." [The] District Court for the Southern District of New York in the New York Times case and the District Court for the District of Columbia and the Court of Appeals for the District of Columbia Circuit in the Washington Post case held that the Government had not met that burden. We agree.

The judgment of the Court of Appeals for the District of Columbia Circuit is therefore affirmed. The order of the Court of Appeals for the Second Circuit is reversed and the case is remanded with directions to enter a judgment affirming the judgment of the District Court for the Southern District of New York. The stays entered June 25, 1971, by the Court are vacated. The judgments shall issue forthwith.

So ordered.

MR. JUSTICE BLACK, with whom MR. JUSTICE DOUGLAS joins, concurring. . . .

[Every] moment's continuance of the injunctions against these newspapers amounts to a flagrant, indefensible, and continuing violation of the First Amendment. [For] the first time in the 182 years since the founding of the Republic, the federal courts are asked to hold that the First Amendment does not mean what it says, but rather means that the Government can halt the publication of current news of vital importance to the people of this country. . . .

In the First Amendment the Founding Fathers gave the free press the protection it must have to fulfill its essential role in our democracy. The press was to serve the governed, not the governors. The Government's power to censor the press was abolished so that the press would remain forever free to censure the Government. The press was protected so that it could bare the secrets of government and inform the people. Only a free and unrestrained press can effectively expose deception in government. . . .

[We] are asked to hold that despite the First Amendment's emphatic command, the Executive Branch, the Congress, and the Judiciary can make laws enjoining publication of current news and abridging freedom of the press in the name of "national security." . . .

The word "security" is a broad, vague generality whose contours should not be invoked to abrogate the fundamental law embodied in the First Amendment. The guarding of military and diplomatic secrets at the expense of informed representative government provides no real security for our Republic.

MR. JUSTICE DOUGLAS, with whom MR. JUSTICE BLACK joins, concurring. . . .

These disclosures may have a serious impact. But that is no basis for sanctioning a previous restraint on the press. [The] dominant purpose of the First Amendment was to prohibit the widespread practice of governmental suppression of embarrassing information. It is common knowledge that the First Amendment was adopted against the widespread use of the common law of seditious libel to punish the dissemination of material that is embarrassing to the powers-that-be. [A] debate of large proportions goes on in the Nation over our posture in Vietnam. That debate antedated the disclosure of the contents of the present documents. The latter are highly relevant to the debate in progress.

Secrecy in government is fundamentally anti-democratic, perpetuating bureaucratic errors. Open debate and discussion of public issues are vital to our national health. On public questions there should be "uninhibited, robust, and wide-open" debate. . . .

The stays in these cases that have been in effect for more than a week constitute a flouting of the principles of the First Amendment. . . .

MR. JUSTICE BRENNAN, concurring.

The error that has pervaded these cases from the outset was the granting of any injunctive relief whatsoever, interim or otherwise. The entire thrust of the Government's claim throughout these cases has been that publication of the material sought to be enjoined "could," or "might," or "may" prejudice the national interest in various ways. But the First Amendment tolerates absolutely no prior judicial restraints of the press predicated upon surmise or conjecture that untoward consequences may result.* Our cases, it is true, have indicated that there is a

---

* Freedman v. Maryland, 380 U.S. 51 (1965), and similar cases regarding temporary restraints of allegedly obscene materials are not in point. For those cases rest upon the proposition that "obscenity is not protected by the freedoms of speech and press." [Here] there is no question but that the material sought to be suppressed is within the protection of the First Amendment; the only question is whether, notwithstanding that fact, its publication may be enjoined for a time because of the presence of an overwhelming national interest.

single, extremely narrow class of cases in which the First Amendment's ban on prior judicial restraint may be overridden. Our cases have thus far indicated that such cases may arise only when the Nation "is at war," [*Schenck*], during which times "[n]o one would question but that a government might prevent actual obstruction to its recruiting service or the publication of the sailing dates of transports or the number and location of troops." Near v. Minnesota, [infra section C2]. Even if the present world situation were assumed to be tantamount to a time of war, or if the power of presently available armaments would justify even in peacetime the suppression of information that would set in motion a nuclear holocaust, in neither of these actions has the Government presented or even alleged that publication of items from or based upon the material at issue would cause the happening of an event of that nature. "[T]he chief purpose of [the First Amendment's] guaranty [is] to prevent previous restraints upon publication." [*Near.*] Thus, only governmental allegation and proof that publication must inevitably, directly, and immediately cause the occurrence of an event kindred to imperiling the safety of a transport already at sea can support even the issuance of an interim restraining order. [Every] restraint issued in this case, whatever its form, has violated the First Amendment — and not less so because that restraint was justified as necessary to afford the courts an opportunity to examine the claim more thoroughly. Unless and until the Government has clearly made out its case, the First Amendment commands that no injunction may issue.

Mr. Justice Stewart, with whom Mr. Justice White joins, concurring.

In the governmental structure created by our Constitution, the Executive is endowed with enormous power in the two related areas of national defense and international relations. This power, largely unchecked by the Legislative and Judicial branches, has been pressed to the very hilt since the advent of the nuclear missile age. . . .

In the absence of the governmental checks and balances present in other areas of our national life, the only effective restraint upon executive policy and power in the areas of national defense and international affairs may lie in an enlightened citizenry — in an informed and critical public opinion which alone can here protect the values of democratic government. . . .

Yet it is elementary that the successful conduct of international diplomacy and the maintenance of an effective national defense require both confidentiality and secrecy. Other nations can hardly deal with this Nation in an atmosphere of mutual trust unless they can be assured that their confidences will be kept. And within our own executive departments, the development of considered and intelligent international policies would be impossible if those charged with their formulation could not communicate with each other freely, frankly, and in confidence. In the area of basic national defense the frequent need for absolute secrecy is, of course, self-evident.

I think there can be but one answer to this dilemma, if dilemma it be. The responsibility must be where the power is. If the Constitution gives the Executive a large degree of unshared power in the conduct of foreign affairs and the maintenance of our national defense, then under the Constitution the Executive must have the largely unshared duty to determine and preserve the degree of internal security necessary to exercise that power successfully. [It] is clear to me that it is the constitutional duty of the Executive — as a matter of sovereign prerogative and not as a matter of law as the courts know law — through the promulgation and enforcement of executive regulations, to protect the confidentiality necessary to carry out its responsibilities in the fields of international relations and national defense.

This is not to say that Congress and the courts have no role to play. Undoubtedly Congress has the power to enact specific and appropriate criminal laws to protect government property and preserve government secrets. . . .

But in the cases before us we are asked neither to construe specific regulations nor to apply specific laws. We are asked, instead, to perform a function that the Constitution gave to the Executive, not the Judiciary. We are asked, quite simply, to prevent the publication by two newspapers of material that the Executive Branch insists should not, in the national interest, be published. I am convinced that the Executive is correct with respect to some of the documents involved. But I cannot say that disclosure of any of them will surely result in direct, immediate, and irreparable damage to our Nation or its people. That being so, there can under the First Amendment be but one judicial resolution of the issues before us. I join the judgments of the Court.

MR. JUSTICE WHITE, with whom MR. JUSTICE STEWART joins, concurring.

I concur in today's judgments, but only because of the concededly extraordinary protection against prior restraints enjoyed by the press under our constitutional system. I do not say that in no circumstances would the First Amendment permit an injunction against publishing information about government plans or operations. Nor, after examining the materials the Government characterizes as the most sensitive and destructive, can I deny that revelation of these documents will do substantial damage to public interests. Indeed, I am confident that their disclosure will have that result. But I nevertheless agree that the United States has not satisfied the very heavy burden that it must meet to warrant an injunction against publication in these cases, at least in the absence of express and appropriately limited congressional authorization for prior restraints in circumstances such as these.

The Government's position is simply stated: The responsibility of the Executive for the conduct of the foreign affairs and for the security of the Nation is so basic that the President is entitled to an injunction against publication of a newspaper story whenever he can convince a court that the information to be revealed threatens "grave and irreparable" injury to the public interest; and the injunction should issue whether or not the material to be published is classified, whether or not publication would be lawful under relevant criminal statutes enacted by Congress, and regardless of the circumstances by which the newspaper came into possession of the information.

At least in the absence of legislation by Congress, based on its own investigations and findings, I am quite unable to agree that the inherent powers of the Executive and the courts reach so far as to authorize remedies having such sweeping potential for inhibiting publications by the press. . . .

[Prior] restraints require an unusually heavy justification under the First Amendment; but failure by the Government to justify prior restraints does not measure its constitutional entitlement to a conviction for criminal publication.

That the Government mistakenly chose to proceed by injunction does not mean that it could not successfully proceed in another way. . . .

The Criminal Code contains numerous provisions potentially relevant to these cases. [Section] 793(e)[8] makes it a criminal act for any unauthorized possessor of a document "relating to the national defense" either (1) willfully to communicate or cause to be communicated that document to any person not entitled to receive it or (2) willfully to retain the document and fail to deliver it to an officer of the United States entitled to receive it. . . .

It is thus clear that Congress has addressed itself to the problems of protecting the security of the country and the national defense from unauthorized disclosure of potentially damaging information. [It] has not, however, authorized the injunctive remedy against threatened publication. It has apparently been satisfied to rely on criminal sanctions and their deterrent effect on the responsible as well as the irresponsible press. I am not, of course, saying that either of these newspapers has yet committed a crime or that either would commit a crime if it published all the material now in its possession. That matter must await resolution in the context of a criminal proceeding if one is instituted by the United States. . . .

MR. JUSTICE MARSHALL, concurring.

I believe the ultimate issue in these cases [is] whether this Court or the Congress has the power to make law. . . .

The problem here is whether in these particular cases the Executive Branch has authority to invoke the equity jurisdiction of the courts to protect what it believes to be the national interest. [I]n some situations it may be that under whatever inherent powers the Government may have, as well as the implicit authority derived from the President's mandate to conduct foreign affairs and to act as Commander in Chief, there is a basis for the invocation of the equity jurisdiction of this Court as an aid to prevent the publication of material damaging to "national security," however that term may be defined.

It would, however, be utterly inconsistent with the concept of separation of powers for this Court to use its power of contempt to prevent behavior that Congress has specifically declined to prohibit. [The] Constitution provides that Congress shall make laws, the President execute laws, and courts interpret laws. [It] did not provide for government by injunction in which the courts and the Executive Branch can "make law" without regard to the action of Congress. [It] is clear that Congress has specifically rejected passing legislation that would have clearly given the President the power he seeks here and made the current activity of the newspapers unlawful. When Congress specifically declines to make con-

8. Section 793(e) of 18 U.S.C. provides that:

(e) Whoever having unauthorized possession of, access to, or control over any document, writing, code book, signal book, sketch, photograph, photographic negative, blueprint, plan, map, model, instrument, appliance, or note relating to the national defense, or information relating to the national defense which information the possessor has reason to believe could be used to the injury of the United States or to the advantage of any foreign nation, willfully communicates, delivers, transmits or causes to be communicated, delivered, or transmitted, or attempts to communicate, deliver, transmit or cause to be communicated, delivered, or transmitted the same to any person not entitled to receive it, or willfully retains the same and fails to deliver it to the officer or employee of the United States entitled to receive it;

is guilty of an offense punishable by 10 years in prison, a $10,000 fine, or both.

duct unlawful it is not for this Court to redecide those issues — to overrule Congress. . . .

MR. CHIEF JUSTICE BURGER, dissenting.

[In] these cases, the imperative of a free and unfettered press comes into collision with another imperative, the effective functioning of a complex modern government and specifically the effective exercise of certain constitutional powers of the Executive. Only those who view the First Amendment as an absolute in all circumstances — a view I respect, but reject — can find such cases as these to be simple or easy.

These cases are not simple for another and more immediate reason. We do not know the facts of the cases. No District Judge knew all the facts. No Court of Appeals Judge knew all the facts. No member of this Court knows all the facts. . . .

I suggest we are in this posture because these cases have been conducted in unseemly haste. [It] seems reasonably clear now that the haste precluded reasonable and deliberate judicial treatment of these cases and was not warranted. The precipitate action of this Court aborting trials not yet completed is not the kind of judicial conduct that ought to attend the disposition of a great issue. . . .

It is not disputed that the Times has had unauthorized possession of the documents for three to four months, during which it has had its expert analysts studying them, presumably digesting them and preparing the material for publication. During all of this time, the Times, presumably in its capacity as trustee of the public's "right to know," has held up publication for purposes it considered proper and thus public knowledge was delayed. No doubt this was for a good reason; the analysis of 7,000 pages of complex material drawn from a vastly greater volume of material would inevitably take time and the writing of good news stories takes time. But why should the United States Government, from whom this information was illegally acquired by someone, along with all the counsel, trial judges, and appellate judges be placed under needless pressure? After these months of deferral, the alleged "right to know" has somehow and suddenly become a right that must be vindicated instanter. . . .

I would affirm the Court of Appeals for the Second Circuit and allow the District Court to complete the trial aborted by our grant of certiorari, meanwhile preserving the status quo in the Post case. I would direct that the District Court on remand give priority to the Times case to the exclusion of all other business of that court but I would not set arbitrary deadlines. . . .

We all crave speedier judicial processes but when judges are pressured as in these cases the result is a parody of the judicial function.

MR. JUSTICE HARLAN, with whom THE CHIEF JUSTICE and MR. JUSTICE BLACKMUN join, dissenting. . . .

With all respect, I consider that the Court has been almost irresponsibly feverish in dealing with these cases.

Both the Court of Appeals for the Second Circuit and the Court of Appeals for the District of Columbia Circuit rendered judgment on June 23. The New York Times' petition for certiorari, its motion for accelerated consideration thereof, and its application for interim relief were filed in this Court on June 24 at about 11 A.M. The application of the United States for interim relief in the Post case was also filed here on June 24 at about 7:15 P.M. This Court's order setting a hearing before us on June 26 at 11 A.M., a course which I joined only to avoid the possibility of even more peremptory action by the Court, was issued less than 24 hours before. The record in the Post case was filed with the Clerk shortly before 1 P.M. on June 25; the record in the Times case did not arrive until 7 or 8 o'clock that same night. The briefs of the parties were received less than two hours before argument on June 26.

This frenzied train of events took place in the name of the presumption against prior restraints created by the First Amendment. Due regard for the extraordinarily important and difficult questions involved in these litigations should have led the Court to shun such a precipitate timetable. . . .

Forced as I am to reach the merits of these cases, I dissent from the opinion and judgments of the Court. [It] is plain to me that the scope of the judicial function in passing upon the activities of the Executive Branch of the Government in the field of foreign affairs is very narrowly restricted. This view is, I think, dictated by the concept of separation of powers upon which our constitutional system rests. . . .

The power to evaluate the "pernicious influence" of premature disclosure is not, however, lodged in the Executive alone. I agree that, in performance of its duty to protect the values of the First Amendment against political pressures, the judiciary must review the initial Executive determination to the point of satisfying itself that the subject matter of the dispute does lie within the proper compass of the President's foreign relations power. Constitutional considerations forbid "a complete abandonment of judicial control." [Moreover], the judiciary may properly insist that the determination that disclosure of the subject matter would irreparably impair the national security be made by the head of the Executive Department concerned — here the Secretary of State or the Secretary of Defense — after actual personal consideration by that officer. . . .

But in my judgment the judiciary may not properly go beyond these two inquiries and redetermine for itself the probable impact of disclosure on the national security.

> [T]he very nature of executive decisions as to foreign policy is political, not judicial. Such decisions are wholly confided by our Constitution to the political departments of the government, Executive and Legislative. They are delicate, complex, and involve large elements of prophecy. They are and should be undertaken only by those directly responsible to the people whose welfare they advance or imperil. They are decisions of a kind for which the Judiciary has neither aptitude, facilities nor responsibility and which has long been held to belong in the domain of political power not subject to judicial intrusion or inquiry.

Chicago & Southern Air Lines v. Waterman Steamship Corp., 333 U.S. 103, 111 (1948) (Jackson, J.).

Even if there is some room for the judiciary to override the executive determination, it is plain that the scope of review must be exceedingly narrow. I can see no indication in the opinions of either the District Court or the Court of Appeals in the Post litigation that the conclusions of the Executive were given even the deference owing to an administrative agency, much less that owing to a co-equal branch of the Government operating within the field of its constitutional prerogative. . . .

Pending further hearings in each case conducted under the appropriate ground rules, I would continue the restraints on publication. I cannot believe that the doctrine prohibiting prior restraints reaches to the point of preventing courts from maintaining the status quo long enough to act responsibly in matters of such national importance as those involved here.

MR. JUSTICE BLACKMUN, dissenting.

The First Amendment, after all, is only one part of an entire Constitution. Article II of the great document vests in the Executive Branch primary power over the conduct of foreign affairs and places in that branch the responsibility for the Nation's safety. Each provision of the Constitution is important, and I cannot subscribe to a doctrine of unlimited absolutism for the First Amendment at the cost of downgrading other provisions. First Amendment absolutism has never commanded a majority of this Court. [What] is needed here is a weighing, upon properly developed standards, of the broad right of the press to print and of the very narrow right of the Government to prevent. Such standards are not yet developed. The parties here are in disagreement as to what those standards should be. But even the newspapers concede that there are situations where restraint is in order and is constitutional. . . .

I therefore would remand these cases to be developed expeditiously, of course, but on a schedule permitting the orderly presentation of evidence from both sides. . . .

The Court, however, decides the cases today the other way. I therefore add one final comment.

I strongly urge, and sincerely hope, that these two newspapers will be fully aware of their ultimate responsibilities to the United States of America. Judge Wilkey, dissenting in the District of Columbia case [concluded] that there were a number of examples of documents that, if in the possession of the Post, and if published, "could clearly result in great harm to the nation," and he defined "harm" to mean "the death of soldiers, the destruction of alliances, the greatly increased difficulty of negotiation with our enemies, the inability of our diplomats to negotiate. . . ." I, for one, have now been able to give at least some cursory study not only to the affidavits, but to the material itself. I regret to say that from this examination I fear that Judge Wilkey's statements have possible foundation. I therefore share his concern. I hope that damage has not already been done. If, however, damage has been done, and if, with the Court's action today, these newspapers proceed to publish the critical documents and there results therefrom "the death of soldiers, the destruction of alliances, the greatly increased difficulty of negotiations with our enemies, the inability of our diplomats to negotiate," to which list I might add the factors of prolongation of the war and of further delay in the freeing of United States prisoners, then the Nation's people will know where the responsibility for these sad consequences rests.

Note: Nebraska Press *and the Pentagon Papers*

1. *Prior restraint.* In these decisions, the Court emphasized repeatedly that the "gag order" in *Nebraska Press* and the injunction in *New York Times* were "prior restraints" and that a prior restraint bears a special "presumption against its constitutional validity." Why is an injunction more threatening to the values underly-

ing the first amendment than a criminal prosecution for publication of the same material? For analysis of the doctrine of prior restraint, see section C2, infra.

2. *Nebraska Press.* It has been suggested that, despite its disclaimers, the Court in *Nebraska Press* "announced a virtual bar to prior restraints on reporting of news about crime." L. Tribe, American Constitutional Law 627 (1978). Is an absolute bar on such prior restraints warranted? Draft a statute that exhausts a state's constitutional power to punish criminally the "reporting of news about crime."

3. *The Pentagon Papers: too much haste?* Publication of the Pentagon Papers offered the public rare and valuable insights into the processes of decisionmaking in government. Moreover, by disclosing, for example, that the Eisenhower administration's attempt to undermine the new communist regime in North Vietnam directly involved the United States in the breakdown of the 1954 Geneva settlement, that the Johnson administration took steps toward waging an overt war against North Vietnam a full year before it disclosed the depth of its involvement to the American public, and that the infiltration of men and arms from North Vietnam into the South was more important as a means of publicly justifying our involvement than for its military effects, publication of the Papers sharpened the public's understanding of the war and altered public attitudes toward a central issue of American policy. At the same time, however, one must ask whether, as the dissenters charged, the Court acted with "unseemly haste" in permitting publication of the documents. In light of the extraordinary seriousness of the government's contentions and the almost overwhelming length of the study, should the Court have permitted the injunctions to remain in effect pending a more thorough judicial determination of the risks? Was the Court, in other words, playing fast and loose with the national security? Consider in this regard Justice Brennan's argument that the very notion of an injunction against expression pending final resolution of the controversy is inherently incompatible with the first amendment.

4. *The Pentagon Papers: injunctions and the national security.* Note that the per curiam opinion did not define the precise circumstances in which a court may enjoin the publication of information relating to the national security. Does the standard enunciated by Justice Stewart, that there must be proof that the disclosure will "surely result in direct, immediate, and irreparable damage to our Nation or its people," come closest to representing the view of the Court? See Emerson, First Amendment Doctrine and the Burger Court, 68 Calif. L. Rev. 422, 456 (1980); Cox, Foreword: Freedom of Expression in the Burger Court, 94 Harv. L. Rev. 1, 7 (1980). Why was that standard not satisfied in the Pentagon Papers case?

5. *The Pentagon Papers: criminal prosecution?* Suppose the New York Times and Washington Post had been criminally prosecuted for their publication of the Pentagon Papers. What standard should govern? Is section 793(e) of the Federal Code, reproduced in footnote 8 of Justice White's opinion, constitutional? Should disclosure of historical information be absolutely protected?

Suppose that in this hypothetical criminal prosecution the government claimed that the newspapers' disclosure of some of the historical information weakened our alliances, increased the difficulty of negotiating with other nations, prolonged the war, and delayed the release of American prisoners of war. Could the newspapers constitutionally be convicted? Are these sorts of issues, as Justice Harlan suggested, beyond the competence of courts? Consider the following arguments:

(a) The executive may consciously or unconsciously err on the side of suppression in order to prevent the revelation of potentially embarrassing information. See generally Blasi, The Checking Value in First Amendment Theory, 1977 A.B.F. Res. J. 521. (b) Newspapers, eager to boost sales, may undervalue the interest in national security.

In considering the Pentagon Papers controversy, recall the problem of the *true* cry of "fire." Even though the true cry may create a clear and present danger that some persons will be injured in the dash for the exit, the benefits of the speech may well outweigh the harm.

6. *Public employees and closed proceedings.* Should government have greater authority to prohibit its employees from disclosing confidential information to the public than to prohibit the press from publishing such information once it comes into its hands? See infra section F3e. Should government, to protect the interests of criminal defendants, have greater authority to exclude the press from trials and pretrial proceedings than to prohibit the press from publishing information about such proceedings and trials once the information comes into its hands? See section F6, infra.

Consider the following argument: The Court's suggestions in *Nebraska Press* and *Pentagon Papers* that the state may keep information from the press by prohibiting government employees to disclose information and by excluding the press from government proceedings is inconsistent with its holdings that the state may not restrict the publisher who causes the real harm by disseminating the information to the public. After all, if an ultimate concern of the first amendment is the "public's right to know," that right is undermined just as much by restrictions on the press' ability to obtain information as by restrictions on its ability to publish.

Consider A. Bickel, The Morality of Consent 79-82 (1975):

> The government is entitled to keep things private and will attain as much privacy as it can get away with politically by guarding its privacy internally; but with few exceptions involving the highest probability of very grave consequences, it may not do so effectively. It is severely limited as to means, being restricted, by and large, to enforcing security at the source. [Yet] the power to arrange security at the source, looked at in itself, is great, and if it were nowhere countervailed it would be quite frightening. [But] there *is* countervailing power. The press, by which is meant anybody, not only the institutionalized print and electronic press, can be prevented from publishing only in extreme and quite dire circumstances. [It] is a disorderly situation surely. But if we ordered it we would have to sacrifice one of two contending values — privacy or public discourse — which are ultimately irreconcilable. If we should let the government censor as well as withhold, that would be too much dangerous power, and too much privacy. If we should allow the government neither to censor nor to withhold, that would provide for too little privacy of decision-making and too much power in the press.

7. *"Technical" information.* Do the decisions examined in this section, taken together, "leave little doubt that, except in cases involving imminent national military catastrophe, the Court will not permit previous restraints upon, or subsequent punishment for, publication in a mass medium of accurate information that the publisher has lawfully acquired"? Cox, supra, at 17.

Suppose that, in addition to general historical information, the Pentagon Papers had disclosed information about present or future military operations, blueprints of secret military weapons, the identity of covert agents abroad, or secret codes? Is the disclosure of such information more readily subject to restriction? See Symposium, National Security and the First Amendment, 26 Wm. & Mary L. Rev. 715 (1985). Do you agree that "the law need not treat differently the crime of one man who sells a bomb to terrorists and that of another who publishes an instructional manual for terrorists on how to build their own bombs out of old Volkswagen parts"? L. Tribe, American Constitutional Law 605 (1978).

Note: The Progressive *Controversy*

In February 1979 Howard Morland, a freelance writer, completed an article for The Progressive magazine, entitled The H-Bomb Secret — How We Got It, Why We're Telling It. The article, which was based on information contained in publicly available literature and Morland's interviews of various scientists and government officials, was designed to demonstrate the ineffectiveness and undesirability of a government system of classification and secrecy. Uncertain of the potential legal consequences of publication, The Progressive delivered a copy of the manuscript to the Department of Energy requesting verification of its "technical accuracy." Officials in the DOE determined that although Morland had relied on no classified documents, the article nonetheless contained information that the Atomic Energy Act required to be classified as "restricted data." They therefore requested The Progressive not to publish the article without first permitting government officials to work with them to recast the manuscript to eliminate the restricted data. The Progressive informed the DOE that it intended to publish the article without alteration.

The following day, March 8, the United States filed suit in federal district court seeking to enjoin publication of the restricted data. The United States maintained that the suit was authorized by the Atomic Energy Act, which authorized injunctive relief to prohibit any person from disclosing restricted data, defined in the act as including any data concerning "design, manufacture, or utilization of atomic weapons," "with reason to believe such data will be utilized to injure the United States or to secure an advantage to any foreign nation." On March 9 the court issued a temporary restraining order against publication of the article. On March 26 the court held a hearing on the issuance of a preliminary injunction.

After considering several complex affidavits submitted by experts on both sides, the court found that at least some of the information in the article may not have been in the public domain. More important, "the article provides a more comprehensive, accurate, and detailed analysis of the overall construction and operation of a thermonuclear weapon than any publication to date in the public literature." The court found further that the article does not "provide a 'do-it-yourself' guide for the hydrogen bomb" but "could possibly provide sufficient information to allow a medium size nation to move faster in developing a hydrogen weapon" and "could provide a ticket to by-pass blind alleys."

The court granted the preliminary injunction. United States v. The Progressive, Inc., 467 F. Supp. 990 (W.D. Wis. 1979). The court noted that, although the purpose of the article was to "alert the people of this country to the false illusion of security created by the government's futile efforts at secrecy" and to "provide the people with needed information to make informed decisions on an urgent issue of public concern," it could "find no plausible reason why the public needs to know the technical details about hydrogen bomb construction to carry on an informed debate on this issue." Moreover, the information at issue, the court observed, deals "with the most destructive weapon in the history of mankind," and an erroneous decision against the government could "involve human life itself and on such an awesome scale." In light of this "disparity of risk," the court held that the injunction was warranted. The court distinguished the Pentagon Papers decision on the grounds that (1) the information disclosed in that case involved "historical data relating to events that occurred some three to twenty years previously"; (2) "no cogent arguments were advanced by the government" in that case "as to why the article affected national security except that publication might cause some embarrassment to the United States"; and (3) there was no specific statutory authorization of the injunction in that case.

The government's suit against The Progressive was dismissed on October 1, 1979, while pending in the U.S. Court of Appeals for the Seventh Circuit, because similar information concerning the construction of the hydrogen bomb was published independently by others.

Consider also Haig v. Agee, 453 U.S. 280 (1981), in which the Court upheld the revocation of Agee's passport because he engaged in activities abroad that caused "serious damage to the national security." Specifically, Agee, a former employee of the CIA, engaged in a campaign "to expose CIA officers and agents and to take the measures necessary to drive them out of the countries where they are operating." Although Agee did not expressly incite "anyone to commit murder," there was evidence that his disclosures resulted in "episodes of violence against the persons and organizations identified." The Court rejected Agee's claim that the passport revocation violated his rights under the first amendment: "Long ago, [this] Court recognized that 'No one would question but that a government might prevent actual obstruction to its recruiting service or the publication of the sailing dates of transports or the number and location of troops.' [Near.] Agee's disclosures [have] the declared purpose of obstructing intelligence operations and the recruiting of personnel. They are clearly not protected by the Constitution."

Is Agee consistent with the Pentagon Papers decision? Are Agee's disclosures "not protected" because they consisted of "technical" rather than "historical" information? Because they were designed to effect change, not through the political process, but by directly obstructing the operations of government? Consider the constitutionality of the Intelligence Identities Protection Act, 50 U.S.C. §421 (1982), which prohibits any person "with reason to believe that such activities would impair or impede the foreign intelligence activities of the United States, [to disclose] any information that identifies an individual as a covert agent, [if the disclosure is part of a] pattern of activities intended to identify or expose covert action."

Consider also the Arms Export Control Act, 22 U.S.C. §2778 (1982), which authorizes compilation of a list of items which may not be exported without a license from the State Department. This list includes not only physical objects, but also information "that can be used or adapted for use" in the production, operation, or maintenance of the armaments listed and "any technology which advances the state of the art or establishes a new art in any area of significant military applicability." Export of technical data is defined to apply to disclosure to foreign nationals in the United States, including disclosure through participation in symposia. For analysis, see Comment, National Security Controls on the Dissemination of Privately Generated Scientific Information, 30 U.C.L.A. L. Rev. 405, 425-428 (1982).

Note: Dangerous Ideas and Information —
Final Thoughts

In what circumstances, if any, may government, consonant with the first amendment, restrict the expression of particular ideas or information of "high" first amendment value because such expression, if left unchecked, might cause some harm to government, private individuals, or society in general? As the foregoing materials illustrate, the Court's efforts to define the perimeters of government power in this regard have focused primarily on the clear and present danger standard. Has that standard served well? In a different context, Justice Holmes, the author of the clear and present danger standard, warned of "the need of scrutinizing the reasons for the rules which we follow, and of not being contented with hollow forms of words merely because they have been used very [often]. We must think things not words, or at least we must constantly translate our words into the facts for which they stand, if we are to keep to the real and the true." O. Holmes, Collected Legal Papers 238 (1920). Has the Court been sensitive to this admonition, or has it "tended to seek [solutions] for problems of freedom of speech by invocation of magic phrases rather than hard rationalizations, if not by way of resolving the issues than by way of covering them up"? Kurland, The Irrelevance of the Constitution: The First Amendment's Freedom of Speech and Freedom of Press Clauses, 29 Drake L. Rev. 1, 5 (1979-1980).

Has the Court, in its results, been underprotective of free speech? Has it been overprotective? A canvass of what the Court has done may be more illuminating than an emphasis on what it has said. The Court has not upheld a restriction on speech because it might induce readers or listeners to engage in criminal activity since *Dennis* (1951) and *Scales* (1961), and it has not upheld a restriction on speech for this reason in the absence of express advocacy of crime since the Espionage Act cases following World War I. The Court has not upheld a restriction on speech because it might provoke a hostile audience response since *Feiner* (1951). It has never upheld a restriction on speech because the ideas expressed might have an improper influence on the judicial process. It has never upheld a restriction on the publication of truthful information because the government would prefer to keep it confidential. Has clear and present danger come to mean absolute protection?

On the other hand, does it really matter what the Court says or does? Consider Nagel, How Useful Is Judicial Review in Free Speech Cases?, 69 Corn. L. Rev. 302, 304–305 (1984):

[It] is not self-evident [that] the legal rules adopted by the Court [have] had any useful systemic consequences. [A] wide range of factors coalesce to determine the amount of tolerance [in a society], including: educational levels, [economic] conditions, international politics, institutional rivalries [and] insecurities caused by flux in social [status]. Adjudication is an unlikely mechanism for controlling such large and complex factors. [The] causes of intolerance and censorship — as well as the cures — lie far beyond the sound and fury of particular cases.

C. OVERBREADTH, VAGUENESS, AND PRIOR RESTRAINT

This section represents a brief interlude in our analysis of content-based restrictions. It focuses not on what speech government may restrict but, rather, on how government may restrict speech. The doctrines examined in this section may be explored either as a distinct unit or as they naturally arise in the course of the preceding and succeeding material.

In interpreting the first amendment, courts have often focused not only on what speech is "protected" but also on what means of suppression are constitutionally permissible. Indeed, "courts have lately come to realize that procedural guarantees play [a] large role in protecting freedom of speech; [for like] the substantive rules themselves, insensitive procedures can 'chill' the right of free expression. Accordingly, wherever first amendment claims are involved, sensitive procedural devices are necessary." Monaghan, First Amendment "Due Process," 83 Harv. L. Rev. 518, 518-519 (1970).

The overbreadth, vagueness, and prior restraint doctrines have played an especially important role in this aspect of first amendment jurisprudence. Under each of these doctrines, courts may invalidate restrictions on expression because the means of suppression are impermissible even though the particular speech at issue might constitutionally be restricted by some other means.

1. Overbreadth and Vagueness

Gooding v. Wilson
405 U.S. 518 (1972)

[During an antiwar demonstration at an army induction center, police attempted to move appellee and his companions away from the door of the center. A scuffle ensued, and appellee said to several of the officers, "You son of a bitch, I'll choke you to death"; "White son of a bitch, I'll kill you"; and "You son of a bitch, if you ever put your hands on me again, I'll cut you all to pieces." Appellee was thereafter convicted of using opprobrious words and abusive language in violation of Georgia Code Ann. §26-6303, which provided: "Any person who shall, without provocation, use to or of another, and in his presence [opprobrious] words or abusive language, tending to cause a breach of the peace [shall] be guilty of a misdemeanor." The Supreme Court affirmed a decision of the U.S. Court of Appeals granting appellee's petition for federal habeas corpus relief.]

MR. JUSTICE BRENNAN delivered the opinion of the Court. . . .

Section 26-6303 punishes only spoken words. It can therefore withstand appellee's attack upon its facial constitutionality only if, as authoritatively construed by the Georgia courts, it is not susceptible of application to speech, although vulgar or offensive, that is protected by the First and Fourteenth Amendments. [Only] the Georgia courts can supply the requisite construction, since of course "we lack jurisdiction authoritatively to construe state legislation." [It] matters not that the words appellee used might have been constitutionally prohibited under a narrowly and precisely drawn statute. At least when statutes regulate or proscribe speech and when "no readily apparent construction suggests itself as a vehicle for rehabilitating the statutes in a single prosecution," [the] transcendent value to all society of constitutionally protected expression is deemed to justify allowing "attacks on overly broad statutes with no requirement that the person making the attack demonstrate that his own conduct could not be regulated by a statute drawn with the requisite narrow specificity." [This] is deemed necessary because persons whose expression is constitutionally protected may well refrain from exercising their rights for fear of criminal sanctions provided by a statute susceptible of application to protected expression. . . .

The constitutional guarantees of freedom of speech forbid the States to punish the use of words or language not within "narrowly limited classes of speech." [*Chaplinsky*.] [Statutes] must be carefully drawn or be authoritatively construed to punish only unprotected speech and not be susceptible of application to protected expression. "Because First Amendment freedoms need breathing space to survive, government may regulate in the area only with narrow specificity." . . .

Appellant does not challenge these principles but contends that the Georgia statute is narrowly drawn to apply only to a constitutionally unprotected class of words — "fighting" words — "those which by their very utterance inflict injury or tend to incite an immediate breach of the peace." [*Chaplinsky*.] In *Chaplinsky*, we sustained a conviction under [a statute] which provided: "No person shall address any offensive, derisive or annoying word to any other person who is lawfully in any street or other public place, nor call him by any offensive or derisive name. . . ." Chaplinsky was convicted for addressing to another on a public sidewalk the words, "You are a God damned racketeer," and "a damned Fascist and the whole government of Rochester are Fascists or agents of Fascists." Chaplinsky challenged the constitutionality of the statute as inhibiting freedom of expression because it was vague and indefinite. The Supreme Court of New Hampshire, however, "long before the words for which Chaplinsky was convicted," sharply limited the statutory language "offensive, derisive or annoying word" to "fighting" words. . . .

In view of that authoritative construction, this Court held: "We are unable to say that the limited scope of the statute as thus construed contravenes the Constitutional right of free expression. It is a statute narrowly drawn and limited to define and punish specific conduct lying within the domain of state power, the use in a public place of words likely to cause a breach of the peace." . . .

Appellant argues that the Georgia appellate courts have by construction limited the prescription of §26-6303 to "fighting" words, as the New Hampshire Supreme Court limited the New Hampshire statute. [We] have, however, made our own examination of the Georgia cases, both those cited and others discovered in research. That examination brings us to the conclusion, in agreement with the courts below, that the Georgia appellate decisions have not construed §26-6303 to be limited in application, as in *Chaplinsky*, to words that "have a direct tendency to cause acts of violence by the person to whom, individually, the remark is addressed."

The dictionary definitions of "opprobrious" and "abusive" give them greater reach than "fighting" words. Webster's Third New International Dictionary (1961) defined "opprobrious" as "conveying or intended to convey disgrace," and "abusive" as including "harsh insulting language." Georgia appellate decisions have construed §26-6303 to apply to utterances that, although within these definitions, are not "fighting" words as *Chaplinsky* defines them. In Lyons v. State, 94 Ga. App. 570, 95 S.E.2d 478 (1956), a conviction under the statute was sustained for [appellee's] awakening 10 women scout leaders on a camp-out by shouting, "Boys, this is where we are going to spend the night." "Get the G—d—bed rolls out . . . let's see how close we can come to the G—d—tents." Again, in Fish v. State, 124 Ga. 416, 52 S.E. 737 (1905), the Georgia Supreme Court held that a jury question was presented by the remark, "You swore a lie." Again, Jackson v. State, 14 Ga. App. 19, 80 S.E. 20 (1913), held that a jury question was presented by the words addressed to another, "God damn you, why don't you get out of the road?" Plainly, although "conveying . . . disgrace" or "harsh insulting language," these were not words "which by their very utterance . . . tend to incite an immediate breach of the peace." [*Chaplinsky.*] Indeed, the Georgia Court of Appeals in Elmore v. State, 15 Ga. App. 461, 83 S.E. 799 (1914), construed "tending to cause a breach of the peace" as [including the possibility that the addressee might retaliate at some time in the future].

Moreover, in Samuels v. State, 103 Ga. App. 66, 67, 118 S.E.2d 231, 232 (1961), the Court of Appeals, in applying another statute, adopted from a textbook the common-law definition of "breach of the peace" [that] makes it a "breach of peace" merely to speak words offensive to some who hear them. [Because] earlier appellate decisions applied §26-6303 to utterances where there was no likelihood that the person addressed would make an immediate violent response, it is clear that the standard allowing juries to determine guilt "measured by common understanding and practice" does not limit the application of §26-6303 to "fighting" words defined by *Chaplinsky*. [Unlike] the construction of the New Hampshire statute by the New Hampshire Supreme Court, the Georgia appellate courts have not construed §26-6303 "so as to avoid all constitutional difficulties." . . .

Affirmed.

Mr. Justice Powell and Mr. Justice Rehnquist took no part in the consideration or decision of this case.

Mr. Chief Justice Burger, dissenting.

I fully join in Mr. Justice Blackmun's dissent against the bizarre result reached by the Court. It is not merely odd, it is nothing less than remarkable that a court can find a state statute void on its face, not because of its language — which is the traditional test — but because of the way courts of that State have applied the statute in a few isolated cases, decided as long ago as 1905 and generally long before this Court's decision in [*Chaplinsky*]. Even if all of those cases had been decided yesterday, they do nothing to demonstrate that the narrow language of the Georgia statute has any significant potential for sweeping application to suppress or deter important protected speech. . . .

The Court apparently acknowledges that the conduct of the defendant in this case is not protected by the First Amendment, and does not contend that the

Georgia statute is so ambiguous that he did not have fair notice that his conduct was prohibited. Nor does the Court deny that under normal principles of constitutional adjudication, appellee would not be permitted to attack his own conviction on the ground that the statute in question might in some hypothetical situation be unconstitutionally applied to the conduct of some party not before the Court. . . .

As the Court itself recognizes, if the First Amendment overbreadth doctrine serves any legitimate purpose, it is to allow the Court to invalidate statutes because their language demonstrates their potential for sweeping improper applications posing a significant likelihood of deterring important First Amendment speech — not because of some insubstantial or imagined potential for occasional and isolated applications that go beyond constitutional bounds. [The] actual and apparent danger to free expression [in] the case at hand is at best strained and remote.* . . .

MR. JUSTICE BLACKMUN, with whom THE CHIEF JUSTICE joins, dissenting. . . .

The Court would justify its conclusion by unearthing a 66-year-old decision [of] the Supreme Court of Georgia, and two intermediate appellate court cases over 55 years old, [broadly] applying the statute in those less permissive days, and by additional reference to (a) a 1956 Georgia intermediate appellate court decision, [which], were it the first and only Georgia case, would surely not support today's decision, and (b) another intermediate appellate court decision [relating], not to §26-6303, but to another statute. . . .

I wonder, now that §26-6303 is voided, just what Georgia can do if it seeks to proscribe what the Court says it still may constitutionally proscribe. The natural thing would be to enact a new statute reading just as §26-6303 reads. But it, too, presumably would be overbroad unless the legislature would add words to the effect that it means only what this Court says it may mean and no more. . . .

Note: Overbreadth

1. *The nature of overbreadth.* The traditional "as applied" mode of judicial review tests the constitutionality of legislation as it is applied to particular facts on a case-by-case basis. Suppose, for example, a state law prohibits any person to "advocate criminal conduct." Under "as applied" review, this law could constitutionally be applied to any expression that satisfies the requirements of *Brandenburg*. That the law fails "on its face" to comport with the strictures of *Brandenburg* is, under this approach, irrelevant.

The first amendment overbreadth doctrine, on the other hand, tests the constitutionality of legislation in terms of its *potential* applications. Under this ap-

---

* Even assuming that the statute, on its face, were impermissibly overbroad, the Court does not satisfactorily explain why it must be invalidated in its entirety. To be sure, the Court notes that "we lack jurisdiction authoritatively to construe state legislation." But that cryptic statement hardly resolves the matter. The State of Georgia argues that the statute applies only to fighting words that *Chaplinsky* holds may be prohibited, and the Court apparently agrees that the statute would be valid if so limited. The Court should not assume that the Georgia courts, and Georgia prosecutors and police, would ignore a decision of this Court sustaining appellee's conviction narrowly and on the explicit premise that the statute may be validly applied only to "fighting words" as defined in *Chaplinsky*. . . .

proach, a state law prohibiting any person to "advocate unlawful conduct" is unconstitutional "on its face" because the law purports to forbid expression that the state may not constitutionally prohibit. That an individual defendant's own speech could constitutionally be restricted under a more narrowly drawn statute is irrelevant.

In effect, then, the overbreadth doctrine is an exception both to the traditional "as applied" mode of judicial review and to the general rule that an individual has no standing to litigate the rights of third persons. See United States v. Raines, 362 U.S. 17 (1960); Barrows v. Jackson, 346 U.S. 249 (1953); see also Note, Standing to Assert Constitutional Jus Tertii, 88 Harv. L. Rev. 423 (1974). For an alternative understanding of overbreadth, see Monaghan, Overbreadth, 1981 Sup. Ct. Rev. 1, suggesting that the doctrine is merely an application in the first amendment context of a more general constitutional principle that an individual has a right to have his interests judged "in accordance with a constitutionally valid rule of law." See also Monaghan, Third Party Standing, 84 Colum. L. Rev. 277 (1984); Sedler, The Assertion of Constitutional Jus Tertii: A Substantive Approach, 70 Calif. L. Rev. 1308 (1982).

2. *Justifications and criticisms of overbreadth.* The overbreadth doctrine is "highly protective of first amendment interests, not only because it sometimes prescribes invalidation of an entire provision but also because of the alacrity with which it can accomplish that result." Note, The First Amendment Overbreadth Doctrine, 83 Harv. L. Rev. 844, 846 (1970). Are you persuaded by Justice Brennan's explanation in *Gooding* that this exception to ordinary standing rules is "necessary because persons whose expression is constitutionally protected may well refrain from exercising their rights for fear of criminal sanctions provided by a statute susceptible of application to protected expression"? For an elaboration of the "chilling effect" rational, see Note, The First Amendment Overbreadth Doctrine, supra, at 852-858. Are you persuaded that "one of the evils of an overly broad statute is its potential for selective enforcement," and that the doctrine is thus justified because "it can minimize [this] danger by restricting the occasions for enforcement"? Karst, Equality as a Central Principle in the First Amendment, 43 U. Chi. L. Rev. 20, 38 (1975).

What are the costs of the overbreadth doctrine? Consider the following objections: (1) Because the doctrine permits an individual whose own rights have *not* been violated to "go free" or to otherwise benefit because the statute might conceivably interfere with the rights of others, it unjustifiably frustrates legitimate state interests. (2) The doctrine enables the Court to act "as if it had a roving commission" to find and to cure unconstitutionality and is thus inconsistent with a fundamental premise of judicial review — that judicial resolution of constitutional controversies is warranted only when unavoidable. A. Cox, The Warren Court 18 (1968). (3) The doctrine necessarily requires the decision of questions not actually presented by the record, and thus results in the resolution of important constitutional issues in a "sterile," abstract context, without the depth and texture ordinarily provided by a concrete factual setting. A. Bickel, The Least Dangerous Branch 115-116 (1962). (4) The doctrine may promote judicial disingenuousness for it invites the Court to escape possibly difficult decisions concerning the constitutionality of the statute "as applied" so long as it can hypothesize potentially unconstitutional applications not actually before the Court. (5) Because the Court may invalidate a statute for overbreadth without explaining precisely how the statute should have been drafted to pass constitutional muster, invocation of the doctrine "lacks intellectual coherence" and may leave legislatures with little or no guidance on how to avoid the Court's objections in the future. Bickel, supra, at 53.

3. *The problem of narrowing construction.* As noted in *Gooding*, the statute at issue in *Chaplinsky* was clearly overbroad on its face but was saved by the state court's narrowing construction. When may a court narrowly construe a facially overbroad statute to save it from invalidation? In affirming the conviction of *Gooding*, could the Georgia Supreme Court have limited the statute to "fighting words" and thus avoided overbreadth invalidation? Was the legislative intent too clear in *Gooding* to permit a narrowing interpretation? Compare Scales v. United States, 367 U.S. 203 (1961), with United States v. Robel, 389 U.S. 258 (1967); see generally Monaghan, supra, at 30-33; Note, The First Amendment Overbreadth Doctrine, supra, at 891-901. Would a narrowing construction by the Georgia Supreme Court have come too late to affect Gooding?

Note that the Supreme Court of the United States had no authority to adopt a narrowing construction in *Gooding*. Is that sensible? Wouldn't a narrowing construction have involved a less drastic exercise of federal power than invalidation?

4. *Broadrick:* requiring *"substantial" overbreadth.* Chief Justice Burger maintained in *Gooding* that the overbreadth doctrine should be invoked only when there is "a significant likelihood of deterring important First Amendment speech." In Broadrick v. Oklahoma, 413 U.S. 601 (1973), the Court, in a five-to-four decision, expressly adopted such a limitation. *Broadrick* involved a state law restricting the political activities of civil servants, an issue examined in section F3a, infra. The plaintiffs conceded that the state could constitutionally prohibit civil servants from doing what they had done — solicit funds for political candidates. They argued, however, that the law was unconstitutionally overbroad because it attempted also to prohibit civil servants from engaging in such relatively innocuous and thus constitutionally protected activities as displaying political bumper stickers and buttons.

The Court, in an opinion by Justice White, observed that under the overbreadth doctrine litigants "are permitted to challenge a statute not because their own rights of free expression are violated, but because of a judicial prediction or assumption that the statute's very existence may cause others not before the court to refrain from constitutionally protected speech or expression." Terming the doctrine "strong medicine," the Court argued that although laws, "if too broadly worded, may deter protected speech to some unknown extent, there comes a point where that effect — at best a prediction — cannot, with confidence, justify invalidating a statute on its face and so prohibiting a State from enforcing the statute against conduct that is admittedly within its power to proscribe." Thus, the Court concluded, "particularly where conduct and not merely speech is involved, we believe that the overbreadth of a statute must not only be real, but substantial as well, judged in relation to the statute's plainly legitimate sweep."

Applying that standard to the statute in *Broadrick*, the Court emphasized that the statute "is not a censorial statute, directed at particular groups or viewpoints. The statute, rather, seeks to regulate political activity in an even-handed and neutral manner." Moreover, the Court maintained, the statute "regulates a substantial spectrum of conduct that [is] manifestly subject to state regulation." Thus, the Court concluded, the act "is not substantially overbroad [and] whatever overbreadth may exist should be cured through case-by-case analysis of the fact situations to which its sanctions, assertedly, may not be applied."

In dissent, Justice Brennan described *Broadrick* "as a wholly unjustified retreat from fundamental and previously well-established [principles]." Although conceding that the Court had "never held that a statute should be held invalid on its face merely because it is possible to conceive of a single impermissible application," and that "in that sense a requirement of substantial overbreadth is already implicit in the doctrine," Brennan faulted the Court for leaving "obscure" the contours of its arguably new conception of overbreadth. The Court, Brennan noted, "makes no effort to define what it means by 'substantial overbreadth'" and "no effort to explain why the overbreadth of the Oklahoma Act, while real, is somehow not quite substantial." Indeed, "no more guidance is provided" on that question "than the Court's conclusory assertion that appellants' showing here falls below the line." Moreover, Brennan criticized the Court for offering "No rationale to explain its conclusion that, for purposes of overbreadth analysis, deterrence of conduct should be viewed differently from deterrence of speech, even where both are equally protected by the First Amendment."

5. *The impact of* Broadrick. Consider Coates v. Cincinnati, 402 U.S. 611 (1971), in which the Court invalidated a city ordinance making it criminal for "three or more persons to assemble [on] any of the sidewalks [and] there conduct themselves in a manner annoying to persons passing by." The Court explained that the ordinance was unconstitutionally overbroad because it might be construed as reaching those individuals whose "exercise of the right of assembly [may] be 'annoying' to some people." Does *Coates* survive *Broadrick?* Does *Gooding* survive *Broadrick?*

In *Broadrick* the Court emphasized that the challenged law regulated "conduct" rather than "speech." Is that sensible? In New York v. Ferber, 458 U.S. 747 (1982), the Court explicitly held the substantial overbreadth doctrine applicable to restrictions on more "traditional forms of expression such as books and films."

In Los Angeles City Council v. Taxpayers for Vincent, — U.S. — , 104 S. Ct. 2118 (1984), the Court offered the following elaboration:

> The concept of 'substantial overbreadth' is not readily reduced to an exact definition. It is clear, however, that the mere fact that one can conceive of some impermissible applications of a statute is not sufficient to render it susceptible to an overbreadth challenge. On the contrary, [there] must be a realistic danger that the statute itself will significantly compromise recognized First Amendment protections of parties not before the Court for it to be facially challenged on overbreadth grounds.

How should "substantiality" be measured: By the total number of unconstitutional applications? By the ratio of possible constitutional to possible unconstitutional applications? Should the state have to justify even an "insubstantial" overbreadth? See Redish, The Warren Court, The Burger Court and the First Amendment Overbreadth Doctrine, 78 Nw. U. L. Rev. 1031, 1067 (1983) (the "logical question [is] whether [a] more narrowly drawn [law] would inadequately achieve the state's goal"). Should it matter whether the law is content-based or content-neutral? See Monaghan, supra, at 23-30 (the overbreadth doctrine should apply with more force when a law is content-based than when it is content-neutral).

The ultimate impact of *Broadrick* remains obscure. Compare Secretary of State of Maryland v. Joseph H. Munson, Co. — U.S. — , 104 S. Ct. 2839 (1984) (applying overbreadth); Schaumburg v. Citizens for a Better Environment, 444 U.S. 620 (1980) (applying overbreadth); Erzonznik v. Jacksonville, 422 U.S. 205 (1975) (applying overbreadth); Lewis v. New Orleans, 415 U.S. 130 (1974) (applying overbreadth) with Los Angeles City Council v. Taxpayers for Vincent, — U.S. — , 104 S. Ct. 2118 (1984) (declining to apply overbreadth); New York v. Ferber, 458 U.S. 747 (1982) (declining to apply overbreadth); Arnett v. Kennedy, 416 U.S. 134 (1974) (declining to apply overbreadth).

6. *Partial invalidation*. May an individual whose own rights are violated by a statute challenge the statute not only "as applied" to him but "on its face"? In Brockett v. Spokane Arcades, Inc., — U.S. — , 105 S. Ct. 2794 (1985), the Court held a Washington obscenity statute unconstitutional because its definition of obscenity was too broad. Without deciding whether the statute was substantially overbroad, however, the Court declined to invalidate the law on its face:

> [An] individual whose own speech [may] validly be prohibited [is] permitted to challenge a statute on its face because it also threatens others not before the court, [and if] the overbreadth is "substantial," the law may not be enforced against anyone [until] it is narrowed to reach only unprotected activity. [But where, as here,] the parties challenging the statute are those who desire to engage in protected speech that the overbroad statute purports to punish, [there is] no want of a proper party to challenge the statute [and it] may forthwith be declared invalid to the extent it reaches too far, but otherwise left intact.

The Court emphasized that such cases are "governed by the normal rule that partial, rather than facial, invalidation is the required course." Justice Brennan, joined by Justice Marshall, dissented on the ground that the statute was "substantially overbroad and therefore invalid on its face."

Compare Secretary of State of Maryland v. Munson, — U.S. — , 104 S. Ct. 2839 (1984), in which the Court held that an individual can challenge a statute on its face, even though it is unconstitutional as applied to him, when the statute "in all its applications directly restricts protected First Amendment activity," for "there is no reason to limit challenges to case-by-case 'as applied' challenges when the statute on its face and therefore in all its applications falls short of constitutional demands." The statute invalidated in *Munson* prohibited any charitable organization, in connection with any fundraising activity, from paying expenses of more than 25 percent of the amount raised. The issue of solicitation of funds is examined in section E4, infra.

Note: Vagueness

1. *The danger of vagueness*. Although not all overbroad laws are vague (e.g., "No person may expressly advocate criminal conduct"), and not all vague laws are overbroad (e.g., "No person may engage in any speech that the state may constitutionally restrict"), there is in most circumstances a close relation between the two doctrines. As a matter of due process, a law is void on its face if it is so vague that persons "of common intelligence must necessarily guess at its meaning and differ as to its application." Connally v. General Construction Co., 269 U.S. 385,

391 (1926). A law that fails to define clearly the conduct it proscribes "may trap the innocent by not providing fair warning" and may in practical effect impermissibly delegate "basic policy matters to policemen, judges and juries for resolution on an ad hoc and subjective basis, with the attendant dangers of arbitrary and discriminatory application." Grayned v. Rockford, 408 U.S. 104, 108-109 (1972).

These concerns are present whenever a law is vague, whether or not it touches on expression. The vagueness doctrine has special bite in the first amendment context, however, for "where First Amendment interests are affected, a precise statute 'evincing a legislative judgment that certain specific conduct [be] proscribed,' assures us that the legislature has focused on the First Amendment interests and determined that other governmental policies compel regulation." Moreover, "where a vague statute '[abuts] upon sensitive areas of basic First Amendment freedoms,' it 'operates to inhibit the exercise of [those] freedoms.' Uncertain meanings inevitably lead citizens to ' "steer far wider of the unlawful zone" [than] if the boundaries of the forbidden areas were clearly marked.' " Id. at 109 & n.5; see also Smith v. Goguen, 415 U.S. 566, 572-573 (1974). In at least some instances, in other words, it may be difficult to determine whether a vague law proscribes — or purports to proscribe — constitutionally protected expression. In such circumstances, vague laws, like overbroad laws, may have a significant chilling effect and may invite selective enforcement. See Amsterdam, The Void-for-Vagueness Doctrine in the Supreme Court, 109 U. Pa. L. Rev. 67 (1960).

2. *How "vague" is "too vague"?* The degree of constitutionally tolerable vagueness "is not calculable with precision; in any particular area, the legislature confronts a dilemma: to draft with narrow particularity is to risk nullification by easy evasion of the legislative purpose; to draft with great generality is to risk ensnarement of the innocent in a net designed for others." L. Tribe, American Constitutional Law 718 (1978). How vague must a law be for it to be held void on its face? Should it matter whether the vagueness is "avoidable"? Whether it is "substantial"? Were the laws at issue in *Gooding* and *Coates* unconstitutionally vague? Consider also the following:

a. A Washington statute requires all state-employed teachers to swear that "I will support the constitution and laws of the United States of America and of the State of Washington, and will by precept and example promote respect for the flag and the institutions of the United States of America and the State of Washington, reverence for law and order and undivided allegiance to the government of the United States." In Baggett v. Bullitt, 377 U.S. 360 (1964), the Court invalidated the oath because it was unclear, for example, whether it prohibited a teacher to refuse "to salute the flag" or to criticize "his state judicial system" or to advocate "the abolition of the Civil Rights Commission" or "foreign aid."

b. A Massachusetts statute requires all public employees to swear that "I will uphold and defend the Constitution of the United States of America and the Constitution of the Commonwealth of Massachusetts [and] oppose the overthrow of the government of the United States of America or of this Commonwealth by force, violence or by any illegal or unconstitutional method." In Cole v. Richardson, 405 U.S. 676 (1972), the Court rejected a claim of vagueness because it would be too "rigidly literal" to "presume that the Massachusetts Legislature intended by its use of such general terms as 'uphold,' 'defend,' and 'oppose' to impose obligations of specific, positive action on oath takers."

c. A city ordinance provides that "no person, while on public or private grounds adjacent to any building in which a school [is] in session, shall willfully make [any] noise or diversion which disturbs or tends to disturb the peace or good order of such school." In Grayned v. City of Rockford, 408 U.S. 104 (1972), the Court, in the expectation that the state courts would interpret the ordinance "to prohibit only actual or imminent interference with the 'peace or good order' of the school," rejected a vagueness challenge because "we think it is clear what the ordinance as a whole prohibits."

d. A Massachusetts statute provides that any person who "publicly mutilates, tramples upon, defaces or treats contemptuously the flag of the United States" shall be guilty of a misdemeanor. In Smith v. Goguen, 415 U.S. 566 (1974), the Court invalidated the statute because nonceremonial use of the flag "for adornment or [to] attract attention" has become common, and the statutory prohibition on treating the flag "contemptuously" failed "to draw reasonably clear lines between the kinds of nonceremonial treatment that are criminal and those that are not."

3. *Vagueness and overbreadth.* The close relation between vagueness and overbreadth is apparent when one recognizes not only that many vague laws are potentially overbroad, but also that many seemingly unambiguous overbroad laws are in fact potentially vague. Although the express terms of an overbroad law may not be vague, "the clarity of its language is delusive," for if the validity of the law is determined in an "as applied" manner "it will have to be recast in order to separate the constitutional from the unconstitutional applications." When, as is often the case, the precise definition of constitutionally protected expression is unclear, the very vagueness of the constitutional doctrine is in effect integrated into the law, thus uncovering "the vagueness that is latent in its terms." P. Freund, The Supreme Court of the United States 67-68 (1961); see also Note, The First Amendment Overbreadth Doctrine, 83 Harv. L. Rev. 844, 871-875 (1970). By declaring overbroad laws unconstitutional on their face, the overbreadth doctrine avoids the vagueness that ordinarily would result from permitting such laws to be enforced up to the limits of their constitutionality.

4. *Vagueness and standing.* When a law is overbroad, or at least substantially overbroad, an individual may assert its unconstitutionality even if his own expression is unprotected. Is a similar waiver of traditional standing rules warranted in the vagueness context? If the law is vague as to its coverage of the individual's own expression, the problem does not arise, for the vagueness in such circumstances violates the individual's own right to due process. Suppose, however, the individual's own expression is so clearly within the statutory prohibition that he could not reasonably have been misled. Consider Smith v. Goguen, supra, in which the defendant was convicted of "contemptuously" treating "the flag of the United States" for wearing a small cloth version of the flag sewn to the seat of his trousers. The Court held that the flag-misuse statute is so vague that "no standard of conduct is specified at all," and that because of the "absence of any ascertainable standard for inclusion and exclusion" the law is inescapably vague in all of its possible applications. Justice White argued in a concurring opinion that the statute was not vague as applied to the defendant, whose own conduct was clearly within the hard-core of the statutory prohibition, because anyone of "reasonable comprehension" should "realize that sewing a flag on the seat of his pants is contemptuous of the flag." If White is right, should the defendant have standing

to challenge the statute on the ground that it is unconstitutionally vague as applied to others? Compare Young v. American Mini Theatres, 427 U.S. 50 (1976) (declining to invalidate ordinances restricting the exhibition of sexually explicit movies on the ground that the ordinances were vague on their face where the ordinances were "unquestionably applicable" to the claimants' speech and the Court was "not persuaded" that the "ordinances [would] have a significant [chilling] effect on the exhibition of films protected by the First Amendment"), with Kolender v. Lawson, 461 U.S. 352 (1983) (invalidating as vague on its face a statute requiring "persons who loiter or wander on the streets to provide 'a credible and reliable' identification and to account for their presence when requested by a peace officer," because the law "[reached] a substantial amount of [protected first amendment] conduct," even though it was not "vague in all of its applications").

2. Prior Restraint

The doctrine of prior restraint has its roots in the sixteenth- and seventeenth-century English licensing systems under which all printing presses and printers were licensed by the state and no book or pamphlet could lawfully be published without the prior approval of a government censor. With the expiration of this system in England in 1695, the right of the press to be free from licensing gradually assumed the status of a common law right. Blackstone's definition of freedom of the press illustrates the importance of the doctrine of prior restraint in eighteenth-century thought: "The liberty of the press is indeed essential to the nature of a free state; but this consists in laying no *previous* restraints upon publications, and not in freedom from censure for criminal matter when published." 4 W. Blackstone, Commentaries *151-152.

Even after adoption of the first amendment, Story and other early American commentators accepted the view that liberty of the press was limited to "the right to publish without any previous restraint or license." J. Story, Commentaries on the Constitution of the United States §1879 (1833); see also 2 J. Kent, Commentaries on American Law 23 (2d ed. 1832). Moreover, in its 1907 decision in Patterson v. Colorado, 205 U.S. 454, 462 (1907), the Court, speaking through Justice Holmes, announced that the Constitution prohibited "all such *previous restraints* upon publications as had been practiced by other governments," but not "the subsequent punishment of such as may be deemed contrary to the public welfare." And although the Court, speaking again through Justice Holmes, recognized a dozen years later in *Schenck* that "the prohibition of laws abridging the freedom of speech is not confined to previous restraints," the doctrine of prior restraint has continued to play a central role in the jurisprudence of the first amendment. As indicated in the *Pentagon Papers* and *Nebraska Press* decisions, supra section B4, the Court has steadfastly held that there is a special presumption under the first amendment against the use of prior restraints.

Like the vagueness and overbreadth concepts, the doctrine of prior restraint is concerned with the permissible means of restricting speech. A prior restraint may thus be invalid even if the particular expression at issue could constitutionally be restricted by some other means, such as subsequent criminal prosecution. Although the historical origins of the doctrine are clear, its analytical and functional underpinnings are often puzzling, at best. Apart from historical considerations, why are prior restraints special? After all, "whether the sanction be fine or imprisonment for criminal violation or fine or imprisonment for violation of [a prior restraint], the judicial sanction takes its bite after the [expression.]" Freund, The Supreme Court and Civil Liberties, 4 Vand. L. Rev. 533, 537-538 (1951).

Lovell v. Griffin
303 U.S. 444 (1938)

MR. CHIEF JUSTICE HUGHES delivered the opinion of the Court.

Appellant, Alma Lovell, was convicted in the Recorder's Court of the City of Griffin, Georgia, of the violation of a city ordinance and was sentenced to imprisonment for fifty days in default of the payment of a fine of fifty dollars. . . .

The ordinance in question is as follows:

> Section 1. That the practice of distributing, either by hand or otherwise, circulars, handbooks, advertising, or literature of any kind, whether said articles are being delivered free, or whether same are being sold, within the limits of the City of Griffin, without first obtaining written permission from the City Manager of the City of Griffin, such practice shall be deemed a nuisance, and punishable as an offense against the City of Griffin. . . .

The violation, which is not denied, consisted of the distribution without the required permission of a pamphlet and magazine in the nature of religious tracts, setting forth the gospel of the "Kingdom of Jehovah." Appellant did not apply for a permit. . . .

The ordinance in its broad sweep prohibits the distribution of "circulars, handbooks, advertising, or literature of any kind." [The] ordinance is not limited to "literature" that is obscene or offensive to public morals or that advocates unlawful conduct. [The] ordinance embraces "literature" in the widest sense.

The ordinance is comprehensive with respect to the method of distribution. It covers every sort of circulation "either by hand or otherwise." There is thus no restriction in its application with respect to time or place. It is not limited to ways which might be regarded as inconsistent with the maintenance of public order or as involving disorderly conduct, the molestation of the inhabitants, or the misuse or littering of the streets. The ordinance prohibits the distribution of literature of any kind at any time, at any place, and in any manner without a permit from the City Manager.

We think that the ordinance is invalid on its face. Whatever the motive which induced its adoption, its character is such that it strikes at the very foundation of the freedom of the press by subjecting it to license and censorship. The struggle for the freedom of the press was primarily directed against the power of the licensor. It was against that power that John Milton directed his assault by his "Appeal for the Liberty of Unlicensed Printing." And the liberty of the press became initially a right to publish "*without* a license what formerly could be published only *with* one." While this freedom from previous restraint upon publication cannot be regarded as exhausting the guaranty of liberty, the prevention of that restraint was a leading purpose in the adoption of the constitutional provision. . . .

Legislation of the type of the ordinance in question would restore the system of license and censorship in its baldest form. . . .

As the ordinance is void on its face, it was not necessary for appellant to seek a permit under it. She was entitled to contest its validity in answer to the charge against her. . . .

Reversed.

MR. JUSTICE CARDOZO took no part in the consideration and decision of this case.

Note: Licensing as Prior Restraint

1. *Standardless licensing.* What is the special vice of the licensing scheme in *Lovell*? Why not simply uphold the scheme on its face but permit any person whose application for a license is unconstitutionally denied to challenge that denial in court? Is the Court's primary concern in *Lovell* the absence of standards to guide the City Manager's discretion? Consider the following arguments: (a) The absence of standards creates a chilling effect similar to that created by a vague or overbroad criminal statute. (b) The absence of standards invites abuse by implicitly empowering the City Manager to discriminate on the basis of content in his administration of the scheme. Do such concerns justify the unwillingness to test the constitutionality of the ordinance "as applied"?

Following *Lovell* the Court has repeatedly held that a state "cannot vest restraining control over the right to speak [in] an administrative official where there are no appropriate standards to guide his action." Kunz v. New York, 340 U.S. 290, 295 (1951) (permit required for religious meetings); see also Shuttlesworth v. City of Birmingham, 394 U.S. 147 (1969) (permit required for parades); Staub v. City of Baxley, 355 U.S. 313 (1958) (permit required to solicit members for dues-paying organization); Saia v. New York, 334 U.S. 558 (1948) (permit required to operate sound amplifiers in public).

2. *Licensing with standards.* Suppose the authority of licensing officials to deny a permit is explicitly limited to only those circumstances in which the proposed expression could constitutionally be punished in a subsequent criminal prosecution. Would such a scheme, like that in *Lovell*, be unconstitutional on its face? Assume, for example, that a state may constitutionally prohibit any person to participate in a parade that would physically interfere with another, ongoing, parade. To prevent such conflicts from occurring, could the state constitutionally prohibit any person to participate in a parade without first obtaining a permit, where the licensing officials are authorized to deny a permit only on a finding that the proposed parade would physically interfere with another, previously authorized parade? Cf. Cox v. New Hampshire, 312 U.S. 569 (1941), infra section E2a. Or assume that a state may constitutionally make criminal the exhibition of "obscene" motion pictures. May the state constitutionally create a licensing board to which all movies must be submitted prior to public exhibition, where the board is authorized to deny a license only on a finding that a movie is "obscene"? So long as the standards are clear, precise, and in conformity with the standards employed in subsequent criminal prosecutions, is there any reason to erect a special presumption against such "prior" restraints?

3. *The objections to licensing.* Consider Emerson, The Doctrine of Prior Restraint, 20 Law & Contemp. Prob. 648, 656-660 (1955):

[(1)] A system of prior restraint normally brings within the complex of government machinery a far greater amount of communication than a system of subsequent punishment. [The] pall of government control is, thus, likely to hang more pervasively over the area of communication.

[(2)] Under a system of subsequent punishment, the communication has already been made before the government takes action. [Under] a system of prior restraint, the communication, if banned, never reaches the market place at all. Or the communication may be withheld until the issue of its release is finally settled, at which time it may have become obsolete.

[(3)] A system of prior restraint is so constructed as to make it easier, and hence more likely, that in any particular case the government will rule adversely to free expression. [A] government official thinks longer and harder before deciding to undertake the serious task of subsequent punishment. [Under] a system of prior restraint, he can reach the result by a simple stroke of the pen.

[(4)] Under a system of prior restraint, the issue of whether a communication is to be suppressed or not is determined by an administrative rather than a criminal procedure. This means that the procedural protections built around the criminal prosecution [are] not applicable to a prior restraint.

[(5)] A system of prior restraint usually operates behind a screen of informality and partial concealment that seriously curtails opportunity for public appraisal and increases the chances of discrimination and other abuse.

[(6)] [As] common experience [shows, the] attitudes, drives, emotions, and impulses [of licensers] all tend to carry them to excesses. [The] function of the censor is to censor. He has a professional interest in finding things to suppress. [These factors combine to produce] unintelligent, overzealous, and usually absurd administration.

[(7)] A system of prior restraint is, in general, more readily and effectively enforced than a system of subsequent punishment. [A] penal proceeding to enforce a prior restraint normally involves only a limited and relatively simple issue — whether or not the communication was made without prior approval. The objection to the content or manner of the communication need not be demonstrated. And furthermore, the violation of a censorship order strikes sharply at the status of the licenser, whose prestige thus becomes involved and whose power must be vindicated.

How weighty are these concerns? In light of these concerns, should licensing ever be permitted?

4. *The* Freedman *case: procedural safeguards.* In Freedman v. Maryland, 380 U.S. 51 (1965), appellant, in violation of a state motion picture censorship statute, exhibited a film, conceded by the state not to be obscene or otherwise violative of the statutory standards, without first submitting it to the State Board of Censors for review. In a unanimous decision, the Court, speaking through Justice Brennan, held the statute invalid. At the outset, the Court emphasized that the statute was unconstitutional not because it might "prevent even the first showing of a film whose exhibition may legitimately be the subject of an obscenity prosecution," but, rather, because the administration of the censorship system "presents peculiar dangers to constitutionally protected speech." The Court explained that,

unlike a prosecution for obscenity, a censorship proceeding puts the initial burden on the exhibitor or distributor. Because the censor's business is to censor, there inheres the danger that he may well be less responsive than a court — part of an independent branch of government — to the constitutionally protected interests in free expression. And if it is made unduly onerous, by reason of delay or otherwise, to seek judicial review, the censor's determination may in practice be final.

The Court thus concluded that "a noncriminal process which requires the prior submission of a film to a censor avoids constitutional infirmity only if it takes place under procedural safeguards designed to obviate the dangers of a censorship system."

The Court then identified and explained several constitutionally required safeguards:

First, the burden of proving that the film is unprotected expression must rest on the [censor]. Second, while the State may require advance submission of all films, in order to proceed effectively to bar all showings of unprotected films, the requirement cannot be administered in a manner which would lend an effect of finality to the censor's determination whether a film constitutes protected expression. [Because] only a judicial determination in an adversary proceeding ensures the necessary sensitivity to freedom of expression, only a procedure requiring a judicial determination suffices to impose a valid final restraint. [To] this end, the exhibitor must be assured, by statute or authoritative judicial construction, that the censor will, within a specified brief period, either issue a license or go to court to restrain showing the film. Any restraint imposed in advance of a final judicial determination on the merits must similarly be limited to preservation of the status quo for the shortest fixed period compatible with sound judicial resolution. Moreover, [the] procedure must also assure a prompt final judicial decision, to minimize the deterrent effect of an interim and possibly erroneous denial of a license. Without these safeguards, it may prove too burdensome to seek review of the censor's determination.

Because the Maryland scheme did not contain these procedural safeguards, the Court held it unconstitutional on its face. Justices Douglas and Black concurred on the ground that no "form of censorship — no matter how speedy or prolonged it may be — is permissible."

5. *The* Freedman *safeguards*. Should the *Freedman* safeguards be deemed a minimum requirement before *any* licensing scheme may pass constitutional muster? What about the parade permit scheme, noted earlier? See Blasi, Prior Restraints on Demonstrations, 68 Mich. L. Rev. 1481, 1536-1552 (1970); Monaghan, First Amendment "Due Process," 83 Harv. L. Rev. 518, 541-543 (1970). See also Southeastern Promotions, Ltd. v. Conrad, 420 U.S. 546 (1975) (*Freedman* applicable to decision of publicly appointed board not to permit performance of musical "Hair" in public auditorium); Blount v. Rizzi, 400 U.S. 410 (1971) (*Freedman* applicable to postal stop orders).

To what extent do the *Freedman* safeguards mitigate the dangers of licensing? Does it follow from *Freedman* that a licensing scheme is always constitutional so long as (a) the licenser's authority to deny a permit is limited to only those circumstances in which the expression could constitutionally be subjected to subsequent criminal prosecution, and (b) the *Freedman* safeguards are employed? *Freedman* involved the licensing of motion pictures. Can government constitutionally require that all *books* be submitted to a board of censors prior to publication in order to screen out those that are obscene? See Bogen, First Amendment Ancillary Doctrines, 37 Md. L. Rev. 679, 685-687 (1978).

Can government constitutionally require that all persons intending to publish "classified" information first obtain a license from a board of censors, so long as the board complies with the *Freedman* safeguards and is authorized to deny a license only on a finding that publication would create a clear and present danger to the national security? Consider the following arguments to distinguish *Freedman*: (a) As suggested by Justice Brennan in the *Pentagon Papers* case, supra section B4, *Freedman* involved efforts to restrict obscenity, which is unprotected by the freedoms of speech and press, whereas classified information is subjected to licensing only "because of the presence of an overwhelming national interest." (b) Whether expression is obscene is purely a definitional question, whereas whether speech threatens the national security involves a prediction of future consequences — a determination best made *after* the expression actually occurs. (c) A minor delay in the exhibition of a motion picture is less critical than a similar delay in the publication of explicitly political speech because motion pictures are less likely to be topical.

Can government constitutionally use licensing to deal with the problem of the hostile audience if the licensing scheme incorporates the *Freedman* safeguards? Recall Kunz v. New York, supra section B3.

6. *Licensing and standing.* Note that both Lovell and Freedman, who were prosecuted for "speaking" without first obtaining a permit, were allowed to assert the unconstitutionality of the licensing schemes on their face. Should they have had standing to raise that issue?

Suppose that in *Freedman* the state court, in affirming Freedman's conviction, had interpreted the licensing scheme as incorporating all the procedural safeguards subsequently required by the Supreme Court. Would Freedman still have been permitted to assert that the law was unconstitutional on its face at the time of his violation? See Shuttlesworth v. City of Birmingham, 394 U.S. 147 (1969), invalidating a conviction for violation of a parade permit ordinance, unconstitutional on its face at the time of violation but subsequently construed by the state courts to satisfy the first amendment because it "would have taken extraordinary clairvoyance" for anyone to have predicted the subsequent narrowing construction. Does this make sense? Should *Shuttlesworth* govern when a state court narrowly construes an overbroad criminal statute after the defendant's violation?

Suppose a licensing scheme is constitutional on its face. May an individual fail to seek a permit and, when prosecuted, interpose as a defense that he could not constitutionally have been denied a permit had he applied for one?

Suppose a licensing scheme is constitutional on its face, an individual applies for a permit, it is denied, and rather than seek judicial review, the individual proceeds to speak without a permit. In a subsequent prosecution, can he assert that the denial of his application was itself unconstitutional? See Poulos v. New Hampshire, 345 U.S. 395 (1953), holding that where a licensing scheme is constitutional on its face, an individual whose permit application is unconstitutionally denied must seek judicial relief and cannot defend against a subsequent criminal prosecution by asserting the invalidity of the permit denial. Is *Poulos* reconcilable with *Lovell* and *Freedman?* See Monaghan, supra, at 542-543. Should *Poulos* apply even when time is of the essence?

Near v. Minnesota

283 U.S. 697 (1931)

[A Minnesota statute provided for the abatement, as a public nuisance, of a "malicious, scandalous and defamatory newspaper, magazine or other periodical." The statute provided further that there "shall be available the defense that the truth was published with good motives and for justifiable ends." In November 1927 a county attorney sought to invoke this statute against The Saturday Press, which had run a series of articles charging "in substance that a Jewish gangster was in control of gambling, bootlegging and racketeering in Minneapolis, and that law enforcing officers and agencies were not energetically performing their duties." The Saturday Press was especially critical of the chief of police, who was charged "with gross neglect of duty, illicit relations with gangsters, and with participation in graft." Pursuant to the statute, a state trial court perpetually enjoined The Saturday Press and its owners from publishing or circulating "any publication whatsoever which is a malicious, scandalous or defamatory newspaper." The Supreme Court reversed.]

MR. CHIEF JUSTICE HUGHES delivered the opinion of the Court. . . .

[The] object of the statute is not punishment, in the ordinary sense, but suppression of the offending newspaper or periodical. The reason for the enactment, as the state court has said, is that prosecutions to enforce penal statutes for libel do not result in "efficient repression or suppression of the evils of scandal." . . .

[The statute provides] that public authorities may bring [the] publisher of a newspaper or periodical before a judge upon a charge of conducting a business of publishing scandalous and defamatory matter [and] unless [the] publisher is able [to prove] that the charges are true and are published with good motives and for justifiable ends, his newspaper or periodical is suppressed and further publication is made punishable as a contempt. This is of the essence of censorship.

The question is whether a statute authorizing such proceedings [is] consistent with the conception of the liberty of the press as historically conceived and guaranteed. In determining the extent of the constitutional protection, it has been generally, if not universally, considered that it is the chief purpose of the guaranty to prevent previous restraints upon publication. [T]he protection even as to previous restraint is not absolutely unlimited. But the limitation has been recognized only in exceptional cases. [No] one would question but that a government might prevent actual obstruction to its recruiting service or the publication of the sailing dates of transports or the number and location of troops. On similar grounds, the primary requirements of decency may be enforced against obscene publications. The security of the community life may be protected against incitements to acts of violence and the overthrow by force of orderly government. [These] limitations are not applicable here. . . .

The fact that for approximately one hundred and fifty years there has been almost an entire absence of attempts to impose previous restraints upon publications relating to the malfeasance of public officers is significant of the deep-seated conviction that such restraints would violate constitutional right. Public officers, whose character and conduct remain open to debate and free discussion in the press, find their remedies for false accusations in actions under libel laws providing for redress and punishment, and not in proceedings to restrain the publication of newspapers and periodicals. [The] fact that the liberty of the press may be abused by miscreant purveyors of scandal does not make any the less necessary the immunity of the press from previous restraint in dealing with official misconduct. Subsequent punishment for such abuses as may exist is the appropriate remedy, consistent with constitutional privilege. . . .

The statute in question cannot be justified by reason of the fact that the publisher is permitted to show, before injunction issues, that the matter published is true and is published with good motives and for justifiable ends. If such a statute, authorizing suppression and injunction on such a basis, is constitutionally valid, it would be equally permissible for the legislature to provide that at any time the publisher of any newspaper could be brought before a court, or even an administrative officer (as the constitutional protection may not be regarded as resting on mere procedural details) and required to produce proof of the truth of his publication, or of what he intended to publish, and of his motives, or stand enjoined. If this can be done, the legislature may provide machinery for determining in the complete exercise of its discretion what are justifiable ends and restrain publication accordingly. And it would be but a step to a complete system of censorship. The recognition of authority to impose previous restraint upon publication in order to protect the community against the circulation of charges of misconduct, and especially of official misconduct, necessarily would carry with it the admission of the authority of the censor against which the constitutional barrier was erected. . . .

For these reasons we hold the statute, so far as it authorized the proceedings in this action [to] be an infringement of the liberty of the press guaranteed by the Fourteenth Amendment. . . .

Judgment reversed.

Mr. Justice Butler, dissenting. . . .

The Minnesota statute does not operate as a *previous* restraint on publication within the proper meaning of that phrase. It does not authorize administrative control in advance such as was formerly exercised by the licensers and censors but prescribes a remedy to be enforced by a suit in equity. In this case there was previous publication made in the course of the business of regularly producing malicious, scandalous and defamatory periodicals. [There] is no question of the power of the State to denounce such transgressions. The restraint authorized is only in respect of continuing to do what has been duly adjudged to constitute a nuisance. [It] is fanciful to suggest similarity between the granting or enforcement of the decree authorized by this statute to prevent *further* publication of malicious, scandalous and defamatory articles and the *previous restraint* upon the press by licensers as referred to by Blackstone and described in the history of the times to which he alludes. . . .

It is well known, as found by the state supreme court, that existing libel laws are inadequate effectively to suppress evils resulting from the kind of business and publications that are shown in this case. The doctrine that measures such as the one before us are invalid because they operate as previous restraints to infringe freedom of press exposes the peace and good order of every community and the business and private affairs of every individual to the constant and protracted false and malicious assaults of any insolvent publisher who may have purpose and sufficient capacity to contrive and put into effect a scheme or program for oppression, blackmail or extortion.

The judgment should be affirmed.

Mr. Justice Van Devanter, Mr. Justice McReynolds, and Mr. Justice Sutherland concur in this opinion.

Note: Injunction as Prior Restraint

1. *Injunctions, criminal prosecutions, and licensing.* Assuming arguendo, as the Court apparently did in *Near*, that the speech prohibited by the injunction could constitutionally be punished in a subsequent criminal prosecution, why is the injunction invalid? Why isn't the injunction a *preferable* means of restraint? After all, unlike a criminal statute, an injunction is directed to a specific individual and is thus less likely to have a broad chilling effect. See Mayton, Toward a Theory of First Amendment Process: Injunctions of Speech, Subsequent Punishment, and the Costs of the Prior Restraint Doctrine, 67 Corn. L. Rev. 245 (1982). Moreover, unlike the licensing schemes in *Lovell* and *Freedman*, the injunctions in *Near*, the *Pentagon Papers* case, and *Nebraska Press* did not require prepublication submission to a censor for review. And, unlike licensing schemes, injunctions are issued and administered by judges rather than by censors whose "business is to censor." In what sense, then, is the injunction a prior restraint?

2. *Injunctions: Are they too effective?* It has been suggested that injunctions are especially threatening to free speech because they are more likely than criminal statutes to be obeyed. Does this make sense? If an injunction prohibits only speech that could constitutionally be punished in a subsequent criminal prosecution, is the greater effectiveness of the injunction a bad thing? Compare Kalven, Foreword: Even When a Nation Is at War, 85 Harv. L. Rev. 3, 34 (1971) (the prior restraint doctrine protects "the chance for civil disobedience") with Schauer, Fear, Risk and the First Amendment: Unraveling the "Chilling Effect," 58 B. U. L. Rev. 685, 729 (1978) ("a *legal* principle can[not] be based upon the value of protecting civil disobedience"). See also Fiss, The Civil Rights Injunction 70-74 (1978).

Suppose an injunction prohibits speech that could not constitutionally be punished in a subsequent criminal prosecution. Is the greater effectiveness of the injunction now a bad thing? Are injunctions especially dangerous because they are more likely to induce compliance with unconstitutional restrictions?

Are injunctions in fact more likely than criminal statutes to be obeyed? It has been argued that injunctions have a special "mystique," causing individuals to accord them an unusually high degree of respect, and that injunctions are more likely to be obeyed because they are more likely to be enforced. Injunctions, after all, are directed at specific individuals, thus increasing the probability that violations will be detected, and violations may be viewed as a direct affront to the issuing judge's authority, thus increasing the likelihood that violations will be punished. On the other hand, punishments imposed for violations of injunctions are typically less severe than those for violations of criminal statutes, thus reducing the potential costs of violation. For analyses of these issues, see Barnett, The Puzzle of Prior Restraint, 29 Stan. L. Rev. 539, 551-552 (1977); Fiss, supra, at 71-73; Blasi, Toward a Theory of Prior Restraint: The Central Linkage, 66 Minn. L. Rev. 11, 24-49 (1981).

3. *The collateral bar rule.* It has been suggested that the critical feature of injunctions, making them far more likely to be obeyed than criminal statutes, and thus appropriately rendering them prior restraints, is the rule, applicable to injunctions generally, that an injunction "must be obeyed until it is set aside, and that persons subject to the [injunction] who disobey it may not defend against the ensuing charge of criminal contempt on the ground that the order was erroneous or even unconstitutional." Barnett, supra, at 552. In the ordinary criminal prosecution, the defendant may assert the unconstitutionality of the statute as a defense. Thus, an individual whose planned expression is prohibited by a statute he believes to be invalid may elect to gamble and speak in defiance of the statute on the assumption that, if prosecuted, he will be able to persuade a court of the statute's unconstitutionality. An individual confronted with an injunction, however, has no such option, for under the "collateral bar" rule, "persons subject to an injunctive order issued by a court with jurisdiction are expected to obey that decree until it is modified or reversed, even if they have proper grounds to object to the order." GTE Sylvania v. Consumers Union, 445 U.S. 375, 386 (1980). This rule, which derives from the notion that "respect for judicial process is a small price to pay for the civilizing hand of law," has been held applicable even to injunctions directed against expression. In Walker v. City of Birmingham, 388 U.S. 307, 321 (1967), for example, a state trial court convicted eight black ministers of criminal contempt for leading mass street parades in violation of a temporary restraining order enjoining them from participating in such parades without first obtaining a permit as required by a city ordinance. The Court, invoking the collateral bar rule, upheld the contempt convictions without passing on the constitutionality of the injunction.

The collateral bar rule may have a significant impact on an individual's willingness to disobey even a patently unconstitutional order, for if the individual violates the injunction he is subject to punishment even if the injunction is invalid. Consider Barnett, supra, at 553:

> [The rule places the individual] in a trilemma of chilling effects unique to a prior restraint situation. [He] can comply with the order and take no legal steps, thereby accepting the suppression. [He] can appeal the order directly, [but] must obey the interim restraint while [he] does so. [Or he] can [speak] in the face of [the] order, but only at the price of forfeiting [his] legal and constitutional objections to the order and thus, in all probability, embracing a contempt conviction.

With the collateral bar rule in force, the state in effect orders the enjoined individual to delay his speech unless and until a court lifts the injunction, whether or not the injunction itself is constitutionally permissible. The rule is thus strong medicine. In *Near*, for example, The Saturday Press was silenced for four years while courts debated the constitutionality of the injunction. In the *Progressive* controversy, supra section B4, the injunction remained in force for seven months, and in the *Skokie* controversy, supra section B3, the injunction prohibited the Nazis from marching for more than eight months before it was set aside.

Does the existence of the collateral bar rule justify the observation that whereas a "criminal statute chills," an injunction "freezes"? A. Bickel, The Morality of

Consent 61 (1975). Does it justify the characterization of injunctions as prior restraints? See Jeffries, Rethinking Prior Restraint, 92 Yale L.J. 409 (1983).

4. *Limits on the collateral bar rule.* The collateral bar rule may not be absolute. In Walker v. City of Birmingham, supra, for example, the Court, in declining to pass on the constitutionality of the injunction, observed that "this is not a case where the injunction was transparently invalid or had only a frivolous pretense to validity," and that the "case would arise in quite a different constitutional posture if the petitioners, before disobeying the injunction, had challenged it in the Alabama courts, and had been met with delay or frustration of their constitutional claims." The Court noted further that there "was an interim of two days between the issuance of the injunction and the [prohibited] march," but "the petitioners give absolutely no explanation of why they did not make some application to the state court during that period." Moreover, the impact of the collateral bar rule may to some extent be softened by the various *Freedman*-like procedural requirements the Court has attached to the issuance and review of injunctions against expression. See Vance v. Universal Amusement Co., 445 U.S. 308 (1980) (statute authorizing injunctions against exhibition of obscene motion pictures held unconstitutional in part because it authorized temporary injunctions of indefinite duration on the basis of a mere showing of probable success on the merits); National Socialist Party v. Skokie, 432 U.S. 43 (1977) (requiring expedited appellate review of injunctions against expression); Carroll v. President & Commissioners of Princess Anne, 393 U.S. 175 (1968) (prohibiting ex parte restraining orders against expression except where it is impossible to notify the opposing parties and to give them an opportunity to participate). Do these procedural safeguards, combined with the above-noted limitations on the collateral bar rule, substantially mitigate the undesirable effects of the rule? See Rendleman, Free Press-Fair Trial: Restrictive Orders after *Nebraska Press*, 67 Ky. L.J. 867, 892-893 (1979) (a contemnor should not "be able to ignore a restrictive order with impunity" as long as he "had reasonable access to review and time to seek it").

5. *When is an injunction not a prior restraint?* Consider the following:

a. Suppose a state holds that, under state law, the collateral bar rule is inapplicable to injunctions against expression. See cases cited in Rendleman, Free Press — Fair Trial: Review of Silence Orders, 52 N.C. L. Rev. 127, 153 n.181, 154 nn. 182-185 (1973). Should injunctions in such a jurisdiction be treated as prior restraints? Consider Blasi, at 87-91:

> [1] [A] major element in the case for a presumption against prior restraint is the undesirably abstract quality of any adjudication that occurs prior to the time the communication at issue is initially disseminated to the public. If the collateral bar rule were no longer to govern injunctions, adjudication of the first amendment claims of enjoined speakers would [still be] somewhat problematic in this regard. [The] issue in a prosecution for violating an injunction is whether the restraint on speaking was unconstitutional at the time it was imposed. That reasonable apprehensions which induced and justified the restraint in the first place failed to materialize does not impeach the state's case for the regulation.
>
> [2] Another major component of the case for linking injunctions with licensing systems is the tendency of both methods of regulation to be used more readily than methods that rely on subsequent punishment. Virtually every argument relating to overuse [would] remain applicable were the collateral bar rule no longer to govern injunctions. A stroke of the pen by a single judge would still be sufficient to create

the legal prohibition. [Moreover, disobedience] of such a personalized prohibition would still be highly visible, and would often be viewed as a test of the judicial system's will. The prospect of expeditious conviction of offenders would continue to spur prosecutorial authorities into action.

[3] An important reason for disfavoring injunctions and licensing systems as methods of speech regulation is that they rest on [the objectionable premise that] the act of speaking is an abnormally hazardous activity that warrants special regulation. [Even with abandonment of the collateral bar rule,] the choice of the injunctive method of regulation represents a judgment that the activity in question requires special, personalized, swift control. The mobilization of judicial authority at the anticipatory stage has symbolic overtones.

b. Suppose a court enjoins an individual from exhibiting any obscene motion picture, expressly defining obscenity according to the Supreme Court's definition. Do you agree that, even with the collateral bar rule in effect, such an injunction should not be treated as a prior restraint because it is "phrased in terms of a constitutionally adequate definition of obscenity" and any particular "motion picture's nonobscenity would [thus] clearly defeat any contempt proceeding [since] if the film were not obscene, there would be no violation of the injunction"? Vance v. Universal Amusement Co., 445 U.S. 308, 322 (1980) (White, J., dissenting).

c. In Pittsburgh Press Co. v. Pittsburgh Commission on Human Relations, 413 U.S. 376 (1973), the Commission, after a hearing, found that Pittsburgh Press had violated a city ordinance by displaying "help wanted" advertisements in its daily newspaper under headings designating job preference by sex. The Commission therefore issued an order prohibiting the newspaper from carrying sex-designated ads in the future. In upholding the order, the Court explained that a criminal statute cast in such terms would be constitutionally permissible and then observed:

[We have] never held that all injunctions are impermissible. [The] special vice of a prior restraint is that communication will be suppressed, either directly or by inducing excessive caution in the speaker, before an adequate determination that it is unprotected by the First Amendment. The present order does not endanger arguably protected speech. Because the order is based on a continuing course of repetitive conduct, this is not a case in which the Court is asked to speculate as to the effect of publication. Cf. [Pentagon Papers case]. Moreover, [because] no interim relief was granted, the order will not have gone into effect before our final determination that the actions of Pittsburgh Press were unprotected.

Consider Redish, The Proper Role of the Prior Restraint Doctrine in First Amendment Theory, 70 Va. L. Rev. 53, 55, 58 (1984):

[Injunctions, like licensing schemes] are appropriately disfavored [because] of the coincidental harm to fully protected expression that results [when] a *preliminary* restraint [is] imposed prior to a decision on the merits of a *final* restraint. To be effective, [an injunction or licensing scheme] must often restrict *all* relevant expression, whether or not fully protected, while the adjudicatory body determines whether the expression should be subjected to a final restraint. Such interim restraints present a threat to first amendment rights not found in subsequent punishment schemes — the threat that expression will be abridged, if only for a short time, prior to a full and fair hearing before an independent judicial forum to determine the scope of the speaker's constitutional right. [Thus,] the doctrine should strike down [injunctions only if they are] imposed *prior* to a full and fair judicial hearing.

6. *Prior restraint revisited.* Consider Freund, The Supreme Court and Civil Liberties, 4 Vand. L. Rev. 533, 539 (1951): "In sum, it will hardly do to place 'prior restraint' in a special category for condemnation. What is needed is a pragmatic assessment of its operation in the particular circumstances. The generalization that prior restraint is particularly obnoxious in civil liberties cases must yield to more particularistic analysis."

D. CONTENT-BASED RESTRICTIONS: "LOW" VALUE SPEECH

As is evident from the analysis in section B, the Court has adhered generally to a "two-level" theory of free expression in its interpretation of the first amendment. Some speech, in other words, is said to possess only "low" first amendment value and is thus accorded less than full constitutional protection. The "two-level" theory has its roots in the famous dictum of Chaplinsky v. New Hampshire, supra section B3:

> There are certain well-defined and narrowly limited classes of speech, the prevention and punishment of which have never been thought to raise any Constitutional problem. These include the lewd and obscene, the profane, the libelous, and the insulting or "fighting" words — those which by their very utterance inflict injury or tend to incite an immediate breach of the peace. It has been well observed that such utterances are no essential part of any exposition of ideas, and are of such slight social value as a step to truth that any benefit that may be derived from them is clearly outweighed by the social interest in order and morality.

This section examines the "low" value theory in depth. In so doing, it poses a number of central first amendment questions: Is the very concept of "low" value speech inherently incompatible with the guarantee of free expression? That is, does the determination that certain types of speech are of "slight social value as a step to truth" compel the Court to make "value judgments concerned with the content of expression, a role foreclosed to it by the basic theory of the First Amendment"? T. Emerson, The System of Freedom of Expression 326 (1970). Is the Court's exercise of this power tolerable so long as it confines itself to defining "low" value speech in terms of discrete categories of expression rather than in terms of particular "good" or "bad" ideas? How is the Court to determine what speech is of "low" first amendment value? What follows from a determination that a certain category of expression is of "low" first amendment value? Is such expression wholly outside the protection of the first amendment, as suggested by *Chaplinsky,* or does such a determination trigger a form of "categorical balancing," according such speech some, but less than "full," first amendment protection?

In exploring these questions, this section examines several categories of potentially "low" value expression — false statements of fact, group defamation, non-newsworthy disclosures of "private" facts, commercial speech, obscenity, and offensive speech.

1. False Statements of Fact

The Supreme Court has long maintained that "[under] the First Amendment there is no such thing as a false idea. However pernicious an opinion may seem, we depend for its correction not on the conscience of judges and juries but on the competition of other ideas." Gertz v. Robert Welch, Inc., infra this section. Government, in other words, may not restrict the expression of an idea or opinion because of *its* determination that the idea or opinion is "false." What, though, of false statements of *fact*? Recall Holmes's example of the "false cry of fire."

The problem of false statements of fact arises most often in the context of defamation. At the time of adoption of the first amendment, civil and criminal actions for defamation were commonplace, and in *Chaplinsky* the Court expressly included libel within the class of utterances that "are no essential part of any exposition of ideas, and are of such slight social value as a step to truth that any benefit that may be derived from them is clearly outweighed by the social interest in order and morality." A decade later, in Beauharnais v. Illinois, infra section D2, the Court announced that libelous utterances are not "within the area of constitutionally protected speech" and, accordingly, that "no one would contend that [they] may be punished only upon a showing" of clear and present danger.

New York Times Co. v. Sullivan

376 U.S. 254 (1964)

MR. JUSTICE BRENNAN delivered the opinion of the Court.

We are required in this case to determine for the first time the extent to which the constitutional protections for speech and press limit a State's power to award damages in a libel action brought by a public official against critics of his official conduct.

Respondent L. B. Sullivan is one of the three elected Commissioners of the City of Montgomery, Alabama. [He] brought this civil libel action against the four individual petitioners, who are Negroes and Alabama clergymen, and against petitioner the New York Times Company, a New York corporation which publishes the New York Times, a daily newspaper. . . .

Respondent's complaint alleged that he had been libeled by statements in a full-page advertisement that was carried in the New York Times on March 29, 1960. Entitled "Heed Their Rising Voices," the advertisement [described the civil rights movement in the South and concluded with an appeal for funds].

Of the 10 paragraphs of text in the advertisement, the third and a portion of the sixth were the basis of respondent's claim of libel. They read as follows:

Third paragraph:

In Montgomery, Alabama, after students sang "My Country, 'Tis of Thee" on the State Capital steps, their leaders were expelled from school, and truckloads of police armed with shotguns and tear-gas ringed the Alabama State College campus. When the entire student body protested to state authorities by refusing to re-register, their dining hall was padlocked in an attempt to starve them into submission.

Sixth Paragraph:

Again and again the Southern violators have answered Dr. King's peaceful protests with intimidation and violence. They have bombed his home almost killing his wife and child. They have assaulted his person. They have arrested him seven times — for "speeding," "loitering" and similar "offenses." And now they have charged him with "perjury" — a *felony* under which they could imprison him for *ten years*. . . .

Although neither of these statements mentions respondent by name, he contended that the word "police" in the third paragraph referred to him as the Montgomery Commissioner who supervised the Police Department, so that he was being accused of "ringing" the campus with police. He further claimed that the paragraph would be read as imputing to the police, and hence to him, the padlocking of the dining hall in order to starve the students into submission. As to the sixth paragraph, he contended that since arrests are ordinarily made by the police, the statement "They have arrested [Dr. King] seven times" would be read as referring to him. . . .

It is uncontroverted that some of the statements contained in the two paragraphs were not accurate descriptions of events which occurred in Montgomery. Although Negro students staged a demonstration on the State Capitol steps, they sang the National Anthem and not "My Country, 'Tis of Thee." Although nine students were expelled by the State Board of Education, this was not for leading the demonstration at the Capitol, but for demanding service at a lunch counter in the Montgomery County Courthouse on another day. Not the entire student body, but most of it, had protested the expulsion. [The] campus dining hall was not padlocked on any occasion. [Although] the police were deployed near the campus in large numbers on three occasions, they did not at any time "ring" the campus. [Dr.] King had not been arrested seven times, but only four. . . .

Respondent made no effort to prove that he suffered actual pecuniary loss as a result of the alleged libel.[3] . . .

The trial judge submitted the case to the jury under instructions that the statements in the advertisement were "libelous per se" and were not privileged, so that petitioners might be held liable if the jury found that they had published the advertisement and that the statements were made "of and concerning" respondent. The jury was instructed that, because the statements were libelous per se, "the law . . . implies legal injury from the bare fact of publication itself," "falsity and malice are presumed," "general damages need not be alleged or proved but are presumed," and "punitive damages may be awarded by the jury even though the amount of actual damages is neither found nor shown." [The jury returned a judgment for respondent in the amount of $500,000].

---

3. Approximately 394 copies of the edition of the Times containing the advertisement were circulated in Alabama. Of these, about 35 copies were distributed in Montgomery County. The total circulation of the Times for that day was approximately 650,000 copies.

We reverse the judgment. We hold that the rule of law applied by the Alabama courts is constitutionally deficient for failure to provide the safeguards for freedom of speech and of the press that are required by the First and Fourteenth Amendments in a libel action brought by a public official against critics of his official conduct. We further hold that under the proper safeguards the evidence presented in this case is constitutionally insufficient to support the judgment for respondent.

I

We may dispose at the outset of [respondent's argument that the judgment of the state court is insulated from constitutional scrutiny because] "The Fourteenth Amendment is directed against State action and not private action." That proposition has no application to this case. Although this is a civil lawsuit between private parties, the Alabama courts have applied a state rule of law which petitioners claim to impose invalid restrictions on their constitutional freedoms of speech and press. It matters not that that law has been applied in a civil action and that it is common law only. [The] test is not the form in which state power has been applied but, whatever the form, whether such power has in fact been exercised. . . .

II . . .

Respondent relies heavily, as did the Alabama courts, on statements of this Court to the effect that the Constitution does not protect libelous publications. Those statements do not foreclose our inquiry here. None of the cases sustained the use of libel laws to impose sanctions upon expression critical of the official conduct of public officials. [In] deciding the question now, we are compelled by neither precedent nor policy to give any more weight to the epithet "libel" than we have to other "mere labels" of state law. [Like] insurrection, contempt, advocacy of unlawful acts, breach of the peace, obscenity, solicitation of legal business, and the various other formulae for the repression of expression that have been challenged in this Court, libel can claim no talismanic immunity from constitutional limitations. It must be measured by standards that satisfy the First Amendment.

[We] consider this case against the background of a profound national commitment to the principle that debate on public issues should be uninhibited, robust, and wide-open, and that it may well include vehement, caustic, and sometimes unpleasantly sharp attacks on government and public officials. See [*Terminiello; De Jonge*]. The present advertisement, as an expression of grievance and protest on one of the major public issues of our time, would seem clearly to qualify for the constitutional protection. The question is whether it forfeits that protection by the falsity of some of its factual statements and by its alleged defamation of respondent.

Authoritative interpretations of the First Amendment guarantees have consistently refused to recognize an exception for any test of truth — whether administered by judges, juries, or administrative officials — and especially one that puts the burden of proving truth on the speaker. [Erroneous] statement is inevitable in free debate, [and] it must be protected if the freedoms of expression are to have the "breathing space" that they "need . . . to survive." . . .

Injury to official reputation affords no more warrant for repressing speech that would otherwise be free than does factual error. Where judicial officers are involved, this Court has held that concern for the dignity and reputation of the courts does not justify the punishment as criminal contempt of criticism of the judge or his decision. [*Bridges.*] If judges are to be treated as "men of fortitude, able to thrive in a hardy climate," [surely] the same must be true of other government officials, such as elected city commissioners. Criticism of their official conduct does not lose its constitutional protection merely because it is effective criticism and hence diminishes their official reputations.

If neither factual error nor defamatory content suffices to remove the constitutional shield from criticism of official conduct, the combination of the two elements is no less inadequate. This is the lesson to be drawn from the great controversy over the Sedition Act of 1798, 1 Stat. 596, which first crystallized a national awareness of the central meaning of the First Amendment. . . .

Although the Sedition Act was never tested in this Court, the attack upon its validity has carried the day in the court of history. Fines levied in its prosecution were repaid by Act of Congress on the ground that it was unconstitutional. [Jefferson], as President, pardoned those who had been convicted and sentenced under the Act and remitted their fines. [These] views reflect a broad consensus that the Act, because of the restraint it imposed upon criticism of government and public officials, was inconsistent with the First Amendment. . . .

What a State may not constitutionally bring about by means of a criminal statute is likewise beyond the reach of its civil law of libel. The fear of damage awards under a rule such as that invoked by the Alabama courts here may be markedly more inhibiting than the fear of prosecution under a criminal statute. [Alabama], for example, has a criminal libel law [which] allows as punishment upon conviction a fine not exceeding $500 and a prison sentence of six months. [The] judgment awarded in this case — without the need for any proof of actual pecuniary loss — was one thousand times greater than the maximum fine provided by the Alabama criminal statute, and one hundred times greater than that provided by the Sedition Act. [Whether] or not a newspaper can survive a succession of such judgments, the pall of fear and timidity imposed upon those who would give voice to public criticism is an atmosphere in which the First Amendment freedoms cannot survive. . . .

The state rule of law is not saved by its allowance of the defense of truth. [A] rule compelling the critic of official conduct to guarantee the truth of all his factual assertions — and to do so on pain of libel judgments virtually unlimited in amount — leads to a comparable "self-censorship." Allowance of the defense of truth, with the burden of proving it on the defendant, does not mean that only false speech will be deterred.[10] [Under] such a rule, would-be critics of official conduct may be deterred from voicing their criticism, even though it is believed to be true and even though it is in fact true, because of doubt whether it can be proved in court or fear of the expense of having to do so. They tend to make only

---

10. Even a false statement may be deemed to make a valuable contribution to public debate, since it brings about "the clearer perception and livelier impression of truth, produced by its collision with error." Mill, On Liberty (Oxford: Blackwell, 1947), at 15; see also Milton, Areopagitica in Prose Works (Yale, 1959), Vol. II, at 561.

statements which "steer far wider of the unlawful zone." [The] rule thus dampens the vigor and limits the variety of public debate. It is inconsistent with the First and Fourteenth Amendments.

The constitutional guarantees require, we think, a federal rule that prohibits a public official from recovering damages for a defamatory falsehood relating to his official conduct unless he proves that the statement was made with "actual malice" — that is, with knowledge that it was false or with reckless disregard of whether it was false or not. . . .

Such a privilege for criticism of official conduct is appropriately analogous to the protection accorded a public official when *he* is sued for libel by a private citizen. In Barr v. Matteo, 360 U.S. 564, 575, this Court held the utterance of a federal official to be absolutely privileged if made "within the outer perimeter" of his duties. The States accord the same immunity to statements of their highest officers. [The] reason for the official privilege is said to be that the threat of damage suits would otherwise "inhibit the fearless, vigorous, and effective administration of policies of government" and "dampen the ardor of all but the most resolute, or the most irresponsible, in the unflinching discharge of their duties." [Analogous] considerations support the privilege for the citizen-critic of government. It is as much his duty to criticize as it is the official's duty to administer. [As] Madison [said,] "the censorial power is in the people over the Government, and not in the Government over the people." . . .

III

We hold today that the Constitution delimits a State's power to award damages for libel in actions brought by public officials against critics of their official conduct. Since this is such an action,[23] the rule requiring proof of actual malice is applicable. . . .

Since respondent may seek a new trial, we deem that considerations of effective judicial administration require us to review the evidence in the present record to determine whether it could constitutionally support a judgment for respondent. [The] proof presented to show actual malice lacks the convincing clarity which the constitutional standard demands. [Although] there is evidence that the Times published the advertisement without checking its accuracy against the news stories in the Times' own files, [we] think the evidence against the Times supports at most a finding of negligence in failing to discover the misstatements, and is constitutionally insufficient to show the recklessness that is required for a finding of actual malice. . . .

We also think the evidence was constitutionally defective in another respect: it was incapable of supporting the jury's finding that the allegedly libelous statements were made "of and concerning" respondent. [The state courts embraced

---

23. We have no occasion here to determine how far down into the lower ranks of government employees the "public official" designation would extend for purposes of this rule, or otherwise to specify categories of persons who would or would not be included. Nor need we here determine the boundaries of the "official conduct" concept. It is enough for the present case that respondent's position as an elected city commissioner clearly made him a public official, and that the allegations in the advertisement concerned what was allegedly his official conduct as Commissioner in charge of the Police Department. . . .

the proposition that criticism of government action could be treated as criticism of the officials responsible for that action for purposes of a libel suit.]

This proposition has disquieting implications for criticism of government conduct. [It would transmute] criticism of government, however impersonal it may seem on its face, into personal criticism, and hence potential libel, of the officials of whom the government is composed. [We] hold that such a proposition may not constitutionally be utilized to establish that an otherwise impersonal attack on governmental operations was a libel of an official responsible for those operations. . . .

Reversed and remanded.

MR. JUSTICE BLACK, with whom MR. JUSTICE DOUGLAS joins, concurring. . . .

"Malice," even as defined by the Court, is an elusive, abstract concept, hard to prove and hard to disprove. The requirement that malice be proved provides at best an evanescent protection for the right critically to discuss public affairs and certainly does not measure up to the sturdy safeguard embodied in the First Amendment. . . .

The half-million-dollar verdict [gives] dramatic proof [that] state libel laws threaten the very existence of an American press virile enough to publish unpopular views on public affairs and bold enough to criticize the conduct of public officials. [There] is no reason to believe that there are not more such huge verdicts lurking just around the corner for the Times or any other newspaper or broadcaster which might dare to criticize public officials. In fact, briefs before us show that in Alabama there are now pending eleven libel suits by local and state officials against the Times seeking $5,600,000, and five such suits against the Columbia Broadcasting System seeking $1,700,000.

In my opinion the Federal Constitution has dealt with this deadly danger to the press in the only way possible without leaving the free press open to destruction — by granting the press an absolute immunity for criticism of the way public officials do their public duty. Compare Barr v. Matteo, 360 U.S. 564. Stopgap measures like those the Court adopts are in my judgment not enough. . . .*

Note: "The Central Meaning" of New York Times v. Sullivan

1. *The central meaning of the first amendment.* Professors Meiklejohn and Kalven maintained that the *New York Times* decision "is [an] occasion for dancing in the streets." Kalven, The *New York Times* Case: A Note on "The Central Meaning of the First Amendment," 1964 Sup. Ct. Rev. 191, 221 n.125. Consider Kalven, supra, at 208-209:

> The Court did not simply, in the face of an awkward history, definitively put to rest the status of the Sedition Act. More important, it found in the controversy over

---

* [In a separate concurring opinion, Justice Goldberg, joined by Justice Douglas, maintained that the first amendment affords "an absolute, unconditional privilege to criticize official conduct," but noted that "defamatory statements directed against the private conduct of a public official or private citizen" may be different, for "purely private defamation has little to do with the political ends of a self-governing society." — EDS.]

seditious libel the clue to "the central meaning of the First Amendment." The choice of language was unusually apt. The Amendment has a "central meaning" — a core of protection of speech without which democracy cannot function, without which, in Madison's phrase, "the censorial power" would be in the Government over the people and not "in the people over the Government." This is not the whole meaning of the Amendment. There are other freedoms protected by it. But at the center there is no doubt what speech is being protected and no doubt why it is being protected. The theory of the freedom of speech clause was put right side up for the first time. [The] central meaning of the Amendment is that seditious libel cannot be made the subject of government sanction.

For Justice Brennan's evaluation of *New York Times*, see Brennan, The Supreme Court and the Meiklejohn Interpretation of the First Amendment, 79 Harv. L. Rev. 1 (1965).

2. *Low value?* Does *New York Times* reject the view of *Chaplinsky* and *Beauharnais* that false statements of fact are of "slight social value" and, hence, not "within the area of constitutionally protected speech"? Consider footnote 19. Is the Court's primary concern with the protection of false statements of fact or with the risk that libel laws might generate a self-censorship that invades the zone of "high" value speech?

3. *Definitional balancing.* Consider Nimmer, The Right to Speak from *Times* to *Time*: First Amendment Theory Applied to Libel and Misapplied to Privacy, 56 Calif. L. Rev. 935, 942-943 (1968):

> [*New York Times*] points the way to the employment of the balancing process on the definitional [level]. That is, the Court employs balancing not for the purpose of determining which litigant deserves to prevail in the particular case, but only for the purpose of defining which forms of speech are to be regarded as "speech" within the meaning of the first amendment. [By] in effect holding that knowingly and recklessly false speech was not "speech" within the meaning of the first amendment, the Court must have implicitly (since no explicit explanation was offered) referred to certain competing policy considerations.

Is such "definitional balancing" an appropriate way to formulate first amendment doctrine? Contrast the "definitional balancing" in *New York Times* with that in *Brandenburg*. How does each treat the issue of intent?

4. *Is* New York Times *overprotective of false speech?* Consider the following views:

a. Even if the first amendment protects libel in the sense that government may not criminally punish such expression, it does not necessarily follow that newspapers should not have to pay for the costs of their speech. The first amendment does not require government — or public officials — to *subsidize* newspapers.

b. *New York Times* rests on the assumption that the marketplace of ideas will function better with the Court's rule than without it. But the opposite assumption seems at least equally plausible. First, self-censorship is not intrinsically a bad thing. It all depends on what speech is discouraged. Although traditional libel law may "chill" more valuable speech than the *New York Times* rule, it also "chills" more false speech. It is by no means clear that the effect of *New York Times* will be to improve the overall quality of public debate. Cf. Sunstein, Hard Defamation Cases, 25 Wm. & Mary L. Rev. 891 (1984). Second, *New York Times* may actually reduce "the quality of information [available to the public by eliminating jury judgments] as to the truth or falsity of some accusations." Nagel, How Useful Is Judicial Review in Free Speech Cases?, 69 Corn. L. Rev. 302, 323 (1984). Finally, *New York Times* may so expose public officials to journalistic abuse that it will drive capable persons away from government service, thus frustrating rather than furthering the political process.

c. *New York Times* undervalues the individual's interest in reputation. In fact, *New York Times* involves a clash of constitutional rights, for the Court has long recognized that the interest in reputation is protected as part of the "liberty" guaranteed by the fourteenth amendment. See Monaghan, Of "Liberty" and "Property," 62 Corn. L. Rev. 405 (1977). The Court too readily exalts the constitutional interest in free expression over the competing constitutional interest in reputation.

d. See Dun & Bradstreet v. Greenmoss Builders, — U.S. — , 105 S. Ct. 2939 (1985) (White, J., concurring):

> The *New York Times* rule [countenances] two evils: first, the stream of information about public officials and public affairs is polluted and often remains polluted by false information; and second, the reputation and professional life of the defeated plaintiff may be destroyed by [falsehoods]. Instead of escalating the plaintiff's burden of proof to an almost impossible level, [the Court] could have achieved [its] stated goal by limiting the recoverable damages to a level that would not unduly threaten the press. Punitive [and presumed damages] might have been prohibited, or limited. Had that course been taken and the common-law standard of liability been retained, the defamed public official, upon proving falsity, could at least have had a judgment to that effect. His reputation would then be vindicated; and to the extent possible, the misinformation circulated would have been countered. He might also have recovered a modest amount, enough perhaps to pay his litigation expenses. [In] this way, both First Amendment and reputational interests would have been far better served.

5. *Is* New York Times *underprotective of false speech?* Consider the following views.

a. Anderson, Libel and Press Self-Censorship, 53 Tex. L. Rev. 422, 424-425, 436 (1975).

> [*New York Times* will not prevent self-censorship because] it does little to reduce the cost of defending against libel claims. Instead, it perpetuates a system of censorship by libel lawyers — a system in which the relevant question is not whether a story is libelous, but whether the subject is likely to sue, and if so, how much it will cost to defend. [The decision] has failed to alleviate this problem primarily because it usually has no effect until a case reaches the trial stage.

For analysis of the use of summary judgment in this context, see Louis, Summary Judgment and the Actual Malice Controversy in Constitutional Defamation Cases, 57 So. Cal. L. Rev. 707 (1984) (observing that 75 percent of all motions for summary judgment by defendants on the issue of actual malice are granted).

b. Smolla, Let the Author Beware: The Rejuvenation of the American Law of Libel, 132 U. Pa. L. Rev. 1, 4-7, 12, 91-93 (1984):

> The data show a trend toward more generous jury awards, and a corresponding trend toward the media settling suits at a substantial cost. [One recent] study showed

that thirty out of forty-seven damage awards included punitive damages, and seven of those punitive damage awards were for $1 million or more. [The] prospect of such lucrative awards is likely to entice more potential defamation plaintiffs to bring [suit]. A failure to adjust defamation doctrine [can] be expected to have a severe impact on the media. [Many] media outlets [defend] libel actions under the peril of shutdown if they lose. [One] alternative to current law is to allow punitive damages only when the plaintiff, in addition to proving actual malice, proves common law ill-will malice. [Preferably,] punitive damages should be [abolished altogether].

See generally, Symposium, Defamation and the First Amendment: New Perspectives, 25 Wm. & Mary L. Rev. 745 (1984).

c. Lewis, *New York Times v. Sullivan* Reconsidered: Time to Return to "The Central Meaning of the First Amendment," 83 Colum. L. Rev. 602, 613, 621 (1983):

[There is now] dramatic evidence [that when] a case goes to a jury, the [*New York Times*] rule means little or nothing. All those phrases designed by the [Court] to protect freedom of speech and press may not in fact be applied. When a judge's charge lasts an hour or more, and one sentence speaks of the need to find "reckless disregard," it rolls right past the [jurors]. The first amendment [should permit] no libel actions against the critics of official conduct."

6. *The limits of* New York Times. What does the Court mean by "reckless disregard"? Does *New York Times* implicitly prohibit criminal prosecutions for libel of public officials? Are all public employees "public officials" within the meaning of *New York Times?* Consider the following decisions, which shed light on these and related issues: McDonald v. Smith, — U.S. — , 105 S. Ct. 2787 (1985) (the petition clause does not provide absolute immunity to an individual sued for expressing libelous falsehoods in petitions to government officials; rather, such an action is governed by *New York Times*); Herbert v. Lando, 441 U.S. 153 (1979) (a libel plaintiff may inquire into the state of mind of publishers and reporters in pretrial discovery in order to make out a case of reckless disregard); Monitor Patriot Co. v. Roy, 401 U.S. 265 (1971) ("a charge of criminal conduct, no matter how remote in time or place, can never be irrelevant to an official's or a candidate's fitness for office for purposes of application of" *New York Times*); St. Amant v. Thompson 390 U.S. 727 (1968) (failure to investigate or otherwise seek corroboration prior to publication is not reckless disregard for the truth unless the publisher acts with a "high degree of awareness of [probable] falsity"); Rosenblatt v. Baer, 383 U.S. 75 (1966) (*New York Times* extends "at the very least to [those] government employees who have, or appear to the public to have, substantial responsibility for or control over the conduct of governmental affairs"); Garrison v. Louisiana, 379 U.S. 64 (1964) (first amendment does not absolutely prohibit criminal prosecution for libel even of public officials, but *New York Times* standard applies). On other issues, see Bloom, Proof of Fault in Media Defamation Litigation, 38 Vand. L. Rev. 247 (1985); Symposium, Defamation in Fiction, 51 Brooklyn L. Rev. 223 (1985).

Perhaps the most important question remaining after *New York Times* was whether the privilege it recognized governed only libel of public officials, or whether it extended to libel of other persons as well. Shortly after the decision, Professor Kalven maintained that the theory of the first amendment expounded in *New York Times* constituted an implicit "invitation to follow a dialectic progression from public official to government policy to public policy to matters in the public domain." Kalven, supra.

CURTIS PUBLISHING CO. v. BUTTS, and ASSOCIATED PRESS v. WALKER, 388 U.S. 130 (1967): In these companion cases, the Court examined the question whether a libel action brought by an individual who is a "public figure" but not a "public official" must also be governed by the *New York Times* standard. Butts brought an action for libel, alleging that the defendant had published an article falsely accusing him of conspiring to "fix" a football game between the University of Georgia and the University of Alabama. At the time of the article, Butts was the athletic director of the University of Georgia, a state university, but was employed by the Georgia Athletic Association, a private corporation. Butts had served previously as head football coach at the university and had an established national reputation. In the companion case, Walker sued the Associated Press for libel, claiming that it had distributed a news dispatch falsely reporting that, when a riot erupted on the campus of the University of Mississippi because of federal efforts to enforce court-ordered desegregation, Walker had taken command of the crowd, encouraged it to use violence, and personally led a charge against the federal marshals. Walker, a private citizen at the time of the riot and publication, had pursued a distinguished military career and was a figure of national prominence. In each case, the jury found the defendant liable under state law, the trial judge approved a damage award of about $500,000, and the defendant maintained that *New York Times* should govern and that it thus could not be held liable without proof that it had published the story either knowing it to be false or with reckless disregard for the truth.

In a sharply divided set of opinions, the Court held the *New York Times* standard applicable to "public figures" as well as to "public officials" and, further, that both Butts and Walker constituted "public figures" for purposes of the rule. Chief Justice Warren, joined by Justices Brennan and White, observed that "increasingly in this country, the distinctions between governmental and private sectors are blurred" and many individuals "who do not hold public office at the moment are nevertheless intimately involved in the resolution of important public questions or, by reason of their fame, shape events in areas of concern to society at large." Moreover, Warren argued, "as a class these 'public figures' have as ready access as 'public officials' to mass media of communication, both to influence policy and to counter criticism of their views and activities." Thus, Warren concluded, "differentiation between 'public figures' and 'public officials' and adoption of separate standards of proof for each have no basis in law, logic, or First Amendment policy." Justice Black, joined by Justice Douglas, maintained that "the First Amendment was intended to leave the press [absolutely] free from the harassment of libel judgments," but accepted the narrower rationale of Chief Justice Warren "'in order for the Court to be able at this time to agree on [a disposition of] this important case.'"

Justice Harlan, joined by Justices Clark, Stewart, and Fortas, reached a somewhat different conclusion. "In *New York Times*," Harlan noted, unlike the situations in *Butts* and *Walker*, "we were adjudicating in an area which lay close to seditious libel, and history dictated extreme caution in imposing liability." At the same time, Harlan observed, "freedom of discussion 'must embrace all issues about which information is needed or appropriate to enable members of society to cope with the exigencies of their period," and because Butts and Walker were both "public figures," "the public interest in the circulation of the materials here involved, and the publisher's interest in circulating them, is not less than that involved in *New York Times*." Thus, in an effort to define an "appropriate accommodation of the conflicting interests at stake," Harlan concluded that "a 'public figure' who is not a public official [may] recover damages for a defamatory falsehood [on] a showing of highly unreasonable conduct constituting an extreme departure from the standards of investigation and reporting ordinarily adhered to by responsible publishers."

Is the extension of *New York Times* to "public figures" mandated by "the central meaning of the first amendment"? For a careful analysis of *Butts* and *Walker*, see Kalven, The Reasonable Man and the First Amendment: *Hill, Butts,* and *Walker,* 1967 Sup. Ct. Rev. 267. How should "public figure" be defined?

Gertz v. Robert Welch, Inc.

418 U.S. 323 (1974)

[In 1968 a Chicago policeman named Nuccio shot and killed a youth named Nelson. The state prosecuted Nuccio and obtained a conviction for murder. The Nelson family retained Gertz, a Chicago attorney, to represent them in civil litigation against Nuccio. In 1969 respondent, publisher of American Opinion, a monthly outlet for the views of the John Birch Society, ran an article in which it accused Gertz of being the architect of a "frame-up" of Nuccio and stated that Gertz had a criminal record and long-standing communist affiliations. Gertz filed this action for libel. After the jury returned a $50,000 verdict for Gertz, the trial court entered judgment n.o.v., concluding that the *New York Times* standard applied to any discussion of a "public issue." The court of appeals affirmed. The Supreme Court reversed.]

MR. JUSTICE POWELL delivered the opinion of the Court. . . .

II

The principal issue in this case is whether a newspaper or broadcaster that publishes defamatory falsehoods about an individual who is neither a public official nor a public figure may claim a constitutional privilege against liability for the injury inflicted by those statements. The Court considered this question on the rather different set of facts presented in Rosenbloom v. Metromedia, Inc., 403 U.S. 29 (1971), [but] no majority could agree on a controlling rationale. . . .

III

We begin with the common ground. Under the First Amendment there is no such thing as a false idea. However pernicious an opinion may seem, we depend for its correction not on the conscience of judges and juries but on the competition of other ideas. But there is no constitutional value in false statements of fact.

Neither the intentional lie nor the careless error materially advances society's interest in "uninhibited, robust, and wide-open" debate on public issues. [New York Times Co. v. Sullivan.] They belong to that category of utterances which "are no essential part of any exposition of ideas, and are of such slight social value as a step to truth that any benefit that may be derived from them is clearly outweighed by the social interest in order and morality." [*Chaplinsky.*]

Although the erroneous statement of fact is not worthy of constitutional protection, it is nevertheless inevitable in free debate. [And] punishment of error runs the risk of inducing a cautious and restrictive exercise of the constitutionally guaranteed freedoms of speech and press. Our decisions recognize that a rule of strict liability that compels a publisher or broadcaster to guarantee the accuracy of his factual assertions may lead to intolerable self-censorship. [The] First Amendment requires that we protect some falsehood in order to protect speech that matters.

The need to avoid self-censorship by the news media is, however, not the only societal value at issue. If it were, this Court would have embraced long ago the view that publishers and broadcasters enjoy an unconditional and indefeasible immunity from liability for defamation. . . .

The legitimate state interest underlying the law of libel is the compensation of individuals for the harm inflicted on them by defamatory falsehood. We would not lightly require the State to abandon this purpose, for [the] individual's right to the protection of his own good name "reflects [our] basic concept of the essential dignity and worth of every human being — a concept at the root of any decent system of ordered [liberty]." Rosenblatt v. Baer, 383 U.S. 75, 92 (1966) (concurring opinion). . . .

The *New York Times* standard defines the level of constitutional protection appropriate to the context of defamation of a public person. [For] the reasons stated below, we conclude that the state interest in compensating injury to the reputation of private individuals requires that a different rule should obtain with respect to them. . . .

[We] have no difficulty in distinguishing among defamation plaintiffs. The first remedy of any victim of defamation is self-help — using available opportunities to contradict the lie or correct the error and thereby to minimize its adverse impact on reputation. Public officials and public figures usually enjoy significantly greater access to the channels of effective communication and hence have a more realistic opportunity to counteract false statements than private individuals normally enjoy.[9] Private individuals are therefore more vulnerable to injury, and the state interest in protecting them is correspondingly greater.

More important than the likelihood that private individuals will lack effective opportunities for rebuttal, there is a compelling normative consideration underlying the distinction between public and private defamation plaintiffs. An individual who decides to seek governmental office must accept certain necessary consequences of that involvement in public affairs. He runs the risk of closer

---

9. Of course, an opportunity for rebuttal seldom suffices to undo harm of defamatory falsehood. Indeed, the law of defamation is rooted in our experience that the truth rarely catches up with a lie. But the fact that the self-help remedy of rebuttal, standing alone, is inadequate to its task does not mean that it is irrelevant to our inquiry.

public scrutiny than might otherwise be the case. And society's interest in the officers of government is not strictly limited to the formal discharge of official duties. . . .

Those classed as public figures stand in a similar position. Hypothetically, it may be possible for someone to become a public figure through no purposeful action of his own, but the instances of truly involuntary public figures must be exceedingly rare. For the most part those who attain this status have assumed roles of especial prominence in the affairs of society. Some occupy positions of such persuasive power and influence that they are deemed public figures for all purposes. More commonly, those classed as public figures have thrust themselves to the forefront of particular public controversies in order to influence the resolution of the issues involved. In either event, they invite attention and comment.

Even if the foregoing generalities do not obtain in every instance, the communications media are entitled to act on the assumption that public officials and public figures have voluntarily exposed themselves to increased risk of injury from defamatory falsehood concerning them. No such assumption is justified with respect to a private individual. He has not accepted public office or assumed an "influential role in ordering society." [He] has relinquished no part of his interest in the protection of his own good name, and consequently he has a more compelling call on the courts for redress of injury inflicted by defamatory falsehood. Thus, private individuals are not only more vulnerable to injury than public officials and public figures; they are also more deserving of recovery.

For these reasons we conclude that the States should retain substantial latitude in their efforts to enforce a legal remedy for defamatory falsehood injurious to the reputation of a private individual. The extension of the *New York Times* test [to defamatory falsehoods relating to private persons if the statements concerned matters of general or public interest] would abridge this legitimate state interest to a degree that we find unacceptable. And it would occasion the additional difficulty of forcing state and federal judges to decide on an ad hoc basis which publications address issues of "general or public interest" and which do not — to determine, in the words of Mr. Justice Marshall, "what information is relevant to self-government." [*Rosenbloom.*]

We doubt the wisdom of committing this task to the conscience of judges. . . .

We hold that, so long as they do not impose liability without fault, the States may define for themselves the appropriate standard of liability for a publisher or broadcaster of defamatory falsehood injurious to a private individual. This approach provides a more equitable boundary between the competing concerns involved here. It recognizes the strength of the legitimate state interest in compensating private individuals for wrongful injury to reputation, yet shields the press and broadcast media from the rigors of strict liability for defamation. At least this conclusion obtains where, as here, the substance of the defamatory statement "makes substantial danger to reputation apparent." This phrase places in perspective the conclusion we announce today. Our inquiry would involve considerations somewhat different from those discussed above if a State purported to condition civil liability on a factual misstatement whose content did not warn a reasonably prudent editor or broadcaster of its defamatory potential. Cf. Time, Inc. v. Hill, 385 U.S. 374 (1967). Such a case is not now before us, and we intimate no view as to its proper resolution.

IV

Our accommodation of the competing values at stake in defamation suits by private individuals allows the States to impose liability on the publisher or broadcaster of defamatory falsehood on a less demanding showing than that required by *New York Times*. This conclusion is not based on a belief that the considerations which prompted the adoption of the *New York Times* privilege for defamation of public officials and its extension to public figures are wholly inapplicable to the context of private individuals. Rather, we endorse this approach in recognition of the strong and legitimate state interest in compensating private individuals for injury to reputation. But this countervailing state interest extends no further than compensation for actual injury. For the reasons stated below, we hold that the States may not permit recovery of presumed or punitive damages, at least when liability is not based on a showing of knowledge of falsity or reckless disregard for the truth.

The common law of defamation is an oddity of tort law, for it allows recovery of purportedly compensatory damages without evidence of actual loss. Under the traditional rules pertaining to actions for libel, the existence of injury is presumed from the fact of publication. Juries may award substantial sums as compensation for supposed damage to reputation without any proof that such harm actually occurred. The largely uncontrolled discretion of juries to award damages where there is no loss unnecessarily compounds the potential of any system of liability for defamatory falsehood to inhibit the vigorous exercise of First Amendment freedoms. Additionally, the doctrine of presumed damages invites juries to punish unpopular opinion rather than to compensate individuals for injury sustained by the publication of a false fact. More to the point, the States have no substantial interest in securing for plaintiffs such as this petitioner gratuitous awards of money damages far in excess of any actual injury.

We would not, of course, invalidate state law simply because we doubt its wisdom, but here we are attempting to reconcile state law with a competing interest grounded in the constitutional command of the First Amendment. It is therefore appropriate to require that state remedies for defamatory falsehood reach no farther than is necessary to protect the legitimate interest involved. It is necessary to restrict defamation plaintiffs who do not prove knowledge of falsity or reckless disregard for the truth to compensation for actual injury. We need not define "actual injury," as trial courts have wide experience in framing appropriate jury instructions in tort actions. Suffice it to say that actual injury is not limited to out-of-pocket loss. Indeed, the more customary types of actual harm inflicted by defamatory falsehood include impairment of reputation and standing in the community, personal humiliation, and mental anguish and suffering. Of course, juries must be limited by appropriate instructions, and all awards must be supported by competent evidence concerning the injury, although there need be no evidence which assigns an actual dollar value to the injury.

We also find no justification for allowing awards of punitive damages against publishers and broadcasters held liable under state-defined standards of liability for defamation. In most jurisdictions jury discretion over the amounts awarded is limited only by the gentle rule that they not be excessive. Consequently, juries assess punitive damages in wholly unpredictable amounts bearing no necessary relation to the actual harm caused. And they remain free to use their discretion selectively to punish expressions of unpopular views. Like the doctrine of presumed damages, jury discretion to award punitive damages unnecessarily exacerbates the danger of media self-censorship, but, unlike the former rule, punitive damages are wholly irrelevant to the state interest that justifies a negligence standard for private defamation actions. They are not compensation for injury. Instead, they are private fines levied by civil juries to punish reprehensible conduct and to deter its future occurrence. In short, the private defamation plaintiff who establishes liability under a less demanding standard than that stated by *New York Times* may recover only such damages as are sufficient to compensate him for actual injury.

V

Notwithstanding our refusal to extend the *New York Times* privilege to defamation of private individuals, respondent contends that we should affirm the judgment below on the ground that petitioner is [a] public figure. [The public figure] designation may rest on either of two alternative bases. In some instances an individual may achieve such pervasive fame or notoriety that he becomes a public figure for all purposes and in all contexts. More commonly, an individual voluntarily injects himself or is drawn into a particular public controversy and thereby becomes a public figure for a limited range of issues. In either case such persons assume special prominence in the resolution of public questions.

Petitioner has long been active in community and professional affairs. He has served as an officer of local civic groups and of various professional organizations, and he has published several books and articles on legal subjects. Although petitioner was consequently well known in some circles, he had achieved no general fame or notoriety in the community. [Absent] clear evidence of general fame or notoriety in the community, and pervasive involvement in the affairs of society, an individual should not be deemed a public personality for all aspects of his life. It is preferable to reduce the public-figure question to a more meaningful context by looking to the nature and extent of an individual's participation in the particular controversy giving rise to the defamation.

In this context it is plain that petitioner was not a public figure. He played a minimal role at the coroner's inquest, and his participation related solely to his representation of a private client. He took no part in the criminal prosecution of Officer Nuccio. Moreover, he never discussed either the criminal or civil litigation with the press and was never quoted as having done so. He plainly did not thrust himself into the vortex of this public issue, nor did he engage the public's attention in an attempt to influence its outcome. We are persuaded that the trial court did not err in refusing to characterize petitioner as a public figure for the purpose of this litigation.

We therefore conclude that the *New York Times* standard is inapplicable to this case and that the trial court erred in entering judgment for respondent. Because the jury was allowed to impose liability without fault and was permitted to presume damages without proof of injury, a new trial is necessary. We reverse and remand for further proceedings in accord with this opinion.

It is so ordered.

MR. JUSTICE BLACKMUN, concurring. . . .

The Court today refuses to apply *New York Times* to the private individual, as contrasted with the public official and the public figure. [I] sense some illogic in this. [Nonetheless] I am willing to join, and do join, the Court's opinion [because by] removing the specters of presumed and punitive damages in the absence of *New York Times* malice, the Court eliminates significant and powerful motives for self-censorship that otherwise are present in the traditional libel action. By so doing, the Court leaves what should prove to be sufficient and adequate breathing space for a vigorous press. . . .

MR. JUSTICE DOUGLAS, dissenting.

The Court describes this case as a return to the struggle of "defin[ing] the proper accommodation between the law of defamation and the freedoms of speech and press protected by the First Amendment." [I] would suggest that the struggle is a quite hopeless one, for, in light of the command of the First Amendment, no "accommodation" of its freedoms can be "proper" except those made by the Framers themselves. . . .

MR. JUSTICE BRENNAN, dissenting. . . .

I adhere to my view expressed in [*Rosenbloom*] that we strike the proper accommodation between avoidance of media self-censorship and protection of individual reputations only when we require States to apply the [*New York Times*] knowing-or-reckless-falsity standard in civil libel actions concerning media reports of the involvement of private individuals in events of public or general interest. . . .

Although acknowledging that First Amendment values are of no less significance when media reports concern private persons' involvement in matters of public concern, the Court refuses to provide, in such cases, the same level of constitutional protection that has been afforded the media in the context of defamation of public persons [because] the private individual does not have the same degree of access to the media to rebut defamatory comments as does the public person and he has not voluntarily exposed himself to public scrutiny.

While these arguments are forcefully and eloquently presented, I cannot accept them, for the reasons I stated in *Rosenbloom*:

> The *New York Times* standard was applied to libel of a public official or public figure to give effect to the [First] Amendment's function to encourage ventilation of public issues, not because the public official has any less interest in protecting his reputation than an individual in private life. While the argument that public figures need less protection because they can command media attention to counter criticism may be true for some very prominent people, even then it is the rare case where the denial overtakes the original charge. Denials, retractions, and corrections are not "hot" news, and rarely receive the prominence of the original story. When the public official or public figure is a minor functionary, or has left the position that put him in the public eye . . . , the argument loses all of its force. [The] unproved, and highly improbable, generalization that an as yet [not fully defined] class of 'public figures' involved in matters of public concern will be better able to respond through the media than private individuals also involved in such matters seems too insubstantial a reed on which to rest a constitutional distinction. . . .

Moreover, the argument that private persons should not be required to prove *New York Times* knowing-or-reckless falsity because they do not assume the risk of defamation by freely entering the public arena "bears little relationship either to the values protected by the First Amendment or to the nature of our society." [Social] interaction exposes all of us to some degree of public view. "[Thus,] the idea that certain 'public' figures have voluntarily exposed their entire lives to public inspection, while private individuals have kept theirs carefully shrouded from public view is, at best, a legal fiction." [*Rosenbloom.*]

Mr. Justice White, dissenting.

For some 200 years — from the very founding of the Nation — the law of defamation and right of the ordinary citizen to recover for false publication injurious to his reputation have been almost exclusively the business of state courts and legislatures. Under typical state defamation law, the defamed private citizen had to prove only a false publication that would subject him to hatred, contempt, or ridicule. Given such publication, general damage to reputation was presumed, while punitive damages required proof of additional facts. The law governing the defamation of private citizens remained untouched by the First Amendment because until relatively recently, the consistent view of the Court was that libelous words constitute a class of speech wholly unprotected by the First Amendment, subject only to limited exceptions carved out since 1964.

But now, using that Amendment as the chosen instrument, the Court, in a few printed pages, has federalized major aspects of libel law by declaring unconstitutional in important respects the prevailing defamation law in all or most of the 50 States. . . .

These are radical changes in the law and severe invasions of the prerogatives of the States. They should at least be shown to be required by the First Amendment or necessitated by our present circumstances. Neither has been demonstrated. . . .

Scant, if any, evidence exists that the First Amendment was intended to abolish the common law of libel, at least to the extent of depriving ordinary citizens of meaningful redress against their defamers. . . . [The] law has heretofore put the risk of falsehood on the publisher where the victim is a private citizen and no grounds of special privilege are invoked. The Court would now shift this risk to the victim, even though he has done nothing to invite the calumny, is wholly innocent of fault, and is helpless to avoid his injury. I doubt that jurisprudential resistance to liability without fault is sufficient ground for employing the First Amendment to revolutionize the law of libel, and in my view, that body of legal rules poses no realistic threat to the press and its service to the public. The press today is vigorous and robust. To me, it is quite incredible to suggest that threats of libel suits from private citizens are causing the press to refrain from publishing the truth. I know of no hard facts to support that proposition, and the Court furnishes none. . . .

In any event, if the Court's principal concern is to protect the communications industry from large libel judgments, it would appear that its new requirements with respect to general and punitive damages would be ample protection. Why it also feels compelled to escalate the threshold standard of liability I cannot fathom, particularly when this will eliminate in many instances the plaintiff's possibility of securing a judicial determination that the damaging publication was indeed false, whether or not he is entitled to recover money damages. Under the Court's new rules, the plaintiff must prove not only the defamatory statement but also some degree of fault accompanying it. The publication may be wholly false and the wrong to him unjustified, but his case will nevertheless be dismissed for failure to prove negligence or other fault on the part of the publisher. I find it unacceptable to distribute the risk in this manner and force the wholly innocent victim to bear the injury; for, as between the two, the defamer is the only culpable party. It is he who circulated a falsehood that he was not required to publish. . . .*

Note: Public and Private Figures, Public and Private Speech

1. *Public figures.* Do you agree that Gertz was not a "public figure"? Consider the following:

a. Plaintiff was divorced by Russell Firestone, the scion of one of America's wealthiest families. Time magazine erroneously reported that the divorce was granted on the ground of adultery. Plaintiff sued Time for libel. In Time, Inc. v. Firestone, 424 U.S. 448 (1976), the Court rejected Time's claim that Mrs. Firestone was a public figure: "[She] did not assume any role of especial prominence in the affairs of society, other than perhaps Palm Beach society, and she did not thrust herself to the forefront of any particular public controversy in order to influence the resolution of the issues involved in it."

b. In the late 1950s, in a widely publicized case, plaintiff was convicted of contempt for his refusal to appear before a grand jury investigating Soviet espionage. Sixteen years later, defendant published a book erroneously identifying plaintiff as a Soviet agent. Plaintiff sued for libel. In Wolston v. Reader's Digest Association, 443 U.S. 157 (1979), the Court rejected the publisher's claim that plaintiff was a "limited-purpose public figure." The Court emphasized that plaintiff had not "engaged the attention of the public in an attempt to influence the resolution of the issues involved" and explained that one who commits a crime does not become a public figure even for the purpose "of comment on a limited range of issues relating to his conviction," for "[to] hold otherwise would create an 'open season' for all who sought to defame persons convicted of a crime."

c. Over the course of several years, various federal agencies spent almost half a million dollars funding plaintiff's research into aggressive monkey behavior. Senator Proxmire awarded the federal agencies his Golden Fleece of the Month Award, an award designed to publicize what Proxmire believed to be the most egregious examples of wasteful government spending. Claiming Proxmire's description of his research to be inaccurate, plaintiff sued for libel. In Hutchinson v. Proxmire, 443 U.S. 111 (1979), the Court rejected Proxmire's argument that plaintiff was a "limited-purpose public figure" for the "purpose of comment on his receipt of federal funds for research projects." The Court concluded that plaintiff "at no time assumed any role of public prominence in the broad question of

---

* [In a separate dissenting opinion, Chief Justice Burger stated: "I am frank to say I do not know the parameters of a 'negligence' [standard] as applied to the news media. [I] would prefer to allow this area of law to continue to evolve as it has up to now with respect to private citizens rather than embark on a new doctrinal theory which has no jurisprudential ancestry." — EDS.]

concern about expenditures" and that "neither his applications for federal grants nor his publications in professional journals can be said to have invited that degree of public attention and comment on his receipt of federal grants essential to meet the public figure level."

2. *Private figures.* Should the *New York Times* standard govern libels of private individuals where the statement concerns matters of public or general concern? Do the "assumption of risk" and "greater access to the media" rationales persuasively distinguish public from private persons?

3. *The need for vindication.* Justice White expressed concern in *Gertz* that the Court's decision would eliminate the private plaintiff's opportunity to vindicate himself by obtaining a judicial declaration of falsity. Is there any way to deal with this concern after *Gertz?* Consider Freund, Political Libel and Obscenity, 42 F.R.D. 491, 497 (1966): "Plaintiffs [should] be permitted to request a special verdict, so that if there is a verdict for the defendant based solely and simply on [the *New York Times* or *Gertz* privileges, the jury could nevertheless find] that the utterances were untrue." Consider also Justice Brennan's suggestion in *Gertz* that states could enact statutes, "not requiring proof of fault, which provide for an action for retraction or for publication of a court's determination of falsity if the plaintiff is able to demonstrate that false statements have been published concerning his activities." Would such a statute violate the first amendment "right" of newspapers not to publish information against their will? See Miami Herald Publishing Co. v. Tornillo, 418 U.S. 241 (1974), infra section F6c.

4. *Inapparent "danger to reputation."* What is the significance of Justice Powell's caveat that the "fault" standard governs "at least [where] the substance of the defamatory statement 'makes substantial danger to reputation apparent'"? Consider Time, Inc. v. Hill, 385 U.S. 374 (1967). In 1952 Hill and his family were held hostage for nineteen hours by escaped convicts who apparently treated them decently. Several years later, Life magazine reported that a Broadway play, "The Desperate Hours," which depicted violence directed against several hostages, was in fact a reenactment of the Hill family's ordeal. Claiming that the suggestion that he and his family had been subjected to violent treatment was false, Hill successfully sued the publisher under a New York "privacy" statute that, as interpreted, created a cause of action for any person whose name or picture was used in a "material and substantial falsification." In a six-to-three decision, the Court held that "the constitutional protections for speech and press preclude the application of the New York statute to redress false reports of matters of public interest in the absence of proof that the defendant published the report with knowledge of its falsity or in reckless disregard of the truth." Does the Court's use of the *New York Times* standard in *Hill* survive *Gertz?* Is *Hill* a situation in which "the substance of the defamatory statement [did not make] substantial danger to reputation apparent"? See also Cantrell v. Forest City Publishing Co., 419 U.S. 245 (1974), in which the Court found it unnecessary to "consider whether [the] constitutional standard announced in Time, Inc. v. Hill applies to all false-light cases."

5. *The limits of* Gertz. Does *Gertz's* "fault" standard govern all libelous statements not involving public officials or public figures, whether or not such statements concern matters of "general or public interest"? Would such an extension of *Gertz* constitute a fundamental "reinterpretation of the first amendment"? Eaton, The American Law of Defamation through *Gertz v. Robert Welch, Inc.* and Beyond: An Analytical Primer, 61 Va. L. Rev. 1349, 1415 (1975).

Is the *Gertz* privilege available only to media defendants? Note Justice Powell's consistent references to the media. Can denial of the privilege to nonmedia defendants be justified on the ground that the "press" is entitled to special constitutional protection? Compare Stewart, Or of the Press, 26 Hastings L.J. 631, 633-635 (1975) with Shiffrin, Defamatory Non-Media Speech and First Amendment Methodology, 25 U.C.L.A. L. Rev. 915, 930-935 (1978).

If the *Gertz* privilege is available to nonmedia libel defendants, what are its limits? Consider whether it should be available (a) only to nonmedia defendants who address a public audience; (b) even to nonmedia defendants who engage in "private" speech if it involves matters of "general or public interest"; or (c) to all nonmedia libelers, as it is to all media libelers, without regard to the subject matter of the statement. For a useful analysis of "private" speech, see Schauer, "Private" Speech and the "Private" Forum: *Givhan v. Western Line School District*, 1979 Sup. Ct. Rev. 217.

DUN & BRADSTREET v. GREENMOSS BUILDERS, — U.S. — , 106 S. Ct. 2939 (1985): Petitioner, a credit reporting agency, provides subscribers with financial information about businesses. All the information is confidential; under the terms of the subscription agreement the subscribers may not reveal it to anyone else. Petitioner sent a report to five subscribers indicating that respondent, a construction contractor, had filed a voluntary petition for bankruptcy. This report was false. In respondent's defamation action against petitioner, the trial judge instructed the jury that it could award presumed and punitive damages without a showing of "actual malice." The jury returned a verdict in favor of respondent and awarded $50,000 in compensatory or presumed damages and $300,000 in punitive damages. The state supreme court upheld the award on the ground that the protections "outlined in *Gertz* are inapplicable to nonmedia defamation defendants." The Supreme Court, in a five-to-four decision, affirmed the judgment.

Justice Powell's plurality opinion was joined by Justices Rehnquist and O'Connor. Although upholding the state court judgment, Justice Powell did not address the nonmedia defendant issue: "In [*Gertz*] we held that [when] a private individual [sues] a publisher for a libel that [involves] a matter of public concern, [the] First Amendment [prohibits] awards of presumed and punitive damages [unless] the plaintiff shows 'actual malice.' [We] have never considered whether the *Gertz* balance obtains when the defamatory statements involve no issue of public concern. To make this determination, we must employ the approach approved in *Gertz* and balance the State's interest in compensating private individuals for injury to their reputation against the First Amendment interest in protecting this type of expression. [The] state interest [here] is identical to the one weighed in *Gertz*. [The] First Amendment interest, on the other hand, is less important than the one weighed in *Gertz*. We have long recognized that not all speech is of equal First Amendment importance. It is speech on '"matters of public concern"' that is 'at the heart of the First Amendment's protection.' In contrast, speech on matters of purely private concern is of less First Amendment concern. [Citing Connick v. Meyers, infra section F3b.] [When the state regulates such expression], 'There is no threat to the free and robust debate of public issues, [and] there is no potential interference with a meaningful dialogue of ideas concerning self-government.' [While] such speech is not totally unprotected by the First Amendment, its protections are less stringent. [In] light of the reduced constitutional value of speech involving no matters of public concern, we hold that the state interest adequately supports awards of presumed and punitive damages — even absent a showing of 'actual malice.'

"The only remaining issue is whether petitioner's credit report involved a matter of public concern. [The report] was speech solely in the individual interest of the speaker and its specific business audience. This particular interest warrants no special protection when [the] speech is wholly false and clearly damaging to the victim's business reputation. Moreover, since the credit report was made available to only five subscribers, who, under the terms of the subscription agreement, could not disseminate it further, it cannot be said that the report involves any 'strong interest in the free flow of commercial information.' [In] addition, the speech here, like advertising, is hardy, [objectively verifiable,] and unlikely to be deterred by incidental state regulation. [Citing Virginia Pharmacy Board v. Virginia Consumer Council, infra section D4.]" Justice Powell thus concluded that, in light of the "content, form, and context" of the speech, it concerned "no public issue."

Chief Justice Burger concurred in the judgment: "I [agree with the plurality opinion that *Gertz* should be] limited to circumstances in which the alleged defamatory expression concerns a matter of general public importance, and that the expression at issue here relates to a matter of essentially private concern." Burger added that "*Gertz* should be overruled."

Justice White also concurred in the judgment: "For either of two reasons, I believe that [*Gertz* should not be applied in this case]. First, I [believe *Gertz*] should be overruled. Second, as Justice Powell indicates, the defamatory publication in this case does not deal with a matter of public importance. [Wisely], Justice Powell does not rest his application of a different rule here on a distinction drawn between media and non-media defendants. On that issue, I agree with [the four dissenting Justices] that the First Amendment gives no more protection to the press in defamation suits than it does to others exercising their freedom of speech."

Justice Brennan, joined by Justices Marshall, Blackmun, and Stevens, dissented. At the outset, Justice Brennan, like Justice White, rejected the media/nonmedia distinction: "The free speech guarantee gives each citizen an equal right to self-expression and to participation in self-government. [Accordingly, a majority of the] Members of this Court agree today that, in the context of defamation law, the rights of the institutional media are no greater and no less than those enjoyed by other individuals or organizations engaged in the same activities."

Justice Brennan then turned to the "public interest" question: "One searches *Gertz* in vain for a single word to support the proposition that limits on presumed and punitive damages obtained only when speech involved matters of public interest. *Gertz* could not have been grounded in such a premise. Distrust of placing in the courts the power to decide what speech was of public concern was precisely the rationale Gertz offered for rejecting the *Rosenbloom* plurality approach. . . .

"Even accepting the notion that a distinction can and should be drawn between matters of public concern and matters of purely private concern, however, the [five Members of the Court voting to affirm the damage award in this case] propose an impoverished definition of 'matters of public concern' that is irreconcilable with First Amendment principles. [Speech] about commercial or economic matters, even if not directly implicating 'the central meaning of the First Amendment,' is an important part of our public discourse. [The] choices we make when we step into the voting booth may well be the product of what we have learned from the myriad of daily economic and social phenomenon that surround us. [Moreover, our] economic system is predicated on the assumption that human welfare will be improved through informed decisionmaking. [Thus, even] if not at 'the essence of self-government,' the expression at issue in this case is important to both our public discourse and our private welfare. That its motivation might be the economic interest of the speaker or listeners does not diminish its First Amendment value. . . .

"Justice Powell also relies in part on the fact that the expression had a limited circulation and was expressly kept confidential by those who received it. [This] argument does not save the analysis. The assertion that the limited and confidential circulation might make the expression less a matter of public concern is dubious on its own terms and flatly inconsistent with our decision in Givhan v. Western Line Consolidated School Dist., 439 U.S. 410 (1979) [rejecting the proposition that "private expression of one's views is beyond constitutional protection"]. Perhaps more importantly, Dun & Bradstreet doubtless provides thousands of credit reports to thousands of subscribers who receive the information pursuant to the same strictures imposed on the recipients in this case. As a systemic matter, therefore, today's decision diminishes the free flow of information because Dun & Bradstreet will generally be made more reticent in providing information to all its subscribers." Justice Brennan concluded that, under *Gertz*, respondent "should be required to show actual malice to receive presumed or punitive damages."

After *Dun & Bradstreet*, consider the following: (a) On the same facts, Greenmoss claims that it is entitled to recover compensatory damages without any showing of "fault." (b) X sues Y for libel arising out of Y's letter to Z stating falsely that X favors abortion and advising Z not to support X's political campaign. (c) X sues Y for libel arising out of Y's letter to Z stating falsely that X is an alcoholic and advising Z not to hire X as a milkman. (d) X sues newspaper Y for publishing a story stating falsely that X, who had been injured in a car accident, was "on parole." In (b), (c), and (d), X claims that he is entitled to recover presumed and punitive damages without any showing of "actual malice."

Note: Other False Statements of Fact

In *Gertz* the Court again made explicit its conclusion that "there is no constitutional value in false statements of fact." Nonetheless, in its *New York Times/Gertz* line of authority, the Court granted substantial first amendment protection to false statements of fact in the libel context to avoid "self-censorship" and "to protect speech that matters." How should false statements of fact be dealt with in other contexts? Consider the following:

a. Suppose an individual falsely asserts that a particular law was enacted because a majority of legislators had been "paid off." In what circumstances, if any, may government criminally punish an individual for factually false utterances that defame government itself?

b. Recall section 3 of the Espionage Act of 1917, supra section B1: "Whoever, when the United States is at war, shall willfully make or convey false reports [with] intent to interfere with [the] success of the military [forces] of the United States [shall be guilty of a felony]." Is the act constitutional in light of the *New York Times/Gertz* line of authority? If not, how might it be redrafted to satisfy the first amendment? Consider Schaefer v. United States, 251 U.S. 466 (1920), in which the Court upheld a conviction under the "false statement" provision of the 1917 act where defendants, in reprinting articles published previously in German newspapers, made minor alterations in the text and, in reprinting a speech by Senator LaFollette, changed LaFollette's statement that the war would lead to "bread lines" to read that it would lead to "bread riots." Brandeis, joined by Holmes, dissented, arguing that even if speech is false, it may not be punished unless it creates a clear and present danger.

c. In Bridges v. California, supra section B2, the Court held that an individual who criticized judges or the judicial process could not constitutionally be held in contempt absent a showing that such criticism created a clear and present danger to the fair administration of justice. What, though, if the criticism includes false statements of fact? Consider Pennekamp v. Florida, 328 U.S. 331 (1946), in which the court reviewed the contempt convictions of the publisher and editor of a newspaper that harshly criticized several local judicial decisions as too favorable to criminals. Although recognizing that the defendants had distorted the facts and that the judge who was the object of the criticism might have had an action for defamation, the Court treated the standard of review as unaffected by the falsity of the speech and thus set aside the convictions because there was no showing of a clear and present danger. See also Craig v. Harney, 331 U.S. 367 (1947).

d. The problem of false statements of fact arises often in the context of political campaigns. Suppose, for example, a supporter of a candidate's opponent falsely accuses the candidate of some impropriety. So long as the candidate can meet the demands of *New York Times*, he can, of course, sue for libel. That may be small consolation, however, if he loses the election. To avoid that result, can the candidate obtain an injunction against further dissemination of the falsehood? Can a state electoral commission prohibit distribution of any campaign literature containing the falsehood? Suppose that, instead of defaming an opponent, a candidate or his supporters falsely inflate the candidate's own qualifications. In what circumstances, and by what means, may such speech be restricted? See Vanasco v. Schwartz, 401 F. Supp. 87 (E.D.N.Y. 1975), summarily aff'd, Schwartz v. Postel, 423 U.S. 1041 (1976) (invalidating on grounds of overbreadth a State Board of Elections' "Fair Campaign Code" that prohibited any "misrepresentation of any candidate's qualifications," of "a candidate's position," or of "any candidate's party affiliation or party endorsement"); Tomei v. Finley, 512 F. Supp. 695 (N.D. Ill. 1981) (granting a preliminary injunction against a candidate's use of a campaign slogan misleadingly suggesting that he was the candidate of a different political party); Developments in the Law — Elections, 88 Harv. L. Rev. 1111, 1272-1286 (1975).

2. Group Defamation

Beauharnais v. Illinois
343 U.S. 250 (1952)

[Beauharnais, president of the White Circle League, organized the distribution of a leaflet setting forth a petition calling on the mayor and city council of Chicago "to halt the further encroachment, harassment and invasion of white people, their property, neighborhoods and persons, by the Negro." The leaflet called for "One million self respecting white people in Chicago to unite," and added that "If persuasion and the need to prevent the white race from becoming mongrelized by the negro will not unite us, then the aggressions, [rapes], robberies, knives, guns and marijuana of the negro surely will." Attached to the leaflet was an application for membership in the White Circle League. As a result of his participation in the distribution of this leaflet, Beauharnais was convicted under an Illinois statute declaring it unlawful for any person to manufacture, publish, sell or exhibit in any public place any publication which "portrays depravity, criminality, unchastity, or lack of virtue of a class of citizens, of any race, color, creed or religion which [publication] exposes the citizens of any race, color, creed or religion to contempt, derision, or obloquy or which is productive of breach of the peace or riots." At Beauharnais's trial, the judge refused to instruct the jury that, in order to convict, they must find "that the article complained of was likely to produce a clear and present danger of a serious substantive evil that rises far above public inconvenience, annoyance or unrest." The trial judge also refused to consider Beauharnais's offer of proof on the issue of truth, for under Illinois law, the defense of truth is unavailable in a prosecution for criminal libel unless "the truth of all facts in the utterance [be] shown together with good motive for publication." The Supreme Court, in a five-to-four decision, affirmed the conviction.]

MR. JUSTICE FRANKFURTER delivered the opinion of the Court. . . .

Libel of an individual was a common-law crime, and thus criminal in the colonies. Indeed, at common law, truth or good motives was no defense. In the first decades after the adoption of the Constitution, this was changed by judicial decision, statute or constitution in most States, but nowhere was there any suggestion that the crime of libel be abolished. [As we have observed, "libelous] utterances are no essential part of any exposition of ideas, and are of such slight social value as a step to truth that any benefit that may be derived from them is clearly outweighed by the social interest in order and morality. . . ." [*Chaplinsky.*]

No one will gainsay that it is libelous falsely to charge another with being a rapist, robber, carrier of knives and guns, and user of marijuana. The precise question before us, then, is whether the protection of "liberty" in the Due Process Clause of the Fourteenth Amendment prevents a State from punishing such libels — as criminal libel has been defined, limited and constitutionally recognized time out of mind — directed at designated collectivities and flagrantly disseminated. [If] an utterance directed at an individual may be the object of criminal sanctions, we cannot deny to a State power to punish the same utterance directed at a defined group, unless we can say that this is a willful and purposeless restriction unrelated to the peace and well-being of the State.

Illinois did not have to look beyond her own borders or await the tragic experience of the last three decades to conclude that wilful purveyors of falsehood concerning racial and religious groups promote strife and tend powerfully to obstruct the manifold adjustments required for free, ordered life in a metropolitan, polyglot community. From the murder of the abolitionist Lovejoy in 1837 to the Cicero riots of 1951, Illinois has been the scene of exacerbated tension between races, often flaring into violence and destruction. In many of these outbreaks, utterances of the character here in question, so the Illinois legislature could conclude, played a significant part. . . .

In the face of this history and its frequent obligato of extreme racial and religious propaganda, we would deny experience to say that the Illinois legislature was without reason in seeking ways to curb false or malicious defamation of racial and religious groups, made in public places and by means calculated to have a powerful emotional impact on those to whom it was presented. . . .

It may be argued, and weightily, that this legislation will not help matters; that tension and on occasion violence between racial and religious groups must be traced to causes more deeply embedded in our society than the rantings of modern Know-Nothings. Only those lacking responsible humility will have a confident solution for problems as intractable as the frictions attributable to differences of race, color or religion. This being so, it would be out of bounds for the judiciary to deny the legislature a choice of policy, provided it is not unrelated to the problem and not forbidden by some explicit limitation on the State's power. That the legislative remedy might not in practice mitigate the evil, or might itself raise new problems, would only manifest once more the paradox of reform. It is the price to be paid for the trial-and-error inherent in legislative efforts to deal with obstinate social issues. . . .

[It] is not within our competence to confirm or deny claims of social scientists as to the dependence of the individual on the position of his racial or religious group in the community. [Moreover, it would be] quite outside the scope of our authority [for] us to deny that the Illinois legislature may warrantably believe that a man's job and his educational opportunities and the dignity accorded him may depend as much on the reputation of the racial and religious group to which he willy-nilly belongs, as on his own merits. This being so, we are precluded from saying that speech concededly punishable when immediately directed at individuals cannot be outlawed if directed at groups with whose position and esteem in society the affiliated individual may be inextricably involved.

We are warned that the choice open to the Illinois legislature here may be abused, [that] prohibiting libel of a creed or of a racial group [is] but a step from prohibiting libel of a political party.[18] Every power may be abused, but the possibility of abuse is a poor reason for denying Illinois the power to adopt measures against criminal libels sanctioned by centuries of Anglo-American law. "While this Court sits" it retains and exercises authority to nullify action which encroaches on freedom of utterance under the guise of punishing libel. Of course discussion cannot be denied and the right, as well as the duty, of criticism must not be be stifled. . . .

____

18. It deserves emphasis that there is no such attempt in this statute. The rubric "race, color, creed or religion" which describes the type of group libel of which is punishable, has attained too fixed a meaning to permit political groups to be brought within it. If a statute sought to outlaw libels of political parties, quite different problems not now before us would be raised. For one thing, the whole doctrine of fair comment as indispensable to the democratic political process would come into play. . . .

As to the defense of truth, Illinois in common with many States requires a showing not only that the utterance state the facts, but also that the publication be made "with good motives and for justifiable ends." Both elements are necessary if the defense is to prevail. [The] teaching of a century and a half of criminal libel prosecutions in this country would go by the board if we were to hold that Illinois was not within her rights in making this combined requirement. Assuming that defendant's offer of proof directed to a part of the defense was adequate,[21] it did not satisfy the entire requirement which Illinois could exact.[22]

Libelous utterances not being within the area of constitutionally protected speech, it is unnecessary, either for us or for the State courts, to consider the issues behind the phrase "clear and present danger." Certainly no one would contend that obscene speech, for example, may be punished only upon a showing of such circumstances. Libel, as we have seen, is in the same class.

We find no warrant in the Constitution for denying to Illinois the power to pass the law here under attack. . . .

Affirmed.

MR. JUSTICE BLACK, with whom MR. JUSTICE DOUGLAS concurs, dissenting. . . .

The Court condones this expansive state censorship by painstakingly analogizing it to the law of criminal libel. As a result of this refined analysis, the Illinois statute emerges labeled a "group libel law." This label may make the Court's holding more palatable for those who sustain it, but the sugar-coating does not make the censorship less deadly. However tagged, the Illinois law is not that criminal libel which has been "defined, limited and constitutionally recognized time out of mind." For as "constitutionally recognized" that crime has provided for punishment of false, malicious, scurrilous charges against individuals, not against huge groups. This limited scope of the law of criminal libel is of no small importance. It has confined state punishment of speech and expression to the narrowest of areas involving nothing more than purely private feuds. Every expansion of the law of criminal libel so as to punish discussions of matters of public concern means a corresponding invasion of the area dedicated to free expression by the First Amendment. . . .

The Court's reliance on [*Chaplinsky*] is also misplaced. New Hampshire had a state law making it an offense to direct insulting words at an *individual* on a public street. Chaplinsky had violated that law by calling a man vile names "face-to-face." We pointed out in that context that the use of such "fighting" words was not an essential part of exposition of ideas. Whether the words used in their context here are "fighting" words in the same sense is doubtful, but whether so or not they are not addressed to or about *individuals*. Moreover, the leaflet used here was also the means adopted by an assembled group to enlist interest in their

21. Defendant offered to show (1) that crimes were more frequent in districts heavily populated by Negroes than in those where whites predominated; (2) three specific crimes allegedly committed by Negroes; and (3) that property values declined when Negroes moved into a neighborhood. It is doubtful whether such a showing is as extensive as the defamatory allegations in the lithograph circulated by the defendant.

22. The defense attorney put a few questions to the defendant on the witness stand which tended toward elaborating his motives in circulating the lithograph complained of. When objections to these questions were sustained, no offer of proof was made, in contrast to the rather elaborate offer which followed the refusal to permit questioning tending to show the truth of the matter. Indeed, in that offer itself, despite its considerable detail, no mention was made of the necessary element of good motive or justifiable ends. In any event, the question of exclusion of this testimony going to motive was not raised by motion in the trial court, on appeal in Illinois, or before us.

efforts to have legislation enacted. And the fighting words were but a part of arguments on questions of wide public interest and importance. Freedom of petition, assembly, speech and press could be greatly abridged by a practice of meticulously scrutinizing every editorial, speech, sermon or other printed matter to extract two or three naughty words on which to hang charges of "group libel." The *Chaplinsky* case makes no such broad inroads on First Amendment freedoms. . . .

If there be minority groups who hail this holding as their victory, they might consider the possible relevancy of this ancient remark: "Another such victory and I am undone."

Mr. Justice Douglas, dissenting. . . .

My view is that if in any case other public interests are to override the plain command of the First Amendment, the peril of speech must be clear and present, leaving no room for argument, raising no doubts as to the necessity of curbing speech in order to prevent disaster. . . .*

Note: Group Defamation

1. *The* Skokie *controversy.* Reconsider the *Skokie* controversy, supra section B3, in light of *Beauharnais.* Does the display of a swastika constitute "group libel"?

2. *Group defamation as "libel."* Central to Justice Frankfurter's analysis was the conclusion that "group libel," as defined in the Illinois statute, is not "within the area of constitutionally protected speech" and thus need not be tested by the clear and present danger standard. In justifying this conclusion, Frankfurter relied primarily on *Chaplinsky*'s characterization of "libelous" utterances as "unprotected" speech. In New York Times v. Sullivan, however, the Court announced that "libel can claim no talismanic immunity from constitutional limitations." Does *New York Times* thus pull the rug out from under *Beauharnais?* See Collin v. Smith, 578 F.2d 1197 (7th Cir. 1978) (the "approach sanctioned implicitly in Beauharnais would [not] pass constitutional muster today").

Note that the concept of "group libel" held in *Beauharnais* to be "unprotected" expression was not limited to false statements of fact. Under the Illinois statute, it was unlawful to portray "depravity, criminality, unchastity, or lack of virtue of a class of citizens, of any race, color, creed, or religion," unless the defendant could prove *both* truth *and* "good motive for publication." As Frankfurter observed, this aspect of the statute was in accord with the historic common law conception of defamation. Do *New York Times* and *Gertz* implicitly hold that "libel" is of "low" first amendment value only insofar as it consists of false statements of fact? For a brief discussion of that question, see Cox Broadcasting Corp. v. Cohn, 420 U.S. 469, 489-491 (1975); id. at 497-500 (Powell, J., concurring).

3. *Other bases for "low" value status.* If the conclusion that group libel constitutes "low" value speech can no longer be sustained solely by invocation of the phrase "libel," is there any other basis for attributing to such expression only "low" first amendment value? Consider the following arguments.

a. The group libel doctrine is a logical extension of the fighting words doctrine. The fighting words doctrine declares the malicious use of personal epithets to be

---

* [Dissenting opinions of Justices Reed and Jackson are omitted — Eds.]

of "low" first amendment value, see supra section B3; the group libel doctrine accords equivalent treatment to the similarly malicious use of what amount to epithets directed against groups.

b. It cannot be seriously maintained that the first amendment was intended to protect speech that maliciously "portrays depravity, criminality, unchastity, or lack of virtue of a class of citizens, of any race, color, creed or religion." Just as express language of incitement is incompatible with the fundamental assumptions of our democratic system, and is thus of "low" first amendment value, group libel is likewise of "low" value because of its incompatibility with our society's fundamental commitment to human dignity and equality. See Beth, Group Libel and Free Speech, 39 Minn. L. Rev. 167 (1955). Consider W. Berns, Freedom, Virtue & First Amendment 152-153 (1957): "[Beauharnais] was punished because he would deprive his fellow citizens of the equal protection of the laws. [To] refer to Illinois' action against Beauharnais as an act of tyrannical government is to falsify the facts; at the very minimum, to do so is to miss something of the essence of the problem."

c. Application of the clear and present danger standard is inappropriate in the context of group libel, and such speech is of especially "low" first amendment value, because it operates not by persuasion but by insidiously undermining social attitudes and beliefs, as evidenced by the experience of Nazi Germany. See Riesman, Democracy and Defamation: Control of Group Libel, 42 Colum. L. Rev. 727 (1942).

4. *False statement of fact.* Suppose the Illinois statute prohibited only false statements of fact that portray "depravity, criminality, unchastity, or lack of virtue of a class of citizens, of any race, color, creed or religion." Are the interests threatened by such expression too diffuse to warrant restriction? Given the statements in the *Beauharnais* leaflet, what sort of showing would be necessary to establish "truth" or "falsity"? Consider Arkes, Civility and the Restriction of Speech: Rediscovering the Defamation of Groups, 1974 Sup. Ct. Rev. 281, 301: "One can think of few things worse than having a jury pronounce on the 'truth' of Beauharnais's charges, with all the solemnity and authority of the legal process. [These] are not the kinds of questions that we typically trust to the judgment of juries."

3. *"Non-Newsworthy" Disclosures of "Private" Information*

Cox Broadcasting Corp. v. Cohn
420 U.S. 469 (1975)

MR. JUSTICE WHITE delivered the opinion of the Court.

The issue before us in this case is whether, consistently with the First and Fourteenth Amendments, a State may extend a cause of action for damages for invasion of privacy caused by the publication of the name of a deceased rape victim which was publicly revealed in connection with the prosecution of the crime.

In August 1971, appellee's 17-year-old daughter was the victim of a rape and did not survive the incident. Six youths were soon indicted for murder and rape.

Although there was substantial press coverage of the crime and of subsequent developments, the identity of the victim was not disclosed pending trial, perhaps because of Ga. Code Ann. §26-9901 (1972), which makes it a misdemeanor to publish or broadcast the name or identity of a rape victim. In April 1972, some eight months later, the six defendants appeared in court. . . .

In the course of the proceedings that day, appellant Wassell, a reporter covering the incident for his employer, learned the name of the victim from an examination of the indictments which were made available for his inspection in the courtroom. That the name of the victim appears in the indictments and that the indictments were public records available for inspection are not disputed. Later that day, Wassell broadcast over the facilities of station WSB-TV, a television station owned by appellant Cox Broadcasting Corp., a news report concerning the court proceedings. The report named the victim of the crime and was repeated the following day.

In May 1972, appellee brought an action for money damages against appellants, relying on §26-9901 and claiming that his right to privacy had been invaded by the television broadcasts giving the name of his deceased daughter. Appellants admitted the broadcasts but claimed that they were privileged under both state law and the First and Fourteenth Amendments.

[The trial court rejected appellants' constitutional claims and granted summary judgment to appellee as to liability, with the determination of damages to await trial by jury. The Georgia Supreme Court reversed the grant of summary judgment. In so doing, the court observed that the first amendment did not, as a matter of law, require judgment for appellants. Moreover, the court rejected appellants' contention that the victim's name was a matter of public interest and could thus be published with impunity, noting that it could discern "no public interest or general concern about the identity of the victim of such a crime as will make the right to disclose the identity of the victim rise to the level of First Amendment protection." At the same time, however, the court remanded to enable the jury to determine whether the public disclosure of the daughter's name actually invaded appellee's "zone of privacy" and whether appellants had invaded appellee's privacy "with willful or negligent disregard for the fact that reasonable men would find the invasion highly offensive."]

We [reverse].

Georgia stoutly defends both §26-9901 and the State's common-law privacy action challenged here. Its claims are not without force, for powerful arguments can be made, and have been made, that however it may be ultimately defined, there *is* a zone of privacy surrounding every individual, a zone within which the State may protect him from intrusion by the press, with all its attendant publicity. Indeed, the central thesis of the root article by Warren and Brandeis, The Right to Privacy, 4 Harv. L. Rev. 193, 196 (1890), was that the press was overstepping its prerogatives by publishing essentially private information and that there should be a remedy for the alleged abuses.[16]

---

16. "Of the desirability — indeed of the necessity — of some such protection [of the right of privacy], there can, it is believed, be no doubt. The press is overstepping in every direction the obvious bounds of propriety and of decency. Gossip is no longer the resource of the idle and of the vicious, but has become a trade, which is pursued with industry as well as effrontery. To satisfy a prurient taste the details of sexual relations are spread broadcast in the columns of the daily papers. To occupy the indolent, column upon column is filled with idle gossip, which can only be procured by intrusion

More compellingly, the century has experienced a strong tide running in favor of the so-called right of privacy. "[I]n one form or another, the right of privacy is by this time recognized and accepted in all but a very few jurisdictions." W. Prosser, Law of Torts 804 (4th ed.). . . .

These are impressive credentials for a right of privacy. [The] version of the privacy tort now before us — termed in Georgia "the tort of public disclosure," [is] that in which the plaintiff claims the right to be free from unwanted publicity about his private affairs, which, although wholly true, would be offensive to a person of ordinary sensibilities. [In] this sphere of collision between claims of privacy and those of the free press, the interests on both sides are plainly rooted in the traditions and significant concerns of our society. Rather than address the broader question whether truthful publications may ever be subjected to civil or criminal liability, [it] is appropriate to focus on the narrower interface between press and privacy that this case presents, namely, whether the State may impose sanctions on the accurate publication of the name of a rape victim obtained from public records — more specifically, from judicial records which are maintained in connection with a public prosecution and which themselves are open to public inspection. We are convinced that the State may not do so.

[In] a society in which each individual has but limited time and resources with which to observe at first hand the operations of his government, he relies necessarily upon the press to bring to him in convenient form the facts of those operations. [With] respect to judicial proceedings in particular, the function of the press serves to guarantee the fairness of trials and to bring to bear the beneficial effects of public scrutiny upon the administration of justice. [The] commission of crime, prosecutions resulting from it, and judicial proceedings arising from the prosecutions [are] without question events of legitimate concern to the public and consequently fall within the responsibility of the press to report the operations of government. . . .

[Moreover, the] interests in privacy fade when the information involved already appears on the public record. [The] publication of truthful information available on the public record contains none of the indicia of those limited categories of expression, such as "fighting" words, which "are no essential part of any exposition of ideas, and are of such slight social value as a step to truth that any benefit that may be derived from them is clearly outweighed by the social interest in order and morality." [*Chaplinsky.*]

By placing the information in the public domain on official court records, the State must be presumed to have concluded that the public interest was thereby being served. Public records by their very nature are of interest to those concerned with the administration of government, and a public benefit is performed by the reporting of the true contents of the records by the media. . . .

We are reluctant to embark on a course that would make public records generally available to the media but forbid their publication if offensive to the sensibilities of the supposed reasonable man. Such a rule would make it very difficult for

---

upon the domestic circle. The intensity and complexity of life, attendant upon advancing civilization, have rendered necessary some retreat from the world, and man, under the refining influence of culture, has become more sensitive to publicity, so that solitude and privacy have become more essential to the individual; but modern enterprise and invention have, through invasions upon his privacy, subjected him to mental pain and distress, far greater than could be inflicted by mere bodily injury. . . ."

the media to inform citizens about the public business and yet stay within the law. The rule would invite timidity and self-censorship and very likely lead to the suppression of many items that would otherwise be published and that should be made available to the public. At the very least, the First and Fourteenth Amendments will not allow exposing the press to liability for truthfully publishing information released to the public in official court records. If there are privacy interests to be protected in judicial proceedings, the States must respond by means which avoid public documentation or other exposure of private information. Their political institutions must weigh the interests in privacy with the interests of the public to know and of the press to publish. Once true information is disclosed in public court documents open to public inspection, the press cannot be sanctioned for publishing it. In this instance as in others reliance must rest upon the judgment of those who decide what to publish or broadcast. . . .

Reversed.*

Note: Invasion of Privacy and the First Amendment

1. *Fact patterns*. In addition to *Cox Broadcasting*, consider the following:

a. William Sidis was a famous child prodigy in 1910. His name and prowess were well known to newspaper readers of the period. At the age of eleven, he lectured to distinguished mathematicians on the subject of four-dimensional bodies, and at the age of sixteen he graduated from Harvard College, amid considerable public attention. Thereafter, Sidis sought to live as unobtrusively as possible, and his name disappeared from public view. In 1937, however, The New Yorker ran a biographical sketch of Sidis in its Where Are They Now? section. The article described Sidis's early achievements, his general breakdown, and his attempts to conceal his identity through his chosen career as an insignificant clerk. The article further described in intimate detail Sidis's enthusiasm for collecting streetcar transfers, his interest in the lore of the Okamakammessett Indians, and his personal lifestyle and habits. Sidis sued for invasion of privacy. Sidis v. F-R Publishing Corp., 113 F.2d 806 (2d Cir. 1940).

b. Dorothy Barber suffered from a rare condition that caused her to lose weight even though she ate often. In its Medicine section, Time magazine reported on Barber's condition, disclosing her name and publishing a photograph that showed "her face, head and arms, with bedclothes over her chest." The article was titled Starving Glutton. Barber sued for invasion of privacy. Barber v. Time, Inc., 348 Mo. 1199, 159 S.W.2d 291 (1942).

c. In 1956 Marvin Briscoe and another man hijacked a truck. After paying his debt to society, Briscoe abandoned his life of crime, led an exemplary life, and made many friends who were unaware of the incident in his earlier life. In 1967 Reader's Digest published an article on The Big Business of Hijacking, which reported that: "Typical of many beginners, Marvin Briscoe and [another man] stole a 'valuable-looking' truck in Danville, Ky., and then fought a gun battle with the local police only to learn that they had hijacked four bowling-pin spotters."

---

* [Concurring opinions of Chief Justice Burger and Justices Powell and Douglas are omitted, as is Justice Rehnquist's dissenting opinion, which argues that there is a "want of jurisdiction." — EDS.]

Briscoe sued for invasion of privacy. Briscoe v. Reader's Digest Association, 4 Cal. 3d 529, 93 Cal. Rptr. 866, 483 P.2d 34 (1971).

2. *Non-newsworthiness and "low" value.* As Justice White suggested in *Cox Broadcasting*, in most states the truthful disclosure of "private" facts concerning an individual constitutes a tort if the disclosure would be "highly offensive" to a reasonable person and is not in itself "newsworthy." See D. Pember, Privacy and the Press (1972). Is the tort of public disclosure compatible with the first amendment? Should it matter that the harm caused by such speech cannot be corrected by counter-speech? That there is no significant "risk that government will [use the tort to] insulate itself from the criminal views of its enemies"? L. Tribe, American Constitutional Law 649-650 (1978).

Is "non-newsworthy" information of "low" first amendment value? Consider Bloustein, The First Amendment and Privacy: The Supreme Court Justice and the Philosopher, 28 Rutgers L. Rev. 41, 56-57 (1974): "[The] weight to be given 'the public interest in obtaining information' should depend on whether or not the information is relevant to the public's governing purposes. 'Public interest,' taken to mean curiosity, must be distinguished from 'public interest,' taken to mean value to the public of receiving information of governing importance. There is [no first amendment] right to satisfy public curiosity and publish lurid gossip about private lives." See also Nimmer, The Right to Speak from *Times* to *Time*: First Amendment Theory Applied to Libel and Misapplied to Privacy, 56 Calif. L. Rev. 935, 962 (1968) ("speech necessary for an effective and meaningful democratic dialogue by and large does not require references to the intimate activities of named individuals").

On the other hand, consider Zimmerman, Requiem for a Heavyweight: A Farewell to Warren and Brandeis's Privacy Tort, 68 Corn. L. Rev. 291, 332-334 (1983):

> [Contemporary] society [uses] knowledge about the private lives of individual members [to] preserve and enforce social norms. [By] providing people with a way to learn about social groups to which they do not belong, gossip increases intimacy and a sense of community among disparate groups and individuals. [It] is a basic form of information exchange that teaches about other lifestyles and attitudes, and through which community values are changed or reinforced. [Perceived] in this way, gossip contributes directly to the first amendment "marketplace of ideas."

Even if "non-newsworthy" information has only "low" first amendment value, might there nonetheless be sound reasons to reject such a standard? Recall that in *Gertz* the Court expressed "doubt" as to "the wisdom of committing [the task of deciding what information is relevant to self-government] to the conscience of judges." Is the "non-newsworthiness" concept simply too vague to protect first amendment rights? Consider Kalven, Privacy in Tort Law — Were Warren and Brandeis Wrong?, 31 Law & Contemp. Prob. 326, 336 (1966): "What is at issue [is] whether the claim of privilege is not so overpowering as virtually to swallow the tort. [Surely] there is force to the simple contention that whatever is in the news media is by definition newsworthy, that the press must in the nature of things be the final arbiter of newsworthiness." But recall *Dun & Bradstreet*.

3. *The interest in "privacy."* Are the interests protected by the public disclosure tort of sufficient importance to justify a restriction of even "low" value expression? How would you compare the gravity of the harm caused by speech that "invades

privacy" with the gravity of the harm in the incitement, fighting words, and libel contexts? Consider Bloustein, supra, at 54: "In [public disclosure] cases the individual has been profaned by laying a private life open to public view. The intimacy and private space necessary to sustain individuality and human dignity has been impaired by turning a private life into a public spectacle. The innermost region of being [has] been bruised by exposure to the world." On the other hand, consider Posner, The Right of Privacy, 12 Ga. L. Rev. 393, 419 (1978): "If what is revealed is something the individual has concealed for purposes of misrepresenting himself to others, the fact that disclosure is offensive to him and of limited interest to the public at large is no better reason for protecting his privacy than if a seller advanced such arguments for being allowed to continue to engage in false advertising of his goods."

4. *Governmental disclosure.* In *Cox Broadcasting* Justice White found it unnecessary to rule directly on the constitutionality of the public disclosure tort, holding more narrowly that "[once] true information is disclosed in public court documents open to public inspection, the press cannot be sanctioned for publishing it." Is this defensible? Recall Landmark Communications v. Virginia, Oklahoma Publishing Co. v. District Court, and Smith v. Daily Mail, supra section B4.

4. Commercial Speech

Although the *Chaplinsky* dictum made no reference to commercial speech, only a month after *Chaplinsky* the Court added commercial advertising to its list of "unprotected" expression in Valentine v. Chrestensen, 316 U.S. 52 (1942). In *Chrestensen* the Court upheld a prohibition on the distribution of any "handbill [or] other advertising matter [in] or upon any street." Although conceding that a similar prohibition on noncommercial expression would violate the first amendment, the Court announced, without explanation or analysis, that the amendment imposed "no such restraint on government as respects purely commercial advertising." *Chrestensen* was expressly reaffirmed in Breard v. Alexandria, 341 U.S. 622 (1951), in which the Court upheld a prohibition on door-to-door solicitation of magazine subscriptions. The Court emphasized that the "selling [brings] into the transaction a commercial feature" and distinguished its prior decision in Martin v. Struthers, infra section E1, invalidating a prohibition on door-to-door distribution of leaflets publicizing a religious meeting, as a case involving "no element of the commercial."

Despite *Chrestensen* and *Breard*, the precise contours and rationale of the commercial speech doctrine remained obscure. The mere presence of a commercial motive, for example, was not deemed dispositive, as evidenced by the Court's continued protection of books, movies, newspapers, and other forms of expression produced and sold for profit. Moreover, in New York Times v. Sullivan, supra section D1, the Court rejected an argument that the paid "political" advertisement there at issue was unprotected commercial expression:

> The publication here was not a "commercial" advertisement in the sense in which the word was used in *Chrestensen*. It communicated information, expressed opinion, recited grievances, [and] protested claimed abuses. [That] the Times was paid

for publishing the advertisement is as immaterial in this connection as is the fact that newspapers and books are sold. [Any] other conclusion would discourage newspapers from carrying "editorial advertisements" of this type, and so might shut off an important outlet for the promulgation of information and ideas by persons who do not themselves have access to publishing facilities.

In the 1970s the Court began to narrow the scope of the commercial speech doctrine. In Pittsburgh Press Co. v. Human Relations Commission, 413 U.S. 376 (1973), for example, the Court upheld an ordinance prohibiting newspapers from listing employment advertisements in gender-designated columns. Although characterizing the advertisements as "classic examples of commercial speech," the Court sustained the ordinance on the narrower ground that the discriminatory hirings proposed by the advertisements were themselves illegal. In Bigelow v. Virginia, 421 U.S. 809 (1975), the Court reversed the conviction of an individual who, prior to the Court's decision in Roe v. Wade, supra Chapter 6, section F2, and in violation of Virginia law, published in his newspaper an advertisement announcing the availability of legal abortions in New York. The Court distinguished *Chrestensen* on the ground that the advertisement in *Bigelow* "did more than simply propose a commercial transaction. It contained factual material of clear 'public interest.'" The Court emphasized that *Chrestensen*'s holding was "distinctly a limited one."

Virginia State Board of Pharmacy v. Virginia Citizens Consumer Council
425 U.S. 748 (1976)

[An organization of prescription drug consumers challenged as violative of the first and fourteenth amendments a Virginia statute providing that a pharmacist licensed in Virginia is guilty of unprofessional conduct if he "publishes, advertises, or promotes, directly or indirectly, in any manner whatsoever, any amount, price, fee, premium, discount, rebate or credit terms [for] any drugs which may be dispensed only by prescription." Although drug prices varied strikingly throughout the state and even within the same locality, the challenged law effectively prevented the dissemination of any prescription drug price information since only licensed pharmacists were authorized to dispense such drugs. A three-judge district court held the law invalid. The Supreme Court affirmed.]

MR. JUSTICE BLACKMUN delivered the opinion of the Court. . . .*

IV

The appellants contend that the advertisement of prescription drug prices is outside the protection of the First Amendment because it is "commercial

* [At the outset, Justice Blackmun rejected a claim that, even if first amendment protection attached to the flow of drug price information, it is a protection enjoyed only by advertisers and not by the appellees, who were mere recipients of such information. Blackmun reasoned that "where a speaker exists [the] protection afforded is to the communication, to its source and to its recipients both." Thus, "if there is a right to advertise, there is a reciprocal [first amendment] right to receive the advertising." — EDS.]

speech." There can be no question that in past decisions the Court has given some indication that commercial speech is unprotected. [Discussing *Valentine, Breard, Pittsburgh Press,* and *Bigelow.*] . . .

[The] question whether there is a First Amendment exception for "commercial speech" is squarely before us. Our pharmacist does not wish to editorialize on any subject, cultural, philosophical, or political. He does not wish to report any particularly newsworthy fact, or to make generalized observations even about commercial matters. The "idea" he wishes to communicate is simply this: "I will sell you the X prescription drug at the Y price." Our question, then, is whether this communication is wholly outside the protection of the First Amendment.

V

We begin with several propositions that already are settled or beyond serious dispute. It is clear, for example, that speech does not lose its First Amendment protection because money is spent to project it, as in a paid advertisement of one form or another. [Citing Buckley v. Valeo, infra section E4; New York Times v. Sullivan, supra section D1.] Speech likewise is protected even though it is carried in a form that is "sold" for profit, [and] even though it may involve a solicitation to purchase or otherwise pay or contribute money. . . .

If there is a kind of commercial speech that lacks all First Amendment protection, therefore, it must be distinguished by its content. Yet the speech whose content deprives it of protection cannot simply be speech on a commercial subject. No one would contend that our pharmacist may be prevented from being heard on the subject of whether, in general, pharmaceutical prices should be regulated, or their advertisement forbidden. Nor can it be dispositive that a commercial advertisement is noneditorial, and merely reports a fact. Purely factual matter of public interest may claim protection. . . .

Our question is whether speech which does "no more than propose a commercial transaction," [*Pittsburgh Press*] is so removed from any "exposition of ideas," [*Chaplinsky*], and from "'truth, science, morality, and arts in general, in its diffusion of liberal sentiments on the administration of Government,'" [Roth v. United States, infra section D5] that it lacks all protection. Our answer is that it is not.

Focusing first on the individual parties to the transaction that is proposed in the commercial advertisement, we may assume that the advertiser's interest is a purely economic one. That hardly disqualifies him from protection under the First Amendment. The interests of the contestants in a labor dispute are primarily economic, but it has long been settled that both the employee and the employer are protected by the First Amendment when they express themselves on the merits of the dispute in order to influence its outcome. [We] know of no requirement that, in order to avail themselves of First Amendment protection, the parties to a labor dispute need address themselves to the merits of unionism in general or to any subject beyond their immediate dispute. . . .

As to the particular consumer's interest in the free flow of commercial information, that interest may be as keen, if not keener by far, than his interest in the day's most urgent political debate. Appellees' case in this respect is a convincing one. Those whom the suppression of prescription drug price information hits the hardest are the poor, the sick, and particularly the aged. A disproportionate amount of their income tends to be spent on prescription drugs; yet they are the least able to learn, by shopping from pharmacist to pharmacist, where their scarce dollars are best spent. When drug prices vary as strikingly as they do, information as to who is charging what becomes more than a convenience. It could mean the alleviation of physical pain or the enjoyment of basic necessities.

Generalizing, society also may have a strong interest in the free flow of commercial information. Even an individual advertisement, though entirely "commercial," may be of general public interest. The facts of decided cases furnish illustrations: advertisements stating that referral services for legal abortions are available, [*Bigelow*]; that a manufacturer of artificial furs promotes his product as an alternative to the extinction by his competitors of fur-bearing mammals, see Fur Information & Fashion Council, Inc. v. E. F. Timme & Son, 364 F. Supp. 16 (S.D.N.Y. 1973); and that a domestic producer advertises his product as an alternative to imports that tend to deprive American residents of their jobs, cf. Chicago Joint Board v. Chicago Tribune Co., 435 F. 2d 470 (C.A.7 1970). [Obviously], not all commercial messages contain the same or even a very great public interest element. There are few to which such an element, however, could not be added. Our pharmacist, for example, could cast himself as a commentator on store-to-store disparities in drug prices, giving his own and those of a competitor as proof. We see little point in requiring him to do so, and little difference if he does not.

Moreover, there is another consideration that suggests that no line between publicly "interesting" or "important" commercial advertising and the opposite kind could ever be drawn. Advertising, however tasteless and excessive it sometimes may seem, is nonetheless dissemination of information as to who is producing and selling what product, for what reason, and at what price. So long as we preserve a predominantly free enterprise economy, the allocation of our resources in large measure will be made through numerous private economic decisions. It is a matter of public interest that those decisions, in the aggregate, be intelligent and well informed. To this end, the free flow of commercial information is indispensable. [And] if it is indispensable to the proper allocation of resources in a free enterprise system, it is also indispensable to the formation of intelligent opinions as to how that system ought to be regulated or altered. Therefore, even if the First Amendment were thought to be primarily an instrument to enlighten public decisionmaking in a democracy, we could not say that the free flow of information does not serve that goal.

Arrayed against these substantial individual and societal interests are a number of justifications for the advertising ban. These have to do principally with maintaining a high degree of professionalism on the part of licensed pharmacists. Indisputably, the State has a strong interest in maintaining that professionalism. . . .

Price advertising, it is argued, will place in jeopardy the pharmacist's expertise and, with it, the customer's health. It is claimed that the aggressive price competition that will result from unlimited advertising will make it impossible for the pharmacist to supply professional services in the compounding, handling, and dispensing of prescription drugs. Such services are time consuming and expensive; if competitors who economize by eliminating them are permitted to advertise their resulting lower prices, the more painstaking and conscientious pharmacist will be forced either to follow suit or to go out of business. It is also claimed that prices might not necessarily fall as a result of advertising. If one pharmacist advertises, others must, and the resulting expense will inflate the cost of drugs. [Finally] it is argued that damage will be done to the professional image of the pharmacist. This image, that of a skilled and specialized craftsman, attracts talent to the profession and reinforces the better habits of those who are in it. Price advertising, it is said, will reduce the pharmacist's status to that of a mere retailer.

The strength of these proffered justifications is greatly undermined by the fact that high professional standards, to a substantial extent, are guaranteed by the close regulation to which pharmacists in Virginia are subject. [At] the same time, we cannot discount the Board's justifications entirely. The Court regarded justifications of this type sufficient to sustain the advertising bans challenged on due process and equal protection grounds. [Citing, e.g., Williamson v. Lee Optical, supra Chapter 6, section D.]

The challenge now made, however, is based on the First Amendment. This casts the Board's justifications in a different light, for on close inspection it is seen that the State's protectiveness of its citizens rests in large measure on the advantages of their being kept in ignorance. The advertising ban does not directly affect professional standards one way or the other. It affects them only through the reactions it is assumed people will have to the free flow of drug price information. . . .

It appears to be feared that if the pharmacist who wishes to provide low cost, and assertedly low quality, services is permitted to advertise, he will be taken up on his offer by too many unwitting customers. They will choose the low-cost, low-quality service and drive the "professional" pharmacist out of business. They will respond only to costly and excessive advertising, and end up paying the price. They will go from one pharmacist to another, following the discount, and destroy the pharmacist-customer relationship. They will lose respect for the profession because it advertises. All this is not in their best interests, and all this can be avoided if they are not permitted to know who is charging what.

There is, of course, an alternative to this highly paternalistic approach. That alternative is to assume that this information is not in itself harmful, that people will perceive their own best interests if only they are well enough informed, and that the best means to that end is to open the channels of communication rather than to close them. If they are truly open, nothing prevents the "professional" pharmacist from marketing his own assertedly superior product, and contrasting it with that of the low-cost, high-volume prescription drug retailer. But the choice among these alternative approaches is not ours to make or the Virginia General Assembly's. It is precisely this kind of choice, between the dangers of suppressing information, and the dangers of its misuse if it is freely available, that the First Amendment makes for us. . . .

VI

In concluding that commercial speech, like other varieties, is protected, we of course do not hold that it can never be regulated in any way. Some forms of commercial speech regulation are surely permissible. We mention a few only to make clear that they are not before us and therefore are not foreclosed by this case.

There is no claim, for example, that the prohibition on prescription drug price advertising is a mere time, place, and manner restriction. We have often approved restrictions of that kind provided that they are justified without reference to the content of the regulated speech, that they serve a significant governmental interest, and that in so doing they leave open ample alternative channels for communication of the information. [Whatever] may be the proper bounds of time, place, and manner restrictions on commercial speech, they are plainly exceeded by this Virginia statute, which singles out speech of a particular content and seeks to prevent its dissemination completely.

Nor is there any claim that prescription drug price advertisements are forbidden because they are false or misleading in any way. Untruthful speech, commercial or otherwise, has never been protected for its own sake. [*Gertz.*] Obviously, much commercial speech is not provably false, or even wholly false, but only deceptive or misleading. We foresee no obstacle to a State's dealing effectively with this problem.[24] The First Amendment, as we construe it today, does not prohibit the State from insuring that the stream of commercial information flow cleanly as well as freely. . . .

Also, there is no claim that the transactions proposed in the forbidden advertisements are themselves illegal in any way. Cf. [*Pittsburgh Press*]. [Finally,] the special problems of the electronic broadcast media are likewise not in this case. . . .

What is at issue is whether a State may completely suppress the dissemination of concededly truthful information about entirely lawful activity, fearful of that information's effect upon its disseminators and its recipients. Reserving other questions,[25] we conclude that the answer to this one is in the negative.

The judgment of the District Court is affirmed.[*]

24. In concluding that commercial speech enjoys First Amendment protection, we have not held that it is wholly undifferentiable from other forms. There are commonsense differences between speech that does "no more than propose a commercial transaction," and other varieties. Even if the differences do not justify the conclusion that commercial speech is valueless, and thus subject to complete suppression by the State, they nonetheless suggest that a different degree of protection is necessary to insure that the flow of truthful and legitimate commercial information is unimpaired. The truth of commercial speech, for example, may be more easily verifiable by its disseminator than, let us say, news reporting or political commentary, in that ordinarily the advertiser seeks to disseminate information about a specific product or service that he himself provides and presumably knows more about than anyone else. Also, commercial speech may be more durable than other kinds. Since advertising is the sine qua non of commercial profits, there is little likelihood of its being chilled by proper regulation and forgone entirely.

Attributes such as these, the greater objectivity and hardiness of commercial speech, may make it less necessary to tolerate inaccurate statements for fear of silencing the speaker. [They] may also make it appropriate to require that a commercial message appear in such a form, or include such additional information, warnings, and disclaimers, as are necessary to prevent its being deceptive. [They] may also make inapplicable the prohibition against prior restraints. . . .

25. We stress that we have considered in this case the regulation of commercial advertising by pharmacists. Although we express no opinion as to other professions, the distinctions, historical and functional, between professions may require consideration of quite different factors. Physicians and lawyers, for example, do not dispense standardized products; they render professional *services* of almost infinite variety and nature, with the consequent enhanced possibility for confusion and deception if they were to undertake certain kinds of advertising.

* [Justice Stevens did not participate. Chief Justice Burger concurred in an opinion emphasizing the reservations set out in n.25. — EDS.]

MR. JUSTICE STEWART, concurring. . . .

[The] Court's decision calls into immediate question the constitutional legitimacy of every state and federal law regulating false or deceptive advertising. I write separately to explain why I think today's decision does not preclude such governmental regulation. . . .

The principles recognized in the libel decisions suggest that government may take broader action to protect the public from injury produced by false or deceptive price or product advertising than from harm caused by defamation. In contrast to the press, which must often attempt to assemble the true facts from sketchy and sometimes conflicting sources under the pressure of publication deadlines, the commercial advertiser generally knows the product or service he seeks to sell and is in a position to verify the accuracy of his factual representations before he disseminates them. The advertiser's access to the truth about his product and its price substantially eliminates any danger that governmental regulation of false or misleading price or product advertising will chill accurate and nondeceptive commercial expression. There is, therefore, little need to sanction "some falsehood in order to protect speech that matters." [Since] the factual claims contained in commercial price or product advertisements relate to tangible goods or services, they may be tested empirically and corrected to reflect the truth without in any manner jeopardizing the free dissemination of thought. Indeed, the elimination of false and deceptive claims serves to promote the one facet of commercial price and product advertising that warrants First Amendment protection — its contribution to the flow of accurate and reliable information relevant to public and private decisionmaking.

MR. JUSTICE REHNQUIST, dissenting.

The logical consequences of the Court's decision in this case, a decision which elevates commercial intercourse between a seller hawking his wares and a buyer seeking to strike a bargain to the same plane as has been previously reserved for the free marketplace of ideas, are far reaching indeed. Under the Court's opinion the way will be open not only for dissemination of price information but for active promotion of prescription drugs, liquor, cigarettes, and other products the use of which it has previously been thought desirable to discourage. Now, however, such promotion is protected by the First Amendment so long as it is not misleading or does not promote an illegal product or enterprise. . . .

The Court speaks of the consumer's interest in the free flow of commercial information, particularly in the case of the poor, the sick, and the aged. It goes on to observe that "society also may have a strong interest in the free flow of commercial information." [One] need not disagree with either of these statements in order to feel that they should presumptively be the concern of the Virginia Legislature, which sits to balance these and other claims in the process of making laws such as the one here under attack. The Court speaks of the importance in a "predominantly free enterprise economy" of intelligent and well-informed decisions as to allocation of resources. While there is again much to be said for the Court's observation as a matter of desirable public policy, there is certainly nothing in the United States Constitution which requires the Virginia Legislature to hew to the teachings of Adam Smith in its legislative decisions regulating the pharmacy profession. E.g., Nebbia v. New York, 291 U.S. 502 (1934); Olsen v. Nebraska, 313 U.S. 236 (1941). . . .

The Court insists that the rule it lays down is consistent even with the view that the First Amendment is "primarily an instrument to enlighten public decision-making in a democracy." I had understood this view to relate to public decision-making as to political, social, and other public issues, rather than the decision of a particular individual as to whether to purchase one or another kind of shampoo. It is undoubtedly arguable that many people in the country regard the choice of shampoo as just as important as who may be elected to local, state, or national political office, but that does not automatically bring information about competing shampoos within the protection of the First Amendment. . . .

There are undoubted difficulties with an effort to draw a bright line between "commercial speech" on the one hand and "protected speech" on the other, and the Court does better to face up to these difficulties than to attempt to hide them under labels. . . .

In the case of "our" hypothetical pharmacist, he may now presumably advertise not only the prices of prescription drugs, but may attempt to energetically promote their sale so long as he does so truthfully. Quite consistently with Virginia law requiring prescription drugs to be available only through a physician, "our" pharmacist might run any of the following representative advertisements in a local newspaper:

> Pain getting you down? Insist that your physician prescribe Demerol. You pay a little more than for aspirin, but you get a lot more relief.

> Can't shake the flu? Get a prescription for Tetracycline from your doctor today.

> Don't spend another sleepless night. Ask your doctor to prescribe Seconal without delay.

Unless the State can show that these advertisements are either actually untruthful or misleading, it presumably is not free to restrict in any way commercial efforts on the part of those who profit from the sale of prescription drugs to put them in the widest possible circulation. But such a line simply makes no allowance whatever for what appears to have been a considered legislative judgment in most States that while prescription drugs are a necessary and vital part of medical care and treatment, there are sufficient dangers attending their widespread use that they simply may not be promoted in the same manner as hair creams, deodorants, and toothpaste. The very real dangers that general advertising for such drugs might create in terms of encouraging, even though not sanctioning, illicit use of them by individuals for whom they have not been prescribed, or by generating patient pressure upon physicians to prescribe them, are simply not dealt with in the Court's opinion. . . .

Note: Virginia Pharmacy *and "the Free Flow of Commercial Information"*

1. *Is commercial speech of "low" first amendment value?* Consider the following:

a. Jackson & Jeffries, Commercial Speech: Economic Due Process and the First Amendment, 65 Va. L. Rev. 1, 17-18, 30-31 (1979):

[The Court's conclusion in *Virginia Pharmacy* that commercial speech is relevant to self-government is] a non sequitur. It apparently rests on the assertion that because regulation of the free enterprise system is a matter of political choice, commercial advertising that plays a part in the functioning of the free enterprise system is *for that reason* politically significant speech. But in terms of relevance to political decision-making, advertising is neither more nor less significant than a host of other market activities that legislatures concededly may regulate. [The] decisive point is the absence of any principled distinction between commercial soliciting and other aspects of economic activity. [In *Virginia Pharmacy*,] economic due process is resurrected, clothed in the ill-fitting garb of the first amendment. [The] Court has reconstituted the values of Lochner v. New York [supra Chapter 6, section D] as components of freedom of speech.

For a thoughtful critique of this argument, see Shiffrin, The First Amendment and Economic Regulation: Away from a General Theory of the First Amendment, 78 Nw. U. L. Rev. 1212, 1225-1239 (1983).

b. Redish, The First Amendment in the Marketplace: Commercial Speech and the Values of Free Expression, 39 Geo. Wash. L. Rev. 429, 433, 441-444 (1971):

If the individual is to achieve the maximum degree of material satisfaction permitted by his resources, he must be presented with as much information as possible concerning the relative merits of competing products. After receiving the competing information, the individual will then be in a position [to] rationally decide which combination of features best satisfies his personal needs. [Moreover,] the theory of political self-government derives to a large extent from the belief in the intelligent free will of the individual, who is capable [of] making his personal decision as to how he should be governed. [Development] of the mind is [thus] an important goal in itself. [Viewed in this light,] informational commercial speech furthers legitimate first amendment purposes. When the individual is presented with rational grounds for preferring one product or brand over another, he is encouraged to consider the competing information [and to] exercise his abilities to reason and think; this aids him towards the intangible goal of rational self-fulfillment.

c. Baker, Commercial Speech: A Problem in the Theory of Freedom, 62 Iowa L. Rev. 1, 3, 14 (1976):

[The] values supported or functions performed by protected speech result from that speech being a manifestation of individual freedom or choice. [Commercial speech, however, is a product of the profit orientation, which, in the United States,] is *externally imposed* on the capitalist enterprise by the market. [Thus,] in our present historical setting, commercial speech is not a manifestation of individual freedom or choice; unlike the broad categories of protected speech, commercial speech does not represent an attempt to create or affect the world in a way which can be expected to represent anyone's private or personal wishes.

d. Coase, Advertising and Free Speech, 6 J. Legal Stud. 1, 2, 14 (1977):

It seems to be believed that [if the government intervened in the market for ideas it] would be inefficient and wrongly motivated. [How] different is the government assumed to be when we come to economic regulation. In this area government is considered to be competent in action and pure in motivation. [Since] we are concerned with [the] same government, why is it that it is regarded as incompetent and untrustworthy in the one market and efficient and reliable in the other? [It] seems to me that the arguments [used] to support freedom in the market for ideas are equally applicable in the market for goods.

Compare Scanlon, Freedom of Expression and Categories of Expression, 40 U. Pitt. L. Rev. 519, 541 (1979): "[Commercial speech deserves less than full first amendment protection because] we regard the government as much less partisan in the competition between commercial firms than in the struggle between religious or political views."

e. Blasi, The Pathological Perspective and the First Amendment, 85 Colum. L. Rev. 449, 486, 488 (1985):

Commercial advertising was never a concern in any of the historical political struggles over freedom of expression. The first amendment claimants in disputes over commercial advertising often are sophisticated and driven by the profit motive. The speech in question is brief and intended to evoke a reflexive, even if somewhat delayed, response from listeners. There is a strong tradition of government regulation of [advertising]. [Perhaps] most important, [the] spectacle of voluminous litigation over [product] advertising, conducted in the name of the first amendment, [would] undercut [society's] belief that first amendment freedoms represent a noble commitment well worth preserving even in the face of serious anxieties, risks, and costs. [Thus, we should] exclude commercial advertising from the protection of the first amendment.

f. Tushnet, Corporations and Free Speech, in The Politics of Law 253, 258-260 (D. Kairys ed. 1982):

In an inversion that would have surprised some of the framers of the Constitution, [*Virginia Pharmacy* declared that] a consumer's interest in receiving accurate price information [is] "as keen, if not keener by far, than his interest in the day's most urgent public debate." [In] some ways, though, [*Virginia Pharmacy*] should not be surprising. After all, one of the classic statements of free-speech theory is found in [Justice Holmes's] dissent in [*Abrams*, which relied on the "free trade in ideas"]. If free speech was defended with the metaphor of the market, it was only a matter of time and political circumstance before the market was defended with the metaphor and substance of free speech. [The] market metaphor [is] powerful precisely because [it] capture[s] important aspects of life in capitalist society, where nearly everything [seems] to be a commodity available for sale and purchase.

2. *What is "commercial" speech?* In *Virginia Pharmacy* the Court reaffirmed that the content of the speech rather than the speaker's commercial or profit motivation is determinative. What matters, in other words, is not whether the speaker is out to make money, but whether the expression does "no more than propose a commercial transaction." Is this definition satisfactory? Does a billboard displaying a cigarette package in a pastoral setting constitute "commercial" speech under this definition? What about corporate-issue advertising that describes the corporation, its activities, or its policies without explicitly identifying any of the corporation's products or services? Consider Comment, First Amendment Protection for Commercial Advertising: The New Constitutional Doctrine, 44 U. Chi. L. Rev. 205, 236 (1976): "[Commercial speech should be defined as] (1)

speech that refers to a specific brand name product or service, (2) made by a speaker with a financial interest in the sale of the advertised product or service, in the sale of a competing product or service, or in the distribution of the speech, (3) that does not advertise an activity itself protected by the first amendment."

In Bolger v. Youngs Drug Products Corp., 463 U.S. 60 (1983), the Court held that various "informational pamphlets" dealing with contraceptives constituted "commercial" speech. "One of [the] pamphlets, 'Condoms and Human Sexuality,' specifically [referred] to a number of Trojan-brand condoms manufactured by [Youngs] and [described] the advantages of each type. [Another], 'Plain Talk about Venereal Disease,' [discussed] condoms without any specific reference to those manufactured by [Youngs]." The Court explained:

> The mere fact that these pamphlets are conceded to be advertisements clearly does not compel the conclusion that they are commercial speech. [Citing New York Times v. Sullivan.] Similarly, the reference to a specific product does not by itself render the pamphlets commercial speech. Finally, the fact that Youngs has an economic motivation for mailing the pamphlets would clearly be insufficient by itself to turn the materials into commercial speech. [The] combination of *all* these characteristics, however, provides strong support for [the] conclusion that the informational pamphlets [are] commercial speech. [Moreover, the pamphlets] constitute commercial speech notwithstanding the fact that they contain discussions of important public issues such as venereal disease and family planning. [Advertising] which "links a product to a current public debate" is not thereby entitled to the constitutional protection afforded noncommercial speech. [Finally, that] a product is referred to generically [and not by brand name] does not [remove] it from the realm of commercial speech. [For] a company with sufficient control of the market for a product may be able to promote the product without reference to specific brand names. [Indeed, in] this case, Youngs describes itself as "the leader in the manufacture and sale" of contraceptives.

Does the commercial speech doctrine logically extend to any expression that relates explicitly to economic or financial affairs? Recall *Dun & Bradstreet*, supra section D1.

3. *The implications of* Virginia Pharmacy. In the years immediately after *Virginia Pharmacy* the Court reaffirmed and expanded its protection of commercial speech. Consider *Bates* and *Linmark*.

BATES v. STATE BAR OF ARIZONA, 433 U.S. 350 (1977): In a five-to-four decision, the Court invalidated a state court rule prohibiting attorney advertising, as applied to a newspaper advertisement stating "DO YOU NEED A LAWYER? Legal Services at Very Reasonable Fees" and listing fees for a variety of services, such as uncontested divorce, uncontested adoption, uncontested nonbusiness bankruptcy, and name change. Justice Blackmun, writing for the Court, emphasized that the issue presented "is a narrow one": "whether lawyers [may] constitutionally advertise the *prices* at which certain routine services will be performed." In rejecting the State's argument that attorney advertising is "inherently misleading," the Court explained that, whatever might be the case with respect to advertising of nonroutine services or advertising directed to the quality of services, advertising disclosing only the price of routine legal services could not be deemed "misleading so long as the attorney does the necessary work at the advertised price." The Court also rejected the state's argument that attorney advertising would adversely affect professionalism and the quality of legal services, stir up unnecessary litigation, increase the overhead costs of lawyers, cause increased fees, and create difficulties in enforcing the line between protected and unprotected advertisements. Without specifying precisely what standard it was applying, the Court concluded that none "of the proferred justifications [rises] to the level of an acceptable reason for the suppression of all advertising by attorneys."

Chief Justice Burger and Justices Powell, Stewart, and Rehnquist dissented. Justice Powell, joined by Justice Stewart, maintained that, unlike the advertising of "prepackaged prescription goods," price advertising of legal services is inherently misleading "because such services are individualized with respect to content and quality and because the lay consumer [usually] does not know in advance the precise nature and scope of the services he requires." Powell also objected that the bar would not be able adequately to police the distinction between deceptive and nondeceptive advertising. Chief Justice Burger stated that he was "in general agreement" with Justice Powell. Justice Rehnquist reiterated his position in *Virginia Pharmacy* that commercial speech is not entitled to first amendment protection.

See also Zauderer v. Office of Disciplinary Counsel, — U.S. — , 105 S. Ct. 2265 (1985) (invalidating disciplinary rules prohibiting the use of illustrations in lawyer advertising and forbidding lawyers to solicit clients through advertisements containing information or advice regarding specific legal problems); In the Matter of R. M. J., 455 U.S. 191 (1982) (invalidating restrictions on lawyer advertising where the advertisements were not "inherently misleading" and the restrictions were not the "least restrictive" means of achieving "substantial" state interests).

LINMARK ASSOCIATES v. TOWNSHIP OF WILLINGBORO, 431 U.S. 85 (1977): Willingboro is a racially integrated residential community in southern New Jersey. From the early 1960s to 1973 the nonwhite population of Willingboro increased from 60 to more than 8,000, or from .005 percent of the population to more than 18 percent. As nonwhites moved into Willingboro, whites began to move out. From 1970 to 1973 the white population declined by some 2,000. In an effort to maintain Willingboro as an integrated community, the township council enacted an ordinance prohibiting the display of "For Sale" or "Sold" signs on all but model homes. Petitioners, an owner of real property and a real estate agent, filed this action seeking to have the ordinance declared invalid. At trial the township presented evidence that "panic selling" by whites who believed that the community was becoming all black and that property values would decline was a major cause in the decline of white population, that the display of "For Sale" and "Sold" signs was a major catalyst of these fears, and that although total home sales had not declined in the nine months following enactment of the ordinance, sales due to racial fear had declined sharply.

In a unanimous decision, Justice Rehnquist not participating, the Court, in an opinion by Justice Marshall, held the ordinance invalid. At the outset, the Court rejected the township's contention that "First Amendment concerns are less directly implicated by Willingboro's ordinance" than by the law at issue in *Virginia*

Pharmacy because the Willingboro ordinance "restricts only one method of communication." Although conceding that "laws regulating the time, place, or manner of speech stand on a different footing from laws prohibiting speech altogether," the Court argued that "the Willingboro ordinance is not genuinely concerned with the place of the speech — front lawns — or the manner of the speech — signs. The township has not prohibited all lawn signs — or all lawn signs of a particular size or shape — in order to promote aesthetic values or any other value 'unrelated to the suppression of free expression.' [Rather], Willingboro has proscribed particular types of signs based on their content because it fears their 'primary' effect — that they will cause those receiving the information to act upon it. That the proscription applies only to one mode of communication, therefore, does not transform this into a 'time, place, or manner' case." Thus, "if the [law] is to be sustained, it must be on the basis of the [government's] interest in regulating the content of the communication."

Turning to that issue, the Court recognized that the goal of "promoting stable, racially integrated housing" is "vital," but nonetheless held that the township had failed to establish that the ordinance "was necessary to achieve this objective." In any event, "the constitutional defect in this ordinance [is] far more basic," for the township "has sought to restrict the free flow of these data because it fears that otherwise homeowners will make decisions inimical to what the [town council] views as the homeowners' self-interest and the corporate interest of the township: they will choose to leave town. [If] dissemination of this information can be restricted, then every locality in the country can suppress any facts that reflect poorly on the locality, so long as a plausible claim can be made that disclosure would cause the recipients of the information to act 'irrationally.' [*Virginia Pharmacy*] denies government such sweeping powers." Quoting Justice Brandeis's concurring opinion in Whitney v. California, supra section B1, the Court concluded that " 'If there be time [to] avert the evil by the process of education, the remedy to be applied is more speech, not enforced silence. Only an emergency can justify suppression.' "

For a further example of the Court's expansive application of *Virginia Pharmacy*, see Carey v. Population Services International, 431 U.S. 678 (1977), in which the Court invalidated a prohibition on the advertising of contraceptives because the state's concerns "that advertisements of contraceptive products would be offensive and embarrassing to those exposed to them, and that permitting them would legitimate sexual activity of young people," are "classically not justifications validating the suppression of expression protected by the First Amendment."

Note: Limitations on the Protection of Commercial Speech

1. *Advertisements for unlawful transactions.* Building on *Pittsburgh Press* the Court has repeatedly stated that commercial advertisements offering to enter into unlawful transactions are not protected by the Constitution. See, e.g., Hoffman Estates v. Flipside, 455 U.S. 489 (1982) ("government may regulate or ban entirely" commercial "speech proposing an illegal transaction"). Recall that under *Brandenburg* express advocacy of unlawful conduct may be prohibited only if it is

likely imminently to bring about such conduct. Should a similar standard govern commercial advertising?

Suppose it is unlawful to purchase, sell, or consume alcoholic beverages in county X. May county X also prohibit all commercial advertising relating to alcoholic beverages? Should it matter whether the prohibited advertisement (a) is displayed on a billboard within county X and says simply "Drink Brand Z Scotch"; (b) is displayed on a billboard within county X and says "Drink at Joe's in County Y"; or (c) is contained in a newspaper printed in county Y but sold also in county X? Cf. Bigelow v. Virginia, 421 U.S. 809 (1975) (invalidating a Virginia prohibition on advertisements for abortion, which were unlawful in Virginia, as applied to a newspaper advertisement offering abortions in New York, where they were lawful).

Suppose county X decides to legalize the purchase, sale, and consumption of alcoholic beverages but, to avoid abuse and to keep potential problems to a minimum, prohibits commercial advertising relating to such beverages. Is the ban on such advertising unconstitutional? Does the greater power — to ban all alcoholic beverages and related advertising — include the lesser — to ban the advertising but not the beverages? Cf. Capital Broadcasting Co. v. Mitchell, 333 F. Supp. 582 (D.D.C. 1971), aff'd sub nom. Capital Broadcasting Co. v. Acting Attorney General, 405 U.S. 1000 (1972) (upholding federal statute prohibiting cigarette advertising on radio and television). See Note, The First Amendment and Legislative Bans of Liquor and Cigarette Advertisements, 85 Colum. L. Rev. 632 (1985).

2. *Overbreadth.* In *Bates* the Court announced in dictum that "the justification for the application of overbreadth analysis applies weakly, if at all, in the ordinary commercial context" and that the Court therefore would not apply the doctrine to commercial advertising. The Court explained that

> there are "commonsense differences" between commercial speech and other varieties. [Since] advertising is linked to commercial well-being, it seems unlikely that such speech is particularly susceptible to being crushed by overbroad regulation. [Moreover], concerns for uncertainty in determining the scope of protection are reduced; the advertiser seeks to disseminate information about a product or service that he provides, and presumably he can determine more readily than others whether his speech is truthful and protected.

3. *Factually false commercial advertising.* In footnote 24 of *Virginia Pharmacy* the Court offered several arguments, further elaborated by Justice Stewart in his concurring opinion, as to why factually false commercial speech may constitutionally be regulated more extensively than other forms of factually false expression. Consider the following criticisms: (a) "Commercial speech is not necessarily more verifiable than other speech. There may well be uncertainty about some quality of a product, such as the health effect of eggs. [On] the other hand, political speech is often quite verifiable by the speakers. A political candidate knows the truth about his own past and present intentions, yet misrepresentations on these subjects are immune from state regulation." Farber, Commercial Speech and First Amendment Theory, 74 Nw. U. L. Rev. 372, 385-386 (1979). (b) "[It] is also incorrect to distinguish commercial from political expression on the

ground that the former is somehow hardier because of the inherent profit motive. It could just as easily be said that we need not fear that commercial magazines and newspapers will cease publication for fear of government regulation, because they are in business for profit." Redish, The Value of Free Speech, 130 U. Pa. L. Rev. 591, 633 (1982).

4. *Deceptive or misleading commercial advertising.* *Virginia Pharmacy* suggests that commercial advertising may be regulated or prohibited, even if it is not factually false, if it is deceptive or misleading. Is this defensible? The Court observed in *Gertz*, supra section D1, that "there is no constitutional value in false statements of fact." Can the same be said of misleading or deceptive expression? Do you agree that since "the First Amendment's concern for commercial speech is based on the informational function of advertising, [there] can be no constitutional objection to the suppression of commercial messages that [are] more likely to deceive the public than to inform it"? Central Hudson Gas v. Public Service Commission, infra this section.

In *Bates* the Court rejected a claim that price advertising of routine legal services was sufficiently "inherently misleading" to justify its prohibition. In Friedman v. Rogers, 440 U.S. 1 (1979), however, the Court upheld a Texas statute prohibiting the practice of optometry under "any trade name" as a permissible restriction on deceptive and misleading advertising. The Court emphasized that a trade name is "a significantly different form of commercial speech from that considered in *Virginia Pharmacy* and *Bates,*" for the advertising in those cases "contained statements about the products or services offered and their prices," whereas "a trade name conveys no information about the price and nature of the services offered [until] it acquires meaning over a period of time by associations formed in the minds of the public between the name and some standard of price or quality." The Court expressed concern that "these ill-defined associations of trade names with price and quality information [could] be manipulated by the users of trade names" and that there was thus "a significant possibility that trade names [could] be used to mislead the public." For example, "the public may be attracted by a trade name that reflects the reputation of an optometrist no longer associated with the practice," or a trade name may free "an optometrist from dependence on his personal reputation [and thus enable] him to assume a new trade name if negligence or misconduct casts a shadow over the old one." For these and similar reasons, the Court concluded that "the State's interest in protecting the public from the deceptive and misleading use of optometrical trade names is substantial and well demonstrated." Justice Blackmun, joined by Justice Marshall, dissented.

In light of *Bates* and *Friedman*, to what extent may a state constitutionally restrict lawyer advertising concerning the *quality* of legal services? Consider ABA Model Rules of Professional Conduct, Rule 7-1, (1983), which prohibits any public communication that "is likely to create an unjustified expectation about the results the lawyer can achieve" or that "compares the lawyer's services with other lawyers' services, unless the comparison can be factually substantiated."

5. *Disclosure.* In Zauderer v. Office of Disciplinary Counsel, — U.S. — , 105 S. Ct. 2265 (1985), an attorney advertised that, in a certain type of case, "if there is no recovery, no legal fees are owed by our clients." The Court upheld a disciplinary rule requiring the attorney to disclose in the advertisement that clients

would have to pay "costs" even if their lawsuits were unsuccessful. The Court explained:

> [There are] material differences between disclosure requirements and outright pro-
> hibitions on speech. [We] have, to be sure, held that in some instances, compulsion
> to speak may be as violative of the First Amendment as prohibitions on speech. [See
> section F5, infra.] [But here, the State has required that lawyers include in their]
> advertising purely factual and uncontroversial information about the terms under
> which [their] services will be available. Because the extension of First Amendment
> protection to commercial speech is justified principally by the value to consumers of
> the information such speech provides, [the advertiser's] constitutionally protected
> interest in *not* providing any particular factual information in his advertising is
> minimal. [We therefore] hold that an advertiser's rights are adequately protected as
> long as disclosure requirements are reasonably related to the State's interest in
> preventing deception of consumers.

The Court emphasized that this standard does not embody a "least restrictive alternative" analysis, and that, under this standard, the challenged disclosure requirement "easily passes muster."

6. *Truthful, nondeceptive commercial speech.* Although *Virginia Pharmacy*, *Bates*, *Linmark*, and *Carey* embodied expansive protection of truthful, nondeceptive commercial speech, subsequent decisions have been somewhat less protective. Consider *Ohralik*, *Central Hudson*, and *Metromedia*.

OHRALIK v. OHIO STATE BAR, 436 U.S. 447 (1978): To place *Ohralik* in proper perspective, it is important first to note the Court's decision in a companion case, In re Primus, 436 U.S. 412 (1978). Primus, an ACLU "cooperating lawyer," was reprimanded by the Disciplinary Board of the South Carolina Supreme Court for writing a letter to a woman who had been sterilized, informing her of the ACLU's willingness to provide free legal representation to women in her position in a proposed lawsuit challenging the constitutionality of an alleged program of sterilizing pregnant mothers as a condition of their continued receipt of Medicaid benefits. Building upon its 1963 decision in NAACP v. Button, infra section E5, the Court held the reprimand unconstitutional. Speaking for the Court, Justice Powell observed that "for the [ACLU], 'litigation is not a technique of resolving private differences'; it is 'a form of political expression' and 'political association.' " To justify a restriction on such " 'core First Amendment rights,' " the state "must demonstrate 'a subordinating interest which is compelling,' " and "that the means employed in furtherance of that interest" are "closely drawn to avoid unnecessary abridgement of associational freedoms.' " Because the record did "not support appellee's contention that undue influence, overreaching, misrepresentation, or invasion of privacy [had] actually occurred," the Court held the reprimand invalid.

In *Ohralik*, appellant, an attorney, after learning about an automobile accident, personally contacted two young women who had been injured in the accident and arranged to represent them in subsequent litigation. As a consequence of this "ambulance chasing," Ohralik was suspended by the Ohio State Bar for violation of a disciplinary rule prohibiting any "lawyer who has given unsolicited advice to a layman that he should obtain counsel or take legal action" from accepting "employment resulting from that advice." Ohralik claimed that his suspension violated the first amendment. The Court, speaking again through Justice Powell, upheld the suspension. The Court explained that *Primus* was distinguishable because *Ohralik* involved only a commercial transaction, and "in rejecting the notion" that expression concerning purely commercial transactions " 'is wholly outside the protection of the First Amendment,' [we] were careful [in *Virginia Pharmacy* not to discard] the 'commonsense' distinction between speech proposing a commercial transaction [and] other varieties of speech." Indeed, "to require a parity of constitutional protection for commercial and noncommercial speech alike could invite dilution, simply by a leveling process, of the force of the Amendment's guarantee with respect to the latter kind of speech. Rather than subject the First Amendment to such a devitalization, we instead have afforded commercial speech a limited measure of protection, commensurate with its subordinate position in the scale of First Amendment values, while allowing modes of regulation that might be permissible in the realm of noncommercial expression." Thus, "a lawyer's procurement of remunerative employment is a subject only marginally affected with First Amendment concerns," and "while entitled to some constitutional protection, [such] conduct is subject to regulation in furtherance of important state interests."

Here, "the State has a legitimate and indeed 'compelling' interest in preventing those aspects of solicitation that involve fraud, undue influence, intimidation, overreaching, and other forms of 'vexatious conduct.' " Moreover, it was unnecessary for the State to prove that Ohralik's own solicitation involved any actual abuse or caused any actual harm to his "clients." Rather, the prohibition could constitutionally be applied whenever, as in *Ohralik*, an attorney for remunerative purposes "personally solicits an unsophisticated, injured, or distressed lay person," for in such circumstances there is great "potential for overreaching" and the solicitation is thus "likely to result in the adverse consequences the State seeks to avert."

Dissenting in *Primus*, Justice Rehnquist maintained that there was no "principled distinction" between *Ohralik* and *Primus* and in effect accused the Court of developing "a jurisprudence of epithets and slogans [in] which 'ambulance chasers' suffer one fate and 'civil liberties lawyers' another." The "constitutional inquiry," Rehnquist argued, "must focus on the character of the conduct which the State seeks to regulate, and not on the motives of the individual lawyers or the nature of the particular litigation involved."

See also Zauderer v. Office of Disciplinary Counsel, — U.S. — , 105 S. Ct. 2265 (1985), in which the Court invalidated a rule forbidding attorneys to solicit clients through advertisements focusing on specific legal problems, and distinguished *Ohralik* on the ground that print advertising "poses much less risk" of "overreaching or undue influence" than in-person solicitation.

CENTRAL HUDSON GAS v. PUBLIC SERVICE COMMISSION OF NEW YORK, 447 U.S. 557 (1980): The Commission permitted electric utilities to engage in institutional and informational advertising but to further the conservation of energy, prohibited such utilities to engage in promotional advertising designed to stimulate the use of electricity. The Court, in an opinion by Justice Powell, held the order invalid. The order, the Court noted, "restricts only commercial speech, that is, expression related solely to the economic interests of the speaker and its audience." Echoing *Ohralik* the Court observed that the "Constitution [accords] a lesser protection to commercial speech than to other constitutionally guaranteed expression." The Court maintained that, in its prior decisions, it had implicitly "developed" a "four-part analysis" for commercial speech cases:

"[First], we must determine whether the expression is protected by the First Amendment. For commercial speech to come within that provision, it at least must concern lawful activity and not be misleading. [Second], we ask whether the asserted governmental interest is substantial. [Third, if] both inquiries yield positive answers, we must determine whether the regulation directly advances the governmental interest. [And fourth], if the governmental interest could be served as well by a more limited restriction on commercial speech, the excessive restrictions cannot survive."

Applying this analysis to the ban on promotional advertising, the Court noted that the "Commission does not claim that the expression at issue is either inaccurate or relates to unlawful activity." Moreover, "in view of our country's dependence on energy resources beyond our control, no one can doubt the importance of energy conservation. Plainly, therefore, the state interest asserted is substantial." Further, "the State's interest in energy conservation is directly advanced by the Commission order." Thus, "the critical inquiry" is whether the Commission's complete suppression of speech ordinarily protected by the First Amendment is no more extensive than necessary to further the State's interest." The Court found the complete ban on promotional advertising to be too "extensive" for two reasons. First, no exception was made for promotional advertising of specific electric products and "services that would [increase the use of electricity but reduce total] energy use by diverting demand from less efficient sources." And second, the Commission "has not demonstrated that its interest in conservation cannot be protected adequately by more limited regulation of [the] format and content of Central Hudson's advertising. It might, for example, require that the advertisements include information about the relative efficiency and expense of the offered service." The Court thus concluded that, "in the absence of a showing that more limited speech regulation would be ineffective, we cannot approve the complete suppression of Central Hudson's advertising."

Justice Blackmun, joined by Justice Brennan, concurred. Although agreeing with the Court that the "level of intermediate scrutiny" embodied in its "four-part analysis" is "appropriate for a restraint on commercial speech designed to protect consumers from misleading or coercive speech, or a regulation related to the time, place or manner of commercial speech," Blackmun maintained that "the test now evolved and applied by the Court is not consistent with our prior cases and does not provide adequate protection for truthful, nonmisleading, noncoercive speech." "Even though 'commercial' speech is involved," the Commission's order "strikes at the heart of the First Amendment," for "it is a covert attempt by the State to manipulate the choices of its citizens, not by persuasion or direct regulation, but by depriving the public of the information needed to make a free choice." Blackmun concluded that "no differences between commercial speech and other protected speech justify suppression of commercial speech in order to influence public conduct through manipulation of the availability of information."

In another concurring opinion, Justice Stevens, also joined by Justice Brennan, concluded that this is not a "commercial speech" case at all. The Commission's order, Stevens argued, "encompasses a great deal more than mere proposals to engage in certain kinds of commercial transactions. It prohibits all advocacy of the immediate or future use of electricity. It curtails expression by an informed and interested group of persons of their point of view on questions [frequently] discussed and debated by our political leaders. For example, an electric company's advocacy of the use of electric heat for environmental reasons, as opposed to wood-burning stoves, would seem to fall squarely within New York's promotional advertising ban and also within the bounds of maximum First Amendment protection." Thus, "if the perceived harm associated with greater electrical usage is not sufficiently serious [for the State directly to prohibit excessive use], surely it does not constitute the kind of clear and present danger that can justify the suppression of speech."

Justice Rehnquist dissented. Rehnquist argued that New York's order is essentially "an economic regulation to which virtually complete deference should be accorded by this Court," for "in terms of constitutional values," the ban on promotional advertising is "virtually indistinguishable" from a decision of the Commission to raise the price of electricity in order to conserve energy. "[Those] who won our independence," Rehnquist emphasized, would not "have viewed a merchant's unfettered freedom to advertise in hawking his wares as a 'liberty' not subject to extensive regulation," for as "our ancestors learned long ago," in a democracy, the economic is subordinate to the political. Moreover, Rehnquist faulted the Court for its application of its own standard. He argued, for example, that in striking down the ban as "more extensive than necessary," the Court engaged in "highly speculative" reasoning. In effect, it conjured "up potential advertisements that a utility might make that conceivably would result in net energy savings" without even suggesting that the Commission had ever confronted such proposals or that, if so confronted, it would actually interpret its order as banning such advertisements. Such speculation, Rehnquist suggested, was simply "inappropriate."

METROMEDIA, INC. v. SAN DIEGO, 435 U.S. 490 (1981): To eliminate hazards to pedestrians and motorists and to preserve and improve the appearance of the city, San Diego enacted an ordinance prohibiting virtually all outdoor advertising display signs. The only exceptions were for "on-site" signs, such as those advertising goods or services produced or offered on the premises, and for signs falling within twelve specified categories, such as temporary political campaign signs, government signs, for-sale signs, and signs on public and commercial vehicles. Although the Court invalidated the ordinance as applied to *noncommercial* advertising, see infra page 1249, it sustained the ordinance as applied to *commercial* messages. Justice White delivered the opinion of the Court:

"[Although *Virginia Pharmacy*] plainly held that speech proposing no more than a commercial transaction enjoys a substantial degree of First Amendment protection, [it] did not equate commercial and noncommercial speech for First Amendment purposes. [The] proper approach to be taken in determining the validity [of] restrictions on commercial speech [is] that which was articulated in *Central Hudson*. . . .

"There can be little controversy [over] the application of the first, second, and fourth criteria. There is no suggestion that the commercial advertising at issue here involves unlawful activity or is misleading. [Nor can there be substantial doubt that the twin goals] of traffic safety and maintaining the appearance of the city are substantial. [Moreover, the ordinance satisfies the] fourth part of the *Central Hudson* test, [for if] the city has a sufficient basis for believing that billboards are traffic hazards and are unattractive, then obviously the most direct and perhaps the only effective approach to solving the problems they create is to prohibit them. The city has gone no farther than necessary in seeking to meet its ends. . . .

"[The critical] question, then, [concerns] the third of the *Central Hudson* criteria: Does the ordinance 'directly advance' governmental interests in traffic safety and in the appearance of the city? [Although appellants assert] that the record is inadequate to show any connection between billboards and traffic safety, [we] hesitate to disagree with the accumulated, common-sense judgments of local lawmakers [that] billboards are real and substantial hazards to traffic safety. There is nothing here to suggest that these judgments are unreasonable. [Similarly, with respect to the] advancement of the city's esthetic interests, [it] is not speculative to recognize that billboards by their very nature, wherever located and however constructed, can be perceived an 'esthetic harm.' [Although] esthetic judgments are necessarily subjective, defying objective evaluation, and for that reason must be carefully scrutinized to determine if they are only a public rationalization of an impermissible purpose, [there] is no claim in this case that San Diego has as an ulterior motive the suppression of speech, and the judgment involved here is not so unusual as to raise suspicions in itself. . . .

"[Finally, we reject the argument] that the city denigrates its interest in traffic safety and beauty and defeats its own case by permitting [the] occupant of property to use billboards located on that property to advertise goods and services offered at that location [while prohibiting occupants of other property to use] identical billboards, equally distracting and unattractive, that advertise goods or services available elsewhere. [The] city may believe that off-site advertising, with its periodically changing content, presents a more acute problem than does on-site advertising. [Or] the city could reasonably conclude that a commercial enterprise [has] a stronger interest in identifying its place of business and advertising the products or services available there than it has in using or leasing its available space for the purpose of advertising commercial enterprises located elsewhere. See Railway Express v. New York [supra Chapter 5, section B] (Jackson, J., concurring). [Thus], insofar as it regulates commercial speech the San Diego ordinance meets the constitutional requirements of *Central Hudson*."

In a separate opinion, Justice Brennan, joined by Justice Blackmun, disagreed with the Court's conclusion that the city could constitutionally ban all commercial billboards. Brennan was especially concerned that an ordinance prohibiting commercial but allowing noncommercial billboards would put city officials "in the position in the first instance of deciding whether the proposed speech is commercial or noncommercial," thus presenting "a real danger of curtailing noncommercial speech in the guise of regulating commercial speech." Pointing, for example, to a United Automobile Workers or Chrysler billboard with the message "Be a patriot — do not buy Japanese-manufactured cars," Brennan argued that "it is one thing for a court to classify in specific cases whether commercial or noncommercial speech is involved, but quite another [for] a city to do so regularly for the purpose of deciding what messages may be communicated by way of billboards." Chief Justice Burger and Justice Rehnquist, in separate opinions, maintained that a ban on *all* billboards — noncommercial as well as commercial — would be constitutional, and thus did not directly address the constitutionality of a ban on only commercial billboards.

Note: Ohralik, Central Hudson, *and* Metromedia — *Retreat on Commercial Speech?*

To what extent do *Ohralik, Central Hudson,* and *Metromedia* retreat from the Court's prior understanding of the first amendment's protection of truthful, nondeceptive commercial speech? Arguably, *Metromedia* represents a low point in the Court's protection of commercial speech since *Virginia Pharmacy.* Compare, for example, *Metromedia*'s reliance on Justice Jackson's concurring opinion in *Railway Express* and its deferential hesitation "to suggest that [the legislative] judgments are unreasonable" with *Linmark*'s reliance on Justice Brandeis's concurring opinion in *Whitney* and its use of a stringent standard of review. Compare also the Court's analysis of the fourth part of the *Central Hudson* test in *Metromedia* with its analysis of that factor in *Central Hudson.* In *Central Hudson* the Court held that the ban on promotional advertising was too "extensive" because the Commission might more narrowly have restricted the "format and content" of the advertising. In *Metromedia,* however, the Court upheld the ban on commercial billboards even though the city, to further its interests in traffic safety and aesthetics, might more narrowly have restricted the size, location and appearance of outdoor signs.

Consider the following bases for distinguishing and hence limiting *Metromedia:* (1) *Metromedia* involved a mere "time, place and manner" restriction of the kind envisioned in *Virginia Pharmacy.* (But recall *Linmark.*) (2) *Metromedia* involved a restriction of *all* commercial messages, rather than a restriction of only particular messages, such as lawyer or electric utility advertising. (3) *Metromedia* involved an ordinance that was justified by interests of traffic safety and aesthetics having nothing to do with "paternalism" or with the "communicative impact" of expression. (On "communicative impact," see supra section B2.)

In Bolger v. Youngs Drug Products Corp., 463 U.S. 60 (1983), the Court invalidated a federal statute prohibiting the mailing of unsolicited advertisements for contraceptives because the interest in shielding "recipients of mail from materials that they are likely to find offensive" is not sufficiently substantial to justify the suppression of "protected speech," and the interest in "aiding parents' efforts to discuss birth control with their children," although "undoubtedly substantial," is not sufficiently furthered by the prohibition to justify the purging of "all mailboxes of unsolicited material that is entirely suitable for adults." *Bolger* suggests that there is still some bite in the Court's protection of commercial speech.

Note: *Labor Disputes and the First Amendment*

Does expression concerning the merits of an on-going labor controversy warrant full first amendment protection? Does such expression, like commercial advertising, hold only "a subordinate position" in the scale of first amendment values?

1. *Labor picketing.* The history of the Court's analysis of labor picketing is traced in Justice Frankfurter's opinion for the Court in International Brotherhood of Teamsters v. Vogt, Inc., 354 U.S. 284 (1957):

[In Thornhill v. Alabama, 310 U.S. 88 (1940), the Court held] unconstitutional a statute that had been applied to ban all [picketing]. As the statute dealt at large with all picketing, so the Court broadly assimilated peaceful picketing in general to freedom of speech, and as such protected against abridgement by the Fourteenth Amendment. [Soon], however, the Court came to realize that the broad pronouncements [of] *Thornhill* had to yield "to the impact of facts unforeseen," or at least not sufficiently appreciated. [The] decisive reconsideration came in Giboney v. Empire Storage & Ice Co., 336 U.S. 490 [1949]. A union, seeking to organize peddlers, picketed a wholesale dealer to induce it to refrain from selling to nonunion peddlers. The state courts, finding that such an agreement would constitute a conspiracy in restraint of trade in violation of the state antitrust laws, enjoined the picketing. This Court [unanimously rejected a contention] that "the injunction [was] an unconstitutional abridgement of free speech because the picketers were attempting peacefully to publicize truthful facts about a labor dispute." [The *Giboney* Court explained that] "the sole immediate object of the [picketing] was to compel [the dealer] to agree to stop selling ice to nonunion peddlers." [The Court concluded that, in] this situation, the injunction did no more than enjoin an offense against Missouri law." [Building] Service Employees v. Gazzam, 339 U.S. 532 [1950], was decided the [following term]. Following an unsuccessful attempt at unionization of a small hotel and refusal by the owner to sign a contract with the union as bargaining agent, the union began to picket the hotel with signs stating that the owner was unfair to organized labor. The State, finding that the object of the picketing was in violation of its statutory policy against employer coercion of employees' choice of bargaining representative, enjoined picketing for such purpose. This Court affirmed, [noting] the unlawful objective of the picketing, namely, coercion by the employer of the employees' selection of a bargaining representative. [This] series of cases, then, established a broad field in which a State, in enforcing some public policy [could] constitutionally enjoin peaceful picketing aimed at preventing effectuation of that policy.

2. *Labor picketing today.* Consider NLRB v. Retail Store Employees Local 1001, 447 U.S. 607 (1980), decided on the same day as *Central Hudson.* During a labor dispute with Safeco, an underwriter of real estate title insurance, Local 1001 picketed the premises of five local title companies that searched titles, performed escrow services and sold only Safeco insurance. The pickets carried signs declaring that Safeco had no contract with the union and distributed handbills asking consumers to support the strike by cancelling their Safeco policies. The board held that the secondary consumer picketing constituted an unfair labor practice. The board reasoned that since the local companies sold only Safeco insurance, the union's action was "reasonably calculated to induce customers not to patronize the neutral parties at all," thus effectively coercing them to pressure Safeco into yielding to the union's demands. The union maintained that this determination violated its rights under the first amendment.

The Court, speaking through Justice Powell, upheld the board's determination on the ground that the union's activity was in furtherance of "unlawful objectives" — that is, inducing customers not to patronize the local companies in order to induce them to join in putting economic pressure on Safeco. Would a similar restriction be constitutional if political rather than economic pressure was involved? Consider Cox, Foreword, Freedom of Expression in the Burger Court, 94 Harv. L. Rev. 1, 36-37 (1980):

> The objectives were "unlawful" only in a Pickwickian sense. The customers violate no law by ceasing to do business with the [local companies]. The [local companies] violate no law by ceasing to do business with [Safeco]. [Safeco] violates no law by settling the dispute upon the union's terms. Congress deemed these consequences undesirable because they extend economic warfare by involving neutrals, but it did not proscribe anything but the appeal to the customers.

Contrast NAACP v. Claiborne Hardware, supra section B1, in which the Court held that an NAACP boycott of white businesses is constitutionally protected activity, with International Longshoremen's Association v. Allied International, 456 U.S. 212 (1982), in which the Court held that a union's refusal to unload cargoes arriving from the Soviet Union as a protest against the Soviet invasion of Afghanistan is a secondary boycott in violation of the NLRA and thus unprotected by the first amendment. Consider L. Tribe, Constitutional Choices 201 (1985): "The contrast between *ILA* and *Claiborne* illustrates the utter manipulability of the political-economic distinction and the Court's hostility [to] the First Amendment rights of labor unions."

Did the Court in *Local 1001* miss "an opportunity to give structure to these aspects of first amendment law" because of its failure to explain that labor picketing should be "classified with commercial advertising as economic speech" subject generally to the "four-part test promulgated in *Central Hudson*"? Cox, supra, at 39. For the argument that "labor speech deserves greater protection than commercial speech," see Goldman, The First Amendment and Nonpicketing Labor Publicity, 36 Vand. L. Rev. 1469 (1983).

3. *Representation elections.* In NLRB v. Gissel Packing Co., 395 U.S. 575 (1969), the International Brotherhood of Teamsters attempted to organize petitioner's employees. On learning of the union's efforts, petitioner's president attempted both in conversation and in writing to dissuade the employees from joining the union. He reminded the employees that a strike some twelve years earlier had shut down the company for three months and described the union as "strike happy." He emphasized that the company was on "thin ice" financially, that the union's "only weapon is to strike," and that a strike "could lead to the closing of the plant." He also pointed out to the employees that because of their age and the limited usefulness of their skills outside their craft, they might not be able to find jobs elsewhere if the company went out of business. Finally, he provided the employees with a long list of firms in the town that had recently gone out of business, impliedly as a result of union demands. The union lost the representation election by a vote of seven to six, but the board set aside the election on the ground that the president's communications with the employees constituted an "unfair labor practice." Petitioner argued that this finding violated the first amendment.

In a unanimous decision, the Court upheld the board. The Court explained that although the NLRA permits an employer to "make a prediction as to the precise effects he believes unionization will have on his company, [the] prediction must be carefully phrased on the basis of objective fact to convey [the] employer's belief as to demonstrably probable consequences beyond his control." Here, "the Board could reasonably conclude that the intended and understood import of [the president's] message was not to predict that unionization would inevitably cause the plant to close but to threaten to throw employees out of work regardless of the economic realities," for the president "had no support for [his] assumption that the union" would have to strike, he "had no basis for attributing other plant closings in the area to unionism," and the Board had "often found that employees, who are particularly sensitive to rumors of plant closings, take such hints as coercive threats rather than honest forecasts." In such circumstances, the president's statement could be deemed "a threat of retaliation based on misrepresentation and coercion, and as such without the protection of the First Amendment."

Could expression analogous to that at issue in *Gissel* be restricted in the context of an ordinary political election? If not, what explains *Gissel*? Is the speech of "low" first amendment value because it concerns a private economic dispute? Is *Gissel* explicable on the ground, suggested by the Court, that the law "must take into account the economic dependence of the employees on their employers, and the necessary tendency of the former, because of that relationship, to pick up intended implications of the latter that might be more readily dismissed by a more disinterested ear"?

4. *Final thoughts.* Consider Pope, The Three-Systems Ladder of First Amendment Values: Two Rungs and a Black Hole, 11 Hast. Const. L.Q. 189, 228-232, 241 (1984):

> The [modern] vision of [constitutional law views] the First Amendment as guarantor of the processes of representative government. [It assumes that in] the well functioning polity, [all] groups are able to press their concerns and make alliances, thereby ensuring that their interests will receive fair consideration. [The critical question is] how far the processes of representation extend. If only the formal processes of representative government are included, then the Supreme Court has gone too far in protecting commercial speech. [However], if the institutions of representative government are inextricably connected to all power relations in society, then the rigid boundaries [between political, commercial, and labor speech] are unjustifiable because labor relations and even commercial competition may be regarded as struggles for power. [Having] recognized the right of selected groups to employ certain forms of economic power [such as the right of corporations to use commercial advertising], the Court is now under pressure to extend those rights to other groups and forms of economic power [such as the right of labor unions to use economic boycotts].

5.   Obscenity

In the first reported obscenity case in the United States, a Pennsylvania court declared it an offense at common law to exhibit for profit a picture of a nude couple. Commonwealth v. Sharpless, 2 Serg. & Rawle 91 (1815). Despite *Sharpless* there were few serious efforts to restrict "obscene" expression prior to the Civil War. In the late 1860s, however, Anthony Comstock, a grocer, initiated a campaign to suppress obscenity. Comstock's efforts resulted in the enactment of anti-obscenity legislation in virtually every state. In applying this legislation, most courts adopted the *Hicklin* definition of obscenity: the "test of obscenity" is "whether the tendency of the matter [is] to deprave and corrupt those whose minds are open to such immoral influences." Regina v. Hicklin, L.R. 3 Q.B. 360, 371 (1868). Under this test, which resulted in the suppression of such works as Theodore Dreiser's An American Tragedy and D. H. Lawrence's Lady Chatterly's Lover, a work could be deemed obscene because of the potential effect of even isolated passages on the most susceptible readers or viewers. See Commonwealth v. Friede, 271 Mass. 318, 171 N.E. 472 (1930) (An American Tragedy); Commonwealth v. DeLacey, 271 Mass. 327, 171 N.E. 455 (1930) (Lady Chatterly's Lover). In an influential decision reviewing the suppression of James Joyce's Ulysses in the early 1930s, a federal court rejected the *Hicklin* test and adopted instead a standard focusing on the effect on the average person of the dominant theme of the work as a whole. United States v. One Book called "Ulysses," 5 F. Supp. 182 (S.D.N.Y. 1933), aff'd, 72 F.2d 705 (2d Cir. 1934).

Throughout this era, it was generally assumed that the first amendment posed no barrier to the suppression of obscenity. Indeed, the *Chaplinsky* dictum prominently featured the "obscene" in its catalogue of "unprotected" utterances. The Supreme Court first considered the obscenity issue in a 1948 case arising out of New York's attempt to suppress Memoirs of Hecate County, a highly regarded book written by Edmund Wilson, America's foremost literary critic. The Court divided equally on the issue, however, and thus affirmed the conviction without opinion. Doubleday & Co. v. New York, 335 U.S. 848 (1948). Nine years later, in *Roth*, the Court finally addressed the obscenity question. There have been two distinct periods in the Court's efforts to come to grips with obscenity. The first period, which lasted from the 1957 decision in *Roth* until 1973, was dominated by the Warren Court's frustrating and largely unsuccessful efforts to define "obscenity." The second period, which began with the Court's 1973 decisions in *Miller* and *Paris Adult Theatre*, has been dominated by the Burger Court's efforts to reformulate the doctrine. This section focuses on three questions: Is obscenity "low" value speech? What is "obscenity"? What interests justify the suppression of obscenity?

ROTH v. UNITED STATES, ALBERTS v. CALIFORNIA, 354 U.S. 476 (1957): Roth was convicted of violating a federal statute prohibiting any person to mail any "obscene" publication. Alberts was convicted of violating a California statute prohibiting any person to write, print, or sell any "obscene" writing. The Supreme Court affirmed the convictions. Justice Brennan delivered the opinion of the Court:

"The dispositive question is whether obscenity is utterance within the area of protected speech and press. [All] ideas having even the slightest redeeming social importance — unorthodox ideas, controversial ideas, even ideas hateful to the prevailing climate of opinion — have the full protection of the guarantees, unless excludable because they encroach upon the limited area of more important interests. But implicit in the history of the First Amendment is the rejection of obscenity as utterly without redeeming social importance. [Thirteen] of the 14 States which by 1792 had ratified the Constitution [provided] for the prosecution of libel, and all of those States made either blasphemy or profanity, or both, statutory crimes. [In] light of this history, it is apparent [that] obscenity, [like] libel, [was] outside the protection intended for speech and press. [We therefore] hold that obscenity is not within the area of constitutionally protected speech or press.

[Accordingly,] obscene material [may be suppressed] without proof [that it will] create a clear and present danger of antisocial conduct. [Citing *Beauharnais*.]

"However, sex and obscenity are not synonymous. Obscene material is material which deals with sex in a manner appealing to prurient interest. The portrayal of sex, e.g., in art, literature, and scientific works, is not itself sufficient reason to deny material the constitutional protection of freedom of speech and press. Sex, a great and mysterious motive in human life, has indisputably been a subject of absorbing interest to mankind through the ages; it is one of the vital problems of human interest and public concern. [It] is therefore vital that the standards for judging obscenity safeguard the protection of freedom of speech and press for material which does not treat sex in a manner appealing to prurient interest. [The proper test is] whether to the average person, applying contemporary community standards, the dominant theme of the material taken as a whole appeals to the prurient interest."

Chief Justice Warren concurred in the result: "It is not the book that is on trial; it is a person. [The] defendants [in] these cases [were] plainly engaged in the commercial exploitation of the morbid and shameful craving for materials with prurient effect. [State] and Federal Governments can constitutionally punish such conduct. That is all that [we] need to decide."

Justice Harlan concurred in the result in *Alberts* but dissented in *Roth*: "In judging the constitutionality of [the] conviction [in *Alberts*], we should remember that our function in reviewing judgments under the Fourteenth Amendment is [limited to inquiring] whether the state action [can] be sustained as [a] rational exercise of power. [The] state legislature has made the judgment that [the] distribution of certain types of literature will induce criminal or immoral sexual conduct. [In] our present state of knowledge, [we cannot say that this judgment is irrational. Moreover,] the State can reasonably [assume] that over a long period of time the indiscriminate dissemination of [obscene material] will have an eroding effect on moral standards. [I] cannot say that [the] suppression [of the materials at issue in these cases would] so interfere with the communication of 'ideas' [that] it would offend the Due Process Clause. . . .

"I dissent in [*Roth*]. We are faced here with the question whether the federal obscenity statute [violates] the First Amendment. [The] Constitution differentiates between those areas of human conduct subject to the regulation of the States and those subject to the powers of the Federal Government. [The] interests which obscenity statutes purportedly protect are primarily entrusted to the care [of] the States. Congress has no substantive power over sexual morality. [Moreover], the dangers of federal censorship in this field are far greater than anything the State may do. [In light of these considerations], I do not think that the federal statute can be constitutionally construed to reach other [than] 'hard-core' pornography. [The] material here involved [is not of that sort]."

Justice Douglas, joined by Justice Black, dissented: "I do not think that the problem can be resolved by the Court's statement that 'obscenity is not expression protected by the First Amendment.' [There] is no special historical evidence that literature dealing with sex was intended to be treated in a special manner by those who drafted the First Amendment. [Moreover,] I reject [the] implication that problems of freedom of speech [are] to be resolved by weighing against the values of free expression, the judgment of the Court that a particular form of expression has 'no redeeming social importance.' The First Amendment [was] designed to preclude courts as well as legislatures from weighing the values of speech against silence. [I] have the same confidence in the ability of our people to reject noxious literature as I have in their capacity to sort out the true from the false in theology, economics, politics, or any other field."

Note: Obscenity and Free Expression

1. *Entertainment, art, literature, and the first amendment.* Does the first amendment protect not only speech that expressly addresses "public" issues but also "speech" in the form of entertainment, art, and literature? Does the latter form of "speech" have a "subordinate position" in the scale of first amendment values? Consider Kalven, The Metaphysics of the Law of Obscenity, 1960 Sup. Ct. Rev. 1, 15-16:

> The classic defense of John Stuart Mill and the modern defense of Alexander Meiklejohn do not help much when the question is why the novel, the poem, the painting, the drama, or the piece of sculpture falls within the protection of the First Amendment. Nor do the famous opinions of Hand, Holmes, and Brandeis. The emphasis is all on truth winning out in a fair fight between competing ideas [and on the] argument that free speech is indispensable to the informed citizenry required to make self-government work. The people need free speech because they vote. [But not] all communications are relevant to the political process. The people do not need novels or dramas or paintings or poems because they will be called upon to vote. Art and belles-lettres do not deal in such ideas — at least not good art or belles-lettres. [Thus] there seems to be a hiatus in our basic free-speech theory.

Consider Meiklejohn's response:

> [There] are many forms of thought and expression within the range of human communications from which the voter derives the knowledge, intelligence, sensitivity to human values: the capacity for sane and objective judgement which, so far as possible, a ballot should express. [The] people do need novels and dramas and paintings and poems, "because they will be called upon to vote." The primary social fact which blocks and hinders the success of our experiment in self-government is that our citizens are not educated for self-government.

Meiklejohn, The First Amendment Is an Absolute, 1961 Sup. Ct. Rev. 245, 256, 263. Does the "self-fulfillment" defense of free expression fill Kalven's "hiatus" and offer a more persuasive rationale for the protection of art, literature, and entertainment?

The Court has generally assumed that nonobscene literature and entertainment are entitled to "full" first amendment protection. In Winters v. New York, 333 U.S. 507, 510 (1948), for example, the Court explained that "The line between the informing and the entertaining is too elusive for the protection of the basic right. Everyone is familiar with instances of propaganda through fiction. What is one man's amusement, teaches another's doctrine." See also Schad v. Borough of Mount Ephraim, 452 U.S. 61 (1981) (holding unconstitutional a prohibition on all live entertainment in the borough).

2. *Is obscenity of only "low" first amendment value?* Does obscenity further any of the values underlying the protection of free expression? Consider the following arguments:

a. As the Court demonstrated in *Roth*, the historical evidence shows that obscenity "was outside the protection intended for speech and press." But consider Kalven, supra, at 9: "[The] Court's use of history was so casual as to be [alarming]. Is it clear, for example, that blasphemy can constitutionally be made a crime today? And what would the Court say to an argument along the same lines appealing to the Sedition Act of 1798 as justification for the truly liberty-defeating crime of seditious libel?"

b. Schauer, Speech and "Speech" — Obscenity and "Obscenity": An Exercise in the Interpretation of Constitutional Language, 67 Geo. L.J. 899, 906, 922, 923, 926 (1979):

> Certain uses of words, although speech in the ordinary sense, clearly are not speech in the constitutional sense. ["Speech" for first amendment purposes is defined by] the idea of cognitive content, of mental effect, of a communication designed to appeal to the intellectual process. This [includes] the artistic and the emotive as well as the propositional. [But] hardcore pornography is [by definition] designed to produce a purely physical effect. [It is] essentially a physical rather than a mental stimulus. [A] pornographic item is in a real sense a sexual surrogate. [Consider] rubber, plastic, or leather sex aids. It is hard to find any free speech aspects in their sale or use. [The] mere fact that in pornography the stimulating experience is initiated by visual rather than tactile means is irrelevant. [Neither] means constitutes communication in the cognitive sense. [Thus,] hardcore pornography *is* sex, [not "speech"].

Is this what the Court meant in *Roth* when it defined obscenity as "material which deals with sex in a manner appealing to prurient interest"? Note that in Brockett v. Spokane Arcades, — U.S. — 105 S. Ct. 2794 (1985), the Court held unconstitutional a statute that defined "appeal to prurient interest" as including material that arouses a normal sexual response. The Court explained that speech "appeals to prurient interest" within the meaning of the constitutional standard only if it incites "a shameful or morbid" sexual response.

c. As the Court observed in *Chaplinsky*, obscenity is "of such slight social value as a step to truth that any benefit that may be derived from [it] is clearly outweighed by the social interest in order and morality." Or as the Court observed in *Roth*, such expression is "utterly without redeeming social importance." But consider Richards, Free Speech and Obscenity Law: Toward a Moral Theory of the First Amendment, 123 U. Pa. L. Rev. 45, 82 (1974):

> [The] First Amendment rests [fundamentally] on the moral liberties of expression, conscience and thought; these liberties are fundamental conditions of the integrity and competence of a person in mastering his life and expressing this mastery to others. [There] is no reason whatsoever to believe that the freedom to determine the sexual contents of one's communications or to be an audience to such communications is not as fundamental to this self-mastery as the freedom to decide upon any other communicative contents. [The] consequence of [laws directed against obscenity] is not only a denial of a reasonable understanding of the varieties of pleasurable sexual function, but also a crippling debasement of the human capacity to master one's sexual life in the light of independent judgment.

d. Laws directed against obscenity are not restrictions on ideas as such, for they limit the *means* of expression rather than the *ideas* expressed. As the Court said in *Chaplinsky*, obscene "utterances are no essential part of any exposition of ideas." Moreover, to the extent that obscenity is associated with a particular ideological message, such as "sexual freedom," it is an especially problematic *means* of expression, for it alters "one's tastes and preferences" not by direct persuasion or rational argument, but by "a process that is, like subliminal advertising, both outside of one's rational control and quite independent of the relevant grounds for preference." Scanlon, Freedom of Expression and Categories of Expression, 40 U. Pitt. L. Rev. 519, 547 (1979). To what extent is this true as well of commercial advertising?

3. *The interests furthered by the suppression of obscenity.* Because the Court in *Roth* accepted the underlying premise of the *Chaplinsky* dictum — that obscene utterances are wholly "unprotected" by the first amendment — the Court found it unnecessary to inquire into the nature or substantiality of the state interests said to justify the suppression of obscene expression. The gradual breakdown of the "two-level" theory and the increased use of "definitional" balancing in such areas as libel and commercial speech, however, may raise doubts about this approach. Do the decisions to "balance" conflicting state and speech interests in the libel and commercial speech contexts suggest a need for similar balancing in the obscenity context? If so, what state interests are sufficiently important to justify restrictions on obscene expression? Consider the following:

a. The state may suppress obscenity because it may cause violent antisocial conduct. Must the state "prove" causation? What must be the nature of the correlation — clear and present danger? Bad tendency? For analysis of the "correlation," see The Report of the Commission on Obscenity and Pornography 26-27 (1970) (finding "no evidence to date that exposure to explicit sexual materials plays a significant role in the causation of delinquent or criminal behavior"). For criticism of the Report, see L. Sunderland, Obscenity: The Court, the Congress and the President's Commission (1975); Clor, Science, Eros and the Law: A Critique of the Obscenity Commission Report, 10 Duq. L. Rev. 63 (1971).

b. The state may suppress obscenity because it "corrupts character," impairs "mental health," and "has a deleterious effect on the individual from which the community should protect him." Henkin, Morals and the Constitution: The Sin of Obscenity, 63 Colum. L. Rev. 391, 394 (1963).

c. The state may suppress obscenity to prevent the erosion of moral standards. Consider Lockhart & McClure, Literature, the Law of Obscenity, and the Constitution, 38 Minn. L. Rev. 295, 374-375 (1954):

> The view that literature may be proscribed because [it] may [change] accepted moral standards [flies] squarely in the face of the [guarantee of free] expression. Back of this fundamental freedom lies the basic conviction that our democratic society must be free to perfect its own standards of conduct and belief [through] the heat of unrepressed controversy and debate. The remedy against those who attack currently accepted standards is [defense] of those standards, not censorship.

d. The state may suppress obscenity because it erodes moral standards not by rational persuasion, but by indirect degradation of values. Consider H. Clor, Obscenity and Public Morality 121, 170-171 (1969):

[Obscene materials] do not make arguments which are to be met by intelligent defense. While they attack moral values, they do not [do so] in any sense relevant to [public debate]. [Rather,] they have an [effect] upon feeling, upon motivations — ultimately upon character and the basic attitudes which arise from character. [Constant] exposure to [obscene] materials which overemphasize sensuality and brutality, reduce love to sex, and blatantly expose to public view intimacies which have been thought [private] must eventually [erode] moral standards. [The] ethical convictions of man do not rest simply upon his explicit opinions. They rest also upon a delicate network of moral and aesthetic feelings, sensibilities, [and] tastes. [These] "finer feelings" [may be eroded] by a steady stream of [obscenity]. Men whose sensibilities are frequently assaulted by prurient and lurid impressions may become desensitized. [This] is what is meant by "an erosion of the moral fabric."

May the state ever use censorship to protect "the moral fabric"? Consider the following views: (1) "Undoubtedly, the general moral standards and social customs prevailing in a community are [influenced by] books. [But the law] cannot be invoked to protect prevailing moral standards, first because this assumes a finality which such standards do not possess, [and] secondly, because [there] is no common agreement on ultimate moral attitudes." N. St. John-Stevas, Obscenity and the Law 196 (1956). See also H. Hart, Law, Liberty, and Morality 21, 57 (1963) (Government may not use law to "enforce morality as such"; it may prohibit acts "which are harmful to others," but it may not prohibit acts "which deviate from accepted morality but harm no one.").

(2) "A society functions only if its members share a common body of values [and] a common ethos. [In] terms of social efficacy, it is not necessary [that the values be "true"]. It is enough that they be held, [for] the holding of some [shared ethos] is needed for the moral solidarity of [a] society. [The society may permit] some divergencies but, [if] it is to remain viable, [it must] protect the essential shared values. [Certainly] the right of censorship is implied." van der Haag, Quia Ineptum, in To Deprave and Corrupt 113-114 (J. Chandos ed., 1962). See also P. Devlin, The Enforcement of Morals 111 (1965) ("[An] individual may by unrestricted indulgence in vice so weaken himself that he ceases to be a useful member of society [and] if a sufficient number of individuals so weaken themselves, society will thereby be weakened").

e. The state may restrict obscenity to protect individuals against the "shock effect" of unwanted exposure to such expression because "a communication of this nature, imposed upon a person contrary to his wishes, has all the characteristics of a physical assault." T. Emerson, The System of Freedom of Expression 496 (1970). May it suppress obscenity to protect individuals against the "shock" of knowing that others are reading or viewing it?

f. The state may suppress the dissemination of obscenity to minors because they are especially vulnerable to its "harmful" effects.

Note: Developments in the Law of "Obscenity" — 1957-1973

1. *The definition of obscenity: the breakdown of consensus.* In *Roth* the Court embraced the view that material is "obscene" if, "to the average person, applying contemporary community standards, the dominant theme of the material taken

as a whole appeals to prurient interest." But agreement on the definition of obscenity was short-lived. Only a decade after *Roth* Justice Harlan aptly observed that "The subject of obscenity has produced a variety of views among the members of the Court unmatched in any other course of constitutional adjudication." As evidence, Harlan noted that in the thirteen obscenity cases decided in the decade after *Roth*, there were "a total of 55 separate opinions among the Justices." Interstate Circuit, Inc. v. Dallas, 390 U.S. 676, 704-705, 705 n.1 (1968) (Harlan, J., dissenting).

By 1968 the following views had emerged:

a. Justices Clark and White adhered to the initial *Roth* formulation. See Memoirs v. Massachusetts, 383 U.S. 413, 441 (1966) (Clark, J., dissenting); id. at 460-462 (White, J., dissenting).

b. Justices Black and Douglas adhered to their view, expressed in *Roth*, that government is wholly powerless to regulate sexually oriented expression on the ground of its obscenity. See Jacobellis v. Ohio, 378 U.S. 184, 196-197 (1964) (Black, J., joined by Douglas, J., concurring).

c. Justice Harlan adhered to his view, expressed in *Roth*, that the federal government could control the distribution of only "hard core" pornography, whereas the states could ban "any material which, taken as a whole, has been reasonably found in state judicial proceedings to treat with sex in a fundamentally offensive manner, under rationally established criteria for judging such material." Jacobellis v. Ohio, supra, at 204 (Harlan, J., dissenting).

d. Justice Stewart "reached the conclusion [that] under the First and Fourteenth Amendments criminal laws in this area are constitutionally limited to hard-core pornography." Stewart continued: "I shall not today attempt further to define the kinds of material I understand to be embraced within that shorthand description; and perhaps I could never succeed in intelligibly doing so. But I know it when I see it, and the motion picture involved in this case is not that." Jacobellis v. Ohio, supra, at 197 (Stewart, J., concurring).

e. Justice Brennan, Chief Justice Warren, and Justice Fortas adopted the view that, for material to be deemed obscene, "three elements must coalesce: it must be established that (a) the dominant theme of the material taken as a whole appeals to a prurient interest in sex; (b) the material is patently offensive because it affronts contemporary community standards relating to the description or representation of sexual matters; and (c) the material is utterly without redeeming social value." Memoirs v. Massachusetts, supra, at 418 (Brennan, J., joined by Warren, C.J. and Fortas, J.). Although this formulation represented the view of only three justices, it was the formulation most often followed by state and federal courts from 1966 until the Court's 1973 decision in Miller v. California, infra. Note the addition of elements b and c to the initial *Roth* formulation.

2. *The definition of obscenity: pandering and variable obscenity.* To complicate matters further, there was substantial disagreement within the Court over the extent to which factors extrinsic to the material itself should be considered in the obscenity determination. Two such factors were especially troublesome — "pandering" and "special" audiences:

a. In Ginzburg v. United States, 383 U.S. 463 (1966), the Court held that "the question of obscenity may include consideration of the setting in which the publications were presented." Here, the publisher had "sought mailing privileges from the postmasters of Intercourse and Blue Ball, Pennsylvania" in order to sell the "publications on the basis of salacious appeal," and the advertising for the publications "openly boasted that the publishers would take full advantage of what they regarded as an unrestricted license allowed by law in the expression of sex and sexual matters." The Court held that such "commercial exploitation of erotica solely for the sake of their prurient appeal [may] support the determination that the material is obscene even though in other contexts the material would escape such condemnation." Justices Black, Douglas, Harlan, and Stewart dissented.

b. In Mishkin v. New York, 383 U.S. 502 (1966), defendant produced books depicting such sexual "deviations as sadomasochism, fetishism, and homosexuality." He maintained that such books "do not satisfy the prurient-appeal requirement [of *Roth*] because they do not appeal to a prurient interest of the 'average person' in sex," and that "'instead of stimulating the erotic, they disgust and sicken.'" The Court rejected this argument, explaining that where "the material is designed for and primarily disseminated to a clearly defined deviant sexual group, rather than the public at large, the prurient-appeal requirement of the *Roth* test is satisfied if the dominant theme of the material taken as a whole appeals to the prurient interest in sex of the members of that group." See also Ward v. Illinois, 431 U.S. 767 (1977).

c. Ginsberg v. New York, 390 U.S. 629 (1968), another "variable obscenity" case, involved the problem of children. The Court had previously addressed the problem of obscenity and children in Butler v. Michigan, 352 U.S. 380 (1957). In *Butler* the Court held invalid a law prohibiting the sale of "lewd" material that might have a deleterious influence upon youth. Justice Frankfurter, speaking for a unanimous Court, explained that the state may not "reduce the adult population of Michigan to reading only what is fit for children."

Ginsberg posed the related, but analytically distinct, question whether a state could constitutionally prohibit "the sale to minors under seventeen years of age of material defined to be obscene on the basis of its appeal to them whether or not it would be obscene to adults." In upholding the doctrine of "variable obscenity" in this context, the Court observed that (1) "the power of the state to control the conduct of children reaches beyond the scope of its authority over adults"; (2) the claim of parents "to direct the rearing of their children is basic in the structure of our society," and the "legislature could properly conclude that parents [are] entitled to the support of laws designed to aid discharge of that responsibility"; and (3) the state "has an independent interest in the well-being of its youth" and in seeing to it "that they are 'safeguarded from abuses' which might prevent their 'growth into free and independent well-developed men and citizens.'" On "variable obscenity," see F. Schauer, The Law of Obscenity 77-95 (1976); Krislov, From *Ginsburg* to *Ginsberg*: The Unhurried Children's Hour in Obscenity Litigation, 1968 Sup. Ct. Rev. 153; Magrath, The Obscenity Cases: Grapes of *Roth*, 1966 Sup. Ct. Rev. 7.

3. *The definition of obscenity*: Redrup. The inability of the Court to articulate a definition of obscenity that could command the allegiance of a majority, compounded by the potential relevance of factors extrinsic to the material itself, led to an era of chaos. In Redrup v. New York, 386 U.S. 767 (1967), the Court began the practice of per curiam reversals of convictions for the sale or exhibition of materials that at least five members of the Court, applying their separate tests, deemed not to be obscene. From 1967 to 1973 some thirty-one cases were disposed of in this fashion. The full opinion of the Court in Walker v. Ohio, 398 U.S. 434 (1970)

is typical: "The judgment of the Supreme Court of Ohio is reversed. [*Redrup.*]" As Justice Brennan later commented: "[The *Redrup* approach] resolves cases as between the parties, but offers only the most obscure guidance to legislation, adjudication by other courts, and primary conduct. By disposing of cases through summary reversal or denial of certiorari we have deliberately and effectively obscured the rationale underlying the decisions. It comes as no surprise that judicial attempts to follow our lead conscientiously have often ended in hopeless confusion." Paris Adult Theatre I v. Slaton, 413 U.S. 49, 83 (1973) (Brennan, J., dissenting).

4. *The interests furthered by the suppression of obscenity: Stanley v. Georgia.* Although debating the definitional issue endlessly, the justices in this era said almost nothing about the nature of the interests that assertedly justified the suppression of obscene expression. As noted earlier, this was due largely to *Roth's* acceptance of the underlying premise of the *Chaplinsky* dictum — obscene utterances are wholly "unprotected" by the first amendment and their restriction thus does not necessitate an inquiry into the nature or substantiality of the state interests.

There was, however, one notable exception to the Court's silence on this issue. In Stanley v. Georgia, 394 U.S. 557 (1969), the Court, speaking through Justice Marshall, held that "the mere private possession of obscene matter cannot constitutionally be made a crime." In reaching this result, the Court announced that the "right to receive information and ideas, regardless of their social worth, [is] fundamental to our free society," and that "in the context of this case — a prosecution for mere possession of printed or filmed matter in the privacy of a person's own home — that right takes on an added dimension," for "also fundamental is the right to be free, except in very limited circumstances, from unwanted governmental intrusions into one's privacy." In light of these interests, "mere categorization of these films as 'obscene' is insufficient justification for such a drastic invasion of personal liberties," for "if the First Amendment means anything, it means that a State has no business telling a man, sitting alone in his own house, what books he may read or what films he may watch."

In defense of its law, Georgia asserted "the right to protect the individual's mind from the effects of obscenity." Treating this as an "assertion that the State has the right to control the moral content of a person's thoughts," the Court declared that although "to some, this may be a noble purpose, [it] is wholly inconsistent with the philosophy of the First Amendment." Thus, "whatever the power of the state to control public dissemination of ideas inimical to the public morality, it cannot constitutionally premise legislation on the desirability of controlling a person's private thoughts." Moreover, the law could not be defended on the ground that "exposure to obscene materials may lead to deviant sexual behavior or crimes of sexual violence," for "given the present state of knowledge, the State may no more prohibit mere possession of obscene matter on the ground that it may lead to antisocial conduct than it may prohibit possession of chemistry books on the ground that they may lead to the manufacture of homemade spirits." Finally, the Court explained that *Roth* and the Court's other obscenity decisions were clearly distinguishable, for they "dealt with public distribution of obscene materials and such distribution is subject to different objections," such as, for example, "the danger that obscene material might fall into the hands of children" or "that it might intrude upon the sensibilities or privacy of the general public." Thus, although "the States retain broad power to regulate obscenity, that power simply does not extend to mere possession by the individual in the privacy of his own home."

Consider Katz, Privacy and Pornography: Stanley v. Georgia, 1969 Sup. Ct. Rev. 203, 213:

> If the government [after *Stanley* may still suppress] commercial distribution, then *Stanley* becomes an intellectually silly case. Stanley himself probably bought his film through some sort of commercial distributor. If so, and if the act of distribution may be proscribed, then Stanley had no "right to receive," only a right to keep whatever he can manage to find. [If] there is a right to receive "information and ideas, regardless of their social worth," then commercial distribution per se is not proscribable.

5. *The implications of* Stanley: Reidel. In United States v. Reidel, 402 U.S. 351 (1971), the Court rejected an expansive lower court interpretation of *Stanley*. In *Reidel* a federal district court, relying on *Stanley*, held a federal statute prohibiting the knowing use of the mails for the delivery of obscene matter unconstitutional as applied to the distribution of such matter to willing recipients who state that they are adults. The district court reasoned that "if a person has the right to receive and possess this material, then someone must have the right to deliver it to him." The Supreme Court reversed. The Court explained that the "focus of [*Stanley*], [was] on freedom of mind and thought and on the privacy of one's home." "Reidel," however, "is in a wholly different position," for "he has no complaints about governmental violations of his private thoughts or fantasies, but stands squarely on a claimed First Amendment right to do business in obscenity and use the mails in the process. [*Stanley*] did not overrule *Roth* and we decline to do so now."

Justice Marshall rejected the Court's interpretation of *Stanley*. He argued that "*Stanley* turned on an assessment of which state interests may legitimately underpin governmental action" and claimed that it was thus "disingenuous to contend that Stanley's conviction was reversed because his home [was] the locus of a search." He concurred in the result, however, for "mail order distribution poses the danger that obscenity will be sent to children." See also United States v. Thirty-Seven Photographs, 402 U.S. 363 (1971).

6. *Reformulation*. By 1973, then, the law of obscenity was in a state of considerable confusion. Two questions were especially troublesome: How should obscenity be defined? When may it be restricted? In its 1973 decisions in *Miller* and *Paris Adult Theatre*, the Court attempted to reformulate and clarify the law.

Miller v. California
413 U.S. 15 (1973)

MR. CHIEF JUSTICE BURGER delivered the opinion of the Court.

This is one of a group of "obscenity-pornography" cases being reviewed by the Court in a re-examination of [the standards] which must be used to identify obscene material that a State may regulate. . . .

[In this case, appellant] conducted a mass mailing campaign to advertise the sale of illustrated books, euphemistically called "adult" material. [Appellant's] conviction was specifically based on his conduct in causing five unsolicited advertising brochures to be sent through the mail. [The] brochures [consist primarily] of pictures and drawings very explicitly depicting men and women in groups of two or more engaging in a variety of sexual activities, with genitals often prominently displayed. [This] case [thus] involves the application of a State's criminal obscenity statute to a situation in which sexually explicit materials have been thrust by aggressive sales action upon unwilling recipients. . . .

II

[Obscene] material is unprotected by the First Amendment. [*Roth.*] [However,] State statutes designed to regulate obscene materials must be carefully limited. [Thus,] we now confine the permissible scope of such regulation to works which depict or describe sexual conduct. That conduct must be specifically defined by the applicable state law, as written or authoritatively construed. . . .

The basic guidelines for the trier of fact must be: (a) whether "the average person, applying contemporary community standards" would find that the work, taken as a whole, appeals to the prurient interest; (b) whether the work depicts or describes, in a patently offensive way, sexual conduct specifically defined by the applicable state law; and (c) whether the work, taken as a whole, lacks serious literary, artistic, political, or scientific value. We do not adopt as a constitutional standard the "*utterly* without redeeming social value" test of [*Memoirs*]. . . .

We emphasize that it is not our function to propose regulatory schemes for the States. [It] is possible, however, to give a few plain examples of what a state statute could define for regulation under part (b) of the standard announced in this opinion, *supra*:

(a) Patently offensive representations or descriptions of ultimate sexual acts, normal or perverted, actual or simulated.

(b) Patently offensive representations or descriptions of masturbation, excretory functions, and lewd exhibition of the genitals.

Sex and nudity may not be exploited without limit by films or pictures exhibited or sold in places of public accommodation any more than live sex and nudity can be exhibited or sold without limit in such public places. At a minimum, prurient, patently offensive depiction or description of sexual conduct must have serious literary, artistic, political, or scientific value to merit First Amendment protection. [In] resolving the inevitably sensitive questions of fact and law, we must continue to rely on the jury system, accompanied by the safeguards that judges, rules of evidence, presumption of innocence, and other protective features provide, as we do with [other] offenses against society and its individual members.

Mr. Justice Brennan [now] maintains that no formulation of this Court, the Congress, or the States can adequately distinguish obscene material unprotected by the First Amendment from protected expression, [*Paris Adult Theatre*, infra]. (Brennan J., dissenting). [But under] the holdings announced today, no one will be subject to prosecution for the sale or exposure of obscene materials unless these materials depict or describe patently offensive "hard core" sexual conduct specifically defined by the regulating state law, as written or construed. We are satisfied that these specific prerequisites will provide fair notice to a dealer in such materials that his public and commercial activities may bring prosecution. See [*Roth*]. . . .

Mr. Justice Brennan also emphasizes "institutional stress" in justification of his change of view. [It] is certainly true that the absence, since *Roth*, of a single majority view of this Court as to proper standards for testing obscenity has placed a strain on both state and federal courts. But today, for the first time since *Roth* was decided in 1957, a majority of this Court has agreed on concrete guidelines to isolate "hard core" pornography from expression protected by the First Amendment. Now we may abandon the casual practice of [*Redrup*] and attempt to provide positive guidance to federal and state courts alike.

This may not be an easy road, free from difficulty. But no amount of "fatigue" should lead us to adopt a convenient "institutional" rationale — an absolutist, "anything goes" view of the First Amendment — because it will lighten our burdens. . . .

III

Under a National Constitution, fundamental First Amendment limitations on the powers of the States do not vary from community to community, but this does not mean that there are, or should or can be, fixed, uniform national standards of precisely what appeals to the "prurient interest" or is "patently offensive." These are essentially questions of fact, and our Nation is simply too big and too diverse for this Court to reasonably expect that such standards could be articulated for all 50 States in a single formulation, even assuming the prerequisite consensus exists. [It] is neither realistic nor constitutionally sound to read the First Amendment as requiring that the people of Maine or Mississippi accept public depiction of conduct found tolerable in Las Vegas, or New York City.[13] [People] in different States vary in their tastes and attitudes, and this diversity is not to be strangled by the absolutism of imposed uniformity. We hold that the requirement that the jury evaluate the materials with reference to "contemporary standards of the State of California" [is] constitutionally adequate.

IV

The dissenting Justices sound the alarm of repression. But, in our view, to equate the free and robust exchange of ideas and political debate with commercial exploitation of obscene material demeans the grand conception of the First Amendment. [The] First Amendment protects works which, taken as a whole, have serious literary, artistic, political, or scientific value, regardless of whether

13. In [*Jacobellis*] two Justices argued that application of "local" community standards would run the risk of preventing dissemination of materials in some places because sellers would be unwilling to risk criminal conviction by testing variations in standards from place to place. [The] use of "national" standards, however, necessarily implies that materials found tolerable in some places, but not under the "national" criteria, will nevertheless be unavailable where they are acceptable. Thus, in terms of danger to free expression, the potential for suppression seems at least as great in the application of a single nationwide standard as in allowing distribution in accordance with local tastes. . . .

the government or a majority of the people approve of the ideas these works represent. [But] the public portrayal of hard-core sexual conduct for its own sake, and for the ensuing commercial gain, is a different matter. [There] is no evidence, empirical or historical, that the stern 19th century American censorship of public distribution and display of material relating to sex [in] any way limited or affected expression of serious literary, artistic, political, or scientific ideas. . . .

In sum, we (a) reaffirm the *Roth* holding that obscene material is not protected by the First Amendment; (b) hold that such material can be regulated by the States, subject to the specific safeguards enunciated above, without a showing that the material is "*utterly* without redeeming social value"; and (c) hold that obscenity is to be determined by applying "contemporary community standards." . . .

Vacated and remanded.

Mr. Justice Douglas, dissenting. . . .

[The] idea that the First Amendment permits punishment for ideas that are "offensive" to the particular judge or jury sitting in judgment is astounding. No greater leveler of speech or literature has ever been designed. . . .

I do not think we, the judges, were ever given the constitutional power to make definitions of obscenity. If it is to be defined, let the people [decide] by a constitutional amendment what they want to ban as [obscene]. Whatever the choice, the courts will have some guidelines. Now we have none except our own predilections.

Mr. Justice Brennan, with whom Mr. Justice Stewart and Mr. Justice Marshall join, dissenting.

In my dissent in [*Paris Adult Theatre*, infra], I noted that I had no occasion to consider the extent of state power to regulate the distribution of sexually oriented material [to] unconsenting adults. [I] need not now decide [that question, for] it is clear that under my dissent in *Paris Adult Theatre* the statute under which the prosecution was brought is unconstitutionally overbroad, and therefore invalid on its face. . . .

Paris Adult Theatre I v. Slaton
413 U.S. 49 (1973)

Mr. Chief Justice Burger delivered the opinion of the Court.

[Petitioners are two Atlanta, Georgia, movie theaters and their owners and managers, operating in the style of "adult" theaters. The theaters have a conventional, inoffensive entrance, without any pictures, but with signs indicating that the theaters exhibit "Atlanta's Finest Mature Feature Films." On the door is a sign saying "Adult Theater — You must be 21 and able to prove it. If viewing the nude body offends you, Please Do Not Enter." The local state district attorney filed civil complaints alleging that petitioners were exhibiting to the public for paid admission two allegedly obscene films, "Magic Mirror" and "It All Comes Out in the End," which depict scenes of simulated fellatio, cunnilingus, and group sex intercourse. Respondent's complaints demanded that the two films be declared obscene and that petitioners be enjoined from exhibiting the films. The trial judge found the films obscene but dismissed the complaints on the ground that "the display of these films in a commercial theatre, when surrounded by requisite notice to the public of their nature and by reasonable protection against the exposure of these films to minors, is constitutionally permissible." The Georgia Supreme Court reversed and held that exhibition of the films should be enjoined. The U.S. Supreme Court vacated and remanded for reconsideration in light of *Miller*.]

We categorically disapprove the theory [that] obscene, pornographic films acquire constitutional immunity from state regulation simply because they are exhibited for consenting adults only. [Although] we have often pointedly recognized the high importance of the state interest in regulating the exposure of obscene materials to juveniles and unconsenting adults, [this] Court has never declared these to be the only legitimate state interests permitting regulation of obscene material. . . .

In particular, we hold that there are legitimate state interests at stake in stemming the tide of commercialized obscenity, even assuming it is feasible to enforce effective safeguards against exposure to juveniles and to passersby.[7] Rights and interests "other than those of the advocates are involved." [These] include the interest of the public in the quality of life and the total community environment, the tone of commerce in the great city centers, and, possibly, the public safety itself. The Hill-Link Minority Report of the Commission on Obscenity and Pornography indicates that there is at least an arguable correlation between obscene material and crime. Quite apart from sex crimes, however, there remains one problem of large proportions aptly described by Professor Bickel:

> It concerns the tone of the society, the mode, or to use terms that have perhaps greater currency, the style and quality of life, now and in the future. A man may be entitled to read an obscene book in his room, or expose himself indecently there. . . . We should protect his privacy. But if he demands a right to obtain the books and pictures he wants in the market, and to foregather in public places — discreet, if you will, but accessible to all — with others who share his tastes, *then to grant him his right is to affect the world about the rest of us, and to impinge on other privacies.* Even supposing that each of us can, if he wishes, effectively avert the eye and stop the ear (which, in truth, we cannot), what is commonly read and seen and heard and done intrudes upon us all, want it or not.

22 The Public Interest 25-26 (Winter 1971). (Emphasis added.) As Mr. Chief Justice Warren stated, there is a "right of the Nation and of the States to maintain a decent society . . ." [*Jacobellis*] (dissenting opinion). . . .

But, it is argued, there are no scientific data which conclusively demonstrate that exposure to obscene material adversely affects men and women or their society. It is urged on behalf of the petitioners that, absent such a demonstration, any kind of state regulation is "impermissible." We reject this argument. It is not for us to resolve empirical uncertainties underlying state legislation, save in the exceptional case where that legislation plainly impinges upon rights protected by

---

7. It is conceivable that an "adult" theater can — if it really insists — prevent the exposure of its obscene wares to juveniles. An "adult" bookstore, dealing in obscene books, magazines, and pictures, cannot realistically make this claim. The legitimate interest in preventing exposure of juveniles to obscene material cannot be fully served by simply barring juveniles from the immediate physical premises of "adult" bookstores, when there is a flourishing "outside business" in these materials.

the Constitution itself. [Although] there is no conclusive proof of a connection between antisocial behavior and obscene material, the legislature of Georgia could quite reasonably determine that such a connection does or might exist. In deciding *Roth*, this Court implicitly accepted that a legislature could legitimately act on such a conclusion to protect *"the social interest in order and morality."* . . .

If we accept the unprovable assumption that a complete education requires the reading of certain books, [and] the well nigh universal belief that good books, plays, and art lift the spirit, improve the mind, enrich the human personality, and develop character, can we then say that a state legislature may not act on the corollary assumption that commerce in obscene books, or public exhibitions focused on obscene conduct, have a tendency to exert a corrupting and debasing impact leading to antisocial behavior? [The] sum of experience, including that of the past two decades, affords an ample basis for legislatures to conclude that a sensitive, key relationship of human existence, central to family life, community welfare, and the development of human personality, can be debased and distorted by crass commercial exploitation of sex. Nothing in the Constitution prohibits a State from reaching such a conclusion and acting on it legislatively simply because there is no conclusive evidence or empirical data. . . .

It is asserted, however, [that] state regulation of access by consenting adults to obscene material violates the constitutionally protected right to privacy enjoyed by petitioners' customers. [Nothing,] however, in this Court's decisions intimates that there is any "fundamental" privacy right "implicit in the concept of ordered liberty" to watch obscene movies in places of public accommodation. [Indeed], we have declined to equate the privacy of the home relied on in *Stanley* with a "zone" of "privacy" that follows a distributor or a consumer of obscene materials wherever he goes. [The] idea of a "privacy" right and a place of public accommodation are, in this context, mutually exclusive. . . .

It is also argued that the State has no legitimate interest in "control [of] the moral content of a person's thoughts," [*Stanley*], and we need not quarrel with this. But we reject the claim that the State of Georgia is here attempting to control the minds or thoughts of those who patronize theaters. Preventing unlimited display or distribution of obscene material, which by definition lacks any serious literary, artistic, political, or scientific value as communication, [is] distinct from a control of reason and the intellect. [The] fantasies of a drug addict are his own and beyond the reach of government, but government regulation of drug sales is not prohibited by the Constitution. . . .

Finally, petitioners argue that conduct which directly involves "consenting adults" only has, for that sole reason, a special claim to constitutional protection. Our Constitution establishes a broad range of conditions on the exercise of power by the States, but for us to say that our Constitution incorporates the proposition that conduct involving consenting adults only is always beyond state regulation, is a step we are unable to take.[15] [The] issue in this context goes beyond whether someone, or even the majority, considers the conduct depicted as "wrong" or

15. The state statute books are replete with constitutionally unchallenged laws against prostitution, suicide, voluntary self-mutilation, brutalizing "bare fist" prize fights, and duels, although these crimes may only directly involve "consenting adults." Statutes making bigamy a crime surely cut into an individual's freedom to associate, but few today seriously claim such statutes violate the First Amendment or any other constitutional provision. . . .

"sinful." The States have the power to make a morally neutral judgment that public exhibition of obscene material, or commerce in such material, has a tendency to injure the community as a whole, to endanger the public safety, or to jeopardize [the] States' "right [to] maintain a decent society." . . .

Vacated and remanded.

Mr. Justice Brennan, with whom Mr. Justice Stewart and Mr. Justice Marshall join, dissenting.*

[I] am convinced that the approach initiated 16 years ago in [Roth], and culminating in the Court's decision today, cannot bring stability to this area of the law without jeopardizing fundamental First Amendment [values]. The vagueness of the standards in the obscenity area produces a number of separate problems, [including a] lack of fair notice, [a] chill on protected expression, and [a severe] stress [on the] judicial machinery. [These concerns] persuade me that a significant change in direction is urgently required. I turn, therefore, to the alternatives that are now open.

1. [One] approach [would] be to draw a new line between protected and unprotected [speech] that resolves all doubt in favor of state [power]. We could hold, for example, that any depiction [of] human sexual organs [is] outside the protection of the First [Amendment]. That formula would [reduce the problems of vagueness]. But [it] would be appallingly [overbroad]. . . .

2. The alternative adopted by the Court [today] adopts a restatement of the Roth-Memoirs definition of obscenity. [This] restatement leaves unresolved the very difficulties that compel our rejection of the underlying Roth approach, while at the same time contributing substantial difficulties of its own. [The] Court today permits suppression if the government can prove that the materials lack "serious literary, artistic, political or scientific value." But [Roth] held that certain expression is obscene, and thus outside the protection of the First Amendment, precisely because it lacks even the slightest redeeming social value. [The] Court's approach [is thus] nothing less than a rejection of the fundamental First Amendment premises [of Roth] and an invitation to widespread suppression of sexually oriented speech. . . .

In any case, [the Court's approach] can have no ameliorative impact on [the] problems that grow out of the vagueness of our current standards. [Although] the Court's [test] does limit the definition of obscenity to depictions of physical conduct and explicit sexual acts, [even] a confirmed optimist could find little realistic comfort in the adoption of such a test. Indeed, the valiant attempt of one lower federal court to draw the constitutional line at depictions of explicit sexual conduct seems to belie any suggestion that this approach marks the road to clarity.[16] . . .

3. I have also considered the possibility of reducing our own role, and the role of appellate courts generally, in determining whether particular matter is obscene. Thus, we might conclude that juries are best suited to determine obscenity vel non and that jury verdicts in this area should not be set aside except in cases of extreme departure from prevailing standards. [But the] First Amendment re-

---

* [A dissenting opinion of Justice Douglas is omitted. — Eds.]

16. Huffman v. United States, 152 U.S. App. D.C. 238, 470 F.2d 386 (1971). The test apparently requires an effort to distinguish between "singles" and "duals," between "erect penises" and "semi-erect penises," and between "ongoing sexual activity" and "imminent sexual activity."

quires an independent review by appellate courts of the constitutional fact of obscenity. [In] any event, even if [such an approach] would mitigate the institutional stress produced by the *Roth* approach, it would [lead] to even greater uncertainty and the consequent due process problems of fair notice. . . .

4. Finally, I have considered the view, urged so forcefully since 1957 by our Brothers Black and Douglas, that the First Amendment bars the suppression of any sexually oriented expression. That position would [strip] the States of power to an extent that cannot be justified by the commands of the Constitution, at least so long as there is available an alternative approach that strikes a better balance between the guarantee of free expression and the States' legitimate interests. . . .

[Given the] inevitable side effects of state efforts to suppress [obscenity], we must scrutinize with care the state interest that is asserted to justify the suppression. For in the absence of some very substantial interest in suppressing such speech, we can hardly condone the ill effects that seem to flow inevitably from the effort. . . .

The opinions in *Redrup* and *Stanley* reflected our emerging view that the state interests in protecting children and in protecting unconsenting adults may stand on a different footing from the other asserted state interests. [But] whatever the strength of [those] interests, [they] cannot be asserted [where, as] in this case, [the] films [were] exhibited only to persons over the age of 21 who viewed them willingly and with prior knowledge of the nature of their contents. [The] justification for the suppression must be found, therefore, in some independent interest in regulating the reading and viewing habits of consenting adults. . . .

In *Stanley* we pointed out that "[t]here appears to be little empirical basis for" the assertion that "exposure to obscene materials may lead to deviant sexual behavior or crimes of sexual violence."[26] [In] any event, we added that "if the State is only concerned about printed or filmed materials inducing antisocial conduct, we believe that in the context of private consumption of ideas and information we should adhere to the view that '[a]mong free men, the deterrents ordinarily to be applied to prevent crime are education and punishment for violations of the law. . . .': . . ."

Moreover, in *Stanley* we rejected as "wholly inconsistent with the philosophy of the First Amendment" [the] notion that there is a legitimate state concern in the "control [of] the moral content of a person's thoughts." [That] is not to say, of course, that a State must remain utterly indifferent to — and take no action bearing on — the morality of the community. The traditional description of state police power does embrace the regulation of morals as well as the health, safety, and general welfare of the citizenry. [But] the State's interest in regulating morality by suppressing obscenity, while often asserted, remains essentially unfocused and ill defined. And, since the attempt to curtail unprotected speech necessarily spills over into the area of protected speech, the effort to serve this speculative interest through the suppression of obscene material must tread heavily on rights protected by the First Amendment. . . .

26. Indeed, since *Stanley* was decided, the President's Commission on Obscenity and Pornography has concluded:

> In sum, empirical research designed to clarify the question has found no evidence to date that exposure to explicit sexual materials plays a significant role in the causation of delinquent or criminal behavior among youth or adults. The Commission cannot conclude that exposure to erotic materials is a factor in the causation of sex crime or sex delinquency. . . .

In short, while I cannot say that the interests of the State — apart from the question of juveniles and unconsenting adults — are trivial or nonexistent, I am compelled to conclude that these interests cannot justify the substantial damage to constitutional rights and to this Nation's judicial machinery that inevitably results from state efforts to bar the distribution even of unprotected material to consenting adults. [I] would hold, therefore, that at least in the absence of distribution to juveniles or obtrusive exposure to unconsenting adults, the First and Fourteenth Amendments prohibit the State and Federal Governments from attempting wholly to suppress sexually oriented materials on the basis of their allegedly "obscene" contents. Nothing in this approach precludes those governments from taking action to serve what may be strong and legitimate interests through regulation of the manner of distribution of sexually oriented material. . . .

Difficult questions must still be faced, notably in the areas of distribution to juveniles and offensive exposure to unconsenting adults. Whatever the extent of state power to regulate in those areas, it should be clear that the view I espouse today would introduce a large measure of clarity to this troubled area, would reduce the institutional pressure on [the] Judiciary, and would guarantee fuller freedom of expression while leaving room for the protection of legitimate governmental interests. . . .

Note: The 1973 Reformulation and Its Aftermath

1. Miller *and* Roth. Does the *Miller* reformulation constitute a "rejection of the fundamental first amendment premises" of *Roth?* Does its elimination of the "utterly without redeeming social value" criterion fatally undermine the notion that obscenity is of only "low" first amendment value?

2. Miller *and vagueness.* Is the *Miller* reformulation likely significantly to reduce the problems generated by the prior vagueness of the definition of obscenity? It is noteworthy that since *Miller* the Court has made clear that the two "plain examples" offered in *Miller* of the sorts of "sexual conduct" that might constitutionally be deemed "patently offensive" are not exhaustive. See Ward v. Illinois, 431 U.S. 767 (1977) (reaffirming the holding in *Mishkin* that materials depicting "sado-masochistic" acts may be held obscene); see also Splawn v. California, 431 U.S. 595 (1977) (reaffirming the holding in *Ginzburg* that "evidence of pandering to prurient interests [is] relevant in determining whether the material is obscene").

Are there any limits on the sorts of "sexual conduct" that might constitutionally be deemed "patently offensive"? In Jenkins v. Georgia, 418 U.S. 153 (1974), the Court, in an opinion by Justice Rehnquist, overturned a state court determination that the highly acclaimed movie "Carnal Knowledge" was obscene. The Court explained that *Miller* "intended to fix substantive constitutional limitations, deriving from the First Amendment, on the type of material subject to [a determination of patent offensiveness]." As an example, the Court observed that "it would be wholly at odds with this aspect of *Miller* to uphold an obscenity conviction based upon a defendant's depiction of a woman with a bare midriff." As for "Carnal Knowledge," the Court noted that "our own viewing of the film satisfies us that [it] could not be found under the *Miller* standards to depict sexual conduct in a patently offensive way." The Court explained that "while the subject of the picture is, in a broader sense, sex, and there are scenes in which sexual conduct including 'ultimate sexual acts' is to be understood to be taking place, the camera does not focus on the bodies of the actors at such times. There is no exhibition of the actor's genitals, lewd or otherwise, during these scenes. There are occasional scenes of nudity, but nudity alone is not enough to make material legally obscene under the *Miller* standards." Thus, "the film could not, as a matter of constitutional law, be found to depict sexual conduct in a patently offensive way, [and] is therefore not outside the protection of the First and Fourteenth Amendments because it is obscene." Does the *Jenkins* gloss on *Miller* significantly reduce the problems of vagueness? For a negative assessment, see Lockhart, Escape from the Chill of Uncertainty: Explicit Sex and the First Amendment, 9 Ga. L. Rev. 533, 546-548 (1975).

Consider also Justice Stevens's post-*Miller*, post-*Jenkins* conclusion that, at least in the context of ordinary criminal prosecutions, an unacceptable level of vagueness is inherent in the obscenity determination:

> The question of offensiveness to community standards [is] not one that the average juror can be expected to answer with evenhanded consistency. The average juror may well have one reaction to sexually oriented materials in a completely private setting and an entirely different reaction in a social context. [Since] obscenity is by no means a neutral subject, and since the ascertainment of a community standard is such a subjective task, the expression of individual jurors' sentiments will inevitably influence the perceptions of other jurors, particularly those who would normally be in the minority. [In] the final analysis, the guilt or innocence of a criminal defendant in an obscenity trial is determined primarily by individual jurors' subjective reactions to the materials in question rather than by the predictable application of rules of law. [In] my judgment, the line between communications which "offend" and those which do not is too blurred [to] delimit the protections of the First Amendment.

Smith v. United States, 431 U.S. 291, 315-316 (1977) (Stevens, J., dissenting).

3. Miller *and appellate review.* One way the Warren Court sought to limit the problems of vagueness was by the active use of independent appellate review of jury determinations of obscenity. This was, of course, a problem in its own right, as well as a solution. After *Miller* what is the appropriate role of appellate courts in reviewing jury determinations of obscenity? In *Jenkins*, supra, the Georgia Supreme Court, in upholding a jury determination that "Carnal Knowledge" was obscene, concluded that "the jury's verdict against appellant virtually precluded all appellate review of the [the movie's patent offensiveness and appeal to prurient interest]." In reversing, the Court observed that "it would be a serious misreading of *Miller* to conclude that juries have unbridled discretion in determining what is 'patently offensive.'" The Court then found the movie nonobscene as a matter of constitutional law "even though a properly charged jury unanimously agreed on a verdict of guilty." Despite *Jenkins* the number of Supreme Court rulings on the obscenity of particular works has declined dramatically since 1973. Is this a good or a bad sign?

4. *Local versus national standards.* What interests are furthered by the Court's conclusion in *Miller* that "appeal to prurient interest" and "patent offensiveness" may be determined according to local rather than national standards? Consider the following objections to local standards:

a. Smith v. United States, 431 U.S. 291, 313-315 (1977) (Stevens, J., dissenting):

The geographic boundaries of [a local] community are not easily defined. They are [thus] subject to elastic adjustment to suit the needs of the prosecutor. Moreover, although a substantial body of evidence and decisional law concerning the content of a national standard could have evolved through its consistent use, the derivation of the relevant community standard for each of our countless communities is necessarily dependent on the perceptions of the individuals who happen to compose the jury in a given case.

b. Hamling v. United States, 418 U.S. 87, 144-145 (1974). (Brennan, J., dissenting):

Under [a local standards approach national], distributors [will] be forced to cope with the community standards of every hamlet into which their goods may wander. [Because] these variegated standards are impossible to discern, national distributors, fearful of risking the expense and difficulty of defending against prosecution in any of several remote communities, must inevitably [retreat] to debilitating self-censorship. [As a result], the people of many communities will be "protected" far beyond government's constitutional power to deny them access to sexually oriented materials.

c. Note, Community Standards, Class Actions, and Obscenity under *Miller v. California*, 88 Harv. L. Rev. 1838, 1844 (1975):

The trier of fact discretion *Miller* permits, in effect, reverses *Redrup*'s institutional distortion. Direct appellate review of findings of prurient appeal and patent offensiveness becomes impossible. If the trier of fact is free to identify and apply [local] community standards, [an] appellate court is left without benchmarks by which to judge the validity of a finding of prurient appeal and patent offensiveness.

5. *Local standards: post-Miller decisions.* The Court has handed down several post-*Miller* rulings concerning the local standards issue:

a. In *Jenkins*, supra, the Court held that "the Constitution does not require that juries be instructed in state obscenity cases to apply the standards of a hypothetical statewide community. [It is constitutionally permissible to instruct] jurors to apply 'community standards' without specifying what 'community' [and] to permit jurors to rely on their understanding of the community from which they come."

b. In Hamling v. United States, 418 U.S. 87 (1974), the Court interpreted a federal statute prohibiting the mailing of obscene materials as permitting a juror to rely, not on national standards, but on his "knowledge of the community or vicinage from which he [comes]." The Court explained that

the fact that distributors of allegedly obscene materials may be subjected to varying community standards in the various federal judicial districts [does] not render a federal statute unconstitutional because of the failure of application of uniform national standards of obscenity, [for] those same distributors may be subjected to such varying degrees of criminal liability in prosecutions by the States for violations of state obscenity statutes.

c. In Smith v. United States, 431 U.S. 291 (1977), the Court upheld a conviction under a federal statute prohibiting the mailing of obscene material where the mailing was entirely intrastate, and where it occurred at a time when the state itself did not prohibit the distribution of obscene material to consenting adults. The Court held that in a federal prosecution, "the jury is entitled to rely on its own knowledge of community standards" and is not bound by the state legislature's declaration as to "what the community standards shall be."

d. In *Paris Adult Theatre*, the Court held that the first amendment does not "require 'expert' affirmative evidence that the materials [are] obscene when the materials themselves [are] actually placed in evidence." The Court explained:

> This is not a subject that lends itself to the traditional use of expert testimony. Such testimony is usually admitted for the purpose of explaining to lay jurors what they otherwise could not understand. [No] such assistance is needed by jurors in obscenity cases; indeed, the "expert witness" practices employed in these cases have often made a mockery out of the otherwise sound concept of expert [testimony]. "Simply stated, hard core pornography [can] and does speak for itself."

See generally F. Schauer, The Law of Obscenity 276-291 (1976).

6. *Intent*. What state of mind must the seller or distributor have in an obscenity prosecution? As the incitement and libel cases make clear, intent can play a central role in "definitional" balancing and can do much to reduce problems caused by the vagueness of the underlying concepts.

In Smith v. California, 361 U.S. 147 (1959), appellant was convicted of violating a city ordinance construed by the state courts as imposing strict liability on the proprietor of any bookstore who possessed in his store any book later judicially determined to be obscene — even if the proprietor had no personal knowledge of the contents of the book. The Court held the imposition of strict liability invalid. This feature of the ordinance, the Court noted, "tends to impose a severe limitation on the public's access to constitutionally protected matter. For if the bookseller is criminally liable without knowledge of the contents [he] will tend to restrict the books he sells to those he has inspected." Such a state of affairs would generate a "self-censorship [affecting] the whole public." Although holding strict liability invalid, the Court emphasized that "[we] do not pass today on what sort of mental element is requisite to a constitutionally permissible prosecution of a bookseller for carrying an obscene book in stock."

In Hamling v. United States, 418 U.S. 87 (1974), which involved a prosecution for mailing obscene materials, the district court instructed the jury that to satisfy its burden on intent, the government must prove that the defendants "knew that the envelopes and packages containing the subject materials were mailed [and] that they had knowledge of the character of the materials." The district court further instructed the jury that the defendants' "belief as to the obscenity or non-obscenity of the material is irrelevant."

The Court, speaking through Justice Rehnquist, affirmed the conviction: "It is constitutionally sufficient that the prosecution show that a defendant had knowledge of the contents of the materials he distributed, and that he knew the character and nature of the materials. To require proof of a defendant's knowledge of the legal status of the materials would permit the defendant to avoid prosecution by simply claiming that he had not brushed up on the law." Is this satisfactory? Is it reconcilable with the Court's analysis of intent in the libel and incitement contexts? Consider Lockhart, supra, at 563: "My suggestion is that [the first amendment establishes] as a defense to a criminal obscenity prosecution that the defendant *reasonably believed* that the material involved was 'not obscene.'"

7. Paris Adult Theatre, Stanley, *and state interests.* In *Paris Adult Theatre,* the Court finally examined in depth the state interests said to support government restrictions on obscenity. Does the Court engage in "definitional" balancing similar to that employed in the libel and commercial speech contexts?

After *Paris Adult Theatre,* what remains of *Stanley?* In two decisions handed down on the same day as *Miller* and *Paris Adult Theatre,* the Court, building on *Reidel,* continued to construe *Stanley* narrowly, holding not only that *Stanley* did not establish a right to sell obscene materials to willing adults but also that it did not prevent the government from punishing an individual for importing such materials or for transporting them across state lines even when intended solely for the individual's own private use. The Court explained that "it is extremely difficult to control the uses to which obscene material is put," and "even single copies, represented to be for personal use, could be quickly and cheaply duplicated by modern technology to enable widespread distribution." United States v. 12 200 Ft. Reels, 413 U.S. 123 (1973) (importation); United States v. Orito, 413 U.S. 139 (1973) (interstate commerce). After *Reidel, Reels,* and *Orito,* what is left of *Stanley?*

Note: Pornography and Feminism

Consider the constitutionality of the following law:

Pornography is the sexually explicit subordination of women, graphically depicted, whether in words or pictures, that also includes one or more of the following: (i) women are presented dehumanized as sexual objects, things or commodities; (ii) women are presented as sexual objects who enjoy pain, humiliation or rape; (iii) women are presented as sexual objects tied up or cut up or mutilated or physically hurt; (iv) women are presented in postures of sexual submission or sexual servility, including by inviting penetration; or (v) women are presented as whores by nature. No person may sell, exhibit, or distribute pornography.

Consider the following views:

a. MacKinnon, Not a Moral Issue, 2 Yale L. & Soc. Pol. Rev. 321, 322-324 (1984):

Obscenity law is concerned with morality, specifically morals from the male point of view, meaning the standpoint of male dominance. The feminist critique of pornography is politics, specifically politics from the women's point of view, meaning the standpoint of the subordination of women to men. Morality here means good and evil; politics means power and powerlessness. Obscenity is a moral idea; pornography is a political practice. The two concepts represent entirely different things. Nudity, explicitness, excess of candor, [these] qualities bother obscenity law when sex is depicted or portrayed. [Sex] forced on real women so that it can be sold at a profit to be forced on other real women; women's bodies trussed and maimed and raped and made into things to be hurt and obtained and accessed and this presented as the nature of women; the coercion that is visible and the coercion that has become invisible — this and more bothers feminists about pornography. Obscenity as such probably does little harm; pornography causes attitudes and behaviors of violence and discrimination which define the treatment and status of half of the population.

b. Clark, Liberalism and Pornography, in Pornography and Censorship 52-57 (D. Copp & S. Wendells eds. 1983):

[Pornography] has very little to do with sex, [but] it has everything to do with [the] use of sexuality as an instrument of active oppression. [Pornography is] a species of hate literature. [It depicts] women [as inviting] humiliating, degrading, and violently abusive [treatment]. [It feeds] traditional male phantasies [and glorifies] the traditional advantages men have enjoyed in relation to exploitation of female sexuality. [Pornography] is a method of socialization; [it] "teaches society to view women as less than human." [It is thus an] affront to [the dignity of women] as equal persons. [Moreover,] role modeling has a powerful effect on human behavior. [People] tend to act out and operationalize the behavior that they see typically acted out around them. [While] the liberal principle behind opposition to censorship is based on a recognition that desirable social change requires public access to information which challenges the beliefs and practices of the status quo, what it does not acknowledge is that information which supports the status quo through providing role models which advocate the use or threat of coercion as a technique of social control directed at a clearly identifiable group depicted as inferior, subordinate, and subhuman, works against the interest both of desirable social change and of the members of the subgroup so identified.

See also A. Dworkin, Pornography: Men Possessing Women (1981); Take Back the Night: Women on Pornography (L. Lederer ed. 1980).

c. MacKinnon, Pornography, Civil Rights, and Speech, 20 Harv. Civ. Rts.-Civ. Lib. L. Rev. 1, 52-54 (1985):

Recent experimental research on pornography shows that [pornographic material may cause] measurable harm to women through increasing men's attitudes and behaviors of discrimination in both violent and nonviolent forms. Exposure to [pornography] increases men's immediately subsequent willingness to aggress against women under laboratory conditions. It [significantly] increases attitudinal measures known to correlate with rape, [such as] hostility toward women, [condoning] rape, and predicting that one would rape [if] one knows one would not get caught. [As] to that pornography [in] which normal research subjects seldom perceive violence, long-term exposure still makes them see women as more worthless, trivial, non-human, and object-like, i.e., the way those who are discriminated against are seen by those who discriminate against them.

d. Note, Anti-Pornography Laws and First Amendment Values, 98 Harv. L. Rev. 460, 470-472, 475 (1984):

The Supreme Court denies [some categories of expression] full first amendment protection because they do not serve the values [of self-government, search for truth, and self-fulfillment that underlie] the first amendment. Pornography may likewise fail to serve such values. [Opponents] of pornography argue that it presents false and degrading images of women [and that it] is as harmful as, and no more valuable than, defamatory falsehoods. Proponents of pornographers' first amendment rights argue that pornography is intended not as a statement of fact, but as an opinion or fantasy about male and female sexuality [that] cannot be prohibited on the basis of its truthfulness or falsity. [But] the argument over whether pornography should be viewed as a statement of fact or an opinion assumes that sexually explicit images communicate "ideas" in the same way that nonsexually explicit words or images do. Feminists argue that men are influenced by pornography not because [it] prompts conscious testing of its depictions of sexuality [but] because [it] conditions men to associate harmful attitudes and actions towards women with sexual excitement. To the extent that any form of expression influences its audience through means that bypass the process of conscious deliberation, [it] cannot be said to [further] self-government [or] the search for truth. Some [argue that the] importance of self-expression as a means of [achieving] individual dignity and choice [supports the pornographer's] right to express his view of the world [and] his [customer's] right to receive those [images]. But the self-expression argument is double-edged. Those who oppose pornography assert that pornography denies women *their* right to individual dignity and choice. They maintain that pornography forces the state to choose whose right to individual dignity and choice it will protect.

e. How would you evaluate the claim that pornography produces harms equal to or greater than those produced by speech falling within existing categories of "low" value expression? Why isn't counterspeech an effective remedy in the pornography context? Note that some defenses of the antipornography ordinance, instead of (or in addition to) operating within the traditional doctrinal framework, reveal ambivalence about conventional approaches to freedom of speech. Such defenses claim that when social power is distributed to dominant groups, free speech, understood in traditional terms, tends to perpetuate the dominance of such groups. In light of widespread social and economic inequality, the notion of a "marketplace of ideas" breaks down. Consider Baat-Ada, Freedom of Speech as Mythology, or Quill Pen and Parchment Thinking in an Electronic Environment, 8 N.Y.U. Rev. L. & Soc. Change 271, 275, 278-279 (1978-1979):

> Contemporary mass media techniques have made the "free marketplace" into American folk mythology. [Were] those [who] oppose pornography able to present [their] case as fully as pornographers present theirs, the pornography industry would be in a precarious position. [Pornography] receives the support it does, however, because [the] pornographic environment is so profitable that [those who oppose pornography are effectively denied equal] access to the public through mass media communication forums.

See also the challenge to "marketplace" theories set out in section A, supra. Would these sorts of arguments compel a substantial rethinking of first amendment doctrine? Would that be a good or a bad idea?

f. In American Booksellers Association v. Hudnut, 771 F.2d 323 (7th Cir. 1985), the Court of Appeals for the Seventh Circuit held unconstitutional an Indianapolis ordinance restricting the distribution of pornography, defined in a manner similar to that suggested above. The Court of Appeals accepted the factual premises of the ordinance, conceding that "depictions of subordination tend to perpetuate subordination" and that the "subordinate status of women in turn leads to affont and lower pay at work, insult and injury at home, battery and rape on the streets." The Court of Appeals observed, however, that "racial bigotry, anti-semitism, violence on television [and other forms of expression also] influence the culture and shape our socialization. [Yet] all is protected speech, however insidious. Any other answer leaves the government in control of all of the institutions of culture, the great censor and director of which thoughts are good for us." Moreover, the Court of Appeals rejected the argument that pornography, as defined in the ordinance, is "low value" speech: "True, pornography and obscenity have sex in common. But Indianapolis left out of its definition any reference to literary, artistic, political, or scientific value. [Moreover, although the Supreme] Court sometimes balances the value of speech against the costs of its restriction, [it] does this by category of speech and not by the content of particular works." The Court emphasized that the Indianapolis ordinance expressly discriminated against a particular viewpoint: "Under the ordinance graphic sexually explicit speech is 'pornography' or not depending on the perspective the author adopts. Speech that 'subordinates' women [is] forbidden, [but speech] that portrays women in positions of equality is [lawful]. This is thought control. [Those] who espouse that approved view may use sexual images; those who do not, may not." The Court of Appeals concluded that because the ordinance "created an approved point of view," it could not be defended as a restriction of only "low value" speech. See also Stone, Anti-Pornography Legislation as Viewpoint Discrimination, 9 Harv. J. L. & Pub. Pol'y — (1986).

NEW YORK v. FERBER, 458 U.S. 747 (1982): Ferber, the proprietor of a Manhattan bookstore specializing in sexually oriented products, was prosecuted for selling two films to an undercover police officer. The films were devoted almost entirely to depicting young boys masturbating. A jury held that the films were not obscene but convicted Ferber of violating a New York statute prohibiting any person knowingly to produce, promote, direct, exhibit, or sell any material depicting a "sexual performance" by a child under the age of sixteen. The statute defined "sexual performance" as any performance that includes "actual or simulated sexual intercourse, deviate sexual intercourse, sexual bestiality, masturbation, sado-masochistic abuse, or lewd exhibition of the genitals." The Court unanimously upheld the conviction. Justice White delivered the opinion:

"In [the *Chaplinsky* dictum], the Court laid the foundation for the excision of obscenity from the realm of constitutionally protected expression. [For the following reasons, we are persuaded that pornographic depiction of children, like obscenity, is unprotected by the first amendment.]

"First. It is evident beyond the need for elaboration that a state's interest in 'safeguarding the physical and psychological well being of a minor' is 'compelling.' [The] use of children as subjects of pornographic materials is harmful to the physiological, emotional, and mental health of the child.

"Second. The distribution of photographs and films depicting sexual activity by juveniles is intrinsically related to the sexual abuse of children in at least two ways. First, the materials produced are a permanent record of the children's participation and the harm to the child is exacerbated by their circulation. Second, the distribution network for child pornography must be closed if the production of material which requires the sexual exploitation of children is to be effectively controlled. . . .

"Third. The advertising and selling of child pornography provides an economic motive for and is thus an integral part of the production of such materials, an activity illegal throughout the nation. [Were] the statutes outlawing the employment of children in these films and photographs fully effective, and the constitutionality of these laws have not been questioned, the First Amendment implications would be no greater than that presented by laws against distribution: enforceable production laws would leave no child pornography to be marketed.

"Fourth. The value of permitting live performances and photographic reproductions of children engaged in lewd sexual conduct is exceedingly modest, if not de minimis. We consider it unlikely that visual depictions of children performing sexual acts or lewdly exhibiting their genitals would often constitute an important and necessary part of a literary performance or scientific or educational work. [If] it were necessary for literary or artistic value, a person over the statutory age who perhaps looked younger could be utilized. Simulation outside of the prohibition of the statute could provide another alternative. Nor is there any question here of censoring a particular literary theme or portrayal of sexual activity. The First Amendment interest is limited to that of rendering the portrayal somewhat more 'realistic' by utilizing or photographing children.

"Fifth. Recognizing and classifying child pornography as a category of material outside the protection of the First Amendment is not incompatible with our earlier decisions. [It] is not rare that a content-based classification of speech has been accepted because it may be appropriately generalized that within the confines of the given classification, the evil to be restricted so overwhelmingly outweighs the expressive interests, if any, at stake, that no process of case-by-case adjudication is required. . . .

"There are, of course, limits on the category of child pornography which, like obscenity, is unprotected by the First Amendment. As with all legislation in this sensitive area, the conduct to be prohibited must be adequately defined by the applicable state law, as written or authoritatively construed. [The] test for child pornography is separate from the obscenity standard enunciated in *Miller*, but may be compared to it for purpose of clarity. The *Miller* formulation is adjusted in the following respects: A trier of fact need not find that the material appeals to the prurient interest of the average person; it is not required that sexual conduct portrayed be done so in a patently offensive manner; and the material at issue need not be considered as a whole. . . .

"It remains to address the claim that the New York statute is unconstitutionally overbroad because it would forbid the distribution of material with serious literary, scientific, or educational value or material which does not threaten the harms sought to be combatted by the State. [The New York Court of Appeals, which invalidated the statute,] was understandably concerned that some protected expression, ranging from medical textbooks to pictorials in National Geographic would fall prey to the statute. [Yet] we seriously doubt, and it has not been suggested, that these arguably impermissible applications of the statute amount to more than a tiny fraction of the materials within the statute's reach. [Under] these circumstances, [the statute] is 'not substantially overbroad and whatever overbreadth exists should be cured through case-by-case analysis of the fact situations to which its sanctions, assertedly, may not be applied.' [Broadrick v. Oklahoma, supra section C1.] As applied to [Ferber] and to others who distribute similar material, the statute does not violate the First Amendment. . . ."

Justice O'Connor filed a concurring opinion: "Although I join the Court's opinion, I write separately to stress that the Court does not hold that New York must except 'material with serious literary, scientific or educational value' from its statute. [The] compelling interests identified in today's opinion suggest that the Constitution might in fact permit New York to ban knowing distribution of works depicting minors engaged in explicit sexual conduct, regardless of the social value of the depictions."

Justice Brennan, joined by Justice Marshall, concurred in the judgment: "I agree with much of what is said in the Court's opinion. [I would make clear, however, that] application of [the New York statute] to depictions of children that in themselves do have serious literary, artistic, scientific, or medical value [would] violate the First Amendment. As the Court recognizes, the limited classes of speech, the suppression of which does not raise serious First Amendment concerns, have two attributes. They are of exceedingly 'slight social value,' and the State has a compelling interest in their regulation. See [*Chaplinsky*]. The First Amendment value of depictions of children that are in themselves serious contributions to art, literature or science, is, by definition, simply not de minimis. At the same time, the State's interest in suppression of such materials is likely to be far less compelling. For the Court's assumption of harm to the child resulting from the 'permanent record' and 'circulation' of the child's 'participation' [lacks] much of its force where the depiction is a serious contribution to art or science."

Justice Stevens filed an opinion concurring in the judgment. Justice Blackman concurred in the result.

Should the Court have analyzed the New York statute, not as a content-based restriction on "unprotected" expression but as a content-neutral restriction on the "means" of expression? Consider the following propositions: (1) There is no first amendment right to violate an otherwise valid criminal law, which is itself unrelated to the suppression of free expression, merely because the violation would render one's speech more effective or "realistic." Cf. United States v. O'Brien, infra section E3. (2) There is no first amendment right to depict the commission of a criminal act where the crime was committed solely to produce the depiction.

In light of the interests underlying the New York statute, could New York constitutionally prohibit the exhibition of a film made entirely in California with only California actors? In *Ferber* the Court noted that "the State is not barred by the First Amendment from prohibiting the distribution of unprotected materials produced outside the State." The Court explained that it "is often impossible to determine where such material is produced" and the "maintenance of the [child pornography] market itself 'leaves open the financial conduit by which the production of such material is funded and materially increases the risk that [local] children will be injured.'" Suppose the film is made in France?

In light of *Ferber*, could the pornography law set out in the preceding Note be justified on the ground that pornography harms women participants in the same way that child pornography harms children? Consider Note, Anti-Pornography Laws and First Amendment Values, 98 Harv. L. Rev. 460, 473 (1984): "Because the Court is probably not disposed to presume that adult models are incapable of refusing to participate in pornographic films or photographs, it is unlikely to reason that adult pornography [can] be banned irrespective of a work's social merit."

Note: The Regulation of Obscenity — A Procedural Perspective

The first amendment is concerned not only with what speech may be suppressed but also with the means by which speech may be suppressed. This problem, explored in depth in section C, supra, has proved especially troublesome in the context of obscenity. This Note examines the constitutionality of several regulatory devices, other than conventional criminal prosecution, designed specifically to control the distribution of obscene materials.

1. *Licensing*. The problem of licensing in this context has focused largely on government censorship of motion pictures prior to exhibition in order to screen out obscene or otherwise offensive films. In the early days of motion pictures, it was questioned whether movies were "speech" at all. See Mutual Film Corp. v. Industrial Commission, 236 U.S. 230 (1915). In Burstyn v. Wilson, 343 U.S. 495 (1952), however, the Court, although noting that the "production, distribution, and exhibition [of motion pictures] is a large-scale business conducted for private profit" and that motion pictures may "possess a greater capacity for evil [than] other modes of expression," nonetheless held that movies are "a form of expression whose liberty is safeguarded by the First Amendment."

In Times Film Corp. v. Chicago, 365 U.S. 43 (1961), the Court upheld a Chicago ordinance requiring the submission of all motion pictures to a licensing board prior to exhibition. Although conceding that the ordinance constituted a prior restraint, the Court observed that there is no "absolute privilege against prior restraint under the First Amendment." The Court emphasized that "we are dealing only with motion pictures," and motion pictures are "not 'necessarily subject to the precise rules governing any other particular method of expression.'" The first amendment, the Court concluded, does not strip the city "of all constitutional power to prevent, in the most effective fashion, the utterance of this class of speech."

Despite *Times Film* the Court has used two doctrines to limit the licensing of motion pictures. First, the Court has consistently invoked the doctrine of Lovell v. Griffin, supra section C2, to invalidate "vague" licensing schemes. See, e.g., Burstyn v. Wilson, supra ("sacrilegious"); Holmby Productions v. Vaughn, 350 U.S. 870 (1955) ("cruel, obscene, indecent, or immoral"); Commercial Pictures Corp. v. Regents, 346 U.S. 587 (1954) ("immoral" and "tend to corrupt morals"). Second, even where the standards employed by the licensing agency are clear, precise, and consistent with the Court's substantive definition of obscenity, the Court has consistently invoked the doctrine of Freedman v. Maryland, supra section C2, to require that licensing schemes employ "procedural safeguards designed to obviate the dangers of a censorship system." Do the *Freedman* safeguards eliminate the objections to licensing in this context? Should motion pictures be treated differently from other means of expression for these purposes?

2. *Injunctions*. Although in cases like Near v. Minnesota, supra section C2, New York Times v. United States, supra section B4, and Nebraska Press v. Stuart, supra section B4, the Court has consistently characterized injunctions against expression as "prior restraints" that bear a "heavy presumption" against their constitutional validity, it has with almost equal consistency upheld injunctions against the exhibition or distribution of obscene materials. In Kingsley Books v. Brown, 354 U.S. 436 (1957), for example, the Court, in a five-to-four decision, sustained the constitutionality of a New York statute designed to deal with obscenity. The statute authorized the issuance of an ex parte injunction pending trial but guaranteed the defendant the right "to a trial of the issues within one day after joinder of issue" and to a decision "by the court within two days of the conclusion of the trial." The statute authorized the issuance of a permanent injunction "against the sale and distribution of written and printed matter found after due trial to be obscene." The Court explained that the New York scheme

"does not differ in essential procedural safeguards from that provided under many state [criminal] statutes making the distribution of obscene publications a misdemeanor." Moreover, the Court maintained that both "modes of procedure provide an effective deterrent against distribution prior to adjudication of the book's content — the threat of subsequent penalization." Finally, the Court distinguished *Near* on the ground that whereas "Minnesota empowered its courts to enjoin the dissemination of future issues of a publication because its past issues had been found offensive," New York "studiously withholds restraint upon matters not already published and not yet found to be offensive." Do you agree with this distinction of *Near?*

In *Paris Adult Theatre*, the Court, building on *Kingsley Books*, expressly approved Georgia's use of injunctions against the exhibition of obscene motion pictures where the state employed "a constitutionally acceptable standard for determining what is unprotected by the First Amendment" and "imposed no restraint on [exhibition] until after a full adversary proceeding and a final judicial determination [that] the materials were constitutionally unprotected."

Consider the constitutionality of a statute authorizing state judges, on finding that a theater has previously exhibited obscene movies, to enjoin the theater's future exhibition of "any obscene motion picture," where "obscene" is defined in accordance with the Court's definition. See Vance v. Universal Amusement Co., 445 U.S. 308 (1980), holding such a statute unconstitutional.

3. *Seizures*. In Marcus v. Search Warrant, 367 U.S. 717 (1961), a Missouri statute authorized the issuance of warrants for the seizure of allegedly obscene materials that, if thereafter found by a court in an adversary hearing to be obscene, were to be burned. Pursuant to this statute, a police officer obtained a warrant on the basis of his own sworn complaint that appellant, a wholesale distributor of magazines, kept on its premises for purposes of sale "obscene publications." Neither the complaint nor the warrant specifically identified the allegedly obscene publications by name. Executing this warrant, the officer seized approximately 11,000 copies of some 280 publications. Two weeks after the seizures, a hearing was held at which appellant was permitted to contest the allegations of obscenity. Seven weeks later, the judge ruled that 100 of the 280 publications were obscene. The Court held this scheme invalid. Noting that the "warrants issued on the strength of the conclusory assertions of a single police officer, without any scrutiny by the judge of any [of the] materials," the Court held that the Missouri procedure "lacked the safeguards which due process demands to assure nonobscene material the constitutional protection to which it is entitled." See also A Quantity of Books v. Kansas, 378 U.S. 205 (1964) (invalidating a similar statutory scheme).

In Heller v. New York, 413 U.S. 483 (1973), a local judge, at the request of an assistant district attorney, went to petitioner's movie theater to view the film "Blue Movie." At the end of the film, the judge, concluding that the movie was obscene, signed a warrant authorizing its seizure. The Court upheld this procedure, but in so doing it expressly interpreted *Marcus* as holding that, in the circumstances there presented, "a prior judicial determination of obscenity in an adversary proceeding was [constitutionally] required." *Heller*, however, was distinguishable:

[Seizing] films to destroy them or to block their distribution or exhibition [as in *Marcus*] is a very different matter from seizing a single copy of a film for the bona fide purpose of preserving it as evidence in a criminal [proceeding]. If such a seizure is pursuant to a warrant, issued after a determination of probable cause by a neutral magistrate, and, following the seizure, a prompt judicial determination of the obscenity issue in an adversary proceeding is available at the request of any interested party, the seizure is constitutionally permissible.

The Court added that "on a showing to the trial court that other copies of the film are not available to the exhibitor, the court should permit the seized film to be copied so that showing can be continued pending a judicial determination of the obscenity issue in an adversary proceeding." See also Roaden v. Kentucky, 413 U.S. 496 (1973); Lo-Ji Sales v. New York, 442 U.S. 319 (1979).

The court has imposed *Freedman*-like safeguards on seizures of obscene materials in other contexts as well. See, e.g., United States v. Thirty-Seven Photographs, 402 U.S. 363 (1971) (upholding a federal statute authorizing customs seizures of obscene materials by interpreting the statute as embodying "explicit time limits of the sort [required by *Freedman*]"); Blount v. Rizzi, 400 U.S. 410 (1971) (holding unconstitutional an "administrative censorship scheme" involving the use of postal stop orders to prevent the mailing of obscene materials).

For an interesting twist on the seizure issue, see Maryland v. Macon, — U.S. — , 105 S. Ct. 2778 (1985), in which the Court held that an undercover agent's purchase of an obscene magazine from a bookseller in the ordinary course of his business did not constitute a "seizure" requiring any special constitutional protections.

4. *Blacklisting*. In Bantam Books v. Sullivan, 372 U.S. 58 (1963), the Court held unconstitutional the activities of the Rhode Island Commission to Encourage Morality in Youth, an agency created by the state legislature "to educate the public" concerning any book containing obscenity and to investigate and recommend prosecutions of all violations of the state's obscenity laws. The commission's practice was to notify book distributors on official commission stationery that it had found certain designated books to be obscene, that it was the commission's duty to recommend prosecution of purveyors of obscenity, and that it circulated lists of "objectionable" publications to local police departments.

In invalidating this scheme, the Court characterized the commission's activities as "a system of prior administrative restraints, since the Commission is not a judicial body and its decisions to list particular publications as objectionable do not follow judicial determinations that such publications may lawfully be banned." The Court rejected as "untenable" the state's contention that procedural safeguards were unnecessary because the commission "does not regulate or suppress obscenity but simply exhorts booksellers and advises them of their legal rights." The Court explained that "though the Commission is limited to informal sanctions [the] record amply demonstrates that the Commission deliberately set about to achieve the suppression of publications deemed 'objectionable' and succeeded in its aim," for as the trial court found, the effect of the commission's notices was "'to intimidate the various book and magazine wholesale distributors and retailers and to cause [the] suppression of the sale and circulation of the books listed in [the] notices.'"

5. *Vagueness and prior civil adjudication*. A recurrent theme in the jurisprudence of obscenity concerns the inherent vagueness of the substantive standard. Although the vagueness issue has several facets, perhaps the most troublesome is

the lack of notice afforded the potential criminal defendant who must guess whether a book or film is "obscene." Several procedural devices have been suggested to mitigate this problem. In *Kingsley Books*, for example, Justice Frankfurter indicated that injunctions might be less threatening to first amendment interests than criminal prosecutions: "Instead of requiring the bookseller to dread that the offer for sale of a book may, without prior warning, subject him to a criminal prosecution, [the] civil procedure assures him that such consequences cannot follow unless he ignores a court order specifically directed to him." Is this advantage of "the civil procedure" sufficient to offset the dangers of injunctions? Would a ban on any obscenity prosecution in the absence of a prior civil adjudication that the particular work is obscene be preferable to the use of injunctions? In such a civil action, should the state be required to prove "obscenity" "beyond a reasonable doubt"? See Cooper v. Mitchell Brothers' Santa Ana Theater, 454 U.S. 90 (1982) ("beyond a reasonable doubt" standard not constitutionally required).

Such a scheme, it should be noted, might pose its own problems. In McKinney v. Alabama, 424 U.S. 669 (1976), for example, a local district attorney, pursuant to an Alabama statutory procedure, brought an in rem equity action against four magazines named as "respondents" and two other parties seeking an adjudication of the magazines' obscenity. After a hearing, the court held the magazines to be obscene. Petitioner, who operated a bookstall, was not a party to that proceeding. Soon after the issuance of the decree, however, he was personally notified of the decision by agents of the state. When petitioner continued to sell one of the magazines, he was prosecuted for selling "matter known [to] have been judicially found to be obscene." At his trial, which resulted in a conviction, petitioner was not permitted to litigate the obscenity of the magazine vel non. Rather, the sole issue for the jury was whether he had sold "matter known [to] have been judicially found to be obscene." In a unanimous decision, the Court set aside his conviction. Despite the state's assertion "that invalidation of petitioner's conviction will seriously undermine the use of civil proceedings to examine the protected character of specific materials," the Court held that the state could not constitutionally declare the issue of obscenity "concluded against him by the decree in a civil proceeding to which he was not a party and of which he had no notice." Is there any way to circumvent this problem? See Note, Community Standards, Class Actions, and Obscenity under *Miller v. California*, 88 Harv. L. Rev. 1838 (1975).

Might there be other objections to the prior civil adjudication device? Consider Lockhart, Escape from the Chill of Uncertainty: Explicit Sex and the First Amendment, 9 Ga. L. Rev. 533, 570-571 (1975):

> Such a universal bar to criminal prosecutions without a prior adjudication would mean giving carte blanche to the distribution of all explicit sexual material, no matter how blatantly offensive and utterly worthless it might be, until the prosecutor learns of the material, gears up to seek a civil adjudication, and then secures a final judgment of obscenity. In the case of some motion pictures and much of the fast-moving periodical and pulp book materials, this would come too late to be of any value, for the principal marketing would have already taken place. This procedure would largely thwart a major role of the criminal law — to encourage compliance with the law — by making the criminal law wholly inapplicable during the major marketing period.

6. *Offensive Speech*

In what circumstances, if any, may government restrict the public use of profane or sexually oriented but nonobscene expression because of its highly offensive character? Recall that in *Chaplinsky* the Court's list of utterances ("the prevention and punishment of which have never been thought to raise any Constitutional problem") expressly included not only "fighting words," the "libelous," and the "obscene," but also the "lewd" and the "profane." Such utterances, the Court observed, "are no essential part of any exposition of ideas, and are of such slight social value as a step to truth that any benefit that may be derived from them is clearly outweighed by the social interest in order and morality." Moreover, in explaining why such utterances are "unprotected," the Court noted not only that they might "tend to incite an immediate breach of the peace" but also that they might "by their very utterance inflict injury." Under *Chaplinsky*, then, the "lewd" and the "profane" were "not considered to be speech in the constitutional sense." The mere "fact that [they were] publicly uttered caused an injury of some sort, [and] it was not necessary for the Court to specify the nature of this injury, or even to indicate whether it was an injury suffered by individual persons or by the public collectively." W. Berns, The First Amendment and the Future of American Democracy 192 (1976).

Is *Chaplinsky*'s treatment of the "lewd" and the "profane" reconcilable with the doctrine, articulated most forcefully in the hostile audience context, that "under our Constitution the public expression of ideas may not be prohibited merely because the ideas are themselves offensive to some of their hearers"? Street v. New York, 394 U.S. 576, 592 (1969). Recall Terminiello v. Chicago, supra section B3. Consider Cox, Foreword: Freedom of Expression in the Burger Court, 94 Harv. L. Rev. 1, 42 (1980):

> The task of accommodation [is] singularly difficult [in this context] because gross offense to the sensibilities usually results only from certain classes of words or symbols, most notably the sexual, scatological, or sacrilegious. To assert that [no] restrictions against the communication of particular ideas is ever constitutional unless the demanding test otherwise applicable to censorship is satisfied implies that the state is powerless to protect the sensibilities of an unconsenting audience against grossly offensive expression. Conversely, any restriction upon expression narrowly tailored to protect sensibility against gross assault is almost by definition tied to content and thus subject to attack as discriminatory.

Cohen v. California

403 U.S. 15 (1971)

MR. JUSTICE HARLAN delivered the opinion of the Court.

This case may seem at first blush too inconsequential to find its way into our books, but the issue it presents is of no small constitutional significance.

Appellant Paul Robert Cohen was convicted in the Los Angeles Municipal Court of violating that part of California Penal Code §415 which prohibits "maliciously and willfully disturb[ing] the peace or quiet of any neighborhood or person . . . by . . . offensive conduct. . . ." He was given 30 days' imprisonment.

The facts upon which his conviction rests are detailed in the opinion of the [state court]:

> On April 26, 1968, the defendant was observed in the Los Angeles County Court-house in the corridor outside [of] the municipal court wearing a jacket bearing the words "Fuck the Draft." There were women and children present in the corridor. The defendant was arrested. The defendant testified that he wore the jacket [as] a means of informing the public of the depth of his feelings against the Vietnam War and the draft.
>
> The defendant did not engage in, nor threaten to engage in, nor did anyone as the result of his conduct in fact commit or threaten to commit any act of violence. The defendant did not make any loud or unusual noise, nor was there any evidence that he uttered any sound prior to his arrest. . . .

[We reverse.]

Not action, merely political speech

I

In order to lay hands on the precise issue which this case involves, it is useful first to canvass various matters which this record does *not* present.

The conviction quite clearly rests upon the asserted offensiveness of the *words* Cohen used to convey his message to the public. The only "conduct" which the State sought to punish is the fact of communication. Thus, we deal here with a conviction resting solely upon "speech." [Further,] the State certainly lacks power to punish Cohen for the underlying content of the message the inscription conveyed. At least so long as there is no showing of an intent to incite disobedience to or disruption of the draft, Cohen could not, consistently with the First and Fourteenth Amendments, be punished for asserting the evident position on the inutility or immorality of the draft his jacket reflected. [Citing *Yates.*]

In the second place, as it comes to us, this case cannot be said to fall within those relatively few categories of instances where prior decisions have established the power of government to deal more comprehensively with certain forms of individual expression simply upon a showing that such a form was employed. This is not, for example, an obscenity case. Whatever else may be necessary to give rise to the States' broader power to prohibit obscene expression, such expression must be, in some significant way, erotic. [*Roth.*] It cannot plausibly be maintained that this vulgar allusion to the Selective Service System would conjure up such psychic stimulation in anyone likely to be confronted with Cohen's crudely defaced jacket.

This Court has also held that the States are free to ban the simple use, without a demonstration of additional justifying circumstances, of so-called "fighting words," those personally abusive epithets which, when addressed to the ordinary citizen, are, as a matter of common knowledge, inherently likely to provoke violent reaction. [*Chaplinsky.*] While the four-letter word displayed by Cohen in relation to the draft is not uncommonly employed in a personally provocative fashion, in this instance it was clearly not "directed to the person of the hearer." [No] individual actually or likely to be present could reasonably have regarded the words on appellant's jacket as a direct personal insult. Nor do we have here an instance of the exercise of the State's police power to prevent a speaker from intentionally provoking a given group to hostile reaction. Cf. [*Feiner*]. There is, as noted above, no showing that anyone who saw Cohen was in fact violently aroused or that appellant intended such a result.

Finally, in arguments before this Court much has been made of the claim that Cohen's distasteful mode of expression was thrust upon unwilling or unsuspecting viewers, and that the State might therefore legitimately act as it did in order to protect the sensitive from otherwise unavoidable exposure to appellant's crude form of protest. Of course, the mere presumed presence of unwitting listeners or viewers does not serve automatically to justify curtailing all speech capable of giving offense. [While] this Court has recognized that government may properly act in many situations to prohibit intrusion into the privacy of the home of unwelcome views and ideas which cannot be totally banned from the public dialogue, e.g., Rowan v. Post Office Dept., 397 U.S. 728 (1970), we have at the same time consistently stressed that "we are often 'captives' outside the sanctuary of the home and subject to objectionable speech." [The] ability of government, consonant with the Constitution, to shut off discourse solely to protect others from hearing it is, in other words, dependent upon a showing that substantial privacy interests are being invaded in an essentially intolerable manner. Any broader view of this authority would effectively empower a majority to silence dissidents simply as a matter of personal predilections.

In this regard, persons confronted with Cohen's jacket were in a quite different posture than, say, those subjected to the raucous emissions of sound trucks blaring outside their residences. Those in the Los Angeles courthouse could effectively avoid further bombardment of their sensibilities simply by averting their eyes. And, while it may be that one has a more substantial claim to a recognizable privacy interest when walking through a courthouse corridor than, for example, strolling through Central Park, surely it is nothing like the interest in being free from unwanted expression in the confines of one's own home. [Given] the subtlety and complexity of the factors involved, if Cohen's "speech" was otherwise entitled to constitutional protection, we do not think the fact that some unwilling "listeners" in a public building may have been briefly exposed to it can serve to justify this breach of the peace conviction where, as here, there was no evidence that persons powerless to avoid appellant's conduct did in fact object to it, and where [the statute] evinces no concern [with] the special plight of the captive auditor, but, instead, indiscriminately sweeps within its prohibitions all "offensive conduct" that disturbs "any neighborhood or person." . . .

II

Against this background, the issue flushed by this case stands out in bold relief. It is whether California can excise, as "offensive conduct," one particular scurrilous epithet from the public discourse, either upon the theory [that] its use is inherently likely to cause violent reaction or upon a more general assertion that the States, acting as guardians of public morality, may properly remove this offensive word from the public vocabulary.

The [first rationale] is plainly untenable. At most it reflects an "undifferentiated fear or apprehension of disturbance [which] is not enough to overcome the right to freedom of expression." [We] have been shown no evidence that substantial numbers of citizens are standing ready to strike out physically at whoever may assault their sensibilities with execrations like that uttered by Cohen. There may be some persons about with such lawless and violent proclivities, but that is an insufficient base upon which to erect, consistently with constitutional values, a governmental power to force persons who wish to ventilate their dissident views into avoiding particular forms of expression. The argument amounts to little more than the self-defeating proposition that to avoid physical censorship of one who has not sought to provoke such a response by a hypothetical coterie of the violent and lawless, the States may more appropriately effectuate that censorship themselves. . . .

Admittedly, it is not so obvious that the First and Fourteenth Amendments must be taken to disable the States from punishing public utterance of this unseemly expletive in order to maintain what they regard as a suitable level of discourse within the body politic. We think, however, that examination and reflection will reveal the shortcomings of a contrary viewpoint.

At the outset, we cannot overemphasize that, in our judgment, most situations where the State has a justifiable interest in regulating speech will fall within one or more of the various established exceptions, discussed above but not applicable here, to the usual rule that governmental bodies may not prescribe the form or content of individual expression. Equally important to our conclusion is the constitutional backdrop against which our decision must be made. The constitutional right of free expression is powerful medicine in a society as diverse and populous as ours. It is designed and intended to remove governmental restraints from the arena of public discussion, putting the decision as to what views shall be voiced largely into the hands of each of us, in the hope that use of such freedom will ultimately produce a more capable citizenry and more perfect polity and in the belief that no other approach would comport with the premise of individual dignity and choice upon which our political system rests. See [*Whitney* (Brandeis, J., concurring)].

To many, the immediate consequence of this freedom may often appear to be only verbal tumult, discord, and even offensive utterance. These are, however, within established limits, in truth necessary side effects of the broader enduring values which the process of open debate permits us to achieve. That the air may at times seem filled with verbal cacophony is, in this sense not a sign of weakness but of strength. We cannot lose sight of the fact that, in what otherwise might seem a trifling and annoying instance of individual distasteful abuse of a privilege, these fundamental societal values are truly implicated. . . .

Against this perception of the constitutional policies involved, we discern certain more particularized considerations that peculiarly call for reversal of this conviction. First, the principle contended for by the State seems inherently boundless. How is one to distinguish this from any other offensive word? Surely the State has no right to cleanse public debate to the point where it is grammatically palatable to the most squeamish among us. Yet no readily ascertainable general principle exists for stopping short of that result were we to affirm the judgment below. For, while the particular four-letter word being litigated here is perhaps more distasteful than most others of its genre, it is nevertheless often true that one man's vulgarity is another's lyric. Indeed, we think it is largely because governmental officials cannot make principled distinctions in this area that the Constitution leaves matters of taste and style so largely to the individual.

Additionally, we cannot overlook the fact, because it is well illustrated by the episode involved here, that much linguistic expression serves a dual communicative function: it conveys not only ideas capable of relatively precise, detached explication, but otherwise inexpressible emotions as well. In fact, words are often chosen as much for their emotive as their cognitive force. We cannot sanction the view that the Constitution, while solicitous of the cognitive content of individual speech, has little or no regard for that emotive function which, practically speaking, may often be the more important element of the overall message sought to be communicated. . . .

Finally, and in the same vein, we cannot indulge the facile assumption that one can forbid particular words without also running a substantial risk of suppressing ideas in the process. Indeed, governments might soon seize upon the censorship of particular words as a convenient guise for banning the expression of unpopular views. We have been able, as noted above, to discern little social benefit that might result from running the risk of opening the door to such grave results.

It is, in sum, our judgment that, absent a more particularized and compelling reason for its actions, the State may not, consistently with the First and Fourteenth Amendments, make the simple public display here involved of this single four-letter expletive a criminal offense. . . .

Reversed.

Mr. Justice Blackmun, with whom The Chief Justice and Mr. Justice Black join.

I dissent. . . .

Cohen's absurd and immature antic, in my view, was mainly conduct and little speech. [Further,] the case appears to me to be well within the sphere of [*Chaplinsky*], where Mr. Justice Murphy, a known champion of First Amendment freedoms, wrote for a unanimous bench. As a consequence, this Court's agonizing over First Amendment values seems misplaced and unnecessary.*

Note: *Offensive Language,* Cohen, *and the Captive Audience*

1. *Offensive language as "low" value speech.* Does *Cohen* repudiate *Chaplinsky*'s assumption that profanity is of only "low" first amendment value? If obscenity has "no redeeming social value," why isn't the same true of profanity? Consider the following proposition: profanity has "high" first amendment value because (a) its use may be necessary to convey "otherwise inexpressible emotions," (b) its suppression creates "a substantial risk of suppressing ideas in the process," and (c) there exists "no readily ascertainable general principle" for distinguishing between prohibitable and nonprohibitable offensive language.

Consider W. Berns, The First Amendment and the Future of American Democracy 200 (1976):

> This country managed to live most of its years under rules, conventional and legal, that forbade the public use of profanity [and] it would be an abuse of language to say

---

* [Justice White dissented on other grounds. — Eds.]

that its freedom was thereby restricted in any important respect. Now, suddenly, and for reasons that ought to persuade no one, we are told that it is a violation of the First Amendment for the law to enforce these rules; that however desirable it might be to see them preserved, there is no way for the law to do this except by threatening the freedom of all speech. [Do] we really live in a world so incapable of communication that it can be said that "one man's vulgarity is another's lyric"?

2. *Offensive language and fighting words.* As evident in *Chaplinsky*, the problems of fighting words and offensive language are closely related. In *Cohen*, however, the Court "made clear that [the phrase 'fighting words'] was no longer to be understood as a euphemism for controversial or dirty talk but was to require instead a quite unambiguous invitation to a brawl." J. Ely, Democracy and Distrust 114 (1980). The Court thus recognized in *Cohen* that the fighting words and offensive language problems are analytically distinct — although fighting words typically involve the use of offensive language, this is not essential; although fighting words usually involve insults directed personally to the addressee, the problem of offensive language is not so limited; and although the fighting words doctrine is designed primarily to forestall an addressee's violent response, government efforts to suppress offensive language are designed primarily to raise the level of public discourse and to protect the sensibilities of an unconsenting audience. The fighting words doctrine is examined in section B3 supra.

3. *Offensive language: manner or content?* Is a law restricting the use of offensive language in public more akin to a law restricting the public expression of an "undesirable" idea or to a law restricting the use of an "undesirable" means of expression? Compare, for example, a law prohibiting the expression of "offensive ideas" in a public park, a law prohibiting the use of profanity in a public park, and a law prohibiting the use of loudspeakers in a public park. Is the prohibition on profanity more akin to the prohibition on loudspeakers because both are directed against "consequences unrelated to content"? Cox, Foreword: Freedom of Expression in the Burger Court, 94 Harv. L. Rev. 1, 40 (1980). Is it more akin to the prohibition on "offensive ideas" because the "harms of shock and offense [flow] entirely from the communicative content of [the] message"? Ely, supra, at 114.

Consider the following views:

a. Haimand, Speech v. Privacy: Is There a Right Not to Be Spoken To?, 67 Nw. L. Rev. 153, 189 (1972):

The problem with the position [that prohibitions on the use of offensive language are merely restrictions on the manner of expression] is that the form and content of communications are so inextricably tied that to control the former is, in fact, to modify the latter. [For] example, it can hardly be maintained that phrases like, "Repeal the Draft," "Resist the Draft," or "The Draft Must Go" convey essentially the same message as "Fuck the Draft." Clearly something is lost in the translation.

b. Stone, Content Regulation and the First Amendment, 25 Wm. & Mary L. Rev. 189, 243-244 (1983):

Governmental efforts to limit speech because it is offensively *noisy* [do] not implicate the same kind of censorial or heckler's veto concerns as governmental efforts to limit speech because the *ideas* are offensive. Analytically, offense at language is more like offense at noise than offense at ideas. [Moreover, although] restrictions on the use of profanity may affect some speakers more than others, [this] is also true of most content-neutral restrictions.

4. *The captive audience.* Does Justice Harlan undervalue the interests of the "audience" in *Cohen?* Consider A. Bickel, The Morality of Consent 72 (1975): "There is such a thing as verbal violence, a kind of cursing, assaultive speech that amounts to almost physical aggression. [The sort of speech at issue in *Cohen*] constitutes an assault." As noted in *Chaplinsky*, such profanities "by their very utterance inflict injury." Why, then, can't such expression be suppressed? Is the interest in protecting the sensibilities of unconsenting individuals against such "assaults" simply too insubstantial to justify restrictions on "offensive" expression? Note Justice Harlan's conclusion in *Cohen* that "The ability of government [to] shut off discourse solely to protect others from hearing it is [dependent] upon a showing that substantial privacy interests are being invaded in an essentially intolerable manner." For analysis of the *Cohen* standard, see Stone, Fora Americana: Speech in Public Places, 1974 Sup. Ct. Rev. 233, 262-272.

Consider the following:

a. Suppose Congress enacts a law authorizing any homeowner who no longer wishes to receive mail from any person or organization to instruct the Postmaster General to direct that person or organization to refrain from further mailings to the homeowner. Consider Rowan v. Post Office Department, 397 U.S. 728 (1970):

> In today's complex society we are inescapably captive audiences for many purposes, but a sufficient measure of individual autonomy must survive to permit every householder to exercise control over unwanted mail. To make the householder the exclusive and final judge of what will cross his threshold undoubtedly has the effect of impeding the flow of ideas, information, and arguments that, ideally, he should receive and consider. [But] nothing in the Constitution compels us to listen to or view any unwanted communication, whatever its merit. [The] ancient concept that "a man's home is his castle" into which "not even the king may enter" has lost none of its vitality, [and we] therefore categorically reject the argument that [an individual] has a right under the Constitution [to] send unwanted material into the home of another.

b. Suppose Congress enacts a law prohibiting any person or organization to mail to another any drawings or photographs portraying or revealing bare human pubic areas without the recipient's prior written consent. In Bolger v. Youngs Drug Products Corp., 463 U.S. 60 (1983), the Court invalidated a federal statute prohibiting the mailing of unsolicited advertisements for contraceptives. The Court explained:

> We [have] recognized the important interest in allowing addresses to give notice to a mailer that they wish no further mailings [citing *Rowan*]. But we have never held that the government itself can shut off the flow of mailings to protect those recipients who might potentially be offended. The First Amendment "does not permit the government to prohibit speech as intrusive unless the 'captive' audience cannot avoid objectionable speech." [The] "short, regular, journey from mail box to trash can [is] an acceptable burden, at least so far as the Constitution is concerned."

See also Consolidated Edison v. Public Service Commission, 447 U.S. 530 (1980) (invalidating a rule prohibiting public utility companies from including in their monthly bills inserts discussing controversial issues).

c. In the mail situation, it is usually possible to "individuate" the audience's decision whether to receive the communication, thus largely avoiding the most difficult captive audience problems. As illustrated by *Cohen*, however, such individuation is not always possible. Consider Rosenfeld v. New Jersey, 408 U.S. 901 (1972), in which appellant addressed a public school board meeting attended by about 150 people, approximately forty of whom were children and twenty-five of whom were women. In the course of his remarks, appellant used the phrase "mother-fucking" on four occasions. He was convicted of using "profane or indecent language in any public [place]." The Court remanded for reconsideration in light of *Cohen*, but Justice Powell maintained in dissent that in these circumstances appellant could constitutionally be convicted for his "willful use of scurrilous language calculated to offend the sensibilities of an unwilling audience." Is this a situation in which "substantial privacy interests are being invaded in an essentially intolerable manner"?

d. Suppose a city operates a public bus system and each bus contains twenty interior advertising spaces available for lease by private persons. May the city, to protect the sensibilities of "captive" commuters, exclude such "highly offensive" messages as "Welfare is Black Theft," "God Is Dead" and "Abortion Is Murder"? Is this a situation in which, as in *Cohen*, the audience "could effectively avoid further bombardment of their sensibilities simply by averting their eyes"? Cf. Lehman v. Shaker Heights, 418 U.S. 298 (1974) (plurality opinion upholding city policy permitting the display of commercial but not generally more "controversial" political or public issue advertisements in the interior of city buses), infra section F1. Note that in the bus situation, unlike the situations in *Cohen* and *Rosenfeld*, the city could protect the "captive" audience by adopting a content-neutral restriction banning *all* speech. Is a content-neutral restriction preferable to a "narrower" restriction based on content? Consider Stone, supra at 280: "If a 'true' captive audience exists, the state may protect the sensibilities of unwilling listeners by banning all speech, regardless of content. It should never, however, be permitted to use the captive audience as a lever for censorship." Should that conclusion, however justified as applied to offensive ideas, apply also to the use of profanity and to the display of "lewd" pictures?

ERZNOZNIK v. JACKSONVILLE, 422 U.S. 205 (1975): In *Erznoznik* the Court invalidated a Jacksonville, Florida, ordinance that declared it a public nuisance for any drive-in movie theater to exhibit any motion picture "in which the human male or female bare buttocks, human female bare breasts, or human bare pubic areas are shown, if such motion picture [is] visible from any public street or place." Justice Powell delivered the opinion of the Court:

"[The city] concedes that its ordinance sweeps far beyond the permissible restraints on obscenity [and] thus applies to films that are protected by the First Amendment. [Nevertheless], it maintains that any movie containing nudity which is visible from a public place may be suppressed as a nuisance. . . .

"[The city's] primary argument is that it may protect its citizens against unwilling exposure to materials that may be offensive. Jacksonville's ordinance, however, does not protect citizens from all movies that might offend; rather it singles out films containing nudity, presumably because the lawmakers considered them especially offensive to passersby. [A] State or municipality may protect individual privacy by enacting reasonable time, place, and manner regulations applicable to all speech irrespective of content. [But] when government [undertakes] selec-

Problem is that it is — content based law

tively to shield the public from some kinds of speech on the ground that they are more offensive than others, the First Amendment strictly limits its power. [Such] selective exclusions have been upheld only when the speaker intrudes on the privacy of the home, see [*Rowan*], or the degree of captivity makes it impractical for the unwilling viewer or auditor to avoid exposure. See [*Lehman*]. [Absent such circumstances, however], the burden normally falls upon the viewer to 'avoid further bombardment of [his] sensibilities simply by averting [his] eyes.' [*Cohen.*] [The] limited privacy interest of persons on the public streets cannot justify this censorship of otherwise protected speech on the basis of its content. . . .

"[The city] also attempts to support the ordinance as an exercise of the city's undoubted police power to protect children. [But] the ordinance is not directed [only] against sexually explicit [nudity]. Rather, it sweepingly forbids display of all films containing *any* uncovered buttocks or breasts, irrespective of context or pervasiveness. [Clearly] all nudity cannot be deemed obscene even as to minors. [Thus], if Jacksonville's ordinance is intended to regulate expression accessible to minors it is overbroad in its proscription. . . .

"[Finally, the city attempts] to justify the ordinance [on the ground] that nudity on a drive-in movie screen distracts passing motorists, thus slowing the flow of traffic and increasing the likelihood of accidents. [But] the legislative classification is strikingly underinclusive. There is no reason to think that a wide variety of other scenes in the customary screen diet, ranging from soap opera to violence, would be any less distracting to the passing motorist."

Justice Douglas filed a concurring opinion.

Chief Justice Burger, joined by Justice Rehnquist, dissented: "Whatever validity the notion that passersby may protect their sensibilities by averting their eyes may have when applied to words printed on an individual's jacket, see [*Cohen*], it distorts reality to apply that notion to the outsize screen of a drive-in movie theater. Such screens [are] designed to [attract and hold] the attention of all observers. [It] is not unreasonable for lawmakers to believe that public nudity on a giant screen, visible at night to hundreds of [drivers], may have a tendency to divert attention from their task and cause accidents. [Moreover], those persons who legitimately desire to [view such films] are not foreclosed from doing so. [Such films may be] exhibited [in] indoor theaters [and in any] drive-in movie theater [whose] screen [is shielded] from public view. Thus, [the challenged] ordinance [is] not a restriction of any 'message.' [The] First Amendment interests involved in this case are trivial at best."

Justice White also dissented.

FCC v. Pacifica Foundation

438 U.S. 726 (1978)

MR. JUSTICE STEVENS delivered the opinion of the Court [all but Part IVB] and an opinion in which THE CHIEF JUSTICE and MR. JUSTICE REHNQUIST joined [Part IVB].

This case requires that we decide whether the Federal Communications Commission has any power to regulate a radio broadcast that is indecent but not obscene.

A satiric humorist named George Carlin recorded a 12-minute monologue entitled "Filthy Words" before a live audience in a California theater. He began by referring to his thoughts about "the words you couldn't say on the public, ah, airwaves, um, the ones you definitely wouldn't say, ever." He proceeded to list those words and repeat them over and over again in a variety of colloquialisms.[*] The transcript of the recording [indicates] frequent laughter from the audience.

At about 2 o'clock in the afternoon on Tuesday, October 30, 1973, a New York radio station, owned by respondent Pacifica Foundation, broadcast the "Filthy Words" monologue. A few weeks later a man, who stated that he had heard the broadcast while driving with his young son, wrote a letter complaining to the Commission. . . .

The complaint was forwarded to the station for comment. In its response, Pacifica explained that the monologue had been played during a program about contemporary society's attitude toward language and that, immediately before its broadcast, listeners had been advised that it included "sensitive language which might be regarded as offensive to some." Pacifica characterized George Carlin as "a significant social satirist" who "[is] not mouthing obscenities, [but] using words to satirize as harmless and essentially silly our attitudes towards those words." Pacifica stated that it was not aware of any other complaints about the broadcast. [The] Commission issued a declaratory order granting the complaint. [It] did not impose formal sanctions, but it did state that the [complaint] would be "associated with the station's license [file]." . . .

The Commission characterized the language used in the Carlin monologue as "patently offensive," though not necessarily obscene, and expressed the opinion that it should be regulated by principles analogous to those found in the law of nuisance where the

> law generally speaks to *channeling* behavior more than actually prohibiting it. [The] concept of "indecent" is intimately connected with the exposure of children to language that describes, in terms patently offensive as measured by contemporary community standards for the broadcast medium, sexual or excretory activities and organs, at times of the day when there is a reasonable risk that children may be in the audience. . . .

Applying these [considerations], the Commission concluded [that] the language as broadcast was indecent and prohibited by 18 U.S.C. [§]1464 [prohibiting the broadcasting of "obscene, indecent or profane language"]. . . .

The United States Court of Appeals for the District of Columbia Circuit reversed. [We reverse and thus sustain the Commission's action.]

IV

B

The question in this case is whether a broadcast of patently offensive words dealing with sex and excretion may be regulated because of its content.[18] Obscene

---

[*] [According to Carlin, there are seven such words: "shit, piss, fuck, cunt, cocksucker, motherfucker, and tits. Those are the ones that will curve your spine [and] grow hair on your hands." — EDS.]

18. A requirement that indecent language be avoided will have its primary effect on the form, rather than the content, of serious communication. There are few, if any, thoughts that cannot be expressed by the use of less offensive language. [Relocated footnote — EDS.]

materials have been denied the protection of the First Amendment because their content is so offensive to contemporary moral standards. [*Roth.*] But the fact that society may find speech offensive is not a sufficient reason for suppressing it. Indeed, if it is the speaker's opinion that gives offense, that consequence is a reason for according it constitutional protection. For it is a central tenet of the First Amendment that the government must remain neutral in the marketplace of ideas. If there were any reason to believe that the Commission's characterization of the Carlin monologue as offensive could be traced to its political content — or even to the fact that it satirized contemporary attitudes about four-letter words[22] — First Amendment protection might be required. But that is simply not this case. These words offend for the same reasons that obscenity offends.[23] Their place in the hierarchy of First Amendment values was aptly sketched by Mr. Justice Murphy when he said: "[S]uch utterances are no essential part of any exposition of ideas, and are of such slight social value as a step to truth that any benefit that may be derived from them is clearly outweighed by the social interest in order and morality." [*Chaplinsky.*]

Although these words ordinarily lack literary, political, or scientific value, they are not entirely outside the protection of the First Amendment. Some uses of even the most offensive words are unquestionably protected. [Indeed], we may assume, arguendo, that this monologue would be protected in other contexts. Nonetheless, the constitutional protection accorded to a communication containing such patently offensive sexual and excretory language need not be the same in every context. It is a characteristic of speech such as this that both its capacity to offend and its "social value," to use Mr. Justice Murphy's term, vary with the circumstances. Words that are commonplace in one setting are shocking in another. To paraphrase Mr. Justice Harlan, one occasion's lyric is another's vulgarity. Cf. [*Cohen*].[25]

In this case it is undisputed that the content of Pacifica's broadcast was "vulgar," "offensive," and "shocking." Because content of that character is not entitled to absolute constitutional protection under all circumstances, we must consider its context in order to determine whether the Commission's action was constitutionally permissible.

22. The monologue does present a point of view; it attempts to show that the words it uses are "harmless" and that our attitudes toward them are "essentially silly." [The] Commission objects, not to this point of view, but to the way in which it is expressed. The belief that these words are harmless does not necessarily confer a First Amendment privilege to use them while proselytizing, just as the conviction that obscenity is harmless does not license one to communicate that conviction by the indiscriminate distribution of an obscene leaflet.

23. The Commission stated: "Obnoxious, gutter language describing these matters has the effect of debasing and brutalizing human beings by reducing them to their mere bodily functions. . . ." Our society has a tradition of performing certain bodily functions in private, and of severely limiting the public exposure or discussion of such matters. Verbal or physical acts exposing those intimacies are offensive irrespective of any message that may accompany the exposure.

25. The importance of context is illustrated by the *Cohen* case. [So] far as the evidence showed, no one in the courthouse was offended by his jacket. . . .

In holding that criminal sanctions could not be imposed on Cohen for his political statement in a public place, the Court rejected the argument that his speech would offend unwilling viewers; it noted that "there was no evidence that persons powerless to avoid [his] conduct did in fact object to it." [In] contrast, in this case the Commission was responding to a listener's strenuous complaint, and Pacifica does not question its determination that this afternoon broadcast was likely to offend listeners. It should be noted that the Commission imposed a far more moderate penalty on Pacifica than the state court imposed on Cohen. Even the strongest civil penalty at the Commission's command does not include criminal prosecution. . . .

IV

C

We have long recognized that each medium of expression presents special First Amendment problems. [The] broadcast media have established a uniquely pervasive presence in the lives of all Americans. Patently offensive, indecent material presented over the airwaves confronts the citizen, not only in public, but also in the privacy of the home, where the individual's right to be left alone plainly outweighs the First Amendment rights of an intruder. [*Rowan.*] Because the broadcast audience is constantly tuning in and out, prior warnings cannot completely protect the listener or viewer from unexpected program content. To say that one may avoid further offense by turning off the radio when he hears indecent language is like saying that the remedy for an assault is to run away after the first blow.[27] . . .

[Moreover], broadcasting is uniquely accessible to children, even those too young to read. Although Cohen's written message might have been incomprehensible to a first grader, Pacifica's broadcast could have enlarged a child's vocabulary in an instant. Other forms of offensive expression may be withheld from the young without restricting the expression at its source. Bookstores and motion picture theaters, for example, may be prohibited from making indecent material available to children. [Citing *Ginsberg,* supra section D5.][28] The ease with which children may obtain access to broadcast material, coupled with the concerns recognized in *Ginsberg,* amply justify special treatment of indecent broadcasting.

It is appropriate, in conclusion, to emphasize the narrowness of our holding. This case does not involve a two-way radio conversation between a cab driver and a dispatcher, or a telecast of an Elizabethan comedy. We have not decided that an occasional expletive in either setting would justify any sanction or, indeed, that this broadcast would justify a criminal prosecution. The Commission's decision rested entirely on a nuisance rationale under which context is all-important. The concept requires consideration of a host of variables. The time of day was emphasized by the Commission. The content of the program in which the language is used will also affect the composition of the audience, and differences between radio, television, and perhaps closed-circuit transmissions, may also be relevant. As Mr. Justice Sutherland wrote, a "nuisance may be merely a right thing in the wrong place, — like a pig in the parlor instead of the barnyard." [We] simply hold that when the Commission finds that a pig has entered the parlor, the exercise of its regulatory power does not depend on proof that the pig is obscene.

[Reversed.]

Mr. Justice Powell, with whom Mr. Justice Blackmun joins, concurring in part and concurring in the judgment. . . .

27. Outside the home, the balance between the offensive speaker and the unwilling audience may sometimes tip in favor of the speaker, requiring the offended listener to turn away. See [*Erznoznik*].

28. The Commission's action does not by any means reduce adults to hearing only what is fit for children. Cf. [Butler v. Michigan, supra section D5]. Adults who feel the need may purchase tapes and records or go to theaters and nightclubs to hear these words. In fact, the Commission has not unequivocally closed even broadcasting to speech of this sort; whether broadcast audiences in the late evening contain so few children that playing this monologue would be permissible is an issue neither the Commission nor this Court has decided.

I [agree] with much that is said in Part IV of Mr. Justice Stevens' opinion, and with its conclusion that the Commission's holding in this case does not violate the First Amendment. Because I do not subscribe to all that is said in Part IV, however, I state my views separately. . . .

[The] Commission sought to "channel" the monologue to hours when the fewest unsupervised children would be exposed to it. [This] consideration provides strong support for the Commission's holding.

The Court has recognized society's right to "adopt more stringent controls on communicative materials available to youths than on those available to adults." [This] recognition stems in large part from the fact that "a child [is] not possessed of that full capacity for individual choice which is the presupposition of First Amendment guarantees." [At] the same time [offensive] speech may have a deeper and more lasting negative effect on a child than on an adult. . . .

The Commission properly held that [the] language involved in this case is as potentially degrading and harmful to children as representations of many erotic acts.

In most instances, the dissemination of this kind of speech to children may be limited without also limiting willing adults' access to it. [The] difficulty is that such a physical separation of the audience cannot be accomplished in the broadcast media. [In] my view, the Commission was entitled to give substantial weight to this difference [between the broadcast and other media] in reaching its decision in this case.

A second difference [is] that broadcasting [comes] directly into the home, the one place where people ordinarily have the right not to be assaulted by uninvited and offensive sights and sounds. [This] is not to say [that] the Commission has an unrestricted license to decide what speech, protected in other media, may be banned from the airwaves in order to protect unwilling adults from momentary exposure to it in their homes. Making the sensitive judgments required in these cases is not easy. But this responsibility has been reposed initially in the Commission, and its judgment is entitled to respect. [Moreover, the] Commission's holding does not prevent willing adults from purchasing Carlin's record, from attending his performances, or, indeed, from reading the transcript reprinted as an appendix to the Court's opinion. On its face, it does not prevent respondent Pacifica Foundation from broadcasting the monologue during late evening hours when fewer children are likely to be in the audience, nor from broadcasting discussions of the contemporary use of language at any time during the day. [On] the facts of this case, the Commission's order did not violate respondent's First Amendment rights. . . .

[I] do not join Part IV-B [of Justice Stevens' opinion] because I do not subscribe to the theory that the Justices of this Court are free generally to decide on the basis of its content which speech protected by the First Amendment is most "valuable" and hence deserving of the most protection, and which is less "valuable" and hence deserving of less protection. [In] my view, the result in this case does not turn on whether Carlin's monologue, viewed as a whole, or the words that constitute it, have more or less "value" than a candidate's campaign speech. This is a judgment for each person to make, not one for the judges to impose upon him.

The result turns instead on the unique characteristics of the broadcast media, combined with society's right to protect its children from speech generally agreed to be inappropriate for their years, and with the interest of unwilling adults in not being assaulted by such offensive speech in their homes. Moreover, I doubt whether today's decision will prevent any adult who wishes to receive Carlin's message in Carlin's own words from doing so. [These] are the grounds upon which I join the judgment of the Court as to Part IV.

Mr. Justice Brennan, with whom Mr. Justice Marshall joins, dissenting. . . .

I

[The] Court refuses to embrace the notion, completely antithetical to basic First Amendment values, that the degree of protection the First Amendment affords protected speech varies with the social value ascribed to that speech by five Members of this Court. [Moreover], all Members of the Court agree that the Carlin monologue [does] not fall within one of the categories of speech, such as "fighting words" [or] obscenity, [that] is totally without First Amendment protection. [Nevertheless] a majority of the Court [finds] that, on the facts of this case, the FCC is not constitutionally barred from imposing sanctions on Pacifica for its airing of the Carlin monologue. This majority apparently believes that the FCC's disapproval of Pacifica's afternoon broadcast of Carlin's "Dirty Words" recording is a permissible time, place, and manner regulation. . . .

A

Without question, the privacy interests of an individual in his home are substantial and deserving of significant protection. [But in] finding these interests sufficient to justify the content regulation of protected speech [the] Court misconceives the nature of the privacy interests involved where an individual voluntarily chooses to admit radio communications into his home [and] it ignores the constitutionally protected interests of both those who wish to transmit and those who desire to receive broadcasts that many — including the FCC and this Court — might find offensive.

"The ability of government, consonant with the Constitution, to shut off discourse solely to protect others from hearing it is . . . dependent upon a showing that substantial privacy interests are being invaded in an essentially intolerable manner. . . ." [Cohen.] [A]n individual's actions in switching on and listening to communications transmitted over the public airways and directed to the public at large do not implicate fundamental privacy interests, even when engaged in within the home. Instead, [these] actions are more properly viewed as a decision to take part, if only as a listener, in an ongoing public discourse. [Moreover], the very fact that [the individual's privacy] interests are threatened only by a radio broadcast precludes any intolerable invasion of privacy; for unlike other intrusive modes of communication, such as sound trucks, "[t]he radio can be turned off." . . .

The [Court] fails to accord proper weight to the interests of listeners who wish to hear broadcasts the FCC deems offensive. It permits majoritarian tastes completely to preclude a protected message from entering the homes of a receptive, unoffended minority. No decision of this Court supports such a result. . . .

B . . .

[The] government unquestionably has a special interest in the well-being of children and consequently "can adopt more stringent controls on communicative materials available to youths than on those available to adults." [But] "[s]peech that is neither obscene as to youths[2] nor subject to some other legitimate proscription cannot be suppressed solely to protect the young from ideas or images that a legislative body thinks unsuitable for them." [*Erznoznik*.] [Thus, today's] result violates in spades the principle of Butler v. Michigan, [supra section D1, that government may not] "reduce the adult population [to] reading only what is fit for children." . . .

C

[T]he factors relied on by [Justices Stevens and Powell are] plagued by a common failing: the lack of principled limits on their use as a basis for FCC censorship. [My] Brother Powell is content to rely upon the judgment of the Commission while my Brother Stevens deems it prudent to rely on this Court's ability accurately to assess the worth of various kinds of speech.[6] [I] would place the responsibility and the right to weed worthless and offensive communications from the public airways where it belongs and where, until today, it resided: in a public free to choose those communications worthy of its attention from a marketplace unsullied by the censor's hand.

II . . .

My Brother Stevens [takes] comfort in his observation[s] that "[a] requirement that indecent language be avoided will have its primary effect on the form, rather than the content, of serious communication," [and] that "[t]here are few, if any, thoughts that cannot be expressed by the use of less offensive language." [The] idea that the content of a message [can] be divorced from the words that are the vehicle for its expression is transparently fallacious. A given word may have a unique capacity to capsule an idea, evoke an emotion, or conjure up an image. [Justice] Harlan, speaking for the Court, recognized [in *Cohen*] that a speaker's choice of words cannot surgically be separated from the ideas he desires to express

2. Even if the monologue appealed to the prurient interest of minors, it would not be obscene as to them unless, as to them, "the work, taken as a whole, lacks serious literary, artistic, political, or scientific value." [*Miller.*] [Relocated footnote. — EDS.]

6. Although ultimately dependent upon the outcome of review in this Court, the approach taken by my Brother Stevens would not appear to tolerate the FCC's suppression of any speech, such as political speech, falling within the core area of First Amendment concern. The same, however, cannot be said of the approach taken by my Brother Powell, which, on its face, permits the Commission to censor even political speech if it is sufficiently offensive to community standards. A result more contrary to rudimentary First Amendment principles is difficult to imagine.

[and that] even if an alternative phrasing may communicate a speaker's abstract ideas as effectively as those words he is forbidden to use, it is doubtful that the sterilized message will convey the emotion that is an essential part of so many communications. . . .

[Moreover, the suggestion] that "[a]dults who feel the need may purchase tapes and records or go to theaters and nightclubs to hear [the tabooed] words," displays] both a sad insensitivity to the fact that these alternatives involve the expenditure of money, time, and effort that many of those wishing to hear Mr. Carlin's message may not be able to afford, and a naive innocence of the reality that in many cases, the medium may well be the message. . . .

WEALTH

III . . .

[There] runs throughout the opinions of my Brothers Powell and Stevens [a] depressing inability to appreciate that in our land of cultural pluralism, there are many who think, act, and talk differently from the Members of this Court, and who do not share their fragile sensibilities. It is only an acute ethnocentric myopia that enables the Court to approve the censorship of communications solely because of the words they contain. . . .

Today's decision will thus have its greatest impact [on] persons who do not share the Court's view as to which words or expressions are acceptable and who [express] themselves using words that may be regarded as offensive by those from different socio-economic backgrounds. In this context, the Court's decision may be seen for what, in the broader perspective, it really is: another of the dominant culture's inevitable efforts to force those groups who do not share its mores to conform to its way of thinking, acting, and speaking. . . .

Mr. Justice Stewart, with whom Mr. Justice Brennan, Mr. Justice White, and Mr. Justice Marshall join, dissenting. . . .

[I] think that "indecent" should properly be read as meaning no more than "obscene." Since the Carlin monologue concededly was not "obscene," I believe that the Commission lacked statutory authority to ban it. . . .

Young v. American Mini-Theatres
427 U.S. 50 (1976)

Mr. Justice Stevens delivered the opinion of the Court.

Zoning ordinances adopted by the city of Detroit [require] that [adult] theaters be dispersed. Specifically, an adult theater may not be located within 1,000 feet of any two other "regulated uses" or within 500 feet of a residential area.[3]

3. In addition to adult motion picture theaters and "mini" theaters, which contain less than 50 seats, the regulated uses include adult bookstores; cabarets (group "D"); establishments for the sale of beer or intoxicating liquor for consumption on the premises; hotels or motels; pawnshops; pool or billiard halls; public lodging houses; secondhand stores; shoeshine parlors; and taxi dance halls.

[A] theater [is classified] as "adult" [if it] is used to present "material distinguished or characterized by an emphasis on matter depicting, describing or relating to 'Specified Sexual Activities' or 'Specified Anatomical Areas.' "[4]

[These] ordinances were amendments to an "Anti-Skid Row Ordinance" which had been adopted 10 years earlier. [In] the opinion of urban planners and real estate experts who supported the ordinances, the location of several [regulated uses] in the same neighborhood tends to attract an undesirable quantity and quality of transients, adversely affects property values, causes an increase in crime, especially prostitution, and encourages residents and businesses to move elsewhere.

Respondents, [two] operators of adult motion picture theaters, [sought] a declaratory judgment that the ordinances were unconstitutional and an injunction against their enforcement. [The Court of Appeals held the ordinances unconstitutional. We reverse.]

I

[Respondents] claim that the ordinances are too vague. They [argue] that they cannot determine how much [focus on "specific sexual"] activity may be permissible before the exhibition is "characterized by an emphasis" on such matter. . . .

We find it unnecessary to consider the validity of [this argument]. For even if there may be some uncertainty about the effect of the ordinances on other litigants, they are unquestionably applicable to these respondents. The record indicates that both theaters propose to offer adult fare on a regular basis. [It] is clear, therefore, that any element of vagueness in these ordinances has not affected these respondents. . . .

Because the ordinances affect communication protected by the First Amendment, respondents argue that they may raise the vagueness issue even though there is no uncertainty about the impact of the ordinances on their own rights. [This doctrine is inapplicable, however, where] the statute's deterrent effect on legitimate expression is not "both real and substantial." [Here, we] are not persuaded that the Detroit zoning ordinances will have a significant deterrent effect on the exhibition of films protected by the First Amendment, [for] there is surely a less vital interest in the uninhibited exhibition of material that is on the borderline between pornography and artistic expression than in the free dissemination of ideas of social and political significance. [We therefore] think this is an inappropriate case in which to adjudicate the hypothetical claims of persons not before the Court. . . .

---

4. These terms are defined as follows:

> For the purpose of this Section, "Specified Sexual Activities" is defined as:
> 1. Human Genitals in a state of sexual stimulation or arousal;
> 2. Acts of human masturbation, sexual intercourse or sodomy;
> 3. Fondling or other erotic touching of human genitals, pubic region, buttock or female breast.
> And "Specified Anatomical Areas" is defined as:
> 1. Less than completely and opaquely covered: (a) human genitals, pubic region, (b) buttock, and (c) female breast below a point immediately above the top of the areola; and
> 2. Human male genitals in a discernibly turgid state, even if completely and opaquely covered.

II

The ordinances are not challenged on the ground that they impose a limit on the total number of adult theaters which may operate in the city of Detroit. There is no claim that distributors or exhibitors of adult films are denied access to the market or, conversely, that the viewing public is unable to satisfy its appetite for sexually explicit fare. Viewed as an entity, the market for this commodity is essentially unrestrained.

[Moreover,] we have held that [a] municipality [whose regulations do not restrain the market for speech] may control the location of theaters as well as the location of other commercial [establishments]. [Thus,] apart from the fact that the ordinances treat adult theaters differently from other theaters and the fact that the classification is predicated on the content of material shown in the respective theaters, the regulation of the place where such films may be exhibited does not offend the First Amendment. We turn, therefore, to the question whether the classification is [unconstitutional because it turns on content].

III

A remark attributed to Voltaire characterizes our zealous adherence to the principle that the government may not tell the citizen what he may or may not say. Referring to a suggestion that the violent overthrow of tyranny might be legitimate, he said: "I disapprove of what you say, but I will defend to the death your right to say it." The essence of that comment has been repeated time after time in our decisions invalidating attempts by the government to impose selective controls upon the dissemination of ideas. . . .

[As] we said in [Mosley v. City of Chicago, 408 U.S. 92 (1972)]: ". . . above all else, the First Amendment means that government has no power to restrict expression because of its message, its ideas, its subject matter, or its content. . . ."

This statement, and others to the same effect, read literally and without regard for the facts of the case in which it was made, would absolutely preclude any regulation of expressive activity predicated in whole or in part on the content of the communication. But [when] we review this Court's actual adjudications in the First Amendment area, we find [that the] question whether speech is, or is not, protected by the First Amendment often depends on the content of the speech. [Citing, e.g., "the line between permissible advocacy and impermissible incitation to crime or violence," the "fighting words" doctrine, the distinction between speech about public officials and speech about private figures in the libel context, the commercial speech doctrine, and the Court's treatment of obscenity.]

[The Detroit ordinances draw a line] on the basis of content without violating the government's paramount obligation of neutrality in its regulation of protected communication. For the regulation of the places where sexually explicit films may be exhibited is unaffected by whatever social, political, or philosophical message a film may be intended to communicate; whether a motion picture ridicules or characterizes one point of view or another, the effect of the ordinances is exactly the same.

Moreover, even though we recognize that the First Amendment will not tolerate the total suppression of erotic materials that have some arguably artistic value, it is manifest that society's interest in protecting this type of expression is of a wholly different, and lesser, magnitude than the interest in untrammeled political debate that inspired Voltaire's immortal comment. Whether political oratory or philosophical discussion moves us to applaud or to despise what is said, every schoolchild can understand why our duty to defend the right to speak remains the same. But few of us would march our sons and daughters off to war to preserve the citizen's right to see "Specified Sexual Activities" exhibited in the theaters of our choice. Even though the First Amendment protects communication in this area from total suppression, we hold that the State may legitimately use the content of these materials as the basis for placing them in a different classification from other motion pictures.

The remaining question is whether the line drawn by these ordinances is justified by the city's interest in preserving the character of its neighborhoods. [The] record discloses a factual basis for the Common Council's conclusion that this kind of restriction will have the desired effect.[34] It is not our function to appraise the wisdom of its decision to require adult theaters to be separated rather than concentrated in the same areas. In either event, the city's interest in attempting to preserve the quality of urban life is one that must be accorded high respect. Moreover, the city must be allowed a reasonable opportunity to experiment with solutions to admittedly serious problems.

Since what is ultimately at stake is nothing more than a limitation on the place where adult films may be exhibited,[35] even though the determination of whether a particular film fits that characterization turns on the nature of its content, we conclude that the city's interest in the present and future character of its neighborhoods adequately supports its classification of motion pictures. . . .

Reversed.

Mr. Justice Powell, concurring.

Although I agree with much of what is said in the Court's opinion, and concur in Parts I and II, my approach to the resolution of this case is sufficiently different to prompt me to write separately.[1] I view the case as presenting an example of innovative land-use regulation, implicating First Amendment concerns only incidentally and to a limited extent. . . .

34. The Common Council's determination was that a concentration of "adult" movie theaters causes the area to deteriorate and become a focus of crime, effects which are not attributable to theaters showing other types of films. It is this secondary effect which these zoning ordinances attempt to avoid, not the dissemination of "offensive" speech. In contrast, in [Erznoznik] the justifications offered by the city rested primarily on the city's interest in protecting its citizens from exposure to unwanted, "offensive" speech. The only secondary effect relied on to support that ordinance was the impact on traffic — an effect which might be caused by a distracting open-air movie even if it did not exhibit nudity.

35. The situation would be quite different if the ordinance had the effect of suppressing, or greatly restricting access to, lawful speech. Here, however, the District Court specifically found that "[t]he Ordinances do not affect the operation of existing establishments but only the location of new ones. There are myriad locations in the City of Detroit which must be over 1000 feet from existing regulated establishments. This burden on First Amendment rights is slight." . . .

1. I do not think we need reach, nor am I inclined to agree with, the holding in Part III (and supporting discussion) that nonobscene, erotic materials may be treated differently under First Amendment principles from other forms of protected expression. I do not consider the conclusions in Part I of the opinion to depend on distinctions between protected speech.

[The] primary concern of the free speech guarantee is that there be full opportunity for expression in all of its varied forms to convey a desired message. Vital to this concern is the corollary that there be full opportunity for everyone to receive the message. . . .

The inquiry for First Amendment purposes [thus] prompts essentially two inquiries: (i) Does the ordinance impose any content limitation on the creators of adult movies or their ability to make them available to whom they desire, and (ii) does it restrict in any significant way the viewing of these movies by those who desire to see them? On the record in this case, these inquiries must be answered in the negative. At most the impact of the ordinance on these interests is incidental and minimal.[2] [The] ordinance is addressed only to the places at which this type of expression may be presented, a restriction that does not interfere with content. Nor is there any significant overall curtailment of adult movie presentations, or the opportunity for a message to reach an audience. . . .

In these circumstances, it is appropriate to analyze the permissibility of Detroit's action under the four-part test of United States v. O'Brien, [infra section E3].* Under that test, a governmental regulation is sufficiently justified, despite its incidental impact upon First Amendment interests, "if it is within the constitutional power of the Government; if it furthers an important or substantial governmental interest; if the governmental interest is unrelated to the suppression of free expression; and if the incidental restriction [on] First Amendment freedoms is no greater than is essential to the furtherance of that interest." . . .

There [is] no question that the ordinance was within the power of the Detroit Common Council to enact. [Nor] is there doubt that the interests furthered by this ordinance are both important and substantial. [Moreover, it is clear] that Detroit has not embarked on an effort to suppress free expression. [Indeed] it is not seriously challenged [that] the governmental interest prompting the [ordinance] was wholly unrelated to any suppression of free expression.[4] Nor is there reason to question that the degree of incidental encroachment upon such expression was the minimum necessary to further the purpose of the ordinance. The evidence presented to the Common Council indicated that the urban deterioration was threatened [only] by a concentration of those [movie theaters] that elected to specialize in adult movies. The case would present a different situation had Detroit brought within the ordinance types of theaters that had not been shown to contribute to the deterioration of surrounding areas.[6]

---

2. The communication involved here is not a kind in which the content or effectiveness of the message depends in some measure upon where or how it is conveyed. . . .

There is no suggestion that [either theatre is] anything more than a commercial purveyor. They do not profess to convey their own personal messages through the movies they show, so that the only communication involved is that contained in the movies themselves. . . .

* [In O'Brien the Court upheld the constitutionality of a conviction for burning a draft card. — EDS.]

4. [The] Common Council simply acted to protect the economic integrity of large areas of its city against the effects of a predictable interaction between a concentration of certain businesses and the responses of people in the area. If it had been concerned with restricting the message purveyed by adult theaters, it would have tried to close them or restrict their number rather than circumscribe their choice as to location.

6. In my view Mr. Justice Stewart's dissent misconceives the issue in this case by insisting that it involves an impermissible time, place, and manner restriction based on the content of expression. It involves nothing of the kind. We have here merely a decision by the city to treat certain movie theaters differently because they have markedly different effects upon their surroundings. . . .

The dissenting opinions perceive support for their position in [*Erznoznik*]. I believe this perception is a clouded one. [The] ordinance in *Erznoznik* was a misconceived attempt directly to regulate the content of expression. The Detroit zoning ordinance, in contrast, affects expression only incidentally and in further-ance of governmental interests wholly unrelated to the regulation of expression. At least as applied to respondents, it does not offend the First Amendment. . . .

MR. JUSTICE STEWART, with whom MR. JUSTICE BRENNAN, MR. JUSTICE MAR-SHALL, and MR. JUSTICE BLACKMUN join, dissenting. . . .

This case does not involve a simple zoning ordinance, or a content-neutral time, place, and manner restriction, or a regulation of obscene expression or other speech that is entitled to less than the full protection of the First Amend-ment. The kind of expression at issue here is no doubt objectionable to some, but that fact does not diminish its protected status any more than did the particular content of the "offensive" expression in [*Erznoznik or Cohen*].

What this case does involve is the constitutional permissibility of selective interference with protected speech whose content is thought to produce distaste-ful effects. It is elementary that a prime function of the First Amendment is to guard against just such interference. By refusing to invalidate Detroit's ordinance the Court rides roughshod over cardinal principles of First Amendment law, which require that time, place, and manner regulations that affect protected expression be content neutral except in the limited context of a captive or juvenile audience. In place of these principles the Court invokes a concept wholly alien to the First Amendment. Since "few of us would march our sons and daughters off to war to preserve the citizen's right to see 'Specified Sexual Activities' exhibited in the theaters of our choice," [the] Court implies that these films are not entitled to the full protection of the Constitution. This stands "Voltaire's immortal com-ment," [on] its head. For if the guarantees of the First Amendment were reserved for expression that more than a "few of us" would take up arms to defend, then the right of free expression would be defined and circumscribed by current popu-lar opinion. The guarantees of the Bill of Rights were designed to protect against precisely such majoritarian limitations on individual liberty.[6] . . .

I can only interpret today's decision as an aberration. [Indeed, the] factual parallels between [*Erznoznik*] and this [case] are striking. There, as here, the ordinance did not forbid altogether the "distasteful" expression but merely re-quired an alteration in the physical setting of the forum. There, as here, the city's principal asserted interest was in minimizing the "undesirable" effects of speech having a particular content. And, most significantly, the particular content of the restricted speech at issue in *Erznoznik* precisely parallels the content restriction embodied [in] Detroit's definition of "Specified Anatomical Areas." [In] short, *Erznoznik* is almost on "all fours" with this case.

The Court must never forget that the consequences of rigorously enforcing the guarantees of the First Amendment are frequently unpleasant. Much speech that seems to be of little or no value will enter the marketplace of ideas, threatening

6. [The] Court stresses that Detroit's content-based regulatory system does not preclude altogether the display of sexually oriented films. But [this] is constitutionally irrelevant, for "'one is not to have the exercise of his liberty of expression in appropriate places abridged on the plea that it may be exercised in some other place.'" [Quoting Schneider v. State, 308 U.S. 147 (1939), infra section E1.]

the quality of our social discourse and, more generally, the serenity of our lives. But that is the price to be paid for constitutional freedom.*

Note: Young and Pacifica

1. *Erotic speech.* Is Justice Stevens's plurality opinion in *Young* an unprincipled "aberration" that "rides roughshod over cardinal principles of First Amendment law," or is it merely a belated yet sensible recognition of the obvious — "that society's interest in protecting [sexually oriented] expression is of a wholly different, and lesser, magnitude than the interest in untrammeled political debate"? Is erotic speech entitled to greater protection than commercial speech?

2. *Nude dancing: the* Schad *case.* In Schad v. Borough of Mt. Ephraim, 452 U.S. 61 (1981), appellants, who operated an adult bookstore, installed a coin-operated mechanism permitting a customer to watch a live dancer, usually nude, performing behind a glass panel. Appellants were convicted of violating a Mount Ephraim zoning ordinance prohibiting all live entertainment within the borough. The Court, in an opinion by Justice White, held the ordinance invalid. The Court noted that, as a form of entertainment, "nude dancing is not without its First Amendment protections from official regulation." The Court found it unnecessary, however, to define precisely how much "First Amendment protection should be extended to nude dancing," holding instead that the ordinance's prohibition on *all* live entertainment was constitutionally overbroad. It explained that "this case is not controlled by *Young*," for unlike the situation in *Young*, there was "no evidence" in *Schad* "that the kind of entertainment appellants wish to provide is available in reasonably nearby areas."

Chief Justice Burger, joined by Justice Rehnquist, dissented. Without deciding the overbreadth question, Burger maintained that, "as applied, the ordinance is valid." "Citizens," he argued, "should be free to choose to shape their community so that it embodies their conception of the 'decent life.'" "Here, as in [*Young*], the zoning ordinance imposes a minimal intrusion on genuine rights of expression," for "Mount Ephraim is a small community on the periphery of two major urban centers where this kind of entertainment may be found acceptable." Moreover, Burger emphasized, the borough "has not attempted to suppress the point of view of anyone or to stifle any category of ideas." Burger concluded: "To say that there is a First Amendment right to impose every form of expression on every community, including the kind of 'expression' involved here, is sheer nonsense. [To] invoke the First Amendment to protect the activity involved in this case trivializes and demeans that great Amendment."

3. *Nude dancing: the* LaRue *case.* In California v. LaRue, 409 U.S. 109 (1972), the Court considered the constitutionality of a series of administrative regulations restricting the type of entertainment that could be presented in bars and nightclubs that were licensed to serve liquor. The regulations, which were premised on administrative findings that explicitly sexual performances in establishments licensed to sell liquor tended to promote rape and prostitution and often resulted in the commission by customers of unlawful public acts of sexuality, prohibited on

---

* [A dissenting opinion of Justice Blackmun, joined by Justices Brennan, Stewart, and Marshall, focusing on the vagueness issue, is omitted. — EDS.]

licensed premises the "actual or simulated 'displaying of the pubic hair, anus, vulva or genitals,'" the "actual or simulated 'touching, caressing or fondling of the breast, buttocks, anus or genitals,'" and the "performance of acts, or simulated acts, of 'sexual intercourse, masturbation, sodomy, bestiality, oral copulation, flagellation or any sexual acts which are prohibited by law.'"

The Court, in an opinion by Justice Rehnquist, upheld the regulations. The Court conceded that "theatrical productions are within the protection of the First [Amendment]" and that the regulations "would proscribe some forms of visual presentation that would not be found obscene." It noted, however, that "as the mode of expression moves from the printed page to the commission of public acts that may themselves violate valid penal statutes, the scope of permissible state regulations significantly increases," and that here the performances "partake more of gross sexuality than of communication." The Court emphasized, moreover, that the state "has not forbidden these performances across the board," but "has merely proscribed [them] in establishments that it licenses to sell liquor." This limitation was "critical," for "the broad sweep of the Twenty-first Amendment has been recognized as conferring something more than the normal state authority over public health, welfare, and morals." The Court thus concluded that, given the rationality of the state's conclusion "that certain sexual performances and the dispensation of liquor by the drink ought not to occur [on the same premises]," and the special "presumption in favor of the validity of the state regulation in this area that the Twenty-first Amendment requires, we cannot hold that the regulations on their face violate the Federal Constitution." Justices Douglas, Brennan, and Marshall dissented. See also New York State Liquor Authority v. Bellanca, 452 U.S. 714 (1981) (upholding a statute prohibiting nude dancing in establishments licensed by the state to sell liquor for on-premises consumption).

4. Cohen *and* Pacifica. Does *Cohen* survive *Pacifica?* Note that *Pacifica* appears to separate the emotive and cognitive aspects of speech — a separation that is at least in tension with *Cohen.* Consider Farber, Civilizing Public Discourse: An Essay on Professor Bickel, Justice Harlan, and the Enduring Significance of *Cohen v. California,* 1980 Duke L.J. 283, 294:

> [The justifications for the restriction in *Pacifica*] turned on the context of the mid-afternoon broadcast, whereas Justice Harlan found that none of the possible context-related justifications were properly presented in *Cohen.* Instead, the issue [Harlan] did find to be properly presented — and therefore the only issue he decided — was whether the state, acting as a paternalistic guardian of public morality, could ban the use of certain words in *all* contexts. Because *Pacifica* dealt with context and *Cohen* dealt only with content, *Cohen* contributed little to the issue presented in *Pacifica.*

Consider also Schauer, Categories and the First Amendment: A Play in Three Acts, 34 Vand. L. Rev. 265, 292-295 (1981):

> After *Young* and *Pacifica,* [it] certainly appears that offensive speech is a subcategory in which restrictions will be permitted so long as those restrictions do not have the effect of a de facto prohibition on dissemination of the material at issue. This subcategory, however, is far more troublesome than the subcategories for either commercial speech or defamation, [for] offensiveness simpliciter as a category is hardly

consistent with most of the antimajoritarian premises of the first amendment, [a] subcategory based [on] offensiveness [is] notoriously vague, [and such a] category is so inherently and extremely indeterminate and so linguistically ill-defined [that] a serious risk exists that the category will in practice be misapplied.

Note: "Low" Value Speech — Final Thoughts

Has the doctrine of "low" value speech injected the Court "into value judgments [foreclosed] to it by the basic theory of the First Amendment"? T. Emerson, The System of Free Expression 326 (1970). Reconsider the various categories of "low" or arguably "low" value expression — express incitement, fighting words, threats, technical military information, false statements of fact, group defamation, nonnewsworthy invasions of privacy, commercial speech, obscenity, offensive language, offensive sexually oriented expression. Has the Court developed a coherent theory of first amendment "value"? What considerations are relevant in deciding whether particular categories of expression constitute "low" value speech?

How would you assess the overall impact of the "low" value doctrine? Have any of the restrictions upheld under this doctrine seriously threatened the system of free expression? Consider the following evaluations: (a) The "low" value doctrine demonstrates the sharply limited efficacy of judicial controls on censorship by the majority, for it defines speech as unworthy of protection in precisely those cases where it most seriously threatens majority values and where protection is thus most needed. (b) The "low" value doctrine has served a salutary function, for it has operated as a critical "safety valve," enabling the Court to deal sensibly with somewhat harmful but relatively insignificant speech without running the risk of diluting the protection accorded expression at the very heart of the guarantee.

E.   CONTENT-NEUTRAL RESTRICTIONS: LIMITATIONS ON THE MEANS OF COMMUNICATION

Content-neutral restrictions limit expression without regard to its content. They turn neither on their face nor as applied on the content or communicative impact of speech. Such restrictions encompass a broad spectrum of limitations on expressive activity, ranging, for example, from a prohibition on the use of loudspeakers, to a ban on billboards, to a limitation on campaign contributions, to a prohibition on the mutilation of draft cards.

To what extent, and in what manner, do content-neutral restrictions implicate the concerns and values underlying the first amendment? How do they differ in this regard from content-based restrictions? Should the doctrines devised to govern content-based restrictions also govern content-neutral restrictions? In exploring these and related questions, this section begins with a search for general principles and then examines four specific problem areas: the right to a public forum; symbolic speech; regulation of the electoral process; and the extent to which other activities, such as litigation and association, constitute "speech" within the meaning of the first amendment.

1. General Principles

SCHNEIDER v. **STATE**, 308 U.S. 147 (1939): In *Schneider* the Court decided a series of companion cases involving the constitutionality of various municipal ordinances restricting leafleting. In one case, for example, the appellants distributed leaflets announcing a protest meeting. Although appellants themselves did not scatter any of the leaflets, some of those to whom the leaflets were handed threw them on the sidewalk and street. Appellants were convicted of violating an ordinance prohibiting any person to leaflet in "any street or way." The Court held the ordinance invalid. Justice Roberts delivered the opinion:

"Municipal authorities, as trustees for the public, have the duty to keep their communities' streets open and available for movement of people and property, the primary purpose to which the streets are dedicated. So long as legislation to this end does not abridge the constitutional liberty of one rightfully upon the street to impart information through speech or the distribution of literature, it may lawfully regulate the conduct of those using the streets. For example, a person could not exercise this liberty by taking his stand in the middle of a crowded street, contrary to traffic regulations, and maintain his position to the stoppage of all traffic; [nor] does the guarantee of freedom of speech or of the press deprive a municipality of power to enact regulations against throwing literature broadcast in the streets. Prohibition of such conduct would not abridge the constitutional liberty since such activity bears no necessary relationship to the freedom to speak, write, print or distribute information or opinion.

"This court has characterized the freedom of speech and freedom of press as fundamental personal rights and liberties. [Mere] legislative preferences or beliefs respecting matters of public convenience may well support regulation directed at other personal activities, but be insufficient to justify such as diminishes the exercise of rights so vital to the maintenance of democratic institutions. And so, as cases arise, the delicate and difficult task falls upon the courts to weigh the circumstances and to appraise the substantiality of the reasons advanced in support of the regulation of the free enjoyment of the rights.

"[The] legislation under attack [is designed to prevent littering]. Although the alleged offenders were not charged with themselves scattering paper in the streets, their convictions were sustained upon the theory that distribution by them [resulted] in such littering. We are of opinion that the purpose to keep the streets clean and of good appearance is insufficient to justify an ordinance which prohibits a person rightfully on a public street from handing literature to one willing to receive it. Any burden imposed upon the city authorities in cleaning and caring for the streets as an indirect consequence of such distribution results from the constitutional protection of the freedom of speech and press. This constitutional protection does not deprive a city of all power to prevent street littering. There are obvious methods of preventing littering. Amongst these is the punishment of those who actually throw papers on the streets. . . .

"It is suggested that the Los Angeles and Worcester ordinances are valid because their operation is limited to streets and alleys and leaves persons free to distribute printed matter in other places. [But] the streets are natural and proper places for the dissemination of information and opinion; and one is not to have the exercise of his liberty of expression in appropriate places abridged on the plea that it may be exercised in some other place."

Justice McReynolds dissented.

MARTIN v. CITY OF STRUTHERS, 319 U.S. 141 (1943): Appellant, a Jehovah's Witness, went to the homes of strangers, knocking on doors and ringing doorbells in order to distribute leaflets advertising a religious meeting. She was convicted of violating a municipal ordinance prohibiting any person "to ring the door bell [or] otherwise summon the inmate [of] any residence [for] the purpose of [distributing] handbills." The Court held the ordinance invalid. Justice Black delivered the opinion of the Court:

"We are faced [with] the necessity of weighing the conflicting interests of the appellant in the civil rights she claims, as well as the right of the individual householder to determine whether he is willing to receive her message, against the interest of the community which by this ordinance offers to protect the interests of all its citizens, whether particular citizens want that protection or not. [In] considering legislation which thus limits the dissemination of knowledge, we [must] 'weigh the circumstances [and] appraise the substantiality of the reasons advanced in support of the regulation.' [*Schneider.*] . . .

"While door to door distributors of literature may be either a nuisance or a blind for criminal activities, they may also be useful members of society engaged in the dissemination of ideas in accordance with the best tradition of free discussion. The widespread use of this method of communication by many groups espousing various causes attests its major importance. [Door] to door distribution of circulars is essential to the poorly financed causes of little people.

"Freedom to distribute information to every citizen whenever he desires to receive it is so clearly vital to the preservation of a free society that, putting aside reasonable police and health regulations of time and manner of distribution, it must be fully preserved. [Traditionally] the American law punishes persons who enter onto the property of another after having been warned by the owner to keep off. [Thus], the city may make it an offense for any person to ring the bell of a householder who has appropriately indicated that he is unwilling to be disturbed. This or any similar regulation leaves the decision as to whether distributors of literature may lawfully call at a home where it belongs — with the homeowner himself. [Because] the dangers of distribution can so easily be controlled by traditional legal methods, [the challenged ordinance] can serve no purpose but that forbidden by the Constitution, the naked restriction of the dissemination of ideas."

Justice Frankfurter filed a separate opinion: "[The] ordinance before us [penalizes only] the distribution of 'literature.' [It does not penalize door-to-door canvassing for other purposes, such as the sale of pots and pans.] The Court's opinion leaves one in doubt whether prohibition of [*all* door-to-door canvassing] would be deemed an infringement of free speech. It would be fantastic to suggest that a city has power [to] forbid house-to-house canvassing generally, but the Constitution prohibits the inclusion in such prohibition of door-to-door [distribution of] printed matter."

Justice Reed dissented.

KOVACS v. COOPER, 336 U.S. 77 (1949): In *Kovacs* the Court, in a five-to-four decision, upheld a city ordinance prohibiting any person to use any sound truck or other instrument that emits "loud and raucous noises" on any public street. Justice Reed, joined by Chief Justice Vinson and Justice Burton, wrote a plurality opinion: "City streets are recognized as a normal place for the exchange of [ideas]. But this does not mean the freedom is beyond all control. We think it is a permissible exercise of legislative discretion to bar sound [trucks], amplified to a loud and raucous volume, from the public ways of municipalities. On the business [streets] such distractions would be dangerous to traffic at all hours useful for the dissemination of information, and in the residential thoroughfares the quiet and tranquility so desirable for city dwellers would likewise be at the mercy of advocates of particular religious, social or political persuasions. . . .

"The right of free speech is guaranteed every citizen that he may reach the minds of willing listeners and to do so there must be opportunity to win their attention. [But the] freedom of speech [does] not require legislators to be insensible to claims by citizens to comfort and convenience. To enforce freedom of speech in disregard of the rights of others would be harsh and arbitrary in itself. That more people may be more easily and cheaply reached by sound trucks [is] not enough to call forth constitutional protection for what those charged with public welfare reasonably think is a nuisance when easy means of publicity are open. [The ordinance does not] restrict the communication of ideas or discussion of issues by the human voice, by newspapers, by pamphlets, by dodgers. We think that the need for reasonable protection in the homes or business houses from the distracting noises of vehicles equipped with such sound amplifying devices justifies the ordinance."

Justice Frankfurter concurred in the result. At the outset, Frankfurter referred to his earlier opinion in Saia v. New York, 334 U.S. 558 (1948), in which he had maintained that "modern devices for amplifying the range and volume of the voice [afford] easy, too easy, opportunities for aural aggression. If uncontrolled, the result is intrusion into cherished privacy. [Surely] there is not a constitutional right to force unwilling people to listen." Frankfurter thus concluded in *Kovacs* that "So long as a legislature does not prescribe what ideas may be noisily expressed, [it] is not for us to supervise the limits it may impose in safeguarding the steadily narrowing opportunities for serenity and reflection." Justice Jackson also concurred in the result.

Justice Black, joined by Justices Douglas and Rutledge, dissented: "The basic premise of the First Amendment is that all present instruments of communication, as well as others that inventive genius may bring into being, shall be free from governmental censorship or prohibition. Laws which hamper the free use of some instruments of communication thereby favor competing channels. Thus, [laws] like [this] ordinance can give an overpowering influence to views of owners of legally favored instruments of communication. [There] are many people who have ideas that they wish to disseminate but who do not have enough money to own or control publishing plants, newspapers, radios, moving picture studios, or chains of show places. [Transmission] of ideas through public speaking is [thus] essential to the sound thinking of a fully informed citizenry. [And] it is an obvious fact that public speaking today without sound amplifiers is a wholly inadequate way to reach the people on a large scale. . . .

"I am aware that the 'blare' of this new method of carrying ideas is susceptible of abuse and may under certain circumstances constitute an intolerable nuisance. But ordinances can be drawn which adequately protect a community from unreasonable use of public speaking devices without absolutely denying to the community's citizens all information that may be disseminated or received through this new avenue for trade in ideas. [A] city ordinance that reasonably restricts the volume of sound, or the hours during which an amplifier may be used, does not, in my mind, infringe the constitutionally protected area of free speech. [But the challenged] ordinance [is] an absolute prohibition of all uses of an amplifier on any of the streets of [the city]."

Justice Murphy also dissented.

METROMEDIA, INC. v. SAN DIEGO, 453 U.S. 490 (1981): A San Diego ordinance banned virtually all outdoor advertising display signs. Four justices concluded that the ordinance was an unconstitutional "content-based" restriction, see infra section F1, and thus found it unnecessary to decide whether a content-neutral ban on *all* outdoor advertising "would be consistent with the first amendment." The five remaining justices did address that question. Justice Brennan, joined by Justice Blackmun, concurred in the invalidation of the ordinance:

"[The] *practical* effect of the San Diego ordinance is to eliminate the billboard as an effective medium of communication. [Thus, it is necessary to assess] the 'substantiality of the governmental interests asserted' and 'whether those interests could be served by means that would be less intrusive on activity protected by the First Amendment.' [*Schneider; Struthers.*] Applying that test to the instant case, I would invalidate the San Diego ordinance. [First], although I have no quarrel with the substantiality of the city's interest in traffic safety, the city has failed to come forward with evidence demonstrating that billboards actually impair traffic safety in San Diego. [Second], the city has failed to show that its asserted interest in aesthetics is sufficiently substantial in the commercial and industrial areas of San Diego. . . .

"It is no doubt true that the appearance of certain areas of the city would be enhanced by the elimination of billboards, but 'it is not immediately [apparent]' that their elimination in all other areas as well would have more than a negligible impact on aesthetics. [A] billboard is not *necessarily* inconsistent with oil storage tanks, blighted areas, or strip development. Of course, it is not for a court to impose its own notion of beauty on San Diego. But before deferring to a city's judgment, a court must be convinced that the city is seriously and comprehensively addressing aesthetic concerns with respect to its environment. Here, San Diego has failed to demonstrate a comprehensive coordinated effort in its commercial and industrial areas to address other obvious contributors to an unattractive environment. In this sense the ordinance is underinclusive.

"I have little doubt that some jurisdictions will easily carry the burden of proving the substantiality of their interest in aesthetics. For example, [a] historical community such as Williamsburg, Va. should be able to prove that its interests in aesthetics and historical authenticity are sufficiently important that the First Amendment value attached to billboards must yield. [And] I would be surprised if the Federal Government had much trouble making the argument that billboards could be entirely banned in Yellowstone National Park, where their very existence would so obviously be inconsistent with the surrounding landscape. [But San Diego has failed to meet its burden here.]"

Justice Stevens dissented: "[The] net effect of the city's ban on billboards will be a reduction in the total quantity of communication in San Diego. [But that does not in itself render the ordinance invalid.] Graffiti [is] an inexpensive means of communicating [to] large numbers of people; some creators of graffiti have no effective alternative means of publicly expressing themselves. Nevertheless, I believe a community has the right to decide that its interests in protecting property from damaging trespasses and in securing beautiful surroundings outweigh the countervailing interest in uninhibited expression by means of words and pictures in public places. If the First Amendment categorically protected the marketplace of ideas from any quantitative restraint, a municipality could not outlaw graffiti.

"I therefore assume that some total prohibitions may be permissible. It seems to be accepted by all that a zoning regulation excluding billboards from residential neighborhoods is justified by the interest in maintaining pleasant surroundings and enhancing property values. The same interests are at work in commercial and industrial zones, [for the] character of the environment affects property values and the quality of life not only for the suburban resident but equally so for the individual who toils in a factory or invests his capital in industrial properties.

"Because the legitimacy of the interests [is] beyond dispute, [the] constitutionality of the prohibition of outdoor advertising involves two separate questions. First, is there any reason to believe that the regulation is biased in favor of one point of view? Second, is it fair to conclude that the market which remains open for the communication [of] ideas is ample and not threatened with gradually increasing restraints? In this case, there is not even a hint of bias or censorship in the city's actions. Nor is there any reason to believe that the overall communications market in San Diego is inadequate. [Thus,] nothing in this record suggests that the ordinance poses a threat to the interests protected by the First Amendment."

Chief Justice Burger also dissented: "[The] uniqueness of the medium, the availability of alternative means of communication, and the public interest the regulation serves are important factors to be weighed; and the balance very well may shift when attention is turned from one medium to another. [Regulating] newspapers, for example, is vastly different from regulating billboards.

"[The city's goals are substantial, and] the means the city has selected to advance these goals are sensible and do not exceed what is necessary to eradicate the dangers seen. [The] authorities reasonably can conclude [that] every large billboard adversely affects the environment, for each destroys a unique perspective on the landscape and adds to the visual pollution of the city. . . .

"[Moreover], the ordinance here in no sense suppresses freedom of expression. [San Diego] has not attempted to suppress any particular point of [view]; it has not censored any information; it has not banned any thought. [It] has not '[attempted] to give one side of a debatable public question an advantage in expressing its view to the people. . . .'

"[Finally, the] messages conveyed on San Diego billboards [can] reach an equally large audience through a variety of other media: newspapers, television, radio, magazines, direct mail, pamphlets, etc. True, these other methods may not be so 'eyecatching' — or so cheap — as billboards, but there has been no suggestion that billboards [advance] any particular viewpoint or issue disproportionately to advertising generally. Thus, the ideas billboard advertisers have been presenting are not relatively disadvantaged vis-à-vis the messages of those who heretofore have chosen other methods of spreading their views. [It] borders on the frivolous to suggest that the San Diego ordinance infringes on freedom of expression, given the wide range of alternative means available."

Justice Rehnquist also dissented.

Note: The Search for Principles

1. *Balancing.* Is "balancing" underprotective of free speech? Should content-neutral restrictions be governed by the same standards as content-based restrictions? Consider Redish, The Content Distinction in First Amendment Analysis, 34 Stan. L. Rev. 113, 128 (1981):

> The most puzzling aspect of the distinction between content-based and content-neutral restrictions is that either restriction reduces the sum total of information or opinion disseminated. That governmental regulation impedes all forms of speech, rather than only selected viewpoints or subjects, does not alter the fact that the regulation impairs the free flow of expression. Whatever rationale one adopts for the constitutional protection of speech, the goals behind that rationale are undermined by *any* limitation on expression, content-based or not.

Is the use of "balancing," rather than the more stringent standards ordinarily associated with content-based restrictions, defensible because (a) content-neutral restrictions do not restrict speech because of its "communicative impact" (that is, because of government's fear of how people will react to the speaker's ideas); (b) content-neutral restrictions are less likely seriously to distort the "marketplace of ideas"; or (c) content-neutral restrictions are less likely to be enacted for the constitutionally impermissible purpose of suppressing "erroneous," "undesirable," or "unpopular" ideas? For commentary on this distinction, see Ely, Flag Desecration: A Case Study in the Roles of Categorization and Balancing in First Amendment Analysis, 88 Harv. L. Rev. 1482 (1975); Farber, Content Regulation and the First Amendment: A Revisionist View, 68 Geo. L. Rev. 727 (1980); Karst, Equality as a Central Principle in the First Amendment, 43 U. Chi. L. Rev. 20 (1975); Redish, supra; Stephan, The First Amendment and Content Discrimination, 68 Va. L. Rev. 203 (1982); Stone, Content Regulation and the First Amendment, 25 Wm. & Mary L. Rev. 189 (1983).

2. *Striking the balance.* If content-neutral restrictions are tested by "balancing," what factors should be weighed in the balance? Consider the following propositions:

a. Although "the purpose to keep the streets clean and of good appearance is insufficient to justify" a prohibition on leafleting, the first amendment does not "deprive a municipality of power to enact regulations against throwing literature broadcast in the streets [since] such activity bears no necessary relationship to the freedom to speak, write, print or distribute information or opinion."

b. "[One] is not to have the exercise of his liberty of expression in appropriate places abridged on the plea that it may be exercised in some other place." Suppose a city permits soapbox orators to make public speeches in only four of its six municipal parks?

c. "That more people may be more easily and cheaply reached by sound trucks [is] not enough to call forth constitutional protection for what those charged with public welfare reasonably think is a nuisance when [alternative] means of publicity are open." Is this consistent with b? Should the existence of alternative means of communication affect the balance?

d. "The dangers of [door-to-door distribution of leaflets] can so easily be controlled by traditional legal methods [that] stringent prohibition can serve no purpose but [the] naked restriction of the dissemination of ideas." Should it matter that the state may be able to achieve part or all of its goals through alternative means that may have a less restrictive effect on expression? See Ely, supra, at 1484-1490; Note, Less Drastic Means and the First Amendment, 78 Yale L.J. 464 (1969).

e. "It would be fantastic to suggest that a city has power [to] forbid house-to-house canvassing generally, but that the Constitution prohibits the inclusion in that prohibition of door-to-door [distribution of] printed matter." Should it matter whether a law is designed specifically to restrict expression or designed to restrict a broader range of activities but has only an incidental effect on free expression?

f. "There has been no suggestion that billboards heretofore have advanced any particular viewpoint or issue disproportionately to advertising generally. Thus, the ideas billboard advertisers have been presenting are not *relatively* disadvantaged vis-à-vis the messages of those who heretofore have chosen other methods of spreading their views." Should it matter whether a content-neutral restriction has "content-differential" effects?

3. *Regulation versus prohibition. Schneider, Struthers, Kovacs,* and *Metromedia* focused primarily on government efforts completely or at least substantially to *prohibit* the use of particular means of communication. Often, however, government attempts merely to *regulate* the use of particular means of communication. Should the same general principles govern? In light of the opinions set out above, how would you rule on the constitutionality of the following laws?

a. "It is unlawful for any person to ring the door bell or otherwise summon the inmate of any residence for the purpose of canvassing unless the inmate has posted a sign stating that canvassers are welcome." Cf. Rowan v. Post Office, 397 U.S. 728 (1970) (upholding a federal statute enabling a householder to direct the postmaster general to forbid persons named by the householder to send correspondence to his home); Lamont v. Postmaster General, 381 U.S. 301 (1965) (invalidating a federal statute requiring the postmaster to detain all communist political propaganda mailed from abroad unless the addressee specifically requests its delivery).

b. "It is unlawful for any person to ring the door bell or otherwise summon the inmate of any residence for the purpose of canvassing between the hours of 8:00 P.M. and 8:00 A.M."

c. "The use of sound amplification equipment is prohibited within fifty yards of any hospital, school, church, courthouse, or residence."

d. "No billboard may be erected within 660 feet of a federal highway unless located in an area zoned for industrial or commercial use." Cf. Highway Beautification Act of 1965, 23 U.S.C. §131.

2. Speech on Public Property: The Public Forum

In what circumstances, if any, does the first amendment guarantee the individual the right to commandeer publicly owned property for the purpose of exercising the freedoms of speech, press, assembly, and petition? The Court has been highly solicitous of the right of owners of *private* property to prevent others from using their property for speech purposes. In *Struthers*, for example, the Court left no doubt that the city could constitutionally "punish those who call at a home in defiance of the previously expressed will of the occupant." More generally, the Court has accepted the view that, in most circumstances, "an uninvited guest may [not] exercise general rights of free speech on property privately owned," for it "would be an unwarranted infringement of property rights to require them to yield to the exercise of First Amendment rights." Lloyd Corp. v. Tanner, 407 U.S. 551, 568, 567 (1972). To what extent, then, does the first amendment supersede the "property rights" of the state? Must the state "subsidize" speech by allowing individuals to use publicly owned property for speech purposes?

"Public forum" theory has evolved along two separate but related lines — one governing streets and parks, the other governing all other publicly owned property. The materials in this section track this distinction.

For commentary on the "public forum," see Cass, First Amendment Access to Government Facilities, 65 Va. L. Rev. 1287 (1979); Kalven, The Concept of the Public Forum: *Cox v. Louisiana*, 1965 Sup. Ct. Rev. 1; Stone, Fora Americana: Speech in Public Places, 1974 Sup. Ct. Rev. 233.

a. The Public Forum: Streets and Parks

COMMONWEALTH v. DAVIS, 162 Mass. 510, 39 N.E. 113 (1895), aff'd sub nom. **DAVIS v. MASSACHUSETTS**, 167 U.S. 43 (1897): Davis, a preacher whose congregation apparently consisted of the crowds on the Boston Common, was convicted under a city ordinance which forbade, among other things, "any public address" on any publicly owned property "except in accordance with a permit from the mayor." The Supreme Judicial Court of Massachusetts, speaking through Justice Holmes, affirmed the conviction. Holmes explained that Davis's argument was premised on the "fallacy" that "the ordinance is directed against free speech generally, [whereas] in fact it is directed toward the modes in which Boston Common may be used." Holmes reasoned that, "as representative of the public," the legislature "may and does exercise control over the use which the public may make of such places," and for "the Legislature absolutely or conditionally to forbid public speaking in a highway or public park is no more an infringement of the rights of a member of the public than for the owner of a private house to forbid it in his house." Since the legislature "may end the right of the public to enter upon the public place by putting an end to the dedication to public uses," it necessarily "may take the lesser step of limiting the public use to certain purposes."

On appeal, the Supreme Court unanimously embraced Holmes's position. Chief Justice White, speaking for the Court, maintained that the federal Constitution "does not have the effect of creating a particular and personal right in the citizen to use public property in defiance of the constitution and laws of the

State." Indeed, the "right to absolutely exclude all right to use, necessarily includes the authority to determine under what circumstances such use may be availed of, as the greater power contains the lesser."*

Is this a satisfactory resolution of the public forum issue? Consider Stone, supra, at 237: "[Under] the Holmes-White approach, the state possessed the power absolutely to prohibit the exercise of First Amendment rights [on] public property simply by asserting the prerogatives traditionally associated with the private ownership of land. [The] problem of the public forum had been 'solved' by resort to common law concepts of private property."

HAGUE v. CIO, 307 U.S. 496 (1939): Forty-two years later, the Court reopened the question. In *Hague*, which arose out of Mayor Hague's efforts to break up the CIO's organizing campaign in Jersey City, the Court considered the constitutionality of a municipal ordinance forbidding all public meetings in the streets and other public places without a permit. The city maintained that the ordinance was clearly constitutional under *Davis*. Although the Court did not directly decide the question, Justice Roberts, in a plurality opinion, flatly rejected the city's contention in a dictum that has played a central role in the evolution of public forum theory:

"Wherever the title of streets and parks may rest, they have immemorially been held in trust for the use of the public and, time out of mind, have been used for purposes of assembly, communicating thought between citizens, and discussing public questions. Such use of the streets and public places has, from ancient times, been a part of the privileges, immunities, rights, and liberties of citizens. The privilege of a citizen of the United States to use the streets and parks for communication of views on national questions may be regulated in the interest of all; it is not absolute, but relative, and must be exercised in subordination to the general comfort and convenience, and in consonance with peace and good order; but it must not, in the guise of regulation, be abridged or denied."

Consider Stone, supra, at 238:

Perhaps the most interesting aspect of the Roberts dictum is its implicit acceptance of the underlying premise of the Holmes-White position — that the public forum issue must be defined in terms of the common law property rights of the state. Rather than challenging that premise head-on, Roberts conveniently adapted it to his own advantage, predicating the public forum right upon established common law notions of adverse possession and public trust. [In effect, Roberts concluded that] the streets, parks, and similar public places are subject to what Professor Kalven has termed "a kind of First-Amendment easement." [Citing Kalven, supra, at 13.] Since such places have been used, "time out of mind," for purposes of speech

---

* [At the time of *Davis* the Court had not as yet held the first amendment applicable to the states, thus undermining the precedential force of *Davis* as a "free speech" decision. It appears that the primary constitutional issue before the Court concerned dictum in Yick Wo v. Hopkins, 118 U.S. 356 (1886), suggesting that the equal protection clause prohibited all forms of standardless licensing. This dictum was rejected more clearly in a series of subsequent decisions. See Lieberman v. Van de Carr, 199 U.S. 552 (1905); Gundling v. Chicago, 177 U.S. 183 (1900); Wilson v. Eureka, 173 U.S. 32 (1899). For a more extensive discussion of *Yick Wo*, see supra Chapter 5, section C2. — Eds.]

and assembly, the Constitution now requires that their continued use for these purposes not "be abridged or denied."

Is this a sound rationale for the right to a public forum? Note that the Roberts rationale creates by implication two distinct classes of public property. Although streets, parks, and similar public places may constitute public fora, publicly owned property that cannot satisfy the "time out of mind" requirement remains subject to the *Davis* dictum, and access to such places for purposes of speech and assembly may thus be denied absolutely upon the state's naked assertion of title. Would it be preferable to base public forum theory on the notion that access to public property for speech purposes is essential to effective exercise of First Amendment rights?

SCHNEIDER v. STATE, 308 U.S. 147 (1939): In *Schneider*, supra section E1, decided only eight months after *Hague*, the Court held that a city's interest in keeping "the streets clean and of good appearance" was "insufficient" to justify a municipal ordinance prohibiting the distribution of leaflets on public property. Although the Court did not explicitly address the status of *Davis*, the impact of *Hague* and *Schneider* was made clear several years later in Jamison v. Texas, 318 U.S. 413 (1943), in which the Court, following *Schneider*, invalidated a city ordinance prohibiting the dissemination of leaflets. Relying on *Davis*, the city maintained that "it has the power absolutely to prohibit the use of the streets for the communication of ideas." The Court responded: "This same argument, made in reliance upon the same decision, has been directly rejected by this Court. [Citing Justice Robert's concurring opinion in *Hague*.]"

Consider Kalven, supra, at 18-21:

> The result [in *Schneider*] had an impressive bite. Leaflet distribution in public places in a city is a method of communication that carries as an inextricable and expected consequence substantial littering of the streets, which the city has an obligation to keep clean. It is also a method of communication of some annoyance to a majority of people so addressed; that its impact on its audience is very high is doubtful. Yet the constitutional balance in *Schneider* was struck emphatically in favor of keeping the public forum open for this mode of communication. [At stake in *Schneider* was] the immemorial claim of the free man to use the streets as a forum. [The state], the Court was telling us, must recognize the special nature and value of that claim to be on the street. [The] operative theory of the Court, at least for the leaflet situation, is that [the] right to use the streets as a public forum [cannot] be prohibited and can be regulated only for weighty reasons.

How does the *Hague/Schneider* theory of the public forum relate to the analysis of content-neutral restrictions generally? Consider the following propositions:

1. Although the *Hague/Schneider* theory holds that the property rights of the state do not in themselves permit the state absolutely to exclude expression from public property that has been used "time out of mind" for speech purposes, it does not hold that government property rights are irrelevant. Thus, content-neutral restrictions governing streets and parks should be tested by more lenient standards of justification than content-neutral restrictions that do not implicate the property rights of the state.

2. The *Hague/Schneider* theory holds that government property rights are irrelevant when the property has been used "time out of mind" for speech purposes. Thus, content-neutral restrictions governing streets and parks should be tested by the same standards of justification that are used to test content-neutral restrictions that do not implicate the property rights of the state.

3. The *Hague/Schneider* theory holds that the streets and parks are "public fora" in which the state must be especially solicitous of free expression. Thus, content-neutral restrictions governing streets and parks should be tested by more stringent standards of justification than content-neutral restrictions that do not implicate "public forum" rights.

Note: Regulating the Public Forum

1. Grace. In United States v. Grace, 461 U.S. 171 (1983), the Court invalidated a federal statute prohibiting any person to display on the public sidewalks surrounding the Supreme Court building "any flag, banner, or device designed [to] bring into public notice any party, organization or movement." The Court explained that the "public sidewalks forming the perimeter of the Supreme Court grounds [are] public forums," and that "the government's ability" to restrict expression in such places "is very limited." Indeed, "the government may enforce reasonable time, place, and manner restrictions" in public forums only if "the restrictions 'are content-neutral, are narrowly tailored to serve a significant government interest, and leave open ample alternative channels of communication,'" and it may absolutely prohibit "a particular type of expression" only if the prohibition is "narrowly drawn to accomplish a compelling governmental interest."

The Court held that the challenged restriction, "which totally bans the specified communicative activity on the public sidewalks around the Court grounds," could not "be justified as a reasonable place restriction" because "it has an insufficient nexus with any of the public interests that may be said to [justify it]." The Court held that the restriction could not be justified as a means "to maintain proper order and decorum" near the Supreme Court, for a "total ban" was not necessary to achieve these ends. And the restriction could not be justified as a means to prevent the appearance "that the Supreme Court is subject to outside influence," for the restriction did not "sufficiently serve" that purpose "to sustain its validity." Indeed, the Court "seriously" doubted that "the public would draw a different inference from a lone picketer carrying a sign on the sidewalks around the [Supreme Court] building than it would from a similar picket on the sidewalks across the street."

Recall Cox v. Louisiana, supra section B2, in which the Court, in dictum, upheld a statute prohibiting any person, "with the intent of interfering with, obstructing, or impeding the administration of justice, or with the intent of influencing any judge, juror, witness, or court officer, in the discharge of his duty," to picket or parade "in or near a building housing a court." Does this aspect of *Cox* survive *Grace?*

2. Grayned. In Grayned v. Rockford, 408 U.S. 104 (1972), approximately 200 demonstrators marched on a public sidewalk about 100 feet from a public high

school to protest the school's racial policies. Appellant, a participant in the demonstration, was convicted of violating a Rockford ordinance prohibiting any "person, while on public or private grounds adjacent to any building in which a school or any class thereof is in session, [to make] any noise or diversion which disturbs or tends to disturb the peace or good order of such school." The Court, in an eight-to-one decision, affirmed the conviction.

At the outset, the Court quoted the *Hague* dictum and noted that the "right to use a public place for expressive activity may be restricted only for weighty reasons." But "reasonable 'time, place and manner' regulations may be necessary to further significant governmental interests, and are permitted." The Court explained that the "crucial question is whether the manner of expression is basically incompatible with the normal activity of a particular place at a particular time." Thus, although "the public sidewalk adjacent to school grounds may not be declared off limits for expressive activity by members of the public, [such] activity may be prohibited if it 'materially disrupts classwork or involves substantial disorder or invasion of the rights of others.'"

Applying these general principles to *Grayned*, the Court observed that the "antinoise" ordinance "is narrowly tailored to further Rockford's compelling interest in having an undisrupted school session conducive to the students' learning"; "punishes only conduct which disrupts or is about to disrupt normal school activities"; requires that the "decision [be] made [on] an individualized basis"; and "gives no license to punish anyone because of what he is saying." The Court concluded that "such a reasonable regulation is not inconsistent with the First and Fourteenth Amendments."

Recall Gregory v. Chicago, supra section B2, in which Gregory led a march of about eighty-five protestors to the home of Chicago Mayor Richard Daley to protest segregation in the city's public schools. Although the Court overturned the demonstrators' convictions for "disorderly conduct" without reaching the first amendment issue, Justice Black observed in a concurring opinion that the Constitution does not leave government powerless to "protect [the] tranquility of spots selected by the people [for] homes, wherein they can escape the hurly-burly of the outside business and political world." In light of *Grace* and *Grayned*, how would you assess the constitutionality of a statute declaring it "unlawful to picket before or about the residence or dwelling of any person in a manner likely to disturb the tranquility of the residents"? See Kamin, Residential Picketing and the First Amendment, 61 Nw. U. L. Rev. 177 (1966).

3. Clark. In Clark v. Community for Creative Non-Violence, 468 U.S. — ,104 S. Ct. 3065 (1983), the National Park Service permitted CCNV to erect symbolic tent cities, consisting of between twenty and forty tents, in Lafayette Park and the Mall in Washington, D.C., for the purpose of conducting a round-the-clock demonstration designed to dramatize the plight of the homeless. Pursuant to a National Park Service regulation prohibiting "camping" in these parks, however, the Service prohibited CCNV demonstrators from sleeping overnight in the tents. The Court assumed arguendo "that overnight sleeping in connection with the demonstration is expressive conduct protected [by] the First Amendment," but upheld the regulation as a "reasonable time, place, and manner restriction."

The Court emphasized that the regulation is "content neutral," that it does not prevent CCNV from demonstrating the "plight of the homeless [in] other ways," and that it "narrowly focuses on the Government's substantial interest in maintaining the parks [in] an attractive and intact condition." The Court rejected CCNV's argument that once the Service decided to permit "the symbolic city of tents," the "incremental benefit to the parks was insufficient to justify the ban on sleeping." The Court explained that it doubted that the Service was in any way obligated to permit the tent cities in the first place and, in any event, that the ban on sleeping was a reasonable, if indirect, way to limit the "size and duration" of such demonstrations once the Service decided to permit them. Finally, the Court rejected CCNV's argument that the regulation was invalid "because there are less speech-restrictive alternatives," such as restrictions on "the size, duration or frequency of demonstrations," that "could have satisfied the government interest." The Court maintained that this argument represents "no more than a disagreement with the Park Service over how much protection [the] parks require" and that the Constitution "does not assign to the judiciary the authority to replace the Park Service as the manager of the Nation's parks."

Justice Marshall, joined by Justice Brennan, dissented. Marshall emphasized that "Lafayette Park and the Mall have served as the sites for some of the most rousing political demonstrations in the Nation's history" and that they thus constitute "'a fitting and powerful forum for political [protest].'" Although Marshall agreed "with the standard enunciated by the majority" and conceded that the government interest in maintaining the parks in an attractive condition is "significant," he did not see how prohibiting CCNV's sleeping would "substantially further that interest." Marshall rejected the Court's argument that because the Park Service was not constitutionally obligated to permit the "tents and the 24-hour vigil," it was not obligated to permit "expressive conduct that supplements these activities." In Marshall's view, the "First Amendment requires the Government to justify *every* instance of abridgement," even if the prohibited expression "is supplementary to other [expression] that the Government [permitted] out of grace but was not constitutionally compelled to allow." Marshall also rejected the majority's argument that the regulation was justified as an indirect means of limiting the "size and duration" of such demonstrations, for there was "no evidence [that] sleeping engaged in as symbolic speech [would] cause *substantial* wear and tear on the park."

Finally, Marshall cautioned that the majority was insufficiently sensitive to the fact that "a content-neutral regulation does not necessarily fall [with] equal force upon different groups or different points of view." To the contrary, a "content-neutral regulation that restricts an inexpensive mode of communication will fall most heavily upon relatively poor speakers and the points of view that such speakers typically espouse." Marshall maintained that this consideration should be taken "into account in adjudicating the First Amendment rights of those [who] are financially deprived. [Citing Martin v. City of Struthers.]"

Is *Clark* consistent with the *Hague/Schneider* approach? Is the Park Service rule a reasonable regulation of "manner"? The symbolic speech issue is examined in section E3 infra.

Consider the following views:

a. Easterbrook, Foreword: The Court and the Economic System, 98 Harv. L. Rev. 4, 20-21 (1984):

> [The Court] had no trouble accepting the constitutionality of a no-camping rule, and it saw the restrictions placed on the CCNV as a neutral application of that rule.

[To] see the burden, the Court asked not what would happen if CCNV's demonstrators took naps, but what would happen if a relaxation on the ban on camping made similar demonstrations more attractive. As the implicit cost of demonstrating fell, more people with less to say would seek initial permits; those who sought permits would stay longer; those whose desire to speak was weaker than the CCNV's would come more frequently; some imposters who simply wanted to sleep and not to speak would use the parks as living quarters. [In] other words, the Court took an ex ante view of the dispute, bypassing for the most part the CCNV's case in order to examine how rules affect future behavior.

b. Tribe, Constitutional Calculus: Equal Justice or Economic Efficiency?, 98 Harv. L. Rev. 592, 601 (1985):

[Easterbrook's] ex ante analysis [pushes] the inquiry back — but only to the point where going any further would uncover issues bearing on the distribution of wealth and power. There is nothing neutral [about] stopping *there*. The depth of field [of] Easterbrook's utilitarian lens is too shallow; [he] fails to ask what would happen if the [demonstration] succeeded in inducing the appropriation of federal relief for [the homeless]. Such demonstrations would then become unnecessary, and the Park Service's purpose in banning such camping — preservation of the park — would be well served.

Note: Devices for Regulating the Public Forum

1. *The "speech-conduct" distinction.* The mass civil rights demonstrations of the 1960s placed considerable strain on the *Hague/Schneider* theory. In Cox v. Louisiana, 379 U.S. 536 (1965), the facts of which are set out at section B3, supra, approximately 2,000 black students, led by Cox, staged a peaceful civil rights protest across the street from the local courthouse. Cox was arrested and subsequently convicted of violating, inter alia, a Louisiana statute providing that "no person shall wilfully obstruct the free, convenient, and normal use of any public sidewalk, street [or] other passageway, or the entrance, corridor or passage of any public building, [by] impeding [passage] thereon or therein." The public forum issue was clear, for as the Court observed, the statute in effect "precludes all street assemblies and parades."

In addressing the public forum issue, the Court rejected the notion that "the First and Fourteenth Amendments afforded the same kind of freedom to those who would communicate ideas by conduct such as patrolling, marching, and picketing on streets and highways, as these amendments afford to those who communicate ideas by pure speech." The Court concluded, however, that it had "no occasion in this case to consider the constitutionality of the uniform, consistent, and nondiscriminatory application of a statute forbidding all access to streets and other public facilities for parades and meetings," for the record disclosed that city officials had in fact permitted other "meetings and parades" to take place "even though they [had had] the effect of obstructing traffic." The Court thus analogized the selective enforcement of the statute to standardless licensing and invalidated it under the doctrine of Lovell v. Griffin, supra section C2.

Is the distinction between communicative "conduct" and "pure speech" meaningful? Consider Kalven, supra, at 23: "The Court's neat dichotomy of 'speech pure' and 'speech plus' will not work. [All] speech is necessarily 'speech plus.' If it is oral, it is noise and may interrupt someone else; if it is written, it may be litter. Indeed, this is why the leaflet cases were an appropriate model: they involved speech with collateral consequences that invited regulation. But the leaflets were not simply litter; they were litter with ideas."

Subsequent decisions have not accepted *Cox*'s speech/conduct distinction. See, e.g., Grayned v. Rockford, 408 U.S. 104 (1972) (subject to such reasonable time, place, and manner regulations as "may be necessary to further significant governmental interests, [peaceful] demonstrations in public places are protected by the First Amendment"); Food Employees Local 590 v. Logan Valley Plaza, 391 U.S. 308 (1968) ("handbilling, like picketing, involves conduct other than speech").

2. *Licensing.* In Cox v. New Hampshire, 312 U.S. 569 (1941), a group of Jehovah's Witnesses were convicted of violating a state statute prohibiting any "parade or procession" upon a public street without first obtaining a permit. The Court, in a unanimous decision, affirmed the convictions. Chief Justice Hughes, speaking for the Court, explained that "as regulation of the use of the streets for parades and processions is a traditional exercise of control by local government, the question in a particular case is whether that control is exerted so as not to deny or unwarrantedly abridge the right of assembly and the opportunities for the communication of [thought] immemorially associated with resort to public places."

The Court emphasized that the state court had "construed the statute" as authorizing "the licensing authority" to take into account only "considerations of time, place and manner so as to conserve the public convenience." Such a limited permit requirement had the "obvious advantage" of "giving the public authorities notice in advance so as to afford opportunity for proper policing," and "in fixing time and place, '[to] prevent confusion by overlapping parades or processions, to secure convenient use of the streets by other travelers, and to minimize the risk of disorder.'" Moreover, the Court emphasized that the state court had stressed that "the licensing board was not vested with arbitrary power [and] that its discretion must be [exercised] 'free [from] unfair discrimination.'" The Court concluded that, under this construction of the statute, it is "impossible to say that the limited authority conferred by the licensing provisions [contravened] any constitutional right."

Consider Baker, Unreasoned Reasonableness: Mandatory Parade Permits and Time, Place, and Manner Regulations, 78 Nw. U. L. Rev. 937, 1013-1018 (1983):

> [The costs of licensing are often underestimated.] The costs fall into three categories: [First, a] permit requirement effectively makes [unlawful] some valuable types of peaceable parades and assemblies, [such as] "spontaneous" demonstrations. [Second, a permit] system requires that those assembling and parading must symbolically and practically bow to the very authorities that [they may believe to be] illegitimate. [And third,] a mandatory permit system [will not] be benign [in operation]. Local authorities consistently have used [the] permit requirement as a means to harass those whom they wish to harass.

For analysis of licensing generally, see supra section C2. Is *Cox* consistent with the general presumption against "prior restraints"? Does *Cox* "symbolize the ideal of Robert's Rules of Order for use of the public forum"? Kalven, supra, 28-29, 26.

For a thorough analysis, see Blasi, Prior Restraints on Demonstrations, 68 Mich. L. Rev. 1481 (1970).

3. *Fees.* To what extent may the state charge for use of the public forum? In Murdock v. Pennsylvania, 319 U.S. 105 (1943), the Court held that the state may not impose a "flat license tax [as] a condition to the pursuit of activities whose enjoyment is guaranteed by the First Amendment" where the tax "is not a nominal fee imposed as a regulatory measure to defray the expenses of policing the activities in question." In Cox v. New Hampshire, supra, the licensing statute provided that "every licensee shall pay in advance" a fee ranging from a nominal amount to $300 per day. The state court construed the statute as requiring "a reasonable fixing of the amount of the fee." That is, the amount of the fee must in each instance turn on the size of the "parade or procession," the size of the crowd, and the "public expense of policing" the event. The state court explained that the fee was "not a revenue tax, but one to meet the expense incident to the administration of the Act and to the maintenance of public order in the matter licensed." The Court held that, in such circumstances, "there is nothing contrary to the Constitution in the charge of a fee limited to the purpose stated." Moreover, the Court rejected "the suggestion that a flat fee should have been charged," explaining that it is difficult to frame "a fair schedule to meet all circumstances," and that there is "no constitutional ground for denying to local governments that flexibility of adjustment of fees which in the light of varying conditions would tend to conserve rather than impair the liberty sought."

Consider Goldberger, A Reconsideration of *Cox v. New Hampshire*: Can Demonstrators Be Required to Pay the Costs of Using America's Public Forums?, 62 Tex. L. Rev. 403, 412-413 (1983):

> The Court's approval of [license fees] in *Cox* results from the Court's erroneous assumption that the relationship between a speaker and the government can be treated like a two-party business relationship. [The Court assumes] that the speaker is the primary beneficiary of his use of a public forum. [This] assumption ignores the benefit of the speaker's activities for the entire society. His activities are part of the process by which a democratic society makes informed decisions. [A] proper distribution of costs [would] allocate the costs generated by speech activities to the society as a whole.

Is there a danger that, if the state "is forced to defray administrative costs, it is likely to be more resistant to permit requests"? Blasi, supra, at 1527.

During the *Skokie* controversy, supra section B3, the village enacted an ordinance requiring applicants for parade or public demonstration permits to procure public liability insurance in the amount of $350,000 and property damage insurance in the amount of $50,000. Is this ordinance constitutional under the doctrine of *Cox*? Consider Gard, Book Review, 32 Hastings L.J. 711, 727 (1981): "[Such a scheme is unconstitutional because] the premium required for the fixed amount of insurance would vary depending upon the existence and extent of hostility threatened by the audience and the past history of the group seeking the insurance, two factors that a municipality generally is proscribed from considering in determining whether to issue a permit." See also Blasi, supra, at 1530-1532; Goldberger, supra, at 440-450; Collin v. Smith, 447 F. Supp. 676 (N.D. Ill. 1978) (invalidating the Skokie ordinance).

b.   The Public Forum: Other Publicly Owned Property

If there is a first amendment right to use streets and parks for purposes of expression, to what extent, if any, is there an analogous right to use other publicly owned property, ranging from a library, to the grounds surrounding a jail, to a military base, to a state fair, for the exercise of first amendment rights? Does the *Hague* dictum's definition of the right to a "public forum" in terms of the common law property rights of the state suggest that the right does not extend to property that has not been used "time out of mind" for speech purposes?

BROWN v. LOUISIANA, 383 U.S. 131 (1966): In 1964 the Audubon Regional Library, which serviced three Louisiana parishes, was operated on a segregated basis. To protest this policy, petitioners, five blacks, entered the reading room of one of the "whites only" libraries. The branch assistant, who was alone in the room, asked if she "could help." One petitioner requested a book, "The Story of the Negro." The branch assistant checked the card catalogue, ascertained that the branch did not have the book, and told the petitioner that she would request the book from the state library and that he would be notified upon its receipt. Although the branch assistant expected petitioners to leave, they did not. One sat down, and the others stood near him. They said nothing. Ten to fifteen minutes after petitioners first entered the library, the sheriff, who had been forewarned of the protest, arrived with his deputies. He asked petitioners to leave. When they refused, he arrested them. Petitioners were convicted of violating Louisiana's breach of the peace statute: "Whoever with intent to provoke a breach of the peace, or under circumstances such that a breach of the peace may be occasioned [thereby] crowds or congregates with others [in a] public place or building [and] fails or refuses to disperse and move on [when] ordered so to do by any law enforcement officer [or] any other authorized person [shall] be guilty of disturbing the peace."

The Court, in a sharply divided set of opinions, reversed the convictions. In a plurality opinion, Justice Fortas, joined by Chief Justice Warren and Justice Douglas, maintained that the convictions violated due process because "there is not the slightest evidence" that the protestors intended "to provoke a breach of the peace" or that a breach of the peace was likely to be "occasioned" by their actions. Fortas did not rest solely on the "no evidence" ground, however:

"[There] is another and sharper answer which is called for. We are here dealing with an aspect of a basic constitutional right — the [freedom] of speech and [the] freedom to petition the Government for a redress of grievances. [These] rights are not confined to verbal expression. They embrace appropriate types of action which certainly include the right in a peaceable and orderly manner to protest by silent and reproachful presence, in a place where the protestant has every right to be, the unconstitutional segregation of public facilities. Accordingly, even if the accused action were within the scope of the statutory instrument, we would [have] to hold that the statute cannot constitutionally be applied to punish petitioners' actions in the circumstances of this case. [The] statute was deliberately and purposefully applied solely to terminate the reasonable, orderly, and limited exercise of the right to protest. [Interference] with this right, so exercised, [is] intolerable under our Constitution."

Justices Brennan and White concurred in the judgment without reaching the first amendment issue.

Justice Black, joined by Justices Clark, Harlan, and Stewart, dissented. Black rejected Fortas's "no evidence" argument, and then turned to the "public forum" issue: "[The plurality's] conclusion that the statute was unconstitutionally applied because it interfered with the petitioners' so-called protest establishes a completely new constitutional doctrine. [The] First Amendment [does not give] any person or group of persons the constitutional right to go wherever they want, whenever they please, without regard to the rights of private or public property or to state law. [The First Amendment] does not guarantee to any person the right to use someone else's property, even that owned by government and dedicated to other purposes, as a stage to express dissident ideas. The novel constitutional doctrine of the prevailing opinion [exalts] the power of private nongovernmental groups to determine what use shall be made of governmental property over the power of the elected governmental officials.

Does Fortas's position suggest that an individual has a constitutional right to distribute leaflets in a library? To make a speech in a library? The issue of "symbolic" speech is examined in section E3 infra.

Adderley v. Florida

398 U.S. 39 (1966)

[About 200 Florida A. & M. students marched to the county jail to protest the arrest the previous day of several of their schoolmates who had engaged in a civil rights demonstration. The protestors went directly to the jail entrance where they were met by a deputy sheriff who explained that they were blocking the entrance to the jail and asked them to move back. The protestors moved back part of the way, where they stood or sat, singing, clapping, and dancing, on the jail driveway and on an adjacent grassy area on the jail premises. This jail entrance and driveway were not normally used by the public but by the sheriff's department for transporting prisoners and by commercial concerns for servicing the jail. Even after their partial retreat, the protestors continued to block vehicular passage over this driveway. Shortly thereafter, the county sheriff, who was legal custodian of the jail and jail grounds, tried to persuade the students to leave. When this failed, he ordered them to leave and informed them that if they did not leave within ten minutes he would arrest them for trespassing. Some protestors left, but 107 others, including petitioners, remained and were arrested. They were convicted of violating a Florida statute declaring unlawful "every trespass upon the property of another, committed with a malicious and mischievous intent." The Court, in a five-to-four decision, affirmed the convictions.]

MR. JUSTICE BLACK delivered the opinion of the Court. . . .

[Petitioners maintain that conviction under the trespass statute] unconstitutionally deprives [them] of their rights to freedom of speech, press, assembly, or petition. We hold that it does not. The sheriff, as jail custodian, had power [to] direct that this large crowd of people get off the grounds. There is not a shred of evidence in this record that this power was exercised [because] the sheriff ob-

jected to what was being sung or said by the demonstrators or because he disagreed with the objectives of their protest. The record reveals that he objected
only to their presence on that part of the jail grounds reserved for jail uses. There
is no evidence at all that on any other occasion had similarly large groups of the
public been permitted to gather on this portion of the jail grounds for any purpose. Nothing in the Constitution of the United States prevents Florida from
even-handed enforcement of its general trespass statute against those refusing to
obey the sheriff's order to remove themselves from what amounted to the curtilage of the jailhouse. The State, no less than a private owner of property, has
power to preserve the property under its control for the use to which it is lawfully
dedicated. For this reason there is no merit to the petitioners' argument that they
had a constitutional right to stay on the property, over the jail custodian's objections, because this "area chosen for the peaceful civil rights demonstration was
not only 'reasonable' but also particularly appropriate. . . ." Such an argument
has as its major unarticulated premise the assumption that people who want to
propagandize protests or views have a constitutional right to do so whenever and
however and wherever they please. [We] reject [that concept]. The United States
Constitution does not forbid a State to control the use of its own property for its
own lawful nondiscriminatory purpose.

These judgments are affirmed.

MR. JUSTICE DOUGLAS, with whom THE CHIEF JUSTICE, MR. JUSTICE BRENNAN,
and MR. JUSTICE FORTAS concur, dissenting. . . .

The jailhouse, like an executive mansion, a legislative chamber, a courthouse,
or the statehouse itself [is] one of the seats of government, whether it be the
Tower of London, the Bastille, or a small county jail. And when it houses political
prisoners or those who many think are unjustly held, it is an obvious center for
protest. The right to petition for the redress of grievances has an ancient history
and is not limited to writing a letter or sending a telegram to a congressman; it is
not confined to appearing before the local city council, or writing letters to the
President or Governor or Mayor. [Conventional] methods of petitioning may be,
and often have been, shut off to large groups of our citizens. [Those] who do not
control television and radio, those who cannot afford to advertise in newspapers
or circulate elaborate pamphlets may have only a more limited type of access to
public officials. Their methods should not be condemned as tactics of obstruction
and harassment as long as the assembly and petition are peaceable, as these were.

There is no question that petitioners had as their purpose a protest against the
arrest of Florida A. & M. students for trying to integrate public theatres. [There]
was no violence; no threat of violence; no attempted jail break; no storming of a
prison; no plan or plot to do anything but protest. The evidence is uncontradicted
that the petitioners' conduct did not upset the jailhouse routine; things went on as
they normally would. None of the group entered the jail. Indeed, they moved
back from the entrance as they were instructed. There was no shoving, no pushing, no disorder or threat of riot. It is said that some of the group blocked part of
the driveway leading to the jail entrance. [But] whenever the students were requested to move they did so. If there was congestion, the solution was a further
request to move to lawns or parking areas, not complete ejection and arrest. . . .

We do violence to the First Amendment when we permit this "petition for
redress of grievances" to be turned into a trespass action. [To] say that a private
owner could have done the same if the rally had taken place on private property is

to speak of a different case, as an assembly and a petition for redress of grievances run to government, not to private proprietors.

The Court forgets that prior to this day our decisions have drastically limited the application of state statutes inhibiting the right to go peacefully on public property to exercise First Amendment rights. [Citing Justice Roberts's plurality opinion in *Hague*. There] may be some public places which are so clearly committed to other purposes that their use for the airing of grievances is anomalous. There may be some instances in which assemblies and petitions for redress of grievances are not consistent with other necessary purposes of public property. A noisy meeting may be out of keeping with the serenity of the statehouse or the quiet of the courthouse. No one, for example, would suggest that the Senate gallery is the proper place for a vociferous protest rally. And in other cases it may be necessary to adjust the right to petition for redress of grievances to the other interests inhering in the uses to which the public property is normally put. [See Cox v. New Hampshire.] But this is quite different from saying that all public places are off limits to people with grievances. . . .

Note: *"No Less Than a Private Owner of Property"?*

1. *Davis revisited?* Does *Adderley* turn on the fact that the protestors "blocked" the jail driveway? Does it turn on Justice Black's assertion that "the State, no less than a private owner of property, has power to preserve the property under its control for the use to which it is lawfully dedicated"? Does *Adderley* undervalue the interest of the speaker in selecting a "particularly appropriate" location for his speech?

2. *The* Grayned *dictum.* In Grayned v. Rockford, supra section B2a, decided in 1972, the Court, although upholding the antinoise ordinance as a reasonable time, place, and manner regulation, offered the following analysis of the public forum issue:

> The nature of a place, "the pattern of its normal activities, dictate the kinds of regulations of time, place, and manner that are reasonable." Although a silent vigil may not unduly interfere with a public library, [*Brown*], making a speech in the reading room almost certainly would. That same speech should be perfectly appropriate in a park. The crucial question is whether the manner of expression is basically incompatible with the normal activity of a particular place at a particular time. Our cases make clear that in assessing the reasonableness of a regulation, we must weigh heavily the fact that communication is involved; the regulation must be narrowly tailored to further the State's legitimate interest.

Note that the Court stated in *Grayned* that "in *Adderley*, the Court held that demonstrators could be barred from jailhouse grounds not ordinarily open to the public, at least where the demonstration obstructed the jail driveway and interfered with the functioning of the jail." Is that an accurate characterization? What are the implications of *Grayned*? Consider Stone, Fora Americana: Speech in Public Places, 1974 Sup. Ct. Rev. 233, 251-252:

> In [the *Grayned* dictum], the right to a public forum came of age. No longer does the right to effective freedom of expression turn on the common law property rights of the state, and no longer does it turn on whether the particular place at issue has

historically been dedicated to the exercise of First Amendment rights. The streets, parks, public libraries, and other publicly owned places are all brought under the same roof. In each case, the "crucial question is whether the manner of expression is basically incompatible with the normal activity of a particular place at a particular time."

GREER v. SPOCK, 424 U.S. 828 (1976): The Fort Dix Military Reservation is a U.S. Army post. Although the federal government exercises exclusive jurisdiction over the base, civilian vehicular traffic is permitted on paved roads within the reservation and civilians are freely permitted to visit unrestricted areas of the base. In 1972 Benjamin Spock, the People's Party's candidate for President of the United States, requested permission to enter the base to hold a meeting to discuss election issues with service personnel and their dependents. The commanding officer of the base rejected the request, citing a Fort Dix regulation providing that "demonstrations, picketing, sit-ins, protest marches, political speeches and similar activities are prohibited and will not be conducted on the Fort Dix Military Reservation."

The Court, in a six-to-two decision, upheld the regulation. In an opinion by Justice Stewart, the Court rejected "the principle that whenever members of the public are permitted freely to visit a place owned or operated by the Government, then that place becomes a 'public forum' for purposes of the First Amendment." Quoting *Adderley*, the Court explained that "'The State, no less than a private owner of property, has power to preserve the property under its control for the use to which it is lawfully dedicated.'" The Court emphasized that it is "the business of a military installation like Fort Dix to train soldiers, not to provide a public forum." Thus, since "the Fort Dix authorities [had not] abandoned [their] interest in regulating [campaign] speeches [on] the [base]," the challenged regulation was not "invalid on [its] face."

Moreover, the regulation was not unconstitutional "as applied": "What the record shows [is] a considered [policy], objectively and evenhandedly applied, of keeping official military activities [free] of entanglement with partisan political campaigns of any kind. Under such a [policy], the military [is] insulated from both the reality and the appearance of acting as a handmaiden for partisan political causes or candidates. Such a policy is wholly consistent with the American constitutional tradition of a politically neutral military establishment under civilian control. [It] is a policy that the military authorities at Fort Dix were constitutionally free to pursue."

Justice Brennan, joined by Justice Marshall, dissented. Brennan maintained that the Court's emphasis on whether the base was a "public forum" was misplaced, for "the determination that a locale is a 'public forum' has never been erected as an absolute prerequisite to all forms of demonstrative First Amendment activity." What is needed, Brennan explained, is a "flexible approach [for] determining when public expression should be protected. [Otherwise], with the rigid characterization of a given locale as not a public forum, there is the danger that certain forms of public speech at the locale may be suppressed, even though they are basically compatible with the activities otherwise occurring at the locale."

Brennan maintained that *Adderley* was distinguishable, for in *Adderley* "the jail custodian 'objected only to [the demonstrators'] presence on that part of the jail grounds reserved for jail uses,'" whereas in *Greer* respondents sought to speak only on the unrestricted areas of the base that were open generally to members of the public. Thus, although the "military certainly [could] exclude civilian traffic, [it] could not choose freely to admit all such traffic save for the traffic in ideas." Finally, Brennan rejected the contention that the interest in "military neutrality" could justify the restriction, for "it borders on casuistry to contend that by even-handedly permitting public expression to occur in unrestricted portions of a military installation, the military will be viewed as sanctioning the causes there espoused."

See also United States v. Albertini, — U.S. — , 105 S. Ct. 2897 (1985) (upholding the exclusion of an individual from a military base where the individual had previously been permanently barred from the base for prior unlawful conduct, even though the individual's purpose in entering the base was to engage in peaceful expressive activity during the base's annual open house).

HEFFRON v. INTERNATIONAL SOCIETY FOR KRISHNA CONSCIOUSNESS, 452 U.S. 640 (1981): The Minnesota State Fair is conducted each year on a 125-acre site. The average daily attendance exceeds 100,000. Minnesota State Fair Rule 6.05 prohibits the sale or distribution of any merchandise, including printed or written material, except from a booth rented from the state. Booths are rented to all comers in a nondiscriminatory manner on a first-come, first-served basis. The rental charge is based on the size and location of the booth. International Society for Krishna Consciousness (ISKCON), an international religious society espousing the views of the Krishna religion, challenged Rule 6.05 on the ground that it would impair its ability effectively to distribute or sell its literature and to solicit donations for the support of the Krishna religion.

The Court upheld the rule. In an opinion by Justice White, the Court observed that "'we have often approved [reasonable time, place, and manner restrictions] provided that they are justified without reference to the content of the regulated speech, that they serve a significant governmental interest, and [that] they leave open ample alternative channels for communication of the information.'"

The Court noted that Rule 6.05 is clearly content-neutral, for it "applies even-handedly to all who wish to distribute and sell written materials or to solicit funds." Moreover, the Court observed that the "principal justification" asserted by the State — "the need to maintain the orderly movement of the crowd given the large number of exhibitors and persons attending the Fair" — is "'a significant governmental interest.'" The Court explained that, in assessing "the significance of the governmental interest," it must consider the "nature and function of the particular forum involved." The Court then rejected ISKCON's effort to analogize "the fairgrounds [to] city streets which have 'immemorially been [used] for purposes [of] assembly [and] discussing public questions'": "A street is continually open, often uncongested, [and] a place where people may enjoy the open air or the company of friends [in] a relaxed environment. The Minnesota Fair [is] a temporary event attracting great numbers of visitors who come to the event for a short period to see [the] host of exhibits [at] the Fair. The flow of the crowd and the demands of safety are more pressing in the context of the Fair. As such, any comparisons to public streets are necessarily inexact." The Court thus concluded that, given the "threat to the State's interest in crowd control if [all] organizations [could] move freely about the fairgrounds distributing and selling literature and soliciting funds at will, [the] State's interest in confining distribution, selling, and fund solicitation activities to fixed locations is sufficient to satisfy the requirement that a place or manner restriction must serve a substantial state interest."

The Court added that, "for similar reasons, we cannot [agree] that Rule 6.05 is an unnecessary regulation because the State could [protect] its interests [by] less restrictive means, such [as] limiting the number of solicitors, or putting more narrowly drawn restrictions on the location and movement of [distributors and solicitors]," for "it is quite improbable that [such] alternative means [would] deal adequately with the [problem]."

Finally, the Court noted that "for Rule 6.05 to be valid as a place and manner restriction, it must [be] clear that alternative forums for the expression [exist] despite the effects of the Rule." The Court concluded that Rule 6.05, is "not vulnerable on this ground": "[The] Rule does not prevent ISKCON from [distributing its literature or soliciting donations] anywhere outside the fairgrounds, [it] does not exclude ISKCON from the fairgrounds, [and it does not] deny that organization the right to conduct [its] desired activity at some point within the forum. Its members may mingle with the crowd and orally propagate their views [and it] may arrange for a booth and [thus] distribute and sell literature and solicit funds from that location on the fairgrounds itself. The Minnesota State Fair is a limited public forum in that it exists to provide a means for a great number of exhibitors temporarily to present their products or views [to] a large number of people in an efficient fashion. Considering the limited functions of the Fair and the confined area within which it operates, we are unwilling to say that Rule 6.05 does not provide ISKCON and other organizations with an adequate means to sell and solicit on the fairgrounds."

Justice Brennan, joined by Justices Marshall and Stevens, concurred in part and dissented in part. Although conceding that "the State has a significant interest in maintaining crowd control on its fairgrounds," Brennan concluded that the "booth rule is an overly intrusive means of achieving [that interest]." "A state fair," Brennan maintained, "is truly a marketplace of ideas and a public forum for the communication of ideas and information." Thus, Rule 6.05 constitutes a "significant restriction on First Amendment rights," for "by prohibiting distribution of literature outside the booths, the fair officials sharply limit the number of fairgoers to whom the proselytizers [can] communicate their messages." Moreover, although "the State contends that if fairgoers are permitted to distribute literature, large crowds will gather, blocking traffic lanes and causing safety problems," it "has failed to provide any support for these assertions." The state, Brennan maintained, may not impose "a significant restriction on [the] ability to exercise core First Amendment rights" on the basis of "a general, speculative fear of disorder." Moreover, this "restriction is not narrowly drawn to advance the State's interests. [If] the State had a reasonable concern that distribution in certain parts of the fairgrounds — for example, entrances and exits — would cause disorder, it could have drafted its rule to prohibit distribution of literature at those points. If the State felt it necessary to limit the number of persons distributing an organization's literature, it could, within reason, have done that as well. It had no right, however, to ban all distribution of literature outside the booths."

On the other hand, Brennan concluded that Rule 6.05's restriction on the sale of literature and the solicitation of funds to fixed booth locations was constitutionally justified as an "antifraud measure." Such a restriction "substantially furthered" the state's interest "in protecting its fairgoers from fraudulent or deceptive solicitation practices," for it provides the state with "the greatest opportunity to police and prevent [such] practices." Justice Blackmun also concurred in part and dissented in part.

U.S. POSTAL SERVICE v. COUNCIL OF GREENBURGH CIVIC AS-SOCIATIONS, 453 U.S. 114 (1981): Title 18 U.S.C. §1725 prohibits the deposit of unstamped "mailable matter" in a letter box approved by the U.S. Postal Service. A local postmaster notified appellee civic association that its practice of delivering messages to residents by placing unstamped notices in the letter boxes of private homes violated section 1725. Thereafter, appellee filed suit seeking declaratory and injunctive relief from the Postal Service's threatened enforcement of the act. The Postal Service offered three justifications for section 1725: (1) it protects mail revenues; (2) it facilitates the efficient and secure delivery of the mails by preventing overcrowding of mailboxes; and (3) it promotes the privacy of mail patrons. The Postal Service argued further that section 1725 left appellees with ample alternative means of delivering their messages: "[They] can deliver their messages [by] paying postage, [by] placing their notices under doors, [or] by telephoning their constituents." The District Court held that section 1725 violated the first amendment. The District Court found that civic associations usually have small cash reserves and cannot afford regularly to mail their notices, that the "slow pace of the mail [would] impede the appellees' ability to communicate quickly with their constituents," that "none of the alternative means of delivery [were] 'nearly as effective as placing [flyers] in approved mailboxes,'" and that this means of expression did not appreciably interfere with any of the government's interests.

The Court, in a seven-to-two decision, reversed. In an opinion by Justice Rehnquist, the Court explained that when a letter box provided by a postal customer is designated an "authorized depository" it becomes an essential "part of the Postal Service's nationwide system for the delivery and receipt of mail." But this did not necessarily convert it into a public forum: "There is neither historical nor constitutional support for the characterization of a letter box as a public forum. [At least since 1934, when section 1725 was promulgated,] access to [letter boxes] has been unlawful except under the terms and conditions specified by Congress and the Postal Service. As such, it is difficult to accept appellees' assertion that because it may be somewhat more efficient to place their messages in letter boxes there is a First Amendment right to do so. [Indeed], it is difficult to conceive of any reason why this Court should treat a letter box differently for First Amendment [purposes] than it has in the past treated the military base in [*Greer* or] the jail [in *Adderley*]."

The Court then turned to the standard to be applied in testing the constitutionality of section 1725: "This Court has long recognized the validity of reasonable time, place, and manner regulations on [public forums] so long as the regulation is content-neutral, serves a significant governmental interest, and leaves open adequate alternative channels for communication. [But] since a letter box is not traditionally such a 'public forum,' [such] elaborate analysis [is] unnecessary.

[While] the analytical line between a regulation of the 'time, place, and manner' in which First Amendment rights may be exercised in a traditional public forum, and the question of whether a particular piece of personal or real property owned or controlled by the government is in fact a 'public forum' may blur at the edges, we think the line is nonetheless a workable one."

The Court explained in a footnote: "What we hold is the principle reiterated by cases such as [*Adderley*] and [*Greer*], that property owned or controlled by the government which is *not* a public forum may be subject to a prohibition of speech, leafleting, picketing, or other forms of communication without running afoul of the First Amendment. Admittedly, the government must act reasonably in imposing such restrictions [and] the prohibition must be content-neutral. [But] §1725 is both a reasonable and content-neutral regulation."

Justice Brennan concurred in the judgment. "For public forum analysis," Brennan argued, "'The crucial question is whether the manner of expression is basically incompatible with the normal activity of a particular place at a particular time.' [*Grayned*.]" In this case, "the mere deposit of mailable matter without postage is not 'basically incompatible' with the 'normal activity' for which a letter box is used, [for] the mails and the letter box are specifically used for the communication of information and ideas, and thus surely constitute a public forum appropriate for the exercise of First Amendment rights." Moreover, the Court's error did not end with its failure to find the letter box a public forum, for "even where property does not constitute a public forum, government regulation that is content-neutral must still be reasonable as to time, place and manner." Brennan concluded, however, that §1725 "is constitutional because it is a reasonable time, place, and manner regulation." In reaching this conclusion, he cited three factors: the statute "is content-neutral," "the burden on expression advances a significant governmental interest — preventing loss of mail revenues," and "there are 'ample alternative channels for communication.'"

Justice White also concurred in the judgment, but for reasons quite different from those offered by either Rehnquist or Brennan: "No one questions [that the Government] may impose a fee on those who would use the [postal system]. A self-evident justification for postage is that the Government may insist that those who use the mails contribute to the expense of maintaining and operating the facility. [It is] bootless [to inquire] whether the postal system is a public forum. For all who will pay the fee, it obviously is, and [because] I am quite sure that the fee is a valid charge, I concur in the judgment."

Justice Marshall dissented, rejecting "the Court's use of the public forum concept to avoid application of the First Amendment." The "concept of a public forum," Marshall maintained, is not "a threshold barrier that must be surmounted before reaching the terrain of the First Amendment." Rather, it "has more properly been used to open varied governmental locations [to] free expression, subject to the constraints on time, place or manner necessary to preserve the governmental function." Given "its pervasive and traditional use as a purveyor of written communication," the "Postal Service [may] properly be viewed as a public forum. [For] the Postal Service's very purpose is to facilitate communication, which surely differentiates it from the military bases [and jails] discussed in cases relied on by the Court."

Justice Marshall also rejected "the Court's assumption that if no public forum is involved, the only [question is] whether the regulation is content-based [and] reasonable": "Even if the Postal System were not a public forum, [§1725] is a law challenged as an abridgement of free expression. [The] question, then, is whether this statute burdens any First Amendment rights enjoyed by appellees [and, if so], whether this burden is justified by a significant governmental interest substantially advanced by the statute." In light of the District Court's findings, Marshall concluded that he could not "join the Court's conclusion that the Federal Government [may] curtail appellees' ability to inform community residents about local civic matters."

Justice Stevens also dissented: "The mailbox is private property; it is not a public forum to which the owner must grant access. [But if] the owner welcomes messages from his neighbors, [it] is presumptively unreasonable to interfere with his ability to receive such communications. The [statute] deprives millions of homeowners of the legal right to make a simple decision affecting their ability to receive communications from others. [The government's asserted justifications for the statute] are insufficient to overcome the presumption that this impediment to communication is invalid."

MEMBERS OF THE CITY COUNCIL OF LOS ANGELES v. TAXPAYERS FOR VINCENT, — U.S. — , 104 S. Ct. 2118 (1984): The Court upheld a Los Angeles ordinance prohibiting the posting of signs on public property, as applied to individuals who tied political campaign signs to public utility poles. Justice Stevens delivered the opinion: "The ordinance [diminishes] the total quantity of [appellees'] communication in the City. [But] the state [may] curtail speech [in a content-neutral manner if the restriction] 'furthers an important or substantial governmental interest; if [that] interest is unrelated to the suppression of free expression; and if the incidental restriction on [free speech] is no greater than is essential to the furtherance of that interest.'

"[It is undisputed that the] state may legitimately [advance] esthetic values, [that] this interest is unrelated to the suppression of ideas, [and that the] problem addressed by this ordinance — the visual assault [on] citizens [presented] by an accumulation of signs posted on public property — constitutes a significant substantive evil. [Moreover, the] restriction on appellees' expressive activity is [no] broader than necessary to protect the City's interest. [By] banning these signs, the City did no more than eliminate the exact source of the evil it sought to remedy.

"It is true that the esthetic interest in preventing [litter] cannot support a prophylactic prohibition against [leafleting. Citing Schneider v. State, supra section E1. But the] rationale of *Schneider* is inapposite in the context of this case. [In *Schneider*,] individual citizens were actively exercising their right to communicate directly with potential recipients of their message. [In] this case, appellees posted [signs that] would remain unattended until removed. As the Court expressly noted in *Schneider*, the First Amendment does not 'deprive a municipality of power to enact regulations against throwing literature broadcast in the streets.' [Characterizing] such an activity as a separate means of communication does not diminish the state's power to condemn it as a public nuisance. [Moreover], in *Schneider*, an anti-littering statute could have addressed the substantive evil without prohibiting expressive activity. [Here], the substantive evil — visual blight — is not merely a possible by-product of the activity, but is created by the medium of expression itself. [Thus, the] ordinance curtails no more speech than is necessary to accomplish its purpose. . . .

"[Appellees argue] that a prohibition against the [posting of signs on public property] cannot be justified on esthetic grounds [unless the ban applies to private property as well. We do not agree]. The private citizen's interest in controlling [his] own property justifies the disparate treatment. Moreover, by not extending the ban to all locations, a significant opportunity to communicate by means of [signs] is preserved, and private property owners' esthetic concerns will keep the posting of signs on their property within reasonable bounds. Even if some visual blight remains, a partial, content-neutral ban may nevertheless enhance the City's appearance. . . .

"[A] restriction on expressive activity may be invalid if the remaining modes of communication are inadequate. [But to] the extent that the posting of signs on public property has advantages over [other] forms of expression, [there] is no reason to believe that these same advantages cannot be obtained through other means. [Indeed, nothing] indicates that the posting of political posters on public property is a uniquely valuable [mode] of communication, or that appellees' ability to communicate effectively is threatened by ever-increasing restrictions on expression. . . .

"Appellees suggest that the public property covered by the ordinance is [a] 'public forum,' [but they] fail to demonstrate the existence of a traditional right of access respecting such items as utility poles for purposes [of] communication comparable to that recognized for public streets and parks. [The] mere fact that government property can be used as a vehicle for communication does not mean that the Constitution requires such uses to be permitted. . . .

"Finally, [appellees] argue that Los Angeles could have written an ordinance that would have had a less severe effect on expressive activity [by] permitting the posting of [signs] in some locations or permitting the posting of signs that meet design specifications. [Any] constitutionally mandated exception to the City's total prohibition [would] necessarily rest on a judicial determination that the City's [interests] in esthetics are not sufficiently important to justify the prohibition in that category. [There is] no basis [in the record for such a judgment. We] accept the City's position that it may decide that the esthetic interest in avoiding 'visual clutter' justifies a removal of [all signs] increasing that clutter."

Justice Brennan, joined by Justices Marshall and Blackmun, dissented: "The posting of signs is [a] time-honored means of communicating. [It] is particularly valuable [because] it entails a relatively small expense in reaching a wide-audience. [There] may be alternative channels of communication, but [for] many speakers those alternatives are far less satisfactory. [There] is no proof, [for example], that a sufficient number of private parties would allow the posting of signs on their property [and, in any event, a] speaker with [unpopular views] is hardly likely to get his message across if forced to rely on this medium. [Similarly], the adequacy of distributing handbills is dubious, [for] a message on a sign will typically reach far more people [and the] average cost of communicating by handbill [is] likely to be far higher than [the] cost of communicating by poster. [Because] the City has completely banned [this] particular medium of communication, and because [there] are no equivalent alternative[s], the Court must examine with particular care the justifications that the City proffers. . . .

"[Moreover, courts] should exercise special care [when] a purely aesthetic objective is asserted to justify a restriction of speech. [Aesthetic] interests are easy for a city to assert and difficult for a court to evaluate. [In some cases, the] asserted interest in aesthetics may be only a facade for content-based suppression, [as where the real objection is to] the messages typically carried by the signs. [In other cases, where the objection is in fact to 'visual clutter'], the government may too easily overstate the substantiality of its goals. [Indeed], when a total ban is justified solely in terms of aesthetics, [the] means may fit the ends only because the ends were defined with the means in mind. In this case, for example, the City has expressed an aesthetic judgment that signs on public property constitute visual clutter [and] that its objective is to eliminate visual clutter. [In such circumstances, the] question whether [the] objective could [be] achieved with less restriction of speech [is completely circular].

"[Because of the] difficulties inherent in judicial review of aesthetics-based restrictions of speech, [there] is a need for more stringent judicial scrutiny than the Court seems willing to exercise. [In] my view, [statements] of aesthetic objectives should be accepted as substantial [only] if the government demonstrates that it is pursuing [its] goal of eliminating visual clutter in a serious and comprehensive manner. Most importantly, [it must] show that it is pursuing its goal through programs other than its ban on signs, that at least some of those programs address the visual clutter problem through means that do not entail the restriction of speech, and that the programs parallel the ban in their stringency, geographical scope, and aesthetic focus. In this case, [there] is no indication that the City has addressed its visual clutter problem in any way other than by prohibiting the posting of signs."

Note: Modern Public Forum Doctrine

1. *Deference to regulators.* Consider Goldberger, Judicial Scrutiny in Public Forum Cases: Misplaced Trust in the Judgment of Public Officials, 32 Buff. L. Rev. 175, 206-207, 217-218 (1983):

> By employing [low] levels of scrutiny in [cases like *Heffron*], the Court [assumes] that regulatory decision making is [generally] trustworthy. [The] Court has failed to recognize [that] public officials [often] have strong incentives to overregulate. [These incentives come] from two sources. First, there is the tendency of forum regulators to be disproportionately sensitive to threats of [disruption]. Second, forum regulators tend to be particularly sensitive toward protecting public services [when] the communication is controversial or is of interest to only a small segment of the population. [To compensate for these incentives, the Court in a case like *Heffron* should have required state] officials to prove that the activities regulated were as disruptive [as] claimed.

2. *Evaluation.* What doctrines and principles emerge from this line of cases? To what extent do these decisions redefine the "right to a public forum"? To what extent do they give appropriate weight to the interest in free expression? Consider the following assessment: The dispute over access to non–public forum property turns on a conflict between two competing views. Under one view, the first amendment requires government to permit the widest possible opportunity for free expression. The greater the opportunity for free expression, the healthier the marketplace of ideas. Thus, any law that restricts free expression must be invalidated unless the government interest served by the restriction outweighs the

effect on free expression. Under the competing view, the traditional means of expression — radio, television, newspapers, speeches, parades, picketing, leaflets, and the like — provide ample opportunity for free expression. Although access to non–public forum public property might make some speech marginally more effective, a denial of access to such property poses no real threat to the marketplace of ideas. Moreover, to require such access would necessarily interfere to some extent with competing government interests and involve the courts in an endless series of highly subjective and inevitably unpredictable judgments. Thus, the costs of such inquiries far exceed the benefits. In recent years, the Court has embraced this second view.

3. *Other nonpublic forums.* For additional decisions holding that various types of public property do not constitute "public forums," see, e.g., Lehman v. City of Shaker Heights, infra section F1 (car card space on the interior of a publicly owned bus is not a public forum); Perry Educators' Association v. Perry Local Educators' Association, infra section F1 (an interschool mail system used to transmit messages within a school is not a public forum); Cornelius v. NAACP Legal Defense and Educational Fund, Inc., infra section F1 (the Combined Federal Campaign, an annual charitable fund-raising drive conducted in the federal work place, is not a public forum).

4. *Equality and public property.* Content-based and other "unequal" exclusions from public property are examined in section F1 infra.

Note: The Right to a "Private" Forum

To what extent, if any, does the first amendment guarantee the individual a right to commandeer some other person's private property for speech purposes? Do the property rights of private owners absolutely preclude such an interpretation of the first amendment? Does the state action requirement foreclose such an interpretation? The state action issue is examined in Chapter 10 infra.

1. *The company town:* Marsh. In Marsh v. Alabama, 326 U.S. 501 (1946), the Court considered whether a state could constitutionally "impose criminal punishment on a person who undertakes to distribute religious literature on the premises of a company-owned town contrary to the wishes of the town's management." The town, a suburb of Mobile, Alabama, known as Chickasaw, was owned by the Gulf Shipbuilding Corporation. The town was freely used by the public and there was "nothing to distinguish [it] from any other town [except] the fact that the title to the property [belonged] to a private corporation." Appellant, a Jehovah's Witness, attempted to distribute literature on one of the town's sidewalks. She was informed that, pursuant to a formal corporation policy, she could not distribute literature without a permit and that no permit would be issued her. When asked to leave, she declined. She was eventually convicted of violating a state statute prohibiting any person to enter or remain on the premises of another after having been warned not to do so.

The Court overturned the conviction. Justice Black, speaking for the Court, observed:

> Had the title to Chickasaw belonged not to a private, but to a municipal corporation [it] would have been clear that appellant's conviction must be reversed. [The] State

urges [that] the corporation's right to control the inhabitants of Chickasaw is coextensive with the right of a homeowner to regulate the conduct of his guests. We cannot accept that contention. Ownership does not always mean absolute dominion. The more an owner, for his advantage, opens up his property for use by the public in general, the more do his rights become circumscribed by the statutory and constitutional rights of those who use it. [In] our view the circumstance that the property rights to the premises where the deprivation of liberty, here involved, took place, were held by others than the public, is not sufficient to justify the State's permitting a corporation to govern a community of citizens so as to restrict their fundamental liberties and the enforcement of such restraint by the application of a state statute.

2. *Privately owned shopping centers:* Logan Valley, Lloyd, *and* Hudgens. In Food Employees Local 590 v. Logan Valley Plaza, 391 U.S. 308 (1968), the Court held that "peaceful [labor] picketing of a business enterprise located within a shopping center" cannot constitutionally be prohibited:

[As this Court held in *Marsh,*] under some circumstances property that is privately owned may, at least for First Amendment purposes, be treated as though it were publicly held. [The] similarities between the business block in *Marsh* and the shopping center in the present case are striking. [The] shopping center premises are open to the public to the same extent as the commercial center of a normal town. [The] shopping center here is clearly the functional equivalent of the business district of Chickasaw involved in *Marsh.* [We therefore hold that, as in *Marsh*], the State may not delegate the power, through the use of its trespass laws, wholly to exclude those members of the public wishing to exercise their First Amendment rights on the premises in a manner and for a purpose generally consonant with the use to which the property is actually put.

In Lloyd Corp. v. Tanner, 407 U.S. 551 (1972), the Court upheld a privately owned shopping center's prohibition on "the distribution of handbills on its property when the handbilling, [concerning a protest against the draft and the Vietnam War, was] unrelated to the shopping center's operations":

[*Marsh*] involved the assumption by a private enterprise of all of the attributes of a state-created municipality [as] a delegate of the State. [In] the instant case there is no comparable assumption [of] municipal functions or power. [Moreover, *Logan Valley* is not controlling, for the opinion in *Logan Valley*] was carefully phrased to limit its holding [to] picketing [that] was "directly related in its purpose to the use to which the shopping center property was being put," [and where] no other reasonable opportunities for the pickets to convey their message to their intended audience were available. Neither of these elements is present [here].

In Hudgens v. NLRB, 424 U.S. 507 (1976), which concerned the right of union members to enter a privately owned shopping center to picket a store located within the center, the Court overruled *Logan Valley:*

The Court in [*Lloyd*] did not say that it was overruling [*Logan Valley*]. [But] the reasoning [of] *Lloyd* cannot be squared [with] *Logan Valley.* [If] a large self-contained shopping center *is* the functional equivalent of a municipality, as *Logan Valley* held, then the [Constitution] would not permit control of speech [to] depend upon [content]. [If] the respondents in [*Lloyd*] did not have a First Amendment right [to] distribute handbills concerning Vietnam, [the] pickets in the present case [cannot] have a First Amendment right to enter [the] shopping center [to advertise] their strike. [The] constitutional guarantee of free expression has no part to play in a case such as this.

For a critical evaluation, see Schauer, *Hudgens v. NLRB* and the Problem of State Action in First Amendment Adjudication, 61 Minn. L. Rev. 433, 444 (1977). Does *Marsh* retain any vitality beyond the limited context of company towns? What about migrant labor camps? See Illinois Migrant Council v. Campbell Soup Co., 519 F.2d 391 (7th Cir. 1975); Petersen v. Talisman Sugar Corp., 478 F.2d 73 (5th Cir. 1973).

3. *Does the appropriation of private property for speech purposes violate the constitutional rights of owners?:* PruneYard. Suppose the state, in an effort to promote free expression, grants the individual a right under state law to enter on private property for speech purposes. Might that in itself violate the property or speech rights of the property owner? In PruneYard Shopping Center v. Robins, 447 U.S. 74 (1980), a group of high school students who sought to solicit support for their opposition to a United Nations resolution against Zionism set up a card table in the PruneYard shopping center and asked passers-by to sign petitions. Pursuant to a policy prohibiting any visitor to engage in any publicly expressive activity not directly related to the shopping center's commercial purposes, a security guard ordered the students to leave. The California Supreme Court held that the California Constitution protects "speech and petitioning, reasonably exercised, in shopping centers even when the centers are privately owned." The U.S. Supreme Court rejected PruneYard's contention that the California Supreme Court's decision violated the federal constitutional rights of the shopping center owner.

The Court explained:

[PruneYard contends] that a right to exclude others underlies the Fifth Amendment guarantee against the taking of property without just compensation. [But] "not every destruction or injury to property by governmental action has been held to be a 'taking' in the constitutional sense." [Here, there] is nothing to suggest that preventing [PruneYard] from prohibiting this sort of activity will unreasonably impair the value or use of [the] property as a shopping center. [PruneYard contends further] that a private property owner has a First Amendment right not to be forced by the State to use his property as a forum for the speech of others. [Although there are circumstances in which] a State may not constitutionally require an individual to participate in the dissemination of an ideological message by displaying it on his private property, [this is not such a case. First, PruneYard is] a business establishment that is open to the public to come and go as they please. The views expressed by members of the public in passing out pamphlets or seeking signatures for a petition thus will not likely be identified with those of the owner. Second, no specific message is dictated by the State to be displayed. [There] consequently is no danger of governmental discrimination for or against a particular message. Finally, [PruneYard] can expressly disavow any connection with the message by simply posting signs in the area where the speakers or handbillers stand.

See also Red Lion Broadcasting Co. v. FCC, 395 U.S. 367 (1969) (upholding the fairness doctrine, requiring broadcast licensees to present "full and fair" coverage of public issues and to provide free reply time to individuals attacked on the air); Miami Herald Publishing Co. v. Tornillo, 418 U.S. 241 (1974) (invalidating a state law granting political candidates a right to reply to criticism and attacks on their record by a newspaper). On the right "not to speak," see infra section F4. On regulation of the media, see infra section F6.

4. *Other "appropriations" of private property for speech purposes:* Zacchini. In Zacchini v. Scripps-Howard Broadcasting Co., 433 U.S. 562 (1977), petitioner's fifteen-second "human cannonball" act, in which he is shot from a cannon into a net some 200 feet away, was, without his consent, filmed in its entirety at a county fair and shown on a television news program later the same day. Petitioner filed a damage action alleging an "unlawful appropriation" of his "professional property." The Court held that the first amendment did not bar petitioner's action: "[The First Amendment does not give the media a right to] broadcast a performer's entire act without his consent. The Constitution no more prevents a State from requiring respondent to compensate petitioner for broadcasting his act on television than it would privilege respondent to film and broadcast a copyrighted dramatic work without liability to the copyright owner." For a useful analysis of *Zacchini*, see Note, Human Cannonballs and the First Amendment, 30 Stan. L. Rev. 1185 (1978).

Similar issues arise in the copyright context. See Harper & Row, Publishers v. Nation Enterprises, — U.S. — , 105 S. Ct. 2218 (1985) (a magazine's unauthorized publication of verbatim quotes from President Ford's unpublished memoirs constituted an actionable copyright infringement). See generally Note, Copyright, Free Speech, and the Visual Arts, 93 Yale L.J. 1565 (1984).

3.   *Symbolic Conduct*

This section explores the use of nonverbal conduct — such as burning a draft card or mutilating a flag — as a means of "symbolic" expression. In what circumstances, if any, does such nonverbal conduct constitute protected "speech" within the meaning of the first amendment? Consider Henkin, Foreword: On Drawing Lines, 82 Harv. L. Rev. 63, 79-80 (1968): "A constitutional distinction between speech and conduct is specious. Speech *is* conduct, and actions speak. There is nothing intrinsically sacred about wagging the tongue or wielding a pen; there is nothing intrinsically more sacred about words than other symbols. [The] meaningful constitutional distinction is not between speech and conduct, but between conduct that speaks, communicates, and other kinds of conduct." In fact, the Court has long recognized that at least some forms of conduct may constitute "speech" within the meaning of the first amendment. In West Virginia State Board of Education v. Barnette, 319 U.S. 624 (1943), for example, Justice Jackson explained that "symbolism is a primitive but effective way of communicating ideas. [It] is a short cut from mind to mind." See also Tinker v. Des Moines Independent Community School District, 393 U.S. 503 (1969) (black armbands); Brown v. Louisiana, supra section E2b (sit-in) (plurality opinion); Stromberg v. California, 283 U.S. 359 (1931) (red flag).

If it is assumed that some forms of nonverbal conduct may constitute "speech," the question remains, how are we to determine what nonverbal conduct merits first amendment protection? At one level, it seems clear that "Everything that one does, every action that one takes or fails to take, 'speaks' to anyone who is interested in looking for a message." That is, "all behavior is *capable of being under-stood* as communication." F. Haiman, Speech and Law in a Free Society 31 (1981). Surely, however, not all behavior that is "capable of being understood as communication" constitutes "speech," for that would bring all conduct within the ambit of the first amendment.

Consider Nimmer, The Meaning of Symbolic Speech under the First Amendment, 21 U.C.L.A. L. Rev. 29, 36 (1973):

> A further element must be added to the mix before conduct may be considered to be speech. Whatever else may or may not be true of speech, as an irreducible minimum it must constitute a communication. That, in turn, implies both a communicator and a communicatee — a speaker and an audience. [Without] an actual or potential audience there can be no first amendment speech right. Nor may the first amend-ment be invoked if there is an audience but no actual or potential "speaker." [Un-less] there is a human communicator intending to convey a meaning by his conduct, it would be odd to think of it as conduct constituting a communication protected by the first amendment.

Does all nonverbal conduct that is intended to communicate constitute "speech"? Note that such a doctrine might create a serious "imposter problem." That is, it would invite fraudulent claims by "criminals" that their actual intent was to communicate. Should courts be in the business of inquiring into the sincerity of individuals who claim to have exercised first amendment rights? Is there any way to avoid such inquiries? The issue of inquiry into sincerity in the religion context is examined in Chapter 8, section C, infra. Note also that, de-pending on the circumstances, nonverbal conduct that is intended to communi-cate may range across the entire spectrum of human behavior. It may include assassination, refusal to pay taxes, public nudity, burning a flag, and urination on the steps of the state capitol. Does all such conduct constitute constitutionally protected "speech" as long as the actor intended to communicate?

United States v. O'Brien

391 U.S. 367 (1968)

MR. CHIEF JUSTICE WARREN delivered the opinion of the Court.

On the morning of March 31, 1966, David Paul O'Brien and three companions burned their Selective Service registration certificates on the steps of the South Boston Courthouse. A sizable crowd, including several agents of the Federal Bureau of Investigation, witnessed the event. Immediately after the burning, [O'Brien] stated to FBI agents that he had burned his registration certificate because of his beliefs, knowing that he was violating federal law.

For this act, O'Brien was indicted, tried, convicted, and sentenced in the United States District Court for the District of Massachusetts. He did not contest the fact that he had burned the certificate. He stated in argument to the jury that he burned the certificate publicly to influence others to adopt his antiwar beliefs, as he put it, "so that other people would reevaluate their positions with Selective Service, with the armed forces, and reevaluate their place in the culture of today, to hopefully consider my position."

The indictment upon which he was tried charged that he "willfully and know-ingly did mutilate, destroy, and change by burning [his] Registration Certificate

[in] violation of [§462(b)(3) of the Universal Military Training and Service Act of 1948]." Section 462(b)(3) [was] amended by Congress in 1965 (adding the words italicized below) so that at the time O'Brien burned his certificate an offense was commited by any person, "who forges, alters, *knowingly destroys, knowingly mutilates,* or in any manner changes any such certificate. . . ." (Italics supplied.) . . .

[T]he Court of Appeals [held] the 1965 Amendment unconstitutional as a law abridging freedom of speech. At the time the Amendment was enacted, a regulation of the Selective Service System required registrants to keep their registration certificates in their "personal possession at all times." 32 C.F.R. §1617.1 (1962). [The] Court of Appeals [was] of the opinion that conduct punishable under the 1965 Amendment was already punishable under the nonpossession regulation, and consequently that the Amendment served no valid purpose; further, that in light of the prior regulation, the Amendment must have been "directed at public as distinguished from private destruction." On this basis, the court concluded that the 1965 Amendment ran afoul of the First Amendment by singling out persons engaged in protests for special treatment. [We] hold that the 1965 Amendment is constitutional both as enacted and as applied. . . .

[The] 1965 Amendment plainly does not abridge free speech on its face, and we do not understand O'Brien to argue otherwise. Amended §12(b)(3) on its face deals with conduct having no connection with speech. It prohibits the knowing destruction of certificates issued by the Selective Service System, and there is nothing necessarily expressive about such conduct. The Amendment does not distinguish between public and private destruction, and it does not punish only destruction engaged in for the purpose of expressing views. Compare Stromberg v. California, 283 U.S. 359 (1931). A law prohibiting destruction of Selective Service certificates no more abridges free speech on its face than a motor vehicle law prohibiting the destruction of drivers' licenses, or a tax law prohibiting the destruction of books and records.

O'Brien nonetheless argues that the 1965 Amendment is unconstitutional in its application to him, and is unconstitutional as enacted because what he calls the "purpose" of Congress was "to suppress freedom of speech." We consider these arguments separately.

II

O'Brien first argues that the 1965 Amendment is unconstitutional as applied to him because his act of burning his registration certificate was protected "symbolic speech" within the First Amendment. His argument is that the freedom of expression which the First Amendment guarantees includes all modes of "communication of ideas by conduct," and that his conduct is within this definition because he did it in "demonstration against the war and against the draft."

We cannot accept the view that an apparently limitless variety of conduct can be labeled "speech" whenever the person engaging in the conduct intends thereby to express an idea. However, even on the assumption that the alleged communicative element in O'Brien's conduct is sufficient to bring into play the First Amendment, it does not necessarily follow that the destruction of a registration certificate is constitutionally protected activity. This Court has held that when "speech" and "nonspeech" elements are combined in the same course of conduct, a sufficiently important governmental interest in regulating the non-speech element can justify incidental limitations on First Amendment freedoms. To characterize the quality of the governmental interest which must appear, the Court has employed a variety of descriptive terms: compelling; substantial; subor-dinating; paramount; cogent; strong. Whatever imprecision inheres in these terms, we think it clear that a government regulation is sufficiently justified if it is within the constitutional power of the Government; if it furthers an important or substantial governmental interest; if the governmental interest is unrelated to the suppression of free expression; and if the incidental restriction on alleged First Amendment freedoms is no greater than is essential to the furtherance of that interest. We find that the 1965 Amendment [meets] all of these requirements, and consequently that O'Brien can be constitutionally convicted for violating it.

The constitutional power of Congress to raise and support armies and to make all laws necessary and proper to that end is broad and sweeping. [Pursuant] to this power, Congress may establish a system of registration for individuals liable for training and service, and may require such individuals within reason to cooperate in the registration system. The issuance of certificates indicating the registration and eligibility classification of individuals is a legitimate and substantial adminis-trative aid in the functioning of this system. And legislation to insure the continu-ing availability of issued certificates serves a legitimate and substantial purpose in the system's administration. . . .

1. The registration certificate serves as proof that the individual described thereon has registered for the draft. The classification certificate shows the eligi-bility classification of a named but undescribed individual. Voluntarily displaying the two certificates is an easy and painless way for a young man to dispel a question as to whether he might be delinquent in his Selective Service obliga-tions. [Additionally] in a time of national crisis, reasonable availability to each registrant of the two small cards assures a rapid and uncomplicated means for determining his fitness for immediate induction, no matter how distant in our mobile society he may be from his local board.

2. The information supplied on the certificates facilitates communication be-tween registrants and local boards, simplifying the system and benefiting all con-cerned. To begin with, each certificate bears the address of the registrant's local board, an item unlikely to be committed to memory. Further, each card bears the registrant's Selective Service number, and a registrant who has his number read-ily available so that he can communicate it to his local board when he supplies or requests information can make simpler the board's task in locating his file. . . .

3. Both certificates carry continual reminders that the registrant must notify his local board of any change of address, and other specified changes in his sta-tus. . . .

The many functions performed by Selective Service certificates establish be-yond doubt that Congress has a legitimate and substantial interest in preventing their wanton and unrestrained destruction and assuring their continuing avail-ability by punishing people who knowingly and wilfully destroy or mutilate them. And we are unpersuaded that the pre-existence of the nonpossession regulations in any way negates this interest.

In the absence of a question as to multiple punishment, it has never been suggested that there is anything improper in Congress' providing alternative statutory avenues of prosecution to assure the effective protection of one and the same interest. [Here], the pre-existing avenue of prosecution was not even statutory. Regulations may be modified or revoked from time to time by administrative discretion. Certainly, the Congress may change or supplement a regulation.

Equally important, a comparison of the regulations with the 1965 Amendment indicates that they protect overlapping but not identical governmental interests, and that they reach somewhat different classes of wrongdoers. The gravamen of the offense defined by the statute is the deliberate rendering of certificates unavailable for the various purposes which they may serve. Whether registrants keep their certificates in their personal possession at all times, as required by the regulations, is of no particular concern under the 1965 Amendment, as long as they do not mutilate or destroy the certificates so as to render them unavailable. . . .

We think it apparent that the continuing availability to each registrant of his Selective Service certificates substantially furthers the smooth and proper functioning of the system that Congress has established to raise armies [and] that the 1965 Amendment specifically protects this substantial governmental interest. We perceive no alternative means that would more precisely and narrowly assure the continuing availability of issued Selective Service certificates than a law which prohibits their wilful mutilation or destruction.

[Moreover,] both the governmental interest and the operation of the 1965 Amendment are limited to the noncommunicative aspect of O'Brien's conduct. The governmental interest and the scope of the 1965 Amendment are limited to preventing harm to the smooth and efficient functioning of the Selective Service System. When O'Brien deliberately rendered unavailable his registration certificate, he wilfully frustrated this governmental interest. For this noncommunicative impact of his conduct, and for nothing else, he was convicted.

The case at bar is therefore unlike one where the alleged governmental interest in regulating conduct arises in some measure because the communication allegedly integral to the conduct is itself thought to be harmful. In Stromberg v. California, 283 U.S. 359 (1931), for example, this Court struck down a statutory phrase which punished people who expressed their "opposition to organized government" by displaying "any flag, badge, banner, or device." Since the statute there was aimed at suppressing communication it could not be sustained as a regulation of noncommunicative conduct. . . .

In conclusion, we find that because of the Government's substantial interest in assuring the continuing availability of issued Selective Service certificates, because amended §462(b) is an appropriately narrow means of protecting this interest and condemns only the independent noncommunicative impact of conduct within its reach, and because the noncommunicative impact of O'Brien's act of burning his registration certificate frustrated the Government's interest, a sufficient governmental interest has been shown to justify O'Brien's conviction.

III

O'Brien finally argues that the 1965 Amendment is unconstitutional as enacted because what he calls the "purpose" of Congress was "to suppress freedom of speech." We reject this argument because under settled principles the purpose of

Congress, as O'Brien uses that term, is not a basis for declaring this legislation unconstitutional.

It is a familiar principle of constitutional law that this Court will not strike down an otherwise constitutional statute on the basis of an alleged illicit legislative motive. . . .

Inquiries into congressional motives or purposes are a hazardous matter. When the issue is simply the interpretation of legislation, the Court will look to statements by legislators for guidance as to the purpose of the legislature, because the benefit to sound decision-making in this circumstance is thought sufficient to risk the possibility of misreading Congress' purpose. It is entirely a different matter when we are asked to void a statute that is, under well-settled criteria, constitutional on its face, on the basis of what fewer than a handful of Congressmen said about it. What motivates one legislator to make a speech about a statute is not necessarily what motivates scores of others to enact it, and the stakes are sufficiently high for us to eschew guesswork. We decline to void [legislation] which could be reenacted in its exact form if the same or another legislator made a "wiser" speech about it. . . .

We think it not amiss, in passing, to comment upon O'Brien's legislative-purpose argument. There was little floor debate on this legislation in either House. Only Senator Thurmond commented on its substantive features in the Senate. [After] his brief statement, and without any additional substantive comments, the [bill] passed the Senate. [In] the House debate only two Congressmen addressed themselves to the Amendment — Congressmen Rivers and Bray. [The] bill was passed after their statements without any further debate by a vote of 393 to 1. It is principally on the basis of the statements by these three Congressmen that O'Brien makes his congressional-"purpose" argument. We note that if we were to examine legislative purpose in the instant case, we would be obliged to consider not only these statements but also the more authoritative reports of the Senate and House Armed Services Committees. [While] both reports make clear a concern with the "defiant" destruction of so-called "draft cards" and with "open" encouragement to others to destroy their cards, both reports also indicate that this concern stemmed from an apprehension that unrestrained destruction of cards would disrupt the smooth functioning of the Selective Service System.

IV

Since the 1965 Amendment to §12(b)(3) of the Universal Military Training and Service Act is constitutional as enacted and as applied, the Court of Appeals should have affirmed the judgment of conviction entered by the District Court. . . .

MR. JUSTICE MARSHALL took no part in the consideration or decision of these cases.

MR. JUSTICE HARLAN, concurring. . . .

I wish to make explicit my understanding that this [decision] does not foreclose consideration of First Amendment claims in those rare instances when an "incidental" restriction upon expression, imposed by a regulation which furthers an "important or substantial" governmental interest and satisfies the Court's other criteria, in practice has the effect of entirely preventing a "speaker" from reaching a significant audience with whom he could not otherwise lawfully communicate. This is not such a case, since O'Brien manifestly could have conveyed his message in many ways other than by burning his draft card.

MR. JUSTICE DOUGLAS, dissenting. . . .

[Douglas maintained that the "underlying and basic [issue] in this case [is] whether conscription is permissible in the absence of a declaration of war." Douglas therefore suggested that "this case should be put down for reargument" on that question. Douglas briefly addressed the symbolic conduct issue in his concurring opinion the following term in Brandenburg v. Ohio, supra section B1: "Action is often a method of expression and within the protection of the First Amendment. Suppose one tears up his own copy of the Constitution in eloquent protest to a decision of this Court. May he be indicted? Suppose one rips his own Bible to shreds to celebrate his departure from one 'faith' and his embrace of atheism. May he be indicted? [This] Court's affirmance of [O'Brien's conviction for burning the draft card] was not, with all respect, consistent with the First Amendment."]

Note: Draft Card Burning and the First Amendment

1. O'Brien *and the Warren Court.* Consider Alfange, Free Speech and Symbolic Conduct: The Draft-Card Burning Case, 1968 Sup. Ct. Rev. 1, 1-3:

> The Warren Court earned much of its libertarian reputation by its concern for First Amendment guarantees of freedom of expression. [It] is ironic, therefore, that in [*O'Brien*] the Court not only rejected a First Amendment claim of a political dissenter that was by no means frivolous but dismissed it in an astonishingly cavalier manner. [Indeed, in upholding O'Brien's conviction, the Court] trivialized the issues and handed down an opinion that has all the deceptive simplicity and superficial force that can usually be achieved by begging the question.

2. *Is draft card burning "speech"?* Did the Court decide that question? How would you decide it? Consider T. Emerson, The System of Freedom of Expression 80, 84, 86, 89 (1970):

> The guiding principle must be to determine which element is predominant in the conduct under consideration. Is expression the major element and the action only secondary? Or is the action the essence and the expression incidental? The answer [must] be based on a common-sense reaction. [The] burning of a draft card is, of course, conduct that involves both communication and physical acts. Yet it seems quite clear that the predominant element in such conduct is expression (opposition to the draft) rather than action (destruction of a piece of cardboard). [On the other hand], other forms of protest [such as blocking traffic or pouring blood over Selective Service files] clearly consist of conduct in which action predominates. [To] attempt to bring such forms of protest within the expression category would rob the distinction between expression and action of all meaning.

Do you agree that any "attempt to disentangle 'speech' from conduct which is itself communicative" is likely to turn "on rather arbitrary classifications" that "will not withstand analysis"? Nimmer, The Meaning of Symbolic Speech under the First Amendment, 21 U.C.L.A. L. Rev. 29, 32, 33 (1973). For commentary on Emerson's "expression-action" distinction, see Baker, Scope of the First Amendment Freedom of Speech, 25 U.C.L.A. L. Rev. 964, 1009-1012 (1978); Ely, Flag Desecration: A Case Study in the Roles of Categorization and Balancing in First Amendment Analysis, 88 Harv. L. Rev. 1482, 1493-1496 (1975); Scanlon, A Theory of Freedom of Expression, 1 Phil. & Pub. Aff. 204, 207-208 (1972).

Why was Chief Justice Warren reluctant in *O'Brien* to "accept the view that an apparently limitless variety of conduct can be labelled 'speech' whenever the person engaging in the conduct intends thereby to express an idea"? Consider the following propositions: (a) If nonverbal conduct that is intended "to express an idea" constitutes "speech," government may not restrict that conduct unless it poses a "clear and present danger" within the meaning of the Holmes/Brandeis formulation. (b) Even if nonverbal conduct that is intended to communicate constitutes "speech," the first amendment does not "afford the same kind of freedom to those who would communicate ideas by conduct [as it affords] to those who communicate by pure speech." Cox v. Louisiana, 379 U.S. 536, 555 (1965).

3. *Symbolic conduct and the content-based/content-neutral distinction.* Should a distinction be drawn between laws that restrict symbolic conduct because of its content and laws that restrict symbolic conduct for reasons unrelated to content? Compare, for example, a law prohibiting "any person to urinate in public" with a law prohibiting "any person to urinate on a public building as a symbolic act of opposition to city government." Does the content-based/content-neutral distinction provide a useful framework for analyzing the constitutionality of such laws? Does *O'Brien* adopt such an analysis?

4. *Restrictions related "to the suppression of free expression":* Stromberg, Tinker, *and* Schacht. In Stromberg v. California, discussed in *O'Brien*, the Court invalidated a statute prohibiting any person to display "a red flag [in] any public place [as] a [symbol] of opposition to organized government." The Court explained that the law might be construed to prohibit "peaceful and orderly opposition to government by legal means" and thus curtailed "the opportunity for free political discussion."

In Tinker v. Des Moines Independent Community School District, 393 U.S. 503 (1969), decided a year after *O'Brien*, school officials, fearing possible disruption of school activities, suspended three public school students because they wore black armbands to school to protest the government's policy in Vietnam. In invalidating the suspensions, the Court observed that "the wearing of an armband for the purpose of expressing certain views is the type of symbolic act that is within the Free Speech Clause of the First Amendment" and is "closely akin to 'pure speech.'" The Court observed further that "the school authorities did not purport to prohibit the wearing of all symbols of political or controversial significance; [rather], a particular symbol — black armbands worn to exhibit opposition to this Nation's involvement in Vietnam — was singled out for prohibition." Consider Ely, supra, at 1498 & n.63: "[In] *Tinker* the state regulated [the armbands] because it feared the effect that the message those armbands conveyed would have on the other children. [*Tinker*] would have been quite a different case had it arisen [in] the context of a school regulation banning armbands in woodworking class along with all other sartorial embellishments liable to become safety hazards." Other aspects of *Tinker* are examined in section F2 infra.

In Schacht v. United States, 398 U.S. 58 (1970), petitioner, who participated in a skit demonstrating opposition to American involvement in Vietnam, was convicted of violating 18 U.S.C. §702, which made criminal the unauthorized wearing of an American military uniform. The Court reversed the conviction. Citing O'Brien, the Court observed that section 702 "is, standing alone, a valid statute on its face." The Court noted, however, that another statute, 10 U.S.C. §772(f), authorized the wearing of an American military uniform in a theatrical production "if the portrayal does not tend to discredit [the armed forces]." Finding that petitioner's skit constituted a "theatrical production" within the meaning of §772(f), the Court concluded: "[Petitioner's] conviction can be sustained only if he can be punished for speaking out against the role of our Army and our country in Vietnam. Clearly punishment for this reason would be an unconstitutional abridgement of freedom of speech. [Section 772(f)], which leaves Americans free to praise the war in Vietnam but can send persons like [petitioner] to prison for opposing it, cannot survive in a country which has the First Amendment."

5. *Restrictions "unrelated to the suppression of free expression."* O'Brien's analysis of restrictions that are "unrelated to the suppression of free expression" applies the general principles of content-neutral balancing to the specific context of symbolic conduct. Is O'Brien's application of those principles sufficiently speech-protective?

Consider Alfange, The Draft-Card Burning Case, 1968 Sup. Ct. Rev. 1, 23, 26:

> [As] the Court's own inventory of possible draft-card uses indicates, [the certificates] serve functions of dispensable convenience rather than urgent necessity. The Court's use of "substantial," therefore, is more appropriate if the term is understood in its sense of "having substance" or "not imaginary," rather than the sense of "considerable" or "large." [Moreover, the Court should have weighed] the importance of the government's interest against the impact of the draft law amendment on freedom of speech.

Should the Court have "balanced" the competing interests in O'Brien? How would you assess the importance of the draft law amendment's impact on free speech? Consider the following arguments:

a. "In view of the fact that the amendment does not punish dissent per se, but merely forbids one very specific means of conveying the expression of dissent, it cannot seriously be contended that the amendment's effect upon speech is anything but minor." Alfange, supra, at 27.

b. "Burning a draft card [is] the ordinary person's way of attracting the attention of the national news media. [To] [prohibit] such an effective form of propagating one's views [is] to greatly diminish the effectiveness of the individual's right [to] make his dissent known." Velvel, Freedom of Speech and the Draft Card Burning Cases, 16 U. Kan. L. Rev. 149, 153 (1968).

c. "[Symbolic] conduct deserves a high degree of constitutional protection. [The] kind of stimulus necessary to activate the political conscience of [the] populace sometimes can be created only by transcending rationality and appealing to more primitive, more basic instincts. [The] communication achieved by the wave of draft-card burnings at the height of the United States involvement in Vietnam represents a paradigm example of the 'speech' with which the First Amendment is concerned." Blasi, The Checking Value in First Amendment Theory, 1977 A.B.F. Res. J. 521, 640.

d. "[Much] of the effectiveness of O'Brien's communication [derived] precisely from the fact that it was illegal. Had there been no law prohibiting draft card [burning], he might have attracted no more attention than he would have by swallowing a goldfish." Ely, supra, at 1489-1490.

e. "As applied to expression, the [*O'Brien*] statute had [a] disparate impact on those who opposed government policy, for who would destroy a draft card as an expression of *support* for government policy? [Indeed], in practical effect, the statute had essentially the same content-differential effect as a law prohibiting any person [to destroy] a draft card 'as a symbolic expression of protest against government policy.'" Stone, Content Regulation and the First Amendment, 25 Wm. & Mary L. Rev. 189, 222-223 (1983).

Is the Court's analysis of symbolic expression in *O'Brien* consistent with its analysis of content-neutral restrictions generally? Consider Ely, supra, at 1488-1489: "What was unconsciously going on in *O'Brien* [was] a reservation [of] serious balancing [for] relatively familiar [means] of expression, such as pamphlets, pickets, public speeches and rallies [and a relegation of] other, less orthodox modes of communication to the [highly deferential approach] that sustained the draft card burning law." Is there anything wrong with this set of priorities?

In Clark v. Community for Creative Non-Violence, 468 U.S. — (1984), the Court, in a seven-to-two decision, upheld a National Park Service regulation prohibiting sleeping in a public park, as applied to individuals engaged in a round-the-clock demonstration designed to call attention to the plight of the homeless. Although the Court assumed arguendo that sleeping in these circumstances constituted "expressive conduct protected to some extent by the First Amendment," it upheld the ban as a permissible "regulation of symbolic conduct." The Court explained that "the four-factor standard of [*O'Brien*] is little, if any, different from the standard applied to time, place, and manner restrictions." The facts and reasoning of *Clark* are set out more fully at section E2a supra.

6. *"Incidental" restrictions on free speech.* Note that, unlike some content-neutral restrictions, such as laws prohibiting leafleting, the law at issue in *O'Brien* was not directed at expressive activity. Its effect on speech was thus merely "incidental." Should it matter whether a content-neutral law is designed specifically to restrict expression or designed to restrict a broader range of activities but has only an incidental effect on free speech? In addition to *O'Brien*, consider Wayte v. United States, — U.S. — , 104 S. Ct. 3065 (1985), in which the Court upheld as an "incidental" restriction on free speech the government's policy of enforcing the selective service registration requirement only against those men who advised the government that they had failed to register or who were reported by others as having failed to register; and United States v. Albertini, — U.S. — , 105 S. Ct. 289 (1985), in which the Court upheld as an "incidental" restriction of free speech a federal statute prohibiting any person to reenter a military base after being ordered not to do so, as applied to an individual who sought to reenter a base for speech purposes.

7. *The problem of legislative motivation.* Should the Court in *O'Brien* have invalidated the 1965 amendment because "the 'purpose' of Congress was 'to suppress freedom of speech'"? As the Court noted, only two members of the House and one senator commented directly on the legislation. Congressman Bray's comments are representative: "The need of this legislation is clear. Beatniks and so-called 'campus cults' have been publicly burning their draft cards to demon-

strate their contempt for the United States and our resistance to Communist takeovers. [If] these 'revolutionaries' are permitted to deface and destroy their draft cards, our entire Selective Service System is dealt a serious blow."

Consider Alfange, supra, at 15, 16: "[What] emerges with indisputable clarity from an examination of the legislative history of the amendment is that the intent of its framers was purely and simply to put a stop to this particular form of antiwar protest, which they deemed extraordinarily contemptible and vicious — even treasonous — at a time when American troops were engaged in combat. [The Court's contrary conclusion blinked] the facts."

The Court has often inquired into the motivation underlying executive and administrative decisions. See, e.g., Cornelius v. NAACP Legal Defense & Educational Fund, — U.S. — , 105 S. Ct. 3439 (1985) ("the existence of reasonable grounds for limiting access to a nonpublic forum [will] not save a regulation that is in reality a facade for viewpoint-based discrimination"); Mt. Healthy City School District Board of Education v. Doyle, 429 U.S. 274 (1977) (although untenured teacher can be dismissed for "no reason whatever," he cannot be fired for exercise of first amendment rights); Keyes v. School District No. 1, 413 U.S. 189 (1973) (Denver schools held unlawfully segregated because school board decisions concerning the location of schools were motivated by racial considerations); Yick Wo v. Hopkins, 118 U.S. 356 (1886) (licensing law invalidated because of discriminatory administration). As indicated in O'Brien, however, the Court has been reluctant to inquire into the motivation underlying legislative actions. Three explanations have usually been offered for this reluctance: the difficulty of ascertaining the "actual" motivation of a collective body; the futility of invalidating a law that could be reenacted with a show of "wiser" motives; and the inappropriateness of impugning the integrity of a coordinate branch of government. Are these explanations sufficiently weighty to justify the conclusion that "the purpose of Congress [is] not a basis for declaring [legislation] unconstitutional"? See generally Alfange, supra, at 27-51; L. Tribe, American Constitutional Law 591-598 (1978); Brest, *Palmer v. Thompson:* An Approach to the Problem of Unconstitutional Legislative Motive, 1971 Sup. Ct. Rev. 95; Ely, Legislative and Administrative Motivation in Constitutional Law, 79 Yale L.J. 1205 (1970); Symposium, Legislative Motivation, 15 San Diego L. Rev. 925 (1978). The issue of legislative motivation is examined more fully in Chapter 5, section C2, supra.

Note: Flag Desecration and Misuse

1. *Flag burning.* In Street v. New York, 394 U.S. 576 (1969), appellant, after hearing a news report that civil rights leader James Meredith had been shot, took his American flag out of a drawer, carried it to a nearby street corner, and lit it with a match. As it burned on the pavement, appellant said to a group of onlookers, "We don't need no damn flag. [If] they let that happen to Meredith we don't need an American flag." Appellant was convicted of violating a New York statute declaring it a misdemeanor "publicly [to] mutilate, deface, defile, trample upon, or cast contempt upon either by words or acts [any flag of the United States]." The Court, in a five-to-four decision, overturned appellant's conviction. The Court found it unnecessary, however, to address appellant's assertion "that New York may not constitutionally punish one who publicly destroys or damages an

Court was from issue of actually burning the flag

American flag as a means of protest," holding instead that the statute "was unconstitutionally applied in appellant's case because it permitted him to be punished merely for *speaking* defiant or contemptuous *words about* the American flag."

Chief Justice Warren and Justices Black, White, and Fortas dissented. Warren chastised the Court for ducking "the basic question presented" — " 'whether the deliberate act of burning an American flag in public as a "protest" may be punished as a crime.' " On that question, Warren concluded that "the States and the Federal Government [have] the power to protect the flag from acts of desecration and disgrace." In a separate dissenting opinion, Justice Fortas elaborated:

> If a state statute provided that it is a misdemeanor to burn one's shirt [on] the public thoroughfare, it could hardly be asserted that the citizen's constitutional right is violated. [And if] the arsonist asserted that he was burning his shirt [as] a protest against the Government's fiscal policies, [it] is hardly possible that his claim to First Amendment shelter would prevail against the State's claim of a right to avert danger to the public and to avoid obstruction to traffic as a result of the fire. [If], as I submit, it is permissible to prohibit the burning of personal property on the public sidewalk, there is no basis for applying a different rule to flag burning. And the fact that the law is violated for purposes of protest does not immunize the violator. [Citing O'Brien.]

Suppose Street had been convicted of violating a law prohibiting any person to make any "open fire in public." Is the flag desecration statute distinguishable? Consider Nimmer, The Meaning of Symbolic Speech under the First Amendment, 21 U.C.L.A. L. Rev. 29, 57 (1973): "To preserve respect for a symbol qua symbol is to preserve respect for the meaning expressed by the symbol. [An] act of flag desecration is a counter symbol, which may express hostility [to] the sanctity of the idea expressed by the flag symbol. A flag desecration statute is, then, in essence a governmental command that one idea (embodied in the flag symbol) is not to be countered by another idea (embodied in the act of flag desecration)."

2. *Contemptuous treatment.* In Smith v. Goguen, 415 U.S. 566 (1974), appellee, who wore a small cloth replica of the United States flag sewn to the seat of his trousers, was convicted of violating a Massachusetts statute prohibiting any person to "publicly mutilate, trample upon, deface or treat contemptuously the flag of the United States." The Court, in a six-to-three decision, overturned the conviction. Justice Powell, speaking for the Court, found it unnecessary to decide whether the statute was unconstitutionally overbroad, holding instead that it was "void for vagueness." Powell emphasized that appellee was charged not "with any act of physical desecration," but with " 'publicly [treating] contemptuously the flag of the United States.' " Powell concluded that this aspect of the statute was "inherently vague" and hence violative of due process:

> [The] flag has become "an object of youth fashion and high camp" [and] casual treatment of the flag in many contexts has become a widespread contemporary phenomenon. [In such circumstances], it could hardly be the purpose of the [state] to make criminal every informal use of the flag. The statutory language under which [appellee] was charged, however, fails to draw reasonably clear lines between the kinds of nonceremonial treatment that are criminal and those that are not. [Legislatures] may not so abdicate their responsibilities for setting the standards of the criminal law.

Justice White concurred. After rejecting the vagueness argument, White concluded that "the 'treats contemptuously' provision of the statute, as applied in this case," violates the first amendment:

[It] is well within the powers of Congress to adopt and prescribe a national flag and to protect the integrity of that flag. [The] flag is an important symbol of nationhood and unity. [I] would not question those statutes which proscribe mutilation, defacement, or burning of the flag or which otherwise protect its physical integrity. [But the] Massachusetts statute [also] makes it a crime if one "treats contemptuously" the flag of the United States, and [appellee] was convicted under this part of the statute. [To] convict on this basis is to convict not to protect the physical integrity [of] the flag, but to punish for communicating ideas about the flag unacceptable to the controlling majority in the legislature.

Justice Rehnquist, joined by Chief Justice Burger, dissented:

I think the [state court] would read the [statute] as carrying the clear implication that the contemptuous treatment, like mutilation, trampling upon, or defacing, must involve some actual physical contact with the flag itself. [If] the statute is thus [limited], the question remains whether the State has sought only to punish those who impair the flag's physical integrity for the purpose of disparaging it as a symbol, while permitting impairment of its physical integrity by those who do not seek to disparage it as a symbol. [Decisions] like [Schacht] suggest that such a law would abridge the right of free expression. But Massachusetts metes out punishment to anyone who publicly mutilates, tramples, or defaces the flag, regardless of his motive or purpose. [These] prohibitions are broad enough that it can be fairly said that the Massachusetts statute [is] designed to preserve the physical integrity of the flag, and not merely to punish those who would infringe that integrity for the purpose of disparaging the flag as a symbol.

Rehnquist maintained that, as so understood, the statute "substantially complies" with the test "established in O'Brien":

Since the statute by this reading punishes a variety of uses of the flag which would impair its physical integrity, without regard to presence or character of expressive conduct in connection with those uses, I think the governmental interest is unrelated to the suppression of free expression. [Moreover,] the governmental interest is sufficient to outweigh whatever collateral suppression of expressive conduct was involved in the actions of [appellee]. [The flag] is not merely cloth dyed red, white, and blue, but also the one visible manifestation of two hundred years of nationhood. [Massachusetts] has not prohibited [appellee] from wearing a sign sewn to the seat of his pants expressing in words his low opinion of the flag [or] anything else. It has prohibited him from wearing there a particular symbol of extraordinary significance and content. [The] flag of the United States in not just another "thing," and it is not just another "idea"; it is not primarily an idea at all. [Appellee] was simply prohibited from impairing the physical integrity of a unique national symbol.

Justice Blackmun, joined by Chief Justice Burger, also dissented.

Was appellee's act intended to communicate? Do you agree with Justice Rehnquist that the state's interest in preserving the physical integrity of the flag is "unrelated to the suppression of free expression"?

3. *Flag misuse.* In Spence v. Washington, 418 U.S. 405 (1974), appellant, to protest the invasion of Cambodia and the killings at Kent State University, displayed a United States flag, which he owned, out of the window of his apartment. Affixed to the flag was a large peace symbol made of removable tape. Appellant was convicted under Washington's "flag misuse" statute, which prohibited the exhibition of a United States flag to which is attached or superimposed "any word, figure, mark, design, drawing, or advertisement." The Court held, in a per curiam opinion, that "as applied to appellant's activity the Washington statute impermissibly infringed free expression."

The Court explained:

> [As] the Court noted in [O'Brien], "[w]e cannot accept the view that an apparently limitless variety of conduct can be labeled "speech" whenever the person engaging in the conduct intends thereby to express an idea." But the nature of appellant's activity, combined with the factual context and environment in which it was undertaken, lead to the conclusion that he engaged in a form of protected expression. [A] flag bearing a peace symbol and displayed upside down by a student today might be interpreted as nothing more than bizarre behavior, but it would have been difficult for the great majority of citizens to miss the drift of appellant's point at the time that he made it. [This] was not an act of mindless nihilism. Rather, it was a pointed expression of anguish by appellant about the then-current domestic and foreign affairs of his government. An intent to convey a particularized message was present, and in the surrounding circumstances the likelihood was great that the message would be understood by those who viewed it.
>
> We are confronted then with a case of prosecution for the expression of an idea through activity. [Accordingly], we must examine with particular care the interests advanced by appellee to support its prosecution. [The state maintains that it] has an interest in preserving the national flag as an unalloyed symbol of our country. [This] interest might be seen as an effort to prevent the appropriation of a revered national symbol by an individual, interest group, or enterprise where there was a risk that association of the symbol with a particular product or viewpoint might be taken erroneously as evidence of governmental endorsement. [Alternatively], the interest [may be understood as] based on the uniquely universal character of the national flag as a symbol. [If] it may be destroyed or permanently disfigured, it [could] lose its capability of mirroring the sentiments of all who view it.
>
> [We] need not decide in this case whether the interest advanced by the [state] is valid. We assume, arguendo, that it is. [But even if] it is valid, [it] is directly related to expression in the context of activity like that undertaken by appellant. For that reason [the] four-step analysis of [O'Brien] is inapplicable. [We hold that the statute is] unconstitutional as applied to appellant's activity. There was no risk that appellant's acts would mislead viewers into assuming that the Government endorsed his viewpoint. [Moreover, appellant] did [not] permanently disfigure the flag or destroy it. [And] his message was direct, likely to be understood, and within the contours of the First Amendment. [The] conviction must be reversed.

Justice Rehnquist, joined by Chief Justice Burger and Justice White, dissented:

> [The] Court's treatment [of the state's interest] lacks all substance. The suggestion that the State's interest somehow diminishes when the flag is decorated with *removable* tape trivializes something which is not trivial. The State [is] hardly seeking to protect the flag's resale value. [The] true nature of the State's interest in this case is [one] of preserving the flag as "an important symbol of nationhood and unity." [It] is the character, not the cloth, of the flag which the State seeks to protect. "[The] flag

is a national property, and the Nation may regulate those who would make, imitate, sell, possess, or use it." . . .

[That] the State has a valid interest in preserving the character of the flag does not mean, of course, that it can employ all conceivable means to enforce it. It certainly could not require all citizens to own the flag or compel citizens to salute one. [It] presumably cannot punish criticism of the flag, or the principles for which it stands, any more than it could punish criticism of this country's policies or ideas. But the statute in this case demands no such allegiance. Its operation does not depend upon whether [the] use of the flag is respectful or contemptuous. [It] simply withdraws a unique national symbol from the roster of materials that may be used as a background for communications. [The] Constitution [does not prohibit] Washington from making that decision.

Is *Spence* consistent with *O'Brien?* Do you agree with the Court that the interests underlying flag misuse statutes are "directly related to expression" and that the *O'Brien* standard thus should not govern? Consider Ely, Flag Desecration: A Case Study in the Roles of Categorization and Balancing in First Amendment Analysis, 88 Harv. L. Rev. 1482, 1503-1504, 1506-1508 (1975):

> [The flag misuse statute is] ideologically neutral on its face, and would proscribe the superimposition of "Buy Mother Fletcher's Ambulance Paint" [as] fully as it would the addition of a swastika. Such "improper use" provisions are [thus] more complicated constitutionally than the ideologically tilted "desecration" provisions. [In the flag misuse context], the state may assert an interest [similar] to that asserted in [defense of a content-neutral law prohibiting any person to interrupt a public speaker]. The state's interest in both of these cases might be characterized as an interest in preventing the [defendant] from interfering with the expression of others. [As with interruption of a public speaker, the] state does not care what message the defendant is conveying by altering the flag: all that matters is that he is interrupting the message conveyed by the flag. [There is, however, an answer to this argument, for] although improper use statutes do not single out certain messages for proscription, they *do* single out one set of messages, namely the set of messages conveyed by the American flag, for protection. That, of course, is not true of a law that generally prohibits the interruption of speakers. [In reality, then, an improper use statute] is, at best, analogous to a law prohibiting the interruption of patriotic speeches, and that is a law that is hardly "unrelated to the suppression of free expression."

Note that the Court in *Spence* emphasized that "the likelihood was great that [appellant's] message would be understood by those who viewed it." Should that matter? Consider Note, Symbolic Conduct, 68 Colum. L. Rev. 1091, 1113-1114 (1968): "If there is to be a doctrine of first amendment protection for symbolic conduct, its cornerstone must be the requirement that others can recognize the conduct as communication. [Otherwise], all conduct might [be] classifiable as speech. [The requirement is thus an effective way to deal with the "imposter problem."] Moreover, [conduct] which is not reasonably calculated to communicate does not aid the free exchange of ideas."

Note: Political Boycotts

Suppose a state prohibits "two or more persons, acting in concert, to refuse to deal with any merchant in an effort to induce such merchant to adopt a practice or policy he would not otherwise choose to adopt." Does such a law violate the first amendment? Is a concerted refusal to deal "speech"?

1. Claiborne Hardware. NAACP v. Claiborne Hardware Co., 458 U.S. 886 (1982), involved an NAACP boycott of white merchants in Claiborne County, Mississippi. The boycott, which was launched in 1966, was intended to induce business and civic leaders to adopt a number of reforms, including the desegregation of all public facilities, the hiring of black policemen, public improvements in black residential areas, and an end to verbal abuse by law enforcement officers. In this action, brought by several merchants against the organizers and the most active participants in the boycott, the Mississippi Supreme Court found that the defendants had used and had "agreed" to use force, violence, and intimidation to coerce nonparticipating blacks to join the boycott. The court therefore held the boycott unlawful and held each of the defendants liable for all of its economic consequences. The Supreme Court reversed.

Justice Stevens delivered the opinion of the Court:

> The boycott [took] many forms. [It] was supported by speeches and nonviolent picketing. Participants repeatedly encouraged others to join in its cause. Each of these elements of the boycott is a form of speech or conduct that is ordinarily entitled to protection under the First and Fourteenth Amendments. . . .
>
> In addition, [the names] of boycott violators were read aloud at meetings [and] published in a local black newspaper. Petitioners admittedly sought to persuade others to join the boycott through social pressure and the "threat" of social ostracism. Speech does not lose its protected character, however, simply because it may embarrass others or coerce them into action. [In] Organization for a Better Austin v. Keefe, 402 U.S. 415, [petitioner] distributed leaflets near respondent's home that were critical of his business practices. A state court enjoined petitioner from distributing the leaflets [on] the ground that the alleged activities were coercive and intimidating, rather than informative, and therefore not entitled to First Amendment protection. This Court reversed. [The Court] explained: "[Petitioner] plainly intended to influence respondent's conduct [by] openly and vigorously [making] the public aware of [his] practices. [This tactic was] no doubt offensive to [some]. But so long as the means are peaceful, the communication need not meet standards of acceptability." . . .
>
> In sum, the boycott clearly involved constitutionally protected activity. [The] presence of protected activity, however, does not end the relevant constitutional inquiry. Governmental regulation that has an incidental effect on First Amendment freedoms may be justified in certain narrowly defined instances. See [O'Brien]. A nonviolent and totally voluntary boycott may have a disruptive effect on local economic conditions. The Court has recognized the strong governmental interest in certain forms of economic regulation, even though such regulation may have an incidental effect on rights of speech and association. [For example, the] right of business entities to "associate" to suppress competition may be curtailed [and secondary] boycotts and picketing by labor unions may be prohibited. [But while] States have broad power to regulate economic activity, we do not find a comparable right to prohibit peaceful political activity such as that found in the boycott in this case. This Court has recognized that expression on public issues "has always rested on the highest rung of the hierarchy of First Amendment values." [It] is not disputed that a major purpose of the boycott in this case was to influence governmental action. [We therefore] hold that the nonviolent elements of petitioners' activities are entitled to the protection of the First Amendment. . . .

The First Amendment does not protect violence. [Although] the extent and significance of the violence in this case is vigorously disputed by the parties, there is no question that acts of violence occurred. [In two instances, for example, shots were fired into the homes of individuals who refused to support the boycott.] No federal rule of law restricts a State from imposing tort liability for business losses that are caused by violence and by threats of violence. When such conduct occurs in the context of constitutionally protected activity, however, "precision of regulation is demanded." . . .

[Thus, while] the State legitimately may impose damages for the consequences of violent conduct, it may not award compensation for the consequences of nonviolent, protected activity. Only those losses proximately caused by unlawful conduct may be recovered. [Here, the state court] awarded respondents damages for all business losses that were sustained during [the boycott, and] all defendants were held jointly and severally liable for these losses. [Such] a damage award may not be sustained, [for] all business losses were not proximately caused by the violence and threats of violence found to be present. . . .

[The] First Amendment similarly restricts the ability of the State to impose liability on an individual solely because of his association with another. In Scales v. United States, [supra section B1], the Court noted that a "blanket prohibition of association with a group having both legal and illegal aims" would present "a real danger that legitimate political expression or association would be impaired." The Court suggested that to punish association with such a group, there must be "clear proof that a defendant 'specifically intend[s] to accomplish [the aims of the organization] by resort to violence.'" [On] the present record no judgment may be sustained against most of the petitioners. Regular attendance and participation at the [meetings of the local branch] of the NAACP is an insufficient predicate on which to impose liability. The [state court's] findings do not suggest that any illegal conduct was authorized, ratified, or even discussed at any of the meetings. . . .

[Moreover, on this record the national NAACP may not be held liable for the specific acts of violence.] The NAACP — like any other organization — of course may be held responsible for the acts of its agents [that] are undertaken within the scope of their actual or apparent authority [and] for other conduct of which it had knowledge and specifically ratified. [Here, however, the state court made no such findings.] To impose liability without [such findings] would impermissibly burden the rights of political association that are protected by the First Amendment. . . .

The taint of violence colored the conduct of some of the petitioners. They, of course, may be held liable for the consequences of their violent deeds. The burden of demonstrating that it colored the entire collective effort, however, is not satisfied by evidence that violence occurred or even that violence contributed to the success of the boycott. A massive and prolonged effort to change the social, political, and economic structure of a local environment cannot be characterized as a violent conspiracy simply by reference to the ephemeral consequences of relatively few violent acts.

Justice Rehnquist concurred in the result. Justice Marshall did not participate.

2. *Evaluation.* Do you agree that the boycotters had a first amendment right to withhold their business from the merchants in an effort to induce the merchants to support their political goals? Do you agree that they had a right to expose the names of nonparticipants as a means of inducing their participation? Would the boycotters have had a right to expose *other* embarrassing facts about the nonparticipants to induce their participation? Consider the following views:

a. Note, The Political Boycott: An Unprivileged Form of Expression, 1983 Duke L.J. 1076 (1983):

A political boycott uses economic coercion to force its victims to speak or act politically in a way that furthers the goals, not necessarily of the [victim], but of the boycotter. Although attempts to persuade individuals to act are usually protected by the first amendment, attempts to *coerce* individuals to act are not so immunized. [Indeed, government has] a strong interest in protecting innocent parties from un- provoked [economic] harm [and] in protecting the free speech and association of individuals from economic coercion. [Moreover, these interests are clearly unre- lated] to the suppression of free expression. [Thus], a law [prohibiting] political boycotts should survive the *O'Brien* test.

b. Harper, The Consumer's Emerging Right to Boycott, 93 Yale L.J. 409, 425 (1984):

The coercive power of a group of consumers who boycott a supporter of a particular [political] cause is limited to the aggregation of those consumers' economic votes. [The] coercion inherent in [such] boycotts is simply an exercise of the influence that citizens as consumers should be encouraged to exercise. [An] analogy to electoral voting is illuminating. By threatening to remove elected officials from office, elec- toral voting may "coerce" those officials to reject political causes in which [they] believe. Yet such "coercion" is an accepted part of governmental decisionmaking. Consumer "coercion" of businessmen [should] also be acceptable.

In International Longshoremen's Association v. Allied International, 456 U.S. 212 (1982), a longshoremen's union, in protest against the Soviet Union's invasion of Afghanistan, refused to handle cargoes arriving from or destined for the Soviet Union. The Court held that the union's conduct constituted a secondary boycott in violation of the NLRA. Characterizing the boycott as "conduct designed not to communicate but to coerce," the Court held that the boycott was not "protected activity under the First Amendment." The Court explained that the "labor laws reflect a careful balancing of interests" and that there "are many ways in which a union and its individual members may express their opposition to Russian foreign policy without infringing upon the rights of others." Is *Claiborne Hardware* con- sistent with *International Longshoremen's Association?*

4. Money and Free Expression: Regulation of Solicitation, Contribution, and Expenditure

It has been suggested that the "critical problem for contemporary First Amend- ment theory is the unequal access that wealth can buy." Carter, Technology, Democracy, and the Manipulation of Consent, 93 Yale L.J. 581 (1984). This section explores that "problem." To what extent is the solicitation, contribution, or expenditure of money "speech" within the meaning of the first amendment? To what extent may government regulate or restrict such activities in order to "enhance" the quality of public debate?

VILLAGE OF SCHAUMBURG v. CITIZENS FOR A BETTER ENVI- RONMENT, 444 U.S. 620 (1980): A Schaumburg ordinance prohibited door- to-door and on-street solicitation of contributions by charitable organizations that do not use at least 75 percent of their receipts for "charitable purposes." The village maintained that the ordinance did not pose a "free speech" issue, for it "deals only with solicitation" and leaves every charity "free to propagate its views [so] long as it refrains from soliciting money." The Court rejected the village's contention:

"[Charitable] appeals for funds [involve] a variety of speech interests — communication of information, the dissemination and propagation of views and ideas, and the advocacy of causes — that are within the protection of the First Amendment. Soliciting financial support is undoubtedly subject to reasonable regulation but the latter must be undertaken with due regard for the reality that solicitation is characteristically intertwined with information and perhaps persuasive speech seeking support for particular causes or for particular views on economic, political, or social issues, and for the reality that without solicitation the flow of such information and advocacy would likely cease. Canvassers in such contexts are necessarily more than solicitors for money."

Consider Marshall, *Village of Schaumburg v. Citizens for a Better Environment* and Religious Solicitation: Freedom of Speech and Freedom of Religion Converge, 13 Loy. L.A. L. Rev. 953, 960, 973 (1980):

The Court's conclusion [does] not follow from [its] premise. [That] there are elements of first amendment concern within a given activity does [not] dictate that the activity as a whole should be construed as protected speech. [A better explanation for holding solicitation protected by the first amendment is that solicitation] is not merely an appeal for money, [but] an exhortation to the person solicited to show his support. [The] grant or denial of a contribution is itself an expression of advocacy.

If solicitation is "speech," is the sale of flowers or the operation of a car wash to raise funds for a charitable or political organization also "speech"?

Assuming that solicitation is "speech," is the Schaumburg ordinance constitutional? The Court invalidated the ordinance:

[The ordinance] is a direct and substantial limitation on protected activity [and] cannot be sustained unless it serves a sufficiently strong, subordinating interest that the Village is entitled to protect. [The Village maintains that] any organization using more than 25 percent of its receipts on fundraising, salaries, and overhead is not a charitable, but [a] for profit enterprise and that to permit it to represent itself as a charity is fraudulent. [Although] such reasoning might apply to charitable organizations whose primary purpose is to provide money or services to the poor or to others worthy of charity, it does not apply to organizations, like CBE, whose primary purpose is [to] advocate positions on matters of public concern, [for such organizations] necessarily spend more than 25 percent of their budget on salaries and administrative expenses. [Although the] Village may serve its legitimate interests, [it] must do [so] without unnecessarily interfering with First Amendment freedoms.

See also Secretary of State of Maryland v. Joseph H. Munson Co., — U.S. — , 104 S. Ct. 2118 (1984) (invalidating a statute prohibiting any charitable organization, in connection with any fundraising activity, from paying expenses of more than 25 percent of the amount raised).

Buckley v. Valeo

424 U.S. 1 (1976)

PER CURIAM.

These appeals present constitutional challenges to the key provisions of the Federal Election Campaign Act of 1971 (Act), and related provisions of the Internal Revenue Code of 1954, all as amended in 1974. . . .

[The] statutes at issue [contain] the following provisions: (a) individual political contributions [and expenditures] "relative to a clearly identified candidate" are limited, [and] campaign spending by candidates for various federal offices [are] subject to prescribed limits; (b) contributions and expenditures above certain threshold levels must be reported and publicly disclosed; (c) a system for public funding of Presidential campaign activities is established; [and] (d) a Federal Election Commission is established to administer and enforce the legislation. . . .

[The Court upheld the constitutionality of the individual contribution limits, the disclosure and reporting provisions, and the public financing scheme. The Court invalidated the composition of the Federal Election Commission and the limitations on expenditures. The following excerpts relate to the contribution and expenditure limitations. For the Court's analysis of the disclosure provisions, see infra section F5a.]

I. CONTRIBUTION AND EXPENDITURE LIMITATIONS

The intricate statutory scheme adopted by Congress to regulate federal election campaigns includes restrictions on political contributions and expenditures that apply broadly to all phases of and all participants in the election process. The major contribution and expenditure limitations in the Act prohibit individuals from contributing more than $25,000 in a single year or more than $1,000 to any single candidate for an election campaign and from spending more than $1,000 a year "relative to a clearly identified candidate." Other provisions restrict a candidate's use of personal and family resources in his campaign and limit the overall amount that can be spent by a candidate in campaigning for federal office. . . .

A. GENERAL PRINCIPLES

The Act's contribution and expenditure limitations operate in an area of the most fundamental First Amendment activities. Discussion of public issues and debate on the qualifications of candidates are integral to the operation of the system of government established by our Constitution. . . .

In upholding the constitutional validity of the Act's contribution and expenditure provisions on the ground that those provisions should be viewed as regulating conduct, not speech, the Court of Appeals relied upon United States v. O'Brien, [supra section E3].

We cannot share the view that the present Act's contribution and expenditure limitations are comparable to the restrictions on conduct upheld in O'Brien. The expenditure of money simply cannot be equated with such conduct as destruction of a draft card. Some forms of communication made possible by the giving and spending of money involve speech alone, some involve conduct primarily, and some involve a combination of the two. Yet this Court has never suggested that the dependence of a communication on the expenditure of money operates itself to introduce a nonspeech element or to reduce the exacting scrutiny required by the First Amendment. . . .

Even if the categorization of the expenditure of money as conduct were accepted, the limitations challenged here would not meet the *O'Brien* test because the governmental interests advanced in support of the Act involve "suppressing communication." The interests served by the Act include restricting the voices of people and interest groups who have money to spend and reducing the overall scope of federal election campaigns. Although the Act does not focus on the ideas expressed by persons or groups subject to its regulations, it is aimed in part at equalizing the relative ability of all voters to affect electoral outcomes by placing a ceiling on expenditures for political expression by citizens and groups. Unlike *O'Brien*, where the Selective Service System's administrative interest in the preservation of draft cards was wholly unrelated to their use as a means of communication, it is beyond dispute that the interest in regulating the alleged "conduct" of giving or spending money "arises in some measure because the communication allegedly integral to the conduct is itself thought to be harmful." . . .

Nor can the Act's contribution and expenditure limitations be sustained, as some of the parties suggest, by reference to the constitutional principles reflected in such decisions as [Cox v. Louisiana, Adderley v. Florida, and Kovacs v. Cooper, supra section E]. Those cases stand for the proposition that the government may adopt reasonable time, place, and manner regulations, which do not discriminate among speakers or ideas, in order to further an important governmental interest unrelated to the restriction of communication. [In] contrast to *O'Brien*, where the method of expression was held to be subject to prohibition, *Cox*, *Adderley*, and *Kovacs* involved place or manner restrictions on legitimate modes of expression — picketing, parading, demonstrating, and using a soundtruck. The critical difference between this case and those time, place, and manner cases is that the present Act's contribution and expenditure limitations impose direct quantity restrictions on political communication and association by persons, groups, candidates, and political parties in addition to any reasonable time, place, and manner regulations otherwise imposed.[17]

A restriction on the amount of money a person or group can spend on political communication during a campaign necessarily reduces the quantity of expression by restricting the number of issues discussed, the depth of their exploration, and the size of the audience reached.[18] This is because virtually every means of communicating ideas in today's mass society requires the expenditure of money. . . .

The expenditure limitations contained in the Act represent substantial rather than merely theoretical restraints on the quantity and diversity of political speech.

17. The nongovernmental appellees argue that just as the decibels emitted by a sound truck can be regulated consistently with the First Amendment, [*Kovacs*], the Act may restrict the volume of dollars in political campaigns without impermissibly restricting freedom of speech. [This] comparison underscores a fundamental misconception. The decibel restriction upheld in *Kovacs* limited the *manner* of operating a soundtruck, but not the *extent* of its proper use. By contrast, the Act's dollar ceilings restrict the extent of the reasonable use of virtually every means of communicating information. . . .

18. Being free to engage in unlimited political expression subject to a ceiling on expenditures is like being free to drive an automobile as far and as often as one desires on a single tank of gasoline.

The $1,000 ceiling on spending "relative to a clearly identified candidate," [for example,] would appear to exclude all citizens and groups except candidates, political parties, and the institutional press from any significant use of the most effective modes of communication.[20] . . .

By contrast with a limitation upon expenditures for political expression, a limitation upon the amount that any one person or group may contribute to a candidate or political committee entails only a marginal restriction upon the contributor's ability to engage in free communication, [for] it permits the symbolic expression of support evidenced by a contribution but does not in any way infringe the contributor's freedom to discuss candidates and issues. While contributions may result in political expression if spent by a candidate or an association to present views to the voters, the transformation of contributions into political debate involves speech by someone other than the contributor.

Given the important role of contributions in financing political campaigns, contribution restrictions could have a severe impact on political dialogue if the limitations prevented candidates and political committees from amassing the resources necessary for effective advocacy. There is no indication, however, that the contribution limitations imposed by the Act would have any dramatic adverse effect on the funding of campaigns and political associations.[23] The overall effect of the Act's contribution ceilings is merely to require candidates and political committees to raise funds from a greater number of persons and to compel people who would otherwise contribute amounts greater than the statutory limits to expend such funds on direct political expression, rather than to reduce the total amount of money potentially available to promote political expression. . . .

In sum, although the Act's contribution and expenditure limitations both implicate fundamental First Amendment interests, its expenditure ceilings impose significantly more severe restrictions on protected freedoms of political expression and association than do its limitations on financial contributions.

B.   CONTRIBUTION LIMITATIONS

Section 608(b) provides, with certain limited exceptions, that "no person shall make contributions to any candidate with respect to any election for Federal office which, in the aggregate, exceed $1,000." . . .

[The] primary First Amendment problem raised by the Act's contribution limitations is their restriction of one aspect of the contributor's freedom of political association. The Court's decisions involving associational freedoms establish that the right of association is a "basic constitutional freedom," [and that] governmental "action which may have the effect of curtailing the freedom to associate is subject to the closest scrutiny." Yet, it is clear that "Neither the right to associate nor the right to participate in political activities is absolute." [Even] a "'significant interference' with protected rights of political association" may be sustained if the

---

20. The record indicates that, as of January 1, 1975, one full-page advertisement in a daily edition of a certain metropolitan newspaper cost $6,971.04 — almost seven times the annual limit on expenditures "relative to" a particular candidate imposed on the vast majority of individual citizens and associations by [the Act].

23. Statistical findings agreed to by the parties reveal that approximately 5.1% of the $73,483,613 raised by the 1,161 candidates for Congress in 1974 was obtained in amounts in excess of $1,000. . . .

State demonstrates a sufficiently important interest and employs means closely drawn to avoid unnecessary abridgment of associational freedoms. . . .

It is unnecessary to look beyond the Act's primary purpose — to limit the actuality and appearance of corruption resulting from large individual financial contributions — in order to find a constitutionally sufficient justification for the $1,000 contribution limitation. [The] increasing importance of the communications media and sophisticated mass-mailing and polling operations to effective campaigning make the raising of large sums of money an ever more essential ingredient of an effective candidacy. To the extent that large contributions are given to secure a political quid pro quo from current and potential office holders, the integrity of our system of representative democracy is undermined. . . .

Of almost equal concern [is] the appearance of corruption stemming from [the] opportunities for abuse inherent in a regime of large individual financial contributions. [Congress] could legitimately conclude that the avoidance of the appearance of improper influence [is] "critical [if] confidence in the system of representative Government is not to be [eroded]." . . .

Appellants contend that the contribution limitations must be invalidated because bribery laws and narrowly drawn disclosure requirements constitute a less restrictive means of dealing with "proven and suspected quid pro quo arrangements." But laws making criminal the giving and taking of bribes deal with only the most blatant and specific attempts of those with money to influence governmental action. And while disclosure requirements serve [many salutary purposes] Congress was surely entitled to conclude that disclosure was only a partial measure, and that contribution ceilings were a necessary legislative concomitant to deal with the reality or appearance of corruption. . . .

We find that, under the rigorous standard of review established by our prior decisions, the weighty interests served by restricting the size of financial contributions to political candidates are sufficient to justify the limited effect upon First Amendment freedoms caused by the $1,000 contribution ceiling.

[Appellants argue further, however,] that the contribution limitations work [an] invidious discrimination between incumbents and [challengers].[33] [But] there is [no] evidence [that] contribution limitations [discriminate] against major-party challengers to incumbents, [and although] the charge of discrimination against minor-party and independent candidates is more troubling, [the] record provides no basis for concluding that the Act invidiously disadvantages such candidates. [Indeed, in some circumstances] the restriction would appear to benefit minor-party and independent candidates relative to their major-party opponents because major-party candidates receive far more money in large contributions. . . .

33. In this discussion, we address only the argument that the contribution limitations alone impermissibly discriminate against nonincumbents. We do not address the more serious argument that these limitations, in combination with the limitation on expenditures [invidiously] discriminate against major-party challengers and minor-party candidates.

Since an incumbent is subject to these limitations to the same degree as his opponent, the Act, on its face, appears to be evenhanded. The appearance of fairness, however, may not reflect political reality. Although some incumbents are defeated in every congressional election, it is axiomatic that an incumbent usually begins the race with significant advantages. [In some circumstances] the overall effect of the contribution and expenditure limitations enacted by Congress could foreclose any fair opportunity of a successful challenge.

However, since we decide in Part I-C, infra, that the ceilings on [expenditures] are unconstitutional under the First Amendment, we need not express any opinion with regard to the alleged invidious discrimination resulting from the full sweep of the legislation as enacted.

In view of these considerations, we conclude that the impact of the Act's $1,000 contribution limitation on major-party challengers and on minor-party candidates does not render the provision unconstitutional on its face.

[For similar reasons, the Court also upheld the $5,000 limit on contributions by "political committees," the limits on volunteers' incidental expenses, and the $25,000 limit on total political contributions by an individual during a single calendar year.]

C. EXPENDITURE LIMITATIONS

The Act's expenditure ceilings impose direct and substantial restraints [on] the quantity of campaign speech by individuals, groups, and candidates. The restrictions, while neutral as to the ideas expressed, limit political expression "at the core of our electoral process and of the First Amendment freedoms." . . .

1. *The $1,000 Limitation on Expenditures "Relative to a
    Clearly Identified Candidate"*

Section 608(e)(1) provides that "[n]o person may make any expenditure . . . relative to a clearly identified candidate during a calendar year [which] exceeds $1,000." [Appellants maintain] that the provision is unconstitutionally vague. [The] use of so indefinite a phrase as "relative to" a candidate fails to clearly mark the boundary between permissible and impermissible [speech]. "Such a distinction offers no security for free [discussion]." [To] preserve the provision against invalidation on vagueness grounds, §608(e)(1) must be construed to apply only to expenditures for communications that in express terms advocate the election or defeat of a clearly identified candidate for federal office.

We turn then to the basic First Amendment question — whether §608(e)(1), even as thus narrowly and explicitly construed, impermissibly burdens the constitutional right of free expression. . . .

The discussion in Part I-A, supra, explains why the Act's expenditure limitations impose far greater restraints on the freedom of speech and association than do its contribution limitations. . . .

We find that the governmental interest in preventing corruption and the appearance of corruption is inadequate to justify §608(e)(1)'s ceiling on independent expenditures. [First], §608(e)(1) prevents only some large expenditures. So long as persons and groups eschew expenditures that in express terms advocate the election or defeat of a clearly identified candidate, they are free to spend as much as they want to promote the candidate and his views. The exacting interpretation of the statutory language necessary to avoid unconstitutional vagueness thus undermines the limitation's effectiveness. . . .

Second, [although the] parties defending §608(e)(1) contend that it is necessary to prevent would-be contributors from avoiding the contribution limitations [by] paying directly for media advertisements or for other portions of the candidate's campaign activities, [such] coordinated expenditures are treated as contributions rather than expenditures under the Act [and are thus limited by the] contribution ceilings. [Thus], §608(e)(1) limits [only] expenditures [made] totally independently of the candidate and his campaign. [But the] absence of [coordination with respect to such expenditures] undermines the value of the expenditure to the candidate [and] alleviates the danger that expenditures will be given as a quid pro quo for improper commitments. [Thus,] §608(e)(1) severely [restricts] independent advocacy despite its substantially diminished potential for abuse. . . .

It is argued [further, however, that the] governmental interest in equalizing the relative ability of individuals [to] influence the outcome of elections [justifies the] expenditure ceiling. But the concept that government may restrict the speech of some [in] order to enhance the relative voice of others is wholly foreign to the First Amendment, which was designed "to secure 'the widest possible dissemination of information from diverse and antagonistic sources.'" [The] First Amendment's protection against governmental abridgment of free expression cannot properly be made to depend on a person's financial ability to engage in public discussion. [Section] 608(e)(1)'s [expenditure] limitation is unconstitutional under the First Amendment.

2. Limitation on Expenditures by Candidates from Personal or Family Resources

The Act also [limits] expenditures by a candidate "from his personal funds, or the personal funds of his immediate family, in connection with his campaigns during any calendar year." . . .

The ceiling on personal expenditures by candidates on their own [behalf] imposes a substantial restraint on the ability of persons to engage in protected First Amendment expression. The candidate, no less than any other person, has a First Amendment right to engage in the discussion of public issues and [to] advocate his own election. . . .

The [interest] in equalizing the relative financial resources of candidates competing for elective office is clearly not sufficient to justify the provision's infringement of fundamental First Amendment rights. . . .

3. Limitations on Campaign Expenditures

Section 608(c) places limitations on overall campaign expenditures by candidates seeking nomination for election and election to federal office. [For example, the] Act imposes blanket $70,000 limitations on both primary campaigns and general election campaigns for the House of Representatives. . . .

No governmental interest that has been suggested is sufficient to justify the restriction on the quantity of political expression imposed by §608(c)'s campaign expenditure limitations. [The] interest in alleviating the corrupting influence of large contributions is served by the Act's contribution limitations and disclosure provisions, [and the] interest in equalizing the financial resources of candidates [is not a] convincing justification for restricting the scope of federal election campaigns. [The] campaign expenditure ceilings appear to be designed primarily to [reduce] the allegedly skyrocketing costs of political campaigns. [But the] First Amendment denies government the power to determine that spending to promote one's political views is wasteful, excessive, or unwise. In the free society ordained by our Constitution it is not the government, but the people — individually as citizens and candidates and collectively as associations and political committees — who must retain control over the quantity and range of debate on public issues in a political campaign.

For these reasons we hold that §608(c) is constitutionally invalid.

In sum, the provisions of the Act that impose a $1,000 [limitation on contributions] are constitutionally valid. These limitations [serve] the basic governmental interest in safeguarding the integrity of the electoral process without directly impinging upon the rights of individual citizens and candidates to engage in political debate and discussion. By contrast, the First Amendment requires the invalidation of the Act's independent expenditure [ceilings]. These provisions place substantial and direct restrictions on the ability of candidates, citizens, and associations to engage in protected political expression, restrictions that the First Amendment cannot tolerate. . . .

[Affirmed] in part and reversed in part.

MR. CHIEF JUSTICE BURGER, concurring in part and dissenting in part. . . .
[The contribution limitations are unconstitutional. Contributions] and expenditures are two sides of the same First Amendment coin. [Limiting] contributions, as a practical matter, will limit expenditures and will put an effective ceiling on the amount of political activity [that] the Government will permit to take place. . . .

The Court's attempt to distinguish the communication inherent in political *contributions* from the speech aspects of political *expenditures* simply "will not wash." We do little but engage in word games unless we recognize that people — candidates and contributors — spend money on political activity because they wish to communicate ideas, and their constitutional interest in doing so is precisely the same whether they or someone else utters the words. [Moreover, the contribution] restrictions are hardly incidental in their effect upon particular campaigns. [Such restrictions] will foreclose some candidacies,[9] [and] alter the nature of some electoral contests drastically.[10]

At any rate, the contribution limits are a far more severe restriction on First Amendment activity than the sort of "chilling" legislation for which the Court has shown such extraordinary concern in the past. See, e.g., [Cohen v. California, supra section D6]. If such restraints can be justified at all, they must be justified by the very strongest of state interests. . . .

MR. JUSTICE WHITE, concurring in part and dissenting in part. . . .
I dissent [from] the Court's view that the expenditure limitations [violate] the First Amendment. . . .

The congressional judgment [was that expenditure limitations are necessary] to counter the corrosive effects of money in federal election campaigns. [The] Court strikes down [§608(e)], strangely enough claiming more [knowledge] as to what may improperly influence candidates than is possessed by the majority of Congress that passed this bill and the President who signed it. [I] would take the word of those who know — that limiting independent expenditures is essential to prevent transparent and widespread evasion of the contribution limits. . . .

The Court also rejects Congress' judgment manifested in §608(c) that the federal interest in limiting total campaign expenditures by individual candidates justifies the incidental effect on their opportunity for effective political speech. I disagree. . . .

9. Candidates who must raise large initial contributions in order to appeal for more funds to a broader audience will be handicapped. . . .
10. Under the Court's holding, candidates with personal fortunes will be free to contribute to their own campaigns as much as they like, since the Court chooses to view the Act's provisions in this regard as unconstitutional "expenditure" limitations rather than "contribution" limitations. . . .

[The] argument that money is speech and that limiting the flow of money to the speaker violates the First Amendment proves entirely too much. Compulsory bargaining [has] increased the labor costs of those who publish newspapers, [and] taxation directly removes from company coffers large amounts of money that might be spent on larger and better newspapers. [But] it has not been suggested [that] these laws, and many others, are invalid because they siphon [off] large sums that would otherwise be available for communicative activities.

[The] judgment of Congress was that reasonably effective campaigns could be conducted within the limits established by the Act. [There] is no sound basis for invalidating the expenditure limitations, so long as the purposes they serve are legitimate and sufficiently substantial, which in my view they are.

[Expenditure] ceilings reinforce the contribution limits and help eradicate the hazard of corruption. [Without] limits on total expenditures, campaign costs will [inevitably] escalate, [creating an incentive to accept unlawful contributions. Moreover,] the corrupt use of money by candidates is as much to be feared as the corrosive influence of large contributions. There are many illegal ways of spending money to influence elections. [The] expenditure limits could play a substantial role in preventing unethical practices. There just would not be enough of "that kind of money" to go around. . . .

It is also important to [restore] public confidence in federal elections. It is critical to obviate [the] impression that federal elections are purely and simply a function of money. [The] ceiling on candidate expenditures represents the considered judgment of Congress that elections are to be decided among candidates none of whom has overpowering advantage by reason of a huge campaign war chest. [This] seems an acceptable purpose and the means chosen a common-sense way to achieve it. . . .

I also disagree with the Court's judgment that §608(a), which limits the amount of money that a candidate or his family may spend on his campaign, violates the Constitution. [By] limiting the importance of personal wealth, §608(a) helps to assure that only individuals with a modicum of support from others will be viable candidates. [This] would tend to discourage any notion that the outcome of elections is primarily a function of money. Similarly, §608(a) tends to equalize access to the political arena, encouraging the less wealthy [to] run for political office. [Congress] was entitled to determine that personal wealth ought to play a less important role in political campaigns than it has in the past. Nothing in the First Amendment stands in the way of that determination. . . .

MR. JUSTICE MARSHALL, concurring in part and dissenting in part.

[The] Court invalidates §608(a), [which limits the amount a candidate may spend from personal or family funds], as violative of the candidate's First Amendment Rights. [I] disagree.

[The] perception that personal wealth wins elections may not only discourage potential candidates without significant personal wealth from entering the political arena, but also undermine public confidence in the integrity of the electoral process.[1]

The concern that candidacy for public office not become, or appear to become,

---

1. "In the Nation's seven largest States in 1970, 11 of the 15 major senatorial candidates were millionaires. The four who were not millionaires lost their bid for election." . . .

the exclusive province of the wealthy assumes heightened significance when one considers the impact of §608(b), which the Court today upholds. That provision prohibits contributions from individuals and groups to candidates in excess of $1,000, and contributions from political committees in excess of $5,000. While the limitations on contributions are neutral there can be no question that large contributions generally mean more to the candidate without a substantial personal fortune to spend on his campaign. Large contributions are the less wealthy candidate's only hope of countering the wealthy candidate's immediate access to substantial sums of money. [Section §608(a) thus provides] some symmetry to a regulatory scheme that otherwise enhances the natural advantage of the wealthy. . . .

MR. JUSTICE BLACKMUN, concurring in part and dissenting in part.

I am not persuaded that the Court makes [a] principled constitutional distinction between the contribution limitations [and] the expenditure limitations. [I] therefore do not join Part I-B of the Court's opinion or those portions of Part I-A that are consistent with Part I-B. As to those, I dissent. . . .

Note: Buckley and Bellotti — Abridging Speech to "Enhance" the Electoral Process

1. *The standard of review.* Is the Court's distinction between the expenditure and contribution limitations persuasive? Do the expenditure limitations demand a more substantial justification than the contribution limitations and the restrictions at issue in such cases as *Kovacs* and *O'Brien* because of their greater potential impact on free expression? Consider Polsby, *Buckley v. Valeo:* The Nature of Political Speech, 1976 Sup. Ct. Rev. 1, 21-22: "[According to the Court], while expenditures are themselves 'speech,' and subject to something like absolute protection in the context of an election campaign, contributions are more nearly like 'association.' They do not express ideas but merely communicate a solidarity between the candidate and contributor. As such, [they are, according to the Court,] entitled to a lesser degree of protection." For a critical assessment of the Court's analysis of the expenditure and contribution limitations, see Nicholson, *Buckley v. Valeo:* The Constitutionality of the Federal Election Campaign Act Amendments of 1974, 1977 Wis. L. Rev. 323, 340-345.

2. Buckley *and the problem of unequal resources.* In upholding the expenditure and contribution limitations in *Buckley*, the Court of Appeals explained: "[The] statute taken as a whole affirmatively enhances First Amendment values. By reducing in good measure disparity due to wealth, the Act tends to equalize both the relative ability of all voters to affect electoral outcomes, and the opportunity of all interested citizens to become candidates for elective federal office. This broadens the choice of candidates and the opportunity to hear a variety of views." 519 F.2d 817, 841 (D.C. Cir. 1975). A fundamental question presented in *Buckley*, then, was "this: in a situation where the speech opportunities of a group in the aggregate, or of the average member of a group, could be maximized, enhanced, or even made initially possible only by abridging the speech of an individual, what (if anything) does the First Amendment command to be done?" Polsby, supra, at 5. Do you agree that, if the purpose and "net effect of the legislation is to enhance freedom of speech, the exacting review reserved for abridgements of free speech

is inapposite"? L. Tribe, American Constitutional Law 802-803 (1978). Do you agree with the Court that "the concept that government may restrict the speech of some elements of our society in order to enhance the relative voice of others is wholly foreign to the First Amendment"?

Note that the *Buckley* case posed a conflict between two conceptions of a properly functioning system of free expression, and between two conceptions of the role of the state. Under one view, government should take the "private" status quo for granted and allow all persons, no matter their resources, to press their interests on the political process. If some people have more money than others, and if their greater resources permit more speech, that result is something for which government is not itself responsible, and that cannot be "remedied" consistently with the first amendment. The role of government is to remain "neutral" as people in the private sphere compete in the political marketplace. Under the competing view, a system of free expression is one in which there is deliberation on what the public good requires, and inequality of resources is itself a product of governmental choices. If government permits the processes of political deliberation to become distorted by inequality of resources, the result is inconsistent with first amendment values. Under this view, government "inaction" amounts to action; and efforts to equalize resources are permitted or perhaps even required. Compare the discussion of the downfall of the *Lochner* period, in Chapter 6, section D, supra, and the discussion of state action, in Chapter 10 infra.

Consider Wright, Politics and the Constitution: Is Money Speech?, 85 Yale L.J. 1001, 1005, 1015-1019 (1976):

> Nothing in the First Amendment prevents us, as a political community, from [choosing] to move closer to the kind of community process that lies at the heart of the First Amendment conception — a process wherein ideas and candidates prevail because of their inherent worth, not because [one] side puts on a more elaborate show of support. [The] picture of the political process that emerges from [*Buckley*] corresponds [to the] pluralist model. [To] the pluralist, the political process consists [of] the pulling and hauling of various competing interest groups. [Force] collides with counterforce, [and] the strongest force [determines] the outcome of [the] process. [By this] line of reasoning, the First Amendment's highest function is to let group pressure run its course unimpeded, lest we skew the process that determines for us the public interest. [This model] gives undeserved weight [to] highly organized and wealthy groups [and drains] politics of its moral and intellectual content. [Unlike the pluralist conception, the First Amendment] is founded on [a] model of how self-governing people [make] their decisions [that emphasizes] considerations of justice and morality — considerations absent from the pluralist approach. [What] the pluralist rhetoric obscures is that *ideas*, and not intensities, form the heart of the expression which the First Amendment is designed to protect.

See also Wright, Money and the Pollution of Politics: Is the First Amendment an Obstacle to Political Equality?, 82 Colum. L. Rev. 609 (1982).

For the opposing point of view, consider BeVier, Money and Politics: A Perspective on the First Amendment and Campaign Finance Reform, 73 Calif. L. Rev. 1045, 1066-1068, 1071, 1076 (1985): "Advocates of judicial deference begin their argument by equating first amendment objectives with a substantive vision of an ideal political process. [They] assert that the actual political process departs significantly from the posited ideal. [They then argue that because the proposed] reforms 'promote' first amendment values, [they] ought not to require strict judicial scrutiny. [But] it is difficult to understand how, without strict judicial scrutiny of the actual effects of the statue, the Court could confidently reach a conclusion that its 'net effect . . . is to enhance freedom of speech.' [Moreover, the] values generally invoked in behalf of reform do not seem capable of generating nonarbitrary, workable criteria for evaluating political reality. When has the public received 'enough' information to satisfy the constitutional value of an 'informed public'? [What] is the constitutional norm against which 'distortions' of election outcomes can be said to occur? [Finally, commentators] who defend lenient scrutiny for campaign finance reform legislation [fail] to acknowledge that regulation of the political process might be a context warranting distrust of elected officials. [They] ignore any systematic possibility that legislators will behave in self- rather than public-interested ways."

3. Bellotti *and the problem of corporate speech.* In First National Bank of Boston v. Bellotti, 435 U.S. 765 (1978), the Court considered the constitutionality of a Massachusetts statute prohibiting any corporation to make contributions or expenditures "for the purpose [of] influencing or affecting the vote on any question submitted to the voters, other than one materially affecting any of the property, business or assets of the corporation." The statute specified further that "No question submitted to the voters solely concerning the taxation of the income, property or transactions of individuals shall be deemed materially to affect the property, business or assets of the corporation." The state court, in upholding the statute, held that the first amendment rights of a corporation are limited to issues that materially affect its business, property, or assets.

The Court, in a five-to-four decision, reversed. Justice Powell, speaking for the Court, explained that the state court "posed the wrong question." The proper question "is not whether corporations 'have' First Amendment rights and, if so, whether they are coextensive with those of natural persons, [but] whether [the statute] abridges expression that the First Amendment was meant to protect." The statute is directed against speech that is "indispensable to decisionmaking in a democracy" and that lies "at the heart of the First Amendment's protection." Moreover, the Court could "find no support in the First [Amendment], or in the decisions of this Court, for the proposition that speech that otherwise would be within the protection of the First Amendment loses that protection simply because its source is a corporation that cannot prove, to the satisfaction of a court, a material effect on its business or property." Indeed, the statute was especially problematic, for it "permits a corporation to communicate to the public its views on certain referendum subjects — those materially affecting its business — but not others." In such circumstances, " 'the State may prevail only upon showing a subordinating interest which is compelling.' "

The state maintained that the statute was necessary to preserve "the integrity of the electoral process." The participation of corporations in the electoral process, the state argued, "would exert an undue influence on the outcome of a referendum vote, and — in the end — destroy the confidence of the people in the democratic process and the integrity of government." Corporations, the state explained, "are wealthy and powerful and their views may drown out other points of view."

The Court gave this argument short shrift:

> To be sure, corporate advertising may influence the outcome of the vote; this would be its purpose. But the fact that advocacy may persuade the electorate is hardly a

reason to suppress it. [As we noted in *Buckley*,] "the concept that government may restrict the speech of some elements of our society in order to enhance the relative voice of others is wholly foreign to the First [Amendment.]" [Moreover,] the people in our democracy are entrusted with the responsibility for judging and evaluating the relative merits of conflicting arguments. They may consider, in making their judgment, the source and credibility of the advocate. But if there be any danger that the people cannot evaluate the information and arguments advanced by [corporations], it is a danger contemplated by the Framers of the First Amendment.

Finally, the Court noted that if the state's "arguments were supported by record or legislative findings that corporate advocacy threatened imminently to undermine democratic processes, thereby denigrating rather than serving First Amendment interests, these arguments would merit our consideration. [But] there has been no showing that the relative voice of corporations has been overwhelming or even significant in influencing referenda in Massachusetts, or that there has been any threat to the confidence of the citizenry in government."

Justice White, joined by Justices Brennan and Marshall, dissented. At the outset, White observed that "what some have considered to be the principal function of the First Amendment, the use of communication as a means of self-expression, self-realization and self-fulfillment, is not at all furthered by corporate speech." Moreover, "the restriction of corporate speech concerned with political matters impinges much less severely upon the availability of ideas to the general public than do restrictions upon individual speech," for even "the complete curtailment of corporate communications concerning political or ideological questions not integral to day-to-day business functions would leave individuals, including corporate shareholders, employees, and customers, free to communicate their thoughts." It is thus "unlikely," White maintained, "that any significant communication would be lost by such a prohibition."

White then turned to the central question:

[The] special status of corporations has placed them in a position to control vast amounts of economic power which may, if not regulated, dominate not only the economy but also the very heart of our democracy, the electoral process. Although [*Buckley*] provides support for the position that the desire to equalize the financial resources available to candidates does not justify the limitation upon the expression of support which a restriction upon individual contributions entails, the interest of Massachusetts [is] quite different. It is not one of equalizing the resources of opposing candidates or opposing positions, but rather of preventing institutions which have been permitted to amass wealth as a result of special advantages extended by the State for certain economic purposes from using that wealth to acquire an unfair advantage in the political process. [The] State need not permit its own creation to consume it.

As an example of the problem, White reported that in "Massachusetts' most recent experience with unrestrained corporate expenditures in connection with ballot questions," a political committee opposed to a proposed amendment to the Massachusetts Constitution spent $120,000, "the bulk of it raised through large corporate contributions," whereas the only political committee supporting the amendment "was able to raise and expend only approximately $7,000." White concluded: "Perhaps these figures reflect the Court's view of the appropriate role which corporations should play in the Massachusetts electoral process, but it nowhere explains why it is entitled to substitute its judgment for that of Massachusetts [which has] acted to correct or prevent similar domination of the electoral process by corporate wealth."

Justice Rehnquist also dissented:

> "A corporation is an artificial being, [existing] only in contemplation of law. Being the mere creature of law, it possesses only those properties which the charter of creation confers upon it, either expressly, or as incidental to its very [existence]." [When] a State charters a corporation for the purpose of publishing a newspaper, it necessarily assumes that the corporation is entitled to the liberty of the press essential to the conduct of its business. [Similarly, the] right of commercial speech [might be] necessarily incidental to the business of a commercial corporation. [But it] cannot be so readily concluded that the right of political expression is equally necessary to carry out the functions of a corporation organized for commercial purposes. A State grants to a business corporation the blessings of potentially perpetual life and limited liability to enhance its efficiency as an economic entity. It might reasonably [conclude] that those properties, so beneficial in the economic sphere, pose special dangers in the political sphere.

For an empirical analysis of the effects of campaign expenditures, see Lowenstein, Campaign Spending and Ballot Propositions: Recent Experience, Public Choice Theory and the First Amendment, 29 U.C.L.A. L. Rev. 505 (1982) ("the power of some groups to raise enormous [sums], without regard to any breadth or depth of popular feeling, seriously interferes with the ability of other groups to use the institutions of direct democracy for their intended purpose"). For general analysis, see Symposium, Campaign Reform, 10 Hastings Const. L.Q. 463 (1983).

4. *Subsidizing speech to "improve" the electoral process:* Buckley *and public financing of campaigns.* Both *Buckley* and *Bellotti* concluded that, absent extraordinary circumstances, government cannot constitutionally *restrict* an individual's or corporation's speech in order to eliminate imbalance in the marketplace. What other means, if any, might government employ to achieve this objective? Consider Powe, Mass Speech and the Newer First Amendment, 1982 Sup. Ct. Rev. 243, 268-269, 282-283: "[To] attempt to tone down a debate [in] the interests of enhancing the marketplace [is] wildly at odds with the normal First Amendment belief that more speech is better. [If the problem is that] the wealthy are too powerful, [we should provide] significant additional public funding [for] electoral campaigns, so that the advantages of wealth can [be] minimized."

In *Buckley* the Court considered the constitutionality of Subtitle H of the Internal Revenue Code, which established a scheme of campaign "subsidies" to equalize the financial resources of political candidates. Under Subtitle H, major political parties (those that had received more than 25 percent of the vote in the preceding presidential election) qualified for subsidies of up to $20 million for their candidate's presidential campaigns. Minor parties (those that had received between 5 and 25 percent of the vote in the preceding presidential election) qualified for subsidies proportional to their share of the vote in the preceding or current election, whichever was higher. All other political parties qualified for subsidies only if they received more than 5 percent of the vote in the current election. Subtitle H provided for public financing of primaries and party nominating conventions on similar terms. All subsidies were indexed to inflation. Major party candidates were eligible for public funding only if they agreed to forgo all private contributions and to limit their expenditures to the amount of the subsidy. Other candidates who accepted subsidies were permitted to supplement their public funding with private contributions as long as they agreed to limit their total expenditures to the amount of the major party subsidy.

The Court upheld the public financing provisions: "Although 'Congress shall make no law [abridging] the freedom of speech, or of the press,' Subtitle H is a congressional effort, not to abridge, restrict, or censor speech, but rather to use public money to facilitate and enlarge public discussion and participation in the electoral process, goals vital to a self-governing people. Thus, Subtitle H furthers, not abridges, pertinent First Amendment values." Is this consistent with the Court's analysis in other parts of the opinion?

The Court held further that Subtitle H's requirement that a candidate who accepts public financing agree to limit total campaign expenditures to the amount of the major party subsidy did not independently violate the first amendment: "Congress [may] condition acceptance of public funds on an agreement by the candidate to abide by specified expenditure limitations. Just as a candidate may voluntarily limit the size of the contributions he chooses to accept, he may decide to forgo private fundraising and accept public funding." Consider Polsby, supra, at 26: "[No] sooner does the Court resolve a most fundamental First Amendment question [concerning the constitutionality of expenditure limitations] in a manner highly favorable to the interest in personal liberty, then it takes it all back again, letting expenditure ceilings in the back door by allowing them as a condition to the candidate's accepting public financing. [The] clash of the holdings is startling."

What other means might government adopt to improve the political process? Compare Columbia Broadcasting System v. FCC, 453 U.S. 367 (1981) (upholding FCC regulation requiring broadcasters "to allow reasonable access [to] a broadcasting station by a legally qualified candidate for Federal elective office on behalf of his candidacy"), and Red Lion Broadcasting Co. v. FCC, 395 U.S. 367 (1969) (upholding the political-editorial and personal attack portions of the FCC's "fairness doctrine"), with Miami Herald Publishing Co. v. Tornillo, 418 U.S. 241 (1974) (invalidating a state statute granting a right of reply to political candidates attacked by newspapers). These decisions are examined more fully in section F6 infra. See generally T. Emerson, The System of Freedom of Expression 627-673 (1970).

5. *Equality and the first amendment.* Another issue posed in *Buckley* was whether "as constructed public financing invidiously discriminates [against non-major party candidates] in violation of the Fifth Amendment." What is the appropriate mode of analysis where government restricts the speech of X but not Y, or grants a subsidy to X but not Y, and the line between X and Y is unrelated to content? Is this a free speech or an equal protection issue? See Karst, Equality as a Central Principle in the First Amendment, 43 U. Chi. L. Rev. 20 (1975).

In *Buckley* the Court rejected the equal protection challenge:

> Subtitle H does not prevent any candidate from getting on the ballot or any voter from casting a vote for the candidate of his choice; the inability, if any, of minor-party candidates to wage effective campaigns will derive not from lack of public funding but from their inability to raise private contributions. [Third parties have

historically been] incapable of matching the major parties' ability to raise money and win elections. Congress was [thus] justified in providing both major parties full funding and all other parties only a percentage of the major-party entitlement. Identical treatment of all [parties] would [make] it easy to raid the United States Treasury [and] artificially foster the proliferation of splinter parties. [Finally, there has been no showing] that the election funding plan disadvantages nonmajor parties by operating to reduce their strength below that attained without any public financing. [We thus] conclude that the general election funding system does not work an invidious discrimination against candidates of nonmajor parties.

Other aspects of the intersection of equal protection and free expression are explored in section F1 infra.

Note: Additional Regulation of the Electoral Process

1. *Expenditures of political action committees.* In Federal Election Commission v. National Conservative Political Action Committee, — U.S. — , 105 S. Ct. 1459 (1985), the Court held unconstitutional a provision of the Presidential Election Campaign Fund Act prohibiting any independent political action committee to spend more than $1,000 to further the election of a presidential candidate receiving public financing. The Court, in an opinion by Justice Rehnquist, explained: "[The] expenditures at issue in this case produce speech at the core of the First Amendment. [In] *Buckley* we struck down [limitations] on individuals' independent expenditures because we found no tendency in such expenditures, uncoordinated with the candidate or his campaign, to corrupt or to give the appearance of corruption. For similar reasons, we [find the] limitation on independent expenditures by political committees to be constitutionally infirm."

Justice White, joined by Justices Brennan and Marshall, dissented:

[The Court] is concerned with the interests of the PAC's contributors. [But] the contributors [are] not engaging in speech to any greater extent than [those] who contribute directly to political campaigns. *Buckley* explicitly distinguished between [using] one's own money to express one's views, [and] giving money to someone else in the expectation that that person will use the money to express views with which one is in agreement. [This] case falls within the latter category. [Exactly] like the contributions limits upheld in *Buckley*, [the challenged provision] "does not in any way infringe the contributor's freedom to discuss candidates and issues." And because it does not limit personal expenditures, it does not "reduce the total amount of money potentially available to promote political expression." Accordingly, *Buckley* indicates that [the challenged provision is constitutional].

The Court responded:

The First Amendment freedom of association is squarely implicated in this case. [Political action committees] are mechanisms by which large numbers of individuals of modest means can join together [to amplify their voices]. To say that [such] collective action [is] not entitled to full First Amendment protection would subordinate the voices of those of modest means as opposed to those sufficiently wealthy to be able to buy expensive media ads with their own resources.

2. *Contributions to "multicandidate political action committees."* The Federal Election Campaign Act of 1971 authorizes the existence of "multicandidate political action committees." Under the act, a "multicandidate political committee" is any political committee "which has received contributions from more than 50 persons, [and] has made contributions to 5 or more candidates for Federal Office." In California Medical Association v. Federal Election Commission, 453 U.S. 182 (1981), the Court upheld a section of the act providing that individuals and unincorporated associations may contribute no more than $5,000 per year to any multicandidate political committee.

In a plurality opinion, Justice Marshall, joined by Justices Brennan, White, and Stevens, explained: "Nothing in [the challenged section] limits the amount [a political action committee] or any of its members may independently expend in order to advocate political views; rather, the statute restrains only the amount that [an individual or association] may contribute to [a political action committee]. [And, as we held in *Buckley*, such contributions are not] entitled to full First Amendment protection."

Moreover, Marshall rejected the claim that because "the contributions here," unlike those at issue in *Buckley*, "flow to a political committee, rather than to a candidate," [the challenged section] "does not further the governmental interest in preventing the actual or apparent corruption of the political process." Marshall explained that this section was necessary "to prevent circumvention of the very limitations on contributions that [the] Court upheld in *Buckley*," for the restrictions limiting annual contributions to a particular candidate to $1,000 and limiting total annual contributions to all candidates to $25,000 could be "easily evaded" if individuals and associations could make unlimited contributions to political action committees.

Justice Blackmun concurred:

> I do not agree [that] the First Amendment test to be applied to contribution limitations is different from the test applicable to expenditure limitations. [Both] can be upheld only "if the State demonstrates a sufficiently important interest and employs means closely drawn to avoid unnecessary abridgment of associational freedoms." [Applying that standard], I conclude that [the challenged section] is a [permissible] means of preventing evasion of the limitations on contributions [upheld] in *Buckley*.

Justice Stewart, joined by Chief Justice Burger and Justices Powell and Rehnquist, dissented on jurisdictional grounds.

Does *CMA* survive *National Conservative Political Action Committee?* In light of *CMA*, could Congress constitutionally limit the *number* of political action committees to which one may contribute? Could it limit the number of political action committees to which one may contribute which support the same candidate?

See also FEC v. National Right to Work Committee, 459 U.S. 197 (1982) (upholding section 441b(b)(4)(C) of the act, which prohibits nonstock corporations from soliciting contributions from persons other than their "members" for the purpose of generating funds to be spent in federal election campaigns).

3. *Contributions to committees supporting or opposing ballot measure referenda: the* Berkeley *case.* In Citizens against Rent Control v. Berkeley, 454 U.S. 290 (1981), the Court invalidated a Berkeley ordinance imposing a $250 limit on

contributions to committees formed to support or oppose ballot measures submitted to a popular vote. The Court maintained that the ordinance imposed a "significant restraint" not only on "freedom of association," but also "on the freedom of expression of [those] who wish to express their views through committees." The Court explained that, in *Buckley*, it had "identified a single narrow exception to the rule that limits on political activity were contrary to the First Amendment. The exception relates to the perception of undue influence of large contributors to a *candidate*. [Referenda, however,] 'are held on issues, not candidates for public office. The risk of corruption perceived in cases involving candidate elections simply is not present in a popular vote on a public issue.' " Justices Rehnquist, Marshall, and Blackmun, who was joined by Justice O'Connor, filed concurring opinions. Justice White dissented.

4. *Regulating campaign promises.* In Brown v. Hartlage, 456 U.S. 46 (1982), petitioner, a candidate for local office in Kentucky, promised the voters that, if elected, he would reduce the salary of the office "to a more realistic level." Petitioner was elected, but a state court declared the election void on the ground that petitioner had violated Kentucky's Corrupt Practices Act. The Court reversed:

> The [Act] prohibits a political candidate from giving, or promising to give, anything of value to a voter in exchange for his vote or support. In many of its possible applications, this provision would appear to present little constitutional difficulty, for a State may surely prohibit a candidate from buying votes. [But] it is equally plain that there are constitutional limits on the State's power to prohibit candidates from making promises in the course of an election campaign. [Candidate] commitments enhance the accountability of government officials [and] assist the voters in predicting the effect of their vote. . . .
>
> [Here, petitioner's promise] was made openly, subject to the comment and criticism of his political opponent and to the scrutiny of the voters. [He] did not offer the voters a payment from his personal funds. His was a declaration of intention to exercise the fiscal powers of government office within what he believed [to] be the recognized framework of office. [Moreover, the] benefit was to extend beyond those voters who cast their ballots for [petitioner], to all taxpayers and citizens. [Thus, like] a promise to lower taxes, to increase efficiency in government, or indeed to increase taxes in order to provide some group with a desired public benefit or public service, [petitioner's] promise to reduce his salary cannot be deemed beyond the reach of the First Amendment, or considered as inviting the kind of corrupt arrangement the appearance of which a State may have a compelling interest in avoiding. See [*Buckley*].

5.   Other Means of Expression: Litigation and Association

NAACP v. BUTTON, 371 U.S. 415 (1963): For more than a decade, the Virginia Conference of the NAACP had financed litigation aimed at ending racial segregation in the public schools of Virginia. Litigation involving public school segregation was typically initiated as follows: A local branch of the NAACP would invite a member of the Conference's legal staff to explain to a meeting of parents and children the legal steps necessary to achieve desegregation. After discussion, the staff member would distribute printed forms authorizing him and other

NAACP attorneys to represent the signers in legal proceedings to achieve desegregation. Although Virginia law had long prohibited the solicitation of legal business, no attempt was made prior to 1956 to prohibit the activities of the NAACP. In 1956, however, the Virginia legislature enacted Chapter 33, which expressly prohibited any organization to retain a lawyer in connection with litigation to which it was not a party and in which it had no pecuniary right or liability. The Supreme Court held that, as applied to the NAACP's activities, Chapter 33 violated the first amendment. Justice Brennan delivered the opinion:

"In the context of NAACP objectives, litigation is not a technique of resolving private differences; it is a means for [achieving] equality of treatment [for] the members of the Negro [community]. It is [a] form of political expression. Groups which find themselves unable to achieve their objectives through the ballot frequently turn to the courts. . . .

"[Moreover,] there is no longer any doubt that the First and Fourteenth Amendments protect certain forms of orderly group activity. Thus we have affirmed the right 'to engage in association for the advancement of beliefs and ideas.' [The] NAACP is not a conventional political party; but [for the group] it assists, [association] for litigation may be the most effective form of political association.

"[Under] Chapter 33, [a] person who advises another that his legal rights have been infringed and refers him to a particular attorney [for] assistance has committed a [crime]. There thus inheres in the statute the gravest danger of smothering all discussion looking to the eventual institution of litigation on behalf of the rights of members of an unpopular minority. [Such] a vague and broad statute lends itself to selective enforcement against unpopular causes. We cannot close our eyes to the fact that the militant Negro civil rights movement has engendered the intense resentment and opposition of the politically dominant white community of Virginia; litigation assisted by the NAACP has been bitterly fought. In such circumstances, a statute broadly curtailing group activity leading to litigation may easily become a weapon of oppression, however even-handed its terms appear. Its mere existence could well freeze out of existence all such activity on behalf of the civil rights of Negro citizens.

"It is apparent, therefore, that Chapter 33 as construed limits First Amendment freedoms. [This] Court has consistently held that only a compelling state interest [can] justify limiting First Amendment freedoms. [However] valid may be Virginia's interest in regulating the traditionally illegal practices of barratry, maintenance and champerty, that interest does not justify the prohibition of the NAACP activities disclosed by this record. Malicious intent was the essence of the common-law offenses of fomenting or stirring up litigation. [The exercise] of First Amendment rights to enforce constitutional rights through litigation, as a matter of law, cannot be deemed malicious. . . .

"[Moreover, there] has been no showing [here] of a serious danger [of] professionally reprehensible conflicts of [interest]. Regulations which reflect hostility to stirring up litigation have been aimed chiefly at those who urge recourse to the courts for private gain, serving no public interest. Here, however, [no] monetary stakes are involved, [and] there is [thus] no danger that the attorney will desert [the] paramount interests of his client to enrich himself or an outside sponsor. And the aims and interests of the NAACP have not been shown to conflict with those of its members and nonmember Negro litigants. . . .

"Resort to the courts to seek vindication of constitutional rights is a different matter from the oppressive, malicious, or avaricious use of the legal process for purely private gain. Lawsuits attacking racial discrimination, at least in Virginia, are neither very profitable nor very popular. They are not an object of general competition among Virginia lawyers; the problem is rather one of an apparent dearth of lawyers who are willing to undertake such litigation. [The] State has failed to advance any substantial regulatory interest, in the form of substantive evils flowing from petitioner's activities, which can justify the broad prohibitions which it has imposed."

Justice White concurred in part and dissented in part.

Justice Harlan, joined by Justices Clark and Stewart, dissented: "Freedom of expression embraces more than the right of an individual to speak his mind. It includes also his right to advocate and his right to join with his fellows in an effort to make that advocacy effective. And just as it includes the right jointly to petition the legislature for redress of grievances, so it must include the right to join together for purposes of obtaining judicial redress. . . .

"But to declare that litigation is a form of conduct that may be associated with political expression does not resolve this case. [For this Court has repeatedly held that] 'general regulatory statutes, not intended to control the content of speech but incidentally limiting its unfettered exercise,' are permissible 'when they have been found justified by subordinating valid governmental interests.' The problem in each such case is to weigh the legitimate interest of the State against the effect of the regulation on individual rights. [Thus, although the State] may not broadly prohibit individuals [from] joining together to petition a court for redress of their grievances, it [may] impose reasonable regulations limiting the permissible form of litigation and the manner of legal representation within its borders. . . .

"The interest which Virginia has asserted is that of maintaining high professional standards among those who practice law within its borders. [The Court's analysis of this interest is] too facile. [With] regard to the claimed absence of the pecuniary element, it cannot well be suggested that the attorneys here are donating their services, since they are in fact compensated for their work. [Moreover,] avoidance of improper pecuniary gain is not the only relevant factor in determining standards of professional conduct. Running perhaps even deeper is the desire [to] prevent any interference with the uniquely personal relationship between lawyer and [client]. When an attorney is employed by an association [to] represent individual litigants, [the] lawyer necessarily finds himself with a divided allegiance — to his employer and to his client — which may prevent full compliance with his basic professional obligations. [For example], it may be in the interest of the [NAACP] in every case [to] press for an immediate breaking down of racial [barriers]. But in a particular litigation, [a] Negro parent, concerned that a continued frontal attack could result in schools closed for years, might prefer to wait [a] longer time for good-faith efforts by the local school board than is permitted by the centrally determined policy of the NAACP. [Is the] lawyer, retained and paid by petitioner and subject to its directions on matters of policy, able to advise the parent with that undivided allegiance that is the hallmark of the attorney-client relation? I am afraid not. . . .

"There remains to [consider the] impact this statute may have on rights of free expression and association. Chapter 33 [does] no more than prohibit petitioner [from] soliciting legal business for its staff attorneys. [The] important function of organizations like petitioner in vindicating constitutional rights is [not] substantially impaired by this statute. [This] enactment [does] not in any way suppress [advocacy] of litigation in general or in particular. [Moreover, it does not] prevent petitioner from recommending the services of attorneys who are not subject to its directions and control. [It] prevents only the solicitation of business for attorneys subject to petitioner's control, and as so limited, should be sustained."

Note: Litigation and the First Amendment

1. Button *in context*. Consider H. Kalven, The Negro and the First Amendment 66-69, 75-79 (1965):

> One of the most distinctive features of the Negro revolution has been its almost military assault on the Constitution via the strategy of systematic litigation. [To] a South hostile to [Brown v. Board of Education], the NAACP has appeared, and accurately, as a militant army led by lawyers determined to see to it that "all deliberate speed" will have some meaning. [Chapter 33 was designed] to slow down [NAACP litigation]. Unless the NAACP goes out and signs up the client, pays for the case, and delivers the client to one of its expert lawyers, it will be unable to recruit the needed flow of litigation. Unless it [can] control the timing and line of attack in the litigation once it is begun, its grand strategy of war by lawsuit will be frustrated. [The] case thus raises a profound question for our scheme of constitutional adjudication.

2. *Litigation as "speech."* Why does *Button* pose a first amendment issue? Because the law might be discriminatorily applied against persons espousing a particular view? Because association for the purpose of litigation is "speech"? Because litigation is "speech"? Because litigation is "speech" when it attempts to enforce constitutional rights?

3. *The reach of* Button: Primus. In In re Primus, 436 U.S. 412 (1978), an ACLU "cooperating lawyer" wrote a letter to a woman who had been sterilized informing her of the ACLU's willingness to provide free legal representation to women in her position in a proposed lawsuit challenging the constitutionality of an alleged program of sterilizing pregnant mothers as a condition of their continued receipt of Medicaid benefits. The Disciplinary Board of the South Carolina Supreme Court reprimanded the ACLU lawyer for violating a disciplinary rule prohibiting any "lawyer who has given unsolicited advice to a layman that he should [take] legal action [to] accept employment resulting from that advice."

The Court held the reprimand unconstitutional. The Court emphasized that, "for the ACLU, as for the NAACP, 'litigation is not a technique of resolving private differences'; it is 'a form of political expression' and 'political association.' " To justify a restriction on such " 'core First Amendment rights,' " the state must demonstrate that the attorney's "activity in fact involved the type of misconduct at which South Carolina's [prohibition on solicitation] is said to be directed." Since the record did "not support [the state's] contention that undue influence, overreaching, misrepresentation, or invasion of privacy [had] actually occurred," the reprimand violated the first amendment.

Suppose Primus was not affiliated with the ACLU, but learned of the alleged Medicaid practice, was offended by it, and decided to challenge it on her own time. Would her solicitation of prospective plaintiffs be protected by the first amendment? Suppose the plaintiffs agreed to pay her a reasonable fee if she won? Does an individual who writes a book lose first amendment protection if she seeks pecuniary gain?

4. *The reach of* Button: Trainmen. The Brotherhood of Railroad Trainmen was founded in the late nineteenth century to promote the welfare of trainmen and their families. One problem facing the Brotherhood was the inability of railroad workers to recover compensatory damages for injuries suffered on the job. This was due, in part, to the inability of the workers' lawyers to deal effectively with the more "able and experienced railroad counsel." To rectify this situation, the Brotherhood established its Department of Legal Counsel. In each of sixteen regions, the Department selected "a lawyer or firm [with] a reputation for honesty and skill in representing plaintiffs in railroad personal injury litigation." When a worker was injured or killed, the Brotherhood advised him or his family to consult a lawyer recommended by the Brotherhood. The Virginia State Bar obtained an injunction in state court against the Brotherhood on the ground that this activity constituted "the solicitation of legal business and the unauthorized practice of law."

In Brotherhood of Railroad Trainmen v. Virginia State Bar, 377 U.S. 1 (1964), the Court, building on *Button*, held the injunction invalid:

> It cannot seriously be doubted that the First [Amendment guarantees] railroad workers the right to gather together for the lawful purpose of helping and advising one another in asserting the rights Congress gave them in the Safety Appliance Act and the Federal Employers' Liability Act. [What] Virginia has sought to halt is not a commercialization of the legal profession which might threaten the moral and ethical fabric of the administration of justice. It is not "ambulance chasing." The railroad workers, by recommending competent lawyers to each other, [are] not themselves engaging in the practice of law, nor are they or the lawyers whom they select parties to any soliciting of business. [For laymen] to associate together to help one another to preserve and enforce rights granted them under federal laws cannot be condemned as a threat to legal ethics. [The] Constitution protects the associational rights of the members of the [Brotherhood] precisely as it does those of the NAACP.

Justice Clark, joined by Justice Harlan, dissented:

> The Court depends upon [*Button*] to support its position. But there the vital fact was that the claimed privilege was a "form of political expression" to secure, through court action, constitutionally protected civil rights. Personal injury litigation is not a form of political expression, but rather a procedure for the settlement of damage claims. No guaranteed civil right is involved. [*Button*] is not apposite.

See also United Transportation Union v. State Bar of Michigan, 401 U.S. 576 (1971) (invalidating an injunction prohibiting the union from recommending attorneys to its members only if the attorneys agreed that their fees would not exceed 25 percent of the recovery); United Mine Workers v. Illinois Bar Association, 389 U.S. 217 (1967) (invalidating an injunction prohibiting the union from employing a salaried attorney to assist its members with workmen's compensation claims).

5. *The reach of* Button: Ohralik. In Ohralik v. Ohio State Bar Association, 436 U.S. 447 (1978), decided on the same day as *Primus*, appellant, an attorney, after learning about an automobile accident, personally contacted two young women who had been injured in the accident and arranged to represent them in subsequent litigation. As a result of this "ambulance chasing," Ohralik was suspended by the Ohio State Bar for violation of a disciplinary rule prohibiting any "lawyer who has given unsolicited advice to a layman that he should obtain counsel" to accept "employment resulting from that advice."

The Court upheld the suspension. The Court explained that *Ohralik* was not governed by *Button* and *Primus*, for appellant's "approaches to the young women [did not involve] political expression or an exercise of associational freedom '[to] secure constitutionally guaranteed civil rights.' " Moreover, *Ohralik* was not governed by *Trainmen*, for "[appellant cannot] compare his solicitation to the mutual assistance in asserting legal rights that was at issue [in *Trainmen*]." Indeed, a "lawyer's procurement of remunerative employment is a subject only marginally affected with First Amendment concerns. It falls within the State's proper sphere of economic and professional regulation." Appellant's conduct, the Court added, was analogous to commercial expression, which occupies only a "subordinate position in the scale of First Amendment values." Accordingly, it was unnecessary for the state to prove that appellant's act of solicitation involved any actual abuse or caused any actual harm to his "clients." Rather, the prohibition could constitutionally be applied wherever, as in *Ohralik*, an attorney for remunerative purposes "personally solicits an unsophisticated, injured, or distressed lay person," for in such circumstances there is present a "potential for overreaching," and the solicitation is thus "likely to result in the adverse consequences the State seeks to avert."

6. *The reach of* Button: Walters. In Walters v. National Association of Radiation Survivors, — U.S. — , 105 S. Ct. 3180 (1985), the Court upheld a federal statute limiting to $10 the fee that may be paid an attorney or agent who represents a veteran seeking benefits from the Veterans' Administration for service-connected disability. The Court held that the challenged provision did not violate the due process clause because veterans had a meaningful opportunity to present their claims even without counsel and significant government interests justified the statutory effort to simplify the administrative process. The Court explained that the first amendment challenge was essentially "inseparable" from the due process claim, and distinguished *Trainmen* on the ground that in *Trainmen* "the First Amendment interest [was] primarily the right to associate collectively for the common good." Justice Stevens, joined by Justices Brennan and Marshall, dissented.

ROBERTS v. U.S. JAYCEES, — U.S. — , 104 S. Ct. 3244 (1984): The Jaycees is a nonprofit membership corporation whose objective is to provide young men with an "opportunity for personal development and achievement and an avenue for intelligent participation [in] the affairs of [the] community." Regular membership in the Jaycees is limited to men between the ages of eighteen and thirty-five. Associate membership is open to older men and to women. Associate members may not vote, hold office, or participate in certain leadership training programs. The Minnesota Department of Human Rights found that the Jaycees' membership policy violated the Minnesota Human Rights Act, which prohibits discrimination on the basis of sex. The Court held that the act does not violate the first amendment right of association. Justice Brennan delivered the opinion of the Court:

"[We have long] recognized a right to associate for the purpose of engaging in those activities protected by the First Amendment, [for an] individual's freedom to speak [and] to petition the Government for the redress of grievances could not be vigorously protected [unless] a correlative freedom to engage in group effort toward those ends were not also guaranteed. [Government] actions that may unconstitutionally infringe upon this freedom can take a number of forms. Among other things, government may seek to impose penalties [on] individuals because of their membership in a disfavored group, [see *Scales*, supra section B1], it may [require] disclosure of [membership] in a group seeking anonymity, [see section F5 infra], and it may try to interfere with the internal organization of [a group]. By requiring the Jaycees to admit women as full voting members, the Minnesota Act works an infringement of the last type. There can be no clearer example of an intrusion into the internal structure [of] an association than a regulation that forces the group to accept members it does not desire. . . .

"The right to associate for expressive purposes is not, however, absolute. Infringements on that right may be justified by regulations adopted to serve compelling state interests, unrelated to the suppression of ideas, that cannot be achieved through means significantly less restrictive of associational freedoms. [We] are persuaded that Minnesota's compelling interest in eradicating discrimination against its female citizens justifies the impact that application of the statute to the Jaycees may have on the male members' associational freedoms. . . .

"[The challenged act] does not aim at the suppression of speech [and it] does not distinguish between prohibited and permitted activity on the basis of viewpoint. [The] Act reflects the State's strong historical commitment to eliminating [discrimination]. That goal, which is unrelated to the suppression of expression, plainly serves compelling state interests of the highest order. . . .

"[Moreover], the Jaycees have failed to demonstrate that the Act imposes any serious burdens on the male members' freedom of expressive association. [To] be sure, [a] 'not insubstantial part' of the Jaycees' activities constitutes protected expression on political, economic, cultural, and social affairs. [There] is, however, no basis [for] concluding that admission of women as full voting members will impede the organization's ability to engage in these protected activities or to disseminate its preferred views. The Act requires no change in the Jaycees' creed of promoting the interests of young men, and it imposes no restrictions on the organization's ability to exclude individuals with ideologies [different] from those of its existing members. . . .

"It [is] arguable that, insofar as the Jaycees is organized to promote the views of young [men], admission of women as voting members will change the message communicated by the group's [speech]. [In] claiming that women might have a different attitude about such issues as the federal budget, school prayer, voting rights, and foreign relations, [the] Jaycees rely solely on unsupported generalizations about the relative interests and perspectives of men and women. Although such generalizations may or may not have a statistical basis in fact with respect to particular positions adopted by the Jaycees, we have repeatedly condemned legal decisionmaking that relies uncritically on such assumptions. [In] the absence of a showing far more substantial than that attempted by the Jaycees, we decline to indulge in the sexual stereotyping that underlies the [contention] that, by allowing women to vote, the [Act] will change the content or impact of the organization's speech."

Justice O'Connor concurred in the judgment: "The Court [neglects] to establish at the threshold that the Jaycees is an association whose activities [should] engage the strong protections of the First Amendment that extends to expressive associations. [An] association engaged exclusively in protected expression enjoys First Amendment protection of both the content of its message and the choice of its members. [But] there is only minimal constitutional protection of the freedom of *commercial* association. [It] is only when the association is predominantly engaged in protected expression that state regulation [raises important first amendment questions]. Determining whether an association's activity is predominantly protected expression will often be difficult, [but it is easy here]. Notwithstanding its protected expressive activities, the Jaycees [is], first and foremost, an organization that [promotes] the art of solicitation and management [and trains] its members [in] business. [The] 'not insubstantial' volume of protected Jaycees activity [is] simply not enough to preclude state regulation of the Jaycees' [primarily] commercial activities." O'Connor therefore concluded that the Minnesota act could constitutionally be applied to the Jaycees even if "the admission of women [would] affect the content of the organization's message."

Justice Rehnquist concurred in the judgment. Chief Justice Burger and Justice Blackmun did not participate.

After *Roberts*, can a state prohibit the Nazi Party of America from excluding Jews? Is that case different because, as suggested by Justice O'Connor, the Nazis, unlike the Jaycees, are "predominantly engaged in protected expression"? Is it different because the admission of Jews would *symbolically* interfere with the essential message of the party? In *Roberts* the Court rejected the argument that the act was invalid as applied to the Jaycees because the admission of women would interfere with the symbolic message inherent in an all-male organization: "[Even] if enforcement of the Act causes some incidental abridgment of the Jaycees' protected speech, that effect is no greater than is necessary to accomplish the State's legitimate purposes. [Like] violence or other types of potentially expressive activities that produce special harms distinct from their communicative impact, [discrimination on the basis of gender is] entitled to no constitutional protection."

After *Roberts*, can a state prohibit Republicans from voting in a Democratic primary? Cf. Rosario v. Rockefeller, 410 U.S. 752 (1973) (upholding a New York statute requiring voters to register their party affiliation eleven months prior to the next party primary in order to inhibit "party raiding"); Storer v. Brown, 415 U.S. 724 (1974) (upholding a California statute forbidding ballot position to an independent candidate who "had a registered affiliation with [any] political parties at any time within one year prior to the immediately preceding primary election"). Regulations of the electoral process are examined in section E4 supra. For a thoughtful analysis of *Roberts*, see Linder, Freedom of Association after *Roberts v. U.S. Jaycees*, 82 Mich. L. Rev. 1878 (1984).

F. ADDITIONAL PROBLEMS

The preceding sections examined general first amendment principles. This section explores the application of those principles in the context of six somewhat distinct problems: the intersection of equality and free expression; the application of the first amendment in such "restricted" environments as schools, prisons, and the military; the free speech rights of public employees; the power of government to "compel" expression; the power of government to compel disclosure of an individual's beliefs or associations; and the special issues posed by freedom of the press.

1. Equality and Free Expression

As we saw in section E, there are some circumstances in which government may restrict expression in a content-neutral manner. To what extent, if any, may government in such circumstances decide *voluntarily* to permit some, but not all, speech? To what extent, if any, may it subsidize some ideas, but not others, by exempting the expression of those ideas from otherwise content-neutral restrictions? Does the constitutionality of such exemptions turn on considerations of "equality" or "free expression"? See Karst, Equality as a Central Principle in the First Amendment, 43 U. Chi. L. Rev. 20 (1974).

Police Department of Chicago v. Mosley
408 U.S. 92 (1972)

Mr. Justice Marshall delivered the opinion of the Court.

At issue in this case is the constitutionality of [a] Chicago ordinance [providing that a] "person commits disorderly conduct when he knowingly [pickets] or demonstrates on a public way within 150 feet of [any] school building while the school is in [session], provided that this subsection does not prohibit the peaceful picketing of any school involved in a labor dispute. . . ."

[For] seven months prior to the enactment of [this ordinance], Earl Mosley, a federal postal employee, [frequently] picketed Jones Commercial High School in Chicago. During school hours and usually by himself, Mosley would walk the public sidewalk adjoining the school, carrying a sign that read: "Jones High School practices black discrimination. Jones High School has a black quota." His lonely crusade was always peaceful, orderly, and quiet, and was conceded to be so by the city of Chicago.

[Mosley brought this action] seeking declaratory and injunctive relief. [We] hold that the ordinance is unconstitutional because it makes an impermissible distinction between labor picketing and other peaceful picketing.

Because Chicago treats some picketing differently from others, we analyze this ordinance in terms of the Equal Protection Clause of the Fourteenth Amendment. Of course, the equal protection claim in this case is closely intertwined with First Amendment interests; the Chicago ordinance affects picketing, which is expressive conduct; moreover, it does so by classifications formulated in terms of the subject of the picketing. As in all equal protection cases, however, the crucial question is whether there is an appropriate governmental interest suitably furthered by the differential treatment. See Reed v. Reed, 404 U.S. 71 (1971); Weber v. Aetna Casualty Co., 406 U.S. 164 (1972); Dunn v. Blumstein, 405 U.S. 330 (1972).

The central problem with Chicago's ordinance is that it describes permissible picketing in terms of its subject matter. Peaceful picketing on the subject of a school's labor-management dispute is permitted, but all other peaceful picketing is prohibited. The operative distinction is the message on a picket sign. But, above all else, the First Amendment means that government has no power to restrict expression because of its message, its ideas, its subject matter, or its content. [Citing Cohen v. California; Street v. New York; New York Times v. Sullivan; NAACP v. Button; Wood v. Georgia; Terminiello v. Chicago.] . . .

Necessarily, then, under the Equal Protection Clause, not to mention the First Amendment itself, government may not grant the use of a forum to people whose views it finds acceptable, but deny use to those wishing to express less favored or more controversial views. And it may not select which issues are worth discussing or debating in public facilities. There is an "equality of status in the field of ideas," and government must afford all points of view an equal opportunity to be heard. Once a forum is opened up to assembly or speaking by some groups, government may not prohibit others from assembling or speaking on the basis of what they intend to say. Selective exclusions from a public forum may not be based on content alone, and may not be justified by reference to content alone. . . .

This is not to say that all picketing must always be allowed. We have continually recognized that reasonable "time, place and manner" regulations of picketing may be necessary to further significant governmental interests. [Cox v. New Hampshire]; [Cox v. Louisiana]; [Adderley v. Florida.] Similarly, under an equal protection analysis, there may be sufficient regulatory interests justifying selective exclusions or distinctions among pickets. Conflicting demands on the same place may compel the State to make choices among potential users and uses. And the State may have a legitimate interest in prohibiting some picketing to protect public order. But these justifications for selective exclusions from a public forum must be carefully scrutinized. Because picketing plainly involves expressive conduct within the protection of the First Amendment, [discriminations] among pickets must be tailored to serve a substantial governmental interest.

In this case, the ordinance itself describes impermissible picketing not in terms of time, place, and manner, but in terms of subject matter. The regulation "thus slip[s] from the neutrality of time, place, and circumstance into a concern about content." This is never permitted. In spite of this, Chicago urges that the ordinance is not improper content censorship, but rather a device for preventing disruption of the school. Cities certainly have a substantial interest in stopping picketing which disrupts a school. "The crucial question, however, is whether [Chicago's ordinance] advances that objective in a manner consistent with the command of the Equal Protection Clause." [It] does not.

Although preventing school disruption is a city's legitimate concern, Chicago itself has determined that peaceful labor picketing during school hours is not an undue interference with school. Therefore, under the Equal Protection Clause, Chicago may not maintain that other picketing disrupts the school unless that picketing is clearly more disruptive than the picketing Chicago already permits. "Peaceful" nonlabor picketing, [however], is obviously no more disruptive than "peaceful" labor picketing. . . .

Similarly, we reject the city's argument that, although it permits peaceful labor picketing, it may prohibit all nonlabor picketing because, as a class, nonlabor picketing is more prone to produce violence than labor picketing. Predictions about imminent disruption from picketing involve judgments appropriately made on an individualized basis, not by means of broad classifications, especially those based on subject matter. [Some] labor picketing is peaceful, some disorderly; the same is true of picketing on other themes. [Given] what Chicago tolerates from labor picketing, the excesses of some nonlabor picketing may not be controlled by a broad ordinance prohibiting both peaceful and violent picketing. Such excesses "can be controlled by narrowly drawn statutes," [focusing] on the abuses and dealing even handedly with picketing regardless of subject matter. [Far] from being tailored to a substantial governmental interest, the discrimination among pickets is based on the content of their expression. Therefore, under the Equal Protection Clause, it may not stand.

Affirmed.

MR. JUSTICE BLACKMUN and MR. JUSTICE REHNQUIST concur in the result.

MR. CHIEF JUSTICE BURGER, concurring.

I join the Court's opinion but with the reservation that some of the language used in the discussion of the First Amendment could, if read out of context, be misleading. Numerous holdings of this Court attest to the fact that the First Amendment does not literally mean that we "are guaranteed the right to express any thought, free from government censorship." This statement is subject to some qualifications, as for example those of [Roth v. United States]; [Chaplinsky v. New Hampshire]. See also [New York Times Co. v. Sullivan].

Note: Mosley *and the* "Equality" *of Ideas*

1. *Equality and underinclusion.* Is the Chicago ordinance, absent the labor picketing exemption, a permissible content-neutral restriction? Compare Grayned v. Rockford, supra section E2. If the ordinance is constitutional absent the labor-picketing exemption, should the exemption render it invalid? Is it anomalous that, under the Court's reasoning, the ordinance would more likely to be constitutional if it restricted *more* speech? Consider the following arguments: (a) The labor exemption undermines the city's asserted justifications for the restriction of nonlabor speech. (b) The standard of review should be higher when the city exempts labor speech than when it acts in a wholly content-neutral manner.

Note that *Mosley* focuses on underinclusion rather than on whether the restricted expression creates a "clear and present danger." Is this focus consistent with the ordinary principles of content-based analysis? Is the Chicago ordinance distinguishable from other content-based restrictions because it attempts to *benefit* rather than to *restrict* a particular class of speech?

Suppose the ordinance in *Mosley* had exempted not "labor picketing" but "any picketing related directly to the operation of the school." Is such an ordinance invalid? Consider Cass, First Amendment Access to Government Facilities, 65 Va. L. Rev. 1287, 1323-1324 (1979):

> The courts [should] consider the context of speech — the relation between the speech and the forum. If a court considers alternative speech forums, it also must take account of the factors that make a given forum more or less suited to the speech involved. [Protesting] decisions where they are made [may] be worth more to the interested speaker than the ability to voice the identical message at another location. The symbolic connection between message and place and the greater likelihood that the message will come to the attention of a particular audience have real value.

2. *Equal protection versus the first amendment.* Note the Court's reliance on the equal protection clause. Does that clause impose more stringent restraints on government's power to restrict speech than the first amendment? Consider Stone, Content Regulation and the First Amendment, 25 Wm. & Mary L. Rev. 189, 206 (1983): "The degree of scrutiny that is appropriate in [testing] content-based restrictions [is] fundamentally a first amendment issue. Invocation of the equal protection clause adds nothing constructive to the analysis. It may, however, by appearing to 'simplify' matters, deflect attention from the central constitutional issue."

3. *Subject-matter restrictions.* Note that in *Mosley* the content-based restriction was directed not against a particular viewpoint, idea, or item of information but against an entire subject of discussion — all nonlabor expression. Should the first amendment's hostility to content-based regulation extend not only to restrictions on particular viewpoints but also to restrictions on entire topics? Is such an extension warranted because to permit "a government the choice of permissible subjects for public debate would be to [allow] government control over the search for political truth"? Consolidated Edison Co. v. Public Service Commission, 447 U.S. 530 (1980).

Consider Stone, Restrictions of Speech Because of its Content: The Peculiar Case of Subject-Matter Restrictions, 46 U. Chi. L. Rev. 81, 83, 108 (1978):

> [Although] "subject-matter" distinctions unquestionably regulate content, they at least appear to do so in a viewpoint-neutral manner. As a consequence, such restrictions do not fit neatly within the Court's general framework for reviewing laws regulating speech; it is unclear whether they should be treated as content-based, content-neutral, or something altogether different. [The] Court's rigorous approach to content-based restrictions stems in part from the realization that such restrictions have an especially potent content-differential impact upon the "marketplace of ideas." [Because] they are at least facially viewpoint-neutral, [however, subject-matter restrictions] do not have the same sort of skewing effect on "the thinking process of the community" as restrictions directed specifically against speech taking a particular side in an ongoing debate. Moreover, because of their apparent viewpoint-neutrality, subject-matter restrictions seem much less likely than other forms of content-based restrictions to be the product of government hostility to the ideas or information suppressed. In general, one is more likely to be hostile to speech espousing a specific point of view than to speech about an entire subject. As a result, one [might] argue that subject-matter restrictions are in general less threatening than other sorts of content-based restrictions and, like content-neutral restrictions, need not be subjected to the most stringent standards of review.

4. *The reach of* Mosley: Carey. In Carey v. Brown, 447 U.S. 455 (1980), appellees participated in a peaceful demonstration in front of the home of the mayor of Chicago, protesting his alleged failure to support the busing of school children to achieve racial integration. As a result of this demonstration, appellees were convicted of violating an Illinois statute declaring it "unlawful to picket before or about the residence or dwelling of any person, except when the residence or dwelling is used as a place of business" or is "a place of employment involved in a labor dispute."

The Court held that the residential picketing statute was "constitutionally indistinguishable from the ordinance invalidated in *Mosley*" and thus declared it "defective on equal protection principles." The Court explained:

> [The] Act accords preferential treatment to the expression of views on one particular subject; information about labor disputes may be freely disseminated, but discussion of all other issues is restricted. [When] government regulation discriminates among speech-related activities in a public forum, the Equal Protection Clause mandates that the legislation be finely tailored to serve substantial state interests, and the justifications offered for and distinctions it draws must be carefully scrutinized. [*Mosley*.] . . .
>
> [The State argues that *Carey* is] distinguishable from *Mosley*, [for] the state interests here are especially compelling and particularly well served by a statute that accords differential treatment to labor and nonlabor picketing. [The State argues, for example, that by] "inviting" a worker into his home and converting that dwelling into a place of employment, [the resident has] "waived" his right to be free from picketing with respect to disputes arising out of the employment relationship, thereby justifying the statute's narrow labor exception at those locations. [But this] proves too little. [Numerous other] actions of a homeowner might constitute "nonresidential" uses of his property and would thus serve to vitiate the right to residential privacy. For example, the resident who prominently decorates his windows [with campaign posters] might be said to "invite" a counter-demonstration, [and] the official who has voluntarily chosen to enter the public arena [might be said to have] "waived" his right to privacy with respect to a challenge to his views on significant issues of social and economic policy. . . .
>
> We are not to be understood to imply [that] residential picketing is beyond the reach of uniform and nondiscriminatory regulation. [Preserving] the sanctity of the home [is] surely an important value. ["The] crucial question, however, is whether [Illinois's statute] advances that objective in a manner consistent with the command of the Equal Protection clause.'" [*Mosley*.] And because the statute discriminates among pickets based on the subject matter of their expression, the answer must be "No."

Justice Rehnquist, joined by Chief Justice Burger and Justice Blackmun, dissented.

5. *The reach of* Mosley: Widmar. The University of Missouri at Kansas City, which officially recognizes more than 100 student groups and routinely permits such groups to meet in university facilities, adopted a regulation prohibiting the use of university buildings for "purposes of religious worship or religious teaching." Several university students who were members of Cornerstone, an organization of evangelical Christian students, challenged the regulation.

In Widmar v. Vincent, 454 U.S. 263 (1981), the Court invalidated the regulation. The Court observed:

[The] campus of a public university, at least for its students, possesses many of the characteristics of a public forum. [At] the same time, however, [a] university differs in significant respects from public forums such as streets or parks. [A] university's mission is education, and [it may] impose reasonable regulations compatible with that mission upon the use of its campus and facilities. [Here, through] its policy of accommodating their meetings, the University has created a forum generally open for use by student groups. [The] Constitution forbids a State to enforce certain exclusions from a forum generally open to the public, even if it was not required to create the forum in the first place. [In] order to justify discriminatory exclusion from a public forum based on the religious content of a group's intended speech, the University [must] show that its regulation is necessary to serve a compelling state interest and that it is narrowly drawn to achieve that end. See [Carey v. Brown]. In this case the University claims a compelling interest in maintaining a strict separation of church and state. [We] agree that the interest of the University in complying with its constitutional obligations may be characterized as compelling. It does not follow, however, that an "equal access" policy would be incompatible with [the Establishment Clause]. It is possible — perhaps even foreseeable — that religious groups will benefit from access to University facilities. But [a] religious organization's enjoyment of merely "incidental" benefits does not violate the prohibition against the "primary advancement" of religion.

Justice Stevens concurred in the judgment. Justice White dissented.

6. *The reach of* Mosley: Metromedia. Although *Mosley*, *Carey*, and *Widmar* all involved access to public property, the equality issue can arise in other contexts as well. In Metromedia, Inc. v. San Diego, 453 U.S. 490 (1981), for example, San Diego, in an effort to eliminate hazards to pedestrians and motorists and improve the appearance of the city, enacted an ordinance prohibiting all outdoor advertising display signs except those falling within twelve specified categories, such as temporary political campaign signs, government signs, for-sale signs, commemorative historical plaques, religious symbols, and signs depicting time, temperature, or news. The Court invalidated the ordinance.

In a plurality opinion, Justice White, joined by Justices Stewart, Marshall, and Powell, found it unnecessary to decide whether a "total ban" on outdoor advertising "would be consistent with the First Amendment," holding instead that the ordinance was invalid because it "restricts the use of certain kinds of outdoor signs [by] reference to the content, or message, of the sign." Citing *Mosley* and *Carey*, White explained that "the city does not have [a broad] range of choice [to] distinguish between various communicative interests," and that it "may not choose the appropriate subjects for public discourse." White thus concluded that because the city permits some messages to be conveyed on billboards, it "must similarly allow billboards conveying [other] messages."

Justice Brennan, joined by Justice Blackmun, concurred in the judgment. Brennan argued, however, that even a content-neutral ban on the use of billboards would be unconstitutional, and thus did not rely "on the exceptions to the ban to invalidate the ordinance." The content-neutral aspect of *Metromedia* is examined at supra section E1.

Justice Stevens dissented:

[It] is difficult to understand why the [twelve] exceptions [present any] threat to the interests protected by the First Amendment. [The] essential concern embodied in the First Amendment is that government may not impose its viewpoint on the public or select the topics on which public debate is permissible. The San Diego ordinance simply does not implicate this concern. [Except] for the provision allowing signs to be used for political campaign [purposes], none of the exceptions even arguably relates to any controversial subject matter. [Moreover], it was surely reasonable for the city to conclude that exceptions for clocks, thermometers, historic plaques, and the like, would have a lesser impact on the appearance of the city than the typical large billboards. [And although] political campaign signs [may] be just as unsightly and hazardous as other off-site billboards, [the community's decision to place] a special value on [political expression] is surely consistent with the interests the First Amendment was designed to protect. [In] the aggregate, therefore, [the] exceptions in this ordinance cause it to have a less serious effect on the communications market than would a total ban. [Ironically, the] plurality invalidates this ordinance — not because it is too broad — [but] because it is not broad enough.

Chief Justice Burger and Justice Rehnquist also dissented.

See also Regan v. Time Inc., — U.S. — , 104 S. Ct. 3262 (1984) (invalidating as an unconstitutional content-based restriction a federal statute prohibiting the publication of any photograph of U.S. currency except "for philatelic, numismatic, educational, historical, or newsworthy purposes"); Consolidated Edison Co. v. Public Service Commission, 447 U.S. 530 (1980) (invalidating as an unconstitutional content-based restriction an order prohibiting public utility companies from including in their monthly bills inserts addressing controversial issues of public policy).

Lehman v. City of Shaker Heights
418 U.S. 298 (1974)

MR. JUSTICE BLACKMUN announced the judgment of the Court and an opinion, in which THE CHIEF JUSTICE, MR. JUSTICE WHITE, and MR. JUSTICE REHNQUIST join.

This case presents the question whether a city which operates a public rapid transit system and sells [commercial and public service] advertising space for car cards on its vehicles is required by the First and Fourteenth Amendments to accept paid political advertising on behalf of a candidate for public office.

[Petitioner, a candidate for the office of state representative,] sought to promote his candidacy by purchasing car card space on the Shaker Heights Rapid Transit System for the months of August, September, and October.

[He] was informed [that], although space was then available, [the] city did not permit political advertising. The system, however, accepted ads from cigarette companies, banks, savings and loan associations, liquor companies, retail and service establishments, churches, and civic and public-service oriented groups. . . .

When petitioner did not succeed in his effort to have his copy accepted, he sought declaratory and injunctive relief in the state courts of Ohio without success. . . .

It is urged that the car cards here constitute a public forum protected by the First Amendment, and that there is a guarantee of nondiscriminatory access to such publicly owned and controlled areas of communication "regardless of the primary purpose for which the area is dedicated." [We] disagree.

[This situation is] different from the traditional settings where First Amendment values inalterably prevail. [Although] American constitutional jurisprudence, in the light of the First Amendment, has been jealous to preserve access to public places for purposes of free speech, the nature of the forum and the conflicting interests involved have remained important in determining the degree of protection afforded by the Amendment to the speech in question. . . .

Here, we have no open spaces, no meeting hall, park, street corner, or other public thoroughfare. Instead, the city is engaged in commerce. It must provide rapid, convenient, pleasant, and inexpensive service to the commuters of Shaker Heights. The car card space, although incidental to the provision of public transportation, is a part of the commercial venture. In much the same way that a newspaper or periodical, or even a radio or television station, need not accept every proffer of advertising from the general public, a city transit system has discretion to develop and make reasonable choices concerning the type of advertising that may be displayed in its vehicles. . . .

Because state action exists, however, the policies and practices governing access to the transit system's advertising space must not be arbitrary, capricious, or invidious. Here, the city has decided that "[p]urveyors of goods and services saleable in commerce may purchase advertising space on an equal basis, whether they be house builders or butchers." This decision is little different from deciding to impose a 10-, 25-, or 35-cent fare, or from changing schedules or the location of bus stops. [Revenue] earned from long-term commercial advertising could be jeopardized by a requirement that short-term candidacy or issue-oriented advertisements be displayed on car cards. Users would be subjected to the blare of political propaganda. There could be lurking doubts about favoritism, and sticky administrative problems might arise in parceling out limited space to eager politicians. In these circumstances, the managerial decision to limit car card space to innocuous and less controversial commercial and service oriented advertising does not rise to the dignity of a First Amendment violation. . . .

[The] city consciously has limited access to its transit system advertising space in order to minimize chances of abuse, the appearance of favoritism, and the risk of imposing upon a captive audience. These are reasonable legislative objectives advanced by the city in a proprietary capacity. [There] is no First or Fourteenth Amendment violation.

[Affirmed.]

MR. JUSTICE DOUGLAS, concurring in the judgment. . . .

[If] the streetcar or bus were a forum for communication akin to that of streets or public parks, considerable problems would be presented. [But] a streetcar or bus is plainly not a park or sidewalk or other meeting place for discussion.

[It] is only a way to get to work or back home. The fact that it is owned and operated by the city does not without more make it a forum.

[If] we are to turn a bus or streetcar into either a newspaper or a park, we take great liberties with people who because of necessity become commuters and at the same time captive viewers or listeners.

In asking us to force the system to accept his message as a vindication of his constitutional rights, the petitioner overlooks the constitutional rights of the commuters. While petitioner clearly has a right to express his views to those who wish to listen, he has no right to force his message upon an audience incapable of declining to receive it. In my view the right of the commuters to be free from forced intrusions on their privacy precludes the city from transforming its vehicles of public transportation into forums for the dissemination of ideas upon this captive audience.

Buses [are] a practical necessity for millions in our urban centers. I have already stated this view in my dissent in Public Utilities Comm'n v. Pollak, 343 U.S. 451 (1952), involving the challenge by some passengers to the practice of broadcasting radio programs over loudspeakers in buses and streetcars: "One who tunes in on an offensive program at home can turn it off or tune in another station, as he wishes. One who hears disquieting or unpleasant programs in public places, such as restaurants, can get up and leave. But the man on the streetcar has no choice but to sit and listen, or perhaps to sit and to try *not* to listen." There is no difference when the message is visual, not auricular. In each the viewer or listener is captive. . . .

I do not view the content of the message as relevant either to petitioner's right to express it or to the commuters' right to be free from it. Commercial advertisements may be as offensive and intrusive to captive audiences as any political message. But the validity of the commercial advertising program is not before us since we are not faced with one complaining of an invasion of privacy through forced exposure to commercial ads. Since I do not believe that petitioner has any constitutional right to spread his message before this captive audience, I concur in the Court's judgment.

MR. JUSTICE BRENNAN, with whom MR. JUSTICE STEWART, MR. JUSTICE MARSHALL, and MR. JUSTICE POWELL join, dissenting. . . .

In the circumstances of this case, [we] need not decide whether public transit cars *must* be made available as forums for the exercise of First Amendment rights. By accepting commercial and public service advertising, the city effectively waived any argument that advertising in its transit cars is incompatible with the rapid transit system's primary function of providing transportation. A forum for communication was voluntarily established when the city installed the physical facilities for the advertisements [and] created the necessary administrative machinery for regulating access to that forum.

The plurality opinion, however, contends that as long as the city limits its advertising space to "innocuous and less controversial commercial and service oriented advertising," no First Amendment forum is created. I find no merit in that position. Certainly, noncommercial public service advertisements convey messages of public concern and are clearly protected by the First Amendment. And while it is possible that commercial advertising may be accorded *less* First Amendment protection than speech concerning political and social issues of public importance, [it] is "speech" nonetheless, often communicating information and ideas found by many persons to be controversial. [Once] such messages have been accepted and displayed, the existence of a forum for communication cannot be gainsaid. To hold otherwise, and thus sanction the city's preference for bland commercialism and noncontroversial public service messages over "uninhibited, robust, and wide-open" debate on public issues, would reverse the traditional priorities of the First Amendment.

Once a public forum for communication has been established, both free speech and equal protection principles prohibit discrimination based *solely* upon subject matter or content. See, e.g., [*Mosley*]. That the discrimination is among entire classes of ideas, rather than among points of view within a particular class, does not render it any less odious. Subject matter or content censorship in any form is forbidden. [Few] examples are required to illustrate the scope of the city's policy and practice.[10]

The city contends that its ban against political advertising is bottomed upon its solicitous regard for "captive riders" of the rapid transit system, who are "forced to endure the advertising thrust upon [them]." Whatever merit the city's argument might have in other contexts, it has a hollow ring in the present case, where the city has voluntarily opened its rapid transit system as a forum for communication. In that circumstance, the occasional appearance of provocative speech should be expected. . . .

The line between ideological and nonideological speech is impossible to draw with accuracy. By accepting commercial and public service advertisements, the city opened the door to "sometimes controversial or unsettling speech" and determined that such speech does not unduly interfere with the rapid transit system's primary purpose of transporting passengers. In the eyes of many passengers, certain commercial or public service messages[11] are as profoundly disturbing as some political advertisements might be to other passengers. There is certainly no evidence in the record of this case indicating that political advertisements, as a class, are so disturbing when displayed that they are more likely than commercial or public service advertisements to impair the rapid transit system's primary function of transportation. . . .

Moreover, even if it were possible to draw a manageable line between controversial and noncontroversial messages, the city's practice of censorship for the benefit of "captive audiences" still would not be justified. [The] advertisements accepted by the city [are] not broadcast over loudspeakers in the transit cars. The privacy of the passengers is not, therefore, dependent upon their ability "to sit and to try *not* to listen." [Rather], all advertisements accepted for display are in

---

10. In declaring unconstitutional an advertising policy remarkably similar to the city's policy in the present case, the California Supreme Court detailed "the paradoxical scope of the [transit] district's policy [banning political advertising]" in the following manner:

A cigarette company is permitted to advertise the desirability of smoking its brand, but a cancer society is not entitled to caution by advertisement that cigarette smoking is injurious to health. A theater may advertise a motion picture that portrays sex and violence, but the Legion for Decency has no right to post a message calling for clean films. A lumber company may advertise its wood products, but a conservation group cannot implore citizens to write to the President or Governor about protecting our natural resources. An oil refinery may advertise its products, but a citizens' organization cannot demand enforcement of existing air pollution statutes. An insurance company may announce its available policies, but a senior citizens' club cannot plead for legislation to improve our social security program. Advertisements for travel, foods, clothing, toiletries, automobiles, legal drugs — all these are acceptable, but the American Legion would not have the right to place a paid advertisement reading, "Support Our Boys in Viet Nam. Send Holiday Packages."

Wirta v. Alameda-Contra Costa Transit District, 63 Cal. 2d 51, 57-58, 434 P.2d 982, 986-987 (1967).

11. For example, the record indicates that *church advertising* was accepted for display on the Shaker Heights Rapid Transit System.

written form. [Should] passengers chance to glance at advertisements they find offensive, they can "effectively avoid further bombardment of their sensibilities simply by averting their eyes." [Cohen v. California.] Surely that minor inconvenience is a small price to pay for the continued preservation of so precious a liberty as free speech.

The city's remaining justification is equally unpersuasive. The city argues that acceptance of "political advertisements [would] suggest [that] the candidate so advertised is being supported or promoted by the government of the City." Clearly, such ephemeral concerns do not provide the city with *carte blanche* authority to exclude an entire category of speech from a public forum. . . .

Moreover, neutral regulations, which do not distinguish among advertisements on the basis of subject matter, can be narrowly tailored to allay the city's fears. The impression of city endorsement can be dispelled by requiring disclaimers to appear prominently on the face of every advertisement. And while problems of accommodating all potential advertisers may be vexing at times, the appearance of favoritism can be avoided by the even-handed regulation of time, place, and manner for all advertising, irrespective of subject matter. . . .

Note: Lehman *and the Limits of* Mosley

1. Lehman. In *Mosley* the Court announced that selective exclusions "must be carefully scrutinized" and "must be tailored to serve a substantial governmental interest." In *Lehman* Justice Blackmun, speaking for the plurality, upheld a selective exclusion because it was not "arbitrary, capricious, or invidious." Is Blackmun's analysis in *Lehman* consistent with *Mosley?* Consider the following:

a. *In its operation of the transit system and its sale of advertising space, "the city is engaged in commerce."* Consider Wells & Hellerstein, The Governmental-Proprietary Distinction in Constitutional Law, 66 Va. L. Rev. 1073, 1116, 1077 (1980):

> As a regulator of the general public, the government must base its proscription of an activity on the premise that the proscription will act to enhance the general welfare. [As] a procurer or provider of goods and services, however, it may assert a different, more specific kind of interest — the interest of an employer who needs an efficient workforce, a landlord who would prefer not to deal with tenants who do not pay rent, or a purchaser who wishes to contract with a trustworthy seller. This quasi-business interest may adequately support regulation that a court might strike down if applied to the public at large and the state supported it with arguments that it promotes the general welfare. [That government acts in a proprietary capacity, however,] legitimately serves only to identify a state interest not present when the state regulates the general public. It should be but one element in the analysis and should not by itself determine the outcome.

For analysis of the state as market participant in the context of the dormant commerce clause, see Chapter 3 supra.

b. *Streetcar passengers are a "captive audience."* Recall Cohen v. California, supra section D6: "The ability of government, consonant with the Constitution, to shut off discourse solely to protect others from hearing it is [dependent] upon a showing that substantial privacy interests are being invaded in an essentially intolerable manner." Is that test satisfied in *Lehman?* If so, is the exclusion of all political and public issue speech an appropriate device for protecting the sensibilities of captive commuters? Suppose that, after polling its commuters, the city finds that although the vast majority do not object to the ideas of Democratic and Republican candidates, they "deeply resent" the views expressed by Socialist candidates. Based on this finding, may the city permit Democratic and Republican candidates to purchase car card space to espouse their "inoffensive" ideas, while excluding the "offensive" Socialist messages? For analysis of the "captive" audience, see supra section D6.

c. *The city's rule avoids "sticky administrative problems."* Consider L. Tribe, American Constitutional Law 693 (1978):

> [The] only alternatives [to the city's policy] would appear to be a constitutional rule requiring the city to offer free space for political ads on its transit cars, and a constitutional rule requiring the city to make space available to the highest political bidder. If imposing the first of these alternatives seems inconceivable, then the city's policy may be defended as preferable to the second, despite the evils of the policy's built-in discriminations, on the theory that discrimination between richer and poorer political candidates would be worse still. [Moreover], the aim of avoiding such economic discrimination [among political candidates is] unrelated to any communicative impact the political ads might have had.

d. *"No First Amendment forum is here to be found."* Do you agree with Justice Brennan that, even if the car card space did not inherently constitute a public forum, the city's acceptance of commercial and public service advertisements "created" such a forum? Recall *Widmar.* Consider Emerson, The Affirmative Side of the First Amendment, 15 Ga. L. Rev. 795, 813 (1981): "The dissenters fail to recognize the complications arising when the government is affirmatively promoting expression by providing facilities for a selected area of expression. They argue that, once the 'forum' has been opened, the government may not regulate on the basis of content. The issue before the Court, however, was what the scope of the forum was."

Would any of these "explanations" of *Lehman* justify a content-based restriction defined in terms of viewpoint rather than subject matter?

2. *The reach of* Lehman: Greer. In Greer v. Spock, 424 U.S. 828 (1976), supra section E2b, the base commander of the Fort Dix Military Reservation, acting under the authority of a regulation prohibiting "demonstrations, picketing, sit-ins, protest marches, political speeches and similar activities" on the base, denied the request of several political candidates to make speeches on the base to discuss election issues with service personnel and their dependents. The candidates maintained that the regulation was invalid because the ban on civilian access to the base for expressive purposes was not content-neutral: "Civilian speakers have occasionally been invited to the base to address military personnel. The subjects of their talks have ranged from business management to drug abuse. Visiting clergymen have, by invitation, participated in religious services at the base chapel. Theatrical exhibitions and musical productions have also been presented on the base."

The Court upheld the regulation. Although the base was generally open to the public, the Court explained that "the business of a military installation [is] to train soldiers, not to provide a public forum." Moreover, the Court emphasized that there was "no claim that the military authorities discriminated in any way among candidates for public office based upon the candidates' supposed political views." In such circumstances, the ban on partisan political expression was not unconstitutional:

> The fact that other civilian speakers and entertainers had sometimes been invited to appear at Fort Dix did not of itself serve to convert [the base] into a public forum or to confer upon political candidates a [free speech or equal protection] right to conduct their campaigns there. The decision of the military authorities that a civilian lecture on drug abuse, a religious service by a visiting preacher at the base chapel, or a rock musical concert would be supportive of the military mission of Fort Dix surely did not leave the authorities powerless thereafter to prevent any civilian from entering Fort Dix to speak on any subject whatever.

Justices Brennan and Marshall dissented.

Is the "implication" of *Greer* that, in regulating access to government-owned facilities that do not constitute "public forums," government may discriminate "among speakers in terms of subject matter, so long as there is no discrimination within any given subject in terms of viewpoint"? L. Tribe, American Constitutional Law 691 n.21 (1978). See also Consolidated Edison Co. v. Public Service Commission, 447 U.S. 530 (1980) (describing *Lehman* and *Greer* as "narrow exceptions to the general prohibition against subject-matter distinctions," justified by "the special interests of a government in overseeing the use of its property").

Is *Greer* reconcilable with *Mosley* and *Widmar* on the ground that the Fort Dix regulation distinguished, not between the speech of different individuals, but between the speech of individuals and the speech of government? That is, was the government, in allowing some expression on the military base in *Greer*, not "creating" a forum, but speaking *itself*? See Shiffrin, Government Speech, 27 U.C.L.A. L. Rev. 565, 577-579 (1980).

3. *The reach of* Lehman: Perry. The school district of Perry Township, Indiana, operates an interschool mail system to transmit messages among the teachers and between the teachers and the school administration. In addition, some private organizations, such as the YMCA and the Cub Scouts, have been permitted to use the system. After the Perry Educators' Association (PEA) was certified as the exclusive bargaining representative of the district's teachers, the school district and PEA entered into a collective bargaining agreement granting PEA, but no other union, access to the mail system. Perry Local Educators' Association (PLEA), a rival union, brought this suit claiming that the district's access policy violated the Constitution.

In Perry Educators' Association v. Perry Local Educators' Association, 460 U.S. 37 (1983), the Court, in a five-to-four decision, upheld the challenged policy. Justice White delivered the opinion:

> The existence of a right of access to public property [depends] on the character of the property at issue. [First, there are the] streets and [parks]. In these quintessential public forums, the government may not [enforce] a content-based exclusion [unless the exclusion] is necessary to serve a compelling state interest and [is] narrowly drawn to achieve that end. [*Mosley; Carey.*] [A] second category consists of public property which the state has [voluntarily] opened for use by the public as a place for

expressive activity. [Although] a state is not required to indefinitely retain the open character of [such facilities], as long as it does so it is bound by the same standards as apply in a traditional public forum. [*Widmar.*] [A third category consists of public] property which is not by tradition or designation a forum for public communication. [The] state may reserve [such property] for its intended purposes, communicative or otherwise, so long as the regulation of speech is reasonable and not an effort to suppress expression merely because public officials oppose the speaker's view. . . .

The school mail facilities [fall] within the third category. [The] interschool mail system is not a traditional public forum [and it] is not held open to the general public. [PLEA argues, however,] that the school mail facilities have become a "limited public forum" from which it may not be excluded because of the periodic use of the system by private non-school connected groups, [such as] the YMCA, Cub Scouts, and other civic and church organizations. [The] use of the [mail system] by [such] groups [is] no doubt a relevant consideration. [Indeed, had the school district] opened its mail system for indiscriminate use by the general public, then PLEA could justifiably argue a public forum [had] been created. [But that] is not the case. [And the] type of selective access [involved here] does not transform government property into a public forum. [*Greer; Lehman.*] Moreover, even if [the grant of] access to the Cub Scouts, YMCAs, and parochial schools [had] created a "limited" public forum, the constitutional right of access [would] extend only to other entities of similar character. While the school mail facilities thus might be a forum generally open for [other] organizations that engage in activities of interest [to] students, they would not [be] open to an organization such as PLEA, which is concerned with the terms and conditions of teacher employment. . . .

[PLEA argues further that by allowing PEA and not PLEA to use the mail facilities,] the access policy [favors] a particular viewpoint, that of the PEA, on labor relations, and consequently must be strictly scrutinized regardless of whether a public forum is involved. There is, however, no indication that the school board intended to discourage one viewpoint and advance another. [It] is more accurate to characterize the access policy as based on the *status* of the respective unions rather than their views. Implicit in the concept of the nonpublic forum is the right to make distinctions in access on the basis of subject matter and speaker identity. These distinctions may be impermissible in a public forum but are inherent and inescapable in the process of limiting a nonpublic forum to activities compatible with the intended purpose of the property. The touchstone for evaluating these distinctions is whether they are reasonable in light of the purpose which the forum at issue serves. [Access to the] mail service [clearly] could be restricted to those with teaching and operational responsibility in the schools. [By] the same token — and upon the same principle — the system was properly opened to PEA, when it [was] designated the collective bargaining agent for all teachers in the Perry schools. PEA thereby assumed an official position in the operational structure of [the schools]. [The] differential access provided PEA and PLEA is reasonable because it is wholly consistent with the district's legitimate interest in "preserv[ing] the property [for] the use to which it is lawfully dedicated."

Justice Brennan, joined by Justices Marshall, Powell, and Stevens, dissented:

In focusing on the public forum issue, the Court disregards the First Amendment's central proscription [against] viewpoint discrimination, in any forum, public or nonpublic. [As the] Court of Appeals [noted], "the access policy [favors] a particular viewpoint on labor relations in the Perry schools: the teachers inevitably will receive from [PEA] self-laudatory descriptions of its activities [and] will be denied the critical perspective offered by [PLEA]." [Indeed], the only reason for [PEA] to seek an exclusive access policy is to deny its rivals access to an effective channel of communication. [In effect, the school district] has agreed to amplify the speech of [PEA], while repressing the speech of [PLEA] based on [PLEA's] point of view. [Such viewpoint discrimination] can be sustained "only if the government can show that the regulation is a precisely drawn means of serving a compelling state interest." [The state interests here] are not sufficient to sustain the [challenged] policy.

4. *The reach of* Perry: Cornelius. The Combined Federal Campaign (CFC) is an annual charitable fund-raising drive conducted in the federal work place during working hours largely through the voluntary efforts of federal employees. In Cornelius v. NAACP Legal Defense & Educational Fund, — U.S. — , 105 S. Ct. 3439 (1985), the Court, in a four-to-three decision, upheld an Executive Order limiting participation in the CFC to voluntary, tax-exempt, nonprofit charitable agencies that provide direct health and welfare services to individuals and expressly excluding legal defense and political advocacy organizations.

In an opinion by Justice O'Connor, the Court first held that the CFC is a nonpublic forum:

> Respondents argue [that] the Government created a limited public forum for use by all charitable organizations to solicit funds from federal employees. [We do not agree.] The Government's consistent policy has been to limit participation in the CFC to "appropriate" voluntary [agencies]. Such selective access, unsupported by evidence of a purposeful designation for public use, does not create a public forum. [Nor] does the history of the CFC support a finding that the Government was motivated by an affirmative desire to provide an open forum for charitable solicitation, [for the] historical background indicates that the Campaign was designed to minimize the disruption to the workplace that had resulted from unlimited ad hoc solicitation activities by *lessening* the amount of expressive activity occurring on federal property. [Finally,] the nature of the government property involved strengthens the conclusion that the CFC is a nonpublic forum, [for the] federal workplace, like any place of employment, exists to accomplish the business of the employer [and] the Government has the right to exercise control over access to the [workplace] to avoid interruptions to the performance of the duties of its employees. [We therefore] conclude that the CFC is a nonpublic forum.

Citing *Perry* the Court next explained that "Control over access to a nonpublic forum can be based on subject matter and speaker identity so long as the distinctions drawn are reasonable in light of the purpose served by the forum and are viewpoint neutral." Here, the Court held that the challenged limitation was reasonable because "the President could reasonably conclude" that (1) "a dollar directly spent on providing food or shelter to the needy is more beneficial than a dollar spent on litigation that might or might not result in aid to the needy"; (2) the participation of legal defense and political advocacy groups would generate controversy and thus "be detrimental to the Campaign and disruptive of the federal workplace"; and (3) the exclusion of legal defense and political advocacy groups would "avoid the reality and the appearance of government favoritism or entanglement with particular viewpoints."

Finally, noting that "the purported concern to avoid controversy excited by particular groups may conceal a bias against the viewpoint advanced by the excluded speakers," the Court remanded for a determination whether the regulation "is in reality a facade for viewpoint-based discrimination."

Justice Blackmun, joined by Justice Brennan, dissented. At the outset, Blackmun maintained that the "Court's analysis empties the limited public forum
concept of meaning, [for if] the Government does not create a limited public
forum unless it intends to provide an 'open forum' for expressive activity, and if
the exclusion of some speakers is evidence that the Government did not intend to
create such a forum, no speaker [will] ever be able to prove that the forum is a
limited public forum."
Blackmun then offered an alternative theory of the limited public forum:

> [In] answering the question whether a person has a right to engage in expressive
> activity on government property, the Court has recognized that the person's right to
> speak [must] be balanced against the "other interests inhering in the uses to which
> the public property is normally put." [Citing *Adderley*.] The Government's acquies-
> cence in the use of property for expressive activity indicates that at least some
> expressive activity is compatible with the intended uses of the property. [If] the
> Government [then attempts to exclude] speech that would be compatible with the
> intended uses of the property, [it] must explain how its exclusion [is] necessary to
> serve [some] compelling governmental interest.

Blackmun concluded that the government's justifications for excluding legal
defense and political advocacy organizations from the CFC "neither reserve the
CFC for expressive activity compatible with the property nor serve any other
compelling governmental interest." Finally, Blackmun argued that the challenged restriction was "blatantly viewpoint-based" because "Government employees may hear only from those charities that think that charitable goals can best be
achieved within the confines of existing social policy and the status quo," and do
not hear from those charitable organizations which seek to change "social policy." Justice Stevens also dissented.

5. *Evaluation.* Consider the Court's categorization of "quintessential," "limited," and "non" public forums. To what extent, if any, do these categories
explain *Mosley*, *Widmar*, *Lehman*, *Greer*, *Perry*, and *Cornelius?* Consider the
following arguments:

a. Subject-matter classifications should be subjected to closer scrutiny in "quintessential" public forums than in "non" public forums for the same reasons that
content-neutral restrictions are subjected to closer scrutiny in quintessential public forums.

b. "[The Court in *Perry*] indulged in a shell game, first throwing out a circular
definition of the public forum, then trying to break the circle by noting the
acceptability of subject-matter restrictions, and, finally, proceeding to apply minimal scrutiny to alleged viewpoint discrimination. [The Court thus] avoided a
rigorous analysis of the viewpoint discrimination issue by focusing on the public
forum analysis." L. Tribe, Constitutional Choices 207 (1985).

c. Whether a particular public facility constitutes a "limited" public forum
rather than a "non" public forum turns on the amount of speech government has
allowed. If the government allows almost all speech, and excludes only a narrow
category, as in *Widmar*, it has created a public forum. If it excludes almost all
speech, and allows only a narrow category, as in *Lehman*, *Greer*, and *Perry*, it has
not created a public forum.

d. "Classification of public places as various types of forums has only confused
judicial opinions by diverting attention from the real first amendment [issues].

Like the fourth amendment, the first amendment 'protects people, not places.' Constitutional protection should depend not on labeling the speaker's physical location but on the first amendment values and governmental interests involved in the case." Farber & Nowak, The Misleading Nature of Public Forum Analysis: Content and Context in First Amendment Adjudication, 70 Va. L. Rev. 1219, 1234 (1984).

6. *Speaker-based restrictions.* Note that *Perry* and *Cornelius* involve "speaker-based" restrictions. Such restrictions, which treat some speakers differently than others, but define the distinction in terms other than content, do not fit neatly within the Court's content-based/content-neutral distinction. In cases like *Perry* and *Cornelius*, the Court sharply distinguished speaker-based from viewpoint-based restrictions and, at least in the nonpublic forum context, tested speaker-based restrictions by a standard of reasonableness. But speaker-based restrictions often have clear viewpoint-differential effects. In *Perry*, for example, the challenged policy unquestionably favored some viewpoints over others, for recognized bargaining agents are likely to take consistent and predictable positions on particular issues. Indeed, in some instances speaker-based restrictions may correlate almost perfectly with viewpoint. Consider, for example, laws granting special subsidies to "veterans' organizations" or denying tax deductions to individuals who contribute to the Communist Party. How should we deal with such restrictions? For discussion, see Stone, Content Regulation and the First Amendment, 25 Wm. & Mary L. Rev. 189, 244-251 (1983). See also Regan v. Taxation with Representation, infra this section.

SOUTHEASTERN PROMOTIONS v. CONRAD, 420 U.S. 546 (1975): Petitioner, a promoter of theatrical productions, applied to a municipal board charged with managing a city auditorium and a city-leased theater, to present the musical "Hair" at the theater. Although no conflicting engagement was scheduled, the board, based on reports that the musical involved nudity and "obscenity," rejected the application because the production would not be "in the best interest of the community." The Court held that this action constituted an unconstitutional prior restraint. Justice Blackmun, speaking for the Court, explained:

"The elements of prior restraint [were] clearly present in the system by which [the] board regulated the use of its theaters. One seeking to use a theater was required to apply to the board. The board was empowered to determine whether the applicant should be granted permission — in effect, a license or permit — on the basis of its review of the content of the proposed production. [The board's] action was no less a prior restraint because the public facilities under [its] control happened to be municipal theaters. The Memorial Auditorium and the [city-leased theater] were public forums designed for and dedicated to expressive activities. [Thus, in] order to be held lawful, [the board's] action [must] have been accomplished with procedural safeguards that reduce the danger of suppressing constitutionally protected speech. [We] held in [Freedman v. Maryland, supra section C2], that a system of prior restraint runs afoul of the First Amendment if it lacks certain safeguards: First, the burden of instituting judicial proceedings, and of proving that the material is unprotected, must rest on the censor. Second, any restraint prior to judicial review can be imposed only for a specified brief period and only for the purpose of preserving the status quo. Third, a prompt final judicial determination must be assured. [Such procedural] safeguards were lacking here."

Justice Douglas dissented in part and concurred in the result in part: "The critical flaw in this case lies, not in the absence of procedural safeguards, but rather in the very nature of the content screening in which respondents have engaged. [A] municipal theater is no less a forum for the expression of ideas than is a public park, or a sidewalk. [As] soon as municipal officials are permitted to pick and choose [between] those productions which are 'clean and healthful and culturally uplifting' in content and those which are not, the path is cleared for a regime of censorship under which full voice can be given only to those views which meet with the approval of the powers that be."

Justice White, joined by Chief Justice Burger, dissented: "[The District Court described] the play as involving not only nudity but repeated 'simulated acts of anal intercourse, frontal intercourse, heterosexual intercourse, homosexual intercourse, and group intercourse.' Given this description of 'Hair,' the First Amendment in my view does not compel municipal authorities to permit production of the play in municipal facilities. Whether or not a production as described by the District Court is obscene and may be forbidden to adult audiences, it is apparent to me that the [State] could constitutionally forbid exhibition of the musical to children, [Ginsberg v. New York, supra section D5], and that [the city] may reserve its auditorium for productions suitable for exhibition to all citizens of the city, adults and children alike."

Justice Rehnquist also dissented: "[Until] this case the Court has not equated a public auditorium, which must of necessity schedule performances by a process of inclusion and exclusion, with public streets and parks. [Moreover, here] we deal with municipal [action], not prohibiting or penalizing the expression of views in dramatic form [in privately owned theaters], but rather managing its municipal auditorium. [If] it is the desire of the citizens of [the city], who presumably have paid for and own the facilities, that the attractions to be shown there should not be of the kind which would offend any substantial number of potential theatergoers, I do not think the policy can be described as arbitrary or unreasonable. [May] an opera house limit its production to operas, or must it also show rock musicals? May a municipal theater devote an entire season to Shakespeare, or is it required to book any potential producer on a first come, first served basis? These questions are real ones in light of the Court's opinion. [A] municipal theater may not be run by municipal authorities as if it were a private theater, free to judge on a content basis alone which plays it wishes to have performed and which it does not. [But] I do not believe fidelity to the First Amendment requires the exaggerated and rigid procedural safeguards which the Court insists upon in this case."

What substantive standards should govern the use of municipal auditoriums? Consider Shiffrin, Government Speech, 27 U.C.L.A. L. Rev. 565, 584 (1980): "*Conrad* does not appreciate the complicated relationships between public forum doctrine and government interests in speech. *Conrad* supposes that the government could not choose between competing applicants on a content basis. Yet such a supposition denies any legitimate government speech interest." What is the city's "speech interest" in *Conrad?* May the city limit use of the auditorium to the presentation of Shakespeare? To "family" productions? To "competently performed" productions?

Suppose a city allocates $50,000 per year to "promote the arts." What factors may it consider in awarding its grants? Are government subsidies of expression less problematic than government restrictions? Is the ordinance in *Mosley* a subsidy or a restriction?

BOARD OF EDUCATION, ISLAND TREES UNION FREE SCHOOL DISTRICT v. PICO, 457 U.S. 853 (1982): In 1975 several members of the petitioner Board of Education attended a conference sponsored by a politically conservative organization at which they obtained lists of books described as "objectionable" and as "improper fare for school students." Thereafter, the board removed eleven of the listed books from the district's school libraries "so that Board members could read them." In a press release justifying this action, the board characterized the books as "anti-American, anti-Christian, anti-Semitic, and just plain filthy." Among the books removed were Slaughterhouse Five, by Kurt Vonnegut, Jr.; The Naked Ape, by Desmond Morris; Best Short Stories of Negro Writers, edited by Langston Hughes; Soul on Ice, by Eldridge Cleaver; and Go Ask Alice, of anonymous authorship. The board appointed a Book Review Committee, consisting of parents and teachers, to recommend whether the books should be retained. Although the committee recommended that most of the books should be retained, the board decided to remove nine of the books and to make one other available subject to parental approval. Respondents, students in the Island Trees school system, brought this action claiming that the board's decision violated the first amendment. The District Court, finding that the board acted not on religious or political principles but "on its belief that the [books] were irrelevant, vulgar, immoral, and in bad taste," granted summary judgment to the board. The Court of Appeals reversed and remanded for a trial on the merits. The Supreme Court affirmed. Justice Brennan delivered an opinion joined by Justices Marshall and Stevens and joined in part by Justice Blackmun:

"We emphasize at the outset the limited nature of the substantive question presented. [This case] does not involve textbooks, or indeed any books that Island Trees students would be required to read. [The] only books at issue in this case are *library* books, books that by their nature are optional rather than required reading. [Furthermore,] even as to library books, the action before us does not involve the *acquisition* of books. [The] only action challenged in this case is the *removal* from school libraries of books originally placed there by school authorities. . . .

"The Court has long recognized that local school boards have broad discretion in the management of school affairs [and] that public schools are vitally important [as] vehicles for 'inculcating fundamental values necessary to the maintenance of a democratic political system.' [At] the same time, however, we have necessarily recognized that the discretion of the States and local school boards in matters of education must be exercised in a manner that comports with the transcendent imperatives of the First Amendment. [We] think that the First Amendment rights of students may be directly and sharply implicated by the removal of books from the shelves of a school library. . . .

"[We] have held that in a variety of contexts 'the Constitution protects the right to receive information and ideas.' [This] right is an inherent corollary of the rights of free speech and press that are explicitly guaranteed by the Constitution, in two senses. First, the right to receive ideas follows ineluctably from the *sender's* First Amendment right to send them. [More] importantly, the right to receive ideas is a necessary predicate to the *recipient's* meaningful exercise of his own rights of speech, press, and political freedom. . . .

"[The] special characteristics of the school *library* make that environment especially appropriate for the recognition of the First Amendment rights of students. [Although petitioners] might well defend their claim of absolute discretion in matters of *curriculum* by reliance upon their duty to inculcate community [values, we] think that [they may not] extend their claim of absolute discretion [into] the school library and the regime of voluntary inquiry that there holds sway. . . .

"[Although petitioners] rightly possess significant discretion to determine the content of their school [libraries, that] discretion may not be exercised in a narrowly partisan or political manner. If a Democratic school board, motivated by party affiliation, ordered the removal of all books written by or in favor of Republicans, few would doubt that the order violated the constitutional rights of the students denied access to those books. The same conclusion would surely apply if an all-white school board, motivated by racial animus, decided to remove all books authored by blacks or advocating racial equality and integration. Our Constitution does not permit the official suppression of *ideas*. Thus, whether petitioners' removal of the books from their school libraries denied respondents their First Amendment rights depends upon the motivation behind petitioners' actions. If petitioners *intended* by their removal decision to deny respondents access to ideas with which petitioners disagreed, and if this intent was the decisive factor in petitioners' decision, then petitioners have exercised their discretion in violation of the Constitution. On the other hand, [an] unconstitutional motivation would *not* be demonstrated if it were shown that petitioners had decided to remove the books at issue because those books were pervasively vulgar [or educationally unsuitable. Such motivations] would not carry the danger of an official suppression of ideas, and thus would not violate respondents' First Amendment rights. . . .

"[On the present record,] we cannot conclude that petitioners were 'entitled to a judgment as a matter of law.' [There remains] a genuine issue of material fact on the critical question of the credibility of petitioners' justifications for their decision."

Justice Blackmun filed a concurring opinion: "[Our decisions] yield a general [first amendment] principle: the State may not suppress exposure to ideas — for the sole *purpose* of suppressing exposure to those ideas — absent sufficiently compelling reasons. [This principle] is both narrower and more basic than the 'right to receive information' identified by the plurality. I do not suggest that the State has any affirmative obligation to provide students with information and ideas, [nor do I] believe, as the plurality suggests, that the right at issue here is somehow associated with the peculiar nature of the school library. [Instead], I suggest that certain forms of state discrimination *between* ideas are improper. [The] State may not act to deny access to any idea simply because state officials disapprove of that idea for partisan or political reasons."

Justice White concurred in the judgment: "[The Court of Appeals concluded] that there was a material issue of fact [concerning the reasons] underlying the school board's removal of the books. I am not inclined to disagree with the Court of Appeals on such a fact-bound issue and hence concur in the judgment of affirmance. Presumably this will result in a trial and the making of a full record and finding on the critical issues. The Court seems compelled to go further and issue a dissertation on the extent to which the First Amendment limits the discretion of the school board to remove books from the school library. I see no necessity for doing so at this point. [We] should not decide constitutional questions until it is necessary to do so, or at least until there is better reason to address them than are evident here."

Chief Justice Burger, joined by Justices Powell, Rehnquist, and O'Connor, dissented: "I agree with the fundamental proposition that 'students do not "shed their rights to freedom of speech or expression at the schoolhouse gate."' [Here,] however, no restraints of any kind are placed on the students. They are free to read the books in question, which are available at public libraries and bookstores. [The] 'right to receive information and ideas' does not carry with it the concomitant right to have those ideas affirmatively provided at a particular place by the government. . . .

"[Moreover, no] amount of 'limiting' language could rein in the sweeping 'right' the plurality would create. The plurality distinguishes library books from textbooks because library books 'by their nature are optional rather than required reading.' [But it] would appear that required reading and textbooks have a greater likelihood of imposing a '"pall of orthodoxy"' over the educational process than do optional reading. [The] plurality also limits the new right by finding it applicable only to the *removal* of books once acquired. Yet if the First Amendment commands that certain books cannot be removed, does it not equally require that the same books be *acquired?*"

Justice Rehnquist, joined by Chief Justice Burger and Justice Powell, also filed a dissenting opinion: "[The] government may act in other capacities than as sovereign, and when it does the First Amendment may speak with a different voice. [When] it acts as an educator, at least at the elementary and secondary school level, the government is engaged in inculcating social values and knowledge in relatively impressionable young people. Obviously there are innumerable decisions to be made as to what courses should be taught, what books should be purchased, or what teachers should be employed. [In my view,] it is 'permissible and appropriate for local boards to make educational decisions based upon their personal, social, political and moral views.' [When the managers of a school district decide to remove a book from a school library,] they are not proscribing it as to the citizenry in general, but are simply determining that it will not be included in [the] library. [Actions] by the government as educator do not raise the same First Amendment concerns as actions by the government as sovereign. . . .

"Justice Brennan would hold that the First Amendment [gives] students a 'right to receive ideas' in the school. [This right] has never been recognized in the decisions of this Court and is not supported by their rationale. [It would be ludicrous] to contend that all authors have a constitutional right to have their books placed [in] school libraries. And yet without such a right our prior precedents would not recognize the reciprocal right to receive information. [Moreover,] the denial of access to ideas inhibits one's own acquisition of knowledge only when that denial is relatively complete. If the denied ideas are readily available from the same source in other accessible locations, the benefits to be gained from exposure to those ideas have not been foreclosed by the State. . . .

"[The] idea that [students] have a right of access, *in the school*, to information other than that thought by their educators to be necessary is contrary to the very nature of an inculcative education. [Contrary to Justice Brennan's assumption, the] libraries of [elementary and secondary] schools serve as supplements to this inculcative role. [They] are not designed for free-wheeling inquiry; they are tailored, as the public school curriculum is tailored, to the teaching of basic skills and ideas. . . .

"[Finally, Justice Brennan limits] his newly discovered right [with] a motive requirement. [But] bad motives and good motives alike deny access to the books removed. If Justice Brennan truly recognizes a constitutional right to receive information, it is difficult to see why the reason for the denial makes any difference."

Justices Powell and O'Connor also filed dissenting opinions.

Do you agree with the plurality that a school board cannot constitutionally remove books "simply because they dislike the ideas" espoused? Consider Justice Powell's evaluation, set forth in his *Pico* dissent: "[Under the plurality's approach, books] may not be removed because they are indecent; extoll violence, intolerance and racism; or degrade the dignity of the individual. [I] would not *require* a school board to promote ideas and values repugnant to a democratic society."

Is the plurality's distinction between removal and acquisition justified? Consider the following argument: "Removal, more than a failure to acquire, is likely to suggest that an impermissible political motivation may be present. There are many reasons why a book is not acquired, the most obvious being limited resources, but there are few legitimate reasons why a book, once acquired, should be removed from a library not filled to capacity." Pico v. Board of Education, 638 F.2d 404, 436 (2d Cir. 1980) (Newman, J., concurring).

Consider the following views:

a. Kreimer, Allocational Sanctions: The Problem of Negative Rights in a Positive State, 132 U. Pa. L. Rev. 1293, 1333-1335 (1984):

> [The] appeal of purpose analysis is manifest, [for it] purports not to constrain the goals or methods chosen by government except insofar as it excludes constitutionally suspect purposes. [But there are difficulties with such an analysis.] The first difficulty lies in identifying those purposes that are proscribed. Granting, in first amendment contexts, that censorship is the paradigm of a constitutionally impermissible action, what characterizes censorship? Is it the purpose of reducing the amount of information available to citizens or the purpose of disfavoring unorthodox views? [Second], there [is] uncertainty about the [way] in which [the impermissible] purpose is to be discovered. [What] can it mean to say that the [school board] acted with hostility to a given viewpoint? Must the hostility have tainted the thinking of a majority of the [board] or only a majority of the proponents of the [board's action]? If the [action was adopted] by a single vote, is it sufficient that a single member harbored hostility to the views at issue?

b. Yudof, Library Book Selection and the Public Schools: The Quest for the Archimedean Point, 59 Ind. L.J. 527, 552-553 (1984):

[Perhaps] the most important limit on school board selection policies will be symbolic. The courts should not be involved in the school's day to day decisionmaking on book selection. [But] if school boards know that the courts will sometimes get involved, even if only in extreme cases, and [thus] restrain themselves accordingly, *Pico* may serve as an effective constitutional limit, even if that limit is poorly defined and mostly symbolic and self-enforced.

REGAN v. TAXATION WITH REPRESENTATION OF WASHING-TON, 461 U.S. 540 (1983): In a unanimous decision, the Court upheld a federal statute providing that contributions to an otherwise tax exempt organization, other than a tax-exempt veterans' organization, are not tax deductible if a substantial part of the organization's activities consists of attempts to influence legislation. Justice Rehnquist delivered the opinion of the Court:

"Congress is not required by the First Amendment to subsidize lobbying. [Respondent contends, however, that the challenged provision is unconstitutional because of its distinction between veterans' and other tax exempt organizations. We do not agree.] The case would be different if Congress were to discriminate invidiously in its subsidies in such a way as to '"aim[] at the suppression of dangerous ideas."' [But] veterans' organizations [receive] tax-deductible contributions regardless of the content of [their speech]. We find no indication that the statute was intended to suppress any ideas or any demonstration that it has had that effect. . . .

"The Court of Appeals nonetheless held that 'strict scrutiny' is required because the statute '*affect[s]* First Amendment rights on a discriminatory basis.' Its opinion suggests that strict scrutiny applies whenever Congress subsidizes some speech, but not all speech. This is not the law. [Congressional] selection of particular entities or persons for entitlement to this sort of largesse 'is [ordinarily] a matter of policy and discretion not open to judicial [review].' [The] reasoning [is] simple: 'although government may not place obstacles in the path of a [person's] exercise [of] freedom of [speech], it need not remove those not of its own creation.' ['Constitutional] concerns are greatest when the State attempts to impose its will by force of law.' [Where] governmental provision of subsidies is not 'aimed at the suppression of dangerous ideas,' its 'power to encourage actions deemed to be in the public interest is necessarily far broader.' . . .

"It [is] not irrational for Congress to decide that, even though it will not subsidize substantial lobbying by charities generally, it will subsidize lobbying by veterans' organizations. Veterans have [made a unique contribution to the nation]. Our country has a long standing policy of compensating veterans for [this contribution] by providing them with numerous advantages. This policy has 'always been deemed to be legitimate.'"

Justice Blackmun, joined by Justices Brennan and Marshall, filed a concurring opinion: "Because [the] discrimination between veterans' organizations and charitable organizations is not based on the content of their speech, [it] does not deny charitable organizations equal protection of the law. [As] the Court says, a statute designed to discourage the expression of particular views would present a very different question."

Consider the following: (a) "No organization, other than a veterans' organization, may demonstrate on a military base." (b) "Contributions to an otherwise tax exempt organization are not deductible if the organization engages in substantial lobbying activities, unless those activities concern the subject of abortion." (c) "Contributions to an otherwise tax exempt organization are not deductible if the organization advocates the violent overthrow of government."

In FCC v. League of Women Voters, — U.S. — , 104 S. Ct. 3106 (1984), the Court invalidated section 399 of the Public Broadcasting Act of 1967, which prohibited any noncommercial educational station that receives a grant from the Corporation for Public Broadcasting to "engage in editorializing." The Court distinguished *Taxation with Representation* on the ground that, under the statute at issue in *Taxation with Representation*, "a charitable organization could create [an] affiliate to conduct its non-lobbying activities using tax-deductible contributions, and, at the same time, establish [a] separate affiliate to pursue its lobbying efforts without such contributions," whereas in *League of Women Voters* "a noncommercial educational station that receives [even] 1% of its overall income from [the CPB] is barred absolutely from all editorializing." Thus, in *Taxation with Representation* the law only prevented the use of *government funds* for lobbying, whereas in *League of Women Voters* the law prohibited any station that accepted government funds from editorializing, whether or not the editorializing was paid for with government funds.

Consider Kreimer, supra, at 1300-1301:

> [In analyzing issues of subsidy and discrimination,] courts must distinguish between threats and offers. Threats are allocations that make a citizen worse off than she otherwise would be because of her exercise of a constitutional right. Offers merely expand her range of options, leaving the citizen better off. For example, an offer by the National Endowment for the Arts to provide grants to citizens who choose to write symphonies rather than jazz differs fundamentally from a threat to withdraw welfare payments if the citizen chooses jazz over symphonies. Both allocations influence a constitutionally protected choice, but a threat abridges first amendment rights in ways an offer does not. The crucial task is to specify an appropriate baseline against which to determine whether the proposed allocation improves or worsens the citizen's situation.

In attempting to specify an appropriate baseline in each case, Kreimer would consider three factors: deviation from the status quo ante (has the complainant lost something she previously had); equality (has the complainant been singled out for treatment less favorable than that accorded most comparable groups); and prediction (what would be the normal course of events if government could not impose the condition or take the exercise of constitutional rights into account).

2. Restricted Environments: The Military, Schools, and Prisons

This section explores the application of first amendment principles in the context of the military, schools, and prisons. To what extent, if any, are such institutions so lacking in the essential prerequisites for free expression that they must be governed by less "speech-protective" principles than society generally?

PARKER v. LEVY, 417 U.S. 733 (1974): Appellee, a captain in the army stationed at Fort Jackson, South Carolina, made several public statements to enlisted personnel, of which the following is representative: "The United States is wrong in being involved in the Viet Nam War. I would refuse to go to Viet Nam if ordered to do so. I don't see why any colored soldier would go to Viet Nam; they should refuse to go [and] if sent should refuse to fight because they are discriminated against [in] the United States, and they are sacrificed and discriminated against in Viet Nam by being given all the hazardous duty." As a consequence of such statements, appellee was convicted by a general court martial of violating articles 133 and 134 of the Uniform Code of Military Justice. Article 133 prohibits "conduct unbecoming an officer and gentleman." Article 134 prohibits "all disorders and neglects to the prejudice of good order and discipline in the armed forces." The Court, in a five-to-three decision, upheld the conviction. Justice Rehnquist delivered the opinion of the Court:

"This Court has long recognized that the military is, by necessity, a specialized society separate from civilian society. [It has] developed laws and traditions of its [own]. 'An army is not a deliberative body. [No] question can be left open as to the right to command in the officer, or the duty of obedience in the soldier.' . . .

"Appellee urges that both Art. 133 and Art. 134 [are] overbroad in violation of the First Amendment. [We do not agree.] While members of the military are not excluded from the protection granted by the First Amendment, the different character of the military community and of the military mission requires a different application of those protections. The fundamental necessity for obedience [may] render permissible within the military that which would be constitutionally impermissible outside it. [While] there may lurk at the fringes of the articles [some] possibility that conduct which would be ultimately held to be protected by the First Amendment could be included within their prohibition, we deem this insufficient to invalidate either of them at the behest of appellee. His conduct, that of a commissioned officer publicly urging enlisted personnel to refuse to obey orders which might send them into combat, was unprotected under the most expansive notions of the First Amendment. Articles 133 and 134 may constitutionally prohibit that conduct, and a sufficiently large [amount] of similar [conduct] so as to preclude their invalidation for overbreadth."

Justice Douglas dissented: "The military by tradition and by necessity demands discipline; and those necessities require obedience in training and action. [I] cannot imagine, however, that Congress would think it had the power to authorize the military to [ban] discussions of public affairs. [Appellee] was uttering his own belief — an article of faith that he sincerely held. [Many] others [share] his views. [Punishing such] utterances is an 'abridgment' of speech in the constitutional sense."

Justice Stewart, joined by Justices Douglas and Brennan, dissented on grounds of vagueness.

In what circumstances, if any, has a soldier a constitutional right to attempt to persuade others not to obey orders? Should *Brandenburg* govern? Consider Imnwinkelried & Zillman, An Evolution in the First Amendment: Overbreadth Analysis and Free Speech within the Military Community, 54 Tex. L. Rev. 42, 80-81 (1975):

> [It is unsatisfactory] to apply an immediacy requirement to calls for disobedience of
> military orders. [The] military has a legitimate interest in conditioning servicemen to
> immediately obey lawful orders by inculcating a positive attitude of obedience to

orders. [Speech] that does not motivate a serviceman to commit an immediate act of disobedience may nevertheless tend to undermine the serviceman's disciplined attitude, impairing a weighty government interest well before the threat of the ultimate, substantive evil becomes imminent. [Thus, the] "stringency of the *Brandenburg* test is not apposite to essential needs of an efficient military."

Consider also Brown v. Glines, 444 U.S. 348 (1980), in which the Court upheld an air force regulation prohibiting any "member of the Air Force [from distributing or posting] any printed or written material [within] an Air Force installation without permission of the commander." In rejecting a serviceman's claim that the regulation constituted an unconstitutional prior restraint, the Court explained that "since a commander is charged with maintaining morale, discipline, and readiness, he must have authority over the distribution of materials that could affect adversely these essential attributes of an effective military force."

Justice Brennan dissented:

The concept of military necessity is seductively broad, and has a dangerous plasticity. [For] that reason, the military-security argument must be approached with a healthy skepticism. [To] be sure, generals and admirals, not federal judges, are expert about military needs. [But] judges, not military officers, possess the competence [to] interpret [the] First Amendment. Moreover, in the context of this case, the expertise of military officials [is] tainted by the natural self-interest that inevitably influences their exercise of the power to control expression. Partiality must be expected when government authorities censor the views of subordinates, especially if those views are critical of the censors. [This] Court abdicates its responsibility to safeguard free expression when it reflexively bows before the shibboleth of military necessity.

For a defense of *Parker*'s "separate community" doctrine, see Hirschhorn, The Separate Community: Military Uniqueness and Servicemen's Constitutional Rights, 62 N.C. L. Rev. 177 (1984) (arguing that a limited judicial role is appropriate, in part, because if judicial intervention inadvertently undermines military discipline and impairs the effectiveness of the armed forces, there may be "no way to determine and correct the mistake until it has produced the substantial and sometimes irreparable cost of failure").

TINKER v. DES MOINES SCHOOL DISTRICT, 393 U.S. 503 (1969): In December 1965 a group of adults and students in Des Moines decided to publicize their objections to the war in Vietnam by wearing black armbands during the holiday season. When the principals of the Des Moines schools learned of this plan, they adopted a policy that any students wearing armbands to school would be suspended until they removed them. Petitioners, several high school and junior high school students, were suspended from school pursuant to this policy. They filed this action seeking to enjoin the school officials from disciplining them further. The Court held the policy unconstitutional. Justice Fortas delivered the opinion of the Court:

"[The] wearing of an armband for the purpose of expressing certain views is the type of symbolic act that is within the Free Speech Clause of the First Amendment. [In] the circumstances of this case, [it] was closely akin to 'pure speech.' . . .

"First Amendment rights, applied in light of the special characteristics of school environment, are available to teachers and students. It can ha argued that either students or teachers shed their constitutional rights to freedom of speech or expression at the schoolhouse gate. [On] the other hand, the Court has repeatedly emphasized the need for affirming the comprehensive authority [of] school officials, consistent with fundamental constitutional safeguards, [to] control conduct in the schools. . . .

"The school officials [sought] to punish petitioners for a silent, passive expression of opinion, unaccompanied by any disorder or disturbance on the part of petitioners. There is here no evidence whatever of petitioners' interference, actual or nascent, with the schools' work or of collision with the rights of other students to be secure and to be let alone. [There] is no indication that the work of the schools or any class was disrupted. Outside the classrooms, a few students made hostile remarks to the children wearing armbands, but there were no threats or acts of violence on school premises.

"The District Court concluded that the action of the school authorities was reasonable because it was based upon their fear of a disturbance from the wearing of the armbands. But, in our system, undifferentiated fear or apprehension of disturbance is not enough to overcome the right to freedom of expression. [In this case], a particular symbol [was] singled out for prohibition. [In] order for the State in the person of school officials to justify prohibition [of] expression of [one particular] opinion, it must be able to show that its action was caused by something more than a mere desire to avoid the discomfort and unpleasantness that always accompany an unpopular viewpoint. Certainly where there is no [showing] that engaging in the forbidden conduct would 'materially and substantially interfere with the requirements of appropriate discipline in the operation of the school,' the prohibition cannot be sustained."

Justice Black dissented: "While I have always believed that [the first amendment prohibits government from censoring] the content of speech, I have never believed that any person has a right to give speeches or engage in demonstrations where he pleases and when he pleases. [The record shows that the] armbands caused comments, warnings by other students, the poking of fun at them, and a warning by an older [student] that other, nonprotesting students had better let them alone. There is also evidence that a teacher of mathematics had his lesson [practically] 'wrecked' [by] disputes with [one of the petitioners]. [The] armbands did exactly what the [school officials] foresaw they would, that is, took the students' minds off their classwork and diverted them to thoughts about the highly emotional subject of the Vietnam war."

Justice Harlan also dissented: "I would, in cases like this, cast upon those complaining the burden of showing that a particular school measure was motivated by other than legitimate school concerns — for example, a desire to prohibit the expression of an unpopular point of view, while permitting expression of the dominant opinion. [Finding] nothing in this record which impugns the good faith of [the school officials], I [dissent]."

Consider Diamond, The First Amendment and Public Schools: The Case against Judicial Intervention, 59 Tex. L. Rev. 477, 493-499 (1981):

Tinker's conception of the relationships between the first amendment and the public schools [and] between the courts and the local school administration was fundamentally incorrect. [Conventional] first amendment analysis is inappropriate in the public school situation for a variety of [reasons]. First, [although] the public school is an institution largely designed for concerns similar to those of the first amendment, [society] strictly controls [the] ideology [and] content of public school teaching, [and] the public schools [thus] embody in all their aspects the denial of first amendment rights. [Second,] the proper functioning of the school is not [an] objectively ascertainable phenomenon. The judiciary cannot know the extent to which any kind of distraction during the course of the day interferes with learning. [Here,] courts should defer to the good faith judgment of the expert authorities. [Finally, although] *Tinker* [assumes] that the first amendment free marketplace of ideas properly belongs in the public school system, [value inculcation], rather than value neutrality, has been the tradition of public education since the beginning, [and value-inculcating] education plainly contradicts [the] free marketplace of ideas.

Consider also Healy v. James, 408 U.S. 169 (1972), in which a local chapter of Students for a Democratic Society (SDS) was denied recognition as a campus organization by a state-supported college. Although the Court remanded for further proceedings, it offered the following views on the issues it resolved:

> [In] 1969-70 [a] climate of unrest prevailed on many college campuses in this country. There had been widespread civil disobedience on some college campuses, accompanied by the seizure of buildings, vandalism, and arson. Some colleges had been shut down altogether, while at others files were looted and manuscripts destroyed. SDS chapters on some of those campuses had been a catalytic force during this period. . . .
>
> [The College argues that its denial of recognition was justified because SDS adheres to] a philosophy of violence and disruption. [But as] repugnant as these views may [be], the mere expression of them would not justify the denial of First Amendment rights. Whether petitioners did in fact advocate a philosophy of "destruction" thus becomes immaterial. The College, acting here as the instrumentality of the State, may not restrict speech or association simply because it finds the views expressed by any group to be abhorrent.
>
> [The College argues further, however,] that this particular group would be a "disruptive [influence]." If this reason, directed at the organization's activities rather than its philosophy, were factually supported by the record, this Court's [decisions] would provide a basis for considering the propriety of nonrecognition. The critical line [is] the line between mere advocacy and advocacy "directed to inciting or producing imminent lawless action and . . . likely to incite or produce such action." [*Brandenburg.*] In the context of the "special characteristics of the school environment," the power of the government to prohibit "lawless action" is not limited to acts of a criminal nature. Also prohibitable are actions which "materially and substantially disrupt the work and discipline of the school." [*Tinker.*] [If] there were an evidential basis to support the conclusion that [the organization] posed a substantial threat of material disruption, [the College's] decision should be affirmed. The record, however, offers no substantial basis for that conclusion.

Suppose that Students for a Homosexual Society seeks recognition from a public university or a high school. Does *Healy* govern? See also Papish v. Board of Curators of the University of Missouri, 410 U.S. 667 (1973), in which the Court, relying upon *Healy*, held that a state university could not constitutionally expel a student for distributing on campus a newspaper containing a political cart depicting policemen raping the Statue of Liberty and an article using the phrase "Mother-fucker."

JONES v. NORTH CAROLINA PRISONERS' UNION, 433 U.S. 119 (1977): Appellee Prisoners' Union was incorporated in 1974 with the alleged goals of seeking "through collective bargaining" to improve working conditions in the state's prisons and jails, working toward the elimination of policies of the Department of Correction with which it disagreed, and serving as a vehicle for the presentation and resolution of inmate grievances. By 1974 the union had attracted 2,000 inmate members in forty different prison units in the state. Unhappy with these developments, the state set out to prevent inmates from forming or operating a union. It therefore prohibited inmate solicitation of other inmates to join the union, meetings between members of the union, and bulk mailings concerning the union from outside sources. The Court upheld these restrictions. Justice Rehnquist delivered the opinion of the Court:

"Because the realities of running a penal institution are complex and difficult, we have [long] recognized the wide-ranging deference to be accorded the decisions of prison administrators. [Here, state] correctional officials uniformly testified that the concept of a prisoners' labor union was itself fraught with potential dangers. [The] Commissioner of the Department of Correction stated in his affidavit: 'The creation of an inmate union will naturally result in increasing the existing friction between inmates and prison personnel. It can also create friction between union inmates and non-union inmates.' [The] Secretary of the Department of Correction stated: 'After the inmate union has become established, there would probably be nothing this Department could do to terminate its existence. [Thus], even if the purposes of the union are as stated in the complaint, the potential for a dangerous situation exists [should the union later change its character].' [The] burden was not on [the Department] to show affirmatively that the Union would be 'detrimental to proper penological objectives' or would constitute a 'present danger to security and order.' Rather, '[s]uch considerations are peculiarly within the province [of] corrections officials, and, in the absence of substantial evidence in the record to indicate that the officials have exaggerated their response to these considerations, courts should ordinarily defer to their expert judgment in such matters.' . . .

"The invocation of the First Amendment [does] not change this analysis. In a prison context, an inmate does not retain those First Amendment rights that are 'inconsistent with his status as a prisoner or with the legitimate penological objectives of the corrections system.' [Associational rights] may be curtailed whenever the institution's officials, in the exercise of their informed discretion, reasonably conclude that such associations [possess] the likelihood of disruption to prison order or stability, or otherwise interfere with the legitimate penological objectives of the prison environment. [Here, the] prison officials concluded that the presence, perhaps even the objectives, of a prisoners' labor union would be detrimental to order and security. [It] is enough to say that they have not been conclusively shown to be wrong in this view."

Justice Marshall, joined by Justice Brennan, dissented: "I realize, of course, that 'the realities of running a penal institution are complex and difficult,' and that correctional officers possess considerably more '"professional expertise,"' in prison management than do judges. [But] 'the realities of running' a school or a city are also 'complex and difficult,' [and] those charged with these tasks — principals, college presidents, mayors, councilmen, and law enforcement personnel — also possess special 'professional expertise.' Yet in no First Amendment case [has] the Court deferred to the judgment of such officials simply because their judgment was 'rational.' [I] do not understand why a different rule should apply simply because prisons are involved. The reason courts cannot blindly defer to the judgment of prison administrators — or any other officials for that matter — is easily understood. Because the prison administrator's business is to maintain order, 'there inheres the danger that he may well be less responsive than a court [to] the constitutionally protected interests in free expression.' A warden seldom will find himself subject to public criticism or dismissal because he needlessly repressed free speech. [But] a warden's job can be jeopardized and public criticism is sure to come should disorder occur. Consequently, prison officials inevitably will err on the side of too little freedom. . . .

"Once it is established that traditional First Amendment principles are applicable in prisoners' rights cases, the dispute here is easily resolved. The [District Court] not only found that there was 'not one scintilla of evidence to suggest that the Union had been utilized to disrupt the operation of the penal institutions,' [it] also found no evidence 'that the inmates intend to operate [the Union] to hamper and interfere with the proper interests of government,' or that the Union posed a 'present danger to security and order.' In the face of these findings, it cannot be argued that the restrictions on the Union are 'imperatively justif[ied].'"

Consider also Bell v. Wolfish, 441 U.S. 520 (1979) (upholding a rule prohibiting inmates to receive hardcover books that are not mailed directly from publishers, book clubs, or bookstores because such a restriction is a "rational response" to an "obvious security problem," operates "without regard to the content of the expression," and leaves open "alternative means of obtaining reading material that have not been shown to be burdensome or insufficient"); Pell v. Procunier, 417 U.S. 817 (1974) (upholding a ban on face-to-face press interviews with inmates in light of the availability of alternative means for inmates to communicate with representatives of the media); Procunier v. Martinez, 416 U.S. 396 (1974) (invalidating prison regulations prohibiting prisoners to write letters that "magnify grievances" or to write or receive letters that are "lewd, obscene, defamatory, [or] otherwise inappropriate," on the ground that such regulations violate the first amendment rights of the persons with whom prisoners correspond).

3. Public Employment

In what circumstances, if any, may government restrict the expression of its employees? In McAuliffe v. Mayor of New Bedford, 155 Mass. 216, 29 N.E. 517 (1892), Justice Holmes, speaking for the Supreme Judicial Court of Massachusetts, upheld a rule prohibiting police officers to "solicit money or any aid, [for] any political purpose whatever." Holmes reasoned: "The petitioner may have a constitutional right to talk politics, but he has no constitutional right to be a policeman. There are few employments for hire in which the servant does not agree to suspend his constitutional rights of free speech, as well as of idleness, by the implied terms of his contract. The servant cannot complain, as he takes the employment on the terms which are offered him." Recall Holmes's articulation of a similar view concerning government's power to control publicly-owned property in Commonwealth v. Davis, supra section E2a. Consider the following criticisms:

a. Frost & Frost Trucking Co. v. Railroad Commission, 271 U.S. 583, 593-594 (1926):

> It would be a palpable incongruity to strike down an act of state legislation which [strips] the citizen of rights guaranteed by the federal Constitution, but to uphold an act by which the same result is accomplished under the guise of a surrender of a right in exchange for a valuable privilege which the state threatens otherwise to withhold. [It] is inconceivable that guarantees embedded in the Constitution [may] thus be manipulated out of existence.

b. Van Alstyne, The Demise of the Right-Privilege Distinction in Constitutional Law, 81 Harv. L. Rev. 1439, 1440-1441, 1461-1462 (1968):

> [Holmes's] tough-minded distinction between constitutionally protected rights [and] unprotected governmental privileges [may] have been influenced by the comparatively small economic role played by governmental units in 1892. Excluding McAuliffe from public employment still left open to him a very large percentage of the available employment in the country. But today the federal and state governments directly or indirectly control a great proportion of the nation's employment; if one is unable to hold public employment, his chances of personal economic success are significantly limited.

c. Kreimer, Allocational Sanctions: The Problem of Negative Rights in a Positive State, 132 U. Pa. L. Rev. 1293, 1315, 1323 (1984):

> Having a constitutional right to perform a given act means, at least, that one may perform that act without governmental interference. The problem, however, is to define "interference." [Holmes's argument fails because the] government as proprietor is no less dangerous to liberty than as sovereign. [Not] only is the magnitude of proprietary sanctions often greater than of sovereign ones, but they are often much more easily brought to bear. [Moreover, allocational sanctions may be especially dangerous, for they enable] the government to circumvent more easily the virtual representation guarantees of the Constitution. By limiting allocative sanctions to particular benefits programs, the government can tailor its inducements to forego constitutional rights so they affect only the least popular or politically efficacious groups.

The Court has not followed *McAuliffe*. In Perry v. Sinderman, 408 U.S. 593, 597 (1972), for example, the Court announced that "even though a person has no 'right' to a valuable government benefit and even though the government may deny him the benefit for any number of reasons, [it may not do so] on a basis that infringes his constitutionally protected interests — especially, his interest in freedom of speech." Government's power to deny a benefit on the basis of other constitutionally impermissible factors, such as race or sex, is examined in Chapter 5 supra.

Does the rejection of *McAuliffe* suggest that the first amendment rights of government employees are coextensive with those of private individuals? Consider Pickering v. Board of Educ., 391 U.S. 563, 568 (1968): "[The] State has interests as an employer in regulating the speech of its employees that differ significantly from those it possesses in [regulating] the speech of the citizenry in general. The problem in any case is to arrive at a balance between the interests of the [employee], as a citizen, in commenting upon matters of public concern and the interests of the State, as an employer, in promoting the efficiency of the public services it performs through its employees."

This section explores five restrictions on the expression of government employees: restrictions on partisan political activity; restrictions on speech criticizing government policy; restrictions relating to the practice of patronage; restrictions on subversive advocacy and associations; and restrictions on the disclosure of "confidential" information.

a. Partisan Political Activity

U.S. Civil Service Commission v. National Association of Letter Carriers
413 U.S. 548 (1973)

Mr. Justice White delivered the opinion of the Court.

[This case presents] the single question whether the prohibition in §9(a) of the Hatch Act, now codified in 5 U.S.C. §7324(a)(2), against federal employees taking "an active part in political management or in political campaigns," is unconstitutional on its face. . . .

A divided three-judge court [held] the section unconstitutional. We reverse. . . .

[Until] after the Civil War, the spoils system under which federal employees came and went depending upon party service and changing administrations, was the prevalent basis for governmental employment and advancement. [That] system did not survive. . . .

[It is now] the judgment of Congress, the Executive, and the country [that] partisan political activities by federal employees must be limited if the Government is to operate effectively and fairly, elections are to play their proper part in representative government, and employees themselves are to be sufficiently free from improper influences. The restrictions [imposed] on federal employees are not aimed at particular parties, groups, or points of view, but apply equally to all partisan activities of the type described. They discriminate against no racial, ethnic, or religious minorities. Nor do they seek to control political opinions or beliefs, or to interfere with or influence anyone's vote at the polls.

[As] the Court held in [Pickering v. Board of Education], the problem in any case is to arrive at a balance between the interests of the [employee] and the [interests] of the [government]. Although Congress is free to strike a different balance than it has, [we] think the balance it [has] struck is sustainable by the obviously important interests sought to be served by [the] Hatch Act.

It seems fundamental [that] employees [of] the Government [should] administer the law in accordance with the will of Congress, rather than in accordance with [the] will of a political party.

[Moreover,] it is not only important that [Government] employees in fact avoid practicing political justice, but [also] that they appear to the public to be avoiding

it, if confidence in the system of representative Government is not to be eroded. . . .

Another major concern [is] the conviction that the rapidly expanding Government work force should not be employed to build a powerful, invincible, and
perhaps corrupt political machine. . . .

A related concern [is] to make sure that Government employees [are] free from
pressure [to] vote in a certain way or perform political chores in order to curry
favor with their superiors rather than to act out of their own beliefs. It may be
urged that prohibitions against coercion are sufficient protection; but for many
years the joint judgment of the Executive and Congress has been that to protect
the rights of federal employees [it] is not enough merely to forbid one employee to
attempt to influence or coerce another. [Perhaps] Congress at some time will
come to a different view of the realities of political life and Government service;
but that is its current view of the matter, and we are not now in any position to
dispute it. . . .

[In light of these interests,] identifiable acts of political management and political campaigning on the part of federal employees may constitutionally be prohibited. . . .

[Appellees argue, however,] that §7324(a)(2) [is] both unconstitutionally vague
and fatally overbroad. . . .

Whatever might be the difficulty with a provision against taking "active part in
political management or in political campaigns," the [Civil Service Commission
has promulgated] regulations specifying the conduct that would be prohibited or
permitted by §7324. . . .

We have set out these regulations in the margin.[21] We see nothing impermissibly vague [or fatally overbroad] in [these regulations].

For the foregoing reasons, the judgment of the District Court is reversed. . . .

---

21. The pertinent regulations, appearing in 5 CFR pt. 733, provide:

PERMISSIBLE ACTIVITIES

§733.111 Permissible activities.

(a) All employees are free to engage in political activity to the widest extent consistent with
the restrictions imposed by law and this subpart. Each employee retains the right to —

(1) Register and vote in any election;

(2) Express his opinion as an individual privately and publicly on political subjects and
candidates;

(3) Display a political picture, sticker, badge, or button;

(4) Participate in the nonpartisan activities of a civic, community, social, labor, or professional organization, or of a similar organization;

(5) Be a member of a political party or other political organization and participate in its
activities to the extent consistent with law;

(6) Attend a political convention, rally, fund-raising function; or other political gathering;

(7) Sign a political petition as an individual;

(8) Make a financial contribution to a political party or organization. . . .

PROHIBITED ACTIVITIES . . .

(a) An employee may not take an active part in political management or in a political
campaign. . . .

(b) Activities prohibited by paragraph (a) of this section include but are not limited to —

(1) Serving as an officer of a political party, a member of a National, State, or local committee
of a political party, an officer or member of a committee of a partisan political club, or being a
candidate for any of these positions; . . .

(3) Directly or indirectly soliciting, receiving, collecting, handling, disbursing, or accounting
for assessments, contributions, or other funds for a partisan political purpose; . . .

(5) Taking an active part in managing the political campaign of a partisan candidate for
public office or political party office;

MR. JUSTICE DOUGLAS, with whom MR. JUSTICE BRENNAN and MR. JUSTICE MAR-SHALL concur, dissenting.

The Hatch Act [prohibits] federal employees from taking "an active part in political management or in political campaigns." [No] one could object if employees were barred from using office time to engage in outside activities whether political or otherwise. But it is of no concern of Government what an employee does in his spare time, [unless] what he does impairs efficiency or other facets of the merits of his job. Some [activities may] affect the employee's job performance. But his political creed, like his religion, is irrelevant. In the areas of speech, like religion, it is of no concern what the employee says in private to his wife or to the public in Constitution Hall. If Government employment were only a "privilege," then all sorts of conditions might be attached. But it is now settled that Government employment may not be denied or penalized "on a basis that infringes [the employee's] constitutionally protected interests — especially, his interest in freedom of speech." See [Perry v. Sindermann]. . . .

I would strike this [law] down as unconstitutional. . . .

Note: Mitchell, Letter Carriers, *and* Broadrick

What standard should govern the constitutionality of the Hatch Act? Did the Court in *Letter Carriers* strike an appropriate "balance"? Compare the Court's analysis in *Letter Carriers* with its analysis in Buckley v. Valeo, supra section E4. Is *Letter Carriers* consistent with *Buckley?*

Letter Carriers specifically reaffirmed United Public Workers v. Mitchell, 330 U.S. 75 (1947), in which the Court upheld section 9(a) of the Hatch Act as applied to a roller in the U.S. Mint who "was a ward executive committeeman of a political party and was politically active on election day as a worker at the polls." The Court explained that "Congress may regulate the political conduct of government employees 'within reasonable limits,' even though the regulation trenches to some extent upon unfettered political action."

Dissenting in *Mitchell*, Justice Black maintained:

Legislation which muzzles several million citizens threatens popular government, not only because it injures the individuals muzzled, but also because of its harmful effect on the body politic in depriving it of the political participation and interest of such a large segment of our citizens. [Laws] which restrict the liberties guaranteed by the First Amendment should be narrowly drawn to meet the evil aimed at and to affect only the minimum number of people imperatively necessary to prevent a grave and imminent danger to the public. [It] is argued that it is in the interest of clean politics to suppress political activities of federal and state employees. [But if a particular practice] is so great an evil as to require legislation, the law could punish those public officials who engage in the practice. [It] would hardly seem to be

---

(6) Becoming a partisan candidate for, or campaigning for, an elective public office;

(7) Soliciting votes in support of or in opposition to a partisan candidate for public office or political party office; . . .

(10) Endorsing or opposing a partisan candidate for public office or political party office in a political advertisement, a broadcast, campaign literature, or similar material;

(11) Serving as a delegate, alternate, or proxy to a political party convention. . . .

imperative to muzzle millions of citizens because some of them, if left their constitutional freedoms, might corrupt the political process.

In Broadrick v. Oklahoma, 413 U.S. 601 (1973), decided on the same day as *Letter Carriers*, the Court upheld Oklahoma's Merit System of Personnel Administration Act, which "serves roughly the same function as the analogous provisions of the other 49 States, and is patterned on §9(a) of the Hatch Act." Appellants, several state employees charged with violating the Oklahoma Act, maintained that the act was unconstitutionally overbroad because it had been construed to prohibit public employees from wearing political buttons and displaying political bumper stickers. Finding that appellants' own activities could clearly be proscribed, and that the act was not "substantially" overbroad, the Court found it unnecessary to decide the overbreadth issue. See supra section C1. Can Oklahoma constitutionally prohibit its public employees from wearing political buttons and displaying political bumper stickers?

b. Criticizing Government Policy

Pickering v. Board of Education
391 U.S. 563 (1968)

MR. JUSTICE MARSHALL delivered the opinion of the Court.

[Appellant], a teacher, [was] dismissed from his position by the appellee Board of Education for sending a letter to a local newspaper in connection with a recently proposed tax increase that was critical of the way in which the Board and the district superintendent of schools had handled past proposals to raise new revenue for the schools. Appellant's dismissal resulted from a determination by the Board, after a full hearing, that the publication of the letter was "detrimental to the efficient operation and administration of the schools of the district." [We conclude] that appellant's rights to freedom of speech were violated. . . .

"[The] theory that public employment which may be denied altogether may be subjected to any conditions, regardless of how unreasonable, has been uniformly rejected." [At] the same time it cannot be gainsaid that the State has interests as an employer in regulating the speech of its employees that differ significantly from those it possesses in connection with regulation of the speech of the citizenry in general. The problem in any case is to arrive at a balance between the interests of the teacher, as a citizen, in commenting upon matters of public concern and the interest of the State, as an employer, in promoting the efficiency of the public services it performs through its employees. . . .

An examination of the statements in appellant's letter objected to by the Board reveals that [they] consist essentially of criticism of the Board's allocation of school funds between educational and athletic programs. [The] statements are in no way directed towards any person with whom appellant would normally be in contact in the course of his daily work as a teacher. Thus no question of maintaining either discipline by immediate superiors or harmony among coworkers is presented here. Appellant's employment relationships with the Board and, to a somewhat lesser extent, with the superintendent are not the kind of close working relationships for which it can persuasively be claimed that personal loyalty and confidence are necessary to their proper functioning. Accordingly, to the extent that the Board's position here can be taken to suggest that even comments on matters of public concern that are substantially correct [may] furnish grounds for dismissal if they are sufficiently critical in tone, we unequivocally reject it.[3]

We next consider the statements in appellant's letter which we agree to be false, [such as appellant's statements substantially overstating the amounts spent by the Board for athletic purposes]. The Board's original charges included allegations that the publication of the letter damaged the professional reputations of the Board and the superintendent and would foment controversy and conflict among the Board, teachers, administrators, and the residents of the district. However, no evidence to support these allegations was introduced at the hearing. So far as the record reveals, Pickering's letter was greeted by everyone but its main target, the Board, with massive apathy and total disbelief. . . .

In addition, the amounts expended on athletics which Pickering reported erroneously were matters of public record on which his position as a teacher in the district did not qualify him to speak with any greater authority than any other taxpayer. The Board could easily have rebutted appellant's errors by publishing the accurate figures [itself]. We are thus not presented with a situation in which a teacher has carelessly made false statements about matters so closely related to the day-to-day operations of the schools that any harmful impact on the public would be difficult to counter because of the teacher's presumed greater access to the real facts. Accordingly, we have no occasion to consider at this time whether under such circumstances a school board could reasonably require that a teacher make substantial efforts to verify the accuracy of his charges before publishing them.

What we do have before us is a case in which a teacher has made erroneous public statements upon issues then currently the subject of public attention, which are critical of his ultimate employer but which are neither shown nor can be presumed to have in any way either impeded the teacher's proper performance of his daily duties in the classroom[5] or to have interfered with the regular operation of the schools generally. In these circumstances we conclude that the interest of the school administration in limiting teachers' opportunities to contribute to public debate is not significantly greater than its interest in limiting a similar contribution by any member of the general public. . . .

[Were] appellant a member of the general public, the State's power to afford the appellee Board of Education or its members any legal right to sue him for writing the letter at issue here would be limited by the requirement that the letter be judged by the standard laid down in [New York Times v. Sullivan, supra section D1]. . . .

3. It is possible to conceive of some positions in public employment in which the need for confidentiality is so great that even completely correct public statements might furnish a permissible ground for dismissal. Likewise, positions in public employment in which the relationship between superior and subordinate is of such a personal and intimate nature that certain forms of public criticism of the superior by the subordinate would seriously undermine the effectiveness of the working relationship between them can also be imagined. We intimate no views as to how we would resolve any specific instances of such situations, but merely note that significantly different considerations would be involved in such cases.

5. We also note that this case does not present a situation in which a teacher's public statements are so without foundation as to call into question his fitness to perform his duties in the classroom. In such a case, of course, the statements would merely be evidence of the teacher's general competence, or lack thereof, and not an independent basis for dismissal.

[We thus] hold that, in a case such as this, absent proof of false statements knowingly or recklessly made by him,[6] a teacher's exercise of his right to speak on issues of public importance may not furnish the basis for his dismissal from public employment. Since no such showing has been made in this case, [appellant's dismissal] cannot be upheld. . . .*

Note: Pickering *and Its Implications*

1. *Speech interests of public employees.* How does one evaluate the "interests of the [public employee], as a citizen, in commenting upon matters of public concern"? Consider Justice Marshall's observations in *Pickering*:

> [The] question whether a school system requires additional funds is a matter of legitimate public concern on which the judgment of the school administration [cannot], in a society that leaves such questions to popular vote, be taken as conclusive. [Teachers] are, as a class, the members of a community most likely to have informed and definite opinions as to how funds allotted to the operation of the schools should be spent. Accordingly, it is essential that they be able to speak out freely on such questions.

See also Blasi, The Checking Value in First Amendment Theory, 1977 Am. B. Found. Res. J. 521, 634 ("Since under the checking value information about the conduct of government is accorded the highest possible valuation, speech critical of public officials by those persons in the best position to know what they are talking about — namely, government employees — would seem to deserve special protection"). Did *Mitchell* and *Letter Carriers* undervalue this interest?

2. *Variations.* Consider the following variations on *Pickering*.

a. Could the Board in *Pickering* justify appellant's dismissal on the ground that, even though appellant's letter played a "substantial" role in its decision to dismiss him, it would in any event have dismissed Pickering for other — constitutionally permissible — reasons? Consider Mt. Healthy City School District Board of Education v. Doyle, 429 U.S. 274 (1977):

> A rule of causation which focuses solely on whether protected conduct played a part, "substantial" or otherwise, in a decision not to rehire, could place an employee in a better position as a result of the exercise of constitutionally protected conduct than he would have occupied had he done nothing. [The] constitutional principle at stake is sufficiently vindicated if such an employee is placed in no worse a position than if he had not engaged in the conduct. [The government agency should be permitted to demonstrate] by a preponderance of the evidence that it would have reached the same decision [even] in the absence of the protected conduct.

b. Kennedy, a field representative in the Chicago Regional Office of the Office of Economic Opportunity, publicly accused his superior, the regional director of

---

6. Because we conclude that appellant's statements were not knowingly or recklessly false, we have no occasion to pass upon the additional question whether a statement that was knowingly or recklessly false would, if it were neither shown nor could reasonably be presumed to have had any harmful effects, still be protected by the First Amendment. . . .

* [Concurring opinions of Justices Douglas and White are omitted. — Eds.]

the OEO, of misusing federal funds in an attempt to bribe a representative of a community action organization. Finding that Kennedy's accusation was false and was made with " 'reckless disregard of the actual facts' known to him or reasonably discoverable by him," the agency discharged him. Is the discharge constitutional? See Arnett v. Kennedy, 416 U.S. 134 (1974) ("[The] appropriate tribunal would infringe no constitutional right of [Kennedy] in concluding that there was 'cause' for his discharge"). Could Kennedy have been discharged if he had not acted "recklessly"?

c. Suppose Kennedy's accusation was true. Could he nonetheless have been discharged on a showing that his "whistle-blowing" substantially undermined his ability to work effectively with his superiors and co-workers? Consider Note, The Nonpartisan Freedom of Expression of Public Employees, 76 Mich. L. Rev. 365, 392-393 (1977): "In [such situations], the public interest is best served if the unscrupulous activity of public officials is disclosed and the efficiency of the governmental agency involved is not permanently impaired. [To achieve these competing objectives, courts] could provide the disclosing employee with damages for dismissal while refusing to reinstate him because his utterance destroyed his working relationship with superiors." See generally Comment, Government Employee Disclosures of Agency Wrongdoing: Protecting the Right to Blow the Whistle, 42 U. Chi. L. Rev. 530 (1975).

3. *Matters of public concern:* Connick. Meyers, an assistant district attorney, was informed by Connick, the district attorney, that she would be transferred to prosecute cases in a different section of the criminal court. After expressing her reluctance to accept the transfer, Meyers circulated a questionnaire soliciting the views of other assistant district attorneys concerning the office transfer policy, office morale, the need for a grievance committee, the level of confidence in their supervisors, and whether they felt pressured to work in political campaigns. Connick fired her for distributing the questionnaire. In Connick v. Meyers, 461 U.S. 138 (1983), the Court held that Meyers's discharge did not violate the first amendment.

Justice White delivered the opinion of the Court:

> The repeated emphasis in *Pickering* on the right of a public employee "as a citizen, in commenting upon matters of public concern," was not accidental. [The] Court has frequently reaffirmed that speech on public issues occupies the "highest rung on the hierarchy of First Amendment values," and is entitled to special protection. [When] employee expression cannot fairly be considered as relating to any matter of political, social, or other concern to the community, [but concerns only matters of personal interest,] officials should enjoy wide latitude in managing their offices, without intrusive oversight by the judiciary in the name of the First Amendment. . . .
>
> Whether an employee's speech addresses a matter of public concern must be determined by the content, form, and context of a given [statement]. In this case, with but one exception, the questions posed [in the questionnaire] do not fall under the rubric of matters of "public concern." We view the questions pertaining to the confidence and trust that Meyers' coworkers possess in various supervisors, the level of office morale, and the need for a grievance committee as mere extensions of [her] dispute over her [transfer]. [Meyers was not seeking] to inform the public that the District Attorney's office was not discharging its governmental responsibilities. [Rather, her purpose was] to gather ammunition for another round of controversy with her superiors. [To] presume that all matters which transpire within a govern-

ment office are of public concern would mean that virtually every remark [would] plant the seed of a constitutional case. . . .

[The inquiry in respondent's questionnaire asking the assistant district attorneys if they] "ever feel pressured to work in political campaigns on behalf of office supported candidates," does touch upon a matter of public concern. [Because this question may have] contributed to Meyers' discharge, we must determine whether Connick was justified in discharging [her]. [Although] there is no demonstration [that] the questionnaire impeded Meyers' ability to perform her responsibilities, [Connick's] judgment [was] that [distribution of the] questionnaire was an act of insubordination which interfered with working relationships. When close working relationships are essential to fulfilling public responsibilities, a wide degree of deference to the employer's judgment is appropriate. Furthermore, we do not see the necessity for an employer to allow events to unfold to the extent that the disruption [is] manifest before taking action. We caution that a stronger showing may be necessary if the employee's speech more substantially involves matters of public concern. [Here, however, respondent's] questionnaire touched upon matters of public concern in only a most limited [sense]. [Moreover, the questionnaire was distributed at work and in the specific context of a personal dispute, thus supporting Connick's] fears that the functioning of his office was endangered. [In such circumstances, the] limited First Amendment interest involved [does] not require that Connick tolerate action which he reasonably believed would disrupt the office [and] destroy working relations.

Justice Brennan, joined by Justices Marshall, Blackmun, and Stevens, dissented:

I would hold that [the] questionnaire addressed matters of public concern because it discussed subjects that could reasonably be expected to be of interest to persons seeking to develop informed opinions about the manner in which the [District Attorney] discharges his responsibilities. [The] Court's adoption of a far narrower conception of what subjects are of public concern [is unwarranted]. [Moreover,] the Court misapplies the *Pickering* test and holds [that] a public employer's mere apprehension that speech will be disruptive justifies suppression of that speech. [Such] extreme deference to the employer's judgment is not [appropriate]. [Here, after] reviewing the evidence, the District Court found that "it [could not] be said that [Connick's] interest in [efficiency] was either adversely affected or substantially impeded by [Meyers'] distribution of the questionnaire." [The] District Court applied the proper legal standard and reached an acceptable accommodation between the competing interests.

Consider Note, Developments in the Law — Public Employment, 97 Harv. L. Rev. 1611, 1757, 1767-1770 (1984):

[The] *Pickering* balancing doctrine [has] inadequately protected public employees' right to free speech. Although courts have fully articulated and usually deferred to employers' interests in efficiency, they have neglected to explicate employees' interests in expression. [Courts] should [scrutinize more critically] the managerial theories underlying asserted efficiency interests. [*Connick*], for example, [was] premised on a particular managerial theory — that rigidly hierarchical management maximizes workplace efficiency. [Under such a theory], when an employee [criticizes] office policy, her speech threatens "the authority of the employer" and thereby impedes efficiency. Yet according to a growing number of [studies], the productivity of the workplace can *increase* when employees are allowed to contribute to the formulation of office policy. [Moreover, the courts should recognize that a] public employee's interests in expression [are] broader than her interests [in] informing the [public]. [Public] employees have legitimate interests in the efficiency and fairness of their working environments, [and] the efforts of employees to address these concerns may merit strong judicial protection. A broader conception of public employees' interests in expression would comport far better with the first amendment's premise of "individual dignity and choice."

c. Patronage

Elrod v. Burns

427 U.S. 347 (1976)

[In December 1970 the Sheriff of Cook County, Illinois, a Republican, was replaced by Richard Elrod, a Democrat. At that time, respondents, all Republicans, were non–civil service employees of the Cook County Sheriff's Office. Respondent Burns was a process server; respondent Vargas was a bailiff and security guard. Following prior practice, Sheriff Elrod discharged respondents from their employment solely because they did not support and were not members of the Democratic Party and had failed to obtain the sponsorship of one of its leaders. The Court held this practice unconstitutional under the first and fourteenth amendments.]

Mr. Justice Brennan announced the judgment of the Court and delivered an opinion in which Mr. Justice White and Mr. Justice Marshall joined. . . .

The Cook County Sheriff's practice of dismissing employees on a partisan basis is but one form of the general practice of political patronage. The practice also includes placing loyal supporters in government jobs that may or may not have been made available by political discharges. Nonofficeholders may be the beneficiaries of lucrative government contracts for highway construction, buildings, and supplies. Favored wards may receive improved public services. [Although] political patronage comprises a broad range of activities, we are here concerned only with the constitutionality of dismissing public employees for partisan reasons.

Patronage practice is not new to American politics. It has existed at the federal level at least since the Presidency of Thomas Jefferson. [More] recent times have witnessed a strong decline in its use, [however, and] merit systems have increasingly displaced the practice. [See *Letter Carriers*.]

The cost of the practice of patronage is the restraint it places on freedoms of belief and association. In order to maintain their jobs, respondents were required to pledge their political allegiance to the Democratic Party, work for the election of other candidates of the Democratic Party, contribute a portion of their wages to the Party, or obtain the sponsorship of a member of the Party, usually at the price of one of the first three alternatives. [An] individual who is a member of the out-party maintains affiliation with his own party at the risk of losing his job. He works for the election of his party's candidates and espouses its policies at the same risk. The financial and campaign assistance that he is induced to provide to another party furthers the advancement of that party's policies to the detriment of his party's views and ultimately his own beliefs. . . .

"[T]he theory that public employment which may be denied altogether may be subjected to any conditions, regardless of how unreasonable, has been uniformly rejected." It is firmly established that a significant impairment of First Amendment rights must survive exacting scrutiny. [The] interest advanced must be paramount, [Buckley v. Valeo, supra section E4], the gain to the subordinating interest [must] outweigh the incurred loss of protected rights, see [United Public Workers v. Mitchell], and the government must "emplo[y] means closely drawn to avoid unnecessary abridgment. . . ."

One interest which has been offered in justification of patronage is the need to insure effective government and the efficiency of public employees. It is argued that employees of political persuasions not the same as that of the party in control of public office will not have the incentive to work effectively and may even be motivated to subvert the incumbent administration's efforts to govern effectively. We are not persuaded. [It] is doubtful that the mere difference of political persuasion motivates poor performance. [At] all events, less drastic means for insuring government effectiveness and employee efficiency are available to the State. Specifically, employees may always be discharged for good cause, such as insubordination or poor job performance, when those bases in fact exist. . . .

The lack of any justification for patronage dismissals as a means of furthering government effectiveness and efficiency distinguishes this case from [*Letter Carriers*] and [*Mitchell*]. In both of those cases, legislative restraints on political management and campaigning by public employees were upheld despite their encroachment on First Amendment rights because, inter alia, they did serve in a necessary manner to foster and protect efficient and effective government. . . .

A second interest advanced in support of patronage is the need for political loyalty of employees [to] the end that representative government not be undercut by tactics obstructing the implementation of policies of the new administration, policies presumably sanctioned by the electorate. The justification is not without force, but is nevertheless inadequate to validate patronage wholesale. Limiting patronage dismissals to policymaking positions is sufficient to achieve this governmental end. Nonpolicymaking individuals usually have only limited responsibility and are therefore not in a position to thwart the goals of the in-party. . . .

It is argued that a third interest supporting patronage dismissals is the preservation of the democratic process. [This] is certainly an interest protection which may in some instances justify limitations on First Amendment freedoms. See [*Buckley; Letter Carriers; Mitchell*]. But however important preservation of the two-party system [may be,] we are not persuaded that the elimination of patronage practice [will] bring about the demise of party politics. Political parties existed in the absence of active patronage practice [and] they have survived substantial reduction in their patronage power through the establishment of merit systems.

Patronage dismissals thus are not the least restrictive alternative to achieving the contribution they may make to the democratic process. The process functions as well without the practice, perhaps even better, for patronage dismissals clearly also retard that process. Patronage can result in the entrenchment of one or a few parties to the exclusion of others. And most indisputably, as we recognized at the outset, patronage is a very effective impediment to the associational and speech freedoms which are essential to a meaningful system of democratic government. Thus, if patronage contributes at all to the elective process, that contribution is diminished by the practice's impairment of the same. [T]he gain to representative government provided by the practice of patronage, if any, would be insufficient to justify its sacrifice of First Amendment rights.[25] . . .

We hold, therefore, that the practice of patronage dismissals is unconstitutional under the First and Fourteenth Amendments. . . .

MR. JUSTICE STEVENS did not participate in the consideration or decision of this case.

MR. JUSTICE STEWART, with whom MR. JUSTICE BLACKMUN joins, concurring in the judgment.

This case does not require us to consider the broad contours of the so-called patronage system, with all its variations and permutations. The single substantive question involved in this case is whether a nonpolicymaking, nonconfidential government employee can be discharged or threatened with discharge from a job that he is satisfactorily performing upon the sole ground of his political beliefs. I agree with the plurality that he cannot. . . .

MR. JUSTICE POWELL, with whom THE CHIEF JUSTICE and MR. JUSTICE REHNQUIST join, dissenting. . . .

The question is [whether] patronage hiring practices sufficiently advance important state interests to justify the consequent burdening of First Amendment interests. [*Buckley.*] It is difficult to disagree with the view, as an abstract proposition, that government employment ordinarily should not be conditioned upon one's political beliefs or activities. But we deal here with a highly practical and rather fundamental element of our political system, not the theoretical abstractions of a political science seminar. In concluding that patronage hiring practices are unconstitutional, the plurality seriously underestimates the strength of the government interest — especially at the local level — in allowing some patronage hiring practices, and it exaggerates the perceived burden on First Amendment rights. . . .

[Patronage] hiring practices have contributed to American democracy by stimulating political activity and by strengthening parties, thereby helping to make government accountable. It cannot be questioned seriously that these contributions promote important state interests. . . .

[For example,] election campaigns for lesser offices [usually] attract little attention from the media. [Unless] the candidates for these offices are able to dispense the traditional patronage that has accrued to the offices, they also are unlikely to attract donations of time or money from voluntary groups. [Thus, the] activities of [patronage supporters] are often the principal source of political information for the voting public. . . .

25. The Court's decision earlier this term in [*Buckley*] is not contrary. It is true that in *Buckley*, as here, the interest to be served was the democratic system, and accordingly in *Buckley*, the infringement of some First Amendment rights was held to be tolerable. In *Buckley*, however, unlike here, the disclosure and contribution limitations on campaign financing, which were upheld, were essential to eliminating the grave evil of improper influence in the political process. With respect to expenditure limitations, however, which were not upheld, the Court found: "These provisions place substantial and direct restrictions on the ability of candidates, citizens, and associations to engage in protected political expression, restrictions that the First Amendment cannot tolerate." The restrictions imposed by patronage dismissals, limiting wholesale an individual's political beliefs, expression, and association, while perhaps less direct, are equally, if not more, substantial, and therefore also intolerable to the First Amendment. . . .

Patronage hiring practices also enable party organizations to persist and function at the local level. Such organizations become visible to the electorate at large only at election time, but the dull periods between elections require ongoing activities: precinct organizations must be maintained; new voters registered; and minor political "chores" performed for citizens who otherwise may have no practical means of access to officeholders. . . .

It is naive to think that these types of political activities are motivated at these levels by some academic interest in "democracy" or other public service impulse. For the most part, as every politician knows, the hope of some reward generates a major portion of the local political activity supporting parties. . . .

[Thus,] patronage hiring practices have been consistent historically with vigorous ideological competition in the political "marketplace." [Indeed,] even after one becomes a beneficiary, the system leaves significant room for individual political expression. Employees, regardless of affiliation, may vote freely and express themselves on some political issues. [The] principal intrusion of patronage hiring practices on First Amendment interests thus arises from the coercion on associational choices that may be created by one's desire initially to obtain employment. This intrusion, while not insignificant, must be measured in light of the limited role of patronage hiring in most government employment. The pressure to abandon one's beliefs and associations to obtain government employment — especially employment of such uncertain duration — does not seem to me to assume impermissible proportions in light of the interests to be served. . . .*

BRANTI v. FINKEL, 445 U.S. 507 (1980): The Court, in a six-to-three decision, held that the first amendment prohibited the discharge of two assistant public defenders solely because they were Republicans and were thus unable to provide the necessary Democratic sponsorship when a Democratic Public Defender took office. Justice Stevens, speaking for the Court, rejected the argument that even if a party affiliation requirement is unconstitutional for nonpolicymaking, nonconfidential employees, such as those involved in *Elrod*, such a requirement is permissible for assistant public defenders:

"*Elrod* [recognized] that party affiliation may be an acceptable requirement for some types of government employment. [But] it is not always easy to determine whether a position is one in which political affiliation is a legitimate factor to be considered. Under some circumstances, a position may be appropriately considered political even though it is neither confidential nor policymaking in character. [For] example, if a State's election laws require that precincts be supervised by two election judges of different parties, a Republican judge could be legitimately discharged solely for changing his party registration. [It] is equally clear that party affiliation is not necessarily relevant to every policymaking or confidential position. The coach of a state university's football team formulates policy, but no one could seriously claim that Republicans make better coaches than Democrats. [In] sum, the ultimate inquiry is not whether the label 'policymaker' or 'confidential' fits a particular position; rather, the question is whether the hiring authority can demonstrate that party affiliation is an appropriate requirement for the effective performance of the public office involved.

"Having thus framed the issue, it is manifest that the continued employment of

---

* [A dissenting opinion of Chief Justice Burger is omitted. — EDS.]

an assistant public defender cannot properly be conditioned upon his allegiance to the political party in control of the county government. The primary, if not the only, responsibility of an assistant public defender is to represent individual citizens in controversy with the State. [Whatever] policymaking occurs in the public defender's office must relate to the needs of individual clients and not to any partisan political interests. [Moreover, we] cannot accept the proposition [that] there cannot be 'mutual confidence and trust' between attorneys [unless] they are both of the same political party. To the extent that [the public defender] lacks confidence in the assistants he had inherited from the prior administration for some reason other than their political affiliations, he is, of course, free to discharge them."

Justices Stewart, Powell, and Rehnquist dissented. The dissenting justices argued that the *Branti* standard is so vague that public officials "no longer will know when political affiliation is an appropriate consideration in filling a position."

How would the *Branti* standard apply to a party affiliation requirement for government prosecutors?

Precisely how does patronage impair the first amendment interests of public employees? In *Elrod* the plurality noted that patronage may both prevent an employee from supporting the party of his choice and "compel" him to support a party he opposes. Which concern, if either, is dominant? Is there a first amendment right *not* to support the promulgation of views with which one disagrees? The right not to speak is examined in section F4 infra.

d. Subversive Advocacy and Associations

[As of 1972,] more than one-sixth of the total civilian labor force was subject to some type of loyalty qualification. The employment loyalty programs imposing these qualifications developed in the years following the Second World War. Those years were marked by an intense fear that Communist and other subversive political organizations were placing agents in sensitive government, military, and industrial positions in an attempt to undermine the nation's defense and destroy its democratic institutions. The federal government and most of the states excluded individuals who either advocated the violent overthrow of the government or were members of "subversive" organizations from a broad range of jobs.

Note, Development of Law — The National Security Interest and Civil Liberties, 85 Harv. L. Rev. 1130, 1160-1165 (1972). See generally Brown, Loyalty and Security (1958); Gellhorn, Individual Freedom and Governmental Restraints (1956); O'Brien, National Security and Individual Freedom (1955).

What interests are served by government's refusal to employ individuals who advocate the violent overthrow of government or belong to organizations that engage in such advocacy? Consider Israel, *Elfbrandt v. Russell*: The Demise of the Oath?, 1966 Sup. Ct. Rev. 193, 219:

[At] least three different state interests are commonly advanced to justify disqualification of individuals from public employment on the basis of membership in organizations advocating the violent overthrow of the government: (1) The elimination of persons who present a potential for sabotage, espionage, or other activities directly injurious to national security. (2) The elimination of persons who are likely to be either incompetent or untrustworthy in the performance of their duties. (3) The elimination of persons who, aside from any question of danger or fitness, simply are not considered deserving of a government position because they oppose the basic principles on which the government is founded.

ADLER v. BOARD OF EDUCATION, 342 U.S. 485 (1952): A New York law provided that no person who becomes a member of any organization that advocates the violent overthrow of government, with knowledge of the organization's proscribed advocacy, "shall be appointed to any [position] in a public school." In enacting this law, the New York legislature found that "members of subversive groups [have] been infiltrating [the] public schools" and that subversive "propaganda [is] sufficiently subtle to escape detection in the classroom." The Court upheld the law:

"A teacher works in a sensitive area in a schoolroom. There he shapes the attitude of young minds towards the society in which they live. [That] the school authorities have the right and the duty to screen [teachers] as to their fitness to maintain the integrity of the schools [cannot] be doubted. One's associates, past and present, as well as one's conduct, may properly be considered in determining [fitness]. If, under [the] New York law, a person is found to be unfit and is disqualified from employment in the public school system because of membership in a [subversive] organization, he is not thereby denied the right of free speech and assembly. His freedom of choice between membership in the organization and employment in the school system might be limited, but [such] limitation is not one the state may not make in the exercise of its police power to protect the schools from pollution and thereby to defend its own existence."

See also Garner v. Board of Public Works, 341 U.S. 716 (1951) (upholding a requirement that every public employee swear that he does not advocate the overthrow of government by force, violence, or other unlawful means or belong to any organization that advocates such overthrow); Wieman v. Updegraff, 344 U.S. 183 (1952) (invalidating an oath requirement because, unlike the loyalty schemes upheld in *Adler* and *Garner*, "under the [challenged] Act, the fact of association alone determines disloyalty and disqualification" even if the individual lacked knowledge of the organization's proscribed advocacy).

Elfbrandt v. Russell
384 U.S. 11 (1966)

Mr. Justice Douglas delivered the opinion of the Court.

This case [involves] questions concerning the constitutionality of an Arizona Act requiring an oath from state employees. . . .

The oath reads in conventional fashion as follows:

I, (type or print name) do solemnly swear (or affirm) that I will support the Constitution of the United States and the Constitution and laws of the State of Arizona; that I will bear true faith and allegiance to the same, and defend them against all enemies, foreign and domestic, and that I will faithfully and impartially discharge the duties of the office of (name of office) according to the best of my ability, so help me God (or so I do affirm).

The Legislature put a gloss on the oath by subjecting to a prosecution for perjury and for discharge from public office anyone who took the oath and who "knowingly and wilfully becomes or remains a member of the communist party of the United States or its successors or any of its subordinate organizations" or "any other organization" having for "one of its purposes" the overthrow of the government of Arizona or any of its political subdivisions where the employee had knowledge of the unlawful purpose. Petitioner, a teacher and a Quaker, decided she could not in good conscience take the oath, not knowing what it meant and not having any chance to get a hearing at which its precise scope and meaning could be determined. This suit for declaratory relief followed. . . .

We recognized in Scales v. United States, [supra section B1], that "quasi-political parties or other groups [may] embrace both legal and illegal aims." We noted that a "blanket prohibition of association with a group having both legal and illegal aims" would pose "a real danger that legitimate political expression or association would be impaired." The statute with which we dealt in *Scales*, the so-called "membership clause" of the Smith Act (18 U.S.C. §2385), was found not to suffer from this constitutional infirmity because, as the Court construed it, the statute reached only "active" membership [with] the "specific intent" of assisting in achieving the unlawful ends of the organization. . . .

The oath and accompanying statutory gloss challenged here [pose a similar problem]. One who subscribes to this Arizona oath and who is, or thereafter becomes, a knowing member of an organization which has as "one of its purposes" the violent overthrow of the government, is subject to immediate discharge and criminal penalties. Nothing in the oath, the statutory gloss, or the construction of the oath and statutes given by the Arizona Supreme Court, purports to exclude association by one who does not subscribe to the organization's unlawful ends. [Thus,] the "hazard of being prosecuted for knowing but guiltless behavior" [is] a reality. [Would] a teacher be safe and secure in [joining] a seminar group predominantly Communist and therefore subject to control by those who are said to believe in the overthrow of the Government by force and violence? Juries might convict though the teacher did not subscribe to the wrongful aims of the organization. And there is apparently no machinery provided for getting clearance in advance.

Those who join an organization but do not share its unlawful purposes and who do not participate in its unlawful activities surely pose no threat, either as citizens or as public employees. Laws such as this which are not restricted in scope to those who join with the "specific intent" to further illegal action impose, in effect, a conclusive presumption that the member shares the unlawful aims of the organization. . . .

This Act threatens the cherished freedom of association protected by the First Amendment, made applicable to the States through the Fourteenth Amendment. [Public] employees of character and integrity may well forgo their calling rather than risk prosecution for perjury or compromise their commitment to intellectual and political freedom. [A] statute touching those protected rights must be "narrowly drawn to define and punish specific conduct as constituting a clear and present danger to a substantial interest of the State." [Legitimate] legislative goals "cannot be pursued by means that broadly stifle fundamental personal liberties when the end can be more narrowly achieved." [A] law which applies to membership without the "specific intent" to further the illegal aims of the organization infringes unnecessarily on protected freedoms. It rests on the doctrine of "guilt by association" which has no place here. [Such] a law cannot stand.

Reversed.

MR. JUSTICE WHITE, with whom MR. JUSTICE CLARK, MR. JUSTICE HARLAN and MR. JUSTICE STEWART concur, dissenting.

According to unequivocal prior holdings of this Court, a State is entitled to condition public employment upon its employees abstaining from knowing membership in the Communist Party and other organizations advocating the violent overthrow of the government which employs them. [*Garner; Adler;* see also *Wieman.*] The Court does not mention or purport to overrule these cases. . . .

[The] crime provided by the Arizona law is not just the act of becoming a member of an organization but it is that membership plus concurrent public employment. [If] a government may remove from office [and] criminally punish [its] employees who engage in certain political activities, [*Mitchell*], it is unsound to hold that it may not, on pain of criminal penalties, prevent its employees from affiliating with the Communist Party or other organizations prepared to employ violent means to overthrow constitutional government. Our Constitution does not require this kind of protection for the secret proselyting of government employees into the Communist Party, an organization [dedicated] to the overthrow of the government by any illegal means necessary to achieve this end. . . .

There is nothing in [*Scales*] dictating the result reached by the Court. *Scales* involved the construction of the Smith Act and a holding that the membership clause did not reach members who knew of the illegal aims of the Party but lacked an active membership and an intent to further the illegal ends. [*Scales*] did not deal with the government employee who is a knowing member of the Communist Party. [It] did not suggest that the State or Federal Government should be prohibited from taking elementary precautions against its employees forming knowing and deliberate affiliations with those organizations who conspire to destroy the government by violent means. . . .

Note: *Loyalty Programs and the First Amendment*

1. *Is* Elfbrandt *overprotective of the right of association?* Is *Elfbrandt's* extension of *Scales* to the public employment context warranted? Does *Elfbrandt* suggest that the state cannot constitutionally refuse to employ an individual because of his subversive advocacy unless such advocacy could constitutionally be declared unlawful? See also Keyishian v. Board of Regents, 385 U.S. 589 (1967), in which the Court, building on *Elfbrandt*, held unconstitutional several sections of the New York law that had been upheld in *Adler*.

2. *The reach of* Elfbrandt: Robel. In United States v. Robel, 389 U.S. 258 (1967), appellee, a member of the Communist Party who had worked at a shipyard for ten years "without incident," was charged with violating section 5(a)(1)(D) of the Subversive Activities Control Act of 1950, which prohibited any member of a

Communist-action organization with knowledge that the organization was under a final order to register with the Subversive Activities Control Board "to engage in any employment in any defense facility." The Court held that section 5(a)(1)(D) was an "unconstitutional abridgment of the right of association protected by the First Amendment."

Chief Justice Warren delivered the opinion of the Court:

> The Government [emphasizes] that the purpose of §5(a)(1)(D) is to reduce the threat of sabotage and espionage in the Nation's defense plants. The Government's interest in such a prophylactic measure is not insubstantial. But [the] means chosen to implement that governmental purpose in this instance cut deeply into the right of association. Section 5(a)(1)(D) [casts] its net across a broad range of associational activities, indiscriminately trapping membership which can be constitutionally punished [see *Scales*] and membership which cannot be so proscribed. [See *Elfbrandt*.] It is made irrelevant to the statute's operation that an individual may be a passive or inactive [member], that he may be unaware of the organization's unlawful aims, or that he may disagree with those unlawful aims. It is also made irrelevant that [the individual] may occupy a nonsensitive position in a defense facility. Thus, §5(a)(1)(D) contains the fatal defect of overbreadth because it seeks to bar employment both for association which may be proscribed and for association which may not be proscribed. [This] the Constitution will not tolerate. [Nothing] we hold today should be read to deny Congress the power under narrowly drawn legislation to keep from sensitive positions in defense facilities those who would use their positions to disrupt the Nation's production facilities. [But] Congress must achieve its goal by means which have a "less drastic" impact on the continued vitality of First Amendment freedoms.

Justice White, joined by Justice Harlan, dissented:

> [The] Court simply disagrees with the Congress and the Defense Department, ruling that [appellee] does not present a sufficient danger to the national security to require him to choose between membership in the Communist Party and his employment in a defense facility. [Given] the characteristics of the Party, its foreign domination, its primary goal of government overthrow, the discipline which it exercises over its members, and its propensity for espionage and sabotage, the exclusion of members of the Party who know the Party is a Communist-action organization from certain defense plants is well within the power of Congress. Congress should be entitled to take suitable precautionary measures. Some Party members may be no threat at all, but many of them undoubtedly are, and it is exceedingly difficult to identify those in advance of the very events which Congress seeks to avoid. [Moreover,] the facilities designated under this standard amount to only about one percent of all the industrial establishments in the United States. [The] impact on associational rights [is thus] minimal. [The] Court says that mere membership in an association with knowledge that the association pursues unlawful aims cannot be the basis for criminal prosecution, [*Scales*]. But denying the opportunity to be employed in some defense plants is a much smaller deterrent to the exercise of associational rights than [a] criminal penalty attached solely to membership, and the Government's interest in keeping potential spies and saboteurs from defense plants is much greater than its interest [in] committing all Party members to prison.

After *Robel*, in what circumstances, if any, may the government refuse to employ an individual in a defense facility because of that individual's membership in a "subversive" organization, where the individual's membership does not meet the requirements of *Scales?*

3. *Is* Elfbrandt *underprotective of the right of association?* In *Elfbrandt* and *Robel*, the Court seemed implicitly to assume that an individual who personally advocates the violent overthrow of government or is a "*Scales* member" of an organization that advocates such overthrow could automatically and without further inquiry be denied government employment. Is such an assumption warranted? Note that, at the time of these decisions, government, under then prevailing doctrine, could constitutionally prohibit *any* person to advocate the violent overthrow of government or to be a "*Scales* member" of an organization advocating such overthrow. See *Dennis* and *Scales,* supra section B1. Two years after *Robel*, however, the Court, in Brandenburg v. Ohio, supra section B1, redefined the circumstances in which government could constitutionally proscribe subversive advocacy, holding that "the constitutional guarantees of free speech and free press do not permit a State to forbid or proscribe advocacy of the use of force or of law violation except where such advocacy is directed to inciting or producing imminent lawless action and is likely to incite or produce such action." How does *Brandenburg* affect the public employment issue?

After *Brandenburg*, may the state deny employment to an individual who personally advocates the violent overthrow of government or is a *Scales* member of an organization that advocates such overthrow only if "such advocacy is directed to inciting or producing imminent lawless action and is likely to incite or produce such action"? May the state deny employment to an individual whose advocacy of unlawful conduct falls short of *Brandenburg* if his employment poses a likely and imminent danger of interference with some substantial government interest? See Comment, *Brandenburg v. Ohio:* A Speech Test for All Seasons?, 43 U. Chi. L. Rev. 151 (1975).

4. *Beliefs.* Should government be *absolutely* prohibited from denying individuals employment because of their "subversive" beliefs? In American Communications Association v. Douds, 339 U.S. 382 (1950), the Court upheld section 9(h) of the National Labor Relations Act, which required union officials to swear that they do "not believe in [the] overthrow of [government] by force or by any illegal or unconstitutional methods." The Court explained: "The principle that one may under no circumstances [suffer] the loss of any right or privilege because of his beliefs [hardly] commends itself to [reason]. If it is admitted that beliefs are springs to action, it becomes highly relevant whether the person who is asked whether he believes in overthrow [is] a general with five hundred thousand men at his command or a village constable. To argue that because the latter may not be asked his beliefs the former must *necessarily* be exempt is to make a fetish out of beliefs."

Justice Jackson dissented:

> [The] issue is whether Congress has power to proscribe [an] opinion or belief which has not manifested itself in any overt act. [I] know of no situation in which a citizen may incur civil or criminal liability [because] a court infers an evil mental state where no act at all has occurred. Our trial processes are [too] clumsy [to] ascertain the thought that has had no outward manifestation. [Only] in the darkest periods of human history has any Western government concerned itself with mere belief, [and] if that practice survives anywhere, it is in the Communist countries whose philoso-

phies we loathe. [Under] our system, it is time enough for the law to lay hold of the citizen when he acts illegally, [or] when his thoughts are given illegal utterance. I think we must let his mind alone.

Justice Black also dissented.

Cf. Baird v. State Bar, 401 U.S. 1 (1971), in which the Court held that an individual could not constitutionally be denied admission to the Bar merely because he "presently entertains the view that a violent overthrow of [government] is something to be sought after."

5. *Loyalty programs and the vagueness doctrine.* As illustrated by *Elfbrandt* and *Robel*, the Court in the 1960s often invalidated state and federal loyalty programs on grounds of overbreadth. The Court also frequently invoked the vagueness doctrine to invalidate such programs. In Cramp v. Board of Public Instruction, 368 U.S. 278 (1961), for example, the Court held unconstitutional a Florida statute requiring every employee of the state to swear that he had never knowingly lent his "aid, support, advice, counsel or influence to the Communist Party." Noting that a citizen "who had ever cast his vote for [a candidate of the Communist Party], a lawyer who had ever represented the [Party, or] a journalist who had ever defended the constitutional rights of the [Party]" could not possibly know whether he could "safely subscribe" to the oath, the Court concluded that the provision was "completely lacking [in] terms susceptible of objective measurement." See also Baggett v. Bullitt, 377 U.S. 360 (1964) (invalidating on vagueness grounds a state law requiring every state employee to swear that he is not a person who "advocates, abets, advises or teaches by any means any person to commit, attempt to commit, or aid in the commission of any act intended to overthrow, destroy or alter [the government] by revolution, force or violence").

Unlike "negative" oaths, such as those involved in *Cramp* and *Baggett*, which require public employees to disclaim certain beliefs, opinions, or associations, "affirmative" oaths usually require such employees to promise to carry out faithfully the functions they are required by law to perform. Article VI of the Constitution requires all federal and state officials to "be bound by Oath or Affirmation to support [the] Constitution," and Article II expressly requires the President to "swear (or affirm) that I will faithfully execute the Office of President of the United States, and will to the best of my Ability, preserve, protect and defend the Constitution of the United States." The Court has upheld the constitutionality of similar oath requirements imposed by the states. See Bond v. Floyd, 385 U.S. 116 (1966).

In some forms, however, even affirmative oaths may pose constitutional problems. In Baggett v. Bullitt, supra, for example, the Court invalidated on vagueness grounds a requirement that all teachers must affirmatively swear that they "will support the constitution and laws of the United States [and] will by precept and example promote respect for the flag and the institutions of the United States [and] reverence for law and order and undivided allegiance to the government of the United States."

More recently, in Cole v. Richardson, 405 U.S. 676 (1972), the Court, in a four-to-three decision, upheld a Massachusetts law requiring all public employees to swear that they "will uphold and defend the Constitution [and] oppose the overthrow of the government [by] force, violence or by any illegal or unconstitutional method." The Court explained that although the second clause of the oath could be construed as imposing "nebulous, undefined responsibilities for action in some hypothetical situations," it would not adopt such a "rigidly literal" interpretation. Rather, the Court construed the second clause as merely "a commitment not to use illegal and constitutionally unprotected force to change the constitutional system."

6. *Bills of attainder.* Another doctrine often invoked by the Court to assess the constitutionality of government loyalty programs centers on Article I's declaration that neither Congress nor the States may pass any "Bill of Attainder." See, e.g., United States v. Brown, 381 U.S. 437 (1965) (invalidating as a bill of attainder a provision of the Labor-Management Reporting and Disclosure Act of 1959 prohibiting any member of the Communist Party to serve as an officer or employee of a labor union); United States v. Lovett, 328 U.S. 303 (1946) (invalidating as a bill of attainder a provision of the Urgent Deficiency Appropriation Act of 1943 prohibiting the payment of any salary or other compensation for any government service to three named individuals who had allegedly engaged in "subversive" activities); Cummings v. Missouri, 71 U.S. (4 Wall.) 277 (1867) (invalidating as a bill of attainder a provision of the Missouri constitution prohibiting any person to serve as an officeholder, lawyer, clergyman, teacher, or corporate official unless he first took an oath that he had never "been in the service [of] the so-called 'Confederate States of America,' [or] manifested [his] sympathy with those engaged in exciting or carrying on rebellion against the United States").

7. *Denial of benefits other than public employment.* In what circumstances, if any, may government deny public benefits other than public employment to individuals because of their "subversive" advocacy or associations? See Communist Party of Indiana v. Whitcomb, 414 U.S. 441 (1974) (invalidating an Indiana statute providing that no political party "shall be permitted [to] have the names of its candidates printed on the ballot [unless] it has filed an affidavit [that] it does not advocate the overthrow [of] government by force or violence," because "burdening access to the ballot [not] because the Party urges others 'to *do* something, now or in the future [but] merely to *believe* in something,' is to infringe interests certainly as substantial as those in public employment, tax exemption, or the practice of law"); Aptheker v. Secretary of State, 378 U.S. 500 (1964) (invalidating section 6 of the Subversive Activities Control Act of 1950, which declared it unlawful for any member of a Communist organization, with knowledge that an order of registration against such organization had become final, to use or attempt to use any U.S. passport, because the statute constituted an "overbroad" restriction on the constitutionally protected right to travel); Speiser v. Randall, 357 U.S. 513 (1958) (invalidating a California statute requiring every claimant for property-tax exemption to sign a statement that he does not advocate the overthrow of government "by force or violence," because the statute placed the burden of proof on the taxpayer to demonstrate that he had not engaged in the prohibited advocacy); Konigsberg v. State Bar, 353 U.S. 252 (1957) (invalidating a decision of the California State Bar to exclude an individual from the practice of law because, some thirteen years earlier, he had been a member of the Communist Party); American Communications Association v. Douds, 339 U.S. 382 (1950) (upholding section 9(h) of the National Labor Relations Act, which expressly withheld the benefits of various provisions of the act from any labor union whose officers failed to execute an affidavit that they were not "[members] of the Communist Party").

e. Confidential Information

Recall that in such decisions as Landmark Communications v. Virginia, Nebraska Press v. Stuart, and New York Times v. United States, examined in section B4 supra, the Court embraced a highly speech-protective approach to government efforts to restrict the publication of "confidential" information. Recall also, however, that in explaining this approach, the Court suggested that, as a "less restrictive means" of achieving its objectives, the government might prohibit its employees from disclosing such information to the public. Should government have greater authority to prohibit its employees from disclosing confidential information than to prohibit the press from publishing it? In what circumstances may government restrict its employees' disclosure of "confidential" information?

Snepp v. United States
444 U.S. 507 (1980)

PER CURIAM. . . .

Based on his experiences as a CIA agent, Snepp published a book about certain CIA activities in South Vietnam. Snepp published the account without submitting it to the Agency for prepublication review. As an express condition of his employment with the CIA in 1968, however, Snepp had executed an agreement promising that he would "not [publish] any information or material relating to the Agency, its activities or intelligence activities generally, either during or after the term of [his] employment [without] specific prior approval by the Agency." The promise was an integral part of Snepp's concurrent undertaking "not to disclose any classified information relating to the Agency without proper authorization." The Government brought this suit to enforce Snepp's agreement. It sought a declaration that Snepp had breached the contract, an injunction requiring Snepp to submit future writings for prepublication review, and an order imposing a constructive trust for the Government's benefit on all profits that Snepp might earn from publishing the book in violation of his fiduciary obligations to the Agency.[2]

The District Court found that Snepp had "willfully [breached] his position of trust with the CIA and the [1968] secrecy agreement" [and] therefore enjoined future breaches of [the] agreement and imposed a constructive trust on Snepp's profits.

The Court of Appeals [agreed] that Snepp had breached a valid contract,[3] [but]

---

2. At the time of suit, Snepp already had received about $60,000 in advance payments. His contract with his publisher provides for royalties and other potential profits.

3. [Snepp] relies primarily on the claim that his agreement is unenforceable as a prior restraint on protected speech.

When Snepp accepted employment with the CIA, he voluntarily signed the agreement that expressly obligated him to submit any proposed publication for prior review. He does not claim that he executed this agreement under duress. Indeed, he voluntarily reaffirmed his obligation when he left the Agency. [Snepp's] agreement is an "entirely appropriate" exercise of the CIA Director's statutory mandate to "protec[t] intelligence sources and methods from unauthorized disclosure," 50 U.S.C. §403(d)(3). Moreover, this Court's cases make clear that — even in the absence of an express agreement — the CIA could have acted to protect substantial government interests by imposing reasonable restrictions on employee activities that in other contexts might be protected by the First Amendment. [Letter Carriers; see Brown v. Glines; Buckley v. Valeo; Greer v. Spock.] The Government has a concluded that the record did not support imposition of a constructive trust. [It] therefore limited recovery to nominal damages and to the possibility of punitive damages if the Government — in a jury trial — could prove tortious conduct.

[We hold] that Snepp breached a fiduciary obligation and that the proceeds of his breach are impressed with a constructive trust.

Snepp's employment with the CIA involved an extremely high degree of trust. . . .

[Whether] Snepp violated his trust does not depend upon whether his book actually contained classified information. The Government does [not] contend — at this stage of the litigation — that Snepp's book contains classified material. The Government simply claims that, in light of the special trust reposed in him and the agreement that he signed, Snepp should have given the CIA an opportunity to determine whether the material he proposed to publish would compromise classified information or sources. . . .

[A] former intelligence agent's publication of unreviewed material relating to intelligence activities can be detrimental to vital national interests even if the published information is unclassified. When a former agent relies on his own judgment about what information is detrimental, he may reveal information that the CIA — with its broader understanding of what may expose classified information and confidential sources — could have identified as harmful. . . . Admiral Turner, Director of the CIA, testified without contradiction that Snepp's book and others like it have seriously impaired the effectiveness of American intelligence operations. "Over the last six to nine months," he said,

> we have had a number of sources discontinue work with us. We have had more sources tell us that they are very nervous about continuing work with us. We have had very strong complaints from a number of foreign intelligence services with whom we conduct liaison, who have questioned whether they should continue exchanging information with us for fear it will not remain secret. I cannot estimate to you how many potential sources or liaison arrangements have never germinated because people were unwilling to enter into business with us.[8]

In view of this and other evidence in the record, both the District Court and the Court of Appeals recognized that Snepp's breach of his explicit obligation to

---

compelling interest in protecting both the secrecy of information important to our national security and the appearance of confidentiality so essential to the effective operation of our foreign intelligence service. The agreement that Snepp signed is a reasonable means for protecting this vital interest.

8. [Mr.] Justice Stevens' dissenting opinion [reflects] a misapprehension of the concern reflected by Admiral Turner's testimony. If in fact information is unclassified or in the public domain, neither the CIA nor foreign agencies would be concerned. The problem is to ensure *in advance*, and by proper procedures, that information detrimental to national interest is not published. Without a dependable prepublication review procedure, no intelligence agency or responsible Government official could be assured that an employee privy to sensitive information might not conclude on his own — innocently or otherwise — that it should be disclosed to the world.

The dissent argues that the Court is allowing the CIA to "censor" its employees' publications. Snepp's contract, however, requires no more than a clearance procedure subject to judicial review. If Snepp, in compliance with his contract, had submitted his manuscript for review and the Agency had found it to contain sensitive material, [an] effort would have been made to eliminate harmful disclosures. Absent agreement in this respect, the Agency would have borne the burden of seeking an injunction against publication. . . .

submit his material — classified or not — for prepublication clearance has irrep-arably harmed the United States Government. . . .

The decision of the Court of Appeals [may] well leave the Government with no reliable deterrent against similar breaches of security. [The] actual damages attributable to a publication such as Snepp's generally are unquantifiable. Nominal damages are a hollow alternative, certain to deter no one. The punitive damages recoverable after a jury trial are speculative and unusual. [Moreover, proof] of the tortious conduct necessary to sustain an award of punitive damages might force the Government to disclose some of the very confidences that Snepp promised to protect. . . .

A constructive trust, on the other hand, protects both the Government and the former agent from unwarranted risks. [If] the agent [breaches] his fiduciary and contractual obligation, the trust remedy simply requires him to disgorge the benefits of his faithlessness. Since the remedy is swift and sure, it is tailored to deter those who would place sensitive information at risk. And since the remedy reaches only funds attributable to the breach, it cannot saddle the former agent with exemplary damages out of all proportion to his gain. [We] therefore reverse the judgment of the Court of Appeals insofar as it refused to impose a constructive trust on Snepp's profits. . . .

MR. JUSTICE STEVENS, with whom MR. JUSTICE BRENNAN and MR. JUSTICE MAR-SHALL join, dissenting. . . .

[Even] assuming that Snepp's covenant to submit to prepublication review should be enforced, the constructive trust imposed by the Court is not an appropriate remedy. If an employee has used his employer's confidential information for his own personal profit, a constructive trust over those profits is obviously an appropriate remedy because the profits are the direct result of the breach. But Snepp admittedly did not use confidential information in his book; nor were the profits from his book in any sense a product of his failure to submit the book for prepublication review. For, even if Snepp had submitted the book to the Agency for prepublication review, the Government's censorship authority would surely have been limited to the excision of classified material. In this case, then, it would have been obliged to clear the book for publication in precisely the same form as it now stands. Thus, Snepp has not gained any profits as a result of his breach; the Government, rather than Snepp, will be unjustly enriched if he is required to disgorge profits attributable entirely to his own legitimate activity.

Despite the fact that Snepp has not caused the Government the type of harm that would ordinarily be remedied by the imposition of a constructive trust, the Court attempts to justify a constructive trust remedy on the ground that the Government has suffered *some* harm. The Court states that publication of "unreviewed material" by a former CIA agent "can be detrimental to vital national interests even if the published information is unclassified." It then seems to suggest that the injury in such cases stems from the Agency's inability to catch "harmful" but unclassified information before it is published. I do not believe, however, that the Agency has any authority to censor its employees' publication of unclassified information on the basis of its opinion that publication may be "detrimental to vital national interests" or otherwise "identified as harmful." [Even] if such a wide-ranging prior restraint would be good national security policy, I would have great difficulty reconciling it with the demands of the First Amendment.

The Court also relies to some extent [on] testimony by the Director of the CIA, Admiral Stansfield Turner, stating that Snepp's book and others like it had jeopardized the CIA's relationship with foreign intelligence services by making them unsure of the Agency's ability to maintain confidentiality. Admiral Turner's truncated testimony does not explain, however, whether these unidentified "other" books actually contained classified information. If so, it is difficult to believe that the publication of a book like Snepp's, which does not reveal classified information, has significantly weakened the Agency's position. Nor does it explain whether the unidentified foreign agencies who have stopped cooperating with the CIA have done so because of a legitimate fear that secrets will be revealed or because they merely disagree with our Government's classification policies. . . .

[The] Court seems unaware of the fact that its drastic new remedy has been fashioned to enforce a species of prior restraint on a citizen's right to criticize his government. Inherent in this prior restraint is the risk that the reviewing agency will misuse its authority to delay the publication of a critical work or to persuade an author to modify the contents of his work beyond the demands of secrecy. The character of the covenant as a prior restraint on free speech surely imposes an especially heavy burden on the censor to justify the remedy it seeks. It would take more than the Court has written to persuade me that that burden has been met.

I respectfully dissent.

Note: Snepp, *Public Employment, and the Disclosure of Confidential Information*

1. *Public employees and confidential information.* Why should the first amendment accord greater protection to the press when it seeks to publish confidential information than to a public employee who seeks to disclose such information? Is the Court's observation in *Pickering* that "the State has interests as an employer in regulating the speech of its employees that differ significantly from those it possesses in connection with regulation of the speech of the citizenry in general" relevant to the disclosure of confidential information? Are there other reasons in this context to grant the state greater control over its employees than over "the citizenry in general"? Consider the following arguments:

a. The public employee gains access to confidential government information only by virtue of his employment. Thus, for government to prohibit an employee's disclosure of such information does not limit any first amendment right the employee would have but for such employment. See Medow, The First Amendment and the Secrecy State: *Snepp v. United States*, 130 U. Pa. L. Rev. 775, 883-884 (1982).

b. Easterbrook, Insider Trading, Secret Agents, Evidentiary Privileges, and the Production of Information, 1981 Sup. Ct. Rev. 309, 345-347:

> Snepp [struck] a bargain. He learned of the CIA's activities by agreeing to limit his speech about them. [So] long as he enters into the agreement without fraud or coercion, he has made a judgment that he is better off with the agreement (and all its restraints) than without; he can hardly complain that his rights have been reduced.

[Constitutional] rights are waived every day. [One] aspect of the value of a right [is] that it can be sold and both parties to the bargain made better off.

c. A. Bickel, The Morality of Consent 79-80 (1975):

The government is entitled to keep things private and will attain as much privacy as it can get away with politically by guarding its privacy internally. [The] power to arrange security at the source, looked at in itself, is great, and if it were nowhere countervailed it would be quite frightening. [But] there *is* countervailing power. The press [can] be prevented from publishing only in extreme and quite dire circumstances. [It] is a disorderly [but practical compromise].

2. *Classified information.* Executive Order No. 12065, 3 C.F.R. 190 (1979), which was in effect when Snepp published his book, required the CIA to classify all information whose disclosure could reasonably be expected to cause "identifiable damage to the national security." May the CIA prohibit its present or former employees from disclosing such "classified" information? Consider the following objections.

a. The classification standard embodied in Executive Order 12065 is "unacceptable as a constitutional standard" because "it completely ignores the elements of likelihood and imminence." Nimmer, National Security Secrets v. Free Speech: The Issues Left Undecided in the *Ellsberg* Case, 26 Stan. L. Rev. 311, 332 (1974).

b. Comment, *Snepp v. United States:* The CIA Secrecy Agreement and the First Amendment, 81 Colum. L. Rev. 662, 690-691 (1981):

Use of "classification" as a suppression standard may be overly restrictive, [for] the classification of a document is hardly conclusive of its threat to national security. [Under the] executive order, authority to classify documents has been delegated to thousands of agency officials [who] exercise substantial discretion in determining how to apply the classification criterion. When there is any doubt about the classifiability of an item, the CIA's interests dictate erring on the side of overclassification. In addition, the CIA is authorized to classify much material that does not, in itself, merit classification status. [For example,] every page of a bound document must be stamped with the classification level of the most sensitive information in the document.

Should government be permitted to restrict the disclosure of classified information only if it is *properly* classified? What problems might arise in administering such a standard? See Alfred A. Knopf, Inc. v. Colby, 509 F.2d 1362 (4th Cir. 1975); United States v. Marchetti, 466 F.2d 1309 (4th Cir. 1972); see also Note, National Security and the Amended Freedom of Information Act, 85 Yale L.J. 401 (1976).

3. *The "value" of disclosure.* In deciding whether government may constitutionally prohibit the disclosure of particular "confidential" information, should courts consider, not only the potential danger, but also the potential value of the disclosure? For example, may an employee disclose "classified" information if it reveals a "substantial abuse of power"? Comment, First Amendment Standards for Subsequent Punishment of Dissemination of Confidential Government Information, 68 Calif. L. Rev. 83, 92-93 (1980).

4. *Confidential information unrelated to the national security*. The problem of confidential government information is not limited to the protection of national security; it implicates a potentially broad range of government interests. For example, in what circumstances may a state, as suggested in *Nebraska Press*, forbid police officers, court officials, and other government officers to disclose confessions, prior crimes, or other "implicative" information about a criminal defendant whose trial is pending? In what circumstances may a state forbid its employees to disclose "confidential" information contained in tax returns? In medical records?

5. *Prior restraint*. Is "some form of prepublication review [warranted because] the government cannot restrain, in advance of publication, material of which it does not have notice prior to communication"? Comment, *Snepp v. United States*: The CIA Secrecy Agreement and the First Amendment, 81 Colum. L. Rev. 662, 695 (1981). Is the case for prepublication review especially strong where, as in *Snepp*, the agency must ultimately bear "the burden of seeking an injunction against publication"? Are there legitimate objections to prepublication review? Consider Comment, Enforcing the CIA's Secrecy Agreement through Postpublication Civil Action: *United States v. Snepp*, 32 Stan. L. Rev. 409, 416 (1980): "The mere threat of censorship may be enough to 'chill' some speech; or the knowledge that CIA censors will be reviewing the proposed publication may be enough to soften criticism of the Agency. Moreover, prior review poses the possibility of long delays in publication." Recall also the objections to prior restraint examined in section C2 supra.

4. Compelled Affirmation, Expression, and Association: The Right Not to Speak

WEST VIRGINIA STATE BOARD OF EDUCATION v. BARNETTE, 319 U.S. 624 (1943): The first amendment right *not* to speak first received articulation in *Barnette*, in which the Court overruled its prior decision in Minersville School District v. Gobitis, 310 U.S. 586 (1940), and held unconstitutional a state law requiring all children in the public schools to salute and pledge allegiance to the flag of the United States. Justice Jackson, speaking for the Court, explained:

"[The] compulsory flag salute and pledge requires affirmation of a belief and an attitude of mind. [It] is now a commonplace that censorship or suppression of expression of opinion is tolerated by our Constitution only when the expression presents a clear and present danger of action of a kind the State is empowered to prevent and punish. It would seem that involuntary affirmation could be commanded only on even more immediate and urgent grounds. [But] here the power of compulsion is invoked without any allegation that remaining passive during a flag salute ritual creates a clear and present danger. [To] sustain the compulsory flag salute we are required to say that a Bill of Rights which guards the individual's right to speak his own mind, left it open to public authorities to compel him to utter what is not in his mind. [But if] there is any fixed star in our constitutional constellation, it is that no official, high or petty, can prescribe what shall be orthodox in politics, nationalism, religion, or other matters of opinion or force citizens to confess by word or act their faith therein. If there are any circumstances which permit an exception, they do not now occur to us."

Justice Frankfurter dissented.

WOOLEY v. MAYNARD, 430 U.S. 705 (1977): In *Wooley* the Court, speaking through Chief Justice Burger, held that New Hampshire could not criminally punish individuals who covered up the state motto "Live Free or Die" on their passenger vehicle license plates because the motto was repugnant to their moral, political, and religious beliefs:

"[The] right of freedom of thought protected by the First Amendment [includes] both the right to speak freely and the right to refrain from speaking at all. See [*Barnette*]. [These] are complementary components of the broader concept of 'individual freedom of mind.' [Here,] as in *Barnette*, we are faced with a state measure which forces an individual, as part of his daily life [to] be an instrument for fostering public adherence to an ideological point of view he finds unacceptable. [Thus, we must] determine whether the State's countervailing interest is sufficiently compelling to justify requiring appellees to display the state motto on their license plates. The two interests advanced by the State are that display of the motto (1) facilitates the identification of passenger [as distinct from other] vehicles, and (2) promotes appreciation of history, individualism, and state pride. [The first argument is insufficient] 'in the light of less drastic means for achieving the same basic purpose.' [The] State's second claimed interest is not ideologically neutral. [The State's interest in disseminating an ideology] cannot outweigh an individual's First Amendment right to avoid becoming the courier for such message."

Justice Rehnquist, joined by Justice Blackmun, dissented: "For First Amendment principles to be implicated, the State must place the citizen in the position of either apparently or actually 'asserting as true' the message. This was the focus of *Barnette*, and clearly distinguishes this case from that one. [Here, the appellees'] 'membership in a class of persons required to display plates bearing the State motto carries no implication and is subject to no requirement that they endorse that motto or profess to adopt it as a matter of belief.' [Indeed,] there is nothing in state law which precludes appellees from displaying their disagreement with the state motto as long as the methods used do not obscure the license plates. Thus appellees could place on their bumper a conspicuous bumper sticker explaining in no uncertain terms that [they] disagree with the connotations of [the] motto. Since any implication that they affirm the motto can be so easily displaced, I cannot agree that the statute may be invalidated under the fiction that appellees are unconstitutionally forced to affirm, or profess belief in, the state motto."

Justice White dissented on other grounds.

PRUNEYARD SHOPPING CENTER v. ROBINS, 447 U.S. 74 (1980): The PruneYard is a privately owned shopping center containing more than seventy-five shops and restaurants. It prohibits any visitors or tenants from engaging in any publicly expressive activity, including the circulation of petitions, that is not directly related to its commercial purposes. Several high school students seeking support for their opposition to a United Nations resolution against Zionism set up a card table in PruneYard's central courtyard. They distributed leaflets and asked passersby to sign petitions. They were asked to leave and thereafter filed suit to enjoin PruneYard from denying them access to the premises for the purpose of circulating their petitions. The California Supreme Court held that the California Constitution protects "speech and petitioning, reasonably exercised, in shopping centers even when the centers are privately owned." Appellants, the owners of PruneYard, maintained that "a private property owner has a

First Amendment right not to be forced by the State to use his property as a forum for the speech of others." The Court, in an opinion by Justice Rehnquist, rejected appellants' claim:

"[In *Wooley*,] the government itself prescribed the message, required it to be displayed openly on appellee's personal property that was used 'as part of his daily life,' and refused to permit him to take any measures to cover up the motto even though the Court found that the display of the motto served no important state interest. Here, by contrast, there are a number of distinguishing factors. Most important, the shopping center [is] a business establishment that is open to the public. [The] views expressed by members of the public in passing out pamphlets or seeking signatures for a petition thus will not likely be identified with those of the owner. Second, no specific message is dictated by the State. [There] consequently is no danger of governmental discrimination for or against a particular message. Finally, [appellants] can expressly disavow any connection with the message by simply posting signs [disclaiming] any sponsorship of the message and [explaining] that the persons are communicating their own messages by virtue of state law. Appellants also argue that their First Amendment rights have been infringed in light of [*Barnette*]. *Barnette* is inapposite because it involved the compelled recitation of a message containing an affirmation of belief. [Appellants here are not] compelled to affirm their belief in any governmentally prescribed position or view, and they are free to publicly dissociate themselves from the views of the speakers or handbillers."

Justice Powell, joined by Justice White, concurred in the result.

ELROD v. BURNS, 427 U.S. 347 (1976), and BRANTI v. FINKEL, 445 U.S. 507 (1980): In *Elrod* and *Branti*, supra section F3c, the Court considered compelled association rather than compelled speech. Are *Elrod* and *Branti* consistent with *PruneYard*? In what sense, if any, did the compelled association in *Elrod* and *Branti* more seriously infringe first amendment values than the compelled "support" of the speech of others in *PruneYard*?

ABOOD v. DETROIT BOARD OF EDUCATION, 431 U.S. 209 (1977): In *Abood* the Court considered another aspect of the right not to associate. *Abood* involved a Michigan statute authorizing union representation of local government employees. The statute permitted "agency shop" arrangements, whereby every government employee represented by a union, even though not a member of the union, was required as a condition of employment to pay the union a service charge equal in amount to union dues. Appellant teachers filed actions against the Detroit Board of Education and the teacher's union on the ground that the agency shop clause in the collective bargaining agreement between the board and the union violated their rights under the first amendment. Specifically, appellants alleged that they were unwilling to pay union dues or the required service charge (1) because they opposed collective bargaining in the public sector and (2) because the union engaged in various political and other ideological activities that appellants did not approve and that were not directly related to the collective bargaining process. The Court rejected the constitutional challenge on the first ground, but sustained it on the second. At the outset, the Court, in an opinion by Justice Stewart, recognized that "to compel employees financially to support their collective-bargaining representative has an impact upon their First Amendment interests":

"An employee may very well have ideological objections to a wide variety of activities undertaken by the union in its role as exclusive representative. His moral or religious views about the desirability of abortion may not square with the union's policy in negotiating a medical benefits plan. One individual might disagree with a union policy of negotiating limits on the right to strike, believing that to be the road to serfdom for the working class, while another might have economic or political objections to unionism itself. [To] be required to help finance the union as a collective-bargaining agent might well be thought, therefore, to interfere in some way with an employee's freedom to associate for the advancement of ideas, or to refrain from doing so, as he sees fit."

Building on Railway Employees' Department v. Hanson, 351 U.S. 225 (1956), and International Association of Machinists v. Street, 367 U.S. 740 (1961), however, the Court concluded that "such interference [with first amendment rights] as exists [in this context] is constitutionally justified." The Court explained:

"The principle of exclusive union representation [is] a central element in the [modern] structuring of industrial relations. [It] avoids the confusion that would result from attempting to enforce two or more agreements specifying different terms and conditions of employment [and] prevents inter-union rivalries from creating dissension within the work force. [Moreover, the] designation of a union as exclusive representative carries with it great responsibilities [and obliges the union] 'fairly and equitably to represent all [employees], union and non-union,' within the relevant unit. A union-shop arrangement has been thought to distribute fairly the costs [among] those who benefit, and it counteracts the incentive that employees might otherwise have to become 'free riders' — to refuse to contribute to the union while obtaining benefits of union representation that necessarily accrue to all employees. [Thus,] insofar as the [challenged] service charge is used to finance expenditures by the Union for the purposes of collective bargaining, contract administration, and grievance adjustment, [the agency shop agreement is not unconstitutional]."

The Court turned next to appellants' argument that the agency shop arrangement unconstitutionally prevented them "from refusing to associate [insofar as the union spends] a part of their required service fees to contribute to political candidates and to express political views unrelated to its duties as exclusive bargaining representative." The Court found this argument "meritorious": "[In *Elrod* we held that the First Amendment prohibits] a State from compelling an individual [to] associate with a political party as a condition of retaining public employment. [This reasoning is] no less applicable to the case at bar, and [thus prohibits] the appellees from requiring any of the appellants to contribute to the support of an ideological cause he may oppose as a condition of holding a job as a public school teacher. We do not hold that a union cannot constitutionally spend funds for the expression of political views, on behalf of political candidates, or toward the advancement of other ideological causes not germane to its duties as collective-bargaining representative. Rather, the constitution requires only that such expenditures be financed from charges, dues, or assessments paid by employees who do not object to advancing those ideas and who are not coerced into doing so against their will by the threat of loss of governmental employment."

Finally, the Court noted that, because the case was still in the pleading stage, it was unnecessary to rule definitively on a remedy. Nonetheless, the Court rejected a suggestion that, to protect the right of dissenters not to support or associate with an organization that espouses views with which they disagree, unions should be required to choose between agency shop arrangements and political expression. The Court explained that "those union members who do wish part of their dues to be used for political purposes have a right to associate to that end without being 'silenced by the dissenters.' " It thus suggested that a more appropriate and more "practical" remedy might provide "for (1) the refund [to dissenters] of a portion of the exacted funds in the proportion that union political expenditures bear to total union expenditures, and (2) the reduction of future exactions by the same proportion."

Justice Powell, joined by Chief Justice Burger and Justice Blackmun, concurred in the judgment.

Consider Cantor, Forced Payments to Service Institutions and Constitutional Interests in Ideological Non-Association, 36 Rutgers L. Rev. 3, 26, 16 (1984):

> Americans often have money extracted from them and used to promote objects which they ideologically oppose. The most obvious example is the taxpayer. Despite moral objections, pacifists' taxes are used to support war efforts, anarchists' funds help support government, and "right to life" advocates' monies are used to further birth control and abortions. [The] explanation is not that freedom of conscience [is] unimportant, [but] that pure peace of mind cannot be accorded high constitutional status in an organized society. [Any other result would cause insurmountable] administrative tangles, [for the] range of conscientious sensibilities is limitless. [The essence of *Barnette* and the other pre-*Abood* decisions is that there is unconstitutionally compelled expression only when the] individual is forced to associate publicly or identify with views in a manner in which observers might perceive some personal endorsement of the views. [That was not the case in *Abood*.]

If taxpayers have no constitutional objection to government use of their tax payments for purposes to which they are ideologically opposed, is there any basis for giving greater protection to the employees in *Abood?* Consider Justice Powell's argument in his concurring opinion in *Abood:* "[The] reason for permitting the Government to compel the payment of taxes and to spend money on controversial projects is that the Government is representative of the people. The same cannot be said of a union, which is representative of only one segment of the population, with certain common interests." See also Ellis v. Brotherhood of Railway, Airline & Steamship Clerks, 466 U.S. 85 (1984) (compelled contributions may constitutionally be used to pay for union conventions, social activities, and publications).

Note: The Right Not *to Speak — Variations*

1. *The right not to publish or broadcast.* In what circumstances, if any, may government constitutionally compel a broadcaster or publisher to broadcast or publish material? See Columbia Broadcasting System v. FCC, 453 U.S. 367 (1981)

(upholding an FCC rule requiring broadcasters "to allow reasonable access [by] a legally qualified candidate for Federal elective office on behalf of his candidacy"); Miami Herald Publishing Co. v. Tornillo, 418 U.S. 241 (1974) (invalidating a "right of reply" statute requiring any newspaper that "assails" the character of a political candidate to print the candidate's reply); Red Lion Broadcasting Co. v. FCC, 395 U.S. 367 (1969) (upholding the FCC's "fairness doctrine"). See section F6 infra.

2. *The right not to speak in the commercial context.* In Zauderer v. Office of Disciplinary Counsel, — U.S. — ,105 S. Ct. 2265 (1985), the Court held that a state may require a commercial advertiser to include in his advertising "factual and uncontroversial information about the terms under which his services will be available" as long as the disclosure requirements are "reasonably related to the State's interest in preventing deception of consumers." In *Zauderer* an attorney advertised that, in a certain type of case, "if there is no recovery, no legal fees are owed by our clients." The Court upheld a disciplinary rule requiring the attorney to disclose in the advertisement that clients would have to pay "costs" even if their suits were unsuccessful. The Court explained that here, unlike *Barnette* and *Wooley*, the state was not attempting to "prescribe what shall be orthodox in politics, nationalism, religion, or other matters of opinion," but was attempting to "prescribe only what shall be orthodox in commercial advertising." The Court added that because "the extension of First Amendment protection to commercial speech is justified principally by the value to consumers of the information such speech provides, [the advertister's] constitutionally protected interest in *not* providing any particular factual information in his advertising is minimal."

3. *State efforts to protect the "right not to speak" from private infringement*: Bellotti. In First National Bank of Boston v. Bellotti, 435 U.S. 765 (1978), the Court held unconstitutional a Massachusetts statute prohibiting any corporation to make contributions or expenditures "for the purpose [of] influencing or affecting the vote on any question submitted to the voters, other than one materially affecting any of the property, business or assets of the corporation." The Court rejected the argument that the restriction was justified because it "protects corporate shareholders [by] preventing the use of corporate resources in furtherance of views with which some shareholders may disagree." The Court explained:

> [*Abood* is] irrelevant to the question presented in this case. In [*Abood*] employees were required to pay dues or a "service fee" to the exclusive bargaining representative. [The] critical distinction here is that no shareholder has been "compelled" to contribute anything. [The] shareholder invests in a corporation of his own volition and is free to withdraw his investment at any time and for any reason. [Finally,] it is by no means an automatic step from the remedy in *Abood*, which honored the interests of the minority without infringing the majority's rights, to [a statute that] would completely silence the majority because [a] minority might object.

Justice White, joined by Justices Brennan and Marshall, dissented:

> [It] is no answer [that] the dissenting "shareholder is free to withdraw his investment at any time and for any reason." The employees [in] *Abood* were also free to seek other jobs where they would not be compelled to finance causes with which they disagreed, but we held in *Abood* that First Amendment rights could not be so

burdened. Clearly the State has a strong interest in assuring that its citizens are not forced to choose between supporting the propagation of views with which they disagree and passing up investment opportunities.

Justice Rehnquist dissented on other grounds.

Consider Brudney, Business Corporations and Stockholders' Rights under the First Amendment, 91 Yale L.J. 235 (1981):

> Under venerable doctrine, expenditure of corporate funds that constitutes waste cannot be made lawfully without the consent of all the stockholders. [The] fact that the wasteful behavior takes the forms of political speech not reasonably related to the corporation's business does not make management's usurpation of corporate funds for that purpose any less wasteful. [Although] the First Amendent protects the [corporation] president's right to express himself, it does not [give him the right] to do so with other people's money. [The crucial question, then, concerns] the state's power to decide *who*, within the corporation, may authorize *it* to [speak].

Other aspects of *Bellotti* are examined at supra section E4.

4. *The right not to listen:* Pollak. If there is a right not to speak, is there also a right not to listen? In Public Utilities Commission v. Pollak, 343 U.S. 451 (1952), the Court held that a publicly regulated street railway that broadcast radio programs in its streetcars did not violate a first amendment right of the passengers "to listen only to such points of view as [they wished] to hear," at least where there was "no substantial claim that the programs [had] been used for objectionable propaganda."

Justice Douglas dissented:

> The First Amendment in its respect for the conscience of the individual honors the sanctity of thought and belief. [The] present case involves a form of coercion to make people listen. [The] streetcar audience is a captive audience. It is there as a matter of necessity, not of choice. [The] man on the streetcar has no choice but to sit and listen, or perhaps to sit and to try *not* to listen. When we force people to listen to another's ideas, we give the propagandist a powerful weapon. [Once] a man is forced to submit to one type of radio program, he can be forced to submit to another. It may be but a short step from a cultural program to a political program. If liberty is to flourish, government should never be allowed to force people to listen to any radio program.

See also Lehman v. City of Shaker Heights, supra section F1 (Douglas, J., concurring).

5.   Compelled Disclosure of Expression, Belief, and Association

For a variety of reasons, government may seek information about an organization's members or about an individual's expression, beliefs, or associations. Although the mere disclosure of such information may not itself "penalize" or otherwise directly limit first amendment freedoms, it may indirectly "chill" the exercise of such freedoms.

a.   General Principles

NAACP v. Alabama
357 U.S. 449 (1958)

MR. JUSTICE HARLAN delivered the opinion of the Court. . . .

Alabama has a statute similar to those of many other States which requires a foreign corporation, except as exempted, to qualify before doing business. [The National Association for the Advancement of Colored People] has never complied with the qualification statute, from which it considered itself exempt.

In 1956 the Attorney General of Alabama brought an equity suit in the State Circuit Court [to] enjoin the Association from conducting further activities within, and to oust it from, the State. [The] State moved for the production of a large number of the Association's records and papers, including bank statements, leases, deeds, and records containing the names and addresses of all Alabama "members" and "agents" of the Association. It alleged that all such documents were necessary [in] view of petitioner's denial of the conduct of intrastate business within the meaning of the qualification statute. Over petitioner's objections, the court ordered the production of a substantial part of the requested records, including the membership lists. . . .

Thereafter petitioner [produced] substantially all the data called for by the production order except its membership lists, as to which it contended that Alabama could not constitutionally compel disclosure. [The Circuit Court then adjudged petitioner in contempt and imposed a fine of $100,000.] . . .

It is beyond debate that freedom to engage in association for the advancement of beliefs and ideas is an inseparable aspect of the "liberty" assured by the Due Process Clause of the Fourteenth Amendment, which embraces freedom of speech. . . .

The fact that Alabama, so far as is relevant to the validity of the contempt judgment presently under review, has taken no direct action [to] restrict the right of petitioner's members to associate freely, does not end inquiry into the effect of the production order. In the domain of these indispensable liberties, whether of speech, press, or association, the decisions of this Court recognize that abridgment of such rights, even though unintended, may inevitably follow from varied forms of governmental action. . . .

It is hardly a novel perception that compelled disclosure of affiliation with groups engaged in advocacy may constitute [an effective] restraint on freedom of association. [There is a] vital relationship between freedom to associate and privacy in one's associations. [Inviolability] of privacy in group association may in many circumstances be indispensable to preservation of freedom of association, particularly where a group espouses dissident beliefs. . . .

We think that the production order, in the respects here drawn in question, must be regarded as entailing the likelihood of a substantial restraint upon the exercise by petitioner's members of their right to freedom of association. Petitioner has made an uncontroverted showing that on past occasions revelation of the identity of its rank-and-file members has exposed these members to economic reprisal, loss of employment, threat of physical coercion, and other manifestations of public hostility. Under these circumstances, we think it apparent that compelled disclosure of petitioner's Alabama membership is likely to affect adversely the ability of petitioner and its members to pursue their collective effort to foster beliefs which they admittedly have the right to advocate, in that it may induce members to withdraw from the Association and dissuade others from joining it because of fear of exposure of their beliefs shown through their associations and of the consequences of this exposure.

It is not sufficient to answer, as the State does here, that whatever repressive effect compulsory disclosure of names of petitioner's members may have upon participation by Alabama citizens in petitioner's activities follows not from *state* action but from *private* community pressures. The crucial factor is the interplay of governmental and private action, for it is only after the initial exertion of state power represented by the production order that private action takes hold.

We turn to the final question whether Alabama has demonstrated an interest in obtaining the disclosures it seeks from petitioner which is sufficient to justify the deterrent effect which we have concluded these disclosures may well have on the free exercise by petitioner's members of their constitutionally protected right of association. [Such] a " . . . subordinating interest of the State must be compelling." . . .

Whether there was "justification" in this instance turns solely on the substantiality of Alabama's interest in obtaining the membership lists. [The] exclusive purpose was to determine whether petitioner was conducting intrastate business in violation of the Alabama foreign corporation registration statute. . . . [We] are unable to perceive that the disclosure of the names of petitioner's rank-and-file members has a substantial bearing on [the issues in the underlying litigation]. As matters stand in the state court, petitioner (1) has admitted its presence and conduct of activities in Alabama since 1918; (2) has offered to comply in all respects with the state qualification statute, although preserving its contention that the statute does not apply to it; and (3) has apparently complied satisfactorily with the production order, except for the membership lists. [Whatever] interest the State may have in obtaining names of ordinary members has not been shown to be sufficient to overcome petitioner's constitutional objections to the production order. [Accordingly], the judgment of civil contempt and the $100,000 fine [must] fall . . . .

Reversed.

TALLEY v. CALIFORNIA, 362 U.S. 60 (1960): Talley, a distributor of handbills protesting employment discrimination, was prosecuted for violating a Los Angeles ordinance prohibiting any person to distribute "any hand-bill [which] does not have printed on [the] face thereof, the name and address of [the] person who printed, wrote, compiled, or manufactured [it]." The Court held the ordinance invalid:

"[It is] urged that this ordinance is aimed at providing a way to identify those responsible for fraud, false advertising and libel. [But] such an identification requirement would tend to restrict freedom to distribute information and thereby freedom of expression. [Anonymous] pamphlets, leaflets, brochures and even books have played an important role in the progress of mankind. Persecuted groups [throughout] history have been able to criticize oppressive practices [either] anonymously or not at all. [Anonymity] has sometimes been assumed for the most constructive purposes. [The] reason for the [decision in NAACP v. Alabama] was that identification and fear of reprisal might deter perfectly peaceful discussions of public matters of importance. This broad Los Angeles ordinance is subject to the same infirmity."

Justice Clark, joined by Justices Frankfurter and Whittaker, dissented: "[Unlike NAACP v. Alabama], there is neither allegation nor proof that Talley [would] suffer 'economic reprisal, loss of employment, threat of physical coercion [or] other manifestations of public hostility.' Talley makes no showing whatever to support his contention that a restraint upon his freedom of speech will result from the enforcement of the ordinance. The existence of such a restraint is necessary before we can strike the ordinance down.'"

BUCKLEY v. VALEO, 424 U.S. 1 (1976): The Federal Election Campaign Act of 1971 requires every political candidate and "political committee" to maintain records of the names and addresses of all persons who contribute more than $10 in a calendar year and to make such records available for inspection by the Commission. Moreover, the act provides that such reports are to be available "for public inspection and copying." The Court, in a per curiam opinion, upheld these provisions:

"The governmental interests sought to be vindicated by the disclosure requirements [fall] into three categories. First, disclosure provides the electorate with information 'as to where political campaign money comes [from]' in order to aid the voters in evaluating those who seek federal office. [Second,] disclosure requirements deter actual corruption and avoid the appearance of corruption by exposing [contributions] to the light of publicity. [Third, such] requirements are an essential means of gathering the data necessary to detect violations of the contribution limitations. [Thus, the] disclosure requirements [directly] serve substantial governmental interests. . . .

"Appellants contend that the Act's requirements are [nonetheless unconstitutional] insofar as they apply to contributions to minor parties [because] the governmental interest in this information is minimal and the dangers of significant infringement on First Amendment rights is greatly increased. [It is true that the] Government's interest in deterring the 'buying' of elections and the undue influence of large contributors on officeholders [may] be reduced where contributions to a minor party [are] concerned, for it is less likely that the candidate will be victorious. [Moreover, these] movements are less likely to have a sound financial base and thus are more vulnerable to falloffs in contributions. In some instances fears of reprisal may deter contributions to the point where the movement cannot survive. [Thus, there] could well be a case, similar to [NAACP v. Alabama,] where the threat to the exercise of First Amendment rights is so serious and the state interest furthered by disclosure so insubstantial that the Act's requirements cannot be constitutionally applied. But no appellant in this case has tendered record evidence of the sort proffered in NAACP v. Alabama.'"

Chief Justice Burger dissented.

In Brown v. Socialist Workers '74 Campaign Committee, 459 U.S. 87 (1982), the Court, building on NAACP v. Alabama and *Buckley*, held that the disclosure provisions of the Ohio campaign reporting law could not constitutionally be applied to the Socialist Workers Party, "a minor political party which historically has been the object of harassment by government officials and private parties."

Consider Stone & Marshall, *Brown v. Socialist Workers:* Inequality as a Command of the First Amendment, 1983 Sup. Ct. Rev. 583, 619:

> In *Buckley*, the Court, applying ordinary content-neutral balancing, held that campaign disclosure requirements are constitutional because they "directly serve substantial governmental interests." In *Brown*, the Court held that such disclosure requirements cannot constitutionally be applied to [the Socialist Workers Party]. What, though, is the appropriate remedy in *Brown?* Is it to leave the disclosure requirements intact for all organizations that do not quality for the constitutionally compelled exemption or is it to invalidate the requirements in their entirety? In *Buckley* and *Brown*, the Court, without explanation, endorsed the former approach. But suppose that, after *Brown*, the Republican Party challenges the disclosure requirements, modified by the constitutionally compelled exemption, as an unconstitutional content-based restriction. Are the requirements, as modified, constitutional?

b. Public Employees and Licensees

In what circumstances may government compel present or prospective public employees and licensees to disclose information about their advocacy, their beliefs, or their associations in order to assess their qualifications? May government compel the disclosure of only that information that would independently justify a finding of disqualification? May government compel the disclosure of any information that might reasonably lead to further inquiry?

SHELTON v. TUCKER, 364 U.S. 479 (1960): The Court, in a five-to-four decision, held unconstitutional an Arkansas statute that compelled "every teacher, as a condition of employment in a state-supported school or college, to file annually an affidavit listing without limitation every organization to which he has belonged or regularly contributed within the preceding five years." Justice Stewart delivered the opinion of the Court:

"[To] compel a teacher to disclose his every associational tie is to impair that teacher's right of free association. [The] statute does not provide that the information it requires be kept confidential. [Even] if there were no disclosure to the general public, the pressure upon a teacher to avoid any ties which might displease those who control his professional destiny would be constant and heavy. Public disclosure, bringing with it the possibility of public pressures upon school boards to discharge teachers who belong to unpopular or minority organizations, would simply operate to widen and aggravate the impairment of constitutional liberty. . . .

"The question to be decided here is not whether the State [can] ask certain of its teachers about all their organizational relationships. It is not whether the State can ask all of its teachers about certain of their associational ties. It is not whether teachers can be asked how many organizations they belong to, or how much time they spend in organizational activity. The question is whether the State can ask every one of its teachers to disclose every single organization with which he has been associated with over a five-year period. [Many] such relationships could have no possible bearing upon the teacher's occupational competence or fitness.

"[This] Court has held that, even though the governmental purpose be legitimate and substantial, that purpose cannot be pursued by means that broadly stifle fundamental personal liberties when the end can be more narrowly achieved. [For example, in *Talley*] we held invalid an ordinance prohibiting the distribution of handbills because the breadth of its application went far beyond what was necessary [to] identify those responsible for fraud, false advertising and libel. [Similarly, Act 10's] comprehensive interference with associational freedom goes far beyond what might be justified in the exercise of the State's legitimate inquiry into the fitness and competency of its teachers."

Justice Frankfurter, who was "authorized to say" that Justices Clark, Harlan, and Whittaker "agree with this opinion," dissented: "[The] Court strikes down [the Act] on the ground that 'Many [of a teacher's] relationships could have no possible bearing upon the teacher's occupational competence or fitness.' Granted that a given teacher's membership in the First Street Congregation is, standing alone, of little relevance to what may rightly be expected of a teacher, is that membership equally irrelevant when it is discovered that the teacher is in fact a member of the First Street Congregation *and* the Second Street Congregation *and* the Third Street Congregation *and* the 4-H Club *and* the 3-H Club *and* half a dozen other groups? Presumably, a teacher may have so many divers associations, so many divers commitments, that they consume his time and energy and interest at the expense of his work or even of his professional dedication. . . .

"Of course, the State might ask: 'To how many organizations do you belong?' or 'How much time do you expend at organizational activity?' But the answer to such questions could reasonably be regarded by a state legislature as insufficient, both because the veracity of the answer is more difficult to test [and] because an estimate of time presently spent in organizational activity reveals nothing as to the quality and nature of that activity. [A] teacher's answers to the questions which [the Act] asks, moreover, may serve the purpose of making known to school authorities persons who come into contact with the teacher in all of the phases of his activity in the community, and who can be questioned, if need be, concerning the teacher's conduct in matters which [may be pertinent] to professional fitness. . . .

"[The] careful and discriminating selection of teachers [is] an intricate affair, [and] if it is to be informed, it must be based upon a comprehensive range of information. I am unable to say [that] Arkansas could not reasonably find that the information which the statute requires [is] germane to that selection. [Of] course, if the information gathered [pursuant to this statute is] used to further a scheme of terminating the employment of teachers solely because of their membership in unpopular organizations, that use will run afoul of the Fourteenth Amendment. It will be time enough, if such use is made, to hold the application of the statute unconstitutional."

Justice Harlan, joined by Justices Frankfurter, Clark, and Whittaker, also dissented: "[This] statute is stricken down because, in the Court's view, it is too broad. [I] am unable to subscribe to this view because I believe it impossible to determine a priori the place where the line should be drawn between what would be permissible inquiry and overbroad inquiry in a situation like this. Certainly the Court does not point that place out."

Shelton, like NAACP v. Alabama, grew out of Southern efforts to restrict the NAACP by compelling disclosure of membership lists. Indeed, a companion

statute to Act 10, held unconstitutional by the District Court, prohibited employment of any member of the NAACP by the state or any of its subdivisions. Is it
relevant that, in *Shelton*, as in NAACP v. Alabama, the Court managed "to defeat
the Southern tactics without violating etiquette by inquiring into the precise
motivation for the statute"? H. Kalven, The Negro and the First Amendment 70
(1976).

KONIGSBERG v. STATE BAR, 366 U.S. 36 (1961): The Committee of
Bar Examiners of California rejected Konigsberg's application for admission to
the bar because he refused to answer questions concerning membership in the
Communist Party. The Committee explained that his refusal to answer obstructed a full investigation into his qualifications. The Court, in a five-to-four
decision, sustained the Committee's action. Justice Harlan delivered the opinion:
"We regard as untenable petitioner's contentions that the questions as to Communist Party membership were made irrelevant either by the fact that bare,
innocent membership is not a ground of disqualification or by petitioner's willingness to answer such ultimate questions as whether he himself believed in violent
overthrow or knowingly belonged to an organization advocating violent overthrow. '[If petitioner] had answered the question[s] that he refused to answer, an
entirely new area of investigation might [have] opened up, and [the] Committee
might [have discovered] that he does advocate the overthrow of government by
force and violence. [The Committee does not] have to take any witness' testimony
as [conclusive].' . . .
"As regards the questioning of [prospective lawyers about] Communist Party
membership, [we] regard the State's interest [in] having lawyers who are devoted
to the law in its broadest sense, including [its] procedures for orderly change, as
clearly sufficient to outweigh the minimal effect upon free association occasioned
by compulsory disclosure in the circumstances here presented. There is here no
likelihood that deterrence of association may result from foreseeable private
action, see [NAACP v. Alabama], for bar committee interrogations [are] conducted in private. [Nor] is there the possibility that the State may be afforded the
opportunity for imposing undetectable arbitrary consequences upon protected
association, see [Shelton v. Tucker], for a bar applicant's exclusion is subject to
judicial review, including ultimate review by this Court, should it appear that
such exclusion has rested [on] factors that do not comport with the Federal
Constitution. [In] these circumstances it is difficult indeed to perceive any solid
basis for a claim of unconstitutional intrusion into rights assured by the [Constitu-
tion]."
Justice Black, joined by Chief Justice Warren and Justice Douglas, dissented:
"The [majority says that the adverse effects of disclosure] will be 'minimal' [be-
cause] Bar interrogations are private [and] because the decisions of Bar admission
committees are subject to judicial review. As to the first ground, the Court simply
ignores the fact that California law does not require its Committee to treat information given it as confidential. And besides, it taxes credulity to suppose that
questions asked an applicant and answers given by him in the highly emotional
area of communism would not rapidly leak out to the great injury of an applicant.
[As] to the second ground given, the Court fails to take into account the fact that
judicial review widens the publicity of the questions and answers and thus tends
further to undercut its first ground. . . . But even if I thought the Court was

correct in its [views of the confidentiality of the interrogations and the utility of judicial review], I could not accept its conclusion that the First Amendment rights involved in this case are 'minimal.' The interest in free association at stake here is not merely the personal interest of petitioner in being free from burdens that may be imposed upon him for his past beliefs and associations. It is the interest of all the people in having a society in which no one is intimidated with respect to his beliefs or associations. [The] inevitable effect of the majority's decision is to condone a practice that will have a substantial deterrent effect upon the associations entered into by anyone who may want to become a lawyer in California. [The] only safe course for those desiring admission would seem to be scrupulously to avoid association with any organization that advocates anything at all somebody might possibly be against."

Justice Brennan dissented on other grounds.

See also In re Anastoplo, 366 U.S. 82 (1961), in which the Court reached a similar result. *Konigsberg* and *Anastoplo* preceded the Court's decisions in *Elfbrandt*, supra this section, and *Brandenburg*, supra section B1. What is the effect, if any, of those decisions?

Note: Baird, Stolar, *and* Wadmond

In three bar admission decisions handed down on the same day in 1971, the Court reexamined *Konigsberg* and *Anastoplo*:

1. Baird. In Baird v. State Bar, 401 U.S. 1 (1971), petitioner, an applicant for admission to the Arizona State Bar, answered most of the questions on her bar application, including Question 25, which called on her to list all organizations with which she had been associated since age sixteen. She refused, however, to answer Question 27: "Are you now or have you ever been a member of the Communist Party or any organization that advocates overthrow of the United States Government by force or violence?" Because of petitioner's refusal to answer this question, the Committee declined to process her application. The Committee explained that "a mere answer of 'yes' would not lead to an automatic rejection of the application, [but] would lead to an investigation [as] to whether or not the applicant presently entertains the view that a violent overthrow of [government] is something to be sought after. [If so,] we would reject the application."

The Court, in a five-to-four decision, held that the Committee's action violated the first amendment. There was, however, no majority opinion. Justice Black, joined by Justices Douglas, Brennan, and Marshall, maintained that "when a State seeks to inquire about an individual's beliefs and associations a heavy burden lies upon it to show that the inquiry is necessary to protect a legitimate state interest." Here, Black argued, by her answers to other questions, petitioner had supplied the Committee with sufficient personal information to enable it to determine her fitness to practice law, and she thus could not be compelled to answer Question 27.

Justice Stewart concurred in the judgment:

> The Court has held that under some circumstances simple inquiry into present or past Communist Party membership [is] not as such unconstitutional. [*Konigsberg*;

Anastoplo.] Question 27, however, goes further and asks applicants whether they have ever belonged to any organization "that advocates overthrow of the [government] by force or violence." Our decisions have been clear that such inquiry must be confined to knowing membership to satisfy the First and Fourteenth Amendments. [See *Robel; Wadmond.*]

Justice Blackmun, joined by Chief Justice Burger and Justices White and Rehnquist, dissented:

To say that because [petitioner] had answered Question 25 and had listed her organization memberships since age 16 she need not respond to Question 27 is no answer at all. [The] questions are not duplicative. [By] her refusal to answer Question 27, she would place on the [Committee] the burden of determining which of the organizations she listed, if any, was an arm of the Communist party or advocated forceful or violent overthrow of the Government. That, however, is not the task of the Committee. [It] is [the applicant's] task.

2. Stolar. In In re Stolar, 401 U.S. 23 (1971), petitioner was denied admission to the Ohio Bar because he refused to answer three questions on the Ohio Bar application. Question 12 instructed the applicant to state "whether you have been, or presently are [a] member of any organization which advocates the overthrow of [government] by force." Question 13 instructed the applicant to list "the names and addresses of all clubs, societies or organizations of which you are or have been a member." Question 7 instructed the applicant to list "the names and addresses of all clubs, societies or organizations of which you are or have been a member since registering as a law student."

As in *Baird* the Court invalidated the Committee's action without a majority opinion. Justice Black, joined by Justices Douglas, Brennan, and Marshall, maintained that Question 12 was unconstitutional under *Baird* and that Questions 7 and 13 were unconstitutional under *Shelton.*

Justice Stewart concurred in the judgment: "Ohio's Questions 7 and 13 are plainly unconstitutional under [*Shelton*]. In addition, Question [12] suffers from the same constitutional deficiency as does Arizona's Question 27 in [*Baird*]."

Chief Justice Burger and Justices Harlan, White, and Blackmun dissented.

3. Wadmond. Law Students Civil Rights Research Council v. Wadmond, 401 U.S. 154 (1971), was a class action challenging Question 26 on the New York Bar application:

(a) Have you ever organized [or] become a member of any organization [which] during the period of your membership [you] knew was advocating or teaching that the [government] should be overthrown [by] force, violence or any unlawful means? If your answer is in the affirmative, state the facts below. (b) If your answer to (a) is in the affirmative, did you, during the period of such membership [have] the specific intent to further the aims of such organizations [to] overthrow the [government] by force, violence or any unlawful means?

The Court, in a five-to-four decision, upheld Question 26. Justice Stewart delivered the opinion of the Court:

Question 26 is precisely tailored to conform to the relevant decisions of this Court. Our cases establish that inquiry into associations of the kind referred to is permissible under the limitations carefully observed here. We have held that knowing membership in an organization advocating the overthrow of the Government by force or violence, by one sharing the specific intent to further the organization's illegal goals, may be made criminally punishable. [*Scales.*] It is also well settled that Bar examiners may ask about Communist affiliations as a preliminary to further inquiry into the nature of the association and may exclude an applicant for refusal to answer. [*Konigsberg.*] Surely a State is constitutionally entitled to make such an inquiry of an applicant for admission to a profession dedicated to the peaceful and reasoned settlement of disputes.

Stewart added in a footnote:

Division of Question 26 into two parts is wholly permissible under [*Konigsberg*], which approved asking whether an applicant had ever been a member of the Communist Party without asking in the same question whether the applicant shared its illegal goals. Moreover, this division narrows the class of applicants as to whom the Committees are likely to find further investigation appropriate. For those who answer part (a) in the negative, that is the end of the matter.

Justice Black, joined by Justice Douglas, dissented:

I do not think that a State can, consistently with the First Amendment, exclude an applicant because he has belonged to organizations that advocate violent overthrow of the Government, even if his membership was "knowing" and he shared the organization's aims. [It] therefore follows for me that governments should not be able to ask questions designed to identify persons who have belonged to certain political organizations.

Justice Marshall, joined by Justice Brennan, also dissented:

Question 26(a) [is] an indiscriminate and highly intrusive device designed to expose an applicant's political affiliations to the scrutiny of screening authorities. [Three] particular difficulties may be mentioned. First, Question 26(a) is undeniably overbroad in that it covers the affiliations of those who do not adhere to teachings concerning unlawful political change, or are simply indifferent to this aspect of an association's activities. [*Elfbrandt.*] Second, no attempt has been made to limit Question 26(a) to associational advocacy of concrete, specific, and imminent illegal acts. [See *Brandenburg.*]. Third, [the] indefinite scope of Question 26(a) expectedly operates to induce prospective applicants to resolve doubts by failing to exercise their First Amendment rights. . . . Part (a) of Question 26 is not rendered harmless by reason of the fact that part (b) limits somewhat the breadth of the question as a whole. [Overreaching] inquiries are not cured simply by adding narrower follow-up questions. [There] is no justification for a requirement of overbroad disclosure that chills the exercise of First Amendment freedoms and is not tailored to serve valid governmental interests. [NAACP v. Alabama.]

4. *Observations.* Consider Note, The Supreme Court, 1970 Term, 85 Harv. L. Rev. 3, 216-217 (1971): "[The *Baird-Stolar-Wadmond* trilogy] produced no clear consensus on the critical issues. [Although the Court held that] demands for blanket disclosure of organizational memberships are proscribed, five Justices found inquiry into Communist Party affiliation unobjectionable, [and] the same

slim majority [seems to have held that] bar associations [may] inquire into *knowing* membership in other subversive organizations."

c. Legislative Investigations

Throughout our history, Congress has used the power of inquiry to obtain information to assist it in the formulation of legislation. Moreover, the Court has recognized that the power of inquiry is "an essential and appropriate auxiliary to the legislative function" and that Congress may thus "compel a private individual to appear before it or one of its committees and give testimony needed to enable it efficiently to exercise a legislative function belonging to it under the Constitution." McGrain v. Daugherty, 273 U.S. 135 (1927). At the same time, however, the Court has emphasized that the power of inquiry is not boundless. In Kilbourn v. Thompson, 103 U.S. 168 (1881), for example, the Court held that Congress could not use the power of inquiry to serve a "judicial" function and that Congress had "no power or authority" to inquire "into the personal affairs of individuals" where the investigation "could result in no valid legislation on the subject." Similarly, in Sinclair v. United States, 279 U.S. 263 (1929), the Court declared that the power of inquiry "must be exerted with due regard for the rights of witnesses" and observed that "a witness rightfully may refuse to answer where the bounds of the power are exceeded or where the questions asked are not pertinent to the matter under inquiry."

It was not until the 1950s that the Court first considered the relationship between the power of inquiry and the first amendment. After World War II, legislative committees at both the state and federal levels launched far-ranging and often highly intrusive investigations into domestic "subversion." The House Un-American Activities Committee, for example, was authorized to investigate "(1) the extent, character, and objects of un-American propaganda activities in the United States, (2) the diffusion within the United States of subversive and un-American propaganda that is instigated from foreign countries or of a domestic origin and attacks the principle of the form of government as guaranteed by our constitution, and (3) all other questions in relation thereto that would aid Congress in any necessary remedial legislation." Not surprisingly, the activities of such committees often brought the power of inquiry into sharp conflict with the first amendment. See generally Taylor, Grand Inquest: The Story of Congressional Investigations (1955); Carr, The House Committee on Un-American Activities, 1945-1950 (1952); Symposium, Congressional Investigations, 18 U. Chi. L. Rev. 421 (1951); Nutting, Freedom of Silence: Constitutional Protection Against Governmental Intrusions in Political Affairs, 47 Mich. L. Rev. 181 (1948).

In its earliest encounters with the practices of these "anti-subversive" committees, the Court invalidated the convictions of several uncooperative witnesses on due process grounds, without reaching the first amendment issue. See, e.g., Sacher v. United States, 356 U.S. 576 (1958); Sweezy v. New Hampshire, 354 U.S. 234 (1957); Watkins v. United States, 354 U.S. 178 (1957).

BARENBLATT v. UNITED STATES, 360 U.S. 109 (1959): Petitioner, an instructor at Vassar College, was subpoenaed to appear as a witness before a subcommittee of the House Committee on Un-American Activities during an inquiry into alleged Communist infiltration into the field of education. After answering a few preliminary questions, petitioner declined to answer five questions concerning past and present membership in the Communist Party. For this refusal, he was convicted of contempt of Congress. The Court, in a five-to-four decision, held that the conviction did not violate the first amendment. Justice Harlan delivered the opinion of the Court:

"Where First Amendment rights are asserted to bar governmental interrogation resolution of the issue [involves] a balancing [of] the competing private and public interests. [Citing NAACP v. Alabama.] That Congress has wide power to legislate in the field of Communist activity in this Country, and to conduct appropriate investigations in aid thereof, is hardly debatable. [This] power rests on the right of self-preservation, 'the ultimate value of any society.' [Dennis.] [Because] the tenets of the Communist Party include the ultimate overthrow of [government] by force and violence, [this] Court has consistently refused to view the Communist Party as an ordinary political party, and has upheld [legislation] aimed at the Communist problem which in a different context would certainly have raised constitutional issues of the gravest order. . . .

"[Petitioner argues, however,] that this particular investigation was aimed not at the revolutionary aspects but at the theoretical classroom discussion of communism. [This] position rests on a too constricted view of the investigatory process, and is not supported by a fair assessment of the record before us. An investigation of advocacy of or preparation for overthrow carefully embraces the right to identify a witness as a member of the Communist Party and to inquire into the various manifestations of the Party's tenets. The strict requirements of a prosecution under the Smith Act, see [Dennis and Yates], are not the measure of the permissible scope of a congressional investigation into 'overthrow,' for of necessity the investigatory process must proceed step by step. . . .

"Nor can we accept [the] contention that [the] true objective of the Committee [was] purely 'exposure.' So long as Congress acts in pursuance of its constitutional power, the Judiciary lacks authority to intervene on the basis of the motives which spurred the exercise of that power. . . .

"Finally, the record is barren of other factors which in themselves might sometimes lead to the conclusion that the individual interests at stake were not subordinate to those of the state. There is no indication [that] the Subcommittee was attempting to pillory witnesses [and] the relevancy of the questions put to [petitioner] is not open to doubt."

Justice Black, joined by Chief Justice Warren and Justice Douglas, dissented: "I do not agree that laws directly abridging First Amendment freedoms can be justified by [a] balancing process. [But] even assuming [that] some balancing is proper in this case, I feel that the Court after stating the test ignores it completely. At most it balances the right of the Government to preserve itself, against Barenblatt's right to refrain from revealing Communist affiliations. Such a balance, however, mistakes the factors to be weighed. [It] completely leaves out the real interest in Barenblatt's silence, the interest of the people as a whole in being able to join organizations, advocate causes and make political 'mistakes' without later being subjected to governmental penalties for having dared to think for themselves. It is this right, the right to err politically, which keeps us strong as a Nation. [It] is these interests of society, rather than Barenblatt's own right to silence, which I think the Court should put on the balance against the demands of the Government. [Instead] they are not mentioned, while on the other side the demands of the Government are vastly overstated and called 'self-preservation.' [Such] a result reduces 'balancing' to a mere play on words. . . .

"Finally, I think Barenblatt's conviction violates the Constitution because the chief aim, purpose and practice of the House Un-American Activities Committee [is] to try witnesses and punish them because they are or have been [Communists]. The punishment imposed is generally punishment by humiliation and public shame. [To] accomplish [this] result, the Committee [calls] witnesses who are suspected of Communist affiliation [and insists] that each tell the name of every person he has ever known at any time to have been a Communist. [These] names are then indexed, published, and reported to Congress, and often to the press. [All] this the Committee [does] to punish by exposure the many phases of 'un-American' activities [that] cannot be reached by legislation. [I] do not question the Committee's patriotism and sincerity in doing all this. I merely feel that it cannot be done by Congress under our Constitution."

Justice Brennan also dissented: "[No] purpose for the investigation of Barenblatt is revealed by the record except exposure purely for the sake of exposure. This is not a purpose to which Barenblatt's rights under the First Amendment can validly be subordinated." . . .

See also Uphaus v. Wyman, 360 U.S. 72 (1959). The New Hampshire legislature constituted the state attorney general a "one-man legislative investigating committee" to determine whether there were any "subversive" persons within the state. In the course of his investigation, the Attorney General called appellant, Executive Director of World Fellowship, Inc., which maintained a summer camp in the state. Appellant refused on first amendment grounds to comply with subpoenas duces tecum calling for the production of the names of all persons who attended the camp during 1954 and 1955. Noting that "Not less than nineteen speakers invited by [appellant] to talk at World Fellowship had either been members of the Communist Party or had connections [with] it," the Court, relying on *Barenblatt*, upheld appellant's conviction for contempt. Consider the following views:

a. Kalven, Meiklejohn and the *Barenblatt* Opinion, 27 U. Chi. L. Rev. 315, 325-326 (1960):

> [*Barenblatt* illustrates] the awkwardness of the Court calling a spade a spade with respect to Congress. [It is clear that] if the House [had] explicitly authorized the Un-American Activities Committee to do exactly what it has done for 20 years, the Court would find totally lacking any predicate for the power to compel testimony. Yet if Congress says it has a legislative purpose and if it occasionally legislates, what can the Court do with its knowledge of real life? How can it hear evidence on — and try the motives of — Congress?

Recall *O'Brien*, supra section E3.

b. T. Emerson, The System of Freedom of Expression 274-275 (1970):

> [The Court has not] attempted to resolve [the legislative investigation] problem by use of the clear and present danger test. The reasons for this are not hard to fathom. The issue posed to the Court is not whether the expression in question has in fact

created a clear and present danger of some substantive evil, but whether the legislature is entitled to obtain the information in aid of its lawmaking or other functions
even though the process "incidentally" infringes on First Amendment rights. [The
Court has thus applied] the balancing of interests test [which is vague]; attempts to
weigh factors that are not comparable; [and] puts the Court in the position of
opposing the legislature on the legislature's own grounds.

**GIBSON v. FLORIDA LEGISLATIVE INVESTIGATING COMMIT-
TEE, 372 U.S. 539 (1963):** The Florida legislature created a committee to investigate the infiltration of Communists into various organizations. Petitioner, who
was president of the Miami Branch of the NAACP, was adjudged in contempt for
refusing to disclose to this committee whether fourteen individuals previously
identified as Communists were members of the NAACP. The Court, in a five-to-
four decision, held that petitioner's conviction violated the first amendment.
Justice Goldberg delivered the opinion of the Court:

"[It] is an essential prerequisite to the validity of an investigation which intrudes
into the area of constitutionally protected rights of speech, press, association and
petition that the State convincingly show a substantial relation between the
information sought and a subject of overriding and compelling state interest.
[This case is not controlled by *Barenblatt*.] In *Barenblatt*, [it] was a refusal to
answer [questions] concerning the witness' *own* past or present membership *in
the Communist Party* which supported his conviction. [The result in *Barenblatt*
was] founded on the holding that the Communist Party is not an ordinary or
legitimate political party [and] that, because of its particular nature, membership
therein is *itself* a permissible subject of regulation and legislative scrutiny. [Here,
however,] the entire thrust of the demands on the petitioner was that he disclose
whether other persons were members of the N.A.A.C.P., itself a concededly
legitimate and nonsubversive organization. Compelling such an organization [to
disclose its membership presents] a question wholly different from compelling the
Communist Party to disclose [its] membership. [Such legitimate and nonsubversive organizations do not] automatically forfeit their rights to privacy of association simply because the general subject matter of the legislative inquiry is
Communist subversion or infiltration. . . .

"[The] record in this case is insufficient to show a substantial connection between the Miami branch of the N.A.A.C.P. and Communist *activities* which [is]
an essential prerequisite to demonstrating the immediate, substantial, and subordinating state interest necessary to sustain [the Committee's] right of inquiry into
the membership lists of the association. [Basically,] the evidence relied upon by
the [Committee] consists of the testimony of [a Committee investigator and a
former NAACP official to the effect that some 14 alleged Communists had either
been members of the NAACP or participated in its meetings]. We do not know
from this ambiguous testimony how many of the 14 were supposed to have been
N.A.A.C.P. members. For all that appears, [each] or all of the named persons
may have attended no more than one or two wholly public meetings of the
N.A.A.C.P. [In] addition, it is not clear whether the asserted Communist affiliations and the association with the N.A.A.C.P., however slight, coincided in time.
Moreover, [there] is no indication that membership carried with it any right to
control over policy or activities, much less that any was sought. [On the basis of
this evidence, and without] any indication [of] subversive infiltration in, or influ-

ence on, the Miami branch of the N.A.A.C.P., [we cannot] find the compelling and subordinating state interest which must exist if essential freedoms are to be curtailed or inhibited. [Of] course, a legislative investigation [must] proceed 'step by step,' [Barenblatt], but step by step or in totality, an adequate foundation for inquiry must be laid before proceeding in such a manner as will substantially intrude upon and severely curtail or inhibit constitutionally protected activities. [No] such foundation has been laid here."

Justice Harlan, joined by Justices Clark, Stewart, and White, dissented: "The Court rests reversal on its finding that the Committee did not have sufficient justification for including the Miami Branch of the N.A.A.C.P. within the ambit of its investigation — that [an] adequate 'nexus' was lacking between the N.A.A.C.P. and the subject matter of the Committee's inquiry. The Court's reasoning is difficult to grasp. [For] unless 'nexus' requires an investigating agency to prove in advance the very things it is trying to find out, I do not understand how it can be said that the information preliminarily developed by the Committee's investigator was not sufficient to satisfy, under any reasonable test, the requirement of 'nexus.'"

See also DeGregory v. Attorney General, 383 U.S. 825 (1966). A 1957 statute authorized the New Hampshire attorney general to investigate subversive activities within the state, to recommend legislation, and "to make public [any] information received by him [as] he deems fit." In 1964 the attorney general initiated an investigation of appellant. This investigation was based "entirely upon a 1955 Report [which connected] appellant with the Communist Party only until 1953, over 10 years prior to the investigation." Although appellant testified that he had not been involved with the Communist Party since 1957 and that he had no knowledge of Communist activities since that date, he refused on first amendment grounds to answer questions concerning his pre-1957 associations. He was thus jailed for one year or until he purged himself of contempt. Noting that there was "no showing of 'overriding and compelling state interest' [that] would warrant intrusion into the realm of political and associational privacy," the Court, relying on Gibson, reversed the conviction.

Consider H. Kalven, The Negro and the First Amendment 112-115 (1965):

[There] are two related but different approaches percolating in [Gibson]. First, there is the idea of [NAACP v. Alabama] that the state must offer some good reason for needing the information. [Second], there is the idea, apparently borrowed from the Fourth Amendment, that invasions of privacy have to be limited to those with some likelihood of success. [It] is here that a foundation, a nexus, a probable cause must be shown. [The] first test is designed to protect anonymity and privacy from disclosure. [The second] is designed to protect the citizen from being bothered, from having his daily privacy upset by governmental action. [What, then, of] Justice Harlan's apparently deadly quip that the announced rule [would] "require an investigating agency to prove in advance the very things it is trying to find [out"?] Is it a proper answer here to say that the same point might be made about requiring the government to arrest only people it "knows" are guilty or only seek evidence it "knows" is there? Can the Fourth Amendment be imported in this fashion into the First?

Note: Intelligence Activities

Although this section focuses on compelled disclosure, there are other means by which government may obtain information about potential "subversives." Suppose, for example, that in an investigation of Communist infiltration of the NAACP in Florida, a government informant infiltrates the organization's leadership and reports regularly on its membership and activities. Or suppose a government official photographs all persons attending a public NAACP rally. In what circumstances, if any, are these and similar forms of surveillance limited by the first amendment?

The question is hardly hypothetical. Consider the 1976 findings of the Senate Select Committee to Study Governmental Operations with Respect to Intelligence Activities:

> The Government has often undertaken the secret surveillance of citizens on the basis of their political beliefs, even when those beliefs posed no threat of violence or illegal acts on behalf of a hostile foreign power. The Government, operating primarily through secret informants, [has] swept in vast amounts of information about the personal lives, views, and associations of American citizens. Investigations of groups deemed potentially dangerous — and even of groups suspected of associating with potentially dangerous organizations — have continued for decades, despite the fact that those groups did not engage in unlawful activity. [FBI] headquarters alone has developed over 500,000 domestic intelligence files. [The] targets of intelligence activity have included political adherents of the right and the left, ranging from activist to casual supporters.
>
> [Although] the FBI has admitted that the Socialist Workers Party has committed no criminal acts, [it] has investigated the [SWP] for more than three decades on the basis of its revolutionary rhetoric [and] its claimed international links. [As] part of their effort to collect information which "related even remotely" to people or groups "active" in communities which had "the potential" for civil disorder, Army intelligence agencies took such steps as: sending agents to a Halloween party for elementary school children [because] they suspected a local "dissident" might be present; monitoring protests of welfare mothers' organizations in Milwaukee; infiltrating a coalition of church youth groups in Colorado; and sending agents to a priests' conference in Washington, D.C., held to discuss birth control measures. [In] 1970 the FBI ordered investigations of every member of the Students for a Democratic Society and of "every Black Student Union and similar group regardless of their past or present involvement in disorders."

Senate Select Committee to Study Governmental Operations with Respect to Intelligence Activities, Final Report, Intelligence Activities and the Rights of Americans, Book II, S. Doc. No. 13133-4, 94th Cong., 2nd Sess. 5-9 (1976). See generally F. Donner, The Age of Surveillance (1980); A. Theoharis, Spying on Americans (1978); Note, Governmental Investigations of the Exercise of First Amendment Rights, 60 Minn. L. Rev. 1257 (1976); Symposium, National Securities and Civil Liberties, 69 Corn. L. Rev. 685 (1984). See also Laird v. Tatum, 408 U.S. 1 (1972) (plaintiffs have no standing to challenge Army's "surveillance of lawful political activities" on ground that their first amendment rights are "chilled" where there is no evidence of "objective" harm).

6. Freedom of the Press

This section examines the first amendment's guarantee of "freedom [of] the press." The focus is on four questions. First, in what circumstances, if any, is the press, because of its constitutionally protected status, exempt from laws of otherwise general application? Second, in what circumstances, if any, may government treat the press differently from other institutions? Third, in what circumstances, if any, may government regulate the press to improve the "marketplace of ideas"? Fourth, to what extent, if any, does the first amendment guarantee a right to "gather" news?

a. A "Preferred" Status for the Press?

The first amendment prohibits any law "abridging the freedom of speech, or of the press." Does the "press" clause confer any rights that would not be conferred by the "speech" clause alone? Consider the views of Justice Stewart and Chief Justice Burger:

a. Stewart, "Or of the Press," 26 Hast. L.J. 631, 633-634 (1975):

[The] Free Press guarantee is, in essence, a *structural* provision of the Constitution. Most of the other provisions in the Bill of Rights protect specific liberties or specific rights of individuals. [The] Free Press Clause extends protection to an institution. The publishing business [is] the only organized private business that is given explicit constitutional protection. [If] the Free Press guarantee meant no more than freedom of expression, it would be a constitutional redundancy. [By] including both [the speech and press] guarantees in the First Amendment, the Founders quite clearly recognized the distinction between the two. [In] setting up the three branches of the Federal Government, the Founders deliberately created an internally competitive system. [The] primary purpose of the constitutional guarantee of a free press was [to] create a fourth institution outside the Government as an additional check on the three official branches. [The] relevant metaphor [is that] of the Fourth Estate. [The first amendment thus protects] the institutional autonomy of the press.

See also Anderson, The Origins of the Press Clause, 30 U.C.L.A. L. Rev. 455 (1983).

b. First National Bank of Boston v. Bellotti, 435 U.S. 765, 797-801 (1978) (Burger, C.J., concurring):

[There are those] who view the Press Clause as somehow conferring special and extraordinary privileges or status on the "institutional press." [I] perceive two fundamental difficulties with [such a] reading of the Press Clause. First, although certainty on this point is not possible, the history of the Clause does not suggest that the authors contemplated a "special" or "institutional" privilege. [Most] pre-First Amendment commentators "who employed the term 'freedom of speech' [used] it synonymously with freedom of the press." [To] conclude that the Framers did not intend to limit the freedom of the press to one select group is not necessarily to suggest that the Press Clause is redundant. [The] liberty encompassed by the Press Clause [merited] special mention simply because it had been more often the object of official restraints. [The] second fundamental difficulty with interpreting the Press

> Clause as conferring special status on a limited group is one of definition. [The] very task of including some entities within the "institutional press" while excluding others [is] reminiscent of the abhorred licensing system [that] the First Amendment was intended to ban. [In my view,] the First Amendment does not "belong" to any definable category of persons or entities: It belongs to all who exercise its freedoms.

Consider also Associated Press v. NLRB, 301 U.S. 103 (1937). The Associated Press is a cooperative organization whose members in 1937 included approximately 1,350 newspapers. It collects, compiles, and distributes news to its members. The NLRB found that the Associated Press discharged an employee in violation of section 7 of the NLRA, which confers on employees the right to organize and to bargain collectively. The Court, in a five-to-four decision, held that application of section 7 to the Associated Press did not violate the first amendment:

> The business of the Associated Press is not immune from regulation because it is an agency of the press. The publisher of a newspaper has no special immunity from the application of general laws. He has no special privilege to invade the rights and liberties of others. He must answer for libel. He may be punished for contempt of court. He is subject to the anti-trust laws. Like others he must pay equitable and nondiscriminatory taxes on his business. The regulation here in question has no relation whatever to the impartial distribution of news.

See also Dun & Bradstreet v. Greenmoss Builders, section D1 supra (the media are not entitled to any greater protection against actions for libel than other speakers); Citizen Publishing Co. v. United States, 394 U.S. 131 (1969) (Sherman Antitrust Act); Oklahoma Press Publishing Co. v. Walling, 327 U.S. 186 (1946) (Fair Labor Standards Act); cf. Grosjean v. American Press Co., 297 U.S. 233 (1936) (taxation).

Are these decisions consistent with Justice Stewart's contention that the "publishing business is [the] only organized private business that is given explicit constitutional protection"? Are there *some* circumstances in which the first amendment exempts the press from tax, labor, antitrust, or other laws of general application?

b. Differential Treatment of the Press

MINNEAPOLIS STAR & TRIBUNE CO. v. MINNESOTA COMMISSIONER OF REVENUE, 460 U.S. 575 (1983): Minnesota imposes a sales tax on retail sales. To avoid double taxation, sales of components to be used in the production of goods that will themselves be sold at retail are exempt from the sales tax. Minnesota also imposes a use tax on the use or consumption of goods that were purchased without payment of the sales tax. The use tax is designed to eliminate the incentive of residents to buy goods in states with lower sales taxes. Until 1971 periodic publications were exempt from both the sales and use tax. In 1971, however, Minnesota imposed a use tax on the cost of paper and ink products consumed in the production of periodic publications. As a result, ink and paper used in such publications became the only components of goods to be sold at retail subject to the use tax. In 1974 Minnesota amended the use tax to exempt the first $100,000 worth of ink and paper consumed by a publication in any calendar year. After enactment of the $100,000 exemption, eleven publishers, producing fourteen of the 388 newspapers in Minnesota, incurred a tax liability in 1974. Appellant was one of the eleven. Because of is size, it paid approximately $600,000, or about two-thirds of the total revenue raised by the tax. The Court held that this taxing scheme violated appellant's rights under the first amendment. Justice O'Connor delivered the opinion of the Court:

"Minnesota has [created] a special tax that applies only to certain publications protected by the First Amendment. [We] must determine whether the First Amendment permits such special taxation. [There] is substantial evidence that differential taxation of the press would have troubled the Framers of the First Amendment. [The] fears of the [framers] were well-founded. [When] a State singles out the press [for special taxation], the political constraints that prevent a legislature from passing crippling taxes of general applicability are weakened, and the threat of burdensome taxes becomes acute. That threat can operate as effectively as a censor to check critical comment by the press. [Differential] taxation of the press, then, places such a burden on the interests protected by the First Amendment and we cannot countenance such treatment unless the State asserts a counterbalancing interest of compelling importance that it cannot achieve without differential taxation. . . .

"Minnesota invites us to look beyond the form of the tax to its substance. The tax is, according to the State, merely a substitute for the sales tax, which, as a generally applicable tax, would be constitutional as applied to the press. [But] the State has offered no explanation of why it chose to use a substitute for the sales tax rather than the sales tax itself.

"[The State argues further] that this scheme actually *favors* the press over other businesses, because the same rate of tax is applied, but, for the press, the rate applies to the cost of components rather than to the sales price. [But we] would be hesitant to fashion a rule that automatically allowed the State to single out the press for a different method of taxation as long as the effective burden was no different from that on other taxpayers or the burden on the press was lighter than that on other businesses. One reason for this reluctance is that the very selection of the press for special treatment threatens the press not only with the current *differential* treatment, but with the possibility of subsequent differentially *more burdensome* treatment. Thus, even without actually imposing an extra burden on the press, the government might be able to achieve censorial effects, for '[t]he threat of sanctions may deter [the] exercise of [First Amendment] rights almost as potently as the actual application of sanctions.' [A] second reason to avoid the proposed rule is that courts as institutions are poorly equipped to evaluate with precision the relative burdens of various methods of taxation. [The] possibility of error inherent in the proposed rule poses too great a threat to concerns at the heart of the First Amendment, and we cannot tolerate that possibility.[13] Minne-

---

13. If a State employed the same *method* of taxation but applied a lower *rate* to the press, so that there could be no doubt that the legislature was not singling out the press to bear a more burdensome tax, we would, of course, be in a position to evaluate the relative burdens. And, given the clarity of the relative burdens, as well as the rule that differential methods of taxation are not automatically permissible if less burdensome, a lower tax rate for the press would not raise the threat that the legislature might later impose an extra burden that would escape detection by the courts.

sota, therefore, has offered no adequate justification for the special treatment of newspapers. . . .

"Minnesota's ink and paper tax violates the First Amendment not only because it singles out the press, but also because it targets a small group of newspapers. The effect of the $100,000 exemption [is] that only a handful of publishers pay any tax at [all]. The State explains this exemption as part of a policy favoring an 'equitable' tax system, [but] there are no comparable exemptions for small enterprises outside the press. [We] think that recognizing a power in the State [to] tailor the tax so that it singles out only a few members of the press presents such a potential for abuse that [Minnesota's interest in an 'equitable' tax system cannot] justify the scheme. [The] tax violates the First Amendment."

Justice Rehnquist dissented: "The Court recognizes [that] Minnesota could avoid constitutional problems by imposing on newspapers [the same] sales tax that it imposes on other retailers. Rather than impose such a tax, however, the Minnesota legislature decided to provide newspapers with an exemption from the sales tax and impose a use tax on ink and paper. [The] problem the Court finds too difficult to deal with is whether this difference in treatment results in a significant burden on newspapers. The record reveals that in 1974 [appellant had total sales of] $46,498,738. Had a 4% sales tax been imposed, [appellant] would have been liable for $1,859,950. [The] record further indicates that [appellant] paid $608,634 in use taxes in 1974. We need no expert testimony [to] determine that the [use tax] is significantly less burdensome than the [sales tax]. Ignoring these calculations, the Court concludes that 'differential treatment' alone [requires] that the [tax] be found 'presumptively unconstitutional' and declared invalid 'unless the State asserts a [compelling justification].' The 'differential treatment' standard [is] unprecedented and unwarranted. [No] First Amendment issue is raised unless First Amendment rights have been infringed. . . .

"Wisely not relying solely on its inability to weigh the burdens of the [tax] scheme, the Court also says that even if the resultant burden on the press is lighter than on others '[t]he very selection of the press for special treatment threatens the press [with] the possibility of subsequent differentially *more burdensome* [treatment].' Surely the Court does not mean what it seems to say. [This] Court is quite capable of dealing with changes in state taxing laws which are intended to penalize newspapers. [Furthermore], the Court itself intimates [in footnote 13 that certain forms of differential treatment are permissible, even though they too have the] potential for 'the threat of sanctions,' because the legislature could at any time raise the taxes to the higher rate. . . .

"[In my view, the] State [in this case] is required to show [only] that its taxing scheme is rational. [In] this case that showing can be made easily. [There] must be few such inexpensive items sold in Minnesota in the volume of newspaper sales. [The] legislature could have concluded that paper boys, corner newsstands, and vending machines provide an unreliable and unsuitable means for collection of a sales tax. [The] reasonable alternative Minnesota chose was to impose [was] the use tax on ink and paper. ["The Court also] finds [that] the exemption newspapers receive for the first $100,000 of ink and paper [used] violates the First Amendment because the result is that only a few of the newspapers actually pay a use tax. I cannot agree. [Absent] any improper motive on the part of the Minnesota legislature in drawing the lines of this exemption, it cannot be construed as violating the First Amendment. [There] is no reason to conclude that the State [acted] other than reasonably and rationally to fit its sales and use tax scheme to its own local needs and usages."

Justice White concurred in part and dissented in part.

Consider Note, The Supreme Court, 1982 Term, 97 Harv. L. Rev. 70, 176-177 (1983):

> Examination of the unusual economics of the newspaper industry demonstrates the wisdom of the majority's [approach]. Because newspaper publishers receive revenue from advertising as well as from the sale of [newspapers], revenues from newspaper sales do not have to cover the cost of producing the newspaper. [Thus, even] if, as Justice Rehnquist argued, Minnesota's [use tax is presently] less burdensome [than] extension of [the] sales tax [would] have been, [the] analysis used by the Court is necessary to ensure that the constitutionality of [the tax] does not turn on the fluctuating price of newsprint.

c. Regulating the Press to "Improve" the Marketplace of Ideas

In what circumstances, if any, is it appropriate for government to regulate the media in order to "improve" the system of free expression? Recall the discussion of this issue in the electoral context in section E4 supra.

MIAMI HERALD PUBLISHING CO. v. TORNILLO, 418 U.S. 241 (1974): In *Tornillo* the Court considered the constitutionality of a Florida "'right of reply' statute which [provided] that if a candidate for [political office] is assailed regarding his personal character or official record by any newspaper, the candidate has the right to demand that the newspaper print, free of cost to the candidate, any reply the candidate may make to the newspaper's charges. The reply must appear in as conspicuous a place and in the same kind of type as the charges which prompted the reply, provided it does not take up more space than the charges." The Court, in a unanimous decision, held the statute invalid. Chief Justice Burger delivered the opinion of the Court:

"[Advocates] of an enforceable right of access to the press [urge] that at the time the First Amendment [was ratified] the press was broadly representative of the people it was serving. [Entry] into publishing was inexpensive [and a] true marketplace of ideas existed in which there was relatively easy access to the channels of communication. Access advocates submit that [the press of today is] very different. [Newspapers] have become big business and [the press] has become noncompetitive and enormously powerful and influential in its capacity to manipulate popular opinion. [The] result of these vast changes has been to place in a few hands the power to inform the American people and shape public opinion. [There] tends to be a homogeneity of editorial opinion, commentary, and interpretative analysis. [The] obvious solution [would] be to have additional newspapers. But [economic factors] have made entry into the marketplace of ideas served by the print media almost impossible. [The] First Amendment interest of the public in being informed is said to be in peril. . . .

"However much validity may be found in these arguments, [the] implementation of a remedy such as an enforceable right of access necessarily [brings] about a confrontation with the express provisions of the First Amendment. [The] argument that the Florida statute does not amount to a restriction of [the newspaper's] right to speak because 'the statute in question here has not prevented [the newspaper] from saying anything it wished' begs the core question. Compelling editors or publishers to publish that which '"reason" tells them should not be published' is what is at issue in this case. The Florida statute operates as a command in the same sense as a statute or regulation forbidding [the newspaper] to publish specified matter. [The] Florida statute exacts a penalty on the basis of the content of a newspaper. The first phase of the penalty [is] exacted in terms of the cost in printing [and] in taking up space that could be devoted to other material the newspaper may have preferred to print. [Faced with such a penalty,] editors might well conclude that the safe course is to avoid controversy. [Thus, government-enforced] right of access inescapably 'dampens the vigor and limits the variety of public debate.' . . .

"[Moreover, even] if a newspaper would face no additional costs to comply with a compulsory access law and would not be forced to forgo publication of news or opinion by the inclusion of a reply, the Florida statute fails to clear the barriers of the First Amendment because of its intrusion into the function of editors. A newspaper is more than a passive receptacle or conduit for news, comment, and advertising. The choice of material to go into a newspaper [constitutes] the exercise of editorial control and judgment. It has yet to be demonstrated how governmental regulation of this crucial process can be exercised consistent with First Amendment guarantees of a free press as they have evolved to this time."

Does *Tornillo* suggest that government may *never* compel "editors or publishers to publish that which '"reason" tells them should not be published'"? Consider B. Schmidt, Freedom of Press v. Public Access 233-235 (1976):

> From the perspective of First Amendment law generally, *Miami Herald* would be a stark and unexplained deviation if one were to read the decision as creating absolute prohibitions on access obligations. [The] principle of *Miami Herald* probably is destined for uncharted qualifications and exceptions. [Although sweeping] access rights will not be [approved, narrow,] specific access guarantees, designed to implement particular and weighty social objectives with the least possible jeopardy to editorial commentary, may be upheld.

In a concurring opinion in *Tornillo*, Justice Brennan asserted that "the Court's opinion [implies] no view upon the constitutionality of 'retraction' statutes affording plaintiffs able to prove defamatory falsehoods a statutory action to require publication of a retraction." Do you agree? Suppose that instead of a "right-of-reply" law, Florida adopted a "right-of-access" law, requiring every newspaper to set aside one page each issue for letters to the editor, not to exceed 500 words, to be selected for publication without regard to content. Would such a law be invalid under *Tornillo?* Recall *PruneYard,* supra section F2.

Red Lion Broadcasting Co. v. FCC
395 U.S. 367 (1969)

[In *Red Lion* the Court considered the constitutionality of the FCC's fairness doctrine and its component regulations governing personal attacks and political editorializing. The fairness doctrine, which originated "very early in the history of broadcasting," imposes "on radio and television broadcasters the requirement that discussion of public issues be presented on broadcast stations, and that each side of those issues must be given fair coverage." The personal attack rule requires that when, "during the presentation of views on a controversial issue of public importance, an attack is made upon the honesty, character, integrity or like personal qualities of an identified person or group," the attacked person or group must be given notice, a transcript, and a reasonable opportunity to respond. The political editorializing rule requires that when, in an editorial, a broadcaster endorses or opposes a political candidate, the broadcaster must notify the opposed candidate or the opponents of the endorsed candidate and give them a "reasonable opportunity" to reply.]

JUSTICE WHITE delivered the opinion of the Court. . . .

The broadcasters challenge the fairness doctrine and its specific manifestations in the personal attack and political editorial rules on conventional First Amendment grounds, alleging that the rules abridge their freedom of speech and press. Their contention is that the First Amendment protects their desire to use their allotted frequencies continuously to broadcast whatever they choose, and to exclude whomever they choose from ever using that frequency. No man may be prevented from saying or publishing what he thinks, or from refusing in his speech or other utterances to give equal weight to the views of his opponents. This right, they say, applies equally to broadcasters.

Although broadcasting is clearly a medium affected by a First Amendment interest, differences in the characteristics of new media justify differences in the First Amendment standards applied to them. . . .

Where there are substantially more individuals who want to broadcast than there are frequencies to allocate, it is idle to posit an unabridgeable First Amendment right to broadcast comparable to the right of every individual to speak, write, or publish. If 100 persons want broadcast licenses but there are only 10 frequencies to allocate, all of them may have the same "right" to a license; but if there is to be any effective communication by radio, only a few can be licensed and the rest must be barred from the airwaves. It would be strange if the First Amendment, aimed at protecting and furthering communications, prevented the Government from making radio communication possible by requiring licenses to broadcast and by limiting the number of licenses so as not to overcrowd the spectrum. . . .

By the same token, as far as the First Amendment is concerned those who are licensed stand no better than those to whom licenses are refused. A license permits broadcasting, but the licensee has no constitutional right to be the one who holds the license or to monopolize a radio frequency to the exclusion of his fellow citizens. There is nothing in the First Amendment which prevents the Government from requiring a licensee to share his frequency with others and to conduct himself as a proxy or fiduciary with obligations to present those views and voices which are representative of his community and which would otherwise, by necessity, be barred from the airwaves.

[The] people as a whole retain their interest in free speech by radio and their collective right to have the medium function consistently with the ends and purposes of the First Amendment. It is the right of the viewers and listeners, not the right of the broadcasters, which is paramount. [It] is the right of the public to receive suitable access to social, political, esthetic, moral, and other ideas and experiences which is crucial here. . . .

[We cannot] say that it is inconsistent with the First Amendment goal of producing an informed public capable of conducting its own affairs to require a broadcaster to permit answers to personal attacks occurring in the course of discussing controversial issues, or to require that the political opponents of those endorsed by the station be given a chance to communicate with the public. Otherwise, station owners and a few networks would have unfettered power to make time available only to the highest bidders, to communicate only their own views on public issues, people and candidates, and to permit on the air only those with whom they agreed. There is no sanctuary in the First Amendment for unlimited private censorship operating in a medium not open to all. . . .

It is strenuously argued, however, that if political editorials or personal attacks will trigger an obligation in broadcasters to afford the opportunity for expression to speakers who need not pay for time and whose views are unpalatable to the licensees, then broadcasters will be irresistibly forced to self-censorship and their coverage of controversial public issues will be eliminated or at least rendered wholly ineffective. Such a result would indeed be a serious matter, for should licensees actually eliminate their coverage of controversial issues, the purposes of the doctrine would be stifled.

At this point, however, as the Federal Communications Commission has indicated, that possibility is at best speculative. [And] if experience with the administration of these doctrines indicates that they have the net effect of reducing rather than enhancing the volume and quality of coverage, there will be time enough to reconsider the constitutional implications. The fairness doctrine in the past has had no such overall effect.

That this will occur now seems unlikely, however, since if present licensees should suddenly prove timorous, the Commission is not powerless to insist that they give adequate and fair attention to public issues. It does not violate the First Amendment to treat licensees given the privilege of using scarce radio frequencies as proxies for the entire community, obligated to give suitable time and attention to matters of great public concern. To condition the granting or renewal of licenses on a willingness to present representative community views on controversial issues is consistent with the ends and purposes of those constitutional provisions forbidding the abridgment of freedom of speech and freedom of the press. . . .

It is argued that even if at one time the lack of available frequencies for all who wished to use them justified the Government's choice of those who would best serve the public interest by acting as proxy for those who would present differing views, or by giving the latter access directly to broadcast facilities, this condition no longer prevails so that continuing control is not justified. To this there are several answers.

Scarcity is not entirely a thing of the past. Advances in technology, such as microwave transmission, have led to more efficient utilization of the frequency spectrum, but uses for that spectrum have also grown apace. [Nothing] in this record, or in our own researches, convinces us that the resource is no longer one for which there are more immediate and potential uses than can be accommodated. . . .

Even where there are gaps in spectrum utilization, the fact remains that existing broadcasters have often attained their present position because of their initial government selection in competition with others before new technological advances opened new opportunities for further uses. Long experience in broadcasting, confirmed habits of listeners and viewers, network affiliation, and other advantages in program procurement give existing broadcasters a substantial advantage over new entrants, even where new entry is technologically possible. These advantages are the fruit of a preferred position conferred by the Government. Some present possibility for new entry by competing stations is not enough, in itself, to render unconstitutional the Government's effort to assure that a broadcaster's programming ranges widely enough to serve the public interest.

In view of the scarcity of broadcast frequencies, the Government's role in allocating those frequencies, and the legitimate claims of those unable without governmental assistance to gain access to those frequencies for expression of their views, we hold the [regulations] constitutional.[28] . . .*

Note: Regulating the Airwaves

1. Buckley *and* Red Lion. Note that *Red Lion*, like Buckley v. Valeo, supra section E4, involves a conflict between competing theories of the role of government and of the appropriate conception of a system of freedom of expression. Under one view, government is permitted and may even have an obligation to intervene in order to prevent the distorting effects on deliberative processes that are created by the operation of the "private" sphere. Under the competing view, government should accept the private sphere "as is" and may not consider inequalities that derive therefrom as "distortions" at all. Why do *Buckley* and *Red Lion* resolve what is in many respects the same dispute in such different ways?

2. *Licensing the airwaves.* In the Communications Act of 1934, the government, "to maintain the control of the United States over [the channels of] radio transmission; and to provide for the use of such channels, but not the ownership therof, by persons for limited periods of time," established the FCC and granted it broad power to license and regulate the broadcast spectrum "as public convenience, interest, or necessity requires." In National Broadcasting Co. v. United States, 319 U.S. 190 (1943), the Court held that such government licensing did not violate the first amendment because, "Unlike other modes of expression, radio inherently is not available to all." Consider the following arguments:

a. Powe, "Or of the [Broadcast] Press," 55 Tex. L. Rev. 39, 55-56 (1976):

As a theory, scarcity begins with the premise [that] information sources do not compete effectively with each other. This premise is not successfully explained, and

---

28. We need not deal with the argument that even if there is no longer a technological scarcity of frequencies limiting the number of broadcasters, there nevertheless is an economic scarcity in the sense that the Commission could or does limit entry to the broadcasting market on economic grounds and license no more stations than the market will support. Hence, it is said, the fairness doctrine or its equivalent is essential to satisfy the claims of those excluded and of the public generally. A related argument, which we also put aside, is that quite apart from scarcity of frequencies, technological or economic, Congress does not abridge freedom of speech or press by legislation directly or indirectly multiplying the voices and views presented to the public through time sharing, fairness doctrines, or other devices which limit or dissipate the power of those who sit astride the channels of communication with the general public. . . .

* [Not having heard argument, Justice Douglas did not participate. — EDS.]

seems contradictory to the normal first amendment assumption. [Moreover,] if one looks to actual numbers [there are more radio and television stations in the United States than daily newspapers].

b. Coase, The Federal Communications Commission, 2 J. L. & Econ. 1, 14-18 (1959):

[The Court] seems to believe that federal regulation is needed because radio frequencies are limited in number and people want to use more of them than are available. But it is a commonplace of economics that almost all resources used in the economic system (and not simply radio and television frequencies) are limited in amount and scarce, in that people would like to use more than exists. [It] is true that some mechanism has to be employed to decide who [should] be allowed to use the scarce resource. But the way this is usually done [is] to employ the price mechanism, and this allocates resources to users without the need for government regulation, [An] administrative agency which attempts to perform the function normally carried out by the pricing mechanism [cannot], by the nature of things, be [fully aware] of the preferences of consumers. [Allocation by means of the pricing mechanism is thus more likely than allocation by administrative action to serve the "public convenience, interest, or necessity."]

c. Van Alstyne, The Mobius Strip of the First Amendment: Perspectives on *Red Lion*, 29 S.C. L. Rev. 539, 562 (1978):

The [Coase] argument is appealing, but it is based on a fatal myopia in its failure to see how clearly freedom of speech [is] abridged by a government policy that adheres only to a private property system and a market-pricing mechanism in determining who shall be able to speak. [Allocation by means of the pricing mechanism would winnow] the field of otherwise eligible applicants strictly according to their ability to pay; it [would eliminate] from the licensing competition those who lack dollars to put in an effective bid.

d. Bollinger, Freedom of the Press and Public Access: Toward a Theory of Partial Regulation of the Mass Media, 75 Mich. L. Rev. 1, 26-36 (1976):

[The] Court's decisions on the question of access [to the print and broadcast media] exhibit fundamental good sense. The good sense, however, derives not from the Court's treatment of broadcasting as being somehow special, but rather from its apparent desire to limit the over-all reach of access regulation. [There] are good first amendment reasons for being both receptive to and wary of access regulation. [Only under a partial regulatory scheme,] with a major branch of the press remaining free of regulation, will the costs and risks of regulation be held at an acceptable level. [By] permitting different treatment of the two institutions, the Court can facilitate realization of the benefits of two distinct constitutional values, both of which ought to be fostered: access in a highly concentrated press and minimal governmental intrusion. [The] Court has imposed a compromise — a compromise, however, not based on notions of expediency, but rather on a reasoned, and principled, accommodation of competing first amendment values.

3. *Regulating the airwaves.* Assuming that licensing of the airwaves is not itself unconstitutional, what factors may the FCC consider in its allocation of licenses?

a. May the FCC prohibit the common ownership of a radio or television station and a daily newspaper located in the same community? In FCC v. National Citizens Committee for Broadcasting, 436 U.S. 775 (1978), the Court sustained such regulations:

> In making [its] licensing decisions between competing applicants, the Commission has long given "primary significance" to "diversification of control of the media of mass communications." [This policy is consistent] with the statutory scheme [and with] the First Amendment goal of achieving "the widest possible dissemination of information from diverse and antagonistic sources." [Petitioners argue that the regulations are invalid because they seriously restrict the opportunities for expression of both broadcasters and newspapers. But as] we stated in *Red Lion*, "to deny a station license because 'the public interest' requires it 'is not a denial of free speech.'" [The] regulations are a reasonable means of promoting the public interest in diversified mass communications; thus they do not violate the First Amendment rights of those who will be denied broadcast licenses pursuant to them.

b. May the FCC compel an applicant for a broadcast license to ascertain the problems, needs, and interests of his community and to provide programming to meet those needs? See Ascertainment of Community Problems by Broadcast Applicants Primer, 57 F.C.C.2d 418 (1976). May the FCC, for example, deny a license to an applicant for a radio station in a community with a substantial black population unless the applicant agrees to devote a substantial portion of his programming to information and entertainment designed specifically for the black community? See generally Canby, Programming in Response to the Community: The Broadcast Consumer and the First Amendment, 55 Tex. L. Rev. 67 (1976). Cf. FCC v. WNCN Listeners Guild, 450 U.S. 582 (1981).

c. May the FCC compel broadcasters to comply with its "fairness doctrine" and its component rules governing "personal attacks" and "political editorializing"? *Red Lion* has been the subject of considerable criticism. See, e.g., Karst, Equality as a Central Principle in the First Amendment, 43 U. Chi. L. Rev. 20, 49 (1975) ("Any process of continuing governmental surveillance over broadcasting content presents truly grave dangers. [Even] the right-of-reply portion of the fairness [doctrine, although] less threatening than the doctrine's more general insistence on fair coverage of issues, [will] give added encouragement to an editorial blandness already promoted by the broadcasters' commercial advertisers; broadcasters will simply minimize the number of newscasts to which a fairness doctrine obligation will attach."); Van Alstyne, supra, at 574 ("In yielding to the fear of licensee abuse, the fairness doctrine may ultimately betray a lack of confidence in the presuppositions of the first amendment itself. [What] can possibly be plainer than that the luminescence of the first amendment itself is dimmed whenever freedom for passionate expression is systematically discouraged by state-imposed duties of fiduciary obligation and the yellow light of self-restraint?"). The literature examining the fairness doctrine and *Red Lion* is voluminous. For a comprehensive list of sources, see Van Alstyne, supra, at 547-548 n.49.

d. May the FCC prohibit broadcasters from airing programs that contain profanity? May it prohibit programs that incite to crime? That are sexually explicit? That depict a racial or religious group in a degrading manner? Recall FCC v. Pacifica Foundation, supra section D6.

4. *Public broadcasting.* In FCC v. League of Women Voters, — U.S. — , 104 S. Ct. 3106 (1984), the Court invalidated section 399 of the Public Broadcasting Act of 1967, which prohibited any noncommercial educational station that receives a grant from the Corporation for Public Broadcasting to "engage in editorializing." The government maintained that the ban was necessary, first, "to protect noncommercial educational broadcasting stations from being coerced, as a result of federal financing, into becoming vehicles for government propagandizing"; and, second, "to keep these stations from becoming convenient targets for capture by private interest groups wishing to express their own partisan viewpoints." Although conceding that section 399, like the rules upheld in *Red Lion*, was designed "to safeguard the public's right to a balanced presentation of public issues," the Court emphasized that, unlike the rules upheld in *Red Lion*, which "[granted] others access to the microphone," section 399 attempted to achieve its objectives by "directly [prohibiting] the broadcaster from speaking out on public issues." And because section 399 was "specifically directed at [expression] that lies at the heart of First Amendment protection," the Court explained that it "must be especially careful in weighing the interests that are asserted [and] in assessing the precision with which the ban is crafted." Applying that standard, the Court held that "the specific interests sought to be advanced by [section 399] are either not sufficiently substantial or are not served in a sufficiently limited manner to justify the substantial abridgement of important journalistic freedoms which the First Amendment [protects]."

Justice Rehnquist, joined by Chief Justice Burger and Justice White, dissented:

> Congress in enacting §399 [has] simply determined that public funds shall not be used to subsidize noncommercial, educational broadcasting stations which engage in "editorializing." [Nothing] in the First Amendment [prevents] Congress from choosing to spend public monies in that manner. [Congress's] prohibition is directly related to its purpose in providing subsidies for public broadcasting, and it is plainly rational for Congress to have determined that taxpayer monies should not be used to subsidize management's views.

The subsidy issue is examined more fully in section F1 supra.

Justice Stevens also dissented.

> [Of] greatest significance for me [is the fact that] the statutory restriction is completely neutral in its operation — it prohibits all editorials without any distinction [concerning] the point of view that might be expressed. [This being so, I believe that the interest] in maintaining government neutrality [outweighs] the impact on expression that results from this statute. Indeed, by simply terminating or reducing funding, Congress could curtail much more expression with no risk whatever of a constitutional transgression.

COLUMBIA BROADCASTING SYSTEM v. DEMOCRATIC NATIONAL COMMITTEE, 412 U.S. 94 (1973): In *CBS* the Court considered a question quite different from that posed in *Red Lion* — whether the first amendment *requires* broadcast licensees to sell advertising time to groups or individuals wishing to express their views on controversial issues of public importance. Respondents, the Democratic National Committee and the Business Executives' Move for Vietnam Peace, maintained that the absolute refusal of licensees to sell advertising time for such purposes violated the first amendment. The Court, in an opinion by Chief Justice Burger, held that, even "assuming governmental action," broadcasters were not constitutionally required "to accept editorial advertisements." Such a requirement would not necessarily further the "public interest in providing access to the marketplace of 'ideas and experiences,'" for it would be "heavily weighted in favor of the financially affluent," it would enable "the time allotted for editorial advertising [to] be monopolized by those of one political persuasion," it would risk "an enlargement of Government control over the content of broadcast discussion of public issues," and it would threaten the interests of listeners and viewers who "in a very real sense [constitute] a 'captive audience.'"

The Court emphasized further that "With broadcasting, where the available means of communication are limited in both space and time, ['what] is essential is not that everyone shall speak, but that everything worth saying shall be said.'" Under the FCC's fairness doctrine, broadcast licenses are already under an affirmative and independent obligation "to provide full and fair coverage of public issues." Thus, the real question "is not whether there is to be discussion of controversial issues of public importance on the broadcast media, but rather who shall determine what issues are to be discussed by whom, and when."

On this question, the Court rejected the "view that every potential speaker is 'the best judge' of what the listening public ought to hear": "[Editing] is what editors are for; and editing is selection and choice of material. In the delicate balancing historically followed in the regulation of broadcasting, Congress and the Commission could appropriately conclude that the allocation of journalistic priorities should be concentrated in the licensee rather than diffused among many. This policy gives the public some assurance that the broadcaster will be answerable if he fails to meet its legitimate needs. No such accountability attaches to the private individual. [Thus, to] agree that debate on public issues should be 'robust, and wide-open' does not mean that we should exchange 'public trustee' broadcasting, with all its limitations, for a system of self-appointed editorial commentators."

Justice Brennan, joined by Justice Marshall, dissented: "[The] broadcast frequencies allotted to the various radio and television licensees constitute appropriate 'forums' for the discussion of controversial issues of public importance. [Indeed,] the electronic media are today 'the public's prime source of information,' [and] any policy that *absolutely* denies citizens access to the airways necessarily [undercuts our 'profound national commitment to the principle that debate on public issues should be uninhibited, robust, and wide-open']."

"[Moreover], the Court's reliance on the Fairness Doctrine as an 'adequate' alternative to editorial advertising seriously overestimates the ability — or willingness — of broadcasters to expose the public to the 'widest possible dissemination of information from diverse and antagonistic sources.' [Under the fairness doctrine], broadcasters retain almost exclusive control over the selection of issues and viewpoints to be covered, the manner of presentation, and, perhaps most important, who shall speak. [In] light of the strong interest of broadcasters in maximizing their audience, and therefore their profits, it seems almost naive to expect the majority of broadcasters to produce the variety and controversiality of material necessary to reflect a full spectrum of viewpoints. [The] genius of the First Amendment [is] that it has always defined what the public ought to hear by permitting speakers to say what they wish. ['Supervised] and ordained discussion' is directly contrary to the underlying purposes of the First Amendment. [Thus, although the] Fairness Doctrine's requirement of full and fair coverage of controversial issues is, beyond doubt, a commendable and, indeed, essential tool for effective regulation of the broadcast [industry, it] simply cannot eliminate the need for a further, complementary airing of controversial views through the limited availability of editorial advertising."

Consider the following observations:

a. "[The] most important access claims may be those that seek to introduce new topics or allegations for public debate, as contrasted with claims to reply to previous communications. [The] contribution of enforced access [would] consist primarily in permitting [speakers] to break through the mist of 'newspeak' that tends to dull almost everyone's response to public events." Blasi, The Checking Value in First Amendment Theory, 1977 A.B.F. Res. J. 521, 628-629.

b. B. Schmidt, Freedom of the Press vs. Public Access 181 (1976):

[CBS] marked a shift in the Court's articulation of the theory of broadcast regulation. In Red Lion, the Court intimated a rationale for regulation that viewed broadcasters as proxies for the public, with no rights of autonomy over their temporarily leased frequencies. [CBS] rests on the view that broadcasters are public trustees rather than proxies designed to serve as a conduit for public expression. Under this trustee theory, broadcasters are obliged to operate in the public interest, [but they are] allowed a considerable degree of trustee discretion and editorial autonomy in day-to-day operations.

c. Bollinger, Elitism, The Masses and the Idea of Self-Government, in Constitutional Government in America 99, 104-105 (Collins ed. 1980):

[CBS] seemed to rely on the problems of administration and the need for journalistic discretion as the primary reasons for its result. It was this latter theory of the case that caused the decision to be hailed by the press [as] representing a substantial shift in the Court's thinking from that found in Red Lion. [But] the opinion is deceptive on that score; for the emphasis on journalistic discretion did not arise from a pure belief in the wisdom of journalists but rather from a perceived need to maintain control of the content of broadcasting in the hands of those who live under the aegis of government scrutiny. [The] difficulty with the claim of [the respondents] was that it opened the broadcast doors to people who were not made "responsible" through the subtle processes of government selection and oversight.

On other aspects of the access issue, see CBS v. FCC, 453 U.S. 367 (1981) (upholding the constitutionality of FCC rules interpreting section 312(a)(7) of the Communications Act, which requires broadcasters to permit "a legally qualified candidate for Federal elective office" to purchase "reasonable amounts of time" on "behalf of his candidacy"); FCC v. Midwest Video Corp., 440 U.S. 689 (1979) (holding that FCC rules requiring that certain cable systems hold out dedicated channels for all users on a first-come, nondiscriminatory basis, violated section 3(h) of the Communications Act, which provides that "a person engaged [in] broadcasting shall not [be] deemed a common carrier").

d.   A Right to "Gather" News?

Branzburg v. Hayes
408 U.S. 665 (1972)

Opinion of the Court by MR. JUSTICE WHITE. . . .

[Three cases were argued and decided together. Branzburg, a newspaper reporter, published several articles describing unlawful drug activities in Frankfort, Kentucky. He refused, on first amendment grounds, to disclose to a state grand jury the identities of the persons whose activities he had described.

Pappas, a television reporter, was given access to Black Panther headquarters in New Bedford, Massachusetts, in anticipation of a police raid. He agreed not to disclose anything he saw or heard except the expected raid. The raid never materialized, and Pappas never broadcast any report. He refused, on first amendment grounds, to disclose to a state grand jury investigating civil disorders anything he observed at the Panther headquarters.

Caldwell, a New York Times reporter, published several articles about the Black Panthers after interviewing their leaders. He refused, on first amendment grounds, to appear before a federal grand jury investigating possible violations of federal laws, including those prohibiting threats against the President. Caldwell maintained that even to appear before the grand jury would destroy his working relationship with the Panthers.

In *Branzburg* and *Pappas*, state courts rejected the constitutional argument. In *Caldwell*, a federal Court of Appeals held that a journalist need not appear before a grand jury in the absence of compelling reasons for requiring his testimony.]

The issue in these cases is whether requiring newsmen to appear and testify before state or federal grand juries abridges the freedom of speech and press guaranteed by the First Amendment. We hold that it does not.

Petitioners Branzburg and Pappas and respondent Caldwell press First Amendment claims that may be simply put: that to gather news it is often necessary to agree either not to identify the source of information published or to publish only part of the facts revealed, or both; that if the reporter is nevertheless forced to reveal these confidences to a grand jury, the source so identified and other confidential sources of other reporters will be measurably deterred from furnishing publishable information, all to the detriment of the free flow of information protected by the First Amendment. Although the newsmen in these cases do not claim an absolute privilege against official interrogation in all circumstances, they assert that the reporter should not be forced either to appear or to testify before a grand jury or at trial until and unless sufficient grounds are shown for believing that the reporter possesses information relevant to a crime the grand jury is investigating, that the information the reporter has is unavailable from other sources, and that the need for the information is sufficiently compelling to override the claimed invasion of First Amendment interests occasioned by the disclosure. [The] heart of the claim is that the burden on news gathering resulting from compelling reporters to disclose confidential information outweighs any public interest in obtaining the information.

We do not question the significance of free speech, press, or assembly to the country's welfare. Nor is it suggested that news gathering does not qualify for First Amendment protection; without some protection for seeking out the news, freedom of the press could be eviscerated. But these cases involve no [restriction] on what the press may publish, and no express or implied command that the press publish what it prefers to withhold. [The] use of confidential sources by the press is not forbidden or restricted. [The] sole issue before us is the obligation of reporters to respond to grand jury subpoenas as other citizens do and to answer questions relevant to an investigation into the commission of crime. . . .

[The] First Amendment does not invalidate every incidental burdening of the press that may result from the enforcement of civil or criminal statutes of general applicability. [Citing Associated Press v. NLRB; Oklahoma Press Publishing Co. v. Walling; Associated Press v. United States.] . . .

It has generally been held that the First Amendment does not guarantee the press a constitutional right of special access to information not available to the public generally. [In Zemel v. Rusk, 381 U.S. 1 (1965)], for example, the Court sustained the Government's refusal to validate passports to Cuba even though that restriction "render[ed] less than wholly free the flow of information concerning that country." The ban on travel was held constitutional, for "[t]he right to speak and publish does not carry with it the unrestrained right to gather information."

Despite the fact that news gathering may be hampered, the press is regularly excluded from grand jury proceedings, our own conferences, the meetings of other official bodies gathered in executive session, and the meetings of private organizations. Newsmen have no constitutional right of access to the scenes of crime or disaster when the general public is excluded, and they may be prohibited from [attending] trials if such restrictions are necessary to assure a defendant a fair trial before an impartial tribunal. . . .

It is thus not surprising that the great weight of authority is that newsmen are not exempt from the normal duty of appearing before a grand jury and answering questions relevant to a criminal investigation. . . .

The prevailing constitutional view of the newsman's privilege is very much rooted in the ancient role of the grand jury. [Because] its task is to inquire into the existence of possible criminal conduct and to return only well-founded indictments, its investigative powers are necessarily broad. [On] the records now before us, we perceive no basis for holding that the public interest in law enforcement and in ensuring effective grand jury proceedings is insufficient to override the consequential, but uncertain, burden on news gathering that is said to result from insisting that reporters, like other citizens, respond to relevant questions put to them in the course of a valid grand jury investigation or criminal trial.

This conclusion [does not] threaten the vast bulk of confidential relationships between reporters and their sources. [Only] where news sources themselves are implicated in crime or possess information relevant to the grand jury's task need they or the reporter be concerned about grand jury subpoenas. Nothing before us indicates that a large number or percentage of *all* confidential news sources falls into either category and would in any way be deterred by our holding. . . .

[Moreover, although the] argument that the flow of news will be diminished by compelling reporters to aid the grand jury in a criminal investigation is not [irrational, we] remain unclear how often and to what extent informers are actually deterred from furnishing information when newsmen are forced to testify before a grand jury. [The] evidence fails to demonstrate that there would be a significant constriction of the flow of news to the public if this Court reaffirms the prior common-law and constitutional rule regarding the testimonial obligations of newsmen.[33]

[Moreover, the] administration of a constitutional newsman's privilege would present practical and conceptual difficulties of a high order. Sooner or later, it would be necessary to define those categories of newsmen who qualified for the privilege, a questionable procedure in light of the traditional doctrine that liberty of the press is the right of the lonely pamphleteer [just] as much as of the large metropolitan publisher. [Almost] any author may [assert] that he is contributing to the flow of information to the public, that he relies on confidential sources of information, and that these sources will be silenced if he is forced to make disclosures before a grand jury.

In each instance where a reporter is subpoenaed to testify, the courts would also be embroiled in preliminary factual and legal determinations with respect to whether the proper predicate had been laid for the reporter's appearance: Is there probable cause to believe a crime has been committed? Is it likely that the reporter has useful information gained in confidence? Could the grand jury obtain the information elsewhere? Is the official interest sufficient to outweigh the claimed privilege? . . .

Finally, as we have earlier indicated, news gathering is not without its First Amendment protections, and grand jury investigations if instituted or conducted other than in good faith, would pose wholly different issues for resolution under the First Amendment. Official harassment of the press undertaken not for purposes of law enforcement but to disrupt a reporter's relationship with his news sources would have no justification. Grand juries are subject to judicial control and subpoenas to motions to quash. We do not expect courts will forget that grand juries must operate within the limits of the First Amendment. . . .

MR. JUSTICE POWELL, concurring.

I add this brief statement to emphasize what seems to me to be the limited nature of the Court's holding. The Court does not hold that newsmen, subpoenaed to testify before a grand jury, are without constitutional rights with respect to the gathering of news or in safeguarding their sources. . . .

As indicated in the concluding portion of the opinion, the Court states that no harassment of newsmen will be tolerated. If a newsman believes that the grand jury investigation is not being conducted in good faith he is not without remedy. Indeed, if the newsman is called upon to give information bearing only a remote and tenuous relationship to the subject of the investigation, or if he has some other reason to believe that his testimony implicates confidential source relationships without a legitimate need of law enforcement, he will have access to the court on a motion to quash and an appropriate protective order may be entered. The asserted claim to privilege should be judged on its facts by the striking of a proper balance between freedom of the press and the obligation of all citizens to give relevant testimony with respect to criminal conduct. The balance of these

33. In his Press Subpoenas: An Empirical and Legal Analysis, Study Report of the Reporters' Committee on Freedom of the Press 6-12, Prof. Vince Blasi [found] that slightly more than half of the 975 reporters questioned said that they relied on regular confidential sources for at least 10% of their stories. Of this group of reporters, only 8% were able to say with some certainty that their professional functioning had been adversely affected by the threat of subpoena; another 11% were not certain whether or not they had been adversely affected. [Relocated footnote. — EDS.]

vital constitutional and societal interests on a case-by-case basis accords with the tried and traditional way of adjudicating such questions.

In short, the courts will be available to newsmen under circumstances where legitimate First Amendment interests require protection.

Mr. Justice Douglas, dissenting. . . .

Today's decision will impede the wide-open and robust dissemination of ideas and counterthought which a free press both fosters and protects and which is essential to the success of intelligent self-government. . . .

I see no way of making mandatory the disclosure of a reporter's confidential source of the information on which he bases his news story. . . .

Mr. Justice Stewart, with whom Mr. Justice Brennan and Mr. Justice Marshall join, dissenting.

The Court's crabbed view of the First Amendment reflects a disturbing insensitivity to the critical role of an independent press in our society. [While] Mr. Justice Powell's enigmatic concurring opinion gives some hope of a more flexible view in the future, the Court in these cases holds that a newsman has no First Amendment right to protect his sources when called before a grand jury. The Court thus invites state and federal authorities to undermine the historic independence of the press by attempting to annex the journalistic profession as an investigative arm of government. . . .

The reporter's constitutional right to a confidential relationship with his source stems from the broad societal interest in a full and free flow of information to the public. It is this basic concern that underlies the Constitution's protection of a free press. . . .

A corollary of the right to publish must be the right to gather news. [The] right to gather news implies, in turn, a right to a confidential relationship between a reporter and his source. [Informants] are necessary to the news-gathering process as we know it today. [And] the promise of confidentiality may be a necessary prerequisite to a productive relationship between a newsman and his informants. . . .

The impairment of the flow of news cannot, of course, be proved with scientific precision, as the Court seems to demand. [But] we have never before demanded that First Amendment rights rest on elaborate empirical studies demonstrating beyond any conceivable doubt that deterrent effects exist. . . .

Rather, on the basis of common sense and available information, we have asked, often implicitly, (1) whether there was a rational connection between the cause (the governmental action) and the effect (the deterrence or impairment of First Amendment activity), and (2) whether the effect would occur with some regularity, i.e., would not be de minimis. [Citing, e.g., NAACP v. Alabama; Shelton v. Tucker; New York Times v. Sullivan; Elfbrandt v. Russell.] Once this threshold inquiry has been satisfied, we have then examined the competing interests in determining whether there is an unconstitutional infringement of First Amendment freedoms. . . .

Surely [the] claim of deterrence here is as securely grounded in evidence and common sense as the claims in the cases cited above. [To] require any greater burden of proof is to shirk our duty to protect values securely embedded in the Constitution. . . .

Posed against the First Amendment's protection of the newsman's confidential relationships in these cases is society's interest in the use of the grand jury to administer justice fairly and effectively. [To] perform these functions the grand jury must have available to it every man's relevant evidence. [But] the longstanding rule making every person's evidence available to the grand jury is not absolute. The rule has been limited by the Fifth Amendment, the Fourth Amendment, and the evidentiary privileges of the common law. . . .

In striking the proper balance between the public interest in the efficient administration of justice and the First Amendment guarantee of the fullest flow of information, we must begin with the basic proposition [that] First Amendment rights require special safeguards. . . .

[When] an investigation impinges on First Amendment rights, the government must not only show that the inquiry is of "compelling and overriding importance" but it must also "convincingly" demonstrate that the investigation is "substantially related" to the information sought.

Governmental officials must, therefore, demonstrate that the information sought is *clearly* relevant to a *precisely* defined subject of governmental inquiry. They must demonstrate that it is reasonable to think the witness in question has that information. And they must show that there is not any means of obtaining the information less destructive of First Amendment liberties. [Citing, e.g., *Gibson*.]

I believe the safeguards developed in our decisions involving governmental investigations must apply to the grand jury inquiries in these cases. Surely the function of the grand jury to aid in the enforcement of the law is no more important than the function of the legislature, and its committees, to make the law. . . .

Accordingly, when a reporter is asked to appear before a grand jury and reveal confidences, I would hold that the government must (1) show that there is probable cause to believe that the newsman has information that is clearly relevant to a specific probable violation of law; (2) demonstrate that the information sought cannot be obtained by alternative means less destructive of First Amendment rights; and (3) demonstrate a compelling and overriding interest in the information. . . .

No doubt the courts would be required to make some delicate judgments in working out this accommodation. But that, after all, is the function of courts of law. Better such judgments, however difficult, than the simplistic and stultifying absolutism adopted by the Court in denying any force to the First Amendment in these cases. . . .

Note: A Right to Gather News?

1. *Newsgathering*. Does the first amendment guarantee the press a right to gather as well as to publish the news? Has the press a first amendment right to gather news through such practices as deception, burglary, wiretapping, and the bribing of sources? Suppose a reporter breaks into a government official's home to uncover evidence of corruption. Can the reporter be prosecuted? Can the newspaper be restrained from publishing the information?

2. Branzburg. Does *Branzburg* recognize a right to gather news? In light of Justice Powell's concurring opinion, is it fair to say that the Court divided "by a vote of four and a half to four and a half"? Stewart, "Or of the Press," 26 Hast. L. Rev. 631, 635 (1975).

On the risk of chilling effect in *Branzburg*, consider Lewis, A Preferred Position for Journalism?, 7 Hofstra L. Rev. 595, 616-617 (1979):

> [It] does not follow that the press will find no confidential sources unless it has an assured testimonial privilege. [The] idea of a testimonial privilege under the first amendment was not even raised in this country until 1958; reporters managed to function without it. My guess is that most confidential sources talk to the press for their own compelling reasons of conscience or ideology or personal animus — and will continue to do so even if an occasional case demonstrates that reporters may come under legal pressure to name their sources.

On the impact of *Branzburg*, see generally Murasky, The Journalist's Privilege: *Branzburg* and Its Aftermath, 52 Tex. L. Rev. 820 (1974). Since *Branzburg* a majority of states have enacted some form of "shield" law to protect the confidentiality of press sources. See Sack, Reflections on the Wrong Question: Special Constitutional Privilege for the Institutional Press, 7 Hofstra L. Rev. 629, 651 n.112 (1979).

3. *Who is the "press"?* Do you agree with Justice White that any effort to define the "press" for purposes of a special "press" privilege "would present practical and conceptual difficulties of a high order"? Consider the following observations:

a. Lange, The Speech and Press Clauses, 23 U.C.L.A. L. Rev. 77, 106 (1975):

> [It is unlikely] that we will succeed in defining the press in ways which will prove satisfactory. [If] the press is defined broadly enough to include the pamphleteer and the underground, the definition also will have to approach speech so closely that the exclusion of speech will often seem arbitrary and unjustified. We will have [a] "structural provision" [with] no distinct structure. If, on the other hand, the pamphleteer and the underground are excluded, the result is perverse.

b. Abrams, The Press *Is* Different: Reflections on Justice Stewart and the Autonomous Press, 7 Hofstra L. Rev. 563, 580-583 (1979):

> In the great preponderance of cases, a court has little difficulty knowing a journalist when it sees one. [Nor] are the definitional difficulties insurmountable. Three approaches to defining "press" may be considered. One would be to afford equivalent "press" protection to all who write, thus treating the occasional pamphleteer precisely the same as the regularly employed journalist. [A] second, narrower, approach is a functional one. [Protection] could be afforded not only to journalists on established newspapers but "to free-lance writers, radio and television stations, magazines, academicians and any other person possessing materials in connection with the dissemination to the public of a newspaper, book, broadcast or other form of communication." The third, narrowest, definition might limit the entities protected by the press clause to [the] "institutional press." [This would] focus on such factors as the regularity of employment of the journalist and the regularity of publication of the newspaper involved. [What] is most important, however, is not the definition

that is chosen; it is the recognition that the conceded definitional difficulty is hardly a basis for affording no press protection at all. [It] is simply unacceptable to say that because a word in the Constitution is difficult to define, it should be afforded no meaning at all.

4. *Newsroom searches:* Zurcher. In Zurcher v. Stanford Daily, 436 U.S. 547 (1978), the Daily, a student newspaper, published articles and photographs concerning a violent clash on campus between demonstrators and police. Thereafter, the police obtained a warrant for an immediate search of the newspaper's offices for negatives, films, and pictures that might enable them to identify some of the demonstrators. The Daily's photographic laboratories, filing cabinets, desks, and wastepaper baskets were searched, but the police found only those photographs that had already been published. The Daily brought this civil action on the theory that the decision of the police to conduct a search, rather than to proceed by subpoena duces tecum, violated the first amendment. The Daily maintained that, unlike subpoenas, "searches of newspaper offices for evidence of crime [will] seriously threaten the ability of the press to gather, analyze, and disseminate news."

Justice White, speaking for the Court, rejected this argument:

> Properly administered, the preconditions for a warrant — probable cause, specificity with respect to the place to be searched and the things to be seized, and overall reasonableness — should afford sufficient protection against the harms that are assertedly threatened by warrants for searching newspaper offices. There is no reason to believe, for example, that magistrates cannot guard against searches of the type, scope, and intrusiveness that would actually interfere with the timely publication of a newspaper [or enable] officers to rummage at large in newspaper files. [Nor] are we convinced, any more than we were in [*Branzburg*], that confidential sources will disappear. [Whatever] incremental effect there may be in this regard [does] not make a constitutional difference.

In a concurring opinion, Justice Powell rejected the argument that "the press [is] entitled to a special procedure, not available to others, when government authorities [require] evidence in its possession." As in *Branzburg*, however, Powell interpreted the opinion of the Court narrowly, construing it as requiring "a magistrate asked to issue a warrant for the search of press offices [to] take cognizance of the independent values protected by the First Amendment."

Justice Stewart, joined by Justice Marshall, dissented:

> A search warrant allows police officers to ransack the files of a newspaper, reading each and every document until they have found the one named in the warrant, while a subpoena would permit the newspaper itself to produce only the specific documents requested. A search, unlike a subpoena, will therefore lead to the needless exposure of confidential information completely unrelated to the purpose of the investigation. The knowledge that police officers can make an unannounced raid on a newsroom is thus bound to have a deterrent effect on the availability of confidential news sources. [Moreover, here, unlike *Branzburg*, the journalists] do not claim that any of the evidence sought was privileged from disclosure; they claim only that a subpoena would have served equally well to produce that evidence. [If the police can demonstrate] that a subpoena would be impracticable, the magistrate [could then] issue a warrant. [Finally, a subpoena, unlike a search warrant,] would allow a newspaper, through a motion to quash, [to] demonstrate [that] the evidence sought did

not exist. The legitimate needs of government would thus [be] served without infringing on the freedom of the press.

Justice Stevens dissented on other grounds. Justice Brennan did not participate.

In the Privacy Protection Act of 1980, 42 U.S.C. §2000aa, Congress prohibited any government officer to search for work product or other documents of any "person reasonably believed to have a purpose to disseminate to the public a newspaper, book, broadcast, or other similar form of public communication," unless there is either probable cause to believe that the person is involved in the crime being investigated or there is otherwise reason to believe that giving notice by subpoena would result in the loss of the evidence.

Pell v. Procunier

417 U.S. 817 (1974)

MR. JUSTICE STEWART delivered the opinion of the Court. . . .

[Three] professional journalists [brought this] suit to challenge the constitutionality [of] §415.071 of the California Department of Corrections Manual, which [prohibits] face-to-face interviews between press representatives and individual inmates whom they specifically name and request to interview. . . .

[Plaintiffs] contend that [members] of the press have a constitutional right to interview any inmate who is willing to speak with them, in the absence of an individualized determination that the particular interview might create a clear and present danger to prison security or to some other substantial interest served by the corrections system. [They] rely on their right to gather news without governmental interference, which [they] assert includes a right of access to the sources of what is regarded as newsworthy information.

We note at the outset that this regulation is not part of an attempt by the State to conceal the conditions in its prisons or to frustrate the press' investigation and reporting of those conditions. [The] Department of Corrections regularly conducts public tours through the prisons for the benefit of interested citizens. In addition, newsmen are permitted to visit both the maximum security and minimum security sections of the institutions and to stop and speak about any subject to any inmates whom they might encounter. . . .

The sole limitation on newsgathering in California prisons is the prohibition in §415.071 of interviews with individual inmates specifically designated by representatives of the press. This restriction [was adopted in 1971]. Prior to the promulgation of §415.071, every journalist had virtually free access to interview any individual inmate whom he might wish. . . .

In practice, it was found that the policy in effect prior to the promulgation of §415.071 had resulted in press attention being concentrated on a relatively small number of inmates who, as a result, became virtual "public figures" within the prison society and gained a disproportionate degree of notoriety and influence among their fellow inmates. Because of this notoriety and influence, these inmates often became the source of severe disciplinary problems. [Section 415.071 was adopted to mitigate the problem.]

[The] media plaintiffs assert that, despite the substantial access to California prisons and their inmates accorded representatives of the [press,] face-to-face interviews with specifically designated inmates is such an effective and superior method of newsgathering that its curtailment amounts to unconstitutional state interference with a free press. We do not agree. . . .

The First and Fourteenth Amendments bar government from interfering in any way with a free press. The Constitution does not, however, require government to accord the press special access to information not shared by members of the public generally. It is one thing to say that a journalist is free to seek out sources of information not available to members of the general public, that he is entitled to some constitutional protection of the confidentiality of such sources, cf. [Branzburg], and that government cannot restrain the publication of news emanating from such sources. Cf. [Pentagon Papers, supra section B4]. It is quite another thing to suggest that the Constitution imposes upon government the affirmative duty to make available to journalists sources of information not available to members of the public generally. That proposition finds no support in the words of the Constitution or in any decision of this Court. Accordingly, since §415.071 does not deny the press access to sources of information available to members of the general public, we hold that it does not abridge the protections that the First and Fourteenth Amendments guarantee. . . .

MR. JUSTICE DOUGLAS, with whom MR. JUSTICE BRENNAN and MR. JUSTICE MARSHALL join, dissenting. . . .

In dealing with the free press guarantee, it is important to note that the interest it protects [is] the right of the people, the true sovereign under our constitutional scheme, to govern in an informed manner. [Prisons,] like all other public institutions, are ultimately the responsibility of the populace. [The] public's interest in being informed about prisons is thus paramount. . . .

It [is] not enough to note that the press [is] denied no more access to the prisons than is denied the public generally. [In my view,] the absolute ban on press interviews with specifically designated [inmates] is far broader than is necessary to protect any legitimate governmental interests and is an unconstitutional infringement on the public's right to know protected by the free press guarantee of the First Amendment.

MR. JUSTICE POWELL, [dissenting]. . . .

For the reasons stated in my dissenting opinion in [Saxbe v. Washington Post Co., 417 U.S. 843 (1974)], I would hold that California's absolute ban against prisoner-press interviews impermissibly restrains the ability of the press to perform its constitutionally established function of informing the people on the conduct of their government. Accordingly, I dissent from the judgment of the Court.

In Saxbe, decided on the same day as Pell, the Court sustained a United States Bureau of Prisons policy virtually identical to the regulation upheld in Pell. Dissenting in Saxbe, Justice Powell, joined by Justices Brennan and Marshall, argued as follows:

> [The journalists] claim a right of access by the press to newsworthy events. [The] Court rejects this claim on the ground that "newsmen have no constitutional right of access to prisons or their inmates beyond that afforded the general public." [I agree]

that neither any news organization nor reporters as individuals have constitutional rights superior to those enjoyed by ordinary citizens. [But] I cannot follow the Court in concluding that *any* governmental restriction on press access to information, so long as it is nondiscriminatory, falls outside the purview of First Amendment concern. . . .

[*Branzburg* does not] compel the majority's resolution of this case. [A] fair reading of the majority's analysis in *Branzburg* makes plain that the result hinged on an assessment of the competing societal interests involved in that case rather than on any determination that First Amendment freedoms were not implicated. . . .

[Although it] goes too far to suggest that the government must justify under the stringent standards of First Amendment review every regulation that might affect in some tangential way the availability of information to the news [media, it] is equally impermissible to conclude that no governmental inhibition of press access to newsworthy information warrants constitutional scrutiny. At some point official restraints on access to news sources, even though not directed solely at the press, may so undermine the function of the First Amendment that it is both appropriate and necessary to require the government to justify such regulations in terms more compelling than discretionary authority and administrative convenience. It is worth repeating our admonition in *Branzburg* that "without some protection for seeking out the news, freedom of the press could be eviscerated." . . .

What is at stake here is the societal function of the First Amendment in preserving free public discussion of governmental affairs. [An] informed public depends on accurate and effective reporting by the news media. No individual can obtain for himself the information needed for the intelligent discharge of his political responsibilities. For most citizens the prospect of personal familiarity with newsworthy events is hopelessly unrealistic. In seeking out the news the press therefore acts as an agent of the public at large. It is the means by which the people receive that free flow of information and ideas essential to intelligent self-government. By enabling the public to assert meaningful control over the political process, the press performs a crucial function in effecting the societal purpose of the First Amendment. [The] Bureau's absolute prohibition of prisoner-press interviews negates the ability of the press to discharge that function and thereby substantially impairs the right of the people to a free flow of information and ideas on the conduct of their Government. The underlying right is the right of the public. . . .

The Bureau's principal justification for its interview ban has become known during the course of this litigation as the "big wheel" phenomenon. [The] Bureau argues that press interviews with "big wheels" increase their status and influence and thus enhance their ability to persuade other prisoners to engage in disruptive behavior. [But] the "big wheel" theory [applies] only to those individuals with both disruptive proclivities and leadership potential. [The] remedy of no interview of any inmate is broader than is necessary to avoid the concededly real problems of the "big wheel" phenomenon.

HOUCHINS v. KQED, 438 U.S. 1 (1978): In 1975 KQED reported the suicide of a prisoner in the Greystone portion of the Santa Rita jail. Thereafter, KQED requested and was denied permission to inspect and take pictures within the Greystone facility. KQED brought this action claiming that the refusal to permit public or media access to the jail violated the first amendment. Shortly after the action was filed, Sheriff Houchins modified his "no-access" policy and instituted a series of monthly tours of the jail. Each tour was limited to twenty-five persons, including representatives of the press. The tours did not include the Greystone facility. No cameras or tape recorders were allowed, and those on the tours were not permitted to interview inmates. The District Court rejected the sheriff's contention that such a restrictive policy was necessary to protect inmate privacy and to minimize security and administrative problems. It therefore preliminarily enjoined the sheriff from denying KQED and other "responsible representatives" of the press "access to the Santa Rita facilities, including Greystone, 'at reasonable times and hours' and 'from preventing [them] from utilizing photographic and sound equipment [and] inmate interviews in providing full and accurate coverage of the Santa Rita facilities.' " The Court of Appeals affirmed. In a three-one-three decision, the Supreme Court, Justices Marshall and Blackmun not participating, affirmed in part and reversed in part. Chief Justice Burger, joined by Justices White and Rehnquist, found *Pell* controlling:

"This Court has never intimated a First Amendment guarantee of a right of access to all sources of information within government control. [*Branzburg's*] observation, in dictum, that 'news gathering is not without its First Amendment protections,' in no sense implied a constitutional right of access to news sources. [There] is an undoubted right to gather news 'from any source by means within the law,' but that affords no basis for the claim that the First Amendment compels others — private persons or governments — to supply information."

Justice Stewart concurred in the judgment: "The First and Fourteenth Amendments do not guarantee the public a right of access to information generated or controlled by government, nor do they guarantee the press any basic right of access superior to that of the public generally. The Constitution does no more than assure the public and the press equal access once government has opened its doors. Accordingly, I agree substantially with [the opinion of the Chief Justice. However, whereas] he appears to view 'equal access' as meaning access that is identical in all respects, I believe that the concept of equal access must be accorded more flexibility in order to accommodate the practical distinctions between the press and the general public.

"When on assignment, a journalist does not tour a jail for his own edification. He is there to gather information to be passed on to others, [and our] society depends heavily on the press for [its] enlightenment. [Thus,] the terms of access that are reasonably imposed on individual members may, if they impede effective reporting without sufficient justification, be unreasonable as applied to journalists who are there to convey to the general public what the visitors see."

Applying this standard, Stewart agreed with the District Court's findings that "the press required access to the jail on a more flexible and frequent basis than scheduled monthly tours if it was to keep the public informed," and that "the media required cameras and recording equipment for effective presentation to the viewing public of the conditions at the jail seen by individual visitors." Stewart found the injunction "overbroad," however, insofar as it "ordered the Sheriff to permit reporters into the [Greystone] facility and [to] interview randomly encountered inmates," for in "both these respects, the injunction gave the press access to areas and sources of information from which persons on the public tours had been excluded, and thus enlarged the scope of what the [sheriff] had opened to public view."

Justice Stevens, joined by Justices Brennan and Powell, dissented. Stevens maintained that this case was not controlled by *Pell*, for in *Pell* the "Court found that the [challenged policy] was 'not part of an attempt by the State to conceal the conditions in its prisons' " and "the record demonstrated that the flow of information to the public [was] adequate [despite] the challenged policy," whereas here, when "the suit was filed, there were no public tours [and the Sheriff] enforced a policy of virtually total exclusion of both the public and the press from those areas within the [jail] where the inmates were confined." Thus, "even though the Constitution provides the press with no greater right of access to information than that possessed by the public," the Sheriff's "no-access" policy violated the independent right of the public "to be informed about conditions within [its prisons]."

Stevens explained that the "preservation of a full and free flow of information to the general public has long been recognized as a core objective of the First Amendment." Moreover, "it is not sufficient [that] the channels of communication be free of governmental restraints. Without some protection for the acquisition of information about the operation of public institutions [by] the public at large, the process of self-governance [would] be stripped of its substance." Although conceding that there are "occasions when governmental activity may properly be carried on in complete secrecy," Stevens observed that "there is no legitimate penological justification for concealing from citizens the conditions in which their fellow citizens are being confined." Moreover, there are especially compelling reasons to allow "a democratic community access to knowledge about how its servants [treat those] of its members who have been committed to their custody." Thus, Stevens concluded, an "official prison policy of concealing [knowledge about the operation of a prison] by arbitrarily cutting off the flow of information at its source abridges the [First Amendment]."

Note: A Press Right of Access to Government Information?

1. *Right of access.* Does the first amendment guarantee the press a right of access to government information? If the right of the press to *publish* information about the activities of government is central to the first amendment, isn't the right of the press to *obtain* such information equally central? Consider the following:

a. BeVier, An Informed Public, An Informing Press: The Search for a Constitutional Principle, 68 Calif. L. Rev. 482, 498-499 (1980):

> The effect on the flow of information [of] government denials of access to information [is] similar to the [effect of such direct restrictions on publication as punishment and censorship. But] the failure of government to [grant] access cannot be credibly argued to be the constitutional equivalent of [such direct restrictions. Punishment and censorship] interfere quite directly with the freedom to publish. When the government denies access to information, however, it poses no threat to freedom, at least if that word is given its ordinary legal meaning. [Punishment and] censorship directly undermine the value of *free* speech, while the denial of access to information undermines [only] the value of *well-informed* speech.

Recall the problem of access to public property for speech purposes, supra section E2.

b. "[Government] may guard mightily against [leaks], and yet must suffer them if they occur. [It] is a disorderly situation, surely. But if we ordered it we would have to sacrifice one of two contending values — privacy or public discourse — which are ultimately irreconcilable. [Thus, to effect a compromise, the First

Amendment] ordains an unruly contest between the press [and] government." A. Bickel, The Morality of Consent 80, 87 (1975). Recall the problem of restrictions on the disclosure of confidential information, supra section F3d.

If there is a first amendment right of press access to government information, what are its limits? Is government under a constitutional obligation to make public all information that might enhance "the ability of our people through free and open debate to consider and resolve their own destiny"? Do you agree that it is "impossible to conceive of a court making case-by-case determinations of the 'necessity' of nondisclosure in any way that would bear even the faintest resemblance [to] 'reasoned elaboration' "? BeVier, supra, at 510.

2. "Offensive" and "defensive" press rights: a theory of press autonomy? Consider Blasi, The Checking Value in the First Amendment, 1977 A.B.F. Res. J. 521, 596:

> [In his opinions in *Branzburg* and *Zurcher*, on the one hand, and *Pell* and *Houchins*, on the other, Justice Stewart] drew a sharp distinction between the claim to freedom from government interference with source relationships that reporters have established on their own and the contention "that the Constitution imposes upon government the affirmative duty to make available to journalists sources of information not available to members of the public generally." Since this [distinction] would not seem to be of pivotal importance if the overriding consideration is the amount and quality of information available to the public, Justice Stewart's heavy reliance on [it] suggests that his principal concern [was] the institutional autonomy of the press.

Does the "institutional autonomy of the press" provide a more satisfactory basis for interpreting the "press" clause than the public's "right to know"? Consider Baker, Press Rights and Government Power to Structure the Press, 34 U. Miami L. Rev. 819, 839-845 (1980):

> Testimonial privileges, protection against searches and seizures, and most protections against regulation are defensive rights: they protect the [press] against destruction, interference, or appropriation by government. Special access to information is an offensive right, a special privilege to engage in activities relevant to press functions. [The] justifications for institutional protection of the press — (1) the need to preserve an outside source that can expose government practices and abuses and (2) the importance of nongovernmentally controlled sources of information [and opinion — suggest] that the press clause rationale is persuasive only for defensive rights. [The] checking function of the press clearly requires independence from government; it requires rights that give the press a defense against government intrusions. [Offensive rights are more problematic. Although] a right of access to government facilities or information furthers the press's capacity to inform and [expose,] constitutionally based access privileges are not as necessary to the protection of the press's integrity [and] neither a separation-of-powers nor a fourth-estate theory requires them.

3. *Are there potential dangers in recognizing a "preferred" status for the press?* Consider Van Alstyne, The First Amendment and the Free Press: A Comment on Some New Trends and Some Old Theories, 9 Hofstra L. Rev. 1, 19-23 (1980):

> [If] journalists may assert access to certain public facilities [in] "first amendment preference" to laypersons, [it] may follow symmetrically that the ensuing published

story must meet a standard of professionalism commensurate with the privileged standing of the reporter. [The press operates] most effectively and most legitimately precisely because it forms no part of government. Each journal, whether trashy and truckling or fearless and admirable, does not now submit its editorial autonomy to public regulation. The point is an important one. It was made most emphatically in [*Tornillo*. This] important security of the fourth estate from the encumbrance of public regulation [may] be at risk if one's accent is not on the freedom of the press but is, rather, on the public's right to know. [We] have already imposed upon radio and television substantial "public" obligations — in exchange for exclusive, cost-free licensing privileges. [There] is no reason to suppose that the matter will be different for newspapers should they, too, "succeed" in securing particular rights, privileges, exemptions, or immunities that [others] cannot claim under a single and indivisible amendment.

See also Bezanson, The New Free Press Guarantee, 63 Va. L. Rev. 731, 732-734 (1977).

4. *Access to judicial proceedings:* Gannett. In Gannett v. DePasquale, 443 U.S. 368 (1979), the defendants in a murder prosecution requested that the public and the press be excluded from a pretrial hearing on a motion to suppress allegedly involuntary confessions. The district attorney did not oppose the request, and the trial judge, finding that the adverse publicity might jeopardize the defendants' right to a fair trial, granted the closure motion. In upholding this order, the Court focused primarily on the claim that the order violated the sixth amendment's guarantee that "In all criminal prosecutions, the accused shall enjoy the right to a [public] trial."

Justice Stewart delivered the opinion of the Court. Although conceding that "there is a strong societal interest in public trials," the Court concluded that the sixth amendment guarantee "is personal to the accused" and that "members of the public" thus "have no constitutional right under the Sixth [Amendment] to attend criminal trials." Turning to the first amendment, the Court found it unnecessary to decide "in the abstract" whether there was a first amendment right of the press or public to attend criminal trials, for "even assuming arguendo, that the [first amendment] may guarantee such access in some situations, [this] putative right was given all appropriate deference by the state [court] in the present case." In reaching this conclusion, the Court noted that (1) none of the spectators present in the courtroom, including a reporter, objected when the defendants moved for closure; (2) the trial judge had concluded that an open proceeding would pose a "reasonable probability of prejudice" to the defendants, so that the closure decision was based "on an assessment of the competing social interests involved [rather] than on any determination that First Amendment freedoms were not implicated"; and (3) "any denial of access [was] only temporary," for once "the danger of prejudice had dissipated, a transcript [was] made available."

Justice Blackmun, joined by Justices Brennan, White, and Marshall, dissented in part. Blackmun argued that the sixth amendment "prohibits the States from excluding the public from a [trial] without affording full and fair consideration to the public's interests in maintaining an open proceeding." Blackmun explained that, under the sixth amendment, "an accused who seeks closure [must] establish that it is strictly and inescapably necessary in order to protect the fair trial guarantee." Blackmun therefore found it unnecessary to "reach the issue of First Amendment access." See Waller v. Georgia, 467 U.S. — (1984) (holding that closure of a pretrial suppression hearing violates the sixth amendment unless, as in *Gannett*, the defendant consents).

Richmond Newspapers v. Virginia
448 U.S. 555 (1980)

MR. CHIEF JUSTICE BURGER announced the judgment of the Court and delivered an opinion, in which MR. JUSTICE WHITE and MR. JUSTICE STEVENS joined.

The narrow question presented in this case is whether the right of the public and press to attend criminal trials is guaranteed under the United States Constitution.

[In 1976 Stevenson was convicted of murder. The conviction was reversed, however, and two subsequent trials ended in mistrials. At the outset of his fourth trial, Stevenson moved that the proceeding be closed to the public. Neither the prosecutor nor anyone else present, including two of appellant's reporters, objected to the motion. The trial judge, acting pursuant to a Virginia statute authorizing the court, "in its discretion," to "exclude from the trial any persons whose presence would impair the conduct of a fair trial," ordered "that the Courtroom be kept clear of all parties except the witnesses when they testify." Later that day, appellant moved to vacate the closure order. In defense of the order, Stevenson argued that he "didn't want information to leak out," be published by the media, perhaps inaccurately, and then be seen by the jurors. The trial judge, noting also that "having people in the Courtroom is distracting to the jury," denied the motion to vacate and ordered the trial to continue "with the press and public excluded." The following day the trial judge excused the jury and found Stevenson "not guilty." As soon as the trial ended, tapes of the proceeding were made available to the public.]

We begin consideration of this case by noting that the precise issue presented here has not previously been before this Court for decision. In [*Gannett*], the Court was not required to decide whether a right of access to *trials*, as distinguished from hearings on *pre*trial motions, was constitutionally guaranteed. . . . .

The origins of the proceeding which has become the modern criminal trial in Anglo-American justice can be traced back beyond reliable historical records. [Throughout] its evolution, the trial has been open to all who cared to observe. [This] is no quirk of history; rather, it has long been recognized as an indispensable attribute of an Anglo-American trial. [Such openness gives] assurance that the proceedings [are] conducted fairly to all concerned, and it [discourages] perjury, the misconduct of participants, and decisions based on secret bias or partiality.

[Moreover,] public trials [have] significant community therapeutic value. [When] a shocking crime occurs, a community reaction of outrage and public protest often follows. Thereafter the open processes of justice serve an important prophylactic purpose, providing an outlet for community concern, hostility, and emotion. . . .

The Bill of Rights was enacted against the backdrop of the long history of trials being presumptively open. [In] guaranteeing freedoms such as those of speech and press, the First Amendment can be read as protecting the right of everyone to attend trials so as to give meaning to those explicit guarantees. "[T]he First Amendment goes beyond protection of the press and the self-expression of individuals to prohibit government from limiting the stock of information from which members of the public may draw." Free speech carries with it some freedom to listen. "In a variety of contexts this Court has referred to a First Amendment right to 'receive information and ideas.'" What this means in the context of trials is that the First Amendment guarantees of speech and press, standing alone, prohibit the government from summarily closing courtroom doors which had long been open to the public at the time that Amendment was adopted. . . .

It is not crucial whether we describe this right to attend criminal trials to hear, see, and communicate observations concerning them as a "right of access,"[11] or a "right to gather information," for we have recognized that "without some protection for seeking out the news, freedom of the press could be eviscerated." [*Branzburg*.] The explicit, guaranteed rights to speak and to publish concerning what takes place at a trial would lose much meaning if access to observe the trial could, as it was here, be foreclosed arbitrarily.[12] . . .

The State argues that the Constitution nowhere spells out a guarantee for the right of the public to attend trials, and that accordingly no such right is protected. The possibility that such a contention could be made did not escape the notice of the Constitution's draftsmen; they were concerned that some important rights might be thought disparaged because not specifically guaranteed. It was even argued that because of this danger no Bill of Rights should be adopted. . . .[15]

But arguments such as the State makes have not precluded recognition of important rights not enumerated. Notwithstanding the appropriate caution against reading into the Constitution rights not explicitly defined, the Court has acknowledged that certain unarticulated rights are implicit in enumerated guarantees. For example, the rights of association and of privacy, the right to be presumed innocent, and the right to be judged by a standard of proof beyond a reasonable doubt in a criminal trial, as well as the right to travel, appear nowhere in the Constitution or Bill of Rights. Yet these important but unarticulated rights have nonetheless been found to share constitutional protection in common with explicit guarantees.[16] . . .

We hold that the right to attend criminal trials[17] is implicit in the guarantees of the First Amendment; without the freedom to attend such trials, which people

11. *Procunier* and *Saxbe* are distinguishable in the sense that they were concerned with penal institutions which, by definition, are not "open" or public places. Penal institutions do not share the long tradition of openness. . . .

12. That the right to attend may be exercised by people less frequently today when information as to trials generally reaches them by way of print and electronic media in no way alters the basic right. Instead of relying on personal observation or reports from neighbors as in the past, most people receive information concerning trials through the media whose representatives "are entitled to the same rights [to attend trials] as the general public."

15. Madison's comments in Congress [reveal] the perceived need for some sort of constitutional "saving clause," which, among other things, would serve to foreclose application to the Bill of Rights of the maxim that the affirmation of particular rights implies a negation of those not expressly defined. Madison's efforts, culminating in the Ninth Amendment, served to allay the fears of those who were concerned that expressing certain guarantees could be read as excluding others.

16. See, e.g., NAACP v. Alabama, 357 U.S. 449 (1958) (right of association); Griswold v. Connecticut, 381 U.S. 479 (1965), and Stanley v. Georgia, 394 U.S. 557 (1969) (right to privacy); Estelle v. Williams, 425 U.S. 501, 503 (1976), and Taylor v. Kentucky, 436 U.S. 478, 483-486 (1978) (presumption of innocence); In re Winship, 397 U.S. 358 (1970) (standard of proof beyond a reasonable doubt); United States v. Guest, 383 U.S. 745, 757-759 (1966), and Shapiro v. Thompson, 394 U.S. 618, 630 (1969) (right to interstate travel).

17. Whether the public has a right to attend trials of civil cases is a question not raised by this case, but we note that historically both civil and criminal trials have been presumptively open.

have exercised for centuries, important aspects of freedom of speech and "of the press could be eviscerated."

Having concluded there was a guaranteed right of the public under the First and Fourteenth Amendments to attend the trial of Stevenson's case, we return to the closure order challenged by appellants. [Despite] the fact that this was the fourth trial of the accused, the trial judge made no findings to support closure; no inquiry was made as to whether alternative solutions would have met the need to ensure fairness; there was no recognition of any right under the Constitution for the public or press to attend the trial. In contrast to the pretrial proceeding dealt with in *Gannett*, there exist in the context of the trial itself various tested alternatives to satisfy the constitutional demands of fairness. There was no suggestion that any problems with witnesses could not have been dealt with by their exclusion from the courtroom or their sequestration during the trial. Nor is there anything to indicate that sequestration of the jurors would not have guarded against their being subjected to any improper information. All of the alternatives admittedly present difficulties for trial courts, but none of the factors relied on here was beyond the realm of the manageable. Absent an overriding interest articulated in findings, the trial of a criminal case must be open to the public.[18] Accordingly, the judgment under review is [reversed].

Mr. Justice Powell took no part in the consideration or decision of this case.

Mr. Justice Brennan, with whom Mr. Justice Marshall joins, concurring in the judgment. . . .

While freedom of expression is made inviolate by the First Amendment, and, with only rare and stringent exceptions, may not be suppressed, the First Amendment has not been viewed by the Court in all settings as providing an equally categorical assurance of the correlative freedom of access to information. . . .[2]

The Court's approach in right-of-access cases simply reflects the special nature of a claim of First Amendment right to gather information. Customarily, First Amendment guarantees are interposed to protect communication between speaker and listener. [But] the First Amendment embodies more than a commitment to free expression and communicative interchange for their own sakes; it has a *structural* role to play in securing and fostering our republican system of self-government. Implicit in this structural role is not only "the principle that

---

18. We have no occasion here to define the circumstances in which all or parts of a criminal trial may be closed to the public, but our holding today does not mean that the First Amendment rights of the public and representatives of the press are absolute. Just as a government may impose reasonable time, place, and manner restrictions upon the use of its streets in the interest of such objectives as the free flow of traffic, see, e.g., Cox v. New Hampshire, [supra section E2a], so may a trial judge, in the interest of the fair administration of justice, impose reasonable limitations on access to a trial. "[T]he question in a particular case is whether that control is exerted so as not to deny or unwarrantedly abridge . . . the opportunities for the communication of thought and the discussion of public questions immemorially associated with resort to public places." It is far more important that trials be conducted in a quiet and orderly setting than it is to preserve that atmosphere on city streets. Moreover, since courtrooms have limited capacity, there may be occasions when not every person who wishes to attend can be accommodated. In such situations, reasonable restrictions on general access are traditionally imposed, including preferential seating for media representatives. . . .

2. A conceptually separate, yet related, question is whether the media should enjoy greater access rights than the general public. But no such contention is at stake here. Since the media's right of access is at least equal to that of the general public, this case is resolved by a decision that the state statute unconstitutionally restricts public access to trials. As a practical matter, however, the institutional press is the likely, and fitting, chief beneficiary of a right of access because it serves as the "agent" of interested citizens, and funnels information about trials to a large number of individuals.

debate on public issues should be uninhibited, robust, and wide-open," but the antecedent assumption that valuable public debate — as well as other civic behavior — must be informed. The structural model links the First Amendment to that process of communication necessary for a democracy to survive, and thus entails solicitude not only for communication itself, but also for the indispensable conditions of meaningful communication.

However, because "the stretch of this protection is theoretically endless," it must be invoked with discrimination and temperance. For so far as the participating citizen's need for information is concerned, "[t]here are few restrictions on action which could not be clothed by ingenious argument in the garb of decreased data flow." An assertion of the prerogative to gather information must accordingly be assayed by considering the information sought and the opposing interests invaded.

[At] least two helpful principles may be sketched. First, the case for a right of access has special force when drawn from an enduring and vital tradition of public entree to particular proceedings or information. Such a tradition commands respect in part because the Constitution carries the gloss of history. More importantly, a tradition of accessibility implies the favorable judgment of experience. Second, the value of access must be measured in specifics. Analysis is not advanced by rhetorical statements that all information bears upon public issues; what is crucial in individual cases is whether access to a particular government process is important in terms of that very process.

To resolve the case before us, therefore, we must consult historical and current practice with respect to open trials, and weigh the importance of public access to the trial process itself. . . .

Tradition, contemporaneous state practice, and this Court's own decisions manifest a common understanding that "[a] trial is a public event. What transpires in the court room is public property." As a matter of law and virtually immemorial custom, public trials have been the essentially unwavering rule in ancestral England and in our own Nation. Such abiding adherence to the principle of open trials "reflect[s] a profound judgment about the way in which law should be enforced and justice administered."

Publicity serves to advance several of the particular purposes of the trial (and, indeed, the judicial) process. Open trials play a fundamental role in furthering the efforts of our judicial system to assure the criminal defendant a fair and accurate adjudication of guilt or innocence. [Moreover, public] access is essential [if] trial adjudication is to achieve the objective of maintaining public confidence in the administration of justice. [Finally,] the trial is more than a demonstrably just method of adjudicating disputes and protecting rights. [Under] our system, judges are not mere umpires, but, in their own sphere, lawmakers — a coordinate branch of *government*. [Public] access to trials acts as an important check, akin in purpose to the other checks and balances that infuse our system of government. "The knowledge that every criminal trial is subject to contemporaneous review in the forum of public opinion is an effective restraint on possible abuse of judicial power." . . .

Popular attendance at trials, in sum, substantially furthers the particular public purposes of that critical judicial proceeding. In that sense, public access is an indispensable element of the trial process itself. Trial access, therefore, assumes structural importance in our "government of laws." . . .

[Thus,] our ingrained tradition of public trials and the importance of public access to the broader purposes of the trial process, tip the balance strongly toward the rule that trials be open. What countervailing interests might be sufficiently compelling to reverse this presumption of openness need not concern us now,[24] for the statute at stake here authorizes trial closures at the unfettered discretion of the judge and parties.[25] Accordingly, [the statute] violates the First and Fourteenth Amendments, and the decision of the Virginia Supreme Court to the contrary should be reversed.

Mr. Justice Stewart, concurring in the judgment. . . .

Whatever the ultimate answer [with] respect to pretrial suppression hearings in criminal cases, the First and Fourteenth Amendments clearly give the press and the public a right of access to trials themselves, civil as well as criminal. [It] has for centuries been a basic presupposition of the Anglo-American legal system that trials shall be public trials. [With] us, a trial is by very definition a proceeding open to the press and to the public.

In conspicuous contrast to a military base, Greer v. Spock, [supra section E2b]; a jail, Adderley v. Florida, [supra section E2b]; or a prison, [*Pell*], a trial courtroom is a public place. Even more than city streets, sidewalks, and parks as areas of First Amendment activity, a trial courtroom is a place where representatives of the press and of the public are not only free to be, but where their presence serves to assure the integrity of what goes on.

But this does not mean that the First Amendment right of members of the public and representatives of the press to attend civil and criminal trials is absolute. Just as a legislature may impose reasonable time, place, and manner restrictions upon the exercise of First Amendment freedoms, so may a trial judge impose reasonable limitations upon the unrestricted occupation of a courtroom by representatives of the press and members of the public. Much more than a city street, a trial courtroom must be a quiet and orderly place. Moreover, every courtroom has a finite physical capacity, and there may be occasions when not all who wish to attend a trial may do so.[3] And while there exist many alternative ways to satisfy the constitutional demands of a fair trial,[4] those demands may also sometimes justify limitations upon the unrestricted presence of spectators in the courtroom.[5]

Since in the present case the trial judge appears to have given no recognition to the right of representatives of the press and members of the public to be present at the Virginia murder trial over which he was presiding, the judgment under review must be reversed. . . .

24. For example, national security concerns about confidentiality may sometimes warrant closures during sensitive portions of trial proceedings, such as testimony about state secrets. Cf. United States v. Nixon, 418 U.S. 683, 714-716 (1974).

25. Significantly, closing a trial lacks even the justification for barring the door to pretrial hearings: the necessity of preventing dissemination of suppressible prejudicial evidence to the public before the jury pool has become, in a practical sense, finite and subject to sequestration.

3. In such situations, representatives of the press must be assured access.

4. Such alternatives include sequestration of juries, continuances, and changes of venue.

5. This is not to say that only constitutional considerations can justify such restrictions. The preservation of trade secrets, for example, might justify the exclusion of the public from at least some segments of a civil trial. And the sensibilities of a youthful prosecution witness, for example, might justify similar exclusion in a criminal trial for rape, so long as the defendant's Sixth Amendment right to a public trial were not impaired.

MR. JUSTICE BLACKMUN, concurring in the judgment.

My opinion and vote in partial dissent last Term in [*Gannett*] compels my vote to reverse the judgment of the Supreme Court of Virginia. . . .

MR. JUSTICE REHNQUIST, dissenting. . . .

[I] do not believe that [the Constitution] requires that a State's reasons for denying public access to a trial, where both the prosecuting attorney and the defendant have consented to an order of closure approved by the judge, are subject to any additional constitutional review at our hands. . . .

The issue here is not whether the "right" to freedom of the press conferred by the First Amendment to the Constitution overrides the defendant's "right" to a fair trial conferred by other Amendments to the Constitution; it is instead whether any provision in the Constitution may fairly be read to prohibit what the trial judge in the Virginia state-court system did in this case. Being unable to find any such prohibition in the First, Sixth, Ninth, or any other Amendment to the United States Constitution, or in the Constitution itself, I dissent.

GLOBE NEWSPAPER CO. v. SUPERIOR COURT, 457 U.S. 596 (1982): To protect the minor victims of sex crimes from further trauma and embarrassment and to encourage such victims to come forward and testify in a truthful and credible manner, section 16A of Chapter 278 of Massachusetts General Laws requires trial judges, at trials for specified sexual offenses involving a victim under age eighteen, to exclude the press and general public from the courtroom during the testimony of the victim. The Court, in a six-to-three decision, held section 16A unconstitutional. Justice Brennan delivered the opinion of the Court:

"*Richmond Newspapers* firmly established for the first time that the press and general public have a constitutional right of access to criminal trials. [Two] features of the criminal justice system, emphasized in the various opinions in *Richmond Newspapers*, together serve to explain why a right of access to *criminal trials* in particular is properly afforded protection by the First Amendment. First, the criminal trial historically has been open to the press and general public. [Second,] the right of access to criminal trials plays a particularly significant role in the functioning of the judicial process and the government as a whole.

"[The Commonwealth] argues that criminal trials have not always been open to the press and general public during the testimony of minor sex victims. [Even] if [this is correct], the argument is unavailing. [Whether] the First Amendment right of access to criminal trials can be restricted in the context of any particular criminal trial [depends] not on the historical openness of that type of criminal trial but rather on the state interests assertedly supporting the restriction. . . .

"Where, as in the present case, the State attempts to deny the right of access in order to inhibit the disclosure of sensitive information, it must be shown that the denial is necessitated by a compelling governmental interest, and is narrowly tailored to serve that interest. . . .

"We agree [that the Commonwealth's interest in] safeguarding the physical and psychological well-being of a minor [is] a compelling one. But as compelling as that interest is, it does not justify a *mandatory*-closure rule, for it is clear that the circumstances of the particular case may affect the significance of the interest. A trial court can determine on a case-by-case basis whether closure is necessary to protect the welfare of a minor victim. Among the factors to be weighed are the minor victim's age, psychological maturity and understanding, the nature of the crime, the desires of the victim, and the interests of parents and relatives. [Section] 16A cannot be viewed as a narrowly tailored means of accommodating the State's asserted interest. . . .

"Nor can §16A be justified on the basis of the Commonwealth's [interest in] the encouragement of minor victims of sex crimes to come forward and provide accurate testimony. The Commonwealth has offered no empirical support for the claim that the rule of automatic closure [will] lead to an increase in the number of minor sex victims coming forward and cooperating with state authorities. [Moreover, this claim is] open to serious question as a matter of logic and common sense. Although §16A bars the press and general public from the courtroom during the testimony of minor sex victims, the press is not denied access to the transcript, court personnel, or any other possible source that could provide an account of the minor victim's testimony. Thus §16A cannot prevent the press from publicizing the substance of a minor victim's testimony, as well as his or her identity. If the Commonwealth's interest in encouraging minor victims to come forward depends on keeping such matters secret, §16A hardly advances that interest in an effective manner.

"[Finally,] even if §16A effectively advanced the State's interest, it is doubtful that the interest would be sufficient to overcome the constitutional attack, for that same interest could be relied on to support an array of mandatory-closure rules designed to encourage victims to come forward: Surely it cannot be suggested that minor victims of sex crimes are the *only* crime victims who, because of publicity attendant to criminal trials, are reluctant to come forward and testify. The State's argument based on this interest therefore proves too much."

Justice O'Connor concurred in the judgment.

Chief Justice Burger, joined by Justice Rehnquist, dissented: "In *Richmond Newspapers*, we [emphasized] that criminal trials were generally open to the public throughout this country's history. [Today] Justice Brennan ignores the weight of historical practice. There is clearly a long history of exclusion of the public from trials involving sexual assaults, particularly those against minors.

"[Moreover, the] Court's wooden application of the rigid standard it asserts for this case is inappropriate. The Commonwealth has not denied the public or the media access to information as to what takes place at trial. As the Court acknowledges, Massachusetts does not deny the press and the public access to the trial transcript or to other sources of information about the victim's testimony. Even the victim's identity is part of the public record. [The] purpose of [Section 16A] was to give assurance to parents and minors that they would have this moderate and limited protection from the trauma, embarrassment and humiliation of having to reveal the intimate details of a sexual assault in front of a large group of unfamiliar spectators — and perhaps a television audience — and to lower the barriers to the reporting of such crimes which might come from the victim's dread of public testimony. [Neither] the purpose of the law nor its effect is primarily to deny the press or public access to information. [We] therefore need only examine whether the restrictions imposed are reasonable and whether the interests of the Commonwealth override the very limited incidental effects of the law on First Amendment rights. . . .

"For me, it seems beyond doubt, considering the minimal impact of the law on First Amendment rights and the overriding weight of the Commonwealth's interest in protecting child rape victims, that the Massachusetts law is not unconstitutional. [Certainly] this law [rationally] serves the Commonwealth's overriding interest in protecting the child from severe — possibly permanent — psychological damage. [The] law also seems a rational response to the undisputed problem of the underreporting of rapes and other sexual offenses. [It] makes no sense to criticize the Commonwealth for its failure to offer empirical data in support of its rule; only by allowing state experimentation may such empirical evidence be produced. [Moreover, the Court's conclusion that Section 16A is not 'effective' because] the press is not prevented from discovering and publicizing both the identity of the victim and the substance of the victim's testimony [is based on a 'misperception']. Section 16A is intended not to preserve confidentiality, but to prevent the risk of severe psychological damage caused by having to relate the details of the crime in front of a crowd which inevitably will include voyeuristic strangers. [Finally, the] Commonwealth's interests are clearly furthered by the mandatory nature of the closure statute. [The] victim might very well experience considerable distress prior to the court appearance, wondering, in the absence of such statutory protection, whether public testimony will be required. The mere possibility of public testimony may cause parents and children to decide not to report these heinous crimes."

Justice Stevens dissented on other grounds.

See also Press-Enterprise Co. v. Superior Court, 464 U.S. 501 (1984), in which the Court held that a state court order closing the voir dire examination of prospective jurors in a criminal trial violated the first amendment. The Court explained that the "presumption of openness may be overcome only by an overriding interest based on findings that closure is essential to preserve higher values and is narrowly tailored to serve that interest. Although conceding that the "jury selection process may, in some circumstances, give rise to a compelling [privacy] interest of a prospective juror when interrogation touches on deeply personal matters," the Court concluded that the trial court in this case had not adequately considered the alternatives to closure.

In what circumstances, if any, does the first amendment guarantee the media a right to televise criminal trials? Cf. Chandler v. Florida, 449 U.S. 560 (1981) (for a state to permit television coverage of a criminal trial does not constitute a per se violation of the defendant's right to a fair trial).

Note: A Public Right of Access to Government Information?

1. *Observations.* Consider the following:

a. Lewis, A Public Right to Know about Public Institutions: The First Amendment as Sword, 1980 Sup. Ct. Rev. 1, 19-20:

> One lingering constitutional argument is surely put to rest by *Richmond Newspapers:* the claim that the Press Clause of the First Amendment gives journalists a distinct and preferred status. As a practical matter it has not been a winning argument anyway: it never commanded a majority in the Court. [Most] future cases

seeking access to government information will probably be brought by press organizations, but they will be based on the rights of the public.

b. Note, The Supreme Court, 1979 Term, 94 Harv. L. Rev. 75, 153-154 (1980):

[In *Richmond Newspapers*, both] Chief Justice Burger and Justice Brennan proceeded from the premise that, in general, a right of access to public institutions will enhance the quality of public discussion about those institutions. [But] they parted company at the critical final step in the analysis: Toward what ultimate constitutional objective is the instrumental value of this access right directed? Chief Justice Burger's plurality opinion [focused] upon the "therapeutic" value to society of seeing its criminal laws in operation. [This] attempt to limit the access analysis strictly to the criminal trial context is [difficult] to reconcile with [the] fact that the first amendment was intended not to mandate the optimal performance of governmental [functions,] but rather to preserve the ultimate personal liberties of the governed. Justice Brennan supplied a principle more readily identified with the purposes of the first amendment: retention by the people of meaningful control over the workings of government. [Under] such a structural vision of the first amendment, all public institutions must be kept within the ambit of the vigorous public debate the framers viewed as necessary to a system of self-government.

2. A *"public" right of access*. What is the source of the public's "right of access"? What are its limits? Consider the following views:

a. Note, The First Amendment Right to Gather State-Held Information, 89 Yale L.J. 923, 933-934 (1980):

The doctrine governing the right to assemble in public areas provides the most appropriate analogy [because both] public forums and state-held information are resources that are necessary for the exercise of First Amendment rights, and resources that the government controls exclusively.

b. Cassell, Restrictions on Press Coverage of Military Operations: The Right of Access, Grenada, and "Off-the-Record Wars," 73 Geo. L.J. 931, 958-959 (1985):

[*Richmond Newspapers*] suggests a narrow right of access, applicable only when three conditions are met: First, a claimant must show that the place "historically had been open to the press and general public." Second, the right of access must "play a particularly significant role" in the functioning of the process in question and of the government as a whole. Finally, if these two elements have been satisfied, access may be denied if the government establishes that "the denial is necessitated by a compelling governmental interest, and is narrowly tailored to serve that interest."

3. *The role of access*. Consider Lewis, supra, at 24-25:

We are not in the age of soapbox orators any more, or of government activity on the margin of society. Government, both federal and state, has grown enormously in size and power. [As] the state takes responsibility for ever larger areas of decision-making, as it penetrates ever deeper into our individual lives, the danger of official abuse grows. The function of the citizen-critic of government is more important now than ever — and harder to perform. If big government is to be effectively criticized and controlled, [it] will take the countervailing force of big newspapers and broadcast networks and public-interest groups and lobbying organizations of all kinds. And they cannot succeed without information. [The] Supreme Court in [*Richmond Newspapers*] vindicated the central purpose of the First Amendment, building on history to find a new remedy for new problems of democratic control.

Note: Conditioned Access to Information

As we have seen, despite *Richmond Newspapers*, government is under no general constitutional obligation to disclose information to the press or public and, indeed, may ordinarily prohibit its employees from disclosing "confidential" information. To what extent, then, may government condition its voluntarily disclosure of information on the press' agreement not to publish? Suppose, for example, government officials agree to disclose to the press all prior convictions of a criminal defendant on condition that the press not publish the information under after a jury is selected. Can a court constitutionally enjoin the breach of such an arrangement?

Consider Seattle Times Co. v. Rhinehart, 467 U.S. — (1984). In a defamation action against the Seattle-Times, a state court ordered the plaintiff to disclose certain information in discovery. The state court entered a protective order pursuant to a state rule modeled on Rule 26(c) of the Federal Rules of Civil Procedure. The order prohibited the newspaper from using the disclosed information, which included the names of contributors to a controversial religious group, for any purpose other than trial of the case.

The Supreme Court unanimously rejected the newspaper's claim that the order violated the first amendment:

[The newspaper] gained the information [only] by virtue of the trial court's discovery processes. [It had] no First Amendment right of access to [the information]. [Moreover, the] protective order prevents [the dissemination only of] information obtained through [discovery. The newspaper is free to] disseminate the identical information [if it obtains it] through means independent of the court's processes. [Thus], continued court control over the discovered information does not raise the same spectre of government censorship that such control might suggest in other situations. . . .

[Moreover,] Rule 26(c) furthers a substantial governmental interest unrelated to the suppression of expression. [Liberal] discovery [has] a significant potential for abuse. [Litigants may] obtain [information] that not only is irrelevant [to the litigation] but if publicly released could be damaging to reputation and privacy. The government clearly has a substantial interest in preventing this sort of abuse. [The] Supreme Court of Washington found that dissemination of [the information in this case] would "result in annoyance, embarrassment and even oppression." It is sufficient for [our purposes] that the highest court in the state found no abuse of discretion. [We] therefore hold that where [a] protective order is entered on a showing of good cause as required by Rule 26(c), is limited to the context of pretrial civil discovery, and does not restrict the dissemination of the information if gained from other sources, it does not offend the First Amendment.

Note: Free Expression — Final Thoughts

Consider Nagel, How Useful Is Judicial Review in Free Speech Cases?, 69 Corn. L. Rev. 302, 303, 335-338 (1984):

The dominant consensus that has prevailed for the last sixty years holds that the adjudication of individual cases can promote the level and quality of public debate. [The] assumptions upon which this [consensus] rests are largely unproven and often doubtful. [Indeed, a] general assessment of free speech cases is not reassuring. [Since 1919], much of the admiration for judges as protectors of free speech is predicated upon eloquent [dissents]. There are numerous major decisions in which the Court has subordinated free speech values to other social [interests]. Even in the cases that ultimately protect free speech, the Court often achieves the protection by [indirection]. In the relatively few decisions resting directly on free speech considerations, the Court often hedges its rulings with enough cautions and limitations to put into question the scope of the Court's commitment to free speech. [Moreover, judicial] efforts — such as those to protect corporate expenditures, nude dancing, and advertising — erode popular support by breeding resentment and bringing into question the utility of free speech. [Indeed,] the Court's program, taken as a whole, has done great damage to the public's understanding and appreciation of free speech by making it seem trivial, foreign, and unnecessarily costly.

VIII

The Constitution
and Religion

The first amendment bars Congress from making laws "respecting an establishment of religion, or prohibiting the free exercise thereof." Judicial supervision of congressional action in this area has a clearer textual basis than judicial activity regarding implied fundamental rights (see Chapter 6 supra) and in this way resembles judicial activity under the free speech provision of the First Amendment (Chapter 7 supra). In addition to discussing doctrinal approaches to church/state issues, this chapter examines whether the relative clarity of the constitutional text, or its history, eases the task of constitutional adjudication or reduces the necessity for other theoretical underpinnings to the constitutional law of religion.

The chapter has three sections. The first provides historical background and outlines the general approaches that courts and commentators have taken to the religion clauses. The second examines problems of establishment, highlighting the tension between the idea that the establishment clause requires some degree of separation between church and state, and a history that includes substantial state support of religious activities. The third section deals with problems of free exercise, focusing on the degree to which government must or may adjust its programs to claims that the programs burden the free exercise of religion.

A. INTRODUCTION: HISTORICAL AND ANALYTICAL OVERVIEW

EVERSON v. BOARD OF EDUCATION, 330 U.S. 1 (1946): New Jersey authorized its local school boards to repay parents with children in private schools for the cost of bus transportation to the schools. Most of the private schools were Roman Catholic parochial institutions. By a 5-to-4 vote, the Court upheld the statute against an establishment clause challenge, concluding that the state could pay the fares "as part of a general program under which it pays the fares of pupils attending public and other schools." This satisfied the first amendment's requirement that "the state [be] neutral in its relations with groups of religious believers and non-believers." Justice Black's opinion for the Court "[reviewed] the background and environment of" the First Amendment:

"A large proportion of the early settlers of this country came here from Europe to escape the bondage of laws which compelled them to support and attend government-favored churches. The centuries immediately before and contemporaneous with the colonization of America had been filled with turmoil, civil strife, and persecutions, generated in large part by established sects determined to maintain their absolute political and religious supremacy. With the power of government supporting them, at various times and places, Catholics had persecuted Protestants, Protestants had persecuted Catholics, Protestant sects had persecuted other Protestant sects, Catholics of one shade of belief had persecuted Catholics of another shade of belief, and all of these had from time to time persecuted Jews. In efforts to force loyalty to whatever group happened to be on top and in league with the government of a particular time and place, men and women had been fined, cast in jail, cruelly tortured, and killed. . . .

"These practices of the old world were transplanted to and began to thrive in the soil of the new America. The very charters granted by the English Crown to the individuals and companies designated to make the laws which would control the destinies of the colonials authorized these individuals and companies to erect religious establishments which all, whether believers or nonbelievers, would be required to support and attend. An exercise of this authority was accompanied by a repetition of many of the old-world practices and persecutions. Catholics found themselves hounded and proscribed because of their faith; Quakers who followed their conscience went to jail; Baptists were peculiarly obnoxious to certain dominant Protestant sects; men and women of varied faiths who happened to be in a minority in a particular locality were persecuted because they steadfastly persisted in worshipping God only as their own consciences dictated. And all of these dissenters were compelled to pay tithes and taxes to support government-sponsored churches whose ministers preached inflammatory sermons designed to strengthen and consolidate the established faith by generating a burning hatred against dissenters.

"These practices became so commonplace as to shock the freedom-loving colonials into a feeling of abhorrence. The imposition of taxes to pay ministers' salaries and to build and maintain churches and church property aroused their indignation. It was these feelings which found expression in the First Amendment. [Virginia,] where the established church had achieved a dominant influence in political affairs and where many excesses attracted wide public attention, provided a great stimulus and able leadership for the movement. The people there, as elsewhere, reached the conviction that individual religious liberty could be achieved best under a government which was stripped of all power to tax, to support, or otherwise to assist any or all religions, or to interfere with the beliefs of any religious individual or group.

"The movement toward this end reached its dramatic climax in Virginia in 1785-86 when the Virginia legislative body was about to renew Virginia's tax levy for the support of the established church. Thomas Jefferson and James Madison led the fight against this tax. Madison wrote his great Memorial and Remonstrance against the law. In it, he eloquently argued that a true religion did not need the support of law; that no person, either believer or non-believer, should be taxed to support a religious institution of any kind; that the best interest of a society required that the minds of men always be wholly free; and that cruel persecutions were the inevitable result of government-established religions. Madison's Remonstrance received stronger support throughout Virginia, and [when] the proposed tax measure [came] up for consideration [it] not only died in committee, but the Assembly enacted the famous 'Virginia Bill for Religious Liberty' originally written by Thomas Jefferson. The preamble to that Bill stated among other things that

> Almighty God hath created the mind free; that all attempts to influence it by temporal punishments or burthens, or by civil incapacitations, tend only to beget habits of hypocrisy and meanness, and are a departure from the plan of the Holy author of our religion, who being Lord both of body and mind, yet chose not to propagate it by coercions on either . . . ; that to compel a man to furnish contributions of money for the propagation of opinions which he disbelieves, is sinful and tyrannical; that even the forcing him to support this or that teacher of his own religious persuasion, is depriving him of the comfortable liberty of giving his contributions to the particular pastor, whose morals he would make his pattern. . . .

And the statute itself enacted

> That no man shall be compelled to frequent or support any religious worship, place, or ministry whatsoever, nor shall be enforced, restrained, molested, or burthened in his body or goods, nor shall otherwise suffer on account of his religious opinions or belief. . . .

"[The] provisions of the First Amendment, in the drafting and adoption of which Madison and Jefferson played such leading roles, had the same objective and were intended to provide the same protection against governmental intrusion on religious liberty as the Virginia statute. . . ."

The opinion summarized the meaning of the establishment clause: "[It] means at least this: Neither a state nor the Federal Government can set up a church. Neither can pass laws which aid one religion, aid all religions, or prefer one religion over another. Neither can force nor influence a person to go to or to remain away from church against his will or force him to profess a belief or disbelief in any religion. No person can be punished for entertaining or professing religious beliefs or disbeliefs, for church attendance or non-attendance. No tax in any amount, large or small, can be levied to support any religious activities or institutions, whatever they may be called, or whatever form they may adopt to teach or practice religion. Neither a state nor the Federal Government can, openly or secretly, participate in the affairs of any religious organizations or groups and vice versa. In the words of Jefferson, the clause was intended to erect 'a wall of separation between Church and State.' Reynolds v. United States [94 U.S. at 164]."

The dissenters agreed with Justice Black's description of the relevant history but argued that the New Jersey statute breached the "wall" of separation. Questions regarding state aid to nonpublic education are discussed in more detail in section B infra.

Note: The History of the Religion Clauses

1. *A challenge to Justice Black's synthesis.* Consider R. Cord, Separation of Church and State 15 (1982):

> [The] First Amendment was intended to [prevent] the establishment of a national church or religion, or the giving of any religious sect or denomination a preferred status, [to] safeguard the right of freedom of conscience in religious beliefs against invasion solely by the national government, [and] to allow the States, unimpeded, to deal with religious establishments and aid to religious institutions as they saw fit. There appears to be no historical evidence that the First Amendment was intended to preclude federal governmental aid to religion when it was provided on a nondiscriminatory basis.

See also Wallace v. Jaffree, — U.S. — 105 S. Ct. 2479 (1985) (Rehnquist, J., dissenting).

Cord relies on the history of drafting and ratification. Does this take adequate account of the broader historical setting that Justice Black emphasized? Cord, at 20-21, argues that Madison's Memorial and Remonstrance was concerned with the proposed statute "as a discriminatory religious dole [to] one religion — Christianity," rather than with nondiscriminatory aid to religion. In a religiously pluralist society, what forms of aid are nondiscriminatory? Should the religion clauses protect the interests of nonbelievers? Can they do so without creating a regime of hostility to religion? Consider whether these questions rest on a false dichotomy between religion and nonreligion. Is there such a thing as "religion" in a generic sense? Cord also shows that between 1800 and 1828 Congress entered into a number of treaties in which it agreed to subsidize education of Native Americans in schools run by a variety of Christian sects.

Is Justice Black's reconstruction of history tenable in light of this evidence? Consider these observations by Justice Brennan, concurring in Abington School District v. Schempp, 374 U.S. 203 (1963), which held unconstitutional the practice of devotional Bible-reading in public schools:

> [The] history which our prior decisions have summoned to aid interpretation of the Establishment Clause permits little doubt that its prohibition was designed comprehensively to prevent those official involvements of religion which would tend to foster or discourage religious worship or belief.
>
> But an awareness of history and an appreciation of the aims of the Founding Fathers do not always resolve concrete problems. [A] more fruitful inquiry [is] whether the practices [threaten] those consequences which the Framers deeply feared; whether, in short, they tend to promote that type of interdependence between religion and state which the First Amendment was designed to prevent. . . .
>
> A too literal quest for the advice of the Founding Fathers upon the issues of [today] seems to me futile and misdirected for several reasons: First, on our precise problem the historical record is at best ambiguous, and statements can readily be found to support either side of the proposition. The ambiguity of history is understandable if we recall the nature of the problems uppermost in the thinking of the statesmen who fashioned the religious guarantees; they were concerned with far more flagrant intrusions of government into the realm of religion than any that our century has witnessed. . . .

Second, the structure of American education has greatly changed since the First Amendment was adopted. In the context of our modern emphasis upon public education available to all citizens, any views of the eighteenth century as to whether the exercises at bar are an "establishment" offer little aid to decision. Education, as the Framers knew it, was in the main confined to private schools more often than not under strictly sectarian supervision. Only gradually did control of education pass largely to public officials. . . .

Third, our religious composition makes us a vastly more diverse people than were our forefathers. They knew differences chiefly among Protestant sects. Today the Nation is far more heterogeneous religiously. [In] the face of such profound changes, practices which may have been objectionable to no one in the time of Jefferson and Madison may today be highly offensive to many persons, the deeply devout and the nonbelievers alike.

2. *Other traditions.* L. Tribe, American Constitutional Law 816-817 (1978), describes other traditions relevant to the interpretation of the religion clauses:

[At] least three distinct schools of thought [influenced] the drafters of the Bill of Rights: first, the evangelical view (associated primarily with Roger Williams) that "worldly corruptions [might] consume the churches if sturdy fences against the wilderness were not maintained"; second, the Jeffersonian view that the church should be walled off from the state in order to safeguard secular interests (public and private) "against ecclesiastical depredations and incursions"; and, third, the Madisonian view that religious and secular interests alike would be advanced best by diffusing and decentralizing power so as to assure competition among sects rather than dominance by any one.

Roger Williams saw separation largely as a vehicle for protecting churches against the state. To the extent that it was possible to accept state aid without state control, he urged cooperation; indeed, he argued that the state must "countenance, encourage, and supply" those in religious service. Thus, his view has been called one of positive toleration, imposing on the state the burden of fostering a climate conducive to all religion. Thomas Jefferson, in contrast, saw separation as a means of protecting the state from the church. [It] was Jefferson's conviction that only the complete separation of religion from politics would eliminate the formal influence of religious institutions and provide for a free choice among political views; he therefore urged the strictest "wall of separation between church and state."

James Madison believed that both religion and government could best achieve their high purposes if each were left free from the other within its respective sphere; he thus urged that the "tendency to a usurpation on one side or the other, or to a corrupting coalition or alliance between them, will be best guarded against by an entire abstinance [sic] of the Government from interference in any way whatever, beyond the necessity of preserving public order, & protecting each sect against trespass on its legal rights by others."

Tribe concludes that these three approaches converge on "a pair of fundamental principles [that animate] the first amendment: voluntarism and separatism." As to voluntarism,

The free exercise clause was at the very least designed to guarantee freedom of conscience by preventing any degree of compulsion in matters of belief. It prohibited not only direct compulsion but also any indirect coercion which might result from subtle discrimination; hence it was offended by any burden based specifically on one's religion. So viewed, the free exercise clause is a mandate of religious voluntarism. The establishment clause [can] be understood as designed in part to assure that the advancement of a church would come only from the voluntary support of its followers and not from the political support of the state. Religious groups, it was believed, should prosper or perish on the intrinsic merit of their beliefs and practices. . . .

Separatism [calls] for much more than the institutional separation of church and state; it means that the state should not become involved in religious affairs and that sectarian differences should not be allowed unduly to fragment the body politic. Implicit in this ideal of mutual abstinence was the principle that under no circumstance should religion be financially supported by public taxation: "for the men who wrote the Religion Clauses [the] 'establishment' of a religion connoted sponsorship, financial support, and active involvement of the sovereign in religious activity."

Is the result in *Everson* consistent with these principles? When might the principles conflict with each other? Consider whether nondiscriminatory aid involves "indirect coercion" or "political support" of "a church" that might displace voluntary support by its members.

3. *Federalism and the first amendment.* Recall that the Bill of Rights was adopted to allay fears that the Constitution's grants of power might authorize Congress to act in matters that should be left to the states. When the first amendment was adopted, several states had churches established by law. See W. Katz, Religion and American Constitutions 8-10 (1964) (religion clauses were designed to bar Congress from interfering with existing establishments in the states); M. Howe, The Garden and the Wilderness 23 (1965) (arguing for a "less radical" view, that the clauses require the courts "to respect state law when it happened to sustain a religious enterprise").

What implications does the drafters' concern with federalism have for the interpretation of the clauses as applied to the states through the fourteenth amendment? Recall Justice Brennan's proposal: to examine whether the practices tend to promote the type of interdependence that threatens the consequences the framers feared. How does the concern with federalism affect the application of this test?

4. *Incorporation.* The framers' concern for federalism and the language of the fourteenth amendment pose some problems for the use of the amendment to make the religion clauses applicable to the states. The free exercise clause protects a "liberty," but what about the establishment clause? Consider Justice Brennan's argument in *Schempp,* supra:

It has been suggested, with some support in history, that absorption of the First Amendment's ban against congressional legislation "respecting an establishment of religion" is conceptually impossible because the Framers meant the Establishment Clause also to foreclose any attempt by Congress to disestablish the existing official state churches. [But] the last of the formal state establishments was dissolved more than three decades before the Fourteenth Amendment was ratified, and thus the problem of protecting official state churches from federal encroachments could hardly have been any concern of those who framed the post-Civil War Amendments. [The] Fourteenth Amendment created a panoply of new federal rights from the protection of citizens of the various States. And among those rights was freedom from such state governmental involvement in the affairs of religion as the Establishment Clause had originally foreclosed on the part of Congress.

It has also been suggested that the "liberty" guaranteed by the Fourteenth Amendment logically cannot absorb the Establishment Clause because that clause is not one of the provisions of the Bill of Rights which in terms protects a "freedom" of the individual. [This] contention [underestimates] the role of the Establishment Clause as a co-guarantor, with the Free Exercise Clause, of religious liberty. The Framers did not entrust the liberty of religious beliefs to either clause alone. . . .

Finally, it has been contended that absorption of the Establishment Clause is precluded by the absence of any intention on the part of the Framers of the Fourteenth Amendment to circumscribe the residual powers of the States to aid religious activities and institutions in ways which fell short of formal establishments. That argument relies in part upon the express terms of the abortive Blaine Amendment — proposed several years after the adoption of the Fourteenth Amendment — which would have added to the First Amendment a provision that "[n]o State shall make any law respecting an establishment of religion. . . ." Such a restriction would have been superfluous, it is said, if the Fourteenth Amendment had already made the Establishment Clause binding upon the States.

The argument proves too much, for the Fourteenth Amendment's protection of the free exercise of religion can hardly be questioned; yet the Blaine Amendment would also have added an explicit protection against state laws abridging that liberty. [Further,] the religious liberty embodied in the Fourteenth Amendment would not be viable if the Constitution were interpreted to forbid only establishments ordained by Congress.

For a discussion of incorporation generally, see Chapter 6, section C supra.

Note: General Approaches to the Religion Clauses

The preceding material indicates that the religion clauses deal with the general area of religious liberty, though in differing ways. Is it useful to develop an overall approach to their interpretation? In considering the following efforts at synthesis, it may help to keep in mind the following questions about each approach: Would the approach permit Congress to exempt from the Social Security or income tax those who base their objections to payment on religious grounds? Would it require Congress to do so? Would the approach permit Congress to subsidize the operation of social services by church-related institutions? Would it require Congress to do so?

1. *Strict separation.* The clauses could be read to erect an absolute barrier to formal interdependence of religion and the state. Religious institutions could receive no aid whatever, direct or indirect, from the state. Nor could the state adjust its secular programs to alleviate burdens the programs placed on believers.

Strict separation has been questioned under both clauses. As to establishment, the Court in *Everson* argued that

state-paid policemen, detailed to protect children going to and from church schools from the very real hazards of traffic, would serve much the same purpose and accomplish much the same result as state provisions intended to guarantee free transportation of a kind which the state deems to be best for the school children's welfare. And parents might refuse to risk their children to the danger of traffic accidents going to and from parochial schools, the approaches to which were not protected by policemen. Similarly, parents might be reluctant to permit their children to attend schools which the state had cut off from such general government services as ordinary police and fire protection, connections for sewage disposal, public highways and sidewalks. Of course, cutting off church schools from these services, so separate and so indisputably marked off from the religious function, would make it far more difficult for the schools to operate. But such is obviously not the purpose of the First Amendment. That Amendment requires the state to be a neutral in its relations with groups of religious believers and non-believers; it does not require the state to be their adversary. State power is no more to be used so as to handicap religions than it is to favor them.

As to free exercise, see Sherbert v. Verner, infra, holding that the free exercise clause sometimes requires states to accommodate their secular programs to the acts of religious believers. Tribe, supra at 822, proposes to deal with this difficulty by relaxing the strictness of the separation: "Actions 'arguably compelled' by free exercise are not forbidden by the establishment clause." On the criteria for required or permissible accommodations, see section C infra.

2. *Strict neutrality.* Kurland, Of Church and State and the Supreme Court, 29 U. Chi. L. Rev. 1, 5 (1961): "[Religion] may not be used as a basis for classification for purposes of governmental action, whether that action be the conferring of rights or privileges or the imposition of duties or obligations." Thus, states must use purely secular criteria as the basis for their actions. Strict neutrality does not permit, much less require, accommodation of secular programs to religious belief. It does permit aid to religious institutions that satisfy the purely secular criteria for participation in the program, at least if the courts are unwilling to conclude that the criteria were not concealed methods of using religion as a basis for the program. Suppose that many religious institutions satisfy the secular criteria for participation and almost no secular institutions do. Is this a Washington v. Davis problem? See Chapter 5, section C2, supra. What if the inference is clear that the legislature desired to aid religious institutions and used secular criteria only out of concern that to do otherwise would violate the neutrality principle?

3. *Voluntarism and noncoercion.* Consider Schwarz, No Imposition of Religion: The Establishment Clause Value, 77 Yale L. J. 692, 693 (1968): The establishment clause prohibits "only aid which has as its motive or substantial effect the imposition of religious belief or practice." More broadly, the religion clauses prohibit the government from influencing religious choice. See Gianella, Religious Liberty, Nonestablishment, and Doctrinal Development, 80 Harv. L. Rev. 1381 (1967), 81 Harv. L. Rev. 513 (1968). Is religious choice voluntary in the first instance? Consider Gianella's argument that a society's institutions provide the structure within which choice is made, that different structures produce different choices, and that in a society in which much is done in collective institutions, voluntarism requires aid to religion. 81 Harv. L. Rev. at 522-526. For example, the system of public education might be said to affect the values students come to acquire and might therefore influence their choices among religions or between religion and nonreligion. Is that an "imposition of religious belief"? If so, does it follow that state aid to religious schools, or a voucher system in which parents receive a specified sum from the state to use for the education of their children in public or private schools, is required by the Constitution? Alternatively, consider

whether the use of taxes to provide aid to religious institutions is coercive or influences religious choice.

4. *Religious pluralism and the political process.* White, J., dissenting in Widmar v. Vincent, 454 U.S. 263 (1981):

> The Establishment Clause [does] not establish what the State is *required* to do. [The] Establishment Clause limits on state action which incidentally aids religion are not as strict as the Court has held. The step from the permissible to the necessary, however, is a long one. In my view, just as there is room under the Religion Clauses for state policies that may have some beneficial effect on religion, there is also room for state policies that may incidentally burden religion. In other words, I believe that the states [have] a good deal [of freedom] to formulate policies that affect religion in divergent ways.

Why should states have that freedom? Consider whether a justification lies in the contemporary political process: The United States is a religiously pluralist society in which most religious groups are tolerant of views that diverge from their own. As proposals work their way through the political process, religiously based interest groups will affect their contours. Some may evoke Roger Williams and Thomas Jefferson to oppose on principle programs affecting religion; others may oppose the religious components on the merits. It might be unlikely that programs that seriously threaten the values with which the religion clauses are concerned will emerge from that process.

This view is discussed in more detail in the remainder of this chapter. Consider whether this sketch of the political process is accurate. Are there programs on which substantial majorities can agree that disregard intense views of religious minorities and that have substantial religious components? Consider the range of programs the Court has examined: state-supported nativity scenes, devotional prayer in public schools, tax support to nonpublic education, tax exemptions for churches. Consider also the implications of the title of a classic study of religious pluralism in the United States, W. Herberg, Protestant, Catholic, Jew (1955).

What might be the limits of a state's freedom to formulate policies that affect religion? Justice White "[did not] suppose that [a state] could prevent students from saying grace before meals in the school cafeteria." Could it require them to do so? Is either the prohibition or the requirement likely to be adopted in any state in the near future? Could the public schools require that students take a course on religion? On Christianity?

Note: Defining Religion

In its decisions under the free speech clause, the Supreme Court has sometimes considered whether a form of expression is "speech" within the meaning of the clause. See Chapter 6, section E3 supra. Similarly, the religion clauses require the courts to determine whether a form of belief is a "religion" within their meaning. If the free exercise clause requires the state to accommodate its secular programs to religious but not to nonreligious, e.g., political, belief, courts must decide whether an objector's belief is religious. The courts may be asked to decide whether the teaching of evolution or of creationism is an establishment of religion. What general considerations might guide the definitional effort?

1. *Unitary or variable definitions?* Rutledge, J., dissenting in *Everson*, supra:

> "Religion" appears only once in the [First] Amendment. But the word governs two prohibitions and governs them alike. It does not have two meanings, one narrow to forbid "an establishment" and another, much broader, for securing "the free exercise thereof." "Thereof" brings down "religion" with its entire and exact content, no more and no less, from the first into the second guaranty, so that Congress and now the states are as broadly restricted concerning the one as they are regarding the other.

Tribe, supra, at 826-828:

> At least through the nineteenth century, religion was given the same fairly narrow reading in the two clauses: "religion" referred to theistic notions respecting divinity, morality, and worship, and was recognized as legitimate and protected only insofar as it was generally accepted as "civilized" by Western standards. . . .
>
> [But religion] in America, always pluralistic, has become radically so in the latter part of the twentieth century. [Even] within a single religion — Christianity — tremendous diversity has occurred, with some Christian groups formally accepting members who regard the concept of "God" as irrelevant or even harmful. This growing diversity in religious belief and practice has been mirrored, and even magnified, by developments in theology. There are, of course, many traditionally theistic American theologians, but for many others there has been a shift in religious thought from a theocentric, transcendental perspective to forms of religious consciousness that stress the immanence of meaning in the natural order. . . .
>
> [Clearly,] the notion of religion in the free exercise clause must be expanded beyond the closely bounded limits of theism to account for the multiplying forms of recognizably legitimate religious exercise. It is equally clear, however, that in the age of the affirmative and increasingly pervasive state, a less expansive notion of religion was required for establishment clause purposes lest all "humane" programs of government be deemed constitutionally suspect. Such a twofold definition of religion — expansive for the free exercise clause, less so for the establishment clause — may be necessary to avoid confronting the state with increasingly difficult choices that the theory of permissible accommodations [could] not indefinitely resolve. . . .
>
> [All] that is *"arguably religious"* should be considered religious in a free exercise analysis [and] anything *"arguably non-religious"* should not be considered religious in applying the establishment clause.

Is Tribe's approach consistent with the language of the Constitution? Is there an alternative solution to the problems Tribe identifies? For a similar approach, see Note, Toward a Constitutional Definition of Religion, 91 Harv. L. Rev. 1056 (1978).

2. *An expansive definition by the Supreme Court: the conscientious objector cases.* The Court's most extended consideration of the definition of religion occurred in a series of cases interpreting a federal statute granting an exemption from compulsory military service to any person "who, by reason of religious training and belief, is conscientiously opposed to participation in war in any form" and defining "religious training and belief" as "an individual's belief in relation

to a Supreme Being involving duties superior to those arising from any human relation, but [not] any essentially political, sociological, or philosophical views or a merely personal moral code." (The reference to a "Supreme Being" was deleted in 1967.)

The Court interpreted these provisions in United States v. Seeger, 380 U.S. 163 (1965). Seeger stated on his draft form that he "preferred to leave the question as to his belief in a Supreme Being open" and that he had a " 'belief in and devotion to goodness and virtue for their own sakes, and a religious faith in a purely ethical creed [without] belief in God, except in the remotest sense.' " The Court unanimously found that Seeger qualified for the statutory exemption. The test was "whether a given belief that is sincere and meaningful occupies a place in the life of its possessor parallel to that filled by the orthodox belief in God of one who clearly qualifies for the exemption. Where such beliefs have parallel positions in the lives of their respective holders we cannot say that one is 'in relation to a Supreme Being' and the other is not." The Court mentioned "the richness and variety of spiritual life in our country. [There] are those who think of God as the depth of our being; others, such as the Buddhists, strive for a state of lasting rest through self-denial and inner purification; in Hindu philosophy the Supreme Being is the transcendental reality which is truth, knowledge and bliss." It cited modern theologians, including Paul Tillich and John Robinson and a leader in the Ethical Culture Movement, who offered definitions of God that differed from traditional theism.

Would denial of an exemption to members of traditional peace churches such as the Amish violate the free exercise clause? Would granting an exemption on religious grounds to a group more narrowly defined than that in Seeger violate the establishment clause? Is the exemption as interpreted in Seeger nondiscriminatory? See Greenawalt, All or Nothing at All, 1971 Sup. Ct. Rev. 31.

Justice Douglas, concurring in Seeger, thought that a broadly defined exemption was required by the free exercise clause and by concepts of equal protection. The plurality in Welsh v. United States, 398 U.S. 333 (1970), applied the Seeger test to grant an exemption to someone who crossed off the word "religious" on the draft form. Justice Harlan concurred only in the result. He argued that Seeger had stretched the statutory language to its limit. "Congress [could eliminate] all exemptions for conscientious objectors. Such a course would be wholly 'neutral.' [However,] having chosen to exempt, it cannot draw the line between theistic or nontheistic religious beliefs on the one hand and secular beliefs on the other." To do so would violate the establishment clause. Justice White, joined by Chief Justice Burger and Justice Stewart, dissented, arguing that the exemption as construed in Seeger was a permissible accommodation of military needs and "free exercise values."

In Gillette v. United States, 401 U.S. 437 (1971), the Court held that the statutory exemption was unavailable to those who had religious objections "relating to a particular conflict." It rejected the claim that the free exercise clause required that the exemption be available to such "selective" objectors, and concluded that an exemption limited to objectors to all wars was sufficiently neutral to avoid establishment clause problems. The "de facto discrimination among religions" was not an establishment of religion because the discrimination "serves a number of purposes having nothing to do with a design to foster or favor any sect, religion, or cluster of religions [such] as the hopelessness of converting a sincere conscientious objector into an effective fighting man." The "interest in maintaining a fair system" might be defeated by requiring the draft system to inquire into the "enormous number of variables" that make selective objection "ultimately subjective." "There is a danger that as between two would-be objectors, both having the same complaint against a war, that objector would succeed who is more articulate, better educated, or better counseled." This danger was greater "the more discriminating and complicated the basis of classification." Justice Douglas dissented.

3. *The futility of definition?* Commentators, drawing on modern theology, have suggested that religion must involve "ultimate concern" or belief in "extra-temporal consequences" or in a "transcendent reality." See, e.g., Note, Toward a Constitutional Definition of Religion, 91 Harv. L. Rev. 1056 (1978); Choper, Defining "Religion" in the First Amendment, 1982 U. Ill. L. Rev. 579. Are the following belief systems religions? Does it matter whether the issue is free exercise or establishment? Recall Tribe's comments, supra. (a) Transcendental meditation (see Malnak v. Yogi, 592 F.2d 197 (3d Cir. 1979), finding that a school board established religion when it authorized the teaching of TM in the public schools); (b) pantheism (see Africa v. Pennsylvania, 662 F.2d 1025 (3d Cir. 1981), finding a system strongly resembling pantheism not a religion when its adherent sought to require prison officials to provide him with a diet of raw foods only); (c) secular humanism (see Grove v. Mead School Dist., 753 F.2d 1528 (9th Cir. 1985), finding no establishment clause violation in allowing public school students to satisfy requirements by reading a book said to advance secular humanism); (d) a belief that eating cat food contributes to spiritual and physical well-being (see Brown v. Pena, 441 F. Supp. 1382 (S.D. Fla. 1977), finding this not a religious belief under statutes prohibiting discrimination on the basis of religion).

Consider Freeman, The Misguided Search for the Constitutional Definition of "Religion," 71 Geo. L.J. 1519, 1553, 1556 (1983): A "religious belief system" has some of the following "relevant features": belief in a supreme being, belief in a transcendent reality, a moral code, a world view accounting for people's role of the universe, sacred rituals, worship and prayer, a sacred text, membership in a social organization. But "there is no single feature or set of features that constitutes the essence of religion." Rather, "a belief system [may] be more or less religious depending on how closely it resembles [the] paradigm" having all eight features.

How can the religion clauses be interpreted unless there is a definition of religion? Consider whether it would be possible to develop doctrines by accepting all sincerely proferred claims that a belief is religious and then determining, in the free exercise context, whether the state's secular goals justify imposing a burden on that belief and in the establishment context, whether the state's secular goals justify its adopting the program at issue. Freeman suggests that such doctrines might be unacceptable because the courts would be unable to distinguish between belief systems at the core of the concept of religion and those at its periphery; distaste for granting a free exercise exemption to the peripheral religion might distort the doctrines dealing with the balance between secular goals and burdens on religion. Consider here the justifications for developing a separate category of free speech doctrine implicating "low value" speech, Chapter 7, section D supra.

4. *Determining sincerity.* In United States v. Ballard, 322 U.S. 78 (1944), the leaders of the "I Am" religion were indicted for mail fraud. The religion, an

offshoot of the theosophy movement, was centered in the Western states. Its founder Guy Ballard was said to have met a Master Saint Germain, who used Ballard as a messenger. (The religion retained a substantial following in 1970. See R. Ellwood, Religious and Spiritual Groups in Modern America 121-125 (1973).) Ballard's widow and son were charged with making representations that they knew were false regarding their power to cure diseases. The Supreme Court held that the jury could not be allowed to determine the truth or falsity of the representations about the Ballards' ability to cure. It could determine only whether or not they believed the representations they made. "Men may believe what they cannot prove. [Religious] experiences which are as real as life to some may be incomprehensible to others. [If] one could be sent to jail because a jury in a hostile environment found [his] teachings false, little indeed would be left of religious freedom." Justice Jackson would have gone further.

> I do not see how we can separate an issue as to what is believed from considerations as to what is believable. [Second,] any inquiry into intellectual honesty in religion raises profound psychological problems. [It] seems to me an impossible task for juries to separate fancied [religious experiences] from real ones, dreams from happenings, and hallucinations from true clairvoyance. [Third,] I do not know what degree of skepticism or disbelief in a religious representation amounts to an actionable fraud. [Religious] symbolism is even used by some with the same mental reservations one has in teaching of Santa Claus or Uncle Sam or Eastern bunnies or dispassionate judges.

Chief Justice Stone, whose dissent was joined by Justices Roberts and Frankfurter, countered, "[If] it were shown that a defendant [had] asserted [that] he had physically shaken hands with St. Germain in San Francisco on a day named, or that [by] the exertion of his spiritual power he 'had in fact cured [hundreds] of persons . . . ,' it would be open to the Government to submit to the jury proof that he had never been in San Francisco and that no such cures had ever been effected." Justice Jackson agreed that a church leader could be prosecuted for fraud if he or she "represents that funds are being used to build a church when in fact they are being used for personal purposes." How does that differ from what the Ballards were charged with? Suppose the leader asserts that, as a matter of his religious belief, he is the embodiment of the religion and that all expenditures for his personal purposes are expenditures for building a church? Cf. Moon v. United States, 718 F.2d 1210 (2d Cir. 1984).

B. THE ESTABLISHMENT CLAUSE

In Lemon v. Kurtzman, 403 U.S. 602 (1971), the Court identified three "tests" for determining whether a statute violates the establishment clause: "First, the statute must have a secular legislative purpose; second, its principal or primary effect must be one that neither advances nor inhibits religion; finally, the statute must not foster 'an excessive government entanglement with religion.' " Are these criteria adequate to deal with the variety of problems that arise under the establishment clause? Can they be sensibly applied? The first part of this section examines the idea that certain purposes are impermissible. The second asks whether there is or ought to be a set of problems that should be examined without regard to the *Lemon* criteria. The third part considers the justifications for and some applications of those criteria.

1. *Impermissible Purposes: The School Prayer Cases*

1. *Determining impermissible legislative purposes.* Stone v. Graham, 449 U.S. 39 (1980), held unconstitutional a Kentucky statute requiring that a copy of the Ten Commandments be posted on the walls of each public classroom. The Court found that this requirement had "no secular legislative purpose": The Commandments were "undeniably a sacred text in the Jewish and Christian faiths," and "if the posted copies [are] to have any effect at all, it will be to induce the school children to read, meditate upon, perhaps to venerate and obey, the Commandments. However desirable this might be as a matter of private devotion, it is not a permissible state objective under the Establishment Clause." Justice Rehnquist's dissent relied on a statement in the statute that its purpose was secular and argued that the requirement had a secular purpose because "the Ten Commandments have had a significant secular impact on the development of secular legal codes of the Western World." Chief Justice Burger and Justices Blackmun and Stewart dissented from the Court's summary action.

Stone shows that a statute that the Court finds has as its sole purpose the promotion of religion is unconstitutional. It relied heavily on the school prayer cases. In Engel v. Vitale, 370 U.S. 421 (1962), the New York Board of Regents drafted and recommended that school districts have classes recite aloud the following prayer: "Almighty God, we acknowledge our dependence upon Thee, and beg Thy blessings upon us, our parents, our teachers and our Country." Justice Black, writing for the Court, stated that "in this country it is no part of the business of government to compose official prayers for any group of the American people to recite as a part of a religious program carried on by government." Quoting from James Madison, he concluded that the prayer's assertedly nondenominational character did not save it because "the same authority which can establish Christianity, in exclusion of all other Religions, may establish with the same ease any particular sect of Christians, in exclusion of all other Sects." Is Madison correct? The Court also argued that "the First Amendment was added to the Constitution to stand as a guarantee that [the] people's religions must not be subjected to the pressures of government for change each time a new political administration is elected to office." Justice Stewart dissented.

In Abington School District v. Schempp, 374 U.S. 203 (1963), the Court held unconstitutional a state law requiring that ten verses from the Bible be read aloud at the opening of each public school day. Justice Clark's opinion for the Court stated the "purpose and effect" test. Bible reading had a religious character, and the state's policies of allowing use of the Douai version of the Bible and of permitting nonattendance were not "consistent with the contention that the Bible is here used either as an instrument for nonreligious moral inspiration or as a reference for the teaching of secular subjects." Justice Stewart dissented, finding "a substantial free exercise claim on the part of those who affirmatively desire to have their children's school day open with the reading of passages from the Bible. [A] compulsory state educational system so structures a child's life that if religious exercises are held to be an impermissible activity in schools, religion is placed at an artificial and state-created disadvantage." This claim was "sufficiently substantial" to justify a state's decision to allow noncoercive Bible-reading.

Wallace v. Jaffree, — U.S. — , 105 S. Ct. 2479 (1985), held unconstitutional an Alabama statute authorizing schools to set aside one minute at the start of the school day "for meditation or voluntary prayer." The statute amended an earlier one authorizing a moment of silence "for meditation." The Court drew on Madison and *Everson* to conclude that "the individual freedom of conscience [embraces] the right to select any religious faith or none at all" because "religious beliefs worthy of respect are the product of free and voluntary choice by the faithful, and [because] the political interest in forestalling intolerance extends beyond intolerance among Christian sects — or even intolerance among 'religions' — to encompass intolerance of the disbeliever and the uncertain." The statute's background demonstrated that it "had *no* secular purpose." The bill's sponsor stated that it was "an 'effort to return voluntary prayer' to the public schools." It served no secular purpose not already served by the "meditation" statute. The Court noted that the statute could not be a permissible accommodation of religion because, prior to its enactment, "there was no governmental practice impeding students from silently praying for one minute at the beginning of the school day. [What] was missing [was] the State's endorsement and promotion of religion and a particular religious practice."

Justice O'Connor concurred in the judgment, on the ground that the statute's "purpose and likely effect [were] to endorse and sponsor voluntary prayer in the public schools." She argued that simple "moment of silence" statutes were constitutional because "a moment of silence is not inherently religious [and because] a pupil who participates in a moment of silence need not compromise his or her belief." Thus, the "State does not necessarily endorse any activity that might occur during the period. Even if a statute specifies that a student may choose to pray silently during a quiet moment, the State has not thereby encouraged prayer over other specified alternatives. [The] crucial question is whether the state has conveyed or attempted to convey the message that children should use the moment of silence for prayer." Answering that question required the Court to engage in a "deferential and limited" inquiry into a statute's purposes as revealed by its text and official legislative history. Here "the conclusion is unavoidable that the purpose of the statute is to endorse prayer in public schools." She also wrote,

> It is not a trivial matter [to] require that the legislature manifest a secular purpose and omit all secretarian endorsements from its laws. That requirement is precisely tailored to the Establishment Clause's purpose of assuring that Government not intentionally endorse religion or a religious practice. [A] legislature [might] enunciate a sham secular [purpose, but] our courts are capable of distinguishing a sham secular purpose from a real one. [The] secular purpose requirement [reminds] government that when it acts it should do so without endorsing a particular religious belief or practice that all citizens do not share.

Chief Justice Burger dissented, arguing that the statute merely amended the prior one to make it clear that prayer was permitted during the moment of silence. He stated that the bill's sponsor testified that "one of his purposes [was] to clear up a widespread misunderstanding that a school-child is legally *prohibited* from [praying] once he steps inside a public school building." Justice Rehnquist's dissent reexamined the history of the religion clauses and concluded that they "forbade establishment of a national religion, and forbade preference among religious sects or denominations." Justice White in dissent also "[supported] a basic reconsideration of our precedents."

Is it accurate to say that each of these statutes had no purpose other than the promotion of religion? Alternatively, do the statutes have no *substantial* secular purposes? Consider whether it is a permissible (nonreligious?) purpose to accommodate the interests of those children who wish to pray in school, or to clarify a misunderstanding about the activities allowed in public schools. For further discussion of statutes designed to accommodate the religious values of those otherwise subject to state regulation (such as attendance in public school), see section C infra. Consider also whether the purposes discussed in Lynch v. Donnelly, infra, are substantial.

In Widmar v. Vincent, 454 U.S. 263 (1981), the Court invoked the free speech clause to require a state university to make its facilities available to a student prayer group, just as it would make them available to other groups seeking to use the public forum it created. See Chapter 6, section F1 supra. Although the Court agreed that the university had a "compelling" interest "in complying with its constitutional obligations," it held that a policy of "nondiscrimination against religious speech" would not violate the establishment clause. Any benefits to religious groups would be "incidental" because "an open forum in a public university does not confer any imprimatur of State approval on religious sects or practices" and "the provision of benefits to [a] broad [spectrum] of groups is an important index of secular effect." Further, "the state interest [in] achieving a greater separation of church and State [under the state Constitution] than is already ensured by the Establishment Clause of the Federal Constitution [is] limited by the Free Exercise Clause and in this case by the Free Speech Clause as well." Thus, the state's interest was not compelling.

The Equal Access Act, 20 U.S.C. §4071 (1984), provides, "It shall be unlawful for any public secondary school which receives Federal financial assistance and which has a limited open forum to deny equal access [to] any students who wish to conduct a meeting within that limited open forum on the basis of the religious, political, philosophical, or other content of the speech at such meetings." A limited open forum is created when the school allows "noncurriculum related student groups to meet on school premises during noninstructional time." Does the act violate the establishment clause? Independent of the act, does *Widmar* imply that high schools must make their facilities available to student-initiated voluntary prayer groups on the same conditions it makes them available to other student groups? In *Widmar* the Court had a footnote to its discussion of the "imprimatur of State approval": "University students are, of course, young adults. They are less impressionable than younger students and should be able to appreciate that the University's policy is one of neutrality toward religion." For further discussion of differences between high schools and universities, see section B3 infra.

2. *Determining legislative purpose: nondiscrimination and gerrymandering.* Larson v. Valente, 456 U.S. 228 (1982), involved a Minnesota statute imposing reporting requirements on religious organizations that solicit more than 50 percent of their funds from nonmembers. The legislative history included one legislator's statement that "what you're trying to get at here is the people who are

running around streets and soliciting people" and another's that he was "not sure why we're so hot to regulate the Moonies anyway." Five members of the Court, in an opinion by Justice Brennan, held that this violated "the clearest command of the Establishment Clause [— that] one religious denomination cannot be officially preferred over another." Such "denominational preferences" must be "justified by a compelling governmental interest, and [be] closely fitted to further that interest." The state's "interest in protecting its citizens from abusive practices" might be compelling, but the 50 percent rule was not closely fitted to preventing abuse. The Court rejected the assumption that over 50 percent support by members assured control over abusive solicitation practices: "[The] need for public disclosure more plausibly rises in proportion with the *absolute amount*, rather than with the *percentage*, of nonmember contributions." Further, the distinctions in the statute "engender a risk of politicizing religion" and "led the Minnesota legislature to discuss the characteristics of various sects with a view towards 'religious gerrymandering.'" Justice White, joined by Justice Rehnquist, dissented on the ground that the statute was not "a deliberate and explicit preference for some religious denominations over others" because it "names no churches or denominations. [Some] religions will qualify and some will not, but this depends on the source of their contributions, not on their brand of religion." A law "does not constitute an establishment of religion merely because it has a disparate impact. An intentional preference must be expressed." Chief Justice Burger and Justice O'Connor joined the other two dissenters in a separate opinion dealing with standing.

2. Permissible Purposes: De Facto Establishments?

Lynch v. Donnelly
465 U.S. 668 (1984)

THE CHIEF JUSTICE [BURGER] delivered the opinion of the Court. . . .

I

Each year, in cooperation with the downtown retail merchants' association, the City of Pawtucket, Rhode Island, erects a Christmas display as part of its observance of the Christmas holiday season. The display is situated in a park owned by a nonprofit organization and located in the heart of the shopping district. The display is essentially like those to be found in hundreds of towns or cities across the Nation — often on public grounds — during the Christmas season. The Pawtucket display comprises many of the figures and decorations traditionally associated with Christmas, including, among other things, a Santa Claus house, reindeer pulling Santa's sleigh, candy-striped poles, a Christmas tree, carolers, cutout figures representing such characters as a clown, an elephant, and a teddy bear, hundreds of colored lights, a large banner that reads "SEASONS GREET-INGS," and the crèche at issue here. All components of this display are owned by the City. . .

[The Court of Appeals held that the crèche violated the establishment clause.]

II

A

This Court has explained that the purpose of the Establishment and Free Exercise Clauses of the First Amendment is "to prevent, as far as possible, the intrusion of either [the church or the state] into the precincts of the other." Lemon v. Kurtzman, 403 U.S. 602, 614 (1971). At the same time, however, the Court has recognized that "total separation is not possible in an absolute sense. Some relationship between government and religious organizations is inevitable." In every Establishment Clause case, we must reconcile the inescapable tension between the objective of preventing unnecessary intrusion of either the church or the state upon the other, and the reality that, as the Court has so often noted, total separation of the two is not possible.

The Court has sometimes described the Religion Clauses as erecting a "wall" between church and state, see, e.g., [Everson]. The concept of a "wall" of separation is a useful figure of speech probably deriving from views of Thomas Jefferson. The metaphor has served as a reminder that the Establishment Clause forbids an established church or anything approaching it. But the metaphor itself is not a wholly accurate description of the practical aspects of the relationship that in fact exists between church and state.

No significant segment of our society and no institution within it can exist in a vacuum or in total or absolute isolation from all the other parts, much less from government. "It has never been thought either possible or desirable to enforce a regime of total separation. . . ." Committee for Public Education & Religious Liberty v. Nyquist, 413 U.S. 756, 760 (1973). Nor does the Constitution require complete separation of church and state; it affirmatively mandates accommodation, not merely tolerance, of all religions, and forbids hostility toward any. See, e.g., Zorach v. Clauson, 343 U.S. 306 (1952); McCollum v. Board of Education, 333 U.S. 203 (1948). Anything less would require the "callous indifference" we have said was never intended by the Establishment Clause. [Zorach.] Indeed, we have observed, such hostility would bring us into "war with our national tradition as embodied in the First Amendment's guaranty of the free exercise of religion." [McCollum.] . . .

C

There is an unbroken history of official acknowledgment by all three branches of government of the role of religion in American life from at least 1789. Seldom in our opinions was this more affirmatively expressed than in Justice Douglas' opinion for the Court validating a program allowing release of public school students from classes to attend off-campus religious exercises. Rejecting a claim that the program violated the Establishment Clause, the Court asserted pointedly: "We are a religious people whose institutions presuppose a Supreme Being." [Zorach.]

Our history is replete with official references to the value and invocation of Divine guidance in deliberations and pronouncements of the Founding Fathers and contemporary leaders. Beginning in the early colonial period long before Independence, a day of Thanksgiving was celebrated as a religious holiday to give thanks for the bounties of Nature as gifts from God. President Washington and his successors proclaimed Thanksgiving, with all its religious overtones, a day of national celebration and Congress made it a National Holiday more than a century ago. That holiday has not lost its theme of expressing thanks for Divine aid any more than has Christmas lost its religious significance.

Executive Orders and other official announcements of Presidents and of the Congress have proclaimed both Christmas and Thanksgiving National Holidays in religious terms. [Thus,] it is clear that Government has long recognized — indeed it has subsidized — holidays with religious significance.

Other examples of reference to our religious heritage are found in the statutorily prescribed national motto "In God We Trust," which Congress and the President mandated for our currency, and in the language "One nation under God," as part of the Pledge of Allegiance to the American flag. That pledge is recited by thousands of public school children — and adults — every year.

Art galleries supported by public revenues display religious paintings of the 15th and 16th centuries, predominantly inspired by one religious faith. . . .

[One] cannot look at even this brief resume without finding that our history is pervaded by expressions of religious beliefs such as are found in *Zorach*. Equally pervasive is the evidence of accommodation of all faiths and all forms of religious expression, and hostility toward none. Through this accommodation, as Justice Douglas observed, governmental action has "follow[ed] the best of our traditions" and "respect[ed] the religious nature of our people." [*Zorach*.]

III

This history may help explain why the Court consistently has declined to take a rigid, absolutist view of the Establishment Clause. [In] our modern, complex society, whose traditions and constitutional underpinnings rest on and encourage diversity and pluralism in all areas, an absolutist approach in applying the Establishment Clause is simplistic and has been uniformly rejected by the Court.

Rather than mechanically invalidating all governmental conduct or statutes that confer benefits or give special recognition to religion in general or to one faith — as an absolutist approach would dictate — the Court has scrutinized challenged legislation or official conduct to determine whether, in reality, it establishes a religion or religious faith, or tends to do so. . . .

In each case, the inquiry calls for line drawing; no fixed, *per se* rule can be framed. . . .

In the line-drawing process we have often found it useful to inquire whether the challenged law or conduct has a secular purpose, whether its principal or primary effect is to advance or inhibit religion, and whether it creates an excessive entanglement of government with religion. [*Lemon*.] But, we have repeatedly emphasized our unwillingness to be confined to any single test or criterion in this sensitive area. . . .

[In] this case, the focus of our inquiry must be on the crèche in the context of the Christmas season. See, e.g., Stone v. Graham, 449 U.S. 39 (1980) (per curiam). In *Stone*, for example, we invalidated a state statute requiring the posting of a copy of the Ten Commandments on public classroom walls. But the Court carefully pointed out that the Commandments were posted purely as a religious admonition, not "integrated into the school curriculum, where the Bible may constitutionally be used in an appropriate study of history, civilization, ethics, comparative religion, or the like." Focus exclusively on the religious component of any activity would inevitably lead to its invalidation under the Establishment Clause.

The Court has invalidated legislation or governmental action on the ground that a secular purpose was lacking, but only when it has concluded there was no question that the statute or activity was motivated wholly by religious considerations. Even where the benefits to religion were substantial, as in *Everson*, we saw a secular purpose and no conflict with the Establishment Clause. . . .

[When] viewed in the proper context of the Christmas Holiday season, it is apparent that, on this record, there is insufficient evidence to establish that the inclusion of the crèche is a purposeful or surreptitious effort to express some kind of subtle governmental advocacy of a particular religious message. In a pluralistic society a variety of motives and purposes are implicated. The City, like the Congresses and Presidents, however, has principally taken note of a significant historical religious event long celebrated in the Western World. . . .

The narrow question is whether there is a secular purpose for Pawtucket's display of the crèche. The display is sponsored by the City to celebrate the Holiday and to depict the origins of that Holiday. These are legitimate secular purposes.[7]

The District Court found that the primary effect of including the crèche is to confer a substantial and impermissible benefit on religion in general and on the Christian faith in particular. Comparisons of the relative benefits to religion of different forms of governmental support are elusive and difficult to make. But to conclude that the primary effect of including the crèche is to advance religion in violation of the Establishment Clause would require that we view it as more beneficial to and more an endorsement of religion, for example, than [expenditure] of public funds for transportation of students to church-sponsored schools. [*Everson*.] . . .

We are unable to discern a greater aid to religion deriving from inclusion of the crèche than from these benefits and endorsements previously held not violative of the Establishment Clause. . . .

The dissent asserts some observers may perceive that the City has aligned itself with the Christian faith by including a Christian symbol in its display and that this serves to advance religion. We can assume, *arguendo*, that the display advances religion in a sense; but our precedents plainly contemplate that on occasion some advancement of religion will result from governmental action. [Here,] whatever benefit to one faith or religion or to all religions, is indirect, remote and incidental; display of the crèche is no more an advancement or endorsement of religion than the Congressional and Executive recognition of the origins of the Holiday itself as "Christ's Mass," or the exhibition of literally hundreds of religious paintings in governmentally supported museums. . . .

[This] Court has not held that political divisiveness alone can serve to invalidate otherwise permissible conduct. [This] case does not involve a direct subsidy to church-sponsored schools or colleges, or other religious institutions, and hence

---

7. Justice Brennan argues that the City's objectives could have been achieved without including the crèche in the display. True or not, that is irrelevant. The question is whether the display of the crèche violates the Establishment Clause. [Relocated footnote. — EDS.]

no inquiry into potential political divisiveness is even called for. In any event, apart from this litigation there is no evidence of political friction or divisiveness over the crèche in the 40-year history of Pawtucket's Christmas celebration. The District Court stated that the inclusion of the crèche for the 40 years has been "marked by no apparent dissension" and that the display has had a "calm history." Curiously, it went on to hold that the political divisiveness engendered by this lawsuit was evidence of excessive entanglement. A litigant cannot, by the very act of commencing a lawsuit, however, create the appearance of divisiveness and then exploit it as evidence of entanglement.

We are satisfied that the City has a secular purpose for including the crèche, that the City has not impermissibly advanced religion, and that including the crèche does not create excessive entanglement between religion and government.

IV

Justice Brennan describes the crèche as a "recreation of an event that lies at the heart of Christian faith." The crèche, like a painting, is passive; admittedly it is a reminder of the origins of Christmas. Even the traditional, purely secular displays extant at Christmas, with or without a crèche, would inevitably recall the religious nature of the Holiday. The display engenders a friendly community spirit of good will in keeping with the season. The crèche may well have special meaning to those whose faith includes the celebration of religious masses, but none who sense the origins of the Christmas celebration would fail to be aware of its religious implications. That the display brings people into the central city, and serves commercial interests and benefits merchants and their employees, does not, as the dissent points out, determine the character of the display. That a prayer invoking Divine guidance in Congress is preceded and followed by debate and partisan conflict over taxes, budgets, national defense, and myriad mundane subjects, for example, has never been thought to demean or taint the sacredness of the invocation.[12]

Of course the crèche is identified with one religious faith but no more so than the [prior] cases in which we found no conflict with the Establishment Clause. It would be ironic, however, if the inclusion of a single symbol of a particular historic religious event, as part of a celebration acknowledged in the Western World for 20 centuries, and in this country by the people, by the Executive Branch, by the Congress, and the courts for two centuries, would so "taint" the City's exhibit as to render it violative of the Establishment Clause. To forbid the use of this one passive symbol — the crèche — at the very time people are taking note of the season with Christmas hymns and carols in public schools and other public places, and while the Congress and Legislatures open sessions with prayers by paid chaplains would be a stilted over-reaction contrary to our history and to our holdings. If the presence of the crèche in this display violates the Establishment Clause, a host of other forms of taking official note of Christmas, and of our religious heritage, are equally offensive to the Constitution.

---

12. Justice Brennan states that "by focusing on the holiday 'context' in which the crèche appear[s]," the Court seeks to "explain away the clear religious import of the crèche," and that it has equated the crèche with a Santa's house or a talking wishing well. Of course this is not true.

The Court has acknowledged that the "fears and political problems" that gave rise to the Religion Clauses in the 18th century are of far less concern today. [*Everson.*] We are unable to perceive the Archbishop of Canterbury, the Vicar of Rome, or other powerful religious leaders behind every public acknowledgment of the religious heritage long officially recognized by the three constitutional branches of government. Any notion that these symbols pose a real danger of establishment of a state church is far-fetched indeed. . . .

[Reversed.]

JUSTICE O'CONNOR, concurring. . . .

I

The Establishment Clause prohibits government from making adherence to a religion relevant in any way to a person's standing in the political community. Government can run afoul of that prohibition in two principal ways. One is excessive entanglement with religious institutions, which may interfere with the independence of the institutions, give the institutions access to government or governmental powers not fully shared by nonadherents of the religion, and foster the creation of political constituencies defined along religious lines. The second and more direct infringement is government endorsement or disapproval of religion. Endorsement sends a message to nonadherents that they are outsiders, not full members of the political community, and an accompanying message to adherents that they are insiders, favored members of the political community. Disapproval sends the opposite message.

Our prior cases have used the three-part test articulated in [*Lemon*] as a guide to detecting these two forms of unconstitutional government action. It has never been entirely clear, however, how the three parts of the test relate to the principles enshrined in the Establishment Clause. Focusing on institutional entanglement and on endorsement or disapproval of religion clarifies the *Lemon* test as an analytical device.

II

In this case, [there] is no institutional entanglement. [Further,] political divisiveness along religious lines should not be an independent test of constitutionality. . . .

[Guessing] the potential for political divisiveness inherent in a government practice is simply too speculative an enterprise, in part because the existence of the litigation, as this case illustrates, itself may affect the political response to the government practice. Political divisiveness is admittedly an evil addressed by the Establishment Clause. Its existence may be evidence that institutional entanglement is excessive or that a government practice is perceived as an endorsement of religion. But the constitutional inquiry should focus ultimately on the character of the government activity that might cause such divisiveness, not on the divisiveness itself. The entanglement prong of the *Lemon* test is properly limited to institutional entanglement.

III

The central issue in this case is whether Pawtucket has endorsed Christianity by its display of the crèche. To answer that question, we must examine both what Pawtucket intended to communicate in displaying the crèche and what message the City's display actually conveyed. The purpose and effect prongs of the *Lemon* test represent these two aspects of the meaning of the City's action.

The meaning of a statement to its audience depends both on the intention of the speaker and on the "objective" meaning of the statement in the community. Some listeners need not rely solely on the words themselves in discerning the speaker's intent: they can judge the intent by, for example, examining the context of the statement or asking questions of the speaker. Other listeners do not have or will not seek access to such evidence of intent. They will rely instead on the words themselves; for them the message actually conveyed may be something not actually intended. If the audience is large, as it always is when government "speaks" by word or deed, some portion of the audience will inevitably receive a message determined by the "objective" content of the statement, and some portion will inevitably receive the intended message. Examination of both the subjective and the objective components of the message communicated by a government action is therefore necessary to determine whether the action carries a forbidden meaning.

The purpose prong of the *Lemon* test asks whether government's actual purpose is to endorse or disapprove of religion. The effect prong asks whether, irrespective of government's actual purpose, the practice under review in fact conveys a message of endorsement or disapproval. An affirmative answer to either question should render the challenged practice invalid.

A

The purpose prong of the *Lemon* test requires that a government activity have a secular purpose. That requirement is not satisfied, however, by the mere existence of some secular purpose, however dominated by religious purposes. In [*Stone*], for example, the Court held that posting copies of the Ten Commandments in schools violated the purpose prong of the *Lemon* test, yet the State plainly had some secular objectives, such as instilling most of the values of the Ten Commandments and illustrating their connection to our legal system. The proper inquiry under the purpose prong of *Lemon*, I submit, is whether the government intends to convey a message of endorsement or disapproval of religion.

Applying that formulation to this case, I would find that Pawtucket did not intend to convey any message of endorsement of Christianity or disapproval of nonChristian religions. The evident purpose of including the crèche in the larger display was not promotion of the religious content of the crèche but celebration of the public holiday through its traditional symbols. Celebration of public holidays, which have cultural significance even if they also have religious aspects, is a legitimate secular purpose. . . .

B . . .

[Under the effect prong, what] is crucial is that a government practice not have the effect of communicating a message of government endorsement or disapproval of religion. It is only practices having that effect, whether intentionally or unintentionally, that make religion relevant, in reality or public perception, to status in the political community.

Pawtucket's display of its crèche, I believe, does not communicate a message that the government intends to endorse the Christian beliefs represented by the crèche. Although the religious and indeed sectarian significance of the crèche [is] not neutralized by the setting, the overall holiday setting changes what viewers may fairly understand to be the purpose of the display — as a typical museum setting, though not neutralizing the religious content of a religious painting, negates any message of endorsement of that content. The display celebrates a public holiday, and no one contends that declaration of that holiday is understood to be an endorsement of religion. The holiday itself has very strong secular components and traditions. Government celebration of the holiday, which is extremely common, generally is not understood to endorse the religious content of the holiday, just as government celebration of Thanksgiving is not so understood. The crèche is a traditional symbol of the holiday that is very commonly displayed along with purely secular symbols, as it was in Pawtucket.

These features combine to make the government's display of the crèche in this particular physical setting no more an endorsement of religion than such governmental "acknowledgments" of religion as [printing] of "In God We Trust" on coins, and opening court sessions with "God save the United States and this honorable court." Those government acknowledgments of religion serve, in the only ways reasonably possible in our culture, the legitimate secular purposes of solemnizing public occasions, expressing confidence in the future, and encouraging the recognition of what is worthy of appreciation in society. For that reason, and because of their history and ubiquity, those practices are not understood as conveying government approval of particular religious beliefs. The display of the crèche likewise serves a secular purpose — celebration of a public holiday with traditional symbols. It cannot fairly be understood to convey a message of government endorsement of religion. It is significant in this regard that the crèche display apparently caused no political divisiveness prior to the filing of this lawsuit, although Pawtucket had incorporated the crèche in its annual Christmas display for some years. For these reasons, I conclude that Pawtucket's display of the crèche does not have the effect of communicating endorsement of Christianity.

JUSTICE BRENNAN, with whom JUSTICE MARSHALL, JUSTICE BLACKMUN and JUSTICE STEVENS join, dissenting. . . .

The principles announced in the compact phrases of the Religion Clauses have, as the Court reminds us, proven difficult to apply. Faced with that uncertainty, the Court properly looks for guidance to the settled test announced in [*Lemon*] for assessing whether a challenged governmental practice involves an impermissible step toward the establishment of religion. Applying that test to this case, the Court reaches an essentially narrow result which turns largely upon the particular holiday context in which the City of Pawtucket's nativity scene appeared. The Court's decision implicitly leaves open questions concerning the constitutionality of the public display on public property of a crèche standing alone, or the public display of other distinctively religious symbols such as a cross. Despite the narrow contours of the Court's opinion, our precedents in my view compel the holding that Pawtucket's inclusion of a life-sized display depicting the biblical description of the birth of Christ as part of its annual Christmas celebration is unconstitutional. Nothing in the history of such practices or the setting in which the City's crèche is presented obscures or diminishes the plain fact that Pawtucket's action amounts to an impermissible governmental endorsement of a particular faith.

I . . .

[After] reviewing the Court's opinion, I am convinced that this case appears hard not because the principles of decision are obscure, but because the Christmas holiday seems so familiar and agreeable. Although the Court's reluctance to disturb a community's chosen method of celebrating such an agreeable holiday is understandable, that cannot justify the Court's departure from controlling precedent. In my view, Pawtucket's maintenance and display at public expense of a symbol as distinctively sectarian as a crèche simply cannot be squared with our prior cases. And it is plainly contrary to the purposes and values of the Establishment Clause to pretend, as the Court does, that the otherwise secular setting of Pawtucket's nativity scene dilutes in some fashion the crèche's singular religiosity, or that the City's annual display reflects nothing more than an "acknowledgment" of our shared national heritage. Neither the character of the Christmas holiday itself, nor our heritage of religious expression supports this result. . . .

Applying the three-part test to Pawtucket's crèche, I am persuaded that the City's inclusion of the crèche in its Christmas display simply does not reflect a "clearly secular purpose." [*Nyquist*.] Unlike the typical case in which the record reveals some contemporaneous expression of a clear purpose to advance religion, or, conversely, a clear secular purpose, here we have no explicit statement of purpose by Pawtucket's municipal government accompanying its decision to purchase, display and maintain the crèche. Governmental purpose may nevertheless be inferred. [The] City claims that its purposes were exclusively secular. Pawtucket sought, according to this view, only to participate in the celebration of a national holiday and to attract people to the downtown area in order to promote pre-Christmas retail sales and to help engender the spirit of goodwill and neighborliness commonly associated with the Christmas season.

Despite these assertions, two compelling aspects of this case indicate that our generally prudent "reluctance to attribute unconstitutional motives" to a governmental body, Mueller v. Allen, should be overcome. First, [all] of Pawtucket's "valid secular objectives can be readily accomplished by other means."[4] Plainly, the City's interest in celebrating the holiday and in promoting both retail sales and goodwill are fully served by the elaborate display of Santa Claus, reindeer, and wishing wells that are already a part of Pawtucket's annual Christmas display. More importantly, the nativity scene, unlike every other element of the Hodgson Park display, reflects a sectarian exclusivity that the avowed purposes of celebrating the holiday season and promoting retail commerce simply do not encompass. To be found constitutional, Pawtucket's seasonal celebration must at least be non-denominational and not serve to promote religion. The inclusion of a distinctively religious element like the crèche, however, demonstrates that a narrower sectarian purpose lay behind the decision to include a nativity scene.

The "primary effect" of including a nativity scene in the City's display is [to] place the government's imprimatur of approval on the particular religious beliefs exemplified by the crèche. Those who believe in the message of the nativity receive the unique and exclusive benefit of public recognition and approval of their views. For many, the City's decision to include the crèche as part of its extensive and costly efforts to celebrate Christmas can only mean that the prestige of the government has been conferred on the beliefs associated with the crèche, thereby providing "a significant symbolic benefit to religion. . . ." [*Larkin*.] The effect on minority religious groups, as well as on those who may reject all religion, is to convey the message that their views are not similarly worthy of public recognition nor entitled to public support. . . .

[As to political entanglement,] the Court should not blind itself to the fact that because communities differ in religious composition, the controversy over whether local governments may adopt religious symbols will continue to fester. In many communities, non-Christian groups can be expected to combat practices similar to Pawtucket's; this will be so especially in areas where there are substantial non-Christian minorities. . . .

B

The Court advances two principal arguments to support its conclusion that the Pawtucket crèche satisfies the *Lemon* test. Neither is persuasive.

First. The Court, by focusing on the holiday "context" in which the nativity scene appeared, seeks to explain away the clear religious import of the crèche. [It] blinks reality to claim, as the Court does, that by including such a distinctively religious object as the crèche in its Christmas display, Pawtucket has done no more than make use of a "traditional" symbol of the holiday, and has thereby purged the crèche of its religious content and conferred only an "incidental and direct" benefit on religion. . . .

[The] City has done nothing to disclaim government approval of the religious significance of the crèche, to suggest that the crèche represents only one religious symbol among many others that might be included in a seasonal display truly

---

4. I find it puzzling, to say the least, that the Court today should find "irrelevant," the fact that the City's secular objectives can be readily and fully accomplished without including the crèche, since only last Term in Larkin v. Grendel's Den, [459 U.S. 116 (1982)] the Court relied upon precisely the same point in striking down a Massachusetts statute which vested in church governing bodies the power to veto applications for liquor licenses. It seems the Court is willing to alter its analysis from Term to Term in order to suit its preferred results.

aimed at providing a wide catalogue of ethnic and religious celebrations, or to disassociate itself from the religious content of the crèche. . . .

Finally, and most importantly, even in the context of Pawtucket's seasonal celebration, the crèche retains a specifically Christian religious meaning. I refuse to accept the notion implicit in today's decision that non-Christians would find that the religious content of the crèche is eliminated by the fact that it appears as part of the City's otherwise secular celebration of the Christmas holiday. The nativity scene is clearly distinct in its purpose and effect from the rest of the Hodgson Park display for the simple reason that it is the only one rooted in a biblical account of Christ's birth. It is the chief symbol of the characteristically Christian belief that a divine Savior was brought into the world and that the purpose of this miraculous birth was to illuminate a path toward salvation and redemption. For Christians, that path is exclusive, precious and holy. But for those who do not share these beliefs, the symbolic re-enactment of the birth of a divine being who has been miraculously incarnated as a man stands as a dramatic reminder of their differences with Christian faith. [To] be so excluded on religious grounds by one's elected government is an insult and an injury that, until today, could not be countenanced by the Establishment Clause.

[Second, the Court relies on the fact that] the Christmas holiday in our national culture contains both secular and sectarian elements. [But to] say that government may recognize the holiday's traditional, secular elements of giftgiving, public festivities and community spirit, does not mean that government may indiscriminately embrace the distinctively sectarian aspects of the holiday. . . .

When government decides to recognize Christmas day as a public holiday, it does no more than accommodate the calendar of public activities to the plain fact that many Americans will expect on that day to spend time visiting with their families, attending religious services, and perhaps enjoying some respite from pre-holiday activities. The Free Exercise Clause, of course, does not necessarily compel the government to provide this accommodation, but neither is the Establishment Clause offended by such a step. Cf. [Zorach]. If public officials [participate] in the *secular* celebration of Christmas — by, for example, decorating public places with such secular images as wreaths, garlands or Santa Claus figures — they move closer to the limits of their constitutional power but nevertheless remain within the boundaries set by the Establishment Clause. But when those officials participate in or appear to endorse the distinctively religious elements of this otherwise secular event, they encroach upon First Amendment freedoms. For it is at that point that the government brings to the forefront the theological content of the holiday, and places the prestige, power and financial support of a civil authority in the service of a particular faith.

The inclusion of a crèche in Pawtucket's otherwise secular celebration of Christmas clearly violates these principles. Unlike such secular figures as Santa Claus, reindeer and carolers, a nativity scene represents far more than a mere "traditional" symbol of Christmas. The essence of the crèche's symbolic purpose and effect is to prompt the observer to experience a sense of simple awe and wonder appropriate to the contemplation of one of the central elements of Christian dogma — that God sent His son into the world to be a Messiah. Contrary to the Court's suggestion, the crèche is far from a mere representation of a "particular historic religious event." It is, instead, best understood as a mystical re-creation of an event that lies at the heart of Christian faith. To suggest, as the Court does, that such a symbol is merely "traditional" and therefore no different from Santa's house or reindeer is not only offensive to those for whom the crèche has profound significance, but insulting to those who insist for religious or personal reasons that the story of Christ is in no sense a part of "history" nor an unavoidable element of our national "heritage." . . .

II . . .

Intuition tells us that some official "acknowledgment" is inevitable in a religious society if government is not to adopt a stilted indifference to the religious life of the people. It is equally true, however, that if government is to remain scrupulously neutral in matters of religious conscience, as our Constitution requires, then it must avoid those overly broad acknowledgments of religious practices that may imply governmental favoritism toward one set of religious beliefs. This does not mean, of course, that public officials may not take account, when necessary, of the separate existence and significance of the religious institutions and practices in the society they govern. Should government choose to incorporate some arguably religious element into its public ceremonies, that acknowledgment must be impartial; it must not tend to promote one faith or handicap another, and it should not sponsor religion generally over non-religion. . . .

[At] least three principles — tracing the narrow channels which government acknowledgments must follow to satisfy the Establishment Clause — may be identified. First, although the government may not be compelled to do so by the Free Exercise Clause, it may, consistently with the Establishment Clause, act to accommodate to some extent the opportunities of individuals to practice their religion. [That] principle would justify government's decision to declare December 25th a public holiday.

Second, our cases recognize that while a particular governmental practice may have derived from religious motivations and retain certain religious connotations, it is nonetheless permissible for the government to pursue the practice when it is continued today solely for secular reasons. [The] mere fact that a governmental practice coincides to some extent with certain religious beliefs does not render it unconstitutional. Thanksgiving Day, in my view, fits easily within this principle, for despite its religious antecedents, the current practice of celebrating Thanksgiving is unquestionably secular and patriotic. . . .

Finally, we have noted that government cannot be completely prohibited from recognizing in its public actions the religious beliefs and practices of the American people as an aspect of our national history and culture. While I remain uncertain about these questions, I would suggest that such practices as the designation of "In God We Trust" as our national motto, or the references to God contained in the Pledge of Allegiance can best be understood, [as] a form a "ceremonial deism," protected from Establishment Clause scrutiny chiefly because they have lost through rote repetition any significant religious content. Moreover, these references are uniquely suited to serve such wholly secular purposes as solemnizing public occasions, or inspiring commitment to meet some national challenge in a manner that simply could not be fully served in our culture if government were limited to purely non-religious phrases. The practices by which the government has long acknowledged religion are therefore probably necessary to serve certain secular functions, and that necessity, coupled with their long history, gives those practices an essentially secular meaning.

The crèche fits none of these categories. . . .

By insisting that such a distinctively sectarian message is merely an unobjectionable part of our "religious heritage, the Court takes a long step backwards to the days when Justice Brewer could arrogantly declare for the Court that "this is a Christian nation." Church of Holy Trinity v. United States, 143 U.S. 457 (1892). Those days, I had thought, were forever put behind us by the Court's decision in Engel v. Vitale, in which we rejected a similar argument advanced by the State of New York that its Regent's Prayer was simply an acceptable part of our "spiritual heritage."

III

The American historical experience concerning the public celebration of Christmas, if carefully examined, provides no support for the Court's decision. . . .

Indeed, the Court's approach suggests a fundamental misapprehension of the proper uses of history in constitutional interpretation. Certainly, our decisions reflect the fact that an awareness of historical practice often can provide a useful guide in interpreting the abstract language of the Establishment Clause. But historical acceptance of a particular practice alone is never sufficient to justify a challenged governmental action, since, as the Court has rightly observed, "no one acquires a vested or protected right in violation of the Constitution by long use, even when that span of time covers our entire national existence and indeed predates it." *Walz*, 397 U.S., at 678. Attention to the details of history should not blind us to the cardinal purposes of the Establishment Clause, nor limit our central inquiry in these cases — whether the challenged practices "threaten those consequences which the Framers deeply feared." [Abington School Dist.] v. Schempp, (Brennan, J., concurring). In recognition of this fact, the Court has, until today, consistently limited its historical inquiry to the particular practice under review. . . .

[The] Court wholly fails to discuss the history of the public celebration of Christmas or the use of publicly-displayed nativity scenes. The Court's complete failure to offer any explanation of its assertion is perhaps understandable, however, because the historical record points in precisely the opposite direction. Two features of this history are worth noting. First, at the time of the adoption of the Constitution and the Bill of Rights, there was no settled pattern of celebrating Christmas, either as a purely religious holiday or as a public event. Second, the historical evidence, such as it is, offers no uniform pattern of widespread acceptance of the holiday and indeed suggests that the development of Christmas as a public holiday is a comparatively recent phenomenon.

The intent of the Framers with respect to the public display of nativity scenes is virtually impossible to discern primarily because the widespread celebration of Christmas did not emerge in its present form until well into the nineteenth century. Carrying a well-defined Puritan hostility to the celebration of Christ's birth with them to the New World, the founders of the Massachusetts Bay Colony pursued a vigilant policy of opposition to any public celebration of the holiday. To the Puritans, the celebration of Christmas represented a "Popish" practice lacking any foundation in Scripture. This opposition took legal form in 1659 when the Massachusetts Colony made the observance of Christmas day, "by abstinence from labor, feasting, or any other way," an offense punishable by fine. Although the Colony eventually repealed this ban in 1681, the Puritan objection remained firm.

During the eighteenth century, sectarian division over the celebration of the holiday continued. As increasing numbers of members of the Anglican and the Dutch and German Reformed churches arrived, the practice of celebrating Christmas as a purely religious holiday grew. But denominational differences continued to dictate differences in attitude toward the holiday. American Anglicans, who carried with them the Church of England's acceptance of the holiday, Roman Catholics, and various German groups all made the celebration of Christmas a vital part of their religious life. By contrast, many nonconforming Protestant groups, including the Presbyterians, Congregationalists, Baptists, and Methodists, continued to regard the holiday with suspicion and antagonism well into the nineteenth century. This pattern of sectarian division concerning the holiday suggests that for the Framers of the Establishment Clause, who were acutely sensitive to such sectarian controversies, no single view of how government should approach the celebration of Christmas would be possible. . . .

[For] those who authored the Bill of Rights, it seems reasonable to suppose that the public celebration of Christmas would have been regarded as at least a sensitive matter, if not deeply controversial. . . .

Furthermore [the] public display of nativity scenes as part of governmental celebrations of Christmas does not come to us supported by an unbroken history of widespread acceptance. It was not until 1836 that a State first granted legal recognition to Christmas as a public holiday. This was followed in the period between 1845 and 1865, by twenty-eight jurisdictions which included Christmas day as a legal holiday. Congress did not follow the States' lead until 1870 when it established December 25th, along with the Fourth of July, New Year's Day, and Thanksgiving, as a legal holiday in the District of Columbia. This pattern of legal recognition tells us only that public acceptance of the holiday was gradual and that the practice [did] not take on the character of a widely recognized holiday until the middle of the nineteenth century. . . .

[The] City's action should be recognized for what it is: a coercive, though perhaps small, step toward establishing the sectarian preferences of the majority at the expense of the minority, accomplished by placing public facilities and funds in support of the religious symbolism and theological tidings that the crèche conveys. . . .

I dissent.

JUSTICE BLACKMUN, with whom JUSTICE STEVENS joins, dissenting. . . .

The crèche has been relegated to the role of a neutral harbinger of the holiday season, useful for commercial purposes, but devoid of any inherent meaning and incapable of enhancing the religious tenor of a display of which it is an integral part. The city has its victory — but it is a Pyrrhic one indeed.

The import of the Court's decision is to encourage use of the crèche in a municipally sponsored display, a setting where Christians feel constrained in acknowledging its symbolic meaning and non-Christians feel alienated by its presence. Surely, this is a misuse of a sacred symbol. . . .

Note: How Are Purpose and Effect Relevant? — De Facto Establishments

The Court's opinion suggests that the *Lemon* criteria may be inapplicable to the problem in *Lynch*. This note examines some possible justifications for adopting a different approach. (Note that Justice Brennan applies a strong form of the *Lemon* tests, while the Court applies a weaker form. Does this suggest difficulties with *Lemon* in general, or only with its application to the kind of problem at issue in *Lynch*?)

1. *Roger Williams versus Thomas Jefferson.* Consider M. Howe, The Garden and the Wilderness 11-12 (1965):

> [Roger Williams's] principle of separation endorsed a host of favoring tributes to faith [so] substantial that they have produced in the aggregate what may fairly be described as a de facto establishment of religion [in which] the religious institution as a whole is maintained and activated by forces not kindled directly by government. [Some] elements of our religious establishment are, of course, reinforced by law. Whenever that situation prevails, as it does, for instance, when the law secures the sanctity of Sunday, the courts are apt to seek out a secular justification for the favoring enactment and, by this evasive tactic, meet the charge that an establishment de jure exists. The ultimate strength of our religious establishment is derived, however, not from the favoring acts of government, but, in the largest measure, from the continuing force of the evangelical principle of separation. The Supreme Court's unwillingness to recognize that this principle has ever been an element in our constitutional tradition — its pretense, that is, that the only theory of separation known in American constitutional history is the Jeffersonian or rationalistic — leaves quite unexplained the persistence of the de facto establishment. Its persistence is owing in large part to the fact that throughout our history the evangelical theory of separation has demanded that the de facto establishment be respected. The hold of that theory is so strong that it is almost inconceivable that any branch of government, whether local, state, or national, could today acknowledge that its objective is the destruction of this establishment. Yet the Supreme Court, by pretending that the American principle of separation is predominantly Jeffersonian and by purporting to outlaw even those aids in religion which do not affect religious liberties, seems to have endorsed a governmental policy aimed at the elimination of de facto establishments.

To what extent does *Lynch* indicate that Williams's evangelical principle of separation has now been acknowledged by the Court? Does *Lynch* extend beyond ceremonial or long-established practices?

In McGowan v. Maryland, 366 U.S. 420 (1961), the Court rejected an establishment clause challenge to laws requiring that most large-scale commercial enterprises remain closed on Sundays. The Court's review of history demonstrated that Sunday closing laws were originally efforts to promote church attendance. "But, despite the strongly religious origin of these laws, nonreligious arguments for Sunday closing began to be heard more distinctly." The Court said that the Constitution "does not ban federal or state regulation of conduct whose reason or effect merely happens to coincide with the tenets of some or all religions." It concluded that, "as presently written and administered, most [Sunday closing laws] are of a secular rather than of a religious character." They "provide a uniform day of rest for all citizens. [To] say that the States cannot prescribe

Sunday as a day of rest for these purposes solely because centuries ago such laws had their genesis in religion would give a constitutional interpretation of hostility to the public welfare rather than one of mere separation of church and State." As of 1961 was Howe's characterization of Sunday closing laws more accurate than the Court's? As of the present?

2. *History as a guide.* Walz v. Tax Commission, 397 U.S. 664 (1970), held constitutional the practice of granting churches exemptions from the property tax. Chief Justice Burger's opinion for the Court said that the "purpose of a property tax exemption is neither the advancement nor the inhibition of religion. [The state] has not singled out one particular church [or] even churches as such; rather, it has granted exemption to all houses of worship within a broad class of property owned by nonprofit, quasi-public corporations [which the state considers] beneficial and stabilizing influences in community life." After describing the ways in which denial of tax exemption would "expand the involvement of government" with religion, the Court said, "The exemption creates only a minimal and remote involvement between church and state. [It] restricts the fiscal relationship between [them], and tends to complement and reinforce the desired separation insulating each from the other." The Court noted that every state had a property tax exemption for churches and that the federal income tax has since its inception exempted religious organizations. It found "significant" that Congress exempted churches from real estate taxes in 1802. "[An] unbroken practice of according the exemption to churches, openly and by affirmative state action, not covertly or by state inaction, is not something to be lightly cast aside." Justice Brennan, concurring, agreed that "the existence from the beginning of the Nation's life of a practice [is] a fact of considerable import in the interpretation of abstract constitutional language. [The] more longstanding and widely accepted a practice, the greater its impact upon constitutional interpretation." He found two "secular purposes" for the exemption: Churches, like other exempt groups, "contribute to the well-being of the community in a variety of nonreligious ways," and they "uniquely contribute to the pluralism of American society." Justice Douglas dissented. Compare the discussion of the role of long-standing practice with that in McCulloch v. Maryland, Chapter 1, section C, supra.

Marsh v. Chambers, 463 U.S. 783 (1983), relied on a "unique history" to uphold the constitutionality of opening legislative sessions with prayers led by a state-employed chaplain. The history ran from colonial times to the present and included the first Congress's hiring a chaplain in 1789, only three days before it reached final agreement on the language of the first amendment.

> [Historical] evidence sheds light not only on what the draftsmen intended the Establishment Clause to mean, but also on how they thought that Clause applied to the practice authorized by the First Congress — their actions reveal their intent. [In] light of the unambiguous and unbroken history of more than 200 years, there can be no doubt that the practice of opening legislative sessions with prayer has become part of the fabric of our society. [It] is simply a tolerable acknowledgment of beliefs widely held among the people of this country. As Justice Douglas observed, "[We] are a religious people whose institutions presuppose a Supreme Being." [*Zorach.*]

The chaplain had held office for sixteen years, but "absent proof [of] an impermissible motive," the long tenure did not "in itself" violate the Constitution.

Justice Brennan, joined by Justice Marshall, dissented. He noted that the Court had not applied the *Lemon* test and that under that test, the purpose and effect were "self-evident" and "clearly religious." He found extensive political entanglement as well. Justice Brennan argued that

> legislative prayer clearly violates the principles of neutrality and separation. [It] intrudes on the right to conscience by forcing some legislators either to participate in a "prayer opportunity" with which they are in basic disagreement, or to make their disagreement a matter of public comment by declining to participate. It forces all residents of the State to support a religious exercise that may be contrary to their own beliefs. It requires the State to commit itself on fundamental theological issues. It has the potential for degrading religion by allowing a religious call to worship to be intermeshed with a secular call to order. And it injects religion into the political sphere by creating the potential that each and every selection of a chaplain, or consideration of a particular prayer, or even reconsideration of the practice itself, will provoke a political battle along religious lines and ultimately alienate some religiously identified group of citizens.

He criticized the Court's reliance on the actions of the first Congress: "Legislators, influenced by the passions and exigencies of the moment, the pressure of constituents and colleagues, and the press of business, do not always pass sober constitutional judgment on every piece of legislation they enact." James Madison, who voted for the bill in the first Congress, later said that the practice was unconstitutional. This "may not have represented so much a change of *mind* as a change of *role*, from a member of Congress engaged in the hurley-burley of legislative activity to a detached observer engaged in unpressured reflection." After summarizing the views he expressed in *Schempp*, supra, Justice Brennan concluded, "the Court's focus [on] a narrow piece of history is, in a fundamental sense, a betrayal of the lessons of history." Justice Stevens's separate dissent emphasized "the preference of one faith over another" inherent in the selection of a chaplain, and the "clearly sectarian content" of the chaplain's prayers.

Does *Lynch* rely on history in an appropriate way? Did *Walz* and *Marsh*? Is Justice Brennan correct in distinguishing *Lynch* from *Walz* and *Marsh*? Is he consistent in seeking the "lessons of history" while insisting that the Court should rely only on the history of the particular practices at issue? In *Walz* the Court stated that tax exemptions had not "given the remotest sign of leading to an established church," and in *Marsh* it said that the fear that "prayer in this context risks the beginning of the establishment the founding Fathers feared [was] not well-founded." Is that the "lesson of history" with respect to de facto establishments? Recall the discussion of interpretivism in Chapter 1, section B, supra.

3. *Religious pluralism and the political process.* What does the Court mean in *Lynch* by saying that the crèche must be considered "in its context"? Is Justice Blackmun correct in his claim that religion's victory is Pyrrhic? Consider Kurland, The Religion Clauses and the Burger Court, 34 Cath. U. L. Rev. 1, 13-14 (1984):

> The crèche opinion was sleazy. [It] would seem that the crèche was really only a device to attract commercial activity, a passive record of an historical event, to be analogized to religious paintings that occupy the walls of many a municipal museum. To suggest that the crèche is unlike the Ten Commandments [in Stone v. Graham] and is not a religious symbol clearly demeans the religion of those who

erected it. If it is not put forth as illustrative of God's miracle, it is surely not merely the portrayal of the birth of any child in Bethlehem two millenia ago. Such treatment of the crèche symbol further detracts from the religious significance of the Christmas holiday, a holiday which every year, at least in this country, pays more homage to Mammon than to God. I would think that devout Christians might take umbrage at the government, in the form of the judiciary, for labeling a depiction of the birth of the Christ child as a nonreligious symbol, like a Christmas tree or a banner proclaiming "Seasons Greetings."

Does the emphasis on context suggest that there is no religious content to the use of the crèche? Or that the undeniable religious content is relatively modest? Should the Court insist that permissible de facto establishments have a low level of religious content? Consider the following argument: Contemporary society is pluralist in religion and in politics. Some religious groups oppose all governmental support of religion, others would support sectarian aid but oppose nondenominational aid, and others support nondenominational aid. As some of these groups seek to secure legislation, they will have to adjust their programs to obtain majority support. The likely outcome of pluralist political bargaining in contemporary society on matters relating to religion is legislation having relatively modest religious content. The political process is therefore sufficient to guard against the evils at which the establishment clause is directed. Does this argument underestimate the degree to which a "least common denominator" religion may raise serious concern about establishment?

Is the "de facto establishment" theory consistent with the Court's disposition of the school prayer cases? As an original matter, does the crèche in *Lynch* demonstrate less governmental support for religion than nondenominational voluntary school prayer? Than student-led prayer groups held in school buildings before or after school hours? Is it sufficient to say that the Court regarded the school prayer cases as involving statutes that had *no* secular purposes?

4. *Nonimposition.* In what sense is the crèche "coercive," as Justice Brennan calls it? *Walz* means that fiscal support of religion through the tax system is not the imposition of religion on nonbelievers. Does the coercion in *Lynch* reside in the psychological impact of the crèche on non-Christians? Would treating that impact as coercive create a "dissenter's veto"? See Chapter 7, section B3 supra.

The school prayer cases discussed coercion. In *Engel* the school allowed those who objected to the prayer to remain silent or be excused from attendance. But the Court said that "When the power, prestige and financial support of government is placed behind a particular religious belief, the indirect coercive pressure upon religious minorities to conform to the prevailing officially approved religion is plain." Presumably, if the "indirect coercive pressure" is sufficiently great, the free exercise clause is violated. See section C infra. If the pressure is insufficient to violate the free exercise clause, why should it violate the establishment clause?

Justice Stewart would have remanded *Schempp* for a development of the facts involving coercion:

[The] dangers of coercion involved in the holding of religious exercises in a schoolroom differ qualitatively from those presented by the use of similar exercises or affirmations in ceremonies attended by adults. Even as to children, however, the duty laid upon government in connection with religious exercises in the public schools is that of refraining from so structuring the school environment as to put any kind of pressure on a child to participate in those exercises; it is not that of providing an atmosphere in which children are kept scrupulously insulated from any awareness that some of their fellows may want to open the school day with prayer, or of the fact that there exist in our pluralistic society differences of religious belief. [Certain] types of exercises would present situations in which no possibility of coercion on the part of secular officials could be claimed to exist. Thus, if such exercises were held either before or after the official school day, or if the school schedule were such that participation were merely one among a number of desirable alternatives, it could hardly be contended that the exercises did anything more than to provide an opportunity for the voluntary expression of religious belief. On the other hand, a law which provided for religious exercises during the school day and which contained no excusal provision would obviously be unconstitutionally coercive upon those who did not wish to participate. And even under a law containing an excusal provision, if the exercises were held during the school day, and no equally desirable alternative were provided by the school authorities, the likelihood that children might be under at least some psychological compulsion to participate would be great. In such a case as the latter, however, I think we would err if we *assumed* such coercion in the absence of any evidence.

Consider Stone, In Opposition to the School Prayer Amendment, 50 U. Chi. L. Rev. 823, 836 (1983): "Social psychologists and sociologists have long observed that children place special importance on how they are regarded by their classmates. The urge to conform [can] often induce children to go along with the majority and do or say things that they are convinced are wrong, or that they would not otherwise do or say." In what sense is the government responsible for this sort of coercion?

5. *Nondiscrimination.* In *Lynch* the Court said that the crèche was not "explicitly discriminatory in the sense contemplated in Larson [v. Valente, supra]," because *Larson* was a case with "substantial evidence of overt discrimination against a particular church." In *Walz* Justice Harlan's concurring opinion stated that "The Court must survey meticulously the circumstances of governmental categories to eliminate [religious] gerrymanders. [The] critical question is whether the circumference of legislation encircles a class [sufficiently] broad." Is the crèche, like the statute in *Larson*, facially neutral? Why is a class including only a specifically Christian symbol broad enough to avoid being a religious gerrymander? Recall the discussion above of the politics of religious pluralism.

6. *Equal protection analysis and Justice O'Connor's approach.* Justice O'Connor's reformulation of the *Lemon* test recasts it in terms familiar from equal protection law. See Chapter 5, section C, supra. On her analysis, the establishment clause prohibits the illicit purposes of "endorsement or disapproval." The purposes can be explicit or implicit. As in equal protection law, sometimes an illicit purpose can be inferred from a statute's effects.

Is this reformulation helpful? Note that it requires Justice O'Connor to accept the claim that the city's crèche was not intended to endorse Christianity and that under her approach, the more those who desire government endorsement of religion support legislation because it endorses a particular religion, the more questionable the legislation becomes. Does her approach thereby contain an underlying hostility toward religion? Justice O'Connor would prohibit actions reasonably perceived as endorsement or disapproval. Perceived by whom? If by religious minorities, is she correct in concluding that reasonable Jews would not perceive the crèche as endorsement of Christianity? Consider Tribe, Constitutional Calculus: Equal Justice or Economic Efficiency, 98 Harv. L. Rev. 592, 611 (1985): "One cannot avoid hearing in *Lynch* a faint echo of the Court that found nothing invidious in the Jim Crow policy of 'separate but equal.'" How likely are religious majorities to see government action that aids their religious preferences as "endorsement" rather than as a sensible submission to the desires of the majority? In *Jaffree* Justice O'Connor said that "individual perceptions, or resentment that a religious observer is exempted from a particular government requirement, would be entitled to little weight" where statutes accommodate free exercise values. Can this position be transferred to the broader establishment clause context?

7. *Purpose in de facto establishments?* Is it helpful to attempt to analyze the problems discussed in this note by using the *Lemon* criteria? Note the Court's suggestion in *Lynch* that they should not be applied in full force, and consider whether Justice Brennan discusses what is really at stake in *Lynch* by using the *Lemon* criteria.

In Harris v. McRae, 448 U.S. 297 (1980), the Court rejected an establishment clause attack on a statute restricting public financing of abortions. The challengers argued that the statute "incorporates into law the doctrines of the Roman Catholic Church." The Court responded that "the fact that the funding restrictions [may] coincide with the religious tenets of the Roman Catholic Church does not, without more, contravene the Establishment Clause." It mentioned that many statutory prohibitions, such as those against larceny, similarly coincided with religious tenets. Are such prohibitions distinguishable on the ground that more religious traditions converge in condemning them than condemn abortion? What more would be needed to establish a first amendment violation? Suppose the challengers showed that religious motivations not broadly shared among many religions played a substantial part in the enactment. Should the burden shift to the state to show a substantial secular purpose? Compare Mt. Healthy v. Doyle, Chapter 7, section F3, supra, and Arlington Heights v. Metropolitan Housing Corp., Chapter 5, section C2, supra. Could a state ever show a substantial secular purpose for a moment-of-silence statute? For de facto establishments in general? What result if the religious motivation is predominant? Consider whether the availability of alternative methods to accomplish secular goals is relevant only if the purpose criterion invalidates legislation substantially motivated by religious concerns.

3. Facially Neutral Statutes That (Incidentally?) Aid Religion

Note: The Problem and Its Background

1. *The basic problem.* The school prayer cases indicate that, de facto establishments aside, legislation with the sole (or predominant?) purpose of aiding religion is unconstitutional. Sometimes the Court will treat legislation that does not use religion as a basis for classification as a religious gerrymander, inferring an impermissible purpose from the statute's structure and history. See, e.g., Larson v. Valente, supra. As with similar issues under the equal protection clause

and the dormant commerce clause, more complex problems arise when the Court is unwilling to infer an impermissible purpose for a statute that does not use religion as a basis for classification, yet the legislation substantially aids religious institutions. (Parallel problems arise when a statute burdens religion. See section C infra.)

The Court has examined this problem most extensively in cases questioning legislative efforts to support nonpublic education. Below the college level, nearly all such education occurs in schools affiliated with churches, so that usually 75 percent or more of the aid goes to church-related schools. The Court's first substantial decision was *Everson*, section A supra, which upheld a program paying the cost of transporting children to public and private schools. The Court said that the first amendment "requires the state to be a neutral in its relations with groups of religious believers and non-believers; it does not require the state to be their adversary." It should not be interpreted "to prohibit [the state] from extending its general state law benefits to all its citizens without regard to their religious belief." The statute "does no more than provide a general program to help parents get their children, regardless of their religion, safely and expeditiously to and from accredited schools."

Four justices dissented. Justice Jackson, joined by Justice Frankfurter, argued that the statute was a religious gerrymander because it excluded private schools operated for profit and the local authority's resolution adopting the program further limited it to students attending public or Catholic parochial schools. Thus, the beneficiaries were selected by "an essentially religious test." Justice Rutledge's dissent was joined by Justices Frankfurter, Jackson, and Burton. He contended that the first amendment "broadly forbids state support, financial or other, of religion in any guise, form or degree. It outlaws all use of public funds for religious purposes." In this case, "parents pay money to send their children to parochial schools and funds raised by taxation are used to reimburse them. This not only helps the children to get to school and the parents to send them. It aids them in a substantial way to get [religious] training and teaching," in part because "transportation [is] as essential to education as any other element." He argued that it was impossible to apportion the expenditures between the parochial schools' religious instruction and their instruction in secular subjects.

On one view, the result in *Everson* produces conceptual and practical difficulties. Without the subsidy for transportation, religious schools would have to raise tuition or pay for transportation by reducing their other activities. The subsidy therefore makes it less expensive for parents to provide their children with a comprehensive religious education. In this sense, the subsidy "supports" or "aids" religion. But if the legislation is truly neutral, should this kind of support violate the Constitution? Is it distinguishable from the provision of general police and fire protection to churches and parochial schools, which could purchase private security services to provide those protections?

2. *Subsequent developments.* Since 1968 the Court has decided over a dozen cases involving public aid to nonpublic education. For earlier decisions, see McCollum v. Board of Education, 333 U.S. 203 (1948) (invalidating program in which public school students were released from their classes to participate in religious education programs conducted in public school classrooms; nonparticipants were required to remain in school); Zorach v. Clauson, 343 U.S. 306 (1952) (upholding program in which students were dismissed from school to attend

religious education classes conducted in nonschool buildings; nonparticipants were required to remain in school).

The Court held the following forms of aid unconstitutional: (a) statutes reimbursing nonpublic schools for salaries, textbooks, and instructional materials used in secular courses and paying teachers of secular subjects in nonpublic schools a 15 percent salary supplement, Lemon v. Kurtzman, 403 U.S. 602 (1971); (b) a tuition tax scheme providing tax credits to low-income parents of children in nonpublic schools and a tax deduction to higher-income parents with children in such schools, Committee for Public Education v. Nyquist, 413 U.S. 756 (1973); (c) a statute reimbursing parents for $75 or $150 in tuition paid to elementary or secondary nonpublic schools, Sloan v. Lemon, 413 U.S. 825 (1973); (d) a statute reimbursing nonpublic schools for their expenses in administering state-required and teacher-prepared tests, Levitt v. Committee for Public Education, 413 U.S. 472 (1973); (e) a statute lending instructional materials and equipment, such as maps and laboratory equipment, to nonpublic schools and providing public school employees to provide services such as remedial reading and counselling at nonpublic schools, Meek v. Pittenger, 421 U.S. 349 (1975); (f) a statute lending instructional equipment to students in nonpublic schools and paying the costs of field trips in secular courses in nonpublic schools, Wolman v. Walter, 433 U.S. 229 (1977).

The Court upheld the following forms of aid: (a) a statute lending textbooks in secular subjects to students in nonpublic schools, Board of Education v. Allen, 392 U.S. 236 (1968) (how can textbooks be distinguished from maps, at issue in *Meek?*); (b) statutes authorizing the use of public school personnel to administer standardized tests and to provide diagnostic speech, hearing, and psychological services at nonpublic schools and to provide therapeutic, remedial, and guidance services at neutral sites, such as public schools and mobile units, for students enrolled in nonpublic schools, Wolman v. Walter, supra; (c) a statute reimbursing nonpublic schools for the cost of administering state-mandated and state-composed tests and for the cost of maintaining state-required records, Committee for Public Education v. Regan, 444 U.S. 646 (1980).

Do the cases form a coherent pattern? Tribe, supra, at 842-843, summarizes the results:

> First, if equipment [is] supplied [at] public expense, [it] must be supplied only to pupils or their parents and not to parochial schools themselves. [Second,] if services are to be supplied at public expense, they must be supplied by personnel not subject to parochial school control, and their content cannot be subject to specification by parochial school teachers or administrators. [Third,] publicly funded services cannot be provided [on] parochial school premises if [they] afford opportunity for anything beyond the most impersonal and limited contact with the child. [Fourth,] services supplied at public expense may be provided on parochial school premises provided the [link] to the educational mission [is] too limited to create any danger that the service-provider, under the subtle pressures of the religious environment, will begin transmitting sectarian views.

Tribe argues that this pattern is justified by the principle that "symbolic identification" of the state with religion should be avoided. See also Justice O'Connor's opinion in Lynch v. Donnelly, supra. Why should symbolism matter more than reality?

Mueller v. Allen

463 U.S. 388 (1983)

[The Minnesota income tax statute permits taxpayers to deduct from their gross income actual expenses incurred for "tuition, textbooks and transportation" for the education of their children in elementary and secondary schools. The deduction is available for expenses incurred in sending children to public as well as nonpublic schools. The deduction is limited to $500 per child in elementary school and $700 per child in secondary school. About 820,000 children attend public schools in Minnesota, while about 91,000 attend nonpublic schools, 95 percent of them in sectarian schools. The court of appeals held that the statute did not violate the establishment clause.]

JUSTICE REHNQUIST delivered the opinion of the Court. . . .

One fixed principle in this field is our consistent rejection of the argument that "any program which in some manner aids an institution with a religious affiliation" violates the Establishment Clause. Hunt v. McNair, 413 U.S. 734, 742 (1973). For example, it is now well-established that a state may reimburse parents for expenses incurred in transporting their children to school, [*Everson*], and that it may loan secular textbooks to all schoolchildren within the state, Board of Education v. Allen, 392 U.S. 236 (1968).

Notwithstanding the repeated approval given programs such as those in *Allen* and *Everson*, our decisions also have struck down arrangements resembling, in many respects, these forms of assistance. In this case we are asked to decide whether Minnesota's tax deduction bears greater resemblance to those types of assistance to parochial schools we have approved, or to those we have struck down. Petitioners place particular reliance on our decision in Committee for Public Education v. Nyquist, where we held invalid a New York statute [granting] thinly disguised "tax benefits," actually amounting to tuition grants, to the parents of children attending private schools. As explained below, we conclude that §290.09, subd. 22, bears less resemblance to the arrangement struck down in *Nyquist* than it does to assistance programs upheld in our prior decisions and those discussed with approval in *Nyquist*.

The general nature of our inquiry in this area has been guided, since the decision in [*Lemon*], by the "three-part" test laid down in that case. [While] this principle is well settled, our cases have also emphasized that it provides "no more than [a] helpful signpos[t]" in dealing with Establishment Clause challenges. [*Hunt.*] . . .

Little time need be spent on the question of whether the Minnesota tax deduction has a secular purpose. Under our prior decisions, governmental assistance programs have consistently survived this inquiry even when they have run afoul of other aspects of the *Lemon* framework. This reflects, at least in part, our reluctance to attribute unconstitutional motives to the states, particularly when a plausible secular purpose for the state's program may be discerned from the face of the statute.

A state's decision to defray the cost of educational expenses incurred by parents — regardless of the type of schools their children attend — evidences a purpose that is both secular and understandable. An educated populace is essential to the political and economic health of any community, and a state's efforts to assist parents in meeting the rising cost of educational expenses plainly serves this secular purpose of ensuring that the state's citizenry is well educated. Similarly, Minnesota, like other states, could conclude that there is a strong public interest in assuring the continued financial health of private schools, both sectarian and nonsectarian. By educating a substantial number of students such schools relieve public schools of a correspondingly great burden — to the benefit of all taxpayers. In addition, private schools may serve as a benchmark for public schools, in a manner analogous to the "TVA yardstick" for private power companies. . . .

We turn therefore to the more difficult but related question whether the Minnesota statute has "the primary effect of advancing the sectarian aims of the nonpublic schools." [Lemon.] In concluding that it does not, we find several features of the Minnesota tax deduction particularly significant. First, an essential feature of Minnesota's arrangement is the fact that §290.09, subd. 22, is only one among many deductions [available] under the Minnesota tax laws. [The] Minnesota legislature's judgment that a deduction for educational expenses fairly equalizes the tax burden of its citizens and encourages desirable expenditures for educational purposes is entitled to substantial deference.[6]

Other characteristics of §290.09, subd. 22, argue equally strongly for the provision's constitutionality. Most importantly, the deduction is available for educational expenses incurred by *all* parents, including those whose children attend public schools and those whose children attend nonsectarian private schools or sectarian private [schools:] "the provision of benefits to so broad a spectrum of groups is an important index of secular effect."

In this respect, as well as others, this case is vitally different from the scheme struck down in *Nyquist*. There, public assistance amounting to tuition grants, was provided only to parents of children in *nonpublic* schools. [Unlike] the assistance at issue in *Nyquist*, §290.09, subd. 22, permits *all* parents — whether their children attend public school or private — to deduct their childrens' educational expenses. [A] program, like §290.09, subd. 22, that neutrally provides state assistance to a broad spectrum of citizens is not readily subject to challenge under the Establishment Clause.

We also agree [that,] by channeling whatever assistance it may provide to parochial schools through individual parents, Minnesota has reduced the Establishment Clause objections to which its action is subject. It is true, of course, that financial assistance provided to parents ultimately has an economic effect comparable to that of aid given directly to the schools attended by their children. It is also true, however, that under Minnesota's arrangement public funds become

---

6. Our decision in [Nyquist] is not to the contrary on this point. We expressed considerable doubt there that the "tax benefits" provided by New York law properly could be regarded as parts of a genuine system of tax laws. Plainly, the outright grants to low-income parents did not take the form of ordinary tax benefits. As to the benefits provided to middle-income parents, the Court said:

> The amount of the deduction is unrelated to the amount of money actually expended by any parent on tuition, but is calculated on the basis of a formula contained in the statute. The formula is apparently the product of a legislative attempt to assure that each family would receive a carefully estimated net benefit, and that the tax benefit would be comparable to, and compatible with, the tuition grant for lower income families.

[While] the economic consequences of the program in *Nyquist* and that in this case may be difficult to distinguish, we have recognized on other occasions that "the form of the [State's assistance to parochial schools must be examined] for the light that it casts on the substance." [Lemon.] The fact that the Minnesota plan embodies a "genuine tax deduction" is thus of some relevance, especially given the traditional rule of deference accorded legislative classifications in tax statutes.

available only as a result of numerous, private choices of individual parents of school-age children. For these reasons, we recognized in *Nyquist* that the means by which state assistance flows to private schools is of some importance: we said that "the fact that aid is disbursed to parents rather than to . . . schools" is a material consideration in Establishment Clause analysis, albeit "only one among many to be considered." It is noteworthy that all but one of our recent cases invalidating state aid to parochial schools have involved the direct transmission of assistance from the state to the schools themselves. The exception, of course, was *Nyquist*, which, as discussed previously is distinguishable from this case on other grounds. Where, as here, aid to parochial schools is available only as a result of decisions of individual parents no "imprimatur of State approval," [*Widmar*], can be deemed to have been conferred on any particular religion, or on religion generally.

We find it useful, in the light of the foregoing characteristics of §290.09, subd. 22, to compare the attenuated financial benefits flowing to parochial schools from the section to the evils against which the Establishment Clause was designed to protect. These dangers are well-described by our statement that "[w]hat is at stake as a matter of policy [in Establishment Clause cases] is preventing that kind and degree of government involvement in religious life that, as history teaches us, is apt to lead to strife and frequently strain a political system to the breaking point." [*Nyquist*.] It is important, however, to "keep these issues in perspective":

> At this point in the 20th century we are quite far removed from the dangers that prompted the Framers to include the Establishment Clause in the Bill of Rights. The risk of significant religious or denominational control over our democratic processes — or even a deep political division along religious lines — is remote, and when viewed against the positive contributions of sectarian schools, any such risk seems entirely tolerable in light of the continuing oversight of this Court.

[*Wolman*] (Powell, J., concurring in part, concurring in the judgment in part, and dissenting in part). The Establishment Clause of course extends beyond prohibition of a state church or payment of state funds to one or more churches. We do not think, however, that its prohibition extends to the type of tax deduction established by Minnesota. The historic purposes of the clause simply do not encompass the sort of attenuated financial benefit, ultimately controlled by the private choices of individual parents, that eventually flows to parochial schools from the neutrally available tax benefit at issue in this case.

Petitioners argue that, notwithstanding the facial neutrality of §290.09, subd. 22, in application the statute primarily benefits religious institutions. Petitioners rely [on] a statistical analysis of the type of persons claiming the tax deduction. They contend that most parents of public school children incur no tuition expenses and that other expenses deductible under §290.09, subd. 22, are negligible in value; moreover, they claim that 96% of the children in private schools in 1978-1979 attended religiously-affiliated institutions. Because of all this, they reason, the bulk of deductions taken under §290.09, subd. 22, will be claimed by parents of children in sectarian schools. Respondents reply that petitioners have failed to consider the impact of deductions for items such as transportation, summer school tuition, tuition paid by parents whose children attended schools outside the school districts in which they resided, rental or purchase costs for a variety of equipment, and tuition for certain types of instruction not ordinarily provided in public schools.

We need not consider these contentions in detail. We would be loath to adopt a rule grounding the constitutionality of a facially neutral law on annual reports reciting the extent to which various classes of private citizens claimed benefits under the law. Such an approach would scarcely provide the certainty that this field stands in need of, nor can we perceive principled standards by which such statistical evidence might be evaluated. Moreover, the fact that private persons fail in a particular year to claim the tax relief to which they are entitled — under a facially neutral statute — should be of little importance in determining the constitutionality of the statute permitting such relief.

Finally, private educational institutions, and parents paying for their children to attend these schools, make special contributions to the areas in which they operate. "Parochial schools, quite apart from their sectarian purpose, have provided an educational alternative for millions of young Americans; they often afford wholesome competition with our public schools; and in some States they relieve substantially the tax burden incident to the operation of public schools." *Wolman*, at 262 (Powell, J., concurring and dissenting). If parents of children in private schools choose to take especial advantage of the relief provided by §290.09, subd. 22, it is no doubt due to the fact that they bear a particularly great financial burden in educating their children. More fundamentally, whatever unequal effect may be attributed to the statutory classification can fairly be regarded as a rough return for the benefits, discussed above, provided to the state and all taxpayers by parents sending their children to parochial schools. In the light of all this, we believe it wiser to decline to engage in the type of empirical inquiry into those persons benefited by state law which petitioners urge.[10]

Thus, we hold that the Minnesota tax deduction for educational expenses satisfies the primary effect inquiry of our Establishment Clause cases.

Turning to the third part of the *Lemon* inquiry, we have no difficulty in concluding that the Minnesota statute does not "excessively entangle" the state in religion. The only plausible source of the "comprehensive, discriminating, and continuing state surveillance" necessary to run afoul of this standard would lie in the fact that state officials must determine whether particular textbooks qualify for a deduction. In making this decision, state officials must disallow deductions taken [for] "instructional books and materials used in the teaching of religious tenets, doctrines or worship, the purpose of which is to inculcate such tenets, doctrines or worship." Making decisions such as this does not differ substantially from making the types of decisions approved in earlier opinions of this Court. In Board of Education v. Allen, 392 U.S. 236 (1968), for example, the Court upheld the loan of secular textbooks to parents or children attending nonpublic schools; though state officials were required to determine whether particular books were or were not secular, the system was held not to violate the Establishment Clause. The same result follows in this case. . . .

[Affirmed.]

---

10. [In] Board of Education v. Allen, 392 U.S. 236 (1968), we approved state loans of textbooks to *all* schoolchildren; although we disapproved, in Meek v. Pittenger and Wolman v. Walter direct loans of instructional materials to sectarian schools, we do not find those cases controlling. First, they involved assistance provided to the schools themselves, rather than tax benefits directed to individual parents. Moreover, we think that state assistance for the rental of calculators, ice skates, tennis shoes, and the like, scarcely poses the type of dangers against which the Establishment Clause was intended to guard.

JUSTICE MARSHALL, with whom JUSTICE BRENNAN, JUSTICE BLACKMUN and JUSTICE STEVENS join, dissenting.

The Establishment Clause of the First Amendment prohibits a State from subsidizing religious education, whether it does so directly or indirectly. In my view, this principle of neutrality forbids not only the tax benefits struck down in [*Nyquist*], but any tax benefit, including the tax deduction at issue here, which subsidizes tuition payments to sectarian schools. . . .

Violates Lemon test.
Advances + endorses religion

I . . .

A

[Direct] government subsidization of parochial school tuition is impermissible because "the effect of the aid is unmistakably to provide desired financial support for nonpublic, sectarian institutions." "[A]id to the educational function of [parochial] schools . . . necessarily results in aid to the sectarian enterprise as a whole" because "[t]he very purpose of those schools is to provide an integrated secular and religious education." [*Meek*.] . . .

Indirect assistance in the form of financial aid to parents for tuition payments is similarly impermissible. [By] ensuring that parents will be reimbursed for tuition payments they make, the Minnesota statute requires that taxpayers in general pay for the cost of parochial education and extends a financial "incentive to parents to send their children to sectarian schools." [*Nyquist*.] . . .

B . . .

1

The majority first attempts to distinguish *Nyquist* on the ground that Minnesota makes all parents eligible. . . .

That the Minnesota statute makes some small benefit available to all parents cannot alter the fact that the most substantial benefit provided by the statute is available only to those parents who send their children to schools that charge tuition. It is simply undeniable that the single largest expense that may be deducted under the Minnesota statute is tuition. The statute is little more than a subsidy of tuition masquerading as a subsidy of general educational expenses. The other deductible expenses are *de minimis* in comparison to tuition expenses.

[The] bulk of the tax benefits afforded by the Minnesota scheme are enjoyed by parents of parochial school children not because parents of public school children fail to claim deductions to which they are entitled, but because the latter are simply *unable* to claim the largest tax deduction that Minnesota authorizes. [Parents] who send their children to free public schools are simply ineligible to obtain the full benefit of the deduction except in the unlikely event that they buy $700 worth of pencils, notebooks, and bus rides for their school-age children. Yet parents who pay at least $700 in tuition to nonpublic, sectarian schools can claim the full deduction even if they incur no other educational expenses.

That this deduction has a primary effect of promoting religion can easily be determined without any resort to the type of "statistical evidence" that the majority fears would lead to constitutional uncertainty. The only factual inquiry necessary is the same as that employed in [*Nyquist*:] whether the deduction permitted for tuition expenses primarily benefits those who send their children to religious schools. In *Nyquist* we unequivocally rejected any suggestion that, in determining the effect of a tax statute, this Court should look exclusively to what the statute on its face purports to do and ignore the actual operation of the challenged provision. In determining the effect of the New York statute, we emphasized that "virtually all" of the schools receiving direct grants for maintenance and repair were Roman Catholic schools, that reimbursements were given to parents "who send their children to nonpublic schools, the bulk of which is concededly sectarian in orientation," that "it is precisely the function of New York's law to provide assistance to private schools, the great majority of which are sectarian, and that "tax reductions authorized by this law flow primarily to the parents of children attending sectarian, nonpublic schools."

2

The majority also asserts that the Minnesota statute is distinguishable from the statute struck down in *Nyquist* in another respect: the tax benefit available under Minnesota law is a "genuine tax deduction," whereas the New York law provided a benefit which, while nominally a deduction, also had features of a "tax credit." . . .

This is a distinction without a difference. Our prior decisions have rejected the relevance of the majority's formalistic distinction between tax deductions and the tax benefit at issue in *Nyquist*. The deduction afforded by Minnesota law was "designed to yield a [tax benefit] in exchange for performing a specific act which the State desires to encourage." [*Nyquist.*] . . .

AGUILAR v. FELTON, — U.S. —, 105 S. Ct. 3232 (1985): Title I of the Elementary and Secondary School Act of 1965 authorizes financial assistance to public and private schools to meet the needs of educationally deprived children living in low-income areas. New York provided Title I services, including remedial reading and arithmetic classes, and guidance services, to parochial-school students in their schools. The services were provided by public-school employees who volunteered to teach in the parochial schools. The teachers were "directed to avoid involvement with religious activities [and] to bar religious materials." They were supervised by a system of unannounced visits. The administrators of the parochial schools were "required to clear the classrooms used by the public school personnel of all religious symbols."

The Court, in an opinion by Justice Brennan, held the program unconstitutional. "[Publicly] funded instructors teach classes composed exclusively of private school students in [religiously affiliated] private schools." The supervisory system used to prevent the program from being used to inculcate religious beliefs "inevitably results in the excessive entanglement of church and state." Entanglement impairs "the freedom of religious belief of those who are not adherents of the denomination [even] when the governmental purpose underlying the involvement is largely secular. In addition, the freedom of even the adherents of the denomination is limited by the governmental intrusion into sacred matters." Here "the aid is provided in a pervasively sectarian environment[, and] because assistance is provided in the form of teachers, ongoing inspection is required to ensure the absence of a religious message." "Agents of the state must visit and inspect the religious school regularly, alert for the subtle or overt presence of religious matter in Title I classes. In addition, the religious school must obey these same agents when they make determinations as to what is and what is not a 'religious symbol' and thus off limits in a Title I classroom." Further, "Administrative personnel of the public and parochial school systems must work together" in scheduling and implementing the program. "As government agents must make these judgments, the dangers of political divisiveness along religious lines increase."

Justice Powell's concurring opinion found

> [the] risk of entanglement [compounded] by the additional risk of political divisiveness. [I] do not suggest that at this point in our history the Title I program or similar parochial aid plans could result in the establishment of a state religion. [Nonetheless,] there remains a considerable risk of continuing political strife over the propriety of direct aid to religious schools and the proper allocation of limited governmental resources. [In] states such as New York that have large and varied sectarian populations, one can be assured that politics will enter into any state decision to aid parochial schools. [Any] proposal to extend direct governmental aid to parochial schools alone is likely to spark political disagreement from taxpayers who support the public schools, as well as from non-recipient sectarian groups, who may fear that needed funds are being diverted from them.

He also believed that Title I had the prohibited effect of "a state subsidy of the parochial [schools,] by relieving those schools of the duty to provide the remedial and supplemental education their children require." Title I "directly [assumed] part of the parochial schools' educational function." But "if [Congress] could fashion a program of evenhanded financial assistance to both public and private schools that could be administered, without governmental supervision in the private schools, so as to prevent the diversion of the aid from secular purposes, we would be presented with a different question."

Chief Justice Burger, Justice White, and Justice Rehnquist filed brief dissents, the latter noting that the Court "[took] advantage of the 'Catch-22' paradox of its own creation, whereby aid must be supervised to ensure no entanglement but the supervision itself is held to cause an entanglement." Justice O'Connor's dissent emphasized that the record contained no evidence that, during the nineteen-year experience with Title I in New York, any Title I teacher had attempted to indoctrinate children in religion. She found the explanation in the fact that the teachers "are professional educators who can and do follow instructions not to inculcate religion in their classes." Thus, "the degree of supervision required to manage [the] risk" of indoctrination "has been exaggerated."

Note: Purpose and Effect in Aid to Nonpublic Education — Benevolent Neutrality?

1. *Certainty or continued confusion?* Do *Mueller* and *Aguilar* substantially clarify the law? Grand Rapids School District v. Ball, — U.S. — , 105 S. Ct. 3216 (1985), a companion case to *Aguilar*, invalidated two programs. In one, public school teachers offered supplementary classes such as remedial reading, during the school day, in parochial school classrooms. In the other, teachers whose basic

salary was paid by the parochial school system, received pay from the public school system to conduct "community education" classes, such as arts and crafts, yearbook production, and chess, after school hours in the parochial school buildings. As to the latter, the Court was concerned that "the religious message [the parochial school teachers] are expected to convey during the regular school day will infuse the supposedly secular classes they teach after school." As to the former, "teachers in [a pervasively religious] atmosphere may well subtly (or overtly) conform their instruction to the environment in which they teach, while students will perceive the instruction provided in the context of the dominantly religious message of the institution, thus reinforcing the indoctrinating effect." This amounted to a "symbolic union of government and religion in one sectarian enterprise."

Which results in the pre-*Mueller* cases invalidating aid survive *Mueller*? Which in the pre-*Mueller* cases upholding aid survive *Aguilar*? *Mueller* distinguishes *Nyquist* on the ground that the Minnesota statute on its face provided aid to parents with children in public and nonpublic schools. How substantially will a requirement of facial neutrality increase the cost of providing aid to nonpublic schools and thereby alter the political dimensions of the issue? Why should facial neutrality be required? Consider this justification for upholding direct appropriations to private schools: Public schools are subsidized through ordinary appropriations; neutrality is achieved by the separate appropriations to private schools. Finding the latter to violate neutrality artificially divides a unitary system of state-supported education that, taken as a whole, is neutral. Is this distinguishable from a voucher system, in which parents receive grants to use for their children's education in either "public" or "private" schools as they choose? Would a voucher system be constitutional? Consider the proposal in Choper, The Establishment Clause and Aid to Parochial Schools, 56 Cal. L. Rev. 260, 266 (1968), that aid should be allowed "so long as such aid does not exceed the value of the secular educational service rendered by the school." How likely is it that a legislature, constrained by pluralist politics and tax limitations, would enact a program that violated this test? Does it simply restate the requirement of neutrality?

2. *Administrative and political entanglement.* Lemon v. Kurtzman, supra, described two forms of excessive entanglement. Administrative entanglement occurs when public officials are required to scrutinize the use of public funds to assure that they are not used for sectarian purposes. Public funds completely devoted to secular purposes make an equal amount of nonpublic funds available for sectarian purposes. Are direct and unrestricted grants to nonpublic schools therefore constitutional? *Lemon* argued that such grants had a "divisive political potential" as partisans would force candidates "to declare" on issues that will lead people to "find their votes aligned with their faith." Although political division is "normal and healthy," division "along religious lines was one of the principal evils against which the First Amendment was intended to protect. [To] have States [divide] on [these] [would] tend to confuse and obscure other issues of great urgency." Political fragmentation is "likely to be intensified" where "successive and very likely permanent annual appropriations that benefit relatively few religious groups" are involved.

Is the idea of political entanglement misconceived? Note its appearance in *Aguilar. Mueller* stated that the language in *Lemon* about political entanglement must be "confined to cases where direct financial subsidies are paid." Is the distinction between direct subsidies and indirect tax benefits consistent with the realities of the legislative process? Note that legislatures must determine annual levels of direct subsidies. Would the use of some formula, for example a stated proportion of the appropriations for public schools, avoid the political entanglement problems raised in *Lemon?* But why will not the determination of the amount of the deductions in Minnesota raise the same problems of political entanglement? Does *Mueller's* suggestion that an aid scheme must cover public as well as nonpublic schools alleviate concern that divisiveness will arise when "relatively few religious groups" receive aid?

Is the use of political divisiveness as a criterion completely misguided? How is political divisiveness to be measured? Recall the comments on this subject in Lynch v. Donnelly. Is there any reason to regard interest groups organized around religion as different, and more suspect, actors in the political process, than interest groups organized around economic interests? What might Roger Williams have said about this question?

3. *Is higher education different?* Tilton v. Richardson, 403 U.S. 672 (1971), upheld a federal statute providing construction grants for buildings used exclusively for secular purposes at church-related colleges; it invalidated a provision allowing the buildings to be used for religious purposes after twenty years, holding that the limitation could not expire "while the building has substantial value." Hunt v. McNair, 413 U.S. 734 (1973), upheld a statute authorizing the state to issue bonds to assist in the financing of buildings used for secular purposes at church-related colleges. Roemer v. Board of Public Works, 426 U.S. 736 (1976), upheld a state program under which qualifying private colleges receive for each full-time student an amount equal to 15 percent of the state's per student appropriations for students in the state college system. The funds could not be used for sectarian purposes; this requirement was enforced by rules requiring separate accounting for the funds and annual reports on planned and actual uses of the funds. Some of the recipients required that their students take courses in theology. Justice Blackmun's plurality opinion noted that the state aid assisted all private colleges, over two-thirds of which had no religious affiliation. In each case the Court applied the *Lemon* test.

In *Tilton* Chief Justice Burger's opinion for the Court said,

> [College] students are less impressionable and less susceptible to religious indoctrination. [Furthermore,] by their very nature, college and postgraduate courses tend to limit the opportunities for sectarian influence by virtue of their own internal disciplines. [Since] religious indoctrination is not a substantial purpose or activity of these church-related colleges and universities, there is less likelihood than in primary and secondary schools that religion will permeate the area of secular education.

What are the implications for this problem of Justice O'Connor's approach in Lynch v. Donnelly?

4. *Course selection: The creationism controversy.* Consider Epperson v. Arkansas, 393 U.S. 97 (1968). In 1928 Arkansas enacted a statute prohibiting "the teaching in its public schools and universities of the theory that man evolved from other species of life." The Court held the statute, "a product of the upsurge of 'fundamentalist' religious fervor of the twenties," unconstitutional. The law "se-

lects from a body of knowledge a particular segment which it proscribes for the sole reason that it is deemed to conflict with a particular religious doctrine. [The] First Amendment does not permit the State to require that teaching and learning must be tailored to the principles or prohibitions of any religious sect or dogma," despite the "State's undoubted right to prescribe the curriculum for its public schools." The Court said that "No suggestion has been made that [the statute] may be justified by considerations of state policy other than the religious views of some of its citizens." Justice Stewart concurred in the result. Justice Black, concurring, would distinguish *Epperson* from the case of "a state law prohibiting all teaching of human development." Suppose such a prohibition was motivated (a) by a new upsurge of fundamentalism that viewed the subject as inculcating antireligious values or (b) by a judgment that, as Justice Black put it, "it would be best to remove this controversial subject from its schools." Is this a case of a "religion-specific" subject, analogous to the "race-specific" classifications discussed in Chapter 5, section C3, supra?

Could a legislature prohibit the teaching of evolution because it was a scientifically questionable theory whose acceptance by many scientists resulted from their antireligious biases? What sort of legislative hearings or findings would be required? Could a judge reassess the legislature's evaluation of the scientific status of the theory of evolution? Suppose the legislature required that "creation-science" and "evolution-science" be given "balanced treatment." See McLean v. Arkansas Board of Education, 529 F. Supp. 1255 (E.D. Ark. 1982) (holding such statute unconstitutional after extensive trial involving testimony about the scientific status of evolution and creationism). In the absence of an illicit motivation of the sort found in *Epperson*, does the Constitution require states to teach only the truth in matters of science? History? Political theory?

Note: Additional Problems

1. *Neutrality in church property disputes.* Differences over religious doctrine have frequently led to schisms and secessions from existing churches. These disputes have generated a large number of cases, as the contending factions claim that each has title to the property of "the church." Adjudicating such claims may enmesh the civil courts in religious disputes. The Court's most recent decision in this area, Jones v. Wolf, 443 U.S. 595 (1979), illustrates both the nature of the problem and the Court's present view of the rules the Constitution requires that the civil courts observe. A church acquired property in conveyances to "the Vineville Presbyterian Church." The church was a member of the Presbyterian Church of the United States (PCUS), a hierarchical church in which decisions by local churches can be reviewed by higher church courts. In 1973 a majority of the Vineville congregation voted to separate from the PCUS and affiliate with another national denomination. After the PCUS courts declared the minority to be the "true congregation," it sued for a declaration that it had the right to use the church property. The Court held that "the First Amendment prohibits secular courts from resolving church property disputes on the basis of religious doctrine and practice. As a corollary, [civil] courts [must] defer to the resolution of issues of religious doctrine or polity by the highest court of a hierarchical church organization." Thus the civil courts could not enforce a rule that treated local church

property as held in trust for the general church unless the latter had abandoned church doctrine as it had existed at the time the local church affiliated with it. See Presbyterian Church v. Mary Elizabeth Blue Hull Church, 393 U.S. 440 (1969). The civil courts may choose to defer to decisions made by higher church authorities in hierarchical churches on nondoctrinal matters. But they may also choose to employ "neutral principles of law" to decide nondoctrinal matters, in both hierarchical and congregational churches. The neutral-principles approach does not require the civil courts to examine church doctrine but "relies exclusively on objective, well-established concepts of trust and property law" and allows churches "flexibility in ordering private rights and obligations to reflect the intentions of the parties" by using "appropriate reversionary clauses and trust provisions." The civil courts may examine religious documents to see if they contain the language that would trigger some neutral principle, but they "must take special care to scrutinize the document in purely secular terms." In *Jones* the Court would allow the civil courts to use the neutral principle that the identity of the local church could be determined by a presumption that majority rule prevailed, "defeasible upon a showing that [it] is to be determined by some other means." Justice Powell's dissent was joined by Chief Justice Burger, Justice Stewart, and Justice White. They would have required the civil courts to defer to decisions of higher church courts in hierarchical churches even if those decisions involved no issue of doctrinal controversy. Which approach better respects the autonomy of religious institutions? Which institution, local or national, is to be given autonomy?

How can church documents be examined "in purely secular terms"? In Avitzur v. Avitzur, 58 N.Y. 2d 108 (1983), the New York Court of Appeals applied the neutral-principles approach. The Avitzurs were married in a Jewish religious ceremony. Prior to the ceremony, they signed a document in which they agreed to appear at the request of either party before a religious tribunal. Under Jewish law, a wife divorced under civil law may not remarry until she and her former husband appear before the tribunal. After obtaining a civil divorce, Mr. Avitzur refused a summons to appear before the religious tribunal. The Court of Appeals held that Mrs. Avitzur could obtain specific performance of the premarital agreement by application of neutral principles of contract law. Three dissenting judges argued that interpreting the premarital agreement would inevitably require an inquiry into religious law. For example, Mr. Avitzur claimed that he was relieved of his duty to appear when summoned because an earlier request by him that the tribunal be convened had been refused. How might similar problems arise under the presumption of majority rule in *Jones?*

2. *Churches as political actors.* Larkin v. Grendel's Den, 459 U.S. 116 (1982), held unconstitutional a statute granting churches and schools the power to veto the issuance of liquor licenses to restaurants within 500 feet of the church or school buildings. The Court acknowledged the "interest in being insulated from certain kinds of commercial establishments," but found that delegating the veto power to churches had the effect of advancing religion and "provides a significant symbolic benefit to religion in the minds of some." Further, the statute "enmeshes churches in the exercise of substantial governmental powers." Justice Rehnquist dissented, arguing that, because the state could prohibit bars within 500 feet of churches, it could adopt the less drastic approach of allowing each church to decide whether it wished "to be unmolested by activities at a neighboring bar."

Note: Concluding Observations

The Court has used a number of metaphors and tests — the "wall of separation," neutrality, the *Lemon* criteria — in dealing with establishment clause issues. Has it developed a sensible approach to the various problems? Which of the Madison/Jefferson/Williams traditions best explains the present state of the law of the establishment clause? Which provides the best resolution of the problems that the courts have addressed?

C.   THE FREE EXERCISE CLAUSE

Religious beliefs and expression are forms of speech and, as such, are protected by the free speech clause of the first amendment. Some early free speech decisions involving religious expression relied on the free exercise clause as well. See, e.g., Cantwell v. Connecticut, Chapter 7, section B3, supra; Lovell v. Griffin, Chapter 7, section C2, supra. What, if anything, does the free exercise clause add to the free speech clause?

Suppose a state prohibited the wearing of chadors (the facial coverings worn, out of religious belief, by certain Moslem women) inside banks because the chadors made it difficult to identify bank customers in the event of a robbery. Would that statute fall within the scope of the free speech clause? The free exercise clause? Note that a statute prohibiting the advocacy of wearing chadors would raise free speech questions.

Until 1963 the Supreme Court had not squarely held that the free exercise clause protects religious beliefs differently, or more extensively, than the free speech clause protects political beliefs. Reynolds v. United States, 98 U.S. 145 (1879), upheld a conviction of a Mormon for bigamy, rejecting a free exercise defense. The Court said that, under the first amendment, "Congress was deprived of all legislative power over mere opinion, but was left free to reach actions which were in violation of social duties or subversive of good order. [Laws] are made for the government of actions, and while they cannot interfere with mere religious belief and actions, they may with practices." In *Cantwell* the Court said that the free exercise clause "embraces two concepts, — freedom to believe and freedom to act. The first is absolute, but in the nature of things, the second cannot be. Conduct remains subject to regulation for the protection of society. [*Reynolds.*] [In] every case the power to regulate must be so exercised as not [unduly] to infringe the protected freedom."

Note the similarity between the *Cantwell* formulation and the contemporaneous approach to problems of picketing and other speech-related conduct, Chapter 7, section E, supra. In reading the materials that follow, consider whether the Court has appropriately adapted the tests of United States v. O'Brien, Chapter 7, section E3, supra, and Washington v. Davis, Chapter 5, section C2, supra, to the free exercise content.

BRAUNFELD v. BROWN, 366 U.S. 599 (1961): Pennsylvania's law requiring that businesses be closed on Sundays was challenged on free exercise grounds by Orthodox Jews whose religion required that they close their stores on Saturdays. They alleged that the Sunday closing laws would place them at a competitive disadvantage so severe as to force them out of business. Chief Justice Warren's plurality opinion rejected the free exercise claim. Citing *Reynolds* it said, "the statute [does] not make criminal the holding of any religious belief or opinion, nor does it force anyone to embrace any religious belief. [It simply] make[s] the practice of their religious beliefs more expensive. [To] strike down [legislation] which imposes only an indirect burden on the exercise of religion [would] radically restrict the operating lattitude of the legislature. [We] are a cosmopolitan nation made up of people of almost every conceivable religious preference. [Consequently,] it cannot be expected, much less required, that legislators enact no law regulating conduct that may in some way result in an economic disadvantage to some religious sects and not to others because of the special practices of the various religions. [If] the State regulates conduct by enacting a general law within its power, the purpose and effect of which is to advance the State's secular goals, the statute is valid despite its indirect burden on religious observance unless the State may accomplish its purposes by means which do not impose such a burden."

Relying on *McGowan*, supra, Chief Justice Warren found that the "family day of rest" purpose was valid. Nor was an exemption for Saturday-observers required because an exemption "might well undermine the State's goal of providing a day that, as best possible, eliminates the atmosphere of commercial noise and activity. [Enforcement] problems would be more difficult [and Saturday-observers] might well [receive] an economic advantage over their competitors who must close on that day. [Competitors might] assert that they have religious convictions which compel them to close their businesses on what had formerly been their least profitable day. This might make necessary a state-conducted inquiry into the sincerity of the individual's beliefs, a practice which a State might well believe would itself run afoul of the spirit of constitutionally protected religious guarantees." Justice Frankfurter, joined by Justice Harlan, submitted a long concurring opinion, agreeing substantially with the plurality's analysis.

Justice Brennan dissented. He described the state's interest as "the mere convenience of having everyone rest on the same day" and called the plurality's concern about a system allowing exemptions "fanciful." This "[exalts] administrative convenience to a constitutional level high enough to justify making one religion economically disadvantageous." Justice Stewart's dissent said that the law "compels an Orthodox Jew to choose between his religious faith and his economic survival. That is a cruel choice. It is a choice which I think no State can constitutionally demand. For me this is not something that can be swept under the rug and forgotten in the interest of enforced Sunday togetherness." Justice Douglas also dissented.

Sherbert v. Verner
374 U.S. 398 (1963)

MR. JUSTICE BRENNAN delivered the opinion of the Court.

Appellant, a member of the Seventh-day Adventist Church, was discharged by her South Carolina employer because she would not work on Saturday, the Sabbath Day of her faith. When she was unable to obtain other employment because from conscientious scruples she would not take Saturday work,[2] she filed a claim for unemployment compensation benefits under the South Carolina Unemployment Compensation Act.

[The state courts found that she was not entitled to benefits because she had failed to accept suitable work without good cause.]

I . . .

[Appellant's] conscientious objection to Saturday work constitutes no conduct prompted by religious principles of a kind within the reach of state legislation. If, therefore, the decision of the [state] Court is to withstand appellant's constitutional challenge, it must be either because her disqualification as a beneficiary represents no infringement by the State of her constitutional rights of free exercise, or because any incidental burden on the free exercise of appellant's religion may be justified by a "compelling state interest in the regulation of a subject within the State's constitutional power to regulate. . . ." [NAACP v. Button.]

II

We turn first to the question whether the disqualification for benefits imposes any burden on the free exercise of appellant's religion. We think it is clear that it does. In a sense the consequences of such a disqualification to religious principles and practices may be only an indirect result of welfare legislation within the State's general competence to enact; it is true that no criminal sanctions directly compel appellant to work a six-day week. But this is only the beginning, not the end, of our inquiry. For "[i]f the purpose or effect of a law is to impede the observance of one or all religions or is to discriminate invidiously between religions, that law is constitutionally invalid even though the burden may be characterized as being only indirect." [Braunfeld.] Here not only is it apparent that appellant's declared ineligibility for benefits derives solely from the practice of her religion, but the pressure upon her to forego that practice is unmistakable. The ruling forces her to choose between following the precepts of her religion and forefeiting benefits, on the one hand, and abandoning one of the precepts of her religion in order to accept work, on the other hand. Governmental imposition of such a choice puts the same kind of burden upon the free exercise of religion as would a fine imposed against appellant for her Saturday worship.

Nor may the South Carolina court's construction of the statute be saved from constitutional infirmity on the ground that unemployment compensation benefits are not appellant's "right" but merely a "privilege." It is too late in the day to doubt that the liberties of religion and expression may be infringed by the denial of or placing of conditions upon a benefit or privilege. . . .

---

2. After her discharge, appellant sought employment with three other mills in the Spartanburg area, but found no suitable five-day work available at any of the mills. In filing her claim with the Commission, she expressed a willingness to accept employment at other mills, or even in another industry, so long as Saturday work was not required. The record indicates that of the 150 or more Seventh-day Adventists in the Spartanburg area, only appellant and one other have been unable to find suitable non-Saturday employment.

III

We must next consider whether some compelling state interest [justifies] the substantial infringement of appellant's First Amendment right. [The] appellees suggest no more than a possibility that the filing of fraudulent claims by unscrupulous claimants feigning religious objections to Saturday work might not only dilute the unemployment compensation fund but also hinder the scheduling by employers of necessary Saturday work. [Even] if the possibility of spurious claims did not threaten to dilute the fund and disrupt the scheduling of work, it would plainly be incumbent upon the appellees to demonstrate that no alternative forms of regulation would combat such abuses without infringing First Amendment rights.[7]

In these respects, then, the state interest asserted in the present case is wholly dissimilar to the interests which were found to justify the less direct burden upon religious practices in [Braunfeld. There] the statute was nevertheless saved by a countervailing factor which finds no equivalent in the instant case — a strong state interest in providing one uniform day of rest for all workers. That secular objective could be achieved, the Court found, only by declaring Sunday to be that day of rest. Requiring exemptions for Sabbatarians, while theoretically possible, appeared to present an administrative problem of such magnitude, or to afford the exempted class so great a competitive advantage, that such a requirement would have rendered the entire statutory scheme unworkable. In the present case no such justifications underlie the determination of the state court that appellant's religion makes her ineligible to receive benefits.

IV

In holding as we do, plainly we are not fostering the "establishment" of the Seventh-day Adventist religion in South Carolina, for the extension of unemployment benefits to Sabbatarians in common with Sunday worshippers reflects nothing more than the governmental obligation of neutrality in the face of religious differences, and does not represent that involvement of religious with secular institutions which it is the object of the Establishment Clause to forestall. See [Schempp]. Nor does the recognition of the appellant's right to unemployment benefits under the state statute serve to abridge any other person's religious liberties. Nor do we, by our decision today, declare the existence of a constitutional right to unemployment benefits on the part of all persons whose religious convictions are the cause of their unemployment. This is not a case in which an employee's religious convictions serve to make him a nonproductive member of society.

Reversed and remanded.

MR. JUSTICE DOUGLAS, concurring. . . .

MR. JUSTICE STEWART, concurring in the result. . . .
[This] case presents a double-barreled dilemma, which in all candor I think the

7. We note that before the instant decision, state supreme courts had, without exception, granted benefits to persons who were physically available for work but unable to find suitable employment solely because of a religious prohibition against Saturday work. . . .

Court's opinion has not succeeded in papering over. The dilemma ought to be resolved.

I . . .

[I] regret that on occasion, and specifically in [*Braunfeld*], the Court has shown what has seemed to me a distressing insensitivity to the appropriate demands of this constitutional guarantee. By contrast I think that the Court's approach to the Establishment Clause has on occasion, and specifically in *Engel* [and] *Schempp*, [been] not only insensitive, but positively wooden, and that the Court has accorded to the Establishment Clause a meaning which neither the words, the history, nor the intention of the authors of that specific constitutional provision even remotely suggests. . . .

[The] result is that there are many situations where legitimate claims under the Free Exercise Clause will run into head-on collision with the Court's insensitive and sterile construction of the Establishment Clause. The controversy now before us is clearly such a case.

Because the appellant refuses to accept available jobs which would require her to work on Saturdays, South Carolina has declined to pay unemployment compensation benefits to her. Her refusal to work on Saturdays is based on the tenets of her religious faith. The Court says that South Carolina cannot under these circumstances declare her to be not "available for work" within the meaning of its statute because to do so would violate her constitutional right to the free exercise of her religion.

Yet what this Court has said about the Establishment Clause must inevitably lead to a diametrically opposite result. . . .

To require South Carolina to so administer its laws as to pay public money to the appellant under the circumstances of this case is [clearly] to require the State to violate the Establishment Clause as construed by this Court. [The] guarantee of religious liberty embodied in the Free Exercise Clause affirmatively requires government to create an atmosphere of hospitality and accommodation to individual belief or disbelief. In short, I think our Constitution commands the positive protection by government of religious freedom — not only for a minority, however small — not only for the majority, however large — but for each of us.

South Carolina would deny unemployment benefits to a mother unavailable for work on Saturdays because she was unable to get a babysitter. Thus, we do not have before us a situation where a State provides unemployment compensation generally, and singles out for disqualification only those persons who are unavailable for work on religious grounds. This is not, in short, a scheme which operates so as to discriminate against religion as such. But the Court nevertheless holds that the State must prefer a religious over a secular ground for being unavailable for work — that state financial support of the appellant's religion is constitutionally required to carry out "the governmental obligation of neutrality in the face of religious differences. . . ."

Yet in cases decided under the Establishment Clause the Court has decreed otherwise. It has decreed that government must blind itself to the differing religious beliefs and traditions of the people. With all respect, I think it is the Court's duty to face up to the dilemma posed by the conflict between the Free Exercise

Clause of the Constitution and the Establishment Clause as interpreted by the Court.

II

My second difference with the Court's opinion is that I cannot agree that today's decision can stand consistently with [*Braunfeld*]. The Court says that there was a "less direct burden upon religious practices" in that case than in this. With all respect, I think the Court is mistaken, simply as a matter of fact. . . .

[We] deal here not with a criminal statute, but with the particularized administration of South Carolina's Unemployment Compensation Act. Even upon the unlikely assumption that the appellant could not find suitable non-Saturday employment, the appellant at the worst would be denied a maximum of 22 weeks of compensation payments. I agree with the Court that the possibility of that denial is enough to infringe upon the appellant's constitutional right to the free exercise of her religion. But it is clear to me that in order to reach this conclusion the court must explicitly reject the reasoning of [*Braunfeld*]. I think the *Braunfeld* case was wrongly decided and should be overruled, and accordingly I concur in the result reached by the Court in the case before us.

Mr. Justice Harlan, whom Mr. Justice White joins, dissenting. . . .

[In] no proper sense can it be said that the State discriminated against the appellant on the basis of her religious beliefs or that she was denied benefits *because* she was a Seventh-day Adventist. She was denied benefits just as any other claimant would be denied benefits who was not "available for work" for personal reasons.

With this background, this Court's decision comes to clearer focus. What the Court is holding is that if the State chooses to condition unemployment compensation on the applicant's availability for work, it is constitutionally compelled to *carve out an exception* — and to provide benefits — for those whose unavailability is due to their religious convictions. Such a holding has particular significance in two respects.

First, despite the Court's protestations to the contrary, the decision necessarily overrules [*Braunfeld*]. [The] secular purpose of the statute before us today is even clearer than that involved in *Braunfeld*. And just as in *Braunfeld* [— so] here, an exception to the rules of eligibility based on religious convictions would necessitate judicial examination of those convictions and would be at odds with the limited purpose of the statute to smooth out the economy during periods of industrial instability. Finally, the indirect financial burden of the present law is far less than that involved in *Braunfeld*. . . .

Second, the implications of the present decision are far more troublesome than its apparently narrow dimensions would indicate at first glance. The State [must] *single out* for financial assistance those whose behavior is religiously motivated, even though it denies such assistance to others whose identical behavior (in this case, inability to work on Saturdays) is not religiously motivated.

It has been suggested that such singling out of religious conduct for special treatment may violate the constitutional limitations on state action. See [Kurland]. My own view, however, is that at least under the circumstances of this case it would be a permissible accommodation of religion for the State, if it *chose* to do so, to create an exception to its eligibility requirements for persons like the appellant. The constitutional obligation of "neutrality," see [*Schempp*], is not so narrow a channel that the slightest deviation from an absolutely straight course leads to condemnation. [The] State violates its obligation of neutrality when, for example, it mandates a daily religious exercise in its public schools, with all the attendant pressures on the school children that such an exercise entails. See [*Engel; Schempp*]. But there is, I believe, enough flexibility in the Constitution to permit a legislative judgment accommodating an unemployment compensation law to the exercise of religious beliefs such as appellant's.

For very much the same reason, however, I cannot subscribe to the conclusion that the State is constitutionally *compelled* to carve out an exception to its general rule of eligibility in the present case. Those situations in which the Constitution may require special treatment on account of religion are, in my view, few and far between. [Such] compulsion in the present case is particularly inappropriate in light of the indirect, remote, and insubstantial effect of the decision below on the exercise of appellant's religion and in light of the direct financial assistance to religion that today's decision requires.

WISCONSIN v. YODER, 406 U.S. 205 (1972): Yoder, a member of the Old Order Amish, was fined $5 for refusing to send his children to school after they had completed the eighth grade. His children were ages fourteen and fifteen; Wisconsin required school attendance until age sixteen. The Amish object to high school education because of their desire to live in a "church community separate and apart from the world." They believe that high schools expose children to worldly matters and emphasize "intellectual and scientific accomplishments, self-distinction, competitiveness, worldly success, and social life with other students," in contrast to the Amish desire for "informal learning-though-doing [and] wisdom, rather than technical knowledge; community welfare, rather than competition." Basic education is acceptable to them because it prepares children "to read the Bible [and] to be good farmers and citizens." The state supreme court held that the conviction violated the free exercise clause, and the Supreme Court affirmed.

Chief Justice Burger's opinion for the Court acknowledged the state's "interest in universal education" but required that it be balanced "when it impinges on fundamental rights and interests" to assure that "there is a state interest of sufficient magnitude to override the [free exercise] interest." "[Only] those interests of the highest order and those not otherwise served can overbalance legitimate claims of free exercise of religion." The Court first asked whether the Amish claim was "rooted in religious belief. [If] the Amish asserted their claims because of their subjective evaluation and rejection of the contemporary secular values accepted by the majority, much as Thoreau rejected the social values of his time and isolated himself at Walden Pond, their claims would not rest on a religious basis. Thoreau's choice was philosophical and personal rather than religious, and such belief does not rise to the demands of the Religion Clauses." But the Amish way of life was "one of deep religious conviction, shared by an organized group and intimately related to daily living." Compulsory high school education required the Amish "to perform acts undeniably at odds with fundamental tenets of their religious beliefs" and "[carried] with it a very real threat of undermining the Amish community."

The Court rejected the state's effort to rely on the distinction between belief and action; "in this context belief and action cannot be neatly confined in logic-tight compartments." Nor was it dispositive that the requirement was facially neutral, for even such regulations "may offend the constitutional requirement for governmental neutrality if it unduly burdens the free exercise of religion [*Sherbert*]." The Court accepted the state's argument that "some degree of education is necessary to prepare citizens to participate effectively and intelligently in our open political system [and] to be self-reliant and self-sufficient participants in society." But the additional one or two years of formal high school education "would do little to serve those interests." The state also argued that the Amish fostered ignorance, but the Court said that the record showed "that the Amish community has been a highly successful social unit within our society, even if apart from the conventional 'mainstream.' Its members are productive and very law-abiding members of society; they reject public welfare in its usual modern forms." The Court also rejected as "highly speculative" the state's claim that its requirement served the interest in providing those Amish children who eventually leave the community with an adequate basis for "making their way in the world." It said that "there is nothing in this record to suggest that the Amish qualities of reliability, self-reliance, and dedication to work would fail to find ready markets in today's society." The Court emphasized that it was "not dealing with a way of life and mode of education by a group claiming to have recently discovered some 'progressive' or more enlightened process for rearing children for modern life." In light of the Amish's "long history as a successful and self-sufficient segment of American society," and their showing of "the adequacy of their alternative mode of continuing informal vocational education in terms of precisely those overall interests that the State advances," a showing "that probably few other religious groups or sects could make, and weighing the minimal difference between what the State would require and what the Amish already accept, it was incumbent on the State to show with more particularity how its admittedly strong interest in compulsory education would be adversely affected by granting an exemption to the Amish."

Justice Douglas's dissent focused on the potential conflict of interest between Amish parents and their children, some of whom might wish to attend high school in order to be in a position to choose whether to adhere to or "to break from the Amish tradition." The Court, and concurring opinions by Justices Stewart and White, said that that issue was not presented on the record. The Court said that, in the absence of evidence of actual conflicts, allowing the state to compel high school attendance because of "the potential" that some parents might "act contrary to the best interests of their children by foreclosing their opportunity to make an intelligent choice between the Amish way of life and that of the outside world," would create "such an intrusion by a State into family decisions in the area of religious training" as itself to raise "grave questions of religious freedom."

UNITED STATES v. LEE, 455 U.S. 252 (1982): Lee, a member of the Old Order Amish, was a self-employed farmer and carpenter. From 1970 to 1977 he had a number of other Amish work for him. He did not pay the social security tax for his employees, claiming that to do so would violate his right to free exercise because "the Amish believe it sinful not to provide for their own elderly and therefore are religiously opposed to the national social security system." The Supreme Court rejected the free exercise claim, without dissent. It accepted Lee's claim that payment of the taxes was forbidden by his religion but found that the limitation on religious liberty was "essential to accomplish an overriding governmental interest." Mandatory participation in the social security system was "indispensable to [its] fiscal vitality." Citing *Braunfeld*, Chief Justice Burger's opinion for the Court said, "Unlike [*Yoder*], it would be difficult to accommodate the comprehensive social security system with myriad exceptions flowing from a wide variety of religious beliefs. The obligation to pay the social security tax initially is not fundamentally different from the obligation to pay income taxes. [There] is no principled way [to] distinguish between general taxes and those imposed under the Social Security Act. If, for example, a religious adherent believes war is a sin, and if a certain percentage of the federal budget can be identified as devoted to war-related activities, such individuals would have a similarly valid claim to be exempt from paying that percentage of the income tax. The tax system could not function if denominations were allowed to challenge the tax system because tax payments were spent in a manner that violates their religious belief."

Justice Stevens concurred in the judgment. He rejected the Court's formulation, which he said imposed a "heavy burden" on government to justify the application of general laws to religious objectors. He argued that the burden should be on the objector to show "that there is a unique reason for allowing him a special exemption." Under the Court's approach, extending the exemption to the Amish would be "relatively simple": because "the Amish have demonstrated their capacity to care for their own, the social cost of eliminating this relatively small group of dedicated believers would be minimal." The Court, he said, "overstated the risk" that "a myriad of other claims" would occur. He noted that "in the typical case [of general taxes], the taxpayer is not in a position to supply to government with an equivalent substitute for the objectionable use of his money." Justice Stevens said that his approach, which would "place an almost insurmountable burden" on religious objectors to neutral laws, "better explains most of [the] Court's holdings," citing *Gillette*, *Braunfeld*, and *Reynolds*. He suggested that *Yoder* was wrongly decided and that *Sherbert* was "arguably" distinguishable on the ground that "laws intended to provide a benefit to a limited class of otherwise disadvantaged persons should be judged by a different standard." He noted that "if tax exemptions were dispensed on religious grounds, every citizen would have an economic motivation to join the favored sects [while no] comparable economic motivation could explain the conduct of the [employee] in *Sherbert*," where employer-dictated changes in work arrangements forced Sherbert out of a job.

Note: Accommodation — Required and Permissible

1. *The Court's position*. *Sherbert* and *Yoder* were followed in Thomas v. Review Board, 450 U.S. 707 (1981), a case essentially identical to *Sherbert*. These three

cases are the only ones in which the Court has held that the free exercise clause requires states to provide an exemption for religious objectors from their general statutes. Do the cases form any coherent pattern?

Note that the Court has been unwilling to exempt the press from regulations applicable to the population generally. See Chapter 6, section F6 supra. Why should government be required to depart from neutrality when a person's conduct is based on religious belief? Recall that United States v. O'Brien, Chapter 6, section E3, supra, held that facially neutral statutes serving important purposes unrelated to suppression of speech are constitutional if the incidental impact on speech is no greater than necessary. Do the principal cases transfer the *O'Brien* approach to the free exercise area? Using *O'Brien*'s formulation, identify the differences between *Yoder* and *Lee*.

2. *Guidelines for accommodation?* Consider Clark, Guidelines for the Free Exercise Clause, 83 Harv. L. Rev. 327, 345 (1969):

> [When] an individual because of compelling conscientious belief refuses to perform any duty of positive action established by the state, there exists a constitutional presumption that the state can satisfy its needs either by performing the act on his behalf or by placing upon him an alternative burden of equal weight, or both. Unless it can overcome this presumption, the state may not attempt to coerce his will by civil contempt or punish his refusal to act by criminal sanctions. If the state can overcome the presumption — that is, if it can show that it has no other way to satisfy its needs — then a balancing of interests must be resorted to. The state may enforce all its laws prohibiting positive actions, except that a similar presumption of privilege exists concerning those actions whose performance an individual's conscience deems an inexcusable duty and which involve directly only himself and other fully consenting persons.

Which cases are consistent with these guidelines? Are the remainder wrongly decided? Consider Frank v. State, 604 P.2d 1068 (Alaska 1969): An Athabascan Indian died in October 1975. The religious funeral celebration culminated in a feast for community members, in which they ate a moose shot out of season. Frank, a member of the hunting party, was prosecuted for illegal transportation of the moose and raised the free exercise defense that the funeral feast was an essential religious ceremony in which the consumption of the moose played an important part. The courts found that the funeral celebration was "the most important institution in Athabascan life," that "food is the cornerstone of the ritual," and that moose meat was perhaps necessary but at least very important in the ritual. Frank's conviction was reversed. In Quaring v. Peterson, 728 F.2d 1121 (8th Cir. 1984), aff'd by an equally divided Court, — U.S. — , 105 S. Ct. 3492 (1985), the court of appeals held it unconstitutional for Nebraska to require that a religious objector have her picture on her driver's license. She believed that taking photographs violated the biblical injunction against graven images. In Callahan v. Woods, 736 F.2d 1269 (9th Cir. 1984), the court of appeals held it unconstitutional for Congress to require that applicants for public assistance obtain Social Security numbers, unless an exemption would impair administrative efficiency. Callahan believed that universal numbers are "the mark of the beast" by which the Antichrist endeavors to control mankind. What result in these cases under Clark's guidelines? Under the Court's approach?

3. *Yoder versus Lee. Lee* refused to require an exemption because of concern that other groups in other contexts would make claims for exemptions. Why was that a special concern in *Lee* but not in *Yoder,* which also involved the Old Order Amish? Consider the proposition that *Lee* demonstrates that *Sherbert* was wrongly decided because *Sherbert* provided the foundation for the claims made in *Lee.* Did *Lee* commit "the error of equating the state's interest in denying a religious exemption with the state's usually much greater interest in maintaining the underlying rule or program for unexceptionable cases"? Tribe, supra at 855. Why is that an error?

4. *Religion versus politics.* Is it correct to say that *Sherbert* creates a rule of required accommodation of religious belief when no such rule requires accommodation of political or other beliefs? What is the point of *Yoder's* discussion of Thoreau and other "progressive" theories of education? Construct the factual parallel to *Sherbert* that would involve a person who sought employment compensation because her political commitments made it impossible to find work. Construct a similar factual parallel for a politically motivated dissenter from public education. Is it obvious that free speech claims in such cases would or should be denied? In response to Justice Stewart, Tribe, supra at 852 n.37, writes, "there is, after all, no 'free choice of babysitter' clause." Is that responsive to the argument that *Sherbert* requires the state to prefer religious over nonreligious belief? Note that if no preference is required, the free exercise clause may be fully subsumed under the free speech clause.

5. *Free exercise and establishment in tension?* Does *Sherbert* create a tension between the religion clauses? By requiring the state to depart from neutrality, *Sherbert* also requires the state to support religion. Could this violate the establishment clause? Consider these positions:

a. There is no tension because the Court will not hold that a regulation that, in its view, promotes free exercise values, also violates anti-establishment values, nor will it hold that a statute promoting anti-establishment values impairs free exercise ones. But consider Thornton v. Caldor, infra.

b. There is no tension. Only those statutory accommodations that are required by the free exercise clause are constitutional, and all other efforts to serve "free exercise values" are unconstitutional. Why should a legislature ever enact a statutory accommodation if this is the test? If we assume that the free exercise clause requires some accommodation, the amount to be determined by applying a balancing test, what reasons are there to think that court-devised accommodations will be more appropriate than legislative ones? Does the balancing test used in *Sherbert* allow the Court to determine the location of the boundary between free exercise requirements and establishment clause prohibitions without sufficient constraint?

c. The tension should be resolved by preferring free exercise values to anti-establishment ones. The expansive role of the modern state creates many opportunities for facially neutral statutes to burden religious belief and reduces the role previously played by many religious institutions. Religious intolerance poses serious threats in a religiously diverse society, so that when legislation advances free exercise values, it should be encouraged. See Tribe, supra, at 833-834. Consider the extent to which the problems discussed in section B, supra, and especially the issue of state aid to religious schools, could be recast as efforts by the state to advance free exercise values.

d. The tension should be resolved by preferring anti-establishment values to free exercise ones. Mainstream religions have a powerful advantage in the political process over marginal religions and over nonreligion. Legislation is likely to enhance the positions of mainstream religions. In the long run, religious minorities will be better off under a regime of strict separation, even though the application of neutral regulations may sometimes affect them adversely.

e. There need be no tension. If states are barred from using religion as a basis for either conferring benefits or imposing burdens, legislators will be required to use neutral rules to accomplish their goals, and the legislation resulting from a political process constrained by a requirement of neutrality will threaten neither free exercise nor anti-establishment values.

6. *Permissible accommodations.* Consider the following statutes.

a. The Equal Access Act, 20 U.S.C. §4071, discussed in section A supra, bars public schools from denying access to student groups "on the basis of the religious, political, philosophical, or other content of the speech" at their meetings.

b. 42 U.S.C. §§2000e-2(a), 2000e(j):

> It shall be an unlawful employment practice for an employer to [discriminate] against any individual with respect to his compensation, terms, conditions, or privileges of employment [because] of such individual's [religion; the] term "religion" includes all aspects of religious observance and practice, as well as belief, unless an employer demonstrates that he is unable to reasonably accommodate an employee's [religious] observance or practice without undue hardship on the conduct of the employer's business.

These provisions were construed in Trans World Airlines v. Hardison, 432 U.S. 63 (1977), as not requiring an employer to adjust its seniority system to allow junior employees to avoid work on their sabbaths by displacing senior employees entitled by the system to work on the other days. "To require TWA to bear more than a de minimis cost in order to give Hardison Saturdays off is an undue hardship."

c. 29 U.S.C. §169: "Any employee [who] is a member of and adheres to established and traditional tenets of a bona fide religion [which] has historically held conscientious objections to [supporting] labor organizations shall not be required to [support] any labor organization as a condition of employment." The employee may be required to choose, from three charities listed in a collective bargaining agreement, one charity to receive an amount equal to union dues.

d. 26 U.S.C. §1402(g): This exempts from the Social Security self-employment tax anyone who is "a member of a recognized religious sect [and] is an adherent of established tenets [by] reason of which he is conscientiously opposed to the acceptance of" benefits from the Society Security system. Those who claim the exemption must waive all benefits under the Social Security Act. The Secretary of the Department of Health and Human Services must find that the religion has the required tenets, that "it is the practice, and has been for a [substantial] period of time [for] the members of such sect [to] make [reasonable] provision for their dependent members," and that the religion "has been in existence at all times since December 31, 1950." In *Lee* the Court noted that "at least one other religious organization [besides the Old Order Amish] has sought an exemption under §1402." It cited a Tax Court decision denying the exemption to a member of Sai Baba. Why is §1402 not a religious gerrymander?

In *Hardison* Justice Marshall, who dissented on statutory grounds, cited *Sherbert*, *Yoder*, *Zorach*, and *Gillette*, to support the proposition that the Court has "found no Establishment Clause problems in exempting religious observers from state-imposed duties even when the exemption was in no way compelled by the Free Exercise Clause." Is that an accurate characterization of the cases? He continued, "If the State does not establish religion over nonreligion by excusing religious practitioners from obligations owed the State, I do not see how the State can be said to establish religion by requiring employers to do the same with respect to obligations owed the employer." Consider the "state action" argument that in cases like *Sherbert* the state's administration of its unemployment system burdens the exercise of religion, while in cases like *Hardison* the burden arises from the employer's decision. Consider this alternative argument: Like private employers, the state may choose not to accommodate religious belief. If it is allowed to alter its own policy without violating the establishment clause, it may do the same as to private employers.

Thornton v. Caldor, — U.S. — , 105 S. Ct. 2914 (1985), held unconstitutional a Connecticut statute providing, "No person who states that a particular day of the week is observed as his Sabbath may be required by his employer to work on that day." Chief Justice Burger's opinion for the Court said that the statute imposes "an absolute duty to conform their business practices to the particular religious practices of the employee. [The] State thus commands that Sabbath religious concerns automatically control over all secular interests at the workplace; the statute takes no account of the convenience or interests of the employer or those of other employees who do not observe a Sabbath." He concluded, "This unyielding weighting in favor of Sabbath observers over all other interests contravenes a fundamental principle of the Religion Clauses, [that] 'no one [has] the right to insist that in pursuit of their own interests others must conform their conduct to his own religious necessities'" (quoting Otten v. Baltimore & Ohio Railway, 205 F.2d 58 (2d Cir. 1953)). The statute's "primary effect [impermissibly] advances a particular religious practice." Justice O'Connor, joined by Justice Marshall, concurred, objecting to the "special and [absolute] protection" given to sabbath observers over those with other "ethical and religious beliefs and practices." "The message conveyed is one of endorsement of a particular religious belief, to the detriment of those who do not share it." Title VII, in contrast, was constitutional because it required reasonable, not absolute, accommodation of all religious beliefs and practices, not just sabbath observance. "[An] objective observer would perceive it as an anti-discrimination law rather than an endorsement of religion or a particular religious practice." Justice Rehnquist dissented without opinion.

Why are the statute's absolute nature and targeting on a particular religious practice impermissible? Note the interaction of *Thornton* with *Sherbert*: When Thornton is discharged, he must receive unemployment benefits. Does *Thornton* therefore mean that the cost of having religious beliefs, where that cost is imposed by private parties, must be borne by the taxpayers generally, rather than by the believer or those imposing costs on belief? Note the interaction of *Thornton* with Sunday closing laws and the politics of majority religious beliefs: In a state with a Sunday closing law, adherents of majority religions do not need the protection provided by a statute like Connecticut's. Having done away with Sunday closing laws, why may not Connecticut recreate some of the benefits of those laws?

Should *Thornton* be seen as a business-oriented case, related importantly to the Court's finding a secular purpose for the crèche in *Lynch?*

On what theory of the establishment clause are statutory accommodations of religious practices permissible? Note that statutory accommodations have the purpose of benefitting religious belief as against nonbelief. Consider these possibilities:

a. "[Government] pursues free exercise values when it lifts a government-imposed burden on the free exercise of religion." O'Connor, J., concurring in the judgment in *Jaffree,* supra. Do the statutes described above satisfy this test? What result under *Thornton* and Justice O'Connor's approach if South Carolina by statute adopted the result in *Sherbert?*

b. Statutory accommodations are permissible solely to alleviate burdens that violate the free exercise clause, but legislatures have some leeway to determine what an appropriate balance is, or to devise accommodations that differ from judicially devised ones because of institutional differences between courts and legislatures. In *Hardison* Justice Marshall said that establishment clause questions would arise if the law required employers "to incur substantial costs to aid the religious observer."

c. Legislatures have substantial discretion to promote "free exercise values" by enacting statutory accommodations. Justice Harlan took this view in *Sherbert,* but he agreed that *Engel* was correctly decided. Why is not voluntary devotional prayer in public schools a permissible accommodation, as Justice Stewart suggested in *Schempp?* Consider also Chief Justice Burger's argument in dissent in *Jaffree* that Alabama's moment of silence statute "accommodates the purely private, voluntary religious choices of the individual pupils who wish to pray while at the same time creating a time for nonreligious reflection for those who do not choose to pray."

7. *Statutory interpretation.* In NLRB v. Catholic Bishop, 440 U.S. 490 (1979), the Court held that the National Labor Relations Act did not apply to lay teachers employed in Catholic schools. Because "the Board's exercise of its jurisdiction [would] give rise to serious constitutional questions," the Court required that "the affirmative intention of the Congress [be] clearly expressed." But in Tony & Susan Alamo Foundation v. Secretary of Labor, — U.S. — , 105 S. Ct. 1953 (1985), the Court held that the Fair Labor Standards Act applied to certain employees of a religious foundation. It did not apply the *Catholic Bishop* test to determine Congress's intention but noted that in the following section of its opinion, it rejected the foundation's first amendment claims on the merits. When would the *Catholic Bishop* test be appropriately invoked?

Note: *Religion as a Form of Belief*

1. *Religion as politics.* Widmar v. Vincent, section A supra, held that the free speech clause required a state university to make its facilities available to a student prayer group, just as it would make them available to other groups seeking to use the public forum it created. Justice White, the only dissenter, rejected the Court's free speech analysis. He criticized the Court for arguing that "religious worship *qua* speech is not different from any other variety of protected speech. [This] proposition is plainly wrong. Were it right, the Religion Clauses would be emptied

of any independent meaning in which religious practice took the form of speech." He would have distinguished between "verbal acts of worship and other verbal acts," saying that "the line may be difficult to draw in many cases" but that doing so was necessary in order to avoid the result that the university could "offer a class entitled 'Sunday Mass,'" which, unless such a line were drawn, would be "indistinguishable from a class entitled 'The History of the Catholic Church.'" He would have treated the case as a free exercise case and, given the availability of facilities near the campus for a prayer group, would have found the burden on free exercise rights minimal and justified by the state's "permissible" interest "in avoiding claims that it is financing or otherwise supporting religious worship."

The Court noted three difficulties with the distinction between worship and speech about religion: It had no "intelligible content" because "there is no indication when 'singing hymns, reading scripture, and teaching biblical principles' cease to be ['speech,'] despite their religious subject matter [and] become 'worship'"; it was doubtful that the courts could administer the distinction because they would have to "inquire into the significance of words and practices to different religious faiths," which would lead to entanglement problems; and the distinction was not relevant because it failed to explain why the Constitution "would require different treatment for religious speech designed to win religious converts than for religious worship by persons already converted."

Are religious beliefs different enough from political beliefs because of their intensity, the fact that they deal with deep questions about human existence, or whatever, to justify different constitutional treatment?

2. *Religion in politics.* Torcaso v. Watkins, 367 U.S. 488 (1961), invalidated a provision in the Maryland constitution that required state officials to declare their belief in the existence of God. "[Neither] a State nor the Federal Government can constitutionally force a person 'to profess a belief or disbelief in any religion' [and] neither can aid those religions based on a belief in the existence of God as against those religions founded on different beliefs." It rejected the state's claim that no one was forced to hold public office, which "cannot possibly be an excuse for barring him from office by state-imposed criteria forbidden by the Constitution [Wieman v. Updegraff, Chapter 7, section F3, supra]."

In McDaniel v. Paty, 435 U.S. 618 (1978), the Court invalidated, without dissent, a provision of the Tennessee Constitution barring ministers from serving as legislators or as delegates to the state's constitutional convention. Chief Justice Burger's plurality opinion reviewed the history of such disqualifications, which were in effect in seven of the original states and which were adopted by six states later admitted to the Union. Disqualification was designed "to assure the success of a new political experiment, the separation of church and state." But "as the value of the dis-establishment experiment was perceived, 11 of the 13 States [gradually] abandoned that limitation," until by 1900 only Maryland and Tennessee retained it. The opinion continued, "the right to the free exercise of religion unquestionably encompasses the right to preach [and] to be a minister." If the disqualification "were viewed as depriving the clergy of a civil right solely because of their religious beliefs," *Torcaso* would control. But the disqualification was triggered by the minister's status, defined "in terms of conduct and activity rather than in terms of belief." Thus, the relevant precedent was *Yoder*, which required an "interest of the highest order." But the state had "failed to demonstrate that [the] dangers of clergy participation in the political process have not lost whatever validity they may once have enjoyed. [The] American experience provides no persuasive support for the fear that clergymen in public office will be less careful of anti-establishment interests or less faithful to their oaths of civil office than their unordained counterparts."

Justice Brennan, joined by Justice Marshall, and Justice Stewart submitted separate concurring opinions arguing that *Torcaso* controlled. Justice Brennan wrote, "freedom of belief [embraces] freedom to profess or practice that belief, even including doing so to earn a livelihood." Tennessee's rule was therefore "absolutely prohibited," and no balancing of interests was required. Further, *Sherbert* establishes that it is unconstitutional to condition "eligibility for office on [abandonment]" of religious activity, despite the state's contention that "the unemployment compensation involved in *Sherbert* was necessary to sustain life while participation in the constitutional convention is a voluntary activity not itself compelled by religious belief." "*Sherbert* and *Torcaso* compel the conclusion that because the challenged provision requires appellant to purchase his right to engage in the ministry by sacrificing his candidacy it impairs the free exercise of his religion." Justice Brennan argued that

> public debate of religious ideas [may] arouse emotion, [but] the mere fact that a purpose of the Establishment Clause is to reduce or eliminate religious divisiveness or strife, does not place religious discussion, association, or political participation in a status less preferred than rights of [political] participation generally. [In] short, government may not as a goal promote "safe thinking" with respect to religion and fence out from political participation those [whom] it regards as overinvolved in religion. Religionists no less than members of any other group enjoy the full measure of protection afforded speech. [The] antidote which the Constitution provides against zealots who would inject sectarianism into the political process is to subject their ideas to refutation in the market-place of ideas and their platforms to rejection at the polls. With these safeguards [and,] with judicial enforcement of the Establishment Clause, any measure of success they achieve must be short-lived, at best.

Justice White concurred in the judgment, relying on the equal protection clause rather than the free exercise clause because he did not see how the minister "has been deterred in the observance of his religious beliefs." Applying "careful scrutiny" to a statute burdening "the right of an individual to seek elective office," he found that the state's interest in maintaining separation of church and state was insufficient because the premise that ministers would subordinate their governmental service to their church duties was unfounded.

What result in *McDaniel* under the free speech clause? Is the confidence expressed by Chief Justice Burger and Justice Brennan in the political process warranted? Should a state be precluded from taking a more jaundiced view of the efficacy of the political process in matters of religion?

Note: Concluding Observations

Do the preceding materials demonstrate that the two religion clauses are incompatible? The establishment clause requires (some sort of) neutrality, while the free exercise clause requires (some sort of) preference to religion and may permit other preferences. Does the concept of benevolent neutrality reconcile

the clauses? When does a permissible benevolence become a prohibited encouragement? Consider whether the religion clauses are incompatible because of
religious pluralism: Any purported benevolent encouragement of some or many
religions will discourage others; given the range of actions required by some
religions and prohibited by others, no regulation can be neutral in its effects as
between some religions and others, or between religion and nonreligion. Are the
religion clauses different from the equal protection clause in this respect?

IX

Economic Liberties and the Constitution: The Contracts and Takings Clauses

In the last few decades, judicial "activism" has — with some notable exceptions — served to advance interests associated with the political agenda of the New Deal coalition, including those of members of minority groups and certain rights of "privacy," most prominently the right to procreative choice. It has operated less frequently to protect "economic" rights. But through much of the nation's history, courts have actively protected economic ordering from governmental intrusion. There is reason to believe that the framers of the Constitution shared a special sympathy for private ordering and that they designed the Constitution, at least in part, as a means of guarding against democratic or collective control of property. See Chapter 1, section A, supra.

During the *Lochner* era the due process clause constrained governmental interference with economic ordering. See Chapter 6, section C, supra. This chapter explores the contracts clause and the eminent domain clause. In reading the materials that follow, consider (1) whether and how interpretation of these seemingly explicit constitutional guarantees has been different from interpretation of another seemingly explicit guarantee, the first amendment, (2) whether there is a difference in the treatment of the seemingly explicit contracts and takings clauses on the one hand and the treatment of "implied" rights, discussed infra, on the other, and (3) what lessons the answers to questions (1) and (2) have for constitutional theory and interpretation in general.

A. The Contracts Clause

The contracts clause provides that "No State shall [pass] any [Law] impairing the Obligation of Contracts." U.S. Const. Art. I, §10, cl. 1.

Note: Early Interpretive Problems

The contracts clause is one of the few "rights-protecting" provisions in the original Constitution, and it is one of the few such provisions that was directly applicable to the states before the adoption of the fourteenth amendment. Moreover, for a long period the contracts clause was one of the most important provision in the Constitution, at least if the structural provisions are excluded. Indeed, in the nineteenth century the clause "was the constitutional justification for more cases involving the validity of state law than all of the other clauses of the Constitution together." B. Wright, The Contract Clause of the Constitution 1 (1938). Some also highly valued the clause for its protection of a form of liberty. Sir Henry Maine claimed that the clause "is the bulwark of American individualism against democratic impatience and socialistic fantasy." H. Maine, Popular Government 247-248 (1885). Why did the framers of the Constitution single out contractual freedom as one of the only rights entitled to protection against abridgement by state governments?

Between the Revolution and the drafting of the Constitution, many states had enacted "debtor relief" laws — provisions that, among other things, postponed the time for payment of private debts, allowed for issuance and required acceptance of paper money, and allowed for payments in installments or at some percentage of the appraised value of commodities. Creditors, well-to-do or otherwise, regarded these measures as an indefensible intrusion on private ordering. The contracts clause was designed to prevent states from enacting such laws. See, for early examples, Sturges v. Crowninshield, 17 U.S. (4 Wheat.) 122 (1819), invalidating a New York law discharging debtors of their obligations upon surrender of their property; Green v. Biddle, 21 U.S. (8 Wheat.) 1 (1823), invalidating a Kentucky law designed to make it harder for landowners to eject good faith squatters. Early controversies over the clause involved three principal issues.

1. *Prospective or retrospective only?* What if a state prohibits people from entering into certain sorts of contracts? In Ogden v. Saunders, 25 (12 Wheat.) 213 (1827), the Court was confronted with the critical question of whether the prohibition of contractual impairments applies only to contracts made before the passage of the allegedly "impairing" law. The case involved a state bankruptcy law passed before the parties had entered into the relevant contract. According to the Court, the law in effect at the time a contract is formed is "the law of the contract," or a part of the contract, and therefore not an impairment at all within the meaning of the clause.

Justice Johnson, writing one of four separate opinions upholding the statute, said that the contract clause was in this respect analogous to the prohibition of bills of attainder and of ex post facto laws. All three were provisions "against arbitrary and tyrannical legislation over existing rights, whether of person or property." Statutory boundaries to contractual freedom, set in advance, were no less defensible here than "in the instances of gaming debts, usurious contracts, marriage, brokage bonds, and various others." The underlying idea is that positive law creates the background against which private parties contract; and there is no vested right to any particular background.

Chief Justice Marshall was in the minority — for the only time, in constitutional cases, during his thirty-four-year tenure as Chief Justice. He emphasized two points. First, in his view the text of the clause did not allow for a distinction between prospective and retrospective impairments. Second, Marshall stressed that the right to contractual freedom was a product of natural law, and that the Court had forgotten that point by allowing positive law to dictate in advance the conditions under which contracts could go forward. The right to contractual freedom was, in his view, prepolitical: "Individuals do not derive from government their right to contract, but bring that right with them into society." Note the correspondence between Marshall's view and that of Justice Chase in Calder v. Bull, Chapter 1 supra.

2. *Interference with contracts under the police power.* What if a state declares unenforceable existing contractual obligations through the exercise of its police power — as, for example, by prohibiting agreements calling for the sale of heroin, or for murder, or for a certain level of pollution? To what extent does the state's reserved authority operate as an implicit "exception" to the contracts clause?

In early cases, the Court ruled that the clause does not prohibit even retroactive contractual impairments if the state is operating pursuant to the police power. In Manigault v. Springs, 199 U.S. 473 (1905), neighboring landowners quarelled over a dam that one of them had built. After negotiations, the landowners agreed that the obstruction might continue for four more months, after which it would be removed, so that there would be a clear passage through the creek. The dam was accordingly removed. Several years later, a statute was enacted that authorized one of the landowners to build a dam on the same creek. The statute of course destroyed the contractual obligation not to build a dam on the creek.

The Court upheld the statute, stating that the police power "is an exercise of the sovereign right of the government to protect the lives, health, morals, comfort, and general welfare of the people, and is paramount to any rights under contracts between individuals." Thus "parties by entering into contracts may not estop the legislature from enacting laws intended for the public good." See also Stone v. Mississippi, 101 U.S. 814 (1880), where the Court said that no "legislature can bargain away the public health or the public morals." (Should the state be required to give compensation in cases like *Manigault* and *Stone*? This question is explored in section B infra.)

A police power "exception" might swallow the contract clause: If any effort that might be described as an attempt to protect the "general welfare" can justify a retroactive interference with rights acquired by contract, the clause furnishes no barrier to contractual impairments. For many years after *Manigault*, however, this risk did not materialize. The reason is that the police power comprehended a relatively narrow category of permissible government ends, and certainly did not include the various forms of redistributive regulation characteristic of modern regulation.

3. *Regulation versus impairment.* In a number of early cases the Court struggled with the issue of whether particular measures were "regulations" interfering with remedies, or genuine impairments of contractual obligations. In this view, delays in time for performance might not interfere with "substantial rights"; they merely affected the remedy. Is a distinction between rights and remedies artificial? The line here was an "obscure" one, Worthen Co. v. Kavanaugh, 295 U.S. 56 (1935), but it did allow for some flexibility on the part of the legislature. See, e.g., Honeyman v. Jacobs, 306 U.S. 539 (1939) (same); Richmond Mortgage & Loan Corp. v. Wachovia Bank & Trust Co., 300 U.S. 124 (1937) (upholding

statute designed to prevent creditor from getting more by remedy than he would have obtained had contract been performed); Curtis v. Whitney, 13 Wall. 68 (1872) (upholding statute providing that a deed may not issue unless a written notice had been served on any previous owner or occupant at least three months before; statute interfered with rights received by plaintiff who had received certificate entitling her to deed before statute had been passed); Bronson v. Kinzie, 1 How. 311 (1843) (noting that state may shorten the statute of limitations period or provide what articles may be liable to execution on judgment). See generally Hale, The Supreme Court and the Contract Clause, 57 Harv. L. Rev. 512, 621, 852 (1944); B. Wright, The Contract Clause of the Constitution (1938).

The following case is the starting point of modern law under the contracts clause.

Home Building & Loan Association v. Blaisdell
290 U.S. 398 (1934)

[In the midst of the depression, Minnesota passed a mortgage moratorium law to provide relief for homeowners threatened with foreclosure. The law, passed in 1933, declared an emergency and said that, during the emergency period, courts may postpone mortgage sales and periods of redemption. Its provisions were to apply "only during the continuance of the emergency and in no event beyond May 1, 1935." Pursuant to the statute, Blaisdell's period of redemption was extended to May 1, 1935, subject in general to the payment by Blaisdell of $40 a month through the extended period. There was no dispute that the extension modified the lenders' contractual rights of foreclosure. The lower court upheld the statute.]

MR. CHIEF JUSTICE HUGHES delivered the opinion of the Court.

In determining whether the provision for this temporary and conditional relief exceeds the power of the State by reason of the clause in the Federal Constitution prohibiting impairment of the obligations of contracts, we must consider the relation of emergency to constitutional power, the historical setting of the contract clause, the development of the jurisprudence of this Court in the construction of that clause, and the principles of construction which we may consider to be established.

Emergency does not create power. Emergency does not increase granted power or remove or diminish the restrictions imposed upon power granted or reserved. The Constitution was adopted in a period of grave emergency. Its grants of power to the Federal Government and its limitations of the power of the States were determined in the light of emergency and they are not altered by emergency. . . .

[In] the construction of the contract clause, the debates in the Constitutional Convention are of little aid. But the reasons which led to the adoption of that clause, and of the other prohibitions of Section 10 of Article I, are not left in doubt and have frequently been described with eloquent emphasis. The widespread distress following the revolutionary period, and the plight of debtors, had called forth in the States an ignoble array of legislative schemes for the defeat of creditors and the invasion of contractual obligations. Legislative interferences had been so numerous and extreme that the confidence essential to prosperous trade had been undermined and the utter destruction of credit was threatened.

"The sober people of America" were convinced that some "thorough reform" was needed which would "inspire a general prudence and industry, and give a regular course to the business of society." The Federalist, No. 44. It was necessary to interpose the restraining power of a central authority in order to secure the foundations even of "private faith." The occasion and general purpose of the contract clause are summed up in the terse statement of Chief Justice Marshall in [*Ogden*]:

> The power of changing the relative situation of debtor and creditor, of interfering with contracts, a power which comes home to every man, touches the interest of all, and controls the conduct of every individual in those things which he supposes to be proper for his own exclusive management, had been used to such an excess by the state legislatures, as to break in upon the ordinary intercourse of society, and destroy all confidence between man and man. This mischief had become so great, so alarming, as not only to impair commercial intercourse, and threaten the existence of credit, but to sap the morals of the people, and destroy the sanctity of private faith. To guard against the continuance of the evil was an object of deep interest with all the truly wise, as well as the virtuous, of this great community, and was one of the important benefits expected from a reform of the government. . . .

The obligation of a contract is "the law which binds the parties to perform their agreement." [This] Court has said that "the laws which subsist at the time and place of the making of a contract, and where it is to be performed, enter into and form a part of it, as if they were expressly referred to or incorporated in its terms. This principle embraces alike those which affect its validity, construction, discharge and enforcement. . . ."

[The] constitutional provision [is] qualified by the measure of control which the State [retains] to safeguard the vital interests of its people. [Not] only are existing laws read into contracts in order to fix obligations as between the parties, but the reservation of essential attributes of sovereign power is also read into contracts as a postulate of the legal order. The policy of protecting contracts against impairment presupposes the maintenance of a government by virtue of which contractual relations are worth while, — a government which retains adequate authority to secure the peace and good order of society. This principle of harmonizing the constitutional prohibition with the necessary residuum of state power has had progressive recognition in the decisions of this Court. . . .

The legislature cannot "bargain away the public health or the public morals." [The] question is not whether the legislative action affects contracts incidentally, or directly or indirectly, but whether the legislation is addressed to a legitimate end and the measures taken are reasonable and appropriate to that end. [It is argued] that the state power may be addressed directly to the prevention of the enforcement of contracts only when these are of a sort which the legislature in its discretion may denounce as being in themselves hostile to public morals, or public health, safety or welfare, or where the prohibition is merely of injurious practices; that interference with the enforcement of other and valid contracts according to appropriate legal procedure, although the interference is temporary and for a public purpose, is not permissible. . . .

Undoubtedly, whatever is reserved of state power must be consistent with the fair intent of the constitutional limitation of that power. The reserved power cannot be construed so as to destroy the limitation, nor is the limitation to be construed to destroy the reserved power in its essential aspects. They must be construed in harmony with each other. This principle precludes a construction which would permit the State to adopt as its policy the repudiation of debts or the destruction of contracts or the denial of means to enforce them. But it does not follow that conditions may not arise in which a temporary restraint of enforcement may be [constitutional]. . . .

[There] has been a growing appreciation of public needs and of the necessity of finding ground for a rational compromise between individual rights and public welfare. The settlement and consequent contraction of the public domain, the pressure of a constantly increasing density of population, the interrelation of the activities of our people and the complexity of our economic interests, have inevitably led to an increased use of the organization of society in order to protect the very bases of individual opportunity. Where, in earlier days, it was thought that only the concerns of individuals or of classes were involved, and that those of the State itself were touched only remotely, it has later been found that the fundamental interests of the State are directly affected; and that the question is no longer merely that of one party to a contract as against another, but of the use of reasonable means to safeguard the economic structure upon which the good of all depends.

It is no answer to say that this public need was not apprehended a century ago, or to insist that what the provision of the Constitution meant to the vision of that day it must mean to the vision of our time. If by the statement that what the Constitution meant at the time of its adoption it means to-day, it is intended to say that the great clauses of the Constitution must be confined to the interpretation which the framers, with the conditions and outlook of their time, would have placed upon them, the statement carries its own refutation. It was to guard against such a narrow conception that Chief Justice Marshall uttered the memorable warning — "We must never forget that it is *a constitution* we are expounding" [McCulloch v. Maryland] — "a constitution intended to endure for ages to come, and consequently, to be adapted to the various *crises* of human affairs." When we are dealing with the words of the Constitution, "we must realize that they have called into life a being the development of which could not have been foreseen completely by the most gifted of its begetters. . . . The case before us must be considered in the light of our whole experience and not merely in that of what was said a hundred years ago."

Nor is it helpful to attempt to draw a fine distinction between the intended meaning of the words of the Constitution and their intended application. When we consider the contract clause and the decisions which have expounded it in harmony with the essential reserved power of the States to protect the security of their peoples, we find no warrant for the conclusion that the clause has been warped by these decisions from its proper significance or that the founders of our Government would have interpreted the clause differently had they had occasion to assume that responsibility in the conditions of the later day. The vast body of law which has been developed was unknown to the fathers, but it is believed to have preserved the essential content and the spirit of the Constitution. With a growing recognition of public needs and the relation of individual right to public security, the court has sought to prevent the perversion of the clause through its use as an instrument to throttle the capacity of the States to protect their fundamental interests. This development is a growth from the seeds which the fathers planted. [The] principle of this development is, as we have seen, that the reservation of the reasonable exercise of the protective power of the State is read into all contracts. . . .

Applying the criteria established by our decisions we conclude:

1. An emergency existed in Minnesota which furnished a proper occasion for the exercise of the reserved power of the State to protect the vital interests of the community. The declarations of the existence of this emergency by the legislature and by the Supreme Court of Minnesota cannot be regarded as a subterfuge or as lacking in adequate basis. [The] finding of the legislature and state court has support in the facts of which we take judicial notice. . . .

2. The legislation was addressed to a legitimate end, that is, the legislation was not for the mere advantage of particular individuals but for the protection of a basic interest of society.

3. In view of the nature of the contracts in question — mortgages of unquestionable validity — the relief afforded and justified by the emergency, in order not to contravene the constitutional provision, could only be of a character appropriate to that emergency and could be granted only upon reasonable conditions.

4. The conditions upon which the period of redemption is extended do not appear to be unreasonable. . .

5. The legislation is temporary in operation. It is limited to the exigency which called it forth. [The] operation of the statute itself could not validly outlast the emergency or be so extended as virtually to destroy the contracts.

We are of the opinion that the Minnesota statute as here applied does not violate the contract clause of the Federal Constitution. Whether the legislation is wise or unwise as a matter of policy is a question with which we are not concerned. . . .

The judgment of the Supreme Court of Minnesota is affirmed.

MR. JUSTICE SUTHERLAND, dissenting.

Few questions of greater moment than that just decided have been submitted for judicial inquiry during this generation. He simply closes his eyes to the necessary implications of the decision who fails to see in it the potentiality of future gradual but ever-advancing encroachments upon the sanctity of private and public contracts. . . .

A provision of the Constitution, it is hardly necessary to say, does not admit of two distinctly opposite interpretations. It does not mean one thing at one time and an entirely different thing at another time. If the contract impairment clause, when framed and adopted, meant that the terms of a contract for the payment of money could not be altered [by] a state statute enacted for the relief of hardly pressed debtors to the end and with the effect of postponing payment or enforcement during and because of an economic or financial emergency, it is but to state the obvious to say that it means the same now. . . .

Following the Revolution, and prior to the adoption of the Constitution, the American people found themselves in a greatly impoverished condition. Their commerce had been well-nigh annihilated. They were not only without luxuries, but in great degree were destitute of the ordinary comforts and necessities of life. In these circumstances they incurred indebtedness in the purchase of imported goods and otherwise, far beyond their capacity to pay. From this situation there arose a divided sentiment. On the one hand, an exact observance of public and private engagements was insistently urged. A violation of the faith of the nation or the pledges of the private individual, it was insisted, was equally forbidden by the principles of moral justice and of sound policy. Individual distress, it was urged, should be alleviated only by industry and frugality, not by relaxation of law or by a sacrifice of the rights of others. Indiscretion or imprudence was not to be relieved by legislation, but restrained by the conviction that a full compliance with contracts would be exacted. On the other hand, it was insisted that the case of the debtor should be viewed with tenderness; and efforts were constantly directed toward relieving him from an exact compliance with his contract. As a result of the latter view, state laws were passed suspending the collection of debts, remitting or suspending the collection of taxes, providing for the emission of paper money, delaying legal proceedings, etc. There followed, as there must always follow from such a course, a long trail of ills, one of the direct consequences being a loss of confidence in the government and in the good faith of the people. Bonds of men whose ability to pay their debts was unquestionable could not be negotiated except at a [discount. Real] property could be sold only at a ruinous loss. Debtors, instead of seeking to meet their obligations by painful effort, by industry and economy, began to rest their hopes entirely upon legislative interference. The impossibility of payment of public or private debts was widely asserted, and in some instances threats were made of suspending the administration of justice by violence. The circulation of depreciated currency became common. Resentment against lawyers and courts was freely manifested, and in many instances the course of the law was arrested and judges restrained from proceeding in the execution of their duty by popular and tumultous assemblages. This state of things alarmed all thoughtful men, and led them to seek some effective remedy. . . .

The defense of the Minnesota law is made upon grounds which were discountenanced by the makers of the Constitution. [That] defense should not now succeed, because it constitutes an effort to overthrow the constitutional provision by an appeal to facts and circumstances identical with those which brought it into existence. With due regard for the processes of logical thinking, it legitimately cannot be urged that conditions which produced the rule may now be invoked to destroy it. . . .

[Hence] the question is not whether an emergency furnishes the occasion for the exercise of that state power, but whether an emergency furnishes an occasion for the relaxation of the restrictions upon the power imposed by the contract impairment clause; and the difficulty is that the contract impairment clause forbids state action under any circumstances, if it have the effect of impairing the obligation of contracts. . . .

It is quite true also that [general] statutes to put an end to lotteries, the sale or manufacture of intoxicating liquors, the maintenance of nuisances, to protect the public safety, etc., although they have the indirect effect of absolutely destroying private contracts previously made in contemplation of a continuance of the state of affairs then in existence but subsequently prohibited, have been uniformly upheld as not violating the contract impairment clause. The distinction between legislation of that character and the Minnesota statute, however, is readily observable. . . . [The Minnesota] statute denies appellant for a period of two years the ownership and possession of the property — an asset which [is] of substantial character, and which possibly may turn out to be of great value. The statute, therefore, is not merely a modification of the remedy; it effects a material and injurious change in the obligation. . . . If the provisions of the Constitution be not upheld when they pinch as well as when they comfort, they may as well be abandoned. Being unable to reach any other conclusion than that the Minnesota statute infringes the constitutional restriction under review, I have no choice but to say so.

[JUSTICES VAN DEVANTER, McREYNOLDS, and BUTLER joined in this dissent.]

Note: Market Ordering and Constitutional Interpretation

1. *The changing scope of the police power.* The Court had long held that the contracts clause did not forbid states from impairing the obligations of contract if the impairment resulted from an exercise of the "police power," the state's traditional authority to protect its citizens from public harms. Thus, for example, the clause did not prevent states from outlawing contracts for murder or for the sale of heroin, even if the impairing law applied retroactively. See, e.g., Manigault v. Springs, 199 U.S. 473 (1905). See generally Hale, The Supreme Court and the Contract Clause, 57 Harv. L. Rev. 621 (1944).

Why, then, was *Blaisdell* such an important case? Consider the possibility that the real shift came in the novel understanding of what the police power allowed, an understanding that resulted in a dramatic expansion of the permissible ends of government that would support a contractual impairment. When government was no longer limited to protection against common law torts or analogous conduct — which is what was involved in the earlier cases — and when it could intervene to protect (for example) mortgagors as a class or subgroups thereof, the police power endangered the contracts clause — a classic case of an exception expanding to eliminate the rule. In this view, the importance of *Blaisdell* lies in the enlargement in the categories of things government might do under the police power. A general if crude way to put the point is that after *Blaisdell*, it may be possible to argue that government might abrogate contracts in the interest of (at least some sorts of) redistribution, and not only in the interest of serving a more "general" end. Is this too broad a reading of Blaisdell? Compare the contemporaneous abandonment of the *Lochner*-era understanding of the permissible ends of government, see Chapter 6, section D, infra, and the similar changes in interpretation of the eminent domain clause, infra. See Sunstein, Naked Preferences and the Constitution, 84 Colum. L. Rev. 1689 (1984), for discussion.

Was the Court correct to broaden the police power? One might criticize the decision on the ground that if the state might impair a contract in order to protect mortgagors, and in so doing be considered to have operated within its police power, it might also be allowed to impair a contract in order to protect creditors or debtors, or any other group, as a class. This might be said to be precisely the evil at which the clause was originally aimed.

Note that in the case of the first amendment, the Court has interpreted the clause expansively in an effort to create a relatively broad constitutional guarantee of free expression. See Chapter 7, supra. In the case of the contracts clause — a similarly "express" constitutional safeguard — the Court has generally taken an opposite tack. Is the Court justified in using the contracts clause to invalidate far less than its drafters intended, while using the first amendment to invalidate far more? Note in particular that the state's "police power" may be used only in very narrow circumstances to justify infringements on freedom of expression. What lessons does this difference suggest for freedom and constraint in adjudication?

2. Blaisdell *and constitutional interpretation.* The Court suggests that the framers' own interpretation of the contracts clause is not controlling. Indeed, it says that the notion that "what the Constitution meant at the time of its adoption it means today [carries] its own refutation." This is one of the most candid statements by the Court that a constitutional decision is not based on the framers' original intent. Is this another way of saying that "it is a Constitution we are expounding," or does it go beyond what Chief Justice Marshall had in mind?

After *Blaisdell,* will contractual impairment be constitutional whenever the Court thinks the impairment a good idea? What constraints apply to a post-*Blaisdell* decision? Consider Epstein, Toward a Revitalization of the Contracts Clause, 51 U. Chi. L. Rev. 703, 735-736 (1984):

> The passage contains some of the most misguided thinking on constitutional interpretation imaginable. The operative assumption seems to be that questions of constitutional law are to be answered according to whether or not we like the Constitution as it was originally drafted. If we do not, we are then free to introduce into the document those provisions that we think more congenial to our time. [By] this standard a court can invest itself with the power of a standing constitutional convention. The importance of a fixed constitutional framework and stable institutional arrangements is necessarily lost once the framework that was designed to place a limit upon politics becomes the central subject of the politics it was designed to limit.

Consider the following responses: (a) A decision to adhere to the original "intent" would have been equally subjective and equally vulnerable. It would have represented adoption of a particular, controversial conception of what a constitution is — in short, a document to be understood by reference to the particular wishes of its authors — a conception that has often and correctly been repudiated elsewhere in the law. (b) In the circumstances of the Depression, it is impossible to decide, except arbitrarily, what the framers' "intent" was. That decision is necessarily constructive, not historical in any simple sense. The framers were not presented with the circumstances of the Depression. Nor were they operating within a society in which contractual freedom had produced the harsh consequences to which the Minnesota legislature had to respond. In applying the framers' understanding to the situation in the 1930s, the notion of "adherence" to an "intent" is not coherent. It is by no means clear what the framers "intended" in such a situation. (c) The contracts clause has always been limited by the police power; that is an uncontroversial limitation, and has been so since the time of ratification. The question is what authority the "police power" includes. The answer to that question properly changes over time. Here, as elsewhere, the framers have set out a general concept, not a particular conception. *Blaisdell* might thus be justified as "interpretation" of the contracts clause, in the same sense as interpretation of other provisions.

3. *The contracts clause after* Blaisdell. After *Blaisdell*, what does the contracts clause prohibit? For a while the answer appeared to be very little. Consider, for example, El Paso v. Simmons, 379 U.S. 497 (1965). The case grew out of a 1910 sale, by contract, from the state of Texas of public land. State law provided for the termination of the contract and forfeiture of the land for nonpayment of interest, and in such a case the purchaser could reinstate his claim on request and with payment of delinquent interest. In 1941 the state amended the law, limiting reinstatement rights to claims asserted five years from the date of forfeiture. The 1941 law operated to impair rights acquired under the 1910 contract.

The Court upheld the law, referring to its purpose "to restore confidence in the stability and integrity of land titles" and to end "the imbroglio over land titles in Texas." Justice Black, in dissent, compared the Court's decision to "balancing away the First Amendment's unequivocally guaranteed rights" and added: "The Court through its balancing process states the case in a way inevitably designed to bypass the Contract Clause and let Texas break its solemn obligation. [Constitutional] adjudication under the balancing method becomes simply a matter of this Court's deciding for itself which result in a particular case seems in the circumstances the more acceptable governmental policy." See also East New York Bank v. Hahn, 326 U.S. 230 (1945) (upholding an extension of mortgage moratorium legislation); Veix v. Sixth Ward, 310 U.S. 32 (1940) (upholding right of states to restrict right of certificate holders to withdraw or recover amounts of certificates).

UNITED STATES TRUST CO. v. NEW JERSEY, 431 U.S. 1 (1977): A New Jersey statute, in conjunction with a parallel New York provision, repealed a statutory covenant, made by the two states in 1962, which limited the ability of the Port Authority of New Jersey and New York to subsidize rail passenger transportation from revenues and reserves. The covenant had been adopted in order to provide special security for the bondholders against competition from rail transportation. But New Jersey and New York later concluded that subsidization was necessary to improve conservation and to advance rail transit. The Court, in an opinion by Justice Blackmun, invalidated the repeal of the covenant:

"The trial court concluded that repeal of the 1962 covenant was a valid exercise of New Jersey's police power because repeal served important public interests in mass transportation, energy conservation, and environmental protection. [Yet] the Contract Clause limits otherwise legitimate exercises of state legislative authority, and the existence of an important public interest is now always sufficient to overcome that limitation. . . .

"[In] applying this standard, [complete] deference to a legislative assessment of reasonableness and necessity is not appropriate [when] the State's self-interest is at stake. A governmental entity can always find a use for extra money, especially when taxes do not have to be raised. If a State could reduce its financial obligations whenever it wanted to spend the money for what it regarded as an important public purpose, the Contract Clause would provide no protection at all. . . .

"Mass transportation, energy conservation, and environmental protection are goals that are important and of legitimate public concern. Appellees contend that these goals are so important that any harm to bondholders from repeal of the 1962 covenant is greatly outweighed by the public benefit. We do not accept this invitation to engage in a utilitarian comparison of public benefit and private loss. Contrary to Mr. Justice Black's fear, expressed in sole dissent in [*El Paso*], the

Court has not "balanced away" the limitation on state action imposed by the Contract Clause. Thus a State cannot refuse to meet its legitimate financial obligations simply because it would prefer to spend the money to promote the public good rather than the private welfare of its creditors. We can only sustain the repeal of the 1962 covenant if that impairment was both reasonable and necessary to serve the admittedly important purposes claimed by the State.

"The more specific justification offered for the repeal of the 1962 covenant was the States' plan for encouraging users of private automobiles to shift to public transportation. The States intended to discourage private automobile use by raising bridge and tunnel tolls and to use the extra revenue from those tolls to subsidize improved commuter railroad service. Appellees contend that repeal of the 1962 covenant was necessary to implement this plan because the new mass transit facilities could not possibly be self-supporting and the covenant's "permitted deficits" level had already been exceeded. We reject this justification because the repeal was neither necessary to achievement of the plan nor reasonable in light of the circumstances.

"The determination of necessity can be considered on two levels. First, it cannot be said that total repeal of the covenant was essential; a less drastic modification would have permitted the contemplated plan without entirely removing the covenant's limitations on the use of Port Authority revenues and reserves to subsidize commuter railroads. Second, without modifying the covenant at all, the States could have adopted alternative means of achieving their twin goals of discouraging automobile use and improving mass transit.

"In the instant case the need for mass transportation in the New York metropolitan area was not a new development, and the likelihood that publicly owned commuter railroads would produce substantial deficits was well known. [It] was with full knowledge of these concerns that the 1962 covenant was adopted. . . .

"During the 12-year period between adoption of the covenant and its repeal, public perception of the importance of mass transit undoubtedly grew because of increased general concern with environmental protection and energy conservation. But these concerns were not unknown in 1962, and the subsequent changes were of degree and not of kind. We cannot say that these changes caused the covenant to have a substantially different impact in 1974 than when it was adopted in 1962. And we cannot conclude that the repeal was reasonable in the light of changed circumstances."

Mr. Justice Brennan, joined by Mr. Justice White and Mr. Justice Marshall, dissented:

"Decisions of this Court for at least a century have construed the Contract Clause largely to be powerless in binding a State to contracts limiting the authority of successor legislatures to enact laws in furtherance of the health, safety, and similar collective interests of the polity. [Today's] decision [remolds] the Contract Clause into a potent instrument for overseeing important policy determinations of the state legislature. At the same time, by creating a constitutional safe haven for property rights embodied in a contract, the decision substantially distorts modern constitutional jurisprudence governing regulation of private economic interests. . . .

"One of the fundamental premises of our popular democracy is that each generation of representatives can and will remain responsive to the needs and desires of those whom they represent. Crucial to this end is the assurance that new legislators will not automatically be bound by the policies and undertakings of earlier days. In accordance with this philosophy, the Framers of our Constitution conceived of the Contract Clause primarily as protection for economic transactions entered into by purely private parties, rather than obligations involving the State itself. The Framers fully recognized that nothing would so jeopardize the legitimacy of a system of government that relies upon the ebbs and flows of politics to 'clean out the rascals' than the possibility that those same rascals might perpetuate their policies simply by locking them into binding contracts. [But Contract] Clause challenges [are] to be resolved by according unusual deference to the lawmaking authority of state and local governments. . . .

"I would not want to be read as suggesting that the States should blithely proceed down the path of repudiating their obligations, financial or otherwise. Their credibility in the credit market obviously is highly dependent on exercising their vast lawmaking powers with self-restraint and [discipline.] [But the] role to be played by the Constitution is at most a limited one. [For] this Court should have learned long ago that the Constitution — be it through the Contract or Due Process Clause — can actively intrude into such economic and policy matters only if my Brethren are prepared to bear enormous institutional and social costs. Because I consider the potential dangers of such judicial interference to be intolerable, I dissent."

ALLIED STRUCTURAL STEEL CO. v. SPANNAUS, 438 U.S. 234 (1978): Allied Structural Steel Co. maintained an office in Illinois with thirty employees. The company operated a general pension plan under which it retained unrestricted rights (1) to amend the plan in whole or in part and (2) to terminate the plan and to distribute the assets at any time and for any reason. Employees were thus entitled to benefits if they worked until reaching age sixty-five and if the company remained in business and elected to continue the plan. The Minnesota legislature enacted a Private Pension Benefits Protection Act, under which employers would be subject to a "pension funding charge" if they terminated the plan or closed a Minnesota office. The charge was assessed if pension funds did not cover full pensions for at least ten years. Under the act, employers must satisfy the deficiency by purchasing deferred annuities, payable to employees at their normal retirement age. Periods of employment prior to the effective date of the act were to be included in the ten-year employment criterion. Allied Structural Steel attempted to terminate its operation in Minnesota; the state informed the company that it owed a pension funding charge of $185,000; and the company brought suit, claiming that the act unconstitutionally impaired its contractual obligations.

The Court, in an opinion by Justice Stewart, responded:

"There can be no question of the impact of the Minnesota Private Pension Benefits Protection Act upon the company's contractual relationships with its employees. The Act substantially altered those relationships by superimposing pension obligations upon the company conspicuously beyond those that it had voluntarily agreed to undertake. [The] Contract Clause remains part of the Constitution. It is not a dead letter. . . .

"[It] is to be accepted as a commonplace that the Contract Clause does not operate to obliterate the police power of the States. [But if] the Contract Clause is to retain any meaning at all, [it] must be understood to impose *some* limits upon the power of a State to abridge existing contractual relationships, even in the exercise of its otherwise legitimate police power. . . .

"In applying these principles to the present case, the first inquiry must be whether the state law has, in fact, operated as a substantial impairment of a contractual relationship. The severity of the impairment measures the height of the hurdle the state legislation must clear. Minimal alteration of contractual obligations may end the inquiry at its first stage. Severe impairment, on the other hand, will push the inquiry to a careful examination of the nature and purpose of the state legislation.

"The severity of an impairment of contractual obligations can be measured by the factors that reflect the high value the Framers placed on the protection of private contracts. Contracts enable individuals to order their personal and business affairs according to their particular needs and interests. Once arranged, those rights and obligations are binding under the law, and the parties are entitled to rely on them.

"Here, the company's contracts of employment with its employees included as a fringe benefit or additional form of compensation, the pension plan. The company's maximum obligation was to set aside each year an amount based on the plan's requirements for vesting. [The] company [had] no reason to anticipate that its employees' pension rights could become vested except in accordance with the terms of the plan. It relied heavily, and reasonably, on this legitimate contractual expectation in calculating its annual contributions to the pension fund.

"The effect of Minnesota's Private Pension Benefits Protection Act on this contractual obligation was severe. The company was required in 1974 to have made its contributions throughout the pre-1974 life of its plan as if employees' pension rights had vested after 10 years, instead of vesting in accord with the terms of the plan. Thus a basic term of the pension contract — one on which the company had relied for 10 years — was substantially modified. The result was that, although the company's past contributions were adequate when made, they were not adequate when computed under the 10-year statutory vesting requirement. The Act thus forced a current recalculation of the past 10 years' contributions based on the new, unanticipated 10-year vesting requirement.

"[Moreover,] the retroactive state-imposed vesting requirement was applied only to those employers who terminated their pension plans or who, like the company, closed their Minnesota offices. The company was thus forced to make all the retroactive changes in its contractual obligations at one time. By simply proceeding to close its office in Minnesota, a move that had been planned before the passage of the Act, the company was assessed an immediate pension funding charge of approximately $185,000.

"Thus, the statute in question here nullifies express terms of the company's contractual obligations and imposes a completely unexpected liability in potentially disabling amounts. [Yet] there is no showing in the record before us that this severe disruption of contractual expectations was necessary to meet an important general social problem. The presumption favoring 'legislative judgment as to the necessity and reasonableness of a particular measure,' simply cannot stand in this case. . . .

"[The statute] clearly has an extremely narrow focus. It applies only to private employers who have at least 100 employees, at least one of whom works in

Minnesota, and who have established voluntary private pension plans, qualified under §401 of the Internal Revenue Code. And it applies only when such an employer closes his Minnesota office or terminates his pension plan. Thus, this law can hardly be characterized, like the law at issue in the *Blaisdell* case, as one enacted to protect a broad societal interest rather than a narrow class.

"Moreover, in at least one other important respect the Act does not resemble the mortgage moratorium legislation whose constitutionality was upheld in the *Blaisdell* case. This legislation, imposing a sudden, totally unanticipated, and substantial retroactive obligation upon the company to its employees, was not enacted to deal with a situation remotely approaching the broad and desperate emergency economic conditions of the early 1930's — conditions of which the Court in *Blaisdell* took judicial notice.

"[This] Minnesota law simply does not possess the attributes of those state laws that in the past have survived challenge under the Contract Clause of the Constitution. [It] did not effect simply a temporary alteration of the contractual relationships of those within its [coverage. And] its narrow aim was leveled, not at every Minnesota employer, not even at every Minnesota employer who left the State, but only at those who had in the past been sufficiently enlightened as voluntarily to agree to establish pension plans for their employees. . . .

"[If] the Contract Clause means anything at all, it means that Minnesota could not constitutionally do what it tried to do to the company in this case."

Justice Brennan, joined by Justices White and Marshall dissented.

"[The] Contract Clause has not [been] applied to state legislation that, while creating new duties, in nowise diminished the efficacy of any contractual obligation owed the constitutional claimant. [The Act] was designed to remedy a serious social problem arising from the operation of private pension plans. [The] impetus for the law must have been a legislative belief [that] private pension plans often were grossly unfair to covered employees. Not only would employers often neglect to furnish their employees with adequate information concerning their rights under the plans, leading to erroneous expectations, but also because employers often failed to make contributions to the pension funds large enough adequately to fund their plans, employees often ultimately received only a small amount of those benefits they reasonably anticipated. Acting against this background, Minnesota [adopted] the Act to remedy, inter alia, what was viewed as a related serious social problem: the frustration of expectation interests that can occur when an employer closed a single plant and terminates the employees who work there. . . .

"I emphasize, contrary to the repeated protestations of the Court, that the Act does not impose 'sudden and unanticipated' burdens. The features of the Act involved in this case come into play only when an employer, after the effective date of the Act, closes a plant. The existence of the Act's duties — which are similar to a legislatively imposed requirement of severance pay measured by the length of the discharged employees' service — is simply one of a number of factors that the employer considers in making the business decision whether to close a plant and terminate the employees who work there. . . .

"The Act does not relieve either the employer or his employees of any existing contract obligation. Rather, the Act simply creates an additional, supplemental duty of the employer, no different in kind from myriad duties created by a wide variety of legislative measures which defeat settled expectations but which have nonetheless been sustained by this Court. For this reason, the Minnesota Act, in my view, does not implicate the Contract Clause in any way. . . .

"Historically, it is crystal clear that the Contract Clause was not intended to embody a broad constitutional policy of protecting all reliance interests grounded in private contracts. [The] Framers never contemplated that the Clause would limit the legislative power of States to enact laws creating duties that might burden some individuals in order to benefit others.

"The terms of the Contract Clause negate any basis for its interpretation as protecting all contract-based expectations from unjustifiable interference. [It] is nothing less than an abuse of the English language to interpret, as does the Court, the term 'impairing' as including laws which create new duties.

"More fundamentally, the Court's distortion of the meaning of the Contract Clause creates anomalies of its own and threatens to undermine the jurisprudence of property rights developed over the last 40 years. The Contract Clause, of course, is but one of several clauses in the Constitution that protect existing economic values from governmental interference. [Decisions] over the past 50 years have developed a coherent, unified interpretation of all the constitutional provisions that may protect economic expectations and these decisions have recognized a broad latitude in States to effect even severe interference with existing economic values when reasonably necessary to promote the general welfare. [At] the same time the prohibition of the Contract Clause, consistently with its wording and historic purposes, has been limited in application to state laws that diluted, with utter indifference to the legitimate interests of the beneficiary of a contract duty, the existing contract [obligation.] . . .

"[Under] the Court's opinion, any law that may be characterized as 'superimposing' new obligations on those provided for by contract is to be regarded as creating 'sudden, substantial, and unanticipated burdens' and then to be subjected to the most exacting scrutiny. The validity of such a law will turn upon whether judges see it as a law that deals with a generalized social problem, whether it is temporary (as few will be) or permanent, whether it operates in an area previously subject to regulation, and, finally, whether its duties apply to a broad class of persons. [The] necessary consequence of the extreme malleability of these rather vague criteria is to vest judges with broad subjective discretion to protect property interests that happen to appeal to them.

"To permit this level of scrutiny of laws that interfere with contract-based expectations is an anomaly. There is nothing sacrosanct about expectations rooted in contract that justify according them a constitutional immunity denied other property rights. Laws that interfere with settled expectations created by state property law (and which impose severe economic burdens) are uniformly held constitutional where reasonably related to the promotion of the general welfare."

Note: United States Trust, Spannaus, and the Possible Revival of the Contracts Clause

1. *"Heightened scrutiny" for a state's abrogation of its own contracts.* Two features of *United States Trust* are noteworthy: first, the willingness to adopt "heightened scrutiny" for a state's abrogation of its own contracts; second, the

willingness to invalidate a state law under the contracts clause. The first element is in one sense familiar in constitutional law. The Court frequently adopts "heightened scrutiny" — in the form of a careful examination of means/ends connections and a search for less restrictive alternatives — when there is special reason for suspicion that an impermissible motivation is at work.

Was there such a special reason in *United States Trust?* Does the fact that a state abrogates a contract to which it is a party give reason to believe that a state's self-interest, rather than some public good, is at stake? Is there a difference between a state's interest and some public good? If so, what is the impermissible end that the Court thought might be at work when a state abrogates its own contract? Note also the possibility that the Court was concerned with effects as well as purpose — the special obligation of government not to break its own promises.

Consider the following view: Careful scrutiny is not properly applied in *United States Trust* because a state does not have an interest independent of that of its citizens. Hence there is no special reason for suspicion of impermissible motivation. When a state operates to help whites at the expense of blacks, or its own citizens at the expense of noncitizens, suspicion is properly triggered; but that analysis is inapplicable to the *United States Trust* situation. For discussion, see Note, Takings Law and the Contract Clause: A Takings Law Approach to Legislative Modification of Public Contracts, 36 Stan. L. Rev. 1447 (1984); Note, A Process-Oriented Approach to the Contract Clause, 89 Yale L.J. 1623 (1980).

2. *The police power and means/ends connections under the contracts clause.* In *United States Trust*, why did the Court conclude that the means/ends connection was too weak? Was *Spannaus* a stronger or weaker case in this regard? Was the end in *Spannaus* any more impermissible than that in *Blaisdell?* Note also that in *Spannaus*, the state was not abrogating its own contract. Why did the Court reject the argument that the pension vesting provision was a reasonable exercise of the police power? Consider L. Tribe, American Constitutional Law 1979 Supplement, at 44-48, criticizing the Court for "mechanically applying the language of the Contract Clause in a manner reminiscent of the *Lochner* era. [The] Court, while avoiding the words 'strict scrutiny,' seems to have applied just such to the Minnesota Act." Is the reference to the *Lochner* era justifiable? Construct an argument that *Spannaus* is inconsistent with the views expressed in *Blaisdell*.

3. *Subsequent developments. United States Trust* and *Spannaus* suggested that the Court would revive the contracts clause as a substantive constraint on legislation. But more recently the Court has returned to its previous, more deferential approach. Consider in this regard Energy Reserves Group v. Kansas Power & Light, 459 U.S. 400 (1983). The contract at issue contained a price escalator clause that provided that if a governmental authority fixes a price for natural gas that is higher than the price specified in the contract, the contract price would be increased to that level. The Kansas statute at issue provided that the increase produced by a federal statute could not be taken into account in determining the contract price. The Energy Resources Group attacked the statute on the ground that it impaired the contractual obligation allowing for increase in the price. In an opinion by Justice Blackmun, the Court responded:

> The threshold inquiry is "whether the state law has, in fact, operated as a substantial impairment of contractual relationship." The severity of the impairment is said

to increase the level of scrutiny to which the legislation will be subjected. [In] determining the extent of the impairment, we are to consider whether the industry the complaining party has entered has been regulated in the past. . . .

If the state regulation constitutes a substantial impairment, the State, in justification, must have a significant and legitimate public purpose behind the regulation, such as the remedying of a broad and general social or economic problem. Furthermore, since *Blaisdell*, the Court has indicated that the public purpose need not be addressed to an emergency or temporary situation. One legitimate state interest is the elimination of unforeseen windfall profits. The requirement of a legitimate public purpose guarantees that the State is exercising its police power, rather than providing a benefit to special interests.

Once a legitimate public purpose has been identified, the next inquiry is whether the adjustment of the rights and responsibilities of contracting parties is based upon reasonable conditions and is of a character appropriate to the public purpose justifying the legislation's adoption. Unless the state is itself a contracting party, "as is customary in reviewing economic and social regulation," [courts] properly defer to legislative judgment as to the necessity and reasonableness of a particular measure.

The Court upheld the statute. First, it suggested that there was no substantial impairment: "Significant here is the fact that the parties are operating in a heavily regulated industry." Thus "ERG knew its contractual rights were subject to alteration by state price regulation. Price regulation existed and was foreseeable as the type of law that would alter contract obligations."

The Court also concluded that any contractual impairment "rests on, and is prompted by, significant and legitimate state interests." The Court referred to two such interests. The first was the protection of consumers from the escalation of prices caused by deregulation. "The State could reasonably find that higher gas prices have caused and will cause hardship among those who use gas heat but must exist on limited fixed incomes." The second interest was "correcting the imbalance between the interstate and intrastate markets by permitting intrastate prices to rise only to the [interstate] level." Justice Powell, joined by the Chief Justice and Justice Rehnquist, concurred, agreeing that there had been no substantial impairment but refusing to reach the question whether any impairment had in the circumstances been justified.

Consider also Exxon Corp. v. Eagerton, 461 U.S. — , 103 S. Ct. 2296 (1983), which involved a state statute prohibiting producers of oil and gas from passing on to consumers the costs of any increase in a state's severance tax. The Court replied that the contracts clause did not prohibit "a generally applicable rule of conduct designed to advance 'broad social interest,' protecting consumers from excessive prices." Do *Energy Reserves* and *Exxon* implicitly overrule *Spannaus?*

4. *Concluding thoughts.* Consider the following evaluation: Modern review under the contract clause is substantially identical to modern rationality review under the due process and equal protection clauses. In all three contexts, the Court engages in the same inquiry, identifying the legitimate state interests and requiring a rough relation between the legitimate state interests and the measure under review. But the class of legitimate state interests is extremely broad; the Court has permitted any justification other than raw political power (the "special interest" problem referred to in the *Energy Reserves* case). Moreover, the fit between the legitimate interest and the measure under review need not be very close.

Is this an accurate picture of the law? Is it troublesome that the Court has adopted the same test in all three areas — even though the contracts clause looks like an explicit limitation of contractual impairments? Is the contracts clause now superfluous? Note in addition the implications, if any, of modern contracts clause jurisprudence for theories of the judicial role. What have been the *sources* of the decisions? What constraints have text and history imposed on the Court?

In recent years, there has been some effort, rooted in principles of neoclassical economics and/or libertarian notions of private autonomy, to revive the contracts clause as a constraint on government action. See, e.g., Epstein, Toward a Revitalization of the Contracts Clause, 51 U. Chi. L. Rev. 703 (1984). Would such a revival be desirable? Because of ordinary principles of constitutional interpretation? Because of the values promoted by the clause? Consider whether the principles underlying the *Blaisdell* decision are a persuasive answer to efforts at revival.

B. THE EMINENT DOMAIN CLAUSE

The eminent domain clause provides "nor shall private property be taken for public use, without just compensation." The clause has two prohibitions: (1) all takings must be for public use, and (2) even takings that are for public use must be accompanied by compensation. Does the takings clause qualify as an "explicit" provision? Consider here, as with the contracts clause, whether and how interpretation of the eminent domain clause differs from interpretation of the first amendment on the one hand and treatment of "implied" fundamental rights on the other.

What is the evil at which the eminent domain clause is aimed? The history of the eminent domain clause is quite sparse, but the answer involves at least some sorts of redistribution of resources. The clause reflects a judgment that if government is seeking to produce some public benefit (the public use requirement), it is appropriate that the payment come from the public at large — taxpayers — rather than from identifiable individuals. The compensation requirement operates as an insurance to that effect. Note, in addition, that compensation tends to reduce the likelihood that a transfer has occurred merely to benefit A at the expense of B. Public willingness to pay for the transfer suggests that some general public good is at work. We begin with the logically prior public use requirement.

HAWAII HOUSING AUTHORITY v. MIDKIFF, — U.S. — , 104 S. Ct. 2321 (1984): This case involved an effort to transfer ownership of property in Hawaii. Justice O'Connor, in her opinion for a unanimous Court, noted that in Hawaii, land had traditionally been concentrated in the hands of few people, and then summarized the facts as follows:

"[The] Land Reform Act of 1967 (Act) [created] a mechanism for condemning residential tracts and for transferring ownership of the condemned fees simple to existing lessees. By condemning the land in question, the Hawaii Legislature intended to make the land sales involuntary, thereby making the federal tax consequences less severe while still facilitating the redistribution of fees simple.

"Under the Act's condemnation scheme, tenants living on single-family residential lots [are] entitled to ask the Hawaii Housing Authority (HHA) to condemn the property on which they live.

"When 25 eligible tenants, or tenants on half the lots in the tract, whichever is less, file appropriate applications, the Act authorizes HHA to hold a public hearing to determine whether acquisition by the State [will] 'effectuate the public purposes' of the Act. If HHA finds that these public purposes will be served, it is authorized to [acquire], at prices set either by condemnation trial or by negotiation between lessors and lessees, the former fee owners' full 'right, title, and interest' in the land. . . .

"After compensation has been set, HHA may sell the land titles to tenants who have applied for fee simple [ownership]. HHA does not sell [or] lease the lot or sell it to someone else, provided that public notice has been given."

The Court upheld the statute against a claim that no "public use" was involved:

"The starting point for our analysis of the Act's constitutionality is the Court's decision in Berman v. Parker, 348 U.S. 26 (1954). In Berman, the Court held constitutional the District of Columbia Redevelopment Act of 1945. That Act provided both for the comprehensive use of the eminent domain power to redevelop slum areas and for the possible sale or lease of the condemned lands to private interests. In discussing whether the takings authorized by that Act were for a 'public use,' [the] Court stated 'We deal [with] what traditionally has been known as the police power. An attempt to define its reach or trace its outer limits is fruitless, for each case must turn on its own facts. The definition is essentially the product of legislative determinations addressed to the purposes of government, purposes neither abstractly nor historically capable of complete definition. Subject to specific constitutional limitations, when the legislature has spoken, the public interest has been declared in terms well-nigh conclusive. In such cases the legislature, not the judiciary, is the main guardian of the public needs to be served by social legislation.' . . .

"There is, of course, a role for courts to play in reviewing a legislature's judgment of what constitutes a public use, even when the eminent domain power is equated with the police power. But the Court in Berman made clear that it is 'an extremely narrow' one. . . .

"To be sure, the Court's cases have repeatedly stated that 'one person's property may not be taken for the benefit of another private person without a justifying public purpose, even though compensation be paid.' [But] where the exercise of the eminent domain power is rationally related to a conceivable public purpose, the Court has never held a compensated taking to be proscribed by the [clause]. . . .

"On this basis, we have no trouble concluding that the Hawaii Act is constitutional. The people of Hawaii have attempted [to] reduce the perceived social and economic evils of a land [oligopoly]. The land oligopoly has, according to the Hawaii Legislature, created artificial deterrents to the normal functioning of the State's residential land market and forced thousands of individual homeowners to lease, rather than buy, the land underneath their homes. Regulating oligopoly and the evils associated with it is a classic exercise of a State's police powers. [We] cannot disapprove of Hawaii's exercise of this power.

"Nor can we condemn as irrational the Act's approach to correcting the land oligopoly problem. The Act presumes that when a sufficiently large number of persons declare that they are willing but unable to buy lots at fair prices the land market is malfunctioning. When such a malfunction is signalled, the Act authorizes HHA to condemn lots in the relevant tract. The Act limits the number of lots any one tenant can purchase and authorizes HHA to use public funds to ensure that the market dilution goals will be achieved. This is a comprehensive and rational approach to identifying and correcting market failure. [When] the legislature's purpose is legitimate and its means are not irrational, our cases make clear that empirical debates over the wisdom of takings — no less than debates over the wisdom of other kinds of socioeconomic legislation — are not to be carried out in the federal courts. Redistribution of fees simple to correct deficiencies in the market determined by the state legislature to be attributable to land oligopoly is a rational exercise of the eminent domain power. Therefore, the Hawaii statute must pass the scrutiny of the Public Use Clause. . . .

"[The] mere fact that property taken outright by eminent domain is transferred in the first instance to private beneficiaries does not condemn that taking as having only a private purpose. The Court long ago rejected any literal requirement that condemned property be put into use for the general public. [A] purely private taking could not withstand the scrutiny of the public use requirement; it would serve no legitimate purpose of government and would thus be void. But no purely private taking is involved in this case."

Note: The Public Use Requirement and the Takings Clause

1. *In general.* The eminent domain clause requires compensation for "takings"; but even with compensation, a taking is prohibited if it is not for a "public use." The "public use" requirement originally operated as a serious independent constraint on government action. For a long period, the requirement was understood to mean that if property was to be taken, it was necessary that it be used by the public; the fact that the taking was "beneficial" was not enough. Eventually, however, courts concluded that a wide range of uses could serve the public even if the public did not in fact have possession. Important examples here are the Mill Acts, which permitted riparian owners to erect and maintain dams which flooded neighboring property. For discussion, see M. Horwitz, The Transformation of American Law, 1780-1860, at 47-53 (1977). Thereafter, so many exceptions were built into the general rule of "use by the public" that the rule itself was abandoned. For discussion, see Dunham, *Griggs v. Alleghany County* in Perspective: Thirty Years of Supreme Court Expropriation Law, 1962 Supreme Court Review 63, 65-71; Note, The Public Use Limitation on Eminent Domain: An Advance Requiem, 58 Yale L.J. 599 (1949).

The decline in the constraints imposed by the public use requirement is parallel to the expansion in the "police power" that has played such an important role in constitutional doctrine under the due process clause after the *Lochner* decision, see infra, and under the contracts clause, see supra. Is it proper for the "public use" requirement to change over time? How does one tell what a "public use" consists of? See R. Epstein, Takings: Private Property and the Law of Eminent Domain (1985).

2. *Public use after* Midkiff. The public use requirement is designed to ensure against what might be called "naked" wealth transfers — takings from A in order

to benefit *B*, supported by no "public" end, and only by a preference for *B*, or by *B*'s political power. Cf. Justice Chase's position in Calder v. Bull, Chapter 1, supra, also complaining about a taking from *A* to benefit *B*.

In the *Midkiff* case, the Court uses two devices to justify a deferential judicial posture in guarding against such transfers. The first involves scrutiny of ends. The Court's broad understanding of public use means that many ends of government will be "public" and thus satisfy constitutional requirements. The second involves scrutiny of means. Here the Court demands very little, requiring only a loose means/ends connection. Was the Court correct in either or both of these approaches? Consider the possibility that, in concert, these devices mean that the "public use" requirement operates as no limitation on government action.

Consider also Epstein, supra, at 181:

> The rational basis test again uses false arguments to negate explicit constitutional guarantees. No antitrust expert thinks "oligopoly" because there are "only" seventy or twenty-two or eighteen landowners in a given market. Why then allow the legislature to so find? [The] case therefore is straightforward. The statute allows tenants as a class to take the reversion from the landlord. These takings do not become something else simply because a large number of tenants is involved. In no individual case is the property used for a pure public good, and in none is there universal right of access. [Land] reform thus runs afoul of the public use limitation, which deserves more respectful treatment than it receives today.

Should "public use" be defined by reference to principles of economic efficiency? Might redistribution be supportable as "public," if it is responsive to some widely held view of what is fair and just? Consider the discussion of the *Lochner* period, Chapter 6, Section D, supra.

Evaluate, after *Midkiff*, Poletown Neighborhood Council v. City of Detroit, 410 Mich. 616, 304 N.W.2d 455 (1981), in which the city of Detroit condemned a neighborhood in order to permit General Motors to build a plant on the land. Was the taking for public use? If a General Motors plant was condemned and transferred for use by the community, would there also be a public use? Is it troublesome if the answer to both questions is yes?

Pennsylvania Coal Co. v. Mahon

260 U.S. 393 (1922)

MR. JUSTICE HOLMES delivered the opinion of the Court.

This is a bill in equity brought by the [plaintiffs] to prevent the Pennsylvania Coal Company from mining under their property in such way as to remove the supports and cause a subsidence of the surface and of their house. The bill sets out a deed executed by the Coal Company in 1878, under which the plaintiffs claim. The deed conveys the surface, but in express terms reserves the right to remove all the coal under the same, and the grantee takes the premises with the risk, and waives all claim for damages that may arise from mining out the coal. But the plaintiffs say that whatever may have been the Coal Company's rights, they were taken away by an Act of Pennsylvania, [commonly] known there as the Kohler Act. . . .

The statute forbids the mining of anthracite coal in such way as to cause the subsidence of, among other things, any structure used as a human habitation, with certain exceptions, including among them land where the surface is owned by the owner of the underlying coal and is distant more than one hundred and fifty feet from any improved property belonging to any other person. As applied to this case the statute is admitted to destroy previously existing rights of property and contract. The question is whether the police power can be stretched so far.

Government hardly could go on if to some extent values incident to property could not be diminished without paying for every such change in the general law. As long recognized, some values are enjoyed under an implied limitation and must yield to the police power. But obviously the implied limitation must have its limits, or the contract and due process clauses are gone. One fact for consideration in determining such limits is the extent of the diminution. When it reaches a certain magnitude, in most if not in all cases there must be an exercise of eminent domain and compensation to sustain the act. So the question depends upon the particular facts. The greatest weight is given to the judgment of the legislature, but it always is open to interested parties to contend that the legislature has gone beyond its constitutional power. . . .

[It] is our opinion that the act cannot be sustained as an exercise of the police power, so far as it affects the mining of coal under streets or cities in places where the right to mine such coal has been reserved. [What] makes the right to mine coal valuable is that it can be exercised with profit. To make it commercially impracticable to mine certain coal has very nearly the same effect for constitutional purposes as appropriating or destroying it. This we think that we are warranted in assuming that the statute does. . . .

The rights of the public in a street purchased or laid out by eminent domain are those that it has paid for. If in any case its representatives have been so short sighted as to acquire only surface rights without the right of support, we see no more authority for supplying the latter without compensation than there was for taking the right of way in the first place and refusing to pay for it because the public wanted it very much. The protection of private property in the Fifth Amendment presupposes that it is wanted for public use, but provides that it shall not be taken for such use without compensation. [When] this seemingly absolute protection is found to be qualified by the police power, the natural tendency of human nature is to extend the qualification more and more until at last private property disappears. But that cannot be accomplished in this way under the Constitution of the United States.

The general rule at least is, that while property may be regulated to a certain extent, if regulation goes too far it will be recognized as a taking. [In] general it is not plain that a man's misfortunes or necessities will justify his shifting the damages to his neighbor's shoulders. We are in danger of forgetting that a strong public desire to improve the public condition is not enough to warrant achieving the desire by a shorter cut than the constitutional way of paying for the change. As we already have said, this is a question of degree — and therefore cannot be disposed of by general propositions.

[We] assume, of course, that the statute was passed upon the conviction that an exigency existed that would warrant it, and we assume that an exigency exists that would warrant the exercise of eminent domain. But the question at bottom is upon whom the loss of the changes desired should fall. So far as private persons or communities have seen fit to take the risk of acquiring only surface rights, we cannot see that the fact that their risk has become a danger warrants the giving to them greater rights than they bought. . . .

Decree reversed.

Mr. Justice Brandeis, dissenting. . . .

[Coal] in place is land; and the right of the owner to use his land is not absolute. He may not so use it as to create a public nuisance; and uses, once harmless, may, owing to changed conditions, seriously threaten the public welfare. Whenever they do, the legislature has power to prohibit such uses without paying compensation; and the power to prohibit extends alike to the manner, the character and the purpose of the use. Are we justified in declaring that the Legislature of Pennsylvania has, in restricting the right to mine anthracite, exercised this power so arbitrarily as to violate the Fourteenth Amendment?

Every restriction upon the use of property imposed in the exercise of the police power deprives the owner of some right theretofore enjoyed, and is, in that sense, an abridgment by the State of rights in property without making compensation. But restriction imposed to protect the public health, safety or morals from dangers threatened is not a taking. The restriction here in question is merely the prohibition of a noxious use. The property so restricted remains in the possession of its owner. The state does not appropriate it or make any use of it. The State merely prevents the owner from making a use which interferes with paramount rights of the public. Whenever the use prohibited ceases to be noxious, — as it may because of further change in local or social conditions, — the restriction will have to be removed and the owner will again be free to enjoy his property as heretofore.

The restriction upon the use of this property cannot, of course, be lawfully imposed, unless its purpose is to protect the public. But the purpose of a restriction does not cease to be public, because incidentally some private persons may thereby receive gratuitously valuable special benefits. [To] keep coal in place is surely an appropriate means of preventing subsidence of the surface; and ordinarily it is the only available means. Restriction upon use does not become inappropriate as a means, merely because it deprives the owner of the only use to which the property can then be profitably put. [Nor] is a restriction imposed through exercise of the police power inappropriate as a means, merely because the same end might be effected through exercise of the power of eminent domain, or otherwise at public expense. Every restriction upon the height of buildings might be secured through acquiring by eminent domain the right of each owner to build above the limiting height; but it is settled that the State need not resort to that power. . . .

[If] by mining anthracite coal the owner would necessarily unloose poisonous gasses, I suppose no one would doubt the power of the State to prevent the mining, without buying his coal fields. And why may not the State, likewise, without paying compensation, prohibit one from digging so deep or excavating so near the surface, as to expose the community to like dangers? . . .

It is said that one fact for consideration in determining whether the limits of the police power have been exceeded is the extent of the resulting diminution in value; and that here the restriction destroys existing rights of property and contract. But values are relative. [For] aught that appears the value of the coal kept in place by the restriction may be negligible as compared with the value of the whole property, or even as compared with that part of it which is represented by the coal remaining in place and which may be extracted despite the statute. [The] defendant has failed to adduce any evidence from which it appears that to restrict its mining operations was an unreasonable exercise of the police power. Where the surface and the coal belong to the same person, self-interest would ordinarily prevent mining to such an extent as to cause a subsidence. It was, doubtless, for this reason that the legislature, estimating the degrees of danger, deemed statutory restriction unnecessary for the public safety under such conditions.

A prohibition of mining which causes subsidence of [structures] and facilities is obviously enacted for a public purpose. [Yet] it is said that these provisions of the act cannot be sustained as an exercise of the police power where the right to mine such coal has been reserved. The conclusion seems to rest upon the assumption that in order to justify such exercise of the police power there must be "an average reciprocity of advantage" as between the owner of the property restricted and the rest of the community; and that here such reciprocity is absent. Reciprocity of advantage is an important consideration, and may even be an essential, where the State's power is exercised for the purpose of conferring benefits upon the property of a neighborhood. [But] where the police power is exercised, not to confer benefits upon property owners, but to protect the public from detriment and danger, there is, in my opinion, no room for considering reciprocity of advantage.

Miller v. Schoene

276 U.S. 272 (1928)

MR. JUSTICE STONE delivered the opinion of the Court.

Acting under the Cedar Rust Act of Virginia, [the] state entomologist ordered the plaintiffs in error to cut down a large number of ornamental red cedar trees growing on their property, as a means of preventing the communication of a rust or plant disease with which they were infected to the apple orchards in the vicinity. The plaintiffs in error appealed from the order to the Circuit Court of Shenandoah county which, after a hearing and a consideration of evidence, affirmed the order and allowed to plaintiffs in error $100 to cover the expense of removal of the cedars. Neither the judgment of the court nor the statute as interpreted allows compensation for the value of the standing cedars or the decrease in the market value of the realty caused by their destruction whether considered as ornamental trees or otherwise. . . .

[On] appeal the Supreme Court of Appeals of Virginia affirmed the judgment. [Cedar] rust is an infectious plant disease in the form of a fungoid organism which is destructive of the fruit and foliage of the apple, but without effect on the value of the cedar. Its life cycle has two phases which are passed alternately as a growth on red cedar and on apple trees. It is communicated by spores from one to the other over a radius of at least two miles. It appears not to be communicable between trees of the same species but only from one species to the other, and other plants seem not to be appreciably affected by it. The only practicable method of controlling the disease and protecting apple trees from its ravages is the destruction of all red cedar trees, subject to the infection, located within two miles of apple orchards.

The red cedar, aside from its ornamental use, has occasional use and value as lumber. It is indigenous to Virginia, is not cultivated or dealt in commercially on any substantial scale, and its value throughout the state is shown to be small as compared with that of the apple orchards of the state. Apple growing is one of the principal agricultural pursuits in Virginia. The apple is used there and exported in large quantities. Many millions of dollars are invested in the orchards, which furnish employment for a large portion of the population, and have induced the development of attendant railroad and cold storage facilities.

On the evidence we may accept the conclusion of the Supreme Court of Appeals that the state was under the necessity of making a choice between the preservation of one class of property and that of the other wherever both existed in dangerous proximity. It would have been none the less a choice if, instead of enacting the present statute, the state, by doing nothing, had permitted serious injury to the apple orchards within its borders to go on unchecked. When forced to such a choice the state does not exceed its constitutional powers by deciding upon the destruction of one class of property in order to save another which, in the judgment of the legislature, is of greater value to the public. It will not do to say that the case is merely one of a conflict of two private interests and that the misfortune of apple growers may not be shifted to cedar owners by ordering the destruction of their property; for it is obvious that there may be, and that here there is, a preponderant public concern in the preservation of the one interest over the other. [Where] the public interest is involved preferment of that interest over the property interest of the individual, to the extent even of its destruction, is one of the distinguishing characteristics of every exercise of the police power which affects property. . . .

We need not weigh with nicety the question whether the infected cedars constitute a nuisance according to the common law; or whether they may be so declared by statute. For where, as here, the choice is unavoidable, we cannot say that its exercise, controlled by considerations of social policy which are not unreasonable, involves any denial of due process.

[Reversed.]

Penn Central Transportation Co. v. New York City
438 U.S. 104 (1978)

Mr. Justice Brennan delivered the opinion of the Court.

The question presented is whether a city may, as part of a comprehensive program to preserve historical landmarks and historic districts, place restrictions on the development of individual historic landmarks — in addition to those imposed by applicable zoning ordinances — without effecting a "taking" requiring the payment of "just compensation." Specifically, we must decide whether the application of New York City's Landmarks Preservation Law to the parcel of land occupied by Grand Central Terminal has "taken" its owners' property in violation of the Fifth and Fourteenth Amendments.

Over the past 50 years, all 50 States and over 500 municipalities have enacted laws to encourage or require the preservation of buildings and areas with historic or aesthetic importance. These nationwide legislative efforts have been precipitated by two concerns. The first is recognition that, in recent years, large numbers of historic structures, landmarks, and areas have been destroyed without adequate consideration of either the values represented therein or the possibility of preserving the destroyed properties for use in economically productive ways. The second is a widely shared belief that structures with special historic, cultural, or architectural significance enhance the quality of life for all. Not only do these buildings and their workmanship represent the lessons of the past and embody precious features of our heritage, they serve as examples of quality for today. . . .

New York City [adopted] its Landmarks Preservation Law in 1965. The city acted from the conviction that "the standing of [New York City] as a world-wide tourist center and world capital of business, culture and government" would be threatened if legislation were not enacted to protect historic landmarks and neighborhoods from precipitate decisions to destroy or fundamentally alter their character. . . .

The New York City law is typical of many urban landmark laws in that its primary method of achieving its goals is not by acquisitions of historical properties, but rather by involving public entities in land-use decisions affecting these properties and providing services, standards, controls, and incentives that will encourage preservation by private owners and users. While the law does place special restrictions on landmark properties as a necessary feature to the attainment of its larger objectives, the major theme of the law is to ensure the owners of any such properties both a "reasonable return" on their investments and maximum latitude to use their parcels for purposes not inconsistent with the preservation goals.

[The Court noted that the law was administered by the Landmarks Preservation Commission, which identified specially important properties as designated "landmarks" and "historic districts."]

[Final] designation as a landmark results in restrictions upon the property owner's options concerning use of the landmark site. First, the law imposes a duty upon the owner to keep the exterior features of the building "in good repair" to assure that the law's objectives not be defeated by the landmark's falling into a state of irremediable disrepair. [Second,] the Commission must approve in advance any proposal to alter the exterior architectural features of the landmark or to construct any exterior improvement on the landmark site, thus ensuring that decisions concerning construction on the landmark site are made with due consideration of both the public interest in the maintenance of the structure and the landowner's interest in use of the property. . . .

In the event an owner wishes to alter a landmark site, [procedures] are available through which administrative approval may be obtained. . . .

Although the designation of a landmark and landmark site restricts the owner's control over the parcel, designation also enhances the economic position of the landmark owner in one significant respect. Under New York City's zoning laws, owners of real property who have not developed their property to the full extent permitted by the applicable zoning laws are allowed to transfer development rights to contiguous parcels on the same city block. . . .

This case involves the application of New York City's Landmarks Preservation Law to Grand Central Terminal (Terminal).

[The Court noted that the terminal is one of New York City's most famous buildings and that it had been designated as occupying a landmark site. Penn

Central submitted two plans to the Commission for construction of an office building atop the terminal. One plan called for a fifty-five-story office building; another called for tearing down some of its facade and constructing a fifty-three-story office building. The Commission denied permission to go forward with the plans. With respect to the second plan, the Commission observed, "To protect a Landmark, one does not tear it down." With respect to the first plan, the Commission referred primarily to the adverse effect of the proposed tower on the dramatic view of the terminal from Park Avenue South. "To balance a 55-story office tower above a flamboyant Beaux-Arts facade seems nothing more than an aesthetic joke. Quite simply, the tower would overwhelm the Terminal by its sheer mass."]

The [issue is whether] the restrictions imposed by New York City's law upon appellants' exploitation of the Terminal site effect a "taking" of appellants' property for a public use within the meaning of the Fifth Amendment. [The] question of what constitutes a "taking" for purposes of the Fifth Amendment has proved to be a problem of considerable difficulty. While this Court has recognized that the "Fifth Amendment's guarantee . . . [is] designed to bar Government from forcing some people alone to bear public burdens which, in all fairness and justice, should be borne by the public as a whole," Armstrong v. United States, 364 U.S. 40, 49 (1960), this Court, quite simply, has been unable to develop any "set formula" for determining when "justice and fairness" require that economic injuries caused by public action be compensated by the government, rather than remain disproportionately concentrated on a few persons. [Indeed,] we have frequently observed that whether a particular restriction will be rendered invalid by the government's failure to pay for any losses proximately caused by it depends largely "upon the particular circumstances [in that] case." United States v. Central Eureka Mining Co., 357 U.S. 155, 168 (1958). . . .

In engaging in these essentially ad hoc, factual inquiries, the Court's decisions have identified several factors that have particular significance. The economic impact of the regulation on the claimant and, particularly, the extent to which the regulation has interfered with distinct investment-backed expectations are, of course, relevant considerations. [So,] too, is the character of the governmental action. A "taking" may more readily be found when the interference with property can be characterized as a physical invasion by government, see, e.g., United States v. Causby, 328 U.S. 256 (1946), than when interference arises from some public program adjusting the benefits and burdens of economic life to promote the common good.

"Government hardly could go on if to some extent values incident to property could not be diminished without paying for every such change in the general law," [Mahon], and this Court has accordingly recognized, in a wide variety of contexts, that government may execute laws or programs that adversely affect recognized economic values. Exercises of the taxing power are one obvious example. A second are the decisions in which this Court has dismissed "taking" challenges on the ground that, while the challenged government action caused economic harm, it did not interfere with interests that were sufficiently bound up with the reasonable expectations of the claimant to constitute "property" for Fifth Amendment purposes. . . .

More importantly for the present case, in instances in which a state tribunal reasonably concluded that "the health, safety, morals, or general welfare" would be promoted by prohibiting particular contemplated uses of land, this Court has upheld land-use regulations that destroyed or adversely affected recognized real property interests. [Zoning] laws are, of course, the classic example, see Euclid v. Ambler Realty Co., 272 U.S. 365 (1926) (prohibition of industrial use). . . .

Zoning laws generally do not affect existing uses of real property, but "taking" challenges have also been held to be without merit in a wide variety of situations when the challenged governmental actions prohibited a beneficial use to which individual parcels had previously been devoted and thus caused substantial individualized harm. . . .

In contending that the New York City law has "taken" their property in violation of the Fifth and Fourteenth Amendments, appellants make a series of arguments, which [urge] that any substantial restriction imposed pursuant to a landmark law must be accompanied by just compensation if it is to be constitutional. Before considering these, we emphasize what is not in dispute. Because this Court has recognized, in a number of settings, that States and cities may enact land-use restrictions or controls to enhance the quality of life by preserving the character and desirable aesthetic features of a city, [appellants] do not contest that [the] restrictions imposed on its parcel are appropriate means of securing the purposes of the New York City law. [Appellants also] accept for present purposes both that the parcel of land occupied by Grand Central Terminal must, in its present state, be regarded as capable of earning a reasonable return, and that the transferable development rights afforded appellants by virtue of the Terminal's designation as a landmark are valuable, even if not as valuable as the rights to construct above the Terminal. . . .

[Appellants] first observe that the airspace above the Terminal is a valuable property interest. [They] urge that the Landmarks Law has deprived them of any gainful use of their "air rights" above the Terminal and that, irrespective of the value of the remainder of their parcel, the city has "taken" their right to this superjacent airspace, thus entitling them to "just compensation" measured by the fair market value of these air rights.

[The] submission that appellants may establish a "taking" simply by showing that they have been denied the ability to exploit a property interest that they heretofore had believed was available for development is quite simply untenable. ["Taking"] jurisprudence does not divide a single parcel into discrete segments and attempt to determine whether rights in a particular segment have been entirely abrogated. In deciding whether a particular governmental action has effected a taking, this Court focuses rather both on the character of the action and on the nature and extent of the interference with rights in the parcel as a whole — here, the city tax block designated as the "landmark site."

Secondly, appellants [argue] that [the law] effects a "taking" because its operation has significantly diminished the value of the Terminal site. Appellants concede that the decisions sustaining other land-use regulations, [reject] the proposition that diminution in property value, standing alone, can establish a "taking," [and] that the "taking" issue in these contexts is resolved by focusing on the uses the regulations permit. [Appellants,] moreover, also do not dispute that a showing of diminution in property value would not establish a "taking" if the restriction had been imposed as a result of historic-district legislation. [But] appellants argue that New York City's regulation of individual landmarks is fundamentally different from zoning or from historic-district legislation because the controls imposed by New York City's law apply only to individuals who own selected properties.

Stated baldly, appellants' position appears to be that the only means of ensuring that selected owners are not singled out to endure financial hardship for no reason is to hold that any restriction imposed on individual landmarks pursuant to the New York City scheme is a "taking" requiring the payment of "just compensation." Agreement with this argument would, of course, invalidate not just New York City's law, but all comparable landmark legislation in the Nation. . . .

[Contrary] to appellants' suggestions, landmark laws are not like discriminatory [zoning:] that is, a land-use decision which arbitrarily singles out a particular parcel for different, less favorable treatment than the neighboring ones. [In] contrast to discriminatory zoning, [the] New York City law embodies a comprehensive plan to preserve structures of historic or aesthetic interest wherever they might be found in the city, and [over] 400 landmarks and 31 historic districts have been designated pursuant to this plan.

Equally without merit is the related argument that the decision to designate a structure as a landmark "is inevitably arbitrary or at least subjective, because it is basically a matter of taste," [thus] unavoidably singling out individual landowners for disparate and unfair treatment. [A] landmark owner has a right to judicial review of any Commission decision, and, [there] is no basis whatsoever for a conclusion that courts will have any greater difficulty identifying arbitrary or discriminatory action in the context of landmark regulation than in the context of classic zoning or indeed in any other context.

Next, appellants observe that New York City's law differs from zoning laws and historic-district ordinances in that the Landmarks Law does not impose identical or similar restrictions on all structures located in particular physical communities. It follows, they argue, that New York City's law is inherently incapable of producing the fair and equitable distribution of benefits and burdens of governmental action [which] they maintain is a constitutional requirement if "just compensation" is not to be afforded. It is, of course, true that the Landmarks Law has a more severe impact on some landowners than on others, but that in itself does not mean that the law effects a "taking." Legislation designed to promote the general welfare commonly burdens some more than others.

In any event, appellants' repeated suggestions that they are solely burdened and unbenefited is factually inaccurate. This contention overlooks the fact that the New York City law applies to vast numbers of structures in the city in addition to the Terminal — all the structures contained in the 31 historic districts and over 400 individual landmarks, many of which are close to the Terminal. . . .

Appellants' final broad-based attack would have us treat the law as an instance, like that in United States v. Causby, [infra,] in which government, acting in an enterprise capacity, has appropriated part of their property for some strictly governmental purpose. [But the] Landmarks Law neither exploits appellants' parcel for city purposes nor facilitates nor arises from any entrepreneurial operations of the city.

[The] Landmarks Law's effect is simply to prohibit appellants or anyone else from occupying portions of the airspace above the Terminal, while permitting appellants to use the remainder of the parcel in a gainful fashion. . . .

[We] now must consider whether the interference with appellants' property is of such a magnitude that "there must be an exercise of eminent domain and compensation to sustain [it]." [*Mahon.*] [That] inquiry may be narrowed to the question of the severity of the impact of the law on appellants' parcel, and its resolution in turn requires a careful assessment of the impact of the regulation on the Terminal site. [The] New York City law does not interfere in any way with the present uses of the Terminal. Its designation as a landmark [contemplates] that appellants may continue to use the property precisely as it has been used for the past 65 years; as a railroad terminal containing office space and concessions. So the law does not interfere with what must be regarded as Penn Central's primary expectation concerning the use of the parcel [or its ability] to obtain a "reasonable return" on its investment.

Appellants, moreover, exaggerate the effect of the law on their ability to make use of the air rights above the Terminal. [First, nothing] the Commission has said or done suggests an intention to prohibit *any* construction above the Terminal.

[Second,] it is not literally accurate to say that they have been denied *all* use of even [pre-existing] air rights. [The] New York courts here supportably found that [the transferable development] rights afforded are valuable. While these rights may well not have constituted "just compensation" if a "taking" had occurred, the rights nevertheless undoubtedly mitigate whatever financial burdens the law has imposed on appellants and, for that reason, are to be taken into account in considering the impact of regulation.

On this record, we conclude that the application of New York City's Landmarks Law has not effected a "taking" of appellants' property. The restrictions imposed are substantially related to the promotion of the general welfare and not only permit reasonable beneficial use of the landmark site but also afford appellants opportunities further to enhance not only the Terminal site proper but also other properties.

Affirmed.

Mr. Justice Rehnquist, with whom The Chief Justice and Mr. Justice Stevens join, dissenting.

Only in the most superficial sense of the word can this case be said to involve "zoning." Typical zoning restrictions may, it is true, so limit the prospective uses of a piece of property as to diminish the value of that property in the abstract because it may not be used for the forbidden purposes. But any such abstract decrease in value will more than likely be at least partially offset by an increase in value which flows from similar restrictions as to use on neighboring properties. All property owners in a designated area are placed under the same restrictions, not only for the benefit of the municipality as a whole but also for the common benefit of one another. In the words of Mr. Justice Holmes, speaking for the Court in [*Mahon,*] there is "an average reciprocity of advantage."

Where a relatively few individual buildings, all separated from one another, are singled out and treated differently from surrounding buildings, no such reciprocity exists. [And] the cost associated with landmark legislation is likely to be of a completely different order of magnitude than that which results from the imposition of normal zoning restrictions. [Under] the historic-landmark preservation scheme adopted by New York, the property owner is under an affirmative duty to *preserve* his property *as a landmark* at his own expense. To suggest that because traditional zoning results in some limitation of use of the property zoned, the New York City landmark preservation scheme should likewise be upheld, represents the ultimate in treating as alike things which are different. The rubric of "zoning" has not yet sufficed to avoid the well-established proposition that the Fifth Amendment bars the "Government from forcing some people alone to be public burdens which, in all fairness and justice, should be borne by the public as a whole." . . .

[Before] the city of New York declared Grand Central Terminal to be a landmark, Penn Central could have used its "air rights" over the Terminal to build a multistory office building, at an apparent value of several million dollars per year. Today, the Terminal cannot be modified in *any* form, including the erection of additional stories, without the permission of the Landmark Preservation Commission, a permission which appellants, despite good-faith attempts, have so far been unable to obtain. . . .

Appellees do not dispute that valuable property rights have been destroyed. [While] the term "taken" might have been narrowly interpreted to include only physical seizures of property rights, "the construction of the phrase has not been so narrow. The courts have held that the deprivation of the former owner rather than the accretion of a right or interest to the sovereign constitutes the taking." . . .

[As] early as 1887, the Court recognized that the government can prevent a property owner from using his property to injure others without having to compensate the owner for the value of the forbidden use. [Thus,] there is no "taking" where a city prohibits the operation of a brickyard within a residential area, [or] forbids excavation for sand and gravel below the water line, see Goldblatt v. Hempstead, 369 U.S. 590 (1962). Nor is it relevant, where the government is merely prohibiting a noxious use of property, that the government would seem to be singling out a particular property owner. . . .

The nuisance exception to the taking guarantee is not coterminous with the police power itself. The question is whether the forbidden use is dangerous to the safety, health, or welfare of others. . . .

Appellees are not prohibiting a nuisance. The record is clear that the proposed addition to the Grand Central Terminal would be in full compliance with zoning, height limitations, and other health and safety requirements. Instead, appellees are seeking to preserve what they believe to be an outstanding example of beaux arts architecture. [The] city of New York, because of its unadorned admiration for the design, has decided that the owners of the building must preserve it unchanged for the benefit of sightseeing New Yorkers and tourists.

Unlike land-use regulations, appellees' action do not merely *prohibit* Penn Central from using its property in a narrow set of noxious ways. Instead, appellees have placed an *affirmative* duty on Penn Central to maintain the Terminal in its present state and in "good repair." . . .

Even where the government prohibits a noninjurious use, the Court has ruled that a taking does not take place if the prohibition applies over a broad cross section of land and thereby "secure[s] an average reciprocity of advantage." [Mahon.] [While] zoning at times reduces *individual* property values, the burden is shared relatively evenly and it is reasonable to conclude that on the whole an individual who is harmed by one aspect of the zoning will be benefited by another.

Here, however, a multimillion dollar loss has been imposed on appellants; it is uniquely felt and is not offset by any benefits flowing from the preservation of some 400 other "landmarks" in New York City. Appellees have imposed a substantial cost on less than one one-tenth of one percent of the buildings in New York City for the general benefit of all its people. It is exactly this imposition of general costs on a few individuals at which the "taking" protection is directed. . . .

As Mr. Justice Holmes pointed out in [*Mahon,*] "the question at bottom" in an eminent domain case "is upon whom the loss of the changes desired should fall." The benefits that appellees believe will flow from preservation of the Grand Central Terminal will accrue to all the citizens of New York City. There is no reason to believe that appellants will enjoy a substantially greater share of these benefits. If the cost of preserving Grand Central Terminal were spread evenly across the entire population of the city of New York, the burden per person would be in cents per year — a minor cost appellees would surely concede for the benefit accrued. Instead, however, appellees would impose the entire cost of several million dollars per year on Penn Central. But it is precisely this sort of discrimination that the Fifth Amendment prohibits.

[A] taking does not become a noncompensable exercise of police power simply because the government in its grace allows the owner to make some "reasonable" use of his property. "[I]t is the character of the invasion, not the amount of damage resulting from it, so long as the damage is substantial, that determines the question whether it is a taking." United States v. Cress, 243 U.S. 316, 328 (1917). . . .

Appellees contend that, even if they have "taken" appellants' property, TDR's constitute "just compensation." [Because] the record on appeal is relatively slim. I would remand to the Court of Appeals for a determination of whether TDR's constitute a "full and perfect equivalent for the property taken."

Note: *"Takings" and the Police Power*

1. *In general.* To what does one look to decide whether there has been a "taking" of private property? Consider Michelman, Property, Utility, and Fairness: Comments on the Ethical Foundations of "Just Compensation" Law, 80 Harv. L. Rev. 1165, 1225 (1967), referring to the

capacity of some collective actions to imply that someone may be subjected to immediately disadvantageous or painful treatment for no other apparent reason, and in accordance with no other apparent principle, than that someone else's claim to satisfaction has been ranked as intrinsically superior to his own. [Avoidance] of this evil is not the same thing as avoidance of all social action having capricious redistributive effects. The reasons begin with the universal acknowledgement that some collective constraint on individual free choice is necessary in order to [lead] to fuller achievement by each of his own ends. [It] is true that collective action which depends for its legitimacy on such understandings must look ultimately to the furtherance of *everyone's* attainment of his own ends, without "discrimination," and that this latter requirement would most obviously be met if a way were found to distribute the benefits and costs associated with each collective measure so that each person would share equally in the net benefits. But such perfection is plainly unattainable. [In] the face of this difficulty, it seems we are pleased to believe that we can

arrive at an acceptable level of assurance that *over time* the burdens associated with
collectively determined improvements will have been distributed "evenly" enough so
that everyone will be a net gainer. The function of a compensation practice, as here
viewed, is to fulfill a stronger felt need to maintain that assurance at an "acceptable"
level — to justify the general expectations of long-run "evenness."

With some such general understanding, the central problem in *Mahon* and
Miller remains: how to distinguish between a "taking" and "regulation." Almost
all government action — to take familiar examples, zoning, the relocation of a
highway, or other land use regulation — diminishes the value of some people's
property and increases the value of the property of other people. Redistribution in
this sense is almost always the result, and often the purpose, of government
action. If compensation was required in all such cases, there would of course be
no redistribution. The fact of compensation would prevent its occurrence. Where
one sets the line between taking and regulation will to a large degree determine
how much redistribution will be permitted through the regulatory process.

2. *Distinguishing takings from regulation.* How does one tell whether there has
been regulation or a taking? Some candidates for a test include the following.

a. *The extent of the intrusion.* Under this view, compensation will be required
if, in Justice Holmes's words, regulation "goes too far." The compensation requirement is triggered by a significant invasion. But this approach raises the
question why the extent of the intrusion is relevant to the question whether
compensation need be paid at all, rather than to the question of the extent of
compensation.

b. *The nature of the intrusion.* Under this approach, the court takes the notion
of "taking" literally, by examining whether property has "actually" been taken.
Has there been, for example, a physical invasion? Compensation may not be
required if the diminution in value produced by a regulatory measure does not
actually "touch" the property in question — for example, relocation of a highway, or a zoning ordinance. Also relevant may be whether government has actually appropriated the property for its own or another's use, rather than simply
destroyed it.

Under this view, physical invasions present a stronger case for requiring compensation than government action that diminishes value without such an invasion. The theme of physical invasion is a prominent one in the law of eminent
domain. But why should government action that actually "invades" be treated
differently from government action that in some other way diminishes value? Is it
persuasive to respond that where there has been a physical invasion, it is easy to
identify those adversely affected, and one need not worry that the costs of identifying those people entitled to compensation will prevent necessary measures from
going forward? Consider the zoning example, where the number of properties
adversely affected may be extremely large, and the costs of identifying them,
calculating their losses, and compensating them may deter socially desirable measures. Cf. R. Posner, Economic Analysis of Law 40-48 (2d ed. 1977).

c. *Balancing.* One might approach the takings versus regulation issue by asking:
How important is the state's interest? How does it compare with the private
interest? Consider, with respect to this approach, the view that "use of the balancing test for such a purpose seems to be a mistake, at best reflecting a careless
confusion of two quite distinct questions. These are, first, whether a given mea-

sure would be in order assuming it were accompanied by compensation payments; and, second, whether the same measure, conceding that it would be proper under conditions of full compensation, ought to be enforced without payment of any compensation. The balancing test may have something to do with the first question, but cannot have anything to do with the second." Michelman, supra, at 1193-1194. But note also a possible defense of a balancing approach as a means of testing whether the measure in question is "so obviously efficient as to quiet the potential outrage of persons 'unavoidably' sacrificed in its interest." Id. at 1235.

d. *The legitimacy of the state's interest: restraining harmful conduct, "mere" redistribution, and public benefit.* Is the state attempting "merely" to redistribute property from one person to another, or is it attempting to promote a more general good? This question is another way of asking whether the action in question falls within the police power. A more particularized version of this approach asks whether the state is preventing the property owner from committing some public harm, or instead demanding some contribution to the public good.

One of the principal purposes of the eminent domain clause, it is commonly thought, is to ensure that public burdens are paid for by the public generally, not by particular individuals; the compensation requirement promotes that goal. But if an individual is committing some kind of harm, the redress or prevention of the harm is something for which the individual, rather than the public, must pay. Someone who is committing a tort can be prevented from doing so, and the state need not furnish compensation.

But how does one know in which category — prevention of tort, or forced contribution to the public good — a particular measure falls? To answer that question, one has to have a background understanding that makes a decision about what is a normal status quo — and that requires a normative theory. Note, for example, the difficulty in *Miller* and *Pennsylvania Coal* of deciding whether there is "private fault" or "public benefit." For a long period the common law furnished the benchmark, but in *Miller*, the Court abandoned that approach, finding a harm that might be prevented without compensation, even though the conduct may not have been tortious at common law.

3. *Action and inaction.* In *Miller* the Court also stated that if government had failed to act, "it would have been none the less a choice. [When] forced to such a choice the state does not exceed its constitutional powers by deciding upon the destruction of one class of property in order to save another." The implication is that government inaction is itself a form of regulation.

What consequences does this insight have for the eminent domain clause and the underlying principle of private property? Consider Sunstein, Naked Preferences and the Constitution, 84 Colum. L. Rev. 1689, 1776 (1984):

> The new conception of the market status quo as neither natural nor inviolate led the way toward a dramatically expanded understanding of the police power. [Indeed], the seeds of a destruction of the eminent domain clause may lie within the *Miller* Court's statement. If government inaction can be understood as government action — if a decision not to act is understood as an intrusion in the same way as "affirmative" regulation — then the traditional notion of private property as natural and prepolitical loses much of its coherence.

4. *"Ordinary observing."* Note finally the approach in B. Ackerman, Private Property and the Constitution (1977). Ackerman distinguishes between two approaches to the issue of takings versus regulation: The first is that of a "scientific policymaker"; the second is that of an "ordinary observer." The former judges the issues by looking at the effects of government action on the property in question. Did it, for example, diminish in value? The latter makes a determination on the basis of a common sense inquiry. Was there a physical invasion on the part of the government? This approach judges takings by reference to common conceptions of whether property has been "taken"; it does not rely on lawyers' references to property as a "bundle of rights," or economists' understanding of property by reference to valuable uses. Ackerman contends that current law reflects the perspective of an ordinary observer.

Note: Penn Central, *Takings, and Related Problems*

1. *The Court's approach.* Note the frank concession by the Court that the issue of whether there has been a "taking" is resolved by an "essentially ad hoc, factual" inquiry. Is that a sensible approach to the problem? Try to outline the elements that go into the inquiry. Can you formulate an alternative approach that would be preferable?

2. *Assorted cases.* Probably the best way to get a sense of eminent domain doctrine is to compare the holdings in different factual settings. In reading these cases, it will be useful to examine the relative weight of the various possible tests referred to on pages 1460-1461, supra. What have been the determinants of the outcomes? Is it possible to construct a coherent body of takings law?

a. Andrus v. Allard, 444 U.S. 51 (1979). The Eagle Protection Act banned the sale of bald or golden eagle parts taken before the effective date of the statute. The act did not ban the possession or transportation of such parts. The Court upheld the statute, saying that government regulation often

> curtails some potential for the use or economic exploitation of private property. To require compensation in all such circumstances would effectively compel the government to regulate by *purchase*. [The] regulations challenged here do not compel the surrender of the artifacts, and there is no physical invasion or restraint upon them. Rather, a significant restriction has been imposed on one means of disposing of the artifacts. But the denial of one traditional property right does not always amount to a taking. At least where an owner possesses a full "bundle" of property rights, the destruction of one "strand" of the bundle is not a taking, because the aggregation must be viewed in its entirety. [It] is, to be sure, undeniable that the regulations here prevent the most profitable use of appellees' property. Again, however, that is not dispositive. When we review regulation, a reduction in the value of the property is not necessarily equated with a taking.

b. Euclid v. Ambler Realty Co., 272 U.S. 365 (1926), involved a zoning ordinance. The tract at issue had been vacant and was held for purpose of sale and development for industrial uses; for such uses, it had a market value of about $10,000 per acre. The zoning ordinance would limit it to residential purposes, thus reducing its market value to $2,500 per acre.

The Court upheld the ordinance. It acknowledged that

the exclusion is in general terms of all industrial establishments, and it may thereby happen that not only offensive or dangerous industries will be excluded, but those which are neither offensive nor dangerous will share the same fate. But this is no more than happens in respect of many practice-forbidding laws which this Court has upheld although drawn in general terms so as to include individual cases that may turn out to be innocuous in themselves.

The Court went on to point to the various benefits of the zoning ordinance:

the segregation of residential, business, and industrial buildings will make it easier to provide fire apparatus suitable for the character and intensity of the development in each section; that it will increase the safety and security of home life; greatly tend to prevent street accidents, especially to children, by reducing the traffic and resulting confusion in residential sections; decrease noise and other conditions which produce or intensify nervous disorders; preserve a more favorable environment in which to rear children, etc.

In the Court's view, these factors were "sufficiently cogent to preclude us from saying, as it must be said before the ordinance can be declared unconstitutional, that such provisions are clearly arbitrary and unreasonable, having no substantial relation to the public health, safety, morals, or general welfare."

Why does the eminent domain clause — as distinguished from, say, the due process clause — require an examination of whether the measure is "clearly arbitrary and unreasonable"? Does this formulation conflate constitutional inquiries under the "public use" and regulation versus taking issues? Note that the deferential approach of Euclid is inapplicable to cases of physical invasion; see, in this regard, the discussion of "ordinary observing" supra.

c. Compare Kaiser Aetna v. United States, 444 U.S. 164 (1979), with PruneYard Shopping Center v. Robins, 447 U.S. 74 (1980). In *Kaiser Aetna* the Army Corps of Engineers attempted to grant public access to Kuapa Pond, a lagoon in Hawaii that was contiguous to a navigable bay. Kaiser Aetna had obtained rights to use the lagoon and had dredged and filled parts of it, erected retaining walls, and built bridges. It also created accommodations for pleasure boats. Eventually there were about 1,500 marina waterfront lot lessees. Kaiser Aetna controlled access to and use of the marina and generally did not permit commercial use. The Army Corps of Engineers contended that Kaiser Aetna was required to allow public access to the lagoon and that no compensation need be paid since there was a federal navigational servitude on the property.

The Court concluded that "the Government's attempt to create a public right to access [goes] so far beyond ordinary regulation or improvement for navigation as to amount to a taking." The Court emphasized that (a) before Kaiser Aetna's improvements, the pond could not be used for navigation in interstate commerce; (b) the body of water was private property under Hawaiian law; (c) the intrusion at issue was on the right to exclude, "universally held to be a fundamental element of the property right"; (d) there was an actual physical invasion.

In *PruneYard*, the California Supreme Court had held that the state constitutional right of free speech compelled shopping center owners to allow picketeers to exercise rights of free speech on shopping center property. The owners contended that there was a "taking" of their property. The Court said:

> Here the requirement that appellants permit appellees to exercise state-protected rights of free expression and petition on shopping center property clearly does not amount to an unconstitutional infringement of appellant's property rights under the Takings Clause. There is nothing to suggest that preventing appellants from prohibiting this sort of activity will unreasonably impair the value or use of their property as a shopping center. [The] decision of the California Supreme Court makes it clear that the PruneYard may restrict expressive activity by adopting time, place, and manner regulations. [Appellees] were orderly, and they limited their activity to the common areas of the shopping center.

What is the relevance of the last two sentences in this passage?

d. In Loretto v. Teleprompter Manhattan CATV Corp, 458 U.S. 419 (1982), the issue was the constitutionality of a New York law providing that a landlord must permit a cable television company to install cable facilities on his property. The cable installation in the relevant case occupied portions of the plaintiff's roof and the side of her building. The Court concluded that the "permanent physical occupation authorized by government is a taking without regard to the public interests that it may serve." The Court added: "An owner suffers a special kind of injury when a stranger directly invades and occupies the owner's property. [The] traditional rule also avoids otherwise difficult line-drawing problems. [Whether] a permanent physical occupation has occurred presents relatively few problems of proof."

e. United States v. Causby, 328 U.S. 256 (1946), raised the question whether frequent flights immediately above a landowner's property constituted a taking. The Court concluded that it did: "If, by reason of the frequency and altitude of the flights, respondents could not use this land for any purpose, their loss would be complete. It would be as complete as if the United States had entered upon the surface of the land and taken exclusive possession of it." See also Griggs v. Allegheny County, 369 U.S. 84 (1962).

3. *Concluding thoughts.* Consider the following view. The confused character of eminent domain doctrine springs from several problems. The Court has recognized since *Miller* that redistribution of resources through regulation is often permissible; the common law is itself a distributive scheme, and efforts to alter the status quo are not for that reason impermissible. That understanding abandons the common law benchmark for deciding whether the property owner has engaged in conduct which a state has a right to prevent without offering compensation. And the abandonment of that benchmark threatens the concept of private property. The police power "exception" to the ordinary compensation requirement becomes extremely expansive — a point we saw earlier in connection with the *Midkiff* case, as well as with rationality review under the due process and equal protection clauses.

At the same time, the Court has taken a "common sense" approach to takings by making physical invasion an important (though neither necessary nor sufficient) factor in deciding whether there has been a taking. But it is unclear why the fact of physical invasion should be so important. Is there any way out of the resulting doctrinal morass?

See Michelman, Property as a Constitutional Right, 38 Wash. & Lee. L. Rev. 1097, 1112-1113 (1981):

> My suggestion is to seek a reapproachement of property and popular sovereignty in the idea that rights under a political constitution, including property rights, are first of all to be regarded as political rights. They are precisely such, I suggest, because and insofar as they are rights affecting the individual's participation in popular sovereignty as something apart from — beyond the reach of — political action.
>
> [If,] to repeat, rights under a constitution are political rights, then what one primarily has a right to is the maintenance of the conditions of one's fair and effective participation in the constituted order, as an individual no less than others to the respect and concern of the community, and also no more entitled than others to any particular outcome save those that bear on the conditions of continued effective participation. Loss — even great loss — of the economic value of one's holdings may not as such violate those conditions. What does, perhaps, violate them is exposure to sudden changes in the major elements and crucial determinants of one's established position in the world, as one has come [to] understand that position.

See also Rose, *Mahon* Reconstructed: Why the Takings Issue Is Still a Muddle, 57 S. Calif. L. Rev. 561 (1984), suggesting that the doctrinal confusion is produced by an inability to decide whether private property is valued because it produces wealth or because it produces citizenship.

Does Michelman's view undervalue the interest in private property? Does it ignore the text and purposes of the eminent domain clause? Would Michelman's view allow too much in the way of redistribution? Note in this regard the difference between judicial treatment of the eminent domain clause and judicial treatment of the first amendment; is it fair to say that the Court has been more receptive to the latter than to the former? For an extended affirmative answer, a criticism of current doctrine as both ad hoc and an unjustifiable emasculation of the eminent domain clause, and a plea for an active judicial role in the protection of private property, see R. Epstein, Takings: Private Property and Eminent Domain (1985).

X

The Constitution and
the Problem of
Private Power

It is a commonplace that the commands of the Constitution are directed to governmental entities rather than private parties. Is there a good reason for this limitation on the Constitution's reach? Does the fact that a constitution is fundamentally about governmental structure and power provide a sufficient reason for the limitation? Is the limitation based on the fact that government generally has more power than private entities and has a monopoly on the use of force to accomplish its objectives?

Note that for at least two reasons, the state action limitation may tell us very little. First, the state action limitation may state no more than a conceptual truth. How could the Constitution, by its own force, govern wholly private conduct? Unless constitutional commands are merely precatory, they must require some governmental entity to respond when rights are invaded. For example, The Civil Rights Cases, infra this section, hold that the thirteenth amendment prohibits purely private acts of enslavement. But to have practical meaning, the amendment must require public entities to do something to outlaw the "prohibited" acts.

Second, the statement that the Constitution controls only government conduct tells us nothing about what the Constitution requires the government to do. Thus, even if the Constitution itself is not directed at private persons, it might require the state to control the conduct of such persons. For example, even if a private person's denial of equal treatment to blacks does not itself violate the fourteenth amendment, the state's decision to permit private persons to deny equal treatment to blacks *might* violate that amendment.

To have meaning, then, the state action doctrine must be supplemented by some substantive constitutional theory about the appropriate limits on governmental power. This chapter examines the Court's efforts to develop such a theory. Section A takes up the possibility of deriving such a theory from principles of federalism and individual autonomy. Section B addresses the problem of defining state "inaction" and explores the theory of governmental neutrality as it intersects the state action problem. Sections C and D examine how departures from and adherence to governmental neutrality relate to findings of state action. Section C concerns situations in which findings of state action are premised on impermissible departures from neutrality by state encouragement, subsidization, or authorization of private conduct that arguably threatens constitutional values. Section D concerns situations in which findings of state action are premised on impermissible adherence to neutrality by state failure to prohibit private conduct threatening such values. The concluding section addresses the ways in which the state action problem relates to broader problems in constitutional theory.

A.　STATE ACTION, FEDERALISM, AND INDIVIDUAL AUTONOMY

One way to think about the state action requirement is that it defines an area that must remain beyond the reach of federal power — both legislative and judicial. Consider, for example, Lugar v. Edmondson Oil Co., 457 U.S. 922, 936 (1982): "Careful adherence to the 'state action' requirement preserves an area of individual freedom by limiting the reach of federal law and federal judicial power. [A] major consequence is to require the courts to respect the limits of their own power as directed against state governments and private interests. Whether this is good or bad policy, it is a fundamental fact of our political order."

The notion that "limiting the reach of federal law" serves to "preserve individual freedom" is a controversial one. The fourteenth amendment, for example, was premised to some degree on the opposite assumption — that an extension of federal law was essential to the preservation of individual rights. See Chapter 5, section A, supra.

Nonetheless, the Court's analysis of the state action issue has long been influenced by the assumed link between individual freedom and restrictions on federal power. Indeed, this "fundamental fact of our political order" was arguably central to the Court's earliest effort to articulate a state action doctrine.

1.　State Action and Federalism

The modern Court has held that state action is a prerequisite to the assertion of rights contained in both the first eight amendments (originally applicable only to the federal government) and in the fourteenth amendment (applicable to the states). But historically, the requirement attracted little attention until passage of the reconstruction amendments after the Civil War.

After the enactment of these amendments, the Court was required to determine the extent to which they changed the traditional balance between state and federal authority. One view was that the new amendments gave the federal government plenary authority to protect individual rights. A second view was that the amendments left untouched the states' traditional functions and authorized federal intervention only when the states defaulted in their primary obligations. See supra Chapter 5, section A2.

Not surprisingly, then, the Court's earliest state action decisions looked to principles of federalism to give content to the doctrine.

The Civil Rights Cases

109 U.S. 3 (1883)

MR. JUSTICE BRADLEY delivered the opinion of the court.

[These cases were brought pursuant to the Civil Rights Act of 1875. The act provided that all persons were "entitled to the full and equal enjoyment of the accommodations, advantages, facilities, and privileges of inns, public conveyances, on land or water, theatres, and other places of public amusement; subject only to the conditions and limitations established by law, and applicable alike to citizens of every race and color, regardless of any previous condition of servitude." Private persons violating these rights were subject to civil damages and criminal penalties.]

Has Congress constitutional power to make such a law? Of course, no one will contend that the power to pass it was contained in the Constitution before the adoption of the [Thirteenth, Fourteenth, and Fifteenth] amendments. . . .

The first section of the Fourteenth Amendment (which is the one relied on), after declaring who shall be citizens of the United States, and of the several States, is prohibitory in its character, and prohibitory upon the States. [Individual] invasion of individual rights is not the subject matter of the amendment. It has a deeper and broader scope. It nullifies and makes void all State legislation, and State action of every kind, which impairs the privileges and immunities of citizens of the United States, or which injures them in life, liberty or property without due process of law, or which denies to any of them the equal protection of the laws. It not only does this, but, in order that the national will, thus declared, may not be a mere brutum fulmen, the last section of the amendment invests Congress with power to enforce it by appropriate legislation. To enforce what? To enforce the prohibition. To adopt appropriate legislation for correcting the effects of such prohibited State laws and State acts, and thus to render them effectually null, void, and innocuous. This is the legislative power conferred upon Congress, and this is the whole of it. It does not invest Congress with power to legislate upon subjects which are within the domain of State legislation; but to provide modes of relief against State legislation, or State action, of the kind referred to. It does not authorize Congress to create a code of municipal law for the regulation of private rights; but to provide modes of redress against the operation of State laws, and the action of State officers executive or judicial, when these are subversive of the fundamental rights specified in the amendment. . . .

An inspection of the law shows that it makes no reference whatever to any supposed or apprehended violation of the Fourteenth Amendment on the part of the States. It is not predicated on any such view. It proceeds ex directo to declare that certain acts committed by individuals shall be deemed offences, and shall be prosecuted and punished by proceedings in the courts of the United States. It does not profess to be corrective of any constitutional wrong committed by the States; it does not make its operation to depend upon any such wrong committed. It applies equally to cases arising in States which have the justest laws respecting the personal rights of citizens, and whose authorities are ever ready to enforce such laws, as to those which arise in States that may have violated the prohibition of the amendment. In other words, it steps into the domain of local jurisprudence, and lays down rules for the conduct of individuals in society towards each

other, and imposes sanctions for the enforcement of those rules, without referring in any manner to any supposed action of the State or its authorities.

If this legislation is appropriate for enforcing the prohibitions of the amendment, it is difficult to see where it is to stop. Why may not Congress with equal
show of authority enact a code of laws for the enforcement and vindication of all
rights of life, liberty, and property? If it is supposable that the States may deprive
persons of life, liberty, and property without due process of law (and the amendment itself does suppose this), why should not Congress proceed at once to
prescribe due process of law for the protection of every one of these fundamental
rights, in every possible case, as well as to prescribe equal privileges in inns, public
conveyances, and theatres? The truth is, that the implication of a power to
legislate in this manner is based upon the assumption that if the States are
forbidden to legislate or act in a particular way on a particular subject, and power
is conferred upon Congress to enforce the prohibition, this gives Congress power
to legislate generally upon that subject, and not merely power to provide modes of
redress against such State legislation or action. The assumption is certainly unsound. It is repugnant to the Tenth Amendment of the Constitution, which
declares that powers not delegated to the United States by the Constitution, nor
prohibited by it to the States, are reserved to the States respectively or to the
people. . . .

In this connection it is proper to state that civil rights, such as are guaranteed
by the Constitution against State aggression, cannot be impaired by the wrongful
acts of individuals, unsupported by State authority in the shape of laws, customs,
or judicial or executive proceedings. The wrongful act of an individual, unsupported by any such authority, is simply a private wrong, or a crime of that
individual; an invasion of the rights of the injured party, it is true, whether they
affect his person, his property, or his reputation; but if not sanctioned in some
way by the State, or not done under State authority, his rights remain in full
force, and may presumably be vindicated by resort to the laws of the State for
redress. An individual cannot deprive a man of his right to vote, to hold property,
to buy and sell, to sue in the courts, or to be a witness or a juror; he may, by force
or fraud, interfere with the enjoyment of the right in a particular case; he may
commit an assault against the person, or commit murder, or use ruffian violence
at the polls, or slander the good name of a fellow citizen; but, unless protected in
these wrongful acts by some shield of State law or State authority, he cannot
destroy or injure the right; he will only render himself amenable to satisfaction or
punishment; and amenable therefor to the laws of the State where the wrongful
acts are committed. Hence, in all those cases where the Constitution seeks to
protect the rights of the citizen against discriminative and unjust laws of the State
by prohibiting such laws, it is not individual offences, but abrogation and denial
of rights, which it denounces, and for which it clothes the Congress with power to
provide a remedy. This abrogation and denial of rights, for which the States alone
were or could be responsible, was the great seminal and fundamental wrong
which was intended to be remedied. And the remedy to be provided must necessarily be predicated upon that wrong. It must assume that in the cases provided
for, the evil or wrong actually committed rests upon some State law or State
authority for its excuse and perpetration. . . .

[The] power of Congress to adopt direct and primary, as distinguished from corrective legislation, on the subject in hand, is sought, in the second place, from the Thirteenth Amendment which abolishes slavery. . . .

This amendment, as well as the Fourteenth, is undoubtedly self-executing without any ancillary legislation, so far as its terms are applicable to any existing state of circumstances. By its own unaided force and effect it abolished slavery, and established universal freedom. Still, legislation may be necessary and proper to meet all the various cases and circumstances to be affected by it, and to prescribe proper modes of redress for its violation in letter or spirit. And such legislation may be primary and direct in its character; for the amendment is not a mere prohibition of State laws establishing or upholding slavery, but an absolute declaration that slavery or involuntary servitude shall not exist in any part of the United States. . . .

The only question [is] whether the refusal to any persons of the accommodations of an inn, or a public conveyance, or a place of public amusement, by an individual, and without any sanction or support from any State law or regulation, [inflicts] upon such persons any manner of servitude, or form of slavery, as those terms are understood in this country? Many wrongs may be obnoxious to the prohibitions of the Fourteenth Amendment which are not, in any just sense, incidents or elements of slavery. Such, for example, would be the taking of private property without due process of law; or allowing persons who have committed certain crimes (horse stealing, for example) to be seized and hung by the posse comitatus without regular trial; or denying to any person, or class of persons, the right to pursue any peaceful avocations allowed to others. . . .

Now, conceding, for the sake of the argument, that the admission to an inn, a public conveyance, or a place of public amusement, on equal terms with all other citizens, is the right of every man and all classes of men, is it any more than one of those rights which the states by the Fourteenth Amendment are forbidden to deny to any person? And is the Constitution violated until the denial of the right has some State sanction or authority? Can the act of a mere individual, the owner of the inn, the public conveyance or place of amusement, refusing the accommodation, be justly regarded as imposing any badge of slavery or servitude upon the applicant, or only as inflicting an ordinary civil injury, properly cognizable by the laws of the State, and presumably subject to redress by those laws until the contrary appears?

After giving to these questions all the consideration which their importance demands, we are forced to the conclusion that such an act of refusal has nothing to do with slavery or involuntary servitude, and that if it is violative of any right of the party, his redress is to be sought under the laws of the State; or if those laws are adverse to his rights and do not protect him, his remedy will be found in the corrective legislation which Congress has adopted, or may adopt, for counteracting the effect of State laws, or State action, prohibited by the Fourteenth Amendment. It would be running the slavery argument into the ground to make it apply to every act of discrimination which a person may see fit to make as to the guests he will entertain, or as to the people he will take into his coach or cab or car, or admit to his concert or theatre, or deal with in other matters of intercourse or business. Innkeepers and public carriers, by the laws of all the States, so far as we are aware, are bound, to the extent of their facilities, to furnish proper accommodation to all unobjectionable persons who in good faith apply for them. If the laws themselves make any unjust discrimination, amenable to the prohibitions of the Fourteenth Amendment, Congress has full power to afford a remedy under that amendment and in accordance with it.

When a man has emerged from slavery, and by the aid of beneficient legislation has shaken off the inseparable concomitants of that state, there must be some stage in the progress of his elevation when he takes the rank of a mere citizen, and ceases to be the special favorite of the laws, and when his rights as a citizen, or a man, are to be protected in the ordinary modes by which other men's rights are protected. There were thousands of free colored people in this country before the abolition of slavery, enjoying all the essential rights of life, liberty and property the same as white citizens; yet no one, at that time, thought that it was any invasion of his personal status as a freeman because he was not admitted to all the privileges enjoyed by white citizens, or because he was subjected to discriminations in the enjoyment of accommodations in inns, public conveyances and places of amusement. Mere discriminations on account of race or color were not regarded as badges of slavery. . . .

MR JUSTICE HARLAN dissenting.

The opinion in these cases proceeds, it seems to me, upon grounds entirely too narrow and artificial. I cannot resist the conclusion that the substance and spirit of the recent amendments of the Constitution have been sacrificed by a subtle and ingenious verbal criticism. . . .

I do not contend that the Thirteenth Amendment invests Congress with authority, by legislation, to define and regulate the entire body of the civil rights which citizens enjoy, or may enjoy, in the several States. But I hold that since slavery, as the court has repeatedly declared, [*Slaughter-House Cases; Strauder*], was the moving or principal cause of the adoption of that amendment, and since that institution rested wholly upon the inferiority, as a race, of those held in bondage, their freedom necessarily involved immunity from, and protection against, all discrimination against them, because of their race, in respect of such civil rights as belong to freemen of other races. Congress, therefore, under its express power to enforce that amendment, by appropriate legislation, may enact laws to protect that people against the deprivation, *because of their race*, of any civil rights granted to other freemen in the same State; and such legislation may be of a direct and primary character, operating upon States, their officers and agents, and, also, upon, at least, such individuals and corporations as exercise public functions and wield power and authority under the State.

[Congress] has not, in these matters, entered the domain of State control and supervision. It does not, as I have said, assume to prescribe the general conditions and limitations under which inns, public conveyances, and places of public amusement, shall be conducted or managed. It simply declares, in effect, that since the nation has established universal freedom in this country, for all time, there shall be no discrimination, based merely upon race or color, in respect of the accommodations and advantages of public conveyances, inns, and places of public amusement.

I am of the opinion that such discrimination practised by corporations and individuals in the exercise of their public or quasi-public functions is a badge of servitude the imposition of which Congress may prevent under its power, by appropriate legislation, to enforce the Thirteenth Amendment; and, consequently, without reference to its enlarged power under the Fourteenth Amendment, the [challenged act] is not, in my judgment, repugnant to the Constitution.

It remains now to consider these cases with reference to the power Congress has possessed since the adoption of the Fourteenth Amendment. . . .

The assumption that this amendment consists wholly of prohibitions upon State laws and State proceedings in hostility to its provisions, is unauthorized by its language. The first clause of the first section — "All persons born or naturalized in the United States, and subject to the jurisdiction thereof, are citizens of the United States, and of the State wherein they reside" — is of a distinctly affirmative character. In its application to the colored race, previously liberated, it created and granted, as well citizenship of the United States, as citizenship of the State in which they respectively resided. [Further] they were brought, by this supreme act of the nation, within the direct operation of that provision of the Constitution which declares that "the citizens of each State shall be entitled to all privileges and immunities of citizens in the several States." Art. 4, §2.

The citizenship thus acquired, by that race, in virtue of an affirmative grant from the nation, may be protected, not alone by the judicial branch of the government, but by congressional legislation of a primary direct character; this, because the power of Congress is not restricted to the enforcement of prohibitions upon State laws or State action. It is, in terms distinct and positive, to enforce "the *provisions* of *this article*" of amendment; not simply those of a prohibitive character, but the provisions — *all* of the provisions — affirmative and prohibitive, of the amendment. . . .

But what was secured to colored citizens of the United States — as between them and their respective States — by the national grant to them of State citizenship? With what rights, privileges, or immunities did this grant invest them? There is one, if there be no other — exemption from race discrimination in respect of any civil right belonging to citizens of the white race in the same State. [Citizenship] in this country necessarily imports at least equality of civil rights among citizens of every race in the same State. It is fundamental in American citizenship that, in respect of such rights, there shall be no discrimination by the State, or its officers, or by individuals or corporations exercising public functions or authority, against any citizen because of his race or previous condition of servitude. . . .

If, then, exemption from discrimination, in respect of civil rights, is a new constitutional right, secured by the grant of State citizenship to colored citizens of the United States — and I do not see how this can now be questioned — why may not the nation, by means of its own legislation of a primary direct character, guard, protect and enforce that right? It is a right and privilege which the nation conferred. It did not come from the States in which those colored citizens reside. It has been the established doctrine of this court during all its history, accepted as essential to the national supremacy, that Congress, in the absence of a positive delegation of power to the State legislatures, may, by its own legislation, enforce and protect any right derived from or created by the national Constitution. . . .

I agree that government has nothing to do with social, as distinguished from technically legal, rights of individuals. No government ever has brought, or ever can bring, its people into social intercourse against their wishes. Whether one person will permit or maintain social relations with another is a matter with which government has no concern. I agree that if one citizen chooses not to hold social intercourse with another, he is not and cannot be made amenable to the law for his conduct in that regard; for no legal right of a citizen is violated by the refusal of others to maintain merely social relations with him, even upon grounds of race. What I affirm is that no State, nor the officers of any State, nor any corporation or individual wielding power under State authority for the public benefit or the public convenience, can, consistently either with the freedom established by the fundamental law, or with that equality of civil rights which now belongs to every citizen, discriminate against freemen or citizens, in those rights, because of their race, or because they once labored under the disabilities of slavery imposed upon them as a race. . . .

My brethren say, that when a man has emerged from slavery, and by the aid of beneficent legislation has shaken off the inseparable concomitants of that state, there must be some stage in the progress of his elevation when he takes the rank of a mere citizen, and ceases to be the special favorite of the laws, and when his rights as a citizen, or a man, are to be protected in the ordinary modes by which other men's rights are protected. It is, I submit, scarcely just to say that the colored race has been the special favorite of the laws. The statute of 1875, now adjudged to be unconstitutional, is for the benefit of citizens of every race and color. What the nation, through Congress, has sought to accomplish in reference to that race, is — what had already been done in every State of the Union for the white race — to secure and protect rights belonging to them as freemen and citizens; nothing more.

[To-day] it is the colored race which is denied, by corporations and individuals wielding public authority, rights fundamental in their freedom and citizenship. At some future time, it may be that some other race will fall under the ban of race discrimination. If the constitutional amendments be enforced, according to the intent with which, as I conceive, they were adopted, there cannot be, in this republic, any class of human beings in practical subjection to another class, with power in the latter to dole out to the former just such privileges as they may choose to grant. The supreme law of the land has decreed that no authority shall be exercised in this country upon the basis of discrimination, in respect of civil rights, against freemen and citizens because of their race, color, or previous condition of servitude. To that decree — for the due enforcement of which, by appropriate legislation, Congress has been invested with express power — every one must bow, whatever may have been, or whatever now are, his individual views as to the wisdom or policy, either of the recent changes in the fundamental law, or of the legislation which has been enacted to give them effect.

For the reasons stated I feel constrained to withhold my assent to the opinion of the court.

Note: Federalism and the Substantive Content of the State Action Doctrine

1. *The meaning of the Civil Rights Cases.* The modern Court has read the Civil Rights Cases to establish "the essential dichotomy [between] deprivation by the State, subject to scrutiny under [the fourteenth amendment] and private conduct [against] which the Fourteenth Amendment offers no shield." Jackson v. Metropolitan Edison Co., 419 U.S. 345, 349 (1974). And, indeed, the Court in the Civil Rights Cases did assert that "Individual invasion of individual rights is not the

subject matter of the [fourteenth] amendment." But does this proposition tell us anything about what should count as a *state* invasion of individual rights? Might it count as a state invasion of individual rights for a state to fail to remedy acts of racial discrimination undertaken by owners of public accommodations who are required by state law to serve the public? Do the Civil Rights Cases hold that a state can constitutionally leave such discrimination unremedied? That it can permit owners of public accommodations to discriminate against blacks even though they are required by state law to serve all whites?

Consider in this regard the Court's argument in the Civil Rights Cases that a wrongful act, unsupported by state authority, cannot by itself violate legal rights so long as the victim can look to state law for redress, and its complaint that the 1875 act "applies equally to cases arising in States which have the justest laws respecting the personal rights of citizens, and whose authorities are ever ready to enforce such laws, as to those which arise in States that may have violated the prohibition of the amendment."

Consider also Justice Bradley's comments on the fourteenth amendment in correspondence with Circuit Judge (later Justice) Wood written twelve years before he authored the majority opinion in the Civil Rights Cases: "[The fourteenth amendment] not only prohibits the making or enforcing of laws which shall abridge the privileges of the citizen; but prohibits the states from denying to all persons within its jurisdiction the equal protection of the laws. [Denying] includes inaction as well as action. And denying the equal protection of the laws includes the omission to protect, as well as the omission to pass laws for protection." (The correspondence is quoted in Bell v. Maryland, 378 U.S. 226, 309-10 (1964) (Goldberg, J. concurring).)

Under this view of the matter, the Civil Rights Cases may stand for the proposition that the states are the primary guarantors of the rights of their citizens, and that the federal government may protect those rights if — but only if — the states fail to do so. Note that this position suggests both a broad and a narrow conception of federal power. It is broad in the sense that it treats state failures to act as state action for purposes of the fourteenth amendment; it is narrow in the sense that it incorporates a federalism-based limit on the federal government's power to act.

2. *The current status of federalism and state action.* Although modern cases occasionally hint that the exercise of federal legislative power is constitutionally permissible only if a state has defaulted in its obligation to protect constitutional rights, this understanding of the Civil Rights Cases and the fourteenth amendment has generally been rejected. The modern Court has read both the thirteenth and fourteenth amendments to give Congress broad power to regulate "private" conduct so as to deal with racial discrimination and the vestiges of slavery. The cases establishing this proposition are discussed in Chapter 2, section F5, supra. Moreover, the issue of congressional power under the Reconstruction amendments has become largely moot because of the Court's expansive reading of the commerce clause which, today, provides Congress with ample power to supplant state law when it wishes to do so. See chapter 2, section E, supra.

In light of these developments, is there anything left of the notion that the state action doctrine operates as a protection of federalism concerns? Recall that many of the modern Court's permissive decisions regarding federal legislative power reflect not so much a judgment "on the merits" as a decision to leave the definition of the constitutional limits on federal power to the political branches. Does the state action doctrine serve to reinforce this division of power between Congress and the Court? See generally Sager, Fair Measure: The Legal Status of Underenforced Constitutional Norms, 91 Harv. L. Rev. 1212 (1978). On this view, Congress is free to define the scope of its own power and to reach private conduct if it reasonably finds that the regulation of such conduct is rationally related to the exercise of one of its delegated powers. In the absence of such a finding, however, the state action doctrine precludes the Court from reading the Constitution in a manner that substantially erodes the traditional function of the states as primary guarantors of the liberty of their citizens.

Does this view of the state action doctrine take adequate account of the fundamental shift in the federal structure arguably intended by the authors of the Reconstruction amendments? See supra Chapter 5, section A2. Does our political history support the view that powerful states serve to protect individual liberty from federal tyranny? Is a federalism-based state action doctrine consistent with the fact that state action is a necessary component of constitutional violations committed by the federal government as well as by the states?

2. State Action and Individual Autonomy

Although the modern Court has largely abandoned the task of policing the federalism limits on the exercise of congressional power, it has been much more active in limiting the authority of both the federal and state governments to invade individual rights. Might one look to principles concerning the appropriate scope of individual autonomy to give content to the state action requirement?

According to this view, the Constitution is designed primarily to protect individual freedom. But in order to realize this goal, individuals must be left free to make choices we would prohibit government from making. Consider, for example the dilemma that would be posed if the Constitution made no distinction between governmental and private action. Without some sort of state action doctrine, private autonomy would be subject to the same limitations as government autonomy. Instead of *protecting* individual rights from legislative interference, the Constitution might *subject* them to judicial interference. It is easy to imagine the extreme consequences that might follow. Newspapers might be prohibited from exclusively promoting a particular point of view. Private home owners might be precluded from choosing their guests on racial or political grounds. Even marriage and divorce decisions might be judicially reviewable for improper motivation.

Does recognition of constitutionally protected individual rights give content to the state action doctrine? Consider Columbia Broadcasting System v. Democratic National Committee, 412 U.S. 94 (1973). Respondents claimed that the refusal of broadcasters to accept their editorial advertisements violated the first amendment. The Federal Communications Commission rejected this contention and refused to require that broadcasters accept such advertisements. The Court agreed with the Commission.

In a portion of his plurality opinion joined by only two other Justices, Chief Justice Burger argued that the first amendment claim failed because the broadcasters' decision could not be attributed to the government.

Were we to read the First Amendment to spell out governmental action in the circumstances presented here, few licensee decisions on the content of broadcasts or the processes of editorial evaluation would escape constitutional scrutiny. . . .

[It] would be anomalous for us to hold, in the name of promoting the constitutional guarantees of free expression, that the day-to-day editorial decisions of broadcast licensees are subject to the kind of restraints urged by respondents. To do so in the name of the First Amendment would be a contradiction. Journalistic discretion would in many ways be lost to the rigid limitations that the First Amendment imposes on Government. Application of such standards to broadcast licensees would be antithetical to the very ideal of vigorous, challenging debate on issues of public interest.

For a discussion of other aspects of *CBS*, see Chapter 7, section F6, supra.

The result in *CBS* maximizes the journalistic freedom of broadcasters, who need not account to a court or government agency for their editorial decisions. But it arguably does so at the expense of the freedom of those wishing to present editorial advertisements, who may be prevented from securing a forum. Can the state action requirement be understood as the Court's technique for balancing the conflicting rights of private individuals in cases such as *CBS*? Consider Glennon & Nowak, A Functional Analysis of the Fourteenth Amendment "State Action" Requirement, 1976 Sup. Ct. Rev. 221, 231, 232:

Confronted with a conflict between individual rights, the court must determine whether the Fourteenth Amendment dictates a preference for one over the other. The court must balance the relative merits of permitting the challenged practice to continue against the limitation which it imposed on the asserted right. If the value of the right clearly outweighs the value of the challenged practice, the Amendment proscribes the practice. If the importance of the right is not clearly greater than that of the challenged practice, the effect of the practice on the right does not violate the Amendment. The impact of the practice on the asserted right is in accordance with the Amendment, not because state action is missing, but because it is permissible for the state to prefer the challenged practice rather than the asserted right.

How should a court go about striking this balance? In cases where some substantive constitutional provision limits the government's power to act, the answer may appear to be easy. For example, it would almost certainly be unconstitutional for the government to dictate editorial policies to newspapers or to oversee marriage decisions. Similarly, Justice Bradley believed that the federal government lacked the constitutional power to regulate the "private" conduct in question in the Civil Rights Cases. If it is unconstitutional for the government to act in these cases, it must be constitutional for it not to act.

Even these "easy" cases raise troubling problems, however. Reliance on substantive constitutional provisions begs the central question: How is the goal of individual autonomy advanced by reading the Constitution to give private entities coercive power that is withheld from government? It is not obvious, for example, that individual freedom is maximized by giving large newspapers and television networks unfettered control over what opinions and information they disseminate.

Moreover, it is important to recognize that the "easy" cases are somewhat atypical. More typically, a finding of no state action means only that the Constitution does not of its own force regulate the privacy activity. It does not follow from such a finding that the private actor is constitutionally immune from legislative regulation.

For example, in *CBS* Chief Justice Burger suggested elsewhere in his opinion that Congress could require networks to accept editorial advertising. Similarly, in Hudgens v. NLRB, 424 U.S. 507 (1976), the Court held that the decision of a privately owned shopping center to exclude peaceful picketers could not be attributed to the government and therefore did not violate the first amendment. But in PruneYard Shopping Center v. Robins, 447 U.S. 74 (1980), the Court rejected a shopping center owner's first amendment objection when a state chose to outlaw such exclusions. And in Moose Lodge No. 107 v. Irvis, 407 U.S. 163 (1972), the Court held that the racially discriminatory policy of a private club was not "state action" and therefore did not violate the fourteenth amendment even though the club benefitted from a state liquor license. But in Roberts v. U.S. Jaycees, 468 U.S. — , 104 S. Ct. 3244 (1984), the Court rejected a constitutional challenge to a state law that, as applied, prohibited a "private" club from engaging in gender discrimination.

Is there a coherent theory of individual autonomy that explains these results? Such a theory would have to explain why the government should not be held accountable for outcomes that it could, but chooses not to change. It would have to distinguish between state "action" that impermissibly interferes with private autonomy, and state "inaction" that allows such interference to go uncorrected.

The next section explores the Court's attempt to formulate such a theory.

B. PURE INACTION AND THE THEORY OF GOVERNMENTAL NEUTRALITY

In Jackson v. Metropolitan Edison Co., 419 U.S. 345 (1974), Justice Rehnquist, writing for the Court, summarized state action jurisprudence as follows:

> While the principle that private action is immune from the restrictions of the Fourteenth Amendment is well established and easily stated, the question whether particular conduct is "private," on the one hand, or "state action" on the other, frequently admits of no easy answer. . . . [The] inquiry must be whether there is a sufficiently close nexus between the State and the challenged action of the regulated entity so that the action of the latter may be fairly treated as that of the State itself. The true nature of the State's involvement may not be immediately obvious, and detailed inquiry may be required in order to determine whether the test is met.

Typically, the Court has organized this "detailed inquiry" under two rubrics. Sometimes the Court finds a sufficiently close nexus when the state delegates a traditional state function to a private entity. On other occasions the nexus is provided when the state becomes entangled with a private entity or when it approves, encourages, or facilitates private conduct. The reach of each of these two strands of state action doctrine, and the way in which they interrelate, is explored below. Note, however, that the nexus inquiry is relevant only if one is attempting to make the state responsible for what is otherwise private conduct. When the state itself is acting — when, in other words, the state's involvement *is* "immediately obvious" — no further inquiry is necessary.

It should be readily apparent, however, that this formulation involves something of an oversimplification. In virtually every "state action" case, it is possible to find some "immediately obvious" conduct of the state that contributes in some way to the alleged constitutional violation. For example, state officials stand ready to enforce background tort and criminal rules that inevitably will favor one party to a dispute rather than the other. If this state involvement "counted" as state action, the state would always be responsible for private conduct. Consequently, before exploring ways in which private conduct is attributed to the state, it is necessary to explore in more detail the concept of state inaction.

1. Pure Inaction

Flagg Bros. v. Brooks
436 U.S. 149 (1978)

Mr. Justice Rehnquist delivered the opinion of the Court.

The question presented by this litigation is whether a warehouseman's proposed sale of goods entrusted to him for storage, as permitted by New York Uniform Commercial Code §7-210, is an action properly attributable to the State of New York. [Section 7-210 provides that after proper notification, a warehouseman may satisfy a lien on goods in his possession by selling the goods.] The District Court found that the warehouseman's conduct was not that of the State, and dismissed this suit for want of jurisdiction. [The] Court of Appeals for the Second Circuit, in reversing the judgment of the District Court, found sufficient state involvement with the proposed sale to invoke the provisions of the Due Process Clause of the Fourteenth Amendment. We agree with the District Court, and we therefore reverse.

I

[When respondent Brooks was evicted from her apartment, the city marshal arranged for storage of her possessions in petitioner's warehouse. After a series of disputes over the validity of petitioner's charges for moving and storage, petitioner sent Brooks a letter threatening sale of the possessions. Brooks thereupon initiated this action, claiming inter alia that the sale pursuant to section 7-210 without a prior judicial hearing would violate the due process clause. She relied upon a series of decisions in which the Court had held that due process requires that debtors be afforded a hearing before a creditor can utilize remedies involving the deprivation of property. See North Georgia Finishing, Inc. v. Di-Chem, Inc., 419 U.S. 601 (1975); Fuentes v. Shevin, 407 U.S. 67 (1972); Sniadach v. Family Finance Corp., 395 U.S. 337 (1969). See supra Chapter 6, section G. Brooks was later joined in her action by respondent Jones, whose goods had also been stored by petitioner following her eviction.]

II

[It] must be noted that respondents have named no public officials as defendants in this action. The city marshal, who supervised their evictions, was dismissed from the case by the consent of all the parties. This total absence of overt official involvement plainly distinguishes this case from earlier decisions imposing procedural restrictions on creditors' remedies such as [*North Georgia Finishing; Fuentes;* and *Sniadach*]. In those cases, the Court was careful to point out that the dictates of the Due Process Clause "attac[h] only to the deprivation of an interest encompassed within the Fourteenth Amendment's protection." [*Fuentes.*] While as a factual matter any person with sufficient physical power may deprive a person of his property, only a State or a private person whose action "may be fairly treated as that of the State itself," [Jackson v. Metropolitan Edison Co., 419 U.S. 345 (1974)], may deprive him of "an interest encompassed within the Fourteenth Amendment's protection," [*Fuentes*]. Thus, the only issue presented by this case is whether Flagg Brothers' action may fairly be attributed to the State of New York. We conclude that it may not.

III

Respondents' primary contention is that New York has delegated to Flagg Brothers a power "traditionally exclusively reserved to the State." [*Jackson.*] They argue that the resolution of private disputes is a traditional function of civil government, and that the State in §7-210 has delegated this function to Flagg Brothers. Respondents, however, have read too much into the language of our previous cases. While many functions have been traditionally performed by governments, very few have been "exclusively reserved to the State." . . .

[The] proposed sale by Flagg Brothers under §7-210 is not the only means of resolving this purely private dispute. Respondent Brooks has never alleged that state law barred her from seeking a waiver of Flagg Brothers' right to sell her goods at the time she authorized their storage. Presumably, respondent Jones, who alleges that she never authorized the storage of her goods, could have sought to replevy her goods at any time under state law. The challenged statute itself provides a damages remedy against the warehouseman for violations of its provisions. This system of rights and remedies, recognizing the traditional place of private arrangements in ordering relationships in the commercial world,[9] can hardly be said to have delegated to Flagg Brothers an exclusive prerogative of the sovereign.[10]

---

9. Unlike the parade of horribles suggested by our Brother Stevens in dissent this case does not involve state authorization of private breach of the peace.

10. It is undoubtedly true, as our Brother Stevens says in dissent, that "respondents have a property interest in the possessions that the warehouseman proposes to sell." But that property interest is not a monolithic, abstract concept hovering in the legal stratosphere. It is a bundle of rights in personalty, the metes and bounds of which are determined by the decisional and statutory law of the State of New York. The validity of the property interest in these possessions which respondents previously acquired from some other private person depends on New York law, and the manner in which that same property interest in these same possessions may be lost or transferred to still another private person likewise depends on New York law. It would intolerably broaden, beyond the scope of any of our previous cases, the notion of state action under the Fourteenth Amendment to hold that the mere

Whatever the particular remedies available under New York law, we do not consider a more detailed description of them necessary to our conclusion that the settlement of disputes between debtors and creditors is not traditionally an exclusive public function.[11] . . .

IV

Respondents further urge that Flagg Brothers' proposed action is properly attributable to the State because the State has authorized and encouraged it in enacting §7-210. [This] Court, however, has never held that a State's mere acquiescence in a private action converts that action into that of the State.

[It] is quite immaterial that the State has embodied its decision not to act in statutory form. If New York had no commercial statutes at all, its courts would still be faced with the decision whether to prohibit or to permit the sort of sale threatened here the first time an aggrieved bailor came before them for relief. [If] the mere denial of judicial relief is considered sufficient encouragement to make the State responsible for those private acts, all private deprivations of property would be converted into public acts whenever the State, for whatever reason, denies relief sought by the putative property owner.

[Here,] the State of New York has not compelled the sale of a bailor's goods, but has merely announced the circumstances under which its courts will not interfere with a private sale. Indeed, the crux of respondents' complaint is not that the State *has* acted, but that it has *refused* to act. This statutory refusal to act is no different in principle from an ordinary statute of limitations whereby the State declines to provide a remedy for private deprivations of property after the passage of a given period of time.

[Reversed.]

MR. JUSTICE BRENNAN took no part in the consideration or decision in these cases.

[JUSTICE MARSHALL'S dissenting opinion is omitted.]

---

existence of a body of property law in a State, whether decisional or statutory, itself amounted to "state action" even though no state process or state officials were ever involved in enforcing that body of law.

This situation is clearly distinguishable from cases such as [*North Georgia Finishing; Fuentes*; and *Sniadach*]. In each of those cases a government official participated in the physical deprivation of what had concededly been the constitutional plaintiff's property under state law before the deprivation occurred. The constitutional protection attaches not because, as in *North Georgia Finishing*, a clerk issued a ministerial writ out of the court, but because as a result of that writ the property of the debtor was seized and impounded by the affirmative command of the law of Georgia. The creditor in *North Georgia Finishing* had not simply sought to pursue the collection of his debt by private means permissible under Georgia law; he had invoked the authority of the Georgia court, which in turn had ordered the garnishee not to pay over money which previously had been the property of the debtor. See Virginia v. Rives, 100 U.S. 313, 318 (1880); Shelley v. Kraemer, 334 U.S. 1 (1948). . . .

11. It may well be, as my Brother Stevens' dissent contends, that "[t]he power to order legally binding surrenders of property and the constitutional restrictions on that power are necessary correlatives in our system." But here New York, unlike Florida in *Fuentes*, Georgia in *North Georgia Finishing*, and Wisconsin in *Sniadach*, has not ordered respondents to surrender any property whatever. It has merely enacted a statute which provides that a warehouseman conforming to the provisions of the statute may convert his traditional lien into good title. There is no reason whatever to believe that either Flagg Brothers or respondents could not, if they wished, seek resort to the New York courts in order to either compel or prevent the "surrenders of property" to which that dissent refers, and that the compliance of Flagg Brothers with applicable New York property law would be reviewed after customary notice and hearing in such a proceeding.

MR. JUSTICE STEVENS, with whom MR. JUSTICE WHITE and MR. JUSTICE MAR-
SHALL join, dissenting. . . .

There is no question in this case but that respondents have a property interest
in the possessions that the warehouseman proposes to sell. It is also clear that,
whatever power of sale the warehouseman has, it does not derive from the consent of the respondents. The claimed power derives solely from the State, and
specifically from §7-210 of the New York Uniform Commercial Code. The question is whether a state statute which authorizes a private party to deprive a person
of his property without his consent must meet the requirements of the Due
Process Clause of the Fourteenth Amendment. This question must be answered
in the affirmative unless the State has virtually unlimited power to transfer interests in private property without any procedural protections.[3] . . .

In determining that New York's statute cannot be scrutinized under the Due
Process Clause, the Court reasons that the warehouseman's proposed sale is
solely private action because the state statute "*permits* but does not compel" the
sale, (emphasis added), and because the warehouseman has not been delegated a
power "*exclusively* reserved to the State" (emphasis added). Under this approach
a State could enact laws authorizing private citizens to use self-help in countless
situations without any possibility of federal challenge. A state statute could authorize the warehouseman to retain all proceeds of the lien sale, even if they far
exceeded the amount of the alleged debt; it could authorize finance companies to
enter private homes to repossess merchandise; or indeed, it could authorize "any
person with sufficient physical power," to acquire and sell the property of his
weaker neighbor. An attempt to challenge the validity of any such outrageous
statute would be defeated by the reasoning the Court uses today: The Court's
rationale would characterize action pursuant to such a statute as purely private
action, which the State permits but does not compel, in an area not exclusively
reserved to the State.

As these examples suggest, the distinctions between "permission" and "compulsion" on the one hand, and "exclusive" and "nonexclusive," on the other, cannot
be determinative factors in state-action analysis. There is no great chasm between
"permission" and "compulsion" requiring particular state action to fall within one
or the other definitional camp. [In] this case, the State of New York, by enacting
§7-210 of the Uniform Commercial Code, has acted in the most effective and
unambiguous way a State can act. This section specifically authorizes petitioner
Flagg Brothers to sell respondents' possessions; it details the procedures that petitioner must follow; and it grants petitioner the power to convey good title to goods
that are now owned by respondents to a third party.

[Cases] such as *North Georgia Finishing* must be viewed as reflecting this
Court's recognition of the significance of the State's role in defining *and controlling* the debtor-creditor relationship. The Court's language to this effect in the
various debtor-creditor cases has been unequivocal. In Fuentes v. Shevin the
Court stressed that the statutes in question "abdicate[d] effective state control
over state power." And it is clear that what was of concern in *Shevin* was the

---

3. It could be argued that since the State has the power to create property interests, it should also
have the power to determine what procedures should attend the deprivation of those interests.
Although a majority of this Court has never adopted that position, today's opinion revives the theory
in a somewhat different setting by holding that the State can shield its legislation affecting property
interests from due process scrutiny by delegating authority to private parties.

private use of state power to achieve a nonconsensual resolution of a commercial dispute. The state statutes placed the state power to repossess property in the hands of an interested private party, just as the state statute in this case places the state power to conduct judicially binding sales in satisfaction of a lien in the hands of the warehouseman.

> Private parties, serving their own private advantage, may unilaterally invoke state power to replevy goods from another. No state official participates in the decision to seek a writ; no state official reviews the basis for the claim to repossession; and no state official evaluates the need for immediate seizure. There is not even a require- ment that the plaintiff provide any information to the court on these matters.

[Yet] the very defect that made the statutes in *Shevin* and *North Georgia Fin- ishing* unconstitutional — lack of state control — is, under today's decision, the factor that precludes constitutional review of the state statute. The Due Process Clause cannot command such incongruous results. If it is unconstitutional for a State to allow a private party to exercise a traditional state power because the state supervision of that power is purely mechanical, the State surely cannot immunize its actions from constitutional *scrutiny* by removing even the mechanical supervi- sion. . . .

It is important to emphasize that, contrary to the Court's apparent fears, this conclusion does not even remotely suggest that "all private deprivations of prop- erty [will] be converted into public acts whenever the State, for whatever reason, denies relief sought by the putative property owner." The focus is not on the private deprivation but on the state authorization. "[W]hat is always vital to remember is that it is the *state's* conduct, whether action or inaction, not the *private* conduct, that gives rise to constitutional attack." Friendly, The Dart- mouth College Case and The Public-Private Penumbra, 12 Texas Quarterly, No. 2, p. 17 (1969) (Supp.) (emphasis in original). The State's conduct in this case takes the concrete form of a statutory enactment, and it is that statute that may be challenged. . . .

Finally, it is obviously true that the overwhelming majority of disputes in our society are resolved in the private sphere. But it is no longer possible, if it ever was, to believe that a sharp line can be drawn between private and public actions. The Court today holds that our examination of state delegations of power should be limited to those rare instances where the State has ceded one of its "exclusive" powers. As indicated, I believe that this limitation is neither logical nor practical. More troubling, this description of what is state action does not even attempt to reflect the concerns of the Due Process Clause, for the state-action doctrine is, after all, merely one aspect of this broad constitutional protection.

In the broadest sense, we expect government "to provide a reasonable and fair framework of rules which facilitate commercial transactions. . . ." [Mitchell v. W. T. Grant. Co., 416 U.S. 600, 624 (1974) (Powell, J., concurring).] This "frame- work of rules" is premised on the assumption that the State will control noncon- sensual deprivations of property and that the State's control will, in turn, be subject to the restrictions of the Due Process Clause. The power to order legally binding surrenders of property and the constitutional restrictions on that power are necessary correlatives in our system. In effect, today's decision allows the State to divorce these two elements by the simple expedient of transferring the implementation of its policy to private parties. Because the Fourteenth Amendment does not countenance such a division of power and responsibility, I respectfully dissent.

LUGAR v. EDMONDSON OIL CO., 457 U.S. 922 (1982): Lugar was indebted to Edmondson Oil, who sued him in state court. Ancillary to that action, and pursuant to state law, Edmondson Oil filed an ex parte petition for prejudgment attachment of certain of Lugar's property. Acting on the petition, the clerk of the state court issued a writ of attachment, which was executed by the county sheriff. This effectively sequestered Lugar's property, although he remained in possession of it. The state court subsequently held a hearing on the propriety of the attachment and ordered it dismissed because Edmondson had failed to establish the statutory grounds for it. Lugar thereupon brought this federal action, alleging that Edmondson had acted jointly with the state to deprive him of his property without due process of law. In a 5-to-4 decision, the Court distinguished *Flagg Brothers* and held that Lugar had alleged sufficient state involvement to make out a due process violation.

Justice White delivered the Court's opinion: "Beginning with [*Sniadach*], the Court has consistently held that constitutional requirements of due process apply to garnishment and prejudgment attachment procedures whenever officers of the State act jointly with a creditor in securing the property in dispute. [In] each of these cases state agents aided the creditor in securing the disputed property; but in each case the federal issue arose in litigation between creditor and debtor in the state courts and no state official was named as a party. Nevertheless, in each case the Court entertained and adjudicated the defendant-debtor's claim that the procedure under which the private creditor secured the disputed property violated federal constitutional standards of due process. Necessary to that conclusion is the holding that private use of the challenged state procedures with the help of state officials constitutes state action for purposes of the Fourteenth Amendment. . . .

"Our cases have [insisted] that the conduct allegedly causing the deprivation of a federal right be fairly attributable to the State. These cases reflect a two-part approach to this question of 'fair attribution.' First, the deprivation must be caused by the exercise of some right or privilege created by the State or by a rule of conduct imposed by the State or by a person for whom the State is responsible. [Second], the party charged with the deprivation must be a person who may fairly be said to be a state actor. This may be because he is a state official, because he has acted together with or has obtained significant aid from state officials, or because his conduct is otherwise chargeable to the State. Without a limit such as this, private parties could face constitutional litigation whenever they seek to rely on some state rule governing their interactions with the community surrounding them. . . .

"*Flagg Brothers* focused on the [second] component of the state-action principle. [Undoubtedly] the State was responsible for the statute [authorizing Flagg Brothers' conduct]. The response of the Court, however, focused not on the terms of the statute but on the character of the defendant: [Action] by a private party pursuant to this statute, without something more, was not sufficient to justify a characterization of that party as a 'state actor.' . . .

"While private misuse of a state statute does not describe conduct that can be attributed to the State, the procedural scheme created by the statute obviously is the product of state action. . . . [We] have consistently held that a private party's joint participation with state officials in the seizure of disputed property is sufficient to characterize that party as a 'state actor' for purposes of the Fourteenth Amendment."

Justice Powell, joined by Justices Rehnquist and O'Connor dissented: "[The Court] holds that respondent, a private citizen who did no more than commence a legal action of a kind traditionally initiated by private parties, thereby engaged in 'state action.' This decision is as unprecedented as it is implausible. It is plainly unjust to the respondent, and the Court makes no argument to the contrary. Respondent, who was represented by counsel, could have had no notion that his filing of a petition in state court, in the effort to secure payment of a private debt, made him a 'state actor' liable in damages for allegedly unconstitutional action by the Commonwealth of Virginia. . . .

"[It] is not disputed that the Virginia Sheriff and Clerk of Court, the state officials who sequestered petitioner's property in the manner provided by Virginia law, engaged in state action. Yet petitioner, while alleging constitutional injury from this action by state officials, did not sue the State or its agents. . . .

"From the occurrence of state action taken by the Sheriff who sequestered petitioner's property, it does not follow that respondent became a 'state actor' simply because the Sheriff was. This Court, until today, has never endorsed this non sequitur."

Chief Justice Burger filed a separate dissenting opinion.

Note: Flagg Brothers *and the Problem of the Passive State*

On what theory is the decision of the New York legislature to vest in warehousemen the power to sell goods in their possession not "state action" subject to constitutional constraints?

1. *"Pure" inaction.* Toward the end of his opinion for the Court, Justice Rehnquist observes that "the crux of respondents' complaint is not that the State *has* acted, but that it has *refused* to act." Assuming arguendo that the state's involvement in this dispute can be fairly characterized as a "mere" refusal to act, why should that fact make a constitutional difference? Does the Constitution always permit the government to acquiesce passively in an existing state of affairs? Note that virtually all equal protection decisions can be characterized as involving state inaction. For example, in Plyler v. Doe, supra Chapter 6, section E5, the Court held that the state's failure to provide public education for "undocumented" immigrant children violated the equal protection clause. Although the Court was narrowly divided on the substantive equal protection issue, not even the dissenters claimed that the challenge should fail because of the absence of state action. Similarly, doesn't the state's failure to provide an adequate hearing in procedural due process cases like *Sniadach, Fuentes,* and *North Georgia Finishing* involve a failure to act? Of course, the state's failure to act in these situations comes in a context where the state is also acting. But is it fair to characterize New York as wholly passive with regard to the dispute between Flagg Brothers and Ms. Brooks?

Consider Brest, State Action and Liberal Theory: A Casenote on *Flagg Brothers v. Brooks*, 130 U. Pa. L. Rev. 1296, 1312-1313 (1982):

> Suppose that the law permits a debtor and creditor to engage in an ongoing game of capture-the-security: Any creditor with a lien against a debtor's property may grab and sell it if he can, and any debtor whose property is seized by a creditor may grab it back and keep it if she can. Within this little state of nature, exempt from the usual rules that forbid us from taking whatever we think is ours or can get away with, one might conceivably say that the State has not acted when the property changes hands. . . .
>
> Suppose, however, that the state intervenes to protect one or the other party's possession, once he or she has gained it. For example, suppose that the state threatens to punish Mrs. Brooks if she engages in some self-help of her own by sneaking into Flagg Brothers' warehouse and liberating her goods, or if she obstructs the public auction at which Flagg Brothers seeks to sell her goods. Although the state did not assist the creditor in gaining possession, it treats his possession as the occasion for transferring to him, and protecting against the debtor, property interests (the rights to possess and dispose of the goods) that were formerly the debtor's. Even if the creditor's *gaining* of possession cannot be characterized as action of the state, the state surely acts when it *protects* the possessory interest once gained.

2. *Statutes as state action.* If, as Brest maintains, mere state acquiescence to the asserted property interest of a possessor implicates constitutional restraints, is there any escape from the conclusion that state action is always present? Would it simplify analysis if the Court acknowledged that fact and directed its attention to whether the state action is constitutional on the merits?

Justice Stevens argues in his dissent in *Flagg Brothers* that it is crucial that "The State's conduct in this case takes the concrete form of a statutory enactment." But isn't the majority correct when it asserts that the existence of the statute is "quite immaterial" because it merely "embodie[s the state's] decision not to act"? On the other hand, cases like *Sniadach* and *Lugar* make clear that judicial enforcement of statutory mandates at the behest of private parties sufficiently implicates the state. So long as courts stand ready to enforce the statutory mandate, why should it matter whether the parties actually resort to judicial enforcement?

Compare the Court's holding regarding statutory embodiments of state refusals to act in *Flagg Brothers* with its decision eleven years earlier in Reitman v. Mulkey, 387 U.S. 369 (1967). Between 1959 and 1963, California enacted various fair housing acts that prohibited racial discrimination in the sale or rental of private dwellings. In 1964, through the initiative process, California voters enacted Proposition 14, which amended the state's constitution to prohibit the state from denying the "right of any person [to] decline to sell, lease or rent [property] to such person or persons as he, in his absolute discretion, chooses." Respondents, alleging that petitioners had refused to rent them an apartment because of their race, brought an action in state court based on the fair housing acts. They contended that Proposition 14, which had the effect of repealing the acts, violated the equal protection clause. The California Supreme Court ruled in their favor and, in a 5-to-4 decision, the U.S. Supreme Court affirmed.

The Court, in an opinion by Justice White, agreed with petitioners that the mere repeal of a statute prohibiting racial discrimination was not sufficient state action to implicate constitutional limits. But the California Supreme Court had not

> read either our cases or the Fourteenth Amendment as establishing an automatic constitutional barrier to the repeal of an existing law prohibiting racial discrimination in housing. [The state court] held the intent of [Proposition 14] was to authorize private racial discrimination in the housing market, to repeal the [fair housing acts] and to create a constitutional right to [discriminate]. . . .
>
> [Private] discriminations in housing were now not only free from [the antidiscrimination statutes] but they also enjoyed far different status than was true before the passage of those statutes. The right to discriminate, including the right to discriminate on racial grounds, was now embodied in the State's basic charter, immune from legislative, executive, or judicial regulation at any level of the state government. Those practicing racial discriminations need no longer rely solely on their personal choice. They could now invoke express constitutional authority, free from censure or interference of any kind from official sources.

Justice Harlan, joined by Justices Black, Clark, and Stewart, dissented:

> [A]ll that has happened is that California has effected a pro tanto repeal of its prior statutes forbidding private discrimination. This runs no more afoul of the Fourteenth Amendment than would have California's failure to pass any such antidiscrimination statutes in the first instance. The fact that such repeal was also accompanied by a constitutional prohibition against future enactment of such laws by the California Legislature cannot well be thought to affect, from a federal constitutional standpoint, the validity of what California has done. The Fourteenth Amendment does not reach such state constitutional action any more than it does a simple legislative repeal of legislation forbidding private discrimination.

Can *Reitman* and *Flagg Brothers* be reconciled? Is it relevant that the two cases involve different substantive constitutional rights? Does the state court's finding of an intent to authorize discrimination in *Reitman* distinguish the two cases? Didn't the New York legislature intend to authorize sales by warehousemen? In *Reitman*, why did the Court think that it mattered that the state had embodied its refusal to correct discriminatory housing practices in a constitutional amendment? Would the result in *Flagg Brothers* have been different if New York had made section 7-210 a part of its constitution? (For a further discussion of the Court's effort to distinguish "mere repeals" of civil rights laws from efforts to "restructure the political process," see Chapter 5, section C3, supra).

3. Flagg Brothers *and* Lugar. Does *Lugar* provide an adequate explanation for the result in *Flagg Brothers?* Is it consistent with *Flagg Brothers?* The Court's opinion in *Lugar* at least has the virtue of recognizing the obvious — i.e., that the conduct of the state legislature in enacting a statute is "state action" for purposes of the Constitution. But according to *Lugar*, the state action problem in *Flagg Brothers* was created by the fact that the actual defendant before the Court was a private actor who was merely invoking his statutory rights. In *Lugar*, of course, the defendant was also a private party. But there, the defendant had relied on state assistance to assert his rights, and this joint conduct was sufficient to make the private party a state actor for constitutional purposes.

Does this distinction make sense? How did the private petitioners in *Reitman* rely upon state assistance in asserting their rights? Recall that the state activity in

Lugar did not involve any actual shift in possession of the property in question. The sheriff merely served on Lugar a piece of paper announcing Lugar's legal obligations. Would the situation be functionally different if these obligations were embodied in a statute and Lugar read of them in a codification printed by the state? Does *Lugar* mean that Ms. Brooks would have been successful if she had sued the state's governor seeking a declaratory judgment that section 7-210 was unconstitutional? If Ms. Brooks had broken into Flagg Brothers warehouse and stolen her furniture, could she have successfully asserted the unconstitutionality of section 7-210 as a defense to a criminal prosecution?

2. Judicial Action and the Theory of Government Neutrality

In *Flagg Brothers*, the Court insists that "It would intolerably broaden [the] notion of state action under the Fourteenth Amendment to hold that the mere existence of a body of property law in a State [itself] amounted to 'state action' even though no state process or state officials were ever involved in enforcing that body of law." On the other hand, it seems to concede that state action is present when judicial or executive officers involve themselves in the enforcement of the law even when the enforcement is at the behest of a private party. Is this concession warranted? If state enforcement of private decisions were always subject to constitutional constraints, would any private conduct remain free from governmental control?

Shelley v. Kraemer
334 U.S. 1 (1948)

MR. CHIEF JUSTICE VINSON delivered the opinion of the Court.

These cases present for our consideration questions relating to the validity of court enforcement of private agreements, generally described as restrictive covenants, which have as their purpose the exclusion of persons of designated race or color from the ownership or occupancy of real property. Basic constitutional issues of obvious importance have been raised. . . .

[In each of the two cases before the Court, black families had purchased homes burdened by restrictive covenants, signed by property owners in the neighborhood, that prohibited occupancy by nonwhites. Respondents brought these actions in state court seeking to specifically enforce the covenant provisions. In each case, the state court upheld the provision and ruled that respondents were entitled to an injunction prohibiting petitioners from occupying the property.]

It cannot be doubted that among the civil rights intended to be protected from discriminatory state action by the Fourteenth Amendment are the rights to acquire, enjoy, own and dispose of property. Equality in the enjoyment of property rights was regarded by the framers of that Amendment as an essential pre-condition to the realization of other basic civil rights and liberties which the Amendment was intended to guarantee. Thus, [42 U.S.C. §1982], derived from §1 of the Civil Rights Act of 1866 which was enacted by Congress while the Fourteenth Amendment was also under consideration, provides:

> All citizens of the United States shall have the same right, in every State and Territory, as is enjoyed by white citizens thereof to inherit, purchase, lease, sell, hold, and convey real and personal property. . . .

It is likewise clear that restrictions on the right of occupancy of the sort sought to be created by the private agreements in these cases could not be squared with the requirements of the Fourteenth Amendment if imposed by state statute or local ordinance. We do not understand respondents to urge the contrary. . . .

But the present cases [do] not involve action by state legislatures or city councils. Here the particular patterns of discrimination and the areas in which the restrictions are to operate, are determined, in the first instance, by the terms of agreements among private individuals. Participation of the State consists in the enforcement of the restrictions so defined. The crucial issue with which we are here confronted is whether this distinction removes these cases from the operation of the prohibitory provisions of the Fourteenth Amendment.

Since the decision of this Court in the Civil Rights Cases, the principle has become firmly embedded in our constitutional law that the action inhibited by the first section of the Fourteenth Amendment is only such action as may fairly be said to be that of the States. That Amendment erects no shield against merely private conduct, however discriminatory or wrongful.

We conclude, therefore, that the restrictive agreements standing alone cannot be regarded as violative of any rights guaranteed to petitioners by the Fourteenth Amendment. So long as the purposes of those agreements are effectuated by voluntary adherence to their terms, it would appear clear that there has been no action by the State and the provisions of the Amendment have not been violated.

But here there was more. These are cases in which the purposes of the agreements were secured only by judicial enforcement by state courts of the restrictive terms of the agreements.

[That] the action of state courts and judicial officers in their official capacities is to be regarded as action of the State within the meaning of the Fourteenth Amendment, is a proposition which has long been established by decisions of this Court. . . .

One of the earliest applications of the prohibitions contained in the Fourteenth Amendment to action of state judicial officials occurred in cases in which Negroes had been excluded from jury service in criminal prosecutions by reason of their race or color. These cases demonstrate, also, the early recognition by this Court that state action in violation of the Amendment's provisions is equally repugnant to the constitutional commands whether directed by state statute or taken by a judicial official in the absence of statute. Thus, in Strauder v. West Virginia, 100 U.S. 303 (1880), this Court declared invalid a state statute restricting jury service to white persons as amounting to a denial of the equal protection of the laws to the colored defendant in that case. In the same volume of the reports, the Court in Ex parte Virginia, [100 U.S. 339 (1880)], held that a similar discrimination imposed by the action of a state judge denied rights protected by the Amendment, despite the fact that the language of the state statute relating to jury service contained no such restrictions.

The action of state courts in imposing penalties or depriving parties of other substantive rights without providing adequate notice and opportunity to defend, has, of course, long been regarded as a denial of the due process of law guaranteed by the Fourteenth Amendment.

In numerous cases, this Court has reversed criminal convictions in state courts for failure of those courts to provide the essential ingredients of a fair hearing. . . .

But the examples of state judicial action which have been held by this Court to violate the Amendment's commands are not restricted to situations in which the judicial proceedings were found in some manner to be procedurally unfair. It has been recognized that the action of state courts in enforcing a substantive common-law rule formulated by those courts, may result in the denial of rights guaranteed by the Fourteenth Amendment, even though the judicial proceedings in such cases may have been in complete accord with the most rigorous conceptions of procedural due process. Thus, in American Federation of Labor v. Swing, 312 U.S. 321 (1941), enforcement by state courts of the common-law policy of the State, which resulted in the restraining of peaceful picketing, was held to be state action of the sort prohibited by the Amendment's guaranties of freedom of discussion. In Cantwell v. Connecticut, 310 U.S. 296 (1940), a conviction in a state court of the common-law crime of breach of the peace was, under the circumstances of the case, found to be a violation of the Amendment's commands relating to freedom of religion. In Bridges v. California, 314 U.S. 252 (1941), enforcement of the state's common-law rule relating to contempts by publication was held to be state action inconsistent with the prohibitions of the Fourteenth Amendment.

The short of the matter is that from the time of the adoption of the Fourteenth Amendment until the present, it has been the consistent ruling of this Court that the action of the States to which the Amendment has reference includes action of state courts and state judicial officials. . . .

Against this background of judicial construction, extending over a period of some three-quarters of a century, we are called upon to consider whether enforcement by state courts of the restrictive agreements in these cases may be deemed to be the acts of those States; and, if so, whether that action has denied these petitioners the equal protection of the laws which the Amendment was intended to insure.

We have no doubt that there has been state action in these cases in the full and complete sense of the phrase. The undisputed facts disclose that petitioners were willing purchasers of properties upon which they desired to establish homes. The owners of the properties were willing sellers; and contracts of sale were accordingly consummated. It is clear that but for the active intervention of the state courts, supported by the full panoply of state power, petitioners would have been free to occupy the properties in question without restraint.

These are not cases, as has been suggested, in which the States have merely abstained from action, leaving private individuals free to impose such discriminations as they see fit. Rather, these are cases in which the States have made available to such individuals the full coercive power of government to deny to petitioners, on the grounds of race or color, the enjoyment of property rights in premises which petitioners are willing and financially able to acquire and which the grantors are willing to sell. The difference between judicial enforcement and nonenforcement of the restrictive covenants is the difference to petitioners between being denied rights of property available to other members of the community and being accorded full enjoyment of those rights on an equal footing.

Respondents urge, however, that since the state courts stand ready to enforce restrictive covenants excluding white persons from the ownership or occupancy of property covered by such agreements, enforcement of covenants excluding colored persons may not be deemed a denial of equal protection of the laws to the colored persons who are thereby affected. This contention does not bear scrutiny. The parties have directed our attention to no case in which a court, state or federal, has been called upon to enforce a covenant excluding members of the white majority from ownership or occupancy of real property on grounds of race or color. But there are more fundamental considerations. The rights created by the first section of the Fourteenth Amendment are, by its terms, guaranteed to the individual. The rights established are personal rights. It is, therefore, no answer to these petitioners to say that the courts may also be induced to deny white persons rights of ownership and occupancy on grounds of race or color. Equal protection of the laws is not achieved through indiscriminate imposition of inequalities.

Nor do we find merit in the suggestion that property owners who are parties to these agreements are denied equal protection of the laws if denied access to the courts to enforce the terms of restrictive covenants and to assert property rights which the state courts have held to be created by such agreements. The Constitution confers upon no individual the right to demand action by the State which results in the denial of equal protection of the laws to other individuals. And it would appear beyond question that the power of the State to create and enforce property interests must be exercised within the boundaries defined by the Fourteenth Amendment. Cf. Marsh v. Alabama, 326 U.S. 501 (1946). . . .

For the reasons stated, the judgment of the Supreme Court of Missouri and the judgment of the Supreme Court of Michigan must be reversed.

Reversed.

MR. JUSTICE REED, MR. JUSTICE JACKSON, and MR. JUSTICE RUTLEDGE took no part in the consideration or decision of these cases.

Note: Shelley v. Kraemer, *State Inaction, and the Theory of Government Neutrality*

1. *State action as a nonissue.* Shelley v. Kraemer is widely regarded as one of the most controversial and problematical decisions in all of constitutional law. See, e.g., Henkin, *Shelley v. Kraemer:* Notes for a Revised Opinion, 110 U. Pa. L. Rev. 473 (1962); Wechsler, Toward Neutral Principles of Constitutional Law, 73 Harv. L. Rev. 1, 29-31 (1959). Do you see why? Chief Justice Vinson devotes virtually all of his opinion to a demonstration that judicial action is "state action" within the meaning of the fourteenth amendment. But how could anyone doubt that there is state action when a state judge issues an injunction enforceable by the state marshal and ultimately supported by the threat of contempt and incarceration in a state institution?

Compare Shelley v. Kraemer with New York Times Co. v. Sullivan, supra Chapter 7, section D, where the Court held that the first amendment required proof of "actual malice" to support libel judgments in favor of public officials. *Sullivan*, like *Shelley*, concerned the constitutionality of a state common law rule invoked in the course of private litigation. Yet in *Sullivan* the Court never doubted that judicial enforcement of the rule was state action and devoted all its attention to the substantive question of its constitutionality. Why is the state action question controversial in *Shelley* but not in *Sullivan?*

2. *The real issue in* Shelley. After completing his lengthy discourse on the state action question, Chief Justice Vinson devotes a single paragraph to petitioners' substantive contention that the enforcement of restrictive covenants violates the equal protection clause. Is his treatment of this issue satisfactory? On what theory does a rule requiring uniform enforcement of any privately made covenant deny equality? Why does Chief Justice Vinson think that it is relevant that only whites have chosen to utilize the rule? What does he mean when he says that the equal protection clause bars the "indiscriminate imposition of inequalities"?

3. *State action and the* Washington v. Davis *problem.* Consider the following argument: In cases such as *Shelley,* focusing analysis on whether or not there is "state action" is unproductive and misleading since, as *Shelley* itself illustrates, it will always be possible to find some state actor implicated in the alleged constitutional violation. The appropriate question to ask is whether, as a substantive matter, this governmental action is unconstitutional. When one asks this question in *Shelley,* the reason for the controversy over the Court's holding becomes clearer. Recall that in Washington v. Davis, supra page 543, the Court held that a statute neutral on its face should not be subject to heightened scrutiny simply because of its disproportionate racial impact. Such statutes need satisfy only low level review unless they were enacted for a discriminatory purpose. See Chapter 5 section C2, supra.

Was Missouri law regarding restrictive covenants neutral on its face in the Washington v. Davis sense? Consider L. Tribe, Constitutional Choices 260 (1985):

> Like other states, Missouri treats most restraints on alienability of real estate as judicially unenforceable: to enforce any such restraint, a state court must first find that the *substance* of the restraining covenant is reasonable and consistent with public policy. Therefore, the issue is not whether *any* judicial enforcement of racially invidious private arrangements constitutes racially invidious state action, but whether a state may *choose* automatically to enforce restrictive covenants that discriminate against blacks *while generally regarding alienability restraints as anathema.* The real "state action" in *Shelley* was Missouri's facially discriminatory body of common and statutory law — the quintessence of a racist state policy.

Do you agree? As long as Missouri classifies some other nonracial restrictive covenants as consistent with public policy, aren't its rules neutral on their face? Are the rules nonetheless race specific and therefore subject to heightened scrutiny because the line between convenants permitted and not permitted was influenced by a racial purpose? Because the disproportionate impact of the rules on blacks creates an inference that this effect was intended?

As you read the remaining material, consider the extent to which the controversy over "state action" is really a controversy concerning the meaning and scope of Washington v. Davis and the principle of governmental neutrality that it embodies. When the Court says that there is no "state action," is it really saying that the state action is facially neutral and therefore not subject to heightened review? In addressing this question, consider the following:

a. Note that the state action question generally seems controversial only in cases like *Shelley* where the "obvious" state action is arguably facially neutral. Where the "obvious" state conduct discriminates on a racial or other suspect basis, the Court tends automatically to find state action. For example, in Plyler v. Doe, Chapter 6, section E5, supra, the state might have argued that its mere failure to provide education for "undocumented" alien children involved no state action. But because the line it drew was quasi-suspect (it was based on alienage and tended to disadvantage children who were not responsible for their illegal entry), the Court did not even discuss the state action issue.

Of course, Washington v. Davis concerned the equal protection clause, where the nature of the line drawn and "neutrality" are central concepts. Is there an analogue to the Washington v. Davis principle that influences the "state action" determination when some other constitutional right — such as free speech or due process — is at issue? The theory of government neutrality may be relevant in two respects. First, an important theme in first amendment jurisprudence is that government regulation of speech that is content-based is subject to heightened scrutiny. In contrast, when the regulation is facially neutral with respect to content, it is more likely to be sustained. See Chapter 7, section E, supra. Consider the state action issue in New York Times v. Sullivan, supra Chapter 7, section D. Was the issue uncontroversial in *Sullivan* because the state common-law rule was "content-based" and was therefore subject to heightened scrutiny under traditional first amendment jurisprudence? Second, as a matter of substantive constitutional law, the Court has sometimes distinguished between obstructing the exercise of a right and the mere failure to subsidize it. For example, although the state is obligated to allow women to secure abortions, it is under no obligation to fund them for women too poor to pay for them. See Chapter 6, section F2, supra. Similarly, although the first amendment guarantees the right of "minor" parties to participate in electoral politics, it does not follow that they also have the right to government subsidies when they do so. See Chapter 7, section E4, supra. Consider whether a finding of "no state action" is really a finding that the government has remained "neutral" in this sense and, therefore, not violated substantive constitutional provisions.

b. If there is this overlap between state action and substantive principles, is the state action doctrine doing any independent work? Note that although the Court always finds "state action" when the line between action and inaction is suspect, it does not follow that it always finds inaction when the line is neutral. Sometimes the Court disposes of such cases by finding "no state action," but on other occasions it upholds the law in question on the merits. Is it possible to formulate a general theory explaining which technique the Court will use? Would anything be lost if the Court always ignored the threshold state action issue and simply asked whether the "obvious" state conduct in the case violated substantive constitutional norms?

c. Just as the *Shelley* problem can be restated in Washington v. Davis terms, the Washington v. Davis principle may be reformulated in terms of the state action doctrine. On this view, Washington v. Davis stands for the proposition that when the state acts in a facially neutral fashion, any inequality in outcomes necessarily results from private forces for which the state bears no legal responsibility. Whichever way the proposition is stated, both the state action doctrine and the Washington v. Davis principle stem from a common assumption that the Constitution does not generally require affirmative government intervention to control private exercises of power arguably threatening constitutional values. (The phrase "constitutional values" might be taken as prejudging the very issue in dispute. That issue is whether certain values *are* constitutionally protected when the threat to them comes from private, rather than government, entities. As used here, the phrase "constitutional value" should be understood as shorthand for values that would be constitutionally protected if they were threatened by government action.) Is there a good reason that "equal" treatment of individuals differently situated with respect to the rule in question should be subject to low level review, while "unequal" treatment of those similarly situated is subject to strict scrutiny? Why government intervention to produce unequal results should be treated differently from government nonintervention producing the same results?

4. *The reach of* Shelley. The Court's decision in *Shelley* demonstrates that the theory of governmental neutrality may not be as universally applicable as cases such as Washington v. Davis suggest. But it would also be a mistake to read some of the more sweeping language in *Shelley* literally. There plainly are situations in which an individual can utilize judicial processes to effectuate a discriminatory intent. For example, it is safe to assume that no court would inquire into the racist motives of an individual invoking state trespass laws against uninvited dinner guests at a private home.

Is there something about *Shelley* that makes the invocation of judicial processes especially troublesome? Do you agree with Tribe that Missouri's refusal to enforce some, but not all, nonracial covenants means that its policy was race specific in the Washington v. Davis sense? Is it relevant that a network of restrictive covenants operates as the functional equivalent of zoning laws and, therefore, serves an essentially "governmental" function? (The "public function" strand of state action jurisprudence is discussed below at section D.) That the state's enforcement of the covenant prevented a willing buyer and seller from dealing with each other?

As you read the material below concerning the reach of *Shelley*, consider the extent to which the distinctions drawn by the Court can be justified under the Washington v. Davis principle.

a. *Governmental neutrality and the problem of money damages.* Although *Shelley* holds that affirmative judicial enforcement of restrictive covenants is unconstitutional, Chief Justice Vinson's opinion states that the mere formation of and voluntary adherence to such agreements do not violate the equal protection clause. There is thus a sense in which *Shelley* is consistent with the principle of governmental neutrality: The government may not enforce such agreements, but neither is it required to invalidate them.

But what are the requirements of neutrality in this context? Here, as elsewhere, judgments about neutrality depend on the baseline from which departures from neutrality are to be measured.

Consider, for example, the award of money damages for violation of restrictive covenants. Does *Shelley* apply if a court imposes damages on a white seller but does not prevent the black purchaser from securing possession? In Barrows v. Jackson, 346 U.S. 249 (1953), respondent entered a restrictive covenant prohibiting the use or occupancy of his property by nonwhites. He then violated the covenant by permitting nonwhites to move into the premises. Petitioners, property owners in the same neighborhood who were also parties to the covenant, sued for damages. The Court held that *Shelley* barred the suit:

> To compel respondent to respond in damages would be for the State to punish her for her failure to perform her covenant to continue to discriminate against non-Caucasians in the use of her property. [If] the State may thus punish respondent for

her failure to carry out her covenant, she is coerced to continue to use her property in a discriminatory manner, which in essence is the purpose of the covenant. Thus, it becomes not respondent's voluntary choice but the State's choice that she observe her covenant or suffer damages. The action of a state court at law to sanction the validity of the restrictive covenant here involved would constitute state action as surely as it was state action to enforce such covenants in [equity].

Chief Justice Vinson, the author of *Shelley*, was the sole dissenter:

The *Shelley* case, resting on the express determination that restrictive covenants are valid between the parties, dealt only with a state court's attempt to enforce them directly against innocent third parties whose right to enjoy their property would suffer immediate harm. [In] this case, the plaintiffs have not sought such relief. The suit is directed against the very person whose solemn promise helped to bring the covenant into existence. The plaintiffs ask only that respondent do what she in turn had a right to ask of plaintiffs — indemnify plaintiffs for the bringing about of an event which she recognized would cause injury to the plaintiffs.

Suppose that respondent had been given $2,500 in exchange for his promise not to allow blacks to use his property. Does *Barrows* mean that respondent can both break the promise and keep the money? Do you agree with the Court that the state is coercing compliance with the covenant when it orders restitution? The Court argues that requiring restitution would discourage sales to blacks. But might it not be argued that by allowing the seller to break his promise while also keeping the money he was given in exchange for the promise, the state is affirmatively encouraging him to breach the covenant?

b. *State enforcement of discriminatory testamentary and inter vivos dispositions of property.* Does *Shelley* prohibit judicial enforcement of all discriminatory transfers of property? Consider Pennsylvania v. Board of Directors of City Trusts, 353 U.S. 230 (1957). In a will probated in 1831, Stephen Girard left a fund to be held in trust for erection and operation of a school for "poor white male orphans." The will named the City of Philadelphia as the trustee, and the school was administered by a state agency. When petitioners were denied admission to the school because of their race, they brought this action. The state court denied relief, but the Supreme Court, in a brief per curiam opinion, reversed: "The Board which operates Girard College is an agency of the State of Pennsylvania. Therefore, even though the Board was acting as a trustee, its refusal to admit [petitioners] to the college because they were Negroes was discrimination by the State."

Would the result in *City Trusts* have been different if the trustees had been private and a court attempted to enforce the terms of the trust? If state executive officials are constitutionally precluded from enforcing the terms of a discriminatory trust, why should state judicial officials be treated differently? Is there a distinction between judicial enforcement of covenants restricting the use of property on racial grounds and judicial enforcement of testamentary provisions having the same effect? Presumably, the Constitution permits individuals to rely on state protection when they utilize their own property for discriminatory purposes during their lifetimes. Should a different rule apply when they attempt an inter vivos transfer of the property with a discriminatory condition? When they attempt to impose discriminatory conditions on use of the property after their death?

On remand in *City Trusts*, the state court appointed private trustees in order to comply with the terms of Girard's will. In Pennsylvania v. Brown, 392 F.2d 120

(3d Cir.), cert. denied, 391 U.S. 921 (1968), the court of appeals held that the substitution was unconstitutional.

Compare *City Trusts* with Evans v. Newton, 382 U.S. 296 (1966). In 1911 U.S. Senator Augustus O. Bacon executed a will that devised to the mayor and city council of Macon, Georgia, a tract of land to be used as a park. The will provided that the park should be used by white people only and was to be under the control of a board of managers, all of whom were to be white. At first, the city ran the park on a segregated basis, but when it began to admit blacks, members of the board of managers brought this suit asking that the city be removed as trustee. The city thereupon resigned as trustee, and the state court appointed new, private trustees to run the park. Black intervenors challenged this decision. The Supreme Court held that the park could not be run on a racially segregated basis. The Court, in an opinion by Justice Douglas, stated:

> If a testator wanted to leave a school or center for the use of one race only and in no way implicated the State in the supervision, control, or management of that facility, we assume arguendo that no constitutional difficulty would be encountered. [This] park, however, is in a different posture. For years it was an integral part of the City of Macon's activities. [The] momentum it acquired as a public facility is certainly not dissipated ipso facto by the appointment of "private" trustees. So far as this record shows, there has been no change in municipal maintenance and concern over this facility. [If] the municipality remains entwined in the management or control of the park, it remains subject to the restraints of the Fourteenth Amendment.

The Court went on to suggest that the park should be treated as a public institution because it was serving a "public function" and was "municipal" in character. (The "public function" strand of the state action doctrine is considered in section D, infra.) Justice White concurred in the result on the ground that the trust was tainted by state legislation that validated racially discriminatory conditions. Justice Black, and Harlan, and Stewart dissented.

On remand, the state court held that Senator Bacon's intention to provide a park for whites only had become impossible to fulfill. Since this limitation was, in the court's view, central to Bacon's intention, it declined to reform the trust and held instead that the trust had failed and that the parkland reverted to the testator's heirs. In Evans v. Abney, 396 U.S. 435 (1970), the Court affirmed in a 6-to-2 decision. Justice Black, a dissenter in *Newton*, wrote for the Court: "We are of the opinion that in ruling as they did the Georgia courts did no more than apply well-settled general principles of Georgia law to determine the meaning and effect of a Georgia will." Justices Douglas and Brennan dissented.

Is *Abney* consistent with *Shelley?* The Court maintained that *Shelley* was "easily distinguishable" because "Here the effect of the Georgia decision eliminated all discrimination against Negroes in the park by eliminating the park itself, and the termination of the park was a loss shared equally by the white and Negro citizens of Macon since both races would have enjoyed a constitutional right of equal access to the park's facilities had it continued." Compare Justice Brennan's dissenting opinion:

> Shelley v. Kraemer stands at least for the proposition that where parties of different races are willing to deal with one another a state court cannot keep them from doing so by enforcing a privately devised racial restriction. . . .

[So] far as the record shows, this is a case of a state court's enforcement of a racial restriction to prevent willing parties from dealing with one another. The decision of the Georgia courts thus, under Shelley v. Kraemer, constitutes state action denying equal protection.

Is *Abney* consistent with *Barrows?* The Court in *Abney* rejected petitioners' argument that

the action of the Georgia court violates the United States Constitution in that it imposes a drastic "penalty," the "forfeiture" of the park, merely because of the city's compliance with the constitutional mandate expressed by this Court in Evans v. Newton. [We] think [that] the will of Senator Bacon and Georgia law provide all the justification necessary for imposing such a "penalty." . . .

[The] Georgia Supreme Court [interpreted] Senator Bacon's will as embodying a preference for termination of the park rather than its integration. Given this, the Georgia court had no alternative under its relevant trust laws, which are long standing and neutral with regard to race, but to end the Baconsfield trust and return the property to the Senator's heirs.

Compare Justice Brennan's views: "When it is as starkly clear as it is in this case that a public facility would remain open but for the constitutional command that it be operated on a nonsegregated basis, the closing of that facility conveys an unambiguous message of community involvement in racial discrimination."

Recall Palmer v. Thompson, supra Chapter 5, section C2, decided only a year after *Abney*. In *Palmer*, Justice Black, again writing for the Court, held that a municipality's decision to close a swimming pool rather than comply with court-ordered integration was constitutionally permissible. Given *Palmer*, does anything turn on the state action analysis in *Abney*, or is the *Abney* decision, once again, fully explicable in terms of substantive equal protection doctrine?

c. *State enforcement of trespass laws.* Does *Shelley* prohibit judicial enforcement of facially neutral trespass laws at the behest of a property owner who attempts to exclude the defendants for racial reasons? This issue was posed in a series of cases involving sit-in demonstrations in racially segregated restaurants in the early 1960s. Although the Court managed to reverse all the resulting convictions, it never reached the *Shelley* issue. See, e.g., Bell v. Maryland, 378 U.S. 226 (1964) (convictions reversed and remanded for consideration of the effect of an intervening change in state law); Peterson v. Greenville, 373 U.S. 244 (1963) (conviction reversed because official state policy encouraged segregation). But although no majority opinion reached the issue, individual justices engaged in spirited debate about the relevance of *Shelley*. Consider, for example, the exchange between Justices Black and Douglas in Bell v. Maryland, supra. Justice Black argued that

The [fourteenth] Amendment does not forbid a State to prosecute for crimes committed against a person or his property, however prejudiced or narrow the victim's views may be. [Such] a doctrine would [severely] handicap a State's efforts to maintain a peaceful and orderly society. Our society has put its trust in a system of criminal laws to punish lawless conduct. [Instead] of attempting to take the law into their own hands, people have been taught to call for police protection to protect their rights wherever possible. It would betray our whole plan for a tranquil and orderly society to say that a citizen, because of his personal prejudices, habits, attitudes, or beliefs, is cast outside the law's protection and cannot call for the aid of officers sworn to uphold the law and preserve the peace.

Justice Black distinguished *Shelley:*

It seems pretty clear that the reason judicial enforcement of the restrictive covenants in *Shelley* was deemed state action was not merely the fact that a state court had acted, but rather that it had acted "to deny to petitioners, on the grounds of race or color, the enjoyment of property rights in premises which petitioners are willing and financially able to acquire and which the grantors are willing to sell." [Quoting from *Shelley.*] [This] means that the property owner may, in the absence of a valid statute forbidding it, sell his property to whom he pleases and admit to that property whom he will; so long as *both* parties are willing [parties]. [But] equally, when one party is unwilling, as when the property owner chooses *not* to sell to a particular person or *not* to admit that person, then [he] is entitled to rely on the guarantee of due process of law, that is, "law of the land," to protect his free use and enjoyment of property and to know that only by valid legislation, passed pursuant to some constitutional grant of power, can anyone disturb this free use.

For Justice Douglas, in contrast, the issue in the sit-in cases was not whether the Constitution overrode the racist preferences of private individuals in the use of their property. He thought it was important that the corporate property owners in the sit-in cases were not acting pursuant to personal preferences. "[The] corporation that owns this restaurant did not refuse service to these Negroes because 'it' did not like Negroes. The reason 'it' refused service was because 'it' thought 'it' could make more money by running a segregated restaurant."

Similarly, Justice Douglas rejected the argument that a finding of state action in this context threatened personal privacy:

The problem with which we deal has no relation to opening or closing the door of one's home. The home of course is the essence of privacy, in no way dedicated to public use, in no way extending an invitation to the public. Some businesses, like the classical country store where the owner lives overhead or in the rear, make the store an extension, so to speak of the home. But such is not this case. The facts of these sit-in cases have little resemblance to any institution of property which we customarily associate with privacy.

Thus, the *Shelley* principle was controlling: "The preferences involved in [*Shelley*] were far more personal than the motivations of the corporate managers in the present case when they decline service to Negroes. Why should we refuse to let state courts enforce *apartheid* in residential areas of our cities but let state courts enforce *apartheid* in restaurants? If a court decree is state action in one case, it is in the other. Property rights, so heavily underscored, are equally involved in each case."

Does Justice Black successfully distinguish *Shelley?* Although the property owner in *Shelley* was presently willing to sell his property to a black, at some previous time, he had agreed not to do so. Why doesn't the right to "free use and enjoyment of property" include the right to bind oneself concerning the future use of the property? Why didn't the adjoining property owners in *Shelley* have an enforcable property interest created by the restrictive covenant?

Does Justice Douglas understate the cost to associational freedoms of his approach? Granted, the restaurant owner is probably motivated by economic concerns rather than personal preferences. But presumably it is economically advantageous to run segregated restaurants because of the associational preferences of the (white) customers. Why shouldn't these preferences be taken into account? (For an argument that "external" preferences should not be taken into account when they are based on a belief that some individuals are not entitled to equal concern and respect, see supra Chapter 5, section B.)

Shortly after *Bell* the public accommodations controversy was mooted when Congress enacted the 1964 Civil Rights Act, which, inter alia, prohibited racial discrimination in most places of public accommodation. In Heart of Atlanta Motel v. United States, 379 U.S. 241 (1964), and Katzenbach v. McClung, 379 U.S. 294 (1964), the Court unanimously upheld the constitutionality of the act. See Chapter 2, section E, supra. The final chapter to the sit-in controversy came in Hamm v. City of Rock Hill, 379 U.S. 306 (1964), in which the Court held that the 1964 act abated state trespass prosecutions for conduct occurring before its passage.

Was the Court wise in "ducking" the constitutional issue posed by the sit-in cases until a political resolution could be achieved? Can the Court's unanimous affirmation of that solution be reconciled with Justice Black's concern for rights of association and private property supposedly threatened by nonenforcement of state trespass laws in this context?

C. CONSTITUTIONALLY IMPERMISSIBLE DEPARTURES FROM NEUTRALITY: STATE SUBSIDIZATION, APPROVAL, AND ENCOURAGEMENT

As discussed in the previous section, the state action doctrine may be premised on the assumption that the Constitution does not normally require departures from governmental neutrality. Under this view, as long as the government does not actively subvert constitutional values, it is generally not under an affirmative obligation to promote them. On the other hand, when the government departs from neutrality in a way that actively discourages or penalizes the exercise of constitutional rights, the Constitution comes into play.

The state can depart from neutrality in many ways — by classifying on a suspect basis, by adopting a content-based restriction on speech, by expressly disadvantaging or benefiting religion, and so on. When a governmental policy is facially nonneutral in this fashion, the state action is usually treated as "obvious," and the Court rarely acknowledges the issue.

As Shelley v. Kramer illustrates, however, there may also be another category of cases in which the Court is sometimes willing to find state action even though the government's policy is facially neutral. In these cases, the state action determination is more controversial, and the Court frequently acknowledges that the state involvement in the private conduct is "nonobvious." Nonetheless, the Court on occasion finds state action to be present, either because the government has so entangled itself with a private entity as to symbolically identify itself with the private conduct in dispute, or because the government has licensed, authorized, or encouraged that conduct.

Shelley itself tells us little about the circumstances under which facially neutral state conduct is nonetheless "state action." This section explores this problem at greater length. As you read the material that follows, consider whether the Court has developed a satisfactory test. Has it successfully distinguished between illicit encouragement of private conduct and the mere failure to prohibit such conduct? Has it adequately explained why governmental neutrality — facial or otherwise — is the appropriate test for determining whether constitutional restrictions should apply? Is the concept of government neutrality coherent?

1. State Subsidization of Private Conduct

Burton v. Wilmington Parking Authority
365 U.S. 715 (1961)

MR. JUSTICE CLARK delivered the opinion of the Court.

In this action for declaratory and injunctive relief it is admitted that the Eagle Coffee Shoppe, Inc., a restaurant located within an off-street automobile parking building in Wilmington, Delaware, has refused to serve appellant food or drink solely because he is a Negro. The parking building is owned and operated by the Wilmington Parking Authority, an agency of the State of Delaware, and the restaurant is the Authority's lessee. Appellant claims that such refusal abridges his rights under the Equal Protection Clause of the Fourteenth Amendment to the United States Constitution. The Supreme Court of Delaware has held that Eagle was acting in "a purely private capacity" under its lease; that its action was not that of the Authority and was not, therefore, state action within the contemplation of the prohibitions contained in that Amendment. [We conclude] that the exclusion of appellant under the circumstances shown to be present here was discriminatory state action in violation of the Equal Protection Clause of the Fourteenth Amendment. . . .

[The city of Wilmington created the Authority for the purpose of constructing parking facilities. Before beginning construction of the facility at issue here, the Authority entered into a series of long-term leases with commercial tenants in order to provide needed capital for its debt service requirements. One such lease was made with Eagle for a period of twenty years, renewable for another ten years. The space leased to Eagle was directly accessible from the street and had no marked public entrance leading from the parking portion of the facility into the restaurant. The Authority agreed to complete construction expeditiously, including decorative finishing of the leased premises and necessary utility connections. Eagle, in turn, spent some $220,000 to make the space suitable for its operation, and to the extent such improvements were attached to the realty, it enjoyed the Authority's tax exemption. The lease contained no requirement that restaurant services be made available to the general public on a nondiscriminatory basis, although the Authority had statutory authority to adopt rules respecting the use of its facilities so long as they would not impair the security of its bondholders. When the building was completed, the Authority placed official signs in appropriate places indicating the public character of the building and flew from mastheads on the roof both the state and national flags.

On being refused service by Eagle because of his race, appellant filed this law suit. The trial court granted his motion for summary judgment, but the Delaware Supreme Court reversed.]

[It] is clear, as it always has been since the Civil Rights Cases, that "Individual invasion of individual rights is not the subject-matter of the amendment," and that private conduct abridging individual rights does no violence to the Equal Protection Clause unless to some significant extent the State in any of its manifestations has been found to have become involved in it. Because the virtue of the right to equal protection of the laws could lie only in the breadth of its application, its constitutional assurance was reserved in terms whose imprecision was necessary if the right were to be enjoyed in the variety of individual-state relationships which the Amendment was designed to embrace. For the same reason, to fashion and apply a precise formula for recognition of state responsibility under the Equal Protection Clause is an "impossible task" which "This Court has never attempted." Kotch v. Pilot Comm'rs, 330 U.S. 552, 556. Only by sifting facts and weighing circumstances can the nonobvious involvement of the State in private conduct be attributed its true significance. . . .

[The] Delaware Supreme Court seems to have placed controlling emphasis on its conclusion [that] only some 15% of the total cost of the facility was "advanced" from public funds; that the cost of the entire facility was allocated three-fifths to the space for commercial leasing and two-fifths to parking space; that anticipated revenue from parking was only some 30.5% of the total income, the balance of which was expected to be earned by the leasing; that the Authority had no original intent to place a restaurant in the building, it being only a happenstance resulting from the bidding; that Eagle expended considerable moneys on furnishings; that the restaurant's main and marked public entrance is on Ninth Street without any public entrance direct from the parking area; and that "the only connection Eagle has with the public facility . . . is the furnishing of the sum of $28,700 annually in the form of rent which is used by the Authority to defray a portion of the operating expense of an otherwise unprofitable enterprise." While these factual considerations are indeed validly accountable aspects of the enterprise upon which the State has embarked, we cannot say that they lead inescapably to the conclusion that state action is not present. Their persuasiveness is diminished when evaluated in the context of other factors which must be acknowledged.

The land and building were publicly owned. As an entity, the building was dedicated to "public uses" in performance of the Authority's "essential governmental functions." 22 Del. Code, §§501, 514. The costs of land acquisition, construction, and maintenance are defrayed entirely from donations by the City of Wilmington, from loans and revenue bonds and from the proceeds of rentals and parking services out of which the loans and bonds were payable. Assuming that the distinction would be significant, the commercially leased areas were not surplus state property, but constituted a physically and financially integral and, indeed, indispensable part of the State's plan to operate its project as a self-sustaining unit. Upkeep and maintenance of the building, including necessary repairs, were responsibilities of the Authority and were payable out of public funds. It cannot be doubted that the peculiar relationship of the restaurant to the parking facility in which it is located confers on each an incidental variety of mutual benefits. Guests of the restaurant are afforded a convenient place to park their automobiles, even if they cannot enter the restaurant directly from the parking area. Similarly, its convenience for diners may well provide additional demand for the Authority's parking facilities. Should any improvements effected in the leasehold by Eagle become part of the realty, there is no possibility of increased taxes being passed on to it since the fee is held by a tax-exempt government agency. Neither can it be ignored, especially in view of Eagle's affirmative allegation that for it to serve Negroes would injure its business, that profits earned by discrimination not only contribute to, but also are indispensable elements in, the financial success of a governmental agency.

Addition of all these activities, obligations and responsibilities of the Authority, the benefits mutually conferred, together with the obvious fact that the restaurant is operated as an integral part of a public building devoted to a public parking service, indicates that degree of state participation and involvement in discriminatory action which it was the design of the Fourteenth Amendment to condemn. It is irony amounting to grave injustice that in one part of a single building, erected and maintained with public funds by an agency of the State to serve a public purpose, all persons have equal rights, while in another portion, also serving the public, a Negro is a second-class citizen, offensive because of his race, without rights and unentitled to service, but at the same time fully enjoys equal access to nearby restaurants in wholly privately owned buildings. [In] its lease with Eagle the Authority could have affirmatively required Eagle to discharge the responsibilities under the Fourteenth Amendment imposed upon the private enterprise as a consequence of state participation. But no State may effectively abdicate its responsibilities by either ignoring them or by merely failing to discharge them whatever the motive may be. It is of no consolation to an individual denied the equal protection of the laws that it was done in good faith. [By] its inaction, the Authority, and through it the State, has not only made itself a party to the refusal of service, but has elected to place its power, property and prestige behind the admitted discrimination. The State has so far insinuated itself into a position of interdependence with Eagle that it must be recognized as a joint participant in the challenged activity, which, on that account, cannot be considered to have been so "purely private" as to fall without the scope of the Fourteenth Amendment.

Because readily applicable formulae may not be fashioned, the conclusions drawn from the facts and circumstances of this record are by no means declared as universal truths on the basis of which every state leasing agreement is to be tested. Owing to the very "largeness" of government, a multitude of relationships might appear to some to fall within the Amendment's embrace, but that, it must be remembered, can be determined only in the framework of the peculiar facts or circumstances present. [Specifically] defining the limits of our inquiry, what we hold today is that when a State leases public property in the manner and for the purpose shown to have been the case here, the proscriptions of the Fourteenth Amendment must be complied with by the lessee as certainly as though they were binding covenants written into the agreement itself. . . .

Reversed and remanded.

MR. JUSTICE STEWART, concurring.

I agree that the judgment must be reversed, but I reach that conclusion by a route much more direct than the one traveled by the Court. In upholding Eagle's right to deny service to the appellant solely because of his race, the Supreme Court of Delaware relied upon a statute of that State which permits the proprietor of a restaurant to refuse to serve "persons whose reception or entertainment by him would be offensive to the major part of his customers. . . ." There is no suggestion in the record that the appellant as an individual was such a person. The highest court of Delaware has thus construed this legislative enactment as authorizing discriminatory classification based exclusively on color. Such a law seems to me clearly violative of the Fourteenth Amendment. I think, therefore, that [the] statute, as authoritatively construed by the Supreme Court of Delaware, is constitutionally invalid.

[A dissenting opinion by JUSTICE FRANKFURTER is omitted.]

MR. JUSTICE HARLAN, whom MR. JUSTICE WHITTAKER joins, dissenting.

The Court's opinion, by a process of first undiscriminatingly throwing together various factual bits and pieces and then undermining the resulting structure by an equally vague disclaimer, seems to me to leave completely at sea just what it is in this record that satisfies the requirement of "state action."

I find it unnecessary, however, to inquire into the matter at this stage, for it seems to me apparent that before passing on the far-reaching constitutional questions that may, or may not, be lurking in this judgment, the case should first be sent back to the state court for clarification as to the precise basis of its decision. . . .

If the Delaware court construed this state statute "as authorizing discriminatory classification based exclusively on color," I would certainly agree, without more, that the enactment is offensive to the Fourteenth Amendment. [If], on the other hand, the state court meant no more than that under the statute, as at common law, Eagle was free to serve only those whom it pleased, then, and only then, would the question of "state action" be presented in full-blown form.

Note: Subsidies, Penalties, and the Search for a Baseline

1. *The meaning of* Burton. Note that in one sense at least, the policy of the Wilmington Parking Authority was "neutral" with regard to racial discrimination by its tenants. While it did not utilize its power to prohibit such discrimination, neither did it deliberately seek tenants who would discriminate or encourage them to do so. One way to restate the holding of *Burton*, then, is that in this context, state inaction in the face of private discriminatory conduct is constitutionally unacceptable. Does the Court identify what it is about this context that triggers this affirmative obligation? The Court states that no general rules in this area are possible and that "Only by sifting facts and weighing circumstances" can "nonobvious" state involvement be detected. But is such "sifting" and "weighing" possible without some normative framework that identifies which facts are relevant and assigns the appropriate weight they should be accorded? As you read the material below, see if you can develop a normative framework that explains the result in *Burton*.

2. *State subsidization.* Does *Burton* stand for the general proposition that state subsidization of discriminatory conduct is unconstitutional? On this view, the state is not obligated to prohibit or penalize such conduct, but neither is it

permitted to accord benefits to those who engage in it. Is this position tenable? Would it be unconstitutional, for example, for the state to provide police and fire protection to establishments that discriminate? Wouldn't the withdrawal of such fundamental services be tantamount to prohibiting the discriminatory conduct?

Any theory that makes subsidization unconstitutional, but does not require penalization, ultimately rests on our ability to distinguish between the withholding of a benefit on the one hand and the imposition of a burden on the other. Is such a distinction possible without a previously established baseline concerning what governmental services individuals have a right to expect?

Consider, for example, Norwood v. Harrison, 413 U.S. 455 (1973), in which the Court confronted a constitutional challenge to a Mississippi statutory program under which textbooks were purchased by the state and lent to students in both public and private schools, without reference to whether any participating private school had racially discriminatory policies. The Court unanimously struck down the program as applied to discriminatory schools. Defenders of the program relied on Pierce v. Society of Sisters, 268 U.S. 510 (1925), which had established the constitutional right of parents to provide private education for their children. They argued that *Pierce* rights would be infringed by lending free textbooks to public school children but withholding them from certain private school children. The Court rejected this argument: "In *Pierce*, the Court affirmed the right of private schools to exist and to operate; it said nothing of any supposed right of private or parochial schools to share with public schools in state largesse, on an equal basis or otherwise. [It] is one thing to say that a State may not prohibit the maintenance of private schools and quite another to say that such schools must, as a matter of equal protection, receive state aids."

Having disposed of appellees' argument that the textbook aid was constitutionally required, the Court went on to hold that it was constitutionally impermissible: "A State may not grant the type of tangible financial aid here involved if that aid has a significant tendency to facilitate, reinforce, and support private discrimination." The Court was careful to note, however, that its holding did not extend to all types of state assistance.

> Textbooks are a basic educational tool and, like tuition grants, they are provided only in connection with schools; they are to be distinguished from generalized services government might provide to schools in common with others. Moreover, the textbooks provided to private school students by the State in this case are a form of assistance readily available from sources entirely independent of the State. [The] State has neither an absolute nor operating monopoly on the procurement of school textbooks; anyone can purchase them on the open market.

Does Norwood successfully distinguish between constitutionally impermissible subsidies for discriminatory conduct and constitutionally permissible failures to penalize such conduct? After *Norwood*, would it be unconstitutional for the state to grant the same tax-exempt status to discriminatory private schools that it grants to other charitable and nonprofit institutions? See McGlotten v. Connally, 338 F. Supp. 448 (D.D.C. 1972) (tax-exempt status of discriminatory fraternal orders unconstitutional). Cf. Bob Jones University v. United States, 461 U.S. 574 (1983) (Internal Revenue Service decision to deny tax-exempt status to private schools engaging in racial discrimination permissible as matter of statutory construction).

Is there a constitutionally relevant distinction between tax exemptions for discriminatory institutions and direct monetary subsidies to them? (For a more detailed discussion of these issues in connection with the establishment and free exercise clauses of the first amendment, see Chapter 8, section B3, supra.)

One year after *Norwood*, the Court again considered whether the provision of "generalized" government services to private discriminatory groups constituted an impermissible departure from neutrality. Gilmore v. City of Montgomery, 417 U.S. 556 (1974), arose out of the fifteen-year struggle of blacks in Montgomery, Alabama, to desegregate the city's public parks. After protracted litigation involving repeated efforts by the city to avoid the original desegregation order, the District Court enjoined the city from allowing use of city-owned recreational facilities by any private group that was racially segregated or had a racially discriminatory admissions policy. The Court of Appeals sustained this order insofar as it restrained the use of city facilities by private schools when the use was "exclusive" and not in common with other citizens. With respect to "nonexclusive" use by private school children and use by nonschool groups, however, the Court of Appeals reversed.

The Supreme Court, in an opinion by Justice Blackmun, affirmed that portion of the Court of Appeals decision prohibiting exclusive use of city facilities by segregated private schools. Emphasizing the city's affirmative duty to desegregate its public schools, the Court argued that "the city's actions significantly enhanced the attractiveness of segregated private schools, formed in reaction against the federal court school order, by enabling them to offer complete athletic programs. [We] are persuaded [that] this assistance significantly tended to undermine the federal court order mandating the establishment and maintenance of a unitary school system in Montgomery."

With regard to nonexclusive use by school groups and use by nonschool groups, however, the Court found that the record was insufficiently developed to render a decision. To guide the District Court on remand, the Court noted that nonexclusive access by segregated school groups might well undermine outstanding school desegregation orders. "For example, all-white private school basketball teams might be invited to participate in a tournament conducted on public recreational facilities with desegregated private and public school teams. [Such] assistance, although proffered in common with fully desegregated groups, might so directly impede the progress of court-ordered school desegregation within the city that it would be appropriate to fashion equitable relief."

Use by segregated nonschool groups might also undermine the outstanding decree to desegregate park facilities.

> For example, the record contains indications that there are all-white private and all-Negro public Dixie Youth and Babe Ruth baseball leagues for children, all of which use city-provided ballfields. [Were] the District Court to determine that this dual system came about as a means of evading the parks decree, or of serving to perpetuate the separate-but-equal use of city facilities on the basis of race, through the aid and assistance of the city, further relief would be appropriate.

The Court cautioned, however, that

> Traditional state monopolies, such as electricity, water, and police and fire protection — all generalized governmental services — do not by their mere provision con-

stitute a showing of state involvement in invidious discrimination. The same is true of a broad spectrum of municipal recreational facilities: parks, playgrounds, athletic facilities, amphitheaters, museums, zoos, and the like. It follows, therefore, that the portion of the District Court's order prohibiting the mere use of such facilities by *any* segregated "private group, club, or organization" is invalid because it was not predicated upon a proper finding of state action.

If, however, the city or other governmental entity rations otherwise freely accessible recreational facilities, the case for state action will naturally be stronger than if the facilities are simply available to all comers without condition or reservation. Here, for example, petitioners allege that the city engages in scheduling softball games for an all-white church league and provides balls, equipment, fields, and lighting. The city's role in that situation would be dangerously close to what was found to exist in *Burton*, where the city "elected to place its power, property and prestige behind the admitted discrimination." We are reminded, however, that the Court has never attempted to formulate "an infallible test for determining whether the State . . . has become significantly involved in private discriminations" so as to constitute state action [quoting *Reitman*].

Justice Marshall wrote a separate opinion concurring in part and dissenting in part; there were separate concurring opinions by Justices Brennan and White, with whom Justice Douglas joined.

Does *Gilmore* provide satisfactory guidelines for distinguishing between subsidies and failures to penalize? How much was the result influenced by the special, affirmative obligation of public entities to remedy the effects of prior segregative acts once a violation of Brown v. Board of Education has been established? See Chapter 5, section A4, supra. In the absence of such a violation, would even exclusive use of public facilities by segregated private entities be unconstitutional?

3. *State dependence on discriminatory conduct.* Was it crucial to the result in *Burton* that the state indirectly profited from Eagle's discriminatory conduct? Justice Clark points out that "profits earned by discrimination not only contribute to, but also are indispensable elements in, the financial success of a governmental agency." Should the result in *Burton* have been different if Eagle were able to show that its refusal to serve blacks resulted in reduced profits? If the Parking Authority had charged it a lower rent so as not to capture any of the profits earned from Eagle's discriminatory conduct? Justice Clark's opinion relies on the "mutual benefits" conferred by Eagle and the Parking Authority on each other. Note that there is a tension between the need to avoid conferring benefits on the private actor and the need to avoid public capture of the benefits from discrimination. For example, the state could avoid benefiting from the discriminatory conduct by not taxing the profits attributable to the discrimination. But by pursuing this policy, the state would in effect subsidize the discriminatory conduct. Does the need to avoid this dilemma explain the constitutional requirement that the state divorce itself entirely from discriminatory private entities when the benefits conferred are "mutual"?

4. *State action as symbolism.* Does the result in *Burton* depend on the "message" sent to the general public when a discriminatory private entity rents space in a public building? Notice Justice Clark's emphasis on the state and federal flags that flew over the parking facility. In these circumstances, is there a risk that the public would interpret Eagle's presence in the building as connoting state approval of its policies? That it would perceive Eagle as a state entity? Should the

Parking Authority prominently post signs stating that it did not approve of the racial policies of its tenants?

Consider the following observation: The "symbolism" argument begs the very question we are attempting to answer. If Eagle's presence in the building subtly communicates state approval of its policies, this must be because we believe that in this context the state has an affirmative obligation to control policies of which it disapproves. But even if this were true, we would still be faced with the task of explaining what it is about this context that triggers this obligation.

Blum v. Yaretsky

457 U.S. 991 (1982)

JUSTICE REHNQUIST delivered the opinion of the Court.

Respondents represent a class of Medicaid patients challenging decisions by the nursing homes in which they reside to discharge or transfer patients without notice or an opportunity for a hearing. The question is whether the State may be held responsible for those decisions so as to subject them to the strictures of the Fourteenth Amendment. . . .

[Under the federal Medicaid program, New York provides Medicaid assistance to eligible persons who receive care in private nursing homes, which are designated either "skilled nursing facilities" (SNFs) or "health related facilities" (HRFs). The latter provide less extensive, and generally less expensive, medical care than the former. Federal regulations require each nursing home receiving Medicaid reimbursements to establish a utilization review committee (URC) of physicians to assess periodically whether each patient is receiving the appropriate level of care.

This suit grew out of a decision by the URC at respondents' nursing home to transfer them from a SNF to an HRF. Medicaid officials were notified of this decision and prepared to terminate payments unless respondents accepted transfer to an HRF. Respondents brought this class action, naming various state officials as defendants. They alleged that the failure to give them adequate notice of the URC decisions and an administrative hearing to challenge those decisions violated the due process clause of the fourteenth amendment. The District Court ruled in respondents' favor, and the Court of Appeals affirmed.]

Faithful adherence to the "state action" requirement of the Fourteenth Amendment requires careful attention to the gravamen of the plaintiff's complaint. In this case, respondents objected to the involuntary discharge or transfer of Medicaid patients by their nursing homes without certain procedural safeguards. They have named as defendants state officials responsible for administering the Medicaid program in New York. These officials are also responsible for regulating nursing homes in the State, including those in which respondents were receiving care. But respondents are not challenging particular state regulations or procedures, and their arguments concede that the decision to discharge or transfer a patient originates not with state officials, but with nursing homes that are privately owned and operated. Their lawsuit, therefore, seeks to hold state officials liable for the actions of private parties, and the injunctive relief they have obtained requires the State to adopt regulations that will prohibit the private conduct of which they complain. . . .

[Although] the factual setting of each case will be significant, our precedents indicate that a State normally can be held responsible for a private decision only when it has exercised coercive power or has provided such significant encouragement, either overt or covert, that the choice must in law be deemed to be that of the State. Mere approval of or acquiescence in the initiatives of a private party is not sufficient to justify holding the State responsible for those initiatives under the terms of the Fourteenth Amendment. . . .

Analyzed in the light of these principles, the Court of Appeals' finding of state action cannot stand. The court reasoned that state action was present in the discharge or transfer decisions implemented by the nursing homes because the State responded to those decisions by adjusting the patient's Medicaid benefits. Respondents, however, do not challenge the adjustment of benefits, but the discharge or transfer of patients to lower levels of care without adequate notice or hearings. That the State responds to such actions by adjusting benefits does not render it *responsible* for those actions. The decisions about which respondents complain are made by physicians and nursing home administrators, all of whom are concededly private parties. There is no suggestion that those decisions were influenced in any degree by the State's obligation to adjust benefits in conformity with changes in the cost of medically necessary care.

Respondents do not rest on the Court of Appeals' rationale, however. They argue that the State "affirmatively commands" the summary discharge or transfer of Medicaid patients who are thought to be inappropriately placed in their nursing facilities. Were this characterization accurate, we would have a different question before us. However, our review of the statutes and regulations identified by respondents does not support respondents' characterization of them. . . .

The regulations cited by respondents require SNF's and HRF's "to make all efforts possible to transfer patients to the appropriate level of care or home as indicated by the patient's medical condition or needs." The nursing homes are required to complete patient care assessment forms designed by the State and "provide the receiving facility or provider with a current copy of same at the time of discharge to an alternate level of care facility or home."

These regulations do not require the nursing homes to rely on the forms in making discharge or transfer decisions, nor do they demonstrate that the State is responsible for the decision to discharge or transfer particular patients. Those decisions ultimately turn on medical judgments made by private parties according to professional standards that are not established by the State.[19] . . .

Respondents next point to regulations which, they say, impose a range of

---

19. The dissent characterizes as "factually unfounded," our conclusion that decisions initiated by nursing homes and physicians to transfer patients to lower levels of care ultimately depend on private judgments about the health needs of the patients. It asserts that different levels of care exist only because of the State's desire to save money, and that the same interest explains the requirement that nursing homes transfer patients who do not need the care they are receiving. We do not suggest otherwise. Transfers to lower levels of care are not mandated by the patients' health needs. But they occur only after an assessment of those needs. In other words, although "downward" transfers are made possible and encouraged for efficiency reasons, they can occur only after the decision is made that the patient does not need the care he or she is currently receiving. The State is simply not responsible for *that* decision, although it clearly responds to it. In concrete terms, therefore, if a particular patient objects to his transfer to a different nursing facility, the "fault" lies not with the State but ultimately with the judgment, made by concededly private parties, that he is receiving expensive care that he does not need. That judgment is a medical one, not a question of accounting.

penalties on nursing homes that fail to discharge or transfer patients whose continued stay is inappropriate. [As] we have previously concluded, however, those regulations themselves do not dictate the decision to discharge or transfer in a particular case. Consequently, penalties imposed for violating the regulations add nothing to respondents' claim of state action.

As an alternative position, respondents argue that even if the State does not command the transfers at issue, it reviews and either approves or rejects them on the merits. The regulations cited by respondents will not bear this construction. [Instead,] the State is obliged to approve or disapprove continued payment of Medicaid benefits after a change in the patient's need for services. Adjustments in benefit levels in response to a decision to discharge or transfer a patient does not constitute approval or enforcement of that decision. As we have already concluded, this degree of involvement is too slim a basis on which to predicate a finding of state action in the decision itself.

Finally, respondents advance the rather vague generalization that such a relationship exists between the State and the nursing homes it regulates that the State may be considered a joint participant in the homes' discharge and transfer of Medicaid patients. For this proposition they rely upon [Burton]. Respondents argue that state subsidization of the operating and capital costs of the facilities, payment of the medical expenses of more than 90% of the patients in the facilities, and the licensing of the facilities by the State, taken together convert the action of the homes into "state" action. But accepting all of these assertions as true, we are nonetheless unable to agree that the State is responsible for the decisions challenged by respondents. [Privately] owned enterprises providing services that the State would not necessarily provide, even though they are extensively regulated, do not fall within the ambit of Burton. That programs undertaken by the State result in substantial funding of the activities of a private entity is no more persuasive than the fact of regulation of such an entity in demonstrating that the State is responsible for decisions made by the entity in the course of its business.

[Reversed.]

[JUSTICE WHITE's opinion, concurring in the judgment in Blum and in Rendell-Baker v. Kohn, page 1511, infra, is omitted.]

JUSTICE BRENNAN, with whom JUSTICE MARSHALL joins, dissenting. . . .

[In] deciding whether "state action" is present in actions performed directly by persons other than government employees, what is required is a realistic and delicate appraisal of the State's involvement in the total context of the action taken. "Only by sifting facts and weighing circumstances can the nonobvious involvement of the State in private conduct be attributed its true significance." [Burton.] See [Lugar]. The Court today departs from the Burton precept, ignoring the nature of the regulatory framework presented by this case in favor of the recitation of abstract tests and a pigeonhole approach to the question of state action.

The Court's analysis in this case [proceeds] upon a premise that is factually unfounded. The Court [describes] the decision to transfer a nursing home resident from one level of care to another as involving nothing more than a physician's independent assessment of the appropriate medical treatment required by that resident. [If] this were an accurate characterization of the circumstances of this case, I too would conclude that there was no "state action" in the nursing home's decision to transfer. A doctor who prescribes drugs for a patient on the basis of his independent medical judgment is not rendered a state actor merely because the State may reimburse the patient in different amounts depending upon which drug is prescribed.

But the level-of-care decisions at issue in this case, even when characterized as the "independent" decision of the nursing home, have far less to do with the exercise of independent professional judgment than they do with the *State's* desire to save money. To be sure, standards for implementing the level-of-care scheme established by the Medicaid program are framed with reference to the underlying purpose of that program — to provide needed medical services. And not surprisingly, the State relies on doctors to implement this aspect of its Medicaid program. But the idea of two mutually exclusive levels of care — skilled nursing care and intermediate care — embodied in the federal regulatory scheme and implemented by the State, reflects no established medical model of health care. On the contrary, the two levels of long-term institutionalized care enshrined in the Medicaid scheme are legislative constructs, designed to serve governmental cost-containment policies. . . .

[In] my view, an accurate and realistic appraisal of the procedures actually employed in the State of New York leaves no doubt that not only has the State established the system of treatment levels and utilization review in order to further its own fiscal goals, but that the State [has] set forth precisely the standards upon which the level-of-care determinations are to be made, and has delegated administration of the program to the nursing home operators, rather than assume the burden of administering the program itself. [Where,] as here, a private party acts on behalf of the State to implement state policy, his action is state action. . . .

[The] degree of interdependence between the State and the nursing home is far more pronounced than it was between the State and the private entity in [*Burton*]. The State subsidizes practically all of the operating and capital costs of the facility, and pays the medical expenses of more than 90% of its residents. And, in setting reimbursement rates, the State generally affords the nursing homes a profit as well. Even more striking is the fact that the residents of those homes are, by definition, utterly dependent on the State for their support and their placement. For many, the totality of their social network is the nursing home community. Within that environment, the nursing home operator is the immediate authority, the provider of food, clothing, shelter, and health care, and, in every significant respect, the functional equivalent of a State. Surely, in this context we must be especially alert to those situations in which the State "has elected to place its power, property and prestige behind" the actions of the nursing home owner. See [*Burton*]. . . .

[We] may safely assume that when the State chooses to perform its governmental undertakings [with] the aid of private parties, not every action of those private parties is state action. But when the State directs, supports, and encourages those private parties to take specific action, that is state action. . . .

Because the State is clearly responsible for the specific conduct of petitioners about which respondents complain, and because this renders petitioners state actors for purposes of the Fourteenth Amendment, I dissent.

RENDELL-BAKER v. KOHN, 457 U.S. 830 (1982): Petitioners were employees of the New Perspectives School, a privately owned institution specializing in "problem" students. Nearly all the school's students were referred to it by public institutions. It was heavily regulated by public authorities, and between 90 and 99 percent of its operating budget came from public funds. Petitioners were discharged after disagreeing with certain school policies. They claimed that their discharge violated their constitutional rights to free speech and procedural due process. Chief Justice Burger wrote the Court's opinion:

"[The] Court of Appeals concluded that the fact that virtually all of the school's income was derived from government funding was the strongest factor to support a claim of state action. But in [*Blum*], we held that the similar dependence of the nursing homes did not make the acts of the physicians and nursing home administrators acts of the State, and we conclude that the school's receipt of public funds does not make the discharge decisions acts of the State.

"The school, like the nursing homes, is not fundamentally different from many private corporations whose business depends primarily on contracts to build roads, bridges, dams, ships, or submarines for the government. Acts of such private contractors do not become acts of the government by reason of their significant or even total engagement in performing public contracts. . . .

"[The] decisions to discharge the petitioners were not compelled or even influenced by any state regulation. Indeed, in contrast to the extensive regulation of the school generally, the various regulators showed relatively little interest in the school's personnel matters. . . .

"[Petitioners] argue that there is a 'symbiotic relationship' between the school and the State similar to the relationship involved in [*Burton*]. Such a claim is rejected in [*Blum*], and we rejected it here. In *Burton*, the Court [stressed] that the restaurant was located on public property and that the rent from the restaurant contributed to the support of the garage. In response to the argument that the restaurant's profits, and hence the State's financial position, would suffer if it did not discriminate, the Court concluded that this showed that the State profited from the restaurant's discriminatory conduct. The Court viewed this as support for the conclusion that the State should be charged with the discriminatory actions. Here the school's fiscal relationship with the State is not different from that of many contractors performing services for the government. No symbiotic relationship such as existed in *Burton* exists here."

Justice White wrote a separate opinion concurring in the judgment.

Justice Marshall, with whom Justice Brennan joined, dissented: "The State has delegated to the New Perspectives School its statutory duty to educate children with special needs. The school receives almost all of its funds from the State, and is heavily regulated. This nexus between the school and the State is so substantial that the school's action must be considered state action. I therefore dissent."

Note: State Action as Coercion or Significant Encouragement

1. Blum *and* Burton. Does *Blum* help explain what factors triggered the finding of state action in *Burton?* The Court argues in *Blum* that *Burton* is inapplicable despite the state's extensive involvement with private nursing homes because the

state was not responsible for the transfer decision under attack. Was the Wilmington Parking Authority responsible for Eagle's decision to discriminate against black customers?

Recall that *Burton* concerns the problem of "nonobvious" state action — i.e., situations where the government's conduct is facially neutral with respect to constitutional values. Where the government's policy discriminates in favor of private individuals threatening constitutional values, the Court generally assumes the presence of state action without discussion. In *Blum*, the Court seems to say that even when private and public entities are closely related, the state is responsible for private decisions that threaten constitutional values only "when it has exercised coercive power or has provided some significant encouragement, either overt or covert" regarding the decision. Does this formulation leave any room for findings of "nonobvious" state action?

2. Rendell-Baker *and* Burton. Does *Rendell-Baker* provide a more satisfactory account of *Burton*? According to *Rendell-Baker*, *Burton* stands for the proposition that the state may not profit from discriminatory conduct. Is that a fair reading of *Burton*? Assuming that it is, might not the school in *Rendell-Baker* pass on to the state some of the savings it realizes from avoiding the cost of due process hearings just as the restaurant in *Burton* passed on some of the profits derived from racial discrimination?

3. Blum *and* Flagg Brothers. Recall that in *Flagg Brothers*, the Court emphasized that plaintiffs had "named no public officials as defendants in [the] action." In *Blum*, however, the suit was directed against public officials. Why doesn't that dispose of the matter? Is it crucial to the result in *Blum* that plaintiffs challenged the transfer decision rather than the adjustment of Medicaid benefits? Given the fact that Medicaid officials were the named defendants, wasn't a challenge to the reduction in benefits at least implicit in their legal theory?

4. Rendell-Baker *and the recognition of public actors.* The Court begins its analysis in *Rendell-Baker* with the assumption that the New Perspectives School is "private." If the school were itself a "public" institution, there would be no doubt that its decision to discharge petitioners would be "state action." But given the fact that the school received virtually all of its funds from public sources, why does the Court begin with the assumption that it is "private"?

Presumably, what makes the New Perspectives School private is the fact that the state exercises less pervasive control over it than it would over a state instrumentality. But the very issue in dispute in *Rendell-Baker* was the degree of control the state was obligated to exercise. Would the acts of state policemen not be attributable to the state if state law left them largely unconstrained in exercising their discretion?

Compare *Rendell-Davis* with Ex parte Virginia, 100 U.S. 339 (1880), where a state judge discriminated against blacks in the selection of juries in violation of state law. The Court rejected the defendant's argument that he was not a state actor because the state had prohibited the conduct in question. "[As] he acts in the name and for the State, and is clothed with the State's power, his act is that of the State. This must be so, or the constitutional prohibition has no meaning." See also Screws v. United States, 325 U.S. 91 (1945) (state police officer who exceeds his authority under state law is nonetheless a state actor acting under color of law).

Is the *Rendell-Baker* "coercion or significant encouragement" test consistent with Ex parte Virginia and *Screws*? If a judge or police officer who acts in the teeth of state statutes is nonetheless acting for the state, why isn't a school official whose conduct is permitted by state law also a state actor?

2. State Licensing and Authorization

PUBLIC UTILITIES COMMISSION v. POLLAK, 343 U.S. 451 (1952): Capital Transit Company was a privately owned corporation providing bus and streetcar service in the District of Columbia under a franchise from Congress. In 1948 it began experimenting with a "music as you ride" program under which radio programs were amplified through loudspeakers in the streetcars and busses. In 1949 the Public Utilities Commission, which regulated Capital, ordered an investigation of the program to determine whether it was "consistent with public convenience, comfort and safety." The Commission concluded that the use of radios was not inconsistent with the public interest and dismissed its investigation. Some of Capital's passengers thereupon appealed the Commission's decision, and the Court of Appeals reversed, holding that the broadcasts deprived passengers of liberty without due process of law. Justice Burton delivered the Court's opinion:

"It was held by the court below that the action of Capital Transit in installing and operating the radio receivers, coupled with the action of the Public Utilities Commission in dismissing its own investigation of the practice, sufficiently involved the Federal Government in responsibility for the radio programs to make the First and Fifth Amendments [applicable] to this radio service. . . .

"[We agree. In reaching this result,] we do not rely on the mere fact that Capital Transit operates a public utility on the streets of the District of Columbia under authority of Congress. Nor do we rely upon the fact that, by reason of such federal authorization, Capital Transit now enjoys a substantial monopoly of street railway and bus transportation in the District of Columbia. We do, however, recognize that Capital Transit operates its service under the regulatory supervision of the Public Utilities Commission of the District of Columbia which is an agency authorized by Congress. We rely particularly upon the fact that that agency, pursuant to protests against the radio program, ordered an investigation of it and, after formal public hearings, ordered its investigation dismissed on the ground that the public safety, comfort and convenience were not impaired thereby.

"We, therefore, find it appropriate to examine into what restriction, if any, the First and Fifth Amendments place upon the Federal Government under the facts of this case, assuming that the action of Capital Transit in operating the radio service, together with the action of the Commission in permitting such operation, amounts to sufficient Federal Government action to make the First and Fifth Amendments applicable thereto."

The Court held that the broadcasts were not unconstitutional.

Moose Lodge No. 107 v. Irvis

407 U.S. 163 (1972)

MR. JUSTICE REHNQUIST delivered the opinion of the Court.

[Appellant Moose Lodge is a local branch of a national fraternal organization. Lodge policy restricts membership to whites and prohibits members from bringing black guests to the Lodge dining room and bar. When appellee, a black, was refused service because of his race, he filed this action, naming as defendants both Moose Lodge and the Pennsylvania Liquor Authority. He claimed that because the Authority had issued Moose Lodge a license that authorized the sale of alcoholic beverages on its premises, the refusal of service was "state action." He sought an injunction requiring the Authority to revoke Moose Lodge's license so long as it continued its discriminatory practices. The Court below ruled in his favor.]

In 1883, this Court in The Civil Rights Cases set forth the essential dichotomy between discriminatory action by the State, which is prohibited by the Equal Protection Clause, and private conduct, "however discriminatory or wrongful," against which that clause "erects no shield," [Shelley]. That dichotomy has been subsequently reaffirmed in [Shelley], and in [Burton].

While the principle is easily stated, the question of whether particular discriminatory conduct is private, on the one hand, or amounts to "state action," on the other hand, frequently admits of no easy answer. . . .

Our cases make clear that the impetus for the forbidden discrimination need not originate with the State if it is state action that enforces privately originated discrimination. [Shelley.] The Court held in [Burton] that a private restaurant owner who refused service because of a customer's race violated the Fourteenth Amendment, where the restaurant was located in a building owned by a state-created parking authority and leased from the authority. . . .

The Court has never held, of course, that discrimination by an otherwise private entity would be violative of the Equal Protection Clause if the private entity receives any sort of benefit or service at all from the State, or if it is subject to state regulation in any degree whatever. Since state-furnished services include such necessities of life as electricity, water, and police and fire protection, such a holding would utterly emasculate the distinction between private as distinguished from state conduct set forth in The Civil Rights Cases and adhered to in subsequent decisions. Our holdings indicate that where the impetus for the discrimination is private, the State must have "significantly involved itself with invidious discriminations," [Reitman], in order for the discriminatory action to fall within the ambit of the constitutional prohibition. . . .

Here there is nothing approaching the symbiotic relationship between lessor and lessee that was present in [Burton]. Unlike Burton, the Moose Lodge building is located on land owned by it, not by any public authority. Far from apparently holding itself out as a place of public accommodation, Moose Lodge quite ostentatiously proclaims the fact that it is not open to the public at large. Nor is it located and operated in such surroundings that although private in name, it discharges a function or performs a service that would otherwise in all likelihood be performed by the State. In short, while Eagle was a public restaurant in a public building, Moose Lodge is a private social club in a private building.

With the exception hereafter noted, the Pennsylvania Liquor Control Board plays absolutely no part in establishing or enforcing the membership or guest policies of the club that it licenses to serve liquor.[3] There is no suggestion in this

---

3. Unlike the situation in [Pollak], where the regulatory agency had affirmatively approved the practice of the regulated entity after full investigation, the Pennsylvania Liquor Control Board has neither approved nor endorsed the racially discriminatory practices of Moose Lodge.

record that Pennsylvania law, either as written or as applied, discriminates against minority groups either in their right to apply for club licenses themselves or in their right to purchase and be served liquor in places of public accommodation. The only effect that the state licensing of Moose Lodge to serve liquor can be said to have on the right of any other Pennsylvanian to buy or be served liquor on premises other than those of Moose Lodge is that for some purposes club licenses are counted in the maximum number of licenses that may be issued in a given municipality. . . .

The District Court was at pains to point out in its opinion what it considered to be the "pervasive" nature of the regulation of private clubs by the Pennsylvania Liquor Control Board. . . .

However detailed this type of regulation may be in some particulars, it cannot be said to in any way foster or encourage racial discrimination. Nor can it be said to make the State in any realistic sense a partner or even a joint venturer in the club's enterprise. The limited effect of the prohibition against obtaining additional club licenses when the maximum number of retail licenses allotted to a municipality has been issued, when considered together with the availability of liquor from hotel, restaurant, and retail licensees, falls far short of conferring upon club licensees a monopoly in the dispensing of liquor in any given municipality or in the State as a whole. We therefore hold that, with the exception hereafter noted, the operation of the regulatory scheme enforced by the Pennsylvania Liquor Control Board does not sufficiently implicate the State in the discriminatory guest policies of Moose Lodge to make the latter "state action" within the ambit of the Equal Protection Clause of the Fourteenth Amendment.

The District Court found that the regulations of the Liquor Control Board adopted pursuant to statute affirmatively require that "[e]very club licensee shall adhere to all of the provisions of its Constitution and By-Laws." . . .

The effect of this particular regulation on Moose Lodge under the provisions of the constitution placed in the record in the court below would be to place state sanctions behind its discriminatory membership rules. . . .

Even though the Liquor Control Board regulation in question is neutral in its terms, the result of its application in a case where the constitution and bylaws of a club required racial discrimination would be to invoke the sanctions of the State to enforce a concededly discriminatory private rule. State action, for purposes of the Equal Protection Clause, may emanate from rulings of administrative and regulatory agencies as well as from legislative or judicial action. [*Shelley*] makes it clear that the application of state sanctions to enforce such a rule would violate the Fourteenth Amendment. . . .

[Appellee] was entitled to a decree enjoining the enforcement of [the] regulations promulgated by the Pennsylvania Liquor Control Board insofar as [they require] compliance by Moose Lodge with provisions of its constitution and bylaws containing racially discriminatory provisions. He was entitled to no more. . . .

Reversed and remanded.

Mr. Justice Douglas, with whom Mr. Justice Marshall joins, dissenting.

My view of the First Amendment and the related guarantees of the Bill of Rights is that they create a zone of privacy which precludes government from interfering with private clubs or groups. The associational rights which our system honors permit all white, all black, all brown, and all yellow clubs to be formed. They also permit all Catholic, all Jewish, or all agnostic clubs to be established. Government may not tell a man or woman who his or her associates must be. The individual can be as selective as he desires. So the fact that the Moose Lodge allows only Caucasians to join or come as guests is constitutionally irrelevant, as is the decision of the Black Muslims to admit to their services only members of their race.

The problem is different, however, where the public domain is concerned. . . .

[The] fact that a private club gets some kind of permit from the State or municipality does not make it *ipso facto* a public enterprise or undertaking, any more than the grant to a householder of a permit to operate an incinerator puts the householder in the public domain. We must, therefore, examine whether there are special circumstances involved in the Pennsylvania scheme which differentiate the liquor license possessed by Moose Lodge from the incinerator permit. . . .

[Liquor] licenses in Pennsylvania, unlike driver's licenses, or marriage licenses, are not freely available to those who meet racially neutral qualifications. There is a complex quota system. [What] the majority neglects to say is that the quota for Harrisburg, where Moose Lodge No. 107 is located, has been full for many years. No more club licenses may be issued in that city.

This state-enforced scarcity of licenses restricts the ability of blacks to obtain liquor, for liquor is commercially available *only* at private clubs for a significant portion of each week. . . .

Thus the State of Pennsylvania is putting the weight of its liquor license, concededly a valued and important adjunct to a private club, behind racial discrimination. . . .

I would affirm the judgment below.

MR. JUSTICE BRENNAN, with whom MR. JUSTICE MARSHALL joins, dissenting.

When Moose Lodge obtained its liquor license, the State of Pennsylvania became an active participant in the operation of the Lodge bar. Liquor licensing laws are only incidentally revenue measures; they are primarily pervasive regulatory schemes under which the State dictates and continually supervises virtually every detail of the operation of the licensee's business. Very few, if any, other licensed businesses experience such complete state involvement. Yet the Court holds that such involvement does not constitute "state action" making the Lodge's refusal to serve a guest liquor solely because of his race a violation of the Fourteenth Amendment. The vital flaw in the Court's reasoning is its complete disregard of the fundamental value underlying the "state action" concept. That value is discussed in my separate opinion in Adickes v. Kress & Co., 398 U.S. 144, 190-191 (1970):

> The state-action doctrine reflects the profound judgment that denials of equal treatment, [are] singularly grave when government has or shares responsibility for them. [Something] is uniquely amiss in a society where the government, the authoritative oracle of community values, involves itself in racial discrimination. Accordingly, . . . the cases [in which] this Court has condemned significant state involvement in racial discrimination, however subtle and indirect it may have been and whatever form it may have taken[,] . . . represent vigilant fidelity to the constitutional principle that no State shall in any significant way lend its authority to the sordid business of racial discrimination.

Plainly, the State of Pennsylvania's liquor regulations intertwine the State with the operation of the Lodge bar in a "significant way [and] lend [the State's] authority to the sordid business of racial discrimination." . . .

I therefore dissent and would affirm the final decree entered by the District Court.

Jackson v. Metropolitan Edison Co.

419 U.S. 345 (1974)

MR. JUSTICE REHNQUIST delivered the opinion of the Court. . . .

[Metropolitan Edison, a privately owned utility, holds a certificate of public convenience issued by a state utility commission authorizing it to provide electricity to its customers. As a condition for holding this certificate, it is subject to extensive state regulation. Under a provision of its general tariff filed with the state commission, it has the right to discontinue service to a customer on reasonable notice of nonpayment of bills. After a lengthy dispute, Metropolitan Edison terminated Jackson's service for alleged nonpayment. Jackson thereupon brought this action, claiming that the termination constituted state action depriving her of property in violation of the due process clause of the fourteenth amendment.]

[The] mere fact that a business is subject to state regulation does not by itself convert its action into that of the State for purposes of the Fourteenth Amendment. Nor does the fact that the regulation is extensive and detailed, as in the case of most public utilities, do so. [*Pollak.*] It may well be that acts of a heavily regulated utility with at least something of a governmentally protected monopoly will more readily be found to be "state" acts than will the acts of an entity lacking these characteristics. But the inquiry must be whether there is a sufficiently close nexus between the State and the challenged action of the regulated entity so that the action of the latter may be fairly treated as that of the State itself. [*Moose Lodge.*] The true nature of the State's involvement may not be immediately obvious, and detailed inquiry may be required in order to determine whether the test is met. [*Burton*]. . . .

[Petitioners] first argues that "state action" is present because of the monopoly status allegedly conferred upon Metropolitan by the State of Pennsylvania. As a factual matter, it may well be doubted that the State ever granted or guaranteed Metropolitan a monopoly.[8] But assuming that it had, this fact is not determinative in considering whether Metropolitan's termination of service to petitioner was "state action" for purposes of the Fourteenth Amendment. In Pollak, [we] expressly disclaimed reliance on the monopoly status of the transit authority. Similarly, although certain monopoly aspects were presented in Moose Lodge No. 107, we found that the Lodge's action was not subject to the provisions of the Fourteenth Amendment. In each of those cases, there was insufficient relationship between the challenged actions of the entities involved and their monopoly status. There is no indication of any greater connection here.

---

8. [As] petitioner admits, such public utility companies are natural monopolies created by the economic forces of high threshold capital requirements and virtually unlimited economy of scale. Regulation was superimposed on such natural monopolies as a substitute for competition and not to eliminate it. . . .

We also reject the notion that Metropolitan's termination is state action because the State "has specifically authorized and approved" the termination practice. In the instant case, Metropolitan filed with the Public Utility Commission a general tariff — a provision of which states Metropolitan's right to terminate service for nonpayment. This provision has appeared in Metropolitan's previously filed tariffs for many years and has never been the subject of a hearing or other scrutiny by the Commission. Although the Commission did hold hearings on portions of Metropolitan's general tariff relating to the general rate increase, it never even considered the reinsertion of this provision in the newly filed general tariff. The provision became effective 60 days after filing when not disapproved by the Commission. . . .

The case most heavily relied on by petitioner is [*Pollak*]. [It] is not entirely clear whether the Court alternatively held that Capital Transit's action was action of the "state" for First Amendment purposes, or whether it merely assumed, arguendo, that it was and went on to resolve the First Amendment question adversely to the bus riders.[16] In either event, the nature of the state involvement there was quite different than it is here. The District of Columbia Public Utilities Commission, on its own motion, commenced an investigation of the effects of the piped music, and after a full hearing concluded not only that Capital Transit's practices were "not inconsistent with public convenience, comfort, and safety," but also that the practice "in fact, through the creation of better will among passengers, . . . tends to improve the conditions under which the public ride." Here, on the other hand, there was no such imprimatur placed on the practice of Metropolitan about which petitioner complains. The nature of governmental regulation of private utilities is such that a utility may frequently be required by the state regulatory scheme to obtain approval for practices a business regulated in less detail would be free to institute without any approval from a regulatory body. Approval by a state utility commission of such a request from a regulated utility, where the commission has not put its own weight on the side of the proposed practice by ordering it, does not transmute a practice initiated by the utility and approved by the Commission into "state action." At most, the Commission's failure to overturn this practice amounted to no more than a determination that a Pennsylvania utility was authorized to employ such a practice if it so desired. Respondent's exercise of the choice allowed by state law where the initiative comes from it and not from the State, does not make its action in doing so "state action" for purposes of the Fourteenth Amendment.

[Affirmed.]

[Dissenting opinions by JUSTICES DOUGLAS and BRENNAN are omitted.]

MR. JUSTICE MARSHALL, dissenting.

When the State confers a monopoly on a group or organization, this Court has held that the organization assumes many of the obligations of the State. Even

---

16. At one point the Court states:

We find in the reasoning of the court below a sufficiently close relation between the Federal Government and the radio service to make it necessary for us to consider those Amendments." Later, the opinion states: "We, therefore, find it appropriate to examine into what restriction, if any, the First and Fifth Amendments place upon the Federal Government . . . *assuming* that the action of Capital Transit . . . amounts to sufficient Federal Government action to make the First and Fifth Amendments applicable thereto." (Emphasis added.)

when the Court has not found state action based solely on the State's conferral of a monopoly, it has suggested that the monopoly factor weighs heavily in determining whether constitutional obligations can be imposed on formally private entities. . . .

The majority distinguishes this line of cases with a cryptic assertion that public utility companies are "natural monopolies." The theory behind the distinction appears to be that since the State's purpose in regulating a natural monopoly is not to aid the company but to prevent its charging monopoly prices, the State's involvement is somehow less significant for state-action purposes. I cannot agree that so much should turn on so narrow a distinction. [It] is far from obvious that an electric company would not be subject to competition if the market were unimpeded by governmental restrictions. . . .

The difficulty inherent in this kind of economic analysis counsels against excusing natural monopolies from the reach of state-action principles. . . .

[The] suggestion that the State would have to "put its own weight on the side of the proposed practice by ordering it" seems to me to mark a sharp departure from our previous state-action cases. From the Civil Rights Cases to Moose Lodge, we have consistently indicated that state authorization and approval of "private" conduct would support a finding of state action.

[I] question the wisdom of giving such short shrift to the extensive interactions between the company and the State, and focusing solely on the extent of state support for the particular activity under challenge. In cases where the State's only significant involvement is through financial support or limited regulation of the private entity, it may be well to inquire whether the State's involvement suggests state approval of the objectionable conduct. But where the State has so thoroughly insinuated itself into the operations of the enterprise, it should not be fatal if the State has not affirmatively sanctioned the particular practice in question.

[It] seems to me in any event that the State *has* given its approval to Metropolitan Edison's termination procedures. The State Utility Commission approved a tariff provision under which the company reserved the right to discontinue its service on reasonable notice for nonpayment of bills.

The majority attempts to make something of the fact that the tariff provision was not challenged in the most recent Utility Commission hearings, and that it had apparently not been challenged before. But the provision had been included in a tariff required to be filed and approved by the State pursuant to statute. That it was not seriously questioned before approval does not mean that it was not approved. . . .

What is perhaps most troubling about the Court's opinion is that it would appear to apply to a broad range of claimed constitutional violations by the company. The Court has not adopted the notion, accepted elsewhere, that different standards should apply to state-action analysis when different constitutional claims are presented. Thus, the majority's analysis would seemingly apply as well to a company that refused to extend service to Negroes, welfare recipients, or any other group that the company preferred, for its own reasons, not to serve. I cannot believe that this Court would hold that the State's involvement with the utility company was not sufficient to impose upon the company an obligation to meet the constitutional mandate of nondiscrimination. Yet nothing in the analysis of the majority opinion suggests otherwise.

I dissent.

Note: Licensing and Authorization as State Action

1. Pollak *and the failure to regulate.* If Congress had chosen not to regulate bus and railway service at all, the Court presumably would have held that the decision of a private company to install radio service was not "state action." Why does the government's refusal to prohibit this practice become state action when it is part of a pervasive pattern of regulation? Does licensing justify a state action finding because it eliminates competitive pressures that otherwise might prevent the private entity from engaging in the challenged conduct? Because the absence of an alternative source for the service increases the costs of the challenged conduct to those objecting to it? Note that *Pollak* rejects Capital Transit's monopoly status as a basis for finding state action.

Is the symbolic significance of the state's affirmative imprimatur on the activity dispositive? Recall that in *Flagg Brothers*, the Court treats a statute authorizing Flagg Brothers' sale as "immaterial" because it merely "embodied [the state's] refusal to act in statutory form."

2. *Licensing and government neutrality.* Is the requirement of government neutrality relevant to the *Pollak* problem? Was the action of the Public Service Commission a departure from neutrality? Does it matter that its statutory mandate required it to prohibit the radio broadcast if it found that the practice was not in the public interest?

In Columbia Broadcasting System v. Democratic National Committee, 412 U.S. 94 (1973), the Federal Communication Commission refused to require broadcast licensees to accept editorial advertising. The Court rejected a first amendment attack on the broadcasters' practice. In a portion of his opinion joined by only two other justices, Chief Justice Burger argued that the Federal Communications Commission decision did not make the actions of the broadcasters "state action." He distinguished *Pollak* as follows: "[In *Pollak*] Congress had expressly authorized the agency to undertake plenary intervention into the affairs of the carrier and it was pursuant to that authorization that the agency investigated the challenged policy and approved it on public interest standards. [Here], Congress has not established a regulatory scheme for broadcast licensees as pervasive as the regulation of public transportation in *Pollak*. More important, [Congress] has affirmatively indicated in the Communications Act that certain journalistic decisions are for the licensee, subject only to the restrictions imposed by evaluation of its overall performance under the public interest standard. In *Pollak* there was no suggestion that Congress had considered worthy of protection the carrier's interest in exercising discretion over the content of communications forced on passengers."

Does this distinction make sense? Why should it matter whether the decision not to regulate is made by Congress directly or by an agency exercising power delegated by Congress? If Pennsylvania liquor laws provided that the liquor control board should apportion licenses in the public interest, but that it should in no event take into account the racially discriminatory policy of applicants in doing so, would this provision make the case for Moose Lodge stronger or weaker? Cf. Reitman v. Mulkey, supra section B1.

Neither *Moose Lodge* nor *Jackson* purport to overrule *Pollak*. Is the Court's distinction between those cases and *Pollak* convincing? Would the result in *Pollak* have been different if the Public Service Commission had concluded that the radio broadcasts were so clearly in the public interest that no investigation was necessary?

Did the regulatory schemes in *Moose Lodge* and *Jackson* depart from the requirement of governmental neutrality? Both schemes are facially neutral in the Washington v. Davis sense. Do government-enforced monopolies in these contexts nonetheless constitute subsidies for conduct that threatens constitutional values? Answering this question presumably involves a comparison between the status quo and the situation that would exist if the government were completely passive. Is such a comparison meaningful?

Consider Justice Marshall's suggestion in his *Jackson* dissent that the Court's decision would allow state-regulated utilities to withhold service from blacks. Do you agree? If the state action inquiry is really about the merits, might not there be differences in the government's obligation depending upon which substantive constitutional right is at stake? Does *Moose Lodge* (which, unlike *Jackson*, involved discrimination against blacks) suggest that Justice Marshall's fears are nonetheless well founded?

D. CONSTITUTIONALLY REQUIRED DEPARTURES FROM NEUTRALITY: THE PUBLIC FUNCTION DOCTRINE

As the previous section illustrates, the Court has sometimes found "state action" when the government impermissibly *departs* from a position of neutrality by *discouraging* the vindication of constitutional values. For example, the Court held in *Shelley* that government enforcement of restrictive covenants impermissibly implicated the state in the perpetuation of segregation. More rarely, the Court has found "state action" when the government impermissibly *adheres* to a position of neutrality when it is obligated to *encourage* the vindication of these values. For example, the Court has held that the government may not remain passive while owners of a "company town" utilize their private power to suppress speech. See Marsh v. Alabama, infra.

This section discusses the circumstances under which departures from neutrality are constitutionally obligated.

Marsh v. Alabama
326 U.S. 501 (1946)

MR. JUSTICE BLACK delivered the opinion of the Court.

In this case we are asked to decide whether a State, consistently with the First and Fourteenth Amendments, can impose criminal punishment on a person who undertakes to distribute religious literature on the premises of a company-owned town contrary to the wishes of the town's management. The town, a suburb of Mobile, Alabama, known as Chickasaw, is owned by the Gulf Shipbuilding Corporation. Except for that it has all the characteristics of any other American town. The property consists of residential buildings, streets, a system of sewers, a sewage disposal plant and a "business block" on which business places are situated. A deputy of the Mobile County Sheriff, paid by the company, serves as the town's policeman. Merchants and service establishments have rented the stores and business places on the business block and the United States uses one of the places as a post office [and] according to all indications the residents use the business block as their regular shopping center. To do so, they now, as they have for many years, make use of a company-owned paved street and sidewalk located alongside the store fronts in order to enter and leave the stores and the post office. Intersecting company-owned roads at each end of the business block lead into a four-lane public highway which runs parallel to the business block at a distance of thirty feet. There is nothing to stop highway traffic from coming onto the business block and upon arrival a traveler may make free use of the facilities available there. In short the town and its shopping district are accessible to and freely used by the public in general and there is nothing to distinguish them from any other town and shopping center except the fact that the title to the property belongs to a private corporation.

Appellant, a Jehovah's Witness, came onto the sidewalk [and] undertook to distribute religious literature. In the stores the corporation had posted a notice which read as follows: "This Is Private Property, and Without Written Permission, No Street, or House Vendor, Agent or Solicitation of Any Kind Will Be Permitted." Appellant was warned that she could not distribute the literature without a permit and told that no permit would be issued to her. She protested that the company rule could not be constitutionally applied so as to prohibit her from distributing religious writings. When she was asked to leave the sidewalk and Chickasaw she declined. The deputy sheriff arrested her and she was charged in the state court with violating [a state statute] which makes it a crime to enter or remain on the premises of another after having been warned not to do so. Appellant contended that to construe the state statute as applicable to her activities would abridge her right to freedom of press and religion contrary to the First and Fourteenth Amendments to the Constitution. This contention was rejected and she was convicted. . . .

Had the title to Chickasaw belonged not to a private but to a municipal corporation and had appellant been arrested for violating a municipal ordinance rather than a ruling by those appointed by the corporation to manage a company town it would have been clear that appellant's conviction must be reversed. [Our] question then narrows down to this: Can those people who live in or come to Chickasaw be denied freedom of press and religion simply because a single company has legal title to all the town?

[We] do not agree that the corporation's property interests settle the question. [Ownership] does not always mean absolute dominion. The more an owner, for his advantage, opens up his property for use by the public in general, the more do his rights become circumscribed by the statutory and constitutional rights of those who use it. Thus, the owners of privately held bridges, ferries, turnpikes and railroads may not operate them as freely as a farmer does his farm. Since these facilities are built and operated primarily to benefit the public and since their operation is essentially a public function, it is subject to state regulation. . . .

Whether a corporation or a municipality owns or possesses the town the public in either case has an identical interest in the functioning of the community in such manner that the channels of communication remain free. [The] managers appointed by the corporation cannot curtail the liberty of press and religion of these people consistently with the purposes of the Constitutional guarantees, and a state statute, as the one here involved, which enforces such action by criminally punishing those who attempt to distribute religious literature clearly violates the First and Fourteenth Amendments to the Constitution.

Many people in the United States live in company-owned towns. These people, just as residents of municipalities, are free citizens of their State and country. Just as all other citizens they must make decisions which affect the welfare of community and nation. To act as good citizens they must be informed. In order to enable them to be properly informed their information must be uncensored. There is no more reason for depriving these people of the liberties guaranteed by the First and Fourteenth Amendments than there is for curtailing these freedoms with respect to any other citizen.

When we balance the Constitutional rights of owners of property against those of the people to enjoy freedom of press and religion, as we must here, we remain mindful of the fact that the latter occupy a preferred position. [In] our view the circumstance that the property rights to the premises where the deprivation of liberty, here involved, took place, were held by others than the public, is not sufficient to justify the State's permitting a corporation to govern a community of citizens so as to restrict their fundamental liberties and the enforcement of such restraint by the application of a state statute.

[Reversed and remanded.]

MR. JUSTICE JACKSON took no part in the consideration or decision of this case. [JUSTICE FRANKFURTER's concurring opinion is omitted.]

MR. JUSTICE REED, dissenting. . . .

What the present decision establishes as a principle is that one may remain on private property against the will of the owner and contrary to the law of the state so long as the only objection to his presence is that he is exercising an asserted right to spread there his religious views. This is the first case to extend by law the privilege of religious exercises beyond public places or to private places without the assent of the owner. . . .

The rights of the owner, which the Constitution protects as well as the right of free speech, are not outweighed by the interests of the trespasser, even though he trespasses in behalf of religion or free speech. We cannot say that Jehovah's Witnesses can claim the privilege of a license, which has never been granted, to hold their meetings in other private places, merely because the owner has admitted the public to them for other limited purposes. . . .

[CHIEF JUSTICE VINSON] and MR. JUSTICE BURTON join in this dissent.

Note: The "Public Function" Theory and the Passive State

1. Marsh *and* Shelley. Note that Justice Black might have written an opinion in *Marsh* that paralleled the Court's analysis one year later in *Shelley*. He might have focused attention on state court enforcement of Alabama's trespass statute and held that this judicial conduct violated the first amendment. But although Justice Black makes brief reference to the state prosecution, his analysis focuses on the

conduct of the company town, rather than the conduct of the state court. Why should decisions of this "private" entity be treated as if they were state decisions? Would the town's actions have been unconstitutional if its owners had physically ejected Marsh without resorting to the state's legal processes?

2. *"Public functions" and private power.* Some language in *Marsh* supports the view that the town was subject to constitutional constraint because it was acting "like" a state. Thus, Justice Black points out that except for its private ownership, Chickasaw had "all the characteristics of any other American town." Why is this relevant?

To the extent that the opinion rests on this premise, it seems to stand for the proposition that there are limits on the extent to which the state may escape constitutional restraints by "delegating" to private parties functions traditionally performed by the state. Does the opinion make clear what those limits are or why they were exceeded in this case?

Even if a "public function" test is workable, why should it matter for state action purposes that the Gulf Shipbuilding Corporation was performing a public function? The Court's concern in Marsh was that citizens in company-owned towns are "free citizens of their State and country" and that "In order to enable them to be properly informed their information must be uncensored." So long as the owners of the town were able to censor information, does it matter whether, in other respects, they were exercising state-like powers?

Some passages in *Marsh* suggest that the difficulty was not with the state's delegation of public functions to a private entity, but with its failure to act in the face of widespread undermining of constitutional values. Viewed in this light, the opinion is a rare acknowledgment that individual freedom may, on occasion, be as threatened by private as by public action. From this perspective, Gulf Shipbuilding's status was "public" because its power rivaled that of the state, rather than because of any particular function it had assumed. Whereas constitutional liberty is normally associated with limits on governmental authority, in *Marsh* the Court arguably thought that the Constitution required the government to intervene actively in order to control exercises of private power.

Of course, when the government so intervenes, there is a risk that it will also restrict liberty. Recall, for example, Chief Justice Burger's argument that imposing first amendment limitations on broadcasters by requiring them to accept editorial advertising would undermine their first amendment rights. In *Marsh*, the Court arguably restricted Gulf Shipbuilding's property and first amendment rights in order to protect the rights of appellant. Does Justice Black offer a convincing rationale for subordinating Gulf Shipbuilding's rights? Is it sufficient to observe that in balancing "constitutional rights of owners of property against those of the people to enjoy freedom of press and religion, [the] latter occupy a preferred position." Why is it relevant that Gulf had, in other respects, opened its property to the public?

3. *The reach of the public function doctrine.* In what other circumstances should the state's delegation of governmental power to private entities or failure to control exercises of private power be subject to constitutional constraint? Consider the following applications of the public function doctrine:

a. *The "white primary" cases.* In a series of cases involving the effective exclusion of blacks from Texas elections, the Court held that the discriminatory policies of "private" political organizations could be attributed to the state. Nixon v.

Herndon, 273 U.S. 536 (1927), held that the fourteenth amendment had been violated when blacks were denied ballots in the state Democratic party primary pursuant to a Texas statute that stated "in no event shall a Negro be eligible to participate in a Democratic Party primary election held in the State of Texas." Texas thereupon rewrote the statute to provide that the State Executive Committee of the party in power could prescribe the qualifications of its members for voting. In Nixon v. Condon, 286 U.S. 73 (1932), the Court once again found that the denial of the franchise to blacks was unconstitutional. Since the Committee was acting under authority expressly delegated by the state, the Court reasoned that its decisions could be attributed to the state.

In Grovey v. Townsend, 295 U.S. 45 (1935), however, where the policy of racial exclusion had been adopted by the state party convention without specific statutory authorization, the Court held that there was no state action and therefore no constitutional violation. In the Court's view, the exclusionary policy was voluntarily adopted by the Democratic Party, which was not an organ of the state. The policy was no more than a refusal of party membership with which "the State need have no concern."

Grovey was overruled in Smith v. Allwright, 321 U.S. 649 (1944). The Court stated that "The privilege of membership in a party may be, as this Court said in [*Grovey*] no concern of a State. But when, as here, that privilege is also the essential qualification for voting in a primary to select nominees for a general election, the State makes the action of the party the action of the State."

Although the Court was unambiguous in holding that the Democratic Party's exclusionary policy could be attributed to the state, the exact basis for the attribution was less clear. In part, the state action finding seemed to rest on the "public function" performed by party officials. Thus, the Court wrote that "the place of the primary in the electoral scheme makes clear that state delegation to a party of the power to fix the qualifications of primary elections is delegation of a state function that may make the party's action the action of the State."

But the state action finding seemed to rest as well on actual state involvement in the primary election process:

> When primaries become a part of the machinery for choosing officials, state and national, as they have here, the same tests to determine the character of discrimination or abridgement should be applied to the primary as are applied to the general election. If the State requires a certain electoral procedure, prescribes a general election ballot made up of party nominees so chosen and limits the choice of the electorate in general elections for state offices, practically speaking, to those whose names appear on such a ballot, it endorses, adopts and enforces the discrimination against Negroes, practiced by a party entrusted by Texas law with the determination of the qualifications of participants in the primary.

Finally, another passage in the opinion suggested that the state had an affirmative constitutional obligation to prevent private organizations from abridging electoral rights:

> The United States is a constitutional democracy. Its organic law grants to all citizens a right to participate in the choice of elected officials without restriction by any State because of race. This grant to the people of the opportunity for choice is not to be

nullified by a State through casting its electoral process in a form which permits a private organization to practice racial discrimination in the election. Constitutional rights would be of little value if they could be thus indirectly denied.

Although the Court maintained virtual unanimity in Smith, controversy over which strand of the opinion was determinative erupted nine years later in Terry v. Adams, 345 U.S. 461 (1953), the last in this series of cases. Terry concerned the exclusion of blacks from "pre-primaries" held by the Jaybird Democratic Association, a Texas political organization. The Jaybirds maintained that they were not a political party at all, but rather, a self-governing voluntary club. Their election was not regulated by the state, and there was no legal connection between victory in that election and nomination by the Democratic Party to run in the subsequent general election. As a practical matter, however, white voters generally abided by the "recommendations" of the Jaybirds, and the Jaybird president testified that a purpose of his organization was to exclude blacks from the voting process. The Jaybirds were so successful in this endeavor that victors in the Jaybird primary had, almost without exception, run and won without opposition in the Democratic primaries and the general election that followed.

Although eight justices agreed that exclusion of blacks from the Jaybird primary violated the fifteenth amendment, no opinion attracted a majority. Writing for three Justices, Justice Black focused on the state's failure to control private conduct that effectively deprived blacks of political power:

> The only election that has counted in this Texas county for more than fifty years has been that held by the Jaybirds from which Negroes were excluded. The Democratic primary and the general election have become no more than the perfunctory ratifiers of the choice that has already been made in Jaybird elections from which Negroes have been excluded. It is immaterial that the state does not control that part of this elective process which it leaves for the Jaybirds to manage. [The] effect of the whole procedure, Jaybird primary plus Democratic primary plus general election, is to do precisely that which the Fifteenth Amendment forbids — strip Negroes of every vestige of influence in selecting the officials who control the local county matters that intimately touch the daily lives of citizens.

Writing only for himself, Justice Frankfurter insisted that "The vital requirement [for a fifteenth amendment violation] is State responsibility — that somewhere, somehow, to some extent, there be an infusion of conduct by officials, panoplied with State power, into any scheme by which colored citizens are denied voting rights merely because they are colored." But here Justice Frankfurter found that state involvement because state election officials had participated in the Jaybird primary.

> As a matter of practical politics, those charged by State law with the duty of assuring all eligible voters an opportunity to participate in the selection of candidates at the primary — the county election officials who are normally leaders in their communities — participate by voting in the Jaybird primary. [If] the Jaybird Association, although not a political party, is a device to defeat the law of Texas regulating primaries, and if the electoral officials, clothed with State power in the county, share in that subversion, they cannot divest themselves of the State authority and help as participants in the scheme.

The four other justices who found the requisite state action joined an opinion by Justice Clark. In his view, the record established that the Jaybirds operated "as part and parcel of the Democratic Party, an organization existing under the auspices of Texas law." It followed that the result was dictated by Smith v. Allright. "[When] a state structures its electoral apparatus in a form which devolves upon a political organization the uncontested choice of public officials, that organization itself, in whatever disguise, takes on those attributes of government which draw the Constitution's safeguards into play."

Justice Minton cast the sole dissenting vote:

> What the Jaybird Association did here was to conduct as individuals, separate and apart from the Democratic Party of the State, a straw vote as to who should receive the Association's endorsement for county and precinct offices. It has been successful in seeing that those who receive its endorsement are nominated and elected. That is true of concerted action by any group. [I] do not understand that concerted action of individuals which is successful somehow becomes state action.

Are the various opinions finding state action in *Terry* sufficiently cognizant of the need to maintain a sphere free from governmental control for those wishing to influence government policy? If the state had attempted to control participation in the Jaybird primary, might not the Jaybirds have had a plausible first amendment complaint? Consider Cover, The Origins of Judicial Activism in the Protection of Minorities, 91 Yale L.J. 1287, 1311 (1982): "Only by protecting the right of [pressure] groups to associate, to communicate, and to seek to influence government can one have a community life that is antecedent and superior to the acts of the state. [If] all political life must pass a test of healthfulness, those who control the testing apparatus have the means to substitute party and state for political society."

Do you agree with Justice Minton that the Jaybirds' success should have no bearing on the state action determination? When private groups effectively secure the power normally associated with the state, why shouldn't they be subject to the same restrictions? Is it relevant that the Jaybirds were able to wield this power only because of the voluntary decision by most white voters to adhere to the result of the Jaybird primary? Recall that, on one theory, this sort of "voluntary" exclusion of discrete and insular minorities from private coalitions is precisely why laws discriminating against such minorities are subject to heightened scrutiny. See chapter 5, section C1, supra. If the results of such exclusionary coalitions are constitutionally suspect, is it reasonable to think that the Constitution places no limits on the ability to form the coalitions in the first place?

b. *Private property and public functions.* Does the public function doctrine help to explain other cases where the Court has placed constitutional limits on the owners of private property? Does it explain *Shelley?*

In Evans v. Newton, supra section B2, the Court's opinion invalidating the exclusion of blacks from the park created by Senator Bacon's will, rested in part on the public character of the facility:

> The service rendered even by a private park of this character is municipal in nature. It is open to every white person, there being no selective element other than race. Golf clubs, social centers, luncheon clubs, schools such as Tuskegee was at least in origin, and other like organizations in the private sector are often racially oriented.

A park, on the other hand, is more like a fire department or police department that traditionally serves the community. Mass recreation through the use of parks is plainly in the public domain; and state courts that aid private parties to perform that public function on a segregated basis implicate the State in conduct proscribed by the Fourteenth Amendment.

Public function analysis also played a role for at least some of the justices in analyzing state responsibility for the racial exclusions at issue in the sit-in cases. See section B2 supra. For example, in a long concurring opinion in Bell v. Maryland, supra section B2, Justice Goldberg argued that restaurants were places of "public accommodation" that the framers of the fourteenth amendment assumed would be subject to governmental control.

> Prejudice and bigotry in any form are regrettable, but it is the constitutional right of every person to close his home or club to any person or to choose his social intimates and business partners solely on the basis of personal prejudice including race. These and other rights pertaining to privacy and private association are themselves constitutionally protected liberties. [But the] broad acceptance of the public in this and in other restaurants clearly demonstrates that the proprietor's interest in private or unrestricted association is slight. The relationship between the modern innkeeper or restaurateur and the customer is relatively impersonal and evanescent. [As] the history of the common law and, indeed, of our own times graphically illustrates, the interests of proprietors of places of public accommodation have always been adapted to the citizen's felt need for public accommodations, a need which is basic and deep-rooted.

Note that the opinion for the Court in *Evans* and Justice Goldberg's concurrent in *Bell* both emphasize the strand in *Marsh* that focused on the "inherently" public or private character of the activity involved. Both opinions tend to underplay the strand that focused on the degree to which private entities exercise the kind of coercive power normally associated with the state. Which version of the public function doctrine is more persuasive?

4. *Retreat from* Marsh? In more recent years, the Court has demonstrated growing reluctance to burden private entities with constitutional requirements through the public function doctrine. Thus, although shopping centers are generally as open to the public as parks, the Court has held that their owners are not bound by the first amendment. See Hudgens v. NLRB, infra this section. And although major utilities arguably exercise coercive power rivalling that of the state, the Court has refused to impose the requirements of procedural due process upon them. See Jackson v. Metropolitan Edison Co., infra this section.

The Court has not completely abandoned public function analysis, however. In *Flagg Brothers*, supra section B1, for example, the Court rejected respondents' argument that "dispute resolution" was a public function. But it found it necessary to warn that

> there are a number of state and municipal functions not covered by our election cases or governed by the reasoning of *Marsh* which have been administered with a greater degree of exclusivity by States and [municipalities]. Among these are such functions as education, fire and police protection, and tax collection. We express no view as to the extent, if any, to which a city or State might be free to delegate to

private parties the performance of such functions and thereby avoid the strictures of the Fourteenth Amendment.

As you read the material below, consider which version of the public function doctrine the modern court has adopted. In its current form, does the doctrine take sufficient account of the need to leave "private space" free from government control? Is it sufficiently attentive to the risk that constitutional values will be undermined by private coercion?

JACKSON v. METROPOLITAN EDISON CO., 419 U.S. 345 (1974): This case, which is summarized in more detail at section C2 supra, arose when Metropolitan, a privately owned utility holding a certificate of public convenience issued by the Pennsylvania Public Utility Commission, terminated Jackson's electrical service for alleged nonpayment of bills. Jackson claimed that her due process rights were violated because she was not accorded a hearing prior to the termination. Justice Rehnquist delivered the Court's opinion:

"Petitioner [urges] that state action is present because respondent provides an essential public service required to be supplied on a reasonably continuous basis by [state law], and hence performs a 'public function.' We have, of course, found state action present in the exercise by a private entity of powers traditionally exclusively reserved to the State. [Nixon v. Condon; *Marsh*; Evans v. Newton]. If we were dealing with the exercise by Metropolitan of some power delegated to it by the State which is traditionally associated with sovereignty, such as eminent domain, our case would be quite a different one. But while the Pennsylvania statute imposes an obligation to furnish service on regulated utilities, it imposes no such obligation on the State. The Pennsylvania courts have rejected the contention that the furnishing of utility services is either a state function or a municipal duty.

"Perhaps in recognition of the fact that the supplying of utility service is not traditionally the exclusive prerogative of the State, petitioner invites the expansion of the doctrine of this limited line of cases into a broad principle that all businesses 'affected with the public interest' are state actors in all their actions.

"We decline the invitation for reasons stated long ago in Nebbia v. New York, 291 U.S. 502 (1934), in the course of rejecting a substantive due process attack on state legislation:

> It is clear that there is no closed class or category of businesses affected with a public interest. . . . The phrase "affected with a public interest" can, in the nature of things, mean no more than that an industry, for adequate reason, is subject to control for the public good. In several of the decisions of this court wherein the expressions "affected with a public interest," and "clothed with a public use," have been brought forward as the criteria . . . it has been admitted that they are not susceptible of definition and form an unsatisfactory test. . . .

"Doctors, optometrists, lawyers, Metropolitan, and Nebbia's upstate New York grocery selling a quart of milk are all in regulated businesses, providing arguably essential goods and services, 'affected with a public interest.' We do not believe that such a status converts their every action, absent more, into that of the State."

Justice Douglas filed a dissenting opinion: "It is said that the fact that respondent's services are 'affected with a public interest' is not determinative. I agree that doctors, lawyers, and grocers are not transformed into state actors simply because they provide arguably essential goods and services and are regulated by the State. In the present case, however, respondent is not just one person among many; it is the only public utility furnishing electric power in the city. When power is denied a householder, the home, under modern conditions, is likely to become unlivable. . . .

"Electrical service, being a necessity of life under the circumstances of this case, is an entitlement which under our decisions may not be taken without the requirements of procedural due process."

Justice Marshall also filed a dissenting opinion: "[The] fact that Metropolitan Edison Co. supplies an essential public service that is in many communities supplied by the government weighs more heavily for me than for the majority. The Court concedes that state action might be present if the activity in question were 'traditionally associated with sovereignty,' but it then undercuts that point by suggesting that a particular service is not a public function if the State in question has not required that it be governmentally operated. This reads the 'public function' argument too narrowly. The whole point of the 'public function' cases is to look behind the State's decision to provide public services through private parties. See [Evans v. Newton; *Terry*; *Marsh*]. In my view, utility service is traditionally identified with the State through universal public regulation or ownership to a degree sufficient to render it a 'public function.' . . .

"Private parties performing functions affecting the public interest can often make a persuasive claim to be free of the constitutional requirements applicable to governmental institutions because of the value of preserving a private sector in which the opportunity for individual choice is maximized. Maintaining the private status of parochial schools [advances] just this value. In the due process area, a similar value of diversity may often be furthered by allowing various private institutions the flexibility to select procedures that fit their particular needs. But it is hard to imagine any such interests that are furthered by protecting privately owned public utility companies from meeting the constitutional standards that would apply if the companies were state owned. The values of pluralism and diversity are simply not relevant when the private company is the only electric company in town."

Note: Public Functions as "Exclusive Prerogatives" of the State

1. *Post*-Jackson *developments*. In a series of decisions since *Jackson*, the Court has rejected "public function" arguments in a number of different contexts:

a. *Shopping centers*. In Amalgamated Food Employees Union v. Logan Valley Plaza, 391 U.S. 308 (1968), a pre-*Jackson* decision, the Court held that shopping centers were covered by the *Marsh* principle. The case arose out of peaceful picketing of a supermarket located in a privately owned shopping mall. Noting that the "similarities between the business block in *Marsh* and the shopping center in the present case are striking," the Court saw "no reason why access to a business district in a company town [should] be constitutionally required, while access for the same purpose to property functioning as a business district should be limited simply because the property surrounding the 'business district' is not under the same ownership." Justice Black, the author of *Marsh*, dissented: "*Marsh* was never intended to apply to this kind of situation. [I] think it is fair to say that the basis on which the [decision] rested was that the property involved encompassed an area that for all practical purposes had been turned into a town. [I] can find very little resemblance between the shopping center involved in this case and Chickasaw, Alabama." Justices Harlan and White also dissented.

Four years later, the Court sharply limited the reach of *Logan Valley*. In Lloyd Corp. v. Tanner, 407 U.S. 551 (1972), the Court held that *Logan Valley* was inapplicable to handbilling protesting the Vietnam war and conducted at a privately owned shopping center. The Court noted that *Logan Valley* was distinguishable because picketers there would have been effectively denied the opportunity to convey their message to patrons of the store in question had they been denied access to the shopping center. The Lloyd Center, in contrast, was surrounded by public sidewalks where handbilling would have been permitted. Moreover, *Logan Valley*, unlike *Lloyd*, involved first amendment activity "directly related [to] the use to which the shopping center property was being put." The Court rejected the argument that owners of the shopping center could not prohibit picketing because the facility was generally open to the public. "Respondents' argument, even if otherwise meritorious, misapprehends the scope of the invitation extended to the public. The invitation is to come to the Center to do business with the tenants." *Marsh* was not apposite because it "involved the assumption by a private enterprise of all of the attributes of a state-created municipality and the exercise by that enterprise of semi-official municipal functions as a delegate of the State." Justice Marshall, the author of *Logan Valley*, filed a dissenting opinion which was joined by Justices Douglas, Brennan, and Stewart.

Lloyd purported merely to distinguish *Logan Valley*. In a post-*Jackson* case, however, the Court announced that "the reasoning [in] *Lloyd* cannot be squared with the reasoning [in] *Logan Valley*." Hudgens v. NLRB, 424 U.S. 507 (1976). The Court "[made] clear, [if] it was not clear before, that the rationale of *Logan Valley* did not survive the [decision] in the Lloyd case." Accordingly, "the constitutional guarantee of free expression has no part to play in a case such as this." Justice Marshall, joined by Justice Brennan, dissented.

b. *Dispute resolution.* As noted above, in Flagg Brothers v. Brooks, supra section B1, the Court held that resolution of disputes between creditors and debtors is not a "public function." The Court focused primarily on the "exclusivity" requirement. "Creditors and debtors have had available to them historically a far wider number of choices than has one who would be an elected public official, or a member of Jehovah's Witnesses who wished to distribute literature in Chickasaw, Ala., at the time *Marsh* was decided."

c. *Schools.* In Rendell-Baker v. Kohn, supra page 1511, the Court held that a private school for "maladjusted" high school students was not subject to constitutional constraints. The Court reached this conclusion despite the fact that students were placed in the program by public officials and virtually all of the school's funding came from public sources. With regard to petitioners' public function argument, the Court conceded that "There can be no doubt that the education of maladjusted high school students is a public function." But in the Court's view, that was "only the beginning of the inquiry." It must further be shown that the function has been "traditionally the *exclusive* prerogative of the State. [Quoting from *Jackson*.]" Here, the state had elected to provide services for these students at public expense, but "That legislative policy choice in no way makes these services the exclusive province of the State. [That] a private entity performs a function which serves the public does not make its acts state action." Justice Marshall, joined by Justice Brennan, dissented.

d. *Nursing homes*. In Blum v. Yaretsky, supra page 1507, a case decided on the same day as *Rendell-Baker*, the Court announced that nursing homes in receipt of federal Medicaid payments were not performing a public function when they decided on the level of care for their patients. The Court rejected respondents' argument that the Medicaid statute and state law made the state responsible for providing every Medicaid patient with nursing home services. Moreover, "Even if respondents' characterization of the State's duties were correct, [it] would not follow that decisions made in the day-to-day administration of a nursing home are the kind of decisions traditionally and exclusively made by the sovereign for and on behalf of the public." Justice Brennan, joined by Justice Marshall, dissented.

2. Jackson *and the legacy of* Marsh. Recall that the public function doctrine, as first articulated in *Marsh*, seemed to rest on two interlocking rationales. First, constitutional restraints were appropriate because company towns had the power to undermine freedom as effectively as the state. Second, state intervention to control this power was not itself subversive of individual liberty because company towns were already open to the public and serving public functions. Much of the confusion in the post-*Marsh* cases arguably stems from disagreement about which of these rationales is dominant. Justice Black seems to have placed the greatest weight on the private power rationale. In *Terry*, for example, he emphasized that the Jaybirds, like the state itself, had the power effectively to disfranchise black citizens. He seemed less concerned than Justice Minton that state regulation of this "private" organization would undermine liberty. Compare Justice Black's position regarding primary elections with his views in the sit-in and shopping center cases. Justices Douglas, Marshall, and Goldberg all emphasized that restaurants and shopping centers were open to the public and not engaged in "private" conduct. Justice Black's refusal to burden these "private entities" with constitutional responsibilities may have stemmed from his perception that restaurants and shopping centers do not exercise the kind of coercive power available to the private parties in *Marsh* and *Terry*.

Does either of the original *Marsh* rationales survive *Jackson*? The emphasis on alternative means of dispute resolution in *Flagg Brothers* arguably relates to the degree of coercive power possessed by creditors. And the "limited invitation" argument in the shopping center cases seems responsive to the "open to the public" rationale. More generally, however, the Court now appears ready to exempt "private" entities from constitutional responsibilities even in situations where both of the *Marsh* requirements are satisfied.

In *Jackson* itself, for example, a public utility serving all customers prepared to pay the fee and subject to pervasive government regulation can hardly advance a convincing claim based on individual autonomy. Moreover, its monopoly status (whether "natural" or not) gives it tremendous power over its customers.

Instead of inquiring into the power of the private entity and its claim to individual autonomy, however, the *Jackson* court asked whether its function has "traditionally" been performed by the state and whether it is the "exclusive" prerogative of the state. Even if this test is workable (see below), why should the "state action" question turn on these factors? Note, for example, that even the municipal functions at stake in Marsh were hardly the "exclusive" prerogatives of the state. Indeed, Justice Black argued that constitutional constraints were necessary precisely because "Many people in the United States live in company-owned towns." Would it have made an important difference if such towns were a new development or had existed for a long time?

3. *Public functions and natural law.* What does it mean for a function to be traditionally the exclusive prerogative of the state? Obviously, the "exclusivity" prong of the requirement cannot be taken literally, since the problem would never arise if state control of the function were altogether exclusive. Note as well that whether or not a function is "exclusively" the state's may depend on how the function is characterized. In *Flagg Brothers*, for example, it may make an important difference whether one thinks of the function as "dispute resolution" (nonexclusive) or as the transfer of property interests (arguably exclusive).

Is the "tradition" component of the *Jackson* test any more helpful? In Garcia v. San Antonio Metropolitan Transit Authority, supra Chapter 2, section E, the Court rejected as unworkable a similar test for measuring federalism limits on congressional authority to interfere with the states. The Court reasoned that a historical test for measuring "traditional governmental functions" would result in "linedrawing of the most arbitrary sort; the genesis of state governmental functions stretches over a historical continuum from before the Revolution to the present, and courts would have to decide by fiat precisely how longstanding a pattern of state involvement had to be."

Nor would a nonhistorical standard be workable. "The essence of our federal system is that within the realm of authority left open to them under the Constitution, the States must be equally free to engage in any activity that their citizens choose for the common weal, no matter how unorthodox or unnecessary anyone else — including the judiciary — deems state involvement to be."

Garcia was written in the context of challenges to federal legislative power vis a vis the states. Are the problems it identifies less acute when the issue is the extent of federal judicial power vis a vis private entities?

Does the *Jackson* test ultimately depend on a platonic or "natural law" view of the functions appropriately attributable to state and individual? Consider in this connection the *Jackson* Court's reliance on Nebbia v. New York, 291 U.S. 502 (1934). In *Nebbia*, which marked the beginning of the end of the "*Lochner* era," the Court upheld the constitutionality of state legislation fixing the price of milk. See Chapter 6, section D, supra. The Court's reliance on *Nebbia* in *Jackson* is doubly ironic. First, in the passage quoted in *Jackson*, the *Nebbia* Court rejected the effort to define a class of private businesses inherently "affected with the public interest." Yet the Court's formulation of the public function doctrine in *Jackson* arguably depends on just such a definition. Second, in *Nebbia*, the Court's contention that there was no "natural" dividing line between the public and private laid the groundwork for an extension of governmental power far beyond what had been permitted during the *Lochner* era. Yet in *Jackson*, the Court relies upon *Nebbia* to establish limits on the reach of government control.

Before the demise of *Lochner*, the Court treated such limits as a preconstitutional given that neither legislature nor court had the power to alter. In more recent years, the Court has generally followed *Nebbia* and, at least in the area of "social and economic legislation," treated the division between public and private as a matter of legislative discretion. See Chapter 6, section D, supra. Does a version of *Lochner* survive as a "natural" barrier to judicial, as opposed to legislative, invasions of the private sphere? Is there good reason to treat legislative and judicial invasions differently?

E. THE CONSTITUTION AND PRIVATE POWER: SOME FINAL THOUGHTS

Does the existence of the "state action" doctrine make any difference in the way that the Court actually decides cases? Is the finding of "no state action" simply another way of announcing the Court's conclusion that the state action, which is always present, is constitutional?

Some commentators have concluded that the "state action" requirement need never prevent a litigant from securing a decision on the merits of a constitutional claim. On this view, it will always be possible to find some government actor and, through clever lawyering, to structure litigation that will challenge the constitutionality of that official's conduct. Consider L. Tribe, Constitutional Choices 255 (1985):

> [State] rules [can be brought] into focus by suing [the] state officials who possess the power, by virtue of the state rules at issue, to put "private" actors in a position to inflict injury — for example, by delegating governmental or monopoly power to private entities. [In *Moose Lodge*, for example,] if the plaintiff had sued the members of the Pennsylvania liquor control board rather than the Moose, he could have directly charged the board members with soborning racism and aggravating its impact by handing out the privilege of a scarce liquor license without regard to the licensee's racist practices. Similarly in [*Jackson*] the plaintiff probably should have sued not Met Ed but the members of the public utility commission that gave Met Ed a monopoly and thus put it in a position to cut plaintiff off from *all* electric power without providing due process in the termination proceeding.

Do you agree that one can always locate a state actor whose responsibility for the challenged conduct can be litigated? Consider Goodman, Professor Brest on State Action and Liberal Theory, and a Postscript to Professor Stone, 130 U. Pa. L. Rev. 1331, 1343 (1982): "Even if one were to conclude [that] private conduct in which the state acquiesces is state action, no such conclusion would be possible with respect to conduct that the state itself makes unlawful."

Note that even if a litigant is able to surmount the state action obstacle, there is no guarantee of success on the merits. Tribe acknowledges that "there are many other ways of slamming the door on the underlying substantive claim. [For] example, the dispossessed would doubtless meet with no success in attacking the constitutionality of private property as an institution. The present Court would presumably deny the existence of an affirmative duty on the part of government to rescue people from their economic [plight]." Constitutional Choices, supra, at 265.

Even if the state action doctrine does not bar suits at the threshold, might not the doctrine influence the result on the merits? To what extent is the "state action" requirement embedded in the substance of constitutional law? Consider the following argument: Much of our thinking about constitutional law is premised on the assumption that personal freedom is linked to the absence of governmental power. The assumption is so basic that it is built into our language of constitutional rights: Speech is said to be "free" when the government passes no laws abridging it; no process is said to be "due" unless the government changes the status quo by depriving individuals of life, liberty, or property.

The state action doctrine is a natural outgrowth of this assumption. It limits government power in two ways: It requires application of constitutional limits when the government acts to restrict individual liberty, and it requires freedom from at least judicially imposed constitutional constraints when individuals act without government assistance or support.

But even if there were no formal state action doctrine, the same attitude toward private and government power would be apparent in the substantive outcome of constitutional litigation. Recall, for example, Linmark Associates v. Township of Willingboro, supra Chapter 7, section D4. In *Linmark*, an integrated, residential community began to lose white residents as the nonwhite population increased. In an effort to maintain the town's integrated status, the township council enacted an ordinance prohibiting display of "For Sale" and "Sold" signs on all but model homes. In a unanimous decision written by Justice Marshall, the Court held that the ordinance violated the first amendment. The Court explained that the law was defective on the ground that the township had "sought to restrict the free flow of [information] because it fears that otherwise homeowners will make decisions inimical to what the [town council] views as the homeowners' self-interest and the corporate interest of the township."

The *Linmark* opinion contains no discussion of the state action doctrine. Was the Court's view of the merits nonetheless influenced by the doctrine? Isn't the Court's first amendment analysis premised on the assumption that individuals are "free" when government power is restricted? Is that premise sound? Arguably, the ordinance invalidated by the Court was a necessary predicate to real freedom. Before its passage, homeowners may well have been effectively forced into speaking by competitive pressure from their neighbors and the feared collapse in the value of their homes as "panic selling" took hold. Although each individual may have wished not to advertise his or her house for sale, this wish could not be achieved so long as each acted individually. Only through collective action pursuant to which all homeowners agreed to refrain from advertising could each individual's desire be realized.

Did the Court fail to pursue this line of analysis because of the assumptions underlying the state action doctrine? Should the competitive pressure not count as "coercion" because the state is not responsible for it? Because self-interest shaped by private behaviour should not be equated with legal obligation?

Is there a good reason why our constitutional law should erect special barriers against collective state action designed to control nongovernmental coercion? Is it a sufficient answer that defects in the political process prevent the accurate aggregating of individual preferences? That unrestrained majoritarianism leads to diminution of minority rights? Aren't these problems also present when resources are distributed by private markets free from government control?

One consequence of abandoning the state action requirement would be to threaten a second fundamental premise upon which much of constitutional law is built: the assumption of governmental neutrality. As long as the government is not held responsible for actual outcomes, "neutrality" is a plausible benchmark against which the constitutionality of its actions can be measured. The government is then permitted to remain passive and is said not to violate constitutional limits so long as it does not actively intervene to aid one group or another. In contrast, if the government were held constitutionally responsible for the actual outcomes produced when its "neutral" policies interacted with private conduct, it would be necessary to decide which groups the government should favor and what outcomes it is constitutionally required to achieve.

Do the difficulties inherent in this analysis suggest that the Court has been wise in insisting on the state action requirement? Does our experience during the *Lochner* era counsel against embarking on the self-conscious effort to define our values through the process of constitutional adjudication? Alternatively, is the lesson of *Lochner* that there also value judgments — albeit, perhaps not self-conscious ones — embedded in the selection of benchmarks against which departures from governmental neutrality are measured? In the assumption that the government is neutral when it is passive? In the assumption that it is passive when it "merely" enforces the allocation of property rights that allow private markets to function?

Is there ultimately any escape from the necessity of using government power to define the values of the community in which we would like to live? Is it possible to concede to government this power while also maintaining the space within which we can lead private and autonomous lives?

Table of Cases

Italic type indicates principal and intermediate cases.

A & P Tea Co. v. Cottrell, 270-271
Abington School Dist. v. Schempp, 1364, 1366, 1374, 1389, 1393-1394, 1413-1415, 1423
Abood v. Detroit Bd. of Educ., 1302
Abrams v. United States, 931, 947, 949, 953-954, 959
Adair v. United States, 740, 745
Adams v. Richardson, 364
Adamson v. California, 705, 713, 724
Adderley v. Florida, 1187
Adickes v. Kress & Co., 1516
Adkins v. Children's Hosp., 612, 740
Adler v. Board of Educ., 110, 1288, 1290
Africa v. Pennsylvania, 1372
Aguilar v. Felton, 1404, 1405-1406
Ake v. Oklahoma, 679
Alamo Found., Tony and Susan, v. Secretary of Labor, 1423
Albertson v. Subversive Activities Control Bd., 984
Alexander v. Holmes County Bd. of Educ., 492
Alexander v. Louisiana, 563
Alfred A. Knopf, Inc. v. Colby, 1299
Allee v. Medrano, 85
Allen v. Wright, 78, 87, 101
Allgeyer v. Louisiana, 146, 728, 734, 745
Allied Stores of Ohio v. Bowers, 513
Allied Structural Steel Co. v. Spannaus, 1439
Amalgamated Meat Cutters v. Connally, 268
Ambach v. Norwick, 662-663
American Booksellers Ass'n v. Hudnut, 1138
American Communications Ass'ns v. Douds, 983, 1292, 1294
American Fed'n of Labor v. Swing, 1490
American Party of Texas v. White, 788
American Textile Mfrs. Inst. v. Donovan, 369

Anastoplo, In re, 1313
Anders v. California, 682
Anderson v. Celebrezze, 791
Anderson v. Martin, 563
Andrus v. Allard, 1462
Apodaca v. Oregon, 722
Aptheker v. Secretary of State, 984, 1294
Armstrong v. United States, 1454
Arnett v. Kennedy, 905-906, 908, 914, 919-920, 1043, 1281
Associated Press v. NLRB, 1323
Association of Data Processing Servs. Orgs. v. Camp, 87
Austin Indep. School Dist. v. United States, 493
Avery v. Georgia, 560
Avery v. Midland County, 775
Avitzur v. Avitzur, 1409

Bacchus Imports v. Dias, 276, 327, 336
Baggett v. Bullitt, 1044, 1293
Bailey v. Drexel Furniture Co., 151, 216, 219
Bailey v. Richardson, 900
Baird v. State Bar, 1293, *1313*
Baker v. Carr, 84, 95, 767-768
Baldwin v. Fish & Game Comm'n, 815
Baldwin v. G. A. F. Seelig, 266, 284, 291-293, 306
Baldwin v. Montana Fish & Game Comm'n, 330-331, 815
Ball v. James, 764-765
Bantam Books v. Sullivan, 1144
Barber v. Time, Inc., 1089
Barenblatt v. United States, 1316
Barron v. Baltimore, 445, 707, 708
Barrows v. Jackson, 1040, 1494-1495, 1497
Bates v. State Bar of Arizona, 1101, 1104-1106

Bearden v. Georgia, 797
Beauharnais v. Illinois, 721, 1059, 1065, *1082*, 1086
Bell v. Maryland, 1475, 1497, 1499, 1528
Bell v. Wolfish, 755, 1273
Bellotti v. Baird, 882-883
Benton v. Maryland, 721
Berea C. v. Kentucky, 455-456
Bernal v. Fainter, 662
Bibb v. Navajo Freight Lines, 298, 300, 308, 310, 312
Bigelow v. Virginia, 1092, 1104
Bi-Metallic Inv. Co. v. State Bd. of Equalization, 923
Bishop v. Wood, 911
Block v. Hirsh, 740
Blount v. Rizzi, 1050, 1144
Blum v. Yaretsky, *1507*, 1509, 1511-1512, 1532
Board of Curators of U. of Mo. v. Horowitz, 290, 920
Board of Educ. v. Allen, 1398-1399, 1402
Board of Educ., Island Trees Union Free School Dist. v. Pico, 1262
Board of Regents of St. C. v. Roth, 901, 908, 910
Bob Jones U. v. United States, 78, 80, 1504
Boddie v. Connecticut, 679, 798, 800-893
Bolger v. Youngs Drug Prod. Corp., 1101, 1111, 1152
Bolling v. Sharpe, 464-465
Bond v. Floyd, 985-986, 990, 1293
Bose Corp. v. Consumers Union of the U.S., 1009
Boston Firefighters Union v. NAACP Boston Ch., 602
Bowles v. Willingham, 190
Boynton v. Virginia, 190
Bradwell v. Illinois, 611
Brandenburg v. Ohio, 946, 985, 987, 990-991, 1039, 1065, 1103, 1268, 1292, 1313
Branti v. Finkel, *1286*, 1302
Branzburg v. Hayes, 1336, 1341
Braunfeld v. Brown, *1410*, 1412-1415, 1418
Breard v. Alexandria, 1091
Breedlove v. Suttles, 757
Bridges v. California, 968, 992, 995-996, 1081, 1490
Briggs v. Elliot, 471, 473
Briscoe v. Reader's Digest Ass'n, 1090
Broadrick v. Oklahoma, 1041-1043, 1277-1278
Brockett v. Spokane Archades, 1043, 1118
Bronson v. Kinzie, 1430
Brooks v. United States, 190
Brotherhood of Locomotive Firemen & Eng'rs v. Chicago R.I. & P.R.R., 296, 304, 308
Brotherhood of R.R. Trainmen v. Virginia St. Bar, 1240, 1241
Brown v. Board of Educ. of Topeka (Brown I), 45, 80, 115, *461*, 463, 469-470, 473, 475-476, 479, 481, 484, 575, 595
Brown v. Board of Educ. of Topeka (Brown II), 467, 468-472, 474-476, 479-481, 485, 490-491, 493-494, 551, 559, 578
Brown v. Glines, 1269

Brown v. Hartlage, 1236
Brown v. Louisiana, *1186*, 1201
Brown v. Maryland, 254
Brown v. Oklahoma, 1013-1014
Brown v. Pena, 1372
Brown v. Socialist Workers '74 Campaign Comm., 1309
Brown v. Thompson, 777
Brunson v. Clarendon School Dist., 491
Buchanan v. Warley, 455-456
Buck v. Bell, 751, 755
Buck v. Kuykendall, 290
Buckley v. Valeo, 202, 389, 1220, 1229, 1232-1233, 1277, *1309*, 1330
Building Serv. Employees v. Gazzam, 1112
Bullock v. Carter, 679, 789
Bunting v. Oregon, 740
Burns v. Fortson, 766
Burstyn v. Wilson, 1142
Burton v. Wilmington Parking Auth., *1500*, 1503, 1506, 1509-1512, 1514, 1517
Bush v. Orleans Parish School Bd., 473, 551
Butler v. Michigan, 1122

Caban v. Mohammed, 636-638, 672
Cabell v. Chavez-Salido, 662-663
Calder v. Bull, 27, 61, 691, 725, 1429, 1448
Califano v. Boles, 820
Califano v. Goldfarb, 305, 640, 645-647, 649-650
Califano v. Jobst, 893
Califano v. Webster, 591, 645, 647, 649-651
Califano v. Westcott, 647
California v. LaRue, 1167-1168
California Med. Ass'n v. Federal Election Comm'n, 1235
Callahan v. Woods, 1419
Cantrell v. Forest City Publishing Co., 1077
Cantwell v. Connecticut, 968, 998, 1000-1001, 1003, 1009, 1011, 1410, 1490
Capital Broadcasting Co. v. Acting Attorney Gen., 1104
Capital Broadcasting Co. v. Mitchell, 1104
Carey v. Brown, 1248-1249
Carey v. Population Servs. Int'l, 853, 884, 991, 1103, 1106
Carmichael v. Southern Coal & Coke Co., 289
Carroll v. President & Comm'rs of Princess Anne, 1005, 1056
Carter v. Carter Coal Co., 143, *160*, 167-168, 172, 177, 230
Carter v. Jury Comm'n, 560
Castaneda v. Partida, 550, 558, 563, 610
CBS v. FCC Central, 1335
Central Hudson Gas v. Public Serv. Comm'n, 1105-1106, *1107*, 1111-1112
Chambers v. Baltimore & O.R.R., 794
Champion v. Ames (Lottery Case), 145, 149-151, 153-154, 178, 181, 190
Chandler v. Florida, 1357
Chaplinsky v. New Hampshire, *1009*, 1012, 1014-1015, 1041, 1058-1059, 1065, 1091, 1115, 1118-1119, 1146, 1150-1152

Chicago, Milwaukee, St. P. Ry. v. Minnesota, 727

Child Labor Case (Hammer v. Dagenhart), 143, 150, 179, 216

Church of Holy Trinity v. United States, 1389

Cipriano v. City of Houma, 676, 764

Citizen Publishing Co. v. United States, 1323

Citizens against Rent Control v. Berkeley, 1235

City of Akron v. Akron Center for Reproductive Health, 874, 886

City of Cleburne v. Cleburne Living Center, 510, 518-519, 522, 585, 687, 689

City of Los Angeles v. Lyons, 82, 94

City of Mobile v. Bolden, 239, 559-560, 568, 777, 784-786

City of Philadelphia v. New Jersey, 263, 269, 275, 286-288, 306, 325, 327

City of Rome v. United States, 239, 244

Civil Rights Cases, 188, 196, 245, 449-450, 454, 1467, 1469, 1474-1475, 1477, 1489, 1501, 1514, 1519

Clark v. Community for Creative Non-Violence, 1181, 1201

Clark v. Paul Gray, Inc., 309

Clements v. Fashing, 789

Cleveland Bd. of Educ. v. LaFleur, 614, 616, 921, 923

Cleveland Bd. of Educ. v. Loudermill, 904-907, 910, 919-920

Coates v. Cincinnati, 1042, 1044

Cohen v. California, 1013, *1146*, 1151-1153, 1168, 1254

Cohen v. Virginia, 44

Colautti v. Franklin, 885

Cole v. Richardson, 1044, 1293

Coleman v. Miller, 95, 103, 106

Colgate v. Harvey, 707

Colgrove v. Green, 767

Collector v. Day, 210

Collin v. Smith, 1016, 1085, 1185

Columbia Broadcasting Sys. v. Democratic Nat'l Comm., 1333, 1476-1478, 1520

Columbia Broadcasting Sys. v. FCC, 1233, 1304

Columbus Bd. of Educ. v. Penick, 487, 558-559, 569

Commercial Pictures Corp. v. Regents, 1142

Committee for Pub. Educ. v. Regan, 1398

Committee for Pub. Educ. & Religious Liberty v. Nyquist, 1378, 1385, 1397, 1399, 1400-1401, 1403, 1406

Commonwealth v. Davis, *1177*, 1179, 1189, 1274

Commonwealth v. DeLacey, 1115

Commonwealth v. Friede, 1115

Commonwealth v. Ives, 438

Commonwealth v. Sharpless, 1114

Commonwealth Edison v. Montana, 262, 271, 287, 290

Communist Party v. Catherwood, 984

Communist Party v. Subversive Activities Control Bd., 984

Communist Party v. United States, 984

Communist Party of Ind. v. Whitcomb, 991, 1294

Complete Auto Transit v. Brady, 287-290

Connally v. General Constr. Co., 1043

Connecticut Gen. Life Ins. Co. v. Johnson, 727

Connick v. Meyers, 1281-1282

Consolidated Edison v. Public Serv. Comm'n, 1152, 1247, 1250, 1256

Cooley v. Board of Port Wardens, 250-252, 255, 258, 298, 320, 416

Cooper v. Aaron, 196, 471-472

Cooper v. Mitchell Brothers' Santa Ana Theater, 1145

Cooper v. Telfair, 27

Coppage v. Kansas, 734, 737, 740, 745

Corfield v. Coryell, 334-335, 735

Cornelius v. NAACP Legal Defense & Educ. Fund, 1198, 1211, 1258-1260

Coronado Coal Co. v. United States Mine Workers, 143-144, 158, 162, 166, 172

Cox v. Louisiana, 995-996, *1006*, 1008-1009, 1180, 1183-1184, 1208

Cox v. New Hampshire, 1048, 1184-1185

Cox Broadcasting Corp. v. Cohn, 1018, *1085*, *1086*, 1090-1091

Coyle v. Oklahoma, 200

Craig v. Boren, 591, *616*, 625-627, 630, 634, 638, 642, 645, 647-649

Craig v. Harney, 995, 1081

Cramp v. Board of Pub. Instruction, 1293

Crandall v. Nevada, 807

Crawford v. Board of Educ., 573, 577-578

Crist v. Bretz, 723

Cumming v. Board of Educ., 454-455, 459

Cummings v. Missouri, 1294

Curtis v. Whitney, 1430

Curtis Publishing Co. v. Butts, *1068*

Dames & Moore v. Regan, 109, *418*

Dandridge v. Williams, 497, 677, *818*, 820-821, 830

Daniel Ball, The, 172

Davis v. Passman, 552

Davis v. School Comm'rs of Mobile County, 480, 487

Day-Brite Lighting v. Missouri, 745

Dayton Bd. of Educ. v. Brinkman (*Dayton I*), 486-487

Dayton Bd. of Educ. v. Brinkman (*Dayton II*), 486-487, 559

Dean Milk Co. v. Madison, 261, 273-275, 277-279, 281-283, 321, 335

Debs, In re, 361

Debs v. United States, 947, 948, 986

De Canas v. Bica, 666

DeFunis v. Odegaard, 111, 581, 602, 605, 608

DeGregory v. Attorney Gen., 1320

DeJonge v. Oregon, 966-967

Dellums v. Powell, 409

Dennis v. United States, 297, 966, 968, 969, 978-981, 985, 994, 1000, 1018, 1035, 1292

DiSanto v. Pennsylvania, 251, 253

Dobbins v. Erie County, 210

Doe v. Bolton, 335

Doe v. Commonwealth's Attorney for Richmond, 896

Doe v. McMillan, 397
Dombrowski v. Eastland, 396
Doubleday & Co. v. New York, 1115
Douglas v. California, 676, 679-680, 683, 792, 795-797, 799, 815, 893
Draper v. Washington, 682
Dred Scott v. Sanford, 440, 443-444, 453, 725
Drummond v. Acree, 493
Duckworth v. Arkansas, 256
Duke Power Co. v. Carolina Envtl. Study Group, 92, 748
Duncan v. Louisiana, 705, 707, 717
Dun & Bradstreet v. Greenmoss Builders, 1066, 1078, 1090, 1323
Dunn v. Blumstein, 654, 765, 809-810, 813

Eaken v. Raub, 29
Eastern Ky. Welfare Rights Org. v. Simon, 81, 83, 91, 93
Eastland v. United States Serv. Servicemen's Fund, 397
East N.Y. Bank v. Hahn, 1437
Edwards v. California, 676, 707, 807
Edwards v. South Carolina, 1005, 1008-1009
EEOC v. Wyoming, 198, 200, 204, 209, 240, 241
Eisenstadt v. Baird, 852, 861, 864, 886, 894, 898
Elfbrandt v. Russell, 1288, 1292-1293, 1313
Elkins v. Moreno, 922
Ellis v. Brotherhood of Ry., Airline & Steamship Clerks, 1304
El Paso v. Simmons, 1437
Elrod v. Burns, 326, 925, 1283, 1287, 1302
Energy Reserves Group v. Kansas Power & Light, 1443
Engel v. Vitale, 1374, 1389, 1394, 1414-1415, 1423
Epperson v. Arkansas, 1407
Erznoznik v. Jacksonville, 1043, 1153
Euclid v. Amber Realty Co., 1455
Evans v. Abney, 1496-1497
Evans v. Newton, 1496, 1527-1530
Everson v. Board of Educ., 1361, 1367, 1370, 1375, 1378, 1380, 1382-1383, 1397, 1399
Evitts v. Lucey, 679
Exxon Corp. v. Eagerton, 1444
Exxon Corp. v. Governor of Md., 253, 276, 285-286, 297, 748

Fairfax's Devisee v. Hunter's Lessee, 38
Farmers Educ. Coop. Union v. WDAY, 319
FCC v. League of Women Voters, 1267, 1333
FCC v. Midwest Video Corp., 1335
FCC v. National Citizens Comm. for Broadcasting, 1332
FCC v. Pacifica Found., 1154, 1167-1168, 1332
FCC v. WNCN Listeners Guild, 1332
FEC v. National Right to Work Comm., 1235
Federal Election Comm. v. National Conservative Political Action Comm., 1234-1235
Federal Energy Regulatory Comm'n v. Mississippi, 208

Federal Power Comm'n v. Hope Nat. Gas Co., 728
Federal Trade Comm'n v. Mandel Bros., 190
Feiner v. New York, 1001, 1004, 1008-1009, 1035
Ferguson v. Skrupa, 747, 749
Fidelity Fed. Sav. & Loan Ass'n v. de la Cuesta, 315
Firefighters Local Union No. 1784 v. Stotts, 606
First Nat'l Bank of Boston v. Bellotti, 1230-1232, 1305-1306, 1322
Fisher v. Hurst, 460
Fiske v. Kansas, 966
Flagg Bros. v. Brooks, 1479, 1484, 1486-1488, 1512, 1520, 1528, 1531-1533
Flast v. Cohen, 89
Flemming v. Nestor, 515
Fletcher v. Peck, 725
Florida Lime & Avocado Growers v. Paul, 315, 320
Foley v. Connelie, 661-662
Food Employees Local 590 v. Logan Valley Plaza, 1184, 1199, 1530-1531
Foster-Fountain Packing Co. v. Haydel, 266, 324
Frank v. State, 1419
Franks v. Bowman Transp. Co., 579, 592
Freedman v. Maryland, 1049-1051, 1054, 1056, 1142, 1144
Friedman v. Rogers, 1105
Frohwerk v. United States, 947, 986
Frontiero v. Richardson, 613, 616-618, 620, 623-624, 640, 642, 644-646
Frost & Frost Trucking Co. v. Railroad Comm'n, 1274
Frothingham v. Mellon, 89
Fuentes v. Shevin, 1479-1483, 1485
Fuller v. Oregon, 680, 796
Fullilove v. Klutznick, 596, 602, 604-607, 650

Gaffney v. Cummings, 777, 785
Gannett v. DePasquale, 1349
Garcia v. San Antonio Metropolitan Transit Auth., 196, 209-211, 230, 1533
Garner v. Board of Pub. Works, 1288
Garrison v. Louisiana, 1067
Gayle v. Browder, 465
Geduldig v. Aiello, 564, 615-616, 651
Geer v. Connecticut, 271
German Alliance Ins. Co. v. Lewis, 740
Gertz v. Robert Welch, Inc., 1059, 1069, 1077-1078, 1080-1081, 1085
Gibbons v. Ogden, 127, 143-145, 148-150, 175, 178, 189, 249-251, 254, 257-258, 294
Giboney v. Empire Storage & Ice Co., 1112
Gibson v. Florida Legis. Investigating Comm., 1319
Gilbert v. Minnesota, 954
Gillette v. United States, 1371, 1418, 1422
Gilmore v. City of Montgomery, 1505-1506
Ginsberg v. New York, 1122
Ginzburg v. United States, 1121, 1132

Gitlow v. New York, 954, 959, 965, 994, 999-1000

Globe Newspaper & Co. v. Superior Court, 1355

Glona v. American Guar. & Liability Ins. Co., 667-668

Goesaert v. Cleary, 612, 618

Goldberg v. Kelly, 676, 900-902, 914, 920

Goldwater v. Carter, 103, 418

Gomez v. Perez, 670-671

Gomillion v. Lightfoot, 550-551, 554, 785

Gong Lum v. Rice, 455

Gooding v. Wilson, 1013-1014, *1036,* 1040-1042, 1044

Gordon v. Lance, 774

Goss v. Board of Educ., 472, 474

Goss v. Lopez, 911-912, 920

Graham v. Richardson, 654-657, 662

Grand Rapids School Dist. v. Ball, 1405

Gravel v. United States, 395

Graves v. O'Keefe, 210

Grayned v. Rockford, 1044-1045, 1180-1181, 1184, 1189, 1246

Green v. Biddle, 1428

Green v. County School Bd., 474-475, 477, 490-491, 579, 592

Greenholtz v. Inmates, 912, 920

Greer v. Spock, 1190, 1255-1256, 1259

Gregory v. City of Chicago, 1007, 1009, 1181

Griffin v. Breckinridge, 246

Griffin v. County School Bd., 472-473

Griffin v. Illinois, 675-676, 679-680, 683-684, 792, 794-795, 796-797, 799, 815, 893

Griffiths, In re, 542, 585, 658

Griswold v. Connecticut, 841, 852-853, 861, 864, 866, 886, 898

Grosjean v. American Press Co., 1323

Grove v. Mead School Dist., 1372

Grovey v. Townsend, 1525

GTE Sylvania v. Consumers Union, 1055

Guilloin v. Walcott, 671

Guinn v. United States, 564

Hadley v. Junior C. Dist., 775

Hague v. CIO, 707, 1178, 1179, *1182-1183,* 1186

Haig v. Agee, 984, 1034

Hamling v. United States, 1134-1135

Hamm v. City of Rock Hill, 1499

Hammer v. Dagenhart (Child Labor Case), 143, 150, 179, 216

Hampton v. Mow Sun Wong, 605, 665-666

Hampton, J. W., Jr., & Co. v. United States, 366

Harlow v. Fitzgerald, 247, 411

Harper v. Virginia State Bd. of Elections, 675-676, 680, 757, 760, 766, 797, 815, 893

Harper & Row v. National Enters., 1201

Harris v. McRae, 684-685, 872, 874, 880, 1396

Hawaii Housing Auth. v. Midkiff, 1475

Healy v. James, 1271

Heart of Atlanta Motel v. United States, 187, 192, 196-197, 215, 217, 1499

Heckler v. Chaney, 364

Heckler v. Mathews, 88

Heffron v. International Soc'y for Krishna Consciousness, 1191

Heisler v. Thomas Colliery, 271

Heller v. New York, 1143

Helvering v. Gerhardt, 210

Henneford v. Silas Mason Co., 292-293

Hennen, Ex parte, 392

Herbert v. Lando, 1067

Hernandez v. Texas, 584

Herndon v. Lowry, 966-968

Hess v. Indiana, 990, 1014

Hicklin v. Orbeck, 331-332, 815, 1114

Hills v. Gautreaux, 489-490

Hines v. Davidowitz, 315, 319

Hipolite Egg Co. v. United States, 150-151, 154, 178, 181

Hirabayashi v. United States, 531, 566, 590

H. L. v. Matheson, 883-884

Hodel v. Virginia Surface Mining Ass'n, 185, 197, 208-209

Hoffman Ests. v. Flipside, 1103

Hoke v. United States, 150-151

Holmby Prods. v. Vaughn, 1142

Holmes v. City of Atlanta, 465

Home Bldg. & Loan Ass'n v. Blaisdell, 35, 155, 1430

Honeyman v. Jacobs, 1429

Hood, H. P., & Sons v. DuMond, 257, 264, 281, 292-293

Hooper v. Bernalillo County Assessor, 520, 809

Houchins v. KQED, 1345

Houston, E. & W. Tex. R.R. Co. v. United States, 141, 144, 154, 165, 175, 180, 235

Hoyt v. Florida, 612, 615

Hudgens v. NLRB, 1199, 1478, 1528, 1531

Hudson v. Palmer, 921

Hudson Distribs. v. Eli Lilly Co., 190

Hudson Water Co. v. McCarter, 271

Hughes v. Alexandria Scrap Co., 278, 322-323, 326, 328

Hughes v. Oklahoma, 270-271, 286, 327

Humphrey's Executor v. United States, 387

Hunt v. McNair, 1399, 1407

Hunt v. Washington State Apple Advertising Comm'n, 249, 260-261, 271, 275, 277-279, 282, 285-287, 321

Hunter v. Erickson, 568-570, 572-577, 681

Hunter v. Underwood, 553

Hutchinson v. Proxmire, 358, 1076

Hylton v. United States, 22

Illinois v. Milwaukee, 27

Illinois Migrant Council v. Campbell Soup Co., 1200

Illinois State Bd. of Elections v. Socialist Workers Party, 113, 789

Industrial Union Dept. v. American Petroleum Inst., 369

Ingraham v. Wright, 910, 920

INS v. Chadha, 108, 201, 371, 408, 410

International Ass'n of Machinists v. Street, 1303

International Bhd. of Teamsters v. United States, 579, 1112
International Bhd. of Teamsters v. Vogt, Inc., 1112
International Longshoremen's Ass'n v. Allied Int'l, 1113, 1218
Interstate Circuit v. Dallas, 1121

Jackson v. Metropolitan Edison Co., 1474, 1478, 1480, *1517*, 1520-1521, 1528, *1529*, 1530-1534
Jackson v. Virginia, 966, 1009
Jacobellis v. Ohio, 1121
James v. Strange, 680, 796
James v. Valtierra, 576, 681
Jamison v. Texas, 1179
Jefferson v. Hackney, 526, 544, 820
Jenkins v. Georgia, 1132-1134
Jenness v. Forston, 788
Jiminez v. Weinberger, 672-673
Johnson v. Board of Educ., 492, 602, 609
Joint Anti-Fascist Comm. v. McGrath, 913
Jones v. Alfred H. Mayer Co., 245-246
Jones v. Helms, 814
Jones v. North Carolina Prisoners' Union, 1272
Jones v. Rath Packing Co., 315
Jones v. Wolf, 1408-1409
Jungerson v. Ostby & Barton Co., 306

Kahn v. Shevin, 591, 615-617, 642-646
Kaiser Aetna v. United States, 1463
Karcher v. Daggett, 766, 786
Karr v. Schmidt, 899
Kassel v. Consolidated Freightways Corp., 269, 298, 312, 321, 527
Katzenbach v. McClung, 191, 196, 215, 285, 1499
Katzenbach v. Morgan, 184, 233, 238-245
Kelley v. Johnson, 898
Kentucky Whip & Collar v. Illinois Cent. Ry., 178
Keyes v. School Dist. No. 1, 482, 486-487, 489-490, 544, 558, 1211
Keyishian v. Board of Regents, 1290
Kilbourn v. Thompson, 1316
Kingsley Books v. Brown, 1142-1143, 1145
Kingsley Int'l Pictures Corp. v. Regents of N.Y., 985, 1145
Kirchberg v. Feenstra, 636
Kirkpatrick v. Preisler, 776
Kleindienst v. Mandel, 985
Knowlton v. Moore, 262
Kolender v. Lawson, 1046
Konigsberg v. State Bar of Calif., 1294, *1312*
Korematsu v. United States, 503, 535, 541-542, 585
Kotch v. Pilot Comm'rs, 1501
Kovacs v. Cooper, 657, *1172*, 1176, 1228
Kramer v. Union Free School Dist., 761, 764, 766, 772
Kunz v. New York, 1003-1004, 1048, 1051
Kusper v. Pontikes, 767

Labine v. Vincent, 668, 674
Laird v. Tatum, 110, 1321

Lalli v. Lalli, 669, 674-675
Lamont v. Postmaster Gen., 985, 1176
Landmark Communications v. Virginia, 979, 995, *1017*, 1091, 1295
Lane Country v. Oregon, 152
Larkin v. Grendel's Den, 1386, 1409
Larson v. Valente, 1376, 1395-1396
Lassiter v. Department of Social Serv., 895
Lassiter v. Northampton County Bd. of Elections, 233-234, 237, 241, 757
Law Students Civil Rts. Research Council v. Wadmond, 1314-1315
Lea v. Washington, 455
Lehman v. City of Shaker Hts., 1153, 1198, *1250*, 1255-1256, 1259, 1306
Lehr v. Robertson, 637, 672
Leisy v. Hardin, 254
Lemon v. Kurtzman, 1373, 1378-1379, 1386, 1391, 1393, 1395-1396, 1398-1400, 1402, 1406-1407, 1410
Levitt v. Committee for Public Educ., 1398
Levy v. Louisiana, 667-668
Lewis v. BT Inv. Mgrs., 258, 260-262, 269, 285-286
Lewis v. City of New Orleans, 1012-1014, 1043
License Cases, 253
Liggett, Louis K., Co. v. Baldridge, 741
Lincoln Fed. Union v. Northwestern Iron & Metal Co., 744-745
Linda R. S. v. Richard D., 90
Lindsey v. Normet, 677, 820
Linmark Assocs. v. Township of Willingsboro, 1101, *1102*, 1106, 1111, 1535
Little v. Streater, 679, 802
Lloyd Corp. v. Tanner, 1177, 1199, 1531
Lochner v. New York, 144, 261, 297, 365, 549, 611, 725-726, 728, 736, 738-741, 744-745, 748-750, 819, 841, 862, 959-960, 1229, 1533-1534, 1536
Lockport v. Citizens for Community Action, 775
Lockwood, In re, 611
Logan v. United States, 450
Logan v. Zimmerman Brush Co., 911, 921
Lo-Ji Sales v. New York, 1144
Loretto v. Teleprompter Manhattan CATV Corp., 1463
Los Angeles City Council v. Taxpayers for Vincent, 1042-1043, *1195*
Lottery Case (Champion v. Ames), *145*, 149-151, 153-154, 178, 181, 190
Louisiana v. United States, 562-563
Lovell v. Griffin, *1047*, 1051, 1054, 1183, 1410
Loving v. Virginia, 565, 575-578, 626
Lubin v. Panish, 679, 789, 852
Lugar v. Edmondson Oil Co., 1468, 1484, 1486-1488, 1509
Luther v. Borden, 97, 105
Lynch v. Donnelly, 1376, *1377*, 1391, 1393, 1395-1396, 1398, 1407, 1423

Madden v. Kentucky, 707
Mahan v. Howell, 776-777
Maher v. Roe, 675, 869, 874, 880

Malloy v. Hogan, 721
Malnak v. Yogi, 1372, 1393
Manigault v. Springs, 1429, 1435
Marbury v. Madison, 18, 45, 72, 101, 202, 209, 242, 244, 443
Marchetti v. United States, 218
Marcus v. Search Warrant, 1143
Marsh v. Alabama, 1198, 1200, 1491, *1521*, 1523-1524, 1528-1532
Marsh v. Chambers, 1392
Marshall v. Lynn, 924
Marshall v. United States, 497, 798
Marston v. Lewis, 766
Martin v. City of Struthers, *1171*, 1177
Martin v. Hunter's Lessee, 38
Martinez v. Bynum, 815, 839-840
Maryland v. Macon, 1144
Maryland v. Wirtz, 181, 183, 186, 198
Massachusetts Bd. of Retirement v. Murgia, 240, 305, 330, 497, 687
Masses Publishing Co. v. Patten, 941, 944-946, 954, 989
Mathews v. Diaz, 664-665
Mathews v. Eldridge, *913*, 918-920
Mathews v. Lucas, 669, 673, 894
Mayor of Baltimore v. Dawson, 465
Mayor of New York v. Miln, 252
Mayor of Philadelphia v. Educational Equality League, 551-552, 558
McAuliffe v. Mayor of New Bedford, 1273, 1274
McCabe v. Atchison, T. & S.F. Ry., 455-456, 458, 465
McCardle, Ex parte, 69
McCarthy v. Philadelphia Civil Service Comm'n, 815
McCollum v. Board of Educ., 1378, 1397
McCray v. United States, 153, 218
McCulloch v. Maryland, 38, 48, 126, 137, 139, 143, 145, 149-150, 161, 181, 210-211, 213, 235, 1392
McDaniel v. Barresi, 579
McDaniel v. Paty, 480, 1424
McDonald v. Board of Election Comm'rs, 766
McDonald v. Smith, 1067
McGinnis v. Royster, 797
McGlotten v. Connally, 1504
McGowan v. Maryland, 504, 1391, 1411
McGrain v. Daugherty, 384, 1316
McKinney v. Alabama, 1145
McLaughlin v. Florida, 542, 566-567
McLaurin v. Oklahoma State Regents, 461-462
McLean v. Arkansas Bd. of Educ., 1408
Meachem v. Fano, 912
Meek v. Pittenger, 1398, 1402-1403
Memoirs v. Massachusetts, 1121
Memorial Hosp. v. Maricopa County, 809, 811, 813
Memphis v. Green, 557
Memphis Bank & Tr. Co. v. Garner, 211, 921
Memphis Light, Gas & Water Div. v. Craft, 921
Metromedia, Inc. v. San Diego, 1106, *1109*, *1173*, 1176, 1249
Metropolitan Life Ins. Co. v. Ward, 336-337, 521-522

Meyer v. Nebraska, 840-841, 861, 886, 898
Miami Herald Publishing Co. v. Tornillo, 1077, 1201, 1233, 1305, *1326*
Michael M. v. Sonoma County Superior Court, 311, 625, 627, 634, 649
Michelin Tire Co. v. Wages, 254, 325
Michigan v. Long, 113
Milk Control Bd. v. Eisenberg Farm Prod., 291-293
Miller v. California, 1115, 1121, *1124*, 1132-1134, 1136
Miller v. Schoene, 744, *1451*
Milliken v. Bradley (*Milliken I*), 488-490
Milliken v. Bradley (*Milliken II*), 490
Mills v. Habluetzel, 670
Minneapolis Star & Tribune Co. v. Minnesota Comm'r of Rev, 1323-1326
Minnesota v. Clover Leaf Creamery Co., 285, 304-305, 506, 526-527
Minnick v. California Dept. of Corrections, 602, 607
Minor v. Happersett, 611
Mishkin v. New York, 1121, 1132
Mississippi v. Johnson, 407
Mississippi U. for Women v. Hogan, 625-626, 638, 648
Missouri v. Holland, 213, 215-216
Missouri ex rel. Gaines v. Canada, 457, 458-460
Missouri, K. & T. Ry. v. May, 225
Mitchell v. W. T. Grant Co., 1483
Mobile County v. Kimball, 172
Monaco v. Mississippi, 198
Monitor Patriot Co. v. Roy, 1067
Monroe v. Board of Comm'rs, 491
Moon v. United States, 1373
Moore v. City of East Cleveland, 886, 889, 892
Moore v. Mead's Fine Bread Co., 190
Moose Lodge No. 107 v. Irvis, 1478, *1513*, 1517, 1519, 1521, 1534
Mora v. McNamara, 108, 427
Morehead v. New York ex rel. Tipaldo, 168
Morton v. Mancari, 535
Mt. Healthy City School Dist. Bd. of Educ. v. Doyle, 552-553, 1211, 1280, 1396
Mueller v. Allen, 1385, *1399*, 1405-1407
Mugler v. Kansas, 727
Muller v. Oregon, 144, 611, 736, 740
Munn v. Illinois, 726-727, 740
Murdock v. Pennsylvania, 1185
Murray v. Hoboken Land & Improvement Co., 709, 725
Mutual Film Corp. v. Industrial Comm'n, 1142
Myers v. United States, 202, 344, 350, 386

NAACP v. Alabama, 1307, 1309, 1311
NAACP v. Button, 1236, 1240-1241, 1412
NAACP v. Claiborne Hardware Co., 990, 1113, 1216-1217
Nader v. Saxbe, 364
Nashville, C. & St. L. Ry. v. Wallace, 78
National Broadcasting Co. v. United States, 1330
National Cable Television Ass'n v. United States, 369

National League of Cities v. Usery, 196, 198,
  200-202, 204-210, 231-232, 320, 329
National Mut. Ins. Co. v. Tidewater Transfer
  Co., 59
National Socialist Party v. Skokie, 1056, 1085
Neagle, In re, 361
Near v. Minnesota, 1052, 1055, 1142-1143
Nebbia v. New York, 155, 165, 291, 293, *741*,
  1529, 1533
Nebraska Press Ass'n v. Stuart, *1019*, 1030-1032,
  1046, 1054, 1142, 1295
New England Power Co. v. New Hampshire,
  270, 327
New Hampshire, Supreme Court of, v. Piper,
  335, 813, 815
New State Ice Co. v. Liebman, 122, 741
New York v. Ferber, 1042-1043, *1139*
New York v. United States, 200, 210
New York City Transit Auth. v. Beazer, *141*,
  496, 502-503
New York State Liquor Auth. v. Ballanca, 1168
New York Times Co. v. Sullivan, *1059*, 1065-
  1067, 1069, 1077, 1080-1081, 1085, 1091, 1491,
  1493
New York Times Co. v. United States, 1023,
  1031-1032, 1034, 1046, 1051, 1054, 1142, 1295
Nixon v. Administrator of General Servs., 403,
  410
Nixon v. Condon, 1525, 1529
Nixon v. Fitzgerald, 410
Nixon v. Herndon, 1525
NLRB v. Catholic Bishop, 1423
NLRB v. Gissel Packing Co., 1113
NLRB v. Jones & Laughlin Steel Corp., 168,
  169, 177, 185, 190, 197
NLRB v. Retail Store Employees Local, 1001,
  1112-1113
Norman v. Baltimore & O. R.R., 155
North American Cold Storage Co. v. Chicago,
  919
North Carolina v. Califano, 231
North Carolina St. Bd. of Educ. v. Swann,
  480, 579
North Georgia Finishing v. Di-Chem, 1479-
  1483, 1485
Norwell v. Cincinnati, 1014
Norwood v. Harrison, 473, 1504-1505
Noto v. United States, 982
Nyquist v. Mauclet, 659, 666

O'Brien v. Skinner, 766
Ogden v. Saunders, 683, 1428
Ohralik v. Ohio St. Bar, *1106*, 1241
Oklahoma Press Publishing Co. v. Walling,
  1323
Oklahoma Publishing Co. v. District Court,
  1019, 1091
Olsen v. Nebraska, 744
Oregon v. Mitchell, 244, 760
Orlando v. Laird, 108, 427
Orr v. Orr, 626, 650
Ortwein v. Schwab, 801
O'Shea v. Littleton, 81
Otten v. Baltimore & O. R.R., 1422

Owen v. City of Independence, 910
Oyama v. California, 659

Pace v. Alabama, 566
*Pacific Gas & Elec. Co. v. State Energy Re-
  sources Conservation Comm'n*, 313, 319-320
Pacific Tel. Co. v. Oregon, 106
Palko v. Connecticut, 711, 721
Palmer v. Thompson, 473, 550-551, 1497
Palmore v. Sidoti, 543, 895
Panama Refining Co. v. Ryan, 155, 367
Papish v. Board of Curators of U. of Mo., 1271
Parham v. Hughes, 627, 635, 637
Parham v. J. R., 894
Paris Adult Theater I v. Slaton, 1115, 1123-
  1124, *1127*, 1135-1136, 1143
Parker v. Levy, *1267*, 1269
Parratt v. Taylor, 921
Pasadena Bd. of Educ. v. Spangler, 490-491
Passenger Cases, 137, 252
Patterson v. Colorado, 1046
Paul v. Davis, 911
Paul v. Virginia, 329, 335-336
Pell v. Procunier, 1273, *1343*
Penn Central Transp. Co. v. New York City,
  1452
Pennekemp v. Florida, 995, 1081
Pennhurst St. School & Hospital. v. Halder-
  man, 231
Pennsylvania v. Board of Directors of City
  Tr., 1495-1496
Pennsylvania v. Brown, 1495
Pennsylvania v. Nelson, 320
Pennsylvania Coal v. Mahon, *1458*
People v. Crane, 655
People v. Fries, 899
People v. Ramirez, 909
People v. Walker, 549
Perez v. Campbell, 317, 319-320
Perez v. United States, 182, *184*, 185
Perry v. Sindermann, 903, 908, 1274
Perry Educators' Ass'n v. Perry Local Educa-
  tors' Ass'n, 1198, 1256, 1258-1260
Personnel Ad. v. Feeney, 548, 554, 556-557,
  564, 569
Petersen v. Tallisman Sugar Corp., 1200
Peterson v. Greenville, 1497
Phalen v. Virginia, 146
Phelps Dodge Corp. v. NLRB, 744
Phoenix v. Kolodziejski, 764
Pickering v. Board of Educ., *1274*, 1278, 1298
Pickett v. Brown, 669, 671
Pierce v. Society of Sisters, 841, 861, 886, 1504
Pierce v. United States, 954
Pike v. Bruce Church Co., 264, 274, 286, 304
Pittsburgh Press Co. v. Pittsburgh Comm'n on
  Human Rel., 1057, 1092, 1103
Planned Parenthood Ass'n of Kansas City of v.
  Ashcroft, 882, 885
Planned Parenthood of Mo. v. Danforth, 868,
  881, 885-886, 894
Plessy v. Ferguson, 451, 454-456, 463, 466
Plyler v. Doe, 660, 666, *831*, 839-840, 1485,
  1492

Poe v. Ullman, 110, 865
Pointer v. Texas, 721-722
Poletown Neighborhood Council v. City of
  Detroit, 1448
Police Dep't of Chicago v. Mosley, 1244, 1247-
  1249, 1254, 1256, 1259
Polish Alliance v. Labor Bd., 193
Poulos v. New Hampshire, 1051
Powell v. McCormack, 102
Presbyterian Church v. Mary Elizabeth Blue
  Hull Church, 1409
Press-Enter. Co. v. Superior Court, 1357
Prigg v. Pennsylvania, 137, 440
Primus, In re, 1106, 1239, 1241
Prize Cases, 425
Process Gas Consumers Group v. Consumers
  Energy Council of America, 383
Procunier v. Martinez, 1273
Pruneyard Shopping Center v. Robins, 748,
  1200, 1301, 1327, 1463, 1478
Public Util. Comm'n v. Pollak, 1306, 1513,
  1514, 1517-1518, 1520

Quantity of Books, A, v. Kansas, 1306
Quaring v. Petersen, 1419
Quilloin v. Walcott, 895-896
Quong Wing v. Kirkendall, 612

Radovich v. National Football League, 190
Rahrer, In re, 255
Railroad Comm'n Cases, 727
Railroad Retirement Bd. v. Alton, 155
Railway Employees Dep't v. Hanson, 1303
Railway Express Agency v. New York, 162, 504,
  1111
Raymond Motor Transp. v. Rice, 300-304, 306,
  307, 311, 313
Red Lion Broadcasting Co. v. FCC, 1200, 1233,
  1305, 1327, 1332-1333
Redrup v. New York, 1122
Reed v. Reed, 612, 613-619, 627, 643-644
Reeves, Inc. v. Stake, 322-323, 326-328
Regan v. Taxation with Representation, 1260,
  1266-1267
Regan v. Time, Inc., 1250
Regents of the University of California v.
  Bakke, 92, 582, 598-599, 601-602, 607, 650
Regina v. Hicklin, 1115
Reid v. Covert, 216
Reitman v. Mulkey, 1486-1488, 1514
Rendell-Baker v. Kohn, 1509, 1511-1512, 1531-
  1532
Rex v. Tutchin, 926
Reynolds v. Sims, 757, 759, 768, 774-777
Reynolds v. United States, 1363, 1410-1411,
  1418
Ribnik v. McBride, 741, 744
Rice v. Santa Fe Elevator Corp., 263, 315, 319
Richardson v. Belcher, 820
Richardson v. Ramirez, 766
Richardson Mortgage & Loan Corp. v. Wacho-
  via Bank & Tr. Co., 1429
Richmond Newspapers v. Virginia, 852, 1350,
  1359

Rinaldi v. Yeager, 628, 680, 796
Rizzo v. Goode, 82, 94
RMG, In the Matter of the Petition of, v.
  EMG No. 79-747, 543
Roaden v. Kentucky, 1144
Roberts v. United States Jaycees, 895-896, 1241,
  1478
Robinson v. California, 721
Roe v. Wade, 111, 243, 854, 862-866, 868-869,
  880, 886, 898, 1092
Roemer v. Board of Pub. Works, 1407
Rogers v. Lodge, 560-561, 795, 786
Rosario v. Rockefeller, 767, 1243
Rose v. Mitchell, 560
Rosenblatt v. Baer, 1067
Rosenfeld v. New Jersey, 1013-1014, 1153
Ross v. Moffitt, 676, 795
Rostker v. Goldberg, 631, 634, 648-649
Roth v. United States, 721, 1115, 1118-1121,
  1132
Roudebush v. Hartke, 105
Rowan v. Post Office Dep't, 1152, 1176
Royster, F. S., Guano Co. v. Virginia, 504, 526
Rutherford v. United States, 899

Sacher v. United States, 1316
Saia v. New York, 1048
St. Amant v. Thompson, 1067
Salyer Land Co. v. Tulare Lake Basin Water
  Storage Dist., 764-765
San Antonio Indep. School Dist. v. Rodriguez,
  678, 821, 831
Santa Clara County v. Southern P. R.R., 727
Santosky v. Kramer, 895
Saxbe v. Washington Post, 1344-1345
Scales v. United States, 981-983, 1035, 1041,
  1292
Scarborough v. United States, 187
Schacht v. United States, 1208-1209
Schad v. Borough of Mt. Ephraim, 1117, 1167
Schaefer v. United States, 954, 1081
Schaumberg v. Citizens for a Better Env't,
  1043, 1218
Schechter Poultry Corp., A. L. A., v. United
  States, 144, 156, 162-164, 166-168, 172, 177,
  222
Schenck v. United States, 943, 945, 947, 959,
  986, 1046
Schlesinger v. Ballard, 616-617, 641-642, 646
Schlesinger v. Reservists to Stop the War, 88
Schneider v. State, 968, 1170, 1176, 1179, 1182-
  1183
Schwartz v. Postel, 1081
Schwegmann v. Calvert Distillers Corp., 190
Schweiker v. Wilson, 524, 527-528, 688
Screws v. United States, 247, 1512
Seattle Times Co. v. Rhinehart, 1359
Second Employers' Liability Cases, 172
Secretary of St. of Md. v. Joseph H. Munson
  Co., 1043, 1219
Securities & Exch. Comm'n v. Ralston
  Purina, 190
Senate Select Comm. on Presidential Cam-
  paign Comms. v. Nixon, 409

Shaffer v. United States, 940, 945
Shapiro v. Thompson, 676, 802, 808-810, 813-815
Sharpless v. Commonwealth, 1114
Shaw v. Delta Air Lines, 319
Sheldon v. Sill, 74
Shelley v. Kraemer, 583, 1481, *1488,* 1491-1500, 1514, 1521, 1523, 1527
Shelton v. Tucker, 1310, 1314
Sherbert v. Verner, 1368, *1411,* 1417-1418, 1420, 1422-1423, 1425
Shilb v. Kuebel, 721
Shreveport Rate Cases (Houston, E. & W.T. R.R.), 141, 144, 154, 165, 175, 180, 235
Shuttlesworth v. City of Birmingham, 1048, 1051
Sidis v. F-R Publishing Corp., 1089
Siebold, Ex parte, 393, 450
Sierra Club v. Morton, 87
Silkwood v. Kerr-McGee Corp., 320
Sinclair v. United States, 1316
Sipuel v. Board of Regents, 460
Skinner v. Oklahoma, 751, 751, 755, 820
Skinner v. State, 755
Skokie v. National Socialist Party of America, 1016, 1055, 1185
Slaughter-House Cases, 445, 447-449, 529, 611, 622, 678, 705, 709, 711, 724-726, 735, 807
Sloan v. Lemon, 1398
Smith v. Allwright, 1525
Smith v. Ames, 728
Smith v. California, 1135
Smith v. Collin, 1016
Smith v. Daily Mail Publishing Co., 1019, 1091
Smith v. Goguen, 1044-1045, 1212-1213
Smith v. Organization of Foster Families, 671
Smith v. United States, 1134-1135
Snepp v. United States, 1295, 1300
Sniadach v. Family Fin. Corp., 1479-1481, 1484-1486
Socialist Labor Party v. Gilligan, 110
Sonzinsky v. United States, 218
Sosna v. Iowa, 801, 809, 812–813
South Carolina v. Katzenbach, 239-240
South Carolina Highway Dep't v. Barnwell Bros., 258, 264, 285-286, 290, 293, 295, 297, 308, 310, 312, 322
South Central Timber Dev. v. Wunnicke, 270, 321, 327, 329
Southeastern Promotions v. Conrad, 1050, 1260, 1262
Southern Pac. Co. v. Arizona, 272, 292, 294, 296-298, 313, 322
Southern Ry. v. United States, 144
Speiser v. Randall, 1294
Spence v. Washington, 1214-1215
Splawn v. California, 1132
Sporhase v. Nebraska, 270-271
Stafford v. Wallace, 142, 144, 154, 157, 172
Stanley v. Georgia, 1123-1124, 1136
Stanley v. Illinois, 614, 616, 893, 898
Stanton v. Stanton, 615, 617-618, 627, 641, 646
State v. Post, 437
Staub v. City of Baxley, 1048

Steward Mach. Co. v. Davis, 225, 226, 228-229, 232
Stolar, In re, 1314
Stone v. Graham, 1374, 1379, 1383, 1385
Stone v. Mississippi, 1429
Storer v. Brown, 789, 1243
Strauder v. West Virginia, 237, 448, 528, 535-536
Street v. New York, 1012, 1146, 1211
Stromberg v. California, 1201, 1208
Stuart v. Laird, 26
Sturges v. Crowninshield, 1428
Sugarman v. Dougall, 653, 658, 661, 663-665
Swain v. Alabama, 535, 551-552, 562-563
Swann v. Charlotte-Mecklenburg Bd. of Educ., 475, 479-481, 484, 487, 492, 558, 579, 592
Sweatt v. Painter, 460-462
Sweezy v. New Hampshire, 1316
Swift & Co. v. United States, 144, 157

Takahashi v. Fish & Game Comm'n, 659
Talley v. California, 1308
Tate v. Short, 679, 797
Taylor v. Louisiana, 615-616
Terminiello v. Chicago, 968, 997, 1146
Terry v. Adams, 1526-1527, 1530, 1532
Testa v. Katt, 209
Texaco v. Short, 748
Thomas v. Review Bd., 1418
Thompson v. Louisville, 966, 1009
Thompson v. Washington, 924
Thornhill v. Alabama, 1112
Thornton v. Caldor, 1420, 1422-1423
Tigner v. Texas, 628
Tilton v. Richardson, 1407
Time, Inc. v. Firestone, 1076
Time, Inc. v. Hill, 1077
Times Film Corp. v. Chicago, 1142
Tinker v. Des Moines Indep. Community School Dist., 1201, 1208, *1269*
Toll v. Moreno, 666
Tomei v. Finely, 1081
Toomer v. Witsell, 329-330, 332-335
Torcaso v. Watkins, 1424-1425
Train v. New York, 363
Trans World Air Lines v. Hardison, 1421-1423
Trimble v. Gordon, 527, 660, 674-675
Truax v. Raich, 659
Twining v. New Jersey, 710
Tyson & Brother v. Banton, 741

United Bldg. & Constr. Trades Council v. Camden, 328, 815
United Jewish Orgs. v. Carey, 561, 580-581, 584, 591, 602, 785
United Mine Workers v. Illinois Bar Ass'n, 1240
United Pub. Workers v. Mitchell, 110, 1277, 1280
United States v. Albertini, 1191, 1210
United States v. American Tel. & Tel., 409
United States v. Ballard, 1372
United States v. Baltimore & O. R.R., 190

United States v. Bass, 186-187
United States v. Belmont, 418
United States v. Brewster, 396
United States v. Brown, 983, 1294
United States v. Butler, 32, 168, 219, 225, 228-229
United States v. Carolene Prods. Co., 193, 507, 537, 539, 571, 583, 590, 654, 657, 660-661, 663, 745, 748-749, 750, 756, 965
United Staes v. Causby, 1454, 1464
United States v. Central Eureka Mining Co., 1454
United States v. Clark, 669
United States v. Cress, 1459
United States v. Cruikshank, 448
United States v. Curtiss-Wright Export Corp., 109, *1414*
United States v. Darby, 177, 181, 183, 185, 190, 193, 196-197, 217, 235, 744
United States v. Doremus, 218-219
United States v. E. C. Knight Co., 139, 143-145, 166, 175, 177
United States v. Grace, 1180-1181
United States v. Guest, 246
United States v. Harris, 449
United States v. Helstoski, 397
United States v. Jefferson County Bd. of Educ., 474
United States v. Kahriger, 218
United States v. Klein, 74
United States v. Kras, 676, 800
United States v. Lee, *1417*, 1419-1421
United States v. Lovett, 383, 1294
United States v. MacCollom, 796
United States v. Marchetti, 1299
United States v. McCullagh, 214
United States v. Montgomery County Bd. of Educ., 579
United States v. New Mexico, 211
United States v. Nixon, 109, 209, 398, 404
United States v. O'Brien, 317, *1202*, 1208-1211, 1215, 1228, 1318, 1410, 1419
United States v. One Book Called "Ulysses," 1115
United States v. Orito, 1136
United States v. Philadelphia, 361
United States v. The Progressive, 1033, 1055
United States v. Ptasynski, 261
United States v. Raines, 1040
United States v. Reese, 448
United States v. Reidel, 1124, 1136
United States v. Richardson, 88
United States v. Robel, 984, 1041, 1290-1293
United States v. Scotland Neck City Bd. of Educ., 491
United States v. SCRAP, 88
United States v. Seeger, 1371
United States v. Shauver, 214
United States v. South-Eastern Underwriters Ass'n, 336
United States v. Texas Educ. Agency, 493
United States v. Thirty-Seven Photographs, 1124, 1144
United States v. Twelve 200-ft. Reels, 1136

United States v. Washington Post Co., 1023
United States v. Women's Sportswear Ass'n, 190
United States Civil Serv. Comm'n v. National Ass'n of Letter Carriers, 1275, 1278, 1280
United States Dep't of Ag. v. Moreno, 498, 519, 522, 679, 820-821
United States Postal Serv. v. Council of Greenburgh Civil Ass'ns, 1193
United States R.R. Retirement Bd. v. Fritz, 305, 311, 513, 518-519, 526, 528
United States Senate v. FTC, 383
United States Trust Co. v. New Jersey, 1437
United Transp. Union v. Long Island R.R., 208
United Transp. Union v. State Bar of Mich., 1240
Uphaus v. Wyman, 1318
Usery v. Turner Elkhorn Mining Co., 922

Valentine v. Chrestensen, 1091-1092
Valley Forge Christian C. v. Americans United For Separation of Church & State, 78, 85, 89, 93
Vanasco v. Schwartz, 1081
Vance v. Bradley, 240, 688
Vance v. Universal Amusement Co., 1056-1057, 1143
Vander Jagt v. O'Neill, 79
Veazie Bank v. Fenno, 153, 178
Veix v. Sixth Ward, 1437
Village of Arlington Heights v. Metropolitan Housing Dev. Corp., 549, 552, 553, 554, 557, 559, 571, 576, 1396
Village of Belle Terre v. Boraas, 888-889
Virginia, Ex parte, 234, 237, 448, 1489, 1512
Virginia v. Rives, 448, 1481
Virginia St. Bd. of Pharmacy v. Virginia Citizens Consumer Council, 1092, 1100-1101, 1103-1104, 1106, 1111
Vitek v. Jones, 910, 912
Vlandis v. Kline, 814, 922

Wabash, St. L. & P. R.R. v. Illinois, 144
Walker v. City of Birmingham, 1055-1056, 1069
Walker v. Ohio, 1122
Wallace v. Jaffree, 1364, 1375, 1395, 1423
Waller v. Georgia, 1349
Walters v. National Ass'n of Radiation Survivors, 918, 1241
Walz v. Tax Comm'n, 1389, 1392-1395
Ward v. Illinois, 1122, 1132
Ware v. Hylton, 27
Warth v. Seldin, 91
Washington v. Davis, 543, 546, 548-549, 551-552, 554, 558, 562-563, 571, 576, 578, 581, 603, 609, 681, 684, 1368, 1410, 1492-1494, 1521
Washington v. Seattle School Dist. No. 1, 567, 573-578
Washington v. United States, 212
Washington v. Yakima Indian Nation, 497
Watkins v. United States, 1316

Watson v. Memphis, 472
Watts v. United States, 985-987, 995
Wayte v. United States, 1210
Weber v. Aetna Cas. & Sur. Co., 591, 668-669, 674, 840
Weeks v. United States, 190
Weinberger v. Salfi, 615, 922
Weinberger v. Wiesenfeld, 305, 507, 526, 615-618, 640-642, 656
Wells v. Rockefeller, 776
Welsh v. United States, 1371
Wengler v. Druggists Mut. Ins. Co., 646-648, 650
Wesberry v. Sanders, 776
West Coast Hotel Co. v. Parrish, 168, 612, 743, 750-751
Western & S. Life Ins. Co. v. State Bd. of Equalization, 337
West Virginia St. Bd. of Educ. v. Barnette, 1201, 1300, 1305
Whalen v. Roe, 899
Wheeling Steel Corp. v. Glander, 727
Whitcomb v. Chavis, 561
White v. Massachusetts Council of Constr. Employers, 322-324, 326-330
White v. Regester, 777
White v. Weiser, 776
Whitney v. California, 959, 960, 965-968, 982, 1111
Wickard v. Filburn, 174, 176-177, 181, 185-187, 190, 196-197, 285
Widmar v. Vincent, 1248-1249, 1255-1256, 1259, 1369, 1376, 1401, 1423
Wieman v. Updegraff, 1288, 1424
Wiener v. United States, 387
Williams v. Florida, 722
Williams v. Illinois, 679, 797
Williams v. Rhodes, 786, 788
Williams v. Standard Oil Co., 740

Williams v. Vermont, 522
Williamson v. Lee Optical of Okla., 503, 506, 510, 513, 746, 748-749
Willson v. Black Bird Creek Marsh Co., 251
Winship, In re, 724
Winters v. New York, 1117
Wisconsin v. Constantineau, 911
Wisconsin v. Yoder, 1416, 1418-1420, 1422, 1424
Wolf v. Colorado, 721
Wolman v. Walter, 1398, 1401-1402
Wolston v. Reader's Digest Ass'n, 1076
Wood v. Georgia, 995
Woods v. Cloyd W. Miller Co., 212, 216, 240
Wooley v. Maynard, 1301, 1305
Worthen Co. v. Kavanaugh, 1429
Wright v. Rockefeller, 544
Wynehamer v. People, 725

Yarbrough, Ex parte, 450
Yates v. United States, 946, 980-982, 985, 990
Yerger, Ex parte, 70
Yick Wo v. Hopkins, 235, 549-551, 554-555, 1211
Young v. American Mini Theatres, 1046, 1161
Youngstown Sheet & Tube Co. v. Sawyer, 104, 109, 346, 404, 420

Zablocki v. Redhail, 890, 893-894
Zacchini v. Scripps-Howard Broadcasting, 1201
Zanderer v. Office of Disciplinary Counsel, 1102, 1105, 1107, 1305
Zemel v. Rusk, 984
Zobel v. Alaska, 520-521
Zobel v. Williams, 333, 809-810
Zorach v. Clauson, 1378-1379, 1387, 1392, 1397, 1422
Zurcher v. Stanford Daily, 1342-1343

Table of Authorities

Abascal & Kramer, Presidential Impoundment: Constitutional Theories and Political Realities, 61 Geo. L.J. 1295 (1973), 363

Abraham, H., Justices and Presidents (1985), 67

Abrams, The Press *Is* Different: Reflections on Justice Stewart and the Autonomous Press, 7 Hofstra L. Rev. 563 (1979), 1341

Ackerman, Beyond *Carolene Products*, 98 Harv. L. Rev. 713 (1985), 537, 539-540, 610, 623

———, Discovering the Constitution (1977), 93 Yale L.J. 1013 (1984), 32

Ackerman, B., Private Property and the Constitution (1977), 1482

Advisory Commission on Intergovernmental Relations, Citizen Participation in the American Federal System (1979), 204

———, The Question of State Government Capability (1985), 123, 124-125

———, Regulatory Federalism (1984), 202, 247

Alfange, Congressional Regulation of the "States Qua States": From *National League of Cities* to *EEOC v. Wyoming*, 1983 Sup. Ct. Rev. 215, 210

———, Free Speech and Symbolic Conduct: The Draft-Card Burning Case, 1968 Sup. Ct. Rev. 1, 1207, 1209, 1211

Alsup, A Policy Assessment of the National Court of Appeals, 25 Harv. L.J. 1313 (1974), 113

Amsterdam, The Void-for-Vagueness Doctrine in the Supreme Court, 109, U. Pa. L. Rev. 67 (1960), 1044

Anderson, Libel and Press Self-Censorship, 53 Tex. L. Rev. 422 (1975), 1066

———, The Origins of the Press Clause, 30 U.C.L.A. L. Rev. 455 (1983), 1322

Arendt, H., On Revolution (1965), 65

Arkes, Civility and the Restriction of Speech: Rediscovering the Defamation of Groups, 1974 Sup. Ct. Rev. 281, 1086

Armor, The Evidence on Busing, Public Interest (Summer 1972), 494

Auerbach, The Communist Control Act of 1954: A Proposed Legal-Political Theory of Free Speech, 23 U. Chi. L. Rev. 173 (1956), 984

———, The Reapportionment Cases: One Person, One Vote—One Vote, One Value, 1964 Sup. Ct. Rev. 1, 773

Baat-Ada, Freedom of Speech as Mythology or "Quill Pen and Parchment Thinking" in an Electronic Environment, 8 N.Y.U. Rev. L. & Soc. Change 271 (1978-1979), 1138

Baker, Commercial Speech: A Problem in the Theory of Freedom, 62 Iowa L. Rev. 1 (1976), 1099

———, Press Rights and Government Power to Structure the Press, 34 U. Miami L. Rev. 819 (1980), 1348

———, Scope of the First Amendment Freedom of Speech, 25 U.C.L.A. L. Rev. 964 (1978), 932, 1208

———, Unreasoned Reasonableness: Mandatory Parade Permits and Time, Place, and Manner Regulations, 78 Nw. U. L. Rev. 937 (1983), 1184

Ball, Judicial Protection of Powerless Minorities, 59 Iowa L. Rev. 1059 (1974), 537

Barber, *National League of Cities v. Usery*: New Meaning for the Tenth Amendment, 1976 Sup. Ct. Rev. 161, 210

Barnett, The Puzzle of Prior Restraint, 29 Stan. L. Rev. 539 (1977), 1054-1055

Bartky, On Psychological Oppressions, in Philosophy and Women (1979), 624

Barton, The General-Election Ballot: More Nominees or More Representative Nominees, 22 Stan. L. Rev. 165 (1970), 788

Bator, Congressional Power over the Jurisdiction of the Federal Courts, 27 Villanova L. Rev. 1030 (1982), 73

Bator, P., P. Mishkin, D. Shapiro, & H. Wechsler, Hart & Wechsler's The Federal Courts and the Federal System (2d ed. 1977), 30, 70, 74-75

Beard, C., An Economic Interpretation of the Constitution of the United States (1913), 2

BeVier, The First Amendment and Political Speech: An Inquiry into the Substance and Limits of Principle, 30 Stan. L. Rev. 299 (1978), 945, 990

————, An Informed Public, An Informing Press: The Search for a Constitutional Principle, 68 Calif. L. Rev. 482 (1980), 1347-1348

————, Money and Politics: A Perspective on the First Amendment and Campaign Finance Reform, 73 Calif. L. Rev. 1045 (1985), 1229

Bell, *Brown v. Board of Education* and the Interest-Convergence Dilemma, 93 Harv. L. Rev. 513, (1980), 466

Bell, D., Race, Racism and American Law (2d ed. 1980), 494

Bennett, The Burger Court and the Poor, in The Burger Court: The Counter-Revolution That Wasn't (Blasi ed. 1983), 830

————, "Mere" Rationality in Constitutional Law: Judicial Review and Democratic Theory, 67 Calif. L. Rev. 1049 (1979), 508-509, 547

————, Objectivity in Constitutional Law, 132 U. Pa. L. Rev. 445 (1984), 693

Bentley, A., The Process of Government (1980), 17

Berger, The Ninth Amendment, 66 Corn. L. Rev. 1 (1980), 852

Berger, R., Congress v. the Supreme Court (1969), 408

————, Government by the Judiciary: The Transformation of the Fourteenth Amendment (1970), 463, 697-698, 706, 715, 760

————, Impeachment (1973), 68, 412

Berns, Freedom of the Press and the Alien and Sedition Laws: A Reappraisal, 1970 Sup. Ct. Rev. 109, 930

Berns, W., The First Amendment and the Future of American Democracy (1976), 1146, 1150

————, Freedom, Virtue and First Amendment (1957), 1086

Beth, Group Libel and Free Speech, 37 Minn. L. Rev. 167 (1955), 1086

Beth, L., The Development of the American Constitution, 1877-1917 (1971), 727

Bezanson, The New Free Press Guarantee, 63 Va. L. Rev. 731 (1977), 1349

Bickel, The Decade of School Desegregation: Progress and Prospects, 64 Colum. L. Rev. 193 (1964), 469

————, The Original Understanding and the Segregation Decision, 69 Harv. L. Rev. 1, 11-40, 61, 65 (1955), 463

Bickel, A., The Least Dangerous Branch (1962), 29-32, 37, 63, 68, 76, 77, 469, 694, 980, 1040-1041

————, The Morality of Consent (1975), 542, 1032, 1055, 1152, 1299, 1348

————, The Supreme Court and the Idea of Progress (1970), 464, 774

Bikle, Judicial Determination of Questions of Fact Affecting the Constitutional Validity of Legislative Action, 38 Harv. L. Rev. 6 (1924), 736

————, The Silence of Congress, 41 Harv. L. Rev. 200 (1927), 256

Bittker, The Case of the Checker-Board Ordinance: An Experiment in Race Relations, 71 Yale L.J. 1387 (1962), 609

Black, C., Decision According to Law (1981), 71

————, The Lawfulness of the Segregation Decisions, 69 Yale L.J. 421 (1960), 465

————, Perspectives in Constitutional Law (1963), 206

————, Structure and Relationship in Constitutional Law (1969), 60

————, The Unfinished Business of the Warren Court, 46 Wash. L. Rev. 3 (1970), 469

Black, H., The Bill of Rights, 35 N.Y.U. L. Rev. 865 (1960), 925, 980

————, A Constitutional Faith (1968), 980

Black & Cahn, Justice Black and First Amendment "Absolutes": A Public Interview, 37 N.Y.U. L. Rev. 549 (1962), 980

Blackstone, W., Commentaries on the Laws of England (1769), 927, 1046

Blasi, The Checking Value in First Amendment Theory, 1977 A.B.F. Res. J. 521, 936, 1032, 1209, 1280, 1335, 1348

————, The Pathological Perspective and the First Amendment, 85 Colum. L. Rev. 449 (1985), 990, 1100

————, Prior Restraints on Demonstrations, 68 Mich. L. Rev. 1481 (1970), 1004, 1009, 1050, 1185

————, Toward a Theory of Prior Restraint: The Central Linkage, 66 Minn. L. Rev. 11 (1981), 1054, 1056

Blasi, V., ed., The Burger Court: The Counterrevolution That Wasn't (1983), 62

Bloom, Proof of Fault in Media Defamation Litigation, 38 Vand. L. Rev. 247 (1985), 1067

Bloustein, The First Amendment and Privacy: The Supreme Court Justice and the Philosopher, 28 Rutgers L. Rev. 41 (1974), 1090–1091

————, The Origin, Validity and Interrelationship of the Political Values Served by Freedom of Expression, 33 Rutgers L. Rev. 372 (1981), 937-938

Bluford, The Lloyd Gaines Story, 1958 J. Ed. Soc. 242 (1959), 459

Bobbitt, P., Constitutional Fate (1982), 210

Bogen, First Amendment Ancillary Doctrines, 37 Md. L. Rev. 679 (1978), 1051

————, The Free Speech Metamorphosis of Mr. Justice Holmes, 11 Hofstra L. Rev. 97 (1982), 952

————, The Supreme Court's Interpretation of the Guarantee of Fredom of Speech, 35 Md. L. Rev. 555 (1976), 1011

Bollinger, Elitism, The Masses and the Idea of Self-Government, in Constitutional Government in America (Collins ed. 1980), 1335

————, Freedom of the Press and Public Access: Toward a Theory of Partial Regulation of the Mass Media, 75 Mich. L. Rev. 1 (1976), 1331

————, The Skokie Legacy: Reflections on an "Easy Case" and Free Speech Theory, 80 Mich L. Rev. 612 (1982), 1017

Bonfield, The Guarantee Clause of Article IV, Section 4: A Study in Constitutional Desuetude, 46 Minn. L. Rev. (1962), 106

Bork, The Impossibility of Finding Welfare Rights in the Constitution, 1979 Wash U. L.Q. 695, 680, 683, 697, 817, 965

————, Neutral Principles and Some First Amendment Problems, 47 Ind. L.J. 1 (1971), 692-693, 760, 934, 936-937, 945, 953

Boudin, "Seditious Doctrines" and the "Clear and Present Danger" Rule, 38 Va. L. Rev. 143 (1952), 983

Brameld, Educational Costs in Discrimination and National Welfare (MacIver ed. 1949), 463

Brennan, The Supreme Court and the Meiklejohn Interpretation of the First Amendment, 79 Harv. L. Rev. (1965), 1065

Brest, The Conscientious Legislator's Guide to Constitutional Interpretation, 27 Stan. L. Rev. 585 (1975), 33, 46, 196

————, Foreword: In Defense of the Antidiscrimination Principle, 90 Harv. L. Rev. 1 (1976), 536, 540, 557

————, The Misconceived Quest for the Original Understanding, 60 B.U. L. Rev. 204 (1980), 693

————, *Palmer v. Thompson:* An Approach to the Problem of Unconstitutional Legislative Motive, 1971 Sup. Ct. Rev. 95, 551, 1211

————, State Action and Liberal Theory: A Case Note on *Flagg Brothers v. Brooks*, 130 U. Pa. L. Rev. 1296 (1982), 1486

————, The Substance of Process, 42 Ohio St. L.J. 131 (1981), 697

————, Who Decides?, 58 S. Cal. L. Rev. 661 (1985), 37

Brilmayer, The Jurisprudence of Article III: Perspectives on the "Case or Controversy" Requirement, 93 Harv. L. Rev. 297 (1979), 94

Brissenden, P., The IWW: A Study of American Syndicalism (1919), 930

Brown, E., Loyalty and Security (1958), 984, 1287

Brown, Emerson, Falk & Freedman, The Equal Rights Amendment: A Constitutional Basis for Equal Rights for Women, 80 Yale L.J. 871 (1971), 624, 639

Brudney, Business Corporations and Stockholders' Rights Under the First Amendment, 91 Yale L.J. 235 (1981), 1306

Bruff, Presidential Power and Administrative Rulemaking, 88 Yale L.J. 451 (1978), 388

Bruff & Gellhorn, Congressional Control of Administrative Regulation: A Study of Legislative Vetoes, 90 Harv. L. Rev. 1369 (1977), 382, 384

Burt, The Constitution of the Family, 1979 Sup. Ct. Rev. 329, 881, 887, 894

————, *Miranda* and Title II: A Morganatic Marriage, 1969 Sup. Ct. Rev. 81, 242

Cahn, Jurisprudence, 30 N.Y.U. L. Rev. 150 (1955), 465

Calabresi, *Bakke* as Pseudo-Tragedy, 28 Cath. U.L. Rev. 427 (1979), 602

Canby, Programming in Response to the Community: The Broadcast Consumer and the First Amendment, 55 Tex. L. Rev. 67 (1967), 1332

Cantor, Forced Payments to Service Institutions and Constitutional Interests in Ideological Non-Association, 36 Rutgers L. Rev. 3 (1984), 1304

Caplan, The History and Meaning of the Ninth Amendment, 69 Va. L. Rev. 233 (1983), 852

Carpeneti, Legislative Apportionment: Multimember Districts and Fair Representation, 120 U. Pa. L. Rev. 666 (1972), 784

Carr, The House Committee on Un-American Activities, 1945-1950 (1952), 1316

———, R., The Warren Court and Desegregation, 67 Mich. L. Rev. 237 (1968), 468

Carter, S., The Constitutionality of the War Powers Resolution, 70 Va. L. Rev. 101 (1984), 433

———, The Political Aspects of Judicial Power, 131 U. Pa. L. Rev. 1341 (1984), 412

———, Technology, Democracy, and the Manipulation of Consent, 93 Yale L.J. 581 (1984), 1218

Casper, Apportionment and the Right to Vote: Standards of Judicial Scrutiny, 1973 Sup. Ct. Rev. 1, 784

———, Constitutional Constraints on the Conduct of Foreign and Defense Policy: A Nonjudicial Model, 43 U. Chi. L. Rev. 463 (1976), 364

———, Jones v. Mayer: Clio Bemused and Confused Muse, 1968 Sup. Ct. Rev. 89, 246

———, Williams v. Rhodes and Public Financing of Political Parties under the American and German Consitutions, 1969 Sup. Ct. Rev. 271, 787

Casper, G., & Posner, R., The Workload of the Supreme Court (1976), 113

Cass, First Amendment Access to Government Facilities, 65 Va. L. Rev. 1287 (1979), 1177, 1247

Cassell, Restrictions on Press Coverage of Military Operations: The Right of Access, Grenada, and "Off-the-Record Wars," 73 Geo. L.J. 931 (1985), 1358

Chafee, Book Review, 62 Harv. L. Rev. 891 (1949), 933

Chafee, Z., Free Speech in the United States (1941), 928, 944, 946, 950, 953-954, 968-969

Chayes, Public Law Litigation and the Burger Court, 96 Harv. L. Rev. 4 (1982), 93

Chein, What Are the Psychological Effects of Segregation under Conditions of Equal Facilities?, 3 Int. J. Opinion & Attitude Res. 229 (1949), 463

Children's Defense Fund, Black and White Children in America: Key Facts (1978), 495

Choper, Congressional Power to Expand Judicial Definitions of the Substantive Terms of the Civil War Amendments, 67 Minn. L. Rev. 299 (1982), 241

———, Defining "Religion" in the First Amendment, 1982 U. Ill. L. Rev. 579, 1372

———, The Establishment Clause and Aid to Parochial Schools, 56 Cal. L. Rev. 260 (1968), 1406

Choper, J., Judicial Review and the National Political Process (1980), 68, 121-122, 199, 247, 345, 413, 697

Clark, Legislative Motivation and Fundamental Rights in Constitutional Law, 15 San Diego L. Rev. 953 (1978), 813

———, Liberalism and Pornography, in Pornography and Censorship (1983), 1137

Clark, K., Effect on Prejudice and Discrimination on Personality Development (Midcentury White House Conference on Children and Youth) (1950), 463

Clark, J. M., Guidelines for the Free Exercise Clause, 83 Harv. L. Rev. 327 (1969), 1419

Clinton, Further Explorations in the Political Thicket: The Gerrymander and the Constitution, 59 Iowa L. Rev. 1 (1973), 785

Clor, Science, Eros and the Law: A Critique of the Obscenity Commission Report, 10 Duq. L. Rev. 63 (1971), 119

Clor, H., Obscenity and Public Morality (1969), 1119

Clune, The Supreme Court's Treatment of Wealth Discriminations under the Fourteenth Amendment, 1975 Sup. Ct. Rev. 289, 794, 800

Coase, Advertising and Free Speech, 6 J. Legal Stud. 1 (1977), 1099

———, The Federal Communications Commission, 2 J. L. & Econ. 1 (1959), 1331

Cohen, Congressional Power to Interpret Due Process and Equal Protection, 27 Stan. L. Rev. 603 (1975), 242, 243

———, Congressional Power to Validate Unconstitutional State Laws, 35 Stan. L. Rev. 387 (1983), 256

———, Equal Treatment for Newcomers: The Core Meaning of National and State Citizenship, 1 Const. Comm. 9 (1984), 814-815

Coleman, Kelly & Moore, Trends in School Segregation 1968-73 (1975), 491

Comment, Brandenburg v. Ohio: A Speech Test for All Seasons?, 43 U. Chi. L. Rev. 151 (1975), 991, 1292

———, Congressional Control of Presidential War-Making under the War Powers Act: The Status of a Legislative Veto after Chadha, 132 U. Pa. L. Rev. 1217 (1984), 432

———, Enforcing the CIA's Secrecy Agreement through Post-Publication Civil Action: United States v. Snepp, 32 Stan. L. Rev. 409 (1980), 1300

———, First Amendment Protection for Commercial Advertising: The New Constitutional Doctrine, 44 U. Chi. L. Rev. 205 (1976), 1100

———, First Amendment Standards for Subsequent Punishment of Dissemination of Confidential Government Information, 68 Cal. L. Rev. 83 (1980), 1299

————, Government Employee Disclosures of Agency Wrongdoing: Protecting the Right to Blow the Whistle, 42 U. Chi. L. Rev. 530 (1975), 1281

————, National Security Controls on the Dissemination of Privately Generated Scientific Information, 30 U.C.L.A. L. Rev. 405 (1982), 1035

————, The Privileges or Immunities Clause of the Fourteenth Amendment: The Original Intent, 79 Nw. U. L. Rev. 142 (1984), 707

————, *Snepp v. United States:* The CIA Secrecy Agreement and the First Amendment, 81 Colum. L. Rev. 662 (1981), 1299, 1300

————, A Strict Scrutiny of the Right to Travel, 22 U.C.L.A. L. Rev. 1129 (1975), 813

————, The Uniformity Clause, 51 U. Chi. L. Rev. 1193 (1984), 262

Cooley, T., Constitutional Limitations (1868), 726

Cord, R., Separation of Church and State (1982), 1364

Corwin, The Basic Doctrine of American Constitutional Law, 12 Mich. L. Rev. 247 (1914), 726

————, The Doctrine of Due Process before the Civil War, 24 Harv. L. Rev. 366 (1911), 726

————, The "Higher Law" Background of American Constitutional Law, 42 Harv. L. Rev. 149 (1928-1929), 694, 726

————, The Steel Seizure Case, 53 Colum. L. Rev. 53 (1953), 382

Corwin, E., The Constitution of the United States of America (1953), 704

————, Liberty against Government (1948), 725

————, The President — Office and Powers (1957), 385

Corwin & Ramsey, The Constitutional Law of Constitutional Amendment, 26 Notre Dame La. 165 (1951), 67

Coulter, J., The Confederate States of America 1861-1865 (1950), 930

Cover, The Origins of Judicial Activism in the Protection of Minorities, 91 Yale L.J. 1287 (1982), 537, 1527

Cover, R., Justice Accused (1975), 439

Cox, Constitutional Adjudication and the Promotion of Human Rights, 80 Harv. L. Rev. 91 (1966), 241

————, Executive Privilege, 122 U. Pa. L. Rev. 1383 (1974), 409

————, Foreword: Freedom of Expression in the Burger Court, 94 Harv. L. Rev. 1 (1980), 1018, 1031-1032, 1113, 1146, 1151

Cox, A., The Role of the Supreme Court in American Government (1976), 64, 865

————, The Warren Court (1968), 1040

Crosskey, Charles Fairman, "Legislative History," and the Constitutional Limitations on State Authority, 22 U. Chi. L. Rev. 1 (1954), 716

Currie, The Constitution in the Supreme Court: Limitations on State Power, 1865-1873, 51 U. Chi. L. Rev. 329 (1983), 704

————, The Constitution in the Supreme Court: The Powers of the Federal Courts, 1801-1835, 49 U. Chi. L. Rev. 646 (1982), 27, 29, 44

————, The Constitution in the Supreme Court: State and National Powers, 1801-1855, 49 U. Chi. L. Rev. 887 (1982), 60

Currie, D., The Constitution in the Supreme Court: The First Hundred Years 1789-1888 (1985), 726

Cutler & Johnson, Regulation and the Political Process, 84 Yale L.J. 1395 (1975), 345

Dahl, R., A Preface to Democratic Theory (1963), 17, 64, 122

————, Who Governs? Democracy and Power in an American City (1961), 955

Dam, The American Fiscal Constitution, 44 U. Chi. L. Rev. 271 (1977), 364

Daniels, R., Concentration Camps: North America, Japanese in the United States and Canada during World War II (rev. ed. 1981), 535

Davis, K., Administrative Law Treatise (1958), 924

Dellapenna, Nor Piety Nor Wit: The Supreme Court on Abortion, 6 Colum. Hum. Rts. L. Rev. 379 (1974-1975), 865

Dellinger, The Legitimacy of Constitutional Change: Rethinking the Amendment Process, 66 Mich. L. Rev. 837 (1968), 67, 107

DeToqueville, A., Democracy in America (J. P. Mayher ed. 1969), 101

Deutsch, Neutrality, Legitimacy, and the Supreme Court: Some Intersections between Law and Political Science, 20 Stan. L. Rev. 169 (1968), 773

————, Precedent and Adjudication, 83 Yale L.J. 1553 (1974), 321

Deutscher & Chein, The Psychological Effects of Enforced Segregation: A Survey of Social Science Opinion, 26 J. Psychol. 259 (1948), 463

Devlin, P., The Enforcement of Morals (1965), 1120

Diamond, The First Amendment and Public Schools: The Case against Judicial Intervention, 59 Tex. L. Rev. 477 (1981), 1270

Donner, F., The Age of Surveillance (1980), 985, 1321

Dowling, Interstate Commerce and State Power, 27 Va. L. Rev. 1 (1940), 257-258, 328
———, Interstate Commerce and State Power — Revised Version, 47 Colum. L. Rev. 547 (1947), 258
Dunham, *Griggs v. Alleghany County* in Perspective: Thirty Years of Supreme Court Expropriation Law, 1962 Supreme Court Review 63, 1447
Dunn, Title VI, The Guidelines, and School Desegregation in the South, 53 Va. L. Rev. 42 (1967), 471, 474
Dunn, J., Western Political Theory in the Face of the Future (1979), 653
Dunne, P., The Supreme Court's Decisions, in Mr. Dooley's Opinions (1900), 68
DuVal, Free Communication of Ideas and the Quest for Truth: Toward a Teleological Approach to First Amendment Adjudication, 41 Geo. Wash. L. Rev. 161 (1972), 932, 937
Dwight, Trial by Impeachment, 6 Am. Leg. Reg. (N.S.) 257 (1867), 412
Dworkin, The Forum of Principle, 56 N.Y.U. L. Rev. 469 (1981), 35, 37, 63, 692, 693
Dworkin, A., Pornography: Men Possessing Women (1981), 1137
Dworkin, R., Taking Rights Seriously (1978), 523

Easterbrook, Foreword: The Court and the Economic System, 98 Harv. L. Rev. 4 (1984), 91, 1182
———, Insider Trading, Secret Agents, Evidentiary Privileges, and the Production of Information, 1981 Sup. Ct. Rev. 309, 1298
———, Legal Interpretation and the Power of the Judiciary, 7 Harv. L. J. & Pub. Policy 87 (1984), 36
———, Substance and Due Process, 1982 Sup. Ct. Rev. 85, 708, 908
Eaton, The American Law of Defamation through *Gertz v. Robert Welch, Inc.* and Beyond: An Analytical Primer, 61 Va. L. Rev. 1349 (1975), 1077
Eisenberg, Congressional Authority to Restrict Lower Federal Court Jurisdiction, 83 Yale L.J. 498 (1974), 75
Elliott, *INS v. Chadha*: The Constitution, The Administrative Constitution, and the Legislative Veto, 1983 Supreme Court Review 125, 383
Ellwood, R., Religious and Spiritual Groups in Modern America (1973), 1373
Ely, The Constitutionality of Reverse Racial Discrimination, 41 U. Chi. L. Rev. 723 (1974), 602
———, Flag Desecration: A Case Study in the Roles of Categorization and Balancing in First Amendment Analysis, 88 Harv. L. Rev. 1482 (1975), 980, 994, 1000, 1175-1176, 1208, 1210, 1215
———, Legislative and Administrative Motivation in Constitutional Law, 79 Yale L.J. 1205 (1970), 547, 1211
———, The Wages of Crying Wolf: A Comment on *Roe v. Wade*, 82 Yale L.J. 920 (1973), 861-862, 864
Ely, J., Democracy and Distrust (1981), 36, 61, 63, 334, 369, 501, 528, 537, 538, 541, 543, 624, 681, 688, 691, 695-697, 709, 715, 734, 760, 774, 851, 965, 978, 989-990, 1151
Emerson, The Affirmative Side of the First Amendment, 15 Ga. L. Rev. 795 (1981), 1255
———, The Doctrine of Prior Restraint, 20 Law & Contemp. Prob. 648 (1955), 1049
———, First Amendment Doctrine and the Burger Court, 68 Calif. L. Rev. 422 (1980), 990, 1031
———, Freedom of Expression in Wartime, 116 U. Pa. L. Rev. 975 (1968), 986
———, Toward a General Theory of the First Amendment, 72 Yale L.J. 877 (1963), 980
———, The War Powers Resolution Tested: The President's Independent Defense Power, 51 Notre Dame Law 187 (1975), 1427
Emerson, T., The System of Freedom of Expression (1970), 937, 945, 990, 1005, 1058, 1120, 1169, 1207, 1233, 1318
Emerson, T., D. Haber & N. Dorsen, Political and Civil Rights in the United States (1967), 980, 984
Epstein, A Common Law for Labor Relations: A Critique of the New Deal Labor Legislation, 92 Yale L.J. 1357 (1983), 738
———, Substantive Due Process by Any Other Name: The Abortion Cases, 1973 Sup. Ct. Rev. 159, 865
———, Toward a Revitalization of the Contracts Clause, 51 U. Chi. L. Rev. 703 (1984), 1436, 1445
Epstein, D., The Political Theory of the Federalist (1984), 344
Epstein, R., Takings: Private Property and the Power of Eminent Domain (1985), 1447, 1448, 1465
Eule, Laying the Dormant Commerce Clause to Rest, 91 Yale L.J. 425 (1982), 249

Fairman, Does the Fourteenth Amendment Incorporate the Bill of Rights? The Original Understanding, 2 Stan. L. Rev. 5 (1949), 706, 716
Fairman, C., Reconstruction and Reunion, 1864-1888, Part One (1971), 698
Fallon, Of Justiciability, Remedies, and Public Law Litigations: Notes on the Jurisprudence of Lyons, 59 N.Y.U. L. Rev. 1 (1984), 93
Farber, Civilizing Public Discourse: An Essay on Professor Bickel, Justice Harlan, and the Enduring Significance of *Cohen v. California*, 1980 Duke L.J. 283, 1168
———, Commercial Speech and First Amendment Theory, 74 Nw. U. L. Rev. 372 (1979), 1104
———, Content Regulation and the First Amendment: A Revisionist View, 68 Geo. L. Rev. 727 (1980), 1175

Farber & Nowak, The Misleading Nature of Public Forum Analysis: Content and Context in First
    Amendment Adjudication, 70 Va. L. Rev. 1219 (1984), 1260
Farrand, M., The Framing of the Constitution of the United States (1913), 2
The Federalist Papers, 7-17, 30-31, 116-117, 120, 122, 194, 203-205, 339-342, 385, 395, 445
Fehrenbacher, D., The *Dred Scott* Case: Its Significance in American Law and Politics (1978), 440
Fiorina, Legislative Choice of Regulatory Forms: Legal Process or Administrative Process, 39 Pub.
    Choice 33 (1982), 366
Fishkin, J., Justice, Equal Opportunity and the Family (1983), 609, 670
Fiske, J., The Critical Period of American History (1888), 2
Fiss, The Fate of an Idea Whose Time Has Come: Antidiscrimination Law in the Second Decade after
    Brown v. Board of Education, 41 U. Chi. L. Rev. 742 (1974), 479
———, Groups and the Equal Protection Clause, 5 J. Phil. & Pub. Affairs 107 (1976), 538-539
———, The Supreme Court, 1978 Term — Foreword: The Forms of Justice, 93 Harv. L. Rev. 1
    (1979), 537
Fiss, O., The Civil Rights Injunction (1978), 1054
Flack, H., The Adoption of the Fourteenth Amendment (1908), 698, 715
Flexner, E., Century of Struggle (1975), 622
Foner, E., Free Soil, Free Labor, Free Men: The Ideology of the Republican Party before the Civil
    War (1970), 439
Frank & Munro, The Original Understanding of "Equal Protection of the Laws," 1972 Wash. U. L.Q.
    421, 463, 535, 698
Frankfurter, John Marshall and the Judicial Function, 69 Harv. L. Rev. 217 (1955), 59
Frantz, The First Amendment in the Balance, 71 Yale L.J. 1424 (1962), 980
———, Is the First Amendment Law?, 51 Calif. L. Rev. 729 (1963), 978, 980
Frazier, The Negro in the United States 674-681 (1949), 463
Fredrickson, G., The Inner Civil War (1968), 138
Freedman, Sex Equality, Sex Differences, and the Supreme Court, 92 Yale L.J. 913 (1983), 635, 639
Freeman, The Misguided Search for the Constitutional Definition of "Religion," 71 Geo. L.J. 1519
    (1983), 1372
Freund, Political Libel and Obscenity, 42 F.R.D. 491 (1966), 1077
———, The Supreme Court and Civil Liberties, 4 Vand. 1. Rev. 533 (1951), 1047, 1058
Freund, E., Police Power (1904), 945
Freund, P., On Understanding the Supreme Court (1949), 736, 968
———, The Supreme Court of the United States (1961), 727, 1045
Friendly, The Bill of Rights as a Code of Criminal Procedure, 53 Calif. L. Rev. 929 (1965), 717
———, The *Dartmouth College* Case and the Public-Private Penumbra, 12 Tex. Q. no. 2, p. 17 (1969)
    (Supp.), 1483
Fuller, The Forms and Limits of Adjudication, 92 Harv. L. Rev. 353 (1978), 819

Gard, Book Review, 32 Hastings L.J. 711 (1981), 1185
———, Fighting Words as Free Speech, 58 Wash. U. L.Q. 531 (1980), 1012, 1014, 1015
Gellhorn, W., Individual Freedom and Governmental Restraints (1956), 1287
Gewirtz, Remedies and Resistance, 92 Yale. L.J. 585, 661 (1983), 492
Gianella, Religious Liberty, Nonestablishment, and Doctrinal Development, 80 Harv. L. Rev. 1381
    (1967), 81 Harv. L. Rev. 513 (1968), 1368
Gibson, W., Aliens and the Law (1940), 659
Ginsburg, Gender in the Supreme Court: The 1973 and 1974 Terms, 1975 Sup. Ct. Rev. 1, 616
———, Sexual Equality under the Fourteenth and Equal Rights Amendments, 1978 Wash. U. L.Q.
    161, 622
Glennon, War Powers Resolution: Sad Record, Dismal Promise, 17 Loy. L.A. L. Rev. 657 (1984), 422
Glennon & Nowak, A Functional Analysis of the Fourteenth Amendment "State Action" Require-
    ment, 1976 Sup. Ct. Rev. 221, 1477
Goebel, J., 1 History of the Supreme Court: Antecedents and Beginnings to 1800 (1971), 250
Goldberger, Judicial Scrutiny in Public Forum Cases: Misplaced Trust in the Judgment of Public
    Officials, 32 Buff. L. Rev. 175 (1983), 1197
———, A Reconsideration of *Cox v. New Hampshire*: Can Demonstrators Be Required to Pay the
    Costs of Using America's Public Forum?, 62 Tex L. Rev. 403 (1983), 1185
Goldman, The First Amendment and Nonpicketing Labor Publicity, 36 Vand. L. Rev. 1469 (1983),
    1113
Goldstein, R., Political Repression in Modern America (1978), 939
Goodman, Professor Brest on State Action and Liberal Theory and a Postscript to Professor Stone,
    130 U. Pa. L. Rev. 1331 (1982), 1534
Graglia, L., Disaster by Decree (1976), 491
Graham, The "Conspiracy Theory" of the Fourteenth Amendment, 47 Yale L.J. 371 (1938), 727

———, Our "Declaratory" Fourteenth Amendment, 7 Stan. L. Rev. 3 (1954), 704
Grano, Judicial Review and a Written Constitution in a Democratic Society, 28 Wayne L. Rev. 1 (1981), 698
Greenawalt, All or Nothing at All, 1971 Sup. Ct. Rev. 31, 1371
———, Criminal Coercion and Freedom of Speech, 78 Nw. U. L. Rev. 1081 (1983), 995
———, Discrimination and Reverse Discrimination (1983), 608
———, Judicial Scrutiny of "Benign" Racial Preference in Law School Admissions, 75 Colum. L. Rev. 559 (1975), 542, 604, 608
———, Speech and Crime, 1980 A.B.F. Res. J. 645, 945, 978
Grey, Do We Have an Unwritten Constitution?, 27 Stan. L. Rev. 703 (1975), 63, 694
———, Eros, Civilization, and the Burger Court, 43 Law & Contemp. Prob. 83 (Summer 1980), 898
———, Origins of the Unwritten Constitution: Fundamental Law in American Revolutionary Thought, 30 Stan. L. Rev. 843 (1978), 63, 694
Gunther, Foreword: In Search of Evolving Doctrine on a Changing Court: A Model for a Newer Equal Protection, 86 Harv. L. Rev. 1 (1972), 508, 616, 821
———, Judicial Hegemony and Legislative Autonomy: The Nixon Case and the Impeachment Process, 22 U.C.L.A. L. Rev. 30 (1974), 407-408
———, Learned Hand and the Origins of Modern First Amendment Doctrine: Some Fragments of History, 27 Stan. L. Rev. 719 (1975), 945, 953, 982, 987
———, Reflections on Robel, 20 Stan. L. Rev. 1140 (1968), 984
———, The Subtle Vices of the Passive Virtues, 64 Colum. L. Rev. 1 (1964), 77
Guthrie, W., The Fourteenth Article of Amendment to the Constitution of the United States (1898), 715
Gwyn, W., The Meaning of the Separation of Powers (1965), 342

Hafen, The Constitutional Status of Marriage, Kinship and Sexual Privacy — Balancing the Individual and Social Interests, 81 Mich. L. Rev. 463 (1983), 890, 895
Haiman, Speech v. Privacy: Is There a Right Not to Be Spoken To?, 67 Nw. U. L. Rev. 153 (1972), 1151
Haiman, F., Speech and Law in a Free Society (1981), 1202
Hale, The Supreme Court and the Contract Clause, 57 Harv. L. Rev. 512, 621, 852 (1944), 1430, 1435
Hall, K., The Politics of Justice (1979), 68
Hamburger, The Development of the Law of Seditious Libel and the Control of the Press, 37 Stan. L. Rev. 661 (1985), 927
Hamilton, Affectation with Public Interest, 39 Yale L.J. 1089 (1930), 741
Hamilton, A., Opinion on the Constitutionality of an Act to Establish a Bank, 8 Papers of Alexander Hamilton 97 (1965), 58
———, Works (1851), 361
Hand, L., The Bill of Rights (1958), 64
———, The Contribution of an Independent Judiciary to Civilization (Dillard ed. 1944), 64
Harper, The Consumer's Emerging Right to Boycott, 93 Yale L.J. 409 (1984), 1218
Harrison, The "Weakened Spring of Government" Revisited: The Growth of Federal Power in the Late Nineteenth Century, in The Growth of Federal Power in American History (R. Jeffreys-Jones & B. Collins eds. 1983), 138
Hart, Herbert, Between Utility and Rights, 79 Colum. L. Rev. 828 (1979), 523
Hart, Henry, The Power of Congress to Limit the Jurisdiction of Federal Courts: An Exercise in Dialectic, 66 Harv. L. Rev. 1362 (1953), 71
———, Law, Liberty and Morality (1963), 1120
Healy, W., The Individual Delinquent (1915), 754
Hearings on Executive Impoundment of Appropriated Funds before the Subcommittee on Separation of Powers of the Senate Committee on the Judiciary, 92d Cong., 1st Sess. (1971), 363
Henkin, Foreword: On Drawing Lines, 82 Harv. L. Rev. 63 (1968), 1201
———, Is There a Political Question Doctrine?, 85 Yale L.J. 597 (1976), 101, 109
———, Morals and the Constitution: The Sin of Obscenity, 63 Colum. L. Rev. 391 (1963), 1119
———, Privacy and Autonomy, 74 Colum. L. Rev. 1410 (1974), 850-851, 866
———, Shelley v. Kraemer: Notes for a Revised Opinion, 110 U. Pa. L. Rev. 473 (1962), 1491
Henkin, L., Foreign Affairs and the Constitution (1972), 414, 417
Herberg, W., Protestant, Catholic, Jew (1955), 1369
Hetherington, State Economic Regulation and Substantive Due Process of Law, 53 Nw. U. L. Rev. 13 (1958), 749
Heymann & Barzelay, The Forest and the Trees: Roe v. Wade and Its Critics, 53 B.U. L. Rev. 765 (1973), 862
Hill, R., The Economic Status of Black Americans (1981), 495
Hirschhorn, The Separate Community: Military Uniqueness and Servicemen's Constitutional Rights, 62 N.C. L. Rev. 177 (1984), 1269

Hirschman, A., Exit, Voice, and Loyalty (1970), 124

Holmes, O., Collected Legal Papers (1920), 43, 1035

———, Justice Oliver Wendell Holmes: His Book Notices and Uncollected Letters and Papers (1936), 739

Horwitz, M., The Transformation of American Law, 1780-1860 (1977), 1447

Horowitz, R., ed., The Moral Foundations of the American Republic (2d ed. 1979), 2

Hough, Due Process of Law — Today, 32 Harv. L. Rev. 218 (1919), 728

Howe, M., The Garden and the Wilderness (1965), 1366, 1391

Hutchinson, More Substantive Equal Protection? A Note on *Plyler v. Doe*, 1982 Sup. Ct. Rev. 167, 839

———, Unanimity and Desegregation: Decisionmaking in the Supreme Court, 1948-1958, Geo. L.J. 1 (1979), 460

Hyman, H., A More Perfect Union (1973), 138

Immwinkelried & Zillman, An Evolution in the First Amendment: Overbreadth Analysis and Free Speech within Military Community, 54 Tex. L. Rev. 42 (1975), 1268

Ingber, The Marketplace of Ideas: A Legitimizing Myth, 1984 Duke L.J. 1, 932

Interpretation Symposium, 58 S. Cal. L. Rev. 1 (1985), 698

Irons, P., Justice at War (1983), 542

———, The New Deal Lawyers (1982), 155

Israel, *Elfbrandt v. Russell:* The Demise of the Oath?, 1966 Sup. Ct. Rev. 193, 1287

———, Selective Incorporation: Revisited, 71 Mich. L. Rev. 253 (1981), 723

Jackson, A., Veto Message of, 1832, on Act to Recharter Bank of the United States, 2 J. Richardson, Messages and Papers of the Presidents (1900), 46

Jackson & Jeffries, Commercial Speech: Economic Due Process and the First Amendment, 65 Va. L. Rev. 1 (1979), 1098

Jacobson, Federalism and Property Rights, 15 N.Y.U. L.Q. 319 (1938), 740

James, J., The Framing of the Fourteenth Amendment (1956), 698

Javits, Who Makes War? (1973), 433

Jefferson, T., Letters to Abigail Adams, Sept. 11, 1804, 7 The Writings of Thomas Jefferson (Ford ed. 1897), 46

———, Letter to Madison, Jan. 30, 1787, in The Portable Thomas Jefferson (M. Peterson ed. 1975), 12, 65

———, Letter to Samuel Kercheval, July 12, 1816, in The Portable Thomas Jefferson (1975), 5, 65

———, Opinion on the Constitutionality of the Bill for Establishing a National Bank, in 19 Papers of Thomas Jefferson (1974), 158

Jeffries, Rethinking Prior Restraint, 92 Yale L.J. 409 (1983), 1056

Jensen, M., Articles of Confederation (1940), 4

———, The New Nation (1940), 4

Johnston, Sex Discrimination and the Supreme Court 1971-1974, 49 N.Y.U. L. Rev. 617 (1974), 616

Kaczorowski, The Politics of Judicial Interpretation: The Federal Courts, Department of Justice and Civil Rights 1866-1876 (1985), 705

Kaden, Federalism in the Courts, in Advisory Commission on Intergovernmental Relations, The Future of Federalism in the 80s (1971), 202

Kadish, Methodology and Criteria in Due Process Adjudication — A Survey and Criticism, 66 Yale L.J. 319 (1957), 716-717

Kalven, The Concept of the Public Forum: *Cox v. Louisiana,* 1965 Sup. Ct. Rev. 1, 1177, 1179, 1183-1184

———, Foreword: Even When a Nation Is at War, 85 Harv. L. Rev. 3 (1971), 1054

———, Meiklejohn and the *Barenblatt* Opinion, 27 U. Chi. L. Rev. 315 (1960), 1318

———, The Metaphysics of the Law of Obscenity, 1960 Sup. Ct. Rev. 1, 1011, 1117

———, The *New York Times* Case: A Note on "The Central Meaning of the First Amendment," 1964 Sup. Ct. Rev. 191, 1064, 1068

———, Privacy in Tort Law — Were Warren and Brandeis Wrong?, 31 Law & Contemp. Probs. 326 (1966), 1090

———, The Reasonable Man and the First Amendment: *Hill, Butts,* and *Walter,* 1967 Sup. Ct. Rev. 267, 1069

———, Upon Rereading Mr. Justice Black on the First Amendment, 14 U.C.L.A. L. Rev. 428 (1962), 980

Kalven, H., The Negro and the First Amendment (1965), 1000-1001, 1239, 1312, 1320

Kamin, Residential Picketing and the First Amendment, 61 Nw. U. L. Rev. 177 (1966), 1181
Kamisar, Poverty, Equality, and Criminal Procedure, in National College of District Attorneys,
    Constitutional Law Deskbook (1977), 796
Kanowitz, "Benign" Sex Discrimination: Its Troubles and Their Cure, 31 Hast. L.J. 1379 (1980), 648
Kaplan, Equal Justice in an Unequal World: Equality for the Negro — the Problem of Special Treat-
    ment, 61 Nw. U. L. Rev. 363 (1966), 543, 609
———, Segregation Litigation and the Schools — Part II: The General Northern Problem, 58 Nw. U.
    L. Rev. 157 (1963), 480
Karst, Book Review, 89 Harv. L. Rev. 1028 (1976), 864
———, Equality as a Central Principle in the First Amendment, 43 U. Chi. L. Rev. 20 (1975), 1040,
    1175, 1233, 1244, 1332
———, Foreword: Equal Citizenship under the Fourteenth Amendment, 91 Harv. L. Rev. 1 (1977),
    623, 756
———, The Freedom of Intimate Association, 89 Yale L.J. 624 (1980), 889, 893
———, Legislative Facts in Constitutional Litigation, 1960 Sup. Ct. Rev. 75, 889, 893
Karst & Horowitz, Affirmative Action and Equal Protection, 60 Va. L. Rev. 955 (1974), 606
Katz, Privacy and Pornography: Stanley v. Georgia, 1969 Sup. Ct. Rev. 203, 1124
Katz, W., Religion and American Constitutions (1964), 1366
Kauper, Penumbras, Peripheries, Emanations, Things Fundamental and Things Forgotten: The
    Griswold Case, 64 Mich. L. Rev. 235 (1965), 850
———, The Steel Seizure Case: Congress, the President, and the Supreme Court, 51 Mich. L. Rev.
    141 (1952), 361
Kauper, P., Civil Liberties and the Constitution (1962), 980
Kennedy, Distributive and Paternalistic Motives in Contract and Tort Law, with Special Reference to
    Compulsory Terms and Unequal Bargaining Power, 41 Md. L. Rev. 563 (1982), 736, 738
———, Form and Substance in Private Law Adjudication, 89 Harv. L. Rev. 1685 (1976), 923
Kent, J., Commentaries on American Law (2d ed. 1832), 1046
King, The Juridical Status of the Fetus: A Proposal for Legal Protection of the Unborn, 77 Mich. L.
    Rev. 1647 (1976), 868
Kitch & Bowler, The Facts of Munn v. Illinois, 1978 Sup. Ct. Rev. 313, 726
Kluger, R., Simple Justice (1976), 456, 463
Kohl, The Civil Rights Act of 1866, Its Hour Come Round at Last, 55 Va. L. Rev. 272 (1969), 246
Komesar, Taking Institutions Seriously: Introduction to a Strategy for Constitutional Analysis, 51 U.
    Chi. L. Rev. 366 (1984), 748
Konvitz, M., The Alien and the Asiatic in American Law (1946), 659
Kreimer, Allocational Sanctions: The Problem of Negative Rights in a Positive State, 132 U. Pa. L.
    Rev. 1293 (1984), 229, 1265, 1267, 1274
Krislov, From Ginzburg to Ginsberg: The Unhurried Children's Hour in Obscenity Litigation, 1968
    Sup. Ct. Rev. 153, 1122
Kronman, Contract Law and Distributive Justice, 89 Yale L.J. 472 (1980), 269
Kurland, Curia Regis: Some Comments on the Divine Right of Kings and Courts to Say What the Law
    Is, 23 Ariz. L. Rev. 582 (1981), 59
———, The Irrelevance of the Constitution: The First Amendment's Freedom of Speech and Free-
    dom of Press Clauses, 29 Drake L. Rev. (1979-1980), 1035
———, Of Church and State and the Supreme Court, 29 U. Chi. L. Rev. 1 (1961), 1368, 1415
———, The Privileges or Immunities Clause: "Its Hour Come Round at Last"?, 1972 Wash. U. L.Q.
    405, 705, 707
———, The Religion Clauses and the Burger Court, 34 Cath. L. Rev. 1 (1984), 1393

Landman, The History of Human Sterilization in the United States — Theory, Statute, and Adjudi-
    cation, 23 Ill. L. Rev. 463 (1929), 755
Lange, The Speech and Press Clauses, 23 U.C.L.A. L. Rev. 77 (1975), 1341
Law, Rethinking Sex and the Constitution, 132 U. Pa. L. Rev. 955 (1984), 640, 649
Lawrence, Eclipse of Liberty: Civil Liberties in the United States during the First World War, 21
    Wayne L. Rev. 33 (1974), 950
Laycock, Due Process and Separation of Powers: The Effort to Make the Due Process Clauses
    Nonjusticiable, 60 Tex. L. Rev. 875 (1982), 909
———, Taking Constitutions Seriously: A Theory of Judicial Review, 59 Tex. L. Rev. 343 (1981), 707
Lederer, L., ed., Take Back the Night: Women in Pornography (1980), 1137
Lempert, The Force of Irony: On the Morality of Affirmative Action and United Steelworkers v.
    Weber, 95 Ethics 86 (1984), 602
Leuchtenberg, The Origins of Franklin D. Roosevelt's Court-Packing Plan, 1966 Sup. Ct. Rev. 347,
    168
Levi, Some Aspects of the Separation of Powers, 76 Colum. L. Rev. 371 (1976), 344

Levin, The Courts, the Congress, and Educational Adequacy: The Equal Protection Predicament, 39 Md. L. Rev. 187 (1979), 831

Levin, H., Education and Earnings of Blacks and the *Brown* Decision (1981), 494

Levmore, Interstate Exploitation and Judicial Intervention, 69 Va. L. Rev. 563 (1983), 262

Levy, L., Emergence of a Free Press (1985), 926-929

——, The Law of the Commonwealth and Chief Justice Shaw, 439

Lewis, *New York Times v. Sullivan* Reconsidered: Time to Return to "The Central Meaning of the First Amendment," 83 Colum. L. Rev. 602 (1983), 1067

——, A Preferred Position for Journalism?, 7 Hofstra L. Rev. 595 (1979), 1341

——, A Public Right to Know about Public Institutions: The First Amendment as Sword, 1980 Sup. Ct. Rev. 1, 1357, 1358

Lincoln, A., First Inaugural Address, March 4, 1861, 6 Messages and Papers 5ff (Richardson ed.), 46

Linde, "Clear and Present Danger" Reexamined: Dissonance in the *Brandenburg* Concerto, 22 Stan. L. Rev. 1163 (1970), 959, 979

Linder, Freedom of Association after *Roberts v. United States Jaycees*, 82 Mich. L. Rev. 1878 (1984), 1243

Lockhart, Escape from the Chill of Uncertainty: Explicit Sex and the First Amendment, 9 Ga. L. Rev. 533 (1975), 1133, 1136, 1145

Lockhart & McClure, Literature, the Law of Obscenity, and the Constitution, 38 Minn. L. Rev. 295 (1954), 1119

Loewy, A Different and More Viable Theory of Equal Protection, 57 N.C. L. Rev. 1 (1978), 814

Lopez, Mexican Migration, 28 U.C.L.A. L. Rev. 615 (1981), 652-653

Louis, Summary Judgment and the Actual Malice Controversy in Constitutional Defamation Cases, 57 S. Cal. L. Rev. 707 (1984), 1066

Lowenstein, Campaign Spending and Ballot Propositions: Recent Experience, Public Choice Theory and the First Amendment, 29 U.C.L.A. L. Rev. 505 (1982), 1232

Lowi, T., The End of Liberalism (2d ed. 1979), 345, 366, 371

Lupu, Untangling the Strands of the Fourteenth Amendment, 77 Mich. L. Rev. 981 (1979), 800, 841, 892

Lusky, Footnote Redux: A *Carolene Products* Reminiscence, 82 Colum. L. Rev. 1083 (1982), 537, 660, 750

——, Racial Discrimination and the Federal Law: A Problem in Nullification, 63 Colum. L. Rev. 1163 (1963), 468

——, The Stereotype: Hard Core of Racism, 13 Buffalo L. Rev. 450 (1964), 469

Maass, A., Congress and the Common Good (1983), 64

MacIntyre, Moral Arguments and Social Contexts, 80 J. Phil. 590 (1983), 694

MacKinnon, Not a Moral Issue, 2 Yale L. & Soc. Pol. Rev. 321 (1984), 1136

——, Pornography, Civil Rights and Speech, 20 Harv. C.R.-C.L. L. Rev. 1 (1985), 1137

——, *Roe v. Wade*: A Study in Male Ideology in Abortion: Moral and Legal Perspectives (J. Garfield ed. 1985), 864

MacKinnon, C., Sexual Harassment of Working Women (1979), 649

Madison, J., A Memorial and Remonstrance (1786), 1362, 1364

Magrath, The Obscenity Cases: Grapes of *Roth*, 1966 Sup. Ct. Rev. 7, 1122

Maine, H., Popular Government (1885), 1428

Marcus, M., Truman and the Steel Seizure Case: The Limits of Presidential Power (1977), 359, 361

Marshall, *Village of Schaumberg v. Citizens for a Better Environment* and Religious Solicitation: Freedom of Speech and Freedom of Religion Coverage, 13 Loy. L.A. L. Rev. 953 (1980), 1219

Mashaw, Administrative Due Process: The Quest for a Dignatary Theory, 61 B.U. L. Rev. 885 (1981), 910

——, The Supreme Court's Due Process Calculus for Administrative Adjudication in *Mathews v. Elridge*: Three Factors in Search of a Theory of Value, 44 U. Chi. L. Rev. 28 (1976), 918

Mashaw, J., Due Process in the Administrative State (1985), 907, 918

Mayton, Seditious Libel and the Lost Guarantees of a Freedom of Expression, 84 Colum. L. Rev. 91 (1984), 928

——, Toward a Theory of First Amendment Process: Injunctions of Speech, Subsequent Punishment, and the Costs of the Prior Restraint Doctrine, 67 Corn. L. Rev. 245 (1982), 1054

McCloskey, Economic Due Process and the Supreme Court: An Exhumation and Reburial, 1962 Sup. Ct. Rev. 34, 26, 748-749

McCloskey, R., The American Supreme Court (1960), 727

McCormack, Race and Politics in the Supreme Court: *Bakke* to Basics, 1979 Utah L. Rev. 491, 607

McCoy, Recent Equal Protection Decisions — Fundamental Right to Travel or "Newcomers" as a Suspect Class?, 28 Vand. L. Rev. 987 (1975), 807, 814

McCurdy, The *Knight Sugar* Decision of 1895 and the Modernization of American Corporation Law, 1869-1903, 53 Bus. Hist. Rev. 304 (1979), 143

McKay, Reapportionment: Success Story of the Warren Court, 67 Mich. L. Rev. 223 (1968), 774

———, "With All Deliberate Speed," 31 N.Y.U. L. Rev. 991 (1956), 470

McLaughlin, A., A Constitutional History of the United States (1936), 3-4

McLure, Incidence Analysis and the Supreme Court: An Examination of Four Cases from the 1980 Term, 1 Sup. Ct. Econ. Rev. 69 (1982), 262

Medow, The First Amendment and the Secrecy State: *Snepp v. United States*, 130 U. Pa. L. Rev. 775 (1982), 1298

Meiklejohn, The First Amendment and Evils That Congress Has a Right to Prevent, 26 Ind. L.J. 477 (1951), 983

———, The First Amendment Is an Absolute, 1961 Sup. Ct. Rev. 245, 934, 1117

Meiklejohn, A., Free Speech and Its Relation to Self-Government (1948), 933, 968

Mendelson, On the Meaning of the First Amendment: Absolutes in the Balance, 50 Calif. L. Rev. 821 (1962), 978, 980

Meyers, M., ed., The Mind of the Founder (1969), 12, 65

Michelman, Foreword: On Protecting the Poor through the Fourteenth Amendment, 83 Harv. L. Rev. 7 (1969), 679, 682, 816-817

———, Formal and Associational Aims in Procedural Due Process, in NOMOS, Due Process (J. Pennock & J. Chapman eds. 1977), 907

———, Politics and Values or What's Really Wrong with Rationality Review?, 13 Creighton L. Rev. 487 (1979), 509, 510

———, Property as a Constitutional Right, 38 Wash. & Lee L. Rev. 1097 (1981), 1464

———, Property, Utility, and Fairness: Comments on the Ethical Foundations of "Just Compensation" Law, 80 Harv. L. Rev. 1165 (1967), 1459-1461

———, Self-Determination: Competing Judicial Models of Local Government Legitimacy, 53 Ind. L.J. 145 (1977-1978), 524

———, The Supreme Court and Litigation Access Fees: The Right to Protect One's Rights — Part I and Part II, 1974 Duke L.J. 527, 791, 799

———, Welfare Rights in a Constitutional Democracy, 1979 Wash. U. L.Q. 659, 679, 815

Mikva & Hertz, Impoundment of Funds — The Courts, the Congress and the President: A Constitutional Triangle, 69 Nw. U.L. Rev. 335 (1974), 363

Mill, J., On Liberty (1859), 931, 989

Miller, *Dames & Moore v. Regan*: A Political Decision by a Political Court, 29 U.C.L.A. L. Rev. 1104 (1982), 423

———, An Inquiry into the Relevance of the Intentions of the Founding Father, with Special Emphasis upon the Doctrine of the Separation of Powers, 27 Ark. L. Rev. 583 (1973), 343

Miller, J., Crisis in Freedom (1951), 930

Miller, L., The Petitioners: The Story of the Supreme Court of the United States and the Negro 351 (1966), 469

Monaghan, Constitutional Adjudication: The Who and the When, 82 Yale L.J. 1381 (1974), 111

———, Constitutional Common Law, 89 Harv. L. Rev. 1 (1975), 242

———, Constitutional Fact Review, 85 Colum. L. Rev. 229 (1985), 1009

———, First Amendment Due Process, 83 Harv. L. Rev. 518 (1970), 946, 1036, 1050, 1051

———, Of "Liberty" and "Property," 62 Corn. L. Rev. 405 (1977), 910-911, 1066

———, Our Perfect Constitution, 56 N.Y.U. L. Rev. 353 (1981), 693

———, Overbreadth, 1981 Sup. Ct. Rev. 1, 1040-1042

———, Presidential Warmaking, 50 B.U. L. Rev. 19 (1970), 427

———, Third Party Standing, 84 Colum. L. Rev. 277 (1984), 94, 1040

Mueller, D., Public Choice (1979), 124

Murasky, The Journalist's Privilege: *Branzburg* and Its Aftermath, 52 Tex. L. Rev. 820 (1974), 1341

Myrdal, G., An American Dilemma (1944), 463

Nagel, Federalism as a Fundamental Value: *National League of Cities* in Perspective, 1981 Sup. Ct. Rev. 81 (1981), 203, 210

———, How Useful Is Judicial Review in Free Speech Cases?, 69 Corn. L. Rev. 302 (1984), 1035, 1066, 1360

Nathanson, The Communist Trial and the Clear-and-Present-Danger Test, 63 Harv. L. Rev. 1167 (1950), 978

Neal, *Baker v. Carr*: Politics in Search of Law, 1962 Sup. Ct. Rev. 252, 773

Nelson, The Impact of the Antislavery Movement upon Styles of Judicial Reasoning in Nineteenth Century America, 87 Harv. L. Rev. 513 (1974), 727

Neuborne, The Myth of Parity, 90 Harv. L. Rev. 1105 (1977), 43

Nichol, Abusing Standing: A Comment on *Allen v. Wright*, 133 U. Pa. L. Rev. 635 (1984), 94

———, Causation as a Standing Requirement: The Unprincipled Use of Judicial Restraint, 69 Ky. L. Rev. 185 (1980-1981), 93

Nicholson, *Buckley v. Valeo:* The Constitutionality of the Federal Election Campaign Act Amendments of 1974, 1977 Wis. L. Rev. 323, 1228

Nimmer, The Meaning of Symbolic Speech under the First Amendment, 21 U.C.L.A. L. Rev. 29 (1973), 994, 1202, 1207, 1212

———, National Security Secrets v. Free Speech: The Issues Left Undecided in the *Ellsberg* Case, 26 Stan. L. Rev. 311 (1974), 1299

———, The Right to Speak from *Times* to *Time:* First Amendment Theory Applied to Libel and Misapplied to Privacy, 56 Calif. L. Rev. 935 (1968), 980, 1065, 1090

Noonan, An Almost Absolute Value in History, in The Morality of Abortion, Legal and Historical Perspectives (1970), 652

Note, Anti-Pornography Laws and First Amendment Values, 98 Harv. L. Rev. 460 (1984), 1137, 1141

———, The Balanced Budget Amendment: An Inquiry into Appropriateness, 96 Harv. L. Rev. 1600 (1983), 66, 365

———, Community Standards, Class Actions, and Obscenity under *Miller v. California*, 88 Harv. L. Rev. 1838 (1975), 1134, 1145

———, Congress, the President, and the Power to Commit Forces to Combat, 81 Harv. L. Rev. 1771 (1968), 427

———, The Constitutional Imperative of Proportional Representation, 94 Yale L.J. 163 (1984), 784

———, Copyright, Free Speech, and the Visual Arts, 93 Yale L.J. 1565 (1984), 1201

———, The Courts, HEW, and Southern School Desegregation, 77 Yale L.J. 321 (1967), 474

———, Developments in the Law — The Constitution and the Family, 93 Harv. L. Rev. 1156 (1980), 889

———, Developments in the Law — Elections, 88 Harv. L. Rev. 1111 (1975), 1081

———, Developments in the Law — The National Security Interest and Civil Liberties, 85 Harv. L. Rev. 1130 (1972), 1287

———, Developments in the Law — Public Employment, 97 Harv. L. Rev. 1611 (1984), 1282

———, Durational Residence Requirements from *Shapiro* through *Sosna:* The Right to Travel Takes a New Turn, 50 N.Y.U. L. Rev. 622 (1975), 812

———, The Equal Treatment of Aliens: Preemption or Equal Protection?, 31 Stan. L. Rev. 1069 (1979), 664

———, The First Amendment and Legislative Bans of Liquor and Cigarette Advertisements, 85 Colum. L. Rev. 632 (1985), 1104

———, The First Amendment Overbreadth Doctrine, 83 Harv. L. Rev. 844 (1970), 1040, 1041, 1045

———, The First Amendment Right to Gather State-Held Information, 89 Yale L.J. 923 (1980), 1358

———, The Future of the War Powers Resolution, 36 Stan. L. Rev. 1427 (1984), 432

———, Governmental Investigations of the Exercise of First Amendment Rights, 60 Minn. L. Rev. 1257 (1976), 1321

———, Human Cannonballs and the First Amendment, 30 Stan. L. Rev. 1185 (1978), 1201

———, The Irrebuttable Presumption Doctrine in the Supreme Court, 87 Harv. L. Rev. 1534 (1974), 922

———, Irrebuttable Presumptions: An Illusory Analysis, 27 Stan. L. Rev. 449 (1975), 922

———, Legislative Purpose, Rationality, and Equal Protection, 82 Yale L.J. 123 (1972), 518

———, Less Drastic Means and the First Amendment, 78 Yale. L.J. 464 (1969), 1176

———, The Mootness Doctrine in the Supreme Court, 88 Harv. L. Rev. 373 (1974), 111

———, National Security and the Amended Freedom of Information Act, 85 Yale L.J. 401 (1976), 1299

———, A Niche for the Guarantee Clause, 94 Harv. L. Rev. 681 (1981), 106

———, The Nonpartisan Freedom of Expression of Public Employees, 76 Mich. L. Rev. 365 (1977), 1281

———, The Political Boycott: An Unprivileged Form of Expression, 1983 Duke L.J. 1076 (1983), 1218

———, Pre-Emption as a Preferential Ground: A New Canon of Construction, 12 Stan. L. Rev. 208 (1959), 320

———, The Preemption Doctrine: Shifting Perspectives on Federalism and the Burger Court, 75 Colum. L. Rev. 623 (1975), 1370, 1372

———, Presidential Impoundment, 61 Geo. L.J. 1295 (1973), 383

———, A Process-Oriented Approach to the Contract Clause, 89 Harv. L. Rev. 373 (1974), 1443

———, The Public Use Limitation on Eminent Domain: An Advance Requiem, 58 Yale L.J. 1623 (1949), 1442

———, Standing to Assert Constitutional Jus Tertii, 88 Harv. L. Rev. 423 (1974), 1040

———, State Economic Substantive Due Process: A Proposed Approach, 88 Yale L.J. 1487 (1979), 749

———, The Supreme Court — 1969 Term, 84 Harv. L. Rev. 1 (1970), 819

———, The Supreme Court — 1970 Term, 85 Harv. L. Rev. 3 (1971), 1315

———, The Supreme Court — 1972 Term, 87 Harv. L. Rev. 57 (1973), 794
———, The Supreme Court — 1973 Term, 88 Harv. L. Rev. 41 (1974), 766, 812
———, The Supreme Court — 1979 Term, 94 Harv. L. Rev. 75 (1980), 784, 1358
———, The Supreme Court — 1982 Term, 97 Harv. L. Rev. 70 (1983), 791, 1326
———, Supreme Court Review of State Findings of Fact in Fourteenth Amendment Cases, 14 Stan. L. Rev. 328 (1962), 1009
———, Symbolic Conduct, 68 Colum. L. Rev. 1091 (1968), 1215
———, Takings Law and the Contract Clause: A Takings Law Approach to Legislative Modification of Public Contracts, 36 Stan. L. Rev. 1447 (1984), 1443
———, Toward a Constitutional Definition of Religion, 91 Harv. L. Rev. 1056 (1978), 1370, 1372
———, The United States and the Articles of Confederation: Drifting Toward Anarchy or Inching Toward Commonwealth, 88 Yale L.J. 142 (1978), 3
Nowak, Due Process Methodology in the Postincorporation World, 70 J. Crim. L. & Criminology 397 (1979), 717
Nozick, Coercion, in Philosophy, Science and Method (S. Morgenbesser ed. 1969), 229
Nutting, Freedom of Silence: Constitutional Protection against Governmental Intrusions in Political Affairs, 47 Mich. L. Rev. 181 (1948), 1316
Nye, R., Fettered Freedom (1949), 931

O'Brien, National Security and Individual Freedom (1955), 1287
Olsen, The Family and the Market: A Study of Ideology and Legal Reform, 96 Harv. L. Rev. 1497 (1983), 623, 651
Olson, M., The Logic of Collective Action (1965), 261, 262
Orfield, G., How to Make Desegregation Work: The Adaptation of Schools to Their Newly Integrated Bodies (1976), 494
———, Public School Desegregation in the United States (1983), 494

Palmer, The Parameters of Constitutional Reconstruction: *Slaughter-House, Cruikshank*, and the Fourteenth Amendment, 1984 U. Ill. L. Rev. 739, 705
Parker, The Past of Constitutional Theory — And Its Future, 42 Ohio St. L.J. 223 (1981), 688
Paul, A., Conservative Crisis and the Rule of Law (1969), 726
Paulsen, The Persistence of Substantive Due Process in the States, 34 Minn. L. Rev. 91 (1950), 749
Peltason, J., Fifty-Eight Lonely Men (1961), 471
Pember, D., Privacy and the Press (1972), 1090
Perry, Abortion, The Public Morals, and the Police Power: The Ethical Function of Substantive Due Process, 23 U.C.L.A. L. Rev. 689 (1976), 863
———, The Authority of Text, Tradition, and Reason: A Theory of Constitutional "Interpretation," 58 S. Cal. L. Rev. 551 (1985), 36, 694
———, The Disproportionate Impact Theory of Racial Discrimination, 125 U. Pa. L. Rev. 540, 558 (1977), 547
———, Freedom of Expression: An Essay on Theory and Doctrine, 78 Nw. U. L. Rev. 1137 (1983), 945
———, Modern Equal Protection: A Conceptualization and Appraisal, 79 Colum. L. Rev. 1023 (1979), 535, 807
———, The Principle of Equal Protection, 32 Hastings L. Rev. 1133 (1981), 540
———, Substantive Due Process Revisited: Reflections on (and Beyond) Recent Cases, 71 Nw. U. L. Rev. 417 (1976), 863
———, Why the Supreme Court Was Plainly Wrong in the Hyde Amendment Case: A Brief Comment on *Harris v. McRae*, 32 Stan. L. Rev. 1113 (1980), 873
Perry, M., The Constitution, the Courts, and Human Rights (1982), 63, 694, 864
Pettigrew & Green, School Desegregation in Large Cities: A Critique of the Coleman "White Flight" Thesis, 46 Harv. Educ. Rev. 1 (1976), 491
Polsby, *Buckley v. Valeo*: The Speech Nature of Political Speech, 1976 Sup. Ct. Rev. 1, 1228, 1233
Pope, The Three-Systems Ladder of First Amendment Values: Two Rungs and a Black Hole, 11 Hast. Const. L.Q. 189 (1984), 1114
Posner, The *DeFunis* Case and the Constitutionality of Preferential Treatment of Racial Minorities, 1974 Sup. Ct. Rev. 1, 509, 605, 608, 739
———, The Right of Privacy, 12 Ga. L. Rev. 393 (1978), 1091
———, The Uncertain Protection of Privacy by the Supreme Court, 1979 Sup. Ct. Rev. 173, 853
Posner, R., Economic Analysis of the Law (2d ed. 1977), 1460
———, Federal Courts: Crisis and Reform (1985), 113
Powe, Mass Speech and the Newer First Amendment, 1982 Sup. Ct. Rev. 243, 1232
———, "Or of the [Broadcast] Press," 55 Tex L. Rev. 39 (1976), 1330
———, The Road to *Swann*: Mobile County Crawls to the Bus, 51 Tex. L. Rev. 505 (1973), 471

Powell, J., The Original Understanding of Original Intent, 99 Harv. L. Rev. 865 (1985), 35, 693

Powell, L., *Carolene Products* Revisited, 82 Colum. L. Rev. 1087 (1982), 537, 539

Powell, T., The Justiciability of Minimum Wage Legislation, 37 Harv. L. Rev. 545 (1924), 740

————, The Still Small Voice of the Commerce Clause, in 3 Selected Essays on Constitutional Law (1938), 258

Prichard, Securing the Canadian Economic Union: Federalism and Internal Barriers to Trade, in Federalism and the Canadian Economic Union 6 (M. Trebilcock et al., eds. 1983), 123-124, 257

Rabban, An Ahistorical Historian: Leonard Levy on Freedom of Expression in Early American History, 37 Stan. L. Rev. 795 (1985), 929

————, The Emergence of Modern First Amendment Theory, 50 U. Chi. L. Rev. 1207 (1983), 945, 952, 953

————, The First Amendment in its Forgotten Years, 90 Yale L.J. 514 (1981), 931

Ragan, Justice Oliver Wendell Holmes, Jr., Zechariah Chafee, Jr., and the Clear and Present Danger Test for Free Speech: The First Year, 1919, 58 J. Am. Hist. 27 (1971), 953

Randall, J., Constitutional Problems under Lincoln (1926), 931

Ratner, Congressional Power over the Appellate Jurisdiction of the Supreme Court, 109 U. Pa. L. Rev. 157 (1960), 72

————, The Coordinated Warmaking Power — Legislative, Executive, and Judicial Roles, 44 S. Cal. L. Rev. 461 (1971), 427

Ravitch, The "White Flight" Controversy, 51 Pub. Interest 135 (1978), 490

Redish, Advocacy of Unlawful Conduct and the First Amendment: In Defense of Clear and Present Danger, 70 Cal. L. Rev. 1159 (1982), 953

————, Constitutional Limitations on Congressional Power to Control Federal Jurisdiction, 77 Nw. U. L. Rev. 143 (1982), 73

————, The Content Distinction in First Amendment Analysis, 34 Stan. L. Rev. 113 (1981), 1175

————, The First Amendment in the Marketplace: Commercial Speech and the Values of Free Expression, 39 Geo. Wash. L. Rev. 429 (1971), 1099

————, The Proper Role of the Prior Restraint Doctrine in First Amendment Theory, 70 Va. L. Rev. 53 (1984), 1057

————, The Value of Free Speech, 130 U. Pa. L. Rev. 51 (1982), 934, 1105, 1175

————, The Warren Court, the Burger Court and the First Amendment Overbreath Doctrine, 78 Nw. U. L. Rev. 1031 (1983), 1042

Regan, Rewriting *Roe v. Wade*, 77 Mich. L. Rev. 1569 (1979), 864, 867, 881

Regan, D. & Singer, R., Animal Rights and Human Obligations (1976), 652

Rehnquist, The Notion of a Living Constitution, 54 Tex. L. Rev. 693 (1976), 693

Reich, The New Property, 73 Yale L.J. 733 (1963), 900, 908

Reinstein, The Welfare Cases: Fundamental Rights, the Poor, and the Burden of Proof in Constitutional Litigation, 44 Temp. L.Q. 1 (1970), 808

Rendleman, Free Press — Fair Trial: Restrictive Orders after *Nebraska Press*, 67 Ky. L.J. 867 (1979), 1056

————, Free Press — Fair Trial: Review of Silence Orders, 52 N.C. L. Rev. 127 (1973), 1056

Reynolds, Testimony before the Subcommittee on Civil and Constitutional Rights of the House Judiciary Committee, 97th Cong., 1st Sess. (1983), 493

Rhoden, The Neonatal Dilemma: Live Births from Late Abortions, 72 Geo. L.J. 1451 (1984), 886

Richards, Free Speech and Obscenity Law: Towards a Moral Theory of the First Amendment, 123 U. Pa. L. Rev. 45 (1974), 935, 1118

————, Interpretation and Historiography, 56 S. Cal. L. Rev. 490 (1985), 851

————, Sexual Autonomy and the Constitutional Right to Privacy: A Case Study in Human Rights and the Unwritten Constitution, 30 Hastings L.J. 957 (1979), 897

Riesman, Democracy and Defamation: Control of Group Libel, 42 Colum. L. Rev. 727 (1942), 1086

Robinson, Slavery in the Structure of American Politics 1765-1820 (1971), 436

Rogat, Mr. Justice Holmes: Some Modern Views — The Judge as Spectator, 31 U. Chi. L. Rev. 213 (1964), 739, 847

Rogat & O'Fallon, Mr. Justice Holmes: A Dissenting Opinion — The Speech Cases, 36 Stan. L. Rev. 1349 (1984), 960

Rosberg, Aliens and Equal Protection: Why Note the Right to Vote?, 75 Mich. L. Rev. 1092 (1977), 661

————, The Protection of Aliens from Discriminatory Treatment by the National Government, 1977 Sup. Ct. Rev. 275, 661, 665

Rose, *Mahon* Reconstructed: Why the Takings Issue Is Still a Muddle, 57 S. Cal. L. Rev. 561 (1984), 1464

Rose-Ackerman, Risk-Taking and Reelection: Does Federalism Promote Innovation?, 9 J. Legal Stud. 593 (1980), 123

Rossell, School Desegregation and White Flight, 90 Pol. Sci. Q. 675 (1975-76), 491

Rostow, Great Cases Make Bad Law: The War Powers Act, 50 Tex. L. Rev. 833 (1972), 427
Rutherglen, Sexual Equality in Fringe-Benefit Plans, 65 Va. L. Rev. 199 (1979), 623, 626
Rutzick, Offensive Language and the Evolution of First Amendment Protection, 9 Harv. C.R.-C.L.
    L. Rev. 1 (1974), 1012

Sack, Reflections on the Wrong Question, Special Constitutional Privilege for the Institutional Press,
    7 Hofstra L. Rev. 629 (1979), 1341
Sager, Fair Measure: The Status of Underenforced Constitutional Norms, 91 Harv. L. Rev. 1212
    (1978), 47, 510, 1476
———, Foreword: Constitutional Limitations on Congress' Authority to Regulate the Jurisdiction of
    the Federal Courts, 95 Harv. L. Rev. 17 (1981), 72
Sandalow, Constitutional Interpretation, 79 Mich. L. Rev. 1033 (1971), 695
———, Racial Preferences in Higher Education: Political Responsibility and the Judicial Role, 42 U.
    Chi. L. Rev. 653 (1975), 602, 605, 607
Scanlon, Freedom of Expression and Categories of Expression, 40 U. Pitt. L. Rev. 519 (1979), 936,
    1100, 1119
———, A Theory of Freedom of Expression, 1 Phil. & Pub. Aff. 204 (1972), 935, 945, 1000, 1208
Schauer, Categories and the First Amendment: A Play in Three Acts, 34 Vand. L. Rev. 265 (1981),
    1168
———, Easy Cases, 58 S. Cal. L. Rev. 399 (1985), 36
———, Fear, Risk and the First Amendment: Unraveling the "Chilling Effect," 58 B.U. L. Rev. 685
    (1978), 1054
———, Hudgens v. N.L.R.B. and the Problem of State Action in First Amendment Adjudication, 61
    Minn. L. Rev. 433 (1977), 1200
———, "Private" Speech and the "Private" Forum: Givham v. Western Line School District, 1979 Sup.
    Ct. Rev. 217, 1078
———, Speech and "Speech" — Obscenity and "Obscenity": An Exercise in the Interpretation of
    Constitutional Language, 67 Geo. L.J. 899 (1979), 1118
Schauer, F., The Law of Obscenity (1976), 1122, 1135
Schmidhauser, J., Judges and Justices (1979), 67
Schmidt, B., Freedom of Press v. Public Access (1976), 1327, 1335
Schwarz, No Imposition of Religion: The Establishment Clause Value, 77 Yale L.J. 692 (1968), 1368
Sedler, The Assertion of Constitutional Jus Tertii: A Substantive Approach, 70 Calif. L. Rev. 1308
    (1982), 1040
———, The Legitimacy Debate in Constitutional Adjudication: An Assessment and a Different Per-
    spective, 44 Ohio St. L.J. 93 (1983), 698
Senate Select Committee to Study Governmental Operations with Respect to Intelligence Activities,
    Final Report, Intelligence Activities and the Rights of Americans, Book II, S. Doc. No. 1313-4,
    94th Cong., 2d Sess. (1976), 1321
Shapiro, M., Freedom of Speech: The Supreme Court and Judicial Review (1966), 38, 978
———, Law and Politics in the Supreme Court (1964), 773
Shea, "Don't Bother to Smile When You Call Me That" — Fighting Words and the First Amend-
    ment, 63 Ky. L.J. 1 (1975), 1012
Shiffrin, Defamatory Non-Media Speech and First Amendment Methodology, 25 U.C.L.A. L. Rev.
    915 (1978), 980, 1078
———, The First Amendment and Economic Regulation: Away from a General Theory of the First
    Amendment, 78 Nw. U. L. Rev. 1212 (1983), 1099
———, Government Speech, 27 U.C.L.A. L. Rev. 565 (1980), 1256, 1261
Sickels, Dragons, Bacon Strips and Dumbbells — Who's Afraid of Reapportionment?, 75 Yale L.J.
    1300 (1966), 784
Siebert, F., Freedom of the Press in England (1952), 926, 927
Siegal, Understanding the Lochner Era: Lessons from the Controversy over Railroad and Utility Rate
    Regulation, 70 Va. L. Rev. 187 (1984), 728
Siegan, B., Economic Liberties and the Constitution (1980), 734-735, 738, 749
Simon, The Authority of the Constitution and Its Meaning: A Preface to a Theory of Constitutional
    Interpretation, 58 S. Cal. L. Rev. 603 (1985), 695
———, The Invention and Reinvention of Welfare Rights, 44 Md. L. Rev. 1 (1985), 908
Simson, Abortion, Poverty and the Equal Protection of the Laws, 13 Ga. L. Rev. 505 (1979), 873
Singer, R., Practical Ethics (1979), 697
Smith, J., Freedom's Fetters (1956), 930, 659
Smolla, Let the Author Beware: The Rejuvenation of the American Law of Libel, 132 U. Pa. L. Rev. 1
    (1984), 1066
Southern Manifesto, 102 Cong. Rec. 3948, 4004 (March 12, 1956), 470
Spann, Simple Justice, 73 Geo. L.J. 1041 (1985), 606

St. John, "The Effects of Desegregation on Children" in Yarmolinsky, Liebman & Schelling, Race and Schooling in the City (1981), 494

St. John-Stevas, N., Obscenity and the Law (1956), 1120

Steel, Nine Men in Black Who Think White, New York Times Magazine, Oct 13, 1968, 469

Stephan, The First Amendment and Content Discrimination, 68 Va. L. Rev. 203 (1982), 1175

Stephen, J., A History of the Criminal Law of England (1883), 927

Stewart, P., Or of the Press, 26 Hastings L.J. 631 (1975), 1078, 1322, 1341

Stewart, R., The Reformation of American Administrative Law, 88 Harv. L. Rev. 1667 (1975), 87, 366, 370, 900

Stewart & Sunstein, Public Programs and Private Rights, 95 Harv. L. Rev. 1193 (1982), 909

Stigler, The Theory of Economic Regulation, 2 Bell J. Econ. & Mgmt. Sci. 3 (1971) 64, 935

Stone, Anti-Pornography Legislation as Viewpoint Discrimination, 9 Harv. J. L. & Pub. Pol — (1986), 1138

———, Content Regulation and the First Amendment, 25 Wm. and Mary L. Rev. 189 (1983), 994, 996, 1000-1001, 1151, 1175, 1210, 1247, 1260

———, Fora Americana: Speech in Public Places, 1974 Sup. Ct. Rev. 233, 1152-1153, 1177-1179, 1189

———, In Opposition to the School Prayer Amendment, 50 U. Chi. L. Rev. 823 (1983), 1395

———, Restrictions of Speech Because of its Content: The Peculiar Case of Subject-Matter Restrictions, 46 U. Chi. L. Rev. 81 (1978), 1247

Stone & Marshall, *Brown v. Socialist Workers:* Inequality as a Command of the First Amendment, 1983 Sup. Ct. Rev. 583, 1310

Storing, H., What the Antifederalists Were For (1981), 5

Story, J., Commentaries on the Constitution of the United States (1883), 1046

Strauss, The Place of Agencies in Government: Separation of Powers and the Fourth Branch, 84 Colum. L. Rev. 573 (1984), 388

———, Was There a Baby in the Bathwater? A Comment on the Supreme Court's Legislative Veto Decision, 1983 Duke L.J. 789, 383

Strickman, Marriage, Divorce, and the Constitution, 22 B.C. L. Rev. 935 (1981), 895

Strong, Fifty Years of "Clear and Present Danger": From *Schenck* to *Brandenburg* — And Beyond, 1969 Sup. Ct. Rev. 41, 968

Struve, The Less-Restrictive-Alternative Principle and Economic Due Process, 80 Harv. L. Rev. 1463 (1967), 749

Sunderland, L., Obscenity: The Court, the Congress and the President's Commission (1975), 1119

Sunstein, Hard Defamation Cases, 25 Wm. & Mary L. Rev. 891 (1984), 1065

———, Interest Groups in American Public Law, 38 Stan. L. Rev. 29 (1985), 541

———, Naked Preferences and the Constitution, 84 Colum. L. Rev. 1689 (1984), 501, 510, 737, 744, 748, 1435, 1461

———, Public Values, Private Interests, and the Equal Protection Clause, 1982 Sup. Ct. Rev. 127, 523, 576

Sutherland, D., Principles of Criminality (4th ed. 1947), 754

Swisher, History of the Supreme Court of the United States; The Taney Period 1836-64 (1974), 440

Symposium, The Article V Convention Process, 66 Mich. L. Rev. 837 (1968), 67

———, Campaign Reform, 10 Hastings Const. L.Q. 463 (1983), 1232

———, Congressional Investigations, 18 U. Chi. L. Rev. 421 (1951), 1316

———, Constitutional Adjudication and Democratic Theory, 56 N.Y.U. L. Rev. 259 (1981), 698

———, The Courts, Social Science and School Desegregation, 39 Law & Contemp. Probs. (Winter/ Spring 1975), 465

———, Defamation and the First Amendment: New Perspectives, 25 Wm. & Mary L. Rev. 745 (1984), 1067

———, Defamation in Fiction, 51 Brooklyn L. Rev. 223 (1985), 1067

———, Judicial Review versus Democracy, 42 Ohio St. L.J. 1 (1981), 698

———, Legislative Motivation, 15 San Diego L. Rev. 925 (1978), 1211

———, National Security and Civil Liberties, 69 Corn. L. Rev. 685 (1984), 1321

———, National Security and the First Amendment, 26 Wm. & Mary L. Rev. 715 (1985), 1033

Tarrow, *Lochner versus New York:* A Political Analysis, 5 Lab. Hist. 277 (1964), 738

Taylor, T., Grand Inquest: The Story of Congressional Investigations (1955), 1316

ten Broek, J., The Antislavery Origins of the Fourteenth Amendment (1951), 439, 716

ten Broek, Barnhart, & Matson, Prejudice, War and the Constitution (1954), 535

Thayer, The Origin and Scope of the American Doctrine of Constitutional Law, 7 Harv. L. Rev. 129 (1883), 33

Thayer, T., John Marshall (1901), 33

Theoharis, A., Spying on Americans (1978), 985, 1321

Thomson, A Defense of Abortion, 1 Phil. & Pub. Affairs 47 (1971), 697, 866

Tiebout, A Pure Theory of Local Expenditures, 64 J. Pol. Econ. 416 (1956), 123-124

Tiedeman, C., A Treatise on the Limitations of the Police Power in the United States (1886), 726

Tiger, The "Political Question" Doctrine and Foreign Relations, 17 U.C.L.A. L. Rev. 1135 (1970), 108

Tooley, M., Abortion and Infanticide (1983), 867

Tribe, Constitutional Calculus: Equal Justice or Economic Efficiency, 98 Harv. L. Rev. 592 (1985), 1183, 1395

——, A Constitution We Are Amending: In Defense of Restrained Judicial Role, 97 Harv. L. Rev. 433 (1983), 108

——, Foreword: Toward a Model of Roles in the Due Process of Life and Law, 87 Harv. L. Rev. 1 (1973), 863, 868

——, Jurisdictional Gerrymandering: Zoning Disfavored Rights out of the Federal Courts, 16 Harv. C.R.-C.L. L. Rev. 129 (1981), 73

——, The Legislative Veto Decision: A Law by Any Other Name?, 21 Harv. J. On Legis. 1 (1984), 383

——, Perspectives on *Bakke*: Equal Protection, Procedural Fairness, or Structural Justice, 92 Harv. L. Rev. 864 (1979), 604

——, The Puzzling Persistence of Process-Based Constitutional Theories, 89 Yale L.J. 1063 (1980), 698, 734

——, Structural Due Process, 10 Harv. C.R.-C.L. L. Rev. 269 (1975), 868, 909, 921, 923

——, Toward a Syntax of the Unsaid: Construing the Sounds of Congressional and Constitutional Silence, 57 Indiana L.J. 515 (1982), 256

Tribe, L., American Constitutional Law (1978), 284, 683, 684, 707, 709, 735-737, 756, 862-863, 866, 937, 965, 979, 995, 1031, 1044, 1090, 1211, 1229, 1255-1256, 1365, 1368, 1370, 1398, 1420

——, American Constitutional Law (1979 Supp.), 1443

——, Constitutional Choices (1985), 327, 864, 874, 1113, 1259, 1492, 1534

——, God Save This Honorable Court (1985), 68

Truman, D., The Governmental Process (1962), 17

Truman, H., Memoirs: Years of Trial and Hope (1956), 360

Tushnet, Corporations and Free Speech, in the Politics of Law (Kairys ed.) (1982), 1100

——, Darkness on the Edge of Town: The Contributions of John Hart Ely to Constitutional Theory, 89 Yale L.J. 1037 (1980), 697, 764

——, Following the Rules Laid Down: A Critique of Interpretivism and Neutral Principles, 96 Harv. L. Rev. 781 (1983), 35, 464, 693

——, The Newer Property: Suggestions for a Revival of Substantive Due Process, 1975 Sup. Ct. Rev. 261, 910

——, The New Law of Standing: A Plea for Abandonment, 62 Corn. L. Rev. 663 (1977), 93

——, The Optimist's Tale, 132 U. Pa. L. Rev. 1257 (1984), 839

——, Segregated Schools and Legal Strategy: The NAACP's Campaign against Segregated Education 1925-1950 (unpublished manuscript), 457

——, The Supreme Court on Abortion, in Abortion, Medicine and the Law (J. Butler & D. Walbert eds.) (1986), 874

Tushnet, M., The American Law of Slavery, 1810-1860 (1981), 253

U.S. Commission on Civil Rights, Fulfilling the Letter and Spirit of the Law: Desegregation of the Nation's Public Schools (1976), 494

U.S. Department of Commerce, Bureau of the Census, the Social and Economic Status of the Black Population in the U.S.: An Historical View, 1790-1978, 495

U.S. Department of Commerce, Current Population Reports Series P-60, No. 145 (1984), 495

U.S. Department of State, Office of Legal Advisor, the Legality of United States Participation in the Defense of Vietnam, 75 Yale L.J. 1085 (1966), 427

Van Alstyne, Congress, The President, and the Power to Declare War: A Requiem for Vietnam, 121 U. Pa. L. Rev. 1 (1972), 433

——, Cracks in the New Property, 62 Corn. L. Rev. 445 (1977), 909

——, A Critical Guide to *Ex parte McCardle*, 15 Ariz. L. Rev. 229 (1973), 71

——, A Critical Guide to *Marbury v. Madison*, 1969 Duke L.J. 1, 28

——, The Demise of the Right/Privilege Distinction in Constitutional Law, 81 Harv. L. Rev. 1439 (1968), 1274

——, The First Amendment and the Free Press: A Comment on Some Trends and Some Old Theories, 9 Hofstra L. Rev. 1 (1980), 1348

——, The Fourteenth Amendment, the "Right" to Vote, and the Understanding of the Thirty-Ninth Congress, 1965 Sup. Ct. Rev. 33, 760

——, A Graphic Review of the Free Speech Clause, 70 Calif. L. Rev. 107 (1982), 980
——, The Mobius Strip of the First Amendment: Perspectives on *Red Lion*, 29 S.C. L. Rev. 539 (1978), 1331-1332
——, Rites of Passage: Race, the Supreme Court, and the Constitution, 46 U. Chi. L. Rev. 775 (1979), 606
Van den Haag, Quia Ineptum, in To Deprave and Corrupt (1962), 1120
——, Social Science Testimony in the Desegregation Cases — A Reply to Professor Kenneth Clark, 6 Vill. L. Rev. 69 (1960), 465
Varat, State "Citizenship" and Interstate Equality, 48 U. Chi. L. Rev. 487 (1981), 334, 814
Velvel, Freedom of Speech and the Draft Card Burning Cases, 16 U. Kan. L. Rev. 149 (1968), 1209
——, The War in Viet Nam: Unconstitutional, Justiciable, and Jurisdictionally Attackable, 16 Kan. L. Rev. 449 (1968), 108
Vile, M., Constitutional and the Separation of Powers (1967), 342
Vining, J., Legal Identity (1978), 87
Vose, Constitutional Change: Amendment Politics and Supreme Court Litigation Since 1900 (1972), 67, 69

Warren, The New "Liberty" Under the Fourteenth Amendment, 39 Harv. L. Rev. 431 (1926), 734
Warren, C., The Supreme Court in United States History 303 (1922), 444
Wasserstrom, R., Philosophy and Social Issues (1980), 623, 625, 639
Wechsler, The Courts and the Constitution, 65 Colum. L. Rev. 1001 (1965), 72
——, The Political Safeguards of Federalism, in H. Wechsler, Principles, Politics, and Fundamental Law (1961), 120-121, 181, 199, 201-202, 247
——, Symposium on Civil Liberties, 9 Am. L. School Rev. 881 (1941), reprinted in Selected Essays on Constitutional Law 1938-1962 (1963), 969
——, Toward Neutral Principles of Constitutional Law, 73 Harv. L. Rev. 1 (1959), 466, 1491
Wellington, Common Law Rules and Constitutional Double Standards: Some Notes on Adjudication, 83 Yale L.J. 221 (1973), 36, 63, 695, 853
——, On Freedom of Expression, 88 Yale L.J. 1105 (1979), 931, 932
Wells & Hellerstein, The Governmental-Proprietary Distinction in Constitutional Law, 66 Va. L. Rev. 1073 (1980), 327, 1254
Westen, The Empty Idea of Equality, 95 Harv. L. Rev. 537 (1982), 500
Westin, Correspondence, 33 Stan. L. Rev. 1187 (1981), 873
Westin, A., The Anatomy of a Constitutional Case (1958), 359
Wharton, F., State Trials (1849), 930
White, T., The Making of the President: 1968 (1969), 492
Whitney & Kotinsky, Personality in the Making (1952), 463
Wiecek, W., The Guarantee Clause of the United States Constitution (1947), 106
Wigmore, *Abrams v. United States*: Freedom of Speech and Freedom of Thuggery in War-Time and Peace-Time, 14 Ill. L. Rev. 539 (1920), 953, 966
Wilkinson, The Supreme Court, the Equal Protection Clause, and the Three Faces of Constitutional Equality, 61 Va. L. Rev. 945 (1975), 775
Wilkinson, J., From *Brown* to *Bakke* (1979), 471, 491, 492
Wilkinson & White, Constitutional Protection for Personal Lifestyles, 62 Corn. L. Rev. 563 (1977), 897, 899
Williams, Liberty and Property: The Problem of Government Benefits, 12 J. Legal Stud. 3 (1983), 909
Williamson, J., The Crucible of Race (1984), 450
Wills, G., Explaining America: The Federalist (1981), 122
Wilson, J., The Politics of Regulation (1980), 259-261, 269
Winter, Poverty, Economic Equality, and the Equal Protection Clause, 1972 Sup. Ct. Rev. 41, 817
Wonnell, Economic Due Process and the Preservation of Competition, 11 Hast. Const. L.Q. 91 (1983), 738
Wood, G., ed., The Confederation and the Constitution (1978), 2
Wood, S., Constitutional Politics in the Progressive Era (1968), 2, 7, 151
Woodward, C., The Strange Career of Jim Crow (1957), 450
——, The Creation of the American Republic, 1776-1787 (1969), 344
Wright, B., The Contract Clause of the Constitution (1938), 1428, 1430
——, The Growth of American Constitutional Law (1942), 740
Wright, C., Law of Federal Courts (4th ed. 1983)
Wright, J., Money and the Pollution of Politics, Is the First Amendment an Obstacle to Political Equality, 82 Colum. L. Rev. 609 (1982), 1229
——, Politics and the Constitution: Is Money Speech, 85 Yale L.J. 1001 (1976), 1229

Yudof, Library Book Selection and the Public Schools: The Quest for the Archimedean Point, 59 Ind. L.J. 527 (1984), 1265

———, School Desegregation: Legal Realism, Reasoned Elaboration, and Social Science Research in the Supreme Court, 42 L. & Contemp. Probs. 57 (1978), 465

Zimmerman, David, Coercive Wage Offers, 10 Phil. & Pub. Affairs 121 (1981), 229, 1090

Zimmerman, Diane, Requiem for a Heavyweight: A Farewell to Warren and Brandeis's Privacy Tort, 68 Corn. L. Rev. 291 (1983), 1090

Index

Abortion, 854-886
  fetus, 865-868, 885-886
  funding, 869-874
  gender discrimination, 864
  governmental financing of, 675, 684-685,
    1396
  Hyde Amendment, 684-685
  parental consent, 881-884
  privacy, 861-864
  regulation of, 874-886
  spousal consent, 881
  viability, 868-869, 885-886
Academic freedom. *See* Education; Freedom of
  association
Adequate state grounds, 113
Administrative state, 365-395
Adoption. *See* Family relations
Advisory opinions, 77-78
Affirmative action
  definition of, 609-610, 649-651
  employment discrimination, 579-580, 602,
    607-608
  gender, 615, 642-643, 645-646, 649-651
  graduate school admissions, 581-596, 601-
    602, 604, 608
  heightened scrutiny for, 581, 583-585, 597,
    599, 600, 602-607, 649
  justifications for, 585-587, 597, 607-609
  minority business enterprises. *See* Affirmative
    action, public works
  public works, 596-601
  race, 547, 548, 578-610
  remedies for school segregation, 578-579
Age, classifications based on, 686-688
Age Discrimination in Employment Act, 209,
  240
Agricultural Adjustment Act, 168, 174, 219
Agriculture, national regulation of, 174-176,
  219-225

Aliens
  admission to practice law, 658
  deportation
    legislative veto, 371-385
  discrimination against, as suspect classifica-
    tion, 652, 654, 659-663
  federal regulation of, 605, 663-667
  formulation and execution of government
    policy, 654, 655, 662-663
  franchise, 655, 661
  government employment, 605, 653-658, 661-
    663, 665-666
  history of discrimination against, 659
  illegal aliens
    right to public education, 660, 666, 831-
      840, 1485, 1493
  public schools, 660, 666
  welfare benefits, 654, 659
Amendments to Constitution
  abortion proposal, 65
  amendment process, 65-67
  democracy and, 65-67
  justiciability, 106-109
  proposal of, 65-67
  ratification, 65-67
  reprisal to Court, 65-67
Antifederalists, 5-6
Appeal
  counsel on. *See* Wealth discrimination; Judi-
    cial process
  filing fees. *See* Wealth discrimination; Judicial
    process
  review by, 111-113
  Supreme Court obligation, 111-113
Apportionment. *See also* Equal protection;
    Voting
  effects on national political process, 120-122,
    202
  political question doctrine and, 75-102

Articles of Confederation, 2-5, 115, 133, 136
Autonomy of coordinate branches, 339-395

Banking, state regulation of, 258, 269
Bar admissions. *See* Freedom of expression
"Belief-action" distinction, 1410-1411
"Benign" classifications. *See* Affirmative action
Bible reading in public schools. *See* Religion
Billboards. *See* Freedom of expression
Bill of attainder, 1294
Bill of rights
    applicability to states, 707-724
    relation to enumerated powers, 116
Birth control. *See* Abortion; Implied fundamen-
        tal rights, contraception
Bituminous Coal Conservation Act of 1935,
        160, 166, 167, 168
Black codes, 445
Blacks. *See* Equal protection; Slavery, thir-
        teenth amendment; Fourteenth
        amendment; Fifteenth amendment;
        Segregation; Affirmative action
Blaine amendments, 1367
Boycott. *See* Freedom of expression
Bricker Amendment, 215
Busing. *See* Segregation; Equal protection

Case or controversy, 76-111
Censorship. *See* Freedom of expression
Certiorari, 111-113
Charitable trusts, discrimination by. *See* State
        action
Child labor
    commerce power, 150-155
    tax power, 216-218
Child Labor Act, 150
Church and state. *See* Religion
Citizens. *See* Privileges and immunities clause
    citizenship of blacks, 441-442, 444, 446, 1473
    corporations as, 335
Civil Rights Act
    of 1866, 245-247, 445-446, 1488
    of 1870, 446, 448
    of 1871, 446, 449, 450
    of 1875, 446, 449, 1469-1474
    of 1964, 186, 187-196, 474, 579-580, 583, 589,
        590, 594, 596, 601, 606, 613, 624, 1499
    of 1965, 562, 580-581
    of 1968, 245, 246
"Clear and present danger" doctrine. *See* Free-
        dom of expression
Commerce clause, dormant. *See* Interstate
        commerce, state regulation of
Communists. *See* Freedom of association;
        Freedom of expression
Compacts. *See* Interstate compacts
Congress. *See also* Separation of powers
    consent to state laws, 254-256, 321-322
    control of federal courts, 69-75
    control over Supreme Court jurisdiction, 69-
        75
    exclusive power to regulate interstate com-
        merce, 250, 252-253

investigations
    power to delegate authority, 365-371
    legislative veto and, 371-385
    power to define scope of Reconstruction
        amendments, 233-247
    power to exclude or expel members, 102-105
    preemption, 251, 254-255, 313-321
Congressional investigations. *See* Freedom of
        expression; Congress, investigations
Constitution
    amendments, 65-67
    compared to Articles of Confederation, 2-5
    political theory underlying, 2-17
    theories of interpretation
        consensus, 695-697
        interpretivism, 31-38, 691-698
        moral philosophy, 694-697, 863-864, 866-
            868
        natural law, 694-696. *See also* Natural law
        noninterpretivism, 31-38, 691-698
        representation/reinforcement, 37-38, 48-61,
            258, 260, 536-539, 571, 583, 590, 603-
            604, 624-625, 647-648, 654, 657, 660-
            661, 663, 668-669, 680, 685-687,
            695-697, 738-739, 760-761
        tradition, 695-697, 889
Constitutional Convention
    consideration of slavery, 436
    Council of Revision, 250, 256
Consumer Credit Protection Act of 1968, 182
Contraception. *See* Implied fundamental rights
Contract clause
    emergencies, as affected by, 1430-1435
    historical background, 1428-1435
    liberty of contract, 724-750, 1427-1445
    mortgage moratoria, application to, 1430-1435
    police power, bargaining away, 1429, 1435-
        1436
Cost/benefit analysis, 260-261, 268, 275, 284,
        296-297, 913-921
"Court-packing plan," 186

Defamation. *See* Freedom of expression, libel
Delegation of legislative powers, 365-371
Deportation, legislative veto of, 371-385
Developmentally Disabled Assistance and Bill
        of Rights Act of 1975, 231
Discrimination. *See* Affirmative action; Age;
        Aliens; Equal protection; Gender
        discrimination; Implied fundamental
        rights; Jurors; Nonmarital children;
        Voting; Wealth discrimination
Divorce. *See* Family relations
Due process of law
    abortion, regulation of, 854-886
    conclusive presumptions, 614-615, 921-923
    economic regulations, 291, 724-750
    equal protection, 464, 514, 519, 791-802
    family relations, 886-900
    incorporation of bill of rights, 707-724
    irrebuttable presumptions, 614-615, 921-923
    privacy, 840-900
    procedural, 900-924
    state action requirement. *See* State action

substantive, 505, 724-750, 840-900, 1529, 1533-1534

Economic efficiency, 500-501, 508-509
Education. *See also* Freedom of expression; Implied fundamental rights; Religion
  academic freedom, 587, 604
  financing of, 678, 821-831
  flag salute, 1300
  fundamental interest, 821-840
  illegal aliens, 831-840. *See also* Aliens
  libraries, 1262-1266
  racial segregation. *See* Segregation
  residence requirements, 839-840
  student rights, 1262-1266, 1269-1272
  teaching of evolution and creationism, 1407-1408
Elections. *See also* Apportionment; Voting
  access to ballot, 786-791
  corporate financing, 1230-1232
  political campaign restrictions, 1220-1236
  public employees, restrictions on political activities of, 1275-1278
Eminent domain
  police power and, 1459-1465
  public use, 1445-1448
  taking, what constitutes, 1448-1465
Employment Retirement Income Security Act, 199, 319
Environmental protection legislation , state, 263-268, 270
Equal Access Act, 1376, 1421
Equal protection. *See also* Affirmative action; Aliens; Discrimination; Due process of law; Education; Elections; Gender discrimination; Implied fundamental rights; Natural law; Nonmarital children
  access to ballot, 786-791
  access to judicial process, 791-802
  balancing tests, 508-509, 542
  due process, overlap with, 791-802
  early interpretation, 448, 449, 528-530
  education, 821-840
  effect, relevance of, 479-480, 483-485, 544-546, 549, 550-551, 557, 558-562, 570, 576, 578, 579, 603-604, 609-610, 639-640, 681, 1492
  facts, review of, 506-508, 542
  freedom of expression, 808, 1233-1234, 1244-1267
  fundamental interests, 751-840
  government employment, 496-499, 543-546, 551-552, 653-658, 661-663, 665-666
  immutable characteristics, 522, 591, 599, 606, 613, 622-623, 636, 639, 659-660, 669
  implied fundamental interests, 751-840
  intermediate standard of review, 511, 547, 591, 599, 617-627, 642, 645, 649, 669
  means/ends analysis, 501-504, 507-510, 541-543, 553, 617-618, 625
  overinclusion, 497, 498, 502, 598, 617-618, 644-645, 650, 662-663, 672

  procreation, 751-756
  public interest requirement, 501, 509-510, 512, 523-524, 540-541, 688
  purpose, need to show illegitimate, 480, 483-485, 487, 498, 511, 519, 520, 521-524, 526, 544-546, 548, 549-550, 552-562, 565, 569, 576, 578, 581, 609-610, 688
  purpose, review based on actual, 506-507, 515, 516-518, 519, 526-528, 649
  racial discrimination, 446, 448, 451-495, 528-610, 622-624, 625-626, 1467, 1485-1486, 1488-1499, 1500-1507, 1513-1517, 1525-1526, 1528
  rational basis review, 452, 453, 495-528, 546, 611-613, 662, 667, 677, 685-687
  representation reinforcement, 536-539, 571, 583, 590, 603-604, 624-625, 647-648, 654, 657, 660-661, 663, 668-669, 680, 685-687, 1527
  state taxes on out-of-state corporations, 336-337
  stigma, 452, 465, 530, 536, 543, 546, 557, 580, 584, 589, 591, 593, 650
  strict scrutiny, 531, 536, 540, 541-543, 547, 553, 563, 566, 574, 575-576, 583-586, 590, 599, 600, 602-607, 613-614, 659-663, 679-680
  suspect classifications, 496, 530-541, 563-565, 571, 576, 583-585, 590, 599, 613-614, 652, 654, 656, 659-663, 675-680, 685-689, 1493
  taxation, state or local, 521-522
  travel, 802-815
  underinclusion, 503-504, 506, 598, 600, 662-663
  voting, 756-791. *See also* Voting
  wealth, 757-761, 789, 791-802, 815-821. *See also* Wealth discrimination
  welfare, 815-821
Equal rights amendment. *See* Gender discrimination
Equality, nature of, 499-501, 548, 651, 683-684
Establishment clause. *See* Religion
Executive power
  domestic, 346-395
  foreign, 413-433
Executive privilege, 398-412

Faction, 6-17, 345
Fair Labor Standards Act, 177, 196
  as applied to state employees, 196-210
  federal power to enact, 177-180
Family relations
  adoption, 543, 614, 636-638, 671-672
  custody, 983-995
  divorce, 543, 650, 798-802, 812-813, 1476
  marriage, 852-853, 890-893
  right to live together, 886-890
Federal Communications Act, 319, 1327-1335
Federal courts, 69-75
Federalists, 6-17
Federal Lottery Act, 145
Federal Safety Appliance Act, 144

, 446, 562, 564, 1524-

See Freedom of association;
...n of expression; Freedom of
...ess; Religion
...rs
...onal and presidential powers, 413-
...24
...24-433
...eenth amendment. See also Due process
    of law; Equal protection; Incorporation
    doctrine; Privileges and immunities
    clause; Procedural due process; State
    action; Substantive due process
  adoption of, 704-707
  as basis for federal legislative power, 1475
  early interpretations, 447-450, 611-612
  economic substantive due process, 724-750
  history, 446, 461-462, 463-464, 535, 622, 656
  intention of framers, 704-707
Framing of Constitution, 1-17
Franchise. See Elections; Equal protection;
    Fifteenth amendment; Voting
Freedom of assembly. See Freedom of expres-
    sion
Freedom of association. See also Freedom of
    expression
  compelled disclosure, 1306-1321
  intimate association, 886-900, 1241-1243
  membership in subversive associations, 965-
    966, 982-983, 1287-1294, 1307-1308,
    1309-1311
  right not to associate, 1283-1287, 1302-
    1304
Freedom of expression. See also Freedom of
    association; Freedom of the press;
    Religion
  absolutism, 925, 979-980
  advocacy of unlawful acts, 939-991, 1287-
    1294, 1312-1321
  anticommunism, 965-985, 1287-1294, 1312-
    1321
  auditoriums, 1260-1262
  bad tendency, 939-949
  balancing, 978-980, 1175-1176, 1209-1210,
    1273-1300
  bar admissions, 1312-1316
  billboards, regulation of, 1173-1175, 1109-
    1111, 1249-1250
  boycotts, 1215-1218
  Brandeis, 960-966
  breach of the peace, 997-1017
  campaigns, 1220-1236
  captive audiences, 997, 1120, 1146-1161,
    1168, 1250-1255, 1306
  checking value, 936-937, 1280
  child pornography, 1139-1141
  classified information, 1023-1035, 1299
  clear and present danger doctrine, 943-944,
    946-947, 949-954, 965, 968-969, 978,
    987-990, 995
  commercial speech, 1091-1114, 1305, 1535
  communicative impact, 994, 1000
  company towns, 1198-1199
  compelled disclosure, 1105-1106, 1306-1321
  compelled speech, 1300-1306

confidential information, 1017-1035, 1295-
    1300
congressional investigations, 1316-1321
contempt by publication, 991-997
copyright, 1201
corporate speech, 1230-1232
courthouse picketing, 995-997, 1180
criticism of the judicial process, 991-997,
    1081, 1180
deference, 958-959, 979-980, 1197
demonstrations and mass protests, 1005-1009
draft card burning, 1202-1211
entertainment, 1117, 1167-1168
equal protection, overlap with, 1233-1234,
    1244-1267
fairness doctrine. See Freedom of the press
false or deceptive advertising, 1104-1105
false statements, 1059-1081, 1086, 1104-1105,
    1278-1281
fees, 1185
feminism and, 1136-1139
"fighting words," 1009-1017
flag desecration, 1211-1215
flag salute, 1300
government employment, limitations on,
    1032, 1273-1300, 1310
group libel, 1082-1086
Hatch Act, 1275-1278
history of, 925-931
Holmes, 943-960, 1035, 1177-1178, 1273-
    1274
home letter boxes, 1193-1195
hostile audience, 997-1017
immorality, 1119-1120
improper motivation, 1000-1001, 1205-1206,
    1210-1211, 1258, 1262-1266
incidental restrictions, 1210
incitement, 941-943, 945-946, 958-959, 989-
    990, 995, 1003-1004
injunctions, 1030-1031, 1052-1058, 1105,
    1142-1143
intelligence activities, 1321
intent of framers, 928-929
interference with judicial process, 991-997,
    1180
interschool mail system, 1256-1258
invasion of privacy, 1018-1019, 1086-1091
labor speech, 1111-1114, 1302-1304
lawyer advertising, 1101-1102, 1106-1107
leafletting, 1170-1171, 1308-1309, 1191-1193
legislative investigations, 1316-1321
libel, 1059-1080, 1085, 1491, 1493
libraries, 1186-1187, 1262-1266
licensing, 925-926, 1004-1005, 1046-1051,
    1142, 1184-1185, 1260-1262, 1330-1332
litigation as expression, 1236-1241
loudspeakers, 1172-1173
loyalty oaths, 1044-1045, 1287-1294
marketplace of ideas, 931-933, 959-960, 965,
    1006, 1099-1100, 1228-1230, 1330-1331
military, 1190-1191, 1255-1256, 1267-1269
obscenity, 1114-1145
offensive speech, 1146-1169
overbreadth, 1036-1043, 1278
patronage, 1283-1287, 1302
Pentagon Papers case, 1023-1033

philosophy of, 931-938
political action committees, 1234-1235
pornography, 1136-1139
prior restraint, 927, 1004-1005, 1030-1031,
    1046-1058, 1142-1145, 1184-1185, 1260-
    1262, 1300, 1327-1333
prisons, 1187-1189, 1272-1273, 1343-1347
private property, 1198-1201, 1521-1524, 1528,
    1530-1531
private speech, 1078-1080, 1281-1283
profanity, 1146-1161
proprietary/governmental distinction, 1254,
    1262-1266, 1273-1275
public employees, 1032, 1273-1300, 1310
public figures, 1059-1077
public forum, 1177-1198, 1244-1262
residential picketing, 1007-1008, 1248
right not to speak, 1300-1306
right to receive ideas and information, 1123-
    1124, 1136, 1262-1266
schools, 1180-1181, 1208, 1248-1249, 1262-
    1266, 1269-1272
seditious libel, 926-927, 929-930
self-fulfillment, 935-936, 965, 1099
self-governance, 933-935, 1006
sexually explicit speech, 1161-1169
shopping centers, 1199-1200, 1301-1302
signs on public property, regulation of, 1195-
    1197
Skokie, 1015-1017, 1085
sleeping in parks, 1181-1183, 1210
Smith Act, 969-985
solicitation of contributions, 1218-1219
sound amplification, 1172-1173
speaker-based restrictions, 1260, 1266-1267
"speech/conduct" distinction, 1183-1184
state fair grounds, 1191-1193
streets and parks, 1177-1186
subject-matter restrictions, 1247, 1254-1255,
    1259
subsidies, 1232-1233, 1260-1262, 1266-1267
subversive advocacy, 939-991, 1287-1294,
    1312-1321
symbolic expression, 1186-1187, 1201-1218
tax exemptions, 1266-1267, 1323-1326
technical information, 1032-1035
theaters, zoning of, 1161-1169
threats, 986-987, 995
underinclusion, 959, 1246-1247
vagueness, 1043-1046, 1162, 1212-1213, 1293-
    1294
Freedom of religion. See Religion
Freedom of speech. See Freedom of expression;
    Freedom of the press
Freedom of the press. See also Freedom of
    expression
access to judicial proceedings, 1349-1359
broadcast regulation, 1267, 1304-1305, 1327-
    1335
differential treatment, 1323-1326
fairness doctrine, 1327-1333
fair trial, free press, 991-997, 1019-1023
gag orders, 1019-1023
newsgathering, 1336-1359
preferred status, 1348-1349
reporter's privilege, 1336-1341

right of reply, 1326-1327
search of newsroom, 1342-1343
taxation of, 1323-1326
Free trade. See Protectionism and free trade
Fugitive Slave Act of 1793, 137
Fugitive slave clause, 436, 440
Fundamental rights. See Equal protection;
    Implied fundamental rights; Privileges
    and immunities clause

Gambling, federal regulation of, 218
Gender discrimination. See also Affirmative
    action; Natural law
    abortion, 864
    administrative convenience as justification
        for, 614, 617, 632, 633, 644, 647
    "archaic and overbroad generalizations," 615,
        617, 625, 628, 641
    armed forces, 613, 616, 631-634, 635
    discrimination against men, 620, 641-642,
        643, 644, 646-649
    early cases, 611-612
    employment, 611-612, 743-744
    equal rights amendment, 613-614, 624-625,
        651-652
    family rights, 614, 615, 635-638, 672
    intermediate scrutiny, 591, 617-627, 642, 645,
        649
    pregnancy, 319, 564, 565, 614-616, 628-629,
        634, 640, 651
    purpose to discriminate, 554-556, 564-565,
        628, 642, 649
    rational basis review, 611-613
    "real" differences, 626, 628-629, 634-640
    segregation 625-626, 1478
    social security, 615, 640-646
    strict scrutiny, 613-614
    veteran's preference, 554-556, 564-565
Gerrymandering. See Voting
Government employees. See also Aliens; Free-
    dom of expression
    Right to notice and hearings before dis-
        charge, 901-910
Government procurement
    State taxes on, 210-212
Grants-in-aid, 218-223

Hearing, right to, 900-924
Homosexuality, 688, 896-898
Housing
    Civil Rights Act of 1866, modern application
        of, 245-247
Housing and Rent Act of 1947, 212
Human life statute, 243

Illegitimacy. See Nonmarital children
Immutable characteristics. See Equal protection
Implied fundamental rights. See also Abortion;
    Incorporation doctrine; Privacy, right
    of; Procedural due process; Procre-
    ation, right of; Substantive due pro-
    cess; Travel; Voting; Welfare

    ṇental rights—(*continued*)
        allot, 786-791
        judicial process, 791-802
        eption, 851-854, 884-885, 1101
        e, 798-802, 812-813
        omic substantive due process, 724-750
        cation, 821-840
        ual protection, 508, 677, 751-840
        amily, 886-900
    Hair length, 898-899
    Homosexuality, 896-898
    Interpretivism, 691-698
    Irrebuttable presumptions, 755
    Marriage, 890-893
    Noninterpretivism, 691-698
    One person/one vote, 767-777
    Privileges or immunities clause, 698-707
    Representation, theories of, 783-784
    Sexual autonomy, 896-898
Implied powers, 48-61
Imports
    original package doctrine, 254
    state regulation of, 271-275
Impoundment, 362-365
Improper motivation. *See* Freedom of expression; Legislators; Voting
Incidence analysis, 262
Incorporation doctrine, 707-724, 1366-1367
Indigent persons. *See also* Wealth discrimination
    abortion, 869-874
    access to judicial process, 791-802
    bankruptcy, 800-801
    counsel, 675-683, 792-796
    divorce, 798-800
    education, 821-831
    housing, 820
    imprisonment for failure to pay fines, 797-798
    suspect classification, 498, 675-685
    transcripts, 792
    travel, 802-808
    voting, 757-760
    welfare, 815-821
Intergovernmental immunity
    regulation, 196-210
    taxation, 210-212
Intermediate scrutiny. *See* Equal protection
Interstate commerce
    definition of, for state regulation, 263, 271
    national regulation of
        agriculture, 174-176
        child labor, 150-155
        crime, 182-184
        Depression and New Deal, 155-156, 166-168
        early developments, 138-139
        exclusive and concurrent power theories, 137
        Fair Labor Standards Act, 177-181, 196-210
        firearms, 186-187
        Interstate Commerce Act, 138, 144, 294
        interstate shipment, 145-155
        labor standards, 177-181, 196-210
        loan sharks, 182-184

    manufacturing, 139-141
    Marshall's view of national power, 127-132
    mining, 160-161, 185-186
    monopolies, 139-141
    navigable waters, 136
    National Labor Relations Act, 169-174
    NRA program, 156-160
    organized crime, 182-184
    police regulations, 139
    political limits on national power, 117-122, 209-210
    prohibition technique, 139, 143-144, 145-150, 177-181
    racial discrimination, 187-196
    railroad rates, 141-142, 144-145
    railroad safety, 144
    stream of commerce theory, 142, 144
    taxation as, 216-218
    tenth amendment as limit, 180, 196-210
state regulation of
    banking, 258, 269
    business
        conducted by state, 321-328, 328-335
        entry into state, 336-337
    concurrent versus exclusive power theories, 250, 252-253, 278-279, 285
    consumer protection laws, 271-275
    cost/benefit analysis, 260-261, 268, 275, 284
    cost-exporting regulations, 261, 262, 268-269
    dams on navigable streams, 251
    early developments, 250-253
    electrical energy, 270, 327
    environmental protection legislation, 263-268, 270
    fishing and hunting, 270
    gasoline sales, 253-254, 276-284
    highways, 293-294, 298-313
    insurance companies, 336-337
    interstate and foreign travel, 252-253, 290
    landfills, 263-268
    liquor control, 254-255
    milk, 275-276, 285-286, 291-292
    motor carriers, 290, 293-294, 298-313
    national consent to, 254-256, 321-322
    natural resources, 270, 287-289
    nuclear power, 313-318, 320
    original package doctrine, 254
    out-of-state corporations, 336-337
    packaging of fruits and vegetables, 271-275
    pilotage regulations, 251-252
    politics of, 259-260
    preemption by federal action, 250, 254, 313-321
    quarantine measures, 266, 268, 269
    railroad safety regulations, 294-297
    reasonable alternatives, 274-275
    retaliatory statutes, 270-271
    state as market participant, 321-328, 328-335
    subsidies as alternative to, 276, 327
    timber, 321-328
    train length limits, 294-296
    trucks, 293-294, 298-313
    underground water, 270-271

waste, solid or liquid, 263-268
Interstate compacts, 167
Irrebuttable presumptions. *See* Due process of
    law

Japanese-Americans, relocation of, 530-535,
    541, 542
Jefferson, Thomas
    views on constitutional amendment, 12
    views on religion, 1363, 1365, 1391
Judicial process
    access to, 791-802
    bankruptcy, 800-801
    criminal justice system, 792-798
    divorce, 798-800
    filing fees, 708-802
    fundamental interest, 791-802
    litigation as expression, 1236-1241
Judicial review
    advisory opinions, 77-78
    antecedents, 2
    authoritativeness, 44-47
    case and controversy, 76-111
    democracy and, 31-38
    establishment of, 18-31
    Hamilton's justification, 30-31
    of legislative findings, 506-508, 548
    legitimacy of, 18-38
    Marshall's justification, 18-31
    natural law and, 61-64
    political questions, 95-109
    ripeness and concreteness, 109-111
    state laws and decisions, 38-44
    theory of, 18-38
Jurisdiction
    congressional control
        over lower federal courts, 74-75
        over Supreme Court, 69-74
    federal courts
        advisory opinion, 77-78
        moot cases, 111
    nonexercise of, 76-77
    Supreme Court, 111-113
        adequate nonfederal ground, 113
        appeal or certiorari, 111-112
Jurors, discrimination in selection of, 448, 528-
    530, 544, 546, 550, 551, 558, 563, 612,
    615, 1489, 1512
Just compensation, 1445-1462
Justiciability, 79-113

Labor relations. *See also* Freedom of expression
    national power, 156-160
    unions and political process, 296, 297
Legislative districting. *See also* Voting
    justiciability, 95-101
Legislative investigations. *See* Freedom of
        expression; Congress, investigations
Legislative veto, 371-385
Legislators
    motives, 480, 483-485, 487, 498, 511, 516,
        520, 521, 527-528, 544-546, 550-551,
        553-562, 1000-1001, 1205-1206, 1210-
        1211, 1258, 1262-1266

obligation to consider constitutionality, 45-46
Legitimacy. *See* Nonmarital children
Libel. *See* Freedom of expression
Liberty of contract, 724-750
Liquor, 616-622, 1513-1517
Literacy tests. *See* Voting
Loyalty oaths. *See* Bill of attainder; Freedom of
    expression

Madison, James
    conceptions of politics, 6-7
    on faction, 7-13
    memorial and remonstrance, 1362, 1364,
        1374
    theory of federalism and national power,
        117-122
    views on property, 16-17
    views on religion, 1362-1363, 1365
Madisonian republicanism, 6-17
Mann Act, 150
Manufacturing as commerce, 139-141, 160-166,
    169-171
Market participant doctrine, 321-328, 333
Marriage, 181, 565-567, 576, 615, 626, 852-853,
    890-893, 1476
Mass media. *See* Freedom of the press
McCarran-Ferguson Act, 336-337
Mental illness, 510-513, 524-526, 686-688
Migratory Bird Treaty Act, 213
Military. *See* Freedom of expression
Military power
    presidential power, 346-362, 413-433
    war-making power, 424-433
Milk, state regulation of, 285-286, 291-292
Mining
    national power, 160-166, 185-186
    state taxation of, 262, 287-289
Miscegenation, 565-567
Missouri Compromise. *See* Slavery
Mootness, 111
Mortgage moratoria, 1430-1435

National Association for the Advancement of
        Colored People
    campaign to end segregation, 456-457, 458-
        459
    effort to suppress, 1236-1239, 1306-1309,
        1318-1321
National citizenship, privileges of, 446, 447,
        448, 698-707
National Health Planning and Resources De-
        velopment Act of 1974, 230
National Industrial Recovery Act, 155, 156,
        166
Nationality, as suspect classification, 530-535
National Labor Relations Act, 168, 169, 199,
        366-368
Naturalization, 441-442
Natural Law. *See also* Constitution, theories of
        interpretation
    equal protection, 548-549, 611, 538-539,
        684
    judicial review and, 61-64
    state action, 1533-1534

es, state control of, 270, 287-

nd proper clause, 48-61
s." *See* Wealth discrimination
endment, 855, 941-952
ital children. *See also* Family relations,
    adoption
suspect classification, 667, 668-669
iological rights, 669-672
intestate succession, 668, 674-675
social security, 672-674
support, 669-671
wrongful death actions, 635-636, 667
Notice and hearing. *See also* Due process of
    law
  as a prerequisite to liberty and property
    deprivations, 900-924
  as a prerequisite to loss of job, 900-907
  distinguishing substance and procedure, 907-
    910
  irrebuttable presumptions and requirement of
    individualized hearings, 921-923
  prior hearing, 900-924
Nullification, 115

Obscenity. *See* Freedom of expression
Occupation of the field, 319. *See also* Preemp-
    tion
Original package doctrine, 254
Overbreadth. *See* Freedom of expression

Packers and Stockyards Act, 142
Parochial schools, aid to, 1361-1363
Pentagon Papers case. *See* Freedom of expres-
    sion
Police power
  contracts clause, 1435-1436
  eminent domain, 1459-1462
Political questions, 95-109
Pornography. *See* Freedom of expression
Prayer in public schools, 1374-1376, 1421, 1423
Preemption,
  in general, 250, 254-255, 313-321
  bankruptcy laws, 319
  pension laws, 319
  sedition laws, 320
Presidency
  amenability to judicial process, 407-408
  domestic affairs, 346-395
  executive privilege, 398-412
  foreign affairs, 413-433
  impeachment, 412-413
Press. *See* Freedom of the press
Presumptions irrebuttable. *See* Due process
    clause
Prices, state regulation of, 291-292
Prior restraint. *See* Freedom of expression
Privacy, Right of. *See* Abortion; Family rela-
    tions; Freedom of expression; Implied
    fundamental rights
Privileges and immunities clause
  of article IV, 328-335, 815

of fourteenth amendment, 446-448, 611, 698-
    707, 1473
Private clubs, discrimination by. *See* State
    action
Procedural due process, 900-924
Procreation, right of, 751-756, 820
Profanity. *See* Freedom of expression
Property rights, 900-924
Protectionism and free trade, 249-250, 257-258
Public choice theory, 524
Public employees. *See* Aliens; Freedom of
    expression
Public schools. *See* Education; Freedom of
    expression; Religion; Segregation
Public use, 1445-1448
Public Utilities Regulatory Policies Act, 208
Pure Food and Drugs Act, 150
Purpose. *See* Equal protection

Race. *See* Equal protection; Segregation; Slav-
    ery; Thirteenth amendment; Four-
    teenth amendment; Fifteenth
    amendment
Railroad Retirement Act of 1934, 156
Railroads
  national regulation of, 141-142
  rate regulation, 141-142, 144-145
  safety regulations, 144, 294-297
Railway Labor Act, 208
Rates, regulation of, 726-728
Rationality review. *See* Equal protection
Reapportionment. *See* Voting
Religion
  establishment of
    abortion, funding of, 1396
    aid to education
      in general, 1361-1363, 1368-1369, 1387-
        1405
      higher education, 1407
      tax credits, 1398-1404
      tuition grants, 1406
    coercion as aspect of, 1394-1395
    creche in public park, 1377-1390
    church property disputes, 1408-1409
    entanglement test, 1382-1383, 1386, 1406-
      1408
    prayer meetings in public facilities, 1376
    prayers
      in public schools, 1374-1376
      in legislature, 1392-1393
    Sunday closing laws, 1391-1392
    tax exemptions, 1392
  free exercise of
    accommodation principle, 1376, 1418-1419,
      1420-1421, 1423
    bigamy statutes, 1410
    compulsory education, 1416-1417
    conscientious objectors, 1370-1372
    employment discrimination statutes as
      protecting, 1421, 1422
    legislature, minister serving in, 1424-1425
    prayer meetings in public facilities, 1421
    prayers in public schools, 1423
    solicitation of funds, 1376-1377

Sunday closing laws, 1410-1411
  tax exemption as required by, 1417-1418
  unemployment compensation, 1411-1416
  work on sabbath, 1422-1423
in general
  antidiscrimination principle, 1368, 1376-1377, 1395
  definition of, 1369-1370, 1372-1373
    as applied in conscientious objector cases, 1370-1372
  relation to free expression, 1420, 1423-1424
Representation/Reinforcement. See Constitution, theories of interpretation
Residency requirements
  divorce, 812-813
  education, 839-840
  medical care, 811-812
  voting, 810-811
  welfare, 802-810
Republicanism
  traditional, 5-6
  Federalist reformulation of, 6-17
Residence, benefits determined by. See Equal protection; Residency requirements; Wealth discrimination; Welfare
Restrictive covenants, state enforcement of. See State action
Ripeness, 110
Roosevelt Court plan, 168

Sales taxes on federal government contractors, 211-212
Schools. See Education; Freedom of expression; Religion; Segregation
Segregation
  attendance zones, creation to achieve integration, 477-478, 579
    busing to achieve integration of schools, 478-479, 484-485, 492-493, 567-575, 577
  de jure/de facto distinction, 479-480, 482-488, 492, 544, 558-559, 567-575
  HEW guidelines, 474
  housing, 489, 553-554, 568, 577, 681, 1486, 1488-1495
  public accommodations, 449, 465, 472, 473, 474, 550-551, 1469-1474, 1497-1499, 1500-1503, 1513-1517, 1528
  public transportation, 451-454, 455, 465
  racial balance or quotas, 476-478, 558, 602
  remedies, 467-470, 471, 473, 475-481, 486, 488-492, 558, 579, 585-586, 592
  schools, 452, 454, 457-458, 460-463, 465, 467-468, 470, 472-473, 474-495, 544, 546, 558-559, 567-575, 578-579, 585-586, 592, 602, 1495-1496, 1504-1506
  separate but equal doctrine, 454-456, 459, 467, 490
  southern resistance to desegregation, 470-475, 481
  social science materials, 463, 465, 491-492, 494
  "white flight," 490-492, 602
Separation of powers
  appointment of officers of the United States, 369-395
  bicameralism, 371-385
  congressional immunities, 395-398
  domestic affairs, 339-412
  executive immunities, 398-412
  faction, 345
  impeachment, 412-413
  legislative veto, 371-385
  limited government, 344-345
  presentment clause, 371-385
  property and, 344-345
  purposes of, 339-345
  seizure of industry by President,
  speech or debate clause, 395-398
  theory of, 339-345
  war and foreign relations, 424-433
  war, conduct or declaration of, 424-433
Severence taxes, 262
Sex discrimination. See Gender discrimination
Sexual autonomy. See Implied fundamental rights
Sherman Antitrust Act, 138, 139, 144, 199
"Sit-in" demonstrations. See State action
Slavery
  abolitionist movement, 437-440
  badges of, 449-450, 557, 1471-1473
  federal regulation of, 137-138
    interstate commerce, 252-253
  Missouri Compromise, validity of, 442-443
  property concept, 441-443
  sanctioned in Constitution, 436, 440, 444, 590
  thirteenth amendment, 445, 449-450, 1471-1473
Smith Act, 320, 965-985
Speech. See Freedom of expression
Speech or debate clause. See Separation of power
Spending power, 219-231
Standing, 78-79
State action
  acts of public officials, 1484-1485, 1488, 1492, 1512
  authorization as, 1481, 1503, 1509, 1513-1521
  California referendum, 1486-1487
  charitable trusts, 1495-1497, 1527-1528
  company towns, 1521-1524
  due process rights, 1479-1485, 1507-1510, 1517-1519, 1528, 1529-1530, 1531
  enforcement of private arrangements, 1488-1499
  and federalism, 1468-1476
  and individual autonomy, 1476-1478
  licensing, 1476-1477, 1513-1517, 1520-1521
  nursing homes, 1507-1510, 1532
  private clubs, 1478, 1513-1517, 1520-1521
  private schools, 1504-1506, 1511, 1512, 1531-1532
  prosecution of "sit-in" demonstrators, 1497-1499, 1528
  public accommodations, 449, 1469-1476, 1497-1499, 1500-1503
  public function theory, 1480, 1496, 1521-1534
  public utilities, 1513, 1517-1519, 1528, 1529-1530

n—(*continued*)
   to act, 1475, 1481, 1485-1486, 1490,
   1502, 1506, 1520
   ictive covenants, 1488-1495, 1498
   pping centers, 1478, 1528, 1530-1531
   itutes as, 1481, 1483, 1486, 1487, 1503
   ubsidization as, 1500-1513
  and substantive constitutional provisions,
    1477, 1493, 1534-1536
  television networks, 1476, 1520, 1524
  theory of government neutrality, 1488, 1492-
    1493, 1499-1500, 1503, 1520-1521, 1535-
    1536
  thirteenth amendment, not required under,
    449-450, 1467, 1471-1473
Stigma. *See* Equal protection
Strict scrutiny. *See* Equal protection
Substantive due process
  abortion, 854-886
  contraception, 841-854, 884-885
  economic substantive due process, 724-750
  modern substantive due process, 840-900
  privacy, 840-900
Subversive advocacy. *See* Freedom of expression
Supreme Court. *See also* Judicial review
  caseload, 113
  congressional control over jurisdiction, 69-74
  jurisdiction, 111-113
  proposals for changes in jurisdiction, 111-113
  reprisal by political branches, 65-74
  review of state court decisions, 111-113
  rules for appeal and certiorari, 111-113
  workload, 113
Surface Transportation Act of 1982, 313
Suspect classifications. *See* Equal protection

Taking of property without just compensation,
   1445-1465
Taxation. *See also* Equal protection
  intergovernmental, 210-212
  of commerce
    corporations, out-of-state, 336-337
    discriminatory, 287-289
    mining, 287-290
    severance, 262, 287-289
    use, 292-293
  of the press, 1323-1326
  regulatory impacts, 216-219
Teachers and loyalty oaths, 1287-1294. *See also*
   Aliens
Thirteenth amendment. *See also* Slavery
  adoption of, 445
  as a basis for federal legislative power, 449-
    450, 1471-1473, 1475
  state action not required, 449, 1471-1472
Titles of nobility, 600
Transportation, state regulation of, 251, 252-
   253, 290, 298-313
Travel, right to
  bona fide residency requirements, 814-815
  fundamental interest, 802-808
  impermissible purposes, 808-810

newcomers as a "suspect" class, 814
  penalty on, 808-814
  passports, 1034, 1294
Treaties
  limitations on, 212-216
  self-executing, 215
Trusts. *See* State action

Uniformity clause, 261
Use tax, 292-293
Utilitarianism, 523

Vagueness. *See* Freedom of expression
Virginia Bill for Religious Liberty (Jefferson),
   1363
Voting
  access to the ballot, 786-791
  absentee ballots, 766
  denial of right, 756-767
  dilution of right, 767-786
  discriminatory purpose, 784-786
  durational residency requirements, 765-766
  equal protection scrutiny, 544, 546, 550, 553,
    559-562, 563, 568, 580-581, 611, 655,
    661, 676, 679, 680, 687, 1524
  felons, 766-767
  free expression, 791
  fundamental interest, 756-791
  gerrymandering, 777-786
  justiciability, 95-101
  literacy tests, 757
  one person/one vote, 767-777
  petition requirements, 788-789
  poll tax, 757-761
  primaries, 767
  property requirement, 864-865
  qualifications of voters, 756-767
  racial discrimination, 784-786
  reapportionment, 767-777
  representation, right of, 772-774, 783-784
  residence requirements, 765-766
  special purpose elections, 764
  state action, 1524
  Voting Rights Act of 1965, 233
  wealth and, 757-761, 789

Wage and hour regulations
  national, 177-180, 196-210
  substantive due process, 740-741
War power
  as source of federal regulatory authority,
    212-213
  separation of powers, 424-433
Wealth discrimination. *See also* Indigent persons
  allocation of scarce resources, 682-683
  as suspect classification, 498, 675-685
  de facto discrimination, 676, 681-683
  necessities, 676, 677, 683
  right to counsel, 675, 677, 679, 680, 682-683